The Consumer Credit and Sales
Legal Practice Series

FORECLOSURES

Defenses, Workouts, and Mortgage Servicing

WITH COMPANION WWW WEBSITE

Third Edition

See *page ix* for information about the companion website.

John Rao
Odette Williamson
Tara Twomey
Geoff Walsh

Contributing Authors: Andrew G. Pizor, Diane E. Thompson,
Margot Saunders, John W. Van Alst

National Consumer Law Center®
7 Winthrop Square, 4th Floor Boston, MA 02110 www.consumerlaw.org

About NCLC® The National Consumer Law Center®, a nonprofit corporation founded in 1969, assists consumers, advocates, and public policy makers nationwide who use the powerful and complex tools of consumer law to ensure justice and fair treatment for all, particularly those whose poverty renders them powerless to demand accountability from the economic marketplace. For more information, go to www.consumerlaw.org.

Ordering NCLC Publications Order securely online at www.consumerlaw.org, or contact Publications Department, National Consumer Law Center, 7 Winthrop Square, 4th Floor, Boston, MA 02110, (617) 542-9595, FAX: (617) 542-8028, e-mail: publications@nclc.org.

Training and Conferences NCLC participates in numerous national, regional, and local consumer law trainings. Its annual fall conference is a forum for consumer rights attorneys from legal services programs, private practice, government, and nonprofit organizations to share insights into common problems and explore novel and tested approaches that promote consumer justice in the marketplace. Contact NCLC for more information or see our web site.

Case Consulting Case analysis, consulting and co-counseling for lawyers representing vulnerable consumers are among NCLC's important activities. Administration on Aging funds allow us to provide free consulting to legal services advocates representing elderly consumers on many types of cases. Massachusetts Legal Assistance Corporation funds permit case assistance to advocates representing low-income Massachusetts consumers. Other funding may allow NCLC to provide very brief consultations to other advocates without charge. More comprehensive case analysis and research is available for a reasonable fee. See our web site for more information at www.consumerlaw.org.

Charitable Donations and Cy Pres *Awards* NCLC's work depends in part on the support of private donors. Tax-deductible donations should be made payable to National Consumer Law Center, Inc. For more information, contact Suzanne Cutler of NCLC's Development Office at (617) 542-8010 or scutler@nclc.org. NCLC has also received generous court-approved *cy pres* awards arising from consumer class actions to advance the interests of class members. For more information, contact Robert Hobbs (rhobbs@nclc.org) or Rich Dubois (rdubois@nclc.org) at (617) 542-8010.

Comments and Corrections Write to the above address to the attention of the Editorial Department or e-mail consumerlaw@nclc.org.

About This Volume This is the Third Edition of *Foreclosures*. Discard all prior editions and supplements. This book includes a companion website. Continuing developments can be found in periodic supplements to and revised editions of this volume, on the companion website, and in NCLC REPORTS.

Cite This Volume As National Consumer Law Center, Foreclosures (3d ed. 2010).

Attention *This publication is designed to provide authoritative information concerning the subject matter covered. Always use the most current edition and supplement, and use other sources for more recent developments or for special rules for individual jurisdictions. This publication cannot substitute for the independent judgment and skills of an attorney or other professional. Non-attorneys are cautioned against using these materials to conduct a lawsuit without advice from an attorney and are cautioned against engaging in the unauthorized practice of law.*

Copyright

ISBN: 978-1-60248-066-7 (this volume)
ISBN: 978-0-943116-10-7 (Series)

Library of Congress Control Number: 2010930058

About the Authors

John Rao is an NCLC attorney focusing on consumer bankruptcy, foreclosures, and credit law. He is co-author of *Bankruptcy Basics* (2007) and editor and contributing author of *Consumer Bankruptcy Law and Practice* (9th ed. 2009). He is also a contributing author to *Collier on Bankruptcy* and the *Collier Bankruptcy Practice Guide*. For 18 years, he had a bankruptcy and consumer law focus at Rhode Island Legal Services and was a managing attorney there. He is a conferee of the National Bankruptcy Conference, fellow of the American College of Bankruptcy, secretary for the National Association of Consumer Bankruptcy Attorneys, a former board member of the American Bankruptcy Institute, an adjunct faculty member at Boston College School of Law, and a member of the federal Judicial Conference Advisory Committee on Bankruptcy Rules, appointed by Chief Justice John Roberts in 2006.

Odette Williamson is an NCLC staff attorney with a focus on sustainable homeownership, consumer credit and foreclosure prevention, and manufactured homes. She is co-author of *Foreclosure Prevention Counseling* (2009). She formerly was an assistant attorney general with the Consumer Protection Division of the Massachusetts attorney general's office.

Tara Twomey is of counsel with NCLC. She is a lecturer in law at Stanford Law School, and was formerly a clinical instructor at the WilmerHale Legal Services Center of Harvard Law School, a lecturer in law at Harvard Law School, and an adjunct faculty member at Boston College Law School. She is co-author of *Bankruptcy Basics* (2007) and a contributing author to *Consumer Bankruptcy Law and Practice* (9th ed. 2009) and *The Cost of Credit* (4th ed. 2009).

Geoff Walsh has been a legal services attorney for over twenty-five years. A contributing author to *Consumer Bankruptcy Law and Practice* (9th ed. 2009) and *Credit Discrimination* (5th ed. 2009), he was a staff attorney with Vermont Legal Aid and with the housing and consumer units of Community Legal Services in Philadelphia. He is currently a staff attorney with NCLC in its Boston office. His practice has focused upon housing and bankruptcy issues, particularly foreclosures of mortgages in government-subsidized housing programs.

Andrew G. Pizor is a staff attorney in NCLC's Washington, D.C., office and co-author of *The Cost of Credit* 2010 Supplement and contributing author to *Truth in Lending* 2009 Supplement. He was formerly an attorney at the Connecticut Fair Housing Center, Consumer Law Group L.L.C., and Legal Services Corp. of Delaware, where he worked on housing and consumer protection issues, focusing on defending foreclosures and fighting predatory lending.

Diane E. Thompson is of counsel with NCLC. She was formerly the homeownership specialist for Land of Lincoln Legal Assistance Foundation, Inc., where she had represented low-income homeowners since 1994. She was a member of the Federal Reserve Board Consumer Advisory Council and is a contributing author to *The Cost of Credit* (4th ed. 2009), *Truth in Lending* (6th ed. 2007), *Stop Predatory Lending* (2d ed. 2007), and *Foreclosure Prevention Counseling* (2d ed. 2009).

Margot Saunders is of counsel with NCLC and was formerly the managing attorney of NCLC's Washington, DC, office. Her areas of focus include predatory lending and mortgage loans, as well as protecting exempt funds and electronic payments. Her publications include *Consumer Banking and Payments Law* (4th ed. 2009), *Access to Utility Service* (1996, 2001), *Energy and the Poor* (1995), *Tenants' Rights to Utility Service* (1994), and *The Manual on*

Water Affordability Programs (1998). She is a former member of the FRB's Consumer Advisory Council and the American Water Works Association Public Advisory Forum, a former consumer specialist for North Carolina Legal Services, and a recipient of the Vern Countryman Consumer Law Award.

John W. Van Alst is an NCLC staff attorney whose focus includes manufactured home issues, deceptive practices law, and automobile fraud. He formerly was an attorney at Legal Aid of North Carolina for seven years, where he handled a broad range of consumer issues, and was also an adjunct clinical professor at the University of North Carolina School of Law. He is also the co-author of *Automobile Fraud* (3d ed. 2007), *Consumer Warranty Law* (3d ed. 2010), and *Consumer Rights for Domestic Violence Survivors*, and is a contributing author to *The Cost of Credit* (4th ed. 2009), *Unfair and Deceptive Acts and Practices* (7th ed. 2008) and *Repossessions* (2009 Supplement).

Acknowledgments

Thanks to Todd Blodgett and Emily Green Caplan for extensive substantive contributions, and Elizabeth De Armond, Allen Agnitti, Kurt Terwilliger, and Mary Kingsley for research and writing. We also want to acknowledge the following who provided sample pleadings added to this edition's appendices: Allison Albert, Lynn Drysdale, Richard Eppink, Daniel Lindsey. O. Max Gardner III, Andrew Neuhauser, Sarah Parady, and Nick Wooten.

Special thanks to Denise Lisio for editorial supervision; Katherine Hunt for editorial assistance; Shirlron Williams for assistance with cite checking; Shannon Halbrook and Microsearch for designing and implementing the companion website; Mary McLean for indexing; and Xylutions for typesetting services. We would also like to thank Diane E. Thompson and Elizabeth Ryan for their significant substantive contributions to earlier editions and to Gary Klein for his groundbreaking work in this area.

What Your Library Should Contain

The Consumer Credit and Sales Legal Practice Series contains 18 titles, updated annually, arranged into four libraries, and designed to be an attorney's primary practice guide and legal resource in all 50 states. Each title includes free access to a companion website, containing the treatise's appendices, sample pleadings, primary sources, and other practice aids, allowing pinpoint searches and the pasting of text into a word processor. Access remains free as long as purchasers keep their titles current.

Debtor Rights Library

2009 Ninth Edition (Two Volumes), and Companion Website, Including NCLC's Bankruptcy Forms Software

Consumer Bankruptcy Law and Practice: the definitive personal bankruptcy manual, from the initial interview to final discharge, including consumer rights when a company files for bankruptcy. The updated ninth edition contains the latest case law interpreting the 2005 Act, and includes such practice aids as the latest Bankruptcy Code, Rules, and fee schedules, a date calculator, over 150 pleadings and forms, software to compute the initial forms, means test data, and a client questionnaire and handout.

2008 Sixth Edition, 2010 Supplement, and Companion Website

Fair Debt Collection: the basic reference, covering the Fair Debt Collection Practices Act and common law, state statutory and other federal debt collection protections. Unique case summaries cover reported and unreported FDCPA cases by category. The companion website contains sample pleadings and discovery, the FTC Commentary, an index to and the full text of *all* FTC staff opinion letters, and other practice aids.

2010 Third Edition and Companion Website

Foreclosures: examines RESPA and other federal and state rights to challenge servicer abuses, as well as details on workout options, loan modification, and mediation programs implemented by federal and state governments. The volume also covers standing and substantive and procedural defenses to foreclosure and tactics after the foreclosure sale. Special chapters cover tax liens, land installment sales contracts, manufactured home foreclosures, and other topics.

2005 Sixth Edition, 2009 Supplement, and Companion Website

Repossessions: a unique guide to motor vehicle and mobile home repossessions, threatened seizures of household goods, statutory liens, and automobile lease and rent-to-own default remedies. The volume examines UCC Article 9 and hundreds of other federal and state statutes regulating repossessions.

2006 Third Edition, 2009 Supplement, and Companion Website

Student Loan Law: collection harassment; closed school, disability, and other discharges; tax intercepts, wage garnishment, and offset of social security benefits; and repayment plans, consolidation loans, deferments, and non-payment of loan based on school fraud.

2008 Fourth Edition, 2010 Supplement, and Companion Website

Access to Utility Service: consumer rights as to regulated and unregulated utilities, including telecommunications, terminations, billing errors, low-income payment plans, utility allowances in subsidized housing, LIHEAP, and weatherization.

Credit and Banking Library

2007 Sixth Edition, 2009 Supplement, and Companion Website

Truth in Lending: detailed analysis of *all* aspects of TILA, the Consumer Leasing Act, the Fair Credit Billing Act, the Home Ownership and Equity Protection Act (HOEPA), and the Credit CARD Act. Appendices and the website contain the Acts, Reg. Z, Reg. M, and their official staff commentaries, numerous sample pleadings, rescission notices, two programs to compute APRs, TIL legislative history, and a unique compilation of *all Federal Register* notices and supplementary information on Regulation Z since 1969.

2006 Sixth Edition, 2009 Supplement, and Companion Website

Fair Credit Reporting: the key resource for handling any type of credit reporting issue, from cleaning up blemished credit records to suing reporting agencies and creditors for inaccurate reports. Covers the new FACTA changes, identity theft, creditor liability for failing to properly reinvestigate disputed information, credit scoring, privacy issues, the Credit Repair Organizations Act, state credit reporting and repair statutes, and common law claims.

2009 Fourth Edition, 2010 Supplement, and Companion Website

Consumer Banking and Payments Law: covers checks, telechecks, electronic fund transfers, electronic check conversions, money orders, and credit, debit, payroll, and stored value cards. The title also covers banker's right of setoff, electronic transfers of federal and state benefit payments, and a special chapter on electronic records and signatures.

2009 Fourth Edition, 2010 Supplement, and Companion Website

The Cost of Credit: Regulation, Preemption, and Industry Abuses: a one-of-a-kind resource detailing state and federal regulation of consumer credit in all 50 states, examines numerous types of predatory lending, federal preemption of state law, credit math calculations, excessive credit charges, credit insurance, and numerous other topics.

2009 Fifth Edition, 2010 Supplement, and Companion Website

Credit Discrimination: analysis of the Equal Credit Opportunity Act, Fair Housing Act, Civil Rights Acts, and state credit discrimination statutes, including reprints of all relevant federal interpretations, government enforcement actions, and numerous sample pleadings.

Consumer Litigation Library

2008 First Edition, 2010 Supplement, and Companion Website

Collection Actions: a complete guide to consumer defenses and counterclaims to collection lawsuits filed in court or in arbitration, with extensive discussion of setting aside default judgments and limitations on a collector's post-judgment remedies. Special chapters include the rights of active duty military, and unique issues involving medical debt, government collections, collector's attorney fees, and bad check laws.

2007 Fifth Edition, 2009 Supplement, and Companion Website

Consumer Arbitration Agreements: successful approaches to challenge arbitration agreements' enforceability and waivers of class arbitration, the interrelation of the Federal Arbitration Act and state law, class actions and punitive damages in arbitration, implications of NAF's withdrawal from consumer arbitrations, the right to discovery, and other topics.

2010 Seventh Edition and Companion Website

Consumer Class Actions: makes class litigation manageable even for small offices, including numerous sample pleadings, class certification memoranda, discovery, class notices, settlement materials, and much more. Includes a detailed analysis of the Class Action Fairness Act, class arbitration, state class action rules and case law, and other topics.

Website and 2009 Index Guide: ALL pleadings from ALL NCLC treatises, including Consumer Law Pleadings Numbers One through Fifteen

Consumer Law Pleadings: over *2000* notable pleadings from all types of consumer cases, including predatory lending, foreclosures, automobile fraud, lemon laws, debt collection, fair credit reporting, home improvement fraud, student loans, and lender liability. Finding aids pinpoint desired pleading in seconds, ready to paste into a word processor.

Deception and Warranties Library

2008 Seventh Edition, 2009 Supplement, and Companion Website

Unfair and Deceptive Acts and Practices: the only practice manual covering all aspects of a deceptive practices case in every state. Special sections on automobile sales, the federal racketeering (RICO) statute, unfair insurance practices, the FTC Holder Rule, telemarketing fraud, attorney fees, and many other topics.

2007 Third Edition, 2010 Supplement, and Companion Website

Automobile Fraud: examination of title law, "yo-yo" sales, odometer tampering, lemon laundering, sale of salvage and wrecked cars, undisclosed prior use, and prior damage to new cars. The website contains numerous sample pleadings and title search techniques.

2010 Fourth Edition and Companion Website

Consumer Warranty Law: comprehensive treatment of new and used car lemon laws, the Magnuson-Moss Warranty Act, UCC Articles 2 and 2A, mobile home, new home, and assistive device warranty laws, FTC Used Car Rule, tort theories, car repair and home improvement statutes, service contract and lease laws, with numerous sample pleadings.

NCLC's Companion Websites

Every NCLC manual includes a companion website, allowing rapid access to appendices, pleadings, primary sources, and other practice aids. Search for documents by category, or with a table of contents or various keyword search options. All documents can be downloaded, printed, and copy and pasted into a word processing document. Pleadings are also available in Word format. Web access is free with each title ordered and remains free as long as a title is kept current.

Website continually subject to update

Consumer Law on the Web: combines *everything* from the 18 other NCLC companion websites. Using *Consumer Law on the Web,* instead of multiple individual companion websites, is often the fastest and most convenient way to pinpoint and retrieve key documents among the thousands available on our individual companion websites.

Other NCLC Publications for Lawyers

issued 24 times a year

NCLC REPORTS, a four-page newsletter, keeps you up to date 24 times a year with the latest consumer law developments. It is also an essential practice tool, with novel ideas, innovative tactics, and key insights from NCLC's experienced consumer law attorneys. Learn the practice implications of new statutes, regulations, cases and trends.

2009 Second Edition and Companion Website

Foreclosure Prevention Counseling: Preserving the American Dream: explains how to obtain a workout, with advice specifically tailored for Fannie Mae, Freddie Mac, subprime, FHA-insured, VA, and Rural Housing Service loans. The book also details new loan modification initiatives from federal and state governments and industry.

2007 First Edition and Companion Website

Bankruptcy Basics: A Step-by-Step Guide for Pro Bono Attorneys, General Practitioners, and Legal Services Offices: provides everything attorneys new to bankruptcy need to file their first case, with a companion website that contains software, sample pleadings, and other practice aids that greatly simplify handling a bankruptcy case.

2007 Second Edition with CD-Rom

STOP Predatory Lending: A Guide for Legal Advocates: provides a roadmap and practical legal strategy for litigating predatory lending abuses, from small loans to mortgage loans. How to analyze the documents, spot issues, raise legal claims, select defendants, and even craft a community response.

2009 First Edition

Instant Evidence: A Quick Guide to Federal Evidence and Objections: facilitates objection by rule number and includes common objections and motions at every stage of a case—all in under 20 pages! Spiral-bound to lay flat, all pages are laminated, allowing new notations for each trial with a dry-erase pen.

2006 Second Edition with CD-Rom

The Practice of Consumer Law: Seeking Economic Justice: contains an essential overview to consumer law and explains how to get started in a private or legal services consumer practice. Packed with invaluable sample pleadings and practice pointers for even experienced consumer attorneys.

National Consumer Law Center Guide Series are books designed for consumers, counselors, and attorneys new to consumer law:

2010 Edition

NCLC Guide to Surviving Debt: a great overview of consumer law. Everything a paralegal, new attorney, or client needs to know about home foreclosures and mortgage modifications, debt collectors, managing credit card debt, whether to refinance, credit card problems, evictions, repossessions, credit reporting, utility terminations, student loans, budgeting, and bankruptcy.

First Edition

NCLC Guide to the Rights of Utility Consumers: explains consumer rights concerning electric, gas, and other utility services: shut off protections, rights to restore terminated service, bill payment options, weatherization tips, rights to government assistance, and much more.

First Edition

NCLC Guide to Consumer Rights for Domestic Violence Survivors: provides practical advice to help survivors get back on their feet financially and safely establish their economic independence.

First Edition

NCLC Guide to Mobile Homes: what consumers and their advocates need to know about mobile home dealer sales practices and an in-depth look at mobile home quality and defects, with 35 photographs and construction details.

First Edition

Return to Sender: Getting a Refund or Replacement for Your Lemon Car: find how lemon laws work, what consumers and their lawyers should know to evaluate each other, investigative techniques and discovery tips, how to handle both informal dispute resolution and trials, and more.

About the Companion Website, Other Search Options

The Companion Website

Purchase of any title in NCLC's Consumer Law Practice Series includes free access to its companion website. Access remains free with continued subscription to that title. Frequently updated, NCLC companion websites offer the treatises' appendices plus hundreds of other documents in PDF and Microsoft Word formats—statutes, regulations, agency interpretations, forms, pleadings, handbooks, reports, and much more—all easily located with flexible, powerful search tools. Documents can be printed, downloaded, and copy/pasted into a word processor.

Accessing the Companion Website

One-time registration is required to access NCLC companion websites. Once registered, users logging in are granted access to all websites they are authorized to use, with only one username and password required.

To register, go to www.consumerlaw.org/webaccess, and click "New users click here to register." Enter the Companion Website Registration Number found on the packing statement or invoice accompanying this publication.[1] Then enter the requested information and click Enter. An email address may be used for the username or a different username may be chosen.

Subscribers do *not* need to register more than once.[2] Subscribers purchasing additional NCLC titles are automatically given access to the new websites under their existing username and password. Registering a second time with the same registration number overrides a prior username and password.

Once registered, go to **www.consumerlaw.org/webaccess**, enter your username and password, and select the desired companion website from the list of authorized sites.

Libraries and others subscribing to the entire 18-volume set can arrange "IP access" so that a username and password are *not* required. Email publications@nclc.org with a list or range of static IP addresses for which access should be permitted *without* entering a username and password.

We encourage users who find mistakes to notify us using the "Report Errors" button, on the left toolbar. Also on the left toolbar, users can click "My Account" to change personal information.

Use of the companion websites with Internet Explorer requires Adobe Reader 7.0 or later or Adobe Acrobat 7.0 or later. Users of other browsers, or those experiencing problems with the websites, should download the latest version of the free Adobe Reader (currently 9.0) from Adobe's website at www.adobe.com. A link to Adobe's site is provided on the NCLC companion website login page.

Locating Documents on the Companion Website

The companion website provides three options to locate documents.

1. The search page (the home page) offers keyword searches to find documents—either full-text searches of all documents on the website or of only the documents' titles.

- Narrow the search to documents of a certain type (such as federal statutes or pleadings) by making a selection from the "Document Type" menu, and then perform a full text or document title search.
- If unsure of a keyword's spelling, type the first few letters and click "See choices."
- To locate a specific appendix section, select the appendix section number (e.g., A.2.3) or a partial identifier (e.g., A) in the search page's "Appendix" drop-down fields.
- Click Search Hints for a quick reference to special search operators, wildcards, shortcuts, and complex searches. Read this closely, as syntax and search operators may be slightly different from those of other websites.

2. The contents page (click on the "Contents" tab at the top of the page) is a traditional "branching" table of contents. Click a branch to expand it into a list of sub-branches or documents. Each document appears once on this contents tree.

1 If you cannot locate this number, contact NCLC Publications at (617) 542-9595 or publications@nclc.org.

2 If all your subscriptions to NCLC treatises are allowed to lapse, your account may be deleted; if this happens, you must re-register if you subsequently purchase a book.

3. The pleading finder page (click on the "Pleading Finder" tab at the top of the page, *if available*) allows pleadings to be located using one or more menus, such as "Type of Pleading" or "Subject." **Select more than one item from one menu, or deselect items, by using the Ctrl key.** For example, make one selection from "Type of Pleading–General," one from "Subject," and three from "Legal Claims" to locate all pleadings of that type and subject that contain one or more of the three legal claims selected. If this search produces insufficient results, simply broaden the search by deselecting "Subject" and/or "Legal Claims" to find pleadings of that type in any subject area or based upon any legal claim. To further narrow search results, this page also includes optional fields to specify terms to be found in the documents' text or titles.

Additional software, related websites, and other information can be located by clicking on links found at the left hand toolbar or on the "Search" page. These links bring you to credit math software, search tips, other websites, tables of contents and indices of all NCLC publications, and other practice aids. Some companion websites have "Software" or "Links" tabs at the top of the page, where this material may also be found.

Finding Word Versions of Website Documents

All documents on the website are in PDF format, and can be copied and pasted into a word processor. Pleadings and certain other documents also are available in Word format, facilitating the opening of entire documents in a word processor. After opening the selected PDF file, click at the top of the page on "Word Version, if available." If a Word version is listed as available, click "DOC Download Document" to save the Word file to your computer.

Documents Found on the Website

The companion website to *Foreclosures* contains sample mortgage foreclosure counseling forms and sample qualified written requests, federal statutes, regulations, handbooks, and agency letters concerning HUD, VA, and Rural Housing Service mortgages, and selected RESPA statutory and regulatory provisions, a GAO report on servicing, a glossary of mortgage servicing terms, and transaction codes. The website also includes summaries of state mortgage servicing, foreclosure, right to cure, condominium, and real estate tax abatement laws.

Of special note are over 160 sample mortgage foreclosure pleadings, including all pleadings found in the manual and many additional pleadings relating to injunction against sale, federally financed housing, RESPA, HOEPA, fraud and UDAP claims, land installment sales contracts, TIL rescission, and bankruptcy. The website also includes a number of pleadings relating to foreclosure rescue scams and debt collection litigation.

Locating Topics in This Treatise

Go to www.consumerlaw.org/keyword to electronically search the full text of every chapter and appendix of this title's main volume and supplement. While the chapters' complete text is not available online, this web-based search engine specifies each page of this title where a word or phrase is found. Select this title, enter a search term or combination of search terms—such as a case name, a regulation cite, or other keywords—and the page numbers containing those terms are listed. Search results are shown with the surrounding text ("hits in context"), facilitating selection of the most relevant pages.

Locating Topics in Other NCLC Manuals or NCLC REPORTS

The full text of all NCLC treatises and supplements, *NCLC REPORTS*, and other publications can be electronically searched to locate relevant topics as described above. Go to www.consumerlaw.org/keyword, and enter a search term or combination of search terms in a similar fashion to performing a keyword search on one title.

Current tables of contents, indices, and other information for all NCLC titles can be found at www.consumerlaw.org/shop. Click *Publications for Lawyers* and scroll down to the book you want. The PDF documents found there can be quickly searched for a word or phrase.

The Quick Reference at the back of this volume lets you pinpoint the correct treatise and treatise sections or appendices that discuss over 1000 different subject areas. These subject areas are listed in alphabetical order and can also be electronically searched at www.consumerlaw.org/qr.

Finding Pleadings

Pleadings relating to this title are found in PDF and Word format on the companion website; search options are discussed above at "Locating Documents on the Website." Over 2000 pleadings are also available at NCLC's *Consumer Law Pleadings* website using the same search techniques discussed above. Pleadings can also be located using *Consumer Law Pleadings*' index guide, which organizes pleadings by type, subject area, legal claim, title, and other categories identical to those on the website.

Summary Contents

Contents

Chapter 3 Foreclosure of Mortgages Held or Insured by the Federal Government

Chapter 6 Mortgage Servicing Abuses

Chapter 11 Manufactured Home Foreclosures and Repossessions

Chapter 13 Tax Liens and Tax Foreclosures

Chapter 14 Issues Arising After a Foreclosure Sale

Chapter 15 Foreclosure Rescue Scams

Appendix A Selected Statutes and Regulations Pertaining to Mortgages Held or Insured by the Federal Government

Appendix I Sample Foreclosure Pleadings and Other Litigation Documents

Appendix J Glossaries

Chapter 1 Introduction

1.1 About This Treatise

1.1.1 Scope

This treatise provides the law and practical advice concerning mortgage servicing and home foreclosures, examining these issues not only in relation to traditional free-standing homes, but also to manufactured homes and condominiums. It covers foreclosure upon private mortgages, government mortgages, and tax liens. A variety of foreclosure rescue scams from equity skimming schemes to phantom help are also addressed.

This introductory chapter provides a practical discussion of how to analyze and defend a foreclosure action. It outlines first steps to take when a client is facing foreclosure, provides an overview of claims and defenses available to homeowners, and just as importantly presents an essential introduction to this nation's mortgage market and the players involved in that market.

Chapter 2 examines loan modifications, workout agreements, mortgage loan mediations, and other negotiation strategies for dealing with delinquencies. Extensive discussion is devoted to the federal government's HAMP program for loan modifications, and also contains tips for obtaining non-litigated resolutions to default. The foreclosure of federally held or guaranteed mortgages is discussed in Chapter 3. Chapter 4 discusses procedural defenses available to prevent or postpone foreclosures, including the lack of standing to foreclose, and Chapter 5 discusses claims and defenses that arise from the loan's origination.

Chapters 6 through 8 address abuses by mortgage servicers—entities that collect the homeowner's payments after the loan has closed. Chapter 6 describes potential abuses and how to approach them. Chapter 7 discusses the challenges to these abuses under a variety of state and federal statutes and state common law. Chapter 8 discusses the application of the Real Estate Settlement Procedures Act to mortgage servicing.

Using bankruptcy to prevent foreclosure is discussed in Chapter 9. Chapter 10 details issues that commonly arise in predatory lending or foreclosure litigation. Chapters 11 through 13 deal with specialized situations where a home may be seized. Chapter 11 examines foreclosure, replevin, and repossession of manufactured homes. Chapter 12 considers forfeiture of land installment contracts and Chapter 13 reviews tax lien foreclosures.

Chapter 14 covers legal issues that arise after a foreclosure sale is completed, including setting aside sales, redemption, defending evictions, and the potential tax consequences of foreclosures. Chapter 15 addresses foreclosure rescue and loan modification scams.

1.1.2 The Appendices

This treatise includes a number of appendices, all of which are also reproduced on the companion website to this treatise. Federal laws, regulations, and other administrative materials that affect mortgage foreclosure are reprinted at Appendices A–C. Appendix A contains laws and regulatory materials relating to federally insured or guaranteed mortgages; Appendix B includes federal agency guidelines on workouts including loan modifications; and Appendix C contains the mortgage servicing provisions of the Real Estate Settlement Procedures Act (RESPA) and related regulations.

An attempt has also been made to identify the statutes relevant to foreclosure in all fifty states and the District of Columbia at Appendices D–G. Appendix D summarizes state laws regulating servicers of mortgage loans; Appendix E summarizes all state foreclosure laws; Appendix F summarizes state real estate tax abatement laws; and Appendix G summarizes state laws governing foreclosures on condominiums. The text of the treatise includes detailed citations listing other relevant state statutes.

The appendices also include a variety of pleadings and practice aids. Appendix H includes sample foreclosure prevention counseling forms, such as a sample intake form, sample authorizations and letters to obtain information and a sample qualified written request.

Appendix I includes sample foreclosure pleadings, discovery, and other litigation materials. These materials include sample affirmative defenses to foreclosure, a motion challenging a mortgage registry's standing to pursue foreclosure, a sample complaint for wrongful foreclosure, a sample action to enjoin a foreclosure, and sample complaints against home improvement contractors, mortgage servicers, and participants in a foreclosure rescue scam.

Discovery, memoranda, motions, and trial documents are also included.

Appendix J is a glossary of mortgage, foreclosure, and mortgage servicing terms. Appendix K explains how to find additional pleadings and primary source materials on the companion website. Appendix L is a list of useful web links.

All the pleadings found in the appendices, plus many additional pleadings from other NCLC treatises and elsewhere, are available on the companion website to this treatise.

1.1.3 The Companion Website

This treatise has a companion website that contains over 350 foreclosure-related files, including all of the treatise's appendices and many additional pleadings and primary sources. The website contains sample mortgage foreclosure counseling forms and sample qualified written requests, and extensive primary source materials concerning HUD, VA, and Rural Housing Service, and reverse mortgages—federal statutes, regulations, handbooks, loss mitigation guidelines, and key agency letters. The website also includes extensive materials concerning FDIC and HAMP loan modifications, and selected RESPA statutory and regulatory provisions, and other key documents concerning mortgage servicing. The website also includes summaries of state mortgage servicing, foreclosure, right to cure, condominium, and real estate tax abatement laws.

Of special note are over 150 sample mortgage foreclosure pleadings, including all pleadings found in this treatise and many additional pleadings relating to injunction against sale, federally financed housing, RESPA, HOEPA, HAMP loan modifications, fraud and UDAP claims, land installment sales contracts, TIL rescission, and bankruptcy. The website also includes a number of pleadings relating to foreclosure rescue scams and debt collection litigation, and two different Windows-based credit math programs, which compute APRs, generate amortization tables, and calculate Rule of 78 rebates.

The website provides many different finding aids, allowing users to pinpoint documents in second. All documents can be saved, printed, or copied and pasted into your own documents. Information on registration and use of the website is found at page ix, *supra*. Appendix K also contains advice on finding documents and using the website.

The website does *not* contain the full text of the treatise's chapters. See § 1.1.4, *infra*, about using Internet-based keyword searches to pinpoint page numbers in the treatise where topics are discussed.

1.1.4 Web-Based Text Search Feature

NCLC offers a unique web-based text search feature for this and all its publications, located at www.consumerlaw.org/keyword. At the website, select this treatise, another NCLC title, or all NCLC publications and specify a search term or a combination of search terms, following the instructions provided on the search page. The website will immediately list all corresponding pages of the specified publication where these terms are found, with hits in context (that is, the surrounding words of the selected key words will be displayed), allowing a quick determination as to the most appropriate pages to read. This search tool can be used to find cases with only a partial name of one of the parties, search for references to a particular statutory or rule citation, or find where a combination of search terms is located. No password or registration is required.

1.1.5 Clearinghouse Citations

Unreported cases with Clearinghouse numbers cited in this and other NCLC treatises are available through the Sargent Shriver National Center on Poverty Law (formerly the National Clearinghouse for Legal Services). The cases may be ordered from the Sargent Shriver National Center on Poverty Law by mail at: 111 N. Wabash St., Suite 500, Chicago, IL 60602; by telephone: (800) 621-3256 or (312) 263-3830; by facsimile: (312) 263-3846; or by e-mail at: admin@povertylaw.org.

1.2 Analyzing a Foreclosure Case

1.2.1 Introduction

Borrowers present many different ways of dealing with financial distress and foreclosure. Some seek legal guidance before the foreclosure process begins, some seek help only when the foreclosure sale is imminent, and others do not seek assistance until after the foreclosure sale has been completed. Some borrowers have detailed records, including loan documents, evidence of payments, and notes of telephone conversations with the servicer. Others may have little information regarding the loan transaction and foreclosure beyond a jumble of bills, collection notices and unopened mail. Some homeowners have little or no understanding of the terms of their mortgage loan. Others may be confused by the foreclosure process.

The most common reason for foreclosure is the failure to make payments when due. However, the causes of nonpayment vary widely from unemployment, divorce, or medical issues to rate resets, loan recasts, or loans that were simply unaffordable from the outset.

Regardless of the unique circumstances of each borrower, there are general methods for analyzing foreclosure cases that will provide a quick preliminary evaluation of the case. When more time permits, a thorough analysis can be performed. This section outlines the first steps that an advocate should consider when a client is facing foreclosure. It provides an overview of claims and defenses that might be available to homeowners and highlights important questions to consider. The claims and defenses are discussed in more detail in later chapters.

1.2.2 *First Steps*

1.2.2.1 Identify the Type of Foreclosure

Foreclosure occurs when real property is sold to satisfy an unpaid debt. The debt is often a home mortgage, but foreclosure can also happen because of other liens, too. Tax liens, mechanics' liens, and other debts can lead to foreclosure. Foreclosure—the process by which the home is sold—is governed by state law. State laws vary widely and different laws may apply to different types of foreclosure. Therefore, an important first step is to identify what type of foreclosure the client is facing.

Mortgages or deeds of trust typically are foreclosed either by judicial or non-judicial process.[1] Judicial foreclosure requires a court action prior to foreclosure in which the borrower can raise defenses to foreclosure. In states permitting non-judicial foreclosure by "power of sale," there is little to no court supervision of the foreclosure process. In order to raise defenses to a non-judicial foreclosure, the borrower must file an action for injunctive relief.

For manufactured homes, state law determines whether the home must be foreclosed upon as real property or repossessed as personal property.[2] Another type of foreclosure (or forfeiture) may occur pursuant to a real estate installment sales contract.[3] Several states regulate land installment sales contracts by statute, detailing procedures for termination, forfeiture, or foreclosure. However, in most states, regulation of installment land sales contracts is left to the common law. Lastly, foreclosures can take place pursuant to tax liens.[4] Tax lien foreclosures generally differ from other types of foreclosure, and the sale process varies by locality.

1.2.2.2 Determine Time Constraints

At the outset, identify any deadlines that the homeowner faces, especially any foreclosure sale date. For example, in judicial foreclosures important deadlines may include: the due date for filing an answer in response to the complaint for foreclosure, the date set for redemption, the foreclosure sale date, and the confirmation sale date.

Nonjudicial foreclosures tend to proceed much more quickly, but there are nevertheless statutory steps a lender must take in order to foreclose. Important events to watch for include: notice of default and/or notice of acceleration; notice of sale; and the auction date. Advocates should be aware of important dates established by state law and local practice when the borrower faces repossession of a manufactured home, a tax sale, or forfeiture on a land sale contract.

1.2.2.3 Understanding the Homeowner's Objectives

Homeowners seek assistance defending foreclosures for many types of reasons. Advocates should provide help consistent with the homeowner's objectives and needs. For example, a homeowner who wants help proving that she has made a particular payment that the servicer claims not to have received needs different legal assistance, and may have different claims, than a borrower with a predatory loan. Borrowers may want to remain in their homes indefinitely, may want to stay for a certain number of years (e.g., until children graduate from high school), or may be willing to give up their homes. Each of these client objectives may suggest a different legal strategy. In addition, if the homeowner's objective is clearly unobtainable, an advocate should be prepared to discuss alternative housing and other resources that might be available.

Homeowners in default on their mortgage loans are often behind on other bills, and may be receiving many calls and letters from debt collectors. These aggressive debt collection tactics may distract homeowners and prevent them from focusing on resolving the pending foreclosure. In these cases, advocates may need to help the client deal with these other debts as well.

1.2.2.4 Gather and Review Loan Documents

In defending mortgage loan foreclosures, it is critical to gather and review the loan documents. These documents tell the story about the particular financial transaction and the players involved. Rarely does a homeowner's story come alive without his own testimony, but sometimes the story found in the paperwork is more complete than that related by the homeowner. Furthermore, what appears in the paper story is usually irrefutable, and cases can be won on the paperwork alone.

While every effort should be made to obtain all the documents that the borrower signed at closing, the six most important are the: note, mortgage, HUD-1 settlement statement, TIL disclosure, the notice of right to cancel (if applicable), and the loan application. A payment history should also be obtained from the servicer to verify that payments have been applied correctly, that escrow accounts

---

1 *See* § 4.2, *infra.*
2 *See* Ch. 11, *infra.*
3 *See* Ch. 12, *infra.*
4 *See* Ch. 13, *infra.*

have been handled correctly, and that improper fees have not been charged to the borrower's account. With these documents in hand a preliminary assessment of the borrower's claims is possible. Chapter 10 provides a detailed discussion of how to obtain documents and tips on handling documents once you receive them.

1.2.2.5 Identify the Critical Parties

Every mortgage transaction brings together a variety of actors. Some are directly involved with the homeowner while others operate behind the scenes. Some appear on the stage at the beginning of the process. Others enter the scene when the homeowner makes payments or defaults. Section 1.3.2, *infra*, provides a detailed description of various parties to a mortgage transaction.

However, for purposes of first steps, it is important to identify the loan originator, the current loan holder and the current servicer. The originator is the financial institution that originally provided the loan to the borrower and is typically listed as the payee on the note. The current loan holder is the party that has the present right to receive payments on the note and initiate a foreclosure. Section 1.3.3.3.2, *infra*, discusses how to compel disclosure of the current loan holder, and § 10.2.5, *infra*, discusses the requirement that the borrower receive a transfer of loan ownership notice. The servicer is the intermediary between the current holder and the borrower. The holder typically delegates significant authority to the servicer to resolve delinquent loans and prosecute foreclosures. Section 8.2.3, *infra*, discusses the requirement that the borrower receive a transfer of servicing notice.

1.2.3 Follow the Money

Before analyzing the legal issues involved in a case, a useful exercise is to consider how the money breaks out in the transaction. Determine into whose pocket each dollar goes. If you are reviewing the origination of the loan, a good way to start is by making four lists.

The first list is for those items that are of value to the borrower: proceeds, purchase price, legitimate pay-offs of debts to third parties, legitimate refinanced balances, etc. In the second list, enumerate items to be paid (or purported to be paid) to third parties. The third list is charges clearly identified as going to the creditor.

On some loans there is a fourth "what's this?" list. If you suspect a problem with the loan servicing, a fifth list can consider what is going into the servicer's pockets. Following the money places a spotlight on those parties with the greatest pecuniary interest in the transaction and therefore the greatest incentive to take advantage of the borrower.

1.2.4 Analyze the Loan for Servicing Claims

Generally, the loan servicer initiates the foreclosure. The servicer may act on its own behalf or as agent for the loan holder. Regardless, the servicer's actions may provide either a defense to the foreclosure or a counterclaim in the foreclosure action. The problems that servicers can cause to homeowners, and the legal claims that flow from these problems, are explained in Chapters 6–8, *infra*.

In almost all cases, the home's foreclosure is based on the servicer's assertion that the homeowner is behind in the payments on the mortgage. This fact alone may be subject to challenge. Questions to consider include:

- Is the debt balance correct? Scrutinize a payment history for added fees and overcharges that are not authorized by the loan contract or state law. If an overcharge appears to be deliberate or if a creditor fails to correct an overcharge after notice, the borrower may have grounds for state UDAP claims and state debt collection law claims. When overcharges involve interest, a usury claim may be available. *See* § 6.4.4, *infra*.
- Did the servicer fail to apply payments properly to an account? A misapplication of payments can occur because there has been a lost payment, an overcharge for an escrow item, an inappropriately charged fee that causes the rest of the payments to be insufficient, or the questionable application of payments to a suspense account. *See* §§ 6.3.2.1, 6.3.3, *infra*. Servicers might also overcharge interest, which can occur in daily accrual contracts. *See* § 6.3.4, *infra*.
- Did the servicer mishandle the borrower's escrow account by overcharging the borrower or by failing to make timely payments on taxes and insurance? Servicers have special statutory duties, and possibly common law duties, to administer escrow accounts appropriately. Failure to do so may result in liability under the Real Estate Settlement Procedures Act, UDAP statutes, or common law theories of breach of contract, breach of implied covenant of fair dealing or breach of fiduciary duty. *See* Chapter 8, §§ 6.3.5, 7.7, 7.8, 7.9, *infra*.
- Did the servicer wrongly charge the homeowner for force placed insurance? There are often misunderstandings, failures of communication, or mistakes that cause servicers to place their own insurance on the property. Force placed insurance is much more expensive than homeowners property insurance and will often create havoc with the payment stream. Unwinding the story back to the placement of force placed insurance may uncover mistakes by the servicer that led to the default, which might be used to stop the foreclosure. *See* § 6.3.5.3, *infra*.
- Has the homeowner been wrongfully charged late fees

or other fees? Under most pooling and servicing agreements, the servicer is permitted to keep the late fees and other fees that are assessed against the homeowner. In some cases, servicers use third-party affiliates to perform inspections or prepare broker's price opinions. The servicers' own financial incentives can lead to the improper assessment of fees or requests for default services to be performed more than is reasonable or necessary. *See* § 6.4.4, *infra.*

- Has the servicer mishandled the account while or after the homeowner was in bankruptcy? Many borrowers who have filed for bankruptcy have found that servicers consistently inflate their claims by miscalculation, misunderstanding the loan contract, or deliberate addition of unauthorized fees. *See* § 6.6, *infra.*
- Did the servicer fail to engage in loss mitigation? Several state and federal programs direct servicers to consider borrowers for loss mitigation alternatives, such as a loan modification, before proceeding to foreclosure. Borrowers may be able to prevent foreclosure, or even unwind a foreclosure, if the servicer did not consider the borrower for these alternatives. *See* § 6.4.5, *infra.*

Determining whether any of these problems exist in the relationship between the homeowner and the servicer can quite often provide grounds for both relief from the foreclosure and for affirmative claims against the servicer and the investor (as the servicer is generally either the agent for the investor or they are engaging in a joint venture).

1.2.5 *Analyze the Loan for Legal Defenses*

1.2.5.1 Potential Legal Defenses

Often defending against foreclosure means challenging unfair lending practices used in originating the loan. Borrowers that have been subjected to unfair lending practices may have a number of state and federal statutory claims as well as common law claims that may be asserted in response to foreclosure. Theses claims and defenses are discussed in more detail in Chapter 5.

The first federal statute to consider is the Truth in Lending Act (TILA). Although TILA is only a disclosure statute, with the major exception of the Home Ownership and Equity Protection Act (HOEPA) amendments, it can be extremely important in predatory lending cases. Its remedies can be useful and powerful, particularly where the right to rescind the transaction applies. HOEPA contains limitations on cost-related terms in covered high-cost home equity loans. Another federal law that contains substantive limitations is the Real Estate Settlement Procedures Act (RESPA).

Several states and localities have enacted home loan protection laws. These provide broader protections than those contained in HOEPA and are an additional source of remedies for the distressed homeowner. Since borrowers of color, older homeowners, and women are often targeted for high-cost loans, fair lending, fair housing, and civil rights statutes provide a source of potential challenge to abusive mortgage lending. One of the most vital and widely available statutory tools in cases of predatory lending is the state unfair and deceptive practices acts (UDAP) statute, which generally prohibits unfair or deceptive business practices. Federal and state RICO statutes may be available when homeowners have been subjected to a broadly defined range of "racketeering activity" or to the collection of an "unlawful debt." Finally, state door-to-door solicitation acts and licensing laws may be raised against various parties to a home loan transaction.

The use of common law theories, including equitable considerations, in the home loan context may be used to address creditor overreaching even where a specific federal or state statute has not been violated. Unconscionability may be used to attack the practices of making unaffordable loans, flipping, and charging outrageous fees. Traditional common law theories of fraud and misrepresentation play powerfully to juries. Breach of fiduciary duty claims are available against brokers who steer borrowers to predatory lenders, and, in limited circumstances, may also be available against lenders. Similarly, lenders may be vulnerable to claims for interference with contractual relations where they seduce brokers into arranging loans based on the brokers' own interest rather than the interests of the brokers' client-borrowers.

1.2.5.2 Specific Law Violations to Investigate

When considering substantive defenses, advocates should ask:

- Did the originator violate the state unfair and deceptive acts and practices (UDAP) statute in making the loan? UDAP violations may include failure to disclose the disadvantageous nature of a loan, "flipping" or continuously refinancing a loan, "overcollateralization," in which a home is taken as security for a small loan, and "loan-padding," in which the loan is structured to increase its size without advancing additional funds to the borrower. *See* § 5.5, *infra.*
- Is the loan usurious under state law? Usurious loans are void in some states, and therefore not enforceable by foreclosure. *See* § 5.13.5, *infra.*
- Did the originator or mortgage broker commit fraud or make misrepresentations in connection with the loan? The loan may be void or subject to reformation by the court. *See* § 5.12, *infra.*
- Do any special circumstances exist which would give rise to a fiduciary duty on the part of the originator? For example, did the originator act as an advisor to the

borrower? If a fiduciary relationship gives rise to a duty to disclose, failure to disclose any disadvantageous financial terms may invalidate the mortgage. *See* § 5.13.2, *infra*.

- Was the originator part of an "enterprise" that has engaged in a "pattern of racketeering" or collection of an "unlawful debt"? A federal Racketeer Influenced and Corrupt Organizations Act (RICO) claim may be available. *See* § 5.13.6, *infra*.
- Did the originator make all disclosures required by the Truth in Lending Act (TILA)? *See* § 5.6, *infra*.
  - If the loan is a home equity loan or other non-purchase money mortgage it may be subject to TIL rescission if the proper disclosures were not made. *See* § 5.6, *infra*.
  - If the loan qualifies as a high-rate home equity loan, special disclosure requirements apply. *See* § 5.8, *infra*.
  - If the loan is a purchase money mortgage, the borrower may still have a claim for damages under TILA if the proper disclosures were not made, even though rescission is not available. *See* § 5.6.7, *infra*.
- If the borrower purchased credit insurance, was there a post-claim denial of coverage by the insurer? If the lender either failed to obtain the policy or if the lender knew at the time it sold the policy that the borrower was not eligible for coverage, then the court may prevent a foreclosure. The borrower may also have claims for damages against either the originator or insurer. *See* § 5.3.3.4, *infra*.
- Did the originator engage in predatory lending or some other home equity scam? Three such scams are home improvement financing scams, refinancing schemes, and foreclosure rescue scams. *See* §§ 5.3.1, 5.3.5, and Chapter 15, *infra*.
- Is the foreclosing mortgage holder the Federal Deposit Insurance Corp. (FDIC) or the Resolution Trust Corp. (RTC)? If so, the borrower may be precluded from raising some claims because of the *D'Oench, Duhme* doctrine and the federal "super holder in due course" doctrine. *See* § 5.14.3, *infra*.
- If there is state action involved in the foreclosure process (for example, if the foreclosing mortgage holder is a state or federal agency) and the foreclosure is by power of sale, it may be subject to a constitutional due process challenge. *See* §§ 3.1.2, 4.7, *infra*.
- Did the originator violate the federal Equal Credit Opportunity Act in making the loan? ECOA violations most often occur when a lender requires a wife's signature on a promissory note even though she is not an applicant on the loan and even though the husband is creditworthy in his own right. *See* § 5.10, *infra*.
- Was the debtor incompetent at the time the mortgage was granted? *See* § 5.13.3, *infra*.
- Are terms unreasonably favorable to the originator, or are certain aspects of the transaction unconscionable? The common law contract defense of unconscionability may apply. *See* § 5.13.4, *infra*.

1.2.6 Analyze the Loan for Procedural Defenses

Borrowers may have defenses to foreclosure where the servicer[5] has not complied with procedures required under state law. In many cases, procedural defects result in an invalid sale and require the servicer to reinitiate the foreclosure process. While this may not provide a permanent solution, it gives borrowers more time to mount a defense or find alternative housing.

When examining the sale for procedural defects, ask:

- Is the entity attempting to foreclose a real party in interest? Generally, the party that possesses the right to collect upon the note is the real party in interest. *See* § 4.4, *infra*.
- Has the servicer waived the right to require that payments be made on time by accepting late payments in the past? *See* § 4.3.3, *infra*.
- Is the servicer improperly attempting to enforce a due on sale provision? *See* § 4.9, *infra*.
- Has the servicer failed to comply with state foreclosure law? State pre-foreclosure notice requirements, as well as contractual requirements, must be strictly followed. *See* §§ 4.2.3, 4.3.2, *infra*.
- Has the servicer violated a state moratorium on foreclosures? *See* § 4.11, *infra*.
- Is the borrower a servicemember entitled to protection under the Servicemembers Civil Relief Act? *See* § 4.12, *infra*.

1.2.7 Negotiating a Workout or Modification

In some cases, a workout or loan modification can achieve a result as good as litigation with the expenditure of far less time and money. In other cases, borrowers may not have strong enough claims to pursue a litigation strategy. In either case, advocates should determine whether a workout agreement or loan modification is possible.

Potential workout terms include a forbearance agreement, temporary interest rate reduction, recasting of missed payments, or permanent modification of loan terms. Chapter 2 details the various workout and modifications that are available.

If no workout agreement is possible, an advocate should determine the following prior to foreclosure:

5 Typically the servicer prosecutes foreclosure actions on behalf of the current holder.

- Does the homeowner have equity and is the homeowner willing to sell the property before foreclosure to preserve its equity? *See* § 2.5, *infra*.
- Is the homeowner able to refinance with a different lender at a lower interest rate? *See* § 2.3.2, *infra*.
- Does the homeowner qualify for a mortgage assistance program? Some states have programs that provide loans to homeowners to make mortgage payments if they meet certain eligibility requirements. *See* § 2.3.3, *infra*.

1.2.8 Should the Homeowner File for Bankruptcy to Protect the Home?

Filing bankruptcy triggers an automatic stay for most debtors, freezing the creditor's ability to foreclose on the home. An emergency filing of a three-page petition, along with certification of compliance with the 2005 Act's credit counseling requirement, stays foreclosure;[6] other bankruptcy forms must be filed within fifteen days thereafter. The consumer's attorney should notify the creditor of the automatic stay. Remedies for violation of the stay include recovery of actual damages, attorney fees, and equitable relief.

Creditors must follow strict procedures in obtaining relief from the stay. Debtors can contest the hearing on the creditor's request for relief from the stay, demonstrate adequate protection for the creditor, and raise defenses and counterclaims. *See* § 9.6, *infra*. The advocate should also consider the following issues:

- Can the homeowner use a chapter 13 bankruptcy to cure the default? A default on a home mortgage can be cured within a reasonable period of time, in some cases even after a foreclosure sale has taken place. *See* § 9.4, *infra*.
- Can the mortgage be "stripped down" to the value of the property? Strip-down is allowed in a chapter 13 case if the mortgage is not secured solely by the debtor's home and by certain "incidental property" related to the home, or when the mortgage is wholly unsecured because the value of the property is less than the amount of senior liens, or when the last payment under mortgage comes due during the chapter 13 case. *See* § 9.7, *infra*.
- Can a judicial lien on the home be avoided in bankruptcy to the extent it impairs an exemption? *See* § 9.8, *infra*.
- When it is not possible to save the home, can it be sold in bankruptcy so that all of the equity is not lost? *See* § 9.10, *infra*.
- Can TIL rescission, or other substantive defenses, be raised in an adversary proceeding to challenge the creditor's proof of claim or respond to a motion for relief from stay? *See* § 9.6, *infra*.

1.2.9 Manufactured Home Foreclosures

State law governs whether a manufactured home must be foreclosed upon as real property or repossessed as personalty. If the property is treated as real estate under state law, then foreclosure procedures are the same as those covered in Chapter 4, *infra*. As with other real estate, a loan workout agreement or modification may be available prior to foreclosure on a manufactured home.

If the property is treated as personalty, then the repossession protections of Article 9 of the Uniform Commercial Code, discussed in NCLC's *Repossessions*[7] apply. Assuming that the manufactured home is considered personal property, some states prohibit self-help repossession of manufactured homes. Even if self-help repossession is allowed, creditors may find it so difficult that they will resort to a judicial remedy such as replevin. Federal law and some state laws afford a special right to cure a default before repossession or to reinstate a contract after repossession of a manufactured home. The advocate should ask:

- Does the buyer have a right to cure or reinstate under state or federal law, and has the creditor complied fully with this right? *See* National Consumer Law Center, *Repossessions* §§ 4.8.2, 9.2 (6th ed. 2005 and Supp.).
- Did the creditor breach the peace while utilizing self-help repossession? *See* National Consumer Law Center, *Repossessions* § 6.4 (6th ed. 2005 and Supp.).
- If the creditor is using replevin to recover the manufactured home, is it complying with all the procedural and substantive requirements for replevin? *See* National Consumer Law Center, *Repossessions* Chapter 5 (6th ed. 2005 and Supp.).
- If the creditor has sold the home, was the sale to an insider? Was the sale commercially reasonable? Was notice of the sale proper? *See* National Consumer Law Center, *Repossessions* §§ 10.6 to 10.8, 11.3.5 (6th ed. 2005 and Supp.). Commercially unreasonable sales to insiders are particularly common with manufactured homes.

Regardless of whether the home is treated as realty or personalty, the advocate should ask:

- Is the home located on a rented manufactured home park lot? If so, to prevent eviction or seizure of the manufactured home, ground rent must be paid. *See* § 11.14, *infra*.
- Does the owner of the manufactured home also own the

6 Several provisions of the Bankruptcy Code limit application of the automatic stay for repeat bankruptcy filers. *See* § 9.3.3.2, *infra*.

7 National Consumer Law Center, Repossessions § 1.3.11 (6th ed. 2005 and Supp.).

land on which the manufactured home is situated? That land may be subject to a mortgage and that mortgage must also be paid, especially if the manufactured home is affixed to the property. *See* §§ 11.2, 11.15, *infra*.

- Did the creditor send the debtor a notice of right to cure at least thirty days before accelerating the debt or commencing foreclosure? If the creditor is claiming the right to extend credit under federal law without regard to state usury ceilings, federal regulations require it to offer this right to cure. *See* § 11.5.2, *infra*.
- Would filing bankruptcy help the debtor? Bankruptcy can be particularly useful as a means of saving a manufactured home. *See* § 11.12, *infra*; National Consumer Law Center, *Repossessions* §§ 8.5.4, 8.6.3, 8.7 (6th ed. 2005 and Supp.).

1.2.10 Real Estate Installment Sales

Real estate installment sales laws in many states provide special consumer protections if the purchaser defaults. Statutory or decisional law may treat real estate installment sales agreements as security agreements in some circumstances. State foreclosure law would then apply. *See* § 12.5, *infra*. Advocates should consider the following:

- Are there equitable defenses to protect against forfeiture of home equity created under an installment sale agreement? *See* § 12.4, *infra*.
- Are bankruptcy precedents available to obtain treatment of the debt created by the installment sale contract as a secured claim in chapter 13? *See* § 12.5, *infra*.

1.2.11 Is the Foreclosure Pursuant to a Tax Lien?

If a homeowner's property taxes are not paid by the date set by statute, the unpaid taxes become a lien on the property. If the tax lien is not satisfied by payment, the taxing authority may initiate the tax sale process. The sale process varies depending on the locality. In some jurisdictions the property is sold; in others a certificate or lien is sold. In other states, no sale occurs at all, and the taxing authority simply takes the property. In all states, however, the taxing authority must follow all statutory requirements.

Generally, after a tax sale, the taxpayer has the right to redeem the property by paying the taxes within the redemption period. In some states, once the redemption period expires, if the taxpayer has not redeemed, title is automatically issued to the tax sale purchaser. In other jurisdictions, the tax sale purchaser must bring a foreclosure action to cut off the right of redemption.

Prior to a tax sale, homeowners can take steps to minimize their tax liability. An assessment may be challenged if the assessment exceeds the property's taxable value. In most states, challenges must be filed immediately after the issuance of the tax bill, and in some states must be accompanied by payment of the tax. Homeowners may also minimize their tax liability by applying for an abatement. *See* § 13.3.1, *infra*.

A homeowner may contest a tax sale. If the tax sale is by judicial process, the taxpayer can raise defenses such as the property's exemption from taxation, lack of statutory authority for the tax, lack of statutory authority for the taxing official's actions, fraud, and payment. *See* § 13.3.2, *infra*.

If the tax sale is a non-judicial process, which most are, the taxpayer must initiate legal action to prevent the sale by injunction. There may be significant procedural obstacles to such an action. Taxpayers may be required to exhaust administrative remedies or to pay the disputed tax and then sue for its return. Nevertheless, there may be grounds to seek an injunction when the tax creditor is fully secured by the equity in the property. *See* § 13.3.2.3, *infra*.

Tax sales involve state action and are therefore subject to due process requirements. Due process requires adequate notice, which means notice by mail in most cases. Due process also requires a full and adequate opportunity to protest, at a hearing. *See* § 13.3.4, *infra*.

After the tax sale an advocate may attempt to overturn the sale. A tax sale may be set aside when there are defects in the sale process. The sale must substantially comply with the state tax sale statute. Advocates should consider the following:

- Can the sale be declared void or collaterally attacked because the taxes are not owed or have already been paid? *See* § 13.3.3.2.3, *infra*.
- Was there fraud or error either in the sale process or in the imposition of the tax that would render the sale void? *See* § 13.3.3.2.4, *infra*.
- Can the tax sale be set aside based on the taxpayer's excusable neglect in failing to respond to a tax sale notice? *See* § 13.3.3.2.6, *infra*.
- Are there equitable grounds to set aside the sale, for example, when a taxpayer has been misled by the taxing authority? *See* § 13.3.3.2.7, *infra*.
- Was there such a gross inadequacy of price or an inadequate price coupled with irregularity or unfairness in the sale process that may be sufficient to justify setting aside the sale? *See* § 13.3.3.2.8, *infra*.
- Does the homeowner still have the right to redeem the property? If so, can the homeowner pay the redemption amount or do so in a chapter 13 bankruptcy? *See* § 13.4, *infra*.

1.2.12 *Is It Possible to Set Aside the Foreclosure Sale?*

Generally, an irregularity in the foreclosure process, including an unconscionably low sales price, may be grounds to invalidate a completed foreclosure sale. If the mortgage was foreclosed upon by power of sale, the homeowner must generally initiate an action to set aside the sale. If the foreclosure was conducted by judicial process, the homeowner may file a motion in the foreclosure action to set aside the foreclosure judgment or to attack the sale. Some states have sale confirmation processes in which objections to the sale must be made. *See* § 14.2, *infra*. An advocate should consider the following:

- Was there any irregularity in the conduct of the sale? *See* § 14.2.3.2, *infra*.
- Did the homeowner receive all the required notices? Was the sale properly advertised? *See* §§ 14.2.3.2, 14.2.3.3.2, *infra*.
- Was the sales price grossly inadequate? Was this inadequate price coupled with some irregularity in the sale, or unfair action by the mortgage holder? *See* § 14.2.3.3, *infra*.
- Is filing bankruptcy advisable? In some states, a debtor can cure a default on a home loan in a chapter 13 bankruptcy, even after a foreclosure auction has taken place. *See* § 14.2.4, *infra*.
- Can the consumer redeem the property? In some states, a right of redemption allows the borrower to retain the home by paying the balance of the mortgage, plus foreclosure costs. Some borrowers can redeem through refinancing the debt or curing the arrearage through a bankruptcy. *See* §§ 9.4.4, 14.1.2, *infra*.

1.2.13 *Is the Consumer Liable for a Deficiency After the Sale?*

If the foreclosure sale price is not sufficient to satisfy the mortgage debt, the lender may be able to obtain a deficiency judgment. Some states have placed restrictions on deficiency judgments, such as requiring that the borrower be given credit for the "fair value" of the property regardless of the foreclosure sale price. Courts have also limited deficiencies on equitable grounds, when the foreclosure sale price was found to be inadequate. Even if a lender obtains a deficiency judgment, it is an unsecured debt which can be discharged in bankruptcy. *See* § 14.3.5, *infra*.

1.3 Understanding the Mortgage Market

1.3.1 *Introduction*

The workings of the mortgage markets are a mystery to most consumers. However, for an advocate, a basic understanding of how mortgage markets function and the players involved has become essential to the effective representation of mortgage borrowers.

Every mortgage transaction brings together a variety of actors. Some are directly involved with the homeowner while others operate behind the scenes. The following subsections describe key players involved in most residential mortgages transactions. The first subsection identifies parties typically involved in the origination of a loan. The second group of players are those that more commonly enter the picture after the parties have entered into a mortgage loan agreement.

1.3.2 *The Players in the Mortgage Origination Process*

1.3.2.1 Mortgage Originator

The mortgage loan originator[8] is the entity that makes the loan and whose name appears as the lender on the loan note and mortgage.[9] The originator may or may not be the party that currently holds the loan and has the right to receive payments on the loan.[10]

Historically, financial institutions that originated loans continued to own the loan. As part of the origination process the financial institution evaluated the risk of the loan, collected payments, and adjusted the payment agreement as circumstances warranted. In this model, lenders made money by making performing loans, borrowers had unmediated access to the holder of their loan, and both lenders and borrowers had in-depth information about local markets. This unity of ownership, with its concomitant transparency, has long since passed. Today, most mortgages are sold or otherwise transferred to another entity shortly after origina-

8 The term, "loan originator," as used in this manner, should not be confused with the same term as used in the SAFE Act. Pub. L. No. 110-289, tit. V, 122 Stat. 2654 (July 30, 2008). Section 1503(3)(A)(i) of the SAFE Act defines "loan originator" as "an individual who (I) takes a residential mortgage loan application and (II) offers or negotiates terms of a residential mortgage loan for compensation or gain." *See* § 5.13.8, *infra* (SAFE Act).

9 For some loans, the Mortgage Electronic Registration System (MERS) appears as the mortgage holder of record or beneficiary of the deed of trust as "nominee" for the loan originator. *See* § 1.3.2.4, *infra*.

10 *See* § 1.3.3.3, *infra*.

tion. As a result, the holder of the mortgage loan at the time a borrower faces foreclosure is not typically the originator.

1.3.2.2 Mortgage Broker

Traditionally, mortgage brokers acted as an intermediary between borrowers and lenders. They did not originate loans. Instead, mortgage brokers were merely middlemen bringing home purchasers or homeowners and lenders together. Brokers operated on behalf of borrowers and attempted to find them the best loans available. This type of arrangement created a special duty on the part of the broker to act in the best interest of the borrower.[11]

Over the years, the role of the mortgage broker has become much more complex. While some brokers continue in the traditional intermediary role, others have taken to originating loans with their own money; by using "table funding"[12] from a prearranged buyer of the loan; or by using a line of credit from a bank, financial institution, or other entity. The fact one person acts as both broker and lender in such transactions complicates the broker-borrower relationship. In these situations, brokers often are working in their own best interest rather than finding the loan product best suited to the borrower's financial needs and abilities.

Home improvement contractors and manufactured home dealers may act as brokers as well. In this capacity, they usually prearrange with a lender to funnel loans to customers who need financing.

Mortgage brokers have been subject to varying degrees of regulation under state law. In response to the recent foreclosure crisis, Congress enacted the Secure and Fair Enforcement Mortgage Licensing Act,[13] also known as the SAFE Act, in 2008. The SAFE Act instituted a nationwide system for licensing and registering "loan originators," including mortgage brokers. Under the SAFE Act, mortgage brokers must participate in pre-licensing and continuing education, must pass a national exam, and must meet specified bonding requirements.

1.3.2.3 Loan Officer

Loan officers are employees of financial institutions who assist home buyers or homeowners in selecting a mortgage loan product offered by their institutions. They are essentially in-house salespeople for banks or mortgage companies. Until recently, loan officers were not required to be individually licensed (although their institutions would generally be licensed entities). Under the SAFE Act,[14] many loan officers will have to obtain an individual license after undergoing pre-licensing training and passing an exam.

1.3.2.4 Mortgage Electronic Registration System (MERS)

The Mortgage Electronic Registration System (MERS) is an electronic registry and clearinghouse established to track ownership and servicing rights in mortgages. For many home loans, MERS, as "nominee" for the lender, is the mortgage holder of record or the beneficiary on a deed of trust. MERS typically has no legal or beneficial interest in the promissory note. Nevertheless, as mortgage holder, MERS frequently initiates foreclosure proceedings. Courts have disagreed over whether MERS has authority to foreclose on a mortgage in its own name.[15]

1.3.2.5 Real Estate Agent

Real estate is often sold through real estate agents or real estate brokers (not to be confused with mortgage brokers, see § 1.3.2.2, *supra*). They list the property in newspapers, circulars, and computer databases. The agents usually represent the seller of the property. However, in some circumstances real estate agents may be buyer's agents or may even undertake representation of both seller and buyer. Real estate agents are typically paid a percentage of the sales price. States commonly require agents to be licensed. Real estate agents frequently recommend mortgage lenders and mortgage brokers to home buyers.

1.3.2.6 Appraiser

Originators, or in some cases mortgages brokers, hire an appraiser or appraisal management company (AMC) to determine the value of the property. AMCs are essentially brokers for appraisal services. They administer networks of independent appraisers to perform appraisals.

Appraisers are subject to state regulation and professional standards, as provided in the Uniform Standards of Professional Appraisal Practice, which is promulgated nationally by the Appraisal Standards Board. In addition, the Home Valuation Code of Conduct (HVCC) establishes standards for solicitation, selection, compensation, conflicts of interest, and appraiser independence for any mortgage loan sold to Fannie Mae or Freddie Mac.[16] The HVCC specifically prohibits lenders from accepting reports completed by an

11 *See* § 5.3.2, *infra.*

12 Table-funding is the process whereby a loan is closed in the name of the original lender, typically a mortgage broker, and the loan funds are provided by an investor who takes assignment of the loan immediately. HUD recognizes that the true lender in this situation is the funder of the loan, meaning the entity to whom the loan is initially assigned after settlement. *See* Regulation X, 24 C.F.R. § 3500.2 (definition of "lender").

13 Pub. L. No. 110-289, tit. V, 122 Stat. 2654 (July 30, 2008). *See* § 5.13.8, *infra.*

14 *Id.*

15 *See* § 4.9, *infra* (detailed discussion of MERS and defenses to foreclosures by MERS).

16 Fannie Mae is the Federal National Mortgage Association; Freddie Mac is the Federal Home Loan Mortgage Corporation.

appraiser selected, retained, or compensated in any manner by mortgage brokers or real estate agents. Under the HVCC borrowers must be provided with a copy of the appraisal at least three days prior to the closing unless the borrowers sign a waiver stating that they do not wish to receive a copy of the appraisal.

For loans not covered by HVCC, originators must furnish borrowers with a copy of the appraisal report upon written request made within a reasonable period of time from the application date.[17] Additionally, effective October 1, 2009, regulations promulgated by the Federal Reserve Board, under the Truth and Lending Act, prohibit creditors and their affiliates from coercing appraisers to misstate property valuation.[18]

Borrowers may pay for appraisal before the closing, or the broker or lender may pay for the appraisal and require the borrower to reimburse the cost of appraisal out of the loan proceeds. In either case, the payment for the appraisal should be listed on the HUD-1 settlement statement.

Obtaining an inflated appraisal is a key element of many mortgage fraud schemes.[19]

1.3.2.7 Closing Agent or Attorney

The mortgage loan closing or settlement is usually conducted by an agent for the lender.[20] Often this agent is an attorney. The name and address of the closing agent is listed on the HUD-1 settlement statement. Homeowners are sometimes under the mistaken impression that the closing agent works for them. This is not surprising since the homeowner pays the agent's bill for conducting the closing and other pre-closing activity, such as searching title and preparing documents. Whether the closing attorney has any duty to the homeowner is a question of state law.[21]

1.3.2.8 Escrow Agent

If all of the monies from the loan proceeds are not distributed at the loan closing, the closing agent is usually responsible for holding the remainder until certain events occur. If it is a home improvement loan, it is common for the remaining proceeds to be paid to a home improvement contractor once work is completed. If the loan is covered by the Home Ownership and Equity Protection Act (HOEPA), the lender cannot (nor can the escrow agent as agent for the lender) pay this money to the contractor in the form of a check or other instrument made out solely to the contractor.[22] The lender or escrow agent may have drafted an escrow agreement that governs to whom and when the remaining funds will be paid.

This type of escrow agent should be distinguished from the role played by loan servicers in managing borrowers' escrow accounts. Under many loan agreements the borrowers' monthly payments include principal, interest, and escrow amounts. Escrow amounts can be used to pay for homeowner's insurance, property taxes, condominium fees, private mortgages insurance, and other similar costs. Loan servicers are typically responsible for collecting, holding, and paying out these monies appropriately. The role of loan servicers as escrow agents is discussed in more detail at Chapter 8, *infra*.

1.3.2.9 Private Mortgage Insurance Companies

Mortgage insurance is common in mortgage transactions involving home purchases. When the borrower's down payment is less than 20% of the purchase price, private mortgage insurance is generally required. The cost of this insurance is added to the borrower's monthly payment and escrowed by the lender. If the borrower defaults, the mortgage insurer will pay the lender some of the monies not recouped in the foreclosure process. The Homeowner's Protection Act of 1998 requires that the insurance be terminated once the equity in the home equals 20%, upon written request, or in any event once the equity reaches 22%.[23]

In many cases, mortgage insurers have an interest in preventing foreclosure, and they can be an ally to the borrower in negotiating a workout or settling claims.

1.3.2.10 Government Mortgage Guarantors

There are special government programs that provide mortgage insurance or guarantees to lenders who make mortgage loans to homebuyers who meet certain criteria. These programs are offered by the federal government (the Federal Housing Administration (FHA), which is part of the U.S. Department of Housing and Urban Development; the Rural Housing Service, which is part of the U.S. Department of Agriculture; and the Department of Veterans Affairs) or by a state housing finance agency. Under these programs, the insurance covers close to 100% of losses. In addition to insurance, these loans come with an obligation on the part of the insured lenders to work with homeowners to cure default.[24]

17 15 U.S.C. § 1691(e).

18 12 C.F.R. § 226.36(b). *See* § 5.3.4.3, *infra*.

19 *See* § 5.3.4, *infra*; National Consumer Law Center, The Cost of Credit § 11.6.6 (4th ed. 2009 and Supp.).

20 *See, e.g.,* Garrett v. Fleet Fin., Inc., 556 S.E.2d 140 (Ga. Ct. App. 2001); Horvath v. Adelson, Golden & Loria, P.C. 773 N.E.2d 478 (Mass. Ct. App. 2002).

21 *See* § 5.3.4.4, *infra*.

22 15 U.S.C. § 1639(i).

23 12 U.S.C. §§ 4901 to 4910. *See* National Consumer Law Center, The Cost of Credit: Regulation, Preemption, and Industry Abuses § 8.3.2.1 (4th ed. 2009 and Supp.). *See also* § 6.3.6, *infra*.

24 *See* Ch. 3, *infra*.

1.3.3 Post-Closing Players

1.3.3.1 Introduction

After a mortgage loan transaction has been consummated a new set of players frequently comes onto the scene. The rise of the secondary mortgage market and the securitization of mortgage loans has created an entirely different cast of characters that play a role during the lifespan of a mortgage loan.

For most of the twentieth century, a mortgage established a long-term relationship between lender and home buyer. The same entity conducted all facets of the home purchase transaction related to obtaining and paying the mortgage loan. Today the vast majority of loans are originated and then sold in whole, so one investor ends up with the entire loan, or securitized. The securitization process, which is discussed in more detail at § 1.3.3.4, *infra*, involves pooling mortgage loans, transferring those obligations to a trust, and then selling fractional interests in the trust's pool of mortgages to investors. Regardless of whether the loan is sold whole or securitized, the end result is that the mortgage holder is typically not the bank or mortgage company that originated the loan.

The right to service mortgage loans may be sold or transferred independently of the loans themselves. The entity with the right to service a mortgage loan is called a servicer. Servicers provide the link between mortgage loan borrowers and mortgage loan holders. They exist to collect and process borrowers' payments, and they handle interest rate adjustments on adjustable rate mortgages, collect and report information to national credit bureaus, and prosecute foreclosures in the event of default. Commonly, the originating lender retains the servicing rights when it sells a mortgage loan. Such a lender would be considered both the originator and servicer, but not the current creditor, or holder, of the loan.

This subsection highlights processes and players that may become involved with mortgage loans after the loan closes.

1.3.3.2 Secondary Mortgage Market

The secondary market is not a place, like Wall Street. Rather, this term describes the phenomenon by which originating lenders sell their loans to buyers (often called investors), usually in bulk. This enables mortgage companies specializing in home equity lending to operate with a small capital base. They can obtain a line of credit from a major bank or firm, originate mortgage loans, and then sell the loans to the secondary market. The secondary market includes "wholesale" lenders who buy loans from smaller lenders, and the securitization market where mortgage loans are pooled and the interest in cash-flows from those loan-pools are sold to investors.

Fannie Mae and Freddie Mac purchase huge numbers of loans in the secondary market. Congress created these entities to provide liquidity or capital in the housing market by purchasing mortgages. This phenomenon puts money back into the hands of the originating lenders so that new loans can be made. The originating lender must follow certain underwriting guidelines specified by Freddie Mac and Fannie Mae when qualifying the borrower for a loan.

1.3.3.3 Mortgage Holder

1.3.3.3.1 In general

The mortgage holder is the entity that currently holds the borrower's note. This is the party that has the present right to receive payments on the note. When the holder is also the mortgage holder or beneficiary of a deed of trust, it has the right to initiate foreclosure proceedings upon default by the borrower.

Many mortgages are sold or otherwise transferred to another entity shortly after origination. As a result, the mortgage holder often is not the bank or mortgage company that made the original loan. Some mortgage loans are pooled and sold (i.e., securitized) pursuant to a trust agreement so that the mortgage holder is a trust. Large financial institutions typically serve as trustees for these trust (e.g., Deutsche Bank National Trust Company as Trustee for the MLMI Trust Series 2005-SL1 or JPMorgan Chase Bank, N.A. as trustee, C-Bass Mortgage Loan Asset Backed Certificates, Series 2004-CB).

1.3.3.3.2 Finding out who owns the mortgage

Sometimes it is difficult to determine who is the present owner of a mortgage loan. A mortgage loan may be assigned several times during its term, and may be held by one entity but serviced by another.

Commonly, a servicer acts as the agent for the holder under the express authority delegated to it under a servicing agreement or, in the case of securitized loans, a pooling and servicing agreement. Occasionally, the servicer will refuse to provide information about its principal—the owner and holder of the note and mortgage. The Truth in Lending Act contains a provision that requires loan servicers to tell borrowers who the actual holder of their mortgage really is.[25] The servicer is required upon written request to provide the homeowner with the name, address, and telephone number of the owner of the mortgage or the master servicer[26] of the mortgage. Unfortunately, there is no time

25 15. U.S.C. § 1641(f). The provision also should require disclosure to the borrower's advocate with a properly signed release form. *See* Appx. H, Form 3, *infra*.

26 If the borrower is provided with the name and address of the master servicer, a second request under § 1641(f) may be sent

frame specified in the statute by which the servicer need respond. The servicer should respond within a reasonable period of time, not to exceed a few weeks. The remedy for failure to comply has also been problematic. However, an amendment to TILA made by the Helping Families Save Their Homes Act of 2009,[27] now states that violations of this notice requirement may be remedied by TILA's private right of action found in 15 U.S.C. § 1640(a), which includes recovery of actual damages, statutory damages, costs, and attorney fees.[28]

A 2009 amendment to TILA also added a provision which requires that if ownership of a mortgage loan is transferred, the new owner or assignee must notify the borrower, within thirty days after the loan is sold or assigned, of its identity, address, telephone number, and the date of transfer, and location where the transfer is recorded.[29] In addition, the new owner must disclose how the borrower may reach an agent or party with authority to act on behalf of the new owner, and any other relevant information regarding the new owner.[30] Failure to comply with these requirements gives rise to a private right of action.[31] This provision is examined in detail at § 10.2.6, *infra*.

Fannie Mae and Freddie Mac have taken steps to enable borrowers to quickly determine whether Fannie Mae or Freddie Mac owns their loan. Borrowers and advocates can either call a toll-free number[32] or enter a street address, unit, city, state, and zip code for the property location on a website set up to provide ownership information.[33] The website information, however, may in some cases refer to Fannie Mae or Freddie Mac as "owners" when in fact their participation may have been as the party that had initially purchased the loans on the secondary market and later arranged for their securitization and transfer to a trust entity which ultimately holds the loan.

to the master servicer to determine the owner of the loan.

27 Pub. Law No. 111-22, tit. IV, § 404, 123 Stat. 1632 (May 20, 2009).

28 *See* 15 U.S.C. § 1640(a). A written request for identification of the mortgage owner sent to the servicer will also be a "qualified written request" under RESPA, which authorizes a private cause of action for violations. *See* § 8.2.2, *infra*.

29 *See* 15 U.S.C. § 1641(g)(1)(A), (B), (D).

30 *See* 15 U.S.C. § 1641(g)(1)(C), (E).

31 See 15 U.S.C. § 1640(a).

32 For Fannie Mae call 1-800-7FANNIE (8:00 a.m. to 8:00 p.m. EST); Freddie Mac call 1-800-FREDDIE (8:00 a.m. to 8:00 p.m. EST).

33 Fannie Maw Loan Lookup, at www.fanniemae.com/homeaffordable; Freddie Mac Self-Service Lookup, https://ww3.freddiemac.com/corporate.

1.3.3.4 Securitization

1.3.3.4.1 In general

Securitization is the process of packaging loans as securities and selling the rights to the future income stream to investors.[34] These rights are pooled in a variety of different ways so that the income stream from a single loan may be divided up and sold as part of two or more different securities. The borrowers' monthly payments on the loan cover both the return to the investors and the profits to the lender. The pools of loans are rated by the various bond-rating agencies.[35] The structure of these transactions attempts to minimize the risk of loss to the investors through insurance and recourse agreements between the trustee and originator.

The securitization of conventional mortgage loans has been around for years. The Government National Mortgage Association (Ginnie Mae), a quasi governmental agency, guarantees pools of loans insured by the Federal Housing Administration (FHA) and the Veteran Administration (VA) for investment purposes. Fannie Mae and Freddie Mac also securitize loans that they purchase through the secondary mortgage market. Typically the loans in these pools must comply with Fannie Mae or Freddie Mac guidelines. Private financial institutions may also securitize loans in what are called "private-label securitizations." The structure of private label securitizations tends to be more diverse than the standardized structures used by Ginnie Mae, Fannie Mae, and Freddie Mac.

For several reasons an understanding of securitization has become essential to the effective representation of mortgage borrowers. First, because securitization results in a transfer of ownership of the underlying loan (usually to a trust), the concept of "real party in interest" is rendered more complex.[36] With a securitized loan the entity pursuing foreclosure may not be the entity that actually holds the loan.

Second, because it is often the case that wrongdoing lenders go out of business or become insolvent, the existence of a consumer remedy may depend on evaluating liability theories against other participants in the securitization transaction. Perhaps more importantly, in defending against foreclosure, the borrower will want to raise defenses

34 *See* Kurt Eggert, *Held Up in Due Course: Predatory Lending, Securitization, and the Holder in Due Course Doctrine*, 35 Creighton L. Rev. 507 (Apr. 2002); Christopher L. Peterson, *Predatory Structured Finance*, 28 Cardozo L. Rev. 2185 (2007). For more technical sources see Frank Fabozzi, The Handbook of Mortgage-Backed Securities (2005); Talcott J. Franklin and Thomas F. Nelson, Mortgage and Asset Backed Securities Litigation Handbook (2010).

35 The rating companies could be Moody's, Standard and Poors or Duff & Phelps Credit Rating Company. *See* National Consumer Law Center, The Cost of Credit: Regulation, Preemption, and Industry Abuses § 11.3 (4th ed. 2009 and Supp.).

36 *See* § 4.3.4, *infra*.

that she could raise against the originating lender.[37] Whether the borrower can raise these defenses and claims against subsequent note holders in a securitization transaction requires thorough analysis, since one of the very purposes of securitization is to insulate participants from legal responsibility for the liability-producing activity of the originating lender.[38]

Third, securitizations generate extensive transactional documentation and extensive ongoing reporting. Reading this paperwork with an understanding of the securitization process can provide important sources of information about the companies involved and about the underlying loans.

Securitization is discussed in more detail in National Consumer Law Center, *The Cost of Credit: Regulation, Preemption, and Industry Abuses* § 11.5 (4th ed. 2009 and Supp.).

1.3.3.4.2 Players

This subsection lists various players in one type of securitization transaction. But it is important to note that securitizations can be structured in many different ways and the parties involved can be given many different names. It is equally important to realize that these different entities are not unrelated or independent of each other. Instead, a complex web of relationships was consciously worked out in an attempt to insulate various parties from the conduct of the originating lender.

Lender. The originator of the loans.

Seller/Wholesale Lender. The Seller is the party that sells the loans to the Issuer. (The term Seller is also used in a different context as the entity that sells securities certificates to investors.) The Seller can be the original Lender, or an affiliate of the original Lender. Alternatively, the original Lender can sell the loans to a Wholesale Lender who, in turn, becomes the Seller of the loans to an Issuer. Where the Seller is a Wholesale Lender, it may sell the loans to an Issuer that is a wholly owned subsidiary of the Seller or of the same parent company that owns the Seller.

Issuer/Depositor. The Seller transfers the notes to an Issuer, also sometimes called a Depositor, or a "Bankruptcy-Remote Entity" or a "Special Purpose Vehicle" (SPV). (Sometimes, though, the Trust is termed the SPV.) The Issuer is a temporary, intermediary owner of the mortgages, and issues securities that represent undivided interests in the cash flows from a particular pool of loans. The Issuer sells the securities and transfers legal title in the loans to a trust entity. Its primary function is to create a legal separation between the entity that is producing the loans (the Lender or Seller) and the Trust, which ultimately holds the loans. This separation is referred to as "bankruptcy remoteness" and the Issuer is often referred to as a "bankruptcy remote entity" in that it is attempting to insulate the financial integrity of the securities from any economic difficulties of the Seller.[39] This separation also is intended to create holder-in-due-course status.[40]

Servicer. The entity that collects monthly payments from borrowers and passes on required cash flows to the Trustee.[41] The Servicer must advance to the Trust payments due from delinquent borrowers, and also must advance the costs of foreclosure. The Servicer retains a fee from borrower payments and can also pocket late charges, bad check charges and other costs. The right to service a portfolio of securitized loans is regarded as a valuable asset and has been traditionally reserved by the Seller for itself, so in many securitized transactions the Seller and the Servicer are the same company. When these companies file bankruptcy, it is often these servicing rights that are their principal assets. But there is also a growing trend to use third party servicers who are not affiliated with the Issuer.

Trustee. Usually a commercial bank, the Trustee acts on behalf of the Trust and the investors. It is essentially an administrative function, to represent the Trust, to monitor the effectiveness of the servicing, to manage and oversee the payments to the bondholders and to administer any reserve accounts. Should the Servicer fail, it is the Trustee's job to step in as temporary servicer until a replacement can be hired.

Custodian. Where a note is bearer paper,[42] and not payable to the order of a named party, a custodian may hold onto the bearer paper for safekeeping as an agent for the Trust. This entity may be the originating Lender or the Servicer, but it does not own the notes, even though it possesses them and the notes are bearer paper.

Underwriter. The Wall Street investment firm (sometimes firms) that provide the initial capital to purchase the securities from the Issuer and then, at a profit, sell them to its customers—institutional investors like insurance companies and mutual funds. As the initial purchaser of all of the bonds, the Underwriter plays a key role in structuring the

37 *See* § 5.14, *infra* (assignee liability).

38 *See* Kurt Eggert, *Held Up in Due Course: Predatory Lending, Securitization, and the Holder in Due Course Doctrine*, 35 Creighton L. Rev. 507 (Apr. 2002); Lynn M. LoPucki, *The Death of Liability*, 106 Yale L.J. 1 23–30 (1996) ("Asset securitization is both a substitute for borrowing and a powerful new strategy for judgment proofing"); Christopher L. Peterson, *Predatory Structured Finance*, 28 Cardozo L. Rev. 2185 (2007); Steven L. Schwarcz, *The Alchemy of Asset Securitization*, 1 Stan. J.L. Bus. & Fin. 133 (1994).

39 *See* Thomas J. Gordon, *Securitization of Executory Future Flows as Bankruptcy-Remote True Sales*, 67 U. of Chi. L. Rev. 1317 (2000); Lynn M. LoPucki, *The Death of Liability*, 106 Yale L.J. 1 23–30 (1996).

40 *See* § 5.14.2, *infra*.

41 *See* § 1.3.3.5, *infra*.

42 Bearer paper is a negotiable instrument that is payable to "bearer" or otherwise indicates that the person in possession of the instrument is entitled to payment. A negotiable instrument that does not state a payee or is payable to "cash" or the like is also bearer paper. U.C.C. § 3-109.

entire transaction, including a role in determining the characteristics of the underlying loans.

Rating agency. Provides supposedly independent evaluation of the credit quality of the securities. There are four rating agencies: Standard & Poors; Moody's; Fitch; and Duff & Phelps. One of them has to rate the bonds as having AAA quality in order for the transaction to be regarded as marketable.[43] The agencies research the characteristics and performance of an ABS, and rating agency websites are a good source of information about ABS transactions.

Insurer. In order for the asset-based securities to be graded as AAA, they have to be "credit enhanced." Often these enhancements come in the form of bond insurance provided by firms that historically insured municipal bonds.[44]

Warehouse Lender/Facility. This financial entity provides the short-term capital that a small lender needs to fund the mortgages initially, until the loans are securitized. Once the Underwriter purchases the securities, there should be enough cash to repay the Warehouse Lender. The warehouse role has been played by large commercial banks, but underwriting firms have provided warehouse funding as well, sometimes taking a security interest in the loans up until they are transferred to the securitization trust.

The existence of all of these entities underscores the complexity of the securitization process. The ability to securitize mortgage loans that become due years in the future provides an effective means by which an originating lender can sell all of its loans and receive cash immediately, allowing it to then seek out new loans. On the other hand, the securitization process attempts to insulate those supplying this capital from any wrongdoing of the originating lender.

1.3.3.4.3 Documentation

The primary contractual document underlying a securitization transaction is the pooling and servicing agreement (PSA). The PSA establishes the securitization loan trust and the various classes of bondholders. It contains the obligations of the servicer and the various "representations and warranties" of the parties to the transaction. In addition, there are other documents associated with the transaction including one or more mortgage loan purchase agreements, an interim servicing agreement, an underwriting agreement, a warehouse agreement, and an insurance agreement.

If the securities are publicly sold, then the pooling and servicing agreement will be publicly available.[45] Searching SEC-filed documents requires the name of the actual loan trust in which the consumer's loan is contained.[46]

These documents often contain interesting information. They may make representations about the characteristics of the borrowers and of the loan pools. A prospectus may list such information as purported default rates. Courts have found that a PSA can show a joint venture between the originator, securitizer, and servicer.[47]

1.3.3.5 Mortgage Servicers

The servicer collects the monthly payments and interacts with the homeowner on the holder's behalf. It may hold monies in escrow to pay the property taxes, homeowner's insurance, or other similar expenses. Servicers are generally responsible for other account maintenance activities such as sending monthly statements, keeping track of account balances, handling interest rate adjustments on adjustable rate mortgages, collecting and reporting information to national credit bureaus, and remitting monies to the owners of the

43 *See* David Reiss, *Subprime Standardization: How Rating Agencies Allow Predatory Lending to Flourish in the Secondary Mortgage Market*, 33 Fla. St. U. L. Rev. 985 (2006) (reviewing the literature on rating agencies and providing detailed explanation of their function in rating loan pools). *See also* Christopher L. Peterson, *Predatory Structured Finance*, 28 Cardozo L. Rev. 2185 (2007) ("Credit ratings on each tranche are essential, since they obviate the need for each individual investor to do due diligence on the underlying mortgages in the pool.").

44 *See* Christopher L. Peterson, *Predatory Structured Finance*, 28 Cardozo L. Rev. 2185 (2007) (discussing internal credit enhancement, for example, dividing the loan pool up into classes which receive payment in descending order of risk, and external enhancement, including insurance). Bond insurance is an example of "external" credit enhancement. Even more common are methods of "internal" enhancement. One example of an internal credit enhancement is a "senior/subordinated structure," in which the securities are divided into *senior* and *subordinate* layers with the subordinate investors assuming a greater risk of loss in return for receiving a higher return than the senior bondholders. By illustration, a $100 million pool of thirty-year fixed rate mortgages might require, in the judgment of a rating agency, a loss coverage of 8%, resulting in the issuance of $8 million in subordinate bonds in order to provide AAA rating to the remaining senior class of $92 million. Often, additional support is created during the early years of the security by diverting the subordinated share of principal repayments into *reserve funds*. When bond insurance is present, the insurers usually are not in first-loss position, often taking a risk position behind the subordinate bondholders.

45 Each securitization trust, once identified, will have web-accessible SEC forms, often with the above documents attached as exhibits. To locate documentation for a particular securitization, start with an "Edgar" search. Go to the SEC's homepage at www.sec.gov and click on "Search for company filings" under the section titled "Filings and Forms (EDGAR)." More detail about finding and analyzing documents in this database may be found at Kevin Byers, *Researching Subprime Residential Loan Securitizations*, The Consumer Advocate vol. 9, no. 1, at 15–20 (Jan./Feb./Mar. 2003) (newsletter of the Nat'l Ass'n of Consumer Advocates). The SEC plans to eventually replace EDGAR with IDEA, which is expected to have greater search capabilities. To use IDEA, click the IDEA link on the SEC's homepage.

46 The name of the loan trust that actually owns a particular loan can be learned by making a demand to the loan servicer under 15 U.S.C. § 1641(f)(2) or through discovery.

47 *See, e.g.*, Short v. Wells Fargo Bank Minn., N.A., 401 F. Supp. 2d 549, 565 (S.D. W. Va. 2005).

loans. The servicer also negotiates any repayment or loss mitigation plan with a defaulting homeowner or hires a foreclosure attorney if necessary. When a mortgage is assigned upon sale in the secondary market, the mortgages are generally serviced by a bank or servicing company. The servicer may be the originating lender if it retained servicing rights when it sold the loan.

Securitized loan pools may have several layers of servicers. For example, the primary servicer will collect monthly payments and interact with the homeowner; the special servicer is often responsible for nonperforming loans and real estate owned assets; and, the master servicer oversees both the primary and special servicer, ensures a smooth transition between the two servicer when a transfer is necessary and is charged overall with protecting the interest of the investors. Primary servicers and special servicers may in turn contract with tax service providers, insurance providers, foreclosure and bankruptcy attorneys, inspection services, and other similar parties to perform different functions in the loan servicing process.

For a detailed discussion of common mortgage servicing abuses, see Chapters 6, 7 and 8, *infra*.

1.3.3.6 Default Services Providers

Mortgage servicers commonly outsource default services to third parties. These third parties, also known as "default service providers," offer a variety of products to servicers, such as electronic information technology products, document preparation (e.g., notices of default or assignments), property inspections, broker's price opinions, bankruptcy proofs of claim preparation, etc. In many cases, the default service providers are divisions, subsidiaries, or affiliates of the servicer.[48]

The use of default service providers by the servicing industry has resulted in more frequent overcharges for improper or unreasonable fees.[49]

1.3.3.7 Lender's Foreclosure Attorney

The lender's foreclosure attorney is also an agent with delegated authority from the mortgage holder, although usually the attorney is hired by the servicer. The attorney appears in the process when the servicer instructs the attorney to accelerate the debt and proceed to foreclosure. The homeowner usually pays the fee for this attorney because the mortgage or loan note specifies that this cost can be passed onto the borrower. However, in most jurisdictions the homeowner cannot be required to pay more than "reasonable" fees.[50]

1.3.3.8 Foreclosing Trustee

In states that use a deed of trust as the underlying security instrument for a home loan, the borrower technically conveys title to the property to a trustee who holds the property for the benefit of the lender. The trustee is typically a title company, escrow company, or other local company specializing in foreclosure services. When the borrower defaults, the servicer will generally instruct the trustee to sell the property under the power of sale provision in the deed of trust. Many times a notice of substitution trustee is filed shortly before foreclosure proceedings are initiated. This substitution merely changes the entity that will pursue the foreclosure on behalf of the servicer/loan owner.

The trustee named on the deed of trust (or later substituted) should not be confused with the owner of the loan, which is commonly a trustee for a trust holding securitized mortgage loans (e.g., Deutsche Bank National Trust Company as Trustee for the MLMI Trust Series 2005-SL1).

1.3.3.9 REO Management

The term "REO" stands for Real Estate Owned. It refers to property that is in possession of the loan holder as a result of foreclosure. Holders and/or servicers may outsource the management of these properties to a specialized company. REO management companies may be responsible for preserving and monitoring property after foreclosure, marketing and selling property, and dealing with homeowners that remain on the property after the foreclosure.

1.4 The Prime, Subprime, and Predatory Markets

1.4.1 Characteristics of the Prime, Subprime, and Predatory Mortgage Markets

Many Americans in the middle- and upper-economic classes are used to receiving competitive interest rates and to paying few fees to buy homes, refinance their mortgages, purchase cars and other consumer goods, take vacations, repair their homes, and send their children to college. The "prime" or "conventional" lending market serves these homeowners. In this market, consumers qualify for the best rate offered by the lender. Lenders in the prime market may allow borrowers to buy down the rate offered by paying

48 *See In re* Stewart, 391 B.R. 327 (Bankr. E.D. La. 2008) (finding that entity which provided broker's price opinions was a corporate division of the servicer and that the true cost incurred by the servicer for broker's price opinions was $50 rather than the $125 charged to the borrower), *aff'd*, 2009 WL 2448054 (E.D. La. Aug. 7, 2009).

49 *See* § 6.4.4.1, *infra*.

50 *See* §§ 6.4.4.7, 6.4.4.6, *infra*.

points in cash or financed as part of the loan.[51] Lenders may also permit the borrower to opt for a higher interest rate rather than pay points or closing costs at the closing.

The prime market serves "A" borrowers with credit scores typically greater than 650.[52] Prime borrowers can access fixed or adjustable long- and short-term mortgage loans to purchase or refinance a home and home equity lines of credit or second mortgages for repairs or other expenses. Underwriting standards are fairly uniform, thanks in large part to Fannie Mae and Freddie Mac.[53]

For those whose credit is blemished to any degree and others who are steered to unconventional lenders, the "subprime" mortgage market can be a very different experience. The subprime market provides credit for "A- to D" borrowers with FICO scores under 650–670. "Alt A" (low or no document loans) may be considered subprime loans even though the FICO scores of the borrowers may be similar to their prime counterparts.[54] The subprime market also makes high loan-to-value (LTV) loans, even where the borrower has relatively good credit.[55]

The subprime market is characterized by a sliding scale of interest rates based, in part, upon credit risk. Typically interest rates run from several percentage points above to almost double the rates offered prime borrowers.[56]

In addition, subprime lenders usually charge higher points and fees than their prime counterparts, and include prepayment penalties more often. A 2004 study showed that about 80% of subprime loans contain prepayment penalties, compared with only 2% of loans in the competitive prime market.[57] Prepayment penalties are especially onerous for this group, since the penalty deters them from refinancing into a prime loan.

The predatory market generally exists as a subset of the subprime market.[58] In this market, price may have more to do with gouging than with risk.[59] There is no single definition for predatory lending, and due to the lack of publicly reported data on this market, it is difficult to quantify the number of predatory loans or the percentage of the subprime market that they represent. One industry-commissioned study found that the 12.4% of first lien loans and 49.6% of second lien loans made by nine lenders between July 1, 1995 and June 30, 2000 were high-cost loans as defined by the federal Home Ownership and Equity Protection Act.[60] These loans are extraordinarily expensive because they either have annual percentage rates of at least 10% above comparable treasury securities or the points and fees exceed 8% of the total loan amount.[61] In addition, an independent researcher estimated that 21% of loans in certain areas of Philadelphia were predatory.[62] Similarly, in Montgomery County, Ohio, an independent study of a random sample of mortgage loans associated with foreclosures revealed that 21% were predatory.[63]

51 One point equals 1% of the principal.

52 U.S. Department of the Treasury and U.S. Department of Housing and Urban Development, Joint Report on Recommendations to Curb Predatory Mortgage Lending 33 (2000), *available at* www.huduser.org/publications/hsgfin/curbing.html; Alan M. White, *Risk-Based Mortgage Pricing: Present and Future Research*, Housing Policy Debate vol. 15, no. 3, at 509 (2004).

53 Kenneth Temkin, Jennifer E. H. Johnson, Diane Levy, U.S. Dep't of Housing and Urban Dev., Office of Policy Development and Research, Subprime Markets, the Role of GSEs, and Risk-Based Pricing, Report Prepared by the Urban Institute 21 (2002); U.S. Department of the Treasury and U.S. Department of Housing and Urban Development, Joint Report on Recommendations to Curb Predatory Mortgage Lending 33 (2000), *available at* www.huduser.org/publications/hsgfin/curbing.html.

54 Kenneth Temkin, Jennifer E. H. Johnson, Diane Levy, U.S. Dep't of Housing and Urban Development, Office of Policy Development and Research, Subprime Markets, the Role of GSEs, and Risk-Based Pricing, Report Prepared by the Urban Institute 21 (2002).

55 Loan-to-value ratio (LTV) is the relationship, expressed as a percentage, between the loan amount and the value of the property securing the loan.

56 *See* Federal Reserve Board at www.federalreserve.gov/releases/h15/data.htm (for historical rates on conventional mortgages); Alan M. White, *Risk-Based Mortgage Pricing—Present and Future Research*, Housing Policy Debate 15:3 (2004).

57 John Farris & Christopher A. Richardson, *The Geography of Subprime Mortgage Prepayment Penalty Patterns*, Housing Policy Debate 15:3, at 688 (2004). *See also* U.S. Department of the Treasury & U.S. Department of Housing and Urban Development, Joint Report on Recommendations to Curb Predatory Mortgage Lending 93 (Washington, D.C. 2000) (showing a 70% rate for subprime loans and a 2% rate for prime loans); Ellen Schloemer, Wei Li, Keith Ernst & Kathleen Keest, Ctr. for Responsible Lending, Losing Ground: Foreclosures in the Subprime Market and Their Cost to Homeowners (showing incidence of prepayment penalties in subprime loans ranging from 54.37% to 71.70% from 1998 to 2005).

58 Prime loans could be predatory, though the likelihood is much smaller in that market.

59 Alan M. White, *Risk-Based Mortgage Pricing—Present and Future Research*, Housing Policy Debate 15:3, at 503 (2004).

60 Michael E. Staten and Gregory Elliehausen, Credit Research Center, The Impact of the Federal Reserve Board's Proposed Revisions to HOEPA on the Number and Characteristics of HOEPA Loans (2001).

61 15 U.S.C. § 1602(aa). The Federal Reserve Board lowered the APR trigger in 2002 to 8% above comparable treasury securities for first lien mortgages. The spread for subordinate lien loans remained at 10%. 66 Fed. Reg. 65,604 (Dec. 20, 2001) (effective Oct. 1, 2002).

62 Ira Goldstein, Reinvestment Fund, Predatory Lending: An Approach to Identify and Understand Predatory Lending (2002).

63 Richard Stock, Center for Business and Economic Growth, Predation in the Sub-Prime Lending Market: Montgomery County (2001). Note that the definitions of predatory lending varied between the Dayton and Philadelphia two studies. In the Goldstein study, predatory lending was defined through the use of property lien data to mean the flipping of mortgage loans resulting in the increasingly larger first liens placed on the properties. Stock examined interest rate, fixed versus adjustable rates, balloon payments, waiver of jury trial, prepayment penalties, excessive fees, and the inclusion of single premium life insurance.

In another study, researchers in North Carolina found that subprime loans with features defined as predatory, i.e., prepay-

1.4.2 Borrower Characteristics in the Subprime Market

Certain borrower characteristics are more prevalent in the subprime than in the prime market. For example, data submitted under the Home Mortgage Data Act revealed that African-American and Latino borrowers in 2005 were much more likely to take out higher-rate loans than non-Latino white borrowers. For purchase-money loans, 54.7% of African-Americans, 46.1% of Latino whites, and only 17.2% of non-Latino whites received higher-priced loans. The gaps were slightly narrower for higher-priced refinance loans, which comprised 49.3% of African-American, 33.8% of Latino white, and 21.0% of non-Latino white borrowers.[64]

Disparities remain even for borrowers with the same income. Controlling for the borrower-related factors available in the HMDA data (i.e., property location, income relied on for underwriting, loan amount, time of year the loan was made, and presence of a co-applicant)[65] accounted for only some of the difference in the incidence of higher-cost loans among racial and ethnic groups. For example, for conventional home-purchase loans, borrower-related factors in the HMDA data accounted for about one-fifth of the difference between blacks and non-Latino whites, bringing the percentage of higher-rate loans down to 47% for blacks (compared to 17.2% for whites).[66] Other studies have also found that African American and Latinos are disproportionately represented in the subprime market, even at upper-income levels.[67]

A Consumer Federation of America study, based on a proprietary database and not on HMDA data, found a similar pattern for risky interest-only and payment option loans. These loans, which can negatively amortize, may be attractive to cash strapped borrowers, but they can negate the wealth-building aspect of homeownership, and if home prices fall, these borrowers could owe more in mortgage debt than their homes are worth. The study found that African American and Latino borrowers were more likely to receive interest-only and payment option mortgages than non-minority borrowers. A further CFA analysis of the data found that this racial disparity remained at all levels of income, debt loads, and credit scores.[68]

---

ment penalties with terms of three years or greater, balloon payments, and loans with combined LTVs of at least 110%, declined in North Carolina after the enactment of an anti-predatory mortgage lending law. Forberto G. Quercia, Michael A. Stegman, & Walter R. Davis, *Assessing the Impact of North Carolina's Anti-Predatory Lending Law*, Housing Policy Debate 15:3, at 593–594 (2004).

64 Robert B. Avery, Kenneth P. Brevoort, Glenn B. Canner, *Higher-Priced Home Lending and the 2005 HMDA Data*, Fed. Reserve Bulletin-2006 A123 (Sept. 8, 2006), *available at* www.federalreserve.gov/pubs/bulletin/2006/hmda/bull06 hmda.pdf.

65 Even if these factors are not directly used in loan underwriting or pricing, they are proxies for at least some of the factors that are considered. *Id.*

66 *Id.* Another study that combined the HMDA data with underwriting information from a large, proprietary subprime loan dataset found that African Americans and Latinos are commonly almost a third more likely to get a high-priced loan than white borrowers with the same credit scores. *See* Debbie Gruenstein Bocian, Keith S. Ernst, Wei Li, Center for Responsible Lending, Unfair Lending: The Effect of Race and Ethnicity on the Price of Subprime Mortgages (May 31, 2006), *available at* www.responsiblelending.org/issues/mortgage/reports/page.jsp?itemID=29371010.

67 U.S. Dep't of Housing and Urban Development, Unequal Burden: Income and Racial Disparities in Subprime Lending in America (2000) (finding, from studies conducted in Atlanta, Baltimore, Chicago, Los Angeles, and New York, that: (1) from 1993–1998, the number of subprime refinancing loans increased ten-fold; (2) subprime loans are more than three times likely in low-income neighborhoods than in high-income neighborhoods; (3) subprime loans are five time more likely in black neighborhoods than in white neighborhoods; (4) homeowners in high-income black areas are twice as likely as homeowners in low-income white areas to have subprime loans); Robert B. Avery, Glenn B. Canner, and Robert E. Cook, Federal Reserve Board, New Information Reported Under HMDA and Its Application in Fair Lending Enforcement (Summer 2005), *available at* www.federalreserve.gov/pubs/bulletin/2005/3-05hmda.pdf (reporting on preliminary analysis of HMDA data); Paul Calem, Kevin Gillen, & Susan Wachter, The Neighborhood Distribution of Subprime Mortgage Lending 14 (Univ. of Penn., Wharton Sch., Zell/Lurie Real Estate Ctr., Working Paper 404, 2002) (finding a "statistically significant relationship such that African-American borrowers, regardless of the neighborhood where they are located, have relatively high likelihood of obtaining a subprime loan compared to a prime loan"); Ira Goldstein, Reinvestment Fund, Predatory Lending: An Approach to Identify and Understand Predatory Lending (2002) (showing that areas within the City of Philadelphia with a higher potential vulnerability to predatory lending tended to have greater concentrations of foreclosure sales; areas that are predominately African American and/or Latino also tended to have higher concentrations of foreclosure sales and were more vulnerable to predatory lending); Debbie Gruenstein and Christopher E. Herbert, Abt Assocs., Inc., Analyzing Trends in Subprime Organizations and Foreclosures: A Case Study of the Boston Metro Area, at i (2000) (showing that the growth of subprime lending in the Boston Metro area was much more significant for properties in low-income and minority neighborhoods than for properties in other neighborhoods; the concentration of subprime lending in minority and low-income neighborhoods was especially striking in the refinance market); Daniel Immergluck and Marti Wiles, Woodstock Institute, Two Steps Back: The Dual Mortgage Market, Predatory Lending, and the Undoing of Community Development (2004) (showing that mortgage refinancing by subprime lenders occurred predominately in African-American neighborhoods in Chicago; refinance lending by subprime lenders in African-American neighborhoods grew by almost thirty times during the period 1993–1998, much faster than in white neighborhoods (only 2.5 times)); Ken Zimmerman, Elvin Wyly, and Hilary Botein, Institute for Social Justice, Predatory Lending in New Jersey: The Rising Threat to Low-Income Homeowners 5–6 (2002) (finding that New Jersey African Americans are 2.5 times more likely than whites to be provided subprime loans).

68 Allen Fishbein, Patrick Woodall, Consumer Federation of America, Exotic or Toxic? An Examination of the Non-Tradi-

High concentrations of subprime lending and racial disparities in subprime lending exist in all regions throughout the United States and in metropolitan areas of all sizes.[69]

The consistency of this data from study to study raises the very real question as to whether discrimination and steering account more for placement in the subprime market (and, hence, higher prices) than risk.

Steering by prime lenders to subprime affiliates may be prevalent. A recent study found that which lending channel a borrower enters—prime or subprime—can have a large impact on the price paid for a home loan. For example, the study found that 75.9% of the loans of Washington Mutual ("WaMu") to African Americans were made though its subprime subsidiary, Long Beach Mortgage Company, and that regardless of race, 90% of Long Beach borrowers received higher-cost home purchase loans. By contrast, WaMu's prime lender, Washington Mutual Bank, accounted for more than 80% of all WaMu's home purchase loans to whites, and less than 1% of the Bank's loans were higher cost.[70] In another study of subprime lending in four cities in California, the authors reported that 25% of the surveyed homeowners took out loans from a subsidiary or affiliate of a financial institution, yet none were referred to the prime lender for lower-cost loans. Interestingly, 60% of all surveyed homeowners believed they had good or excellent credit.[71]

Other disparities also exist in the subprime market. Females appear to be more likely to receive subprime mortgages, even when controlling for income, although the studies are not completely consistent.[72] Older borrowers are also overrepresented in the subprime market.[73] Another study found significant subprime refinance variation between regions. Borrowers on the West Coast and Northwest were half as likely to receive subprime refinance loans as borrowers in the Southwest or Great Plains, and there were also large variations among Metropolitan Statistical Areas, with the highest subprime MSAs concentrated in the Southeast, Southwest and Midwest regions.[74]

1.4.3 Foreclosure Rates

The rate at which loans go into foreclosure is significantly higher in the subprime market than in the prime market. As of the last quarter of 2009, 15.58% of subprime mortgage loans—more than one of every seven loans—were in foreclosure. This stands in stark contrast to the rate for prime

tional Mortgage Market for Consumers and Lenders (May 24, 2006), *available at* www.consumerfed.org/pdfs/Exotic_Toxic_Mortgage_Report0506.pdf.

69 *See, e.g.,* Calvin Bradford, Center for Community Change, Risk or Race? Racial Disparities and the Subprime Refinance Market 6–7 (Washington, D.C. 2002); Paying More for the American Dream: A Multi-State Analysis of Higher Cost Home Purchase Lending (Mar. 2007) (a joint report by California Reinvestment Coalition, Community Reinvestment Association of North Carolina, Empire Justice Center, Massachusetts Affordable Housing Alliance, Neighborhood Economic Development Advocacy Project, Woodstock Institute), *available at* www.nedap.org/pressroom/documents/2007_Report-2005_HMDA.pdf; National Community Reinvestment Coalition, Fair Lending Helps Community Prosperity: An Analysis of Fair lending Disparities in the New Orleans Metro Area (Apr. 2007), *available at* www.ncrc.org/pressandpubs/documents/New%20Orleans%20MSA%20Home%20Lending%20Final.pdf; Kevin Stein, California Reinvestment Coalition, Who Really Gets Higher-Cost Home Loans? Home Loan Disparities By Income, Race and Ethnicity of Borrowers and Neighborhoods in 14 California Communities in 2005 (Dec. 2006), *available at* www.calreinvest.org/system/assets/39.pdf.

70 *See* Paying More for the American Dream: A Multi-State Analysis of Higher Cost Home Purchase Lending (Mar. 2007) (a joint report by California Reinvestment Coalition, Community Reinvestment Association of North Carolina, Empire Justice Center, Massachusetts Affordable Housing Alliance, neighborhood Economic Development Advocacy Project, Woodstock Institute), *available at* www.nedap.org/pressroom/documents/2007_Report-2005_HMDA.pdf.

71 Kevin Stein and Margaret Libby, California Reinvestment Committee, Stolen Wealth: Inequities in California's Subprime Mortgage Market 41, 47, 50 (2001).

72 The Federal Reserve Board analysis of the 2005 HMDA data found little difference in pricing or credit denials when borrowers in the 2005 data were distinguished by gender. Robert B. Avery, Kenneth P. Brevoort, Glenn B. Canner, Federal Reserve, *Higher-Priced Home Lending and the 2006 HMDA Data*, Fed. Reserve Bulletin-2006 A123 (Sept. 8, 2006), *available at* www.federalreserve.gov/pubs/bulletin/2006/hmda/bull06hmda.pdf. In contrast, a Consumer Federation of America study based on the 2005 HMDA data found that, controlling for income, women are more likely than men to receive higher-cost mortgages. Allen J. Fishbein, Patrick Woodall, Consumer Federation of America, Women are Prime Targets for Subprime Lending: Women Are Disproportionately Represented in High-Cost Mortgage Market (Dec. 2006), *available at* www.consumerfed.org/pdfs/WomenPrimeTargetsPressRelease.pdf. Unlike the Board's analysis, the CFA study looked not only at loans with a single female borrower, but also at those with a male co-applicant when the female was listed as the primary borrower. Most likely, when the female was listed first, the female's income was higher than that of the male co-applicant and was the primary support for the loan. Another study found that female borrowers accounted for 29% of subprime refinance mortgages compared to 19% of all refinance mortgages. *See* National Community Reinvestment Coalition, The 2005 Fair Lending Disparities: Stubborn and Persistent II (May 2006), *available at* www.ncrc.org/policy/analysis/policy/2006/2006-05-23_2005HMDAreport.pdf (data on gender bias and racial/ethnic and socioeconomic disparities in provision of high-rate subprime loans).

73 *See* Howard Lax, Michael Manti, Paul Raca, & Peter Zorn, *Subprime Lending: An Investigation of Economic Efficiency*, Housing Policy Debate 15:3, at 545 (2004) (30% of borrowers getting subprime loans are aged 55 and older as compared with 17% of prime borrowers in this age category).

74 *See* Allen J. Fishbein, Patrick Woodall, Consumer Federation of America, Subprime Locations: Patterns of Geographic Disparity in Subprime Lending (Sept. 5, 2006), *available at* www.consumerfed.org/pdfs/SubprimeLocationsStudy090506.pdf. The study also found that African-American and Latino borrowers were more Likely to receive subprime loans.

loans—3.31% during the same period.[75] Nationally, from 1998 to 2007, the percentage of prime loans in foreclosure was consistently about 0.50%, while the percentage of subprime loans in foreclosure ranged from 3.5% to over 9%.[76]

When foreclosures occur, families are evicted, neighborhoods suffer, and tax bases decline. The homeowner not only loses stable housing and a major wealth-building asset, but also suffers a reduced credit rating that will make it harder to buy or even rent a home in the future. In addition, the average foreclosure results in $7200 in administrative charges to the borrower.[77] A city can lose up to almost $20,000 in lost property taxes, unpaid utility bills, property upkeep, sewage, and maintenance for each house abandoned in foreclosure.[78] Neighbors also bear the costs of foreclosure: a single-family home foreclosure lowers the value of homes located within one-eighth of a mile by an average of almost 1%.[79]

It is important to note that high foreclosure numbers occur even when the economy is booming. When a downturn befalls us, such as the recession that began in December 2007, the devastation can skyrocket.[80] The advent of new mortgage products, combined with the recent collapse of the housing market and the lending industry's subsequent tightening of mortgage credit, have caused dramatic increases in foreclosures and delinquencies.[81]

75 Mortgage Bankers Ass'n, National Delinquency Survey 3 (Fourth Quarter 2009).

76 Mortgage Bankers Association, National Delinquency Survey 3 (Fourth Quarter 2006). *See also* Daniel Immergluck and Geoff Smith, Woodstock Institute, Risky Business—An Econometric Analysis of the Relationship Between Subprime Lending and Neighborhood Foreclosures 17, 23 (2004). *See also* Debbie Gruenstein & Christopher E. Herbert, Abt Assocs., Inc., Analyzing Trends in Subprime Organizations and Foreclosures: A Case Study of the Boston Metro Area, at i (2000) (found that the volume of foreclosures started by subprime lenders in the Boston area grew by 154% during 1995–1999 while the overall volume of foreclosures dropped by 30%).

77 U.S. Senate, Joint Economic Committee, Sheltering Neighborhoods from the Subprime Foreclosure Storm 14 (Apr. 11, 2007), *available at* http://jec.senate.gov/reports.htm.

78 *Id.* at 15.

79 *Id.*

80 Floyd Norris, *Recession, Far From Over, Already Setting Records*, N.Y. Times, Apr. 25, 2009, at B3 (correction *available at* www.nytimes.com/2009/04/25/business/economy/25charts.html); Center for Responsible Lending, Soaring Spillover (May 2009), *available at* www.responsiblelending.org/mortgage-lending/research-analysis/soaring-spillover-3-09.pdf (predicting foreclosures will cost neighbors $509 billion in 2009).

81 In the last quarter of 2009, 4.58% of all loans were in foreclosure compared to 1.19% at the same time in 2006. By the end of 2009, the number of subprime loans in foreclosure had increased from 4.53% in 2006 to 15.58%. Prime loan foreclosures increased from 0.5% to 1.88% over the same period. Mortgage Bankers Ass'n, National Delinquency Survey 3 (Fourth Quarter 2006).

1.4.4 The Role of Nontraditional Mortgages

In recent years, one significant factor contributing to default and foreclosure risk is the expansion of the "nontraditional" or "alternative" loan product market. Such products include interest-only loans, payment option adjustable rate mortgages, and hybrid adjustable rate mortgages, such as "2-28s" and "3-27s."[82] On the one hand, abuses in this area are just another form of lending without regard to ability to pay. On the other hand, these products are a new and hazardous path to foreclosure.

With interest-only loans, the borrower is required to pay only the interest due on the loan for an initial period such as three or five years. During this time, the interest rate may fluctuate or be fixed. After the interest-only period, the borrower's payments must include both principal and interest.

A payment option adjustable rate mortgage (ARM) is a nontraditional adjustable rate mortgage that allows the borrower to choose from a number of different payment options. For example, each month the borrower may be able to choose a minimum payment option that does not even pay all the interest on the loan, an interest-only payment, or a payment large enough to pay off the principal and interest over either fifteen or thirty years. If the borrower chooses the minimum payment option, the loan will negatively amortize. After a specified number of years, or if the loan reaches a certain negative amortization cap, the required monthly payment amount is recast to require payments that will fully amortize the outstanding balance over the remaining loan term.[83]

In "2-28" and "3-27" loans, also known as "exploding ARMs," the interest rate is fixed at an artificially low rate for a brief period of two or three years. They then switch to an adjustable rate for the remaining twenty-eight or twenty-seven years, with rate increases as often as every six months.[84]

Significant payment shock is a common feature of all of these types of loans. Even if the interest rate index is unchanged, a 2-28 subprime ARM carries an average payment shock of 29% over the teaser-rate payment. With

82 For a discussion of these products, see *Testimony of Michael Calhoun Before the Senate Committee on Banking, Housing and Urban Affairs, Subcommittee on Housing and Transportation and Subcommittee on Economic Policy, on Calculated Risk: Assessing Non-Traditional Mortgage Products* (Sept. 20, 2006), *available at* www.responsiblelending.org/pdfs/Testimony-Calhoun092006.pdf.

83 *See* Statement on Subprime Mortgage Lending 22 (Mar. 2, 2007), *available at* http://a257.g.akamaitech.net/7/257/2422/01jan20071800/edocket.access.gpo.gov/2007/pdf/07-1083.pdf.

84 U.S. Senate, Joint Economic Committee, Sheltering Neighborhoods from the Subprime Foreclosure Storm 1–2 (Apr. 11, 2007), *available at http://jec.senate.gov/reports.htm.*

interest rate increases, many borrowers have experienced payment shocks of 50%.[85]

From 2004 to 2007, these alternative mortgage products—especially interest-only loans—moved from a marginal role in the mortgage market to a place of dominance. In 2005, interest-only loans constituted 27% of loans nationwide and 30% of subprime loans.[86] In the secondary market, 23.5% of all securitized subprime originations in 2005 were interest-only loans.[87] Almost three-quarters of securitized subprime mortgages originated in 2004 and 2005 were exploding ARMs.[88]

The fact that this has occurred in an environment of low interest rates raises serious questions about how and why consumers are receiving these products. Interest-only loans generally are suitable for households expecting significant increases in income, for those with fluctuations in income where the borrower is able to pay down principal during certain periods, or for investors seeking to maximize cash flow. Subprime borrowers generally do not fit any of these criteria. Many are on fixed incomes, and those with fluctuating incomes do not see substantial upswings in incoming funds. Accordingly, these loans can only be made to such borrowers if the lender dispenses with underwriting that analyzes whether the borrower can afford the loan beyond the initial teaser rate, if then. Indeed, roughly half of all subprime borrowers in the past two years were given "stated income" loans (also called "no doc" loans), in which they were qualified for the loan based simply on statements on the loan application regarding their income, or "reduced documentation" (also called "low doc") loans.[89]

Because many nontraditional mortgage products, and adjustable rate mortgages in general, have been made without adequate underwriting, they present major risks to consumers and to the economy. The growth of ARMs and interest-only products in a low-rate environment means that rate increases hold the potential of leading to huge increases in defaults and foreclosures. Such a result would devastate individual consumers, their families, and communities. Moreover, consumers show extreme sensitivity to interest rate variations; upward adjustments in rates often result in unaffordable monthly payments.

Many lenders underwrote adjustable rate loans only for the teaser rate, making default highly likely.[90] Even prime lenders do not underwrite the loan for the maximum possible payment, but generally only for the fully indexed payment, at best. The result is that neither consumers nor the market are taking the risk of interest rate increases into account, leading to major safety and soundness concerns. This is evidenced by Standard & Poor's requiring increased credit enhancements for option-ARMs.[91] Further, lenders do not disclose to the borrower that the borrower has not been qualified for the eventual payments she will need to make. In 2006, the federal banking regulators issued an Interagency Guidance on Nontraditional Mortgage Product Risks to address some of these problems,[92] and in 2007 they proposed a second guidance on subprime lending.[93] These documents, which serve as guides for bank examinations, only apply to financial institutions regulated by the federal banking agencies.[94]

Delinquency rates for subprime ARMs demonstrate the huge risk posed by nontraditional products. At the end of 2009, 42.70% of subprime ARMs nationwide were seriously delinquent, approximately 2.3 times the rate for prime ARMs.[95] In some metropolitan areas, over 20% of subprime mortgages were delinquent in February 2007.[96] In 2006,

---

85 *Id.* at 2.

86 Greg McBride, CFA, www.bankrate.com, Presentation to FRB Consumer Advisory Council (Oct. 26, 2005) (on file with authors). *See also Kirstin Downey,* Interest-Only: Borrower Beware: Popular but Risky Mortgage Draws Government Scrutiny, Wash. Post, Dec. 21, 2005, at D1 (23% of borrowers in 2005 chose interest-only mortgages, compared to 1% in 2000); Kenneth Harney, *Banks Warned They Must Scale Back on Payment-Option Mortgage,* S.F. Chron., Dec. 11, 2005, at K12 (payment option mortgages account for roughly a third of new home loans issued by some major lenders in 2005).

Thirty percent of purchase loans were interest-only as of March 2006. Loan Performance, *Interest-Only, Neg AM and Investor Activity for Purchase Loans,* The Market Pulse 3 (Mar. 2006 data).

87 *What Else Is New? ARMS Dominate Subprime MSB Mix*, Inside B&C Lending (Jan. 20, 2006).

88 Sheila C. Bair, Chairman, Federal Deposit Insurance Corporation, Possible Responses to Rising Mortgage Foreclosures 1 (Apr. 17, 2007), *available at* www.house.gov/apps/list/hearing/financialsvcs_dem/ht041707.shtm.

89 U.S. Senate, Joint Economic Committee, Sheltering Neighborhoods from the Subprime Foreclosure Storm 2 (Apr. 11, 2007), *available at* http://jec.senate.gov/reports.htm.

90 *See, e.g.,* Fremont Investment and Loan Prospectus, Fremont Home Loan Trust 2006-1 424B5 (Apr. 4, 2006) *available at* www.sec.gov/Archives/edgar/data/1357374/000088237706001254/d486451_all.htm; Option One Prospectus, Option One Mortgage Loan Trust 2006-3 424B5 (Oct. 19, 2006), *available at* www.sec.gov/Archives/edgar/data/1378102/000088237706003670/d581063_424b5.htm.

91 Remarks by Federal Reserve Governor Susan Schmidt Bies (Oct. 12, 2005), *available at* www.federalreserve.gov/BoardDocs/Speeches/2005/200510122/default.htm.

92 Interagency Guidance on Non-Traditional Mortgage Product Risks (Sept. 29, 2006), *available at* www.federalreserve.gov/boarddocs/srletters/2006/SR0615a2.pdf. *See also* Conference of State Bank Supervisors & American Association of Residential Mortgage Regulators, Guidance on Nontraditional Mortgage Product Risks (Jan. 31, 2007).

93 Statement on Subprime Mortgage Lending (Mar. 2, 2007), *available at* http://a257.g.akamaitech.net/7/257/2422/01jan20071800/edocket.access.gpo.gov/2007/pdf/07-1083.pdf.

94 At least one court has cited these guidelines as a partial basis for finding certain mortgage loans unfair. Commonwealth v. Fremont Inv. & Loan, 897 N.E.2d 548 (Mass. 2008).

95 10.45% of prime ARMs were seriously delinquent. Mortgage Bankers Ass'n, National Delinquency Survey 2 (Fourth Quarter 2008). The MBA defines "seriously delinquent" as ninety days or more delinquent, or in the process of foreclosure.

96 U.S. Senate, Joint Economic Committee, Sheltering Neighbor-

one in every 21 households in Detroit experienced foreclosure.[97]

As of the end of 2005, 2.2 million households in the subprime market either had lost their homes to foreclosure or held subprime mortgages that likely will fail over the next several years.[98] These foreclosures will cost homeowners as much as $164 billion, primarily in lost home equity.[99] It is projected that one out of five (19%) subprime mortgages originated during 2005 and 2006 will end in foreclosure.[100] As of March 2007, foreclosures were at a record high—13.33% for all subprime loans and 14.44% for subprime ARMs.[101]

An increase in interest rates can only magnify this problem. Some local studies attribute a significant fraction of the increase in local foreclosure rates since the mid-1990s to subprime ARMs.[102] In addition, borrowers may find that falling home prices make it impossible to refinance their mortgage loans to avoid foreclosure, particularly where a negatively amortizing loan has eaten into any home equity they had.

hoods from the Subprime Foreclosure Storm 20–28 (Apr. 11, 2007), *available at* http://jec.senate.gov/reports.htm (21.3% for Michigan as a whole, 23.9% for Detroit, 20.3% for Flint, 21.3% for Jackson, Mississippi, 22.7% for the Boston metropolitan area, 24.1% for the Cleveland metropolitan area, 21.4% for the Youngstown area).

97 *Id.* at 7.

98 Center for Responsible Lending, Losing Ground: Foreclosures in the Subprime Market and Their Cost to Homeowners (2006), *available at* www.responsiblelending.org/pdfs/FC-paper-12-19-new-cover-1.pdf.

99 *Id.*

100 *Id.*

101 Amy Hoak, New Foreclosures at Record High: Mortgage Delinquencies Rise Across the Board in Fourth Quarter, Market Watch (Mar. 13, 2007).

102 *See, e.g.,* Lynne Dearborn, Mortgage Foreclosures and Predatory Practices in St. Clair County, Illinois, 1996–2000, at 23 (July 2003) (from 1996 to 2000, the proportion of foreclosure judgments attributable to adjustable rate mortgages rose from 11% to 30%; at the same time, the proportion of fixed rate foreclosure judgments decreased almost 20%).

Chapter 2 Pre-Foreclosure Workout and Modification Agreements

2.1 Introduction

2.1.1 The Changing Climate for Workouts

In the past several years the dynamic for negotiating pre-foreclosure workout agreements for low- and moderate-income homeowners has changed dramatically. Workouts have become increasingly popular as the foreclosure crisis has escalated, the lending industry has liberalized its approach to homeowner defaults, and federal, state, and local governments seek to respond to the growing number of foreclosures.

In the past, lenders were extraordinarily reluctant to evaluate any but the simplest proposals for straightforward repayment agreements to avoid foreclosure. In many cases, due to confusion about mortgage servicing responsibilities and lack of accountability, it was impossible to determine whom to contact to discuss a workout. Even when an appropriate representative of the lender could be reached, that person generally had little flexibility to consider postponing a foreclosure sale or arranging reasonable workout terms. While borrowers with huge debts were getting significant concessions, individual homeowners with small mortgages were generally told that only full payment with fees and costs would suffice. The best general advice for homeowners was that a chapter 13 bankruptcy would achieve a better result than a negotiated agreement.

More recently, with the rapid increase in the number of homes entering foreclosure, the environment for doing workouts has changed markedly. To a large extent, the change is attributed to the growing foreclosure crisis and the realization in the industry and government that large numbers of foreclosures on low- and moderate-income property owners do not make sense. With a glut of properties on the market, lenders were left with the problem of managing large portfolios of deteriorating properties.

The desire to avoid the management headaches of ownership of foreclosed property led some in the industry to reevaluate foreclosure practices. Fannie Mae, Freddie Mac, and other large institutional mortgage holders encourage and provide financial incentives to servicers to do workouts on residential mortgage loans. The federal government has launched several initiatives, including the Making Home Affordable Modification program (HAMP), to encourage the rewriting of loan terms. The industry, in general, is devoting more resources to responsible foreclosure avoidance. The system is far from perfectly responsive, but homeowners now have an alternative to filing for bankruptcy, and may do better with a negotiated agreement than with a straightforward cure of arrears in chapter 13.

2.1.2 Organization of This Chapter

No chapter in this treatise is more subject to change than this chapter. The last several years has seen the creation of a number of new federal or industry programs for loan modifications or other workouts—Hope for Homeowners, HOPE NOW, Project Lifeline, Home Affordable Modification Program (HAMP), Second Lien Modification Program (2MP), Home Affordable Foreclosure Alternatives (HAFA), Home Affordable Unemployment Program (UP), and Home Affordable Refinance Program (HARP). Some of these programs are temporary and will end soon. Workouts also continue to occur outside these programs. Moreover, special rules apply to loans purchased by Fannie Mae or Freddie Mac, loans insured by HUD (FHA), VA, or the Rural Housing Service, and loans where the home has been affected by a natural disaster.

No one set of rules applies to modifications and workouts for all mortgages and the type of workout that is available for a particular type of mortgage may change over time. Right now HAMP and to a lesser extent HARP dominate the loan modification arena, but this may not be the case in the future.

This chapter begins with some general advice about loan modifications and other workouts and then turns to specific programs and specific types of mortgages. Section 2.2 provides initial steps an advocate should take in evaluating a homeowner's workout options and understanding the nature of the mortgage obligation. Section 2.3 then considers the major alternatives to a workout—bankruptcy, refinancing, government mortgage assistance programs, selling the home, and seeking someone to assume the mortgage.

Sections 2.4 and 2.5 summarize the types of workouts that lenders may offer. Not all of these workouts are available for every type of mortgage or mortgage modification program, and terminology will vary significantly from lender to lender in describing these types. Section 2.6 then provides general advice about the process of seeking a modification or other workout from a mortgage servicer, and § 2.7 considers some of the potential adverse consequences of a workout.

The remainder of the chapter discusses specific loan modification or workout programs. Section 2.8 analyzes HAMP, § 2.8.9 reviews 2MP, § 2.8.10 reviews UP, § 2.8.11 reviews HAFA, and § 2.9 reviews HARP. Section 2.10 summarizes some of HAMP's predecessors that still may have some vitality: Hope for Homeowners (H4H), HOPE NOW, and Project Lifeline. Fannie Mae and Freddie Mac provide guidelines for loan workouts and these are examined at § 2.11. Workout options for HUD (FHA), VA, and Rural Housing Service loans are set out at § 2.12. Finally, § 2.13 reviews special options where a home is in an area affected by a natural disaster.

An advocate may jump directly to a section describing a particular mortgage program, such as HAMP. Nevertheless, it is recommended that the reader also review the initial sections discussing workouts in general—such as how to evaluate a case, alternatives to a workout, how to deal with a recalcitrant servicer, and pitfalls to avoid in a modification agreement.

2.2 Getting Started

2.2.1 Client Needs for Representation

Obtaining a loan modification or other workout can be a complex process, with confusing guidelines, daunting paperwork, and servicer recalcitrance. Homeowners on their own may grasp for any workout option offered, even one that will not work in the long term and may make matters worse. Even more damaging, homeowners can fall easy victims to foreclosure rescue or loan modification scammers. Foreclosure rescue schemes can steal a home from the consumer and loan modification scammers can take much needed money from the homeowner, and prevent homeowners until it is too late from pursuing viable options on their own to save a home. Such abusive practices are examined at Chapter 15, *infra*, and a homeowner receiving proper counseling is more likely to avoid such traps.

Legal representation is one option for homeowners in financial distress. A housing counselor is another. In addition, the National Consumer Law Center's *Foreclosure Prevention Counseling*[1] contains much of the material in this chapter in a format designed for counselors and consumers looking to negotiate an affordable workout agreement. The *NCLC Guide to Surviving Debt*[2] is another helpful resource for consumers and counselors looking for advice to help families deal with a foreclosure or other debt problems. Several chapters provide advice to homeowners on foreclosure issues, and other chapters deal with debt collection, which debts to pay first, budgeting, credit reports, student loans, car repossessions, credit cards, finding effective credit counseling, and other topics.

2.2.2 Preparation Tips

As with any negotiation, an important key to success is extensive preparation. Begin with a clear understanding of your client's financial situation. Detailed information should be obtained about debts, income, assets, and expenses.[3] Realistic income and expenses projections are particularly important.

A rough budget should be prepared to determine how much money is available for a possible workout. It makes little sense to advocate for a proposed workout which the client cannot afford in the short and long term. For this reason, a plan must also be devised to deal with other significant expense problems.[4] Workouts on purchase money mortgages have little benefit, for example, if no plan is in place to deal with the second mortgage or to keep utility services flowing.

Sympathetic elements of your client's situation should be developed and documented. If possible, your client should document his or her hardship in writing. Such written statements or "hardship letters" may be useful later. Documents which provide proof of the hardship (e.g., death certificates, divorce decrees) should be collected. Lender loss mitigation specialists will often work harder to find a solution when they feel some sympathy for the borrower in default.

It is also important to obtain information about the subject property, particularly its conditions and fair market value. When appropriate, an appraisal or broker's price opinion (BPO) should be ordered.[5] The lender's willingness to discuss a deal may depend in large part on the real value of the property in the event of foreclosure. Physical problems with the property, including deterioration or liability associated with ownership (such as lead paint liability), make foreclosure a less desirable option for the lender. As discussed below, such information may be an important bargaining chip.

1 (2d ed. 2009), *available at* www.consumerlaw.org/shop.

2 (2010 ed.), *available at* www.consumerlaw.org/shop.

3 A sample intake form for this purpose is included as Appendix H.1, Form 1, *infra.*

4 *See generally* NCLC Guide to Surviving Debt (2010 ed.).

5 In some communities, appraisers will consider working for low-income clients on a reduced fee or pro bono basis. Other potential sources of information about value include sales of neighboring homes, tax assessments and realtor's estimates. Many realtors will provide a free estimate of value (often called a "broker's price opinion") because they are hoping to earn a commission if the homeowner decides to sell.

2.2.3 Understanding the Client's Objectives

As with any case, the client's needs and goals must be fully explored. For example, clients experiencing temporary lay-offs may have a legitimate expectation of increased future income upon return to work. For them, a period of temporary forbearance on mortgage payments might be the most appropriate bargaining objective. Other clients, particularly older clients upon retirement, may have a permanent income reduction. They will require a complete refinance or loan restructuring. Still others may prefer to sell their homes because of an expected permanent decrease in income. Their bargaining objective would be time to arrange a fair market sale to obtain the benefit of accumulated equity. Some clients may have multiple debt problems and multiple objectives. In those cases, bankruptcy still may be the first choice.[6]

2.2.4 Knowing the Players

It is important to understand the roles of several key players in a workout negotiation. More detail on all of the players in a mortgage transaction is found at § 1.3.2, *supra*.

The mortgage holder owns the borrower's mortgage and has the right to foreclose. Usually it did not originate the loan and may be a trust that holds title to securitized pools of loans. Section 1.3.3.3.2, *supra*, sets out ways to determine the mortgage holder's identity. The mortgage holder has ultimate authority to decide whether or not to accept a workout, but this authority is often initially delegated to a mortgage servicer.

The servicer may or may not be the originating lender. Frequently, the servicer will be the only party with whom the borrower has had any contact. Loan modifications and other workouts are typically arranged through the servicer, who will have workout specialists. Unfortunately, it is often hard to communicate with loan servicers, they may have inadequate resources to meet the needs of addressing a national portfolio,[7] and may have less to gain from a mortgage workout than does the mortgage holder.

If the servicer has already hired an attorney to initiate foreclosure proceedings on a home, the homeowner may have to deal with that attorney, at least initially, instead of with the servicer. As with the servicer, such attorneys may not be interested in negotiating a workout, even one beneficial to the mortgage holder. When necessary, attorneys should be reminded of their ethical responsibility to communicate offers of settlement to their client.

6 *See* Ch. 9, *infra*.

7 Some may remember the problems which arose several years ago, when one of the largest servicers centralized all of its operations in Texas without providing a toll-free number for borrower's telephone calls and without providing borrowers its new address for payments.

A mortgage insurer generally will pay some or all of the monies not recouped in the foreclosure process, so that the mortgage insurer may have a greater interest in preventing foreclosure than the mortgage holder. Thus the mortgage insurer may be helpful in negotiating a workout or may even agree to pay a small arrearage or provide other limited relief in order to keep the borrower in the home. If a homeowner is paying for private mortgage insurance, it is a good idea to find out the name of the insurer and to keep its loss mitigation department informed of the progress of workout negotiations.[8] Just informing the mortgage insurer may keep the servicer or mortgage holder on its best behavior. In addition, special service requirements apply to mortgages insured by HUD (FHA-insured mortgages), the VA, or the Rural Housing Service (RHS).

2.2.5 Breaking Down the Amount of the Default

2.2.5.1 Overview

An understanding of existing loan terms and the amount of the default is essential to a workout negotiation. A high interest rate, for example, might be negotiated down to a market rate.

Obtaining a breakdown of the default between principal, interest, insurance escrow, tax escrow, and foreclosure fees and costs is also important. It is easier to negotiate forgiveness of interest than of legitimate costs like escrow advances expended by the lender. Additionally, in some cases, a breakdown of the default will reveal that some charges claimed are not proper.[9] Foreclosure fees and costs, for example, may be excessive or not earned. The lender should recover unexpended fees and costs and deduct them from the arrears if a workout is achieved.

Another cost which should be scrutinized with purchase money mortgages is private mortgage insurance (PMI). PMI protects the lender against a deficiency in the event of a default. Many lenders require PMI on a purchase money mortgage when the borrower's down payment is less than 20% of the purchase price. The cancellation of unnecessary

8 This may be difficult to figure out. A charge for mortgage insurance should appear in the RESPA statement or other document itemizing disbursements. It may be necessary to obtain more information about the mortgage insurer directly from the lender or servicer (as your clients are paying for it, they are entitled to know who is providing it).

9 *See In re* Maxwell, 281 B.R. 101, 123 (Bankr. D. Mass. 2002) (according to the court the servicer fabricated the amount the debtor owed "out of thin air"; there is no other explanation for the wildly divergent payoff figures); Dwyer v. J.I. Kislak Mortgage Corp., 13 P.3d 240 (Wash. Ct. App. 2000) (lender violated the state consumer protection statute when it presented borrower with a payoff statement that included amounts that were not necessary to pay off the mortgage).

PMI, as well as other grounds on which to challenge the amount of the default, are discussed at § 7.11.7, *infra*.

More invidiously, it is common for some lenders to include fees and costs paid out as an element of a claimed escrow deficiency, and additionally to break them out as charges necessary to cure a default. Obviously, those amounts are double counted and should be deducted from the balance.

2.2.5.2 Seeking Information About the Amount Claimed Due

Obtaining a workout requires cooperation between the homeowner and the servicer or lender. This means that it is best to start the process of obtaining information from the lender in an informal way. It is best to begin by asking politely for information, before demanding it based on the lender's legal obligations discussed in the next section.

A responsible lender or servicer will want authorization from the borrower before releasing account information to an advocate. It is thus important to obtain an information release authorization form from clients early in the counseling process. A sample authorization release form for this purpose is contained at Appendix H.1.2, *infra*.

It is also important to get all of the information you may need about your clients' account status at the outset of workout discussions. It is impossible to evaluate any strategy to address the default without knowing how much is claimed due. A form request for information from the lender or servicer is contained at Appendix H.1.3, *infra*.

2.2.5.3 RESPA Provision Requires Lenders to Provide Information About Loan Accounts and to Correct Errors

The Real Estate Settlement Procedures Act (RESPA) mandates that lenders or loan servicers must respond to consumers who have disputes about their accounts and must make corrections to their accounts when appropriate.[10] By invoking the protections of this statute, known as the Servicer Act, borrowers in default can challenge the amount of the claimed default and require the lender to respond promptly to the dispute.[11] If the lender fails to meet its obligations, it will face liability for statutory damages and attorney fees.[12]

When a consumer has a question or a dispute concerning the account, including the escrow, a written inquiry (called a "qualified written request") triggers certain obligations on the part of the servicer, as long as the consumer provides identifying information and a statement of the reasons why the account is in error or clear information about the consumer's question.[13] The servicer must acknowledge the request within twenty days of receipt.[14] Within sixty days after receipt of a qualified written request from the consumer, the servicer must: conduct an investigation if an error is alleged; provide the information requested, if available; make any necessary correction to the account; and inform the consumer of its actions.[15] During this sixty-day period, the servicer cannot give any information to a credit reporting agency if a payment related to the inquiry is overdue.[16] Chapter 8, *infra*, includes a complete discussion of qualified written requests.

2.2.6 *Determining Whether Your Client Has Defenses to Repayment*

In some cases, obtaining loan paperwork or talking to your client may uncover potential consumer defenses to collection, such as Truth in Lending violations, usury, fraud, or unfair and deceptive practices.[17] Whenever possible, the client should not make an agreement to repay money to a lender when there is a substantial defense to repayment. When appropriate, legal claims can be used as bargaining chips for workouts either before or after legal action is commenced. A "qualified written request," under RESPA, provides an opportunity to obtain informal discovery and, if the error is correctable, to have the situation resolved without litigation.[18]

---

10 12 U.S.C. § 2605. *See also* § 8.2.2, *infra*. The loan "servicer" includes the entity responsible for servicing the loan (accepting payments, maintaining escrow accounts, etc.) and the holder of the loan if the holder also services the loan.

11 12 U.S.C. § 2605(f). The statute of limitations is three years. 12 U.S.C. § 2614. Certain governmental agencies, for example, the Resolution Trust Corp. and the Federal Deposit Insurance Corp., or governmentally sponsored entities, for example, Fannie Mae, Ginnie Mae, and others, are exempted in certain circumstances from coverage. 12 U.S.C. § 2605(i)(2). The Department of Housing and Urban Development has also promulgated regulations under § 2605 and created form notices. Reg. X, 24 C.F.R. § 3500.21 and appendices. This section also places a substantive duty upon servicers to pay the taxes, insurance, and other escrowed monies to the appropriate recipients.

12 *See* Ploog v. HomeSide Lending, Inc., 209 F. Supp. 2d 863 (N.D. Ill. 2002). An individual consumer may recover actual damages, costs, and reasonable attorney fees for "each such failure." If the evidence also reveals a pattern or practice of noncompliance, the court may award "additional" damages for each violation up to $1000. Arguably, the "additional" damages which fall under the $1000 limitation do not include punitive damages.

13 The consumer must include their name and account number, reasons why the account is in error or some detail about the nature of the information sought. 12 U.S.C. § 2605(e)(1)(A), (B); Reg. X, 24 C.F.R. § 3500.21(e)(1), (2) *See* Rawlings v. Dovenmuehle Mortgage, Inc., 64 F. Supp. 2d 1156 (M.D. Ala. 1999).

14 12 U.S.C. § 2605(e)(1)(A); Reg. X, 24 C.F.R. § 3500.21(e)(1).

15 12 U.S.C. § 2605(e)(1)(B)(2); Reg. X, 24 C.F.R. § 3500.21(e)(3).

16 12 U.S.C. § 2605(e)(3); Reg. X, 24 C.F.R. § 3500.21(e)(4).

17 These defenses are discussed in more detail in Ch. 5, *infra*.

18 *See* § 8.2.2, *infra*.

2.2.7 Timing

There are significant advantages to beginning a workout discussion as early as possible after the default. There is the obvious advantage of negotiating a workout on a smaller default. Getting involved early also avoids the difficulty of negotiating at the last minute with a potential foreclosure sale date pending; it makes the debtor appear more responsible in trying to prevent the problem from getting out of hand; and in some cases, it avoids the extra layer of complexity when a foreclosure lawyer is involved on behalf of the lender.

It may even be better to start before default. It may be easier to negotiate an affordable loan modification if foreclosure fees and costs, which can total thousands of dollars, have not been added to the account. Homeowners must demonstrate that though they are still current, default is imminent or reasonably foreseeable. What is considered an imminent default will vary from servicer to servicer, based on their internal policy or investor guidelines. Servicers take different approaches to determining imminent default but have generally been willing to modify the loans of homeowners who face payment shock due to an upcoming interest rate reset on their adjustable rate mortgage, if they are able to demonstrate that their current income does not support a higher payment. At a minimum the servicer must evaluate the borrower's financial condition in light of his or her stated hardship and inquire as to the condition of the property. Common reasons that a borrower may be in imminent danger of default include death of co-borrower, divorce, illness, and unemployment or underemployment.

The industry is tightening its standards on imminent default. Freddie Mac, Fannie Mae, and the FHA have issued new guidelines on imminent default with respect to HAMP. In the case of Freddie Mac and Fannie Mae, the companies have developed servicing software that takes into account the borrower's cash reserves (must have non-retirement liquid assets of $25,000 or less), FICO score, debt-to-income ratio, and property value.[19]

When the client has not acted quickly and does not seek help from you before the foreclosure sale process has commenced, it may still be possible to negotiate a workout. However, at least for lawyers, once the lender has legal representation, ethical responsibilities require negotiating with the lawyer or obtaining permission to negotiate with the lender or servicer directly. Although some lawyers will not grant this permission, others will readily do so. It is worth asking. Alternatively, lawyers must transmit settlement offers to their client, so it is possible to negotiate through the lawyer to achieve a favorable result.

As discussed below, when a foreclosure is pending, careful attention must be given to preventing the sale. A foreclosure sale will cut off the homeowner's rights to the property, the ability (in most cases) to cure the default in bankruptcy, and the right to raise most defenses to the validity of the mortgage. In such cases, it is important to focus on preventing the sale as a short-term goal, before focusing on the workout as a long-term solution.

If bankruptcy is contemplated, workouts should generally be discussed, if at all, prior to the filing. Once bankruptcy is filed, most lenders will not seriously negotiate an agreement which goes beyond the best potential result under the Bankruptcy Code. However some anti-foreclosure programs, such as the Making Home Affordable Program, do require that servicers consider borrowers in bankruptcy for loan modifications and other workout options.

2.2.8 Relevance of the Homeowner's Equity Position

Workout discussions can be counterintuitive. Mortgage holders tend to be most willing to discuss favorable workout terms for borrowers who have the least amount invested in their property.

If there is substantial equity, lenders are generally eager to foreclose because they can buy the property at below market rates, resell for fair market value, and keep the difference. Conversely, if there is little equity, foreclosure is likely to be a losing proposition for the lender, so that a workout is a better option.

The upshot is, in some cases, new homeowners who have defaulted relatively early in their mortgages may be better candidates for favorable workout terms than homeowners (including older homeowners) who have responsibly made payments for a long period of time. Certainly, when representing a homeowner who can take advantage of that dynamic, it is appropriate to do so. When representing a homeowner with substantial equity, arguments about fairness may need to be pressed.

Whatever the circumstances, it is a good idea to know the amount of your client's equity in the property as well as the salability of the property, because it is a good clue to how the mortgage holder will react to proposed terms.

2.2.9 Lump Sum As Incentive

One further incentive to build upon for a workout discussion is the availability of a lump-sum payment toward the workout. Many mortgage holders will provide much more favorable workout terms to borrowers who have a lump sum saved toward curing the default. Perversely, over a period of time, the incentive for a workout may increase based on a lump sum, even if the homeowner is actually further behind.

19 Freddie Mac Bulletin, No. 2010-1 (Jan. 26, 2010), *available at* http://freddiemac.com/sell/guide/bulletins/; Fannie Mae, Lender Announcement SVC-2010-02 (Feb. 1, 2010), *available at* www.efanniemae.com/sf/guides/ssg/annltrs/pdf/2010/svc1002.pdf.

Thus, borrowers should be encouraged to save anything possible toward the mortgage while a workout is being discussed. (If possible, those funds should be placed in escrow.) Even if the mortgage holder has refused partial payments, after several months the accumulated lump sum may be an important bargaining chip toward a workout.

Saving money toward a workout also demonstrates for the lender that the homeowner is committed to the loan workout process. It demonstrates for you, as an advocate, that your clients have established a workable budget. And in the event that foreclosure prevention plans go awry, money that has been put aside can be used to pay for moving expenses and for alternative housing.

2.3 Alternatives to a Workout or Modification

2.3.1 Bankruptcy

The best alternative to a workout is often a chapter 13 bankruptcy filing. Moreover, if workout discussions are commenced but proceed unfavorably, the chapter 13 bankruptcy option remains available for exploration up until the time of sale. In many instances borrowers can continue to negotiate a workout option while they are in an active chapter 13 bankruptcy proceeding.

Chapter 9, *infra*, examines in some detail how a bankruptcy filing can slow or prevent a foreclosure. Even more detail is found in another National Consumer Law Center publication, *Consumer Bankruptcy Law and Practice* (9th ed. 2009) with a companion website containing pleadings, software, and other practice aids. Attorneys new to bankruptcy may prefer National Consumer Law Center's *Bankruptcy Basics*, also with a companion website. Finally, a chapter explaining the bankruptcy process for consumers is found in National Consumer Law Center's *Surviving Debt*.

Nevertheless, if the major reason to file a bankruptcy is to prevent foreclosure, a comparison between the best possible outcome on an overdue mortgage debt after a chapter 13 bankruptcy filing and under a loan workout plan illustrates that a voluntary workout may sometimes be a cheaper alternative for a homeowner. Note that this example does not evaluate some of the obvious ancillary advantages of bankruptcy, such as the automatic stay, that a cure in installments may usually be implemented over creditor objection, and that the chapter 13 process may be less expensive with respect to other debts that impact the debtor's budget.

It also does not consider the significant benefit gained by the possible strip-off of completely underwater junior mortgages,[20] or the ability to avoid judicial liens,[21] which are other encumbrances on the property that may prevent a voluntary workout on the first mortgage. Moreover, this example does not review the potential advantages of combining bankruptcy relief with a voluntary workout. On the other hand, some likely costs of bankruptcy are not considered. These include filing and attorney fees, and potential obligations to priority and unsecured creditors under the Bankruptcy Code.[22]

Consider the following scenario:

Mr. and Mrs. Wilson have a thirty-year first mortgage obtained in 2005. The interest rate is 9.75%. Monthly payments are $1300 (including $220 monthly escrow for taxes and insurance). Mr. Wilson lost his job ten months ago, was unemployed for nine months, and has generated mortgage arrears of $14,000 including foreclosure fees and costs.

Mr. Wilson recently returned to work at a job which pays about 60% of his prior income. The Wilsons will have about $2100 in monthly take home pay and $1000 in expenses for necessities other than the mortgage.

The current situation is as follows:

- $195,000 principal balance due;
- $114,000 total arrears;
- $106,000 payoff including interest and costs;
- Debt is secured by a $175,000 property;
- Income available for mortgage: $1100 per month.

If the Wilsons file bankruptcy, they will be entitled to cure their arrears by resuming their current monthly mortgage payments and paying down the arrears in the plan at present value interest.[23] Monthly payments to cure the arrears in bankruptcy will thus include:

$1300.00	ongoing payment[24]
$ 233.33	payment on arrears[25]
$ 57.28	interest on arrears[26]
$ 32.25	trustee's fee[27]

It will thus cost the Wilsons $1622.86 monthly to cure the arrears. It looks like the Wilsons will not be able to keep this home by filing a chapter 13 case. They need to pay $1622.86 to cure the arrears even before considering other required

20 *See* § 9.7, *infra.*

21 *See* § 9.8, *infra.*

22 *See* Ch. 9, *infra* (more complete discussion of using bankruptcy to prevent foreclosure).

23 11 U.S.C. § 1322(b)(3), (5).

24 This includes the existing escrow payment. It also assumes that the payment can be made outside the bankruptcy process (directly to the creditor) without the trustee's fee.

25 This assumes that the plan will be allowed to extend to sixty months and that the cure can be effectuated over the full term of the plan.

26 This is the interest on arrears payment required by the Supreme Court decision in Rake v. Wade, 508 U.S. 464, 113 S. Ct. 2187, 124 L. Ed. 2d 424 (1993). That holding has been legislatively overruled for mortgages dated after October 22, 1994. 11 U.S.C. § 1322(e).

27 This is the trustee's commission at 10% of the amount paid into the plan on account of this claim.

payments in chapter 13.[28] However, their available income is only $1100.

If the lender will agree to a loan workout, available loan modification terms might include interest rate reductions, extension of loan term to 360 months from the date of the modification, and capitalization of arrears.[29] Lenders consider these types of loan workouts because, on the whole, foreclosures generate losses. Interest rate reductions to market rate do not cost the lender money when compared with making a new loan with the funds recovered in foreclosure, because recovered funds can only be lent out at market rate. Extension of the loan term has little impact on the lender because the lender will receive interest over the entire term of the loan as modified. Capitalization of arrears allows the lender to collect all outstanding past-due interest payments and fees with additional interest over the term of the modified loan.

The total principal balance after capitalization of arrears would be $106,000. Even if this loan were then modified to an above-market interest rate (at a rate of 8.5%) over a new 360-month term, payments would be lower at $815 per month plus escrow for a total payment of $1035.[30]

Clearly, at least on a monthly basis, this workout alternative is cheaper for the Wilsons (by $500 per month) than a chapter 13 bankruptcy. It appears to be the only option which will allow the Wilsons to keep their home.[31] However, if the Wilsons are struggling with other non-mortgage debt problems or could benefit from bankruptcy relief in other ways, an even better strategy for the Wilsons may be to pursue a workout or loan modification as part of the bankruptcy proceeding. Policies at major national institutions such as HUD, Fannie Mae, Freddie Mac, and the Department of Treasury (for its Home Affordable Modification Program) now allow workout agreements with homeowners that have filed bankruptcy.[32] For the HAMP loan modification program, Treasury guidelines specify that a borrower in an active chapter 7 or chapter 13 bankruptcy case must be considered for HAMP if the borrower submits a request to the servicer.[33]

2.3.2 *Refinancing*

If the home was financed at a high interest rate, refinancing at a lower interest rate and/or with a longer payment period can greatly reduce monthly payments. Moreover, refinancing a low interest first mortgage and high interest second mortgage into a low interest first mortgage can also reduce payments.

For example, a family with a twenty-five-year, $10,000 first mortgage at 8% interest and a fifteen-year, $30,000 second mortgage at 18% interest has combined monthly payments of $399.26. Refinancing those two mortgages with a twenty-five-year, $30,000 first mortgage at 10% will result in new monthly payments of $272.61. This is $126.65 per month less than the prior combined monthly payments.

On the other hand, some refinancing schemes are frauds.[34] Even legitimate refinancing options that look like an improvement on closer inspection are far more costly than the existing mortgage. In order to evaluate the cost and value of refinancing it is imperative to carefully review the proposed loan terms.[35]

The major disadvantages in refinancing residential mortgage debts are the increased finance charges that result from extending the repayment period, the possibility of having to pay points, the additional closing costs, and prepayment penalties on the old mortgages. The feasibility of refinancing depends on whether the homeowner can obtain a loan at a reasonable rate, usually from a savings bank, a commercial bank, a credit union, or a legitimate mortgage company. Most finance companies and certain mortgage companies do not make residential loans at reasonable rates and terms.[36] Another disadvantage which must be explored carefully is whether the borrowers will lose their right to raise defenses to the original loan if it is refinanced with a new lender.

The availability of special mortgage programs should also be explored, such as reverse mortgages (for older homeowners),[37] federal FHA-guaranteed loans,[38] state

28 Such payments would include their obligation for payments on unsecured and priority debts.

29 *See* § 2.4.6, *supra*.

30 Some lenders charge one time modification fees of up to $750. This analysis assumes that the modification fees and the bankruptcy fees (including filing fees and a higher attorney fee) will effectively net out.

31 A similar outcome might be available if the Wilsons could refinance. However, their poor credit record associated with a mortgage delinquency makes refinancing unlikely.

32 *See* § 2.8.6, *infra*.

33 *See* Dep't of the Treasury, Home Affordable Modification Program, Supplemental Directive 10-02, at 7 (Mar. 24, 2009); § 2.8.6, *infra*.

34 This treatise's companion website contains a complaint which outlines an abusive refinancing scheme. *See also* Appx. K, *infra* (information on finding foreclosure and home defense pleadings on this treatise's companion website and in National Consumer Law Center's *Consumer Credit and Sales Legal Practice Series*).

35 *See* National Consumer Law Center, The Cost of Credit: Regulation, Preemption, and Industry Abuses § 6.5 (4th ed. 2009 and Supp.) (further discussion of the refinancing process); NCLC Guide to Surviving Debt Ch. 6 (2010 ed.) (a set of refinancing "do's and don'ts" for clients).

36 *See* National Consumer Law Center, The Cost of Credit: Regulation, Preemption, and Industry Abuses § 6.5 (4th ed. 2009 and Supp.).

37 *See generally* § 5.3.7.2, *infra*.

38 The FHA has a "streamline" refinance program for mortgages on which it has already issued a guarantee. A prerequisite for qualification is that the borrower be current or nearly current. Thus, this program benefits homeowners that foresee a coming financial problem and those who have defaulted but can catch

bonded mortgage funds, or local neighborhood development funds available through banks' community reinvestment programs. New programs are being developed on the federal and state level to aid homeowners who are in default or in danger of defaulting on their loan. Most of the programs allow homeowners with adjustable rate mortgages to refinance into thirty-year fixed rate loans.[39] Typically, borrowers must meet income- and mortgage-limit guidelines. Most states focus their efforts on borrowers who are current on their mortgage or less than sixty days delinquent. Thus, despite the proliferation of these programs, borrowers have difficulty qualifying for the loans.

Homeowners that apply for refinancing and are rejected should obtain the reasons for their rejection and determine whether the reasons are legitimate. Under the Equal Credit Opportunity Act, lenders who reject a credit application must explain their reasons.[40] The Act prohibits lenders from engaging in discrimination based on several factors including denying credit based on the applicant's receipt of government benefits.[41] To the extent a lender offers a legitimate explanation, the consumer should try to cure the problem so that the next application will be successful.[42]

2.3.3 Federal, State, and Local Mortgage Assistance Programs

States and municipalities have long-standing programs to help homeowners in financial distress. Pennsylvania[43] has developed a mortgage assistance program in response to multiple plant closings and consequent high rates of foreclosures against laid-off workers. The program provides for loans to homeowners to pay part of the monthly mortgage payment for several years. Homeowners who are behind in their payments for reasons beyond their control (for example, lay-offs) and who are likely to be able to resume full home loan payments in several years are eligible. Some unions and corporations also have mortgage assistance programs.

Notice to the homeowner of this assistance is a prerequisite to foreclosure in Pennsylvania. Lenders in Pennsylvania must also delay foreclosure proceedings once they receive notice that a homeowner has been approved for assistance from the program.[44]

The federal government has established a mortgage relief program for borrowers unemployed as a result of a military base closing. Under this program, the federal government temporarily makes payments on behalf of distressed homeowners.[45] These and other assistance programs should be explored whenever a homeowner is in default.

States and the federal government have created a number of new mortgage assistance or refinance programs in response to the foreclosure crisis.[46] Minnesota, for example, created a loan fund as part of its Foreclosure Prevention Assistance Program. Borrowers receive counseling and they may apply for an emergency loan of up to $5500 to reinstate their mortgage. The loans are offered on a one-time basis and are deferred with no interest. Lenders are required to notify borrowers about the availability of assistance under the program.

Delaware's Emergency Mortgage Assistance Program helps homeowners who are sixty or more days delinquent get caught up on their mortgage or make future mortgage payments. Homeowners may borrow up to $15,000 to pay off delinquent principal, interest, escrow, and reasonable foreclosure fees and costs. The loan has a 3% interest rate and borrowers must make a minimum monthly payment of $40. As the foreclosure crisis evolves, new programs will be created on the state level and the terms of existing programs may change. Advocates should keep abreast of program development.

2.3.4 Selling the Home

When a property can be sold for more than the balance owed on the mortgage, the loan will be fully paid from the sale proceeds. This is typically known in the industry as a "full" sale. The proceeds of the sale that exceed the mortgage balance are retained by the homeowner.

In many cases it is in the homeowner's interest to sell the property rather than to have it foreclosed, as the property is likely to sell for a higher price through a realtor than in the foreclosure process. This is especially true for homeowners who have substantial equity and little likelihood of being able to afford reinstatement or modification of their loan.

---

up on the arrears as well as homeowners that want a lower interest rate or other change in terms. *See generally* § 2.12.1.3, *infra*; HUD Handbook 4155.1, rev. 4. The handbook is available on HUD's website (www.hud.gov) and on this treatise's companion website.

39 *See* The Pew Charitable Trusts, Defaulting on the Dream: States Respond to America's Foreclosure Crisis (Apr. 2008) (summary of state initiatives).

40 Reg. B, 12 C.F.R. § 202.9. *See* Newton v. United Companies Fin. Corp., 24 F. Supp. 2d 444 (E.D. Pa. 1998).

41 15 U.S.C. § 1691(a)(2); Reg. B, 12 C.F.R. §§ 202.2(z), 202.4.

42 *See* National Consumer Law Center, Repossessions § 14.7.9.1 (6th ed. 2005 and Supp.) (more information on the federal Equal Credit Opportunity Act); National Consumer Law Center, Credit Discrimination (5th ed. 2009 and Supp.) (more information on the federal Equal Credit Opportunity Act).

43 35 Pa. Stat. Ann. §§ 1680.401c to 1680.410c (West).

44 *See* NBD Mortgage Co. v. Pa. Hous. Fin. Agency Homeowner Emergency Assistance Program, 651 A.2d 237 (Pa. Commw. Ct. 1994) (lender which proceeded to foreclosure after it learned that application had been approved was not entitled to recover costs).

45 12 U.S.C. § 1735g.

46 *See* The Pew Charitable Trusts, Defaulting on the Dream: States Respond to America's Foreclosure Crisis (Apr. 2008) (summary of state initiatives).

Of course, if the property can be sold for more than the amount due *before foreclosure is complete*, the homeowner can tender full payment on the claim from the sale proceeds in order to prevent the foreclosure auction. Permission from the lender to do so is not required.

However, if the full sale cannot be completed before the foreclosure sale date, the homeowner must seek and obtain a sufficient postponement of the sale. If substantial equity is available, the mortgage holder is not hurt by the delay because the equity in the property means that the mortgage will be paid in full with interest from the sale proceeds even if the property takes a short while to sell.[47] The lender also may readily agree to postpone a sale if very little equity is present. That is because the lender may be fully paid only by an arm's length fair market value sale. It may incur losses if it is forced to proceed to foreclosure and then obtains a lower price.

2.3.5 *Mortgage Assumption*

Some mortgages can be assumed (taken over) by a third party. When a mortgage is assumable, the property can be transferred, and the person to whom it is transferred can pick up the payments on the mortgage. If payments were behind when the mortgage was assumed, absent a workout agreement, the person assuming the mortgage will be in default and subject to the same collection activity as the transferring homeowner. The advantage may be that the assuming party is in a better position to deal with the default than the original homeowner.

A mortgage is always assumable if the contract documents say it is or, in most states, if the documents are silent on this issue. Other loan contracts contain a "due on sale" provision, a clause specifying that transfer of the property accelerates the full loan balance.[48]

There are a number of situations in which assumption can take place despite attempts by the mortgage holder to enforce a due on sale provision. For example, mortgage holders generally cannot block a transfer from parent to child.[49] Additionally, mortgage holders will sometimes agree to otherwise impermissible assumptions so that they can start getting payments from someone.

After a mortgage assumption, the transferor generally remains personally liable on the loan note. Of course, the lender can release the borrower from this obligation, but rarely will do so unless there is a financial incentive to do so, or the borrower can demonstrate some type of extreme hardship.

2.4 Types of Workouts

2.4.1 *General*

There are many different ways to modify or temporarily change mortgage payments to alleviate a homeowner's difficulty making payments. Each mortgage holder's standards for agreeing to these different possible workouts (and its jargon for identifying them) are likely to be different. Not every mortgage holder will consider a workout on each basis described below, but it does not hurt to ask and solicit a counterproposal.[50] If the servicer participates in the federal Home Affordable Modification Program (HAMP), the servicer is required to evaluate the borrower for a modification under the terms of that program before offering the borrower any non-program options discussed below. See the discussion of HAMP at § 2.8, *infra*.

The best workout for a homeowner may be some combination of different types of workout arrangements. For example, if an unemployed homeowner has found a lower paying job which will not start for three months, that homeowner may need a temporary moratorium on payments and a permanent interest rate reduction.

Many of the options described below parallel those offered under Fannie Mae and Freddie Mac guidelines, discussed at § 2.11, *infra*. Even if an option described below differs from those guidelines, advocates may still use it as a basis of a workout proposal on a loan held by Fannie Mae or Freddie Mac. Both companies will consider proposals that vary from their guidelines if it is the best way of resolving the delinquency.

2.4.2 *Repayment Plans*

A repayment plan (also known as reinstatement agreement or deferral agreement) involves curing a default by making regular monthly mortgage payments as they are due, together with partial monthly payment on the arrears (including fees and costs). For example, a typical agreement might call for making one-and-a-quarter monthly payments until the default is resolved. This type of agreement is similar to a cure of arrears in the context of a chapter 13 bankruptcy.

47 Some lenders may be reluctant to give up the potential windfall which a cheap purchase at foreclosure creates. Those lenders might be given a nudge toward a consensual sale through litigation to stay the foreclosure on equitable grounds, based on the forfeiture of equity which results from a below market foreclosure. If the lender, in bad faith, refuses to grant a reasonable request for a delay in the foreclosure sale, they may be liable. *See* Snowden v. Chase Manhattan Mortgage Corp., 2003 WL 22519518 (Mass. Super. Ct. Nov. 5, 2003).

48 Due on sale provision are discussed at § 4.9, *infra*.

49 *See* 12 C.F.R. pt. 590.

50 One issue that may be negotiable which can be included as part of a workout proposal is the mortgage holder's report on the homeowner's credit history. At a minimum, any negative reference should be removed or clarified once the terms of the agreement are met. Alternatively this issue can be raised in the process of drafting the documents to implement a workout.

The homeowners most likely to benefit from this type of payment agreement are those who have experienced temporary financial difficulties which are now resolved. The homeowners need to have some excess income in their budget to commit to the mortgage beyond the regular monthly payment.

A short-term repayment plan allows a homeowner to repay the arrears over a three- to six-month period. These repayment plans are typically informal and servicers verbally approve the plan. In the past, most mortgage holders limited repayment plans to no more than one year for reinstatement. Agreements up to twenty-four months are now common, though these longer term arrangements may be referred to as forbearance plans and a written agreement is usually required. Time periods of thirty-six and even forty-eight months are also possible; the servicer, however, must generally get special approval from the mortgage holder.

One pitfall to this type of arrangement is that it may fail to account for the extra initial expenses associated with recovery from temporary financial difficulties. Homeowners often have substantial budgetary pressures for several months after dealing with a temporary financial problem. Other bills, including utilities, may have fallen into arrears and expenses, such as urgent car repairs may have been deferred. The agreement must realistically take these expenses into account—perhaps by proposing graduated payments on the arrears.

2.4.3 *Forbearance Plans*

A forbearance plan is generally a more formal agreement that allows homeowners who have missed several loan payments due to a serious event (illness, divorce, natural disaster, etc.) to repay the arrears over a period of time while concurrently making their regular monthly mortgage payments. While similar to a repayment plan, a forbearance plan is usually long-term, and offers options unavailable in a repayment plan, such as a period of reduced or suspended payment to allow the homeowner to recover from the event that caused the financial hardship. A written agreement is usually required.

2.4.4 *Temporary Interest Rate Reduction*

A temporary interest rate reduction may be available to help homeowners who have ongoing financial problems which are likely to be temporary in nature, but which preclude full payment of the mortgage for a foreseeable period of time. The borrower generally must have a feasible plan for increasing income to make full payments at the expiration of the rate-reduction period.

The theory behind a temporary rate reduction is that if someone gets help by lowering payments in the short term, he or she will be able to keep from falling further behind while waiting, for example, for a recall from a lay-off. Some mortgage holders want assurance that if the borrower cannot return to paying the full rate within a reasonable time, foreclosure will go forward unopposed.

Typically, rates can be reduced fairly easily to the market rate of interest or, with some cause shown, below market.[51]

2.4.5 *Recasting of Missed Payments*

A similar provision for temporary mortgage relief is known as recasting (also known as deferral). Recasting involves canceling missed payments and adding the obligation to make those payments to the end of the loan term. It is a method of allowing someone who can start making monthly payments again to do so without the need to address the default. Thus, it is available for some homeowners who have addressed their temporary financial difficulties, but cannot afford to get caught up on their mortgage default.

Recasting is generally available as to retroactive (already missed) payments rather than to payments due in the future. Because of changes in mortgage accounting practices, most large institutional lenders (including Fannie Mae and Freddie Mac) no longer consider recasting. When it remains available, the mortgage holder is usually unwilling to recast more than six monthly payments.

2.4.6 *Permanent Modification of Loan Terms*

2.4.6.1 Overview

Loan modifications have emerged as a primary strategy for addressing the foreclosure crisis. A loan modification is a written agreement between the servicer and the homeowner to change one or more of the original terms of the note to ease the homeowner's burden of making timely mortgage payments, reducing the interest rate or principal amount, changing the mortgage product (for example, from an adjustable to a fixed rate), extending the loan term, or capitalizing delinquent payments. The modification can be short-term (less than two years), long-term (two to five years) or for the life of the loan. Some plans, such as HAMP, call for a three-month trial modification before a more permanent modification.

51 Advocates should make certain that the paperwork on a temporary interest rate reduction specifies that the loan will amortize during the period of the rate reduction at the lower rate. This proviso will prevent a problem with the foregone interest being carried on the lender's books or rolled into the loan principal to change the amortization of the loan.

An agreement of this type occurs most frequently when the borrower can no longer afford the original loan terms due to a permanent change in circumstances, and it is not in the mortgage holder's financial interest to foreclose.[52] A permanent modification may also be available if the homeowner has counterclaims or other leverage to exchange (by way of release) for the change in loan terms.

The biggest loan modification initiative to date is the federal Home Affordable Modification Program (or HAMP). This program has superseded a patchwork of prior industry and government sponsored loan modification initiatives and is now the standard used by the industry. Most servicers participate in the program and are obligated to evaluate eligible borrowers for HAMP modifications before proceeding to consider non-HAMP modifications, other workout options, or foreclosure. HAMP is discussed in detail at § 2.8, *infra*.

Modifications are permitted under Fannie Mae and Freddie Mac servicing guidelines. For the most part, many other prime and subprime mortgage-backed securities' pooling and servicing agreements (PSAs) permit loan modifications if the loan is in default or if the servicer determines that default is reasonably foreseeable.[53]

Prior to the development of HAMP, the financial services industry and the federal government launched a series of voluntary efforts to modify loans *en masse*. In December 2007, the Treasury Department announced an industry-sponsored plan to streamline the modification of securitized subprime mortgages.[54] Major lenders and servicers, such as Bank of America, Citi, and JPMorgan Chase, followed by creating their own loan modification programs primarily aimed at streamlining the modification process. Loan modification programs were also instituted by the Federal Reserve and by the FDIC, after its takeover of Indy Mac Federal Bank.[55]

Many of these earlier modification programs actually increased monthly payments, by simply adding the arrears to principal, without further adjustments in interest, the loan term, or the principal, even when the principal due exceeded the home's value.[56] Other modifications only offered temporary relief, with interest rates reduced for between one to five years, or reduced payments in the short run by creating balloon payments in the future. Not surprisingly, many homeowners re-defaulted under these unrealistic and burdensome modification terms.

2.4.6.2 Types of Permanent Loan Modifications

A loan modification can be accomplished with any of the following five changes to the loan terms or by some combination of these five:

1. Interest Rate Reductions. The most common scenario for a permanent interest rate reduction is when the existing rate is above market, and is unaffordable for the homeowner. In some cases, this may involve converting a variable rate to a fixed rate loan. The mortgage holder may recognize that if it forecloses on the property and finances the subsequent disposition, it can obtain no more than the market rate of interest.

2. Extension of the Loan Payment Period. Extending the loan repayment period helps homeowners by allowing them to repay the principal over a longer term, thereby reducing the monthly payment. For example, an older homeowner who borrowed $100,000 in 1990 on a thirty-year mortgage might owe only $20,000 today. Payments might be $750 monthly based on the original note. By extending the term back out to 360 months on the $20,000 balance, monthly payments can be reduced to $175 dollars. The mortgage holder does not lose out as long as the rate is at least as high as the market rate, because the entire principal will be repaid with the applicable interest.

3. Reamortization with Capitalization of Arrears. If a loan is reamortized, the existing interest rate is applied to the amount due on the loan over the remaining loan term as if there is no default. Payments are recalculated accordingly. Reamortization is generally combined with other permanent modifications to the interest rate or terms. However, reamortizing, even without extending the period or changing the interest rate, can help some homeowners who have defaulted because it allows them to take missed payments and have them spread out over the remaining balance of the loan (i.e., "capitalized"). This cancels the arrears. If there is no adjustment to the rate, period, or principal, payments will go up slightly. However, if reamortization is combined with an interest rate reduction, an extension of the period of the loan, or a cancellation of principal, payments can be significantly reduced.

4. Reduction of Principal Balance. Reduction may be available in some cases when the loan amount is more than the value of the property due to depreciation for reasons

---

52 The lender may be uninterested in foreclosure for a variety of reasons including depreciation of the property, potential liabilities associated with the property such as lead paint exposure, the existence of a large balance on a higher priority lien, or realization that the property is unmarketable for some other reason.

53 Fitch Ratings, Residential Mortgage Special Report: Residential Mortgage Loss Mitigation Strategies (Oct. 14, 2003), *available at* www.fitchratings.com.

54 American Securitization Forum, Streamlined Foreclosure and Loss Avoidance Framework for Securitized Subprime Adjustable Rate Mortgage Loans, *available at* www.treas.gov/prss/releases/hp7066.htm.

55 A summary of industry and government sponsored loss mitigation programs initiated since 2008 is available on National Consumer Law Center's website at www.consumerlaw.org/issues/financial_distress/loan_modification.shtml.

56 *See* Alan M. White, Rewriting Contracts, Wholesale: Data on Voluntary Mortgage Modifications from 2007 and 2008 Remittance Reports (Aug. 26, 2008), *available at* papers.ssrn.com/sol3/papers.cfm?abstract_id=1259538.

beyond the borrower's control.[57] (It also may be available as a negotiated result in litigation.) The mortgage holder may agree to reduce the principal when it recognizes that its best potential result in foreclosure is to obtain the current value of the property less its foreclosure and disposition costs.[58] Most mortgage holders will require an appraisal before considering an agreement to modify the principal. Once the principal is reduced, if the loan is reamortized, payments should be lower.

5. *Deferred Junior Mortgages*. Some mortgage holders are willing to think about reductions in principal to the value of the property only if they are allowed to keep deferred junior mortgages in the amount of the principal reduction. This protects the mortgage holder in the event that the property value later goes up.[59] Terms of the deferred junior mortgage typically would not require payment except on transfer of property. Providing for such a mortgage may be a bargaining chip to obtain a modification agreement.

2.4.7 *Other Creative Workout Terms*

Some mortgage holders will consider other offers of workouts involving temporary or permanent relief, even if they are highly creative, such as deferral or subordination of a portion of the principal in favor of a home equity loan for emergency home repairs,[60] cancellation of accrued arrears, or substitution or surrender of alternative collateral in exchange for a modification. However, some mortgage holders may be uninterested if the proposal is too complicated.

2.5 Presales and Other Transfers of the Property

2.5.1 *Short Sales*

Some mortgage holders, particularly in a depressed real estate market, will agree to allow property to be sold through a realtor rather than foreclose, even if the proceeds of the sale will not cover the amount due on the mortgage. This is called a "short" sale. A short sale may help the mortgage holder avoid a portion of its potential foreclosure losses. The sale also avoids a foreclosure notation on the homeowner's credit report.

If there are multiple liens on the property, the process of arranging a short sale may be complicated. Any lender whose interest will be cut off in whole or in part must approve the sale and release its lien. This may mean that while the proceeds of the sale fully pay the first mortgage, there is a short sale with respect to the second. In that scenario only the second mortgage holder must approve the sale.

It rarely makes sense for a consumer to complete a short sale if the lender does not agree to waive any deficiency.[61] However, all lenders will request a financial statement to make sure that the deficiency claim it is releasing has limited economic value. When other assets are truly at risk, the borrower may want to make a cash contribution in addition to the sale price in exchange for a waiver of the balance of the deficiency. Once the lender agrees, advocates should confirm in writing that the deficiency has been waived.

Some lenders that own properties for which foreclosure makes little sense (particularly in neighborhoods where resale would be time consuming and expensive) will provide incentives for the homeowner to arrange a short sale. HUD's short sale program, for example, provides latitude for a servicer to make payments to the homeowner in order to encourage short sales.[62] Under Fannie Mae's pre-foreclosure (short sale) option, borrowers are eligible for up to $5000 in relocation assistance.[63] As lenders do not volunteer this information, it is a good idea to ask when the process is being arranged.

In most communities there are realtors that specialize in arranging short sales. In order to earn a sales commission, these realtors will often deal with the details necessary to obtain lender approval. The lender may impose strict time limits.

2.5.2 *Deeds in Lieu of Foreclosure*

It may be possible to negotiate to have the lender accept voluntary return of the property as an alternative to foreclosure. This is usually called a "deed in lieu of foreclosure." Deeds in lieu will not be accepted by the mortgage holder if there are junior liens on the property, because in that case foreclosure is necessary for the mortgage holder to obtain clear title.

---

57 Most lenders are very concerned about providing this relief to defaulted borrowers who have caused the depreciation to their property by misconduct.

58 This alternative closely approximates the result of a bankruptcy strip-down under 11 U.S.C. § 506(d). Lenders may consider this relief because they recognize the economic realities of foreclosure, despite the Supreme Court's affording them special protection from strip-down in the *Nobelman* case. Nobelman v. Am. Sav. Bank, 508 U.S. 324, 113 S. Ct. 2106, 124 L. Ed. 2d 228 (1993).

59 In drafting such instruments a distinction should be made between equity created by appreciation and equity created by the homeowner's payments. The homeowner should also be made aware of the potential difficulties which a deferred junior mortgage creates for home equity borrowing.

60 The lender may agree to this approach when the value of the collateral would decline if the emergency home repairs are not made.

61 The servicer is required to waive the deficiency if the short sale is being done under the alternative to foreclosure program that is part of the Home Affordable Modification Program.

62 *See* § 2.12.1.7, *infra*.

63 *See* § 2.11.3.4, *infra*.

Deeds in lieu should not be offered unless the lender agrees to some consideration for the agreement, such as forgiveness of deficiency claims[64] or an extra period of time for the homeowner to remain in the property before eviction. Some lenders, including those servicing HUD-guaranteed loans, may even provide a small amount of cash in exchange for a deed in lieu in order to help pay moving expenses.[65] The lender may agree to these terms in order to save the time and expense of foreclosure.

Deeds in lieu can be a poor choice for a homeowner if there is significant equity in the property. That equity can only be realized by a sale rather than a voluntary transfer—even, perhaps, a foreclosure sale.

2.6 Seeking a Modification or Other Workout

2.6.1 Knowing What Terms to Request

The most important part of a workout negotiation may be deciding what terms to request. Of course, HAMP and other mortgage programs may have narrow guidelines as to what terms are available under the program.

Section 2.3, *supra*, describes various workout terms, although the industry utilizes a wide array of terminology to describe those terms. A borrower should propose terms at least sufficient to address the economic problem which caused the default. As with any negotiation, it may be necessary to begin with a bargaining position which goes beyond the homeowner's real needs in order to get to a fallback position which is within the borrower's ability to pay. There is little value to either the homeowner or the mortgage holder in negotiating terms which, if accepted, will not resolve the homeowner's problems for both the long and short term.

2.6.2 Knowing the Parameters of the Mortgage Holder's Policies

2.6.2.1 General

When crafting a loan modification or other workout proposal, first determine who holds or insures the mortgage. The servicer should tell you who owns or insures the mortgage. For instructions on obtaining this information from recalcitrant servicers, see §§ 1.3.3.3.2, *supra*, and 10.2.5, *infra*.

Workout options vary depending on the guidelines or programs developed by the mortgage holder, insurer or servicer. Most of these guidelines are written. If the loan servicer participates in the Home Affordable Modification Program, it must consider a modification under the terms of that program first. Government insurers, such as the FHA, have detailed instructions on how and when the loans that they insure can be modified.

The holder or servicer may have developed its own loan modification program, the parameters of which will be applied to your client's loan. Sometimes these programs are the result of an enforcement action by a state or federal agency. Others in the industry follow workout guidelines established by Fannie Mae which, as the leading purchaser of mortgages on the secondary market, sets the standard for many servicers.

2.6.2.2 Workout Limits Based Upon a Loan's Securitization

Servicers often claim that when a mortgage has been securitized, its modification is governed by a pooling and servicing agreement (PSA), and spelled out in servicing contracts and/or in servicing guidebooks and policies which are distributed and incorporated by reference in the servicing contract.[66] Some PSAs give servicers the ability to modify loans, while others cap loan modifications by a number or percentage of the outstanding balance in the loan pool.[67] If the modification is pursuant to the HAMP program, the servicer must take reasonable steps to remove such restrictions.[68]

---

64 Such forgiveness is not helpful in states which prohibit deficiency judgments following residential foreclosures. Any agreement to forgive a deficiency claim in consideration for a deed in lieu must be explicit and in writing to avoid further action by the lender. For example, in Nash Finch Co. v. Corey Dev., Ltd., 669 N.W.2d 546 (Iowa 2003) a forbearance agreement provided that the lender could file deed in lieu of foreclosure in *partial* satisfaction of the note. The court upheld the lender's right to file a deed of foreclosure and pursue a deficiency judgment after the mortgagor defaulted on the forbearance agreement, as the parties did not agree that by filing deed in lieu of foreclosure, the mortgagor's original debt on the promissory note was completely extinguished.

65 *See* § 2.7.1.1.6, *infra*.

66 The Fannie Mae Servicing Guide and Freddie Mac's Single Family Seller/Servicer Guides are available on-line at www.allregs.com. Fannie Mae provides free access to its Single-Family Servicing Guide at www.allregs.com/efnma (be sure to turn off any pop-up blockers). Lender Announcements and Letters, which update the Fannie Mae guides, are available on Fannie Mae's website at www.efanniemae.com. Freddie Mac's Single-Family Seller/Servicer Guide, and its Bulletins and Industry Letters are also available on-line at www.freddiemac.com/singlefamily/#.

67 If the PSA contains such a restriction, and if the servicer has hit the cap, the modified loan may have to be removed from the loan pool.

68 *See* § 2.8.3.4.3, *infra*.

Most PSAs, however, impose no meaningful restrictions on loan modifications and give servicers the discretion to modify loans so long as it is the "usual and customary" industry practice or in the best interest of investors.[69] To determine what is in the best interest of investors, servicers can perform a net present value test.[70] Once the terms of the proposed modification are established, the net present value of the money the investor would receive under the proposed modification is compared with what would be received if no modification were made. If the servicer can expect a greater return from modifying the mortgage, then the modification is in the best interests of the investors. In other words, a modification will be less costly to investors than foreclosing on the property.

2.6.2.3 Net Present Value As a Predictor of Modification Success

As described at § 2.8.2.2, *infra*, the net present value or NPV test is often key to determining if a workout proposal is in the mortgage holder's best interest. More information on the NPV tests used by the FDIC and under HAMP, including the FDIC's public calculator to determine NPV, are described at § 2.8.2.2.2, *infra*. This subsection provides a brief overview of the concept.

To determine the NPV, one compares the value to investors of a loan modification as compared to a foreclosure. These are "net" calculations because the value of a foreclosure is subtracted from the value of the loan modification and "present value" because the value of the loan modification and the value of the foreclosure are both stated in present dollars. The present value calculation discounts the future cash stream of the loan modification or the future payoff from a foreclosure by a standard interest rate (sometimes called the "discount rate"), applied over the projected length of time the foreclosure will take or the loan modification will last. The modification is also discounted for the probability that it will not perform, or, in other words, that the borrower will "redefault."

Embedded in any net present value calculation are assumptions about how much will be recovered after a foreclosure. These assumptions include a reasonable estimate of foreclosure costs, the actual current value of the home, and a forecast as to the value of the home when sold following foreclosure. The amount of time to foreclose and the amount of time to sell a home post-foreclosure are also critical elements. Most net present value calculations also make assumptions as to whether or not a loan modification will perform. The redefault rate assumptions critically affect the approval or denial of a loan modification.

NPV does not take account of claims a consumer may have, or the cost and time of litigation, or any of the larger societal costs of a preventable foreclosure. There will be many cases when a borrower may fail the NPV test but should still be offered a loan modification.

2.6.3 Requesting Delay of Foreclosure Sales

At the outset, the most important request may be for a delay of the foreclosure sale process long enough to make a workout application. A completed foreclosure sale will generally cut off all workout possibilities.[71] In addition, as the foreclosure process moves forward, the mortgage holder continues to incur costs that will eventually have to be reimbursed by the borrower. These costs increase the amount the borrower must raise to cure the delinquency, and efforts should be made to keep costs to a minimum.[72]

A request for delay is more likely to be granted when preliminary information is provided about the homeowner's ultimate potential to make a reasonable workout proposal.[73] For example, if a homeowner has recently returned to work, documentation of employment would almost always justify postponing a sale. Similarly, an offer of partial payment may help obtain several months' delay.

Mortgage holders have different approaches to handling requests for delay. One pitfall to avoid is leaving the decision to grant a delay in the mortgage holder's hands to the very last minute. The risk is that the advocate and the homeowner will assume that the application is being acted upon and will lose the opportunity to pursue other strategies prior to sale. When a timely request is made, agreements to delay should be granted at least seven days before the foreclosure sale date if the mortgage holder is considering a workout proposal in good faith. With the significant uptick in call volume due to the foreclosure crisis, servicers may take at least thirty days to respond to any request for a

69 *See* Credit Suisse, Fixed Income Research, The Day After Tomorrow: Payment Shock and Loan Modifications (Apr. 5, 2007).

70 *See* American Securitization Forum, Statement of Principles, Recommendations and Guidelines for the Modification of Securitized Subprime Residential Mortgage Loans (June 2007), *available at* www.americansecuritization.com/uploadedFiles/ASF%20Subprime%20Loan%20Modification%20Principles_060107.pdf.

71 In some circumstances, usually involving third-party financing or serious defects in the foreclosure sale process, lenders will agree to resell a property to the prior homeowner after foreclosure. In a few states, where post-sale redemption is allowed, workout negotiations may continue after a foreclosure sale based on the homeowner's right to reacquire the property by payment. *See* Ch. 14, *infra*.

72 It may be possible to negotiate a delay in the foreclosure process which may reduce costs. For example, the mortgage holder may agree to wait thirty days before referring the case to a foreclosure attorney.

73 Under the federal Home Affordable Modification Program (HAMP), the servicer cannot complete the sale until the borrower has been determined ineligible for the program or failed to perform under the terms of the program. The HAMP guidelines also require the servicer to suspend foreclosure procedings in certain situations. *See* § 2.8.7, *infra*.

workout or delay of sale. There have also been reports of lost paperwork and busy call-centers.[74] Given this limitation, advocates must be prepared to take other action to immediately stop the sale.

A mortgage holder acting in bad faith may be liable for refusing to grant a reasonable request to delay a foreclosure sale. The holder may have a duty to provide the homeowner with a reasonable delay to conduct a market sale of the property. Ideally, the homeowner should produce a buyer with a legally binding commitment to purchase the property at a price that would result in a full recovery of all money due to the holder, including costs.[75]

When an agreement to delay a sale is reached, it is essential to reduce it to writing. In most cases, a confirming letter should suffice unless the sale is a court-supervised process, for which applicable procedural requirements must be met.[76] In addition, if the loan is transferred to a new servicer, any agreement with the former servicer should be reaffirmed in writing.[77] If an agreement to delay the foreclosure sale to allow the borrower to arrange a private sale is breached, the borrower may not have a remedy unless he or she can prove actual damages (such as reduced sale price) caused by the breach.[78] Whatever the process, it is a good idea to check and make sure that the sale is actually canceled.

If there is no sale date, or if it is a good way off when workout negotiations are commenced, it is important nevertheless to keep an eye on the sale process. It is not unheard of for a property to be sold, without notice to an advocate, while a workout application is pending.

2.6.4 Where The Servicer Initiates a Modification

Some mortgage modification programs, such as HAMP, involve the servicer initiating contact with borrowers to offer modifications. If the homeowner receives a pre-approved modification offer, it should be reviewed carefully. The offers are based on the information that the servicer has on file regarding the homeowner's income, debt level, and property value, among other factors. If the information the servicer has on file is incorrect, the modification offered may be unrealistic. Homeowners need to calculate independently the level of monthly payments they can afford and determine whether the modification fits the program's parameters, as well as run an analysis under the net present value test.[79] If the servicer's initial offer is based on misinformation, homeowners should promptly correct that information and negotiate a modification that best fits their needs.

Depending on the mortgage modification program, the workout process may be streamlined. In that case, to accept an offer to modify a loan, the homeowner sends in a modification agreement, proof of current income, and the modified payment. If the homeowner's income is verified and is comparable to what the servicer has on file, the loan will be modified. Other times, more paperwork is involved. Some programs include a three- or four-month trial period where the homeowner is required to make payments under the proposed modification. The Home Affordable Modification Program, discussed at § 2.8.4, *infra*, follows this basic model.

2.6.5 The Homeowner's Application for a Workout

Different mortgage holders and their servicers have different workout application processes and forms. All of them involve obtaining financial information about the borrower's debts, assets, income, expenses and reasons for default, with appropriate verification. Additionally, mortgage servicers will obtain a property appraisal and/or a credit report. It is usually a good idea to get the forms prior to submitting a workout application to avoid duplication of work, and to submit the forms with a cover letter explaining the workout being requested and the reasons why it should be provided.

Many lenders and servicers will ask for proof of involuntary hardship leading to the default, though this has been deemphasized as lenders recognize that workout agreements generally benefit their bottom line. In general, it is to the homeowners' advantage to send a letter and documentation of hardship, whenever hardship is present. Sympathetic elements of the situation should be emphasized.

When proof of hardship is required, the standards for establishing hardship are more liberal than in the past, and now include events like divorce and virtually any health problem or termination from employment no matter what the reason. A few lenders continue to look askance at parenting choices (one parent choosing to remain at home with children) when they feel more income would be available if both parents worked. When this issue arises it is helpful to show the cost of alternative child care arrangements if they help establish that remaining at home is a sensible financial choice.

---

74 *See* State Foreclosure Prevention Working Group, Analysis of Subprime Mortgage Servicing Performance, Data Report No. 2 (Apr. 2008).

75 *See* Snowden v. Chase Manhattan Mortgage Corp., 2003 WL 22519518 (Mass. Super. Ct. Nov. 5, 2003).

76 This will vary on a state-by-state basis.

77 *See* Walker v. Midland Mortgage Co., 935 So. 2d 519 (Fla. Dist. Ct. App. 2006) (oral agreement with former servicer did not prevent new servicer from instituting foreclosure proceedings).

78 *In re* Pa. Footwear Corp., 204 B.R. 165 (Bankr. E.D. Pa. 1997). *See also* Peoples Heritage Bank v. Pease, 838 A.2d 354 (Me. 2003) (lender who breached terms of oral repayment agreement by foreclosing on borrower's property liable for damages).

79 Advocates may use the FDIC's calculator to determine NPV, as discussed at § 2.8.2.2.2, *infra*.

Verification requirements typically include income verification like pay stubs, unemployment compensation award letters, back tax forms, and the like. Similarly, documentation of expenses like utility bills, tax payments, and other fixed costs of homeownership may also be required. Because a workout involves giving a borrower a second chance on a defaulted loan, it is not unreasonable for the lender to expect information similar to that required for qualifying for a mortgage. This may include budget information and related verification when the mortgage holder is being asked to forebear on enforcing the terms of the loan. Additionally, it is not unfair for a lender whose collateral is at risk to want an appraisal or, at minimum, a property inspection.

Some workout plans are more difficult to document than others. For example, if the homeowner expects to pay off the default based on anticipated settlement of a lawsuit or resolution of a child support claim, it may be difficult to document the basis for that expectation. Creative solutions to these problems can sometimes be worked out. The homeowner might proffer the complaint in a lawsuit together with an opinion by the lawyer of the amount and date of the expected settlement. The lender may be willing to postpone foreclosure for a short period to let the attorney try to settle the case. Similarly, part of the settlement in a child support case might be to have the child support debtor write a letter which can be used as proof that future child support payments will be made.

While it is reasonable for a lender to insist on some documentation of the homeowner's future prospects, perverse or unnecessary documentation requirements should be resisted. It is a good idea to pin down exactly what will be required from the beginning in order to avoid the constant imposition of new requirements. For some mortgage holders there is a "bring me the broomstick of the Wicked Witch of the West" mentality so that they can avoid dealing with the merits of a proposal.

2.6.6 Workout and Foreclosure Fees

Many mortgage holders purport to charge a workout or modification fee for handling workout applications. Some want this up front regardless of the application's outcome. Fees can run as high as $600 plus costs. There are a number of approaches to take, including the possibility of simply having the homeowner pay. A $600 fee may be a small price to pay for an agreement to halve the principal, or otherwise make serious modifications to the mortgage.

When possible, however, modification fees should be minimized. This can involve requesting a waiver or asking for a fee reduction to make the modification affordable. Remember that a modification can in some cases save the mortgage holder thousands of dollars in foreclosure fees, loss of principal and resale costs after foreclosure. In addition, mortgage holders compensate servicers for their time and costs in arranging workout plans. Charging a fee to the borrower may be double dipping.

Hard costs of a modification, such as appraisal fees and credit report charges should be scrutinized for padding. When legitimate, however, it is difficult to argue that they should not be paid. A homeowner can request an agreement to pay some or all modification fees in installments or to have the fee lumped together with the loan balance if the modification involves reamortization.

Identical problems arise when the mortgage holder has begun to incur foreclosure fees and costs. They should be scrutinized to make sure that they are legitimate and they should be minimized if possible. A typical problem is an attorney's retainer for foreclosure which is not fully expended, due to the workout agreement preventing foreclosure. Any amount not actually expended should be credited back to the homeowner. To the extent foreclosure fees and costs are valid, they need to be accounted for in the modification process.

2.6.7 Dealing with an Unresponsive Servicer

Once the application is made, follow up may be necessary. It is not uncommon for applications to be swallowed up as if by a black hole. It is a good idea to find out whom has the application at any given time (as well as the name of that person's superior) and to make polite but regular follow up phone calls.

There are several structural barriers that discourage servicers from offering workouts or even bothering to respond to workout requests.[80] Servicers make money by lifting profits off the top of what they collect from borrowers—servicing fees (a fixed percentage of the unpaid principal balances), ancillary fees (like late fees), and interest income on borrower payments held until turned over to investors. On the other hand, performing large numbers of modifications or other workouts comes with attendant costs including staffing, physical infrastructure, out-of-pocket expenses for property valuations, credit reports, and financing costs. The incentives offered to servicers by many loan modification programs are not enough to encourage servicers to assume these costs. Moreover, servicers do not face significant costs or penalties for failing to make modifications.[81]

The securitization process can also lead to mismatched interest among the investors in any given loan pool. The

80 *See* Diane Thompson, National Consumer Law Center, Why Servicers Foreclose When They Should Modify and Other Puzzles of Servicer Behavior: Servicer Compensation and its Consequences (2009).

81 *See* Diane Thompson, National Consumer Law Center, Why Servicers Foreclose When They Should Modify and Other Puzzles of Servicer Behavior: Servicer Compensation and its Consequences (2009).

typical securitization process results in different classes of securities, called tranches. Loan modifications can have different effects on different tranches, giving rise to a conflict of interest between investors. Servicers may be reluctant to engage in significant loss mitigation for fear of being sued by disgruntled investors.

These disincentives are manifested to the homeowner by the lack of adequate staff to properly respond to consumers' requests for a modification or workout, or even to simply answer the telephone to respond to questions. Homeowners have a difficult time finding a live person who can provide reliable information about the loan account and who has authority to make modification decisions. Stories abound about exasperated homeowners attempting to navigate vast voicemail systems, being bounced around from one department to another and receiving contradictory information from different servicer representatives.

When a servicer is unresponsive to a workout proposal, it is appropriate to go over its head and complain directly to the mortgage holder or insurer. Fannie Mae, Freddie Mac, and some institutional investors have loss mitigation departments which will intervene, if pushed, to address a proposed workout. The applicable Fannie Mae offices are regional.[82] Freddie Mac's loss mitigation is done on a national basis.[83] It is a good idea to learn the location of the applicable office and to find a person in that office to call or write when a servicer is unresponsive. It is best to ask to speak with someone in "loss mitigation," or "workouts." Contacts with helpful employees should be fostered and assiduously maintained.

In addition, the Home Affordable Modification Program requires servicers to establish an in-house escalation process to address some of the problems that consumers may face with the implementation of that program. The Department of Treasury, separately, has set up its own case escalation process for advocates and housing counselors who believe that a servicer is not following the program's guidelines.[84]

The scope of a servicer's authority to arrange workout terms may be less than clear. Although most servicers have substantial delegated authority, complicated or unusual workout terms generally have to be cleared with the mortgage holder. It may be necessary to push the servicer to take a proposal to the mortgage holder rather than simply to refuse the proposal as the path of least resistance.

Sometimes a loan servicer will state that a particular option is not available because of a pooling agreement or securitization arrangement.[85] This is a particularly common assertion regarding loan modifications. Probing this assertion may sometimes lead to the discovery that the option remains available, if the servicer takes an extra step. Other times, the servicer's hands may really be tied and it will be necessary to work around the restriction or avoid it entirely by proceeding with bankruptcy.

In general, dealing with the servicer may require some give-and-take. Remember that proposals are subject to a negotiation process. As with any negotiation, a record should be made of contacts with the servicer and significant communications should be confirmed in writing.

2.6.8 Evaluating a Workout Offer

To achieve an affordable monthly payment, the servicer may offer a workout that requires that extends the loan term, such as from thirty years to forty years. While a forty-year mortgage may achieve a lower monthly payment, it should be the last option used to achieve an affordable modification, as it significantly decreases a homeowner's chance at building equity. In the example below, the relatively *small* decrease in the monthly payment as a result of a forty year mortgage at a 7% interest rate is compared to huge extra expense incurred over the long term.

Comparison Between 30- and 40- Year Terms

	30	40
Loan Amount	$200,000	$200,000
Interest Rate	7%	7%
Monthly Payments	$1330.60	$1242.86
Finance Charge	$279,017.80	$396,574.03
Balance End Year 5	$188,263.18	$194,544.91
Balance End Year 10	$171,624.77	$186,811.65
Balance End Year 20	$114,600.16	$160,307.53

In this example, the forty-year amortization saves $87 a month, but the homeowner will pay over $100,000 extra over the term of the loan and will pay down principal must

82 The Midwestern Regional Office, (312) 368-6200, serves Illinois, Indiana, Iowa, Michigan, Minnesota, Nebraska, North Dakota, Ohio, South Dakota, and Wisconsin.

The Northeastern Regional Office, (215) 575-1400, serves Connecticut, Delaware, Maine, Massachusetts, New Hampshire, New Jersey, New York, Pennsylvania, Puerto Rico, Rhode Island, Vermont, and the Virgin Islands.

The Southeastern Regional Office, (404) 398-6000, serves Alabama, the District of Columbia, Florida, Georgia, Kentucky, Maryland, Mississippi, North Carolina, South Carolina, Tennessee, Virginia, and West Virginia.

The Southwestern Regional Office, (972) 773-HOME (4663), serves Arizona, Arkansas, Colorado, Kansas, Louisiana, Missouri, New Mexico, Oklahoma, Texas, and Utah.

The Western Regional Office, (626) 396-5100, serves Alaska, California, Guam, Hawaii, Idaho, Montana, Nevada, Oregon, Washington, and Wyoming.

83 To lodge a complaint about a Freddie Mac servicer, it is necessary to call 800-FREDDIE and access the customer service representative from the initial menu. Ask the customer service representative for the name and number of someone in the loss mitigation department who can review your workout proposal.

84 A description of the Home Affordable Modification Program's case escalation process is available on the program's administrative website at www.hmpadmin.com/portal/resources/escalation.html.

85 *See* § 2.4.2.2, *supra*.

slower. However, these downsides to a forty-year mortgage over a thirty-year term lessen when the interest rate is lowered. The difference in the monthly payment rises, and the difference in the balance at points along the term is reduced.

Any plan to modify the loan to cure the default must also address any junior liens on the property or those lenders will foreclose. A reduction in the monthly payment on the first mortgage may free up resources to enable the homeowner to make payments on the second mortgage. Most likely, however, the homeowner is also struggling on the second mortgage, and advocates must come up with a plan to deal with the second mortgage. The junior mortgage holder may understand its precarious lien position, as most second mortgage holders receive little if anything from the proceeds of a foreclosure sale. The junior mortgage holder may agree to modify its mortgage to reduce the monthly payment or take a portion of the amount owed now or opt to receive a payoff in the future to release the lien. The homeowner may be required to sign an (unsecured) promissory note for the negotiated amount. If the homeowner is receiving an incentive payment under a modification program, that payment can be promised to the junior mortgage holder to release its lien.

2.6.9 Documenting an Agreement

2.6.9.1 General

The mortgage holder generally has forms which it requires for executing a workout agreement. These should be scrutinized carefully to make sure they are consistent with the agreement. Many such forms include a release term for all legal claims which the borrower may have against the mortgage holder. The terms of the waiver may be inappropriately broad, and the homeowner may be required to release a wide range of claims in exchange for a simple workout agreement.[86] Advocates representing clients, especially in loan modification negotiations, should only agree to waivers that are limited in scope and commensurate with the benefit clients obtain. The homeowner's advocate should make sure all the forms are properly signed by the mortgage holder (or a servicer with the necessary authority) and recorded, if necessary, with the registry.[87]

2.6.9.2 Watch Out for Waiver Clauses

Many loan modification agreements, from simple repayment plans to litigation settlements, contain waiver provisions that purpose to release the servicer and holder from any past or future claims that a borrower may have. Often the waiver appears in "legalese" at the end of the agreement or is buried in a long list of acknowledgments made by the borrower.[88] The breadth of these waivers is astonishing and not likely understood by the borrower executing the agreement.

Servicers have argued that such waivers are effective even if the underlying loan modification fails and the borrower redefaults. This is particularly troubling given the large number of borrowers that have been pushed into unaffordable repayment plans or loan modifications in the last few years.

The scope of waivers is generally not limited to the loan modification process, and may preclude borrowers from later raising a vast range of legitimate federal and state law claims against servicers, holders, and originators. Covered claims encompass causes of action against the holder or originator under consumer protection statutes such as the Truth in Lending Act or the Home Ownership Equity Protection Act. Claims barred under these waivers also include actions against the servicer for the misapplication of payments, the assessment of illegal fees, or the improper accounting of escrow funds. Servicers specifically insulate themselves from liability under the Electronic Funds Transfer Act, the Real Estate Settlement Procedures Act, the Fair Credit Reporting Act and the Fair Debt Collection Practices Act. In essence, servicers are using the loan modification process to scrub loans of liability for the bad conduct of both themselves and the loan originators.

Advocates representing clients in loan modification negotiations should only agree to waivers of claims commensurate with the relief the clients obtain. For example, a short-term repayment plan should not require any waiver of rights; the voiding of a loan probably requires at least some. To the extent releases are part of the agreement, they should

86 Some mortgage holders have a pernicious practice in which they require a release of all claims as a precondition to entering into workout discussions at all. Signing such a release should be resisted, because entering into negotiations is no consideration for a release of claims.

87 Changes to terms of the mortgage should be filed as addenda to the mortgage. However, most modifications of loan terms are not modifications of the mortgage, but rather changes to the loan contract (the note). These changes may not need to be recorded. *See* United States v. Omdahl, 104 F.3d 1143 (9th Cir. 1997) (government not estopped from foreclosure by FmHA employee's erroneous proposal to write-down the mortgage, given no detrimental reliance, and mere negligence of supervisor).

88 For example, one of the largest subprime servicer includes the following paragraph in its loan modification agreements: "BY EXECUTING THIS MODIFICATION, YOU FOREVER IRREVOCABLY WAIVE AND RELINQUISH ANY CLAIMS, ACTIONS OR CAUSES OF ACTION, STATUTE OF LIMITATIONS OR OTHER DEFENSES, COUNTERCLAIMS, OR SETOFFS OF ANY KIND WHICH EXIST AS OF THE DATE OF THIS MODIFICATION, WHETHER KNOWN OR UNKNOWN, WHICH YOU MAY NOW OR HEREAFTER ASSERT IN CONNECTION WITH THE MAKING, CLOSING, ADMINISTRATION, COLLECTION OR THE ENFORCEMENT BY OCWEN OF THE LOAN DOCUMENTS, THIS MODIFICATION OR ANY OTHER RELATED AGREEMENTS."

be mutual. If the servicer is asking the client to release all of the servicer's agents, attorneys, and assignees, make sure the client's agents, attorneys, and assignees are also released. Given the how frequently loans in the secondary market change hands, it would be prudent for the agreement to bind everyone in the creditor's assignment chain, past and present, as well as all servicers and other agents. If needed, waivers can be limited to preserve claims against parties, such as brokers, that may be pursued independently.

Sometimes clients seek assistance after a repayment plan or previous loan modification has failed. In many cases, these borrowers have signed an agreement that contains a waiver of claims. Such a waiver is almost certainly not effective to waive TIL rescission rights[89] and may not be enforceable at all. When faced with a one-sided waiver, review standard contract defenses, such as lack of consideration, lack of mutuality, and unconscionability. Only rarely should such a waiver be enforceable as a result of arm's length negotiation.

2.6.9.3 Make Sure You Can Enforce the Agreement

Enforceability is another area in which settlement agreements and loan modifications present similar concerns. Advocates must be sure that everything that has been agreed upon is documented in writing, that all necessary parties are bound, and that attorney fees and costs may be recovered in the event of a breach of the agreement.

2.6.9.4 Limit Confidentiality Clauses

Confidentiality clauses are traps waiting to spring years later on a client who mentions her workout to a minister, tax advisor, or family friend. Advocates should approach confidentiality requirements of loan modifications as they would in settlement agreements.[90]

2.6.9.5 Change the Account Number

Most servicers use automated record-keeping systems. Unless a thorough purge of the existing computer records is done, it is likely that, at some point, when the servicer generates a payment statement or history, some of the forgiven fees in the loan modification may get picked up and swept into your client's current information. Changing the loan's account number helps give the loan a fresh start, without the history of the fees, charges, and principal that have been forgiven in the loan modification.

2.6.9.6 Forbid Future Solicitation of Your Client

Forbidding future solicitation of your client by the current holder and all of its assignees and agents can help give your clients peace of mind and prevent your practice from becoming a revolving door.[91]

2.7 A Workout's Potential Adverse Consequences

2.7.1 Tax Consequences of Workout Options

The IRS generally, with certain exceptions, treats forgiven mortgage debt, whether after a foreclosure, short sale, or settlement of litigation, as taxable income.[92] Thus, a deed in lieu, short sale, or workout that reduces the principal balance can have significant tax consequences for the homeowner.[93] These tax consequences and the exceptions to the general rule are discussed in detail at § 14.6, *infra*. Practitioners should, as part of negotiating the workout agreement, confirm with the lender how much will be reported to the IRS as cancelled debt and advise the homeowner accordingly.[94]

2.7.2 Credit Reporting Consequences

Loan modifications and other workouts may have a relatively minor adverse impact on homeowner's credit rating. But this has to be put into context that a foreclosure will have a very serious adverse effect on a consumer's credit score and credit report. In fact any existing default or even delinquency on a mortgage payment will already have adversely impacted a credit rating.

A special problem exists when homeowners current on their mortgage payments seek a HAMP modification. Ap-

89 Vermurlen v. Ameriquest Mortgage Co., 2007 WL 2963637 (W.D. Mich. Oct. 9, 2007) (holding that preprinted form forbearance agreement could not waive TIL rescission rights); Wrobel v. S.L. Pope & Assocs., 2007 WL 2345036 (S.D. Cal. Aug. 15, 2007) (finding "fair chance of success" for TIL rescission where "Forbearance and Release Agreement" did not comply with requirements for waiver of rescission rights); Mills v. Home Equity Group, Inc., 871 F. Supp. 1482 (D.D.C. 1994) (negotiated settlement agreement that contained waiver of TIL claims not effective to waive TIL rescission rights since no explicit mention of TIL rescission).

90 *See* § 10.9.2, *infra*.

91 *See* § 10.9.9.2, *infra*.

92 26 U.S.C. § 108(e)(1).

93 For example, HUD, in its Loss Mitigation Program, requires that servicers report any discharge of indebtedness for short sales (pre-foreclosure sales) or deeds in lieu to the IRS. Dep't of Hous. & Urban Dev., Mortgagee Letter 00-05 (Jan. 19, 2000), *available at* www.hud.gov/offices/adm/hudclips/letters/mortgagee/files/00-05.doc.

94 *See* § 14.6.3.5, *infra* (information on how a taxpayer should proceed upon receiving a 1099-C).

parently, during the three-month trial modification period, the servicer reports the mortgage payments in a way that can seriously lower a homeowner's credit score. Nevertheless, this may be the better of two options where foreclosure is the alternative.

There are no easy answers for clients who are worried about how workout agreements or foreclosure will affect their credit record. Most adverse information about a consumer's credit history is reported for seven years. Bankruptcy can be reported for ten years. A wealth of information about credit reporting can be found in National Consumer Law Center, *Fair Credit Reporting*.[95] There is also substantial information for clients about credit reporting and how to improve a bad credit report in the *NCLC Guide to Surviving Debt*.[96]

Unfortunately, there are no hard and fast rules about how any individual credit granting decision will be made based on a particular notation on a credit report. Each creditor evaluates credit reports differently. A notation which is fatal to an application for credit with one creditor may not preclude credit on reasonable terms from a different creditor.

Here is some general information which may be useful to clients who are worried about their credit:

- Concerns about future credit should rarely influence how homeowners address their current problem. A consumer cannot control how the credit report is evaluated by those who check credit reports. Any delinquency will usually mean "bad credit risk" to most creditors even if it is paid in full relatively quickly. There are generally more important concerns in the foreclosure avoidance process than the potential future impact on a consumer's credit rating which will result from one type of foreclosure avoidance plan over another.
- A foreclosure avoidance plan of any type is likely to look better on the credit report than a completed foreclosure. Any effort which prevents a foreclosure from being completed will show a creditor that the homeowner has made an effort. Repayment plans and loan modifications, if they cure the arrears, will show that the homeowners have gotten back on their feet.
- A completed foreclosure is usually fatal to applications for new mortgages from reputable lenders for about two years. Bankruptcy is also usually fatal for two years. The completed foreclosure will be an important consideration for most lenders even after the two years has expired until the notation is deleted from the credit record after seven years.
- A deed in lieu of foreclosure is not a big improvement over foreclosure. One myth about credit reporting is that a deed in lieu of foreclosure is going to keep a borrower in good standing on their credit record. A deed in lieu of foreclosure is a strong black mark on a credit record; it is viewed only slightly less negatively than a foreclosure. A deed in lieu should be considered when appropriate, but it should not be seen as a "silver bullet" for future credit.
- In a modification that is part of a litigation settlement, the consumer can and should require creditors to help repair your client's credit.[97]
- Unsecured credit, such as a credit card, is often available even to people with a recent foreclosure on their credit records. There is a great deal of competition in the credit card business. Companies even compete for borrowers with bad credit records. It is a good idea for the consumer to shop around for reasonable terms, rather than simply accepting the first offer. Lower interest rates and fees may be available. Many finance companies and other "hard money" lenders prey on people's beliefs that they have no other potential source of credit.
- The consumer should avoid credit repair scams. For-profit credit repair is almost always a scam. No one can clean a credit record entirely if there have been delinquencies on debts within the past seven years. Some credit repair companies recommend credit "fixes" which are illegal. Others charge a great deal of money to write letters to credit reporting agencies that a consumer can write just as easily for free.

2.7.3 *Consequences for Receipt of Public Benefits*

While not common, loan modifications may affect a borrower's eligibility for public benefits. Because of the wide variation in public benefit eligibility from state to state, a public benefits expert should be consulted. Any detrimental effects should be considered before the loan modification agreement is executed.[98]

2.8 The Home Affordable Modification Program (HAMP)

2.8.1 *The Basics*

2.8.1.1 Overview of the Making Home Affordable Program

The Obama Administration announced the Making Home Affordable Program in February 2009. The program is slated to end December 31, 2012. The program consists of

95 (6th ed. 2006 and Supp.).
96 (2005 ed.).

97 *See* § 10.9.3, *infra*.
98 *See* § 10.9.8, *infra*.

two components. Section 2.9, *infra*, discusses the Home Affordable Refinance Program (HARP), the program component set up to refinance loans owned or securitized by Fannie Mae or Freddie Mac.

This section examines the other component, created to modify all eligible mortgages to lower their monthly payment to an affordable level. The centerpiece of the program is the modification plan—now known as the Home Affordable Modification Program or HAMP—which applies to loans originated on or before January 1, 2009. This program was designed to standardize industry practices regarding mortgage loan modifications. In fact, most servicers now participate in the program and are obligated to first evaluate eligible borrowers for HAMP modifications before proceeding to consider non-HAMP modifications, other workout options, or foreclosure. Section 6.4.5, *infra*, discusses the servicer's failure to comply with HAMP as a foreclosure defense.

2.8.1.2 HAMP Described

Homeowners who are behind on their mortgages may be offered the opportunity to modify the terms of their first mortgage under the Home Affordable Modification Program (HAMP) developed by the U.S. Department of the Treasury. Homeowners will be offered a modification that lowers their monthly mortgage payment to a targeted 31% of their monthly gross income. This level of payment may be achieved by reducing the interest rate, extending the term of the loan, or deferring payment on a part of the principal.

HAMP is now the largest mortgage loan modification program in the nation in terms of its size and scope. The program covers loans held or insured by Fannie Mae, Freddie Mac, FHA, VA, and privately securitized mortgages. Though servicer participation is voluntary, most servicers participate in the program. Financial institutions receiving assistance under the Financial Stability Plan were required to implement the program. Servicers of non-GSE mortgages entered into agreements with the Department of Treasury which required them to review all eligible mortgages for inclusion in the program if doing so would not violate investor servicing agreements. Over one hundred servicers have now signed agreements with Treasury to modify first lien mortgages under the program.[99] Detailed program guidelines and a list of participating servicers are available on the Treasury's website at www.financialstability.gov.

Aside from modifying first lien mortgages, the program was expanded to further assist borrowers in reducing their debt burden by making second lien mortgage loans more affordable. A second lien mortgage program was added to HAMP that requires participating servicers to modify or pay off such mortgages. For those borrowers who do not qualify for a HAMP modification or fall off the program, the Home Affordable Foreclosure Alternatives portion of the program offers a streamlined short sale or deed in lieu of foreclosure process. A new program focuses on unemployed borrowers, and a new plan is due out soon to encourage loan principal write-downs, which are not currently required under the program.[100]

The program sought to streamline and standardize industry practices regarding mortgage loan modifications. However, since its launch the modification program has had a series of well publicized setbacks. Most notably, the program has helped far fewer homeowners than projected, with many people stuck in the trial portion of the plan. In addition, borrowers and advocates reported a high degree of noncompliance among servicers with program guidelines, including wrongful denials, offers of unsustainable modifications that did not comply with program guidelines, and premature foreclosure sales held without a proper HAMP review. In response, Treasury has increased emphasis on timelines and notice to borrowers. Legal advocates are also bringing cases challenging servicer noncompliance with the program.[101] The details of the program and Treasury's response to its implementation, however, are constantly evolving and advocates are advised to keep abreast of program developments.

2.8.1.3 Obtaining Current Information on HAMP

The Home Affordable Modification Program has undergone several key changes since its introduction in February 2009. General information about the modification portion of the program is available on the Making Home Affordable Program's official website, www.makinghomeaffordable.gov. This site includes a list of participating servicers, program forms and calculators, as well as a loan look up feature to determine if a loan is held by Fannie Mae or Freddie Mac. In theory, all covered operating subsidiaries will also be listed on the official website.

Detailed program guidelines are available on the administrative website designed for the servicers of non-GSE mortgages that participate in the program at www.hmpadmin.com/portal/programs/hamp.html. This website contains so-called "Supplemental Directives" and other documents (such as

99 A copy of the Servicer Participation Agreement can be obtained on the program's administrative website at www.hmpadmin.com. Copies of executed agreements with participating servicers can be obtained from the Department of Treasury's website at http://financialstability.gov/impact/contracts_list.htm. Servicers had until December 31, 2009 to sign the agreement. Servicers of second lien mortgages have until October 3, 2010 to sign an amended or new agreement to participate in that portion of the program.

100 *See Testimony of Phyllis Caldwell, Chief Homeownership Preservation Officer, U.S. Department of Treasury, Before the House Financial Services Subcommittee on Housing and Community Opportunity* (Apr. 14, 2010), *available at* http://makinghomeaffordable.gov/pr_04152010.html.

101 *See* § 6.4.5, *infra*.

FAQs) issued by the Department of Treasury to help servicers implement the program. Model forms are posted on this site as well.

The supplemental directives and other documents on the HAMP administrative website provide general guidance to servicers of non-GSE loans. Fannie Mae and Freddie Mac issue their own HAMP-related guidance through industry announcements or bulletins on their respective websites. Information on FHA and VA HAMP is available on their respective websites as well.

Another useful site is the HAMP section of Treasury's Financial Stability website. This site, www.financialstability.gov/roadtostability/homeowner.html, has program reports, fact sheets, and case examples.

2.8.2 HAMP Eligibility

2.8.2.1 General Program Eligibility

The program has a two tier eligibility process. Borrowers and the properties securing the loans to be modified must meet the basic program requirements. If the basic eligibility requirements are satisfied, then servicers will perform a key evaluation—called a net present value test—to determine whether it is more cost effective to modify the loan or foreclose.

In general, borrowers who are current on their mortgage or in foreclosure are eligible for a modification under HAMP. For borrowers who are current or less than sixty days delinquent, the servicer must determine whether a payment default is imminent based on its own standards so long as those standards are consistent with applicable contractual agreements with investors and accounting rules. At a minimum, however, the servicer must evaluate the borrower's financial condition in light of the borrower's stated hardship and inquire as to the condition of the property.[102] Common reasons that a borrower may be in imminent danger of default include illness, unemployment or underemployment, divorce, or scheduled interest rate increase within 120 days. Other key eligibility requirements include:

- The borrower's monthly mortgage payment, before modification, must be greater than 31% of his monthly gross income.[103]
- The loan is a first lien mortgage originated on or before January 1, 2009.[104]
- The loan is secured by a one-to-four unit property which is the borrower's principal residence. Cooperative share mortgages and loans on manufactured homes and condominiums are eligible.
- The property may not be vacant or condemned. Borrowers temporarily absent from their home (due to military service or incarceration for example) may qualify for HAMP so long as the house is not vacant.
- The loan has not been previously modified under HAMP.

A borrower in active litigation regarding the mortgage loan may qualify for HAMP. As discussed at § 2.8.6, *infra*, borrowers in an active chapter 13 or 7 bankruptcy may also qualify for HAMP.

Eligible first lien mortgages must have an unpaid principal balance (prior to capitalization of the arrears) equal to or less than:

- One unit: $729,750;
- Two units: $934,200;
- Three units: $1,129,250;
- Four units: $1,403,400.

2.8.2.2 Net Present Value Test

2.8.2.2.1 General

The core eligibility requirement under HAMP is the net present value (NPV) test. The NPV test compares the net present value of the money the servicer would receive if the loan were modified with what would be received if no modification were made. Servicer guidelines require servicers to first combine the present value of the unmodified payment stream with the value realized after a foreclosure prior to comparing the result with the value of a modification. Servicers are also expected to include the risk of prepayment in determining the value of a loan modification (but not, apparently, in setting the value of the payment stream pre-modification).

If the servicer can expect a greater return from modifying the mortgage (the NPV of the modified loan is higher than the NPV of the loan before modification), then the modification is considered to be "NPV Positive" and the servicer must modify the mortgage absent fraud or a prohibition in the securitization contracts.

102 *See* Dep't of Treasury, Supplemental Directive 09-01 (Apr. 6, 2009), *available at* www.hmpadmin.com//portal/programs/hamp/servicer.html.

103 Monthly mortgage payment includes principal, interest, property taxes, hazard insurance, flood insurance, condominium association fees and homeowners' association fees (including any escrow payment shortage amounts subject to a repayment plan). The monthly mortgage payment amount does not include payment for mortgage insurance premiums or junior mortgages. If the mortgage payment will change due to an interest rate reset on an adjustable rate mortgage, servicers will use the higher of either the borrower's current scheduled monthly payment or a fully amortizing payment based on the note reset rate using the index value as of the date of the evaluation. *See* Dep't of Treasury, Supplemental Directive 09-01 (Apr. 6, 2009), *available at* www.hmpadmin.com//portal/programs/hamp/servicer.html.

104 *See* § 2.8.9, *infra* (the Second Lien Mortgage Program).

If the test produces a "NPV Negative" because the projected return would be greater without a modification, the servicer has the option to modify the loan at its discretion. If the mortgage is serviced for a third-party investor, the servicer in this situation must obtain the investor's express permission.

Details of the specific factors to be considered under the program's NPV test are not available to the public.[105] The FDIC, when it developed its own loan modification program, developed a calculator that is publicly available, and that is often a useful tool in evaluating whether a homeowner should pursue a HAMP modification or other workout. The FDIC NPV analysis and its relation to the HAMP NPV is discussed later in this section. Several private, for-profit companies are now pushing their own versions of the NPV test. Advocates should be cautious in using these for-profit services. Treasury has not disclosed the NPV test or the assumptions to any company, other than servicers, and servicers are barred from redisclosing the NPV test or the assumptions built into the NPV test to any third party, on pain of criminal prosecution. Worse, the public documentation of the NPV test is itself inaccurate, according to a report by the Special Inspector General for TARP.[106]

2.8.2.2.2 The FDIC's spreadsheet

Shortly after its takeover of IndyMac Federal Bank, the FDIC created a model loan modification program for the financial services industry. As part of that program, the FDIC created a spreadsheet for the industry to use when performing the net present value test. Unlike the HAMP NPV analysis, the FDIC's spreadsheet is publicly available at www.fdic.gov/consumers/loans/loanmod/NPV.xls. The FDIC spreadsheet is a useful tool in a HAMP application, for a foreclosure mediation, or for other workout negotiations. It provides fast and objective results, with very few inputs from the homeowner; since most of the information is publicly available or within the knowledge of both the servicer and the homeowner. It is also verifiable, uses conservative assumptions, and has been recommended in several states for use in foreclosure mediation programs.

The FDIC's spreadsheet evaluates the following features:

- *Affordability*: The FDIC uses a range of affordability ratios, from 31% to 38% of income. The "affordability ratio" is the ratio between the homeowner's gross monthly income and the monthly mortgage payment (PITI).[107] A homeowner will not be approved for a loan modification where the modification contains an affordability ratio of less than 31% or more than 38%. If a homeowner is already paying less than 31% of her income for PITI, a loan modification will not be approved. What ratio the homeowner ends up with depends on how much the payment is reduced. In general, only if the homeowner is currently paying 38% or less of her income will her ratio be reduced below 38%. In no circumstances will the final ratio be less than 31%. The target affordability ratio, once determined, drives the rest of the calculations.
- *Reduction of Payment*: Payments under the FDIC program must be reduced by at least 10%. If a 10% reduction of the payment puts the homeowner below a 31% affordability ratio, the modification will be denied. Only homeowners who are currently paying more than 38% of their income in PITI will have their payments reduced by more than 10%.
- *Modified Payment*: The modified payment is calculated after the affordability standard is set. The program follows a standard modification waterfall, which is a sequence of steps designed to reduce the borrower's monthly mortgage payment to no more than 31% of their gross monthly income.[108] Interest is reduced first, to a floor of 3%, holding the length of the loan current; next the amortization and payments are extended out to forty years;[109] and finally, if nothing else works to get the payment low enough, principal forbearance necessary to reduce the modified payment to its target is calculated. No interest is charged on the forborne principal. Under the FDIC program and similar to Making Home Affordable Modification Program, the payments stay low for five years and then step up a percentage point every year, until the Freddie Mac rate effective at the time the loan modification was made is reached.

105 The Department of Treasury did prepare a document describing the base NPV model, and has published an illustrative spreadsheet. The document describing the base model allows servicers to change key inputs, including the discount rate, default rate, and the REO stigma. The servicer must, however, use the home price appreciation provided in the base NPV model. They do not have the discretion to substitute a different projection. *See* Dep't of Treasury, Home Affordable Modification Program, Base Net Present Value (NPV) Model Specifications (June 11, 2009), *available at* www.hmpadmin.com//portal/programs/hamp/servicer.html.

106 Office of the Special Inspector General for the Troubled Asset Relief Program, Factors Affecting Implementation of the Home Affordable Modification Program (Mar. 25, 2010), *available at* www.sigtarp.gov/reports/audit/2010/Factors_Affecting_Implementation_of_the_Home_Affordable_Modification_Program.pdf.

107 PITI means a payment that covers principal, interest, taxes, and insurance, the latter two portions of the payment being escrowed to pay property taxes, condominium fees, hazard insurance, and the like.

108 *See* § 2.8.5, *infra*.

109 If the loan has an existing schedule of longer than forty years, that existing schedule of payments will be maintained. Earlier versions of the spreadsheet did not extend the payments, only the amortization term, due to concerns that pooling and securitization agreements—and REMIC and FASB rules—prohibited the extension of the repayment term of the loan.

- *Foreclosure Scenario*: An REO value[110] is determined by discounting the current value by the price appreciation forecast (an estimate of future value for the property), the stigma of being sold as REO property rather than owner-occupied, and the estimated months to foreclosure. Assumed foreclosure costs (estimated by state) and interest losses (based on the note rate) are subtracted from the discounted current value to arrive at the REO value. The difference between this REO value and the current unpaid principal balance is then discounted to present value, using the current Freddie Mac rate for the expected rate of return. The FDIC further assumes that some percentage of foreclosures will cure on their own. If a servicer assumes that most loans in foreclosure will cure on their own, either through refinancing, or sale, or the homeowner coming up with the funds on their own to reinstate the loan, then the cost of doing a foreclosure becomes very small, and few loans will be modified. The more costly a foreclosure (the larger the negative number), the more likely a loan modification will be made.
- *Value of Modification*: The value of the modification (LMV) is based on two numbers: (1) the present value of the payment schedule (PVP—present value of payments)[111] and (2) the anticipated loss from foreclosure in the event the borrower redefaults (RFL—redefault foreclosure loss).[112] Both the present value of the payments (PVP) and the loss after a foreclosure (RFL) are then multiplied by the chance they will happen: the present value of the payments (PVP) is multiplied by the chance that the loan modification will be successful (C1); the loss suffered if there is a foreclosure after the loan modification (RFL) is multiplied by the chance that the loan modification will fail (C2). Those two probabilistic calculations are added together to give the value of the modification. (PVP x C1 + RFL x C2 = LMV).
- *Does the Modification Pass?*: The value of the modification (cell E28) is compared to the present value of the anticipated foreclosure loss (cell B41). Both the results of the foreclosure scenario and the value of the loan modification will often be stated as negative numbers, particularly when the potential loss from a foreclosure is high (remember that the value of a modification includes the risk of a delayed foreclosure). The value of the modification may be a positive number, when, for example, the loss from a foreclosure is relatively small compared to the potential payment stream from a loan modification. As long as the value of the loan modification is greater—or represents a smaller loss—than the present value of the anticipated foreclosure, the net present value test is passed, and a modification, on the payment terms worked out by the program, is deemed to be in the best interests of the investor.

Most of the assumptions embedded in the spreadsheet are conservative and cut against the homeowner. Key areas for advocacy when using the spreadsheet to get a loan modification include the following:

- Home price appreciation forecast (cells B32, E22);
- REO stigma discount (cell B33);
- Months to foreclosure (cell B34);
- Months to REO sale (cell B35);
- Foreclosure costs (cell B36);
- Months to redefault (cell E20);
- Redefault rate (cell E21).

2.8.2.2.3 *Spreadsheet's auto-completion feature*

The FDIC spreadsheet auto-completes several fields, including the homeowner's current monthly payment and taxes and insurance escrow amounts, as well as the Freddie Mac weekly mortgage rate. You can and should override these fields with the actual current information. The auto-completed information is often wrong and can lead to homeowners being improperly denied loan modifications. In addition to filling out the gray shaded cells, you *must* update with current information the following cells:

- Current Freddie rate (cell B5);[113]
- Current monthly mortgage payment (cell B19);
- Current interest payment (cell B20);[114]
- Monthly taxes and insurance (cell B27).

2.8.2.2.4 *Comparison between HAMP's NPV and the FDIC spreadsheet*

How different the results will be in practice from the FDIC spreadsheet is difficult to determine without seeing the formulae.

110 REO stands for real estate owned and refers to real estate which is purchased by the mortgage holder at a foreclosure sale.

111 The present value calculation does not currently include the forborne principal, which appears to be a mistake.

112 The loss suffered after a foreclosure is calculated in a similar manner as in the foreclosure scenario, allowing for the additional delay in prosecuting the foreclosure and the payments received before the loan modification fails.

113 Find the current Freddie Mac Weekly Primary Mortgage Market Survey at www.freddiemac.com/dlink/html/PMMS/display/PMMSOutputYr.jsp. The relevant rate is the thirty-year mortgage rate.

114 An easy way to get the correct amount for a fully amortizing loan is to change the reference in the formula in cell B20 from B11, the original interest rate, to B14, the current interest rate.

	HAMP	FDIC Program
Affordability target	31%	38%
Redefault rate	Will be based on actual performance of modified loans; however, servicers are free to use their own numbers, even if higher than the average	40%
Past-due escrow and interest	Capitalized	Capitalized
Interest rate floor	2%	3%
Interest rate cap	Freddie Mac Weekly Primary Market Mortgage Rate	Freddie Mac Weekly Primary Market Mortgage Rate
Waterfall	1) Interest rate reduction 2) Extend term to 480 months 3) Principal forbearance	1) Interest rate reduction 2) Extend term to 480 months 3) Principal forbearance
Principal forgiveness permitted	Yes	No
Required reduction in payment	6%	10%
Discount rate (rate used for present value calculations)	Freddie Mac Weekly Primary Market Mortgage Rate plus as much as 250 basis points	Freddie Mac Weekly Primary Market Mortgage Rate
Home price appreciation fore-cast	Special, nonpublic, dataset prepared by FHFA	Case-Shiller Home Price Index (propri-etary dataset)
REO stigma	Fannie Mae and Freddie Mac REO sales	Servicer's history, if adjusted, or National Association of Realtors Existing Home Sales Data

2.8.3 *The Procedure to Seek a HAMP Modification*

2.8.3.1 Participating Servicers Must Consider Eligible Loans for Modification

As described above, while participation in HAMP is voluntary, most servicers are participating.[115] Participating servicers must consider all eligible mortgage loans for modification unless prohibited under investor guidelines. If contractual agreements, such as pooling and servicing agreements restrict participation in the program, servicers are required to use reasonable efforts to obtain waivers or approvals from the parties.[116] These efforts include contacting the investor in writing at least once to encourage the investor to permit modifications under HAMP.[117]

Servicers must actively pre-screen all first lien mortgages with two or more payments due and owing to determine if they meet the basic criteria for HAMP.[118] The servicer is required to perform a NPV test on eligible loans that are at least sixty days delinquent or at risk of default. Then servicers must proactively solicit any borrower whose loan passes the pre-screen, unless the servicer has documented that the investor is not willing to participate in HAMP.

2.8.3.2 Initiating the Application Process

Frequently, the servicer will be the only party with whom the borrower has had any contact. Only on investigation will it become apparent that the servicer is acting on another entity's behalf. It is appropriate to begin the workout process with the servicer. The servicer should have workout specialists who will take applications and provide information on the prerequisites and standards for a workout. As with any negotiation, a record should be made of contacts with the servicer and significant communications, including any agreement to delay the foreclosure sale, should be confirmed in writing.

A borrower who is two or more payments behind and whose loan meets basic HAMP guidelines, should receive written letters, telephone calls, or other solicitations from the servicer offering a HAMP workout. Borrowers who are current on their mortgage or in bankruptcy will need to contact the servicer to initiate a review under program guidelines. Following contact with the servicer, the borrower will be sent an initial package which includes a Request for Modification and Affidavit (RMA) or similar

115 *See* § 2.8.1.2, *supra*.

116 These efforts include contacting an investor in writing at least once to encourage them to permit modifications under HAMP. *See* Dep't of Treasury, Supplemental Directive 10-02 (Mar. 24, 2010), *available at* www.hmpadmin.com//portal/programs/hamp/servicer.html.

117 *See* Dep't of Treasury, Supplemental Directive 10-02 (Mar. 24, 2010), *available at* www.hmpadmin.com//portal/programs/hamp/servicer.html.

118 *See* Dep't of Treasury, Supplemental Directive 10-02 (Mar. 24, 2010), *available at* www.hmpadmin.com//portal/programs/hamp/servicer.html.

form requesting basic financial information. The process for entering this trial period has changed.[119] Now servicers must fully verify that a borrower is eligible for HAMP prior to offering them a trial period plan.[120]

Before the borrower can be offered a trial period plan, he or she must sign and return the RMA form, IRS Form 4506-T (Request for Transcript of Tax Return), and provide proof of income. Income will be verified with copies of two recent pay stubs, not more than ninety days old, and the most recent federal tax return. Other documentation may be requested for self-employed borrowers and those who receive child support, Social Security, disability, public assistance, rental and other forms of income.[121] Non-borrower income may be considered if the servicer believes the income can reasonably be relied on to support the mortgage payment.

At their option, applicants may ask servicers to consider certain types of income in the HAMP evaluation. The borrower may choose to have income from alimony, maintenance, or child support considered.[122] Effective July 1, 2010, unemployment insurance benefits and other sources of temporary income related to unemployment will no longer be considered a source of income for HAMP.[123]

The borrower may include income from a non-borrower that is reasonably likely to continue, but this is risky in case that income stops being directed to the borrower. Inclusion of additional income may help borrowers whose low income otherwise produces a negative NPV test result. On the other hand, including the optional income may preclude eligibility because the borrower will be pushed under the 31% debt-to-income ratio that is a threshold requirement for HAMP or result in an unsustainable modification, when the alimony, child support, or income from the non-borrower ceases (since homeowners can only receive one HAMP modification and may not be re-evaluated even if their income drops through no fault of their own). In any case, borrowers are entitled to have their application considered with and without the optional income and must receive a modification if they qualify under either scenario.

Practitioners may wish to run their clients through the FDIC Loan-Mod-in-a-Box before submitting the income documentation to the servicer. The FDIC Loan-Mod-in-a-Box will give practitioners a rough estimate as to whether the optional income is necessary for a positive NPV. If it is not necessary, it should not be included in the submission to the servicer. In cases where a homeowner is denied for failure to pass the NPV, advocates should assess whether there is additional "optional" income that could be included in a resubmission.

The RMA contains a hardship affidavit. Every borrower and co-borrower seeking modification, whether in default or not, must sign a hardship affidavit which describes any current or anticipated hardship, such as a reduction or loss of income, change in household financial circumstances, increase in monthly mortgage payment or other expenses, lack of sufficient cash reserves, excessive debt payments, or overextension with creditors. A hardship affidavit and the RMA are on the HAMP administrative website. The forms contain simple check off boxes and neither has to be notarized. Submission of the standard RMA is all that is needed to trigger the servicer's duty to evaluate the homeowner for a HAMP modification, although the servicer may request additional information is required by its contractual agreements with investors.

Borrowers should be mindful that anyone who signed the original loan document will be required to sign all the modification documents, including the RMA, and the income of the co-borrower will be included in all calculations. Only if the co-borrower is deceased or divorced are absent co-borrowers necessarily excluded from the HAMP loan modification documents, although the servicer may use its discretion in other cases where the co-borrower is absent from the household or cannot sign, due to disability, military deployment, or incarceration, for example.[124] If the co-borrower is deceased or is no longer part of the household, the borrower will need to provide proof with a death certificate or divorce decree. Quitclaim deeds from one borrower to another may also be useful, particularly in the case of never-married and now-separated borrowers.

119 The initial Treasury Supplemental Directive 09-01 (Apr. 6, 2009) authorized services to initiate trial modification plans based on verbal or "stated" income information from borrowers. Servicers would then verify this information during the trial plan period. Effective June 1, 2010 this option is no longer permitted. Servicers must evaluate borrowers for trial modifications using documentation of income and other eligibility standards. Dep't of Treasury, Supplemental Directive 10-01 (Jan. 28, 2010), *available at* www.hmpadmin.com//portal/programs/hamp/servicer.html.

120 *See* Dep't of Treasury, Supplemental Directive 10-01 (Jan. 28, 2010), *available at* www.hmpadmin.com//portal/programs/hamp/servicer.html.

121 For a complete list of acceptable proofs of income see Dep't of Treasury, Supplemental Directive 10-01 (Jan. 28, 2010), *available at* www.hmpadmin.com//portal/programs/hamp/servicer.html.

122 Dep't of Treasury, Supplemental Directive 09-07 (Oct. 8, 2009), *available at* www.hmpadmin.com//portal/programs/hamp/servicer.html; Supplemental Directive 09-01 (Apr. 6, 2009), *available at* www.hmpadmin.com//portal/programs/hamp/servicer.html.

123 Dep't of Treasury, Supplemental Directive 10-04 (May 11, 2010), *available at* www.hmpadmin.com//portal/programs/hamp/servicer.html.

124 *See* Dep't of Treasury, Supplemental Directive 10-01 (Jan. 28, 2010), *available at* www.hmpadmin.com//portal/programs/hamp/servicer.html; Dep't of Treasury, Supplemental Directive 09-01 (Apr. 6, 2009), *available at* www.hmpadmin.com//portal/programs/hamp/servicer.html.

2.8.3.3 Servicer's Review of the Application

Once the initial package of information is submitted, servicers are required to acknowledge receipt within ten business days and review the documentation provided by the borrower for completeness within thirty calendar days. During that time the servicer will be evaluating the borrower's credit report to verify debts, liens and occupancy status. The servicer will also obtain the property's value from an automated system or other source.

Borrowers often have to submit the same documents over and over again, leading to substantial delays in the conversion of active trial modifications to permanent modifications.[125] Aside from the new requirement that servicers must acknowledge receipt of the initial package of information within ten business days, if the documentation is incomplete servicers must make at least two attempts to contact the borrower in writing, the first attempt should be within thirty calendar days of receiving the initial documents.[126] The first notice must give the borrower at least thirty calendar days to provide the designated information. A second notice must give the borrower an additional fifteen calendar days.[127]

Once the servicer receives a complete set of documents, the borrower should either be approved for a trial period plan and sent the relevant notice, or denied a HAMP modification.

2.8.3.4 Where an Application Is Denied

2.8.3.4.1 Notice requirement

Supplemental Directive 09-08[128] requires notice if a borrower is not offered a trial period plan, a permanent HAMP modification, or if the servicer contends that eligibility may be denied because the borrower did not provide required financial information.

With the exception of the incomplete information notice, all notices must be mailed no later than ten business days from the date the servicer determines that a HAMP modification will not be offered. The non-approval notice should clearly specify why the borrower is not being offered a HAMP modification,[129] providing the primary reason or reasons for the non-approval.[130] Importantly, if the notice discusses other non-HAMP loss mitigation options that are being considered or offered to the borrower, it must clearly state that the borrower was considered, but is not eligible, for HAMP. The absence of the borrower notices required by Supplemental Directive 09-08 should be used to argue that the borrower is still being considered for HAMP, and that a foreclosure sale must therefore not take place.[131]

2.8.3.4.2 Denial based on a negative NPV analysis

If the borrower is rejected for a HAMP modification because the test is "NPV Negative," the notice must give the borrower the option of receiving certain data inputs that went into the NPV calculation, including the interest rate, borrower's gross income, real estate taxes, insurance, and other information that that was used in the analysis.[132] Treasury does not require other key inputs, including the amount of foreclosure fees claimed or the home valuation, to be disclosed to the borrower, but servicers do sometimes disclose these inputs, and advocates should be sure to request all inputs.

The borrower (or her representative) has thirty calendar days from the date of the notice of non-approval to request the NPV data. The servicer must provide it within ten business days of the request. Once the borrower receives the

125 A twin problem is servicers rejecting documents for minor imperfections. Treasury addressed this issue in Supplemental Directive 10-01 by calling on servicers to use good business judgment in accepting documents with imperfections (blank fields, erasures, inaccurate dates, etc.) if there is no indication of fraud.

126 *See* Dep't of Treasury, Supplemental Directive 10-02 (Mar. 24, 2010), *available at* www.hmpadmin.com//portal/programs/hamp/servicer.html (discussion of servicer standards regarding borrower outreach and communication); Dep't of Treasury, Supplemental Directive 10-01 (Jan. 28, 2010), *available at* www.hmpadmin.com//portal/programs/hamp/servicer.html (discussion of servicer standards regarding borrower outreach and communication).

127 *See* Dep't of Treasury, Supplemental Directive 10-02 (Mar. 24, 2010), *available at* www.hmpadmin.com//portal/programs/hamp/servicer.html (discussion of servicer standards regarding borrower outreach and communication); Dep't of Treasury, Supplemental Directive 10-01 (Jan. 28, 2010), *available at* www.hmpadmin.com//portal/programs/hamp/servicer.html (discussion of servicer standards regarding borrower outreach and communication).

128 Mandatory for servicers as of Jan. 1, 2010.

129 *See* Dep't of Treasury, Supplemental Directive 09-08 (Nov. 3, 2009), *available at* www.hmpadmin.com//portal/programs/hamp/servicer.html.

130 The notices must comply with the Equal Credit Opportunity Act, when applicable. Dep't of Treasury, Supplemental Directive 09-08, at 1 (Nov. 3, 2009), *available at* www.hmpadmin.com//portal/programs/hamp/servicer.html.

131 *See* Dep't of Treasury, Supplemental Directive 09-01, at 14 (Apr. 6, 2009), *available at* www.hmpadmin.com//portal/programs/hamp/servicer.html; Supplemental Documentation—Frequently Asked Questions Home Affordable Modification Program ("HAMP FAQs") Q53, *available at* www.hmpadmin.com/portal/docs/hamp_servicer/hampfaqs.pdf.

132 The available NPV inputs include the: unpaid balance on the original loan; interest rate before modification; months delinquent; next ARM reset date (if applicable); next ARM reset rate (if applicable); principal and interest before modification; monthly insurance payment; monthly real estate taxes; monthly HOA fee (if applicable); monthly gross income; borrower's total monthly obligations; borrower/ co-borrower FICO; zip code; and state. *See* Dep't of Treasury, Supplemental Directive 09-08 (Nov. 3, 2009), *available at* www.hmpadmin.com//portal/programs/hamp/servicer.html.

input data from the servicer, the borrower can review the information to ensure it is correct. If the information is inaccurate, the borrower has thirty calendar days to provide the servicer with the correct information. During that thirty-day period, the servicer is not allowed to proceed to a foreclosure sale. However, as with other HAMP provisions forbidding foreclosure sales during various stages of the evaluation process, advocates should not rely on servicers to comply with the thirty-day ban automatically. Advocates should take steps to ensure that the foreclosure sale is indeed cancelled and other foreclosure action suspended.

If the borrower finds "material" errors, the servicer must redo the NPV test. The material standard probably means that they are likely to change the outcome of the NPV test. Since the test score is not public, consumers will have to proceed using their best guess as to whether the error is significant enough to have made a difference.

Another option to obtain complete NPV information, as well as other records of the servicer's eligibility determination, is to send a Qualified Written Request (QWR) under RESPA, which imposes requirements on servicers to respond to borrower requests for information or correction of account errors.[133] Using a QWR in this manner is discussed at § 6.4.5.9, *infra*. Chapter 8, *infra*, also includes a complete discussion of qualified written requests. Discovery is another option to obtain this information. The administration has opined that servicers' NPV analyses are proprietary, which may be raised in any discovery request.

2.8.3.4.3 Denial based on investor not participating in the HAMP program

If the borrower is sent a non-approval notice as required by Supplemental Directive 09-08 stating that the investor is simply not participating in the program, there are a number of steps borrowers and advocates can take to challenge that assertion. HAMP requires servicers, not investors, to participate in the program. Nonetheless, in certain limited situations existing contracts between servicers and the trusts that own the mortgages may limit servicers' authority to modify loans. These terms in pooling and servicing agreements are the exception rather than the rule. Large investors like Fannie Mae and Freddie Mac require that their mortgages be modified under HAMP guidelines, as do insurers like the FHA and VA under their respective HAMP programs.

Supplemental Directive 10-02 requires servicers to provide Fannie Mae (in its role as program administrator) with a list of investors who choose not to modify their mortgages according to program guidelines. The list should be available after September 1, 2010. Though there are no plans to make this list publicly available, it could be obtained in discovery or a FOIA request. This list should be checked to find out if an investor is truly not willing to modify the loan under HAMP. The borrower must first obtain the name of the holder of their mortgage. A written request under 15 U.S.C. § 1641(f)(2) to the servicer asking for the identify of the holder should be sufficient, if the request is not honored verbally.[134] The servicer is liable for statutory damages and attorney fees under TILA if it does not provide the information. In addition, if there is mortgage insurance on the loan, the borrower should contact the mortgage insurance company. Private mortgage insurers may be involved in evaluating loans for modification, and unlike the servicer, they stand to lose money if the loan forecloses.

Servicers should also be asked to identify the document which indicates that the loan prohibits modification. Investors do not make these decisions on a case-by-case basis; servicers are typically given broad discretion to modify mortgages in pooling and servicing agreements (PSAs). Few PSAs forbid all modifications. If there is a conflict between the PSA and a HAMP modification, HAMP guidelines allow the servicer to skip steps in the modification process (the waterfall) if required by the PSA or to substitute amortization extension for term extension. The guidelines also require that servicer make "reasonable efforts" to get the investors to waive the restrictions on HAMP modifications contained in the PSAs. Reasonable efforts include, but are not limited to, writing the investor at least once to request a waiver. Servicers should be able to document the reasonable steps they have taken to obtain a waiver. Advocates should not rely on a servicer's representation as to what the PSA says, but should insist on reviewing it themselves.[135] In particular, advocates should be aware that most PSAs contain multiple clauses governing PSAs, often including one that forbids modifications except where modifications are specifically allowed elsewhere in the document. A common example of the type of clause that freely allows modification is regarding loans in default or at imminent risk of default.

If the servicer refuses answer questions, borrowers and advocates should escalate the matter through the servicer's in-house escalation team or Treasury if necessary by e-mailing escalations@hmpadmin.com. Discovery is, of course, another option for acquiring information from servicers.

2.8.4 The Trial Period Plan

If the application is accepted, the homeowner, prior to obtaining a permanent loan modification, will be required to participate in a trial period plan, by making monthly pay-

133 12 U.S.C. § 2605. *See also* Regulation X, the implementing regulation for RESPA, especially 24 C.F.R. § 3500.21.

134 *See* § 1.3.3.3.2, *supra*; National Consumer Law Center, Truth in Lending §§ 2.3.5.2, 6.6.2.4.2, 8.6.5.2 (6th ed. 2007 and Supp.).

135 How to locate and review a PSA is detailed at § 1.3.3.4.3, *supra* (documentation).

ments based on the proposed new loan terms for an initial three-month period (or longer if necessary to comply with investor guidelines). The homeowner will be sent a notice that will outline the terms of the trial modification and payment due dates. Borrowers are not required to sign and return the notice; instead they need only send in the first payment by the due date.

The HAMP trial period is essentially a period of forbearance where the servicer is agreeing to temporarily take less than the full payment due under the terms of the note and mortgage (which are not altered during the trial period). This means that at the end of the trial period borrowers will owe more on their loans than when they started. If the borrower receives a permanent modification, these arrears (interest, escrow advances to third parties, fees, etc.) will be capitalized. If the borrower falls off the trial period plan, however, the borrower will be deeper in arrears. This is especially problematic for borrowers who were current prior to entering a trial period plan. Servicers have used the arrears accumulated during the trial period as the basis for initiating foreclosures. Moreover, the reporting of trial period payments to credit bureaus means that borrowers who are current will experience a negative mark on their credit report, even if they make every trial period payment in full and on time.

If a borrower is not eligible for HAMP, or if they fall off the trial period plan, the servicer should consider the borrower for other workout options, including non-HAMP modifications, forbearance, short sales, deeds in lieu of foreclosure (including those under the program's Home Affordable Foreclosure Alternatives) and refinance programs. Borrowers may be re-evaluated under the program guidelines if their financial circumstances change.[136]

2.8.5 The Permanent Modification

To receive a permanent loan modification, the borrower must be current at the end of the trial period. Current means that the borrower has made each trial period payment by the last day of the month in which it was due. Borrowers who do not make the trial period payments when due are considered to have failed the trial period, and are not eligible for HAMP, though servicers have the discretion to make exceptions for mitigating circumstances.[137]

The permanent modification will become effective the first day of the month following the trial period. The effective date of the permanent modification is specified in the trial plan agreement; the servicer's delay in executing the final permanent modification cannot alter the effective date of the permanent modification or the amount of unpaid principal due under the permanent modification. The conversion is not automatic however, and servicer delays in converting trial modifications to permanent modifications have been one of the problems most cited by advocates.

The terms of the HAMP modification are determined by a standard process. To reach the targeted monthly payment, servicers must follow a sequence of steps (referred to as the "standard modification waterfall") to reduce the borrower's monthly mortgage payment to no more than 31% of their gross monthly income. Note that servicers under HAMP are not precluded from agreeing to a modification that reduces the borrower's monthly payment to below 31%, so long as the modification otherwise complies with the program's guidelines.

The modification sequence first requires the servicer to capitalize any accrued interest, escrow advances to third parties, and servicing advances paid to third parties (not retained by the servicer) related to the preservation of the property and enforcement of the mortgage, if allowed by state law. Only third-party fees that are "reasonable and necessary" should be capitalized. Late fees may not be capitalized and must be waived by the servicer if the borrower completes the initial three-month trial period.

Next the interest rate is reduced. It can be reduced to as low as 2% to reach the affordability target. The interest rate on the modified loan will be fixed for five years and then adjust upwards 1% per year (or less) until it reaches the interest rate cap. The interest rate cap is the lesser of (1) the fully indexed and fully amortizing contract rate or (2) the Freddie Mac Primary Mortgage Market Survey rate for thirty-year fixed rate mortgage loans (on the date the modification is prepared).[138] Once capped, the rate is fixed for the remainder of the term.

If a 2% interest rate does not result in an affordable payment (31% of the homeowner's gross monthly income) then the servicer will extend the term of the loan (to a maximum of forty years); and if necessary, defer payment on a portion of the principal.[139] If term extension is not permitted by an applicable pooling and servicing agreement, the servicer may reamortize the mortgage based on an amortization schedule of up to 480 months with a balloon due at maturity under the original term of the mortgage.

136 *See* Dep't of Treasury, Supplemental Directive 10-01 (Jan. 28, 2010), *available at* www.hmpadmin.com//portal/programs/hamp/servicer.html.

137 Mitigating circumstances are not defined. Instead servicers must use good business judgment. *See* Dep't of Treasury, Supplemental Directive 10-01 (Jan. 28, 2010), *available at* www.hmpadmin.com//portal/programs/hamp/servicer.html.

138 The Freddie Mac Primary Mortgage Market Survey rate is available at www.freddiemac.com.

139 Treasury guidelines set limits on the portion of loan principal that may be deferred under the forbearance waterfall step. The forbearance amount is limited to the greater of 30% of the unpaid principal balance or an amount that leaves an interest-bearing principal of at least 100% of the property's current fair market value. If forbearance must exceed these levels in order to produce the affordable payment, the borrower fails the NPV test. Dep't of Treasury Supplemental Directive 10-01 (Jan. 28, 2010), *available at* www.hmpadmin.com//portal/programs/hamp/servicer.html.

However, negative amortization after the effective date of the modification is prohibited.

If payment on a portion of the principal is deferred, no interest will accrue on the forbearance amount. This amount will be a balloon payment, that is, it will be due at the end of the loan term or when the loan is paid off or refinanced. Mortgage holders and servicers are not required to forgive a portion of the principal under program guidelines. However, servicers are permitted to forgive principal before any steps in the waterfall process described above (though subsequent steps may not be skipped).

The 31% payment target is based on the borrower's housing expense payment (principal, interest, taxes, property insurance, homeowner's or condominium association fees). The servicer is also required to determine the borrower's total monthly debt ratio ("back-end ratio") by considering the borrower's payments on other installment debt and liens. Counseling is required only for homeowners whose debt-to-income ratio is equal to or greater than 55%. There is no cost for any required counseling.

There is also no cost for the modification and servicers cannot require that homeowners make a cash contribution. If the mortgage account does not have an escrow for taxes and insurance, the borrower must agree to set up an escrow account before the initial trial period. Presumably, the no cash contribution policy should mean that any initial escrow deposit will be capitalized in the new principal amount.

2.8.6 Borrowers in Bankruptcy

Borrowers with active chapter 7 or chapter 13 bankruptcy cases must be considered for HAMP if the borrower, borrower's counsel, or the bankruptcy trustee (with the borrower's permission) submits a request to the servicer.[140] Though servicers are not required to solicit these borrowers for HAMP, they must work with the borrower or the borrower's counsel to obtain the approval of the court or trustee in keeping with local court rules and procedures. This includes extending the trial period plan as necessary to accommodate delays in obtaining court approval or receiving trial period payments from the trustee. However, servicers are not required to extend the trial period beyond two additional months.[141]

Borrowers who file for bankruptcy after entering a HAMP trial period plan may not be denied a permanent modification on the basis of a bankruptcy filing. Borrowers who received a chapter 7 discharge of personal liability on the mortgage are eligible for HAMP.[142] It is irrelevant whether the borrower reaffirmed the debt in bankruptcy, and the servicer cannot ask the borrower to reaffirm as part of the HAMP approval process.

A servicer cannot object to confirmation of a chapter 13 plan, move for relief from the automatic stay, or move for dismissal of the chapter 13 case on the basis that the borrower paid amounts due under the trial period plan (as opposed to the non-modified mortgage payment). Servicers may waive the HAMP trial period altogether and offer eligible chapter 13 debtors a permanent modification if:

- The borrower makes all post-petition payments that are due on the first lien mortgage prior to the effective date to the HAMP agreement, and at least three of the payments are equal to or greater than the modified payment;
- The modification is approved by the bankruptcy court, if required; and
- The waiver of the trial period plan is permitted by investor guidelines;

This waiver to the trial period plan, however, is at the discretion of the servicer and it depends on whether the servicer has developed the systems capability to process the waiver.

The procedure for requesting a HAMP is slightly modified for borrowers in active bankruptcy. Servicer may accept copies of bankruptcy schedules and tax returns, instead of the standard Request for a Modification and Affidavit (or similar form) and IRS Form 4506T-EZ. The bankruptcy schedules must be current (less than ninety days old) or updated evidence of income must be provided. A hardship affidavit must be provided if one was not completed earlier. These procedures are optional for servicers. Borrowers in bankruptcy may submit HAMP application documents in the same manner as borrowers not in bankruptcy. Unless the servicer has clearly authorized the alternative procedures, the better practice may be for bankruptcy debtors to follow the general HAMP application process.

140 *See* Dep't of Treasury, Supplemental Directive 10-02 (Mar. 24, 2010), *available at* www.hmpadmin.com//portal/programs/hamp/servicer.html. This is a change in policy. Previously, borrowers in active bankruptcy proceedings were only eligible for HAMP at the servicer's discretion. *See* Dep't of Treasury, Supplemental Directive 09-01 (Apr. 6, 2009), *available at* www.hmpadmin.com//portal/programs/hamp/servicer.html.

141 This would result in a total trial period of five months. *See* Dep't of Treasury, Supplemental Directive 10-02 (Mar. 24, 2010), *available at* www.hmpadmin.com//portal/programs/hamp/servicer.html.

142 For borrowers who obtained a prior chapter 7 discharge, the HAMP Modification Agreement will be amended to insert the following language in section 1: "I was discharged in Chapter 7 bankruptcy proceeding subsequent to the execution of the Loan Documents. Based on this representation, Lender agrees that I will not have personal liability on the debt pursuant to this Agreement." *See* Dep't of Treasury, Supplemental Directive 10-02 (Mar. 24, 2010), *available at* www.hmpadmin.com//portal/programs/hamp/servicer.html.

2.8.7 *Restrictions on Foreclosure Actions*

The initiation or continuation of foreclosure proceedings during the HAMP modification process has generated an avalanche of complaints about the program. Many foreclosure sales have been completed while a HAMP request was pending, in violation of the servicer's contract with Treasury and program guidelines.

In response, Treasury tightened some requirements regarding the foreclosure process. Servicers are prohibited from referring a loan to foreclosure or conducting a scheduled sale until the borrower: has been evaluated for HAMP and determined ineligible for the program; failed to make a required trial period plan payment by the last day of the month in which the payments is due; provide the required documents after at least two written requests; or failed to respond entirely to the servicer's outreach efforts.[143] Additionally, once the borrower is in a trial modification based on verified income, the servicer may not refer the loan to foreclosure or proceed with a pending foreclosure. If a loan was already referred to foreclosure prior to the borrower entering a trial period based on verified income, the servicer must take steps to stop the foreclosure process, including taking action to ensure that a judgment does not enter in a state with a judicial foreclosure process.

The sale is delayed slightly for borrowers who receive notice that they are not approved for HAMP. Servicers must wait thirty calendar days after the date of the non-approval notice, or longer if necessary to review additional material provided by the borrower in response to the notice, to conduct a foreclosure sale. They do not have to wait thirty days if the reason the borrower was not approved for the program was due to the ineligibility of the property or mortgage loan or if the borrower does not accept the offer. Practitioners report that many servicers are routinely sending borrowers notice that the borrower has declined to participate in the program; borrowers should be advised to contest such notices immediately.

A servicer does not have a duty to suspend a scheduled foreclosure sale unless the borrower's request for a HAMP modification is received by midnight seven business days prior to the sale date.[144] In addition to meeting the deadline, the borrower's submission must be complete—meaning the servicer must receive an RMA form, an IRS Form 4506T, and a required proof of income. Servicers are allowed to impose other requirements on the submission process up to thirty days before the scheduled sale. For example, the servicer may require that the documents be sent certified or express mail or to either the servicer or foreclosure attorney/foreclosure trustee. These requirements must be posted on the servicer's website and sent to the borrower in writing. Borrowers who contact the servicer before the deadline should be told the submission requirements. Given that servicers can vary the submission requirements, borrowers are advised to check with the servicer prior to submitting any documentation which will be relied on to postpone a scheduled sale.

143 *See* Dep't of Treasury, Supplemental Directive 10-02 (Mar. 24, 2010), *available at* www.hmpadmin.com//portal/programs/hamp/servicer.html. Note that the policy with respect to temporary suspension of foreclosure proceedings completely supersedes earlier section in Dep't of Treasury, Supplemental Directive 09-01 (Apr. 6, 2009), *available at* www.hmpadmin.com//portal/programs/hamp/servicer.html.

144 Borrowers who were denied a HAMP modification and request reconsideration are subject to the same deadline. *See* Dep't of Treasury, Supplemental Directive 10-02 (Mar. 24, 2010), *available at* www.hmpadmin.com//portal/programs/hamp/servicer.html.

2.8.8 *HAMP Incentives to Servicers, Holders, and Homeowners*

HAMP has an extensive incentive compensation programs for servicers, holders, and homeowners, but as of yet no penalty for servicer noncompliance. If the borrower completes the three-month trial period, the servicers will receive an incentive payment of $1000 for each loan modification, plus an additional $500 if the homeowner was current when the loan was modified. The servicer will receive an incentive payment of up to $1000 each year the homeowner remains in the program for up to three years.

If the homeowner was current with payments when the loan was modified, the lender or investor receives a one-time $1500 bonus. If the lender or investor reduces the monthly payment to 38% of the homeowner's gross monthly income, then the program will share in the cost of any further reduction to the affordability target of 31% of the homeowner's gross monthly income.

Borrowers will receive an incentive payment that will be applied towards reducing the principal balance of the mortgage. So long as the homeowner is current on the modified mortgage, he or she will receive $1000 each year for up to five years. The incentive payment is to be applied first to the interest bearing unpaid principal balance (before being applied to any deferred principal forbearance).

2.8.9 *The Second Lien Modification Program (2MP)*

2.8.9.1 2MP Described

After implementing HAMP, Treasury announced a separate program to deal with second liens in August 2009. The Second Lien Modification Program (referred to as 2MP) is intended to complement HAMP by providing borrowers with sustainable monthly payments or complete extinguishment of second lien mortgage loans. The program was temporarily shelved and reintroduced in March 2010, and servicers must sign a new or amended agreement with Treasury by October 3, 2010 to participate in the program.[145] Servicers who do not currently participate in the first lien program under HAMP are eligible to participate in the second lien program. The four largest servicers, Bank of America, Chase, Citi, and Wells Fargo, have signed agreements to participate in 2MP.

Modification of a second lien mortgage will not become effective unless the modification of the corresponding first lien mortgage is effective under HAMP. Participating servicers are required to offer to modify a borrower's second lien mortgage and dismiss any outstanding foreclosure action. The offer to modify the second lien mortgage may be made during the HAMP trial period, or later on the date the HAMP modification becomes effective.

Only mortgages in the second lien position originated on or before January 1, 2009 are eligible to be modified or extinguished under the program. A mortgage lien that would be in the second position but for a tax lien, a mechanic's lien, or other non-mortgage related lien is eligible. A second mortgage on which no interest is charged and no payments are due until the first lien is paid in full (e.g., a FHA partial claim) is not eligible. A loan with a small balance (less than $5000), or scheduled monthly payment of less than $100 may not be modified, though the loan itself could be extinguished under program guidelines.[146]

In general, servicers of second mortgages may rely on information and documents provided to the servicer of the first lien mortgage under HAMP and are not required to verify any financial information provided by the borrower in connection with that process. They may conclude that if the borrower faced imminent default or was delinquent on the first mortgage, then default is reasonably foreseeable with respect to the second mortgage. Moreover, the servicer is not required to perform a net present value test on the second mortgage as it is assumed that modification of the first and second mortgage under HAMP guidelines will result in a positive net present value.

To qualify for the program, the second lien mortgage may be current or delinquent. Mortgages insured, guaranteed, or held by the federal government, (e.g., FHA, VA, Rural Development) are not eligible. If the borrower is evaluated for the program and not offered a modification, the servicer should mail a notice within ten days of that evaluation. If borrowers enter into second lien modification agreements, they must do so by December 31, 2012.

145 The details for this program are contained in Dep't of Treasury, Supplemental Directive 09-05 Revised, issued on Mar. 26, 2010, and subsequent announcements and are available at www.hmpadmin.com//portal/programs/hamp/servicer.html.

146 *See* Dep't of Treasury, Supplemental Directive 09-05R (Mar. 26, 2010), *available at* www.hmpadmin.com//portal/programs/hamp/servicer.html.

2.8.9.2 The 2MP Trial Period Plan

A three-month trial period may be required under the program if the borrower is delinquent on a second lien mortgage when offered the modification. A trial plan is not required if the borrower is current on the mortgage and the amount of the borrower's monthly payment is equal to or greater than the amount that will be due after modification. If the borrower is delinquent they must enter a trial period plan with payments as proposed under the second lien modification. The plan may run concurrently or overlap the HAMP trial period.[147] Additionally, if the HAMP-modified first lien falls out of good standing while the second lien is in a trial period, the servicer is not required to offer a modification on the second lien.

Borrowers must make each trial period payment no later than thirty days from the due date. The servicer may, however, extend the trial period for one additional month if the borrower did not make the final trial period payment on time.

2.8.9.3 2MP Modification/Extinguishment Steps

The program provides two alternatives for servicers of second lien mortgages: modify the loan, or receive a payment in exchange for releasing the lien (extinguishment). Servicers may partially extinguish or forgive a portion of the principal and then modify the loan. However, the converse is not allowed; if the second lien mortgage is modified under 2MP, the loan is not eligible later for a full or partial extinguishment of the loan.

The standard to modify a second lien mortgage requires the servicer to first capitalize any accrued interest and advances to third parties. Only those third-party fees that are reasonable and necessary may be capitalized.[148] Late fees and other ancillary fees (e.g., insufficient fund fees, over limit fees, annual fees) may not be capitalized and must be waived by the servicer unless the borrower fails to complete the 2MP trial period and the second lien is not modified.

Next the borrower's interest rate must be reduced to 1% for amortizing loans (payment of both principal and interest). For interest only loans servicers have the option of

147 Since the modification of the second lien cannot be effective until the HAMP modification of the first lien is effective, the trial period on the second lien may be longer than three months if there is an overlap in the trial periods. The borrower must continue to make payments during the trial period regardless of its length. *See* Dep't of Treasury, Supplemental Directive 09-05R (Mar. 26, 2010), *available at* www.hmpadmin.com//portal/programs/hamp/servicer.html.

148 These are described as the costs and expensed incurred in servicing the second lien, including costs related to the preservation and protection of property and enforcement of the mortgage. *See* Dep't of Treasury, Supplemental Directive 09-05R (Mar. 26, 2010), *available at* www.hmpadmin.com//portal/programs/hamp/servicer.html.

converting the loan to an amortizing loan at 1% or keeping the interest only feature and reducing the interest rate to 2%. For partially amortizing loans (such as convertible HELOCs), if 50% or more of the lien (based on the unpaid principal balance) is amortizing, the servicer may reduce the interest rate to 1%. If less than 50% of the loan is amortizing then the servicer will use the same options available for interest only loans.

After five years, the interest rate on the second lien mortgage will reset to the then current interest rate on the modified first mortgage, with the same interest rate cap as on the first lien mortgage.[149] Servicers, however, do have the discretion to offer an interest rate lower than the interest on the HAMP modified first mortgage.

The next step involves extending the term of the mortgage. For amortizing second lien mortgages, the term is extended to match (at a minimum) the term of the first lien mortgage modified under HAMP. The term can be extended up to forty years if allowed by applicable servicing agreements. If a term extension is not permitted, then the second lien mortgage may be reamortized (with a new amortization period that matches the first mortgage or up to forty years); reamortization in this manner will result in a balloon payment at the maturity of the loan. With an interest only mortgage that is not converted, the amortization will begin after year five.[150]

Finally, if there was principal forbearance or forgiveness on the HAMP-modified first lien mortgage, the servicer must *forbear* principal on the second lien in the same proportion. There is no requirement that the servicer forgive principal on the second lien. However, if the servicer chooses to forgive principal, it may elect this option in lieu of an interest rate reduction.

All loans modified under the program must result in a closed-end second mortgage. If the mortgage is an open-end line of credit, the servicer must terminate the borrower's ability to draw additional amounts on the credit line while the modification becomes effective.

A servicer may elect to get a payoff (extinguishment) of the second lien mortgage as an alternative to or in conjunction with the modification of the mortgage. A portion or the entire amount of the second mortgage may be paid off based on a formula. To exercise this option, the servicer may not charge the borrower a fee or require the borrower to sign a promissory note.

The formula for compensating investors to extinguish the lien is based on the borrower's combined loan-to-value (CLTV) ratio and the degree of delinquency on the mortgage.[151] For loans that are more than six months past due, the lender or investor will be paid six cents per dollar of unpaid principal balance extinguished. For loans that are less than or equal to six months past due, a higher range of payments is allowed depending on the borrower's CLTV, ranging from ten cents per dollar of unpaid principal balance extinguished for a second lien with greater than 140% CLTV to twenty-one cents per dollar of unpaid principal balance extinguished for a second lien with less than 115% CLTV.

2.8.9.4 2MP and Borrowers in Bankruptcy

The guidelines regarding borrowers in bankruptcy in 2MP parallel those of the first lien modification program.[152] Borrowers with active chapter 7 or chapter 13 bankruptcy cases are eligible for 2MP if the borrower, borrower's counsel or the bankruptcy trustee (with the borrower's permission) submits a request to the servicer. Servicers must work with the borrower or the borrower's counsel to obtain any court or trustee approvals. Borrowers who are in a trial period plan and subsequently file for bankruptcy may not be denied a 2MP permanent modification on the basis of a bankruptcy filing.

2.8.9.5 2MP Incentives

Servicers of second liens modified or extinguished under the program receive a $500 fee. If the amount of the borrower's monthly payment on the second lien is reduced by six percent or more, the servicer will also receive a fee of $250 for up to three years as long as both the HAMP modification and second lien modification remain in good standing and the loan has not been paid in full. This is in addition to any incentive compensation the servicer may have received for modifying the first lien under HAMP. The borrower will receive a fee of up to $250 for up to five years under the same terms. However the fee will be applied to reduce the principal balance owed on the mortgage.

No incentives will be paid to servicers for modifying the second lien unless both the first and second liens are in good standing. If the borrower misses three consecutive payments at any time the account is no longer in good standing and that status cannot be restored. Servicers and borrowers are

149 In the alternative, servicers may do a gradual interest rate step up after five years if a pooling and servicing or other agreement calls for it. At no time, however, may the interest rate on the second lien exceed the interest rate on the modified first lien mortgage. *See* Dep't of Treasury, Supplemental Directive 09-05R (Mar. 26, 2010), *available at* www.hmpadmin.com//portal/programs/hamp/servicer.html.

150 For partially amortizing loans, if 50% or more of the lien is amortizing, it is treated as a fully amortizing loan; if less than 50% of the loan is amortizing the loan may be treated like a fully amortizing loan or interest-only loan. *See* Dep't of Treasury, Supplemental Directive 09-05R (Mar. 26, 2010), *available at* www.hmpadmin.com//portal/programs/hamp/servicer.html.

151 The combined loan-to-value ratio (CLTV) is the ratio of the current total unpaid principal balance of the HAMP-modified first lien and the current total unpaid principal balance of the unmodified second lien divided by the property value (which was obtained in connection with the HAMP modification).

152 *See* § 2.8.6, *supra*.

no longer eligible to receive further incentive payments. Borrowers will lose incentive payments already accrued.

2.8.10 *Home Affordable Unemployment Program (UP)*

The Department of Treasury on May 11, 2010 announced the Home Affordable Unemployment Program (UP), effective July 1, 2010.[153] For three months, participants have their monthly mortgage payment reduced to less than or equal to 31% of the borrowers gross monthly household income and may be suspended in full. Servicers are given discretion to extend the three-month period according to their investor/regulatory guidelines.

Homeowners seeking to participate must meet HAMP eligibility requirements and be unemployed when applying, be entitled to receive unemployment benefits in the month of the UP forbearance effective date, and request a UP forbearance plan before missing three monthly mortgage payments. In addition, servicers have discretion to require a borrower to have received three months of unemployment benefits before commencement of the plan. Eligibility ceases if the homeowner is re-employed during the three months of reduced payments. Homeowners in a permanent HAMP modification are not eligible for an UP forbearance, but can convert from a trial plan to UP forbearance, and are still eligible for UP forbearance if they have previously been found ineligible for HAMP.

Even if an unemployed homeowner requests assistance for HAMP, the homeowner must first be evaluated for an UP forbearance plan and offered the UP forbearance before they can be considered for HAMP. Borrowers in an UP forbearance plan will be evaluated for HAMP at either reemployment or thirty days prior to the UP period expiring. The forbearance period under UP does not count toward the HAMP three-month trial plan.

It is possible that this new program will actually make things worse for homeowners. Since the program requires forbearance for only three months, it will not address the needs of those unemployed for longer terms. In addition, the plan requires evaluation for a HAMP modification thirty days before the end of the forbearance, possibly only eight weeks into the borrower's unemployment, long before most unemployed workers have found re-employment.

Unlike a regular HAMP trial plan, that portion of the three monthly payments that are reduced get added into the principal amount due. Additionally, late fees will continue to accrue during the processing of the forbearance request and during the forbearance itself. These late fees will only be waived in the unlikely event of a permanent HAMP modification.

153 Dep't of Treasury, Supplemental Directive 10-04 (May 11, 2010), *available at* www.hmpadmin.com//portal/programs/hamp/servicer.html.

Another drawback of the program is that many homeowners have used unemployment benefits to support HAMP modified mortgage payments. The Treasury supplemental directive announcing UP states that unemployment insurance benefits and other sources of temporary income related to unemployment will no longer be considered a source of income for HAMP.[154] Now unemployment benefits are no longer to be counted as income, regardless of how long the homeowner expects to receive unemployment benefits.

Homeowners must request a forbearance under this plan before they are three months delinquent, but servicers may require them to receive three months of unemployment benefits before approving them for a forbearance. Care must be taken in coordinating these timing requirements.

2.8.11 *Home Affordable Foreclosure Alternatives (HAFA)*

2.8.11.1 HAFA Described

Assistance is available for borrowers who do not qualify for HAMP, who are offered a modification but decline it, who default on a HAMP modification, or who do not successfully complete the terms of a trial period plan. Under the Home Affordable Foreclosure Alternatives (HAFA) portion of the program, borrowers are offered a short sale or a deed in lieu of foreclosure as a means of avoiding foreclosure. The program is part of HAMP and servicers may not solicit a borrower for the program until he or she has been evaluated for a HAMP modification. In addition, before offering a HAFA alternative, servicers must consider other (non-HAMP) loan modifications or workout options that will help the borrower keep his or her home. The details for this program are contained in Supplemental Directive 09-09 Revised, issued on March 26, 2010, and subsequent announcements.[155]

As with HAMP, this program's aim is to simplify and streamline the process for obtaining a short sale or deed in lieu of foreclosure with a standard process and compressed timeframe. Borrowers must first meet the basic eligibility criteria for HAMP.[156] Any financial and hardship informa-

154 *Id.*

155 Note that this replaces in its entirely, Dep't of Treasury, Supplemental Directive 09-09 (Nov. 30, 2009). Both supplemental directives are available at www.hmpadmin.com//portal/programs/hamp/servicer.html.

156 These include that the one to four unit property is the borrower's principal residence; the current unpaid principal balance is equal to or less than $729,750; the borrower's total monthly payment exceed 31% of the borrower's gross monthly income; and the loan was originated on or before January 1, 2009. The HAMP NPV test does not project investor cash flow from either a short sale or deed in lieu of foreclosure and will not be performed as part of HAFA. *See* Dep't of Treasury, Supplemental Directives 09-09R (Mar. 26, 2010) and 09-01 (Apr. 6, 2009),

tion collected from the borrower as part of that process will be used to evaluate the borrower for HAFA options. A servicer may, however, request updated financial information to comply with investor guidelines. While the short sale or deed in lieu is being implemented, the borrower's total monthly payment should be reduced to no more than 31% of his or her gross monthly income.

Every potentially eligible borrower must be considered for HAFA before the loan is referred to foreclosure or a pending sale is conducted. This evaluation must take place within thirty calendar days of the date the borrower does not qualify for HAMP, does not complete the trial period plan, misses two consecutive payments on a HAMP modification (and is therefore delinquent), or simply requests a short sale or deed in lieu of foreclosure. If the loan was already referred to foreclosure before evaluation, the foreclosure process may continue during the evaluation under HAFA, but the sale itself cannot be completed. Once the HAFA evaluation is complete, the loan may be referred to foreclosure, although the sale cannot take place while the borrower is still within the HAFA processing timeframe. Borrowers with active chapter 7 or chapter 13 bankruptcy cases may be considered for HAFA if the borrower, borrower's counsel, or the bankruptcy trustee submits a request to the servicer.

Under both HAFA options, the borrower, working with real estate professionals, is required to deliver clear and marketable title. A portion of the gross proceeds from the short sale may be used to pay junior lien holders to release their liens. Each lien holder, in order of priority, may be paid no more than six percent of the unpaid principal balance of their loan, up to an aggregate cap of $6000. Servicers may, but are not required to, negotiate with junior lien holders on behalf of borrowers.

To participate in HAFA, investors are required to waive all rights to seek a deficiency judgment with respect to the first mortgage and they may not require the borrower to sign a promissory note for the deficiency. In addition, servicers may not charge borrowers administrative processing fees for HAFA, though they may require the borrower to waive reimbursement for escrow surplus or other items. Upon successful completion of the HAFA short sale or deed in lieu the borrower will receive $3000 to pay moving costs; the servicer will be paid $1500; and investors will be paid up to $2000 for allowing a portion of the short sale proceeds to be used to pay off junior lien holders.

2.8.11.2 HAFA Short Sales

With a HAFA short sale, the servicer allows the borrower to sell the property for less than the total amount due on the mortgage. The servicer will accept the net proceeds from the sale of the property in full satisfaction of the total amount due on the first mortgage. The transaction costs that may be deducted from the gross sales proceeds to determine the minimum net proceeds depend on the reasonable and customary real estate transaction costs in a community, but typically include real estate commissions, title and attorney fees, taxes, etc. The servicer is allowed to set the policy (consistent with investor guidelines) regarding net sales proceeds, though that policy should be in writing and applied consistently across all loans serviced for that investor.

Servicers have ten business days to respond after receiving a request for approval of a short sale. The approval notice will state the minimum net sales proceeds. That approval notice, and corresponding threshold for net sales proceeds, is effective for 120 calendar days but may be extended an additional eight months at the discretion of the servicer. Borrowers will have at least forty-five days from the date of the sales contract to close the transaction.

2.8.11.3 HAFA Deeds in Lieu of Foreclosure

With a deed in lieu of foreclosure the borrower voluntarily transfers ownership of mortgaged property to the servicer in full satisfaction of the total amount due on the first mortgage. The borrower must provide marketable title, free of any mortgages, liens, or other encumbrances. Servicers will usually require that the borrower attempt to sell the property through a short sale before agreeing to accept a deed in lieu of foreclosure.

2.9 Making Home Affordable Refinance Program (HARP)

The Making Home Affordable Refinance Program (known as HARP) is designed to assist homeowners who are current on their mortgage but wish to refinance into a more affordable loan. The program also targets homeowners who are unable to refinance because of declining property values. Homeowners will be offered fixed-rate mortgage with a fifteen- or thirty-year term. Only homeowners with loans that are owned or securitized by Fannie Mae or Freddie Mac will qualify for this program. The program's sunset date was extended and the program is now slated to end on June 30, 2011.

To qualify the homeowner must be the owner occupant of a one to four unit property. The homeowner must be current on his or her mortgage. Current means the homeowner has not been more than thirty days late in the past twelve months. The refinancing program applies only to first mortgages that do not exceed 125% of the current market value of the property.

Both Fannie Mae and Freddie Mac have established toll-free telephone numbers and a website to provide information on the loans they own or securitize.

---

available at www.hmpadmin.com//portal/programs/hamp/servicer.html.

- For Fannie Mae, call 1-800-7FANNIE (8:00 a.m. to 8:00 p.m. EST) or check www.fanniemae.com/homeaffordable.
- For Freddie Mac, call 1-800-FREDDIE (8:00 a.m. to 8:00 p.m. EST) or check www.freddiemac.com/avoidforeclosure.

The interest rate on the refinanced loan will be based on the market rate in effect at the time of the refinance. The loan will not include prepayment penalties or balloon payments, and the borrower cannot receive cash from the loan. Only transaction costs, such as the cost of an appraisal or title report, may be included in the refinanced amount.

2.10 Hope for Homeowners, HOPE NOW, and Project Lifeline

2.10.1 Hope for Homeowners (H4H)

The HOPE for Homeowners (H4H) program was created in 2008 to allow eligible homeowners to refinance into FHA-insured thirty-year fixed rate mortgages.[157] Any type of mortgage is eligible to be refinanced under the program including prime mortgages, subprime mortgages (e.g., interest only, payment-option adjustable rate mortgages) and government-backed mortgages. The program was substantially overhauled in 2009 to increase its flexibility and eliminate certain features, such as the requirement that homeowners share a portion of any future appreciation with the FHA. The program is temporary and will end on September 30, 2011, unless extended.[158]

Homeowners who are current or delinquent on their mortgage at the time of the refinance are eligible for the program if they have not intentionally defaulted on their mortgage or any other substantial debt within the last five years. An intentional default means that the homeowner had available funds that could pay the mortgage and other debts without hardship. Disputed debts may be excluded from consideration. In addition, if delinquent on the mortgage, the borrower must have made a minimum of six full payments on the first mortgage and spend more than 31% of their gross monthly income on making all mortgage payments. Borrowers convicted of fraud under state or federal law in the past ten years do not qualify under program guidelines. The borrower must also certify that they did not knowingly or willfully provide false information to obtain the mortgage being refinanced under the program. Borrowers in bankruptcy may participate in the program.

Only mortgages originated on or before January 1, 2008 are eligible to be refinanced. They must secure a property that is the homeowner's primary and only residence. This means the homeowner cannot have an ownership interest in other residential real estate, including second homes or rental properties. Also, homeowners with a net worth of over $1,000,000 (including retirement assets) are excluded from the program.

The amount of the H4H mortgage cannot exceed a nationwide maximum mortgage limit as follows:

One-unit property	$ 550,440
Two-units property	$ 704,682
Three-units property	$ 851,796
Four-units property	$1,058,574

The new FHA-insured mortgage will have a loan-to-value (LTV) of between 90% and 105% of the current appraised value of the property (excluding the upfront mortgage insurance premium (UFMIP)) depending on the status of the loan being refinanced. If the homeowner was current on the loan being refinanced, the LTV on the new H4H loan will be 105% of the current appraised value of the property (excluding UFMIP). If the homeowner was delinquent, the LTV will be either 90% or 96.5% of the current appraised value of the property, depending on the borrower's debt-to-income ratio. For homeowners with credit scores below 500 the maximum LTV is 90% of the current appraised value of the property.

Holders of the primary or secondary mortgage to be refinanced are required to waive all prepayment penalties and late fees (including insufficient fund fees) and accept reduced payoff amounts as payment in full. The homeowner will be required to pay an annual premium of not more than 0.75% of the remaining principal balance of the new insured mortgage. The 0.75% annual premium will be collected for the life of the H4H mortgage.[159] An upfront mortgage insurance premium of 2% of the base loan amount is also charged.

The H4H program creates an equity-sharing system between the homeowner and HUD.[160] Now called an "exit premium," the homeowners must share with HUD a portion of the initial equity in the property. The initial equity is the lesser of: (1) the appraised value of the property at the time of the H4H origination less the original principal balance on the H4H mortgage or (2) the outstanding amount due under all existing mortgages, less the original principal balance on the H4H mortgage. If the homeowner sells the property or refinances the loan, HUD and the homeowner will share in the equity as shown in the chart below:

157 12 U.S.C. § 1715z-23. Additional statutory changes to the H4H program were made by the Helping Families Save Their Homes Act of 2009, Pub. Law No. 111-22, § 202 (May 20, 2009).

158 The program is described in Dep't of Hous. & Urban Dev. Mortgagee Letter 2009-43 (Oct. 20, 2009).

159 *Id.*

160 12 U.S.C. § 1715z-23(k).

	Shared Equity: If the homeowner sells the property or refinances the loan, HUD and the homeowner share in equity created as a result of the sale or refinancing as follows:	
If sale or refinancing occurs during year:	HUD is entitled to:	Homeowner is entitled to:
1	100%	0%
2	90%	10%
3	80%	20%
4	70%	30%
5	60%	40%
After year 5	50%	50%

The homeowner is not permitted to give a second mortgage or other secondary lien on the property during the first five years of the new loan. However, exceptions to this rule may be made for secondary liens necessary to ensure maintenance of the property.

This program still is voluntary. However, servicers that participate in the federal Home Affordable Modification Program (HAMP) must consider the borrower for a H4H refinance, when feasible. Consideration for a H4H refinance should not delay the modification process under that program. It is unclear from the current HAMP guidelines however, how much effort servicers should take in evaluating homeowners for this refinance program.

2.10.2 HOPE NOW Alliance Plan

In 2007, the mortgage industry created a voluntary program to help consumers who have securitized subprime adjustable rate mortgages avoid foreclosure by temporarily freezing their interest rate at the initial level.[161] The mortgage industry players forming this alliance, called HOPE NOW, have expanded the program to include workouts on other loans and have created a consumer hotline.[162] The servicing guidelines for the HOPE NOW alliance provide that servicers are to consider stopping the foreclosure process for up to thirty days (or longer if necessary) for borrowers who are ninety days or greater past due, and in imminent danger of losing their home to foreclosure.[163] During this foreclosure delay, servicers are to consider loss mitigation options, including a loan modification.

The rate reset plan sets up a streamlined procedure for processing loan modifications for borrowers who are current on their loan payments but in danger of default after the initial interest rate resets. These borrowers may be offered a limited modification under which the interest rate will be kept at the existing rate, generally for a period of five years following the upcoming reset. Since the modification offered under the plan is a temporary rate freeze, attorneys are likely to obtain more substantial loan modifications for their clients in an individualized workout, litigation settlement, or even the federal Home Affordable Modification Program.

The plan applies to securitized subprime residential ARM loans originated between January 1, 2005 and July 31, 2007 with an initial interest rate reset between January 1, 2008 and July 31, 2010. The subprime loan must be a first lien ARM with an initial fixed-rate period of thirty-six months or less. Loans referred to as "2/28s" and "3/27s" meet this description.

Only borrowers who are current with loan payments are eligible for help. Under the plan a borrower is defined as current if he or she was not more than thirty days delinquent and the borrower has not been more than sixty days delinquent in the prior twelve-month period. In addition the borrower must currently occupy the property as a primary residence; have a mortgage payment which will go up by more than 10% at the upcoming reset; and meet the "FICO test," which is that the borrower must have a current FICO score less than 660 and which is less than a score 10% higher than the FICO score at origination. Finally, the loan-to-value ratio (LTV) must be greater than 97% (based on first lien only).

Some borrowers may receive this temporary rate freeze modification without signing a written agreement. The plan provides that if the servicer is unable to obtain a written agreement, the borrower's payment of two payments under the loan as modified, after receiving notice of the modified terms, will be deemed consent. Borrowers who unwittingly receive this limited temporary freeze modification may be precluded from later obtaining another modification.[164] The pooling and servicing agreement or the servicer's guidelines

161 The plan was announced on December 6, 2007 by Treasury Secretary Paulson and the American Securitization Forum (ASF). The ASF's summary of the plan titled Streamlined Foreclosure and Loss Avoidance Framework for Securitized Subprime Adjustable Rate Mortgage Loans (ASF Plan) is available at www.americansecuritization.com/uploadedFiles/FinalASFStatementonStreamlinedServicingProcedures.pdf. A detailed analysis of the plan is available in 26 NCLC REPORTS, *Bankruptcy & Foreclosures Ed.* 13–16 (Jan./Feb. 2008).

162 Information about HOPE NOW services is available at: www.hopenow.com/index.php.

163 The servicing guidelines are available at: www.hopenow.com/press_release/files/Mortgage%20Servicing%20Guidelines.pdf.

164 However, borrowers may argue that they are not precluded from

may limit the borrower to one modification during the life of the loan.[165] Advocates attempting to negotiate a more meaningful modification for the borrower may wish to avoid this issue by taking steps to ensure that the borrower is not automatically put into a fast track modification. If the borrower has already "consented" to the modification by making the two payments before the advocate gets involved, the advocate should advise the servicer that the plan provides that the "fast track option is non-exclusive."[166] Issues related to state law contract formation requirements and statute of frauds should also be raised.

2.10.3 Project Lifeline

On February 12, 2008, six HOPE NOW alliance members announced creation of Project Lifeline.[167] The project grants eligible borrowers a thirty-day delay in the foreclosure proceedings. The borrower must be at least ninety days delinquent, and not less than thirty days from a scheduled foreclosure sale, or in bankruptcy. Any type of loan product including subprime, Alt-A, and prime loans qualify for the program. Second liens and home equity loans are eligible. The project does not apply to properties that are vacant or bought as investment.

The stated purpose of the project is to pause the foreclosure process so the borrower can be evaluated for a loan modification. The modification the borrower may receive is a "trial modification" where the borrower must make three payments under the workout plan before the loan is formally modified.

Project guidelines emphasize that the project is not a moratorium and borrowers will be evaluated for a delay of the proceedings or workout on an individual basis. Given that the delay is not automatic, borrowers should negotiate with the servicer for a more substantial delay of the foreclosure proceedings earlier in the process.[168] Given that many servicers are currently taking at least thirty days to respond to a submitted workout proposal, a sixty-day delay of the proceedings may be more effective in reaching a workout. In addition, as discussed earlier at § 2.3.3, *supra*, an early suspension of the foreclosure proceedings may minimize the costs and fees associated with the process. Any agreement to delay the foreclosure proceedings should be confirmed in writing.

2.11 Workout Options for Fannie Mae and Freddie Mac Loans

2.11.1 Overview

Fannie Mae and Freddie Mac are the common names for two government-sponsored entities (GSEs) created by Congress to provide liquidity in the housing market by purchasing and investing in mortgage loans. Fannie Mae, more formally known as the Federal National Mortgage Association, is the largest of the two corporations and one of the biggest investors in the mortgage marketplace. Like its sister corporation, Freddie Mac, the Federal Home Loan Mortgage Corporation, it buys mortgages from lending institutions and then either holds them in investment portfolios or resells them as mortgage-backed securities to investors. The two corporations suffered significant losses during the financial crisis and were taken over by the federal government in September 2008. Congress created a new agency, the Federal Housing Finance Agency (FHFA), to oversee Fannie Mae, Freddie Mac and the Federal Home Loan Banks.[169]

Fannie Mae and Freddie Mac, as the largest investors in the mortgage marketplace, set the industry standards on workout options. Fannie Mae's workout policy is outlined in the company's *Selling and Servicing Guides* together with their periodic updates. The Fannie Mae *Single-Family Servicing Guide*, which includes a copy of the servicing contract between Fannie Mae and its vendors, is available on-line at www.allregs.com/efnma.[170] As Fannie Mae is the biggest purchaser of mortgages on the secondary market, their guides and workout policies tend to be used generically

---

getting a modification under the federal Home Affordable Modification Program.

165 Freddie Mac's servicer guide, for example, states that to be eligible for a loan modification, the mortgage must "not have been previously modified under our loan modification workout option." *See* Freddie Mac Servicer Guide, vol. 2, § B65.15 (Apr. 14, 2000) (existing mortgage requirements).

166 *See* American Securitization Forum, Streamlined Foreclosure and Loss Avoidance Framework for Securitized Subprime Adjustable Rate Mortgage Loans 5 (Dec. 6, 2007), *available at* www.americansecuritization.com/uploadedFiles/FinalASFStatementonStreamlinedServicingProcedures.pdf.

167 The alliance members are Bank of America, Chase, Citigroup, Countrywide, Washington Mutual, and Wells Fargo. A fact sheet is available at www.fsround.org/hope_now/pdfs/February12-ProjectLifelineOverview.pdf.

168 In Massachusetts for example, the Division of Banks will help homeowners negotiate a sixty-day delay of the foreclosure proceedings. *See* www.mass.gov/?pageID=ocasubtopic&L=6&L0=Home&L1=Consumer&L2=Housing+Information&L3=Foreclosure+Resources&L4=Information+for+Homeowners&L5=If+you+have+received+a+foreclosure+notice+or+a+foreclosure+date+has+been+set&sid=Eoca.

169 On September 6, 2008, the Director of the Federal Housing Finance Agency appointed FHFA as conservator of the GSEs. At that time of the takeover Fannie Mae and Freddie Mac owned or guaranteed almost thirty-one million mortgages, about 58% of all single-family mortgages. These mortgages represented approximately 20% of loans that were seriously delinquent at that time.

170 When using the allregs site, be sure to turn off any pop-up blockers. The guide is updated periodically through Lender Announcements and Lender Letters. These are available at www.efanniemae.com/sf/guides/ssg.

by many servicers, as well as by some lenders acting for themselves. Freddie Mac has its own multi-volume industry publication called the Single-Family Seller/Servicer Guide. This guide is now available on-line at http://freddiemac.com/sell/guide.[171] It is not unreasonable to use the Fannie Mae or Freddie Mac publications as background for making workout proposals to servicers of non-GSE loans.

In addition to the options discussed below, in certain circumstances both Fannie Mae and Freddie Mac will consider a charge-off of the loan instead of foreclosure.[172] A charge-off ceases collection efforts on a mortgage when the debt is deemed to be uncollectible. A small monetary delinquency that is deemed uncollectible accompanied by serious, uninsured damage to the property (i.e., natural disaster, presence of hazardous substance) may lead to a charge-off. All other workout options must be explored before a recommendation for a charge-off is considered.[173]

2.11.2 Fannie Mae and Freddie Mac Home Affordable Modification Programs

Both Fannie Mae and Freddie Mac have implemented their own version of the Home Affordable Modification Program (HAMP).[174] All servicers must evaluate eligible Fannie Mae and Freddie Mac held loans for the program. The structure, requirements, and timeline of the GSEs' programs parallel the first lien portion of HAMP; there is, as yet, no second lien program or alternative to foreclosure program. However, as discussed below, both companies offer other workout options, including options that may be used to address junior liens. In addition, Fannie Mae has established an alternative modification program for those borrowers who were accepted into a HAMP trial period plan, but not offered a HAMP permanent modification because of eligibility restrictions.[175] Freddie Mac developed a similar program, called the HAMP Backup Modification, for borrowers who were initially eligible for a HAMP trial plan, based on stated income, but were subsequently determined ineligible due to underwriting and documentation requirements.[176]

The requirements of Fannie Mae and Freddie Mac HAMP closely track the program developed by the Department of Treasury. Only first-lien mortgages originated on or before January 1, 2009 are eligible.[177] Those mortgages must secure a one to four unit property which is the borrower's principal residence. The home cannot be vacant or condemned.

Borrowers who are current or in danger of defaulting on their mortgage are eligible so long as their monthly mortgage payment is greater than 31% of their monthly gross income.[178] Servicers will use the NPV test developed under the federal HAMP to determine the value of a modification as compared to not modifying the mortgage.

To reach the affordability target of 31% the servicer will employ a standard modification process that capitalizes the arrears, reduces the interest rate (to a floor of 2%), extends the term of the loan by up to forty years; and provides for principal forbearance. The interest rate on the modified loan is capped at the Freddie Mac Primary Mortgage Market Survey rate for thirty-year fixed rate mortgage loans. If the rate on the modified loan is initially reduced below the cap it will be fixed for five years and then adjust upwards 1% per year (or less) until it reaches the interest rate cap at which time it will be fixed for the remaining term of the loan.

The requirements for GSE-HAMP do differ, however, with regard to the determination of imminent default. Servicers must evaluate the borrower's financial condition in light of their stated hardship. Borrowers who are current or less than thirty or thirty-one days delinquent will be assessed using a servicing software that will consider their credit scores, debt-to-income ratios, and property values. Borrowers with cash reserves (non-retirement funds) equal to or exceeding $25,000 are not considered in imminent default.

Like federal HAMP, GSE-HAMP will end December 31, 2012. Servicers must evaluate borrowers for HAMP eligibility before they are considered for the options outlined below.

171 The Single-Family Servicer/Servicer Guide is updated with Bulletins and Industry Letters which are available at http://freddiemac.com/sell/guide/bulletins/.

172 *See* Freddie Mac Single-Family Seller/Servicer Guide, vol. 2, § B65.50; Fannie Mae Single-Family Servicing Guide § VII, 508 (applies to second mortgages).

173 Freddie Mac Single-Family Seller/Servicer Guide, vol. 2, § 65.14.

174 *See* Fannie Mae Single-Family Servicing Guide § VII, 610; Freddie Mac Single-Family Seller/Servicer Guide, vol. 2, § B65.1. For a discussion of HAMP, see § 2.8, *supra*.

175 Fannie Mae Lender Letter, LL-2010-04 (Mar. 18, 2010), *available at* www.efanniemae.com/sf/guides/ssg/annltrs/pdf/2010/ll1004.pdf. To be eligible for this alternative modification, the HAMP trial period plan must have been initiated prior to March 1, 2010, and the borrower must have made all the required payments including subsequent payments that may have been due while the servicer attempted to convert the trial period to a permanent modification.

176 Freddie Mac Bulletin, Number 2010-11 (May 17, 2010), *available at* http://www.freddiemac.com/sell/guide/bulletins/pdf/bll1011.pdf.

177 This includes Fannie Mae's jumbo conforming mortgages which are conventional mortgages sold to Fannie Mae between July 2007 to December 2008 that exceeded the company's loan limits ($417,000 for a one unit property).

178 At least for Fannie Mae's program the items which are included in the monthly mortgage payment are slightly different from the regular program. They include principal, interest, property taxes, hazard insurance, flood insurance, condominium and homeowners association fees (as applicable) and any escrow payment shortage amounts subject to a sixty-month repayment plan.

2.11.3 Other Workout Options for Fannie Mae Loans

2.11.3.1 General

The Fannie Mae *Single-Family Servicing Guide* outlines workout options for loans held by Fannie Mae. Workout options are divided into two classes: (1) special relief measures, for borrowers experiencing a temporary hardship and (2) loss mitigation alternatives, for those experiencing a long-term term or permanent reduction in their ability to support the mortgage. Fannie Mae delegates considerable discretion to its servicers to implement most of these options and servicers are charged with evaluating each borrower's circumstance on a case-by-case basis.[179]

2.11.3.2 The Hardship Requirement

Fannie Mae requires that certain special relief and loss mitigation workout options be offered only to borrowers experiencing a financial hardship. While "hardship" is not specifically defined, the *Single-Family Servicing Guide* gives numerous examples.

In general, the borrower's financial hardship must be the result of an involuntary reduction in income or an unavoidable increase in his or her expenses. Examples include: unemployment or long-term job layoff; mandatory pay reduction; disability or illness that results in a decrease in income or in major medical expenses; death of a family member who made a significant contribution toward the mortgage payment; natural disaster; or decline in a self-employed borrower's earnings. In addition, the servicer should consider any substantial reduction in income that the borrower could not prevent, or other unusual circumstances that are well-documented.[180] However, a borrower may not be eligible if his or her financial hardship results from circumstances that he or she can control or plan ahead for—such as experiencing a normal seasonal layoff, voluntarily quitting a job or reducing the number of hours worked, or reducing (or eliminating) income as a result of returning to school. A further discussion on documenting hardship is included at § 2.6.5, *supra*.

2.11.3.3 Special Relief Measures

Special relief measures are available to borrowers who are experiencing temporary hardship. These workout options are generally granted to borrowers who can quickly bring the mortgage current, or to borrowers who will have a reasonable opportunity to avoid foreclosure by selling their property.[181]

Careful attention should be paid to workouts on second mortgages. Before setting up a special relief plan for a second mortgage, Fannie Mae requires that servicers contact the servicer of the first mortgage to determine the status of that mortgage and any action that servicer is contemplating. The plan will automatically terminate if the first mortgage holder institutes a foreclosure action.

Special relief measures include the following:

Temporary Indulgence. A temporary indulgence is a thirty-day "grace period" to enable the borrower to repay all past-due installments at once. This may be appropriate when the sale of the home is pending or the borrower is expecting a lump-sum settlement from insurance or assistance from a social service agency. The servicer does not need to obtain Fannie Mae's approval before granting this option.[182]

Repayment Plan. Under a repayment plan a borrower must be able to resume regularly scheduled payments and pay additional amounts at scheduled intervals to cure the delinquency. Generally, servicers will limit repayment plans to twelve months, though for certain loans they are allowed to offer repayment terms of up to eighteen months or even longer. A repayment plan lasting more than six months must be in writing.[183] Servicers are expected to waive late fees accrued during the repayment period as long as the borrower remains current on the plan.

Forbearance. A forbearance is a written agreement to reduce or suspend a borrower's monthly payments for a specific period. Forbearance may be offered by itself or in combination with other options, such as a repayment plan or modification. Generally, the forbearance should period should last no longer than six months from the date of the first reduced or suspended payment, though for some mortgages servicers are allowed to offer plans of up to twelve

179 *See* Fannie Mae, Lender Announcement 04-04 (July 30, 2004), *available at* www.efanniemae.com/sf/guides/ssg/annltrs/pdf/2004/04-04.pdf (servicers must apply appropriate judgment in dealing with borrowers and loans on a case-by-case basis, consistent with servicing policy). With respect to special relief measures, the guide states, "we will not object to any reasonable relief plan the servicer develops as long as it does not jeopardize our lien position or reduce the amount of any future claim that we might file with [the mortgage insurer]." Fannie Mae Single-Family Servicing Guide § VII.

180 Fannie Mae provides the following as an example of an unusual circumstance which should be considered favorably: individuals who are not eligible for relief under the Servicemembers Civil Relief Act, but who are nonetheless affected by a call-up of reservists or members of the National Guard—such as individuals who rent their properties to one of these servicemembers, or individuals who receive a substantial portion of their mortgage payment from an individual who has been called-up, but who is not a party to the mortgage.

181 Fannie Mae Single-Family Servicing Guide § VII. Loans in Fannie Mae's MBS pool may be granted forbearance for no more than six consecutive months. Fannie Mae, Lender Announcement 08-07 (Mar. 28, 2008), *available at* www.efanniemae.com/sf/guides/ssg/annltrs/pdf/2008/0807.pdf.

182 Fannie Mae Single-Family Servicing Guide § VII, 301.

183 *Id.* § VII, 404.

months (or longer with Fannie Mae's permission). After the forbearance period is over, the borrower must resume regular monthly payments as well as pay additional funds toward the delinquency at scheduled intervals. If the forbearance is combined with a repayment plan, the combined period may not exceed thirty-six months.[184]

Another type of forbearance agreement—called the Payment Reduction Plan—temporarily reduces a borrower's monthly payment while the servicer works to put a permanent foreclosure prevention option in place. The borrower's monthly principal and interest payment is reduced by up to 30% for up to six months.[185] Only borrowers ineligible for HAMP are offered this option. The mortgage must be a first-lien conventional mortgage originated no less than six months prior to the plan's effective date. The servicer is not allowed to charge any late fees, penalties, stop payment, or similar fees during the term of the plan.

2.11.3.4 Loss Mitigation Alternatives

Loss mitigation alternatives should be considered where the reason for default appears to be long-term or too serious for short-term relief measures. All conventional mortgages are eligible for loss mitigation—including those held by Fannie Mae in portfolio, those purchased for its portfolio but subsequently sold to back a mortgage-backed security (MBS) issue, and those originally delivered as part of an MBS pool. Fannie Mae and the mortgage insurer must approve all loss mitigation alternatives.[186]

Loss mitigation alternatives include the following:

Modification. A loan modification is a written agreement between the servicer and the borrower that permanently changes one or more of the original terms of the note in order to help the borrower bring a defaulted loan current and prevent foreclosure. Fannie Mae will consider modifications that reduce the interest rate on the mortgage, that change the mortgage product (for example, from an adjustable rate mortgage to a fixed rate mortgage at the current market rate), that extend the term of the mortgage, and that capitalize delinquent payments.[187] An MBS pool mortgage can be modified if the borrower is at least four payments behind; loans that Fannie Mae holds in portfolio appear to have no such requirement.[188]

Fannie Mae allows adjustable rate mortgages to remain adjustable rate mortgages when modified, as opposed to changing to fixed rate mortgages.[189] The newly modified mortgage will retain the same adjustable rate features, such as the index, change dates, and limits on interest rate changes, as contained in the original mortgage. However, servicers can recommend modifications of adjustable rate mortgages that extend the term of the mortgage or capitalize delinquent amounts. Fannie Mae does not allow fixed rate mortgages to be modified into adjustable rate mortgages.[190]

The interest rate on the newly modified loan may be reduced to the current market rate or to a below-market interest rate.[191] The interest rate may also be temporary reduced to a below-market interest rate on a fixed rate mortgage, and then gradually increased to a fixed, current market interest rate in a series of steps. The interest rate on adjustable rate mortgages may be gradually increased to a fixed, current market interest rate.[192]

Fannie Mae requires the borrower to make a cash contribution to reduce the delinquency, if financially feasible, before it will agree to modify a conventional mortgage.[193] The servicer can charge the borrower actual out-of-pocket costs to cover expenses for credit report, title, or other documents, if permitted under the terms of the note, security instrument, and applicable law. If the borrower is unable to pay all or a portion of the processing fee, Fannie Mae will consider reimbursing the servicer the difference between what the borrower can pay and the amount of the fee for a portfolio mortgage, or capitalizing all or a part of the fee.[194]

According to Fannie Mae guidelines, a servicer should consider a modification for a delinquent borrower who has experienced a permanent or long-term reduction in income and is unable to continue making the mortgage payments; or if the terms of the mortgage (such as those imposed by a nonstandard adjustable rate mortgage) contribute toward a greater risk of borrower default; or *any other* situation in which changing the terms of the mortgage would cure the delinquency, avoid foreclosure, or prevent future delinquencies.[195]

184 Fannie Mae Single-Family Servicing Guide, § VII, 403.

185 *Id.* § VII, 403.01.

186 With respect to a pre-foreclosure sale, if the proceeds from the transaction and the contribution of the mortgage insurer will fully compensate Fannie Mae, the servicer may negotiate and complete the pre-foreclosure sale without Fannie Mae's involvement. However, a servicer must obtain Fannie Mae's prior approval of any pre-foreclosure sale that will result in a loss to the company. Fannie Mae Single-Family Servicing Guide § VII, 504.

187 Fannie Mae Single-Family Servicing Guide § VII, 502.02; Fannie Mae, Lender Announcement 06-18 (Oct. 4, 2006), *available at* www.efanniemae.com/sf/guides/ssg/annltrs/pdf/2006/06-18.pdf.

188 Fannie Mae Single-Family Servicing Guide § VII, 502.02. *See also* Fannie Mae, Lender Announcement 06-18 (Oct. 4, 2006), *available at* www.efanniemae.com/sf/guides/ssg/annltrs/pdf/2006/06-18.pdf.

189 Fannie Mae Single-Family Servicing Guide § VII, 602. *See also* Fannie Mae, Lender Announcement 06-18 (Oct. 4, 2006), *available at* www.efanniemae.com/sf/guides/ssg/annltrs/pdf/2006/06-18.pdf.

190 Fannie Mae, Lender Announcement 06-18 (Oct. 4, 2006), *available at* www.efanniemae.com/sf/guides/ssg/annltrs/pdf/2006/06-18.pdf.

191 *Id.*

192 *Id.*

193 Fannie Mae Single-Family Servicing Guide § VII, 602.

194 *Id.* § VII, 602.02.

195 *Id.* § VII, 602.

Assumption. Mortgage assumption permits a qualified applicant to assume both the title to the property and the mortgage obligation from a borrower who is currently delinquent in the mortgage payments. An assumption may be considered if the current market value of the property equals or exceeds the unpaid principal balance of the loan plus interest due and expected sales costs. Fannie Mae will also consider granting permission for an assumption when the current market value of the property is slightly less than the outstanding indebtedness since the property purchaser may be willing to make up the difference in cash because of the lower closing costs associated with a mortgage assumption. In all cases, the property purchaser must qualify for the mortgage under Fannie Mae's current underwriting guidelines.[196]

The servicer can charge the purchaser a fee of 1% of the unpaid principal balance with a minimum of $400 and up to a maximum of $900. Servicers, however, cannot charge the purchaser an assumption fee unless it is permitted under the terms of the note, security instrument, and applicable law. Fannie Mae will not approve an assumption on a property with subordinate liens unless they will be paid off.[197]

Pre-Foreclosure Sale. A pre-foreclosure sale is a sale of the property in which Fannie Mae and the borrower agree to accept the proceeds of the sale to satisfy the defaulted mortgage, even though this may be less than the amount owed on the mortgage, in order to avoid foreclosing on the property. The borrower must have experienced some permanent involuntary loss in income and no other relief options will succeed.[198] It is in Fannie Mae's interest to agree to such a sale when the value of the property has declined to less than the amount owed on the mortgage since a market-rate sale is likely to bring a higher return than a foreclosure sale. However, all other workout options must be considered prior to the use of a pre-foreclosure sale procedure.[199] In addition, subordinate lien holders must agree to the pre-foreclosure sale.

When appropriate, the homeowner should request a delay of the foreclosure sale to complete a market sale of the property. Unless a delay is approved, the servicer will continue the foreclosure process even if the property is listed for sale. However, the terms of any pre-foreclosure sale agreement will be honored as long as the property is sold before the foreclosure sale date.[200] Fannie Mae and the insurer must approve the delay of the foreclosure proceedings.[201]

Fannie Mae will pay the servicer an incentive fee of between $750 to $1250 for each pre-foreclosure sale. The amount of the fee the servicer receives will depend on the net proceeds of the sale. In addition, the borrower may receive between $2500 to $5000 in relocation assistance.

Deed in Lieu. Deed in lieu of foreclosure is a workout option in which a borrower voluntarily conveys clear property title to the lender in exchange for a discharge of the debt. Fannie Mae views this as a last resort. Fannie Mae may agree to a deed in lieu when the property has been on the market as a pre-foreclosure sale for at least three months without a reasonable sales offer; there are legal impediments to pursuing foreclosure; or acceptance of a deed in lieu will allow Fannie Mae to obtain title earlier than if a foreclosure action is pursued. The mortgage insurer or guarantor must also agree to acceptance of the deed in lieu.[202]

For each completed deed in lieu for a conventional mortgage, the servicer receives a $1000 incentive fee. The servicer is reimbursed for attorney fees (up to $350) and for the costs for obtaining a title update if the borrower is unable to pay.[203] Borrower are eligible to receive between $2500 to $5000 in relocation assistance.

The company also started a Deed-for-Lease program (called D4L) that allows qualified borrowers of properties transferred through a deed in lieu of foreclosure to remain in their home by executing a twelve month lease.[204] Tenant-occupied properties qualify under this program. To qualify the former homeowner or tenant must be able to pay market rent, not to exceed 31% of his or her monthly gross income. Fannie Mae will set the rent and terms of the lease.

2.11.3.5 Fannie Mae HomeSaver Advance Loan

Under Fannie Mae's HomeSaver Advance program borrowers may receive an unsecured personal loan to bring a delinquent mortgage loan current.[205] The loan can be used to pay delinquent principal, interest, taxes and insurance, and other advances and fees on a first mortgage. The interest rate is fixed at 5% with no payments or interest accruing for the first six months, with a term of fifteen years. Borrowers currently in bankruptcy or who have had debt previously discharged from bankruptcy are not eligible. In addition, borrowers must have surplus income to support an additional monthly payment of at least $200, but not the ability to cure the delinquency through a repayment plan within a nine-month period.

The loan amount is capped: the lesser of $15,000 or 15% of the original unpaid principal balance for delinquent principal, interest, taxes, insurance, escrow advances, advances for attorney fees and costs, and up to six months of unpaid

196 *Id.* § VII, 603.
197 *Id.*
198 *Id.* § VII, 604.01.
199 *Id.* § VII, 604.
200 *Id.* § VII, 604.02.
201 *Id.* § VII, 604.

202 *Id.* § VII,606.
203 *Id.*
204 Fannie Mae, Lender Announcement 09-33 (Nov. 5, 2009), *available at* www.efanniemae.com/sf/guides/ssg/annltrs/pdf/2009/0933.pdf.
205 Information about Fannie Mae's HomeSaver Advance program is available at www.efanniemae.com/sf/servicing/homesaver advance.jsp. The program began in April 2008.

homeowner association fees (twelve months if the association's fees are paid once a year). Late charges and other "ancillary" fees and costs cannot be rolled into the loan. The servicer will receive a $700 workout fee from Fannie Mae for each Advance loan that brings the mortgage current.

The HomeSaver Advance loan can be made in connection with any mortgage loan that is at least six months old and purchased or securitized by Fannie Mae. Investment properties and second homes qualify; owner occupancy is not required. There are also no loan-to-value restrictions or property valuation requirements. This option may only be used once during the term of a first-lien mortgage.

2.11.3.6 Waiver of Late Charges

Under Fannie Mae guidelines the servicer has the discretion, in certain hardship cases, to waive late charges or defer late charges to a future date.[206] If, for example, the interest rate of a mortgage has been reduced to 6% under the terms of the Servicemembers Civil Relief Act, the servicer is expected to waive the collection of late charges during the period for which the reduced interest rate remains in effect.[207]

2.11.4 Freddie Mac Loans

2.11.4.1 In General

Freddie Mac divides its workout options into three broad categories: reinstatements, relief options, and workout options. Relief options provide a borrower with temporary relief and will cure a delinquency over a defined period of time. The workout options lead to a long-term cure of the delinquency or transfer of property other than through a foreclosure sale. Freddie Mac compensates servicers for implementing certain options.[208]

2.11.4.2 The Hardship Requirement

In general, to be considered for a workout, a borrower must be delinquent in his or her mortgage payments, or be in imminent danger of default. In most instances, workout options may be offered only to borrowers experiencing an involuntary reduction of income or increase in expenses. Borrowers do not have to demonstrate hardship for relief options with repayment plans twelve months or less in duration.[209] Manufactured-home owners are also not required to demonstrate hardship for many relief or workout options.

Examples of an involuntary reduction in income include unemployment or a mandatory pay reduction,[210] underemployment following a previous job loss, death of a borrower or primary wage earner in the household, decline in business earnings for a self-employed borrower, incarceration of a spouse or co-borrower, illness, disability, separation, divorce, and natural or man-made disaster.[211]

Unavoidable increase in expenses may result from an unanticipated repair that affects the value or habitability of the property, overextension on credit resulting from a borrower using credit to pay his or her mortgage payments, medical debt, food expenses or utility bills.[212]

2.11.4.3 Reinstatement

Servicers are required to pursue reinstatement as the first option for resolving a delinquency.[213] A reinstatement occurs when a borrower pays all delinquent mortgage payments and past-due amounts, making the mortgage current. A borrower may reinstate a delinquent mortgage at any time, even after foreclosure proceedings begin or while a relief or workout plan is in progress. In general, the servicer need not seek Freddie Mac's approval to process a reinstatement. However, the servicer must follow Freddie Mac guidelines which do not give the servicer the discretion to reject a reinstatement if the borrower meets the terms outlined by the company in the *Single-Family Seller/Servicer Guide*.[214]

In a *full reinstatement*, the borrower restores a delinquent mortgage to current status by paying the total amount delinquent (including advances, accrued interest, legal costs, and other expenses allowed by the security agreement and state law).[215] Under Freddie Mac guidelines, the servicer

206 If the servicer chooses to defer late charges, it cannot foreclose the mortgage later if the only delinquent amount is unpaid late charges. Fannie Mae Single-Family Servicing Guide § VII, 201.

207 Fannie Mae Single-Family Servicing Guide § VII, 201.

208 Freddie Mac Single-Family Seller/Servicer Guide, vol. 2, § 65.42. Servicer compensation was increased. *See* Freddie Mac Bulletin (July 31, 2008), *available at* www.freddiemac.com/sell/guide/bulletins/pdf/bll073108.pdf.

209 Freddie Mac Single-Family Seller/Servicer Guide, vol. 2, § 65.15.

210 The mandatory pay reduction could result from elimination of overtime, reduction in regular working hours, or a reduction in base pay.

211 Freddie Mac Single-Family Seller/Servicer Guide, vol. 2, § 65.17.

212 *Id.*

213 *Id. at* vol. 2, § 65.6.

214 *See id.* at vol. 2, § A65.8.

215 A servicer may not refuse to accept a full reinstatement if the borrower offers to pay all amounts due except for the cost of the BPO, inspection fees and accrued late charges. Freddie Mac requires the servicer to make arrangements with the borrower to pay the late charges after the mortgage is reinstated. If the borrower can pay all arrearages, inspection fees and costs, except for the cost of the BPO, Freddie Mac may waive collection of the BPO costs. *See* Freddie Mac Single-Family Seller/Servicer Guide, vol. 2, § A65.8.

In addition, the fees that the servicer can pass on to the homeowner are capped. *See* Freddie Mac Single-Family Seller/

does not have the discretion to reject a full reinstatement if the payment includes the total amount delinquent (including accrued interest, unpaid principal, actual legal costs and advances), but not other expenses incurred such as the cost of a broker's price opinion (BPO), inspection fees, and accrued late charges.[216]

In a *partial reinstatement*, the borrower pays an amount less than the total due, including advances, legal fees, and expenses (except accrued late charges), and executes a repayment plan for the remainder.[217] The repayment period may last up to twelve months if there is an escrow account on the mortgage. If there is no escrow account the servicer must establish one and then may extend the repayment period up to eighteen months without Freddie Mac's approval. The borrower completely reinstates the mortgage when he or she pays all of the payments specified in the repayment plan. The servicer must accept partial reinstatement of the mortgage if the borrower pays, at a minimum, all outstanding legal fees and related expenses, plus the first payment due under the repayment plan. In addition, the borrower must execute a written repayment plan for the remaining delinquent interest, principal and escrow (if applicable) and the scheduled monthly payments.[218]

2.11.4.4 Relief Options

Relief options allow borrowers to gradually pay back delinquent amounts or temporarily reduce the amount of the mortgage payment or temporarily stop making mortgage payments. All relief options must result in the borrower bringing his or her mortgage current or paying the mortgage in full. Freddie Mac will consider proposals from borrowers who do not meet the eligibility requirements for a proposed relief option if the relief option is the best possible solution to cure the delinquency.[219]

Relief Options include the following:

Repayment Plan. A repayment plan is an agreement that gives the borrower a fixed amount of time to bring delinquent mortgage payments current by paying the normal monthly payment plus an additional amount.[220] A repayment plan can stand alone as a relief option or can be combined with short-term forbearance, long-term forbearance, or a partial reinstatement. If a repayment plan stands alone, the repayment period must not last longer than twelve months from the date of the agreement, unless approved by Freddie Mac. If the repayment period lasts more than three months and the borrower is ninety or more days delinquent, the borrower must be experiencing (or have experienced) financial hardship or have a signed sales contract to sell the home. If a repayment plan is combined with another relief option, the maximum repayment period can vary. Servicers are compensated $250 for successful plans on mortgages that are sixty or more days delinquent.[221]

Short-term forbearance. A short-term forbearance is a written agreement to temporarily let a borrower reduce or suspend monthly payments during the forbearance period. Payments may be suspended for up to three months or reduced for up to six months from the date of the agreement. At the end of the forbearance period, the borrower must bring the mortgage current through payment in full or begin a repayment plan (lasting no longer than twelve months from the due date of the last paid installment), or pay off the mortgage in full.[222] To qualify, a borrower must meet the financial hardship criteria or have a signed sales contract for the sale of the home. Freddie Mac's approval is not necessary.

Long-term forbearance. A long-term forbearance is an agreement to temporarily let a borrower reduce or suspend mortgage payments during the forbearance period which may last up to twelve months from the date of the agreement. At the end of the forbearance period, the borrower must either bring the mortgage current, begin a repayment plan (lasting no longer than twelve months from when the forbearance ends), or pay off the mortgage in full. Long-term forbearances are typically granted when the property was damaged by a disaster, causing financial hardship; a borrower is waiting for an outstanding major medical claim, causing financial hardship; a borrower is deceased and the estate is in probate; or a law suit is pending that may jeopardize Freddie Mac's lien position. Freddie Mac must approve this option.[223]

2.11.4.5 Workout Options

A workout option enables the borrower to address a long-term or permanent reduction in income which may make homeownership not sustainable or to complete a transfer of the home short of foreclosure. Freddie Mac will consider workout proposals that do not meet published guidelines if the option is the best solution to resolve the delinquency. Approval from Freddie Mac and the mortgage insurer is required for most workout options.

Servicer Guide, vol. 2, § A65.7, Exhibits 57 and 57A (approved attorney fees and title expenses).

216 Freddie Mac Single-Family Seller/Servicer Guide, vol. 2, § A65.8.

217 *Id. at* vol. 2, § A65.7.

218 *Id. at* vol. 2, § A65.9.

219 *Id. at* vol. 2, § A65.1.

220 The plan must be in writing if it exceeds three months. The plan may include accrued late charges. The servicer cannot accrue or collect late charges from the borrower during the repayment plan if the borrower is paying as agreed. Freddie Mac Single-Family Seller/Servicer Guide, vol. 2, § A65.16.

221 Freddie Mac Bulletin No. 2006-5 (Dec. 15, 2006), *available at* www.freddiemac.com/sell/guide/bulletins/pdf/bll065.pdf.

222 Freddie Mac Single-Family Seller/Servicer Guide, vol. 2, § A65.18.

223 *Id. at* vol. 2, § A65.24.

Workout options include the following:

Modification. A loan modification is a written agreement between the servicer and the borrower that permanently changes one or more of the original terms of the note. Freddie Mac will consider reducing the interest rate, changing the term or type of mortgage, and capitalizing the arrears. However, no write-off or permanent reduction of the unpaid principal balance is allowed.[224] Freddie Mac will consider a modification for first-lien loans at least twelve months old at the time of application. Freddie Mac will also consider a loan modification on a second mortgage if the existing lien status will be maintained.[225] The borrower must show financial hardship or an allowable reason to warrant the modification. The borrower must have a stable income to support some level of monthly payment.[226] Servicers may not charge the borrower a fee for modifying the loan.[227] In addition, the prohibition against modifying a mortgage that has been previously modified under Freddie Mac's guidelines, has been removed.[228] Approval from Freddie Mac and the mortgage insurer is required.

Assumption. A mortgage assumption permits a qualified applicant to assume both the title to the property and the mortgage obligation from a borrower who is currently delinquent in the mortgage payments (or in imminent danger of default). The current borrower must show financial hardship.[229] The servicer may charge the applicant a fee not to exceed the greater of $400 or 1% of the unpaid principal balance of the mortgage, to a maximum fee of $900. The applicant must pay a down payment of at least 5% of the total indebtedness.[230] Approval from Freddie Mac and the mortgage insurer is required.

Short Payoff. A short payoff is the sale of the property for less than the total amount necessary to satisfy the mortgage obligation. The borrower must have the property listed for sale at the current market price and show financial hardship.[231] Freddie Mac will also consider this option if the borrower defaults on a modification plan. Approval from Freddie Mac and the mortgage insurer is required.[232]

Deed in Lieu. A deed in lieu of foreclosure is a workout option in which a borrower voluntarily conveys clear property title to Freddie Mac in exchange for a discharge of the debt. The servicer must determine that no other relief or workout options are appropriate and the property has not significantly deteriorated.[233] Approval from Freddie Mac and the mortgage insurer is required.

2.11.4.6 Charge-Offs

Freddie Mac will consider a charge-off of a mortgage loan that has an unpaid principal balance of $5000 or less and is 120 days or more delinquent.[234] Properties that have been condemned due to deterioration, a disaster, or a hazardous substance are also eligible if it is not economically feasible to repair the property and the land has little or no value. Generally, a charge-off ends collection efforts on the mortgage but does not cancel the note or release the lien on the property. However, the borrower can negotiate an amount for the release of the lien. Freddie Mac may agree to charge-off the debt and release the lien.[235]

2.11.4.7 Late Charges and Other Fees

The servicer is prohibited from charging additional fees to the borrower other than those approved by Freddie Mac for each relief or workout option. In addition, the servicer may not refuse to consider a workout option or require payment of accrued late charges as a condition of doing a workout.[236]

2.12 Workout Options for HUD, VA, and RHS Loans

2.12.1 HUD Loans

2.12.1.1 General

Regulations and guidelines issued by the Department of Housing and Urban Development (HUD) require that HUD-approved lenders consider alternatives to foreclosure within ninety days of the date of default.[237] However, HUD does

224 *Id. at* vol. 2, § B65.11.

225 *Id. at* vol. 2, § B65.15.

226 Loan modification expenses include fees for notary, title, recordation, legal assistance, home inspection and BPO. Some of these fees are capped. The borrower is generally expected to pay half of the expenses and other amounts due, or reduce the amount to three months of delinquent interest payments. However, if the borrower is unable to pay the expenses, the amount can be capitalized and in some instances the mortgage insurer may pay all or a portion of the amount due. Freddie Mac Single-Family Seller/Servicer Guide, vol. 2, §§ B65.14, 23.

227 Freddie Mac Bulletin (July 31, 2008) *available at* www.freddiemac.com/sell/guide/bulletins/pdf/bll073108.pdf.

228 *Id.*

229 Freddie Mac Single-Family Seller/Servicer Guide,vol. 2, § B65.49.

230 *Id. at* vol. 2, § B65.29.

231 *Id. at* vol. 2, § B65.36.

232 The servicer does not need to obtain Freddie Mac's approval for this option if the sale proceeds are less than the total amount due, but a mortgage insurance claim payment or a borrower contribution results in the company receiving all sums owed on the mortgage. Freddie Mac Single-Family Seller/Servicer Guide, vol. 2, § B65.35.

233 *Id. at* vol. 2, § B65.43.

234 Freddie Mac Single-Family Seller/Servicer Guide, vol. 2, § B65.50.

235 *Id.*

236 *Id. at* vol. 2, § 65.43.

237 Notice to the homeowner on foreclosure prevention options together with a HUD brochure on that topic must be sent

not require that lenders actually accomplish workouts with homeowners. Lenders need only consider foreclosure avoidance tools. Once they do so, lenders can then proceed to foreclosure if they so choose.[238]

The requirements of HUD's Loss Mitigation Program are outlined in detail in a January 2000 letter HUD sent to all approved lenders and servicers to clarify the program's policy and procedures.[239] Although portions of this letter have been updated by subsequently issued letters, Mortgagee Letter 00-05 still contains the most comprehensive and detailed outline of current workout requirements for FHA-insured loans.[240] Advocates should consult Mortgagee Letter 00-05 and other letters updating its provisions when assisting a homeowner with a FHA-insured loan.

2.12.1.2 Special Forbearance

Homeowners may be eligible for two types of special forbearance if they experienced a verifiable reduction in income or an increase in living expenses, and the lender determines the borrower has a reasonable ability to pay under the terms of such an agreement. Lenders may enter into these agreements with homeowners without prior approval by HUD.[241] For both types of forbearance, borrowers must be a minimum of three payments behind.

A Type I special forbearance allows homeowners to reduce or suspend payments for a defined period of time so long as the arrearage does not exceed the equivalent of twelve monthly mortgage payments. At the end of the forbearance period, the homeowner must typically begin paying at least the full amount of the monthly mortgage payment due under the mortgage. The repayment period must last at least four months, but otherwise lenders and homeowners are free to agree to any repayment plan for the accumulated arrears throughout the remaining term of the loan.[242] There is no maximum length of time to repay.

The repayment plan may include accrued foreclosure costs and late fees. However, these fees may only be collected after the loan has been reinstated through collection of principal, interest, and escrow advances. The loan cannot be considered delinquent because the borrower has not paid late fees or other foreclosure costs.[243]

HUD updated the special forbearance option to make it easier for homeowners who are unemployed and have a reasonable prospect of reemployment to use this option. Lenders may now enter special forbearance agreements with homeowners who have good payment records and a stable employment history, but have not received a commitment of employment at the time the lender reviews their financial information. Homeowners may be required to make partial payments based on their ability to pay and they are required to actively seek employment during the term of the reduced payments.[244] The lender is required to verify the homeowner's employment status monthly and renegotiate the terms of the special forbearance plan when the homeowner's employment status changes.

---

between the thirty-fifth and the forty-fifth day of delinquency. *See* Dep't of Hous. & Urban Dev., Mortgagee Letter 00-05 (Jan. 19, 2000), *available at* www.hud.gov/offices/adm/hudclips/letters/mortgagee/files/00-05.doc; Dep't of Hous. & Urban Dev., Mortgagee Letter 97-44 (Sept. 29, 1997), *available at* www.hud.gov/offices/adm/hudclips/letters/mortgagee/files/97-44ml.txt. *See also* 12 U.S.C. § 1715u (requiring lenders to engage in loss mitigation activities specified by HUD).

The mortgagee letters and other HUD materials referenced in this section and periodic updates are currently available on the Internet at www.hud.gov.

238 Denial of a request to participate in the loss mitigation program is not subject to judicial review. Dean v. Dep't of Hous. & Urban Dev., 2000 WL 575576 (W.D.N.Y. Mar. 14, 2000).

239 Dep't of Hous. & Urban Dev., Mortgagee Letter 00-05 (Jan. 19, 2000), *available at* www.hud.gov/offices/adm/hudclips/letters/mortgagee/files/00-05.doc. *See also* periodic updates to this letter contained in: Dep't of Hous. & Urban Dev., Mortgagee Letter 2005-18 (Apr. 26, 2005), *available at* www.hud.gov/offices/adm/hudclips/letters/mortgagee/files/05-18ml.doc; Dep't of Hous. & Urban Dev., Mortgagee Letter 2003-19 (Nov. 20, 2003), *available at* www.hud.gov/offices/adm/hudclips/letters/mortgagee/files/03-19ml.doc; Dep't of Hous. & Urban Dev., Mortgagee Letter 2002-17 (Aug. 29, 2002), *available at* www.hud.gov/offices/adm/hudclips/letters/mortgagee/files/ml02-17.doc (supersedes portion of Mortgagee Letter 00-05 which discusses special forbearance); Dep't of Hous. & Urban Dev., Mortgagee Letter 2002-13 (June 7, 2002), *available at* www.hud.gov/offices/adm/hudclips/letters/mortgagee/files/02-13ml.doc; Dep't of Hous. & Urban Dev., Mortgagee Letter 2001-14 (May 23, 2001), *available at* www.hud.gov/offices/adm/hudclips/letters/mortgagee/files/01-14ml.doc.

240 *See* § 3.2.2, *infra* (discussing Mortgagee Letter 2008-32 (Oct. 17, 2008) making significant revisions to provisions of Mortgagee Letter 2000-05 related to the availability of FHA loss mitigation to homeowners in bankruptcy).

241 24 C.F.R. § 203.614 was completely altered to eliminate the previous *regulatory* conditions to granting a special forbearance. The new version of § 203.614 simply gives the mortgage holder the authority to grant special forbearance if the default is due to circumstances beyond the control of the homeowner upon the conditions "prescribed by HUD." This leaves HUD the latitude to change the provisions of this tool through mortgagee letters without first going through the notice and comment process required to change regulations. Thus, advocates should look to: Dep't of Hous. & Urban Dev., Mortgagee Letter 2002-17 (Aug. 29, 2002), *available at* www.hud.gov/offices/adm/hudclips/letters/mortgagee/files/ml02-17.doc; Dep't of Hous. & Urban Dev., Mortgagee Letter 2001-14 (May 23, 2001), *available at* www.hud.gov/offices/adm/hudclips/letters/mortgagee/files/01-14ml.doc; Dep't of Hous. & Urban Dev., Mortgagee Letter 00-05 (Jan. 19, 2000), *available at* www.hud.gov/offices/adm/hudclips/letters/mortgagee/files/00-05.doc; as well as any updates to determine the conditions under which a special forbearance can be granted.

242 Dep't of Hous. & Urban Dev., Mortgagee Letter 2002-17 (Aug. 29, 2002), *available at* www.hud.gov/offices/adm/hudclips/letters/mortgagee/files/ml02-17.doc.

243 *Id.*

244 *Id.*

A Type II special forbearance combines a short-term special forbearance plan, typically three months, and a modification or partial claim. This short-term special forbearance is used by HUD to assess the homeowner's ability to support the debt. During this "trial period" the amount of the monthly payment will generally not exceed the homeowner's normal monthly payment.

All special forbearance agreements must be in writing. A homeowner can negotiate a special forbearance agreement even if foreclosure proceedings have started.[245]

2.12.1.3 Streamline Refinance

Borrowers who are current on an existing FHA-insured loan may be able to refinance with a new FHA-insured loan and reduce monthly payments through the streamline refinance option.[246] The new FHA insured loan may be made by the original lender or a different lender who participates in the FHA insurance program. An eligible refinance must provide some net tangible benefit to the homeowner. The benefit can be in the form of a reduction in the total payment for principal and interest, replacement of an adjustable rate mortgage with a fixed rate mortgage, or reduction of the term of the mortgage.[247] Refinance may be approved without an appraisal and without consideration of loan-to-value ratio. The borrower cannot receive any funds out of the refinance, either directly or for payment of other debts. There is no new risk to the lender or to HUD as guarantor in this type of refinancing because it replaces one guaranteed loan with another having essentially the same principal balance. There is, however, a significant limitation on eligibility for the streamline refinance. Borrowers who have been paying on their loan for at least one year must have experienced no more than one thirty-day late payment in the preceding twelve months and have made all payments within the month due for the three months prior to the date of application.[248] This option may work well for borrowers who are current in payments and whose original interest rate was higher than current market levels. Some closing costs may be financed.

245 In order for a lender to be eligible for an incentive payment from HUD, it must execute the special forbearance no earlier than after three missed payments. Dep't of Hous. & Urban Dev., Mortgagee Letter 2002-17 (Aug. 29, 2002), *available at* www.hud.gov/offices/adm/hudclips/letters/mortgagee/files/ml02-17.doc; Dep't of Hous. & Urban Dev., Mortgagee Letter 2001-14 (May 23, 2001), *available at* www.hud.gov/offices/adm/hudclips/letters/mortgagee/files/01-14ml.doc.

246 HUD Handbook 4155.1 Ch. 6.C; Dep't Hous. & Urban Dev., Mortgagee Letter 2009-32 (Sept. 18, 2009), *available at* www.hud.gov/offices/adm/hudclips/letters/mortgagee/files/09-32ml.doc (revised streamline refinance transactions).

247 Dep't Hous. & Urban. Dev., Mortgagee Letter 2009-32 (Sept. 18, 2009), *available at* www.hud.gov/offices/adm/hudclips/letters/mortgagee/files/09-32ml.doc.

248 *Id.*

2.12.1.4 Partial Claims

Lenders may make a claim to HUD in the amount of no more than the equivalent of twelve monthly mortgage payments accumulated during a period of forbearance.[249] To be eligible for a partial claim: the homeowner must be at least four months behind; the amount of the arrearage cannot exceed the equivalent of twelve monthly mortgage payments; the homeowner must be able to resume making full monthly mortgage payments; and a special forbearance or loan modification will not resolve the delinquency. Legal fees and costs related to a canceled foreclosure action can be incorporated into a partial claim.[250] However, these fees and costs must reflect work actually completed and meet HUD guidelines for reasonable attorney fees. Although lenders do not have to seek HUD's approval prior to advancing funds to the homeowner, they must follow the guidelines outlined in HUD's Mortgagee Letters.[251]

If eligible, HUD will then pay the arrearage to the lender. The homeowner must give HUD an interest-free mortgage in the amount of the arrears which generally will not require repayment until a transfer of ownership of the property or payoff of the first mortgage. The mortgage to secure the partial claim amount need not be a second mortgage. HUD will accept subordination to any other valid liens on the property.

A partial claim may be utilized as a stand alone tool or may be combined with the special forbearance option. In addition, an existing special forbearance plan may be converted to a partial claim if the homeowner's circumstances change and he or she is unable to meet the terms of the agreement. However, a partial claim cannot be combined with a mortgage modification.[252]

2.12.1.5 Mortgage modification

As an option distinct from the FHA-HAMP loan modification program discussed at § 2.12.1.6, *infra*, HUD has traditionally offered loan modification as a standard fore-

249 24 C.F.R. § 203.371; Dep't of Hous. & Urban Dev., Mortgagee Letter 2003-19 (Nov. 20, 2003), *available at* www.hud.gov/offices/adm/hudclips/letters/mortgagee/files/03-19ml.doc; Dep't of Hous. & Urban Dev., Mortgagee Letter 00-05 (Jan. 19, 2000), *available at* www.hud.gov/offices/adm/hudclips/letters/mortgagee/files/00-05.doc; Dep't of Hous. & Urban Dev., Mortgagee Letter 2001-14 (May 23, 2001), *available at* www.hud.gov/offices/adm/hudclips/letters/mortgagee/files/01-14ml.doc.

250 Dep't of Hous. & Urban Dev. Mortgagee Letter 2008-21 (Aug. 14, 2008), *available at* www.hud.gov/offices/adm/hudclips/letters/mortgagee/files/08-21ml.doc.

251 *See* Dep't of Hous. & Urban Dev., Mortgagee Letter 2003-19 (Nov. 20, 2003), *available at* www.hud.gov/offices/adm/hudclips/letters/mortgagee/files/03-19ml.doc.

252 Dep't of Hous. & Urban Dev., Mortgagee Letter 2003-19 (Nov. 20, 2003), *available at* www.hud.gov/offices/adm/hudclips/letters/mortgagee/files/03-19ml.doc.

closure avoidance tool. The intent of a modification is to eliminate an arrearage and to reduce monthly mortgage payments for homeowners who have recovered from financial distress but whose net income has been reduced to a level lower than it was before the default.[253] Borrowers must be three or more monthly payments behind.

Lenders may reamortize the arrearage over the remaining term of the loan, or may extend the term not more than ten years beyond the original maturity date or thirty years, whichever is less.[254] In recent directives, HUD has set new requirements designed to ensure that a modification under this option actually reduces monthly payments instead of simply capitalizing past due amounts and creating a higher payment.[255] To ensure future affordability, a mortgage holder's eligibility for an incentive payment for modification is now tied to reduction of the interest rate to a level not more than fifty basis points above the Freddie Mac Weekly Primary Market Survey Rate.[256] In addition, the mortgage holder must extend the reamortization period to 360 months from the due date of the first installment under the modified loan.[257]

A mortgage modification may not, however, be used in conjunction with a partial claim.[258] A modification may be used in conjunction with a special forbearance. The previous requirement that a homeowner can be eligible for a loan modification only if the default is caused by circumstances beyond the control of the homeowner has been deleted.[259] Thus, a lender can now agree to a loan modification regardless of the reason for the delinquency.

253 Dep't of Hous. & Urban Dev., Mortgagee Letter 00-05 (Jan. 19, 2000), *available at* www.hud.gov/offices/adm/hudclips/letters/mortgagee/files/00-05.doc.

254 23 C.F.R. § 203.616; Dep't of Hous. & Urban Dev., Mortgagee Letter 00-05 (Jan. 19, 2000), *available at* www.hud.gov/offices/adm/hudclips/letters/mortgagee/files/00-05.doc.

255 Dep't of Hous. & Urban Dev., Mortgagee Letter 2009-23 (Sept. 23, 2009), *available at* www.hud.gov/offices/adm/hudclips/letters/mortgagee/files/09-23ml.doc and http://www.hud.gov/offices/adm/hudclips/letters/mortgagee/files/09-25mlatch.doc; Mortgagee Letter 2008-22 (Aug. 14, 2008), *available at* www.hud.gov/offices/adm/hudclips/letters/mortgagee/files/08-21ml.doc.

256 Dep't of Hous. & Urban Dev., Mortgagee Letter 2009-23 (Sept. 23, 2009), *available at* www.hud.gov/offices/adm/hudclips/letters/mortgagee/files/09-23ml.doc and http://www.hud.gov/offices/adm/hudclips/letters/mortgagee/files/09-25mlatch.doc.

257 *Id.*

258 Dep't of Hous. & Urban Dev., Mortgagee Letter 00-05 (Jan. 19, 2000), *available at* www.hud.gov/offices/adm/hudclips/letters/mortgagee/files/00-05.doc. *But see* § 2.12.1.6, *infra* (allowing partial claim and modification within the parameters of this special program).

259 Compare the former 24 C.F.R. § 203.616 with the amended version.

2.12.1.6 FHA-HAMP

The Department of Treasury's guidelines for the Home Affordable Program (HAMP) are discussed earlier in this chapter. While most home mortgage servicers signed on to participate in HAMP during 2009, the Treasury Department's general HAMP guidelines do not apply to mortgages originated under federally guaranteed loan programs such as those administered by FHA, VA, and RHS. Instead, the Treasury guidelines indicated that these agencies would implement their own versions of the HAMP loan modification program.[260] HUD announced its version, called FHA-HAMP, in July 2009.[261] The program applies only to FHA-insured mortgages. FHA-HAMP combines two of FHA's existing loss mitigation tools—mortgage modification and the partial claim. To be eligible, the homeowner must be at least one, but not more than twelve, monthly mortgage payment in arrears. The current payment for interest, principal, taxes, and insurance must take up at least 31% of the borrowers' gross monthly income. Other FHA loss mitigation options, including special forbearance, loan modification, and partial claim, must be ineffective for preserving homeownership.

FHA-HAMP modifies a loan by creating a new kind of partial claim. As with the lien created under the traditional FHA partial claim, the FHA-HAMP lien does not bear interest. It consists of two components.[262] One part includes the arrearage due on the mortgage (unpaid interest, principal, and foreclosure costs). The other part is an additional lien created by reducing the interest-bearing loan principal to an amount needed to lower the new mortgage payment so that it will not take up more than 31% of the household's gross monthly income. This interest-free FHA-HAMP lien must be paid off through a later refinancing or sale of the property. The total amount of the FHA-HAMP lien cannot exceed an amount equal to 30% of the outstanding principal balance at the time the partial claim is created.

FHA-HAMP has features in common with Treasury's basic HAMP program. For example, the FHA-HAMP modification achieves an affordable payment by putting part of the mortgage principal in "forbearance," by reducing the interest rate, and by extending the loan term. A later HUD Mortgagee Letter sets an interest rate cap for FHA-HAMP. The cap is tied to the Freddie Mac Weekly Primary Mortgage Market Survey Rate for thirty-year fixed rate mortgages at the time of the FHA-HAMP modification.[263] Be-

260 Dep't of Treasury, HAMP Supplemental Directive 09-01, at 3 (Apr. 6, 2009), *available at* www.hmpadmin.com//portal/programs/hamp/servicer.html.

261 Dep't of Hous. & Urban Dev., Mortgagee Letter 2009-23 (July 30, 2009), *available at* www.hud.gov/offices/adm/hudclips/letters/mortgagee/files/09-23ml.doc and www.hud.gov/offices/adm/hudclips/letters/mortgagee/files/09-23mlatach.doc.

262 *Id.*

263 Dep't of Hous. & Urban Dev., Mortgagee Letter 2009-35 (Sept.

fore the FHA-HAMP modification is made permanent, the homeowner must make payments on time at the new payment level for a three-month trial period. Servicers receive a financial incentive payment from HUD in the amount of $1250 when they implement a modification under FHA-HAMP. In addition, servicers who sign participation agreements with the Treasury Department's agent (Fannie Mae) are entitled to receive additional incentive payments of up to $1000 annually for the initial three years of a borrower's successful performance under the modified loan.[264] Borrowers receive similar incentives applied to principal reduction if they satisfy payment requirements during the first three years.

There are, however, differences between the two programs. FHA-HAMP does not involve a net present value analysis that compares the relative costs of a loan modification to the costs of a foreclosure. An FHA-HAMP modification will not be approved if, after modification, the homeowner's payments on the first mortgage plus any junior liens and all other installment debts take up more than 55% of the household's gross monthly income.[265] This difference can be important because under the Treasury's HAMP program this total post-modification debt-to-income ratio is only relevant in triggering a requirement that the homeowner receive credit counseling. Another difference between FHA-HAMP and the Treasury's HAMP program is that the interest rate set at the beginning of the FHA-HAMP modification remains the fixed rate for the full term of the loan. The rate does not increase in steps after five years, as occurs under the Treasury program.

2.12.1.7 Pre-Foreclosure Sale

Lenders have the option of resolving incurable defaults by offering homeowners who cannot meet their monthly obligations the opportunity to sell their property through pre-foreclosure sales.[266] Other home retention alternatives such as forbearance, modification, and partial claim should have been considered and determined unlikely to succeed due to the borrower's financial condition. The proceeds of the sale will satisfy the mortgage debt even if the proceeds are less than the amount owed. If the homeowner completes the sale within the required timeframe, they will be paid a cash consideration of up to $1000. Unlike other options, homeowners wishing to use this option must submit an application and receive permission from HUD to conduct a pre-foreclosure sale. To be eligible for a pre-foreclosure sale HUD requires the following:[267]

- The home's "as is" appraised value must be at least 63% of the total amount due on the mortgage (minimum sales proceeds amounts are based on a tiered schedule depending on length of time the property is marketed);
- The borrower must have negative equity, meaning an "as is" appraisal that indicates a property value less than 100% of the outstanding mortgage balance, including any outstanding partial claim amounts.
- The net sales price must be at least 84% of the home's "as is" appraised value;[268]
- The loan need only be thirty days in arrears; and
- The homeowner has four months to sell but this may be extended an additional two months if the lender scores in the top twenty-fifth percentile on its annual performance reviews or if the borrower has a signed contract of sale but closing has not occurred by the end of the initial four months.[269]

A pre-foreclosure sale will be reported to the national credit bureaus as a "short sale" and the lender is required to file Form 1099-A with the Internal Revenue Service (IRS) and report any discharge of indebtedness.

2.12.1.8 Deed in Lieu

A voluntary transfer of the property can be considered when the homeowner is in default and does not qualify for any other loss mitigation option, or upon a failure of a pre-foreclosure sale. As with any deed in lieu, an important prerequisite is that there are no other junior liens on the property. The homeowner will be paid $2000 after leaving the property, assuming there are no junior liens on the property. If there are liens, the $2000 to be paid to the homeowner may be diverted to pay off junior liens in order to clear the title.[270]

23, 2009), *available at* www.hud.gov/offices/adm/hudclips/letters/mortgagee/files/09-35ml.doc.

264 Dep't of Hous. & Urban Dev., Mortgagee Letter 2010-04 (Mar. 26, 2010), *available at* www.hud.gov/offices/adm/hudclips/letters/mortgagee/files/10-04ml.pdf; Dep't of Treasury, HAMP Supplemental Directive 10-03 (Mar. 26, 2010), *available at* www.hmpadmin.com/portal/docs/fha_hamp/sd1003.pdf.

265 Dep't of Hous. & Urban Dev., Mortgagee Letter 2009-23 (July 30, 2009), *available at* www.hud.gov/offices/adm/hudclips/letters/mortgagee/files/09-23ml.doc and www.hud.gov/offices/adm/hudclips/letters/mortgagee/files/09-23mlatach.doc (attachment—guidelines for the fha-home affordable modification program).

266 Dep't of Hous. & Urban Dev. , Mortgagee Letter 2008-43 (Dec. 24, 2008), *available at* www.hud.gov/offices/adm/hudclips/letters/mortgagee/2008ml.cfm.

267 Dep't of Hous. & Urban Dev., Mortgagee Letter 2008-43 (Dec. 24, 2008), *available at* www.hud.gov/offices/adm/hudclips/letters/mortgagee/2008ml.cfm.

268 This puts a premium on minimizing real estate broker fees and other costs of sale.

269 Dep't of Hous. & Urban Dev., Mortgagee Letter 2008-43 (Dec. 24, 2008), *available at* www.hud.gov/offices/adm/hudclips/letters/mortgagee/2008ml.cfm. *See* § 2.7.1.3, *supra* (loss mitigation performance reviews).

270 Dep't of Hous. & Urban Dev., Mortgagee Letter 00-05 (Jan. 19, 2000), *available at* www.hud.gov/offices/adm/hudclips/letters/

2.12.1.9 Incentives for Lenders

The regulations and the mortgagee letter provide incentives to lenders who use mortgage foreclosure alternatives. HUD will pay the lenders $100 for each special forbearance agreement executed, whether or not it is successful.[271] This amount can increase to $200 if the lender ranks in the top 25% in relation to other lenders, based upon its overall loss mitigation performance.[272] Lenders will receive $750 for each completed loan modification; $500 for each partial claim; and $1000 each time the lender facilitates a successful pre-foreclosure sale.[273] This payment is in addition to reimbursement for expenses such as the cost of an appraisal, title search or recording fee.[274]

2.12.1.10 Uncooperative Lenders or Servicers

When a lender or servicer does not cooperate in workout discussions with a homeowner, HUD wants to hear about it. HUD will often review a workout proposal and press a reluctant lender or servicer to agree. Getting help from HUD is best achieved through HUD's national oversight office for loss mitigation in Oklahoma City.[275]

In 1998, Congress gave HUD authority to penalize lenders that do not engage in loss mitigation.[276] In order to avoid assessment of penalties the mortgage holder must ensure that loss mitigation evaluations are completed for all mortgages more than four monthly installments in arrears. The mortgage holder must take appropriate actions based on the evaluations and document both the evaluation and the subsequent actions taken in accordance with the evaluations.[277] Subservicers, including special default servicers, tend to be particularly flagrant in their abuses of loss mitigation considerations. HUD has emphasized that, while servicers may employ subservicers in connection with foreclosure of guaranteed loans, these subservicers must be approved by FHA and must follow FHA loss mitigation guidelines.[278] The penalty can be three times the amount of any insurance claim available to the lender.[279] The existence of the penalty increases the importance of notifying HUD when you are working with an unreasonably uncooperative lender.

2.12.2 *VA Loans*

2.12.2.1 Overview

The Department of Veterans Affairs (VA) guarantees loans made by private lenders to veterans for the purchase, construction, or refinancing of homes owned and occupied by veterans.[280] Recently the VA completed a multi-year initiative to redesign its loan servicing system.[281] The main focus of the initiative is the establishment of a new computer-based loan tracking system called VA Loan Electronic Reporting Interface or VALERI. As part of this process the VA overhauled some of the regulations and guidelines which govern the servicing of guaranteed loans. Many of the new rules are substantively similar to existing regulations with the exception of rules governing the computer-based loan tracking system.[282] The new rules will be phased in over an

mortgagee/files/00-05.doc. *See also* Dep't of Hous. & Urban Dev., Mortgagee Letter 2002-13 (June 7, 2002).

271 Dep't of Hous. & Urban Dev., Mortgagee Letter 00-05 (Jan. 19, 2000), *available at* www.hud.gov/offices/adm/hudclips/letters/mortgagee/files/00-05.doc.

272 HUD has devised a loss mitigation scoring system to rank mortgage holders' performance in order of cost savings for HUD. The formula gives a lower score (lower is better) to a lender who is able to prevent defaults from turning into claims for reimbursement from the FHA insurance funds. These scores are then weighted to favor lenders whose portfolio includes first-time homeowners, minority homeowners, and new loans based upon the assumption that these are riskier loans. The results are posted on HUD's loss mitigation website, www.hud.gov/offices/hsg/sfh/nsc/nschome.cfm. HUD will be switching to a different system for ranking lenders in the near future. *See* Dep't of Hous. & Urban Dev., Mortgagee Letter 2005-18 (Apr. 26, 2005), *available at* www.hud.gov/offices/adm/hudclips/letters/mortgagee/files/05-18ml.doc.

273 Dep't of Hous. & Urban Dev., Mortgagee Letter 2005-18 (Apr. 26, 2005), *available at* www.hud.gov/offices/adm/hudclips/letters/mortgagee/files/05-18ml.doc.

274 Dep't of Hous. & Urban Dev., Mortgagee Letter 00-05 (Jan. 19, 2000), *available at* www.hud.gov/offices/adm/hudclips/letters/mortgagee/files/00-05.doc.

275 Call (888) 297-8685 or write to the Oklahoma City office at the following address, with a copy to the servicer: Dep't of Housing & Urban Development, National Servicing Center, 301 N.W. 6th St., Suite 200, Oklahoma City, OK 73102.

276 12 U.S.C. § 1735f-14.

277 Dep't of Hous. & Urban Dev., Mortgagee Letter 2008-27 (Sept. 26, 2008), *available at* www.hud.gov/offices/adm/hudclips/letters/mortgagee/files/08-27ml.doc.

278 Dep't of Hous. & Urban Dev., Mortgagee Letter 2009-42 (Oct. 19, 2009), *available at* www.hud.gov/offices/adm/hudclips/letters/mortgagee/files/09-42ml.doc.

279 *See* Dep't of Hous. & Urban Dev., Mortgagee Letter 2008-27 (Sept. 26, 2008), *available at* www.hud.gov/offices/adm/hudclips/letters/mortgagee/files/08-27ml.doc (summarizing treble damages penalty assessments). *See also* 24 C.F.R. § 203.605(c) (assessment of civil money penalty); 24 C.F.R. § 30.35(c)(2) (amounts of penalty for failure to engage in loss mitigation); 70 Fed. Reg. 21,572 (Apr. 26, 2005) (background and comments on penalty regulation).

280 38 U.S.C. ch. 37.

281 *See* 73 Fed. Reg. 6294 (Feb. 1, 2008).

282 Compare the current regulations at 38 C.F.R. §§ 36.4300 to 36.4393 (redesignated subpart B) with the new series of regulations for the Loan Guaranty Program established under a new subpart F: 38 C.F.R. §§ 36.4800 to 36.4893. A new website for VALERI was established at www.homeloans.va.gov/valeri.htm. This website contains the most up-to-date information on the program including a copy of U.S. Dep't of Veterans Affairs, Veterans Benefit Administration, VA Loan Electronic Reporting Interface: VA Servicer Guide, Version 1.1 (Apr. 2008) (hereinafter "VALERI Guide"). Other materials on the VA's policy may also be available at http://homeloans.va.gov/service.htm.

eleven-month period. During the phase-in period the servicing industry will be divided into several segments, with each segment given a deadline for implementation of the new rules.[283] Servicers who have not yet implemented the new rules will be governed by existing regulations (38 C.F.R. §§ 36.4300 to 36.4393, inclusive).

Several changes to the regulations relate to the servicing and foreclosure of guaranteed loans in default. In general, the new rules delegate more authority to servicers to implement loss mitigation options, increase incentive payments to servicers for using various options, establish a system for measuring servicer performance, establish a time frame for when foreclosure should be completed, and set limits on the amount of interest and other fees and costs that can be included in a guaranty claim.[284] The final rule allows the servicer to decrease or increase the interest rate on modified loans, and removes the 1% cap on interest rate increases that had been in the proposed rules.[285] Servicers will receive an incentive fee for implementing various workout options. The amount of the fee will be based on their tier ranking which is determined after an evaluation of their performance in servicing the loans.

The VA expects the holder of the mortgage to exhaust all possible alternatives before pursing foreclosure. There are three options for reinstatement of the loan: a repayment plan, special forbearance, and a loan modification. The servicer must consider a loan modification after it determines that a repayment plan or period of forbearance is not feasible. Homeowners who cannot sustain home ownership may be eligible for a compromise claim or deed in lieu of foreclosure. Other options, such as refinancing or an assumption may also be considered.

2.12.2.2 Repayment Plan

A repayment plan is a written agreement between the borrower and the lender to reinstate a loan that is at least sixty-one days delinquent by paying the regular monthly payment plus a portion towards the delinquency each month.[286] The repayment plan must last at least three months for servicers to receive an incentive. The period of repayment is not limited. Plans may be renegotiated at any time. Servicers ranked in the top three tiers of the VA's performance evaluation are paid an incentive fee of between $120 and $200 for each repayment plan.

2.12.2.3 Special Forbearance

With a special forbearance, the mortgage holder agrees to suspend payments or accept reduced payments for one or more months.[287] The period of forbearance is followed by repayment of the arrears in a lump-sum repayment or through a payment plan. In underwritten repayment or forbearance plans, lenders must accept partial payments of installments.[288] Special forbearance plans have no maximum duration. Top ranked servicers are paid an incentive fee of between $120 and $200 for each special forbearance.

2.12.2.4 Modification

A lender may modify a VA-guaranteed loan by changing one or more of the terms of the loan, including the interest rate or term or reamortizing the balance due. Under the new regulations, lenders are now allowed to increase the interest rate on a modified mortgage.[289] The loan term may extended the maturity date to the shorter of 360 months from the due date of the first installment required under the modification, or 120 months after the original maturity date of the loan.[290] Loans must be at least twelve months old and in default to qualify. The borrower must be considered a good credit risk based on a review of a current credit report and other factors outlined in 38 C.F.R. § 36.4840. The fact of the default will not preclude the borrower from being judged as creditworthy; the decision is mostly based on review of the borrowers' current and expected income, expenses, and other obligations. Unpaid interest, taxes, insurance, and advances needed to preserve the lien position (such as homeowner association fees, special assessments, water and sewer liens, etc.) may be added to the newly modified balance. Late fees and other charges may not be included.[291] The loan may be modified up to three times without VA approval and an unlimited number of times with VA approval. Servicers will receive an incentive fee of between $300 and $700 for modification depending on their ranking.

2.12.2.5 VA-HAMP

The VA, like FHA, implemented its own version of the Treasury Department's Making Home Affordable Program (HAMP).[292] VA-HAMP became effective February 1, 2010

283 *See* 73 Fed. Reg. 6294 (Feb. 1, 2008); 73 Fed. Reg. 30,505 (June 1, 2008).

284 *See* 73 Fed. Reg. 6294 (Feb. 1, 2008).

285 The majority of VA-guaranteed loans are securitized in Government National Mortgage Association (GNMA) insured pools, which require the holder to purchase the loan from the pool in order to modify the loan. The VA is allowing for an increase in the interest rate on modification because servicers had difficulty resecuritizing loans with interest rates below market average.

286 38 C.F.R. § 36.4801; VALERI Guide § 5.2.1, *available at* www.homeloans.va.gov/valeri.htm.

287 38 C.F.R. § 36.4801; VALERI Guide § 5.2.2, *available at* www.homeloans.va.gov/valeri.htm.

288 38 C.F.R. § 36.4816.

289 38 C.F.R. § 36.4815; the old regulations, which will still be in effect for some servicers, do not allow the increase (38 C.F.R. § 36.4311(c)).

290 38 C.F.R. § 36.4815. The modified loan must bear a fixed interest rate.

291 38 C.F.R. § 36.4815(f). Borrowers should not be charged a processing fee.

292 VA Circular 26-10-02 (Jan. 8, 2010), *available at* www.homeloans.va.gov/circulars/26_10_2.pdf.

and authorizes loan modifications until December 31, 2012. Before a VA-HAMP modification will be reviewed, the lender must consider the borrower for all other options for preserving homeownership under VA guidelines, including a repayment plan, special forbearance, and a traditional VA loan modification. VA-HAMP requires that the servicer conduct two loan modification analyses, one assuming a VA guaranty is in place and one assuming there is no guaranty. The likely effect of the guaranty is to make foreclosure, rather than a loan modification, a more favorable option for the mortgage holder. If a VA-HAMP modification could be approved only without the VA guaranty, VA states that it will consider taking over the loan itself under its refunding option. Under the alternative calculation, if the homeowner is found eligible for a modification under the standard Treasury HAMP analysis even when the VA guaranty is taken into account, the lender is to implement the modification.

2.12.2.6 Compromise Sale

A compromise sale is a sale of the property to a third party for an amount that is insufficient to pay off the loan.[293] The servicer may file a claim with the VA to recoup the debt owed by the borrower. To qualify for a compromise sale the net proceeds of the sale and any waiver of deficiency must equal or exceed the net value of the property. Borrowers must obtain the servicer's written approval prior to executing the sale. Top ranked servicers are paid an incentive fee of between $600 and $1000 for each compromise sale.

2.12.2.7 Refinance

A borrower may refinance a high interest rate loan at a current, lower rate with the VA's interest rate reduction refinancing loan.[294] The new loan could also be used to obtain a shorter term, a fixed interest rate, or fund energy efficient improvements. However the term of the refinance loan may not exceed the term of the original loan plus ten years or thirty years, whichever is shorter. If the current loan is delinquent or if foreclosure is imminent, VA approval is necessary to refinance. The balance of the new loan can include the unpaid installments, plus late fees.

2.12.2.8 Deed in Lieu of Foreclosure

A deed in lieu of foreclosure is a voluntarily transfer of the property to the holder of the VA-guaranteed loan.[295] Servicers are required to consider other workout options, including a compromise sale, before accepting a deed in lieu of foreclosure. The deed in lieu of foreclosure will usually not be accepted if there are any junior liens on the property. Servicers ranked in the top three tiers are paid an incentive fee of between $150 and $350 for each deed in lieu.

2.12.2.9 Assumption

If a workout is unsuccessful, a lender may grant a borrower forbearance for a reasonable period of time to permit the sale or transfer of the property. For loans made prior to March 1, 1988, a borrower may transfer property to a third party without the approval of the VA.[296] The original borrower remains liable, however, unless he or she obtains a release from the VA permitting such an assumption. For loans made on or after March 1, 1988, the approval of the VA is needed for an assumption.[297] In addition, the transaction is subject to a funding fee and a processing charge.[298] The funding fee is equal to one-half of 1% of the loan balance as of the date of transfer. However, certain buyers are exempt from paying this fee. The maximum charge for processing an assumption application is the lesser of: (1) $300 and the cost of a credit report or (2) the maximum fee prescribed by state law.

2.12.2.10 Refunding

The VA has the authority to buy a loan in default from the lender and take over its servicing.[299] However, this option, called "refunding," is to be exercised at the discretion of the VA. Though the VA makes very limited use of this option, the VA claims to review every loan in default to determine whether to refund the loan.[300] There is no formal application process.[301] The objective of refunding is to avoid foreclosure when it is determined by the VA that the default can be cured through various relief measures and the lender is unable or unwilling to grant further relief.[302] Other loss mitigation options may then be available to the homeowner.

The failure of the VA to exercise the latter authority has been the subject of unsuccessful litigation. Courts have held that the taking of assignments of defaulted mortgages is a matter committed to the agency's discretion and was therefore not judicially reviewable.[303]

---

293 *See* 38 C.F.R. § 36.4801; VALERI Guide § 5.2.4, *available at* www.homeloans.va.gov/valeri.htm. This option is similar to a "short sale."

294 38 C.F.R. § 36.4807.

295 38 C.F.R. § 36.4819; VALERI Guide § 5.2.5, *available at* www.homeloans.va.gov/valeri.htm.

296 VA Handbook H26-94-1, at § 1.13 (1994).

297 *Id.* § 1.14.

298 *Id.*

299 38 U.S.C. § 3732(a)(2). *See also* 38 C.F.R. § 36.4820.

300 VA Circular 26-02-7 (May 7, 2002), *available at* www.mortgagebankers.org/files/Residential/2002/va26_02_7.pdf.

301 VA Handbook H26-94-1, at § 3.06 (1994).

302 *Id.* The VA often reamortizes the delinquency and the unpaid loan balance, resulting in a higher monthly payment. *See* VA Circular 26-02-7 (May 7, 2002), *available at* www.mortgagebankers.org/files/Residential/2002/va26_02_7.pdf.

303 *E.g.*, Gatter v. Nimmo, 672 F.2d 343 (3d Cir. 1982), *aff'g* Gatter

2.12.3 RHS Loans

2.12.3.1 Overview

The Section 502 Single-Family Housing Program[304] provides direct loans to very low and low-income individuals for the purchase, construction, or rehabilitation of single family homes located in rural areas. The program is administered by the Rural Housing Service (RHS), an agency of the United States Department of Agriculture (USDA).[305] Under section 502, the RHS also guarantees loans made by private lenders to low- and moderate-income individuals living in rural areas.[306] These loans may be made for up to 102% of the value of the property that secures the loan.

When the Treasury Department announced guidelines for the Home Affordable Modification Program (HAMP) in April 2009, it indicated that RHS, along with HUD (FHA), and the VA, would be developing HAMP programs for the home loans they regulated.[307] Over the subsequent year, HUD (FHA) and the VA announced their own versions of HAMP, discussed above. As of the time of preparation of this treatise, RHS had not yet announced any guidance for a HAMP program applicable to RHS direct or guaranteed loans.

2.12.3.2 Section 502 Direct Loans

2.12.3.2.1 General

RHS's Section 502 Single-Family Housing Program provides assistance to homeowners facing foreclosure. RHS, with some assistance from local rural development field offices, services section 502 direct loans through its Centralized Servicing Center in St. Louis, Missouri.[308] There is no third-party servicer. RHS will not initiate special servicing until a homeowner is at least two months delinquent.[309] The options offered to delinquent homeowners are discussed in the following subsections.

2.12.3.2.2 Interest credit and payment assistance

RHS offers two types of payment subsidies to section 502 direct loan homeowners under its interest credit and payment assistance options (also referred to as the interest credit option or the Payment Assistance option). Many borrowers receive these subsidies at the time the loan is initially made and may continue to receive the subsidies throughout the life of the loan, if they remain eligible. To be eligible to receive a payment subsidy during the term of the loan, the borrower must have an adjusted income at or below the income guidelines established by the agency.

With the interest credit option, the agency subsidizes the interest portion of a borrower's monthly payment in an effort to reduce the monthly payment to an affordable amount.[310] A borrower currently receiving subsidized interest will continue to receive it for the initial loan and for any subsequent loan for as long as the borrower is eligible for and remains on the interest credit option. A borrower who has never received the interest credit option, or who has stopped receiving subsidized interest and at a later date again qualifies for a payment subsidy, will receive the payment assistance option. The payment assistance option is used to reduce the borrower's required payment.[311]

Both types of payment subsidies are subject to recapture; the borrower will be required to repay the subsidy when he or she sells the property, moves out of the property, or pays off the loan in full.[312] The interest credit and payment assistance options are recalculated annually, and the homeowner must notify RHS of household, employment, and income changes.[313] For both programs, RHS will send a notice of review ninety days before the expiration of the agreement.[314]

2.12.3.2.3 Payment moratorium

A payment moratorium is available when a homeowner can show that due to circumstances beyond his or her control, the homeowner is unable to continue making payments of principal and interest when due without "unduly

v. Cleveland, 512 F. Supp. 207 (E.D. Pa. 1981); United States v. Harvey, 659 F.2d 62 (5th Cir. 1981). Courts have also held there is no private action for damages for the VA's failure to forebear from foreclosure. Bright v. Nimmo, 756 F.2d 1513 (11th Cir. 1985). According to the VA, the refunding program "is not a veteran's benefit, but rather an administrative option established by the regulation to enable VA to assist a veteran when VA makes the determination that the option is appropriate." 73 Fed. Reg. 6294 (Feb. 1, 2008).

304 The Section 502 Single-Family Housing Program was created by the Housing Act of 1949. Pub. L. No. 81-171 ch. 338, tit. V, § 502, 63 Stat. 433 (July 15, 1949) (codified at 42 U.S.C. § 1472). The regulations for the direct single-family housing program is provided in 7 C.F.R. pt. 3550.

305 The RHS was formerly known as the Farmers Home Administration (FmHA). The Rural Housing Service is one of three agencies comprising the United States Department of Agriculture's (USDA) Rural Development Mission.

306 42 U.S.C. § 1472(h).

307 Dep't of Treasury, Home Affordable Modification Program, Supplemental Directive 09-01, at 3 (Apr. 6, 2009), *available at* www.hmpadmin.com//portal/programs/hamp/servicer.html.

308 That office can be reached at (800) 793-8861.

309 United States Dep't of Agric., Direct Single Family Housing Programs Centralized Servicing Center Handbook § 5.1(B) (1996).

310 7 C.F.R. § 3550.68.

311 *Id.*

312 *Id.*

313 7 C.F.R. § 3550.68(e).

314 United States Dep't of Agric., Direct Single Family Housing Programs Centralized Servicing Center (CSC) Handbook § 4.6 (1996).

impairing his standard of living."[315] With a moratorium, the homeowner's scheduled monthly payments may be deferred for up to two years.[316] At the end of two years, or at an earlier date if it is determined that the homeowner no longer needs moratorium assistance, the loan will be reamortized.[317] If the homeowner is unable to afford the new payments on the reamortized loan, all or part of the interest that accrued during moratorium may be forgiven.[318] The loan will be accelerated at the end of two years if the homeowner is unable to resume monthly payments and maintain the loan.[319] Eligibility for moratorium is reviewed every six months, and the homeowner should be provided with sixty days' notice before the moratorium is terminated.[320]

2.12.3.2.4 Delinquency workout agreement

A delinquency workout agreement allows a borrower to cure a delinquency, either by making a single lump payment or by paying the delinquent amount, in addition to the scheduled mortgage payment, through monthly installments not to exceed two years.[321]

2.12.3.2.5 Protective advances

RHS also has the ability to advance funds to cover the cost of taxes, insurance, and emergency repairs necessary to protect the government's interest in the property.[322] The payments are then charged to the borrower's account. Repayment terms are to be consistent with the borrower's ability to repay or the loan can be reamortized to include the amount of the advance.

315 42 U.S.C. § 1475(a). *See* United States v. Larson, 76 Fed. Appx. 742 (8th Cir. 2003) (discussing the inability to continue making payments, and finding that the borrower was not entitled to a moratorium because she had not experienced a 20% reduction in her income in the past twelve months and her inability to pay was not temporary); United States v. Asken, 2002 WL 32175416 (E.D. Pa. Oct. 28, 2002) (RHS's denial of an application for a moratorium will not be overturned when evidence was presented that mortgagor was fired from employment and thus his financial situation was not due to circumstances beyond his control). *See also* 7 C.F.R. § 3550.207(a)(1).

316 7 C.F.R. § 3550.207(c).

317 7 C.F.R. § 3550.207(c).

318 7 C.F.R. § 3550.207(c).

319 7 C.F.R. § 3550.207(d).

320 7 C.F.R. § 3550.207(b).

321 7 C.F.R. § 3550.205; United States Dep't of Agric., Direct Single Family Housing Programs Centralized Servicing Center Handbook § 5.2 (1996). *See also* 7 C.F.R. § 3550.201.

322 7 C.F.R. 3550.206.

2.12.3.3 Section 502 Guaranteed Loans

2.12.3.3.1 In general

The Rural Housing Service's (RHS) Section 502 Single-Family Housing Guaranteed Loan Program provides loans, through private lenders, to eligible low- to moderate-income borrowers in rural areas.[323] RHS has a loss mitigation program designed to address serious defaults—generally those loans ninety or more days past due. The agency issued loss mitigation guidelines. The guidelines, published in the *Loss Mitigation Guide*, outline the agency's workout options and policies.[324] The *Loss Mitigation Guide* updates the workout options offered by the agency in the past. These options are almost identical to many of the options offered by HUD under its Loss Mitigation Program.[325]

Under program guidelines, the lender is required to evaluate each delinquent loan within ninety days to determine if a loss mitigation option is appropriate. In addition, the lender should inform borrowers of the availability of loss mitigation and housing counseling assistance before the end of the second month of delinquency.[326] The options fall into two broad categories: options to cure a default, such as a special forbearance or loan modification; and disposition options that result in the homeowner transferring the property, such as pre-foreclosure sale or a deed in lieu of foreclosure. An option may be used alone or in combination with another option. There are, however, limitations on combining options.

To qualify for a workout options the borrower must be generally three or more months delinquent for reinstatement options and more than thirty days delinquent for disposition options, as well as occupy the property as a primary resi-

323 Pub. L. No. 81-171, ch. 338, tit. V, § 502, 63 Stat. 433 (July 15, 1949) (codified at 42 U.S.C. § 1472). The RHS was formerly known as the Farmers Home Administration (FmHA).

324 RD AN No. 4433 (1980-D) (Apr. 17, 2009), *available at* www.rurdev.usda.gov/regs/an/an4433.pdf (single family housing guaranteed loan program loss mitigation comprehensive policy clarification). The Loss Mitigation Guide is attached to RD AN No. 4433 (1980-D) as Exhibit A, USDA Rural Development Loss Mitigation Guide, Single Family Housing Guaranteed Loan Program. This notice updates RD AN No. 4321 (1980-D) (Dec. 18, 2007) (Single Family Housing Guaranteed Loan Program Loss Mitigation Comprehensive Policy Clarification). *See also* RD AN No. 4434 (1980-D) (Apr. 30, 2009), *available at* http://www.rurdev.usda.gov/regs/an/an4434.pdf (single family housing guaranteed loan program acceptable foreclosure time frames); RD AN No. 4429 (1980-D) (Apr. 14, 2009), *available at* www.rurdev.usda.gov/regs/an/an4429.pdf (single family housing guaranteed loan program acceptable liquidation fees and costs).

325 Notably, the agency did not adopt HUD's partial claim option, which provides for an interest-free loan to delinquent homeowners.

326 Lenders can satisfy this requirement by mailing HUD Publication PA-426-H to borrowers.

dence.[327] Borrowers who have had their bankruptcy case dismissed or discharged may also qualify for a workout options.[328] Those with a bankruptcy case pending are unlikely to qualify under program guidelines.

2.12.3.3.2 Special forbearance

A special forbearance is a written agreement to cure the mortgage arrears. The agreement may include a plan to reduce or suspend payments for one or more months to allow the borrower to recover from the cause of the default or an agreement to allow the borrower to resume making full monthly payments while delaying repayment of the arrears. The period of reduced or suspended payment is followed by a repayment plan. There is no time limit on the repayment plan, so long as during the term of the plan, the accumulated arrears do not exceed the equivalent of twelve monthly mortgage payments.[329]

Special forbearance may be offered to borrowers who have experienced a verifiable loss of income or increase in living expenses, but who will have sufficient income to repay the arrears during the term of the plan. The borrower must be at least three months behind and committed to occupying the property as a primary residence during the term of the special forbearance agreement. RHS allows for the repayment of foreclosure costs and late fees through the special forbearance plan. Such costs and late fees are collected after payment of all principal, interest, and escrow advances. The loan will not be considered delinquent only because the borrower has not paid late fees or other foreclosure costs.

Borrowers who defaulted because of unemployment, and have no immediate prospect for reemployment, may take advantage of this option. The special forbearance can be extended to borrowers, who are currently unemployed, but have a good payment and stable employment history. Borrowers will be required to make partial payments based on financial ability. The servicer will verify the borrower's employment status monthly and restructure the forbearance agreement when the borrower's employment status changes.

A special forbearance may be used alone or combined with a loan modification. If the special forbearance plan results in a modification, foreclosure costs and fees are collected in accordance with the requirements applicable to that option. A borrower may also use a special forbearance to reduce or suspend payments pending the sale of the property.

327 The borrower is required to occupy the property as a principal residence to qualify for a special forbearance or loan modification. The requirement may be waived for other options. USDA Rural Development/Rural, Housing Service, Loss Mitigation Guide 4.

328 *Id.*

329 USDA Rural Development Loss Mitigation Guide 2-32.

2.12.3.3.3 Modification

A modification is a permanent change in one or more terms of the loan. A modification is appropriate for borrowers who have experienced a permanent or long-term reduction in income or an increase in expenses, or who have recovered from the cause of the default but do not have sufficient surplus income to repay the arrears through a repayment plan. A loan that is not delinquent, but in danger of default, can be modified. RHS eliminated the requirement that the loan be at least twelve months old before it can be modified.

Lenders may reamortize the arrearage over the remaining term of the loan, capitalize delinquent principal, interest and escrow advances, or reduce the interest rate (even to below market). Foreclosure costs, late fees, and other administrative expenses may not be capitalized. These and other fees may be collected through a repayment plan. The modification must result in a fixed rate, fully amortizing loan, and the modified principal balance may exceed the loan's original principal balance and 100% loan-to-value.[330] The term of the modified loan should not exceed thirty years. If the loan has been modified within the last two years, RHS's approval is required to do a second modification.[331]

2.12.3.3.4 Pre-foreclosure sale

A pre-foreclosure sale allows a borrower to satisfy the mortgage debt with the proceeds of a market sale, even if the proceeds of the sale are less than the amount owed.[332] The borrower must submit an application for this option. RHS requires that:

- The home's "as is" appraised value must be at least 63% of the total amount due on the mortgage;[333]
- The net sales price must be at least 82% of the home's "as is" appraised value;
- The loan need only be more than thirty days in arrears;[334]
- The homeowner has ninety days to sell but this may be extended an additional thirty days if a sale is likely;
- If the property is under contact, the servicer may extend the pre-foreclosure sale period for sixty days, but not more than 180 days total; and
- Any junior liens on the property must be discharged.

330 USDA Rural Development Loss Mitigation Guide 2-41.

331 USDA Rural Development Loss Mitigation Guide 2-44.

332 USDA Rural Development Loss Mitigation Guide 2-47.

333 A pre-foreclosure sale may be considered if the property's appraised value slightly exceeds the mortgage payoff figure, but net proceeds, after deducting the costs of the sale, will fall short of the amount needed to discharge the mortgage by more than $1000. *Id.* at 15.

334 The servicer has the discretion to accept an application from a borrower who is facing imminent default. USDA Rural Development Loss Mitigation Guide 2-48.

A pre-foreclosure sale will be reported to the national credit bureaus as a "short sale" and the lender is required to file Form 1099-A with the IRS and report any discharge of indebtedness. Servicers will receive a $1000 incentive fee for each pre-foreclosure sale.

2.12.3.3.5 Deed in lieu of foreclosure

A deed in lieu of foreclosure allows the borrower to voluntarily transfer the property in exchange for a release from obligations under the mortgage. Other loss mitigation options should be considered, including marketing the property through a pre-foreclosure sale process. The loan need only be more than thirty days delinquent. As with any deed in lieu, there should be no junior liens on the property. Unlike HUD, RHS does not pay the homeowner an incentive for leaving the property. The borrower, however, will not be pursued for a deficiency judgment by either the lender or RHS.[335] Any discharge of indebtedness will be reported to the IRS. Servicers will receive a $250 incentive fee for each deed in lieu of foreclosure.

2.13 Assisting Homeowners Facing Foreclosure After a Natural Disaster

2.13.1 In General

When a natural disasters strikes, low-income consumers face a vast array of problems. Homeowners who are victims of natural disasters are not only faced with the task of rebuilding or repairing their properties, but also possible unemployment and extraordinary expenses related to finding alternative living accommodations. In many cases homeowners will deplete their savings and use credit cards to make their mortgage payments. In the months and years following the disaster, advocates should expect a growing number of foreclosure cases, consumer debt cases, and bankruptcy matters.[336]

To stem the tide of expected foreclosures from a natural disaster, the federal agencies that insure or guarantee loans for low- and moderate-income individuals may issue ninety-day moratoriums on the initiation of new foreclosures. State or local governments may, if pressed, enact moratoriums on foreclosures as well. Mortgage lenders and servicers can also provide broad-based relief from the threat of foreclosure by exercising flexibility in implementing investor guidelines on workout or loss mitigation options. These options include the temporary suspension or reduction of mortgage payments, or the permanent modification of the terms of the mortgage.[337] Below is a brief summary of the relief options that homeowners and their advocates should explore. Of course, assistance making mortgage payments and repairing the home is available from the Federal Emergency Management Agency (FEMA).[338] In addition, there are numerous programs run by private and government organizations to help victims of natural disasters.

2.13.2 Government Imposed Moratoriums on Foreclosure

Some states enact moratorium laws postponing foreclosure sales of homes or farms during times of natural disasters or widespread economic distress.[339] The statutes generally allow for relief when the governor declares an emergency. Advocates in states affected by natural disasters should keep current on state foreclosure laws as foreclosures conducted in violation of a moratorium may be invalid.

2.13.3 Moratoriums and Other Relief for Federally Guaranteed or Insured Loans

In light of the devastation caused by Hurricanes Katrina, Rita, and Wilma, the agencies that insure or guarantee loans to low- and moderate-income homeowners, including U.S. Department of Housing and Urban Development (HUD), the Department of Veterans Affairs (VA), and Rural Housing Service (RHS), each imposed moratoriums, on the initiation of new foreclosures or in some instances the continuation of a foreclosure proceeding, in the counties declared disaster areas.[340] All the federal agencies recommended that servicers extend forbearance and other workout options to

335 USDA Rural Development Loss Mitigation Guide 2-61.

336 The number of low- and moderate-income families in New York who were seriously behind on their mortgage payments soared after September 11th. *See* Sarah Kershaw, *Failing Mortgages Soar in New York*, N.Y. Times, Mar. 27, 2002, at A1, B6.

337 *See generally* § 2.4, *supra* (complete discussion of workout and loss mitigation options).

338 *See* Coble, Terry, *Disaster Assistance Guide for Legal Services Practitioners*, Clearinghouse Review (May 1995) (description of various FEMA programs).

339 *See* § 4.11, *infra* (discussion of moratorium statutes).

340 The VA imposed two exceptions to the moratorium if the default was "clearly insoluble" and there was no likelihood of reinstatement, and when a foreclosure sale was already scheduled prior to the disaster. *See* Department of Veterans Affairs, VA Loan Guaranty Policy Regarding Natural Disasters, *available at* www.homeloans.va.gov/docs/va_policy_regarding_natural_disasters.doc. *See also* Dep't of Hous. & Urban Dev., Mortgagee Letter 2005-33 (Aug. 31, 2005), *available at* www.hud.gov/offices/adm/hudclips/letters/mortgagee/files/05-33ml.doc; August 31, 2005 memorandum from Russell T. Davis, Administrator, RHS to Rural Development Single Family Guaranteed Loan Holders and Servicers. A list of counties declared disaster areas and the date of declaration generally is available from FEMA's website at www.fema.gov/disasters.

homeowners affected by the hurricanes;[341] HUD and RHS recommended that servicers waive late charges and suspend delinquency reporting to the credit bureaus.

Due to the large scale of the devastation caused by the storms, the agencies extended their moratoriums on foreclosure for certain borrowers whose homes were moderately or severely affected by the hurricanes.[342] The moratorium was not automatically extended for everyone. HUD and the VA, for example, required borrowers to contact the lender before the deadline and make a written plan to resolve the delinquency.[343] HUD also extended the foreclosure moratorium deadline for those who were eligible to apply for funds under the Louisiana or Mississippi assistance programs.[344]

2.13.4 *Lender or Servicer Imposed Moratoriums and Other Relief Options*

Both Fannie Mae and Freddie Mac authorized the suspension of foreclosure proceedings immediately after Hurricanes Katrina and Rita.[345] Servicers were instructed to work closely with homeowners to develop workout or relief plans to cure the delinquency. After the blanket moratorium on foreclosures expired, servicers were authorized to continue moratoriums and extend other relief to affected homeowners on a case-by-case basis, based on individual assessment.[346] Among other relief options, servicers were permitted to temporarily reduce or suspend mortgage payments, or modify the mortgage by changing the interest rate, extending the term of the loan, or capitalizing delinquent payments.[347] In addition, for affected homeowners, servicers were directed to discontinue reporting delinquencies, preforeclosure sales, deeds in lieu of foreclosure, short payoffs, and other adverse actions to the credit bureaus,[348] and waive the assessment of penalties or late fees.[349]

Though there is no longer a blanket prohibition on foreclosures, Freddie Mac under its temporary servicing guidelines, required that servicers seek its permission prior to initiating foreclosure on the most severely damaged prop-

341 For FHA loss mitigation guidelines, refer to: Dep't of Hous. & Urban Dev., Mortgagee Letter 2005-18 (Apr. 26, 2005), *available at* www.hud.gov/offices/adm/hudclips/letters/mortgagee/files/05-18ml.doc; Dep't of Hous. & Urban Dev., Mortgagee Letter 2003-19 (Nov. 20, 2003), *available at* www.hud.gov/offices/adm/hudclips/letters/mortgagee/files/03-19ml.doc; Dep't of Hous. & Urban Dev., Mortgagee Letter 2002-17 (Aug. 29, 2002); Dep't of Hous. & Urban Dev., Mortgagee Letter 2002-13 (June 7, 2002); Dep't of Hous. & Urban Dev., Mortgagee Letter 2001-14 (May 23, 2001); Dep't of Hous. & Urban Dev., Mortgagee Letter 00-05 (Jan. 19, 2000), *available at* www.hud.gov/offices/adm/hudclips/letters/mortgagee/files/00-05.doc.

For VA loans, 38 C.F.R. §§ 36.4300 to 36.4393; VA Handbook H26-94-1, at § 3.06(a) (1994). The handbook and updates available at http://homeloans.va.gov/service.htm.

RHS's Loss Mitigation Guide is published as an attachment to an administrative notice, RD AN No. 4333 (1980-D) (Apr. 17, 2009) (Single Family Housing Guaranteed Loan Program Loss Mitigation Comprehensive Policy Clarification), *available at* www.rurdev.usda.gov/regs/an/an4433.pdf.

342 *See, e.g.*, Dep't of Hous. & Urban Dev., Mortgagee Letter 2006-18 (June 30, 2006), *available at* www.efanniemae.com/sf/guides/ssg/annltrs/pdf/2006/06-18.pdf; Veterans Benefit Admin., Dep't of Veterans Affairs, Circular 26-06-3, *available at* www.vba.va.gov/ro/south/spete/RLC/IB/pdf/Circular_26-06-03.pdf.

RHS imposed a six month moratorium for Section 502 direct loans. *See* www.rurdev.usda.gov/rd/disasters/katrina.html#regs.

343 *See, e.g.*, Dep't of Hous. & Urban Dev., Mortgagee Letter 2006-05 (Feb. 23, 2006), *available at* www.hud.gov/offices/adm/hudclips/letters/mortgagee/files/06-05ML.doc; Dep't of Hous. & Urban Dev., Mortgagee Letter 2006-12 (May 24, 2006), *available at* www.hud.gov/offices/adm/hudclips/letters/mortgagee/files/06-12ML.doc; Dep't of Hous. & Urban Dev., Mortgagee Letter 2006-18 (June 30, 2006), *available at* www.hud.gov/offices/adm/hudclips/letters/mortgagee/files/06-18ML.doc.

344 Dep't of Hous. & Urban Dev., Mortgagee Letter 2006-18 (June 30, 2006), *available at* www.hud.gov/offices/adm/hudclips/letters/mortgagee/files/06-18ML.doc.

345 In fact, for victims of Hurricanes Katrina and Rita, Freddie Mac suspended payments for three and two months respectively; suspended all late fee, collection and foreclosure activities; and authorized servicers to refund one month's payment upon the request of the homeowner. Also, under Fannie Mae guidelines a servicer should not begin or continue a foreclosure action against a borrower who is current or less than ninety days delinquent. The servicer has more discretion for a seriously delinquent mortgage. *See* Fannie Mae Single-Family Servicing Guide, pt. III, § 1102.01.

Under Freddie Mac guidelines, eviction and other collection action may also be suspended. The servicer must get the approval of the insurer. Freddie Mac Single-Family Seller/Servicer Guide, vol. 2, §§ 58.11, 67.29.

346 *See* Freddie Mac Bulletin to All Freddie Mac Sellers and Servicers (Aug. 4, 2006), *available at* www.freddiemac.com/sell/guide/bulletins/pdf/bll080406.pdf (effective Sept. 1, 2006, blanket foreclosure moratorium for mortgages secured by properties in the most severely affected areas ends); Fannie Mae, Lender Letter 04-06 (Aug. 8, 2006), *available at* www.efanniemae.com/sf/guides/ssg/annltrs/pdf/2006/ll0406.pdf (hurricane-related special relief measures).

347 *See* § 2.6, *supra* (discussion of workout options on Fannie Mae and Freddie Mac loans).

348 Fannie Mae, Lender Letter 03-06 (May 11, 2006), *available at* www.efanniemae.com/sf/guides/ssg/annltrs/pdf/2006/ll0306.pdf; Fannie Mae Announcement 05-06 (Aug. 24, 2005), *available at* https://www.efanniemae.com/sf/guides/ssg/annltrs/pdf/2005/05-06.pdf; Freddie Mac Bulletin to All Freddie Mac Sellers and Servicers (Mar. 1, 2007), *available at* www.freddiemac.com/sell/guide/bulletins/pdf/bll030107.pdf.

349 Fannie Mae Single-Family Servicing Guide, pt. III, § 1101.

erties.[350] In addition, Freddie Mac relaxed documentation requirements for its long-term forbearance option, streamlined its underwriting process for loan modifications and required servicers to waive prepayment penalties if the mortgage is paid off in connection with a workout or default.[351] Fannie Mae also, required that servicers seek its permission prior to initiating or continuing a foreclosure in selected counties or parishes in Louisiana and Mississippi.[352] Servicers did not need to obtain standard documentation when considering workout proposals, such as repayment plans. In addition, they had the discretion to modify a mortgage less than a year old and increase its term up to forty years.[353] The company encouraged lenders to waive all or a part of the prepayment penalties if the mortgage was paid off.[354]

Both Fannie Mae and Freddie Mac delegate many decisions to servicers. Although servicers are expected to aggressively work with the homeowner to prevent foreclosure, it is still the case that good advocacy is required to obtain the best outcome for the homeowner. Servicers may go beyond written guidelines to prevent or cure a mortgage default.[355] As stated by Fannie Mae in its guidelines, when it comes to assisting victims of natural disasters, "there can be no hard-and-fast rules—instead compassion, flexibility, and common sense must be used to determine how a policy should best be applied."[356]

Servicers were also required to expedite the release of insurance proceeds to assist homeowners in repairing or rebuilding their property.[357] If a property cannot be legally rebuilt, the insurance proceeds must be used to reduce the amount of the outstanding mortgage debt.

2.13.5 State Assistance

After a natural disaster, states often develop new programs to aid victims. The state of Louisiana used federal Community Development Block Grant (CDBG) disaster funds to assist homeowners whose homes suffered flood or wind damage as a result of hurricanes Katrina or Rita. Under the state plan, eligible homeowners received a one-time grant payment of up to $150,000, for damage to the home not covered by property insurance, FEMA grants, or other federal, state, or local government programs. In exchange for the grant, homeowners were required to agree to covenants and restrictions running with and encumbering the property. The covenants include requirements that the property be rebuilt and repaired according to housing codes and ordinances, elevation of the building in compliance with FEMA standards, and the homeowner occupying the property for three years. More information about the program is available at www.road2la.org.

The state of Mississippi had a similar program, using CDBG funds to assist homeowners whose primary residence suffered flood damage as a result of Hurricane Katrina. Eligible homeowners whose homes were located outside a FEMA designated 100-year flood zone were eligible

350 Freddie Mac Bulletin to All Freddie Mac Sellers and Servicers (Mar. 1, 2007), *available at* www.freddiemac.com/sell/guide/bulletins/pdf/bll030107.pdf.

Freddie Mac divides the disaster area into three zones (Zone One: minimal to no damage; Zone Two: moderate damage; and Zone Three: significant damage) and varies its level of assistance based on the zone. The requirement that servicers obtain Freddie Mac's written approval before beginning foreclosure on properties in designated areas ended December 31, 2007. Freddie Mac Bulletin (Dec. 5, 2007), *available at* www.freddiemac.com/sell/guide/bulletins/pdf/bll120507.pdf and www.freddiemac.com/sell/guide/bulletins/pdf/bll120507xA.pdf and www.freddiemac.com/sell/guide/bulletins/pdf/bll120507xB.pdf.

351 The newly modified loan term could be extended to forty years. Freddie Mac Bulletin to all Freddie Mac Sellers and Servicers (Mar. 1, 2007), *available at* www.freddiemac.com/sell/guide/bulletins/pdf/bll030107.pdf. The requirements regarding loan modifications and long-term forbearance ended December 31, 2007. Freddie Mac Bulletin (Dec. 5, 2007), *available at* www.freddiemac.com/sell/guide/bulletins/pdf/bll120507.pdf and www.freddiemac.com/sell/guide/bulletins/pdf/bll120507xA.pdf and www.freddiemac.com/sell/guide/bulletins/pdf/bll120507xB.pdf. A summary of Freddie Mac's current policies are available on its website at www.freddiemac.com/singlefamily/service/disastermgmt.html.

352 Fannie Mae Lender Letter 06-06 (Nov. 21, 2006), *available at* www.efanniemae.com/sf/guides/ssg/annltrs/pdf/2006/ll0606.pdf; Fannie Mae Lender Letter 04-06 (Aug. 8, 2006), *available at* www.efanniemae.com/sf/guides/ssg/annltrs/pdf/2006/ll0406.pdf. This requirement ends on March 31, 2007. The requirement that servicers obtain written approval before beginning foreclosure on properties in designated parishes ended December 31, 2007. However, servicers should not pursue foreclosure if the borrower is awaiting grant funds from Louisiana's The Road Home program. Fannie Mae Lender Letter 01-07 (Mar. 29, 2007), *available at* www.efanniemae.com/sf/guides/ssg/annltrs/pdf/2007/ll0107.pdf; Fannie Mae Lender Letter 08-07 (Dec. 21, 2007), *available at* www.efanniemae.com/sf/guides/ssg/annltrs/pdf/2007/ll0807.pdf.

353 Fannie Mae Lender Letter 03-05 (Dec. 2, 2005), *available at* www.efanniemae.com/sf/guides/ssg/annltrs/pdf/2005/ll0305.pdf.

354 Fannie Mae Lender Letter 01-06 (Feb. 14, 2006), *available at* www.efanniemae.com/sf/guides/ssg/annltrs/pdf/2006/ll0106.pdf.

355 *See* Fannie Mae Single-Family Servicing Guide, pt. III, § 1102.

356 *Id. at* pt. III, Ch. 11.

357 For Fannie Mae loans that are current, servicers must use their discretion to determine the amount of insurance proceeds to disburse; for loans thirty to ninety days delinquent, servicers are authorized to release up to 20% but not more than $15,000; and for loans ninety or more days delinquent, servicers are authorized to release up to 10% but not more than $10,000. Fannie Mae Announcement 05-06 (Aug. 24, 2005), *available at* https://www.efanniemae.com/sf/guides/ssg/annltrs/pdf/2005/05-06.pdf.

For Freddie Mac loans, if the mortgage is current, the servicer may release an unlimited amount of insurance proceeds, but only up to $40,000 for loans thirty to ninety days delinquent. Freddie Mac Bulletin (October 7, 2005), *available at* http://freddiemac.com/sell/guide/bulletins.

to receive a one-time grant payment of up to $150,000, for flood damage not covered by property insurance or FEMA grants. In exchange for the grant payment, homeowners were required to agree to covenants on their property that required compliance with building codes, elevation of the building, and flood insurance. The Mississippi Development Authority, which administered the program, appointed lenders to manage the grant distribution process for their customers. As part of that process lenders were permitted to reduce the amount homeowners receive by any past-due installments on the mortgage or taxes owed. More information about the program is available at http://mshomehelp.gov.

2.13.6 Post-Foreclosure Eviction Relief

If, as the result of a disaster, there is a lack of comparable alternative housing available (at reasonable rates) in the immediate vicinity of the borrower's current residence, Fannie Mae requires that servicers contact the eviction attorney to discuss whether or not to begin (or complete) eviction proceedings. If Fannie Mae and the eviction attorney agree not to pursue eviction proceedings, the servicer may be authorized to offer the borrower a month-to-month lease (at whatever rent the borrower can reasonably afford) to enable the borrower to remain in a property that Fannie Mae has acquired by foreclosure or a deed in lieu.[358]

358 Fannie Mae Single-Family Servicing Guide, pt. III, § 1102.2.

Chapter 3 Foreclosure of Mortgages Held or Insured by the Federal Government

3.1 Introduction

3.1.1 In General

The Department of Housing and Urban Development (HUD), the Department of Veterans Affairs (VA), and the Rural Housing Service (RHS) (formerly the Farmers Home Administration) make, insure, or guarantee loans, mostly on behalf of low- to moderate-income individuals. Homeowners facing foreclosure of mortgages held, insured, or guaranteed by the federal government have many protections not available to individuals with conventional mortgages. Each agency has implemented a loss mitigation or foreclosure avoidance program to assist individuals who are delinquent on their mortgages and in danger of foreclosure. The options available under these programs may allow a homeowner the flexibility to restructure a mortgage or delay repayment of a delinquency. Subsidies, or other assistance, may be available to further assist homeowners. Moreover, denial of these options is often subject to agency review.

In addition to these options, HUD, VA, and RHS have also established standards as to a number of different types of mortgage loan workouts and modifications, examined at § 2.12, *supra*. These include temporary forbearance on mortgage payments, refinancing options, permanent loan modifications, and deed in lieu of foreclosure. HUD also has implemented guidelines to apply the Home Affordable Mortgage Program (HAMP) to loans that it insures.[1]

Failure to offer this assistance, or to properly service a loan held or guaranteed by HUD, VA, or RHS may provide an equitable basis to postpone a foreclosure sale and, in some cases, may constitute a full legal defense to foreclosure. In addition, all of the foreclosure defense strategies discussed in Chapter 4, *infra*, are available to advocates challenging foreclosures of federally held or guaranteed loans.

1 *See* § 2.12.1.6, *supra.*

3.1.2 Due Process Challenges to Foreclosure of Federally Held Mortgages

3.1.2.1 The Government As Foreclosing Mortgage Holder

Due process requires adequate notice and a meaningful opportunity for a hearing prior to deprivation of a significant property interest.[2] A foreclosure by power of sale of a mortgage held by the federal government would seem to violate this standard, because personal notice of a foreclosure sale is not required in all states,[3] and no state which permits power of sale foreclosure requires a court hearing prior to foreclosure.

Under the Supreme Court's state action doctrine, there is no federal due process protection without a state actor, and most power of sale foreclosure proceedings involve two private parties.[4] However, when the foreclosing party is an

2 *See* Sniadach v. Family Fin. Corp., 395 U.S. 337, 89 S. Ct. 1820, 23 L. Ed. 2d 349 (1969) (hearing must be aimed at establishing the validity, or at least the probable validity, of the underlying claim); Mullane v. Cent. Hanover Trust, 339 U.S. 306, 70 S. Ct. 652, 94 L. Ed. 865 (1950) (notice must be reasonably calculated under the circumstances to apprise interested parties of the pendency of the action).

The Due Process Clause of the Fifth Amendment applies to the federal government, while the Due Process Clause of the Fourteenth Amendment applies to the states.

3 *See, e.g.*, Mich. Comp. Laws §§ 600.3101 to 600.3180.

4 In the mid to late 1970s, there was a wave of assaults on the power of sale foreclosure as a violation of due process. Almost all foundered on the lack of state action. Courts cited, among other decisions, the Supreme Court's opinion in Flagg Bros., Inc. v. Brooks, 436 U.S. 149, 98 S. Ct. 1729, 56 L. Ed. 2d 185 (1978). In *Flagg Bros.*, the Supreme Court upheld a New York state statute that authorized the sale of stored goods to satisfy a warehouseman's lien. The Court found no due process violation because there was no state action implicated by the sale. No state officials participated in the sale, and because the settlement of disputes between debtors and creditors is not a traditional, exclusive function of the state, the mere fact that the state authorized the sale through a statute does not create state action.

For more recent examples rejecting due process challenges to state non-judicial foreclosure statutes, see Apao v. Bank of N.Y.,

instrumentality of the government, the state action requirement is satisfied and full due process protections apply. The majority of courts which have considered this issue have had no trouble finding state action when the foreclosing party is a direct instrumentality of the federal government, such as the Rural Housing Service or the Department of Veterans Affairs.[5]

324 F.3d 1091 (9th Cir. 2003) (private foreclosure sale did not involve state action); Waller v. Life Bank, 2008 WL 495486 (E.D. Mich. Feb. 21, 2008) (citing cases from Michigan Appeals and Supreme Courts and the Sixth Circuit holding that Michigan's foreclosure by advertisement procedure is not state action); Curlee v. Wells Fargo Home Mortgage, 2007 WL 4287544 (N.D. Miss. Dec. 5, 2007) (Mississippi's non-judicial foreclosure procedure is not state action); Parker v. Bancorp-South Bank, 253 S.W.3d 918 (Ark. 2007) (Arkansas Statutory Foreclosure Act is constitutional; no state action, so no due process requirement under U.S. or state constitution); Parks v. Bank of New York, 614 S.E.2d 63 (Ga. 2005). *But see* Griffin v. Bierman, 941 A.2d 475 (Md. 2008) (parties agree that foreclosure constitute state action, and process must satisfy due process requirements).

5 *See* Boley v. Brown, 10 F.3d 218 (4th Cir. 1993) (foreclosures of VA-guaranteed loan must comply with due process); Vail v. Derwinski, 946 F.2d 589 (8th Cir. 1991), *amended by* 956 F.2d 812 (8th Cir. 1992); Johnson v. U.S. Dep't of Agric., 734 F.2d 774 (11th Cir. 1984) (foreclosure of Farmers Home Admin. (FmHA) mortgage subject to due process constraints); United States v. Whitney, 602 F. Supp. 722 (W.D.N.Y. 1985) (VA foreclosure subject to due process requirements); Rau v. Cavanaugh, 500 F. Supp. 204 (D.S.D. 1980) (notice by publication constitutionally defective; administrative hearing may satisfy due process); Ricker v. United States, 417 F. Supp. 133 (D. Me. 1976) (notice by publication under Maine statute insufficient); Garner v. Tri-State Dev. Corp., 382 F. Supp. 377 (E.D. Mich. 1974); Law v. U.S. Dep't of Agric., 366 F. Supp. 1233 (N.D. Ga. 1973). *See also* Williams v. Conner, 522 F. Supp. 2d 92 (D.D.C. 2007) (farmer stated due process claim; fact issue whether Rural Housing Service complied with its own rules to notify farmer of deficiency after foreclosure sale); United States v. Asken, 2002 WL 32175416 (E.D. Pa. Oct. 28, 2002) (FmHA regulations provide adequate notice and opportunity for hearing). *But see* Vail v. Brown, 39 F.3d 208 (8th Cir. 1994) (hearing on deficiency not required by due process because foreclosure notice permitted veterans to participate in foreclosure sales).

Courts have generally refused to find state action in cases in which the foreclosure is being conducted by a federally-owned corporation, such as the Federal National Mortgage Ass'n (FNMA), Government National Mortgage Ass'n (GNMA), or Federal Home Loan Mortgage Corp. (FHLMC). *See* Warren v. Gov't Nat'l Mortgage Ass'n, 611 F.2d 1229 (8th Cir. 1980); Hoffman v. Dep't of Hous. & Urban Dev., 519 F.2d 1160 (5th Cir. 1975) (court rejected argument that foreclosure by FNMA by power of sale violates due process); Northrip v. Fed. Nat'l Mortgage Ass'n, 527 F.2d 23 (6th Cir. 1975) (foreclosure by FNMA is not state action, power of sale foreclosure is privately created contractual remedy); Liberty Mortgage Banking Ltd. v. Fed. Home Loan Mortgage Corp., 822 F. Supp. 956 (E.D.N.Y. 1993) (Freddie Mac is not state actor). *See generally* Blegen, Daniel E., *The Constitutionality of Power of Sale Foreclosures by Federal Government Entities*, 62 Mo. L. Rev. 425 (Spring 1997).

Although courts have consistently imposed due process requirements on foreclosing federal agencies, no court has held that federal agencies cannot use the power of sale process, only that whatever method of foreclosure is used must meet the minimal due process standards of notice and hearing. Thus, when federal agencies have foreclosed under state statutes which only require notice by publication, courts have invalidated the sales on the grounds that the notice was not "reasonably calculated under all the circumstances to apprise interested parties of the pendency of the action and afford them an opportunity to present their objections."[6] And with respect to the hearing requirement, courts have suggested that an administrative hearing within the foreclosing agency may satisfy due process as long as the hearing officer is neutral and hearing procedures comport with due process standards.[7]

3.1.2.2 Due Process Requirements

Once state action has been established, due process protections apply. Exactly what this protection means for borrowers, however, is not entirely clear. Generally, due process requires notice reasonably calculated to apprise interested parties of the pendency of the action,[8] and a pre-deprivation hearing aimed at establishing the validity of the underlying claim.[9] In light of the Supreme Court's decision in *Mennonite Board of Mission v. Adams*,[10] notice by publication or posting (constructive notice) is probably invalid. Notice must be served personally, either by mail or by other means necessary to insure actual notice.[11] As a

6 Mullane v. Cent. Hanover Trust, 339 U.S. 306, 314–315, 70 S. Ct. 852, 94 L. Ed. 865, 873 (1950).

7 Johnson v. U.S. Dep't of Agric., 734 F.2d 774 (11th Cir. 1984); United States v. Ford, 551 F. Supp. 204 (D.S.D. 1980). *But see* Sutton v. U.S. Small Bus. Admin. 92 Fed. Appx. 112 (6th Cir. 2003) (unpublished) (foreclosure by SBA did not violate borrower's due process rights where foreclosure complied with Michigan advertisement procedure; prior hearing not necessarily required to satisfy due process; court used a balancing test, and borrowers had ample opportunity to discuss the defaulted mortgage with the SBA and to attempt to arrive at a compromise prior to foreclosure).

8 Mullane v. Cent. Hanover Trust, 339 U.S. 306, 70 S. Ct. 852, 94 L. Ed. 865 (1950). *See also* Williams v. Conner, 522 F. Supp. 2d 92 (D.D.C. 2007) (farmer stated due process claim; fact issue whether Rural Housing Service complied with its own rules to notify farmer of deficiency after foreclosure sale).

9 Sniadach v. Family Fin. Corp., 395 U.S. 337, 89 S. Ct. 1820, 23 L. Ed. 2d 349 (1969).

10 462 U.S. 791, 798, 103 S. Ct. 2706, 77 L. Ed. 2d 180 (1982) (applying due process notice requirements to a tax sale and holding that notice by publication was insufficient). *See* § 13.3.4.2, *infra*.

11 Mennonite Bd. of Mission v. Adams, 462 U.S. 791, 103 S. Ct. 2706, 77 L. Ed. 2d 180 (1982). *See* Henderson v. Kingpin Dev. Co., 859 So. 2d 122 (La. Ct. App. 2003) (notice required if identity of subsequent owner of property was ascertainable from conveyance records); Freeman v. City of Kingsport, 926 S.W.2d

general matter, notice must be timely and must adequately detail the reasons for the proposed action (the foreclosure).[12]

With respect to the hearing requirement, courts which have applied due process standards to governmental foreclosures have not required agencies to foreclose by judicial process. An administrative hearing may be sufficient, if it provides a meaningful and timely opportunity to contest the foreclosure.[13] One court has stated that an administrative hearing which meets the requirements of *Goldberg v. Kelly*[14] is necessary.[15] In *Goldberg* the Supreme Court found that before welfare benefits could be terminated, a recipient must be given a hearing which satisfies due process. While the Court stated that due process hearing requirements could vary depending on the nature of the property right at stake, the Court articulated some basic criteria for a fair hearing. The hearing provided must give the recipient an effective opportunity to defend by confronting witnesses and presenting arguments and evidence orally.[16] The recipient must be given the right to be represented by counsel, though at her own expense.[17] The decision maker's conclusion must be based solely on legal rules and evidence adduced at the hearing.[18] In order to insure compliance with this requirement, the decision maker must put the decision in writing, state the reasons for the decision and detail the evidence relied upon.[19] And the decision maker must be impartial.[20] It would seem also that an opportunity to appeal the decision must be available.

One final consideration which has been addressed to some extent by the courts is: assuming due process protections of notice and a hearing apply, can a borrower validly waive these protections in a mortgage or otherwise? While courts have held that these protections can be waived, such a waiver must be knowing and voluntary.[21] When the waiver provision[22] is contained in the mortgage itself, it is unlikely to be honored by the court.[23] One court termed the mortgage a "contract of adhesion" and found that the purported waiver was ineffective because "the Government has 'made no showing whatever that the [borrowers] were actually aware or made aware of the significance of the fine print now relied upon as a waiver of constitutional rights.' "[24] Other factors relevant to the voluntariness of the waiver were the borrowers' lack of education, their lack of familiarity with legal documents and foreclosure proceedings, the fact that they did not read the mortgage and had no understanding that they were foregoing their rights to due process protections, their lack of legal representation, and the fact that no one explained the waiver they were signing.[25]

A borrower, however, may be held to have waived her right to a hearing by conduct. In *United States v. Ford*,[26] the court found that while the borrowers' waiver of their due process rights in the note and deed of trust was not voluntary because of the inequality of bargaining power between them and the Farmers Home Administration (FmHA) (now RHS), they waived their right to a hearing by failing to respond to notices sent by the FmHA advising them that they had the right to a meeting before the foreclosure took place.[27]

3.2 Mortgages Insured by the Federal Housing Authority

3.2.1 Pre-Foreclosure Servicing Requirements on FHA-Insured Mortgages

3.2.1.1 In General

Congress created the Federal Housing Administration (FHA) in 1934 to help define federal housing policy during the Depression. The FHA's primary public purpose is now to expand homeownership and rental housing opportunities for people not adequately served by the private mortgage markets.

The FHA is now part of the Department of Housing and Urban Development (HUD) and administers a variety of single family mortgage insurance programs designed to

247 (Tenn. Ct. App. 1996) (whether heirs' identity and addresses were ascertainable in order to require mailed notice as a matter of due process is a question of fact to be determined at trial). *But see* Miss. Farm Bureau Ins. Co. v. Coleman, 876 F. Supp. 111, 114 (S.D. Miss. 1995) (actual receipt of notice not required, service of notice by mail is per se sufficient to comply with due process whether or not such notice ultimately resulted in actual notice); Cheff v. Edwards, 203 Mich. App. 557, 513 N.W.2d 439, 441 (1994) (foreclosure by advertisement does not violate due process; foreclosure is a matter of private contract rights, not judicial action).

12 Goldberg v. Kelly, 397 U.S. 254, 90 S. Ct. 1011, 25 L. Ed. 2d 287 (1970).

13 Ricker v. United States, 417 F. Supp. 133, 138 (D. Me. 1976).

14 397 U.S. 254, 90 S. Ct. 1011, 25 L. Ed. 2d 287 (1970).

15 United States v. Ford, 551 F. Supp. 1101 (N.D. Miss. 1982).

16 *Goldberg*, 397 U.S. at 267.

17 *Id.*, 397 U.S. at 270.

18 *Id.*, 397 U.S. at 271.

19 *Id.*

20 *Id.*

21 *See* United States v. Ford, 551 F. Supp. 1101, 1105 (N.D. Miss. 1982); Rau v. Cavanaugh, 500 F. Supp. 204 (D.S.D. 1980); Ricker v. United States, 417 F. Supp. 133, 139 (D. Me. 1976).

22 Or in most cases, a provision allowing foreclosure by power of sale, without a hearing.

23 *See* United States v. Ford, 551 F. Supp. 1101, 1105 (N.D. Miss. 1982); Rau v. Cavanaugh, 500 F. Supp. 204 (D.S.D. 1980); Ricker v. United States, 417 F. Supp. 133, 139 (D. Me. 1976).

24 Ricker v. United States, 417 F. Supp. 133, 139 (D. Me. 1976) (citing Fuentes v. Shevin, 407 U.S. 67, 95, 92 S. Ct. 1983, 32 L. Ed. 2d 556 (1972)).

25 *Id.* at 140.

26 551 F. Supp. 1101, 1105 (N.D. Miss. 1982).

27 *Id.*

make homeownership more readily available.[28] These programs operate through HUD-approved lending institutions such as banks, savings and loan associations, and mortgage companies. These lenders fund the mortgage, which HUD insures. HUD does not provide direct loans or financial assistance to purchase a home. (However, HUD does acquire a small number of mortgages, for one reason or another, after they are made. Special issues that arise when HUD itself is the foreclosing mortgage holder are covered at § 3.2.3, *infra.*)

Homeowners pay premiums for the insurance by which HUD guarantees the lender it will earn a return for taking the risk of lending money to the homeowner.[29] If the lender forecloses, it receives compensation for most of any losses due to the foreclosure.[30]

For the most part, the procedures to foreclose on a FHA-insured or guaranteed mortgage are the same as those applicable to other mortgages. State law will govern.[31]

However, families facing foreclosure of FHA-insured mortgages have some protections not available to persons with conventional loans. For example, a lender under these programs may not commence to foreclose for a default in payment unless at least three full monthly installments are past due;[32] the lender may not foreclose when the only default is an inability to pay an escrow shortage in a lump sum;[33] the lender must give notice of the default no later than at the end of the second month of delinquency;[34] the lender must make reasonable efforts to arrange or hold a face-to-face interview with the homeowner before three monthly installments are due and unpaid;[35] and the lender must accept partial payments in many circumstances.[36] The lender must also permit reinstatement of the mortgage, even after foreclosure proceedings have been initiated, if the borrower tenders in a lump sum all amounts required to bring the account current, including foreclosure costs and reasonable attorneys fees.[37] This reinstatement right does not apply if the lender has previously accepted reinstatement within the preceding two years.

In addition, homeowners, including those with conventional mortgages, are entitled to notice of the availability of housing counseling and notice of their rights under the Servicemembers Civil Relief Act (SCRA). The SCRA notice must be sent: (1) to all homeowners who are in default on a residential mortgage; (2) include a toll-free number (800-342-9647) to call if servicemembers or their dependents require further assistance; and (3) be made within forty-five days from the date a missed payment was due, unless the homeowner pays the overdue amount before the expiration of the forty-five-day period.[38] In addition, within the same time period, the lender must notify all eligible homeowners in default of the availability of housing counseling provided by HUD-approved agencies and the lender.[39]

---

28 *See* 12 U.S.C. §§ 1701 to 1701z-15. Some of the FHA insurance programs which are currently active are:
Mortgage Insurance Section 203(b);
Mortgage Insurance for Disaster Victims Section 203(h);
Mortgage Insurance for Outlying Areas Section 203(i);
Rehabilitation Mortgage Insurance Section 203(k);
Cooperative Program Section 203(n):
Mortgage Insurance for Low- and Moderate-Income Buyers Section 221(d)(2);
Mortgage Insurance for Condominium Units Section 234(c);
Mortgage Insurance for Adjustable Rate Mortgages;
Energy Efficient Mortgage Insurance.
A complete list of HUD's current single-family housing programs can be found at www.hud.gov/offices/hsg/sfh/ins/singlefamily.cfm. For the purposes of this treatise, these programs will be lumped together and called "FHA-insured" or "HUD-insured" loans.

29 FHA requires a one time upfront mortgage insurance premium of 1.50% for a thirty-year fixed rate mortgage. In addition to the upfront fee there is a yearly fee of .50% of the unpaid balance of the loan which is divided into twelve equal payments and paid monthly. If the loan is paid in full within the first seven years there may be a prorated refund of the upfront premium paid. For loans made after December 8, 2004, the FHA eliminated the refund of upfront mortgage premiums except when the borrower refinances to another FHA-insured mortgage. In that circumstance, the borrower will be entitled to a prorated refund within the first three years. *See* Dep't of Hous. & Urban Dev., Mortgagee Letter 2005-03 (Jan. 6, 2005). The monthly mortgage insurance premium may not be waived regardless of the loan to value.

30 When HUD pays out a claim to a foreclosing lender, it succeeds to that lender's interest, and may attempt to collect from the former homeowner. *See, e.g.*, *In re* Bourne, 262 B.R. 745 (Bankr. E.D. Tenn. 2001) (IRS offset tax refund against debt owed to HUD).

31 Note that HUD-insured mortgages are not held by the federal government, but by private entities. The relatively small number of mortgages that are actually held by HUD may be subject to a special federal provision governing HUD foreclosures. *See* § 3.2.3, *infra*. It is unclear whether the special procedures for foreclosures by HUD are being used at this time.

32 24 C.F.R. § 203.606(a).

33 24 C.F.R. § 203.550(d) (when shortage is due to adjustment after analysis).

34 24 C.F.R. § 203.602. *See also* 24 C.F.R. § 201.50(b) (applicable to manufactured home loans); CitiMortgage, Inc. v. Ferguson, 2008 WL 376380 (Ohio Ct. App. Feb. 7, 2008) (denying summary judgment for lender in foreclosure action based on borrower's statement that lender failed to comply with notice requirement under 24 C.F.R. § 201.50).

35 24 C.F.R. § 203.604(b). *See* Washington Mut. Bank v. Mahaffey, 796 N.E.2d 39 (Ohio Ct. App. 2003) (mortgage holder is required to have a face-to-face interview with the borrower, or make a reasonable effort to arrange an interview, before bringing foreclosure action on FHA-insured mortgage). *See also* 24 C.F.R. § 201.50(a) (applicable to manufactured home loans).

36 24 C.F.R. § 203.556(b). *See also* 24 C.F.R. § 201.41 (applicable to manufactured home loans).

37 24 C.F.R. § 203.608.

38 12 U.S.C. § 1701x(c)(5)(A)(ii)(IV), (B); Dep't of Hous. & Urban Dev., Mortgagee Letter 2006-28 (Nov. 20, 2006).

39 12 U.S.C. § 1701x(c)(5)(A)(ii) (I), (III); Dep't of Hous. & Urban Dev., Mortgagee Letter 2002-12 (May 23, 2002). The notice can either list the HUD-approved agencies or provide

Appendix A.2, *infra*, includes selected statutes, regulations, and mortgagee letters for HUD insured loans. These materials and additional HUD interpretations and guidelines are available on the companion website.

3.2.1.2 The HUD Assignment Program

Until 1996, the HUD Home Mortgage Assignment Program was the primary method for low-income homeowners with FHA-insured mortgages to prevent foreclosure during periods of temporary financial hardship.[40] Homeowners facing foreclosure for reasons beyond their control applied directly to HUD for relief.[41] If the homeowner qualified, HUD accepted assignment of the mortgage from the insured lender and provided temporary forbearance (for up to thirty-six months) and other relief to allow the homeowner an opportunity to regain firm financial footing. HUD held all assigned mortgages in its own portfolio.

As of the beginning of 1995 more than 82,000 assigned loans were in HUD's portfolio.[42] In 1996, HUD reported to Congress that performance on those loans was very poor, with more than 50% of the homeowners not making required payments despite forbearance.[43] Subsequently, on April 26, 1996, Congress terminated the HUD assignment program.[44]

After terminating the assignment program, HUD urged lenders to utilize other existing foreclosure avoidance/loss mitigation tools to reduce FHA foreclosure costs and help address the needs of borrowers facing temporary financial hardship.[45] HUD has issued revised regulations and developed educational efforts aimed at lenders, issued a written clarification of the potential workout options, and created an incentive program to encourage lenders to help HUD mitigate its losses by working with homeowners when appropriate.[46]

3.2.1.3 Foreclosure Requirements for Lenders of FHA-Insured Loans

To cure defaults, lenders must either use a foreclosure prevention tool or begin foreclosure within six months of default.[47] Before a loan has been in default for four months, a lender must conduct a review to determine if any of the loss mitigation tools are appropriate.[48] Lenders must document that they have considered all loss mitigation options to determine which, if any, are appropriate before initiating foreclosure.[49] In addition, HUD guidelines require lenders to provide special relief for military personnel on active duty, including postponement of payment on the principal, and protections during foreclosure.[50] Decisions by HUD to exercise or forego exercising options offered under the loss mitigation program, 12 U.S.C. § 1715u, are not subject to

---

HUD's toll-free telephone number where homeowners can obtain information about local agencies. *But see* Castrillo v. American Home Mortgage Servicing, Inc., 670 F. Supp. 2d 516, 527 (E.D. La. 2009) (no private right of action for affirmative claim based on notice requirement; does not address failure to comply as defense to foreclosure).

40 The HUD assignment program was originally created as a result of the settlement in Ferrell v. Pierce in 1976. See Ferrell v. Pierce, 743 F.2d 454 (7th Cir. 1984) for a description of the history of this litigation. The resulting consent decree obligated HUD to operate a mortgage assignment program or equivalent program for all homeowners with single-family home mortgages insured by HUD. Since that time, HUD has tried on occasion to divest itself of this obligation. These attempts have resulted in court decisions holding HUD in contempt. Plaintiffs' attorneys reopened the *Ferrell* case and filed a new motion to hold the defendants in contempt.

41 24 C.F.R. § 203.651 (repealed).

42 Approximately 15,000 families per year were receiving relief under the program and were thereby avoiding loss of their homes. U.S. Dep't of Hous. & Urban Dev., Providing Alternatives to Mortgage Foreclosure: A Report to Congress 86 (Mar. 1996).

43 *Id.* at 89. The reasons for this poor performance are unclear. Some blame poor management of the mortgages by HUD after assignment.

44 The Balanced Budget Downpayment Act I, Pub. L. No. 104-99, 110 Stat. 26 (1996); The Omnibus Consolidated Rescissions and Appropriations Act of 1996, Pub. L. No. 104-134, 110 Stat. 1321–1329 (codified at 12 U.S.C. § 1715u and titled "Authority to assist mortgagors in default"). Anticipated changes to the HUD Assignment program were discussed in *Good News and Bad News On HUD Guaranteed Mortgages*, 14 NCLC REPORTS *Bankruptcy and Foreclosures Ed.* 13 (Jan./Feb. 1996).

Applications in the pipeline at the time the program was terminated were processed. In addition, HUD allowed late applications in some cases for good cause. *See* 62 Fed. Reg. 60,124 (Nov. 6, 1997) (comment on Assignment Program grace period).

This savings clause has since been repealed, however. In Ferrell v. U.S. Dep't of Hous. & Urban Dev., 186 F.3d 805 (7th Cir. 1999), the Seventh Circuit reversed a preliminary injunction reinstating the assignment program. The court reasoned that Congress's intent was clearly to eliminate the assignment program.

45 Dep't of Hous. & Urban Dev., Mortgagee Letter 00-05 (Jan. 19, 2000).

46 *Id.*

47 12 U.S.C. § 1715u(a); 24 C.F.R. § 203.355.

48 24 C.F.R. § 203.605(a). *See also* Dep't of Hous. & Urban Dev., Mortgagee Letter 2002-13 (June 7, 2002); Dep't of Hous. & Urban Dev., Mortgagee Letter 00-05 (Jan. 19, 2000).

49 24 C.F.R. § 203.605(a).

50 *See, e.g.*, 24 C.F.R. §§ 203.345, 203.346 and 203.610. Mortgage holders are also required to comply with the Servicemembers Civil Relief Act (SCRA). Mortgagee Letter 2003-04 (Mar. 24, 2003); Mortgagee Letter 2001-22 (Sept. 24, 2001) (discussing mortgage holders' responsibility under the Soldiers' and Sailors' Civil Relief Act of 1940, a predecessor of the Act).

In addition, homeowners must get notice of their rights under the SCRA and of the availability of housing counseling within forty-five days of missing a payment. 12 U.S.C. § 1701x(c)(5)(A)(ii)(IV); Dep't of Hous. & Urban Dev., Mortgagee Letter 2006-28 (Nov. 20, 2006); Dep't of Hous. & Urban Dev., Mortgagee Letter 2002-12 (May 23, 2002). *See* § 4.12, *infra* (discussion of the Servicemembers Civil Relief Act).

judicial review.[51] HUD may impose sanctions on lenders for failing to engage in loss mitigation activities, in the form of a penalty in the amount of three times the amount of any HUD-insurance benefit the lender is entitled to receive.[52]

3.2.2 Foreclosure Defense Based on Lender's Failure to Comply with HUD Servicing Guidelines

In addition to the foreclosure defense strategies discussed in Chapter 4, *infra*, some courts have held that failure to abide by the regulations governing the servicing of HUD loans is a legal defense to foreclosure.[53] The language of the statute creating the pre-foreclosure servicing requirements and the relevant regulations support the argument that a lender's compliance with these requirements is a prerequisite to foreclosure. In pertinent part, the statute provides: "Upon default of any mortgage insured under this title [12 U.S.C. § 1707 *et seq.*], mortgagees *shall* engage in loss mitigation actions for the purpose of providing an alternative to foreclosure."[54] The relevant regulations use similar language,[55] and make clear that the lender cannot foreclose until all servicing requirements have been met.[56]

Under the prior version of these regulations, in effect when the assignment program was in operation, several courts held that the mortgage holder's failure to comply with servicing regulations, including the sending of required notices, constituted an affirmative defense to foreclosure.[57] For example, in *Federal National Mortgage Ass'n v. Moore*,[58] a borrower raised as a defense to a foreclosure the fact that the lender had not provided a notice of default that complied with HUD's regulations in effect at the time, because it was not on a form "approved by the Secretary [of HUD]" and it was not timely.[59] In *Bankers Life v. Denton*,[60] the borrower alleged as a defense that the mortgage holder had failed to comply with the provisions of the servicing regulations, namely, by failing to hold a face-to-face interview with the borrower before three loan installments had become past due, to seek that face-to-face interview through a certified mail request and a visit to the borrower at the mortgaged property, and to review its file to determine compliance with the appropriate servicing requirements. The court held that the borrower had a valid defense to foreclosure based on the lender's failure to meet these

51 12 U.S.C. § 1715u(d). *See* Dean v. U.S. Dep't of Hous. & Urban Dev., 2000 U.S. Dist. LEXIS 6361 (W.D.N.Y. Mar. 14, 2000).
This provision was included presumably to prevent courts from requiring HUD to set up an alternative to foreclosure program, such as the assignment program which was the result of the litigation in Ferrell. *See also* Miller v. GE Capital Mortgage Servs., Inc. (*In re* Miller), 124 Fed. Appx. 152 (4th Cir. 2005) (no implied private right of action to enforce loss mitigation requirements of 24 C.F.R. §§ 203.600 to 203.660).

52 Veterans Affairs and HUD Appropriations Act, Pub. L. No. 105-276, § 601(g), 112 Stat. 2461 (1998).

53 *See* Kersey v. PHH Mortgage Corp., ___ F. Supp. 2d ___, 2010 WL348380 (E.D. Va. Jan. 22, 2010) (refusing to dismiss declaratory judgment action seeking ruling that mortgage holder failed to comply with pre-foreclosure requirement for face-to-face interview set forth in mortgage documents incorporating terms of 24 C.F.R. § 203.604); Ghervescu v. Wells Fargo Home Mortgage, 2008 WL 660248 (Cal. Ct. App. Mar. 13, 2008) (unpublished) (borrower may assert lender's failure to apply FHA mandatory loss mitigation procedures defensively either to preclude or set aside sale); ABN AMRO Mortgage Group, Inc. v. Tullar, 770 N.W.2d 851 (Iowa Ct. App. 2009) (table) (stating that borrower may assert defensively lender's failure to comply with contractually incorporated HUD regulations, but concluding that in this case lender complied with regulations); Wells Fargo Home Loan Mortgage v. Neal, 922 A.2d 538 (Md. 2007); GMAC v. Grey, 1991 Ohio App. LEXIS 6004 (1991). *See also* Countrywide Home Loans v. Wilkerson, 2004 WL 539983 (N.D. Ill. Mar. 12, 2004) (lender not entitled to summary judgment in foreclosure action where it had not established that it complied with 24 C.F.R. § 203.604, requiring face-to-face meeting with mortgagor, or reasonable efforts to arrange a meeting); Mellon Mortgage Co. v. Larios, 1998 U.S. Dist. LEXIS 7988 (N.D. Ill. May 19, 1998) (failure to comply with HUD servicing requirements is a defense to foreclosure); Fed. Nat'l Mtg. Ass'n v. Moore, 609 F. Supp. 194 (N.D. Ill. 1985); Brown v. Lynn, 392 F. Supp. 559 (N.D. Ill. 1975); Nat'l City Mortgage v. Pope, 2002 Conn. Super. LEXIS (Conn. Super. Ct. Mar. 13, 2002) (lender did not comply with HUD regulations as described in mortgage); Bankers Life v. Denton, 120 Ill. App. 3d 576, 458 N.E.2d 203 (1983); Fed. Nat'l Mortgage Ass'n v. Ricks, 83 Misc. 2d 814, 372 N.Y.S.2d 485 (Sup. Ct. 1975); GMAC v. Grey, 1991 Ohio App. LEXIS 6004 (1991); Fleet Real Estate Funding v. Smith, 530 A.2d 919 (Pa. Super. Ct. 1987). *Cf.* Cross v. Fed. Nat'l Mortgage Ass'n, 359 So. 2d 464 (Fla. Dist. Ct. App. 1978). *Contra* Manufacturers Hanover Mortgage Corp. v. Snell, 370 N.W.2d 401 (Mich. Ct. App. 1985); Fed. Nat'l Mortgage Ass'n v. Prior, 381 N.W.2d 558 (Wis. Ct. App. 1988).

54 12 U.S.C. § 1715u(a) (emphasis added).

55 24 C.F.R. § 203.500 ("It is the intent of the Department that no mortgagee shall commence foreclosure or acquire title to a property until the requirements of this subpart have been followed."). *See, e.g.*, 24 C.F.R. § 203.606 ("[b]efore initiating foreclosure, the mortgagee *must ensure that all* servicing requirements of this subpart have been met") (emphasis added); 24 C.F.R. § 203.605(a) ("Before four full monthly installments due on the mortgage have become unpaid, the mortgagee *shall* evaluate on a monthly basis all of the loss mitigation techniques provided at § 203.501 to determine which is appropriate.") (emphasis added).

56 *See* Bankers Life Co. v. Denton, 120 Ill. App. 3d 576, 458 N.E.2d 203 (1983) (discussion of mandatory nature of similar regulations in effect in 1983); Wells Fargo Home Loan Mortgage, Inc. v. Neal, 922 A.2d 538 (Md. 2007) (discussion of the mandatory language in statute and mortgagee letter).

57 *See* Fed. Nat'l Mortgage Ass'n v. Moore, 609 F. Supp. 194 (N.D. Ill. 1985); Bankers Life Co. v. Denton, 120 Ill. App. 3d 576, 458 N.E.2d 203 (1983); GMAC v. Grey, 1991 Ohio App. LEXIS 6004 (Ohio Ct. App. 1991) (holding that the failure of a mortgage holder to adhere to the HUD servicing requirements set forth in the regulations and handbook constitutes an affirmative defense to foreclosure).

58 609 F. Supp. 194 (N.D. Ill. 1985).

59 *Id.* at 196.

60 120 Ill. App. 3d 576, 458 N.E.2d 203 (1983).

requirements because the language contained in the servicing requirements is mandatory and expressly requires compliance.[61] The court noted that the servicing requirements have the force and effect of law, having been adopted as regulations pursuant to the authority conferred on HUD by Congress.[62] The court rejected the argument that the ability of HUD to bar a lender from the insurance program for failure to comply with the servicing requirements was adequate remedy for the borrower.[63]

Although the regulations in effect at the time these cases were decided have been changed, and the authorizing statute has been amended, the mandatory nature of the language is exactly the same, and many of the requirements, namely the sending of pre-foreclosure notices and the pre-foreclosure review, are the same. One case decided since 12 U.S.C. § 1715u was amended and the new regulations were issued, *Mellon Mortgage Co. v. Larios*,[64] concluded that the result should be the same under the revised standards. Citing cases decided under the assignment program era regulations which held that the lender's failure to comply with servicing guidelines was a defense to foreclosure, the court ruled that failure to comply with the new servicing regulations was also a defense.[65] Other cases have put the burden on the lender to comply with HUD regulations prior to foreclosure.[66]

Several courts have allowed borrowers to raise a lender's noncompliance with HUD guidelines as an equitable defense to a foreclosure.[67] In *Washington Mutual Bank v. Mahaffey*,[68] a foreclosing lender was denied summary judgment based on its failure to arrange a face-to-face interview with the borrower. Even though a representative of the lender visited the borrower's property, the lender failed to establish that it made a reasonable effort to arrange an interview with the borrower because it did not satisfy the HUD regulations' minimum requirement of one letter sent to the borrower via certified mail. Earlier cases have denied the lender the right to foreclose on similar grounds. These courts have reasoned that the guidelines provide "sensible, equitable standards of conduct, consistent with and issued in furtherance of the national housing goals,"[69] and that a lender who disregards these standards violates reasonable expectations of good faith and fair dealing.[70] Lenders have an incentive to participate in the HUD-insured mortgage program and to receive a significant benefit from the program because the loans are virtually risk free due to the federal government guarantee.[71] It would be inconsistent with both the spirit and purpose of the HUD program and with the equitable doctrine of clean hands to allow lenders to accept the benefits of the program while ignoring the features which distinguish it from traditional mortgages.[72]

Borrowers may be rebuffed, however, in their efforts to bring an affirmative action to challenge the lack of pre-foreclosure servicing. In *Miller v. G.E. Capital Mortgage Servs., Inc.*, the Fourth Circuit held that a borrower with an FHA mortgage had no private right of action to sue for violation of the loss mitigation provisions under 12 U.S.C.

---

61 *Id.*, 458 N.E.2d at 204.

62 *Id.*, 458 N.E.2d at 204–205.

63 "HUD's withdrawal of a mortgagee's approval to participate in the mortgage insurance program after repeated violations of the servicing requirements is a useless remedy for the individual faced with the immediate problem of the foreclosure action; an action which could possibly be avoided by either assignment of the mortgage to HUD or further efforts to arrange a revised payment plan." *Id.* at 205.

64 1998 U.S. Dist. LEXIS 7988 (N.D. Ill. May 19, 1998).

65 *Id.* at *5. See also GMAC Mortgage of Penn. v. Gray, 1991 WL 268742 (Ohio Ct. App. Dec. 10, 1991) (failure to comply with servicing requirements is an affirmative defense to foreclosure).

66 *See, e.g.*, Countrywide Home Loans v. Wilkerson, 2004 WL 539983 (N.D. Ill. May 12, 2004) (unreported) (lender not entitled to summary judgment in foreclosure action where it had not established that it complied with 24 C.F.R. § 604, requiring face-to-face meeting with the borrower, or reasonable efforts to arrange a meeting).

67 *See, e.g.*, Ghervescu v. Wells Fargo Home Mortgage, 2008 WL 660248 (Cal. Ct. App. Mar. 13, 2008) (unreported); ABN AMRO Mortgage Group, Inc. v. Tullar, 770 N.W.2d 851 (Iowa Ct. App. 2009) (table) (stating that borrower may assert defensively lender's failure to comply with contractually incorporated HUD regulations, but concluding that in this case lender complied with regulations); Wells Fargo Home Loan Mortgage, Inc. v. Neal, 922 A.2d 538 (Md. 2007).

Cases decided under the previous version of the statute and regulations that may be helpful include: Cross v. Fed. Nat'l Mortgage Ass'n, 359 So. 2d 464 (Fla. Dist. Ct. App. 1978); Associated E. Mortgage Co. v. Young, 163 N.J. Super. 315, 394 A.2d 899 (Super. Ct. Ch. Div. 1978); Fed. Nat'l Mortgage Ass'n v. Ricks, 83 Misc. 2d 814, 372 N.Y.S.2d 485 (Sup. Ct. 1975) (lender's failure to follow HUD's requirements may "constitute unconscionable conduct so as to deny the mortgagee the foreclosure relief it is seeking"); Fleet Real Estate Funding v. Smith, 530 A.2d 919 (Pa. Super. Ct. 1987). *See also* Manufacturers Hanover Mortgage Corp. v. Ballard, 1985 WL 3075 (N.D. Ill. Oct. 11, 1985); Brown v. Lynn, 392 F. Supp. 559 (N.D. Ill. 1975); Bankers Life Co. v. Denton, 120 Ill. App. 3d 576, 458 N.E.2d 203 (1983); Banc Plus Mortgage Corp. v. McClaskey, Clearinghouse No. 43,736A (Ohio C.P. Franklin County Mar. 28, 1988) (No. 87CV-05-3052); Pa. Sch. Employees Retirement Fund v. Terrel, 582 A.2d 367 (Pa. Super. Ct. 1990). *But see* Heritage Bank v. Ruh, 465 A.2d 547 (N.J. Super. Ct. Ch. Div. 1983) (borrower negligent for failure to make payments, failing to contact mortgage holder, failing to notify mortgage holder it was sending notice to the wrong address and failing to make escrow payments; under these circumstances, violation of servicing guidelines not a defense).

68 154 Ohio App. 3d 44, 796 N.E.2d 39 (2003). *See also* LaSalle National Bank v. Johnson, 2006 WL 551563 (N.J. Super. Ct. Ch. Div. Mar. 3, 2006) (unpublished) (denying lender summary judgment). *But see* Washington Mut. Bank v. Teodorescu, 2005 WL 3108231 (N.J. Super. Ct. App. Div. Nov. 22, 2005) (no equitable relief where *pro se* defendant failed to show how lender's failure to follow HUD guidelines was unconscionable).

69 Brown v. Lynn, 392 F. Supp. 559, 563 (N.D. Ill. 1975).

70 *Id.*

71 *Id.*

72 Associated E. Mortgage Co. v. Young, 163 N.J. Super. 315, 394 A.2d 899 (Super. Ct. Ch. Div. 1978).

§ 1715u.[73] The borrower, a chapter 7 bankruptcy debtor, brought an adversary proceeding against the lender to avoid the pre-petition foreclosure of his home. Citing the lack of "rights-creating" language, the court reasoned that Congress did not intend to create such a right for borrowers and the focus of the law was on regulating lenders.

The Maryland Court of Appeals, the state's highest court, rejected a breach of contract claim based on a servicer's noncompliance with language contained in the deed of trust. The language in the deed of trust required compliance with FHA regulations before the loan is accelerated or foreclosure initiated. The court in *Wells Fargo Home Mortgage, Inc. v. Neal* held that this contractual language was not a bargained for term between the homeowner and servicer, but rather an FHA-imposed form drafted by that agency, and the language did not give rise to a private right of action for breach of contract.[74] The court went on to say, however, that foreclosure proceedings are equitable in nature, and failure to comply with HUD servicing guidelines may be asserted as a defense. Indeed, the court noted the mandatory nature of the loss mitigation requirements in the statute and mortgagee letters and stated that "under the principles of equity, a mortgagee's commencement of a foreclosure proceeding on an FHA-insured mortgage, without first having adhered to the mandatory loss mitigation regulations, may invalidate the mortgagee's declaration of default."[75] For a more detailed discussion of courts' application of equitable principles to deny foreclosure relief under unfair circumstances, both inside and outside the context of government-related loans, *see* Chapter 6, *infra*.

In a mortgagee letter issued in October 2008 HUD substantially revised its directives to participating FHA mortgage holders regarding treatment of homeowners in bankruptcy.[76] Prior to this letter, HUD had generally prohibited mortgage holders from offering loss mitigation options to borrowers in bankruptcy. The agency was acting under the erroneous belief that a mortgage holder's discussion of loss mitigation options with debtor's counsel might violate the automatic bankruptcy stay. Under the new directives, mortgage holders and servicers are encouraged to contact debtor's counsel and offer loss mitigation options after a bankruptcy has been filed. The letter recognizes that "waiting until a bankruptcy is discharged or dismissed before offering loss mitigation may be injurious to the interests of the borrower, the mortgagee and the FHA insurance funds."[77] In chapter 7 cases the mortgage holder should not require reaffirmation of the debt as a condition to offering appropriate loss mitigation options.[78]

3.2.3 Foreclosure of Mortgages Held by HUD

3.2.3.1 HUD Foreclosure Statute Applies When HUD Holds the Mortgage

Congress has enacted legislation authorizing foreclosure by non-judicial power of sale for HUD-held single family mortgages. This provision applies only to mortgages actually held by HUD (in other words, when HUD is the foreclosing mortgage holder) and not to mortgages which are insured or guaranteed by HUD.[79]

The statute, entitled "Single Family Mortgage Foreclosure,"[80] appears to preempt state foreclosure law by implication, so that even in states where judicial foreclosure is otherwise required, HUD may follow the non-judicial foreclosure procedure established by the statute.[81] In fact, the statute seems to go so far as to grant HUD a power of sale without any regard to whether a power of sale is contained in the mortgage contract.[82] Some of the other key aspects of the foreclosure provision are:[83]

73 124 Fed. Appx. 152 (4th Cir. 2005). *See also* Leggette v. Washington Mut. Bank, 2005 WL 2679699 (N.D. Tex. Oct. 19, 2005) (unlikely that Congress created private right of action under statute or regulations).

74 Wells Fargo Home Loan Mortgage, Inc. v. Neal, 922 A.2d 538 (Md. 2007). *See also* Mitchell v. Chase Home Fin., L.L.C., 2008 WL 623395 (N.D. Tex. Mar. 4, 2008) ("[R]egulations promulgated under the National Housing Act govern relations between the mortgagee and the government, and give the mortgagor no claim for duty owed or for the mortgagee's failure to follow said regulations."); Hayes v. M&T Mortgage Corp., 906 N.E.2d 638, 642 (Ill. Ct. App. 2009). *But see* Kersey v. PHH Mortgage Corp., ___ F. Supp. 2d ___, 2010 WL 348380 (E.D. Va. Jan. 22, 2010) (borrower may assert breach of contract claim based on mortgage holder's failure to comply with FHA servicing requirements incorporated into deed of trust); Baker v. Countrywide Home Loans, Inc., 2009 WL 1810336 (N.D. Tex. June 24, 2009) (failure to comply with HUD regulations incorporated in agreement may give rise to liability on breach of contract theory); Buis v. Wells Fargo Bank, N.A., 401 F. Supp. 2d 612, 616 (N.D. Tex. 2005).

75 Wells Fargo Home Loan Mortgage, Inc. v. Neal, 922 A.2d 538, 551 (Md. 2007).

76 Dep't of Hous. and Urban Dev. Mortgagee Letter 2008-32 (Oct. 17, 2008).

77 *Id.* at 1.

78 *Id. See also* § 9.11.2, *infra.*

79 *See, e.g.,* Gutierrez v. Wells Fargo Bank, 2009 WL 322915 (N.D. Cal. Feb. 9, 2009); Rice v. Wells Fargo Home Mortgage, 2007 WL 4126525 (E.D. Mich. Nov. 19, 2007); Mubeidin v. Homecomings Fin. Network, Inc., 2006 WL 44326 (W.D. Va. Jan. 9, 2006).

80 12 U.S.C. §§ 3751–3768.

81 HUD is not *required* to use this process, however, so that in a state where the state foreclosure process has even less protection for the borrower, HUD might use the state process.

82 12 U.S.C. § 3754(b) of the Act. "A foreclosure commissioner designated under this section shall have a non-judicial power of sale." Most state power of sale laws allow foreclosure by power of sale when the power of sale is contained in the mortgage.

83 The Act appears to be modeled on the Multifamily Mortgage Foreclosure Act of 1981, 12 U.S.C. §§ 3701–3717, which

- HUD must designate a foreclosure commissioner to carry out foreclosures in accordance with the statute;
- The borrower must be given a "Notice of Default and Foreclosure Sale" at least twenty-one days prior to the sale;
- The foreclosure commissioner may cancel the sale if the borrower cures the default (in other words, pays the installments which are then due) before the sale, though the commissioner has discretion to refuse to cancel a foreclosure sale if the borrower has cured a default previously;
- The borrower has no right of redemption after foreclosure;
- If the foreclosure sale price is less than the outstanding mortgage debt, the foreclosure commissioner can ask the attorney general to seek a deficiency judgment, unless the mortgage prohibits such an action.[84]

3.2.3.2 Challenges to the Law

This law raises serious due process issues, particularly for borrowers in states which otherwise require a lender to foreclose by judicial process. No provision is made for a pre-foreclosure hearing, which due process would seem to require.[85]

Regulations promulgated under the act do not appear to rectify these apparent defects.[86] The regulations do not provide for any pre-foreclosure hearing, either administrative or otherwise. The act appears to be modeled on the Multifamily Mortgage Foreclosure Act of 1981,[87] which authorizes HUD to foreclose by power of sale on multifamily residences of more than four units.[88] Regulations issued under the Multifamily Foreclosure Act, however, require that HUD provide the mortgagor with an opportunity informally to present reasons why the mortgage should not be foreclosed.[89]

Because it appears to broadly preempt state foreclosure law, the statute raises issues as to what other foreclosure protections are preempted. For example, will state-mandated notices of intention to foreclose be required? Will such notices be sent voluntarily? Will state-required post-foreclosure accountings of sale proceeds be provided? Are state-mandated cure rights entirely preempted? Are state standards concerning gross inadequacy of price entirely preempted? What law will apply to deficiency claims made by HUD? These questions and numerous others remain open. If HUD acts on its rights under the statute, substantial litigation is likely to result.

It should be noted that HUD currently owns very few mortgages to which this statute would apply.[90] There have been no reports that the statute has been widely used to effectuate foreclosures.

3.2.4 *The Sale of HUD Mortgages*

3.2.4.1 Foreclosure Defense and Counseling for Loans Sold by HUD

In 1995, as a cost cutting measure, HUD began divesting itself of approximately 90,000 mortgage loans which it acquired through the HUD assignment[91] and other programs.[92] Aggressive collection activities by the lenders who

authorizes HUD to foreclose by power of sale on multifamily residences of more than four units. *See* Certified Enterprises, L.L.C. v. Dauphin Creek Apts., L.L.C., 2009 WL 2870506 (S.D. Ala. Sept. 3, 2009) (stating that the Single Family Mortgage Foreclosure Act represents an extension of the Multifamily Mortgage Foreclosure Act, and the former is a "sister" of the latter).

One district court has rejected a constitutional challenge to the Multifamily Mortgage Foreclosure Act. *See* Lisbon Square v. United States, 856 F. Supp. 482 (E.D. Wis. 1994).

84 *See also* Ingram v. Cuomo, 51 F. Supp. 2d 667 (M.D.N.C. 1999) (HUD was not required to obtain deficiency judgment after repossession of manufactured home in order for debt to be subject to referral to Internal Revenue Service (IRS) for collection and tax refund offset).

85 *See* Johnson v. U.S. Dep't of Agric., 734 F.2d 774 (11th Cir. 1984); United States v. Ford, 551 F. Supp. 1101 (N.D. Miss. 1982); § 3.1.2, *supra*.

86 24 C.F.R. §§ 27.100 to 27.123.

87 12 U.S.C. §§ 3701 to 3717. *See* Certified Enterprises, L.L.C. v. Dauphin Creek Apts., L.L.C., 2009 WL 2870506 (S.D. Ala. Sept. 3, 2009) (stating that the Single Family Mortgage Foreclosure Act represents an extension of the Multifamily Mortgage Foreclosure Act, and the former is a "sister" of the latter).

88 One district court has rejected a constitutional challenge to this statute. *See* Lisbon Square v. United States, 856 F. Supp. 482 (E.D. Wis. 1994).

89 24 C.F.R. § 27.5(b). These regulations do not, however, establish any procedures for the administrative hearing, therefore making it difficult to say that this process satisfies due process. *But see* Lisbon Square v. United States, 856 F. Supp. 482 (E.D. Wis. 1994) (holding that the Multifamily Mortgage Foreclosure Act does not violate borrower's due process rights); Carada Ltd. v. McAuliffe, 1993 WL 117525 (W.D.N.Y. Apr. 6, 1993) (due process does not require prior hearing under Multifamily Mortgage Foreclosure Act or judicial foreclosure; borrower had ample opportunity to present reasons why foreclosure should not go forward).

90 HUD has sold virtually all loans in its portfolio. *See* § 3.2.4.1, *infra*.

91 In the HUD assignment program, homeowners facing foreclosure for reasons beyond their control applied to HUD for relief. If the homeowner qualified, HUD accepted assignment of the mortgage from the insured lender and provided temporary forbearance (for up to thirty-six months) and other relief to allow the homeowner an opportunity to regain their financial footing and to begin to pay the full monthly mortgage payment again. Until the recent sales, HUD held all assigned mortgages in its own portfolio. The assignment program was ended by Congress on April 26, 1996. *See* 24 C.F.R. § 203.601; § 3.2.1.2, *supra*.

92 These include assistance payment contracts under 24 C.F.R. § 235.375 and mortgages acquired as automatic assignments under 12 U.S.C. § 1715l. This subsection focuses only upon

purchased the mortgages from HUD have created substantial confusion and anxiety. In many cases, the entities collecting on the loans asserted defaults of tens of thousands of dollars without recognizing the forbearance and other relief which was provided as a matter of law in HUD's assignment program.[93] Further, because the FHA insurance on the loans ended at the time of sale,[94] these homeowners are unable to insist on the use of one of the loss mitigation tools which HUD provides[95] if a default occurs.

Most of HUD's loan portfolio has been sold in a series of auctions, which began in October 1995.[96] Purchasers of these loans and their servicers must follow all requirements set forth in the mortgage loan sale agreement they enter into with HUD when they purchase the loans.[97] In addition, by regulation, when at the time of the sale the homeowner is still within the thirty-six month forbearance period provided by the assignment program, the purchaser must allow the homeowner to continue payment under any forbearance agreement that existed between the homeowner and HUD, and must allow reinstatement of the loan in the event of default if the homeowner pays all or a substantial part of arrearage accrued under the forbearance agreement.[98]

If thirty-six months have passed since the homeowner entered the assignment program, however, the purchaser may require a minimum monthly payment equal to the full monthly payment due under the mortgage. A homeowner must pay more than the full monthly payment due under the mortgage to reduce the arrearage that accumulated during the thirty-six month forbearance period if the homeowner has available income to support the higher payment. The homeowner has the right to reinstate upon default[99] by paying the additional amount that accrued since the time the homeowner failed to make a required payment under any outstanding forbearance agreement, or under the terms of the mortgage if the forbearance agreement has expired.[100]

3.2.4.2 The Importance of the Terms of the Loan Sale Agreement: Enforcement by Borrowers

The purchasers of the loans are also bound by the terms of their loan sale agreements, each of which has important protective provisions for the affected homeowners. HUD inserted a provision in every loan sale agreement which confirms that homeowners have third party beneficiary status to enforce the servicing requirements. Thus, in addition to making complaints to HUD if servicers are not following these mandates, homeowners have the right to sue to enforce the loan sale agreement.

On other important points, however, the loan sale agreements differ and cannot be easily summarized. For that reason, it is critical for advocates to obtain the appropriate sale agreement that governs a particular client's loan.[101] Copies of some of the agreements can be obtained from the National Center on Poverty Law.[102]

Following the first few sales, HUD became more precise in the language it used in the loan sale agreements and made improvements to respond to complaints it received from its field offices, from housing counseling agencies, and from homeowners.[103] For example, the loan sale agreement for the first sale incorporated portions of the HUD Handbook entitled "Mortgage Assignment and Processing Secretary-Held Servicing."[104] HUD changed this method for the next three loan sales by, instead, describing the servicing requirements in the text of the agreements in a more general but less cumbersome way. This change was an improvement in

---

mortgages acquired by HUD through the assignment program.

93 HUD has acknowledged that internal audits by HUD's Inspector General found significant deficiencies with HUD's management of its portfolios. 60 Fed. Reg. 45,331 (Aug. 31, 1995).

94 *Id.* at 45,332.

95 *See* § 2.12, *supra* (discussion of these tools).

96 Purchasers include: EMC Mortgage, Inc.; BCGS L.L.C.; Ocwen National Bank; Salomon Brothers; CS First Boston; and Commercial Finance Service. Wendover Funding, Inc. services many of the loans. Some of the loans may have since been resold, securitized, and/or assigned, presumably with the same level of homeowner protection.

97 24 C.F.R. § 291.307(b).

98 24 C.F.R. § 291.307(c)(1).

99 Note that a homeowner who accumulated an arrearage during the thirty-six month forbearance period allowed by the assignment program, because HUD agreed in forbearance contracts that the homeowner could make reduced payments, while delinquent, is not in default for that reason alone. *See* 12 U.S.C. § 1715u(b).

100 24 C.F.R. § 291.307(c)(2). Some purchasers have threatened foreclosure and demanded the number of payments which the homeowner has not made under a forbearance agreement plus all missed pre-assignment payments, and all amounts forborne and suspended during the thirty-six months of the assignment program and thereafter. This approach is clearly wrong. *In re* Epps, 110 B.R. 691, 707 (E.D. Pa. 1990) (defines difference between payoff amount and cure amount). *See also In re* Santos, 97 B.R. 227 (Bankr. E.D. Pa. 1989).

101 The sales occurred on October 25, 1995, March 20, 1996, September 4, 1996, January 28, 1997, and September 9, 1997. Homeowners whose loans were sold received a letter from HUD informing them of the sale and the name and address of the new holder/servicer. Comparing the dates of these letters to the sale dates gives the advocate the information needed to determine which loan sale agreement applies. For example, if the client's letter explaining the transfer is dated November 1995, the loan was sold in the first sale.

102 FHA Single Family Mortgage Loan Sale #1, Clearinghouse No. 51,971 (Sept. 11, 1995); FHA Single Family Mortgage Loan Sale #2, Clearinghouse No. 51,972 (Apr. 29, 1996); FHA Single Family Mortgage Loan Sale #3, Clearinghouse No. 51,973 (July 18, 1996); FHA Single Family Mortgage Loan Sale #4, Clearinghouse No. 51,974 (Nov. 27, 1996). *See* § 1.1.5, *supra* (information on ordering Clearinghouse documents).

Exhibit L of the FHA Single Family Loan Sale #5 (Sept. 9, 1997) is available on the companion website to thitreatise.

103 *See Good News and Bad News on HUD Guaranteed Mortgages,* 14 NCLC REPORTS *Bankruptcy & Foreclosures Ed.* (Jan./Feb. 1996) (discussion of complaints).

104 HUD Handbook 4330.2 REV-1.

two important ways. First, these loan sale agreements acknowledge that a forbearance agreement with HUD could have been made orally[105] and, if so, the purchaser must honor it.[106] Second, the purchaser is obligated to renew forbearance agreements at least through the original term of the mortgage and thereafter for up to ten years, if it is within the homeowner's reasonable ability to pay a monthly payment which would amortize the mortgage loan in full in that period despite the arrearage.

The third loan sale agreement was improved further because HUD more clearly limited the amount which the purchaser could demand to reinstate a loan in default to any amount the homeowner had not paid under an existing forbearance agreement (if any) for the six months immediately preceding the sale of the loan.[107] HUD further provided that the homeowner must be given at least sixty days to pay this reinstatement amount.[108]

The fourth sale agreement delineated the servicing requirements in much greater detail than the previous three agreements. For the first time, HUD listed what must be included in the forbearance agreements that are required through the life of the loan. The agreement clearly distinguished the servicing requirements for loans still in the initial thirty-six month forbearance period from those sold after this period. The timing and content of default notices and acceleration warnings were also specified. In addition, HUD defined how to calculate the amount necessary to cure a default under various scenarios, late fees, and monthly amounts due under forbearance agreements.

Finally, the fifth sale agreement was structured in the same manner as the fourth agreement and contained all of the features described above. The fifth sale agreement makes clear that the loans may be modified or refinanced. However, the servicer must disclose to the borrower in writing that the right to forbearance terminates once the loan is modified, except if the modification solely extends the maturity date of the loan.[109] In addition, the special servicing guidelines outlined in the agreement are no longer applicable if the loan is brought current any time after the initial thirty-six month period expires.

Advocates have identified numerous problems with the servicing of these loans following the sales. According to the allegations of a class action filed against Wendover Funding, Inc., for example, many homeowners received notices of intent to foreclose even though they were current under a forbearance agreement they had with HUD.[110] Wendover allegedly sent the class members additional notices of intent to foreclose and refused to accept payment. Homeowners became anxious and, believing that foreclosure was imminent, refinanced their loans, paying high closing costs and fees. Furthermore, Wendover charged late fees on the assignment arrearage even when the homeowners were current with their monthly payments. The complaint also alleges violations of the Fair Debt Collection Practices Act.[111]

3.2.4.3 Negotiating Strategies for Affected Homeowners

A serious problem with the HUD assignment program which continues to haunt homeowners is that once arrears have accumulated it is difficult, if not impossible, to pay them off. One reason is that HUD applies the monthly payment first to interest that accrues on advances on escrow payments, then to the advances themselves, then to FHA service charges, then to late fees, then to the escrow, then to interest, and finally to the principal. This practice has resulted in long periods of negative amortization because the reduced or suspended payments were insufficient to cover even all the interest and therefore never reduced the principal. Accordingly, many low-income homeowners allegedly owe $10,000 to $30,000 in arrears in addition to the principal balance due. Despite resuming payments after forbearance, many homeowners will owe more at the end of the term of the mortgage than at the beginning.

Given the difficulty of paying these arrears (even in installments over a long term), negotiating a loan modifi-

105 These agreements state that the oral agreement can be gleaned from the payment history (such as HUD's acceptance of a certain payment amount over time), other information in the servicing file, and, presumably, information provided by the homeowner.

106 HUD was responding to complaints from housing counseling agencies and others that HUD sometimes did not send the homeowner a written forbearance agreement after orally agreeing to accept a certain monthly payment. For loans sold at the first sale, at least one of the servicers attempted to foreclose even though a homeowner had made all monthly payments that HUD had required, but there was no recent written forbearance agreement to document the oral agreement. The payment history, however, made the payment agreement clear and substantiated the homeowner's understanding.

107 Technically the applicable date is the "servicing transfer date" and not the actual date of sale. This date is designated by HUD in each of the loan sale agreements.

108 In addition, if there is a default under a forbearance agreement that requires the homeowner to pay the full monthly mortgage payment and an additional sum to be applied to the assignment arrears, the default can be cured if: the homeowner demonstrates a loss of income or other reasonable justification for the default; the homeowner demonstrates that it is within the homeowner's reasonable ability to pay at least the full monthly payment due under the mortgage; and the homeowner pays the amount that would be due under the new forbearance agreement (i.e., the monthly mortgage payment) times the number of months the homeowner is behind under the current agreement.

109 The maturity date of the loan may be extended up to ten years.

110 The complaint is available at Peoples v. Wendover Funding, Inc., Clearinghouse No. 51,970 (D. Md. filed Jan. 17, 1997) (No. K-97-158). Class certification has been granted. Peoples v. Wendover Funding, 179 F.R.D. 492 (D. Md. 1998).

111 15 U.S.C. §§ 1692–1692o.

cation or paying the loan off through refinancing[112] may be the only viable options for many homeowners. In negotiating a workout or refinancing, advocates should be aware that HUD sold these loans for 74% to 91% of the outstanding principal balance.[113]

What this statistic means for homeowners is that the profit margin for investors is high if homeowners refinance and pay the entire amount due, that is, the unpaid principal plus the assignment arrears.[114] The negotiating room in a given case is likely to be the difference between what the investor paid to purchase the loan and the total amount owed, because any amount higher than the amount the investor paid plus post-sale interest is profit to the investor.

Another issue to consider is that account records in many cases are fragmentary or nonexistent. These records should always be requested in the loan negotiation process in order to make certain that the amount claimed to be due is accurate given the loan payment and forbearance history.

3.3 Mortgages Guaranteed by the Department of Veterans Affairs

3.3.1 Pre-Foreclosure Servicing Requirements for VA-Guaranteed Mortgages

The Department of Veterans Affairs (VA) Home Loan Guaranty Program[115] allows eligible veterans to purchase homes without any down payment at relatively low interest rates. The VA guarantees the loans made by private lenders. The VA's guaranty on the loan protects the lender against loss if the loan goes into default.[116] The amount of guaranty on the loan depends on the loan amount and whether the veteran used some of his or her entitlement previously.

A homeowner whose mortgage is guaranteed by the VA has a variety of options not available to homeowners with private conventional mortgages.[117] These rights are more limited, however, than those available under the HUD or Rural Housing Service programs. The holder of the mortgage may not foreclose unless the borrower fails to make three full monthly payments;[118] may allow the borrower to reinstate prior to sale by tender of the amount of the delinquency, including installment payments, late charges, and reasonable expenses incurred and paid by the lender if foreclosure has begun;[119] and must provide thirty days' advance notice to the VA of its intention to foreclose.[120] The holder must extend all reasonable forbearance, including consideration of a temporary suspension of payments, or the holder may modify the terms by extension or reamortization of the loan.

Prior to initiating a foreclosure action, the VA encourages holders to consider alternative relief and measures to reinstate the loan, including accepting partial payments pursuant to a written repayment plan.[121] The foreclosure action may be stayed or dismissed pending appropriate action by the lender. In addition, under the Servicemembers Civil Relief Act, a court order is required prior to a foreclosure, sale or

---

112 One housing counseling agency in Maryland obtained an agreement with a bank to refinance those homeowners who had been in the assignment program but who had a good payment history for at least a year at market interest rate and market points.

113 This amount varied from sale to sale. Again, it is critical to know when the loan was sold. The loans were sold for $.74 on the dollar (or 74%) of unpaid principal balance for the first and second sales. The sale price increased to $.91 on the dollar (or 91%) of the unpaid principal balance at the third sale and went up slightly to $.92 on the dollar (92%) at the fourth sale. *See* FHA Single Family Mortgage Loan Sale #1, Clearinghouse No. 51,971 (Sept. 11, 1995); FHA Single Family Mortgage Loan Sale #2, Clearinghouse No. 51,972 (Apr. 29, 1996); FHA Single Family Mortgage Loan Sale #3, Clearinghouse No. 51,973 (July 18, 1996); FHA Single Family Mortgage Loan Sale #4, Clearinghouse No. 51,974 (Nov. 27, 1996).

114 For example, if the unpaid principal balance on a loan sold at the first or second sale was $100,000 with an arrears of $30,000, the investor paid only $74,000 (74% of $100,000) for the right to collect $130,000, producing a profit of $56,000 if the homeowner refinances and pays the full amount due of $130,000.

115 38 U.S.C. § 3710. The Home Loan Guaranty Program was established by the Servicemen's Readjustment Act of 1944. The purpose of the program was to enable veterans to obtain loans and to obtain them with the least risk of foreclosure, to both the veteran and the Veterans Administration as guarantor of the veteran's indebtedness. United States v. Shimer, 367 U.S. 374, 81 S. Ct. 1554, 6 L. Ed. 2d 908 (1961).

The VA also has a direct loan program. *See* 38 U.S.C. § 3711.

116 Under the VA's program, a lender is required to collect an up-front one-time fee at closing called the "funding fee." This amount is between .50% and 3.30% of the loan amount depending upon the status of the veteran and if the veteran has used his or her VA benefits previously to purchase a home. There is no monthly premium and there is no refund of the funding fee when the loan-to-value is reduced below 80% or if the loan is paid off early.

117 *See* 38 C.F.R. §§ 36.4300 to 36.4393. *See also* VA Handbook H26-94-1 (1994). Loan servicing handbooks and other resources for information about VA-guaranteed mortgages are available on the VA website at www.homeloans.va.gov.

The VA recently issued a new series of regulations for its Loan Guaranty Program as part of its establishment of a new computer-based loan tracking system. The new regulations, which are substantially similar to existing regulations, were established under a new subpart F: 38 C.F.R. §§ 36.4800 to 36.4893. A new website for the computer-based loan tracking system, called the VA Loan Electronic Reporting Interface (VALERI), is available at www.homeloans.va.gov/valeri.htm. This website contains up to date information on the program including a copy of U.S. Dep't of Veterans Affairs, Veterans Benefit Administration, VA Loan Electronic Reporting Interface: VA Servicer Guide, Version 1.1 (Apr. 2008).

118 VA Handbook H26-94-1, at § 4.05 (1994).

119 38 C.F.R. § 36.4308(h); VA Handbook H26-94-1, at § 4.10 (1994).

120 38 C.F.R. § 36.4317; VA Handbook H26-94-1, at § 4.08 (1994).

121 The VA's loan workout policies are discussed in detail at § 2.12.2, *supra*.

seizure of property while the servicemember is on active duty or within ninety days after the end of active duty.[122]

Although authority exists for the VA to refund the unpaid balance of a loan to the lender, and take assignment of the loan and the mortgage,[123] in reality the VA rarely exercises this power.[124] The failure of the VA to take assignment of guaranteed mortgages has been the subject of unsuccessful litigation. Courts have held that the failure of the VA to take foreclosure avoidance measures or to take assignment of defaulted mortgages is a matter committed to agency discretion and is therefore not subject to judicial review.[125]

The VA recently established a new computer-based loan tracking system called VA Loan Electronic Reporting Interface or VALERI. As part of this process the VA overhauled some of the regulations and guidelines which govern the servicing of guaranteed loans. Many of the new rules are substantively similar to existing regulations with the exception of rules governing the computer-based loan tracking system. In general, the new rules which relate to the servicing and foreclosure of guaranteed loans delegate more authority to servicers to implement loss mitigation options, increase incentive payments to servicers for using various options, establish a system for measuring servicer performance, establish a time frame for when foreclosure should be completed, and set limits on the amount of interest and other fees and costs that can be included in a guaranty claim.[126]

Appendix A.3, *infra*, contains for VA-guaranteed loans selected statutes regulations, a loan foreclosure fee schedule and time frames, and policies toward natural disasters. The companion website has these materials and additional interpretations and guidelines for VA-guaranteed mortgages.

3.3.2 *Foreclosure of VA-Guaranteed Mortgages*

Foreclosure of VA-guaranteed mortgages are generally conducted in accordance with the laws of the state in which the property is located.[127] However, some courts have held that VA regulations preempt or override state foreclosure law.[128] To the extent that VA regulations offer more protection than the application of weaker state laws, borrowers may benefit. Other courts hold that the only state laws nullified are those inconsistent with VA regulations or their purposes.[129] For example, where an original mortgagor was not been made a party to the foreclosure of an assumed mortgage, the original mortgagor is not liable for any deficiency.[130]

---

122 50 U.S.C. app. § 533(c). Temporary amendments to the SCRA, codified at 50 U.S.C. § app. 533(b) and (c), effective September 30, 2008 through December 31, 2010, affect two provisions of the SCRA. First, under the pre-amendment version of subsection (b) of section 533 a court had the authority to enter an order to stay foreclosure proceedings or to adjust the terms of the mortgage obligation if it found that military service materially affected the servicemember's ability to comply with the obligation. Prior to the amendment, a court could enter such an order with respect to an action filed during the period of military service and up to ninety days from the conclusion of active service. The temporary amendment allows a court to enter such orders for cases filed during the period of military service and up to nine months after the end of active duty. The second temporary provision applies to the requirement in subsection (c) of section 533, which requires a court order before a valid foreclosure sale may take place while the servicemember is on active duty. The amendment temporarily extends this protection to nine months from the end of active duty, from ninety days in the pre-amendment version.

123 38 U.S.C. § 1816(a).

124 Neither homeowners nor lenders are informed of the criteria for relief or the basis for or nature of the decision; homeowners are not offered the opportunity to apply for relief, present facts and evidence in support of a request for relief, or contest a denial. *See* First Family Mortgage Corp. of Fla. v. Earnest, 851 F.2d 843 (6th Cir. 1988) (assignment is within the discretion of the VA and not reviewable under the Administrative Procedure Act); Rank v. Nimmo, 677 F.2d 692 (9th Cir. 1982); Gatter v. Nimmo, 672 F.2d 343 (3d Cir. 1982), *aff'g* Gatter v. Cleveland, 512 F. Supp. 207 (E.D. Pa. 1981); United States v. Harvey, 659 F.2d 62 (5th Cir. 1981).

125 *E.g.*, First Family Mortgage Corp. of Fla. v. Earnest, 851 F.2d 843 (6th Cir. 1988) (assignment is within the discretion of the VA and not reviewable under the Administrative Procedure Act); Rank v. Nimmo, 677 F.2d 692 (9th Cir. 1982); Gatter v. Nimmo, 672 F.2d 343 (3d Cir. 1982), *aff'g* Gatter v. Cleveland, 512 F. Supp. 207 (E.D. Pa. 1981); United States v. Harvey, 659 F.2d 62 (5th Cir. 1981).

126 The new regulations are now codified at 38 C.F.R. §§ 36.4800 to 36.4893 (2008). *See also* § 2.12.2, *supra* (discussing new VA servicing/loss mitigation regulations for, *inter alia*, repayment plans, forbearance agreements, loan modifications, refinancings, loan assumptions, and various sale options as loss mitigation tools).

127 *See* Grant v. United States Dep't of Veterans' Affairs, 827 F. Supp. 418 (S.D. Tex. 1993). *See also* Anderson v. United States, 85 Fed. Cl. 532, 544 (Ct. Cl. 2009) ("State laws and general property law principles, when not in conflict with federal law, are controlling for the law of mortgages in relation to the home loan guarantee program.").

128 United States v. Wells, 403 F.2d 596 (5th Cir. 1968) (under program similar to loan guaranty; federal law should be applied to questions of federal rights and liabilities stemming from a federal program to assure uniform administration of nationwide VA program); United States v. Rossi, 342 F.2d 505 (9th Cir. 1965) (terms of guaranty governed by federal law).

129 Federal Home Loan Mortgage Corp. v. Dutch Lane Assocs., 810 F. Supp. 86 (S.D.N.Y. 1992) (VA held bound to comply with notice requirements of state deficiency judgment statute); Unites States v. Whitney, 602 F. Supp. 722 (W.D.N.Y. 1985). *See also* Yunis v. United States, 118 F. Supp. 2d 1024 (C.D. Cal. 2000) (pursuant to federal rule of decision that only the VA could dispose of property that it acquired through administration of its home loan guaranty program, non-judicial foreclosure sale of property owned by VA, under the program, was void, even though sale complied with state law). *Cf.* Jensen v. Turnage, 782 F. Supp. 1527 (M.D. Fla. 1990).

130 Unites States v. Whitney, 602 F. Supp. 722 (W.D.N.Y. 1985) (VA could not recover deficiency judgment against mortgagor

3.3.3 Foreclosure Defense Based on Lender's Failure to Comply with VA Servicing Guidelines

Several state courts have held that a borrower can raise inadequate loan servicing as an equitable defense to foreclosure.[131] In *Union National Bank of Little Rock v. Cobbs*, the court held that the lender's alleged failure to comply with the mortgage servicing provisions of the VA Lender's Handbook could be raised as an equitable defense in a foreclosure action.[132] In *Cobbs*, the lender failed to respond to a borrower's letters regarding his repayment problems and failed to try to help resolve the problems, as required by the Handbook. The court held that although foreclosure is an action at law in Pennsylvania, equitable relief can be granted, if consistent with principles of law.[133]

Thus, advocates should review the VA servicing requirements for lender noncompliance. A lender's deviation from VA procedures which is in bad faith or which has the effect of denying the borrower full participation in forbearance programs, may be grounds to postpone or prevent foreclosure.

3.3.4 Administrative Appeals of Adverse Decisions

3.3.4.1 In General

Veterans who are denied a request for relief under some of the options the VA offers as an alternative to foreclosure may appeal those decisions to the Board of Veterans' Appeals. The Board of Veterans' Appeals (BVA) is an administrative body within the Department of Veterans Affairs. It has jurisdiction to review determinations by the Secretary of Veterans Affairs on all questions of law and fact regarding the provision of benefits to veterans.[134] The enabling regulation specifically grants the BVA jurisdiction to consider an appeal involving a veteran's basic eligibility for guaranteed home loans, as well as waiver of payment of the loan guaranty indebtedness after foreclosure.[135] The statute and regulation outlining the BVA's jurisdiction are silent on the BVA's authority to review decisions disapproving a compromise claim, refunding and assignment of the mortgage, or acceptance of a deed in lieu. However, advocates should appeal adverse decisions regarding these options as they fall within the court's general grant of jurisdiction.[136]

A claim may be appealed from the BVA to the United States Court of Appeals for Veterans Claims. The U.S. Court of Appeals for Veterans Claims was created by Congress in 1988[137] to exercise exclusive jurisdiction over the decisions by the Board of Veterans' Appeals on the motion of claimants. This federal court is not a part of the Department of Veterans Affairs. The court has jurisdiction to review final decisions issued by the BVA.[138] Only veteran-claimants may seek the review of the court; the VA may not appeal BVA decisions.[139] The court's decisions are subject to limited review by the U.S. Court of Appeals for the Federal Circuit.

A notice of appeal must be received by the court within 120 days after the BVA mails its final decision.[140] The court does not hold trials, hear testimony by witnesses, or receive new evidence. In making its decision, the court reviews the BVA decision, the briefs submitted by the parties, and the record that was considered by VA and was available to the BVA.[141] Oral argument is held only at the discretion of the court. Either party may appeal the decision of the court to the U.S. Court of Appeals.

where it chose not to make mortgagor a party to the foreclosure proceeding; state law not "inconsistent state law" displaced by VA regulations).

131 Fed. Nat'l Mortgage Ass'n v. Ricks, 83 Misc. 2d 814, 372 N.Y.S.2d 485 (Sup. Ct. 1975) (failure to follow handbook would constitute unconscionable conduct on part of mortgage holder); Union Nat'l Bank of Little Rock v. Cobbs, 389 Pa. Super. 509, 567 A.2d 719 (1989) (borrower may raise lender's failure to comply with servicing provision of Handbook as an equitable defense). *But see* Bright v. Nimmo, 756 F.2d 1513 (11th Cir. 1985) (VA's failure to follow manuals and guidelines designed to help the veteran avoid foreclosure does not create a private action for damages for wrongful foreclosure; veteran not entitled to equitable relief under state law).

132 Union Nat'l Bank of Little Rock v. Cobbs, 389 Pa. Super. 509, 567 A.2d 719 (1989). *See also* Prudential Ins. Co. of Am. v. Jackson, 270 N.J. Super. 510, 637 A.2d 573 (Super. Ct. App. Div. 1994).

133 Union Nat'l Bank of Little Rock v. Cobbs, 389 Pa. Super. 509, 567 A.2d 719 (1989).

134 38 U.S.C. § 7104; 38 C.F.R. § 20.101.

135 38 C.F.R. § 20.101(a)(18).

136 *See* 38 U.S.C. § 7104; 38 C.F.R. § 20.101. *See also* Donovan v. West, 11 Vet. App. 481 (1998) (considering the BVA's jurisdiction to review VA denial of acceptance of a deed in lieu).

137 The court was created by the Veterans' Judicial Review Act of 1988, Pub. L. No. 100-687, 102 Stat. 4105 (codified at 38 U.S.C. §§ 7251–7269). Originally named the United States Court of Veterans Appeals, its name was changed effective March 1, 1999, by the Veterans Programs Enhancement Act of 1988, Pub. L. No. 105-368, 112 Stat. 3315. The court's seven judges are appointed by the President, and confirmed by the Senate, for fifteen year terms. The court's address is 625 Indiana Ave., N.W., Suite 900, Washington, D.C. 20004. Its telephone number for case-related matters is (202) 501-5970.

138 *See* 38 U.S.C. § 7261 (scope of court's review of BVA decisions). *See also* Frison v. Principi, 2003 WL 22097797 (D.C. Cir. Aug. 28, 2003) (district court lacked subject matter jurisdiction to review veteran's claims).

139 38 U.S.C. § 7266.

140 38 U.S.C. § 7266.

141 *See* 38 U.S.C. § 7261(b), (c).

3.3.4.2 Post-Foreclosure Waiver of Indebtedness

A veteran will be liable to the VA through either indemnification or subrogation for any claim paid by the VA to a lender due to default and foreclosure on the veteran's guaranteed mortgage.[142] The obligation remains even if the veteran transfers the property encumbered by the VA-guaranteed mortgage, and allows the new owner to assume payment of the mortgage.[143] The veteran may apply for a waiver of this indebtedness.[144] The Court of Appeals for Veterans Claims applies an "arbitrary and capricious" standard when reviewing decisions by the BVA to deny a waiver. Thus, in most cases the court defers to the BVA and rarely overturns decisions denying waivers.[145]

The veteran may also challenge the validity of the debt in an effort to avoid payment. In reviewing the validity of the debt the court considers, among other issues, lack of servicing on the loan,[146] lack of proper notice of foreclosure,[147] and other factors that may render the debt invalid.

3.4 Mortgages Held or Guaranteed by the Rural Housing Service

3.4.1 Rural Housing Mortgages

Two different mortgage loan programs are administered by the Rural Housing Service (RHS), an agency of the United States Department of Agriculture (USDA).[148] The Rural Housing Service was briefly named the Rural Housing and Community Development Service (RHCDS) and is the successor agency to the Farmers Home Administration (FmHA), which was eliminated in 1994 when the USDA was reorganized.

The Section 502 Single-Family Housing Program[149] provides for direct loans from RHS to very low and low-income individuals for the purchase, construction, or rehabilitation of single family homes located in rural areas. The standard term for a RHS direct loan is thirty-three years. However, a loan may be made for a shorter term, or in certain cases for thirty-eight years. Loans are made to individuals who are unable to obtain sufficient credit from private lenders. Payment subsidies are available to some borrowers to reduce monthly loan payments and make the loan affordable.

Appendix A.4, *infra*, contains for RHS direct loans, selected statutes and regulations. These are also available on the companion website, as are additional RHS interpretations and guidelines. The RHS, under Section 502, also guarantees loans made by private lenders to low- and moderate-income individuals living in rural areas.[150]

Appendix A.5, *infra*, contains for RHS guaranteed loans selected regulations and administrative notices. These are also available on the companion website, as are additional RHS interpretations and guidelines.

---

142 38 U.S.C. §§ 36.4323, 3732. *See also* Anderson v. United States, 85 Fed. Cl. 532 (Ct. Cl. 2009) (VA has no obligation to return to former homeowner the profit the agency retained after it purchased home at judicial foreclosure sale and later sold it for $65,000 more than the indebtedness owed by former homeowner).

143 Buzinski v. Brown, 6 Vet. App. 360 (1994).

144 If the VA determines that collection of a debt owed to the VA by a veteran as a result of default on a VA-guaranteed home loan "would be against equity and good conscience," the VA must waive collection of the debt. 38 U.S.C. § 5302(b); 38 C.F.R. § 1.964(a)(3).

The elements that may be considered in applying the "equity and good conscience" standard are: (1) whether the debtor was at fault in creating the debt; (2) the weight of the debtor's fault against the VA's fault; (3) whether collection of the debt would deprive the debtor or his or her family of basic necessities; (4) whether withholding of a benefit would defeat the purpose of the benefit; (5) whether the debtor was unjustly enriched; and (6) whether the debtor's reliance on VA benefits resulted in relinquishment of a valuable right or incurrence of a legal obligation. 38 C.F.R. § 1.965(a).

In addition, "there cannot be any indication of fraud, misrepresentation or bad faith on the part of the person seeking the waiver." Mueller v. Nicholson, 20 Vet. App. 447 (Jan. 11, 2006); Kaplan v. Brown, 9 Vet. App. 116 (1996). *See also* Bousquet v. Principi, 2002 WL 31256175 (Vet. App. 2002).

145 For one example of a decision denying a waiver that was overturned, see Coyote v. Brown, 14 Vet. App. 317 (1994). *See also* Steward v. Nicholson, 20 Vet. App. 227 (Vet. App. 2005) (Board denied waiver; remand to the Board to consider whether veteran should be granted waiver because the VA failed to comply with servicing guidelines regarding notice and counseling); Bousquet v. Principi, 18 Vet. App. 161 (Table), 2002 WL 31256175 (Vet. App. 2002) (Board decision denying waiver was remanded because in finding bad faith, Board failed to adequately analyze evidence and testimony regarding efforts of borrower to sell the property to avoid foreclosure). *But see* Mueller v. Nicholson, 20 Vet. App. 447 (Vet. App. 2006) (denying full waiver; facts found by Board not clearly erroneous); Harris v. Principi, 19 Vet. App. 160 (Table), 2004 WL 3106503 (Vet. App. 2004) (unpublished) (Board's decision as to validity of debt in waiver application is reviewed de novo).

146 Howe v. West, 2000 WL 750256 (Vet. App. June 8, 2000).

147 Berotti v. West, 11 Vet. App. 194 (1998); Larsen v. Brown, 15 Vet. App. 133 (1996); East v. Brown, 8 Vet. App. 34 (1995). *See also* Buzinski v. Brown, 6 Vet. App. 360 (1994) (VA right of indemnity may be defeated if veteran did not receive adequate notice that transferee defaulted on notice).

148 The Rural Housing Service is one of three agencies comprising the United States Department of Agriculture's (USDA) Rural Development Mission.

149 The Section 502 Single-Family Housing Program was created by the Housing Act of 1949. Pub. L. No. 171, ch. 338, tit. V, § 502, 63 Stat. 433 (codified at 42 U.S.C. § 1472). The regulations for the direct single-family housing program are provided in 7 C.F.R. pt. 3550.

150 42 U.S.C. § 1472(h).

3.4.2 *Section 502 Direct Single-Family Housing Loans*

3.4.2.1 Pre-Foreclosure Servicing Requirements for Section 502 Direct Loans

The RHS, under its Section 502 Direct Single-Family Housing Program, provides a number of options to help borrowers avoid foreclosure, including moratoriums, payment assistance, delinquency workout agreements, and payment advances.[151] A moratorium is available if a borrower is temporarily unable to continue making monthly payments due to circumstances beyond her control.[152] A borrower's scheduled monthly payments may be deferred for up to two years. Although RHS regulations purport to bar consideration of a moratorium after loan acceleration, this regulation is inconsistent with the statute and subject to challenge.[153] At the end of the moratorium, the borrower must make a lump payment of the deferred interest or the loan will be reamortized. At the end of a moratorium period RHS also has the authority to forgive interest accrued during the moratorium where future payments would otherwise be unaffordable.[154]

A delinquency workout agreement (DWA) allows a borrower to make a delinquent account current, either by making a single payment or by paying the delinquent amount, in addition to the scheduled mortgage payment, in monthly installments over a period not to exceed two years.[155] The RHS also has the ability to advance funds to cover the cost of taxes, insurance, and emergency repairs necessary to protect the government's interest in the property.[156] The payments are then charged to the borrower's account. Repayment terms are to be consistent with the borrower's ability to repay or the loan can be reamortized to include the amount of the advance.

These options are in addition to the payment subsidies, called interest credit and payment assistance, which are available to borrowers with Section 502 direct loans.[157] The interest portion of a borrower's monthly payment is subsidized through the interest credit and payment assistance. The borrower's income is reviewed annually to determine if the borrower is eligible for continued payment subsidy.

3.4.2.2 Acceleration and Foreclosure of Section 502 Direct Loans

Foreclosure of a Section 502 direct loan is a two-step process: acceleration of the note and sale of the property, if the note is not paid upon acceleration. A Section 502 mortgage can be accelerated when there has been a default under the terms of the mortgage. Most often acceleration results from a failure to make payments due under the mortgage. A single missed payment does not warrant acceleration. The account must be delinquent in an amount equal to three scheduled payments or an amount equal to two scheduled payments that have been delinquent for at least three consecutive months.[158] Once the mortgage is accelerated the borrower is not eligible for loan servicing and will not be allowed to cure unless given such a right by state law.[159]

When the decision to accelerate the loan is based on nonpayment, the account should be examined to verify that the necessary delinquency exists. Special attention to ac-

151 *See* United States Dep't of Agric., Direct Single Family Housing Programs Centralized Servicing Center Handbook HB-2-3550 Ch. 5 (1998). The handbook is available on the RHS website at www.rurdev.usda.gov/rhs. Loans made by RHS are serviced centrally at its Centralized Servicing Center in St. Louis, Missouri. Local offices provide backup servicing if needed. The RHS delinquency resolution (loan workout) policies are discussed in more detail at § 2.12.3.2, *supra. See generally* Susan A. Reif & Jennifer Ide, *The Section 502 Single-Family Housing Program: Does It Still Meet the Needs of Rural Borrowers?,* Clearinghouse Rev. Nov.–Dec. 1998) (discussing framework of RHS program and its foreclosure relief options).

152 7 C.F.R. § 3550.207. *See* United States v. Larson, 76 Fed. Appx. 742 (8th Cir. 2003) (discussing inability to continue making payments, finding that borrower was not entitled to moratorium because she had not experienced a 20% reduction in her income in the past twelve months and her inability to pay was not temporary). *See also* United States v. Martinez, 2004 WL 2827045 (E.D. Pa. Dec. 9, 2004) (summary judgment for RHS denied, where borrower alleged that she had attempted more than once to apply for moratorium and was prevented from doing so by RHS employees; court said that right to moratorium not guaranteed, but noted that "[t]he statutory language [of Section 1475(a)] requiring a borrower to demonstrate his or her eligibility for moratorium relief presupposes that a borrower who requests such relief will be given the opportunity to make the required demonstration."), *citing* United States v. Childers, 152 Ohio App. 3d 622, 789 N.E.2d 691, 695 (2003)); United States v. Asken, 2002 WL 32175416 (E.D. Pa. Oct. 28, 2002) (RHS's denial of an application for a moratorium will not be overturned when evidence was presented that mortgagor was fired from employment and thus his financial situation was not due to circumstances beyond his control).

153 United States v. Shields, 733 F. Supp. 776 (D. Vt. 1989) (addressing older codification of regulation in effect today, holding that moratorium statute, 42 U.S.C. § 1475, places no time limit on homeowner's right to apply for a moratorium and regulatory bar on post-acceleration application is invalid).

154 7 C.F.R. § 3550.207(c).

155 7 C.F.R. § 3550.205.

156 7 C.F.R. § 3550.206.

157 7 C.F.R. § 3550.68. *See also* United States Dep't of Agric., Direct Single Family Housing Programs Centralized Servicing Center Handbook HB-2-3550 Ch. 4 (1998). In a foreclosure action, the agency will seek to recapture the subsidy.

158 7 C.F.R. § 3550.202(b) (2002). *See* United States Dep't of Agric., Direct Single Family Housing Programs Centralized Servicing Center Handbook HB-2-3550 § 5.1 (1998).

159 7 C.F.R. § 3550.211(h). *But see* United States v. Shields, 733 F. Supp. 776 (D. Vt. 1989).

counting procedures is warranted if a borrower has ever made a payment in cash rather than by check, money order, or bank draft, which are the approved forms of payment.[160] The RHS requires that any cash payment be accompanied by a fee to cover the cost of conversion to a money order. If the conversion fee is not included in the payment, it will be deducted from the payment.[161] Be aware that a late fee is assessed when a full scheduled payment is not received by the fifteenth day after its due date.[162] The RHS has the discretion to waive such fees under limited circumstances, such as when late payment is due to circumstances beyond the borrower's control or to facilitate servicing of a delinquency.[163]

In reviewing the account to determine if a delinquency justifying acceleration exists, be aware that when a borrower submits less than the full scheduled payment amount, the RHS holds the payment in "suspense"; the payment is cashed but not credited to the borrower's account.[164] Only when a subsequent payment is received and combined with the partial payment to equal the scheduled payment is the amount credited to the borrower's account.[165] This accounting procedure could result in the appearance of the requisite two payment delinquency over three months necessary to justify acceleration of the account.

The borrower must also be given proper notice of acceleration. If the notice is not proper, the acceleration can be challenged and, if the notice is found to be defective, rescinded, opening the door to servicing options which were closed by the acceleration.[166] A proper notice of acceleration must contain a demand for full payment of the amount due on the account including unpaid principal and interest, protective advances, and any subsidy subject to recapture.[167] It must notify the borrower of the reason for the acceleration, the method of payment, the opportunity for an informal discussion with the decision maker and the process for requesting an administrative hearing.[168] Notice of acceleration must be given to the borrower and any cosigner simultaneously by regular and certified mail, return receipt requested.[169] If a borrower's address differs from the property address, the acceleration notice must also be sent to property address.[170]

In foreclosing on the mortgage, the RHS must follow the foreclosure procedures of the state in which the property is located to the extent such procedures are more favorable to the borrower than the foreclosure procedures that would otherwise be followed by the agency.[171] Prior to the adoption of this standard, the Third Circuit held that RHS (at that time called FmHA) need not comply with a state statute when it chooses to foreclose on a mortgage in federal court.[172] Although the court compared the procedural protections offered under state and federal law, the case turned on whether commercial interests or third parties are affected by the utilization of RHS's foreclosure process. If these interests are not affected, then RHS may use whatever procedure it selects.[173] Subsequent to this decision, however, 42 U.S.C. § 1475 was amended and states that RHS must follow the procedure in the state if it is more beneficial to the borrower.[174]

3.4.2.3 Default Based on Failure to Refinance

While failure to make timely payments under the mortgage is the most common cause of acceleration and foreclosure, any default under the terms of the mortgage can result in foreclosure. Unique to the Section 502 direct loan program is the requirement that the Rural Housing Service may require that a borrower refinance using private credit if it determines that the borrower has the ability to secure private financing and, thus, is no longer eligible for Section 502 assistance. The obligation to refinance is a term of the mortgage and failure to do so can result in foreclosure.[175] A Section 502 direct loan is not intended to replace private credit: as a result the RHS will periodically review a borrower's ability to refinance using private credit. A borrower

160 7 C.F.R. § 3550.152(a).

161 7 C.F.R. § 3550.152(a). *See also* United States Dep't of Agric., Direct Single Family Housing Programs Centralized Servicing Center Handbook HB-2-3550 § 2.7 (1998).

162 7 C.F.R. § 3550.153 (1998). *See* United States Dep't of Agric., Direct Single Family Housing Programs Centralized Servicing Center Handbook HB-2-3550 § 2.10 (1998).

163 United States Dep't of Agric., Direct Single Family Housing Programs Centralized Servicing Center Handbook HB-2-3550 § 2.10 (1998).

164 7 C.F.R. § 3550.152(b). *See* United States Dep't of Agric., Direct Single Family Housing Programs Centralized Servicing Center Handbook HB-2-3550 § 2.9 (1998).

165 United States Dep't of Agric., Direct Single Family Housing Programs Centralized Servicing Center Handbook HB-2-3550 § 2.9 (1998).

After acceleration, however, RHS will not accept partial payments. *See* United States v. Asken, 2002 WL 32175416 (E.D. Pa. Oct. 28, 2002).

166 *See* United States v. Rinehart, 2005 WL 2922181 (N.D.N.Y. Nov. 4, 2005) (summary judgment denied where the agency's record was "unclear and confusing," and court could not determine when borrower defaulted and if he received the proper notice).

167 United States Dep't of Agric., Direct Single Family Housing Programs Centralized Servicing Center Handbook HB-2-3550 § 6.5(b) (1998).

168 *Id.*

169 *Id.*

170 *Id.*

171 42 U.S.C. § 1475(b).

172 *See* United States v. Spears, 859 F.2d 284 (3d Cir. 1988).

173 *Id.*

174 42 U.S.C. § 1475(b). *But see* United States v. Asken, 2002 WL 32175416 (E.D. Pa. Oct. 28, 2002) (where no commercial interest or third party involved, RHS not required to comply with state notice requirements); United States v. Jones-Williams, 870 F. Supp. 90 (M.D. Pa. 1994) (HUD, like RHS, need not comply with state notice requirements).

175 7 C.F.R. § 3550.160.

undergoing review has thirty days after notice to provide the RHS with financial information for purposes of evaluating the borrower's ability to obtain private credit.[176] A borrower who fails to respond may be found in default and face foreclosure.

If the RHS finds that the borrower is eligible for private credit, the borrower is given ninety days to refinance.[177] The borrower has thirty days to contest the RHS's determination by providing information to document her inability to refinance with private credit.[178] If the borrower fails to demonstrate an inability to refinance and fails to refinance, foreclosure action can be initiated.[179]

3.4.2.4 Administrative Challenges to Acceleration of Section 502 Direct Loans

Borrowers can challenge acceleration of a Section 502 direct loan if they have not been informed of all the servicing options available to them. Similarly, if an option was requested and improperly denied, acceleration of the loan is open to a challenge. The decision of the RHS to accelerate a borrower's loan, or any decision adverse to the borrower, can be contested by requesting either an informal review by the Centralized Servicing Center, mediation, or a formal appeal with the National Appeals Division.[180]

The National Appeals Division (NAD) was established in 1994[181] to review adverse decisions issued by USDA agencies, including the RHS. Borrowers have the right to challenge agency decisions to deny requests for further assistance, or agency steps that will adversely affect the borrower's situation.[182] Borrowers who wish to appeal an adverse decision must submit a written request to the NAD within thirty days of receiving the decision. The NAD will conduct a hearing in person or by telephone, or the borrower-appellant may request a review of the record. The hearing officer will review the agency record, together with evidence submitted by the appellant and the agency. Decisions are issued within thirty days if the hearing was conducted in-person or by telephone. If the borrower-appellant requested a record review, a determination is issued within forty-five days of receipt of the request for a record review. The burden of proof is on the appellant to prove that the agency erred in its adverse decision. Both the borrower and the RHS can appeal the hearing officer's decision to the director of NAD.[183]

Final decisions of the NAD can be reviewed and enforced by any United States district court of competent jurisdiction. Actions are brought under the Administrative Procedures Act, 7 U.S.C. § 6999, which allows district courts to set aside final agency determinations that are arbitrary, capricious, or not in accordance with the law.[184] If an appeal or review is not requested, the RHS may begin the foreclosure within thirty days after an acceleration notice is sent. If an appeal or review is requested, foreclosure may begin as soon as the NAD upholds the decision to foreclose.[185]

3.4.2.5 Foreclosure Defense Based on RHS's Failure to Comply with Servicing Guidelines

The failure of the RHS to properly service Section 502 direct loans in accordance with the applicable regulations is a defense to foreclosure.[186] Courts have refused to foreclose

176 7 C.F.R. § 3550.160(c)(1).

177 7 C.F.R. § 3550.160(c)(2).

178 7 C.F.R. § 3550.160(c)(3).

179 7 C.F.R. § 3550.160(d)(2).

180 *See also* 7 C.F.R. § 3550.4. For a description of the informal and formal appeals process, see United States Dep't of Agric., Direct Single Family Housing Programs Field Office Handbook HB-1-3550, at Ch. 1 (1998). The handbook is available on the RHS website at www.rurdev.usda.gov/handbooks.html.

181 The Federal Crop Insurance Reform and Department of Agriculture Reorganization Act of 1994, Pub. L. No. 103-354, §§ 271–283, 108 Stat. 3178. The regulations are published in 7 C.F.R. pt. 11.

182 The regulations are applicable to adverse decisions made by an agency with respect to "denial of participation in, or receipt of benefits under, any program of any agency." 7 C.F.R. § 11.3. For example, the agency's decision to deny the homeowner moratorium assistance may be challenged.

183 Decisions of the director of the National Appeals Division (NAD), and those of its hearing officers, are now available in a searchable database on the NAD's website at www.nad.usda.gov. You can also file and request an appeal electronically.

184 *See, e.g.*, Clark v. U.S. Dep't of Agri.-Rural Hous. Serv., 2007 WL 3112458 (W.D.N.C. Oct. 22, 2007) (complaint which seeks to enjoin foreclosure and to cancel the note and deed of trust did not state a claim under the Administrative Procedures Act; relief sought went beyond judicial review of final determination by NAD), *aff'd*, 282 Fed. Appx. 263 (4th Cir. 2008). *See also* Dawson Farms, L.L.C. v. Farm Serv. Agency, 504 F.3d 592 (5th Cir. 2007) (discussing conflict among circuits on exhaustion requirement for district court jurisdiction over APA challenges to USDA decisions); Deaf Smith County Grain Processors, Inc. v. Glickman, 162 F.3d 1206 (D.C. Cir. 1998) (district courts have authority to review NAD appeal decisions under APA standards).

185 United States Dep't of Agric., Direct Single Family Housing Programs Centralized Servicing Center Handbook HB-2-3550 § 6.5 (1998).

186 *See* Curry v. Block, 738 F.2d 1556 (11th Cir. 1984); Johnson v. U.S. Dep't of Agric., 734 F.2d 774 (11th Cir. 1984); United States v. Martinez, 2004 WL 2827045 (E.D. Pa. Dec. 9, 2004) (same as *Childers*); United States v. Shields, 733 F. Supp. 776 (D. Vt. 1989); United States v. Gomiller, 545 F. Supp. 17 (N.D. Miss. 1981); United States v. Trimble, 86 F.R.D. 435 (S.D. Fla. 1980); United States v. Villanueva, 453 F. Supp. 17 (E.D. Wash. 1978); United States v. Childers, 152 Ohio App. 3d 622, 789 N.E.2d 691, 695 (2003) (genuine issue of material fact as to whether mortgagor requested payment moratorium relief, so as to be entitled to an opportunity to demonstrate her eligibility for such relief, precluded summary judgment for mortgage holder in foreclosure action). *But see In re* Cottrell, 213 B.R. 33 (M.D. Ala. 1997) (servicing errors were not grounds for appeal of

on Section 502 direct loans when the borrower was not informed of a servicing option she qualified for under the regulations; was improperly denied a servicing option; was dissuaded from applying for an option; or was not informed of her right to appeal a denial of the option or other adverse decision. Any irregularity in the servicing may be grounds to challenge the acceleration of the loan in a foreclosure action. Thus, advocates reviewing Section 502 direct loan accelerations should review the borrower's record to determine if she was offered servicing to avoid foreclosure and if her eligibility for such servicing was properly calculated.[187]

3.4.3 Section 502 Guaranteed Loans

The Section 502 guaranteed loan program assists rural residents with modest incomes obtain housing through conventional financing.[188] Lenders, who must be approved to participate in the program, agree to service the loans in accordance with agency regulations.[189] The regulations require that the lender give the borrower a reasonable opportunity to bring the account current before foreclosure proceedings are commenced;[190] contact the borrower if payment is not received by the twentieth day after it is due;[191] make a reasonable attempt to interview the borrower before the loan becomes sixty days delinquent;[192] and not commence foreclosure until the loan is ninety days delinquent.[193]

Unlike loans offered directly by the RHS, borrowers with Section 502 guaranteed loans do not have the right to a moratorium or to most of the servicing options discussed above.[194] Instead, RHS' loss mitigation program for guaranteed loans offers the following options: special forbearance; modification; pre-foreclosure sale; and deed in lieu of foreclosure.[195] Interest assistance is also available to eligible low-income borrowers to help them repay the loan.[196] The borrower's eligibility for interest assistance must be established at the time the loan guarantee is authorized. Borrowers may appeal the RHS' decision to deny, reduce, cancel, or refuse to renew interest assistance.[197]

The right of Section 502 guaranteed loan borrowers to appeal adverse decisions to the National Appeals Division (NAD) is limited. A borrower may not appeal a lender's decision to deny servicing relief.[198] A lender's decision to accelerate a borrower's loan is also not subject to appeal to the NAD.[199] Thus, the first opportunity advocates may have to challenge a lender's servicing action may be in the foreclosure proceeding. Advocates should assert that the lack of servicing is as an equitable defense in the foreclosure action, especially because, as a requirement to participate in the loan guarantee program, lenders must agree to service the loan in accordance with agency regulations.[200]

3.5 Debts Owed to the Federal Government

When loans guaranteed by FHA/HUD, the VA, or RHS are foreclosed, borrowers typically end up with a debt owed to the federal agency that originated the loan or paid out the insurance claim to a private lender. These debts can be for significant sums. RHS, for example, typically adds to the deficiency debt sums for the "recapture" of subsidies for interest reduction it paid out during the life of the loan.[201] Debts owed to federal agencies can be assigned to the Treasury Department for further collection action. Under the Debt Collection Improvement Act[202] the federal government has enhanced authority to collect debts arising out of these federal housing programs. The Treasury Department can snatch federal income tax refunds. To a limited extent the federal government can also conduct offsets against certain federal public benefits, such as Title II Social Security payments. Under the RHS direct loan program the agency initiates tax refund offsets before foreclosure and applies the seized amounts to the loan account.

---

foreclosure when the RHS did not provide an illiterate borrower with a form requesting moratorium relief, orally denied her a moratorium, and failed to notify her of her right to appeal the decision).

187 For an example of improper servicing, see *In re* Cottrell, 213 B.R. 33 (Bankr. M.D. Ala. 1997) (finding that the RHS violated its servicing duties by failing to provide a borrower who inquired about a moratorium with a form to apply; orally denying a moratorium; giving grounds for that denial which were inaccurate; and not telling the borrower she could appeal the denial of the moratorium). *But see* United States v. Anderson, 2007 WL 2126871 (D.N.D. July 23, 2007) (notice to borrower of "available primary loan service programs, debt settlement programs, appeal procedures, applicable time limits, recommendations for low-cost or no-cost legal representation as well as acceleration and foreclosure procedures" satisfied notice requirements); United States v. Sodders, 2006 WL 1765414 (N.D. Ind. June 21, 2006) (notice sent to borrower which was missing pages with instructions on how to apply for special servicing options substantially complied with RHS's notice requirements).

188 42 U.S.C. 1472(h). The regulations for the RHS guaranteed loan program are at 7 C.F.R. §§ 1980.301 to 1980.399.

189 7 C.F.R. § 1980.309(b)(2)(ii).

190 7 C.F.R. § 1980.371.

191 7 C.F.R. § 1980.371(a).

192 7 C.F.R. § 1980.371(b).

193 7 C.F.R. § 1980.371(d).

194 *See* 7 C.F.R. § 1980.370; § 3.4.2.1, *supra.*

195 For a discussion of the options offered under the loss mitigation program, see § 2.12.3, *supra.*

196 7 C.F.R. § 1980.390.

197 7 C.F.R. § 1980.390(l).

198 7 C.F.R. § 1980.399(b)(2).

199 7 C.F.R. § 1980.399(b)(3).

200 *See* 7 C.F.R. § 1980.309(b)(2)(ii).

201 *See, e.g.,* Allen v. U.S. Dep't of Agriculture, 698 F. Supp. 669 (S.D. Miss. 1988).

202 31 U.S.C. §§ 3701 to 3720E. *See* National Consumer Law Center, Collection Actions Ch. 11 (2008 and Supp.).

For advocates working with homeowners who participate in these various federal programs, it is important to advise them about the potential for these future harsh collection efforts. With respect to tax refunds, it may be possible for the debtor to structure employment compensation in a way that minimizes the exposure to seizures. In many cases, filing for chapter 7 bankruptcy relief may be the best option for dealing with these debts over the long term. For the most part, debts owed to the federal government are dischargeable just like any other debt. The few exceptions, such as certain tax and student loan debts, do not apply to mortgage loan deficiency debts.[203] A bankruptcy discharge may also be an effective means to prevent tax assessments due to the writing-off of a former mortgage debt. Issues related to debt write-offs and debt forgiveness are discussed in more detail at Chapter 14, *infra*.

203 *See* National Consumer Law Center, Consumer Bankruptcy Law and Practice Ch. 14 (9th ed. 2009 and Supp.).

Chapter 4 Legal Defenses to Home Foreclosures

4.1 Introduction

Few events are more devastating to a family than the loss of a home to foreclosure. Children may be forced to change schools and leave friends. A family may be distanced from workplaces and social support. The homeowner's equity is often lost as a result of a foreclosure sale, and it is not unusual for the foreclosed homeowner to find that he or she is personally liable for a large deficiency. Wages may be threatened to pay the deficiency judgment, further contributing to the family's financial distress.

Shortly after the foreclosure, the family may be summarily evicted from the home, although some states provide a waiting period (redemption period) before an eviction can take place. Affordable replacement housing can be difficult to find, particularly for a family already in financial straits. Moving and furniture storage costs can also exacerbate the financial difficulties facing the family.

This chapter discusses procedural and equitable defenses to prevent foreclosures, and if prevention is not possible to postpone a foreclosure long enough to allow the family to find appropriate housing. Chapter 5, *infra*, discusses substantive challenges to the validity of the mortgage agreement, and other claims that may be raised based on lender misconduct in the making of the loan. This chapter also discusses protections from foreclosure available to military members on active duty under the Servicemembers Civil Relief Act. Chapters 6, 7, and 8, *infra*, discuss claims and defenses that may be raised based on servicer misconduct in the servicing of the mortgage.

It is important to note from the outset that none of these strategies *alone* is likely to save a home. While it is natural for attorneys to resort to litigation in response to a threatened foreclosure, rarely will litigation fully resolve the family's problem. Some defenses may reduce the amount owed or may cause a delay in the foreclosure process.

Eventually, however, the homeowner will probably be left with some debt which must be paid. At that point, the homeowner must be able to cure the default, to arrange a negotiated restructuring, to refinance, or to force a cure through the bankruptcy process. To be effective, an advocate must be familiar with the home financing process, who the players are in the process, and what their interests are. Chapter 2, *supra*, is a practical discussion of the real estate lending process, negotiated strategies to deal with delinquencies, and practice tips for obtaining non-litigated resolutions of default.[1]

Techniques for using bankruptcy to prevent foreclosures are discussed in Chapter 9, *infra*. As is always true when representing a client who is in debt, the attorney must be familiar with the benefits that may be gained by the filing of bankruptcy when foreclosure is threatened. In many cases, a bankruptcy filing will be the only way to force a lender to accept payments on a default over time.

Chapter 14, *infra*, discusses some of the legal issues that arise after a foreclosure sale is completed. These include bidding at the foreclosure sale, post-sale redemption, setting aside a completed foreclosure sale, deficiencies and surpluses, defending evictions, and rights of tenants when the landlord's building is foreclosed. The potential tax consequences of foreclosure and workouts are also discussed.

4.2 Introduction to the Foreclosure Process

4.2.1 Overview

Foreclosure procedures are wholly determined by state law, the details of which vary from state to state.[2] The two most common methods of foreclosure in this country are judicial foreclosure and non-judicial foreclosure by "power of sale."[3] All states have a procedure for judicial foreclosure, and some states require that mortgages be foreclosed only by judicial process.[4] States which permit foreclosure

---

1 *See also* NCLC Guide to Surviving Debt (2010 ed.).

2 *See* Harbor Funding Corp. v. Kavanagh, 666 A.2d 498 (Me. 1995) (law of situs of property governs foreclosure; mortgage provision choosing foreign state's law did not govern foreclosure of real property located in Maine); Appx. E, *infra* (summary of state foreclosure laws). *See also* National Consumer Law Center, Foreclosing a Dream: State Laws Deprive Homeowners of Basic Protections (Feb. 2009). This report included a survey of state foreclosure laws and is available on NCLC's website, www.consumerlaw.org.

3 Other less common foreclosure procedures are discussed at § 4.2.4, *infra*.

4 *E.g.*, Iowa Code § 654.1; Del. Code Ann. tit. 10, § 5061.

by power of sale have enacted statutes regulating such foreclosures.

Most states have added varying levels of protection for the homeowner to the statutory foreclosure process. Some states permit a homeowner to "cure" a default by paying the installments due and any costs of the foreclosure to reinstate the loan. All states allow the homeowner to "redeem" the mortgage by paying off the total outstanding debt before the sale, or in some states by paying the purchase price, plus costs and interest, to the purchaser within a time certain after the sale. If a state has a requirement that foreclosure sales be confirmed by the court, the court must allow the homeowner's objections to be heard. A few states, such as Pennsylvania and Maryland, have developed mortgage assistance programs in response to plant closings and high rates of foreclosures involving laid-off workers.

4.2.2 Judicial Foreclosure

In less than half of the states, mortgages are always foreclosed by judicial action, either because of state law requirements or local custom. In these states, the lender must file an action in court, usually in the county where the property is located, to obtain a judicial decree authorizing a foreclosure sale. Generally, to obtain a judgment, the lender must prove that there is a valid mortgage between the parties, that the borrower is in default of the mortgage, and that the proper procedure has been followed.[5] The homeowner then has an opportunity to raise procedural and substantive defenses to the foreclosure, such as tender of the payments due, the lender's fraud, usury, invalidity of the mortgage, and Truth in Lending Act violations.[6]

In addition, certain technical procedural defenses may be available such as lack of jurisdiction, lack of joinder of necessary parties, insufficiency of service of process and improper pleading. If the court concludes, after considering any defenses, that there has in fact been a default and that the lender has the legal right to foreclose, the court will determine the total amount owed and may set a deadline for a redemption, if redemption is available under state law. If this amount is not paid by the deadline set by the court, the foreclosure will proceed, usually according to local rules or statutes governing foreclosure sales.

The court's decree of foreclosure may provide that additional notice of the foreclosure sale be given according to the decree. Typically, the sale is conducted by the sheriff or other public officer appointed by the court. In many states, after the sale the court must review the sale procedures and confirm the sale.

4.2.3 Non-Judicial, "Power of Sale" Foreclosure

In thirty states and the District of Columbia, foreclosing lenders are permitted to sell the mortgaged property at a foreclosure sale without filing a court action.[7] In these jurisdictions, foreclosures are accomplished by the lender's exercise of the "power of sale" contained in the mortgage (or deed of trust). That is, the original mortgage contains a power of sale clause stating that in the event of a default in payments or other breach, the holder of the mortgage may conduct a sale of the property after giving notice as required by the terms of the mortgage or applicable statute.[8] Generally, notice of the sale is followed by a sale by an auctioneer, a sheriff, or a public official.

Notice requirements differ from state to state. Most states require that notice of the sale be mailed, by registered or certified mail, to the homeowner, though some do not. Nearly all states require some form of public notice either by legal advertisement in a newspaper or posting in a public place. Some states require that notice also be given to junior lien holders, taxing authorities and other persons with an interest in the property. Of the thirty states where non-judicial foreclosures predominate, only five require personal service of the foreclosure notice upon the homeowner.[9]

Because notice requirements vary so much from state to state it is important to check the local notice requirements carefully, as well as any notice requirements contained in the mortgage. Courts have held that a lender's failure to comply strictly with notice requirements may render the sale void.[10]

5 If a lender establishes these elements and the borrower offers no defenses, the lender may be entitled to summary judgment. DiNardo v. Patcam Serv. Station, Inc., 644 N.Y.S.2d 779 (App. Div. 1996). *But see* Republic Nat'l Bank v. Zito, 721 N.Y.S.2d 244 (App. Div. 2001) (no summary judgment when lender failed to produce proof of the unpaid note).

6 In at least one state (Delaware) mortgages are foreclosed by *scire facias* process, in which the mortgagor is ordered to show cause why the foreclosure should not be allowed. Del. Code Ann. tit. 10, § 5061.

7 *See* Appx. E, *infra* (summary of state foreclosure laws).

8 When the mortgage or deed of trust does not contain a power of sale clause, or does not incorporate a statutory power of sale, judicial foreclosure may be required.

9 Maryland, Minnesota, Oklahoma, Oregon, and South Dakota. *See* Appx. E, *infra*.

10 *See In re* Gatlin, 357 B.R. 519 (Bankr. W.D. Ark. 2006) (sale invalid because notice did not include correct property address); *In re* Kitts, 274 B.R. 491 (Bankr. E.D. Tenn. 2002) (foreclosure sale void where there was a failure to comply with notice provisions in deed of trust); *In re* Cummings, 173 B.R. 959 (Bankr. N.D. Ga. 1994) (advertisement of sale by assignor of note violated statutory notice requirements because assignor did not conduct sale; sale set aside); LeDesma v. Pioneer Nat'l Title Ins. Co., 629 P.2d 1007 (Ariz. Ct. App. 1981) (strict compliance with notice requirements is essential to valid sale under deed of trust); Abdel-Kafi v. Citicorp Mortgage, Inc., 772 A.2d 802 (D.C. 2001) (notice of foreclosure sale invalid when mortgagee sent notice to wrong address); Independence Fed. Sav. Bank v. Huntley, 573 A.2d 787 (D.C. 1990) (borrower's actual receipt of

To contest a foreclosure by power of sale, the homeowner must file an affirmative action and request an injunction to stop the sale. Otherwise there is no judicial involvement at all in the foreclosure.[11] Most courts require that a bond be posted prior to the issuance of any injunctive relief.[12]

A further disadvantage faced by consumers required to file an action to stop a foreclosure, rather than defend against a lender's action, is that some claims may be beyond the applicable statute of limitations. When a foreclosure is by judicial action, even time-barred claims can arguably be raised defensively to reduce the amount of the plaintiff's claim.[13] These arguments may not be equally available in an affirmative injunctive action to prevent a foreclosure. However, some courts have allowed borrowers to raise time-barred claims in affirmative suits in power of sale jurisdictions on the theory that these actions are actually "defensive" in nature.[14] That is, they are brought not in response to a lender's foreclosure, but because the foreclosure is conducted extra judicially it is the borrowers who have to initiate court action. Additionally, a number of courts have allowed debtors in bankruptcy to raise time-barred claims in response to a lender's proof of claim.[15]

4.2.4 Other Methods of Foreclosure

There are two other, less common methods of foreclosure: strict foreclosure and foreclosure by entry and possession.

Strict foreclosure is allowed in only two states, Connecticut and Vermont.[16] The lender in these jurisdictions must go

foreclosure notice did not excuse bank's failure to strictly comply with statutory notice requirements); Fleischer Co. v. Grice, 226 A.2d 153 (Md. 1967) (requirements of rule in regard to foreclosure sale are to be strictly complied with); Chace v. Morse, 189 Mass. 559, 561 (1905); Moore v. Dick, 187 Mass. 207 (1905) (advertising in the *Lynn Bee* rather than the *Lynn Reporter* was an invalid exercise of the power of sale, even though both papers were published in the same office by the same company); Myrad Properties, Inc. v. LaSalle Bank Nat'l Ass'n, 300 S.W.3d 746 (Tex. 2009) (defect in property description involving omission of separate parcel of land was beyond scope of corrective deed, warranting rescission of trustee's deed); Deep v. Rose, 364 S.E.2d 228 (Va. 1988) (sale conducted in violation of mandatory time periods contained in statute governing advertisement is void—not voidable; result is to render sale ineffectual, no title passes to purchaser), *partially overruled by* 1992 Va. Legis. Serv. 550 (West) (amending Va. Code Ann. § 55-59.2—failure to comply with advertising requirements renders sale voidable). *See also In re* Kekauoha-Alisa, 2008 WL 4181347 (Bankr. D. Haw. Sept. 3, 2008) (failure to comply with statutory requirement to provide notice of sale's postponement by public announcement voided sale); Federal Home Loan Mortgage Corp. v. Appel, 137 P.3d 429 (Idaho 2006). *But see* Worthy v. World Wide Fin. Serv., 347 F. Supp. 2d 502 (E.D. Mich. 2004) (improper notice did not invalidate sale where mortgagor not prejudiced), *aff'd without op.*, 192 Fed. Appx. 369 (6th Cir. 2006); Knapp v. Doherty, 20 Cal. Rptr. 3d 1 (Cal. Ct. App. 2004) (notice not in compliance with statute did not invalidate sale where deviation was slight and did not cause injury to borrower); Myrad Props., Inc. v. LaSalle Bank N.A., 252 S.W.3d 605 (Tex. App. 2008) (erroneous and inconsistent property description in notice of substitute trustee's sale did not invalidate sale where notice provided to prospective bidder contact information that could clear up confusion), *rev'd*, 252 S.W.3d 605 (Tex. 2008) (use of corrective deed to convey an additional parcel of land is beyond the appropriate scope of a correction deed) ; Bailey v. Pioneer Fed. Sav. & Loan Ass'n, 172 S.E.2d 730 (Va. 1970) (substantial compliance with requirements set forth in deed of trust sufficient so long as rights of parties are not affected in material way). *See generally* §§ 4.3.2 (discussing procedural requirements to foreclosure), 4.3.4 (other procedural defenses), *infra*.

11 *See* Plein v. Lackey, 67 P.3d 1061 (Wash. 2003) (obtaining restraining order or injunction to restrain a trustee's sale is the only means by which a homeowner may stop a sale once foreclosure has begun). *See generally* Julia Patterson Forrester, *Constructing a New Theoretical Framework for Home Improvement Financing*, 75 Or. L. Rev. 1095 (1996) (recommending prior judicial process for foreclosure of home improvement loans).

12 *But see* Wells Fargo Home Mortgage, Inc. v. Neal, 922 A.2d 538 (Md. 2007) (no requirement to post bond where lender allegedly did not meet regulatory pre-condition to foreclosure of FHA insured mortgage); Gordonville Corp. N.V. v. LRI 1-A Ltd. P'ship, 856 A.2d 746 (N.H. 2004) (failure to post bond did not preclude plaintiff from challenging validity of foreclosure).

13 *See, e.g.*, Maynard v. Household Fin. Corp. III, 861 So. 2d 1204 (Fla. Dist. Ct. App. 2003) (foreclosure defendant could raise compulsory counterclaim in recoupment even though claim would have been time-barred if brought as an independent cause of action); Consumer Household Disc. Co. v. Vespaziani, 415 A.2d 689 (Pa. 1980) (TIL damages claim can be raised defensively as a recoupment in lender's suit on debt, despite expiration of limitations period, because claim arose out of the same transaction). *Cf.* § 5.6.6, *infra* (special limits on assertion of TIL rescission claims).

14 Hill v. Hawes, 144 F.2d 511 (D.C. Cir. 1944) (usury claim raised affirmatively beyond statute of limitations); *In re* Bishop, 79 B.R. 94 (Bankr. D.D.C. 1987) (a "defensive use" of a usury claim permitted beyond statute of limitations in extrajudicial foreclosure jurisdiction); Richlin v. Schleimer, 7 P.2d 711 (Cal. 1932) (usury case: "we deem it immaterial that by reason of the nature of foreclosure proceedings under a deed of trust, it becomes necessary in such case for the borrower to assert his right as a plaintiff in an action seeking to enjoin the threatened foreclosure rather than as a defendant urging his defense in an action brought by the [lender]"); King v. Kitchen Magic, Inc., 391 A.2d 1184 (D.C. 1978) (suit to nullify the mortgage based on fraud was an equitable action filed as a defensive measure against the foreclosure allowed despite statute of limitations).

15 *E.g.*, *In re* Coxson, 43 F.3d 189 (5th Cir. 1995); *In re* Jones, 122 B.R. 246 (W.D. Pa. 1990); Werts v. Fed. Nat'l Mortgage Ass'n, 48 B.R. 980 (E.D. Pa. 1985); *In re* Dangler, 75 B.R. 931 (Bankr. E.D. Pa. 1987); *In re* Hanna, 31 B.R. 424 (Bankr. E.D. Pa. 1983); *In re* Galea'i, 31 B.R. 629 (Bankr. D. Haw. 1981). *But see In re* Smith, 737 F.2d 1549 (11th Cir. 1984) (TIL claim not a recoupment).

16 *See* Appx. E, *infra* (summary of state foreclosure laws). *See also In re* Bartlett, 353 B.R. 398 (Bankr. D. Vt. 2006) (explaining Vermont's strict foreclosure process); Ocwen Fed. Bank v. Charles, 898 A.2d 197 (Conn. App. Ct. 2006) (explaining the Connecticut strict foreclosure process).

to court to get a court order declaring the borrower to be in default of the mortgage. Full legal and equitable title to the property then vests in the lender unless the borrower can redeem by paying the balance of the loan by a date set by the court. With strict foreclosure there is no sale. The results of a strict foreclosure are grossly unfair to borrowers when the property is worth more than the amount of the debt. The foreclosing lender gets title without regard to the amount owed. The borrowers lose all of their equity and the lender gets a windfall. Bankruptcy court decisions from Connecticut and Vermont have upheld challenges to those states strict foreclosure practices on fraudulent transfer grounds.[17] These rulings, which led to amendment of the Vermont statute, allow homeowners to request a sale and require additional judicial scrutiny of the sale process.[18]

With foreclosure by entry and possession, the lender physically enters on to the property and takes constructive possession of the property. Although permitted in Rhode Island[19] and New Hampshire,[20] and in Massachusetts[21] in conjunction with foreclosure by power of sale, this method of foreclosure is rarely used. Massachusetts law requires continued possession for three years to foreclose the owner's equity of redemption. If used, entry and possession is usually invoked as a supplemental procedure along with termination of an owner's rights by exercise of a power of sale.

4.2.5 Right to Cure a Default

Twenty-two states, the District of Columbia , and Puerto Rico provide by statute that the borrower can cure a default in payments by paying the amount due, plus any permissible costs and fees, by a time certain before the sale.[22] This amount would only include payments due up to the date of the cure (including interest), but not future payments or accelerated payments.[23] If the borrower becomes current in his or her obligations by the cure deadline, the foreclosure is stopped and the mortgage is reinstated. Some states place limits on the number of times a homeowner can take advantage of the right to cure.[24] Other state statutes provide that the foreclosure action shall be stayed upon payment of the installments due, but that if a new default occurs within a certain time period the action may be reinstated.[25] The time period during which the homeowner can cure the default varies from state to state.[26]

Failure to give notice of a statutory right to cure, even when the homeowner has actual notice of the amount needed to cure, may render the foreclosure defective as a matter of law.[27]

Some mortgages also provide a contractual right to cure a default in payments within a specified period of time.[28]

---

17 *In re* Chase, 2005 WL 189711 (Bankr. D. Vt. Jan. 27, 2005), *subsequent decision* 328 B.R. 675 (Bankr. D. Vt. Aug. 2, 2005) (sale may be voided under "reasonably equivalent value" standard applicable to fraudulent transfers); *In re* Fitzgerald, 237 B.R. 252 (Bankr. D. Conn. 1999), *subsequent decision*, 255 B.R. 807 (Bankr. D. Conn. 2000).

18 Vt. Stat. Ann. tit. 12, §§ 4531(a) (borrower may request foreclosure by sale), 4528(a) (foreclosure decree to make finding of property value before sale).

19 R.I. Gen. Laws § 34-23-3.

20 N.H. Rev. Stat. Ann. § 479:19.

21 Mass. Gen. Laws ch. 244, §§ 1 to 10.

22 *See* Appx. E, *infra* (summary of state foreclosure laws).

23 *See generally* National Consumer Law Center, Foreclosing a Dream: State Laws Deprive Homeowners of Basic Protections (Feb. 2009) (discussing cure requirements under state statutes).

24 *See, e.g.*, Okla. Stat. tit. 46, § 44 (cannot cure more than three times in twenty-four months).

25 *See, e.g.*, Neb. Rev. Stat. § 25-2149.

26 *See* Appx. E, *infra* (summary of state foreclosure laws).

27 Bank-Fund Staff Fed. Credit Union v. Cuellar, 639 A.2d 561 (D.C. 1994) (notice fatally defective, foreclosure laws are to be construed in favor of homeowners); Marra v. Stocker, 615 A.2d 326 (Pa. 1992) (failure to comply with state statutory obligation to provide notice describing right to cure renders sale invalid); Mills v. Haggard, 58 S.W.3d 164 (Tex. App. 2001) (foreclosure sale set aside for failure to send notice to cure). *See also In re* Cunningham, 2008 WL 1696756 (Bankr. N.D. Tex. Apr. 9, 2008) (foreclosure sale did not comply with statutory two-step process, which includes notice of a right to cure; damages awarded for wrongful foreclosure); Camden Nat'l Bank v. Peterson, 948 A.2d 1251 (Me. 2008) (summary judgment order on foreclosure vacated; genuine issue of material fact created as to whether statutory requirement of providing notice to cure was met where bank did not produce certificate of mailing); Douglass v. Country Wide Home Loans, Inc., 2005 WL 1542658 (Tex. App. June 30, 2005), *appeal after remand,* 2006 WL 3028924 (Tex. App. Oct. 26, 2006) (judgment affirmed). *But see* Mortgage Elec. Registration Sys. v. Ronghi, 2008 WL 4092824 (N.J. Super. Ct. App. Div. Sept. 5, 2008) (even if right to cure was not received, motion to vacate is properly denied where "defendants were well apprised of the foreclosure proceedings" and waited ten months to move to vacate judgment).

28 Fed. Deposit Ins. Corp. v. Cantore, 2001 Conn. Super. LEXIS 1597 (Conn. Super. Ct. June 6, 2001) (notice to cure invalid when it did not conform to the requirements of the mortgage deed); G.E. Capital Mortgage Serv. v. Baker, 1999 Conn. Super. LEXIS 1791 (Conn. Super. Ct. July 2, 1999) (failure to provide a sixty-day cure period as required by the mortgage is a special defense to foreclosure); O'Malley v. Chevy Chase Bank, 766 A.2d 964 (D.C. 2001) (when mortgage contract provides for right to cure, contract will govern over statutory right to cure); Moet II Inc. v. McCarthy, 646 N.Y.S.2d 64 (N.Y. App. Div. 1996); Mortgage Elec. Registration Sys. v. Akpele, 2004 WL 1462540 (Ohio Ct. App. June 30, 2004) (no certified mail receipt or other evidence that letter required by note and mortgage was ever mailed); Douglass v. Country Wide Home Loans, Inc., 2005 WL 1542658 (Tex. App. June 30, 2005), *appeal after remand,* 2006 WL 3028924 (Tex. App. Oct. 26, 2006) (judgment affirmed) (lender not entitled to order of foreclosure where notice of right to cure required by security instrument not given). *See also* Camden Nat'l Bank v. Peterson, 957 A.2d 591 (Me. 2008) (summary judgment order on foreclosure vacated; genuine issue of material fact as to whether notice was sufficient under the terms of the mortgage contract where the notice did not provide, at a minimum, the correct description of the

Certain manufactured home loans are covered by a federal thirty-day right to cure.[29]

When a borrower cannot cure within the statutory period, but can cure in installments within a "reasonable time" while also making current payments, a chapter 13 bankruptcy may be advisable.[30] As bankruptcy is governed by federal law, this option is available in all states.

Several states provide for a distinct pre-acceleration right to cure. Massachusetts, New Jersey, and Pennsylvania statutes set limits on default fees that can be charged before acceleration during a specified cure period.[31] Statutes in approximately ten other states provide for a fixed period of time for a homeowner to cure before formal foreclosure proceedings may begin.[32] The advantage to these pre-acceleration cure statutes is that the notify homeowners of a time period to cure before substantial legal fees are incurred and arrearages grow to be unmanageable.

4.2.6 Redemption

All states allow the homeowner to redeem the mortgage by paying the total outstanding balance, including costs, prior to the sale. The homeowner may be able to exercise the equitable right of redemption by taking a new loan to pay off the defaulted loan, selling the home and repaying the mortgage from the proceeds, or by selling the redemption right.[33]

In some states, homeowners also have a "statutory right of redemption" from the sale under which the right of redemption continues for a set period of time after the sale.[34] The borrower redeems under the statutory right of redemption by paying (or finding a buyer to pay) the total purchase price, plus interest and any allowable costs to the foreclosure sale purchaser.[35] Some statutes also permit lien holders or other interested parties to redeem the mortgage.[36] In most "power of sale" foreclosure jurisdictions, any right of redemption is foreclosed by the sale of the property.

4.3 Procedural Defenses

4.3.1 Introduction

Before a legally valid foreclosure sale can take place, there must be a valid mortgage between the parties, a default by the borrower, proper foreclosure procedure, and no cure (if permitted) or redemption by the borrower.[37] This section and Chapter 5, *infra*, will outline various legal challenges which the homeowner may mount to the foreclosure—including challenging the validity of the mortgage, raising lender misconduct as a defense, and asserting noncompliance with required procedures. The foreclosure of federally insured, guaranteed or direct loan program mortgages are discussed in Chapter 2, *supra*. And again, it is essential that in addition to these legal defenses, the advocate review the negotiation strategies discussed in Chapter 2 in order to be prepared to deal with any debt owed which cannot be eliminated by litigation or to be in a position to negotiate a settlement of these claims.

The procedure by which defensive claims can be raised will depend on the method of foreclosure used. If the foreclosure is by judicial process, the homeowner/borrower will have the opportunity to raise defenses and counterclaims to the foreclosure in the answer to the foreclosure

---

property subject to foreclosure). *But see* Mortgage Elec. Registration Sys. v. Goduto, 955 A.2d 544 (Conn. App. Ct. 2008) ("Any possible discrepancy between the terms of the mortgage and the plaintiff's notices caused no harm to the defendant because he had sixty-five days of actual notice in which to protect his property rights."); Fidelity Bank v. Krenisky, 807 A.2d 968 (Conn. App. Ct. 2002) (notice of default was legally sufficient to permit action for foreclosure even though it did not inform the mortgagors of their right to reinstate the mortgage, where the mortgagors had actual notice of that right).

29 National Consumer Law Center, The Cost of Credit: Regulation, Preemption, and Industry Abuses § 10.5.2.3 (4th ed. 2009 and Supp.). *See* National Consumer Law Center, Repossessions § 4.8.3 (6th ed. 2005 and Supp.).

30 *See* § 9.4.4, *infra.*

31 *See* Appx. E, *infra.*

32 Hawaii, Iowa, Maine, Maryland, Nevada, North Carolina, North Dakota, Oklahoma, Texas, and West Virginia. *See* Appx. E, *infra.*

33 *But see* Flynn v. Korneffel, 547 N.W.2d 249 (Mich. 1996) (payment of redemption amount into escrow account was not redemption under statute).

34 *See* § 14.1.2, *infra.*

The redemption period may be extended for members of the military on active duty. *See* § 206(b) (50 U.S.C. app. § 526(b)); § 4.12, *infra* (discussion of the Servicemembers Civil Relief Act).

35 *See In re* Poe, 477 F.3d 1317 (11th Cir. 2007) (under Alabama law, mortgagors that sold one of two parcels subject to mortgage remained liable on mortgage debt, as required for them to qualify as debtors with right of redemption as to the remaining parcel); Watts v. Rudulph Real Estate, 675 So. 2d 411 (Ala. 1996) (when foreclosure sale purchaser did not act with due diligence in providing itemized statement of costs to owner of right to redeem, owner was excused from compliance with ten-day limit on surrendering property in order to redeem). *See also* Benefield v. Graham, 992 So. 2d 717 (Ala. Civ. App. 2008) (holder of mortgagor's right to redemption was not required to pay to purchaser the foreclosure sale property mortgage-deficiency debt since bank, not purchaser, had owned that debt).

36 *See* Appx. E, *infra* (summary of state foreclosure laws).

37 For example, see Mason v. S. Mortgage Co., 828 So. 2d 735 (Miss. 2002), in which a lender attempted to foreclose an invalid mortgage. The lender had erroneously disbursed funds to pay off the consumer's former mortgage. The lender could not recoup these funds through foreclosure as there was no mortgage; it was canceled by mutual agreement. *See also* Mortgage Elec. Registration Sys. v. Richard, 889 So. 2d 1126 (La. Ct. App. 2004) (summary judgment denied where lender failed to produce payment schedule in support of allegation that mortgagor missed payment; mortgagor produced copy of cancelled check).

complaint.[38] A trial will then be held to resolve the claims and counterclaims.

With the more common foreclosure by power of sale, however, the foreclosure may take place entirely outside the judicial process. There is no court hearing, no opportunity to raise defenses or counterclaims, no judgment or decision by a court. Thus, to contest a power of sale foreclosure, the homeowner must file an affirmative action to raise these claims and enjoin the foreclosure. This action should be accompanied by a motion for a temporary restraining order and preliminary injunction to prevent a foreclosure sale while the homeowner's claims are being litigated. In most states, the posting of a bond is a prerequisite to a temporary restraining order or preliminary injunction. Courts in most jurisdictions may waive this requirement, however, in appropriate circumstances including indigence. Often the foreclosure is imminent when the homeowner first seeks legal advice, so the advocate must work very quickly to prevent the foreclosure.

Whether the foreclosure is by judicial or non-judicial process, sometimes filing a bankruptcy petition is the easiest way to stop an imminent foreclosure and allow the homeowner time to initiate these claims.[39] Substantive and procedural defenses are not waived when a homeowner files bankruptcy.

4.3.2 *Failure to Meet Procedural Prerequisites*

In most jurisdictions, foreclosures are seldom contested by the homeowner. As a result, lenders are often careless about complying with procedural foreclosure requirements, such as the proper and timely service of notice, service on the proper parties, or advertisement in the appropriate place and manner. Practitioners who represent homeowners in foreclosures have found that statutory requirements are not met in many cases. By raising a lack of compliance, the homeowner can force the lender to start the foreclosure process over again, or at least to correct the defect, providing the homeowner with additional time to arrange a workout, refinancing or a private sale.

Because of the variations among state foreclosure procedures, the practitioner must first scrutinize the mortgage contract, applicable state statutes, and case law interpreting those statutes to determine whether the lender has fully complied. Because a mortgage is a contract, its terms must be strictly followed to validly foreclose. Most state foreclosure procedures are designed to produce a swift sale of real estate. Some state statutes, however, contain protections for homeowners. Because foreclosure is such a harsh remedy, some courts take the position that strict compliance with statutory procedure, and the terms of the mortgage, is required before the foreclosure is permitted. Failure to strictly comply with statutory requirements can be a defense to foreclosure.

Where the notice of default is defective with respective to either content or timing, such defect may serve as grounds to defend against an action for foreclosure.[40]

Improper notice concerning the right to cure may also serve as the basis of a challenge to foreclosure in instances where a lender either fails to give the required notice or accelerates a loan prior to the termination of a prescribed curative period. These challenges may arise with respect to state laws governing notice of the right to cure[41] or to

38 *See, e.g.*, Mortgage Elec. Registration Sys. v. Alicea, 2006 WL 1149236 (M.D. Pa. Apr. 26, 2006) (mortgagor can bring counterclaim against a lender who failed to pay real estate taxes; the property was sold at a tax sale).

39 See Ch. 9, *infra* and National Consumer Law Center, Consumer Bankruptcy Law and Practice Ch. 9 (9th ed. 2009) for discussion of using bankruptcy to stop a foreclosure.

40 Cameron v. US Bank Home Mortgage, 2009 WL 3431392 (Cal. Ct. App. Oct. 27, 2009) (unpublished) (notice of default invalid where amount identified as necessary to cure was much greater than amount of past-due obligations and included fees to which bank was not legally entitled; notice deemed "necessarily defective" and not in compliance with letter or purpose of statute); Anolik v. EMC Mortgage Corp., 28 Cal. Rptr. 3d 759 (Cal. Ct. App. 2005) (unpublished) (notice of default failed to provide valid identification of debtor's breach of obligation "actually known" as required by statute; because nonjudicial foreclosure is "drastic sanction" and "draconian remedy," statutory requirements require strict compliance); Miller v. Cote, 179 Cal. Rptr. 753 (Cal. Ct. App.1982) (notice of default defective as to both timing and content; strict compliance is required); Bank-Fund Staff Fed. Credit Union v. Cuellar, 639 A.2d 561 (D.C. 1994); Bank v. Kim, 825 A.2d 566 (N.J. Super. Ct. App. Div. 2003) (court could not waive or modify requirements of foreclosure statute when mortgagee compliance was incomplete); S. Atl. Fin. Servs., Inc. v. Middleton, 590 S.E.2d 27 (S.C. 2003); Ulery-Williams, Inc. v. First Wyoming Bank, 748 P.2d 740 (Wyo. 1988) (holding that the clear requirements of the statute governing notice of default and intent to foreclose must be met, and noting that because provisions of the statute are mandatory in relevant texts, "the necessity of strict compliance with a notice requirement is emphasized"). *See also* Manufacturers & Traders Trust Co. v. Korngold, 618 N.Y.S.2d 744, 745 (1994) (notice of default sent by lender's agent failed to comply with mortgage requirement that notice be sent by "lender"; agency cannot be "proven out of the mouth of the agent," so notice containing no proof of agency was ineffective). *But see* Pantoja v. Countrywide Home Loans, Inc., 640 F. Supp. 2d 1177 (N.D. Cal. 2009) (notice of default was deficient since it did not properly identify beneficiary, as required by statute, but it could not serve as the basis for a wrongful foreclosure claim where the plaintiff did not allege prejudice resulting from the defect); Chase Manhattan v. Smith, 2000 WL 195095 (Conn. Super. Ct. Feb. 7, 2000) (where notice of default was provided in accordance with terms of mortgage documents, actual receipt was not required).

41 *See, e.g.*, Iowa Code § 654.2D; Me. Rev. Stat. Ann. tit. 14, § 6111; Tenn. Code Ann. § 45-20-104; Chase Home Fin. L.L.C. v. Higgins, 985 A.2d 508 (Me. 2009) (vacating judgment of foreclosure and order of sale; bank improperly accelerated note before giving required notice of default and right to cure under

mortgage documents that contain contractual provisions regarding acceleration and the right to cure.[42]

A lender's failure to comply with applicable notice of sale provisions may also provide grounds for defense against foreclosure. Some courts have refused to allow foreclosures to proceed where a lender fails to demonstrate that notice was properly served and received,[43] sent to or served upon the correct parties,[44] mailed or published within the prescribed time frame,[45] sent to a homeowner's last known

statute); American Money Ctrs., Inc. v. Lauletta, 2001 WL 1734203 (Me. Super. Ct. 2001) (where homeowner denied receiving notice of right to cure and bank cannot provide a post office certificate of mailing to establish conclusively owner's receipt, a genuine issue of fact exists and precludes summary judgment in foreclosure action). *See also* note 10, *supra*.

42 *See In re* Sharpe, 425 B.R. 620 (Bankr. N.D. Ala. 2010) (lender failed to give borrower proper notice of default, right to cure and opportunity to cure; "Because the defendant here failed to give the plaintiffs proper notice of the acceleration, its acceleration failed. Because the acceleration failed, the foreclosure is void."); Martenson v. RG Fin., 2010 WL 334648 (D. Ariz. Jan. 22, 2010) (lender gave notice of default and stated amount to cure, but set deadline for date to cure only one week later instead of providing thirty-day minimum; stating that lenders must strictly comply with deed of trust statutes, court finds that borrower had likelihood of success on wrongful foreclosure claim, which would invalidate trustee's sale); Schaeffer v. Chapman, 861 P.2d 611 (Ariz. 1993) (deed of trust provision requiring lender to provide notice and thirty-day period to cure before acceleration must be strictly construed in favor of borrower); Hicks v. Callan, 2008 WL 4098979 (Ariz. Ct. App. Sept. 2, 2008) (strict compliance with notice requirements in deed of trust is as much a precondition to enforcing a default as compliance with statutory notice provisions); Sovereign Bank v. Bradley, 2002 WL 653317 (Conn. Super. Ct. Mar. 26, 2002); Fed. Deposit Ins. Corp. v. Cantore, 2001 Conn. Super. LEXIS 1597 (Conn. Super. Ct. June 6, 2001) (acceleration of loan ineffective when purported notice to cure did not conform to the requirements of the mortgage deed); G.E. Capital Mortgage Serv. v. Baker, 1999 WL 511156 (Conn. Super. Ct. July 7, 1999); Bank-Fund Staff Fed. Credit Union v. Cuellar, 639 A.2d 561 (D.C. 1994) (foreclosure notice erroneously stating that mortgagors did not have right to cure and lacking amount needed to cure as required by recorder of deeds standard form was defective as a matter of law even though mortgagors had actual notice of amount needed to cure); Frost v. Regions Bank, 15 So. 3d 905 (Fla. Dist. Ct. App. 2009) (summary judgment of foreclosure precluded due to bank's failure to present facts to refute mortgagors' affirmative defense that bank did not provide requisite notice and opportunity to cure); Bank of New York v. Parnell, 2010 WL 291752 (La. Ct. App. Jan. 26, 2010) (summary judgment for bank reversed; under contractual terms of mortgage, bank was required to take affirmative act of mailing specified notice before accelerating the note, and right to accelerate thus did not arise until act was taken); Butler Capital Corp. v. Cannistra, 891 N.Y.S.2d 238 (N.Y. Sup. Ct. 2009) (mere conclusory assertions from someone without personal knowledge, including those contained in an attorney's affirmation, are insufficient to establish that lender complied with pre-acceleration requirements; failure to submit proper proof requires denial of requested relief); Norwest Bank Minnesota. v. Sabloff, 747 N.Y.S.2d 559 (App. Div. 2002) (bank failed to give requisite notice to cure as expressly required in mortgage documents); State Bank of Kenmare v. Lindberg, 436 N.W.2d 12 (N.D. 1989) (notice before foreclosure improperly accelerated debt); Wells Fargo Bank, N.A. v. Shalvey, 2007 WL 2205762 (Ohio Ct. App. July 26, 2007) (summary judgment for bank reversed; condition precedent to acceleration clause is a notice of default, and lender provided no evidence verifying that such notice was received); Federal Nat'l Mortgage Ass'n v. Robilio, 2008 WL 2502114 (Tenn. Ct. App. June 24, 2008) (reversing summary judgment in unlawful detainer action in which plaintiff raised defense of wrongful foreclosure; where trustee fails to comply with foreclosure terms that "are sufficiently clear and originate in the deed of trust, the law demands strict compliance for the conveyance to be valid"); CitiFinancial Mortgage Co. v. Beasley, 2007 WL 77289 (Tenn. Ct. App. Jan. 11, 2007) (summary judgment for lender reversed; undisputed date of foreclosure sale was within thirty-day curative period specified in deed of trust); Sauceda v. GMAC Mortgage Corp., 268 S.W.3d 135 (Tex. App. 2008) (bank's own evidence showed that it did not perform notice obligations of deed of trust). *But see* Mortgage Elec. Registration Sys., Inc. v. Goduto, 955 A.2d 544 (Conn. App. Ct. 2008) (substantial compliance with notice requirements in mortgage document is sufficient; courts look primarily to actual notice received rather than whether there has been "punctilious adherence" to formality); Ocwen Loan Serv. V. Graley, 2007 WL 3088081 (Conn. Super. Ct. Oct. 9, 2007).

43 *See, e.g.*, Security Pac. Fin. Corp. v. Bishop, 704 P.2d 357 (Idaho Ct. App. 1985) (absent showing that mortgagor received notice of all details of sale required by statute, such as time, date, place, and amount owing on debt, sale was invalid even though mortgagor had actual notice); Principal Residential Mortgage, Inc. v. Nash, 606 N.W.2d 120 (N.D. 2000) (order confirming foreclosure sale vacated when homeowner did not receive notice of the sale even though she was actively involved in the foreclosure process); Ohio Sav. Bank v. Hawley, 2001 Ohio App. LEXIS 702 (Ohio Ct. App. Feb. 16, 2001) (foreclosure sale vacated when mortgagor did not receive actual notice of the sale; notice by publication was inadequate); Sauceda v. GMAC Mortgage Corp., 268 S.W.3d 135 (Tex. App. 2008) (lower court erred in granting summary judgment on borrower's claim of wrongful foreclosure where fact issue remained as to whether notice was properly served in accordance with statute); Harwath v. Hudson, 654 S.W.2d 851 (Tex. App. 1983) (notice of sale was in accordance with minimum statutory requirements, but was not listed in three places as required by deed of trust; "the right of the grantor of a deed of trust to have its provisions strictly complied with to effect a valid foreclosure sale is absolute"). *See also* §§ 4.3.2, 4.3.4, *supra*.

44 *See, e.g.*, Williams v. Kimes, 996 S.W.2d 43 (Mo. 1999) (failure to provide notice of sale to contingent remainder owners of property was substantial defect sufficient to render sale void); Option One Mortgage Corp. v. Wall, 977 P.2d 408 (Or. Ct. App. 1999).

45 Dews v. District Ct., 648 P.2d 662 (Colo. 1982) (rule relating to notice of hearing on foreclosure under power of sale required strict compliance; sale set aside where notice did not comply with rule that notice be sent fifteen days prior to hearing); Independence Fed. Sav. Bank v. Huntley, 573 A.2d 787, 788 (D.C. 1990) (affirming judgment against bank on claim of wrongful foreclosure where owner was not given written notice of certified mail thirty days in advance of foreclosure notwithstanding actual notice to owner sixteen days before sale and owner's presence at sale); First Fed. Sav. & Loan Ass'n of Ottawa v. Chapman, 452 N.E.2d 600 (Ill. App. Ct. 1983) (sales vacated; bank's notice of continued sale dates was given more

address,[46] or sent in accordance with provisions governing the publication of notice in newspaper advertisements.[47] However, it is possible that courts may not require strict compliance with notice of sale requirements where actual notice was received or where no prejudice is deemed to have occurred with respect to the owner's rights.[48] Similarly, courts may refuse to enforce foreclosure where a bank violates a statute governing the rescheduling of sales,[49] but may allow them to proceed where such violation does not result in prejudice.[50]

4.3.3 *Default: Waiver and Estoppel*

The terms of the note and mortgage or deed of trust generally will define what constitutes default by the homeowner and gives the lender the right to *accelerate*, or to claim that the remaining payments are due at once. While the provisions regarding default and acceleration in the contract documents should be checked for errors or ambiguities, almost all mortgages provide that the failure to pay any installment on its due date is a default that entitles the lender to accelerate the balance of the debt without notice to the homeowner.[51] Some states, however, require that a notice be sent to the borrower indicating the lender's intent to accelerate and providing the borrower an opportunity to cure the default.[52]

Some courts have refused to enforce an acceleration provision strictly when the lender has previously accepted late payments from the homeowner and has not insisted on timely future payments.[53] These courts generally hold that

than maximum of four weeks before date of sale, as set forth in statute); Fleisher Co. v. Grice, 226 A.2d 153 (Md. 1967) (requirements of rule in regard to foreclosure sale are to be strictly complied with). *But see* Knapp v. Doherty, 20 Cal. Rptr. 3d 1 (Cal. Ct. App. 2004) (sale notice was serviced prematurely, but defect regarded by court as "slight deviation from statutory notice requirements" that did not cause injury); Option One Mortgage Corp. v. Corman, 835 N.Y.S.2d 608 (App. Div. 2007) (fact that letter terminating forbearance agreement and notice of foreclosure sale were not mailed to mortgagors at least ten days prior to first date of publication of sale, as required by law, did not justify setting aside sale); Key Bank of N.Y. v. Van Dev. Corp., 619 N.Y.S.2d 835 (1994) (sale conducted one day before expiration of twenty-eight-day notice period not set aside; court said this was a mere irregularity which did not prejudice the substantial right of any party).

46 *See, e.g.,* Abdel-Kafi v. Citicorp. Mortgage, Inc., 772 A.2d 802 (D.C. 2001) (reversing judgment of possession in eviction action where lender failed to comply with statute's directive to provide owner with notice of sale at his last known address; "In cases of doubt, we have construed the statute in favor of the homeowner and have adopted the principle of strict compliance by lenders with the rules governing trust deed foreclosures."). *But see* SunTrust v. Wright, 2003 WL 23573448 (Va. Cir. Ct. Nov. 12, 2003) ("last known address" requirement does not call for perfect compliance; defective notice will not invalidate sale).

47 *In re* Burke, 98 B.R. 746 (Bankr. W.D. Va. 1989); Stanley v. Robinson, 822 So. 2d 406 (Ala. 2001) (date of sale in notice advertised in newspaper contradicted date in notice sent to mortgagor); Wayman v. Zmyewski, 629 N.Y.S.2d 871 (App. Div. 1995).

48 *See, e.g.,* Riley v. Robey (*In re* Riley), 25 Fed. Appx. 149 (4th Cir. 2002) (unpublished) (substantial compliance with notice requirements of statute is sufficient so long as parties' rights are not adversely affected in a material way); Cross v. Downey Sav. & Loan Ass'n, 2009 WL 481482 (C.D. Cal. Feb. 23, 2009); Amos v. Aspen Alps 123, L.L.C., 2010 WL 27401 (Colo. Ct. App. Jan. 7, 2010) (upholding sale since actual notice was received and no lack of prejudice resulted from defect); Macon-Atlanta State Bank v. Gall, 666 S.W.2d 934 (Mo. Ct. App. 1984); Mortgage Elec. Registration Sys., Inc. v. Schotter, 857 N.Y.S.2d 592 (App. Div. 2008) (publication of notice of sale in New York Law Journal rather than local county newspaper was mere irregularity and not a jurisdictional defect causing prejudice of a substantial right); Amresco New England II v. Denino, 725 N.Y.S.2d 78 (App. Div. 2001); Cano v. Berkeley Fed. Bank & Trust, 2002 WL 397002 (Tex. App. Mar. 14, 2002); Koegel v. Prudential Mut. Sav. Bank, 752 P.2d 385 (Wash. Ct. App. 1988).

49 *See, e.g.,* Federal Home Loan Mortgage Corp. v. Appel, 137 P.3d 429 (Idaho 2006) (summary judgment for bank was improper where it was doubtful that statute governing rescheduling of sale as affected by an automatic stay was complied with; strict compliance required).

50 *See, e.g.,* Gianotta Properties, Inc. v. Barbaccia, 146 Fed. Appx. 97 (9th Cir. 2005) (failure to give notice of postponement of sale did not warrant setting aside sale absent showing of prejudice or surprise); *In re* Kekauoha-Alisa, 407 B.R. 442 (B.A.P. 9th Cir. 2009) (table; text available at 2009 WL 1080708) (failure to comply with statutory requirement that postponement of sale be made by public announcement did not lead to setting aside sale; lower court applied erroneous standard by construing case law to require strict compliance).

51 *But see* Citimortgage, Inc. v. Lovelett, 2001 Conn. Super. LEXIS 581 (Conn. Super. Ct. Feb. 27, 2001) (notice of default may be required in order to accelerate and foreclose even when the mortgage note does not require such notice); Sarasota, Inc. v. Ballew, 2001 Tex. App. LEXIS 1262 (Tex. App. Feb. 28, 2001) (note and deed of trust do not require automatic acceleration of note upon default and mortgagee who did not clearly and unequivocally express intent to accelerate the note cannot foreclose).

Advocates should also find out whether a loan has been properly accelerated. Aames Capital Corp. v. Lockwood, 2002 Conn. Super. LEXIS 170 (Conn. Super. Ct. Jan. 15, 2002) (summary judgment denied when mortgagor may have cured default prior to acceleration); Fed. Deposit Ins. Corp. v. Cantore, 2001 Conn. Super. LEXIS 1597 (Conn. Super. Ct. June 6, 2001) (acceleration of loan ineffective when purported notice to cure did not conform to the requirements of the mortgage deed).

52 *See, e.g.,* Nev. Rev. Stat. § 107.080; Or. Rev. Stat. § 86.705. *See generally* Appx. E, *infra* (summary of state foreclosure laws).

53 *See, e.g.,* Smith v. Gen. Fin. Corp. of Georgia, 255 S.E.2d 14 (Ga. 1979); Mayo v. Bank of Carroll County, 276 S.E.2d 660 (Ga. Ct. App. 1981) (if bank had expressly waived timely payment of installment of promissory note secured by deed of trust, late payment could not constitute proper grounds for acceleration of loan); Dunn v. General Equities of Iowa, 319 N.W.2d 515 (Iowa 1982) (acceleration options in installment notes can be waived by a course of dealing of accepting late payments); Foundation Prop. Inv., L.L.C. v. CTP, L.L.C., 159 P.3d 1042 (Kan. Ct. App. 2007) (lender's acceptance of late

the acceptance of late payments by the lender modifies or waives the strict acceleration provisions or estops the lender from strictly enforcing the acceleration provisions. Thus, when there has been an acceleration without notice and subsequent foreclosure, the homeowner may be entitled to have the foreclosure dismissed and be given the opportunity to make timely future payments on the mortgage after notice that late payments will no longer be accepted. A pattern of acceptance of late payments at least creates a factual question as to whether a new agreement had been created.[54] Waiver and estoppel are generally not available as defenses where late or partial payments are made and accepted after notice of default has been given and/or a foreclosure action has been filed.[55]

Some mortgages contain a provision that a waiver of any breach shall not constitute a waiver of any other or subsequent breach or default.[56] Most courts, however, have found such clauses do not bar the borrower from claiming waiver or estoppel.[57]

Estoppel may also provide a defense when a lender has agreed to delay foreclosure while the borrower attempts to refinance or to catch up payments, and the borrowers have relied to their detriment on the lender's promise.[58] Acceptance of a partial payment by a lender in some states may constitute a waiver of the right to foreclose, by virtue of state statute.[59] A Maine statute provides that acceptance of

---

payments over a period of nine months established a course of dealing such that it waived the right to accelerate the note; no evidence that lender ever objected to late payments, and borrower "reasonably relied on [lender] accepting late payments without exercising the acceleration clause"); Nolan J. Cunningham Apts., Inc. v. Dupre, 428 So. 2d 1046 (La. Ct. App. 1983) ("When a series of installments are due and the payee customarily permits payments to be made after the due date, a course of conduct is established whereby the payee, by acquiescence therein, is deemed to have waived his right to demand that an acceleration clause be enforced without first placing the payor in default, thereby signaling and end to such conduct."); Meehan v. Cable, 523 S.E.2d 419 (N.C. Ct. App. 1999) (note holder who repeatedly accepted late payments waived the right to accelerate debt without first notifying mortgagor that prompt payment would be expected in the future); Driftwood Manor Investors v. City Fed. Sav. & Loan Ass'n, 305 S.E.2d 204 (N.C. Ct. App. 1983) (note holder waived prompt payment of installment when it had repeatedly accepted late payments). *See also* 55 Am. Jur. 2d *Mortgages* §§ 388–392 (1971); Annotation, 97 A.L.R. 2d 997 (1964); 59 C.J.S. *Mortgages* § 388 (1971); Law of Distressed Real Estate Appx. D (Clark Boardman Callaghan) (summary of state case law authority on lender waiver and estoppel). *But see* Chem. Bank v. Dippolito, 897 F. Supp. 221, 224 (E.D. Pa. 1995) (acceptance of mortgage payments after due date of balloon payment did not estop bank from foreclosure, when bank maintained foreclosure proceedings even while accepting payments and made no representations that it would not enforce balloon payments, and borrower was not harmed because payments were applied to outstanding debt); Ocwen Fed. Bank v. Weinberg, 1999 Conn. Super. LEXIS 2204 (Conn. Super. Ct. Aug. 11, 1999) (when mortgage expressly contains nonwaiver clause, mortgagee did not waive right to accelerate mortgage by accepting late payment); LRB Holding Corp. v. Bank of Am., 944 So. 2d 1113 (Fla. Dist. Ct. App. 2006) (commercial mortgage; lender did not waive right to accelerate mortgage without notice to mortgagor by accepting 39 late payments out of the 84 payments due on the mortgage); Barker v. Agee, 378 S.E.2d 566 (N.C. Ct. App. 1989) (no waiver where lender accepted only two late installments before electing to accelerate; "Generally no waiver results from isolated instances of acceptance of late payments; only a consistent course of conduct will preclude the noteholder from exercising the right to accelerate the debt").

54 Liberty Bank v. New London Ltd. P'ship, 2007 WL 1416944 (Conn. Super. Ct. May 1, 2007) (genuine issue of material fact as to defenses of waiver and estoppel given lender's consistent pattern of accepting late payments; nonwaiver clause did not necessarily bar defenses); Mayo v. Bank of Carroll County, 276 S.E.2d 660 (Ga. Ct. App. 1981). *But see* Price v. Bustamante, 2001 Tex. App. LEXIS 5251 (Tex. App. July 26, 2001) (acceptance of late payments does not preclude acceleration of loan).

55 *See, e.g.,* Old Saybrook Auto Mall, Inc. v. Import Motors of Old Saybrook, 2008 WL 1868372 (Conn. Super. Ct. Apr. 8, 2008) (accepting late payments on delinquent note does not constitute waiver of right to accelerate); First Knox Nat'l Bank v. Peterson, 2009 WL 3086583 (Ohio Ct. App. Sept. 24, 2009) (bank's acceptance of payments after it filed foreclosure action did not constitute waiver of rights under the mortgage where borrowers had never been current with mortgage obligations). *Cf.* Caulder v. Lewis, 338 S.E.2d 837 (S.C. 1986) (holding that lender's acceptance of one or two late payments after notifying mortgagors that mortgagee would foreclose if future payments were in default did not amount to waiver, and acceleration of debt could proceed).

56 *See generally* National Consumer Law Center, Repossessions § 4.3.3 (6th ed. 2005 and Supp.).

57 *Id. See also* § 12.4.2, *infra* (discussing nonwaiver clauses in land installment sales contracts). *But see In re* Krueger, 192 F.3d 733 (7th Cir. 1999) (mortgagee did not waive timely payments requirement when it accepted one late payment pursuant to a note with a nonwaiver clause); *In re* Sharpe, 391 B.R. 117 (N.D. Ala. 2008) (acceptance of late payments does not alter the terms of the acceleration or the nonwaiver of acceleration clause of the security agreement); Ohio Sav. Bank v. Wage, 2007 WL 1297159 (Conn. Super. Ct. Apr. 4, 2007) (prior election to accept late payments rather than to enforce acceleration did not constitute waiver where contract contained anti-waiver clause); Ocwen Fed. Bank v. Weinberg, 1999 Conn. Super. LEXIS 2204 (Conn. Super. Ct. Aug. 11, 1999) (when mortgage expressly contains nonwaiver clause, mortgagee did not waive right to accelerate mortgage by accepting late payment); United Cos. Lending Corp. v. Candela, 740 N.Y.S.2d 543 (App. Div. 2002) (acceptance of late payments did not constitute waiver due to anti-waiver provisions in loan documents); First Nat'l Bank of Am. v. Pendergrass, 2009 WL 1865127 (Ohio Ct. App. June 30, 2009) (bank allowed appellants to continue making payments with 5% increase in interest rate for several months after a balloon payment had become due; court finds that acceptance of late loan payments does not constitute waiver of the right to accelerate and foreclose following a subsequent default where loan documents contain anti-waiver provisions); Buckeye Retirement Co. v. Walling, 2006 WL 3849863 (Ohio Ct. App. Dec. 29, 2006) (anti-waiver provision precluded defense of waiver).

58 Nassau Trust Co. v. Montrose Concrete Prods. Corp., 56 N.Y.2d 175, 436 N.E.2d 1265 (1982).

59 Casco N. Bank v. Edwards, 640 A.2d 213 (Me. 1994). *But see* Associated Bank-Milwaukee v. Wendt, 625 N.W.2d 359 (Wis. Ct. App. 2001) (mortgagee's acceptance of partial payment

value towards the mortgage after commencement of foreclosure proceedings but before the expiration of the right of redemption is a waiver of the right to foreclose unless there is a signed agreement to the contrary or unless the bank returns the payment within ten days of receipt.[60]

4.3.4 Other Procedural Defenses

Like foreclosure procedures, procedural defenses to foreclosures will vary from state to state, and can only be determined by reference to state statutes and case law. In general, in states that require a legal proceeding to foreclose, service of process and other procedural requirements must be met as in any other case.[61] Foreclosure pleadings may be subject to rules set by case law or rule. Similarly, rules may require that relevant documents be attached to the complaint. Failure to comply may be grounds to object to foreclosure or to move for dismissal resulting in temporary delays.

Other examples of successful procedural defenses may include the failure of the lender to introduce the original note in the foreclosure proceeding,[62] failure of the lender to obtain an enforceable security interest in the property,[63] failure of the lender to follow state licensing requirements,[64] failure to abide by the terms of the mortgage note,[65] the misjoinder of a claim for personal liability on the note, mortgage or deed of trust in the foreclosure proceeding,[66] failure to join indispensable parties,[67] violation of the statute of limitations,[68] or the improper or ineffective assignment of the mortgage.[69] Defects such as the failure to join a necessary party,[70] or the failure to comply with pre-foreclosure notice requirements may be defenses to a foreclosure.[71]

In some states additional notice requirements apply when the property being foreclosed upon is residential property. In Pennsylvania, for example, the lender must provide a notice stating the exact sum necessary to cure to owners of moderately priced homes, defined as properties for which the original principal amount borrowed was $50,000 or less.[72] The failure to comply with this notice requirement deprives the court of jurisdiction.[73] Pennsylvania also requires that lenders provide homeowners with notice of the Homeowners' Emergency Mortgage Assistance program.[74]

---

does not waive right to foreclose).

60 Me. Rev. Stat. Ann. tit. 14, § 6321.

61 *See, e.g.*, Hutchison v. Chase Manhattan Bank, 922 So. 2d 311 (Fla. Dist. Ct. App. 2006) (mortgagor was not served with a summons or named as a party in foreclosure proceedings; he did not receive adequate notice or have an opportunity to be heard in accordance with due process under the state constitution); Mortgage Elec. Registration Sys., Inc. v. Crutchfield, 144 P.3d 196 (Okla. Civ. App. 2006) (personal service of mortgagor failed; court lacked personal jurisdiction over mortgagor).

62 Emerald Plaza W. v. Salter, 466 So. 2d 1129 (Fla. Dist. Ct. App. 1985). *But see* Ocwen Fed. Bank v. Harris, 2000 U.S. Dist. LEXIS 16649 (N.D. Ill. Oct. 23, 2000) (lost promissory note not needed to foreclose); New England Sav. Bank v. Bedford Realty Corp., 680 A.2d 301 (Conn. 1996) (lost note will not preclude foreclosure action); Mitchell Bank v. Schanke, 676 N.W.2d 849 (Wis. 2004) (lender not required to produce note in physical form if it could establish the note's existence, terms and condition through other evidence, or otherwise establish the existence of outstanding debt secured by the mortgage). *See generally* § 4.4.4, *infra*.

63 *See In re* Marsh, 245 B.R. 536 (Bankr. M.D. Tenn. 2000) (omitted notary seal rendered deed of trust null and void); *In re* Buchholz, 224 B.R. 13 (Bankr. D.N.J. 1998) (a mortgage which was not executed in the presence of a notary public and not acknowledged under state law was insufficient to perfect a lender's security interest); Nicholson v. Wash. Mut., 2001 Tex. App. LEXIS 6119 (Tex. App. Aug. 31, 2001) (servicer not authorized to conduct sale of property as deed of trust authorized the holder of the note and deed to appoint a substitute trustee to foreclose on the property). *See also In re* Kitts, 274 B.R. 491 (Bankr. E.D. Tenn. 2002).

64 Solomon v. Gilmore, 731 A.2d 280 (Conn. 1999) (second mortgage issued by an unlicensed lender was not enforceable); Antuna v. Nescor, Inc., 2002 Conn. Super. LEXIS 1003 (Conn. Super. Ct. Apr. 1, 2002) (home improvement contract entered into by unlicensed salesman not enforceable and mortgagee cannot foreclose); Beneficial Haw., Inc. v. Kida, 30 P.3d 895 (Haw. 2001) (nullifying mortgage contract entered into by unlicensed broker). *But see* Staley v. Americorp Credit Corp., 164 F. Supp. 2d 578 (D. Md. 2001) (licensing provision did not create a private right of action); McDonnell v. Von Feldt, 604 N.W.2d 305 (Wis. Ct. App. 1999) (state licensing statute does not prohibit unlicensed mortgagees from bringing foreclosure actions).

65 Morequity, Inc. v. Dunn, 2000 Conn. Super. LEXIS 2485 (Conn. Super. Ct. Sept. 12, 2000) (no summary judgment in foreclosure action when mortgagor was denied right given by mortgage note to reinstate the mortgage); Nicholson v. Wash. Mut., 2001 Tex. App. LEXIS 6119 (Tex. App. Aug. 31, 2001) (attempt to foreclose was ineffective because servicer not authorized by deed of trust to foreclose on property).

66 Meco Realty Co. v. Burns, 200 A.2d 869 (Pa. 1964).

67 Agricola Partners Inc. v. Parker, 655 So. 2d 967 (Ala. 1995) (note holder's brother, to whom note holder had allegedly assigned her one half interest in a mortgage which was security for the note, was indispensable party to action on note and therefore must be joined). *See also* § 4.4.2.4, *infra*.

68 Bingham v. Lechner, 45 P.3d 562 (Wash. Ct. App. 2002) (statute of limitation barred non-judicial foreclosure proceeding).

69 *See In re* Cummings, 173 B.R. 959 (Bankr. N.D. Ga. 1994) (security deed not effectively assigned before foreclosure sale; foreclosure by purported assignee set aside); Family Fin. Servs. Inc. v. Spencer, 677 A.2d 479 (Conn. App. Ct. 1996) (plaintiff in foreclosure action was not real party in interest because it did not make the loan, nor was loan properly assigned to it; foreclosure claim dismissed for lack of standing). *But see* Ocwen Fed. Bank v. Harris, 2000 U.S. Dist. LEXIS 16649 (N.D. Ill. Oct. 23, 2000) (assignee did not need lost promissory note to foreclose); New England Sav. Bank v. Bedford Realty Corp., 680 A.2d 301 (Conn. 1996) (assignee of mortgage which could not produce the note could still bring equitable foreclosure). *See generally* § 4.4.5, *infra*.

70 Agricola Partners Inc. v. Parker, 655 So. 2d 967 (Ala. 1995).

71 *Id. See* § 4.3.2, *supra*.

72 Bankers Trust Co. v. Foust, 621 A.2d 1054 (Pa. Super. Ct. 1993) (citing Pennsylvania's "loan interest and protection law").

73 *Id.*

74 *But see* Wells Fargo Bank, N.A. v. Monroe, 966 A.2d 1140 (Pa.

4.4 Who Has the Right to Foreclose?

4.4.1 Introduction

The securitization of mortgage debt has created significant new issues for advocates to consider in defending a foreclosure. Before the rise of securitization, advocates seldom raised questions about the foreclosing party's authority to proceed. The familiar name of the loan originator routinely appeared on the face of foreclosure documents. Today, however, it is not unusual for a homeowner to receive a notice of sale or foreclosure complaint bearing the name of a hitherto unknown entity claiming to be the holder of the mortgage and promissory note. Mortgages are often bought and sold many times between the loan origination and the commencement of a foreclosure. New entities now play critical roles in the foreclosure process. These include trusts owning securitized mortgage debt, loan servicers, and private electronic databases for recording mortgage assignments. The players themselves are constantly changing. Servicing rights are bought and sold. Mergers of large financial institutions transfer ownership of the trusts that own mortgages and notes from one entity to another. All of these developments add new complexities to the question of who has authority to foreclose in a particular case.

Foreclosure laws have been built on a foundation of state real property, contract, and commercial laws. The explosion in securitized mortgage debt occurred with little regard for the details of these fundamental state laws. Today, when mortgage holders and servicers are questioned about their authority to foreclose, they often struggle to assemble documents showing that in acquiring ownership of the underlying obligations they complied with state property and commercial law. Their efforts can be haphazard, and the documentation they produce frequently turns out to be defective. Homeowners have a legitimate interest in ensuring that the party seeking to foreclose, and not some other entity, is the proper one to proceed under a state's foreclosure laws. Similarly, purchasers at a foreclosure sale need to know that the sale is conveying valid title to the real property. Servicers' lack of care in conducting foreclosures can harm the interests of investors as well by impairing title in properties subject to foreclosure sales. For all of these reasons, issues pertaining to standing to foreclose are critical in contemporary foreclosure practice. Chapter 1, *supra*, discusses how a practitioner can compel disclosure of the owner and holder of a mortgage.[75] This information can assist in evaluating whether a defense may be raised on standing grounds.

4.4.2 Judicial Foreclosures—Who Has Authority to Foreclose?

4.4.2.1 Overview

In judicial foreclosures the plaintiff must typically allege in its complaint that it is the current owner of the mortgage and the note being enforced. The court must make findings to this effect before allowing a foreclosure to proceed. Homeowners may challenge judicial foreclosures on a number of grounds related to the authority of the named plaintiff to foreclose. These challenges may go to the court's subject matter jurisdiction over the case and involve standing questions that have constitutional implications. In bankruptcy proceedings similar issues arise. A servicer or mortgage holder moving for relief from the bankruptcy stay must satisfy constitutional and related judicial standing requirements. The bankruptcy rules incorporate equivalents to Federal Rule of Civil Procedure 17 (requiring that proceedings be brought in name of the real party in interest) and Federal Rule of Civil Procedure 19 (requiring joinder of all necessary parties).[76] Because they frequently apply these important procedural rules in the context of foreclosures of securitized mortgages, bankruptcy court decisions on standing, real party in interest, and necessary party issues are highly relevant for state court proceedings in which similar rules apply.[77]

Super. 2009) (even if notice of homeowners' emergency mortgage assistance, which is prerequisite to any mortgage foreclosure action, was defective, mortgagors suffered no prejudice, where mortgagors were given the opportunity to pursue mortgage assistance, mortgagors met with a credit counseling agency within thirty days as provided by the Notice of Homeowners' Emergency Mortgage Assistance, and applied for mortgage assistance).

75 *See* § 1.3.3.3.2, *supra*.

76 *See In re* Kang Jin Hwang, 396 B.R. 757 (Bankr. C.D. Cal. 2008) (discussing applicability of Fed. R. Civ. P. 17 and 19 in context of securitized mortgage holder's motion for relief from bankruptcy stay).

77 *See In re* Minbatiwalla, 424 B.R. 104 (Bankr. S.D.N.Y. 2010) (in addition to establishing rights of the mortgage holder, a servicer seeking stay relief must show it has authority to act as the holder's agent); *In re* Canellas, 2010 WL 571808 (Bankr. M.D. Fla. Feb. 9, 2010) (motion for relief from stay denied after movant produced no evidence of ownership of note; *allonge* dated inconsistently with trust documents); *In re* Lee, 2009 WL 1917010 (Bankr. C.D. Cal. Jan. 26, 2009) (sanctioning attorney who pursued stay relief motion knowing named party lacked ownership interest in note); *In re* Jacobson, 402 B.R. 359 (Bankr. W.D. Wash. 2009) (servicer's declaration in support of motion for relief from stay did not establish that it had beneficial interest in note); Mortgage Elec. Registration Sys., Inc. v. Medina, 2009 WL 4823387, at *3 (D. Nev. Dec. 4, 2009) (MERS cannot be real party in interest because has no concrete interest in debt obligation); *In re* Mitchell, 2009 WL 1044368 (Bankr. D. Nev. Mar. 31, 2009) (no evidence MERS had any ownership interest in promissory note such as would make it real party in interest), *aff'd on other grounds,* 423 B.R. 914 (D. Nev. 2009) (because MERS cannot comply with court rule requiring participation in settlement negotiations through rep-

4.4.2.2 Constitutional Standing Requirements

Standing is a basic element of any civil action. A foreclosing plaintiff may be barred from all relief if it fails this basic test. For federal courts, which include the bankruptcy courts, standing has a constitutional foundation. Article III of the U.S. Constitution limits a federal court to jurisdiction over "cases" or "controversies" between parties.[78] As the Supreme Court recently defined the requirement, "[t]o qualify for standing, a claimant must present an injury that is concrete, particularized, and actual or imminent; fairly traceable to the defendant's challenged behavior; and likely to be redressed by a favorable ruling."[79] The law of standing mandates that the plaintiff have suffered a concrete injury (an "injury in fact") caused in some way by the defendant, and the injury must be subject to remedy by the court.[80] As a threshold matter in any federal lawsuit it is the responsibility of the plaintiff to allege facts clearly demonstrating that it is a proper party to invoke the exercise of a court's remedial powers.[81]

Standing issues in foreclosure cases can arise in several ways, particularly when the underlying claim is based on securitized mortgage debt. Even if a payment default unquestionably occurred, a party that cannot show any ascertainable rights in the particular debt has suffered no concrete injury and cannot seek relief from the courts.[82] In order to have standing, the named plaintiff must have either current ownership rights in the note and mortgage or have documented authority to conduct a foreclosure from the entity that presently owns those rights. Standing also takes on importance when assessing the role of an electronic database system such as MERS.[83] An entity that serves solely as a "nominee" or placeholder in a data recording system does not have a concrete or "beneficial" interest in receiving payments on the debt obligation. It suffers no injury from the borrower's nonpayment.

In the federal courts the named plaintiff must have standing at the time it files the complaint. A plaintiff who acquires an interest in the mortgage debt only after filing the complaint will be precluded from all relief.[84] The same is true for the plaintiff who had the requisite interest when it filed the complaint but loses it later by a transfer of rights to a different entity. In the federal courts standing to foreclose is a threshold question in every case and the court may raise standing questions on its own.[85] However, the entry of a final judgment may preclude further challenges to a court's assumption of jurisdiction over the case.[86]

In state courts standing is not always a jurisdictional threshold. Not all state constitutions contain an equivalent to Article III's case or controversy requirement. As will be discussed in more detail below, state laws vary in the extent to which they consider a standing objection waived if a

resentative with authority to confer on behalf of true owner, MERS is precluded from filing motion in bankruptcy court); *In re* Fitch, 2009 WL 1514501 (Bankr. N.D. Ohio May 28, 2009) (MERS was never in chain of title for mortgage and note; had no standing); *In re* Sheridan, 2009 WL 631355 (Bankr. D. Idaho Mar. 12, 2009) (MERS failed to show standing to bring motion); *In re* Wilhelm, 407 B.R. 392 (Bankr. D. Idaho 2009) (MERS lacked authority to transfer note; stay relief denied); *In re* Wells, 407 B.R. 873 (Bankr. N.D. Ohio 2009) (the standing requirements a creditor must meet to file a proof of claim and to seek relief from stay are the same); *In re* Waring, 401 B.R. 906 (Bankr. N.D. Ohio 2009) (servicer with no interest in note or authority to act on behalf of owner did not have standing to enter into reaffirmation agreement); *In re* Kang Jin Hwang, 396 B.R. 757 (Bankr. C.D. Cal. 2008) (denying motion for relief from stay filed by servicer that still possessed note but had sold rights to enforce it to unknown entity); *In re* Vargas, 396 B.R. 511 (Bankr. C.D. Cal. 2008) (servicer's evidence in form of written declaration and testimony of clerical staff not admissible to establish mortgage holder's standing); *In re* Gilbreath, 395 B.R. 356 (Bankr. S.D. Tex. 2008) (entity lacked standing to file proof of claim in bankruptcy case because it failed to file documents showing it was present holder of note); *In re* Nosek, 386 B.R. 374 (Bankr. D. Mass. 2008) (imposing sanctions on creditor for misrepresenting status of holder of note during protracted litigation), *aff'd in part rev'd in part*, 406 B.R. 434 (D. Mass. 2009) (upholding sanctions against original creditor and two law firms involved, but not against assignee creditor); *In re* Hayes, 393 B.R. 259 (Bankr. D. Mass. 2008) (trustee for investment trust failed to provide evidence that debtor's mortgage was included in trust; no evidence that servicing agreement authorized servicer to file proof of clam for an identified mortgage holder); *In re* Maisel, 378 B.R. 19 (Bankr. D. Mass. 2007) (servicer bringing stay relief motion failed to document standing as of time motion filed); *In re* Parrish, 326 B.R. 708 (Bankr. N.D. Ohio 2005) (objection to proof of claim sustained where claimant failed to produce competent evidence it was current holder of note or authorized agent of holder).

78 Warth v. Seldin, 422 U.S. 490, 498 (1975).

79 Davis v. Fed. Election Comm'n, ___ U.S. ___, 128 S. Ct. 2759, 2768 (2008).

80 Ass'n of Data Processing Serv. Orgs. v. Camp, 397 U.S. 150, 152 (1970).

81 Warth v. Seldin, 422 U.S. 490, 518 (1975).

82 *In re* Wilhelm, 407 B.R. 392, 398 (Bankr. D. Idaho 2009) (party seeking relief from bankruptcy stay to foreclose must show it has interest in note and injury from non-payment in order to meet constitutional standing requirement); *In re* Hayes, 393 B.R. 259, 266–267 (Bankr. D. Mass. 2008) (movant in motion for relief from stay must establish it meets constitutional and prudential standing requirements); *In re* Maisel, 378 B.R. 19, 22 (Bankr. D. Mass. 2007) (claimant has burden to bring forward information showing how it acquired enforceable rights in mortgage debt so as to have standing to proceed).

83 *See* § 4.6, *infra* (discussing litigation over MERS's standing in foreclosure cases).

84 *See* § 4.4.6.2, *infra*.

85 *See, e.g.*, *In re* Hayes, 393 B.R. 259, 267 (Bankr. D. Mass. 2008) (defect in standing cannot be waived).

86 Reusser v. Wachovia Bank, N.A., 525 F.3d 855 (9th Cir. 2008) (borrower may not collaterally attack unappealed bankruptcy court order that granted relief from stay to servicer despite failure to name the owner of the debt as party). *See also* Travelers Indemnity Co. v. Bailey, 129 S. Ct. 2195, 2205–2206 (2009) (res judicata principles of finality apply to a court's exercise of subject matter jurisdiction implicit in a final judgment).

homeowner fails to raise it in a timely manner. For example, New York courts have held that standing is not a precondition to invoking the court's subject matter jurisdiction in a foreclosure action.[87] The homeowner may waive standing objections by failing to raise them in an answer or by motion. However, once the standing issue has been raised in an appropriate manner in a New York proceeding, the foreclosing plaintiff must prove its standing in order to be entitled to any relief.[88] States do not follow a uniform rule in allowing a plaintiff to amend a complaint to cure a standing defect that existed when the action was filed.[89]

4.4.2.3 Real Party in Interest

In addition to the constitutional "case or controversy" requirement, federal standing jurisprudence recognizes a "prudential" limit on the exercise of a court's jurisdiction. The "prudential" standing doctrine requires that the party bringing the lawsuit assert its own rights and interests and not those of some other party.[90] Federal Rule of Civil Procedure 17 embodies this prudential standing principle. Under Rule 17 "[a]n action must be prosecuted in the name of the real party in interest."[91] Most state rules of civil procedure include a similar provision. In a foreclosure case, such a rule ensures that the defendant is not later subject to suit for the same claim by some other party who actually had the right to enforce the obligation.

According to some courts, a challenge to the plaintiff's status as the real party in interest does not raise a question addressing the court's subject matter jurisdiction.[92] Rather, a question about who is the real party in interest addresses the capacity of the named plaintiff to bring the action.[93] Therefore, objections to the plaintiff's status as a real party in interest are waived if the defendant does not raise them in a timely manner.[94] For this reason the homeowner should avoid any admissions to the plaintiff's status in responsive pleadings. The plaintiff's failure to bring the action in the name of the correct party in interest should be raised with the answer as an affirmative defense.[95] A motion under a rule analogous to Federal Rule of Civil Procedure 12(b)(7) alleging failure to join a necessary party may be appropriate as well.

After an objection has been raised, Rule 17 expressly allows for a reasonable delay in a proceeding for the joinder, ratification, or substitution of the correct party in interest.[96] However, before an amendment to cure the initial filing is allowed, the plaintiff must demonstrate that there was a reasonable mistake or that it will suffer an unavoidable forfeiture by the dismissal of the action.[97] In foreclosure

87 Countrywide Home Loans, Inc. v. Delphonse, 883 N.Y.S.2d 135 (N.Y. App. Div. 2009); HSBC Bank USA v. Dammand, 875 N.Y.S. 2d 490 (App. Div. 2009); HSBC Guyerzeller Bank A.G. v. Chascona N.V., 841 N.Y.S.2d 11 (N.Y. App. Div. 2007) (concurring decision: action commenced by party without standing tolled statute of limitations); Wells Fargo Bank Minnesota, N.A. v. Mastropaolo, 837 N.Y.S.2d 247 (App. Div. 2007) (challenge to foreclosure plaintiff's status as holder of note and mortgage goes to capacity to sue, and unlike challenge to subject matter jurisdiction, may be waived if not raised by defendant); Done v. Wells Fargo Bank, N.A., 2009 WL 2959619 (N.Y. Sup. Ct. Sept. 14, 2009) (same). *But see* Deutsche Bank Nat'l Trust Co. v. McRae, 894 N.Y.S.2d 720 (N.Y. Sup. Ct. 2010) (when defendant does not appear or file answer, it has not waived challenge to standing and court may dismiss action for lack of evidence of plaintiff's standing); Citigroup Global Mkts. Realty Corp. v. Bowling, 2009 WL 4893940 (N.Y. Sup. Ct. Dec. 18, 2009) (same); Deutsche Bank Nat'l Trust Co. v. Abbate, 2009 WL 3384474 (N.Y. Sup. Ct. Oct. 6, 2009) (standing goes to subject matter jurisdiction, allowing post-judgment challenge to foreclosure).

88 Wells Fargo Bank Minnesota, N.A. v. Mastropaolo, 837 N.Y.S.2d 247, 250 (N.Y. App. Div. 2007).

89 *See* § 4.4.6.2, *infra*.

90 Gladstone Realtors v. Village of Bellwood, 441 U.S. 91, 100 (1979); Benjamin v. Aroostook Med. Ctr., Inc., 57 F.3d 101, 104 (1st Cir. 1995).

91 Fed. R. Civ. P. 17(a).

92 Washington Mut. Bank v. Beatley, 2008 WL 928424 (Ohio Ct. App. Apr. 8, 2008) (reversing lower court dismissal of complaint pursuant to Ohio Rule 12(b)(6) because lack of standing involves capacity to sue, not jurisdiction of court); First Union Nat'l Bank v. Hufford, 767 N.E.2d 1206 (Ohio Ct. App. 2001).

93 *See generally* 13A Charles A. Wright, Arthur R. Miller, Federal Practice & Procedure § 3531 (summarizing cases that distinguish between constitutional standing and real party in interest in context of federal jurisdiction).

94 First Union Nat'l Bank v. Hufford, 767 N.E.2d 1206 (Ohio Ct. App. 2001).

95 *See generally* 6A Charles A. Wright, Arthur R. Miller, Federal Practice & Procedure § 1554.

96 Fed. R. Civ. P. 17(a)(3) provides: "The court may not dismiss an action for failure to prosecute in the name of the real party in interest until, after an objection, a reasonable time has been allowed for the real party in interest to ratify, join, or be substituted into the action. After ratification, joinder, or substitution, the action proceeds as if it had been originally commenced by the real party in interest." *See, e.g.*, Haw. R. Civ. P. 17(a); Idaho R. Civ. P. 17(a); Iowa R. Civ. P. 2; Miss. R. Civ. P. 17(a); Or. R. Civ. P. 26A; W. Va. R. Civ. P. 17(a). *See also* Whittiker v. Deutsche Bank Nat'l Trust Co., 605 F. Supp. 2d 914, 942, n.18 (N.D. Ohio 2009) (not an FDCPA violation to have brought an action in name of entity that was not real party in interest; under Ohio law standing is not jurisdictional and defect may be cured by later amendment); IndyMac Bank v. Miguel, 184 P.3d 821 (Haw. 2008) (initial lack of standing to foreclose can be corrected by later amendment; Hawaii law does not adopt the federal Article III case and controversy jurisdictional requirement). *See generally* Washington Mut. Bank, F.A. v. Krishna, 2006 WL 3719437 (Conn. Super. Ct. Nov. 28, 2006) (unpublished) (allowing substitution of assignee after complaint filed although the assignment to assignee occurred two years before complaint filed).

97 *In re* Foreclosure Cases, 2007 WL 3232430 (N.D. Ohio Oct. 31, 2007) (applying Fed. R. Civ. P. 17(a)). *See also* Aurora Loan Servs., L.L.C. v. Nuzzo, 2008 WL 5220682, at *4 (Conn. Super. Ct. Nov. 13, 2008) (denying foreclosing plaintiff's motion for summary judgment, noting that negligence of the plaintiff may be a factor for the court to weigh in determining whether to allow substitution under real-party-in-interest rule).

cases some courts do not permit real party in interest status to be acquired through an assignment made to the plaintiff after the complaint was filed, requiring instead that the case be dismissed and a new action filed.[98] Rulings vary among the states, and even within a jurisdiction, over the question of allowing lenders to cure real party in interest defects after commencement of a foreclosure action.[99] The degree to which the plaintiff exercised due diligence in attempting to identify the proper party before filing the complaint is often determinative. Dismissal is certainly appropriate where the court has given the plaintiff an opportunity to amend to add the real party in interest, but the plaintiff fails to do so.[100]

4.4.2.4 Joinder of All Necessary Parties

Leaving essential parties out of a foreclosure action may be just as harmful to a foreclosure defendant as bringing the case in the name of the wrong party. In order to raise appropriate defenses and counterclaims it is essential to have the right parties before the court. Obtaining complete relief for the homeowner who has been the target of a predatory loan scheme or other abusive lending practice often requires looking beyond a trust, servicer, or databank system initially named as plaintiff.[101]

Federal Rule of Civil Procedure 19 and analogous state rules require that an additional person be joined as a party in an action if "in the person's absence complete relief cannot be accorded among those already parties."[102] The failure to join a party needed for a just adjudication may be raised in the answer or by motion.[103]

4.4.3 Non-Judicial Foreclosures—Who Has the Right to Foreclose?

The standing issue in non-judicial foreclosures, while lacking the constitutional dimension of the case or controversy requirement, nevertheless presents the same concern that an entity foreclosing the mortgage must be the proper party with authority to foreclose. States enacted non-judicial foreclosure statutes as a boon to creditors, giving them a speedier alternative to the more cumbersome judicial procedures. Because they operate in derogation of the traditional judicial alternative, non-judicial foreclosure statutes often set out detailed procedural requirements. Lenders must strictly comply with these procedures. For example, a non-judicial foreclosure statute may require that a chain of title be properly recorded prior to the sale date evidencing the assignment of the mortgage to the party foreclosing the mortgage.[104] Some non-judicial foreclosure statutes explicitly define who may use the procedures and specify who must serve required notices, advertise, and conduct the sale. Failure of the appropriate entity to comply with these procedures may lead to a defective sale that must be set aside by a court.[105]

---

98 Jeff-Ray Corp. v. Jacobson, 566 So. 2d 885 (Fla. Dist. Ct. App. Sept. 12, 1990) (plaintiff required to file new action because mortgage assignment not made until four months after case filed); Aurora Loan Servs. v. Grant, 851 N.Y.S.2d 56 (N.Y. Sup. Ct. Aug. 29, 2007) (complaint dismissed for lack of standing because note and mortgage assigned to plaintiff after foreclosure proceeding commenced). *See also* Saxon Mortgage Servs., Inc. v. Hillery, 2008 WL 5170180 (N.D. Cal. Dec. 9, 2008) (dismissing foreclosure action for lack of subject matter jurisdiction because plaintiff failed to allege note had been assigned to it before it filed complaint; leave to file amended complaint granted); *In re* Schwartz, 366 B.R. 265 (Bankr. D. Mass. 2007) (movant could not obtain relief from bankruptcy stay after foreclosure because movant had not received valid assignment until after the non-judicial foreclosure sale took place); Wells Fargo Bank, N.A. v. Byrd, 897 N.E.2d 722 (Ohio Ct. App. 2008) (under Ohio law, standing defect cannot be cured by later amendment); Everhome Mortgage Co. v. Rowland, 2008 WL 747698 (Ohio Ct. App. Mar. 20, 2008) (affidavit which failed to prove that plaintiff was holder of note could not be cured by submission of documents on appeal); Wells Fargo Bank, N.A. v. Janosik, Allegheny Common Pleas No. GD08-2561 (Pa. C.P. Allegheny Cty. Mar. 23, 2009) (trial decision), *available at* www.consumerlaw/unreported (rejecting foreclosing plaintiff's "relation back" argument and dismissing foreclosure action filed prior to assignment to named plaintiff). *But see* WM Specialty Mortgage, L.L.C. v. Salomon, 874 So. 2d 680 (Fla. Dist. Ct. App. May 26, 2004) (reversing dismissal because plaintiff not given opportunity to prove that although assignment was executed after complaint filed, an equitable transfer of the mortgage may have occurred before action commenced); Bank of New York v. Stuart, 2007 WL 936706 (Ohio Ct. App. Mar. 30, 2007) (assignment of mortgage made after action commenced, but filed with court before foreclosure judgment entered, properly conferred standing to plaintiff). *See generally* § 4.4.6.2, *infra*.

99 *See* § 4.4.6.2, *infra*.

100 *In re* Kang Jin Hwang, 396 B.R. 757 (Bankr. C.D. Cal. 2008) (motion for relief from stay dismissed where servicer given two chances to amend to add current owner of obligation, but servicer failed to do so).

101 *See* Christopher L. Peterson, *Predatory Structured Finance*, 28 Cardozo L. Rev. 2185 (Apr. 2007) (discussing role of securitization of mortgages as means of separating entities responsible for misconduct in originating loans from entities that ultimately benefit from the transaction and who enforce the obligation against the borrower); Kathleen C. Engel & Patricia A. McCoy, *Turning a Blind Eye: Wall Street Finance of Predatory Lending*, 75 Fordham L. Rev. 2039 (Mar. 2007). *See also* § 10.3, *infra* (potential parties in foreclosure and abusive lending cases).

102 *See generally In re* Kang Jin Hwang, 396 B.R. 757, 770–771 (Bankr. C.D. Cal. 2008) (dismissing servicer's motion for relief from bankruptcy stay because, *inter alia*, the servicer failed to join the current owner of note as necessary party as required by Fed. R. Civ. P. 19).

103 Fed. R. Civ. P. 12(b)(7); 7 Charles A. Wright, Arthur R. Miller, et al., Federal Practice & Procedure § 1609.

104 *E.g.*, Mich. Comp. Laws § 600.3204.

An attorney general opinion in Michigan also provides that in a foreclosure by advertisement, an assignee who holds the mortgage at the time the foreclosure proceedings are commenced must be named in the published notice of sale. *See* 2004 WL 79109 (Mich. A.G. 2004).

105 *E.g.*, *In re* Schwartz, 366 B.R. 265 (Bankr. D. Mass. 2007) (finding non-judicial foreclosure invalid because foreclosing

In *U.S. Bank National Association v. Ibanez,* a Massachusetts state court set aside a non-judicial foreclosure sale on standing grounds.[106] The Massachusetts power of sale statute authorizes the "holder of the mortgage"[107] to give notice, advertise, and conduct a foreclosure sale when non-judicial foreclosure is authorized by the loan documents. The creditor who conducted the foreclosure sale of the Ibanez's home held the borrowers' promissory note indorsed in blank. However, when it sent out the foreclosure notices, advertised, and conducted the foreclosure sale the creditor had not been assigned the mortgage. Instead, it took an assignment of the mortgage ten months after the sale, as it prepared to convey the property it had acquired though the sale to a post-sale purchaser.

In invalidating the Ibanez's sale the Massachusetts court focused on two points. First, the state statute defined who had authority to conduct a non-judicial foreclosure sale that effectively extinguished a borrower's interest in real property. Only a "holder of the mortgage" could conduct such a sale. Because the creditor in question had not been the holder of the mortgage when it conducted the sale, the creditor failed to comply with this most basic statutory requirement. The creditor's reliance on an "industry standard and practice" of delaying assignment of the mortgage until after a sale could not supersede the plain statutory language. Second, the court considered the terms of the pooling and servicing agreement that allowed the servicer to foreclose on behalf of the investors who owned the obligation. The pooling and servicing agreement required that a specific form of mortgage assignment be given to the trust in recordable form at the time a loan was transferred to the trust.[108] Contrary to the terms of the pooling and servicing agreement, such an assignment to the trust had not been made before the Ibanez's foreclosure sale. The foreclosing servicer's sloppy practices had exposed not only the borrower to risks associated with a sale by the wrong party, but the conduct also posed a risk to the trust's investors, potentially depriving them of the benefit of a valid sale. The practices could also impair rights of purchasers at foreclosure sales, undermining confidence in the entire foreclosure sale system.[109]

Federal courts in several non-judicial foreclosure states, particularly Arizona, California, and Nevada, have summarily rejected standing challenges contained in complaints filed against foreclosing creditors.[110] In several of these decisions the federal courts appeared to be reacting to an influx of actions filed by homeowners, often appearing *pro se*, using form complaints that included a "where's the note" challenge among a plethora of other bare bones claims. These courts took only a cursory glance at the laws governing negotiable instruments and deeds of trust in their respective states. Instead, they viewed their states' non-judicial foreclosure statutes as creating an exclusive and self-contained system of remedies that did not allow challenges based on legal grounds arising outside of the statutes. The courts lumped standing challenges together with general equitable attacks on foreclosure sales, a form of relief they considered precluded by the sale statutes.[111] In virtually ignoring state negotiable instruments and real property laws, these rulings seem particularly short-sighted. Not all courts

---

party had not received valid mortgage assignment until after the foreclosure sale took place); Davenport v. HSBC Bank, 739 N.W.2d 383 (Mich. Ct. App. 2007) (foreclosure sale void where foreclosing party was not current record holder of mortgage as required by Michigan foreclosure by advertisement statute; mortgage had been assigned four days after sale).

106 U.S. Bank National Ass'n v. Ibanez, 2009 WL 3297551 (Mass. Land Ct. Oct. 14, 2009), *denying motion to vacate earlier decision* at 2009 WL 795201 (Mass. Land Ct. Mar. 26, 2009) (application for direct appellate review granted by Mass. Supreme Judicial Court, Docket No. 2010-P-0123 (Mar. 23, 2010)).

107 Mass Gen. Laws Ann. ch. 244, § 14.

108 U.S. Bank N.A. v. Ibanez, 2009 WL 3297551, at *8 (Mass. Land Ct. Oct. 14, 2009).

109 *Id.* at *12.

110 Cilluffo v. Washington Mut. Bank, 2010 WL 431896 (N.D. Cal. Feb. 2, 2010) (rejects applicability of U.C.C. to California non-judicial foreclosure); Newbeck v. Washington Mut. Bank, 2010 WL 291821, at *7 (N.D. Cal. Jan. 19, 2010) (no California requirement that trustee produce original note, distinguishing *Ibanez* (incorrectly) as arising from judicial foreclosure; properly conducted sale preclusive on rights of borrower and lender); Wood v. Aegis Wholesale Corp., 2009 WL 1948844 (E.D. Cal. July 6, 2009) (assertion that foreclosing entity did not have physical possession of the original note insufficient to render foreclosure proceeding invalid); Pantoja v. Countrywide Home Loans, Inc., 640 F. Supp. 2d 1177, 1186 (N.D. Cal. 2009) (no requirement under California law to produce original promissory note); Sicairos v. NDEX West, L.L.C., 2009 WL 385855 (S.D. Cal. Feb. 13, 2009) (California non-judicial foreclosure statute does not require production of note); Goodyke v. BNC Mortgage, Inc., 2009 WL 2971086 (D. Ariz. Sept. 11, 2009) (U.C.C. provisions not applicable in state's non-judicial foreclosures); Ernestberg v. Mortgage Investors Group, 2009 WL 160241 (D. Nev. June 22, 2009) (deferring to California federal court decisions on issue of standing in non-judicial foreclosures); Diessner v. Mortgage Elec. Registration Sys., 2009 WL 1457624 (D. Ariz. May 18, 2009) (rejecting applicability of U.C.C. to Arizona non-judicial foreclosure system); Mansour v. Cal-Western Reconveyance Corp., 2009 WL 1066155 (D. Ariz. Apr. 21, 2009) (adopting holdings of Nevada and California federal cases to effect there is no requirement for presentment of note in non-judicial foreclosures). *See also In re* Weisband2010 WL 1253182, at *7 (Bankr. D. Ariz. Mar. 29, 2010) (production of underlying promissory note not required to foreclose under Arizona non-judicial foreclosure statute and "[i]t would make no sense to require a creditor to demonstrate more to obtain stay relief"; court finds servicer lacked standing on other grounds).

111 In rejecting standing challenges, the California federal courts rely heavily upon the state court decision in Moeller v. Lien, 30 Cal. Rptr. 2d 777 (Cal. Ct. App. 1994). The *Moeller* court rejected a borrower's action to set aside a non-judicial sale on general equitable grounds, alleging an inadequate sale price. *Moeller* did not discuss any questions of standing or authority to foreclose. It did not consider the applicability of negotiable instruments law or any aspects of California real property law.

within these jurisdictions have limited their analyses of standing-related challenges to non-judicial foreclosures in this manner.[112]

4.4.4 Enforceability of the Note

4.4.4.1 Relationship Between Notes and Mortgages

In what we loosely refer to as a "mortgage" transaction there are typically two distinct documents: (1) the borrower's obligation to pay the debt in the form of a promissory note, and (2) the security interest in the borrower's property as evidenced by the mortgage or deed of trust. The transfer of the mortgage is a transfer of the security interest in land, which is generally governed by the law of conveyances and the real property recording system. The transfer of the promissory note, on the other hand, is governed by the law of contracts and by the Uniform Commercial Code (UCC).[113] Traditionally, a party transferred the mortgage and note together to an assignee. In securitized mortgage transactions this practice is not always followed. Instead, the note and mortgage may be transferred to different entities at different times. For servicers and the entities they represent, many standing and real party in interest problems arise as a consequence of the diverging paths these two essential documents follow after loan origination. An assignee's authority to foreclose may be challenged when the note and mortgage were not properly transferred or assigned. Because different rules apply to transfers of notes and mortgages, it is important to examine each set of rules in turn.

4.4.4.2 The Primacy of the Note

Before a foreclosure action can be maintained, the foreclosing entity is often required to allege that it has the original promissory note. The party can be required to present the original note or account for its absence.[114] The debt manifested by the promissory note is the principal obligation; the mortgage only secures payment of the debt and typically cannot be transferred independently.[115] However, the law of many states treats negotiation of a note as an equitable assignment of the mortgage, even when the mortgage is not assigned or delivered.[116] The converse, however, is not true. Without an interest in the debt, as evidenced by a properly assigned note, the lender who has been assigned a mortgage alone does not have the authority to foreclose.[117] In *Fleet National Bank v.*

112 *In re* Mitchell, 2009 WL 1044368, at *4 (Bankr. D. Nev. Mar. 31, 2009) (rejecting as "designed out of whole cloth" the distinction between standing requirements of judicial and non-judicial foreclosure systems; both require the foreclosing party to have authority to enforce the note), *aff'd on other grounds,* 2009 WL 5868512 (D. Nev. Dec. 30, 2009) (noting bankruptcy court's divergence from other federal courts' rulings on non-judicial foreclosures, affirms on ground that MERS cannot proceed with motion for relief from stay because it cannot comply with court rule requiring participation in settlement negotiations by representative with authority to confer on behalf of true owner). *See also* Saxon Mortgage Servs., Inc. v. Hillery, 2008 WL 5170180 (N.D. Cal. Dec. 9, 2008) (to participate in lawsuit, purported lender must show that note had been assigned to it; leave to amend granted), *subsequent op. at* 2009 WL 2435926 (N.D. Cal. Aug. 3, 2009) (finding servicer could enforce note under negotiable instruments law); *In re* Vargas, 396 B.R. 511 (Bankr. C.D. Cal. 2008) (in context of motion for relief from stay, discussing applicability of U.C.C. negotiable instruments law to enforcement of deed of trust under California law); Mortgage Elec. Registration Sys. v. Southwest Homes of Arkansas, 301 S.W. 3d 1 (Ark. 2009) (MERS, as entity without any legal interest in property recognized under state law, had no basis on which to challenge its exclusion from notice of non-judicial foreclosure sale).

113 For further discussion of negotiable instruments, see National Consumer Law Center, The Cost of Credit: Regulation, Preemption, and Industry Abuses § 10.6.1.3 (4th ed. 2009 and Supp.); National Consumer Law Center, Unfair and Deceptive Acts and Practices § 11.7.2 (7th ed. 2008 and Supp.).

114 *See also* Dasma Invs., L.L.C. v. Realty Assocs. Fund III, L.P., 459 F. Supp. 2d 1294 (S.D. Fla. 2006) (plaintiff has no standing to foreclosure when it possesses only a one page addendum to note and not the complete original promissory note); State Street Bank & Trust Co. v. Lord, 851 So. 2d 790, 51 U.C.C. Rep. Serv. 2d 191 (Fla. Dist. Ct. App. 2003). *See generally U.C.C.* § 3-501(b)(2) (party asked to make payment on note may demand that claimant exhibit instrument).

115 Kluge v. Fugazy, 536 N.Y.S.2d 92 (N.Y. App. Div. 1988) (plaintiff assigned mortgage and not the note could not bring an action for foreclosure; absent transfer of debt, the assignment of the mortgage alone is a nullity). On the other hand, if the lender transfers the note only, the general rule is that the security interest belongs, in equity, to the assignee even if there was not a formal assignment or delivery of the security interest or document. *See* U.C.C. § 9-203(g); Baxter Dunaway, Law of Distressed Real Estate § 24:18 (West 2009).

116 Carpenter v. Longan, 83 U.S. 271, 275 (1872) ("All the authorities agree that the debt is the principal thing and the mortgage an accessory"); Restatement Third of Property (Mortgages) § 5.4 (a) ("A transfer of an obligation secured by a mortgage also transfers the mortgage unless the parties to the transfer agree otherwise."); U.C.C.§ 9-203(g), cmt. 9 (codifying common law rule that transfers of obligations secured by security interest in real property also transfer security interest or lien). Restatement of Property (Mortgages) § 5.4(b) asserts a corollary position that the "transfer of a mortgage also transfers the obligation the mortgage secures unless the parties to the transfer agree otherwise." This rule, however, is preceded by an important qualification. The rule applies "[e]xcept as otherwise required by the Uniform Commercial Code." Thus, compliance with U.C.C. requirements for a valid transfer of a negotiable instrument and acquisition of a current right to enforce the instrument take precedence over the general rule stated in § 5.4(b).

117 *See In re* Leisure Time Sports, Inc., 194 B.R. 859 (B.A.P. 9th Cir. 1996) (applying California law and concluding that assignment of mortgage without assignment of debt which it secured was not valid); Crofford v. Green Tree Servicing, L.L.C., 2006 WL 3734929 (Ark. Ct. App. Dec. 20, 2006) (rejecting creditor's

Nazareth,[118] for example, a subsidiary of a lender that had been assigned the mortgage, but not the note, had no standing to foreclose. A state statute allowed the holder of the note to foreclose on the property without having been assigned the mortgage, but did not allow the converse.[119]

Some courts, however, have been willing to impute intent by the assignor to transfer the note where the note was not transferred with the mortgage. Generally that intention must be expressed clearly in a validly assigned mortgage, and there should be a subsequent proper transfer of the note.[120] Once the assignee transfers its interest in the note to a third party, it no longer possesses the right to foreclose.[121]

4.4.4.3 The Promissory Note As a Negotiable Instrument Under the UCC

The Uniform Commercial Code defines a negotiable instrument, determines how it is transferred, and limits who may enforce it. Some familiarity with basic UCC concepts is essential in fashioning an appropriate response to a servicer's or assignee's claim that it has the right to foreclose based on a note and mortgage originated by someone else.

The UCC defines a negotiable instrument as "an unconditional promise or order to pay a fixed amount of money, with or without interest or other charges described in the promise or order."[122] For participants in the lending industry, much of the utility of negotiable instruments derives from the ease and reliability with which they can be bought and sold, or transferred from one party to another. The UCC defines the transfer of a negotiable instrument as "negotiation."[123] The original promisor, or maker of the note (e.g., homeowner), is the "issuer" of the instrument.[124] The issuer delivers the negotiable instrument to an initial transferee who may then make subsequent transfers of the obligation following the rules for negotiation under UCC Article 3.

---

argument that, because foreclosure was an "in rem" remedy, it could foreclose without introducing note into evidence, but reversing grant of summary judgment for creditor on other grounds); McKay v. Capital Res., 940 S.W.2d 869 (Ark. 1997) (assignee could not enforce note as it did not produce the note or satisfy the U.C.C. requirements for lost negotiable instruments); Fleet v. Nazareth, 818 A.2d 69 (Conn. Ct. App. 2003) (mortgagee's subsidiary lacked standing to bring foreclosure action where mortgagee was only assigned interest in the mortgage and not the note); State Street Bank and Trust Co. v. Lord, 851 So. 2d 790, 51 U.C.C. Rep. Serv. 2d 191 (Fla. Dist. Ct. App. 2003) (mortgagee that never had actual or constructive possession of the promissory note could not maintain a cause of action to enforce the note or foreclose the mortgage); Kluge v. Fugazy, 536 N.Y.S.2d 92 (N.Y. App. Div. 1988) (mortgagee who received assignment of mortgage without note could not maintain an action for foreclosure; the note was expressly excluded from transfer); Shepard v. Boone, 99 S.W.3d 263 (Tex. App. 2003) (mortgage company assigned deed of trust, but not the note, had no authority to foreclose); Mitchell Bank v. Schanke, 676 N.W.2d 849 (Wis. 2004) (mortgage does not exist without underlying debt). *See also* 5-Star Mgmt., Inc. v. Rogers, 940 F. Supp. 512, 520 (E.D.N.Y. 1996) (collecting cases from various jurisdictions, noting that the decisive weight of authority holds that "an assignment of a mortgage without the underlying debt is a nullity, unless the promissory note in question has been lost or destroyed, or the original contracting parties intended the mortgage to be independently enforceable"); *In re* Vargas, 396 B.R. 511, 516-517 (Bankr. C.D. Cal. 2008) (MERS had no standing to proceed with motion for relief from bankruptcy stay because it had transferred note to unidentified entity prior to filing the motion). *See also* Provident Bank v. Community Home Mortgage Corp., 498 F. Supp. 2d 558, 571 (E.D.N.Y. 2007) (in order to perfect security interest in note under New York's U.C.C., the secured party must take possession of the note; secured party not required to file the assignment in real estate records in order to enforce remedies for payment of debt); Federal Nat'l Mortgage Ass'n v. Youkelsone, 755 N.Y.S.2d 730 (App. Div. 2003) (in order to prove standing plaintiff must demonstrate that it was the owner of the note and mortgage at the time it commenced the foreclosure proceeding).

118 818 A.2d 69 (Conn. Ct. App. 2003).

119 *See* Conn. Gen. Stat. § 49-17.

120 Ingomar Ltd. P'ship v. Packer, 2007 WL 1675846 (Conn. Super. Ct. May 23, 2007) (unpublished) (although mortgage and note were not assigned to plaintiff until after foreclosure action filed, plaintiff was real party in interest because it had contractual relationship with note holder; contract gave plaintiff beneficial interest in note and mortgage at time action filed); Connecticut Bank & Trust Co. v. Katske, 535 A.2d 836 (Conn. Super. Ct. 1986) (assignor inadvertently failed to assign note along with the mortgage), *aff'd*, 535 A.2d 818 (Conn. App. Ct. 1988). *See also* Harmony Homes v. United States *ex rel.* Small Bus. Admin., 936 F. Supp. 907 (M.D. Fla. 1996) (note and mortgage were effectively assigned to bank, even though note was not endorsed or delivered to the bank; the language of the assignment is evidence of the assignor's intent to surrender control of the note and mortgage, and therefore the bank, not the assignor had standing to file the foreclosure action), *aff'd without op.*, 124 F.3d 1299 (11th Cir. 1997) (table); Lawyers Title Ins. Co. v. Novastar Mortgage, Inc., 862 So. 2d 793 (Fla. Dist. Ct. App. 2003) (assignee of note and mortgage as collateral security was the proper party to foreclose even though assignor improperly retained possession of the note; assignment constituted constructive delivery of the note). *Cf.* Kluge v. Fugazy, 536 N.Y.S.2d 92 (N.Y. App. Div. 1988) (assignment and written agreement clearly indicate that the parties did not intend to assign the note).

121 *See* Harmony Homes v. United States *ex rel.* Small Bus. Admin., 936 F. Supp. 907 (M.D. Fla. 1996) (lender who assigned interest in property to bank was not the proper party to file suit to foreclose a mortgage), *aff'd without op.*, 124 F.3d 1299 (11th Cir. 1997) (table). *See also* Associates of Selma, Inc. v. Whetstone, 628 So. 2d 578 (Ala. 1993) (vendor that unconditionally assigned note and mortgage to bank as security could not sue for deficiency; bank was a necessary party); McKay v. Capital Res., 940 S.W.2d 869 (Ark. 1997) (assignee could not enforce note as it did not produce the note or satisfy the U.C.C. requirements for lost negotiable instruments).

122 U.C.C. § 3-104(a). *See* § 5.14.2.3, *infra*.

123 U.C.C. § 3-201 (" 'Negotiation' means a transfer of possession, whether voluntary or involuntary, of an instrument by a person other than the issuer to a person who thereby becomes its holder."). *See generally In re* Lee, 408 B.R. 893, 899 (Bankr. C.D. Cal. 2009) (discussing U.C.C.'s negotiation provisions in connection with securitized mortgage loan).

124 U.C.C. § 3-105(a).

Negotiable instruments may be payable in two forms. They can be payable "to order" or "to bearer."

When a negotiable instrument is made payable to the order of an identified person it is referred to as "order paper." Sometimes order paper is called "specially" indorsed paper.[125] To be negotiated, order paper must be signed or "indorsed" payable to the specific person and the note must be transferred to that person.[126] Upon acquiring possession, the designated person becomes the "holder" of the note.[127] The holder of a negotiable instrument is entitled to certain desirable rights established by UCC Article 3.

A negotiable instrument may also be made payable to "bearer." "Bearer paper" includes a note made payable in blank or to no identified person.[128] Bearer paper can be negotiated simply by transferring possession of the instrument.[129] The transferor's signature is not necessary. The person in possession of bearer paper becomes the "holder" of the note.

A common pattern in securitized mortgage transactions is for a note to be made out initially to the order of the originating lender. A subsequent indorsement then coverts this order paper to bearer paper when a later transferee indorses the note in blank. From that point on the note is negotiated as bearer paper. Freddie Mac and Fannie Mae recommend that servicers handling their uniform notes follow this procedure.[130]

Participants in transactions involving mortgage-backed securities have a strong interest in seeing their promissory notes treated as negotiable instruments. A creditor derives two major benefits when it qualifies under the UCC as the holder of a negotiable instrument. First, it gains a presumptive right to enforce the obligation.[131] Second, and more important, the holder of a negotiable instrument is entitled to claim "holder in due course" status.[132] This status shields the transferee from claims related to misconduct by the loan originator and prior holders of the debt.[133] For owners of negotiable instruments today, the protection they derive from their status as the holders in due course of negotiable instruments is critical.

In certain situations the promissory note may fail to meet the UCC's technical requirements for creation of a negotiable instrument. For example, the note must establish an obligation to pay a sum certain or be payable on demand or at a definite time.[134] A note obligating the promisor to pay for open-end credit would thus not be a negotiable instrument. With limited exceptions a note cannot contain undertakings beyond payment of money.[135] For any of these reasons, the note may not qualify as a negotiable instrument. However, simply because the note fails to meet the UCC's technical requirements of a negotiable instrument may not mean that the obligation itself is unenforceable. The owner of the obligation or the entity in possession of the note may still be able to prove a right to enforce it.[136] However, the purported owner may lose the benefit of the presumption of enforceability that accrues to negotiable instruments and the holders of negotiable instruments. More significantly, the party will not enjoy holder-in-due-course protection.

4.4.4.4 Who Can Enforce a Negotiable Instrument?

4.4.4.4.1 General

Assuming that the note is a negotiable instrument as defined by the UCC, the "holder" has a presumptive right to enforce it.[137] The UCC defines a "holder" as "the person

---

125 U.C.C. § 3-205(a) ("If an indorsement is made by the holder of an instrument, whether payable to an identified person or payable to bearer, and the indorsement identifies a person to whom it makes the instrument payable, it is a 'special indorsement.' When specially indorsed, an instrument becomes payable to the identified person and may be negotiated only by the indorsement of that person.")

126 U.C.C. § 3-201(b) (". . . if an instrument is payable to an identified person, negotiation requires transfer of possession of the instrument and its indorsement by the holder.").

127 U.C.C. § 3-201(a).

128 U.C.C. § 3-205(b) ("When indorsed in blank, an instrument becomes payable to bearer and may be negotiated by transfer of possession alone until specially indorsed."). *See also* U.C.C. § 3-109(a) (bearer promise or order is "payable to bearer or to the order of bearer or otherwise indicates that the person in possession of the promise or order is entitled to payment." A note is also a bearer instrument when it "does not state a payee").

129 U.C.C. § 3-201(b) ("If an instrument is payable to bearer, it may be negotiated by transfer of possession alone.").

130 *See, e.g.*, Freddie Mac Document Custody Procedure Handbook Ch. 5 (Dec. 2009), *available at* www.freddiemac.com/cim/handbook.html.

131 *See, e.g.*, U.C.C. § 3-308 cmt. 2 ("Once signatures are proved or admitted a holder, by mere production of the instrument, proves 'entitlement to enforce the instrument' ").

132 To be a holder in due course, the holder must take the instrument for value, in good faith, without notice that the instrument is in default, and without notice of other defects specified in of U.C.C. § 3-302(a)(2). *See* § 5.14.2, *infra* (discussing assignee liability and holder-in-due-course rule).

133 *See* § 5.14.2, *infra*.

134 *See* § 5.14, *supra;* National Consumer Law Center, Unfair and Deceptive Acts and Practices § 11.7.2 (7th ed. 2008 and Supp.).

135 U.C.C. § 3-104(a)(3).

136 *See, e.g.*, Von Frank v. Hershey Nat'l Bank, 306 A.2d 207 (Md. 1973) (notes at issue were not negotiable instruments; "simple contract law," not the U.C.C., determines enforceability); G.E. Capital Mortgage Servicers, Inc. v. Neely, 519 S.E.2d 553 (N.C. Ct. App. 1999) (plaintiff need not rely solely on law of negotiable instruments to recover debt, but can also recover under general contract law); Lawson v. Finance Am. Private Brands, Inc., 537 S.W.2d 483 (Tex. App. 1976) (transferee of non-bearer instrument which is payable to other party is not holder and not entitled to presumption of enforceability, but must prove transaction through which it acquired note).

137 U.C.C. § 3-308(b) (authenticity of the signatures is admitted unless specifically denied in the pleadings; if validity of the

in possession of a negotiable instrument that is payable either to bearer or to an identified person that is the person in possession."[138] Whether the entity in possession of a promissory note is a "holder" depends in part upon compliance with rules for transfer of bearer paper and order paper.

The creditor's status as the holder of the negotiable instrument carries important implications for the borrower. The UCC provides that the borrower satisfies the obligation to the extent payment is made "to a person entitled to enforce the instrument."[139] A holder is clearly a person entitled to enforce a negotiable instrument.[140] Conversely, payment to a person who is *not* entitled to enforce the instrument does *not* satisfy the obligation. If the borrower pays the wrong party, a proper holder could demand payment in the future, exposing the borrower to double liability.[141] For this reason, the borrower has more than an academic interest in ensuring that a claimant is truly a person entitled to enforce the instrument. The Third Circuit recognized this concern in *Adams v. Madison Realty & Development.*[142] The creditor in *Adams* claimed the right to enforce a negotiable instrument despite a defective indorsement. The creditor argued that the UCC's rule requiring physical attachment of an indorsement to the promissory note was overly technical and should not bar it from claiming holder status as against the borrower, the "maker" of the note. In rejecting the creditor's argument, the court noted the significant policy reasons behind the requirement of strict compliance with rules for proper indorsement of a negotiable instrument:

> From the maker's standpoint, therefore, it becomes essential to establish that the person who demands payment of a negotiable note, or to whom payment is made, is the duly qualified holder. Otherwise the obligor is exposed to the risk of double payment, or at least to the expense of litigation incurred to prevent duplicative satisfaction of the instrument. These risks provide makers with a recognizable interest in demanding proof of the chain of title. Consequently, plaintiffs here, as makers of the notes, may properly press defendant to establish its holder status.[143]

4.4.4.4.2 *Enforcement of order paper: a party in possession of a properly indorsed note*

A negotiable instrument payable to the order of an identified person is "order paper."[144] For effective negotiation of order paper, there must be a proper indorsement to a transferee plus delivery of the instrument to the designated transferee.[145] If there were defects in either indorsement or delivery, the party seeking to enforce the note is not a "holder" of the instrument.

To be effective, the indorsement must be by a person with authority to transfer the note. A purported indorsement by a transferor who was not a proper holder undercuts subsequent indorsements. This potential makes inquiry into the chain of past indorsements a highly relevant inquiry.[146] Typically a corporate officer or someone exercising a power of attorney for the corporation must indorse a note. A pooling and servicing agreement, the loan documents themselves, or state law may define who has authority to make an indorsement. Indorsement by a person without authority is ineffective.[147]

---

signatures is admitted or proved, a party producing a negotiable instrument is entitled to payment so long as the party has a right to enforce under one of the three categories in § 3-301). *See e.g.* Citicorp Int'l Trading Co. v. Western Oil & Ref. Co, Inc. , 790 F. Supp. 428 (S.D.N.Y. 1992) (promissory note is "self-standing" and proof of note and failure to make payments makes out prima facie case for payment).

138 U.C.C. § 1-201(21).

139 U.C.C. § 3-602(a).

140 U.C.C. § 3-301.

141 *See, e.g.,* Equity Bank v. Gonsalves, 691 A.2d 1143, 1145–1146 (Conn. Super. Ct. 1996) ("The rule as to the payment and discharge of negotiable instruments is that the payment of the bill or note must be made to the rightful holder or his authorized agent . . . Paying the wrong party does not discharge a negotiable note"); Jackson v. 2109 Brandywine, L.L.C. , 952 A.2d 304 (Md. Spec. Ct. App. 2008) (payment of note to unauthorized agent did not satisfy obligation); Madison-Hunnewell Bank v. Hurt, 903 S.W.2d 175 (Mo. Ct. App. 1995) (payment to someone other than holder exposes payor of note to double liability).

142 853 F.2d 163 (3d Cir. 1988).

143 *Id.,* 853 F.2d at 168.

144 U.C.C. § 3-109(b).

145 U.C.C. §§ 3-201(b), 3-204; Provident Bank v. MorEquity, Inc., 585 S.E.2d 625 (Ga. Ct. App. 2003); Citizens Bank v. Cross, 57 U.C.C. Rep. Serv. 2d 876, 879–880 (R.I. Super. Ct. 2005).

146 Foster Poultry Farms, Inc. v. Suntrust Bank, 2008 WL 160960 (E.D. Cal. Jan. 14, 2008 (applying New York U.C.C., finding broken chain of indorsements of order paper due to defective *allonge*); New Haven Sav. Bank v. Follins, 431 F. Supp. 2d 183 (D. Mass. 2006) (party not holder of note where it had not produced documentary evidence of the chain of indorsements or documentation evidencing that the note was in bearer form at the time the party took possession of it); *In re* Parrish, 326 B.R. 708, 720 (Bankr. N.D. Ohio 2005) (to withstand challenge to bankruptcy proof of claim, claimant must produce evidence that traces loan from originator to current claimant); 6 Hawkland UCC Series § 3-202:4 ("If any indorsement written by someone other than a holder has been forged or is unauthorized, none of the transferees subject to the unauthorized or forged indorsement qualifies as a holder"); James J. White & Robert S. Summers, Uniform Commercial Code § 17.3 (5th ed. 2008) (successive transferees downstream from non-holder transferor of order paper do not become holders; non-holder cannot effectively negotiate order instrument). *But see In re* Weisband, 2010 WL 1253182, at *7 (Bankr. D. Ariz. Mar. 29, 2010) (court declines to impose blanket requirement that all movants for relief from stay must offer proof of note's entire chain of assignments, "although there may be circumstances where, in order to establish standing, the movant will have to do so.").

147 *See* § 4.4.5.3, *infra.*

Another common mistake defeating proper negotiation is for a transferor to forget to indorse the instrument, or for the wrong party to indorse the instrument. If a note is made payable to a lender, and is then put into a securitization trust without indorsement by the lender to the trust, the securitization trust is not a holder.[148] After it has obtained the note, the trust might be able to go back and obtain the missing indorsement. By then, however, it may have notice of the note being overdue and cannot become a holder in due course (although it may acquire the rights of a holder in due course under the shelter rule).[149] On a more basic level, it is not unusual for servicers or mortgage holders to file court complaints with notes attached that are indorsed to a party other than the named plaintiff. In identifying the current holder of the note, the pleading and the exhibits may be in flagrant conflict. These defects may contravene a plaintiff's obligation under a court rule or statute to attach accurate copies of controlling loan documents referred to in the complaint.

If a note is not payable to bearer and lacks the words "to the order of," it is not a negotiable instrument.[150] A common mistake defeating negotiability occurs when the drafter of the instrument is attempting to create order paper but forgets the "to the order of" language. So, for example, if a promissory note said "payable to First National Bank," this would not be payable to *order*. It must state "payable to the order of First National Bank."[151]

Stamps and seals for signatures are generally permissible. State laws will govern notarization formalities. The UCC does not require dating of indorsements.[152] However state laws establishing judicial foreclosure procedures often require that the foreclosing party satisfy pleading requirements. These may include requirements for averments specifying when the foreclosing plaintiff acquired the rights it seeks to enforce.[153] Failure to comply with these rules may lend further support to standing or real party in interest challenges.[154] The timing of an entity's acquisition of the right to enforce a note may also be relevant to determining whether that entity has the right to use a state's non-judicial foreclosure procedures. Finally, timing of indorsements is relevant to the inquiry as to whether the loan is properly included in a trust.[155]

Other common errors that can prevent a transferee from being a holder of order paper relate to the location of the indorsement on the instrument. A holder of a negotiable instrument payable to order must obtain that instrument via an indorsement either written on the instrument itself or on a paper affixed to the instrument.[156] Such a separate paper for an indorsement is called an *allonge*.[157]

For instruments governed by the pre-1990 version of UCC Article 3, the *allonge* must be "a paper so firmly affixed thereto as to become a part thereof."[158] The 1990 amendments to Article 3, in effect in all states other than New York, still require that the indorsement be "made on [the] instrument" but add that "a paper affixed to the instrument is a part of the instrument."[159] The Official Comment to UCC § 3-204 states that under this language an *allonge* is valid even though there is sufficient space on the instrument for an indorsement.[160] The 1990 amendments do not appear to eliminate the requirement that the paper containing the indorsement be attached to the instrument in a permanent way, although it no longer must be affixed so firmly "as to become a part thereof." While there have been few decisions interpreting the 1990 language, it is probably insufficient to fold a promissory note around the indorsements[161] or include the indorsements in a separate assignment document.[162]

148 See Kurt Eggert, *Held Up In Due Course: Predatory Lending, Securitization, and the Holder in Due Course Doctrine*, 35 Creighton L. Rev. 503, 566–570 (2002).

149 *See* § 11.7.2.4, *infra.*

150 *See* Universal Premium Acceptance Corp. v. York Bank & Trust Co., 69 F.3d 695 (3d Cir. 1995) (drafts that stated "pay and deposit only to credit of" were not negotiable); Tamman v. Schinazi, 54 U.C.C. Rep. Serv. 2d 287 (S.D.N.Y. 2004); Stone v. Mehlberg, 728 F. Supp. 1341 (W.D. Mich. 1989); Tompkins Printing Equip. Co. v. Almik, Inc., 725 F. Supp. 918 (E.D. Mich. 1989); Hall v. Westmoreland, Hall & Bryan, 182 S.E.2d 539 (Ga. Ct. App. 1971); Sirius L.C. v. Erickson, 156 P.3d 539 (Idaho 2007); Leavings v. Mills, 175 S.W.3d 301 (Tex. App. 2004). *Cf.* Lakhaney v. Anzelone, 788 F. Supp. 160 (S.D.N.Y. 1992) (note was negotiable where it was payable to "[plaintiff] or order"); Coop. Centrale Raiffeisen-Boerenleenbank B.A. v. Bailey, 710 F. Supp. 737 (C.D. Cal. 1989) (note was negotiable where it obliged the maker to "pay to the order to payee;" the phrase could be construed only to mean "pay to the order of" payee).

151 This rule does not apply to checks, which under U.C.C. §§ 3-104(c) and 3-104(f) are negotiable even if they do not have order language.

152 *In re* Roberts, 367 B.R. 677, 683 (Bankr. D. Colo. 2007) (applying Colorado law).

153 *See, e.g.,* Vt. R. Civ. P. 80.1(b) (a complaint in foreclosure must set forth, "any assignment of the mortgage"; the names of all parties in interest and, as to each party in interest, the date of record of the instrument upon which the interest is based").

154 *See* § 4.4.6.1, *infra.*

155 *See* § 4.4.5.2, *infra.*

156 U.C.C. §§ 3-201(b), 3-204(a). Note that if it is bearer paper, only delivery of the instrument is necessary.

157 *See* U.C.C. § 3-204 cmt. 1.

158 U.C.C. § 3-202(1), (2) (pre-1990 version). Note that if it is bearer paper, only delivery of the instrument is necessary.

159 U.C.C. § 3-204(a).

160 U.C.C. § 3-204 cmt. 1.

161 Adams v. Madison Realty & Dev., Inc., 853 F.2d 163 (3d Cir. 1988) (decided under pre-1990 language, but interpreting language that the 1990 amendments did not change).

162 *See, e.g., In re* Weisband, 2010 WL 1253182, at *4 (Bankr. D. Ariz. Mar. 29, 2010) (movant for relief from stay failed to show it was holder of note and real party in interest where indorsement to movant was on a separate sheet of paper and there was no evidence that it was stapled or otherwise attached to the rest of the note); Big Builders, Inc. v. Israel, 709 A.2d 74 (D.C. 1998) (claimant would not be holder under either version of U.C.C. because indorsement was on separate unattached docu-

Allonges governed by the pre-1990 version of Article 3 must meet even stricter requirements: they must be so firmly attached to the instrument as to become a part of it,[163] and many cases held that an *allonge* could only be used if there was no room on the instrument itself for an indorsement.[164] These stricter requirements still apply to notes made in New York, and for notes made prior to the effective date of the 1990 Article 3 revisions in the relevant state.

4.4.4.4.3 *Enforcement of bearer paper: a party must be in possession*

Bearer paper is issued in blank, payable to no identified person or to "bearer." Indorsement to the current holder is not necessary. The entity seeking to enforce bearer paper need only produce evidence of possession. Provided the authenticity of signatures is not disputed, possession establishes the party as a holder who is presumptively entitled to enforcement by mere production of the instrument.[165]

For securitized mortgage transactions, the terms of a pooling and servicing agreement (PSA) typically set up a custodial system for holding negotiable instruments. The PSA may require delivery of the note to the trustee within a fixed period of time after the trust acquires the obligation. In other cases the PSA designates a custodial entity which holds the original document for the trust.[166] The custodian retains possession of the note, and under some agreements transfers the note to a servicer after default. The servicer then holds the note during the foreclosure. Despite the terms of PSAs, servicers often proceed to foreclose without pos-

---

ment); Town of Freeport v. Ring, 727 A.2d 901 (Me. 1999); NAB Asset Venture II v. Lenertz, Inc., 1998 WL 422207 (Minn. Ct. App. July 28, 1998) (stapling *allonge* to instrument is proper indorsement under U.C.C. § 3-204(a)); Becker v. Nat'l Bank & Trust Co., 284 S.E.2d 793 (Va. 1981) (decided under pre-1990 language, but interpreting language that the 1990 amendments did not change).

The following decisions under the comparable language of the pre-1990 version which precluded separate assignment documents should not be affected by the 1990 changes: *In re* Governor's Island, 39 B.R. 417 (Bankr. E.D.N.C. 1984) (where there is separate assignment and no indorsement on note, assignee is not holder in due course); Wear v. Farmers & Merchants Bank of Las Cruces, 605 P.2d 27 (Alaska 1980) (Texas law; separate assignment not sufficient where actual note was not attached to the assignment agreement); Security Pac. Nat'l Bank v. Chess, 129 Cal. Rptr. 852 (Cal. Ct. App. 1976) (separate assignment agreement did not serve as an indorsement; thus, assignee did not become holder in due course); Billas v. Dwyer, 232 S.E.2d 102 (Ga. Ct. App. 1976) (where purported transfer and assignment of note had never been attached to the note, it did not serve as an effective indorsement); Duxbury v. Roberts, 446 N.E.2d 401 (Mass. 1983); Dyck-O'Neal, Inc. v. Pungitore, 52 U.C.C. Rep. Serv. 2d 717 (Mass. App. Ct. 2003) (unpublished) (plaintiff not a holder where assignment not affixed to note, but still obtained transferor's rights); Bremen Bank & Trust Co of St. Louis. v. Muskopf, 817 S.W.2d 602 (Mo. Ct. App. 1991) (instrument was not effectively negotiated where separate assignment agreement was not attached to the note).

163 *See* pre-1990 U.C.C. § 3-202(2).

Decisions finding *allonges* defective under the pre-1990 version of Article 3 include: Foster Poultry Farms, Inc. v. Suntrust Bank, 2008 WL 160960 (E.D. Cal. Jan. 14, 2008) (applying New York U.C.C., not a valid negotiation where *allonge* used despite space for indorsement on face of note); Tallahassee Bank & Trust Co. v. Raines, 187 S.E.2d 320 (Ga. Ct. App. 1972) (a separate paper pinned or clipped to an instrument is an insufficient indorsement); Illinois State Bank of Quincy v. Yates, 678 S.W.2d 819 (Mo. Ct. App. 1984) (assignment stapled to note did not constitute negotiation of note); Estrada v. River Oaks Bank & Trust Co., 550 S.W.2d 719 (Tex. App. 1977) (one indorsement stapled to four notes not sufficient); Crossland Sav. Bank v. Constant, 737 S.W.2d 19 (Tex. App. 1987) (stapling separate piece of paper to back of two long sets of loan documents insufficient where there was room on note for indorsement). *But see In re* Nash, 49 B.R. 254 (Bankr. D. Ariz. 1985), *aff'd on other grounds*, 60 B.R. 27 (B.A.P. 9th Cir. 1986) (physical separation of note and assignment within company's file did not prevent assignee from becoming a holder in due course given the parties' clear intent that the note and the assignment were to be physically attached); Lamson v. Commercial Credit Corp., 531 P.2d 966 (Colo. 1975) (a two-page indorsement stapled to two checks was sufficient to constitute an *allonge* for both checks).

164 Official Comment 1 to the 1990 version of U.C.C. § 3-204 repudiates this position. *See* NAB Asset Venture II v. Lenertz, Inc., 1998 WL 422207 (Minn. Ct. App. July 28, 1998) (stapling *allonge* to instrument is proper indorsement under U.C.C. § 3-204(a)); Winfield v. Dosohs I, 1998 Tex. App. LEXIS 4674 (July 30, 1998) (unpublished) (upholding indorsement in light of 1990 amendments where *allonge* was a paper "sticky" attached to note, even though note had room for indorsement).

Decisions enforcing the restrictions of the pre-1990 version of Article 3 include: *In re* Nash, 49 B.R. 254 (Bankr. D. Ariz. 1985), *aff'd on other grounds*, 60 B.R. 27 (B.A.P. 9th Cir. 1986); Pribus v. Bush, 173 Cal. Rptr. 747 (Cal. Ct. App. 1981) (an *allonge* should only be used when there is no room for the indorsement on the note itself); Tallahassee Bank & Trust Co. v. Raines, 187 S.E.2d 320 (Ga. Ct. App. 1972); Bremen Bank & Trust Co of St. Louis. v. Muskopf, 817 S.W.2d 602 (Mo. Ct. App. 1991); Fed. Fin. Co. v. Delgado, 1 S.W.3d 181 (Tex. App. 1999) (indorsement on *allonge* invalid under pre-1990 version of Article 3 where adequate space on original note, therefore holder was mere "transferee," not "holder in due course"); Estrada v. River Oaks Bank & Trust Co., 550 S.W.2d 719 (Tex. App. 1977). *But cf.* Southwestern Resolution Corp. v. Watson, 964 S.W.2d 262 (Tex. 1997) (staples can be used as an *allonge* under pre-1990 version of Article 3 where no more room on note).

165 U.C.C. § 3-308, cmt 2; Vandegriff v. Hamilton, 519 S.E.2d 702 (Ga. Ct. App. 1999); The Cadle Co. v. Shearer, 69 S.W.3d 122 (Mo. Ct. App. 2002); U.S. National Bank Ass'n v. Marcino, 908 N.E.2d 1032 (Ohio Ct. App. 2009) (indorsement of order paper in blank converted it to bearer paper; foreclosing lender established right to foreclose by possession of note without documenting chain of prior transfers).

166 *See e.g.* Freddie Mac Form 1035 (rev 2/08.2), Custodial Agreement Single Family Mortgages, *available at* www.freddiemac.com/cim/pdf/Form1035.pdf (transfer of original notes and mortgage from servicer to custodian); Fannie Mae Single Family Servicing Guide pt. I, ch. 4, § 403 (2006), *available at* www.efanniemae.com/sf/guides/ssg/index.jsp#ssg.

session of the note and without proof that the trust they purport to represent possesses the note.

4.4.4.4.4 *Others who can enforce a negotiable instrument: non-holders and those not in possession of note*

The general rule is that in order to enforce a negotiable instrument, an entity must be a "holder" of the note in accordance with the UCC's definition of that term.[167] For both bearer paper and order paper possession of the note is an essential element of holder status. However, there are exceptions. In defining parties who are entitled to enforce a negotiable instrument, the UCC describes two categories of claimants who may enforce although they are not holders in possession of the note.[168] The first is a "nonholder in possession of the instrument who has the rights of a holder." The second is a "person not in possession of the instrument who is entitled to enforce the instrument pursuant to Section 3-309 [lost instruments] or 3-418(d) [payment or acceptance by mistake]."[169] Claims of enforceability under these non-holder categories defined in section 3-301 turn up with some regularity in foreclosures of securitized mortgages.

"A nonholder in possession of an instrument who has the rights of the holder" can occur in different situations, including where the FDIC or RTC acts as the receiver for a failed bank, or where one corporate entity acquires the assets of another. A non-holder in possession with the rights of a holder also includes those who acquire rights by subrogation and "any other person who under applicable law is a successor to the holder or otherwise acquires the holder's rights."[170] As the result of an acquisition, the FDIC may be in possession of a negotiable instrument indorsed to the order of a defunct entity, and no further valid indorsements can be made. The FDIC can not be a true "holder" because the note it possesses is order paper that is not indorsed to the order of the FDIC. However, contractual and statutory terms governing bulk transfers may make the FDIC the legal "owner" of the note. In this situation the FDIC is entitled to enforce the instrument as a "non-holder in possession with the rights of a holder."

A party seeking to enforce a note who does not qualify as a holder should be required to produce evidence showing that it acquired the right to enforce the obligation from a transferor who had the right to enforce it.[171] The question of whether a non-holder can exercise the rights of a holder may not present a standing question that can be resolved by review of the face of notes and indorsements. Instead, the proponent of the claim must meet its burden of proof by presenting evidence on a wider range of transactional issues related to its own status and the rights held by former transferors and transferees of the obligation.[172]

The second significant category of non-holders who can enforce negotiable instruments consists of claimants who concede that they are not in possession of the instrument. These claimants unambiguously assert that they are not in possession because the note has been "lost, destroyed, or stolen."[173] In cases involving securitized mortgage obligations servicers sometimes make little or no effort to ascertain the whereabouts of notes. Instead they file documents claiming in conclusory terms that the notes were lost or destroyed and anticipate that no one will scrutinize this claim. These types of pro forma lost note claims should be challenged. The UCC's requirements for establishing the right to enforce a lost note are exacting.[174]

If the note is lost, impaired, or destroyed, the amount of the debt may be established by extrinsic evidence.[175] The claimant must submit an affidavit showing its right to collect and the terms of the instrument. The evidence must show that the claimant was entitled to enforce the instrument when loss of possession occurred or has directly or indirectly acquired ownership of the instrument from a person who was entitled to enforce it when loss of possession

167 U.C.C. § 1-201(21).

168 U.C.C. § 3-301. *See also* § 5.14.2.6, *infra.*

169 U.C.C. § 3-301.

170 U.C.C. § 3-301 cmt.

171 U.C.C. § 3-203 cmt. 2 ("If the transferee is not a holder because the transferor did not indorse, the transferee is nevertheless a person entitled to enforce the instrument under Section 3-301 if the transferor was a holder at the time of transfer. Although the transferee is not a holder, under subsection (b) [of § 3-203] the transferee obtained the rights of the transferor as holder. Because the transferee's rights are derivative of the transferor's rights, those rights must be proved.").

172 *See, e.g.,* Federal Deposit Ins. Corp. v. Houde, 90 F.3d 600 (1st Cir. 2000) (FDIC not entitled to enforce a note because it failed to prove any transfers, bank insolvency proceedings, or testimony forming the basis for its claimed ownership of the note); New Haven Sav. Bank v. Follins, 431 F. Supp. 2d 183 195–196 (D. Mass. 2006) (nonholder showed itself to be owner of note and entitled to enforce it although note not indorsed to it or payable to bearer); *In re* Carlyle, 242 B.R. 881 (Bankr. E.D. Va. 1999) (lack of indorsement on promissory note did not deprive party in possession of right to enforce it, but merely stripped party of its presumed right to payment and required it to prove the transaction by which it acquired instrument); Ninth RMA Partners, L.P. v. Krass, 746 A.2d 826, 830–831 (Conn. App. Ct. 2000) (transferees of note from FDIC succeeded to FDIC's right to enforce obligation although neither FDIC nor subsequent transferees were "holders" of note).

173 U.C.C. § 3-301, incorporating the provisions of § 3-309 (Enforcement of Lost, Destroyed, or Stolen Instrument).

174 U.C.C. § 3-309.

175 *See* New England Sav. Bank v. Bedford Realty Corp., 680 A.2d 301 (Conn. 1996), *rev'd after remand,* 717 A.2d 713 (1998) (assignee of lost note can use other evidence to establish the amount of the debt); Bobby D. Assocs. v. DiMarcantonio, 751 A.2d 673 (Pa. Super. Ct. 2000) (lost note established where current creditor's transferor was holder of note when it was lost and transferred all its right to current creditor); Mitchell Bank v. Schanke, 676 N.W.2d 849 (Wis. 2004) (lender not required to produce note so long as it can prove the underlying debt secured by the mortgage).

occurred.[176] This requires specific evidence about the circumstances of the holder of the obligation at the time it was allegedly lost.[177] The affidavit should also establish that the note cannot be located. The court should not allow the party to proceed without the original note unless the court is satisfied that the homeowner is adequately protected against a potential claim by another person to enforce the note.[178] Affidavits should be scrutinized carefully and challenged when appropriate.[179]

4.4.5 Transfer of the Mortgage—Who Is the Current Assignee and Was There a Proper Assignment of Mortgage?

4.4.5.1 General

In addition to scrutinizing the note and its indorsements for compliance with negotiable instruments law, practitioners should check for the existence of and the validity of assignments of the mortgage. Unless the entity seeking to foreclose was the loan originator, it must show that it is the current holder of a valid assignment of the mortgage. Courts have dismissed foreclosure cases brought by an alleged assignee of a mortgage when the party failed to produce a written assignment of the mortgage.[180] Some of these decisions are based in part on state law requirements that mortgage assignments be recorded.[181] Without a valid mortgage, a holder of the note has no lien on the property and generally can only institute a collection action, not foreclose on the home.[182] Of course, a successful collection action might give rise to a judgment lien, so defeating the mortgage and not the note may only delay the inevitable if the property cannot be protected by a state homestead exemption.[183]

The statute of frauds requires that any interest in real estate be in writing.[184] Mortgages are now widely considered to create an interest in real estate.[185] Transferring the interest created by a mortgage via assignment should also be covered by the statute of frauds. Thus, the failure to create, retain, or produce a written assignment may mean that the assignee has no legal interest in the property and therefore cannot foreclose.

The absence of a separate written assignment of a mortgage will not always defeat a foreclosure. Some courts look to the general rule that a mortgage follows the note.[186] Where there is no written assignment of the mortgage, but

---

176 U.C.C. § 3-309(a). *See, e.g.,* YYY Corp. v. Gazda, 761 A.2d 395 (N.H. 2000) (sustaining lost claim on obligation passing through FDIC receivership).

177 *See, e.g., In re* Gavin, 319 B.R. 27, 32 (B.A.P. 1st Cir. 2004) (construing U.C.C. § 3-309 to require direct evidence of past ownership and terms of loan; court will not make inferences from circumstantial evidence).

178 *See* U.C.C. § 3-309(b). *See also* McKay v. Capital Res., 940 S.W.2d 869 (Ark. 1997) (assignee could not enforce note as it did not produce the note or satisfy the U.C.C. requirements for lost negotiable instruments).

179 *Cf.* Am. Sav. Bank v. Fernandez, 78 P.3d 339 (Haw. 2003) (unpublished) (denying summary judgment for lender that relied on hearsay affidavit to establish amount of debt).

180 *See In re* Foreclosure Cases, 521 F. Supp. 2d 650 (S. D. Ohio 2007); *In re* Foreclosure Cases, 2007 WL 4034554 (N.D. Ohio Nov. 14, 2007); *In re* Foreclosure Cases, 2007 WL 3232430 (N.D. Ohio Oct. 31, 2007); Wells Fargo Bank, N.A. v. Reyes, 867 N.Y.S.2d 21 (N.Y. Sup. Ct. 2008) (table) (foreclosure dismissed where no evidence of assignment of mortgage to plaintiff); DJL Mortgage Capital, Inc. v. Parsons, 2008 WL 6974000 (Ohio Ct. App. Mar. 13, 2008) (lower court improperly entered judgment for plaintiff without evidence plaintiff had assignment of mortgage); Everhome Mortgage Co. v. Rowland, 2008 WL 747698 (Ohio Ct. App. Mar. 20, 2008) (reversing summary judgment in favor of assignee in foreclosure action since assignee failed to demonstrate it had an interest in either the note or the mortgage); Keybank N.A. v. Wright, 2006 WL 2578757 (Ohio Ct. App. Sept. 1, 2006) (denying Countrywide leave to intervene and assert prior lien in mortgage foreclosure action since it had not produced or recorded an assignment of the prior mortgage); Washington Mut. Bank, F.A. v. Green, 806 N.E.2d 604 (Ohio Ct. App. 2004) (summary judgment for plaintiff reversed where defendant raised disputed issue as to identity of current assignee of mortgage); First Union Nat'l Bank v. Hufford, 767 N.E.2d 1206 (Ohio Ct. App. 2001) (denying plaintiff relief because failed to document how it obtained rights under mortgage). *See also In re* Jacobson, 402 B.R. 359 (Bankr. W.D. Wash. 2009) (no standing shown to move for relief from stay where servicer could not identify current holder of mortgage and note).

181 *See In re* Dimmings, 386 B.R. 199, 205 (Bankr. N.D. Ohio 2008) (denying motion for relief from stay in part since original creditor and subsequent assignee failed to record mortgage). *But cf.* Martin v. Select Portfolio Serving Holding Corp., 2008 WL 618788 (S.D. Ohio Mar. 3, 2008) (holding that failure to record or produce assignment until requested by plaintiff in FDCPA action does not invalidate assignment).

182 *But see* Conn. Gen. Stat. § 49-17 (permitting foreclosure where the note is validly transferred even if the mortgage is not assigned); U.C.C. § 9-203(g) (right to foreclose belongs in equity to owner of the debt).

183 *See* § 9.8, 11.10, 14.3.5, *infra.*

184 The Statute of Frauds was enacted in English law in 1677 and carried over, either by statute or common law, to all of the states except Louisiana. Restatement (Second) of Contracts ch. 5, statutory n. (1981) (listing the corresponding state statutes).

185 *See, e.g.,* Manir Properties v. Resolution Trust Corp., 1993 WL 381445 (E.D. Pa. Sept. 29, 1993) (explaining that nineteenth century Pennsylvania common law treated mortgages as a "chose in action" and therefore not subject to the statute of frauds but that Pennsylvania law now clearly treats mortgages as interests in real property).

186 Carpenter v. Longan, 83 U.S. 271, 275 (1872) ("All the authorities agree that the debt is the principal thing and the mortgage an accessory"); Bankers Trust Co. of California, N.A. v. Vaneck, 899 A.2d 41 (Conn. App. Ct. 2006) (state statute codifies common law principle). *See* Becker v. Dramin, 6 Conn. Supp. 33 (Conn. Super. Ct. 1938) (holding that mortgage follows note and so assignment of mortgage is not covered by the statute of frauds, provided there is a valid transfer of the note). Levy v. McGill, 137 Fed. Appx. 613 (5th Cir. 2004) (holding that asset purchase agreement, in lieu of assignment, was in any

a party is clearly entitled to enforce the promissory note secured by a mortgage, courts may be inclined to allow foreclosure to proceed.[187] Using the statute of frauds to defeat a foreclosure action may be easiest when there is no writing transferring either the note or the mortgage to the foreclosing entity. Practitioners should remember that in many jurisdictions, the statute of frauds can be waived, either by failure to plead or failure to object to parole testimony.[188]

Several courts have barred borrowers from asserting the failure of the assignment to comply with the statute of frauds primarily because they find that the borrower is not a third-party beneficiary of the assignment contract.[189] As a general rule, only the parties to the contract transferring the interest in land are able to assert a defense of the statute of frauds.[190] This of course overlooks much of the reason for the statute of frauds: to prevent fraud, to protect title to land, and to prevent multiple claims. Borrowers in today's world of securitization, where mortgages are sold often and early, with correspondingly frequent false claims[191] have reason to demand that any foreclosing entity demonstrate the validity of the documents relied on to assert the claim.

4.4.5.2 Is the Mortgage Properly Included in the Trust?

The terms of a pooling and servicing agreement govern when and how a trust may acquire mortgages. For example, some PSAs permit the trust to acquire only mortgages that are current, precluding the trustee from accepting loans that are in default. A trust agreement may set a closing date after which new mortgages may not be added to the trust pool. Given that a trustee may exercise only powers granted by the trust agreement, the trustee arguably has no authority to bring a defaulted mortgage into the trust or acquire a mortgage after the closing date. It is unclear what the ultimate effect of such an unauthorized transfer of a loan to the trust may be. Some advocates have raised these acquisition defects as a challenge to the trust's standing to pursue a foreclosure, arguing that the invalid transfer gave the trust no valid claim to enforce.[192] The language of particular PSAs may support these arguments more than others. The terms of the pooling and servicing agreement may also define which entities have authority to transfer mortgages to the trust. For example, the PSA may provide that only a designated "depositor" may assign a mortgage to the trust. A mortgagee's direct assignment of a mortgage to the trust, bypassing the depositor, may violate such a term of the PSA. Few courts have addressed the question of whether the homeowner may assert a violation of the PSA's loan acquisition terms as an objection to the trust's standing to enforce a particular loan obligation. However, some courts have ruled that borrowers have no right to assert violations of the PSA as defenses to enforcement of the mortgage claims.[193]

---

case definite enough and did not need to be delivered to transfer trust deed).

187 *In re* Minbatiwalli, 424 B.R. 104 (Bankr. S.D.N.Y. 2010); *In re* Lewis, 2009 WL 3614763 (Bankr. E.D. Tenn. Oct. 26, 2009) (transfer of note secured by deed carries right to enforce security instrument); *In re* Hill, 2009 WL 1956174 (Bankr. D. Ariz. July 6, 2009) (production of original note indorsed in blank sufficient to proceed with motion for relief from stay; no need to establish assignment of deed of trust); *In re* Conde-Dedonato, 391 B.R. 247 (Bankr. E.D. N.Y. 2008); U.S. Bank National Ass'n v. Marcino, 908 N.E.2d 1032 (Ohio Ct. App. 2009) (negotiation of note operates as an equitable assignment of the mortgage); U.S. Bank Nat'l Ass'n v. Wiegand, 2009 WL 1623764 (Conn. Super. Ct. May 14, 2009) (applying state statute, plaintiff had right to enforce mortgage based on pre-complaint transfer of note); LaSalle Bank National Ass'n v. Street, 2009 WL 1040300 (Ohio Ct. App. Apr. 17, 2009) (transfer of note secured by mortgage operates as equitable assignment of mortgage even though mortgage not assigned or delivered).

188 Gramatan Home Investors Corp. v. Whittemore, 518 A.2d 32 (Vt. 1986) (overturning trial court's dismissal of foreclosure action for plaintiff-assignee's failure to produce documentary evidence of assignment since defendant borrowers did not object to oral testimony of the assignment and thus waived the statute of frauds defense).

189 *See* Countrywide Home Loans, Inc. v. Brown, 223 Fed. Appx. 13 (2d Cir. 2007) (holding that borrower cannot raise failure to comply with statute of frauds defense in foreclosure since the defense is "personal" to the assignor); Austin v. Countrywide Homes Loans, 261 S.W.3d 68 (Tex. App. 2008) (holding that *pro se* homeowner was not a party to the assignment and so, as a third party, has no right to invoke the statute of frauds with respect to the assignment). *Cf.* Levy v. McGill, 137 Fed. Appx. 613 (5th Cir. 2004) (holding that statute of frauds may not cover assignments and that asset purchase agreement, in lieu of assignment, was in any case definite enough and did not need to be delivered to transfer trust deed); Conradt v. Lepper, 81 P. 307 (Wyo. 1905) (finding that borrower could not assert illegal assignment of mortgage as a defense to foreclosure if the underlying mortgage was valid).

190 Restatement (Second) of Contracts § 144 (1981).

191 *See, e.g.,* Impac Warehouse Lending Group v. Credit Suisse First Boston L.L.C., 270 Fed. Appx. 570 (9th Cir. 2008) (litigation by warehouse lender against securitizer and mortgage broker; mortgage broker sold same loans to both warehouse lender and securitizers, apparently creating fake documentation for the sale to the warehouse lender).

192 *See, e.g.,* HSBC Bank USA, N.A. v. Perez, No. EQ4870 (Iowa Dist. Ct. Nov. 19, 2009), *available at* www.consumerlaw.org/unreported (unpublished trial court decision) (defendant raised disputed issue of material fact, precluding summary judgment for plaintiff, where alleged loan assigned to trust one month after default and PSA precluded trustee from acquiring loans in default). *See generally In re* Canellas, 2010 WL 571808 (Bankr. M.D. Fla. Feb. 9, 2010) (denying motion for relief from stay where *allonge* to note referred to a trust that had not come into existence until two months after purported indorsement).

193 *In re* Samuels, 415 B.R. 8 (Bankr. D. Mass. 2009) (even if direct assignment from loan originator to trust, as opposed to assignment to from depositor to trust, violated PSA and gave rise to unfavorable tax, regulatory, contractual, and tort consequences for trust's investors, this would not render the assignment itself invalid); *In re* Almeida, 417 B.R. 140 (Bankr. D. Mass. 2009)

4.4.5.3 Power of Attorney from Authorized Agent to Assign Mortgage

A corporate officer with authority to assign the mortgage typically signs off on the assignment document. In some states, a person who executes an assignment of a mortgage or otherwise acts as authorized agent for the current owner of the mortgage must do so under a valid power of attorney.[194] A power of attorney documents that the agent was vested with the authority to perform the designated tasks on behalf of the owner of the obligation.[195] In many cases, the power of attorney forms that the foreclosing parties submit for the record raise more questions than they answer.

New York courts have been particularly vigilant in scrutinizing mortgage assignment documents to ensure that foreclosing plaintiffs meet the threshold test for standing. In a number of cases the courts noted that the same individual appeared without explanation as representative of multiple entities in a series of assignments.[196] In one case the same individual had executed two assignments contemporaneously on behalf of two different assignors.[197] In other cases the same individual executed a power of attorney for the assignor and the assignee in the same transaction.[198] It did not escape the court's attention in yet another case that a particular law firm appeared as the "attorney in fact" for MERS in the execution of a prior assignment of the mortgage.[199] The same law firm then appeared as attorney for the plaintiff bank in foreclosing upon a junior mortgage held by MERS. The law firm had thus "transferred ownership rights of the subject property from its former client [MERS] to its current client [the bank] and then sued the former client [MERS] for the benefit of the current client [the bank]."[200] These and other discrepancies, inconsistencies, and potential conflicts have led courts to withhold granting defaults or summary judgment to foreclosing plaintiffs.

4.4.6 *Scrutinizing the Proffered Loan Documents*

4.4.6.1 Is There a Prima Facie Showing That the Foreclosing Party Is the Current Holder of the Note and Mortgage?

A party against whom a negotiable instrument is being enforced is entitled to demand that the claimant give reasonable identification and "exhibit the instrument" it seeks to enforce[201] If enforcement of a note is sought on behalf of

(same). *But see In re* Weisband, 2010 WL 1253182, at *6 (Bankr. D. Ariz. Mar. 29, 2010) (trust documents failed to establish that debtor's loan was included in trust for which servicer acted as agent); *In re* Jones, 2008 WL 4539486 (Bankr. D. Mass Oct. 3, 2008) (rejecting mortgage servicer's proof of claim due to lack of evidence that debtor's mortgage was added to trust by assignment in accordance with agreement transferring loans to trust); *In re* Hayes, 393 B.R. 259, 268 (Bankr. D. Mass. 2008) (lack of evidence of assignment of mortgage to trust precludes standing for claimant).

194 *E.g.*, HSBC Bank, U.S.A., N.A. v. Valentin, 859 N.Y.S. 2d 895 (N.Y. Super. Ct. 2008) (table) (if power of attorney refers to PSA, there must be a copy of the PSA to determine if servicing agent may proceed on behalf of plaintiff); HSBC Bank USA, N.A. v. Cherry, 2007 WL 4374284 (N.Y. Super. Ct. Dec. 17, 2007) (if power of attorney in support of verification refers to pooling and servicing agreement, the PSA must be attached); Deutsche Bank Nat'l Trust Co. v. Clouden, 851 N.Y.S.2d 57 (N.Y. Super. Ct. 2007) (defective power of attorney to assign mortgage); EMC Mortgage Corp. v. Batista, 841 N.Y.S.2d 819 (N.Y. Super. Ct. 2007) (power of attorney for affidavit failed to specify authority under pooling and service agreement to make verification); Deutsche Bank Nat'l Trust Co. v. Lewis, 831 N.Y.S.2d 358 (N.Y. Super. Ct. 2006) (same).

195 *See, e.g., In re* Samuels, 415 B.R. 8 (Bankr. D. Mass. 2009) (one limited power of attorney form authorized servicer to assign mortgages only in repurchase and refinance situations; second power of attorney gave morc general authority); *In re* Wells, 407 B.R. 873 (Bankr. N.D. Ohio 2009) (no authority shown under pooling and servicing agreement for servicer or its employee to file proof of claim in bankruptcy court for mortgage holder); *In re* Hayes, 393 B.R. 259, 268 (Bankr. D. Mass. 2008) (servicer's limited power of attorney did not give it authority to assign mortgage to trust on behalf of originator); HSBC Bank U.S.A., N.A. v. Yeasman, 866 N.Y.S.2d 92 (N.Y. Sup. Ct. 2008) (table) (purported assignment of mortgage and note without evidence of power of attorney or corporate resolution to authorize assignment was not valid; plaintiff lacked standing to foreclose based on current record).

196 Indymac Bank, F.S.B. v. Bethley, 880 N.Y.S. 2d 873 (N.Y. Super. Ct. 2009) (table) (same affiant appears on numerous affidavits in different cases before same court); HSBC Bank USA, N.A. v. Vasquez, 2009 WL 2581672 (N.Y. Super. Ct. Aug. 21, 2009) (noting conflict of interest in assignments). *See also* U.S. Bank N.A. v. Bernard, 2008 WL 383814 (N.Y. Super. Ct. Feb. 14, 2008); Wells Fargo Bank, N.A. v. Farmer, 2008 WL 307454 (N.Y. Super. Ct. Feb. 4, 2008); Deutsche Bank Nat'l Trust Co. v. Castellanos, 2008 WL 123798 (N.Y. Super. Ct. Jan. 14, 2008); Wells Fargo Bank, N.A. v. Davilmar, 847 N.Y.S.2d 906 (N.Y. Super. Ct. 2007). *See also* HSBC Bank USA, N.A. v. Yeasmin, 866 N.Y.S.2d 92 (N.Y. Sup. Ct. 2008) (table).

197 U.S. Bank N.A. v. Merino, 836 N.Y.S.2d 853 (N.Y. Super. Ct. 2007).

198 Wells Fargo Bank, N.A. v. Farmer, 859 N.Y.S.2d 900 (Table), 2008 WL 307454 (N.Y. Super. Ct. Feb. 4, 2008); Deutsche Bank Nat'l Trust Co. v. Clouden, 851 N.Y.S.2d 57 (N.Y. Super. Ct. 2007).

199 U.S. Nat'l Bank Ass'n v. Kosak, 2007 WL 2480127 (N.Y. Super. Ct. Sept. 4, 2007).

200 U.S. Nat'l Bank Ass'n v. Kosak, 2007 WL 2480127, at *2 (N.Y. Super. Ct. Sept. 4, 2007).

201 U.C.C. § 3-501(b)(2); Mckay v. Capital Res. Co., Ltd., 940 S.W.2d 869 (Ark. 1997) (applying best evidence rule; plaintiff must produce original note, not copy, otherwise maker may face double liability); Ferris v. Nichols, 245 So. 2d 660 (Fla. Dist. Ct. App. 1971) (original note and supporting affidavits must be in summary judgment record); Affiliated Acceptance Corp. v. Boggs, 917 S.W.2d 652 (Mo. Ct. App. 1996) (discussing presentment requirement); Liles v. Myers, 248 S.E.2d 385 (N.C. Ct. App.1978) (copy of note attached to summary judgment record does not establish prima facie case that plaintiff is holder;

another person, reasonable evidence of the claimant's authority to enforce on behalf of that person must be produced.[202] In addition, in judicial foreclosures, a statute or court rule often requires the plaintiff to make specific averments as to its interest in the obligation or produce as attachments to a pleading copies of the documents that form the basis of its claim.[203] Similar rules apply for motions for relief from the stay and proofs of claims filed in bankruptcy cases.[204] The most common failure to make out a prima facie case occurs when a plaintiff in a judicial foreclosure attempts to move for summary judgment or a default based on a record that incorporates as exhibits a mortgage, note, or both which identify holders inconsistently with the averments of the complaint.[205]

When the lender moves for summary judgment in a judicial foreclosure, the current loan documents must be included in the record. If there are unexplained inconsistencies among the creditors named in pleadings and the parties whose names appear on supporting loan documents, the plaintiff has not made out a prima facie case. These gaps indicate unspecified transfers of negotiable instruments and assignments of mortgages. In the face of these inconsistencies many courts will dismiss foreclosure actions or refuse to grant other forms of relief to servicers or purported mortgage holders.[206]

A similar failure to make out a prima facie case occurs when a servicer or MERS takes legal action in its name and fails to disclose the current owner of the note and mortgage.[207] The servicer or MERS may purport to act on behalf of the owner of securitized mortgage debt, but in reality have made no effort to investigate the facts of current ownership.[208] Without naming the principal and providing proof of authority to act on behalf of that principal, the servicer cannot meet the most basic showing of standing and real party in interest.[209]

Production of an original note, properly indorsed or payable to the bearer, entitles the holder to a presumptive right to enforce the instrument. However, this presumption may be rebutted, and the standard for rebuttal is not high.[210] Facial defects in indorsements, lack of authorization for indorsements, and unresolved contradictions among essential loan documents suffice to rebut the presumption of enforceability and require the lender to produce evidence establishing its right to enforce the obligation.

---

distinguishing documentation burdens of proof for motions to dismiss/summary judgment); Sherer v. Bench, 549 S.W.2d 57 (Tex. App. 1977) (for summary judgment movant must provide original note with proper certification).

202 U.C.C. § 3-501(b)(2).

203 *See, e.g.,* Me. Rev. Stat. Ann. tit. 14, § 6321 ("The mortgagee shall certify proof of ownership of the mortgage note and produce evidence of the mortgage note, mortgage and all assignments and endorsements of the mortgage note and mortgage."); N.Y. Real Prop. Acts. Law § 1302 (McKinney) (plaintiff in a foreclosure of high-cost loan must affirmatively allege that it owns and holds the note and mortgage, or has been delegated authority by the owner to foreclose); Pa. R. Civ. P. 1147 (in a foreclosure complaint the plaintiff must set forth "the parties to and the date of the mortgage and of any assignments, and a statement of the place of record of the mortgage and assignments"); Vt. R. Civ. P. 80.1(b) (complaint in foreclosure must set forth, "any assignment of the mortgage" and "the names of all parties in interest and, as to each party in interest, the date of record of the instrument upon which the interest is based").

204 Fed. R. Bankr. P. 3001(c), (d) (documentation requirements for proof of claim); *See generally In re* Parrish, 326 B.R. 708, 720 n.33 (Bankr. N.D. Ohio 2005) (referring to local court rule requiring showing of chain of title of note and security agreement for motion for relief from stay).

205 *See, e.g.,* BAC Funding Consortium, Inc. v. Jean-Jacques 28 So. 3d 936 (Fla. Dist. Ct. App. 2010) (no attachments to complaint showed plaintiff owned note or mortgage, reversing grant of summary judgment to plaintiff).

206 *See, e.g., In re* Wells, 407 B.R. 873 (Bankr. N.D. Ohio 2009) (note attached to bankruptcy proof of claim still in name of original lender; no documentation of transfer of note to creditor); *In re* Wilhelm, 407 B.R. 392 (Bankr. D. Idaho 2009) (standing is part of prima facie case and burden on movant in motion for relief from stay); *In re* Kang Jin Hwang, 396 B.R. 757 (Bankr. C.D. Cal. 2008) (dismissal of motion for relief from stay for failure to join current owner of note in motion brought by prior owner); *In re* Parrish, 326 B.R. 708 (Bankr. N.D. Ohio 2005) (conflicting documents showed entity filing proof of claim in bankruptcy case was neither current holder of note or authorized agent for a holder); Citigroup Mkts. Realty Corp. v. Randolph Bowling, 2009 WL 4893940 (N.Y. Sup. Ct. Dec. 18, 2009) (court raises prima facie lack of standing *sua sponte* and dismisses foreclosure action); Wells Fargo Bank, N.A. v. Reyes, 867 N.Y.S.2d 21 (N.Y. Sup. Ct. 2008) (foreclosure dismissed where no evidence of assignment of mortgage to plaintiff); Washington Mut. Bank, F.A. v. Green, 806 N.E.2d 604 (Ohio Ct. App. 2004) (summary judgment for plaintiff reversed where defendant raised disputed issue as to identity of current assignee of mortgage).

207 *In re* Mitchell, 2009 WL 1044368 (Bankr. D. Nev. Mar. 31, 2009) (MERS not real party in interest as was not beneficial owner and failed to show authority to act for current owner), *aff'd on other grounds,* 423 B.R. 914 (D. Nev. 2009); *In re* Sheridan, 2009 WL 631355 (Bankr. D. Idaho Mar. 12, 2009) (MERS lacked standing to bring motion because failed to produce any evidence of who was current note holder); *In re* Vargas, 396 B.R. 511 (Bankr. C.D. Cal. 2008) (MERS cannot seek relief from stay on behalf of undisclosed real party in interest).

208 *In re* Jacobson, 402 B.R.359 (Bankr. W.D. Wash. 2009) (servicer failed to produce competent evidence of authority from present holder of note to enforce obligation); *In re* Hayes, 393 B.R. 259 (Bankr. D. Mass. 2008).

209 *See* § 4.5, *supra.*

210 *In re* Oakmore Ranch Mgmt., 337 B.R. 222, 228 (B.A.P. 9th Cir. 2006) (under California law, virtually any admissible evidence that the holder of the note is *not* the owner is sufficient to rebut the presumption); Ohio Citizens Bank of Toledo v. Venture Metal Prods. Co., 622 N.E.2d 758 (Ohio Ct. App. 1993) (indorsements enjoy a presumption of validity which can be rebutted; presumption exists only until evidence to contrary is produced).

4.4.6.2 Can Foreclosing Parties Retroactively Fix Defective Filings?

It is not unusual for a servicer to produce documents showing an assignment of a mortgage or a transfer of a note made after a foreclosure began. The assignments and transfers may be dated well after the filing of the court complaint or the commencement of a non-judicial foreclosure. They may even be dated long after the foreclosure sale. These belated transfers can result from isolated careless acts, or they may represent a servicer's standard business practice. Some servicers engage in these practices on the assumption that no one will notice or care about the timing discrepancies. Their practices come under scrutiny only in the relatively rare instances when a borrower brings a challenge or an alert court raises questions on its own initiative. Whether the untimely documents are the product of a servicer's routine practice or its last minute scrambling to correct an isolated error, the servicer will likely argue that the assignments should be given retroactive effect, making them effective to a date prior to the initiation of foreclosure. In judicial proceedings a servicer will likely argue that Federal Rule of Civil Procedure 17 or an equivalent state rule allows for liberal amendment of pleadings to correct an error in identification of the party initially named as plaintiff.

Federal courts have strictly enforced the rule that a party invoking the judiciary's power must have standing to do so at the time it files a lawsuit.[211] These courts reject servicers' reliance on assignments of mortgages and transfers of notes executed after the filing of a lawsuit or motion with the court. State courts in New York,[212] Ohio,[213] and elsewhere[214] have similarly rebuffed foreclosing plaintiff's attempts to correct legal claims that were jurisdictionally defective when filed. In the non-judicial foreclosure context state law may require that a sale be conducted only when the creditor has a statutorily defined interest in the property. Otherwise, the sale can be invalidated despite post-sale efforts to cure a standing defect.[215]

---

211 HSBC Mortgage Serv., Inc. v. Horn, 2008 WL 4449497 (S.D. Ohio Sept. 30, 2008) (dismissal where notice of filing of assignment of mortgage occurred five days after complaint filed); *In re* Foreclosure Cases, 521 F. Supp. 2d 650 (S.D. Ohio 2007) (Rose, J.); *In re* Foreclosure Actions, 2007 WL 4034554 (N.D. Ohio Nov. 14, 2007) (O'Malley J.); *In re* Foreclosure Cases, 2007 WL 3232430 (N.D. Ohio Oct. 31, 2007) (Boyko, J.). *See also* Saxon Mortgage Servs., Inc. v. Hillery, 2008 WL 5170180 (N.D. Cal. Dec. 9, 2008) (dismissing foreclosure action for lack of subject matter jurisdiction because plaintiff failed to allege note had been assigned to it before it filed complaint; leave to file amended complaint granted).

212 U.S. Bank N.A. v. Collymore, 890 N.Y.S.2d 578 (N.Y. App. Div. 2009) (affirming denial of plaintiff's summary judgment motion where evidence insufficient to show it held assignment of mortgage or physical possession of note indorsed prior to filing complaint); Wells Fargo Bank, N.A. v. Marchione, 887 N.Y.S.2d 615 (N.Y. App. Div. 2009) (no standing to foreclose where mortgage assigned to plaintiff before service of summons and complaint but after complaint filed); Lasalle Bank N.A. v. Ahearn, 875 N.Y.S.2d 595 (N.Y. App. Div. 2009) (averment in complaint stating that mortgage is to be assigned to plaintiff after commencement of action does not satisfy standing requirement); Countrywide Home Loans, Inc. v. Gress, 888 N.Y.S.2d 914 (N.Y. App. Div. 2009) (post-complaint assignment not given retroactive effect); Deutsche Bank Nat'l Trust v. Abbate, 2009 WL 3384474 (N.Y. Sup. Ct. Oct. 6, 2009) (no retroactive effect to assignment, standing objection not waived); New Century Mortgage Corp. v. Durden, 2009 WL 264134 (N.Y. Sup. Ct. Feb. 2, 2009) (no retroactive effect to assignment); Deutsche Bank Nat'l Trust Co. v. Bailey, 880 N.Y.S.2d 872 (N.Y. Sup. Ct. 2009) (table) (order for sale denied unless plaintiff submits documents proving it had note at time it commenced case); U.S. Bank N.A. v. White, 880 N.Y.S.2d 227 (N.Y. Sup. Ct. 2009) (table) (no standing where assignment to plaintiff made 202 days after action filed); IndyMac Bank, F.S.B. v. Boyd, 2009 WL 142572 (N.Y. Sup. Ct. Jan. 22, 2009) (retroactive assignment cannot cure standing defect); Indymac Bank v. Bethley, 880 N.Y.S.2d 873 (N.Y. Sup. Ct. 2009) (table) (assignment of mortgage two days after complaint filed defeats standing); Credit-Based Asset Servicing & Securitization, L.L.C. v. Akitoye, 880 N.Y.S.2d 223 (N.Y. Sup. Ct. 2009) (table) (no standing where note and mortgage assigned ninety-eight days after complaint filed); Washington Mut. Bank v. Patterson, 875 N.Y.S.2d 824 (N.Y. Sup. Ct. 2008) (table) (refusing to give retroactive effect to post-complaint assignment); Nomura Credit & Capital, Inc. v. Washington, 866 N.Y.S.2d 93 (N.Y. Sup. Ct. 2008) (table) (no standing where mortgage was assigned after complaint filed); Deutsche Bank Trust Co. Americas v. Peabody, 866 N.Y.S.2d 91 (N.Y. Super. Ct. 2008) (for a post-complaint assignment of note and mortgage to be effective, must be evidence documents had been delivered to assignee before compliant filed); Countrywide Home Loans, Inc. v. Taylor, 843 N.Y.S.2d 495 (N.Y. Super. Ct. 2007) (labeling post-complaint assignment as applying retroactively does not cure standing defect); U.S. Nat'l Bank Ass'n v. Kosak, 2007 WL 2480127 (N.Y. Super. Ct. Sept. 4, 2007) (rejecting retroactive assignment of mortgage); Countrywide Home Loans, Inc. v. Hovanec, 839 N.Y.S.2d 432 (N.Y. Super. Ct. 2007) (rejecting attempt to label assignment of mortgage as effective before action commenced); Aurora Loan Servs. v. Grant, 2007 WL 2768915 (N.Y. Super. Ct. Aug. 29, 2007) (documents showed mortgage and note assigned after complaint filed, fails to meet standing requirement).

213 Wells Fargo Bank, N.A. v. Jordan, 2009 WL 625560 (Ohio Ct. App. Mar. 12, 2009) (assignment of mortgage three weeks after complaint filed does not cure standing defect); Wells Fargo Bank, N.A. v. Byrd, 897 N.E.2d 722 (Ohio Ct. App. 2008) (rejecting servicer's "ratification" argument for allowing retroactive cure of filing without standing).

214 Jeff-Ray Corp. v. Jacobson, 566 So. 2d 885 (Fla. Dist. Ct. App. Sept. 12, 1990) (plaintiff required to file new action because mortgage assignment not made until four months after case filed);Wells Fargo Bank, N.A. v. Janosik, Allegheny Common Pleas No. GD08-2561 (Pa. C.P. Allegheny Cty. Mar. 23, 2009) (trial decision), *available at* www.consumerlaw/unreported (rejecting foreclosing plaintiff's "relation back" argument and dismissing foreclosure action filed prior to assignment to named plaintiff). *But see* U.S. Bank NA v. Mallory, 982 A.2d 986 (Pa. Super. Ct. 2009) (plaintiff complied with statutory requirement to plead current interest in loan by stating in complaint it was in process of finalizing assignment of mortgage).

215 *In re* Schwartz, 366 B.R. 265 (Bankr. D. Mass. 2007) (movant

Federal Rule of Civil Procedure 17(a) does not give foreclosing servicers unlimited freedom to correct jurisdictional defects through post-complaint amendments to show curative assignments or transfers of notes. For example, the district court in *In re Foreclosure Cases*[216] acknowledged the role of Rule 17(a) in allowing amendments to avoid dismissals of actions for technical grounds. While it is true that Rule 17 provides for a liberal opportunity to amend a complaint to substitute the correct party in interest after an objection has been raised, the rule should not be construed as creating a blank check for substitution of parties in all cases.[217] Courts have discretion to dismiss actions filed without naming the real party in interest. The court in *In re Foreclosure Cases* refused to allow amendments and instead dismissed a series of pending foreclosures in large part because the servicers before the court had demonstrated a pattern of indifference to compliance with real party in interest and standing rules. In the court's view, the provisions of Rule 17(a) allowing amendment and substitution were intended to prevent injustice to parties who brought actions in the wrong name as the result of honest and understandable mistakes, not to condone reckless practices that were becoming routine for mortgage servicers. Mortgage servicers are directly and indirectly affiliated with some of the largest financial institutions in the world. They have no reasonable excuse for repeated failures to implement practices that ensure accurate documentation of the ownership of claims at the inception of a foreclosure.

4.4.7 Rule 11 Sanctions for Misrepresentation of Standing and Real Party in Interest

Counsel preparing foreclosure complaints have an obligation to make a reasonable inquiry to ensure that factual contentions set forth in pleadings have evidentiary support.[218] This duty certainly includes investigation into the facts related to current ownership of notes and mortgages, as these facts form the very basis for the foreclosure action. Courts have become increasingly vigilant in exercising their own authority under Rule 11 to scrutinize mortgage servicers' filings for blatantly inconsistent content related to standing and real party in interest.[219] Careless foreclosure practices undermine the functioning of the courts and harm property rights of homeowners, investors, and purchasers of properties at foreclosure sales. Although Rule 11 does not function primarily as a fees-shifting provision, it does authorize a court to order that the offending creditor pay the objecting homeowner's attorney fees.[220]

Bankruptcy Rule 9011 incorporates Federal Rule of Civil Procedure 11 into bankruptcy proceedings. Thus, when servicers, lenders, and their attorneys file motions for relief from the bankruptcy stay and proofs of claim, they must comply with Rule 9011's reasonable investigation requirement. The bankruptcy courts have been particularly active in enforcing Rule 9011 against servicers and lenders who brought matters before the courts without reasonable investigation of the creditor's standing.[221] The analyses from

could not obtain relief from bankruptcy stay after foreclosure because movant had not received valid assignment until after the non-judicial foreclosure sale had taken place); U.S. Bank N.A. v. Ibanez, 2009 WL 3297551 (Mass. Land Ct. Oct. 14, 2009) (vacating non-judicial sale where mortgage assigned to foreclosing lender ten months after foreclosure sale).

216 *In re* Foreclosure Cases, 2007 WL 3232430 (N.D. Ohio Oct. 31, 2007).

217 *See, e.g.*, Summit Office Park v. U.S. Steel, 639 F.2d 1278 (5th Cir. 1981) (where plaintiff originally did not have standing to assert claim against defendant, it does not have standing to amend complaint and control litigation by substituting new plaintiff); Delor v. Intercosmos Media Group, Inc. 232 F.R.D. 562, 566–567 (E.D. La. 2005); Metal Forming Technologies, Inc. v. Marsh & McLennan Co., 224 F.R.D. 431 (S.D. Ind. 2004); Lans v. Gateway 2000, Inc., 84 F. Supp. 2d 112, 120 (D.D.C. 1999), *aff'd*, 252 F.3d 1320 (D.C. Cir. 2001) (rejecting plaintiff's argument for amendment; plaintiff claimed it had forgotten about a pre-complaint assignment; Rule 17 designed to remedy "honest and understandable mistake," not to create standing where none existed when action filed); 6A Charles A. Wright, Arthur R. Miller, et al., Federal Practice and Procedure Civ. 2d § 1555 ("[t]hus, it has been held that when the determination of the right party to bring the action was not difficult and when no excusable mistake had been made, then the last sentence of Rule 17(a) was not applicable and the action should be dismissed").

218 Fed. R. Civ. P. 11.

219 Bank of New York v. Williams, 979 So. 2d 347 (Fla. Dist. Ct. App. 2008) (attorney fee awarded to homeowner under Florida prevailing party statute after dismissal of foreclosure complaint on standing grounds); Mainsource Bank v. Winafeld, 2008 WL 4061415 (Ohio Ct. App. Sept. 2, 2008) (upholding imposition of Rule 11 sanctions against plaintiff who filed foreclosure action when it was not real party in interest). *See also* Wells Fargo Bank, N.A. v. Reyes, 867 N.Y.S.2d 21 (N.Y. Sup. Ct. 2008) (table) (scheduling hearing to consider sanctions for frivolous litigation conduct in bringing foreclosure action when public records indicated that mortgage had never been assigned to named plaintiff when action filed); Countrywide Home Loans, Inc. v. Taylor, 843 N.Y.S.2d 495 (N.Y. Sup. Ct. 2007) (sanctions appropriate if plaintiff continues to bring actions accompanied by similar defective documentation of standing).

220 Fed. R. Civ. P. 11(c)(4). *See* Kirk Capital Corp, 16 F.3d 1485, 1490 (8th Cir. 1994); *In re* Kunstler, 914 F.2d 505, 522–523 (4th Cir. 1990); White v. Gen. Motors Corp. 675, 684 (10th Cir. 1990).

221 *In re* Nosek, 406 B.R. 434 (D. Mass. 2009) (affirming imposition of sanctions of $250,000 on creditor for misrepresenting status of holder of note during protracted litigation); *In re* Lee, 408 B.R. 893 (Bankr. C.D. Cal. 2009) (Rule 9011 sanctions imposed on creditor's attorney for failure to disclose transfer of ownership of note, failure to join true owner in motion for relief from bankruptcy stay, and for submitting copy of note with motion that was not true and correct copy of the original note). *See also In re* Fitch, 2009 WL 1514501 (N.D. Ohio May 28,

these bankruptcy court decisions can provide strong support for advocates seeking to enforce Rule 11 standards under similar state rules.

The bankruptcy courts have raised additional ethical concerns over the relations between large national default servicing firms and local counsel who appear in routine bankruptcy matters.[222] Some of these concerns focus on the servicers' chronically poor accounting practices, but the servicing relationships also implicate standing issues. In *In re Taylor*[223] a Pennsylvania bankruptcy court reviewed the practices of a large nationwide default servicer, Lender Processing Services, Inc. (LPS, formerly Fidelity Mortgage Servicing). LPS/Fidelity represents most of the largest banks in the United States and provides default services for more than 50% of all home mortgages in foreclosure.

The *Taylor* court conducted its review concurrently with an ongoing investigation of LPS/Fidelity by the Department of Justice's Executive Office for U.S. Trustees (hereinafter U.S. Trustee). The U.S. Trustee's investigation focused on concerns that LPS/Fidelity, rather than law firms supposedly retained by the servicers, improperly directed legal actions in bankruptcy cases. The evidence presented to the bankruptcy court in *Taylor* indicated some disturbing practices that were standard in cases that HSBC, a large primary mortgage servicer, referred to attorneys for foreclosure or bankruptcy work. Upon a default, HSBC uploaded data and loan documents to an LPS/Fidelity computer platform. The platform selected attorneys to file specific legal pleadings in courts around the country. These attorneys communicated almost exclusively with one of the LPS/Fidelity computer platforms. Direct communication between attorneys and HSBC was discouraged, and attorneys' requests for information could negatively affect a law firm's prospects for receiving future referrals from LPS/Fidelity. LPS/Fidelity relied almost exclusively on computerized data and imposed little human oversight over the data it forwarded to counsel. For example, the law firm that filed a proof of claim for HSBC in the *Taylor* case relied almost entirely on non-attorney staff who prepared documents using LPS/Fidelity data, including downloaded notes and mortgages. The firm filed the documents in court under an attorney's electronic signature. The law firm filed 90% of its proofs of claims without any attorney review. The proof of claim filed in the *Taylor* case included the wrong promissory note as an exhibit.

The bankruptcy court in *Taylor* raised significant questions about how foreclosure attorneys could comply with ethical obligations to investigate facts and exercise independent judgment when the LPS/Fidelity data systems created a virtual wall between attorneys and the owners of the obligations.[224] A district court decision reversed the bankruptcy court's imposition of Rule 11 sanctions against the attorneys directly involved in the *Taylor* ruling.[225] Due to the ongoing U.S. Trustee's investigation, the bankruptcy court had not ruled on the conduct of all law firms involved or on the role of LPS/Fidelity itself. Familiarity with the operation of these default servicing systems, as described in the *Taylor* bankruptcy court decision, can provide useful background for discovery or to support a motion for Rule 11 sanctions.

Rule 11 incorporates a "safe harbor" provision.[226] A party intending to file a motion for Rule 11 sanctions must first serve the opposing party with a copy of the motion. The motion must not be filed with the court unless the targeted party fails to withdraw or correct the challenged filing within twenty-one days after service of the motion. When a

2009) (not reaching a sanctions ruling, but reprimanding attorney who signed false affidavits of authority to file motion for entity that never authorized the filing); *In re* Wilhelm, 407 B.R. 392, 403 n.20 (Bankr. D. Idaho 2009) (in light of servicer's counsel's "helter-skelter" submissions, court warns "counsel should gather the appropriate documents and factual data *before* filing (as required by Rule 9011 in any event), rather than attempting to cure patently defective motions with serial supplemental filings"); *In re* Sheridan, 2009 WL 631355, at *6 n.19 (Bankr. D. Idaho Mar. 12, 2009) (suggesting potential for Rule 9011 violation in filing motion and characterizing movant as real party in interest based solely on undocumented representations made to attorney by servicer); *In re* Vargas, 396 B.R. 511, 521 n.13 (Bankr. C.D. Cal. 2008) (declarant's "total lack of competence" to testify as to real party in interest raised "serious question as to the good faith of counsel for MERS under Rule 9011"); *In re* Hayes, 393 B.R. 259, 269 (Bankr. D. Mass. 2008) ("[i]naccurate representations about the moving party's status as the holder may constitute a violation of Fed. R. Bankr. P. 9011").

222 *In re* Taylor, 407 B.R. 618 (Bankr. E.D. Pa. 2009), *rev'd,* 2010 WL 624909 (E.D. Pa. Feb. 18, 2010) (setting aside bankruptcy court's findings of Rule 11 violations by specific local counsel, but noting concerns about wider LPS practices that were the subject of lengthy critical analysis by bankruptcy court). *See also In re* Stewart, 391 B.R. 327 (Bankr. E.D. La. 2008) (finding Rule 11 violations in arrangement between national law firm that hired local firm to conduct bankruptcy litigation, effectively shielding local firm from contact with major servicer client).

223 407 B.R. 618 (Bankr. E.D. Pa. 2009), *rev'd,* 2010 WL 624909 (E.D. Pa. Feb. 18, 2010).

224 *Taylor*, 407 B.R. at 645, *rev'd,* 2010 WL 624909 (E.D. Pa. Feb. 18, 2010). *See also In re* Waring, 401 B.R. 906 (Bankr. N.D. Ohio 2009) (critiquing servicer's practice of farming out legal work on bankruptcy reaffirmation agreements in manner that precluded debtors and their attorneys from communicating with owner of obligation); *In re* Parsley, 384 B.R. 138 (Bankr. S.D. Tex. 2008) (local counsel's restricted relationship with national counsel effectively barred local counsel from communication with client); *In re* Ulmer, 363 B.R. 777 (Bankr. D.S.C. 2008) (sanctions imposed against law firm that allowed out-of-state paralegals to prepare stay relief motions filed electronically with court without attorney review); *In re* Rivera, 342 B.R. 435 (Bankr. D. N.J. 2006), *subsequent decision at* 369 B.R. 193 (Bankr. D. N.J. 2007), *aff'd,* 2007 WL 1946656 (D.N.J. June 27, 2007) ($125,000 penalty under Rule 9011 assessed against law firm for attaching pre-signed supporting affidavits to 150 stay relief motions).

225 2010 WL 624909 (E.D. Pa. Feb. 18, 2010).

226 Fed. R. Civ. P. 11(c)(2).

foreclosing plaintiff cannot provide evidence of standing and real party in interest after a reasonable request, serving a motion under Rule 11 is appropriate. It may be helpful to review other pleadings and court decisions involving the same servicer or the same foreclosure firm, as these may show that the same party or attorneys have engaged in a pattern of filing unsupported claims.

4.4.8 Avoiding Summary Judgment

4.4.8.1 General

Entities that foreclose through judicial proceedings typically move for summary judgment after the homeowner has filed an answer or otherwise appeared in the case. Under Federal Rule of Civil Procedure 56 and analogous state rules the party moving for summary judgment must produce evidence to establish that it is entitled to judgment as a matter of law.[227] A plaintiff in a foreclosure case who cannot produce evidence that it holds a valid assignment of the underlying mortgage and a right to enforce the promissory note is not entitled to judgment.[228] In addition, to obtain summary judgment the foreclosing plaintiff must show that no genuine disputed issues as to any material fact remain to be litigated.[229] Evidence of the existence of other entities with documented rights to the loan obligation raises precisely this kind of dispute over an essential fact.[230] In ruling on summary judgment the court must construe any inferences from evidence presented against the moving party and in favor of the respondent. Supporting affidavits must be unequivocal and cannot call upon the court to make inferences about the existence of an assignment to the named plaintiff.[231]

4.4.8.2 Challenging Summary Judgment Affidavits—Are They Based upon the Affiant's Personal Knowledge?

Rule 56 sets out strict requirements for affidavits filed in support of or in opposition to summary judgment. The affidavits must be (1) made on personal knowledge; (2) set forth facts that would be admissible in evidence; and (3) show that the affiant is competent to testify on the subject matter.[232] In a foreclosure action the plaintiff's affidavits must verify essential facts, including the current assignment of the mortgage and ownership and possession of the promissory note. Affidavits cannot refer loosely to the documents needed to establish these claims. Rather, Rule 56 provides, "[i]f a paper or part of a paper is referred to in an affidavit, a sworn or certified copy must be attached to or served with the affidavit."[233] Thus, where past assignments of a mortgage and transfers of a note are elements of the plaintiff's claim, certified copies of all relevant documents must accompany the affidavit. Similarly, claims that a servicer has "authority" to act for a trust under the terms of a pooling and servicing agreement or some other document cannot be considered without properly certified copies of those documents. In foreclosures arising out of securitized mortgage transactions, the plaintiff's affidavits frequently fail to comply with these basic standards mandated by Rule 56.

The "personal knowledge" requirement applicable to the content of a summary judgment affidavit is the same as applies to testimony a witness gives in court.[234] An affidavit is inadmissible if the affiant could not actually have perceived or observed the subject of his or her testimony.[235] Affidavits attested to by attorneys should be routinely stricken on this basis. Affidavits purporting to state facts based on "information and belief" cannot be considered.[236] A foreclosing plaintiff may not use affidavits to assert legal

227 Fed. R. Civ. P. 56(c)(2).

228 Wells Fargo Bank, N.A. v. Jordan, 2009 WL 625560 (Ohio Ct. App. Mar. 12, 2009) (moving party in foreclosure action bears burden of identifying parts of the record which demonstrate the absence of a genuine issue of material fact).

229 Fed. R. Civ. P. 56(c)(2). *See, e.g.*, Washington Mut. Bank, F.A. v. Green, 806 N.E.2d 604 (Ohio Ct. App. 2004) (reversing summary judgment for lender where defendant raised disputed issues of fact as to identity of current assignee of mortgage).

230 *See, e.g.,* BAC Funding Consortium, Inc. v. Jean-Jacques, 28 So. 3d 936 (Fla. Dist. Ct. App. 2010) (inconsistencies in identities of entities claiming ownership interests as identified in pleadings and supporting documents precluded summary judgment for foreclosure); Flagstar Bank, F.S.B. v. Moore, 2010 WL 403846 (Ohio Ct. App. Feb. 5, 2010) (record showing variety of entities claiming enforcement rights related to mortgage presented disputed issues of fact precluding summary judgment).

231 *E.g.*, First Union Nat'l Bank v. Hufford, 767 N.E.2d 1206 (Ohio Ct. App. 2001) (plaintiff cannot prevail on summary judgment because failed to document how it obtained note and mortgage).

232 Fed. R. Civ. P. 56(e).

233 *Id.*

234 Fed. R. Evid. 602 (witness "may not testify to a matter unless evidence is introduced sufficient to support a finding that the witness has personal knowledge of the matter"). *See* Charles A. Wright, Arthur R. Miller, et al., Federal Practice & Procedure § 6024 (discussing applicability of Fed. R. Evid. 602 personal knowledge standard to summary judgment affidavits).

235 Charles A. Wright, Arthur R. Miller, et al., Federal Practice & Procedure § 6024 n.2; Argo v. Blue Cross and Blue Shield of Kansas, Inc. 452 F.3d 1193 (10th Cir. 2006). *See* United Nat'l Bank Ass'n v. Kosak, 2007 WL 2480127 (N.Y. Super. Ct. Sept. 4, 2007) (rejecting affidavit by attorney in fact, employee of non-party servicer); Wells Fargo Bank, N.A. v. Davilmar, 847 N.Y.S.2d 906 (N.Y. Sup. Ct. 2007) (affidavit of non-party servicer does not make claim for plaintiff).

236 Sellers v. M.C. Floor Crafters, Inc., 842 F.2d 639 (2d Cir. 1988) (rejecting affidavit based on both personal knowledge and information and belief where content did not distinguish between the two); Londrigan v. Federal Bureau of Investigation, 670 F.2d 1164, 1174 (D.C. Cir. 1981) (affidavit based merely on information and belief not acceptable).

conclusions, for example that it is the "holder" of a negotiable instrument.[237] The facts and documents that support holder status must be set out in properly verified form.

Servicers who prepare foreclosure documents on behalf of trusts tend to use canned affidavits loaded with vague and often contradictory content. These affidavits often parrot language of the rules of evidence for authentication of documents or paraphrase the elements of a foundation for admissibility of business records as evidence.[238] A close reading of the affidavits often exposes glaring defects. For example, in a strained effort to cover as many eventualities as possible, the affidavits frequently employ the disjunctive, with the affiant purporting to have personal knowledge of the records of the servicer *or* the mortgage holder *or* past or future assignees of the servicer or mortgage holder. In bankruptcy cases the affiant may simply purport to have personal knowledge of all records of "the Movant" without identifying specifically who that movant is.[239] These statements do not satisfy the Rule 56 requirement that the affiant affirmatively show the basis for any first-hand knowledge of facts alleged in an affidavit. Consistent with the rule of construction against the movant, these sloppy and evasive affidavits should never serve as the basis for granting summary judgment.

Servicers' affidavits run into a problem with lack of personal knowledge when the affiant swears to facts about practices in an office where the affiant does not work or transactions that took place when the affiant's company had no interest in the obligation. The affiant may not claim personal knowledge of records that are admitted to be kept at a location far from where the affiant works and provide no explanation of how that personal knowledge was obtained.[240] Despite bald assertions that the affiant is familiar with the records, the realities of time and place may simply make personal knowledge of the stated facts impossible. If there is nothing in the affidavit indicating that the affiant is a custodian of the account he or she swears to be familiar with, the affidavit should be stricken. Similarly, personal knowledge cannot be "delegated." A trust, for example, cannot appoint a servicer's officer or employee to execute declarations attesting to personal knowledge of the trust's record keeping practices.

The supporting affidavit of a servicing agent could potentially suffice, but it must include documents showing that the servicing agent had authority from the holder of the obligation to make the verification.[241] The servicer's employee will only have first-hand knowledge of facts involving the servicer's records and practices and not those of the trust. If the authority to verify facts comes from a pooling and servicing agreement, the servicer must produce the agreement in order to establish that the scope of the affiant's agency includes the authority to verify the stated facts for the trust.[242] When the same individual appears as agent or "attorney in fact" for multiple entities, this raises additional questions about the authority of the designated individual to attest to the truth of the facts based on personal knowledge.[243]

237 *See, e.g., In re* Wilhelm, 407 B.R. 392 (Bankr. D. Idaho 2009) (declaration improperly asserted legal conclusion that movant was "holder" of note).

238 *See, e.g., In re* Jacobson, 402 B.R. 359 (Bankr. W.D. Wash. 2009).

239 *See In re* Jacobson, 402 B.R. 359, 368–369 (Bankr. W.D. Wash. 2009) (not clear from declaration whether affiant worked for servicer, owner of obligation, or assignee); *In re* Sheridan, 2009 WL 631355, at *4 (Bankr. D. Idaho Mar. 12, 2009) (motion used terms movant, claimant, and petitioner "without definition or evident consistency"); BAC Funding Consortium , Inc. v. Jean-Jacques, 28 So. 3d 936 (Fla. Dist. Ct. App. 2010) (summary judgment record failed to include proper authentication of documents alleged to support assignment of mortgage). *See also* Mortgage Elec. Registration Sys., Inc. v. Zeigler, Case No. 2:09-CV-0676 RLH-RJJ (D. Nev. Dec. 4, 2009) (unpublished), *available on this treatise's companion website* (MERS employee who verified affidavit and who purportedly reviewed files had no personal knowledge of who possessed promissory note at relevant time).

240 *See In re* Jacobson, 402 B.R. 359 (Bankr. W.D. Wash. 2009) (declarant works in California and signs declaration in California, records are in Minnesota).

241 Deutsche Bank Nat'l Trust Co. v. Clouden, 851 N.Y.S.2d 57 (N.Y. Super. Ct. 2007) (servicer's employee executing affidavit to support referral to foreclosure must act pursuant to power of attorney that authorizes the individual to execute the affidavit on behalf of owner of obligation).

242 HSBC Bank, U.S.A., N.A. v. Valentin, 859 N.Y.S.2d 895 (N.Y. Super. Ct. 2008) (table) (if power of attorney refers to PSA, there must be a copy of the PSA to determine if servicing agent may proceed on behalf of plaintiff); HSBC Bank USA, N.A. v. Cherry, 2007 WL 4374284 (N.Y. Super. Ct. Dec. 17, 2007) (if power of attorney in support of verification refers to a PSA, the PSA must be attached); Deutsche Bank Nat'l Trust Co. v. Clouden, 851 N.Y.S.2d 57 (N.Y. Super. Ct. 2007) (must be power of attorney and, if applicable, PSA authority, for declarant to execute supporting affidavit); EMC Mortgage Corp. v. Batista, 841 N.Y.S.2d 819 (N.Y. Super. Ct. 2007) (power of attorney for affidavit failed to specify authority under PSA to make verification); Deutsche Bank Nat'l Trust Co. v. Lewis, 831 N.Y.S.2d 358 (N.Y. Super. Ct. 2006) (same).

243 HSBC Bank v. Vasquez, 2009 WL 2581672 (N.Y. Sup. Ct. Aug. 21, 2009) (table) (court will not grant summary judgment to foreclosing plaintiff unless provides explanation of appearance of same attorney as representative of both assignor and assignee of mortgage); Deutsche Bank Nat'l Trust Co. v. Castellanos, 856 N.Y.S.2d 497 (N.Y. Super. Ct. 2008) (concurrent affidavits by same person as vice president of different entities); Wells Fargo Bank, N.A. v. Davilmar, 847 N.Y.S.2d 906 (N.Y. Super. Ct. 2007) (same attorney with no personal knowledge of facts executing affidavits on behalf of multiple parties); U.S. Bank N.A. v. Merino, 836 N.Y.S.2d 853 (N.Y. Super. Ct. 2007) (two assignments for two different entities executed by same individual).

4.4.8.3 Authentication of Documents

Documents without a proper foundation to authenticate them cannot support a motion for summary judgment.[244] The same authentication requirements for admission of a document into evidence at trial apply when a document is used to support a motion for summary judgment.[245] These requirements apply to a promissory note, deed, and related assignment and negotiation documents referenced in the plaintiff's summary judgment record.

Assuming there are no challenges to the validity of signatures, an original promissory note meets requirements for self-authentication under Federal Rule of Evidence 902(9).[246] However, admission of the note into evidence may only establish a prima facie case, as in the case of bearer paper. For order paper, where holder status may depend on the validity of prior indorsements, or for enforcement by non-holders or parties not in possession of notes, considerably more properly verified documentary evidence must accompany an affidavit supporting a motion for summary judgment.[247]

Mortgages and deeds of trust are typically self-authenticating.[248] However, mortgages and deeds must be "accompanied by a certificate of acknowledgment executed in the manner provided by law by a notary public or other officer authorized by law to take acknowledgments."[249] In *In re* Vargas[250] the bankruptcy court denied the servicer's motion for relief from the bankruptcy stay because, among other defects, the deed of trust presented to the court had not been properly authenticated. Authentication does not dispose of additional proof requirements related to standing to enforce a mortgage or deed of trust. A plaintiff with an authenticated mortgage may still need to prove a chain of assignments.[251] Many assignments are not recorded, and those assignments may require further extrinsic evidence to prove.

4.4.8.4 Business Records

Assuming that the plaintiff can produce a properly authenticated note and mortgage, the extrinsic evidence needed to show a party's current right to enforce the documents may have to meet additional requirements for admissibility. The extrinsic evidence typically consists of hearsay. Before they can be considered for summary judgment purposes, business records must be authenticated by a person who could admit the documents into evidence at trial.[252] The business records exception to the hearsay rule requires testimony of a custodian or other qualified witness. The witness's bare assertion that he or she works for the company and is familiar with its recordkeeping procedures is insufficient.[253] For business records to be properly qualified there must be "enough information presented to demonstrate that the person is sufficiently knowledgeable about the subject of the testimony."[254] This rule applies to summary judgment affidavits. Any records mentioned in affidavits filed in support of a motion for summary judgment must be included in the motion and properly certified.[255]

In cases involving securitized mortgage obligations, it may prove difficult for the movant to certify business records properly. An employee of a servicer will likely not have the personal knowledge necessary to certify a prior owner's records. The servicer's employee may not be able to certify the trust's records, even if those records were allegedly shipped to the servicer for review. This is because a written certification necessary to introduce business records into evidence under the hearsay exception of Federal Rule of Evidence 802(6) must meet certain requirements. The certification must state, based on the declarant's first-hand knowledge, that the records were made at or near the time of the occurrence of the matters set forth, and the records must be kept in the course of a regularly conducted business

244 Canada v. Blain's Helicopters, Inc., 831 F.2d 920, 925 (9th Cir. 1987).

245 10A Charles A. Wright, Arthur R. Miller, et al., Federal Practice & Procedure § 2722. n.40.

246 "Extrinsic evidence of authenticity as a condition precedent to admissibility is not required with respect to . . . [c]ommercial paper, signatures thereon, and documents relating thereto to the extent provided by general commercial law." Fed. R. Evid. 902(9). *See* United States v. Varner, 13F.3d 1503, 1509 (11th Cir. 1994); Smith v. Weindrop 833 P.2d 856, 858 (Colo. Ct. App. 1992).

247 *See* §§ 4.4.4.4.2, 4.4.4.4.4, *supra.*

248 Fed. R. Evid. 902(8).

249 *Id. See also* Fed. R. Evid. 901(b)(7):

> (a) General provision: The requirement of authentication or identification as a condition precedent to admissibility is satisfied by evidence sufficient to support a finding that the matter in question is what its proponent claims.
>
> (b) Illustrations. By way of illustration only, and not by way of limitation, the following are examples of authentication or identification confirming with the requirements of this rule: . . .
>
> (7) Public records or reports. Evidence that a writing authorized by law to be recorded or filed and in fact recorded or filed in a public office, or purported public record, report, statement, or data compilation, in any form, is from the public office where items of this nature are kept.

250 396 B.R. 511, 520–521 (Bankr. C.D. Cal. 2008).

251 *In re* Hayes, 393 B.R. 259 (Bankr. D. Mass. 2008) (record must include chain of ownership of the mortgage).

252 IBP, Inc. v. Mercantile Bank of Topeka, 6 F. Supp. 2d 1258 (D. Kan. 1998).

253 *In re* Mitchell, 2009 WL 1044368, at *6 (Bankr. D. Nev. Mar. 31, 2009) (affiant's "bald assertion that she reviewed the loan file" is inadequate to show that she is personally knowledgeable of the facts), *aff'd on other grounds*, 423 B.R. 914 (D. Nev. 2009).

254 *In re* Jacobson, 402 B.R. 359, 368 (Bankr. W.D. Wash. 2009).

255 Fed. R. Civ. P. 56(e).

activity.[256] A servicer's employee cannot make these representations regarding the record keeping practices of some other entity at some other time. To the extent that a plaintiff relies on computer records to establish its claim to enforce the note or mortgage, the plaintiff must meet the evidentiary requirements for introduction of computer records.[257]

4.4.8.5 Summary: Defeating Summary Judgment

The following techniques may help the homeowner to defeat summary judgment on grounds that appear routinely in the lender's evidence:

- If there are any inconsistencies between parties identified in transactional documents attached to the complaint and the averments in the pleading, deny in the answer that the plaintiff holds the note and mortgage and raise the real party in interest issue as an affirmative defense or by motion. Hold to this position consistently throughout the proceeding. Many foreclosure defendants unwittingly admit to the plaintiff's status as the real party in interest, waiving the defense, or binding themselves to a judicial admission on the issue.
- Check the local recorder's office and submit evidence showing recorded assignments to others and the absence of any recorded assignment to the named plaintiff. Even when recording is not essential to the validity of an assignment, the evidence of other entities with recorded interests in the same obligation, coupled with the lack of any recorded interest for the named plaintiff, should create a disputed issue of fact and shift the burden squarely to plaintiff to establish its interest.
- Challenge the conclusory nature of plaintiffs' supporting affidavits. These declarations may merely state that the affiant is an officer of the plaintiff corporation or an officer of a servicing entity, that he or she is familiar with the loan account, and knows that the documents themselves are in the plaintiff's records. However, the documents attached to the complaint and "verified" by the officer may be only copies of the original loan documents and in the name of a non-party. In moving for summary judgment based upon these sketchy facts the plaintiff is asking the court to make impermissible inferences as to how the documents came to be in the plaintiffs' records.
- Demand supporting evidence showing how, when, and whether the mortgage and note had been assigned and transferred to the plaintiff. Courts should consider these to be valid demands and require that the plaintiffs connect all the links from the original loan documents up to the plaintiff's acquisition of rights in the obligation. Challenge undated documents as potentially executed after commencement of the foreclosure action.
- Produce recent correspondence, notices, and dunning letters in which entities other than the named plaintiff claim a right to collect on the obligation. These documents, like the original loan papers in the name of a non-party, raise disputed issues of fact regarding the named plaintiff's interest in the underlying obligation.

4.5 Challenging a Servicer's Standing to Foreclose

If a loan has been securitized, the real party interest is the trustee of the securitization trust, not the servicing agent.[258] However, under certain circumstances, a servicer may be able to meet standing requirements to initiate a foreclosure action in its name. The servicers' standing to bring an action depends mainly on state statutes and case law. In order to be able to conduct a foreclosure proceeding, a servicer must do two things. First, it must identify the entity that currently holds the obligation. Second, it must show it has authority to act for that entity.[259] Servicers may fall short on either count. For example, courts will deny relief where the servicer is unable to disclose the current holder and instead

256 Fed. R. Evid. 803(6), 902(11).

257 *In re* Vargas, 396 B.R. 511 (Bankr. C.D. Cal. 2008) (discussing eleven step foundation requirements for admissibility of computer records, finding creditor's witness failed to meet requirements).

258 LaSalle Bank N.A. v. Nomura Asset Capital Corp., 180 F. Supp. 2d 465, 469–471 (S.D.N.Y. 2001); LaSalle Bank N.A. v. Lehman Brother Holdings, Inc., 237 F. Supp. 2d 618, 631–634 (D. Md. 2002); *In re* Kang Jin Hwang, 396 B.R. 757, 766 (Bankr. C.D. Cal. 2008).

If the servicer files suit in its own name instead of in the name of the holder, an argument could be made that this is a fraud on the court. On the other hand, if the creditor files suit in the name of the actual holder, it may be the unauthorized practice of law for a servicer to retain counsel to represent the holder. At least one court has come to such a conclusion. *In re* Morgan, 225 B.R. 290 (Bankr. E.D.N.Y. 1998).

The court in *Morgan* also held that servicers have no pecuniary interest in either the outcome of the proceedings or in the underlying mortgage. The district court, however, vacated the *Morgan* decision based in part on the fact that the judge issued the opinion after the bankruptcies had been resolved. Once the controversies were moot, the judge had no authority to issue a decision. *In re* Nunez, 2000 WL 655983 (E.D.N.Y. Mar. 17, 2000), *vacating In re* Morgan, 225 B.R. 290 (Bankr. E.D.N.Y. 1998). *See also* Webster Bank v. Flanagan, 725 A.2d 975 (Conn. App. Ct. 1999); Family Fin. Servs. Inc. v. Spencer, 677 A.2d 479 (Conn. App. Ct. 1996).

259 *In re* Minbattiwalla, 424 B.R. 104 (Bankr. S.D.N.Y. 2010) (claimant who is a servicer must, in addition to establishing the rights of the holder, identify itself as an authorized agent for the holder, citing *In re* Parrish, 326 B.R. 708, 720 (Bankr. N.D. Ohio 2005)); *In re* Waring, 401 B.R. 906 (Bankr. N.D. Ohio 2009) (because it had no interest in note and no proof of authority to act on behalf of noteholder, servicer did not have standing to enter into reaffirmation agreement); *In re* Hayes, 393 B.R. 259 (Bankr. D. Mass. 2008) (no evidence of servicing agreement authorizing servicer to file proof of claim for an identified mortgage holder).

relies on a purported general authority to represent an undefined current or future assignee.[260] In other cases, the servicer will be denied standing because it claims to act for a named holder but cannot show the requisite contractual authority from that holder to do so.[261]

Borrowers are most successful in challenging a servicer's standing where state law clearly defines the holder of the note and mortgage as the real party in interest. For example, in order to make out a prima facie case in Connecticut for strict foreclosure, the plaintiff must prove by a preponderance of the evidence that it is the owner of the note and mortgage and the borrower defaulted on the note.[262]

There may be stronger grounds to challenge a servicer's standing, especially with regards to manufactured homes, when the creditor's interest is not properly perfected. In *Leake v. Oakwood Acceptance Corp.* (*In re* Wuerzberger),[263] a creditor assigned all of its interest in a retail installment contract and lien to a securitized trust, but was still noted as the secured party on the certificate of title. The court reasoned that the creditor's retention of contractual rights to service the loan, and the fact that its name remained on the title, did not give it a legal interest in the lien.[264]

Courts have allowed a servicer to file a foreclosure action in its own name when the servicer's agreement with the holder specifically gives the servicer a right to collect and foreclose on the mortgage.[265] This language, which may be contained in a pooling and servicing agreement, gives the servicer the authority to collect on the obligation and enforce the security instrument. One court has held that the deed of trust must delegate such authority to the servicer.[266] In *Nicholson v. Washington Mutual* the court, strictly construing the language of the deed of trust, held that only the lender or trustee was authorized to appoint a substitute trustee and foreclose.[267] There was no authority in the deed of trust for the lender to delegate these tasks to the servicer. A number of bankruptcy courts have held that servicers lacked the requisite interest or authority to participate in proceedings related to a bankruptcy case, including filing a motion for relief from the stay, entering into a reaffirmation agreement, or filing a proof of claim.[268] Other courts have

260 *In re* Sheridan, 2009 WL 631355, at *4 (Bankr. D. Idaho Mar. 12, 2009) (rejecting contention that MERS may pursue stay relief for unidentified successors and assigns under deed of trust); *In re* Kang Jin Hwang, 396 B.R. 757 (Bankr. C.D. Cal. 2008) (motion for relief from stay denied where servicer did not know identify of current noteholder); *In re* Vargas, 396 B.R. 511 (Bankr. C.D. Cal. 2008) (MERS acting as purported agent for current note holder denied relief from stay on grounds, *inter alia,* that it offered no evidence as to who was the holder of the promissory note and entitled to enforce it).

261 *In re* Jacobson, 402 B.R. 359, 369 (Bankr. W.D. Wash. 2009) (dismissing motion for relief from stay where servicer failed to produce competent evidence of agency relationship: "At a minimum, there must be an unambiguous representation or declaration setting forth the servicer's authority from the present holder of the note to collect on the note and enforce the deed of trust. If questioned, the servicer must be able to produce and authenticate that authority."). *See also In re* Weisband, 2010 WL 1253182, at *6 (Bankr. D. Ariz. Mar. 29, 2010) (among several grounds for lack of standing, servicer could not show that the debtor's loan was included in the trust for which it acted as servicer).

262 Webster Bank v. Flanagan, 725 A.2d 975 (Conn. App. Ct. 1999); Family Fin. Servs. Inc. v. Spencer, 677 A.2d 479 (Conn. App. Ct. 1996).

With strict foreclosure, there is no sale and the foreclosing entity receives title to the property. *But see* Connecticut Nat'l Mortgage Co. v. Knudsen, 2007 WL 2834610 (Conn. Super. Ct. Sept. 17, 2007 (unpublished) (defendant waived objection to plaintiff's standing by raising issue more than one year after she had opportunity to do so in post-judgment proceedings).

263 271 B.R. 778 (Bankr. W.D. Va. 2002).

264 *See also In re* Wuerzberger, 284 B.R. 814 (Bankr. W.D. Va. 2002) (later opinion in same case holding that bank to which the obligation was assigned held perfected security interest even though assignor was still listed as lienholder on certificate of title).

265 Bankers Trust v. 236 Beltway Inv., 865 F. Supp. 1186 (E.D. Va. 1994) (both lender and servicer had standing to sue on mortgage in default); First Nat'l City Bank v. Burton M. Saks Constr. Corp., 70 F.R.D. 417 (D. V.I. 1976) (servicer the proper party under Rule 17(a) when contract with holder gave it the authority to bring a foreclosure action); *In re* Tainan, 48 B.R. 250 (Bankr. E.D. Pa. 1985) (servicer, in capacity as representative of Fannie Mae for collection purposes, was the party in interest for Rule 17(a) purposes in a relief from stay proceeding); Green Tree Servicing L.L.C. v. Sanders, 2006 WL 2033668 (Ky. Ct. App. July 21, 2006) (under terms of pooling and servicing agreement, servicer became the real party in interest once the loan was automatically assigned to it at the commencement of a foreclosure action). *But see* Roberts v. LaConey, 650 S.E.2d 474 (S.C. 2007) (applying South Carolina law, holds that debt collector engaged in unauthorized practice of law by collecting on behalf of original creditor while the original creditor retained ownership interest in the debt; debt collector was not assignee of the original creditor and did not collect on a debt that it owned). *See generally* National Consumer Law Center, Fair Debt Collection § 11.5 (6th ed. 2008 and Supp.) (on subject of unauthorized practice of law by debt collectors and by attorneys).

266 For an example of the language which may be contained in the pooling and servicing agreement, see Green Tree Servicing L.L.C. v. Sanders, 2006 WL 2033668 (Ky. Ct. App. July 21, 2006). *But see* Brock v. Green Tree Servicing, L.L.C., 2009 WL 2415854 (Ky Ct. App. Aug. 7, 2009) (after new entity acquired partial ownership of company, Green Tree failed to show it had standing to foreclose based on prior PSA).

267 Nicholson v. Washington Mut., 2001 WL 1002418 (Tex. App. Aug. 31, 2001) (unpublished) (deed of trust must be strictly construed). *See also* Weingartner v. Chase Home Fin., L.L.C., __ F. Supp. 2d __, 2010 WL 1006708 (D. Nev. Mar. 15, 2010) (deed of trust arguably authorized MERS as an agent to substitute a trustee to foreclose, but deed of trust language did not authorize MERS to assign to a servicer the authority to select a trustee to foreclose).

268 *In re* Sheridan, 2009 WL 631355, at *3 (Bankr. D. Idaho 2009); *In re* Jacobson, 402 B.R. 359, 366 (Bankr. W.D. Wash. 2009) ("Even if a servicer or agent has authority to bring the motion on behalf of the holder, it is the holder, rather than the servicer, which must be the moving party, and so identified in the papers and in the electronic docketing done by the moving party's

found that the servicer appearing in a bankruptcy proceeding has a pecuniary interest in the mortgage sufficient to confer standing or that it is the agent of the holder.[269]

If the servicer forecloses on the borrower, the attorney should examine the agreement between the servicer and holder to determine whether there is any contractual right to release the security interest or to foreclose. A contract that confers insufficient authority may negate any interest the servicer can claim in the proceeding. When the servicer brings an action in its own name, without disclosing the true holder of the mortgage, the foreclosure may be delayed by requiring that the servicer add information identifying the real party in interest.[270]

counsel."); *In re* Wilhelm, 407 B.R. 392 (Bankr. D. Idaho 2009) (denying stay relief where movant failed to establish proof of possession of note); *In re* Waring, 401 B.R. 906 (Bankr. N.D. Ohio 2009) (because it had no interest in note and no proof of authority to act on behalf of noteholder, mortgage servicer did not have standing to enter into reaffirmation agreement); *In re* Kang Jin Hwang, 396 B.R. 757, 767 (Bankr. C.D. Cal. 2008) (noteholder, not servicer, is real party in interest in motion for relief from bankruptcy stay); *In re* Jones, 2008 WL 4539486 (Bankr. D. Mass. Oct. 3, 2008) (servicer's proof of claim rejected for lack of supporting documentation establishing complete chain of assignments); *In re* Hayes, 393 B.R. 259 (Bankr. D. Mass. 2008) (trustee for investment trust failed to provide evidence that debtor's mortgage was included in trust; no evidence of servicing agreement authorizing servicer to file proof of clam for an identified mortgage holder); *In re* Maisel, 378 B.R. 19 (Bankr. D. Mass. 2007) (servicer bringing stay relief motion failed to document standing as of time motion filed). *See also In re* Lee, 408 B.R. 893 (Bankr. C.D. Cal. 2009) (imposing Rule 9011 sanctions upon attorney for failure to disclose movant's lack of current ownership of note).

269 Greer v. O'Dell, 305 F.3d 1297 (11th Cir. 2002) (loan servicer is a "real party in interest" entitled to defend claim on behalf of holder and take all required action through counsel to protect its interests and those of the holder); *In re* Woodberry, 383 B.R. 373 (Bankr. D.S.C. 2008) (servicer has standing to file stay relief motion in bankruptcy); *In re* Viencek, 273 B.R. 354 (Bankr. N.D.N.Y. 2002) (servicer a party in interest because of its pecuniary interest in the mortgages it services; servicer was also authorized to file proof of claim as agent of the holder); Fairbanks Capital Corp. v. Nagel, 735 N.Y.S.2d 13 (N.Y. App. Div. 2001) (servicer had standing as agent of trustee).

270 *In re* Viencek, 273 B.R. 354 (Bankr. N.D.N.Y. 2002) (delay granted for servicer to amend proof of claim to identify actual creditor).

4.6 Defenses to Foreclosure by the Mortgage Electronic Registration System

4.6.1 The Mortgage Electronic Registration System (MERS)

4.6.1.1 What Is MERS?

Approximately two-thirds of all newly-originated residential mortgages in the United States are recorded in the name of Mortgage Electronic Registration Systems, Inc. (MERS).[271] However, MERS is not a mortgage lender, servicer, or investor. MERS is a corporation that administers an electronic registry (the Mortgage Electronic Registration System) which tracks ownership interests and servicing rights in mortgages for its members, who are mortgage lenders, servicers, investors, and other members of the mortgage lending industry.[272]

Industry members such as Fannie Mae, Freddie Mac, and the Mortgage Bankers Association of America began developing MERS in 1993 and incorporated its parent company MERSCORP in 1995.[273] Their stated goal was to reduce the costs and administrative burdens associated with recording assignments and otherwise tracking interests in mortgage loans that are sold through bulk transfers on the secondary market.[274] The basic premise is that MERS will serve as the permanent "mortgagee of record," as a common designee for the successive owners of a mortgage loan. Transfers of ownership or servicing rights in a mortgage loan will be tracked electronically on the MERS system rather than in public land records.[275]

271 *Process Loans, Not Paperwork,* MERS brochure, *available at* www.mersinc.org/newsroom/brochures.aspx.

272 *Id.*

273 For a general background on the development of MERS, see Slesinger and Mclaughlin, *Mortgage Electronic Registration System*, 31 Idaho L. Rev. 805 (1995). *See also* R.K. Arnold, *Yes, There Is Life on MERS*, Prob. & Prop. (Aug. 1997).

274 Slesinger and Mclaughlin, *Mortgage Electronic Registration System*, 31 Idaho L. Rev. 805 (1995). *See also* R.K. Arnold, *Yes, There Is Life on MERS*, Prob. & Prop. (Aug. 1997).

275 Slesinger and Mclaughlin, *Mortgage Electronic Registration System*, 31 Idaho L. Rev. 805 (1995). *See* R.K. Arnold, *Yes, There Is Life on MERS*, Prob. & Prop. (Aug. 1997). *See also* MERSCORP Inc. v. Romaine, 861 N.E.2d 81, 83 (N.Y. 2006) ("[i]n the MERS system, the mortgagor is notified of transfers of servicing rights pursuant to the Truth in Lending Act, but not necessarily of assignments of the beneficial interest in the mortgage").

However, when a MERS member transfers ownership or servicing rights to a non-MERS member, an assignment from the MERS member to the non-MERS member is supposedly recorded in local property records. *Id.*

Under the MERS system, mortgage originators, lenders, servicers and investors "register" their mortgage loans with MERS.[276] In order to register a mortgage loan with MERS, an entity must be a MERS "member" and pay an annual membership fee which varies depending upon the number of loans that will be registered throughout the year.[277] MERS then charges a one-time, flat fee of $6.95 for each individual loan that is registered on the MERS system.[278]

MERS becomes the mortgagee of record in one of two ways. For a loan that has already been originated and recorded, the lender may execute and record an assignment of the mortgage to MERS. For a newly originated loan, a mortgage or deed of trust can be prepared with MERS named as the original mortgagee (or beneficiary in a deed of trust).[279] These mortgages are often referred to as MOMs, an acronym for "MERS as original mortgagee."[280] In either case, MERS serves as mortgagee or beneficiary solely in the capacity as "nominee" for the lender and the lender's successors and assigns. MERS as nominee for the lender has been approved by Fannie Mae, Freddie Mac, Ginnie Mae, FHA, and the VA.[281]

A typical MOM mortgage contains the following language or something substantially similar thereto:

> "MERS" is Mortgage Electronic Registration Systems, Inc. MERS is a separate corporation that is acting solely as nominee for Lender and Lender's successors and assigns. MERS is the mortgagee under this Security Instrument.[282]

After MERS becomes the mortgagee of record,[283] subsequent transfers of ownership or servicing rights in a mortgage loan are tracked within the MERS system. Though recording fees vary from county to county, MERS's one time $6.95 per loan registration fee is significantly less than the cost of recording even a single assignment of mortgage in most county land records.[284] A loan registered with MERS receives a permanent 18-digit mortgage identification number (MIN) which serves as the loan's identifier throughout the life of the loan. The rights and obligations of various users of MERS are determined by contracts between the users and the rules of MERS. However, it is worth noting that it is the MERS members who access the system and record transfers; MERS itself does not play an active role in identifying or recording transfers of mortgage interests.[285]

Because MERS serves as mortgagee of record for the successive owners of the mortgage loan, it is the only entity with a publicly recorded interest in the mortgage. MERS does not provide consumers with access to information about the true owner of the mortgage loan. Rather, consumers contacting MERS's toll-free telephone number or utilizing its public website will only learn the name of their mortgage servicer.[286]

Unlike a servicer, which may have an economic interest in the debt or be the actual or constructive holder of the note, MERS has no legal or beneficial interest in the promissory note. While MERS is often specifically designated as mortgagee or beneficiary in the mortgage or deed of trust (as nominee for the original lender who is also identified in the document), the accompanying promissory note refers only to the lender and generally does not identify MERS or grant MERS any interest whatsoever in the mortgage debt. MERS does not become holder of the promissory notes which accompany mortgages for which it serves as mortgagee.[287]

---

276 *Process Loans, Not Paperwork,* MERS brochure, *available at* www.mersinc.org/newsroom/brochures.aspx.

277 *Id.*

278 The fee as of May 2010, however, may vary with different packages offered to users.

279 *MERS Membership Rules, available at* www.mersinc.org/Foreclosures/index.aspx.

280 *Process Loans, Not Paperwork,* MERS brochure, *available at* www.mersinc.org/newsroom/brochures.aspx.

281 *Id.*

282 *Id.*

283 There has been some resistance to recording mortgages and other documents in the name of MERS. In April 2001 the Suffolk County (NY) Clerk announced that, as of May 1, 2001, instruments which listed MERS as mortgagee or nominee of record would not be accepted unless MERS was in fact the actual mortgagee. MERS and its parent company MERSCORP, Inc. filed an action for declaratory relief seeking to compel the clerk to accept its instruments. In December 2006 the New York Court of Appeals held that the clerk had a statutory duty to record duly acknowledged MERS mortgages, assignments and releases.

284 It is designed to be cheaper than recording an assignment of mortgage. MERS markets itself, in part, by comparing the cost to record one or two (or more) assignments of mortgage with the one time cost of registering a mortgage on its system. *See Process Loans, Not Paperwork, available at* www.mersinc.org/newsroom/brochures.aspx.

285 *Id.*

286 The telephone number for the automated system is 888-679-6377. When calling MERS to obtain information on a loan, you must supply MERS with the MIN number or a Social Security number. The MIN number should appear on the face of the mortgage. You may also search by property address or by other mortgage identification numbers by using MERS's on-line search tool at www.mers-sericerid.org.

287 *See* Fannie Mae Single Family Servicing Guide pt. I, ch. 4, § 407 (2006) ("MERS will have no beneficial interest in the mortgage, even if it is named as the nominee for the beneficiary in the security instrument."). *See also In re* Fitch, 2009 WL 1514501 (Bankr. N.D. Ohio May 28, 2009) (summarizing MERS witness's testimony to effect that MERS never owns or holds promissory notes); Gemini Servs., Inc. v. Mortgage Elec. Registration Sys., Inc. (*In re* Gemini), 350 B.R. 74 (Bankr. S.D. Ohio 2006) (although MERS held legal title to mortgage, it could not hold beneficial interest because it did not hold note); Taylor, Bean & Whitaker Mortgage Corp. v. Brown, 583 S.E.2d 844 (Ga. 2003); Mortgage Elec. Registration Sys., Inc. v. Nebraska Dep't of Banking, 704 N.W.2d 784 (Neb. 2005) (accepting MERS's claims that it does not hold interests in notes); Nelson & Whitman, Real Estate Finance Law § 5.34 (4th ed. 2002) (West Group).

In those cases in which MERS does take possession of the note, often endorsed in blank, it continues to disclaim any beneficial interest.[288]

Similarly, and though it serves as mortgagee of record, MERS holds no beneficial interest in the mortgage itself.[289] The commonly accepted meaning of nominee is one who acts in a representative or nominal capacity only, and who does not acquire any property or ownership rights.[290] In an action involving MERS, the Seventh Circuit noted that because MERS acts in furtherance of its principal's interests and not its own, its role is distinct from that of a trustee, and described MERS's status as follows: "It is a nominee only, holding title to the mortgage but not the note. Each lender appears to be entitled not only to payment as the note's equitable (and legal) owner but also to control any litigation and settlement."[291]

4.6.1.2 The Role of MERS in Foreclosure

Despite the numerous limitations on MERS's role and authority, MERS claims that as the lender's nominee, it has the right to foreclose in its own name. Thus, in many jurisdictions, foreclosure actions are commenced in the name of MERS rather than the holder of the promissory note or the servicer. MERS's recommended foreclosure procedures are available on its website at www.mersinc.org/foreclosures/index.aspx. However, as explored more fully at § 4.6.2, *infra*, MERS's status as the nominal mortgagee without an interest of its own in the promissory note may not be sufficient to meet the standing requirements necessary to prosecute a judicial foreclosure action or to satisfy the elements of a particular state's non-judicial foreclosure laws. At least with respect to mortgages where Fannie Mae is the investor, MERS can no longer bring an action its name. In 2006 Fannie Mae amended its servicing guide to make clear that that MERS must not be named as a plaintiff in any judicial foreclosure action on a mortgage owned or securitized by Fannie Mae.[292] On March 30, 2010 Fannie Mae further amended its servicing guide to provide: "Effective with foreclosures referred on or after May 1, 2010, MERS must not be named as a plaintiff in any foreclosure action, whether judicial or non-judicial, on a mortgage loan owned or securitized by Fannie Mae."[293] This action will likely have a substantial long-term effect on industry-wide practice.

MERS and its members do not always employ transparent practices in creating and handling the documents that are necessary for the foreclosure or that relate to the assignment of interests that occur in preparation for or prosecution of the foreclosure. There is considerable potential for error in this realm, in part because MERS authorizes its members to execute mortgage related documents in its name. For example, a mortgage loan that is recorded in the name of MERS but is owned by the MERS member could be assigned from MERS to the member (or another entity) by an employee of the member executing the assignment as a MERS signatory. Thus, despite MERS's status as mortgagee on any given group of mortgages, the process used to foreclose upon or transfer each mortgage can vary greatly depending upon the actions of the MERS member entity controlling the transaction.

A 2008 New York case illustrates this point. In *Deutsche Bank Nat'l Trust Co. v. Maraj*,[294] the court denied the plaintiff's motion for a default foreclosure judgment because of questions about the relationship between MERS (the nominee for original lender Indymac Bank) and the plaintiff. The court noted that the person who executed the assignment by MERS, on behalf of Indymac, to Deutsche Bank, was the same person who executed Deutsche Bank's application for a default judgment in the foreclosure proceedings. In the assignment to Deutsche Bank, the assignor claimed to be Vice President of MERS and, in a later affidavit, she claimed to be an officer of Deutsche Bank. The affidavits and assignment of mortgage indicated that Indymac, MERS, and Deutsche Bank all shared the same business address.[295]

---

288 *See, e.g., MERS Recommended Foreclosure Procedures*, generally, available at www.mersinc.org/Foreclosures/index.aspx.

289 *Id. See also* Mortgage Elec. Reg. Sys., Inc. v. Neb. Dep't of Banking & Fin., 704 N.W.2d 784, 786–787 (Neb. 2005) (MERS "only holds legal title to members' mortgages in a nominee capacity and is contractually prohibited from exercising any rights with respect to the mortgages (i.e., *foreclosure*) without the authorization of the members" and that "MERS merely tracks the ownership of the lien" for its members); Fannie Mae Single Family Servicing Guide pt. I, ch. 4, § 407 (2006).

290 *See* Weingartner v. Chase Home Fin., L.L.C., 2010 WL 1006708, at *1 (D. Nev. Mar. 15, 2010) (reviews various definitions of "nominee" and concludes term may give MERS authority to appoint substitute trustee to conduct foreclosure sale, but does not give MERS authority to delegate that task to a servicer); Winters Nat'l Bank & Trust Co. v. Saker, 419 N.E.2d 890 (Ohio Ct. App. 1979). *Black's Law Dictionary* defines "nominee" as one designated to act for another as his representative in a rather limited sense. Black's Law Dictionary 727 (6th ed. 1991).

291 Mortgage Elec. Registration Sys., Inc. v. Estrella, 390 F.3d 522, 525 (7th Cir. 2004). The court's inquiry into MERS's legal status was for the purpose of determining diversity jurisdiction.

292 Fannie Mae Announcement 06-24 (Dec. 7, 2006), *available at* www.efanniemae.com/sf/guides/ssg/annltrs/pdf/2006/0624.pdf. Freddie Mac requires foreclosure in the name of MERS or a transfer of the mortgage from MERS to servicer and foreclosure in the servicer's name. Freddie Mac Single-Family Seller/Servicer Guide § 66.17.

293 Fannie Mae Announcement SVC-2010-05 (Mar. 30, 2010), *available at* www.efanniemae.com/sf/guides/ssg/annltrs/pdf/2010/svc1005.pdf.; Fannie Mae Single Family Servicing Guide pt. VIII, ch. 1, § 105 (2010).

294 2008 N.Y. Slip. Op. at 50176(U), 2008 WL 253926, at *1 (N.Y. Sup. Ct. 2008).

295 *Id. See also* Aurora Loan Servs. v. Sattar, 851 N.Y.S.2d 62 (Table), 2007 WL 2917245 (N.Y. Sup. Ct. Oct. 9, 2007) (trial court *sua sponte* dismisses action to foreclose where MERS member cannot prove ownership of note and mortgage through assignments in the MERS system); Lasalle Bank N.A. v. Lamy,

4.6.2 Challenging MERS's Standing and Related Defenses

4.6.2.1 MERS Cannot Act on Behalf of Undisclosed "Successors and Assigns"

At the heart of the MERS scheme is the fiction that it acts at all times as the representative of the current owner of the underlying mortgage obligation. In MERS-sponsored transactions, the original lender and the borrower sign a security agreement which purports to authorize MERS to act on behalf of the original lender and the original lender's "successors and assigns." When the borrower signs off on such a document it is impossible to know who these successors and assigns will be. In the past, servicers have pursued judicial and non-judicial foreclosures in the name of MERS without disclosing the identities of the current holders of the notes and mortgages or showing any specific authority for MERS to act on behalf of those holders.

In a judicial foreclosure or bankruptcy proceeding MERS's amorphous agency status runs contrary to the requirement to bring a proceeding in the name of the real party in interest and to join in the proceeding all necessary parties.[296] The "nominee" status of MERS toward its members does not resemble a true agency relationship between an agent and a principal. Nor can MERS act on its own, untethered to any entity that owns the particular mortgage debt. Many courts have rejected MERS's contention that it can be a legitimate representative to assert legal rights on behalf of unidentified successors and assigns of an originating lender.[297] For example, in finding MERS did not have standing to challenge a non-judicial foreclose sale that extinguished the property interests of a MERS "member," the Arkansas Supreme Court stated, "[w]e specifically reject the notion that MERS may act on its own, independent of the directions of the specific lender who holds the repayment interest in the security instrument at the time MERS purports to act."[298] In order to represent some other entity in a foreclosure, MERS must produce evidence of a specific agency relationship with an identified principal. This evidence would have to include including properly authenticated documents, witnesses competent to testify based on personal knowledge, and the compliance with rules for admission of business records.[299]

4.6.2.2 MERS Is Not a True Beneficiary of the Note or Other Concrete Obligation

MERS deliberately drafts security instruments that purport to give it contradictory rights. In a deed of trust or mortgage MERS includes a term to the effect that MERS takes an interest "solely as nominee" for the lender and the lender's successors and assigns.[300] At the same time MERS deed of trust documents typically provide that "MERS is the beneficiary under this Security Instrument."[301] The standard MERS security instrument goes on to state that MERS

> holds only legal title to the interests granted by Borrower to this Mortgage; but, if necessary to comply with law or custom, MERS, (as nominee for Lender and Lender's successors and assigns), has the right: to exercise any and all of those interests, including but not limited to, the right to foreclose and sell the Property; and to take any action required of Lender including, but not limited to, releasing or cancelling this Mortgage.[302]

These clauses allow MERS to pick and choose its role, depending upon which characterization furthers its legal position in a particular situation. If it advances a legal argument, MERS claims to be a mere a placeholder, a neutral data entry. When asserting broad legal rights to foreclose or assign a wide range of legal rights, MERS points to the security instrument's virtually unlimited delegation of authority to MERS take a wide range of actions "necessary to comply with local law or custom." In *Mortgage Electronic Registration Systems, Inc. v. Nebraska Dep't of Banking & Finance,*[303] MERS stressed its limited place-

---

824 N.Y.S.2d 769 (N.Y. Sup. Ct. 2006) (trial court refused to order default where MERS member submitted undated assignment of mortgage and note by MERS).

296 Fed. R. Civ. P. 17(a), 19(a). *See generally In re* Kang Jin Hwang, 396 B.R. 757 (Bankr. C.D. Cal. 2008).

297 Mortgage Elec. Registration Sys. v. Medina, 2009 WL 4823387 (D. Nev. Dec. 4, 2009); *In re* Mitchell, 2009 WL 1044368 (Bankr. D. Nev. Mar. 31, 2009) (MERS must show evidence of true agency relationship in order to file motion for relief from bankruptcy stay), *aff'd on other grounds,* 423 B.R. 914 (D. Nev. 2009) (MERS precluded from filing motion for relief from stay because MERS cannot comply with court rule requiring participation in settlement negotiations by representative with authority to confer on behalf of true owner); *In re* Sheridan, 2009 WL 631355, at *5–6 (Bankr. D. Idaho Mar. 12, 2009) (MERS cannot act for unnamed successors and assigns; must show authority from identified principal); *In re* Vargas, 396 B.R. 511 (Bankr. C.D. Cal. 2008) (MERS cannot proceed with motion for relief from stay on behalf of unnamed parties without evidence of who currently owns note).

298 Mortgage Elec. Registration Sys. v. Southwest Homes of Arkansas, 301 S.W.3d 1, 2 (Ark. 2009).

299 *In re* Sheridan, 2009 WL 631355, at * 5–6 (Bankr. D. Idaho Mar. 12, 2009); *In re* Jacobson, 402 B.R. 359, 368 (Bankr. W.D. Wash. 2009); *In re* Vargas, 396 B.R. 511; 517–520 (Bankr. C.D. Cal. 2008). *See generally* § 4.4.8, *supra.*

300 Landmark National Bank v. Kesler, 216 P.3d 158, 164 (Kan. 2009).

301 *In re* Sheridan, 2009 WL 631355, at *2 (Bankr. D. Idaho Mar. 12, 2009). *See generally* Weingartner v. Chase Home Fin., L.L.C., 2010 WL 1006708, at *2 (D. Nev. Mar. 15, 2010) (MERS's "beneficiary" designation is "confusing, unorthodox, and usually unnecessary").

302 *Id.* at 165.

303 704 N.W.2d 784 (Neb. 2005).

holder role when faced with the threat of regulation as a mortgage lending institution by the state of Nebraska. The Nebraska court summarized MERS characterization of its functions as follows:

> MERS argues that it does not acquire mortgages loans and is therefore not a mortgage banker under § 45-702(6) because it only holds legal title to members' mortgages in a nominee capacity and is contractually prohibited from exercising any rights with respect to the mortgages (i.e., foreclosure) without the authorization of the members. Further, MERS argues that it does not own the promissory notes secured by the mortgages and has no right to payments on the notes.

The court went on describe the functions of a typical mortgage lender or servicer, accepting MERS contention that it did not perform any of these roles: "MERS does not take applications, underwrite loans, make decisions on whether to extend credit, collect mortgage payments, hold escrows for taxes and insurance or provide any loan servicing functions whatsoever." MERS emphasized before the Nebraska court that it never acquired any loans or extensions of credit and did not acquire rights to any payments or receive payments. According to MERS, other entities retained promissory notes and servicing rights at all times while it merely held legal tile to the mortgage for recordation purposes. What is typically understood to be the "beneficial" interest in a mortgage, the right to collect payments and enforce the obligation—is exactly the interest MERS assured the Nebraska court it never held. In this way MERS successfully avoided regulation as a lender.

In arguments in recent cases decided by appellate courts in Arkansas and Kansas, MERS characterized its interests quite differently.[304] In Arkansas and Kansas MERS attempted to intervene in post-sale proceedings to set aside foreclosure sales. In both cases other lienholders had foreclosed, wiping out liens originally recorded in the names of MERS members. In both cases, after the initial land record recordings, the MERS members' mortgages had been assigned to other entities. In accordance with MERS's practice, these subsequent assignments were not recorded. Later, when other lienholders foreclosed, they provided notice of sale only to the lenders identified in the MERS mortgage documents as originally recorded. The current assignees of the MERS mortgages did not receive notice of the sale and lost their interest in the properties through foreclosure. Although the original MERS members admittedly no longer held any interest in the properties, MERS claimed that it held an interest in the properties and should have been notified of the foreclosure sales. Essentially, MERS claimed that as beneficiary under the security instruments it was entitled to notice like any other mortgage holder.

In both cases the appellate courts held that MERS lacked standing to seek judicial relief to set the sales aside.[305] The courts rejected MERS's contention that it should have been notified of the pending foreclosures. MERS had no enforceable rights in the property that could be affected by a foreclosure. MERS lacked the minimal concrete interest that would give it standing to challenge the sales. The current noteholders, not MERS, were the beneficial owners of the obligations at issue. These noteholders had failed to record their interests in the mortgages and were not parties to the challenges.

In focusing on MERS's lack of any enforceable rights in the underlying loan obligations, the Arkansas and Kansas courts hit upon the major flaw in MERS's claim to have a beneficial interest in mortgage transactions. The Missouri court of appeals in *Bellistri v. Ocwen Loan Servicing*[306] similarly focused upon MERS lack of any true beneficial interest in loans when it denied a MERS member's standing claim. In *Bellistri,* a MERS member sought to intervene in a quiet title action following a tax sale. The MERS member claimed standing as the grantee of a deed of trust assigned to it by MERS. Purporting to act in its capacity as "nominee" for an originating lender, MERS had assigned the deed of trust to the MERS member. MERS had never been a holder of the promissory note or held any kind of beneficial interest in the note. Under Missouri law, MERS's assignment of a deed of trust to the MERS member without the promissory note conveyed no cognizable interest. It did not matter that the purported assignment stated that it transferred the deed of trust "together with any and all notes and obligations" described in the security instrument. Since MERS could present no evidence that it ever held the promissory note or had authority from the holder to transfer it, the MERS member, as purported transferee, received nothing from MERS upon which to base a claim for standing to challenge a tax sale.

A series of decisions from the Nevada federal courts further examined MERS's contention that the boilerplate language of its security instruments gave it standing to pursue legal remedies in its own name. In 2009, the Nevada bankruptcy courts denied a total of twenty-seven stay relief motions brought by MERS. Eighteen cases were consolidated for appeal to the U.S. district courts, and all the bankruptcy court decisions were affirmed.[307] Despite the

304 Mortgage Elec. Registration Sys. v. Southwest Homes, 301 S.W.3d 1 (Ark. 2009); Landmark Nat'l Bank v. Kesler, 216 P.3d 158 (Kan. 2009). The Kansas foreclosure sale in *Kesler* involved a judicial foreclosure and the sale in *Southwest Homes* involved a non-judicial foreclosure.

305 Mortgage Elec. Registration Sys. v. Southwest Homes, 301 S.W.3d 1, 7 (Ark. 2009); Landmark Nat'l Bank v. Kesler, 216 P.3d 167–169 (Kan. 2009).

306 284 S.W.3d 619 (Mo. Ct. App. 2009).

307 *See* Mortgage Elec. Registration Sys., Inc. v. Medina, 2009 WL 4823387, at *3 (D. Nev. Dec. 4, 2009) ("Since MERS admits that it does not actually receive or forfeit money when borrowers fail to make their payments, MERS must at least provide

language of its security instruments purporting to give it a beneficial interest in loans, MERS admitted in these proceedings that it had no beneficial interest in the promissory notes themselves. It had no right to receive or forfeit money related to the obligations. In finding MERS lacked standing to proceed in bankruptcy courts, the courts focused upon MERS's inability to show that it had any authority to act on behalf of an entity that did in fact have the right to enforce the obligations. The district courts in particular looked to a local bankruptcy court rule which required that a creditor communicate in good faith with a debtor before the creditor could file a motion for relief from stay. Because MERS had no authority to negotiate on behalf of the true owners of the obligations, MERS could not possibly comply with this local rule.[308] Courts should apply a similar analysis whenever there is a state or local mediation or conference requirement that directs an authorized representative of the foreclosing party to negotiate with the homeowner before taking an action leading to foreclosure.

A number of state courts have applied rationales similar to those described above to bar MERS from proceeding in judicial foreclosures.[309] Federal courts have denied MERS the right to foreclose, both on standing grounds[310] and for failure to meet the requirement of complete diversity of citizenship.[311] MERS often brings foreclosure actions as nominee for the actual owner of the note. In these situations, the citizenship of the note owner rather than of MERS should control determination of whether diversity of citizenship exists.[312] These state and federal courts emphasize the inherent conflicts that arise when parties attempt to use the MERS contract language contrary to essential requirements of state contract and property law. Regardless of what the documents say, MERS cannot transfer interests in negotiable instruments contrary to the UCC and other state laws governing transfer of debt obligations.[313] If state law does not permit the practice, MERS cannot transfer a deed of trust as an enforceable obligation separate from the promissory note.[314] In judicial proceedings, MERS cannot assert rights belonging to another party contrary to procedural rules pertaining to the real party in interest and indispensible parties.[315]

---

evidence of its alleged agency relationship with the real party in interest in order to have standing to seek relief from stay."); Mortgage Elec. Registration Sys., Inc. v. Zeigler, Case No. 2:09-CV-0676 RLH-RJJ (D. Nev. Dec. 4, 2009) (unpublished), *available on this treatise's companion website* (neither MERS nor the entity for whom MERS purported to act as nominee had ownership interest in promissory note when motion filed); *In re* Mitchell, 2009 WL 1044368 (Bankr. D. Nev. Mar. 31, 2009) (no evidence MERS had any ownership interest in promissory note such as would make it real party in interest), *aff'd on other grounds,* 423 B.R. 914 (D. Nev. 2009) (because MERS cannot comply with court rule requiring participation in settlement negotiations by representative with authority to confer on behalf of true owner, MERS precluded from filing motion in bankruptcy court); *In re* Hawkins, 2009 WL 901766 (Bankr. D. Nev. Mar. 31 2009) (same analysis as *Mitchell*).

308 *In re* Mitchell, 423 B.R. 914 (D. Nev. 2009); Mortgage Elec. Registration Sys., Inc. v. Medina, 2009 WL 4823387 (D. Nev. Dec. 4, 2009).

309 Aurora Loan Servs. v. Sattar, 851 N.Y.S.2d 62 (table), 2007 WL 2917245 (N.Y. Sup. Ct. Oct. 9, 2007) (trial court *sua sponte* dismisses action to foreclose where MERS member cannot prove ownership of note and mortgage through assignments in the MERS system); LaSalle Bank N.A. v. Lamy, 824 N.Y.S.2d 769 (N.Y. Sup. Ct. 2006) (trial court refused to order default where MERS member submitted undated assignment of mortgage and note by MERS); Mortgage Elec. Registration Sys. v. Bastian, 824 N.Y.S.2d 764 (N.Y. Sup. Ct. 2006) (table) (default judgment denied where no evidence note and mortgage were assigned to MERS); Mortgage Elec. Registration Sys., Inc. v. Burek, 798 N.Y.S.2d 346 (N.Y. Sup. Ct. 2004) (trial court denied summary judgment based on material questions of fact as to MERS proof of ownership of note and mortgage); Mortgage Elec. Registration Sys., Inc. v. Rees, 2003 WL 22133834 (Conn. Super. Ct. Sept. 4, 2003) (summary judgment denied because MERS failed to provide proof of ownership of note; discrepancy between MERS's affidavit and note); Mortgage Elec. Registration Sys., Inc v. Johnston, Docket No. 420-6-09 Rdcv (Vt. Super. Ct. Oct. 28, 2009) (unpublished), *available on this treatise's companion website* (MERS "nominee" status not equivalent to agency and insufficient for standing to foreclose). *But see* Mortgage Elec. Registration Sys., Inc. v. Coakley, 838 N.Y.S.2d 622 (N.Y. Sup. Ct. 2007) (appellate court upholds denial of homeowner's motion to dismiss foreclosure action where MERS alleged ownership and possession of promissory note indorsed in blank); Mortgage Elec. Registration Sys., Inc. v. Azize, 965 So. 2d 151 (Fla. Dist. Ct. App. 2007) (where homeowner did not contest allegations in foreclosure complaint that MERS was owner of note dismissal of complaint for lack of proper party was error); Mortgage Elec. Registration Sys., Inc. v. Revoredo, 955 So. 2d 33 (Fla. Dist. Ct. App. 2007) (adopting *Azize* reasoning); Mortgage Elec. Registration Sys., Inc. v. Ventura, 2006 WL 1230265 (Conn. Super. Ct. Apr. 20, 2006) (summary judgment proper where MERS brings action in its own name and "c/o" the mortgage servicer and the servicer actually holds the note).

310 *See* § 4.6.2.1, *supra.*

311 Mortgage Elec. Registration Sys., Inc. v. Estrella, 390 F.3d 522 (7th Cir. 2004); *In re* Foreclosure Cases, 521 F. Supp. 2d 650 (S.D. Ohio 2007).

312 Mortgage Elec. Registration Sys., Inc. v. Estrella, 390 F.3d 522 (7th Cir. 2004).

313 Landmark National Bank v. Kesler, 216 P.3d 158, 167 (Kan. 2009). *See also* Weingartner v. Chase Home Fin., L.L.C., 2010 WL 1006708 (D. Nev. Mar. 15, 2010) (language of MERS deed of trust did not allow MERS to transfer beneficial interest in the underlying debt to servicer that appointed trustee to conduct non-judicial foreclosure sale; refusing to dismiss action for wrongful foreclosure against trustee).

314 Bellistri v. Ocwen Loan Servicing, L.L.C., 284 S.W.3d 619, 623 (Mo. Ct. App. 2009).

315 *In re* Wilhelm, 407 B.R. B.R. 392 (Bankr. D. Idaho 2009); *In re* Vargas, 396 B.R. 511 (Bankr. N.D. Cal. 2008); Saxon Mortgage Services, Inc. v. Hillery 2008 WL 5170180 (N.D. Cal. Dec. 9, 2008).

4.6.2.3 Challenging MERS's Standing in Bankruptcy Proceedings

If the consumer files bankruptcy, MERS advises its members that proofs of claim should be filed in the name of both MERS and the servicer, and that motions for relief from the stay may be filed either solely in the name of MERS or jointly with the servicer.[316] Several bankruptcy courts have rejected MERS's claim that it has standing to pursue a motion for relief from the stay solely in its name and without competent evidence of its status as agent for an identified note holder.[317] All the real party in interest and general standing principles discussed above in relation to non-MERS claimants who bring motions for relief from the stay and file proofs of claim in bankruptcy court apply with equal force to MERS.[318]

In *Greer v. O'Dell*,[319] the Eleventh Circuit held that a servicer's pecuniary interest in loan obligations it serviced was sufficient to confer standing on it to file proofs of claim on behalf of its principal, a credit card issuer. Although the court relied upon some questionable factual findings, the key to the court's holding is that the servicer is a "creditor" having a "claim" against the debtor, as those terms are defined by the Bankruptcy Code.[320] The court specially noted that under its agreement with the card issuer, the servicer was authorized to collect payments on the debts and entitled to obtain fees based on the amounts it collected.

Because MERS is not authorized or permitted to collect payments, it does not possess a "claim" against a debtor in bankruptcy. Even using the broadest construction of "claim" as adopted by the Supreme Court in *Johnson v. Home State Bank*, MERS does not have a " 'right to payment' in the form of its right to the proceeds from the sale of the debtor's property,"[321] since it has no legal or equitable ownership rights in such proceeds. Alternatively, MERS's naked right to foreclose under the mortgage cannot be "viewed as a 'right to an equitable remedy' for the debtor's default on the underlying obligation,"[322] since the true lenders and holders have this right and again have not delegated to MERS the "right to payment" on the underlying note. For these reasons, it is doubtful that MERS has standing to file a proof of claim or stay relief motion in its own right.[323]

316 In its foreclosure legal opinions, MERS states as to proofs of claim: "It is advised to file in both names in order to disclose to the court the relationship of MERS and the servicer. The address to be used is the servicer's address so that all trustee payments go directly to the servicer, not to MERS." *See* www.mersinc.org/foreclosures/index.aspx.

317 Mortgage Elec. Registration Sys., Inc. v. Medina, 2009 WL 4823387, at *3 (D. Nev. Dec. 4, 2009) (MERS must provide evidence of its alleged agency relationship with the real party in interest in order to have standing to seek relief from stay."); Mortgage Elec. Registration Sys., Inc. v. Zeigler, Case No. 2:09-CV-0676 RLH-RJJ (D. Nev. Dec. 4, 2009) (unpublished), *available on this treatise's companion website* (neither MERS nor the entity for whom MERS purported to act as nominee had ownership interest in promissory note when motion filed); *In re* Mitchell, 2009 WL 1044368 (Bankr. D. Nev. Mar. 31, 2009) (no evidence MERS had any ownership interest in promissory note such as would make it real party in interest), *aff'd on other grounds,* 423 B.R. 914 (D. Nev. 2009) (because MERS cannot comply with court rule requiring participation in settlement negotiations by representative with authority to confer on behalf of true owner, MERS precluded from filing motion in bankruptcy court); *In re* Hawkins, 2009 WL 901766 (Bankr. D. Nev. Mar. 31 2009) (same analysis as *Mitchell*); *In re* Fitch, 2009 WL 1514501 (Bankr. N.D. Ohio May 28, 2009) (MERS cannot file motion for relief from stay unless it was entitled to enforce note under negotiable instruments law and was current mortgagee; MERS's witness testified that MERS members are prohibited from pleading ownership of note); *In re* Sheridan, 2009 WL 631355 (Bankr. D. Idaho Mar. 12, 2009) (MERS may not bring stay relief motion on behalf of "successors and assigns" when it cannot show authority to proceed on behalf of an identified beneficial owner of obligation); *In re* Vargas, 396 B.R. 511 (Bankr. C.D. Cal. 2008) (MERS cannot proceed on behalf of unnamed parties). *See also In re* Jacobson, 402 B.R. 359, 367 n.9 (Bankr. W.D. Wash. 2009) (finding "problematic" MERS's identification as the beneficiary of obligation "solely as nominee"; denying motion for relief from stay). *But see In re* Relka, 2009 WL 5149262 (Bankr. W.D. Wyo. Dec. 22, 2009) (creditor, a servicer, allowed to proceed with motion for relief from stay where MERS assigned mortgage to creditor and creditor's witness testified from personal knowledge that she copied note indorsed to creditor from the original in creditor's vault); *In re* Scott, 376 B.R. 285 (Bankr. D. Idaho 2007) (for purposes of motion to dismiss a complaint court assumes as true allegation that MERS is "beneficiary" under deed of trust); *In re* Huggins, 357 B.R. 180 (Bankr. D. Mass. 2006) (MERS may proceed with motion for relief from stay as nominee for original lender where original lender continued to hold note and mortgage had not been assigned).

318 *See* § 4.5, *supra*.

319 305 F.3d 1297 (11th Cir. 2002).

320 11 U.S.C. § 101(10)(A) (" 'creditor' means entity that has a claim against the debtor that arose at the time of or before the order for relief concerning the debtor"); 11 U.S.C. § 101(5) (" 'Claim' means—(A) right to payment, whether or not such right is reduced to judgment, liquidated, unliquidated, fixed, contingent, matured, unmatured, disputed, undisputed, legal, equitable, secured, or unsecured; or (B) right to an equitable remedy for breach of performance if such breach gives rise to a right to payment, whether or not such right to an equitable remedy is reduced to judgment, fixed, contingent, matured, unmatured, disputed, undisputed, secured, or unsecured.").

321 Johnson v. Home State Bank, 501 U.S. 78, 111 S. Ct. 2150, 2154, 115 L. Ed. 2d 66 (1991).

322 *Id.*

323 *See In re* Wilhelm, 407 B.R. 392 (Bankr. D. Idaho 2009) (movants lack standing to bring motion for relief from stay; deed did not authorize MERS to transfer note); *In re* Sheridan, 2009 WL 631355 (Bankr. D. Idaho Mar. 12, 2009) (MERS may not bring stay relief motion when it cannot identify the beneficial owner of obligation and has no pecuniary interest of its own in the debt). *See also In re* Jones, 2008 WL 4539486 (Bankr. D. Mass. Oct. 3, 2008) (in non-MERS case, rejecting improperly supported proof of claim arising from securitized mortgage transaction); *In re* Gilbreath, 395 B.R. 356 (Bankr. S.D. Tex. 2008) (same); *In re* Hayes, 393 B.R. 259 (Bankr. D. Mass. 2008) (same). *But see In re* Huggins, 357 B.R. 180 (Bankr. D. Mass. 2006) (MERS as nominee was authorized by the mort-

4.6.2.4 Decisions Holding MERS Has Standing to Foreclose

When courts have allowed MERS to foreclose, their analysis typically relied on questionable interpretations of one of three standard terms of the MERS security agreement. These are: (1) the designation of MERS as a "nominee" of the current note holder, equating this term incorrectly with a broad agency status; (2) the reference to MERS as the "beneficiary" of the obligation, despite MERS own disavowal of this status; and (3) the grant of authority in the document for MERS to take any action "if necessary to comply with law or custom." To allow MERS to foreclose in its name, the court must apply one or more of these terms in a way that overrides basic state property law and commercial law, as well as the real party in interest and necessary party rules applicable in judicial proceedings.[324]

The Minnesota Supreme Court's decision in *Jackson v. Mortgage Electronic Registration Systems, Inc.*[325] is characteristic of rulings that treat the MERS deed of trust language as controlling and give short shrift to state property and negotiable instruments law. Minnesota's non-judicial foreclosure statute contains a requirement that before a mortgage holder can foreclose by advertisement all assignments of the mortgage must be recorded. The *Jackson* homeowners challenged MERS's authority to foreclose in its name under the Minnesota statute after ownership of the obligation secured by the mortgage (the promissory note) had been transferred to another party and this transfer had not been recorded. The homeowners argued that the transfer of the note, representing a transfer of the true ownership interest secured by the mortgage, was an assignment that must be recorded in order to comply with the statute.

The Minnesota Supreme Court rejected this argument, choosing to label the transfers of ownership interests among MERS members as assignments of "equitable" rights under the mortgages rather than true mortgage assignments. According to the court, the statutory requirement to record "all assignments" of mortgages as a condition to foreclosure did not apply to recording of these "equitable" assignments. For purposes of its decision the court assumed MERS did not assign mortgages, but left the lien in land records in MERS's name. As the dissent pointed out, the majority's reasoning ignored the plain statutory language requiring recording of *all* assignments of the right to enforce the mortgage. Most significantly, the majority decision undermined the entire purpose of recording transfers of property interests in land records. These records are a source of information for the public about ownership interests in mortgages. MERS is the antithesis of a public recording system, allowing concealment of the identities of the parties who own mortgages and disclosing only a meaningless placeholder name to homeowners and the public.[326]

A Michigan court similarly construed MERS's rights under that state's non-judicial foreclosure statute without regard to MERS's lack of ownership of the underlying debt. Michigan's foreclosure by advertisement statute allows "the owner of the indebtedness or of an interest in the indebtedness secured by the mortgage or the servicing agent of the mortgage" to foreclose.[327] MERS can never be the owner of the indebtedness, and it is clearly not a servicing agent. Yet, in an action brought by an unrepresented homeowner, a federal district court in Michigan found that MERS was entitled to foreclose under the statute.[328] The court appears to have equated MERS's "nominee" designation with the right to act as an agent with a broad but completely undefined scope of authority. The placeholder or straw man role that MERS serves does not create anything like a traditional agency relationship.[329] As with the Minnesota court, the Michigan court again did not consider the role of negotiable instruments law, even though this appears to be contemplated in the Michigan statutory references to the "owner of indebtedness" as the party entitled to foreclose by advertisement.

In other non-judicial foreclosure jurisdictions, notably Arizona, California, and Nevada, some courts have ruled that the UCC rules governing enforcement of negotiable instruments do not play any role in foreclosures conducted under these states' non-judicial foreclosure statutes.[330] These courts rejected borrowers' challenges to foreclosures based on demands that foreclosing parties provide proof of the ownership and possession of promissory notes. Extending this analysis further, several Arizona and California courts rejected challenges to MERS's standing to foreclose using non-judicial foreclosure statutes.[331] Not all courts have

---

gage to conduct the foreclosure and had standing to seek relief from stay).

324 *See generally* Weingartner v. Chase Home Fin., L.L.C., 2010 WL 1006708 (D. Nev. Mar. 15, 2010) (rejecting view that terms "nominee" and "beneficiary" in MERS deed of trust authorize MERS to transfer beneficial interest in debt obligation to entity that appoints trustee to conduct non-judicial foreclosure).

325 770 N.W.2d 487 (Minn. 2009).

326 Jackson v. Mortgage Elec. Registration Sys., Inc., 770 N.W.2d 487, 503–504 (Minn. 2009).

327 Mich. Comp. Laws § 600.3204.

328 Hilmon v. Mortgage Elec. Registration Sys., Inc., 2007 WL 1218718 (E.D. Mich. Aug. 23, 2007).

329 *See e.g.* Landmark National Bank v. Kesler, 216 B.R. 158, 166 (Kan. 2009) (contrasting MERS's "nominee" status with a true agency relationship).

330 *See* § 4.4.3, *supra.*

331 Swanson v. EMC Mortgage Corp., 2009 WL 3627925 (E.D. Cal. Oct. 29, 2009) (a "beneficiary" under a deed of trust may foreclose under California power of sale statute; deed of trust labels MERS as a beneficiary); Blau v. America's Servicing Co., 2009 WL 3174823 (D. Ariz. Sept. 29, 2009) (deed of trust authorized MERS to convey all of original lender's interest to assignee who could foreclose through private sale); Pantoja v. Countrywide Home Loans, Inc., 640 F. Supp. 2d 1177 (N.D. Cal. 2009) (deed of trust language effective to make MERS a "beneficiary" entitled to foreclose under non-judicial foreclo-

shared this view. While the real party in interest requirement embodied in Federal Rule of Civil Procedure 17 does not apply to non-judicial foreclosures, other courts have ruled that an entity foreclosing non-judicially must nevertheless meet UCC standards showing that it is a proper party entitled to enforce a negotiable instrument.[332] Without a clear directive to the contrary, state non-judicial foreclosure statutes should not be construed inconsistently with basic UCC and state property law principles.

4.6.2.5 Challenging the Validity of Transfers of Notes and Assignments of Mortgages by MERS

The structure of MERS transactions violates the fundamental notion that the promissory note and mortgage cannot be separated,[333] and assignment of the promissory note operates as an assignment of the mortgage.[334] A lien recorded in the name of MERS remains in public records while MERS members transfer ownership of notes among themselves. The practical effect of splitting the note from the mortgage is to make it impossible for the lienholder (MERS) to foreclose without express authority from the note holder (typically the trustee for a group of securitized loans).[335]

Because MERS is a purely nominal lienholder it cannot enforce any rights in the underlying note. MERS cannot transfer or assign an enforceable obligation to another entity.[336] MERS attempts to get around these flaws by pointing to the language of its form security agreement authorizing it to take any actions necessary to comply with law or custom. Courts, however, have rejected this argument, noting that it conflicts with basic property and commercial law.[337] The

---

sure statute); Adams v. SCME Mortgage Bankers, Inc., 2009 WL 1451715 (E.D. Cal. May 22, 2009) (MERS authorized by its own loan documents to foreclose as trustee on behalf of current owner of obligation, no requirement under California law that foreclosing party have possession of note).

332 Mortgage Elec. Registration Sys., Inc. v. Zeigler, No. 2:09-CV-0676 (D. Nev. Dec. 4, 2009) (unpublished), *available on this treatise's companion website* (in judicial proceeding seeking relief from bankruptcy stay MERS lacks standing because not entitled to enforce promissory note); Mortgage Elec. Registration Sys., Inc. v. Medina, 2009 WL 4823387 (D. Nev. Dec. 4, 2009) (MERS lacks standing to pursue stay relief motion without proof it is owner of beneficial interest or authorized agent for identified owner); *In re* Mitchell, 2009 WL 1044368, at *4 (Bankr. D. Nev. Mar. 31 2009) (no distinction between judicial and non-judicial foreclosures in requirement that foreclosing party have right to enforce note), *aff'd on other grounds and legal analysis questioned,* 423 B.R. 914 (D. Nev. 2009); *In re* Vargas, 396 B.R. 511, 520 (Bankr. C.D. Cal. 2008) (under California law only holder of negotiable instrument or party authorized under U.C.C. § 3-301 may enforce negotiable instrument)

333 *See* Grant S. Nelson & Dale A. Whitman, Real Estate Finance Law § 5.27 (5th ed. 2007); George E. Osborne, Handbook on the Law of Mortgages § 223 (West 1970); 1 Garrard Glenn, Mortgages, Deeds of Trust, and Other Security Devices As to Land § 249 (1943).

334 Numerous courts have affirmed this basic hornbook principle. *See, e.g.*, Brewer v. Atkeison, 25 So. 992, 993 (Ala. 1899) ("[t]he principle underlying this and our other decisions to the same effect is, that an assignment by the mortgagee of one of the mortgage notes operates as an assignment pro tanto of the lien upon the lands"); Parkhurst v. Watertown Steam Engine Co., 8 N.E. 635, 635 (Ind. 1886) ("[i]t is settled in this state that the assignment of one or more notes made to the same person, and secured by a mortgage, operates as an assignment, *pro tanto*, of the mortgage"); Martindale v. Burch, 10 N.W. 670, 671 (Iowa 1881) ("[t]hat an assignment or transfer of a note, secured by a mortgage, operates as an assignment of the mortgage lien, is a settled rule of the law"); Robinson Female Seminary v. Campbell, 55 P. 276, 277 (Kan. 1898) ("[t]he assignment of the note operated as an assignment of the mortgage made to secure the note"); W. Md. R.R., Land & Improvement Co. of Baltimore City v. Goodwin, 26 A. 319, 321 (Md. 1893) ("[t]he law in this state is well settled 'that an assignment of a debt secured by mortgage operates as an assignment of the mortgage.' "); Hatlestad v. Mutual Trust Life Ins. Co., 268 N.W. 665, 668 (Minn. 1936) ("mere transfer of the note secured by a mortgage is in law an assignment of the latter"); Studebaker Bros. Mfg. Co. v. McCurgur, 30 N.W. 686, 687 (Neb. 1886) ("the assignment of one of the notes by itself, without any accompanying transfer of the mortgage, is an assignment *pro tanto* of the mortgage"); Page v. Pierce, 26 N.H. 317, 1853 WL 2428, at *4 (1853) ("[i]t is settled in this State, that the assignment of a debt secured by a mortgage of land, is *ipso facto* an assignment of the security also").

335 Landmark National Bank v. Kesler, 216 P.3d 158, 166–167 (Kan. 2009) (separating interests of note and deed of trust can leave mortgage unenforceable); Bellistri v. Ocwen Loan Servicing, L.L.C., 284 S.W. 3d 619, 623 (Mo. Ct. App. 2009) (mortgage loan becomes ineffectual when note holder does not also hold the deed of trust). *See also In re* Vargas, 396 B.R. 511, 516–517 (Bankr. C.D. Cal. 2008) (separation of note and mortgage leaves titular mortgage holder with no enforceable rights absent express agency relationship with noteholder).

336 *In re* Weisband, 2010 WL 1253182, at *5 (Bankr. D. Ariz. Mar. 29, 2010) (assignees from MERS take only the rights and remedies available to MERS, and since MERS has no beneficial interest in debt obligation, an assigne cannot acquire standing that passes constitutional muster by assignment from MERS); Weingarter v. Chase Home Fin., L.L.C., 2010 WL 1006708, at *4 (D. Nev. Mar. 15, 2010) (refusing to dismiss wrongful foreclosure action against foreclosing trustee appointed by entity to whom MERS purported to transfer debt obligation; MERS could not transfer beneficial interest in debt to any entity acting solely under deed of trust language because "[o]ne cannot transfer the beneficial interest in underlying debt merely by assigning the security instrument").

337 *In re* Wilhelm, 407 B.R. 392, 404 (Bankr. D. Idaho 2009) (MERS as a "nominal beneficiary" of security instrument not authorized to transfer promissory notes); Bellistri v. Ocwen Loan Servicing, L.L.C., 284 S.W.3d 619, 623–624 (Mo. Ct. App. 2009) (document under which MERS purported to transfer note along with mortgage had no effect as different entity, not MERS, possessed note at the time); Saxon Mortgage Services, Inc. v. Hillery, 2008 WL 5170180, at *5 (N.D. Cal. Dec. 9, 2008) (assignment of deed of trust without note ineffective); LaSalle Bank N.A. v. Lamy, 824 N.Y.S.2d 769 (N.Y. Sup. Ct. 2006) (table) (MERS cannot make effective transfer of note

verbiage of MERS security instruments and other form loan documents does not set in place a structure through which a current note holder authorizes MERS to transfer ownership of the note from one party to another. MERS is prohibited by its own program rules from claiming ownership of promissory notes. Therefore, individuals purporting to act as MERS's representatives have no ability to transfer notes.[338] Nevertheless, this fact has not hindered some courts from holding that MERS can make a valid transfer of a note even though it neither owns nor possesses a note.[339] Advocates, therefore, should pay close attention to the note transfer issues in states where the holder of the note is an essential party to the foreclosure.

4.6.3 Other Challenges to MERS

In addition to challenging MERS's right to foreclose in its name or its standing to bring a foreclosure lawsuit, advocates should also consider challenges to MERS's foreclosure practices and other activities including whether they violate any state laws related to banking, mortgage lending, foreclosure, or debt collection,[340] whether they violate state licensing regulations,[341] and whether MERS's prosecution of foreclosures without any beneficial interest in the note gives rise to causes of action such as wrongful foreclosure.

Additionally, MERS's status as nominal mortgagee may be incompatible with state recording acts. In 2001, a county clerk's office in New York state refused to record mortgages or other documents naming MERS as "nominee" for the lender on the basis that because MERS has no interest in the property or the mortgage loan it is not a proper mortgage holder, and thus a document recorded in its name cannot be a proper "conveyance" within the meaning of the state's recording statute.[342] MERS filed suit to compel the clerk to accept its filings, and the state's highest court ultimately ruled in favor of MERS.[343] However, while the court held that documents naming MERS as nominee for the lender were entitled to be recorded,[344] it did not grant MERS's request for a declaration that its instruments were "lawful in all respects."[345] Moreover, the concurring and dissenting opinions express concern about problems this system creates for consumers, and specifically note that the issues of whether MERS can legally separate the promissory note from the mortgage and whether MERS would have standing to foreclose are reserved for another day.[346]

4.6.4 New Statutory Requirements Related to Identifying Mortgage Holders

Several states have enacted legislation that requires mortgage holders to provide identifying information about themselves and their interest in the property when they foreclose. While these provisions are typically designed to facilitate settlement negotiations, the disclosure requirements can also serve as a basis for ascertaining claims related to the standing and real party in interest status of the foreclosing party. For example, Maryland has enacted a statute which requires that the notice of intent to foreclose list identifying information about the mortgage holder and servicer, including contact information for a person who has authority to modify the loan.[347] In addition, the notice must give the license number of the mortgage originator and mortgage lender. The statute requires that a complaint or "order to

because it is never holder of the negotiable instrument).

338 *See In re* Fitch, 2009 WL 1514501 (Bankr. N.D. Ohio May 28, 2009) (summarizing testimony of MERS witness); Mortgage Elec. Registration Sys., Inc. v. Nebraska Dep't of Banking, 704 N.W.2d 784 (Neb. 2005). *See also* Wiengartner v. Chase Home Fin., L.L.C., 2010 WL 1006708, at *3 n.3 (D. Nev. Mar. 15, 2010) ("The financial institution owns the beneficial interest in the underlying debt. MERS does not own a bank's underlying debt simply because MERS's agent physically touches a blank-endorsed promissory note in the back room of the bank any more than a teller owns the bank's cash simply because he has it in his hands at the front desk.").

339 Blau v. American's Servicing Co., 2009 WL 3174823 (D. Ariz. Sept. 29, 2009) (construing deed of trust language to authorize MERS to convey all of original lender's interests to assignee); Crum v. LaSalle Bank, N.A., 2009 WL 2986655 (Ala. Civ. App. Sept. 18, 2009) (MERS's assignment of mortgage transferred rights under note; issues related to U.C.C. negotiable instruments law raised for first time on appeal are not addressed); U.S. Bank, N.A. v. Flynn 897 N.Y.S.2d 855 (N.Y. Sup. Ct. 2010) (giving effect to MERS assignment of note and mortgage based on MERS authority under security agreement to act as nominee for lender, ignoring MERS lack of ownership of note); Bank of New York v. Dobbs, 2009 WL 2894601 (Ohio Ct. App. Sept. 8, 2009) (MERS's assignment of mortgage to creditor brought with it the right to enforce the note, overlooking lack of indorsement of note to plaintiff).

340 *But see* Robey v. Shapiro, Marianos & Cejda, L.L.C., 434 F.3d 1208 (10th Cir. 2006) (dismissing FDCPA claim and state law claims against MERS); Trent v. Mortgage Elec. Registration Sys., 618 F. Supp. 2d 1356 (M.D. Fla. 2007) (dismissing complaint alleging that MERS violated state debt collection and UDAP statutes by misrepresenting itself as a creditor, by failing to comply with state regulations pertaining to debt collectors and mortgage lenders, and by using other deceptive means to collect debts), *aff'd*, 288 Fed. Appx. 571 (11th Cir. 2008).

341 *But see* Mortgage Elec. Registration Sys., Inc. v. Nebraska Dep't of Banking, 704 N.W.2d 784 (Neb. 2005) (reversing lower court decision and finding MERS not a mortgage broker under the Mortgage Bankers Registration and Licensing Act).

342 Mortgage Elec. Registration Sys., Inc. v. Romaine, 861 N.E.2d 81 (N.Y. 2006).

343 *Id.*

344 After the New York controversy began, MERS successfully lobbied for passage of legislation expressly authorizing recordation of mortgage related documents in the name of a nominee in at least one state. *See* Minn. Stat. § 507.413 (2006).

345 Mortgage Elec. Registration Sys., Inc. v. Romaine, 861 N.E.2d 81, 87 (N.Y. 2006) (dissent, noting that lower court denied MERS's request for declaration and issue not addressed on appeal above).

346 *Id.* at 85, 87.

347 Md. Code Ann., Real Prop. § 7-105.1(c).

docket" for a foreclosure sale be accompanied by an original or certified copy of the mortgage or deed of trust and a copy of the debt instrument accompanied by an affidavit certifying ownership of the debt. This certification must include a certified copy of the assignment or deed of appointment of a substitute trustee authorizing the party to foreclose.[348]

Several other recent state enactments require that foreclosure notices identify contacts with the foreclosing entity who have authority to negotiate over loan terms.[349] The foreclosing party's failure to comply with these notification requirements should strengthen challenges raising standing and real party in interest claims. The homeowner's inability to communicate with authorized loss mitigation staff of the mortgage holder can be used to highlight concerns over lack of standing in a very concrete way.

4.7 Due Process Challenges to Foreclosure by Power of Sale

4.7.1 Introduction

Due process requires that deprivation of a significant property interest be preceded by both adequate notice and a meaningful opportunity for a hearing.[350] Foreclosure by power of sale would seem to violate this standard in two ways: personal notice of a foreclosure sale is not required in all states,[351] and no state which permits power of sale foreclosure requires a hearing before a judge prior to foreclosure. In the mid- to late-1970s, there was a wave of assaults on the power of sale foreclosure as a violation of due process. Almost all foundered at the circuit court level, however, because of the Supreme Court's insistence that there can be no constitutional deprivation without a state actor, and because most power of sale foreclosure proceedings are between two private parties.

Chief among the Supreme Court cases that are responsible for these losses is *Flagg Brothers, Inc. v. Brooks*.[352] In *Flagg Brothers*, the Supreme Court upheld a New York state statute that authorized the sale of stored goods to satisfy a warehouseman's lien. The Court found no due process violation because there was no state action implicated by the sale. No state officials participated in the sale, and because the settlement of disputes between debtors and creditors is not a traditional, *exclusive* function of the state, the mere fact that the state authorized the sale through a statute does not create state action.

Without state action there is no due process protection.[353] There are at least two foreclosure situations, however, in which state action may be established: when the state foreclosure process requires the participation of a government official, and when the foreclosing mortgage holder is a gov-

348 Md. Code Ann., Real Prop. § 7-105.1(d).

349 Cal. Civ. Code § 2923.5 (pre-foreclosure notice must identity means to contact mortgagee or agent in timely manner, including toll-free number for access to live representative; applies until 2013 for loans made from 2003 to 2007); Colo. Rev. Stat. § 38-38-102.5 (foreclosure notice must include direct phone to holder's loss mitigation department or representative); Ga. Code Ann. § 44-14-162.2 (notice at initiation of foreclosure proceedings must include name, address, and phone number of individual or entity having full authority to negotiate and modify mortgage); Me. Rev. Stat. Ann. tit. 14, § 6111 (pre-foreclosure notice must include contact information for "persons having authority to modify a mortgage" including the mortgagee and servicer); Mass. Gen. Laws ch. 244, § 35A (on notice of default holder must provide name and address of mortgage holder, phone number of representative of mortgagee whom borrower should contact to dispute claims); N.J. Stat. Ann § 2A:50-56 (pre-foreclosure notice must give name and address of lender and phone number of representative for dispute resolution); N.C. Gen. Stat. Ann. § 53-243.11(21) (pre-foreclosure notice must provide address, phone number and other contact information for lender, servicer, or agent for either who is authorized to work with borrower to avoid foreclosure).

350 *See* Sniadach v. Family Fin. Corp., 395 U.S. 337, 89 S. Ct. 1820, 23 L. Ed. 2d 349 (1969) (hearing must be aimed at establishing the validity, or at least the probable validity, of the underlying claim); Mullane v. Cent. Hanover Trust, 339 U.S. 306, 70 S. Ct. 652, 94 L. Ed. 865 (1950) (notice must be reasonably calculated to under the circumstances to apprise interested parties in the pendency of the action). *See also* Griffin v. Bierman, 941 A.2d 475 (Md. 2008) (due process does not require actual notice; notice by mail is constitutionally sufficient).

The Due Process Clause of the Fifth Amendment applies to the federal government, while the Due Process Clause of the Fourteenth Amendment applies to the states.

351 *See, e.g.*, Mich. Comp. Laws §§ 600.3101 to 600.3180.

352 436 U.S. 149, 98 S. Ct. 1729, 56 L. Ed. 2d 185 (1978).

353 Ray v. Oakland County Drain Comm'n, 115 Fed. Appx. 775 (6th Cir. 2004) (unpublished) (foreclosure by advertisement valid; no state action existed for Fourteenth Amendment purposes); Waller v. Life Bank, 2008 WL 495486 (E.D. Mich. Feb. 21, 2008) (citing cases from Michigan Appeals and Supreme Courts and the Sixth Circuit holding that Michigan's foreclosure by advertisement procedure is not state action); Curlee v. Wells Fargo Home Mortgage, 2007 WL 4287544 (N.D. Miss. Dec. 5, 2007) (Mississippi's non-judicial foreclosure procedure is not state action); Parker v. BancorpSouth Bank, 253 S.W.3d 918 (Ark. 2007) (Arkansas Statutory Foreclosure Act is constitutional; no state action, so no due process requirement under U.S. or state constitution); Parks v. Bank of New York, 614 S.E.2d 63 (Ga. 2005) (no state action; statute's notice provision challenged as it does not provide for actual receipt of foreclosure sale notice). *See* Apao v. Bank of N.Y., 324 F.3d 1091 (9th Cir. 2003) (extensive regulation of the secondary mortgage market does not convert private foreclosure procedures into state action); Russell v. Standard Fed. Bank, 2000 WL 1923513 (E.D. Mich. Nov. 27, 2000) (power of sale foreclosure does not involve the requisite state action to bring a prima facie constitutional claim); Bullock v. Resolution Trust Corp., 918 F. Supp. 1001 (S.D. Miss. 1995) (non-judicial foreclosure sale was not state action as required to support plaintiff's claims under the Fourteenth Amendment and § 1983); Northup v. Poling, 761 A.2d 872 (Me. 2000) (ministerial actions of the register of deeds in recording notice did not constitute state action such as to give rise to a due process claim under state and federal constitution).

ernment agency. The participation of a state official is discussed below. Cases in which the foreclosing mortgage holder is a government agency are discussed in Chapter 3, *supra*.

4.7.2 Participation by State Official

In some states, statutory foreclosure procedures require the participation of a state official for the proper conduct of the foreclosure.[354] In these states, a strong argument may be made that the involvement of the state official constitutes state action for due process purposes. A number of courts have reached this conclusion.[355]

In *Dieffenbach v. Attorney General of Vermont*,[356] the Second Circuit found state action in Vermont's strict foreclosure statute as the mortgage holder must obtain a decree of foreclosure from the court; the clerk or the court must render an accounting and can extend the redemption period; and then the court will issue a writ of possession which the sheriff will execute. The court interpreted the portion of the *Flagg Brothers* decision referring to the "total absence of overt official involvement" to mean that "an automatic ministerial act suffices to transform what would be private action to the 'affirmative command' of the state."

A federal district court in *New Destiny Development Corp. v. Piccone*,[357] relying on *Flagg Brothers*, found state action in a *lis pendens* statute when the town clerk was required to record a *lis pendens* on property during a foreclosure. The court concluded that state action is present when a town clerk facilitates the deprivation of property by placing a notice in the land records. The court describes *Flagg Brothers* as holding that the "state action element is met in cases where a government official participates in the physical deprivation of property."

The participation of a clerk was also critical in *Turner v. Blackburn*,[358] in which a three-judge panel of a federal district court found state action in a statute regulating power of sale foreclosures. The scheme required that the court clerk: (1) administer, with some discretion as to how to do so, upset bid provisions which are incorporated into all deeds of trust; (2) audit the proceeds from the foreclosure sale; and (3) receive petitions for eviction. The court held "that the direct participation by the clerk in the procedure by which plaintiff was deprived of ownership, and threatened to be deprived of possession, of her property constituted state action." The court noted that, having found state action, a party to a mortgage can only waive due process rights if the waiver is voluntarily, intelligently, and knowingly given (it was not in this case).[359]

The Supreme Court has never defined the extent of state participation required to implicate state action. There is a limited discussion in a footnote of *Flagg Brothers*, which reads as follows:

> In each of those cases [*North George Finishing, Fuentes, Sniadach*] a government official participated in the physical deprivation of what had concededly been the . . . plaintiff's property. . . . The constitutional protection attaches not because, as in *North Georgia Finishing*, a clerk issued a ministerial writ out of the court, but because as a result of that writ the property of the debtor was seized. . . .[360]

As is apparent, the Supreme Court has not established in this footnote a test of what is "minor" participation versus "major" participation. Nor does it establish that a governmental official must do something more than issue orders or stamp a document. Rather, it establishes that if a deprivation follows from the government action, then constitutional protection attaches. Thus, it could be plausibly argued that *any action* of any government official, without which a foreclosure would not be enforceable or have the effect of law, is the state action which *Flagg Brothers* envisions.

It is probably unrealistic to argue that the mere recording of a deed constitutes state action. Indeed, at that point, the deprivation suffered under a foreclosure would already have taken place. But when it is required by state law that a clerk issue a writ, or receive documents such as an accounting of sales results in order to finalize a foreclosure, or that a sheriff execute a foreclosure, it is consistent with constitutional law to find the presence of state action.

Once state action has been established, due process protections apply. What due process requires is generally discussed at § 3.1.2.2, *supra*.

4.8 Foreclosure of a Deed of Trust

In some jurisdictions, a deed of trust is used as security for a loan, instead of a mortgage. Under a deed of trust, legal title to the property is transferred from the property owner to a trustee to be held for the benefit of the lender, to secure repayment of the loan.[361] If the loan is not repaid, the lender can direct the trustee to sell the property to satisfy the outstanding debt, in accordance with the power of sale in the deed of trust and any applicable statutory provisions.[362] In

354 *See, e.g.*, Colo. Rev. Stat. § 38-39-101 (foreclosure by power of sale by public trustee).

355 *But see* Northrip v. Fed. Nat'l Mortgage Ass'n, 527 F.2d 23 (6th Cir. 1975) (no state action when statute required participation of sheriff in foreclosure); Lawson v. Smith, 402 F. Supp. 851, 855 (N.D. Cal. 1975) (use of county recorder in non-judicial foreclosure sale not state action).

356 604 F.2d 187 (2d Cir. 1979).

357 802 F. Supp. 692, 696 (D. Conn. 1992).

358 389 F. Supp. 1250 (W.D.N.C. 1975).

359 *Id.* at 1257–1258.

360 Flagg Bros. v. Brooks, 436 U.S. 149, 160 n.10, 98 S. Ct. 1729, 56 L. Ed. 2d 185 (1978).

361 *See* Milton R. Friedman, Friedman on Contracts & Conveyances of Real Prop. § 6.1 (2001).

362 *Id.*

many states, the deed of trust was developed as an alternative to the mortgage, which traditionally had to be foreclosed judicially.[363] Although today there is little practical difference between the two, because a deed of trust is held by a trustee who has an independent duty to protect the rights of the borrower (as well as the lender), borrowers in foreclosure under a deed of trust may be able to raise breach of the trustee's duty as a defense to a foreclosure sale or, after foreclosure, when seeking to set aside a sale.

In most jurisdictions "a trustee under a deed of trust owes fiduciary duties both to the lender and to the borrower."[364] Because of this fiduciary relationship, the trustee must be "scrupulously fair and impartial" in carrying out these duties, including the foreclosure sale.[365] The nature of the fiduciary relationship, however, is more limited than a conventional trustee.[366] The trustee's powers are generally limited to the power to conduct a foreclosure sale and to convey title under prescribed circumstances.[367] The trustee's fiduciary obligations are limited to carrying out the sale with "fidelity to ethical principles" and to the statutory and contractual requirements, but do not extend beyond those requirements.[368] Thus the trustee must comply strictly with the terms of the power of sale and with the statute.

Failure to comply with statutory requirements may subject the trustee to liability for wrongful foreclosure and may constitute grounds to set aside the sale.[369] In addition, a trustee who has actual knowledge of anything which should legally prevent the foreclosure may have a duty to investigate.[370] For example, in a case in which a homeowner filed an action against a deed of trust grantee/pool company after the pipes connected to the pool failed, causing extensive damage to the borrower's home, the trustee breached his duty to the borrower by proceeding with a foreclosure sale after learning of the lawsuit.[371] By contrast, the West Virginia Supreme Court, in *Lucas v. Fairbanks Capital Corp.*,[372] held that such a fiduciary duty does not include reviewing the account records to ascertain the actual amount due or considering borrower's objections to the foreclosure sale.[373] In *Lucas*, the homeowners alleged numerous wrongful act by Fairbanks in servicing the loan including failing to post

363 *See In re* Krohn, 52 P.3d 774, 777 (Ariz. 2002) ("The deed of trust provisions were added to Arizona law in 1971 following complaints by representatives of the mortgage industry that the 'mortgage and foreclosure process in Arizona [was] unnecessarily time-consuming and expensive.' " (footnote omitted)).

364 Perry v. Va. Mortgage & Inv. Co., 412 A.2d 1194, 1197 (D.C. 1980) (citing S&G Inv. Inc. v. Home Fed. Sav. & Loan Ass'n, 505 F.2d 370, 377 n.21 (D.C. Cir. 1974)). *See* Nat'l Life Ins. Co. v. Silverman, 454 F.2d 899 (D.C. Cir. 1971); Maynard v. Sutherland, 313 F.2d 560, 565 n.16 (D.C. Cir. 1962); Spruill v. Ballard, 58 F.2d 517 (D.C. Cir. 1932); Murray v. Wells Fargo Home Mortgage, 953 A.2d 308 (D.C. 2008); Killion v. Bank Midwest, 987 S.W.2d 801, 813 (Mo. Ct. App. 1998) (a fiduciary relationship exists between the trustee of a deed of trust and the debtor and creditor; the trustee is considered to be the agent of both debtor and creditor and should perform the duties of the trust with impartiality and integrity); Sloop v. London, 219 S.E.2d 502, 504, 505 (N.C. 1975) ("The clear language of the deed of trust as well as North Carolina law, imposes upon the trustee a Fiduciary duty to use diligence and fairness in conducting the sale and to receive and disburse the proceeds of the sale."); Paul v. Hanson, 2008 WL 353226 (Wash. Ct. App. Feb. 11, 2008). *But see* Heritage Oaks Partners v. First Am. Title Ins. Co., 66 Cal. Rptr. 3d 510 (Cal. Ct. App. 2007).

365 Sheridan v. Perpetual Bldg. Ass'n, 322 F.2d 418, 421 (D.C. Cir. 1963) (trustee breached duty by releasing first purchaser at foreclosure sale who had bid higher amount, then selling to second buyer for less, without consulting borrower). *But see* Paul v. Hanson, 2008 WL 353226 (Wash. Ct. App. Feb. 11, 2008) (no breach of fiduciary duty where trustee acted in accordance with terms of agreement).

366 Perry v. Va. Mortgage & Inv. Co., 412 A.2d 1194, 1197 (D.C. 1980).

367 *Id. See also* 2 Baxter Dunaway, The Law of Distressed Real Estate § 17:23 (2003).

368 Wheeler v. McBlair, 5 App. D.C. 375, 381, 382 (D.C. Cir.), *aff'd*, 172 U.S. 643 (1895) (trustees' powers and duties are measured by terms of instrument appointing them; they do not have same discretion in exercise of duties as other trustees); Lewis v. Jordan Inv., Inc., 725 A.2d 495, 499 (D.C. 1999) (a trustee under a deed of trust has the fiduciary obligation to comply with the powers and duties of the trust instrument, as well as the applicable statute under the District of Columbia Code); Perry v. Va. Mortgage & Inv. Co., 412 A.2d 1194, 1197 (D.C. 1980) (citing S&G Inv. Inc. v. Home Fed. Sav. & Loan Ass'n, 505 F.2d 370, 377 n.21 (D.C. Cir. 1974) (trustees of deeds have only those powers and duties imposed by the trust instrument itself, coupled with the applicable statute governing foreclosure sales in the District of Columbia)).

369 *In re* Worcester, 811 F.2d 1224 (9th Cir. 1987) (trustee's failure to accurately describe property in notice of sale and in trustee's deed was grounds for setting aside sale); Sloop v. London, 219 S.E.2d 502, 505 (N.C. 1975) (trustee's failure to attend sale and signing of sale "report" before sale occurred were breaches of duty).

370 *See* Killion v. Bank Midwest, 987 S.W.2d 801 (Mo. Ct. App. 1998) (finding no breach of duty, but noting "the trustee may proceed without making any affirmative investigation unless the trustee has actual knowledge 'of anything which should *legally* prevent the foreclosure.' " (citation omitted)). *But see* Lewis v. Jordan Inv., Inc., 725 A.2d 495, 500 (D.C. 1999) ("Absent fraud, misrepresentation, or self-dealing, we do not impose any additional duties upon the trustee."); 2 Baxter Dunaway, The Law of Distressed Real Estate § 17:25 (2003) (no duty to investigate absent unusual circumstances).

371 Cox v. Helenius, 693 P.2d 683 (Wash. 1985) (also noting grossly inadequate sale price when grantors' home, with an equity of at least $100,000 existing in the grantors, was sold for $11,784).

Under Washington's deed of trust statute, a prerequisite to foreclosure is that no action be pending on an obligation secured by the deed of trust. Wash. Rev. Code § 61.24.030(4).

The court noted in *Cox*, however, that "even if the statutory requisites to foreclosure had been satisfied and the Coxes had failed to properly restrain the sale, this trustee's actions, along with the grossly inadequate purchase price, would result in a void sale." 693 P.2d at 686 (citing Lovejoy v. Americus, 111 Wash. 571, 574, 191 P. 790 (1920)). *See* Miebach v. Colasurdo, 685 P.2d 1074 (Wash. 1984).

372 618 S.E.2d 488 (W. Va. 2005).

373 *Id.* at 497–498.

or improperly posting payments, charging unlawful fees, and illegally pursuing foreclosure.[374] Two justices disagreed with the majority and in a well-written dissent arguing that trustees to deeds of trust have the right and the duty to consider the legitimate objections to the parties to the trust, and to make inquiries where necessary.[375]

Trustees who have any potential conflicts of interest in acting as trustee must disclose this fact or will be required to prove that they were faithful to their duties.[376] Acting as an agent of the creditor by purchasing the property at the foreclosure sale is a conflict of interest that has been held to be a breach of duty, though some statutes specifically allow an employee or agent of the creditor to serve as trustee.[377] Any actions of the trustee that could "chill" bidding at a foreclosure sale could constitute a breach of duty.[378]

Finally, selling the property at a price that is shockingly low may amount to a breach of the trustee's duty,[379] though courts usually look for some irregularity or unfairness in addition to a low price.[380]

374 *Id.* at 491.

375 *Id.* at 505.

376 Sheridan v. Perpetual Bldg. Ass'n, 322 F.2d 418, 421 (D.C. Cir. 1963) (because of their close connection with the lender, the trustees were not qualified to act as trustees unless borrower, after full and fair disclosure to him of the facts, acquiesced; one trustee was an officer of the lender, one managed a partner of the lender; trustees' continual consultation with and dominance by lender breached duty to borrower); Lewis v. Jordan Inv., Inc., 725 A.2d 495, 500 (D.C. 1999) ("[w]here it is shown that a fiduciary has conflicting interests, the burden is on the fiduciary to prove that he has been faithful to his duties."); Perry v. Va. Mortgage & Inv. Co., 412 A.2d 1194, 1197 (D.C. 1980); Mills v. Mut. Bldg. & Loan Ass'n, 6 S.E.2d 549, 552 (N.C. 1940) (trustee who both acted as trustee and bid at sale on behalf of creditor breached duty of impartiality).

377 *See* Mills v. Mut. Bldg. & Loan Ass'n, 6 S.E.2d 549, 552 (N.C. 1940); Cox v. Helenius, 693 P.2d 683 (Wash. 1985) (though statute allows an employee, agent, or subsidiary of a beneficiary to be a trustee, when an actual conflict of interest arises, the person serving as trustee and beneficiary should prevent a breach by transferring one role to another person).

378 *In re* Worcester, 811 F.2d 1224, 1230 (9th Cir. 1987) (as a result of misdescription of property, bidders interested in a smaller lot would have been deterred from attending the sale); Biddle v. Nat'l Old Line Ins. Co., 513 S.W.2d 135 (Tex. 1974) (trustee or mortgagee has duty not to chill bidding; court found no breach of duty).

379 Lewis v. Jordan Inv., Inc., 725 A.2d 495, 500 (D.C. 1999) (finding that the foreclosure sale price was not shockingly low). *See In re* Krohn, 52 P.3d 774, 777, 781 (Ariz. 2002) ("We believe *gross* inadequacy *is* proof of unfairness, and as we have seen, gross inadequacy, as defined in comment b to RESTATEMENT § 8.3, is more than inadequacy"; adopting Restatement (Third) of Property view that *gross* inadequacy of sale price is sufficient justification for setting aside sale in both judicial and non-judicial foreclosure).

380 *See* § 14.2.3, *infra*. *See also In re* Worcester, 811 F.2d 1224, 1232 (9th Cir. 1987) (inadequate price plus irregularity in sale constitute grounds to set aside sale).

4.9 Enforceability of Due on Sale Contract Provisions

4.9.1 Overview

Due on sale clauses are common contract provisions which give a lender the option to immediately call due, or accelerate, a real estate secured loan when the borrower sells or transfers all or part of the security to a third party.[381] Almost all consumer mortgage loans contain such a provision in the loan notė or mortgage. Many lenders seek to enforce this right (which can lead to foreclosure proceedings) even when the transfer is between family members or in the probate process upon death of the debtor.

The enforceability of such clauses now is largely a matter of federal law, another example of the sweeping federal preemption of mortgage credit laws that took place in the early 1980s.[382] State common law or statutory limits on the enforceability of due on sale clauses have been for the most part preempted by the Garn-St. Germain Depository Institutions Act of 1982 (DIA),[383] which makes such clauses generally enforceable.

The DIA is broad in its scope. It applies to any lender, which is defined to include individuals, state and federal

381 *See In re* Jordan, 2008 WL 1746737 (Bankr. M.D. Ala. Apr. 11, 2008) (lender brought action to foreclose under due-on-sale clause after discovering that borrower transferred property under a 'bond for title' contract); Haynes v. First Fed. Bank of Cal., 2008 WL 4226100 (Cal. Ct. App. Sept. 17, 2008) (party who assumed loan without consent of lender triggered due-on-sale clause entitling foreclosing lender to attorney fees); Levine v. First Nat'l Bank of Commerce, 948 So. 2d 1051 (La. 2007) (lender brought action to foreclose, pursuant to due-on-sale clause in mortgage, after borrower executed a bond for deed contract with unrelated third party); Am. Investors, Inc. v. King, 796 So. 2d 955 (Miss. 2001) (lender may foreclose when mortgagor deeded interest to third party without prior written consent of lender); Kirshenbaum v. Fidelity Fed. Bank, 941 A.2d 213 (R.I. 2008) (successor mortgagee notifies mortgagor of intent to foreclose under due-on-sale clause after mortgagor's transfer of property without consent). *See also* Rader v. Danny Darby Real Estate, Inc., 2001 WL 1029355 (Tex. App. Sept. 10, 2001) (unpublished) (seller's failure to disclose existence of due on sale provision to buyer who agreed to assume mortgage could constitute UDAP violation or fraud). *Cf.* Whitty v. First Nationwide Mortgage Corp., 2006 WL 3570169 (Cal. Ct. App. Dec. 11, 2006) (loan servicer not liable for wrongful foreclosure when it denied borrower's request to waive due on sale clause so as to facilitate sale to third party; "A party does not breach a tort duty merely by exercising an express contractual right.").

382 *See generally* National Consumer Law Center, The Cost of Credit: Regulation, Preemption, and Industry Abuses §§ 2.4.2, 3.10, 3.11 (4th ed. 2009 and Supp.).

383 12 U.S.C. § 1701j-3. *See, e.g.*, R & G Props. v. Column Fin., Inc., 968 A.2d 286 (Vt. 2008) (DIA validates due-on-sale clauses and preempts state law). *See generally* National Consumer Law Center, The Cost of Credit: Regulation, Preemption, and Industry Abuses § 3.11 (4th ed. 2009 and Supp.) (background information).

banks, state and federal credit unions, and finance companies,[384] and every loan, mortgage, advance, or credit sale secured by a lien on real property,[385] whether consummated before or after the Act's effective date.[386]

The Act provides that notwithstanding state law, the exercise of a due on sale clause by a lender is governed exclusively by the terms of the contract, subject only to the limitations contained in the Act. Most importantly, the DIA prohibits the exercise of due on sale rights with respect to certain non-substantive or non-sale transactions, including intra-family transfers.[387] The DIA also exempts transfers in states that previously restricted due on sale rights when the loans fall within "window periods"[388] created by the Act. State laws in states with window periods continued to apply for three years following the effective date of the Act.[389] These states were also authorized to pass legislation within the three years following the DIA's enactment to continue state restrictions with respect to some loans. Five states exercised the right to continue state restrictions, though this right has lapsed in two of those states and been repealed in another.[390]

In addition, the Act makes clear that it does not prohibit mortgage assumption. In fact, it specifically encourages lenders to permit an assumption of a mortgage, either at the contract rate of interest or at a rate between the contract rate and the market rate.[391]

4.9.2 Federal Exemptions

Under the DIA and Office of Thrift Supervision (OTS)[392] regulations issued pursuant to the DIA, valid due on sale contract provisions are enforceable by lenders subject to nine specific exemptions.[393] The Act provides that a lender may *not* enforce a due on sale clause with respect to residential real property upon:

(1) the creation of a lien or other encumbrance subordinate to the lender's security instrument which does not relate to the transfer of rights of occupancy, provided that such encumbrance is not created pursuant to a contract for deed;
(2) the creation of a purchase money security interest for household appliances;
(3) a transfer by devise, descent or operation of law on the death of a joint tenant or tenant by the entirety;
(4) the granting of a leasehold interest for three years or less with no option to purchase;
(5) a transfer, resulting from the borrower's death, to a relative who will occupy the property;
(6) a transfer to the borrower's spouse or children where they will occupy the property;
(7) a transfer resulting from a decree of dissolution of marriage, legal separation agreement or incidental property settlement agreement where the transferee becomes the owner and occupier of the property;
(8) a transfer into an *inter vivos* trust in which the borrower is a beneficiary and which does not affect a transfer of occupancy rights, provided that the borrower does not refuse to provide the lender with reasonable means to receive timely notice of a transfer of the beneficial interest or a change in occupancy;
(9) any other transfer or disposition described in regulations proscribed by the Federal Home Loan Bank Board.

These prohibitions preempt state law, so that even if state law would allow a lender to accelerate a loan under these circumstances, federal law controls.

The DIA created no private cause of action which would give rise to federal subject matter jurisdiction.[394] However, as enforcement of due on sale usually takes place within

384 12 C.F.R. § 591.2(g). *But see In re* Black, 221 B.R. 38 (Bankr. S.D. Fla. 1998) (private banking institution did not qualify as a "lender," within meaning of DIA; statutory definition of lender as a "person" or "governmental agency" was not broad enough to include a private bank).

385 12 U.S.C. § 1701j-3(a)(1).

386 Courts have found that the Act has no retroactive effect, but applies only to cases in which the transfer occurred after its passage.

387 12 U.S.C. § 1701j-3 (d).

388 The "window period" under the DIA begins on the date the state adopted a law which prohibited the unrestricted exercise of due on sale clauses (or the date on which the state's highest court rendered a decision prohibiting the unrestricted exercise of due on sale clauses) and ends on October 15, 1982 (the effective date of the DIA). Any loans recorded during the window period are considered "window period loans." 12 C.F.R. § 591.2(p).

389 The DIA became effective October 15, 1982. The Act does not apply retroactively. *See* Freedom Sav. & Loan Ass'n, Inc. v. LaMonte, 448 So. 2d 51 (Fla. Dist. Ct. App. 1984) (section of DIA which purports to authorize unrestricted enforcement of due on sale clause in mortgages by any lender does not have retroactive effect); Viereck v. Peoples Sav. & Loan Ass'n, 343 N.W.2d 30 (Minn. 1984) (policy underlying the inclusion of the "window period" in the DIA authorizing exercise of due on sale clauses by federal savings and loan institutions is to ensure that mortgagors who relied upon state law prohibiting or limiting loan acceleration prior to the enactment of the Act are protected by state law during the period of transition between October 15, 1982 and October 15, 1985).

390 *See* Ariz. Rev. Stat. Ann. § 33-1571 (extending protection to 1987); Mich. Comp. Laws § 445.1622 (extending protection indefinitely for residential loans); Minn. Stat. § 47.20(6c) (extending protection until 1990); N.M. Stat. Ann. § 48-7-15 (Michie) (extending protection indefinitely); Utah Code Ann. § 57-15-11 (extending protection indefinitely) (repealed in 2008).

391 12 U.S.C. § 1701j-3(b)(3).

392 The Federal Home Loan Bank Board initially issued the regulations. In 1989, it was abolished and replaced by the Office of Thrift Supervision.

393 12 U.S.C. § 1701j-3(d); 12 C.F.R. §§ 591.3 to 591.5.

394 Dupuis v. Yorkville Fed. Sav. & Loan Ass'n, 589 F. Supp. 820 (D.C.N.Y. 1984).

state foreclosure proceedings, the federal regulations and their preemption of state law can be raised defensively to prevent foreclosure if one of these exemptions applies. (Of course, the availability of an exemption will not prevent a foreclosure based on another default on the mortgage such as failure to make payments.)

4.9.3 Intra-Family Transfers

As is evident from the earlier list of exempt transfers, federal law aims to protect intra-family transfers from triggering acceleration. These include transfers to the borrower's relative on the borrower's death, transfers to the borrower's children and spouse,[395] and transfers resulting from a marriage dissolution or property settlement.

The OTS regulations provide that these intra-family transactions are only exempt from enforcement of due on sale provisions if the transferee will occupy the property.[396] The Act, however, contains no such limitation.[397] Although the OTS is given authority to issue regulations governing the implementation of the Act and courts often defer to an agency's interpretation, when the language of a statute is clear, its plain meaning will usually be enforced. Thus the agency's occupancy requirement may be an *ultra vires* act subject to challenge.

4.9.4 Exemption for "Window Period" Loans

The DIA also created complex exceptions for states which restricted the enforcement of due on sale clauses prior to the effective date of the Act.[398] In order to protect the reasonable expectations of borrowers in these "window period" states, the Act provided that state restrictions would continue for three years after the effective date of the Act, or until October 15, 1985.[399] The Act also authorized window period states to continue these restrictions beyond the three year period, with respect to certain loans, by passing legislation within that three year period. Five window period states elected to continue state restrictions. Of these five, three states extended state restrictions permanently, and two extended restrictions to a cut-off date which has now passed. Of the three states that extended the state restrictions permanently, one state (Utah) has since repealed its law in 2008. Thus the window period exception is relevant today in only two states: Michigan and New Mexico. In these two states, state law will continue to apply to certain mortgage loans, subject to some limitations.

First, state restrictions apply only to "window period loans," that is, loans made after the enactment of the state law that restricts due on sale rights but before October 15, 1982. Second, state law does not apply to loans made by federally chartered institutions, which includes national banks, federal savings and loans and federal credit unions.[400] And third, even if state law applies, lenders may require that any proposed transferee meet credit standards customarily applied by the lending institution and may accelerate if the borrower transfers the property to someone who fails to meet such standards, or if the transferee fails to provide credit information requested by the lender.[401] The lender may, however, waive this right if it fails to respond in writing within thirty days of receiving a valid notice of sale by the borrower and the completed credit application of the transferee.[402]

---

395 A Florida bankruptcy court has found that even a post-foreclosure judgment transfer from mother to son did not violate the due-on-sale clause of the mortgage because the transfer was an intra-family transfer, exempt from the due-on-sale provision under 12 U.S.C. § 1701j-3(d). *In re* Jordan, 199 B.R. 68 (Bankr. S.D. Fla. 1996). *See also In re* Alexander, 2007 WL 2296741 (N.D. Fla. Apr. 25, 2007); *In re* Griffith, 183 Misc. 2d 210, 702 N.Y.S.2d 789 (Sur. Ct. 2000).

396 The preamble to the regulations states that this requirement is consistent with the congressional intention to restrict due on sale rights to protect consumers. 48 Fed. Reg. 21,559. *See generally* Grant Nelson & Dale Whitman, Real Estate Finance Law § 5.24.

397 *Cf. In re* Saunders, 2008 WL 724770 (Bankr. E.D. Pa. Mar. 17, 2008) (mortgagor able to tender mortgage payments under 12 U.S.C. § 1701j-3(d) where title to property was held in name of deceased son at time of mortgagor's bankruptcy petition). *Compare* 12 U.S.C. § 1701j-3(d)(5)–(7) *with* 12 C.F.R. § 591.5(b)(v).

398 The DIA became effective October 15, 1982.

399 *See, e.g.*, Miranda v. Macias, 191 Cal. Rptr. 177 (Cal. Ct. App. 1983) (loan was within the "window period" created by the Act and lender not permitted to enforce due on sale clause); Viereck v. Peoples Sav. & Loan Ass'n, 343 N.W.2d 30 (Minn. 1984) (no federal preemption permitted original state-chartered mortgagees to accelerate due on sale clauses contained in mortgage instruments on borrower-occupied residences executed prior to June 1, 1979 when mortgagees, subsequent to execution, acquired a federal charter or assigned the mortgage instrument to a federally chartered savings and loan institution; policy evinced by the inclusion of the "window period" in the DIA is to ensure that mortgagors who relied upon state law prohibiting or limiting loan acceleration prior to the enactment of the Act are protected by state law during the period of transition between October 15, 1982 and October 15, 1985). *See also* Phillips v. Super. Ct., 692 P.2d 1038 (Ariz. Ct. App. 1984) (Arizona statute regarding enforceability of due on sale clauses was not preempted by this section with respect to promissory note executed in 1982 because note was a "window period" real property loan which remained subject to state law restrictions on enforcement until 1985).

400 *See* First Fed. Sav. & Loan Ass'n of Morrilton v. Stacha, 688 S.W.2d 269 (Ark. 1985) (Act's "window period" exception, which permits state laws on due on sale clauses to remain in force for a limited time, applies only to non-federal loans); State *ex rel.* Bardacke v. N.M. Fed. Sav. & Loan Ass'n, 699 P.2d 604 (N.M. 1985) (Act did not make due on sale clauses enforceable by state-chartered savings and loan association during period in which state law made due on sale clauses unenforceable).

401 12 U.S.C. § 1701j-3(c)(2)(A); 12 C.F.R. § 591.4(d)(1), (2).

402 12 C.F.R. § 591.4(d)(3).

4.9.5 Additional Limitations on the Exercise of Due on Sale Clauses

4.9.5.1 Lender Waiver by Agreement

In all other states, an additional limitation imposed by the DIA applies. If, before a transfer occurs, a lender and the proposed transferee enter a written agreement for the latter to assume the loan, the lender waives its option to exercise a due on sale clause with respect to that transfer.[403] Under these conditions the regulations provide that the lender "*shall* release the existing borrower from all obligations under the loan instruments."[404] Notwithstanding the seemingly mandatory and unambiguous nature of this language, it appears that at least one court, and two agencies in opinion letters, have taken the position that a lender may continue to hold the original borrower liable for the loan after such an assumption.[405]

4.9.5.2 Contractual Limits on Due on Sale Clauses Are Not Preempted

With respect to all loans, including window period loans, contractual limits on the lender's right to accelerate still apply. Both parties are bound by the contract and the statute does not change that. For example, some contract provisions require that the borrower obtain the written consent from the lender prior to a transfer, but state that consent cannot be withheld unreasonably.[406] Courts are required to give effect to these provisions.[407] On the other hand, a Washington court construed a no-waiver provision in the contract to bar the borrower's argument that the bank had waived the due-on-sale clause by accepting payments.[408]

The principle of contract construction that ambiguous language will be construed against the drafting party should work in favor of borrowers when disputes arise as to whether or not the contract requires that the lender act reasonably.[409] The scope of the clause itself may also be subject to interpretation in favor of the borrower.[410]

---

403 12 C.F.R. § 591.5(b)(4). Lenders may also waive their option to exercise the due on sale clause by accepting payments from the transferee. *See* Brown v. Powell, 648 N.W.2d 329 (S.D. 2002) (after original purchaser assigned his interest in a contract for deed to his attorney, vendor for a while accepted and then refused attorney's payment under contract, and after refusing payment commenced foreclosure action against purchaser alleging default; court held that vendor was aware that purchaser had assigned his interest to attorney while accepting payments on contract from attorney, thus vendor waived non-assignment clause and forfeiture of contract was inequitable); *In re* Mini, 2009 WL 3756827 (Bankr. N.D. Cal. Nov. 9, 2009) (finding that lender waived its rights under due on sale clause by its conduct prior to homeowner's bankruptcy petition, namely requiring her to make $10,000 in payments in order to continue loan modification negotiations). *But see* Kings Langley, Ltd. v. Fed. Deposit Ins. Corp., 108 F.3d 338 (9th Cir. 1996) (table) (text available at 1996 WL 733190) (no waiver by acceptance of payments after transfer when lender not aware of transfer and manner of payment designed to conceal transfer); *In* re Tewell, 355 B.R. 674, 684 (Bankr. N.D. Ill. 2006) (lender's failure to invoke due on sale clause immediately following transfer of property and its continued acceptance of payments from debtor did not constitute "clear, unequivocal, and decisive act" of waiver; due on sale language indicating that lender could invoke clause "at its option" allowed for enforcement of rights "at a later date"); *In re* Martin, 176 B.R. 675, 676 (Bankr. D. Conn. 1995) (lender does not waive its right to enforce a due on sale provision when it does not specify violation of due on sale provision at the time it accelerated the mortgage because the lender was not aware of the transfer at the time); Stipek v. Reg'l Tr. Servs. Corp., 1999 WL 1215321 (Wash. Ct. App. Dec. 20, 1999) (unpublished) (bank's ability to enforce due-on-sale clause was protected by an express no-waiver provision even where it accepted payments for five years after the plaintiff's purchase of the property).

404 12 C.F.R. § 591.5(b)(4) (emphasis added).

405 *See* Grant Nelson & Dale Whitman, Real Estate Finance Law § 5.24, nn.129, 130 (citing Bank USA v. Sill, 221 Ill. App. 3d 598, 164 Ill. Dec. 102, 582 N.E.2d 310 (1991)); Federal Home Loan Bank Board General Counsel Opinion Letter No. 1090 (Nov. 26, 1984); Dep't of Hous. & Urban Dev., Mortgagee Letter 88-2 (Feb. 5, 1988). *See also* Cadlerock Joint Venture v. Alvarez, 1999 WL 619588 (S.D.N.Y. Aug. 16, 1999) (unpublished) (enforcing clause that continued original buyer's liability after assumption; no discussion of federal regulation).

406 *See* W. Life Ins. Co. v. McPherson K.M.P., 702 F. Supp. 836 (D. Kan. 1988) (court found duty to act reasonably based on contract provision, but found that lender acted reasonably); Sec. First Fed. Sav. & Loan Ass'n v. Jarchin, 479 So. 2d 767 (Fla. Dist. Ct. App. 1985) (when bank frustrated assumption of mortgage, it cannot accelerate based on language of mortgage contract, which DIA does not affect). *But see* Rubin v. Centerbanc Fed. Sav. & Loan Ass'n, 487 So. 2d 1193 (Fla. Dist. Ct. App. 1986) (it is reasonable for a lender to withhold consent to an assumption unless the parties agree to increase the interest rate to the prevailing market rate).

407 *See* Sec. First Fed. Sav. & Loan Ass'n v. Jarchin, 479 So. 2d 767 (Fla. Dist. Ct. App. 1985) (rights and remedies of both parties are fixed and governed by the contract).

408 Stipek v. Reg'l Tr. Servs. Corp., 1999 WL 1215321 (Wash. Ct. App. Dec. 20, 1999).

409 As a matter of general contract law, some courts hold that the covenant of good faith is implied even when the express terms of the contract do not limit either party from acting unreasonably. *See, e.g.*, Duffield v. First Interstate Bank, 13 F.3d 1403 (10th Cir. 1993). *But see* State Street Bank & Trust Co. v. Inversiones Errazuriz Limitada, 374 F.3d 158, 170 (2d Cir. 2005) ("the duties imposed by an implied covenant of good faith and fair dealing are not without limits. . . . [W]here a contract allows a bank to withhold consent for particular conduct and sets no express restrictions on the bank's right to do so, the bank is not prohibited from unreasonably or arbitrarily withholding such consent.") (citations and quotation marks omitted).

410 Levine v. First Nat'l Bank, 738 So. 2d 133 (La. Ct. App. 1999) (interpreting due on sale clause not to apply to bond for deed, which is a type of land installment contract).

4.9.5.3 Debtor May Cure Default Arising from Due on Sale Clause in Bankruptcy

When a transfer has occurred in violation of a due on sale clause, and the transferee subsequently files for bankruptcy, the transferee-debtor may be able to cure this non-monetary default through a chapter 13 plan. The court in *In re Garcia* reasoned that due on sale default can be cured by monetary compensation, or perhaps by a higher interest rate, if the market warrants.[411] A default arising from a violation of a due on sale clause can be cured without impermissibly modifying the lender's lien rights.[412] If the transferor files for bankruptcy, the debt may not be dischargeable under chapter 7.[413]

411 *In re* Garcia, 276 B.R. 627 (Bankr. D. Ariz. 2002).
The court reasoned that the lack of a debtor-creditor relationship between the debtors and lender had no bearing on debtors' right to cure the pre-petition default. *See also In re* Mini, 2009 WL 3756827 (Bankr. N.D. Cal. Nov. 9, 2009) (as long as there is no bad faith on the part of the debtor, a due on sale clause does not prevent modification of a loan even when the debtor is not the named borrower; violation of due on sale clause gives lender "a right to compensation for any economic loss, not a right to void any attempt at reorganization"); *In re* Ramos, 357 B.R. 669 (Bankr. S.D. Fla. 2006) (agreeing with *Garcia's* "well reasoned" analysis that breach of due on sale clause does not constitute cause to grant a motion for relief from stay; and declining to address whether non-borrower debtor had ability to cure default as lender waived objection to reinstatement and cure by debtor of defaults under the mortgage); Keith M. Lundin, Chapter 13 Bankruptcy § 132.1, at 132–136 (3d ed. 2000 and Supp.) ("Garcia is carefully reasoned and convincing. If the power to cure 'any default' at § 1322(b)(3) and (b)(5) means anything, it is not an invitation for the bankruptcy courts to pick and choose which defaults are curable and which are not. Instead, the issue is, what constitutes a cure for a nonmonetary default such as a transfer in violation of the due-on-sale clause. The suggested monetary cures in Garcia are clever and translate into plan provisions that mortgage holders might find palatable despite having to deal with a debtor not of their choosing.").

412 *But see In re* Allen, 300 B.R. 105 (D.D.C. 2003) (debtor who acquired interest in property by virtue of deed executed by her son in violation of a due-on-transfer clause could not cure and reinstate the deed of trust in her chapter 13 bankruptcy case; the attempt by debtor to cure the default to prevent loss of property to foreclosure would result in modification of the lender's rights in violation of the anti-modification provisions of the bankruptcy code, § 1322(b)(2)); *In re* Tewell, 355 B.R. 674, 681 (Bankr. N.D. Ill. 2006) (debtor who obtained residential property from original mortgagor in violation of due on sale clause may not cure default through chapter 13 plan over the mortgage holder's objection; treatment of mortgage under chapter 13 plan "would be an impermissible modification of the Creditor's right to, at its option, enforce the due-on-sale clause in violation of § 1322(b)(2)"); *In re* Martin, 176 B.R. 675 (Bankr. D. Conn. 1995) (debtor's chapter 13 bankruptcy plan to waive default due to an unauthorized transfer was an impermissible modification of the lender's secured claim in violation of § 1322(b)(2)).

413 *See, e.g., In re* Jordan, 2008 WL 1746737 (Bankr. M.D. Ala. Apr. 11, 2008) (chapter 7 debtor's pre-petition transfer of property and retention of proceeds with knowledge of due-on-sale provision and without lender's consent was willful and malicious under 11 U.S.C. § 523(a)(6)).

4.9.6 Failing to Respond to a Credit Application by the Transferee As Implicit Waiver of Due on Sale Rights

The extent of a lender's obligation under the regulations to respond to a prospective transferee's completed credit application in a timely manner is not entirely clear. Pursuant to 12 C.F.R. § 591.4(d)(3), a lender who fails to respond in writing within thirty days to a valid notice of sale and receipt of the transferee's completed credit application loses its right to enforce an otherwise valid due on sale clause. This provision clearly applies to window period loans, which are not affected by preemption, but which are subject to the lender's determination of creditworthiness.[414] The Act specifically provides that with respect to window period loans, lenders may require that prospective transferee's meet customary credit standards.[415] This regulation imposes a duty on the lender to promptly respond to the proposed transferee's credit application.

What is not clear is whether this obligation to respond applies to non-window period loans also.[416] The plain language of section 591.4(d)(3) does not limit the obligation to respond to window period loans. An argument can be made, therefore, that even with non-window period loans, the lender must accept and respond to a prospective transferee's credit application within thirty days or lose its rights. It must be noted, however, that the placement of the section suggests otherwise about its intended application. The other provisions of section 591.4(d) all relate to "window-period" loans.[417] However, the paragraph is included within section 591.4 entitled "Loans originated by lenders other than Federal savings associations" rather than section 591.5 entitled "Limitation on exercise of due on sale clauses."

4.9.7 Prepayment Fees and Loan Acceleration

Some mortgages include provisions that require a borrower to pay a penalty if the loan is repaid before it is legally due.[418] When the prepayment is not voluntary, as when the lender enforces a due on sale clause, imposing a prepayment

414 That is, it is clear that it still applies in Michigan and New Mexico to loans made during the respective window periods.

415 12 U.S.C. § 1701j-3(c)(2)(A).

416 That is, it is arguable, but not clear, that it applies in other states as well, and to loans outside the window period.

417 12 C.F.R. § 591.4(d)(1), (2), (4).

418 *E.g.*, Manpearl v. Abba Indus., 2002 WL 273656 (Cal. Ct. App. Feb. 26, 2002) (unpublished) (mortgagee cannot enforce a due on sale clause and collect a prepayment penalty when mortgagee did not comply with state law which provided that any waiver of the right to prepay without penalty must be separately signed or initialed by the obligor).

penalty is unfair. Thus the federal regulations prohibit the charging of such fees when the lender seeks to enforce a due on sale clause by written demand or formal proceedings on loans secured by the borrower's home.[419]

Moreover, lenders cannot get around this prohibition by simply not responding to a credit application submitted in accordance with the terms of the loan.[420] If a lender fails to approve a credit application within thirty days from a transferee who would meet the lenders' underwriting standards, and the borrower transfers the property and repays the loan in full within 120 days, the lender is prohibited from charging a prepayment penalty.[421]

4.10 Using Equitable Grounds to Prevent a Foreclosure

4.10.1 Generally

Foreclosure actions at common law were actions in equity.[422] Many state statutes retain the equitable character of the foreclosure process, even when the foreclosure is by power of sale, through provisions granting the mortgagor the right to petition the court to enjoin the foreclosure sale.[423]

A number of courts have relied solely on equitable considerations to prohibit foreclosure, despite the lender's legal right to foreclose. In these cases courts have barred foreclosure when the foreclosure proceedings were commenced after a one day delay in payment,[424] when the mortgage holder knew of the default and failed to inquire about it during personal dealings with the mortgagor but immediately thereafter brought an action to foreclose,[425] when the foreclosure was brought five days after the grace period on a $175.00 principal payment and eight days after the grace period on $153.00 interest payment and the mortgagor mistakenly believed the grace period to be thirty days,[426] when a mortgage payment was not made due to an inadvertent error of a bookkeeper who had been ill, when the mortgage holder had been advised of the bookkeeper's illness and had made no mention of late payment to mortgagor.[427] In at least one case, a family court stayed a foreclosure proceeding filed in another branch of the court to allow a party's defenses to the note to be litigated in the context of a divorce and property distribution case.[428] In each of these and similar cases, the court has found that the conduct of the lender to be unconscionable or so lacking in good faith as to warrant the court's intervention to prevent the foreclosure.

The court's inherent equitable power to prohibit unfair foreclosures played a role in many of the cases that barred foreclosure on grounds of waiver and estoppel[429] and on the basis of the mortgage holder's failure to engage in reasonable loss mitigation.[430] Equitable principles should bar foreclosure pending a servicer's consideration of a request for a loan modification under the various crisis-driven programs such as HAMP. Application of equitable principles to claims under these programs is discussed in more detail at § 6.4.5.3, *infra*.

---

419 12 C.F.R. § 591.5(b)(2).

420 Some lenders tried to use that ploy to force a pay off when the prepayment penalty could be collected. *See* National Consumer Law Center, The Cost of Credit: Regulation, Preemption, and Industry Abuses § 5.8.6 (4th ed. 2009 and Supp.).

421 12 C.F.R. § 591.4(b)(3).

422 *See* Deutsche Bank Nat'l Trust Co. v. Angle, 933 A.2d 1143 (Conn. 2007); LaSalle Nat'l Bank v. Freshfield Meadows, 798 A.2d 445 (Conn. 2002); Randall v. Bisbee-Baldwin Corp., 995 So. 2d 1004 (Fla. Dist. Ct. App. 2008); Beneficial Haw., Inc. v. Kida, 30 P.3d 895 (Haw. 2001); Bank of Haw. v. Horwworth, 787 P.2d 674 (Haw. 1990); Idaho First Nat'l Bank v. Bliss Valley Foods, Inc., 824 P.2d 841 (Idaho 1991); Wells Fargo Home Mortgage, Inc. v. Neal, 922 A.2d 538 (Md. 2007); 2301 Jerome Ave. Realty Corp. v. Di Paolo, 737 N.Y.S.2d 816 (Sup. Ct. 2002); Bank of Wilson v. Hartman, 785 P.2d 338 (Okla. Civ. App. 1989); C.J.S. *Mortgages* § 386, at 607–608.

423 *See, e.g.*, Wells Fargo Home Mortgage, Inc. v. Neal, 922 A.2d 538, 552 (Md. 2008) (court may apply general equitable principles in enjoining non-judicial foreclosure; homeowner alleged servicer's failure to comply with FHA loss mitigation guidelines); Redding v. Gibbs, 280 N.W.2d 53 (Neb. 1979) (court of equity has the power to relieve a mortgagor from the effect of an operative acceleration clause, when the default of the mortgagor was the result of some unconscionable or inequitable conduct of the mortgagee); Ruotolo v. Benjamin Franklin Corp., 441 A.2d 1185 (N.H. 1982) (superior court has equitable powers under New Hampshire statute to enjoin a foreclosure if the equities of the situation warrant; citing Meredith v. Fisher, 435 A.2d 536 (N.H. 1981) (because mortgage foreclosure is essentially a right to equitable relief, the element of fairness must pervade the entire foreclosure process)); Larson v. W. Underwriters Inc., 87 N.W.2d 883 (S.D. 1958) (equity court has power to relieve mortgagor from effect of acceleration clause when default was result of some inequitable conduct by mortgagee); C.J.S. *Mortgages* § 495(6). *But see* Freeman v. Wozniak, 617 N.W.2d 46 (Mich. Ct. App. 2000) (when mortgagee followed proper foreclosure procedure, a court cannot use its equitable powers to set aside a foreclosure sale when an older homeowner suffers from dementia).

424 Bisno v. Sax, 346 P.2d 814 (Cal. Ct. App. 1959).

425 Redding v. Gibbs, 280 N.W.2d 53 (Neb. 1979).

426 Damus Realty Corp. v. 3440 Realty Corp., 40 N.Y.S.2d 69 (Sup. Ct.), *aff'd*, 41 N.Y.S.2d 940 (App. Div. 1943) (court found mortgagee's conduct to be unconscionable, slight delay would not prejudice mortgagee, and mortgagor had made substantial payments).

427 Ariz. Coffee Shops, Inc. v. Phoenix Downtown Parking Ass'n, 387 P.2d 801 (Ariz. 1963) (court found mortgagee not prejudiced and that default was entirely out of proportion to the harshness of plaintiff's action in declaring entire debt due). *See also* Cherry v. Chase Manhattan Mortgage Corp., 190 F. Supp. 2d 1330 (M.D. Fla. 2002) (foreclosure denied when lender rejected mortgagor's attempted payment because it erroneously filed satisfaction of the mortgage).

428 *See* Glade v. Glade, 45 Cal. Rptr. 2d 695 (Ct. App. 1995).

429 *See* § 4.3.3, *supra*.

430 *See* Ch. 3, *supra* (foreclosure of mortgages held or insured by the federal government), § 6.4.5, *infra*.

4.10.2 *Mortgagee's/Trustee's Duty of Good Faith*

A trustee under a deed of trust, or a mortgagee under a mortgage, has a duty to exercise good faith and diligence in conducting a foreclosure sale of property.[431] The lender must protect the rights of the mortgagor under the terms of the power of sale.[432] The mortgagee or trustee must remain at arm's length with the buyer,[433] must conduct the sale fairly and limit expenses within reasonable bounds,[434] and must exert a reasonable effort to obtain a fair price.[435]

In reality, however, this duty is not scrupulously honored. The foreclosing creditor generally has little financial incentive to widely advertise residential foreclosures or to encourage meaningful competitive bidding. It is estimated that more than 75% of properties foreclosed by sale are purchased by the mortgage holder, also the sole bidder at the sale, for no more than the amount of indebtedness.[436] As a result, the foreclosed homeowner loses any equity in the property and the lender receives a windfall.

The inequity of this practice is highlighted in the case of *Murphy v. Financial Development Corp.*[437] The homeowner in this case had $19,000 in equity in the property at the time of foreclosure. The bid at the foreclosure sale (by the lender) covered the balance due on the mortgage ($27,000) but did not provide for a return of any of the homeowner's substantial equity. On the day of the sale, the lender offered to sell the property to a third party for $40,000. It sold the property to the third party two days later for $38,000.

The New Hampshire Court of Appeals found that the fact that the lender offered, on the day of the sale, to sell the property at a price higher than its bid showed that the lender knew it could get more for the property. Knowing this, the lender should have taken measures to ensure receiving a higher price at the sale, such as establishing an upset bid or advertising the property commercially to reach more prospective buyers. The court found that the lender in this case had a duty to secure at least a portion of the debtor's equity when the debtor had substantial equity, the lender knew of the appraised value of the property, and the borrower had made efforts to forestall the foreclosure by making partial payments. This action was brought after the foreclosure was completed. The homeowner was awarded damages in an amount equal to the difference between the fair price of the property and the price obtained at the foreclosure sale.

The lender is also obligated to exercise good faith and diligence to protect the interests of the homeowner before the foreclosure sale. This may include postponing the foreclosure sale to allow the homeowner to conduct a market sale of the property and retain some of the equity in the property. A Massachusetts trial court held that a lender did not exercise good faith when it refused to postpone a

431 *In re* Strayton, 360 B.R. 8 (Bankr. D. Mass. 2007); Scappaticci v. G.E. Capital Mortgage Servs., Inc., 2000 Conn. Super. LEXIS 3319 (Conn. Super. Ct. Nov. 27, 2000); Brown v. Freedman, 474 S.E.2d 73 (Ga. Ct. App. 1996) (mortgagee has duty to exercise the power of sale so as to protect his security—not to gain as much as possible regardless of mortgagor's rights); Pearman v. W. Point Nat'l Bank, 887 S.W.2d 366 (Ky. Ct. App. 1994) (covenant of good faith and fair dealing implied in all mortgage contracts; duty continues after default and throughout foreclosure process); Am. First Fed., Inc. v. Battlefield Ctr., L.P., 2009 WL 112439 (Mo. Ct. App. Jan. 20, 2009) (when foreclosing on mortgaged property, a mortgagee is a trustee for the mortgagor and is required to act in good faith and with absolute fairness in making the sale so as to protect the mortgagor); Mills v. Mut. Bldg. & Loan Ass'n, 6 S.E.2d 549 (N.C. 1940). *See also In re* Yoyo, 2007 WL 4268768 (Bankr. D. Mass. Nov. 30, 2007) (lender breached duty of good faith and fair dealing by failing to produce documents and other evidence related to the foreclosure sale). *But see* Johnstone v. Bank of Am., 173 F. Supp. 2d 809 (N.D. Ill. Nov. 15, 2001); Storek & Storek, Inc. v. Citicorp Real Estate, Inc., 122 Cal. Rptr. 2d 267 (Ct. App. 2002) (implied covenant of good faith and fair dealing did not prohibit lender from determining whether the contract's provisions had been satisfied prior to distribution of loan proceeds as expressly permitted by the contract); LaSalle Nat'l Bank v. Freshfield Meadows, Ltd. Liab. Co., 798 A.2d 445 (Conn. Ct. App. 2002) (no breach of implied covenant when mortgage and note do not require that lender accept less than the amount due); Voyles v. Sandia Mortgage Corp., 751 N.E.2d 1126 (Ill. 2001) (no independent cause of action for breach of the duty of good faith and fair dealing).

432 Hood v. Adams, 124 Mass. 481 (1978). *But see* Lucas v. Fairbanks Capital Corp., 618 S.E.2d 488 (W. Va. 2005) (holding that such a trustee's duty does not include reviewing the account records to ascertain the actual amount due or considering borrower's objections to the foreclosure sale).

433 Holman v. Ryon, 61 App. D.C. 10, 56 F.2d 307 (1932) (sale by trustee to his wife at less than adequate price is breach of duty).

434 *See* Am. Jur. 2d *Mortgages* § 758.

435 *In re* Strayton, 360 B.R. 8 (Bankr. D. Mass. 2007) (foreclosure sale likely to result in significant loss of value where lender did not market, appraise or inspect the property); White v. MacQueen, 195 N.E. 832 (Ill. 1935); Bascom Constr. Inc. v. City Bank & Trust, 629 A.2d 797 (N.H. 1993) (mortgagee's duty of good faith requires that it take all reasonable steps under the circumstances to insure that a fair and reasonable price is obtained); Harper v. Interstate Brewery Co., 120 P.2d 757 (Or. 1942).

At least one court has borrowed the U.C.C. standard of commercially reasonable sale and has applied it to foreclosure sales when the foreclosing lender sought a deficiency judgment, Wansley v. First Nat'l Bank of Vicksburg, 566 So. 2d 1218 (Miss. 1990) (citing Rankin County Bank v. McKinnnon, 531 So. 2d 822, 825 (Miss. 1988)); Lake Hillside Estates Inc. v. Galloway, 473 So. 2d 461 (Miss. 1985). *But see* Andrews v. Nationsbank, 903 F. Supp. 128 (D.D.C. 1995) (under Va. law, there is no independent cause of action for breach of duty of good faith and fair dealing; foreclosure sale conducted in accordance with state law was commercially reasonable), *aff'd*, Andrews v. NationsBank, N.A. 107 F.3d 922 (D.C. Cir. 1996).

436 *See* Steven Wechsler, *Through the Looking Glass: Foreclosure by Sale as De Facto Strict Foreclosure—An Empirical Study of Mortgage Foreclosure and Subsequent Resale*, 70 Cornell L. Rev. 850, 875–876 (1985). According to Wechsler, some put this figure closer to 95%.

437 495 A.2d 1245 (N.H. 1985).

foreclosure sale, even though the homeowner produced a buyer that made a legally binding commitment to purchase the property and was willing to pay a price that would result in a full recovery of all money due to the lender, including costs, and net $50,000 to the homeowner. The lender's compliance with state foreclosure statutes did not relieve it of liability for breach of its duty.[438]

Another argument may be made for pre-foreclosure equitable relief when the sale is not likely to bring a fair price, as for example, when it is not widely advertised or is scheduled for a holiday or in a manner that would chill the bidding. Finally, the loss mitigation protocols incorporated into government sponsored programs such as HAMP require that servicers consider options related to short sales and deeds in lieu before conducting a foreclosure sale. Servicers must review these alternatives when a borrower does not qualify for a loan modification. Failure to consider and implement these options when appropriate violates a servicer's duty to act in good faith.[439] The property disposition options related to the federal loan modification initiatives are discussed at Chapter 2, *supra*.

4.10.3 Enjoining a Foreclosure Sale When There Is Sufficient Equity in the Property to Satisfy the Mortgage Debt

Prior to a sale, a homeowner with substantial equity may be able to enjoin a foreclosure to allow a sale on the open market. A foreclosure sale is virtually guaranteed to bring no more than the balance due on the note.[440] A sale on the open market, however, should allow the homeowner to retain some of the equity in the property. Such a sale presents no risk to the lender; it will be paid in full from the sale proceeds.

The argument is analogous to the concept of adequate protection in bankruptcy. A secured creditor is prohibited from foreclosing in bankruptcy by the automatic stay, unless the creditor can show that it is not "adequately protected," or that its interest will be impaired by the continuation of the stay. Courts have found adequate protection when the value of the secured property exceeds the secured debt.[441] Even if the stay is continued for a substantial time, the creditor will be able to satisfy its claim fully when the stay is lifted.

Similarly, as long as there is sufficient equity in the property to satisfy the mortgage, the lender is fully protected and would not be prejudiced by the delay which listing and selling the home on the open market would cause.

In an unpublished order, a New Hampshire trial court enjoined the foreclosure of a home to allow the homeowner to secure mortgage assistance payments from the Welfare Department.[442] The court ruled that the delay caused "no unreasonable consequences to the defendant [mortgage company]." The homeowner had argued that the foreclosure, scheduled for the dead of winter at a time when the market was flooded with similar properties for sale, was likely to bring only a fraction of the amount owned on the mortgage.[443] A postponement of the sale, it was suggested, would in all likelihood increase the sale price and the amount ultimately realized by the mortgage company.[444]

Because the lender has a duty to the borrower to obtain the highest price when selling the property, it theoretically should have no objection to selling the home in the manner most likely to bring the highest price.[445] This was not the case in *Snowden v. Chase Manhattan Mortgage Corp.*, however, where a lender refused to postpone a foreclosure sale to allow the homeowner to conduct a market sale that would have satisfied the lender's lien and costs and netted the homeowner $50,000 from the equity in his property. The trial court held that the lender's compliance with state foreclosure laws could not overcome its fiduciary duty to the

438 Snowden v. Chase Manhattan Mortgage Corp., 17 Mass. L. Rptr. 27, 2003 WL 22519518 (Mass. Super. Ct. Nov. 5, 2003). *See also In re* Strayton, 360 B.R. 8 (Bankr. D. Mass. 2007) (foreclosing lender must do more than comply with procedures in state statute). *But cf.* Farm Credit Servs. of Am. v. Dougan 704 N.W.2d 24 (S.D. 2005) (lender did not breach the implied covenant of good faith and fair dealing when it refused to grant borrower an extension to make the first payment on the note; express provisions of the loan documents required timely installment payments, and no provision entitled borrowers to extensions as a matter of right).

439 *See generally* § 6.4.5, *infra*.

440 Steven Wechsler, *Through the Looking Glass: Foreclosure by Sale as De Facto Strict Foreclosure—An Empirical Study of Mortgage Foreclosure and Subsequent Resale*, 70 Cornell L. Rev. 850, 875–876 (1985).

441 An equity cushion exists when the value of the secured property exceeds the amount of the mortgage. Bankruptcy cases applying this principle include: *In re* Schuessler, 386 B.R. 458 (Bankr. S.D.N.Y. 2008); *In re* Heath, 79 B.R. 616 (Bankr. E.D. Pa. 1987) (39% equity in property appraised at $32,000); *In re* Breuer, 4 B.R. 499 (Bankr. S.D.N.Y. 1980) (debtor's agreement to cure a default promptly plus cushion of $21,000 were adequate protection); *In re* McAloon, 1 B.R. 766 (Bankr. E.D. Pa. 1980) ($20,000 mortgage on $28,000 property has adequate protection); *In re* Rogers Dev. Corp., 2 B.R. 679 (Bankr. E.D. Va. 1980) (15 to 20% equity cushion gave adequate protection); *In re* Shockley Forest Industries, 5 B.R. 160 (Bankr. N.D. Ga. 1980) (additional security provided collateral which far exceeded claim). *See generally* National Consumer Law Center, Consumer Bankruptcy Law and Practice § 9.7.3.2.2 (9th ed. 2009).

442 Chase Home Mortgage Corp., Clearinghouse No. 49,957 (N.H. Super. Ct. Feb. 24, 1992) (No. 92-E-00026).

443 *See* Chase Home Mortgage Corp., Clearinghouse No. 49,957 (N.H. Super. Ct. Jan. 29, 1992) (No. 92-E-00026) (verified petition to enjoin foreclosure sale and for *ex parte* restraining order).

444 *Id.*

445 Of course, the lender will object. It stands to make a fast profit from a quick turnaround sale.

homeowner to consider a market sale that would obtain the highest price for the property.[446]

If it is not possible to get an injunction from the court to stop the foreclosure to allow a more orderly sale, a chapter 13 bankruptcy filing providing for liquidation of the property may provide a solution.[447] In most cases, filing the petition will stay all proceedings against the property, allowing time for a sale.[448] This option is discussed further in Chapter 9, *infra*.

4.11 State and Local Moratorium and Mediation Programs

4.11.1 General

State and local governments have at various times authorized stays of foreclosures to last for the duration of a particular economic crisis or a natural disaster. Foreclosure moratorium legislation was common during the Great Depression of the 1930s, when twenty-seven states enacted such laws.[449] Property values fell sharply during the Depression and foreclosure sales were producing abysmally low prices. The moratorium laws were seen as a way to delay foreclosure sales, often for several years, until property values improved or other financing options became available.

Moratorium laws are most effective when they work in conjunction with other programs that can produce a concrete solution to the homeowner's payment problem. Many states have established programs that provide direct financial assistance to struggling homeowners. This assistance may be in the form of funds to reinstate a loan in default or the opportunity to refinance into a state guaranteed loan program offering more favorable terms. Some states and localities have authorized across-the-board moratoriums on foreclosures while these financial assistance programs were being implemented. Once the programs are in place, they typically provide for a delay of foreclosure proceedings while the homeowner applies for assistance. These state financial aid programs for homeowners in distress are discussed at § 2.3.3, *supra*.

Another way in which a moratorium can provide concrete help to borrowers is to stay proceedings to allow for mediation between the homeowner and the mortgage holder. Sometimes referred to as a foreclosure "diversion" program, this type of mediation system requires a delay of proceedings in order to allow the negotiations to run their course. Foreclosure mediation programs are discussed in more detail in this section.

Because a foreclosure conducted in violation of a moratorium or mediation requirement should be invalid, it is important that practitioners keep current on the status of any state laws of these types. Also, when seeking to set aside a foreclosure, the practitioner should review the applicable statutory provisions regarding any moratorium or mediation requirement that may have been in effect at the time of the foreclosure.

4.11.2 Constitutional Issues Related to State Moratorium and Mediation Laws—the Supreme Court's **Blaisdell** *and* **Energy Resources** *Decisions*

Moratorium laws alter the preexisting contractual relations between a homeowner and a mortgage holder. They suspend the mortgage holder's right to enforce terms of the note and mortgage as originally negotiated. They may deny access to the state foreclosure remedies that were in effect when the parties entered into the loan transaction. These impositions led some mortgage holders to challenge several of the moratorium statutes enacted during the Great Depression. Mortgage holders argued that these state laws violated the Contracts Clause of the United States Constitution.[450]

The Depression-era foreclosure relief statutes applied in non-judicial as well as in judicial foreclosure states. In traditionally non-judicial foreclosure states, such as California and Minnesota, a homeowner could apply to a court for an order staying a foreclosure. In judicial foreclosure states the statutes gave the courts hearing foreclosure cases authority to grant long-term stays of proceedings on a case-by-case basis. The laws typically allowed courts to stay a scheduled foreclosure sale, or if the sale had already taken place, to stay the post-sale redemption period for an extended time. Many Depression-era statutes authorized the court to require the borrower to pay some form of compensation to the lender as a condition to a long-term stay. The courts could set this compensation in the form of ongoing payments of some or all of the interest coming due, or as payments based on the rental value of the property or its income.[451]

446 Snowden v. Chase Manhattan Mortgage Corp., 17 Mass. L. Rptr. 27, 2003 WL 22519518 (Mass. Super. Ct. Nov. 5, 2003).

447 *See* National Consumer Law Center, Consumer Bankruptcy Law and Practice § 12.6.5 (9th ed. 2009).

448 *See id.* at Ch. 9 (discussion of automatic stay).

449 Osborne on Mortgages § 331 (2d ed. 1979). *See generally Powell on Real Property*, § 37.49 (1968 ed.); G. Glenn, *Mortgages,* vol. II §§ 15–167 (1943); Poteat, *State Legislative Relief for the Mortgage Debtor During the Depression,* 5 Law & Contemp. Probs. 517 (1938); Feller, *Moratory Legislation: A Comparative Study,* 46 Harv. L. Rev. 1061 (1933).

450 "No state shall . . . pass any . . . Law impairing the Obligation of Contracts." U.S. Const. art. I, § 10. *See generally* William L. Prosser, *The Minnesota Mortgage Moratorium*, 7 So. Cal. L. Rev. 353 (1934); Clifford C. Hynning, *Constitutionality of Moratory Legislation,* 12 Chicago-Kent L. Rev. 182 (1934).

451 *See generally* G. Glenn, Mortgages, vol. II, § 154.1 (1943);

In its 1934 ruling in *Home Bldg. & Loan Ass'n v. Blaisdell* the United States Supreme Court upheld a Minnesota foreclosure moratorium statute, and in doing so proclaimed a major revision of Contracts Clause jurisprudence.[452] The Minnesota statute authorized courts to stay non-judicial foreclosure sales and toll the running of the state's post-sale redemption period for up to two years. During this time the state court could set terms of compensation to be paid to the mortgagee as it determined to be fair and equitable.

In *Blaisdell* the Supreme Court ruled that Minnesota's enactment of the moratorium legislation was a valid exercise of the state's police power during a temporary economic crisis. Significantly, the court emphasized that each state had the inherent authority under its police power to alter contract remedies in order to protect the public and the state itself from the harm brought on by widespread economic insecurity. As the court noted, "the reservation of the reasonable exercise of the protective power of the State is read into all contracts."[453]

According to the *Blaisdell* court, the pertinent question to ask when assessing the validity of a particular exercise of a state's police power was "whether the legislation is addressed to a legitimate end and the means taken are reasonable and appropriate to that end."[454] With respect to the Minnesota foreclosure moratorium statute the court considered it a reasonable measure, particularly because it included significant protections for the mortgagees.[455] In addition, the existence of emergency conditions was undisputed and the legislation was limited in time to the period of the crisis.

The standard enunciated by the *Blaisdell* court was a pragmatic, fact-based one that would allow courts to exercise substantial discretion in reviewing Contracts Clause challenges. Courts must weigh the severity of a particular impairment of private contracts against the need to protect the economic and social interests of a much broader public. In later reviews of Depression-era state laws enacted to protect borrowers from the effects of foreclosures, the Supreme Court showed great deference to state legislatures' determinations of the need for particular protections.[456]

One common theme running through the Supreme Court's decisions upholding state statutes that limited lenders' foreclosure remedies was its view that these laws were extensions of the role that state courts had always played in policing mortgage foreclosures.[457] The court emphasized that for centuries state courts had been engaged in a well-recognized practice of applying equitable principles to foreclosures in order to prevent harsh and unfair results. The 1930s state legislation built upon this tradition of active judicial supervision over foreclosures. Therefore, lenders could not justly characterize the new laws as drastic new forms of state regulation.

The Supreme Court revised its *Blaisdell* standard for Contracts Clause review a few decades later in its decision in *Energy Reserves Group, Inc. v. Kansas Power & Light Co.*[458] Here the court upheld a Kansas statute that regulated the prices for intrastate sales of natural gas. The state law did not arise from any particular economic emergency and was not designed to be temporary. The standard that the court outlined in upholding the constitutionality of the Kansas statute remains the controlling test for any Contracts Clause analysis today.[459]

This test asks three questions:

Comment, Moratoria and Stay Laws: Mortgage Moratorium Legislation in California, 30 Cal. L. Rev. 172 (1942); M. Litton, Suits for Interest Under the New York Mortgage Moratorium, 25 Cornell L. Q. 401 (1940); William L. Prosser, The Minnesota Mortgage Moratorium, 7 So. Cal. L. Rev. 353 (1934).

452 290 U.S. 398 (1934). *See* Samuel L. Olken, *Charles Evans Hughes and the Blaisdell Decision: A Historical Study of Contract Clause Jurisprudence*, 72 Or. L. Rev. 513 (1993).

453 Home Bldg. & Loan Ass'n v. Blaisdell, 290 U.S. 398, 443–444, 54 S. Ct. 231 (1934).

454 *Id.* 290 U.S. at 438.

455 *Id.* at 425 (noting that the statute did not "impair the integrity of the mortgage indebtedness," the obligation for interest remained intact, and the mortgagors were required to pay the rental value of the property while they remained in possession).

456 E. New York Sav. Bank v. Hahn, 326 U.S. 230 (1945) (deferring to New York's determination that the need for Depression-related moratorium relief remained effective into the wartime housing conditions). *See also* Gelfert v. Nat'l City Bank of New York, 313 U.S. 221 (1941) (upholding state statute limiting assessment of deficiency judgments after mortgage foreclosures); Honeyman v. Jacobs, 306 U.S. 539 (1939) (same); Richmond Mortgage & Loan Corp. v. Wachovia Bank & Trust Co., 300 U.S. 124 (1937) (same). *But see* W.B. Worthen Co. v. Kavanaugh, 295 U.S. 56 (1935) (striking down Arkansas statute as violative of Contracts Clause, noting that provisions of the statute included: (1) an increase in the minimum period after default and before foreclosure could be initiated from sixty-five days to two and one-half years; (2) a decrease in the statutorily allowed "default penalty" rate from 20% to 3%; (3) suspension of the mortgagor's obligation to pay attorney fees and costs in connection with a foreclosure; and (4) a provision allowing the debtor to remain in possession of the property for four years after foreclosure with no interim protections for lenders).

457 Gelfert v. Nat'l City Bank of New York, 313 U.S. 221, 232, 233 (1941) (upholding New York antideficiency legislation, and observing that "for about two centuries there has been a rather continuous effort through general rule or by appeal to the chancellor in specific cases to prevent the machinery of judicial sales from becoming an instrument of oppression. And so far as mortgage foreclosures are concerned, numerous devices have been employed to safeguard mortgagors from sales which will or may result in mortgagees collecting more than their due."). *See also* Honeyman v. Jacobs, 306 U.S. 539, 543, 544 (1939); Richmond Mortgage Corp. v. Wachovia Bank, 300 U.S. 124, 129, 130 (1937); Home Bldg. & Loan Ass'n v. Blaisdell, 290 U.S. 398, 446, 447 (1934).

458 459 U.S. 400 (1983).

459 *See generally* Alex McBride, *The Constitutionality of and Need for Mortgage Moratoria in the Context of Hurricane Katrina*, 81 Tul. L. Rev. 1303 (Mar. 2007) (discussing development of Contracts Clause jurisprudence up to modern analysis).

(1) Is there in fact a substantial impairment of the creditor's contractual rights?
(2) If yes, is there a significant and legitimate public purpose behind the regulation, such as remedying a broad and general social and economic problem? and
(3) If there is a significant and legitimate public purpose, is the adjustment of the rights and responsibilities of the contracting parties based upon reasonable conditions and of a character appropriate to the public purpose supporting the legislation?[460]

The second and third *Energy Reserves* criteria become part of the evaluation only if the answer to the first threshold question is affirmative—that is, only if the state law does in fact impose a substantial impairment on contract rights.[461] Thus under the three-part standard taken as a whole, a state law *can* significantly impair substantive contract rights and still survive a constitutional challenge. The older distinction in Contracts Clause jurisprudence between impairments of substantive contract rights and impairments that affect only contract remedies is no longer controlling.

Similarly, a finding that the state enacted the law impairing contract rights as a temporary emergency measure may help to sustain the legislation, but the temporary emergency justification is no longer required in order to pass muster under the *Energy Reserves* standard.

Finally, the *Energy Reserves* court emphasized that in deciding whether an impairment to contract rights is substantial, courts should consider whether the area of regulation is one that was already subject to significant government regulation before the new enactment.[462] The longer-standing and more involved the past regulation, the less likely the new statutory limitations will be considered as working a substantial impairment.[463] As mortgage foreclosures have historically been subject to state regulation, particularly by the courts, not all new restrictions on foreclosure rights should even qualify as "substantial" impairments under the first prong of the *Energy Reserves* test.[464]

460 *Id.* 459 U.S. at 411.
461 *Id.* 459 U.S. at 411, 412.
462 *Id.* 459 U.S. at 413.
463 *See, e.g.*, CFCU Cmty. Credit Union v. Hayward, 552 F.3d 253, 267, 268 (2d Cir. 2009) (impairment of creditor's rights by retroactive increase in state's homestead exemption may not be considered substantial because of long history of state regulation of exemptions).
464 *See generally* Richmond Mortgage & Loan Corp. v. Wachovia Bank & Trust Co., 300 U.S. 124, 128, 129 (1937) (mortgage holders have no constitutionally protected right to continuing reliance on a state providing a particular form of mortgage foreclosure remedy; state has power to direct foreclosures from a non-judicial into judicial system regardless of the form of foreclosure allowed when the mortgage was created).

4.11.3 State Moratorium and Mediation Enactments During the 1980s

During the 1980s a rise in farm foreclosures in the Midwest and widespread spikes in unemployment led a number of states and localities to take action to slow foreclosures. Minnesota and Iowa enacted mandatory mediation statutes which required lenders to negotiate with borrowers and certify compliance with the mediation requirement before they could proceed with foreclosures.[465] The Minnesota mediation law allowed a court to authorize a stay of a non-judicial foreclosure for a period of ninety days or until mediation could be concluded. When lenders brought a challenge to the statute on Contracts Clause grounds, an appellate court had little difficulty in sustaining the law.[466]

During the same period state appellate courts struck down three state laws that attempted to place severe limitations on foreclosures of farm properties. Oklahoma had enacted a statute that created an across-the-board prohibition on foreclosures by farm banks. The prohibition lasted for one year. In a narrowly divided opinion, the Oklahoma Supreme Court voided the law, noting that the bar applied across the board to all farm-lending bank foreclosures without a provision for exercise of judicial discretion to set the length of a stay and fashion conditions of payment during the stay.[467] Similarly, the Kansas Supreme Court struck down a statute which set a series of limits on farm foreclosures.[468] These restrictions included a one-year stay of foreclosures and a substantial modification of post-sale redemption standards. These retroactive changes were applicable to cases in which judgments had been entered. Under other new provisions of the Kansas law, borrowers could acquire the properties free and clear after a sale under significantly more lenient terms than existed before. Finally, the Iowa Supreme Court invalidated a state statute applicable to farm homesteads which attempted to create a two-year post-sale redemption period and give debtors more favorable redemption terms after judgment and sale.[469]

465 Iowa Code § 654.15; Minn Stat. Ann. § 583.01 (former citation, repealed as temporary measure). *See generally* Robert M. Lawless, *The American Response to Farm Crises: Procedural Debtor Relief*, 1988 U. Ill. L. Rev. 1037 (1988); Roland C. Amundson & Lewis J. Rotman, *Depression Jurisprudence Revisited: Minnesota's Moratorium on Mortgage Foreclosure*, 10 Wm. Mitchell L. Rev. 805 (1984); Note, 12 Real Est. L.J. 366 (1984); Timothy D. Benton, *Iowa's Mortgage Moratorium Statute: A Constitutional Analysis*, 33 Drake L. Rev. 303 (1983/1984).
466 Laue v. Production Credit Ass'n of Blooming Prairie, 390 N.W.2d 823 (Minn. Ct. App. 1986). *See also* First Nat'l Bank v. Heimke, 407 N.W.2d 344 (1987) (recognizing that the Iowa mandatory mediation statute, like the recent Minnesota law, applied retroactively to existing mortgages, but declining to reach merits of appeal on ripeness grounds).
467 Fed. Land Bank of Wichita v. Story, 756 P.2d 588 (Okla. 1988).
468 Fed. Land Bank of Wichita v. Bott, 732 P.2d 710 (Kan. 1987).
469 Fed. Land Bank of Omaha v. Arnold, 426 N.W.2d 153 (Iowa 1988).

A Connecticut statute enacted in 1983, and still in effect today, allows an unemployed or "underemployed" homeowner against whom a foreclosure action has been brought to apply to a court for an order restructuring a mortgage loan.[470] In restructuring a loan the court may order reduced payments for a period of six months. In directing the restructuring of a loan the court may add to the principal any earned but unpaid interest, taxes, and foreclosure costs and fees. The court may also establish a new "composite interest rate" based on a weighted combination of the original note rate and a "prevailing interest rate" for the debt added to the loan principal. However, there are significant limitations on the relief available under these provisions.[471] They authorize a court to restructure mortgage debt only for homeowners who meet specific criteria for reduced household income, and the statute limits the loan-to-value ratio of any restructured loan.

Finally, in Philadelphia during the early 1980s the county sheriff and presiding judge ordered a stay of foreclosure sales in response to an upsurge in unemployment and foreclosures.[472] Local community groups, labor organizations, and legal services attorneys worked to support the effort as a means to delay foreclosures until the state could enact a comprehensive financial assistance program for distressed homeowners.[473] More recently, a similar coalition worked with the Philadelphia courts to implement a stay of foreclosure sales in conjunction with the development of a foreclosure mediation program.[474]

4.11.4 State and Local Responses to the Current Foreclosure Crisis

The subprime foreclosure crisis that grew with unprecedented severity beginning in 2007 created momentum for state and local governments to look anew at moratoriums and other temporary foreclosure relief measures. Several states enacted laws that added time and notice requirements to existing foreclosure procedures.[475] Other states enacted statutes which added protections for homeowners at risk of foreclosure of high-cost home mortgages.[476]

Beginning in mid-2008 and with increasing frequency thereafter, courts and state legislatures in many parts of the country implemented new residential foreclosure mediation programs designed to encourage parties to agree to alternatives to foreclosure. These programs vary in the degree to which they mandate participation by mortgage holders. They also vary in the manner in which they stay foreclosure proceedings to allow for the completion of negotiations. These aspects of state and local programs are discussed in the subsections that follow.

An effective foreclosure mediation program has the potential to address one of the most troublesome features of the current foreclosure crisis, namely the inability of homeowners to reach a live person with whom they can communicate about options other than foreclosure. The process of mortgage securitization has created a substantial gulf between homeowners and the investment entities that now own many home mortgages. It has become apparent that large-scale modifications of mortgages are essential to controlling the foreclosure crisis. Yet, policymakers and advocates at the federal and state levels repeatedly cite the intransigence of mortgage servicers as a major barrier to increasing the availability of effective loan modifications. State and local mediation programs have attempted with varying degrees of success to implement procedures to address this problem. The mediation programs have been authorized in three basic ways: by state statutes, by directives from the state judiciary, and by administrative orders from local courts. Regardless of the authority for their implementation, all were implemented as temporary measures, due to expire within a fixed number of years.

4.11.5 State Statutes Requiring Foreclosure Mediation

4.11.5.1 General

During 2008, Connecticut and California enacted statutes that required mortgage holders to engage in some form of negotiations with homeowners before proceeding with foreclosures. Under a statute enacted in the same year, New York required a settlement conference before foreclosures

470 Conn. Gen. Stat. § 49-31f.

471 *See, e.g.*, GMAC Mortgage Corp. v. Glenn, 931 A.2d 290 (Conn. App. Ct. 2007) (denying relief to homeowner under Act's provision barring assistance to applicants who had foreclosure action filed against them for any reason over the past seven years).

472 *See generally* NCLC REPORTS *Bankruptcy and Foreclosures Ed.* (July/Aug. 2008) (discussing history of Philadelphia foreclosure moratorium initiatives of 1983, 2004, and 2008).

473 *See* § 2.3.3, *supra* (discussing Pennsylvania Homeowners' Emergency Mortgage Assistance Program (HEMAP)).

474 *See* § 4.11.7, *infra*.

475 *See, e.g.*, Md. Code Ann., Real Prop. § 7-105.1(b)(1), (c)(1) (West) (foreclosure action may not be commenced until later of ninety days after default or forty-five days after service of a notice of intent to foreclose); Mass Gen. Laws ch. 244, § 35A (ninety-day pre-acceleration notice required); N.Y. Real Prop. Acts. Law § 1304 (applicable to certain high-cost, subprime, and nontraditional loans, lender must send notice with required information ninety days before commencement of legal action); N.C. Gen. Stat. § 53-243.11(21) (new notice requirement forty-five days before initial foreclosure filing). *See also* Indymac Fed. Bank FSBV v. Black, 22 Misc. 3d 1115(A), 2009 WL 211787 (table) (N.Y. Sup. Ct. Jan. 23, 2009) (dismissing foreclosure action for failure to comply with New York's new ninety-day notice requirement applicable to certain high-cost loan).

476 *See* § 5.11, *infra* (discussing high-cost loan legislation at the state level).

of certain loans designated under the law as "high cost." In late 2009, New York amended this statute to require settlement conferences in all residential foreclosures. During 2009, Indiana, Maine, Michigan, Nevada, and Oregon also enacted statutes that require servicers to attempt to engage in some form of loss mitigation review before proceeding with foreclosure. Maryland and Vermont enacted foreclosure mediation or conference statutes in early 2010. The circumstances under which negotiations take place under these state enactments vary a great deal from program to program. Their structures are discussed in more detail below. At the time this treatise was published, a number of foreclosure mediation and conference bills were pending in state legislatures around the country. It is likely that more of these laws will appear.

4.11.5.2 California

The California statutory provision, effective September 6, 2008, applies to the state's non-judicial foreclosures.[477] Under the law, the mortgage holder must send a notice to a homeowner thirty days before it takes the initial step in the foreclosure sale process—the filing a notice of default. The notice informs the homeowner of the opportunity for a phone conference with a mortgage holder or its agent. The procedure does not involve a mediator or require participation of a housing counselor. The mortgage holder may proceed with foreclosure thirty days after giving the notice by indicating either that it conferred with the homeowner or made good-faith attempts to do so. The statute does not require that any particular options be considered in a phone conference and does not specify any consequences for the lender's bad-faith noncompliance.

In February 2009 another new California statute added ninety days to the three-month statutory time period that must pass after the filing of a notice of default and before the foreclosure sale.[478] A mortgage holder may be exempted from this supplemental ninety-day waiting period if the state's commissioner of corporations certifies that the lender developed a loan modification system that meets criteria set forth in the statute.[479] This new enactment, like the phone conference requirement, does not create any enforcement mechanism that homeowners can assert against noncomplying mortgage holders. In addition, most large servicers have been able to obtain exemptions from the ninety-day delay requirement.

4.11.5.3 Connecticut

The Connecticut statute directs the state's chief court administrator to implement a statewide foreclosure mediation program, including development of standard forms and rules.[480] Under the initial program rules, the foreclosing mortgage holder was required to attach to the front of a foreclosure complaint a notice to the homeowner describing mediation rights and include a mediation request form. The homeowner had to file the foreclosure mediation request form not more than fifteen days after the return date on the summons, unless the court extended the time. Under the 2009 amendments to the foreclosure mediation statute, borrowers are deemed automatically eligible for mediation. However, to preserve this participation right they must still submit documents indicating an intent to participate in the proceedings. A judgment may not be entered while mediation is pending. Counsel for the mortgage holder must certify compliance with the notice provisions before proceeding with foreclosure. Participation is mandatory for counsel representing the mortgage holder, and the holder's counsel must appear at a mediation session with authority to settle. The mortgage holder must be available by phone or electronic means. The mediation program framework also allows homeowners to pursue applications for financial help under the state's program that provides financial assistance to homeowners in distress.[481]

4.11.5.4 Indiana

Indiana's statute went into effect in July 2009 and provides homeowners with the opportunity to request a settlement conference with the servicer within thirty days of service of a judicial foreclosure complaint.[482] The conference is to take place within sixty days of service of the notice. The statute does not require mediation supervised by a third party. Instead, it allows for a conference during which a servicer or authorized representative of the foreclosing plaintiff confers with a homeowner by phone. The homeowner may appear with counsel or a housing counselor. The statute does not establish specific guidelines for matters to be considered at a conference.

477 Cal. Civ. Code § 2923.5 (operative from Sept. 6, 2008, to Jan. 1, 2013, for residential mortgages made from Jan. 1, 2003, through Dec. 31, 2007). *See generally In re* Morgan-Austin, 2009 WL 780457 (Bankr. N.D. Cal. Feb. 14, 2009) (under express exemption in statute for homeowners in bankruptcy, negotiation requirement does not apply to lender proceeding with foreclosure after bankruptcy court granted relief from stay, but while bankruptcy case still pending).

478 Bill ABX27, signed Feb. 20, 2009, adding Cal. Civ. Code § 2923.52–53, effective May 21, 2009, until Jan. 1, 2011, for first mortgages recorded between Jan. 1, 2003, and Jan. 1, 2008.

479 Cal. Civ. Code § 2923.53.

480 Conn. Gen. Stat. Ann. § 8-265ee, effective July 1, 2008, to July 1, 2010. Information and forms related to program are available at www.jud.ct.gov and www.jud.ct.gov/foreclosure.

481 Conn Gen. Stat. Ann. § 8-265dd.

482 Ind. Code § 32-30-10.5-8.

4.11.5.5 Maine

Maine passed foreclosure mediation legislation in early 2009.[483] The program went into effect on a limited local basis in late 2009 and statewide beginning in January 2010. Maine is a judicial foreclosure state.

Under the Maine statute, a homeowner who has been served with a foreclosure complaint may request a mediation supervised by a court-approved mediator. The statute requires that parties to the mediation conduct a loan modification analysis using the FDIC "loan mod in a box" calculation. Similar to the HAMP methodology but using transparent data entries, this calculation produces a monetary result indicating whether the estimated loss to investors will be greater from completing foreclosure or implementing an affordable loan modification.[484] The statute requires that homeowners participating in mediation receive a copy of this calculation. A mediator's certification that the lender or servicer participated in good faith in mediation, including compliance with the loan modification analysis, is required before foreclosure may proceed.

4.11.5.6 Michigan

Michigan's statutory conference law applies to the state's foreclosure by advertisement proceedings.[485] Under the law, the servicer must give the borrower a notice of the right to request a conference before initiating a foreclosure. The homeowner has fourteen days to request a conference. Homeowners must work through approved housing counselors in order to participate in a conference. Foreclosure is delayed for up to ninety days if a conference is requested. The statute does not provide for third-party supervision over conferences. Servicers have interpreted the statute to permit the conferences to take place by phone. The statute sets general parameters for consideration of a loan modification. If application of these standards produces a recommendation for a specific loan modification and the servicer refuses to implement the modification, the servicer must foreclose through judicial proceedings.

The statutory provisions are not self-enforcing. Instead, they depend upon a homeowner instituting judicial proceedings to enjoin a sale if a servicer proceeds to foreclose without serving the required notice. The homeowner would also have to initiate a lawsuit for an injunction if a servicer proceeds to sale without implementing a loan modification found appropriate under the statutory guidelines.

483 Me. Rev. Stat. Ann. tit. 14, § 6321-A.

484 *See* www.fdic.gov/consumers/loans/loanmod/loanmodguide.html (description and guide to the FDIC loan modification calculation tool).

485 Mich Comp. Laws § 600.3205a.

4.11.5.7 Nevada

Nevada is a non-judicial foreclosure state. The state's foreclosure mediation legislation went into effect in July 2009.[486]

Under the law a trustee foreclosing on a residential property must serve the homeowner with a notice of the availability of mediation. The state judiciary manages the foreclosure mediation program, including training and supervision of mediators. If a homeowner requests mediation, a trustee may not proceed with a sale unless a mediator's certification of the servicer's good faith participation in mediation has been filed in land records. The statute lists several items constituting good faith participation by a servicer. These include submission to the mediator of a loan modification analysis and proof of standing to foreclose. The statute establishes a system for referral of cases to the courts for the imposition of contempt sanctions against mortgage holders who do not participate in good faith.

4.11.5.8 New York

Effective September 1, 2008, a New York court rule required settlement conferences before certain residential foreclosure actions could proceed.[487] The law applied to loans the statute defined as "high cost," "subprime," and "non-traditional."[488] In late 2009 the New York legislature amended the statute to make the conference requirement applicable to all residential foreclosures. The amendments added a good faith participation requirement and prohibited shifting of the servicer's attorney fees for legal work related to a foreclosure settlement conference. Under the law, conferences are mandatory and are to be scheduled within sixty days after filing of the proof of service of the foreclosure complaint.[489] The plaintiff must appear for the conference with an attorney authorized to settle and the mortgage holder must be available by phone or video conference. The court may appoint counsel for unrepresented defendants.

4.11.5.9 Oregon

An Oregon statute went into effect in June 2009 requiring foreclosing servicers to notify homeowners that they may request a loan modification.[490] The notice informs homeowners of a procedure for submitting the request and sets a

486 Nev. 2009 Enacted Assembly Bill No. 149 (2009).

487 N.Y. C.P.L.R. 3408 (McKinney), applicable to loans created between Jan. 1, 2003, and Sept. 1, 2008.

488 *See* N.Y. Real Prop. Acts. Law § 1304 (defining thresholds for high-cost, subprime, and nontraditional loans).

489 *See* Indymac Fed. Bank F.S.B. v. Black, 22 Misc. 3d 1115(A), 2009 WL 211787 (table) (N.Y. Sup. Ct. Jan. 23, 2009) (dismissing foreclosure action due to plaintiff's failure to comply with conference and notice requirements).

490 Or. Enrolled Senate Bill 628 (2009).

timeline for the servicer's response. The servicer must file an affidavit in land records describing compliance with this requirement before a sale may take place. The statute does not create a system for supervision over conferences by any neutral third parties. There is no requirement for in-person appearances, so that phone contact between a servicer and homeowner would constitute a conference. The statute gives servicers a degree of unilateral discretion to exempt homeowners from the conference requirement.

4.11.6 Statewide Judicial Directives for Foreclosure Mediation

4.11.6.1 General

During 2008, in response to the surge in foreclosures filed in their respective states, the supreme courts of Ohio and New Jersey promulgated general rules or protocols authorizing local courts to develop foreclosure mediation programs. The supreme courts developed model rules and forms but left discretion to county courts to modify the recommended procedures as they saw fit. Generally, these protocols diverted foreclosures into the local courts' established mediation programs used in a wide variety of civil cases.[491] In 2009, the Supreme Court of Florida and the president judge of the Delaware Superior Court also issued administrative orders creating uniform statewide foreclosure mediation systems.

4.11.6.2 Delaware

Effective August 31, 2009 an administrative order of the president judge of the Delaware Superior Court set in place a statewide system for foreclosure mediation.[492] Under the program guidelines homeowners may request a mediation conference which stays entry of judgment in a judicial foreclosure case for up to sixty days. The homeowner must work with a counselor to formulate a loan modification proposal. If, based on factors such as the borrower's income, the homeowner and counselor cannot propose a modification that meets program guidelines, the process terminates and foreclosure can proceed. If the homeowner can make a proposal meeting the guidelines, the servicer must respond. The system anticipates a period of negotiations, with an actual mediation session scheduled only after negotiations have deadlocked. Eligibility for the state's homeowner relief program (DEMAP) can be considered in the context of mediations.

4.11.6.3 Florida

During 2008 and 2009, several Florida circuit courts implemented foreclosure mediation and conference programs. These programs varied in structure, with some ordering mediation in all cases and others requiring a homeowner to opt in. The Florida Supreme Court conducted reviews of these programs during 2009 with the goal of coming up with a uniform protocol to be mandated statewide. The Florida Supreme Court issued this directive at the end of 2009.[493] The court's accompanying report noted that as of the end of 2009 there were 456,000 foreclosure cases pending in the Florida courts. Under the model procedure homeowner participation is automatic, with exclusion occurring if the homeowner does not submit information to a counselor in preparation for a scheduled mediation session. The program anticipates court supervision over mediations, with courts having authority to sanction servicers who do not appear with appropriate authority to settle. Servicers must pay a $750 fee that goes toward costs of the program and mediator fees. This cost, in turn, may be included in a judgment as costs assessed against the homeowner. A mediation manager must certify compliance with mediation before a judgment may be entered. Mediation is to be concluded within 120 days of the filing of the complaint. The directive does not require consideration of any specific loan modification analysis, but does require that the servicer produce evidence of current ownership of the note and mortgage.

4.11.6.4 New Jersey

New Jersey's program went into effect for cases filed after January 5, 2009.[494] The New Jersey procedure requires that a notice of the right to request mediation be served with the summons and complaint. Along with these documents the homeowner receives financial forms to complete and referral information for housing counselors. Mediation is scheduled when the homeowner completes the financial information. New Jersey homeowners can request mediation up to the time of sale. However, ongoing proceedings, including

491 The chief judge of the New York State Unified Courts issued report in June 2008 establishing a "Statewide Program for Residential Owner-Occupied Foreclosures." *See* www.courts.state.ny.us/press/pr2008_4.shtml. These procedures were not fully implemented after the legislature enacted the mandatory settlement conference provisions for high-cost loans, discussed in the preceding subsection.

492 Administrative Directive of the President Judge of the Superior Court of the State of Delaware No. 2009-3 (Aug. 31, 2009), *available at* http://courts.delaware.gov/Courts/Superior%20Court/pdf/?Administrative_Directive_2009-3.pdf.

493 *In re* Final Report and Recommendations on Residential Mortgage Foreclosure Cases, No. AOSC09-54 (Fla. Sup. Ct. Admin. Order Dec. 28, 2009), *available at* www.floridasupremecourt.org/clerk/adminorders/2009/AOSC09-54.pdf.

494 Administrative Office of the Courts, New Jersey Foreclosure Mediation (Oct. 2009), *available at*www.judiciary.state.nj.us/civil/foreclosure/11290_foreclosure_med_info.pdf.

entry of judgment, are not stayed automatically pending mediation. Homeowners may obtain a stay of the sale by motion.

4.11.6.5 Ohio

The Ohio Supreme Court promulgated a foreclosure mediation model for county common pleas courts to use as a basis for developing their own mediation programs.[495] Several Ohio county courts have adopted procedures under these guidelines. These include programs for Cuyahoga County (Cleveland), Franklin County (Columbus), Lucas County (Toledo), and Summit County (Akron).[496] Under the statewide guidelines, a form for requesting mediation is served with the complaint. Upon receipt of a borrower's request for mediation, the court sends questionnaires to the borrower and the mortgage holder. The borrower completes and returns the forms along with required financial documentation. The mortgage holder must provide a payment history and evidence of its standing to proceed. The local court's mediation department monitors the collection of data needed to evaluate the case for mediation. When questionnaires and documents have been received, a judge or magistrate may review the request for mediation and the documents submitted with the questionnaires. At this stage, based on its document review, the court may decline to schedule the case for mediation. If the court orders mediation, the case will proceed along the court's alternative dispute resolution procedures. The mortgage holder and its attorney must participate in the sessions. During the pendency of mediation there is no automatic stay of the homeowner's time to answer the complaint. Instead, the homeowner must formally request a stay by filing a routine motion.

4.11.7 Local Court Initiatives

The rules of certain state court systems allow local courts considerable leeway in scheduling related to cases on their dockets. Some local courts have used this authority to initiate their own procedures for stays and mediation in residential foreclosures. The Philadelphia courts have led the way in using this authority to promote the resolution of foreclosure cases. Pennsylvania law gives the president judge of a county common pleas court broad authority to "supervise the judicial business of the court" and "promulgate all administrative rules and regulations" related to adjudication of civil cases.[497] As discussed above, in 1983 the Philadelphia courts used this authority to stay foreclosures pending the implementation of a statewide financial assistance program for homeowners facing foreclosure. In 2004 the court again stayed foreclosures for a limited time under this rule. Most recently, by an order of April 16, 2008, the president judge of the Philadelphia Common Pleas Court implemented a "Residential Mortgage Foreclosure Diversion Pilot Program."[498] Under the order, sheriff sales were stayed pending completion of conciliation conferences.[499] Mortgage holders must file certificates of completion of conciliation before a foreclosure sale can proceed.

Under the current Philadelphia procedure conciliation sessions are scheduled automatically when the foreclosing plaintiff lists on an initial civil court cover sheet that the property is owner-occupied. This designation triggers a case management order. A conciliation hearing notice is then served upon the homeowner along with the complaint. The homeowner is expected to work with a housing counselor to complete and share documents. The housing counselor helps the homeowner to prepare a proposal for the mortgage holder to review before the conciliation conference. For cases not resolved before a session, a civil case manager appointed by the court conducts the conciliation meeting. So long as the homeowner complies with the conciliation procedures, foreclosure proceedings, including entry of judgment and sheriff sale, are stayed until a certification is filed that the conciliation process has concluded. If an agreement is not reached at the conference, an order issues setting an additional session or authorizing the mortgage holder to proceed with the foreclosure. The program has produced significant rates of participation by homeowners, due in part to a system for direct door-to-door contacts by community groups to reach out to homeowners who have received notices of conciliation sessions.

In addition to Philadelphia, county common pleas courts in other Pennsylvania counties have instituted their own foreclosure mediation programs.[500] Acting under similar authority granted to local courts, judicial districts serving Santa Fe, New Mexico and Lousville, Kentucky initiated their own foreclosure mediation programs during 2009. New Mexico and Kentucky are judicial foreclosure states. The city of Providence, Rhode Island established a mediation program by ordinance in 2009. This program applies to non-judicial foreclosures on properties in that city.[501] The

495 Foreclosure Mediation Resources, www.supremecourtofohio.gov/foreclosure (model procedures and forms).

496 *See, e.g.,* Cuyahoga County Common Pleas court program documents at www.cp.cuyahogacounty.us/internet/CourtDocs/ForeclosureMediation.pdf. As of early 2010 state legislation was under consideration to make similar programs mandatory statewide in Ohio.

497 42 Pa. Cons. Stat. Ann. § 325(e) (West).

498 *See* http://fjd.phila.gov/mfdp.

499 *Id. See* Joint Gen. Court Regulation No. 2008-01. *See generally* NCLC REPORTS *Bankruptcy and Foreclosures Ed.* (July/Aug. 2008) (describing history and procedures under Philadelphia's foreclosure moratorium and mediation programs).

500 These include the courts for Allegheny County (Pittsburgh), Northampton County (Easton/Bethlehem), and Bucks County (suburban Philadelphia).

501 Text of the Providence, Rhode Island ordinance is available at: www.psh.com/stuff/contentmgr/files/0/c86431439116cc

city requires filing of certification of compliance with mediation as a condition to transfer of title of foreclosed properties.

4.11.8 *Assessing the Effectiveness of Foreclosure Mediation Programs*

4.11.8.1 General

Foreclosure mediation programs have the potential to address some of the major problems related to the current foreclosure crisis, particularly in forcing servicers to consider reasonable alternatives to the foreclosure of overvalued securitized mortgages. Mediation programs typically receive strong support from the judiciary, from local pro bono attorney organizations, and from the general public. With the increased role of the federal government in promoting loan modifications, an effective mediation program can be a useful means to hold mortgage holders and servicers accountable for compliance with their obligations under these federal programs as well as with their own public relations pronouncements. To date there has been little data produced to show how effective any of the ongoing mediation programs have been in providing lasting solutions for homeowners facing foreclosure. Participation rates vary significantly from program to program. Few programs keep data on the specific nature of the agreements reached through mediation. Particularly with respect to loan modifications, no programs have kept systematic track of the details of modifications reached through mediation. It has not yet been possible to assess whether the modification agreements reached through mediation programs are truly helping to reduce indebtedness and monthly payment obligations of homeowners.

Some of the more recent statewide programs, such as those implemented by statutes in Maine and Nevada, have included concrete obligations for participating servicers. For example, the Maine program mandates use of a transparent net present value test to evaluate the option of an affordable loan modification. The Nevada program, operating in a state with a high foreclosure rate and a non-judicial foreclosure law, incorporates potentially strong enforceable standards for consideration of loan modifications. The Vermont statute requires a review of HAMP eligibility through mediation. The Maine, Nevada, Vermont, and the recently amended New York statute now all incorporate a good faith participation requirement along with some form of judicial oversight over this obligation.

27543693ca686b2082/formdocs/prov_foreclosure_and_eviction_odinances.pdf (Deutsche Bank filed a lawsuit against the City of Providence in early 2010 seeking to invalidate the ordinance based on the claim that the City lacked authority under its local government powers to regulate foreclosures contrary to the uniform statewide procedures enacted by the legislature.).

When advocates seek to develop and implement a foreclosure mediation program, they may wish to focus on certain components that will make favorable outcomes more likely. These features include: (1) a clear set of obligations placed upon all participating servicers and mortgage holders; (2) procedures that encourage homeowners to participate; and (3) a method to evaluate the concrete results reached in cases that have gone through the mediation system.

4.11.8.2 The Mortgage Holder/Servicer Obligations

Among the crucial obligations that the program must place upon servicers is the production of all relevant documents in their control. These include the documentation necessary to show that the entity claiming the right to foreclose actually has standing to do so. The servicer must provide all pertinent payment history, origination, assignment, and valuation documents. A major focus of mediation should be upon determining whether an affordable loan modification will impose a less severe loss on the mortgage holder than a foreclosure. For this reason, the mediation rules should require the mortgage holder to prepare a net present value analysis similar to those used in federal programs, such as under the FDIC or HAMP guidelines.[502] Finally, the program must impose consequences on mortgage holders who do not cooperate in good faith to ensure full consideration of a loan modification and other options. At a minimum, mortgage holders who do not cooperate in good faith to provide data for these calculations or who fail to have authorized representatives available for negotiations should not be permitted to proceed with foreclosures.

4.11.8.3 Encouraging Homeowner Participation

Mediation programs can incorporate several procedures that facilitate the broadest possible participation by homeowners. The rules should not restrict homeowners to a narrow window of time for making a request for mediation. For example, limiting the time for requests to the inception of the foreclosure proceeding unnecessarily excludes many homeowners. Instead the rules should permit homeowners to request mediation until the time of sale. Stays of proceedings should be automatic, lasting until the mortgage holder shows it has complied with its obligations under the mediation program. Based on the experiences in programs such as Philadelphia's, the better procedure appears to be to issue an order initiating the mediation process automatically at the commencement of the foreclosure proceeding and simultaneously schedule a session for a specific date. Similarly, in Philadelphia a practice of follow-up door-to-door

502 *See* § 2.8.1.1, *supra*.

contact with eligible homeowners has contributed to high homeowner participation rates. Finally, programs need to ensure that mediators, housing counselors, and pro bono attorneys have adequate training. Implementing these procedures can bring with it a substantial cost to financially strapped government entities. However, these costs need to be considered in relation to the significant external costs, including the burdens imposed upon state and local government, when waves of foreclosures proceed unchecked.

4.11.8.4 Tracking Results of Mediation

The mediation system should require that participants consider a list of specific alternatives to foreclosure. These alternatives may include the standard loss mitigation options of a repayment or forbearance agreement and a short sale, but must also include consideration of loan modifications for homeowners who wish to keep their homes. By the conclusion of the mediation period the participants should be able to complete a checklist and document that they have considered each of these options. If a settlement is reached, the participants should have a record of the terms agreed upon. If the settlement involved a loan modification, the parties should be required to provide a summary of the terms. For cases in which a servicer or mortgage holder rejected a loan modification that would have produced a less severe loss for investors than a foreclosure, the homeowner should come out of the mediation with a record of the servicer's decision. This record can serve as the basis for the homeowner's argument that a court should exercise its equitable powers to restrain a foreclosure that is grossly unfair and unnecessarily harms investors and the homeowner. If the servicer is a participant in the HAMP program, the rejection of a modification that is appropriate under the program guidelines should clearly preclude that servicer from foreclosing.

4.11.9 Judicial Enforcement of Conference Statutes: New York and California

State laws mandating foreclosure mediations, conferences, or settlement discussions will benefit homeowners facing foreclosure so long as lenders know that courts will enforce the requirements. If statutes are drafted without express language prohibiting foreclosures in the event of noncompliance with program rules, courts must decide whether the legislature intended that the statutes be judicially enforceable. In judicial foreclosure states, questions of enforceability arise in the context of opposition to entry of judgment or a motion to dismiss a foreclosure action. In non-judicial foreclosure states, the homeowner will be forced to file an action for injunctive relief to stop or set aside a foreclosure sale, or possibly to recover monetary damages after an improperly conducted foreclosure. Over the past year courts in New York, a judicial foreclosure state, and California, where non-judicial foreclosures predominate, addressed some of these issues, with conflicting results.

As originally enacted, Rule 3408 of the New York Civil Practice Rules and Laws, effective October 1, 2008, applied only to high-cost, subprime, or "nontraditional" loans as defined by New York Real Property Actions and Proceedings Law § 1304. Amendments to Rule 3408 enacted in late 2009 expanded the conference requirement to apply to all foreclosures of borrowers' residences. New York courts strictly enforced the pre-amendment version of Rule 3408. For example, in *Indymac Federal Savings Bank F.S.B. v. Black,* the court refused to allow entry of a foreclosure judgment and *sua sponte* dismissed the lender's action because the application for judgment did not include an affirmation detailing the basis for the lender's claim that the loan was exempt from the conference requirement.[503] The court viewed Rule 3408 as a remedial statute to be liberally construed to carry out its purpose. Accordingly, a borrower should be deemed to qualify for a conference absent conclusive evidence to the contrary. Similarly, in *Butler Capital Corporation v. Cannistra,*[504] the court refused to allow a foreclosure sale and ordered a settlement conference where the lender's application to proceed to sale did not include "evidentiary proof" that the loan in question was not subprime and that the property was not the borrower's residence. According to the court, conclusory statements from the lender's attorney that the loan was exempt would not suffice. The clear legislative intent favored denial of foreclosure and ordering a conference: "In keeping with the obvious homeowner-protective legislative intent of the relevant foreclosure statutes, the Court errs on the side of those protections."[505]

In the non-judicial foreclosure context California Civil Code § 2923.5 requires that a lender attempt to contact a defaulted borrower prior to foreclosure and explore alternatives that might avoid the loss of the home. Specifically, the "mortgagee, beneficiary or authorized agent" must "contact the borrower in person or by telephone in order to assess the borrower's financial situation and explore options for the borrower to avoid foreclosure."[506] The statute goes on to

503 Indymac Fed. Bank F.S.B. v. Black, 2009 WL 211787 (N.Y. Sup. Ct. Jan. 23, 2009).

504 891 N.Y.S.2d 238, 2009 WL 3834395 (N.Y. Sup. Ct. Oct. 8, 2009).

505 *Id.* at *5. *See also* GRP Loan, L.L.C. v. Ivery, 886 N.Y.S.2d 317 (Sup. Ct. 2009) (noting the benefits to courts and the community from the conferences, holding that a request for a conference in a foreclosure action "should be carefully considered on its merits regardless of whether it falls within the ambit of the Subprime Lending Reform Act."). *But see* Onewest Bank F.S.B. v. Berry, 2009 WL 3417852 (N.Y. Sup. Ct. Oct. 23, 2009) (declining to vacate default judgment based on homeowner's request for conference in case involving non-subprime, high-cost loan).

506 Cal. Civ. Code § 2923.5(a)(2) (West).

require that the lender's notice of default filed in land records include a declaration "from the mortgagee, beneficiary, or authorized agent" of compliance with section 2923.5, including that the lender attempted "with due diligence to contact the borrower as required by this section."[507]

The California courts, unlike those in New York, have divided over the question of whether a homeowner may assert noncompliance with the conference statute as grounds to prevent or overturn a foreclosure sale.[508] Looking beyond the question of direct enforceability of the statute, the court in *Nool v. HOMEQ Servicing*,[509] suggested an alternative that may offer an appropriate option for enforcing the conference requirement. While the *Nool* court held that the statutory provisions standing alone were not enforceable through a private right of action, the court appropriately pointed out that the borrower could have brought an action under California Business and Professions Code § 19200, which supports a private right of action for "any practices forbidden by law."[510]

Some California courts have placed further limits on enforcement of the conference requirement of section 2923.5, holding that California's tender rule applies to any action to enforce the conference statute.[511] The tender rule requires that borrowers challenging a non-judicial foreclosure sale in California must tender the amount of the lender's secured indebtedness in order to maintain a cause of action asserting any irregularity in sale procedures. Another California court improperly held that the Home Owner's Act of 1933 (HOLA) preempts section 2923.5 as to federal savings associations regulated by the Office of Thrift Supervision.[512] Section 2923.5 clearly deals with foreclosure procedures. It does not mandate changes to loan terms. As part of the state's traditional regulation of mortgage foreclosures, the statute is not preempted by federal statutes or by actions of agencies acting under federal banking laws.

A useful discussion of court enforcement of an order for participation in mediation is set forth in the bankruptcy court's decision in *In re A.T. Reynolds & Sons, Inc.*[513] Wells Fargo, the creditor in *Reynolds,* appeared for a court-ordered mediation through a representative who did not have authority to consider a full range of settlement options. The representative attended the mediation "prepared only to repeat a pre-conceived mantra that indicated that Wells Fargo was not open to any compromise that would involve 'taking a single dollar out of their pocket.' "[514] The court found that the refusal to consider the costs and benefits of various options and the creditor's general obstructionist behavior constituted a violation of the court's mediation referral order and sanctioned the creditor.

4.12 Protections from Foreclosure Available Under the Servicemembers Civil Relief Act

4.12.1 Introduction

The Servicemembers Civil Relief Act (SCRA)[515] provides special protections for military service personnel on active duty and their dependents. The SCRA was signed into law on December 19, 2003, and is a complete revision of the Soldiers' and Sailors' Civil Relief Act (SSCRA)of 1940.[516] The new law preserves or expands many of the protections available under the original law and restates or clarifies certain key issues. A number of states have similar laws.[517]

Among the most significant protections that the Act provides are limitations on the foreclosure of real property owned by servicemembers on active duty. The Act also provides for protections against default judgments, tolling of the statute of limitations, a reduction of the interest rate on pre-active duty obligations to 6%, restrictions on eviction from residential property, and the right to terminate residential or vehicle leases. The military is responsible for providing written notice to servicemembers of the benefits available under the Act.[518] Lenders are also responsible for

507 Cal. Civ. Code § 2923.5(b) (West).

508 *Compare* Ortiz v. Accredited Home Lenders, Inc., 639 F. Supp. 2d 1159, 1166 (S.D. Cal. 2009) (refusing to dismiss borrower's action for monetary damages, agreeing with borrower that "the California legislature would not have enacted this 'urgency' legislation, intended to curb high foreclosure rates in the state, without any accompanying enforcement mechanism.") *with* Kuoha v. Equifirst Corp., 2009 WL 3248105 (S.D. Cal. Oct. 7, 2009) (no private right of action for damages resulting from alleged violation of § 2923.5); Gaitan v. Mortgage Elec. Registration Sys., 2009 WL 3244729 (C.D. Cal. Oct. 5, 2009) (rejecting claims for monetary damages and an order setting sale aside, holding statute "contains no language that indicates any intent whatsoever to create a private right of action."); Nool v. HOMEQ Servicing, 653 F. Supp. 2d 1047 (E.D. Cal. 2009) (dismissing claim for money damages); Anaya v. Advisors Lending Group, 2009 WL 2424037 (E.D. Cal. Aug. 5, 2009) (rejecting claims for damages and order enjoining sale).

509 653 F. Supp. 2d 1047 (E.D. Cal. 2009).

510 *Id.* at n.2.

511 Delgada v. Bank of Am. Corp., 2009 WL 4163525 (E.D. Cal. Nov. 23, 2009); Keen v. American Home Mortgage Servicing, 664 F. Supp. 2d 1086 (E.D. Cal. 2009).

512 Murillo v. Aurora Loan Servs. L.L.C., 2009 WL 2160579 (N.D. Cal. July 17, 2009).

513 424 B.R. 76 (Bankr. S.D.N.Y. 2010).

514 *Id.* at *3.

515 50 U.S.C. app. §§ 501–596.

516 50 U.S.C. app. §§ 501–593. *See, e.g.*, Watkins v. Sands, 2005 WL 1377419 (Cal. Ct. App. June 10, 2005) (unpublished) (the 2003 law, unlike the 1940 version, applies to administrative as well as judicial proceedings).

517 *See* National Consumer Law Center, Collection Actions, Chapter 7, note 13 (2008 and Supp.) (listing and summarizing similar state laws).

518 50 U.S.C. app. §§ 515, 515a.

providing written notice of the SCRA's mortgage-related provisions to borrowers who are forty-five days late on their mortgage.[519] Courts construed the original SSCRA liberally to protect members of the armed forces, and courts have been interpreting the SCRA with similar liberality.[520] As of the printing of this treatise, several bills proposing to add to or enhance SCRA protections for military service personnel and their spouses had been referred to committee for review.[521]

Since the rewritten law preserves the substance of the original SSCRA, decisions under this former law remain relevant. A detailed discussion of the Servicemembers Civil Relief Act is contained in Chapter 7 of NCLC's *Collection Actions* (2008 and Supp.). This discussion will focus on sections of the Act providing relief to servicemembers facing foreclosure of mortgages or deeds of trust, or forfeiture of land installment contracts.

4.12.2 Who Is Protected by the Act?

The Act applies to members of the uniformed services on active duty. The uniformed services include the armed forces (Army, Navy, Air Force, Marine Corps, and Coast Guard), and the commissioned corps of both the National Oceanic and Atmospheric Administration and the Public Health Service.[522] Members of the National Guard who are called to active service authorized by the President or Secretary of Defense for more than thirty consecutive days for the purpose of responding to a national emergency,[523] reservists ordered to report for military service,[524] persons ordered to report for induction under the Military Selective Service Act (50 U.S.C. app. §§ 451–473),[525] and United States citizens serving with allied forces[526] are also entitled to the Act's protections.

Active duty includes full-time training, annual training duty, and attendance at a military school while in active military service.[527] Active duty also includes periods of time that a servicemember is absent from duty on account of sickness, wounds, leave, or other lawful cause,[528] but not periods of time the servicemember is AWOL or confined to military prison.[529]

The dependents and co-obligors of servicemembers are entitled to many of the protections of the Act.[530] In many cases, however, the dependent or co-obligor must obtain a court order for protections that are automatic for service-

519 Dep't of Hous. & Urban Dev., Mortgagee Letter 06-28 (Nov. 20, 2006).

520 *See, e.g.*, Bank of Nova Scotia v. George, 2008 WL 501263 (D. V.I. Feb. 15, 2008); Merrill v. Beard, 2007 WL 461469 (N.D. Ohio Feb. 7, 2007) (in setting aside default judgments courts strictly construe requirements of Act in favor of servicemembers); Miller v. Beard, 2007 WL 461469 (N.D. Ohio Feb. 7, 2007) (in setting aside default judgment courts strictly construe requirements of Act in favor of servicemembers); Sprinkle v. SB&C Ltd., 472 F. Supp. 2d 1235 (W.D. Wash. 2006) (acknowledging expansive purpose of protections under Act; construing requirement for affidavit of non-military service to apply to garnishment proceeding); Linscott v. Vector Aerospace, 2006 WL 240529 (D. Or. Jan. 31, 2006) (citing principle of liberal construction and finding private right of action under § 537 of the Act, barring enforcement of chattel liens); State *ex rel.* Estate of Perry, 168 S.W.3d 577 (Mo. Ct. App. 2005) (Act's provisions on tolling of statutes of limitations are to be liberally construed).

521 One bill proposes to amend § 303 of the SCRA, which currently allows a court to invalidate a sale of foreclosure of the servicemember's property made within ninety days after the termination of military service. The proposed amendment would additionally allow surviving spouses of servicemembers killed in Operation Iraqi Freedom or Operation Enduring Freedom the benefit of a one-year moratorium on sale or foreclosure of their property. *See* H.R. 4664, 111th Cong. (introduced and referred to House Committee on Veterans' Affairs, Feb. 23, 2010).

Another bill proposes to allow the U.S. Attorney General to commence a civil action regarding patterns or practices of violating SCRA and a private right of action for any person to intervene in the civil action. *See* H.R. 3949, 111th Cong. (received in Senate Nov. 4, 2009 and referred to Committee on Veteran's Affairs).

522 50 U.S.C. app. § 511. *But see In re* Gaddy, 2004 WL 2044107 (Bankr. D. Kan. Apr. 12, 2004) (Act's protections do not apply to civilian employees of a private contractor engaged in support of uniformed servicemembers in Iraq).

523 50 U.S.C. app. § 511(2)(A)(ii).

524 50 U.S.C. app. § 516; *In re* Marriage of Brazas, 662 N.E.2d 559 (Ill. App. Ct. 1996) (trial court abused discretion under the pre-2003 version of the Act by entering judgment against defendant reservist while he was on duty). *See* Hurley v. Deutsche Bank Trust Co., 2009 WL 701006, at *5 (W.D. Mich. Mar. 13, 2009) (servicemember entitled to SCRA protection from non-judicial mortgage foreclosure from time when his National Guard unit was ordered to active duty, not from when he received his individual order).

525 *Id.*

526 50 U.S.C. app. § 514.

527 10 U.S.C. § 101(d)(1). *But cf.* Donahou v. Presidential Limousine & Auto Sales, Inc., 2007 WL 1229342 (W.D. Ark. Apr. 24, 2007) (active duty does not include eight-month "Delayed Entry" period between time servicemember enlisted and time he reported for duty; he had no military duties during this time and was able to maintain civilian employment).

528 50 U.S.C. app. § 511(2)(C). *See, e.g.*, Secretary of Hous. & Urban Dev. v. McClenan, 4 Misc. 3d 1027(A), 798 N.Y.S.2d 348 (Civ. Ct. N.Y. 2004) (active duty servicemember receiving medical treatment pending deployment is protected by Act).

529 Reed v. Albaaj, 723 N.W.2d 50 (Minn. Ct. App. 2006) (Act does not apply to servicemember while incarcerated in military prison for crime committed while on active duty); *In re* Marriage of Hampshire, 934 P.2d 58 (Kan. 1997) (interpreting pre-2003 version of Act not to protect soldier who was AWOL or in military prison at the time of proceedings which led to default judgment for child support).

530 50 U.S.C. app. § 538 (general extension of protections to dependents); 50 U.S.C. app. § 513 (protections for comakers, guarantors, and persons secondarily liable). *See, e.g.*, Small v. Kulesa, 204 S.W.3d 99 (Ark. Ct. App. 2005) ("[T]he protection Congress intended would be a sham if it did not extend to the co-tenant spouse of a service member whose property taxes are delinquent.").

members.[531] The Act's definition of "dependent" includes not only a spouse or child, but also any individual for whom the servicemember provided more than one-half of the individual's support for 180 days immediately preceding an application for relief.[532] Thus, the dependent does not have to be an individual who resided in the servicemember's household prior to active duty and need not be a family member. Dependents may seek the basic protections under the Act related to mortgages, installment contracts, and evictions.[533] To be eligible for relief, the dependent must show that his or her ability to comply with a contractual obligation has been materially affected by the servicemembers military duty.[534] The extension of the Act's protections to co-obligors is subject to the court's discretion. A court that limits enforcement of an obligation or proceeding for the benefit of a servicemember may do the same for a comaker or any other person primarily or secondarily liable for the obligation.[535] The Act may also protect a small business owned by a servicemember.[536]

4.12.3 Protections Against Foreclosure

The Act provides important protections for servicemembers facing foreclosure while on active duty. The relief provided by the Act applies to a servicemember who originated a mortgage, trust deed or security in the nature of a mortgage prior to beginning active duty, and for which the servicemember is still obligated.[537] Under the pre-2003 version of the Act, ownership was interpreted to include an equitable or legal interest.[538]

Unless the protection is waived by a servicemember, a court order is required prior to a foreclosure, sale or seizure of property while the servicemember is on active duty or within ninety days after the end of active duty.[539] In 2008, Congress temporarily amended this provision to extend the period of time required for a court order. Lenders must obtain a court order within nine months, instead of ninety days, after the end of active duty.[540] Unless extended, this provision expires December 31, 2010, after which the previous ninety-day period is reinstated.[541]

SCRA section 553(c)'s prohibition on foreclosure sales without court approval is especially helpful in the states where lenders are permitted to foreclose on the mortgage without court action. In these jurisdictions, a court order provides added protection as foreclosure in these states tends to proceed swiftly. In addition, a creditor or debt collector who threatens to foreclose in violation of the Act is likely to be in violation of the FDCPA or a state debt collection or UDAP statute.[542] A foreclosure in violation of this provision may render the sale invalid and subject the lender to criminal prosecution.[543]

A U.S. district court recently enforced the provisions of section 533(c) strictly in invalidating a non-judicial foreclosure sale conducted while the mortgagor was on active military duty in Iraq.[544] In declaring the sale void the court rejected a number of creditor defenses. First, the creditor pointed out that the servicemember failed to show that he had given the creditor notice of his active duty status before the sale. The servicemember had taken no affirmative steps to stop the sale before it took place. In response, the court contrasted section 553(c) with other SCRA sections which expressly require that the servicemember give a creditor notice of the call to military duty.[545] Moreover, it would contravene the clear purpose of section 553(c) to require a servicemember to seek judicial relief to stop a foreclosure sale that the SCRA expressly declares to be invalid.[546]

531 *See* Umstead v. Chase Manhattan Mortgage Co., 2005 WL 2233554 (W.D. Va. Sept. 13, 2005) (family member has standing to seek stay or modified payment schedule for servicemember's mortgage if she can show that she is a dependent, and that her ability to comply with payment schedule has been "materially affected" by homeowner's service). *But see* Rodriguez v. American Express, 2006 WL 908613 (E.D. Cal. Apr. 7, 2006) (provisions for reduction of interest protects spouse only if account is joint); *In re* Cockerham, 336 B.R. 592 (Bankr. S.D. Ga. 2005) (co-debtor spouse of servicemember not entitled to stay where court did not stay creditor's attempt to repossess vehicle of servicemember).

532 50 U.S.C. app. § 511(4).

533 50 U.S.C. app. § 538 (dependents may apply to courts to seek all forms of relief provided under §§ 531-537 of the Act).

534 50 U.S.C. app. § 538.

535 50 U.S.C. app. § 513.

536 Linscott v. Vector Aerospace, 2006 WL 1310511 (D. Or. May 12, 2006) (subchapter S corporation; servicemember owner had personally guaranteed his company's debts). *See also* Rodriquez v. American Express, 2006 WL 908613 (E.D. Cal. Apr. 7, 2006) (sole proprietor of "small construction company").

537 50 U.S.C. app. § 533(a).

538 *See* Fourth Nat'l Bank v. Hill, 314 P.2d 312 (Kan. 1957) (the term "owned" includes equitable as well as legal interest in the property); Title Guarantee & Trust Co. v. Zenker, 48 N.Y.S.2d 338 (Sup. Ct. 1944). *But see* Goodwin v. Gerling, 239 S.W.2d 352 (Mo. 1951) (soldier had a claim assertable in equity against record owner of property as opposed to an "equitable ownership").

539 50 U.S.C. app. §§ 107, 533(c).

540 50 U.S.C. app. § 533(c)

541 Pub. L. No. 110-289 (2008); 50 U.S.C. app. § 533 (note).

542 *See, e.g.*, Sprinkle v. SB&C Ltd., 472 F. Supp. 2d 1235 (W.D. Wash. 2006) (debt collector violated FDCPA and state UDAP statute by garnishing servicemember's bank account without filing affidavit of non-military service required by Act).

543 50 U.S.C. app. § 533(c) (sale or foreclosure "shall not be valid" if carried out contrary to Act); 50 U.S.C. app. § 533(d) (criminal sanctions for foreclosure in knowing violation of Act).

544 Hurley v. Deutsche Bank Trust Co. Americas, 2009 WL 701006 (W.D. Mich. Mar. 13, 2009), *later op.*, 2009 WL 1067314 (W.D. Mich. Apr. 21, 2009).

545 2009 WL 1067314, at *1 (W.D. Mich. Apr. 21, 2009) (referring to § 527 of the SCRA, which reduces the interest rate on a servicemember's pre-active duty obligations to 6% and expressly requires that the servicemember provide a copy of the military order to the lender).

546 2009 WL 701006, at *6 (W.D. Mich. Mar. 13, 2009).

Second, the creditor contended that section 553(c) contained an implicit requirement that the servicemember show how military service materially affected his or her ability to make mortgage payments. This showing is required in order to obtain a stay of judicial foreclosures under SCRA section 553(b).[547] The servicemember in this action failed to make this showing. However, the court noted that Congress did not include such a requirement in section 553(c), applicable to non-judicial mortgage foreclosures.[548] Finally, the federal court rejected the creditor's argument that a state court's approval of an eviction order after the non-judicial sale barred the federal court's involvement under the *Rooker-Feldman* doctrine. In the federal court's view, the improper non-judicial foreclosure gave rise to a distinct injury, separate from the later eviction action.[549] Regardless of the state court eviction judgment, the servicemember had a private cause of action for damages, including punitive damages, for violation of the SCRA prohibition on non-judicial sales, as well as for violation of the SCRA's provision extending the right to redeem after a foreclosure sale.[550]

In another significant recent ruling, a court held that the SCRA imposes strict liability on creditors who enforce liens against servicemembers without court approval.[551] The *B.C. Enterprises* decision involved a violation of section 537 of the SCRA. Section 537, like section 553(b), prohibits foreclosure and other enforcement of liens against active duty servicemembers unless a court has approved the action. The creditor in *B.C. Enterprises* violated section 537 by enforcing storage liens against motor vehicles owned by servicemembers and selling the vehicles at auction. In finding the creditor liable for violating the SCRA the court rejected arguments that it was impractical for anyone to find out whether a vehicle was owned by an active duty servicemember before selling it at auction. The SCRA statutory scheme placed the burden of investigation squarely on the creditor. A creditor who found this burden too severe always had the option of requesting court approval before conducting a sale.[552] The *B.C. Enterprises* court's strict liability holding applies fully to mortgage servicers and lenders who proceed under non-judicial foreclosure statutes. Particularly during periods of significant military deployment, they proceed with non-judicial foreclosure sales at their own peril.

Servicemembers may waive the protections provided by a court ordered sale, but the waiver must be in writing and executed during or after the servicemember's period of active duty.[553] Assuming a sale was properly performed, the period of time the servicemember was on active duty does not count toward any period that state law provides for redeeming the property after the foreclosure sale.[554] The extension is mandatory and automatic.[555] It does not require a showing of service-related financial prejudice or an impairment of the servicemember's ability to participate in litigation.[556]

In addition, a court may, on its own or upon application by a servicemember, impose a stay of foreclosure proceedings or fashion such equitable relief as may be appropriate to protect the interests of all parties.[557] The relief can include adjusting the substantive payment obligation under a mortgage.[558] Under the similar provision of the SSCRA, courts suspended mortgage payments or reduced payments during the period of military service.[559] Some courts limited payments to interest or to an amount sufficient to cover taxes

547 50 U.S.C. app. § 553(b).

548 2009 WL 701006, at *6 (W.D. Mich. Mar. 13, 2009).

549 2009 WL 701006, at *8 (W.D. Mich. Mar. 13, 2009).

550 50 U.S.C. app. § 526(b).

551 United States v. B.C. Enters., Inc., 667 F. Supp. 2d 650 (E.D. Va. 2009).

552 United States v. B.C. Enters., Inc., 667 F. Supp. 2d 650, 663 (E.D. Va. 2009).

553 50 U.S.C. app. §§ 533(c)(2), 517. *See also* § 4.12.6, *infra*.

554 50 U.S.C. app. § 526(b). *See* Peace v. Bullock, 40 So. 2d 82 (Ala. 1949) (extending period allowed for redemption of real estate under a prior version of the Act); Ill. Nat'l Bank of Springfield v. Gwinn, 107 N.E.2d 764 (Ill. App. Ct. 1952) (Soldiers' and Sailors' Civil Relief Act extended the time for borrower to redeem). *See also* Wilkin v. Shell Oil Co., 197 F.2d 42 (10th Cir. 1952) (three-year post-sale redemption period stayed under SSCRA, allowing redemption by servicemember who sought relief promptly after end of military service); Small v. Kulesa, 204 S.W.3d 99 (Ark. Ct. App. 2005) (decided under similar provision of the SSCRA, two-year period for payment of overdue property taxes to prevent tax sale began with date career servicemember left military service). *But see* Farran v. Wayne County, 2005 WL 2219417 (Mich. Ct. App. Sept. 14, 2005) (unpublished) (period of military service not counted in calculating redemption period after tax sale).

555 Hendrick v. Bigby, 305 S.W.2d 674 (Ark. 1957); Peace v. Bullock, 40 So. 2d 82 (Ala. 1949).

556 Conroy v. Aniskoff, 507 U.S. 511, 113 S. Ct. 1562, 123 L. Ed. 2d 229 (1993).

557 50 U.S.C. app. § 533(b). *See* Scranton Lackawanna Trust Co. v. Griffith, 51 Pa. D. & C. 475 (C.P. 1945) (under Soldiers' and Sailors' Civil Relief Act, court in the exercise of its sound discretion may stay foreclosure, upon condition that interest and taxes be paid promptly when due, when title to the mortgaged premises is in name of the dependent mother of servicemember, who had previously assisted in making payments on the mortgage and to whom in return his mother had promised to convey title to the property).

Under a temporary amendment to 50 U.S.C. app. § 533(b), the court may impose a stay of the foreclosure proceeding for any action filed during or within nine months after the end of active duty. The Act was amended in 2008 to temporarily extend the post-active-duty protection to nine months. This extension will expire December 31, 2010, and the previous ninety-day post-active-duty protection period will be reinstated. Pub. L. No. 108-289 (2008).

558 *See, e.g.*, Fed. Nat'l Mortgage Ass'n v. Deziel, 136 F. Supp. 859 (E.D. Mich. 1956).

559 *See* Brown Serv. Ins. Co. v. King, 24 So. 2d 219 (Ala. 1945) (conditioning stay upon payment of ongoing taxes and insurance); R.R. Fed. Sav. & Loan Ass'n v. Morrison, 40 N.Y.S.2d 319 (Sup. Ct. 1943) (applying reduced payments to taxes, then interest); Nassau Sav. & Loan Ass'n v. Ormond, 39 N.Y.S.2d 92 (Sup. Ct. 1942) (reduced payments applied to current taxes, then payment arrears).

and insurance. The court's broad equitable power to reform mortgage obligations continues under the SCRA.[560] It should allow a court faced with a foreclosure to fashion other appropriate adjustments to an obligation, such as shifting the timing of a balloon payment or reamortizing an arrearage. However, courts may fashion equitable relief or grant a stay under the Act only when military service materially affects the servicemember's ability to pay the mortgage or meet the obligations under the mortgage.[561]

Courts that have considered whether military service materially affects the servicemember's ability to meet her obligations under the mortgage under the SSCRA often considered the income of the servicemember before and after entry into military service, and the history of payment or default on the mortgage.[562] Generally, to obtain a stay, the servicemember must provide the court with sufficient financial information so that the court can adequately assess the effect of military service upon the servicemember's ability to meet her financial obligations. The burden is on the party seeking foreclosure to show that military service has not materially affected the servicemember's ability to pay the mortgage.[563]

In addition to providing for the adjustment of a mortgage obligation that is already subject to a foreclosure proceeding, the Act authorizes a court to grant anticipatory relief.[564] A servicemember may apply to a court for relief from any mortgage liability or similar obligation incurred before the military service began. It is not necessary that there be a pending foreclosure proceeding or that a breach or default have occurred.

The Act's provision for anticipatory relief requires judicial intervention. In the absence of a timely application by the servicemember to a court, the Act does not impose an enforceable duty upon a mortgagee to negotiate a modification of an obligation.[565] The servicemember must apply to a court for relief during military service or within 180 days of the end of service. If the servicemember's ability to comply with the mortgage obligation has been materially affected by military duty, the court may stay enforcement of the obligation or suspend payments during the period of military service.[566] In connection with the stay, the court may modify the loan repayment terms to allow repayment of the balance of principal and accumulated interest during the remaining loan term extended by a period equal to the length of military service.[567] If the servicemember complies with any court-approved modification of payment terms, the mortgagee may not assess penalties under any contractual provision.[568]

A court order is also required for tax sales of certain real property.[569] Before a court may authorize a tax sale, it must determine that military service does not materially affect the servicemember's ability to pay the unpaid tax or assessment.[570] The court may stay a sale of the property or any proceeding to collect the unpaid tax during the period of active duty and for 180 days after active duty.[571]

If the property has already been sold, section 561 of the Act extends the servicemember's period for redemption until 180 days after the end of active duty.[572] In addition, section 526 of the Act, tolling statutes of limitation and redemption periods generally, applies to tax sales.[573] Under section 526(b), the entire period of military service is excluded from computation of a tax sale redemption period.[574] Depending upon which provision is more beneficial in a particular case, either section 526 or section 561 of the Act may be used to set aside a tax sale based upon the extended redemption period.[575]

560 50 U.S.C. app. § 533(b)(2).

561 50 U.S.C. app. § 533(b). *See* Umstead v. Chase Manhattan Mortgage Co., 2005 WL 2233554 (W.D. Va. Sept. 13, 2005) (dependant may obtain stay or modified payment schedule for servicemember's mortgage if she can show that her ability to comply with payment schedule has been "materially affected" by homeowner's service). *See also* Fed. Home Loan Mortgage Corp. v. Taylor, 318 So. 2d 203 (Fla. Dist. Ct. App. 1975) (under the SSCRA, court in mortgage foreclosure action was within discretion in determining that acceleration of entire mortgage debt would be unconscionable, on basis of a technical default of one month's installment which could have arisen from excusable misunderstanding and lack of effective and timely communications because mortgagors were in the Philippines in connection with mortgagor husband's military duty).

562 *See, e.g.*, Fed. Nat'l Mortgage Ass'n v. Deziel, 136 F. Supp. 859 (E.D. Mich. 1959) (finding a pattern of pre-service defaults and conditioning stay on fulfillment of future payment obligations); Brown Serv. Ins. Co. v. King, 24 So. 2d 219 (Ala. 1945); Queens County Sav. Bank v. Thaler, 44 N.Y.S.2d 4 (Sup. Ct. 1943) (ability to pay mortgage not materially impaired by military service when evidence of default on mortgage prior to entering military service); O'Leary v. Horgan, 179 Misc. 518, 39 N.Y.S.2d 555 (Sup. Ct. 1943) (finding reduced income related to military service and granting stay conditioned upon spouse of servicemember reporting income status annually); Jamaica Sav. Bank v. Bryan, 25 N.Y.S.2d 17 (Sup. Ct. 1941).

563 Fleet Mortgage Corp. v. Hansen, 1991 U.S. Dist. LEXIS 9526 (N.D. Ill. July 11, 1991); Meyers v. Schmidt, 46 N.Y.S.2d 420 (N.Y. County Ct. 1944).

564 50 U.S.C. app. § 591. *See generally* Application of Marks, 181 Misc. 497, 46 N.Y.S.2d 755 (Sup. Ct. 1944) (applying similar anticipatory relief provision of SSCRA to reduce mortgage payments for duration of military service and allowing extended repayment period).

565 *See* Koenig v. Waukesha State Bank, 2006 WL 2334841 (E.D. Wis. Aug. 10, 2006).

566 50 U.S.C. app. § 591(b)(1).

567 50 U.S.C. app. § 591(b)(1)(B). *See* N.Y. Life Ins. Co. v. Litke, 181 Misc. 32, 45 N.Y.S.2d 576 (Super Ct. 1943) (under similar SSCRA section, allowing affordable repayment of arrears to avoid foreclosure).

568 50 U.S.C. app. §§ 523, 591(c).

569 50 U.S.C. app. § 561.

570 50 U.S.C. app. § 561(b)(1).

571 50 U.S.C. app. § 561(b)(2).

572 50 U.S.C. app. § 561(c).

573 50 U.S.C. app. § 526(b).

574 *See* Small v. Kulesa, 204 S.W.3d 99 (Ark. Ct. App. 2005).

575 LaMaistre v. Leffers, 333 U.S. 1, 68 S. Ct. 371, 92 L. Ed. 429

The Act limits other consequences of nonpayment of property taxes. It prohibits assessment of penalties on unpaid property taxes during the period of active service and limits the rate of interest accruing on delinquent property taxes during military duty to 6%.[576]

These limitations do not require court approval or a finding of prejudice. Given the exorbitant penalties and interest rates authorized by some state schemes for collection of delinquent property taxes, these reductions can provide a significant benefit.

In addition to those provisions that specifically pertain to mortgages and foreclosures, the Act creates general procedural protections for all servicemembers who are parties to civil litigation. These protections include restrictions on entry of default judgments and authorization for stays of proceedings in all forms of civil litigation, including judicial foreclosures. The Act prohibits entry of default judgment against an active duty servicemember unless an attorney has been appointed.[577] The Act authorizes the courts to stay proceedings, initially for ninety days, and then, upon a sufficient showing of prejudice, for the duration of military service plus ninety days.[578] These procedural protections incorporate a "material effect" test related to military service. However, in the context of the Act's procedural relief, the "material effect" standard does not consider the financial impact of military service. Rather, the focus is upon the effect that active duty has on the servicemember's ability to participate in litigation.[579]

Thus, a servicemember may move under the Act to open a foreclosure judgment that was entered by default during active duty or within sixty days after the end of active duty.[580] The servicemember's ability to defend the action must have been materially affected by military service and she must aver a meritorious defense.[581] The right to redeem, as extended by the Act, can be a meritorious defense.[582] The servicemember must move to vacate the default judgment no later than ninety days after release from active duty.[583]

4.12.4 *Protections Against Forfeiture of Land Installment Contracts*

The Act also provides protections against the forfeiture of land installment contracts similar to those provided for mortgages.[584] While the servicemember is on active duty, a land installment contract may not be terminated for breach of its terms occurring before or while on active duty. The property may not be forfeited without a court order.[585] A deposit or an installment on the contract must have been paid prior to active duty to obtain the protections of this section.

A court is authorized to issue a stay of the forfeiture or provide equitable relief to preserve the interests of all parties.[586] In addition, a court may order repayment to the servicemember of all or part of the prior installments or deposits as a condition of terminating the contract and resuming possession of the property.[587]

4.12.5 *Interest Rate Reduction Under the Act*

The Act requires that a lender reduce the interest rate to 6% on any loan obligation incurred prior to active duty.[588]

(1948) (SSCRA's two provisions extending redemption periods supplement one another); Small v. Kulesa, 204 S.W.3d 99 (Ark. Ct. App. 2005) (setting aside tax sale under former version of § 526, holding that two-year period for payment of overdue property taxes to prevent sale began with date servicemember left military service); Farran v. Wayne County, 2005 WL 2219417 (Mich. Ct. App. Sept. 13, 2005) (section 526(b) of SCRA, unlike § 561, tolls redemption period for non-residential property). *See also* Hendrick v. Bigby, 305 S.W.2d 674 (Ark. 1957) (same, under SSCRA).

576 50 U.S.C. app. § 561(d).

577 50 U.S.C. app. § 521.

578 50 U.S.C. app. §§ 522, 525. *See* Atkins v. County of Alameda, 2004 WL 444105 (N.D. Cal. Mar. 8, 2005) ("Courts have long construed the 'stay' provision of the Act liberally, retaining broad discretion to consider any and all stay-related factors."); Hernandez v. Hernandez, 906 A.2d 429 (Md. Ct. Spec. App. 2006) (when servicemember has complied with documentation requirements of § 522(b)(2), the Act leaves no room for judicial discretion and court must grant the initial ninety-day stay). *But see* White v. Black, 190 F.3d 366 (5th Cir. 1999) (SSCRA authorizes courts to stay proceedings but not to dismiss pending action against servicemember).

579 50 U.S.C. app. §§ 521(g), 522(d).

580 50 U.S.C. app. § 521(g). *See* Kramer v. Ginger, 93 N.E.2d 437 (Ill. App. Ct. 1950) (when persons affected by foreclosure proceedings alleged that at time of service of summons they were both in military service, and plaintiff had not filed proper affidavit of military service and had not had attorney appointed to protect interests of defendants, petition filed within ninety days from time defendant first received knowledge of proceedings to set aside decree of sale and decree confirming sale was timely under the Soldiers' and Sailors' Civil Relief Act). *See also* Merrill v. Beard, 2007 WL 461469 (N.D. Ohio Feb. 7, 2007) (in setting aside default judgments courts strictly construe requirements of Act in favor of servicemembers); Bernhardt v. Alden Café, 864 A.2d 421 (N.J. Super. Ct. App. Div. 2005) (although trial court's decision to vacate default judgment under § 521(g) is discretionary, it abused that discretion when it refused to set aside default for servicemember whose military status was undisputed and who alleged a meritorious defense).

581 50 U.S.C. § 521(g).

582 Flagg v. Sun Inv. & Loan Corp. 373 P.2d 226, 229 (Okla. 1962).

583 *See* Collins v. Collins, 805 N.E.2d 410 (Ind. Ct. App. 2006) (enforcing ninety-day time limit to bar motion to open judgment under Act).

584 50 U.S.C. app. § 532. Land installment contracts are discussed in Chapter 12, *infra*.

585 50 U.S.C. app. § 532(a)(1).

586 50 U.S.C. app. § 532(c).

587 *Id.*

588 Additionally, as this treatise goes to press, Congress was considering a bill to provide mortgage assistance payments, on behalf of households of eligible Armed Forces members, in the

The loan shall not bear a rate higher than 6% during the period of active duty and one year thereafter,[589] unless a court decides, on application by the lender, that the servicemember's ability to pay the higher interest rate is not materially affected by military service.[590] For mortgages, trust deeds, or other security instrument in the nature of a mortgage, the 6% interest rate limitation will continue through the period of military service and for one year after active duty ends.[591] Interest in excess of 6% must be forgiven, not simply deferred.[592] In addition, the amount of the periodic payments must be reduced by the amount of the interest forgiven.[593] This prevents lenders from requiring the same monthly payment from the servicemember but simply shifting a greater portion of that payment to pay off the principal. The Act's definition of "interest" includes contractual penalties and late payment fees.[594]

To benefit from the interest rate reduction, the servicemember must provide written notice to the lender and a copy of the military orders calling the servicemember to active duty and any other orders further extending military service.[595] This notice must be given no later than 180 days after the servicemember's termination or release from active duty.[596] The interest rate reduction is effective as of the date on which the servicemember is called to active duty.[597] A lender does not comply with the Act by making an offer to the servicemember to adjust the interest rate. Rather, upon notice of the debtor's military service the lender must proceed to adjust the account and credit any sums overpaid since the call to service.[598] The interest reduction requirement also applies to debts where a corporation is the primary obligor, so long as the servicemember is personally liable.[599]

4.12.6 Waiver of Rights Under the Act

A servicemember may waive any of the rights or protections provided by the Act.[600] In certain circumstances, the agreement to waive protections under the Act must be in writing and executed during or after the servicemember's period of active duty. The agreement must specify the legal instrument to which the waiver applies and, if the servicemember is not a party to that instrument, the servicemember concerned must be specified.[601]

A written agreement is required if the servicemember is modifying, terminating or canceling a contract, lease, or obligation secured by a mortgage, trust, deed, lien, or other security interest in the nature of a mortgage.[602] A written waiver agreement is also required for repossession, retention, foreclosure, sale, forfeiture, or taking possession of property that is security for any obligation, or was purchased or received under a contract, lease, or bailment.[603] The SCRA provides no authority for a court to imply a waiver of a servicemember's rights under the Act.[604]

4.12.7 Remedies for Violation of the Act

As of the printing of this treatise, a private cause of action has not yet been directly established under the Act.[605] However, the Act expressly preserves the servicemember's right to pursue a claim for wrongful conversion.[606] In addition, courts have held that the former version of the Act creates a private cause of action for violations.[607] The debtor

form of grants or zero interest loans. *See* H.R. 4156, 111th Cong. (introduced and referred to House Committee on Financial Services, Nov. 19, 2009).

589 Housing and Economic Recovery Act of 2008, Pub. L. No.110-289, § 2203, 122 Stat. 2849 (2008) (amending SCRA § 207 to extend period to which prohibition on interest rates exceeding 6% is applied).

590 50 U.S.C. app. § 527(c). *See* Linscott v. Vector Aerospace, 2006 WL 1310511 (D. Or. May 12, 2006) (where lump-sum judgment against servicemember could not be broken down into principal, permissible interest, and excess interest, entire judgment was tainted by 18% interest rate; enforcement must be enjoined), *later op. at* 2007 WL 2220357 (D. Or. July 27, 2007) (denying SCRA relief because servicemember failed to send creditor a copy of his military orders).

591 50 U.S.C. app. § 527(a)(1)(A); Pub. L. No. 110-289, 122 Stat. 2849 (2008) (amending the SCRA with addition of provision specifying its application to a "mortgage, trust deed, or other security in the nature of a mortgage").

592 50 U.S.C. app. § 527(a)(2). *See* Rodriquez v. American Express, 2006 WL 908613 (E.D. Cal. Apr. 7, 2006).

593 50 U.S.C. app. § 527(a)(3).

594 50 U.S.C. app. § 527(d)(1); Pub. L. No. 110-289, 122 Stat. 2849 (2008). *See* Koenig v. Waukesha State Bank, 2006 WL 2334841, at *4 (E.D. Wis. Aug. 10, 2006).

595 50 U.S.C. app. § 527(b)(1).

596 *Id.*

597 50 U.S.C. app. § 527(b)(2).

598 *See* Rodriguez v. American Express, 2006 WL 908613 (E.D. Cal. Apr. 7, 2006).

599 *See* Linscott v. Vector Aerospace, 2006 WL 1310511 (D. Or. May 12, 2006) (where corporation's obligations were personally guaranteed by servicemember, Act barred enforcement against corporation of foreign judgment which included interest in excess of 6%), *later op. at* 2007 WL 2220357 (D. Or. July 27, 2007) (denying SCRA relief because servicemember failed to send creditor a copy of his military orders); Cathey v. First Republic Bank, 2001 U.S. Dist. LEXIS 13150 (W.D. La. July 6, 2001).

600 50 U.S.C. app. § 517(a).

601 50 U.S.C. app. § 517(a).

602 50 U.S.C. app. § 517(b)(1).

603 50 U.S.C. app. § 517(b)(2).

604 *See, e.g.*, Sedler v. Select Props., Inc., 2004 WL 3392897 (Va. Cir. Ct. June 18, 2004) (finding no implied waiver of the Act's provision tolling statute of limitations).

605 As this treatise goes to press, a bill has been introduced in Congress, that would expressly provide for a private cause of action to enforce the SCRA. *See* H.R. 3949, 111th Cong. (introduced Oct. 28, 2009, received in Senate and referred to Committee on Veterans' Affairs).

606 50 U.S.C. app. § 531(d)(2).

607 Marin v. Citibank, N.A., 208 F.3d 203 (2d Cir. 2000) (unpublished, text available at 2000 U.S. App. LEXIS 3789) (reversing

is not confined to raising the violation of the Act defensively, in response to a foreclosure, but can sue affirmatively.[608] These rulings should remain good law under the current Act.[609]

A federal district court recently reviewed decisions under the SSCRA and held that, as under the prior law, a servicemember may assert a private right of action to enforce the SCRA.[610] The court ruled that a servicemember could sue a creditor to recover monetary damages related to the creditor's retention of the servicemember's property under a mechanic's lien contrary to section 537 of the Act. In a later decision in the same case the court granted injunctive relief in favor of the servicemember, enjoining the creditor from registering its foreign money judgment in the state.[611] The court barred registration because the judgment included interest that had been assessed at a rate of 18% while the servicemember was on active duty.

Violations of the SCRA may also lead to FDCPA violations. For example, a debt collector violated the SCRA, the FDCPA, and state consumer protection statutes when it entered judgment against a garnishee bank and seized a servicemember's military pay without the filing of an affidavit of non-military service.[612] The court held that by doing so the collector was proceeding with an action it had no lawful right to take and using false representations and deceptive means to collect a debt in violation of the FDCPA.[613]

4.12.8 The SCRA in Bankruptcy

The SCRA applies in bankruptcy cases.[614] For example, in adversary actions and in proceedings to lift the automatic stay the bankruptcy courts must enforce the Act's protections against default and may grant stays of proceedings.[615] Bankruptcy courts must apply the reduction of interest rates to 6% for pre-military service obligations.[616] One bankruptcy court held that the interest rate reduction to 6% must be applied to reduce payments on allowed claims under a confirmed chapter 13 plan for the duration of the debtor/servicemember's active duty.[617] As a supplement to the relief generally available to homeowners in chapter 13, the bankruptcy courts may employ the full range of powers under the SCRA to stay, suspend, or reschedule mortgage obligations for active duty servicemembers.[618]

---

dismissal of affirmative suit and remanding for consideration of existence of private cause of action); Cathey v. First Republic Bank, 2001 U.S. Dist. LEXIS 13150, at *14 (W.D. La. July 6, 2001); Moll v. Ford Consumer Fin. Co., 1998 U.S. Dist. LEXIS 3638 (N.D. Ill. Mar. 23, 1998). *See also* Marin v. Citibank, 208 F.3d 203 (2d Cir. 2000) (unpublished, text available at 2000 WL 268582) (remanding for consideration of existence of private cause of action).

608 Moll v. Ford Consumer Fin. Co., 1998 U.S. Dist. LEXIS 3638 (N.D. Ill. Mar. 23, 1998).

609 *See* Hurley v. Deutsche Bank Trust Co. Americas, 2009 WL 701006 (W.D. Mich. Mar. 13, 2009), *later op.*, 2009 WL 1067314, at *3 (W.D. Mich. Apr. 21, 2009 (in latter opinion, noting "at this juncture, all courts that have considered whether an implied right of action exists under the SCRA or the SSCRA . . . have concluded that a private right of action should be implied."); Batie v. Subway Real Estate Corp., 2008 WL 5136636 (N.D. Tex. Mar. 12, 2008) (vacating on reconsideration court's prior ruling in same case, 2008 WL 413627 (N.D. Tex. Feb. 15, 2008), which held no private right of action to enforce SCRA); Linscott v. Vector Aerospace, 2006 WL 240529 (D. Or. Jan. 31, 2006) ("[t]here is no indication that in enacting and renewing the Act, Congress intended to create rights without remedies").

610 Linscott v. Vector Aerospace, 2006 WL 240529 (D. Or. Jan. 31, 2006) ("There is no indication that in enacting and renewing the Act, Congress intended to create rights without remedies.").

611 Linscott v. Vector Aerospace, 2006 WL 1310511 (D. Or. May 12, 2006).

612 15 U.S.C. § 1692e(5), (10).

613 Sprinkle v. SB&C Ltd., 472 F. Supp. 2d 1235 (W.D. Wash. 2006).

614 *In re* A.H. Robins, Co., 996 F.2d 716 (4th Cir. 1993) (allowing servicemember to file claim in corporate debtor's chapter 11 case after bar date based on tolling of time limit by SSCRA).

615 *See In re* Templehoff, 339 B.R. 49 (Bankr. S.D.N.Y. 2005) (creditor must review debtor's statements and schedules for evidence of military service as an "essential step" in preparing an affidavit of non-military service filed with a motion for relief from stay); *In re* Lewis, 257 B.R. 431 (Bankr. D. Md. 2001) (staying an adversary proceeding brought against chapter 7 debtor/servicemember to determine dischargeability of debt); *In re* Burrell, 230 B.R. 309 (Bankr. E.D. Tex. 1999) (declining to grant stay of lender's motion for relief from stay where servicemember presented no evidence showing that military service affected debtor's ability to defend); *In re* Montano, 192 B.R. 843 (Bankr. D. Md. 1996) (denying creditor's application for default judgment in adversary action because affidavit of non-military service failed to set forth detailed facts to support allegations).

616 50 U.S.C. app. § 527.

617 *In re* Watson, 292 B.R. 441 (Bankr. S.D. Ga. 2003).

618 50 U.S.C. app. §§ 533(b), 591.

Chapter 5 Defending Foreclosures by Challenging Unfair Lending Practices

5.1 Introduction

Often defending against foreclosures means challenging unfair lending practices used in originating the loan. Unfair lending practices refer both to substantive terms of a contract and to the process by which the contract is struck and enforced. It encompasses excessive cost in relation to the value of goods and services purchased; excessive cost of credit itself; taking financial advantage of vulnerable or unsophisticated borrowers and buyers; and engaging in unfair or deceptive conduct at any stage of the mortgage loan transaction.

In some cases unfair lending practices, such as fraudulent conduct, may lead to a finding that the mortgage or deed of trust is not valid or legally enforceable. In cases where there are material violations of the Truth in Lending Act or the mortgage loan is unconscionable, borrowers may have the ability to rescind the mortgage transaction. Courts using their equitable powers may also rescind mortgage transactions based on numerous other statutory and common law claims. Other types of misconduct by the lender, or its agents, may give rise to damages or setoff against the amount owed on the loan.

This chapter considers common types of unfair loan origination practices, such as creditor overreaching, loan packing, property flipping, loan churning, and problems associated with broker originated loans. The chapter also reviews federal and state statutory and common law claims that may be used in challenging such practices and defending against foreclosure. Another important section discusses the holder-in-due-course doctrine and whether the homeowner can raise origination-related claims and defenses against the mortgage holder.

Consumer claims concerning loan origination are examined in even more detail in another NCLC treatise, *Cost of Credit* (4th ed. 2009 and Supp.). Claims concerning lender and servicer practices *after* the loan origination are considered in chapters 6–8, *infra*.

5.2 Market Incentives for Unfair Lending

For most of the twentieth century, a mortgage established a long-term relationship between lender and home buyer.[1] All facets of home purchase transactions related to obtaining and paying the mortgage loan were conducted with the same entity. Banks and savings and loan institutions sought out mortgage loan applicants, prepared and processed applications, and performed servicing functions for the life of the loan. Profits on mortgage loan transactions were primarily derived from the difference between the interest rate charged to the borrower for the loan and lower interest rate paid by the lender on short-term deposits.

In the 1970s, the advent of mortgage securitization commenced a disintegration in the structure of the mortgage industry as it had existed for more than half a century.[2] With the growth of securitization, mortgage lenders moved away from their longstanding practice of retaining mortgage loans in-house and began to originate loans for sale on the secondary mortgage market. As a result, lenders' primary source of income has shifted and is now derived from fees related to the origination of the loan and the proceeds of selling the loans into the secondary market. A greater volume of loans (even bad loans) and loans in higher amounts lead to more income for the lender. This market mechanism creates an incentive for lenders to relax underwriting standards, and in some cases, engage in unfair lending practices in order to close as many loans as possible. Since origination fees are usually based on a percentage on the loan value, lenders also have an incentive to encourage

1 In 1934 the Fair Housing Administration developed the thirty-year fixed rate loan program to provide homeowners with lower payments and mortgage stability. Prior to this development, and at the time when Congress enacted the Home Owners' Loan Act, the vast majority of mortgages were short-term loans that needed to be refinanced every five years. During the Great Depression homeowners were unable to refinance these short-terms loans, and as a result as many as half of the home loans in the country were in default.

2 Michael G. Jacobides, *Industry Change Through Vertical Disintegration: How and Why Markets Emerged in Mortgage Banking*, 48 Acad. of Mgmt. J. 465, 475 (2005).

homeowners to borrow more money than they can afford. Similarly, mortgage or loan brokers have financial incentives to close as many loans as possible without regard to whether the loan is in the best interest of the borrower.

Loans that are unsuitable for the borrower can quickly lead to foreclosure. Defending against these foreclosures requires both an understanding of unfair lending practices and the claims that may be raised to challenge them.

5.3 Common Types of Misconduct

5.3.1 Creditor Overreaching

Creditor overreaching is one of the most common types of unfair lending practice. Often credit transactions, especially those secured by the borrower's home, are made at considerable expense and risk to the consumer, but with little or no true benefit.[3] A number of legal claims may be available to consumers who have been extended credit that was disadvantageous to their financial interest.

Some creditor overreaching is substantive, as in gross disparities between the price of a product or service and its value; some is procedural, as in misrepresentation about terms or benefits, or a failure to disclose material information. Of course, the two often go hand in hand, for a legitimate creditor with a valuable service to offer at a reasonable price has less need to misrepresent. Thus, while it is important to be aware of the distinction between substance and process in judicial analysis of these cases, abuses of both types are often present in overreaching cases and advocates may be able to utilize both types of precedent in challenging particular conduct.[4]

Consolidation loans frequently are the result of both substantive and procedural overreaching. Examples include:

- Consolidation loans with monthly payments about the same or higher than the combined monthly payments of the credit transactions consolidated;[5]
- Consolidation loans paying off no interest debts (e.g., medical bills, utility bills) or a debt with a significantly lower interest rate (for example, a low-rate first mortgage);[6]
- Refinancing a loan that requires monthly escrow payments with a new loan that lacks an escrow account but has the same monthly payment;[7]
- Refinancing a loan with prepayment or rebate penalties with another loan having about the same APR and installments;[8]
- Extending credit to a financially overburdened consumer on terms which make default and foreclosure the likely result;[9]
- Providing variable-rate/variable-payment loans to consumers with fixed income or income with little growth potential;[10]
- Making a loan to a consumer for a different amount than the consumer requested without explaining why the loan in the amount requested was not provided;[11]
- Making a loan to a consumer at a higher interest rate than the consumer was originally promised;[12]

---

3 *See generally* Julia Patterson Forrester, *Mortgaging the American Dream: A Critical Evaluation of the Federal Government's Promotion of Home Equity Financing*, 69 Tul. L. Rev. 373 (1994).

4 This treatise's companion website contains sample pleadings for use in abusive mortgage lending cases, including pleadings from a home improvement financing fraud case and pleadings dealing with predatory mortgage lending. Both chapters include complaints and a number of other papers. *See also* Appx. K, *infra*.

5 *See In re* Miner, 369 B.R. 655 (Bankr. D. Kan. 2007) (refinance loan converted unsecured debt into secured debt and extended length of repayment on debt).

6 *See In re* Barker, 251 B.R. 250 (Bankr. E.D. Pa. 2000); *In re* Stepanski, 20 B.R. 399 (Bankr. D.N.J. 1982) (although the loan was voided on the basis of usury, Beneficial Finance's paying off a 9 1/4% mortgage with the proceeds of a 17% mortgage was criticized as "high handed conduct" and "sharp dealing").

7 This conceals the cost of the new loan because the monthly payments no longer include property taxes and insurance, which the borrower must pay separately.

8 *Cf. In re* Milbourne, 108 B.R. 522 (Bankr. E.D. Pa. 1989) (series of refinancings cost borrower over $3000 more than obtaining separate new loans, lender's failure to disclose how refinancing was advantageous to lender but disadvantageous to borrower violated state UDAP statute).

9 *See* Williams v. First Gov't Mortgage & Investors Corp., 225 F.3d 738 (D.C. Cir. 2000) (older borrower on fixed income requested $1400 to pay delinquent taxes and was given a thirty-year mortgage which paid off the balance of his first mortgage); Bankers Trust Co. of Cal. v. Payne, 730 N.Y.S.2d 200 (Sup. Ct. 2001); Beneficial Mortgage Co. of Ohio v. Leach, 2002 WL 926759 (Ohio Ct. App. May 9, 2002) (issue of material fact existed as to whether lender's conduct in refinancing loan after borrower defaulted on a prior loan was unconscionable as defense to lender's foreclosure action; lender did not inform borrower that mortgage was variable rate, rate was potentially much greater than prior mortgage on house, loan agreement was one of adhesion, lender purportedly threatened borrower with "other action" if she failed to sign the new note and mortgage, and borrower was in a worse financial position after refinancing); Vern Countryman, *Improvident Credit Extensions*, 27 Me. L. Rev. 1 (1975); Hersbergen, *The Improvident Extension of Credit as an Unconscionable Contract*, 23 Drake L. Rev. 225 (1974). *See also* U.C.C.C. § 5-108(4)(a) (1974) (one factor in determining unconscionability is belief by seller, lessor, or lender at consummation, that there is no reasonable probability of payment in full of the obligation by the consumer or debtor).

10 Dwight Golann, *Developments in Consumer Financial Services Litigation*, 43 Bus. Law. 1081, 1083–1085 (May 1988).

11 Carr v. Home Tech Co., 476 F. Supp. 2d 859 (W.D. Tenn. 2007) (borrower requested $5000 for home repairs and received $51,000 which includes credit card consolidations and closing costs); Newton v. United Companies Fin. Corp., 24 F. Supp. 2d 444 (E.D. Pa. 1998); Bankers Trust Co. of Cal. v. Payne, 730 N.Y.S.2d 200 (Sup. Ct. 2001).

12 Johnson v. Equity Title & Escrow Co., 476 F. Supp. 2d 873 (W.D. Tenn. 2007) (loan promised at 5–6%, but borrower received loan at 9.639%).

- Extending a balloon payment transaction or a demand transaction to a consumer who does not have the resources to meet the balloon or demand.[13]

Some of these variations may be found in "equity skimming" schemes, in which an unscrupulous lender makes a high-cost loan secured by the equity in the borrower's home on onerous terms the lender knows the borrower has no reasonable probability of repaying. The lender then acquires the property through foreclosure[14] or merely profits from the origination fees.

Many consumers are unable to protect themselves from such practices. Credit transactions even in their simplest form are complex and beyond comprehension to some consumers. Even the basic credit concept of calculating interest on a declining balance of an installment credit transaction can be difficult to comprehend. When loan transactions are made more complex by the addition of complicated terms, such as balloon payments, variable rates, negative amortization, prepaid finance charges, and prepayment penalties, a proper evaluation of the credit terms requires a skill beyond the grasp of most consumers.[15]

For simple credit transactions, federally mandated Truth in Lending Act (TILA) disclosures provide the most basic information upon which an evaluation can be made—the APR and the finance charge. Even these basic disclosures, however, are seldom made available until after the consumers have made a decision about accepting the loan using whatever information the lender has already given them. Moreover, TIL disclosures may fail to alert consumers to the significant disadvantages built into many of these complex credit transactions, particularly in the home loan area.

Unfair lending practices inevitably lead to many defaults. With a large number of loans secured by the borrowers' homes, the consequences of default can be dire. Overreaching creditors may be subject to a number of legal claims including violations of state unfair and deceptive acts and practices laws, the Truth in Lending Act, the Equal Credit Opportunity Act, and the Racketeer Influenced and Corrupt Organizations Act. Creditors may also be liable based on common law causes of action such as fraud, misrepresentation, estoppel, breach of fiduciary duty, unconscionability, and usury. Each of these claims is discussed at §§ 5.5 to 5.13, *infra.*

5.3.2 Broker Originated Loans

5.3.2.1 The Role of the Loan Broker

Mortgage brokers have made an important contribution to the rise in unfair lending practices and loan defaults over the past decade.[16] While many borrowers believe mortgage brokers are required to act in the borrower's best interest, this is not always true. Instead brokers have too often favored their own and lenders' interests. Any time a broker is involved in a mortgage loan, the transaction should be examined carefully for potential claims and defenses.

Traditionally mortgage brokers have acted as intermediaries by checking with various lenders for different loan terms and connecting borrowers with lenders. In recent years, however, some brokers have acted in far different roles by originating loans with their own money;[17] by using "table funding" from a prearranged buyer of the loan;[18] or by using a line of credit from a bank, financial institution, or other entity.[19] In these situations the relationship of the broker to the borrower is complicated by the fact that the broker appears to act as both broker and lender in the loan transaction.

5.3.2.2 The Legal Status of Brokers

When defending a foreclosure it is important to determine whether the broker was an agent for the borrower or the

13 For further discussion of some of these practices, *see* Gary Klein, *Preventing Foreclosures: Spotting Scams Involving Low-Income Homeowners*, 27 Clearinghouse Rev. 116 (1993). *See* Maxwell v. Fairbanks Capital Corp., 281 B.R. 101 (Bankr. D. Mass. 2002); Associates Home Equity Servs. v. Troup, 778 A.2d 529 (N.J. Super. Ct. App. Div. 2001).

14 *Cf.* U.C.C.C. § 5-108(a) (1974) (especially cmt. ¶ 4: selling goods to low-income consumers without expectation of payment, but with expectation of repossessing goods and reselling at a profit, is an example of an unconscionable transaction). For another example of equity skimming, see *In re* Jackson, 245 B.R. 23 (Bankr. E.D. Pa. 2000).

15 *See* A. Mechele Dickerson, The Myth of Home Ownership and Why Home Ownership Is Not Always a Good Thing 84 Ind. L.J. 189, 216 (2009); National Consumer Law Center, The Cost of Credit: Regulation, Preemption, and Industry Abuses § 11.2 (4th ed. 2009 and Supp.).

16 For a more detailed discussion of mortgage brokers, see National Consumer Law Center, The Cost of Credit: Regulation, Preemption, and Industry Abuses § 11.6.4 (4th ed. 2009 and Supp.).

17 National Ass'n of Mortgage Brokers, Inc. v. Donovan, 641 F. Supp. 2d 8, 10 n.2 (D.D.C. 2009) ("an entity may call itself a mortgage broker but provide funding for a loan that it originates.").

18 *Table funding* means a settlement at which a loan is funded by a contemporaneous advance of loan funds and an assignment of the loan to the person advancing the funds. Reg. X, 12 C.F.R. § 3500.2(b). *See* Easter v. American West Fin., 381 F.3d 948 (9th Cir. 2004) (defines a table-funded transaction and holds that state usury laws do not apply to the correspondent lender if a three-part test is met); England v. MG Invs., Inc., 93 F. Supp. 2d 718 (S.D. W. Va. 2000) (court denied assignee's motion for summary judgment on regarding agency and on the holder-in-due course defense where the assignee and correspondent broker entered into a sixteen-page master agreement containing over twenty-eight detailed requirements which the assignee imposed on the broker, suggesting that the broker was making the loan for the assignee).

19 *See* Elizabeth Renuart, *An Overview of the Predatory Lending Process*, 15 Housing Pol'y Debate, 467 (2004).

lender. Absent evidence to the contrary, the loan broker is traditionally the borrower's agent for purposes of arranging the transaction.[20] This relationship imposes a fiduciary duty upon the broker.[21] In other cases, however, close scrutiny of the broker-lender relationship may show that the broker actually functions as the lender's agent, thereby making the lender liable for the broker's conduct.[22] Such circumstances may include where the broker also funds the loan, where the broker and lender are the same entity acting under a different trade names, or where two corporate entities exist but with identical or common principals. The payment of fees by the lender to the broker, whether a yield spread premium or other compensation, may help establish that the broker is the lender's agent. Boilerplate language in a contract disclaiming agency or a fiduciary duty should not deter a closer examination of the actual relationship between the entities.

5.3.2.3 Potential Claims

To the extent the broker is considered an agent of the lender or was in fact the originator of the loan, claims arising from broker misconduct may give rise to defenses against foreclosure.[23] Where the broker has a fiduciary duty to the borrower, advocates should explore whether the lender induced the broker to breach that duty, for example, by the payment of a yield spread premium or other incentives.[24] Such payments may also give rise to a claim against the lender for interference with a contractual relationship. Brokers may misrepresent or fail to explain their role or their fee.[25] They may misrepresent the nature or value of the credit they obtain for the borrower.[26] Such misrepresentations or omissions may constitute fraud, intentional misrepresentation, negligent representation, or support a UDAP claim.[27] In some cases kickbacks, such as yield spread premiums paid from the lender to the broker, may violate the anti-kickback provisions of RESPA.[28] The manner in which the broker's fee is treated for Truth in Lending (TIL) purposes may create grounds for TIL rescission.[29] Brokers' fees also may be included in the "fees and charges" trigger for determining whether the loan is subject to HOEPA.[30]

Borrowers may also be able to raise UDAP, fraud, misrepresentation, and other claims when a broker puts false information on a loan application regarding the borrower's income, employment, or intention to occupy the property securing the loan.[31] Falsifying such information can result in a borrower being approved for a loan that he or she would not otherwise qualify for. While some may perceive this as helping the borrower get a loan, this misconduct is more likely intended to enrich the broker and lender, which earn additional origination fees, and increase the risk of foreclosure. According to study produced by a mortgage industry consultant, between half and three-quarters of early defaults on mortgages can be traced back to false information on the loan application.[32]

Some states have passed legislation specifically regulating mortgage brokers,[33] and the SAFE Mortgage Licensing Act of 2008 requires states to impose minimum licensing and registration requirements on individual loan originators,

---

20 National Consumer Law Center, The Cost of Credit: Regulation, Preemption, and Industry Abuses § 11.6.4.3 (4th ed. 2009 and Supp.).

21 National Consumer Law Center, The Cost of Credit: Regulation, Preemption, and Industry Abuses § 11.6.4.3 (4th ed. 2009 and Supp.).

22 National Consumer Law Center, The Cost of Credit: Regulation, Preemption, and Industry Abuses § 11.6.4.3 (4th ed. 2009 and Supp.).

23 *See* National Consumer Law Center, The Cost of Credit: Regulation, Preemption, and Industry Abuses § 11.6.4.4 (4th ed. 2009 and Supp.).

24 BasePoint Analytics, Broker-Facilitated Fraud: The Impact on Mortgage Lenders 4 (2007) ("Broker incentives such as Yield Spread Premiums . . . and rebates from lenders create an environment where brokers are tempted to line their own pockets at the expense of lenders and borrowers.").

25 Young v. First Am. Fin. Servs., 992 F. Supp. 440 (D.D.C. 1998) (motion for summary judgment of lender granted on fraud claim where homeowner alleged that they were never informed that the broker was not the lender because no evidence of agency was presented; summary judgment on fraud claim against broker denied); Noel v. Fleet Fin., Inc., 971 F. Supp. 1102 (E.D. Mich. 1997) (similar allegations withstood a motion to dismiss).

26 Barker v. Altegra Credit Co., 251 B.R. 250 (Bankr. E.D. Pa. 2000) (broker assisted in the arranging of the refinancing of a special state-sponsored mortgage loan resulting in the doubling of the interest rate and a balloon payment; breach of fiduciary duty and fraud stated against the broker). *See, e.g.*, Hays v. Bankers Trust Co., 46 F. Supp. 2d 490 (S.D. W. Va. 1999) (a 9.7% conventional thirty-year mortgage turned into a 10.65% balloon note).

27 *See* §§ 5.5, 5.12, *infra*. *See generally* National Consumer Law Center, Unfair and Deceptive Acts and Practices § 6.2.1 (7th ed. 2008 and Supp.); National Consumer Law Center, The Cost of Credit: Regulation, Preemption, and Industry Abuses § 12.2 (4th ed. 2009 and Supp.).

28 *See* § 5.9.3, *infra*.

29 *See* National Consumer Law Center, Truth in Lending § 3.7.4 (6th ed. 2007 and Supp.).

30 *See* National Consumer Law Center, Truth in Lending § 3.7.4 (6th ed. 2007 and Supp.).

31 Ware v. Indymac Bank, F.S.B., 534 F. Supp. 2d 835 (N.D. Ill. 2008) (inflated income and assets); Martinez v. Freedom Mortgage Team, Inc., 527 F. Supp. 2d 827 (N.D. Ill. 2007) (inflated income and appraisal); Matthews v. New Century Mortgage Corp., 185 F. Supp. 2d 874 (S.D. Ohio 2002) (falsified income and employment status); BasePoint Analytics, White Paper: A Study on Mortgage Fraud and the Impacts of a Changing Financial Climate 16 (2007) (study of three million loans involving 50,000 brokers showed "employment, income and occupancy fraud represented about 80% of identified fraud, and that these are often facilitated by brokers.").

32 BasePoint Analytics, White Paper: A Study on Mortgage Fraud and the Impacts of a Changing Financial Climate 16 (2007).

33 A list of state broker laws appears in National Consumer Law Center, The Cost of Credit: Regulation, Preemption, and Industry Abuses Appx. B (4th ed. 2009 and Supp.).

including mortgage brokers and lender employees.[34] Even before the SAFE Act, certain states had imposed licensing requirements,[35] or other more specific requirements.[36] Some states had already required brokers to purchase a surety bond to compensate borrowers injured by broker misconduct.[37] This is especially important where the broker may be judgment-proof. It may be possible to argue that a contract arranged by a broker who fails to obtain a required license is void,[38] or at least that the broker was not entitled to a fee.[39] If the statute itself provides no remedy, a violation may give rise to a UDAP claim.[40] State credit repair statutes may apply to mortgage brokers and provide significant remedies.[41]

34 *See* § 5.13.9, *infra.*

35 *E.g.*, Ariz. Rev. Stat. § 6-903.

36 *See, e.g.*, State v. Western Capital Corp., 290 N.W.2d 467 (S.D. 1980) (South Dakota statute requires a three-day cooling-off period and certain disclosures; violation of these provisions constitutes a deceptive practice); Opportunity Mgmt. Co. v. Frost, 1999 Wash. App. LEXIS 336 (Wash. Ct. App. Feb. 16, 1999) (statute was violated where broker did not place loan on terms agreed upon with broker but, nevertheless, received a broker fee; lenders are covered as well); Idaho Admin. Code r. 04.02.01.200 (Idaho regulation prohibits brokers from receiving any fee either directly or indirectly until the loan is made or a written commitment is made to the consumer; broker must furnish a written contract to the consumer containing certain information); Mass. Regs. Code tit. 940, § 8.01–8.08 (promulgating regulations under state UDAP statute, e.g., failure to disclose facts which may have induced borrower not to enter into transaction; charging fees which significantly deviate from industry standard or are unconscionable).

37 *See, e.g.*, Conn. Gen. Stat. § 36a-492(a).

38 *See, e.g.*, Beneficial Hawaii, Inc. v. Kida, 30 P.3d 895 (Haw. 2001) (mortgage and loan note void when arranged by an unlicensed mortgage broker; mortgage holder may be entitled to equitable lien on the property if it could prove that it paid consideration for the mortgage and note; lender failed to offer this proof in this case).

39 *See, e.g.*, Steinberg v. Brickell Station Towers Inc., 625 So. 2d 848 (Fla. Dist. Ct. App. 1993) (unlicensed mortgage broker not entitled to fee under Florida Mortgage Brokerage Act).

40 *See* South Dakota v. Western Capital Corp., 290 N.W.2d 467 (S.D. 1980) (a violation of South Dakota broker law constitutes a UDAP violation and triggers restitution and civil penalties); National Consumer Law Center, Unfair and Deceptive Acts and Practices § 3.2.7 (7th ed. 2008 and Supp.).

41 *See, e.g.*, Lewis v. Delta Funding Corp. (*In re* Lewis), 290 B.R. 541 (Bankr. E.D. Pa. 2003) (lender and assignee may be liable for broker's violation of the state credit repair statute when the assignee funded the transaction knowing of the illegal payment of the broker fee); Barker v. Altegra Credit Co., 251 B.R. 250 (Bankr. E.D. Pa. 2000) (Pennsylvania's credit repair statute applies to the broker in this case; it enhances the principle that the broker's conduct constitutes a violation of the state UDAP, triggering treble damages).

5.3.3 Credit Insurance

5.3.3.1 Introduction

Another unfair lending practice is "packing" loans with expensive credit insurance products that have limited or no benefit to the borrower. Sometimes borrowers are signed up and charged for these products without their knowledge. Because these products are so profitable to both the creditor and insurance industry, there is enormous pressure to sell these products.[42] Credit insurance can present problems for borrowers that knowingly obtain it as well. Borrowers may not fully appreciate the cost or may have difficulty collecting benefits. This subsection provides a general overview of credit insurance products and summarizes defenses to a foreclosure where the borrower's valid claim on a credit insurance policy remains unpaid.[43] For a more detailed discussion of credit insurance see National Consumer Law Center, *The Cost of Credit: Regulation, Preemption, and Industry Abuses* Chapter 8.

5.3.3.2 Credit Insurance Basics

The two most common types of credit insurance are credit life insurance and credit disability or accident and health (A&H) insurance. Credit life pays off an outstanding obligation in the event of the borrower's death. The coverage provided by credit life insurance policies varies in both who is covered (single debtors or joint debtors) and the amount of the coverage (declining or level). Declining coverage may not cover the loan's principal balance at the time of loss. Credit disability insurance is an indemnity insurance to cover payments in the event that the borrower's income is interrupted for health reasons. Indemnity coverage means that the insurer will make the monthly payments while the insured borrower is unable to work due to a disability covered under the policy—a "covered loss." The two critical components of credit disability insurance are the "waiting period," the number of continuous days a person is required to be "disabled" before the coverage provisions apply, and the "elimination period," the initial number of days in the period of disability for which there are no benefits payable. The elimination period, if there is one, operates like a deductible.

42 Jack Gillis, James Hunt, D.J. Powers, Birny Birnbaum, Consumer Federation of America, Center for Economic Justice, Credit Insurance Overcharges Hit $2.5 Billion Annually (Nov. 2001), *available at* www.consumerfed.org/pdfs/credins.pdf (in 2000, consumers paid about $6 billion for the traditional credit insurance products).

43 *See generally* Rita Gordon Pereira, *Credit Insurance: Obtaining Relief for Postclaim Ineligibility Determinations*, 28 Clearinghouse Rev. 891 (1994).

Credit insurance may be written as an individual policy, sold directly to the borrower. More often, however, it is a group policy, issued by the insurer to the creditor. The actual terms of the policy are set forth in the master policy between the creditor and the insurer. The group eligible to be insured under this policy is the creditor's borrowers, who are "enrolled" as members of the group if they purchase the insurance. Instead of receiving an insurance policy, a borrower receives a certificate of insurance.

The impetus for selling credit insurance comes from the important ways in which the creditor benefits from its sale. Creditors usually receive significant compensation from the sale of the insurance from the insurer. Because lenders typically receive commissions at a specified percentage of the premium, insurers often compete to offer the most expensive (rather than least expensive) insurance so that they can offer the highest commissions. Insurers may offer creditors dividends or retrospective rate credits based on a favorable claim experience. Creditors also benefit from the added security provided by the insurance. Lastly, if the credit insurance purchase is voluntary, the cost of the premium may in some cases be added to the principal or amount financed. Interest can then be charged on the premium thereby inflating the amount of interest earned. As a result of these market incentives borrowers may be involuntarily saddled with credit insurance, may be pressured into purchasing it, or may be overcharged for it. In some cases, borrowers have even been sold coverage under which they are ineligible to receive benefits under the terms of the policy.

Sources governing the sale of credit insurance include: insurance statutes and regulations; state insurance department bulletins; state licensing laws; and, credit laws, including the Truth in Lending Act. Abuses in the sale of these insurance products may also give rise to claims under state UDAP statutes, usury laws, or other common law claims such as fraud or misrepresentation.

5.3.3.3 Inappropriate Grounds for Denial of Coverage

Denial of a credit insurance claim often leads to foreclosure. The event triggering the borrower's insurance claim also causes a significant loss of income (e.g., lost employment because of disability or death), and the denial of insurance coverage means that the loan cannot be repaid.

There are at least four ways that a valid credit insurance claim can be improperly denied, the first three involving the lender:

1. The insurer rejects a claim because, at the time of application, the borrower was not eligible for the insurance that the lender sold;
2. The originating lender fails to submit or properly process the application so that coverage never goes into effect;
3. The current lender takes on responsibility to submit the insurance claim, but fails to do so; or
4. The insurer determines that a covered loss has not occurred.

While the insurer determines if the borrower was eligible for insurance at the time of application, the lender is often the one at fault for selling insurance to someone it knows or should know does not qualify. The lender makes a significant profit selling the insurance whether or not the borrower qualifies. For example, a preexisting condition may limit the applicability of a disability policy, but the lender may sell the policy despite its knowledge of the condition.[44] Alternatively, the lender may simply not inquire about relevant facts such as health or age. On occasion, the lender deliberately misstates information on the insurance application.

The lender can also fail to submit the borrower's application to the insurance company, or may submit it improperly, so that the coverage never goes into effect. This can just be negligence on the lender's part or it could be a deliberate scam to keep all of the premium instead of sharing it with the insurance company.

Similarly, the lender or servicer can take on the responsibility to submit the borrower's claim to the insurance company and fail to do so. Again, this may be negligence. It is harder to see why this would be intentional, because the lender will be the prime beneficiary of any claim. On the other hand, where an originating lender is also the servicer, that lender may receive rebates based on claims experience, and it is the investor, not the servicer, who will suffer because of the loss of insurance proceeds.

The insurance company may also be at fault for denying a claim. The insurance company, of course, has the greatest incentive not to pay the claim. It can falsely allege that a disability is not serious enough to lead to loss of employment, that a condition fully disclosed in the application still disqualifies a claim, or that it never received the application,

44 *See* Hardy v. Am. S. Life Ins. Co., 211 So. 2d 559 (Fla. 1968) (consumer could recover because there was a "sound health" clause and creditor had actual knowledge of the borrower's poor health); Shoup v. Union Sec. Life Ins. Co., 124 P.3d 1028 (Idaho 2005) (reversing summary judgment in favor of insurer where insured could have reasonably relied on lender and insurer representations that insurance was effective); Simonson v. Mich. Life Ins. Co., 194 N.W.2d 446 (Mich. Ct. App. 1971) (consumer could recover where policy contained a "sound health" clause and the insured was obviously paralyzed in one arm and one leg; the creditor therefore had a duty to inquire further). *But see* Rouse v. Household Fin. Corp., 156 P.3d 569 (Idaho 2007) (lender and credit life disability insurer did not breach duty to deal fairly, honestly and in good faith with borrowers where lender encouraged borrowers to refinance, refinance cancelled borrowers' credit disability insurance, and new policy was declined).

premium payment, or claims form. Alternatively, the insurer may just stall and refuse to pay.

5.3.3.4 Available Legal Claims to Challenge Nonpayment of Credit Insurance

Foreclosure is an equitable action, and equity should deny foreclosure where the lender has unclean hands and could have prevented the foreclosure by acting properly.[45] While an appeal to equity based on the handling of a credit insurance claim is appropriate, it is also helpful to raise various legal claims, either as an aid to stop a foreclosure or in an affirmative action before a foreclosure is threatened.

Legal claims to challenge a denial of credit insurance benefits are discussed in detail in another treatise in this series.[46] These include a misrepresentation or negligence claim where a lender fails to submit an application or claim to an insurer.[47] Once the lender undertakes to perform an action (submit claims on borrower's behalf), the lender has a duty to the borrower, and is negligent if it breaches that duty by failing to submit a timely claim.[48]

There is also a contract action for the lender's breach of an implied or express contract to obtain insurance coverage for the borrower. Where the obligation to purchase the credit insurance is part of the loan agreement, the lender's material breach can also lead to the borrower being excused from performance.[49] Moreover, the practice is clearly a violation of the state unfair and deceptive acts and practices statute, as long as lenders are not exempted from a particular state's statute.[50] There are thus statutory, tort, and contract claims that will hold a creditor liable for all damage accruing from its failure to obtain insurance or submit a claim.[51]

The same claims should apply where the lender obtains insurance for the borrower, but knows or should have known that the coverage is worthless. The lender represented it was obtaining insurance coverage, and it did not do so.

Where an insurer fails to pay a valid claim, the consumer, depending on state law, should have one or more of the following claims: breach of contract; bad faith refusal to pay a claim; violation of a state unfair insurance practices statute; and violation of a state deceptive practices statute. An insurer may not be able to deny benefits because of a preexisting condition, where its agent, the originating lender, knew or should have known about the condition.[52] Insurers also in some cases have been estopped from denying coverage when they have accepted premium payments.[53]

5.3.4 *Property Flipping and Inflated Appraisals*

5.3.4.1 Introduction

Inflating appraisals and property flipping are two deceptive activities that often go hand-in-hand but can also occur independently.[54] Inflated appraisals can be used by mortgage brokers and loan officers to earn extra fees and commissions or to otherwise increase lending volume. Where a property has a higher loan-to-value ratio than permitted by the lender's underwriting guidelines, inflating the appraised value of the house may get the transaction approved.

Property flipping scams typically involve speculators who buy dilapidated residential properties at low prices and use

45 *See* § 4.10, *supra*.

Borrowers may need to allege some misconduct on the part of the lender with respect to the credit insurance in order to enjoin foreclosure or repossession upon denial of a claim. *See* Bank of Coushatta v. Hodges, 525 So. 2d 581 (La. Ct. App. 1988) (where borrower alleged no negligent or wrongful act by lender, lender could not be precluded from foreclosing even where borrower disputed credit insurer's denial of coverage).

46 *See* National Consumer Law Center, The Cost of Credit: Regulation, Preemption, and Industry Abuses § 8.5.5.3 (4th ed. 2009 and Supp.).

47 *See* Exchange Bank of Midgeville v. Hill, 224 S.E.2d 23 (Ga. 1976).

48 Musgrave v. Mut. Sav. & Loan Ass'n, 174 S.E.2d 820 (N.C. Ct. App. 1970).

49 *See* Allied Elevator, Inc. v. E. Tex. State Bank of Buna, 965 F.2d 34 (5th Cir. 1992).

50 *See* Fort Worth Mortgage Corp. v. Abercrombie, 835 S.W.2d 262 (Tex. App. 1992) (unconscionable and deceptive practice to switch credit disability policy to less favorable one).

51 Beiter v. Decatur Fed. Sav. & Loan Ass'n, 150 S.E.2d 687 (Ga. 1966).

52 Hardy v. Am. S. Life Ins. Co., 211 So. 2d 559 (Fla. 1968) (insurance company liable for benefits because there was a "sound health" clause and the creditor had actual knowledge of the borrower's poor health); Simonson v. Mich. Life Ins. Co., 194 N.W.2d 446 (Mich. Ct. App. 1971) (insurance company was liable because the policy contained a "sound health" clause and the insured was obviously paralyzed in one arm and one leg; the creditor therefore had a duty to inquire further). *See also* Ginocchio v. Am. Bankers Life Assur. Co., 889 F. Supp. 1078 (N.D. Ill. 1995) (creditor's representation regarding ambiguous term in credit disability policy at issue); Grimm v. USLIFE Credit Life Ins. Co., 1999 Ohio App. LEXIS 2445 (Ohio Ct. App. May 19, 1999) (Ohio statute makes the person who solicits and procures insurance the agent of the company issuing the insurance); Justus v. Mountain Life Ins. Co., 1999 Tenn. App. LEXIS 702 (Tenn. Ct. App. Oct. 15, 1999) (bank employee's representation that insurance policy is in full force and effect is binding on insurance company). *But see* Sadtler v. John Hancock Mut. Life Ins. Co., 291 A.2d 500 (D.C. 1972) (creditor acts as agent of insured rather than insurer when selling credit insurance).

53 Puerto Rico v. Pan Am. Life Ins. Co., 307 F. Supp. 1065 (D. P.R. 1969); Larr v. Minn. Mut. Life Ins. Co., 567 So. 2d 239 (Miss. 1990). *But see* Minn. Mut. Life Ins. Co. v. Morse, 487 S.W.2d 317 (Tex. 1972); Hocutt v. Prudential Ins. Co. of Am., 501 S.W.2d 347 (Tex. App. 1973).

54 *See* National Consumer Law Center, The Cost of Credit: Regulation, Preemption, and Industry Abuses § 11.6.6 (4th ed. 2009 and Supp.).

inflated appraisals and other forms of deception to resell them at huge markups to unsophisticated first-time homebuyers. Often these flipping schemes are targeted at low- or moderate-income racial minorities.[55] Buyers are often persuaded to enter into purchase agreements only after the seller has promised to make necessary or agreed upon repairs to the property. When the closing date arrives, however, the seller has made few, if any, of the repairs. Once at the closing table, buyers are threatened with the loss of their earnest money deposit and the "opportunity to be a homeowner" if they do not complete the transaction.

The end result is that the buyer has purchased property in questionable condition and is saddled with a debt load that exceeds the market value of the property. These homeowners will be unable to resell the home in an arms-length transaction because the mortgage indebtedness exceeds the fair market value of the property. Ultimately, the homeowners may lose their homes due to foreclosure sales because the home's condition is much worse than represented, promised repairs are not performed, and the consumer's mortgage payments may be higher than the consumer can afford.[56]

When a lender or broker refinances an existing mortgage based on an inflated appraisal, the homeowner will face a similar problem. The lender or broker will profit from commissions and other fees that are often based on the size of the loan, but the homeowner will have lost their equity and will owe more than the home is worth. When the value of a home is less than the amount owed on debts secured by it, the homeowner is said to be "under water" or "upside down."[57] Even if the homeowner can afford the monthly payments, he or she will not be able to sell the home or refinance the loan until the balance is reduced or the home appreciates in value.

It is possible through the use of aggressive litigation and advocacy to preserve homeownership, depending on the condition of the property, or alternatively, to force a discharge of the debt and payment of sufficient damages to allow the homeowner to move on. Practitioners should always explore what the homeowner wants (whether to keep the home or to move), the actual condition of the house, and the cost of repairs. As discussed at § 5.3.4.3, *infra,* lenders may be liable for the damages arising from the inflated appraisal or property flipping. In some cases, lenders may be willing to settle a property flipping or fraudulent appraisal case by writing the debt down to the actual value of the property.[58] Sometimes, this is enough to make the loan affordable. If extensive repairs to the home are needed, practitioners almost always must develop claims against parties to the transaction other than the lender and seller in order to preserve homeownership.

Another pressure point, particularly for HUD-insured loans, may be the mortgage insurer. The mortgage insurer will be on the hook if there is a foreclosure and the home is worth less than the outstanding debt; if the lender is recalcitrant to settle, contact with the mortgage insurer may bring forward movement. HUD in particular has devoted considerable resources to investigating appraisal fraud in FHA-insured loans and is often receptive to information about fraud in FHA lending.

Sellers, appraisers, mortgage brokers, and closing agents frequently conspire to mislead the buyer as to the property's market value, the condition of the property, and the mortgage financing terms.[59] Commonly, fraudulent documents and bogus appraisals are used to secure a loan for the inflated purchase price. Lenders may also actively participate in the flipping scheme, particularly when the loans are insured by the federal government (e.g., FHA or VA),[60] or where the lender has a preexisting agreement to sell its loans for securitization.[61] Actual damages in property flipping cases can be significant.[62] Generally, if the homebuyer has

55 *See, e.g.,* Vaughn v. Consumer Home Mortgage Inc., 2003 WL 21241669 (E.D.N.Y Mar. 23, 2003) (alleging HUD had actual knowledge that "hot zone" for property flipping schemes was a low-income, minority neighborhood). *See also* Martinez v. Freedom Mortgage Team, Inc., 527 F. Supp. 2d 827 (N.D. Ill. 2007) (alleging that broker and lender targeted Hispanics); Barkley v. Olympia Mortgage Co., 2007 WL 2437810 (E.D.N.Y. Aug. 22, 2007) (claims under Fair Housing Act, 42 U.S.C. §§ 1981 and 1983, survive motion to dismiss).

56 *See, e.g.,* Martinez v. Freedom Mortgage Team, Inc., 527 F. Supp. 2d 827 (N.D. Ill. 2007) ("finding damages as an element of fraud pleaded sufficiently because 'Martinez' injury is that he owes more on his home than it worth and is therefore trapped in [an] adjustable, negatively amortizing loan").

57 The phrase "upside down" refers to the loan-to-value ratio for a property. Traditional underwriting guidelines require the loan amount (the numerator) to be less than the property value (the denominator).

58 The loan holder may treat this as forgiving the debt for tax purposes and issue an IRS Form 1099-C to the borrower. The forgiven debt may be considered taxable income and can create a significant tax liability for the homeowner if not handled properly. *See* § 14.6.3, *infra* (discussion of handling "discharge of indebtedness income").

59 *See, e.g.,* United States. v. Sloan, 505 F.3d 685 (7th Cir. 2007); Hoffman v. Stamper, 867 A.2d 276, 293–295 (Md. 2005).

60 *See, e.g.,* M&T Mortgage Corp. v. Miller, 323 F. Supp. 2d 405 (E.D.N.Y. 2004) (plaintiffs alleged FHA insurance served several purposes: (1) allowed mortgage to be sold to a bulk purchaser on the secondary market; (2) guaranteed payment in the event of the borrower's default; and (3) was used to further deceive buyers that purchase price was fair and transaction was legitimate).

61 Under a common type of agreement called an asset purchase and forward flow agreement, a lender contracts with a "sponsor" to automatically sell all mortgage products of a specific type to the sponsor. As a result, the lender has an incentive to originate as many mortgages of that type as possible with little regard for traditional underwriting concerns.

62 *See, e.g.,* Vaughn v. Consumer Home Mortgage, 293 F. Supp. 2d 206 (E.D.N.Y. 2003) (offer of judgment for $500,000 accepted on behalf of four victims of property flipping scheme); Boone v. Bownes, Civ. Action No. 02-143-MJR (S.D. Ill. Aug. 26, 2005) (actual damages for victim homebuyer $112,587); Hoffman v. Stamper, 843 A.2d 153 (Md. Ct. Spec. App. 2003), *aff'd in*

lost the home in a foreclosure, all monies spent by the homeowner, for moving in and out, for inspections, repairs, and all payments on the mortgage should be recoverable.[63] If the homebuyer has been able to keep the home, actual damages may include monies spent on repairs, the difference between the appraised value and the actual value, and the excess mortgage payments, calculated based on the difference between the monthly payments assuming the true value of the home and the actual monthly payments using the inflated appraised valuation.[64] Where recoverable, a claim for emotional distress should also be developed.

5.3.4.2 Appraiser Liability

While sellers are obvious defendants in property flipping schemes,[65] appraisers, with whom consumers may have had little contact, are essential to the scam. An inflated appraisal is the linchpin of these transactions.[66] As a result, advocates should carefully examine the appraisal and investigate the appraiser in these cases. Inflated values are typically achieved by misrepresenting the condition of the property or by using false comparables, such as sales of other flipped properties, or omitting key information about the sales transactions, such as a sale of the property within the previous year. Appraisers may overstate how many square feet are within a building, attach pictures of a different house, or provide a false or misleading floor plan. Appraisers may also falsely describe the neighborhood, as one that is stable or has high home values, when in fact home values are low and falling in the neighborhood. A description of the house that is false on its face or that suggests that there is no deferred maintenance when, for example, the client says the home needs a new roof or furnace, may be enough to warrant closer scrutiny of an appraisal.

The sales history of the property is a matter of public record, and usually the sales price can be easily ascertained. Practitioners should always check how much the property flipper bought the property for. A large run-up suggests appraisal fraud, may have been enough to put the lender on notice, and if not explained in the appraisal report, probably sufficient in itself to state a claim for appraisal fraud. Appraisals in sub-prime transactions may be inflated by over 1000% above the actual fair market value in order to create a loan-to-value ratio of between 60% and 75% to satisfy the underwriting requirements of the lender and secondary market.[67] Federal Housing Administration (FHA) appraisals typically are inflated by 30% to 50% because FHA-insured loans are made at close to 100% of the appraised value.

Proof of the actual value of the home is usually done through the introduction of a retrospective appraisal.[68] Such an appraisal, sanctioned by the Uniform Standards of Professional Appraisal Practice, looks at comparables in the market at the time the original appraisal was done. The weak point of a retrospective appraisal is that the home's condition may have changed. Sometimes the homeowner will have documented evidence of the condition of the home at purchase; that information is helpful for the retrospective appraisal as well as the foreclosure defense. A retrospective appraisal, or a review appraisal, can also be helpful in identifying factual misstatements on the original appraisal and failure to follow accepted industry practices. The Seventh Circuit has recently questioned the use of a review appraiser, finding that the review appraiser's values came in too low.[69] Instead, the Seventh Circuit suggested a statistical analysis, comparing the appraised value of the home and price that the property flipper purchased the home for to "normal variation of honest estimates in the appraisal business."[70]

There can be little question that the preparation of a falsified appraisal is misrepresentation that will support a fraud claim[71] and falls within the scope of most state UDAP

relevant part, 867 A.2d 276 (Md. 2004) (economic damages ranging from $3000 to $49,000 upheld).

63 Hoffman v. Stamper, 843 A.2d 153 (Md. Ct. Spec. App. 2003), *aff'd in relevant part*, 867 A.2d 276 (Md. 2004).

64 Pence v. ABN AMRO Mortgage Group, Civ. Action. No. 3-:02-CV-398, at 2 (S.D. Ohio Apr. 18, 2005) ("Damages for fraudulent or negligent appraisal consist of the difference between the actual value of the appraised property and the price paid, plus any special damages naturally and proximately cause by the fraud or negligence before it is discovered."); Posner v. Davis, 395 N.E.2d 133 (Ill. App. Ct. 1979). *See also* McGlawn v. Pa. Human Relations Comm'n, 891 A.2d 757 (Pa. Commw. Ct. 2006) (upholding damages valuation based on difference between interest due under predatory mortgage versus interest if homeowner had received a fairly priced loan).

65 *See, e.g.,* Bird v. Delacruz, 411 F. Supp. 2d 891 (S.D. Ohio 2005) (property flipping allegations against seller supported claims for breach of contract and unjust enrichment).

66 *See* United States v. Owens, 301 F.3d 521 (6th Cir. 2002) (describing appraiser's key role in a property flipping scheme); Vaughn v. Consumer Home Mortgage Inc., 2003 WL 21241669, at *6 (E.D.N.Y. Mar. 23, 2003).

67 *See* Mortgage Foreclosure Filings in Pennsylvania: A Study of The Reinvestment Fund for the Pennsylvania Department of Banking 83 (Mar. 2005), *available at* www.trfund.com/policy/pa-foreclosures.htm (reporting significantly higher concentrations of inflated appraisals in subprime loan pools than in prime loan pools).

68 *See* Kinsey v. Scott, 463 N.E.2d 1359 (Ill. App. Ct. 1984) (finding appraiser's retrospective valuation of property nine years previously not based on guess or conjecture and therefore admissible). *Cf.* Munjal v. Baird & Warner, Inc., 485 N.E.2d 855 (Ill. App. Ct. 1985) (upholding use of appraisal nine months after sales date as reasonably close in time to tort, particularly since appraisal close to sales price of property).

69 Decatur Ventures, L.L.C. v. Daniel, 485 F.3d 387, 391 (7th Cir. 2007).

70 *Id.*

71 *See* Vaughn v. Consumer Home Mortgage, Inc., 2003 WL 21241669 (E.D.N.Y. Mar. 23, 2003); Banks v. Consumer Home Mortgage, Inc., 2003 WL 21252584 (E.D.N.Y. Mar. 28, 2003);

statutes.[72] UDAP clams may be particularly promising since in most states the consumer does not have to show reliance,[73] privity of contract is unnecessary,[74] and nondisclosure is just as actionable as affirmative deception.[75] Practitioners should also consider a negligent misrepresentation claim against the appraiser, since claims sounding in negligence will ordinarily be covered by the appraiser's errors and omissions insurance policy, but fraud claims will not. A negligent misrepresentation claim can present two hurdles: generally, the borrower must show that the misrepresentation was factual[76] and that the appraiser either intended that the borrower rely on the appraisal or knew that the appraiser's client (usually the lender) intended that the borrower rely on the appraisal.[77] Form contracts used by the FHA or by Fannie Mae sometimes require the appraiser to certify that borrowers may rely on the appraisal, even if the borrower never sees the appraisal.[78]

Appraisers may also be liable for fraudulent concealment, civil conspiracy,[79] civil RICO violations,[80] and violations of state licensing laws. Under pressure from the New York Attorney General, Fannie Mae adopted the Home Valuation Code of Conduct for all loans originated after May 1, 2009 in an attempt to reduce the manipulation of appraisals. The Code prohibits commissioned loan officers and mortgage brokers from selecting, retaining, or providing for payment to the appraiser. Lenders selling loans to Fannie Mae must comply with the Code.[81]

Moore v. Mortgagestar, Inc. (S.D. W. Va. Dec. 18, 2002) (Civ. Action No. 2:01-0226), *available at* www.consumerlaw.org/unreported. *See also* Barkley v. Olympia Mortgage Co., 2007 WL 2437810 (E.D.N.Y. Aug. 22, 2007). *But see* Decatur Ventures, L.L.C. v. Daniel, 485 F.3d 387, 391 (7th Cir. 2007) (while trainee appraiser likely had intention to mislead, no evidence that supervising appraiser was aware of, rather than indifferent to, fraud).

72 Vaughn v. Consumer Home Mortgage, Inc., 2003 WL 21241669, at *6 (E.D.N.Y. Mar. 23, 2003); Banks v. Consumer Home Mortgage, Inc., 2003 WL 21252584, at *5 (E.D.N.Y. Mar. 28, 2003); Commonwealth v. Percudani, 844 A.2d 35 (Pa. Commw. Ct. 2004), *op. amended on reconsideration,* 851 A.2d 987 (Pa. Commw. Ct. 2004).

73 National Consumer Law Center, Unfair and Deceptive Acts and Practices § 4.2.12 (7th ed. 2008 and Supp.). *But cf.* Commonwealth v. Percudani, 844 A.2d 35, 48 (Pa. Commw. Ct. 2004), *op. amended on reconsideration,* 851 A.2d 987 (Pa. Commw. Ct. 2004) (reliance unnecessary in attorney general suit, but stating in dictum that for private UDAP action home buyer must show reliance on falsified appraisal).

74 *See* National Consumer Law Center, Unfair and Deceptive Acts and Practices § 4.2.19.3 (7th ed. 2008 and Supp.).

75 *See id.* § 4.2.14.

76 Brushwitz v. Ezell, 757 So. 2d 423 (Ala. 2000). *Cf.* United States v. Owens, 301 F.3d 521, 528 (6th Cir. 2002) (an appraisal inflated by 340% is beyond any normal range and probably proof of the subjective intent to defraud). *But cf.* Private Mortgage Inv. Servs. v. Hotel & Club Assocs., 296 F.3d 308 (4th Cir. 2002) (relying on Comment b to Restatement (2d) of Torts § 552 to find that South Carolina would find negligent misrepresentation in the misrepresentation of opinion as well as facts).

77 Restatement (2d) of Torts, § 552; Decatur Ventures, L.L.C. v. Daniel, 485 F.3d 387, 390 (7th Cir. 2007) (actual knowledge by appraiser of reliance required to state a case for negligence). *Compare* Private Mortgage Inv. Servs. v. Hotel & Club Assocs., 296 F.3d 308 (4th Cir. 2002) (finding negligent misrepresentation by an appraiser); Soderberg v. McKinney, 52 Cal. Rptr. 2d 635, 640 (Cal. Ct. App. 1996) (acknowledging negligent misrepresentation claim against real estate appraiser and collecting cases); Kelley v. Carbone, 837 N.E.2d 438, 441–443 (Ill. App. 2005), *appeal denied,* Kelley v. Corbone, 217 Ill. 2d 603 (Ill. Jan. 25, 2006) (finding negligent misrepresentation where appraiser failed to comply with the Uniform Standard of Professional Appraisal Practice); West v. Inter-Financial, Inc., 139 P.3d 1059, 1065–1066 (Utah Ct. App. 2006) (acknowledging negligent misrepresentation claim against appraiser by homebuyers, finding appraiser has a duty of honesty toward all users of the appraisal report, and collecting cases) *with* Zanaty Realty, Inc. v. Williams, 2005 Ala. LEXIS 208 (Ala. Nov. 18, 2005) (no cause of action for negligence where appraiser did not intend homebuyer to rely on appraisal); Kuehn v. Stanley, 91 P.3d 346, 349–351 (Ariz. Ct. App. 2004) (not finding negligent misrepresentation by an appraiser).

78 *See* Hoffman v. Stamper, 867 A.2d 276, 293–295 (Md. 2005) (FHA contracts permit buyers to rely on the value as being at least equal to the appraised value; this is sufficient to state reliance for the purposes of fraud, even if the buyer never reads the appraisal); Fannie Mae's Revised Appraisal and Property Report Forms, Frequently Asked Questions, at 3, *available at* www.efanniemae.com/sf/formsdocs/forms/pdf/sellingtrans/appraisalfaqs.pdf.

79 *See* Adcock v. Brakegate, Ltd., 645 N.E.2d 888 (1994). *See also* Banks v. Consumer Home Mortgage, Inc., 2003 WL 21252584, at *5 (E.D.N.Y. Mar. 28, 2003) (home flipping case involving inflated appraisals); Moore v. Mortgagestar, Inc. (S.D. W. Va. Dec. 18, 2002) (Civ. Action No. 2:01-0226), *available at* www.consumerlaw.org/unreported (denying motion to dismiss conspiracy claim against appraiser in predatory lending scheme); Commonwealth v. Parisi, 873 A.2d 3 (Pa. 2005) (denying motions to dismiss complaint for acting in concert where appraisals were either inflated or misled borrowers). *But see* Whitley v. Taylor Bean & Whitacker Mortgage Corp., 607 F. Supp. 2d 885 (N.D. Ill. 2009) (appraiser not liable for conspiracy where acting as agent for lender and mortgage broker because Illinois intra-corporate conspiracy doctrine prohibits finding conspiracy between corporation and its own agents). *See generally* National Consumer Law Center, Unfair and Deceptive Acts and Practices §§ 11.5.3.3, 11.5.3.3.1, 11.5.3.3.2 (7th ed. 2008 and Supp.).

80 *Compare* Matthews v. New Century Mortgage Corp., 185 F. Supp. 2d 874 (S.D. Ohio 2002) (denying motion to dismiss RICO claim where broker submitted false information to lender) *with* Honorable v. Easy Life Real Estate Sys., Inc., 182 F.R.D. 553 (N.D. Ill. 1998) (granting motion to dismiss RICO claim on ground that banks, not consumers, were victims of realtors' falsification).

81 Fannie Mae Announcement 09-01 (Jan. 7, 2009) (amending Selling Guide); Fannie Mae Home Valuation Code of Conduct Frequently Asked Questions, *available at* www.efanniemae.com/sf/guides/ssg/relatedsellinginfo/appcode/pdf/hvccfaqs.pdf. The guide and related materials are available at www.efanniemae.com/sf/guides/ssg/relatedsellinginfo/appcode.

5.3.4.3 Lender Liability

While the ultimate holder of the mortgage loan may stand to lose in these property flipping schemes (except to the extent the loan is federally insured), loan originators can stand to make significant profits on these transactions.[82] As a result, lenders may also engage in fraudulent conduct in documenting and underwriting the loan.[83] Lenders sometimes encourage the preparation of a false appraisal or overlook evidence that an appraisal is falsified.[84]

Since October 1, 2009, regulations enacted by the Federal Reserve Board, under the Truth in Lending Act, have prohibited creditors and their affiliates from coercing appraisers to misstate property valuations.[85] Creditors may not rely on appraisals with knowledge that the anti-coercion rule has been violated unless the creditor documents efforts to determine the accuracy of the appraisal.[86] The regulation includes both examples of conduct that violates the rule and examples of conduct that and does not violate the rule.[87] Remedies include actual and statutory damages as well as attorney fees and costs under TILA.[88] The HOPE for Homeowners program also prohibits influencing appraisers.[89]

Credit applications and down payments also are routinely falsified in both "sub-prime" and FHA-financed transactions.[90] For example, in *M&T Mortgage Corporation v. Miller*,[91] the plaintiffs alleged that the lender falsified and inflated their income level on the loan application to deceive HUD and FHA into believing that the loan was affordable. In another recent case, a loan officer helped the seller evade HUD requirements and then actively participated in defrauding the consumer.[92] Even where the lender does not actively participate in the scheme, lenders have often been indifferent to the incidence of property flipping in their portfolios.[93]

In addition to fraud, negligent supervision,[94] conspiracy, UDAP, and civil RICO claims, advocates should investigate potential claims for reverse redlining under federal discrimination laws[95] and claims under the federal False Claims Act in cases where the lender or holder submits an insurance claim.[96] The lender's failure to comply with federal regulations, guidance, or requirements from its investors in underwriting may support various tort claims.[97] In particular, there is extensive regulation and guidance as to the lender's use and review of appraisals.[98] Practitioners should also be

---

82 *See* Gaudie v. Countrywide Home Loans, Inc., ___ F. Supp. 2d ___, 2010 WL 181648, at *4–5 (N.D. Ill. Jan. 14, 2010) (rejecting argument that lender "had no incentive to inflate the appraisal" and noting "fact that a lender may be more incentivized by the increased fees and commission rate").

83 *See* Consumer Prot. Div. v. Morgan, 874 A.2d 919, 928–930, 934 (Md. 2005) (describing how the fraud works with FHA insurance and one lender's complicity in the fraud). *Cf.* California v. Ameriquest, at 10 H (Cal. Super. Ct. Mar. 21, 2006) (complaint), *available at* http://ag.ca.gov/newsalerts/cms06/06-005_0a.pdf (alleging that Ameriquest obtained inflated appraisals).

84 Zimmerman v. Logemann, 2009 WL 4407205, at *10 (W.D. Wis. Nov. 30, 2009) (observing that appraisal was so obviously inaccurate that lenders "were [either] very foolish in accepting the appraisal or they knew it was false and accepted it because they were part of the fraud"). *See* Martinez v. Freedom Mortgage Team, Inc., 527 F. Supp. 2d 827 (N.D. Ill. 2007) (lender's knowledge of falsified appraisal sufficient to state claim for UDAP, fraud, and civil conspiracy); People v. First Am. Corp. (N.Y. Sup. Ct. 2007) (complaint), *available at* www.oag.state.ny.us/press/2007/nov/EA%20Complaint.pdf (alleging appraiser caved to pressure from its largest lender client to come in at higher target numbers on appraisals).

85 12 C.F.R. § 226.36(b); 73 Fed. Reg. 44,604 (July 30, 2008); National Consumer Law Center, Truth in Lending § 9.9.2 (6th ed. 2007 and Supp.).

86 Reg. Z, 12 C.F.R. § 226.36(b)(2).

87 Reg. Z, 12 C.F.R. § 226.36(b)(1)(i)–(ii).

88 *See* National Consumer Law Center, Truth in Lending § 9.9.4 (6th ed. 2007 and Supp.).

89 12 U.S.C. § 1715z-23(g)(1).

90 False second notes and mortgages (often in favor of the seller and called "seller carry-back" notes and mortgages) and falsified gift letters are two common techniques for falsifying down payments. *E.g.*, Hoffman v. Stamper 867 A.2d 276 (Md. 2005). *See also* United States v. Owens, 301 F.3d 521 (6th Cir. 2002) (loan officer "created false documents . . . includ[ing] W-2 tax forms, check stubs, employment verifications, and other documents"); United States v. Agboola, 2006 WL 2521624 (D. Minn. Aug. 30, 2006) (defendant engaged in property flipping scheme using false seller-carry back promissory notes, fraudulent down payments, and other false documents and devices).

91 M&T Mortgage Corp. v. Miller, 323 F. Supp. 2d 405 (E.D.N.Y. 2004).

92 *See* Hoffman v. Stamper, 867 A.2d 276 (Md. 2005).

93 *See, e.g.*, Michael Moss and Andrew Jacobs, *Blue Skies and Green Yards, All Lost to Red Ink*, N.Y. Times, Apr. 11, 2004, at sec. 1, p.1 (division of Chase Manhattan continued lending on suspect home loans arranged by builder until Freddie Mac notified Chase that it was beginning an investigation).

The lender's condonation of such practices may give rise to claims against the lender and assignee under various theories, including fraud, UDAP, and aiding and abetting. *See also* M. Diane Pendley, Glenn Costello & Mary Kelsch, Fitch Ratings, *The Impact of Poor Underwriting Practices and Fraud in Subprime RMBS Performance* 4–5 (Nov. 28, 2007), *available at* www.fitchratings.com/corporate/reports/report_frame.cfm?rpt_id=356624 (reporting that 51% of a sample of subprime purchase loan files showed an inflated appraisal and 16% had evidence of either a straw-buyer or a flip).

94 Carroll v. Fremont Inv. & Loan, 636 F. Supp. 2d 41, 54 (D.D.C. 2009).

95 *See, e.g.*, Barkley v. Olympia Mortgage Co., 2007 WL 2437810 (E.D.N.Y. Aug. 22, 2007); Honorable v. Easy Life Real Estate Sys., 100 F. Supp. 2d 885 (N.D. Ill. 2000).

96 A private individual bringing a claim under the False Claims Act may receive 15–30% of the amount recovered for the government. *See* National Consumer Law Center, Unfair and Deceptive Acts and Practices § 9.4.13 (7th ed. 2008 and Supp.).

97 *Cf.* Commonwealth v. Fremont Inv. & Loan, 2008 WL 517279, at *13 (Mass. Super. Ct. Feb. 25, 2008), *aff'd*, 2008 WL 2312648 (Mass. App. Ct. May 2, 2008) (relying on *Statement on Subprime Mortgage Lending*, 72 Fed. Reg. 37,569 (July 10, 2007) in finding that loans that cannot be repaid are per se unfair).

98 Financial Institutions Reform, Recovery, & Enforcement Act of

alert to the relationships among the parties and what knowledge may be imputed to the lender. For example, the closing agent is nearly always the lender's agent, and the closing agent's knowledge of fraud may be imputed to the lender.[99] Common ownership or control among corporations may also be a basis for imputed knowledge or an agency relationship, such as where the lender owns the appraisal company.[100]

5.3.4.4 Liability of Other Parties

In addition to the seller, appraiser and lender, other parties may be liable for their participation in a flipping scheme or obtaining an inflated appraisal. For example, building contractors that were hired to perform renovations but either did not do the work or misrepresented the extent of the work have been implicated.[101] Consumers have also sufficiently pleaded claims against mortgage brokers,[102] closing attorneys, property inspectors, and title companies.[103] TILA's prohibition on influencing appraisers specifically applies to mortgage brokers and their affiliates.[104] While TILA does not include a private right of action against brokers, violations, nevertheless, should constitute unfair or deceptive acts or practices under state UDAP laws.

5.3.4.5 Anti-Flipping Regulation

In an attempt to curb the increasing number of property flipping schemes, the FHA recently implemented property flipping guidelines. These guidelines seek to hold lenders accountable for the quality of appraisals on properties secured by FHA-insured mortgages.[105] The final rule requires that:

- Only owners of record can sell properties that will be financed using FHA-insured mortgages (the transaction may not involve any sale or assignment of the sales contract);
- Any re-sale of a property may not occur 90 or fewer days from the last sale to be eligible for FHA financing;
- For re-sales that occur between 91–180 days where the new sales price exceeds the previous sales price by 100%, FHA will require additional documentation validating the property's value.[106]

1989, Pub. L. No. 101-73, 103 Stat. 183 (Aug. 9, 1989) (codified as amended at 12 U.S.C. §§ 1811–1835a); 12 C.F.R. pt. 34 (appraisals in federally related transactions for properties with a value greater than $250,000 must meet certain requirements); Interagency Independent Appraisal and Evaluation Functions, Financial Institution Letter 84-2003 (Oct. 27, 2003) (regulated entities are supposed to maintain procedures to "establish and maintain . . . independent real estate appraisal and evaluation for . . . asset securitization and sales units," thus extending the reach of responsibility to federally regulated lenders acting in their roles as securitizers and even, arguably, trustees of securitized pools); Interagency Appraisal and Evaluation Guidelines, Financial Institution Letter, FIL-74-94 (Nov. 11, 1994); Dep't of Housing & Urban Development Mortgagee Letter 94-54 (Nov. 7, 1994) (appraisal review requirements for FHA insured loans). *See also* § 5.3.4.5 *infra* (FHA anti-flipping regulations).

Fannie Mae's guidelines may be accessed at www.efanniemae.com. Freddie Mac's guidelines can be accessed, at least partially, at www.freddiemac.com/sell/guide/bulletins/#. Freddie Mac's official guide is available on-line at allregs.com, a subscription-only website. *See also* M. Diane Pendley, Glenn Costello & Mary Kelsch, Fitch Ratings, *The Impact of Poor Underwriting Practices and Fraud in Subprime RMBS Performance*, at 7 (Nov. 28, 2007), *available at* www.fitchratings.com/corporate/reports/report_frame.cfm?rpt_id=356624 (describing techniques lenders should use to monitor the accuracy of appraisals).

99 *See, e.g.*, Dawson v. Thomas (*In re* Dawson), 2008 WL 1700419 (Bankr. D.D.C. Apr. 9, 2008) (charging lender with knowledge that loan was residential, not commercial, since homeowner told closing attorney that she lived in home); Home Loan Corp. v. Texas Am. Title Co., 191 S.W.3d 728 (Tex. App. 2006) (finding material issue of fact whether title company had a duty to tell lender facts indicating fraud and collusion between seller and mortgage broker; duty could have existed whether title company was an escrow agent or closing agent).

100 *See* Gaudie v. Countrywide Home Loans, Inc., ___ F. Supp. 2d ___, 2010 WL 181648 (N.D. Ill. Jan. 14, 2010).

101 *See* Polonetsky v. Better Homes Depot, Inc., 760 N.E.2d 1274 (N.Y. 2001) (UDAP claim against speculator for misrepresenting that contractors and attorneys to whom it steered the consumer were FHA-approved).

102 *See* § 5.3.2, *supra*.

103 Barkley v. Olympia Mortgage Co., 2007 WL 2437810 (E.D.N.Y. Aug. 22, 2007) (denying motions to dismiss third party claims against sellers and closing attorneys in property flipping case). *See, e.g.*, Coveal v. Consumer Home Mortgage, Inc., 2005 WL 704835 (E.D.N.Y Mar. 29, 2005) (denying attorney's motion to dismiss fraud claim); M&T Mortgage Corp. v. Miller, 323 F. Supp. 2d 405 (E.D.N.Y. 2004) (denying motions to dismiss third party claims in property flipping case; claims asserted against lender, seller, real estate broker, appraiser, closing attorneys, inspector, and title company); Hoffman v. Stamper, 843 A.2d 153 (Md. Ct. Spec. App. 2004) (entering judgment for purchasers and finding evidence sufficient to support finding against loan officer, lender and appraiser under UDAP statute), *remanded on appeal*, 867 A.2d 593 (Md. 2005) (remanding for redetermination of damages); Child v. Charske, 822 N.E.2d 853 (Ohio C.P. Montgomery Cty. 2004) (finding title company may owe duty in tort to all parties to a real estate transaction); *In re* Brown, 605 S.E.2d 509 (S.C. 2004) (disbarring lawyer for, among other things, his involvement in property flipping schemes as closing agent); *In re* Lattimore, 604 S.E.2d 369 (S.C. 2004) (lawyer disbarred, in part, for ignoring indicia of property flipping).

104 12 C.F.R. § 226.36(b).

105 The regulations permit administrative action against a mortgage holder for "[s]ubmitting, or causing to be submitted, with an application for FHA mortgage insurance an appraisal, valuation condition sheet, or any other documentation relating to an appraisal that does not satisfy FHA requirements." 24 C.F.R. § 25.9(ee). *See also* 24 C.F.R. § 203.5(e).

106 24 C.F.R. § 203.37a.

The ninety-day no-flip prohibition is waived when the sellers of the property are:

- HUD itself, disposing of property in its REO[107] portfolio;
- Sales of properties that were acquired by the seller through inheritance;
- Fannie Mae, Freddie Mac or other federally-chartered financial institutions are disposing of REO;
- Local or state housing agencies;
- Nonprofit organizations that have previous approvals to purchase HUD REO properties at a discount; and
- Properties located in a presidentially-declared disaster area, provided FHA has issued an announcement of eligibility.

In addition to the specific limitation set forth in the regulation, the rules provide flexibility for FHA to examine and require additional evidence of appraised value when properties are re-sold within twelve months.[108]

5.3.5 *Home Improvement Financing Schemes*

Unscrupulous home improvement contractors and the lenders that finance them often prey on low-income homeowners who do not have access to traditional financing sources. Using high-pressure sales tactics, and sometimes fraudulent inducements, they persuade unsophisticated homeowners to sign contracts for overpriced repairs financed at exorbitant interest rates, knowing that the owner cannot afford to pay back the loan.[109] In some cases, the contractor may receive the loan proceeds directly or indirectly from the lender without providing any services to the homeowner. When contractors actually perform some work, the quality of the repairs often falls well below acceptable standards.[110]

For example, in *United States Finance Co. v. Jones*,[111] an Alabama widow, who could barely read or write, was visited at night by two salesmen from a Florida home improvement company.[112] The salesmen offered to put aluminum siding and a new roof on her home and then persuaded her to sign a mortgage providing for payments of $30.66 per month for eighty-four months (for a total of $2575.44). Instead of the aluminum siding, the contractors put tar paper on the sides of the house and sprayed it with aluminum paint. The other contracted-for repairs were not properly done. In fact, it was undisputed that the contractors did more harm than good to the house. Additionally, the signature of Ms. Jones's deceased husband was forged on the mortgage, and the forgery was notarized.

Ms. Jones sued the contractor and the assignee of the mortgage. The assignee filed a cross bill for foreclosure, claiming to be a holder in due course.[113] The Alabama court held that the assignee was not a holder in due course, and therefore it was subject to the claims and defenses Jones had against the contractor. The court then affirmed the trial court's decision to set aside the mortgage.

Besides payment on the contract, contractors may also receive a commission for "arranging" the loan (which is not disclosed to the borrower).[114] When there is large amount of equity in the property, the bank or finance company may get back much more than the amount of the loan when it ultimately forecloses.[115]

Any home improvement loan should be scrutinized closely for evidence of consumer fraud, breach of warranty, and other defenses to foreclosure,[116] such as TIL violations. The

107 Real Estate Owned (REO) most commonly refers to property which is in the possession of a lender as a result of foreclosure or forfeiture.

108 24 C.F.R. § 203.37a.

109 *See* Westfield Group v. Campisi, 2006 WL 328415 (W.D. Pa. Feb. 10, 2006) (describing various home improvement lending schemes in the context of litigation over the scope of loan brokers insurance coverage).

110 *See* Johnson v. Equity Title & Escrow Co., 476 F. Supp. 2d 873 (W.D. Tenn. 2007) (denying motion to dismiss numerous claims where, among other things, loan proceeds paid directly to home improvement contractor and subsequent repairs were substandard); Jackson v. CIT Group/Consumer Finance, Inc., 2006 WL 3098767 (W.D. Pa. Oct. 30, 2006) (denying motion to dismiss claims against lender based on allegations that homeowners were induced to enter a home improvement contract for greater amount than requested, were required to use builders specified by broker, and work actually performed was poorly done and had a negative value because it ruined the infrastructure of home); Collier v. Batiste, 2006 WL 1560739 (E.D. La. May 23, 2006) (denying motion by holder of home improvement loans to dismiss fraud claims based on allegation that holder benefited from fraudulent conduct of builder/broker).

111 229 So. 2d 495 (Ala. 1969).

112 *Id.* at 496.

113 Note that this case was decided prior to the enactment of the FTC Holder Rule in 1975 which requires credit-sellers to include in consumer credit contracts a notice that any assignees are subject to the claims and defenses against the assignor. This effectively defeats the assignee's status under the U.C.C. as a holder in due course, and also subjects the assignee, as a matter of contract law, to the consumer's claims and defenses. *See* National Consumer Law Center, Unfair and Deceptive Acts and Practices § 11.6 (7th ed. 2008 and Supp.).

114 *See* Pizzo v. Florida, 916 So. 2d 828 (Fla. Dist. Ct. App. 2005) (description of one home improvement and credit arranging scam).

115 *See* Gary Klein, *Preventing Foreclosure: Spotting Loan Scams Involving Low Income Homeowners*, 27 Clearinghouse Rev. 116 (1993).

116 *See* Chrysler First Fin. Servs. Corp. v. De Premis, 639 N.Y.S.2d 496 (table) (N.Y. 1996) (denying summary judgment in foreclosure action to assignee of mortgage where genuine issue of material fact existed as to whether homeowner was fraudulently induced to execute a mortgage instead of a retail sales installment agreement for windows); Green Tree Consumer Discount Co. v. Newton, 909 A.2d 811 (Pa. Super. Ct. 2006) (mortgagors permitted to raise counterclaim for recoupment in foreclosure action brought by mortgage holder's assignee arising from home improvement installment contract and mortgage). *See*

bankruptcy court in Rhode Island, for example, allowed a borrower to rescind a mortgage made nominally by a home improvement contractor on the grounds that the disclosures were not given at the time the home improvement contract was signed.[117] The contract stated that it was "pending financing." The court found that the contractor intended to and agreed to provide financing. The loan which financed the contract closed weeks later and the disclosures were given at the closing. The loan was immediately assigned to another lender. The court found that the borrowers had an extended three-year right to rescind under TILA.

Whenever the home improvement contractor is the originating creditor or when the contractor refers the consumer to the lender or has some other business arrangement with the lender, then the FTC Holder Rule Notice must be included in the note, which as a matter of contract law will make any holder of the note subject to all claims and defenses the consumer could raise against the contractor.[118]

In addition, advocates should not overlook grounds for affirmative suits against contractors, lenders or other parties to the transaction[119] who have engaged in these predatory practices.[120] Juries have returned multi-million dollar verdicts to victims of unfair lending practices involving home improvement contracts.[121] Advocates should also look to state home improvement statutes for an independent remedy when contractor fraud is involved.[122] Many states have enacted home improvement statutes that require licensing or registration of contractors and regulate their behavior.[123]

5.3.6 *Foreclosure Rescue and Loan Modification Scams*

Foreclosure rescue scams revolve around various types of schemes targeted at homeowners already facing foreclosure and in financial distress. Foreclosure rescue scams typically come in three varieties. The first might be called "phantom help," where a rescuer charges outrageous fees for little or no assistance. A common form of this scam is to falsely promise assistance in obtaining a mortgage loan modification for a hefty up-front fee.

A second variety is a bait-and-switch scam where the homeowner does not realize he or she is giving up ownership of the house. A third version is a bailout that typically involves the homeowners surrendering title to their homes with the belief that they will be able to repurchase them at a later time. In the later two scenarios, homeowners often become tenants in their own homes on terms that are often oppressive and unaffordable.

---

also National Consumer Law Center, Truth in Lending (6th ed. 2007 and Supp.); National Consumer Law Center, The Cost of Credit: Regulation, Preemption, and Industry Abuses (4th ed. 2009 and Supp.); National Consumer Law Center, Unfair and Deceptive Acts and Practices (7th ed. 2008 and Supp.). *See generally* Julia Patterson Forrester, *Constructing a New Theoretical Framework for Home Improvement Financing*, 75 Or. L. Rev. 1095 (1996) (general discussion of the home improvement financing process and available defenses).

117 *In re* Lombardi, 195 B.R. 569 (Bankr. D.R.I. 1996). *See also* Bynum v. Equitable Mortgage Group., 2005 WL 818619 (D.D.C. 2005); Newton v. United Companies Fin. Corp., 24 F. Supp. 2d 444 (E.D. Pa. 1998) (allowing borrowers to rescind home improvement loans and awarding statutory damages based on finding that lender failed to make timely HOEPA disclosures); Gramatan Home Investors Corp., 470 A.2d 1157 (Vt. 1983) (affirming trial court's decision that installment sales contracts for vinyl siding were properly rescinded under Vermont Consumer Fraud Act and therefore unenforceable).

118 *See* § 5.12.2, *infra*; National Consumer Law Center, Unfair and Deceptive Acts and Practices § 11.6 (7th ed. 2008 and Supp.).

119 In addition to the contractor and lender, the borrower may also have claims against other parties involved in the transaction such as mortgage brokers or settlement service providers. *See* Beard v. Worldwide Mortgage Corp., 354 F. Supp. 2d 789 (W.D. Tenn. 2005) (denying motion to dismiss RICO, FHA and state law conspiracy claims against settlement agent and notary); Equicredit Corp. of Am. v. Jackson, 2004 WL 2726115 (Ohio Ct. App. Nov. 24, 2004) (both home improvement contractor and broker must comply with home solicitation sales act).

120 For example, homeowners have successfully pleaded violations of the Racketeer Influenced and Corrupt Organizations Act, 18 U.S.C. §§ 1961–1968, the Fair Housing Act, 42 U.S.C. §§ 3601–3619, the Equal Credit Opportunity Act, 15 U.S.C. §§ 1691–1691f, state unfair and deceptive practices acts, and state conspiracy laws. *See, e.g.*, Beard v. Worldwide Mortgage Corp., 354 S. Supp. 2d 789 (W.D. Tenn. 2005) (denying motion to dismiss RICO, FHA and state law conspiracy claims); Newton v. United Companies Fin. Corp., 24 F. Supp. 2d 444 (E.D. Pa. 1998) (allowing rescission of the loan and awarding damages for violations of HOEPA and ECOA). Sample pleadings regarding home improvement fraud, foreclosure, and home defense can be found on this treatise's companion website.

121 *See, e.g.*, Union Mortgage Co. Inc. v. Barlow, 595 So. 2d 1335 (Ala. 1992) ($6 million awarded in punitive damages against a lender engaged in pattern and practice of fraud in funding loans arranged by home improvement contractor); Baker v. Harper, Civ. No. 90-048 (Ala. Cir. Ct. Barbour Cty. July 24, 1991) ($45 million awarded to five families who had been victimized by a lender and a contractor that failed to do required work in a high interest rate mortgage transaction); Williams v. Aetna Fin. Co., 700 N.E.2d 859 (Ohio 1998) (1.5 million in punitive damages). *See also* National Consumer Law Center, The Cost of Credit: Regulation, Preemption, and Industry Abuses § 12.9 (4th ed. 2009 and Supp.); Gene A. Marsh, *Lender Liability for Consumer Fraud Practices of Retail Dealers and Home Improvement Contractors*, 45 Ala. L. Rev. 1 (1993). Class action pleadings from a case involving abusive home improvement practices can be found on this treatise's companion website.

122 *See, e.g.*, Barber v. Fairbanks Capital Corp., 266 B.R. 309 (Bankr. E.D. Pa. 2001) (Pennsylvania Home Improvement Finance Act applied to unscrupulous home improvement loan made to eighty-six-year-old widow). *See also* Blacker v. Crapo, 964 A.2d 1241 (Conn. App. Ct. 2009) (home improvement contract unenforceable due to violations of state Home Solicitation Sales Act and Home Improvement Act).

123 Am. Ass'n of Retired Persons, Home Improvement Financing: A Model State Law (2000), *available at* www.aarp.org/research/legis-polit/legislation/aresearch-import-165-D17165.html. Summaries of state home improvement financing laws can be found in Volumes II and III of this report.

A variety of federal and state causes of action, under both statutory and common law, can be used to attack foreclosure rescue scams. Attacks on those that involve loss of title to the home often begin with the premise that the homeowner's transfer of title to the property was not absolute and intended to provide security for a loan (i.e., an equitable mortgage). Once the transaction is seen as a loan, then the homeowner can invoke a variety of lending laws, including those governing usury, mortgage lending, and foreclosures.

A detailed discussion of foreclosure rescue scams and the legal theories available to attack such scams can be found in Chapter 15 of this treatise.

5.3.7 *Special Circumstances for Older Homeowners*

5.3.7.1 Introduction

Older homeowners are particularly vulnerable to, and often targets of, unfair lending practices. Many have lived in their homes for decades, have paid down their mortgages, and have accumulated substantial equity in their homes. In addition to those types of misconduct described above, older homeowners may stand to lose their homes as a result of two other types of misconduct: reverse mortgage abuses and exploitation by family members.

5.3.7.2 Reverse Mortgage Abuses

Many older homeowners have trouble paying debts including rising medical bills and other age-related expenses. In certain circumstances, reverse mortgages can be an appropriate financial solution. However, these mortgages, which by design tap into the homeowner's equity, can also present unscrupulous lenders with an opportunity for abuse.[124]

Reverse mortgages (sometimes called reverse annuity mortgages or RAMs) are rising debt loans made to older homeowners which are secured by equity in the home.[125] There are two principal types of reverse mortgages: Home Equity Conversion Mortgages (HECMs)[126] and proprietary reverse mortgages. HECMs are subject to HUD regulations that offer consumers some protection.[127] HECMs are FHA insured but also protect the homeowner in the event that the lender cannot meet its obligations.[128] Private loans, in contrast, are not regulated at the federal level.

Repayment of a reverse mortgage loan is generally not required until certain events occur, such as the homeowner's death, the home is sold, or the homeowner fails to occupy the home for at least a year, such as after moving to a nursing home. Typically, reverse mortgage loans are paid out to the homeowner in monthly installments. The amount of the monthly proceeds received by the homeowner is determined by the value of the home, the interest rate and other fees charged, the loan term, the amount of any initial lump sum disbursed to the homeowner, and the homeowner's age.[129] The homeowner remains responsible for keeping the home in good repair as well as paying property taxes and hazard insurance.[130] A homeowner in default for failing to make these payments may be able to reinstate the loan and cure the default through a chapter 13 bankruptcy plan even where the lender has opted to accelerate the loan.[131]

Reverse mortgages are subject to some additional disclosure requirements under the federal Truth in Lending Act,[132] such as payment disclosures which reflect that a single payment is due when one of the specified events occurs. A number of states have also enacted laws designed to protect against abuses in reverse mortgages. These protections include:

- *Limits on Liability*. Limitation of the borrower's or the estate's liability to the lesser of the proceeds of the sale of the home or the amount of the debt,[133] as well as prohibition of prepayment penalties.[134]
- *Disclosure Requirements*. Full disclosure of costs, fees, and terms of reverse mortgages is required.[135]

---

124 *See* National Consumer Law Center, Subprime Revisited: How Reverse Mortgage Lenders Put Older Homeowners' Equity at Risk (Oct. 2009), *available at* www.consumerlaw.org/reports/content/ReverseMortgages1009.pdf; Victoria Wong and Norma Paz Garcia, Consumers Union of U.S., Inc., There's No Place Like Home: The Implications of Reverse Mortgages on Seniors in California (Aug. 1999), *available at* www.consumersunion.org/pdf/reverse.pdf (detailing some common reverse mortgage abuses).

125 *See* National Consumer Law Center, The Cost of Credit: Regulation, Preemption, and Industry Abuses § 11.6.8 (4th ed. 2009 and Supp.) (describing reverse mortgages).

126 12 U.S.C. § 1715z-20.

127 24 C.F.R. pt. 206.

128 12 U.S.C. § 1715z-20(i)(A).

129 For a general discussion of reverse mortgage loans, see *Reverse Mortgages: Mandatory Counseling and Other Protections for the Elderly Homeowner*, 27 Clearinghouse Rev. 622 (1993); *Home Equity Conversion Programs: A Housing Option for the "House-Rich, Cash-Poor" Elderly*, 23 Clearinghouse Rev. 481 (1989).

130 24 C.F.R. § 206.27(b)(5), (6). HECM lenders may elect to pay property taxes or hazard insurance premiums by withholding funds from monthly payments or charging funds to a line of credit. 24 C.F.R. § 206.205.

131 *In re* Boudreax, 2010 WL 724355 (Bankr. E.D. La. Feb. 24, 2010).

132 15 U.S.C. § 1648; 12 C.F.R. § 226.33. *See* National Consumer Law Center, Truth in Lending § 5.10.4.5.6 (6th ed. 2007 and Supp.).

133 Some states do this by defining a reverse mortgage as a non-recourse loan while others explicitly limit payment to the proceeds of the sale. *E.g.*, Mont. Code Ann. § 90-6-506(5); N.C. Gen. Stat. § 53-257(6).

134 *See, e.g.*, Colo. Rev. Stat. § 11-38-103; Conn. Gen. Stat. § 36-9g(c); 205 Ill. Comp. Stat. § 5/6.1(b)(1).

135 *See, e.g.*, Colo. Rev. Stat. § 11-38-109; 205 Ill. Comp. Stat. § 5/6.1(c)(3).

- *Protection from Default*. Homeowners are protected from being considered in default for temporary absences from the home,[136] such as a temporary stay in a nursing home.
- *Minimum Time Requirements Between Loan Maturity and Default*. After the loan matures, as a result of either the death of the borrower or the borrower's default of an obligation under the contract, a reasonable time must be allowed for the borrower or the estate to arrange for repayment.[137]
- *Required Counseling*. Counseling by a third party is a precondition to receipt of a reverse mortgage under many reverse mortgage programs and some state laws.[138]

Some of the abuses among reverse mortgage lenders are similar to those committed in the market for subprime traditional mortgages.[139] Reverse mortgage lenders have begun using financial incentives to reward brokers for arranging deals that boost lenders' profits and raise the costs paid by borrowers.[140] By adjusting reverse mortgage loan terms, such as interest rates, servicing fees, rate adjustment intervals and distributions, brokers and lenders can maximize their profits at the expense of older homeowners.

Older homeowners are also vulnerable to other abuses associated with reverse mortgages. Some older homeowners have been persuaded to sink proceeds from reverse mortgages into complicated annuity contracts or expensive long-term care insurance products.[141] These products generate large commissions for sellers, but frequently prove financially toxic for older homeowners. While Congress has banned the sale of some financial and insurance products, such as annuities, in conjunction with HECM loans,[142] those prohibitions do not apply to other reverse mortgage programs.

5.3.7.3 Exploitation by Family Members

Exploitation of older homeowners by family members can take many forms. For example, these scenarios have been reported as the basis for a foreclosure:

- A son prevails upon his older parent to convey property to him at an exceedingly low price. The son uses the property to secure loans and then proceeds to default upon them. The maker of the loans brings a foreclosure action against the property.[143]
- A mother agrees to use her good credit history to purchase property in her own name for the use of her son. They agree that the son will reside on the property, assume all financial obligations associated with the property, and eventually obtain financing in his own name. The mother places the son on the title as joint tenant. The son then forges his mother's signature to use the property as security to obtain a bank loan, and he subsequently defaults on the loan. The bank brings a foreclosure action.[144]
- A bereaved widow, whose deceased husband had always handled the family's financial affairs, finds herself confused and unable to manage her affairs after her husband's death. She welcomes the assistance of an apparently concerned relative who diverts the mortgage money for his own use.
- An older parent cosigns a bank loan for a son with a poor credit history. The parent's home is pledged as collateral for the loan. When the son fails to repay the loan, the bank threatens to foreclose on the parent's home.

Situations such as these add another, sometimes sensitive, dimension to foreclosure defense litigation.

Issues which must be thoroughly considered include:

- Does the older homeowner have a cause of action against the relative for fraud, duress, or undue influence?[145] If there is a potential claim, is the homeowner willing to assert it against a relative?
- Did the lender participate in the relative's fraud? Or, did the lender acquiesce in the fraud? In either case, the lender may be equally liable.[146]

---

136 205 Ill. Comp. Stat. § 5/6.1(c); Mont. Code Ann. § 11-38-107(2).

137 *See, e.g.*, N.C. Gen. Stat. § 53-268.

138 *See* Mass. Gen. Laws ch. 167E, § 2(i); Minn. Stat. § 47.58(8); Mont. Code Ann. § 90-5-503; N.C. Gen. Stat. § 53-270(6).

139 *See* National Consumer Law Center, Subprime Revisited: How Reverse Mortgage Lenders Put Older Homeowners' Equity at Risk, NCLC Special Report (Oct. 2009), *available at* www.consumerlaw.org/reports/content/ReverseMortgages1009.pdf.

140 *See, e.g.*, Labrador v. Seattle Mortgage Co., ___ F. Supp. 2d ___, 2010 WL 289296 (N.D. Cal. Jan. 15, 2010) (class action alleging improper assessment of broker fees).

141 *See, e.g.*, Liebig v. Farley, 2009 WL 567059 (Conn. Super. Ct. Feb. 13, 2009) (alleging extensive misconduct by financial consultant).

142 12 U.S.C. § 1715z-20(o).

143 *See Estate of* Bontkowski, 785 N.E.2d 126, 133 (Ill. Ct. App. 2003) (in action by estate to recover property, court finds that deed by which mother allegedly conveyed property was properly set aside given inadequacy of consideration ($10) and circumstances indicating oppression, fraud and duress; grantor was eighty-five years old, had a sixth grade education and limited ability to speak English, and was not represented by independent legal counsel; deed was apparently signed on date that another deed was forged and was not properly notarized, and grantor's alleged signature on deed was extremely feeble).

144 *See* Spear v. Wells Fargo Bank, 2006 WL 2917411 (Cal. Ct. App. Oct. 12, 2006) (negligence claims against bank fail, as court finds that bank had no duty to discover and report son's forgery, and that mother was in best position to monitor son's activities).

145 *See generally* National Consumer Law Center, Automobile Fraud Ch. 7 (3d ed. 2007 and Supp.); National Consumer Law Center, Collection Actions § 10.5.3.1 (2008 and Supp.).

146 *But see* Family First Fed. Sav. Bank v. De Vincentis, 665 A.2d

- Was the transaction consummated when the homeowner was incapacitated? Lack of mental capacity is grounds to rescind a contract.[147]
- Was the homeowner's signature on the loan documents forged? Obviously a homeowner who never signed the documents is not liable for the loan.[148] Similarly, a homeowner is not liable for a loan if she is unaware that she signed a contract for a mortgage.[149]
- In the case of a cosigner, the FTC Trade Regulation Rule Concerning Credit Practices[150] requires that lenders provide cosigners with special warnings regarding the potential obligations of a cosigner.[151] If these warnings were not provided, the cosigner may have a claim against the lender. Though there is no private cause of action under the FTC Rule, in most states violation of an FTC Rule constitutes an actionable unfair and deceptive trade practice.[152] While the FTC Rule does not apply to banks, savings and loans, and federal credit unions, which are excluded from the FTC's jurisdiction,[153] the federal agencies regulating those institutions have enacted somewhat comparable regulations.[154]

1119 (N.J. Super. Ct. App. Div. 1995) (lender had no duty to inquire into what appeared to be routine transaction, just because borrower was older and was not independently represented in mortgage transaction with son when son got proceeds of loan; son's fraud did not invalidate transaction because bank not involved in fraud).

147 *See generally* National Consumer Law Center, Collection Actions § 5.4.1 (2008 and Supp.).

148 Century Mortgage Co. v. George, 35 Conn. App. 326, 646 A.2d 226, 229–230 (1994) (foreclosure denied when deed defective because signature of older owner was forged by son; no ratification of mortgage by owner because owner did not receive any of proceeds, owner was an older homeowner and dying of cancer at time; court granted relief in part because foreclosure is an equitable action); Northgate Elec. Profit Sharing Plan v. Hayes, 620 N.Y.S.2d 418 (App. Div. 1994).

149 Jones v. Adams Fin. Servs., 71 Cal. App. 4th 831 (1999) (older homeowner who is legally blind and suffers from dementia will not be compelled to arbitrate claim that she was tricked into signing loan documents).

150 16 C.F.R. § 444. *See generally* National Consumer Law Center, Unfair and Deceptive Acts and Practices §§ 6.11, 6.13 (7th ed. 2008 and Supp.).

151 National Consumer Law Center, Unfair and Deceptive Acts and Practices § 6.11.9 (7th ed. 2008 and Supp.).

152 *See* National Consumer Law Center, Unfair and Deceptive Acts and Practices § 6.11.10 (7th ed. 2008 and Supp.).

153 15 U.S.C. § 46(a).

154 *See* 15 U.S.C. § 57(f); 12 C.F.R. §§ 227.11–227.16; 12 C.F.R. § 706. These regulations are discussed in National Consumer Law Center, Unfair and Deceptive Acts and Practices § 6.11.2 (7th ed. 2008 and Supp.).

5.4 Raising Origination Misconduct to Stop a Foreclosure Substantive Claims and Defenses

How a homeowner raises origination misconduct in response to a foreclosure will depend on whether the foreclosure is being conducted by judicial action or by power of sale. With a judicial foreclosure, the borrowers will have an opportunity to raise these claims as defenses to the foreclosure action. When the foreclosure is by power of sale, however, there is no court action and the borrowers will have to bring an affirmative action for injunctive relief to stop the foreclosure.[155]

These claims may possibly be raised post-foreclosure in an action to set aside the sale, depending on state law and on who purchased at the sale, but obviously it is preferable to raise any available claims before the foreclosure has taken place.[156] After a foreclosure sale, the borrower may be unable to set aside the sale, although he or she might still have a claim for damages against the original lender.

While origination misconduct in certain cases can act as a defense to a foreclosure, often the misconduct will lead only to a damage action. But such damage claims can also stop a foreclosure.

For example, in an action to foreclose a mortgage securing a home improvement loan, the homeowner was allowed to offset damages awarded on a breach of contract counterclaim against the mortgage debt and thereby discharge the mortgage.[157] In a repossession case a Georgia court found that a debtor was not in default because the amount due was more than offset by the statutory penalty for a usurious credit agreement.[158]

A Wisconsin court has similarly held that in a replevin action to determine a creditor's right to possession, the debtor's Truth in Lending and other counterclaims should be heard because the creditor has no right of possession if the allowable counterclaims exceed the amount in default.[159]

155 *See* § 4.2, *supra*.
Many courts require the posting of a bond as a condition to obtaining injunctive relief. *See* § 10.5, *infra*.

156 *See* § 14.2, *infra* (discussion of setting aside a completed foreclosure).

157 Retrovest Assocs., Inc. v. Bryant, 573 A.2d 281 (Vt. 1990). *See also* Proctor Trust Co. v. Upper Valley Press, Inc., 405 A.2d 1221, 1223 (Vt. 1979) (consolidated judgment granted plaintiff a decree of foreclosure, but set off against the mortgage note the amount of defendants' verdict on their counterclaim for fraud and deceit).

158 Ford Motor Credit Co. v. Spann, 265 S.E.2d 863 (Ga. Ct. App. 1980). *See also* Hill v. Hawes, 144 F.2d 511 (D.C. Cir. 1944) (suit for cancellation of a note and deed of trust on the ground that if payments of usurious interest are credited to the plaintiff the note has been fully paid; usury as complete defense to the note).

159 Car Credit, Inc. v. Fredette, Case No. 82-SC-8148 (Wis. Cir. Ct., Dane Cty. Nov. 30, 1982). *But see* Gen. Motors Acceptance

These claims may eliminate the delinquency or reduce it to an amount that the borrower could afford to pay to redeem the mortgage.

Key to deciding on available claims for origination misconduct is to review of all documents connected with the original mortgage transaction. This includes the mortgage (or deed of trust), the promissory note, the Truth in Lending disclosure statement, the settlement sheet, the deed, and any other documents signed by or given to the client in the course of the transaction.[160]

5.5 Unfair and Deceptive Acts and Practices (UDAP) Statutes

5.5.1 Applying UDAP Statutes to Creditor Overreaching

Abusive lending practices typically can be challenged under state unfair and deceptive acts and practices (UDAP) statutes[161] that broadly prohibit deceptive and often unfair practices. The major reason a UDAP statute might not apply is that some states limit the generally broad scope of these statutes.

Where a UDAP statute applies to "trade or commerce," this certainly encompasses lending.[162] Even a statute that only applies to "goods or services" is often interpreted to apply to loans.[163] If not, services in connection with a loan are certainly covered.[164] Also look to see if certain entities are exempted from a UDAP statute's scope, such as banks, financial institutions, or regulated industries.[165] A state-by-state analysis as to whether a UDAP statute applies to credit transactions and creditors is found at NCLC's *Unfair and Deceptive Acts and Practices* § 2.2.1.8 (7th ed. 2008 and Supp.).

UDAP statutes generally prohibit both deceptive and unfair practices. Unfairness is a broader standard than deception. Even the deception standard is broader than mere affirmative misrepresentations. A practice can be deceptive even if the defect is simply a failure to disclose the disadvantageous cost or nature of the loan.[166]

For example, when a loan broker failed to disclose the approximate amount of his high broker fee at the time the consumer engaged the broker, or that he already had a prearranged lender, the broker violated the state UDAP statute.[167] In that case, the court considered the consumer's lack of sophistication, the amount of the broker fee ($1344) compared to the net loan amount of $3656, and the broker's lack of an active search for a lender.

A homeowner may also have a UDAP claim for "churning" or "loan flipping."[168] Churning occurs when lenders or brokers reap significant income from convincing homeowners to frequently refinance their mortgages without a tangible, net benefit to the homeowner.[169] "Overcollateralizing" also may be vulnerable to a UDAP challenge, as when a home is taken as security for a relatively small

Corp. v. Cobrera, 459 N.Y.S.2d 665 (N.Y. Sup. Ct. 1982).

160 *See* § 10.2, *infra* (more discussion on gathering the information needed to defend foreclosures or challenge unfair lending practices).

161 The companion website to this treatise contains a complaint which includes a UDAP claim in a predatory home mortgage lending case. *See also* Appx. K, *infra* (finding foreclosure and home defense pleadings in NCLC's Consumer Credit and Sales Legal Practice Series). *See generally* National Consumer Law Center, Unfair and Deceptive Acts and Practices (7th ed. 2008 and Supp.).

162 See National Consumer Law Center, Unfair and Deceptive Acts and Practices § 2.2.1.4 (7th ed. 2008 and Supp.).

163 *Id.* § 2.2.1.2.

164 *Id.* § 2.2.1.3.

165 *Id.* § 2.2.1.5.

166 Besta v. Beneficial Loan Co., 855 F.2d 532 (8th Cir. 1988); Marks v. Chicoine, 2007 WL 1056779 (N.D. Cal. Apr. 6, 2007) (allegation that broker misstated interest rate and failed to disclose that loan had forty-year term states UDAP claim); *In re* Barker, 251 B.R. 250 (Bankr. E.D. Pa. 2000); *In re* Milbourne, 108 B.R. 522 (Bankr. E.D. Pa. 1989). *See* Chandler v. Am. Gen. Fin., Inc., 768 N.E.2d 60 (Ill. App. Ct. 2002). *See also* Cohen v. JP Morgan Chase & Co., 498 F.3d 111, 126–127 (2d Cir. 2007) (reversing dismissal of UDAP claim; charging of illegal fee may constitute deception even if it was disclosed). *See generally* National Consumer Law Center, Unfair and Deceptive Acts and Practices Ch. 6, §§ 2.2.1, 2.2.5 (7th ed. 2008 and Supp.).

167 *In re* Dukes, 24 B.R. 404 (Bankr. D. Mich. 1982). *See also* Pierce v. NovaStar Mortgage, Inc., 422 F. Supp. 2d 1230 (W.D. Wash. 2006) (state consumer protection act applied to allegations that broker failed to disclose the yield spread premium); Russell v. Fidelity Consumer Discount Co., 72 B.R. 855 (Bankr. E.D. Pa. 1987) (charging a broker fee for a broker who did not participate in arranging the loan violates UDAP).

168 *See* National Consumer Law Center, The Cost of Credit: Regulation, Preemption, and Industry Abuses §§ 6.1.1, 12.10.2.4 (4th ed. 2009 and Supp.).

169 *See In re* Milbourne, 108 B.R. 522 (Bankr. E.D. Pa. 1989) (series of refinancings cost borrower over $3000 more than obtaining new separate loans; lender's failure to disclose the advantage to the lender and disadvantage to consumer of refinancing is a UDAP violation); Villegas v. Transamerica Fin. Servs., 708 P.2d 781 (Ariz. Ct. App. 1985) (when borrower sought to refinance loan to lower payments and new loan was more expensive, borrower stated a UDAP claim, but not a violation of the duty of good faith). *See also In re* Tucker, 74 B.R. 923 (Bankr. E.D. Pa. 1987) (dicta suggests frequent flipping may state UDAP claim even in absence of usury); Bd. of Governors of the Fed. Reserve Sys. & U.S. Dep't of Hous. & Urban Dev., Joint Report to Congress Concerning Reform to the Truth in Lending Act and the Real Estate Settlement and Procedures Act 59 (July 1998), *available at* www.federalreserve.gov/boarddocs/RptCongress/tila.pdf (discussing problems with loan flipping); National Consumer Law Center, The Cost of Credit: Regulation, Preemption, and Industry Abuses § 11.6.6 (4th ed. 2009 and Supp.) (discussing flipping in greater detail). *But see* Trevino v. Sample, 565 S.W.2d 93 (Tex. Civ. App. 1978) (no fraud in refinancing migrant worker's mortgage with higher installments and interest rate).

loan.[170] An allegation of "loan-padding"—structuring a loan to increase its size without advancing additional funds to borrowers, thereby increasing lender profit or giving a larger loan on which to foreclose—has been held to state a cause of action under a state UDAP statute.[171]

5.5.2 How UDAP Statutes Can Stop a Foreclosure

All states and the District of Columbia authorize a private cause of action under their UDAP statute.[172] Many states allow consumers to recover not only actual damages, but also statutory damages, minimum damages, multiple damages, equitable relief, and/or attorney fees.[173]

A number of state UDAP statutes provide for enhanced penalties where the victim is an older, including Arkansas, California, Delaware, Florida, Georgia, Hawaii, Illinois, Indiana, Iowa, Louisiana, Minnesota, Nevada, New York, Pennsylvania, Wisconsin, and Wyoming.[174] These statutes generally provide extra private or state remedies for specified types of violations, such as if a seller willfully disregards the rights of the older person and if the older person was more vulnerable by reason of age or health than other persons.

UDAP claims can help defend a foreclosure action in three ways: the consumer can seek equitable relief under the UDAP statute to stop a foreclosure; the borrower may assert that the lender should not be allowed to foreclose because the UDAP violation caused the default or otherwise interfered with the borrower's ability or intent to pay the loan; or the borrower can assert that UDAP damages offset the amount of delinquent payments. This claim is stronger if the borrower has complained to the creditor prior to default.[175]

When state UDAP statutes authorize equitable relief, a UDAP claimant may seek to void or rescind the contract based on illegality. A Florida court found its authority to extend to voiding a note, mortgage and agreement in a UDAP case, when the transaction was unfair and voiding the transaction restored the status quo.[176] Before voiding a mortgage because of a UDAP violation, however, courts may require some showing of deception in connection with the taking of a security interest in the home. Similarly, unfair or deceptive acts in the foreclosure process may provide equitable grounds to set aside a sale.[177] Even where a UDAP statute does not explicitly authorize equitable relief, many states consider foreclosure to be an equitable

---

170 McRaid v. Shepard Lincoln Mercury, 367 N.W.2d 404 (Mich. Ct. App. 1985) (exchange of home worth $43,000 for a car and $10,000 cash violated UDAP). *But cf.* Victoria Bank & Trust Co. v. Brady, 779 S.W.2d 893 (Tex. App. 1989) (after loan had been paid, bank retained security interest in order to force payment of another loan that bank had previously told borrower he would not be liable for), *rev'd in part*, 811 S.W.2d 931 (Tex. 1991).

171 Therrien v. Resource Fin. Group, 704 F. Supp. 322 (D.N.H. 1989) (lender required a payment escrow which they advanced as part of the loan, adding nearly $12,000 to the principal at 20 1/4% interest, placed the payment escrow in an interest-bearing account on which they credited borrowers with 5% interest and retained any excess; also lenders double-charged for closing costs).

172 National Consumer Law Center, Unfair and Deceptive Acts and Practices § 13.2.1 (7th ed. 2008 and Supp.).

173 *See generally* National Consumer Law Center, Unfair and Deceptive Acts and Practices Ch. 13, Appx. A (7th ed. 2008 and Supp.) (describing private UDAP remedies and analysis of each state UDAP statute).

174 *See* Ark. Code Ann. §§ 4-88-201 to 4-88-207; Cal. Bus. & Prof. Code § 17206.1; Del. Code Ann. tit. 6, § 2581; Fla. Stat. Ann. § 501.2077; Ga. Code Ann. § 10-1-851; Haw. Rev. Stat. § 480-13.5; 815 Ill. Comp. Stat. Ann. § 505/7; Iowa Code Ann. § 714.16A; La. Rev. Stat. Ann. § 51:1407(D); Minn. Stat. § 325F.71; Nev. Rev. Stat. § 598.0933, 598.0973; N.Y. Gen. Bus. Law § 349-c (McKinney); 73 Pa. Cons. Stat. § 201-8(b); Tenn. Code Ann. § 47-18-125; Tex. Bus. & Com. Code Ann. § 17.47(c)(2) (Vernon) (additional civil penalty up to $250,000 for initial violation if victim is over 65); Wis. Stat. § 100.264; Wyo. Stat. Ann. § 40-12-111.

In addition, North Dakota provides those over sixty-five years of age with a special right to cancel door-to-door sales. Instead of three days, in North Dakota the merchant must give the older consumer either a fifteen-day cancellation notice or a thirty-day money back guarantee (except for intentional damage or misuse). N.D. Cent. Code § 51-18-02. For a discussion of enhanced penalties for older consumers, *see generally* National Consumer Law Center, Unfair and Deceptive Acts and Practices § 15.5.3.6 (7th ed. 2008 and Supp.).

175 Fannie Mae's uniform mortgage (Form 3001) includes a notice of grievance clause that prohibits the borrower and lender from taking judicial action based on the mortgage without first notifying the other party of the breach and giving a reasonable time to cure.

176 Hinton v. Brooks, 820 So. 2d 325 (Fla. Dist. Ct. App. 2001) (sellers' misrepresentation regarding lack of termite damage is fraud in the inducement and is a defense to foreclosure); McLendon v. Metro. Mortgage Co., Clearinghouse No. 43,703G (Fla. Cir. Ct. Dade County May 20, 1988); EBC Amro Asset Mgmt., Ltd. v. Kaiser, 681 N.Y.S.2d 539, 540 (App. Div. 1998) (fraud as defense to mortgage foreclosure when mortgage holder dissipated investment fund that served as security for loan); Green Tree Acceptance, Inc. v. Anderson 981 P.2d 804 (Okla. 1999) (both fraud and misrepresentation are legal bases for rescission of a mortgage in an action by the mortgage holder to foreclose; summary judgment denied lender when lender's agent told borrower that the mortgage document was an "affidavit of clear title" and convinced him to execute the document based on that false description of the document's legal effect); Rader v. Danny Darby Real Estate, Inc., 2001 WL 1029355 (Tex. Sept. 10, 2001) (failure of seller to disclose existence of due on sale provision when buyer assumed mortgage, which led to foreclosure, was issue of fact precluding summary judgment in favor of lender in foreclosure). *See also* Morgera v. Chiappardi, 74 Conn. App. 442, 813 A.2d 89 (2003) (in strict foreclosure case court can use equity to withhold foreclosure when the plaintiff's conduct is inequitable); Fidelity v. Kreniskey, 807 A.2d 968 (Conn. App. Ct. 2002) (when plaintiff's conduct is inequitable, a court may withhold foreclosure on equitable grounds).

177 *See* § 14.2.3, *infra*.

proceeding in which a lender's unfair or deceptive conduct during origination could be used to raise equitable defenses such unclean hands.[178]

5.6 Truth in Lending Rescission and Damage Claims

5.6.1 Truth in Lending Rescission Rights

The Truth in Lending Act (TILA) is designed to provide consumers with accurate information about loan transactions in order to facilitate informed use of credit.[179] TILA requires a creditor to disclose certain important information about the credit terms to the consumer in writing prior to consummation of a credit transaction.

The provision of TILA that is most relevant to foreclosure defense is the right of rescission.[180] This right applies to consumer credit transactions in which a nonpurchase money lien or security interest is or will be placed on the consumer's principal dwelling.[181] Home equity loans, transactions that refinance purchase money mortgages, home improvement loans, and credit sales secured by the consumer's home are common examples of rescindable transactions.[182] The right to rescind does not apply, however, to transactions for the purchase of the home.[183]

The rescission right is absolute for three business days,[184] but it is extended for up to three years[185] if certain "material" TIL disclosures were not provided correctly at the time of the original credit transaction or a proper notice of the right to cancel was not given.[186] Therefore, any credit transaction involving a home (other than for its purchase) should be examined for TIL violations, which may provide a continuing opportunity to rescind the transaction.

Inaccuracies in certain disclosures can lead to rescission only if they exceed tolerances set by the statute—in most cases, a finance charge error must exceed 1/2 of 1% of the total loan amount (or 1% in some refinancing transactions).[187] A highly important exception to this rule establishes a lower tolerance for errors when a homeowner is asserting rescission in response to a foreclosure. If the holder of the mortgage has initiated "any judicial or non-judicial foreclosure process on the principal dwelling of an obligor," the tolerance for errors in the finance charge is just $35.[188] Case law is not clear what constitutes "initiation" of a non-judicial foreclosure, but this determination is likely to be state-specific. In any event, in some cases, to take advantage of this lower tolerance, homeowners in financial trouble might delay rescission until foreclosure proceedings are initiated.

When evaluating a mortgage transaction for TIL rescission, timing is critical. The right to rescind expires three years after consummation of the transaction, with almost no exceptions.[189] If the loan is almost three years old, the possibility of rescinding the transaction should be determined without delay.

The TIL rescission provisions reflect Congress's desire to keep homeowners from placing their homes in jeopardy without a clear understanding of the risks and benefits of the transaction.[190] TIL rescission can be a powerful tool, providing an extremely beneficial remedy for consumers facing foreclosure or struggling to meet payments on a home equity loan with onerous terms. The Truth in Lending Act, including rescission, is discussed in detail in NCLC's *Truth in Lending* (6th ed. 2007 and Supp.).

5.6.2 Grounds for Extended Rescission

The right to rescind normally lasts three business days after consummation of the transaction, but can be extended for up to three years under a number of circumstances:

178 *See, e.g.*, Boretz v. Segar, 199 A. 548, 549 (Conn. 1938). *See generally* § 4.10, *supra*.

179 *See generally* National Consumer Law Center, Truth in Lending (6th ed. 2007 and Supp.).

180 *See* National Consumer Law Center, Truth in Lending Ch. 6 (6th ed. 2007 and Supp.).

181 15 U.S.C. § 1635(a).

182 The companion website to this treatise includes a sample rescission letter, an objection to a secured claim in Bankruptcy Court, and many other helpful papers. *See also* Appx. K, *infra* (finding foreclosure and home defense pleadings in NCLC's Consumer Credit and Sales Legal Practice Series).

183 15 U.S.C. § 1635(a). *See* National Consumer Law Center, Truth in Lending § 6.2.6.1 (6th ed. 2007 and Supp.).

184 15 U.S.C. § 1635(a). Under certain circumstances, the consumer may waive the three-day period. *See* National Consumer Law Center, Truth in Lending § 6.2.9 (6th ed. 2007 and Supp.).

185 The Massachusetts statute of limitations on Truth in Lending claims is four years for damages and rescission. Mass. Gen. Laws ch. 140D, § 10(f) and ch. 260, § 5A.

186 15 U.S.C. § 1635(a), (f). *See* National Consumer Law Center, Truth in Lending § 6.3.2 (6th ed. 2007 and Supp.).

187 15 U.S.C. § 1605(f). *See* National Consumer Law Center, Truth in Lending § 4.6.3.2 (6th ed. 2007 and Supp.).

188 15 U.S.C. § 1635(i)(1), (2); National Consumer Law Center, Truth in Lending § 6.3.2.2 (6th ed. 2007 and Supp.). *See* Payton v. New Century Mortgage Corp., 2003 WL 22349118 (N.D. Ill. Oct. 14, 2003) (consumer has extended right to rescind where finance charge is underdisclosed by more than $35); Layell v. Home Loan & Inv. Bank, 244 B.R. 345 (E.D. Va. 1999) (applying $35 tolerance in suit challenging non-judicial foreclosure). *But cf.* Stump v. WMC Mortgage Corp., 2005 WL 645238, at *8 n.3 (E.D. Pa. Mar. 16, 2005) ($35 tolerance did not apply where no foreclosure had been initiated and bankruptcy automatic stay prohibited initiation of foreclosure).

189 15 U.S.C. § 1635(f). *See* § 5.6.6, *infra*. The right lasts for four years in Massachusetts. Mass. Gen. Laws ch. 140D, § 10(f) and ch. 260, § 5A.

190 S. Rep. No. 96-368, at 28, *reprinted in* 1980 U.S.C.C.A.N. 236, 264 ("This provision was enacted to give the consumer the opportunity to reconsider any transaction which would have the serious consequence of encumbering the title to his home.").

- *Closed-end credit:* the creditor fails to give the consumer all "material" disclosures or fails to provide each consumer with two copies of a notice describing the right to rescind.[191] For closed-end credit, the "material" disclosures are defined as the annual percentage rate, the finance charge, the amount financed, the total of payments, and the payment schedule.[192] The Federal Reserve Board's regulations specify the content of the notice of right to cancel. Many courts have held that errors or omissions in the notice, or failure to provide the proper number of copies, extend the right to rescind.[193]
- *Higher-priced mortgage loans:*[194] the loan includes a prepayment penalty but does not comply with the list of requirements specified in the Board's regulations.[195]
- *High-rate loan covered by HOEPA:*[196] the lender fails to make the special "advance look" disclosures or includes a prohibited term.[197]

5.6.3 *Effect of Rescission on Creditor's Right to Foreclose*

Once notice of rescission is given, the lien on the consumer's home becomes void,[198] taking away the creditor's foreclosure remedy, and its leverage. The homeowner is entitled to a return, or a credit against the balance of the debt, of all finance, interest, and other charges, such as closing costs and broker fees.[199] This can dramatically reduce the consumer's debt if the interest rate or charges were high or substantial payments had been made. In certain circumstances the consumer may even have the right to retain the proceeds or goods purchased.[200]

Rescission is a complete defense to foreclosure on the property because it voids the security interest.[201] A foreclosure sale is improper after the consumer has sent a rescission notice, even if a court has not yet ruled on the validity of the consumer's rescission.[202]

The consumer may bring suit in federal district court, bankruptcy court or state court to enforce these rights. Federal courts can enjoin state non-judicial foreclosure proceedings during the pendency of a TIL rescission claim, and may, depending on the stage of the foreclosure, be able to

191 15 U.S.C. § 1635(a); 12 C.F.R. § 226.23(b).

192 12 C.F.R. § 226.23 n.48. The material disclosures for home equity lines of credit are defined in 12 C.F.R. § 226.15 n.36.

193 *See* National Consumer Law Center, Truth in Lending § 6.4.3 (6th ed. 2007 and Supp.).

194 *See* § 5.7, *infra*; 12 C.F.R. § 226.35(a).

195 12 C.F.R. § 226.32(d)(6).

196 *See* § 5.8, *infra*.

197 15 U.S.C. § 1639(j); 12 C.F.R. § 226.23 n.48.

198 15 U.S.C. § 1635(b); 12 C.F.R. §§ 226.15(d)(2), 226.23(d)(2); Official Staff Commentary §§ 226.15(d)(1)-1, 226.23(d)(1)-1. *See* National Consumer Law Center, Truth in Lending § 6.6.3 (6th ed. 2007 and Supp.). *See also* 69 Fed. Reg. 16,796, 16,771–16,772 (Mar. 31, 2004) (reiterating that security interest becomes void when consumer rescinds); Lippner v. Deutsche Bank Nat'l Trust Co., 544 F. Supp. 2d 695 (N.D. Ill. 2008) (security interest becomes void upon mailing rescission letter); Willis v. Friedman (Md. Ct. Spec. App. May 2, 2002), *available at* www.consumerlaw.org/unreported ("[o]nce the right to rescind is exercised, the security interest in the debtor's property becomes void ab initio").

199 15 U.S.C. § 1635(b); 12 C.F.R. §§ 226.15(d)(2), 226.23(d)(2); Official Staff Commentary § 226.23(d)(2)-1. *See* Semar v. Platte Valley Fed. Sav. & Loan Ass'n, 791 F.2d 699 (9th Cir. 1986) (in a successful rescission action, consumer not responsible for any finance charges, including interest, or for any loan expenses (which exceeded $11,000)); Ramirez v. Household Fin. Corp. (*In re* Ramirez), 329 B.R. 727, 734 (Bankr. D. Kan. 2005) (affirming bankruptcy court order voiding consumer's obligation to pay finance charges and closing costs); Robertson v. Strickland (*In re* Robertson), 333 B.R. 894, 898, 904 n.14 (Bankr. M.D. Fla. 2005) (after rescission, consumer is not responsible for loan discount fee, mortgage broker fee, closing fee, recording fees, mortgage note stamps, or intangible tax); Williams v. BankOne (*In re* Williams), 291 B.R. 636 (Bankr. E.D. Pa. Apr. 3, 2003); *In re* Jackson, 245 B.R. 23 (Bankr. E.D. Pa. 2000) (summary of the consequences of a rescission violation by a creditor); *In re* Michel, 140 B.R. 92 (Bankr. E.D. Pa. 1992) (finance charges and other charges, including filing fees and costs and credit insurance, must be eliminated). *But see* Coleman v. Equicredit Corp., 2002 WL 88750 (N.D. Ill. Jan. 22, 2002) (erroneously rejecting consumer's claim that upon rescission all payments made should be returned or credited to principal); Mortgage Source, Inc. v. Strong, 75 P.3d 304 (Mont. 2003) (borrower who rescinded is still liable for loan broker fee; court appears to be unaware of contrary Commentary provision); Gen. Home Capital Corp. v. Campbell, 800 N.Y.S.2d 917 (Dist. Ct. 2005) (application fee and appraisal fee need not be refunded because they are not part of finance charge; court ignores "any amount" language and is apparently unaware of Official Staff Commentary § 226.23(d)(2)-1). *See generally* National Consumer Law Center, Truth in Lending § 6.6.4 (6th ed. 2007 and Supp.).

200 15 U.S.C. § 1635(b); Reg. Z, 12 C.F.R. §§ 226.15(d)(3), 226.23(d)(3). *See* National Consumer Law Center, Truth in Lending § 6.9.5 (6th ed. 2007 and Supp.).

If the creditor does not take possession of the money or property within twenty calendar days after the consumer's tender, the consumer may keep it without further obligation. *See, e.g.*, Arnold v. W.D.L. Inv., Inc., 703 F.2d 848 (5th Cir. 1983) (consumer offered to tender proceeds, but creditor failed to cancel note and mortgage; creditor's noncompliance resulted in forfeiting rights to proceeds); Basnight v. Diamond Developers, Inc., 146 F. Supp. 2d 754 (M.D.N.C. 2001) (lender forfeited rights to home improvement materials by failing to take possession within twenty days).

201 Albano v. Norwest Fin. Haw., Inc., 244 F.3d 1061 (9th Cir. 2001) (TIL rescission claim); Family Fin. Servs. v. Spencer, 677 A.2d. 479 (Conn. App. Ct. 1996) (creditor's failure to accept rescission notice nullified the mortgage, barring the creditor from foreclosure); Yslas v. D.K. Guenther Builders, Inc., 342 So. 2d 859 (Fla. Dist. Ct. App. 1977); Cmty. Nat'l Bank & Trust v. McClammy, 525 N.Y.S.2d 629 (App. Div. 1988) (if rescission claim established, would be defense to a foreclosure on a nine-year-old mortgage). *See also* Fed. Deposit Ins. Corp. v. Ablin, 532 N.E.2d 379 (Ill. App. Ct. 1988).

202 Willis v. Friedman (Md. Ct. Spec. App. May 2, 2002), *available at* www.consumerlaw.org/unreported.

enjoin judicial foreclosure proceedings as well.[203] Rescission can also be raised in state court in response to the foreclosure. It is, however, important to assert rescission before the foreclosure is complete.[204]

The creditor's failure to perform its rescission obligations under TILA may be a separate TIL violation, entitling the consumer to actual and statutory damages and attorney fees.[205] This award can make a substantial reduction in the balance. If the creditor disputes the consumer's right to rescind, the creditor's proper course of action is to file a declaratory judgment action within twenty days after receiving the rescission notice, before the deadline for returning the consumer's money or property and recording a termination of the security interest.[206]

If the loan is a higher-priced mortgage loan, as described at § 5.7, *infra*, or is covered by the Home Ownership and Equity Protection Act (HOEPA), which is discussed at § 5.8, *infra*, the consumer is entitled to not only statutory damages and actual damages, but also special enhanced damages in the amount of all finance charges and fees paid by the consumer.[207] The consumer may also recover damages for other TIL violations even when the transaction is canceled.[208] The one-year statute of limitations for TIL damage claims runs from the date of the violation in the case of violations of the creditor's rescission obligations, but it runs from the date of consummation of the transaction for disclosure violations.[209]

5.6.4 The Consumer's Tender Obligation

5.6.4.1 Nature of the Tender Obligation

When the consumer rescinds a transaction, and after the creditor takes the required steps to void the mortgage and return certain payments, the consumer is then obligated to tender the loan proceeds, or the fair market value of any property received. If the loan that was rescinded was a refinancing of another loan with the same creditor, and new money is advanced, only the amount of the new advance is subject to rescission, and the tender obligation is based on the amount of the new advance.[210]

The consumer's tender obligation is the net amount owed after voiding all finance charges, interest, and other charges, and after crediting all the consumer's payments directly to the principal.[211] If the consumer received property in the transaction, the tender obligation is its fair market value, which may be less than the original credit obligation. For example, the fair market value of a home improvement may

203 *See* § 10.6, *infra* (discussion of obstacles to injunctive relief in federal court against state court foreclosure).

204 *See, e.g.*, Fonua v. First Allied Funding, 2009 WL 816291 (N.D. Cal. Mar. 27, 2009) (claim for rescission mooted by completed foreclosure). *See* National Consumer Law Center, Truth in Lending § 6.9.6 (6th ed. 2007 and Supp.) (raising rescission as a defense to foreclosure).

205 15 U.S.C. § 1640. *See, e.g.*, Gerasta v. Hibernia Nat'l Bank, 575 F.2d 580 (5th Cir. 1978); Moore v. Cycon Enters., Inc. 2007 WL 475202 (W.D. Mich. Feb. 9, 2007); Canty v. Equicredit Corp., 2003 WL 21243268 (E.D. Pa. May 8, 2003); Fairbanks Capital Corp. v. Jenkins, 225 F. Supp. 2d 910 (N.D. Ill. 2002); Gibbons v. Interbank Funding Group, 208 F.R.D. 278 (N.D. Cal. 2002) (claim for statutory damages for failure to recognize the plaintiff's right to rescind was not barred by the statute of limitations when the claim was brought within one year after the expiration of the twenty-day period after rescission); Aquino v. Pub. Fin. Consumer Discount Co., 606 F. Supp. 504 (E.D. Pa. 1985) (consumer could recover statutory damages for creditor's failure to rescind and obtain rescission despite earlier recovery of TIL statutory damages for other disclosure violations); Bell v. Parkway Mortgage, Inc. (*In re* Bell), 309 B.R. 139 (Bankr. E.D. Pa. 2004) (awarding statutory damages for disclosure violations as setoff), *modified in part on other grounds*, 314 B.R. 54 (Bankr. E.D. Pa. 2004); *In re* Armstrong, 288 B.R. 404 (Bankr. E.D. Pa. 2003) (a consumer who is entitled to rescission may also recover a statutory damage award for the creditor's failure to rescind voluntarily); Williams v. Gelt Fin. Corp., 239 B.R. 728 (Bankr. E.D. Pa. 1999), *aff'd*, 237 B.R. 590 (E.D. Pa. 1999); Murray v. First Nat'l Bank of Chicago, 239 B.R. 728 (Bankr. E.D. Pa. 1999); Ralls v. Bank of N.Y. (*In re* Ralls), 230 B.R. 508 (Bankr. E.D. Pa. 1999) (statutory damages awarded for disclosure violations and for failure to respond properly to rescission notice); Bourgeois v. Mortgage Funding Corp. (*In re* Bourgeois) (Bankr. D. Mass. Mar. 16, 1998) (No. 95-12036-WCH, A.P. No. 95-1541), *available at* www.consumerlaw/unreported (consumer awarded $2000 for mortgagee's failure to respond to rescission notice). *See also* National Consumer Law Center, Truth in Lending § 6.9.3 (6th ed. 2007 and Supp.).

206 *See* 15 U.S.C. § 1635(b); American Mortgage Network, Inc. v. Shelton, 486 F.3d 815 (4th Cir. 2007) (affirming award of declaratory judgment to lender in suit lender brought to resolve issues regarding consumer's rescission); Decision One Mortgage Co. v. Fraley, 2000 WL 1889700 (6th Cir. Dec. 19, 2000) (unreported) (affirming award of declaratory judgment to lender in suit lender brought to resolve issues regarding consumer's rescission); Aquino v. Public Fin. Consumer Discount Co., 606 F. Supp. 504 (E.D. Pa. 1985) (suggesting the creditor can petition court for declaration of rights and duties within twenty-day time for response).

207 15 U.S.C. § 1640(a)(4). *See* § 5.8.1, *infra*. The regulation for higher-priced mortgage loans does not state whether violations entitle consumers to special enhanced damages, but the Supplementary Information accompanying the proposed regulation describes the remedies for violations. This is discussed in greater detail in National Consumer Law Center, Truth in Lending § 9.8.4 (6th ed. 2007 and Supp.).

208 15 U.S.C. § 1635(g). *See also* S. Rep. No. 96-368, at 29, *reprinted in* 1980 U.S.C.C.A.N. 236, 265 ("Finally, the bill explicitly provides that a consumer who exercises his right to rescind may also bring suit under the act for other violations not relating to rescission."); National Consumer Law Center, Truth in Lending § 6.9.3 (6th ed. 2007 and Supp.).

209 15 U.S.C. § 1640(e). *See* National Consumer Law Center, Truth in Lending § 7.2 (6th ed. 2007 and Supp.).

210 Reg. Z, 12 C.F.R. §§ 226.23(a)(1)-5. *See* National Consumer Law Center, Truth in Lending § 6.2.3.2 (6th ed. 2007 and Supp.).

211 *See* § 5.6.3, *supra*.

be an amount drastically lower than the cash price, particularly when the improvements were inadequately performed.[212]

The Act provides that the creditor forfeits the right to any property the consumer tenders if it fails to accept the consumer's tender within twenty days.[213] In addition, according to some courts, the creditor may lose the right to the debt balance if it does not perform its statutory obligations even if the consumer did not tender.[214]

5.6.4.2 Does the Court Have the Authority to Condition Rescission on Tender?

The Act provides that the security interest becomes void upon rescission, that the creditor must return the consumer's money or property within twenty days, and that the consumer's duty to tender arises only "upon the performance of the creditor's obligations."[215] Thus, the normal rule is that the creditor must void the security interest before the consumer is required to perform this tender obligation.

The Act also, however, gives courts the authority to modify "the procedures prescribed by" the rescission provision.[216] Whether this provision gives a court the authority to reverse the statutory steps, and require the consumer to tender before the creditor voids the security interest and returns the consumer's money or property, has been much debated.

There is a strong argument that the court's modification authority does not extend to placing a precondition on the voiding of the security interest, which the Act makes an automatic consequence of the consumer's rescission.[217] The sequence of rescission and tender set forth in TILA reorders the common law rules governing rescission.[218] The Act limits the court's modification authority to the procedural aspects of rescission and does not give courts equitable authority to alter substantive provisions. The voiding of the security interest is the substance of the consumer's rescission right, and thus cannot be altered by the courts. Regulation Z, adopted by the Federal Reserve Board to implement and interpret the Act, also makes clear that the voiding of the security interest is not subject to modification by the court.[219] These arguments are presented in greater detail in National Consumer Law Center, *Truth in Lending* § 6.7 (6th ed. 2007 and Supp.).

Despite these arguments, however, most courts have concluded that they have the authority to modify the rescission sequence by conditioning the voiding of the security interest upon the consumer's tender.[220] Some courts, most notably in the Ninth Circuit, have gone further by dismissing rescission claims unless the consumer's complaint alleges ability to tender.[221] This interpretation of the court's power to modify the rescission process is erroneous and has been rejected by the Federal Reserve Board.[222]

Even if a court concludes that it has authority to condition rescission upon tender, this authority is discretionary and the court need not exercise it. Decisions suggest that equitable principles such as the severity of the creditor's TIL violations and the borrower's ability to repay the tender amount should be considered when deciding whether to impose conditions on the right to rescind.[223] Even courts that have concluded that they have the authority to condition rescission upon tender recognize the rule that "*the creditor must ordinarily tender first*," and that "while the goal should always be to 'restor[e] the parties to the status quo ante,' . . . rescission must also maintain its vitality as an enforcement tool."[224] Thus, it is inappropriate to routinely grant modification, absent special equitable circumstances which it should be the creditor's burden to prove.[225]

---

212 15 U.S.C. § 1635(b); Reg. Z, 12 C.F.R. §§ 226.15(d)(3), 226.23(d)(3). *See* National Consumer Law Center, Truth in Lending § 6.6.5 (6th ed. 2007 and Supp.).

213 15 U.S.C. § 1635(b). *See, e.g.*, Sosa v. Fite, 498 F.2d 114 (5th Cir. 1984); Arnold v. W.D.L. Invs., Inc., 703 F.2d 848 (5th Cir. 1983). *See generally* National Consumer Law Center, Truth in Lending § 6.9.5 (6th ed. 2007 and Supp.).

214 *In re* Celona, 90 B.R. 104 (Bankr. E.D. Pa. 1988), *aff'd*, 98 B.R. 705 (E.D. Pa. 1989); *In re* Tucker, 74 B.R. 923 (Bankr. E.D. Pa. 1987). *See* Basnight v. Diamond Developers, Inc., 146 F. Supp. 2d 754 (M.D.N.C. 2001) (borrower had no duty to return the property, as creditor refused to cancel the security interest); National Consumer Law Center, Truth in Lending § 6.9.5 (6th ed. 2007 and Supp.).

215 15 U.S.C. § 1635(b).

216 *Id.*

217 *See, e.g.*, Williams v. Bank One (*In re* Williams), 291 B.R. 636 (Bankr. E.D. Pa. 2003) (no authority for equitable modification); *In re* Myers, 175 B.R. 122 (Bankr. D. Mass. 1994) (conditional rescission inappropriate in bankruptcy context under identical provisions in Mass. TIL statute). *Cf.* Bell v. Parkway Mortgage, Inc., 314 B.R. 54 (Bankr. E.D. Pa. 2004).

218 Williams v. Homestake Mortgage Co., 968 F.2d 1137, 1140 (11th. Cir. 1992); Velazquez v. HomeAmerican Credit, Inc., d/b/a Upland Mortgage, 254 F. Supp. 2d 1043, 1045 (N.D. Ill. 2003) (TILA's rescission "scheme is contrary to the rule under common law rescission, where the rescinding party must tender first.").

219 12 C.F.R. §§ 226.15(d)(4), 226.23(d)(4).

220 *See, e.g.,* American Mortgage Network, Inc. v. Shelton, 486 F.3d 815 (4th Cir. 2007); Yamamoto v. Bank of New York, 329 F.3d 1167 (9th Cir. 2003); Decision One Mortgage Co. v. Fraley, 238 F.3d 420 (Table), 2000 WL 1889700 (6th Cir. Dec. 19, 2000).

221 *See, e.g.*, Yamamoto v. Bank of New York, 329 F.3d 1167 (9th Cir. 2003); Del Valle v. Mortgage Bank of Cal., 2009 WL 3786061 (E.D. Cal. Nov.10, 2009).

222 *See* § 5.6.4.3, *infra*; National Consumer Law Center, Truth in Lending § 6.7.2.3 (6th ed. 2007 and Supp.).

223 Williams v. Homestake Mortgage Co., 968 F.2d 1137 (11th Cir. 1992).

224 *Id.* at 1140, 1142.

225 That it should be the creditor's burden flows from the fact, recognized by the Eleventh Circuit, that the creditor must ordinarily tender first, and that the TIL rescission remedy was designed to be "a painless remedy," with all burdens placed on the creditor to facilitate compliance with the statute. 968 F.2d at

To prepare for the likely tender battle, the consumer should not present the TIL violations in a vacuum, but should relate the creditor's TIL violations to violations of other laws and other oppressive practices. Creditor behavior such as excessive refinancings or "flippings," refusing to pick up the property tendered by the consumer, overreaching, deception, or targeting vulnerable individuals should be stressed. The nature and severity of the creditor's TIL violations, and whether the creditor ignored the consumer's rescission, should also weigh against modification. The effect of foreclosure on the consumer—loss of the family home—should also be a factor, particularly if the loan was predatory. As discussed in the next subsection, it is critical to establish a record as to the borrower's ability to repay the proceeds.

If the goal of equitable modification is to make sure that the parties return to the *status quo ante*, it is important to look at the consumer's situation before entering into the loan in question. What were the consumer's monthly payments? How much equity did the consumer have in the home? What was the total of the consumer's other secured debt? If the court's attention is focused on the consumer's *status quo ante* it may be apparent that the remedy the consumer seeks is not at all inequitable.

It is important to remember that a court's equitable authority to modify the rescission process is not limited to protecting creditors. A court may also modify a consumer's responsibility to tender in a way that is affordable and manageable for the consumer. This is especially appropriate where the creditor's misconduct, or circumstances beyond either party's control (such as a collapse in the mortgage market), make it harder for the consumer to tender. For example, lending based on inflated appraisals or without regard to ability to repay may leave a consumer with a tender obligation that exceeds what more honest creditors may be willing to refinance. Under such circumstances, the court should use its equitable authority to adjust the tender process in a way that preserves the consumer's rights under TILA.

5.6.4.3 Planning for Tender

It is essential to begin planning for tender at the outset of a TIL rescission case. The homeowner must be prepared for the court to condition rescission upon tender, and must develop a realistic plan for meeting the tender obligation.[226]

There are a variety of options available to meet the tender obligation, once that amount has been determined. The homeowner may be able to tender in cash from available funds, especially if the homeowner had already made a number of payments and the principal has been significantly reduced due to the elimination of finance charges, interest, and fees. The homeowner may be able to refinance with another (affordable) lender. Some state agencies or nonprofit organizations may make funds available to help homeowners refinance out of abusive loans. For older homeowners, a reverse mortgage may be an option.

Some courts have allowed consumers to repay the value of the credit in installments.[227] Others have permitted the value to be repaid as an unsecured claim at a few cents on the dollar in a chapter 13 bankruptcy or to be discharged completely in a chapter 7 bankruptcy.[228] Other courts have simply left the creditor in the position of an unsecured creditor for the debt balance.[229]

The importance of developing and documenting a plan for tender is illustrated by *Yamamoto v. Bank of New York*.[230] There, the Ninth Circuit upheld a trial court's discretion to condition rescission on the consumer's tender, and held that voiding of a security interest was not automatic upon sending a rescission notice. The court required the consumer to tender as a pre-trial matter, prior to adjudicating the validity of the rescission. In 2004 the Federal Reserve Board explicitly rejected this position in an amendment to the Official Staff Commentary.[231]

1140. And modification thus would be on the creditor's motion, and thus it should have the burden of proof.

226 *See generally* National Consumer Law Center, Truth in Lending § 6.8 (6th ed. 2007 and Supp.).

227 *See, e.g.*, Shepeard v. Quality Siding & Window Factory, Inc., 730 F. Supp. 1295 (D. Del. 1990); Mayfield v. Vanguard Sav. & Loan Ass'n, 710 F. Supp. 143 (E.D. Pa. 1989); Fed. Deposit Ins. Corp. v. Hughes Dev. Co., 684 F. Supp. 616 (D. Minn. 1988); Bookhart v. Mid-Penn Consumer Discount Co., 559 F. Supp. 208 (E.D. Pa. 1983); Sterten v. Option One Mortgage Corp., 352 B.R. 380 (Bankr. E.D. Pa. 2006). *See also* Smith v. Capital Roofing Co., 622 F. Supp. 191 (S.D. Miss. 1985) (after canceling lien on residence, court ordered consumer to repay principal only in reasonable monthly payments). *But see* Reese v. Hammer Fin. Corp., 1999 U.S. Dist. LEXIS 18812 (N.D. Ill. Nov. 29, 1999) (declining to allow installment payments). *See generally* National Consumer Law Center, Truth in Lending § 6.8.2 (6th ed. 2007 and Supp.).

228 *In re* Williams, 291 B.R. 636 (Bankr. E.D. Pa. 2003) (debtor allowed to repay tender balance over life of chapter 13 plan); Williams v. Gelt Fin. Corp., 239 B.R. 728 (Bankr. E.D. Pa. 1999), *aff'd*, 237 B.R. 590 (E.D. Pa. 1999); Murray v. First Nat'l Bank of Chicago, 239 B.R. 728 (Bankr. E.D. Pa. 1999); Bourgeois v. Mortgage Funding Corp. (*In re* Bourgeois) (Bankr. D. Mass. Mar. 16, 1998) (No. 95-12036-WCH, A.P. No. 95-1541), *available at* www.consumerlaw/unreported. *See* § 5.6.5, *infra* (further discussion of rescission in bankruptcy).

229 *See, e.g.*, Harris v. Tower Loan, Inc. 609 F.2d 120 (5th Cir. 1980); Williams v. Gelt Fin. Corp., 237 B.R. 590 (E.D. Pa. 1999), *aff'g* 232 B.R. 629 (Bankr. E.D. Pa. 1999); *In re* Rodrigues, 278 B.R. 683 (Bankr. D.R.I. 2002); Ralls v. Bank of N.Y. (*In re* Ralls), 230 B.R. 508 (Bankr. E.D. Pa. 1999); *In re* Celonia, 90 B.R. 104 (Bankr. E.D. Pa. 1988), *aff'd*, 98 B.R. 705 (E.D. Pa. 1989); *In re* Gurst, 79 B.R. 969 (Bankr. E.D. Pa. 1987).

230 329 F.3d 1167 (9th Cir. 2003). *See* National Consumer Law Center, Truth in Lending § 6.7.2.3 (6th ed. 2007 and Supp.).

231 Official Staff Commentary §§ 226.15(d)(4)-1, 226.23(d)(4)-1. *See also* Comptroller of Currency, OCC Bulletin 2004-19 (May 7, 2004) (instructing banks that "a consumer's right to rescind

Despite the Federal Reserve Board's rejection of *Yamamoto*'s holding, other courts have expressed similar concerns about the consumer's ability to tender.[232] According to the Ninth Circuit, the consumer in *Yamamoto* did not dispute the tender amount; did not ask the trial court for extra time to pay the tender amount; did not propose any tender options such as refinancing or sale of the property; and indicated no ability to pay *any* tender amount. Nor, in the court's opinion, did the consumer present evidence of lender overreaching that would have guided the trial court's discretion in determining whether equitable modification was warranted.

The key to avoiding these issues is to plead and make a record that shows that the consumer has a realistic plan for tender[233] and that there are questions of fact that preclude summary judgment in favor of the creditor. In particular:

- The debtor should never indicate no ability to pay any amount. If the debtor has no hope of paying the tender amount in cash, the debtor should propose another plan, or several alternate plans such as paying the tender amount over time or refinancing.[234] At deposition, the consumer should expect questions about the ability to tender and should be prepared to answer them.
- The debtor should plead any grounds that exist for reducing the tender amount, particularly if these make tender more realistic. The debtor should submit evidence showing that there are issues of fact regarding these claims and that they should go to trial.
- If available, the debtor should submit evidence showing the egregious nature of the creditor's TIL violations and other misconduct.

It is strongly advisable for the consumer to continue making mortgage payments while the right to rescind is litigated. First, if the consumer continues to make payments, the creditor will be less likely to succeed in portraying the consumer as a deadbeat, and the court will be less likely to feel that the equities favor the creditor. Second, if the consumer has made payments steadily, the court may agree that the consumer can tender just by continuing the installment payments. Continuing to make payments may also protect the consumer's credit rating.

If the consumer makes payments to the creditor while rescission is being litigated, the consumer should make it clear that the payments are made without prejudice to the rescission claim. Otherwise, the creditor may argue that the consumer waived rescission by making payments after sending the cancellation notice. Alternatively, the consumer could make payments into a trust or escrow account.

Even if the consumer cannot make the full monthly payment, it is important that the consumer stay in the habit of making a monthly payment in an affordable amount. This practice will build up a fund for tender, plus make it more likely that the consumer will be able to attract a reputable lender to refinance the debt.

5.6.5 TIL Rescission Rights in Bankruptcy

5.6.5.1 In General

The consumer has the option of enforcing Truth in Lending and other rescission rights in federal district, state, or bankruptcy court. Of course, the relative advantages and disadvantages of federal court, state court, and bankruptcy court vary from jurisdiction to jurisdiction. But some advantages of bankruptcy court may be particularly relevant in rescission cases.[235]

A bankruptcy case can be prepared and filed quite quickly with a "bare bones" petition.[236] With some exceptions particularly applicable to repeat filers, the filing of the petition stops any collection activity immediately—including both judicial and non-judicial foreclosures.[237] TIL rescission can be raised in an adversary proceeding to challenge the validity of the creditor's proof of claim.[238] Moreover, rescission is a defense which may be raised in contesting any motion for relief from stay which the lender files.[239] Another advantage of bankruptcy court is that there is a strong argument that an arbitration clause is ineffective in bankruptcy litigation.[240]

The merits of the TIL rescission and other consumer defenses can be litigated in an adversary proceeding within

is not affected by the sequence of the rescission procedures or a court order modifying those procedures in both open and closed-end credit").

232 *See, e.g.*, Del Valle v. Mortgage Bank of Cal., 2009 WL 3786061 (E.D. Cal. Nov.10, 2009).

233 *See* Kakogui v. American Brokers Conduit, 2010 WL 1265201, at *4–5 (N.D. Cal. Mar. 30, 2010) (requiring consumer to "either the present ability to tender the loan proceeds or the expectation that he will be able to tender within a reasonable time."). In a footnote, *Kakogui* observed that "a TILA plaintiff might be able to allege that while he lacks the liquidity to tender the loan proceeds at the time he files the rescission claim, he has sufficient equity in the home and a willingness to sell that would render it likely that he could tender the loan proceeds if given a reasonable period of time."

234 *See id.*

235 *See generally* Ch. 9, *infra* (discussion of the role of bankruptcy in foreclosure defense).

236 *See* National Consumer Law Center, Consumer Bankruptcy Law and Practice § 7.2.2 (9th ed. 2009).

237 A federal court could enjoin a non-judicial foreclosure sale and a state court could enjoin a foreclosure, but that outcome is not automatic, as it is in bankruptcy. Moreover, many courts require a bond as a prerequisite to issuing an injunction. Although there is a bankruptcy filing fee, no bond is required to obtain a stay in bankruptcy.

238 11 U.S.C. § 502(b)(1). *See* National Consumer Law Center, Truth in Lending § 6.9.7 (6th ed. 2007 and Supp.).

239 *See* § 9.6.1, *infra. See also* National Consumer Law Center, Consumer Bankruptcy Law and Practice Ch. 9 (9th ed. 2009).

240 *See generally* National Consumer Law Center, Consumer Arbitration Agreements § 4.2.3 (5th ed. 2007 and Supp.).

the debtor's bankruptcy case.[241] Discovery and other relevant procedures are quite similar to what is available under the federal rules, although the case is likely to be resolved on a faster timeline.[242] Debtors intending to bring a TIL claim during or after the bankruptcy proceeding should be sure to list the claim (and any other potential claims) on their schedule of assets. Failure to list the claim may deprive the debtor of standing to bring the claim or the debtor may be estopped from bringing the claim after the case is closed.[243] If possible the cause of action should be claimed as exempt.

While individual courts vary, in general bankruptcy courts may be more accustomed to laws which level the playing field between debtors and creditors. Bankruptcy courts have been more comfortable in recognizing that under the prescribed TIL scheme, a valid rescission reduces the creditor to unsecured status.[244] Damage claims, to the extent exempt from claims of creditors, abandoned by the trustee, or pursued as a set-off to the creditor's claim, are also available.[245]

While transfer of all the consumer's interest in the property terminates the right to rescind,[246] filing a bankruptcy case does not transfer all the debtor's interest in the property, so rescission can be exercised after filing.[247] Nonetheless, it is best, if possible, to rescind before filing bankruptcy, to avoid the need to resolve the question of whether the right to rescind has passed to the trustee.[248]

5.6.5.2 Tender in Bankruptcy

Another significant advantage to raising a rescission claim in bankruptcy court is that the debtor may have more options to manage any required TIL tender obligation.[249] A successful Truth in Lending rescission suit may void the creditor's lien entirely and leave the creditor with an unsecured claim.[250] In chapter 13 cases, the creditor with an unsecured claim often only receives a small percentage of the claim.

There are sound reasons for treating the tender obligation as an unsecured debt. In the bankruptcy context, courts not only must be mindful to protect the integrity of Truth in

241 A fuller discussion of how to raise consumer defenses in a bankruptcy case is contained at § 9.6, *infra*. *See also* National Consumer Law Center, Consumer Bankruptcy Law and Practice Chs. 11–13 (9th ed. 2009) (especially § 13.4.4).

242 Fed. R. Bankr. P. 7001–7087.

243 *See* National Consumer Law Center, Consumer Bankruptcy Law and Practice § 13.3.2.6 (9th ed. 2009).

244 *See* § 5.6.5.2, *infra*.

245 *See* National Consumer Law Center, Truth in Lending § 6.9.7 (6th ed. 2007 and Supp.).

246 12 C.F.R. §§ 226.15(a)(3), 226.23(a)(3).

247 *See* National Consumer Law Center, Truth in Lending § 6.3.2.2.2 (6th ed. 2007 and Supp.).

248 *See id.* §§ 6.3.2.2.2, 6.9.7.

249 For discussion of consumer's tender obligation under TILA, see National Consumer Law Center, Truth in Lending § 6.8 (6th ed. 2007 and Supp.). For a further discussion of tender in bankruptcy, see *id.* § 6.12.3.

250 Bilal v. Household Fin. Corp. (*In re* Bilal), 296 B.R. 828 (D. Kan. 2003); *In re* Williams, 291 B.R. 636 (Bankr. E.D. Pa. 2003) (debtor allowed to repay tender amount, after deduction for damages, over life of chapter 13 plan as unsecured claim separately classified); *In re* Rodrigues, 278 B.R. 683 (Bankr. D.R.I. 2002) (mortgage rendered void and creditor's claim treated as an unsecured claim); Wolfe v. IMC Mortg. Co. (Bankr. D. Md. May 19, 2000) (No. 99-12837PM), *available at* www.consumerlaw/unreported (claim is unsecured); Murray v. First Nat'l Bank of Chicago, 239 B.R. 728 (Bankr. E.D. Pa. 1999); Ralls v. Bank of N.Y. (*In re* Ralls), 230 B.R. 508 (Bankr. E.D. Pa. 1999); *In re* Whitley, Inc., 177 B.R. 142 (Bankr. D. Mass. 1995) (judicial preconditioning of cancellation of lien upon tender in bankruptcy is inappropriate); *In re* Myers, 175 B.R. 122 (Bankr. D. Mass. 1994) (following *Celona*); *In re* Brown, 134 B.R. 134 (Bankr. E.D. Pa. 1991) (TIL rescission rendered debt unsecured; application of TIL recoupment penalty for disclosure violations eliminated debt); *In re* Perkins, 106 B.R. 863, 874 (Bankr. E.D. Pa. 1989); *In re* Celona, 90 B.R. 104 (Bankr. E.D. Pa. 1988), *aff'd*, 98 B.R. 705 (E.D. Pa. 1989); *In re* Tucker, 74 B.R. 923 (Bankr. E.D. Pa. 1987) (consumers also entitled to $1000 TIL statutory damages by recoupment; $1000 damages for the creditor's failure to respond properly to the rescission demand; and attorney fees); *In re* Chancy, 33 B.R. 355 (Bankr. N.D. Okla. 1983) (creditor received 8% payout); *In re* Wright, 11 B.R. 590 (Bankr. S.D. Miss. 1981) (consumer also entitled to TIL statutory damages and attorney fees). *Cf.* Clay v. Johnson, 77 F. Supp. 2d 879 (N.D. Ill. 1999) (court orders conditional rescission, but allows debtors to repay obligation in installments in their separate chapter 13 case); Williams v. Gelt Fin. Corp., 239 B.R. 728 (Bankr. E.D. Pa. 1999), *aff'd*, 237 B.R. 590 (E.D. Pa. 1999). *But see* Quenzer v. Advanta Mortgage Corp., USA, 288 B.R. 884 (D. Kan. 2003) (court has discretion to require payment of principal as condition of voiding lien); Ray v. Citifinancial Inc., 228 F. Supp. 2d 664 (D. Md. 2002) (bankruptcy court may condition TIL rescission upon tender but also has discretion to reduce or eliminate creditor's lien without requiring tender based on equitable considerations); Reese v. Hammer Fin. Corp., 1999 U.S. Dist. LEXIS 18812 (N.D. Ill. Nov. 29, 1999) (allowing consumer ninety days to tender); Ramirez v. Household Fin. Corp. (*In re* Ramirez), 329 B.R. 727 (Bankr. D. Kan. 2005) (fact that debt would be unsecured in bankruptcy justifies modification); Webster v. Centex Home Equity Corp. (*In re* Webster), 300 B.R. 787 (Bankr. W.D. Okla. 2003) (requiring tender within sixty days in chapter 13 bankruptcy); *In re* Wepsic, 231 B.R. 768 (Bankr. S.D. Cal. 1998) (cancellation of lien dependent on borrower's tender of amounts due to the lender, subject to offsets authorized by TILA; it would be inequitable to void the lien as borrower has enough equity in the property to satisfy the lien and could avoid paying an unsecured claim); *In re* Cox, 175 B.R. 266 (Bankr. C.D. Ill. 1994) (creditor held a secured claim; court influenced by its opinion that debtors were "holding creditor at bay" by litigating TIL claim in bankruptcy court, and then retaining ability to return to state court if unsuccessful in the current case); *In re* Lynch, 170 B.R. 26 (Bankr. D.N.H. 1994) (making creditor an unsecured creditor would allow the consumers a windfall: they would retain their residence; have a unencumbered homestead right; and be obligated only for a fraction of the creditor's claim; court ordered security interest in the amount of the claim as reduced by rescission credits and the damages for which the creditor was liable).

Lending, but also to implement the purposes of the bankruptcy system. Thus courts have held that judicial preconditioning of cancellation of the creditor's lien on the consumer's tender is inappropriate in bankruptcy, distinguishing the seminal cases to the contrary as not involving bankruptcy proceedings in which the policies of the Bankruptcy Code come into play. These cases are consistent with the general preference in the Bankruptcy Code for the discharge of unsecured claims to insure the fresh financial start bankruptcy is meant to provide, as well as the policy in favor of fairness and equality of treatment among unsecured creditors. Finally, according to these courts, it would be unfair to force consumers to choose between bankruptcy and the exercise of their rights under TILA.[251]

Even in those courts that do not adopt the position that the tender obligation is unsecured in bankruptcy, a debtor has the separate argument in cases in which the creditor failed to comply with its rescission obligations,[252] that the debtor has no obligation to tender at all (either secured or unsecured).[253] In these cases, the right to retain loan proceeds might be vested in the consumer, leaving the creditor without any claim, secured or unsecured, for the proceeds.

One bankruptcy court used its authority under chapter 13 and TILA to order a compromise result. The consumer's tender obligation was unsecured, and the court did not make rescission conditional upon tender. The court did, however, order the consumer to classify the tender obligation separately from other unsecured claims and to pay it in full over the life of the chapter 13 plan.[254] Presumably, if the debtor failed to pay the tender amount, the result would be dismissal of her chapter 13 bankruptcy, but the loan would still be rescinded. The tender amount in this case was less than $10,000, an amount that a low-income debtor could conceivably pay over the life of a chapter 13 plan. With a higher tender amount, however, this approach could result in unaffordable payments since the plan would have to be completed within five years.

Another bankruptcy court agreed with this general approach but went one step farther, granting the debtor a reasonable time to pay the tender obligation even if that period exceeded the five-year duration of her chapter 13 plan.[255] Yet another court concluded that treating the tender obligation as unsecured was too severe, but the debtor would be allowed to pay, through the chapter 13 plan, an amount to be determined by the court.[256] The creditor would retain its lien until the plan amount was paid.

Even if the creditor is deemed entitled to retain a secured claim after a successful rescission in bankruptcy, that claim is subject to the provisions of the Code affecting secured claims. These include the right to cure any default by payments under the plan,[257] the right to pay off in full at present value,[258] and the myriad of other special debtor protections applicable under the Bankruptcy Code.[259] If the rescission claim is rejected, these bankruptcy rights also function as alternative strategies to help the homeowner remain in place.

Rescission claims in chapter 13 may also be brought together with stripdown claims when the right to strip down remains available.[260] A judge may be more willing to permit stripdown or to accept an especially low valuation of the property if the debtor has consumer claims raised in the alternative. Similarly, rescission may be easier to fully effectuate, if it is clear to the judge and the secured creditor that the creditor's lien has no real economic value.

5.6.6 Time Limit for Rescission

In *Beach v. Ocwen Federal Bank,*[261] the Supreme Court ruled that extended rescission rights under the Truth in Lending Act must be exercised within the three year period provided under the statute. The court barred use of TIL rescission by recoupment as a defense to a collection action after expiration of the three year period. Until the *Beach* case was decided, courts had been virtually unanimous in concluding that rescission by recoupment consistent with state law was allowable when raised defensively to the

251 *See, e.g.*, Celona v. Equitable Nat'l Bank, 98 B.R. 705 (E.D. Pa. 1989); *In re* Myers, 175 B.R. 122 (Bankr. D. Mass. 1994); *In re* Chancy, 33 B.R. 355 (Bankr. N.D. Okla. 1983); *In re* Piercy, 18 B.R. 1004, 1007 (Bankr. W.D. Ky. 1982) ("It would be palpably unfair to deny the relief to which a consumer is entitled under TIL because that consumer has also availed himself of bankruptcy relief.").

252 *See* § 5.6.2, *supra* (full discussion of creditor's obligations after rescission); National Consumer Law Center, Truth in Lending § 6.6.4 (6th ed. 2007 and Supp.) (same).

253 *See* National Consumer Law Center, Truth in Lending § 6.6.5 (6th ed. 2007 and Supp.).

254 Williams v. BankOne (*In re* Williams), 291 B.R. 636 (Bankr. E.D. Pa. 2003). *Accord* Wile v. Household Bank (*In re* Wile), 304 B.R. 198 (Bankr. E.D. Pa. 2004) (requiring chapter 13 bankruptcy cases seeking TIL rescission to follow rule announced in Williams v. BankOne); Bell v. Parkway Mortgage, Inc. (*In re* Bell), 309 B.R. 139 (Bankr. E.D. Pa. 2004) (finding similar orders appropriate here, although not necessarily in every case), *modified in part*, 314 B.R. 54, 61–62 (Bankr. E.D. Pa. 2004) (allowing debtor a reasonable time to make tender, even if it goes beyond duration of chapter 13 plan).

255 Bell v. Parkway Mortgage, Inc. (*In re* Bell), 314 B.R. 54, 60–61 (Bankr. E.D. Pa. 2004).

256 Cruz v. Household Fin. Consumer Discount Co. (*In re* Cruz) (Bankr. E.D. Pa. Nov. 1, 2004) (Bankr. No. 03-17888), *available at* www.consumerlaw/unreported.

257 11 U.S.C. § 1322(b)(3), (5).

258 11 U.S.C. § 1325(a)(5).

259 *See generally* National Consumer Law Center, Consumer Bankruptcy Law and Practice Ch. 11 (9th ed. 2009).

260 *See id.* § 17.5.

261 Beach v. Ocwen Fed. Bank, 523 U.S. 410, 118 S. Ct. 1408, 140 L. Ed. 2d 566 (1998). *See* National Consumer Law Center, Truth in Lending § 6.3.3.3 (6th ed. 2007 and Supp.) (extensive discussion of *Beach*).

extent of the lender's claim even if the statutory three-year period for rescission had expired.[262]

However, *Beach* does not prevent use of claims other than rescission in foreclosure cases and bankruptcy when consistent with state law governing limitations periods. For example, TIL damage claims will continue to be available in foreclosure cases and bankruptcy by way of recoupment even after the one-year time limit for raising that claim has expired.[263]

The Court in *Beach* also gave a nod to an exception to the three-year rule in a cryptic footnote which states: "Since there is no claim before us that Florida law purports to provide any right to rescind defensively on the grounds relevant under the Act, we have no occasion to explore how state recoupment law might work when raised in a foreclosure proceeding outside the 3-year period."[264] At its broadest, the language in the Court's footnote arguably means that in states which have a clear doctrine permitting recoupment in the foreclosure context, TIL rescission claims still may be permitted beyond three years. A more narrow reading of the Court's footnote focuses on states that have independent state law grounds for rescission. A few states have adopted their own versions of TILA.[265] The Court's footnote in *Beach* at least gives its imprimatur to rescission by recoupment under state TILA-type statutes.[266]

Rescission is available after the three-year period despite *Beach* in some circumstances when an agency has commenced a proceeding to enforce TIL rescission rights within the three-year period.[267] Bankruptcy law may also give a short extension of the three-year period for debtors who file bankruptcy just before the rescission period expires.[268] Other theories for asserting a rescission claim after the three-year period are discussed in National Consumer Law Center, *Truth in Lending* § 6.3.3 (6th ed. 2007 and Supp.).

5.6.7 Truth in Lending Damages Claims

Nearly all home mortgages, when the lender is in the business of making loans to consumers, are subject to the disclosure requirements of the Truth in Lending Act. The creditor must disclose, *inter alia*, the annual percentage rate (APR),[269] the finance charge,[270] the amount financed,[271] and any security interest taken.[272] Failure to disclose these items as required may give rise to claims for actual damages,[273] statutory damages,[274] and attorney fees.[275] Statutory damages are limited to twice the finance charge, but not less than $400 and not more than $4000. (Prior to July 1, 2008 statutory damages were limited to $200 and $2000, respectively.[276]) While these claims will not defeat the mortgage, they may be used to reduce the amount of indebtedness. Such claims are discussed fully in National Consumer Law Center, *Truth in Lending*.[277]

5.7 TILA Rights Concerning Higher-Priced Mortgage Loans

Truth in Lending Regulation Z now provides certain additional requirements for "higher-priced mortgage loans," defined as a first mortgage with an APR at least 1.5 percentage points over the "average prime offer rate" (APOR) or a second mortgage that is at least 3.5 percentage points over the APOR.[278] The APOR is based on a weekly survey of market interest rates.[279] The higher-priced loan category

262 *See, e.g.*, Dawe v. Merchants Mortgage & Trust Co., 683 P.2d 796 (Colo. 1984); Westbank v. Maurer, 276 Ill. App. 3d 553, 658 N.E.2d 1381 (1995); Cmty. Nat'l. Bank & Trust v. McClammy, 525 N.Y.S.2d 629 (App. Div. 1988).

263 *See* National Consumer Law Center, Truth in Lending § 6.3.3.3 (6th ed. 2007 and Supp.).

The Supreme Court deliberately distinguished recoupment of damage claims from recoupment of rescission based on the existence of protections for recoupment of damages in 15 U.S.C. § 1640(e).

264 Beach v. Ocwen Fed. Bank, 523 U.S. 410, 118 S. Ct. 1408, 140 L. Ed. 2d 566 n.6 (1998).

265 Those states are Connecticut, Maine, Massachusetts, Oklahoma, and Wyoming.

266 *See In re* Fidler, 210 B.R. 411 (Bankr. D. Mass., 1997), *reaffirmed on motion to vacate* 226 B.R. 734 (1998) (Massachusetts law permitted rescission after three year period permitted by Truth in Lending Act). *Accord* Maxwell v. Fairbanks Capital Corp. (*In re* Maxwell), 281 B.R. 101 (Bankr. D. Mass. 2002) (allowing rescission to be asserted by recoupment under state TIL eleven years after consummation). *But see* Green Tree Acceptance, Inc. v. Anderson, 981 P.2d 804 (Okla. Ct. App. 1999) (applying *Beach* reasoning to bar rescission by recoupment after three-year period under Oklahoma disclosure law); Roberson v. Cityscape Corp., 262 B.R. 312 (Bankr. E.D. Pa. 2001) (under Pennsylvania law, homeowner cannot assert claim for rescission defensively after three-year bar).

267 15 U.S.C. § 1635(f). *See* National Consumer Law Center, Truth in Lending § 6.3.3.7 (6th ed. 2007 and Supp.).

268 11 U.S.C. § 108(b). *See* National Consumer Law Center, Truth in Lending § 6.3.3.6 (6th ed. 2007 and Supp.).

269 15 U.S.C. § 1638(a)(4); Reg. Z, 12 C.F.R. § 226.18(e).

270 15 U.S.C. § 1638(a)(3); Reg. Z, 12 C.F.R. § 226.18(d).

271 15 U.S.C. § 1638(a)(2)(A); Reg. Z, 12 C.F.R. 226.18(b).

272 15 U.S.C. § 1638(a)(9); Reg. Z, 12 C.F.R. § 226.18(m).

273 15 U.S.C. § 1640(a)(1).

274 15 U.S.C. § 1640(a)(2)(A).

275 15 U.S.C. § 1640(a)(3).

276 Housing and Economic Recovery Act of 2008, Pub. L. No. 110-289, § 2502(b), 122 Stat. 2654, 2857 (2008) (codified at 15 U.S.C. § 1640(a)(2)(A)(ii)). *See* National Consumer Law Center, Truth in Lending § 8.6.2.1 (6th ed. 2007 and Supp.) (discussion of the reach of the effective date).

277 Chs. 4, 8 (5th ed. 2003 and Supp.).

278 12 C.F.R. § 226.35(a). Home equity lines of credit are not subject to the rule.

279 73 Fed. Reg. 44,522 (July 30, 2008). *See* Higher-Priced Mortgage Loans and the Average Prime Offer Rate Trigger, 28 NCLC REPORTS *Consumer Credit and Usury Ed.* 1 (Jan./Feb. 2010). The Federal Financial Institutions Examination Council has posted links to the fixed and adjustable rate APOR tables and a rate spread calculator to assist in determining whether or not a loan is covered at www.ffiec.gov/ratespread.

is designed to match the subprime market and uses rate triggers lower than high-cost loans under HOEPA.[280]

For loan applications received after September 30, 2009, the regulations prohibit lending without regard to ability to pay and restrict the use of prepayment penalties for more than two years.[281] For applications received after March 31, 2010, first mortgages meeting the APR trigger must have escrow accounts for taxes and insurance.[282] For manufactured homes, the effective date of the escrow requirement is October 1, 2010.[283]

Remedies for violations include actual damages, statutory damages, special statutory damages consisting of the sum of all finance charges and fees paid by the consumer, and attorney fees and costs.[284] Loans violating the prepayment penalty requirements are subject to the extended right of rescission.[285] These provisions are discussed in detail in National Consumer Law Center, *Truth in Lending* § 9.8 (6th ed. 2007 and Supp.).

5.8 The Home Ownership and Equity Protection Act (HOEPA)

5.8.1 Overview

The Home Ownership and Equity Protection Act (HOEPA)[286] seeks to prevent predatory lending practices in high-cost loans,[287] preventing predatory lenders from skimming equity from borrowers' homes, particularly older, minority, and low-income homeowners.[288] HOEPA carves out a class of high-rate closed-end loans and subjects them to special regulation. For these loans, rather than capping interest rates, HOEPA requires additional disclosures, prohibits certain abusive loan terms and practices, imposes additional penalties, and extends the potential liability of assignees. Whether a loan is a high-cost loan subject to these restrictions depends on whether it meets either of two triggers, one based on the annual percentage rate and the other based on the points and fees charged.[289]

Violations of HOEPA, which amends the Truth in Lending Act, trigger the usual TIL monetary damages. For violations deemed "material,"[290] the consumer may also recover enhanced damages of the sum of all finance charges and fees paid by the consumer.[291] More critically, violation of HOEPA's disclosure provisions or inclusion of a prohibited term (whether invoked or not) triggers the extended rescission right.[292] The law also limits the right of assignees of high-cost mortgages to assert holder-in-due-course status to cut off consumer claims and defenses.[293]

As is true under TILA generally, the extended rescission right under HOEPA expires three years after consummation, with few exceptions.[294] However, a claim for the HOEPA enhanced damage award can be a significant sum, making HOEPA coverage and violations worth investigating even for loans more than three years old. While these damage claims are subject to TILA's one-year statute of limitations, in most jurisdictions damage claims can be raised by way of recoupment after the statute of limitations has passed. Fraudulent concealment may also extend the statute of limitations for HOEPA damage claims.[295]

An important HOEPA provision is that assignees of high-cost mortgages are subject to all claims and defenses, whether arising under TILA or under other statutory or common law, that the consumer could assert against the original creditor.[296] The purpose of this restriction is two-fold: to protect the consumers and to encourage the second-

280 *See* § 5.8, *infra.*

281 12 C.F.R. § 226.35(b)(1)-(2); 73 Fed. Reg. 44,522 (July 30, 2008).

282 12 C.F.R. § 226.35(b)(3); 73 Fed. Reg. 44,522, 44,557 (July 30, 2008).

283 73 Fed. Reg. 44,522, 44,557 (July 30, 2008).

284 National Consumer Law Center, Truth in Lending § 9.8.4 (6th ed. 2007 and Supp.).

285 Reg. Z, 12 C.F.R. § 226.23 n.48; 73 Fed. Reg. 44,522, 44,601 (July 30, 2008).

286 The majority of the law is codified in 15 U.S.C. § 1639. The definition of covered mortgages is at 15 U.S.C. § 1602(aa).

287 Riegle Community Development and Regulatory Improvement Act, Pub. L. No. 103-325, tit. I, subtit. B, 108 Stat. 2160 (1994). For a discussion of HOEPA, see generally National Consumer Law Center, Truth in Lending Ch. 9 (6th ed. 2007 and Supp.).

288 *See* National Consumer Law Center, The Cost of Credit: Regulation, Preemption, and Industry Abuses §§ 11.1–11.3.1 (4th ed. 2009 and Supp.) (discussion of predatory home equity mortgage lending).

The congressional hearings also have background on equity-skimming lending. *See, e.g., Equity Predators: Stripping, Flipping and Packing Their Way to Profits: Hearings Before the Senate Special Comm. on Aging*, 105th Cong. (Mar. 16, 1998), *available at* www.senate.gov/~aging/hr14.htm; *Problems in Community Development Banking, Mortgage Lending Discrimination, Reverse Redlining, and Home Equity Lending: Hearings Before the Senate Comm. on Banking, Hous. and Urban Affairs*, 103d Cong. (Feb. 3, 17, 24, 1993).

289 *See* § 5.8.2, *infra.*

290 The standard for whether a violation is material for purposes of HOEPA enhanced damages is a common law standard, not the restricted statutory definition of "material" for purposes of TIL rescission.

291 15 U.S.C. § 1640(a). *See* H.R. Conf. Rep. No. 103-652, at 13, 159, 162 (1994) (accompanying H.R. 3474). The creditor has the burden of demonstrating that the violation is not material. The congressional intent that "materiality" as used in this section be a common law standard, not the TIL standard as defined in 15 U.S.C. § 1602(u) and Reg. Z, 12 C.F.R. § 226.23 n.48 is a bit confusing as other sections of HOEPA deem violations to be material for TIL rescission purposes.

292 15 U.S.C. §§ 1602(u), 1635, 1639(j); Reg. Z, 12 C.F.R. § 226.23(a)(3). *See generally* National Consumer Law Center, Truth in Lending Ch. 6 (6th ed. 2007 and Supp.).

293 *See generally* National Consumer Law Center, Truth in Lending § 9.7 (6th ed. 2007 and Supp.).

294 *See* § 5.6.6, *supra.*

295 *See* National Consumer Law Center, Truth in Lending § 7.2 (6th ed. 2007 and Supp.).

296 15 U.S.C. § 1641(d). *See* § 5.8.5, *infra.*

ary market to do more self-policing.[297] Without a market to sell their loans, disreputable contractors and other originators cannot survive long.

For several years after HOEPA became effective, lenders continued to make loans without attempting to hide the fact that they met the HOEPA triggers. Few lenders now identify their loans as HOEPA loans. Nonetheless, a loan that the lender characterizes as falling below the HOEPA triggers may actually, upon close analysis of the documents, be a HOEPA loan.[298] Lenders often purport to avoid the HOEPA triggers by mischaracterizing loan fees or concealing the fact that the fees are padded or paid to an affiliate. Foreclosure rescue scams should also be reviewed for HOEPA coverage.[299]

This subsection provides an overview of HOEPA. The Act, the regulations, and the cases interpreting them are discussed in detail in Chapter 9 of National Consumer Law Center, *Truth in Lending*.[300]

5.8.2 Covered Mortgages

A loan subject to HOEPA is one which meets the following criteria:[301]

- Is closed-end consumer credit;[302]
- Is not a "residential mortgage transaction," i.e., is not used for the acquisition or construction of the property;[303]
- Is secured by the borrower's principal dwelling;[304] and
- Meets one of two alternative costs-triggers:

1) *APR Trigger.* The loan has an APR that is at least 8%, for first mortgages or 10% for junior liens, above the rate for Treasury securities of a comparable term. For example, if the yield on a fifteen-year Treasury security is 6%, an APR of 14% on a fifteen-year first mortgage will meet the trigger.[305]

or

2) *Points and Fees Trigger.* The loan has upfront fees and charges (including broker fees, credit insurance premiums, and other charges for credit insurance[306]) which are 8% of the loan amount[307] or $400 (an amount which changes annually with the CPI), whichever is greater.[308]

297 *See, e.g.*, Bryant v. Mortgage Capital Res. Corp., 197 F. Supp. 2d 1357 (N.D. Ga. 2002) (discussion of assignee liability); Rodrigues v. U.S. Bank (*In re* Rodrigues), 278 B.R. 683, 688 (Bankr. D.R.I. 2002) ("The legislative history indicates Congress's intent to establish a strict liability standard for assignees of such loans. . . .").

The 2001 revision of the Commentary reinforces the plain language of the statute. Official Staff Commentary to Reg. Z, 12 C.F.R. § 226.34(a)(2)-3. The new language states: "For such loans, a purchaser's or other assignee's liability for all claims and defenses that the consumer could assert against the creditor is not limited to violations of the act."

298 National Consumer Law Center, Truth in Lending § 9.2.6.3.7 (6th ed. 2007 and Supp.) and National Consumer Law Center, Stop Predatory Lending Ch. 7 (2d ed. 2007) both provide step-by-step analyses of sample loan documents to illustrate the HOEPA calculations.

299 *See* Ch. 15, *infra*.

300 (6th ed. 2007 and Supp.).

301 15 U.S.C. § 1602(aa).

302 Consumer credit is defined by TILA, 15 U.S.C. § 1602(e), (f), (h). *See* National Consumer Law Center, Truth in Lending §§ 2.2, 2.3 (6th ed. 2007 and Supp.).

Closed-end credit is that repayable on specific repayment terms over a specified term, in contrast to open-end credit, which is defined at 15 U.S.C. § 1602(i).

303 As defined in TILA, 15 U.S.C. § 1602(w). This tracks the exclusion from TILA's rescission right. 15 U.S.C. § 1635. *See* National Consumer Law Center, Truth in Lending § 6.2.6 (6th ed. 2007 and Supp.).

304 Dwelling is defined at 15 U.S.C. § 1602(v). This, too, tracks TILA's definitions for rescission purposes. 15 U.S.C. § 1635; Reg. Z, 12 C.F.R. § 226.23; National Consumer Law Center, Truth in Lending § 6.2.4 (6th ed. 2007 and Supp.).

305 The statute specifies the relevant date to use in determining the Treasury yield. The Federal Reserve Bank's website provides the necessary history of Treasury yield rates. Go to www.federalreserve.gov/releases, scroll down to "Weekly Releases" and under "H.15" click on "historical data." Scroll down to "Treasury constant maturities," find the comparable term, and then click on "weekly." Reg. Z, 12 C.F.R. § 226.32(a)(1)(i) (as amended).

306 After October 1, 2002, premiums and other charges for credit life, accident, health, or loss of income insurance or debt-cancellation coverage, written in connection with the loan, are included in the points and fees trigger. Reg. Z, 12 C.F.R. § 226.32(b)(1)(iv) (as amended effective Oct. 1, 2002). *See* National Consumer Law Center, The Cost of Credit: Regulation, Preemption, and Industry Abuses § 8.3 (4th ed. 2009 and Supp.) (discussion of the different types of credit insurance).

307 Fees and charges are specifically defined by 15 U.S.C. § 1602(aa)(4) and 12 C.F.R. § 226.32(b)(1) to include: a) all components of the TIL finance charge except interest and time price differential (Reg. Z, 12 C.F.R. § 226.4); b) all compensation paid to mortgage brokers; c) real-estate related fees as itemized in 12 C.F.R. § 226.4(c)(7) unless (i) the charge is reasonable, (ii) the creditor does not receive direct or indirect compensation, and (iii) the charge is are paid to unaffiliated third parties; and d) premiums for credit insurance written in connection with the transaction.

It is the creditor's burden to establish that the criteria for excluding these closing costs are met, because it, not the consumer, has the information readily available. H.R. Conf. Rep. No. 103-652, at 13, 159 (1994) (accompanying H.R. 3474).

308 The $400 floor changes annually on January 1 by the amount of the annual percentage rate change in the consumer price index as reported on June 1 of the year before the adjustment. In 2000 the floor was $451 (65 Fed. Reg. 17,129, 17,132 (Mar. 31, 2000)); $465 for 2001 (65 Fed. Reg. 70,465 (Nov. 24, 2000)); $480 for 2002 (66 Fed. Reg. 57,849 (Nov. 19, 2001)); $488 for 2003 (67 Fed. Reg. 61,769 (Oct. 2, 2002)); $499 for 2004 (68 Fed. Reg. 50,965 (Aug. 25, 2003)); $510 for 2005 (69 Fed. Reg. 50,298 (Aug. 16, 2004)); $528 for 2006 (70 Fed. Reg. 46,066 (Aug. 9, 2005)); $547 for 2007 (71 Fed. Reg. 46,388 (Aug. 14, 2006)); $561 for 2008 (72 Fed. Reg. 44,032 (Aug. 7, 2007)); and $583 for 2009 (73 Fed. Reg. 46,190 (Aug.8, 2008)).

The major exclusion from HOEPA's scope is open-end credit. However, the Federal Reserve Board's rules prohibit attempts to circumvent HOEPA by structuring home loans as open-end lines of credit.[309] Reverse mortgages are also excluded, although TILA requires special disclosures for reverse mortgages.[310]

5.8.3 *Advance Look Disclosures*

Covered loans are subject to additional disclosure requirements. The consumer must be given special "advance look" HOEPA disclosures at least three business days prior to consummation,[311] to assure that the consumer has time to reflect. Failure to make the advance-look disclosures gives rise to an extended right to rescind.[312] In addition to warning the consumer that the loan need not be consummated simply because the application has been made or disclosures received, the disclosure must warn that the home and any equity in it might be lost in the event of nonpayment.

The "advance look" notice must also disclose several items of important information about the cost of the loan:

- The APR;
- The amount of regular monthly payments for fixed rate loans, and, for variable rate loans, both the regular and maximum possible monthly payment and a statement that the interest rate and the monthly payment may increase;[313]
- The amount of any balloon payment;[314] and
- For a mortgage refinancing, the total amount the consumer will borrow, defined to be the face amount of the note (also known as the principal), and, if the amount borrowed includes premiums or charges for optional credit insurance or debt cancellation coverage, a statement to that effect.[315]

The creditor must make new advance look disclosures if the terms change.[316] The FRB has promulgated a rule allowing waiver of the three-day waiting period if necessary to permit a homeowner to meet a bona fide personal financial emergency,[317] but there are strong arguments that this exception should be interpreted narrowly.[318]

5.8.4 *Substantive Prohibitions*

Covered loans are also subject to prohibitions on certain mortgage terms: prepayment penalties (with a complex exception),[319] balloon payments in loans with terms of less than five years, negative amortization, requiring more than two payments to be paid in advance from the loan proceeds, and default interest rates.[320] Effective for new applications on or after October 1, 2009, it is also a violation to make a loan without regard to the homeowner's ability to pay.[321] Before that date, it is a violation to have a pattern or practice of making covered loans without regard to ability to pay.[322] Further, the proceeds of a HOEPA loan cannot be paid out by a check made out solely to a home improvement contractor.[323]

In addition, due on demand provisions or call provisions that permit the creditor to terminate the loan in advance of the original maturity date and to accelerate the entire loan balance are prohibited except in limited circumstances.[324] The Board's rules also prohibit a lender from refinancing a HOEPA loan into a new HOEPA loan within one year of the origination date, unless the refinancing is in the borrower's best interest.[325] This prohibition extends to assignees of the

309 Reg. Z, 12 C.F.R. § 226.34(b). *See also* Official Staff Commentary to Reg. Z, 12 C.F.R. § 226.34(b)-1.

310 15 U.S.C. § 1648.

311 15 U.S.C. § 1639(a). *See In re* Jackson, 245 B.R. 23 (Bankr. E.D. Pa. 2000) (loan was rescindable because creditor failed to give timely advance disclosures); Newton v. United Companies Fin. Corp., 24 F. Supp. 2d 444 (E.D. Pa. 1998); Williams v. Gelt Fin. Corp. (*In re* Williams), 232 B.R. 629 (Bankr. E.D. Pa. 1999), *aff'd*, 237 B.R. 590 (E.D. Pa. 1999) (court found HOEPA notice was not given based on consumer's testimony and creditor's failure to rebut it). *See also* Payne v. Equicredit Corp., 2002 WL 1018969 (E.D. Pa. May 20, 2002) (though HOEPA notice was dated almost a year after settlement, court rejected lender's claim that the date contained the wrong year and that the consumer must testify and cannot rely on the document alone to prove a timing violation; consumer established a prima facie case and lender failed to rebut it with any other evidence), *aff'd*, 2003 WL 21783757 (3d Cir. Aug. 4, 2003).

312 15 U.S.C. §§ 1602(u), 1635; Reg. Z, 12 C.F.R. §§ 226.23, n.48, 226.23(a)(3).

313 15 U.S.C. § 1639(a),(b). Variable rate loans must also disclose the APR, and a statement that the rate and monthly payment may increase.

314 12 C.F.R. § 226.32(c)(3).

315 12 C.F.R. § 226.32(c)(5).

316 15 U.S.C. § 1639(b)(2).

317 12 C.F.R. § 226.31(c)(1)(iii). *See also* 15 U.S.C. § 1639(b)(3).

318 *See* National Consumer Law Center, Truth in Lending § 9.3.8 (6th ed. 2007 and Supp.).

319 *See In re* Williams, 232 B.R. 629 (Bankr. E.D. Pa. 1999) (violation when lender included prepayment penalties in a "high cost" loan).

320 15 U.S.C. § 1639(c)–(h).

321 73 Fed. Reg. 44,522, 44,545–44,546 (July 30, 2008); National Consumer Law Center, Truth in Lending § 9.5.2.3 (6th ed. 2007 and Supp.).

322 After October 1, 2002, a presumption is created that a creditor violates this prohibition if the creditor does not verify and document the borrower's ability to repay. Reg. Z, 12 C.F.R. § 226.34(a)(4) (as amended). This treatise's companion website reprints a sample complaint in a case alleging the creditor extended credit without the ability to repay.

323 15 U.S.C. § 1639(i).

324 Reg. Z, 12 C.F.R. § 226.32(b)(1)(iv) (as amended effective Oct. 1, 2002).

325 Reg. Z, 12 C.F.R. § 226.34(a)(3) (as amended effective Oct. 1, 2002).

original loan. In addition, a lender cannot structure a home-secured loan as an open-end plan to evade HOEPA.[326]

5.8.5 Assignee Liability Under HOEPA

5.8.5.1 General

Under HOEPA, assignees of covered mortgages are liable for *all* claims and defenses with respect to the assigned mortgage that the consumer could assert against the originator.[327] The statute does not limit assignee liability to TILA or HOEPA violations. If the consumer could assert UDAP, RICO, fraud, or other claims against the originating mortgage lender, these claims can be asserted against the assignee.[328] The statute gives the consumer this right regardless of whether the assignee is a holder in due course or has inserted a waiver-of-defense clause in the contract.

The assignee's maximum liability for claims and defenses to which it is subject by virtue of the HOEPA provision is the remainder of the mortgage indebtedness plus the total amount paid by the consumer in the transaction.[329] This cap, however, does not limit the assignee's liability for its own actions. Further, if the assignee would be liable for the assignor's actions even in the absence of the HOEPA provision, the HOEPA cap does not limit liability.

5.8.5.2 Exemption Where Assignee Is Unaware of HOEPA Coverage

Assignees are exempt from HOEPA's assignee liability provision if the assignee "demonstrates, by a preponderance of the evidence, that a reasonable person exercising ordinary due diligence" could not have determined that the loan was covered by HOEPA.[330]

In some cases, whether the loan is covered or not will be apparent on the face of the documents. The maker of a covered transaction is required to prominently place in the loan documents notice of the fact that assignees are potentially liable.[331] In other cases, such as sale-leaseback transactions arranged by foreclosure rescue scammers, the assignee will not receive that notice. But, due diligence also compels assignees to examine all documentation required by TILA, the itemization of the amount financed, and other disclosures of disbursements.[332] This must be more than a mechanical comparison of the loan documents and the disbursement statement.[333] For example, if the loan documents show unfamiliar fees, the assignee must look into them to make sure that they are bona fide, reasonable in amount, and otherwise legitimate.[334] In addition, the assignee is responsible for any other information it actually possesses at the time of assignment.[335]

In litigation over a sale-leaseback transactions, debate over the extent of the assignee's knowledge will often

326 Reg. Z, 12 C.F.R. § 226.34(b) (as amended effective Oct. 1, 2002).

327 15 U.S.C. § 1641(d)(1).

328 *See, e.g.*, Short v. Wells Fargo Bank Minn., N.A., 401 F. Supp. 2d 549 (S.D. W. Va. 2005) (assignee is subject to all federal or state claims and defenses if loan is covered by HOEPA), *subsequent proceedings*, 2006 WL 1589611 (S.D. W. Va. June 8, 2006); Cooper v. First Gov't Mortgage & Inv. Corp., 238 F. Supp. 2d 50, 55 (D.D.C. 2002) (denying assignee's motion for summary judgment; "Congress made assignees subject to all claims and defenses, whether under TILA or other law, that could be raised against the original lender."); Bryant v. Mortgage Capital Res. Corp., 197 F. Supp. 2d 1357 (N.D. Ga. 2002); Mason v. Fieldstone Mortgage Co., 2000 U.S. Dist. LEXIS 16515 (N.D. Ill. 2000); Rodrigues v. U.S. Bank (*In re* Rodrigues), 278 B.R. 683, 688 (Bankr. D.R.I. 2002) ("The legislative history indicates Congress's intent to establish a strict liability standard for assignees of such loans. . . ."); Barber v. Fairbanks Capital Corp. (*In re* Barber), 266 B.R. 309 (Bankr. E.D. Pa. 2001) (however, ECOA claim dismissed against assignee on grounds that ECOA assignee provisions trump HOEPA's); Murray v. First Nat'l Bank of Chicago (*In re* Murray), 239 B.R. 728 (Bankr. E.D. Pa. 1999). *See also* Dash v. FirstPlus Home Loan Trust 1996-2, 248 F. Supp. 2d 489, 505 (M.D.N.C. 2003) (Congress made assignees of mortgages subject to all claims and defenses, whether under TILA or other law, that could be raised against the original lender; case dismissed due to a standing issue); Pulphus v. Sullivan, 2003 WL 1964333 n.11 (N.D. Ill. Apr. 28, 2003) (HOEPA subjects assignee to suit for the creditor's violations of state law); Vandenbroeck v. ContiMortgage Corp., 53 F. Supp. 2d 965 (W.D. Mich. 1999), *aff'd on other grounds*, 210 F.3d 696 (6th Cir. 2000) (state law claims raised against assignee by virtue of HOEPA abrogation of holder-in-due-course status remanded to state court). *Cf.* Harvey v. EMC Mortgage Corp. (*In re* Harvey), 2003 WL 21460063 (Bankr. E.D. Pa. June 9, 2003) (HOEPA abrogates holder-in-due-course defense and makes assignee liable for all claims except under laws that have conflicting assignee liability provisions). *But see* Dowdy v. Bankers Trust, 2002 U.S. Dist. LEXIS 3978 (N.D. Ill. Feb. 7, 2002) (erroneously confusing derivative liability created by HOEPA with the standard for liability for one's own acts under state UDAP statute). *But cf.* Faircloth v. National Home Loan Corp., 313 F. Supp. 2d 544 (M.D.N.C. 2003) (HOEPA does not extend liability to assignee for UDAP violation where state law limits liability to alleged perpetrator), *aff'd on other grounds*, 87 Fed. Appx. 314 (4th Cir. 2004); Canty v. Equicredit Corp., 2003 WL 21243268 (E.D. Pa. May 8, 2003) (consumer conceded that holder was not liable derivatively for a UDAP claim, though it is unclear why).

329 15 U.S.C. § 1641(d)(2).

330 15 U.S.C. § 1641(d)(1); Cazares v. Pacific Shore Funding, 2006 WL 149106 (C.D. Cal. Jan. 3, 2006) (burden of proof is on assignee); Cooper v. First Gov't Mortgage & Investors Corp., 238 F. Supp. 2d 50 (D.D.C. 2002) (assignee failed to meet burden); Rodrigues v. U.S. Bank, 278 B.R. 683, 688 (Bankr. D.R.I. 2002) (assignee has burden).

331 15 U.S.C. § 1641(d)(4). *See* Reg. Z, 12 C.F.R. § 226.32(e)(3). Failure to include this notice should be grounds for enhanced damages and civil liability under 15 U.S.C. § 1640.

332 15 U.S.C. § 1641(d)(1).

333 Cooper v. First Gov't Mortgage & Investors Corp., 238 F. Supp. 2d 50 (D.D.C. 2002).

334 *Id.*

335 *Id.*

overlap with the question of whether the assignee can use the bona fide purchaser defense to avoid the consequences of a claim that the sale-leaseback arrangement was an equitable mortgage.[336] If the assignee establishes that it was a bona fide purchaser, it cannot be subject to HOEPA liability.

5.9 Real Estate Settlement Procedures Act (RESPA)

5.9.1 In General

The express purpose of the Real Estate Settlement Procedures Act (RESPA)[337] is to protect consumers from unnecessarily high settlement charges and certain abusive practices that have developed in the residential real estate industry.[338] It attempts to achieve this goal primarily by controlling the manner by which settlement services for residential real estate loan transactions are provided and compensated. It also requires advance disclosure of settlement costs, designed to enable a borrower to make an informed decision as to whether the offered terms are reasonable and acceptable. This section provides a brief overview of RESPA provisions that apply prior to or at the loan closing. A more detailed discussion of these provisions may be found in National Consumer Law Center, *The Cost of Credit: Regulation, Preemption, and Industry Abuses* § 12.2.2 (4th ed. 2009 and Supp.). For an in-depth treatment of RESPA provisions applicable to loan servicing and a chart summarizing all of RESPA's requirements, see Chapter 8, *infra.*

5.9.2 RESPA's Disclosure Requirements

5.9.2.1 Introduction

HUD recently adopted amendments to RESPA's Regulation X that significantly changed the rules for cost disclosures effective January 1, 2010.[339] The old and new disclosure requirements are discussed in detail in National Consumer Law Center, *The Cost of Credit: Regulation, Preemption, and Industry Abuses* § 12.2.1.3 (4th ed. 2009 and Supp.). Private remedies under these disclosure requirements vary significantly from requirement to requirement.

336 *See* §§ 15.4.1.2–15.4.1.3, *infra* (discussing equitable mortgage doctrine and bona fide purchaser defense).

337 12 U.S.C. §§ 2601–2617.

338 Wanger v. EMC Mortgage Corp., 127 Cal. Rptr. 2d 685 (Cal. Ct. App. 2002) (RESPA is a consumer protection statute and should be liberally construed).

339 73 Fed. Reg. 68,204 (Nov. 17, 2008). *See* Real Estate Settlement Procedures Act (RESPA): Proposed Rule to Simplify and Improve the Process of Obtaining Mortgages and Reduce Consumer Settlement Costs, 73 Fed. Reg. 14,030 (Mar. 14, 2008).

5.9.2.2 Disclosure Violations Without an Explicit RESPA Remedy

No remedies are prescribed for violations of the following disclosure requirements,[340] but failure to comply may constitute a violation of state unfair and deceptive acts and practices statutes.[341] No later than three business days after application, the consumer must be given a "good faith estimate" of settlement costs.[342] Prior to 2010, Regulation X permitted the good faith estimate (GFE) to disclose estimates of the amount or range for each charge, as long as

340 *Several courts have held that there is no private right of action under 12 U.S.C. § 2604*: Collins v. FMHA-USDA, 105 F.3d 1366 (11th Cir. 1997); Beard v. Worldwide Mortgage Corp., 354 F. Supp. 2d 789 (W.D. Tenn. 2005); Wingert v. Credit Based Asset Serv. & Securitization, L.L.C., 2004 WL 2915306 (W.D. Pa. Aug. 26, 2004); Chow v. Aegis Mortgage Corp., 286 F. Supp. 2d 965 (N.D. Ill. 2003); Reese v. 1st Metro. Mortgage Co., 2003 WL 22454658 (D. Kan. Oct. 28, 2003); Marbury v. Colonial Mortgage Co., 2001 U.S. Dist. LEXIS 1632 (M.D. Ala. Jan. 12, 2001); Mentecki v. Saxon Mortgage Inc., 1997 U.S. Dist. LEXIS 1374 (E.D. Va. Jan. 10, 1997); Campbell v. Machias Sav. Bank, 865 F. Supp. 26 (D. Me. 1994).

Courts have also held there is no private right of action under 12 U.S.C. § 2603: Morrison v. Brookstone Mortgage Co., 415 F. Supp. 2d 801 (S.D. Ohio 2005); Reese v. 1st Metro. Mortgage Co., 2003 WL 22454658 (D. Kan. Oct. 28, 2003).

341 *See, e.g.*, Chow v. Aegis Mortgage Corp., 286 F. Supp. 2d 965 (N.D. Ill. 2003); Anderson v. Wells Fargo Home Mortgage, Inc., 259 F. Supp. 2d 1143 (W.D. Wash. 2003) (failure to disclose the yield spread premium proves one element of a UDAP claim); Gardner v. First Am. Title Ins. Co., 2003 WL 221844 (D. Minn. Jan. 27, 2003); Brophy v. Chase Manhattan Mortgage Co., 947 F. Supp. 879 (E.D. Pa. 1996) (borrowers could pursue state law claims in state court on issue of whether disparities between good faith estimate and HUD-1 settlement statement violated Pennsylvania's UDAP statute); Stewart Title Guar. Co. v. American Abstract & Title Co., 363 Ark. 530 (Ark. 2005) (referral fees in violation of RESPA sufficient to establish "improper conduct" in claim for tortious interference with business expectancy under UDAP statute); Wash. Mut. Bank v. Super. Ct., 89 Cal. Rptr. 2d 560 (Ct. App. 1999) (court specifically held that RESPA and Reg. X do not expressly preempt private rights of action under state laws for violations of their provisions). *See also* National Consumer Law Center, Unfair and Deceptive Acts and Practices § 3.2.7 (7th ed. 2008 and Supp.); National Consumer Law Center, The Cost of Credit: Regulation, Preemption, and Industry Abuses § 12.2.1.9 (4th ed. 2009 and Supp.) (discussion regarding preemption issues). *But see In re* Noyes, 382 B.R. 561 (Bankr. D. Mass. 2008) (mere technical violation of RESPA—failure to provide timely good faith estimate—did not support state UDAP claim); Koch v. First Union Corp., 2002 WL 372939 (Pa. Ct. Com. Pl. 2002) (violation of good faith estimate provisions of RESPA not actionable under state UDAP statute); Herrod v. First Republic Mortgage Corp., Inc., 625 S.E.2d 373 (W. Va. 2005) (affirming summary judgment for lender on state UDAP claim because nothing in UDAP statute makes yield spread premiums specifically illegal and failure to provide good faith estimate not actionable under UDAP statute because nothing in UDAP statute imposes liability on lender for broker's violation).

342 12 U.S.C. § 2604(d).

they bore a reasonable relationship to the borrower's ultimate cost for each charge and were based upon experience in the area in which the property was located.[343] As amended, Regulation X now requires the loan originator to disclose actual costs, using a new form mandated by HUD, as well as a summary of the specific loan terms including the initial loan amount, the term, negative amortization, adjustable rates, prepayment penalties, balloon payments, the maximum interest rate, the monthly payment, and whether an escrow account is required (but not the amount of the escrow payment). The new GFE is generally binding for ten business days.[344] In addition to the GFE, a booklet explaining these costs must be provided.[345]

For any loan covered by RESPA, settlement agents must use the HUD-1 settlement statement at the closing to clearly and conspicuously itemize all charges actually imposed on the borrower.[346] The amendments also changed the HUD-1 form. Beginning January 1, 2010, the form is three pages long and must include information about the loan term, the monthly payments, interest rate adjustments, and any changes from the amounts disclosed on the GFE. Unfortunately, many of these changes risk causing greater confusion and the ARM disclosures are nearly impenetrable.[347] Finally, section 10 of RESPA requires that the borrower receive a written escrow account statement at the time the account is opened.[348]

5.9.2.3 Disclosures with Explicit RESPA Remedies

RESPA requires disclosure at the time of a mortgage loan application as to whether the servicing of the loan may be assigned, sold, or transferred at any time during the term of the mortgage. Because this requirement is contained within RESPA section 2605, borrowers have a private right of action if the lender fails to give the disclosure.[349] Similarly, when a so-called "affiliated business arrangement" is involved, a statement disclosing the nature of the relationship between the provider of the settlement service and the person or entity making the referral, and a written estimate of the charge or range of charges is generally made by such provider.[350] The disclosure of an affiliated business arrangement is mandated by section 2607 of RESPA, which also contains a private right of action.

5.9.3 *Substantive RESPA Prohibitions*

Kickbacks and referrals are prohibited by RESPA section 2607(a) which provides that no person shall give and no person shall accept any fee, kickback, or other thing of value pursuant to any oral or written agreement or understanding for the referral of a settlement service in the scope of loans described above.[351] The private remedy for a violation of this provision is treble damages and attorney fees.[352] One of the most prevalent kickbacks founds in residential real estate transactions is the "yield spread premium." This fee, which is paid from the lender to the loan broker for getting a borrower to sign on to a loan with a higher interest rate, is a quintessential kickback, and one that is frequently not explained to the borrower.

Nevertheless, the Department of Housing and Urban Development (HUD), the agency designated to promulgate regulations under and to enforce RESPA, has condoned this practice. The standard articulated by HUD for determining whether such a payment is illegal requires an evaluation of the total compensation paid to the broker from any source (not just lender-paid fees) and the goods, services, or facilities provided.[353] According to HUD, a violation occurs if the total compensation is not reasonable for the services provided.

Section 2607(b) prohibits the giving or accepting of any portion, split, or percentage of any charge for services not actually performed. Since virtually every mortgage transaction involves an array of "settlement services" this section was intended to prevent abuse of unwary and vulnerable consumers by eliminating excessive, duplicative, and unearned fees. However, in evaluating whether excessive fees violate RESPA, several appellate courts have distinguished between "mark ups" and "overcharges," finding the former a violation but not the later. Mark-ups occur when the lender outsources the settlement service to a third party, pays the vendor its fee, inflates the costs without itself performing any additional service, and passes the padded fee on to the homeowner. An overcharge occurs when the lender itself performs the settlement services and pads the cost.

---

343 Reg. X, 24 C.F.R. § 3500.7(a), (c)(2).

344 73 Fed. Reg. 68,239, 68,240, *codified at* 24 C.F.R. § 3500.7(a).

345 12 U.S.C. § 2604; Reg. X, 24 C.F.R. § 3500.6 (not required for refinancings, subordinate lien or reverse mortgages).

346 12 U.S.C. § 2603(a), (b); Reg. X, 24 C.F.R. § 3500.8(a), (b).

347 *See* 27 NCLC REPORTS *Consumer Credit and Usury Ed.* 11 (describing problems with new requirements).

348 12 U.S.C. § 2609; Reg. X, 24 C.F.R. § 3500.17.

349 *See* § 8.2.3, *infra.*

350 12 U.S.C. § 2607(c)(4); Reg. X, 24 C.F.R. § 3500.15(a).

This document is useful in determining whether any of the closing costs count towards the points and fees trigger for Home Ownership and Equity Protection Act purposes. *See* National Consumer Law Center, Truth in Lending § 9.2.6.3.5 (6th ed. 2007 and Supp.). For a more detailed discussion of affiliated business arrangements, see National Consumer Law Center, Cost of Credit: Regulation, Preemption, and Industry Abuses § 12.2.1.6.7 (4th ed. 2009 and Supp.).

351 Reg. X, 24 C.F.R. § 3500.14(b).

A historical overview of the law related to kickbacks and referral fees, as well as a review of current case law may be found in National Consumer Law Center, The Cost of Credit: Regulation, Preemption, and Industry Abuses § 12.2.1.6 (4th ed. 2009 and Supp.).

352 12 U.S.C. § 2607(d).

353 *See* 66 Fed. Reg. 53,052 (Oct. 10, 2001).

A third category of charges referred to as "undivided unearned fees," or more aptly called "no service fees," may also violate section 2607(b).[354] These charges do not involve a third party settlement provider, but differ from "overcharges" because they involve charges where no, nominal, or duplicative work is done.

In addition to the prohibitions of section 2607 dealing with kickbacks, referral fees, fee splitting, and unearned fees, RESPA contains two other restrictions related to settlement charges. RESPA makes it illegal for a lender to require borrowers to purchase title insurance from a particular title insurance company. RESPA also prohibits charging for the preparation of the Truth in Lending disclosure or the HUD-1 settlement statement.

5.10 Fair Lending Statutes

Fair lending statutes generally prohibit discrimination against certain groups of people. For example, the Equal Credit Opportunity Act (ECOA) prohibits discrimination in any aspect of credit on the basis of race, color, national origin, religion, sex or gender, marital status, age, or public assistance status.[355] The federal Fair Housing Act and its state counterparts prohibit discrimination on the basis of race, color, religion, sex or gender, disability or handicap, familial status, or national origin in the sale rental, or advertising of housing and in housing-related financing.[356] In addition, the civil rights acts provide that the same right to contract, purchase, and hold property available to white citizens must be extended to all citizens.[357] These statutes are discussed in detail in National Consumer Law Center, *Credit Discrimination*,[358] but they are briefly discussed here to alert the practitioner to their use as potential defenses or counterclaims to foreclosure actions.

Equitable and declaratory relief is available under all the federal credit discrimination statutes. Not only is it clear that such relief is available for a violation of the federal civil rights acts, but the Fair Housing Act specifically states that the court "may grant as relief, as the court deems appropriate, any permanent or temporary injunction, temporary restraining order, or other order."[359] Similarly, the ECOA states that an aggrieved credit applicant may obtain "such equitable and declaratory relief as is necessary to enforce the requirements" of the ECOA.[360]

A number of courts have allowed homeowners to raise a lender's violation of the ECOA and the FHA as a defense to foreclosure. For example, the Maine Supreme Judicial Court has used its equitable power under the ECOA to bar a lender from foreclosing on property owned by joint tenancy when the wife's signature on the mortgage was obtained in violation of that Act.[361] Claims of reverse redlining under either the ECOA or the FHA may also be raised defensively in foreclosure actions.[362] Reverse redlining is the practice of targeting protected groups (e.g., minorities) for particularly predatory loans. More recently, the ECOA has been used affirmatively to combat the predatory practice of making loans to consumers for a larger amount than they applied for and without a formal loan denial and statement of reasons why the loan in the amount requested was not provided.[363] Other recent credit discrimination cases have alleged that giving brokers and others discretion as to the size of interest rate upcharges has a disparate impact on protected groups.

As a general rule, both the ECOA and the FHA have a two-year statutes of limitation for affirmative claims.[364]

354 *See* Cohen v. JP Morgan Chase & Co., 498 F.3d 111 (2d Cir. 2007).

355 15 U.S.C. § 1691.

The ECOA also prohibits discrimination against consumers who exercise their rights under the Consumer Credit Protection Act. *See generally* National Consumer Law Center, Credit Discrimination Ch. 3 (5th ed. 2009 and Supp.).

356 42 U.S.C. §§ 3604, 3605.

State fair lending laws are compiled in National Consumer Law Center, Credit Discrimination Appx. E (5th ed. 2009 and Supp.).

Section 3605 of the FHA specifically applies to real-estate-related financing transactions. It is less clear whether courts will also apply § 3604 to home equity lending. *See* National Consumer Law Center, Credit Discrimination § 2.3.3.1.2 (5th ed. 2009 and Supp.).

357 42 U.S.C. §§ 1981, 1982.

358 *See generally* National Consumer Law Center, Credit Discrimination Ch. 3 (5th ed. 2009 and Supp.).

359 42 U.S.C. § 3613(c).

360 15 U.S.C. § 1691e(c).

361 Calaska Partners Ltd. v. Corson, 672 A.2d 1099 (Me. 1996).

Like *Calaska,* many ECOA cases involve lenders that that have required a spouse's signature on a promissory note, not just the mortgage, even though he or she is not an applicant on the loan. *See* 15 U.S.C. § 1691b(a); 12 C.F.R. § 202.7(d)(1) (prohibiting creditor's from requiring spouse's signature unless spouse is a joint applicant).

These courts have held that the obligation may not be enforced against a party who became an obligor in violation of ECOA. *See, e.g.,* Integra Bank v. Freeman, 839 F. Supp. 326 (E.D. Pa. 1993); Still v. Cunningham, 94 P.3d 1104 (Alaska 2004); Banco Popular N. Am. v. *In re* Smith, 2004 WL 1664236 (Conn. Super. Ct. June 29, 2004) (ECOA claim may form basis of valid foreclosure defense).

362 *See* National Consumer Law Center, Credit Discrimination § 8.3 (5th ed. 2009 and Supp.).

363 *See* Newton v. United Co. Fin. Corp., 24 F. Supp. 2d 444 (E.D. Pa. 1998).

Counteroffers that are accepted or used are not considered to be "adverse actions" under the ECOA. There is a split amount the courts whether written notice is required if there is no adverse action. *Cf.* Riccardi v. Ameriquest Mortgage Co., 164 Fed. Appx. 221 (3d Cir. 2006) (no ECOA violation where written notice of change in terms provided at closing); Diaz v. Va. Hous. Dev. Auth., 117 F. Supp. 2d 500 (E.D. Va. 2000) (notice of counteroffer does not have to be in writing); *In re* United Cos. Fin. Corp., 277 B.R. 596 (Bankr. D. Del. 2002) (denying class certification in case based on ECOA counteroffer notice requirements and citing *Diaz* with approval that written notice of counteroffer not required).

364 *See* National Consumer Law Center, Credit Discrimination § 11.8.2 (5th ed. 2009 and Supp.).

However claims usually can be brought by way of set-off or recoupment.[365] The majority of reported ECOA cases that have addressed the issue have permitted recoupment claims after the limitations period has run.[366] Similarly, courts have allowed recoupment claims in FHA cases.[367] In addition to equitable relief discussed above, consumer remedies for violation of fair lending statutes in affirmative or defensive cases include actual damages, punitive damages, and attorney fees and costs.[368]

Significantly, both the ECOA and the FHA may allow consumers to reach assignees and secondary market players. The ECOA definition of creditor explicitly includes assignees as long as they regularly participate in credit decisions, including setting the terms of the credit.[369] The FHA explicitly applies to the selling, brokering, or appraising of residential real estate and to any other entity providing financial assistance related to a loan covered by the Act.[370] The FHA also applies to the activities of secondary market players in the purchasing of loans, debts, or securities, the pooling and packaging of these instruments, and the marketing and sale of securities issues on the basis of loans or debts.[371]

5.11 State High-Cost Mortgage Statutes

State anti-predatory lending laws also can be powerful tools for challenging unfair lending practices and defending against foreclosure. The scope and content of these state laws varies widely.[372] Some like HOEPA provide a private right of action for borrowers, while other limit enforcement to government agencies. Some permit double or treble damages, while others limit relief to compensatory damages. Several jurisdictions have adopted anti-predatory lending laws that do not significantly increase, and may even reduce existing protections by overriding ordinances by political subdivisions that are more protective.[373] However, many states that have enacted high-cost mortgage laws have expanded on HOEPA by covering more loans and by prohibiting more abusive loan terms.

States with strong anti-predatory lending laws often include provisions such as: prohibitions on refinancing a mortgage without providing a net tangible benefit to the consumer; loan counseling requirements for certain loans; and bans or restrictions on lending without regard to ability to repay, prepayment penalties, balloon payments, and negative amortization. The scope of these restrictions varies but such laws often exempt prime loans and home equity lines of credit. Growing anger in the wake of the recent foreclosure crisis has led many state legislatures to consider enacting new laws to reduce predatory lending. Therefore, it is important to monitor legislative developments in your state.

When planning to raise claims based on state anti-predatory lending laws it is necessary to first investigate whether the law has been preempted by federal law. Federal preemption has significantly undermined state consumer protections regarding credit charges and lending. Nevertheless, state laws that have not been preempted have been shown to protect homeowners far better than existing federal protections and weak regulators.[374] The subject of preemption and how to determine whether a state law has been preempted is discussed in National Consumer Law Center, *The Cost of Credit: Regulation, Preemption, and Industry Abuses* Chapter 3 (4th ed. 2009 and Supp.).

5.12 Fraud or Misrepresentation

The elements of fraud[375] are more difficult to establish than the elements of a deception claim under a UDAP

365 *Id.* § 11.8.2.2.

366 *See, e.g.*, Mayes v. Chrysler Credit Corp, 167 F.3d 675 (1st Cir. 1999); Bolduc v. Beal Bank, 167 F.3d 667 (1st Cir. 1999); Silverman v. Eastrich Multiple Investor Fund, L.P., 51 F.3d 28 (3d Cir. 1995); Federal Deposit Ins. Corp. v. Medmark, Inc., 897 F. Supp. 511 (D. Kan. 1995); Marine Am. State Bank v. Lincoln, 433 N.W.2d 709 (Iowa 1998). *But see* Riggs Nat'l Bank v. Linch, 36 F.3d 370 (4th Cir. 1994).

367 *See, e.g.*, Assoc. Home Equity Servs., Inc. v. Troup, 778 A.2d 529, 539 (N.J. Super Ct. App. Div. 2001).

368 *See* National Consumer Law Center, Credit Discrimination § 11.7 (5th ed. 2009 and Supp.).

369 Regulation B, 12 C.F.R. § 202.2(*l*)-(1). The Commentary further clarifies that the definition of creditor includes an assignee or a potential purchaser of the obligation who influences the credit decision by indicating whether or not it will purchase the loan if the transaction is consummated. Official Staff Commentary, 12 C.F.R. § 202.2(*l*)-(1).

370 42 U.S.C. § 3605.

371 24 C.F.R. § 100.125.

372 *See* National Consumer Law Center, The Cost of Credit: Regulation, Preemption, and Industry Abuses § 12.2.4 (4th ed. 2009 and Supp.) (overview of many of the state high-cost mortgage laws and their key provisions).

373 *See, e.g.*, Colo. Rev. Stat. §§ 5-3.5-101 to 303; Fla. Stat. §§ 494.0078 to 494.00797; Ind. Code § 24-9; Mich. Comp. Laws § 445.1631-1645; Md. Code Ann., Com. Law §§ 12.124.1, 12.127, 12.409.1, 12.1029; Nev. Rev. Stat. 598D.010 to 598D.150; 63 Pa. Cons. Stat. §§ 456.501 to 456.524; S.C. Code Ann. §§ 37-23-10 to 37-23-85; Utah Code Ann. §§ 61-2d, 70D-1-21; Wis. Stat. § 428.

For example, in 2001, the Pennsylvania legislature enacted a weak high-cost mortgage statute that preempted Philadelphia Municipal Ordinance, 00-715(A) (2000) which afforded borrowers greater protection from predatory lending.

374 *See* Lei Ding, et al., The APL Effect: The Impacts of State Anti-Predatory Lending Laws on Foreclosures (Mar. 23, 2010); Ctr. for Community Capital, Univ. of North Carolina at Chapel Hill, The Preemption Effect: The Impact of Federal Preemption of State Anti-Predatory Lending Laws on the Foreclosure Crisis (Mar. 29, 2010).

375 The elements of fraud and misrepresentation are matters of state law. The elements of fraud generally include: (1) misrepresentation (such as false representation, concealment, or nondisclosure); (2) knowledge of the falsity (or scienter); (3) intent to

statute.[376] However, four home foreclosure cases illustrate the effective use of a fraud or misrepresentation approach.[377]

In *Peoples Trust & Savings Bank v. Humphrey*,[378] consumers went to their own bank for a home construction loan. The bank promised them a "good loan" at a 9 1/2% rate. That, however, was merely the initial rate. The permanent financing (after two temporary construction loans) was actually a then novel, variable-rate loan and contained a demand clause allowing the bank to demand payment of the balance of the loan at its discretion. Quoting from an old, respected legal treatise, the court held: "[w]hen parties to a contract have a prior understanding about the contract's terms, and the party responsible for drafting the contract includes contrary terms and then allows the other party to sign it without informing him of the changes, the drafter's conduct is fraudulent."[379] The court in *Humphrey* dismissed the lender's foreclosure, reformed the contract by deleting the demand and variable-rate clauses, and awarded $1000 actual and $40,000 punitive damages. It should be noted, however, that variable-rate clauses in residential mortgages have become much more common in the period since this decision, so that their inclusion is likely to be less alarming to the courts. Further, the 1987 requirement for variable-rate caps, along with the required TIL disclosures, should make variable-rate terms more apparent to borrowers.[380] Nonetheless, the principle articulated in *Humphrey* should still hold true when any contrary terms included by the lender are not obvious.

Greene v. Gibraltar Mortgage Investment Corp.[381] is another misrepresentation case. The court found the failure to disclose an unconscionably high broker fee and the lender's charging of interest on that fee to be a misrepresentation.[382] The lender also falsely represented the loan amount and claimed to offer a market interest rate. Accordingly, the court voided the promissory note and deed of trust and permanently enjoined foreclosure proceedings.[383]

Mahaffey v. Investors National Security Co.[384] involved a common home improvement fraud. The borrowers were promised home insulation which would cut fuel consumption in half, the borrower's home would be used for promotional purposes, and the total cost would be $5300. Work was begun before the three-day cooling-off period, but never completed; what was done was done improperly. The contractors induced borrowers to sign a completion certificate despite the incomplete work by threatening them with "sky-rocketing interest rates" and "troubles." The assignee tried to foreclose, but the Nevada Supreme Court found the contract to be null and void because of the fraudulent inducement and failure of consideration on the contractor's part. The assignee was liable because the required FTC Notice of Preservation of Claims and Defenses[385] clause appeared in the contract.

Fraud may also be available as a defense when a borrower is tricked by a family member into signing mortgage documents. In *First Charter National Bank v. Ross*,[386] a wife was allowed to assert fraud as a special defense to a foreclosure action when her husband had given her loan documents to sign with the signature page on top, had discouraged her from looking at the documents, and had told her that the documents had nothing to do with their home. The court ruled that the defense of fraud was not barred by the general rule that a person has a duty to read what they sign and that notice of the content of signed documents is imputed. The court said the rule does not apply when there is fraud or artifice, and applies only if nothing is said or done to

defraud or to induce reliance; (4) justifiable reliance; and (5) resulting damage. Spencer v. DHI Mortgage Co., Ltd., 642 F. Supp. 2d 1153, 1164 (E.D. Cal. 2009). The elements of negligent misrepresentation generally require proof that: (1) the party justifiably relied to his detriment; (2) on information provided without reasonable care; (3) by one who owed relying party duty of care. Swarich v. OneWest Bank, F.S.B., 2009 WL 4041947 (E.D. Mich. Nov. 20, 2009).

376 *See* National Consumer Law Center, Unfair and Deceptive Acts and Practices § 3.2.4 (7th ed. 2008 and Supp.).

377 *See also* Manufacturers and Traders Trust v. Hughes, 2003 WL 21780956 (N.D. Ill. July 31, 2003) (traditional equitable defenses such as fraud may be raised against assignee's foreclosure claim); *In re* Miner, 369 B.R. 655 (Bankr. D. Kan. 2007) (lender's failure to inform borrowers of effects of converting unsecured debt to secured debt and failure to disclose payments on secured debt would extend for a longer period of time than payments on unsecured debt could support a fraud claim through omission); Home Loan & Inv. Bank v. Sebjan, 2000 Conn. Super. LEXIS (Conn. Super. Ct. July 24, 2000) (summary judgment denied and mortgagee cannot foreclose when mortgagee negligently misrepresented the amount of the mortgage); King v. Kitchen Magic, Inc., 391 A.2d 1184 (D.C. 1978) (home improvement mortgage case in which true price of the improvements was not disclosed to homeowners; nine years after original transaction court allowed claim to nullify the lien based on fraud); Mitchell v. Dahlberg, 547 N.W.2d 74 (Mich. Ct. App. 1996) (when there is fraud or other unusual circumstances, equitable remedies may be appropriate to prevent foreclosure); Harrel v. Solt, 2000 Ohio App. LEXIS 6312 (Ohio Ct. App. Dec. 27, 2000) (summary judgment denied and lender cannot foreclose on a home that mortgagors were fraudulently induced to purchase). The companion website to this treatise contains complaints containing fraud claims against mortgage lenders.

378 451 N.E.2d 1104 (Ind. Ct. App. 1983).

379 *Id.* at 1112.

380 *See* 12 U.S.C. § 3806; Reg. Z, 12 C.F.R. §§ 226.6(a) n.12, 226.18, 226.19, 226.30.

381 488 F. Supp. 177 (D.D.C. 1980), *later proceeding at* 529 F. Supp. 186 (D.D.C. 1981). *See also* Faison v. Nationwide Mortgage Corp., 839 F.2d 680 (D.C. Cir. 1987).

382 *See* National Consumer Law Center, The Cost of Credit: Regulation, Preemption, and Industry Abuses § 12.7 (4th ed. 2009 and Supp.) (discussing unconscionability).

383 488 F. Supp. at 181.

384 747 P.2d 890 (Nev. 1987).

385 16 C.F.R. § 433. *See* National Consumer Law Center, Unfair and Deceptive Acts and Practices § 11.6.2 (7th ed. 2008 and Supp.).

386 29 Conn. App. 667, 617 A.2d 909 (1992). *See also* Jones v. Adams Fin. Servs., 71 Cal. App. 4th 831 (1999) (legally blind older homeowner tricked into signing loan documents).

mislead the person signing. The court had discretion to determine whether the wife was negligent and whether the defense of fraud could be raised. It should be noted, however, that some courts have refused to invalidate a mortgage when the fraud was committed by a party other than the lender and the lender was not involved in or aware of the fraud.[387]

5.13 Other Defenses

5.13.1 Estoppel

When various and conflicting promises in the loan origination process were made by a lender, a court may find that the effect of some of the promises is to estop the lender from enforcing others. In *First State Bank v. Phillips*,[388] for example, the court held that a bank was estopped from enforcing a balloon payment clause in a note and dismissed the foreclosure.

The consumer in *Phillips* had assumed a mortgage extended by the bank to the person from whom the consumer brought the house. The mortgage indicated it would be fully paid with monthly payments. A separate promissory note provided that after a period of regular monthly payments, the balance of the note would be due in a single lump-sum balloon payment. The mortgage which the consumer saw did not contain the balloon payment; the consumer never saw the note which did. When the consumer talked to bank employees about assuming the mortgage, the balloon payment was not disclosed. In dismissing the foreclosure, the court found that the nondisclosure of the balloon payment forfeited the bank's right to enforce it.[389]

Under the right circumstances, promissory estoppel can also be used to enforce a mortgage servicer's promise to delay a foreclosure. In *Vissuet v. Indymac Mortgage Services*,[390] for example, a mortgage servicer was bound by promissory estoppel when it told a borrower that it would postpone a trustee sale if she completed and submitted an application for a loan modification.[391] Promissory estoppel requires a borrower to prove: that the servicer made a promise; the borrower relied to her detriment on the promise; and that reliance was both reasonable and foreseeable.[392] Making a partial payment toward an amount past due, however, does not qualify as reliance because the borrower was already obligated to make the payment.[393]

5.13.2 Fiduciary Duty

Traditionally, a credit transaction has been considered an arm's length transaction in which there has been no special duty read into the creditor-debtor relationship. Most courts, however, have held that the presence of certain factors in the creditor-debtor relationship may give rise to a fiduciary duty. A fiduciary owes its principal a duty of loyalty.[394] As the agent in a principal-agent relationship, the fiduciary has a duty to act in the best interests of the principal.

For example, a fiduciary relationship can arise when a party—generally a "weaker" party in the sense of the ability to protect itself—places trust and confidence in another.[395]

387 *See* Family First Fed. Sav. Bank v. De Vincentis, 284 N.J. Super. 503, 665 A.2d 1119 (1995) (mortgagor's son's fraud not imputed to bank because bank did not participate in fraud); Gizzi v. Hall, 754 N.Y.S.2d 373 (App. Div. 2002) (fraud of the builder not a defense to foreclosure by the lender); G.E. Capital Mortgage Servs., Inc. v. Holbrooks, 666 N.Y.S.2d 175 (App. Div. 1997) (fraud by mortgage broker not imputed to lender because court found broker had to have withheld knowledge of forgery from lender, and the broker was not the agent of the lender); Melton v. Family First Mortgage Corp., 576 S.E.2d 365 (N.C. 2003) (mortgagor not entitled to rescind loan based on "fraud in the treaty" rather than fraud in the factum; mortgagor claimed that she entered into loan based on misrepresentations made by granddaughter, lender not aware of misrepresentations, and not under duty to inquire), *aff'd without op.*, 597 S.E.2d 672 (N.C. 2003). *See also* David v. Financial One, 2007 WL 3202995 (E.D. Mich. Oct. 30, 2007) (holder, as bona fide purchaser of mortgage, not liable for fraud of broker or lender where holder had no knowledge of fraudulent conduct).

388 681 S.W.2d 408 (Ark. Ct. App. 1984).

389 *See also* Argent Mortgage v. Wyrick, 2007 WL 1053412 (Conn. Super. Ct. 2007) (homeowner had right to assert equitable estoppel defense to foreclosure where lender failed to notify homeowners of a requirement in force placed insurance policy to start rebuilding within a year of casualty and as a result full amount of mortgage not covered by policy). *But cf.* Chem. Bank v. Dippolito, 897 F. Supp. 221, 224 (E.D. Pa. 1995) (acceptance of mortgage payments after due date of balloon payment did not estop bank from foreclosure, when bank maintained foreclosure proceedings even while accepting payments and made no representations that it would not enforce balloon payments, and borrower was not harmed because payments were applied to outstanding debt).

390 2010 WL 1031013 (S.D. Cal. Mar. 19, 2010).

391 *Id.* at *1. The court also found the same facts to support a breach of contract claim with the act of completing and returning the form to be adequate consideration. *Id. See* Garcia v. World Sav., F.S.B., 2010 WL 1031013 (S.D. Cal. Mar. 19, 2010) (finding promissory estoppel where servicer promised to postpone sale if borrower got financing to cure default; borrower got financing but servicer allowed sale to proceed).

392 *See* Garcia v. World Sav., F.S.B., ___ Cal. Rptr. 3d ___, 2010 WL 1408927, at *3 (Cal. Ct. App. Apr. 9 ,2010); Healy v. Brewster, 380 P.2d 817 (Cal. 1963).

393 Newgent v. Wells Fargo Bank, N.A., 2010 WL 761236 (S.D. Cal. Mar. 2, 2010).

394 *See, e.g.*, Frey v. Fraser Yachts, 29 F.3d 1153 (7th Cir. 1994). *See also* National Consumer Law Center, The Cost of Credit: Regulation, Preemption, and Industry Abuses § 12.9 (4th ed. 2009 and Supp.).

395 Garrett v. BankWest, 459 N.W.2d 833 (S.D. 1990); Mark Budnitz, *The Sale of Credit Life Insurance: The Bank as Fiduciary*, 62 N.C. L. Rev. 295 (1984). *See* Smith v. Jenkins, 626 F. Supp. 2d 155, 171 (D. Mass. 2009) (borrower with mental illness sufficiently pleaded claim for breach of fiduciary duty where

Such a "duty of confidence"[396] arguably can arise if a lender acts in the role of advisor and knows or should have known the borrower trusted him.[397] When such a relationship exists it gives rise to a duty to disclose. For example, one court has held that a fiduciary duty arose between bank and borrower after the initial negotiation of the loan terms, such that subsequent inaccurate, untimely and incomplete information provided by the loan officer to the borrowers constituted a breach of fiduciary duty.[398] Mortgage loan brokers may also owe a fiduciary duty to borrowers arising from either an agency relationship or a confidential relationship.[399]

In *Wyatt v. Union Mortgage Co.*,[400] a loan broker arranging a home loan was held to have a financial duty to counsel the borrower and disclose the disadvantageous financial aspects of a loan transaction. The broker failed to counsel the borrower about the interest rate, late charges, a balloon payment, and their consequences—terms particularly important, given the consumer's income and other financial obligations.[401]

If established, the existence of a fiduciary duty gives rise to a duty of fair and honest disclosure of all facts which might be presumed to influence the consumer to act.[402] When there is a duty to disclose, failure to do so should give rise to a tort claim for nondisclosure,[403] or the silence may qualify as misrepresentation.[404] Such claims can be used to invalidate the underlying mortgage transaction or to recover money damages to offset any delinquency.[405]

Similarly, if a fiduciary relationship is used to induce a homeowner to make a voluntary transfer of property to the fiduciary (in lieu of foreclosure, for example), there is ample precedent to have that transfer set aside.[406] Alternatively, a constructive trust may be imposed on the property so that the homeowner can recover the property.[407]

In the foreclosure process the lender has a fiduciary duty to ensure that the homeowner obtains the highest price possible from the sale of the property. A lender's refusal to postpone a foreclosure sale, for example, to allow the homeowner to conduct a market sale to a willing and financially capable buyer is a violation of its fiduciary duty. The pre-auction sale would have satisfied the lender's lien and costs and netted the homeowner a surplus.[408]

5.13.3 Incompetence

Contracts entered into by persons who are deemed incompetent are generally voidable.[409] This basic principle of contract law may be used to invalidate mortgage contracts made by persons who are too young to form valid contracts, or who suffer from temporary or permanent mental incapacity at the time the mortgage is made.[410] Mental incapacity can also be grounds for equitably tolling a statute of limitations.[411]

A bankruptcy court in Massachusetts, for example, has allowed a debtor to put on evidence as to whether she was entitled to rescind a note and mortgage based on incompetence.[412] The debtor was allowed to raise the claim post-foreclosure because the lender was also the foreclosure purchaser and therefore there was no intervening bona fide purchaser.[413] Moreover, the court held that it was no defense for the lender to assert that it was not aware that the debtor was incompetent.[414]

---

defendants knew he was novice at real estate transactions, could not understand underlying details, and took advantage of his trust).

396 J. Shephard, The Law of Fiduciaries 31 n.70 (1981).

397 Stewart v. Phoenix Nat'l Bank, 49 Ariz. 34, 64 P.2d 101, 106 (1937). *But see* Strong v. First Family Fin. Servs., Inc. 202 F. Supp. 2d 536 (S.D. Miss. 2002) (lenders and borrowers typically not in a fiduciary relationship); Dicicco v. Willow Grove Bank, 2004 WL 2150980 (E.D. Pa. Sept. 21, 2004) (lender not fiduciary of borrower—law presumes the relationship between lender and borrower is conducted at arms-length and the parties are each acting in their own interest).

398 Callahan v. First Merit Mortgage Corp. 2005 WL 3867346 (Ohio Mun. Sept. 22, 2005) (lender created relationship of trust and confidence by assuring borrowers that they would receive specified loan terms).

399 *In re* Barker, 251 B.R. 250 (Bankr. E.D. Pa. 2000) (broker as agent of borrower owed her a fiduciary duty); Arnold v. United Companies Lending Corp., 511 S.E.2d 854 (W. Va. 1998) (distinguishing loan broker with fiduciary duties to borrower from "mere middleman" with no fiduciary obligations). *See* § 5.3.2.2, *supra*.

400 598 P.2d 45 (Cal. 1979).

401 *Id. See also* Ware v. Indymac Bank, F.S.B., 534 F. Supp. 2d 835 (N.D. Ill. 2008) (denying mortgage broker's motion to dismiss breach of fiduciary duty claim where borrower alleged loan flipping, charging of exorbitant fees and falsification of documents); Zimmer v. Nawabi, 2008 WL 2073956 (E.D. Cal. May 14, 2008) (failing to disclose loan terms orally, and instructing borrower to sign loan documents without reading them, breached broker's fiduciary duty); High v. McLean Fin. Corp., 659 F. Supp. 1561 (D.D.C. 1987).

402 Barrett v. Bank of Am., 229 Cal. Rptr. 16 (Ct. App. 1986).

403 Restatement (Second) of Torts § 551.

404 First Nat'l Bank of Md. v. Brown, 181 N.W.2d 178, 182 (Iowa 1970) (if the misrepresentation amounts to fraud in the inducement "whether innocent or not" that may give the defrauded party the right to avoid the contract in an action in equity).

405 *See* discussion at § 5.5.2, *supra*.

406 *E.g.*, Clark v. Tibbetts, 167 F.2d 397 (1948).

407 Chiu v. Wong, 16 F.3d 306 (8th Cir. 1994).

408 Snowden v. Chase Manhattan Mortgage Corp., 17 Mass. L. Rptr. 27, 2003 WL 22519518 (Mass. Super. Ct. Nov. 5, 2003).

409 *See* Krasner v. Berk, 319 N.E.2d 897 (Mass. 1974). *See generally* 41 Am. Jur. 2d *Incompetent Persons* § 65-103 (1995).

410 *See* United Companies Lending Corp. v. Coates, 520 S.E.2d 236 (Ga. Ct. App. 1999) (a deed to secure a debt was not enforceable against a minor's property as the guardian who executed the deed had not obtained court approval).

411 Stoll v. Runyon, 165 F.3d 1238 (9th Cir. 1999).

412 *In re* Hall, 188 B.R. 476 (Bankr. D. Mass. 1995).

413 *Id.*

414 *Id.* (citing Reed v. Mattapan Deposit & Trust Co., 198 Mass. 306 (1908) (it is no defense to avoidance of the contract that one party did not know the other was incompetent)).

5.13.4 Unconscionability

The common law contract defense of unconscionability may be applied to stop a foreclosure, when either the mortgage terms are unreasonably favorable to the lender or certain aspects of the transaction render it unconscionable.[415] For example, a Connecticut court found a second mortgage contract to be unconscionable based on the facts that: (1) the defendant had a limited knowledge of English, was uneducated and did not read very well; (2) the defendant's financial situation made it apparent that she could not reasonably expect to repay the mortgage (her monthly income was $1126 and the payment on her first mortgage was $1011); (3) at the closing, the defendant was not represented by an attorney and was rushed by plaintiff's attorney to sign the loan documents; (4) the defendant was not informed until the last minute that, as a condition of credit, she was required to pay one year's interest in advance; and (5) there was an absence of meaningful choice on the part of the defendant.[416] In addition, the court found that the contract was substantively unconscionable, because it contained a large balloon payment that the borrower had no means of paying, and that the borrower had no reasonable opportunity to understand the terms of the contract.[417]

5.13.5 Usury

Federal preemption of state usury laws has limited usury as a possible defense to foreclosure actions.[418] However, when a lender is foreclosing on a second mortgage,[419] when a lender is not covered by any of the federal preemption laws,[420] or when the state has opted out of the federal preemption provisions,[421] usury laws may provide a viable defense. Even when state (or federal) law places no restrictions on interest rates, other than that the interest rate shall be as the contract provides, the loan may be usurious if there is "hidden interest." Hidden interest may be found when unauthorized charges for lender services are not included in the stated interest rate. For example, inclusion of an inflated appraisal fee may be a hidden finance charge, if the law only permits the "bona fide actual cost" of such a fee to be excluded from interest. In some circumstances, excessive "points" or similar charges may give rise to a challenge as hidden interest.[422] When a mortgage broker acts as an agent for the lender and retains a broker fee, the fee may be deemed "interest" for purposes of usury.[423] When there is hidden interest, the actual interest rate is higher than the stated contract rate, and therefore the loan is usurious.[424]

The remedies available when usury can be established will vary from state to state. Often a statute will declare a usurious loan void as to all or part of the interest while

415 *See In re* Maxwell, 281 B.R. 101 (Bankr. D. Mass. 2002) (refinancing of mortgage loan unconscionable where homeowner received nothing of value but had her monthly mortgage increased to over 98% of her income); Hager v. American Gen. Fin., Inc., 37 F. Supp. 2d 778 (S.D. W. Va. 1999) (denying lender's summary judgment on unconscionability claim where borrowers alleged that the defendants induced them to enter into and refinance transaction with high interest rate); Beneficial Mortgage Co. of Ohio v. Leach, 2002 WL 926579 (Ohio Ct. App. May 9, 2002) (reversing foreclosure judgment based on unconscionability). *See generally* National Consumer Law Center, The Cost of Credit: Regulation, Preemption, and Industry Abuses § 12.7 (4th ed. 2009 and Supp.).

416 Family Fin. Servs. v. Spencer, 677 A.2d 479, 485 (Conn. Ct. App. 1996).

417 *Id.*. *See also* Maxwell v. Fairbanks Capital Corp., 281 B.R. 101 (Bankr. D. Mass. 2002); Swayne v. Beebles Invests., Inc., 891 N.E.2d 1216 (Ohio Ct. App. 2008) (procedural unconscionability based on gross disparity in bargaining power and substantive unconscionability based on one-year balloon note with an APR of 41.657% where borrower clearly had no ability to make final balloon payment); Benefit Mortgage Co. of Ohio v. Leach, 2002 WL 926759 (Ohio Ct. App. May 9, 2002). *But see* Emigrant Mortgage, Co. v. D'Agostino, 896 A.2d 814 (Conn. App. Ct. 2006) (borrower failed to provide any evidence to support assertion that default interest rate of 18% was unconscionable).

418 Depending on the circumstances, state usury laws may be preempted by one of several federal laws including: the National Bank Act, 12 U.S.C. § 85; the Depository Institutions Deregulation and Monetary Control Act, 12 U.S.C. § 1735f-7a, (DIDA); the Alternative Mortgage Transactions Parity Act, 12 U.S.C. §§ 3801–3805; and the Home Owners' Loan Act, 12 U.S.C. §§ 1461, 1463, 1464. *See* National Consumer Law Center, The Cost of Credit: Regulation, Preemption, and Industry Abuses Ch. 3 (4th ed. 2009 and Supp.).

419 DIDA generally preempts state limitations on the rate or amount of interest, discount points, finance charges, or other charges applicable to loans secured by a "first lien" on residential real property. National Consumer Law Center, The Cost of Credit: Regulation, Preemption, and Industry Abuses § 3.10.3 (4th ed. 2009 and Supp.). The term "first lien" has been construed to include both purchase money security interests as well as lien resulting from refinancing. *See id.* § 3.10.3.1.

420 DIDA applies only to "federally related mortgage loans" as described by the National Housing Act. 12 U.S.C. 1735f-5(b); 12 U.S.C. § 1735f-7a. *See* Jackson v. Mundaca Fin. Servs., Inc., 76 S.W.3d 819 (Ark. 2002) (holding that Arkansas's usury statute not preempted by federal law, because lender not regulated by Dep't of Hous. and Urban Dev., and protections from predatory lending practices did not apply). *See also* Sweeney v. Sav. First Mortgage, L.L.C., 879 A.2d 1037 (Md. 2005) (holding Maryland's Finder Fee Law regulating fees charged by mortgage brokers not preempted by DIDA).

421 As a result of DIDA's opt-out provisions, not all DIDA preemptions apply in all states. *See* National Consumer Law Center, The Cost of Credit: Regulation, Preemption, and Industry Abuses § 3.10.4 (4th ed. 2009 and Supp.).

422 *See id.* § 7.2.2. *See also id.* § 9.2.8 (points as interest in deregulated state).

423 Rumbaut v. Reinhart, 628 N.Y.S.2d 756 (App. Div. 1995). *But see In re* Bryant, 39 B.R. 313 (Bankr. Nev. 1984) (holding mortgage broker fee not includable as "interest" for purposes of state usury statute).

424 *See* National Consumer Law Center, The Cost of Credit: Regulation, Preemption, and Industry Abuses Ch. 7 (4th ed. 2009 and Supp.) (further discussion of hidden interest).

leaving the principal obligation intact.[425] Under such statutes, the widely accepted rule is that all payments already made on the contract will be applied to the principal debt until the debt has been paid off.[426] Thus, in a foreclosure case, a borrower may be able to raise a usury claim to reduce or eliminate the amount of a default.

Some statutes declare usurious transactions to be completely void and prohibit any creditor recovery whether or not the principal has been repaid.[427] Voiding of loans is another remedy in some states, particularly for violation of state small loan laws.[428]

A borrower in a foreclosure situation can also seek an equitable remedy for usury to enjoin the foreclosure. The main obstacle is the rule that a party seeking equity must do equity which, in the case of a borrower facing foreclosure of a usurious mortgage, may mean tendering the principal balance owed on the debt.[429] One way to avoid a tender obligation for the full balance of the loan is to seek alternative equitable rescission and reformation remedies. Courts in some states may address usury by reforming the consumer's obligations under the note so that there is no default going forward.

In some cases, a loan might violate a criminal usury statute.[430] Even some states that repealed other caps on interest rates left criminal usury caps in place. In this case, a court may invoke its equitable authority to reform the contract to a legal rate, void the loan in appropriate circumstances,[431] invoke the clean hands doctrine to refuse relief to the lender,[432] or hold that the lender has forfeited the right to collect interest and charges.[433]

5.13.6 Civil RICO

The federal Racketeer Influenced and Corrupt Organizations Act (RICO)[434] provides powerful civil remedies, including attorney fees and treble damages, to victims subjected to a broadly defined range of "racketeering activity"

425 *E.g., In re* Vehm Eng'g Corp., 521 F.2d 186 (9th Cir. 1975); Speare v. Consolidated Assets Corp., 367 F.2d 208 (2d Cir. 1966); Patterson v. Green, 474 So. 2d 725 (Ala. Civ. App. 1985); Metcalf v. Bartrand, 491 P.2d 747 (Alaska 1971); Westman v. Dye, 4 P.2d 134 (Cal. 1931); So. Discount Co. of Georgia v. Ector, 268 S.E.2d 621 (Ga. 1980); Bjornstad v. Perry, 443 P.2d 999 (Idaho 1968); Saskill v. 4-B Acceptance, 453 N.E.2d 761 (Ill. App. Ct. 1983); Bonfanti v. Davis, 487 So. 2d 165 (La. Ct. App. 1986); Waldorf v. Zinberg, 307 N.W.2d 749 (Mich. Ct. App. 1981); Thomas Lakes Owners Ass'n v. Riley, 612 N.W.2d 529 (Neb. Ct. App. 2000) (obligation to pay interest is void, and creditor cannot replace usurious interest with interest at legal rate); *In re* Castillian Apartments, Inc., 190 S.E.2d 161 (N.C. 1972); First State Bank of Bedford v. Miller, 563 S.W.2d 572 (Tex. 1978). *See* National Consumer Law Center, The Cost of Credit: Regulation, Preemption, and Industry Abuses §§ 10.8.2.1–10.8.2.4 (4th ed. 2009 and Supp.).

426 *See, e.g., In re* Vehm Eng'g Corp., 521 F.2d 186 (9th Cir. 1975) (Cal. law); Speare v. Consolidated Assets Corp., 367 F.2d 208 (2d Cir. 1966) (N.J. law); *In re* Bogan, 281 F. Supp. 242 (W.D. Tenn. 1968) (Tenn. law); Westman v. Dye, 4 P.2d 134 (Cal. 1931); Tauber v. Johnson, 291 N.E.2d 180 (Ill. App. Ct. 1972); *In re* Castillian Apartments, Inc., 190 S.E.2d 161 (N.C. 1972). *But see* Bjornstad v. Perry, 443 P.2d 999 (Idaho 1968) (rule does not apply when statute provides for borrower's recovery of interest paid); Negaard v. Miller Constr. Co., 396 N.W.2d 833 (Minn. Ct. App. 1986) (payments are applied first to interest as a matter of law).

427 *See, e.g.,* Equity Mortgage, Inc. v. Niro, 690 A.2d 407 (Conn. App. Ct. 1997) (applying Conn. Gen. Stat. § 37-8; court addressed the apparent usury violation on the face of the document even though the issue was not raised below); Rea v. Breakers Ass'n, 674 So. 2d 496 (Miss. 1996) (finance charge 100% in excess of amount allowed triggers forfeiture of principal and interest as well as repayment of any amounts paid); Seidel v. 18 E. 17th St. Owners, 598 N.E.2d 7 (N.Y. 1992) (N.Y. Gen. Oblig. Law § 5-511(2) (McKinney) voids usurious loans; borrow relieved of further interest and principal payment and mortgages securing the loan are canceled); Hilal v. Lipton, 642 N.Y.S.2d 78 (App. Div. 1996) (payment of $10,000 origination fee in addition to legal interest on note rendered loan usurious; entire loan was voided even though one of the two lenders did not benefit from the payment of the origination fee).

428 *See* Bailey v. Defenbaugh & Co. of Cleveland, 513 F. Supp. 232 (N.D. Miss. 1981); *In re* Perry, 272 F. Supp. 73 (D. Me. 1967); *In re* Harrington, 6 B.R. 655 (Bankr. D.R.I. 1980); McNish v. Gen. Credit Corp., 83 N.W.2d 1 (Neb. 1957) (statute since amended); Conrad v. Home & Auto Loan Co., 385 N.Y.S.2d 979 (App. Div. 1976); Smashed Ice v. Lee, 200 N.W.2d 236 (S.D. 1972). *See generally* Hubachek, Annotations on Small Loan Laws (Russell Sage Found. 1938) (complete compilation of small loan act cases decided through 1938); Hubachek, *The Development of Regulatory Small Loan Laws*, 8 Law & Contemp. Problems 108 (1941) (including supplemental list of small loan cases through 1941).

429 Speare v. Consolidated Assets Corp., 367 F.2d 208 (2d Cir. 1966) (N.J. law); Metcalf v. Bartrand, 491 P.2d 747 (Alaska 1971); Winnett v. Roberts, 225 Cal. Rptr. 82 (Cal. Ct. App. 1986) (proper tender made; foreclosure sale set aside); Feemster v. Schurkman, 291 So. 2d. 622 (Fla. Dist. Ct. App. 1974); Citizens & S. DeKalb Bank v. Watkins, 225 S.E.2d 266 (Ga. 1976); Naumburg v. Pattison, 711 P.2d 1387 (N.M. 1985); Bohlinger v. Am. Credit Co., 594 S.W.2d 710 (Tenn. Ct. App. 1979). *But see* Williams v. Macchio, 329 N.Y.S.2d 405 (Sup. Ct. 1972) (no tender necessary when usurious contract signed under duress). *See also* National Consumer Law Center, The Cost of Credit: Regulation, Preemption, and Industry Abuses § 10.8.3 (4th ed. 2009 and Supp.).

430 *See In re* Tavares, 298 B.R. 195 (Bankr. D. Mass. 2003) (holding, in part, that private refinancing transaction violated state criminal usury statute and was therefore per se violation of state consumer protection statute).

431 Begelfer v. Najarian, 409 N.E.2d 167 (Mass. 1980).

432 *E.g.,* Brabson v. Valentine, 804 S.W.2d 451 (Tenn. Ct. App. 1990).

433 *E.g.,* Moore v. Comfed Sav. Bank, 908 F.2d 834 (11th Cir. 1990); Norris v. Sigler Daisy Corp., 392 S.E.2d 242 (Ga. 1990).

434 18 U.S.C. §§ 1961–1968. *See* National Consumer Law Center, Unfair and Deceptive Acts and Practices § 14.2 (7th ed. 2008 and Supp.) (detailed analysis of RICO); National Consumer Law Center, The Cost of Credit: Regulation, Preemption, and Industry Abuses § 10.8.5.3 (4th ed. 2009 and Supp.) (detailed analysis of RICO).

or to the collection of an "unlawful debt," which is defined as any usurious debt bearing interest of at least twice the "enforceable rate."[435] The companion website contains a sample complaint against a mortgage lender which includes a civil RICO count.

In order to state a claim under RICO, a plaintiff must allege either the conduct of an "enterprise" through a "pattern" of "racketeering activity"[436] or the conduct of an enterprise through the collection of an "unlawful debt."[437] Racketeering activity is conduct which violates any of a list of state and federal statutes. Most notably for consumer purposes, this list includes mail fraud, wire fraud, and extortion.[438] A pattern comprises a minimum of two incidents of racketeering activity.[439] Collection of an "unlawful debt" can entail either illegal gambling debts or usury under state or federal law, at a rate at least twice the enforceable rate.[440] For a claim based on collection of an unlawful debt, the plaintiff need only show one instance of collection of an unlawful debt; the plaintiff need not show any pattern of racketeering activity nor any pattern of abuse.[441]

Several RICO cases involving allegedly fraudulent creditor overcharges have been litigated.[442] In one common situation, involves a bank contracts which after contracting to lend sums to a business borrower at the "prime rate" that it charges its most creditworthy customers, but then in fact lends at a higher rate.[443] Plaintiffs have alleged that the mailing of interest statements assessing excessive interest constitutes mail fraud and provides the underlying "predicate offense" to support the RICO action. Similarly, a RICO claim survived dismissal in a class action by alleging that a lender fraudulently induced borrowers involving fraudulent inducements to repeatedly refinance home mortgage loans survived dismissal in a class action.[444]

Equity-stripping scams can also give rise to viable RICO claims. A federal district court refused to dismiss a RICO claim against a mortgage company and its associates that alleged a predatory lending scheme designed to strip homeowners of their equity.[445] The plaintiffs claimed that the defendants had misrepresented loan terms, inflated home

---

435 18 U.S.C. § 1961(6). *See generally* National Consumer Law Center, Unfair and Deceptive Acts and Practices § 14.2 (7th ed. 2008 and Supp.).

436 *See* Sedima, S.P.R.L. v. Imrex Co., 473 U.S. 479, 105 S. Ct. 3275, 87 L. Ed. 2d 346 (1985).

437 *See, e.g.*, Durante Bros. & Sons, Inc. v. Flushing Nat'l Bank, 755 F.2d 239, 248 (2d Cir. 1985) (overruled as to "racketeering injury" requirement by implication of *Sedima*), *on remand*, 652 F. Supp. 101 (E.D.N.Y. 1986).

438 18 U.S.C. § 1961(1).

The Eleventh Circuit, in the case of Sikes v. Teleine, Inc., 281 F.3d 1350, 1360–1361 (11th Cir. 2002) aggregated the requirements for a civil RICO claim predicated upon mail or wire fraud as follows: (1) that the defendant intentionally participated, (2) in a scheme to defraud, (3) the plaintiff of money or property, (4) by means of material misrepresentations, (5) using the mails or wires, (6) and that the plaintiff relied on a misrepresentation made in furtherance of the fraudulent scheme, (7) that such misrepresentation would have been relied upon by a reasonable person, (8) that the plaintiff suffered injury as a result of such reliance, and (9) that the plaintiff incurred a specifiable amount of damages. Courts, however, are split on whether the plaintiff's reliance on the misrepresentation (#6) is a requirement. The majority holds that it is not. *See* Phoenix Bond & Indem. Co. v. Bridge, 477 F.3d 928, 932–933 (7th Cir. 2007), and cases cited.

439 18 U.S.C. § 1961(5).

The Supreme Court has noted that the requirement of two incidents of racketeering activity is a minimum only, and has hinted that more elaborate proof of a true "pattern" may be required. *See* Sedima, S.P.R.L. v. Imrex Co., 473 U.S. 479, 105 S. Ct. 3275, 87 L. Ed. 2d 346 (1985). Advocates should plead as many incidents as possible to demonstrate the existence of a pattern. Alternatively, RICO claims based on the allegation of collection of unlawful debt need not establish a "pattern" but must show that the defendant was in the business of lending money or a thing of value at a usurious rate. *See* 18 U.S.C. § 1961(6); Durante Bros. & Sons Inc. v. Flushing Nat'l Bank, 755 F.2d 239 (2d Cir. 1985) (overruled as to "racketeering injury" requirement by implication of *Sedima*), *on remand*, 652 F. Supp. 101 (E.D.N.Y. 1986). *See also* H.J., Inc. v. Northwestern Bell Tel. Co., 492 U.S. 229 (1989).

440 18 U.S.C. § 1961(6).

441 18 U.S.C. §§ 1961(6), 1962(c) (pattern of racketeering *or* collection of unlawful debt).

442 *See* Matthews v. New Century Mortgage Corp., 185 F. Supp. 2d 874 (S.D. Ohio 2002) (plaintiffs adequately alleged pattern in state RICO claim brought against defendants who had allegedly been part of a fraudulent home improvement loan scheme targeting older women); Faircloth v. Certified Fin. Inc., 2001 U.S. Dist. LEXIS 6793 (E.D. La. May 16, 2001) (court accepted settlement in class action alleging defendant had lent funds to plaintiffs with pending personal injury actions and then flipped the loans to create unlawful interest; judge approved attorney fee of more than $530,000).

443 *See* Am. Nat'l Bank & Trust Co. of Chicago v. Haroco, Inc., 473 U.S. 606, 105 S. Ct. 3291, 87 L. Ed. 2d 437 (1985), *aff'g* 747 F.2d 384 (7th Cir. 1984) (fraudulent overcharging stated RICO claim); Morosani v. First Nat'l Bank, 703 F.2d 1220 (11th Cir. 1983).

444 Emery v. Am. Gen. Fin., Inc., 71 F.3d 1343 (5th Cir. 1995).

After remand, however, the district court dismissed an amended complaint for failure to plead sufficient facts to state a RICO claim, 952 F. Supp. 602 (N.D. Ill. 1977), and the Seventh Circuit affirmed, 134 F.3d 1321 (7th Cir. 1998). *See* National Consumer Law Center, The Cost of Credit: Regulation, Preemption, and Industry Abuses § 12.6 (4th ed. 2009 and Supp.) (extensive discussion of *Emery* case). *See also* Stewart v. Associates Consumer Discount Co., 183 F.R.D. 189 (E.D. Pa. 1998) (class certification granted where allegations involve a scheme targeting borrowers who had difficulty obtaining credit from banks, sending them "live" checks, charging excessive points, upselling loans from consumer loans to home-secured loans, and repeatedly refinancing loans); Cannon v. Nationwide Acceptance Corp., 1997 WL 779086 (N.D. Ill. Dec. 12, 1997); Parish v. Beneficial Illinois, Inc., 1996 WL 172127 (N.D. Ill. Apr. 10 1996) (pleading a loan flipping scheme can constitute "racketeering activity"; case dismissed without prejudice on issue of pleading a "pattern"; plaintiffs permitted to conduct limited discovery on this issue).

445 Eva v. Midwest Nat'l Mortgage Banc, Inc., 143 F. Supp. 2d 862 (N.D. Ohio 2001).

appraisals, established impossible repayment terms, and charged undisclosed fees. Likewise, a foreclosure rescue scheme may be framed as the collection of an unlawful debt, based on a single transaction without any need to show a pattern of racketeering activity.[446] RICO has also been used to combat home improvement loan schemes,[447] foreclosure rescue scams,[448] and other mortgage-related fraud.[449]

The practice of lenders paying brokers yield spread premiums to obtain business has been challenged under RICO.[450] The Real Estate Settlement and Procedures Act requires the disclosure of such payments and prohibits the payment of illegal referral fees. In one example of a classic scam, borrowers successfully alleged that a broker represented a mortgage as having the lowest rate available, but had already agreed with the settlement agent, who funded the loan at the outset, and the subsequent assignee of the loan, to share sums charged to the borrowers.[451] In that case, the borrowers theorized that the rate was too high, artificially inflated by the hidden kickbacks, and negotiation may have yielded a lower rate.[452] A borrower can successfully

446 In one example, a foreclosure rescue arrangement nominally transferred title from the sellers to the foreclosure rescue firm, allowed the sellers to stay in the home in exchange for rent, and required the sellers to "repurchase" the home at the end of one year or face eviction. Proctor v. Metropolitan Money Store Corp., 645 F. Supp. 2d 464, 481–482 (D. Md. 2009) (citing Md. Code Ann. Real Prop. § 7-101(a)). In a class action brought in Maryland, a federal district court construed the arrangement as creating an equitable mortgage under Maryland law, characterizing the rent as interest. *Id.* at 482. Accordingly, the sellers stated a class action RICO claim for collection of an unlawful debt by alleging that the loans made entailed interest in excess of twice Maryland's usury limit. *Id. See also In re* Eyler, 2008 WL 4833096, at *4–5 (Bankr. D. Md. Oct. 28, 2008) (amended proposed findings of fact and conclusions of law) (concluding that transaction structured as a sale from distressed homeowners to foreclosure-rescue firm was actually a loan that called for interest exceeding state's maximum rate by more than double, and thus calling for collection of an unlawful debt under RICO); Palmer v. Roberts, 2005 WL 1631267 (E.D. Mich. July 6, 2005) (denying motion for summary judgment on RICO claim where plaintiffs facing foreclosure alleged that defendants, who purportedly helped them through sale-repurchase agreements, were engaged in the business of collecting unlawful debts); Rowland v. Haven Properties, L.L.C., 2005 WL 1528264 (N.D. Ill. June 24, 2005) (finding plaintiff involved in sale-leaseback transaction sufficiently alleged RICO claim). Foreclosure rescue and equity-stripping schemes are discussed further in Ch. 15, *infra*.

447 Johnson v. Equity Title & Escrow Co. of Memphis, L.L.C., 476 F. Supp. 2d 873 (W.D. Tenn. 2007) (denying motion to dismiss RICO claim in case alleging predatory lending scheme targeted toward African-American homeowners); Carr v. Home Tech Co., 476 F. Supp. 2d 859 (W.D. Tenn. 2007) (borrowers sufficiently pleaded RICO claim alleging defendants engaged in predatory lending practices designed to lure unsuspecting and unsophisticated African-American homeowners into exploitive mortgage loans for purposes of home improvements or debt consolidation); Beard v. Worldwide Mortgage Corp., 354 F. Supp. 2d 789 (W.D. Tenn. 2005) (denying motion to dismiss RICO claim against settlement against where borrowers alleged scheme of predatory lending practices); Pulphus v. Sullivan, 2003 WL 1964333 (N.D. Ill. Apr. 28 2003) (RICO claim arising from home improvement loan scheme; plaintiff sufficiently alleged conduct by assignees of loans by pleading they had reviewed loan documents of originating lenders, underwrote the loans, and approved loan applications, and sufficiently alleged conduct by loan originator by pleading that employee of title company closed fraudulent loan on originator's behalf).

448 *See* § 15.4.12, *infra*.

449 Meeks-Owens v. Indymac Bank, F.S.B., 557 F. Supp. 2d 566, 569, 574 (M.D. Pa. 2008) (denying lender's motion to dismiss RICO claim where plaintiff alleged: (1) mortgage loan issued by defendant exceeded market value of property at time of purchase by more than 30%; (2) defendant misrepresented a subprime mortgage as a conventional loan; (3) defendant lent plaintiff money without investigating her ability to repay loan; and (4) defendant made loan based on an incomplete mortgage application and "patently defective" appraisal that inflated value of plaintiff's home); Lester v. Percudani, 556 F. Supp. 2d 473 (M.D. Pa. 2008) (upholding use of RICO by group of homebuyers who claimed that a real estate developer, an appraiser, and a mortgage lender schemed together to create incentive programs that encouraged the plaintiffs to buy real estate at artificially inflated values and to finance the purchases with loans that they could not afford to repay); Thomas v. Ross & Hardies, 9 F. Supp. 2d 547 (D. Md. 1998) (court refused to dismiss complaint against an attorney who participated in scheme by which financial services company convinced homeowners to mortgage their homes for maximum amount possible in return for paying off prior loans and extending a line of credit).

In Bridge v. Phoenix Bond & Indem. Co., the U.S. Supreme Court held that it was not, writing that "a plaintiff asserting a RICO claim predicated on mail fraud need not show, either as an element of its claim or as a prerequisite to establishing proximate causation, that it relied on the defendant's alleged misrepresentations." 128 S. Ct. 2131, 2145 (2008).

450 Mulligan v. Choice Mortgage Corp., USA, 1998 WL 1031495 (D.N.H. Sept. 30, 1998) (denying motion to dismiss RICO claim based on lender's kickback to mortgage broker). *See* National Consumer Law Center, The Cost of Credit: Regulation, Preemption, and Industry Abuses § 12.2.1.6 (4th ed. 2009 and Supp.).

451 Kerby v. Mortgage Funding Corp., 992 F. Supp. 787, 790–791 (D. Md. 1998).

452 *Id.* at 791. The borrowers alleged mail fraud as the predicate acts giving rise to a pattern of racketeering activity. *Id.* at 798–799. *See also* Briggs v. Countrywide Funding Corp., 931 F. Supp. 1545 (M.D. Ala. 1996) (scheme to defraud as predicate act for RICO was that arrangement induced brokers to steer borrowers to higher priced loans in exchange for hidden commission payments from the lender), *vacated on other grounds*, 949 F. Supp. 812 (M.D. Ala. 1996). *But see* Vandenbroeck v. CommonPoint Mortgage Co., 22 F. Supp. 2d 677 (W.D. Mich. 1998) (borrowers' allegations that mortgage lender formed association-in-fact with investors and lenders who purchased their loans were insufficient to establish RICO "enterprise," since they did not show that alleged association-in-fact exhibited any sort of decision making mechanism for conducting the group's affairs; court also found no allegation that demonstrated existence of an enterprise separate and apart from alleged pattern of racketeering), *aff'd*, 210 F.3d 696 (6th Cir. 2000) (affirming dismissal without leave to amend on grounds that representation regarding loan discount fees included a written statement given to consumers which included two different definitions, only one of which was accurate, and therefore no intent to defraud can be shown).

plead a RICO claim when the payment of the premium is not disclosed, the cost of the premium is passed on to the borrower in the form of a higher interest rate, the broker represented that it would provide the lowest rate available, or money flowed between the assignee, the funding lender, the broker, and its related title company, and the mail was used in furtherance of the scheme.[453]

5.13.7 Invalid Security Instruments

If the mortgage (or deed of trust) is not a legally enforceable instrument then there can be no valid foreclosure.[454] A deed or mortgage that is forged is void ab initio.[455] As a result, forgery of a mortgage is generally an absolute defense to foreclosure.[456] Similarly, where a deed has been forged and the new title holder then encumbers the property, courts have held both the deed and the mortgages are nullities.[457]

The validity of security instruments in some community property states may require both spouses to execute instruments encumbering a homestead. For example, under Wisconsin law, a court found that a mortgage on a married couple's homestead that was not signed by both spouses was void as to both spouses, regardless of their respective ownership interests.[458]

The failure to follow the formal requisites in acknowledging deeds or mortgages may also result in a void instrument. Many deed and mortgage fraud cases involve situations in which the person whom the notary certified as having appeared did not, in fact, appear.[459] In fraudulent mortgage cases, borrowers are often instructed to sign a stack of documents that are then taken elsewhere for notarization.[460] Alternatively, improper notarizations may result from the taking of an actual acknowledgment from an imposter, taking an acknowledgment from an incompetent person, or the taking of an acknowledgment over the telephone. Regardless, of the reason for the defective acknowledgment, practitioners should investigate whether such defects may render the instrument invalid or result in an equitable mortgage.[461]

5.13.8 SAFE Act Licensing

Federal and state SAFE Act requirements may be another source of potential defenses. In July 2008, Congress passed the SAFE Mortgage Licensing Act which requires states to impose minimum licensing and registration requirements on individual loan originators, including mortgage brokers and lender employees.[462] Previously, most licensing and registration laws applied to organizations rather than individuals. While each state must enact its own laws and regulations to implement the Act, HUD is required to establish minimum standards and to impose a licensing and registration regime for any state that fails to do so.[463] The SAFE Act also requires states to participate in the Conference of State Bank

453 National Consumer Law Center, Unfair and Deceptive Acts and Practices § 14.2 (7th ed. 2008 and Supp.).

454 *See, e.g. In re* Hudson, 642 S.E.2d 485 (N.C. Ct. App. 2007) (contention that property is not secured may be raised as defense to foreclosure).

455 *See, e.g.,* Ala. Code § 7-3-401 (person not liable on instrument unless person signed the instrument); *Ex parte* Floyd, 796 So. 2d 303 (Ala. 2001) (forged instrument—satisfaction of mortgage—is void); Wutzke v. Bill Reid Painting Serv., Inc., 151 Cal. App. 3d 36 (1984) (fact that deed of trust conveys more limited property interest than grant deed irrelevant distinction is considering validity; forged deed of trust, like forged deed, is void); McGinn v. Tobey, 28 N.W. 818 (Mich. 1886) (in Michigan, courts do not distinguish between forged instruments and instruments procured by fraud, both are void).

456 While finding such instruments void, some courts have allowed lenders equitable liens on property to the extent the true homeowner may have benefited from the transaction.

457 *See, e.g.,* Flagstar v. Gibbons, 238 S.W.3d 912 (Ark. 2006); Altegra Credit Co. v. Tin Chu, 816 N.Y.S.2d 140 (App. Div. 2006); Chand v. Steuben Hill Mgmt. Corp., 798 N.Y.S.2d 521 (App. Div. 2005) (holding deed was forgery and all other recorded subsequent instruments void ab initio); Sorenson v. Pyatt, 146 P.3d 1172 (Wash. 2006).

458 *See In re* Larson, 346 B.R. 486 (Bankr. E.D. Wis. 2006) (mortgage signed by husband, but not wife, invalid; but lender entitled to equitable subrogation of previous lender's rights because it satisfied previous loan).

459 Most courts distinguish between defective acknowledgments and failure to acknowledge. Courts are more likely to find instruments valid where defect is technical in nature. *See, e.g., In re* Fisher, 320 B.R. 52 (E.D. Pa. 2005); Poole v. Hyatt, 689 A.2d 82 (Md. 1997). *But see In re* Biggs, 377 F.3d 515 (6th Cir. 2004) (failure to include mortgagor's name in notarization section rendered the deed of trust invalid under state law).

460 *See* Goldome Credit Corp. v. Hardy, 503 So. 2d 1227 (Ala. Civ. App. 1987) (affirming trial court's determination that the mortgage not executed before a notary was invalid and setting aside foreclosure). *See also In re* Miller, 320 B.R. 203 (N.D. Ala. 2006) (stating, but not deciding, mortgage invalid for lack of proper acknowledgment and therefore insufficient to transfer legal title in the collateral to lender); *In re* Fisher, 320 B.R. 52 (E.D. Pa. 2005) (permitting chapter 13 bankruptcy trustee to avoid mortgage where notary was not present to acknowledge mortgagor's identity and voluntary acquiescence to be bound by terms of the agreement); *In re* Bowling, 314 B.R. 127 (Bankr. S.D. Ohio 2004) (same). *But see In re* Nichols, 265 B.R. 831 (B.A.P. 10th Cir. 2001) (distinguishing between validity and perfection of improperly notarized mortgage and affirming denial of debtor's motion to avoid mortgagee's lien).

461 *See, e.g., In re* Wilkinson, 186 B.R. 186 (Bankr. D. Md. 1995) (improperly acknowledged deed of trust void against subsequent bona fide purchaser, under W. Va. law); Taylor Elec. Co. v. First Mariner Bank, ___ A.2d ___, 2010 WL 1172939 (Md. Ct. Spec. App. Mar. 29, 2010) (equitable mortgage). *See also In re* Andrews, 404 B.R. 275 (Bankr. S.D. Ohio 2008) (discussing doctrine of substantial compliance).

462 Secure and Fair Enforcement for Mortgage Licensing Act of 2008, Pub. L. No. 110-289, §§ 1501–1517 (codified at 12 U.S.C. §§ 5101–5116).

463 *See* 74 Fed. Reg. 66,548 (Dec. 15, 2009) (notice of proposed

Supervisors' Nationwide Mortgage Licensing System (NMLS)[464] which will facilitate the sharing of licensee information.

The federal Act does not create any private right of action; however, in many states a violation of the licensing rules will give rise to a UDAP claim.[465] It may be possible to argue that a contract with an unlicensed or unregistered originator is void.[466]

5.13.9 Miscellaneous

Under a California statute, a cosigner on a consumer credit transaction is entitled to a statutory notice from the lender at the time the loan is made.[467] Failure to provide this notice has been held to be a defense to foreclosure.[468]

5.14 Raising Origination-Related Claims and Defenses Against Assignees

5.14.1 Holders of HOEPA Loans Are Liable for Origination Misconduct

The Home Ownership Equity Protection Act (HOEPA) allows consumers to raise all claims and defenses against assignees that they could against the original lender of a HOEPA loan, whether or not the HOEPA notice on assignee liability is included in the note.[469] This right is not limited to HOEPA claims or to TIL claims, but applies to *any* claim or defense the consumer has against the originating lender.

The only exception to assignee liability is where the assignee could not reasonably have known that HOEPA applied to the note, such as being unaware that hidden fees triggered HOEPA coverage. But if the APR rate or fees on their face are high enough to trigger HOEPA coverage, then the trust is subject to all claims and defenses the consumer has against the originating lender, even though the loan itself is not identified as a HOEPA loan and the HOEPA notice is not in the loan.

A number of states have also enacted mini-HOEPA statutes that cover certain high-cost loans not within HOEPA's scope and that, like HOEPA, make assignees subject to origination-related defenses. Good examples are Arkansas,[470] Georgia,[471] Maine,[472] New Jersey,[473] New Mexico,[474] New York,[475] and Oklahoma.[476] Nevertheless, some of these statutes' assignee liability provisions are more restrictive than HOEPA, and each provision must be parsed carefully.

5.14.2 The Holder-in-Due Course Doctrine

5.14.2.1 Overview

The common law rule is that an assignee is subject to all defenses that the consumer could raise against the assignor.[477] Thus a consumer could raise as defenses to a foreclosure all defenses that the consumer has against the originating lender. But Uniform Commercial Code (UCC) § 3-305 generally allows the assignee of a promissory note or other negotiable instrument to be free from those defenses if it has the rights of a holder in due course.[478] Thus key to raising origination misconduct as a defense in a foreclosure is to challenge the mortgagee's claim that it has the rights of a holder in due course. The assignee bears the burden of asserting and proving it has holder-in-due-course

rulemaking). HUD's regulations had not yet been finalized at the time of publication.

464 12 U.S.C. § 5104. The NMLS is located at www.stateregulatoryregistry.org.

465 *See* South Dakota v. Western Capital Corp., 290 N.W.2d 467 (S.D. 1980) (a violation of South Dakota broker law constitutes a UDAP violation and triggers restitution and civil penalties); National Consumer Law Center, Unfair and Deceptive Acts and Practices § 3.2.7 (6th ed. 2004 and Supp.).

466 *See, e.g.*, Beneficial Hawaii, Inc. v. Kida, 30 P.3d 895 (Haw. 2001) (mortgage and loan note void when arranged by an unlicensed mortgage broker; mortgagee may be entitled to equitable lien on the property if it could prove that it paid consideration for the mortgage and note; lender failed to offer this proof in this case). *See also* Solomon v. Gilmore, 731 A.2d 280 (Conn. 1999) (barring enforcement of second mortgage by unlicensed lender; discussing why result is appropriate even if it appears to create windfall for borrower); National Consumer Law Center, The Cost of Credit: Regulation, Preemption, and Industry Abuses § 11.6.4.4 (4th ed. 2009 and Supp.).

467 Cal. Civ. Code §§ 1799.90(a)(5), 1799.91 (West); Cal. Bus. & Prof. Code §§ 10240(a), (b), 10241 (West).

468 Engstrom v. Kallons, 49 Cal. App. 4th 773, 56 Cal. Rptr. 2d 842 (1996).

469 *See* § 5.8.5, *supra*.

470 Ark. Code Ann. § 23-53-101.

471 Ga. Code Ann. §§ 7-6A-1 to 7-6A-13.

472 Me. Rev. Stat. Ann. tit. 9-A, § 8-206-A.

473 N.J. Stat. Ann. § 46:10B-22.

474 N.M. Stat. §§ 58-21A-1 to 58-21A-14.

475 N.Y. Banking Law § 6-1 (McKinney); N.Y. Real Prop. Acts. Law § 1302 (McKinney); N.Y. Gen. Bus. Law § 771-a (McKinney).

476 Okla. Stat. tit. 14A, §§ 1301(10), 3-309.4, 3-410, 3-411, 3-413.

477 9 Corbin, Corbin on Contracts § 892 (interim ed. 2002); 29 Lord, Williston on Contracts §§ 74.47, 74.49 (4th ed. 2003); Farnsworth, Farnsworth on Contracts § 11.8 (2d ed. 1998); Restatement (Second) of Contracts § 336 (1981).

478 As revised, U.C.C. § 3-305 also says that the right to enforce an instrument is subject to "a claim in recoupment" against the original payee, so long as the claim arose from the transaction that gave rise to the claim. U.C.C. § 3-305(a)(3). This might appear at first glance to reduce the scope of the holder-in-due-course doctrine, but a later section provides that a holder in due course is only subject to claims in recoupment that arise against it, not those that are based on the actions of the assignee. U.C.C. § 3-305, cmts. 2, 3.

status—the burden is not on the consumer to show the opposite.[479]

Section 5.14.2.1, *supra*, provides an overview of the holder-in-due-course doctrine as it applies to foreclosure defenses. The doctrine is discussed in more detail in the National Consumer Law Center, *Unfair and Deceptive Acts and Practices* § 11.7 (7th ed. 2008 and Supp.).

Even a holder-in-due course is subject to certain defenses as described at § 5.14.2.1, *supra*. In addition under TILA a consumer may exercise the right of rescission against an assignee, even a holder in due course.[480] A holder in due course is also liable for its own conduct, either by its direct actions or on a theory such as civil conspiracy.[481] Alternatively, a state consumer statute or the close-connectedness doctrine may provide grounds for finding assignees liable even if they would not be so under the UCC.[482] Moreover, as described at § 5.4, *supra*, all holders are also subject to origination defenses in HOEPA loans.

5.14.2.2 Origination Misconduct That Can Be Raised As a Defense Even Against a Holder in Due Course

Certain defenses are available even if the party enforcing the note has the rights of a holder in due course.[483] These defenses include incapacity, infancy, duress, illegality, and fraud in the factum. Illegality might include usury and making a loan while the originating lender is unlicensed.

5.14.2.3 Holder-in-Due-Course Status Can Only Be Raised Where the Note Is a Negotiable Instrument

According to UCC § 3-302, an assignee only attains holder-in-due-course status if it is assigned a negotiable instrument.[484] There can be no holder-in-due-course status if the loan does not qualify as a negotiable instrument. The seven basic requirements for a note to be a negotiable instrument are outlined in UCC § 3-104(a).

The note must:

1. Be a writing that is signed.
2. Contain an unconditional promise to pay.
3. Be a fixed amount.
4. Of money.
5. Payable to bearer or to order.
6. Payable on demand or at a definite time.
7. Contain no other undertaking except as authorized by UCC § 3-104(a)(3). (This last requirement has been called a requirement that the instrument be a "courier without baggage.")

If the note fails to meet any one these requirements, it is not a negotiable instrument, and there cannot be a holder in due course of that instrument.

Few if any manufactured home loans or home improvement loans originated or arranged by the seller will qualify as negotiable instruments.[485] The loans often include undertakings not authorized by UCC § 3-104(a)(3). Moreover, such contracts typically include the FTC Holder Notice, and that notice states that consumers can raise dealer-related claims and defenses against the holder.[486] The FTC Holder Rule requires even a negotiable instrument to include the FTC Holder Notice when it is given in connection with the purchase of goods or services and the seller referred the consumer to the lender or has a formal or formal business relationship with the lender. Such a note can be a negotiable instrument, but there cannot be a holder in due course of such an instrument.[487]

Another important limit on a loan being a negotiable instrument is that the amount of the note and the payment schedule must be definite.[488] Where a note has a payment schedule to be determined later or the size of the payment is contingent on a future event, the note is not a negotiable instrument. Home equity lines of credit and other open-end loans cannot be negotiable instruments because the amount of credit extended, by definition, changes over time.[489]

Even a home improvement loan where the seller neither originates nor arranges the loan cannot be a negotiable instrument if the amount of the loan is left uncertain, depending on charges assessed by the contractor. Certain exotic option ARMs may not have a fixed principal amount, because various payment options lead to varying amounts of negative amortization, even if all payments are made. Arguably, then these varying amounts of negative amortization built into a loan mean that the principal amount during the term of the loan is not fixed.

The 1990 Revision to UCC Article 3 made it clear that most variable rate notes meet the requirement that the instrument be for a fixed sum of money. If a note was made before the relevant state enacted these revisions, then the

479 U.C.C. § 3-308, cmt. 2.

480 15 U.S.C. § 1641(c).

481 *See* National Consumer Law Center, Unfair and Deceptive Acts and Practices § 11.5 (7th ed. 2008 and Supp.).

482 *See* National Consumer Law Center, Unfair and Deceptive Acts and Practices §§ 11.6.5.5.4, 11.6.5.5.5 (7th ed. 2008 and Supp.).

483 U.C.C. § 3-305. *See* National Consumer Law Center, Unfair and Deceptive Acts and Practices § 11.7.2.5 (7th ed. 2008 and Supp.).

484 *See* generally National Consumer Law Center, Unfair and Deceptive Acts and Practices § 11.7.2 (7th ed. 2008 and Supp.).

485 *See* National Consumer Law Center, Unfair and Deceptive Acts and Practices § 11.7.2.2 (7th ed. 2008 and Supp.).

486 *See* National Consumer Law Center, Unfair and Deceptive Acts and Practices § 11.6 (7th ed. 2008 and Supp.).

487 U.C.C. § 3-106(d).

488 *See* National Consumer Law Center, Unfair and Deceptive Acts and Practices § 11.7.2.2.2 (7th ed. 2008 and Supp.).

489 *See id.*

holder might not be a holder in due course of a variable rate note.[490]

Also consider whether a loan instrument contains undertakings not listed in UCC § 3-104(a)(3). For example, a requirement that the consumer purchase insurance not related to protecting the home can be viewed as such an undertaking, defeating the note's status as a negotiable instrument. It has even been argued that the standard Fannie Mae/Freddie Mac mortgage notes contain such undertakings that defeat holder-in-due-course status.[491]

5.14.2.4 A Holder in Due Course Must First Be a Holder

Holder-in-due-status requires not just a negotiable instrument, but that the assignee be a "holder" of such an instrument.[492] Holder is a technical term meaning that the instrument has been "negotiated" to that entity either as "bearer" paper or "to order" paper. A negotiable instrument can be payable either "to the order of" an identified person, or to "bearer."[493] Many notes do not identify a payee, showing only a blank line after the "pay to the order of" language. This makes the instrument payable to the bearer.[494]

If an instrument is payable to bearer, simply transferring physical possession is sufficient to negotiate the instrument, making the entity in possession a holder. To transfer a negotiable instrument that is payable to an identified person, the payee must properly indorse it to the order of the new holder and deliver it to the new holder. Any slip up in the chain of indorsements means that no assignee after that slip-up can be a holder.

The indorsement must be either on the note itself or on an "*allonge*"—a paper actually "affixed" to the note, not just accompanying the note. Article 3 prior to the 1990 revisions was even stricter regarding indorsements found on an *allonge*. If a note was made before the relevant state enacted these revisions, then the note's negotiation might be improper if these stricter *allonge* requirements were not followed.[495]

490 *See* National Consumer Law Center, Unfair and Deceptive Acts and Practices § 11.7.2.3.2 (7th ed. 2008 and Supp.).

491 R. Mann, *Searching for Negotiabilty in Payment and Credit Systems*, 44 UCLA L. Rev. 951 (Apr. 1997).

492 *See* U.C.C. § 3-302; National Consumer Law Center, Unfair and Deceptive Acts and Practices § 11.7.2.3 (7th ed. 2008 and Supp.).

493 U.C.C. § 3-109.

494 U.C.C. § 3-109(a).

495 *See* National Consumer Law Center, Unfair and Deceptive Acts and Practices § 11.7.2.3.2 (7th ed. 2008 and Supp.).

5.14.2.5 Preconditions to Assignee of Negotiable Instrument Acquiring Holder-in-Due-Course Status

Being a holder of a negotiable instrument is necessary to acquire holder-in-due-course status, but it is not sufficient. In addition, the assignee must take the instrument:

(1) For value;
(2) In good faith, and;
(3) Without notice of a number of things delineated in UCC § 3-302(a)(2), including that the loan was overdue or that the consumer had a defense.[496]

A key requirement here relates to notice that the loan was overdue. An assignee buying a note with knowledge the consumer is delinquent cannot be a holder in due course. (Nevertheless § 5.14.3, *infra*, examines the shelter rule that may give such an assignee the *rights* of a holder in due course.)

If a note includes illegal or unfair terms, TIL violations, or other law violations apparent on the face of the document, this may also be grounds to challenge the holder-in-due course status. The transferee had notice of consumer defenses.

Another example might be a variable rate loan where the underwriting is based upon the teaser rate and not the eventual level of monthly payments. A purchaser of such a note who also receives the loan application and other underwriting materials should be on notice of homeowner defenses concerning the improvident extension of credit.

5.14.2.6 The Shelter Rule: Acquiring the Rights of a Holder in Due Course Even When Not Qualifying for That Status

5.14.2.6.1 The general rule

Even if an entity is not a holder in due course itself, it can still acquire the *rights* of a holder in due course. This "shelter rule" is an important roadblock to a consumer's ability to defeat holder-in-due course status, but the rule is not always fatal to a consumer's defenses.

The shelter rule applies if at least one person in the negotiable instrument's chain of title attains the status of a holder in due course. (The loan originator is not a holder in due course.) Then with certain exceptions, those taking the note in the chain of title after the holder in due course acquire the *rights* of a holder in due course.

Consider the fifth transferee on a note who does not qualify as a holder in due course in its own right because it knew the loan was in default. It still can acquire the *rights*

496 *See* National Consumer Law Center, Unfair and Deceptive Acts and Practices § 11.7.2.3 (7th ed. 2008 and Supp.).

of a holder in due course if one of the prior transferors was a holder in due course, and then transferred that status down the ownership chain to the fifth transferee.

The foreclosing entity thus has the burden of proving that at least one entity took the instrument as a holder in due course. It cannot meet this burden if every transferee was on notice of the delinquency, where the originating lender did not sell the note until after the consumer was in default.

Similarly, bearer paper often is held by the originating lender, and not transferred to the foreclosing entity until after default, if at all. If the foreclosing entity obtains physical possession after the default, it is on notice of the delinquency, and cannot be a holder in due course. Importantly for the operation of the shelter rule, no other entity had possession of the bearer note and thus no other entity could be a holder in due course. Thus the foreclosing entity cannot acquire the rights of a holder in due course.

Consider another example, where a note is made out to the order of an originating lender and then is transferred from the originating lender to a wholesale lender, and then to an issuer, and finally to the trust. (These terms are defined at § 1.3.3.4, *supra*.) For the trust to be a holder in due course, there must be a proper indorsement to the trust. This means that there must be proper indorsement from the originating lender to the wholesale lender, and then from the wholesale lender to the issuer, and finally from the issuer to the trust. If any of those indorsements is missing or not proper, then the trust is not a holder in due course. Sometimes, the transfer from the wholesale lender to the issuer or at least from issuer to the trust will not include a proper indorsement, because the volume of notes involved encourages parties to skip this step. Order paper is only properly negotiated if the transferor signs the note or an "*allonge*"—a paper actually "affixed" to the note, not just accompanying the note. Revisions to Article 3 in 1990 made it clear that variable rate notes meet the requirement that the instrument be for a fixed sum of money. If a note was made before the relevant state enacted these revisions, then the holder might not be a holder in due course of a variable rate note.[497]

Nevertheless, the trust still has the *rights* of a holder in due course if it is a transferee from someone who is a holder in due course (or has the rights of a holder in due course). Thus if the wholesale lender is a holder in due course, then the issuer and the trust have the rights of a holder in due course, even though there is no proper indorsement from seller to issuer and from issuer to the trust.[498] Only if the improper indorsement occurred between the originating lender and the wholesale lender (the first transferee) will no subsequent assignee have a chance to become a holder in due course. Nor will it help for the foreclosing entity to ask the originating lender to indorse the note over properly, because by that time any indorsee will have notice of the default.

5.14.2.6.2 Important exception to the shelter rule

There is an important exception to the shelter rule. A party cannot acquire the rights of a holder in due course if it engaged in fraud or illegality affecting the instrument.[499] This means that if an entity engaged in fraud, it cannot obtain the rights of a holder in due course and cannot pass those rights on to a subsequent assignee. While the subsequent assignee may (or may not) qualify as a holder in due course in its own right, it cannot acquire those rights from an entity engaged in fraud affecting the instrument.

Since securitizations often involve interconnected and affiliated parties, it may be possible to show that the issuer aided and abetted a pattern of fraud by the originating lender, and thus the issuer cannot acquire the rights of a holder in due course.[500] In such cases, no assignee from the issuer can acquire the rights from the issuer and must achieve holder-in-due-course status independently.

5.14.3 Damage Claims Against Assignees of Mortgage Loans

The prior subsections examine defenses consumers can raise against enforcement of mortgage loans. This subsection considers affirmative claims for damages for origination misconduct that can be brought against the foreclosing entity.

In the case of HOEPA loans, federal law allows the consumer to raise all affirmative claims (up to a cap) against the note holder (in a securitized loan, this is usually the trust) that the consumer could raise against the loan originator.[501] State mini-HOEPA statutes also may allow such affirmative claims, even where the federal statute does not apply.[502]

In addition, various parties that aid and abet in the fraud can be held liable for their participation. Where the original lender sells the loan to a wholesale lender, which, in turn, securitizes the loan, the ultimate holder, while being more remote from the wrongdoing of the original lender, may still be liable, particularly where the original lender was making

497 *See* National Consumer Law Center, Unfair and Deceptive Acts and Practices § 11.7.2.3.2 (7th ed. 2008 and Supp.).

498 U.C.C. § 3-203. *See* National Consumer Law Center, Unfair and Deceptive Acts and Practices § 11.7.2.4 (7th ed. 2008 and Supp.).

499 *See* U.C.C. § 3-203; National Consumer Law Center, Unfair and Deceptive Acts and Practices § 11.7.2.4 (7th ed. 2008 and Supp.).

500 *See* National Consumer Law Center, Unfair and Deceptive Acts and Practices §§ 11.6.5.3, 11.7 (7th ed. 2008 and Supp.) (close-connectedness and raising lender-related defenses against assignees).

501 15 U.S.C. § 1641(d).

502 *See* § 5.4, *supra*.

loans to the specifications of the purchaser.[503] Once it can be shown that the financial institutions that are providing the lending capital for a predatory lending scheme are dictating loan terms or, at least, are aware of the predatory characteristics of the loans, participation theories should be able to reach those entities, even where they do not take legal title to the loans.

In one decision, a federal district court held that the Wall Street underwriters for a bankrupt predatory lender could be liable to injured consumers on an aiding and abetting theory where consumers alleged that the underwriters knew of the lender's fraud and provided substantial assistance to the lender's scheme.[504] Civil conspiracy and RICO theories have also been upheld in such circumstances.[505] While those who construct securitization transactions go to great lengths to attempt to insulate participants in the transactions from liability for lender malfeasance, those very efforts can establish the absence of an arms-length relationship.[506]

5.14.4 *Raising Claims and Defenses Against the FDIC*

5.14.4.1 Overview

The wave of bank failures that began in 2008 brings with it a set of additional hurdles to borrowers who are attempting to defend against a foreclosure. First are the *D'Oench, Duhme* doctrine and its statutory counterpart, which operate to bar claims based on agreements that are not in writing or that do not meet certain formalities. Second is the requirement that persons with claims against a failed bank exhaust an administrative claims process as a precondition of any litigation. An understanding of these issues is critical whenever the Federal Deposit Insurance Corporation (FDIC) is acting or has acted as the receiver for a failed banking institution.[507]

These issues are discussed briefly in the following subsections. A thorough analysis of the statutory and common law *D'Oench* doctrines and the implications of the administrative claims process may be found in NCLC's *The Cost of Credit: Regulation, Preemption, and Industry Abuses* § 10.7 (4th ed. 2009 and Supp.).

5.14.4.2 *D'Oench* and Related Doctrines

A federal statute, 12 U.S.C. § 1823(e), gives the FDIC broad immunity from many claims unless the agreement upon which the claim is based is in writing and meets certain formal requirements:

> No agreement which tends to diminish or defeat the interest of the Corporation in any asset acquired by it under this section or section 1821 of this title, either as security for a loan or by purchase or as receiver of any insured depository institution, shall be valid against the Corporation unless such agreement—
>
> (A) is in writing,
>
> (B) was executed by the depository institution and any person claiming an adverse interest thereunder, including the obligor, contemporaneously with the acquisition of the asset by the depository institution,
>
> (C) was approved by the board of directors of the depository institution or its loan committee, which approval shall be reflected in the minutes of said board or committee, and
>
> (D) has been, continuously, from the time of its execution, an official record of the depository institution.[508]

This statute is a partial codification of a somewhat similar common law protection articulated by the Supreme Court in a 1942 case, *D'Oench, Duhme & Co. v. Fed. Deposit Ins. Corp.*[509] In addition, some courts have fashioned another common law doctrine that gives the FDIC "super holder-in-due-course" or "federal holder-in-due-course" status, protecting it against borrower claims and defenses even when it does not meet the usual UCC requirements for holder-in-due-course status.[510] However, although the cir-

503 England v. MG Invs., Inc., 93 F. Supp. 2d 718 (S.D. W. Va. 2000) (original lender could be viewed as agent of secondary purchaser where master loan purchase agreement contained detailed requirements for loans and a purchase commitment regarding loans that met these requirements, despite language in agreement that attempted to create appearance of arms-length relationship between the two parties).

504 Aiello v. Chisik, 2002 U.S. Dist. LEXIS 5858 (C.D. Cal. Jan. 10, 2002) (denying motion to dismiss of *Lehman Bros.*).

505 *See, e.g.*, Smith v. Berg, 247 F.3d 532 (3d Cir. 2001) (RICO); Williams v. ITT Aetna Fin. Co., 700 N.E.2d 859 (Ohio 1998). *See generally* National Consumer Law Center, Unfair and Deceptive Acts and Practices § 11.5 (7th ed. 2008 and Supp.).

506 England v. MG Invs., Inc., 93 F. Supp. 2d 718 (S.D. W. Va. 2000). *See also* Short v. Wells Fargo Bank Minnesota, N.A., 401 F. Supp. 2d 549 (S.D. W. Va. 2005) (issues of fact regarding whether pooling and servicing agreement showed existence of joint venture among lender, loan servicer, and assignee).

507 Many of the decisions in this area involve the former Resolution Trust Corporation, which acted as receiver for many savings and loan associations that failed in the 1980s, and which was entitled to the same special protections as the FDIC.

508 *See also* 12 U.S.C. § 1787(p)(2) (substantively identical provision applicable to credit unions); Gulfstream Dev. Group, L.L.C. v. Schwartz, 2009 WL 1107751 (M.D. Fla. Apr. 22, 2009) (decisions interpreting § 1823(e) are applicable to credit union statute).

509 315 U.S. 447, 62 S. Ct. 676, 86 L. Ed. 956 (1942) (holding ineffective any secret or implied agreements that would tend to diminish or defeat the interest of the FDIC).

510 *See, e.g.*, Fed. Deposit Ins. Corp. v. Wood, 758 F.2d 156 (6th Cir. 1985). *See generally* National Consumer Law Center, The Cost of Credit: Regulation, Preemption, and Industry Abuses § 10.7.8 (4th ed. 2009 and Supp.).

cuit courts are split on the question, a number of courts have held that the two common law doctrines are displaced by the statute.[511]

The statutory and common law *D'Oench* doctrines have been applied to bar a wide variety of claims, including claims of fraud in the inducement when the fraudulent misrepresentations were not contained in a writing meeting the formal standards set by the doctrines.[512] In addition, most courts have held that successor institutions that purchase the assets of failed banks and thrifts from the FDIC can invoke the same protections.[513] However, these doctrines are not limitless. Some of the exceptions to these doctrines that might be of use to homeowners in foreclosure are:

- *The FTC Holder Rule.* The Federal Trade Commission Rule Concerning the Preservation of Consumer's Claims and Defenses (the "FTC Holder Rule") was created by Congress to preserve consumer claims and defenses from holder-in-due-course immunity.[514] The FTC Holder Rule requires sellers of goods and services to include in consumer credit contracts a notice (the "FTC Holder Notice") that any assignees are subject to the consumer's claims and defenses against the assignor.[515] The FTC Holder Rule will apply in cases in which the mortgage loan is related to a sales transaction, such as in a home improvement contract.[516] When the FTC Holder Notice appears in the loan notice or credit contract, the claim is not based on an agreement not found in the bank's records, and therefore *D'Oench* and its statutory codification should not apply.[517]
- *Rescission Claims.* A consumer raising a Truth in Lending rescission claim against a foreclosing lender should not be subject to the *D'Oench* bar and related doctrines.[518] The "super-defendant" status of the FDIC under *D'Oench* and section 1823(e) has been held not to protect a lender from the successful assertion of a consumer's rescission right.[519] The Truth in Lending Act specifically provides that rescission is available against assignees, without exception.[520]
- *Void Transactions.* Section 1823(e) provides that no agreement which diminishes or defeats the FDIC's interest in an asset acquired by it shall be valid. If the transaction is void, however, there is no asset in which the FDIC can acquire an interest. If the FDIC acquires no interest, its interest cannot be diminished or defeated. Thus, an obligation rendered void by fraud in the factum is not an asset protected by section 1823(e).[521] A usurious obligation may be void under state law and therefore not protected by section 1823(e). Similarly, an obligation that a borrower has discharged

511 *Statute has displaced the common law doctrines*: Fed. Deposit Ins. Corp. v. Deglau, 207 F.3d 153 (3d Cir. 2000); Kessler v. Nat'l Enters., Inc., 165 F.3d 596 (8th Cir. 1999); Murphy v. Fed. Deposit Ins. Corp., 61 F.3d 34 (D.C. Cir. 1995); DiVall Insured Income Fund v. Boatmen's First Nat'l Bank, 69 F.3d 1398 (8th Cir. 1995). *See also* Gens v. Resolution Trust Corp., 112 F.3d 569 (1st Cir. 1997) (suggesting that "FDIC's right to invoke [either *D'Oench* or federal holder-in-due-course] doctrine[s] . . . is open to serious question" without deciding the issue); Ledo Fin. Corp. v. Summers, 122 F.3d 825, 829 n.2 (9th Cir. 1997) (*D'Oench* doctrine not applicable in light of *O'Melveny* and *Atherton*; declining to reach question whether *D'Oench* overruled).

Common law doctrines continue to exist: Nat'l Enters., Inc. v. Barnes, 201 F.3d 331, 333 n.4 (4th Cir. 2000) (*D'Oench* is a separate and independent ground for decision); Murphy v. Fed. Deposit Ins. Corp., 208 F.3d 959 (11th Cir. 2000) (FIRREA does not preempt *D'Oench*, reasonable interpretation is that Congress intended *D'Oench* to coexist with FIRREA); Young v. Fed. Deposit Ins. Corp., 103 F.3d 1180 (4th Cir. 1997) (*D'Oench* remains separate and independent ground for decision).

512 *See, e.g.*, Langley v. Fed. Deposit Ins. Corp., 484 U.S. 86, 91, 108 S. Ct. 396, 98 L. Ed. 2d 340 (1987); Fed. Deposit Ins. Corp. v. Deglau, 207 F.3d 153 (3d Cir. 2000) (section 1823(e) bars fraud in the inducement defense); Fed. Deposit Ins. Corp. v. Hatmaker, 756 F.2d 34 (6th Cir. 1985) (refusing to allow borrower to assert claim that bank inserted an amount in blank note that was five times greater than amount orally agreed to; § 1823(e) bars claim based on such an agreement); Gulfstream Dev. Group, L.L.C. v. Schwartz, 2009 WL 1107751 (M.D. Fla. Apr. 22, 2009) (*D'Oench* bars claim that a bank's misrepresentations, which were contrary to the written agreement, fraudulently induced plaintiffs to enter into contract).

513 *See* National Consumer Law Center, The Cost of Credit: Regulation, Preemption, and Industry Abuses § 10.7.9.4 (4th ed. 2009 and Supp.).

514 16 C.F.R. pt. 433 (Preservation of Consumers' Claims and Defenses) (authorized by 15 U.S.C. §§ 41–58).

515 *See generally* National Consumer Law Center, Unfair and Deceptive Acts and Practices § 11.6 (7th ed. 2008 and Supp.) (discussing the FTC Holder Rule).

516 When the notice is required but not included, in violation of the rule, the consumer's rights against the creditor are less clear. For a discussion of the consumer's possible remedies, see National Consumer Law Center, Unfair and Deceptive Acts and Practices § 11.6.4 (7th ed. 2008 and Supp.).

517 *See* Leavings v. Mills, 175 S.W.3d 301, 312 n.9 (Tex. App. 2004) (FDIC and RTC take notes free only of terms or agreements that are not apparent from face of instrument, so FTC Holder Notice preserved claims even if current holder acquired note from one of those agencies).

518 *See* New Me. Nat'l Bank v. Gendron, 780 F. Supp. 52, 54 (D. Me. 1991) (*D'Oench* asserted by bridge bank); Kasket v. Chase Manhattan Mortgage Corp., 695 So. 2d 431, 435 (Fla. Dist. Ct. App. 1997) (FDIC and RTC not liable for civil or criminal penalties under TILA, but exemption could not be raised by assignee in a voluntary assignment by government agency; nor were *D'Oench* doctrine and § 1823(e) available as defenses as any alleged TIL violations would be evident from the face of the documents). *Cf.* Fed. Deposit Ins. Corp. v. Monterrey, Inc., 847 F. Supp. 997, 1004 n.9 (D. P.R. 1994) (suggesting that TIL rescission is available against FDIC, but not other TIL remedies).

519 New Me. Nat'l Bank v. Gendron, 780 F. Supp. 52, 57 (D. Me. 1991).

520 15 U.S.C. § 1641(c).

521 *See* Langley v. Fed. Deposit Ins. Corp., 484 U.S. 86, 93 (1987) (when instrument is rendered void before being acquired by FDIC, instrument is not an asset protected by § 1823(e)) (dicta).

by payment, but that remains on the bank's books, is not an asset in which the FDIC can acquire a protected interest.[522]

- *Fraud in the Factum.* While it is clear that fraudulent inducement claims do not fall within an exception to *D'Oench* and related doctrines, it is equally clear that the doctrines do not bar claims of fraud in the factum.[523] Fraud in the factum is not limited to forgeries, but applies whenever a party reasonably relies on a misrepresentation as to the character or essential terms of a contract.[524] Alteration of a document is fraud in the factum.[525]

A number of other consumer claims or defenses have survived *D'Oench* or related defenses in at least some courts. These include:

- Breach of fiduciary duty;[526]
- State consumer fraud (UDAP) claims;[527]
- Failure of consideration;[528]
- Wrongful acceleration and unreasonable sale at foreclosure;[529] and

---

522 Fed. Deposit Ins. Corp. v. Bracero & Rivera, Inc., 895 F.2d 824, 830 (1st Cir. 1990) (note not an asset protected by § 1823 because legal obligation extinguished by payment); Commerce Fed. Sav. Bank v. Fed. Deposit Ins. Corp., 872 F.2d 1240, 1245 (6th Cir. 1989) (since note secured by mortgage that FDIC sought to enforce had been paid in full, security was extinguished prior to takeover and accordingly did not exist for FDIC to acquire); Grubb v. Fed. Deposit Ins. Corp., 868 F.2d 1151, 1158–1159 (10th Cir. 1989). *See also* Salgado v. Fed. Deposit Ins. Corp., 2004 WL 2584689, at *3 (E.D. Pa. Nov. 15, 2004) (paid note was not an asset acquired by FDIC for purposes of 15 U.S.C. § 1821(d)(9)(A), denying defendant's motion for summary judgment on plaintiff's defamation claim arising from agency's negative report to a credit reporting agency); Note, *Ways Around the Wrath: Exploring the Remaining Exceptions to the D'Oench, Duhme Doctrine and Section 1823(e)*, 54 U. Pitt. L. Rev. 1127 (1993).

523 Langley v. Fed. Deposit Ins. Corp., 484 U.S. 86, 93 (1987) (dicta); Fed. Deposit Ins. Corp. v. Turner, 869 F.2d 270, 275 (6th Cir. 1989) (section 1823(e) did not bar defense based on guaranty fraudulently altered by bank officer). *See also* Fed. Deposit Ins. Corp. v. Kagan, 871 F. Supp. 1522, 1526 (D. Mass. 1995) (FDIC subject to defense of fraud in the factum); Resolution Trust Corp. v. Davies, 824 F. Supp. 1002, 1012 (D. Kan. 1993) (dicta).

524 *See* Restatement (Second) of Contracts § 163 (1981) (defining fraud in the factum as misrepresentation as to character or essential terms of a contract that induces a party to sign it, as long as party did not have a reasonable opportunity to know its character or essential terms); Anderson v. Ashby, 873 So. 2d 168, 181–185 (Ala. 2003) (misrepresentation of essential nature or existence of contract may be fraud in the factum even if party fails to take advantage of opportunity to read contract); Amsterdam v. DePaul, 175 A.2d 219 (N.J. Super. Ct. App. Div. 1961) (good discussion of expansive nature of fraud in the factum).

525 Fed. Deposit Ins. Corp. v. Turner, 869 F.2d 270 (6th Cir. 1989) (bank officer fraudulently altered guaranty).

526 Cent. Nat'l Bank v. Fed. Deposit Ins. Corp., 771 F. Supp. 161 (E.D. La. 1991) (*D'Oench* does not bar an action based on breach of fiduciary duty); F.E. Appling Interests v. McCamish, Martin, Brown & Loeffler, 953 S.W.2d 405 (Tex. App. 1997), *aff'd*, 991 S.W.2d 787 (Tex. 1999) (attorney subject to negligent misrepresentation claim for inaccurate representation that settlement agreement in lender liability suit met requirements of § 1823(e)). *See also* Tuxedo Beach Club Corp. v. City Fed. Sav. Bank, 749 F. Supp. 635 (D.N.J. 1990) (claim of breach of fiduciary duty not barred, but it fails on other grounds).

527 *See* Tuxedo Beach Club Corp. v. City Fed. Sav. Bank, 749 F. Supp. 635 (D.N.J. 1990) and cases cited therein. *See also* Fed. Sav. & Loan Ins. Corp. v. Mackie, 962 F.2d 1144 (5th Cir. 1992) (UDAP and breach of duty of good faith claims not barred if based on obligations in written agreement; would be barred if based on oral promises and representations); Fed. Deposit Ins. Corp. v. Rusconi, 808 F. Supp. 30 (D. Me. 1992) (UDAP claim not barred if not based on oral representations); Desmond v. Fed. Deposit Ins. Corp., 798 F. Supp. 829 (D. Mass. 1992) (breach of duty of good faith and fair dealing also survived; noting that breach of that duty violates Mass. UDAP statute, a claim which also survived); First Commerce of Am. v. Mr. Travel Agent, Inc., 1995 Conn. Super. LEXIS 986 (Mar. 28, 1995) (unpublished) (UDAP claim survives motion for summary judgment when based on actions of bank in attempting to coerce refinancing and threatening interest rate higher than allowed by note). *But see* Sweeney v. Resolution Trust Corp., 16 F.3d 1 (1st Cir. 1994). *But cf.* FDIC Guidelines for Use of *D'Oench* and Statutory Provisions, 62 Fed. Reg. 5984, 5987 (Feb. 10, 1997) (stating that assertion of *D'Oench* or § 1823(e) may be appropriate as to a UDAP claim based on a misrepresentation or omission by the failed bank).

528 DiVall Insured Income Fund, Ltd. P'ship v. Boatmen's First Nat'l Bank, 69 F.3d 1398 (8th Cir. 1995); Fed. Deposit Ins. Corp. v. O'Flahaven, 857 F. Supp. 154 (D.N.H. 1994) (failure of consideration defense based upon nondisbursement of funds is not barred because fact of whether or not funds were disbursed should be contained in bank records); Fed. Deposit Ins. Corp. v. Sather, 468 N.W.2d 347 (Minn. Ct. App. 1991), *aff'd*, 488 N.W.2d 260 (Minn. 1992); Cinco Enters., Inc. v. Benso, 995 P.2d 1080 (Okla. 1999) (state law defense of failure of consideration available to avoid liability on certain notes; no secret agreement barring defense under either *D'Oench* or § 1823(e)); Bank of New Glarus v. Swartwood, 297 Wis. 2d 458, 725 N.E.2d 944 (Wis. Ct. App. 2006) (*D'Oench* does not bar a failure of consideration defense based upon nondisbursement of funds). *But see* Fed. Deposit Ins. Corp. v. McCullough, 911 F.2d 593 (11th Cir. 1990) (defenses of fraudulent inducement and failure of consideration barred because never memorialized and made part of bank records); Fed. Deposit Ins. Corp. v. McClanahan, 795 F.2d 512 (5th Cir. 1986) (claims of failure of consideration and fraudulent inducement are barred).

529 Resolution Trust Corp. v. Carr, 13 F.3d 425 (1st Cir. 1993); Texas Refrigeration Supply, Inc. v. Fed. Deposit Ins. Corp., 953 F.2d 975 (5th Cir. 1992) (claims arising from the U.C.C. are not precluded by *D'Oench*, but noting that only claims or defenses *not based* on agreements are not barred; thus if basis for wrongful acceleration claim was an oral agreement, *D'Oench* would bar it); Fed. Deposit Ins. Corp. v. Blue Rock Shopping Ctr., Inc., 766 F.2d 744 (3d Cir. 1985) (if FDIC acted improperly to impair collateral, *D'Oench* does not prevent borrower from discharge of debt under Uniform Commercial Code); S&S Diversified Servs., L.L.C. v. Arguello, 911 F. Supp. 498 (D. Wyo. 1995) (where debtor claims Article 9 notice provisions violated before FDIC stepped in, no right to deficiency acquired); New Bank of New England N.A. v. Callahan, 798 F.

- A challenge to the validity of a lien under Texas homestead law.[530]

For a detailed discussion of issues relating to *D'Oench, Duhme*, see NCLC's *The Cost of Credit: Regulation, Preemption, and Industry Abuses* § 10.7.[531]

5.14.4.3 Requirement to Exhaust FDIC's Administrative Claims Process

Another issue that arises when a federal receiver is appointed for a failed bank is the requirement to exhaust the administrative claims process that the receiver sets up.[532] In many instances, a claim will be barred if the litigant did not exhaust the administrative claims process. Some courts have recognized an exception for affirmative defenses, but the exact contours of this exception remain undefined, particularly where an affirmative defense could also have been asserted as an independent claim.

If a litigant filed suit before the federal receiver was appointed, most courts have held that the case can resume in that court once the litigant exhausts the claims process. If suit was not filed before the receiver was appointed, the consumer can file suit within sixty days after exhausting the administrative claims process, but suit must be filed in the United States district court where the failed bank had its principal place of business or in the United States district court for the District of Columbia.[533]

Supp. 73 (D.N.H. 1992); Wansley v. First Nat'l Bank of Vicksburg, 566 So. 2d 1218 (Miss. 1990). *Cf.* Commc'n Sys., Inc. v. Ironwood Corp., 930 F. Supp. 1162 (S.D. Tex. 1996) (because acceleration clause in note is not "agreement" within meaning of *D'Oench* or § 1823(e) it is admissible to show when assignee's cause of action accrued). *But see* Fed. Deposit Ins. Corp. v. Bathgate, 27 F.3d 850 (3d Cir. 1994) (wrongful acceleration defense barred where it depends upon allegations relating to an unrecorded agreement); Burns v. Resolution Trust Corp., 880 S.W.2d 149 (Tex. 1994).

530 Patterson v. Fed. Deposit Ins. Corp., 918 F.2d 540, 544 (5th Cir. Tex. 1990) (homestead rights exist independently of any agreement between the parties); *In re* Napier, 144 B.R. 719, 725 (Bankr. W.D. Tex. 1992); Mundaca Inv. Corp. v. Espinoza, 1996 WL 671267, at *2–3 (Tex. App. Nov. 20, 1996) (unpublished).

531 (4th ed. 2009 and Supp.).

532 12 U.S.C. § 1821(d). *See* National Consumer Law Center, The Cost of Credit: Regulation, Preemption, and Industry Abuses § 10.7 (4th ed. 2009 and Supp.) (detailed analysis of claims process and its implications).

533 12 U.S.C. § 1821(d)(6)(A).

Chapter 6 Mortgage Servicing Abuses

6.1 Introduction

6.1.1 Overview

Mortgage servicing is the management of mortgage loans from the time they are originated until they are satisfied or foreclosed. The vast majority of residential mortgage loans are managed by "servicers" for the benefit of the holders of the loan. Servicers exist primarily to collect and process payments. They are also responsible for sending monthly statements, keeping track of account balances, handling escrow accounts, engaging in loss mitigation and prosecuting foreclosures. In effect, servicers provide the critical link between mortgage borrowers and mortgage holders.

Despite the important role played by mortgage servicers, they typically do not have a significant stake in the performance of mortgage loans. Instead, servicers make money through investment choices: purchases of the right pool of mortgage servicing rights and the correct interest hedging decisions.[1] They are also compensated through a complex web of direct payments on the principal balance of loan pools, fees charged to borrowers, interest paid on short-term deposits ("float income"), and amounts paid from affiliated businesses. This compensation structure too often incentivizes mortgage servicers to engage in abusive conduct towards borrowers. Unfortunately, borrowers, who have no voice in selecting which servicers handle their loans, have few market mechanisms they can employ to deter abuses.

In general terms, abusive servicing occurs when a servicer seeks to collect unwarranted fees or other costs from borrowers, engages in unfair collection practices, or through its own improper behavior precipitates borrower default or foreclosure.[2] An explosion of litigation against mortgage servicers has exposed the frequency and scope of mortgage servicing abuses. Some well documented examples include:

- Misapplying payments;[3]
- Charging unauthorized or unreasonable fees;[4]
- Disregarding qualified written requests under the Real Estate Settlement Procedures Act;[5]
- Refusing to consider loss mitigation options;[6]
- Improperly forceplacing insurance;[7]
- Failing to make timely and proper escrow disbursements;[8] and
- Engaging in coercive collection practices.

The effect of mortgage servicing abuses can be severe. The stress of facing foreclosure and battling with a mortgage servicer, even if the situation is eventually resolved, can be overwhelming for the average homeowner. Negative credit ratings can make it more difficult for borrowers to refinance their homes, obtain other credit, or even get a job. The most devastating result of mortgage servicing abuses is unwarranted foreclosure of the borrower's home. Foreclosures uproot families and children, destroy credit histories, and may limit future homeownership opportunities. Foreclosures often consume a life's savings and all of a family's assets. They present a serious threat to neighborhood stability and community well-being.[9]

This chapter describes common mortgage servicing abuses and provides a guide for determining the proper amount due on consumer mortgage loans. The next chapter will focus on the rights and remedies available to borrowers under federal and states statutes and the common law. Chapter 8, *infra*, considers challenges to servicing abuses based on the Real Estate Settlement Procedures Act, and Chapter 7, *infra*, discusses challenges based on non-RESPA legal claims.

---

1 Diane E. Thompson, National Consumer Law Center, Why Servicers Foreclose When They Should Modify and Other Puzzles of Servicer Behavior: Servicer Compensation and its Consequences (Oct. 2009), *available at* www.consumerlaw.org/issues/mortgage_servicing/content/Servicer-Report1009.pdf.

2 Kurt Eggert, Fannie Mae Foundation, Limiting Abuse and Opportunism by Mortgage Servicers, Housing Policy Debate 15(3), at 756 (2004). These practices are distinguishable from appropriate servicer actions that may nevertheless harm borrowers, such as collecting appropriate late fees or foreclosing on borrowers who have not made their payments despite proper loss mitigation efforts.

3 *See* § 6.3.2, *infra.*

4 *See* §§ 6.4.3, 6.4.4, *infra.*

5 *See* § 8.2.2, *infra.*

6 *See* § 6.4.5, *infra.*

7 *See* § 6.3.5.2, *infra.*

8 *See* § 6.3.5.3, *infra.*

9 Joint Economic Committee, U.S. Senate, Sheltering Neighborhoods from the Subprime Foreclosure Storm (Apr. 11, 2007), *available at* http://jec.senate.gov/Documents/Reports/subprime11apr2007.pdf.

6.1.2 Servicing Compensation Structure

Customarily, the servicer collects a monthly fee in return for the services provided. This fee is based on the outstanding principal loan balance and typically ranges from 25 basis points (prime loans) to 50 basis points (subprime loans).[10] For example, a securitized loan pool with an outstanding balance of $900 million and a 38 basis point servicing fee would generate yearly income of approximately $3.42 million for the servicer. In addition, the servicer is entitled to keep "float income" and ancillary fees. Float income is the amount earned on funds invested between the collection of the payment from the borrower and the disbursement to the owner.[11] For loans with escrow accounts, float income may also be earned on collected funds until they are disbursed to the taxing authority or insurance provider. Important factors affecting float earnings include escrow disbursement timing and escrow analysis and cushion requirements.

Ancillary fees consist of late fees and other "service" fees. Such fees are a crucial part of servicers' income. For example, one servicer's CEO reportedly stated that extra fees, such as late fees, appeared to be paying for all of the operating costs of the company's entire servicing department, leaving the conventional servicing fee almost completely profit.[12] Consequently, servicers have perverse incentives to charge borrowers as much in fees, both legitimate and illegitimate, as they can. For example, just one improper late fee of $15 on each loan in one average size loan pool (3500 loans) would generate an additional $52,500 in income for the servicer.

Default services, such as property inspections, broker's price opinions and appraisals, present another revenue generating opportunity for servicers. In some instances the costs of services provided by third-party vendors may be marked-up by the servicer resulting in additional costs to borrowers and additional profits for the servicer. In other cases, default services are performed by the servicer's own subsidiaries or "in-sourced vendors."[13] Profits from these entities or units flow to the servicer, and mark up may likewise occur.[14] As a result, the servicer has an incentive to order services provided by these entities more than may be necessary and reasonable.

6.2 Opportunities for Servicing Abuse

6.2.1 General

The life of a mortgage loan presents many opportunities for servicer error and abuse. There are four potential stages in which servicing problems arise described briefly below. Common abuses in each stage are discussed in more detail in the following sections.

6.2.2 Before Default

In this stage, the homeowner is not currently considered to be in default on any obligations under the mortgage loan documents. Despite the current status of the loan, questions may arise regarding the proper application of payments or the handling of the borrower's escrow account. For example, in *Rawlings v. Dovenmuehle Mortgage, Inc.*,[15] the servicing of the homeowners mortgage loan was transferred, and the new servicer claimed that the homeowner failed to make two payments for the months just prior to the transfer. The homeowners responded by sending the new servicer copies of the canceled checks showing that the payments had been timely made to the old servicer. The new servicer then sent a letter stating that the homeowners owed $38.20 in late fees and that the account was in default. The homeowners again sent copies of the canceled checks and a copy of their account history with the old servicer. Along with the copies, they requested in writing that the error be corrected and sought a copy of their loan history. The servicer then

10 Kurt Eggert, Fannie Mae Foundation, *Limiting Abuse and Opportunism by Mortgage Servicers*, Housing Policy Debate 15(3), at 758 (2004).

11 In 2007, one of the nation's largest servicers reported an additional $30 million in revenue from float income which made up 9% of its servicing income. Ocwen Financial Corporation, Form 10-K, at 28 (Mar. 13, 2008), *available at* www.sec.gov/Archives/edgar/data/873860/000101905608000419/ocn_10k07.htm.

12 *Id.* Ocwen Financial Corporation reported that in 2007 nearly 12% (just over $40 million) of its servicing income was derived from late fees and other loan collection fees. Ocwen Financial Corporation, Form 10-K, at 27 (Mar. 13, 2008), *available at* www.sec.gov/Archives/edgar/data/873860/000101905608000419/ocn_10k07.htm.

In 2006, Countrywide reported $285 million in revenue from late fees alone. Gretchen Morgenson, *Dubious Fees Hit Borrowers in Foreclosures*, New York Times, Nov. 6, 2007.

13 For example, executives from the largest servicers in the country have reported that increased operating expenses from increased delinquencies and loss mitigation efforts "tend to be fully offset by increases to ancillary income in our servicing operation, greater fee income from items like late charges, and importantly from in-sourced vendor functions." *See* Countrywide Financial Q3 2007 Earnings Call Transcript (Oct. 26, 2007), *available at* http://seekingalpha.com/article/51626-countrywide-financial-q3-2007-earnings-call-transcript?page=-1.

14 *See In re* Stewart, 391 B.R. 327 (Bankr. E.D. La. 2008) (finding that although servicer's testimony at trial stated that entity which provided broker's price opinions was an independent affiliate of servicer, servicer later revealed in another court proceeding that entity is actually a corporate division of the servicer and that the true cost incurred by the servicer for broker's price opinions is $50 rather than the $125 charged to the borrower), *aff'd*, 2009 WL 2448054 (E.D. La. Aug. 7, 2009).

15 64 F. Supp. 2d 1156 (M.D. Ala. 1999).

sent an account history, but it was not for their account but for some other borrowers' account. The homeowners then made several telephone calls to the servicer and were told they needed to contact the old servicer. Two more notices of default were sent. Even after the homeowners hired an attorney who also sent a letter to the servicer, they received five more default notices. Eventually, after battling for over seven months to resolve the error, the old servicer admitted it had applied the payments to the wrong account and the new servicer corrected the account.

In another case, *Choi v. Chase Manhattan Mortgage Co.*,[16] the servicer failed to pay taxes on the homeowners' property over a two-year period because a tax notification company it contracted with provided erroneous information. The city eventually sold the home at tax sale. The homeowners informed the servicer that they had received notice that the property had been sold and that it could still be redeemed. Although the servicer apparently attempted to redeem, it later claimed that the taxing authority lost the payment check. The servicer also failed to petition the court to have the tax sale deed voided and the homeowners lost their home.

As demonstrated in these two examples, pre-default servicing errors are often compounded once the mortgage loan goes into default and can lead to foreclosure.

6.2.3 *After Default, but Before Foreclosure*

Here, the servicer has made a determination the borrower is in default on one or more obligations under the mortgage loan documents. The most common reason for default is nonpayment of amounts contractually due. A right to cure notice has likely been sent to the borrower and foreclosure proceedings may have been initiated. In some cases, foreclosure may be imminent. The servicer, in most cases, will retain local counsel to assist with the foreclosure. It is at this point that late fees have been assessed, other mysterious fees have been charged to the borrower's account, and the borrower's payments are being placed in a "suspense account" or are being returned. Frequently neither the servicer nor the local foreclosure attorney respond to requests for information regarding the borrower's account. When the servicer or local attorney do provide information regarding the borrower's account it is often confusing, internally inconsistent, and sometimes simply undecipherable.

In *Maxwell v. Fairbanks Capital Corp.*,[17] the servicer acquired the servicing rights in a portfolio of so-called "non-performing loans." Shortly after receiving notice of the servicing transfer, the homeowner and a housing counselor assisting her made numerous attempts to get information about the account and an itemized payoff figure. The servicer first sent a letter stating that the total payoff amount was $264,603.13, but then one week later claimed that it was owed $363,603.38. During the next two-year period, the servicer and its attorneys quoted six different payoff figures on the mortgage ranging from a low of $121,948.38 to a high of $430,707.28. It was also revealed during the course of the litigation that the servicer could not locate or produce, and had never obtained, a payment history on the account, a set of original TIL disclosures, or a copy of the note. The court found that the servicer had "in a shocking display of corporate irresponsibility, repeatedly fabricated the amount of the Debtor's obligation to it out of thin air."[18]

6.2.4 *Post-Payoff or Foreclosure*

At this stage, the loan has either been paid in full or the home has been sold pursuant to a foreclosure sale. Where a loan has been paid in full, servicer abuses may continue to wreak havoc upon borrowers. Most commonly, the servicer's failure to provide a timely release of the security instrument and/or update credit report information may jeopardize the borrower's ability sell or refinance the property or to obtain future credit. Servicers also may falsely assert that amounts are still due and owing on a mortgage loan despite full payment. For homes that have been sold pursuant to a foreclosure sale, the servicer may have breached its duty of care to the borrower in wrongfully foreclosing or the sale may have been defective or illegal under state law. Although homes rarely sell at foreclosure for more than is owed on the mortgage account, the servicer may fail to properly account for and provide a credit to the borrower for any surplus.

In *Islam v. Option One Mortgage Corp.*,[19] the homeowners asserted that the servicer's failure to properly credit the payoff funds resulted in aggressive collection efforts by the servicer and false reports to credit reporting agencies. Nearly three weeks after refinancing their mortgage loan, the borrowers were contacted by a representative of the servicer who demanded payment of an alleged past due mortgage payment and threatened foreclosure of the home. After over a year of phone calls and written requests, the servicer finally informed the credit reporting agencies that the mortgage had been paid in full. However, as a result of the delay, the borrowers were denied credit on two occasions.

6.2.5 *In Bankruptcy or After Bankruptcy*

Often one of the primary objectives of borrowers filing for bankruptcy protection is to cure mortgage arrears. Many times borrowers efforts are hampered by mortgage servicers who consistently inflate their claims by miscalculation, misunderstanding of the loan contract and their obligations

16 63 F. Supp. 2d 874 (N.D. Ill. 1999).
17 281 B.R. 101 (Bankr. D. Mass. 2002).
18 *Id.* at 117.
19 432 F. Supp. 2d 181 (D. Mass. 2006).

under the Bankruptcy Code, or deliberate addition of unauthorized fees. Escrow overcharges, interest overcharges, late charge abuses and the imposition of "junk fees" are common servicing abuses in bankruptcy. In addition, the absolute breakdown of many servicers' accounting procedures when the homeowner files for bankruptcy has led to unfounded claims of post-petition delinquency and unsupported motions for relief from the automatic stay.

In *In re Gorshtein*,[20] the court determined that sanctions were warranted against several servicers for filing motions to lift the automatic stay based upon attorney affidavits certifying material post-petition defaults, when in fact, there were no material defaults by the debtors. The court rejected what it termed as the mortgage servicers' "dog ate my homework" excuses, such as those relating to "the Servicing Agent's defective computer system, which could not cope with payments by the debtor except in the exact amount programmed into the computer, or the Bank's mistake in taxing the debtor with the premium on a $1 million property insurance policy for a $100,000 house."[21] The court emphasized the damage to the judicial process that occurs when a court is asked to rule on incorrect or baseless facts. It also noted that in each instance, the mortgage servicers' actions had created a danger that a debtor would lose his or her home without just cause and in violation of the debtor's rights under the Bankruptcy Code.[22]

In *In re Nosek*,[23] the bankruptcy court was outraged at the servicer's poor accounting practices for homeowners in bankruptcy. The servicer used a variety of excuses for failing to properly account for the homeowner's payments during bankruptcy, all of which the court found to be unacceptable. As the court said: "Even if Ameriquest must manually account for these payments . . . Ameriquest is not excused from doing it right, even if it is an administrative burden. . . . Ameriquest is simply unable or unwilling to conform its accounting practices to what is required under the Bankruptcy Code, something this Court can encourage by assessing punitive damages under Section 105(a)."[24] The court awarded the consumer $250,000 in emotional distress damages and $500,000 in punitive damages for Ameriquest's violation of section 1322(b) of the Bankruptcy Code. On appeal the First Circuit Court of Appeals reversed the decision finding no violation of the debtor's right to cure under chapter 13 because the debtor had failed to include a provision in her plan directing how payments should be applied.[25]

20 285 B.R. 118 (Bankr. S.D.N.Y. 2002).

21 *Id.* at 126.

22 *Id.* at 120.

23 363 B.R. 643 (Bankr. D. Mass. 2007).

24 *Id.* at 650.

25 *In re* Nosek, 544 F.3d 34 (1st Cir. 2008). The First Circuit's opinion should not be applicable where debtor's plan specifies how payments received by the servicer from the debtor and/or trustee should be applied.

6.3 Common Abuses Arising Before Default

6.3.1 Overview

Servicing abuses can occur at any time during the life of the loan including before default. Many times pre-default abuses such as the misapplication of payments or improper force placed insurance, if not corrected by the servicer, can lead the borrower down the path to default. While these abuses may be common before default, they can occur at any time. As a result, advocates are encouraged to engage in a rolling analysis of the potential abuses regardless of the borrower's exact situation. Often, a series of abusive behaviors can be traced back to one of the following issues. In such cases, it may be possible to completely unwind the transaction, eliminating subsequent fees and reinstating the loan.

In some cases, the servicer's failure to provide an accounting or inability to explain how it calculated the amount due may be grounds for denying the servicer's right to foreclose or claims for other relief. Requests for an accounting might be made pursuant to a qualified written request under RESPA,[26] or in the context of disputing a creditor's claim in a bankruptcy proceeding.[27]

6.3.2 Misapplication of Payments

6.3.2.1 In General

The misapplication of payments is one of the most common problems that borrowers are reported to have with servicers. The reasons for misapplication of payments range from sloppy procedures to more insidious efforts to generate more revenue. Servicers may purposefully ignore grace periods, may fail to apply funds in the order specified by the contract,[28] or may improperly charge late fees.[29] Trouble

26 *See* Ch. 8, *infra* (more information on qualified written requests).

27 *See In re* Sanders, 2007 WL 188676 (Bankr. D. Mass. Jan. 23, 2007); *In re* Nosek, 363 B.R. 643 (Bankr. D. Mass. 2007), *vacated on other grounds*, 544 F.3d 34 (1st Cir. 2008).

28 For example, the Fannie Mae/Freddie Mac uniform instruments include language mandating how payments are to be applied. When the servicer fails to apply payments as required by the instrument, the contract has been breached. *See, e.g.,* Fannie Mae/Freddie Mac Uniform Instruments, First Lien Security Instruments, Form 3022: Massachusetts Mortgage (Jan. 2001), *available at* www.freddiemac.com/uniform/unifsecurity.html.

29 *See In re* Ocwen Fed. Bank F.S.B. Mortgage Servicing, 2006 WL 794739 (N.D. Ill. Mar. 22, 2006), *aff'd*, 491 F.3d 638 (7th Cir. 2007) (denying motion to dismiss state law claims including fraudulent concealment, unjust enrichment, breach of contract, breach of good faith and fair dealing, conversion, negligence, misrepresentation, defamation, and fraud and deceit

often arises when servicing rights are transferred from one servicer to another.[30] Account information may not be accurately transferred or payments may be misapplied by the old or new servicer. Servicers frequently compound payment application problems by then reporting the homeowner late to the credit rating agencies.

In *Nosek v. Ameriquest Mortgage Co.*,[31] the servicer persisted in its inability to provide an accurate accounting of the amounts actually paid by the borrower and amounts remaining due. In discussing the absurdity of the servicers' position, the court stated:

> To credit back late charges but be unable to properly bill the borrower or provide an accurate statement on her account or apply payments from the chapter 13 trustee is unconscionable for a large sophisticated national lender. The Defendant has breached its duty of good faith and fair dealing by inadequately applying, tracking, and crediting payments made by the Plaintiff.

Unfortunately, these problems are more typical than unusual. The failure to properly apply even a single payment can have a snowballing effect that leaves homeowners fighting foreclosure and struggling to repair their credit for months, or even years. In many cases, borrowers attempting to correct errors in their accounts are met with the servicer's callous indifference, compounding the effect of the problem. For example, in *Hukic v. Aurora Loan Servicing*,[32] a clerical error, in which the borrower's payment was recorded as $1135, instead of $1335, left the homeowner battling with subsequent servicers and fending off foreclosure for nearly five years. Despite the fact that every payment was for the correct amount and timely, the failure to correct the clerical error caused each month's payment to be credited to the prior month, along with late fees, and the remaining balance was placed in an escrow account. More than five years later, a state court ordered reinstatement of the monthly payments and waiver of all fees, costs, and penalties against the borrower, and then dismissed the complaint for foreclosure.

The problem of sloppy accounting procedures is not limited to for-profit mortgage servicers. In *In re Sanders*,[33] the Massachusetts Housing Finance Agency was unable to provide a consistent statement of amounts due or an adequate explanation of the legal basis under which it was attempting to collect these various amounts. The court said that "[t]he Agency's evidence in support of these ever-morphing sums and grounds is decidedly unpersuasive—the shifting origins of the claim components, the Agency's inconsistent application of funds paid by the Debtor, the accounting paid by the Debtor, the account requested by the Debtor and largely unfurnished by the Agency, taken together, portray a lender profoundly confused about its rights, obligations and activities with respect to its loan to the Debtor."[34] Because the agency was unable to prove its claim, the court declared the debtor's mortgage current as of the trial date. Unfortunately, this behavior—by a state authorized agency, the purpose of which is to foster homeownership—is far from atypical.

A range of legal claims are available to challenge the misapplication of payments, including:

- Breach of contract;
- Breach of the implied covenant of good faith and fair dealing;
- Unjust enrichment;
- Negligent and intentional infliction of emotional distress;
- Negligent credit reporting;
- Defamation, to the extent not preempted by FCRA;
- Negligent servicing;
- Negligent accounting;
- Conversion;
- Tortuous interference with credit expectancy;
- State Unfair and Deceptive Practices (UDAP);
- Fair Credit Reporting Act (FCRA);
- Fair Debt Collection Practices Act (FDCPA); and
- Real Estate Settlement Procedures Act (RESPA).

Discussion of these claims against servicers is provided in detail in Chapters 7 and 8 of this treatise.

6.3.2.2 Determining the Amount Due

Determining and proving mistakes in the application of payments can be challenging because of the complexity and murkiness of most servicers' payment histories. The courts seem generally confused about which party should bear the burden of proving the amount due and propriety of assessed fees.[35] The question of who has the burden of proof may

based on federal preemption grounds; allegations in the multi-district litigation assert that the servicer ignored grace period, misapplied payments, failed to apply payments, improperly charging late fees, improperly force-placed insurance, assessed unwarranted fees, declared loans in default prematurely and initiated unfair and illegal foreclosure proceedings).

30 *See* § 8.2.3, *infra*.

31 2006 WL 1867096 (Bankr. D. Mass. June 30, 2006), *rev'd*, 354 B.R. 331 (D. Mass. 2006) (reversed on preemption grounds).

32 2006 WL 1457787 (N.D. Ill. May 22, 2006) (denying motion to dismiss claim for tortuous interference with credit, allowing tort claim for negligent credit reporting pending a new definite statement, dismissing claims for negligent and intentional infliction of emotional distress and credit defamation as untimely, and dismissing FCRA claim for lack of private right of action against furnisher).

33 2007 WL 188676 (Bankr. D. Mass. Jan. 23, 2007).

34 *Id.* at *1.

35 *Compare In re* Sanders, 2007 WL 188676 (Bankr. D. Mass. Jan. 23, 2007) (court disallows claim for fees which are not adequately shown to be due) *with* Dowling v. Litton Loan Ser-

very well turn on the procedural posture of the case. For example, if the servicer is asserting amounts due in the course of a bankruptcy proceeding, courts have generally placed the burden on the servicer to prove the amount due including the legality of any fees charged. The allowance of fees should require at least a showing that:

1. The fees are authorized by the contract and applicable state and federal law;
2. The statutory and contractual events that trigger the fees have in fact occurred;
3. The fees were properly assessed to the homeowner (i.e., the homeowner was notified in the legally required manner of the events that triggered the fees); and
4. The homeowner has not paid the fees.

On the other hand, if the homeowner is mounting an affirmative action against the servicer, the burden of proving the misapplication of payments or improper assessment of fees may lie with the homeowner.[36]

One way to approach the questions of what is due and what has been paid, is set out below. This framework is designed primarily for fixed rate, scheduled payment loans. While the general principles outlined here can be applied to adjustable rate or daily accrual loans, those types of loans require some additional considerations and computations.

I. Establishing the Framework

A. Obtain adequate supporting documentation to begin the analysis.[37]

B. Determine the type of loan involved, (e.g., FHA, VA, conventional uninsured, conventional insured).

C. READ and UNDERSTAND the note and security instrument, including any riders. Determine the following contract terms:

1. What is method of charging interest?[38]
2. What is the ORDER in which payments are to be applied?[39]
3. Is a suspense account authorized by the contract?
4. Are late fees authorized by the contract? If so, determine amount of the late fee (e.g., $10 or 5% of principal and interest payment) and when a payment is deemed late.[40]
5. Is an escrow account for taxes, insurance, and other items authorized by the contract and has such an account been established?

D. Determine the existence of any events that could alter the amount due.

1. Are there any applicable loan modifications or forbearance agreements?
2. Have there been any bankruptcy filings by the homeowner? Is there a confirmed chapter 13 plan or other order that modifies payment requirements?[41]

E. Understand the servicer's responsibilities to the owner of the loan.

1. Do the Fannie Mae/Freddie Mac servicing guidelines apply?
2. Is there a pooling and servicing agreement that governs the servicer's relationship with the owner of the loan and outlines the servicer's authority and responsibility?

F. Obtain adequate documentation from the homeowner, if questioning the posting of payments by the servicer, that payments in question were actually made.

G. Review transfer of servicing notices to determine if either new servicer or old servicer indicated that loan was in default?[42]

II. Run a Sample Amortization.

A. Figure out what the loan principal should have looked like at a particular point in the loan history based on the total of payments to that date.

B. Compare this amount with what the servicer claims was the loan principal on that same date.

III. Scrutinize the Payment History[43]

A. Were payments applied to principal, interest, and other items in the order specified by the contract when the payment was received?

---

vicing, L.P., 2006 WL 3498292 (S.D. Ohio Dec. 1, 2006) (court appears to indicate that the homeowner has burden of proving that fees charged were improper).

36 *See, e.g.,* Dowling v. Litton Loan Servicing, L.P., 2006 WL 3498292 (S.D. Ohio, Dec. 1, 2006).

37 At a minimum the note, security instrument, any forbearance agreement, and a payment history should be gathered. In addition any other written communications with the servicer will be helpful in determining the proper amount due. These may include, for example, monthly statements, servicing transfer letters, payoff statements, and notices of default. Homeowners should also provide, to the extent, possible evidence of any payments made. *See* § 10.2.6, *infra.*

38 There are several accounting methods used for calculating the amount of interest due on mortgage loans. Conventional mortgage loans generally use what is called the scheduled method of accounting. Other loans may use the daily accrual method of accounting. *See* § 6.3.4.2, *infra.*

39 Typically a provision of the security instrument will specify the order in which payments should be applied. For example, on post-January 2001 Fannie Mae/Freddie Mac uniform security instruments, the order of application of payments is (1) interest; (2) principal; (3) escrow; (4) late fees; and (5) any other charges due under the security instrument.

40 *See* § 6.4.3, *infra.*

41 *See* § 9.4, *infra.*

42 Under the FDCPA a servicer who takes a mortgage loan for servicing is a "debt collector" if the loan is delinquent at the time of transfer. *See* § 7.4, *infra.* If no FDCPA validation notice was provided, this may serve as the servicer's statement that the loan was not in default at transfer.

43 Remember that payment histories reflect the books of the servicers and not borrowers. Suspense and escrow balances will be a liability for the servicer (a credit balance) and an outstanding corporate advance will be a receivable for the servicer (a debit balance).

B. Were any payments or portions of a payment placed in a suspense account?
C. Were payments pulled out of suspense and applied in accordance with the contract terms?[44]
D. Determine when fees were charged and whether the fees were proper.
  1. When were fees charged?
  2. Were those fees permitted under the contract?
  3. Were fees paid before interest and principal? If so, is the order of payment consistent with the note?
  4. Has the servicer reversed some of the charges?
  5. Is there an explanation in the transaction notes?

It might be helpful to workup a simple spreadsheet by manually entering the payments that were made by your client and late fees that you agree were proper. Your spreadsheet can be used to show the court how payments *should* have been applied and the current amount due.[45]

6.3.3 Use of Suspense Accounts

Servicers use suspense accounts to place payments received from borrowers that, for whatever reason, are not applied to the outstanding loan balance. There is no strong accounting justification for suspense accounts, but they are widely used in the mortgage servicing industry.[46] The ostensible excuse for their use is that the consumer has not provided enough funds to cover a single payment. A major national servicer explained the use of suspense account this way: "If the amount received was not sufficient to pay the contractual obligation according to the loan servicing program, the payment was placed in suspense. When the next payment was received, it was placed in suspense and if the total in suspense then equaled a contractual obligation, then the oldest outstanding contractual obligation was deemed paid, at least in theory."[47]

As the name "suspense account" implies, borrowers funds held in such accounts are in legal limbo—they are not credited to the loan, the borrower does not receive interest on them, and the account is not a trust account.[48] In most cases, borrowers are unaware that a suspense account even exists and are confused when payments made are not reflected in the accounting that the homeowner receives from

44 Note the language on Application of Payments in the Fannie Mae/Freddie Mac uniform instruments. Paragraph 2 of the Security Instrument:

> 2. Application of Payments or Proceeds. Except as otherwise described in this Section 2, all payments accepted and applied by Lender shall be applied in the following order of priority: (a) interest due under the Note; (b) principal due under the Note; (c) amounts due under Section 3. Such payments shall be applied to each Periodic Payment in the order in which it became due. Any remaining amounts shall be applied first to late charges, second to any other amounts due under this Security Instrument, and then to reduce the principal balance of the Note. If Lender receives a payment from Borrower for a delinquent Periodic Payment which includes a sufficient amount to pay any late charge due, the payment may be applied to the delinquent payment and the late charge. If more than one Periodic Payment is outstanding, Lender may apply any payment received from Borrower to the repayment of the Periodic Payments if, and to the extent that, each payment can be paid in full. To the extent that any excess exists after the payment is applied to the full payment of one or more Periodic Payments, such excess may be applied to any late charges due. Voluntary prepayments shall be applied first to any prepayment charges and then as described in the Note.

45 This is exactly what the homeowners did in McAdams v. Citifinancial Mortgage Co., 2007 WL 141128 (M.D. La. Jan. 16, 2007). The court denied summary judgment for lender, construing the contract prepared by the lender against it, and found that a plain reading of the allocation provision required payments to be applied to interest and principal, not late payments.

46 Some loan documents do not appear to authorize the creation and maintenance of a suspense account. At least one court, however, has rejected a borrower's claim that holding excess partial payments in suspense, rather than crediting the partial payment, was unfair. *See* Fasanaro v. The First Nat'l Bank of Chicago, 920 So. 2d 103 (Fla. Dist. Ct. App. 2006) (affirming final judgment of foreclosure).

The current Fannie Mae/Freddie Mac uniform instruments appear to allow for the use of suspense accounts: "Lender is not obligated to apply such payments at the time such payments are accepted. If each Periodic Payment is applied as of its scheduled due date, then Lender need not pay interest on unapplied funds. Lender may hold such unapplied funds until Borrower makes payment to bring the Loan current. If Borrower does not do so within a reasonable period of time, Lender shall either apply such funds or return them to Borrower." *See* Fannie Mae/Freddie Mac Single-family Uniform Instruments, Form 3200: Multistate Fixed Rate Note (Jan. 2001), *available at* www.freddiemac.com/uniform/unifnotes.html.

47 Nosek v. Ameriquest Mortgage Co., 2006 WL 1867096 (Bankr. D. Mass. June 30, 2006), *rev'd* 354 B.R. 331 (D. Mass 2006) (reversed on preemption grounds), *subsequent decision,* 363 B.R. 643 (Bankr. D. Mass. 2007), *vacated on other grounds,* 544 F.3d 34 (1st Cir. 2008). *See also* Fannie Mae Single Family Servicing Guide, pt. III: General Servicing Functions, ch. 1: Mortgage Payments (Nov. 1, 2004), ch. 101: Scheduled Mortgage Payments (Jan. 31, 2003), ch. 101.03: Payment Shortages (Jan. 31, 2003) ("Sometimes payments received from the borrower are less than the total amount due. The servicer should not automatically return these payments to the borrower. Instead, the servicer should base its decision to process partial payments on the amount of the shortage and on any special circumstances that might justify the lesser amount. If the servicer decides to accept the payment, any portion of it that equals one or more full installments should be applied. Any remaining portion should be held as 'unapplied funds' until enough money to make a full installment is received.").

48 *See* O. Max Gardner, III, *Mortgage Securitization, Servicing, and Consumer Bankruptcy*, American Bar Association, GP Solo Law Trends and News—Business Law, vol. 2, no. 1 (Sept. 2005), *available at* www.abanet.org/genpractice/newsletter/lawtrends/0509/business/mortgagesecuritization.html.

the servicer. The shrouded nature of these accounts and uncertain status of the funds they contain, make them ripe for abuse.

In some cases servicers have been known to hold more than a month's payment in suspense.[49] In other cases, servicers have raided suspense accounts to pay unauthorized fees. Use of suspense accounts can also cause borrowers to be charged more interest.[50] Servicers may fail to credit borrowers for funds held in suspense when providing payoff statements or filing proofs of claim in bankruptcy.[51] In bankruptcy cases, servicers may also create a trustee suspense account where payments from the trustee are held prior to being applied to the borrower's account.

Some state laws may limit the use of suspense accounts by creditors. A clear statutory mandate to apply payments when received to the loan installment payments due makes the use of such accounts illegal.[52] In addition, the use of suspense accounts to extract additional fees from the homeowner can be challenged on grounds similar to those available for misapplication of payments.[53]

6.3.4 Interest Overcharges

6.3.4.1 In General

Interest overcharges can result when servicers inappropriately claim unaccrued interest or calculate interest in ways that are not authorized by the contract.[54] Even as consumers have become more aware of the cost savings benefit of having lower interest rates on loans—especially those like home mortgages which are for large amounts and have long terms—many in the financial industry have found creative ways to extract more money from borrowers.

There are several accounting methods used for calculating the amount of interest due on mortgage loans. Conventional mortgage loans generally use what is called the scheduled method of accounting. On a "scheduled loan," for purposes of determining how much interest is due on the loan, each payment is counted as made on the date that it is scheduled to be paid. This means that whether the payment is received on the first day, the third day, or the seventeenth day of the month, the same amount of interest is charged for that month. For scheduled loans, the interest to be paid over the life of the loan is determined when the loan is made. The only events that will alter the predicted amortization of the mortgage will be prepayments of principal.

In contrast, under the daily accrual method of accounting the amount of interest due is determined during the term of the loan, rather than at the time the loan is established, or at the time of prepayment. Lenders who use this method charge interest based upon the actual number of days between payments. In other words, the actual annual note rate of the loan is be divided by 360[55] to determine the daily rate, and this daily rate is multiplied by the number of days that have lapsed between payments.

In certain circumstances some methods are significantly more disadvantageous to the consumer than others. For example, the daily accrual method can be especially problematic to consumers who consistently make late payments and payments at odd intervals. While daily accrual loans have been used by some subprime lenders to extract more money from borrowers, it is important to note that this method of charging interest is not per se unfair or unlawful. In fact, for borrowers who consistently make payments early this accounting method can be beneficial.

6.3.4.2 Which Accounting Method Applies?

The first hurdle facing practitioners who are considering claims based on interest overcharges is determining the applicable accounting method. The language of the note and mortgage (or deed of trust) govern the applicable accounting method. For example, the Fannie Mae/Freddie Mac Uniform Note includes the following language: "Each monthly payment will *be applied as of its scheduled due date* and will be applied to interest before Principal."[56] (emphasis

49 *See In re* Fagan, 376 B.R. 81 (Bankr. S.D.N.Y. 2007) (finding at one point servicer held an amount in excess of the monthly mortgage payment in suspense).

50 *See* Jefferson v. Chase Home Fin. L.L.C., 2007 WL 1302984 (N.D. Cal. May 3, 2007); *In re* Jones, 366 B.R. 584 (Bankr. E.D. La. 2007) (use of suspense account contributed to addition of significant interest charges that were not really due), *aff'd in relevant part, and rev'd in part on other grounds*, 391 B.R. 577 (E.D. La. 2008).

51 *See In re* Sanchez, 372 B.R. 289 (Bankr. S.D. Tex. 2007).

52 *See, e.g.,* W. Va. Code § 46A-2-115(c) (stating that "[a]ll amount paid to a creditor arising out of any consumer credit sale or consumer loan shall be credited upon receipt against payments due . . .").

53 *See* Jefferson v. Chase Home Fin. L.L.C., 2007 WL 1302984 (N.D. Cal. May 3, 2007) (granting borrower's motion for judgment on the pleadings on conversion claim where lender put mid-monthly prepayments in suspense account instead of crediting to loan). *But see* Margulies v. Chase Manhattan Mortgage Corp., 2005 WL 2923580 (N.J. Super. App. Div. Nov. 7, 2005) (no fiduciary duty exists between servicer and homeowner based upon escrow or suspense accounts, even if improper disbursements made; breach of contract claim remanded).

54 *See* Cortez v. Keystone Bank, 2000 WL 536666 (E.D. Pa. May 2, 2000) (allegation of overcharge of interest in home equity line of credit state claim for breach of contract and violation of RESPA); Allenson v. Hoyne Sav. Bank, 272 Ill. App. 3d 939 (1995) (plaintiff's allegations of misamortization scheme resulting in overcharges sufficient to support RICO claim).

55 Rather than divide the annual rate by 365, creditors often prefer to divide the annual rate by 360 days, and assume that all monthly periods have thirty days. *See* National Consumer Law Center, The Cost of Credit: Regulation, Preemption, and Industry Abuses § 4.6.4 (4th ed. 2009 and Supp.).

56 *See* Fannie Mae/Freddie Mac Single-family Uniform Instruments, Form 3200: Multistate Fixed Rate Note, at 3 (Jan. 2001), *available at* www.freddiemac.com/uniform/unifnotes.html.

added) This or similar language indicates that the loan is a "scheduled loan." Daily accrual loans will typically contain the following or similar language: "Interest will be calculated assuming a 360-day year and will be charged on that part of [t]he principal which has not been paid, for the actual number of days elapsed." In rare cases, the note or security instrument may not give any indication of which accounting method should be used. This situation requires a careful analysis of the loan history to determine the method used by the servicer.[57]

In addition to determining the method of accounting, challenging the interest charged on a mortgage loan may also require a determination of the use of a 360- versus 365-day year, the extent of proper rounding, and whether compounding interest is permissible. There may also be questions about whether interest can be charged on items not included in the original loan balance, such as late fees, escrow advances and attorney fees.[58] Many of these issues are discussed in detail in National Consumer Law Center, *The Cost of Credit: Regulation, Preemption, and Industry Abuses* Chapter 4 (4th ed. 2009 and Supp.).

6.3.5 Escrow Account Issues

6.3.5.1 Overview

Escrow accounts are generally required by lenders to ensure payment of taxes, insurance, or other charges. These accounts are most commonly established and initially funded at the time of the loan settlement. After settlement, a portion of the borrower's mortgage payment is typically allocated to the escrow account. While escrow accounts are common in conventional mortgage loans, until recently[59] they were found less often in loans made by subprime lenders.[60]

Even in the absence of abusive servicing, the existence of an escrow account creates a complex set of issues and potential pitfalls for homeowners. The most common problems relate to the changing amount of the monthly payment and the timely and accurate disbursement of funds to taxing authorities and insurance providers.[61] In addition, the presence of an escrow account complicates the accounting process—leading to questions about whether particular payments should have been applied to the interest and principal of the loan, or to the escrow account.

The Real Estate Settlement Procedures Act (RESPA) closely governs the amounts required to be paid by borrowers into an escrow account, the disbursement of payments from the escrow account, and the proper method for addressing surpluses, shortages and deficiencies in escrow accounts. These issues are more fully described at § 8.3, *infra*. State laws may augment the requirements of RESPA.[62] The mortgage instruments should also be carefully scrutinized to determine any additional obligations of the servicer or prohibitions related to the maintenance of the borrower's escrow account.[63]

In addition, when the servicer has stated that there is a negative escrow balance, but refuses to provide an accounting and is unable to explain how it determined the balance due, that may be sufficient grounds for dismissing the servicer's claims for money due.[64]

57 *See* National Consumer Law Center, The Cost of Credit: Regulation, Preemption, and Industry Abuses Ch. 4 (4th ed. 2009 and Supp.).

58 *In re* Crowley, 293 B.R. 628 (Bankr. D. Vt. 2003) (clause in note providing that "the Maker must pay interest on all amounts not paid when due, at the legal rate" did not entitle lender to interest on late fees since there is no due date for late fees).

59 Regulations issued by the Federal Reserve Board, effective April 1, 2010, require servicers to establish escrow accounts for the payment of property taxes and premiums for required mortgage-related insurance for all "higher-priced" first lien mortgage loans. Reg. Z, 12 C.F.R. § 226.35(b)(3); 73 Fed. Reg. 44,522, 44,604 (July 30, 2008). For a detailed discussion of this requirement, see National Consumer Law Center, Truth in Lending § 9.8 (6th ed. 2007 and Supp.).

60 One of the hallmarks of a predatory mortgage loan was the refinancing of a low interest rate mortgage with an escrow account into a higher rate mortgage without an escrow account. The homeowner was led to believe that the payments on the new mortgage are lower than on the previous mortgage, only to find out months later that the "reduced" payment does not include any amounts for taxes or insurance premiums. The homeowner then is in the difficult position of either having to find sufficient funds to pay the property tax or insurance bill or facing default and higher monthly payments when the servicer advances funds to cover the taxes or forceplaces insurance on the property.

61 *See also* Sarsfield v. Citimortgage, Inc., 667 F. Supp. 2d 461 (M.D. Pa. 2009) (denying motion to dismiss negligence claim based on a failure to provide a reasonable estimate of the escrow expenses).

62 *See, e.g.,* Cal. Civ. Code § 2954 (West) (limiting the circumstances under which an impound account can be required); Kirk v. Source One Mortgage Servs. Corp., 46 Cal. App. 4th 483 (1996) (lender may not continue escrow account without borrower's consent).

63 For example, some versions of the Fannie Mae/Freddie Mac Uniform Deeds of Trust include the following limitation:

> Lender shall apply the Funds to pay the Escrow Items. Lender may not charge Borrower for holding and applying the Funds, annually analyzing the escrow account or verifying the Escrow Items, unless the Lender pays the Borrower interest on the Funds and applicable law permits the Lender to make such a charge.

Despite this language in the mortgage or deed of trust, servicers have been quite willing to charge borrowers escrow management or analysis fees. Other types of abuses, which are discussed below, include the failure to make timely disbursements and the improper use of force placed insurance.

64 *See In re* Price, 403 B.R. 775 (Bankr. E.D. Ark. 2009) (alleging that servicer diverted payments to unauthorized escrow account and failed to send notice of rate adjustment); *In re* Sanders, 2007 WL 188676 (Bankr. D. Mass. Jan. 23, 2007); *In re* Nosek,

6.3.5.2 Failure to Make Timely and Proper Escrow Disbursements

There have been numerous instances in which servicers have failed to make timely disbursements from borrowers' escrow accounts for real estate taxes, insurance or other charges. In the most devastating cases, homeowners have lost their homes to tax foreclosure after the servicer failed to make real estate tax payments,[65] while other homeowners have been left to deal with uninsured property damage after the servicer failed to pay insurance premiums.[66] More commonly penalties assessed by the taxing authorities or reinstatement fees imposed by insurance companies as a result of late payments are simply passed on to the borrower.[67] While such fees or penalties may be relatively small, they can nevertheless lead to escrow account shortages or deficiencies, which in turn may cause the borrowers' mortgage payments to increase.

Servicers have also been known to make tax payments on the wrong property altogether or forceplace insurance rather than pay the homeowner's property insurance with escrow account funds.[68]

Failure of the servicer to make timely payments may give rise to claims such as breach of fiduciary duty, breach of contract, and may violate state UDAP laws.[69] Statutory protections may provide an additional remedy.[70] The Servicer Act, contained in section 6 of RESPA,[71] also creates an express right of action for a servicer's failure to make payment from an escrow account for taxes, insurance, and other charges "in a timely manner as such payments become due."[72]

6.3.5.3 Force Placed Insurance

Mortgage lenders routinely require homeowners to purchase property insurance to protect the lender's interest in the home in case of fire or other casualty. Homeowners whose property is located is certain federally designated flood zones are also required to maintain flood insurance. The loan instruments will authorize the lender to purchase such insurance on behalf of the homeowner if the homeowner fails to present evidence of continuous coverage or if the coverage lapses during the term of the loan.[73] This

363 B.R. 643 (Bankr. D. Mass. 2007), *vacated on other grounds*, 544 F.3d 34 (1st Cir. 2008).

65 *See, e.g.*, Marks v. Quicken Loans, Inc., 561 F. Supp. 2d 1259 (S.D. Ala. 2008) (alleging servicers failed to make timely payment of hazard insurance premium; holding servicer at time bill issued, but before payment was due was not liable under RESPA); Mortgage Elec. Registration Sys., Inc. v. Alicea, 2006 WL 1149236 (M.D. Pa. Apr. 26, 2006); Choi v. Chase Manhattan Mortgage Co., 63 F. Supp. 2d 874 (N.D. Ill. 1999).

66 *See, e.g.*, First Fed. Sav. & Loan Assoc. v. Savage, 435 S.W.2d 67 (Ky. 1968); Monahan v. GMAC Mortgage Corp., 893 A.2d 298 (Vt. 2005) (affirming $43,380 jury award for consequential and compensatory damages for servicer's conduct in failing to renew flood insurance policy and subsequent uninsured property damage). *See also* Whitfield v. Countrywide Home Loans, Inc., 252 Fed. Appx. 654 (5th Cir. 2007) (servicer not liable for failing to pay insurance premium after renewal notice sent only to borrower, borrower did not forward notice, policy lapsed and home destroyed in hurricane); Randy R. Koenders, *Duty of Mortgagee of Real Property with Respect to Obtaining or Maintenance of Fire or Other Casualty Insurance Protecting Mortgagor*, 42 A.L.R.4th 188 (1985 and Supp.).

67 *See, e.g.*, Settlement Agreement by and Between the United States Department of Housing and Urban Development and Mellon Mortgage Company (Sept. 30, 1999), *available at* www.hud.gov/offices/hsg/sfh/res/paul/rsamello.pdf (describing HUD's investigation into Mellon's handling of borrower escrow accounts).

68 *See, e.g.*, U.S. Bank Nat'l Ass'n v. James, 2009 WL 2448578 (D. Me. Aug. 9, 2009) (denying motion to dismiss claims based on servicer failure to timely pay insurance); Smith v. GMAC Mortgage Corp., 2007 WL 2593148 (W.D.N.C. Sept. 5, 2007); Booker v. Washington Mut. Bank, F.A., 2007 WL 475330 (M.D.N.C. Feb. 9, 2007).

69 *But see* Parks v. Wells Fargo Home Mortgage, 398 F.3d 937 (7th Cir. 2005) (homeowner did not have claim for emotional distress or punitive damages under Illinois state law for servicer's failure to pay county real estate taxes); Margulies v. Chase Manhattan Mortgage, 2005 WL 2923580 (N.J. Super. Ct. App. Div. Nov. 7, 2005) (no fiduciary duty exists between servicer and homeowner based upon escrow or suspense accounts, even if improper disbursements made; breach of good faith and fair dealing claim also disallowed; breach of contract claim allowed for servicer's failure to credit payments when received and for charging late fees when payments had been received but not processed on a timely basis).

70 *See, e.g.*, Ky. Rev. Stat. Ann. § 367.320 (West) (requiring timely payments from escrow accounts on high-cost loans even if account is in default unless account funds are insufficient); Me. Rev. Stat. Ann., tit. 9-A, §§ 9-305-A, 9-405 (mandating timely payments from escrow accounts and making creditor, assignee or servicer liable for actual damages for violation); Minn. Stat. § 47.205, Subd. 3 (same); N.C. Gen. Stat. § 45-92; N.Y. Banking Law § 6-k (McKinney); N.Y. Real Prop. Tax Law § 953 (McKinney); Vt. Stat. Ann. tit. 8, § 10404(d).

71 11 U.S.C. § 2605.

72 11 U.S.C. § 2605(g). *See* § 8.2.4, *infra*.

73 For example, the Fannie Mae/Freddie Mac uniform instruments include the following language:

> **Property Insurance.** Borrower shall keep the improvements now existing or hereafter erected on the Property insured against loss by fire, hazards included within the term "extended coverage," and any other hazards including, but not limited to, earthquakes and floods, for which Lender requires insurance.... If Borrower fails to maintain any of the coverages described above, Lender may obtain insurance coverage, at Lender's option and Borrower's expense. Lender is under no obligation to purchase any particular type or amount of coverage. Therefore, such coverage shall cover Lender, but might or might not protect Borrower, Borrower's equity in the Property, or the contents of the Property, against any risk, hazard or liability and might provide greater or lesser coverage than was previously in effect. Borrower acknowledges that the cost of the insurance coverage so obtained might significantly exceed the

coverage is called "forceplaced" or "collateral protection" insurance.

Typically an insurer will issue a master policy to the servicer or lender under which coverage for individual properties can be added, deleted, or modified. The lender, not the borrower, is named as the insured and coverage is often limited to the lender's interest in the property, that is, the loan balance.[74] When an individual property is added to the master policy, the creditor pays the premium and then seeks reimbursement from the consumer. The cost of such insurance is almost always much higher than a standard homeowner's insurance policy.

This type of insurance presents extraordinary potential for abuse.[75] Insurers often provide lenders with refunds, kickbacks or other compensation in relation to force placed insurance policies. In some cases, commissions are paid to affiliates of the lender.[76] Because the lender makes the decision about which insurer to use, and since the lender does not eventually have to pay for the premium, there is a built-in incentive for the lender to select the insurer that pays the lender, or its affiliates, the most in the form of kickbacks or other compensation.

Unfortunately the practice of force placing insurance on homeowners is a significant problem with very serious consequences. The placement of this insurance and the lender's efforts to obtain reimbursement from the consumer frequently necessitates a huge increase in the homeowner's monthly payments. As a result, the homeowner may be unable to make the new monthly payments in full (assuming proper notice has been given to the borrower),[77] may incur late payment penalties or other fees, and may eventually face foreclosure.

Servicers have been known to improperly forceplace flood insurance or to obtain force placed insurance coverage in an amount greater than the outstanding balance due on the mortgage.[78] The preemption provisions of the National Flood Insurance Act, however, severely limit homeowners' ability to challenge these practices.[79] One court has held that, based on federal preemption, all claims—both federal and state—are barred against the mortgage holder and the servicer.[80] The mistakes of an independent third party, who falsely certified to the servicer that the property was in a flood zone, triggering the incorrect forceplacing of the flood insurance,

---

> cost of insurance that Borrower could have obtained. Any amounts disbursed by Lender under this Section 5 shall become additional debt of Borrower secured by this Security Instrument. These amounts shall bear interest at the Note rate from the date of disbursement and shall be payable, with such interest, upon notice from Lender to Borrower requesting payment.

See, e.g., Fannie Mae/Freddie Mac Uniform Instruments, First Lien Security Instruments, Form 3005: California Deed of Trust *available at* www.freddiemac.com/uniform/unifsecurity.html.

While this language permits a servicer or lender to force-place insurance, standing alone, it does not impose a duty on the servicer or lender to procure insurance in the event borrowers allow their policies to lapse. *See, e.g., In re* Riccitelli, 14 Fed. Appx. 57 (2d Cir. 2001); Caplen v. Security Nat'l Servicing Corp., Inc., 514 F. Supp. 2d 746 (E.D. Pa. 2007).

74 *See* Caplen v. Security Nat'l Servicing Corp., Inc., 514 F. Supp. 2d 746 (E.D. Pa. 2007) (force placed insurance for benefit of lender not borrower), *aff'd*, 343 Fed. Appx. 833 (3d Cir. 2009). *See also* Edwards v. Homeq Servicing Corp., 2008 WL 544180 (E.D. La. Feb. 25, 2008)(force placed flood insurance protects lenders interests not those of borrower).

Some insurers may offer dual interest policies issued to the borrower and containing a standard mortgage clause in favor of the lender. In such cases, coverage may extend beyond the loan balance up to the replacement value of the home. Unlike regular homeowner's insurance, forceplaced insurance also does not generally cover the contents of the home or liability for personal injury occurring on the property.

75 *See, e.g.,* American Bankers Ins. Co. of Florida v. Alexander, 818 So. 2d 1073 (Miss. 2001), *overruled on other grounds by* Capital City Ins. Co. v. G.B. "Boots" Smith Corp., 889 So. 2d 505 (Miss. 2004). *See generally* National Consumer Law Center, Unfair and Deceptive Acts and Practices § 10.5.10 (7th ed. 2008 and Supp.) (more details about the abuses in force placed insurance).

76 *See* Abels v. JPMorgan Chase Bank, N.A., 2009 WL 5342768 (S.D. Fla. Nov. 23, 2009) (breach of implied covenant of fair dealing sufficiently pleaded where lender purchased force placed insurance from affiliate at excessive rate).

77 The Fannie Mae/Freddie Mac uniform instruments provide that force placed insurance costs are payable by the borrower, with interest, but only "upon notice from Lender to Borrower requesting payment." *See* 11 U.S.C. § 2605.

78 *See* Hayes v. Wells Fargo Home Mortgage, 2006 WL 3193743 (E.D. La. Oct. 31, 2006) (mortgage assignee permitted under contract to unilaterally require increase in amount of flood insurance coverage to value of property rather than amount of outstanding loan balance). *See also* 42 U.S.C. § 4012a(e) (amount of insurance coverage must be "at least equal to the lesser of the outstanding balance or the designated loan or the maximum limit of coverage available for the particular type of property, whichever is less").

79 Further, courts have held that borrowers have no private right of action against mortgage lenders or servicers under the NFIA. *See, e.g.,* Wentwood Woodside I, L.P. v. GMAC Commercial Mortgage Corp., 419 F.3d 310 (5th Cir. 2005); Arvai v. First Fed. Sav. & Loan Ass'n of South Holland, 737 F.2d 638, 642 (7th Cir. 1984) ("Congress specifically placed the responsibility of administering and enforcing those aspects of the Flood Program dealing with mortgage lenders with those federal agencies which supervise the lenders").

Courts have routinely denied homeowners claims based upon the failure of mortgage lenders to require flood insurance or to notify borrowers that their property is located in a covered flood zone in accordance with NFIA. *See, e.g.,* Hofbauer v. Northwestern Nat'l Bank of Rochester, Minn., 700 F.2d 1197 (8th Cir. 1983); Nicholson v. Countrywide Home Loans, 2008 WL 731032 (N.D. Ohio Mar. 17, 2008); Callahan v. Countrywide Home Loans, Inc., 2006 WL 2993178 (N.D. Fla. Oct. 20, 2006); *In re* Schweizer, 354 B.R. 272 (Bankr. D. Idaho 2006).

80 Clark v. AmSouth Mortgage Co., 474 F. Supp. 2d 1249 (M.D. Ala. 2007) (NFIA expressly provides that mortgage holder and servicer can rely on and cannot be liable for, properly guaranteed determination of need for flood insurance).

are not protected by the preemptive provisions of the National Flood Insurance Act, however.[81]

Unwinding the mortgage problems back to the initial placement of such insurance can often identify the point that the payment problems began for a homeowner. If the placement of the insurance was improper—the servicer had adequate proof of existing coverage[82] or it was the servicer's fault that the coverage lapsed[83]—then the homeowner may have a defense to the default and foreclosure.[84]

Remedies for wrongful force placed insurance include:

- State statutory law protections;[85]
- State UDAP claims;[86]
- Breach of fiduciary duty;[87]
- Breach of contract;[88]
- Unjust enrichment;
- RESPA;[89]
- TILA.[90]

6.3.6 Private Mortgage Insurance

Private mortgage insurance (PMI), which protects the lender in the event of a default, is required on many purchase money mortgage loans when the borrower's down payment is less than 20% of the sale price.[91] If there is a foreclosure and the foreclosure sale price is less than the

81 *Id.*

82 The borrower's failure to provide adequate proof of existing coverage upon request of the servicer will likely insulate the servicer from claims related to placement of force placed insurance. *See* Webb v. Chase Manhattan Mortgage Corp., 2008 WL 2230696 (S.D. Ohio May 28, 2008) (finding not liable because servicer took reasonable measures to obtain current insurance information from borrower, even though servicer's predecessor in interest failed to pay insurance premium from escrowed funds); Mills v. Equicredit Corp., 344 F. Supp. 2d 1071 (E.D. Mich. 2004) (dismissing breach of contract claim for wrongly placing homeowner insurance on property where borrowers failed to ensure servicer received borrower's proof of insurance), *aff'd on other grounds*, 172 Fed. Appx. 652 (6th Cir. 2006).

83 The servicer may be at fault for the coverage lapse where, for example, the servicer maintained an escrow account for the payment or renewal of the homeowner's insurance policy, but failed to make the required payments. *See* U.S. Bank Nat'l Ass'n v. James, 2009 WL 2448578 (D. Me. Aug. 9, 2009); Smith v. GMAC Mortgage Corp., 2007 WL 2593148 (W.D.N.C. Sept. 5, 2007); Booker v. Washington Mut. Bank, F.A., 2007 WL 475330 (M.D.N.C. Feb. 9, 2007) (servicer disbursed $800 from homeowner's escrow account to pay property taxes on land other than plaintiff's, failed to pay property insurance bill, then purchased and charged homeowners for much more expensive force placed insurance). *See also In re* Ocwen F.S.B. Mortgage Servicing Litig., 2006 WL 794739 (N.D. Ill. Mar. 22, 2006), *aff'd*, 491 F.3d 638 (7th Cir. 2007) (numerous complaints filed alleging, *inter alia,* wrongful placement of force placed insurance); Vician v. Wells Fargo Home Mortgage, 2006 WL 694740 (N.D. Ind. Mar. 16, 2006) (denying servicer's motion to dismiss claims for breach of contract, breach of fiduciary duty, unjust enrichment, and violations of state UDAP statute and TILA, based on allegations of improper force placed insurance); Dowling v. Select Portfolio Servicing, Inc., 2006 WL 571895 (S.D. Ohio Mar. 7, 2006) (denying servicer's motion to dismiss RICO and fraud claims where servicer improperly force placed insurance on homeowners' property, then attempted to collect cost of premiums, and eventually initiated foreclosure proceedings); Barbera v. WMC Mortgage Corp., 2006 WL 167632 (N.D. Cal. Jan. 19, 2006) (dismissing TIL and RESPA claims as time-barred and remanding state claims to state court where servicer, among other things, initially ignored homeowner's proof of insurance and then failed to credit homeowner's account for premium charges during period of overlapping coverage); Hyderi v. Washington Mut. Bank, FA, 235 F.R.D. 390 (N.D. Ill. 2006) (challenging servicer's policy of not paying insurance bills out of escrow unless it received bill from insurer; class certification denied); Stevens v. Citigroup, Inc., 2000 WL 1848593 (E.D. Pa. Dec. 15, 2000) (finding claims brought regarding force placed insurance not barred by the filed rate doctrine); Johnson v. HomeEq Servicing Corp., 2005 WL 2899632 (Ky. Ct. App. Nov. 4, 2005) (reversing lower court decision and holding that lender, by force placing insurance, waived right to claim homeowner in default for failure to obtain insurance); American Bankers Ins. Co. of Florida v. Alexander, 818 So. 2d 1073 (Miss. 2001) (filed-rate doctrine not bar to plaintiff claims that lender overcharged for force placed insurance), *overruled on other grounds by* Capital City Ins. Co. v. G.B. "Boots" Smith Corp., 889 So. 2d 505 (Miss. 2004).

84 Advocates should be aware that certain claims, including improper forced placed insurance, asserted against Fairbanks Capital Corp., a.k.a., Select Portfolio Servicing, may be precluded by the class settlement in Curry v. Fairbanks Capital Corp., No 03-1095 (D. Mass. 2003). *See, e.g.,* Dowling v. Select Portfolio Servicing, Inc., 2007 WL 928639 (S.D. Ohio Mar. 27, 2007).

85 Some states have specific protections applicable to consumers for force placed insurance, which provide proscriptions regarding placement, cost, payment of premiums, and occasionally private rights of actions. *See, e.g.,* W. Va. Code § 46A-3-109a.

86 Booker v. Washington Mut. Bank, F.A., 2007 WL 475330 (M.D.N.C. Feb. 9, 2007) (statutory violations need to be pleaded with particularity; breaches of contract are not grounds for state UDAP claim). *See also* National Consumer Law Center, Unfair and Deceptive Acts and Practices § 10.5.10 (7th ed. 2008 and Supp.).

87 *See* Vician v. Wells Fargo Home Mortgage, 2006 WL 694740 (N.D. Ind. Mar. 16, 2006); § 7.9, *infra*.

88 *See* Vician v. Wells Fargo Home Mortgage, 2006 WL 694740 (N.D. Ind. Mar. 16, 2006); § 7.7, *infra. See also* Abels v. JPMorgan Chase Bank, 2009 WL 5342768 (S.D. Fla. Nov. 23, 2009) (denying motion to dismiss claim for breach of implied covenant of good faith and fair dealing where borrowers alleged impermissible self-dealing by lender that purchased insurance from one of its affiliates at excessive rates).

89 *See* § 8.2.4, *infra*.

90 Several courts have held that a servicer's actions in placing unauthorized insurance and then charging borrower's account for such insurance may trigger new disclosures under section 226.18 of Regulation Z. *See* Vician v. Wells Fargo Home Mortgage, 2006 WL 694740 (N.D. Ind. Mar. 16, 2006); Travis v. Boulevard Bank, N.A., 880 F. Supp. 1226, 1230 (N.D. Ill. 1995). *See also* National Consumer Law Center, Truth in Lending § 3.9.4.4.2 (6th ed. 2007 and Supp.).

91 *See* National Consumer Law Center, The Cost of Credit: Regulation, Preemption, and Industry Abuses § 8.3.2.1 (4th ed. 2009 and Supp.).

balance due on the loan, PMI will pay some or all the difference to the lender. Once the borrower has more than 20% equity in the property, the equity cushion should adequately protect the lender in the event of foreclosure. As a result, the justification for PMI no longer exists and it should be cancelled.

For single-family home mortgage loans originated on or after July 29, 1999 in which the home is the borrower's principal residence, federal law requires the automatic termination of PMI policies when the homeowner's mortgage balance first becomes less than 78% of the original value of the property securing the loan, or at the midpoint of the mortgage amortization period,[92] whichever is first.[93] However, automatic termination is available only if the borrower is "current" on mortgage payments.[94] Consumer-initiated voluntary cancellation is permitted after the mortgage balance is 80% of the original value.[95] Disclosures regarding the borrower's cancellation rights are also required.[96] A private right of action for actual and statutory damages together with attorney fees and costs allows individuals or classes to enforce the statute.[97]

Single-family home mortgage loans closed before the effective date of the federal law must have their PMI cancelled at the midpoint of the mortgage amortization period.[98] The midpoint rule also applies to mortgage loans closed on or after July 29, 1999 and secured by a one-to-four family investment property or a two-to-four family principal residence.

Borrowers may also obtain relief from PMI obligations based upon the terms of the loan[99] or upon state law. In recent years a few states have enacted legislation to regulate PMI. For example, in California, if PMI is required as a condition of securing a loan, the lender must notify the borrower whether he or she has a right to cancel the insurance and under what conditions the insurance can be cancelled.[100] In Minnesota, borrowers have the right to cancel PMI when the unpaid principal balance of the loan falls below 80% of the current fair market value of the property.[101] These state statutes, however, are enforceable only to the extent that they are not preempted by federal law.[102]

6.3.7 *Payoff Fees or Fax Fees*

Many lenders charge a borrower a fee for calculating the amount needed to pay off the loan in full, when for example the borrower is refinancing the loan or selling the home.[103] These payoff fees range from $25 to $100. Fax fees, which range from $10 to $20, are charged for faxing a payoff statement to the consumer.

Courts have routinely rejected the argument that these fees constitute prepayment penalties under the terms of the loan documents.[104] However, it may still be possible to

92 The midpoint of the original amortization period for adjustable rate mortgages and most fixed rate mortgages occurs upon expiration of seven and a half years if the mortgage had an original amortization period of fifteen years; upon expiration of ten years if the mortgage had an original amortization period of twenty years; and upon expiration of fifteen years if the mortgage had an original amortization of thirty years.

93 12 U.S.C. §§ 4901(18), 4902(b) (effective July 29, 1999).

There is an exception in the law that relieves loans defined as high risk from these standards. 12 U.S.C. § 4902(g). However, it does not appear that any loans have been designated as high risk by either Fannie Mae or Freddie Mac.

94 12 U.S.C. §§ 4901(16), 4902(b).

According to Fannie Mae, "[a] borrower's payments will be considered 'current' if the payment due in the month preceding the scheduled termination date (or the mid-point of the amortization period, as applicable) and all outstanding late charges were paid by the end of the month in which the payment was due. For example, if the schedule termination date for a mortgage is 10/01/02, the borrower's mortgage payments will be considered current if the amount due on 09/01/02 (which includes the payment and all outstanding late charges) is paid by 9/30/02." Fannie Mae Singly Family Servicing Guide, pt. II: Mortgage and Property Insurance, ch. 1: Mortgage Insurance (Jan. 31, 2003), ch. 102: Conventional Mortgage Insurance (Jan. 31, 2003), ch. 102.03: Automatics Termination of Mortgage Insurance (June 1, 2005).

95 12 U.S.C. §§ 4901(2), 4902(a).

96 12 U.S.C. § 4903.

97 12 U.S.C. § 4907.

98 12 U.S.C. § 4902(c).

99 *Compare* Kochin v. Norwest Mortgage, Inc., 2001 WL 856206 (Minn. Ct. App. July 31, 2001) (unpublished decision) (affirming judgment in favor of homeowners where servicer failed to terminate PMI in contradiction to loan-approval conditions document) *with* Bennett v. Bank United, 114 S.W.3d 76 (Tex. App. 2003) (note and deed of trust contemplated life-of-loan PMI and conferred no right of cancellation).

100 Cal. Civ. Code § 2954.6 (West). *See also* Conn. Gen. Stat. §§ 36a-725 to 36a-726 (lender must notify borrower under what conditions borrower has right to cancel); 765 Ill. Comp. Stat. § 930/15 (same); Md. Code Ann., Fin. Inst. § 5-508 (West) (incorporating federal law); N.Y. Ins. Law § 6503(d) (McKinney) (mortgagor not required to pay PMI if loan-to-value ratio less than 75%, but no private right of action).

101 Minn. Stat. § 47.207.

102 *See* 12 U.S.C. § 4908 (describing protections for state laws).

103 For a discussion of the general requirements imposed by Regulation Z on mortgage creditors for providing payoff statements, *see* National Consumer Law Center, Truth in Lending § 9.9.3 (6th ed. 2007 and Supp.).

104 Watt v. GMAC Mortgage Corp., 457 F.3d 781 (8th Cir. 2006) (holding RESPA permitted servicer to charge fee for payoff statement); Curran v. Washington Mut. Bank, N.A., 2006 WL 516846 (W.D. Ark. Mar. 2, 2006), *aff'd,* 471 F.3d 857 (8th Cir. 2006); Capellini v. Mellon Mortgage Co., 991 F. Supp. 31 (D. Mass 1997); Krause v. GE Capital Mortgage Serv., Inc., 314 Ill. App. 3d 376 (2000); Colangelo v. Norwest Mortgage, Inc., 598 N.W.2d 14 (Minn. Ct. App. 1999).

The *Curran* court also rejected the argument that the payoff fee was impermissible under RESPA, which does not explicitly authorize the servicer to charge a fee for responding to a qualified written request. *See also* Smith v. Chase Manhattan Mortgage Corp., 2006 WL 353975 (W.D. Ark. Feb. 16, 2006), *aff'd,* 222 Fed. Appx. 533 (8th Cir. 2007).

challenge such charges as unreimbursable expenses under the provisions of the note.[105] A federal district court in Florida ruled that such fees are prohibited by the standard loan contract that allowed full or partial prepayment without imposition of a prepayment fee. The court rejected the lender's argument that the fee was authorized by a provision of the note which allowed the note holder "the right to be paid back for all costs and expenses in enforcing the note." The court held that this provision applied only to actual out-of-pocket expenses the lender paid to a third party.[106]

It is also not clear that a mortgage holder can legitimately withhold a discharge of the mortgage based on the consumer's failure to pay these charges.[107] For example, in *Orser v. Select Portfolio Servicing, Inc.*,[108] the court denied defendant's motion to dismiss claims of breach of contract and unjust enrichment based on the servicer's imposition of a payoff quote fee. The payoff statement obtained by the plaintiff provided an amount to be paid "in order to obtain a reconveyance of the Deed of Trust," and included a $50 payoff fee. The parties agreed that the fee was not a sum secured by the deed of trust and therefore, the court held that allegations that the payment of such fee was required for reconveyance of the deed of trust sufficiently supported a claim for breach of contract.

In response to frequent consumer complaints about payoff and fax fees, some states have recently enacted legislation governing the timing and fees for payoff statements.[109] A summary of these statutes is provided at Appendix D.2, *infra*. Note that some state laws governing mortgage-related fees may be preempted by federal law.[110]

6.4 Abuses Occurring After Default

6.4.1 Introduction

Although all homeowners should have the same right to quality service, response to questions regarding the loan account, and freedom from improper and unreasonable fees regardless of the status of their loan, that is not always the case. Loans in default are often treated very differently from "performing loans." Servicers often inflate their claims by miscalculation, misunderstanding of the loan contract, or deliberate addition of unauthorized fees.[111] In addition it is often impossible for borrowers to obtain timely, competent, and consistent information from mortgage servicers. Borrowers are rarely able to speak with a real person that has sufficient knowledge to discuss the amount of the default or sufficient authority to resolve disputes.

Though the following abusive practices typically occur after default, in many instances abuses, such as misapplication of payments, interest overcharges and escrow account problems, described at § 6.3, *supra*, may continue (or even begin) after default. As a result, advocates should review § 6.3, *supra*, for other improper conduct by the servicer.

6.4.2 When Is Default?

The concept of a default on the mortgage loan is both technical and somewhat slippery. Technically a borrower is in default when the borrower fails to comply with any one of the requirements of the contract. Failure to make a mortgage payment on the exact day it is due is a technical

105 *See* Sandlin v. Shapiro & Fishman, 919 F. Supp. 1564, 1569 (M.D. Fla. 1996) (payoff fee for determining payoff amount violated mortgage provision prohibiting prepayment charge); *In re* Montano, 2007 WL 1837714 (Bankr. D. Ariz. June 25, 2007) (finding separate $50 payoff fee to be unreasonable and not compensable). *But see* Smith v. Chase Manhattan Mortgage Corp., 2006 WL 353975 (W.D. Ark. Feb. 16, 2006) (breach of contract claim for fax fee barred under voluntary payment doctrine), *aff'd*, 222 Fed. Appx. 533 (8th Cir. 2007).

106 *See also* Krause v. G.E. Capital Mortgage Servs., 1998 WL 831896 (N.D. Ill. Nov. 20, 1998) (class certification in payoff fee case; dismissal of federal claims); Dougherty v. N. Fork Bank, 753 N.Y.S.2d 130 (App. Div. 2003) (under state law lender prohibited from charging a quote fee of $100).

107 *See* Davis v. Homecomings Fin., 2006 WL 2927701 (W.D. Wash. Oct. 10, 2006) (denying servicer's motion for summary judgment on breach of contract and UDAP claim; questions of fact existed as to whether servicer required payment of payoff fee for release of security instrument); Cappellini v. Mellon Mortgage Co., 991 F. Supp. 31 (D. Mass. 1997); Stephens v. Omni Ins. Co., 204 P.3d 885 (Wash. 2009) (practice of including miscellaneous service charges such as fax fees on mortgage payoff statement has the capacity to deceive because it creates the misleading appearance that mortgage cannot be released unless the miscellaneous charges are paid). *See also* Brinton v. Haight, 125 Idaho 324, 870 P.2d 677 (1994) (holding that reconveyance fee constituted trustee's administrative expense which is not part of secured debt and which, therefore, was not required to be paid to obtain a deed of reconveyance). *But see* Beyer v. Countrywide Home Loans Servicing, 2009 WL 3229308 (9th Cir. Oct. 8, 2009) (inclusion of expedited payoff service fee in payoff demand statement was not deceptive within meaning of consumer protection statute because statement twice unambiguously disclosed that payment of fee was not required to release the mortgage lien).

108 2005 WL 3478126 (W.D. Wash. Dec. 20, 2005).

109 *E.g.*, Ga. Code Ann. § 7-6A-3 (4) (payoff balances must be provided within reasonable time "but in any event no more than five business days after the request"; no fee may be charged except that $10 processing fee may be charged if information provided by facsimile or within sixty days of previous request); Me. Rev. Stat. tit. 9-A, § 9-305-B (charge may not be assessed for first two payoff requests in any calendar year, and charges for each subsequent request may not exceed $5).

110 *See, e.g.*, Tombers v. Federal Deposit Ins. Corp., 2009 WL 3170298 (S.D.N.Y. Sept. 30, 2009) (class action suit alleging that $20 fax/quote fee required for payoff statement violated New York Real Property Law § 274-a was preempted by federal law); Molosky v. Wash. Mut. Bank, 2008 WL 183634 (E.D. Mich. Jan. 18, 2008) (payoff fees and recording fees preempted as "loan-related" fees).

111 *See* Wienert v. GMAC Mortg. Corp., 2009 WL 3190420 (E.D. Mich. 2009).

default. Yet, practically, lenders do not consider a mortgagor to be in default until after the late fee is triggered—generally either ten or fifteen days after the payment due date. While nonpayment is the most common event of default, the borrower's noncompliance with other terms of the note or mortgage can also constitute a default, such as the failure to maintain property insurance.

The question of whether the borrower is, or was, in default on a particular day is important because default can trigger coverage under,[112] or exemption from,[113] some law. It can explain (although imperfectly) why the servicer is treating payments in a certain way and it will often determine whether certain rights under the note and the mortgage or deed of trust are applicable.

The Fannie Mae/Freddie Mac Uniform Notes and Security Instruments generally contain a right to notice of the default and a right to cure the default prior to acceleration[114] of the loan.[115] State laws may also provide for notice of and the right to cure mortgage loan defaults.[116] Failure to give notice of the default and right to cure, when required by the contract or state law, may render a foreclosure defective as a matter of law or give rise to a breach of contract claim.[117]

In addition, the acceptance of late payments by the servicer has been held to modify or waive the strict acceleration provisions of the contract, or work as an estoppel against the servicer from strictly enforcing the acceleration provisions. A pattern of acceptance of late payments at least raises factual questions as to whether a new agreement has been created.[118] This common law rule, which exists in most states, is probably the reason that servicers often return payments made by borrowers after the loan is deemed to be in default. It may also serve as the justification, albeit a flawed one, for the maintenance of suspense account.

6.4.3 The Morass of Late Fees

6.4.3.1 Overview

Mortgage loan contracts typically provide a grace period, e.g., ten or fifteen days, beyond the due date of an installment payment, during which time borrowers may pay the installment without penalty. When the payment is made after the expiration of the grace period, the note may authorize the imposition of a late fee on the borrower.

Late charges may only be assessed to the borrower if the contract specifically authorizes them. Even where late fees are permitted under the agreement, the servicer must still comply with any applicable state law before assessing the fee to the borrower's account.

---

112 For example, the Fair Debt Collection Practices Act only applies to mortgage servicers if they obtained the mortgage after the borrower was in default. 15 U.S.C. § 1692a(1)(F); § 7.4, *infra.*

There is an extensive line of decisions parsing the issue of whether a servicer is considered a debt collector. Some of these cases turn on the question of whether the servicer treated the loan as covered by the FDCPA, regardless of whether the loan was actually in default. *See, e.g.,* Schlosser v. Fairbanks Cap. Corp., 323 F.3d 534 (7th Cir. 2003); Dowling v. Litton Loan Servicing, 2006 WL 3498292 (S.D. Ohio Dec. 1, 2006) (FDCPA applies to servicer who claims to be debt collector even though may not be under statutory provisions because loan was not in default at time of change of servicer). *But see* Walcker v. SN Commercial, L.L.C., 2006 WL 3192503 (E.D. Wash. Nov. 2, 2006), *aff'd on other grounds,* 28 Fed. Appx. 455 (9th Cir. 2008) (finding under terms of loan borrower not in default until ten days after servicer sent notice of default and granting summary judgment for servicer under state collection agency statute because servicer obtained the loan during that ten-day period).

113 For example, Regulation X, which is promulgated by HUD and supplements RESPA, states that a servicer's obligation to make timely payments from escrow for taxes and insurance are suspended if the borrower is thirty days or more in default. *See* Reg. X, 24 C.F.R. § 3500.17(k)(1), (2).

This regulation, however, is not supported by the language of the statute and its validity is uncertain. *See* § 8.2.4, *infra.*

114 To accelerate a loan is to demand full and immediate payment of the entire unpaid balance of the loan, including principal, interest, late charges, and other fees (not just the delinquent portion).

115 *See, e.g.,* Fannie Mae/Freddie Mac Uniform Instrument, Form 3044: Texas, Single-Family, *available at* www.freddiemac.com/uniform/unifsecurity.html ("Lender shall give notice to Borrower prior to acceleration following Borrower's breach of any covenant or agreement in this Security Instrument. . . . The notice shall specify: (a) the default; (b) the action required to cure the default; (c) a date, not less than thirty days from the date the notice is given to Borrower, by which the default must be cured; and (d) that failure to cure the default on or before the date specified in the notice will result in acceleration of the sums secured by this Security Instrument and sale of the Property. The notice shall further inform Borrower of the right to reinstate after acceleration and the right to bring a court action to assert the non-existence of a default or any other defense of Borrower to acceleration and sale. If the default is not cured on or before the date specified in the notice, Lender at its option may require immediate payment in full of all sums secured by this Security Instrument without further demand and may invoke the power of sale and any other remedies permitted by Applicable Law.").

116 *See* § 4.2.5, *supra,* and Appx. E, *infra* (summarizing state foreclosure laws).

117 *See* § 4.2.5, *supra.*

In practice, advocates should always obtain a copy of the notice of default from either the borrower or the servicer. If the borrower claims not to have received a copy and the servicer cannot produce a copy, it may be possible to eliminate any foreclosure fees or costs incurred subsequent to when the notice should have been provided.

118 *See, e.g.,* Mayo v. Bank of Carroll County, 276 S.E.2d 660 (Ga. Ct. App. 1981) (if bank expressly waived timely payment of installment of promissory note secured by deed of trust, late payment could not constitute proper grounds for acceleration of loan); Meehan v. Cable, 523 S.E.2d 419 (N.C. Ct. App. 1999) (note holder who repeatedly accepted late payments waived right to accelerate debt without first notifying mortgagor that prompt payment would be expected in the future). *See* § 4.3.3, *supra.*

Late fees are closely regulated and often charged incorrectly. There are a myriad of overlapping, and occasionally conflicting, limits on the assessment and collection of late fees. This subsection provides an overview of the issues which are more fully developed later.

There are several types of limits on late fees:

- Limit on the *dollar amount* charged for a late fee (maximum $10 or $15) in some contracts or some states;
- Limit on the *percentage*—4 or 5%, or occasionally up to 6% of the payment which is late;
- Limit on the *payment amount* on which the late charge is calculated (i.e., the entire amount of the payment, or only that part of the payment which is actually late);
- Limit on the *date* on which the late charge can be assessed;
- Limit on the *triggering* event (i.e., do all sums due, including fees, have to be paid to avoid a late fee, or only principal and interest?).

Which limit applies? In some situations, more than one limit may apply to the imposition of late fees. Suppose for example that the note sets one limit (say 5% of the payment), state law at the time of the contract permitted a maximum $25 late fee, and state law at the time the late fee is imposed (based on a change in the law) allows a maximum $50 late fee. When more than one limit may apply to the imposition of late fees, the general rule is that the state law limit as of the date of the contract applies.[119]

On what amount is the late fee based? Where the late fee is determined as a percentage, the question arises as to whether the fee is based on the entire payment due or just the portion that is late. For example, if the principal and interest due on the first of the month is $550, and only $540 is paid on time, is the fee calculated on the whole $550, or only on the $10 that is late? Most contracts specify that if the entire payment is not made then the entire payment is deemed to be late,[120] so that the fee would be calculated on the entire $550. But some, especially older, contracts can be read to only permit the fee to be calculated on the amount which is unpaid. State law on late charges can also provide guidance on this issue.

Other contracts may limit the payment amount on which the late charge is calculated to "principal and interest." In these cases the calculation of late fees should exclude escrow amounts or other fees.

6.4.3.2 Late Fees As Hidden Interest

Late fees, like any other payments made to a lender, are a potential source of hidden interest and should be closely scrutinized. A servicer's ability to exclude late charges from interest on a contract varies widely from state to state. Further complexity is added if a national bank or federal savings bank is involved in the transaction.[121] However, even if the interest rate charged for the loan is not subject to a usury cap because of deregulation[122] or the interest rate is preempted because the lender is a financial institution,[123] the *over*charging of a late fee may still be a breach of contract or a violation of state law.[124]

6.4.3.3 Pyramiding Late Fees

Pyramiding of late fees is a term used to describe the practice of taking assessed late fees from the regular pay-

---

119 The usury saving clause in most notes will prevent the imposition of a late fee which may be authorized by the contract, but is in excess of state law. The Usury Savings Clause in the Fannie Mae/Freddie Mac Uniform Note states:

> **Applicable Law.** This Note shall be governed by federal law and, to the extent not inconsistent with or more restrictive than federal law or regulation governing the Lender, the laws of the jurisdiction in which the property defined in the Security Instrument as the "Property" is located. In the event of a conflict between any provision of this Note and any such law or regulation in effect *as of the date of this Note, such law or regulation shall control to the extent of such conflict and the conflicting provision contained in this Note shall be without effect.* All other provisions of this Note will remain fully effective and enforceable.

120 With respect to determining the amount on which the late fee is based the Fannie Mae/Freddie Mac Uniform Note states:

> The amount of the charge will be ________% of *my overdue payment of principal and interest*. I will pay this late charge promptly but only once on each late payment. Freddie Mac specifically prohibits the charging of more than 5% on any late payment. On first mortgages, the fee is assessed if the payment has not been received within 15 days after the due date; on second mortgages it is 10 days.

Freddie Mac Single Family Servicing Guide 64.3(a).

121 The general rule of thumb is that if the loan is originally made by a financial institution that has preemption status, then that preemption status stays with the loan, even if it is assigned to an institution or serviced by an institution with*out* that status; and the converse of this is true as well. *See* National Consumer Law Center, The Cost of Credit: Regulation, Preemption, and Industry Abuses § 3.4.5.1.3 (4th ed. 2009 and Supp.) (full discussion of the preemption status of loans as they are assigned and serviced).

122 *See generally* National Consumer Law Center, The Cost of Credit: Regulation, Preemption, and Industry Abuses Ch. 3 (4th ed. 2009 and Supp.).

123 *See* National Consumer Law Center, The Cost of Credit: Regulation, Preemption, and Industry Abuses Ch. 3 (4th ed. 2009 and Supp.) (thorough discussion of the preemption of state interest rate limits in loans made by financial institutions).

124 Armstrong v. Steppes Apartments, Ltd., 57 S.W.3d 37 (Tex. App. 2001) (late charge is not authorized by law, plus interest, is usury; usury savings clause does not save the contract from being usurious if note is usurious on its face).

ment and leaving part of the scheduled payment overdue resulting in the assessment of another late charge.[125] Federal regulations, state law, and the payment application provisions found in mortgage documents generally prohibit this practice.

The FTC's Credit Practices Rule (FTC rule) prohibits the pyramiding of late charges.[126] The FTC rule prohibits attributing a borrower's current payment first to outstanding late charges or overdue amounts and then to the installment that is currently due. The FTC rule declares that this practice (along with others in installment contracts) is "unfair" under section 5 of the Federal Trade Commission Act.[127] Under the FTC rule, it is an "unfair act or practice" for a creditor to impose a late charge "when the only delinquency is attributable to late fee(s) or delinquency charge(s) assessed on earlier installments."[128] Agencies regulating banks, savings banks and credit unions have adopted similar rules applicable to their regulated entities.[129]

The Federal Reserve Board's Regulation Z, which implements the Truth in Lending Act (TILA), also prohibits the pyramiding of late fees for mortgages covered by TILA.[130] A servicer cannot impose any late or delinquency fee when the only delinquency is attributable to the late or delinquency fee itself and the payment is otherwise a full payment for the applicable period and is paid on its due date or during an applicable grace period.[131] The Federal Reserve Board intends that this rule be construed consistently with the FTC Credit Practices Rule.[132]

Similarly, Freddie Mac prohibits the collection of a late charge from a regular monthly payment: deducting a late fee from a payment made to cure a delinquency is not allowed. Most importantly, the servicer guide also prohibits causing the mortgage to become delinquent or placed in foreclosure because of an unpaid late charge.[133]

Despite the clear prohibitions of the FTC Credit Practices Rule and Regulation Z, it appears that Fannie Mae's servicing guides (Fannie Mae guidelines) specifically authorize a servicer to "hold as unapplied" a payment that is only missing a late fee due.[134] However, a servicer should not be able to rely on Fannie Mae guidelines as a defense to the specific rules of the FTC—or the rules of the applicable federal financial institution regulator. The Fannie Mae guidelines are written to provide instructions to servicers for the protection of the investors. These guidelines do not overrule applicable laws and federal regulations. The issue of whether a particular servicer has violated the FTC's Credit Practices Rule will turn on whether the servicer charges a late fee for a payment which is otherwise timely and in the correct installment amount, and which does not include a late payment fee assessed for the previous payment.[135]

Many state laws prohibit other types of pyramiding. For example, if there is a missed payment, but regular payments are made after that missed payment, a state statute may prohibit the charging of more than one late charge.[136] Under the accounting method that is prohibited here, every payment is viewed as one month late and late charges are validly assessed every month. This practice is prohibited in states that adopted the 1974 draft of the Uniform Consumer Credit Code.[137]

In addition, imposing a late charge under these circumstances may violate the payment application provision found in the mortgage documents. As is discussed more fully at § 6.3.3, *supra*, servicers create havoc with homeowners' payments by placing them into suspense accounts. If a payment has been placed in suspense (because it was late, not in full amount, failed to include fees assessed, or for no reason at all), the servicer *cannot* call subsequent payments

125 *See* National Consumer Law Center, Cost of Credit § 7.2.4.3 (4th ed. 2009 and Supp.).

126 *See* 16 C.F.R. § 444.4.

127 15 U.S.C. § 45(a).

Although there is no private right of action under the Federal Trade Commission Act, violations of the Act and FTC Rules may be per se violations of state UDAP statutes. *See* National Consumer Law Center, Unfair and Deceptive Acts and Practices Ch. 3 (7th ed. 2008 and Supp.).

128 16 C.F.R. § 444.4.

129 *See, e.g.,* 12 C.F.R. § 560.33 (OTS).

130 For coverage of TILA, *see* National Consumer Law Center, Truth in Lending Ch. 2 (6th ed. 2007 and Supp.).

131 Reg. Z, 12 C.F.R. § 226.36(c)(1)(ii); 73 Fed. Reg. 44,522, 44,604 (July 30, 2008). For purposes of this Regulation Z provision, "servicer" has the same meaning as in the regulations promulgated under the Real Estate Settlement Procedures Act. *See* § 8.2.1, *infra*.

For a discussion of the remedies available for violation this regulation, see National Consumer Law Center, Truth in Lending § 9.9.4 (6th ed. 2007 and Supp.).

132 Official Staff Commentary to Reg. Z § 226.36(c)(1)(ii)-1; 73 Fed. Reg. 44,522, 44,614 (July 30, 2008).

133 Freddie Mac Single Family Servicer Guide 64.3(b).

134 Fannie Mae Single Family Servicing Guide, pt. III: General Servicing Functions, ch. 1: Mortgage Payments, ch. 101.03: Payment Shortages (Jan. 31, 2003): "[I]f a servicer chooses to do so, it may hold as 'unapplied' a payment that does not include late charges (or any allowable prepayment premiums) that are due. The servicer may then use a portion of the subsequent payment to make up the shortage so that the payment can be applied." *See also* Fannie Mae Single Family Servicing Guide, pt. I: Lender Relationships, ch. 2: Contractual Relationship (Jan. 31, 2003), ch. 203: Servicing Compensation (Jan. 31, 2003), ch. 203.03: Late Charges (Nov. 1, 2004).

135 *See* 16 C.F.R. § 444.4(a) ("[I]t is an unfair act or practice within the meaning of section 5 of that Act for a creditor, either directly or indirectly, to levy or collect any delinquency charge on a payment, which payment is otherwise a full payment for the applicable period and is paid on its due date or within an applicable grace period, when the only delinquency is attributable to late fee(s) or delinquency charge(s) assessed on earlier installment(s).").

136 *See, e.g.,* Ky. Rev. Stat. Ann. § 367.320 (West) (applicable to high-cost loans only); N.C. Gen. Stat. § 24-10.1; W. Va. Code § 46A-3-112.

137 U.C.C.C. § 2.502 (1974). *See* National Consumer Law Center, The Cost of Credit: Regulation, Preemption, and Industry Abuses § 2.3.3.10 (4th ed. 2009 and Supp.) (discussion of the U.C.C.C.).

late just because the subsequent payment failed to include enough to make up past amounts wrongfully applied to fees.[138] The first place to look to determine this rule is the application of payments section of security agreement. Paragraph 2 of the Uniform Security Instrument sets out the rules for applying payments:

> All payments accepted and applied by Lender shall be applied in the following order of priority: *interest* due under the Note; *principal* due under the Note; amounts due under Section 3 (*escrow*). Such payments shall be applied to each Periodic Payment in the order in which it became due. Any remaining amounts shall be applied first to late charges, second to any other amounts due under this Security Instrument, and then to reduce the principal balance of the Note. If Lender receives a payment from Borrower for a delinquent Periodic Payment which includes a sufficient amount to pay any late charge due, the payment may be applied to the delinquent payment and the late charge. If more than one Periodic Payment is outstanding, Lender may apply any payment received from Borrower to the repayment of the Periodic Payments if, and to the extent that, each payment can be paid in full. To the extent that *any excess exists after the payment is applied to the full payment of one or more Periodic Payments*, such excess may be applied to any late charges due.

There is generally nothing in the contract between the homeowner and the lender that permits the servicer to apply payments intended for principal, interest, and escrow to anything other than principal, interest, and escrow. Only if all these amounts are paid in full does the contract permit late charges to be deducted from the payment. Any ambiguity in the contract terms should be resolved in the homeowner's favor where the lender has prepared the mortgage loan contract.[139]

6.4.3.4 Other Contractual and State Law Limitations on Late Fees

Practitioners should closely study the exact terms of the contract. The limits of the contract itself must be complied with before late charges can be validly assessed.[140] Most state statutes authorizing late fees make them contingent upon what is disclosed to the consumer in the contract. If, for example, the contract only permits late charges after the payment is paid fifteen days past the due date and even though the state law would have permitted the imposition of a late charge after ten days, the lender is still not permitted to charge until the payment is fifteen days late.

Additionally, the general rule in state statutes and contracts is that late fees may be imposed only *after* the payment has not been received a certain number of days *after* it was due. For example, suppose a contract includes this language:

> (A) Late Charges for Overdue Payments
>
> If the Note Holder has not received the full amount of any monthly payment by the end of 15 calendar days *after* the date it is due, I will pay a late charge to the Note Holder. The amount of the charge will be 5% of my overdue payment of principal and interest. I will pay this late charge promptly but only once on each payment.[141]

Many servicers will impose the late fee on day 16, but this would be improper under this language. The language specifically only permits the late fee to be charged *after* fifteen days *after* the payment was due. So if the payment is due on day 1, then the end of fifteen days after day 1 is day 16, which means that the fee for the failure to make a timely payment can only be imposed on day 17, because the borrower should theoretically have the entire day of day 16 in which to make the payment.

A related issue is whether the servicer has promptly credited the payment to the borrower's account. Regulation Z, which implements the Truth in Lending Act (TILA), requires that a servicer credit payments to the borrower's loan account as of the date of receipt.[142] The servicer need only credit the payment as of the date of receipt. It need not actually post the payment on the date of receipt.[143]

---

138 *See* McAdams v. Citifinancial Mortgage Co., 2007 WL 141128 (M.D. La. Jan. 16, 2007) (payments allowed to be applied only to interest and principal, not to late fees; in summary judgment motion construed contract against the party who prepared it—the lender).

139 *See* McAdams v. Citifinancial Mortgage Co., 2007 WL 141128 (M.D. La. Jan. 16, 2007) (finding nothing in mortgage loan agreement permitted late fees to be captured before interest and principal).

140 *See In re* Parsley, 384 B.R. 138 (Bankr. S.D. Tex. 2008) (servicer unable to explain why proof of claim in bankruptcy case claimed $243.36 in late fees, but master servicing loan history only indicated $101.40 in late fees); Bank of Crockett v. Cullipher, 752 S.W.2d 473 (Tenn. Ct. App. 1988) (imposing substantial late charges in absence of contractual authorization to pressure repayment was unconscionable conduct under state statute); Bowman Plumbing, Heating and Elec. v. Logan, 2002 WL 31119669 (Va. Cir. Ct. Sept. 12, 2002) (Virginia late payment statute requires late payment fee to be specified in the contract); Metro Hauling, Inc. v. Daffern, 723 P.2d 32 (Wash. Ct. App. 1986).

141 This is standard language from the Fannie Mae/Freddie Mac Uniform Note.

142 Reg. Z, 12 C.F.R. § 226.36(c)(1)(i); 73 Fed. Reg. 44,522, 44,604 (July 30, 2008). For purposes of this Regulation Z provision, "servicer" has the same meaning as in the regulations promulgated under the Real Estate Settlement Procedures Act. *See* § 8.2.1, *infra*.

For a discussion of the remedies available for violation this regulation, see National Consumer Law Center, Truth in Lending § 9.9.4 (6th ed. 2007 and Supp.).

143 Official Staff Commentary to Reg. Z § 226.36(c)(1)(i)-1; 73

There are two exceptions to this "same-day" requirement: (1) when a delay in posting does not result in any charge to the consumer or in the reporting of negative information to a consumer reporting agency;[144] and (2) when a servicer specifies in writing requirements for the consumer to follow in making payments but accepts a payment that does not conform to these requirements.[145] In this latter case, the servicer must credit the nonconforming payment within five days after receipt.

The date of receipt is the date when the payment (in whatever form) reaches the servicer.[146] For example, payment by check is received when the check reaches the servicer, not when the funds are collected. Electronic fund transfers, preauthorized payment arrangements, and the like are received when the servicer receives the transfer.

Payments should be credited based on the legal obligations between the parties to the transaction which are determined by applicable state or other law.[147] In addition, the servicer may specify reasonable requirements for making payments in writing. The Commentary lists some examples: setting a cut-off hour for payment to be received; requiring that the payment be accompanied by the account number or payment coupon; specifying that only checks or money orders be sent by mail; requiring that payments be in U.S. dollars; specifying that the consumer use a particular address.[148] However, such requirements must not be difficult for most consumers to follow. The Commentary mentions that a cut-off time of 5:00 p.m. for receipt of a mailed check is reasonable.[149]

The amount of the late fees that can be collected is also limited. Most prime, conventional loans permit late fees equal to 5% of the amount of the payment that was missed. However, state laws may place limits on these allowed amounts, allowing only 4%[150] rather than 5%, or an amount no greater than $15, or some other fixed dollar amount.[151] In these cases the lower authorization should apply.

Another important limitation is the question of when the late fee is imposed, and whether the consumer must be notified of its imposition within a certain amount of time after the late payment which triggered it.[152] The servicer may be prohibited from assessing late charges after the loan has been accelerated.[153] Again, these issues are governed by state law and the contract.

6.4.3.5 Putting It All Together

To sum up, a consumer can only be charged late fees when the contract permits those fees. Late fees may not violate state law. To illustrate how state law and contractual limitations[154] work together, envision the following example:

Day Allowed

- The mortgage note authorizes the collection of a late charge if the payment is not received by the end of fifteen days after the date it is due. So if the payment is due on day 1, the late fee can only be assessed on day 17.
- The state law permits the collection of a late charge properly disclosed and authorized in the contract, after it is ten days late, permitting the imposition on day 12.
- In this case, the limitation imposed in the note would prevail—because this is the one disclosed and authorized in the contract—and the late charge could only be assessed on day 17.

Amount allowed

- The mortgage note authorizes the collection of a late charge equal to 5% of the payment, so that the charge would be an amount greater than $10. (The mortgage also includes a usury savings clause, as described above, limiting the amount to the applicable amount allowed under state law.)
- The state law *at the time the note was signed* only permitted late charges equal to $10. The law has since been changed to permit late charges equal to $15.
- In this case, the limitation imposed by the state law as of the date the note was signed would prevail, and the

Fed. Reg. 44,522, 44,614 (July 30, 2008).

144 Reg. Z, 12 C.F.R. § 226.36(c)(1)(i); 73 Fed. Reg. 44,522, 44,604 (July 30, 2008); Official Staff Commentary to Reg. Z § 226.36(c)(1)(i)-1; 73 Fed. Reg. 44,522, 44,614 (July 30, 2008).

145 Reg. Z, 12 C.F.R. § 226.36(c)(2); 73 Fed. Reg. 44,522, 44,604 (July 30, 2008).

146 Official Staff Commentary to Reg. Z § 226.36(c)(1)(i)-3; 73 Fed. Reg. 44,522, 44,614 (July 30, 2008).

147 Official Staff Commentary to Reg. Z § 226.36(c)(1)(i)-2; 73 Fed. Reg. 44,522, 44,614 (July 30, 2008).

148 Official Staff Commentary to Reg. Z § 226.36(c)(2)-1; 73 Fed. Reg. 44,522, 44,614 (July 30, 2008).

149 Official Staff Commentary to Reg. Z § 226.36(c)(2)-2; 73 Fed. Reg. 44,522, 44,614 (July 30, 2008). In the absence of servicer guidelines for making payments, payments may be made at any location where the servicer conducts business, at any time during normal business hours, and by cash, money order, draft, or other similar instrument in a properly negotiable form, or by electronic fund transfer if so agreed by the consumer and the servicer. Official Staff Commentary to Reg. Z, 12 C.F.R. § 226.36(c)(2)-3; 73 Fed. Reg. 44,522, 44,614 (July 30, 2008).

150 *See, e.g.*, N.C. Gen. Stat. § 24-10.1. *See also* 24 C.F.R. § 203.25 (FHA-insured loans; 4% late fee allowed on installments more that fifteen days late).

151 *See, e.g.*, W. Va. Code § 46A-3-112.

152 *See, e.g.*, Cal. Civ. Code § 2954.5.

153 *See, e.g.*, James v. Olympus Servicing, L.P., 2002 WL 31307540 (N.D. Ill. Oct. 9, 2002); *In re* Guarnieri, 297 B.R. 365 (Bankr. D. Conn. 2003).

154 *See* National Consumer Law Center, The Cost of Credit: Regulation, Preemption, and Industry Abuses § 7.2.4.2.2 (4th ed. 2009 and Supp.) (more detailed discussion of these multiple limitations).

maximum amount that could be charged for a late fee would be $10.

Limitation on Pyramiding

- The mortgage note simply states that "I will pay this late charge promptly but only once on each payment."
- The state law includes language prohibiting the pyramiding based on a missed payment: "If a late payment charge has been once imposed with respect to a particular late payment, no such charge shall be imposed with respect to any future payment which would have been timely and sufficient but for the previous default."
- The consumer misses a payment in one month, but makes every other monthly payment on a timely basis.
- The servicer has imposed a late fee for every payment made since the first payment was missed, justifying this by asserting that each payment applies to the one due in the previous month, so that each payment is actually late.
- The key to this scenario is the strength of the limitation in state law prohibiting the pyramiding of late fees. In this scenario the language quoted above would permit only one late fee charge.

Claims that result from the overcharge of late fees can include:

- Breach of contract;
- Usury;[155]
- Unfair and deceptive acts and practices;
- Unjust enrichment;
- Breach of good faith and fair dealing; and,
- Breach of fiduciary duty.

6.4.4 Challenging Other Fee Abuses

6.4.4.1 Overview

One of the most difficult problems facing a borrower attempting to sort out a servicer's accounting is the piling on of all the fees that are added to the principal and interest. The analysis for the legality of these fees should be similar to that employed for the imposition of late fees. The fees have to be authorized by both the contract and by the applicable state law. Even when fees are authorized by the contract, they should be limited by reasonableness, the duty of good faith and fair dealing,[156] and the standards of the industry.[157] Some states limit the amount of fees that can be charged pursuant to a default to those specifically authorized.[158]

The propriety of these fees is complicated by the fact that national mortgage servicers commonly outsource default services to third parties. These third parties, also known as "default service providers," offer a variety of products to servicers, such as electronic information technology products, document preparation (e.g., notices of default or assignments), property inspections, broker's price opinions, bankruptcy proofs of claim preparation, etc.). In many cases, the default service providers are divisions, subsidiaries, or affiliates of the servicer.[159]

Previously, servicers performed many of these default-related functions in-house and the costs for such services were considered general operating expenses. With the outsourcing of this work came the practice of charging debtors fees for these services. In some instances the costs of services provided by third-party vendors may be marked-up by the servicer resulting in additional costs to borrowers and additional profits for the servicer. Alternatively, the servicer may receive a kickback from the third-party vendor.[160] Servicers may also benefit by being able to recover out-of-pocket expenses from investors under the terms of applicable pooling and servicing agreements, whereas they are not permitted to do so if the expense is part of the servicer's general overhead and labor costs.[161] As a result, the servicer

155 *See* National Consumer Law Center, The Cost of Credit: Regulation, Preemption, and Industry Abuses § 7.2.4.2 (4th ed. 2009 and Supp.) (discussion of late fees as interest).

156 *See* § 7.8, *infra*.

157 The requirements imposed on servicers by Fannie Mae and Freddie Mac do not provide specific rights for the homeowner (except if the requirements have been incorporated into the note and mortgage or deed of trust as enforceable contract clauses); they are intended to simply establish standards that servicers handling loans owned by these two companies are required to follow. As the majority of mortgage loans existing in the United States are held by one of these two companies, and many of the balance were entered into using the uniform instruments developed by them, their requirements on servicers do establish at least minimum industry standards.

158 *See, e.g.*, W. Va. Code § 46A-2-115:

> (a) Except for reasonable expenses including costs and fees authorized by statute incurred in realizing on a security interest, the agreement with respect to a consumer credit sale or a consumer loan may not provide for charges as a result of default by the consumer other than those authorized by this chapter.

159 *See In re* Stewart, 391 B.R. 327 (Bankr. E.D. La. 2008) (finding that entity which provided broker's price opinions was a corporate division of the servicer and that the true cost incurred by the servicer for broker's price opinions was $50 rather than the $125 charged to the borrower), *aff'd*, 2009 WL 2448054 (E.D. La. Aug. 7, 2009).

160 *E.g.*, Kenty v. Bank One, Columbus, N.A., 1992 WL 170605 (S.D. Ohio Apr. 23, 1992) (where bank charges higher premium on force placed insurance than it actually pays, excess is interest; thus if bank received kick-backs or rebates from premium charged to consumer's account with crediting that account, that constitutes interest), *aff'd in part and rev'd in part*, 92 F.3d 384 (6th Cir. 1995) (though excessive premium may be interest, usury cap not applicable by virtue of state law and most favored lender statute). *See generally* National Consumer Law Center, Unfair and Deceptive Acts and Practices § 10.5.10 (7th ed. 2008 and Supp.).

161 *See* Larry Cordell, Karen Dynan, Andreas Lehnert, Nellie Liang, & Eileen Mauskopf, *The Incentives of Mortgage Servicers:*

has an incentive to order services provided by these entities more than may be necessary and reasonable.[162]

Older cases dealing with excess fees being treated as interest, leading to a usury claim, should be useful in support of a breach of contract theory.[163] As the contract establishes the maximum amount of interest to be charged to the consumer, and the consumer is presumably paying that interest in the regular payments, fees that are not authorized are excess interest, in violation of the contract terms.

As noted in the previous section on late fees, it is improper under the payment application provisions of many notes, most state laws and the FTC Credit Practices Rule for late fees to be deducted from payments prior to interest, principal, and escrow. Assuming other fees charged by the servicer are legal, the same analysis, which prohibits payments from being deemed inadequate because of the failure to include the late fee, should apply equally to the failure to pay other charges that may be imposed by the servicer.[164]

Claims that can be made for overcharging of fees include:

- Breach of contract;
- Breach of the implied covenant of good faith and fair dealing;
- Unjust enrichment;
- Negligent servicing;
- State unfair and deceptive practices (UDAP);
- Fair Debt Collection Practices Act (FDCPA).

The subsections that follow provide more detail on fees frequently charged by servicers that may be subject to challenge.

6.4.4.2 Property Preservation Fees

Most standard mortgage contracts authorize lenders to do and pay for whatever is necessary to protect the value of the property securing the loan and the lender's rights in the property. To the extent lender's actions include payment of money, such funds generally become additional secured debt. Servicers and lenders point to this language to justify a variety of property inspection and preservation fees.

Property inspection fees are charged to borrowers for inspections (usually drive-by) to determine the physical condition or occupancy status of the mortgage property. Inspections are frequently ordered automatically by the servicer's software system once the loan is placed in default status.[165] Inspections can be ordered repeatedly sometimes as often as once a week. While the amount charged for property inspections tends to be relatively small, the repetitive nature of the fee can result in charges to the borrower's account of several hundred dollars.

Drive-by inspections primarily serve to notify the servicer of the occupancy of the property and neither protect the property's value nor affect the lender's rights in the property.[166] Repeated inspections done weekly or monthly when the servicer is in contact with the homeowner, knows the property is occupied, and has no reason to be concerned about the condition of the property, are not "necessary."[167] Courts have found that property inspections are neither reasonable nor necessary and that such inspections without advance notice to the borrower do not comply with the underlying mortgage loan contract.[168] Thus, it is questionable whether such fees may legitimately be charged to the

Myths and Realities 17 (Fed. Reserve Bd. Fin. & Econ. Discussion Series Div. Research & Statistical Affairs Working Paper No. 2008-46).

162 *See* Young v. Wells Fargo & Co., 671 F. Supp. 2d 1006 (S.D. Iowa 2009) (denying motion to dismiss RICO claim where borrowers alleged servicer and default services provider systematically charged unwarranted, improper and unreasonable property inspection and late fees).

163 *See* National Consumer Law Center, The Cost of Credit: Regulation, Preemption, and Industry Abuses Ch. 7 (4th ed. 2009 and Supp.).

164 *See* McAdams v. Citifinancial Mortgage Co., 2007 WL 141128 (M.D. La. Jan. 16, 2007) (payments allowed to be applied only to interest and principal, not to late fees; in summary judgment motion construed contract against the party who prepared it—the lender.).

165 *See* Young v. Wells Fargo & Co., 671 F. Supp. 2d 1006 (S.D. Iowa) (alleging that servicer's computer system ordered drive-by property inspections, that no one at the servicer reviewed inspections and that such inspections were unreasonable).

166 *See, e.g.*, Porter v. Fairbanks Capital Corp., 2003 WL 21210115 (N.D. Ill. May 21, 2003) (plaintiff's sufficiently alleged FDCPA violation claiming that BPO was not "necessary to the protect the value of the Property"); *In re* Zunner, 396 B.R. 265 (Bankr. W.D.N.Y. 2008) (broker's price opinion in preparation of foreclosure was not allowable charge to protect mortgage holders' interest in property). *But see* Walker v. Countrywide Home Loans, Inc., 98 Cal. App. 4th 1158, 121 Cal. Rptr. 2d 79 (2002).

167 *In re* Stewart, 391 B.R. 327 (Bankr. E.D. La. 2008) (finding that automatically generated property inspections conducted on wrong property, and even when conducted on correct property, were never reviewed by servicer); *In re* Jones, 366 B.R. 584 (Bankr. E.D. La. 2007), *aff'd in relevant part, and rev'd in part on other grounds*, 391 B.R. 577 (E.D. La. 2008) (where servicer presented no evidence concerning its policy guidelines on inspections and could not state any reasons why continuous monthly property inspections were necessary, particularly when inspection reports showed little or no change in the property's condition from month to month and gave lender no cause for concern, property inspections were unreasonable). *But see In re* Hight, 393 B.R. 484 (Bankr. S.D. Tex. 2008) (rejecting homeowner's general objection and finding that property inspection proper means of ensuring property is not depreciating).

168 In addition to the "do whatever is necessary" clause, servicers may attempt to rely upon the standard clause in many mortgages and deeds of trust dealing with inspections, which typically states that the lender or its agent "may make reasonable entries upon and inspections of the Property. . . . Lender shall give Borrower notice at the time of or prior to an inspection specifying reasonable cause for the inspection." However, servicers normally do not provide any notice to the homeowner of drive-by or curbside property inspections. *See* Liberty Lending Servs. v. Canada, 668 S.E.2d 3 (Ga. Ct. App. 2008) (affirming class certification; borrower alleged servicer charged for inspec-

borrower. When the servicer cannot, or simply does not, provide information to substantiate the reason, the amount, and the nature of the charges, homeowners can claim that the charges were not actually incurred pursuant to the contract.[169]

Property inspection fees are distinguishable from property protection costs incurred to preserve the value of the property.

Courts have given lenders wide discretion to charge property protection fees, but those fees must be actually incurred[170] and necessary to preserve the value of the property or the lender's rights in the property.[171] Most courts have also held that such fees must be reasonable.[172] Legitimate expenses may include amounts reasonable and necessary to winterize a home, to replace or repair locks, restore utilities, and the like.[173]

6.4.4.3 Broker's Price Opinions

Broker's price opinions (BPOs) are determinations of property value typically based on drive-by exterior examination, public data sources, and recent comparable sales. A servicer may obtain a BPO as an alternative to a full appraisal after a loan is placed in default status. As with property inspections, BPOs are often ordered automatically by the servicer's software system.

Servicers argue that BPOs are necessary to protect the value of the property securing the loan and the lender's rights in the property. This assertion, however, has been

---

tions but failed to provide notice as required by the security instrument).

Additionally, this clause should not be construed to cover inspections where there is no actual entry on the property. *See* Ladd v. Equicredit Corp. of Am., 2001 WL 1033618 (E.D. La. Sept. 7, 2001) (property inspection provision does not apply to drive-by inspections).

169 Scott v. Fairbanks Capital Corp., 284 F. Supp. 2d 880 (S.D. Ohio 2003) (when homeowners alleged they were unable to obtain substantiation of charges, court construed claim as challenge to whether the charges were actually incurred or were permitted by contract); *In re* Sacko, 394 B.R. 90 (Bankr. E.D. Pa. 2008) (disallowing fees for property inspection when servicer did not present evidence regarding the nature of charges or why it was necessary to incur these expenses).

170 Scott v. Fairbanks Capital Corp., 284 F. Supp. 2d 880 (S.D. Ohio 2003) (costs for protecting mortgaged property may not be charged unless they were actually incurred for the purposes stated in security instrument). *See, e.g., In re* Stewart, 391 B.R. 327 (Bankr. E.D. La. 2008) (disallowing charges for broker's price opinions and finding it unlikely several were in fact performed given that the property was under an evacuation order due to Hurricane Katrina); *In re* Parrish, 326 B.R. 708 (Bankr. N.D. Ohio July 6, 2005) (stating that lender has obligation to keep a full and accurate accounting of payments made and charges accrued and should be able to document charges such as inspection fees).

171 *See, e.g.,* Scott v. Fairbanks Capital Corp., 284 F. Supp. 2d 880, 890 (S.D. Ohio 2003); Porter v. Fairbanks Capital Corp., 2003 WL 21210115 (N.D. Ill. May 21, 2003) (complaint sufficiently alleged claim under FDCPA that charges for property preservation services and broker's price opinions were not permitted under mortgage clause covering costs to protect value of property); Chatman v. Fairbanks Capital Corp., 2002 WL 1338492 (N.D. Ill. June 13, 2002); *In re* Zunner, 396 B.R. 265 (Bankr. W.D.N.Y. 2008) (broker's price opinion in preparation of foreclosure was not allowable charge to protect mortgage holders' interest in property); *In re* Liberty Constr. & Dev. Corp., 106 B.R. 458, 460 (Bankr. E.D. Va. 1989).

172 *See, e.g., In re* Jones, 366 B.R. 584 (Bankr. E.D. La. 2007), *aff'd in relevant part, and rev'd in part on other grounds*, 391 B.R. 577 (E.D. La. 2008) (servicer failed to show that property inspections were necessary and reasonable).

Incredibly however, one court has stated that such fees need not be reasonable, economical, or fair to the borrower. *See* Majchrowski v. Norwest Mortgage, Inc., 6 F. Supp. 2d 946, 950 (N.D. Ill. 1998).

The settlement between the Federal Trade Commission and Fairbanks Capital Corporation strongly supports the view that property preservation fees must be actual, necessary, and reasonable. Specifically, the settlement enjoins Fairbanks from assessing or collecting:

> B. Fees for property inspections, provided that Defendants may impose reasonable fees for property inspections actually performed if: 1) the customer's loan payment has not been received within forty-five (45) calendar days of the due date; and 2) the inspections are limited to the initial inspections and to additional inspections during the period of delinquency not more frequent than every thirty (30) calendar days and only if the Defendants (a) have been unable to contact the consumer for the previous thirty (30) calendar days or (b) have been able to contact the consumer but have determined that the mortgaged property is vacant;
>
> C. Fees for broker's price opinions, provided that Defendants may impose reasonable fee for a broker's price opinion ordered and actually performed if: (1) the consumer's loan payment has not been received within sixty-three (63) calendar days of the due date; and (2) the broker's price opinions are limited to the initial's broker's price opinion and additional broker's price opinions during the period of continued delinquency not more frequent than every six (6) months . . .

See Stipulated Final Judgment and Order As to Fairbanks Capital Corp. entered in United States of Am. v. Fairbanks Capital Corp., Fairbanks Capital Holding Corp., and Thomas D. Basmajian, File No. 032 3014 (D. Mass. 2003), *available at* www.ftc.gov/os/2003/11/0323014order.pdf.

173 These types of services are most commonly required for properties that have been abandoned. Servicers will often argue that inspections are necessary to determine if the property is vacant. To the contrary, a telephone call to the borrower will frequently establish that the property is occupied thereby negating the need for the inspection. For example, HUD regulations governing FHA-insured mortgages state that inspections are permitted only when (1) the mortgage is in default (payment is not received within forty-five days of the due date) and efforts to reach the borrower by telephone during that forty-five-day period have been unsuccessful, or (2) the property is vacant or abandoned. *See* 24 C.F.R. § 203.377.

rejected by a number of courts.[174] For example, in *In re Zunner*, the court found the BPO "really does nothing to protect value."[175] Further, the *Zunner* court reasoned that a post-closing valuation was meaningless for purposes of limiting the lender's risk and did nothing to protect the lender's rights under the contract.

6.4.4.4 Foreclosure Fees and Costs

Foreclosure fees and costs is a broad category of charges that may include attorney fees and other costs associated with collection or foreclosure. Attorney fees are discussed in more detail at § 6.4.4.6, *infra*. Foreclosure costs other than attorney fees may include costs for auction advertisements, sheriff's costs, filing fees, service of process, certified mail, etc. Foreclosure costs may vary depending on whether a state is a judicial or non-judicial foreclosure state and on state law itself. Generally, foreclosure costs must be reasonable and actually incurred before they are recoverable against the borrower.[176]

Within the category of foreclosure costs, failure to credit the borrower with refunds from a cancelled sheriff's sale is an area ripe for abuse. In some jurisdictions, the sheriff's department will require an advance deposit from the servicer before initiating a foreclosure sale. The servicer charges the deposit as a foreclosure cost against the borrower's account. If the sale is cancelled, the sheriff returns the portion of the deposit that represents unexpended funds. However, servicers frequently do not credit the refund back to the borrower's account.[177]

6.4.4.5 Corporate Advances

Corporate advance is a catch-all category for servicing-related expenses (not escrow expenses) paid with servicer funds rather than escrow funds, to be recovered from borrower. Corporate advances may include foreclosure expenses, attorney fees, bankruptcy fees, force placed insurance, and so forth. Borrowers should seek an itemization of corporate advance amounts so that a determination can be made as to whether each charge is appropriate.

174 Porter v. Fairbanks Capital Corp., 2003 WL 21210115 (N.D. Ill. May 21, 2003) (complaint sufficiently alleged claim under FDCPA that charges for property preservation services and broker's price opinions were not permitted under mortgage clause covering costs to protect value of property); *In re* Wasson, 402 B.R. 561 (Bankr. W.D.N.Y. 2009); *In re* Zunner, 396 B.R. 265 (Bankr. W.D.N.Y. 2008).

175 396 B.R. 265, 266 (Bankr. W.D.N.Y. 2009).

176 *See* Korea First Bank v. Lee, 14 F. Supp. 2d 530 (S.D.N.Y. 1998) (lender not entitled to recover more than it paid its attorney or more than what was reasonable); *In re* Riser, 289 B.R. 201 (Bankr. M.D. Fla. 2003).

177 *In re* Hannon, 421 B.R. 728 (Bankr. M.D. Pa. 2009) (servicer failed to adjust proof of claim in bankruptcy to reflect refund of sheriff's deposit).

6.4.4.6 Attorney Fees

Most standard mortgage contracts require that the borrower pay the lender's attorney fees in any action to enforce or collect sums due under the note. Generally, however, these fees must be reasonable, and must be actually incurred by the lender.[178] In some cases, the lender will charge a flat fee for attorney fees as soon as a case is referred to an attorney for foreclosure, even if the foreclosure is not completed or even commenced.[179] In other cases, foreclosure firms will bill for projected costs before incurring them. When borrowers seek to bring their accounts current, the arrearage amount often includes an unaccrued portion of attorney fees.

In general, foreclosure fees and costs are highly inflated. The lender has little incentive to minimize them because they can be passed on to the borrower. Many foreclosure attorneys and law firms use in-house paralegals or outsourced default service providers (which may be affiliated with the law firm) to generate form documents that may take as little as fifteen minutes of time on a computer. In some cases, the borrower may be charged a fee for this work even though it may not involve the provision of legal services.[180] The borrower may contest such a fee as unreasonable or not

178 *See* Korea First Bank v. Lee, 14 F. Supp. 2d 530 (S.D.N.Y. 1998) (lender was not entitled to recover more than it paid its attorney or what was reasonable); *In re* Watson, 384 B.R. 697 (Bankr. D. Del. 2008) (rejecting lender's argument that fees did not have to be reasonable); *In re* Riser, 289 B.R. 201 (Bankr. M.D. Fla. 2003) (attorney fee assessment to debtors' mortgage account when no lender attorney ever appeared in case was "both illegal and fraudulent"). *See also In re* Coates, 292 B.R. 894 (Bankr. C.D. Ill. 2003) (creditor required to disclose agreement between itself and law firm so that court can determine exactly how much creditor is actually being charged for services); *In re* 1095 Commonwealth Ave. Corp., 204 B.R. 284 (Bankr. D. Mass. 1997) (secured creditor fraudulently overstated its claim for legal fees by failing to disclose two-tiered fee arrangement with its attorneys in which attorneys granted bank a discount but bank billed debtors at full standard rate), *aff'd in relevant part, modified in part on other grounds*, 236 B.R. 530 (D. Mass. 1999).

179 *In re* McMullen, 273 B.R. 558 (Bankr. C.D. Ill. 2001) (flat fee covering attorney fees for entire foreclosure proceeding found excessive where not pro-rated to cover only services actually performed prior to bankruptcy filing). *See also In re* Hight, 393 B.R. 484 (Bankr. S.D. Tex. 2008) (disallowing creditor's pre-petition attorney fees for preparation of foreclosure sale when creditor failed to provide evidence pertaining to what work was done, who did the work, hourly rate, and time spent).

180 *E.g., In re* Crowder, Case No. 06-36030-H4-13 (Bankr. S.D. Texas filed June 8, 2009) (Declaration of Stephanie Jeffries, Exhibit A to Moss Codilis' Response to Order to Show Cause) (declaration stating that law firm affiliate provides several "non-legal functions" for servicers, including preparing foreclosure notices, bankruptcy proofs of claims and reviewing bankruptcy plans, and that it "did not provide legal services" to the servicer in the case and did not have an "attorney-client relationship with the servicer.").

authorized by the underlying loan documents.[181] When the attorney has been paid a retainer, but a cure takes place before the foreclosure is completed, the unexpended fees should be returned by the attorney and credited to the account. If not, the fees passed on are not bona fide and can be challenged on that basis. A refusal to credit an account for unexpended attorney fees can also be challenged under many state unfair trade practice statutes.[182] Some states specifically limit attorney fees in the event of foreclosure.[183]

6.4.4.7 Wrongful Foreclosure

Wrongful foreclosure is a tort generally available at common law.[184] While initially the claim was meant to address improprieties in the sale itself or the notice, in recent years it has been used to deal with servicer improprieties that lead to foreclosure. For example, in the case of *Hauf v. HomEq Servicing Corp.*,[185] the court denied the servicer's motion to dismiss after the homeowner tried for years to send in their payments after a successful completion of a forbearance agreement. The homeowner's efforts included numerous attempts by their attorney to prove to the servicer that there was no default, despite which the servicer initiated a foreclosure proceeding. The sheer size of the servicer's operations[186] appeared to be proffered as the excuse. The defendant's vice president "guessed . . . that HomeEq continued with the foreclosure, despite the Haufs' communications, because 'either the correspondence did not get to the right location in our organization for it to be addressed, or if it did, it wasn't sufficiently addressed.' "[187] The court allowed the case to proceed on both tort and contract claims, including wrongful foreclosure, breach of contract, punitive damages, and emotional distress damages resulting from an intentional tort.

In some states, borrowers may need to allege that they were not in default on the mortgage loan in order to maintain a claim for wrongful foreclosure.[188]

6.4.5 *Servicer's Failure to Engage in Appropriate Loss Mitigation As a Foreclosure Defense*

6.4.5.1 Introduction

Most everyone loses when a home is sold through a foreclosure—the homeowner,[189] the family,[190] the lender,[191] the investor,[192] and the community.[193] As a result, numerous private and government sponsored programs encourage and require servicers to affirmatively consider loan modifications before foreclosures may be completed.[194]

This subsection discusses the obligations of servicers to affirmatively consider loss mitigation options before foreclosure, and the extent to which the servicer's refusal to consider those options can be a defense to foreclosure. It also discusses, at § 6.4.5.3, *infra*, servicers' obligations to honor loan modifications and forbearance agreements entered into by previous servicers.

181 National Consumer Law Center, Fair Debt Collection § 15.2 (5th ed. 2004 and Supp.).

182 *See* § 7.2, *supra*.

183 *See, e.g.*, Mont. Code Ann. § 71-1-320 (limiting trustees' fees and attorney fees in non-judicial foreclosure to 5% of obligation).

184 *See also* § 14.5, *infra*.

185 2007 WL 486699 (M.D. Ga. Feb. 9, 2007).

186 Other courts have been similarly unimpressed with the excuse of "too big to do it right." *See* Nosek v. Ameriquest Mortgage Co., 2007 WL 682581 (Bankr. D. Mass. Mar. 6, 2007) (rejecting Ameriquest's excuse for not tracking bankruptcy payments correctly).

After a summary affirmance by the district court, the First Circuit Court of Appeals vacated the judgment and remanded with direction to dismiss the debtor's adversary proceeding. The First Circuit held that the creditor failed to establish a violation of either a specific Bankruptcy Code section or her confirmed plan necessary to invoke the Bankruptcy Court's authority under § 105 to award relief. *In re* Nosek, 544 F.3d 34 (1st Cir. 2008).

187 2007 WL 486699, at *7 (M.D. Ga. Feb. 9, 2007).

188 *See* Larson v. Homecomings Fin., L.L.C., 2009 WL 5538536 (D. Nev. 2009).

189 Ellen Schloemer, Wei Li, Keith Ernst, and Kathleen Keest, Center for Responsible Lending, Losing Ground: Foreclosures in the Subprime Market and Their Cost to Homeowners 2 (Dec. 2006) ("As this year ends, 2.2 million households in the subprime market either have lost their homes to foreclosure or hold subprime mortgages that will fail over the next several years. These foreclosures will cost homeowners as much as $164 billion, primarily in lost home equity.").

190 The loss of the family home can have a devastating emotional impact on children. The change itself is damaging, the forced move is traumatic, and the change in schools can precipitate academic difficulties.

191 Pooling and servicing agreements, which detail the arrangements between the parties to the securitization process, generally require the original lender to repurchase defaulted loans from the trusts under certain conditions. Because many originators are thinly capitalized, these repurchase requirements can cause the originator to become insolvent.

192 Investor loss severity can vary dramatically depending on economic conditions. Losses may be limited in appreciating real estate markets because property can be sold in foreclosure for more than what is owed on the mortgage loan. By contrast, depreciating real estate markets can dramatically increase the loss severity on foreclosed loans.

193 The neighborhood effects of foreclosure include lower home values, decreased property taxes, and increased vandalism and crime. *See, e.g.*, Dan Immergluck & Geoff Smith, *The External Costs of Foreclosures: The Impact of Single-Family, Mortgage Foreclosures on Property Values*, Housing Policy Debate vol. 17, issue 1 (2006).

194 *See* Ch. 2, *supra* (full discussion of different loss mitigation and loan modification programs).

Currently, homeowners who are behind on their mortgage may be offered the opportunity to modify the terms of their first mortgage under the Home Affordable Modification Program (HAMP) developed by the United States Department of the Treasury and implemented on March 4, 2009. Under specified conditions, homeowners are to be offered a modification that lowers their monthly mortgage payment to a targeted 31% of their monthly gross income. The terms of this program are described in detail at § 2.8, *supra*.

While servicer participation in HAMP is technically voluntary, most servicers participate. All financial institutions receiving assistance under the Financial Stability Plan are required to implement the program.[195] The federal government offers incentives to servicers, lenders, and borrowers for loan modifications made under the auspices of the program. Participating servicers must *review the eligibility of any borrower who asks to be considered for the program.*

Fannie Mae, Freddie Mac, the FHA, and the VA have similar loss mitigation programs. Other options, such as short sales, deeds in lieu, forbearance, etc., may also be available to the borrower through government-sponsored or privately created programs. For a thorough description of the different loss mitigation programs, see Chapters 2 and 3, *supra*. NCLC's website has ongoing descriptions of the various loan modification programs currently available.[196]

6.4.5.2 Net Present Value As the Critical Test in Loan Modification Programs

The driving force behind the current loan modification programs is the net present value (NPV) analysis. Under HAMP a modification must be made when the net present value test is passed.[197] Leading investor representatives have also stated that servicers should perform loan modifications when a proposed loan modification "passes" an NPV test.[198]

Net present value calculations compare, from the perspective of the investor, the value of a loan modification as compared to a foreclosure. These are "net" calculations because the value of a foreclosure is subtracted from the value of the loan modification and "present value" because the value of the loan modification and the value of the foreclosure are both stated in present dollars. The present value calculation discounts the future cash stream of the loan modification or the future payoff from a foreclosure by a standard interest rate (sometimes called the "discount rate"), applied over the projected length of time the foreclosure will take or the loan modification will last. The modification is also discounted for the probability that it will not perform—that the borrower will "redefault."

Thus the *NPV analysis evaluates whether the investor will do better financially from a loan modification than a foreclosure.* Assuming the answer is yes, there is little justification for a foreclosure to proceed when *both* the investor and the homeowner will be better off from a loan modification. If a servicer fails to evaluate a homeowner's eligibility for a loan modification prior to initiating foreclosure proceedings, the homeowner should be able to assert an equitable defense to foreclosure.

6.4.5.3 Equitable Nature of Foreclosure Requires Prior Loss Mitigation

Foreclosure is an equitable remedy. Despite the mortgage industry's general attitude that foreclosure remedies exist exclusively to provide relief to the lender, the majority rule is that default does not automatically entitle the mortgage holder to foreclosure on the property.[199] A court sitting in equity is obligated to evaluate its various options and seek a fair and reasonable result under the circumstances.[200] The

195 A list of participating servicers and executed participation agreements are available through the HAMP administrative website at www.hmpadmin.com.

196 Go to www.consumerlaw.org and click on "Lenders in Financial Distress" and then "Loan Modification Programs."

197 *See* § 2.8.2.2, *supra*.

198 *See* American Securitization Forum, Statement of Principles, Recommendations and Guidelines for the Modification of Securitized Subprime Residential Mortgage Loans (June 2007), *available at* www.americansecuritization.com/uploadedFiles/ASF%20Subprime%20Loan%20Modification%20Principles_060107.pdf.

199 *See, e.g.*, Woods v. Monticello Dev. Co., 656 P.2d 1324 (Colo. Ct. App. 1982) ("Equitable remedies are not automatic—the term itself implies a balancing."); M & T Mortgage Corp. v. Foy, 858 N.Y.S.2d 567 (N.Y. Sup. Ct. 2008) ("The courts are not merely automatons mindlessly processing paper motions in mortgage foreclosure actions most of which proceed on default."); Sovereign Bank, F.S.B. v. Kuelzow, 687 A.2d 1039 (N.J. Super. Ct. App. Div. 1997) ("Foreclosure is a discretionary remedy."); Rosselot v. Heimbrock, 561 N.E.2d 555 (Ohio Ct. App. 1988) ("simply because appellant defaulted on the terms of his obligation to appellees does not automatically entitle them to foreclose because foreclosure of a mortgagor's equity of redemption is a separate question from the existence of a default on the underlying obligation"). *See also* 30A C.J.S. *Equity* § 69 (2007) ("The granting of relief against forfeiture is generally discretionary, the controlling principle being that it will be granted where, and only where, it is equitable under the circumstances.").

200 *See, e.g.*, Bisno v. Sax, 346 P.2d 814 (Cal. Ct. App. 1959) (foreclosure sale precluded upon acceptance of delinquent payments; "California recognizes that: 'Equity does not wait upon precedent which exactly squares with the facts in controversy, but will assert itself in those situations where right and justice would be defeated but for its intervention.' ") (citation omitted); New Alliance Bank v. Win Holdings Int'l, Inc., 2008 WL 732036 (Conn. Super. Ct. Feb. 27, 2008) (finding that equity precluded lender from foreclosing on mortgages based on alleged default for failure to pay real estate taxes; " 'An action of foreclosure is peculiarly equitable and the court may entertain all questions which are necessary to be determined in order that complete justice may be done between the parties.' ") (citation omitted); Rosselot v. Hembrock, 561 N.E.2d 555 (Ohio Ct.

rules of equity apply whether the foreclosure is initiated in a judicial foreclosure state or in a non-judicial foreclosure state.[201]

In addition, the party seeking to obtain the benefits of an equitable remedy must have clean hands.[202] A number of courts have relied upon the equitable considerations of "unclean hands" to prevent foreclosure, despite a lender's legal right to foreclose.[203] As one court articulated the point:

> It is a fundamental principle of equity jurisprudence that for a complainant to show that he is entitled to the benefit of equity he must establish that he comes into court with clean hands. . . . The clean hands doctrine is applied not for the protection of the parties but for the protection of the court. . . . It is applied not by way of punishment but on considerations that make for the advancement of right and justice.[204]

Courts have often recognized the harshness of forfeiture in real estate contracts and leases and have, under the maxim "equity abhors a forfeiture," refused in equity to uphold strict forfeiture provisions in contracts.[205] The maxim, equity abhors a forfeiture, is a longstanding principle of common law and has been recognized to apply to foreclosures in various jurisdictions:

> The court also relies upon the general equitable principles which apply to the remedy of foreclosure. Foreclosure is a harsh remedy and equity abhors a forfeiture. A court of equity may invoke its inherent equitable powers to avoid a forfeiture and deny the remedy of foreclosure.[206]

A court may be particularly attentive to this issue when the forfeiture seems disproportionate or oppressive and unconscionable under the circumstances.[207]

App. 1998) ("once a court has determined that a default on a mortgage has occurred, it must then consider the equities of the situation in order to decide whether foreclosure is appropriate.").

201 *See, e.g.*, Lo v. Jensen, 106 Cal. Rptr. 2d 443 (Cal. Ct. App. 2001) ("The law has long provided that if a non-judicial foreclosure sale has been unfairly or unlawfully conducted, or is tainted by fraud, the trial court has the power to set it aside"); Gilroy v. Ryberg, 667 N.W.2d 544 (Neb. 2003) ("Although the Act [authorizing non-judicial foreclosure] does not provide a remedy for a defective trustee's sale, the trustor can sue in equity to set the sale aside."). *See also* Molly F. Jacobson-Greany, *Setting Aside Nonjudicial Foreclosure Sales: Extending the Rule to Cover Both Intrinsic and Extrinsic Fraud or Unfairness,* 23 Emory Bankr. Dev. J. 139 (2006) (and cases cited therein) ("Actions to set aside a non-judicial foreclosure sale are equitable in nature. The overwhelming majority of states that permit non-judicial foreclosure adhere to some version of the same general rule regarding set asides. The general rule is that the court has the equitable power to set aside a non-judicial foreclosure sale if (1) the property was purchased for an inadequate price at auction; and (2) the debtor can show irregularity, unfairness or fraud in connection with the sale.").

202 *See* IndyMac Bank, F.S.B. v. Yano-Horoski, 890 N.Y.S.2d 313 (N.Y. Sup. Ct. 2009) (holding servicer's action in refusing to consider reasonable loss mitigation alternatives were unconscionable and demonstrated unclean hands). *See also* Wells Fargo Home Mortgage, Inc. v. Neal, 922 A.2d 538, 552 (Md. 2007) ("[T]he venerated equity doctrine of clean hands . . . requires that 'he who comes into equity must come with clean hands,' is applicable in foreclosure proceedings such as one implicated in the present case.") (citations omitted).

203 LaSalle v. Bank Nat'l Ass'n v. Bardales, 2009 WL 1312509 (Conn. Super. Ct. Apr. 14, 2009) (denying motion to strike special defense of unclean hands on several grounds); New Alliance Bank v. Win Holdings Int'l, Inc., 2008 WL 732036 (Conn. Super. Ct. Feb. 27, 2008) (doctrine of clean hands requires that plaintiff seeking equitable relief must show that conduct has been fair, equitable and honest as to the particular controversy at issue; here, court concluded that equitable considerations barred foreclosure where it appeared plaintiff, wanting to use foreclosure to extricate itself from a loan with "stormy history," forced the default and thus did not have clean hands); Monetary Funding Group, Inc. v. Pluchino, 867 A.2d 841 (Conn. App. Ct. 2005); Marin v. Seven of Five Ltd., 921 So. 2d (Fla. Dist. Ct. App. 2006); Prudential Ins. Co. of Am. v. Jackson, 637 A.2d 573 (N.J. Super. Ct. App. Div. 1994) (reversing judgment of foreclosure in case presenting issue of fact as to whether mortgage holder complied with Veterans' Administration recommendations in foreclosing on VA-insured mortgage; requiring a plenary hearing to balance conduct of mortgage holder who acted with unclean hands in disregarding VA's recommendations with action of defaulting mortgagor seeking to avoid foreclosure); M & T Mortgage Corp. v. Foy, 858 N.Y.S.2d 567 (N.Y. Sup. Ct. 2008) (high interest rate on thirty-year mortgage granted to minority buyer in minority area created rebuttable presumption of discriminatory practice, which would constitute unclean hands and preclude equitable relief of foreclosure).

204 *See, e.g.*, Thompson v. Orcutt, 777 A.2d 670, 676 (Conn. 2001) (citations omitted).

205 *See, e.g.*, Warner v. Haught, Inc., 329 S.E.2d 88, 95–96 (W. Va. 1985) (principle applies to oil and gas lease payments to a landowner); Bailey v. Savage, 236 S.E.2d 203 (W. Va. 1977) (harshness of forfeiture in the context of land installment contracts is recognized, forfeiture prevented when the borrower who had not made payments for three months tendered the amount due and acceptance was refused).

206 Sovereign Bank, F.S.B. v. Kuelzow, 687 A.2d 1039, 1044 (N.J. Super. Ct. App. Div. 1997) (citations and quotations omitted). *Accord* Honeyman v. Jacobs, 306 U.S. 539, 543–544 (1939); Richmond Mortgage Corp. v. Wachovia Bank, 300 U.S. 124, 129–130 (1937); Home Bldg. & Loan Ass'n v. Blaisdell, 290 U.S. 398, 446–447 (1934); *In re* 2435 Plainfield Ave., Inc., 223 B.R. 440, 451 (Bankr. D.N.J. 1998); Yates v. Halford, 73 P.3d 1236, 1241 (Alaska 2003); Bright v. Gass, 831 S.W.2d 149, 153 (Ark. Ct. App. 1992); Scarberry v. Bill Patch Land & Water Co., 7 Cal. Rptr. 408, 418 (Cal. Ct. App. 1960); Rivers v. Amara, 40 So. 2d 364 (Fla. 1949); Fleet Mortgage Corp. v. Deale, 678 N.E.2d 35, 37 (Ill. App. Ct. 1997); Quigley v. Acker, 955 P.2d 1377, 1384–1385 (Minn. 1998); Albertson v. Leca, 447 A.2d 383, 389 (R.I. 1982); Madison Tire Co. v. Weaver, 1986 WL 12493 (Tenn. Ct. App. 1986). *See generally* Gelfert v. National City Bank of New York, 313 U.S. 221, 232–233 (1941) (upholding constitutionality of New York anti-deficiency statute and noting that such remedial legislation builds upon well established judicial traditions of regulating foreclosures to prevent inequitable results).

207 Vonk v. Dunn, 775 P.2d 1088 (Ariz. 1989) (genuine issue of

6.4.5.4 Loss Mitigation for FHA Loans As a Prerequisite to Foreclosure

The FHA has long had extensive rules requiring servicers to engage in loss mitigation before foreclosing on property, as detailed at § 3.2.1, *supra*. The prime objective of the National Housing Act is to preserve homeownership and avoid the devastating financial consequences of foreclosure.[208] Although homeowners do not have a private right of action against the servicer for failing to follow the FHA loss mitigation guidelines,[209] many courts have held that the servicer's failure to follow these guidelines provides a defense to the foreclosure.[210]

In *Wells Fargo v. Neal*,[211] the Maryland Supreme Court held that a servicer's failure to follow FHA-required loss mitigation guidelines means that the homeowner cannot be considered in default:

> A mortgagor seeking to raise a violation of the HUD loss mitigation regulations as a defense to foreclosure . . . is not required to pay his or her debt in full in order to be granted an injunction [to stop a non-judicial foreclosure]. This is because, under the principles of equity, a mortgage holder's commencement of a foreclosure proceeding on an FHA-insured mortgage, without first having adhered to the mandatory HUD loss mitigation regulations, may invalidate the mortgage holder's declaration of default.[212]

6.4.5.5 HAMP Review As a Prerequisite to Foreclosure

The Department of Treasury's HAMP guidelines—explicitly adopted by Congress in the Helping Families Save Their Home Act[213]—are directly analogous to the FHA rules requiring servicers to engage in loss mitigation. In keeping

---

material fact as to whether foreclosure due to $66 tax arrearage was oppressive or unconscionable; "Because foreclosure is an equitable proceeding, the plaintiff must do more than merely establish that the defendant has violated the strict terms of the mortgage or the note. The plaintiff must additionally show that some purpose of the [acceleration clause] is . . . being circumvented or that the mortgage holder's security is jeopardized"); Arizona Coffee Shop, Inc. v. Phoenix Downtown Parking Ass'n, 387 P.2d 801 (Ariz. 1963); Baypoint Mortgage Corp. v. Crest Premium Real Estate etc. Trust, 214 Cal. Rptr. 53 (Cal. Ct. App. 1985) (affirming order issuing preliminary injunction and refusing to allow foreclosure to go forward where debtor failed to pay on the first of the month; "One of the most important functions of the law is to maintain a proper balance between creditor and debtor. To this end, it attempts to match the creditor's remedy to the debtor's default. Major defaults justify drastic remedies, minor defaults only warrant lesser remedies."); Petterson v. Weinstock, 138 A. 433 (Conn. 1927) (foreclosure denied where it was unconscionable and would render hardship upon mortgagor but where mortgage holder's security was not impaired); Caspert v. Anderon Apartments, 94 N.Y.S.2d 521 (N.Y. Sup. Ct. 1949) (action to foreclose denied; where there was no damage to mortgage holder but irreparable damage to mortgagor, the disproportionate inequity was deemed unconscionable and oppressive). *See also* 30A C.J.S. *Equity* § 69 (2007) ("The granting of relief against forfeiture is generally discretionary, the controlling principle being that it will be granted where, and only where, it is equitable under the circumstances.").

208 *See* Topa Equities, Ltd. v. City of Los Angeles, 342 F.3d 1065, 1072 (9th Cir. 2003) (quoting 12 U.S.C. § 1701t (1994)); Pozzie v. U.S. Dep't of Hous. & Urban Dev., 48 F.3d 1026, 1028 (7th Cir. 1995) (same); Conille v. Sec'y of Hous. & Urban Dev., 840 F.2d 105, 116 (1st Cir. 1988) (same); Wells Fargo Home Mortgage, Inc. v. Neal, 922 A.2d 538 (Md. 2007); Fleet Real Estate Funding Corp. v. Smith, 530 A.2d 919, 923–924 (Pa. Super. Ct. 1987); U.S. Dep't of Hous. & Urban Dev., Loss Mitigation Program—Comprehensive Clarification of Policy and Notice of Procedural Changes, Mortgagee Letter 00-05, at 1 (Jan. 19, 2000).

209 Wells Fargo Home Mortgage, Inc. v. Neal, 922 A.2d 538 (Md. 2007).

210 *Id. See also* Countrywide Home Loans, Inc. v. Wilkerson, 2004 WL 539983 (N.D. Ill. Mar. 12, 2004) ("It is undisputed here that under Illinois law that failure to comply with HUD's mortgage services requirements is a complete defense to a mortgage foreclosure action."); Williams v. Nat'l Sch. of Health Tech., Inc., 836 F. Supp. 273, 283 (E.D. Pa. 1993) ("Pennsylvania courts have recognized a mortgage holder's failure to comply with HUD forbearance regulations as an equitable defense to foreclosure"), *aff'd,* 37 F.3d 1491 (3d Cir. 1994); Fed. Nat'l Mortgage Ass'n v. Moore, 609 F. Supp. 194, 196 (N.D. Ill. 1985) ("In Illinois, a mortgage holder's failure to comply with the mortgage servicing regulations can be raised in a foreclosure proceeding as an affirmative defense."); Ghervescu v. Wells Fargo Home Mortgage, 2008 WL 660248 (Cal. Ct. App. Mar. 13, 2008) (unpublished) (holding that borrower may assert lender's failure to apply FHA mandatory loss mitigation procedures defensively, either to preclude or to set aside a foreclosure sale); ABN AMRO Mortgage Group, Inc., 770 N.W.2d 851 (Iowa Ct. App. Apr. 22, 2009) (table) (stating that borrower may assert failure to comply with contractually incorporated HUD regulations defensively, but concluding that because lender complied with regulations in this matter foreclosure could go forward); Fed. Land Bank of St. Paul v. Overboe, 404 N.W.2d 445, 449 (N.D. 1987) (stating that "various courts have held that the failure of a lender to follow HUD regulations governing mortgage servicing constitutes a valid defense sufficient to deny the lender the relief it seeks in a foreclosure action" and cataloguing cases).

211 Wells Fargo Home Mortgage, Inc. v. Neal, 922 A.2d 538 (Md. 2007).

212 *Id.* at 551. *See also* LaSalle Nat'l Bank v. Johnson, 2006 WL 551563 (N.J. Super. Ct. Ch. Div. Mar. 3, 2006) (unpublished) (lender failed to provide borrower with face-to-face interview and review loss mitigation evaluation prior to initiating foreclosure; motion for summary judgment denied); Washington Mut. Bank v. Mahaffrey, 154 Ohio App. 3d 44, 796 N.E.2d 39 (2003) (foreclosing lender denied summary judgment due to failure to arrange face-to-face interview with borrower required by HUD regulations). *But see* Washington Mut. Bank v. Teodorescu, 2005 WL 3108231 (N.J. Super. Ct. App. Div. Nov. 22, 2005) (no equitable relief where *pro se* borrower failed to show how lender's failure to follow HUD guidelines was unconscionable).

213 Pub. L. No. 111-22, § 129, 123 Stat. 1632 (2009).

with the National Housing Act's stated purpose, HAMP's primary objective is to keep Americans in their homes by preventing avoidable foreclosures.[214] Participating servicers must sign a contract with the Treasury Department's financial agent agreeing to review every potentially eligible borrower who asks to be considered for the program.[215] Thus HAMP creates a contractual obligation on the part of servicers to review the loans of all eligible homeowners according to the guidelines set forth by the Department of the Treasury.[216]

The newly created HAMP contractual obligation to consider borrowers for loan modification is markedly similar to the established FHA's HUD regulations requiring loss mitigation analysis prior to initiating foreclosure proceedings. Thus HAMP can be interpreted analogously to require a loan modification analysis prior to foreclosure. The well-established principles of equity articulated in the court's analysis in *Neal* apply equally to the HAMP modification scenario.

The court of equity's requirement for fairness and reasonableness are not met if servicers forego HAMP's guidelines and required analysis.[217] Similarly, any servicer not complying with the HAMP guidelines should be adjudged to have "unclean hands" that preclude foreclosure.

It is a widely acceptable truism in the post-meltdown mortgage industry that "[w]hen properly done, modifications can benefit both homeowners and . . . investors."[218] In practical terms, a loan modification NPV analysis simply evaluates whether the investor will benefit to a greater extent with a loan modification than from a foreclosure. HAMP loan modifications have the clear potential to obviate the need for a forfeiture and lead to more balanced results for both the investor and the homeowner. Under the maxim equity abhors a forfeiture, courts should also accept a servicer's failure to properly evaluate the homeowner for a loan modification as a valid defense to foreclosure.

HAMP program guidelines establish that a servicer may not refer a loan to foreclosure or conduct a scheduled foreclosure sale until either (a) the borrower is evaluated for HAMP and determined to be ineligible, or (b) reasonable attempts to solicit the borrower have been unsuccessful.[219] In a change from prior HAMP guidance, all foreclosure activity must cease once a borrower is in a trial period plan, even if the loan had previously been referred to foreclosure.[220] The servicer must make all reasonable efforts to take actions within its authority to halt further activity in the foreclosure process, whether judicial or non-judicial, once the borrower enters into a trial period plan based on verified income. In other words, servicers are no longer permitted to accept trial plan payments and simultaneously go forward with foreclosure proceedings on a separate track.

6.4.5.6 HAMP Creates an Industry Standard Requiring Loan Modification Analysis Prior to Foreclosure

Industry standards generally provide the guiding principles for a determination of whether or not a particular industry practice is valid, even when a law has not specifically delineated the practice.[221] The failure of a servicer to comply with an industry standard set forth in federal law should establish a defense to foreclosure where that servicer has failed to properly engage in the loan modification analysis prior to initiating foreclosure proceedings.

Congress has specifically articulated that the loan modification analysis required by the HAMP program is *the*

214 *See* Dep't of the Treasury, Supplemental Directive 09-01 (Apr. 6, 2009), *available at* www.hmpadmin.com/portal/index.html.

215 For details on HAMP eligible borrowers, see § 2.8.2, *supra*.

216 Deutsche Bank Nat'l Trust v. Hass, 2009-2627-AV (Mich. Cir. Ct., Macomb Cty. Sept. 30, 2009) (reversing district court's granting of possession where material fact remained as to whether servicer was obligated to consider borrower for HAMP before foreclosing); BAC Home Loans Servicing v. Bates, CV 2009-06-2801 (Ohio Ct. Comm. Pl., Butler Cty. Mar. 8, 2010) (finding that equitable principles require HAMP evaluation for eligible borrowers before foreclosure).

217 *See* BAC Home Loans Servicing v. Bates, CV 2009-06-2801 (Ohio Ct. Com. Pleas, Butler Cty., Mar. 8, 2010) (finding that equitable principles require HAMP evaluation for eligible borrowers before foreclosure).

218 Diane Pendley, Thomas Crowe, U.S. RMBS Servicers' Mitigation and Modification Efforts, Fitch Ratings: Structured Finance 1 (May 26, 2009).

219 Dep't of Treasury, Supplemental Directive 10-02 (effective June 1, 2010). A servicer may refer a loan to foreclosure or continue with a planned foreclosure sale for other reasons, including if the borrower fails to make payments under an offered trial period plan, or declines to participate in the HAMP program. *See* § 2.8.7, *supra*.

220 Dep't of Treasury, Supplemental Directive 10-02 (effective June 1, 2010). If the borrower fails to make a payment, the servicer may proceed with the foreclosure process.

221 *See, e.g.*, Ladco Props. XVII v. Jefferson-Pilot Life Ins. Co., 531 F.3d 718 (8th Cir. 2008) (evidence in the record supported the lower court's conclusion that a 3% liquidated damages provision in a loan commitment agreement was reasonable, valid and enforceable in part because it fell within accepted industry standards); Federal Deposit Ins. Corp. v. Transworld Mortgage, 120 F.3d 266 (5th Cir. 1997) (affirming award to FDIC for defendant's failure to collect advances as required by collection agreement, which in turn imposed duty to comply with all laws, rules and regulations applicable to its servicing of loans; defendant violated both governmental regulations and industry standards); Puentes v. Wells Fargo Home Mortgage, Inc., 72 Cal. Rptr. 3d 903 (Cal. Ct. App. 2008) (lender's interest calculation based on reasonable interpretation of the term "yearly rate" in the note comported with industry standards; court found that "lenders nationwide employ the same practice"); Bank of New York v. Nat'l Funding, 2005 WL 527749 (Conn. Super. Ct. Jan. 21, 2005) (mortgage broker's misrepresentation of loan to value ratio was deceptive and violated public policy because conduct undermined banking principles and mortgage industry standards).

standard of the residential mortgage servicing industry under both federal and state law.[222] Section 129 provides:

> Standard Industry Practice—The qualified loss mitigation plan guidelines issued by the Secretary of the Treasury under the Emergency Economic Stabilization Act of 2008 shall constitute standard industry practice for purposes of all Federal and State laws.

HAMP guidelines are required to be used unless specifically prohibited by the governing pooling and servicing agreements, and even then, the servicers are required to use "reasonable efforts" to remove those obstacles.[223] Some pooling and servicing agreements, which govern the relationship between the servicer and owner of the loan, include mandatory loss mitigation efforts before foreclosure is pursued.[224] These requirements are intended to protect the investors with additional benefits to homeowners from fewer foreclosures.[225]

6.4.5.7 Due Process Rights Under HAMP

Procedural due process claims under the Fifth Amendment arise when the government has deprived a person of a protected liberty or property interest[226] without proper notice or an opportunity to be heard. Though the government does not have a direct role in modifying loans, servicers, based on the HAMP participation agreements, have an affirmative duty to review loans of eligible homeowners for possible modification. In essence, servicers are acting as the government's agents in executing HAMP. As a result, there may be a sufficiently close nexus between the government and conduct of the servicer to assert violations of the borrowers' procedural due process rights when a servicer fails to follow the HAMP guidelines.[227]

6.4.5.8 Third-Party Beneficiary Rights Under HAMP

Under most state law a person who is not a party to a contract may nevertheless bring a breach of contract claim where the party was the intended beneficiary of a contract between two other parties. To plead a cause of action for breach of a third-party beneficiary contract, borrower must allege:

- A contract between A and B;
- An intent, either expressed by the parties or in the provisions of the contract, that the contract primarily and directly benefit C, the third party;
- Breach of contract by either A or B; and
- Damages to C resulting from the breach.

Under HAMP, most servicers have executed participation agreements with the federal government. Courts are currently divided on whether borrowers are intended beneficiaries, as opposed to incidental beneficiaries, of these participation agreements. At least one court has denied a servicer motion to dismiss a third-party beneficiary claim

---

222 Helping Families Save Their Homes Act of 2009, Pub. L. No. 111-22, 123 Stat. 1632 (2009).

223 *See* Home Affordable Modification Program, Supplemental Directive 09-01 (Apr. 6, 2009), *available at* www.hmpadmin.com/docs/Supplemental_Directive_09-01.pdf.

224 As an illustration, the following is typical loss mitigation language from a 2006 ACE Securities (Deutsche Bank) securitization:

> The Servicer shall make reasonable efforts to collect all payments called for under the terms and provisions of the related Mortgage Loans, and shall, to the extent such procedures shall be consistent with this Agreement and Accepted Servicing Practices, follow such collection procedures as it would follow with respect to mortgage loans comparable to the Mortgage Loans and held for its own account. Consistent with the foregoing, the Servicer may in its discretion (i) waive any late payment charge or, if applicable, penalty interest or (ii) extend the due dates for the Monthly Payments due on a Mortgage Note related to a Mortgage Loan for a period of not greater than 180 days; provided that any extension pursuant to this clause shall not affect the amortization schedule of any Mortgage Loan for purposes of any computation hereunder. Notwithstanding the foregoing, in the event that any Mortgage Loan is in default or, in the judgment of the Servicer, such default is reasonably foreseeable, the Servicer, consistent with Accepted Servicing Practices may waive, modify or vary any term of such Mortgage Loan (including, but not limited to, modifications that change the Mortgage Rate, forgive the payment of principal or interest or extend the final maturity date of such Mortgage Loan), accept payment from the related Mortgagor of an amount less than the Stated Principal Balance in final satisfaction of such Mortgage Loan, or consent to the postponement of strict compliance with any such term or otherwise grant indulgence to any Mortgagor if in the Servicer's determination such waiver, modification, postponement or indulgence is not materially adverse to the interests of the certificate holders (taking into account any estimated Realized Loss that might result absent such action).

See Pooling & Servicing Agreement, ACE Securities Corp., Home Equity Loan Trust, Series 2006-ASAP3 Asset Backed Pass-Through Certificates, *available at* www.sec.gov/Archives/edgar/data/1363656/000088237706002126/d511339_ex4-1.htm.

225 For example, in the 2004 Ameriquest pooling and servicing agreement, the loss mitigation alternatives are outlined in detail, including waiver of interest and overdue principal. *See* www.sec.gov/Archives/edgar/data/1363656/000088237706002126/d511339_ex4-1.htm.

226 *See* Williams v. Geithner, 2009 WL 3757380 (D. Minn. 2009) (denying preliminary injunction and finding HAMP does not create sufficient property interest for due process claim).

227 *See* Huxtable v. Geithner, 2009 WL 5199333 (S.D. Cal. Dec. 23, 2009).

because arguably the purpose of the participation agreements is to help homeowners who are facing foreclosure.[228] Other courts have held that borrowers are only incidental beneficiaries that do not possess third-party rights under the contracts.[229]

6.4.5.9 Improper Denial of a Loan Modification Is Equivalent to No Analysis

HAMP guidelines obligate a servicer to *evaluate* the homeowner, the loan, and the home, to see if the net present value analysis will return a sustainable loan modification. Implicit in that requirement is that the evaluation be based on the program guidelines. Servicers are required to provide notices to "every borrower that has been evaluated for HAMP but is not offered a Trial Period Plan, is not offered an official HAMP modification, or is at risk of losing eligibility for HAMP because they have failed to provide required financial documentation."[230] The notice must provide the primary reason or reasons for the non-approval. Importantly, if the notice discusses other non-HAMP loss mitigation options that are being considered or offered to the borrower, it must clearly state that the borrower was considered for but is not eligible for HAMP.

What happens if the homeowner seeking a loan modification provides all the requested information and is denied? How is that denial to be tested for compliance with the guidelines? Unfortunately, each servicer is permitted to develop its own specific NPV analysis, which must be consistent with the model developed by the Department of the Treasury. However, neither the individual servicers' NPV formulas nor the Treasury's NPV model are publicly available.[231]

One somewhat imperfect test is to use the publicly available FDIC Loan Mod in a Box.[232] In addition to specific guidelines, the FDIC has made available a spreadsheet analysis easily used on most spreadsheet software on personal computers.[233] While many of the specific criteria to qualify for the FDIC loan modification are different than those in the HAMP program,[234] the differences are generally *less* friendly to homeowners.[235] As a result, a finding that a homeowner does qualify for an FDIC loan modification should be a valid basis to challenge the servicer's denial of a loan modification under the HAMP program.

When the reason for non-approval of a trial or permanent HAMP modification is a negative result on the NPV test, the servicer must inform the borrower in writing that she has the option of requesting certain data related to the NPV test.[236] The borrower (or her representative) has thirty calendar days from the date of the notice of non-approval to request the NPV data. The servicer must provide it within ten business days of the request. Servicers are only required to provide some of the NPV values—notable exceptions include the market value of the property and how it was determined, the terms of the modified loan that were used for the test, and the numerical values of the NPV results for modification versus rejection (critical for knowing how far the borrower is from qualifying).[237] The servicer is not allowed to proceed to a foreclosure sale until thirty calendar days after the NPV data is given to the borrower, to allow the borrower time to identify potential errors. If the borrower finds "material" errors, the servicer must redo the NPV test. By triggering a thirty-day period of ostensible protection from foreclosure sale, a request for the NPV inputs provides an opportunity for borrowers and their advocates to discover whether errors have been made.

Complete NPV information, as well as other records of the servicer's eligibility determination should be obtainable under the Real Estate Settlement Procedures Act (RESPA), which imposes requirements on servicers to respond to borrower requests for information or correction of account

228 *See* Reyes v. Saxon Mortg. Servs., Inc., 2009 WL 3738177 (S.D. Cal. Nov. 5, 2009).

229 *See* Villa v. Wells Fargo Bank, N.A., 2010 WL 935680 (S.D. Cal. Mar. 15, 2010); Escobedo v. Countrywide Home Loans, Inc., 2009 WL 4981618 (S.D. Cal. 2009).

230 *See* Dep't of Treasury, Supplemental Directive 09-08 (effective Jan. 1, 2010). All Supplemental Directives are available at www.hmpadmin.com/portal/programs/hamp/servicer.html.

231 The Obama administration has opined that NPV formulas used by servicers are proprietary.

232 *See* FDIC website at www.fdic.gov/consumers/loans/loanmod/loanmodguide.html. *See* § 2.8.2.2.2, *supra.*

233 The FDIC spreadsheet allows for rapid and objective determinations as to whether or not any individual homeowner is eligible for a loan modification and requires very few inputs from the homeowner; most of the information is publicly available or within the knowledge of both the servicer and the homeowner and could easily be brought to a mediation conference. Also, it incorporates an example of the ubiquitous net present value (NPV) calculation to determine if a loan modification is in the interests of the mortgage holder.

234 The FDIC uses a range of affordability ratios, from 31% to 38% of income. The "affordability ratio" is the ratio between the homeowner's gross monthly income and the monthly mortgage payment (PITI). A homeowner will not be approved for a loan modification with an affordability ratio of less than 31% or more than 38%. In contrast, the targeted affordability ratio for HAMP loan modifications is 31%.

235 The FDIC spreadsheet is verifiable: anyone can check to see whether or not a homeowner is eligible for modification.

236 *See* Dep't of Treasury, Supplemental Directive 09-08 (effective Jan. 1, 2010).

237 Available NPV inputs are: a. Unpaid balance on the original loan as of [Data Collection Date]; b. Interest rate before modification as of [Data Collection Date]; c. Months delinquent as of [Data Collection Date]; d. Next ARM reset date (if applicable); e. Next ARM reset rate (if applicable); f. Principal and interest payment before modification; g. Monthly insurance payment; h. Monthly real estate taxes; i. Monthly HOA fees (if applicable); j. Monthly gross income; k. Borrower's total monthly obligations; l. Borrower FICO; m. Co-borrower FICO (if applicable); n. Zip code; and o. State. *See* Dep't of Treasury, Supplemental Directive 09-08 (effective Jan. 1, 2010).

errors in the form of a "qualified written request."[238] The information available through a qualified written request is limited to information "relating to the servicing" of the loan.[239] HAMP activities should qualify because loss mitigation has become a routine function of servicers in the servicing of mortgage loans, and the only method of obtaining a HAMP modification based on the design of the program is through a participating servicer. But some servicers resist providing anything other than payment and escrow information.[240]

In the case of a wrongful HAMP denial, it may be possible to seek "correction" of a borrower's account in the form of a loan modification consistent with the HAMP guidelines. A threshold question is whether wrongful denial of a HAMP modification or incorrect application of the HAMP modification guidelines would constitute an account error within the meaning of RESPA. The statute and Regulation X do not specify the types of errors that borrowers may seek to correct.[241] Given that RESPA is a remedial consumer protection statute that should be construed liberally,[242] and that the handling of loss mitigation requests is a customary task of servicers in servicing mortgages, errors related to processing loan modification requests should be subject to the dispute procedures in RESPA.[243]

6.4.5.10 Requirements of Servicers to Honor Loan Modification and Forbearance Agreements

A homeowner having difficulty making payments, in default, or facing foreclosure is generally much relieved to have the opportunity to enter into a loan modification or forbearance agreement which will deal with the past-due payments and fees and should have affordable payments.[244] Unfortunately, sometimes servicers fail to honor the loan modifications or forbearance agreements entered into by their predecessor servicers.[245]

The failure of a servicer to recognize and honor the terms of a loan modification or forbearance agreement previously entered into with the homeowner is actionable. In *Hauf v. HomeQ Servicing Corporation*,[246] the court refused to dismiss the homeowners' claim against the servicer for its repeated and frustrating refusal to honor the forbearance agreement entered into between the homeowners and the previous servicer. Similarly, in *Wright v. Litton Loan Servicing L.L.P.*,[247] the court found that the servicer continually refused to honor the loan modification agreement, repeatedly sent the homeowner "incomprehensible" and unsubstantiated demands for large amounts supposedly due, and failed to respond to homeowner's counsel. The *Wright* court held that the homeowner was entitled to actual and statutory damages for failing to comply with RESPA's qualified written request rules and to actual damages for non-economic losses, such as pain, suffering, and emotional distress, plus statutory penalties under the Fair Debt Collection Practices Act for "each of the 20 written communications which constituted a separate violation of the statute," plus attorney fees.[248]

6.5 Post-Payoff or Foreclosure Abuses

6.5.1 Overview

A number of servicing issues may continue even after borrowers have paid their mortgage loan in full. These abuses can limit borrowers' ability to obtain future credit and to sell or refinance the property. When there is substantial equity in the property, servicers may prefer to foreclose in order to realize a portion of the windfall from the below market foreclosure sale and reduce the number of nonperforming loan in their portfolio. Wrongful foreclosure by a servicer may permit the borrower to set aside the sale and other aggressive efforts to collect on the debt may give rise to a host of other claims. In cases where the outstanding

---

238 12 U.S.C. § 2605. *See also* § 8.2.2, *infra*.

239 12 U.S.C. § 2605(e)(1)(A). *See also* 24 C.F.R. § 3500.21(e)(2)(i).

240 *See* § 8.2.2.2, *infra* (discussion of what constitutes a QWR).

241 *See* §§ 8.2.2.2, 8.2.2.6, *infra*.

242 Ploog v. HomeSide Lending, Inc., 209 F. Supp. 2d 863 (N.D. Ill. 2002) (holding RESPA is remedial in nature); Johnstone v. Bank of Am., N.A., 173 F. Supp. 2d 815 (N.D. Ill. 2001) (same); Rawlings v. Dovenmuehle Mortgage, Inc., 64 F. Supp. 2d 1156 (M.D. Ala. 1999) (same).

243 To the extent a borrower is charged late fees or penalties resulting from a delay in the conversion from Trial Plan to permanent modification or is charged any improper fees in relation to the modification, an even stronger argument can be made that the account should be "corrected." *See* 12 U.S.C. § 2605(e)(2)(A) (defining correction of account to include crediting of late charges and penalties).

244 *See, e.g.*, Freddie Mac, Single Family Seller Servicer Guide, vol. II, ch. B65.

245 *See, e.g.*, Hauf v. HomeQ Servicing Corp., 2007 WL 196857 (M.D. Ga. Jan. 23, 2007); Wright v. Litton Loan Servicing L.P., 2006 WL 891030 (E.D. Pa. Apr. 4, 2006); JP Morgan Chase Bank v. Murdock, 2007 WL 549561 (Ohio Ct. App. Feb. 23, 2007). *Cf.* Morgan Chase Bank v. Rodrigues, 952 A.2d 56 (Conn. App. Ct. 2008) (finding that because allegations regarding servicer's failure to honor predecessor's forbearance agreement related to servicer's conduct after the mortgage note and to documents other than the mortgage note, lower court properly struck foreclosure action counterclaim for emotional distress; court left "for another day" the issue "whether an abrogation of a forbearance agreement may properly constitute a special defense to a foreclosure action on the ground that it related to the enforcement of the note").

246 2007 WL 196857 (M.D. Ga. Jan. 23, 2007).

247 2006 WL 891030 (E.D. Pa. Apr. 4, 2006).

248 *Id. But see* JP Morgan Chase Bank v. Murdock, 2007 WL 549561 (Ohio Ct. App. Feb. 23, 2007) (authorizing foreclosure to proceed and ignoring the homeowner's affidavit that the servicer refused to honor a loan modification).

amount of the debt is far greater than the property value, servicers may continue to aggressively pursue the borrower for a deficiency after the sale.

6.5.2 Failure to Provide a Timely Release

Payment in full of a mortgage loan extinguishes the security interest in the property. However, unless the mortgage holder records a release or discharge in the local land records office evidencing satisfaction of the loan, the mortgage remains a cloud on the homeowners' title and may limit their ability to sell or refinance the property.[249] The widespread sale and securitization of home mortgages has made the process of obtaining a release of a mortgage much more complicated. Payoff amounts are often directed to the servicer, who must either obtain and record a release from the holder of the obligation or pass that responsibility to the holder itself. Identifying the holder, however, sometimes leads to a game of "Who owns the loan?" in which the chain of title from the originator to the ostensible current holder is uncertain or not properly documented.

While most states have enacted statutes that deal specifically with the recordation of releases upon payment in full, the time allowed from payoff to recording varies widely, as do damages available to the homeowner.[250] Where the penalties for non-compliance are relatively small, lenders may have limited incentives to comply.[251] Additionally, some states require a demand notice before statutory penalties will apply.[252] At least two courts have considered and rejected servicers' argument that state mortgage satisfaction statutes are preempted by federal law.[253]

In addition to statutory claims, borrowers may be able to assert common law claims for breach of contract, breach of good faith and fair dealing as well as equitable relief.[254]

6.5.3 Credit Reporting Issues

Servicers have been known to damage borrowers' credit histories even after borrowers have fully paid their loans. Prior servicers or holders of the obligation may continue to report the debt due and owing. In some cases, the entity receiving the payoff may continue to report the account as open or delinquent.[255] These credit reporting errors can limit the borrower's ability to obtain future credit. As with incorrect credit reporting during the loan period, claims under the Fair Credit Reporting Act should be explored. Additionally, claims for negligent servicing, slander of title, and defamation have also been maintained.

6.5.4 Foreclosure Sale and Beyond

The servicing abuses discussed in the sections above may ultimately result in the wrongful foreclosure of the borrowers' home. For example, in *Chedick v. Nash*,[256] the servicers' fraudulent failure to provide accurate information about the payoff amount led to an unnecessary foreclosure sale. In cases where the servicers negligence or malfeasance

---

249 *See, e.g.*, Pierce v. Bank One, Oklahoma, N.A., 24 P.3d 381 (Okla. Civ. App. 2001) (affirming award of $22,000 for bank's failure to record a proper discharge within the time period specified by statute).

250 For example, in Massachusetts, an entity that has accepted payment of a mortgage pursuant to its payoff statement must record or provide a proper discharge and supporting documentation (assignments, mergers, etc.) within forty-five days of receiving payment. If a mortgage holder or servicer fails to comply with the statute, the mortgagor is entitled to statutory damages of $2500 or actual damages, whichever is greater, plus attorney fees and costs. *See* Mass. Gen. Laws ch. 183, § 55. *See also* Alaska Stat. § 34.20.050 (release required within ten days of payoff; damages of $300 plus actual damages); Conn. Gen. Stat. § 49-8 (release required within sixty days from payoff; damages in the amount of $200 per week up to $5000 or actual damages, whichever is greater, and attorney's fees); 33 Me. Rev. Stat. tit. 33, § 551; N.Y. Real Prop. Law § 275 (McKinney) (requiring release to be presented for recording within thirty days of payoff and authorizing increasing statutory damages depending on the length of delay beyond thirty days); Vt. Stat. Ann. tit. 27, § 464 (thirty days; damages of $25 per day up to $5000); Currier v. Huron, 940 A.2d 1085 (Me. 2008) (awarding $5000 in exemplary damages for failure to provide a timely release).

A summary of these statutes is provided at Appx. D.2, *infra*.

251 *In re* Consol Mortgage Satisfaction Cases, 780 N.E.2d 556 (Ohio 2002) (certifying class challenge to lenders' failure to comply with Ohio statute governing timely recordation of releases). *But see* Alexander v. Wells Fargo Fin. Ohio 1, Inc., 2009 WL 2963770 (Ohio Ct. App. Sept. 17, 2009) (arbitration clause in conjunction with mortgage transaction blocks right to class action for failure to file entry of satisfaction within statutory time period).

252 Mo. Rev. Stat. § 443.130. *Compare* Glass v. First Nat'l Bank, 191 S.W.3d 662 (Mo. 2006) (borrowers letters satisfied statutory requirement even though statute not explicitly referenced in letter) *with* Garr v. Countrywide Home Loans, Inc., 137 S.W.3d 457 (Mo. 2004) (finding borrowers letter insufficient to invoke statutory penalties for failure to release mortgage); Murray v. Fleet Mortgage Corp., 936 S.W.2d 212 (Mo. Ct. App. 1996).

253 Santana v. CitiMortgage, Inc., 2006 WL 1530083 (Conn. Super. Ct. May 22, 2006) (unpublished) (Home Owners' Loan Act (HOLA) did not preempt Connecticut statute requiring proper release of mortgage upon full payment and within a specified time period); Pinchot v. Charter One Bank, F.S.B., 792 N.E.2d 105 (Ohio 2003) (neither HOLA nor OTS regulation on preemption encompasses activity that necessarily occurs after the debt is satisfied).

254 *See* Nationsbanc Mortgage Corp. v. Hopkins, 190 S.W.3d 299 (Ark. Ct. App. 2004) (denying Nationsbanc request for $77,393.78 in interest, costs, penalties, and attorney fees in foreclosure action on later mortgage where it failed to provide a timely release for previous mortgage; relief based on the "clean-hands" equitable doctrine).

255 *See, e.g.*, Islam v. Option One Mortgage Corp., 432 F. Supp. 2d 181 (D. Mass. 2006).

256 151 F.3d 1077 (D.C. Cir. 1998).

has led to a foreclosure borrowers may have a claim for wrongful foreclosure in addition to the claims discussed in this chapter and at Chapter 5, *supra*.[257] Improper conduct by the servicer in the foreclosure proceeding itself may also allow borrowers to set aside the foreclosure sale.[258]

After the foreclosure sale, servicers may deprive homeowners of excess proceeds by attempting to add still more unauthorized fees and costs. Servicers and their local counsel have also been known to harass homeowners and engage in deceptive or abusive conduct in attempting to collect deficiency judgments. In *Heim v. California Savings Bank*,[259] the court held that the borrower had sufficiently stated a claim for violations of the Fair Debt Collection Practices Act. In April 1997, the borrower executed a deed in lieu of foreclosure to the then holder of the obligation. Two years later the same entity and its affiliates initiated a foreclosure action against the homeowner and later filed a motion to obtain a deficiency judgment. At the time of the foreclosure, the purported outstanding debt was approximately $20,000 higher than it had been in April 1997. The motion for deficiency judgment was later dismissed after the parties failed to prosecute it. The court held that the plaintiff sufficiently alleged that the defendants had engaged in false, deceptive, abusive, or misleading actions.

In addition to claims for violations of FDCPA, homeowners may also be able to assert claims for violations of state UDAP statutes, for abuse of process, negligence, and intentional (or negligent) infliction of emotional distress.

6.6 In Bankruptcy or After Bankruptcy

6.6.1 Introduction

In addition to all of the servicing abuses discussed above, borrowers who have filed for bankruptcy face even more challenges.[260] Some servicers consistently inflate their claims filed in the bankruptcy case by miscalculation, misunderstanding the loan contract, or deliberate addition of unauthorized fees.[261] When an overcharge appears deliberate, or in situations involving inadvertent overcharges which the servicer fails to correct after due notice, debtor's attorneys should consider claims for unfair trade practices (and attorney fees),[262] breach of contract, breach of the duty of good faith and fair dealing, and in egregious cases, intentional infliction of emotions distress and sanctions under Bankruptcy Rule 9011.[263] Remedies may also be available under various sections of the Bankruptcy Code.[264]

6.6.2 Interest Charge Abuses

Several problems related to interest charges can arise, most often in chapter 13 cases in which the debtor is proposing to cure a mortgage default.[265] A common problem arises when servicers itemize or otherwise include in the proof of claim for the cure amount interest on arrears[266] that will accrue post-petition under the plan. In jurisdictions where the trustee automatically calculates and pays that interest, some debtors end up paying double.

In order to prevent this problem, the Code requires that claims for unmatured interest be disallowed.[267] An objection to claim may be necessary. Although many trustees are conscientious about not double paying interest, debtor's counsel cannot rely on the trustee to catch this error.

Another interest charge abuse can involve the filing of a secured proof of claim for the entire amount of precomputed interest (for a loan on which the balance is calculated to include precomputed interest for the entire term of the loan under state law). That practice, which includes in the bal-

257 *See* § 14.4.1, *infra* (discussion on wrongful foreclosures).

258 *See* § 14.2.3, *infra*. *But see* Cuauhtli v. Chase Home Fin. L.L.C., 2007 WL 548759 (N.D. Tex. Feb. 22, 2007), *aff'd on other grounds*, 252 Fed. Appx. 690 (5th Cir. 2007) (under Texas state law, a debtor may recover for common law wrongful foreclosure only if the mortgage holder either (1) fails to comply with the statutory or contractual terms, or (2) complies with such terms, yet takes affirmative action that detrimentally affects the fairness of the foreclosure process).

259 828 A.2d 129 (Conn. App. Ct. 2003) (reinstating negligence claim and affirming dismissal of intentional infliction of emotional distress claim).

260 A more detailed discussion of mortgage servicing abuses in bankruptcy is found at National Consumer Law Center, Consumer Bankruptcy Law and Practice § 14.4.3 (9th ed. 2009).

261 *See, e.g.*, *In re* Prevo, 394 B.R. 847, 851 (Bankr. S.D. Tex. 2008) (reviewing servicers' practices of inflating proofs of claim with undocumented and excessive fees, court concludes, "[b]ased upon hearings in this and other cases, the Court believes that certain members of the mortgage industry are intentionally attempting to game the system by requesting undocumented and potentially excessive fees and then reducing those fees in amended proofs of claim only after being exposed by debtor's counsel."). *See also* Katherine M. Porter, *Misbehavior and Mistake in Bankruptcy Mortgage Claims,* 87 Tex. L. Rev. 121 (2008) (analyzing data from lender and servicer claims in 1700 chapter 13 cases, finding lack of documentation of costs and misleading categorizations in substantial portion of claims).

262 *See generally* National Consumer Law Center, Unfair and Deceptive Acts and Practices (7th ed. 2008 and Supp.).

263 Fed. R. Bankr. P. 9011. *See In re* Berghoff, 2006 WL 1716299 (Bankr. N.D. Ohio 2006) (violation of Rule 9011 to include impermissible fees in claims).

264 *See generally* National Consumer Law Center, Consumer Bankruptcy Law and Practice (9th ed. 2009).

265 *See* § 9.4, *infra*.

266 This interest is required to be paid based on Rake v. Wade, 508 U.S. 464, 113 S. Ct. 2187, 124 L. Ed. 2d 424 (1993). The requirement of payment of interest on arrears is not applicable to secured claims related to mortgages which were consummated after October 22, 1994 unless the parties' agreement requires that payment. 11 U.S.C. § 1322(e).

267 11 U.S.C. § 502(b)(2).

ance interest not yet earned, can undermine plans which propose to modify the secured claim and pay it on an amortization schedule different from that contained in the contract,[268] and it can distort the amount of interest on arrears to which that creditor is entitled.

Even if the credit contract allows precomputed interest, the filing of a claim including such interest should be challenged in bankruptcy as inconsistent with 11 U.S.C. §§ 1325(a)(5) and 502(b)(2). At a minimum, the debtor is entitled to have appropriate interest rebates calculated. In some transactions creditors may argue that these calculations must be made under the very unfair Rule of 78, but depending upon the contract and state or federal law, these arguments can often be defeated, as the Rule of 78 may be abrogated by statute or applicable only in the event of prepayment or other specified event.[269] If interest on arrears is permitted, the debtor and the trustee will also need to carefully calculate the appropriate interest on arrears payment so that only the arrears generate interest.

6.6.3 Misapplication of Payments

It has become increasingly common for mortgage servicing companies to make errors in crediting bankruptcy debtors' payments and to file motions for relief from the automatic stay when the debtor is current in post-petition payments. This occurs due to the industry practice of crediting payments received to the oldest outstanding installment. The effect is that timely payments received post-petition are treated as if they were late. Although this practice may be appropriate if there is no bankruptcy pending, it is not appropriate in situations in which the pre-petition arrears are being paid according to a proof of claim (which may already include late charges for those payments) and the debtor's chapter 13 plan. Bankruptcy courts have become more forceful in requiring servicers to correct their accounting practices to ensure that payments will be credited in accordance with the terms of confirmed plans.[270] Hidden late charges are also a pervasive problem with miscrediting payments made to cure a default under a chapter 13 plan.[271]

Problems related to the misapplication of payments may not be easily detectable without reviewing loan payment records.[272] At a minimum, when a debtor has cured a default, payment records should be reviewed at the close of the case to make sure that they reflect the cure. In cases of baseless motions for relief from stay due to errors in misapplying plan payments, sanctions against the servicer or its attorney may be warranted.[273] The bankruptcy courts and the U.S. Trustee also have authority to investigate the practices of a particular servicer whose faulty accounting

268 *See* § 7.6, *infra* (discussion of modification of secured claims).

269 *In re* McMurray, 218 B.R. 867 (Bankr. E.D. Tenn. 1998) (Rule of 78 was only authorized, and was not required, when debtor prepaid loan). *See* National Consumer Law Center, The Cost of Credit: Regulation, Preemption, and Industry Abuses § 5.6.3 (4th ed. 2009 and Supp.) (discussion of the rule and the limited situations in which it continues to be legal).

270 *In re* Boday, 397 B.R. 846 (Bankr. N.D. Ohio 2008) (creditor violated plan confirmation order and discharge order by failing to apply portions of debtor's ongoing post-petition payments to reduce principal balance as if loan were not in default); *In re* Hudak, 2008 WL 4850196, at *5 (Bankr. D. Colo. Oct. 24, 2008) (Bankruptcy Code, not language of deed of trust determines how ongoing payments will be applied while debtor cures default in chapter 13); *In re* Rodriguez, 396 B.R. 436 (Bankr. S. D. Tex. 2008) (private right of action under § 105 may proceed to remedy servicers' errors in applying payments contrary to plan terms); *In re* Myles, 395 B.R. 599 (Bankr. M.D. La. 2008) (debtor may assert claims for breach of contract and stay violation against creditor who improperly treated post-petition payments as if loan in default); *In re* Payne, 387 B.R. 614 (Bankr. D. Kan. 2008) (imposing sanctions upon servicer who improperly created a post-petition escrow arrearage by applying debtors' payments to pre-petition debt rather than to the currently due monthly installments); *In re* Collins, 2007 WL 2116416 (Bankr. E.D. Tenn. July 19, 2007) (upon plan confirmation, creditor must update accounting system so that post-petition maintenance of payment installments are treated as contractually current).

271 *See, e.g., In re* Jones, 366 B.R. 584 (Bankr. E.D. La. 2007), *rev'd in part on other grounds*, 391 B.R. 577 (E.D. La. 2008); Nosek v. Ameriquest Mortgage Co., 363 B.R. 643 (Bankr. D. Mass. 2007), *vacated on other grounds*, 544 F.3d 34 (1st Cir. 2008); *Debtors Force Mortgage Servicer to Remedy Chapter 13 Violations*, 12 NCLC REPORTS *Bankruptcy and Foreclosures Ed.* 43 (Mar./Apr. 1994).

272 *See In re* Wines, 239 B.R. 703 (Bankr. D.N.J. 1999) (example of case reconciling payments made and proof of claim).

273 *In re* Schuessler, 386 B.R. 458 (Bankr. S.D.N.Y. 2008) (ordering creditor to pay attorneys fees and debtors' costs and barring recoupment of any costs as a result of filing of unwarranted motion for relief from stay); *In re* Parsley, 384 B.R. 138 (Bankr. S.D. Tex. 2008) (finding servicer filed baseless motion for relief from stay, but denying sanctions absent clear and convincing evidence of bad faith); *In re* Ulmer, 363 B.R. 777 (Bankr. D.S.C. 2007) (awarding sanctions and finding that affidavits of default related to motions for relief from stay were not executed before a notary public as indicated in the document and affidavits may not have been reviewed and signed by attorney purported to have signed the paper); *In re* Allen, 2007 WL 115182 (Bankr. S.D. Tex. Feb. 9, 2007) (memorandum opinion regarding sanction of creditor's attorneys) (finding sanctions under Rule 9011 warranted against creditor's counsel for failing to perform an adequate investigation prior to filing pleadings); *In re* Thompson, 350 B.R. 842 (Bankr. E.D. Wis. 2006) (servicer failed to identify allegedly missed payments on which affidavit of default was based); *In re* Rivera, 342 B.R. 435 (Bankr. D.N.J. 2006), *aff'd*, 2007 WL 1946656 (D.N.J. June 29, 2007) (sanctioning individual attorney and law firm for submitting pre-signed certifications in support of relief from stay); *In re* Gorshtein, 285 B.R. 118 (Bankr. S.D.N.Y. 2002); *In re* Kilgore, 253 B.R. 179 (Bankr. D.S.C. 2000). *See also In re* Cabrera-Mejia, 402 B.R. 335 (Bankr. C.D. Cal. 2008) (sanctioning law firm under Rule 9011 and Bankr. Rule 105(a) after it filed twenty-one motions for relief from stay with the court without factual investigation and without properly authenticated documents to support claims).

technique affect numerous debtors with cases pending in the court.[274] Carefully drafted plan terms can also deter misapplication of payments.[275]

6.6.4 Escrow Overcharges

One of the most common problems found in reviewing mortgage claims in bankruptcy is abuse in the collection of escrow arrears. Often, this occurs because servicers use the total amount of escrow arrears in annually reevaluating the borrower's escrow account. This annual review is then used as the basis for calculating the borrower's new escrow payment going forward. However, in most cases pre-petition escrow arrears have already been included in the bankruptcy proof of claim and are being paid through a chapter 13 plan. Because those arrears are being paid under the plan, this practice can lead to double or sometimes triple payments.[276]

Mortgage servicers are required under the Real Estate Settlement Procedures Act to reevaluate each borrower's escrow account on an annual basis.[277] When a chapter 13 case is filed to cure a mortgage default, the servicer should conduct an escrow account analysis to determine the debtor's new escrow payment before the first post-petition payment is due.[278] The Real Estate Settlement Procedures Act permits the servicer to conduct such an analysis in this situation before the end of debtor's normal escrow account year.[279] Importantly, to give effect to the cure plan, the servicer must treat all unpaid pre-petition escrow payments as if they have been paid in conducting this analysis. These unpaid pre-petition escrow payments are part of mortgage holder's arrearage claim to be paid under the plan and cannot be collected in post-petition maintenance payments.[280] Thus, pre-petition escrow account shortages and deficiencies, often representing amounts disbursed by the servicer for taxes, insurance, and other escrow items when there were insufficient funds in the debtor's escrow account, are largely paid as part of the mortgage holder's arrearage claim during the longer cure period under the plan rather than recovered in the shorter one-year period following the case filing as part of debtor's escrow portion of the post-petition maintenance payments. If done correctly, in most cases this will produce a lower monthly escrow payment to be included as part of the debtor's total post-petition maintenance payments.

Another variation on the theme entails the servicer paying off pre-petition debts, such as real estate taxes, after the bankruptcy filing and then significantly increasing debtor's post-petition payments. Servicers have asserted that they are contractually entitled to make such advances and adjust the debtor's payment upwards. However, courts have held that paying off such pre-petition debts merely allows the mortgage holder to stand in the shoes of the third party creditor and be paid through the chapter 13 plan.[281]

Escrow overcharges may also arise where the servicer includes foreclosure fees in the borrower's escrow account balance.[282] At the same time, the fees may also be broken out as a separate element of the claim. Again, this practice results in the double counting of these fees.

Proofs of claims should be reviewed for these problems. When the line item for escrow arrears appears to be out of line, (for example, if it is more than the amount of the

274 *See, e.g., In re* Countrywide Home Loans, Inc., 384 B.R. 373 (Bankr. W.D. Pa. 2008) (U.S. Trustee had good cause to order lender to appear for inquiry into its proof of claim practices in pending cases); *In re* Stewart, 2009 WL 2448054 (E.D. La. Aug. 7, 2009) (ordering Wells Fargo to provide court with accountings for pending chapter 13 cases after finding servicer failed to notify debtors of payment changes and misapplied debtors' payments to pre- and post-petition charges).

275 *See* § 9.4.4.6, *infra. See also In re* Nosek, 544 F.3d 34, 48–49 (1st Cir. 2008) (chapter 13 plan may set procedures requiring notice of creditor's assessment of fees and payment changes, require proper allocation of payments, and have method for court to resolve disputes, but debtor's plan in this case lacked specificity to enforce such obligations under § 105(a)). *See generally* John Rao, *A Fresh Look at Curing Mortgage Defaults in Chapter 13*, 27 American Bankr. Inst. J. 14 (Feb. 2008) (proposing chapter 13 plan provisions that specifically direct allocation of post-petition payments in accordance with plan and code).

276 *See In re* Pitts, 354 B.R. 58 (Bankr. E.D. Pa. 2006) (incongruity of proof of claim that seemed to claim taxes as a separate item as well as escrow deficiency satisfied debtor's burden of challenging validity of claim and mortgage company failed to meet burden of presenting evidence justifying taxes claimed); *In re* Wines, 239 B.R. 703, 708 n.5 (Bankr. D.N.J. 1999).

277 *See* 12 U.S.C. § 2609(c); § 8.3.2, *infra. See also In re* Laskowski, 384 B.R. 518 (Bankr. N.D. Ind. 2008) (bankruptcy exemption in Regulation X relating to escrow statement does not relieve servicer of duty to conduct annual escrow analysis).

278 Chapter 13 plan payments generally begin no later than thirty days after the case is filed. *See* 11 U.S.C. § 1326(a).

279 RESPA's implementing regulation, Regulation X, provides that in certain situations the servicer need not wait until the end of the twelve-month escrow computation year to perform an escrow analysis. If the analysis is done before the end of the twelve-month computation year, the servicer is required to send the borrower a "short year statement" which will change one escrow account computation year to another, and establish the beginning date of the new computation year. *See* Reg. X, 24 C.F.R. § 3500.17(i)(4).

280 Campbell v. Countrywide Home Loans, Inc., 545 F.3d 348 (5th Cir. 2008).

281 Campbell v. Countrywide Home Loans, Inc., 361 B.R. 831 (Bankr. S.D. Tex. 2007), *aff'd in part, rev'd in part* 545 F.3d 348 (5th Cir. 2008) (borrower's missed pre-petition escrow payments must be included in proof of claim and collected through proof of claim process, even though servicer paid the underlying tax bills post-petition; however the act of listing the shortfall in proof of claim did not violate automatic stay).

282 Fees paid to third-party vendors who provide foreclosure services are often referred to as "corporate advances." Although these advances are not typically treated as an escrow item, servicers occasionally disburse funds from the borrower's escrow account to pay for these foreclosure expenses.

monthly payment for taxes and insurance multiplied by the number of months the debtor is in arrears) then more information should be obtained through a qualified written request or discovery, if necessary. Servicers' obligation to respond to qualified written requests under the RESPA timeframe should apply in all bankruptcy cases.[283]

6.6.5 Undisclosed Fees and Payment Changes

In curing a default under section 1322(b)(5), the debtor makes payments under the plan on the pre-petition arrearage and provides for the "maintenance of payments while the case is pending."[284] For a cure plan to be successful there must be full disclosure of all post-petition "maintenance" payments.[285] Unfortunately, it has become common for mortgage creditors to add fees and charges to mortgage accounts without notice to the borrower, trustee, or bankruptcy court while the bankruptcy case is pending, and without disclosing the fees in a proof of claim or amended claim, and without seeking court approval. Some creditors secretly maintain these charges on the debtor's account while the bankruptcy is pending and wait to collect the fees once the bankruptcy case is closed or when the loan is paid off or refinanced. In some cases, post-petition fees assessed prior to plan confirmation are included in the arrearage amount on the proof of claim but are not separately listed or itemized. Some servicers refuse to provide normal escrow account statements and payment change notices to debtors in bankruptcy, depriving these debtors of the opportunity to pay the amounts due during the chapter 13 case and subjecting them to later collection efforts.[286]

As a result of these practices, debtors who complete their plans often emerge from a chapter 13 case only to have the servicer begin foreclosure anew based on claims of unpaid fees for such items as escrow shortages, attorney fees, property inspections, broker's price opinions, and other charges allegedly incurred during the chapter 13 case. The fundamental unfairness of these practices has led a number of courts to find that mortgage holders and servicers who fail to disclose fees, payment increases, and account deficiencies waive their right to collect these amounts.[287] Moreover, the bankruptcy filing does not exempt the servicer from RESPA's duty to manage escrow accounts appropriately, notify the debtor of account shortages, and ensure that timely disbursements are made.[288]

6.6.6 Bankruptcy Monitoring and Proof of Claim Fees

Many mortgage holders and servicers charge borrowers who file bankruptcy a fee for monitoring the bankruptcy case, even in chapter 7 cases in which the borrower is current on monthly mortgage payments and plans to continue to make monthly payments as they come due. These "monitoring" fees may be $250 or more and are automatically assessed to the borrower's account as soon as the bankruptcy is filed. They may include fees for periodic inspections of the property or broker's price opinions.[289] Mortgage holders generally assert that these fees are authorized by language in their loan notes that obligates the borrower to pay any costs incurred in defending its security interest.

Holders and servicers often claim a right to fees for filing a proof of claim. Proof of claim fees may be charged alone

283 *See* § 8.2.5.2, *infra. See also In re* Payne, 387 B.R. 614 (Bankr. D. Kan. 2008); *In re* Moffitt, 390 B.R. 368 (Bankr. E.D. Ark. 2008); *In re* Laskowski, 384 B.R. 518 (Bankr. N.D. Ind. 2008); *In re* Thompson, 350 B.R. 842 (Bankr. E.D. Wis. 2006).

284 11 U.S.C. § 1322(b)(5). *See* § 9.4, *infra.*

285 *In re* Sanchez, 372 B.R. 289, 297 (Bankr. S.D. Tex. 2007) ("in order for the bankruptcy system to function—every entity involved in a bankruptcy proceeding must fully disclose all relevant facts"); *In re* Jones, 366 B.R. 584, 602–603 (Bankr. E.D. La. 2007) ("Bankruptcy courts can not function if secured lenders are allowed to assess post-petition fees without disclosure and then divert estate funds to their satisfaction without court approval"), *aff'd in part, rev'd in part*, 391 B.R. 577 (E.D. La. 2008).

286 *E.g., In re* Dominique, 368 B.R. 913 (Bankr. S.D. Fla. 2007) (servicer failed to provide escrow statements during chapter 13 plan and just before plan completion provided debtors with an escrow account review indicating a $6397 escrow deficiency); *In re* Rizzo-Cheverier, 364 B.R. 532 (Bankr. S.D.N.Y. 2007) (servicer allowed deficiency in escrow account to accrue and then, without notice to debtor, applied trustee plan payments intended for pre-petition arrears to post-petition escrow deficiency).

287 Craig-Likely v. Wells Fargo Home Mortgage, 2007 U.S. Dist. LEXIS 29042 (E.D. Mich. Mar. 2, 2007); Chase Manhattan Mortg. Corp. v. Padgett, 268 B.R. 309 (S.D. Fla. 2001) (servicer waived right to collect escrow account deficiency because it failed to notify borrowers of deficiencies as required by RESPA); *In re* Armstrong, 394 B.R. 794, 798–799 (Bankr. W.D. Pa. 2008) (servicer waived right to increased mortgage payments by failing to give notice of payment changes on an adjustable rate mortgage in violation of local rule); *In re* Payne, 387 B.R. 614, 637 (Bankr. D. Kan. 2008) ("When a lender silently accepts payments for over three years without notifying the borrower the payments are insufficient, when the borrower believes his taxes and insurance are being paid by his monthly payments to his lender, and when the borrower has no reason to know the lender is advancing taxes and insurance and thereby increasing borrower's indebtedness, the lender waives his right to recover the advances from the borrower."); *In re* Johnson, 384 B.R. 763 (Bankr. E.D. Mich. 2008) (even though debtor's chapter 13 case was dismissed, court found that creditor waived its right to recover arrearage for taxes and insurance by failing over five year period to comply with RESPA and local rule requiring disclosure of payment increases); *In re* Dominique, 368 B.R. 913, 921 (Bankr. S.D. Fla. 2007) (creditor who failed to perform annual escrow analysis and give annual notice of any escrow deficiency waived its right to recover deficiency).

288 *See* § 8.2.5.2, *infra.*

289 *See* § 6.4.4.2, *supra.*

or combined with "monitoring" fees, and are generally in the range of $150 to $400.[290] Additional fees may be charged for pursuing motions for relief from stay, objections to confirmation, or for responding to a debtor's objection to claim.[291]

There are several possible bases on which creditors' bankruptcy monitoring fees can be challenged. However, the first problem in some cases is discovering that they exist, because the fees are charged to the debtor's escrow account or to a suspense account, and collected on a going forward basis by adjustment to future payments rather than as elements of a proof of claim. Clients should be alerted to report any correspondence reflecting significant escrow payment changes to determine whether this problem has arisen.

Typically, the contract clause on which the mortgage holder relies is a general provision which does not expressly authorize the imposition of "bankruptcy monitoring fees," but which applies more generally to attorney fees and other costs of defending the mortgage in a court action.[292] For example, one large loan servicing company that routinely imposes these fees relies upon the following provision contained in its standard mortgage:

> Litigation. Borrower shall defend this mortgage in any action purporting to affect such property whether or not it affects the lien hereof, or purporting to affect the lien hereof or purporting to affect the rights or powers of Lender, and shall file and prosecute all necessary claims and actions to prevent or recover for any damage to or destruction of such property; and Lender is hereby authorized, without obligation to do so, to prosecute and defend any such action, whether brought by or against Borrower or Lender, or with or without suit, to exercise or enforce any other right, remedy, or power available or conferred hereunder, whether or not judgment be entered in any action or proceeding; and Lender may appear or intervene in any action or proceeding, and retain counsel therein, and take such action therein, as either may be deemed necessary or advisable, and may settle, compromise or pay the same or any other claims and, in so doing, may expend and advance such sums of money as either may deem necessary. Whether or not Borrower so appears or defends, Borrower on demand shall pay all costs and expenses, including but not limited to reasonable attorney fees of Lender including costs of evidence of title, in any such action or proceeding in which Lender may appear by virtue of being made a party defendant or otherwise, and irrespective of whether the interest of Lender in such property or their respective powers hereunder may be affected by such action, . . .

In addition to being an unbargained-for term which is imposed in the boilerplate, this language, upon close reading, does not appear to authorize a bankruptcy monitoring fee. The provision appears to apply only where the borrower or lender defends the mortgage in a case that purports to affect the property, the lien, or the lender's powers or rights, or in actions to enforce the lender's rights, or in actions to recover for damage to or destruction of the property. A borrower's chapter 13 bankruptcy, because of the anti-modification provision in 11 U.S.C. § 1322(b)(2), does not affect the property or the lien and is not an action to enforce the holder's rights.[293]

According to the quoted paragraph, whether or not the borrower defends the action, the borrower is required to pay all of the lender's costs and expenses of any such action *in which the lender appears*, including reasonable attorney fees. Monitoring to determine whether an appearance is necessary does not appear to be covered.

Some mortgages contain provisions for recovery of fees which refer to bankruptcy proceedings. For example, a common mortgage and deed of trust provision states that if "there is a legal proceeding that may significantly affect Lender's rights in the property (such as a proceeding in bankruptcy, . . .), then Lender may do and pay whatever is reasonable or appropriate to protect the value of the Property and Lender's rights in the Property. . . ." Because this language refers to "a proceeding *in* bankruptcy," it may be construed as applying only when an adversary proceeding within the bankruptcy case is filed against the holder rather than the filing of a bankruptcy case itself, and therefore would not generally permit recovery of monitoring and proof of claim fees.[294]

Often mortgage provisions relating to recovery of fees such as those quoted here are ambiguous. It is a basic

290 *In re* Collins, 2009 WL 1607737 (Bankr. S.D. Tex. June 8, 2009) ($250 fee charged for initial set-up work including both internal administrative tasks and filing of initial proof of claim).

291 *See* National Consumer Law Center, Consumer Bankruptcy Law and Practice § 11.6.2.7.1 (9th ed. 2009).

292 It is clear that bankruptcy monitoring fees can never be allowed without contractual authorization for charging those fees. *See In re* Hatcher, 208 B.R. 959 (B.A.P. 10th Cir. 1997) (no post-petition attorney fees allowed absent mortgage provision authorizing fees); *In re* LaRoche, 115 B.R. 93 (Bankr. N.D. Ohio 1990).

293 *In re* Thomas, 186 B.R. 470 (Bankr. W.D. Mo. 1995).

Even if there is a default, and a case is brought under chapter 13, the bankruptcy arguably does not affect the lender's rights, if the Code protects the lender's claim from being modified under 11 U.S.C. § 1322(b)(2). *In re* Rangel, 408 B.R. 650 (Bankr. S.D. Tex. 2009) (chapter 13 case is not a proceeding that might substantially affect mortgage holder's security interest because § 1322(b)(2) preserves holder's rights); *In re* Romano, 174 B.R. 342 (Bankr. M.D. Fla. 1994). *But see In re* Holland, 374 B.R. 409 (Bankr. D. Mass. 2007) (finding similar language unambiguously permitted lender to assess post-petition attorney fees against the debtor).

294 *In re* Rangel, 408 B.R. 650 (Bankr. S.D. Tex. 2009) (deed of trust language construed as applying to proceeding brought within bankruptcy case).

principal of contract law that any ambiguity in a contract is construed against the drafter, in this case the lender (and its assignees).[295] Equally importantly, courts have strictly construed contractual provisions providing for fees and costs.[296]

Of course, the analysis of any particular case will depend on the language of the loan contract at issue. As the language quoted here illustrates, advocates should review the language of the contract closely to determine whether it actually says what the holder or servicer claims that it says, and whether it is ambiguous.[297]

If a holder or servicer attempts to collect a bankruptcy fee from property of the estate while the automatic stay is in effect by adding the fee to the debtor's account, it has violated Code section 362(a)(3). Section 362(a)(3) prohibits "any act to obtain possession of property of the estate or of property from the estate or to exercise control over property of the estate" while the stay is in effect. In a chapter 13 case, all property the debtor acquires during the entire time the case is pending is property of the estate pursuant to section 1306(a). By seeking payment of this fee directly from the debtor, the lender violates the stay.[298] Similarly, by collecting fees not provided for by the plan and therefore failing to credit payments in accordance with the plan, the lender also violates section 524(i).[299]

In addition, it is an unfair and deceptive practice to state that a fee is authorized by the contract when it is not.[300] It is also unfair and deceptive to impose a fee that is not authorized.[301] Relying on confusing, ambiguous, or misleading contract clauses (which the above-quoted contract clause certainly is) may also be a unfair or deceptive act or practice (UDAP) violation.[302]

There may also be questions about whether the monitoring or proof of claim fee represents a charge for the provision of legal services. If all the attorney for the holder is doing is "monitoring" the bankruptcy, that is, receiving court notices, reading them, keeping them, and so forth, then these activities do not constitute the practice of law and should not be compensable as an attorney fee.[303] These routine administrative services are generally not compen-

295 *In re* Stark, 242 B.R. 866 (Bankr. W.D.N.C. 1999) (bankruptcy monitoring fees disallowed as ambiguous mortgage contract construed against lender). *See also In re* Williams, 1998 WL 372656 (Bankr. N.D. Ohio June 10, 1998).

296 *See, e.g., In re* Sublett 895 F.2d 1381 (11th Cir. 1990); First Brandon Nat'l Bank v. Kerwin-White, 109 B.R. 626 (D. Vt. 1990). *See also In re* Williams, 1998 WL 372656 (Bankr. N.D. Ohio June 10, 1998) (ambiguous contract term inadequate basis to support creditor's request for fees for motion for relief from stay); *In re* Romano, 174 B.R. 342 (Bankr. M.D. Fla. 1994) (interpreting loan note's ambiguous attorney fee provision against the lender/drafter). *Cf. In re* Majchrowski, 6 F. Supp. 2d 946 (N.D. Ill. 1998) (standard form mortgage provision allows lender to charge a fee for filing proof of claim and is not ambiguous so as to require construction against the drafter).

297 *See In re* Hatala, 295 B.R. 62 (Bankr. D.N.J. 2003) (mortgage provided for fees only in foreclosure and not for fees incurred after foreclosure judgment; fees limited to those permitted by state rules); *In re* Woodham, 174 B.R. 346 (Bankr. M.D. Fla. 1994) (analysis of provision which does not specifically provide for attorneys fees in bankruptcy).

298 Wells Fargo Bank v. Jones, 391 B.R. 577 (E.D. La. 2008) (mortgage creditor's assessment and collection of undisclosed and improper post-petition inspection fees and other charges violated automatic stay); *In re* Sanchez, 372 B.R. 289 (Bankr. S.D. Tex. 2007) (creditor's failure to disclose post-confirmation fees charged to the debtor and to file fee application under Rule 2016 violated automatic stay); *In re* Stark, 242 B.R. 866 (W.D.N.C. 1999) (sanctions imposed for violating stay by attempting to collect inspection and monitoring fees); *In re* Banks, 31 B.R. 173 (Bankr. N.D. Ala. 1982). *See also In re* Payne, 387 B.R. 614 (Bankr. D. Kan. 2008) (servicer violated stay and plan confirmation order by applying post-petition payments to late fees, excessive interest, legal costs, and escrow deficiencies during pendency of confirmed plan); *In re* Myles, 395 B.R. 599 (Bankr. M.D. La. 2008) (allowing debtor to proceed with claims for violation of stay and breach of contract based on creditor's misapplication of debtor's post-petition payments to undisclosed fees and charges). *But see* Mann v. Chase Manhattan Mortgage Corp., 316 F.3d 1 (1st Cir. 2003) (mortgage company did not violate automatic stay by adding fees to debtor's account if it never attempted to collect those fees from debtor; court glossed over fact that addition of fees increased lien on debtor's property).

In order to avoid unknown charges being assessed against a debtor's mortgage account, it may be advisable to file a motion at the end of a chapter 13 case seeking an order that the mortgage default has been cured and the mortgage is current. An example of such a motion can be found in National Consumer Law Center, Consumer Bankruptcy Law and Practice Appx. G.12, Form 146 (9th ed. 2009). If the debtor does not discover improper charges until after they have been paid, the debtor should still be able to challenge the fees. *See In re* Staggie, 255 B.R. 48 (Bankr. N.D. Idaho 2000) (bankruptcy court has authority under § 506 to review attorney fees of secured creditor even if the collateral has been sold and the fees paid by debtor).

In an opinion that was wrongly decided, and may be avoided by counsel through careful drafting of the chapter 13 plan, the Eleventh Circuit rejected a debtor's challenge to a mortgage lender's collection of attorney fees and expenses from mortgage payments made outside the plan because it held that such payments were not property of the estate protected by the automatic stay after confirmation. Telfair v. First Union Mortgage Corp., 216 F.3d 1333 (11th Cir. 2000).

299 *See* § 9.4.4.6, *infra*. Section 524(i) applies to cases filed on or after October 17, 2005.

300 *See generally* National Consumer Law Center, Unfair and Deceptive Acts and Practices § 5.6.4.2 (7th ed. 2008 and Supp.).

301 *See generally* National Consumer Law Center, Unfair and Deceptive Acts and Practices § 6.10.7 (7th ed. 2008 and Supp.).

302 *See* Michaels v. Amway Corp., 522 N.W.2d 703 (Mich. Ct. App. 1994).

303 *In re* Thomas, 186 B.R. 470 (Bankr. W.D. Mo. 1995) (lender that filed proof of claim without attorney assistance not entitled to attorney fee). *See* State Unauthorized Practice of Law Comm. v. Paul Mason, 46 F.3d 469 (5th Cir. 1995). *See also In re* Porter, 399 B.R. 113 (Bankr. D.N.H. 2008) (no special legal knowledge required for routine reviews of debtors' schedules and financial qualifications to determine whether reaffirmation agreements were appropriate; denying claim for attorney fees related to this work).

sable under any reading of typical mortgage provisions.[304] Moreover, while proof of claim preparation in many cases has been outsourced to large national firms that purport to be law firms, the actual work is often not performed by paralegals or other legal professionals, and it may not be done under the supervision of an attorney.[305]

Several holders and servicers charge a flat rate monitoring fee to all borrowers in bankruptcy. This uniform charge is obviously not based on actual costs or expenses in "monitoring" the borrower's bankruptcy. Instead, it is an attempt to spread costs among all borrowers who file bankruptcy. Contract provisions providing for attorney fees are only enforceable "to the extent that it is shown that the creditor has been damaged by having to pay, or assume the payment of attorney fees or other collection expenses."[306] These provisions often allow the holder or servicer to recover only fees and costs that have been actually "disbursed" to a third party to protect the collateral or the holder's rights.[307] Similarly, if a holder and servicer is charging for other costs based on a contract provision, it should be required to justify the costs and show that they were actually incurred.[308]

In addition to being actually incurred by the holder or servicer, the fee must be reasonable and properly documented.[309] If the servicer cannot document the basis for a charge after a debtor's good faith request to do so through formal discovery or other informal means, the court should disallow the charge.[310] If the fee is for services that are unnecessary, then it is not reasonable.[311] In most cases it is not necessary for the mortgage holder to do anything to protect its interest in a bankruptcy case.[312] A holder can adequately monitor a case simply by making sure that it continues to receive payments (which is what the lender does in any event). The Bankruptcy Code and Rules expressly provide for notice if any action is taken which affects its mortgage.[313] A creditor can rely on receiving those notices without any affirmative action to monitor the case.

The fee also may be unreasonable if it exceeds the cost of the services performed.[314] Unreasonable or excessive charges

---

304 *See In re* Thomas, 186 B.R. 470 (W.D. Mo. 1995); *In re* Banks, 31 B.R. 173 (Bankr. N.D. Ala. 1982); *In re* Cipriano, 8 B.R. 697 (Bankr. D.R.I. 1981). *But see In re* Majchrowski, 6 F. Supp. 2d 946 (N.D. Ill. 1998) (standard form mortgage provision allows lender to charge a fee for filing proof of claim and for property inspections associated with foreclosure).

The latter court appears to have been hostile to pursuit of these claims in this case as a RICO class action. Incredibly, the court states that the contract authorizes fees even if they are not "reasonable, economical or fair to the borrower."

305 *In re* Taylor, 407 B.R. 618 (Bankr. E.D. Pa. 2009) (finding that proofs of claim filed by national firm were prepared by clerks who are not legally trained and are not paralegals, and that attorney for firm reviews only a random sample of 10% of filed claims), *sanctions rev'd on other grounds,* 2010 WL 624909 (E.D. Pa. Feb. 18, 2010).

306 *In re* Banks, 31 B.R. 173, 178 (Bankr. N.D. Ala. 1982) (citing Annotation, 17 A.L.R.2d 288 § 8, at 298 (1951)).

307 *In re* Rangel, 408 B.R. 650, n.11 (Bankr. S.D. Tex. 2009) (proof of claim fee disallowed because servicer did not produce any evidence that fee was actually disbursed to law firm and fee application merely stated that it had been invoiced).

308 *See* Korea First Bank v. Lee, 14 F. Supp. 2d 530 (S.D.N.Y. 1998) (lender can collect no more than it agreed to pay its counsel).

309 *In re* Good, 207 B.R. 686 (Bankr. D. Idaho 1997) (assessing reasonableness of fees charged by mortgage lender). *See In re* Williams, 1998 WL 372656 (Bankr. N.D. Ohio June 10, 1998) (bank failed to meet burden of proving its fees are reasonable, by failing to provide adequate documentation). *Cf. In re* Maywood, Inc., 210 B.R. 91 (Bankr. N.D. Tex. 1997) (fees disallowed for lender's bankruptcy monitor in chapter 11 case when the monitor spent the bulk of his time playing games on his laptop computer, reading the newspaper, and practicing his putting).

If fees or expenses are to be collected from property of the estate, they should be itemized and requested in an application filed pursuant to Fed. R. Bankr. P. 2016.

310 *In re* Prevo, 394 B.R. 847 (Bankr. S.D. Tex. 2008) (disallowing foreclosure fees and costs, late charges, and BPO fees where servicer did not comply with basic supporting documentation requirements of Official Form B10 and Bankr. Rule 3001); *In re* Sacko, 394 B.R. 90 (Bankr. E.D. Pa. 2008) (disallowing servicer's charges for property inspections, property preservation costs, and escrow advances, and limiting assessment of sheriff's sale costs and attorney fees due to servicer's failure to meet burden of production in documenting need for the charges).

311 *See In re* Dalessio, 74 B.R. 721 (B.A.P. 9th Cir. 1987); Wells Fargo Bank v. Jones, 391 B.R. 577 (E.D. La. 2008) (mortgage creditor failed to show that monthly property inspections during chapter 13 case were necessary and reasonable); *In re* Stewart, 391 B.R. 327 (Bankr. E.D. La. 2008) (finding no reasonable basis for assessing multiple drive by inspection charges and paying for BPO opinion when borrower was current in long term chapter 13 case and servicer was regularly in contact with borrower); *In re* Payne, 387 B.R. 614 (Bankr. D. Kan. 2008) (rejecting servicer's attempt to charge debtor for twenty-three drive by inspections made during period when debtor was in open and clear occupancy of home and in constant contact with servicer).

312 *In re* Stewart, 391 B.R. 327 (Bankr. E.D. La. 2008) (finding no reasonable basis for assessing multiple drive by inspection charges and paying for broker's price opinion when borrower was current in long-term chapter 13 case and servicer was regularly in contact with borrower); *In re* Payne, 387 B.R. 614 (Bankr. D. Kan. 2008) (rejecting servicer's attempt to charge debtor for twenty-three drive by inspections made during period when debtor was in open and clear occupancy of home and in constant contact with servicer).

313 Fed. R. Bankr. P. 3015, 7004, 9014.

314 *See also In re* Stewart, 391 B.R. 327, 346 (Bankr. E.D. La. 2008) (servicer falsely represented BPO as pass through of a charge of between $90 and $125, when it actually paid $50 for each inspection; servicer also improperly compounded late fees to charge $360.23 over thirteen months for one $554.11 missed payment). *See generally* Franks v. Associated Air Ctr. Inc., 663 F.2d 583 (5th Cir. 1982) (gross overcharges violate UDAP); *In re* Staggie, 255 B.R. 48 (Bankr. D. Idaho 2000) (excessive attorney fees sought under § 506(b) disallowed as not reasonable); Russell v. Fid. Consumer Discount Co., 72 B.R. 855 (Bankr. E.D. Pa. 1987) (grossly excessive fee was unconscionable).

may also violate the requirement of good faith and fair dealing implied in any contractual relationship.[315]

Some state debt collection statutes or regulations apply to creditors as well as debt collectors.[316] (The federal Fair Debt Collection Practices Act applies only to third party collectors.[317]) Most debt collection statutes and regulations prohibit the collection of any amount not authorized by contract or applicable law.[318] In addition, there may be a state statute which limits the extent of the creditor's attorney fees that may be shifted under contract terms. This state law limitation will be binding upon the creditor in bankruptcy court as well.[319]

315 Burnham v. Mark IV Homes, Inc., 441 N.E.2d 1027, 1031 (Mass. 1982). *See* U.C.C. § 1-203.

316 *See* National Consumer Law Center, Collection Actions Ch. 11 (2008 and Supp.).

317 However, the FDCPA does apply if the debt was acquired by the debt collector or mortgage lender (or servicer) at a time when the debt was in default. *See* National Consumer Law Center, Fair Debt Collection (6th ed. 2008 and Supp.).

318 *See, e.g.*, Martinez v. Albuquerque Collection Servs., 867 F. Supp. 1495 (D.N.M. 1994) (collection agency violated FDCPA by collecting inflated charges for attorney fees); West v. Costen, 558 F. Supp. 564 (W.D. Va. 1983) (imposition of service charge on bad check violated FDCPA because no contract or statute permitted charge).

319 *See, e.g.*, *In re* Doty, 2008 WL 4104485 (Bankr. D. Mont. Aug. 28, 2008) (applying Montana statute limiting attorney fees to 1% of amount due on obligation at time of default, reducing fees from creditor's claim of $7843.75 to $456.00).

Chapter 7 Non-RESPA Challenges to Mortgage Servicing Abuses

7.1 Introduction

Chapter 6, *supra*, details common mortgage servicer abuses. This chapter considers legal theories and statutory remedies for mortgage servicing abuse other than those provided by RESPA. These options may be particularly useful when the practices violate a provision of RESPA that does not include an express right of action or when the practice may not be covered by RESPA. RESPA claims are discussed in more detail in Chapter 8, *infra*.

One of the most vital statutory bodies in cases of mortgage servicing abuses is state unfair and deceptive practices acts (UDAP) laws. When state UDAP laws apply to servicers, they can be powerful tools for borrowers. The Fair Debt Collection Practices Act is broad in the scope of proscribed conduct but its applicability to servicers is limited by a specific exemption. Similarly, the Truth in Lending Act creates a special exemption for servicers. Nevertheless, servicers may be proper parties where the borrower asserts a TIL claim against the owner of the obligation. The Fair Credit Reporting Act should also be explored whenever servicers improperly report homeowners as in default on the mortgage obligation.

In addition to these statutory claims, a number of common law claims may be asserted against the servicer. Breach of contract and breach of fiduciary duty are two of the most common claims asserted against servicers. In addition, a number of tort law claims may be available.

7.2 State Unfair and Deceptive Acts and Practices Statutes

Every state has a deceptive practices or UDAP (unfair and deceptive acts and practices) statute.[1] The typical statute includes a broad prohibition against deceptive acts and practices, and many states prohibit unfair acts as well. All states except Iowa offer a private cause of action to consumers, and the typical statute allows enhanced remedies such as statutory damages, treble damages, punitive damages, or attorney fees.[2]

The main question in asserting a UDAP claim against a servicer is whether the statute applies to servicers. Many UDAP statutes apply broadly to all transactions in trade or commerce, but some apply more narrowly to consumer transactions as defined by the statute or to sales or leases of goods or services.[3] Some UDAP statutes do not apply to land transactions, some exclude credit transactions, and some exclude certain types of entities such as financial institutions or regulated industries.[4] In a few states there is a question about the extent to which the UDAP statute applies to acts that occur after the consumer enters into the transaction. UDAP coverage issues are discussed in detail in Chapter 2 of National Consumer Law Center, *Unfair and Deceptive Acts and Practices* (7th ed. 2008 and Supp.).

Assuming that the UDAP statute applies, misrepresentation of the amount due in an escrow account statement can be both unfair and deceptive and may violate the statute.[5] A servicer violated the Massachusetts UDAP statute by misapplying the consumer's mortgage payments and initiating foreclosure when the consumer was complying with a forbearance agreement.[6]

1 *See* National Consumer Law Center, Unfair and Deceptive Acts and Practices Appx. A (7th ed. 2008 and Supp.) (state-by-state summaries of UDAP statutes).

2 Some state UDAP statutes also provide for equitable relief. *E.g.*, Wright v. Litton Loan Servicing, L.P., 2006 WL 891030 (E.D. Pa. Apr. 4, 2006) (borrower entitled to equitable relief requiring servicer to correct its records).

3 *See, e.g.*, Ky. Rev. Stat. Ann. § 367.170; Eversole v. EMC Mortgage Corp., 2005 WL 3018755 (E.D. Ky. Nov. 9, 2005) (dismissing UDAP claim because servicer did not sell or lease consumer goods or services).

4 *But see* Dowling v. Litton Loan Servicing, L.P., 2006 WL 3498292 (S.D. Ohio Dec. 1, 2006) (loan servicing agent was not a "financial institution" exempted from state UDAP statute).

5 *E.g.*, Mark v. Keycorp Mortgage Inc., 1996 WL 465400 (N.D. Ill. Aug. 8, 1996); Sanders v. Lincoln Serv. Corp., 1993 WL 211358 (N.D. Ill. June 15, 1993); Aitken v. Fleet Mortgage Corp., 1992 WL 33926 (N.D. Ill. Feb. 12, 1992). *See also* Birkholm v. Washington Mut. Bank, F.A., 447 F. Supp. 2d 1158 (W.D. Wash. 2006) (denying motion to dismiss UDAP claim where plaintiffs alleged servicer used escrow funds to pay late charges, corporate advances, force place insurance premiums, property inspection fees and payoff fees).

6 *See, e.g.*, *In re* Hart, 246 B.R. 709 (Bankr. D. Mass. 2000) (servicer liable for UDAP violation based on its misapplication of mortgage payment and initiation of foreclosure even though

Many courts have held that a violation of another consumer protection statute is a per se UDAP violation.[7] Accordingly, a number of courts have held that consumers can assert a UDAP claim for violations of the Real Estate Settlement Procedures Act (RESPA).[8] Even where RESPA itself does not create a federal cause of action for violation of a requirement,[9] as in the case of the requirements for disclosure of settlement charges, the violation may be actionable under the state UDAP statute.[10] RESPA expressly preempts state laws only to the extent they are inconsistent with it,[11] so the use of a state UDAP statute as a vehicle for enforcing RESPA's disclosure requirements is not preempted.[12] Courts interpreting UDAP statutes that exempt practices authorized by another law may find compliance with RESPA's disclosure requirements sufficient to defeat a UDAP claim involving disclosure, however.[13]

7.3 Truth in Lending Claims

Claims under the Truth in Lending Act (TIL) can be a powerful response to an actual or threatened foreclosure.[14] Whether TIL claims can be asserted against a servicer depends on whether the obligation itself, rather than just the servicing rights, have been assigned to it, and whether the assignment was solely for administrative convenience.

The general rule is that Truth in Lending damage claims can be asserted against an assignee of the obligation if the violation is apparent on the face of the documents.[15] Moreover, rescission claims can be asserted against an assignee regardless of whether the violation is apparent on the face of the documents.[16] However, the Truth in Lending Act creates a special exemption for servicers. A servicer is not treated as an assignee for purposes of TIL liability unless it is or was the owner of the obligation.[17] In addition, even if it does own the obligation, the servicer is not treated as the owner if it acquired the obligation solely for its administrative convenience in servicing the obligation.[18] Nevertheless, the servicer is required to identify, upon written request of the borrower, the true owner of the obligation.[19]

Holding an interest in the loan is sufficient for TIL liability if the holder acquired the interest at least in part for reasons other than administrative convenience.[20] In addition, a servicer may be liable as an assignee if it holds itself out as the owner or holder of a loan.[21]

---

it was aware that consumer was complying with terms of forbearance agreement; Fannie Mae vicariously liable for servicer's acts). *See also* National Consumer Law Center, Unfair and Deceptive Acts and Practices Ch. 2 (7th ed. 2008 and Supp.) (general discussion of UDAP coverage).

7 *See* National Consumer Law Center, Unfair and Deceptive Acts and Practices § 3.2.7 (7th ed. 2008 and Supp.).

8 Munoz v. Int'l Home Capital Corp., 2004 WL 3086907, at *11 (N.D. Cal. May 4, 2004) (denying motion to dismiss); Chow v. Aegis Mortgage Corp., 286 F. Supp. 2d 956 (N.D. Ill. 2003); Jenkins v. Mercantile Mortgage Co., 231 F. Supp. 2d 737 (N.D. Ill. Sept. 27, 2002); Fardella v. Downey Sav. & Loan Ass'n, 2001 WL 492442 (N.D. Cal. May 9, 2001); Gardner v. First Am. Title Ins. Co., 2001 U.S. Dist. LEXIS 21839 (D. Minn. Dec. 10, 2001) (plaintiff's allegations that defendants created sham intermediary companies which paid kickbacks stated both RESPA and UDAP claims); Christakos v. Intercounty Title Co., 196 F.R.D. 496 (N.D. Ill. 2000). *See also* Johnson v. Matrix Fin. Servs. Corp., 820 N.E.2d 1094 (Ill. App. Ct. 2004) (violation of RESPA's anti-kickback provisions is UDAP violation, but not shown here). *But cf.* Shafer v. GSF Mortgage Corp., 2003 WL 21005793 (Minn. Ct. App. May 6, 2003) (unpublished) (RESPA violations not admissible as evidence of consumer fraud). *See generally* Ch. 8, *supra*, (detailed discussion of RESPA's mortgage servicing requirements); National Consumer Law Center, The Cost of Credit: Regulation, Preemption, and Industry Abuses § 12.2 (4th ed. 2009 and Supp.) (detailed discussion of other provisions of RESPA).

9 The statute affords a private cause of action for violation of the servicer obligations (12 U.S.C. § 2605), the anti-kickback provisions (12 U.S.C. § 2607), the title insurance company steering rules (12 U.S.C. § 2608), the escrow payment rules (§ 2605(g)), and the duty to respond to a qualified written request (§ 2605(e)). *See* National Consumer Law Center, The Cost of Credit: Regulation, Preemption, and Industry Abuses § 12.2 (4th ed. 2009 and Supp.).

10 Tandiama v. Novastar Mortgage, Inc., 2005 WL 1287996 (W.D. Wash. May 31, 2005); Anderson v. Wells Fargo Home Mortgage, 259 F. Supp. 2d 1143, 1147–1148 (W.D. Wash. 2003); Washington Mut. Bank v. Superior Court, 75 Cal. App. 4th 773, 89 Cal. Rptr. 2d 560 (1999). *See also* Brazier v. Security Pac. Mortgage Inc., 245 F. Supp. 2d 1136 (W.D. Wash. 2003) (RESPA requirements are incorporated into state UDAP statute). *See generally Using UDAP Statutes to Fill the Gaps in RESPA Violations*, 21 NCLC REPORTS *Deceptive Practices and Warranties Ed.* 9 (Nov./Dec. 2002).

11 12 U.S.C. § 2616; 24 C.F.R. §§ 3500.13(a), (b)(2) (RESPA does not preempt state laws that provide greater protection to consumers), 3500.21(h) (RESPA preempts state laws that require certain notices to borrowers); § 8.4, *infra*. *See* Blair v. Source One Mortgage Servs. Corp., 925 F. Supp. 617 (D. Minn. 1996). *See also* Fardella v. Downey Sav. & Loan Ass'n, 2001 U.S. Dist. LEXIS 6037 (N.D. Cal. May 8, 2001).

12 Washington Mut. Bank v. Superior Court, 75 Cal. App. 4th 773, 89 Cal. Rptr. 2d 560 (1999).

13 Weatherman v. Gary-Wheaton Bank, 186 Ill. 2d 472, 713 N.E.2d 543, 239 Ill. Dec. 12 (1999). *See also* National Consumer Law Center, Unfair and Deceptive Acts and Practices §§ 2.2.16, 2.5.3.7 (7th ed. 2008 and Supp.).

14 *See* § 5.6, *supra*.

15 15 U.S.C. § 1641(a). *See* National Consumer Law Center, Truth in Lending § 7.3.2 (6th ed. 2007 and Supp.).

16 15 U.S.C. § 1641(c). *See* National Consumer Law Center, Truth in Lending § 7.3.3 (6th ed. 2007 and Supp.).

17 15 U.S.C. § 1641(f). *See* National Consumer Law Center, Truth in Lending § 7.3.6 (6th ed. 2007 and Supp.).

18 15 U.S.C. § 1641(f)(2). *See* National Consumer Law Center, Truth in Lending § 7.3.6 (6th ed. 2007 and Supp.).

19 15 U.S.C. § 1641(f)(2). In addition, 15 U.S.C. § 1641(g), which became effective May 20, 2009, requires creditors to provide notice to borrowers when the ownership of their mortgage loans is transferred or assigned to another party. *See also* § 10.2.5, *infra*.

20 *See* National Consumer Law Center, Truth in Lending § 7.3.6 (6th ed. 2007 and Supp.).

21 *See id.*

Even when the statutory exemption protects a servicer from TIL liability, it may still be proper to join the servicer as a party to a TIL rescission action.[22] Rule 19(a) of the Federal Rules of Civil Procedure allows joinder of parties under several circumstances. First, a person may be joined if, without that person, complete relief cannot be accorded among the existing parties. The rule also allows joinder of any person who claims an interest relating to the subject matter and is so situated that the disposition of the action in the person's absence may as a practical matter (1) impair or impede the person's ability to protect that interest or (2) leave any of the existing parties subject to a substantial risk of incurring double, multiple, or inconsistent obligations. Where foreclosure is either underway or has been threatened, joinder of the servicer may be proper under this rule. Otherwise, the servicer could improperly report to credit bureaus or attempt to foreclose on the loan that the debtor is attempting to rescind. Dismissing the servicer in such a case would impair the consumers' ability to protect their interests and also might prejudice the interests of the other parties.[23] Some courts have found that servicers are not a proper party under Rule 19(a), but those cases are generally distinguishable from cases in which the servicer has the authority to foreclose and has, in fact, initiated the foreclosure process.[24]

In some situations, a TIL violation may occur based on the actions of the servicer while servicing the account. For example, a servicer who improperly charges servicing-related fees to the borrower's mortgage account may cause a violation of TILA by improperly disclosing account balances or other variable rate adjustment disclosures on periodic statements or change notices required for adjustable rate loans and home equity lines of credit (HELC).[25] In addition, a servicer may violate the TIL requirements concerning disclosure of ownership of the mortgage loan,[26] duty to promptly credit payments to the account,[27] and prohibiting the pyramiding of late fees.[28]

22 *See id.*

23 *Id.*

24 *See* Hubbard v. Ameriquest Mortgage Co., 624 F. Supp. 2d 913 (N.D. Ill. 2008) (previous servicer not indispensible party); Walker v. Gateway Fin. Co, 286 F. Supp. 2d 965 (N.D. Ill. 2003) (homeowners not threatened with foreclosure and any concern of improper reporting to credit agencies was speculative).

25 *See* Chatman v. Fairbanks Capital Corp., 2002 WL 1338492 (N.D. Ill. June 13, 2002) (homeowner's complaint properly alleged TIL violation based on lender's inaccurate statement of loan balance resulting from alleged improper charging of "property preservation" fees). *See also* McAdams v. Citifinancial Mortgage Co. of New York, 2008 WL 577559 (M.D. La. Mar. 3, 2008) (post-closing misapplication of payment may give rise to TIL violation); National Consumer Law Center, Truth in Lending Chs. 4, 5 (6th ed. 2007 and Supp.).

26 *See* § 1.3.3.2, *supra.*

27 *See* § 6.4.3.4, *supra.*

28 *See* § 6.4.3.3, *supra.*

7.4 Fair Debt Collection Practices Act and State Debt Collection Laws

7.4.1 *Introduction*

The Fair Debt Collection Practices Act (FDCPA)[29] offers potent remedies against abusive debt collection tactics such as fee padding, demands for incorrect amounts, and harassment. The Act is applicable to some but not all servicers. The key question is whether the servicer acquired the debt before or after it went into default.

The following subsections analyze the applicability of the FDCPA to mortgage servicers, and review the substantive prohibitions that are most likely to apply to servicers. It concludes with an outline of FDCPA remedies and an overview of state debt collection laws. A comprehensive discussion of the FDCPA and state debt collection laws may be found in National Consumer Law Center, *Fair Debt Collection* (6th ed. 2008 and Supp.).

7.4.2 *FDCPA Coverage*

The Fair Debt Collection Practices Act covers the activities of debt collectors.[30] The basic definition of "debt collector" is any person whose principal business is debt collection or who regularly collects or attempts to collect debts that are owed or due to another.[31] Servicers meet this basic definition in that they regularly collect or attempt to collect debts that were originally owed to the creditor who originated the loan or the creditor's assignee. However, the statute creates an exemption for any person collecting or attempting to collect a debt that was not in default at the time the person obtained it.[32] Servicers fall within this exemption when the servicing rights are assigned prior to the borrower's default.[33] Servicers will be covered by the

29 15 U.S.C. §§ 1692 to 1692o.

30 15 U.S.C. § 1692a(6).

31 *Id. See* Oppong v. First Union Mortgage Corp., 215 Fed. Appx. 114 (3d Cir. 2007) (servicer was "debt collector" regardless of whether a significant portion of business is from debt collection); Carter v. Countrywide Home Loans, Inc. 2009 WL 2742560 (E.D. Va. 2009); National Consumer Law Center, Fair Debt Collection §§ 4.2, 4.3 (6th ed. 2008 and Supp.).

32 15 U.S.C. § 1692a(6)(F)(iii). *See* National Consumer Law Center, Fair Debt Collection § 4.3.10 (6th ed. 2008 and Supp.).

33 *See, e.g.*, Downs v. Clayton Homes, Inc., 88 Fed. Appx. 851 (6th Cir. 2004) (servicer exempt because loan was not in default at time of acquisition); Perry v. Stewart Title Co., 756 F.2d 1197, 1208 (5th Cir.), *as amended on rehearing by* 761 F.2d 237 (5th Cir. 1985); Bridge v. Ocwen Fed. Bank, 669 F. Supp. 2d 853 (N.D. Ohio 2009); Dolan v. Fairbanks Capital Corp., 2005 WL 1971006 (E.D.N.Y. Aug. 16, 2005); Scott v. Wells Fargo Home Mortgage Inc., 326 F. Supp. 2d 709 (E.D. Va. 2003), *aff'd*, 67 Fed. Appx. 238 (4th Cir. 2003). *See also* Brown v. Morris, 243 Fed. Appx. 31 (5th Cir. 2007) (FDCPA not applicable where creditor obtained loan through merger rather than assignment or transfer).

FDCPA if they obtain the servicing rights after the loan is in default.[34] Courts commonly dismiss FDCPA claims against servicers where the borrower fails to plead that the loan was in default at the time servicing rights were transferred.[35]

Whether a debt was in default at the time a servicer acquired it will be a question of fact.[36] "Default" is not defined by the FDCPA, but probably does not occur immediately after a debt becomes due.[37] Whether a debt is in default depends at least in part on any definition of default in the parties' contract.[38] The fact that the creditor or servicer does not consider the debt to be in default may be irrelevant.[39] On the other hand, the Seventh Circuit has held that, even though a debt was not actually in default when the servicer obtained it, the FDCPA applied where the servicer treated it as in default.[40]

34 *See* Portley v. Litton Loan Servicing, L.P., 2010 WL 1404610 (E.D. Pa. Apr. 5, 2010) (servicing transfer notice stating debtor in default sufficient to establish servicer was debt collector); Castrillo v. American Home Mortg. Serv., Inc., 2010 WL 1424398 (E.D. La. Apr. 5, 2010) (exemption does not apply because servicing rights obtained after loan in default); Martin v. Select Portfolio Serv. Holding Corp., 2008 WL 618788 (S.D. Ohio Mar. 3, 2008) (using two-part test to determine whether servicer was "debt collector": 1) did servicer acquire servicing rights after loan was in default, or 2) did servicer acquire servicing right "as a debt in default," even if not actually in default, such that the servicer's understanding was that it would be a "debt collector"; holding neither prong applied on fact presented).

35 Motley v. Homecomings Fin., L.L.C., 557 F. Supp. 2d 1005 (D. Minn. 2008) (no allegation that loan in default when servicer obtained servicing rights); Porter v. Fairbanks Capital Corp., 2002 WL 31163702 (N.D. Ill. 2002); *In re* Price, 403 B.R. 775 (Bankr. E.D. Ark. 2009).

36 Schlosser v. Fairbanks Capital Corp., 323 F.3d 534, 536 (7th Cir. 2003) (servicer was debt collector under FDCPA where it treated debt as in default when it acquired it); Dawson v. Dovenmuehle Mortgage, Inc., 2002 WL 501499 (E.D. Pa. Apr. 3, 2002). *See generally* § 6.4.2, *supra* (discussion of what constitutes a default).

37 Alibrandi v. Financial Outsourcing Servs., Inc., 333 F.3d 82, 87 (2d Cir. 2003); Walcker v. SN Commercial, L.L.C., 2006 WL 3192503 (E.D. Wash. Nov. 2, 2006), *aff'd on other grounds*, 286 Fed. Appx. 455 (9th Cir. 2008) (granting summary judgment for servicer under state collection agency statute and finding under terms of loan borrower not in default until ten days after servicer sent notice of default).

38 Alibrandi v. Financial Outsourcing Servs., Inc., 333 F.3d 82, 87 n.5 (2d Cir. 2003); Hartman v. Meridian Fin. Servs., Inc., 191 F. Supp. 2d 1031, 1043–1044 (W.D. Wis. 2002). *See also* Skerry v. Mass. Higher Educ. Assistance Corp., 73 F. Supp. 2d 47, 52 (D. Mass. 1999) (using federal regulation's definition of default for student loan debt); Jones v. Intuition, Inc., 12 F. Supp. 2d 775, 779 (W.D. Tenn. 1998) (same).

39 Hartman v. Meridian Fin. Servs., Inc., 191 F. Supp. 2d 1031, 1044 (W.D. Wis. 2002).

40 Schlosser v. Fairbanks Capital Corp., 323 F.3d 534 (7th Cir. 2003); Dowling v. Litton Loan Servicing, L.P., 2006 WL 3498292 (S.D. Ohio Dec. 1, 2006) (mislabeling loan as in default when it is not is type of misrepresentation FDCPA intended to address).

Where a servicer was attempting to collect on a forbearance agreement rather than on the original, defaulted loan, the servicer was not a debt collector.[41] Since the homeowners were current on their obligations set forth in the forbearance agreement at the time the servicer began collecting the obligation, the debt was not in default at the time the servicer acquired it.

Some servicers use subservicers for loans in default. The exemption will not apply to the subservicer that obtains servicing rights after default. The servicer exception also does not extend to an attorney hired by the servicer to pursue a foreclosure proceeding or other collection efforts against the borrower on the mortgage or deed of trust.[42]

The FDCPA does not cover a creditor's servicing of a loan it originated, because the FDCPA only covers collection of debts that are "owed or due another."[43] Even if the original creditor assigns the debt to another entity and retains only the servicing rights, it will fall into an exemption for entities collecting debts that they originated.[44]

7.4.3 Substantive Prohibitions

The FDCPA includes broad, general prohibitions of:

- Any false, deceptive, or misleading representation;[45]
- Use of any unfair or unconscionable means to collect a debt;[46] and

41 Bailey v. Security Nat'l Servicing Corp., 154 F.3d 384 (7th Cir. 1998).

42 *See* Kaltenbach v. Richards, 464 F.3d 524 (5th Cir. 2006) (foreclosure attorney subject to general requirements of FDCPA); Wilson v. Draper & Goldberg, P.L.L.C., 443 F.3d 373 (4th Cir. 2006) (rejecting foreclosure firm's argument that it was merely enforcing a lien on real property in an *in rem* proceeding and not collecting a debt); Miller v. McCalla, Raymer, Padrick, Cobb, Nichols, and Clark, L.L.C., 214 F.3d 872 (7th Cir. 2000) (suit against law firm that was collecting mortgage debt); National Consumer Law Center, Fair Debt Collection § 4.2.8 (6th ed. 2008 and Supp.). *But see* Brown v. Morris, 243 Fed. Appx. 31 (5th Cir. 2007) (attorney involved primarily in non-judicial foreclosure, i.e., enforcing security interest, not a debt collector per se); Mansour v. Cal-Western Reconveyance Corp., 618 F. Supp. 2d 1178 (D. Ariz. 2009) (non-judicial foreclosure not an attempt to collect a debt); Fouche v. Shapiro & Massey, L.L.P., 575 F. Supp. 2d 776 (S.D. Miss. 2008) (distinguishing between prosecuting non-judicial foreclosure as enforcement of security instrument not covered by FDCPA and judicial foreclosure as debt collection); Hulse v. Ocwen Fed. Bank, F.S.B., 195 F. Supp. 2d 1188, 1204 (D. Or. 2002) (foreclosing on property pursuant to deed of trust is not the collection of a debt within the meaning of the FDCPA).

43 15 U.S.C. § 1692a(6).

44 15 U.S.C. § 1692a(6)(F)(ii). *See* McAnaney v. Astoria Fin. Corp., 357 F. Supp. 2d 578, 592–593 (E.D.N.Y. 2005).

45 15 U.S.C. § 1692e. *See* Hartman v. Meridian Fin. Servs., Inc., 191 F. Supp. 2d 1031, 1044 (W.D. Wis. 2002) (granting summary judgment to debtors on claim that servicer's collection letters were deceptive).

46 15 U.S.C. § 1692f.

- Any conduct the natural consequence of which is to harass, oppress, or abuse any person.[47]

In addition, the statute prohibits a number of specific practices. The prohibitions most likely to come into play in the context of loan servicing are:

- Falsely representing the character, amount, or legal status of any debt;[48]
- Threatening to take action that cannot legally be taken;[49]
- Threatening to take action that is not intended to be taken;[50]
- Reporting or threatening to report false information to a credit bureau;[51]
- Communicating information about a disputed debt to a credit bureau without reporting that it is disputed;[52]
- Using simulated process or official documents;[53]
- Collecting any amount unless it is explicitly authorized by the agreement or permitted by law;[54]
- Communicating with a consumer whom the servicer knows to be represented by an attorney;[55]
- Calling the debtor at an unusual time or at a time or place that the servicer knows or should know is inconvenient to the consumer;[56]
- Communicating about the debt with third parties (with certain specified exceptions);[57]
- Venue abuse.[58]

These substantive provisions are discussed in extensive detail in National Consumer Law Center, *Fair Debt Collection* Chapter 5 (6th ed. 2008 and Supp.).

The FDCPA's validation notice requirement is particularly significant in the context of mortgage servicing. Within five days after the initial communication[59] with the debtor, the loan servicer (if it qualifies as a debt collector), must send the debtor a notice that states the amount of the debt and identifies the creditor to whom the debt is owed.[60] (The validation notice can be part of the initial collection letter.) It is a violation if the validation notice does not include an accurate statement of the full amount due as of the date of the notice.[61] Stating an amount that does not include all interest, late charges, attorney fees, and other charges due on the date of the notice is insufficient, even if those charges change daily.[62] The notice must also set forth important rights the debtor has, including the right to dispute the debt and request that the collector provide verification of it.[63] Collection activities may continue during the thirty-day period that the consumer has the right to request debt validation, as long as the collection activities are not inconsistent with the consumer's right to debt validation or overshadow the right.[64] If the consumer disputes the debt, the

47 15 U.S.C. § 1692d.

48 15 U.S.C. § 1692e(2)(a). *See In re* Maxwell, 281 B.R. 101 (Bankr. D. Mass. 2002) (servicer demanded amounts borrower did not owe); *In re* Hart, 246 B.R. 709 (Bankr. D. Mass. 2000) (servicer misrepresented that consumer was obligated to repay amounts in "negative suspense account").

49 15 U.S.C. § 1692e(5). *But see* Whittaker v. Deutsche Bank Nat'l Trust Co., 605 F. Supp. 2d 914 (N.D. Ohio 2009) (filing of foreclosure action without immediate means of proving amount or ownership of debt not FDCPA violation because no "deception" involved).

50 15 U.S.C. § 1692e(5).

51 15 U.S.C. § 1692e(8).

52 15 U.S.C. § 1692e(8).

53 15 U.S.C. § 1692e(9), (13).

54 15 U.S.C. § 1692f(1). *See* Scott v. Fairbanks Capital Corp., 284 F. Supp. 2d 880 (S.D. Ohio 2003) (denying motion to dismiss as complaint sufficiently alleged FDCPA violation that "padded" fees not permitted by contract); Porter v. Fairbanks Capital Corp., 2003 WL 21210115 (N.D. Ill. May 21, 2003) (complaint adequately alleged claim under FDCPA that charges for property preservation services and broker's price opinions were not permitted under mortgage clause covering costs to protect value of the property); *In re* Maxwell, 281 B.R. 101 (Bankr. D. Mass. 2002) (servicer attempted to collect interest on mortgage even though it did not have possession of note and could not determine whether it was entitled to demand interest).

55 15 U.S.C. § 1692c(a)(2). *See* Hartman v. Meridian Fin. Servs., Inc., 191 F. Supp. 2d 1031 (W.D. Wis. 2002) (granting summary judgment to consumers against servicer who continued to communicate with them after learning they were represented by counsel).

56 15 U.S.C. § 1692c(a)(1).

57 15 U.S.C. § 1692c(b).

58 15 U.S.C. § 1692i.

59 *See* Thompson v. BAC Home Loans Servicing, L.P., 2010 WL 1286747 (N.D. Ind. Mar. 26, 2010) (notice of transfer of servicing rights did not constitute initial communication where it did not provide status of debt or attempt to collect past-due amounts); National Consumer Law Center, Fair Debt Collection § 5.7 (6th ed. 2008 and Supp.).

State debt collection laws may provide a broader definition of an initial communication. *See* Ray v. Int'l Bank, Inc., 2005 WL 2305017 (D. Colo. Sept. 21, 2005) (no Colorado law supports proposition that documents initiating court proceedings cannot constitute an "initial communication").

60 15 U.S.C. § 1692g(a). *See* Hartman v. Meridian Fin. Servs., Inc., 191 F. Supp. 2d 1031, 1044 (W.D. Wis. 2002) (granting summary judgment against servicer that did not send validation notice).

61 Miller v. McCalla, Raymer, Padrick, Cobb, Nichols, & Clark, L.L.C., 214 F.3d 872 (7th Cir. 2000) (suit against law firm that was collecting mortgage debt). *See* National Consumer Law Center, Fair Debt Collection § 5.7.2.6.4 (6th ed. 2008 and Supp.).

62 Miller v. McCalla, Raymer, Padrick, Cobb, Nichols, & Clark, L.L.C., 214 F.3d 872 (7th Cir. 2000). *See also* Person v. Stupar, Schuster & Cooper, S.C., 136 F. Supp. 2d 957 (E.D. Wis. 2001); Bawa v. Bowman, Heintz, Boscia & Vician, 2001 WL 618966 (S.D. Ind. May 30, 2001); Wilkerson v. Bowman, Heintz, Boscia & Vician, 200 F.R.D. 605, 607 (N.D. Ill. 2001).

63 15 U.S.C. § 1692g(a). *See* Schlosser v. Fairbanks Capital Corp., 323 F.3d 534, 536 (7th Cir. 2003) (reversing dismissal of suit alleging that servicer failed to give notice of right to dispute debt).

64 15 U.S.C. § 1692g(b), *as amended by* Pub. L. No. 109-351 (2006).

servicer must cease its attempts to collect the debt, or the disputed portion of the debt, until it mails verification of the debt to the consumer.[65]

7.4.4 FDCPA Remedies

The FDCPA is a strict liability statute.[66] In the case of any violation, the consumer may recover actual damages, statutory damages up to $1000, attorney fees, and costs.[67] There are specific provisions for class actions, including factors for courts to use in determining the amount of a statutory damage award in a class action.[68] A collector is not liable if the violation resulted from a bona fide error, but the collector has the burden of showing not only that the error was unintentional but also that it occurred despite reasonable procedures to avoid errors.[69] Federal and state courts have jurisdiction over suits under the Act.[70]

7.4.5 Claims Under State Debt Collection Statutes

Many states have their own debt collection practices statutes that may apply to servicers.[71] These statutes are particularly worth investigating because many of them have a broader scope than the FDCPA. For example, in a number of states the state debt collection practices statute covers creditors who are collecting or servicing their own debts. State debt collection practices statutes are discussed in detail in National Consumer Law Center, *Fair Debt Collection* § 11.2, Appendix E (6th ed. 2008 and Supp.).

65 15 U.S.C. § 1692g(b). *See* McDaniel v. South & Associates, P.C., 325 F. Supp. 2d 1210 (D. Kan. 2004) (law firm's filing of judicial foreclosure action after consumer disputed claim and requested verification of debt, in response to FDCPA validation letter, was debt collection activity covered by FDCPA). *See also* National Consumer Law Center, Fair Debt Collection § 5.7.2.7 (6th ed. 2008 and Supp.).

66 National Consumer Law Center, Fair Debt Collection § 5.2.3 (6th ed. 2008 and Supp.).

67 15 U.S.C. § 1692k(a). *See* National Consumer Law Center, Fair Debt Collection §§ 6.3, 6.4, 6.5, 6.8 (6th ed. 2008 and Supp.).

68 15 U.S.C. § 1692k(b)(2). *See* National Consumer Law Center, Fair Debt Collection § 6.6 (6th ed. 2008 and Supp.).

69 15 U.S.C. § 1692k(c). *See* National Consumer Law Center, Fair Debt Collection Ch. 7 (6th ed. 2008 and Supp.).

70 15 U.S.C. § 1692k(d).

71 *See, e.g.,* Hartman v. Meridian Fin. Servs., Inc., 191 F. Supp. 2d 1031, 1049–1050 (W.D. Wis. 2002) (granting summary judgment to consumers against servicer for violations of state debt collection law); Wright v. Litton Loan Servicing, L.P., 2006 WL 891030 (E.D. Pa. Apr. 4, 2006) (plaintiff awarded statutory damages of $2000 based on amount of $100 for each of 20 written communications that violated state debt collection act).

7.5 Fair Credit Reporting Act

The possibility of a claim under the Fair Credit Reporting Act (FCRA) should be explored whenever the servicer inaccurately reports information regarding the borrower's account to a credit reporting agency.[72] Such disputes are not uncommon.[73] For example, the servicer may incorrectly report that the consumer has defaulted on a mortgage obligation. The consumer may have made all payments on time, but the servicer misapplied them, failed to record them, or delayed in posting them. Or the claim of default may be based on a charge that the servicer had no right to impose. If the servicer claims that the consumer is in default, typically it will report that default to one or more credit reporting agencies. A false report that the consumer is in default may trap the consumer in a bad loan by making it impossible to refinance out of it.

While the FCRA creates standards of accuracy that creditors and other entities must follow when they furnish information to credit reporting agencies,[74] it does not create a private cause of action for consumers to enforce these duties.[75] Instead, the consumer has a private cause of action only after invoking the FCRA's reinvestigation procedure.

72 The Fair Debt Collection Practices Act (FDCPA) also places some obligations on entities that furnish information to credit reporting agencies. It prohibits entities that meet the definition of "debt collector" from reporting or threatening to report false information to a credit bureau, or reporting information about a disputed debt without reporting that it is disputed. *See* 15 U.S.C. § 1692e(8).

The reinvestigation procedure under FCRA is not required before a consumer can assert these FDCPA claims. *See* National Consumer Law Center, Fair Debt Collection § 9.6.7 (6th ed. 2008 and Supp.); § 7.4, *supra.*

73 *See, e.g.,* Calloway v. Green Tree Servicing, L.L.C., 607 F. Supp. 2d. 669 (D. Del. 2009) (denying motion to dismiss FCRA claim where servicer was incorrectly reporting two outstanding mortgages when borrowers had only one mortgage); Sites v. Nationstar Mortgage, L.L.C., 2009 WL 117844 (M.D. Pa. Jan. 16, 2009) (servicer reported borrowers as delinquent because of typographical error in processing payment); Islam v. Option One Mortgage Corp., 432 F. Supp. 2d 181 (D. Mass. 2006) (alleging false reports to credit reporting agencies after failure to properly credit payoff funds); Hukic v. Aurora Loan Servs., Inc., 2006 WL 1457787 (N.D. Ill. May 22, 2006) (reporting borrower delinquent based on clerical error in which payment recorded as $1135 instead of $1335); Gordon v. Greenpoint Credit, 266 F. Supp. 2d 1007 (S.D. Iowa 2003) (alleging servicer falsely alleged late payments on manufactured home contract). *See also* Miller v. Wells Fargo & Co., 2008 WL 793676 (W.D. Ky. Mar. 24, 2008) (servicer falsely reporting bankruptcy of borrower).

74 15 U.S.C. § 1681s-2(a).

75 15 U.S.C. § 1681s-2(c). *See* Dvorak v. AMC Mortgage Servs., Inc., 2007 WL 4207220 (E.D. Wash. Nov. 26, 2007); Gibbs v. SLM Corp., 336 F. Supp. 2d 1, 11 (D. Mass. 2004) (no private cause of action against student loan servicer for initial furnishing of inaccurate information); Gordon v. Greenpoint Credit, 266 F. Supp. 2d 1007 (S.D. Iowa 2003).

A consumer invokes the reinvestigation procedure by disputing the completeness or accuracy of the information furnished to the credit reporting agency.[76] This dispute must be communicated to the credit reporting agency.[77] Disputing the debt with the entity that furnished the information is insufficient,[78] although it is often wise to send a copy of the dispute and supporting documentation to the furnisher.

Once the credit reporting agency receives the dispute, it is required to conduct a reinvestigation within thirty days.[79] As part of its reinvestigation, the credit reporting agency is required to notify the furnisher of the information of the dispute.[80] The furnisher is then required to conduct its own investigation and report back to the credit reporting agency.[81] The furnisher can be held liable under the FCRA if it fails to perform these duties in accordance with the statute.[82]

In the case of willful noncompliance, the FCRA offers a private cause of action for actual damages, or, in the alternative, statutory damages of $100 to $1000, plus attorney fees.[83] In addition, the statute authorizes the consumer to seek punitive damages.[84] For negligent violations the FCRA authorizes actual damages plus attorney fees.[85]

To determine whether a potential FCRA claim exists, the first step is to obtain the consumer's credit report. Consumers are entitled to one free credit report per year from each of the three nationwide credit reporting agencies.[86] If inaccurate information appears on the report, a demand letter to the furnisher may be sufficient to obtain its removal. If not, the consumer should dispute the information with the credit reporting agency and request a reinvestigation. If the furnisher agrees to remove the disputed information, the consumer should re-check the credit report a few months later to make sure that the inaccurate information has not reappeared.

Advocates should be aware that the FCRA may preempt state law claims against servicers for their actions affecting the credit status of the borrower.[87] The FCRA also establishes a limited qualified immunity for the furnisher of information from liability under several tort theories unless the conduct involves malice or willful intent.[88] Several courts have parsed through the relationship between FCRA and state law claims and have found that if the state claim avoids reference to credit reporting issues, and instead concentrates on collection issues, breach of contract, state UDAP claims, or that the conduct was potentially willful and malicious, that it survives FCRA preemption.[89]

7.6 State Mortgage Servicing Laws

Many states have enacted laws for consumers to use to combat servicing abuses. A summary of these laws is contained at Appendix D, *infra*. While many of these statutes contain provisions similar to RESPA, some provide even greater rights to consumers.[90] For example, some statutes require that a lender or servicer respond to borrower inquiries in a shorter time period than the sixty-day period allowed under RESPA,[91] or afford borrowers more time to repay escrow shortages and deficiencies.[92] Significantly, several of these statutes provide a private right of action for certain violations that may not exist under RESPA, or provide more substantial remedies.[93] Generally if the state

76 15 U.S.C. § 1681i(a)(1)(A).

77 *Id.*

78 Dumas v. Dovenmuehle Mortgage Inc., 2005 WL 1528262 (N.D. Ill. June 23, 2005) (holding plaintiff must show that the furnisher received notice from credit reporting agency, not consumer). *See also* Dvorak v. AMC Mortgage Servs., Inc., 2007 WL 4207220 (E.D. Wash. Nov. 26, 2007).

79 15 U.S.C. § 1681i(a)(1)(B) (allows a fifteen-day extension in some circumstances); Dumas v. Dovenmuehle Mortgage Inc., 2005 WL 1528262 (N.D. Ill. June 23, 2005) (holding plaintiff must show that the furnisher received notice from credit reporting agency, not consumer). *See also* Dvorak v. AMC Mortgage Servs., Inc., 2007 WL 4207220 (E.D. Wash. Nov. 26, 2007).

80 15 U.S.C. § 1681i(a)(2).

81 15 U.S.C. § 1681s-2(b).

82 *See* Gordon v. Greenpoint Credit, 266 F. Supp. 2d 1007 (S.D. Iowa 2003) (complaint adequately alleged furnisher liability claim under FCRA based on false reporting of late payments on manufactured home contract). *See also* National Consumer Law Center, Fair Credit Reporting Ch. 6 (6th ed. 2006 and Supp.) (detailed discussion of furnisher liability under the FCRA).

83 15 U.S.C. § 1681n(a)(1), (3).

84 15 U.S.C. § 1681n(a)(2).

85 15 U.S.C. § 1681o.

86 15 U.S.C. § 1681j. *See* National Consumer Law Center, Fair Credit Reporting § 3.3 (6th ed. 2006 and Supp.).

87 *See* National Consumer Law Center, Fair Credit Reporting § 10.7 (6th ed. 2006 and Supp.).

88 *See* National Consumer Law Center, Fair Credit Reporting § 10.4 (6th ed. 2006 and Supp.).

89 *See, e.g.*, Calloway v. Green Tree Servicing, L.L.C., 607 F. Supp. 2d 669 (D. Del. 2009) (claim based on defamatory conduct with malice or intent to injure not preempted by FCRA); Sites v. Nationstar Mortgage, L.L.C., 2009 WL 117844 (M.D. Pa. Jan. 16, 2009) (FCRA preempted UDAP claim, but not fraud, defamation, and interference with future contractual relations claims); Islam v. Option One Mortgage Corp., 432 F. Supp. 2d 181 (D. Mass. 2006) (FCRA preempted claim under state law that governed procedures to ensure accuracy of information reported to credit agencies and negligence claim); Hutchinson v. Delaware Sav. Bank F.S.B., 410 F. Supp. 2d 374 (D.N.J. 2006) (FCRA did not preempt consumers' state law claims based on servicer's malicious and wrongful attempt to collect on loan after bankruptcy discharge); Hukic v. Aurora Loan Servs., Inc., 2006 WL 1457787 (N.D. Ill. May 22, 2006) (FCRA does not preempt state law tort claims relating to credit reporting if malice is alleged).

90 State laws that provide greater protections to consumers generally are not preempted. *See* § 8.4, *infra*.

91 The servicing statutes in Alaska, Kansas, Maryland, Minnesota, Utah, Washington, and Wisconsin allow servicers only a fifteen-day period to respond to borrower inquiries. *See* Appx. D, *infra*.

92 *See, e.g.*, Conn. Gen. Stat. § 36a-716 (one year to repay shortage); N.H. Rev. Stat. Ann. § 397-B:5 (same).

93 Several statutes provide for an award of statutory damages in addition to actual damages, without the need to prove a pattern or practice of noncompliance as required by § 2605(f) of

law provides greater protections to borrowers than RESPA, and it is not preempted under some other federal law that is not inconsistent with RESPA, then the law is not preempted.[94]

7.7 Breach of Contract

An obvious claim in most servicing abuse cases is breach of contract. The most common claims against servicers for breach of contract relate to misapplication of payments, charging unauthorized fees, improperly using escrow funds and the imposition of forced-placed insurance.[95] The basic elements of a breach of contract claim are: 1) the existence of a valid contract between the parties;[96] 2) borrowers have performed their obligations under the contract or have an excuse for non-performance;[97] 3) servicer-holder failed to perform an obligation created by the contract; and, 4) the borrowers suffered damages as a result of the breach.

A critical step in asserting a successful breach of contract claim is establishing the obligations of the servicer or holder under the contract.[98] Advocates should carefully review the note and the mortgage agreement as well as any other attendant documents[99] the homeowner may have to determine the express terms of the agreement.

For example, the Fannie Mae/Freddie Mac Single-Family Uniform Instrument for a mortgage or deed of trust requires the servicer to maintain the escrow account in compliance with RESPA.[100] A servicer that requires escrow payments in an amount that causes the escrow account balance to exceed the maximum amount set by RESPA breaches the terms of the contract.[101] As a result, a breach of contract claim should be available to enforce RESPA provisions that do not have a private right of action, such as many of the escrow account provisions.[102] Borrowers may also consider bringing a breach of contract claim where the contract expressly incorporates servicing guidelines promulgated by HUD, Fannie Mae or Freddie Mac.[103]

Where the terms of the contract are subject to more than one meaning, the language should be construed strongly against the servicer-holder.[104] Residential mortgage agreements are classic contracts of adhesion. The loan documents are frequently preprinted forms offered by lenders on a take-it-or-leave-it basis that deprive prospective borrowers

---

RESPA. *See, e.g.*, Colo. Rev. Stat. § 38-40-104 ($1000 statutory damages); Minn. Stat. § 47.205 ($500 per violation); N.J. Stat. Ann. § 17:16F-18 (West) ($500).

94 *See* § 8.4, *infra*. *See also* National Consumer Law Center, The Cost of Credit: Regulation, Preemption, and Industry Abuses Ch. 3 (4th ed. 2009 and Supp.) (detailed discussion of federal preemption of state laws applicable to mortgage lenders and servicers).

95 *See* Chapter 6, *supra* (description of each problem).

96 Some courts have held the breach of contract claim does not lie against the servicer because it is not a party to the contract. *See* Conder v. Home Sav. of Am., 680 F. Supp. 2d 1168 (C.D. Cal. 2010); Ruff v. America's Serv. Co., 2008 WL 1830182 (W.D. Pa. 2008).

97 *See* Hukic v. Aurora Loan Servs., 588 F.3d 420 (7th Cir. 2009) (affirming summary judgment for lender on breach of contract claim because borrower had not performed in accordance with the contract).

98 *See* Motley v. Homecomings Fin., L.L.C., 557 F. Supp. 2d 1005 (dismissing breach of contract claim because borrower failed to attach contract or plead terms of the contract that were breached).

99 *See* Walker v. Washington Mut. Bank, 2007 WL 1953130 (Cal. Ct. App. July 5, 2007) (unpublished) (reversing summary judgment on breach of contract claim where borrower alleged servicer failed to credit payments in accordance with repayment plan).

100 The Fannie Mae/Freddie Mac Single-Family Uniform Instrument typically includes in section 3, entitled "Funds for Escrow Items," the following contractual language:

> Lender may, at any time, collect and hold Funds in an amount (a) sufficient to permit Lender to apply the Funds at the time specified under RESPA, and (b) not to exceed the maximum amount a lender can require under RESPA. Lender shall estimate the amount of Funds due on the basis of current data and reasonable estimates of expenditures of future Escrow Items or otherwise in accordance with Applicable Law. . . . Lender shall apply the Funds to pay the Escrow Items no later than the time specified under RESPA. . . . If there is a surplus of Funds held in escrow, as defined under RESPA, Lender shall account to Borrower for the excess funds in accordance with RESPA. If there is a shortage of Funds held in escrow, as defined under RESPA, Lender shall notify Borrower as required by RESPA, and Borrower shall pay to Lender the amount necessary to make up the shortage in accordance with RESPA, but in no more than twelve monthly payments. If there is a deficiency of Funds held in escrow, as defined under RESPA, Lender shall notify Borrower as required by RESPA, and Borrower shall pay to Lender the amount necessary to make up the deficiency in accordance with RESPA, but in no more than twelve monthly payments.

101 *See* Mark v. Keycorp Mortgage Inc., 1996 WL 465400 (N.D. Ill. Aug. 8, 1996); Sanders v. Lincoln Serv. Corp., 1993 WL 211358 (N.D. Ill. June 15, 1993); Aitken v. Fleet Mortgage Corp., 1992 WL 33926 (N.D. Ill. Feb. 12, 1992).

102 *See* § 8.3.6, *supra*. *See also* Monet v. Chase Home Fin., L.L.C., 2010 WL 1240973 (N.D. Cal. Mar. 26, 2010) (denying motion to dismiss breach of contract claim against loan owner for failure to provide notice of change of servicer).

103 *But see In re* Thorien, 2008 WL 5683488 (Bankr. D. Idaho Nov. 6, 2008) (rejecting claim that borrower was third-party beneficiary of contract between servicer and Freddie Mac based on Idaho law); Wells Fargo Home Loan Mortgage, Inc. v. Neal, 922 A.2d 538 (Md. 2007) (failure to comply with FHA regulations before loan accelerated or foreclosure initiated not breach of contract because contractual language was not a bargained-for term between homeowner and servicer).

104 *See* McAdams v. Citifinancial Mortgage Co., 2007 WL 141128 (M.D. La. Jan. 16, 2007) (ambiguity should be resolved in the homeowner's favor where the lender has prepared the mortgage loan contract); *In re* Romano, 174 B.R. 342 (Bankr. M.D. Fla. 1994) (construing loan note's ambiguous attorney fee provision against the lender/drafter).

the opportunity to negotiate terms effectively.[105] While the principle of construing ambiguities against the drafter is a potentially powerful doctrine for consumers, many courts considering breach of contract claims have failed to reach the issue by finding that the term in question is not in fact ambiguous.[106] Thus, careful attention must be paid to establishing the potential double-meaning of challenged terms.

7.8 Breach of the Implied Covenant of Good Faith and Fair Dealing

The duty of good faith and fair dealing between parties[107] to a contract is based in both common law and the UCC.[108] This implied contractual obligation is recognized in every state and is imposed on parties to an existing contract "to prohibit improper behavior in the performance and enforcement" of that contract.[109] Typically, a breach of the duty of good faith and fair dealing arises in connection with performance under the loan documents rather than the making or origination of the loan. Consequently, such a claim may be particularly useful in challenging servicing abuses in the later stages of the relationship.

Whether conduct violates the duty of good faith and fair dealing varies with the circumstances. Lack of good faith may be overt or the result of inactions and fair dealing may require more than honesty.[110] A breach of the duty is commonly characterized by conduct that violates the standards of decency, fairness, or reasonableness.

In the context of loan servicing, violations of this duty frequently relate to decisions to accelerate and foreclose, forceplace insurance and improperly assess fees.[111] Servicers may also breach this duty by improperly applying payments to the homeowners account.[112] For example, one court held that a mortgage holder breaches its duty of good faith by refusing to postpone a foreclosure sale when the homeowner had a binding unconditional contract to sell.[113] Another court held that a breach occurred when the mortgage holder failed to accept a deed in lieu of foreclosure resulting in additional interest charges, fees and costs.[114]

105 Flagg v. Yonkers Sav. And Loan Ass'n, 307 F. Supp. 2d 565 (S.D.N.Y. 2004), *aff'd*, 396 F.3d 178 (2d Cir. 2005).

106 *See, e.g.*, Ford v. Dovenmuehle Mortgage, Inc., 273 Ill. App. 3d 240 (1995) (holding that term "installment" was not ambiguous and servicer could charge a late fee on "installment" consisting of principal, interest, taxes and insurance, rather than merely principal and interest); Heist v. Eastern Sav. Bank, F.S.B., 884 A.2d 1224 (Md. Ct. Spec. App. 2005) (finding that homeowners agreement to prepayment penalty addendum was unequivocal).

107 This cause of action may also extend to attorneys acting on behalf of the mortgage servicer. *See* Whittingham v. Mortgage Elec. Registration Servs., Inc., 2007 WL 1456196 (D.N.J. May 15, 2007) (attorney representing servicer also bound by duty of good faith and fair dealing even though not a party to the contract). *But see* Rivera v. Washington Mut. Bank, 637 F. Supp. 2d 256 (D.N.J. 2009) (no contractual relationship between borrower and attorney for servicer in foreclosure action).

108 Restatement (Second) of Contracts § 205 (1979). *See also* Carreau & Co. v. Security Pac. Bus. Credit, Inc., 272 Cal. Rptr. 387, 398 (Ct. App. 1990); Cadle Co. v. Vargas, 771 N.E.2d 179 (Mass. App. Ct. 2002); Am. Bankers' Ins. Co. v. Wells, 819 So. 2d 1196, 1206–1207 (Miss. 2001) (lender's purchase of force placed insurance on gross rather than net balance may be a violation); GMAC v. Baymon, 732 So. 2d 262, 269 (Miss. 1999) (duty exists in all contracts, but lender's purchase of force placed insurance here was not a breach); Noonan v. First Bank Butte, 740 P.2d 631 (Mont. 1987) (tortious breach of covenant of good faith and fair dealing requires action which is arbitrary, capricious or unreasonable and exceeds plaintiff's justifiable expectations); Kirke La Shelle Co. v. Paul Armstrong Co., 188 N.E. 163, 167 (N.Y. 1933) ("in every contract there exists an implied covenant of good faith and fair dealing"); Southface Condo. Owners Ass'n, Inc. v. Southface Condo. Ass'n, 733 A.2d 55, 58 (Vt. 1999). *But see* Lovell v. Western Nat'l Life Ins. Co., 754 S.W.2d 298 (Tex. 1988) (no duty of good faith and fair dealing between mortgagor and mortgage holder absent special circumstances or explicit agreement).

109 In some states, a breach of good faith and fair dealing is not an independent claim, but rather a theory upon which a breach of contract claim may be based. *See* Webb v. Chase Manhattan Mortgage Corp., 2007 WL 709335 (S.D. Ohio Mar. 5, 2007). *See also* Harris v. Provident Life and Accident Ins. Co., 310 F.3d 73, 80 (2d Cir. 2002); Tornow v. Stanford Bros., Inc., 2005 WL 4135450 (Mich. Cir. Ct. Apr. 21, 2005) (unpublished).

110 Restatement (Second) of Contracts § 205 (1979) (describing conduct which may constitute bad faith as "evasion of the spirit of the bargain, lack of diligence and slacking off, willful rendering of imperfect performance, abuse of a power to specify terms, and interference with or failure to cooperate in the other party's performance.").

111 Improper handling of the transfer of servicing right may also give rise to a breach of duty. *See* Hilgeman v. Am. Mortgage Sec., Inc., 994 P.2d 1030 (Ariz. 2000) (affirming trial court's award for compensatory damages for failure to forward payments to purchaser of loan).

112 *In re* Nosek, 2006 WL 1867096 (Bankr. D. Mass. June 30, 2006), *appeal allowed and case remanded*, 354 B.R. 331 (D. Mass. 2006) (Bankruptcy Code preempts state law claim of breach of implied covenant of good faith and fair dealing), *vacated*, 544 F.3d 34 (1st Cir. 2008). *But see* Marguiles v. Chase Manhattan Mortgage Corp., 2005 WL 2923580 (N.J. Super. Ct. App. Div. Nov. 7, 2005) (absent bad faith misapplication of payments did not constitute breach of duty of good faith and fair dealing).

113 Snowden v. Chase Manhattan Mortgage Corp., 2003 WL 22519518 (Mass. Super. Ct. Nov. 5, 2003). *See also* Wells Fargo v. Sinott, 2008 WL 474131 (D. Vt. Feb. 20, 2008) (denying lender's motion for summary judgment where borrower sought to negotiate with the bank but the legal foreclosure process outpaced the informal workout process). *But see* Farm Credit Servs. of Am. v. Dougan, 704 N.W.2d 24 (S.D. 2005) (no breach duty of good faith and fair dealing in bringing foreclosure action on oversecured property).

114 Citicorp. Mortgage, Inc. v. Upton, 616 A.2d 1179 (Conn. Super. Ct. 1992). *See also In re* Peterson, 93 B.R. 323 (Bankr. D. Vt. 1988) (refusing to dismiss claim for breach of covenant and good faith dealing arising out of purported unlawful declaration of acceleration and overreaching in obtaining modification of original agreement); Monahan v. GMAC Mortgage Corp., 893 A.2d 298 (Vt. 2005) (affirming judgment in favor of homeowner who claimed servicer/lender breached its duty of good

Failure to modify a loan as contemplated by the parties may also breach the duty.[115]

In *Charleswell v. Chase Manhattan Bank, N.A.*,[116] the court held that plaintiff homeowners had sufficiently stated a claim for breach of good faith and fair dealing by alleging that the mortgage holder misled owners as to the extent of their insurance coverage, treated Virgin Island homeowners differently than mainland customers, and billed owners for excessive and unnecessary insurance after a hurricane damaged their property.[117] The duty of good faith and fair dealing may also be breached where the lender consistently overstates the payoff amount or improperly capitalizes certain costs that should have been assessed as separate fees. Courts have held that conduct preventing consumers from refinancing or paying off the mortgage may breach the implied covenant of good faith and fair dealing.[118]

In *In re Nosek*,[119] the court found that the servicer breached the implied covenant of good faith and fair dealing by its inability, or unwillingness, to account for and properly distinguish between pre-petition and post-petition payments made by the borrower during the course of her chapter 13 bankruptcy, by failing to promptly credit the borrower's account from funds held in suspense, and by "dragg[ing] its feet" when asked by the plaintiff, and the court, for a detailed accounting.[120] In awarding the borrower $250,000 in damages on this claim, the court noted that the servicer's behavior was "diametrically opposite good faith behavior." It should be noted that the servicer's conduct giving rise to this significant damage award is not unusual, particularly in bankruptcy cases. On appeal, the district court concluded that the debtor's claim for breach of duty of good faith and fair dealing was preempted by the Bankruptcy Code. However, it is not clear that the district court was correct in finding the borrower's state law claim preempted, and for borrowers who are not in bankruptcy, misapplication of payments may give rise to a breach of the duty of good faith and fair dealing.

In sorting through the conflicting cases on the duty of good faith in lender liability cases, it is important to note the distinction between those sounding in tort and those sounding in contract. While the contractual obligation is firmly established and applies to every contract, tort liability for breach of the covenant of good faith is less widely recognized. Tort liability may require a showing of some special relationship, beyond that of lender and customer, such as special circumstances giving rise to a fiduciary or quasi-fiduciary relationship or other indicia of a heightened duty.[121] Where tort liability is recognized, damages for breach of duty may include consequential, and in some states, punitive damages.

7.9 Breach of Fiduciary Duty

Absent special circumstances, most courts have held that the mere existence of a debtor-creditor relationship does not give rise to a fiduciary duty. However, special circumstances may exist where a disparity of bargaining power is coupled with the weaker party placing trust and confidence in the stronger party.

In the servicing context, a fiduciary duty most commonly arises when the servicer acts as escrowee for the borrower's escrow account.[122] In many residential loan transactions,

faith and fair dealing where despite its knowledge that plaintiffs were unable to make their mortgage payments without rental income from the property, and the fact that the loss of rental income was due, in part, to GMAC's own breach of contract and lack of assistance in remedying the breach, GMAC moved ahead with foreclosure proceedings against plaintiffs).

115 *In re* Thorian, 2008 WL 767024 (Bankr. D. Idaho Mar. 21, 2008) (denying lender's summary judgment motion on breach of covenant of good faith and fair dealing).

116 308 F. Supp. 2d 545 (D. V.I. 2004).

117 *Id.* at 561–562. *See also* Am. Bankers' Ins. Co. v. Wells, 819 So. 2d 1196, 1206–1207 (Miss. 2001) (jury question whether lender violated duty of good faith by forceplacing insurance on gross rather than net balance for borrowers whose own insurance lapsed).

118 *See* Chedick v. Nash, 151 F.3d 1077 (D.C. Cir. 1998) (recognizing tort of promissory fraud, i.e., misrepresentation of present intent to perform an act in the future; the act here was its duty to act in good faith); *In re* Hart, 246 B.R. 709 (Bankr. D. Mass. 2000) (servicer breached duty when after having been alerted to potential problem with homeowner's account, it did nothing and instead abandoned him to the "ambiguities and vagaries of its computer system and muddled internal operations."); Security Pac. Nat'l Bank v. Evans, 878 N.Y.S.2d 732 (N.Y. App. Div. 2009) (servicer's failure to confirm its letters, and not credit report, reflected accurate payment history sufficiently stated cause of action).

119 354 B.R. 331 (D. Mass. 2006) (Bankruptcy Code preempts state law claim of breach of implied covenant of good faith and fair dealing), *subsequent decision*, *In re* Nosek, 363 B.R. 643 (Bankr. D. Mass. 2007).

120 *See also In re* Hart, 246 B.R. 709 (Bankr. D. Mass. 2000) (servicer breached duty when after having been alerted to potential problem with homeowner's account, it did nothing and instead abandoned him to the "ambiguities and vagaries of its computer system and muddled internal operations").

121 *See, e.g.*, Foley v. Interactive Data Corp., 765 P.2d 373 (Cal. 1988) (tort for breach of implied covenant of good faith and fair dealing not available in employment contract cases; suggesting tort will only be recognized in insurance cases); Mitsui Mfrs. Bank v. Superior Court, 260 Cal. Rptr. 793 (Ct. App. 1989) (no tort liability for breach of duty of good faith); Bankers Trust Co. v. Brown, 107 P.3d 609 (Okla. Civ. App. 2004) (tort liability for breach of implied covenant of good faith and fair dealing does not extend to mortgage holder/mortgagor relationship). *See also* § 5.13.2, *supra* (discussion of fiduciary duty).

122 *See* Smith v. GMAC Mortgage Corp., 2007 WL 2593148 (W.D.N.C. Sept. 5, 2007) (denying motion to dismiss breach of fiduciary duty claim where servicer failed to pay insurance premium from escrow and then force-placed insurance); Webb v. Chase Manhattan Mortgage Corp., 2007 WL 709335 (S.D. Ohio Mar. 5, 2007) (following *Cairns* and finding no fiduciary duty based on escrow account). *But see* Marguiles v. Chase Manhattan Mortgage Corp., 2005 WL 2923580 (N.J. Super. Ct.

borrowers are required to pay, in advance monthly installments, amounts for real estate taxes and/or hazard insurance. These funds are held in an escrow account controlled by the servicer. RESPA imposes limits on how much a servicer may collect and hold in the account for such items.[123] The servicer is then required to disburse monies in a timely manner from the escrow account for tax and insurance payments as they become due.

Borrowers have sufficiently alleged claims for breach of fiduciary duty against servicers and lenders in cases where the servicer failed to make timely disbursements[124] and failed to refund or credit excess escrow funds as required by RESPA.[125] Servicers may also be liable for improper disbursements from borrowers escrow account. For example, in *McDonald v. Washington Mutual Bank, NA*,[126] the borrower alleged that the servicer had improperly used tax escrow funds to pay for force placed insurance. As a result, borrowers were required to pay additional funds into their tax escrow account and were charged various late fees. In denying the servicer's motion to dismiss, the court stated that as escrowee, the servicer owed a fiduciary duty to borrowers to act only in accordance and in strict compliance with the escrow agreement.[127]

7.10 Tort Liability

7.10.1 Introduction

While contract law theories and statutory remedies often predominate in cases of abusive servicing practices, it is also possible that such conduct may give rise to liability based on common law torts.

App. Div. Nov. 7, 2005) (unpublished) (existence of mortgage loan escrow account does not give rise to fiduciary duty); Cairns v. Ohio Sav. Bank, 672 N.E.2d 1058 (Ohio Ct. App. 1996) (rejecting breach of fiduciary duty claim based on lender's administration of escrow account).

123 *See* § 8.3.2, *supra*.

124 *See* Choi v. Chase Manhattan Mortgage Co., 63 F. Supp. 2d 874 (N.D. Ill. 1999) (denying motion to dismiss breach of fiduciary duty claims against lender and servicers); Valenza v. Heine, 1986 WL 15000 (E.D. Pa. Dec. 31, 1986), *aff'd without op.*, 831 F.2d 288 (3d Cir. 1987).

125 Heller v. First Town Mortgage Corp., 1998 WL 614197 (S.D.N.Y. Sept. 14, 1998); Mark v. Keycorp Mortgage, Inc., 1996 WL 465400 (N.D. Ill. Aug. 8, 1996). *See also* Birkholm v. Washington Mut. Bank, F.A., 447 F. Supp. 2d 1158 (W.D. Wash. 2006) (denying motion to dismiss breach of fiduciary duty claim where plaintiffs alleged servicer used escrow funds to pay late charges, corporate advances, force placed insurance premiums, property inspection fees, and payoff fees rather than taxes and insurance).

126 2000 WL 967994 (N.D. Ill. July 11, 2000).

127 *See also* Vician v. Wells Fargo Home Mortgage, 2006 WL 694740 (N.D. Ind. Mar. 16, 2006) (denying servicer's motion to dismiss, *inter alia*, breach of fiduciary duty claim based on allegations of improper force placed insurance).

7.10.2 Negligence

Borrowers seeking to assert tort claims based in negligence have met with mixed results. Whether styled as a claim for negligence or negligent servicing, courts have applied the same traditional four-part test. In order for plaintiffs to prevail in such an action, they must show: (1) a duty of care owed by the defendant to the plaintiff; (2) breach of that duty by the defendant; (3) injury to the plaintiff; and (4) that the defendant's breach caused the plaintiff's injury.[128]

The first hurdle for plaintiffs asserting a cause of action based in negligence is establishing a duty of care owed by the servicer to the homeowner. Generally a breach of contract alone will not give rise to a duty of care.[129] A contract can provide the basis for a tort claim only if a duty exists independently of the performance of the contract.[130] Thus a negligence claim may be available when the law imposes some other duty of affirmative care. For example, a servicer's violation of the duty imposed by RESPA to respond to a qualified written request can provide the basis for a negligence claim.[131] One court has found a duty of care in servicing loans "to maintain proper and accurate loan records

128 *See, e.g.*, Riley v. Fairbanks Capital Corp., 2006 WL 317242 (M.D. Ala. Feb. 9, 2006), *vacated and remanded*, 222 Fed. Appx. 897 (11th Cir. 2007) (to be dismissed for lack of subject matter jurisdiction); Hutchinson v. Delaware Sav. Bank F.S.B., 410 F. Supp. 2d 374 (D.N.J. 2006).

129 *See, e.g.*, Lawrence v. Aurora Loan Servs. L.L.C., 2010 WL 36427 (E.D. Cal. 2010) (servicer "owed plaintiffs no legal duty of care by virtue of acting as their loan servicer").

130 Many states have adopted the "economic loss rule" which creates a line between tort law, which allocates risk by imposing a reasonable duty of care, and contract law, which is meant to enforce the risk allocation created by the agreement. *See, e.g.*, Foster v. Argent Mortg. Co., L.L.S., 2010 WL 1136807 (E.D. Mich. Jan. 25, 2010) (applying economic-loss rule in holding that tort claim for intentional infliction of emotional distress must rest on breach of duty distinct from breach of contract); Davis v. Wells Fargo Home Mortgage, 2007 WL 2039077 (Wash. Ct. App. July 17, 2007) (unpublished) (economic-loss rule prevented recovery in tort).

Pennsylvania has adopted the "gist of the action doctrine" which limits parties from asserting tort claims where the crux of the claim is governed by a contract between parties. *See also In re* Figard, 382 B.R. 695 (Bankr. W.D. Pa. 2008).

131 Rawlings v. Dovenmuehle Mortgage, Inc., 64 F. Supp. 2d 1156 (M.D. Ala. 1999). *See also* Whittingham v. Mortgage Elec. Registration Servs., Inc., 2007 WL 1456196 (D.N.J. May 15, 2007) (under New Jersey law and in limited situations, attorney may have independent duty to non-client such as borrower); Johnson v. Citimortgage, Inc. 351 F. Supp. 2d 1368 (N.D. Ga. 2004) (plaintiff sufficiently pleaded claim for negligent performance of contract alleging defendant failed to maintain proper and accurate loan records); Barber v. National Bank of Alaska, 815 P.2d 857 (Alaska 1991) (reversing directed verdict for servicer where plaintiff alleged servicer was negligent in postponing mortgage sale while homeowner assistance loan application was pending and after servicer's agent informed borrower that sale would be postponed).

and to discharge and fulfill the other incidents attendant to the maintenance, accounting and servicing of loan records."[132]

A second significant challenge for homeowners is demonstrating that the servicer's conduct was the proximate cause of their injuries.[133] Proximate cause is the act that sets off a natural chain of events that produces the injury. However, an "unforeseeable" intervening cause may break the causal relationship. For example, at least one court has stated that numerous other negative credit items on the homeowner's credit report, precluded a finding that the servicer's incorrect reporting of her account status caused her to be denied later refinancing.[134]

7.10.3 Negligent Misrepresentation

Negligent misrepresentation generally occurs when: (1) the defendant makes a false statement of material fact; (2) the defendant failed to exercise reasonable care in obtaining or communicating the false information; (3) the plaintiff justifiably relied on the false information; and (4) injury to the plaintiff exists. As with traditional negligence claims, the plaintiff must also demonstrate that the misrepresentation caused the injury.[135] Claims for negligent misrepresentation must satisfy the heightened pleading standards of Federal Rule of Civil Procedure 9(b) and courts have routinely dismissed claims that are not accompanied by the "who, what, when, where, and how" of the alleged misconduct.[136]

7.10.4 Intentional Infliction of Emotional Distress

To state a claim for intentional infliction of emotional distress, the homeowner must allege that the defendant's conduct was extreme and outrageous, that the conduct was intentional or reckless and, that the conduct actually caused severe emotional distress. Extreme and outrageous conduct has often been described as conduct that is so extreme in degree, as to go beyond all possible bounds of decency, and to be regarded as atrocious, and utterly intolerable in a civilized community.[137]

For example, a court has denied defendant's motion to dismiss a borrower's claim for intentional infliction of emotional distress where the borrower alleged that the defendant/mortgagor forcibly entered the borrower's property, changed the locks, and removed his personal possessions prior to the date that the mortgagor was entitled to possession.[138] However, many courts have dismissed claims for intentional infliction of emotional distress against a mortgage servicer for foreclosing on a mortgage,[139] or even for shoddy customer service in responding to borrower inquiries and requests.[140]

7.10.5 Intentional Interference with Contractual Relations

The elements of this tort are: the existence of a contractual relationship; the defendant's knowledge of the contract; the intent to interfere; and the existence of damages suffered by the plaintiff. This tort has been asserted in challenging alleged excess coverage and inflated premiums in relation to force placed insurance.[141]

---

132 *See* Islam v. Option One Mortgage Corp., 432 F. Supp. 2d 181 (D. Mass. 2006) (noting that negligence in the context of debt collection has been recognized in state law for decades).

133 *See* Hutchinson v. Delaware Sav. Bank F.S.B., 410 F. Supp. 2d 374 (D.N.J. 2006). *See also* Burch v. Chase Manhattan Mortgage Corp., 2008 WL 4265180 (N.D. Ga. 2008) (borrower failed to demonstrate causation and damages).

134 Riley v. Fairbanks Capital Corp., 2006 WL 317242 (M.D. Ala. Feb. 9, 2006), *vacated and remanded,* 222 Fed. Appx. 897 (11th Cir. 2007) (to be dismissed for lack of subject matter jurisdiction). *See also* Burch v. Chase Manhattan Mortgage Corp., 2008 WL 4265180 (N.D. Ga. 2008) (borrowers failed to demonstrate that tax lien as a result of untimely tax payment by servicer caused blemished credit ratings where borrower has several other tax liens on other properties).

135 *See* Tobin v. BC Bancorp, 2010 WL 431437 (S.D. Cal. Feb. 1, 2010) (denying defendant's motion for judgment on the pleadings where servicer told plaintiffs that foreclosure sale was on hold "indefinitely" but proceeded with sale); Barber v. National Bank of Alaska, 815 P.2d 857 (Alaska 1991); Ghervescu v. Wells Fargo Home Mortgage, 2008 WL 660248 (Cal. Ct. App. Mar. 13, 2008) (unpublished) (reversing dismissal of negligent misrepresentation claim where servicer represented earliest date for foreclosure sale was May 4, but property was, in fact, sold at foreclosure on March 27).

136 *See, e.g.,* Barkho v. Homecomings Fin., L.L.C., 657 F. Supp. 2d 857, 863 (E.D. Mich. 2009) (dismissing negligent misrepresentation claim for failure to identify specific misrepresentations made to plaintiff); Hudson v. American Home Mortgage Servicing, Inc., 2009 WL 3353312 (N.D. Cal. Oct. 16, 2009) (dismissing claim where plaintiff failed to allege any misrepresentations of material fact).

137 *See* Restatement (Second) Tort § 46 cmt. d.

138 Matthews v. Homecoming Fin. Network, 2005 WL 2387688 (N.D. Ill. Sept. 26, 2005). *See also* Citifinancial Mortgage Co. v. Frasure, 63 U.C.C. Rep. Serv. 2d 942 (N.D. Okla. 2007) (denying lender's motion for summary judgment on intentional infliction of emotional distress claim).

139 *See, e.g.,* Hinton v. Wachovia Bank of Delaware Nat'l Ass'n, 189 Fed. Appx. 394 (6th Cir. 2006) (finding plaintiff did not demonstrate severe emotional distress and that servicer's conduct in foreclosing after borrower defaulted on mortgage and forbearance agreement not so outrageous in character); Mills v. Equicredit Corp., 344 F. Supp. 2d 1071 (E.D. Mich. 2004) (dismissing borrower's intentional infliction of emotional distress claim and stating that a "tort claim based on a failure to perform obligations that are covered by the express contract is inappropriate"), *aff'd on other grounds,* 172 Fed. Appx. 652 (6th Cir. 2006).

140 Rodrigues v. J.P. Morgan Chase Bank, 2009 WL 3710688 (D. Conn. Nov. 3, 2009) (servicer had "serious administrative and customer service problems" but did not "intend to cause or recklessly cause Plaintiffs anguish").

141 *See* Kenty v. Transamerica Premium Ins. Co., 650 N.E.2d 863

Some courts have also recognized the tort of interference with future or prospective contractual relations. This tort requires a prospective contractual relationship, purpose to harm the plaintiff, absence of privilege, and actual damages.[142] In cases involving a negative consumer credit report one court has held that a valid or reasonable expectancy of credit can satisfy the requirement of a prospective contractual relationship, although a pending credit application was not necessary.[143]

7.10.6 Unjust Enrichment

Unjust enrichment is a theory of legal liability based not on contract or statute, but upon equity and justice. Thus, a person who has been unjustly enriched at the expense of another is required to make restitution to the other. The elements of an unjust enrichment claim can vary by state, but generally are: (1) a benefit conferred on the defendant by the plaintiff; (2) an appreciation or knowledge by the defendant of the benefit; and (3) the acceptance or retention by the defendant of the benefit under such circumstances as to make it inequitable for the defendant to retain the benefit without making restitution.[144] Acknowledgment of a valid express contract does not necessarily preclude the possibility of an unjust enrichment claim.[145] However, as with negligence claims, unjust enrichment cannot be predicated on the defendant's failure to fulfill contract terms.

For example, in *Vician v. Wells Fargo Home Mortgage*,[146] the plaintiff alleged that the servicer had been unjustly enriched by collecting money for improper force placed insurance to which it was not entitled. The court held that the plaintiff's unjust enrichment claim was not barred by the existence of a specific contract. Instead the court found unjust enrichment to be an alternative theory of liability. Homeowners may also want to consider an unjust enrichment claim where the servicer has improperly collected late fees or attorney fees.[147]

In another case, *Walters v. Fidelity Mortgage of Cal.*,[148] the court denied the servicer's motion to dismiss the plaintiff's unjust enrichment claim. The plaintiff alleged that despite her compliance with the servicer's demand that she enter into a "reinstatement quote" to avoid foreclosure, the servicer proceeded with a trustee's sale and retained the benefit of the sale at the plaintiff's expense. Homeowners and advocates might rely on this theory where a servicer agrees to accept payments to cure a default or enters into a reinstatement agreement, but proceeds with a foreclosure on a separate track.

7.10.7 Libel

The tort of libel[149] has been the traditional non-statutory remedy for inaccurate consumer reports.[150] Libel is the written, printed publication of defamatory language. It requires prejudice to the consumer's reputation or livelihood, resulting from a communication to a third party, such as a credit reporting agency. Malice may be presumed,[151] but must be pleaded.[152] A federal district court has held that a borrower stated a claim for libel where he alleged that his mortgage servicer made false statements to credit reporting agencies that his account was delinquent.[153]

(Ohio 1995) (construing facts in favor of plaintiff on denial of motion to dismiss, overcharge could have been breach of contract induced by insurer; civil conspiracy claim also survived dismissal).

142 Zions First Nat'l Bank, N.A. v. Limited Health Club, 704 F.2d 120, 123 (3d Cir. 1983).

143 Bell v. May Dep't Stores Co., 6 S.W.3d 871 (Mo. 1999) (en banc). *See also* Sites v. Nationstar Mortgage, L.L.C., 2009 WL 117844 (M.D. Pa. Jan. 16, 2009) (denying motion to dismiss intentional interference with future contractual relations claim based on false statement made to credit reporting agencies and holding FCRA did not preempt claim).

144 *See* Restatement (First) of Restitution § 1 (2005).

145 *See, e.g.,* Pierce v. Emigrant Mortgage Co., 2008 WL 349191 (D. Conn. Feb. 6, 2008); Orser v. Select Portfolio Serv., Inc., 2005 WL 3478126 (W.D. Wash. Dec. 20, 2005) (unjust enrichment claim for collecting $50 payoff fee not precluded by existence of valid mortgage loan where loan documents did not expressly authorize fee); Pomykala v. PCFS Mortgage Res., 2005 WL 2149411 (D. Mass. Sept. 1, 2005) (denying defendant's motion to dismiss, *inter alia*, unjust enrichment claim); *In re* Nosek, 354 B.R. 331 (Bankr. D. Mass. 2006), *vacated on other grounds*, 544 F.3d 34 (1st Cir. 2008). *But see* Lum v. New Century Mortgage Corp., 19 A.D.3d 558, 800 N.Y.S.2d 408 (App. Div. 2005).

146 2006 WL 694740 (N.D. Ind. Mar. 16, 2006).

147 *See* Whittingham v. Mortgage Elec. Registration Servs., Inc., 2007 WL 1456196 (D.N.J. May 15, 2007) (borrower allegations that she was overcharged for work actually performed by foreclosure attorney sufficiently stated claim for unjust enrichment). *See also* Pierce v. Emigrant Mortgage Co., 2008 WL 349191 (D. Conn. Feb. 6, 2008) (failure of bank's attorney to respond to borrower's attempts to bring loan current leading to application of default interest rate unjustly enriched bank).

148 2010 WL 1493131 (E.D. Cal. Apr. 14, 2010).

149 Historically, the tort of defamation consisted of slander and libel. Slander is defamation by speaking, and libel is defamation by writing.

150 *See* National Consumer Law Center, Fair Credit Reporting § 10.5.2 (6th ed. 2006 and Supp.).

151 Johnson v. Citimortgage, Inc., 351 F. Supp. 2d 1368 (N.D. Ga. 2004) (malice inferred from the nature of the defamation); Matthews v. Deland State Bank, 334 So. 2d 164 (Fla. Dist. Ct. App. 1976) (bank's knowledge that the amount it reported as due was wrong, coupled with repeated refusal to correct it, is libel per se pursuant to which malice is presumed). *But see* Denney v. Northwestern Credit Ass'n, 104 P. 769, 770 (Wash. 1909) (words contained in report were innocent when considered in their natural sense without special knowledge, malice not implied).

152 Thornton v. Equifax, 619 F.2d 700 (8th Cir. 1980); Mitchell v. Surety Acceptance Corp., 838 F. Supp. 497 (D. Colo. 1993).

153 Johnson v. Citimortgage, Inc., 351 F. Supp. 2d 1368 (N.D. Ga. 2004). *See also* Sites v. Nationstar Mortgage, L.L.C., 2009 WL 117844 (M.D. Pa. Jan. 16, 2009) (denying motion to dismiss

The Fair Credit Reporting Act, however, prohibits any action in the nature of defamation, invasion of privacy, or negligence with respect to reporting of information against reporting agencies, users, and furnishers of information unless the conduct involves malice or willful intent to injure.[154] For more information on this important limitation see National Consumer Law Center, *Fair Credit Reporting* Chapter 10 (6th ed. 2006 and Supp.).

7.10.8 Conversion

The tort of conversion is any act of dominion or control over another's personal property inconsistent with her rights therein. This includes assuming control or ownership over the property, or applying the property to one's own use.[155] The elements of a conversion claim are: (1) the plaintiff's right to ownership or possession of personal property; (2) the defendant's use of the property in a way inconsistent with the plaintiff's rights; and (3) damages.[156] In general, the plaintiff must show that the defendant intentionally took the plaintiff's property and intentionally exercised dominion and control over it in defiance of the plaintiff's rights.[157]

In one case, *Williamson v. Ocwen Loan Servicing, L.L.C.*,[158] the court denied Ocwen's motion to dismiss the plaintiff's conversion claim, where the plaintiff alleged that Ocwen had no legal right to foreclose on the property and converted her personal property that was stored at the foreclosed home.

defamation claim based on false statement made to credit reporting agencies and holding FCRA did not preempt claim).

154 *See* 15 U.S.C. § 1681h(e).

155 *See* Restatement (Second) of Torts, § 22A (1965).

156 Fremont Indemnity Co. v. Fremont Gen. Corp., 55 Cal. Rptr. 3d 621, 638 (Cal. Ct. App. 2007).

157 *See, e.g., In re* Prince, 414 B.R. 285, 296–296 (Bankr. M.D. Tenn. 2009) (dismissing conversion claim where servicer misapplied cure payments, causing loan to go into default and leading to foreclosure, because debtor could not show that servicer "intentionally" took the property and exercised control over it).

158 2009 WL 5205405 (M.D. Tenn. Dec. 23, 2009).

Chapter 8 Challenging Mortgage Servicing Abuses—The Real Estate Settlement Procedures Act

8.1 Introduction

8.1.1 Overview

The Real Estate Settlement Procedures Act (RESPA), originally enacted in 1974, was designed to ensure that consumers in real estate transactions would receive timely information on the nature and costs of the settlement process and would be protected from abusive practices, such as kickbacks. In addition, RESPA placed limitations upon the use of escrow accounts. The National Affordable Housing Act of 1990 amended RESPA to require detailed disclosures for the transfer, sale, or assignment of mortgage servicing rights. It also mandated disclosures for mortgage escrow accounts at closing and annually, thereafter, itemizing the charges to be paid by the borrower and from the account by the servicer. The Department of Housing and Urban Development (HUD) is the agency designated to promulgate regulations under and enforce RESPA.[1]

Appendix C, *infra*, reprints selected provisions of the Act and regulations under the Act. This material and additional RESPA interpretations are found on the companion website. Sample qualified written requests are found at Appendix H.2, *infra*, and also on the companion website in MS Word format.

This chapter focuses on the obligations imposed on servicers under the Real Estate Settlement Procedures Act, and the remedies available under RESPA to redress breaches of these obligations.[2] There are limitations, however to the practices covered by RESPA and to the remedies available under RESPA, so advocates should consider other non-RESPA claims when challenging servicing abuses. Other claims are discussed in Chapter 7, *supra*, and in other NCLC publications. Common servicer abuses that can be challenged under RESPA and other law are detailed at Chapter 6, *supra*.

1 Regulation X is HUD's implementing regulation for RESPA. 24 C.F.R. pt. 3500.

2 *See* National Consumer Law Center, The Cost of Credit: Regulation, Preemption, and Industry Abuses § 12.2.1 (4th ed. 2009 and Supp.) (detailed discussion of settlement issues such as kickbacks, fee splitting and yield spread premiums).

8.1.2 Scope

RESPA applies to loans secured by a first or subordinate lien on residential real property of one to four units.[3] In addition, RESPA's scope is limited to "federally related mortgage loans," which are defined as loans made by federally-insured depository lenders (other than for temporary financing, such as a construction loan) or by creditors who make or invest more than one million dollars a year in residential secured loans, HUD-related loans, or loans intended to be sold on the secondary market to Fannie Mae or Freddie Mac.[4] Thus most home mortgage transactions are subject to RESPA requirements. Manufactured and mobile home purchase loans are also usually covered by RESPA if the loan will be secured by the real property upon which the manufactured home is or will be placed.[5]

Consistent with other consumer protection laws, RESPA's implementing regulation, Regulation X, exempts "business purpose loans" from the statute's coverage.[6] Loans on

3 12 U.S.C. § 2602(1)(A).

Prior to October 28, 1992, RESPA's application was limited to loans secured by first liens on residential real property of one to four units. *See* Housing and Community Development Act of 1992, Pub. L. No. 102-550, § 908, 106 Stat. 3672 (Oct. 28, 1992) (amending section 2602(1)(A) to include loans secured by subordinate liens as well). *See also* 59 Fed. Reg. 6506, 6511 (Feb. 10, 1994).

In contradiction to the plain language of the statute, Regulation X excludes subordinate mortgage loans from the servicing provisions. *See* § 8.2.1, *infra*.

4 12 U.S.C. § 2602(1)(B).

In the latter category, "creditors" are defined by reference to the Truth in Lending Act's definition. *See* 15 U.S.C. § 1602(f). *See also* National Consumer Law Center, Truth in Lending § 2.3 (6th ed. 2007 and Supp.).

5 Regulation X states that a loan can be a "federally related mortgage loan" if it is secured by residential real property upon which there is "located or, following settlement, will be placed using the proceeds of the loan, a manufactured home." Reg. X, 24 C.F.R. § 3500.2(b)(i)(B).

6 Reg. X, 24 C.F.R. § 3500.5(b)(2) ("business purpose loans" defined as "[a]n extension of credit primarily for a business, commercial, or agricultural purpose, as defined by Regulation Z, 12 C.F.R. 226.3(a)(1)" are excluded from RESPA's coverage). Regulation X directs that individuals may rely upon the "business purpose loans" exclusion found in Regulation Z,

property of twenty-five acres or more,[7] and temporary financing transactions (such as construction loans)[8] are also exempted from RESPA coverage. Additional limitations on coverage of the RESPA servicing provisions are discussed at § 8.2.1, *infra*.

8.2 The Servicer Act Provisions of RESPA

8.2.1 General

In 1990, Congress imposed new requirements on servicers of federally related mortgage loans through amendments to RESPA.[9] These amendments followed reports of a substantial number of consumer complaints about mortgage servicing problems.[10] The amendments generally require servicers to respond to borrower inquiries and correct account errors,[11] disclose information relating to the transfer of servicing operations,[12] and make timely payments out of escrow accounts.[13] These provisions are included in section 6 of RESPA, and are known as the "Servicer Act," or the Cranston-Gonzales Amendments to RESPA.

The requirements of the Act apply to "servicers."[14] A servicer is defined as the entity responsible for the servicing of the loan (accepting payments, maintaining escrow accounts, and so forth), which can be the maker or holder of the loan if such entity also services the loan.[15] The Federal Deposit Insurance Corp. (FDIC) and the Resolution Trust Corp. (RTC) generally are not subject to the Servicer Act, and Ginnie Mae (Government National Mortgage Ass'n), Freddie Mac (Federal Home Loan Mortgage Corp.), and Fannie Mae (Federal National Mortgage Ass'n) are not "servicers" for the purposes of the Act if they assume the servicing obligations on a loan following the termination of a servicing contract for cause or due to the insolvency of the prior servicer.[16] In addition, Regulation X expands the list of entities that are not covered "servicers" to include: the Federal Housing Administration (FHA) (including cases in which a mortgage insured under the National Housing Act[17] is assigned to HUD), the National Credit Union Administration (NCUA), the Rural Housing Service (RHS) (successor agency to the Farmers Home Administration (FmHA)), and the Department of Veterans Affairs (VA), if these entities assume the servicing obligations of the mortgage loan following the termination of a servicing contract for cause or due to the insolvency of the prior servicer.[18]

Despite unambiguous statutory language, HUD has construed the Servicer Act not to apply to subordinate liens and home equity lines of credit covered by the Truth in Lending Act and Regulation Z.[19] It is questionable whether this exemption from the Servicer Act coverage is enforceable, and at least one court had held that the regulation is not entitled to deference because it clearly conflicts with the statute.[20]

---

which implements the Truth in Lending Act. *Id. See* National Consumer Law Center, Truth in Lending § 2.4 (6th ed. 2007 and Supp.). *See also* Johnson v. Wells Fargo Home Mortg., Inc., 2007 WL 3226153 (D. Nev. Oct. 29, 2007) (RESPA did not apply to loan borrower used to acquire rental property that was not owner-occupied).

7 Reg. X, 24 C.F.R. § 3500.5(b)(1).

8 Reg. X, 24 C.F.R. § 3500.5(b)(3). The temporary financing exemption does not apply if the loan finances construction of one- to four-family residential property and the loan is used, or may be converted to, permanent financing by the same lender.

9 Cranston-Gonzalez National Affordable Housing Act, Pub. L. No. 101-625, 104 Stat. 4079 (1999) (codified at 12 U.S.C. § 2605).

As HUD is responsible for the regulatory oversight of RESPA, the implementing regulations for the Servicer Act are contained in Regulation X. 24 C.F.R. § 3500.21.

10 *See* U.S. Gen. Accounting Office, Report, Home Ownership—Mortgage Servicing Transfers Are Increasing and Causing Borrower Concern (1989) (available on this treatise's companion website). *See also* Wanger v. EMC Mortgage Corp., 103 Cal. App. 4th 1125, 127 Cal. Rptr. 2d 685 (2002).

11 12 U.S.C. § 2605(e).

12 12 U.S.C. § 2605(a), (b).

13 12 U.S.C. § 2605(g).

14 Gonzalez v. First Franklin Loan Servs., 2010 WL 144862 (E.D. Cal. Jan. 11, 2010)(only a loan servicer has a duty to respond to borrower inquiries under RESPA § 2605(e)); Lopez v. GMAC Mortgage Corp., 2007 WL 3232448 (N.D. Cal. Nov. 1, 2007) (motion to dismiss RESPA claim granted as to foreclosure trustee company which was not alleged to be a loan servicer); *In re* Madera, 363 B.R. 718, *aff'd on other grounds*, 388 B.R. 586 (E.D. Pa. 2008) (Bankr. E.D. Pa. 2007) (RESPA § 2605(e) applies only to servicers).

15 12 U.S.C. § 2605(i)(2).

The term "servicing" is defined as "receiving any scheduled periodic payments from a borrower pursuant to the terms of any loan, including amounts for escrow accounts . . ., and making the payments of principal and interest and such other payments with respect to the amounts received from the borrower as may be required pursuant to the terms of the loan." 12 U.S.C. § 2605(i)(3). *See also* McCarley v. Household Fin. Corp., III, 2008 WL 4195152 (11th Cir. Sept. 15, 2008) (applying RESPA definition of the term "servicing").

Regulation X further distinguishes between a "master" servicer (the owner of the right to service) and a "subservicer" (a servicer who performs the servicing on behalf of the master servicer). Reg. X, 24 C.F.R. § 3500.21(a).

16 12 U.S.C. § 2605(i)(2)(A), (B).

17 12 U.S.C. §§ 1701–1701z-15.

18 Reg. X, 24 C.F.R. § 3500.2(b).

19 Regulation X states that the Servicer Act provisions apply to a "mortgage servicing loan," which generally includes all "federally related mortgage loans," but does not include "subordinate lien loans or open-end lines of credit (home equity plans) covered by the Truth in Lending Act and Regulation Z, including open-end lines of credit secured by a first lien." Reg. X, 24 C.F.R. § 3500.21(a).

20 Cortez v. Keystone Bank, 2000 U.S. Dist. LEXIS 5705 (E.D. Pa. May 2, 2000).

8.2.2 Servicer's Duty to Provide Information and Correct Account Errors

8.2.2.1 Overview

Section 2605(e) provides consumers with important rights to help them resolve disputes with servicers. This provision, which was added to RESPA by the Servicer Act, permits consumers to obtain information about the servicing of their mortgage and escrow accounts by providing a written inquiry to the servicer. When the written inquiry questions a servicer's actions on the account, this provision requires the servicer to respond to the specific dispute and take corrective action when appropriate. A borrower inquiry made under this provision is referred to as a "qualified written request," which "includes a statement of the reasons for the belief of the borrower, to the extent applicable, that the account is in error or provides sufficient detail to the servicer regarding other information sought by the borrower."[21]

8.2.2.2 What Is a Qualified Written Request?

The servicer's obligation to respond to consumer inquiries is triggered by its receipt of a "qualified written request."[22] To qualify as a qualified written request, the inquiry must be addressed to a servicer of the mortgage loan and not other parties related to the loan.[23] RESPA defines a "servicer" to mean "the person responsible for servicing of a loan (including the person who makes or holds a loan if such person also services the loan)."[24] The term "servicing" is defined to mean "receiving any scheduled periodic payments from a borrower pursuant to the terms of any loan, including amounts for escrow accounts . . . and making the payments of principal and interest and such other payments with respect to the amounts received from the borrower as may be required pursuant to the terms of the loan."[25] Thus, a loan originator or the entity that is the current holder of the note and mortgage may be a servicer if it handles servicing functions related to the loan, such as accepting and disbursing payments. However, a servicer's attorney or the trustee on a deed of trust is generally not a servicer for purposes of RESPA.[26] A borrower inquiry sent to a third party who is not a servicer within the RESPA definition therefore will not be a qualified written request unless the servicer authorizes the third party to receive requests on its behalf.

The inquiry must be in the form of a written correspondence.[27] Any written document should suffice, though the request may not be made on a payment coupon or other "payment medium supplied by the servicer."[28]

A qualified written request must also include the name and account of the borrower, or provide sufficient information to enable the servicer to identify the borrower's name and account.[29] Arguably, a letter containing the borrower's name and property address, without a specific reference to an account number, should enable the servicer to identify the account.[30] The letter does not need to be signed by the borrower.[31]

21 12 U.S.C. § 2605(e)(1)(B).

22 A sample qualified written request is contained at Appx. H.2, *infra.* HUD's website also provides a model qualified written request that can be used by borrowers: www.hud.gov/offices/hsg/sfh/res/reslettr.cfm.

23 *See* Gardner v. American Home Mortg. Servicing, Inc., 2010 WL 582117 (E.D. Cal. Feb. 11, 2010) (dismissing RESPA claim because borrower failed to plead facts showing that entity she sent inquiry to was the servicer of the loan); Moon v. Countrywide Home Loans, Inc., 2010 WL 522753 (D. Nev. Feb. 9, 2010) (same); Gonzalez v. First Franklin Loan Servs., 2010 WL 144862 (E.D. Cal. Jan. 11, 2010)(only a loan servicer has a duty to respond to borrower inquiries under § 2605(e)); *In re* Madera, 363 B.R. 718 (Bankr. E.D. Pa. 2007), *aff'd on other grounds,* 388 B.R. 586 (E.D. Pa. 2008) (RESPA § 2605(e) applies only to servicers).

24 12 U.S.C. § 2605(i)(2).

25 12 U.S.C. § 2605(i)(3). Regulation X clarifies the statutory definition by noting that the "making of payments" of principal and interest and other payments by the servicer from payments received from the borrower is to the "owner of the loan or other third parties." Reg. X, 24 C.F.R. § 3500.2(b).

26 Castrillo v. American Home Mortg. Servicing, Inc., 2010 WL 1424398 (E.D. La. Apr. 5, 2010) (summary judgment granted because no evidence offered that trustee for securitized trust was a servicer of the borrower's loan); Carter v. Countrywide Home Loans, Inc., 2009 WL 2742560 (E.D. Va. Aug. 25, 2009)(letter sent to servicer's agent was not QWR); Lopez v. GMAC Mortgage Corp., 2007 WL 3232448 (N.D. Cal. Nov. 1, 2007) (motion to dismiss RESPA claim granted as to foreclosure trustee company which was not alleged to be a loan servicer); Griffin v. Citifinancial Mortgage Co., 2006 WL 266106 (M.D. Pa. Feb. 1, 2006) (holding no duty under § 2605(e) to respond to qualified written request that borrower sent to servicer's bankruptcy counsel instead of servicer). *See also* §§ 8.1.1, 8.1.2, *infra.*

27 12 U.S.C. § 2605(e)(1)(B); Reg. X, 24 C.F.R. § 3500.21(a), (e)(2). *See, e.g.,* Hunter v. Wash. Mut. Bank, 2008 WL 4206604 (E.D. Tenn. Sept. 10, 2008) (facsimile sent by homeowner listing his name, account number, and reasons he believed servicer was in error may be a qualified written request). *See also* McCarley v. Household Fin. Corp., III, 2008 WL 276330 (M.D. Ala. Jan. 30, 2008) ("call logs" detailing plaintiff's oral communications with servicer are not qualified written requests), *aff'd on other grounds,* 2008 WL 4195152 (11th Cir. Sept. 15, 2008).

28 Reg. X, 24 C.F.R. § 3500.21(e)(2).

29 12 U.S.C. § 2605(e)(1)(B)(i); Reg. X, 24 C.F.R. § 3500.21(e)(2).

30 *See* Kee v. Fifth Third Bank, 2009 WL 735048 (D. Utah Mar. 18, 2009) (absent evidence showing that servicer was unable to determine who sent letters, letters containing borrower's name and address were sufficient); Wright v. Litton Loan Servicing, 2006 WL 891030 (E.D. Pa. Apr. 4, 2006) (statute requires sufficient information to allow servicer to identify the account; the account number is not necessary). *But see* Gorham-DiMaggio v. Countrywide Home Loans, Inc., 592 F. Supp. 2d 283 (N.D.N.Y. 2008) (request sent by e-mail to servicer's attorney which lacked the borrower's last name and account number was not a qualified written request).

31 *See* Moon v. GMAC Mortg. Corp., 2009 WL 3185596 (W.D. Wash. Oct. 2, 2009).

Finally, a written inquiry must be treated as a qualified written request if it (1) includes the "reasons for the belief of the borrower, to the extent applicable, that the account is in error," or (2) "provides sufficient detail to the servicer regarding other information sought by the borrower."[32] While a written inquiry can both dispute a servicer action and seek information, either request alone can be a qualified written request.

For writings that seek to dispute an account error, courts have refused to find a RESPA violation if the communication does not state any reasons why the borrower believes that the account is in error.[33] However, because the statute provides that the borrower shall state the reasons "to the extent applicable," courts should not require that qualified written requests include a detailed explanation of the reasons for the dispute when, for example, the borrower does not have the information needed to discover the error or is unable to decipher the servicer's accounting procedures. It should be sufficient for the borrower to state simply: "We dispute the amount claimed to be owed because we have made all required payments."

For writings that seek information about the borrower's account, Regulation X limits the "other information" referred to in the statute to consist of "information related to the servicing of the loan."[34] As a result, courts have denied liability under RESPA where the written request from the borrower did not relate to the "servicing" of the loan.[35] For example, courts have uniformly held that a letter seeking to rescind a mortgage loan under the Truth in Lending Act based on loan origination violations, which addresses only the validity of the loan and not its servicing, is not a qualified written request.[36] On the other hand, a borrower inquiry seeking the identity of the mortgage note holder is related to the servicing of the loan and may be a qualified written request.[37] This information assists the borrower in determining whether mortgage payments have been paid to the proper party and in identifying the party to receive a TILA notice of rescission.[38]

A request for information related to the status of a loan modification application also should be treated as a proper qualified written request.[39] Loss mitigation has become a routine function of servicers in the servicing of mortgage loans.[40] In particular, an inquiry related to the Home Affordable Modification Program (HAMP) should qualify because the only method of obtaining a HAMP modification based on the design of the program is through a participating servicer.[41] In fact, Congress has specifically stated that the loan modification analysis required by the HAMP program is the standard of the residential mortgage servicing industry under both federal and state law.[42]

One court has incorrectly held that a borrower inquiry seeking information about the amounts claimed as due on a

32 12 U.S.C. § 2605(e)(1)(B)(ii).

Regulation X limits "other information" to "information related to the servicing of the loan." Reg. X, 24 C.F.R. § 3500.21(e)(2).

33 Gorham-Dimaggio v. Countrywide Home Loans, Inc., 2010 WL 883683 (N.D.N.Y. Mar. 8, 2010) (letter stating simply that the borrower was "disputing the escrow" was not a qualified written request); Pettie v. Saxon Mortgage Servs., 2009 WL 1325947 (W.D. Wash. May 12, 2009) (finding that letter which failed to give specific reasons for claiming the account was in error and which stated that "we dispute the amount that is owed according to the Monthly Billing Statement" was not a qualified written request).

34 Reg. X, 12 C.F.R. § 3500.21(e)(2). *See* Kee v. Fifth Third Bank, 2009 WL 735048 (D. Utah Mar. 18, 2009) (letter from borrower concerning private mortgage insurance charge was qualified written request); Powell v. Aegis Mortgage Corp., 2007 WL 98372 (D. Md. Jan. 11, 2007) (letter from borrower referring to amounts paid into escrow account related to servicing and considered qualified written request).

35 *See* Kee v. Fifth Third Bank, 2009 WL 735048 (D. Utah Mar. 18, 2009) (letter addressing the validity of the loan agreement rather than servicing was not qualified written request); Harris v. Am. Gen. Fin., 2005 WL 1593673 (D. Kan. July 6, 2005); MorEquity, Inc. v. Naeem, 118 F. Supp. 2d 885 (N.D. Ill. 2000) (if written request does not relate to "servicing" of the loan, the protections at § 2605 are not triggered).

36 Morris v. Bank of Am., 2010 WL 761318 (N.D. Cal. Mar. 3, 2010); Chevy Chase Bank, F.S.B. v. Carrington, 2010 WL 745771 (M.D. Fla. Mar. 1, 2010) (TILA rescission letter did not assert that the account is in error or seek any information); Sipe v. Countrywide Bank, 2010 WL 596322 (E.D. Cal. Feb. 16, 2010); Petracek v. American Home Mortg. Servicing, 2010 WL 582113 (E.D. Cal. Feb. 11, 2010); Keen v. American Home Mortg. Servicing, Inc., 664 F. Supp. 2d 1086 (E.D. Cal. 2009); Taylor v. Nelson, 2006 WL 266052 (E.D. Pa. Jan. 31, 2006); Steele v. Chase Manhattan Mortgage Corp., 2005 WL 2077271 (E.D. Pa. Aug. 26, 2005) (letter regarding rescission demand not related to "servicing" therefore § 2605 inapplicable).

37 *See* Diamond v. One West Bank, 2010 WL 1742536 (D. Ariz. Apr. 29, 2010). *But see* DeVary v. Countrywide Home Loans, Inc., 2010 WL 1257647 (D. Minn. Mar. 25, 2010) (court improperly combined the separate information production and dispute prongs of § 2605(e) and found that request for name of note owner was not submitted as part of an account dispute and therefore was not a QWR).

38 *See* Woods v. Greenpoint Mortg. Funding, Inc., 2010 WL 1729711 (E.D. Cal. Apr. 28, 2010) (information regarding on whose behalf the servicer is accepting loan payments is related to servicing and a proper subject of a QWR; by failing to give borrower a "straight answer" to request for identity of owner of mortgage, servicer harmed borrower by preventing him from rescinding the loan).

39 *See* Diamond v. One West Bank, 2010 WL 1742536 (D. Ariz. Apr. 29, 2010). *But see* Williams v. Wells Fargo Bank, N.A., Inc., 2010 WL 1463521 (N.D. Cal. Apr. 13, 2010) (request for loan origination documents as part of borrowers' inquiry about "options" for loan modification or short sale was not a QWR).

40 *See* § 6.4.5, *supra*.

41 *See* § 2.8.1.2, *supra*.

42 *See* Helping Families Save Their Homes Act of 2009, Pub. L. No. 111-22, 123 Stat. 1632 (2009) ("The qualified loss mitigation plan guidelines issued by the Secretary of the Treasury under the Emergency Economic Stabilization Act of 2008 shall constitute standard industry practice for purposes of all Federal and State laws"). *See also* § 6.4.5.6, *supra*.

mortgage account is not related to servicing.[43] After receiving a letter from the servicer's attorney claiming that the account was in arrears, the borrowers sent a letter requesting information about reinstatement of the mortgage and the charges alleged to be due. The court narrowly applied the statutory definition of servicing and found that the request did not relate to the servicer's receipt of a "scheduled periodic payment." Certainly a request concerning a demand for payment of amounts due on the account relates to the servicer's receipt of scheduled periodic payments on the account. In the ordinary course, it is the servicer that determines the amount of the scheduled payments and how the payments are applied to the account, thus also determining whether periodic payments have been made, whether amounts are owed, and whether the account is in default. In fact, the servicer in most instances is the only entity that would have the ability to respond to such an inquiry, particularly if the mortgage loan is owned by a securitized trust which has no direct knowledge of payment and default status information. In addition to misapplying the statute and regulation, the court's decision would leave borrowers without recourse to obtain essential information which RESPA was intended to make available.

Though not contained in the Act, Regulation X imposes one other condition. A written request need not be treated as a qualified written request if it was delivered to the servicer more than one year after either (1) the "date of transfer of servicing," or (2) "the date that the mortgage servicing loan amount was paid in full," whichever date applies.[44]

Apart from the question of whether this condition conflicts with the purpose of the Act, servicers have been misapplying the regulation by arguing that compliance with the Act is not required anytime a written request is sent more than one year after the servicer first began servicing the account or one year after the disputed act or omission occurred. Clearly, the one-year limitation was not intended to apply to current servicers.[45] The only reasonable interpretation of the regulation is that when the servicing of a mortgage has been transferred, the prior servicer need not respond to requests sent more than one year after it ceased being responsible for servicing the account. Disputes against the current servicer can be raised at any time while the loan is being paid and for a period of one year after the loan is paid in full.[46] In addition, the regulation should not preclude a qualified written request directed to the current servicer that disputes an action or omission of the former servicer or seeks information in the current servicer's files that relates to the actions or omissions of the prior servicer dating back more than one year after the servicing transfer.[47]

Regulation X provides an exception to the one-year limitation for qualified written requests seeking information about escrow accounts. Servicers are required to maintain records in a retrievable format related to escrow accounts for a period of at least five years after the servicer last serviced the account.[48] Regulation X specifies that borrowers may obtain this information in the servicer's escrow records by sending a qualified written request.[49] While the borrower should be able to obtain escrow information dating back five years from the current servicer, this provision ensures that the borrower will have recourse against the prior servicer, who must provide the information in response to a qualified written request even if the request is sent more than one year after the servicing transfer.

In sum, the qualifying conditions for treatment as a qualified written request are easily met in most cases.[50] The

43 Moore v. Federal Deposit Ins. Corp., 2009 WL 4405538 (N.D. Ill. Nov. 30, 2009).

44 Reg. X, 24 C.F.R. § 3500.21(e)(2)(ii).

45 Davidson v. Countrywide Home Loans, Inc., 2010 WL 962712 (S.D. Cal. Mar. 16, 2010) (servicer interpretation of regulation is unsupported by language of statute); Campiglia v. Saxon Mortgage Servs., Inc., 2010 WL 958025 (N.D. Cal. Mar. 12, 2010) (given that many mortgages have payment periods of thirty or forty years, Congress could not have intended for duty to comply with § 2605(e) to extend for only first year that servicer is servicing loan).

46 *See also In re* Sánchez-Rodríguez, 377 B.R. 1 (Bankr. D. P.R. 2007) (servicer required to comply with § 2605(e) even after foreclosure judgment).

47 When there has been a transfer of servicing and post-transfer payments have not been properly applied to the borrower's account, it may not be clear which servicer is at fault. Regardless of where fault lies for the error, the new servicer is required to take corrective action in response to a qualified written request (and comply with 12 U.S.C. § 2605(d) as described at § 8.2.3, *infra*). Rawlings v. Dovenmuehle Mortgage, Inc., 64 F. Supp. 2d 1156 (M.D. Ala. 1999) (new servicer required to comply with § 2605(e) even though needed information and misapplied payments not received from prior servicer until after sixty-day response period.).

In addition, the prior servicer cannot escape liability under § 2605(e) by arguing that it is not the current servicer. Williamson v. Advanta Mortgage Corp., 1999 WL 1144940 (N.D. Ill. Oct. 8, 1999) (servicer who failed to forward payments to new servicer and provided adverse credit information required to respond to qualified written request). In this situation, it may be advisable to send a qualified written request to both the former and current servicer.

48 Reg. X, 24 C.F.R. § 3500.17(l)(2).

49 Reg. X, 24 C.F.R. § 3500.17(l)(4). One court has held that the regulation does not require the servicer to provide the information in the same format as the escrow analysis and escrow statements the borrower may have received. *See* Gorham v. Bank of Am., N.A., 2010 WL 1704829 (N.D.N.Y. Apr. 28, 2010) (regulation recognizes that retention of records includes "computerized storage" of information intended to "reflect[ ] the service's handling of each borrower's escrow account" and therefore does not require a servicer to keep actual photocopies, or the equivalent).

50 *E.g.*, Jeffries v. Dutton & Dutton, P.C., 2006 WL 1343629 (N.D. Ill. May 11, 2006); Wright v. Litton Loan Servicing, L.P., 2006 WL 891030 (E.D. Pa. Apr. 4, 2006) (qualified written request not required to contain name and account number, only information sufficient to identify the account); Vician v. Wells Fargo Home Mortgage, 2006 WL 694740 (N.D. Ind. Mar. 16, 2006); McDonald v. Wash. Mut. Bank, 2000 U.S. Dist. LEXIS 11496

correspondence need not indicate that it is being sent pursuant to the Servicer Act or contain the magic words "qualified written request." As a result, an advocate may wish to review copies of any prior correspondence sent by the client to the servicer, particularly when the dispute has been long-standing, to determine if they should have been treated by the servicer as qualified written requests.[51]

8.2.2.3 Where to Send a Qualified Written Request?

The servicer's obligation to respond is triggered by its receipt of a qualified written request. Regulation X provides that a servicer can establish, upon notice to borrower, a separate and "exclusive" office and address for receipt and processing of qualified written requests.[52] Notice of the "exclusive" office may be contained in a "Notice of Transfer"[53] or separately delivered by first-class mail.[54] Failure to send a qualified written request to the "exclusive" address may preclude the servicer's liability under section 2605(e).[55] However, the servicer has the burden to prove that proper written notice of the designated address was provided to the borrower.[56]

Moreover, because the obligation to comply with section 2506(e) is triggered by the servicer's "receipt" of a qualified written request, it may be argued that a servicer who has acknowledged receipt of the request, even if it had not been sent to the designated address, is liable for any failure to respond to the request. For example, if the borrower has received a letter from the servicer in response to a qualified written request, thereby acknowledging its receipt of the request, this should preclude a defense by the servicer in subsequent litigation that the request was invalid when sent to the wrong address. Moreover, the borrower may be able to prove that the qualified written request was forwarded within the servicer's operation to the correct address or department that handles such requests. In this instance, the fact that the request was not initially sent to the designated address may only affect the time when the statutory compliance periods commence following actual receipt at the designated address,[57] if there had been a delay while the request was being forwarded internally.

If the debtor cannot locate a notice of transfer or separate notice, or if the servicer has not designated a specific address for receipt of qualified written requests, it is generally not advisable to send the request to the address on a payment coupon. These "lock box" addresses are often the post office box for a third-party vendor hired by the servicer to process payments. When in doubt, the best course of action is to call the servicer and request the appropriate address.

Another issue that arises frequently is where to send the qualified written request when the servicer is represented by outside counsel in a foreclosure case or bankruptcy proceeding. Several courts have held that sending a qualified written request to the servicer's counsel alone was insufficient.[58] This ruling sets up a potential conflict with the ethical rule limiting communications with a party represented by coun-

---

(N.D. Ill. June 26, 2000) ("§ 2605(e)(1)(B) does not require much for a correspondence to constitute a 'qualified written request' "); Cortez v. Keystone Bank, 2000 U.S. Dist. LEXIS 5705 (E.D. Pa. May 2, 2000); Rawlings v. Dovenmuehle Mortgage, Inc., 64 F. Supp. 2d 1156 (M.D. Ala. 1999); *In re* Tomasevic, 275 B.R. 103 (Bankr. M.D. Fla. 2001). *But see* Harris v. American General Fin., Inc., 2005 WL 1593673 (D. Kan. July 6, 2005) (attorney's letter regarding mortgage holder's collection practices was not a qualified written request because it failed to include account numbers and did not state account was in error or request any information); MorEquity, Inc. v. Naeem, 118 F. Supp. 2d 885 (N.D. Ill. 2000) (information sought did not relate to the "servicing" of the loans and therefore inquiry was not a "qualified written request").

The plaintiff has the burden to prove that a correspondence is a "qualified written request." Ploog v. Homeside Lending, Inc., 2001 U.S. Dist. LEXIS 15697 (N.D. Ill. Sept. 28, 2001).

51 As discussed at § 8.2.6.1, *infra*, the statute of limitations for claims brought under § 2605 is three years.

52 Reg. X, 24 C.F.R. § 3500.21(e)(1).

53 *See* § 8.2.3, *infra*.

54 Reg. X, 24 C.F.R. § 3500.21(e)(1).

55 *See* Bally v. Homeside Lending, Inc., 2005 WL 2250856, at *1 (N.D. Ill. Sept. 8, 2005) (granting summary judgment for servicer where borrower was sent a separate "Borrower Notification Attachment Per RESPA Act" which stated that "[i]f you want to send a 'qualified written request' regarding the servicing of your loan, it must be sent to HomeSide at the address shown on the reverse side of this page."); ABN AMRO Mortgage Group, Inc. v. Tullar, 770 N.W.2d 851 (Iowa Ct. App. Apr. 22, 2009) (table).

56 McLean v. GMAC Mortgage Corp., Inc., 2008 WL 5246149 (S.D. Fla. Dec. 16, 2008) (statement on reverse side of mortgage statement listing four separate mailing addresses, including one for "General Inquiries," was insufficient to provide borrowers with notice of the exclusive address for qualified written requests); Catalan v. RBC Mortgage Co., 2008 WL 2741159, at *7, 8 (N.D. Ill. July 8, 2008) ("to comply with the applicable regulation, at a minimum, the notice must be 'separate' and must advise customers of a 'separate and exclusive address' that they must use for the mailing of inquiries regarding the servicing of their mortgage loans"; debt collection letter sent to borrower which listed address for directing communication "regarding this notice" did not satisfy regulation's requirements).

57 *See* § 8.2.2.5, *infra*.

58 *See* Kee v. Fifth Third Bank, 2009 WL 735048 (D. Utah Mar. 18, 2009) (because section 2605 explicitly states that qualified written requests may be sent by borrower's agent, but does not similarly provide that request may be sent to servicer's agent, letter sent to servicer's attorney was not qualified written request); Griffin v. Citifinancial Mortgage Co., 2006 WL 266106 (M.D. Pa. Feb. 1, 2006) (holding that servicer had no duty to respond where request was sent to servicer's outside counsel). *But see* McLean v. GMAC Mortgage Corp., Inc., 2008 WL 5246149 (S.D. Fla. Dec. 16, 2008) (letter sent to servicer's bankruptcy attorney was valid qualified written request because attorney did not refuse acceptance of letter or advise borrower to contact servicer directly).

sel.[59] To avoid this potential conflict, attorneys may want to consider having clients send the qualified written request to the servicer. Alternatively, attorneys should notify servicer's counsel of the request and send copies to both counsel and the servicer.

In some cases, servicers defend their failure to respond to qualified written requests by disclaiming receipt of the request. Generally, there is a presumption of receipt where the debtor provides evidence that a properly addressed letter was placed in a U.S. Post Office mail receptacle.[60] In most cases, this evidence will consist of a copy of the letter and the borrower's testimony regarding when and where the letter was mailed.

8.2.2.4 Who May Send a Qualified Written Request?

A qualified written request may be sent by the borrower's "agent."[61] A letter seeking an itemized payoff on a mortgage sent by a non-attorney housing counselor that did not specifically identify the counselor as the agent of the borrower was held to be a qualified written request when the servicer had previously received the borrower's authorization for release of information to the counseling agency.[62] There is also no requirement in the Act that a borrower actually prepare a qualified written request sent in her name, or understand its contents and purpose.[63]

Servicers often demand that a letter sent by the borrower's attorney be accompanied by an authorization or release from the borrower. Attorneys may consider providing such an authorization to facilitate processing of the request. However, this is not a requirement under RESPA and a letter does not lose its status as a qualified written request simply because it is not accompanied by a client authorization.[64]

59 *See, e.g.*, Model Rules of Prof'l Conduct R. 4.2.

60 *See* James v. New Century Mortgage Corp., 2006 WL 2989242 (E.D. La. 2006), *citing* United States v. Wilson, 322 F.3d 353 (5th Cir. 2003).

61 12 U.S.C. § 2605(e)(1)(A). *See* Ortega v. Wells Fargo Bank, 2010 WL 696749 (S.D. Cal. Feb. 23, 2010) (letter sent by borrower's attorney was qualified written request); Harris v. American Gen. Fin., Inc., 2005 WL 1593673 (D. Kan. July 6, 2005) (attorney's letter referencing account error based on misapplication of funds was qualified written request); *In re* Laskowski, 384 B.R. 518 (Bankr. N.D. Ind. 2008) (chapter 13 bankruptcy trustee, as agent of the consumer debtor, and the debtor each have standing to send a qualified written request).

62 Maxwell v. Fairbanks Capital Corp., 281 B.R. 101 (Bankr. D. Mass. 2002).

63 *Id.* The court in *Maxwell* found the servicer's defense that the borrower did not understand the qualified written request to be "shameless" and unsupported by the Act and its underlying remedial purpose.

64 Moon v. GMAC Mortgage Corp., 2009 WL 3185596 (W.D. Wash. Oct. 2, 2009) (letter sent by borrower's attorney that was not signed by the borrower and did not contain an authorization was a qualified written request).

8.2.2.5 Servicer Obligations upon Receipt of a Qualified Written Request

The receipt of a qualified written request triggers certain obligations on the part of the servicer.[65] The servicer must initially provide a written response acknowledging receipt of the request within twenty days (excluding holidays, Saturdays, and Sundays).[66] The servicer need not provide this acknowledgment if it takes the requested action within the twenty day period and provides notice of that action to the borrower.[67]

Within sixty days (excluding holidays, Saturdays, and Sundays) of receipt of a qualified written request from the borrower, depending upon the nature of the request, the servicer must:

- Make any necessary corrections to the borrower's account, including crediting any late charges or penalties resulting from the error, and provide written notification of the correction;[68] or
- After conducting an investigation, provide the borrower with a written explanation or clarification as to why the servicer believes the account is correct;[69] or
- After conducting an investigation, provide the borrower with the information requested, or an explanation why the information sought is unavailable.[70]

In all three forms of response, the written notification to the borrower must also include the name and telephone number of a servicer representative that can provide assistance to the borrower.[71]

65 *In re* Cooley, 365 B.R. 464 (Bankr. E.D. Pa. 2007) (refusing to dismiss RESPA claim which alleged that owner of loan rather than servicer responded to qualified written request).

66 12 U.S.C. § 2605(e)(1)(A); Reg. X, 24 C.F.R. § 3500.21(e)(1). *See* Rawlings v. Dovenmuehle Mortgage, Inc., 64 F. Supp. 2d 1156 (M.D. Ala. 1999) (notices of default sent to homeowner during twenty day period which did not acknowledge receipt of qualified written request failed to satisfy § 2605(e)(1)); *In re* Tomasevic, 275 B.R. 103 (Bankr. M.D. Fla. 2001) (servicer failed to acknowledge receipt of qualified written request).

67 12 U.S.C. § 2605(e)(1)(A); Reg. X, 24 C.F.R. § 3500.21(e)(1).

68 12 U.S.C. § 2605(e)(2)(A); Reg. X, 24 C.F.R. § 3500.21(e)(3)(i). *See In re* Tomasevic, 275 B.R. 103 (Bankr. M.D. Fla. 2001) (servicer failed to correct account after being notified in qualified written request that payments made by borrower had not been properly credited).

69 12 U.S.C. § 2605(e)(2)(B)(i); Reg. X, 24 C.F.R. § 3500.21(e)(3)(ii)(A).

70 12 U.S.C. § 2605(e)(2)(C)(i); Reg. X, 24 C.F.R. § 3500.21(e)(3)(ii)(B). *See* Rubenstein v. Dovenmuehle Mortgage, Inc., 2009 WL 3467769 (E.D. Pa. Oct. 28, 2009) (servicer complied with RESPA by stating in QWR response that it could not provide a loan accounting because it was unable to obtain payment histories for period before it began servicing the loan); Loan Pettie v. Saxon Mortgage Servs., 2009 WL 1325947 (W.D. Wash. May 12, 2009) (no RESPA violation when servicer explained in its response to QWR why it could not provide the requested information).

71 12 U.S.C. § 2605(e)(2); Reg. X, 24 C.F.R. § 3500.21(e)(3).

During the sixty-day response period to a qualified written request relating to a payment dispute, the servicer cannot give any adverse information to a credit reporting agency concerning the payments subject to the request.[72] When several qualified written requests have been provided to a servicer, the improper reporting with respect to each request can be a separate violation of section 2605(e)(3).[73]

By misapplying a general statute providing that the "validity and enforceability" of loan agreements and mortgages is not affected by RESPA,[74] the Department of Housing and Urban Development (HUD), in Regulation X, has emasculated RESPA's more specific statutory provision dealing with the potential impact of servicer errors by providing that a servicer or lender is not prohibited from pursuing collection remedies, including foreclosure, during the sixty-day period.[75] Under HUD's ill-conceived interpretation, a lender or servicer in receipt of a qualified written request disputing the existence of a default based on a misapplication of payments by the servicer is precluded from reporting the alleged default to a credit reporting agency, but can nevertheless take the more drastic step of initiating foreclosure. It remains to be seen whether this regulation can withstand a judicial challenge.

The servicer obligations in the Act are mandatory and demand strict compliance. Even an "unintentional" act or omission can be a violation of section 2605(e)(2), as in the case of a servicer who claimed to be unable to respond to a qualified written response because a prior servicer had not forwarded evidence of misapplied payments made by the borrower and other necessary information to the servicer until after the sixty-day response period had passed.[76]

Similarly, a servicer should not be relieved of its obligations under the Act simply because a qualified written request is sent while litigation is pending between the parties. Nothing in the Act or Regulation X precludes a qualified written request from being sent during litigation or while a borrower's bankruptcy is pending, even if the information sought might be obtained under applicable discovery rules.[77]

8.2.2.6 Adequate Investigation

Significantly, section 2605(e) is not simply a disclosure statute; it requires that servicers take affirmative action to correct a servicing error if an account dispute is asserted in a qualified written request.[78] By invoking the protections of the Servicer Act, borrowers can challenge the misapplication of payments, escrow overcharges, improper late fees or other charges, or any erroneous claim of default.[79] It can be a powerful tool in challenging abuses by establishing a clear cause of action against a recalcitrant or incompetent servicer.

Servicers have argued that section 2605(e) is not violated, if in response to a notice of dispute contained in a qualified written request, the servicer simply provides the borrower with a written explanation as to why it believes the account is correct, even though the account is in fact incorrect. Servicers ignore, however, that section 2605(e) requires that they conduct an investigation before sending such a response. Courts may conclude that compliance with section 2605(e) is not met either when the servicer has failed to conduct an investigation (or the response does not respond to the specific inquiry)[80] or when the servicer should have discovered the error through reasonable investigation and made an appropriate correction. The servicer's "subjective belief" that it has properly responded is immaterial.[81]

8.2.2.7 Servicer Charges for Responding to a Qualified Written Request

Section 6 of RESPA does not explicitly address whether lenders may charge a fee for responding to a qualified written request and Regulation X is silent on the question.[82]

---

72 12 U.S.C. § 2605(e)(3); Reg. X, 24 C.F.R. § 3500.21(e)(4)(i).

73 *See* Holland v. GMAC Mortgage Corp., 2006 WL 1133224 (D. Kan. Apr. 26, 2006) (summary judgment granted against servicer for four separate violations of § 2605(e)(3) by reporting borrower to credit reporting agencies after receiving qualified written requests).

74 12 U.S.C. § 2615.

75 Reg. X, 24 C.F.R. § 3500.21(e)(4)(ii). *See also* Cardiello v. The Money Store, Inc., 2001 U.S. Dist. LEXIS 7107 (S.D.N.Y. June 1, 2001) (servicer's sending of collection letters to borrowers relating to disputed payoff amount on mortgage during sixty-day period not prohibited by § 2605(e)), *aff'd*, 29 Fed. Appx 780 (2d Cir. 2002) (unpublished).

76 Rawlings v. Dovenmuehle Mortgage, Inc., 64 F. Supp. 2d 1156 (M.D. Ala. 1999).

77 Chatman v. Fairbanks Capital Corp., 2002 U.S. Dist. LEXIS 10945 (N.D. Ill. June 13, 2002) (court rejected servicer's argument that plaintiff's qualified written request was "litigation strategy" and that information requested was subject to Federal Rules of Civil Procedure); *In re* Figard, 382 B.R. 695 (Bankr. W.D. Pa. 2008) (servicer compliance with qualified written request required even though borrower could obtain information under discovery provisions of Bankruptcy Rules). *See* § 8.2.5.2, *infra* (discussion of RESPA compliance when the borrower is in bankruptcy proceeding).

78 Carter v. Countrywide Home Loans, Inc., 2009 WL 2742560 (E.D. Va. Aug. 25, 2009) (servicer's duty to investigate under RESPA is not triggered if the borrower seeks only information in a QWR and does not also assert an account dispute).

79 Courts have held that a violation of § 2605(e) may not be raised as a "special defense" to foreclosure, although a RESPA violation may give rise to a proper counterclaim. Webster Bank v. Linsley, 2001 WL 1042581 (Conn. Super. Ct. Aug. 14, 2001); Security Pac. Nat'l Bank v. Robertson, 1997 WL 561235 (Conn. Super. Ct. Aug. 28, 1997).

80 Holland v. GMAC Mortgage Corp., 2006 WL 1133224 (D. Kan. Apr. 26, 2006).

81 *Id.* at *9 ("defendant did not cite, nor could the court locate, authority supporting the proposition that defendant's subjective belief is the appropriate standard to apply").

82 HUD likely determined that regulation was not necessary because servicers would not charge for complying with a borrower

However, lenders should not take the absence of an express prohibition as a license to charge borrowers for their compliance with the statute. Both the remedial nature of the Servicer Act[83] and its legislative history[84] suggest that lenders should not be allowed to assess fees for responding to qualified written requests.

Not only is the charging of such fees inconsistent with the purpose of the Act, it would have a chilling effect on borrowers' use of this important statutory right. The procedure initiated by the borrower's qualified written request is not unlike the dispute resolution provisions of the Truth in Lending Act (TILA),[85] the Fair Debt Collection Practices Act (FDCPA),[86] and the Fair Credit Reporting Act (FCRA)[87] in which creditors appropriately do not charge for investigating disputes or correcting errors. In addition, servicers presently do not charge for complying with the cost of other RESPA requirements.[88] There is no sound reason why the servicer's duty to respond to a qualified written request should be treated differently than servicer's other obligations under RESPA simply because the borrower initiates the process.

In addition, fees assessed to the borrower for routine servicing activities, such as responding to borrower inquiries, are generally not permissible under the terms of the loan agreement, particularly if the fees are not expressly authorized and conspicuously disclosed in the loan instruments.[89] Such fees also may be prohibited by state law.

Despite the remedial nature of RESPA and the chilling effect lenders' charges will have on consumers seeking to resolve account disputes, the Eighth Circuit Court of Appeals recently held that RESPA does not prohibit lenders from charging a fee for information provided in response to a qualified written request.[90] In the class action case, the plaintiffs asserted that the lenders imposition of a $20 fee each time plaintiffs requested their payoff amount violated section 2605(e). In reaching its decision the court paid little attention to the purpose behind the enactment of the Servicer Act in 1990. Instead the court focused on the intent of

---

inquiry. This was the position HUD adopted in regard to an issue raised during a rulemaking proceeding concerning escrow accounts:

> Several States Attorneys General commented that they were concerned that "lenders, in the absence of . . . an express provision will try to circumvent the express limits on profiteering contained in the proposed rule by charging consumers annual maintenance fees." In response, the Department considered whether servicers would charge borrowers escrow account maintenance fees or document storage fees to defray lost revenue resulting from changes in accounting practices required by this final rule. . . . The Department has not seen evidence that servicers, as a common practice, currently charge maintenance or storage fees in conjunction with escrow accounts. . . . If the Department sees such fees develop with respect to any other loans to thwart the statutory and regulatory limitations, then HUD is likely to reconsider this issue in conjunction with applicable State law provisions. At this time, the Department intends to monitor the servicing industry carefully to insure compliance with Sections 8 and 10 of RESPA.

See 59 Fed. Reg. 53,902 (Oct. 26, 1994).

83 *See* Ploog v. HomeSide Lending, Inc., 209 F. Supp. 2d 863 (N.D. Ill. 2002) (holding RESPA is remedial in nature); Johnstone v. Bank of Am., N.A., 173 F. Supp. 2d 815 (N.D. Ill. 2001) (same); Rawlings v. Dovenmuehle Mortgage, Inc., 64 F. Supp. 2d 1156 (M.D. Ala. 1999) (same); Wagner v. EMC Mortgage Corp., 127 Cal. Rptr. 2d 685 (Cal. Ct. App. 2002) (same). *But see* Katz v. Dime Sav. Bank, F.S.B., 992 F. Supp. 250 (W.D.N.Y. 1997) (finding § 2605 not a consumer protection statute).

84 The legislative history of the Servicer Act explains that its purpose was "to authorize a comprehensive, new housing policy that can mobilize sustained national effort to provide more affordable housing for all Americans." S. Rep. No. 101-316, at 5 (1990), *reprinted in* 1990 U.S.C.C.A.N. 5793.

Charging fees for compliance with RESPA requirements is inconsistent with this purpose and with Congress's concern about affordable housing. In addition, widespread complaints on abusive servicing practices, including unresponsiveness to inquiries, prompted the congressional enactment of section 2605. *See* U.S. Gen. Accounting Office, Report, Home Ownership—Mortgage Servicing Transfers Are Increasing and Causing Borrower Concern (1989) (available on this treatise's companion website). *See also* Wanger v. EMC Mortgage Corp., 103 Cal. App. 4th 1125, 127 Cal. Rptr. 2d 685 (2002).

85 12 C.F.R. § 226.13.

86 15 U.S.C. § 1692g(b).

87 15 U.S.C. § 1681i.

88 Servicers are expressly prohibited from charging fees for escrow account statements. *See* § 8.3.5, *infra*.

89 In a complaint filed against Fairbanks Capital Holding Corp. and its wholly-owned subsidiary Fairbanks Capital Corp., the Federal Trade Commission alleged that Fairbanks had engaged in a variety of unfair, deceptive, and illegal practices in the servicing of subprime mortgage loans, including the failure to post consumers' mortgage payments in a timely manner and the charging of illegal late fees and other unauthorized fees. Under the terms of a settlement with the FTC, Fairbanks is enjoined from assessing or collecting any fee "unless it is for services actually rendered and is: (a) expressly authorized, and clearly and conspicuously disclosed, by the loan instruments and not prohibited by law; (b) expressly permitted by law and not prohibited by the loan instruments; or (c) a reasonable fee for a specific service requested by a consumer that is assessed and/or collected only after clear and conspicuous disclosure of the fee is provided to the consumer and explicit consent is obtained from the consumer to pay the fee in exchange for the service, and such fee is not otherwise prohibited by law or the loan instruments." *See* Stipulated Final Judgment and Order as to Fairbanks Capital Corp. entered in United States of America v. Fairbanks Capital Corp., Fairbanks Capital Holding Corp., and Thomas D. Basmajian, District of Massachusetts, File No. 032 3014, *available at* www.ftc.gov/os/2003/11/0323014order.pdf.

90 Watt v. GMAC Mortgage Corp., 457 F.3d 781 (8th Cir. 2006). *See also* Curran v. Washington Mut. Bank, F.A., 471 F.3d 857 (8th Cir. 2006) (per curiam) (summarily holding that RESPA does not prohibit the imposition of fees for response to qualified written request seeking loan payoff); Smith v. Chase Manhattan Mortgage Corp., 2006 WL 353975 (W.D. Ark. Feb. 16, 2006), *aff'd*, 222 Fed. Appx. 533 (8th Cir. 2007) (same).

Congress to give consumers more information about settlement costs and protect them from unnecessarily high settlement charges.[91] The court found that these purposes would not be undermined by allowing lenders to charge a fee for information provided in response to qualified written requests. The court did not address whether the fees charged by the lender for responding to qualified written requests were authorized by the mortgage loan documents,[92] permitted by state law, or reasonable.

8.2.2.8 Class Action Issues for Qualified Written Requests

Despite clear congressional intent that class actions should be available for violations of the Servicer Act,[93] courts have generally denied class certification in cases involving servicers' failure to respond to qualified written requests. Courts considering the issue have held that borrowers failed to satisfy the burden of showing numerosity[94] and that a determination of whether correspondence is a qualified written request is an "individualized inquiry" precluding class certification.[95] Despite these opinions to the contrary, identifying qualified written requests upon examination of the servicer's records should not be an insurmountable task for the parties in class actions given that the statutory requirements are so minimal.

8.2.3 Transfer of Servicing

8.2.3.1 Overview

Typically, a mortgage loan will be assigned or sold several times during its term, and may be held by one entity but serviced by another. Section 2605(a) provides that the originating lender of a mortgage loan must disclose whether servicing of the loan may be assigned during the term of the mortgage. In addition, the borrower must be notified if servicing of the loan is transferred from one entity to another after the loan is made.

Section 2605(a) is limited to the transfer of servicing. RESPA does not require notice of any transfers of ownership of the note and mortgage.[96] However, a provision in the Truth in Lending Act requires that if ownership is transferred, the new owner or assignee of a mortgage loan must notify the borrower within thirty days after the loan is sold or assigned of its identity, address, and telephone number, as well as information about any agent or party with authority to act on behalf of the new owner and other relevant information.[97]

8.2.3.2 Notice at Time of Loan Application

To ensure that borrowers know the identity of the lender or servicer, the Servicer Act requires that at the time of application for a mortgage loan, any person who makes a mortgage loan covered by RESPA must disclose to each applicant whether the servicing of the loan may be assigned, sold or transferred at any time during the term of the mortgage.[98] The servicer may adopt the format for this notice provided by HUD in a model form, though the precise language in the model form need not be used.[99] In

91 The court noted that at the time § 2605 was enacted in 1990, Congress also amended § 2610 to prohibit servicers and lenders from charging fees for escrow account statements, but had not included a similar provision concerning requests for payoff amounts.

92 *See, e.g.,* Krause v. G.E. Capital Mortgage Servs., 1998 U.S. Dist. LEXIS 18863 (N.D. Ill. Nov. 18, 1998) (court rejected lender's argument that the payoff fee was authorized by provision of note which allowed the note holder "the right to be paid back for all costs and expenses in enforcing the note," noting that this provision applied only to actual out-of-pocket expenses lender paid to a third party).

93 12 U.S.C. § 2605(f)(2). *See also* § 8.2.6.3, *infra.*

94 Chase Manhattan Mortgage Corp. v. Nuehring, 2002 U.S. Dist. LEXIS 1823 (N.D. Ill. Feb. 4, 2002) (borrowers failed to satisfy burden of showing numerosity in relation to servicer's alleged violations of § 2605(e)).

95 Ploog v. Homeside Lending, Inc., 2001 U.S. Dist. LEXIS 15697 (N.D. Ill. Sept. 28, 2001). *But see* McDonald v. Wash. Mut. Bank, 2000 U.S. Dist. LEXIS 11496 (N.D. Ill. June 26, 2000) (subclass certified as to alleged violations of § 2605(e)(3) for servicer's reporting of adverse credit information within sixty days of receiving qualified written requests).

96 *See, e.g.,* Daw v. Peoples Bank & Trust Co., 5 Fed. Appx. 504 (7th Cir. 2001).

97 *See* 15 U.S.C. 1641(g); 10.2.6, *infra.*

Violations of this notice requirement may be remedied by TILA's private right of action, which includes recovery of actual damages, statutory damages, and attorney fees. *See* 15 U.S.C. § 1640(a).

98 12 U.S.C. § 2605(a); Reg. X, 24 C.F.R. § 3500.21(b). Regulation X, however, allows the disclosure statement to be given within three business days after submission of the application, if the application is taken by telephone, or not at all if the loan application is denied within three business days following receipt of the application. Reg. X, 24 C.F.R. § 3500.21(b)(1); § 3500.21(c)(1), (2).

The servicing disclosure statement may be the first indication borrowers have that the loan is a table-funded transaction or that they are dealing with a mortgage broker. *See* Rochester Home Equity, Inc. v. Upton, 767 N.Y.S.2d 201 (Sup. Ct. 2003) (borrower who refused to complete mortgage transaction based on servicing disclosure statement indicating that her mortgage would be assigned not liable for rate lock-in fee because lender failed to provide statement before lock-in agreement was signed).

99 Reg. X, 24 C.F.R. § 3500.21(b), app. MS-1.

The regulation calls the notice a "servicing disclosure statement." Section 2605(a) was considerably shortened in 1996 by the Omnibus Consolidated Appropriations Act, Pub. L. No. 104-208, 110 Stat. 3009 (1996). Prior to 1996, under § 2605(a), the lender not only had to disclose that the mortgage loan might be transferred but also reveal the percentage of its loans for which servicing had been transferred over a specified period of time. This information at least gave the consumer some gauge

addition to the required transfer information, the notice must include a statement of the borrower's rights under section 2605 to dispute and obtain information about the account, as well as information about the consumer's right to notice in the event of future transfers of servicing.[100] Failure to provide this notice gives rise to a private right of action.[101]

8.2.3.3 Notice at Time of Transfer

If the servicing of a mortgage is actually transferred after the mortgage loan is made, the former (transferor) servicer must notify the consumer in writing fifteen days before the effective date of the transfer.[102] Such a notice need not be given, however, if the lender provided it at closing.[103] In addition, the new (transferee) servicer must provide the identical notice to the consumer not more than fifteen days after the effective date of the transfer.[104] The notices from the old and new servicer can be combined into one notice as long as it is sent to the consumer no later than fifteen days before the effective date of the transfer.[105] The term "effective date of transfer" is defined in the statute to mean the date on which the mortgage payment of the borrower is first due to the new (transferee) servicer pursuant to the assignment, sale, or transfer of the servicing of the mortgage loan.[106] In addition to RESPA, the requirement to provide a notice of servicing transfer is often included as a contract term in the mortgage instrument.[107]

The notice of transfer should be mailed to the borrower at the address stated in the loan application or in other information submitted to or obtained by the lender or settlement agent, except that a revised address shall be used when the lender or settlement agent has been expressly informed in writing of a change in address.[108] The lender or servicer is deemed to have satisfied the delivery requirement for the transfer notice if it is sent in this manner, whether or not the notice is actually received by the borrower.[109] Notification of a change of address provided by the borrower to a former (transferor) servicer should be binding on a new (transferee) servicer.[110]

The notice of transfer must include the following information:

---

as to the likelihood of a transfer. HUD created a model form for both the required disclosures and the optional information. Reg. X, 24 C.F.R. § 3500.21(b), app. MS-1. Although HUD has not yet revised this form or amended Regulation X to delete the portion relating to the optional information, it did propose a rule to implement the amended statute that was never finalized. *See* 62 Fed. Reg. 25,740 (May 9, 1997).

100 Reg. X, 24 C.F.R. § 3500.21(b)(3)(iv), (d), (e).

101 *See* Catencamp v. Cendant Timeshare Resort Group-Consumer Fin., Inc., 471 F.3d 780 (7th Cir. 2006).

102 12 U.S.C. § 2605(b)(2)(A).

The regulation creates certain exemptions to this notice requirement, for example, when the transfer is between affiliates, when the transfer results from mergers or acquisitions of servicers, and when the transfer is between master servicers as long as the subservicer remains the same. Reg. X, 24 C.F.R. § 3500.21(d)(1)(i)(A)–(C). The transfer notice is not required when transfer of the ownership of the loan is transferred unless the servicing of the loan is also transferred. *See* Salomon Bros. Realty Corp. v. Bourgeois, 2006 WL 2116591 (E.D. La. July 27, 2006).

103 12 U.S.C. § 2605(b)(2)(C).

In addition, a different notice period is allowed if any one of three, somewhat unusual, events occur: (1) the contract for servicing was transferred for cause; (2) the servicer files bankruptcy; or (3) the Fed. Deposit Ins. Corp. or the Resolution Trust Corp. commences proceedings for receivership of the servicer. 12 U.S.C. § 2605(b)(2)(B); Reg. X, 24 C.F.R. § 3500.21(d)(2)(ii). In these instances, the notice must be sent no later than thirty days after the date of the transfer.

104 12 U.S.C. § 2605(c).

Here again, the timing of the notice is altered if any of the three situations noted above occur or if the notice was provided at settlement. 12 U.S.C. § 2605(c)(2)(B), (C); Reg. X, 24 C.F.R. § 3500.21(d)(2)(ii). *But see* Daw v. Peoples Bank & Trust Co., 5 Fed. Appx. 504 (7th Cir. 2001) (lender not required to give borrower advance notice of assignment because, once borrower defaulted, there were no longer any scheduled periodic payments to make or collect and, thus, there were no servicing rights to assign, sell, or transfer).

105 Reg. X, 24 C.F.R. § 3500.21(d)(2)(C).

106 12 U.S.C. § 2605(i)(1).

107 The Fannie Mae/Freddie Mac Single-Family Uniform Instrument typically includes in section 20, entitled "Sale of Note; Change of Loan Servicer; Notice of Grievance," the following contractual language:

> If there is a change of the Loan Servicer, Borrower will be given written notice of the change which will state the name and address of the new Loan Servicer, the address to which payments should be made and any other information RESPA requires in connection with a notice of transfer of servicing.

108 Reg. X, 24 C.F.R. § 3500.11.

109 Reg. X, 24 C.F.R. § 3500.11.

However, in order for the presumption of delivery to apply, the servicer must produce an authenticated copy of the transfer notice and provide testimony from someone with personal knowledge that the letter was, in fact, placed in a U.S. Postal Service mail receptacle or of the procedures in place at the time of mailing. *See* Modelist v. Deutsche Bank. Nat'l Trust Co., 2006 WL 2792196 (S.D. Tex. Aug. 25, 2006) (denying lender's motion for summary judgment), *subsequent proceeding,* 2006 WL 2792197 (S.D. Tex. Sept. 26, 2006) (district court modified magistrate's report to grant summary judgment after lender filed affidavit of mailing which was not controverted by borrower).

110 *See* Wanger v. EMC Mortgage Corp., 103 Cal. App. 4th 1125, 127 Cal. Rptr. 2d 685 (2002) (servicer must exercise reasonable care and diligence in determining the correct address of borrower when mailing notice of transfer).

The *Wanger* court did not apply § 3500.11 of Regulation X because it was not in effect at the time the borrower mailed the change of address notice to the lender. For this reason, the *Wanger* court relied upon an analogous Regulation X provision, 24 C.F.R. § 3500.17(b), which requires that escrow account statements be sent to the borrower's last known address and concluded that a determination of the borrower's last known address can include the servicer's actual and constructive knowledge.

- The effective date of the transfer;
- The name, address, and toll-free or collect call telephone number of the transferee servicer;
- A toll-free or collect call telephone number for a particular individual employed by the new servicer or the department that the consumer can contact to answer questions;
- The date on which the former servicer will stop accepting loan payments and the date on which the new servicer will begin accepting the payments;
- Any information concerning the effect, if any, that the transfer may have upon the terms of mortgage life, disability or other types of optional insurance;
- What action, if any, the consumer must take to maintain insurance coverage.[111]

8.2.3.4 Treatment of Payments During Transfer Period

Many servicing problems occur at or near the time of transfer of servicing, often caused by the old and new servicer's inability to communicate with each other and reconcile accounting records with respect to borrower payments made during the transition period. Errors involving even just one or two payments can spiral into a threatened foreclosure despite borrower efforts to prove that payments were in fact made.[112] Fortunately, RESPA provides some protection to borrowers by providing a grace period for borrower payments at the time of transfer.

If a consumer mistakenly sends a payment during the sixty-day period following the effective date of transfer to the old servicer which it receives before the due date under the terms of the note, a late fee cannot be imposed nor can the payment be treated as late for any other purposes.[113] This grace period provides some protection to the consumer not only when the payment is sent to the incorrect servicer but also in the event that the old servicer fails to send the payment in a timely way to the new servicer.[114] A servicer's failure to provide the borrower with a transfer notice or the grace period for payments gives rise to a private right of action.[115]

8.2.4 Servicer's Duty to Make Timely Escrow Disbursements

If a borrower is required under the terms of the mortgage to make payments to the servicer for deposit in an escrow account, RESPA limits the amount servicers can require to be deposited in the escrow account, requires the servicer to provide borrowers with initial and annual account statements, and imposes certain other requirements on the servicer.[116] Most of these requirements are not found in the Servicer Act.[117] The Servicer Act, however, creates an express right of action for a servicer's failure to make payments from an escrow account for taxes, insurance and other charges "in a timely manner as such payments become due."[118]

The Act does not specify when a payment is deemed to have been made in a "timely manner." The implementing regulation states that the timely payment requirement for this section of the Act shall be governed by the timeframes and requirements contained in another Regulation X provision dealing with comparable servicer obligations under section 10 of RESPA.[119] This regulation provides that a payment shall be considered timely if it is made on or before the deadline to avoid a penalty.[120] Regulation X defines a "penalty" as a "late charge imposed for paying after the disbursement is due."[121]

A special rule for the payment of property taxes requires the servicer to make disbursements on an installment basis

---

111 12 U.S.C. § 2605(b)(3); Reg. X, 24 C.F.R. § 3500.21(d)(3).
A sample notice is provided in Appendix MS-2 to Regulation X. If the new servicer changes either the monthly payment amount for an escrow account or the accounting method used by the former servicer to calculate the escrow payment, the new servicer must also provide the borrower with an initial escrow account statement within sixty days of the date of servicing transfer. Reg. X, 24 C.F.R. § 3500.17(e); § 8.3, *infra*.

112 *E.g.*, Rawlings v. Dovenmuehle Mortgage, Inc., 64 F. Supp. 2d 1156 (M.D. Ala. 1999).

113 12 U.S.C. § 2605(d); Reg. X, 24 C.F.R. § 3500.21(d)(5). *See* Holland v. GMAC Mortgage Corp., 2006 WL 1133224, at *6 (D. Kan. Apr. 26, 2006) ("purpose of § 2605(d) is to prohibit lenders or servicers from imposing a fee in the sixty-day window from the time a mortgage loan is transferred from one servicer to another").

114 Bibler v. Arcata Invs. 2, L.L.C., 2005 WL 3304127 (Mich. Ct. App. Dec. 6, 2005) (finding that failure to send transfer letter gave rise to equitable defense of laches limiting assignees attempts to collect where borrower paid loan in full, but previous servicer failed to forward payoff funds to new servicer).

115 12 U.S.C. § 2605(f); § 8.2.6.2, *infra*.

116 Escrow accounts are generally required by lenders and servicers to ensure payment of taxes, insurance or other charges. Although nearly ubiquitous in the conventional consumer mortgage market, they are rarely found in loans made by subprime lenders.

117 *See* § 10 of RESPA, 12 U.S.C. § 2609, *discussed at* § 8.3, *infra*. Section 10 does not provide for an express right of action.

118 12 U.S.C. § 2605(g).

119 *See* Reg. X, 24 C.F.R. § 3500.21(g) (which in turn references Reg. X, 24 C.F.R. § 3500.17(k)).

120 Reg. X, 24 C.F.R. § 3500.17(k)(1).
Regulation X also requires the servicer to advance funds in order to make disbursements in a timely manner as long as the "borrower's payment is not more than 30 days overdue." *See* Reg. X, 24 C.F.R. § 3500.17(k)(2); § 8.3.2, *infra*.

121 Reg. X, 24 C.F.R. § 3500.17(b).
The definition also specifies that a penalty does not include "any additional charge or fee imposed by the payee associated with choosing installment payments as opposed to annual payments or for choosing one installment plan over another." Reg. X, 24 C.F.R. § 3500.17(b).

if the taxing authority offers a choice between annual and installment payments, and does not provide a discount for lump sum annual payments or impose an additional charge or penalty for installment payments.[122] If the taxing authority does provide a discount for lump sum annual payments, or imposes additional charges for installment payments, the servicer at its discretion may make a lump sum annual disbursement.[123]

Servicer errors in making timely disbursements, often blamed on computer glitches or problems related to the transfer of servicing, may result in additional costs being passed on to consumers. Rather than absorb these costs caused by their errors, servicers have been known to simply pay them out of borrower escrow accounts. A comparison between a homeowner's initial tax bill and the actual escrow disbursements made, as shown on the annual escrow account statement, may reveal that the homeowner paid additional interest or late charges as a result of the servicer's negligence.[124] Late payment or cancellation of homeowner insurance policies can also produce unnecessary interest charges or reinstatement fees or, far worse, an actual loss during a period without coverage.[125] In addition to other applicable claims, the Act allows for the recovery of damages resulting from a servicer's failure to make timely disbursements.[126]

Regrettably, HUD has taken some of the teeth out of the statutory requirement with its interpretation of the timely escrow disbursement obligation. Regulation X provides that the obligation does not apply when the "borrower's payment is more than 30 days overdue."[127] Though the regulation contains no further explanation of this limitation, it apparently means that a servicer is relieved of the timely disbursement requirements whenever the homeowner's mortgage payment is more than thirty days late at the time the disbursement becomes due, even if there are sufficient funds in the escrow account to cover the disbursement. The regulation should not, however, protect a servicer who has wrongly claimed that the borrower is late with payments.

As long as the borrower's mortgage payment is not more than thirty days late, the servicer must pay escrow items such as taxes and insurance in a timely manner even if there are not sufficient funds in the escrow account to cover the items.[128] For example, a servicer cannot obtain force placed insurance from another carrier in this situation and must instead pay the insurance premium on the borrower's policy when due by advancing its own funds. Any escrow deficiency resulting from the advance is then paid by the borrower through an adjustment to future escrow payments following an escrow account analysis.[129]

8.2.5 Servicer Defenses

8.2.5.1 The "Safe Harbor" Statutory Defense

The Act creates a safe harbor from liability for servicers who timely correct an account error.[130] A servicer can avoid liability by making an appropriate adjustment to an account within sixty days of discovering an error.[131] The correction must also occur before commencement of an action under section 2605(f) and the receipt of a written notice of the error from the borrower.[132]

During the sixty-day period, the servicer must also notify the borrower of the error and make "whatever adjustments" are necessary to ensure that the borrower will not be required to pay any charges that would not otherwise be

122 Reg. X, 24 C.F.R. § 3500.17(k)(3).
The servicer and borrower may mutually agree to a disbursement arrangement, either installment or lump sum, that differs from that required by Regulation X, but the agreement must be voluntary and neither loan approval nor any of the loan terms may be conditioned on the acceptance by the borrower of the different disbursement arrangement. Reg. X, 24 C.F.R. § 3500.17(k)(4).

123 Reg. X, 24 C.F.R. § 3500.17(k)(3).
This subsection states that a servicer may make disbursements on an annual basis in this situation, "but is not required by RESPA to." Reg. X, 24 C.F.R. § 3500.17(k)(3). HUD added this language to make clear that a servicer could be required by state law to make annual disbursements when there is a discount for annual payments or an additional charge for installment payments. *See* 63 Fed. Reg. 3214 (Jan. 21, 1998).

124 When comparing an aggregate or annual tax bill to an annual escrow account statement, advocates should ensure that the same time period is being compared or should make any necessary adjustment to reflect different time periods covered by the escrow statement. Annual escrow statements use a twelve-month computation year which may not correspond to the tax year dates used by the taxing authorities.

125 Servicers have even been known to purchase force placed insurance after a homeowner's policy has been canceled due their own negligence in making the escrow disbursement.

126 12 U.S.C. § 2605(f).
In pleading a claim under this section, the borrower must allege some actual damages were incurred directly from the untimely disbursements. *See* Stevens v. Citigroup, Inc., 2000 WL 1848593 (E.D. Pa. Dec. 15, 2000).

127 Reg. X, 24 C.F.R. § 3500.17(k)(1), (2).

128 Reg. X, 24 C.F.R. § 3500.17(k)(2); § 8.3.4, *infra*.

129 *See* § 8.3, *infra*.

130 12 U.S.C. § 2605(f)(4); Reg. X, 24 C.F.R. § 3500.21(f)(4).

131 Rogers v. First Nationwide Mortgage Corp., 2001 WL 1276223 (Cal. Ct. App. Oct. 23, 2001) (unpublished) (no violation of § 2605 as servicer corrected errors within statutory sixty-day period).

132 12 U.S.C. § 2605(f)(4); Reg. X, 24 C.F.R. § 3500.21(f)(4).
This safe harbor applies to both the former (transferor) and current (transferee) servicers. In addition, Congress created a safe harbor for violations that occurred from the date of passage of § 2605 to the date the regulations were promulgated. 12 U.S.C. § 2605(j). This subsection required HUD to publish regulations by April 20, 1991. 12 U.S.C. § 2605(j)(3). HUD failed to meet this deadline by over three years. *See* 59 Fed. Reg. 65,448 (Dec. 19, 1994) (effective date of the regulations was June 19, 1995).

payable.[133] For instance, a servicer who has applied a borrower's payment to the wrong account or paid property taxes from the borrower's escrow account for the wrong property must not only correct the error but must also reverse or provide a credit for any late charges or other penalties stemming from the error.

The safe harbor defense provided by section 2605(f) should be contrasted with the statutory defenses available to a creditor under the Truth in Lending Act (TILA). Under the TILA, a creditor is provided with a correction of error defense similar to that under the Servicer Act.[134] However, the TILA also provides a bona fide error defense, which permits a creditor to avoid liability by showing that the violation was not intentional and resulted from a bona fide error notwithstanding the maintenance of procedures reasonably adapted to avoid any such error.[135] Because section 2605(f) does not contain a bona fide error defense, servicers are liable for unintentional violations of the Servicer Act and it should be no defense that a servicer had reasonable procedures in place that failed to correct a bona fide error.

The servicer may also have a defense when it waives any claim to a disputed payment obligation.[136] However, a waiver under these circumstances should only have an impact on the amount of damages a borrower may recover. It should not be a defense to liability that falls outside the safe harbor and should not affect the borrower's entitlement to statutory damages under the Act.[137]

8.2.5.2 Borrower in Bankruptcy Proceeding

8.2.5.2.1 No bankruptcy exemption under Servicer Act or Regulation X

With increasing frequency, servicers have been arguing that compliance with the Servicer Act is not required if the borrower is a debtor in a bankruptcy proceeding, and that no liability exists for violations that occur while the bankruptcy is pending. These servicers rarely articulate any grounds for this position and instead simply refer to a non-existent bankruptcy "exemption." Neither the Servicer Act nor the applicable sections of Regulation X contain any reference to bankruptcy or create an exemption for the servicing of an account in bankruptcy.[138]

Significantly, the Department of Housing and Urban Development (HUD) has recognized that servicers may treat borrowers who are in bankruptcy differently with regard to other provisions of RESPA.[139] So HUD's decision to omit any special bankruptcy provisions or exemptions in the Servicer Act regulations clearly indicates that HUD intended for there to be full compliance with the Servicer Act regardless of whether the borrower has filed bankruptcy.[140]

8.2.5.2.2 No conflict between RESPA and Bankruptcy Code

Servicers have also attempted to rely upon a troubling line of cases which have held that some state consumer protection laws are preempted by the Bankruptcy Code.[141] While these cases are wrongly decided,[142] they are of questionable application to the mortgage servicing situation in which the requirements in question are imposed by

133 12 U.S.C. § 2605(f)(4). *See* Reg. X, 24 C.F.R. § 3500.21(f)(4).

134 15 U.S.C. § 1640(b).

135 15 U.S.C. § 1640(c). *See* National Consumer Law Center, Truth in Lending § 7.4.4 (6th ed. 2007 and Supp.) (detailed discussion of the bona fide error defense under the TILA).

136 Cardiello v. The Money Store, Inc., 2001 U.S. Dist. LEXIS 7107 (S.D.N.Y. June 1, 2001) (no liability when servicer waived claim for disputed remaining balance on mortgage); 29 Fed. Appx. 780 (2d Cir. 2002) (unpublished).

137 *See* § 8.2.6.2, *infra*.

138 Servicers have also sought withdrawal of the reference by the district court to the bankruptcy court in matters involving the adjudication of RESPA claims. *See* 28 U.S.C. § 157(d); National Consumer Law Center, Consumer Bankruptcy Law and Practice § 14.2.5 (9th ed. 2009).

One court has held that withdrawal of the reference was not compelled because the bankruptcy court's consideration of a RESPA claim in connection with an adversary proceeding objecting to a servicer's proof of claim, based on noncompliance with a qualified written request, was "merely tangential" and furthers judicial economy. *See* Alfonseca-Baez v. Doral Fin. Corp., 376 B.R. 70 (D. P.R. 2007).

139 *E.g.*, Reg. X, 24 C.F.R. § 3500.17(b)(i)(2) (dealing with annual escrow statements).

140 *See* Chase Manhattan Mortgage Corp. v. Padgett, 268 B.R. 309 (S.D. Fla. 2001) (although servicer was not required to provide borrowers who filed bankruptcy with annual escrow account statements based on the Regulation X bankruptcy exemption found in § 3500.17(i)(2), servicer was required to notify borrowers of escrow account shortages because no bankruptcy exemption exists for that requirement under § 3500.17(f)(5)); *In re* Dominique, 368 B.R. 913 (Bankr. S.D. Fla. 2007).

141 *See* Cox v. Zale Del. Inc., 239 F.3d 910 (7th Cir. 2001); Pertuso v. Ford Motor Credit Co., 233 F.3d 417 (6th Cir. 2000).

142 *See Claims Available for Violations of Discharge Injunction*, 18 NCLC REPORTS, *Bankruptcy and Foreclosures Edition* 17 (Mar./Apr. 2000) (critique of the cases finding preemption).

The Eighth Circuit's more enlightened analysis of the issue is worth noting. In Sears, Roebuck & Co. v. O'Brien, 178 F.3d 962 (8th Cir. 1999), the debtor alleged that a creditor had violated a state "mini-FDCPA" statute, which prohibits creditor contact with a debtor who is represented by counsel, by sending a copy of a letter soliciting a reaffirmation agreement directly to the debtor. In rejecting the creditor's argument that the state statute was preempted, the Eighth Circuit held that Congress did not intend to "exclusively" regulate the bankruptcy area so that there could not be "field" preemption, and that the state law requirement did not conflict with the Bankruptcy Code. *See also* Greenwood Trust Co. v. Smith, 212 B.R. 599, 603 (B.A.P. 8th Cir. 1997) (state collection law does not impede creditor's rights under Bankruptcy Code to negotiate reaffirmation agreements); Sturm v. Providian Nat'l Bank, 242 B.R. 599 (S.D. W. Va. 1999) (enforcement of state statute prohibiting direct communications with a debtor represented by counsel "in no way impedes administration of bankruptcy case").

another federal statute (RESPA), one that is not in conflict with the Bankruptcy Code.

In addition to the cases involving Bankruptcy Code preemption of state law claims, servicers have relied on some initial decisions which held that a debtor is precluded from pursuing claims under the federal Fair Debt Collection Practices Act (FDCPA) for violations of the bankruptcy discharge injunction.[143] As in the debt collection situation, servicers have argued that the requirements of RESPA are "preempted" by the Bankruptcy Code.

The Seventh Circuit in *Randolph v. IMBS, Inc.*[144] correctly rejected this characterization of the issue when two federal statutes come into play. The *Randolph* court noted that "[o]ne federal statute does not preempt another," and that the proper question is whether one of the statutes has been expressly or implicitly repealed:

> When two federal statutes address the same subject in different ways, the right question is whether one implicitly repeals the other—and repeal by implication is a rare bird indeed. (*citations omitted.*) It takes either irreconcilable conflict between the statutes or a clearly expressed legislative decision that one replace the other.[145]

Applying this correct analysis, the *Randolph* court held that although there may be some "operational differences" between the FDCPA and the Bankruptcy Code, there is no "irreconcilable conflict" between the two statutes. In fact, the Seventh Circuit found that the two statutes can work together harmoniously, permitting a debtor for example to obtain the more significant remedy of punitive damages when a willful collection action violates both the FDCPA and the bankruptcy automatic stay. Significantly, the *Randolph* court concluded that both statutes can be easily enforced and that debt collectors "can comply with both simultaneously."[146]

Similarly, the exercise of substantive RESPA rights requiring the production of information and correction of servicing errors is not an attempt to supplant the Code procedure for adjudication of claims.[147] On the contrary, the information sought in a qualified written request will assist rather than hinder the bankruptcy court in adjudicating claims if and when a debtor or trustee objects to claim filed by a mortgage servicer.

Although the Servicer Act and the Bankruptcy Code are certainly capable of coexistence, one court has found that the RESPA requirements for compliance with a "qualified demand letter" are in conflict with the Bankruptcy Code.[148] The court's decision is based in part on a misunderstanding of the potential interplay between section 2605(e) and the bankruptcy claims process set out in 11 U.S.C. § 502 and Federal Rule of Bankruptcy Procedure 3007.

The court in *Nosek* correctly observes that the Bankruptcy Code and rules set up a "different process [] to determine the propriety of claims and to resolve disputes," and that the bankruptcy court is given the authority to determine the amount of the claim.[149] These differences, however, do not equate to an irreconcilable conflict. Nothing in the Servicer Act addresses the allowance or disallowance of a claim in bankruptcy or deprives a bankruptcy court of the exclusive authority to make determinations concerning bankruptcy claims. A dispute in a qualified written request simply requests that the servicer correct errors it may have made on the mortgage account, thereby potentially avoiding a dispute under the bankruptcy claims process. The bankruptcy judge still remains the final arbiter of any claim dispute that may arise in a bankruptcy case.

Compliance with RESPA would also not be asking the servicer to do anything more than it would need to do in a chapter 13 case in order to prepare and file a proof of claim. Certainly the servicer must conduct a reasonable investiga-

143 *See* National Consumer Law Center, Fair Debt Collection § 2.2.5 (6th ed. 2008 and Supp.).

These decisions are based in part on the view that a debtor should not be permitted to create a private right of action for a violation of the Code's discharge injunction, when none exists under the Bankruptcy Code, by using another federal statute, and that the Code provides an exclusive remedy for discharge injunction violations in the form of contempt proceedings. *See, e.g.*, Walls v. Wells Fargo Bank, 276 F.3d 502 (9th Cir. 2002) ("To permit a simultaneous claim under the FDCPA would allow through the back door what [the debtor] cannot accomplish through the front door—a private right of action.").

However, violations of substantive RESPA requirements, such as the obligation to correct servicing errors, provide transfer of servicing notices, and make timely disbursements out of escrow, are not simply the reformulation of Bankruptcy Code violations as the Code does not provide for these servicer obligations nor does it provide an exclusive remedy for such violations.

144 368 F.3d 726 (7th Cir. 2004).

145 *Randolph*, 368 F.3d at 730.

The Supreme Court has stated: "The courts are not at liberty to pick and choose among congressional enactments, and when two statutes are capable of coexistence, it is the duty of the courts, absent a clearly expressed congressional intention to the contrary, to regard each as effective." Morton v. Mancari, 417 U.S. 535, 551 (1974). *See also* Traynor v. Turnage, 485 U.S. 535 (1988).

146 *Randolph*, 368 F.3d at 730. *See also* Dougherty v. Wells Fargo Home Loans, Inc., 425 F. Supp. 2d 599 (E.D. Pa. 2006); *In re* Gunter, 334 B.R. 900 (Bankr. S.D. Ohio 2005).

147 *See* Conley v. Central Mortgage Co., 414 B.R. 157 (E.D. Mich. 2009) (RESPA permits debtor to obtain information when no adversary proceeding or contested matter is pending or when debtor does not yet have enough information to know whether to object to a proof of claim); *In re* Figard, 382 B.R. 695 (Bankr. W.D. Pa. 2008) (RESPA is not in conflict with the claims objection procedure set out in the Bankruptcy Code and Bankruptcy Rules).

148 *In re* Nosek, 354 B.R. 331 (D. Mass. 2006), *vacated on other grounds*, 544 F.3d 34 (1st Cir. 2008). *But see In re* Laskowski, 384 B.R. 518 (Bankr. N.D. Ind. 2008) (finding no irreconcilable conflict between Bankruptcy Code and RESPA); *In re* Figard, 382 B.R. 695 (Bankr. W.D. Pa. 2008) (same).

149 *Id.* at 339.

tion before filing a bankruptcy claim concerning the facts alleged in the claim, including the correct amount owing on the mortgage account.[150] If an error is found in the course of this investigation, the servicer would need to correct the account and file an accurate claim. This response should be no different than what is expected of a servicer with respect to a borrower-initiated inquiry or dispute contained in a qualified written request.

Rather than conflict with the claims allowance process in bankruptcy, the ability to dispute servicer errors in a qualified written request instead promotes judicial economy by averting unnecessary litigation over an objection to an erroneous proof of claim filed by a servicer.[151] Litigation may also be avoided when the servicer's actions are not in error, as the borrower may obtain a sufficient explanation of the dispute in response to a qualified written request and thereafter decide not to file a formal objection to the servicer's bankruptcy proof of claim. Similarly, the borrower's ability to obtain account information through a qualified written request can obviate the need under the Federal Rules of Bankruptcy Procedure to file an objection to a proof of claim in order to initiate formal discovery.[152] To the extent that a servicer does not correct an account error or provide the requested information, the borrower may then initiate an objection to the servicer's proof of claim and pursue remedies for Servicer Act violations in the same bankruptcy proceeding. The availability of different and "overlapping" remedies under the RESPA and the Code, especially when these statutes further a common purpose, does not create an inescapable conflict.[153]

The *Nosek* court also expressed concern based on the timeframes for servicer compliance under section 2605(e) and the Bankruptcy Rules of Civil Procedure. It noted that an objection to a bankruptcy claim must be filed at least thirty days prior to the hearing under Bankruptcy Rule 3007. The court then incorrectly suggests that the servicer has only twenty days to comply with qualified written requests under section 2605(e). In fact the servicer simply needs to acknowledge receipt of the request within twenty days, and has sixty days (excluding holidays, Saturdays, Sundays) to actually respond.[154] Bankruptcy Rule 3007 on the other hand simply requires that a claim objection be filed at least thirty days before a hearing on the objection, but does not dictate when the hearing shall occur or how much time the bankruptcy court may take to schedule and conduct the hearing. It is unclear how these procedural timeframes create an unavoidable conflict for servicers. To the extent any "operational differences" exist, as the Seventh Circuit in *Ranolph* would suggest, the bankruptcy court would certainly have the authority to set a timetable for compliance.

As an example of how the "preemption" of Servicer Act requirements in bankruptcy proceedings would lead to absurd results, surely the requirement that servicers make timely payments out of escrow accounts must be enforceable in chapter 13 cases.[155] Typically chapter 13 cases extend for periods of three to five years. Certainly Congress could not have intended that a debtor's ability to cure a mortgage default in chapter 13 should be frustrated by the complete chaos which would ensue if servicers are permitted to ignore RESPA and not make timely disbursements out of escrow for taxes and insurance while a debtor is in a chapter 13 case.

In addition, servicer compliance with the Servicer Act in providing information or correcting errors at the request of the borrower, or by making timely payments out of escrow, is not prohibited by the automatic stay in bankruptcy.[156] By expressly exempting servicers from some of RESPA's requirements when a homeowner is in bankruptcy but not others, HUD has also recognized that the two federal statutes can be read in harmony so that both can be given proper effect. Based on the Seventh Circuit's analysis in *Randolph*, courts should conclude that the Servicer Act and the Bankruptcy Code can both be complied with and enforced simultaneously.[157] In fact, most courts have rejected servicer

150 The failure to do so would subject the servicer to sanctions under Bankruptcy Rule 9011. *See In re* Ulmer, 363 B.R. 777 (Bankr. D.S.C. 2007); *In re* Thompson, 350 B.R. 842 (Bankr. E.D. Wis. 2006); *In re* Rivera, 342 B.R. 435 (Bankr. D.N.J. 2006), *aff'd,* 2007 WL 1946656 (D.N.J. June 29, 2007); *In re* Gorshtein, 285 B.R. 118 (Bankr. S.D.N.Y. 2002); *In re* Kilgore, 253 B.R. 179 (Bankr. D.S.C. 2000).

151 *See* National Consumer Law Center, Consumer Bankruptcy Law and Practice § 14.4.3 (9th ed. 2009) (discussion of the claims objection process in bankruptcy).

152 *See* Chatman v. Fairbanks Capital Corp., 2002 U.S. Dist. LEXIS 10945 (N.D. Ill. June 13, 2002) (compliance with plaintiff's qualified written request was required after litigation initiated even though information requested was available under Federal Rules of Civil Procedure).

153 Randolph v. IMBS, Inc., 368 F.3d 726, 731 (7th Cir. 2004) ("overlapping statutes do not repeal one another by implication; as long as people can comply with both, then courts can enforce both").

154 *See* 12 U.S.C. § 2605(e)(1)(A); §§ 8.2.2.5, 8.2.2.6, *supra*.

155 *See* § 8.2.4, *supra*.

156 *See, e.g.*, Chase Manhattan Mortgage Corp. v. Padgett, 268 B.R. 309 (S.D. Fla. 2001) (§ 362(a) of the Bankruptcy Code does not prevent servicer from merely providing RESPA notice of an escrow advance or deficiency; violation occurs only when servicer "exert[s] pressure" to collect advances); *In re* Dominique, 368 B.R. 913 (Bankr. S.D. Fla. 2007); *In re* Draper, 237 B.R. 502 (Bankr. M.D. Fla. 1999). *See also In re* Ramirez, 280 B.R. 252 (C.D. Cal. 2002) (mere mailing by a creditor of informational billing statements not a violation of stay).

157 Some servicers have also relied upon the Supreme Court decision in Kokoszka v. Belford, 417 U.S. 642 (1974) in arguing that they need not comply with RESPA. This pre-Bankruptcy Code decision is completely inapposite as it did not involve RESPA in any way. In *Kokoska*, the Supreme Court considered the interplay between the Consumer Credit Protection Act's (CCPA) wage garnishment provisions and the Bankruptcy Act. In finding that Congress did not intend to alter bankruptcy law with the enactment of the CCPA, the Court noted that the CCPA

arguments on this point and have required compliance with section 2605 when the borrower is in bankruptcy.[158]

8.2.6 *Private Remedies for Violation of the Servicer Act Requirements*

8.2.6.1 In General

In contrast with other sections of RESPA, section 2605(f) provides an express private right of action.[159] The consumer may recover actual damages, statutory damages, costs, and reasonable attorney fees.[160] An action seeking relief under section 2605 may be brought in federal or state court.[161] Unlike other RESPA claims that must be brought within one year,[162] the statute of limitations for actions brought under section 2605 is three years.[163] In the case of an action for violations of a servicer's duty to respond to a qualified written request,[164] the action may not be filed before the time period for servicer compliance has expired.[165]

8.2.6.2 Actual Damages

The Servicer Act does not provide for an award of treble damages,[166] and the availability of punitive damages is uncertain.[167] When a claim for statutory damages cannot be established, the borrower will be limited to an award of actual damages for each violation of the Act, plus costs and attorney fees.[168] There is a growing trend among courts to treat damages as an element of a claim under section 2605(e). As a result several courts have held that to avoid dismissal or summary judgment, plaintiffs must sufficiently

---

was passed under both the bankruptcy and commerce powers of Congress. RESPA is not one of the statutes passed as part of the CCPA and it was not enacted under the bankruptcy clause of the Constitution. In addition, the specific issue raised in *Kokoska* was whether the wage garnishment provisions of the CCPA constrained the trustee's recovery of an income tax refund as property of the debtor's bankruptcy estate. Since the debtor's assertion of the CCPA provisions presented a direct conflict with the Bankruptcy Act's definition of property of the debtor's estate, the Supreme Court found that the Act controls. A debtor's exercise of rights under RESPA, however, does not involve conflicts with Bankruptcy Code provisions as in *Kokoska*. *See* Randolph v. IMBS, Inc., 368 F.3d 726, 731 (7th Cir. 2004) (criticizing application of *Kokoska* to interplay between FDCPA and Bankruptcy Code).

158 Conley v. Central Mortgage Co., 414 B.R. 157 (E.D. Mich. 2009); *In re* Laskowski, 384 B.R. 518 (Bankr. N.D. Ind. 2008); *In re* Figard, 382 B.R. 695 (Bankr. W.D. Pa. 2008); *In re* Sánchez-Rodríguez, 377 B.R. 1 (Bankr. D. P.R. 2007) (debtors who filed chapter 13 bankruptcy to save home from foreclosure entitled to seek information about mortgage in qualified written request). *See also In re* Padilla, 379 B.R. 643, 666–667 (Bankr. S.D. Tex. 2007) (concluding that "[n]othing in the Bankruptcy Code immunizes mortgagees from causes of action based on RESPA.").

159 12 U.S.C. § 2605(f); Reg. X, 24 C.F.R. § 3500.21(f). *See* National Consumer Law Center, The Cost of Credit: Regulation, Preemption, and Industry Abuses §§ 12.2.1.3–12.2.1.4 (4th ed. 2009 and Supp.) (discussion of other sections of RESPA for which a private right of action was not specifically included).

160 The language of § 2605(f) authorizing an award of attorney fees in the case of a "successful" action brought to enforce compliance with the section's provisions suggests that fee awards are limited to successful plaintiffs and not defendants. The Servicer Act's fee provision is similar to the pre-1983 version of another RESPA fee provision, § 2607(d), which had been construed as authorizing only costs and attorney fees for successful plaintiffs. *See* Lane v. Residential Funding Corp., 323 F.3d 739 (9th Cir. 2003).

161 12 U.S.C. § 2614. *See also* Yeiser v. GMAC Mortgage Corp., 535 F. Supp. 2d 413 (S.D.N.Y. 2008) (finding that because RESPA claim involving qualified written request was available to homeowners as defense or counterclaim in state foreclosure action pursuant to § 2614, res judicata barred litigation of claim in subsequent federal court action).

162 For example, the one-year statute of limitations applies to actions brought under section 8, 12 U.S.C. § 2607 (prohibition against kickbacks and unearned fees), and section 9, 12 U.S.C. § 2608 (prohibition against requiring that title insurance be purchased from a particular vendor). *See* 12 U.S.C. § 2614; § 8.6, *infra* (chart).

163 12 U.S.C. § 2614.

An untimely RESPA damage claim may be asserted by way of recoupment in the bankruptcy process as an objection to a lender or servicer's proof of claim. *See In re* Thompson, 350 B.R. 842 (Bankr. E.D. Wis. 2006); *In re* Harvey, 2003 WL 21460063 (Bankr. E.D. Pa 2003); National Consumer Law Center, Consumer Bankruptcy Law and Practice § 14.3.2.4 (9th ed. 2009).

164 *See* §§ 8.2.2.5, 8.2.2.6, *supra*.

Additionally, advocates should be aware that certain RESPA claims asserted against Fairbanks Capital Corp., a.k.a., Select Portfolio Servicing, may be precluded by the class settlement in Curry v. Fairbanks Capital Corp., No. 03-10895 (D. Mass. 2003). *See, e.g.*, Slezak v. Fairbanks Capital Corp., 186 Fed. Appx. 732 (9th Cir. 2006); § 8.2.2.7, *supra*.

165 *See* Harris v. American Gen. Fin., Inc., 259 Fed. Appx. 107 (10th Cir. 2007) (unpublished) (claims based on noncompliance with qualified written request were not ripe).

166 Other sections of RESPA, such as sections 8 and 9, do provide for an award of treble damages. 12 U.S.C. §§ 2607(d), 2608(b). *See also* § 8.6, *infra* (chart).

167 *In re* Tomasevic, 273 B.R. 682 (Bankr. M.D. Fla. 2002) (punitive damages may not be awarded).

Arguably, as § 2605(f) is silent on the availability of punitive damages and its provision for "additional" damages subject to the $1000 limitation does not include punitive damages, Congress could not have intended that $1000 should be the maximum "punitive" award when a servicer's conduct is particularly abusive. *See* National Consumer Law Center, Fair Debt Collection § 6.5.1 (6th ed. 2008 and Supp.) (more detailed discussion of this argument in a similar context).

168 12 U.S.C. § 2605(f)(1), (3); Ploog v. Homeside Lending, Inc., 209 F. Supp. 2d 863 (N.D. Ill. 2002) (actual damages available for each violation); Katz v. The Dime Sav. Bank, 992 F. Supp. 250 (W.D.N.Y. 1997) (plaintiff entitled to recover actual damages "suffered due to each violation").

In a class action, there may be an award of actual damages to each of the borrowers in the class. 12 U.S.C. § 2605(f)(2)(A).

allege that actual damages were caused by the servicer's failure to comply.[169] Courts have been willing to broadly define the scope of actual damages available under the statute.

169 *See, e.g.,* Sam v. American Home Mortgage Servicing, 2010 WL 761228 (E.D. Cal. Mar. 3, 2010) (refusing to grant motion to dismiss where complaint alleged that failure to respond to qualified written request resulted in plaintiffs being unable to rescind their loan); Morris v. Bank of Am., 2010 WL 761318 (N.D. Cal. Mar. 3, 2010) (dismissing RESPA claim for failure to allege actual damages); Gates v. Wachovia Mortgage, F.S.B., 2010 WL 902818 (E.D. Cal. Feb. 19, 2010) (complaint dismissed which contained mere allegation that servicer failed to acknowledge request, and did not plead any facts showing how the borrower was harmed); Saldate v. Wilshire Credit Corp., 2010 WL 582074 (E.D. Cal. Feb. 12, 2010) (claim dismissed where plaintiff failed to allege "identifiable damages attributable" to RESPA violation); Pelayo v. Home Capital Funding, 2009 WL 1459419 (S.D. Cal. May 22, 2009) (finding that plaintiff had sufficiently pleaded damages by alleging in complaint the following: "as a proximate result of the negligent conduct of Defendants and their failures as herein alleged, the Plaintiff has sustained damages, including monetary loss. . . ."); McCutcheon v. America's Servicing Co., 2007 WL 2287675 (E.D. Pa. July 31, 2007) (same), *aff'd on other grounds*, 560 F.3d 143 (3d Cir. 2009); Spencer v. Hutchens, 471 F. Supp. 2d 548 (M.D.N.C. 2006) (granting summary judgment because borrower failed to provide any evidence that he suffered injury from servicer's failure to provide transfer of servicing notice); Hutchinson v. Del. Sav. Bank F.S.B., 410 F. Supp. 2d 374 (D.N.J. 2006) (allegations of actual damages required and satisfied by claim that failure to respond to qualified written request resulted in "negative credit ratings" and "the inability to obtain and borrow another mortgage loan."); Collier v. Wells Fargo Home Mortgage, 2006 WL 1464170 (N.D. Tex. May 26, 2006) (dismissing RESPA claim where plaintiff failed to plead damages were caused by lender's failure to respond or inadequate response to QWR); Caddell v. Citimortgage, Inc., 59 U.C.C. Rep. Serv. 2d 181, n.9 (D. Kan. 2006); Byrd v. Homecomings Fin. Network, 407 F. Supp. 2d 937 (N.D. Ill. 2005) (stating that § 2605(f) requires party to show actual damage from violation of § 2605(e)(2)); *In re* Price, 403 B.R. 775 (Bankr. E.D. Ark. 2009) (finding that borrowers had adequately pleaded actual damages by alleging that they expended time and expenses in seeking to obtain requested documents); *In re* Holland, 2008 WL 4809493, at *10 (Bankr. D. Mass. Oct. 30, 2008) (entering summary judgment in favor of servicer because borrower "failed to establish any causal link between [servicer's] failure to respond to [qualified written request] and any harm."). *But see In re* Nosek, 2006 WL 1867096 (Bankr. D. Mass. June 30, 2006) (awarding $1 in damages on RESPA claim even though plaintiff failed to establish causation between emotional distress and lender's RESPA violation), *appeal allowed and case remanded*, 354 B.R. 331 (D. Mass. 2006) (Bankruptcy Code preempts RESPA's dispute resolution provisions as to disputed claim in ongoing bankruptcy proceeding), *on remand*, 363 B.R. 643 (Bankr. D. Mass. 2007).

After a summary affirmance by the district court, the First Circuit Court of Appeals vacated the judgment and remanded with direction to dismiss the debtor's adversary proceeding. The First Circuit held that the creditor failed to establish a violation of either a specific Bankruptcy Code section or her confirmed plan necessary to invoke the Bankruptcy Court's authority under § 105 to award relief. *In re* Nosek, 544 F.3d 34 (1st Cir. 2008).

At a minimum, actual damages for a Servicer Act violation should include all of the homeowner's economic injuries that directly flow from the servicer's failure to respond to the qualified written request, make appropriate corrections to the account, or otherwise comply with the Act's requirements.[170] For example, these damages may encompass:

- Cost of photocopies and postage in sending a qualified written request;[171]
- Time spent in obtaining compliance, transportation costs, and inconvenience;[172]
- Additional interest, late fees, and foreclosure costs;[173]
- Payments made to former servicer after effective date of transfer;[174]
- Loss of home through foreclosure;[175]
- Denial of right to rescind loan by failing it identify note holder;[176]
- Denial of access to full amount of credit line;[177] and
- Damage to credit rating.[178]

170 Stevens v. CitiGroup, Inc., 2000 U.S. Dist. LEXIS 18201 (E.D. Pa. Dec. 15, 2000) (§ 2605(b) claim dismissed when borrower failed to plead existence of damages flowing directly from servicer's failure to provide servicing transfer notice); Katz v. The Dime Sav. Bank, 992 F. Supp. 250 (W.D.N.Y. 1997); *In re* Tomasevic, 273 B.R. 682 (Bankr. M.D. Fla. 2002).

171 Cortez v. Keystone Bank, 2000 U.S. Dist. LEXIS 5705 (E.D. Pa. May 2, 2000); *In re* Tomasevic, 273 B.R. 682 (Bankr. M.D. Fla. 2002).

172 Johnstone v. Bank of Am., 173 F. Supp. 2d 809 (N.D. Ill. 2001); Cortez v. Keystone Bank, 2000 U.S. Dist. LEXIS 5705 (E.D. Pa. May 2, 2000) (actual damages include time spent away from job preparing correspondence to servicer); Rawlings v. Dovenmuehle Mortgage, Inc., 64 F. Supp. 2d 1156 (M.D. Ala. 1999) ($75 for "secretarial service correspondence" and $40 for traveling to post office).

173 Padgett v. OneWest Bank, F.S.B., 2010 WL 1539839 (N.D. W. Va. Apr. 19, 2010) (allegation of inaccurate imposition of late fees satisfied pleading requirement for damages under RESPA); Johnstone v. Bank of Am., 173 F. Supp. 2d 809 (N.D. Ill. 2001); *In re* Tomasevic, 273 B.R. 682 (Bankr. M.D. Fla. 2002) (additional interest caused by servicer's misapplication of chapter 13 plan payments to pre-petition arrearage recoverable as actual damages, though debtor failed to prove charges for additional interest).

174 Wanger v. EMC Mortgage Corp., 103 Cal. App. 4th 1125, 127 Cal. Rptr. 2d 685 (2002).

175 *Id.* (foreclosure may be included in actual damages awarded under § 2605(f)(1), regardless of whether foreclosure was wrongful, if borrower can show that foreclosure occurred as a result of the servicer's failure to deliver notice of servicing transfer).

176 Woods v. Greenpoint Mortgage Funding, Inc., 2010 WL 1729711 (E.D. Cal. Apr. 28, 2010) (by failing to give borrower a "straight answer" to request for identity of owner of mortgage, servicer harmed borrower by preventing him from rescinding the loan).

177 Cortez v. Keystone Bank, 2000 U.S. Dist. LEXIS 5705 (E.D. Pa. May 2, 2000).

178 Hutchinson v. Delaware Sav. Bank F.S.B., 410 F. Supp. 2d 374 (D.N.J. 2006); Williamson v. Advanta Mortgage Corp., 1999 U.S. Dist. LEXIS 16374 (N.D. Ill. Oct. 8, 1999) (damages

Given the frustration and anguish that homeowners often experience in attempting to resolve disputes with unresponsive servicers, most courts have fortunately held that a plaintiff is entitled to recover actual damages for emotional distress. However, the first court to address this issue, *Katz v. The Dime Savings Bank*,[179] held that actual damages did not include emotional distress based on the dubious finding that the Servicer Act was not a consumer protection statute.[180] Most courts have since rejected the *Katz* holding and construed RESPA's actual damages provision to include damages for emotional distress on the basis that RESPA is a remedial consumer protection statute that should be construed liberally.[181] Although proof of emotional distress damages will often be aided by expert testimony, courts have held that borrowers may rely upon their own testimony.[182]

resulting from inability to refinance mortgage at lower interest rate based on servicer's failure to take corrective action and negative reporting sufficiently pleaded).

The borrower may at a minimum need to show that information received by a credit reporting agency from the servicer was reported to a third party. *See* Johnstone v. Bank of Am., 173 F. Supp. 2d 809 (N.D. Ill. 2001).

179 992 F. Supp. 250 (W.D.N.Y. 1997).

180 It is remarkable that the *Katz* court have reached this conclusion despite its reference to the legislative history of the Servicer Act, which explains that its purpose was "to authorize a comprehensive, new housing policy that can mobilize sustained national effort to provide more affordable housing for all Americans." S. Rep. No. 101-316, at 5 (1990), *reprinted in* 1990 U.S.C.C.A.N. 5763, 5769.

Apparently, the *Katz* court did not view Congress' efforts to facilitate homeownership as a consumer protection purpose.

181 Moon v. GMAC Mortgage Corp., 2009 WL 3185596 (W.D. Wash. Oct. 2, 2009); McLean v. GMAC Mortgage Corp., 595 F. Supp. 2d 1360 (S.D. Fla. 2009); Wright v. Litton Loan Servicing L.P., 2006 WL 891030 (E.D. Pa. Apr. 4, 2006) (concluding actual damages include non-economic losses such as suffering and emotional distress and awarding plaintiff $25,000); Ploog v. Homeside Lending, Inc., 209 F. Supp. 2d 863 (N.D. Ill. 2002); Johnstone v. Bank of Am., 173 F. Supp. 2d 809 (N.D. Ill. 2001); Rawlings v. Dovenmuehle Mortgage, Inc., 64 F. Supp. 2d 1156 (M.D. Ala. 1999); *In re* Thompson, 350 B.R. 842 (Bankr. E.D. Wis. 2006); *In re* Nosek, 2006 WL 1867096 (Bankr. D. Mass. June 30, 2006) (recognizing actual damages includes emotional distress but finding that plaintiff had not sufficiently demonstrated causation between servicer's failure to respond to QWR and emotional distress), *appeal allowed and case remanded*, 354 B.R. 331 (D. Mass. 2006) (Bankruptcy Code preempts RESPA's dispute resolution provisions as to disputed claim in ongoing bankruptcy proceeding), *vacated on other grounds*, 544 F.3d 34 (1st Cir. 2008). *See also* Wanger v. EMC Mortgage Corp., 103 Cal. App. 4th 1125, 127 Cal. Rptr. 2d 685 (2002) (RESPA construed as having remedial consumer protection purpose in context of transfer of servicing notice requirements). *But see In re* Tomasevic, 273 B.R. 682 (Bankr. M.D. Fla. 2002).

182 *See* McLean v. GMAC Mortgage Corp., 595 F. Supp. 2d 1360 (S.D. Fla. 2009) (borrowers may establish causation between RESPA violation and their emotional distress damages through lay testimony; however, court concluded that borrowers' testimony concerning mental distress was insufficient).

8.2.6.3 Statutory Damages

The Servicer Act provides that in addition to actual damages, a court may award "additional" damages in an amount not to exceed $1000 if the evidence reveals a "pattern or practice of noncompliance."[183] As in the case of actual damages, a borrower should be entitled to an award of up to $1000 per violation, not a total award of $1000 for all "pattern and practice" violations.[184] Recovery of statutory damages in class actions is capped at $500,000 or 1% of the net worth of the servicer, whichever is less.[185]

The availability of statutory damages is obviously limited by the evidentiary burden of showing a "pattern and practice" of noncompliance. It is conceivable that this requirement can be established through evidence of the servicer's dealings simply with the named plaintiff in an action. In *Ploog v. Homeside Lending, Inc.*,[186] the plaintiff alleged that the servicer failed to respond to five separate qualified written requests. For purposes of ruling on a motion to dismiss, the court concluded that the plaintiffs would be entitled to statutory damages for the servicer's pattern and practice of noncompliance based on the five violations.[187]

183 12 U.S.C. § 2605(f)(1)(B); Reg. X, 24 C.F.R. § 3500.21(f)(1)(i).

184 The language of § 2505(f) ("[w]hoever fails to comply with any provision of this section shall be liable to the borrower for each such failure") can be distinguished from that in the Fair Debt Collection Practices Act (FDCPA), 15 U.S.C. § 1692k(a) ("any debt collector who fails to comply with any provision of this subchapter with respect to any person is liable to such person in an amount equal to"). Under the FDCPA, some courts have held that multiple violations trigger only one statutory damage recovery of up to $1000. *See* National Consumer Law Center, Fair Debt Collection § 6.4.7.2.2 (6th ed. 2008 and Supp.).

The language of § 2605(f) is clear on its face that multiple violations trigger multiple penalties when a pattern or practice exists. Nevertheless, the court in Ploog v. Homeside Lending, Inc., 209 F. Supp. 2d 863 (N.D. Ill. 2002), relying upon dicta in Katz v. The Dime Sav. Bank, 992 F. Supp. 250 (W.D.N.Y. 1997), ignored the Act's plain language and held that the "pattern and practice" language somehow conflicts with the "for each such violation" phrase, and that the statute should be construed as permitting recovery of only actual damages for each violation. *See also* Serfass v. CIT Group/Consumer Fin., Inc., 2008 WL 4200356 (D.S.C. Sept. 10, 2008) (statutory damages limited to $1000 awarded despite multiple violations).

185 12 U.S.C. § 2605(f)(2); Reg. X, 24 C.F.R. § 3500.21(f)(1)(ii). Regulation X makes clear that the class action damages cap does not apply to actual damages. In determining the amount of a class action award, the conference report issued at the time of enactment of this provision states that the court shall consider, among other relevant factors, the amount of any actual damages awarded, the frequency and persistence of failure of compliance by the creditor, the resources of the creditor, the number of persons adversely affected, and the extent to which the creditor's failure to comply was intentional. *See* H.R. Conf. Rep. No. 101-943, at 512 (1990), *reprinted in* 1990 U.S.C.C.A.N. 6070, 6217.

186 209 F. Supp. 2d 863 (N.D. Ill. 2002).

187 *See also* Serfass v. CIT Group/Consumer Fin., Inc., 2008 WL 4200356 (D.S.C. Sept. 10, 2008) (pattern and practice of non-

But the more common approach would be for the plaintiff to conduct discovery and present evidence about the servicer's policies and procedures for compliance with the Act's requirements, and its conduct in a representative sample of servicing accounts.[188]

Although current case law has not explored the extent of proof that must be presented to satisfy the "pattern and practice" requirement under section 2605(f), courts may look to case law on similar requirements under Title VII (involving employment discrimination) and the Home Ownership and Equity Protection Act (HOEPA).[189] One court has noted that the "pattern and practice" language in RESPA and other federal statutes is not a "term of art but rather is defined according to the usual meaning of the words," and that it suggests a "standard or routine way of operating."[190]

8.3 Other RESPA Servicing Requirements—Escrow Accounts

8.3.1 Introduction

Escrow accounts are generally required by lenders to ensure payment of taxes, insurance, or other charges. These accounts are most commonly established and initially funded at the time of the loan settlement. After settlement, a portion of the borrower's mortgage payment is typically allocated to the escrow account.

Although nearly ubiquitous in the conventional consumer mortgage market, escrow accounts are found less frequently in loans made by subprime lenders. However, subprime lenders or servicers may later seek to create an escrow or similar account if the borrower has defaulted on payments or has failed to make tax payments. It is questionable whether lenders (or servicers) may force escrow accounts on borrowers without their consent. One court has held that the lender was not authorized under the note or deed of trust to unilaterally create an account where one had not existed before the borrower failed to pay property taxes.[191]

---

compliance established by servicer's failure to respond to five qualified written requests sent by the plaintiff); Wright v. Litton Loan Servicing, L.P., 2006 WL 891030 (E.D. Pa. Apr. 4, 2006) (awarding statutory damages in view of the numerous violations with respect to the plaintiff). *But see* McLean v. GMAC Mortgage Corp., 595 F. Supp. 2d 1360 (S.D. Fla. 2009) (evidence of two RESPA violations was insufficient to support a pattern or practice); *In re* Thompson, 350 B.R. 842 (Bankr. E.D. Wis. 2006) (failure to respond to five qualified written requests from same borrower did not constitute "pattern and practice"); *In re* Maxwell, 281 B.R. 101 (Bankr. D. Mass. 2002) (failing to respond to two qualified written requests not sufficient to establish "pattern and practice").

However, the failure of a servicer to respond to a series of inquiries that are substantially similar and raise the same dispute may not constitute a pattern and practice. *See* Cortez v. Keystone Bank, 2000 U.S. Dist. LEXIS 5705 (E.D. Pa. May 2, 2000).

188 The plaintiff should not be required to present evidence based on a statistical analysis. For violations based on the servicer's response to qualified written requests, one potential difficulty in conducting discovery may involve the servicer's lack of adequate record keeping for requests that it deems not to be formal qualified written requests but which actually do meet the broad definition of such requests under the Servicer Act. This lack of records may necessitate discovery concerning the servicer's general procedures for responding to written correspondence from borrowers and its specific maintenance of adequate procedures for identifying and responding to qualified written requests. Advocates should explore whether the servicer has a designated exclusive office and address for receipt of qualified written requests (*see* §§ 8.2.2.3, 8.2.2.4, *supra*), as this may aid in identifying records related to the servicer's procedures and compliance.

189 In Newton v. United Companies Fin. Corp., 24 F. Supp. 2d 444 (E.D. Pa. 1998), the court applied a somewhat stringent standard of proof borrowed from employment discrimination cases to an action brought under HOEPA alleging that the lender had engaged in a "pattern and practice" of making loans without considering borrowers' ability to repay the loans. In recent regulations and commentary interpreting the "pattern and practice" requirement under HOEPA, the Federal Trade Commission (FTC) has clarified that such an exacting standard is not required. The FTC Commentary now states that the issue of whether a creditor is engaging in a "pattern or practice" depends on the "totality of the circumstances." Official Staff Commentary, 12 C.F.R. § 226.34(a)(4)-2. More explicitly, this Commentary section states: "While a pattern or practice is not established by isolated, random, or accidental acts, it can be established without the use of statistical process. In addition, a creditor might act under a lending policy (whether written or unwritten) and that action alone could establish a pattern or practice of making loans in violation of this section." For a more detailed discussion of this HOEPA provision, see National Consumer Law Center, Truth in Lending § 10.4.7 (6th ed. 2007 and Supp.).

190 Cortez v. Keystone Bank, 2000 U.S. Dist. LEXIS 5705 (E.D. Pa. May 2, 2000).

191 Anolik v. EMC Mortgage Corp., 28 Cal. Rptr. 3d 759, (Cal. Ct. App. 2005) (as modified on denial of rehearing, review denied and ordered not to be officially published).

The lender in *Anolik* relied on the following language, commonly found in mortgages and deeds of trust, to support its argument that it was authorized to create an escrow account at any time:

> Subject to applicable law or to a written waiver by Lender, Borrower shall pay to Lender on the day monthly payments are due under the Note, until the Note is paid in full, a sum ("Funds") for: (a) yearly taxes and assessments which may attain priority over this Security Instrument as a lien on the Property. . . . These items are called "Escrow Items." Lender may, at any time, collect and hold Funds in an amount not to exceed the maximum amount a lender for a federally related mortgage loan may require for Borrower's escrow account under . . . 12 U.S.C. Section 2601 et seq. ("RESPA"), unless another law that applies to the Funds sets a lesser amount. If so, Lender may, at any time, collect and hold Funds in an amount not to exceed the lesser amount. Lender may estimate the amount of Funds due on the basis

If an escrow account has been properly established, Section 10 of the Real Estate Settlement Procedures Act (RESPA) limits the amount of money a lender or servicer can require the borrower to deposit into an escrow account to pay "taxes, insurance premiums, or other charges with respect to the property."[192] This section of RESPA requires that the borrower receive a written escrow account statement at the time the account is opened, and annually thereafter.[193] In addition, Regulation X, the regulation implementing section 10, describes the procedure to be used for conducting an escrow account analysis and the formula for calculating how much of a cushion the servicer can legitimately maintain in the account.[194] The Regulation X provisions also establish rules on how the servicer should handle surpluses, shortages, and deficiencies.[195]

Congress enacted section 10 of RESPA in response to reports of lender and servicer abuses concerning the "over-escrowing" of consumer mortgage accounts. One court described the problem as follows:

> [A]n unscrupulous lender has the opportunity to extract an involuntary interest free loan by requiring the borrower to pay more than is necessary to cover the borrower's tax and insurance obligations. A lender with numerous customers could realize substantial profits from the use of funds gained through small individual overcharges.[196]

The discussion that follows provides an overview of the escrow accounting process. However, the Regulation X rules covering escrow accounts are arcane, and are best understood through application in an actual account transaction. Fortunately, the Department of Housing and Urban Development (HUD) has provided several illustrations of the proper method for conducting account calculations as an appendix to the rules.[197] Advocates may wish to review these examples before attempting to verify the accuracy of a client's escrow account analysis.

8.3.2 Escrow Account Analysis

8.3.2.1 Overview

RESPA requires that a lender or servicer perform an escrow account analysis at the time an account is established and annually thereafter.[198] An "escrow account analysis" means the accounting that a servicer conducts to determine: (1) the appropriate target balances for the items to be paid under the account; (2) the borrower's monthly escrow payments for the upcoming twelve-month period; and (3) whether any surpluses, shortages, and deficiencies exist.[199] The accounting process is referred to as a "trial running balance" in which the servicer makes projections of "target balances" over the course of an "escrow account computation year."[200] Regulation X defines a "target balance" as the "estimated month end balance in an escrow account that is just sufficient to cover the remaining disbursements from the escrow account in the escrow account computation year, taking into account the remaining scheduled periodic payments, and a cushion, if any."[201]

> of current data and reasonable estimates of expenditures of future Escrow Items or otherwise in accordance with applicable law.

The court, however, found that the quoted language did not authorize the lender to establish a forced escrow account and increase the borrower's monthly payment. *Id.*, 28 Cal. Rptr. 3d at 769–770 (ordered not published).

192 12 U.S.C. § 2609; Reg. X, 24 C.F.R. § 3500.17.

RESPA does not cover prepaid or advance mortgage payments that are withheld from the loan proceeds to cover mortgage payments that would otherwise be paid over the course of the loan. Limitations on such prepaid payments may be imposed under state law. In addition, under the Home Ownership and Equity Protection Act, a lender may not require prepayment of more than two periodic payments in a covered loan. *See* 15 U.S.C. § 1639(g); National Consumer Law Center, Truth in Lending § 10.4.6 (6th ed. 2007 and Supp.).

193 12 U.S.C. § 2609(c); Reg. X, 24 C.F.R. § 3500.17(g), (h), (i).

194 Reg. X, 24 C.F.R. § 3500.17(c), (d).

The Department of Housing and Urban Development (HUD) issued several escrow rules during 1994–1995 to implement section 10 of RESPA. *See* 59 Fed. Reg. 53,890 (Oct. 26, 1994); 60 Fed. Reg. 8812 (Feb. 15, 1995); 61 Fed. Reg. 13,241 (Mar. 26, 1996).

It then issued amendments to its October 1994 rule in 1998. *See* 63 Fed. Reg. 3214 (Jan. 21, 1998).

195 Reg. X, 24 C.F.R. § 3500.17(f).

196 Aitken v. Fleet Mortgage Corp., 1992 WL 33926, at *1 (N.D. Ill. Feb. 12, 1992). The incentive to "overescrow" described in *Aitken*, however, may be limited by state law requirements that interest be paid to consumers on escrow balances. *See* Appx. D, *infra* (summary of state laws requiring that interest be paid on escrow accounts).

Advocates should note that in the opinion of the Office of Thrift Supervision, state laws that require federal savings associations to pay interest on mortgage escrow accounts are preempted by the Home Owners' Loan Act (12 U.S.C. §§ 1461–1470). 12 C.F.R. § 560.2. *See also* 12 C.F.R. § 34.4 (similar preemption regulation applicable to national banks); Flagg v. Yonkers Sav. And Loan Ass'n, FA, 396 F.3d 178 (2d Cir. 2005) (state escrow interest statute preempted by HOLA regulations that were found not to be inconsistent with RESPA); First Fed. Sav. and Loan Ass'n of Boston v. Greenwald, 591 F.2d 417 (1st Cir. 1979); Wis. League of Fin. Insts., Ltd. v. Galecki, 707 F. Supp. 401 (W.D. Wis. 1989).

197 *See* Appendix E to 3500: Arithmetic Steps to Aggregate Analysis, *reprinted at* Appendix C.3, *infra*.

198 12 U.S.C. § 2609(c).

199 Reg. X, 24 C.F.R. § 3500.17(b).

200 Reg. X, 24 C.F.R. § 3500.17(b).

The "escrow account computation year" is the twelve-month period that the servicer establishes for the account, beginning with the borrower's initial payment date under the loan agreement, and continues each twelve-month period thereafter. Reg. X, 24 C.F.R. § 3500.17(b). The servicer may alter the computation year only if the servicer elects to issue a "short year" statement as provided for in 12 C.F.R. § 3500.17(i)(4), or upon transfer of servicing as provided for in 12 C.F.R. § 3500.17(e).

201 Reg. X, 24 C.F.R. § 3500.17(b).

Following the enactment of section 10 of RESPA, there was considerable controversy over the methodology used to calculate projected target balances, and litigation ensued. Lenders and servicers argued that RESPA and Regulation X permitted the use of a "single-item" accounting method in which a separate account was established for each of the individual items to be paid under an escrow account.[202] Consumers argued that this accounting method produced excess escrow charges and that RESPA required the use of an "aggregate" accounting method.[203] HUD eventually responded in 1994 by promulgating a rule requiring an aggregate accounting method in which escrow accounts are analyzed as a whole.[204]

8.3.2.2 General Limits on Escrow Deposits

Once an escrow account has been established, RESPA prohibits a servicer from requiring a borrower to pay into the escrow account a monthly amount greater than one-twelfth of the total of all disbursements payable during the computation year.[205] The servicer may also require a "cushion" on the account which may not exceed an amount equal to one-sixth of the total disbursements for the year (the equivalent of two months of escrow payments). RESPA does not require the use of a cushion, and servicers may use a smaller cushion than allowed by RESPA.[206] In addition, state laws requiring less than a two-month cushion are not preempted by RESPA.[207]

8.3.2.3 Aggregate Analysis

To conduct an escrow account analysis, the servicer must first estimate the amounts of the various disbursements. If the servicer knows what the charge for a particular escrow item will be in the next computation year, then that amount is to be used.[208] If the charge is unknown to the servicer, the servicer may base the estimate on the charge from the preceding year, or use the preceding year's charge as adjusted by the most recent year's change in the Consumer Price Index.[209]

Errors sometimes occur when servicers fail to take into account changes in disbursement items from year-to-year, most often when there have been property tax bill adjustments based on reassessments or tax rate increases. When these amount changes are significant, a borrower may face an escrow shortage or deficiency. While a servicer may profess to lack knowledge of the change, the servicer may have been provided the correct amount in tax bills or notices sent by the taxing authority or notified of the changes by a company it contracts with to provide tax billing and payment services.[210]

Another problem can occur when the servicer knows that there will be a substantial increase in an escrow disbursement, but the change will not take effect until after the current computation year. For example, a substantial increase in property taxes may be anticipated in the second year after purchase of a newly constructed home because the first year's taxes were based on an unimproved lot. Regulation X does not permit the servicer to require additional payments to cover such an anticipated increase because the servicer can only consider changes that will occur during the upcoming twelve-month computation period.[211]

Although HUD considered different proposed rule changes to avoid this borrower "payment shock," it ultimately concluded in the 1998 rulemaking proceeding that several of the proposed changes under consideration were likely to cause "overescrowing" and that the existing regulations sufficiently addressed the problem.[212] HUD noted at that time that servicers could make use of permissible alternatives to avoid payment shock, including conducting an escrow analysis mid-year, without waiting to the end of the computation year, through the use of a short-year statement.[213]

---

202 The lending industry found some support for their position in an informal HUD Opinion which the agency later withdrew. *See* Mark v. Keycorp Mortgage Inc., 1996 WL 465400 (N.D. Ill. Aug. 8, 1996).

203 The plain language of section 10 appears to mandate an aggregate accounting method as it provides that servicers may maintain a cushion "not to exceed one-sixth of the estimated *total* amount of such taxes, insurance premiums and other charges to be paid." 12 U.S.C. § 2609(2) (emphasis added).

204 *See* 59 Fed. Reg. 53,890 (Oct. 26, 1994).

The initial impact of the rule was somewhat blunted, however, as HUD elected to phase-in implementation over a three-year period. The rule was made to apply to all federally related mortgage loans settled on or after May 24, 1995 ("post-rule accounts"), but servicers were permitted to use the single-item method for existing mortgages ("pre-rule accounts") during a phase-in period that ended October 27, 1997.

205 12 U.S.C. § 2609(a); Reg. X, 24 C.F.R. § 3500.17(c).

The servicer may require the payment of an additional sum to cover a shortage on the account as described at § 8.3.4.3, *infra*.

206 Reg. X, 24 C.F.R. § 3500.17(d).

207 *See* § 8.4, *infra*.

The mortgage documents may provide for a lower cushion amount or contemplate that a lower amount imposed by state law shall be used. *See* Miller v. Chevy Chase Bank, 1998 U.S. Dist. LEXIS 3651 (N.D. Ill. Mar. 24, 1998) (mortgage provided that lender would limit cushion to lower amount than under RESPA if imposed by "another law"); Aitken v. Fleet Mortgage Corp., 1992 WL 33926 (N.D. Ill. Feb. 12, 1992) (mortgage provided for one-month cushion).

208 Reg. X, 24 C.F.R. § 3500.17(c)(7).

209 Reg. X, 24 C.F.R. § 3500.17(c)(7).

210 One of the largest of these companies is Transamerica Real Estate Tax Service, Inc. Transamerica and other similar companies also provide services relating to property and flood insurance.

211 Reg. X, 24 C.F.R. § 3500.17(c).

212 *See* 63 Fed. Reg. 3214 (Jan. 21, 1998).

Among other matters, HUD indicated that the comments it received suggested that there was not agreement among industry representatives that a "problem" actually existed.

213 *See* § 8.3.4.1, *infra*.

In addition to the estimated disbursement amounts, the servicer must next create a time-line for when the disbursements will be made during the computation year. Regulation X requires that the servicer use as the disbursement date a date on or before any applicable penalty deadline.[214] Thus, the disbursement date should be timed to avoid the imposition of any penalties for late payments.

The Regulation X provisions issued in 1994 prohibited the practice of "pre-accrual," which involved requiring borrowers to deposit escrow funds needed for disbursements and maintenance of a cushion "some period before the disbursement date."[215] At the same time, HUD adopted a special rule for the payment of property taxes. Servicers are required to make disbursements on an installment basis if the taxing authority offers a choice between annual and installment payments, and the authority does not provide a discount for lump sum annual payments or impose an additional charge or penalty for installment payments.[216] If the taxing authority does provide a discount for lump sum annual payments, or imposes additional charges for installment payments, the servicer at its discretion may make a lump sum annual disbursement.[217]

Once the estimated disbursement amounts and dates have been set for the escrow items, the servicer must use an aggregate analysis in completing the escrow account analysis. This involves the following arithmetic steps:

Step 1: The servicer first projects a trial balance for the account as a whole over the next computation year. The servicer assumes disbursement dates and amounts as per the rules discussed above. The servicer also assumes that the borrower will make monthly payments equal to one-twelfth of the estimated total annual escrow account disbursements.[218]

Step 2: The servicer then examines the monthly trial balances and adds to the first monthly balance an amount just sufficient to bring the lowest monthly trial balance to zero, and adjusts all other monthly balances accordingly.[219]

Step 3: The servicer then adds to the monthly trial balances the permissible cushion, which is either two months of the borrower's escrow payments or a lesser amount set by state law or the mortgage.[220]

If the aggregate analysis is done correctly, the lowest monthly target balance for the account shall be less than or equal to one-sixth of the estimated total annual escrow account disbursements (the two-month cushion), or a lesser amount set by state law or the mortgage documents. This is illustrated in the examples provided at Appendix E to section 3500 of Regulation X.[221]

8.3.2.4 Charges at Settlement or upon Creation of the Account

When a servicer creates an escrow account, the servicer may require the borrower to make an initial deposit into the account. The servicer may not charge the borrower more than an "amount sufficient to pay" the charges for the escrow items covering the period from the date the items were last paid until the initial payment date.[222] The "amount sufficient to pay" is to be computed so that the lowest month end target balance projected for the escrow account computation year is zero, as in Step 2 described in the previous section.[223] The servicer may also charge the borrower a cushion that shall not be greater than one-sixth of the estimated total annual disbursements from the account.[224]

An example provided by HUD as Appendix E to Regulation X, 24 C.F.R. § 3500, helps to illustrate how the escrow payment and initial deposit is calculated on a new account. In the example, it is assumed that the first payment on the mortgage is due on July 1 and that a disbursement of $500 for property taxes is due that month.[225] There is also another $700 property tax disbursement due in December and a $360 school tax due in September. The total of these

---

HUD also pointed out that some servicers were providing disclosures to borrowers about potential problems with anticipated payment increases and permitting borrowers to make voluntary overpayments to escrow accounts. HUD encouraged this approach as a "best practice" for servicers. *See* 63 Fed. Reg. 3214 (Jan. 21, 1998).

214 Reg. X, 24 C.F.R. § 3500.17(c), (k).
Regulation X defines a "penalty" as a "late charge imposed for paying after the disbursement is due." Reg. X, 24 C.F.R. § 3500.17(b). The definition specifies that a penalty does not include "any additional charge or fee imposed by the payee associated with choosing installment payments as opposed to annual payments or for choosing one installment plan over another." Reg. X, 24 C.F.R. § 3500.17(b).

215 Reg. X, 24 C.F.R. § 3500.17(b), (c)(6).

216 Reg. X, 24 C.F.R. § 3500.17(k)(3). The servicer and borrower may mutually agree to a disbursement arrangement, either installment or lump sum, that differs from that required by Regulation X, but the agreement must be voluntary and neither loan approval nor any of the loan terms may be conditioned on the acceptance by the borrower of the different disbursement arrangement. Reg. X, 24 C.F.R. § 3500.17(k)(4).

217 Reg. X, 24 C.F.R. § 3500.17(k)(3).
This subsection states that a servicer may make disbursements on an annual basis in this situation, "but is not required by RESPA to." Reg. X, 24 C.F.R. § 3500.17(k)(3). HUD added this language to make clear that a servicer could be required by state law to make annual disbursements when there is a discount for annual payments or an additional charge for installment payments. *See* 63 Fed. Reg. 3214 (Jan. 21, 1998).

218 Reg. X, 24 C.F.R. § 3500.17(d)(i)(A).

219 Reg. X, 24 C.F.R. § 3500.17(d)(i)(B).

220 Reg. X, 24 C.F.R. § 3500.17(d)(i)(C).
The cushion amount used in this step is net of any increases or decreases resulting from prior year shortages or surpluses.

221 *See* Appx. C.3, *infra*.
Once again, advocates are encouraged to review these examples in order to comprehend the trial running balance methodology. One of the examples is discussed at § 8.3.2.4, *infra*.

222 Reg. X, 24 C.F.R. § 3500.17(c)(1)(i).

223 *Id.*

224 *Id.*

225 The example described here is reprinted at Appendix C.3, *infra*.

annual escrow disbursements is $1560, so the borrower would need to make escrow payments of $130 per month ($1560 divided by 12 equals $130). If the borrower begins making the $130 escrow payment with the first mortgage payment due in July, and assuming the above disbursement dates, the initial trial balance (Step 1) for the account shows that the account will have a negative $780 balance in December. Thus, in order to bring the lowest monthly trial balance amount to zero (Step 2), the lender or servicer can demand that the borrower make an initial deposit of $780 at settlement or upon creation of the account. If the lender or servicer also requires a two-month cushion (Step 3), then it can demand that the borrower pay an additional $260 as a deposit (1/6 of $1560 equals $260), bringing the total initial deposit to $1040.

8.3.3 Escrow Account Statements

8.3.3.1 Initial Account Statement

The initial escrow account statement provides the borrower with notice of the escrow payment amount and an itemization of the estimated taxes, insurance premiums, and other charges anticipated to be paid from the escrow account during the first twelve months of the loan. The statement shall be given to the borrower at closing if the account is established when the loan is made, or within forty-five days of the establishment of the account.[226] It may be incorporated into the HUD-1 or HUD-1A settlement statement, attached as an additional page to the HUD-1 or HUD-1A, or provided as a separate document.[227]

The initial escrow account statement must contain the following information:[228]

- The amount of the borrower's monthly mortgage payment and the portion of the monthly payment going into the escrow account;
- An itemization of the estimated taxes, insurance premiums, and other charges the servicer reasonably anticipates to be paid from the escrow account during the escrow account computation year;[229]
- The anticipated disbursement dates of those charges;[230]
- The amount that the servicer selects as a cushion; and
- A trial running balance for the account.

8.3.3.2 Annual Account Statement

The annual escrow account statement provides the borrower with a summary of all of the account deposits and disbursements made during the servicer's twelve-month computation year. It also notifies the borrower of any surpluses, shortages, and deficiencies that exist and the action the servicer intends to take in response. The statement must be provided not less than once per year, within thirty days of the completion of the escrow account computation year.[231]

The annual escrow account statement must contain the following information:[232]

- The amount of the borrower's current monthly mortgage payment and the portion of the monthly payment going into the escrow account;[233]
- The amount of the past year's monthly mortgage payment and the portion of the monthly payment that went into the escrow account;
- The total amount paid into the escrow account during the past computation year;
- The total amount paid out of the escrow account during the same period for taxes, insurance premiums, and other charges (as separately identified);
- The balance in the escrow account at the end of the period;
- An explanation of how any surplus is being handled by the servicer;

226 12 U.S.C. § 2609(c)(1)(B).

Regulation X differs from the statutory language by providing that the initial escrow statement may be submitted to the borrower within forty-five days of "settlement for escrow accounts that are established as a condition of the loan." Reg. X, 24 C.F.R. § 3500.17(g)(1). If a lender is authorized to establish an escrow account subsequent to closing, see § 8.3.1, *supra*, and does in fact create an account, the lender is required to provide the borrower with an initial escrow account statement. There is no exemption from the initial account statement requirement if the account is overdue or if the borrower has filed bankruptcy.

227 Reg. X, 24 C.F.R. § 3500.17(h)(2).

228 Reg. X, 24 C.F.R. § 3500.17(g)(1)(i). Sample formats for an initial escrow account statement and a completed example are provided as part of the HUD Public Guidance Documents and are entitled "Initial Escrow Account Disclosure Statement-Format" (Appendix G-1) and "Initial Escrow Account Disclosure Statement-Example" (Appendix G-2). They were published at different times in the Federal Register (60 Fed. Reg. 24,736 (May 9, 1995) and 60 Fed. Reg. 8812 (Feb. 15, 1995)), and are available on HUD's website at www.hud.gov.

229 The statement does not need to identify each payee by name if it provides sufficient information to determine the use of the funds. Notations such as "county taxes" or "hazard insurance" are permitted. Reg. X, 24 C.F.R. § 3500.17(h)(3).

230 If the escrow item is to be paid in installments, such as property taxes paid on a quarterly basis, the statement shall indicate each payment amount and disbursement date. Reg. X, 24 C.F.R. § 3500.17(h)(3).

231 12 U.S.C. § 2609(c)(2); Reg. X, 24 C.F.R. § 3500.17(i).

232 Reg. X, 24 C.F.R. § 3500.17(i)(1).

Sample formats for an annual escrow account statement and a completed example are provided as part of the HUD Public Guidance Documents and are entitled "Annual Escrow Account Disclosure Statement-Format" (Appendix I-1) and "Annual Escrow Account Disclosure Statement-Example" (Appendix I-3). They were published at different times in the Federal Register (60 Fed. Reg. 24,737 (May 9, 1995) and 60 Fed. Reg. 8824 (Feb. 15, 1995)), and are available on HUD's website at www.hud.gov.

233 The first four items on this list are to be "clearly itemized." Reg. X, 24 C.F.R. § 3500.17(i)(1).

- An explanation of how any shortage or deficiency is to be paid by the borrower; and
- If applicable, the reason(s) why the estimated low monthly balance was not reached, as indicated by noting differences between the most recent account history and last year's projection.

Despite the mandatory language found in section 10 of RESPA and the lack of any statutory exemption, HUD has provided in Regulation X that a servicer need not provide the borrower with an annual escrow statement if the borrower is more than thirty days overdue at the time the servicer conducts the escrow analysis.[234] This exemption also applies when the mortgage account is in foreclosure or when the borrower is in a bankruptcy proceeding.[235] If the servicer does not provide an annual account statement because of this exemption and the account is subsequently "reinstated or otherwise becomes current," the servicer is then required to provide the statement within ninety days of the date the account was brought current.[236]

This regulation is inconsistent with both the purpose behind section 10 of RESPA and the policy of promoting homeownership through loss mitigation efforts aimed at avoiding foreclosure. For borrowers who are experiencing temporary financial difficulties and barely more than a month behind in payments, the exemption provides little incentive for them to become current and instead deprives them of critical information about their account, such as the new monthly payment amount, which may ultimately cause them to fall further behind.[237]

The exemption is even less rational in the bankruptcy setting, in which HUD failed to distinguish between borrowers who are current with their mortgage payments at the time of the bankruptcy filing and intend to remain current, with those who are in default.[238] Nor does the rule treat differently borrowers who are curing a mortgage default in a chapter 13 bankruptcy. As a borrower could conceivably go three to five years under a chapter 13 plan without receiving annual escrow account statements, the exemption serves only to undermine the potential for successful plan completion and jeopardizes the debtor's fresh start even if the plan is completed.[239] Borrowers who are curing a default in a chapter 13 may argue, however, that the exemption should not apply after their chapter 13 plan is confirmed, as the effect of plan confirmation is that the account is deemed reinstated.[240] The borrower may also seek to avoid the exemption by including a provision in the chapter 13 plan requiring the servicer to comply with the RESPA escrow account statement requirements during the life of the plan.[241]

Finally, the exemption in section 3500.17(i)(2) of Regulation X applies only to the submission of the annual account statement to the borrower and does not excuse the servicer from its obligation to conduct an escrow account analysis at the end of the twelve-month computation year.[242] Arguably, a borrower who is more than thirty days overdue or in foreclosure or bankruptcy may attempt to obtain the information provided in the annual escrow statement by sending a qualified written request to the servicer.[243]

8.3.3.3 Delivery of Escrow Account Statements

A lender or servicer may satisfy the delivery requirement for escrow account statements by sending them to the borrower by first-class mail, postage prepaid, at the borrow-

234 Reg. X, 24 C.F.R. § 3500.17(i)(2).

It is interesting to note that during the rulemaking proceeding, HUD received twenty-five comments from the servicing industry requesting an exclusion for loans in foreclosure or that were sixty days or more delinquent. Although the industry actually sought the more reasonable sixty-day period, HUD opted for the shorter period in the final rule. *See* 59 Fed. Reg. 53,902 (Oct. 26, 1994).

235 Reg. X, 24 C.F.R. § 3500.17(i)(2).

236 Reg. X, 24 C.F.R. § 3500.17(i)(2).

The statement shall contain a history of the account since the last statement, which is likely to be longer than one year.

237 In negotiating forbearance, reinstatement, or deferral agreements to avoid foreclosure, borrowers and their advocates may wish to make clear in the agreement that the account is deemed "reinstated or otherwise current" for purposes of the RESPA servicing requirements and specifically provide that the servicer shall provide annual escrow account statements.

238 As evidence that the bankruptcy exemption was not well-reasoned, it is worth noting that § 3500.17(i)(2) did not include any discussion of bankruptcy when first promulgated under the notice and comment rulemaking procedure. Prior to the regulation's effective date, however, HUD added the bankruptcy exemption as a "technical correction" to the rule language without soliciting comment. *See* 60 Fed. Reg. 8812 (Feb. 15, 1995).

239 *E.g., In re* Dominique, 368 B.R. 913 (Bankr. S.D. Fla. 2007) (just before completion of the chapter 13 plan, servicer provided debtors with an escrow account review indicating a $6397 escrow deficiency).

240 *See* 11 U.S.C. § 1322(b)(5); § 9.4.4.5, *infra*. *See also In re* Jones, 366 B.R. 584 (Bankr. E.D. La. 2007), *aff'd on other grounds*, 391 B.R. 577 (E.D. La. 2008) (plan confirmation "recalibrates" the amounts due as of the petition date); *In re* Wines, 239 B.R. 703 (Bankr. D.N.J. 1999) (post-petition mortgage debt treated like a current mortgage and consists of those payments which come due after the bankruptcy petition is filed).

241 If the provision is incorporated into the chapter 13 confirmation order, the servicer shall be bound by the provision on res judicata grounds. *E.g., In re* Collins, 2007 WL 2116416, at *18 (E.D. Tenn. July 19, 2007) (approving plan provision requiring servicer to provide sixty-days' notice of any escrow payment change). *See* National Consumer Law Center, Consumer Bankruptcy Law and Practice § 12.11 (9th ed. 2009).

242 *In re* Laskowski, 384 B.R. 518 (Bankr. N.D. Ind. 2008) (bankruptcy exemption in Regulation X applies only to sending of annual statement and does not relieve servicer of obligation to conduct annual escrow analysis).

243 *See* § 8.2.2, *supra*.

There is no default, foreclosure, or bankruptcy exemption for servicer compliance with a qualified written request. *See* § 8.2.5.2, *supra*.

er's last known address.[244] One court has held that a determination of "last known address" for purposes of compliance with Regulation X includes a servicer's actual and constructive knowledge, and therefore a servicer must exercise reasonable care and diligence in determining the correct address for the borrower.[245] At a minimum, this standard should require a servicer to search its own records and the records of prior servicers for any written notices of address change, and to review records of phone conversations or other communications with the borrower for other evidence of an address change.[246]

8.3.4 Surpluses, Shortages, and Deficiencies

8.3.4.1 Overview

As part of the escrow account analysis to be conducted at the end of the twelve-month computation year, the servicer is required to determine if there is a surplus, shortage, or deficiency.[247] While this determination is generally made only at year-end, a servicer may have an incentive to conduct an escrow account analysis mid-year if it has advanced funds to the borrower.

As long as the borrower's mortgage payment is not more than thirty days late, the servicer must pay escrow items such as taxes and insurance in a timely manner even if there are not sufficient funds in the escrow account to cover the items.[248] A servicer cannot obtain force placed insurance from another carrier in this situation and must instead pay the insurance premium on the borrower's policy when due. If there are insufficient funds in the account not caused by a borrower's payment default, and the servicer advances funds to pay an escrow disbursement, the servicer must perform an escrow account analysis before seeking repayment of the deficiency.[249] In this situation, the servicer need not wait until the end of the twelve-month computation year to perform an escrow analysis.[250]

The existence of a surplus, shortage, or deficiency triggers certain obligations for the servicer which are discussed in the next sections.

8.3.4.2 Requirements for Surpluses

If the escrow analysis indicates that a surplus exists,[251] the servicer is required to refund to the borrower any surplus equal to or greater than fifty dollars.[252] By requiring a "refund," the regulation does not permit a servicer to simply credit the surplus directly to principal on the loan, though the borrower may agree to use the refund in this manner.[253] If the surplus is less than fifty dollars, the servicer may provide a refund to the borrower or credit the amount against the next year's escrow payments.[254] Any required refunds must be made within thirty days after the escrow account analysis.[255]

This rule governing surpluses applies only if the borrower is current with payments at the time the escrow analysis is conducted. If the borrower's payment is more than thirty days overdue, the servicer may keep the surplus in the escrow account pursuant to the terms of the mortgage loan documents.[256] As the Regulation X surplus rule is not applicable to an account in default, the lender or servicer may apply the surplus as payment towards the amount in default if that is authorized by the loan documents or state law.

8.3.4.3 Requirements for Shortages

If the escrow analysis indicates that the account has a shortage of less than one month's escrow payment,[257] the servicer has three options. It can: (1) do nothing and simply allow the shortage to exist; (2) require the borrower to repay the shortage within thirty days; or (3) require the borrower to repay the shortage in equal monthly payments over at least a twelve-month period.[258]

If the escrow analysis indicates that the account has a shortage that is equal to or greater than one month's escrow payment, the servicer has two options. It can: (1) do nothing

---

244 Reg. X, 24 C.F.R. § 3500.17(b).
Hand delivery of the statements is also acceptable. Reg. X, 24 C.F.R. § 3500.17(b).

245 Wanger v. EMC Mortgage Corp., 103 Cal. App. 4th 1125, 127 Cal. Rptr. 2d 685 (2002).
Although the issue in *Wanger* involved transfer of servicing notice requirements, the court applied and construed the "last known address" provision of § 3500.17(b) of Regulation X.

246 *See* § 13.3.4.2, *infra* (cases dealing with the last known address notice requirement in relation to tax sale procedures).

247 Reg. X, 24 C.F.R. § 3500.17(f).

248 Reg. X, 24 C.F.R. § 3500.17(k)(2).

249 Reg. X, 24 C.F.R. § 3500.17(f)(2)(ii).

250 Reg. X, 24 C.F.R. § 3500.17(f)(1)(ii).
If the analysis is done before the end of the twelve-month computation year, the servicer is required to send the borrower a "short year statement" which will change one escrow account computation year to another, and establish the beginning date of the new computation year. Reg. X, 24 C.F.R. § 3500.17(i)(4). The servicer must send the short year statement to the borrower within sixty days from the end of the short year. Reg. X, 24 C.F.R. § 3500.17(i)(4)(i).

251 A surplus is defined as an "amount by which the current escrow account balance exceeds the target balance for the account." Reg. X, 24 C.F.R. § 3500.17(b).

252 Reg. X, 24 C.F.R. § 3500.17(f)(2)(i).

253 *See* 60 Fed. Reg. 8812 (Feb. 15, 1995).

254 Reg. X, 24 C.F.R. § 3500.17(f)(2)(i).

255 Reg. X, 24 C.F.R. § 3500.17(f)(2)(i).

256 Reg. X, 24 C.F.R. § 3500.17(f)(2)(ii).

257 A "shortage" is defined as an "amount by which a current escrow account balance falls short of the target balance at the time of the escrow analysis." Reg. X, 24 C.F.R. § 3500.17(b).

258 Reg. X, 24 C.F.R. § 3500.17(f)(3)(i).

and simply allow the shortage to exist; or (2) require the borrower to repay the shortage in equal monthly payments over at least a twelve-month period.[259] The servicer cannot demand full payment in a lump sum of a shortage equal to or greater than one month's escrow payment.

In contrast with the surplus and deficiency provisions, Regulation X does not contain any language limiting the shortage requirements in the event the borrower's payment is more than thirty days overdue at the time of the escrow analysis.[260] A servicer should thus be required to comply with the shortage requirements even if the borrower is not current with payments on the account.[261]

8.3.4.4 Requirements for Deficiencies

In order to determine whether the deficiency requirements apply, it is necessary to distinguish between a shortage and a deficiency. Regulation X defines a deficiency as the "amount of a negative balance in an escrow account."[262] Unlike a shortage when there still remains a positive balance in the escrow account at the time of the escrow analysis (though the balance is less than originally projected), a deficiency exists when the servicer has advanced funds to cover disbursements, which in turn produces a negative balance in the account. For example, if the escrow analysis projected a target balance of $240 at the end of the twelve-month computation year, and the account actually has a balance of $140 at that time, there exists a $100 shortage. On the other hand, if this same account has a negative balance of $550 at the end of the twelve-month computation year, because the servicer advanced funds to cover a disbursement, there exists a shortage of $240 and a deficiency of $550.

If the escrow analysis indicates that the account has a deficiency of less than one month's escrow payment, the servicer has three options. It can: (1) do nothing and simply allow the deficiency to exist; (2) require the borrower to repay the deficiency within thirty days; or (3) require the borrower to repay the deficiency in two or more equal monthly payments.[263]

If the escrow analysis indicates that the account has a deficiency that is equal to or greater than one month's escrow payment, the servicer has two options. It can: (1) do nothing and simply allow the deficiency to exist; or (2) require the borrower to repay the deficiency in two or more equal monthly payments.[264] In the case of a large deficiency, some borrowers may find little comfort in the rule's two-month repayment requirement. Borrowers experiencing financial hardships and advocates on their behalf may attempt to negotiate a longer repayment period than provided under the rule.

Like the rule governing surpluses, the rule governing deficiencies applies only if the borrower is current with payments at the time the escrow analysis is conducted. If the borrower's payment is more than thirty days overdue, the servicer may collect the deficiency pursuant to the terms of the mortgage loan documents.[265]

8.3.4.5 Notice of Shortage or Deficiency

A servicer is required to notify the borrower at least once during the twelve-month computation year if there is a shortage or deficiency.[266] The notice may be included as part of the annual escrow statement or it may be sent as a separate document.[267]

The notice requirement in this section of Regulation X does not contain an exemption from compliance when the debtor is in default, foreclosure, or bankruptcy.[268] This has led several courts to conclude that although a servicer may not be required by RESPA to provide annual escrow account statements to chapter 13 debtors in bankruptcy, it is required to provide debtors with escrow shortage and deficiency notices during the pendency of their chapter 13 plan.[269]

8.3.5 No Fee for Account Statements

RESPA prohibits the imposition or charging of any fees to borrowers for the preparation or submission of initial and annual escrow account statements, or any statement re-

259 Reg. X, 24 C.F.R. § 3500.17(f)(3)(ii).

260 *See* Reg. X, 24 C.F.R. § 3500.17(f)(2)(ii), (4)(iii). *See also* §§ 8.3.4.2, 8.3.4.4, *supra* (discussing these provisions).

261 This compliance may be of little consequence, however, because a servicer is not required to provide an annual account statement if the borrower is more than thirty days overdue. *See* Reg. X, 24 C.F.R. § 3500.17(i)(2); § 8.3.4, *supra* (discussing this provision).

262 Reg. X, 24 C.F.R. § 3500.17(b).

263 Reg. X, 24 C.F.R. § 3500.17(f)(4)(i).

264 Reg. X, 24 C.F.R. § 3500.17(f)(4)(ii).

265 Reg. X, 24 C.F.R. § 3500.17(f)(4)(iii).

266 Reg. X, 24 C.F.R. § 3500.17(f)(5). *See In re* Payne, 387 B.R. 614, 637 (Bankr. D. Kan. 2008) (servicer violated RESPA by failing to provide chapter 13 debtors with notice that mortgage payment was insufficient to cover annual escrow shortages).

267 Reg. X, 24 C.F.R. § 3500.17(f)(5).

268 The exemption contained in § 3500.17(i)(2) explicitly states that it only applies to the provisions of § 3500.17(i)(1) which deal with the furnishing of annual escrow statements.

269 Chase Manhattan Mortgage Corp. v. Padgett, 268 B.R. 309 (S.D. Fla. 2001); *In re* Payne, 387 B.R. 614, 637 (Bankr. D. Kan. 2008); *In re* Johnson, 384 B.R. 763 (Bankr. E.D. Mich. 2008); *In re* Laskowski, 384 B.R. 518 (Bankr. N.D. Ind. 2008); Craig-Likely v. Wells Fargo Home Mortgage (*In re* Craig-Likely), 2007 U.S. Dist. LEXIS 29042 (E.D. Mich. Mar. 2, 2007) (servicer's failure to send escrow account notices concerning payment changes during plan resulted in waiver of right to seek payment of post-petition deficiency); *In re* Dominique, 368 B.R. 913 (Bankr. S.D. Fla. 2007).

The *Padgett* and *Dominique* courts additionally found that the notices were required to be sent by Florida state law. *See* Fla. Stat. § 501.137(2).

quired to be sent to borrowers under section 2609(c).[270] As the statutory authority for the Regulation X requirement to send notices of shortages and deficiencies is derived from section 2609(c), a servicer should not charge a fee for such notices, even if they are sent separately from the annual escrow account statement.

8.3.6 No Private Enforcement

Section 10 of RESPA does not provide an express private right of action. While a few courts have found that an implied cause of action exists for enforcement of the RESPA sections that lack an express right of action,[271] the majority of courts have refused to do so.[272] Borrowers who have been harmed by an overcharge on an escrow account or the failure to receive an account statement may seek damages under a breach of contract theory or as a violation of an unfair and deceptive acts and practices statute.[273]

Most escrow violations may be pursued as a breach of contract because the RESPA escrow requirements have been incorporated into the vast majority of mortgages and deeds of trust. The Fannie Mae/Freddie Mac Single-Family Uniform Instrument for a mortgage or deed of trust requires the servicer to maintain the escrow account in compliance with RESPA.[274] As a result, a breach of contract claim should be available to enforce RESPA provisions that do not have a private right of action.

HUD has been given authority under RESPA to assess penalties against lenders and servicers who fail to comply with the escrow account statement requirements.[275]

8.4 RESPA Preemption

The general RESPA provision relating to preemption expressly provides that state laws are preempted only to the extent of their inconsistency with RESPA.[276] If the state law provides greater protections to borrowers than RESPA, and it is not preempted under some other federal law that is not inconsistent with RESPA,[277] then the law is not pre-

---

270 12 U.S.C. § 2610.
This statute also prohibits the charging of fees for the preparation of the HUD-1 settlement statement and the TIL disclosure statement.

271 *See* Vega v. First Fed. Sav. & Loan Ass'n, 622 F.2d 918 (6th Cir. 1980) (holding that a private right of action exists briefly mentioned in footnote 8 of the opinion); Heller v. First Town Mortgage Corp., 1998 U.S. Dist. LEXIS 14427 (S.D.N.Y. Sept. 14, 1998) (finding a private right of action).

272 *E.g.*, Hardy v. Regions Mortgage, Inc., 449 F.3d 1357 (11th Cir. 2006); Louisiana v. Litton Mortgage, Co., 50 F.3d 1298 (5th Cir. 1995); Allison v. Liberty Sav., 695 F.2d 1086 (7th Cir. 1982); Birkholm v. Washington Mut. Bank, F.A., 447 F. Supp. 2d 1158 (W.D. Wash. 2006); Clayton v. Raleigh Fed. Sav. Bank, 194 B.R. 793 (M.D.N.C. 1996), *aff'd*, 107 F.3d 865 (4th Cir. 1997) (table); Hermann v. Meridian Mortgage Corp., 901 F. Supp. 915 (E.D. Pa. 1995).

273 *See* National Consumer Law Center, Unfair and Deceptive Acts and Practices § 3.2.7 (7th ed. 2008 and Supp.); § 8.5, *infra*. *See also* Heller v. First Town Mortgage Corp., 1998 U.S. Dist. LEXIS 14427 (S.D.N.Y. Sept. 14, 1998); Markowitz v. Ryland Mortgage Co., 1995 U.S. Dist. LEXIS 11323 (N.D. Ill. Aug. 9, 1995) (lender's motion for summary judgment on consumer fraud claim denied when borrowers alleged it retained escrow greater than permitted by the contract); Sanders v. Lincoln Serv. Corp., 1993 U.S. Dist. LEXIS 4454 (N.D. Ill. Apr. 5, 1993) (class plaintiffs stated a claim for breach of contract and state UDAP violation when creditor alleged to maintain unauthorized surpluses in customers' escrow accounts). *But see* McMaster v. CIT Group/Consumer Fin. Inc., 2006 WL 1314379 (E.D. Pa. May 11, 2006) (RESPA violation under section without private right of action was not per se violate state UDAP statute).

274 The Fannie Mae/Freddie Mac Single-Family Uniform Instrument typically includes in section 3, entitled "Funds for Escrow Items," the following contractual language:

> Lender may, at any time, collect and hold Funds in an amount (a) sufficient to permit Lender to apply the Funds at the time specified under RESPA, and (b) not to exceed the maximum amount a lender can require under RESPA. Lender shall estimate the amount of Funds due on the basis of current data and reasonable estimates of expenditures of future Escrow Items or otherwise in accordance with Applicable Law.... Lender shall apply the Funds to pay the Escrow Items no later than the time specified under RESPA.... If there is a surplus of Funds held in escrow, as defined under RESPA, Lender shall account to Borrower for the excess funds in accordance with RESPA. If there is a shortage of Funds held in escrow, as defined under RESPA, Lender shall notify Borrower as required by RESPA, and Borrower shall pay to Lender the amount necessary to make up the shortage in accordance with RESPA, but in no more than twelve monthly payments. If there is a deficiency of Funds held in escrow, as defined under RESPA, Lender shall notify Borrower as required by RESPA, and Borrower shall pay to Lender the amount necessary to make up the deficiency in accordance with RESPA, but in no more than twelve monthly payments.

275 Section 2609(d) provides that the Department of Housing and Urban Development (HUD) may assess a penalty of $50 for each failure of a lender or servicer to provide an escrow account statement, though the total amount imposed in any twelve-month period may not exceed $100,000. The penalty amount is $100 for any "intentional disregard of the requirement to submit the statement," without any cap on the total penalty amount allowed. 12 U.S.C. § 2609(d).

276 12 U.S.C. § 2616; Reg. X, 24 C.F.R. § 3500.13(a). *See In re* Dominique, 368 B.R. 913 (Bankr. S.D. Fla. 2007).

277 *E.g.*, Flagg v. Yonkers Sav. & Loan Ass'n, FA, 396 F.3d 178 (2d Cir. 2005) (state law requiring interest on escrow accounts preempted by Home Owners' Loan Act (HOLA) regulations that were found not to be inconsistent with RESPA); McKell v. Washington Mut., Inc., 142 Cal. App. 4th 1457 (2006) (HOLA did not preempt action under California's Unfair Competition Law). *See generally* National Consumer Law Center, The Cost of Credit: Regulation, Preemption, and Industry Abuses Ch. 3 (4th ed. 2009 and Supp.) (detailed discussion of federal preemption of state laws applicable to mortgage lenders and servicers).

empted.[278] For example, a state law requiring a servicer to maintain less than a two-month cushion on an escrow account would not be preempted.[279] Similarly, one court has held that a state law requiring servicers to notify borrowers of escrow deficiencies did not conflict with RESPA and was therefore not preempted.[280]

Similarly, state laws that provide a private enforcement mechanism for violations of RESPA or similar state law servicer requirements are not preempted. In one recent case involving the overcharging of settlement costs and the inaccurate disclosure of these charges on the HUD-1 settlement statement, the servicer argued that RESPA preempted claims based on the state deceptive practices act and state tort law because RESPA provides no private right of action for violations of the kind alleged in the complaint.[281] The court disagreed, specifically upholding the right of consumers to sue under state statutory or common law theories for violations of RESPA.

In addition to the general preemption provision covering RESPA,[282] the Servicer Act contains a specific provision relating to the preemption of conflicting state laws.[283] It states that a servicer who "complies with the requirements of this section regarding timing, content, and procedures for notification of the borrower" shall be considered to have complied with any state laws or regulations "requiring notice to a borrower at the time of application for a loan or transfer of the servicing of a loan." While this provision arguably covers all of the Servicer Act requirements found in section 6 of RESPA, the precise wording of the statute suggests that it only preempts state laws that conflict with the transfer of servicing notification requirements found in sections 2605(a) and (b). The corresponding regulation provides little clarification, though it does seem to support the more limited view of the provision's scope.[284] A separate Regulation X provision, however, makes clear that section 2605(h) only preempts the transfer of servicing requirements, and that the general RESPA preemption statute that preempts only conflicting state laws applies to the other Servicer Act requirements.[285]

8.5 Using Other Consumer Protection Laws to Combat Servicing Abuses

Borrowers who have been harmed by abusive servicing practices may look to other statutes than RESPA for redress, particularly when the practice violates a provision of RESPA that does not include an express right of action. Because abusive servicer practices are far reaching in scope, borrowers may consider a wide range of legal theories and claims under other federal consumer protection statutes and state law. These claims are discussed in Chapter 6 of this treatise and in other NCLC publications.

8.6 RESPA Chart

The chart below lists citations to each obligation imposed by RESPA on lenders and servicers throughout a mortgage transaction, grouped in presettlement, settlement, and post-settlement stages. The chart then indicates whether the statute specifies a remedy, provides a description of the remedy, and states the applicable statute of limitations.

278 Johnson v. Matrix Fin. Servs. Corp., 354 Ill. App. 3d 684, 696, 820 N.E.2d 1094, 1105 (Ill. App. Ct. 2004) ("section 2616 can be characterized as a consumer-friendly 'anti-preemption' provision"; it is possible for a defendant to comply with RESPA and still be liable under state law).

The Secretary of HUD is authorized to determine upon request of "any person" whether and to what extent inconsistencies exist between RESPA and state law. 12 U.S.C. § 2616; Reg. X, 24 C.F.R. § 3500.13(b), (c).

279 Reg. X, 24 C.F.R. § 3500.17(d)(1)(ii). *See also* § 8.3.2.1, *supra*.

280 Chase Manhattan Mortgage Corp. v. Padgett, 268 B.R. 309 (S.D. Fla. 2001). *See* Appx. D, *infra* (summary of state laws requiring similar escrow account deficiency notifications).

281 Wash. Mut. Bank v. Super. Ct., 75 Cal. App. 4th 773 (1999), *further proceedings at* 15 P.3d 1071 (Cal. 2001) (nationwide class certification in a mortgage loan case reversed and remanded due to trial court's failure to adjudicate effect of choice of law provision in the mortgages), *further proceedings at* 115 Cal. Rptr. 2d 765 (Cal. Ct. App. 2002) (Home Owners' Loan Act (HOLA) preempts certain claims based on state law).

282 12 U.S.C. § 2616.

283 12 U.S.C. § 2605(h); Reg. X, 24 C.F.R. § 3500.21(h).

284 Borrowing from the words of the statute, Regulation X states: "Any State law requiring notice to the borrower at the time of application or at the time of transfer of servicing of the loan is preempted, and there shall be no additional borrower disclosure requirements." Reg. X, 24 C.F.R. § 3500.21(h). Regulation X also provides that certain provisions of state law, such as those requiring additional notices to insurance companies or taxing authorities, are not preempted, and may be added to notices sent under the Act.

285 Section 3500.13(d) of Regulation X, interpreting 12 U.S.C. § 2616, states that a "specific preemption of conflicting State laws regarding notices and disclosures of mortgage servicing transfers is set forth n 3550.21(h)."

REAL ESTATE SETTLEMENT PROCEDURES ACT (RESPA)

CLAIM	CITATIONS	RIGHT OF ACTION	REMEDY[286]	STATUTE OF LIMITATIONS	DEFAULT OR BANKRUPTCY EXEMPTION
Presettlement					
Duty to Provide Good Faith Estimate, Information Booklet	Section 5 12 U.S.C. § 2604 Reg. X § 3500.7; Reg. X § 3500.6				
Duty to Provide Servicing Statement	Section 6 12 U.S.C. § 2605(a) Reg. X § 3500.21(b)	Yes § 2605(f) § 2614	actual damages, costs and attorney fees; plus $1000 per violation if pattern and practice of non-compliance	3 years § 2614	
Duty to Provide "Controlled Business Arrangement" Notice	Section 8 12 U.S.C. § 2607 Reg. X § 3500.15	Yes § 2607(d) § 2614	3 times amount paid for settlement service, attorney fees, and costs	1 year § 2614	
Settlement					
Duty to Provide HUD-1 Settlement Statement	Section 4 12 U.S.C. § 2603 Reg. X § 3500.8				
Duty to Provide Initial Escrow Account Statement	Section 10 12 U.S.C. § 2609(c) (1) Reg. X § 3500.17(g)				
Prohibition Against Kickbacks, Fee Splitting and Unearned Fees	Section 8 12 U.S.C. § 2607 Reg. X § 3500.14(b)	Yes § 2607(d) § 2614	3 times amount paid for settlement service, attorney fees, and costs	1 year § 2614	
Prohibition Against Requiring Purchase of Title Insur. from Particular Title Co.	Section 9 12 U.S.C. § 2608 Reg. X § 3500.16	Yes § 2608(b) § 2614	3 times all charges for title insurance	1 year § 2614	
Prohibition Against Charging Fee for Preparing Escrow and HUD-1 Statements, and TIL Disclosures	Section 12 12 U.S.C. § 2610 Reg. X § 3500.12				
Post-Settlement					
Duty to Make Timely Payments Out of Escrow	Section 6 12 U.S.C. § 2605(g) Reg. X § 3500.21(g) and § 3500.17(k)	Yes § 2605(f) § 2614	actual damages, costs and attorney fees; plus $1000 per violation if pattern and practice of non-compliance	3 years § 2614	If borrower more than 30 days overdue; Reg. X, § 3500.17(k) (1), (2)
Duty to Provide Annual Escrow Statements	Section 10 12 U.S.C. § 2609(c) (2) Reg. X § 3500.17(i)				If borrower more than 30 days overdue, or in foreclosure or bankruptcy; Reg. X, § 3500.17(i)(2)
Duty to Perform Escrow Analysis and Calculate Proper Escrow Payment	Section 10 12 U.S.C. § 2609(a) Reg. X § 3500.17(c)				No
Requirements for Escrow Surpluses	Reg. X § 3500.17(f)				If borrower more than 30 days overdue; Reg. X, § 3500.17(f)(2)(ii)

CLAIM	CITATIONS	RIGHT OF ACTION	REMEDY[286]	STATUTE OF LIMITATIONS	DEFAULT OR BANKRUPTCY EXEMPTION
Requirements for Escrow Shortages	Reg. X § 3500.17(f)				No
Requirements for Escrow Deficiencies	Reg. X § 3500.17(f)				If borrower more than 30 days overdue; Reg. X, § 3500.17(f)(4)(iii)
Duty to Provide Notice of Escrow Shortage or Deficiency	Section 10 12 U.S.C. § 2609(b) Reg. X, 24 C.F.R. § 3500.17(f)(5)				No
Duty to Respond to Qualified Written Request	Section 6 12 U.S.C. § 2605(e) Reg. X § 3500.21(e)	Yes § 2605(f) § 2614	actual damages, costs and attorney fees; plus $1000 per violation if pattern and practice of non-compliance	3 years § 2614	No
Duty to Provide Transfer of Servicing Statement and 60-day Payment Safe Harbor	Section 6 12 U.S.C. § 2605(b)-(d) Reg. X § 3500.21(d)	Yes § 2605(f) § 2614	actual damages, costs and attorney fees; plus $1000 per violation if pattern and practice of non-compliance	3 years § 2614	No

286 Where a remedy or right of action is not listed, the failure to comply with a RESPA provision may possibly be pursued as a breach of contract or state UDAP statute violation. *See* Ch. 6, *supra*.

Chapter 9 Using Bankruptcy to Prevent Foreclosure

9.1 Introduction

A consumer facing the loss of his or her home through foreclosure or execution on a judgment may be able to secure temporary or permanent relief in the bankruptcy court. A complete discussion of the bankruptcy process can be found in *Consumer Bankruptcy Law and Practice*[1] and we recommend that treatise for those considering using bankruptcy to assist their clients. In addition, many of the topics discussed in this chapter have been affected by amendments made to the Bankruptcy Code by the 2005 Bankruptcy Act.[2] While many of these changes are covered in this chapter, readers are encouraged to review the more detailed discussion of these amendments in the National Consumer Law Center's *Consumer Bankruptcy Law*.[3] Attorneys who have not filed a bankruptcy case will also find NCLC's *Bankruptcy Basics* to be a helpful step-by-step instructional guide.

This chapter will address only selected bankruptcy topics that have particular relevance to the foreclosure prevention process. Several topics that are also quite important are discussed in more detail in other chapters of this treatise (as well as in *Consumer Bankruptcy Law and Practice*). These include:

- *Discharge of a Deficiency Judgment*. A deficiency judgment is an unsecured debt and is subject to discharge in bankruptcy, whether the debtor files under chapter 7 or 13.[4]
- *Truth in Lending Rescission*. Section 5.6, *supra*, discusses bringing a Truth in Lending rescission action and other consumer claims in bankruptcy court against a creditor who holds a security interest in the debtor's home. If the action is successful, the security interest will be released, in whole or in part, and the debtor is not liable for any finance charges.[5] In several jurisdictions, after rescission, the debt may be treated as a wholly unsecured claim.[6]
- *Tax Consequences of a Bankruptcy Discharge*. Although cancellation of indebtedness may have tax consequences, debt discharged in bankruptcy is generally not taxable.[7] More complicated tax issues may arise if debt is canceled as part of a loan workout agreement, before the borrower files bankruptcy, because the taxable event may have already occurred.[8]
- *Setting Aside a Foreclosure Sale in Bankruptcy*. It is still possible to set aside a mortgage foreclosure or tax sale in bankruptcy, although grounds to do so have been limited by a 1994 Supreme Court decision.[9]
- *Using Bankruptcy Law to Void Transfers of Homes to Foreclosure Rescue Scammers*. Bankruptcy law provides several important avenues of relief for homeowners who have deeded their homes to foreclosure rescue scammers.[10]

The seven primary topics which are included in this chapter are:

1 (9th ed. 2009). Attorneys just getting started in bankruptcy should also consider reviewing National Consumer Law Center, Bankruptcy Basics (2007).

2 Pub. L. No. 109-8 (Apr. 20, 2005).

3 (9th ed. 2009).

4 11 U.S.C. §§ 727, 1328. *See* § 14.3, *infra*; National Consumer Law Center, Consumer Bankruptcy Law and Practice Ch. 15 (9th ed. 2009).

5 *See* § 5.6.6, *supra* (discussion of rescission rights in bankruptcy); National Consumer Law Center, Consumer Bankruptcy Law and Practice § 15.4.4 (9th ed. 2009); National Consumer Law Center, Truth in Lending § 6.8.4 (6th ed. 2007 and Supp.).

6 *In re* Rodrigues, 278 B.R. 683 (Bankr. D.R.I. 2002) (mortgage rendered void and creditor's claim treated as an unsecured claim); *In re* Celona, 90 B.R. 104 (Bankr. E.D. Pa. 1988), *aff'd*, 98 B.R. 705 (E.D. Pa. 1989); *In re* Myers, 175 B.R. 122 (Bankr. D. Mass. 1994); *In re* Tucker, 74 B.R. 923 (Bankr. E.D. Pa. 1987) (consumers also entitled to $1000 TIL statutory damages by recoupment; $1000 damages for the creditor's failure to respond properly to the rescission demand; and attorney fees); *In re* Chancy, 33 B.R. 355 (Bankr. N.D. Okla. 1983) (creditor received 8% payout); *In re* Wright, 11 B.R. 590 (Bankr. S.D. Miss. 1981) (consumer also entitled to TIL statutory damages and attorney fees). *But see* Wells Fargo Bank, N.A. v. Jaaskelainen, 407 B.R. 449 (D. Mass. 2009); Quenzer v. Advanta Mortgage Corp. USA, 288 B.R. 884 (D. Kan. 2003); *In re* Wepsic, 231 B.R. 768 (Bankr. S.D. Cal. 1998); *In re* Cox, 175 B.R. 266 (Bankr. C.D. Ill. 1994); *In re* Lynch, 170 B.R. 26 (Bankr. D.N.H. 1994).

7 *See* § 14.6.4.3, *infra*.

8 *See* § 9.3, *infra*.

9 BFP v. Resolution Trust Co., 511 U.S. 531, 114 S. Ct. 1757, 128 L. Ed. 2d 556 (1994). *See* §§ 13.3.3.2.8, 14.2.4, *infra* (more complete discussion of setting aside foreclosure sales in bankruptcy).

10 *See* § 15.5, *infra*.

- *Automatic Stay*. The filing of a petition in bankruptcy automatically prevents almost all creditor actions against the debtor and the debtor's property, including foreclosure, foreclosure sales, and the filing of liens against the property.[11] A foreclosure conducted in violation of the automatic stay is generally void.[12] Depending on the circumstances of the case, this protection may be permanent or temporary.[13]
- *Curing a Mortgage Default in Chapter 13*. Until the foreclosure sale process is complete, a borrower can file a petition under chapter 13 and propose a plan to pay off the mortgage arrearage within a reasonable time. Sections 9.3 and 9.4 address many of the issues that arise when the debtor plans to address a mortgage default in chapter 13.[14]
- *Raising Consumer Defenses to Prevent Relief from the Automatic Stay*. Section 9.5 covers the use of consumer defenses to defeat a creditor's motion for relief from the automatic stay. This defensive use of consumer claims may be necessary in order to obtain a determination of the legitimate balance of the creditor's secured claim in the bankruptcy process.
- *Voiding Mortgage Liens in Chapter 13*. Although Congress and the Supreme Court have limited the availability of the strip down remedy with respect to home mortgages, § 9.7, *infra* discusses situations in which home mortgages may still be voided, in whole or in part, when they exceed the value of the underlying collateral. When this bankruptcy remedy remains available, it can prevent a foreclosure sale by making a mortgage entirely void, or by reducing the amount owed and secured by the lien to a manageable sum.
- *Avoiding Judgment Liens*. If a creditor sues a homeowner and gets a judgment, if unpaid, the judgment may become a lien against the debtor's home. The creditor may later execute on that lien by seeking to force a sale of the home to obtain proceeds to satisfy the amount of the judgment lien. Section 9.7 discusses how exemptions from execution under state or federal law may be used in bankruptcy to avoid or nullify a judgment lien. The underlying debt may then be paid or discharged as an unsecured claim.[15]
- *Preserving Equity by Liquidating Property in Bankruptcy*. Sometimes homeowners may not be able to prevent the loss of their home because of overwhelming financial burdens. The homeowners, however, would be better off selling their home themselves, at a higher price than would be obtained at a foreclosure sale, and thereby protecting their equity. It may be possible to do this in a chapter 13 bankruptcy (and sometimes in chapter 7 too). As discussed at § 9.10, *infra*, filing bankruptcy can give the homeowner needed time to arrange the private sale.
- *The Impact of Bankruptcy on Later Foreclosure Defense Proceedings*. Bankruptcy does not always provide a permanent resolution to foreclosure problems. For example, a chapter 7 case does not provide any significant opportunity to permanently cure a mortgage default. Section 9.11 is an introduction to the potential impact of bankruptcy on later foreclosure prevention efforts.

9.2 Bankruptcy Basics

9.2.1 Two Common Types of Bankruptcy for Consumers

9.2.1.1 General

Bankruptcy law provides for two main types of consumer cases: chapter 7 and chapter 13. Both types are generally effective at stopping a pending foreclosure action. Similarly, debtors may seek to void certain property transfers under both chapters. However, if an outstanding mortgage on the homeowner's property is in default, chapter 13 will frequently be the better choice.

9.2.1.2 Chapter 7 (Straight Bankruptcy)

In bankruptcy cases under chapter 7, the debtors file a petition asking the court to discharge their debts. The basic idea in a chapter 7 bankruptcy is to wipe out (discharge) debts in exchange for giving up property, except for "exempt" property that the law allows the debtor to keep. In most cases, all of the debtor's property will be exempt. But property that is not exempt is sold, with the money distributed to creditors.

11 11 U.S.C. § 362; National Consumer Law Center, Consumer Bankruptcy Law and Practice Ch. 9 (9th ed. 2009).

12 *See* Kalb v. Feuerstein, 308 U.S. 433, 60 S. Ct. 343, 84 L. Ed. 370 (1940); *In re* Smith, 224 B.R. 44 (Bankr. E.D. Mich. 1998) (void sale is not a post-petition transaction subject to 11 U.S.C. § 549); *In re* Nail, 195 B.R. 922 (Bankr. N.D. Ala. 1996) (foreclosure conducted after bankruptcy reinstated was void even though creditor was not aware of the reinstatement—it was on notice of the hearing on the motion to reinstate and chose not to attend or inquire as to results). *But see In re* Jones, 63 F.3d 411 (5th Cir. 1995) (sale in violation of stay is voidable rather than void and can be ratified if court annuls the automatic stay). *See generally* National Consumer Law Center, Consumer Bankruptcy Law and Practice § 9.6 (9th ed. 2009).

13 More information on the automatic stay can be found at § 9.2, *supra*.

14 11 U.S.C. § 1322(b)(3)(5). *See also* National Consumer Law Center, Consumer Bankruptcy Law and Practice § 6.3.4 (9th ed. 2009).

15 11 U.S.C. § 522(f). *See also* National Consumer Law Center, Consumer Bankruptcy Law and Practice Ch. 10 (9th ed. 2009).

If there is an outstanding mortgage in default, a chapter 7 case probably will not be the right choice because it does not eliminate the right of mortgage holders (or other secured creditors) to take the debtor's property to enforce the mortgage obligation. Even though the debtor's underlying personal obligation on the secured debt will be discharged, security interests on property generally pass through a bankruptcy unaffected if not dealt with in the bankruptcy. If the debtor's personal obligation on a secured debt is discharged, a secured creditor has no right to seek a deficiency judgment or to collect money from the debtor, but may pursue its rights under state law solely to enforce the lien. So while the debtor will gain the protection of the automatic stay while the chapter 7 case is pending and ultimately the discharge of personal liability on a secured debt, a chapter 7 bankruptcy may not provide any long-term help if the debtor's intention is to retain the collateral securing the debt.

9.2.1.3 Chapter 13 (Reorganization)

In chapter 13 cases, the debtor must file a "plan" showing how she will pay off past-due and current debts over a period of up to five years. The most important fact about chapter 13 bankruptcy for homeowners facing foreclosure is that it allows debtors to cure defaults on secured loans such as home mortgages.[16] In most cases, payments to the mortgage holder will be at least as much as the regular monthly payments, with some additional payment to get caught up on the delinquent amount. Chapter 13 cases also allow debtors to keep both exempt property, which would be protected in chapter 7, and non-exempt property, which would be sold in chapter 7. For a chapter 13 plan to be a viable option, homeowners will need to have enough income to pay for their necessities and to keep up with the required payments as they come due.

9.2.2 Gathering the Necessary Information

While the primary purpose in filing for bankruptcy may be to stop a home foreclosure, homeowners will be required to complete a significant amount of paperwork detailing their financial situation. Homeowners must provide the attorney with the information necessary to accurately prepare the bankruptcy petition and schedules.[17] The attorney will need to obtain a complete list of creditors and current addresses, account numbers, and balances owed for each debt. It is more important in chapter 13 than in chapter 7 to know the precise amount owed on each debt, as this may affect the feasibility of the plan. Particularly in cases where the homeowners are proposing to pay less than 100% to unsecured creditors, to avoid a judicial lien, or to strip off a wholly unsecured junior mortgage,[18] the attorney also should try to obtain a copy of a recent appraisal of the home. The trustee or secured creditor simply may not rely upon the tax assessment value. It also is very important that homeowners provide a realistic budget of expenses so that the attorney can determine the amount of excess income available to make monthly plan payments.

9.2.3 Credit Counseling Requirements

Bankruptcy law requires that debtors receive budget and credit counseling within 180 days *before* the bankruptcy case is filed.[19] If time is critical in the foreclosure case, homeowners should immediately be referred to an approved credit counseling agency. The counseling requirement may be temporarily or permanently waived, but only in very limited circumstances.[20] Organizations providing this counseling must be approved by the United States Trustee Program (or the Bankruptcy Administrator in North Carolina and Alabama). Agencies must also provide the bankruptcy counseling and necessary certificates without regard to ability to pay. If homeowners cannot afford the fee, they should ask for a fee waiver or reduced fee.

To receive a discharge in a chapter 7 or chapter 13 case, the debtor must complete a financial education course. This course is different from the budget and credit counseling that must be completed prior to filing.

9.2.4 Litigating in a Bankruptcy Case

Lawsuits within a bankruptcy case are called "adversary proceedings." The proceedings are initiated by a complaint and are governed by rules that closely parallel the Federal Rules of Civil Procedure. Depending on the specific circumstances of the case, the bankruptcy court may be a preferable forum for litigating foreclosure related claims and defenses.[21] In many districts, the bankruptcy judges and federal judges may be a good deal more sympathetic to the homeowner's case than judges in local courts. Not only do bankruptcy judges regularly see the problem of debtors in trouble, but also they are generally more aware of the unfair creditor practices that often take place. Many bankruptcy judges are pleased to be presented with novel and creative cases that provide both a change of pace from routine

16 *See* §§ 9.4, 9.5, *supra*.

17 National Consumer Law Center, Consumer Bankruptcy Law and Practice Appx. F (9th ed. 2009) (sample bankruptcy questionnaire).

18 *See* § 9.7, *supra*.

19 11 U.S.C. § 109(h).
A list of approved agencies is available on the website for the Executive Office of the United States Trustee, at www.usdoj.gov/ust/eo/bapcpa/ccde/cc_approved.htm.

20 *See In re* Gee, 332 B.R. 602 (Bankr. W.D. Mo. 2005); National Consumer Law Center, Consumer Bankruptcy Law and Practice § 3.2.1.4 (9th ed. 2009).

21 *See generally* National Consumer Law Center, Consumer Bankruptcy Law and Practice Ch. 13 (9th ed. 2009).

bankruptcy matters and a means for ruling on unfair practices.

In addition, most bankruptcy judges are far more knowledgeable in commercial law, and often in consumer law (such as the Truth in Lending Act), than the average state judge. Bankruptcy judges and federal appellate judges may be more disposed, because of lower case loads and greater availability of law clerk assistance, to give careful consideration to bona fide legal arguments on behalf of debtors.

9.3 Obtaining the Automatic Stay

9.3.1 Stays Obtained by Filing for Bankruptcy

9.3.1.1 The Automatic Stay

One of the most important weapons in the consumer bankruptcy arsenal is the automatic stay provision of the Bankruptcy Code.[22] Few other legal steps that may be taken by a consumer can effectuate relief so simply, so effectively, and so dramatically. The instant that a bankruptcy case is filed, the automatic stay takes effect, freezing almost all actions against the debtor and the debtor's property, including a foreclosure or sale of secured property.

The 2005 Bankruptcy Act (2005 Act) imposes a number of new restrictions on repeat bankruptcy filings. These new provisions, discussed at § 9.3.3.2, *infra*, must be considered in determining whether the debtor's bankruptcy filing will invoke the automatic stay and stop a pending foreclosure or sale of secured property.

The power of the automatic stay extends to almost all actions that may be taken against the debtor's secured property.[23] For debtors who seek legal assistance just prior to some serious adverse action against their secured property, the automatic stay may provide the only practical solution. For others, for whom other legal steps have failed, the stay may provide at least temporary relief by postponing a crisis while more permanent relief is sought through the bankruptcy process.

It is sometimes necessary to file a bankruptcy immediately in order to utilize the automatic stay to stop an imminent foreclosure or repossession. In those cases the debtor may commence a case by filing only the three-page bankruptcy petition, along with a list of the debtor's creditors and their addresses.[24] Based on a requirement imposed by the 2005 Act, the debtor must receive budget and credit counseling from an approved credit counseling agency within the 180 days before the bankruptcy is filed.[25] If the debtor needs to file a petition in an emergency, such as to stop a foreclosure, the debtor must submit a certification describing the "exigent circumstances" and stating that the debtor requested counseling services from an approved agency but was unable to obtain the services during the seven-day period following the request.[26] This certification and request for deferral of the counseling, if approved by the court, affords the debtor a period of thirty days after the petition is filed to obtain the counseling.[27] It is almost never advisable, however, to seek a delay of the counseling under this provision because the required briefing can usually be completed over the telephone or Internet within an hour or two. Also, some courts have strictly interpreted the exigent circumstances requirement.[28]

The filing must be accompanied by the filing fee of $274 for chapter 13 ($299 for a case under chapter 7) or an application to pay the fee in installments.[29] In an important positive change from prior law,[30] the 2005 Act provides for the waiver of chapter 7 filing fees for debtors with incomes less than 150% of the applicable official poverty line based on family size.[31] In addition to the income test, the debtor must be unable to pay the filing fee in installments.[32]

---

22 11 U.S.C. § 362.

23 *See* National Consumer Law Center, Repossessions § 8.2.4.2 (6th ed. 2005 and Supp.).

24 Fed. R. Bankr. P. 1007(a); Official Bankruptcy Form 1.

Blank forms suitable for copying may be found on the companion website to National Consumer Law Center, Consumer Bankruptcy Law and Practice (9th ed. 2009).

25 11 U.S.C. §§ 109(h), 521(b). *See also* Interim Bankruptcy Rule 1007(b)(3). *See generally* National Consumer Law Center, Consumer Bankruptcy Law and Practice §§ 3.2.1.4, 7.3.5 (9th ed. 2009) (discussion of the counseling requirements).

26 11 U.S.C. § 109(h)(3)(A).

The debtor must summarize the exigent circumstances on Exhibit D of the bankruptcy petition (Official Form 1). For a sample certification in support of request for delay of the briefing, see National Consumer Law Center, Consumer Bankruptcy Law and Practice, Form 7, Appx. G.3 (9th ed. 2009).

27 11 U.S.C. § 109(h)(3)(B).

28 *E.g., In re* Dixon, 338 B.R. 383 (B.A.P. 8th Cir. 2006) (no abuse of discretion by bankruptcy court in denying motion for deferral based on finding that debtor had been given sufficient twenty-day advance notice of pending foreclosure under Missouri law); *In re* LaPorta, 332 B.R. 879 (Bankr. D. Minn. 2005). *But see In re* Cleaver, 333 B.R. 430, 435 (Bankr. S.D. Ohio 2005) (pending foreclosure sale "exactly the sort of exigent circumstance contemplated by the statute").

29 An application to pay filing fees in installments is governed by Fed. R. Bankr. P. 1006. The actual application is Official Form 3.

30 *See* former 28 U.S.C. § 1930(a) (codifying United States v. Kras, 409 U.S. 434 (1973)).

31 28 U.S.C. § 1930(f)(1). *See* National Consumer Law Center, Consumer Bankruptcy Law and Practice § 14.6.2 (9th ed. 2009).

32 Bankruptcy Rule 1006(c) provides that a voluntary chapter 7 petition shall be accepted for filing if accompanied by a debtor's application requesting a fee waiver prepared using Official Form 3B. Fed. R. Bankr. P. 1006(c). A copy of Official Form 3B is *reprinted in* National Consumer Law Center, Consumer Bankruptcy Law and Practice Appx. D.2 (9th ed. 2009).

After these few documents are filed, the rules require that the remainder of the usual forms be filed within fourteen days.[33] This deadline may be further extended upon application, for cause shown.[34] Further discussion about the necessary forms for filing a case and instructions for filling them out can be found in National Consumer Law Center, *Consumer Bankruptcy Law and Practice* § 7.3 (9th ed. 2009).

As soon as the petition is filed, whether or not it is accompanied by the balance of the necessary forms, the automatic stay goes into effect.

9.3.1.2 The Codebtor Stay

In addition to the automatic stay available in every bankruptcy case, chapter 13 provides a special automatic stay of creditor actions against most people who are codebtors with the debtor.[35] This codebtor stay, which can relieve creditor pressure on friends or relatives of the debtor, may be an important reason to file a chapter 13 case.

Because of the codebtor stay, a chapter 13 bankruptcy filing by one joint debtor obligated on a mortgage protects his or her codebtor from foreclosure as well—even if the codebtor is not a party to the bankruptcy filing. The codebtor stay only applies to consumer debts.[36] It may be lifted[37] to the extent that:

- The debtor's plan does not propose to pay the debt;[38]
- The codebtor received the consideration for the debt;[39] or
- The creditor's interest would be irreparably harmed by the continuation of the stay.

9.3.2 Purpose of the Automatic Stay

The main purpose of the automatic stay is to protect the debtor and the debtor's property. As stated in the House Report for the 1978 Bankruptcy Code:

> The automatic stay is one of the fundamental debtor protections provided by the bankruptcy laws. It gives the debtor a breathing spell from creditors. It stops all collection efforts, all harassment, and all foreclosure actions. It permits the debtor to attempt a repayment or reorganization, or simply to be relieved of the financial pressures caused by over-extension of credit.[40]

Functionally, the stay also freezes the debtor's assets as of the date of filing the petition. In chapter 7 bankruptcies, this guarantees protection of the debtor's property, including any equity; the exempt property will provide the debtor with a fresh start while the non-exempt property can be distributed fairly to creditors. In chapter 13 plans, the stay protects the debtors' property, provides an opportunity to effectuate a debt adjustment plan, and if the plan is successful, gives the debtor a fresh start.

The stay allows the bankruptcy court to deal with the debtor's situation in an orderly manner. It prevents, at least until the bankruptcy court allows otherwise, other parties and courts from interfering with or complicating the bankruptcy process.

9.3.3 Duration of the Automatic Stay

9.3.3.1 General Rule

Depending upon the circumstances, the duration of the automatic stay varies significantly. If the circumstances require, the stay can be ended by the court almost immediately, although such immediate relief is very unusual in consumer bankruptcy cases. As a practical matter, the stay is usually not lifted in less than thirty days after the petition has been filed. Indeed, the stay may last for the duration of the case, three to six months in straight chapter 7 cases and up to five years in chapter 13 cases.[41]

Technically, the statute provides that the stay continues until the following dates:[42]

- To the extent the stay is based upon provisions barring an act against property of the estate:

33 Fed. R. Bankr. P. 1007(c).

34 *Id.*

35 *See* National Consumer Law Center, Consumer Bankruptcy Law and Practice § 9.4.4 (9th ed. 2009) (discussion of the codebtor stay, which is also available in chapter 12 cases).

36 11 U.S.C. § 1301(a). *See In re* Stovall, 209 B.R. 849 (Bankr. E.D. Va. 1997) (personal property tax not a consumer debt).

37 11 U.S.C. § 1301(c).

38 *See In re* Zersen, 189 B.R. 732 (Bankr. W.D. Wis. 1995) (stay may be lifted only as to the portion of the debt that will not be paid in the chapter 13 plan).

39 *See In re* Motes, 166 B.R. 147 (Bankr. E.D. Mo. 1994) (codebtor stay not lifted as to mortgage on jointly owned motor home, even though debtor had moved out of the home, because original consideration was to both debtor and his non-debtor wife).

40 11 U.S.C. § 362(e); H.R. Rep. No. 95-595, at 340 (1977).

41 Courts have differed about the scope of stay protection for property in chapter 13 cases following confirmation of the debtor's plan. The issue may turn on the language of the confirmed plan. *See In re* Clark, 207 B.R. 559 (Bankr. S.D. Ohio 1997) (post-confirmation wages were property of estate protected from IRS levy for post-petition taxes when plan clearly provided that property of estate did not revest in debtors upon confirmation). *See also In re* Kolenda, 212 B.R. 851 (W.D. Mich. 1997) (automobile acquired post-confirmation was property of the estate protected by stay); National Consumer Law Center, Repossessions § 8.2.4.2.1 (6th ed. 2005 and Supp.). *But see In re* Fisher, 203 B.R. 958 (N.D. Ill. 1997) (vesting of property of estate in debtor at confirmation deprives that property of stay protection afforded to property of the estate), *rev'g* 198 B.R. 721 (Bankr. N.D. Ill. 1996).

42 11 U.S.C. § 362(c)–(e).

(i) The date such property is no longer property of the estate (usually the date property is abandoned) or the date it is deemed abandoned at the close of the case under 11 U.S.C. § 554(c);[43]
(ii) The date on which the stay is terminated by order of the court, or by inaction of the court upon a request for relief from the stay.[44]

- To the extent the stay is against any other act, the earliest of the following:
  (i) The date the case is closed;[45]
  (ii) The date the case is dismissed;[46]
  (iii) The date a discharge is granted or denied;[47]
  (iv) The date on which the stay is terminated by order of the court, or by inaction of the court upon a request for relief from the stay.[48]

In a practical sense, the benefits of the stay may last much longer. A creditor may not pay attention to the date the bankruptcy ends, especially as there is no specific notice that the stay is terminated at the end of the case. With respect to debts discharged in the bankruptcy case, the automatic stay is replaced by the discharge injunction which protects the debtor from acts to collect on the discharged debt.[49]

9.3.3.2 Limitations Based on Repeat Filings

The 2005 Act creates a number of new exceptions and limitations to the automatic stay, several of which apply if there have been prior dismissed bankruptcy cases. If the debtor has had one prior bankruptcy case dismissed within the year before the petition is filed, the automatic stay will terminate thirty days after the case is filed.[50] Because the stay terminates under this provision only with respect to the debtor and only as to actions taken[51] in relation to a debt or property securing such a debt, or to a lease, the automatic stay provided under section 362(a) of the Code continues to apply in the later case to property of the estate and to actions not taken in relation to a debt.[52] If the debtor's home remains estate property, for example, this should mean that a secured creditor cannot proceed with a home foreclosure after the thirty-day period has expired without first seeking stay relief.

The debtor may file a motion within the thirty-day period requesting that the court extend the stay as to all or some creditors.[53] The debtor must demonstrate that the case has been filed in good faith, typically by showing that circumstances have changed. The 2005 Act does not define good faith for purposes of this stay limitation, but good faith has been given a recognized meaning by case law with respect to the filing of a case.[54] In addition, this stay limitation provision sets forth several circumstances in which a case is presumed to be filed in bad faith, and the debtor may need to rebut such a presumption if it arises with clear and convincing evidence to the contrary.[55]

If a debtor has had two or more cases dismissed within the year before the petition, the automatic stay does not go into effect upon the filing of the case.[56] On a motion filed by the debtor within thirty days after filing of the later case, the court may order the stay to take effect as to all or some creditors upon a showing by the debtor that the case has been filed in good faith.[57]

---

43 *See, e.g., In re* Cruseturner, 8 B.R. 581 (Bankr. D. Utah 1981) (when the trustee abandons property in which the debtor had an interest prior to filing the petition, such property becomes property of the debtor and is subject to the automatic stay pursuant to 11 U.S.C. § 362(a)(5)).

44 Unlike many orders, an order granting relief from the stay takes effect immediately, unless it provides otherwise. Fed. R. Bankr. P. 7062.

45 *See In re* Bryant, 95 B.R. 857 (Bankr. M.D. Ga. 1989) (court will not reopen closed case to consider motion for relief from stay).

46 *In re* De Jesus Saez, 721 F.2d 848 (1st Cir. 1983) (ten-day stay of enforcement of judgments, applicable to adversary proceedings, does not serve to preserve stay for ten days after petition has been dismissed).

47 *See, e.g., In re* Cornist, 7 B.R. 118 (Bankr. S.D. Cal. 1980).

48 11 U.S.C. § 362(e). Fed. R. Bankr. P. 7062.

49 11 U.S.C. § 524(a). *See* National Consumer Law Center, Consumer Bankruptcy Law and Practice § 15.5.1.4 (9th ed. 2009).

50 11 U.S.C. § 362(c)(3); National Consumer Law Center, Consumer Bankruptcy Law and Practice § 9.3.3 (9th ed. 2009).

51 *In re* Stanford, 373 B.R. 890 (Bankr. E.D. Ark. 2007) (prepetition state court replevin action is the type of formal, judicial proceeding described in § 362(c)(3)(A)); *In re* Paschal, 337 B.R. 274 (Bankr. E.D.N.C. 2006) ("action taken" construed to mean that stay termination under § 362(c)(3) applies only as to creditors who have taken some type of pre-petition formal action against the debtor, such as a "judicial, administrative, governmental, quasi-judicial, or other essentially formal activity or proceeding"). *But see In re* James, 358 B.R. 816 (Bankr. S.D. Ga. 2007).

52 *In re* Holcomb, 380 B.R. 813 (B.A.P. 10th Cir. 2008); *In re* Jumpp, 356 B.R. 789 (B.A.P. 1st Cir. 2006); *In re* Stanford, 373 B.R. 890 (Bankr. E.D. Ark. 2007); *In re* McFeeley, 362 B.R. 121 (Bankr. D. Vt. 2007); *In re* Harris, 342 B.R. 274 (Bankr. N.D. Ohio 2006); *In re* Jones, 339 B.R. 360 (Bankr. E.D.N.C. 2006); *In re* Johnson, 335 B.R. 805 (Bankr. W.D. Tenn. 2006). *But see In re* Daniel, 404 B.R. 318 (Bankr. N.D. Ill. 2009); *In re* Jupiter, 344 B.R. 754 (Bankr. D.S.C. 2006).

53 11 U.S.C. § 362(c)(3)(B). A motion to extend the stay must be filed and heard by the court before the thirty-day period expires.

54 *See* National Consumer Law Center, Consumer Bankruptcy Law and Practice §§ 9.7.3.1.5, 12.3.3, 12.3.4, 12.10 (9th ed. 2009). *See also In re* Sarafoglou, 345 B.R. 19 (Bankr. D. Mass. 2006); *In re* Baldassaro, 338 B.R. 178 (Bankr. D.N.H. 2006) (good faith found based on changed circumstances).

55 11 U.S.C. § 362(c)(3)(C). *See* National Consumer Law Center, Consumer Bankruptcy Law and Practice § 9.3.3.2.2 (9th ed. 2009) (discussion of the circumstances giving rise to the presumption). *See also In re* Whitaker, 341 B.R. 336 (Bankr. S.D. Ga. 2006) (primary way debtor may rebut presumption of bad faith is to show substantial change in financial or personal affairs or other reason why current case will be successful).

56 11 U.S.C. § 362(c)(4); National Consumer Law Center, Consumer Bankruptcy Law and Practice § 9.3.3.3 (9th ed. 2009).

57 The debtor may need to rebut a presumption, based on circum-

In addition, the automatic stay is not applicable as to the enforcement of a lien against, or security interest in, real property if the debtor files a case during a period when the debtor is ineligible to be a debtor under section 109(g) or in violation of a prior court order prohibiting the debtor from being a debtor in another case.[58] If there are co-debtors on a real-estate-secured debt, this stay exception would not apply in a case filed by one of the co-debtors if that co-debtor is not ineligible under section 109(g) or was not named in the prior court order, and the stay under section 1301 would protect the interest of the nonfiling co-debtor. In a joint case, this provision would apply as to real property jointly held by both debtors only if both debtors are ineligible under section 109(g) or subject to the prior court order.[59]

Under section 109(g), a debtor is not eligible for relief under the Bankruptcy Code if, within 180 days before the filing of the petition, the debtor had a prior case dismissed for willful failure to abide by orders of the court or to prosecute the case, or the debtor requested and obtained the voluntary dismissal of the case following the filing of a request for relief from the automatic stay.[60] However, it is often not clear whether section 109(g) was invoked in the prior case. Courts rarely make express findings, in dismissing the prior case, that the debtor willfully failed to prosecute the case or willfully failed to obey a court order. The clerk normally accepts the petition filed in the later case because no determination has been made that the debtor is ineligible under section 109(g).

Thus, it is not likely that real-estate-secured creditors will rely upon this stay exception if the debtor's filing status is unclear. A creditor who proceeds with enforcement of a real property lien in reliance on the exception based on section 109(g) may act at its peril. There may be factual or legal disputes about whether the debtor is eligible for relief. If the debtor prevails, the creditor's action is likely to be found a willful violation of the stay, since a mistake does not vitiate the willfulness of an action in violation of the stay.[61]

Significantly, the 2005 Act did not amend the codebtor stay provisions found in 11 U.S.C. § 1301, and no reference to the codebtor stay is made in 11 U.S.C. § 362(c). To the extent that the stay provided under 11 U.S.C. § 1301 is applicable, as discussed at § 9.3.1.2, *supra*, the repeat filing stay limitation provisions do not prevent the application of the codebtor stay as to any actions taken against a codebtor on a consumer debt of the debtor. Thus, a creditor will still need to file a motion for relief in most cases in which a codebtor exists.[62]

9.3.3.3 *In Rem* Stay Relief

Another provision of the 2005 Act allows creditors with claims secured by real property to seek *in rem* stay relief in certain limited circumstances.[63] If the court enters an *in rem* order and the order is properly recorded, the stay does not apply with respect to the property in a later case filed within two years after the date of the order.[64]

An *in rem* order may be granted if the secured creditor proves that:

- The filing of the petition was part of a scheme to hinder, delay, and defraud creditors; *and*
- The scheme involved either (1) transfer of full or partial interests in the property without creditor or court approval *or* (2) multiple bankruptcy filings involving the same property.[65]

By requiring that the scheme to hinder, delay and defraud a creditor[66] must involve either an unauthorized transfer of the property or multiple bankruptcy filings affecting the property, section 362(d)(4) requires the court to determine whether the specific conduct was an abusive filing, gener-

stances similar to those found in § 362(c)(3)(C), that the case was not filed in good faith. 11 U.S.C. § 362(c)(4)(D).

58 11 U.S.C. § 362(b)(21); National Consumer Law Center, Consumer Bankruptcy Law and Practice § 9.3.3.6 (9th ed. 2009).

59 Section 362(b)(21) should be compared with the refiling provision in § 362(c)(3), which expressly states that the provision is applicable in a single or joint case filed by an individual debtor.

60 *See* National Consumer Law Center, Consumer Bankruptcy Law and Practice §§ 3.2.12, 9.7.3.1.5 (9th ed. 2009).

61 *See* National Consumer Law Center, Consumer Bankruptcy Law and Practice § 9.6 (9th ed. 2009).

62 *In re* Lemma, 393 B.R. 299 (Bankr. E.D.N.Y. 2008) (although automatic stay applicable to debtors was terminated by operation of § 362(c)(3)(A), mortgage creditor's scheduling of foreclosure sale violated codebtor stay under § 1301); *In re* King, 362 B.R. 226 (Bankr. D. Md. 2007) (although no stay went into effect as to debtor based on prior dismissed case, post-petition foreclosure sale violated the codebtor stay under § 1301 and was therefore void).

63 11 U.S.C. § 362(d)(4); National Consumer Law Center, Consumer Bankruptcy Law and Practice § 9.4.5.5.2 (9th ed. 2009).

64 11 U.S.C. § 362(b)(20).

65 11 U.S.C. § 362(d)(4). *See In re* McCray, 342 B.R. 668 (Bankr. D. Col. 2006) (relief under section 362(d)(4) not available to purchaser of property at foreclosure whose claim is not secured by interest in real property).

66 Courts may rely upon case law construing the "hinder, delay or defraud a creditor" language found in § 727(a)(2) in applying § 362(d)(4). However, it is important to note that the words in the § 362(d)(4) phrase are joined by the conjunction "and" rather than "or," thus ensuring that *in rem* orders will be infrequently entered only in cases in which a creditor can prove the debtor's petition was part of a scheme not only to hinder and delay, but also to defraud the creditor. *See In re* Poissant, 405 B.R. 267, 273 (Bankr. N.D. Ohio 2009); *In re* Smith, 395 B.R. 711 (Bankr. D. Kan. 2008) (debtor was a plodder, not a plotter, so there was no scheme to defraud); *In re* Gould, 348 B.R. 78, 80, (Bankr. D. Mass. 2006) (use of "and" in § 362(d)(4) must be deliberate "since Congress clearly knew how to use the disjunctive form when it wishes to do so"); *In re* Abdul Muhaimin, 343 B.R. 159 (Bankr. D. Md. 2006) (creditor satisfied burden of proving scheme to hinder, but failed to prove fraud).

ally in relation to a real property foreclosure. For example, a court may find that the transfer of a fractional interest of property to a bankruptcy debtor by a property owner facing foreclosure, done to gain the automatic stay, was part of a scheme to hinder, delay or defraud a foreclosing creditor. However, an innocent transfer of property, such as a court ordered transfer of a former spouse's property interest to a debtor as part of a domestic court proceeding, should not by itself form the basis for an *in rem* order under section 362(d)(20).

Similarly, if an *in rem* order is sought based on the provision regarding multiple filings involving the same property, the order cannot be imposed during the first bankruptcy filing involving the property given the "multiple" filing requirement. However, it could be used as the basis for an order if a spouse, co-owner, or former owner had previously filed in the recent past. A filing in the more distant past would not likely be considered a part of a scheme to hinder, delay, and defraud creditors.

A debtor in a later case may move for relief from the order based on changed circumstances or other good cause.[67] The stay exception in section 362(b)(20) also does not affect the applicability of the section 1301 codebtor stay.

Since the Bankruptcy Code now sets a bright line rule for *in rem* stay relief, courts should not grant such orders in other circumstances.[68] Certainly, it should not be granted in the first bankruptcy filing involving a property. It should also not be granted in a later bankruptcy case unless the case meets the requirements of being part of a scheme to hinder, delay, or defraud creditors.

9.3.4 Scope of the Automatic Stay

9.3.4.1 Stay of Legal Proceedings

The acts prohibited by the automatic stay are set out in a series of overlapping statutory provisions.[69] Almost all forms of legal actions[70] are brought to an immediate halt by filing the petition. Replevin actions, foreclosures, deficiency actions, attachments,[71] garnishments,[72] and executions are among the many types of legal proceedings affected by this provision. Even proceedings on admittedly nondischargeable debts are enjoined until the stay is lifted.[73] No further steps may be taken in stayed proceedings without the permission of the bankruptcy court.[74] Thus, the act of continuing the date of a foreclosure sale violates the stay, although several appellate courts have held otherwise on the theory that such a postponement merely preserves the status quo.[75] In addition, the failure of a creditor to dismiss or stay a pending court proceeding against the debtor, once notified of the debtor's bankruptcy, can be a willful violation of the stay.[76]

---

67 11 U.S.C. § 362(d)(4). For a sample Motion for Relief from *In Rem* Order Entered in Prior Case, see National Consumer Law Center, Consumer Bankruptcy Law and Practice Appx. G.4, Form 48 (9th ed. 2009).

68 Some of the grounds used to justify such orders in decisions prior to the 2005 Act may no longer be valid. *See* National Consumer Law Center, Consumer Bankruptcy Law and Practice § 9.7.3.1.5 (9th ed. 2009).

69 11 U.S.C. § 362(a).

70 11 U.S.C. § 362(a)(1).

The stay bars "the commencement or continuation, including the issuance or employment of process, of a judicial or other proceeding against the debtor that was or could have been commenced before the commencement of the case . . . or to recover a claim against the debtor that arose before the commencement of the case." *See* Ohio v. Kovacs, 469 U.S. 928 (1985).

71 *In re* Matthews, 184 B.R. 594 (Bankr. S.D. Ala. 1995) (IRS levy notices and tax refund seizures violated stay and discharge injunction).

72 *See In re* Roberts, 175 B.R. 339 (B.A.P. 9th Cir. 1994) (state franchise tax board violated stay by continuing to accept payments from debtor's employer pursuant to pre-petition garnishment).

73 *In re* Byrne, 5 B.R. 556 (Bankr. W.D. Pa. 1980). *See In re* Merchant, 958 F.2d 738 (6th Cir. 1992) (actions to collect nondischargeable student loan violate stay); *In re* Arneson, 282 B.R. 883 (B.A.P. 9th Cir. 2002) (stay applies to bar enforcement of debt found nondischargeable in earlier bankruptcy case). *But see In re* Cady, 315 F.3d 1121 (9th Cir. 2002) (creditor may proceed against property of the debtor after it obtains judgment of nondischargeability, but not against property of the estate); *In re* Embry, 10 F.3d 401 (6th Cir. 1993) (once creditor obtained determination that debt was nondischargeable in chapter 7 case due to false pretenses, creditor could proceed against property that was not property of the estate without violating the automatic stay).

Note, however, that exempted property is protected during and after the case. 11 U.S.C. § 522(c).

74 *See, e.g.,* Dean v. Trans World Airlines, 72 F.3d 754 (9th Cir. 1996) (involuntary dismissal of action against debtor violated the stay); *In re* Tampa Chain Co., 835 F.2d 54 (2d Cir. 1987) (appeal of defendant in adversary proceeding cannot be dismissed after that defendant became debtor in his own bankruptcy case); Pope v. Manville Forest Prods. Corp., 778 F.2d 238 (5th Cir. 1985) (even dismissal of case against debtor is precluded by the stay); *In re* Weed, 6 Bankr. Ct. Dec. (CRR) 606, 2 Collier Bankr. Cas. 2d (MB) 994 (S.D. Iowa 1980) (discovery in district court case not allowed without lifting of stay); *In re* Lobherr, 282 B.R. 912 (Bankr. C.D. Cal. 2002) (renewal of judgment violated stay and was void); *In re* Vierkant, 240 B.R. 317 (B.A.P. 8th Cir. 1999) (docket entry noting default judgment entered after stay became effective is subject to stay and therefore void ab initio).

75 Taylor v. Slick, 178 F.3d 698 (3d Cir. 1999) (postponement of foreclosure sale to new date does not violate stay); *In re* Peters, 101 F.3d 618 (9th Cir. 1996) (creditor did not violate stay by continuing foreclosure sale date after plan confirmation). *Cf. In re* Derringer, 375 B.R. 903 (B.A.P. 10th Cir. 2007) (filing and serving notice of foreclosure was more than mere postponement or continuance of sale and thus violated stay); *In re* Lynn-Weaver, 385 B.R. 7, 11 (Bankr. D. Mass. 2008) (while a one-time postponement is permitted as a temporary place-holding measure, repeated rescheduling of sale violated stay).

76 Eskanos & Adler, Prof'l Corp. v. Leetien, 309 F.3d 1210 (9th Cir. 2002); *In re* Scroggin, 364 B.R. 772 (B.A.P. 10th Cir. 2007) (creditor willfully violated stay when it waited twelve weeks

The Bankruptcy Code stay requirements bar only actions against the debtor, and not those brought by the debtor.[77] The debtor's actions may be continued after commencement of the case, although the trustee may acquire an interest in some of them and a party may be able to remove an action to the bankruptcy court. Occasionally, it is not clear whether an action is against the debtor or brought by the debtor, for example, when a debtor's counterclaim predominates or when the debtor has filed an appeal. Several courts of appeals have held that the answer to this question turns on whether the action was brought initially by or against the debtor.[78]

9.3.4.2 Stay of Acts Directed at Debtor's Property (Including Foreclosure)

Several Bankruptcy Code provisions protect the property owned by the debtor at the time the petition is filed. Those provisions prohibit:

- The enforcement, against the debtor or against property of the estate, of a judgment obtained before the commencement of the case;[79]
- Any act to obtain possession of property of the estate;[80]
- Any act to create, perfect, or enforce any lien against property of the estate;[81] and
- Any act to create, perfect, or enforce any lien to the extent that such lien secures a claim that arose before the commencement of the case.[82]

Thus, repossession and any sale of repossessed property are clearly enjoined.[83] Post-petition retention of previously repossessed property of the estate is also a violation of the automatic stay.[84] This means that creditors must promptly return property in their possession which they had repossessed pre-petition.[85] Failure to do so is a willful violation of the stay which gives rise to damages, attorney fees and other potential relief.[86]

The provisions prohibiting acts to obtain possession of or to enforce liens against property of the estate apply regardless of when the claim arose. This is because property of the estate is essentially frozen, to be administered only by the bankruptcy court. In a chapter 13 case, this can be very important because all property the debtor acquires for the entire time the case is pending may become property of the estate.[87] These provisions also prevent the creation, perfection, or the enforcement of any pre-petition lien against

before it sent release of wage garnishment to employer); *In re* Braught, 307 B.R. 399 (Bankr. S.D.N.Y. 2004) (creditor willfully violated stay by failing to take affirmative action to vacate state court judgment entered in violation of stay).

77 11 U.S.C. § 362(a); Martin-Trigona v. Champion Fed. Sav., 892 F.2d 575 (7th Cir. 1989) (automatic stay inapplicable to debtor's lawsuit); Carley Capital Group v. Fireman's Fund Ins. Co., 889 F.2d 1126 (D.C. Cir. 1989) (debtor's appeal of judgment in action filed by debtor not stayed).

78 Ingersoll-Rand Fin. Corp. v. Miller Mining Co., 817 F.2d 1424 (9th Cir. 1987); Teachers Ins. & Annuity Ass'n of Am. v. Butler, 803 F.2d 61 (2d Cir. 1986); Freeman v. I.R.S., 799 F.2d 1091 (5th Cir. 1986); Commerzanstalt v. Telewide Sys., Inc., 790 F.2d 206 (2d Cir. 1986); Cathey v. Johns-Manville Sales Corp., 711 F.2d 60 (6th Cir. 1983); Ass'n of St. Croix Condo. Owners v. St. Croix Hotel Corp., 682 F.2d 446 (3d Cir. 1982). *See also* Ellision v. Northwest Eng'g Co., 709 F.2d 681 (11th Cir. 1983). *But see* Mason v. Okla. Turnpike Auth., 115 F.3d 1442 (10th Cir. 1997) (code does not prevent debtor's appeal in action originally brought against debtor, but did stay creditor's cross-appeal); Koolik v. Markowitz, 40 F.3d 567 (2d Cir. 1994) (appeal by debtor plaintiff from adverse judgment on defendant's counterclaim was stayed); Maritime Elec. Co. v. United Jersey Bank, 959 F.2d 1194 (3d Cir. 1991) (claims and counterclaims could be disaggregated so that a defendant-debtor's counterclaims could proceed); Accredited Assocs., Inc. v. Shottenfeld, 292 S.E.2d 417 (Ga. Ct. App. 1982) (holding that result turned on which party filed appeal); Kessel v. Peterson, 350 N.W.2d 603 (N.D. 1984) (appeal by debtor plaintiff from adverse judgment on defendant's counterclaim was stayed).

79 11 U.S.C. § 362(a)(2).

80 11 U.S.C. § 362(a)(3).

81 11 U.S.C. § 362(a)(4).

82 11 U.S.C. § 362(a)(5).

Perfection of certain types of liens is permitted under 11 U.S.C. § 362(b)(3).

83 *In re* Reed, 102 B.R. 243, 10 U.C.C. Rep. Serv. 2d 611 (Bankr. E.D. Okla. 1989) (post-petition repossession and sale violates automatic stay); *In re* Koresko, 91 B.R. 689 (Bankr. E.D. Pa. 1988) (debtor retains right to redeem vehicle after repossession; post-petition sale violates stay).

84 *See* National Consumer Law Center, Repossessions § 8.2.6 (6th ed. 2005 and Supp.).

85 *See* National Consumer Law Center, Repossessions §§ 8.2.5, 8.2.6, 8.3 (6th ed. 2005 and Supp.).

86 *See* National Consumer Law Center, Repossessions § 8.2.6 (6th ed. 2005 and Supp.).

87 11 U.S.C. § 1306(a); Sec. Bank of Marshalltown, Iowa v. Neiman, 1 F.3d 687 (8th Cir. 1993) (property acquired by chapter 13 debtor during case continues to be property of the estate protected by the stay after it vests in the debtor upon confirmation); *In re* Kolenda, 212 B.R. 851 (W.D. Mich. 1997) (automobile acquired post-confirmation was property of the estate protected by stay). *See In re* Clark, 207 B.R. 559 (Bankr. S.D. Ohio 1997) (post-confirmation wages were property of estate protected from IRS levy for post-petition taxes when plan clearly provided that property of estate did not revest in debtors upon confirmation). *But see In re* Rangel, 233 B.R. 191 (Bankr. D. Mass. 1999) (cataloging cases and advantages and disadvantages of various approaches); *In re* Fisher, 203 B.R. 958 (N.D. Ill. 1997), *rev'g* 198 B.R. 721 (Bankr. N.D. Ill. 1996) (vesting of property of estate in debtor at confirmation deprives that property of stay protection afforded to property of the estate); *In re* Adams, 12 B.R. 540 (Bankr. D. Utah 1981) (all of debtor's property except that used to fund plan is no longer property of the estate after confirmation, under 11 U.S.C. § 1327(b)).

One possible way to avoid the problem of property losing its character as property of the estate is to provide in the plan for such property to vest in the debtor at the end of the case, as § 1327(b) provides that confirmation vests property in the estate only if the plan does not provide otherwise. *See In re* Denn, 37 B.R. 33 (Bankr. D. Minn. 1983).

property of the debtor that is not part of the bankruptcy estate, such as exempt property in a chapter 7 case.[88]

The applicability of the stay to acts against property of the estate often turns on difficult questions as to whether the debtor had a property interest at the time the case was filed. Generally, however, even a very limited interest will bring a stay into effect. Thus, the stay may halt even foreclosures, sales of repossessed property, or other transactions which are nearly complete, depending upon the state law as to the debtor's interest.[89] The stay also applies when the debtor has only an equitable or possessory interest, but not a legal interest in the property.[90]

9.3.5 Notice of the Automatic Stay

Effective and early notice to creditors of the existence of the automatic stay is critical for two reasons. First, a creditor without notice may take actions against the debtor or her property, because it is not aware that such actions are precluded. Although these actions are generally void, it may cost the debtor and her advocate substantial time and expense to have these actions reversed. Second, once a creditor has notice, almost any creditor activity in violation of the stay will be illegal and actionable for the debtor.[91]

Creditors do receive official notice of the automatic stay in the notice of the first meeting of creditors.[92] Unfortunately, from the debtor's perspective, this notice is not always adequate for several reasons. The notice is not mailed until weeks after the petition is filed and then it goes only to creditors listed in the schedules or statement. A repossession company or other entity to whom no debt is owed would not be included in these lists. Although the notice mailed to creditors by the court explains the automatic stay to some extent, few unsophisticated creditors who receive it have a clear understanding of all of the acts that are prohibited.

The only solution to this problem, at least as to creditors and others who might violate the stay without prompt, clear notice, is for the debtor's advocate to give immediate additional notice of the stay after the petition is filed.[93] This notice should be sent, if possible, by certified mail, return receipt requested. If time is a critical factor, a telephone call or facsimile preceding the mailed notification may be appropriate.[94]

When time is especially short, such as when a bankruptcy is filed immediately before a scheduled foreclosure sale, a special effort to provide notice should be made. This might include advance notice of the filing to the creditor or the creditor's attorney as long as threatened action cannot be taken early to thwart the debtor's purpose in filing bankruptcy.[95]

If a foreclosure is imminent, the debtor may choose to provide personal notice by sending via facsimile or electronic mail a letter containing the debtor's bankruptcy filing information to the lender's attorney (or trustee if there is a deed of trust). Similarly, appearing at or near the property involved and posting notice of the bankruptcy on the property about to be foreclosed, or providing notice to the clerk or auctioneer at the designated foreclosure site, are additional steps that should be taken if the debtor is unable to

---

88 *In re* Glasply Marine Indus., 971 F.2d 391 (9th Cir. 1992) (stay prohibits creation of new property tax liens after petition filed); *In re* Parr Meadows Racing Ass'n, 880 F.2d 1540 (2d Cir. 1989); *In re* Hunter's Run Ltd. P'ship, 875 F.2d 1425 (9th Cir. 1989); *In re* Brooks, 871 F.2d 89 (9th Cir. 1989) (creditor cannot re-record deed after bankruptcy to perfect by changing incorrect property description). *But see In re* Knightsbridge Dev. Co., 884 F.2d 145 (4th Cir. 1989) (creditor did not violate stay by amending its *lis pendens* post-petition); *In re* Morton, 866 F.2d 561 (2d Cir. 1989) (provision does not preclude actions to renew or extend existing liens).

Perfection of certain types of liens is permitted under 11 U.S.C. § 362(b)(3). Equibank v. Wheeling Pittsburgh Steel, 884 F.2d 80 (3d Cir. 1989) (application of § 362(b)(3)).

89 Jordan-Starr v. Norwest Bank-Region VIII, 163 B.R. 838 (D. Colo. 1994) (debtor's right to redeem properly repossessed vehicle was property of the estate as it constituted an equitable interest in the vehicle); *In re* Jenkins, 19 B.R. 105 (D. Colo. 1982) (debtors retained interest in property subject to deed of trust foreclosure until redemption period had run); *In re* Cooper, 273 B.R. 297 (Bankr. D.D.C. 2002) (resale of debtor's property after first foreclosure sale purchaser failed to comply with terms of sale was stayed by bankruptcy petition filed before resale occurred because debtor had right of redemption); *In re* Evans, 22 B.R. 608 (Bankr. D. Neb. 1982) (debtor retained interest in pawned goods during redemption period). *See* Fish Mkt. Nominee Corp. v. Pelofsky, 72 F.3d 4 (1st Cir. 1995) (stay prevented state court order terminating debtor's right of redemption during bankruptcy case); *In re* Garber, 129 B.R. 323 (Bankr. D.R.I. 1991) (state law right of redemption comes into the estate precluding sale of seized property by creditor).

90 *In re* Sielaff, 164 B.R. 560 (Bankr. W.D. Mich. 1994) (debtor had equitable interest which was included in property of the estate and protected by automatic stay, in automobile which he drove and on which he had made the majority of payments, notwithstanding debtor's father had signed credit application and installment contract and was listed owner on vehicle's title). *See also In re* Di Giorgio, 200 B.R. 664 (C.D. Cal. 1996) (declaring unconstitutional state statute which permitted execution on writ of possession despite tenant's bankruptcy filing).

91 *See* National Consumer Law Center, Consumer Bankruptcy Law and Practice § 9.6 (9th ed. 2009).

92 Official Bankruptcy Form 9.

93 The notice should be given after filing. Pre-petition notice of the intention to file may not suffice. *In re* Flack, 239 B.R. 155 (Bankr. S.D. Ohio 1999).

94 *In re* Cepero, 226 B.R. 595 (Bankr. S.D. Ohio 1998) (verbal notice sufficient to make failure to return repossessed automobile willful violation of stay); *In re* Coons, 123 B.R. 649 (Bankr. N.D. Okla. 1991) (phone call from debtor's attorney to creditor is sufficient notice of stay).

95 Advance notice might also provide a later basis to challenge unnecessary costs, such as an auctioneer's fee for a canceled sale. Early notice of a bankruptcy case should cause the creditor to eliminate any avoidable costs related to a stayed proceeding or sale in order to minimize the claim which will later be filed in the case.

confirm that the sale has been canceled. If any of these latter actions are taken, a witness is helpful in the event of a later case based on a creditor's violation of the stay.

Notice provided by the debtor or her advocate can be much more specific than the official notice, tailored to the action the recipient is likely to take. If appropriate, the notice can advise that the debtor will seek damages and attorney fees based on contempt and an unfair practices claim in the event that the stay is violated.[96]

Of course, the stay is applicable regardless of whether the creditor has actual notice of the filing. Actions taken in violation of the stay can be set aside whether or not the creditor had notice of the stay prior to taking action.[97] The purpose of giving notice then is actually twofold.

The 2005 Act adds complicated and confusing notice requirements with which both debtors and courts must comply based on a creditor's pre-petition request to the debtor,[98] or post-petition request to the court[99] for notice at a specified address. These amendments provide that notice given to a creditor other than in accordance with 11 U.S.C. § 342 is not "effective notice" unless "brought to the attention of" the creditor.[100] For reasons discussed more fully at § 9.6.3.2 of NCLC's *Consumer Bankruptcy Law and Practice* (9th ed. 2009), many notices given directly by a debtor as discussed above, especially those provided early in the case, are not subject to the new notice requirements because they are not notices required by the Bankruptcy Code or Rules, court order, or other applicable laws.[101] In addition, the debtor may be able to establish that a nonconforming notice is nevertheless "effective" because it has been "brought to the attention of" the creditor.[102]

In any event, the only apparent relevance of lack of "effective notice" based on the 2005 amendments is that no "monetary penalty" can be imposed on a creditor for violation of the section 362 automatic stay or the section 542 and 543 turnover requirements if the creditor has not received "effective notice" of the order for relief.[103] This provision does not affect the discharge of a debt or violations of the discharge injunction. Nor does it preclude other remedies, such as claims for actual damages and attorney fees, or remedies against other entities, such as a creditor's attorney.[104]

96 *See* National Consumer Law Center, Consumer Bankruptcy Law and Practice Appx. G.3, Form 33 (9th ed. 2009) (sample Letter to Creditors Giving Notice of Stay).

97 *See* National Consumer Law Center, Consumer Bankruptcy Law and Practice § 9.6.1 (9th ed. 2009).

98 11 U.S.C. § 342(c)(2).

99 11 U.S.C. § 342(e), (f).

100 11 U.S.C. § 342(g).

101 11 U.S.C. § 342(c).

102 *See* National Consumer Law Center, Consumer Bankruptcy Law and Practice § 9.6.3.3 (9th ed. 2009).

103 11 U.S.C. § 342(g)(2).

104 *See* National Consumer Law Center, Consumer Bankruptcy Law and Practice § 9.6.2 (9th ed. 2009).

9.3.6 Enforcing the Stay

9.3.6.1 Remedies for Violations of the Stay

It has long been held that actions taken in violation of the stay are void.[105] This means that any actions taken after the bankruptcy filing, including foreclosure sales, repossessions and judgments are without legal effect.[106] This is true whether or not the violation occurred with knowledge of the stay, though there are limited exceptions to this general rule.[107]

Courts have the power to undo violations of the stay by injunction, by avoiding post-petition transfers under 11 U.S.C. § 549,[108] and, if appropriate, by ordering other

105 Kalb v. Feuerstein, 308 U.S. 433, 60 S. Ct. 343, 84 L. Ed. 370 (1940). *See, e.g., In re* Knightsbridge Dev. Co., 884 F.2d 145 (4th Cir. 1989) (arbitration award entered in violation of stay is void); Borg-Warner Acceptance Corp. v. Hall, 685 F.2d 1306 (11th Cir. 1982). *See also In re* Smith, 876 F.2d 524 (6th Cir. 1989); *In re* Holman, 92 B.R. 764 (Bankr. S.D. Ohio 1988). *But see* Riley v. United States, 118 F.3d 1220 (8th Cir. 1997) (responsible party tax assessment was not invalid due to notice of proposed assessment that was issued in violation of stay); Sikes v. Global Marine Co., 881 F.2d 176 (5th Cir. 1989) (court has power to annul stay to ratify post-petition filing of personal injury case against debtor); Matthews v. Rosene, 739 F.2d 249 (7th Cir. 1984) (when debtor inexcusably and unreasonably delayed contempt petition for almost three years, ordinary rule that orders issued in violation of stay are void would not be applied due to laches); *In re* Schwartz, 119 B.R. 207 (B.A.P. 9th Cir. 1990) (failure to challenge tax assessment made in violation of the stay during case in which stay violation occurred precludes debtor from challenging the assessment as void in a later case; assessment was not void, but only voidable).

106 *E.g., In re* Shamblin, 878 F.2d 324 (9th Cir. 1989) (tax sale held in violation of the stay is void); *In re* Ward, 837 F.2d 124 (3d Cir. 1988) (foreclosure sale occurring in violation of the stay is void). *See also* Lampe v. Xouth, Inc., 952 F.2d 697 (3d Cir. 1991) (legal action commenced in violation of the stay is void and cannot be referred to the bankruptcy court). *But see* Easley v. Pettibone Michigan Corp., 990 F.2d 905 (6th Cir. 1993) (actions in violation of stay are voidable and shall be voided absent limited equitable circumstances).

107 *E.g., In re* Smith, 876 F.2d 524 (6th Cir. 1989) (post-petition sale of repossessed car is void even though bank had no notice of stay; debtor found not to have remained "stealthily silent"); Zestee Foods, Inc. v. Phillips Foods Corp., 536 F.2d 334 (10th Cir. 1976). *See also In re* Mauck, 287 B.R. 219 (Bankr. E.D. Mo. 2002) (notice to mortgage servicing agent at payment address sufficient to render later notice of foreclosure a willful violation by both servicing agent and mortgage holder). *See generally* Kennedy, The Automatic Stay in Bankruptcy, 11 U. Mich. J.L. Reform 177 (1978).

108 *See* National Consumer Law Center, Consumer Bankruptcy Law and Practice § 10.4.2.6.6 (9th ed. 2009) (discussion of that section).

However, under § 549(c) a debtor or trustee may not be able to avoid a transfer of real property to a good faith purchaser without knowledge of the bankruptcy and for fair equivalent value, unless a copy or notice of the bankruptcy petition has been filed in the county recording office before the transfer has

statutory and equitable remedies as discussed below. Numerous courts have held, for example, that post-petition credit union deductions or repossessed property must be returned.[109] In most jurisdictions, unsold repossessed property must be returned even if the repossession occurred pre-petition.[110] Even in jurisdictions that do not follow this rule, property must generally be returned upon provision of adequate protection by the debtor.[111]

The Bankruptcy Code contains a specific cause of action against a creditor who causes injury to an individual[112] by a willful violation of the stay.[113] A willful violation is one committed knowingly; no malice need be shown.[114] Even when a violation begins innocently, refusal to rectify it after notice of the case renders it willful.[115] For example, courts have held that failure to return an automobile repossessed pre-petition (or post-petition without notice of the stay), is a willful violation once notice of the stay is given.[116] Simi-

become so far perfected that it could not be overturned by bona fide purchaser. *Compare In re* McGowan, 19 B.R. 952 (Bankr. E.D. Pa. 1982) (sale completed and therefore valid) *with In re* Ward, 837 F.2d 124 (3d Cir. 1988) (sale not perfected and therefore not within exception). *See also* 40235 Wash. St. Corp. v. Lusardi, 329 F.3d 1076 (9th Cir. 2003) (§ 549(c) does not create exception to protect transfers that are void under § 362(a)).

109 *In re* Smith, 876 F.2d 524 (6th Cir. 1989) (post-petition sale of repossessed car is void); *In re* Hellums, 772 F.2d 379 (7th Cir. 1985) (post-petition payroll deductions must be returned); *In re* Taylor, 7 B.R. 506 (E.D. Pa. 1980); *In re* Putnam, 167 B.R. 737 (Bankr. D.N.H. 1994) (post-petition repossession without notice of stay); *In re* Brooks, 132 B.R. 29 (Bankr. W.D. Mo. 1991) (post-petition payroll deductions); *In re* Fry, 122 B.R. 427 (Bankr. N.D. Okla. 1990) ($25,000 in punitive damages awarded for failure to return repossessed manufactured home); *In re* Miller, 10 B.R. 778 (Bankr. D. Md. 1981); *In re* Newman, 1 B.R. 428 (Bankr. E.D. Pa. 1979).

110 Thompson v. GMAC, L.L.C., 566 F.3d 699 (7th Cir. Ill. 2009) (refusal to return car that was repossessed pre-petition is violation of stay); *In re* Rozier, 376 F.3d 1323 (11th Cir. 2004), *relying upon answer to certified question*, Motors Acceptance Corp. v. Rozier, 278 Ga. 52, 597 S.E.2d 367 (Ga. 2004) (repossession did not terminate debtor's interest under Georgia law); *In re* Moffett, 356 F.3d 518 (4th Cir. 2004) (no termination of debtor's interest under Virginia law); *In re* Knaus, 889 F.2d 773 (8th Cir. 1989) (property seized pre-petition must be returned because the automatic stay prohibits acts to "exercise control over property of the estate"; failure to return it constitutes an actionable violation of the stay); *In re* Sharon, 234 B.R. 676 (B.A.P. 6th Cir. 1999); *In re* Colortran Inc., 210 B.R. 823 (B.A.P. 9th Cir. 1997); *In re* Abrams, 127 B.R. 239 (B.A.P. 9th Cir. 1991); GMAC v. Ryan, 183 B.R. 288 (M.D. Fla. 1995); *In re* Sanders, 291 B.R. 97 (Bankr. E.D. Mich. 2003); *In re* Robinson, 285 B.R. 732 (Bankr. W.D. Okla. 2002); *In re* Greene, 248 B.R. 583 (Bankr. N.D. Ala. 2000); *In re* Berscheit, 223 B.R. 579 (Bankr. D. Wyo. 1998) (adequate protection not required as a prerequisite to turnover); Turner v. Dekalb Bank, 209 B.R. 558 (Bankr. N.D. Ala. 1997) (chapter 13 debtor retained property rights in vehicle repossessed pre-petition); *In re* Holman, 92 B.R. 764 (Bankr. S.D. Ohio 1988). *See also In re* Del Mission Ltd., 98 F.3d 1147 (9th Cir. 1996) (failure to turn over property of the estate is a violation of the stay). *But see In re* Lewis, 137 F.3d 1280 (11th Cir. 1998) (property need not be returned because under Alabama law, debtor no longer has possessory right or title to an automobile after repossession; only a right of redemption comes into the estate).

111 *In re* Brown, 237 B.R. 316 (Bankr. E.D. Va. 1999) (while declining to determine whether adequate protection is required, court notes that plan proposing to pay claim in full together with proof of insurance is sufficient to constitute adequate protection); *In re* Nash, 228 B.R. 669 (Bankr. N.D. Ill. 1999) (creditor could retain automobile; adequate protection required as a prerequisite to turnover); *In re* Fitch, 217 B.R. 286 (Bankr. C.D. Cal. 1998); *In re* Young, 193 B.R. 620 (Bankr. D.D.C. 1996) (section 362(a)(3) does not require the return of automobile repossessed pre-petition absent provision of adequate protection); *In re* Richardson, 135 B.R. 256 (Bankr. E.D. Tex. 1992) (section 362(a)(3) does not require the return of automobile repossessed pre-petition). *See generally* National Consumer Law Center, Repossessions § 7.3 (6th ed. 2005 and Supp.) (further discussion of turnover).

112 Several courts have held that use of the term "individual" in the statute does not preclude an award of damages to a corporate debtor. *E.g., In re* Chateaugay Corp., 112 B.R. 526 (S.D.N.Y. 1990); *In re* Bair Island Marina & Office Ctr., 116 B.R. 180 (Bankr. N.D. Cal. 1990).

113 11 U.S.C. § 362(k) (formerly § 362(h)). *See* Pettitt v. Baker, 876 F.2d 456 (5th Cir. 1989).

114 *See In re* Lansdale Family Restaurants, Inc., 977 F.2d 826 (3d Cir. 1992) (willfulness does not require an intent to violate the stay, it requires only that acts which violate the stay be intentional acts); *In re* Ketelsen, 880 F.2d 990 (8th Cir. 1989); *In re* Bloom, 875 F.2d 224 (9th Cir. 1989); Haile v. New York State Higher Educ. Servs. Corp., 90 B.R. 51 (W.D.N.Y. 1988); *In re* Brooks, 207 B.R. 738 (Bankr. N.D. Fla. 1997) (creditor willfully violated automatic stay by requiring debtor to retrieve pre-petition repossessed vehicle forty miles away from where it was repossessed; held that creditor retained vehicle for unreasonable period of time where five days elapsed from the time of notice of bankruptcy until debtors received vehicle); *In re* Coons, 123 B.R. 649 (Bankr. N.D. Okla. 1991) (knowledge of bankruptcy case makes action taken by creditor willful). *Cf.* 11 U.S.C. § 523(a)(6) (referring to willful and malicious acts); *In re* Lafanette, 208 B.R. 394 (Bankr. W.D. La. 1996) (IRS did not willfully violate stay when it diverted debtor's tax refund to child support agency, because IRS had no notice of bankruptcy case).

115 *In re* Abrams, 127 B.R. 239 (B.A.P. 9th Cir. 1991) (retention of repossessed automobile after receiving notice of the stay is willful); Carr v. Sec. Sav. & Loan Ass'n, 130 B.R. 434 (D.N.J. 1991) (refusal to return repossessed automobile); *In re* Brooks, 132 B.R. 29 (Bankr. W.D. Mo. 1991) (refusal to return post-petition payroll deductions); *In re* Holman, 92 B.R. 764 (Bankr. S.D. Ohio 1988); *In re* Maas, 69 B.R. 245 (Bankr. M.D. Fla. 1986); *In re* Stephen W. Grosse, P.C., 84 B.R. 377 (Bankr. E.D. Pa. 1988), *aff'd*, 96 B.R. 29 (E.D. Pa.), *aff'd*, 879 F.2d 857 (3d Cir. 1989) (table).

116 *See In re* Knaus, 889 F.2d 773 (8th Cir. 1989) (failure to return, pursuant to § 542, property seized pre-petition after receipt of notice of the stay constitutes a willful violation of the stay); Motors Acceptance Corp. v. Rozier, 290 B.R. 910 (M.D. Ga. 2003), *aff'd*, 376 F.3d 1323 (11th Cir. 2004) (court found that creditor was in contempt of automatic stay); *In re* Rutherford, 329 B.R. 886 (Bankr. N.D. Ga. 2005) (debtor may recover actual damages, including attorney fees for filing turnover complaint, but not punitive damages); *In re* Ryan, 183 B.R. 288 (M.D. Fla. 1993) (willful violation in not returning vehicle seized pre-petition upon receipt of notice of stay); *In re* Cepero,

larly, a willful violation occurs when a creditor fails to act affirmatively to prevent an action prohibited by the stay, e.g., by failing to prevent the sheriff from selling a property post-petition at sheriff sale.[117] The same theory would apply to failing to call off the repo man.

Section 362(k)(1) provides for actual damages,[118] costs and attorney fees[119] as well as, in appropriate cases, punitive damages.[120] For damages to be available, the debtor must show that the creditor received notice of the stay.[121] Amendments to the Bankruptcy Code made by the 2005 Act provide that a "monetary penalty" may not be imposed on a creditor under section 362(k) for violation of the stay if the creditor has not received "effective notice" of the order for relief as provided under section 342.[122] This provision appears to preclude only the recovery of punitive damages under section 362(k)(1), so actual damages or other relief that is not a monetary penalty should still be recoverable.[123] This limitation also applies only to a creditor who has not received effective notice, not others who may have violated the stay such as the creditor's attorney or a repossessions company.

Amendments made by the 2005 Act also provide that if a violation of the stay is based on an action taken by a creditor in the good faith belief that the stay had been terminated as

---

226 B.R. 595 (Bankr. S.D. Ohio 1998); *In re* Belcher, 189 B.R. 16 (Bankr. S.D. Fla. 1995); *In re* Putnam, 167 B.R. 737 (Bankr. D.N.H. 1994) (post-petition repossession without notice of stay is rendered willful upon failure to return property after receipt of notice); *In re* Holman, 92 B.R. 764 (Bankr. S.D. Ohio 1988) (willful violation in failure to return auto seized post-petition without notice of the stay once notice is received). *See also In re* Diviney, 211 B.R. 951 (Bankr. N.D. Okla. 1997) (compensatory damages and $40,000 in punitive damages awarded when lender failed to return repossessed automobile after the dismissal of debtors' chapter 13 case was vacated). *But see In re* Barringer, 244 B.R. 402 (Bankr. E.D. Mich. 1999) (passive retention of lawfully repossessed automobile does not constitute violation of stay).

117 *In re* Galmore, 390 B.R. 901 (Bankr. N.D. Ind. 2008) (creditor that failed to request recall of civil bench warrant after notice of bankruptcy willfully violated stay); *In re* Mims, 209 B.R. 746 (Bankr. M.D. Fla. 1997) (creditor had duty to dismiss garnishment proceeding after bankruptcy filed); *In re* Sams, 106 B.R. 485 (Bankr. S.D. Ohio 1989).

118 *In re* See, 301 B.R. 549 (Bankr. N.D. Iowa 2003) (debtor awarded actual damages consisting of lost wages and travel expenses); *In re* Brown, 237 B.R. 316 (Bankr. E.D. Va. 1999) (compensatory and punitive damage award satisfied by court ordered cancellation of debt owed on repossessed truck); *In re* Seal, 192 B.R. 442 (Bankr. W.D. Mich. 1996) (debtor can recover damages from payments due to the creditor in other chapter 13 cases if necessary).

An award of actual damages under § 362(k)(1) includes damages for emotional distress. *In re* Dawson, 390 F.3d 1139 (9th Cir. 2004); Fleet Mortgage Group, Inc. v. Kaneb, 196 F.3d 265 (1st Cir. 1999); *In re* Covington, 256 B.R. 463 (Bankr. D.S.C. 2000) (emotional distress damages awarded without need for medical testimony). *But see* Aiello v. Providian Fin. Corp., 239 F.3d 876 (7th Cir. 2001) (debtor could not recover for "purely emotional injury" when there were no other damages); *In re* Stinson, 295 B.R. 109 (B.A.P. 9th Cir. 2003) (to be entitled to emotional distress damages, debtor must have suffered significant economic loss caused by the willful violation of the automatic stay).

119 Consejo de Titulares del Condominio Carolina Court Apts., 405 B.R. 24, 26 (B.A.P. 1st Cir. 2009) (fees should not be reduced simply because damages are small); *In re* Roman, 283 B.R. 1 (B.A.P. 9th Cir. 2002) (attorney fees allowed for work necessary to obtain or protect an award under former § 362(h) on appeal); *In re* Walsh, 208 B.R. 949 (Bankr. N.D. Cal. 1997) (debtor also entitled to attorney fees for work done on appeal).

120 *See, e.g., In re* Bloom, 875 F.2d 224 (9th Cir. 1989) (punitive damages upheld on appeal when creditor continued to violate stay after being warned by debtor's attorney that his conduct violated the stay); *In re* Ocasio, 272 B.R. 815 (B.A.P. 1st Cir. 2002) (ratio of 9-to-1 between punitive damages and compensatory damages was not excessive); *In re* Smith, 296 B.R. 46 (Bankr. M.D. Ala. 2003) ($25,000 punitive damages assessed against seller for repossession of manufactured home while debtor was physically inside it); *In re* Kortz, 283 B.R. 706 (Bankr. N.D. Ohio 2002) ($51,000 punitive damages and equitable subordination of mortgage to remedy mortgage company's "belligerent" violations of stay); *In re* Shade, 261 B.R. 213 (Bankr. C.D. Ill. 2001) (punitive damages may be awarded even if there are no compensatory damages); *In re* Meeks, 260 B.R. 46 (Bankr. M.D. Fla. 2000) ($35,000 in punitive damages awarded when a creditor experienced in bankruptcy matters repossessed debtor's automobile despite having notice of automatic stay); *In re* Baker, 140 B.R. 88 (D. Vt. 1992) ($10,000 punitive damages for repossession of debtor's car in violation of stay); *In re* McCormack, 203 B.R. 521 (Bankr. D.N.H. 1996) (punitive damages of $10,000 assessed against mortgage company that repeatedly sent statements and demands to chapter 13 debtor for fees that had been disallowed by court); *In re* Timbs, 178 B.R. 989 (Bankr. E.D. Tenn. 1994) (punitive damages awarded against attorney who failed to take affirmative steps to end wage garnishment; actions were willful even if attorney had not understood the law); *In re* Markey, 144 B.R. 738 (Bankr. S.D. Mich. 1992) ($12,500 punitive damages awarded against attorney who filed foreclosure action in violation of stay); *In re* Fry, 122 B.R. 427 (Bankr. N.D. Okla. 1990) (punitive damages of $25,000 awarded for repossession of manufactured home in knowing violation of stay); *In re* Carrigan, 109 B.R. 167 (Bankr. W.D.N.C. 1989) ($5000 in punitive damages and disallowance of arrearage claim awarded against secured creditor who "visited" debtors at 9:00 p.m. on Sunday night to "discuss" a debt in violation of the stay); Mercer v. D.E.F., Inc., 48 B.R. 562 (Bankr. D. Minn. 1985) ($5000 punitive damages awarded against appliance rental company for repossession in violation of stay). *See also* Nissan Motors Acceptance Corp. v. Baker, 239 B.R. 484 (N.D. Tex. 1999) (debtors had no obligation to mitigate damages as a prerequisite to obtaining actual or punitive damages for creditor's retention of repossessed automobile).

121 *See* Price v. Rochford, 947 F.2d 829 (7th Cir. 1991) (commencing lawsuits without notice of the stay is not actionable under § 362); *In re* Abt, 4 B.R. 527 (Bankr. E.D. Pa. 1980) (repossession of automobile by several creditors without notice of stay was not contempt). *See generally* National Consumer Law Center, Consumer Bankruptcy Law and Practice § 9.5 (9th ed. 2009) (further discussion of notice of the stay).

122 11 U.S.C. § 342(g)(2); § 9.3.5, *supra*.

123 *See* § 9.3.5, *supra*.

to the debtor under section 362(h),[124] any recovery under section 362(k)(1) shall be limited to actual damages.[125] As provided in section 362(k)(1), actual damages may include an award of emotional distress damages, attorney fees and costs.[126]

In addition to remedies under section 362(k)(1), the debtor also has remedies for violation of the automatic stay as contempt of a court order.[127] The legislative history of section 362(k) (formerly section 362(h)) makes clear that Congress was granting an additional remedy to debtors beyond those already in existence.[128] The sanctions that may be imposed for contempt are similar to those available under section 362(k), except that punitive damages are not available.[129] Remedies for contempt may include fines and attorney fees,[130] as well as compensatory damages.[131]

The duty is on creditors, especially those regularly involved with bankruptcy cases, to establish procedures that assure compliance with the stay, in order that bankruptcy cases proceed smoothly.[132] Indeed, if either a creditor or its collection agent has knowledge of the case, the creditor may be held liable for any post-filing collection attempts by its agent.[133] Additionally, reliance in good faith on the advice of an attorney that actions are not barred by the stay is no defense,[134] neither is "computer error" a valid defense.[135]

Note also that the same actions which can be penalized as violations of the automatic stay might also be unfair trade practices under state law.[136] In some cases it may be a good idea to seek this remedy in the alternative because of the availability of enhanced damages.

9.3.6.2 Violations of the Stay by Government Entities

Another issue which unfortunately often arises are the remedies available against government entities for violations of the stay. If the stay is violated through state action as defined for purposes of the civil rights laws,[137] remedies

124 Section 362(h) provides for the termination of the stay as to personal property based on the debtor's failure to take certain action related to the statement on intention under section 521(a)(2). *See* § 9.9.2, *infra*; National Consumer Law Center, Consumer Bankruptcy Law and Practice § 11.4.2.3 (9th ed. 2009).

125 11 U.S.C. § 362(k)(2).

126 *See* note 119, *supra*.

127 It is quite clear that a violation of the stay's prohibitions constitutes contempt of court. *In re* Del Mission Ltd., 98 F.3d 1147 (9th Cir. 1996) (government failure to turn over property of the estate is a violation of the stay justifying contempt remedy); Jove Eng'g Inc. v. Internal Revenue Serv., 92 F.3d 1539 (11th Cir. 1996) (contempt remedy available when § 362(h) not applicable); *In re* Carter, 691 F.2d 390 (8th Cir. 1982); Fid. Mortgage Investors v. Camelia Builders, 550 F.2d 47 (2d Cir. 1976).

Contempt proceedings in bankruptcy cases are governed by Fed. R. Bankr. P. 9020. *See* National Consumer Law Center, Consumer Bankruptcy Law and Practice § 14.2.8 (9th ed. 2009). *See also In re* Del Mission Ltd., 98 F.3d 1147 (9th Cir. 1996) (state found in contempt for failing to promptly return taxes it had been ordered to repay debtor after violation of stay).

128 130 Cong. Rec. H1942 (daily ed. Mar. 26, 1984) (remarks of Rep. Rodino). *See also In re* Skinner, 917 F.2d 444 (10th Cir. 1990); *In re* Wagner, 74 B.R. 898 (Bankr. E.D. Pa. 1987).

129 *In re* Dyer, 322 F.3d 1178 (9th Cir. 2003) (punitive penalties not available for civil contempt).

130 *See* Hubbard v. Fleet Mortgage Co., 810 F.2d 778 (8th Cir. 1987) (upholding imposition of $7649 fine, plus attorney fees, plus cancellation of mortgage); Borg-Warner Acceptance Corp. v. Hall, 685 F.2d 1306 (11th Cir. 1982); *In re* Gustafson, 111 B.R. 282 (B.A.P. 9th Cir. 1990) (attorney fees awarded to recompense debtor for action necessary to obtain school transcript withheld in violation of stay); *In re* Newlin, 27 B.R. 781 (E.D. Pa. 1983); *In re* Stephen W. Grosse, P.C., 84 B.R. 377 (Bankr. E.D. Pa. 1988), *aff'd*, 96 B.R. 29 (E.D. Pa.), *aff'd*, 879 F.2d 857 (3d Cir. 1989) (table).

131 *In re* Zartun, 30 B.R. 543 (B.A.P. 9th Cir. 1983); *In re* Batla, 16 B.R. 392 (Bankr. N.D. Ga. 1981); *In re* Reed, 11 B.R. 258 (Bankr. D. Utah 1981); Springfield Bank v. Caserta, 10 B.R. 57 (Bankr. S.D. Ohio 1981); *In re* Walker, 7 B.R. 216 (Bankr. D.R.I. 1980).

However, damages may be denied when no notice of the stay is given. *In re* Smith Corset Shops, 696 F.2d 971 (1st Cir. 1982). *See In re* Ketelsen, 880 F.2d 990 (8th Cir. 1989) (no damages proved when FmHA seized the debtor's tax refund in violation of the stay; however attorney fees awarded). *But see In re* Walters, 868 F.2d 665 (4th Cir. 1989) (award for damages for emotional distress resulting from contempt is impermissible).

Disallowance of a secured claim may also be an appropriate sanction. *In re* Carrigan, 109 B.R. 167 (Bankr. W.D.N.C. 1989) (secured creditor's pre-petition arrearage claim of nearly $5000 disallowed and punitive damages awarded). The debtor may wish to argue against such a sanction when the only benefit would be to other unsecured creditors.

132 *In re* Price, 103 B.R. 989 (Bankr. N.D. Ill. 1989) (IRS threat to levy against debtor violates stay even though notice was generated by computer; IRS had no procedures in place to prevent notices from being sent out in violation of the stay); *In re* Stucka, 77 B.R. 777 (Bankr. C.D. Cal. 1987) (failure to adopt procedures to prevent stay violations rendered violations "willful" and "wanton"); *In re* Stalnaker, 5 Bankr. Ct. Dec. (CRR) 203 (Bankr. S.D. Ohio 1978).

133 *In re* Fultz, 18 B.R. 521 (Bankr. E.D. Pa. 1982) (creditor had notice); *In re* Fowler, 16 B.R. 596 (Bankr. S.D. Ohio 1981) (agent's knowledge imputed to creditor).

134 *In re* Taylor, 884 F.2d 478 (9th Cir. 1989).

However, under such circumstances punitive damages may not be available. *In re* Ketelsen, 880 F.2d 990 (8th Cir. 1989).

135 *In re* Campion, 294 B.R. 313 (B.A.P. 9th Cir. 2003) (failure of debt collector's computer to match debtor's name with name in its database did not render violation nonwillful); *In re* Rijos, 263 B.R. 382 (B.A.P. 1st Cir. 2001) (rejecting creditor's "computer did it" defense); *In re* Chateaugay Corp., 112 B.R. 526 (S.D.N.Y. 1990); *In re* McCormack, 203 B.R. 521 (Bankr. D.N.H. 1996) (computer error defense called a "non-starter").

136 *See* Vahlsing v. Commercial Union Ins. Co., 928 F.2d 486 (1st Cir. 1991) (damages for abuse of process, negligence and other theories unsuccessfully sought); *In re* Aponte, 82 B.R. 738 (Bankr. E.D. Pa. 1988).

Relief under other theories should also be considered.

137 Judges and similar officials, however, have immunity for their violations of the stay. *See In re* 1736 18th Street, N.W., 97 B.R. 121 (Bankr. D.D.C. 1989) (city rent administrator has judicial

under 42 U.S.C. § 1983 may be available against officials who violate the stay under color of law. This is because a violation of 11 U.S.C. § 362 would be denial of rights secured by federal law.[138] If such an action were successful, then attorney fees would also be proper under the Civil Rights Attorney's Fees Award Act, 42 U.S.C. § 1988.[139]

In light of Supreme Court cases taking a narrow view of the Bankruptcy Code's waiver of sovereign immunity,[140] there was some doubt about whether damages were available against state and federal governmental entities for violating the automatic stay. These questions should be put to rest, with respect to the federal government, by the 1994 amendments to the Bankruptcy Code which include an unambiguous abrogation of sovereign immunity as to claims for violations of the automatic stay in amended 11 U.S.C. § 106(a).[141]

Although the same amendment attempted to abrogate states' Eleventh Amendment immunity, the Supreme Court has cast doubt on whether Congress may do so.[142] A few courts have found that section 106 was enacted pursuant to the privileges and immunities clause of the Fourteenth Amendment and is therefore valid,[143] but several appellate courts have found that *Seminole Tribe* invalidates section 106 insofar as it authorizes damage suits against a state.[144]

However, although the Supreme Court has not decided the question of whether Congress has validly abrogated state immunity in section 106, the Court has clearly held that the Eleventh Amendment does not apply to certain bankruptcy proceedings. Because bankruptcy is an *in rem* matter, affecting the debtor's property, the bankruptcy case itself is not a suit against the state and the discharge of a debt to the state is not barred by the Eleventh Amendment.[145] Similarly, court proceedings about the debtor's property, such as proceedings to avoid liens on the property or to compel turnover of preferential transfers, are not suits against the state that implicate a state's sovereign immunity because they are ancillary to a bankruptcy court's *in rem* jurisdiction.[146] One court of appeals has held that a proceeding to enforce the automatic stay seeking sanctions against the state for contempt, which may include an award of attorney fees, is the type of proceeding "necessary to effectuate the *in rem* jurisdiction of the bankruptcy court" and not barred by the Eleventh Amendment.[147]

9.3.6.3 Procedure

Although several courts have held that relief under section 362(k) may be available by motion,[148] it may be

immunity for conducting rent proceeding in violation of the stay).

138 Maine v. Thiboutot, 448 U.S. 1, 100 S. Ct. 2502, 65 L. Ed. 2d 555 (1980).

139 *Id. See also* National Consumer Law Center, Consumer Bankruptcy Law and Practice Ch. 15 (9th ed. 2009).

140 United States v. Nordic Vill., 503 U.S. 30, 112 S. Ct. 1011, 117 L. Ed. 2d 191 (1992); Hoffman v. Conn. Dep't of Income Maint., 492 U.S. 96, 109 S. Ct. 2818, 106 L. Ed. 2d 76 (1989).

141 This amendment applies to all cases filed after October 22, 1994. Pub. L. No. 103-394, § 702(a). 11 U.S.C. § 106(a).

However, punitive damages may not be awarded under this provision, and there are limitations on attorney fees, at least against the federal government. *See generally* National Consumer Law Center, Consumer Bankruptcy Law and Practice § 14.3.2.2 (9th ed. 2009).

142 *See* Seminole Tribe of Florida v. Florida, 517 U.S. 44, 116 S. Ct. 1114, 134 L. Ed. 2d 252 (1996).

However, a state that files a claim is generally found to have waived sovereign immunity under 11 U.S.C. § 106(b), at least as to a claim by the debtor arising from the same transaction. *In re* Burke, 146 F.3d 1313 (11th Cir. 1998) (state waived Eleventh Amendment by filing proofs of claim in debtors' cases); *In re* Straight, 143 F.3d 1387 (10th Cir. 1998); *In re* Rose, 187 F.3d 926 (8th Cir. 1999) (state waived Eleventh Amendment protection from being sued to determine dischargeability of student loan by filing claim for student loan debt); *In re* Barrett Ref. Corp., 221 B.R. 795 (Bankr. W.D. Okla. 1998) (state could not undo waiver by withdrawing proof of claim). *See also In re* Platter, 140 F.3d 626 (7th Cir. 1998) (state waived Eleventh Amendment immunity by filing dischargeability complaint); *In re* Innes, 207 B.R. 953 (Bankr. D. Kan. 1997) (state consented to litigation in federal court by signing participation agreement with U.S. Department of Education agreeing to oppose dischargeability complaints). *But see In re* Creative Goldsmiths of Washington, 119 F.3d 1140 (4th Cir. 1997) (Eleventh Amendment immunity not waived by filing unrelated claim).

143 *E.g.*, Hood v. Tenn. Student Assistance Corp., 319 F.3d 755 (6th Cir. 2003), *aff'd on other grounds*, 541 U.S. 440 (2004) (Congress validly abrogated states' sovereign immunity under Constitution's Bankruptcy Clause and Fourteenth Amendment); *In re* Headrick, 200 B.R. 963 (Bankr. S.D. Ga. 1996); *In re* S. Star Foods, Inc., 190 B.R. 419 (Bankr. E.D. Okla. 1995).

144 *E.g.*, Nelson v. La Crosse County Dist. Att'y, 301 F.3d 820 (7th Cir. 2002) (Constitution's Bankruptcy Clause not valid authority for abrogating states' sovereign immunity); *In re* Sacred Heart Hosp. of Norristown, 133 F.3d 237 (3d Cir. 1998); *In re* Estate of Fernandez, 123 F.3d 241 (5th Cir. 1997); *In re* Creative Goldsmiths of Wash., 119 F.3d 1140 (4th Cir. 1997); *In re* Martinez, 196 B.R. 225 (D. P.R. 1996).

145 Tenn. Student Assistance Corp. v. Hood, 124 S. Ct. 1905, 158 L. Ed. 2d 764 (2004).

146 Central Virginia Cmty. College v. Katz, 546 U.S. 356, 126 S. Ct. 990 (2006).

147 *In re* Omine, 485 F.3d 1305, 1313–1314 (11th Cir. 2007).

148 Fed. R. Bankr. P. 9014. *See In re* Zumbrun, 88 B.R. 250 (B.A.P. 9th Cir. 1988); *In re* Karsh Travel, Inc., 102 B.R. 778, 780–781 (N.D. Cal. 1989); *In re* Hooker Invs., 116 B.R. 375, 378 (Bankr. S.D.N.Y. 1990); *In re* Forty-Five Fifty-Five, Inc., 111 B.R. 920, 922–923 (Bankr. D. Mont. 1990). *See also In re* Rijos, 263 B.R. 382 (B.A.P. 1st Cir. 2001) (debtors denied due process when bankruptcy court denied motion to stay sanctions without conducting evidentiary hearing); *In re* Elegant Concepts Ltd., 67 B.R. 914, 917 (Bankr. E.D.N.Y. 1986) (court, approving procedure of filing motion for sanctions, suggested that adversary proceeding might be more appropriate, but noted that adverse party raised no procedural objections and thereby waived any procedural irregularity); *In re* Herbert, 61 B.R. 44, 45 (Bankr. W.D. La. 1986) (as creditor was properly served under Rule

preferable to proceed by complaint pursuant to the adversary rules, especially if injunctive relief or a contempt remedy is sought.[149] This will eliminate any potential issues about the due process rights of the party defending.

In many, if not all cases, careful practice will require seeking statutory remedies together with relief for contempt in the alternative.[150] Expeditious action to protect the debtor's rights is generally advisable, especially if damages may be mitigated, but a remedy is available even after the bankruptcy case is terminated.[151]

9.3.7 Proceedings Seeking Relief from Stay

9.3.7.1 Overview

Another issue that may come up in a bankruptcy case which is filed to address a foreclosure is a motion by the creditor for relief from the automatic stay in order to proceed with the foreclosure process. In some cases the creditor will be seeking permission from the bankruptcy court to proceed with the sale of property which has already been foreclosed. In others, the creditor will seek relief from stay in order to foreclose or otherwise enforce the lien.

The material in this subsection contains basic information about motions for relief from stay and the appropriate debtor response. More information is available in National Consumer Law Center, *Consumer Bankruptcy Law and Practice* § 9.7 (9th ed. 2009).

9.3.7.2 Form of Proceeding

The rules provide that the proper method of proceeding for relief from the automatic stay "shall" be by motion under Rule of Bankruptcy Procedure 9014.[152] Indeed, the stay may not be eliminated without court approval even if the parties agree to relief.[153] The trustee and, if the court orders, other creditors are entitled to notice of any agreement to terminate the stay before it is approved, if a motion for relief from stay was not previously served.[154] For the same reason, a pre-petition agreement by the debtor that the stay will not apply to a particular creditor cannot be enforced.[155]

Rule 9014 specifically provides that no answer is required to a motion, unless specifically ordered by the court.[156] Nonetheless, it is often useful to file an answer in order to frame the issues to be presented as defenses to the motion. Moreover, some courts have adopted local rules requiring a response or grant relief by default in cases in which answers are not filed, despite the clear contrary language of the rules. As Rule 9014 provides only that there be "notice and opportunity for hearing," it is usually wise to file at least a request for a hearing on the motion.[157] Local rules and practices should be checked carefully in this area.

Under extraordinary circumstances, the bankruptcy court may, upon a creditor's petition, grant relief from the automatic stay without providing for notice and a hearing. Such *ex parte* relief may be allowed if the creditor seeking relief can show that it would suffer irreparable damage from the stay before there is an opportunity for notice and a hearing. The bankruptcy rules set forth the standards related to *ex parte* relief.[158]

9014 and creditor failed to raise any procedural objections, motion for sanctions was appropriate, even if, as court suggested, adversary proceeding was more appropriate).

149 Fed. R. Bankr. P. 7001–7087.

150 *See, e.g.*, National Consumer Law Center, Consumer Bankruptcy Law and Practice Appx. G.4, Forms 34, 35, 37 (9th ed. 2009). *See also id.* § 14.2.8 (contempt power of the bankruptcy court).

151 Price v. Rochford, 947 F.2d 829 (7th Cir. 1991); *In re* Davis, 177 B.R. 907 (B.A.P. 9th Cir. 1995). In some instances the case may need to be reopened pursuant to 11 U.S.C. § 350(b).

152 Fed. R. Bankr. P. 4001(a)(1).

Normally this motion should be heard in the bankruptcy court in which the bankruptcy case is pending, although other courts may have concurrent jurisdiction over some of the issues that arise. *In re* Baldwin-United Corp. Litig., 765 F.2d 343 (2d Cir. 1985). *See also* NLT Computer Servs. Corp. v. Capital Computer Sys., Inc., 755 F.2d 1253 (6th Cir. 1985) (fact that monies had been paid into district court registry did not remove them from jurisdiction of bankruptcy court once a bankruptcy was filed).

One court of appeals had held that, at least in some cases in which a motion for relief has been filed, an oral order granting relief from the stay is sufficient, even if it is not memorialized by a subsequent written order. Noli v. Comm'r, 860 F.2d 1521 (9th Cir. 1988).

153 *In re* Fugazy Express, 982 F.2d 769 (2d Cir. 1992).

154 Fed. R. Bankr. P. 4001(d).

155 Farm Credit of Cent. Fla., ACA v. Polk, 160 B.R. 870 (M.D. Fla. 1993). *See also In re* Riley, 188 B.R. 191 (Bankr. D.S.C. 1995) (pre-petition agreement to waive protections of automatic stay could not be enforced after cure of default that gave rise to agreement); *In re* Madison, 184 B.R. 686 (Bankr. E.D. Pa. 1995) (pre-petition agreement not to file a bankruptcy case for 180 days was void because it violated public policy).

156 *In re* Allstar Bldg. Prods., 809 F.2d 1534 (11th Cir. 1987), *rev'd on other grounds*, 834 F.2d 894 (11th Cir. 1987) (en banc). Some courts have local rules or standing orders which require answers to motions for relief from stay. In most other respects, proceedings under Rule 9014 are covered by the same rules as adversary proceedings, which in general conform to the Federal Rules of Civil Procedure. *See* Fed. R. Bankr. P. 9014, 7001–7087.

157 It is, of course, also inappropriate for a court to enter relief from the stay on the basis of an *ex parte* affidavit, except in the limited circumstances described in Fed. R. Bankr. P. 4001(a)(3). *See* First Republicbank Dallas v. Gargyle Corp., 91 B.R. 398 (N.D. Tex. 1988).

158 Fed. R. Bankr. P. 4001(a)(2).

9.3.7.3 Standing of Moving Party to Seek Stay Relief and Indispensable Parties

In a proceeding for relief from the stay, the failure to serve both the debtor and the trustee should lead to a motion to dismiss for lack of an indispensable party.[159] The debtor usually has possession of property and will be a defendant in legal proceedings if the stay is lifted. The trustee is also an indispensable party because the trustee has at least a possible interest in almost every case involving property. Moreover, the Bankruptcy Code provides that the trustee appear and be heard at any hearing that concerns the value of property subject to a lien, a frequent issue in stay litigation.[160] The stay should not automatically expire under 11 U.S.C. § 362(e) until at least thirty days after all proper parties have been joined in the action.

In some cases there may also be questions about the standing of the moving party to seek relief from the automatic stay.[161] Some courts have held that a mortgage servicing company with no beneficial interest in the underlying mortgage did not have standing to file a motion for relief from the stay and that only the holder of the note and mortgage could file such a motion.[162]

As the selling and securitization of mortgages has become commonplace, it has become harder for mortgage holders and servicers to keep track of which party holds the mortgage. Bankruptcy courts have become increasingly aware of such issues and have more frequently denied motions for relief from stay based upon lack of standing.[163] In some instances courts have denied motions for relief when the movant failed to provide true copies of documents establishing assignment of the note.[164] To comply with federal court standing and real party in interest requirements,[165] the creditor must have been assigned the note and have the right to enforce it at the time a motion for relief from the stay is filed.[166]

9.3.7.4 Time Limits for Court Actions

The Bankruptcy Code sets out strict time limits for stay litigation.[167] Section 362(e) provides that there must be a preliminary hearing on a request for relief from the stay within thirty days; if that hearing is not held, the stay is automatically terminated.

If the court at the preliminary hearing finds that there is a "reasonable likelihood that the party opposing relief" from the stay will prevail in the stay litigation, the stay can be continued until a final hearing. This finding may sometimes

---

159 *See* Fed. R. Civ. P. 19; Fed. R. Bankr. P. 7019. *See also* Fed. R. Bankr. P. 9014.

160 11 U.S.C. § 1302.

161 *See* § 4.4, *supra* (more detailed discussion of standing and real party in interest issues).

162 Mortgage Elec. Registration Sys., Inc. v. Medina, 2009 WL 4823387 (D. Nev. Dec. 4, 2009) (MERS cannot be real party in interest because has no concrete interest in debt obligation); *In re* Minbattiwalla, 2010 WL 694166 (Bankr. S.D.N.Y. Mar. 1, 2010) (in addition to establishing rights of the holder, servicer seeking stay relief must show it has authority to act as holder's agent); *In re* Canellas, 2010 WL 571808 (Bankr. M.D. Fla. Feb. 9, 2010) (motion for relief from stay denied after movant produced no evidence of ownership of note; *allonge* dated inconsistently with trust documents); *In re* Lee, 408 B.R. 893 (Bankr. C.D. Cal. 2009) (sanctioning attorney who pursued stay relief motion knowing named party lacked ownership interest in note); *In re* Wells, 407 B.R. 873 (Bankr. N.D. Ohio 2009) (the standing requirements a creditor must meet to file a proof of claim and to seek relief from stay are the same); *In re* Wilhelm, 407 B.R. 392 (Bankr. D. Idaho 2009) (MERS lacked authority to transfer note; stay relief denied); *In re* Jacobson, 402 B.R. 359 (Bankr. W.D. Wash. 2009) (servicer's declaration in support of motion for relief from stay did not establish that it had beneficial interest in note); *In re* Mitchell, 2009 WL 1044368 (Bankr. D. Nev. Mar. 31, 2009) (no evidence MERS had any ownership interest in promissory note such as would make it real party in interest), *aff'd on other grounds,* 2009 WL 5868512 (D. Nev. Dec. 30, 2009) (because MERS cannot comply with court rule requiring participation in settlement negotiations through representative with authority to confer on behalf of true owner, MERS is precluded from filing motion in bankruptcy court); *In re* Fitch, 2009 WL 1514501 (Bankr. N.D. Ohio May 28, 2009) (MERS was never in chain of title for mortgage and note; had no standing); *In re* Sheridan, 2009 WL 631355 (Bankr. D. Idaho Mar. 12, 2009) (MERS failed to show standing to bring motion); *In re* Kang Jin Hwang, 396 B.R. 757 (Bankr. C.D. Cal. 2008) (servicer who is not holder of the note may not seek relief from stay in its own name); *In re* Morgan, 225 B.R. 290 (Bankr. E.D.N.Y. 1998), *vacated on other grounds sub nom., In re* Nunez, 2000 WL 655983 (E.D.N.Y. Mar. 17, 2000).

163 *E.g., In re* Hayes, 393 B.R. 259 (Bankr. D. Mass. 2008) (trustee of securitized trust who submitted documents which failed to establish it was holder of mortgage lacked standing to file stay relief motion or proof of claim); *In re* Maisel, 378 B.R. 19 (Bankr. D. Mass. 2007) (assignee who filed motion before mortgage was assigned to it did not have standing).

164 *In re* Lee, 408 B.R. 893 (Bankr. C.D. Cal. 2009) (attorney sanctioned for pursuing stay relief motion knowing named party lacked ownership interest in note); *In re* Jacobson, 402 B.R. 359 (Bankr. W.D. Wash. 2009) (servicer's declaration did not establish that it had beneficial interest in note); *In re* Kang Jin Hwang, 396 B.R. 757 (Bankr. C.D. Cal. 2008) (servicer who is not holder of the note may not seek relief from stay in its own name); *In re* Vargas, 396 B.R. 511 (Bankr. C.D. Cal. 2008) (evidence by written declaration and from clerical staff testimony not admissible to establish mortgage holder's standing); *In re* Hayes, 393 B.R. 259 (Bankr. D. Mass. 2008). *See also In re* Nosek, 386 B.R. 374 (Bankr. D. Mass. 2008) (imposing sanctions on creditor for misrepresenting status of holder of note during protracted litigation), *aff'd in part, rev'd in part,* 406 B.R. 434 (D. Mass. 2009).

165 *See* Fed. R. Civ. P. 17(a), made applicable in bankruptcy by Fed. R. Bankr. P. 7017.

166 *In re* Maisel, 378 B.R. 19 (Bankr. D. Mass. 2007) (servicer bringing stay relief motion failed to document standing as of time motion filed).

167 *In re* River Hills Apartments Fund, 813 F.2d 702 (5th Cir. 1987). *See also In re* Looney, 823 F.2d 788 (4th Cir. 1987) (overcrowded docket does not excuse failure to meet time limits).

be made without the taking of evidence.[168] But there must be at least an opportunity for the movant to be heard.[169] The hearing must be concluded within thirty days after the preliminary hearing unless the parties consent to an extension or the court finds that an extension is required by "compelling circumstances."[170]

An additional time limit was added by the 2005 Act. If a party in interest files a motion for relief, the stay automatically terminates sixty days after the motion is filed, unless:

- The court decides the motion before that time; or
- The time period is extended by agreement of the parties or by the court for a specific period of time for good cause based on findings of the court.[171]

It is unlikely that this provision will significantly change practice with respect to stay relief motions. Under pre-2005 Act practice, stay motions had normally been decided within sixty days. In the few cases where they had not been, the delay beyond sixty days had usually been based either on an agreement of the parties or for good cause. However, attorneys should be careful not to allow the sixty-day period to run through inadvertence.

Two important points must be remembered with respect to these time limits. First, they apply only to the automatic stay. A judge may always reinstate the stay by order or issue a separate injunction staying certain acts.[172] Second, only that aspect of the creditor's pleading seeking relief from the stay is subject to the time limits. If the creditor's pleading seeks other relief, such as reclamation, which might require a more extensive final determination of rights, a slower pace is permitted for the other proceedings. The time limits may also be waived, either explicitly or implicitly, by the party seeking relief.[173]

9.3.7.5 Grounds for Relief from Stay

The stay may be lifted "for cause"[174] or through a court's exercise of discretion to grant equitable relief to prevent undue harm. Thus, courts may lift stays of litigation affecting the debtor's financial condition or a nondischargeable debt when the debt would clearly be nondischargeable or when proceedings elsewhere have already significantly progressed.[175] But the bankruptcy court may instead decide to determine a dischargeability issue itself before allowing another court to proceed.

Another type of cause for relief from the stay is the failure of a debtor to make current payments on a secured obligation. Generally, if the creditor's interest is adequately protected (as discussed in the next few paragraphs), the stay should not be lifted solely for this reason.[176] Obviously, a creditor's refusal to accept payments or inaccuracies in crediting payments should preclude it from obtaining relief under this theory.[177] However, if the failure to pay is prolonged or the collateral is depreciating, and there is no prospect for cure, a court may decide that there is no purpose in maintaining the stay.

The most common ground creditors allege when seeking relief from the stay is that the creditor has not been provided with "adequate protection" of its interest in the collateral. Adequate protection must give the creditor the "indubitable equivalent" of the creditor's interest in the property.[178]

---

168 Salter v. KDT Indus., 28 B.R. 374 (S.D.N.Y. 1982).

169 *In re* Looney, 823 F.2d 788 (4th Cir. 1987).

170 11 U.S.C. § 362(e)(1).

171 11 U.S.C. § 362(e)(2).

172 *See, e.g., In re* Wedgewood Realty Group, Ltd., 878 F.2d 693 (3d Cir. 1989) (stay can be reimposed on grounds similar to those which would warrant a preliminary injunction); *In re* Williams, 346 B.R. 361 (Bankr. E.D. Pa. 2006) (court may invoke stay under § 105(a) even though debtor did not request stay extension within thirty days of petition as required by § 362(c)(3)(B)); *In re* Kozak Farms, 47 B.R. 399 (W.D. Mo. 1985); *In re* Whitaker, 341 B.R. 336 (Bankr. S.D. Ga. 2006); *In re* Fulghum Constr. Corp., 5 B.R. 53 (Bankr. M.D. Tenn. 1980) (preliminary injunction issued by court prior to automatic expiration of stay prevented order of possession to creditors); *In re* Walker, 3 B.R. 213 (Bankr. W.D. Va. 1980) (stay renewed pursuant to the court's powers under 11 U.S.C. § 105(a) on assumption it had expired due to time limits); *In re* Feimster, 3 B.R. 11 (Bankr. N.D. Ga. 1979).

173 *In re* Alderson, 144 B.R. 332 (Bankr. W.D. La. 1992) (creditor waived benefit of time limits when it set the hearing date beyond thirty days itself and because its motion sought additional relief, abandonment, in addition to relief from stay); *In re* Small, 38 B.R. 143 (Bankr. D. Md. 1984) (party who files discovery requests after the thirty-day period and seeks other relief implicitly waives the thirty-day hearing requirement); *In re* Wilmette Partners, 34 B.R. 958 (Bankr. N.D. Ill. 1983).

174 11 U.S.C. § 362(d)(1).

175 *See, e.g., In re* Holtkamp, 669 F.2d 505 (7th Cir. 1982) (personal injury action allowed to go forward when insurer assumed full financial responsibility); *In re* Harris, 4 B.R. 506 (S.D. Fla. 1980), *aff'd in part and rev'd in part*, 7 B.R. 284 (action allowed to proceed after declaratory judgment that judgment for plaintiff would be res judicata on all facts necessary to show nondischargeability).

176 Household Fin. Corp. v. Adams, 27 B.R. 582 (D. Del. 1983); *In re* Phoenix Pipe & Tube, Ltd. P'ship, 154 B.R. 197 (Bankr. E.D. Pa. 1993) (nonpayment alone not sufficient cause for relief from automatic stay; nonpayment combined with lack of equity will result in sufficient cause); *In re* Mannings, 47 B.R. 318 (Bankr. N.D. Ill. 1985); *In re* Davis, 11 B.R. 680 (Bankr. E.D. Pa. 1981). *See In re* Mathews, 208 B.R. 506 (Bankr. N.D. Ill. 1997) (stay relief inappropriate after debtor missed two post-petition mortgage payments, especially given an $8000 equity cushion). *See also In re* Can-Alta Properties, Ltd., 87 B.R. 89 (B.A.P. 9th Cir. 1988) (when creditor is protected by equity, debtor must be given a reasonable opportunity to propose and implement a confirmable plan); *In re* Raymond, 99 B.R. 819 (Bankr. S.D. Ohio 1989) (sporadic post-confirmation payments alone are not ground for relief from stay when no evidence established amount of post-confirmation arrears or value of collateral); *In re* Heath, 79 B.R. 616 (Bankr. E.D. Pa. 1987) (relief denied when creditor protected by equity cushion).

177 *In re* Alvarez, 101 B.R. 176 (B.A.P. 9th Cir. 1989).

178 11 U.S.C. § 361(3).

Adequate protection exists, however, if there is no foreseeable way that the creditor can be economically harmed by continuation of the stay.

The Bankruptcy Code contemplates that the debtor will propose methods of providing adequate protection that will satisfy the creditor. Adequate protection is defined in the Bankruptcy Code only by example.[179] Two examples provided in the Bankruptcy Code are cash payments compensating for the collateral's depreciation and additional or replacement liens.[180] Other possibilities are a cash security deposit, a guarantor, or insurance.[181]

An important example of adequate protection is an equity "cushion" on a secured debt. Consider a $65,000 unpaid balance on a $100,000 home, with $35,000 in equity thus protecting the creditor. Even if the stay is continued for quite a while, the creditor should be able to fully satisfy its claim by foreclosure if necessary when the stay ends.[182] As long as insurance protects against the danger of the collateral's destruction, the creditor's claim is not at risk, unless the collateral will depreciate in value to less than the outstanding debt. With depreciating collateral, such as motor vehicles, it may be necessary to provide for periodic cash payments which will reduce the creditor's claim at least as fast as the value of the collateral decreases.[183] The Supreme Court has held that in determining whether the creditor has "adequate protection," the creditor is not entitled to interest that might have been earned from foreclosing on the collateral.[184] Thus in the example of the $100,000 home, the creditor could not claim the cushion was inadequate because if it immediately foreclosed on the home it could earn more than $35,000 during the course of the stay from investing the proceeds of the foreclosure sale. This lost "opportunity cost" may not be considered.

The court may monitor or reconsider the situation at later dates to assure that the creditor is protected.[185] The creditor, however, is not necessarily entitled to an equity "cushion" as great as it originally bargained for; the court decides what is adequate to protect the creditor's interest, even if the creditor once had better than "adequate" protection.[186]

Perhaps the most useful definition of adequate protection in the foreclosure or repossession context of a depreciating manufactured home is the concept of cash payments to compensate the creditor for the collateral's depreciation, because the debtor will often have little or no equity in the property at issue.[187] It is this provision of the Bankruptcy Code which allows the debtor to propose a plan in a chapter 13 case which, in effect, will cure or pay off the debt on a

---

179 11 U.S.C. § 361 (1981). *See, e.g., In re* Rash, 149 B.R. 430 (Bankr. E.D. Tex. 1993) (factors which demonstrate undersecured creditor is adequately protected are that vehicle is insured and maintained, and that debtor is current in payments); *In re* Anchorage Boat Sales, Inc., 4 B.R. 635 (Bankr. E.D.N.Y. 1980).

The following factors should be taken into consideration in determining what constitutes adequate protection: the resulting harm to the creditor if the stay was continued, the possibility of reorganization and the necessity of the property for effective reorganization, the debtor's equity in the property, and the value the creditor would receive if the stay were lifted.

180 11 U.S.C. § 361(1), (2).

Adequate protection is also required in situations other than stay litigation; however, the discussion here will concentrate on automatic stay cases.

181 The 2005 amendments to the Bankruptcy Code added other requirements for providing adequate assurance to personal property secured creditors in chapter 13 cases, which are discussed in National Consumer Law Center, Consumer Bankruptcy Law and Practice § 12.8.2 (9th ed. 2009).

182 Cases applying this principle include *In re* Schockley Forest Industries, 5 B.R. 160 (N.D. Ga. 1980) (additional security provided collateral which far exceeded claim); *In re* Heath, 79 B.R. 616 (Bankr. E.D. Pa. 1987) (39% equity cushion in property appraised at $32,000); *In re* Breuer, 4 B.R. 499 (Bankr. S.D.N.Y. 1980) (debtor's agreement to cure promptly plus cushion of $21,000 was adequate protection); *In re* Rogers Dev. Corp., 2 B.R. 679 (Bankr. E.D. Va. 1980) (15–20% equity cushion gave adequate protection); *In re* McAloon, 1 B.R. 766 (Bankr. E.D. Pa. 1980) ($20,000 mortgage on $28,000 property was adequate protection). *See also In re* McKillips, 81 B.R. 454 (Bankr. N.D. Ill. 1987) (adequate protection payments necessary when equity cushion eroding, but only to the extent of the erosion).

183 *See* 11 U.S.C. § 361(1), (2). *But see In re* Rose, 21 B.R. 272 (Bankr. D.N.J. 1982) ("bankruptcy default" clause is invalid and unenforceable under both federal and state law; GMAC also waived its right to enforce the clause by accepting installment payments and failing to accelerate after the petition was filed—no relief would be granted from the automatic stay as long as payments and required insurance continue).

184 United Sav. Ass'n v. Timbers of Inwood Forest Assocs. Ltd., 484 U.S. 365, 108 S. Ct. 626, 98 L. Ed. 2d 740 (1988).

185 *See In re* Pitts, 2 B.R. 476 (Bankr. C.D. Cal. 1979) (small equity cushion with court monitoring every few months sufficient to provide adequate protection). *See also In re* Johnson, 10 B.R. 741 (Bankr. E.D. Pa. 1981) (the trustee in chapter 13 case withheld $600 from debtor which was to be turned over to creditor holding a security interest in debtor's automobile if plan were not confirmed; the $600 was held to be adequate to protect creditor's interest pending confirmation or denial of confirmation).

186 *In re* San Clemente Estates, 5 B.R. 605 (Bankr. S.D. Cal. 1980). *See also In re* Ahlers, 794 F.2d 388 (8th Cir. 1986) (considering the extent to which a creditor is entitled to adequate protection for potential delays associated with foreclosure). *But see In re* Lake Tahoe Land Co., 5 B.R. 34 (Bankr. D. Nev. 1980) (dicta stating that for land a 40–50% cushion is necessary); *In re* Tucker, 5 B.R. 180 (Bankr. S.D.N.Y. 1980) ($6500 cushion on $88,000 property inadequate when liens increasing at $25 per day, no payments offered, no insurance in existence, and no successful plan likely).

187 11 U.S.C. § 361(1).

When the creditor's interest in the property is declining because of the accrual of more senior liens, such as property taxes, adequate protection may consist of payments in the amount of the debtor's monthly property tax liability. *In re* Busconi, 135 B.R. 192 (Bankr. D. Mass. 1991). *See In re* Self, 239 B.R. 877 (Bankr. E.D. Tex. 1999) (maintenance of plan payments in chapter 13 together with proof of insurance establish that the creditor holding lien on the debtor's truck is adequately protected).

car or home. As long as the plan payments are being made, the creditor is adequately protected within the meaning of the Bankruptcy Code.

Alternatively, when the debtor cannot afford the necessary payments, it may occasionally be an option to provide an additional or replacement lien which will constitute adequate protection.[188] For example, if the debtor owns unencumbered land upon which a manufactured home is located, a lien on the land may be offered to the secured creditor as adequate protection. Of course, the risk in doing so is that the creditor will then have a security interest in both properties. If payments cannot be made the debtor might lose both. For this reason, the strategy is advisable only in the most extreme cases.

Unless payments on a secured debt are current, in most chapter 7 cases in which liens cannot be avoided,[189] and in which there is no capacity to redeem,[190] there is little likelihood of providing a secured creditor with adequate protection unless there is equity in the property. For this reason, when secured creditors do move for relief from stay in chapter 7 cases, it is usually granted. However, many creditors will not move for relief quickly, if at all, because of the cost and time involved. Even when they do, the debtor may have bought several weeks or months of delay as well as an opportunity to get caught up outside bankruptcy if circumstances have changed.

No matter which type of adequate protection the debtor proposes to provide, proof of sufficient insurance for the collateral is likely to be required.[191] In a chapter 13 case, the 2005 Act requires that a debtor who is retaining personal property subject to a lease or securing a purchase money claim must provide to the lessor or creditor, not later than sixty days after the case is filed, reasonable evidence of the maintenance of any required insurance coverage.[192] The debtor is also required to continue to provide evidence of coverage "for as long as the debtor retains possession of the property."[193]

Finally, debtors' attorneys should point out to the court that the Bankruptcy Code does not require termination of the stay when there is no adequate protection.[194] All that is required is that the stay be modified to provide a time limit for some action or that the stay be conditioned, for example, on monthly payments being made or other risks to the property being eliminated.[195] The bankruptcy court can also allow state court litigation of certain rights to continue while retaining for itself the final issue of possession.

The remaining basis for relief from the automatic stay[196] is available when the debtor has no equity in the property and the property is not necessary for an effective reorganization. This basis does not apply if the property is exempt, because allowing a creditor to proceed could jeopardize the debtor's fresh start.[197]

This basis should not apply at all in chapter 7 cases as no reorganization is contemplated. It is even arguable that this basis for lifting a stay is not applicable to consumer cases at all because the term "reorganization" is used in the Bankruptcy Code only when dealing with corporate bankruptcies. Chapter 13 refers to "rehabilitation" or "adjustment of debts" rather than "reorganization."[198] Nevertheless, the view that chapter 13 cases, at least, were meant to be included within the term "reorganization" has been judicially adopted.[199]

Even if the debtor has no equity in the collateral, the debtor's testimony is usually sufficient to establish that the collateral is necessary for an effective reorganization in chapter 13.[200] Debtors may testify that saving the property is a prime motivation for the plan, thus making retention of the property necessary for an effective reorganization.[201]

9.3.7.6 Debtor Must Conduct Speedy Discovery

Discovery is available concerning motions for relief from stay based on Federal Rule of Civil Procedure 9014. Obtaining discovery on a motion for relief from stay may provide an early opportunity not just to obtain materials related to the motion, but also to obtain other items which may be useful if litigation against the creditor is contemplated.

As a result of the short time limits, discovery must be completed with great speed. The thirty days allowed by the rules to provide requested documents and answers to requests for admissions or interrogatories is always too long unless the parties agree that the stay can continue pending

188 11 U.S.C. § 361(2).

189 *See* § 9.8, *infra*.

190 *See* National Consumer Law Center, Consumer Bankruptcy Law and Practice § 11.5 (9th ed. 2009).

191 *See In re* Self, 239 B.R. 877 (Bankr. E.D. Tex. 1999) (full coverage insurance on debtor's truck is an essential element of adequate protection).

192 11 U.S.C. § 1326(a)(4).

193 *Id.*

194 11 U.S.C. § 362(d).

195 *See, e.g., In re* Polvino, 4 B.R. 677 (Bankr. W.D.N.Y. 1980) (stay modified to continue, provided debtors obtained confirmation of plan, paid back real estate taxes, mortgage payments, and arrearages, and avoided other liens within six weeks).

196 11 U.S.C. § 362(d)(2).

197 The bankruptcy liquidation process, however, could include a release to a secured creditor later in the case if it were in the interest of the estate. 11 U.S.C. § 725.

198 *In re* Feimster, 3 B.R. 11 (Bankr. N.D. Ga. 1979).

199 *In re* Pittman, 8 B.R. 299 (Bankr. D. Colo. 1981); *In re* Zellman, 6 B.R. 497 (Bankr. M.D. Ill. 1980); *In re* McAloon, 1 B.R. 766 (Bankr. E.D. Pa. 1980). *See also In re* Purnell, 92 B.R. 625 (Bankr. E.D. Pa. 1988).

200 *See In re* Stewart, 3 B.R. 24 (Bankr. N.D. Ohio 1980) (property in question could not be necessary to an effective reorganization in a chapter 7 straight bankruptcy liquidation).

201 *See In re* McAloon, 1 B.R. 766 (Bankr. E.D. Pa. 1980) (court found property necessary upon debtor's testimony that he would not remain in chapter 13 if it were lost).

discovery. The most expeditious discovery method may be a deposition with a subpoena *duces tecum* to bring relevant documents. Under the Federal Rules of Civil Procedure, the deposition may be tape recorded. An order for expedited discovery will be needed if any discovery other than by deposition is needed.[202] One positive result of such a motion is often a quick stipulation by the creditor that the hearing (and stay) may be continued beyond the thirty day deadline.

9.3.7.7 Burden of Proof

The Bankruptcy Code provides that the burden of proof in stay litigation is on the party seeking relief from the stay as to the issue of the debtor's equity in property. In other words, if the question of equity is central to whether a creditor's interest is adequately protected from harm due to the stay, the creditor must prove that the debtor lacks sufficient equity to provide adequate protection.[203] The burden of proof for all other issues is on the party opposing relief from the stay.[204] Regardless of which party has the ultimate burden of proof on a motion for relief from stay, the creditor always must carry an initial burden of production on the grounds alleged in the motion. Failure by the creditor to carry the initial burden to show cause should result in a decision for the debtor.[205]

9.3.7.8 Raising Defenses in Response to a Motion for Relief from Stay

A common problem in bankruptcy cases involving disputed secured claims arises when the creditor files an early motion for relief from stay. For example, suppose a chapter 13 debtor has a strip-down, Truth in Lending, or unlawful foreclosure defense (or offset) to a home secured loan. Your client's plan may be to dispute the validity or amount of the creditor's claim. For some clients, having enough income to cure the loan default depends on obtaining a determination that the claim is wholly or partially void. Using consumer defenses in response to a motion for relief is discussed at § 9.6, *infra*.

9.3.7.9 Stays Pending Appeal

It is important to remember that once the automatic stay is terminated by order of the court or otherwise, if an appeal is contemplated, it may be essential to obtain a stay pending appeal. Absent a stay, property may be sold, litigation terminated unfavorably or both.[206] In that event, an appeal may be rendered moot.[207]

9.4 Curing Defaults on Home Loans

9.4.1 Generally

At some point after default, some homeowners resolve their financial problems and are able to resume making their monthly mortgage payments. Others may be able to reprioritize their debts and ongoing expenses in order to free up sufficient funds to make payments. However, a big hurdle for low- and moderate-income homeowners is that most cannot afford to pay their accumulated mortgage arrears in a lump sum.

Under state law, if the mortgage holder will not agree to accept an affordable plan to pay the arrears over time,[208] the homeowner is at risk of foreclosure despite being able to make future payments. However, federal law, under chapter 13 of the Bankruptcy Code, provides a homeowner with an opportunity to impose a plan on the mortgage holder to accept a cure of the default in installments over a reasonable period of time.[209]

If a chapter 13 bankruptcy plan proposes to cure a default, prospective monthly payments must be made starting within thirty days after filing bankruptcy. In addition, the chapter 13 debtor has a right to pay the delinquent amount (the

202 The procedure to obtain expedited or emergency relief is usually set by local rules. The pleading might be termed "Debtor's Request for Expedited Discovery Concerning Motion for Relief From Stay and Request for Expedited Treatment of This Motion." The pleading can seek, in the alternative, an early deadline for discovery responses by the party seeking relief from stay or continuation of the stay past the thirty-day expiration period under 11 U.S.C. § 362(e). Many courts will want to see that the discovery is reasonable and necessary in the circumstances of the case. A creditor will often consent to the relief requested in order to obviate the need for a court appearance on the request for expedited relief.

203 Collier on Bankruptcy ¶ 362.10 (Lawrence P. King, ed., 15th ed. 1992). *But see In re* Gauvin, 24 B.R. 578 (B.A.P. 9th Cir. 1982) (debtor always has burden on adequate protection).

204 11 U.S.C. § 362(g). *See In re* Allstar Bldg. Prods., Inc., 834 F.2d 898 (11th Cir. 1987) (en banc) (party opposing creditor's motion for relief has burden on claim that security interest is not properly perfected).

205 *In re* Sonnax Indus., Inc., 907 F.2d 1280 (2d Cir. 1990). *See In re* Rogers, 239 B.R. 883 (Bankr. E.D. Tex. 1999) (debtor could have obtained judgment at close of creditor's case as it was only her evidence that established that the collateral's value was declining, thereby giving rise to an obligation to establish that her payments constitute adequate protection).

206 *See* Fish Mkt. Nominee Corp. v. Pelofsky, 72 F.3d 4 (1st Cir. 1995) (automatic stay ended immediately upon dismissal of case).

207 *See* Fed. R. Bankr. P. 7062, 8005; Fed. R. Civ. P. 62. *See also In re* Highway Truck Drivers & Helpers Local 107, 888 F.2d 293 (3d Cir. 1989).

208 *See* Ch. 2, *supra*.

209 A general discussion of the operation of chapter 13 of the Bankruptcy Code is beyond the scope of this chapter. All of the details for filing and following through on a case under chapter 13 are included in National Consumer Law Center, Consumer Bankruptcy Law and Practice (9th ed. 2009).

arrearage) in installments over a reasonable period of time.[210] Non-monetary defaults also may be addressed under a plan.[211] The cure provision in section 1322(b)(5) has been construed to cover not only the right to cure pre-petition default amounts but also any arrears which accrue post-petition during the plan.[212]

It is well-established by case law and an amendment to the statute that defaults on home loans may be cured under section 1322(b)(5) even if there has already been an acceleration of the payments by the creditor or a judgment which has caused the entire amount to become due.[213] A homeowner retains the right to cure until the foreclosure sale process is complete under state law.[214] It is also possible to pay off a loan on which a default has occurred even if the mortgage matured before bankruptcy was filed, or if it will mature during the case.[215]

The Code does not define what period of time is "reasonable" for purposes of section 1322(b)(5). This necessarily depends to some extent on the facts and the circumstances of each case. It is not safe to assume that a cure over the entire length of the plan will be found to be reasonable,[216] although in appropriate cases that long a time period has been allowed.[217] It may be possible to obtain a longer period of time to cure by arguing that the time for a plan to run does not begin until confirmation of the plan. Several courts have held that the plan can run for sixty months from that date.[218]

An owner that is not personally liable on the loan note generally has the right to cure a default on the property in chapter 13.[219] This issue arises when property is transferred from the person who obtained the mortgage to another person that files bankruptcy. Often the transfer occurs upon the death of the original mortgagor. In many such cases, a due on sale provision is unenforceable, particularly for interfamily transfers.[220] The transfer itself is not then a default, but the lender may argue that the monetary default cannot be addressed in installments unless the new owner takes on all of the obligations of the mortgage.

If you practice in a jurisdiction that does not allow a non-mortgagor to cure a default, and you cannot persuade the mortgage holder to accept a cure from a non-mortgagor as in its best interests (to avoid foreclosure losses), you may be able to negotiate for a formal mortgage assumption. Upon assumption, there is no doubt that the new mortgagor can use the bankruptcy process to cure the default.

Finally, most courts permit current payments on long-term obligations which are to be cured to be paid by the debtor directly to the lender rather than made through the chapter 13 trustee.[221] These payments are often incorrectly

---

210 11 U.S.C. § 1322(b)(5); *In re* Glenn, 760 F.2d 1428 (6th Cir. 1985); *In re* Terry, 764 F.2d 1558 (11th Cir. 1985); *In re* Clark, 738 F.2d 869 (7th Cir. 1984); Grubbs v. Houston First Am. Sav. Ass'n, 730 F.2d 236 (5th Cir. 1984) (en banc); *In re* Taddeo, 685 F.2d 24 (2d Cir. 1982) (to deprive debtors of the right to cure after an acceleration would undermine the purpose of the cure provisions). *See generally* National Consumer Law Center, Consumer Bankruptcy Law and Practice § 11.6.2 (9th ed. 2009).

211 For example, the plan may provide for purchase of homeowner's insurance to remedy a breach arising from failure to meet insurance requirements under the mortgage and loan note. However, the 2005 Act requires that a debtor who is retaining personal property subject to a lease or securing a purchase money claim must provide to the lessor or creditor, not later than sixty days after the case is filed, reasonable evidence of the maintenance of any required insurance coverage. 11 U.S.C. § 1326(a)(4).

Similarly, the plan may provide for amelioration of physical problems which the lender claims are a material breach of the loan terms. *But see In re* Martin, 176 B.R. 675, 676 (Bankr. D. Conn. 1995) (breach of due-on-sale clause may not be cured in chapter 13).

212 *See In re* Mendoza, 111 F.3d 1264 (5th Cir. 1997); *In re* Hoggle, 12 F.3d 1008 (11th Cir. 1994).

213 11 U.S.C. § 1322(c)(1); *In re* Thompson, 894 F.2d 1227 (10th Cir. 1990); *In re* Metz, 820 F.2d 1495 (9th Cir. 1987).

214 11 U.S.C. § 1322(c)(1). *See* § 9.4.4.3, *infra*, (discussion of curing mortgage defaults after a foreclosure sale is conducted but before the sale process is complete).

215 11 U.S.C. § 1322(c)(2).

Pay-off of secured debts is contemplated under 11 U.S.C. § 1325(a)(5). *See generally* National Consumer Law Center, Consumer Bankruptcy Law and Practice Ch. 11 (9th ed. 2009).

216 *In re* Coleman, 5 B.R. 812 (Bankr. W.D. Ky. 1980) (reasonable time not synonymous with three-year duration of typical plan).

217 *In re* King, 23 B.R. 779 (B.A.P. 9th Cir. 1982) (cure over duration of plan not unreasonable); *In re* Sidelinger, 175 B.R. 115 (Bankr. D. Me. 1994) (thirty-six months to cure mortgage default was reasonable length of time); Philadelphia Sav. Fund Soc'y v. Steward, 16 B.R. 460 (Bankr. E.D. Pa. 1981) (three years, four months); *In re* Johnson, 6 B.R. 34 (Bankr. N.D. Ill. 1980) (three years).

218 *E.g.*, West v. Costen, 826 F.2d 1376 (4th Cir. 1987); *In re* Serna, 193 B.R. 537 (Bankr. D. Ariz. 1996). *See also In re* Black, 78 B.R. 840 (Bankr. S.D. Ohio 1987) (no dismissal when payments extend over sixty-six months, if plan complied with duration requirements of the Code at the time of confirmation).

219 11 U.S.C. § 102(2); *In re* Rosa, 261 B.R. 136 (Bankr. D.N.J. 2001) (debtor could cure default on mortgage on her property even though mortgage was in name of her spouse); *In re* Rutledge, 208 B.R. 624 (Bankr. E.D.N.Y. 1997); *In re* Wilcox, 209 B.R. 181 (Bankr. E.D.N.Y. 1996) (debtor could pay off mortgage on inherited home even though under "reverse mortgage" provisions mortgage came due when debtor's father died). *See In re* Parks, 227 B.R. 20 (Bankr. W.D.N.Y. 1998) (cure would be permitted, but new owner does not have any greater rights than father would have had). *See also* Johnson v. Home State Bank, 501 U.S. 78, 111 S. Ct. 2150, 115 L. Ed. 2d 66 (1991). *But see In re* Lippolis, 228 B.R. 106 (E.D. Pa. 1998) (transfer of property to debtors in contemplation of chapter 13 bankruptcy solely in order to frustrate foreclosure is bad faith which precludes cure).

220 *In re* Trapp, 260 B.R. 267 (Bankr. D.S.C. 2001) (debtor could cure mortgage with due on sale clause on property she had purchased from mortgagors). *See* § 4.9.3, *supra*.

221 If the debtor is the disbursing agent for ongoing mortgage payments, the payments generally are not made through the trustee and the trustee receives no commission for distribution. *In re* Aberegg, 961 F.2d 1307 (7th Cir. 1992); *In re* Donald, 170

referred to as payments "outside the plan." In fact, the debtor is simply serving as the disbursing agent for these payments, which are provided for and paid under the plan. Because the payments on long-term obligations are often higher than on any others, the debtor may seek whenever possible to be the disbursing agent to avoid adding to them the substantial cost of the trustee's percentage fees and expenses (usually 10%).[222]

9.4.2 *Creditors' Attorney Fees and Costs*

Another question is the extent to which creditors may collect attorney fees and costs as part of the amount needed to cure in bankruptcy. The answer will usually turn on the precise language of the contract and on state law. Section 506(b) of the Code provides for collection of such charges only if provided for by the parties' agreement or by applicable state statute.[223] Similarly, for agreements entered into after October 22, 1994, section 1322(e) provides that if a chapter 13 plan proposes to cure a pre-petition default, the amount necessary to cure the default shall be determined by the underlying agreement and applicable nonbankruptcy law.[224] Agreements departing from the standard "American Rule" that each party must bear its own attorney fees are to be strictly construed, especially when drafted by the party trying to collect the fees (usually the creditor).[225]

In addition, many state statutes place significant limitations on fee arrangements[226] or prohibit them entirely.[227] Such state laws are usually read in to any contract to which they are applicable as implied terms. In any case, fees should be allowed under section 506(b) and section 1322(e) only to the extent that they are reasonable, necessary and actually paid.[228] The reasonableness requirement is imposed directly by section 506(b) of the Code and therefore the issue is a question of federal law.[229] The creditor and its counsel have the burden of proving that the fees requested are reasonable.[230]

B.R. 579 (Bankr. S.D. Miss. 1994); *In re* Burkhart, 94 B.R. 724 (Bankr. N.D. Fla. 1988); *In re* Wright, 82 B.R. 422 (Bankr. W.D. Va. 1988). *See In re* Bettger, 105 B.R. 607 (Bankr. D. Or. 1989) (proceeds of sale of real estate could be paid directly to creditors). *See also* Collier on Bankruptcy ¶ 1302.05[1][c] (Lawrence P. King, ed., 15th ed.).

222 *See In re* Land, 96 B.R. 311 (D. Colo. 1989); *In re* Lopez, 350 B.R. 868 (Bankr. C.D. Cal. 2006) (overruling trustee's objection to debtor acting as disbursing agent on current payments), *aff'd*, 372 B.R. 40 (B.A.P. 9th Cir. 2007); *In re* Vigil, 344 B.R. 624 (Bankr. D.N.M. 2006) (debtor need not demonstrate special circumstances to make current payments directly); *In re* Burkhart, 94 B.R. 724 (Bankr. N.D. Fla. 1988).

223 Under section 506(b), such costs are recoverable as part of an allowed secured claim only if the creditor's collateral is greater than the amount claimed.

224 In seeking allowance of a secured claim which includes fees and expenses as part of a cure amount, on agreements entered into after October 22, 1994, a creditor must first satisfy the requirements of § 506(b) and then must also show that the expenses are permitted under § 1322(e). *In re* Evans, 336 B.R. 749 (Bankr. S.D. Ohio 2006) (in adding § 1322(e), Congress did not intend to "supplant but to supplement" the requirements of § 506(b)). *See also In re* Madison, 337 B.R. 99 (Bankr. N.D. Miss. 2006) (section 1322(e) does not permit undersecured creditor to collect attorney fees for preparation and filing of proof of claim; despite "ambiguity" in § 1322(e), § 506 controls as to requested fees). *But see In re* Plant, 288 B.R. 635 (Bankr. D. Mass. 2003) (section 1322(e) rather than § 506(b) determines creditor's entitlement to pre-petition fees in chapter 13 cure situation).

225 *In re* Hatcher, 208 B.R. 959 (B.A.P. 10th Cir. 1997) (creditor had no right, under § 506(b) or otherwise, to post-petition attorney fees in addition to fees provided for in mortgage contract); *In re* Lake, 245 B.R. 282 (Bankr. N.D. Ohio 2000) (fees not permitted under Ohio law as made applicable by section 1322(e)); *In re* Kennedy Mortgage Co., 23 B.R. 466 (Bankr. D.N.J. 1982) (instrument did not allow fees when collection was by way of set-off); *In re* Roberts, 20 B.R. 914 (Bankr. E.D.N.Y. 1981) (participation in chapter 13 proceeding was not included in the attorney fees provision of the mortgage). *See also In re* United Nesco Container Corp., 68 B.R. 970 (Bankr. E.D. Pa. 1987); National Consumer Law Center, Collection Actions Ch. 6 (2008 and Supp.).

226 *In re* Doty, 2008 WL 4104485 (Bankr. D. Mont. Aug. 28, 2008) (applying Montana statute limiting attorney fees to 1% of amount due on obligation at time of default, reducing fees from creditor's claim of $7843.75 to $456.00); *In re* Wilder, 22 B.R. 294 (Bankr. M.D. Ga. 1982) (statutory attorney fees could not be collected for work that could have been performed by non-lawyers).

227 *In re* Bertsch, 17 B.R. 284 (Bankr. N.D. Ohio 1982) (assessment of bank's attorney fees against debtor disallowed as contrary to Ohio public policy).

228 *In re* E. Side Investors, 702 F.2d 214 (11th Cir. 1983); *In re* Brooks, 2007 WL 1114091 (Bankr. D.N.J. Apr. 12, 2007) (reimbursement above amount set by "no look" fee for stay relief motions denied because no itemization of services justifying higher fee was provided and no complex issues were raised in motions); *In re* Porcheddu, 338 B.R. 729 (Bankr. S.D. Tex. 2006) (foreclosure law firm sanctioned for filing false fee applications and misrepresenting that fee statements were based on contemporaneous time records); *In re* Jemps, 330 B.R. 258 (Bankr. D. Wyo. 2005) (attorney "thoroughness to the point of overzealousness" not compensable, even if creditor approves, particularly if creditor is oversecured and services not needed to protect its interest); *In re* Crowley, 293 B.R. 628 (Bankr. D. Vt. 2003) (excessive time spent by creditor attorney in drafting default letters, a modification agreement, and for pursuing new legal theory in stay relief proceeding found to be unnecessary and not recoverable under note); *In re* Staggie, 255 B.R. 48 (Bankr. D. Idaho 2000) (excessive attorney fees sought under § 506(b) disallowed as not reasonable); *In re* Harmon, 72 B.R. 458 (Bankr. E.D. Pa. 1987); *In re* Trombly, 31 B.R. 386 (Bankr. D. Vt. 1983); *In re* Bailey, 23 B.R. 222 (Bankr. E.D. Pa. 1982) (attorney fees and costs denied for unsuccessful proceeding for relief from automatic stay); *In re* Banks, 31 B.R. 173 (Bankr. N.D. Ala. 1982).

229 *In re* Welzel, 275 F.3d 1308 (11th Cir. 2001) (en banc) (bankruptcy court must independently determine reasonableness of fees as a matter of federal law because § 506(b) preempts state law); *In re* Hudson Shipbuilders, Inc. 794 F.2d 1051 (5th Cir. 1986).

230 *In re* Prevo, 394 B.R. 847 (Bankr. S.D. Tex. 2008) (disallowing

Some courts have held that the inclusion in a proof of claim of any attorney fee incurred in connection with the bankruptcy case is improper unless the fee has been sought and approved under Federal Rule of Bankruptcy Procedure 2016, because the fee would be paid from the property of the bankruptcy estate.[231] Other courts have held that a creditor may include an attorney fee demand in a proof of claim without filing an application under Rule 2016 if the claim is sufficiently detailed and provides adequate notice to the debtor.[232]

Unfortunately, one court of appeals has concluded that creditor's attorney fees arising after confirmation of a chapter 13 plan to cover, for example, the costs of collecting a post-confirmation default, are not subject to court approval under section 506(b) or the automatic stay.[233] The decision does not adequately address whether the confirmed plan itself[234] or the underlying contract makes such fees inappropriate.[235] It also fails to consider that amounts required to be paid by the debtor post-confirmation in a case in which the debtor is curing a default are subject to the bankruptcy court's jurisdiction because they involve the "maintenance of payments while the case is pending" as set out in section 1322(b)(5).[236] And in any event, this problem can probably

foreclosure fees and costs, late charges, and BPO fees where servicer did not comply with basic supporting documentation requirements of proof of claim form and Rule 3001); *In re* Hight, 393 B.R. 484 (Bankr. S.D. Tex. 2008) (disallowing creditor's pre-petition attorney fees for preparation of foreclosure when creditor failed to provide evidence pertaining to what work was done, who did the work, hourly rate, and time spent); *In re* Jones, 366 B.R. 584 (Bankr. E.D. La. 2007), *aff'd in relevant part, and rev'd in part on other grounds,* 391 B.R. 577 (E.D. La. 2008) (post-confirmation attorney fees denied because no evidence presented as to what services were provided or whether they were necessary); *In re* Brooks, 2007 WL 1114091 (Bankr. D.N.J. Apr. 12, 2007) (reimbursement above amount set by "no look" fee for stay relief motions denied where no itemization of services rendered to justify higher fee was provided and no complex issues were raised in motions); *In re* Coates, 292 B.R. 894 (Bankr. C.D. Ill. 2003) (claim of mortgage servicer for attorney fees, foreclosure expenses, and other charges denied as servicer failed to produce evidence that would satisfy its burden of proving reasonableness); *In re* Staggie, 255 B.R. 48 (Bankr. D. Idaho 2000) (burden of proof not satisfied because counsel's billing summary failed to provide detailed breakdown of time entries). *See also In re* Porcheddu, 338 B.R. 729 (Bankr. S.D. Tex. 2006) (foreclosure law firm sanctioned for filing false fee applications and misrepresenting that fee statements were based on contemporaneous time records).

231 *In re* Moffitt, 408 B.R. 249 (Bankr. E.D. Ark. 2009) (Rule 2016 application required when fees to be paid by estate); *In re* Padilla, 379 B.R. 643 (Bankr. S.D. Tex. 2007); *In re* Tate, 253 B.R. 653 (Bankr. W.D.N.C. 2000). *See also In re* Jones, 366 B.R. 584 (Bankr. E.D. La. 2007) (legal fees incurred post-petition and preconfirmation must be approved by court as reasonable under § 506(a) and upon application filed under Rule 2016), *aff'd,* 391 B.R. 577 (E.D. La. 2008); *In re* Plant, 288 B.R. 635 (Bankr. D. Mass. 2003) (Rule 2016 application required if creditor's claim for fees contested by debtor); *In re* Powe, 281 B.R. 336 (Bankr. S.D. Ala. 2001) (nationwide class of debtors certified to challenge creditor's failure to adequately disclose attorney fees charged to debtors); *In re* Noletto, 281 B.R. 36 (Bankr. S.D. Ala. 2000) (fees that are not properly claimed or disclosed with specificity, or omitted from an arrearage claim to be paid under debtor's plan, are per se unreasonable); *In re* Gifford, 256 B.R. 661 (Bankr. D. Conn. 2000) (court noted that in future cases it would follow Tate and require oversecured creditors to seek approval of fees under Rule 2016).

232 *In re* Madison, 337 B.R. 99 (Bankr. N.D. Miss. 2006) (attorney fees and costs may be requested in proof of claim if disclosure is specific and fees are itemized); *In re* Powe, 281 B.R. 336 (Bankr. S.D. Ala. 2001). *See also In re* Atwood, 293 B.R. 227 (B.A.P. 9th Cir. 2003) (proof of claim lacking specific detail fails to meet creditor's evidentiary burden on reasonableness of fees).

233 Telfair v. First Union Mortgage Corp., 216 F.3d 1333 (11th Cir. 2000) (defendant's post-confirmation appropriation of attorney fees by including them in debtors' escrow balance without court approval does not implicate sections 506(b) or 362(a)). *Cf. In re* Tate, 253 B.R. 653 (Bankr. W.D.N.C. 2000) (including attorney fee incurred in connection with the bankruptcy case in proof of claim is improper unless fee has been sought and approved under Federal Rule of Bankruptcy Procedure 2016, because fee would be paid from property of the bankruptcy estate); *In re* Gifford, 256 B.R. 661 (Bankr. D. Conn. 2000) (court noted that in future cases it would follow Tate and require oversecured creditors to seek approval of fees under Rule 2016); *In re* Nield, 95 B.R. 259 (Bankr. D. Me. 1989) (use of escrow funds to pay creditor's attorney fees for motion for relief from stay, without court approval, violates automatic stay). *See also* Mann v. Chase Manhattan Mortgage Corp., 316 F.3d 1 (1st Cir. 2003) (mortgage company adding charges to debtor's account in its internal bookkeeping, absent any overt attempt to collect the fees, did not violate automatic stay).

234 *See* § 9.4.4.5, *infra. See also In re* Echevarria, 212 B.R. 185 (B.A.P. 1st Cir. 1997), *aff'd,* 141 F.3d 1149 (1st Cir. 1998) (creditor cannot seek interest payments that are inconsistent with confirmed plan).

235 One difficulty is determining whether any such fees have been charged. A request for information under the Servicer Act, 12 U.S.C. § 2605, may be necessary to determine if the creditor has included any hidden fees in the debtor's account. *See* § 8.2.2, *supra.*

In addition, it may be advisable to file a motion or adversary proceeding at the end of a chapter 13 case seeking an order that the mortgage default has been cured and that the mortgage is current. An example of such a motion can be found in National Consumer Law Center, Consumer Bankruptcy Law and Practice Appx. G.12, Form 146 (9th ed. 2009).

If the debtor does not discover improper charges until after they have been paid, the debtor should still be able to challenge the fees. *See In re* Staggie, 255 B.R. 48 (Bankr. D. Idaho 2000) (bankruptcy court has authority under § 506 to review attorney fees of secured creditor even if the collateral has been sold and the fees paid by debtor).

236 *In re* Padilla, 365 B.R. 492 (Bankr. E.D. Pa. 2007). *See also In re* Padilla, 379 B.R. 643 (Bankr. S.D. Tex. 2007) (disclosure of post-confirmation attorney fees through Rule 2016 fee application is required to ensure debtors can exercise their right to cure post-confirmation defaults and to receive their "fresh start"; court can order under § 105(a) disgorgement of fees charged to debtors without a proper Rule 2016 application or in violation of confirmed plan); *In re* Sanchez, 372 B.R. 289 (Bankr. S.D. Tex. 2007) (creditor's failure to disclose post-confirmation fees

be addressed by a carefully drafted plan provision.[237] In addition, an amendment made by the 2005 Act provides a statutory remedy in the bankruptcy court if a mortgage lender has misapplied payments under a chapter 13 plan and thereby caused the debtor to incur unnecessary and improper fees.[238]

Bankruptcy courts have struggled with the question of whether they have jurisdiction to address bankruptcy overcharges by a national creditor against a class of affected consumers. The better reasoned cases hold that the district court can hear such claims and can refer the authority to hear them to the bankruptcy court.[239]

9.4.3 Payment of Interest on the Arrears

Another important question is whether additional interest must be computed during the bankruptcy case on the unpaid portion of the arrears. As the bulk of the arrears is usually accumulated interest, the question in large part amounts to whether a debtor is required to pay interest on unpaid interest claims.

In 1993 the Supreme Court resolved a conflict among the circuits and required the payment of interest on arrearages. In *Rake v. Wade*[240] the Court held that homeowners seeking to cure a default by paying the arrears in installments in chapter 13 also have to pay interest on the arrears at present value.[241]

In 1994 Congress overruled the Supreme Court's decision in *Rake*, but only for mortgages made after October 22, 1994.[242] This means that if there is a default on a mortgage made after that date, payment of interest on arrears will only be necessary to the extent required under the underlying mortgage as limited by state law.[243] Consequently, in many cases, interest cannot be charged on the arrears (or at least on the interest portion of arrears), because it would be inconsistent with the contract or state law.[244] The operative date is the date the mortgage was signed, not the date of the default.

9.4.4 Curing a Default in Bankruptcy After a Foreclosure Judgment or Foreclosure Auction

9.4.4.1 Generally

The Bankruptcy Code now makes clear that a mortgage default can be cured under 11 U.S.C. § 1322(b)(3) and (5) until a valid foreclosure sale is completed.[245] This reverses

charged to the debtor and to file fee application under Rule 2016 violated automatic stay); *In re* Jones, 366 B.R. 584 (Bankr. E.D. La. 2007) (post-confirmation fees are subject to state law and contract between the parties, and must be disclosed to the debtor so as to afford the debtor an opportunity to pay the fees by seeking plan modification), *aff'd in part and rev'd in part,* 391 B.R. 577 (E.D. La. 2008).

237 An example of such a plan provision can be found in National Consumer Law Center, Consumer Bankruptcy Law and Practice Appx. G.3, Form 18 (9th ed. 2009). *See also Challenging Mortgage Servicer "Junk" Fees and Plan Payment Misapplication: Making Use of New Section 524(i)*, 25 NCLC REPORTS *Bankruptcy and Foreclosures Ed.* 11 (Nov/Dec. 2006).

238 11 U.S.C. § 524(i). *See* § 9.4.4.6, *infra.*

239 Bank United v. Manley, 273 B.R. 229 (N.D. Ala. 2001) (affirming certification of nationwide class of debtors challenging mortgage overcharges); *In re* Cano, 410 B.R. 506 (Bankr. S.D. Tex. 2009); *In re* Harris, 280 B.R. 876 (Bankr. S.D. Ala. 2001) (in case challenging attorney fees improperly posted to debtors' mortgage accounts, class certification under Rule 7023(b)(2) was appropriate as most fees had not yet been collected or only partially paid by debtors and declaratory and injunctive relief removing fees from accounts and providing restitution for those paid was predominant form of relief); *In re* Noletto, 244 B.R. 845 (Bankr. S.D. Ala. 2000) (nationwide class relief available). *Cf. In re* Williams, 244 B.R. 858 (S.D. Ga. 2000) (class action permitted if limited to debtors in judicial district where case filed).

240 508 U.S. 464, 113 S. Ct. 2187, 124 L. Ed. 2d 424 (1993).

241 Citing 11 U.S.C. § 1322(a)(5).

242 11 U.S.C. § 1322(e).
That section was made applicable to agreements made after the effective date of the Bankruptcy Reform Act only. Pub. L. No. 103-394, § 702(b)(2)(D). *See also* 140 Cong. Rec. 10,770 (Oct. 4, 1994). The legislative history provides that for this purpose a refinancing is considered a new agreement. H.R. Rep. No. 103-835, at 55 (1994), *reprinted in* 1994 U.S.C.C.A.N. 3340. *See In re* Harding, 274 B.R. 173 (Bankr. D. Md. 2002) (modification agreement entered into after October 22, 1994, that modified terms of 1986 mortgage was refinancing and governed by § 1322(e)).

243 *In re* Young, 310 B.R. 127 (Bankr. E.D. Wis. 2003) (note provision that interest due until paid in full not sufficient to require interest on arrearage under § 1322(e)); *In re* Bumgarner, 225 B.R. 327 (Bankr. D.S.C. 1998) (interpreting contract signed in 1996 as not authorizing interest on bankruptcy arrears). *See also In re* Trabal, 254 B.R. 99 (D.N.J. 2000) (interest on arrears required since mortgage "significantly more specific" than in Bumgarner by providing for payment of "all other sums, with interest"; no specific reference to bankruptcy arrears required); *In re* Koster, 294 B.R. 737 (Bankr. E.D. Mo. 2003) (note language required payment of interest on portion of arrearage attributable to principal and attorney fee advances but not late charges and "additional charges").

244 Because many states prohibit contracts calling for interest on interest (compound interest), even contracts with clear provisions for interest on arrears may not be interpreted as allowing interest on that portion of the arrears representing accrued (past-due) interest. *See In re* Jones, 366 B.R. 584 (Bankr. E.D. La. 2007) (additional interest cannot accrue on the repayment of interest under Louisiana law), *aff'd,* 391 B.R. 577 (E.D. La. 2008).

245 11 U.S.C. § 1322(c)(1). *See In re* Jordan, 199 B.R. 68 (Bankr. S.D. Fla. 1997); *In re* Ross, 191 B.R. 615 (Bankr. D.N.J. 1996).
The issues are somewhat murkier in the few states which allow strict foreclosure without an auction. *See In re* Stephens, 221 B.R. 290 (Bankr. D. Me. 1998) (chapter 13 cure not allowed in Maine after debtor's rights in property are terminated

decisions which had held that a state law foreclosure judgment terminates the bankruptcy right to cure a default.[246]

In addition, it is now clear that a cure may be effectuated for mortgages that have matured at the time of filing and for those that will mature during the course of the debtors' plan.[247] Moreover, because the Code does not define when a property must be considered "sold," there is still room to argue, in both judicial and non-judicial foreclosure jurisdictions, that a debtor may cure a default after the foreclosure auction until the sale process is fully completed in accordance with state law process.[248] Some examples of situations in which this argument has been made successfully are discussed below.

9.4.4.2 Post-Foreclosure Sale Rights of Redemption

Courts have held that a debtor may cure a default or pay off the balance owed on a mortgage in bankruptcy even after a completed foreclosure auction, when there is a state law unexpired right of redemption.[249] Under those precedents, state law post-foreclosure redemption rights come into the debtors' bankruptcy estate.

However, the Eleventh Circuit Court of Appeals reversed a bankruptcy case allowing cure of a mortgage default after a valid foreclosure sale under Alabama law.[250] The district court case had permitted the debtors to reinstate their mortgage based on the state law right to post-foreclosure redemption.[251] The district court held that the foreclosure sale did not cut off the debtor's redemption right, and that the debtor could exercise this right through his chapter 13 plan.[252]

On appeal, the Eleventh Circuit concluded that although the debtor retained his state law right to redeem after the foreclosure sale, the right to redeem does not encompass a right to cure the arrears in installments in order to reinstate the mortgage. The court was not prepared to find that the right to modify a mortgage under section 1322(b)(2) creates the potential to modify the state law right to redeem. Other circuit courts have similarly held that the debtor may not cure a default in a chapter 13 case filed during the post-sale redemption period.[253]

Because the court reaffirmed that the right to redeem is a property interest which comes into the bankruptcy estate, the decision leaves open the possibility that debtors can redeem under their plans if they pay the full lump sum due on the mortgage. The decision leaves unclear, however, whether debtors would have to pay the entire balance due in a lump sum or whether the balance could be paid in installments.[254] Regardless, the deadline for doing so would be extended by the Bankruptcy Code under 11 U.S.C. § 108(b).[255]

---

without sale by strict foreclosure); *In re* Munger, 1998 WL 470410 (Bankr. D. Vt. July 23, 1998) (debtor not permitted to cure in Vermont under strict foreclosure process after end of redemption period and recording of a certified copy of the judgment).

One court has held that a default on a real estate installment sale agreement cannot be cured after a state court determination that the buyers' rights under that contract have been terminated, even when the buyers remain in possession of the property. *In re* Belmonte, 240 B.R. 843 (Bankr. E.D. Pa. 1999). *But see In re* Brown, 249 B.R. 193 (Bankr. N.D. Ill. 2000) (buyer under real estate installment sales agreement still had right to cure after seller declared forfeiture because buyer had right to cure and reinstate contract under state law).

246 H.R. Rep. No. 103-385, at 52 (1994), *reprinted in* 1994 U.S.C.C.A.N. 3340, 3361.

247 11 U.S.C. § 1322(c)(2). *See In re* Jones, 188 B.R. 281 (Bankr. D. Or. 1995).

248 *See* H.R. Rep. No. 103-385, at 52 (1994), *reprinted in* 1994 U.S.C.C.A.N. 3340, 3361 (debtor's rights are safeguarded "at least" through foreclosure sale and may be extended beyond that date to the extent additional opportunities to cure are available under state law). This passage specifically mentions rights of redemptions as one way in which state law might extend the right to cure.

249 *In re* Ragsdale, 155 B.R. 578 (Bankr. N.D. Ala. 1993); *In re* Dickerson, 130 B.R. 110 (Bankr. S.D. Ala. 1991) (may exercise statutory right of redemption in chapter 13 plan); *In re* Ivory, 32 B.R. 788 (Bankr. D. Or. 1983) (may cure after foreclosure sale and before running of statutory redemption period).

250 *In re* Smith, 85 F.3d 1555 (11th Cir. 1996).

251 Commercial Fed. Mortgage Corp. v. Smith, 170 B.R. 708 (N.D. Ala. 1994).

252 Alabama law allows redemption of a foreclosed mortgage up to one year from the date of the foreclosure sale. Ala. Code § 6-5-248(b). *See In re* Saylors, 869 F.2d 1434 (11th Cir. 1989) (right of redemption is a property right within the jurisdiction of the bankruptcy court).

253 *In re* Connors, 497 F.3d 314 (3d Cir. 2007) (debtor no longer had right to cure under New Jersey law after hammer fell at foreclosure sale); *In re* Cain, 423 F.3d 617 (6th Cir. 2005) (no right to cure default in chapter 13 filed after foreclosure sale but within six-month redemption period); Colon v. Option One Mortgage Corp., 319 F.3d 912 (7th Cir. 2003) (right to cure under Illinois law is cut off upon completion of sale if time for redemption has run and does not continue until order confirming sale); *In re* Canney, 284 F.3d 362 (2d Cir. 2002); (under Vermont strict foreclosure law, automatic stay does not permit debtor to redeem property after end of redemption period, except as extended for sixty days by 11 U.S.C. § 108(b); court did not consider application of section 1322(c)(1)). *See also In re* Froehle, 286 B.R. 94 (B.A.P. 8th Cir. 2002) (redemption period following tax sale under Iowa law not tolled beyond sixty-day period provided for in section 108(b), and debtor may not use cure provisions under chapter 13 to redeem property); *In re* McCarn, 218 B.R. 154 (B.A.P. 10th Cir. 1998) (debtor's right to cure ends at time of foreclosure sale regardless of state law redemption periods).

254 Alabama law requires that post-foreclosure redemption be made in a lump sum. Ala. Code § 6-5-253(a).

In dicta, the court implies that installment redemption would not be permitted, by stating that the Code does not allow the debtors to modify the terms of the statutory right of redemption. *In re* Smith, 85 F.3d 1555, 1560 (11th Cir. 1996).

255 If bankruptcy is filed before the end of the redemption period, 11 U.S.C. § 108(b) extends the time to take actions such as redemption until at least sixty days after the order for relief.

9.4.4.3 Cure Rights When the Sale Process Is Not Yet Completed Under State Law

Some courts have found that a debtor retains an interest in foreclosed property under state law until the appropriate person (in most states, the mortgage holder, the trustee, the sheriff or another public official) executes a deed to the foreclosure sale purchaser (or similar memorandum that satisfies the statute of frauds),[256] and the consideration (purchase price) has been paid,[257] or the sale has not been confirmed by the court when confirmation is required.[258] If the borrower files bankruptcy during this time period, the interest of the debtor becomes property of the bankruptcy estate. A *subsequent* execution of a deed (post-filing) would be void because of the automatic stay.[259] A debtor can then cure the default on the mortgage through the chapter 13 plan.

Other courts have found that under state law, the sale is complete when the gavel falls at the foreclosure auction.[260] Research under the applicable state's foreclosure law may be required to pursue a cure after the auction.

This might provide additional time for a debtor who seeks to redeem to obtain the necessary lump sum. *See In re* Connors, 497 F.3d 314 (3d Cir. 2007) (chapter 13 filed during ten-day redemption period under New Jersey law extends period sixty days from filing of petition).

256 *In re* Gomez, 388 B.R. 279 (Bankr. S.D. Tex. 2008) (legal title never passed to purchaser at foreclosure sale under Texas law because substitute trustee's deed was not prepared or delivered before debtors' bankruptcy filing); *In re* Love, 353 B.R. 216 (Bankr. W.D. Tenn. 2006) (Tennessee non-judicial foreclosure not complete until trustee's deed signed); *In re* Grassie, 293 B.R. 829 (Bankr. D. Mass. 2003) (debtor retains equity of redemption when bankruptcy petition filed minutes after foreclosure sale and memorandum of sale signed by purchaser but before memorandum of sale signed by auctioneer); *In re* Dow, 250 B.R. 6 (Bankr. D. Mass. 2000) (under Massachusetts law, sale is not final until purchaser executes memorandum of sale); *In re* Beeman, 235 B.R. 519 (Bankr. D.N.H. 1999) (sale not complete under New Hampshire law until title is transferred by recorded deed); *In re* Ross, 191 B.R. 615 (Bankr. D.N.J. 1996) (cure can be effectuated after sale until sheriff's deed is delivered). *See also In re* Hernandez, 244 B.R. 549 (Bankr. D. P.R. 2000) (title is transferred under Puerto Rican law when deed of judicial sale is executed; upon colorable showing that property had been effectively transferred pre-petition, court should grant relief from stay to allow Puerto Rican courts to address specific arguments with respect to technical defects). *But see In re* Connors, 497 F.3d 314 (3d Cir. 2007) (section 1322(c) refers to a "discrete event" rather than entire foreclosure process and therefore debtor does not have right to cure between time home sold at foreclosure sale and time deed is delivered); *In re* Bebensee-Wong, 248 B.R. 820 (B.A.P. 9th Cir. 2000) (relief from stay granted to foreclosure sale purchaser was not abuse of discretion because, under California law, recording of trustee's deed related back to date of sale, which occurred before bankruptcy); *In re* McKinney, 344 B.R. 1 (Bankr. D. Me. 2006) (§ 1322(c)(1) extends right to cure beyond expiration of pre-sale redemption period under state law, but does not extend cure right beyond fall of hammer at auction sale; filing of post-auction report of sale is not a condition to effective transfer of title by foreclosure sale under Maine law); *In re* Eagles, 193 B.R. 23 (Bankr. S.D. Cal. 1996) (trustee's sale is final upon acceptance of last and highest bid, regardless of when deed is recorded). *Compare In re* Bland, 227 B.R. 163 (Bankr. E.D. Ark. 1998) (Arkansas foreclosure sale complete when auctioneer accepts bid) *with In re* Tomlin, 228 B.R. 916 (Bankr. E.D. Ark. 1999) (sale not complete under Arkansas law until foreclosure deed recorded).

257 *See* Fed. Deposit Ins. Corp. v. Dye, 642 F.2d 837, 843 (5th Cir. 1981) (foreclosure sale is not final until the deed is transferred); *In re* Related Partners Properties, Inc, 163 B.R. 213 (S.D. Fla. 1993) (expiration of the Florida redemption period is accomplished only when clerk of court files certificate of title and serves copy); *In re* Benson, 293 B.R. 234 (Bankr. D. Ariz. 2003) (trustee's sale is not complete until bid price is paid); *In re* Bradley, 75 B.R. 198 (Bankr. W.D. Va. 1987) (under Virginia law debtor still had an interest in property after foreclosure sale when no deed was executed prior to filing petition). *But see In re* Hurt 158 B.R. 154 (B.A.P. 9th Cir. 1993) (can cure default up to sale of property, cannot cure during period of statutory redemption; summarizing decisions from other jurisdictions); *In re* Johnson, 171 B.R. 613 (Bankr. M.D. Tenn. 1994) (debtors could not reinstate mortgage after foreclosure sale even though trustee's deed had not been recorded when bankruptcy petition filed).

258 *See In re* Crawford, 217 B.R. 558 (N.D. Ill. 1998) (cure permitted until confirmation by court completes sale); Christian v. Citibank, 214 B.R. 352 (N.D. Ill. 1997) (same); *In re* Wescott, 309 B.R. 308 (Bankr. E.D. Wis. 2004) (under Wisconsin law, foreclosure sale was not complete until state court entered order confirming sale; homeowner may cure under § 1322(c)(1) so long as petition filed before post-sale confirmation order entered); *In re* Pellegrino, 284 B.R. 326 (Bankr. D. Conn. 2002) (discussing when debtor's rights in the property are exhausted under strict foreclosure process); *In re* Brown, 282 B.R. 880 (Bankr. E.D. Ark. 2002) (because judicial foreclosure not complete under Arkansas law until sale is confirmed by court, debtor may cure default when bankruptcy filed after sale but one day before sale was confirmed); *In re* Jones, 219 B.R. 1013 (Bankr. N.D. Ill. 1998) (same); *In re* Rambo, 199 B.R. 747 (Bankr. W.D. Okla. 1996) (debtor may cure default under § 1322 after foreclosure but before confirmation of sale by the court). *See also In re* Kane, 236 B.R. 131 (Bankr. D. Conn. 1999) (foreclosure sale complete under Connecticut law upon judicial confirmation of sale and not when appeal period expires). *But see* Colon v. Option One Mortgage Corp., 319 F.3d 912 (7th Cir. 2003) (chapter 13 debtor's right to cure a mortgage default expires under Illinois law upon completion of the foreclosure sale and does not continue during the period between sale and judicial confirmation by state court); *In re* Crawford, 232 B.R. 92 (Bankr. N.D. Ohio 1999) (sale complete when gavel falls even though court confirmation is required).

259 *In re* Benson, 293 B.R. 234 (Bankr. D. Ariz. 2003) (when bankruptcy filed after fall of auctioneer's hammer, but before high bidder paid bid price, bidder's subsequent payment of bid price violated stay as "act to obtain possession of property of the estate").

260 *E.g., In re* Connors, 497 F.3d 314 (3d Cir. 2007) (debtor lost right to cure under New Jersey law when hammer fell at foreclosure sale); *In re* Bobo, 246 B.R. 453 (Bankr. D. Colo. 2000); *In re* Denny, 242 B.R. 593 (Bankr. D. Md. 1999) (foreclosure sale complete under Maryland law when gavel falls).

9.4.4.4 If the Sale Can Be Set Aside

As discussed in Chapter 14, *infra*,[261] there are a variety of grounds on which a foreclosure sale can be set aside, depending on state law. If a court will set aside the sale for a procedural defect, inadequacy of price under state law, or other invalidity, cure rights are reinstated.[262] Occasionally a sale may be set aside on bankruptcy grounds alone. For example, if the sale violated the automatic stay in the current or a prior bankruptcy case, the transfer is generally void regardless of whether the sale process complied with state law.[263]

In these cases, curing the default in bankruptcy requires a two-step process. Step one involves having the sale set aside or declared void. This can be accomplished in either state court or in bankruptcy court. If the bankruptcy court is the preferred forum, that court has jurisdiction to make the necessary determination because it has authority to order turnover of property to the estate.[264] If the sale is set aside, then the property must be turned over to the estate and the debtor's cure rights are reinstated.[265] These latter actions must take place in the bankruptcy court.

9.4.4.5 Effect of a Cure

The effect of a cure under section 1322(b)(5) is to nullify all consequences of the default.[266] Thus, in the case of a long-term mortgage, the debtor would normally be returned to the original amortization schedule once the default has been cured.[267] In fact, once the plan is confirmed, the debtor's ongoing mortgage payments should be applied from the petition date in accordance with the original loan amortization as if no default exists, with all pre-petition arrears being paid separately under the plan as a component of the mortgage holder's proof of claim.[268] Unfortunately, holders of long-term mortgages do not always comply with this principle, and debtors' attorneys may have to bring proceedings at the end of a chapter 13 plan to ensure that the cure is fully effectuated and not subverted by a mortgage holder's contrary bookkeeping practices.[269] Damages and attorney fees may be available in a cause of action to

261 *See* § 14.2, *infra*.

262 *See In re* Schwartz, 366 B.R. 265 (Bankr. D. Mass. 2007) (sale not valid because assignment of mortgage to party that conducted sale did not occur until after sale); *In re* Cooper, 317 B.R. 500 (Bankr. E.D. Tenn. 2004) (errors in advertisements rendered sale invalid).

263 *E.g., In re* Glendenning, 243 B.R. 629 (Bankr. E.D. Pa. 2000). *Cf. In re* Syed, 238 B.R. 133 (Bankr. N.D. Ill. 1999) (automatic stay annulled retroactively to validate sale when bankruptcy filing was in bad faith). *See generally* National Consumer Law Center, Consumer Bankruptcy Law and Practice § 9.6 (9th ed. 2009).

264 28 U.S.C. § 157(b)(2)(E); 11 U.S.C. §§ 541, 542. *But see In re* Hernandez, 244 B.R. 549 (Bankr. D. P.R. 2000) (upon colorable showing that property had been effectively transferred prepetition, court should grant relief from stay to allow Puerto Rican courts to address specific arguments with respect to technical defects).

Hernandez can be distinguished because the court was evaluating a defense to a motion for relief from the stay, rather than determining whether to set aside a transfer of property of the estate. When a sale is invalid and the buyer is seeking relief from the stay, the best practice is to seek to have the sale invalidated in a separate proceeding. Similar issues are discussed at § 9.6, *infra*.

265 11 U.S.C. § 1322(c)(1).

266 The House Report to the Bankruptcy Reform Act of 1994 reaffirms that this is the intent of Congress. "It is the Committee's intention that a cure pursuant to a plan should operate to put the debtor in the same position as if the default had never occurred." H.R. Rep. No. 103-835, at 55 (1994), *reprinted in* 1994 U.S.C.C.A.N. 3340. *See also In re* Southeast Co., 868 F.2d 335 (9th Cir. 1989) (chapter 11 cure); *In re* Epps, 110 B.R. 691 (E.D. Pa. 1990) (debtor did not lose the benefit of HUD forbearance agreement when prebankruptcy default on agreement was cured under chapter 13 plan).

267 *See In re* Wines, 239 B.R. 703 (Bankr. D.N.J. 1999).

Similar issues sometimes arise when a creditor files a timely proof of claim that is inconsistent with the debtor's confirmed chapter 13 plan. Courts have differed how to resolve the inconsistency, though the majority appear to hold that the plan is binding with respect to everything other than the amount of a claim, as long as the claim is timely filed. *Compare In re* Hobdy, 130 B.R. 318 (B.A.P. 9th Cir. 1991) (timely filed claim controls) *with In re* Sanders, 243 B.R. 326 (Bankr. N.D. Ohio 2000) (confirmed plan controls).

Note that this issue is unlikely to arise in those jurisdictions which delay confirmation until after the claims bar date.

268 *In re* Jones, 366 B.R. 584 (Bankr. E.D. La. 2007) (plan confirmation "recalibrates" the amounts due as of the petition date), *aff'd in relevant part, and rev'd in part on other grounds,* 391 B.R. 577 (E.D. La. 2008). *See also* Rake v. Wade, 508 U.S. 464, 473 (1993) ("As authorized by § 1322(b)(5), the plans essentially split each of respondent's secured claims into two separate claims-the underlying debt and the arrearages. While payments of principal and interest on the underlying debts were simply 'maintained' according to the terms of the mortgage documents during the pendency of petitioners' cases, each plan treated the arrearages as a distinct claim to be paid off within the life of the plan pursuant to repayment schedules established by the plans.") (*superseded by statute on other grounds*).

269 *In re* Rathe, 114 B.R. 253 (Bankr. D. Idaho 1990); *In re* Ward, 73 B.R. 119 (Bankr. N.D. Ga. 1987) (late charges may not be added to current payments made pursuant to plan unless those payments are not made on time). *Cf.* Telfair v. First Union Mortgage Corp., 216 F.3d 1333 (11th Cir. 2000) (defendant's charge for post-confirmation attorney fees by including it in debtors' escrow balance without court approval does not implicate sections 506(b) or 362(a)).

A carefully drafted plan can probably avoid the potential pitfalls associated with the Telfair decision. *See* § 9.4.2, *supra*.

An example of a motion that can be filed by the debtor at the end of a chapter 13 case, seeking an order that the mortgage default has been cured and that the mortgage is current, can be found in National Consumer Law Center, Consumer Bankruptcy Law and Practice Appx. G.12, Form 146 (9th ed. 2009). *See In re* Chess, 268 B.R. 150 (Bankr. W.D. Tenn. 2001) (mortgage holder that did not respond to trustee's customary motion to deem mortgage current at end of plan could not assert debtor was in arrears at end of plan).

enforce the binding terms of the plan[270]—generally in a contempt proceeding for a violation of the confirmation order or the discharge.[271]

9.4.4.6 Proper Crediting of Plan Payments

The Code was amended in 2005 to provide that the creditor's willful failure to credit payments received under a confirmed plan in accordance with the plan constitutes a violation of the injunction of section 524(a).[272] The section does not apply, however, if confirmation of the plan has been revoked, the plan is in default, or the creditor has not received the plan payments as required by the plan. The provision is also limited to cases in which the failure to credit payments has caused material injury to the debtor.

This provision is in response to decisions which had questioned whether the Code provided authority to remedy a creditor's failure to credit payments properly. For example, section 524(i) provides a remedy that the Court of Appeals for the Eleventh Circuit found missing in *Telfair v. First Union Mortgage Corp.*,[273] when a chapter 13 debtor challenged a creditor's application of plan payments to charges not contemplated by the plan. It also makes clear that a failure to properly credit plan payments that results in a post-discharge assertion that the debtor is in default is not simply a matter for state courts to resolve, but rather a critical issue that must be resolved by the bankruptcy court to ensure that the provisions and purposes of a plan are effectuated.

The provision also establishes that there can be a discharge injunction violation even without an act to collect on a dischargeable debt. Prior to the enactment of section 524(i), mortgage holders and servicers often argued that since a long-term mortgage debt that is cured under section 1322(b)(5) is not subject to discharge, based on section 1328(a)(1), there could be no discharge violation for a post-discharge attempt to collect improper cure-related fees. Although arguably section 524(a) does apply in that situation even without the amendment, section 524(i) makes clear that there can be a discharge violation if material injury is caused by the servicer's failure to credit payments under the plan, even though the underlying mortgage debt has not been discharged.

The willfulness requirement of section 524(i) should not be a significant obstacle for debtors. As in section 362(k)(1), willfulness should be interpreted to mean simply that the creditor intended to commit the act, i.e., credit the payment in the manner it did; the debtor should not need to prove that the creditor intended to violate the Code or the plan provisions.[274] Absent a creditor's proof that the improper crediting was a mistake in conflict with the creditor's normal procedures, the creditor should be presumed to have intended its acts.

The material injury requirement should be met in virtually every case involving a secured creditor. The failure to properly credit payments will almost always result in a higher payoff balance for the debtor and therefore a larger lien on the debtor's property than if the payments were credited properly. A creditor that has collected the payments made by the debtor under the plan and credited them in a manner leading to a higher balance remaining on a debt has caused a material injury to the debtor. Similarly, a creditor who has reported negative information on the debtor's credit report about nonpayment or collection efforts with respect to fees resulting from the improper crediting of payments has caused a material injury to the debtor.

In any action seeking to establish a violation of section 524(i), and correspondingly the injunction of section 524(a), the debtor will need to prove that the creditor failed to credit payments "in the manner required by the plan." Thus, to invoke the protections of section 524(i), the debtor's chapter 13 plan must contain precise language directing how payments are to be applied.[275] If the court's local rules contain

270 11 U.S.C. § 1327(a). *See In re* Riser, 289 B.R. 201 (Bankr. M.D. Fla. 2003) (mortgage holder not entitled to payments for charges incurred before or during bankruptcy that were not provided for in confirmed plan); *In re* Rathe, 114 B.R. 253 (Bankr. D. Idaho 1990) (mortgage holders attempt to collect fees resulting from its flawed accounting procedure for applying post-petition payments in chapter 13 violates debtor's plan and Bankruptcy Code).

271 *See In re* McCormack, 203 B.R. 521 (Bankr. D.N.H. 1996) (mortgage holder bank held liable for $10,000 punitive damages when it did not adjust its computer records to reflect effect of plan confirmation and sent debtor demand letter expressing intent to collect fees that were not due under plan); *In re* Ronemus, 201 B.R. 458 (Bankr. N.D. Tex. 1996) (creditor assessed $10,000, plus $3000 attorney and accountants' fees after discharge due to mortgage holder charging late charges on current payments made during bankruptcy and for charging filing fee, attorney fees and expenses to debtor's escrow account without permission of court). *See also In re* Turner, 221 B.R. 920 (Bankr. M.D. Fla. 1998) (attorney fees and costs awarded as sanctions for discharge violation based on mortgage holder's accounting inconsistent with completion of confirmed chapter 11 plan).

272 11 U.S.C. § 524(i).

273 216 F.3d 1333 (11th Cir. 2000). *See* § 9.4.2, *supra*.

274 *See* National Consumer Law Center, Consumer Bankruptcy Law and Practice § 9.6 (9th ed. 2009).

275 *In re* Nosek, 544 F.3d 34 (1st Cir. 2008) (chapter 13 plan may set procedures requiring notice of creditor's assessment of fees and payment changes, require proper allocation of payments, and have method for court to resolve disputes). *See also* John Rao, *A Fresh Look at Curing Mortgage Defaults in Chapter 13*, 27 Am. Bankr. Inst. L.J. 14 (Feb. 2008) (proposing chapter 13 plan provisions that specifically direct allocation of post-petition payments in accordance with plan and Code); *Making Use of Section 524(i) Revisited*, 26 NCLC REPORTS *Bankruptcy and Foreclosures Ed.* 16 (Jan./Feb. 2008).

An example of such a plan provision can be found in National Consumer Law Center, Consumer Bankruptcy Law and Practice Appx. G.3, Form 18 (9th ed. 2009). *See also Challenging Mortgage Servicer "Junk" Fees and Plan Payment Misapplication: Making Use of New Section 524(i)*, 25 NCLC RE-provisions which sufficiently direct how payments are to be applied by mortgage creditors, the debtor may simply incorporate these local rule provisions by reference in the plan.[276]

Several courts have recently provided guidance on what types of plan provisions implementing section 524(i) may be approved.[277] A plan term may require that upon entry of the confirmation order, the debtor's mortgage account is to be deemed current for purposes of application of ongoing post-petition payments.[278] Courts have uniformly approved plan provisions that require the mortgage holder or servicer to make appropriate adjustments to the ongoing maintenance payments based on the note and security agreement and applicable nonbankruptcy law, including payment changes based on escrow account analysis and interest rate provisions in an adjustable rate mortgage, and to notify the debtor, debtor's attorney and trustee of such payment changes.[279] A plan term may require a servicer to give notice to the debtor (and the trustee) before it attempts to impose fees and charges that may affect the debtor's post-petition payments.[280] Local court rules can establish a similar requirement.[281] A plan term or local rule should provide that the servicer's claims for post-petition fees will be disallowed if the servicer fails to comply with the notice requirement.[282]

9.5 Paying Secured Claims in Full

There are several reasons to consider paying off a home mortgage in full during the bankruptcy process, rather than curing the default and reinstating according to the loan's original terms. Perhaps the most important is that when a secured claim is paid in full pursuant to section 1325(a)(5), the debtor may pay present value interest rather than contract rate interest and may reamortize the loan over the full length of the plan.[283] If the loan is at a high rate or would have matured before the end of the plan, the effect of these changes is likely to be lower monthly payments for housing costs.

Additionally, upon completion of the plan, the loan will be fully paid so that no relationship between the lender and the debtor remains. Foreclosure then will be permanently averted.

PORTS *Bankruptcy and Foreclosures Ed.* 11 (Nov/Dec. 2006).

276 *In re* Anderson, 382 B.R. 496 (Bankr. D. Or. 2008) (finding that certain plan provisions were "surplusage" because addressed in either contract between the parties or in local rules).

277 *E.g., In re* Emery, 387 B.R. 721 (Bankr. E.D. Ky. 2008) (proposed special mortgage provision does not violate section 1322(b)(2)); *In re* Watson, 384 B.R. 697 (Bankr. D. Del. 2008); *In re* Aldrich, 2008 WL 4185989 (Bankr. N.D. Iowa Sept. 4, 2008) (discussing plan provisions that would be presumptively acceptable in future plans); *In re* Andrews, 2007 WL 2793401 (Bankr. D. Kan. Sept. 26, 2007); *In re* Collins, 2007 WL 2116416 (Bankr. E.D. Tenn. July 19, 2007). *See also In re* Jones, 2007 WL 2480494 (Bankr. E.D. La. Aug. 29, 2007) (describing procedures related to payment application and notification of fees mortgage servicer would need to implement to avoid imposition of sanctions), *rev'd in part on other grounds,* 391 B.R. 577 (E.D. La. 2008).

278 *In re* Ramsey, 421 B.R. 431 (Bankr. M.D. Tenn. 2009); *In re* Booth, 399 B.R. 316 (Bankr. E.D. Ark. 2009); *In re* Patton, 2008 WL 5130096 (Bankr. E.D. Wis. Nov. 19, 2008); *In re* Emery, 387 B.R. 721 (Bankr. E.D. Ky. 2008); *In re* Collins, 2007 WL 2116416 (Bankr. E.D. Tenn. July 19, 2007). *But see In re* Segura, 2009 WL 416847 (Bankr. D. Colo. 2009) (refusing to approve plan term deeming payments current upon confirmation).

Some courts have approved similar provisions only if qualifying language is added which specifies that the "deeming current" is contingent upon successful completion of the plan. *See, e.g., In re* Nelson, 408 B.R. 394 (Bankr. D. Colo. 2009); *In re* Winston, 2009 WL 2883158 (Bankr. N.D.N.Y. May 7, 2009); *In re* Hudak, 2008 WL 4850196 (Bankr. D. Colo. Oct. 24, 2008).

279 *See, e.g., In re* Ramsey, 421 B.R. 431 (Bankr. M.D. Tenn. 2009); *In re* Segura, 2009 WL 416847 (Bankr. D. Colo. Jan. 9, 2009); *In re* Emery, 387 B.R. 721 (Bankr. E.D. Ky. 2008); *In re* Watson, 384 B.R. 697 (Bankr. D. Del. 2008); *In re* Hudak, 2008 WL 4850196 (Bankr. D. Colo. Oct. 24, 2008); *In re* Anderson, 382 B.R. 496 (Bankr. D. Or. 2008); *In re* Patton, 2008 WL 5130096 (Bankr. E.D. Wis. Nov. 19, 2008); *In re* Aldrich, 2008 WL 4185989 (Bankr. N.D. Iowa Sept. 4, 2008). *See also In re* Herrera, 422 B.R. 698 (B.A.P. 9th Cir. 2010) (accounting and notice requirements imposed under local form chapter 13 plan do not violate the anti-modification provision in § 1322(b)(2)); *In re* Booth, 399 B.R. 316 (Bankr. E.D. Ark. 2009) (provision requiring payment change notice approved but only as to debtor, not trustee and debtor's counsel).

This type of plan provision requires mortgage creditors to service the loan in the customary manner as they would for homeowners outside of bankruptcy. Based on the Real Estate Settlement Procedures Act, this would mean performing an annual escrow analysis and notifying borrowers of any changes in escrow deposits and balances at least once per year within thirty days of the analysis. 12 U.S.C. § 2609. For adjustable rate mortgages based on the Truth in Lending Act, it would require notification of payment amount changes at least twenty-five days before the due date for the new payment amount. 12 C.F.R. § 226.20(c).

280 *In re* Segura, 2009 WL 416847 (Bankr. D. Colo. Jan. 9, 2009); *In re* Watson, 384 B.R. 697 (Bankr. D. Del. 2008); *In re* Patton, 2008 WL 5130096 (Bankr. E.D. Wis. Nov. 19, 2008); *In re* Aldrich, 2008 WL 4185989 (Bankr. N.D. Iowa Sept. 4, 2008) (finding plan term requiring annual notice and notice ninety days before final payment be "presumptively acceptable" to the court). *See also In re* Armstrong, 394 B.R. 794 (Bankr. W.D. Pa. 2008) (servicer waived interest rate increase by failure to give notice to debtor during pendency of chapter 13 case as required by local rule); *In re* Payne, 387 B.R. 614 (Bankr. D. Kan. 2008); Chase Manhattan Mortgage Corp. v. Padgett, 268 B.R. 309 (S.D. Fla. 2001).

281 *See, e.g., In re* Armstrong, 394 B.R. 794 (Bankr. W.D. Pa. 2008); *In re* Payne, 387 B.R. 614 (Bankr. D. Kan. 2008).

282 *In re* Aldrich, 2008 WL 4185989 (Bankr. N.D. Iowa Sept. 4, 2008) (plan provision providing for waiver of any undisclosed fees would be "presumptively acceptable" to the court).

283 11 U.S.C. § 1325(a)(5). *See generally* National Consumer Law Center, Consumer Bankruptcy Law and Practice § 11.6.1 (9th ed. 2009) (discussion of paying off a mortgage in full in chapter 13).

The right to modify and pay off the terms of a home mortgage that would have matured during the chapter 13 bankruptcy case is now clear.[284] The Code, as amended in 1994, does not distinguish between older purchase-money mortgages that are coming due and new short term mortgages such as home equity loans. Thus, perhaps the most advantageous use of this provision will be to pay off high rate home equity loans at a lower rate and over a longer term in a bankruptcy plan. Additionally, balloon payments can be spread out over the entire term of the plan.

A few courts had concluded that the present value interest rate for purposes of section 1325(a)(5) should be the same as the contract rate, however, the majority had held otherwise.[285] The Supreme Court largely resolved this dispute in *Till v. SCS Credit Corp.*[286] The Court held that a formula method is to be used, with the prime rate of interest[287] as the starting point, adjusted by a factor for risk. Although not setting any specific amount for the risk factor, the Court cited cases adding 1% to 3% to the interest rate, and noted that the rate selected should be "high enough to compensate the creditor for its risk but not so high as to doom the plan."[288] The Court also held that an objecting creditor has the burden of going forward with evidence that the interest rate proposed by the debtor is inadequate.[289]

More difficult questions arise when the debtor's plan seeks to pay off a home mortgage that will not mature during the plan period. If the debtor seeks to modify the interest rate or monthly payment amounts, courts may see this as a modification of the mortgage within the meaning of section 1322(b)(2).[290] Some basis for an exception to section 1322(b)(2) must be found in order to overcome the protection for home mortgage lenders. These issues are discussed at § 9.7, *infra*. If no basis to allow a modification is available, the mortgage can nevertheless be paid off in the plan without an extension of the mortgage term (i.e., by the original due date) or a change to the existing interest rate.

Paying off the mortgage during the plan is generally best suited to situations in which there is a low balance remaining on the mortgage. Otherwise, it is unlikely that the homeowner would be able to afford the payments required to pay off the debt in full within the maximum five year period of a chapter 13 plan.[291]

Another related issue arises when debtors seek to pay off secured claims from the proceeds of a court approved sale of property or refinancing of debt.[292] These issues are discussed at § 9.9, *infra*.

9.6 Using Consumer Defenses in Response to a Motion for Relief from Stay in Chapter 13

9.6.1 How This Issue Arises

A common problem in bankruptcy cases involving disputed secured claims arises when the creditor files an early motion for relief from the automatic stay to proceed with a foreclosure. For example, suppose you file a chapter 13 case for a client who has defaulted on both a first mortgage and a home equity loan. Suppose further that the home equity loan involved fraud, usury, disclosure violations or other conduct which gives rise to consumer defenses to that

284 11 U.S.C. § 1322(c)(2) permits a chapter 13 debtor to modify a mortgage that will mature during the plan period. Permissible modifications would include payment over the period of the plan and payment of interest at present value under section 1325(a)(5)(B)(ii). *In re* Paschen, 296 F.3d 1203 (11th Cir. 2002) (statutory exception to Code's anti-modification provision permits debtors to bifurcate and cram down undersecured, short-term home mortgages); *In re* Eubanks, 219 B.R. 468 (B.A.P. 6th Cir. 1998) (short-term mortgage subject to modification based on plain language of (§ 1322(c)(2)); *In re* Petrella, 230 B.R. 829 (Bankr. N.D. Ohio 1999) (mortgage holder's objection to confirmation denied, because evidence established that mortgage would mature during plan and could be modified); *In re* Mattson, 210 B.R. 157 (Bankr. D. Minn. 1997) (§ 1322(b)(2) protections did not apply to loans maturing before end of plan); *In re* Young, 199 B.R. 643 (Bankr. E.D. Tenn. 1996) (debtors could strip down mortgage if last payment was due before final scheduled plan payment). *See* 8 Collier on Bankruptcy, ¶ 1322.16, at 1322–1351 (Lawrence P. King, ed., 15th ed.). *See also In re* Nepil, 206 B.R. 72 (Bankr. D.N.J. 1997) (loan on which creditor had obtained foreclosure judgment could be treated as loan on which final payment due before end of plan). *But see In re* Witt, 133 F.3d 508 (4th Cir. 1997) (stripdown not permitted under § 1322(c)(2), because it provides for modification of payments and not claims).

The *Witt* court misreads § 1322(c)(2) because the statute plainly refers to "claims as modified."

285 *Compare In re* Valenti, 105 F.3d 55 (2d Cir. 1997) (present value rate is current rate for treasury bills with term comparable to plan plus 1% to 3% risk factor) *with In re* Smithwick, 121 F.3d 211 (5th Cir. 1997) (contract rate is rebuttably presumed to be present value rate).

286 541 U.S. 465 (2004).

287 The prime rate of interest may be found at http://federalreserve.gov/releases/h15/data.htm#top.

288 124 S. Ct. at 1962. *See* National Consumer Law Center, Consumer Bankruptcy Law and Practice § 11.6.1.3.3.6 (9th ed. 2009) (discussion of the risk factor).

To the extent that the application of *Till* does not produce a lower rate, debtors who are on active duty in the armed forces may obtain plan confirmation of a present value interest rate of 6% based pursuant to the Servicemembers Civil Relief Act. *See* 50 U.S.C. app. § 527(c); *In re* Watson, 292 B.R. 441 (Bankr. S.D. Ga. 2003) (plan modified to reduce interest rate from 12% to 6% while debtor on active duty).

289 124 S. Ct. at 1961.

290 *See* Nobelman v. Am. Sav. Bank, 508 U.S. 324, 113 S. Ct. 2106, 124 L. Ed. 2d 228 (1993).

291 *See* 11 U.S.C. § 1322(d).

292 *See In re* Martin, 232 B.R. 29 (Bankr. D. Mass. 1999) (discussing concerns when debtor seeks to pay off claims with the proceeds of a refinanced loan).

creditor's claim.[293] Your client's plan may be to cure the default on the first mortgage and to dispute the validity of the second mortgage securing the home equity loan note. For low-income clients, having enough income to cure the first mortgage default often depends on obtaining a determination that a home equity loan obligation is wholly or partially void.

Problems arise when the junior secured creditor attempts to frustrate your client's plan by moving quickly for relief from stay, before issues about the amount and validity of the claim are fully joined. The creditor may seek relief on the ground that the plan does not adequately protect its interest in the property because the plan does not provide for full payment of its claim. Similarly, the creditor may claim an entitlement to relief based on the debtor's lack of equity in the property. In either case the essence of your response may be that the creditor has no claim, that its claim is unsecured or that the claim is allowable only in an amount far lower than the amount asserted.

9.6.2 Responding to the Motion

Although it is generally true that you cannot raise counterclaims directly to a motion for relief from stay, it is clear that defenses are permitted.[294] It is thus possible to plead that the motion should be denied because the creditor has no cognizable claim or has a claim which is substantially less than the amount asserted. It is helpful, if possible, to set out the actual defenses fully and to explain how they would reduce or eliminate the creditor's claim in an accompanying memorandum of law.

If an objection to the creditor's claim has already been filed, or when an adversary proceeding is pending to void the mortgage or reduce the amount of the claim, the existence of that proceeding should be referenced in the answer to the motion for relief. If the objection or adversary proceeding has not been filed, it should be filed quickly after answering the motion. The argument on the motion for relief can then be framed as a need to deny or defer the motion until the validity and extent of the underlying secured claim is decided.

293 Some advocates have been particularly successful with Truth in Lending rescission defenses in this context. There are a number of helpful cases concluding that rescission makes the mortgage void so that the home equity loan creditor has only an unsecured claim in bankruptcy. *See generally* National Consumer Law Center, Consumer Bankruptcy Law and Practice § 14.4.4 (9th ed. 2009); National Consumer Law Center, Truth in Lending Ch. 6 (6th ed. 2007 and Supp.).

294 *See* National Consumer Law Center, Consumer Bankruptcy Law and Practice § 9.7.3.1.3 (9th ed. 2009).

9.6.3 The Applicable Legal Standard for Evaluating Consumer Defenses to a Motion for Relief

A number of courts have held that the existence of defenses to a creditor's claim is relevant to a determination of that creditor's motion for relief.[295] Commonly, upon a showing of "likelihood of success on the merits" courts will continue the stay until the objection to claim can be heard and finally determined.[296] These courts liken the process of continuing the automatic stay to a request for preliminary injunctive relief.

Therefore, the debtor must be prepared to make a showing of likelihood of success on the merits as to any consumer defenses at the hearing on a motion for relief. As some courts also want to balance the hardships or otherwise consider issues normally relevant to preliminary injunctions, debtors must be prepared on those issues as well.

A creditor's argument that there is no subject matter jurisdiction in the bankruptcy court to evaluate state law consumer defenses to validity or amount of claims is generally meritless. It is clear that the bankruptcy court has core jurisdiction to decide objections to claims pursuant to 28 U.S.C. § 157(b)(2)(C). Similarly, there is core jurisdiction to determine the validity, extent or priority of liens pursuant to 28 U.S.C. § 157(b)(2)(K).[297]

In some courts, though, there is a certain amount of judicial hostility to disputes based on state law defenses to claims. Judges who feel that way, however, are plainly wrong. 11 U.S.C. § 502(b)(1) contemplates that claims be disallowed to the extent that they are unenforceable against the debtor under "applicable law." Applicable law includes

295 Payment Plans, Inc. v. Strell, 717 F.2d 25 (2d Cir. 1983) (fact that creditor's lien was unperfected considered in denying relief from stay); *In re* Bialac, 694 F.2d 625, 627 (9th Cir. 1982) (when debtor's defenses and counterclaims directly involve question of debtor's equity, they should be heard in stay proceeding); Societa Internazionale Turismo v. Lockwood, 14 B.R. 374 (Bankr. E.D.N.Y. 1981) (creditor denied relief on ground that it had "no real claim" even though it had state court default judgment).

296 *See, e.g., In re* Fitzgerald, 237 B.R. 252 (Bankr. D. Conn. 1999); *In re* Moore & White Co., 83 B.R. 277 (Bankr. E.D. Pa. 1988); *In re* Davenport, 34 B.R. 463 (Bankr. M.D. Fla. 1983). *See also In re* Rice, 82 B.R. 623 (Bankr. S.D. Ga. 1987) (relief from stay must be denied if evidence supports conclusion that lien will be held invalid in a collateral proceeding); *In re* Gellert, 55 B.R. 970 (Bankr. D.N.H. 1985) (continuing the stay on the ground of an available defense to the claim requires a showing analogous to the showing necessary for a preliminary injunction including "likelihood of success on the merits").

297 In addition to retaining jurisdiction in bankruptcy court, consumer defenses and claims brought as a core proceeding provides the debtor with an additional ground for defeating the enforcement of a mandatory arbitration agreement. *See* National Consumer Law Center, Consumer Arbitration Agreements § 4.2.3 (5th ed. 2007 and Supp.).

the law governing the contract, including state law. In some courts, these defenses are even considered mandatory counterclaims to the proof of claim.[298]

It is also essential in chapter 13 cases for the court to determine the validity and extent of liens because they affect the feasibility of the debtor's plan. Moreover, proper distributions on claims cannot be made in either chapter 13 or chapter 7 (if property is liquidated in that chapter) unless the trustee knows the amount of the valid claims.[299]

9.6.4 Practice Tips

1. *Make sure the underlying issues are joined quickly.* Often the court is more comfortable continuing the stay if it is convinced that the underlying issues can be resolved relatively quickly. Thus, it is a good idea to file an adversary proceeding challenging the creditor's claim at an early stage, preferably before the hearing on the motion for relief. You can then point to the existence of that proceeding and your willingness to expedite it as evidence that the creditor will not be required to wait too long before a determination of its rights.

If the creditor has not yet filed a claim at all, it is still possible to join the issues by filing a claim on its behalf,[300] or, for secured creditors, by seeking a determination of the validity and extent of their lien.

2. *Seek discovery.* A debtor is entitled to discovery on a motion for relief from stay pursuant to Federal Rule of Bankruptcy Procedure 9014 which incorporates the adversary proceeding discovery rules. A motion for relief provides a good opportunity to obtain discovery to flesh out the grounds supporting an underlying objection to claim. As response times are generally short, it may be necessary to move for an expedited discovery schedule.[301]

298 Siegel v. Fed. Home Loan Mortgage Corp., 143 F.3d 525 (9th Cir. 1998).

299 With a particularly hostile judge, however, other strategies such as a motion to withdraw the reference might be considered. If grounds for withdrawal are available, an objection to claim might be heard in district court. *See* National Consumer Law Center, Consumer Bankruptcy Law and Practice § 14.2.5 (9th ed. 2009).

In extreme cases, a debtor might even want to consent to relief from the stay in order to allow determination of the amount or validity of the claim in another forum as long as the debtor reserves the right to deal with any claim which is ultimately determined to be valid in the bankruptcy process.

300 Fed. R. Bankr. P. 3004.

The claim should be filed in the amount which the debtor believes is legitimate. The creditor than has an opportunity to supersede it within thirty days. As it is unclear that the failure of a secured creditor to supersede a debtor-filed claim limits the lien to the amount of the claim, it may be a good idea to combine this strategy with a request for a declaratory judgment on the validity and extent of the creditor's lien.

301 Many creditors will voluntarily agree to an expedited schedule, because they know that the court generally will not grant a motion without at least a minimal opportunity for discovery.

3. *Use the hearing on the motion for relief from stay as an opportunity to educate the judge.* The hearing on motion for relief from stay can offer a relatively unfettered opportunity to explain the important issues underlying your client's consumer defenses.

4. *Join other defenses to relief from stay with your client's consumer defenses.* Do not forget that your client may have more traditional defenses to relief from stay which should be pleaded in addition to the existence of the consumer defenses. The existence of an equity cushion, for example, is an independent ground for denying relief from stay.[302] The availability of equity in the property also serves as the basis to argue that a lender will not be hurt by a short delay necessary to resolve consumer defenses in the context of an adversary proceeding objecting to the creditor's claim.

In addition, a motion for relief from the stay based on an alleged default by the debtor in making post-petition mortgage payments may be frivolous. It has become increasingly common for mortgage servicing companies to make errors in crediting bankruptcy debtors' payments and to file motions for relief from the stay even though debtors are current with post-petition payments. In such cases, sanctions against the lender or servicer may be warranted.[303]

302 *See* National Consumer Law Center, Consumer Bankruptcy Law and Practice § 9.7.3.2.2 (9th ed. 2009).

303 *In re* Cabrera-Mejia, 402 B.R. 335 (Bankr. C.D. Cal. 2008) (sanctioning law firm under Rule 9011 and Code § 105(a) after it filed twenty-one motions for relief from stay without factual investigation and without properly authenticated documents to support claims); *In re* Scheussler, 386 B.R. 458 (Bankr. S.D.N.Y. 2008) (ordering creditor to pay attorney fees and debtor costs and barring recoupment of any costs as a result of filing of unwarranted motion for relief from stay); *In re* Parsley, 384 B.R. 138 (Bankr. S.D. Tex. 2008) ("simplified" loan histories provided by national law firm, through a separate entity employing 300–350 legal assistants, to local firm for use in prosecuting stay relief motions are not reviewed for accuracy by attorneys for the national firm before they are provided to the local firm); *In re* Ulmer, 363 B.R. 777 (Bankr. D.S.C. 2007) (awarding sanctions and finding that affidavits of default related to motions for relief from stay were not executed before a notary public as indicated in the document and affidavits may not have been reviewed and signed by attorney purported to have signed the paper); *In re* Thompson, 350 B.R. 842 (Bankr. E.D. Wis. 2006) (servicer failed to identify allegedly missed payments on which affidavit of default was based); *In re* Rivera, 342 B.R. 435 (Bankr. D.N.J. 2006), *aff'd,* 2007 WL 1946656 (D.N.J. June 29, 2007) (sanctioning individual attorney and law firm for submitting pre-signed certifications in support of relief from stay); *In re* Brown, 319 B.R. 876 (Bankr. N.D. Ill. 2005) ($10,000 sanction imposed on mortgage holder for groundless stay relief motion); *In re* Gorshtein, 285 B.R. 118 (Bankr. S.D.N.Y. 2002); *In re* Williams, 2001 WL 1804312 (Bankr. D.S.C. Nov. 19, 2001) (actual damages for lost wages, additional blood pressure medication, and emotional distress, plus punitive damages and attorney fees, awarded to debtor based on mortgage servicer's violation of the automatic stay by filing a false affidavit accusing debtor of noncompliance with consent order and triggering relief from the stay when debtor was not in default); *In re* Kilgore, 253 B.R. 179 (Bankr. D.S.C. 2000).

5. *Join consumer defenses with other lien avoidance strategies.* In some cases you may find that the debtor has bankruptcy lien avoidance opportunities as well as consumer defenses. For example, in a challenge to a second mortgage holder's claim, the debtor may have an argument that the mortgage may be "stripped off" the property pursuant to 11 U.S.C. § 506(a), (d)[304] together with defenses under the Truth in Lending Act or Home Ownership Equity Protection Act (HOEPA).[305] On one hand, it may be easier to establish the low property valuation necessary to strip off the security interest and render it wholly unsecured and dischargeable. On the other, it may be simpler to establish that there is a strong legal basis for rescission and cancellation of the mortgage. Both can be raised in an adversary proceeding challenging the claim and both may be raised defensively to a motion for relief from stay.

6. *Ask the creditor to withdraw the motion or to postpone it pending resolution of the underlying issues.* Often creditors will agree to postpone hearings on their motion for relief or to withdraw them entirely in order to avoid the expense and duplication of two separate hearings. Some sophisticated creditors may also recognize the disadvantage of allowing you an opportunity to put on a part of your case to establish "likelihood of success on the merits" before the creditor is fully prepared.

7. *Be prepared to meet your burden at the hearing on the motion for relief.* The court is likely to want, at a minimum, some showing that your client's defenses to the claim have merit. You may need to present testimony or other evidence.

8. *If necessary file an appeal and obtain a stay pending appeal.* If a judge ignores consumer defenses and grants relief from stay to allow a creditor to pursue your client outside bankruptcy, consider filing an appeal. Grant of relief from stay is a final order for purposes of appeal.[306] Remember though that a stay pending appeal may be necessary so that the issues are not rendered moot by, for example, a completed foreclosure.[307]

9. *If relief is granted and a stay pending appeal is denied, all is not lost.* It is still possible to raise the underlying consumer defenses outside the bankruptcy process. Unless your client's objections to claim have been fully litigated and decided in the bankruptcy court, there is no res judicata effect of the grant of relief from stay which restricts the right to raise defenses when the creditor seeks to enforce its claim outside bankruptcy.[308]

10. *If necessary, consider amending the plan.* If your client's defenses are considered and the claim is ultimately allowed in an amount different from the amount included for that creditor in the debtor's plan, it may nevertheless be possible to amend the plan.[309] The plan, as amended, may adequately protect the creditor's rights so that relief from stay can be denied.[310]

11. *Consider removing the state court foreclosure proceeding or a pending affirmative claim against the lender to the bankruptcy court.* Removal of a claim to bankruptcy court is permitted by statute.[311] The procedures and time deadlines for removal are provided by rule.[312] Removal of the state court proceeding may not be necessary to adjudication of your client's defenses to the claim, but it does provide an alternative means for bringing the matter before the bankruptcy forum. Federal rules will then apply.[313]

Some courts may choose to remand a foreclosure action to state court, but the presence of a significant federal consumer claim weighs against that course of action.[314] In addition, the residence may be the estate's single most important asset, so resolution of the matters related to foreclosure may be within the court's core jurisdiction.[315]

If the foreclosure proceeding is removed, the lender's argument that it needs relief from stay to adjudicate the foreclosure in state court will be obviated. Removing an affirmative claim will show the bankruptcy court that the consumer claims you intend to litigate have already been joined. In addition, if there have been any positive rulings in the state court proceedings, such as denial of a motion to dismiss, upon removal, those rulings will continue to be law governing the case.

Fees may be awarded to debtor's counsel when imposed as a sanction against an opposing party or counsel for violation of Bankruptcy Rule 9011, which was amended in 1997 to conform substantially to Fed. R. Civ. P. 11. A motion for sanctions may not be filed until twenty-one days have passed after it has been served on the respondent, who may withdraw or correct the challenged pleading or paper during that time. *See* Fed. R. Bankr. P. 9011(c)(1)(A).

304 *See* § 9.7, *infra*.

305 *See* Ch. 5, *supra*.

306 *E.g.*, *In re* Sun Valley Foods Co., 801 F.2d 186 (6th Cir. 1986).

307 Fed. R. Bankr. P. 7062, 8005; Fed. R. Civ. P. 62. *See In re* Weston, 110 B.R. 452 (E.D. Cal. 1989) (appeal held moot after foreclosure sale), *aff'd*, 967 F.2d 596 (9th Cir. 1992).

308 Grella v. Salem Five Cent Sav. Bank, 42 F.3d 26 (1st Cir. 1994) (trustee's later counterclaim in separate proceeding on bank's complaint for determination of secured status not barred when trustee did not object to relief from stay); *In re* Vitreous Steel Prods. Co., 911 F.2d 1223 (7th Cir. 1990).

309 11 U.S.C. §§ 1323, 1329.

310 *See* National Consumer Law Center, Consumer Bankruptcy Law and Practice § 9.7.3.2.2 (9th ed. 2009).

311 28 U.S.C. § 1452. *See generally* National Consumer Law Center, Consumer Bankruptcy Law and Practice § 14.4.1 (9th ed. 2009).

312 Fed. R. Bankr. P. 9027. For cases pending when the bankruptcy case is commenced, parties have ninety days to remove. In addition, an action can be removed for up to thirty days after relief from stay is granted with respect to that action.

313 Fed. R. Bankr. P. 9027(g).

314 *See* Gandy v. Peoples Bank & Trust Co., 224 B.R. 340 (S.D. Miss. 1998) (presence of federal claim important reason not to remand case removed by lender).

315 *Compare In re* Jackson Brook Inst., Inc. 227 B.R. 569 (D. Me. 1998) (refusal to remand) *with In re* Chapman, 132 B.R. 153 (Bankr. N.D. Ill. 1991) (discretionary abstention granted).

The *Chapman* case may be distinguishable because the debtor's counterclaims had already been litigated, in whole or in part.

9.7 Stripping Down Residential Mortgages to the Value of the Collateral

9.7.1 Home Secured Loans

11 U.S.C. § 506 provides that a secured claim in bankruptcy may be limited to the amount of the value of the creditor's collateral.[316] The statute further provides that a lien may be voided to the extent it exceeds the value of the collateral to which it is attached.[317] The process of voiding liens under this provision has come to be called "strip down."

This Bankruptcy Code provision recognizes economic reality outside the bankruptcy process. If a creditor seizes collateral and sells it, the creditor can realize no more than the collateral's value. To the extent the claim exceeds the value of the collateral, the creditor is unsecured.

Despite relatively clear statutory language the Supreme Court has held that liens may not be stripped down in a chapter 7 bankruptcy case.[318] Additionally, the Court has concluded that creditors whose sole security is a mortgage on the debtor's residential real property are protected from strip down in chapter 13 cases by the provisions of 11 U.S.C. § 1322(b)(2).[319] Nevertheless there are a variety of situations in which strip down remains a viable option in chapter 13, even after the 2005 Bankruptcy Code amendments.[320] These include situations in which:

- The collateral involved is not the debtor's principal residence (e.g., a vacation home or a rental property);[321]
- The collateral is the debtor's principal residence, but the creditor has taken additional security (e.g., appliances or other personal property located in the residence);[322]
- The collateral is the principal residence, but the lien of the creditor involved is not secured by any portion of the debtor's principal residence (e.g., a $40,000 second mortgage on a $100,000 home subject to a first mortgage of $105,000);[323]

316 11 U.S.C. § 506(a).

317 11 U.S.C. § 506(d).

318 Dewsnup v. Timm, 502 U.S. 410, 112 S. Ct. 773, 116 L. Ed. 2d 903 (1992).

Several courts have limited *Dewsnup* to its facts and allowed mortgages to be voided in certain situations. *In re* Smith, 247 B.R. 191 (W.D. Va. 2000), *aff'd sub nom.* Warthen v. Smith, 1 Fed. Appx. 178 (4th Cir. 2001); *In re* Yi, 219 B.R. 394 (E.D. Va. 1998) (totally unsecured mortgage lien may be stripped off in chapter 7), *overruled by* Ryan v. Homecomings Fin. Network, 253 F.3d 778 (4th Cir. 2001); *In re* Farha, 246 B.R. 547 (Bankr. E.D. Mich. 2000); *In re* Zempel, 244 B.R. 625 (Bankr. W.D. Ky. 1999); *In re* Howard, 184 B.R. 644 (Bankr. E.D.N.Y. 1995) (unsecured judgment lien can be stripped off). *But see In re* Talbert, 344 F.3d 555 (6th Cir. 2003) (wholly unsecured lien may not be stripped off in chapter 7 case); Ryan v. Homecomings Fin. Network, 253 F.3d 778 (4th Cir. 2001) (same); *In re* Laskin, 222 B.R. 872 (B.A.P. 9th Cir. 1998); *In re* Cunningham, 246 B.R. 241 (Bankr. D. Md. 2000).

319 Nobelman v. Am. Sav. Bank, 508 U.S. 324, 113 S. Ct. 2106, 124 L. Ed. 2d 228 (1993).

320 *See* National Consumer Law Center, Consumer Bankruptcy Law and Practice § 11.6.1.2 (9th ed. 2009); *Impact of BAPCPA on Ability to Strip Down Home Mortgages*, 25 NCLC REPORTS *Bankruptcy and Foreclosures Ed.* 5 (Sept/Oct. 2006). *See also Homeowners Get No Break: Supreme Court Makes it Harder to Save a Home in Bankruptcy*, 11 NCLC REPORTS *Bankruptcy and Foreclosures Ed.* 21 (May/June 1993); *More Developments on* Nobelman, 12 NCLC REPORTS *Bankruptcy and Foreclosures Ed.* 45 (May/June 1994); *More Ways to Strip Down Residential Mortgages*, 13 NCLC REPORTS *Bankruptcy and Foreclosures Ed.* 16 (Jan./Feb. 1995); *Latest Developments on Stripdown*, 14 NCLC REPORTS *Bankruptcy and Foreclosures Ed.* 18 (Mar./Apr. 1996).

321 *E.g., In re* Lee, 162 B.R. 217 (D. Minn. 1993).

322 *See, e.g., In re* Hammond, 27 F.3d 52 (3d Cir. 1994) (personal property as additional security); *In re* Thomas, 344 B.R. 386 (Bankr. W.D. Pa. 2006) (additional security in "Miscellaneous Proceeds," which included any compensation, settlement, award of damages, or proceeds, other than hazard insurance proceeds, paid by a third party); *In re* Pedigo, 283 B.R. 493 (Bankr. E.D. Tenn. 2002) (creditor's right to cancel credit life and disability policy and claim unearned premium was additional security).

The *Hammond* case was cited favorably by Congress in the legislative history to the 1994 Bankruptcy Amendments in the section-by-section analysis on section 206. That section conforms the treatment of mortgages in chapter 11 to that in chapter 13. The 2005 Act attempts to limit modification on these grounds by adding a definition of "debtor's principal residence" in § 101 of the Code. *See* § 9.7.3, *infra*; National Consumer Law Center, Consumer Bankruptcy Law and Practice § 11.6.1.2 (9th ed. 2009).

323 *See, e.g., In re* Zimmer, 313 F.3d 1220 (9th Cir. 2003); *In re* Lane, 280 F.3d 663 (6th Cir. 2002) (adopting majority position that wholly unsecured mortgage may be stripped off); *In re* Pond, 252 F.3d 122 (2d Cir. 2001); *In re* Dickerson, 222 F.3d 924 (11th Cir. 2000); *In re* Tanner, 217 F.3d 1357 (11th Cir. 2000); *In re* Bartee, 212 F.3d 277 (5th Cir. 2000); *In re* McDonald, 205 F.3d 606 (3d Cir. 2000); *In re* Mann, 249 B.R. 831 (B.A.P. 1st Cir. 2000); *In re* Lam, 211 B.R. 36 (B.A.P. 9th Cir. 1997), *appeal dismissed*, 192 F.3d 1309 (9th Cir. 1999); *In re* Sette, 164 B.R. 453 (Bankr. E.D.N.Y. 1994); *In re* Moncrief, 163 B.R. 492 (Bankr. E.D. Ky. 1994); *In re* Williams, 161 B.R. 27 (Bankr. E.D. Ky. 1993); *In re* Lee, 161 B.R. 271 (Bankr. W.D. Okla. 1993); *In re* Plouffe, 157 B.R. 198 (Bankr. D. Conn. 1993). For an extended discussion of this issue see *Stripdown Allowed When Residential Mortgage Creditor is Completely Unsecured*, 12 NCLC REPORTS *Bankruptcy and Foreclosures Ed.* 33 (Nov./Dec. 1993). *But see In re* Barnes, 207 B.R. 588 (Bankr. N.D. Ill. 1997); *In re* Neverla, 194 B.R. 547 (Bankr. W.D.N.Y. 1996).

However, the *Neverla* court acknowledges that its position is inconsistent with the statutory language.

Although the overwhelming majority of courts have held that chapter 13 debtors may use § 506(d) to strip off wholly unsecured liens, it is not so clear that such right exists for chapter 7 debtors. *See In re* Lavelle, 2009 WL 4043089 (Bankr. E.D.N.Y. Nov. 19, 2009); *In re* Zempel, 244 B.R. 625 (Bankr. W.D. Ky. 1999); *In re* Howard, 184 B.R. 644 (Bankr. E.D.N.Y. 1995).

- The collateral is the principal residence, but the lien of the creditor involved is not secured by real property, such as in the case of a manufactured home that is treated as personal property under state law;[324]
- The collateral is the principal residence, but the lien involved is not a security interest under the Code's definition because it is not a consensual lien (e.g., judicial liens, tax liens, most mechanics' liens and any other involuntary encumbrance);[325]
- The mortgage will mature during the course of a chapter plan or has been reduced to judgment before bankruptcy;[326] and
- The claim is not secured only by real property that is the debtor's principal residence because the collateral serves both as the residence and as an income producing property (e.g., a multifamily property).[327]

Each of these situations takes the secured claim out of the category of claims which are protected from modification under the Code[328] and thus out of the protections described in the *Nobelman* opinion. Thus not only is strip down available for those claims, but also any other modification permissible under the Code may be undertaken through the debtor's plan. This may include changes to the loan term and reduction of the interest rate to present value.[329]

When strip down is available, it is a valuable strategy to prevent foreclosure because it eliminates some or all of a mortgage. If the mortgage is entirely void (e.g., as it may be in the case of some junior mortgages), then obviously foreclosure is no longer a relevant concern. If the mortgage is partially void, there is a smaller balance on which the debtor is obligated, thus increasing the potential to cure the default, pay off, achieve a workout or refinance.

9.7.2 Manufactured Home Loans

If the creditor's claim is not secured solely by a security interest in "real property" that is the debtor's principal residence, the secured loan may be modified. Before the 2005 Code amendments, it was clear that a lien secured by real estate upon which a manufactured home was situated, or a lien secured by the manufactured home itself, were not secured solely by real property that was the debtor's principal residence and could be stripped-off if the manufactured home was treated as personalty under state law.[330]

But see Ryan v. Homecomings Fin. Network, 253 F.3d 778 (4th Cir. 2001); *In re* Laskin, 222 B.R. 872 (B.A.P. 9th Cir. 1998) (chapter 7 debtors may not use § 506(d) to strip off wholly unsecured liens); *In re* Cater, 240 B.R. 420 (M.D. Ala. 1999); *In re* Grano, 422 B.R. 401 (Bankr. W.D.N.Y. 2010); *In re* Bessette, 269 B.R. 644 (Bankr. E.D. Mich. 2001); *In re* Keltz, 261 B.R. 845 (Bankr. W.D. Pa. 2001); *In re* Fitzmaurice, 248 B.R. 356 (Bankr. W.D. Mo. 2000); *In re* Cunningham, 246 B.R. 241 (Bankr. D. Md. 2000); *In re* Virello, 236 B.R. 199 (Bankr. D.S.C. 1999); *In re* Swiatek, 231 B.R. 26 (Bankr. D. Del. 1999).

324 *See* § 9.7.2, *infra* (discussion of manufactured homes). *See also In re* Bradshier, 2010 WL 545967 (Bankr. M.D.N.C. Feb. 16, 2010) (additional security interest in escrow account treated as personal property under state law).

325 *See, e.g., In re* McDonough, 166 B.R. 9 (Bankr. D. Mass. 1994); *In re* Cullen, 150 B.R. 1 (Bankr. D. Me. 1993).

326 Section 1322(c)(2) permits modification, despite § 1322(b)(2), of mortgages for "which the last payment on the original payment schedule . . . is due before the date on which the final payment under the plan is due." *In re* Paschen, 296 F.3d 1203 (11th Cir. 2002) (statutory exception to Code's anti-modification provision permits debtors to bifurcate and cram down undersecured, short-term home mortgages); *In re* Eubanks, 219 B.R. 468 (B.A.P. 6th Cir. 1998); *In re* Reeves, 221 B.R. 756 (Bankr. C.D. Ill. 1998); *In re* Mattson, 210 B.R. 157 (Bankr. D. Minn. 1997) (§ 1322(b)(2) protections did not apply to loans maturing before end of plan); *In re* Young, 199 B.R. 643 (Bankr. E.D. Tenn. 1996) (debtors could strip down mortgage if last payment was due before final scheduled plan payment). *See also In re* Nepil, 206 B.R. 72 (Bankr. D.N.J. 1997) (loan on which creditor had obtained foreclosure judgment could be treated as loan on which final payment due before end of plan). *But see In re* Witt, 113 F.3d 508 (4th Cir. 1997) (stripdown not permitted under § 1322(c)(2), because it provides for modification of payments and not claims); *In re* Rowe, 239 B.R. 44 (Bankr. D.N.J. 1999) (pre-petition acceleration alone does not bring a mortgage under this provision).

The *Witt* court misreads § 1322(c)(2) because the statute plainly refers to "claims as modified."

Modification allows the debtor to strip-down and then to pay off the present value of the allowed secured claim as modified at present value during the pendency of the plan. *See* § 9.5, *supra*.

327 *In re* Scarborough, 461 F.3d 406 (3d Cir. 2006) (based on plain language of § 1322(b)(2), namely use of the word "is" in the phrase "real property that is the debtor's principal residence," court held that anti-modification protection does not apply to claim secured by both debtor's principal residence and other rental property that is not debtor's principal residence); Lomas Mortgage Inc. v. Louis, 184 B.R. 630 (D. Mass. 1995), *aff'd*, 82 F.3d 1 (1st Cir. 1996) (debtor can strip down mortgage secured by multi-family residence); *In re* Del Valle, 186 B.R. 347 (Bankr. D. Conn. 1995); *In re* Legowski, 167 B.R. 711 (Bankr. D. Mass. 1994); *In re* Adebanjo, 165 B.R. 98 (Bankr. D. Conn. 1994) (§ 1322(b)(2) "protects claims secured only by a security interest in real property that is the debtor's principal residence, and not the real property in which the debtor resides."); *In re* McGregor, 172 B.R. 718 (Bankr. D. Mass. 1994); *In re* McVay, 150 B.R. 254 (Bankr. D. Or. 1993) (residential property used in part as bed and breakfast); *In re* Ramirez, 62 B.R. 668 (Bankr. S.D. Cal. 1986).

The *Ramirez* case was cited favorably by Congress in the legislative history to the 1994 Bankruptcy Amendments in the section-by-section analysis on section 206. That section conforms the treatment of mortgages in chapter 11 to that in chapter 13. Ramirez was cited as an existing substantive limit on the anti-modification provision. *But see In re* Guilbert, 165 B.R. 88 (Bankr. D.R.I. 1994), *rev'd on other grounds*, 176 B.R. 302 (D.R.I. 1995).

328 11 U.S.C. § 1322(b)(2).

329 *See* § 9.5, *supra*.

330 *In re* Thompson, 217 B.R. 375 (B.A.P. 2d Cir. 1998) (loan may be modified as manufactured home personalty under New York law); *In re* Tirey, 350 B.R. 62 (Bankr. S.D. Tex. 2006); *In re* Nowlin, 321 B.R. 678 (Bankr. E.D. Pa. 2005); *In re* Colver, 13

A new definition added by the 2005 Act may have been intended to protect manufactured home lenders from strip down, by defining "debtor's principal residence" to mean a residential structure, "without regard to whether it is attached to real property."[331] The definition further provides that debtor's principal residence includes "an individual condominium or cooperative unit, a mobile or manufactured home, or trailer."[332] However, these amendments did not accomplish this result, if that was the purpose, because no change was made to section 1322(b)(2) and the "real property" requirement remains in that provision. While a mobile or manufactured home may be the debtor's principal residence under the Code definition, it would still be personal property if state law so provides and therefore the debt would not be secured "only by a security interest in real property" that is the debtor's principal residence. Thus, the anti-modification provision in section 1322(b)(2) does not apply to a security interest in a mobile or manufactured home, cooperative, or other residence that is treated as personal property under state law.[333]

9.7.3 Mortgages with Additional Security

A claim that is not secured *"only"* by the debtor's principal residence, such as when additional security is provided, may be modified. The 2005 Act attempts to limit modification on these grounds by adding a definition of "debtor's principal residence" as a residential structure which includes "incidental property."[334] A separate definition of "incidental property" is also added by the 2005 Act, which refers to property rights going beyond ownership of the structure. The term "incidental property" is specifically defined to mean:

- Property commonly conveyed with a principal residence in the area where the property is located;
- All easements, rights, appurtenances, fixtures, rents, royalties, mineral rights, oil or gas rights or profits, water rights, escrow funds, or insurance proceeds; and
- All replacements or additions.[335]

Courts had differed prior to the 2005 Act on whether some of the rights enumerated in the new definition of "incidental property" were additional collateral which removed a secured claim from the protection against modification in section 1322(b)(2). Claims secured by the debtor's principal residence and also household goods,[336] proceeds from credit insurance,[337] appliances,[338] rents,[339] bank ac-

B.R. 521 (Bankr. D. Nev. 1981); *In re* Plaster, 101 B.R. 696 (Bankr. E.D. Okla. 1989). *See In re* Johnson, 269 B.R. 246 (Bankr. M.D. Ala. 2001) (creditor with mortgage on real estate where manufactured home was situated but not on manufactured home did not have lien on debtor's principal residence). *See also* National Consumer Law Center, Consumer Bankruptcy Law and Practice § 11.6.1.2.2.6 (9th ed. 2009); National Consumer Law Center, Consumer Warranty Law § 17.2.2 (3d ed. 2006 and Supp.).

331 11 U.S.C. § 101(13A).

332 11 U.S.C. § 101(13A)(B).

333 *In re* Reinhardt, 563 F.3d 558 (6th Cir. 2009) (anti-modification provision did not prevent stripdown of loan secured by manufactured home treated as personal property even though creditor also held security interest in real estate upon which home was situated); *In re* Ennis, 558 F.3d 343 (4th Cir. 2009); Green Tree Servicing, L.L.C. v. Harrison, 2009 WL 82565 (W.D. La. Jan. 12, 2009); *In re* Coleman, 392 B.R. 767 (B.A.P. 8th Cir. 2008); *In re* Davis, 386 B.R. 182 (B.A.P. 6th Cir. 2008) (manufactured home which is personal property under state law is not subject to § 1322(b)(2) protection); *In re* Shepherd, 381 B.R. 675 (E.D. Tenn. 2008); Moss v. GreenTree-Al, L.L.C., 378 B.R. 655 (S.D. Ala. 2007); *In re* Jordan, 403 B.R. 339 (Bankr. W.D. Pa. 2009); *In re* Gearheart, 2007 WL 4463342 (Bankr. E.D. Ky. Dec. 14, 2007); *In re* Fuller, 2007 WL 3244113 (Bankr. M.D.N.C. Nov. 2, 2007); *In re* Oliviera, 378 B.R. 789 (Bankr. E.D. Tex. 2007); *In re* Bartolome, 2007 WL 2774467 (Bankr. M.D. Ala. Sept. 21, 2007); *In re* Manning, 2007 WL 2220454 (Bankr. N.D. Ala. Aug. 2, 2007); *In re* McLain, 376 B.R. 492 (Bankr. D.S.C. 2007); *In re* Cox, 2007 WL 1888186 (Bankr. S.D. Tex. June 29, 2007). *But see In re* Lunger, 370 B.R. 649 (Bankr. M.D. Pa. 2007).

334 11 U.S.C. § 101(13A)(A).

335 11 U.S.C. § 101(27B).

336 *In re* Hammond, 27 F.3d 52 (3d Cir. 1994); *In re* Bouvier, 150 B.R. 24 (Bankr. D.R.I. 1993).

The *Hammond* case was cited favorably as representing current law by the legislative history to the 1994 amendments to the Code. 140 Cong. Rec. H10, 764 (daily ed. Oct. 4, 1994).

337 Transouth Fin. Corp. v. Hill, 106 B.R. 145 (W.D. Tenn. 1989); *In re* Pedigo, 283 B.R. 493 (Bankr. E.D. Tenn. 2002); *In re* Selman, 120 B.R. 576 (Bankr. D.N.M. 1990); *In re* Stiles, 74 B.R. 208 (Bankr. N.D. Ala. 1987). *But see In re* Washington, 967 F.2d 173 (5th Cir. 1992) (mere fact that debtor obtained credit life and disability insurance was not additional security, at least in case where insurance was voluntary and could be canceled by the debtors, and there was no language pledging the policy as security for the loan or assigning its proceeds to the creditor).

338 Sapos v. Provident Inst. of Sav., 967 F.2d 918 (3d Cir. 1992) (anti-modification protection does not apply because security interest included personal property such as household appliances and wall-to-wall carpeting); Wilson v. Commonwealth Mortgage Corp., 895 F.2d 123, 128 (3d Cir. 1990) (appliances and furniture); *In re* Escue, 184 B.R. 287 (Bankr. M.D. Tenn. 1995) ("refrigerator, space heater, and similar items" additional security even though described as "fixtures" in mortgage documents); *In re* Jablonski, 70 B.R. 381 (Bankr. E.D. Pa. 1987) (security interest covered appliances and also rents, issues, and profits), *aff'd on other grounds*, 88 B.R. 652 (E.D. Pa. 1988); *In re* Reeves, 65 B.R. 898 (Bankr. N.D. Ill. 1986) (security interest also covered fixtures).

339 Lutz v. Miami Valley Bank, 192 B.R. 107 (W.D. Pa. 1995) (security interest in rents); Secor Bank v. Dunlap, 129 B.R. 463 (E.D. La. 1991) (security interest also covered easements, rights, appurtenances, rents, royalties, mineral, oil and gas rights, water rights, stock, and all fixtures); *In re* Heckman, 165 B.R. 16 (Bankr. E.D. Pa. 1994) (security interest in rents placed mortgage outside scope of § 1322(b)(2)); *In re* Jackson, 136 B.R. 797 (Bankr. N.D. Ill. 1992) (modification permitted because rents are additional security). *But see In re* Davis, 989 F.2d 208 (6th Cir. 1993).

counts,[340] or escrow accounts established for payment of taxes and insurance[341] were held to be subject to modification. Some courts, however, focused on whether the additional collateral provided something more to the creditor than might already exist as a component of its security interest in the real property, often by considering whether the security interest was contained in "boilerplate" language commonly found in mortgage documents.[342] These courts often followed a two-part test developed by the court in *In re French*,[343] which considered whether the additional items of collateral were (1) merely enhancements that can be made component parts of the real property, and (2) of little or no independent value. If the collateral met both of these elements, the mortgage could not be modified.

Rather than adopt a test similar to that set out in *In re French*, the 2005 Act provides an exclusive list of items that shall be deemed "incidental property." Significantly, the definition does not use the nonexclusive term "include" or "includes" in listing the items in section 101(27B),[344] nor does it state that similar items are to be considered. The specificity in the new definition of "incidental property" clarifies that security interests in types of property not enumerated, such as appliances, furniture, bank accounts, motor vehicles, or property of entities other than the debtor, will permit the mortgage loan to be modified, as under pre-2005 Act law.[345] An additional security interest in any type of property not commonly conveyed with a principal residence in the area where the property is located, or not expressly described in the new definition, should permit modification.

The new definition of incidental property should overrule decisions which had permitted modification, for example, based on additional security in rents and profits from the property,[346] insurance proceeds,[347] and mortgage escrow accounts.[348] However, if the additional security is personalty under state law, such as mortgage escrow accounts in some states, Congress' failure to eliminate the "real property" requirement in section 1322(b)(2) may mean that decisions which turned on the real property versus personalty distinction still control.[349]

9.8 Avoiding Judicial Liens—Section 522(f)(1)

In bankruptcy, the debtor may "avoid" (i.e., nullify) many types of prebankruptcy transfers of exempt property.[350] The power to avoid transfers is expansive, due, in part, to the broad definition of the word "transfer" in the Code.[351] The debtor, with some limitations, may invalidate numerous types of transfers, and recover valuable interests in property, as long as the interest in the property can be claimed as exempt.[352] Exemptions may be established by the Code or by state law.[353]

Section 522(f) gives the debtor an unqualified right to avoid any judicial lien that impairs an exemption. Because the term "judicial lien" is itself defined very broadly[354] to include levies, judgment liens (including confessed judg-

---

340 *In re Libby*, 200 B.R. 562 (Bankr. D.N.J. 1996) (mortgage included additional security in debtor's account at the creditor bank); *In re* Crystian, 197 B.R. 803 (Bankr. W.D. Pa. 1996) (right to setoff against checking account constituted additional security).

341 *In re* Donadio, 269 B.R. 336 (Bankr. M.D. Pa. 2001) (security interest also covered escrow account for taxes and insurance); *In re* Stewart, 263 B.R. 728 (Bankr. W.D. Pa. 2001) (same, even though collateral not in hands of mortgage holder on petition date). *But see In re* Ferandos, 402 F.3d 147 (3d Cir. 2005) (funds in escrow account do not constitute additional collateral as a matter of New Jersey law); *In re* Davis, 989 F.2d 208 (6th Cir. 1993) (requirement that debtor obtain fire insurance, absent the existence of proceeds from such insurance due to a fire, was not additional security for purposes of § 1322(b)(2)).

342 *In re* Ferandos, 402 F.3d 147 (3d Cir. 2005) (security interest in rents did not constitute interest in additional collateral because real property is defined to include "rents" under New Jersey law); *In re* Davis, 989 F.2d 208 (6th Cir. 1993) (holding that benefits which are merely incidental to an interest in real property do not remove mortgage from anti-modification protection); *In re* French, 174 B.R. 1 (Bankr. D. Mass. 1994).

343 174 B.R. 1 (Bankr. D. Mass. 1994).

344 *See* 11 U.S.C. § 102(3) ("'include' or 'includes' are not limiting").

345 *E.g.,* Sapos v. Provident Inst. of Sav., 967 F.2d 918 (3d Cir. 1992) (wall-to-wall carpeting additional security); *In re Libby*, 200 B.R. 562 (Bankr. D.N.J. 1996) (mortgage included additional security in debtor's account at the creditor bank); *In re Bouvier*, 160 B.R. 24 (Bankr. D.R.I. 1993) (claim secured not only by mortgage but also by personal property of debtors' corporation).

346 *In re* Heckman, 165 B.R. 16 (Bankr. E.D. Pa. 1994) ("rents of the premises" are additional collateral); *In re DeCosta*, 204 B.R. 1 (Bankr. D. Mass. 1996).

347 It is arguable whether a security interest that applies only to unearned insurance premiums, rather than proceeds from an insurance claim, are covered by the new definition. *See In re* Pedigo, 283 B.R. 493 (Bankr. E.D. Tenn. 2002) (creditor's right to cancel credit life and disability policy and claim unearned premium was additional security).

348 *In re* Donadio, 269 B.R. 336 (Bankr. M.D. Pa. 2001) (security interest also covered escrow account for taxes and insurance); *In re* Stewart, 263 B.R. 728 (Bankr. W.D. Pa. 2001).

349 *E.g., In re* Ferandos 402 F.3d 147 (3d Cir. 2005); *In re* Bradshier, 2010 WL 545967 (Bankr. M.D.N.C. Feb. 16, 2010) (additional security interest in escrow account treated as personal property under state law); *In re* Thomas, 344 B.R. 386 (Bankr. W.D. Pa. 2006) (escrow account is personal property under Pennsylvania law and modification was therefore permitted).

350 11 U.S.C. § 522.

351 11 U.S.C. § 101(54).

352 *See In re* Dardar, 3 B.R. 641 (Bankr. E.D. Va. 1980) (§ 522(f) only applicable to property claimed exempt).

353 National Consumer Law Center, Consumer Bankruptcy Law and Practice Ch. 10 (9th ed. 2009).

354 11 U.S.C. § 101(36).

ments)[355] and liens obtained by sequestration or any other legal or equitable proceeding,[356] this section provides a powerful tool for the debtor. When there is a dispute as to whether a particular lien is a judicial lien, for example when a lien is granted in divorce proceedings, careful analysis of the Code's definition is required.[357]

The power to avoid judicial liens extends to every type of exempt property without limitation. Even if the lien has caused the property to be removed from the debtor's possession, the lien can be avoided, forcing the return of the property.[358] If the lien only partially impairs the exemption, only that part may be avoided. On the other hand, when the total value of the property subject to the lien could be claimed as exempt, any amount of liens can be avoided because even if only a few dollars of liens remained, they would impair the exemption. Hence, if a house with $25,000 in equity is claimed as totally exempt, a judgment lien against the home of $100,000 may be totally avoided under this section.[359] When only some liens may be avoided, the most junior avoidable liens are the ones which impair the debtor's exemption.[360] In addition, the mathematical formula provided in section 522(f)(2)(A) can result in the partial avoidance of a judicial lien.[361]

The Bankruptcy Rules prescribe the procedure to be followed for lien avoidance by the debtor. Bankruptcy Rule 4003(d) provides that lien avoidance under 11 U.S.C. § 522(f) shall be by motion in accordance with Bankruptcy Rule 9014.[362] The burden is on the debtor to file a lien avoidance proceeding.[363] If none is filed, all liens on the property of the debtor, including otherwise exempt property, will normally survive the bankruptcy.

Once the avoidance is accomplished, the debtor's advocate should be sure to obtain an order granting complete relief, including a requirement that the lienholder take all steps necessary to reflect the avoidance of the lien in state and local recording offices. Alternatively, the debtor's advocate should obtain a court order suitable for filing where the lien is recorded. Failure to record cancellation of the lien may result in inadvertent payment when the property is sold or otherwise transferred.

9.9 Debtor's Statement of Intention Regarding Secured Property

9.9.1 Requirements of Section 521(a)(2)

Section 521(a)(2)[364] requires the debtor to file a statement of intentions with respect to property securing consumer debts. The debtor need not state all of his or her plans regarding the property on this statement (e.g., lien avoidance, continuing payments in accordance with 11 U.S.C. § 524(j), etc.). All that is required is a declaration that the

355 *In re* Gardner, 685 F.2d 106 (3d Cir. 1982). *See also In re* Bistansin, 95 B.R. 29 (Bankr. W.D. Pa. 1989) (lien created by sheriff's levy is avoidable judicial lien). *Cf. In re* Duden, 102 B.R. 797 (D. Colo. 1989) (lien which would impair debtor's ability to alienate property post-petition is avoidable even though it may not presently attach to debtor's property as a judicial lien because of homestead exemption).

356 *But see In re* Lucas, 21 B.R. 794 (Bankr. W.D. Mich. 1982) (lien given to secure appeal bond held to be security interest and not judicial lien).

357 11 U.S.C. § 522(f)(1)(A). *See also* Farrey v. Sanderfoot, 500 U.S. 291, 111 S. Ct. 1825, 114 L. Ed. 2d 337 (1991).

358 *In re* Bagley, 1 B.R. 116 (Bankr. E.D. Pa. 1979) (sheriff ordered to return automobile seized under levy). *See also In re* Brown, 734 F.2d 119 (2d Cir. 1984) (debtor could exempt and avoid judicial lien on cash proceeds of execution sale of property when proceeds still in hands of state court commissioner); Bryant v. Gen. Elec. Credit Corp., 58 B.R. 144 (N.D. Ill. 1986); *In re* Buzzell, 56 B.R. 197 (Bankr. D. Md. 1986).

359 11 U.S.C. § 522(f)(2)(A).

Some difficult issues arise if the exempt property is jointly owned and the lien involved is against only one owner. *See In re* Lehman, 205 F.3d 1255 (11th Cir. 2000) (overriding language of the statute to count only one half the amount of jointly owed senior debts against the debtor's interest in the property); Nelson v. Scala, 192 F.3d 32 (1st Cir. 1999) (same). *Cf. In re* Cozad, 208 B.R. 495 (B.A.P. 10th Cir. 1997); *In re* Piersol, 244 B.R. 309 (Bankr. E.D. Pa. 2000). *See generally Update on Bankruptcy Exemptions*, 18 NCLC REPORTS *Bankruptcy and Foreclosure Ed.* 25 (May/June 2000).

360 Although § 522(f)(2)(A) does not specify the order of priority in which multiple judicial liens on the property may be avoided, courts have held that the most junior judicial liens should be avoided first. *See* Owen v. Owen, 500 U.S. 305, 111 S. Ct. 1833, 114 L. Ed. 2d 250 (1991) (if property would be exempt "but for" the lien, lien can be avoided); *In re* Hanger, 217 B.R. 592 (B.A.P. 9th Cir. 1997), *aff'd*, 196 F.3d 1292 (9th Cir. 1999); *In re* Jochum, 309 B.R. 327 (Bankr. E.D. Mo. 2004); *In re* Dolan, 230 B.R. 642 (Bankr. D. Conn. 1999) (state law priority determines order in which judicial liens are avoided); *In re* Hoffman, 28 B.R. 503 (Bankr. D. Md. 1983).

361 *See In re* Silveira, 141 F.3d 34 (1st Cir. 1998) (debtor sought to avoid a judicial lien in the amount of $209,500 on homestead property valued at $157,000 that was encumbered by a $117,680 mortgage; as the sum of all liens on the property plus the debtor's $15,000 exemption was $342,180, amount of impairment that could be avoided was $185,180, resulting in the creditor retaining a lien in the amount of $24,320); *In re* Falvo, 227 B.R. 662 (B.A.P. 6th Cir. 1998).

362 The adversary proceeding service of process rules contained in Bankruptcy Rule 7004 apply to a motion to avoid a lien. These rules contain special requirements for serving insured depository institutions. *See In re* Hamlett, 322 F.3d 342 (4th Cir. 2003) (lien avoidance judgment vacated when officer of financial institution not properly served).

Information about whether a particular entity is an insured depository institution may be obtained on the Federal Deposit Insurance Corporation's website at www2.fdic.gov/structur/search/findoneinst.asp.

363 Issues concerning the avoidance of judicial liens are discussed more fully in National Consumer Law Center, Consumer Bankruptcy Law and Practice § 10.4.2 (9th ed. 2009). Sample forms are included in Appendix G of that treatise as well as on this treatise's companion website.

364 11 U.S.C. § 521(a)(2)(A).

debtor intends to retain or to surrender the collateral, and, if applicable, to claim it as exempt, to redeem it, to reaffirm the secured debt, or assume an unexpired lease on the property.

The statement must be filed within thirty days of the filing of a chapter 7 petition or before the first meeting of the creditors, whichever is earlier; the court within that period may extend the deadline. The statement is not required in chapter 13 cases.[365]

Within thirty days after the date first set for the meeting of creditors, the debtor "shall perform his intention."[366] In most cases performance is quite simple, as the intention to retain or exempt property has long since been accomplished. The provision can be seen as setting a guideline as to when redemption is to be accomplished; however, section 521(a)(2)[367] also expressly provides that it does not affect substantive rights, so it should not bar redemption if it is not achieved by the deadline.[368]

The chapter 7 trustee is supposed to "ensure that the debtor shall perform" the stated intention,[369] but the Code provides no mechanism for the trustee to use. As a practical matter, trustees will probably become involved only if a secured creditor wants the debtor to carry out the stated intention of redemption or reaffirmation. Presumably, the trustee could then ask the court to resolve the matter, something the secured creditor could just as easily do on its own. The statement of intention thus seems designed primarily as a way for secured creditors to obtain notice of what the debtor plans to do, and as a guideline of when redemption and reaffirmation should occur. The thirty-day guideline may even prove helpful to a debtor who has no other way of stopping a foreclosure or repossession, as it may extend the time a debtor may retain possession of property.[370]

The bankruptcy rules provide that the statement of intention shall be prepared as prescribed by Official Form Number 8.[371] That form requires a specific listing of all property subject to security interests securing consumer debts, and the names of the creditors holding liens on the property.[372] The rules also require that the statement be served on the trustee and each creditor named in the statement on or before the date the statement is filed.[373] The statement of intention may be amended by the debtor at any time before the time period for performance of the intention expires.[374]

It is important to note what this section does and does not require. It requires only that the debtor state: (1) whether the property will be surrendered or retained; (2) whether it will be claimed as exempt; (3) whether the debtor intends to redeem the property; (4) whether the debtor intends to reaffirm the debt secured by the property; and (5) whether the debtor intends to assume an unexpired lease on the property.[375]

Before the 2005 Act, there had been a split of opinion as to whether the debtor must choose one of the options provided under the Bankruptcy Code or in the Official Form, and whether the debtor could retain secured property without reaffirming the debt by continuing to make payments (often referred to as the "fourth option").[376] Despite the lack of a material change in the statutory language of section 521(a)(2), most courts have held that the 2005 amendments to the Code eliminated the "fourth option" with respect to personal property because of the newly enacted sections 362(h), 521(a)(6) and 521(d), as discussed at § 9.9.2, *infra*.[377] However, some secured creditors have continued to permit the debtor to choose to retain the property subject to the creditor's security interest and state law rights whatever they may be. For example, a debtor may choose to simply continue paying an automobile loan or home mortgage without either redeeming or reaffirming the debt.[378] In fact, with respect to a home mortgage, the 2005 Act amendments lend further support for the continuing

365 Fed. R. Bankr. P. 1007(b)(2).

366 11 U.S.C. § 521(a)(2)(B).
The court may also provide additional time for performance.

367 11 U.S.C. § 521(a)(2)(C). *See In re* Eagle, 51 B.R. 959 (Bankr. N.D. Ohio 1985) (debtors who stated intention to reaffirm debt not barred from redeeming property instead).

368 *In re* Rodgers, 273 B.R. 186 (Bankr. C.D. Ill. 2002) (redemption not barred by expiration of former forty-five day period from statement of intention).

369 11 U.S.C. § 704(3).

370 *See In re* Simpson, 147 B.R. 14 (Bankr. E.D.N.C. 1992) (debtor's counsel was justified in refusing to consent to relief from stay for creditor to complete foreclosure before expiration of the statutory period).

371 Fed. R. Bankr. P. 1007(b)(2).

372 In addition, Official Form 8 requires the debtor to list personal property subject to a lease, and to name the lessor.

373 *Id.*

374 Fed. R. Bankr. P. 1009(b); *In re* Crooks, 148 B.R. 867 (Bankr. N.D. Ill. 1993) (debtor's statement which erroneously stated intention to retain car did not preclude debtor from later surrendering it).

375 11 U.S.C. § 521(a)(2)(A).

376 *See In re* Price, 370 F.3d 362 (3d Cir. 2004) (Code does not limit debtor to choice between redemption or reaffirmation); *In re* Parker, 139 F.3d 668 (9th Cir. 1998); *In re* Boodrow, 126 F.3d 43 (2d Cir. 1997); *In re* Belanger, 962 F.2d 345 (4th Cir. 1992); Lowry Fed. Credit Union v. West, 882 F.2d 1543 (10th Cir. 1989); *In re* Windham, 136 B.R. 878 (Bankr. M.D. Fla. 1992); *In re* Stefano, 134 B.R. 824 (Bankr. W.D. Pa. 1991). *See also In re* Sokolowski, 205 F.3d 532 (2d Cir. 2000) (default on filing clause in credit contract is unenforceable under the Boodrow ruling). *But see In re* Burr, 160 F.3d 843 (1st Cir. 1998); *In re* Johnson, 89 F.3d 249 (5th Cir. 1996) (debtor who was in default on secured debt did not have right to retain collateral without either redeeming or reaffirming debt); *In re* Taylor, 3 F.3d 1512 (11th Cir. 1993); *In re* Edwards, 901 F.2d 1383 (7th Cir. 1990); *In re* Bell, 700 F.2d 1053 (6th Cir. 1983).

377 *In re* Dumont, 581 F.3d 1104 (9th Cir. 2009) ("ride through" option as recognized in *Parker* was effectively overruled by 2005 amendments); *In re* Husain, 364 B.R. 211 (Bankr. E.D. Va. 2007); *In re* Blakeley, 363 B.R. 225 (Bankr. D. Utah 2007); *In re* McFall, 356 B.R. 674 (Bankr. N.D. Ohio 2006); *In re* Steinhaus, 349 B.R. 694 (Bankr. D. Idaho 2006).

378 *See* National Consumer Law Center, Consumer Bankruptcy Law and Practice § 11.5.4 (9th ed. 2009).

payment option by clarifying that a mortgage creditor can accept regular payments after the case is completed without violating the discharge injunction even if the debt is not reaffirmed.[379]

In jurisdictions in which the debtor is limited to the options of redemption, reaffirmation or surrender, problems arise because debtors cannot unilaterally exercise any of those three options. Redemption requires agreement about the value of the item, in order to set the proper price. Reaffirmation requires a bilateral agreement on terms negotiated between the parties. And even surrender requires that the creditor and the debtor jointly agree on a plan to transfer the property.

In each case, it is sufficient that the debtor make a good faith effort to effectuate the option chosen on the statement of intention. Thus, if redemption is chosen, the debtor may make an offer of redemption based on the reasonable replacement value of the property.[380] For reaffirmation, an offer of terms is probably sufficient.[381] And for surrender of property that is not easily moved, offering to make it available for the creditor to pick up is all that is required. The issues are somewhat more difficult for vehicles, but as most automobile creditors do not run vehicle sales lots, even a car cannot simply be dropped off somewhere unilaterally with a transfer of title.

Ultimately, the creditor is left to state law rights with respect to the collateral. The lien passes through the bankruptcy process unaffected. The bankruptcy court cannot order turnover of property to the creditor, replevin or foreclosure.[382] And the creditor is not permitted to take steps toward repossession or foreclosure that violate the automatic stay,[383] even if the debtor fails to carry out her intention as designated on the statement.

9.9.2 Stay Relief Based on Noncompliance with Statement of Intention

9.9.2.1 General

Prior to the 2005 Act, there was no sanction provided for failing to carry through on stated intentions, which reflected the view that the statement of intention was designed primarily as a notice provision for secured creditors. Thus, court decisions prior to the 2005 amendments held that a debtor's failure to follow through on a stated intention at best gave the secured creditor an additional argument in seeking relief from the automatic stay.[384] A series of overlapping and conflicting provisions in the 2005 Act codifies these cases and provides that relief from the stay is the proper remedy for other violations relating to the statement of intention. These provisions are limited to security interests in personal property, and therefore would apply to home secured loans only if the security is treated as personal property (such as manufactured homes in some states).

9.9.2.2 Stay Relief Under Section 362(h)

Section 521(a)(2)(C) was amended in 2005 to add an exception for relief from the stay as permitted by section 362(h). Section 362(h) terminates the automatic stay with respect to personal property of the estate securing a claim, and renders that property no longer property of the estate, if the debtor fails to (1) timely file a statement of intention, or to state an intention to surrender the property, redeem the property, enter into a reaffirmation agreement with respect to the underlying claim, or assume an unexpired lease on the property, and (2) fails to take timely action to carry out the stated intention.[385] Thus, the provision has no applicability if the debtor has timely entered into a reaffirmation agreement, even if that agreement is later disapproved by the court.[386] Importantly, section 362(h) does not apply to resi-

379 11 U.S.C. § 524(j). *See In re* Caraballo, 386 B.R. 398 (Bankr. D. Conn. 2008) (2005 Act did not eliminate ride-through option recognized in *Boodrow* as to real property); *In re* Wilson, 372 B.R. 816 (Bankr. D.S.C. 2007) (debtor may elect ride-through option as to real property; option still available after 2005 amendments); § 9.11.2, *infra*.

380 *See* National Consumer Law Center, Repossessions § 8.5 (6th ed. 2005 and Supp.).

381 *See* National Consumer Law Center, Repossessions § 8.8 (6th ed. 2005 and Supp.).

382 *In re* Steinhaus, 349 B.R. 694 (Bankr. D. Idaho 2006) (creditor not entitled to order directing that debtor turn over vehicle; rather, creditor left only with state law rights); *In re* Donnell, 234 B.R. 567 (Bankr. D.N.H. 1999) (denying injunctive relief to enforce security interest and refusing to deny discharge of debt or dismiss case); *In re* Weir, 173 B.R. 682 (Bankr. E.D. Cal. 1994).

383 *See* National Consumer Law Center, Repossessions § 8.2 (6th ed. 2005 and Supp.).

384 *In re* Rathbun, 275 B.R. 434 (Bankr. D.R.I. 2001) (adopting opinion in Donnell); *In re* Donnell, 234 B.R. 567 (Bankr. D.N.H. 1999) (denying injunctive relief to enforce security interest and refusing to deny discharge of debt or dismiss case); *In re* Weir, 173 B.R. 682 (Bankr. E.D. Cal. 1994) (no implied cause of action or other remedy, except possibly relief from stay if debtors are in monetary default on obligation, if creditor believes debtors have not filed adequate statement of intentions). *See also* National Consumer Law Center, Consumer Bankruptcy Law and Practice § 11.4 (9th ed. 2009).

385 If a creditor violates the stay based on a good faith belief that the stay had been terminated as to the debtor under §§ 362(h), 362(k)(2) provides that the recovery under § 362(k)(1) shall be limited to actual damages.

386 *In re* Baker, 390 B.R. 524 (Bankr. D. Del. 2008), *aff'd* 400 B.R. 136 (D. Del. 2009) (bankruptcy ordered return to debtor of automobile repossessed by creditor after court refused to approve reaffirmation; creditor had no right under Delaware law to repossess automobile); *In re* Chim, 381 B.R. 191 (Bankr. D.

dential mortgages or deeds of trust, unless the security interest is a lien on a manufactured home that is treated as personal property under state law.

Section 362(h) does not affect the debtor's substantive rights in relation to the creditor, but merely creates a possible early termination of the automatic stay. The 2005 Act reinforces this conclusion by adding, as the sole exception to section 521(a)(2)(C), language making clear that the only effect of failing to take certain actions under the provision is relief from the automatic stay in some cases slightly earlier than would ordinarily occur without the application of section 362(h).

Section 362(h)(1)(B) provides that the stay of section 362(a) is terminated if the debtor does not take timely the action specified in the statement of intention, unless the statement states an intention to reaffirm the debt on its original terms and the creditor refuses to agree to such reaffirmation.[387] There may be a question as to what the original contract terms were or how much is owed on the contract. For example, it is not clear whether "original contract terms" mean that default rates, late charges or other fees that have been assessed due to events subsequent to the contract, or other subsequent modifications in terms, should be eliminated. If there is a dispute regarding the current balance, a debtor may maintain that the creditor has refused to reaffirm on the original contract terms. If a creditor fails to provide a debtor sufficient information to determine the precise balance, the debtor may be able to take the position that he or she is willing to reaffirm on the original terms but has not been given sufficient information to do so.

9.9.2.3 Stay Relief Under Section 521(a)(6)

Section 521(a)(6) provides that the debtor shall not retain possession of personal property as to which a creditor has an allowed secured claim for the purchase price secured by that personal property, unless the debtor, not later than forty-five days after the meeting of creditors, enters into a reaffirmation agreement or redeems the property. If the debtor fails to "so act," the stay under section 362(a) is terminated and the property is no longer property of the estate. The creditor may then take whatever action is permitted with respect to the property under applicable nonbankruptcy law.[388] Once again, section 521(a)(6) does not apply to residential mortgages or deeds of trust, unless the security interest is a lien on a manufactured home that is treated as personal property under state law. Like section 362(h), this provision also does not apply if the debtor timely redeems or enters into a reaffirmation agreement, even if the reaffirmation is disapproved by the court.[389]

Section 521(a)(6) raises a host of issues in addition to those raised by section 362(h). First, the time period stated is inconsistent with that in section 521(a)(2)(B). The former requires the debtor to perform the stated intention within thirty days of the first date set for the meeting of creditors.[390] Section 521(a)(6) sets a period for reaffirmation or redemption of forty-five days after the meeting of creditors, which not only is a different length of time, but probably should run from the conclusion of the meeting, which could be well after the first date set for the meeting. However, the time period set by section 521(a)(6) is not a deadline for such acts. It simply is a time period after which the property is no longer estate property protected by the section 362(a) stay. Because, as discussed below, this provision applies to a more specific category of secured debts, the forty-five-day time period may override the shorter thirty-day time period incorporated in section 362(h).

Second, the reach of section 521(a)(6) is more limited than section 521(a)(2). The former applies only to allowed claims and only to purchase money security interests, while the latter applies to any secured debt or lease covered by the statement of intention.[391] Generally, in order for a claim to be allowed, it must be filed in accordance with section 501.[392] Few creditors file proofs of claim in chapter 7 no asset cases. Whether they will begin to do so to come within the ambit of section 521(a)(6) remains to be seen. Even if a creditor files a proof of claim in a no asset chapter 7 case, the debtor may file an objection to the claim and it is then not allowed unless the court overrules the objection.

Third, the provision does not authorize a creditor to repossess property. It leaves that issue to applicable non-

Md. 2008); *In re* Moustafi, 371 B.R. 434 (Bankr. D. Ariz. 2007) (permitting ride-through after denying approval of reaffirmation agreement); *In re* Husain, 364 B.R. 211 (Bankr. E.D. Va. 2007); *In re* Blakely, 363 B.R. 225 (Bankr. D. Utah 2007); *In re* Quintero, 2006 WL 1351623 (Bankr. N.D. Cal. May 17, 2006) (automatic stay does not terminate under § 362(h) if debtor enters into reaffirmation agreement that court later disapproves because creditor failed provide required reaffirmation disclosures under § 524(k)).

387 *See In re* Hinson, 352 B.R. 48 (Bankr. E.D.N.C. 2006) (stay did not terminate when debtor offered to reaffirm on original terms and creditor insisted on including attorney fees in reaffirmation).

388 Such creditor action is not permitted if the court determines, on a motion filed by the trustee before the forty-five-day period expires and after notice and a hearing, that the property is of consequential value or benefit to the estate, and orders adequate protection for the creditor's interest and delivery of any "collateral" to the trustee's possession. 11 U.S.C. § 362(h)(2).

389 *In re* Baker, 390 B.R. 524 (Bankr. D. Del. 2008), *aff'd*, 400 B.R. 136 (D. Del. 2009); *In re* Quintero, 2006 WL 1351623 (Bankr. N.D. Cal. May 17, 2006) (section 521(a)(6) does not require reaffirmation agreement to be approved).

390 11 U.S.C. § 521(a)(2)(B).

391 *See* Coastal Fed. Credit Union v. Hardiman, 398 B.R. 161 (E.D.N.C. 2008); *In re* Donald, 343 B.R. 524 (Bankr. E.D.N.C. 2006) (plain meaning construction of the term "claim for the purchase price" suggests that § 521(a)(6) is limited to a claim for the full purchase price of the personal property).

392 11 U.S.C. § 502(A).

bankruptcy law.[393] There are likely to be serious questions under nonbankruptcy law about whether repossession from a debtor who is current in payments is in good faith, whether a creditor has waived a default by accepting later payments, or whether other provisions of state law would prohibit repossession.

In any event, the ultimate effect of section 521(a)(6), in most cases in which it applies and in which the debtor has neither entered into a reaffirmation agreement or redeemed the property, is to terminate the section 362(a) stay with respect to the property approximately fifteen days earlier than it would otherwise be terminated. In most chapter 7 cases, the court promptly closes chapter 7 cases once the sixty-day deadline for objections to discharge has run.[394]

9.10 Sale of Property

In some cases, homeowners may have no choice but to sell their home on which mortgage payments are no longer possible. Typically, the price at a private market sale is much higher than the price obtained at foreclosure. This means that the homeowner can preserve more equity.

By preventing a foreclosure auction while the automatic stay remains in place,[395] bankruptcy can help homeowners get enough time to arrange a private market sale. However, in the case of a chapter 7, delay of foreclosure may be quite limited, especially if the mortgage holder quickly seeks relief from the automatic stay.

In a chapter 7 case, if the debtor wishes to sell property in the period before the case is completed, that sale can only be effectuated with the cooperation of the chapter 7 trustee and the permission of the bankruptcy court. Because the trustee has an interest in the property during the bankruptcy case even if the equity is fully exempt, the trustee may need to abandon that interest[396] (something he or she should be willing to do if there is no non-exempt equity) or to join in a motion explaining the details of the sale and seeking permission to allow the sale to go forward. If there is non-exempt equity, the trustee will want to recover that amount for the benefit of creditors. If the sale is completed after the chapter 7 case is completed, but before the foreclosure auction, the lender has no right to object if it is paid in full from the proceeds of the sale. And the trustee will have abandoned the estate's interest, by operation of law at the close of the case.[397]

A more thorough way to achieve the same result is to file a chapter 13 plan which includes a provision to liquidate the property.[398] As the debtor retains more control of property of the estate during a chapter 13 case,[399] it is somewhat easier to manage a chapter 13 sale process. In order to have the plan confirmed though, the debtor may need to establish the value of the property, steps taken toward achieving a sale, and the plan for distributing the sale proceeds.[400] It is helpful to have the trustee and the mortgage holder supporting the plan, or at least agreeing not to oppose it.

Before any sale of the property, it is advisable to obtain a specific order authorizing the sale free and clear of liens to satisfy any title insurers, specifying the distribution of the proceeds, and setting the compensation of any real estate broker.[401] This can generally be accomplished by a motion seeking such an order, with service on all lienholders and other affected parties.[402]

Another scenario for sale of property in chapter 13 arises when the debtor has sought to cure a default on a home mortgage and is prevented from doing so by further financial problems. If trustee payments are not made, the debtor is likely to face a motion to dismiss the case. If monthly mortgage payments are the problem, then a motion for relief from stay by the affected creditor is likely.[403]

If the debtor has substantial equity in the property, the debtor's best option may be to seek to modify the chapter 13 plan in order to sell the property under the plan.[404] The

393 *In re* Steinhaus, 349 B.R. 694 (Bankr. D. Idaho 2006); *In re* Rowe, 342 B.R. 341 (Bankr. D. Kan. 2006) (provision does not compel turnover of property but merely recognizes creditor's right to exercise its state law remedies).

394 Bankruptcy Rule 4004(c) requires that the court normally grant a discharge forthwith after the deadline for objections to discharge (sixty days after the first date set for the meeting of creditors) has run. Unless there are assets to administer, the case is then closed and the automatic stay ends.

395 *See* § 9.3, *supra*.

396 11 U.S.C. § 554(a).

397 11 U.S.C. § 554(c).

398 *See* 11 U.S.C. § 1322(b)(8). *See also* Williams, Non-Business Liquidation under chapter 13 of the Bankruptcy Code, 59 Am. Bankr. L.J. 283 (1985).

399 11 U.S.C. §§ 1303, 1306(b).

400 *See, e.g., In re* Anderson, 18 B.R. 763 (Bankr. S.D. Ohio 1982) (plan not feasible when its success contingent on sale of realty in adverse market).

401 In some districts, it may be necessary to obtain an order appointing the broker as a professional person in the case pursuant to § 327(a). *See In re* Haley, 950 F.2d 588 (9th Cir. 1991) (refusing commission to broker who had not been given approval to act as broker for debtor's property in chapter 11 case).

Probably, a chapter 13 debtor who retains a broker is not subject to the provisions governing employment of professionals by the trustee. However, some courts may feel otherwise if estate assets are to be used to pay the broker. *See* National Consumer Law Center, Consumer Bankruptcy Law and Practice § 12.6.5 (9th ed. 2009).

402 *See* National Consumer Law Center, Consumer Bankruptcy Law and Practice Appx. G, Form 72 (9th ed. 2009).

403 Grounds to defend such a motion are discussed in Ch. 9 of National Consumer Law Center, Consumer Bankruptcy Law and Practice (9th ed. 2009).

There may be other ways to defend such a motion without selling the property, particularly if there is only a small post-petition default.

404 Confirmed chapter 13 plans may be modified, with limitations, pursuant to 11 U.S.C. § 1329. If the plan has not yet been

debtor then can seek to pay the trustee from the proceeds of the sale or to defend the motion for relief on the ground that the creditor is adequately protected by the equity and by the anticipated full payment of the debt from the proceeds of sale.

One issue that has occasionally prevented execution of such a modified plan is whether the debtor must reevaluate the best interests of the creditors[405] (and/or the debtor's ability to pay)[406] in the modified plan.[407] If the property has appreciated in value, reevaluation under these tests may require larger payments to unsecured creditors than originally anticipated. If faced with an objection to the plan as modified, a debtor should argue that the property is valued to determine its liquidation value to creditors under the Code as of the date of filing.[408] It follows that equity accruing post-petition then belongs to the debtor rather than the estate.

If the court does not accept that argument, the debtor has a right to dismiss the bankruptcy case (if it has not previously been converted from chapter 7) and to sell the property outside the bankruptcy process without court supervision.[409] Point out to the court that in such an event, unsecured creditors will get no additional dividend. In making this choice, of course, the debtor must balance the amount of the sale proceeds that would be paid to unsecured creditors under the plan as modified, against the potential lost opportunity to obtain a chapter 13 discharge.

confirmed, the plan may be freely modified under 11 U.S.C. § 1323.

405 11 U.S.C. § 1325(a)(4).

406 11 U.S.C. § 1325(b).

407 Barbosa v. Solomon, 235 F.3d 31 (1st Cir. 2000).

Similar issues may arise when a debtor seeks to modify a plan to pay off a mortgage with the proceeds of a refinancing loan. *In re* Martin, 232 B.R. 29 (Bankr. D. Mass. 1999) (debtor cannot pay off plan early with proceeds of home mortgage refinancing without plan modification reanalyzing obligations to other creditors under § 1325). *But see In re* Murphy, 474 F.3d 143 (4th Cir. 2007) (debtors' early payoff of plan with proceeds from refinancing did not result in improvement in debtors' "financial condition" sufficient to warrant plan modification); *In re* Sunahara, 326 B.R. 768 (B.A.P. 9th Cir. 2005) (debtor may modify plan, despite local rule and model plan, to provide for early termination without full payment of all claims, since plain language of § 1329(b) does not require application of disposable income test in § 1325(b)(1)(B) with respect to modified plans).

408 11 U.S.C. § 522(a)(2).

409 11 U.S.C. § 1307(b).

Timing of the exercise of this right to dismiss should take account of the time needed to sell the property outside bankruptcy. The debtor may need to maximize the period in which the creditor is prevented from foreclosing by the automatic stay or the confirmed chapter 13 plan in order to have sufficient opportunity to arrange the details of the sale of the property.

9.11 Impact of Bankruptcy on Later Foreclosure Prevention Efforts

9.11.1 In General

Filing a bankruptcy which does not fully address a mortgage delinquency may impact future legal proceedings and negotiated agreements seeking to avoid foreclosure. Even when the bankruptcy does nothing more than create temporary delay, either because the mortgage holder gets relief from the stay or the case is completed without resolving the delinquency,[410] it may nevertheless have an impact on future efforts to prevent foreclosure.

9.11.2 Impact of Bankruptcy on Negotiated Workout Plans and Loan Modifications

9.11.2.1 Effect of Prior Discharge

As a completed bankruptcy normally discharges a borrowers' personal liability to pay a loan, even while the mortgage remains in place, some lenders are wary of negotiating a workout agreement following bankruptcy. Because mortgage holders' policies differ on this question, it does not hurt to try to pursue a loan workout or modification even after bankruptcy.

Some mortgage holders may insist that personal liability be reaffirmed as a precondition to a loan workout after bankruptcy. As the Bankruptcy Code precludes reaffirmation agreements that are not made and filed with the court before the discharge is entered,[411] postbankruptcy reaffirmation is not possible. Mortgage holders should be told that this is the case and asked about alternatives. One method to satisfy the holder in this situation might be to structure the workout as a refinance with a new note and mortgage so that the owner agrees to accept personal liability going forward as part of the deal.[412]

410 The lien associated with a mortgage will pass through the bankruptcy unaffected if it is not avoided or paid. *See* Dewsnup v. Timm, 502 U.S. 410, 112 S. Ct. 773, 116 L. Ed. 2d 903 (1992).

411 11 U.S.C. § 524(c).

412 This may not be possible if there are junior liens on the property as the lender, upon refinancing, would lose its priority. In addition, the refinancing may be viewed as a void reaffirmation despite the homeowner's willingness to enter into the new agreement. *See In re* Lopez, 345 F.3d 701 (9th Cir. 2002) ("asset retention agreement" which required debtors to pay discharged debt was void reaffirmation); *In re* Zarro, 268 B.R. 715 (Bankr. S.D.N.Y. 2001) (post-petition settlement agreement that included reaffirmation of debt was unenforceable). *But see* DuBois v. Ford Motor Credit Co., 276 F.3d 1019 (8th Cir. 2002) (creditor did not violate discharge injunction when debtors

The 2005 amendments make it easier to convince a mortgage holder to enter into a workout agreement if the debtor has not signed a reaffirmation agreement. Section 524(j) provides that certain actions of creditors holding security interests in real property of the debtor, such as seeking periodic payments in a ride-through situation,[413] do not violate the discharge injunction. The lien retained by the creditor must be on real property that is the debtor's principal residence.[414]

The exception to the discharge injunction created by this provision applies to creditor acts that are in the ordinary course of business between the creditor and the debtor.[415] The acts must also be limited to seeking or obtaining periodic payments on a valid lien "in lieu of pursuit of *in rem* relief to enforce the lien."[416] This provision is consistent with court opinions in ride-through jurisdictions that have found section 524(a)(2) is not violated if the creditor does not attempt to collect on the discharged debt as a personal liability of the debtor, and if the collection efforts do not involve coercion or harassment by the creditor.[417]

9.11.2.2 Bankruptcy Policies of Loss Mitigation Programs

Policies at major national institutions such as HUD, Fannie Mae, Freddie Mac, and the Department of Treasury (for its Home Affordable Modification Program) now allow workout agreements with homeowners that have filed bankruptcy, even without reaffirmation of the underlying debt, because significant losses may be mitigated by working with the existing borrower.[418] In some cases workout discussions are possible even while a debtor is in a bankruptcy proceeding.[419] For the HAMP loan modification program, Treasury guidelines specify that a borrower in an active chapter 7 or chapter 13 bankruptcy case must be considered for HAMP if the borrower, borrower's counsel or bankruptcy trustee submits a request to the servicer.[420] In addition, borrowers who are in a trial period plan and subsequently file for bankruptcy may not be denied a permanent HAMP modification on the basis of the bankruptcy filing.[421]

In a pending chapter 13 case, if the debtor is able to obtain approval of a loan modification or workout agreement before confirmation of the plan, the debtor may propose a plan which incorporates the terms of the modification or workout.[422] In some cases, this may also be possible post-confirmation, though the debtor may need to seek bankruptcy court approval of the modification or workout and possibly a modification of the chapter 13 plan.[423] Under Treasury guidelines for the HAMP loan modification program, servicers are required to work with the debtor and debtor's counsel to obtain any court or trustee approvals required in accordance with local court rules and procedures.[424] The Treasury guidelines also provide that if a debtor in an active chapter 13 case is in a trial period plan and makes postpetition payments in the amount required by the trial plan, the servicer may not object to confirmation, move for stay relief, or move for dismissal of the bankruptcy case on the grounds that the debtor did not pay the non-modified mortgage payments.[425]

Some loss mitigation programs seek to take advantage of the extensive financial information that the debtor submits in the required bankruptcy schedules filed with the court, to avoid the debtor having to compile and resubmit this same information as part of the workout application process. For

---

voluntarily entered into and paid new car lease that included excess usage charges from previous lease that had been discharged without any coercion by creditor; court did not address question of whether new lease was a void reaffirmation).

413 Debtors in some circuits are permitted to retain secured property without reaffirming the debt if payments continue to be made post-discharge. *E.g.*, *In re* Price, 370 F.3d 362 (3d Cir. 2004); *In re* Parker, 139 F.3d 668 (9th Cir. 1998); Capital Communications Fed. Cred. Union v. Boodrow, 126 F.3d 43 (2d Cir. 1997). *See also* National Consumer Law Center, Consumer Bankruptcy Law and Practice § 11.4 (9th ed. 2009).

414 11 U.S.C. § 522(j)(1).

415 11 U.S.C. § 522(j)(2).

416 11 U.S.C. § 522(j)(3).

417 *In re* Garske, 287 B.R. 537 (B.A.P. 9th Cir. 2002) (telephone calls from secured creditor about whether debtor intended to continue payments in a ride-through jurisdiction did not violate discharge injunction); *In re* Ramirez, 280 B.R. 252 (C.D. Cal. 2002). *But see In re* Henry, 266 B.R. 457 (Bankr. C.D. Cal. 2001).

418 *See, e.g.*, Dep't of the Treasury, Home Affordable Modification Program, Supplemental Directive 09-01 (Apr. 6, 2009) and Dep't of the Treasury, Supplemental Directive 10-02 (Mar. 24, 2009) ("If the borrower previously received a Chapter 7 bankruptcy discharge but did not reaffirm the mortgage debt under applicable law, the following language must be inserted in . . . the Agreement: 'I was discharged in a Chapter 7 bankruptcy proceeding subsequent to the execution of the Loan Documents. Based on this representation, Lender agrees that I will not have personal liability on the debt pursuant to this Agreement.' "); Fannie Mae Announcement 08-03 (Dec. 12, 2008) (same); Dep't of Hous. & Urban Dev. Mortgagee Letter 2008-32 (Oct. 17, 2008).

419 *See, e.g.*, Dep't of Hous. & Urban Dev. Mortgagee Letter 2008-32 (Oct. 17, 2008) (advising mortgage holders and servicers of FHA mortgages that they must send information about the availability of loss mitigation to debtor's counsel upon receipt of notice of a bankruptcy filing, and that that they "may offer appropriate loss mitigation options prior to discharge or dismissal, without requiring relief from the automatic stay and in the case of a Chapter 7 bankruptcy, without requiring reaffirmation of the debt.").

420 *See* Dep't of the Treasury, Home Affordable Modification Program, Supplemental Directive 10-02, at 7 (Mar. 24, 2009). *See also* § 2.8.6, *supra*.

421 *Id.*

422 If the debtor has already filed a chapter 13 plan, the debtor may modify the plan at any time before confirmation. 11 U.S.C. § 1323.

423 11 U.S.C. § 1329.

424 *See* Dep't of the Treasury, Home Affordable Modification Program, Supplemental Directive 10-02, at 7 (Mar. 24, 2009).

425 *Id.* at 8.

purposes of determining income eligibility, the Treasury guidelines for HAMP provide that the servicer may accept copies of the bankruptcy schedules and tax returns (if required to be filed) in lieu of the normal application documents (RMA and Form 4506T-EZ).[426] If the bankruptcy schedules are more than ninety days old, the debtor must provide the servicer with updated income information.[427] Similarly, a HUD mortgagee letter advises that the debtor's bankruptcy schedules will often include sufficient financial information for the mortgage holder to properly evaluate the debtor's eligibility for loss mitigation.[428] Using this financial information, mortgage holders are instructed that they may complete the loss mitigation evaluation before the debtor's chapter 13 plan is confirmed and may offer a pre-approved loan modification agreement.[429]

9.11.3 Impact of Bankruptcy on Legal Defenses to Foreclosure

The res judicata impact of bankruptcy is clear in some circumstances and less clear in others. Most obviously, if an issue is fully and actually litigated in a bankruptcy adversary proceeding, and the bankruptcy case proceeds to conclusion, that issue cannot then be relitigated in another forum.[430] Slightly less clear is whether a bankruptcy order resolving a claim has res judicata impact if the bankruptcy case is dismissed prior to discharge.[431] However, if the issue was fully litigated during the bankruptcy process, either claims preclusion or issue preclusion is likely to apply.

Most problematic is that a few courts have held that defenses to a loan transaction are mandatory counterclaims to a proof of claim filed in bankruptcy, so that a debtor is later precluded from raising those claims.[432] As most bankruptcy lawyers sometimes or always ignore proofs of claims filed in chapter 7 bankruptcy cases, the decisions finding res judicata impact in failing to object to claims may pose a problem for later litigation of defenses. Whenever possible, the cases invoking res judicata should be distinguished as inapplicable to consumer chapter 7 cases—especially cases in which proofs of claims were not supposed to be filed because no distribution on claims was anticipated.

When the cases cannot be distinguished, it is easy to argue that they are wrongly decided. An unopposed proof of claim is typically "deemed allowed" often without any formal court order. It is incorrect to treat this as the equivalent of a final judgment on the merits, particularly when no party had any reason to challenge the claim, because no distributions on the claim were being made. And finally, as a last resort, a bankruptcy can be reopened in order to have a claim reconsidered for cause.[433]

Finally, if a debtor has affirmative claims against a mortgage holder that predate the bankruptcy filing, they must have been listed in the debtor's bankruptcy schedules as an asset of the estate. Although most often the trustee will abandon those claims by inaction through the close of the case,[434] whereupon they revert to the debtor, failure to list the claims means that they were never administered and so never passed back from the estate to the debtor.[435] Mortgage holders often raise the failure to list affirmative claims as an asset during bankruptcy in a later case by the debtor to defeat the debtor's claims based on the doctrine of judicial estoppel.[436] The failure to schedule an asset may sometimes

426 *Id.*

427 Debtors are still required to provide a hardship affidavit.

428 *See* Dep't of Hous. & Urban Dev. Mortgagee Letter 2008-32 (Oct. 17, 2008).

429 *Id.*

430 *See, e.g., In re* Grossinger's Assocs., 184 B.R. 429 (Bankr. S.D.N.Y. 1995) (bankruptcy court order entered after full litigation on claim, barred later relitigation of same issues). *See also In re* Dominelli, 820 F.2d 313 (9th Cir. 1987) (litigation by bankruptcy trustee of debtor's usury claim precluded later suit on same ground by junior lienholder).

431 11 U.S.C. § 349(b) reinstates most liens voided in bankruptcy and vacates some orders entered during the case.

432 *See* Siegel v. Fed. Home Loan Mortgage Corp., 143 F.3d 525 (9th Cir. 1998); *In re* Baudoin, 981 F.2d 736 (5th Cir. 1993). *But see* County Fuel v. Equitable Bank Corp., 832 F.2d 290 (4th Cir. 1987) (allowance of proof of claim does not preclude claims that could have been raised by objection).

433 11 U.S.C. §§ 350, 502(j).

434 11 U.S.C. § 554(c).

435 *See* National Consumer Law Center, Consumer Bankruptcy Law and Practice § 14.3.2.6 (9th ed. 2009).

436 *See* Burnes v. Pemco, 291 F.3d 1282 (11th Cir. 2002) (debtor who intentionally failed to disclose employment discrimination case in schedules barred from pursuing claim for monetary damages but not claim for injunctive relief); Hamilton v. State Farm Fire & Cas. Co., 270 F.3d 778 (9th Cir. 2001) (debtor judicially estopped from bringing insurance claims not listed in schedules); *In re* Coastal Plains, Inc., 179 F.3d 197 (5th Cir. 1999); Wolfork v. Tackett, 273 Ga. 328, 540 S.E.2d 611 (2001) (failure to list tort claim that arose during pendency of chapter 13 judicially estopped debtor from pursing claim in state court). *But see* Stallings v. Hussmann Corp., 447 F.3d 1041 (8th Cir. 2006) (no judicial estoppel because debtor gained no advantage from a bankruptcy case that was dismissed and claim arose after petition was filed); Ajaka v. Brooksamerica Mortgage Corp., 453 F.3d 1339 (11th Cir. 2006) (lower court dismissal based on judicial estoppel reversed and remanded as evidence suggested debtor who failed to list potential Truth in Lending rescission claim did not intend to conceal the claim or "manipulate the judicial system"); Eubanks v. CBSK Fin. Group, 385 F.3d 894 (6th Cir. 2004) (judicial estoppel did not apply when debtors made good faith mistake in not scheduling claim and made numerous attempts to advise the bankruptcy court and the trustee of the claim); *In re* Barger, 348 F.3d 1289 (11th Cir. 2003) (employment discrimination case not barred when debtor's counsel inadvertently failed to schedule claim; trustee could substitute for debtor in seeking damages and debtor could seek injunctive relief); *In re* Baldwin, 307 B.R. 251 (M.D. Ala. 2004) (judicial estoppel did not apply because debtor was not aware of lender liability claim when bankruptcy filed and later promptly amended schedules); *In re* Smith, 293 B.R. 786 (Bankr. D. Kan. 2003) (when symptoms of injury from weight reduction drug did not appear until after bankruptcy was filed,

be cured by reopening the bankruptcy case and amending the debtor's schedules, thereby allowing the trustee an opportunity to administer the asset or abandon it to the debtor.[437]

9.11.4 *Impact of Prior Bankruptcy on Later Bankruptcy Filing*

If a debtor pursues a chapter 7 case or fails to cure a default under chapter 13, one avenue for foreclosure prevention may be to file another case under chapter 13. If there has been a change in circumstances, the second chapter 13 case might work out better than the first.

In general, a completed chapter 7 case does not prevent a debtor from filing under chapter 13 to cure a mortgage default or obtain other relief under the chapter 13 provisions.[438] This is true even if the debtor is unable to obtain a discharge in the later case. For example, a discharge obtained in a chapter 7 case that was filed within four years of a chapter 13 petition will prevent the debtor from getting a discharge in the subsequent chapter 13 case.[439] Similarly, if the debtor's circumstances have changed, a debtor may usually file another chapter 13 after either a successful or unsuccessful previous chapter 13 case.[440] The debtor will not be granted a discharge in a chapter 13 case filed within two years of a prior chapter 13 case in which a discharge was received.[441] In chapter 13 cases in which the debtor is precluded from obtaining a discharge, some courts have held that the debtor may not make use of lien avoidance Code provisions such those which permit the strip-off of a wholly unsecured mortgage.[442]

However, there are certain circumstances in which a chapter 13 case after a previous bankruptcy case is precluded by statute.[443] For more information, see § 9.3.3.2, *supra* and National Consumer Law Center, *Consumer Bankruptcy Law and Practice* § 12.10.[444] In addition, the dismissal of prior bankruptcy cases within the preceding year may limit the application of the automatic stay in the subsequent case, as discussed at § 9.3.3.2, *supra.*

---

debtor's claim accrued post-petition and was not estate property); *In re* Carter, 258 B.R. 526 (Bankr. S.D. Ga. 2001) (chapter 13 debtors' failure to list tort claim that arose post-confirmation and not necessary for maintenance of plan did not judicially estop them from pursing claim); Hoffman v. Truck Driving Academy, Inc., 777 So. 2d 151 (Ala. Civ. App. Ct. 2000) (no judicial estoppel where creditor failed to show it was prejudiced by debtor's failure to disclose claims in bankruptcy); Period Homes, Ltd. v. Wallick, 569 S.E.2d 502 (Ga. 2002); IBF Participating Income Fund v. Dillard-Winecoff, L.L.C. 573 S.E.2d 58 (Ga. 2002) (fact that claim was not scheduled produced no advantage for debtor because bankruptcy case was ultimately dismissed); Chicon v. Carter, 573 S.E.2d 413 (Ga. Ct. App. 2002) (tort claim that arose after confirmation of plan not part of bankruptcy estate and debtors obtained no unfair advantage by not disclosing it); Johnson v. Si-Cor, 28 P.3d 832 (Wash. Ct. App. 2001) (no evidence that failure to disclose claim benefited debtor).

The debtor's failure to schedule a cause of action should not preclude the trustee from pursuing the action. Parker v. Wendy's Intern., Inc., 365 F.3d 1268 (11th Cir. 2004).

437 11 U.S.C. § 350; Fed. R. Bankr. P. 1009. *In re* Riazuddin, 363 B.R. 177 (B.A.P. 10th Cir. 2007); *In re* Lopez, 283 B.R. 22 (B.A.P. 9th Cir. 2002) (debtor should have been permitted to reopen and amend to schedule a cause of action because, even if claim had been intentionally concealed, asset could be administered to benefit creditors); *In re* Rochester, 308 B.R. 596 (Bankr. N.D. Ga. 2004) (debtor allowed to reopen bankruptcy case to add products liability claim as debtor's failure to list in original schedules was not intentional or in bad faith). *But see* Burnes v. Pemco, 291 F.3d 1282 (11th Cir. 2002) (reopening to amend not allowed when debtor intentionally failed to disclose claim in schedules).

438 Johnson v. Home State Bank, 501 U.S. 78, 111 S. Ct. 2150, 115 L. Ed. 2d 66 (1991).

439 11 U.S.C. § 1328(f)(1).

440 *See In re* Smith, 43 B.R. 319 (Bankr. E.D.N.C. 1984) (plan confirmed, with conditions, even though there had been three prior unsuccessful chapter 13 cases).

Although a debtor may file a chapter 13 bankruptcy to cure a mortgage default or obtain some other relief under the chapter 13 provisions, the debtor will not be granted a discharge in a chapter 13 case filed within two years of a prior chapter 13 case in which a discharge was received. 11 U.S.C. § 1328(f)(2).

441 11 U.S.C. § 1328(f)(2).

442 *See* § 9.7.1, *supra. See also In re* Mendoza, 2010 WL 736834 (Bankr. D. Colo. Jan. 21, 2010) (chapter 13 plan must be completed and discharge entered before mortgage may be stripped off); *In re* Blosser, 2009 WL 1064455 (Bankr. E.D. Wis. 2009); *In re* Jarvis, 390 B.R. 600 (Bankr. C.D. Ill. 2008). *But see In re* Picht, 2009 WL 1766820 (Bankr. D. Kan. June 20, 2009) (strip-off permitted).

443 11 U.S.C. § 109(g).

444 (9th ed. 2009).

Chapter 10 Litigating Mortgage Defenses and Claims

10.1 Introduction

This chapter provides general guidance on litigating abusive lending or servicing claims in the context of foreclosure defense. The chapter is intended to be used in conjunction with all chapters in this treatise that relate to substantive claims that may be raised by a homeowner.[1] The chapter discusses how to obtain the necessary information to effectively defend a homeowner against foreclosure. It then considers who may be potential defendants, issues related to forum selection, and bonding requirements when the consumer seeks preliminary relief. Many times the homeowner's ability to challenge a mortgage transaction or foreclosure in federal court may be limited based on a related state court proceeding. This chapter reviews the *Rooker-Feldman* doctrine, the Anti-Injunction Act and other barriers to federal court that may be faced by homeowners. Section 10.7, *infra*, reviews the effect of a mandatory arbitration clause, and § 10.8, *infra*, considers tax consequences of damage awards or settlements in favor of the homeowner. Lastly, the chapter looks at issues that are important in settling cases.

Practitioners should also review the numerous sample pleadings found at Appendix I, *infra*. All of these pleadings and a large number of additional pleadings are found on the companion website, in PDF and Word formats. Appendix I, *infra*, includes several sample answers to judicial foreclosures, and several complaints to enjoin non-judicial foreclosures, including related pleadings seeking temporary or preliminary relief. Several of these pleadings involve such new issues as enjoining a foreclosure after a servicer fails to review applications for loan modification or where the homeowner is satisfying the requirements of a trial loan modification.

Other sample pleadings in Appendix I, *infra*, include a complaint to enforce permanent modification for a borrower in a trial modification plan, and answers, complaints, discovery, and other documents relating to standing to foreclose and servicer misconduct. Another sample complaint deals with a servicer's accounting practices and federal law violations. The appendix also includes additional pleadings related to loan broker and loan origination abuses and a complaint against a fraudulent home improvement company. The companion website includes all of these and many additional pleading in PDF and Word formats.

10.2 Gathering Information

10.2.1 Client Interview

The client interview process is critical in evaluating the homeowner's potential defenses to foreclosure and affirmative claims. The initial interview commonly defines the scope of the legal services needed based on both the problem and the homeowner's goals. In addition, the initial interview shapes the homeowner's perception of the lawyer.

Regardless of whether the homeowner may have origination or servicing claims, a good place to start is with some background information about the homeowners and the acquisition of their home. After establishing the basic homeownership history, it is useful to know about the homeowner's past and current financial condition. A future financial picture will also be important in evaluating the homeowner's potential options.

Next, the homeowner can be walked through the transaction or series of transactions in chronological order. It is important ask questions about what the homeowner understood was happening. This frequently differs from what actually happened. In some cases homeowners are confused or unable to remember the details of the transaction. This is especially true where the homeowners are moved through a transaction, such as a loan closing, very rapidly. In mortgage servicing cases, homeowners' difficulty in getting reliable information from servicers may leave them in the dark as to what is happening with their accounts.

Homeowners' testimony can make their story come alive. Advocates should evaluate how well potential clients are able to relate their stories and whether they would be good witnesses if required to testify at trial.

1 *See, e.g.*, Ch. 5, *supra* (for claims related to origination), Ch. 6, supra (description of servicer abuses), Ch. 7, *supra* (for non-RESPA claims related to mortgage servicing abuses), Ch. 8, *supra* (RESPA claims related to mortgage servicing abuses), and Ch. 15, *infra* (for claims related to foreclosure rescue scams).

10.2.2 Obtaining and Storing Documents

10.2.2.1 Overview

Mortgage loans typically involve a thick stack of paperwork. Some of these documents are required by federal or state law. Others are used because of industry custom or lender practice. Some documents, such as a pooling and servicing agreement or an assignment, may be generated after the loan closing as the loan travels through the secondary mortgage market. Mortgage servicers also generate records, such as payment history and escrow account information, that may be relevant to a homeowner's claims.

These documents are a critical source of information when litigating mortgage claims. They generally provide detailed information about the financial transaction and the players involved. In some cases, the story found in the paperwork is more complete than that related by a homeowner.

10.2.2.2 Document Sources

The most common sources of documents are: the homeowner; the lender or owner of the loan; the settlement agent; the title insurance company; the broker; the servicer; and the registry of deeds or other public office where security interests are recorded. A copy of the owner's entire file should be obtained, even if the homeowner has a "complete set." Many times the borrower is provided with the "duplicate" set of blank documents at a loan closing. It is important to obtain copies of the documents that contain the borrower's signature. The executed copies may differ from what is in the borrower's file as a result of post-closing "doctoring."

Often, a call or letter to the mortgage owner or servicer along with a release of information form signed by the borrower will be sufficient to get copies. If the mortgage owner or servicer refuses to turn over the file, a qualified written request under the Real Estate Settlement Procedures Act sent to the servicer may prompt a response.[2]

10.2.2.3 Storing Documents

Documents in mortgage lending cases may come from a number of different sources. In addition, what is not included in a set of documents may be more important than what is included. For this reason document handling procedures and chain of custody issues may be important if a case goes to trial.

When original documents are received, regardless of the source, they should be Bates stamped[3] and then scanned or copied. The originals should then be placed in a file, labeled with the source and date received, and put away for safe keeping. Preferably these tasks should be done by an office assistant who could, if necessary, testify at trial. Copies of the documents can then be highlighted or marked up in performing an analysis of possible claims.

10.2.3 Mortgage Loan Documents

Mortgage loan documents should be reviewed in all foreclosure cases for indications of abusive lending or other claims that may provide significant remedies. Certain types of home loans trigger additional disclosure requirements. For example, variable rate disclosures are required for variable rate loans.[4] An "early warning" notice must be given for high-cost loans.[5] At a minimum, advocates should obtain copies of the loan note, mortgage or deed of trust, Truth in Lending (TIL) disclosure, HUD-1 settlement statement, and the notice of right to cancel, if applicable.

Loan Note: The loan note creates an obligation (debt) of the borrower (the mortgagor) to pay the lender (the mortgagee or mortgage holder). The loan note also specifies the essential terms under which the loan is to be repaid, including, interest rate, payment term and due dates, balloon payments, variable rate provisions, maximum interest rate cap, prepayment penalties, late fees, etc. The loan note is a fairly short instrument that rarely exceeds four pages. Examples of sample fixed and adjustable rate mortgage promissory notes are found at Appxs. H.3.2 and H.3.3, *infra*.

Mortgage or Deed of Trust: The mortgage or deed of trust creates the lender's security interest in the property. The mortgage also specifies the lender's and borrower's rights and responsibilities regarding the property. It often specifies the order of application for payments, lists the borrower's rights to notice of default, acceleration and foreclosure, and authorizes the use of escrow accounts. Riders, which are typically a separate document attached to the back of the instrument, contain important amendments to the standard language in most mortgages and deeds of trust. Common mortgage riders include adjustable rate riders, balloon riders, prepayment penalty riders, one-to-four family riders, and condominium riders. Copies of mortgages or deeds of trust, along with any applicable riders, can usually be found at the local land records office. A sample mortgage is found at Appendix H.3.1, *infra.*

2 *See* § 8.2.2, *supra*.

3 Some new software packages will automatically place a Bates stamp on scanned documents.

4 15 U.S.C. § 1638(a)(4); Official Staff Commentary § 226.17(c)(1)-8. *See* National Consumer Law Center, Truth in Lending §§ 4.6.4.1, 4.6.4.4 (6th ed. 2007 and Supp.).

5 15 U.S.C. § 1639. *See* National Consumer Law Center, Truth in Lending § 9.3 (6th ed. 2007 and Supp.).

TIL Disclosure and Rescission Notice: The TIL disclosure is required for most residential mortgage loans. The document provides key price, payment and term information. The form and contents of the disclosure may vary depending on whether the transaction is considered an open-end or closed-end credit transaction. A notice of the right to cancel must also be provided in most transactions for which the home is taken as collateral, other than transactions for the purchase of the home.[6] While the Truth in Lending Act (TILA) does not generally limit interest rate or fees that can be charged, the statute is nevertheless frequently called upon to carry the day in an abusive lending case where violations appear on the face of the document. The failure to provide accurate disclosures gives borrowers powerful remedies against abusive lending and even a defense to foreclosure. Similarly, the failure to provide borrowers the requisite number of properly completed notices of the right to cancel violates TILA. As a result, it is important to obtain and review the TIL disclosure and the notice of right to cancel, if applicable, for accuracy.[7]

HUD-1 Settlement Statement: In most residential real estate transactions, settlement agents are required to provide the borrower with a HUD-1 settlement statement. The statement must clearly and conspicuously itemize all charges actually imposed on the borrower.[8] A review of the HUD-1 provided at the settlement will reveal whether the estimate of the costs provided in the good faith estimate of closing costs[9] was at all close to the actual charges. If the charges are significantly different the borrower may have been baited with better terms and then switched into a disadvantageous loan. In addition, the HUD-1 is critical to evaluating whether the lender provided accurate information on the TIL disclosure.

Other Documents: Other documents the borrower may have been given during the application process may help reveal problems with the loan. These include the loan application, credit insurance application, and credit report. There are usually two loan applications. One is hand-written and filled in by the broker or lender at the time of application. At closing, the borrower is asked to sign a typed version. Sometimes the information in these two applications varies. Particular attention should be paid to the terms of the loan and the homeowner's income indicated on the application. The appendices also reprint a sample change rate notice for an adjustable rate mortgage note and a sample annual escrow account statement.[10]

Some lenders routinely sell vulnerable borrowers unnecessary and expensive credit insurance. The credit insurance application provides valuable information about the terms, exclusions, and limitations to the policy.

Credit reports are also a useful source of information. The report not only contains information about the borrower's creditworthiness, it also provides information about other debts that the homeowner may have financed into the new loan. Reviewing the monthly payment amounts, the original balance, and the term of these other obligations will assist in determining whether the loan was in the borrower's best interest. The report will also include information about who requested the borrower's credit information and when.

10.2.4 Appraisal

A determination of the current fair market value of the client's home is important for determining what claims the homeowner may be able to assert as well as what outcomes are realistic for the homeowner. When dealing with abusive lending, property flipping, or foreclosure rescue scams it is also a good idea to obtain an estimate of the home value at the time of the transaction.

Most mortgage lenders usually require an appraisal before they will make a loan. A copy of the appraisal can often be obtained from the closing agent or even the appraiser. However, these appraisals should be viewed with caution as, in some cases, they are artificially inflated to allow the borrower to take out a larger loan. The most accurate estimate of past and current fair market value is available from a reliable appraiser. Alternatively, a broker's price opinion or Internet valuation services[11] may provide a ballpark value that will be sufficient to evaluate the case and will be much less expensive than a full appraisal.

10.2.5 Mortgage Transfer of Ownership Notices

10.2.5.1 General

When defending against a foreclosure or challenging servicing abuses it is important to know, not only who the servicer is, but also who is the current owner of the mortgage. The identity of the current mortgage owner, however, may not always be apparent. Many mortgages today are

6 *See* National Consumer Law Center, Truth in Lending § 6.4.3 (6th ed. 2007 and Supp.).

7 *See* National Consumer Law Center, Truth in Lending (6th ed. 2007 and Supp.).

8 12 U.S.C. § 2603(a); Reg. X § 3500.8(a).

9 No later than three business days after application, the consumer must be given a "good faith estimate" of the settlement costs. 12 U.S.C. § 2603; Reg. X § 3500.7.

HUD released amendments to Regulation X, most of which are effective January 1, 2010, that significantly alter RESPA disclosure requirements. 73 Fed. Reg. 68,204 (Nov. 17, 2008). The new rules, among other things, standardize the good faith estimates, limit increases on most fees, unless circumstances change, and revamp settlement statements. *See* § 5.9.2, *supra*.

10 *See* Appxs. H.3.4, H.3.5, *infra*.

11 Information on valuation or real estate may be obtained from websites such as www.zillow.com, www.homegain.com, and www.realtor.com.

assigned by the loan originator to a purchaser on the secondary market. Very often the mortgage owner at the time of foreclosure (or even shortly after the loan closing) is not the bank or mortgage company that originated the loan. When mortgages are pooled and sold through the securitization process, the ownership of the loan is typically transferred to a trust. A trustee, usually a commercial bank, acts on behalf of the trust and investors.

The Helping Families Save Their Homes Act of 2009 (the "2009 Act") amended the Truth in Lending Act to require that borrowers be notified whenever ownership of their mortgage loan is transferred.[12] The new owner or assignee must notify the borrower in writing, within thirty days after the loan is sold or assigned, of its identity, address, telephone number, and the date of transfer and location where the transfer is recorded. In addition, the new owner must disclose how the borrower may reach an agent or party with authority to act on behalf of the new owner, and any other relevant information.[13]

The law became effective upon enactment, May 20, 2009. Failure to comply with these requirements gives rise to a private right of action, which includes recovery of actual damages, statutory damages, costs, and attorney fees.[14] Borrowers may be entitled to multiple statutory damages of up to $4000 per violation each time the rule is not complied with.

To implement the statutory requirements for mortgage transfer notices, the Federal Reserve Board issued an interim final rule on November 20, 2009, which initially became effective on an optional basis on that date.[15] Compliance with the interim final rule became mandatory on January 19, 2010.[16]

10.2.5.2 Persons Subject to the Notice Requirement

The 2009 Act's new transfer notice requirement is intended to apply to persons who acquire ownership of mortgage debt. Thus, the rule uses the term "covered person" rather than "creditor" to describe persons subject to its requirements. To be a "covered person" under the rule, a person must become the owner of the mortgage loan by acquiring legal title to the debt obligation.[17] The person must also acquire more than one mortgage loan in any twelve-month period.[18] The rule applies even if ownership is transferred to a different legal entity based on a merger, acquisition, or reorganization.[19]

By specifying that legal title must be acquired, the rule does not apply to a person who acquires only a beneficial interest or security interest in the loan.[20] For example, if the owner of a mortgage loan uses the loan as security to obtain financing, the lender providing the financing is not a "covered person" under the rule. It is not clear whether the rule will permit evasion of the statutory requirement when there have been transfers of the debt obligation, but legal title is purportedly retained by the Mortgage Electronic Registration System (MERS).[21] However, as a nominee only, MERS generally claims to hold title to the mortgage, but not the note.[22] Therefore transfers of the note's ownership within the MERS system should be subject to the rule. In any event, the Board should clarify in a final rule that transfers between members in the MERS system are subject to the disclosure requirements.

A party that assumes credit risk without acquiring legal title to loans is not covered by the rule.[23] Thus, an investor that acquires mortgage-backed securities, pass-through certificates, or participation interests and does not directly acquire legal title in the underlying mortgage loans is not covered. This was apparently intended to exempt entities such as Ginnie Mae when it serves as a guarantor of securities and obtains equitable title to loans. However, if the issuer of the securities defaults and Ginnie Mae then acquires legal title to the loans, Ginnie Mae would be required to comply with the rule.

The rule also provides an exception for mortgage servicers in certain situations, consistent with the TILA assignee liability provision in 15 U.S.C. § 1641(f)(2). If the servicer holds legal title to the loan or the obligation is assigned to the servicer "solely for the administrative convenience of the servicer in servicing the obligation," the servicer is not a "covered person" under the rule.[24] This servicer exemption should not apply to transfers to MERS, however, since MERS is not a servicer and claims no rights to any payments made on the mortgage loans or to any servicing rights related to mortgage loans.[25] Servicers remain obligated, however, to respond to borrower requests under section 1641(f)(2) for the name, address, and telephone number of the loan owner.

As for the type of mortgage transaction covered, the rule applies to any consumer credit transaction that is secured by the principal dwelling of a consumer.[26] This includes loans

12 15 U.S.C. § 1641(g)(1)(A)–(E).
13 15 U.S.C. § 1641(g)(1)(C), (E).
14 15 U.S.C. § 1640(a).
15 *See* 74 Fed. Reg. 60,143 (Nov. 20, 2009).
16 The FRB has sought comments on the interim final rule, which were due by January 19, 2010. Any additional changes to the rule based on comments received will be reported in future NCLC publications.
17 Reg. Z, 12 C.F.R. § 226.39(a)(1).
18 *Id.*
19 Official Staff Commentary to Reg. Z § 226.39(a)(1)-4.
20 Official Staff Commentary to Reg. Z § 226.39(a)(1)-2.
21 *See* § 4.6, *supra* (information about MERS).
22 Mortgage Elec. Registration Sys., Inc. v. Estrella, 390 F.3d 522, 524–525 (7th Cir. 2004).
23 *Id.*
24 Reg. Z, 12 C.F.R. § 226.39(a)(1).
25 *See* § 4.6, *supra.*
26 Reg. Z, 12 C.F.R. § 226.39(a)(2).

secured by manufactured homes that are a consumer's principal dwelling. The TIL Commentary makes clear that closed-end mortgage loans as well as home equity lines of credit are covered by the rule.[27] The disclosure requirements do not apply to mortgage loans on investment property and those not primarily for personal, family, or household purposes.

10.2.5.3 The Disclosure Requirement

The disclosures required by the 2009 Act must be mailed or delivered on or before the 30th calendar day following the date the covered person acquires the loan.[28] For example, if a covered person acquires a mortgage loan on March 1, the disclosure must be mailed or delivered on or before March 31. The acquisition date is the date that is recognized in the books and records of the acquiring person.[29]

The rule provides that if there is more than one consumer liable on the mortgage, disclosures may be sent to any consumer who is "primarily liable."[30] No definition of "primarily liable" is provided. As a result, a transfer notice could be sent to one spouse even though the other spouse is paying all the bills. This is particularly problematic if joint obligors are not living together. Hopefully, the FRB will revise this in the final rule and require that transfer notices be provided to all consumers on the note.

The rule provides an exception for temporary holders of mortgage loans. If a covered person sells or transfers legal title to the mortgage loan on or before the 30th calendar day after the covered person acquired the mortgage loan, the covered person is not required to provide the disclosure.[31] The transferee in that situation who subsequently becomes a covered person would be required to give the disclosure if the loan is not transferred again within thirty days. The FRB suggests this exception will prevent borrowers from being confused by multiple disclosures they would receive if the various entities that might briefly hold a mortgage loan during the securitization process were required to comply. Unless this provision is changed by the FRB in the final rule, practitioners may need to investigate intermediate transfers to determine who should receive rescission notices or whether a proper chain of title leads to the current holder.[32]

10.2.5.4 Content of Required Disclosures

10.2.5.4.1 Identification of the loan

The notice sent to the borrower must identify the loan that was acquired or transferred. The covered person is given flexibility on how to disclose this, such as by providing the property address along with the pre-transfer account number, or the date when the credit was extended and the original loan amount or credit line.[33] In addition to identifying the loan, the notice sent to the borrower must contain disclosure of four categories of information discussed in the following subsections.

10.2.5.4.2 New owner's identity, address, and telephone number

The covered person under the rule who is the party acquiring the loan must disclose its name, address, and telephone number.[34] This information must be provided even if there is another party who is servicing the loan.[35] If there is more than one covered person, the information shall be provided for each of them. The covered person may, at its option, provide an e-mail or website address but is not required to do so.

10.2.5.4.3 Acquisition date

The covered person must disclose the date that the loan was acquired.[36] The acquisition date is the date that is recognized in the books and records of the acquiring person.[37]

10.2.5.4.4 Agent's contact information

The notice sent to the borrower must disclose how to reach an agent or party having authority to act on behalf of the covered person.[38] The notice must identify a person (or persons) authorized to receive legal notices on behalf of the covered person and resolve issues concerning the consumer's payments on the loan.[39] The rule does not require the

27 Official Staff Commentary to Reg. Z § 226.39(a)(2)-1.

28 Reg. Z, 12 C.F.R. § 226.39(b).

29 Reg. Z, 12 C.F.R. § 226.39(b)(1).

30 Reg. Z, 12 C.F.R. § 226.39(b)(2).

31 Reg. Z, 12 C.F.R. § 226.39(c)(1).

32 Similarly, there is an exception for repurchase agreements. If a mortgage loan is transferred to a covered person in connection with a repurchase agreement and the transferor that is obligated to repurchase the loan continues to recognize the loan as an asset on its own books for accounting purposes, the covered person acquiring the loan is not required to provide the disclosures. However, if the transferor does not repurchase the mortgage loan, the acquiring party must make the disclosures within thirty days after the date that the transaction is recognized as an acquisition in its books. Reg. Z, 12 C.F.R. § 226.39(c)(2).

33 Official Staff Commentary to Reg. Z § 226.39(d)-1.

34 Reg. Z, 12 C.F.R. § 226.39(d)(1).

35 A different statute, the Real Estate Settlement Procedures Act, requires the borrower to be notified if servicing of the loan is transferred from one entity to another. 12 U.S.C. § 2650(b). *See* § 8.2.3.3, *supra*.

36 Reg. Z, 12 C.F.R.§ 226.39(d)(2).

37 Reg. Z, 12 C.F.R.§ 226.39(b)(1).

38 Reg. Z, 12 C.F.R. § 226.39(d)(3).

39 *Id.*

covered person to appoint persons for these purposes if they do not exist when the loan is acquired. The FRB's position in including agents for receipt of legal notice is helpful in carrying out at least one purpose of the 2009 Act, which is to provide the borrower with the identity of persons to whom the borrower may wish to send notice of the extended right of rescission.

If the owner authorizes separate parties to act on its behalf for different purposes, the notice must provide contact information for each agent. When multiple agents are listed, the notice should describe how the authority for each agent differs, noting for example that one agent is authorized to receive legal notice and another to resolve payment disputes.

A covered person may comply by simply providing the phone number for the agent, if the consumer can use the phone number to obtain the agent's address.[40] This is unfortunate since borrowers may not be aware that an oral communication with the agent listed as dealing with payment disputes, which is the servicer in most cases, will not be treated as a qualified written request under the Real Estate Settlement Procedures Act.[41] Hopefully the FRB will reconsider this position after receiving comments and require that servicer's address for receipt of qualified written requests be listed and information about RESPA rights be provided.

10.2.5.4.5 Recording location

The 2009 Act provides that the notice disclose "the location of the place where transfer of ownership of the debt is recorded."[42] Because the statute refers to ownership of the debt, the Board has construed the requirement as applying only if transfer of the debt's ownership has been recorded. This interpretation renders it meaningless since transfers of debt ownership are generally not recorded in public land records. The FRB at a minimum should require disclosure of the location where the covered person's security interest in the property is located.

10.2.5.4.6 Optional disclosures

The 2009 Act provides that the party acquiring a loan shall notify the borrower of "any other relevant information regarding the creditor."[43] The FRB interprets the statutory language as giving it authority to impose additional requirements by regulation after notice and comment, and seeks comment on whether the rule should include additional requirements. At least until the FRB receives comment, the FRB has taken the position that the statute does not require covered persons to "determine independently what additional information a reviewing court might subsequently determine to be legally relevant in order to avoid liability."[44]

10.2.6 Servicing Records

10.2.6.1 Payoff Amount

The payoff amount is typically the amount the homeowner is required to pay to satisfy the loan and obtain a release of the mortgage or reconveyance of the deed of trust. In addition to principal and interest owed on the loan, the payoff amount will include any prepayment penalties, late fees or other fees that the servicer believes are due. It may be useful to compare the current payoff amount to any previous payoff statements that the homeowners obtained to determine if any improper fees or charges have been assessed. The payoff amount also is useful to know for purposes of workout options[45] or settlement negotiations.

Regulation Z, which implements the Truth in Lending Act (TILA), requires that a servicer must provide an accurate statement of the amount necessary to pay off an account in full as of a specific date, within a reasonable time of the receipt of a request from a borrower or the consumer's representative.[46] Under most circumstances, a "reasonable" response time is within five business days of receipt. However, the response time may be longer when the servicer is experiencing an unusually high volume of refinancing requests.[47]

10.2.6.2 Payment History

A complete life-of-the-loan payment history should be obtained from the current servicer. The payment history should provide a complete breakdown of all transactions from the date of the original loan closing to the present. The payment history should show each payment received as well as how that payment was credited.

Payment histories often contain numerical codes and other cryptic notations used by servicers to identify particular types of transactions. Advocates should request that account histories and statements be provided in a complete and comprehensible format in which all the codes are translated, or request that a separate explanation of all

40 *Id.*
41 12 U.S.C. § 2605(e).
42 15 U.S.C. § 1641(g)(1)(D).
43 15 U.S.C. § 1641(g)(1)(E).

44 *See* 74 Fed. Reg. 60,148 (Nov. 20, 2009).
45 *See* Chapter 2, *supra*.
46 Reg. Z, 12 C.F.R. § 226.36(c)(1)(iii); 73 Fed. Reg. 44,522, 44,604 (July 30, 2008). For a discussion of the general requirements imposed by Regulation Z on mortgage creditors for providing payoff statements, see National Consumer Law Center, Truth in Lending § 9.9.3 (6th ed. 2007 and Supp.).
47 Official Staff Commentary § 226.36(c)(1)(iii)-1; 73 Fed. Reg. 44,522, 44,614 (July 30, 2008).

transaction codes used by the servicer be provided. A glossary of mortgage servicing terms is located at Appendix J, *infra*.

10.2.6.3 Contact History

Most servicers maintain a contact history detailing communications with the homeowner and other third parties. The contact history may also list important events in the loan's history such as the date letters were sent to the borrower or the date the loan was referred to a default servicer. Automated calls to the borrower may also be recorded in the contact history.

The contact history may be useful for putting together a timeline of important events in the life of the loan. This timeline can be used to supplement the homeowners' story. The contact history also frequently provides a behind-the-scene look at what was happening with the loan. Because of the wealth of information provided in a contact history, servicer's may be reluctant to voluntarily provide it to homeowners or their counsel. In many cases, it can only be obtained through discovery. When possible, advocates should attempt to obtain an unredacted version of the contact history.

10.2.6.4 Pooling and Servicing Agreement

Pooling and servicing agreements (PSA) broadly govern the securitization of residential mortgage loans including the formation of the trust (which becomes the owner of the loans), the servicing of the loans in the trust, and the duties of various parties to the trust agreement. The PSA may outline the loss mitigation or workout options available to the servicer and the parameters of the servicer's authority to implement those options. The PSA may be used to establish whether or not the servicer was an agent of a lender. If the security was publicly sold, then the PSA is publicly available on the U.S. Securities and Exchange Commission's website (www.sec.gov).[48]

10.2.6.5 Transfer of Servicing Notice

Lenders are required at the time of application for most mortgage loans to disclose to each applicant whether the servicing of the loan may be assigned, sold, or transferred at any time during the term of the mortgage.[49] If the servicing of a mortgage is transferred after the mortgage loan is made, both the former and the new servicer must notify the borrower in writing of the transfer.[50] Since many servicing problems occur at or near the time of transfer of servicing, the information contained in the notice, especially the effective date of the transfer, are helpful in discovering servicing errors. A sample notice as to change of servicer is reprinted at Appendix H.3.6, *infra*.

48 *See* § 1.3.3.3.2, *supra*.

49 12 U.S.C. § 2605(a); Reg. X, 24 C.F.R. § 3500.21(b). *See also* § 8.2.3, *supra*.

50 12 U.S.C. §§ 2605(b)(2)(A), 2605(c). *See also* § 8.2.3, *supra*.

10.2.7 Public Records

10.2.7.1 Land Records

Local land records can be checked to determine: the number of loans a particular lender made in that locality; the names and addresses of the affected homeowners; whether a lender has an unusually high number of foreclosures or is repeatedly flipping loans. In property flipping cases, the land records will identify the seller of the property, and in foreclosure rescue cases, the land records will show who acquired title to the property from the homeowner. Many land record offices provide public access to their indices over the Internet.

10.2.7.2 Consumer Complaints

Through state freedom of information acts, records of consumer complaints to local consumer protection agencies, attorney general offices, and licensing divisions can be obtained to see whether similar complaints have been made about the potential defendants in the past. The Better Business Bureau should also be contacted for copies of any complaints. In addition, the Federal Trade Commission's website has a search function that allows users to identify Federal Trade Commission (FTC) complaints filed against any entity. Even if the FTC has not filed a complaint against an entity, it will provide copies of complaints that consumers have made to it (after redacting identifying information about the complainant) in response to a federal Freedom of Information Act request.[51]

10.2.7.3 Newspaper Articles/Internet Searches

Using the Internet and other electronic database services to conduct a search on a topic of interest or to discover information about a particular lender or party involved in the transaction can prove fruitful.[52] Similarly, searches of

51 Request can be emailed to the FTC at foia@ftc.gov. The FTC charges fees for searching its records plus a per-page copying charge.

52 Websites often contain important information that advocates may want to preserve as evidence. Because websites can be modified or removed at any time it is important to "capture" a webpage as it appears on a certain date and time. At a minimum, webpages that may be used as evidence should be printed by someone who will be able to testify as to their authenticity. *See* Michael Fontham, Trial Technique and Evidence §§ 6.9, 8.10 (2d ed. 2002).

newspapers and other periodicals are often a useful source for information about potential defendants.

10.2.7.4 Corporate and Business Documents

Every state requires corporations and other businesses to file certain documents at the time the company begins operation in that state and periodically thereafter. The filing typically consists of the articles of incorporation and annual reports. When dealing with corporations, this information is helpful to figure out who stands behind the corporation or business in the event the corporate veil can be pierced or to sue these individuals separately. Further, formal links between the various parties to the transaction can establish a wide net of liability. Some states may permit you to obtain a copy of the part of the company's state tax return that shows the names and addresses of the current officers. Another way to find out who is behind a corporation or other fictitious name is to get the form that the U.S. Postal Service requires a person to file when getting a post office box.[53] The form requires a real person and a street address.

10.2.7.5 Securities and Exchange Commission Documents

Publicly traded corporations must file periodic reports with the Securities and Exchange Commission (SEC).[54] Entities that must file with the SEC also include the trusts that are frequently involved in the securitization process. Reports filed with the SEC include information about the financial viability of the company to pay a judgment. They may also provide default and foreclosure data and reveal company policies that may be helpful in proving pattern and practice claims.

10.2.7.6 Rating Agencies

Credit rating agencies provide opinions on the creditworthiness of particular companies, securities, or obligations. The growth of complex financial products in the mortgage market has meant that the rating agencies play a bigger role in this sector. As a result, the agencies collect a tremendous amount of data related to lenders, servicers, insurers, and other parties involved in mortgage transactions. This data includes both financial and operational information.

The date and time should be printed on the page. Webpages for a given date may also be available from web archiving services, such as www.archive.org.

53 This information may be obtained by an attorney for purposes of serving process on a party in litigation. *See* 39 C.F.R. § 265.6(d).

54 The SEC website is located at www.sec.gov. Go to "Filings and Forms (EDGAR)."

10.2.7.7 Other Lawsuits

Obtaining complete information about other lawsuits against the same defendants is not an easy or inexpensive task. On the bright side, the existence of lawsuits filed in federal courts can be found by using the Public Access to Court Electronic Records (PACER).[55] This is an electronic public access service that allows users to obtain case information from federal courts. PACER, which includes a nationwide party/case index, allows the user to request information about case file documents, listings of all case parties, the case docket, and case status information. There is a small per page cost for using the PACER system.[56]

On the state level the situation is vastly different. There is no nationwide access to state court dockets and filed documents. In those state courts that have begun accepting electronic documents, access to court filing information may be possible over the Internet. Otherwise, obtaining this information will usually require manual file and docket searches based on plaintiff and defendant party name indexes in the court clerk's office.

10.2.8 Information Obtained Through Discovery

10.2.8.1 List of Items to Ask for in Discovery

Once a case has been filed, additional documents will be available through discovery requests to the lender, mortgage owner, servicer, or other parties. Depending upon the nature of the action, documents to request may include:

- Canceled checks from the settlement agent showing all disbursements made from the loan proceeds and any other payments made.
- Written agreements between:
  - Home improvement contractor and lender;
  - Broker and lender;
  - Lender and assignee;
  - Lender, servicer, and trustee, if loans are securitized; and
  - Servicer and any subservicer.
- Rate sheets from lender and broker showing the interest rates available from the lender at the time of the loan (if a yield spread premium was paid).
- Underwriting guidelines.
- Any servicing records that cannot be obtained voluntarily from the servicer, such as:
  - Payment history;

55 Access to the PACER system is available at www.pacer.gov.

56 The per page cost applies to the number of pages that result from any search and applies to documents whether or not the pages are viewed, downloaded, or printed.

- Transfer of servicing notices;
- Transfer of loan ownership notices;
- Payment change notices on adjustable rate mortgages;
- Escrow account statements; and
- Default notices.

- Entire creditor file.
- Entire assignee file.
- Settlement or escrow agents file.
- Entire mortgage broker file.
- Entire home improvement contractor file.
- Complaints to lender/assignee from other borrowers about a bad actor involved in the transaction.
- Information regarding number of loans originated by the same lender in default and in foreclosure, foreclosure numbers and rates over a period of time.
- The files of other borrowers, when alleging a pattern and practice claims.
- Names and addresses of former employees.
- Employee training manuals.
- Correspondence with any regulatory agency involving similar bad acts.
- Lender's appraisal manuals or guidelines.
- Any broker or appraiser watch lists or stop lists[57] maintained by lender or servicer.

10.2.8.2 Confidentiality/Protection Orders

Frequently defendants argue that materials sought by homeowners in discovery contain confidential commercial information. As a result, advocates can expect that defendants will ask for a confidentiality agreement before producing the discovery or that defendants will file a motion for a protective order. Since it is not clear that defendants are entitled to the broad, sweeping confidentiality they frequently request, it is generally recommended that a court determine what, if any, of the discovery materials should be protected.

10.3 Choosing Defendants

10.3.1 Introduction

Whether defending a foreclosure or bringing an affirmative case, there are often numerous potential parties against whom claims and defenses can be raised. For example, in abusive lending transactions potential parties might include mortgage brokers, real estate brokers, appraisers,[58] sellers, home improvement contractors, title insurers, loan officers, originators, and owners. In mortgage servicing cases potential parties might include mortgage owners, master servicers, subservicers, servicer's employees, and any other entities involved in the loan servicing, such as force placed insurance providers or property inspection companies.

When bringing an affirmative suit, as a general rule, homeowners are better off naming as defendants any party that was involved in the abusive conduct. Homeowners frequently benefit from the finger pointing that ensues between defendants. Importantly, joining multiple parties also alleviates third party discovery problems. Casting a wide net may compensate for the fact that some of the defendants may be judgment proof, may have filed for bankruptcy, or may have disappeared altogether. On the other hand, naming extra parties as defendants complicates and delays the litigation and increases the amount of legal talent for the opposition.

Foreclosure actions in which the homeowner is the defendant are often brought in the name of the loan servicer. When the homeowner is challenging the validity of the mortgage, raising servicer misconduct as a defense, or asserting noncompliance with required loss mitigation procedures, the owner of the loan, as the real party in interest, should be joined in the action.[59] However, state law may limit the type of counterclaims that may be asserted by the homeowner and the parties that may be joined in a foreclosure action.

10.3.2 Mortgage Owner Liability

10.3.2.1 In General

The most critical player in foreclosure defense cases is the mortgage loan owner. The owner is the party that has the right to foreclose on the mortgage or deed of trust. In some cases, the owner may be the entity that originated the loan. However, more commonly, mortgages are pooled and sold through the securitization process in which the ultimate owner is a trust, which holds the mortgage loan for the benefit of investors. Owners may be liable for abusive lending practices based on their own involvement in the improper conduct. Alternatively, owners may be liable for the conduct of third parties, such as the originator, based on theories of assignee liability. Owners may also be liable for the conduct of servicers, or other players involved in servicing the loan, under various agency theories.

Only the mortgage owner has the final legal authority to modify the terms of the note and mortgage. While this authority may be delegated to a servicer or subservicer, the power of the servicer to modify loan terms may be constrained by the owner. Accordingly, a full resolution of

57 Many lenders maintain "watch lists" or "stop lists" of brokers or appraisers with whom they will not do business based on fraud detection systems.

58 Appraisers and sellers are common defendants in property flipping scams. *See* § 5.3.4, *supra*.

59 *See* Ch. 4, *supra* (procedural defenses).

abusive lending or servicing claims requires identification and joinder of the actual owner of the obligation.

10.3.2.2 Liability for Originator Conduct

If the loan has been assigned, the homeowner will generally want to raise against the current mortgage owner the defenses that could have been raised against the originating lender.[60] If an assignee has the rights of a holder in due course, however, it may be shielded from some liability for the actions of the loan originator.

The common law rule is that an assignee is subject to all the defenses that the consumer could raise against the assignor.[61] Uniform Commercial Code (UCC) § 3-305 modifies this common law rule and permits the assignee of a negotiable instrument to be free from those defenses if it has attained the status or acquired the rights of a holder in due course. There are technical requirements as to when an assignee becomes a holder in due course, and an important initial question is whether the assignee has met those requirements.[62] Even if the assignee is a holder in due course, the homeowner may still be able to raise certain defenses.[63]

In addition, under TILA a homeowner may exercise the right of rescission against any assignee.[64] The Home Ownership and Equity Protection Act (HOEPA) makes assignees of covered mortgage loans liable for all claims and defenses that the consumer could raise against the originating lender, up to a cap.[65]

Alternatively, the assignee's own conduct may make it liable based on civil conspiracy or joint venture theories.[66] State lending statutes or the close-connectedness doctrine may also provide grounds for finding assignees liable even if they would not be so under the UCC or HOEPA.[67]

10.3.2.3 Liability for Mortgage Servicing Abuses

10.3.2.3.1 In general

Whether the mortgage owner can be held liable for servicing abuses will turn on whether the servicer is considered an agent of the mortgage owner. Where an agency relationship exists, the mortgage owner generally is liable. The question of whether an agency relationship exists between the mortgage owner and a servicer is usually one of fact.[68] An agency relationship arises as a result of actual or apparent authority. Absent one or the other type of authority the principal cannot be liable under an agency theory.

Actual or express authority is defined by the conduct of the principal towards the agent.[69] It may be expressed or implied. Express authority exists when the principal intentionally confers authority upon the agent, when the principal allows the agent to believe it has authority,[70] or when, by want of ordinary care, the principal allows the agent to believe that it possesses authority. Implied authority includes the power to take actions that are incidental and necessary to carry out the agent's express authority. In the mortgage servicing context, express authority is usually found in the servicing agreement between the owner and servicer or in the pooling and servicing agreement for a loan that has been securitized.[71] A servicer who initiates a foreclosure action[72] or files a proof of claim[73] or motion for relief from stay[74] in a bankruptcy case should be considered an agent of the owner.[75]

Apparent authority exists when a reasonable person would suppose the servicer has the authority it is purporting to exercise. Where the owner has granted the servicer express authority to act, apparent authority may cover circumstances in which the servicer is acting beyond the scope of its actual

60 *See* § 5.14, *supra*.

61 9 Corbin, Corbin on Contracts § 892 (interim ed. 2002); 29 Lord, Williston on Contract §§ 74.47, 74.49 (4th ed. 2003); Farnsworth, Farnsworth on Contract § 11.8 (2d ed. 1998); Restatement (Second) of Contract § 336 (1981).

62 *See* § 5.12.2, *supra*.

63 *See* § 5.12.2.2, *supra*.

64 15 U.S.C. § 1641(c). *See* National Consumer Law Center, Truth in Lending § 6.9.2 (6th ed. 2007 and Supp.).

65 15 U.S.C. § 1641(d)(1). *See also* National Consumer Law Center, Truth in Lending § 9.7 (6th ed. 2007 and Supp.).

66 *See* National Consumer Law Center, Unfair and Deceptive Acts and Practices § 11.5 (7th ed. 2008 and Supp.).

67 *See* National Consumer Law Center, Unfair and Deceptive Acts and Practices §§ 11.6.5.5.4, 11.6.5.5.5 (7th ed. 2008 and Supp.).

68 Circumstantial evidence may be used to establish the agency relationship and the scope of the agent's authority. Aquaduct, L.L.C. v. McElhenie, 116 S.W.3d 438 (Tex. App. 2003).

69 Restatement (Third) of Agency § 2.01 (2006).

70 *See* Aquaduct, L.L.C. v. McElhenie, 116 S.W.3d 438 (Tex. App. 2003) (loan servicer had implied actual authority to accept final payment on mortgage note).

71 *See In re* Mortgage Lenders Network, USA, Inc., 380 B.R. 131 (Bankr. D. Del. 2007) (detailing provisions in the PSA that support owner-servicer agency relationship).

72 Bankers Trust v. 236 Beltway Inv., 865 F. Supp. 1186 (E.D. Va. 1994) (both lender and servicer had standing to sue on mortgage in default).

73 Fed. R. Bankr. P. 3001(b) (proof of claim may be filed by creditor or its authorized agent); *In re* Viencek, 273 B.R. 354 (Bankr. N.D.N.Y. 2002) (mortgage servicing agent has standing to defend against objection to claim). *See also* Green v. O'Dell, 305 F.3d 1297 (11th Cir. 2002) (servicing agent had standing to file proof of claim).

74 *In re* Woodberry, 383 B.R. 373 (Bankr. D.S.C. 2008); *In re* Tainan, 48 B.R. 250 (Bankr. E.D. Pa. 1985) (servicer, in capacity as representative of Fannie Mae for collection purposes, was the party in interest in a relief from stay proceeding).

75 *See* Dupuis v. Federal Home Loan Mortgage Corp., 879 F. Supp. 139 (D. Me. 1995) (holding servicer was agent for holder, but precluding holder liability based on *Merrill* doctrine); *In re* Kline, 420 B.R. 541 (Bankr. D.N.M. 2009) (knowledge of loan servicer can be imputed to lender-owner for purposes of determining violation of the stay); *In re* Crawford, 388 B.R. 506 (Bankr. S.D.N.Y. 2008) (loan owner liable for conduct of servicing agent and various subagents).

authority.[76] As a result, the owner may be liable for the tortious conduct of or statutory violations committed by the servicer.[77]

10.3.2.3.2 Liability for conduct of subagents

A subagent is an entity appointed by the agent of the principal. In order for a subagency to exist the appointing agent must have either actual or apparent authority to create the subagent relationship. A subagent that acts for multiple principals that are hierarchically stratified is under the "primary control" of the appointing agent, but it is under the ultimate control of the appointing agent's principal.[78] As a result, the principal is equally liable for the conduct of subagents.

In the mortgage servicing industry there are typically three types of servicers: the master servicer, the subservicer, and the special servicer. The master servicer oversees the servicing operations, but the homeowner is unlikely to have much contact with the master servicer. The subservicer is generally the entity that collects payments and maintains borrowers' escrow accounts. The special servicer may come into the picture when a loan becomes more than sixty days past due. Subservicers or special servicers are generally responsible for engaging in loss mitigation and, if that fails, foreclosing on the loan. Subservicers and special servicers may in turn contract with tax service providers, insurance providers, foreclosure and bankruptcy attorneys, inspection services, and other similar parties to perform different functions in the loan servicing process.

Can the mortgage owner be liable for the improper conduct of all these parties? Generally, the mortgage owner may be liable based on either a direct agency relationship or a subagency relationship. When a mortgage owner designates a servicing agent, whether it be a subservicer or a special servicer, the mortgage owner is forming a direct agency relationship subject to the traditional rules of agency discussed above. For example, if the owner appoints both the master servicer and the special servicer, then these two entities are considered co-agents of the mortgage owner and the mortgage owner would have liability for the conduct of both. However, the servicers themselves would not have vicarious liability for wrongs committed by the other servicer.

By contrast, if the master servicer appoints a special servicer, then the special servicer is a subagent of the master servicer. In this case, the special servicer has two principals that may be liable for its conduct, the master servicer and the mortgage owner. The same rules should apply all the way down the chain to include parties such as foreclosure attorneys that may be hired by the subservicer or special servicer.[79]

10.3.2.3.3 Liability limitations for government agency owners

One exception to owner liability is based on the *Merrill* doctrine, which may limit liability of a government agency for the acts of it agents.[80] Several courts have held that Freddie Mac was immune from liability for the unauthorized acts of its loan servicing agents.[81] However, a Connecticut court in *Federal National Mortgage Association v. Alves*,[82] considered and rejected Fannie Mae's argument that it was protected from liability based on the *Merrill* doctrine. The homeowners brought counterclaims in a foreclosure action against Fannie Mae based on the conduct of its servicer, who wrongfully accelerated the mortgage debt and wrongfully instituted the foreclosure action. The homeowners' claims included breach of contract, breach of good faith and fair dealing, violation of the state unfair and deceptive acts and practices (UDAP) statute, and negligence. Fannie Mae argued that it could not be found liable for the authorized actions of the mortgage servicer under the *Merrill* doctrine because it would undermine an important governmental purpose. The court first assumed that Fannie Mae was a federal instrumentality for purposes of applying the *Merrill* doctrine, and then held that the doctrine was limited to equitable estoppel situations in which a party relies on an unauthorized misrepresentation of a government agent. The court concluded that the *Merrill* doctrine could not be read so broadly as to allow federal agencies through their agents to violate contractual rights or common law duties with impunity.[83]

76 Restatement (Third) of Agency § 2.03 (2006), cmt. a (apparent authority "applies to actors who appear to be agents but are not, as well as to agents who act beyond the scope of their actual authority").

77 Restatement (Third) of Agency § 7.08 (2006). *See* Jones v. Federated Fin. Reserve Corp., 144 F.3d 961 (6th Cir. 1998) (principal could be liable for FCRA violation committed by agent); *In re* Hart, 246 B.R. 709 (Bankr. D. Mass. 2000) (owner liable for servicer's UDAP violation); Thrash v. Credit Acceptance Corp., 821 So. 2d 968 (Ala. 2001) (denying summary judgment for creditor on issue of whether it was liable for negligence and trespass as a result of conduct by third-party hired by creditor repossess vehicle).

78 Restatement (Third) of Agency §§ 3.14, cmt. b, 3.15.

79 *See In re* Crawford, 388 B.R. 506 (Bankr. S.D.N.Y. 2008) (awarding $60,0000 in punitive damages against loan owner for conduct of servicing agent and various agents and subagents in violating the automatic stay).

80 Federal Crop Ins. Corp. v. Merrill, 332 U.S. 380 (1947).

81 Paslowski v. Standard Mortgage Corp., 129 F. Supp. 2d 793 (W.D. Pa. 2000); Siradas v. Chase Lincoln First Bank, N.A., 1999 WL 787658 (S.D.N.Y. Sept. 30, 1999); Deerman v. Federal Home Loan Mortgage Corp., 955 F. Supp. 1393 (N.D. Ala. 1997); Dupuis v. Federal Home Loan Mortgage Corp., 879 F. Supp. 139 (D. Me. 1995).

82 2002 WL 1138322 (Conn. Super. Ct. May 6, 2002) (unpublished).

83 *See also In re* Hart, 246 B.R. 709 (Bankr. D. Mass. 2000)

10.3.3 Liability of Servicers and Others Involved in Servicing Loans

When a hierarchical agency relationship exists, advocates should consider every party in the chain as a potential defendant. While it is advisable to sue the owner of the obligation, there is no requirement that the owner be included. At the bottom of the chain is usually an individual or employee.[84] There may be tactical, evidentiary, or discovery reasons to include such individuals as defendants. Traditionally, the employees may not escape liability for their own bad conduct by claiming to be only an agent of another entity.[85] Thus an individual may be liable for UDAP or other common law tort claims.[86] Similarly corporate entities may not typically avoid liability for torts or statutory violations because they acted in conformance with directives from the owner or other principal. A servicer also may not escape liability for its own conduct by transferring servicing rights to another party.[87]

While the mortgage owner should be liable for all the acts of the servicer as its agents, the servicer is generally not liable for problems arising at the origination of the loan.[88] Nevertheless, it may be proper to join a servicer as an indispensable party because the servicer could attempt to foreclose while the debtor is litigating abusive lending claims.[89]

10.4 Forum Selection

10.4.1 Federal Jurisdiction

10.4.1.1 In General

A federal forum is potentially available whenever the homeowner has a claim under the Truth in Lending Act (TILA), the Real Estate Settlement Procedures Act (RESPA), Fair Debt Collection Practices Act (FDCPA), Fair Credit Reporting Act (FCRA), or federal Racketeer Influenced and Corrupt Organizations Act (RICO). State courts also have jurisdiction over claims under these federal statutes. Federal jurisdiction is also available when there is diversity of citizenship among the parties and the homeowner's claim exceeds the federal jurisdictional threshold.[90]

10.4.1.2 Advantages and Disadvantages of Federal Court

A number of factors should be considered in determining whether federal or state court provides the better forum for the homeowner. Some of the typical considerations are:

- In which forum is the case likely to suffer the longest delays before trial?
- Are claims being brought affirmatively or is the homeowner attempting to stop a foreclosure?
- How difficult is it to obtain an injunction against a pending foreclosure?
- Will the federal court require a disproportionate investment of time at the pre-trial stage?
- Are state discovery rules as liberal as the federal discovery rules?
- Are there differences in attitude toward homeowners or consumers on the part of the federal and state judges?
- Is there a risk that the federal court will consider the case too minor to justify its attention?
- From what locality are the jury pools drawn for state and federal court?[91]
- Do state rules allow non-unanimous verdicts in civil cases?
- It is more likely that the homeowner will win or lose if non-unanimous verdicts are allowed?

10.4.1.3 Supplemental Jurisdiction

A number of potential state law claims are available in unfair lending or abusive servicing cases—breach of contract, fraud, UDAP, state collection statutes, and other specialized statutes dealing with mortgage brokers and lenders. All of these state claims may be brought in federal court along with a federal claim so long as they "are so related to [federal claims] that they form part of the same case or controversy under Article III of the United States Constitution."[92] Even when this test for supplemental jurisdiction is met, the statute gives the federal district court discretion to decline supplemental jurisdiction over a claim in certain

(holding Fannie Mae vicariously liable for violation of state UDAP statute by its servicer without discussion of *Merrill*).

84 Employers may be responsible for the misconduct of their employees under the doctrine of *respondeat superior*. *See* Restatement (Third) of Agency §§ 2.04, 7.07 (2006).

85 Vazquez v. Sears Roebuck & Co., 221 B.R. 222, 231 (Bankr. N.D. Ill. 1998) ("A creditor and its attorney are jointly and severally liable for their violations of the discharge injunction because under general principles of agency law, an agent whose tortious conduct renders the principal liable is also liable for his own tortious acts.").

86 *See* National Consumer Law Center, Unfair and Deceptive Acts and Practices § 11.2 (7th ed. 2008 and Supp.).

87 *In re* Noletto, 280 B.R. 868 (Bankr. S.D. Ala. 2001).

88 A servicer is not considered an assignee for purposes of TIL liability unless it is or was the owner of the obligation. *See* 15 U.S.C. § 1641(f); National Consumer Law Center, Truth in Lending § 7.3.6 (6th ed. 2007 and Supp.).

89 *See* § 7.3, *supra*.

90 28 U.S.C. § 1332.

91 Jury verdicts must be unanimous in federal court unless the parties stipulate otherwise. Fed. R. Civ. P. 48.

92 28 U.S.C. § 1367(a).

circumstances.[93] If the federal district court dismisses state law claims by declining to exercise supplemental jurisdiction, the period of limitations for these claims is tolled while they are pending in federal court and for a period of thirty days after dismissal, unless state law provides for a longer tolling period.[94]

10.4.1.4 Removal of Foreclosure Actions

While homeowners may prefer a federal forum in some instances, federal courts generally do not have jurisdiction over foreclosure or eviction actions that the mortgage holder has originally filed in state court. Foreclosure and subsequent eviction actions typically involve only questions of state law. Because removal may not be based on a federal defense, counterclaims based on TILA, RESPA, or other federal statutes are insufficient to permit removal of the original action.[95] Diversity jurisdiction is also not available to the homeowner if the homeowner is a citizen of the state in which the original action was brought.[96] Homeowners that seek removal of such actions without an "objectively reasonable" basis may be assessed cost and fees.[97]

10.4.2 Staying in State Court

Homeowners preferring a state forum must anticipate that one or more of the defendants will prefer a federal forum. Consequently, homeowners and their counsel will have to weigh the relative merits of a state court action in which only state statutory and common law claims are pursued as compared with a federal court action that includes claims under federal statutes and potential state law claims. While homeowners have the right to bring many federal statutory claims, such as Truth in Lending or Fair Debt Collection Practices Act claims, in state courts, defendants frequently seek to remove these actions to federal court.[98]

A defendant has the right to remove a state court action if the action could initially have been brought in the federal court. Defendants seeking removal of an action in which a TIL or a RESPA claim has been raised, for example, typically argue that the federal court would have original jurisdiction over the homeowner's action had the case been filed in federal court based on federal question jurisdiction.[99] Alternatively, defendants may seek removal based on diversity jurisdiction. The defendant must prove[100] that the parties have diverse citizenship and the controversy exceeds $75,000.[101] In actions seeking declaratory or injunctive relief, such as to prevent the defendant from going forward with a foreclosure, the amount in controversy is measured by the value of the object of the litigation.[102] When the object of the litigation is the loan itself, the value will be equal to the outstanding amount due on the loan.[103] Attorneys fees are typically excluded from the jurisdictional amount but are counted when mandated by a contract or statute.[104]

Fannie Mae claims that its charter confers independent grounds for federal jurisdiction. The D.C. Circuit has endorsed this view, as have the majority of district courts to address the topic.[105]

---

93 28 U.S.C. § 1367(c).

94 28 U.S.C. § 1367(d).

95 *See* Beneficial Nat'l Bank v. Anderson, 539 U.S. 1, 6 (2003).

96 28 U.S.C. § 1441(b).

97 *See* 28 U.S.C. § 1447(c); Chase Manhattan Mortgage Corp. v. Smith, 507 F.3d 910 (6th Cir. 2007) (affirming award of $6513.16 in fees and costs against homeowner).

98 28 U.S.C. § 1441.

99 *See* 28 U.S.C. §§ 1331, 1441(b). Section 1331 grants jurisdiction to federal courts over disputes "arising under the Constitution, law or treaties of the United States." Federal courts may also exercise jurisdiction over state law claims that implicate significant federal issues. *See* Grable & Sons Metal Prods., Inc. v. Darue Eng'g & Mfg., 545 U.S. 308, 312 (2005); Brunson v. American Home Mortgage Servicing, Inc., 2009 WL 2524336, at *3 (D. Utah Aug. 14, 2009) (denying remand because plaintiff's complaint alleging violations of TILA and RESPA raised a federal question); Moore v. Chase Bank, 2008 WL 314664 (N.D. Cal. Feb. 4, 2008) (denying remand where state UDAP claims based on violation of federal law, e.g., TILA and HOEPA). *But see* Coleman v. Beazer Homes Corp., 2008 WL 1848653, at *4 (W.D.N.C. Apr. 23, 2008) (remanding to state court where plaintiffs' claims did not "present a substantial dispute or controversy regarding the validity, construction, or application of any federal law"); Beard v. Aurora Loan Servs., L.L.C., 2006 WL 1350286 (S.D. Tex. May 17, 2006) (using a three-prong test to establish federal jurisdiction and holding that fact that RESPA, TILA, and FDCPA governed some conduct complained of was insufficient to confer jurisdiction); King v. Provident Bank, 428 F. Supp. 2d 1226, 1231 (M.D. Ala. 2006) (remanding because state law claims requiring interpretation of RESPA did not create federal question jurisdiction); Cavette v. Mastercard Int'l, 282 F. Supp. 2d 813, 819 (W.D. Tenn. 2003) (remanding because credit card holder's claim did not involve "substantial" or "necessary" interpretation of TILA or related federal regulations).

100 The defendant bears the burden of establishing, by a preponderance of the evidence, that removal is proper is light of the strong presumption against removal.

101 28 U.S.C. § 1332.

102 Hunt v. Washington State Apple Adver. Comm'n, 432 U.S. 333, 347, 97 S. Ct. 2434 (1977).

103 Garfinkle v. Wells Fargo Bank, 483 F.2d 1074, 1076 (9th Cir. 1973); Henderson v. Nationstar Mortgage Co., L.L.C., 2008 WL 302374 (W.D. Wash. Jan. 31, 2008).

104 Helmers v. Countrywide Home Loans, Inc., 2008 WL 191306 (E.D. La. Jan. 22, 2008); Rembert v. Cadle Co., 2008 WL 163670 (N.D. W. Va. Jan. 16, 2008).

105 Pirelli Armstrong Tire Corp. Reitiree Med. Benefits Trust *ex rel.* Federal Nat'l Mortgage Ass'n v. Raines, 534 F.3d 779, 784–785 (D.C. Cir. 2008) (collecting cases and holding that Sallie Mae's charter provides for federal jurisdiction). *Cf.* Knuckles v. RBMG, Inc., 481 F. Supp. 2d 559, 563 (S.D. W. Va. 2007) (rejecting argument that Sallie Mae's charter confers original jurisdiction); Federal Nat'l Mortgage Ass'n v. Sealed, 457 F. Supp. 2d 41 (D.D.C. 2006).

If the state court action is removed, the homeowner can try to have the action remanded to state court[106] if the notice of removal was untimely or by asking the federal court to exercise its discretion to remand "all matters in which State law predominates."[107] If the homeowner is successful in having a removed action remanded to state court based on a lack of subject matter jurisdiction, the homeowner may be awarded costs and expenses, including reasonable attorney fees.

A notice of removal must be filed within thirty days after the defendant receives a copy of the initial pleading. The Seventh Circuit has held that the right to removal can not be revived by assigning the mortgage to another party after the thirty-day time period had expired.[108]

A homeowner intent on remaining in state court may seek to avoid removal by limiting the complaint to state law causes of action. In doing this the homeowner takes advantage of the "well-pleaded complaint rule" which allows plaintiffs to have control over the claims alleged in a complaint and to avoid federal court jurisdiction by relying exclusively on state law claims.[109] An action removed to federal court on the basis that the plaintiff could have raised federal claims instead of or in addition to state law claims should be remanded by the federal court.[110]

It is black-letter law that a case may not be removed to federal court based on a federal defense, even if the plaintiff anticipates a federal defense.[111] Thus, a mortgage owner or servicer who has filed a state court foreclosure action may not later remove the action to federal court simply because the homeowner has raised defenses and counterclaims under federal law. Similarly, courts have held that third party defendants, such as mortgage brokers and home improvement contractors brought into a foreclosure action by the homeowner, may not remove the action because the homeowner's third party claims are viewed as defensive in nature.[112]

10.4.3 Personal Jurisdiction over Out-of-State Defendants

Given the rise of mortgage securitization, it is now very common for out-of-state entities to be involved in cases related to residential home mortgages. If the homeowner brings an affirmative action against out-of-state entities, the court must have personal jurisdiction over those defendants. For cases brought in both state and federal court, jurisdiction over out-of-state parties will be governed by the state long-arm statute.[113] Courts must also determine whether exercise of jurisdiction satisfies due process requirements. Generally, out-of-state defendants must have certain minimum contacts with a state such that maintaining the suit in that state does not offend traditional notions of fair play and substantial justice.[114]

In most cases, parties (even non-residents) to a real property transaction are subject to the personal jurisdiction of the courts where the property is located. Recently, however, courts have been faced with the question of whether they may exercise personal jurisdiction over non-resident trust companies asserting that they have no contact with the forum state other than taking assignment of a mortgage note secured by real property in the state.[115] In *Johnson v. Long Beach Mortgage Loan Trust 2001-4*,[116] the court found sufficient minimum contacts based on two specific contacts: (1) the trust took an assignment of the homeowner's mortgage note, and (2) the trust drew a revenue stream from the homeowner's mortgage payments, even though it did not directly collect the payments.

Other courts have disagreed with the *Johnson* holding, finding that such contacts are insufficient to meet the due process requirements for personal jurisdiction.[117] The most

106 28 U.S.C. § 1441(c).
A motion to remand on grounds other than lack of subject matter jurisdiction must be filed within thirty days after the filing of the notice of removal. 28 U.S.C. § 1447(c). *See* National Consumer Law Center, The Cost of Credit: Regulation, Preemption, and Industry Abuses § 13.16 (4th ed. 2009 and Supp.) (discussion of removal of preemption issues to federal court).

107 *See* 28 U.S.C. § 1441(c).

108 Boyd v. Phoenix Funding Corp., 366 F.3d 524 (7th Cir. 2004).

109 Caterpillar Inc. v. Williams, 482 U.S. 386, 392 (1987); Jaimes v. Dovenmuehle Mortgage, Inc., 2008 WL 536644 (S.D. Tex. Feb. 27, 2008); McCrae v. Commercial Credit Corp., 892 F. Supp. 1385 (M.D. Ala. 1995).

110 An exception to this doctrine may be raised by defendants where the state law claims are completely preempted by federal law. Beneficial Nat'l Bank v. Anderson, 539 U.S. 1 (2003) ("complete preemption" found in usury action against national bank).

111 Caterpillar Inc. v. Williams, 482 U.S. 386, 393 (1987).

112 *E.g.*, Thomas v. Shelton, 740 F.2d 478, 497 (7th Cir. 1984); Associates Home Equity Servs., Inc. v. Kay, 1999 WL 1270969 (N.D. Ill. Dec. 22, 1999). *Cf.* New Venture Gear, Inc. v. Fonehouse, 982 F. Supp. 892, 893 (N.D. N.Y. 1997) (third-party defendant may remove entire action pursuant to 28 U.S.C. § 1441(c) where the claim against the third-party defendant is "separate and independent").

113 *See* Fed. R. Civ. Pro. 4(k) (incorporating state law long-arm statutes). *See* National Consumer Law Center, Unfair and Deceptive Acts and Practices § 12.6.2 (7th ed. 2008 and Supp.) (discussion of long-arm jurisdiction in UDAP cases).

114 Int'l Shoe v. Wash., 326 U.S. 310, 66 S. Ct. 154, 90 L. Ed. 95 (1945).

115 While trusts acknowledge they can be sued in their home states, forcing financially distressed homeowner to bring suit in another state presents a formidable barrier to defending foreclosures or challenging other mortgage abuses.

116 Johnson v. Long Beach Mortgage Loan Trust 2001-4, 451 F. Supp. 2d 16 (D.D.C. 2006). *See also* Easter v. American West Fin., 381 F.3d 948 (9th Cir. 2004) (trusts subject to specific personal jurisdiction as beneficiaries of Washington deeds of trust who receive income streams from loans negotiated and delivered in Washington and secured by Washington real property).

117 Williams v. Firstplus Home Loan Owner Trust 1998-4, 310 F. Supp. 2d 981 (W.D. Tenn. 2004). *See, e.g.*, Frazier v. Preferred Credit, 2002 WL 31039856 (W.D. Tenn. July 31, 2002); Skinner v. Preferred Credit, 638 S.E.2d 203 (N.C. 2006) (the state legislature overruled this decision in 2007 by adopting N.C.

troubling aspect of these cases is that the courts have found that the existence of "an independent servicer [with] exclusive power to perform all acts in connection with administering loans" militates against a finding of personal jurisdiction for the trust.[118] Given the relationship evidenced in most pooling and servicing agreements between the trust and the servicer, it is difficult to see how a trust circumvents personal jurisdiction merely by hiring an agent to collect payments and enforce performance of the loans.

A bankruptcy proceeding may offer a way around personal jurisdiction problems presented by non-resident trusts. Generally, any case within the district court's bankruptcy jurisdiction (relates in any way to the bankruptcy debtor's property) may be filed in the bankruptcy court in which the bankruptcy case has been filed.[119] This is true regardless of whether the state or federal courts in that state would otherwise have had "long-arm jurisdiction" over the defendant.[120] There is also no "minimum contacts" test that must be satisfied before an out-of-state defendant can be sued in the forum district's bankruptcy court.[121]

10.5 Bond Requirements

The Federal Rules of Civil Procedure and many state rules of civil procedure permit courts to issue preliminary injunctions or temporary restraining orders only if the movant gives security in an amount the court considers proper.[122] To the extent such security is required it usually takes the form of a judicial or court bond. These bonds guarantee payment of the costs and damages that may be sustained by the mortgage holder in the event that it was wrongfully enjoined or restrained. In some cases, the cost of a bond presents a significant barrier to relief for the homeowner.[123]

Courts generally have the authority to waive the bond requirement. A waiver should be granted when the delay required to litigate the borrower's claims will not cause unreasonable harm to the lender, or when the validity of the security instrument is in question.[124] For example, if the value of the homeowner's property exceeds the amount of the debt, the lender's interest is protected even if there is some delay in resolving the underlying dispute. In the alternative, the borrower may propose a bond in the amount of reasonable monthly payments, either at the amount of the regular monthly mortgage payment or in an amount calculated to offset any expense caused by the delay.[125] One court has held that indigent homeowner-plaintiffs, who were asserting rescission claims, were not required to post a bond under Federal Rule of Civil Procedure 65(c).[126]

Homeowners may also face bond requirements where they seek to stay a judgment of foreclosure pending appeal,[127] set aside a foreclosure sale,[128] or enjoin an eviction after a foreclosure sale. Many courts have held that failure to post a bond on appeal renders the challenge moot.[129]

Laws S.L. 2007-351, which amended the state long-arm statute and the state lending laws applicable to assignees of loans made in the state to state residents that are secured by real property in the state).

118 Frazier v. Preferred Credit, 2002 WL 31039856, at *6 (W.D. Tenn. July 31, 2002).

119 *See* National Consumer Law Center, Consumer Bankruptcy Law and Practice § 14.3.2.1 (9th ed. 2009).

120 28 U.S.C. § 1409(a).

121 *See In re* Fed'l Fountain, Inc., 165 F.3d 600 (8th Cir. 1999) (en banc) (nationwide service is constitutional); *In re* Hogue, 736 F.2d 989 (4th Cir. 1984) (finding nationwide service of process constitutional).

122 Fed. R. Civ. Pro. 65(c). Borrowers may avoid the bond requirements of Rule 65(c) and other similar state rules by proceeding immediately for a permanent injunction rather than seeking a preliminary injunction or temporary restraining order.

123 *See, e.g.*, Ferguson v. Commercial Bank, 578 So. 2d 1234 (Ala. 1991) (court entered restraining order against mortgage holder prohibiting foreclosure; ordered homeowners to post $250,000 surety bond; parties agreed to reduce bond amount to $30,000; homeowners failed to post bond because premium equaled the bond amount).

124 *See* Avila v. Stearns Lending, Inc., 2008 WL 1378231 (C.D. Cal. Apr. 7, 2008) (issuing preliminary injunction and denying defendants request for bond where strong likelihood of success on the merits); Phleger v. Countrywide Home Loans, Inc., 2007 WL 4105672 (N.D. Cal. Nov. 16, 2007) (foreclosure enjoined but no bond required because mortgage adequately protected by property value); Thomas v. F.F. Fin., Inc., 1989 WL 37658 (S.D.N.Y. Apr. 12, 1989) (preliminary injunction granted to homeowner-plaintiff who alleged she had rescinded loan; no bond required since no prior mortgage on property meant that sufficient equity existed to protect creditor against damages arising from injunction).

125 Rioux v. C.F. Inv., Inc. (D.N.H. Jan. 4, 1990), *available at* www.consumerlaw.org/unreported (order granting preliminary injunction; borrowers to pay $400 per month pending final decision [original contract payments $1050 per month]).

Courts may also condition injunctions upon borrowers continued maintenance of hazard insurance and a prohibition against further encumbrances. *See* Jetton v. Caughron, No. 3-87-0126 (M.D. Tenn. Apr. 4, 1987).

126 Lopez v. Delta Funding Corp., 1998 WL 1537755 (E.D.N.Y. Dec. 23, 1998).

127 These post-judgment bonds are often referred to as appeal or *supersedeas* bonds. *See* Metfirst Fin. Co. v. Price, 991 F.2d 414 (7th Cir. 1993) (interpreting Illinois statute and holding that motion to set aside foreclosure must be accompanied by bond or other security); Fla. Stat. Ann. § 45.045 (West); Mass. Gen. L. c. 239, §§ 5,6 (requiring *supersedeas* bond on appeal but providing for waiver if defense is not frivolous and appellee is indigent); Wells Fargo Home Mortg., Inc. v. Neal, 922 A.2d 538 (Md. 2007).

128 Illinois requires the posting of a bond contemporaneously with the filing of a motion to set aside a foreclosure sale. 735 Ill. Comp. Stat. 5/15-1508(c). *See also* Baltrotsky v. Kugler, 910 A.2d 1089 (Md. 2006) (challenge to foreclosure sale ratification moot where borrower failed to post a *supersedeas* bond or other security).

129 *See* Fincher v. Fleet Mortgage, Group, Inc., 555 S.E.2d 120 (Ga. Ct. App. 2001) (appeal of denial of injunction to stop dispossession post-foreclosure deemed moot as homeowner failed to post *supersedeas* bond).

When lenders, servicers, and other defendants appeal an adverse judgment, homeowners are well within their rights to request that these defendants post a bond on appeal. In *In re Hoopai*,[130] the court, citing ongoing mortgage market turbulence and signs of the defendant's financial weakness, ordered the mortgage lender to post a $150,000 bond pending the appeal.[131]

10.6 Issues Posed by Separate Court Proceedings

10.6.1 Introduction

Several issues complicate the homeowner's ability to challenge a mortgage transaction or foreclosure in federal court when there is a related state proceeding. These issues are most likely to arise when the homeowner files an action in federal court to rescind or challenge a mortgage transaction and there is a threatened, pending, or concluded action in state court to foreclose on the home or to evict the homeowner. They do not arise when there has been only a non-judicial foreclosure sale, without any state court judicial proceeding for foreclosure or eviction, and the homeowner is not seeking to enjoin a potential future state court proceeding.[132]

Defendants often raise *Younger* abstention, the Anti-Injunction Act, and the *Rooker-Feldman* doctrine, in addition to res judicata and collateral estoppel. These issues should be evaluated as part of the homeowner's decision whether to file an independent action or whether to seek relief in the foreclosure or eviction case. They should also be considered when choosing between state and federal court to initiate an action, since *Younger*, the Anti-Injunction Act, and *Rooker-Feldman* only apply in federal court (though states might have similar doctrines).

Timing is critical. In general, the farther the existing state court proceeding is from a final judgment the more likely a federal or state court is to reach the merits and grant relief in an independent action. If a state court judgment has already been entered against the homeowner, it may prove a serious impediment to federal litigation, and the possibility of obtaining relief from the judgment in state court should be evaluated. Another option is to file a bankruptcy proceeding, because the bankruptcy court may have greater powers to deal with pending state court actions.

10.6.2 Younger *Abstention*

The *Younger* abstention doctrine prevents a federal court from issuing declaratory or injunctive relief that would interfere with pending state proceedings.[133] *Younger* abstention applies when: (1) there are ongoing state proceedings that are judicial in nature; (2) the state proceedings implicate state interests so important that exercise of the federal judicial power would disregard the comity between the states and the national government; and (3) the state proceedings afford an adequate opportunity to raise the federal claims.[134] Even if all three of these criteria are met, abstention can be avoided if the state proceedings are undertaken in bad faith or for purposes of harassment, or some other extraordinary circumstances exist, such as proceedings pursuant to a flagrantly unconstitutional statute. If the federal plaintiff does not ask the federal court to interfere with the state court proceeding, but seeks some other type of relief, *Younger* abstention is inapplicable.[135]

The first and third requirements for *Younger* abstention are fairly straightforward. If the state case is merely threatened rather than filed, *Younger* does not bar declaratory relief because there is no ongoing state proceeding and the first *Younger* requirement is not met.[136] In foreclosure cases, the third requirement for *Younger* abstention—an adequate opportunity to raise federal claims—is sometimes not met, because some jurisdictions sharply curtail the homeowner's ability to raise consumer law claims such as TILA in response to foreclosure or eviction actions.[137] Claims that can be asserted in bankruptcy court may also be unavailable in state court.[138]

The second requirement for *Younger* abstention—important state interests—has evolved over time, bringing more state interests within its ambit. *Younger* involved pending state *criminal* prosecutions, and the doctrine has since been applied in other contexts, such as civil contempt proceedings, that involve enforcement actions by the state or state courts and are akin to criminal prosecutions.[139]

---

130 2007 WL 2460762 (Bankr. D. Haw. Aug. 27, 2007).

131 *See also* Leff v. First Horizon Home Loan, 2007 WL 2572362 (D.N.J. 2007) (requiring lender to post both *supersedeas* bond and cost bond, pursuant to Fed. R. App. P. 7, pending appeal).

132 *See, e.g.*, Johnson v. LaSalle Bank, 663 F. Supp. 2d 747 (D. Minn. 2009) (*Rooker-Feldman* doctrine inapplicable where foreclosure was non-judicial).

133 Younger v. Harris, 401 U.S. 37, 53–54, 91 S. Ct. 746, 27 L. Ed. 2d 669 (1971).

134 Middlesex County Ethics Comm. v. Garden State Bar Ass'n, 457 U.S. 423, 432, 102 S. Ct. 2515, 73 L. Ed. 2d 116 (1982).

135 Whittiker v. Deutsche Bank Nat'l Trust Co., 605 F. Supp. 2d 914 (N.D. Ohio 2009).

136 Steffel v. Thompson, 415 U.S. 452, 475, 94 S. Ct. 1209, 39 L. Ed. 2d 505 (1974). *See also* Hicks v. Miranda, 422 U.S. 332, 349, 95 S. Ct. 2281, 45 L. Ed. 2d 223 (1975) (holding that *Younger* applies where state criminal proceeding is filed after federal suit but before any proceedings of substance on merits in federal suit).

137 *See* National Consumer Law Center, Truth in Lending § 7.6.8 (6th ed. 2007 and Supp.).

138 *See, e.g.* Funches v. Household Fin. Consumer Discount Co. (*In re* Funches), 381 B.R. 471 (Bankr. E.D. Pa. 2008) (avoidance rights of third parties cannot be asserted in state court proceedings, so *Younger* abstention inapplicable).

139 *See* Ohio Civil Rights Comm'n v. Dayton Christian Sch., Inc.,

In 1987, in *Pennzoil Co. v. Texaco, Inc.*,[140] the Supreme Court extended the doctrine to bar a company's federal challenge to a state requirement that a bond be posted as a condition of an appeal of a state civil case. The Court characterized the case as involving a challenge to the process by which the state compels compliance with the judgments of courts, similar to civil contempt proceedings.[141] It held that the state's interests in this civil proceeding were so important that exercise of federal judicial power would disregard the comity between the states and the federal government. The Court took pains, however, to state that it was not announcing a rule that would be applicable to all civil cases between private parties.[142]

Eviction or foreclosure proceedings that may be pending in state court in foreclosure cases involve only private parties, and TIL and other claims do not generally challenge a state's enforcement efforts. Therefore, these cases are not likely to implicate important state interests under *Younger*. For example, a New York federal district court hearing a challenge to a foreclosure rescue scam transaction enjoined the parties from proceeding with the eviction action.[143]

Since *Pennzoil*, when the state court suit is a civil case between private parties, courts have been more likely to abstain if the federal suit is a constitutional challenge to the state court's procedures.[144] If the federal suit does not challenge the state court's procedures, but instead seeks a ruling on some issue between the private parties, a state eviction or foreclosure proceeding is less likely to be seen as implicating the important state interests that the *Younger* doctrine requires.[145]

If the state case has gone to judgment and a sheriff's sale or a writ of possession to enforce that judgment is pending, enjoining the enforcement of the judgment comes closer to *Pennzoil*.[146] However, it still may be possible to argue that

---

477 U.S. 619, 628, 106 S. Ct. 2718, 91 L. Ed. 2d 512 (1986) (administrative agency action commenced by state civil rights commission); Middlesex Co. Ethics Comm. v. Garden State Bar Ass'n, 457 U.S. 423, 432, 102 S. Ct. 2515, 73 L. Ed. 2d 116 (1982) (state bar disciplinary proceedings); Moore v. Sims, 442 U.S. 415, 430–435, 99 S. Ct. 2371, 60 L. Ed. 2d 994 (1979) (action by governmental agency for temporary custody of allegedly abused child); Trainor v. Hernandez, 431 U.S. 434, 445–447, 97 S. Ct. 1911, 52 L. Ed. 2d 486 (1977) (civil action by the state to collect fraudulently obtained welfare benefits); Juidice v. Vail, 430 U.S. 327, 335, 97 S. Ct. 1211, 51 L. Ed. 2d 376 (1977) (civil contempt proceeding); Huffman v. Pursue, Ltd., 420 U.S. 592, 607, 95 S. Ct. 1200, 43 L. Ed. 2d 482 (1975) (public nuisance proceeding brought by the state).

140 481 U.S. 1, 107 S. Ct. 1519, 95 L. Ed. 2d 1 (1987).

141 481 U.S. at 13.

142 *Id.* at 14 n.12.

143 Calvagno v. Bisbal, 430 F. Supp. 2d 95, 101 (E.D.N.Y. 2006). *But see* Novak v. Washington Mut. Bank, F.A., 2008 WL 423511 (N.D. Ohio Feb. 14, 2008) (*Younger* abstention bars challenge to pending state foreclosure action); Daniels v. Superior Court, 2008 WL 427302 (E.D. Cal. Feb. 14, 2008) (*Younger* abstention bars challenge to ongoing state court proceedings to evict homeowner from foreclosed home); Allen v. Nat'l City Bank, 2007 WL 2341010 (D. Colo. Aug. 14, 2007) (same).

144 *See* Schall v. Joyce, 885 F.2d 101, 108–110 (3d Cir. 1989) (identifying special state interest in enforcing orders and judgments where judgment debtor sought to challenge confession of judgment procedures in federal court). *See also* Scott v. Mortgage Elec. Registration Sys., 2004 WL 1925008, at *4 (E.D. Pa. Aug. 27, 2004) (holding that *Younger* abstention bars due process challenge in federal court to state foreclosure procedures); Fisher v. Fed. Nat'l Mortgage Ass'n, 360 F. Supp. 207, 210 (D. Md. 1973) (invoking *Younger* abstention, pre-*Penzoil*, to refuse to hear constitutional challenge to state foreclosure procedures); Ungar v. Isaias, 336 F. Supp. 1233, 1234 (S.D.N.Y. 1972) (same).

145 *See* Schall v. Joyce, 885 F.2d 101, 109 (3d Cir. 1989) (explaining that "Pennzoil's limiting principle is its focus on the special interest that a state has in enforcing the orders and judgments of its courts"); Schumacher v. ContiMortgage Corp., 2000 WL 34030847, at *5 (N.D. Iowa June 21, 2000) (unpublished) (relying on *Rowland* to find abstention unwarranted, despite TIL affirmative defense in state foreclosure suit); Rowland v. Novus Fin. Corp., 949 F. Supp. 1447, 1456, n.8 (D. Haw. 1996) (noting that, while *Pennzoil* "directly implicat[ed] the state judiciary process itself," the plaintiff's "federal suit does not directly attack the validity of the state foreclosure proceeding per se, but rather involves a claim for rescission that could ultimately affect the final distribution of the bankruptcy estate"). *But see* Doscher v. Menifee Circuit Court, 2003 WL 22220534 (6th Cir. Sept. 24, 2003) (unpublished) (affirming district court dismissal under *Younger* where *pro se* debtor sought federal court order reopening foreclosure judgment); Beeler Props., L.L.C. v. Lowe Enters. Residential Investors, L.L.C., 2007 WL 1346591 (D. Colo. May 7, 2007) (applying *Younger* abstention without discussing whether state court foreclosure proceeding implicates important state interests); Hedrick v. Coleman, 2005 WL 2671327, at *2 (E.D. Mich. Oct. 19, 2005) (unpublished) (abstaining from hearing TIL Regulation Z challenge to state foreclosure action under both *Younger* and Anti-Injunction Act); Smith v. Litton Loan Servicing, L.P., 2005 WL 289927, at *7 (E.D. Pa. Feb. 4, 2005) (unpublished) (abstaining from considering action for mortgage rescission and damages and finding that foreclosure and ejectment were important state interests under *Younger* and *Penzoil*).

146 *See* Gray v. Pagano, 287 Fed. Appx. 155 (3d Cir. 2008) (unpublished) (concluding that federal suit to nullify state court foreclosure judgment and enjoy foreclosure sale implicated important state interests); DCR Fund I, L.L.C. v. TS Family Ltd. P'ship, 261 Fed. Appx. 139 (10th Cir. 2008) (unpublished) (*Younger* abstention bars federal challenge to foreclosure sale that state court allowed to proceed); Burlinson v. Wells Fargo Bank, 2009 WL 646330 (D. Colo. Mar. 9, 2009) (applying *Younger* abstention to suit seeking order that state court foreclosure judgment was void; state foreclosure proceedings involve important state interests); Madera v. Ameriquest Mortgage Co. (*In re* Madera), 2008 WL 447497 (E.D. Pa. Feb. 7, 2008) (*Younger* abstention prevents injunction against enforcement of state court foreclosure judgment), *on appeal*, 2008 WL 447497 (E.D. Pa. Feb. 7, 2008) (denying motion to stay sale: *Younger* abstention precludes injunction); Hicks v. Superior Court, 2008 WL 638544 (E.D. Cal. Mar. 5, 2008) (magistrate's recommendation) (*Younger* abstention bars federal suit seeking to enjoin state post-foreclosure eviction action), *adopted by* 2008 WL 795132 (E.D. Cal. Mar. 25, 2008); Daniels v. Superior Court, 2008 WL 638509 (E.D. Cal. Mar. 5, 2008) (magistrate's recommendation) (applying *Younger* abstention to foreclosure and eviction actions), *adopted by* 2008 WL 795566 (E.D. Cal. Mar. 24, 2008).

the plaintiff's federal challenge is not to the state court procedures themselves. The *Rooker-Feldman* doctrine, discussed at § 10.6.4, *infra*, is likely to be an additional impediment, though. Some courts have also invoked the related *Colorado River* abstention doctrine[147] as grounds for refusing to issue orders enjoining state court foreclosure or eviction proceedings, or to hear federal cases that parallel ongoing state court cases.[148]

10.6.3 The Anti-Injunction Act

Another potential impediment to federal court relief when there is an ongoing state court proceeding is the Anti-Injunction Act, which prohibits federal courts from granting injunctions to stay proceedings in state courts.[149] For example, federal courts may refuse to enjoin state court foreclosure proceedings based on the Anti-Injunction Act.[150] This prohibition cannot be evaded by addressing the injunction to a party rather than the state court.[151]

The Anti-Injunction Act only prohibits injunctions against *pending* state proceedings. It does not preclude injunctions against the *institution* of state proceedings.[152] There is a disagreement among the circuits about the meaning of this limitation, however. The Seventh Circuit Court of Appeals, followed by the First and Eighth, has held that the jurisdiction of the federal court is determined at the time that its injunctive powers are invoked, whether in the complaint or by motion.[153] The Fourth, Fifth, and Sixth Circuit Courts of Appeals have held that the Anti-Injunction Act applies whenever the state action is filed before the federal court *rules* on a request for injunctive relief,[154] and the Second Circuit has indicated agreement with this rule.[155]

The Anti-Injunction Act contains three explicit exceptions, all of which are to be narrowly construed.[156] First, a federal court may enjoin state proceedings "as expressly authorized by Act of Congress."[157] To invoke this exception, the other law need not expressly refer to the Anti-Injunction Act, or expressly authorize an injunction against a state court proceeding.[158] The question is whether the other law creates a federal right or remedy, enforceable in a federal court of equity, that can be given its intended scope only by the stay of a state court proceeding.[159] Some courts have held that TILA does not fall within this exception.[160]

A second explicit exception to the Anti-Injunction Act is that a federal court can enjoin a state proceeding where necessary in aid of its jurisdiction. This rule applies when "necessary to prevent a state court from so interfering with a federal court's consideration or disposition of a case as to seriously impair the federal court's flexibility and authority to decide the case."[161] This exception has been applied to cases in which a federal court obtains *in rem* jurisdiction prior to a state court suit, to removal cases, and to multidistrict litigation.[162]

The mere fact that a state court might rule first on an issue before the federal court (and expose the homeowner to res judicata or collateral estoppel) is not enough to invoke this exception.[163] But if the state action threatens not simply to reach judgment first, but also to interfere with the federal

147 Colorado River Water Conservation Dist. v. United States, 424 U.S. 800, 96 S. Ct. 1236, 47 L. Ed. 2d 483 (1976).

148 *See, e.g.*, Scherbenske v. Wachovia Mortgage, F.S.B., 626 F. Supp. 2d 1052 (E.D. Cal. 2009); Credit-Based Asset Servicing & Securitization, L.L.C. v. Lichtenfels, 658 F. Supp. 2d 355 (D. Conn. 2009); St. Clair v. Wertzberger, 637 F. Supp. 2d 251 (D.N.J. 2009).

149 28 U.S.C. § 2283.

150 *See* Foster v. Argent Mortgage Co., L.L.C., 2007 WL 2109558 (E.D. Mich. July 23, 2007).

151 Atl. Coast Line R.R. Co. v. Bhd. of Locomotive Eng'rs, 398 U.S. 281, 287, 90 S. Ct. 1739, 26 L. Ed. 2d 234 (1970).

152 Dombrowski v. Pfister, 380 U.S. 479, 485 n.2, 85 S. Ct. 1116, 14 L. Ed. 2d 22 (1965); Tropf v. Fid. Nat'l Title Ins. Co., 289 F.3d 929, 941–942 (6th Cir. 2002).

153 Hyde Park Partners, L.P. v. Connolly, 839 F.2d 837, 842 n.6 (1st Cir. 1988); Nat'l City Lines, Inc. v. L.L.C. Corp., 687 F.2d 1122, 1127 (8th Cir. 1982); Barancik v. Investors Funding Corp., 489 F.2d 933, 937 (7th Cir. 1973). *See also* Hruby v. Larsen, 2005 WL 1540130, at *2 (D. Minn. June 30, 2005) (following *National City Lines* in foreclosure rescue scam case).

154 Denny's Inc. v. Cake, 364 F.3d 521, 531 (4th Cir. 2004); Royal Ins. Co. of Amer. v. Quinn-L Capital Corp., 3 F.3d 877, 885 (5th Cir. 1993); Roth v. Bank of the Commonwealth, 583 F.2d 527, 533–534 (6th Cir. 1978).

155 Denny's Inc. v. Cake, 364 F.3d 521, 531 (4th Cir. 2004); Royal Ins. Co. of Amer. v. Quinn-L Capital Corp., 3 F.3d 877, 885 (5th Cir. 1993); Roth v. Bank of the Commonwealth, 583 F.2d 527, 533–534 (6th Cir. 1978). *See* Standard Microsystems Corp. v. Tex. Instruments Inc., 916 F.2d 58, 61–62 (2d Cir. 1990).

156 Chick Kam Choo v. Exxon Corp., 486 U.S. 140, 146, 108 S. Ct. 1684, 100 L. Ed. 2d 127 (1988).

157 28 U.S.C. § 2283.

158 Mitchum v. Foster, 407 U.S. 225, 237, 92 S. Ct. 2151, 32 L. Ed. 2d 705 (1972).

159 *Id. See also* Vendo Co. v. Lektro Vend Corp., 433 U.S. 623, 631–635, 97 S. Ct. 2881, 53 L. Ed. 2d 1009 (1977) (plurality opinion) (holding that Clayton Act was not express authorization for injunction, since neither statute nor legislative history mentioned § 2283 or the enjoining of state court proceedings).

160 Clark v. U.S. Bank Nat'l Ass'n, 2004 WL 1380166, at *3 (E.D. Pa. June 18, 2004) (holding, in case where plaintiff raised TIL and other claims, that none of the exceptions to Anti-Injunction Act applied). *See also* Tropf v. Fid. Nat'l Title Ins. Co., 289 F.3d 929, 942 n.21 (6th Cir. 2002) (stating, where plaintiffs raised TIL and many other claims, that no statute authorized the injunction plaintiffs sought).

161 Atl. Coast Line R.R. Co. v. Bhd. of Locomotive Eng'rs, 398 U.S. 281, 295, 90 S. Ct. 1739, 26 L. Ed. 2d 234 (1970).

162 *See In re* Diet Drugs, 282 F.3d 220, 235 (3d Cir. 2002) (multidistrict litigation); James v. Bellotti, 733 F.2d 989, 993 (1st Cir. 1984) (*in rem* jurisdiction); 1975 Salaried Ret. Plan for Eligible Employees of Crucible, Inc. v. Nobers, 968 F.2d 401, 407 (3d Cir. 1992) (*in rem* jurisdiction and removal cases).

163 Ret. Sys. of Ala. v. J.P. Morgan Chase & Co., 386 F.3d 419, 429 (2d Cir. 2004). *See* Atl. Coast Line R.R. Co. v. Bhd. of Locomotive Eng'rs, 398 U.S. 281, 294–296, 90 S. Ct. 1739, 26 L. Ed. 2d 234 (1970); Signal Props., Inc. v. Farha, 482 F.2d 1136, 1137 (5th Cir. 1973).

court's own path to judgment—such as by preventing relief on the federal claims even if they are proven—then a preliminary injunction may be necessary in aid of the federal court's jurisdiction.[164] This exception might allow a federal court to enjoin the actual eviction of the homeowner or sale of the property (through foreclosure or otherwise) in order to protect the ability of the federal court to grant the homeowner the relief sought on a TIL rescission claim.[165]

The final exception is that a federal court can enjoin state court proceedings as necessary to protect or effectuate its judgments. This exception is intended to prevent relitigation of an issue that was presented to and decided by the federal court, and is similar to the doctrines of res judicata and collateral estoppel.[166] This exception would allow a federal court that had issued a final judgment in a foreclosure rescue scam case, for example, to enjoin the rescuer from filing or pursuing an eviction action in state court to relitigate the issues.

164 *See In re* Diet Drugs, 282 F.3d 220, 235 (3d Cir. 2002); Piper v. Portnoff Law Assocs., 262 F. Supp. 2d 520, 529–530 (E.D. Pa. 2003).

165 *See* Piper v. Portnoff Law Assocs., 262 F. Supp. 2d 520, 529–531 (E.D. Pa. 2003) (applying this exception to enjoin sheriff's sale); Cottonwood Christian Ctr. v. Cypress Redevelopment Agency, 218 F. Supp. 2d 1203, 1217–1218, 1232 (C.D. Cal. 2002) (enjoining state condemnation proceeding where condemnation would hamper federal court's ability to rule on landowner's challenge to city's land use decisions). *But see* Madera v. Ameriquest Mortgage Co. (*In re* Madera), 2008 WL 447497 (E.D. Pa. Feb. 7, 2008) (Anti-Injunction Act bars federal court injunction against state court foreclosure proceeding; if federal court grants TIL rescission, it can reverse the conveyance of the debtor's home to the foreclosure purchaser), *on appeal*, 2008 WL 447497 (E.D. Pa. Feb. 7, 2008) (denying motion to stay sale; bankruptcy case is not an *in rem* proceeding so Anti-Injunction Act prohibits injunction against foreclosure sale ordered by state court); Smith v. ABN AMRO Mortgage Group, Inc., 2007 WL 2029044 (S.D. Ohio July 10, 2007) (exception inapplicable where federal suit was not *in rem* and not removed from state court); Armstrong v. Real Estate Int'l, Ltd., 2006 WL 354983, at *4–5 (E.D.N.Y. Feb. 14, 2006) (concluding that injunction not necessary in aid of federal court's jurisdiction in TIL challenge to foreclosure rescue scam because state court, which could hear TIL claims, had already entered judgment); Clark v. U.S. Bank Nat'l Ass'n, 2004 WL 1380166, at *3 (E.D. Pa. June 18, 2004) (unpublished) (denying TIL plaintiff's prayer for injunction against sheriff's sale scheduled to enforce state court foreclosure judgment).

166 Chick Kam Choo v. Exxon Corp., 486 U.S. 140, 146–147, 108 S. Ct. 1684, 100 L. Ed. 2d 127 (1988); Tropf v. Fid. Nat'l Title Ins. Co., 289 F.3d 929, 942 n.21 (6th Cir. 2002); Scherbenske v. Wachovia Mortg., F.S.B., 626 F. Supp. 2d 1052 (E.D. Cal. 2009) (Anti-Injunction Act precludes injunction against state court post-foreclosure eviction proceeding; mere filing of suit in federal court is insufficient to invoke exception); Smith v. ABN AMRO Mortgage Group, Inc., 2007 WL 2029044 (S.D. Ohio July 10, 2007) (exception does not apply where federal suit has not yet gone to judgment).

10.6.4 The **Rooker-Feldman** *Doctrine*

10.6.4.1 Summary of Doctrine

Under the *Rooker-Feldman* doctrine, a federal court lacks subject matter jurisdiction over a claim that is the functional equivalent of an appeal from a state court judgment.[167] The doctrine arose in two cases. In *Rooker v. Fidelity Trust Co.*,[168] the plaintiff's federal suit asked for a declaration that a state court judgment was null and void. The Supreme Court held that Congress had empowered only the Supreme Court, not federal district courts, to exercise appellate authority over state court judgments. It affirmed dismissal of the suit for lack of jurisdiction.

In the second case, *District of Columbia Court of Appeals v. Feldman*,[169] two law graduates brought suit in federal court after the District of Columbia Court of Appeals refused to waive a court rule that required bar applicants to have graduated from an ABA-approved law school. The Supreme Court held that the federal court could take jurisdiction over claims that the court rule was unconstitutional, but not over claims that the District of Columbia court had erred in refusing to grant a waiver.

In two decisions in 2005 and 2006, the Supreme Court has made clear that the doctrine is extremely narrow and that lower courts were interpreting it too broadly.[170] In 2005, in *Exxon Mobil Corp. v. Saudi Basic Indus. Corp.*,[171] the Court reversed a lower court's dismissal of a federal suit that was brought while a state court suit was pending, but before it had gone to judgment. The Court held that the doctrine did not prevent the federal court from assuming concurrent jurisdiction over the federal case when it was filed, and the later entry of judgment by the state court did not operate to vanquish the jurisdiction the federal court had properly assumed. It defined the *Rooker-Feldman* doctrine as "confined to . . . cases brought by state-court losers complaining of injuries caused by state-court judgments rendered before the district court proceedings commenced and

167 *See* District of Columbia Court of Appeals v. Feldman, 460 U.S. 462, 482–486, 103 S. Ct. 1303, 75 L. Ed. 2d 206 (1983); Rooker v. Fid. Trust Co., 263 U.S. 413, 416, 44 S. Ct. 149, 68 L. Ed. 362 (1923).

168 263 U.S. 413, 44 S. Ct. 149, 68 L. Ed. 362 (1923).

169 460 U.S. 462, 103 S. Ct. 1303, 75 L. Ed. 2d 206 (1983).

170 *See* Lance v. Dennis, 546 U.S. 459, 126 S. Ct. 1198, 1201, 163 L. Ed. 2d 1059 (2006) (noting that the Court has never applied the doctrine since *Rooker* and *Feldman* and listing the cases in which the Court rejected application of the doctrine); Marshall v. Marshall, 547 U.S. 293, 126 S. Ct. 1735, 1752, 164 L. Ed. 2d 480 (2006) (Stevens, J., concurring in part and concurring in the judgment) (referring to the grave in which *Rooker Feldman* was buried).

171 Exxon Mobil Corp. v. Saudi Basic Indus. Corp., 544 U.S. 280, 284, 125 S. Ct. 1517, 161 L. Ed. 2d 454 (2005) (emphasis added).

inviting district court review and rejection of those judgments."[172]

The Court reiterated the narrowness of the doctrine in 2006 in *Lance v. Dennis*.[173] There, the Court held that the doctrine does not apply if the federal plaintiff was not a party to the state case, even if it was in privity with a party.

Despite these limiting rulings, a number of federal courts have continued to apply the doctrine to refuse to hear cases filed after a state foreclosure action has gone to judgment, so practitioners should expect to have to address the issue.[174] A substantial percentage of these post-foreclosure federal suits were litigated by *pro se* plaintiffs with poorly-framed and sometimes unintelligible claims. Competent drafting will reduce—although it will not eliminate—the likelihood of a *Rooker-Feldman* dismissal.

Even without the *Rooker-Feldman* doctrine, res judicata or collateral estoppel may prevent the consumer from litigating issues in federal court that were or could have been raised in the state court proceedings. A federal court is required to give a state court judgment the same preclusive effect as a state court would.[175] Thus, while the *Rooker-Feldman* doctrine is narrower than the doctrines of res judicata and collateral estoppel,[176] cases that clear the *Rooker-Feldman* hurdle may face additional procedural challenges. In addition, comity or abstention may allow or require a federal court to stay or dismiss a federal court action so that state court litigation may take precedence.[177]

The following subsections focus on situations in which the *Rooker-Feldman* doctrine may not be a bar to federal court jurisdiction.

10.6.4.2 Cases Removed from State Court

The *Rooker-Feldman* doctrine does not restrict a federal court's jurisdiction to adjudicate claims in a case removed from state court. Such a case invokes the federal court's original jurisdiction, and cannot be characterized as an appeal of a state court judgment. The federal court's authority to manage its own cases allows it to review orders entered prior to removal, even if the result would be to void a determination made by the state court.[178]

10.6.4.3 Where State Case Had Not Reached Final Judgment Before Federal Case Filed

Parallel cases in state and federal court are unaffected by the *Rooker-Feldman* doctrine.[179] Thus, a case in federal

172 *Id.*, 544 U.S. at 284.

173 Lance v. Dennis, 546 U.S. 459, 126 S. Ct. 1198, 1200, 163 L. Ed. 2d 1059 (2006).

174 *See, e.g.*, Silva v. Massachusetts, 351 Fed. Appx. 450 (1st Cir. 2009) (*Rooker-Feldman* doctrine bars federal suit challenging statutory scheme under which defendant obtained state court judgment granting foreclosure title to home); Ashby v. Polinsky, 2009 WL 1262962 (2d Cir. May 6, 2009) (barring *pro se* post-foreclosure federal suit); Pease v. First Nat'l Bank, 335 Fed. Appx. 412 (5th Cir. 2009) (barring *pro se* post-foreclosure suit against bank, bank officer, substitute trustee, sheriff, and state court judge); Stanley v. Hollingsworth, 307 Fed. Appx. 6 (7th Cir. 2008) (*Rooker-Feldman* doctrine bars federal claim that aspects of state court foreclosure judgment were wrong, and claim that creditor committed malicious prosecution in obtaining that judgment, but not claims based on acts that preceded the state court proceeding, including forced placement of insurance); Givens v. Homecomings Fin., 278 Fed. Appx. 607 (6th Cir. 2008) (unpublished) (*Rooker-Feldman* doctrine bars FDCPA, conspiracy, and RICO claims where primary relief sought was injunction against enforcement of state court post-foreclosure eviction order); Stack v. Mason & Assocs., 245 Fed. Appx. 920 (11th Cir. 2007) (*Rooker-Feldman* doctrine bars suit that challenged fees charged as part of state court foreclosure judgment); Garvin v. Bank of N.Y., 227 Fed. Appx. 7 (2d Cir. 2007) (*Rooker-Feldman* doctrine bars *pro se* plaintiff's federal suit asking that state court foreclosure judgment "be overruled and reversed"); Knapper v. Bankers Trust Co. (*In re* Knapper), 407 F.3d 573 (3d Cir. 2005); Hunter v. U.S. Bank, 2010 WL 1037945 (D.D.C. Mar. 22, 2010) (*Rooker-Feldman* doctrine bars jurisdiction over *pro se* suit that challenged validity of state court foreclosure judgment); Sherk v. Countrywide Home Loans, Inc., 2009 WL 2412750 (E.D. Pa. Aug. 5, 2009) (*Rooker-Feldman* doctrine bars relief predicated on a finding that the state court wrongly entered a foreclosure judgment); Burlinson v. Wells Fargo Bank, 2009 WL 646330 (D. Colo. Mar. 9, 2009) (barring FDCPA claim alleging that creditor's attorney foreclosed on home without legal right to do so); Book v. Mortgage Elec. Registration Sys., 608 F. Supp. 2d 277 (D. Conn. 2009) (*Rooker-Feldman* doctrine bars claims alleging injuries arising out of post-foreclosure ejectment and out of actions that related to implementation of state foreclosure judgment); Hoodenpyle v. Deutsche Nat'l Bank Holding Trust, 2009 WL 564278 (D. Colo. Mar. 5, 2009) (*Rooker-Feldman* doctrine bars federal suit to stay state court foreclosure); Johnson v. EMC Mortgage Corp., 2008 WL 2437434 (D. Minn. June 12, 2008) (*Rooker-Feldman* doctrine bars claim to quiet title and order reconveyance of foreclosed home); Ramseur v. Fed. Nat'l Mortgage Ass'n, 2007 WL 2421523 (E.D. Mich. Aug. 24, 2007) (construing *pro se* complaint as seeking redress for injuries arising from state court foreclosure judgment, so it is barred by *Rooker-Feldman* doctrine); Moncrief v. Chase Manhattan Mortgage Corp., 2007 WL 3170694 (M.D. Pa. Sept. 28, 2007) (refusing jurisdiction over fraud claims where state foreclosure action had already gone to judgment), *aff'd*, 275 Fed. Appx. 149 (3d Cir. 2008). *See also* §§ 10.6.4.9.2, 10.6.4.9.3, *infra*.

175 *See* § 10.6.5, *infra* (discussion of res judicata and collateral estoppel).

176 Exxon Mobil Corp v. Saudi Basic Indus. Corp., 544 U.S. 280, 125 S. Ct. 1517, 1522, 1527, 161 L. Ed. 2d 454 (2005).

177 125 S. Ct. at 1527. *See* § 10.6.2, *supra*.

178 Motley v. Option One Mortg. Corp., 620 F. Supp. 2d 1297 (M.D. Ala. 2009); 4 B's Realty 1530 CR 39, L.L.C. v. Toscano, 2009 WL 702011 (E.D.N.Y. Mar. 12, 2009).

179 Exxon Mobil Corp v. Saudi Basic Indus. Corp., 544 U.S. 280, 125 S. Ct. 1517, 1526–1527, 161 L. Ed. 2d 454 (2005); Kougasian v. TMSL, Inc., 359 F.3d 1136, 1140 (9th Cir. 2004); Noel v. Hall, 341 F.3d 1148 (9th Cir. 2003); St. Clair v. Wertzberger, 637 F. Supp. 2d 251 (D.N.J. 2009); Bey v. Wells Fargo, N.A., 2009 WL 367963 (E.D. Mich. Feb. 10, 2009) (*Rooker-Feldman* doctrine inapplicable where federal com-

court may proceed concurrently with a state case, although, when one reaches judgment, it may have res judicata effect on the other.[180]

Accordingly, the *Rooker-Feldman* doctrine has no application at all if the state court case has not gone to judgment at the time the federal suit is filed.[181] Even if the state court case has gone to final judgment, some courts hold that the *Rooker-Feldman* doctrine is inapplicable if the appeal time has not run[182] or a state court appeal is pending[183] at the time the federal suit is filed.

Whether a state foreclosure judgment is truly final should be carefully explored. Foreclosure cases typically go through a number of stages. The consumer may be able to avoid the doctrine by arguing that whatever ruling the state court has rendered is not a final state court judgment. For example, in Illinois there is some authority that there is a final and appealable judgment in a foreclosure case only after the home has been sold and the state court has confirmed the sale after a hearing at which the homeowner can raise certain defenses. In this situation, the existence of the interlocutory foreclosure judgment may not trigger *Rooker-Feldman* concerns.[184] A state court judgment that is void may also escape the *Rooker-Feldman* doctrine, although if it is merely voidable the doctrine may apply.[185]

---

plaint was filed six days before judgment of eviction was entered in state court action). *See also* Scarpone v. Dionisio, 2007 WL 1237836 (D.N.J. Apr. 26, 2007) (*Rooker-Feldman* doctrine does not bar fraudulent transfer claim against entity that purchased foreclosure judgment, where state court proceedings to enforce that judgment did not address whether entity was bona fide purchaser); National Consumer Law Center, Truth in Lending § 7.6.4 (6th ed. 2007 and Supp.) (concurrent litigation of TIL cases in state and federal courts).

180 *See* National Consumer Law Center, Truth in Lending § 7.6.4 (6th ed. 2007 and Supp.) (concurrent litigation of TIL cases in state and federal courts). *See also* Lyons v. WM Specialty Mortgage L.L.C., 2008 WL 2811810 (D. Colo. July 18, 2008) (finding it unnecessary to decide whether state court foreclosure suit became final upon issuance of order approving sale or only upon later issuance of deed, as res judicata would bar suit even if *Rooker-Feldman* doctrine did not).

181 Exxon Mobil Corp v. Saudi Basic Indus. Corp., 125 S. Ct. 1517 (2005); Brown v. JPMorgan Chase Bank, 2008 WL 711721 (N.D. Ind. Mar. 13, 2008) (*Rooker-Feldman* doctrine inapplicable where no final judgment had been entered in state court foreclosure case), *aff'd*, 2009 WL 1761101 (7th Cir. June 23, 2009); Willis v. U.S. Bank, 2007 WL 3313669 (D. Minn. Nov. 6, 2007) (*Rooker-Feldman* doctrine does not bar federal suit that was filed before state court foreclosure judgment was rendered, but res judicata bars it); Lund v. Citibank (West) F.S.B., 2007 WL 3408468 (E.D. Mich. Nov. 14, 2007) (*Rooker-Feldman* doctrine does not bar federal suit that was filed before state court foreclosure judgment was rendered, but res judicata and collateral estoppel bar it).

182 Bear v. Patton, 451 F.3d 639, 642 (10th Cir. 2006); Dornheim v. Sholes, 430 F.3d 919 (8th Cir. 2005); Allen v. United Properties & Constr., Inc., 2008 WL 4080035 (D. Colo. Sept. 3, 2008) (*Rooker-Feldman* doctrine inapplicable where federal suit was filed before state court appeal period expired). *But cf.* Federacion de Maestros de Puerto Rico v. Junta de Relaciones del Trabajo de Puerto Rico, 410 F.3d 17 (1st Cir. 2005) (state court judgment is final for *Rooker-Feldman* purposes if all proceedings have ended with regard to the issues that the federal plaintiff seeks to litigate, even if other issues remain to be resolved); Schuh v. Druckman & Sinel, L.L.P., 2008 WL 542504, at *5 (S.D.N.Y. Feb. 29, 2008) (magistrate's recommendation) (*Rooker-Feldman* doctrine may apply even though appeal of state court judgment was pending).

183 Guttman v. Khalsa, 446 F.3d 1027, 1032 (10th Cir. 2006) (doctrine inapplicable where petition for certiorari to state supreme court was pending at time plaintiff filed federal suit). *But see* Schuh v. Druckman & Sinel, L.L.P., 2008 WL 542504, at *5 (S.D.N.Y. Feb. 29, 2008) (magistrate's recommendation) (*Rooker-Feldman* doctrine may apply even though appeal of state court judgment was pending).

184 *In re* Hodges, 350 B.R. 796 (N.D. Ill. 2006). *See also* Coleman v. America's Wholesale Lender, 2009 WL 761169 (E.D. Pa. Mar. 18, 2009) (foreclosure judgment not final, and *Rooker-Feldman* doctrine inapplicable, where homeowners filed federal suit after foreclosure judgment and sale of home but before ejectment portion of foreclosure case was concluded); McMahon v. Prudential Ins. Co., 2007 WL 2463343 (E.D. Mich. Aug. 30, 2007) (*Rooker-Feldman* doctrine does not bar claims that arise out of post-foreclosure accounting action that was still pending in state court at time federal suit was filed, but collateral estoppel bars these claims); Woodsbey v. Easy Mortgage (*In re* Woodsbey), 375 B.R. 145 (Bankr. W.D. Pa. 2007) (existence of foreclosure judgment does not prevent bankruptcy court from hearing claims where state law allows debtor to cure mortgage default up to one hour before sheriff's sale). *Cf.* Bear v. Patton, 451 F.3d 639 (10th Cir. 2006) (whether state court order requiring property to be partitioned and sold was final is state law question where sale had not yet occurred and accounting and distribution of proceeds would take place only after sale); Beeler Props., L.L.C. v. Lowe Enters. Residential Investors, L.L.C., 2007 WL 1346591 (D. Colo. May 7, 2007) (discussing whether state court foreclosure judgment was final, but finding it unnecessary to decide the question, as *Younger* abstention would bar plaintiff's claim even if *Rooker-Feldman* doctrine did not). *But see* Spencer v. Mortgage Acceptance Corp., 2006 WL 1302413 (N.D. Ill. May 4, 2006) (state court judgment of foreclosure was final judgment and *Rooker-Feldman* doctrine applied, even though home had not been sold and court had not approved foreclosure report of sale and distribution and order for possession and deed). *But cf.* Federacion de Maestros de Puerto Rico v. Junta de Relaciones del Trabajo de Puerto Rico, 410 F.3d 17 (1st Cir. 2005) (state court judgment is final for *Rooker-Feldman* purposes if all proceedings have ended with regard to the issues that the federal plaintiff seeks to litigate, even if other issues remain to be resolved).

185 Dougal v. Saxon Mortgage (*In re* Dougal), 395 B.R. 880 (Bankr. W.D. Pa. 2008).

10.6.4.4 Where Federal Parties Are Not the Same As the State Parties

10.6.4.4.1 Where federal plaintiff was not a party to the state court action

The Supreme Court has made it clear that the *Rooker-Feldman* doctrine does not apply if the federal plaintiff was not a party to the state case. Even if the federal plaintiff is in privity with a party to the state case, the doctrine does not apply.[186] Thus, a prior state court judgment against one of two co-owners of a home will not be a basis for invoking the doctrine to bar a federal suit by the other co-owner.[187] Likewise, the doctrine does not bar a bankruptcy trustee from asserting a claim, where the trustee was not a party to the prior state court judgment.[188]

10.6.4.4.2 Where federal defendants were not parties to the state court action

Some courts have suggested that if the federal defendants were not parties to the state court proceedings, this may be a reason not to apply the *Rooker-Feldman* doctrine even though the federal plaintiff was a party. The Second Circuit has stated that one requirement of the *Rooker-Feldman* doctrine is that "the parties in the state and federal suits must be the same."[189] However, in a different part of the same opinion the court described a hypothetical situation in which suing people who were not parties to the state court case would not avoid the doctrine.[190] In addition, the Tenth Circuit has held that adding defendants beyond those involved in the state court case does not avoid the doctrine.[191] In that case the court held that the doctrine barred claims against both the old and the new defendants.

Even if there is no per se rule that the *Rooker-Feldman* doctrine does not apply to claims that are asserted in federal court against entities who were not parties in the previous state court case, these claims are more likely to be considered independent claims, to which the *Rooker-Feldman* doctrine does not apply.[192] A federal district court decision has held that a state court foreclosure judgment did not bar claims against the foreclosure attorney, as the homeowner had neither sought a remedy in state court nor suffered an adverse judgment as to the attorney.[193] Another decision holds that a judgment in a state court foreclosure action brought by the mortgagee did not prevent the homeowner from bringing federal claims against a servicer and a broker.[194] A decision in the second suit would not be directed at the judgment holder, so could not negate the foreclosure judgment. Nor did a judgment in a state court foreclosure action brought by MERS as "nominee" for a servicer bar a federal claim against the servicer.[195] In a non-judicial foreclosure state, if the prior state court proceeding is an eviction action brought by the buyer at the foreclosure sale, the judgment may not bar jurisdiction over a suit against the mortgage holder.

10.6.4.5 Claims the Homeowner Could Not Have Raised in the State Court Case

The *Rooker-Feldman* doctrine does not apply to claims that the homeowner could not have raised in the state court proceeding.[196] The federal suit cannot be characterized as an

186 Lance v. Dennis, 546 U.S. 459, 126 S. Ct. 1198, 1200, 163 L. Ed. 2d 1059 (2006).

187 *See* Bannister v. Coronado Fin., Inc., 2008 WL 4104067 (D.N.M. Mar. 28, 2008) (*Rooker-Feldman* doctrine inapplicable where federal plaintiff who apparently claimed an interest in a home upon which a judgment creditor foreclosed had not been allowed to intervene in foreclosure case).

188 Ameriquest Mortgage Co. v. Kekauoha-Alisa (*In re* Kekauoha-Alisa), 407 B.R. 442 (B.A.P. 9th Cir. 2009); Prior v. Zerbo (*In re* Zerbo), 397 B.R. 642 (Bankr. E.D.N.Y. 2008).

189 Hoblock v. Albany County Bd. of Elections, 422 F.3d 77, 89 (2d Cir. 2005).

190 *Id.* at 88 (suing state officials who implemented court order will not avoid *Rooker-Feldman*).

191 Tal v. Hogan, 453 F.3d 1244, 1257 (10th Cir. 2006). *See also* Carter v. Countrywide Home Loans, Inc., 2008 WL 803035 (E.D. Va. Mar. 20, 2008) (rejecting argument that *Rooker-Feldman* doctrine is inapplicable where federal defendant was not a party to state court suit).

192 *See* § 10.6.4.8, *infra*.

193 Bell v. JP Morgan Chase Bank, 2007 WL 107833 (E.D. Mich. Jan. 8, 2007) (*Rooker-Feldman* doctrine does not bar claim against foreclosure attorney, but res judicata does). *But see* Dockter v. Deutsche Bank Nat'l Trust Co., 2009 WL 88912 (D.N.D. Jan. 12, 2009) (*Rooker-Feldman* doctrine bars suit against attorneys for state court plaintiffs, as these claims are inextricably intertwined with the claims against the state court plaintiff).

194 *In re* Faust, 353 B.R. 94 (Bankr. E.D. Pa. 2006). *See also* Estate of Keys v. Union Plants Bank, 578 F. Supp. 2d 629 (S.D.N.Y. 2008) (key question is causation; *Rooker-Feldman* doctrine bars claim where injury was caused by state court foreclosure judgment).

195 Fritz v. GMAC Mortgage Corp., 2008 WL 2783218 (E.D. Wis. July 17, 2008).

196 Hansford v. Bank of Am., 2008 WL 4078460 (E.D. Pa. Aug. 22, 2008) (*Rooker-Feldman* doctrine does not bar damages claims that could not have been asserted in state court foreclosure case); Laychock v. Wells Fargo Home Mortgage, 2008 WL 2890962 (E.D. Pa. July 23, 2008) (TIL rescission claim barred, but not claim for damages for TIL, HOEPA, and RESPA violations that could not have been asserted in state court foreclosure case); *In re* Denaro, 383 B.R. 879 (Bankr. D.N.J. 2008) (*Rooker-Feldman* doctrine does not bar claim that debt should have been reduced by property's market value rather than foreclosure sale price, as this claim matured only after state court issued its judgment and the property was sold); Kaliner v. Mortgage Elec. Registration Sys., Inc. (*In re* Reagoso), 2007 WL 1655376 (Bankr. E.D. Pa. June 6, 2007) (*Rooker-Feldman* doctrine bars claim seeking revision in terms of mortgage but not claims for money damages that could not have been raised as foreclosure counterclaims); Brown v. Grant Holding, L.L.C.,

appeal on an issue that the state court not only did not reach, but could not have reached.

A number of states restrict the claims and defenses that a homeowner can raise in a foreclosure action or in an eviction action filed after a foreclosure sale in a non-judicial foreclosure state.[197] In these states, the *Rooker-Feldman* doctrine does not prevent federal litigation of claims that the homeowner could not have raised in the state court case.

10.6.4.6 Where Homeowner Is Defendant in Federal Court Case

According to the Supreme Court's formulation, the doctrine applies only to federal cases "brought by" state court losers.[198] Occasionally the homeowner will be the defendant rather than the plaintiff in the federal suit. For example, if the homeowner attempts to rescind the loan under the Truth in Lending Act after the foreclosure judgment is entered, the creditor may bring an action in federal court seeking a declaratory judgment that the rescission is invalid. In this admittedly atypical situation, the federal suit is brought by the state court winner, so the *Rooker-Feldman* doctrine should not be applicable.

10.6.4.7 Where Federal Plaintiff Was Also the Plaintiff in State Court

There is some authority that the *Rooker-Feldman* doctrine does not apply if the federal plaintiff was not the defendant in the state court proceeding. For example, before filing in federal court the homeowner may have brought suit in state court to try to stop a non-judicial foreclosure. In a pre-*Exxon* decision, the Seventh Circuit held a state court plaintiff who loses and then tries again in federal court encounters the law of preclusion, not the *Rooker-Feldman* doctrine.[199] This view is consistent with *Exxon*'s requirement that the injury of which the federal plaintiff complains must result from the state court judgment itself. Two post-*Exxon* decisions have applied this principle to hold that the *Rooker-Feldman* doctrine did not bar a federal suit that was filed after a similar state court challenge to a non-judicial foreclosure had failed.[200]

10.6.4.8 Claims Asserted in Bankruptcy

Many courts have held that the *Rooker-Feldman* doctrine is inapplicable to certain types of actions in bankruptcy court. These courts rely on the fact that federal bankruptcy courts have original jurisdiction that explicitly allows them to avoid, modify, and discharge state judgments in certain circumstances. For example, a bankruptcy court can avoid a transfer of the debtor's property, avoid a preference, avoid a fraudulent transfer, and avoid certain post-petition transactions.[201] It may nullify a judgment obtained in violation of the automatic stay.[202] It may modify a judgment in certain circumstances[203] and, of course, can discharge debts.[204] Since the *Rooker-Feldman* doctrine is grounded not on any constitutional rule, but on the federal statutes that vest review of state supreme court decisions solely in the U.S. Supreme Court, it has no application to claims brought in

---

394 F. Supp. 2d 1090 (D. Minn. 2005) (*Rooker-Feldman* inapplicable when housing court only decided whether former owner of home could remain in possession and could not decide equitable mortgage claim). *See also* Madera v. Ameriquest Mortgage Co. (*In re* Madera), 586 F.3d 228 (3d Cir. 2009) (dismissing TIL rescission claim but addressing merits of TIL damages claim); Beth-El All Nations Church v. City of Chicago, 486 F.3d 286 (7th Cir. 2007) (recognizing exception, but finding that federal plaintiff had opportunity to raise claims in state court case); Long v. Shorebank Dev. Corp., 182 F.3d 548, 558 (7th Cir. 1999) (eviction judgment does not bar FDCPA claim; "an issue cannot be inextricably intertwined with a state court judgment if the plaintiff did not have a reasonable opportunity to raise the issue in state court proceedings"); Doyle v. Town of Litchfield, 372 F. Supp. 2d 288, 300 n.8 (D. Conn. 2005) ("a claim cannot be 'inextricably intertwined' unless the plaintiff had an opportunity to present it in the state court"); Bush v. SA Mortgage Serv. Co., 2005 WL 1155851 (E.D. La. May 9, 2005) (tax sale case; when notice of state court proceeding was alleged to be constitutionally inadequate, plaintiff did not have reasonable opportunity to raise federal claim, so *Rooker-Feldman* doctrine is inapplicable); *In re* Cooley, 365 B.R. 464 (Bankr. E.D. Pa. 2007) (rescission barred, but not money damage claims, since state law precluded the homeowner from raising the latter in foreclosure case); *In re* Randall, 358 B.R. 145 (Bankr. E.D. Pa. 2006) (foreclosure judgment precludes rescission claim, but not money damage claims that could not have been litigated in foreclosure case). *Cf.* Reusser v. Wachovia Bank, 2006 WL 2334844 (D. Or. Aug. 10, 2006) (*Rooker-Feldman* bars claims that could have been raised as defenses in state court eviction action, even though they could not have been raised as counterclaims), *aff'd on other grounds,* 525 F.3d 855 (9th Cir. 2008).

197 *See* National Consumer Law Center, Truth in Lending § 7.6.8 (6th ed. 2007 and Supp.).

198 *Exxon*, 125 S. Ct. at 1517.

199 Homola v. McNamara, 59 F.3d 647, 650 (7th Cir. 1995).

200 Thad-Marine v. Mortgage Elec. Registration Sys., Inc., 2007 WL 2004861 (E.D. Mich. July 9, 2007) (*Rooker-Feldman* doctrine inapplicable, but res judicata bars federal suit); Walker v. Seldman, 471 F. Supp. 2d 106 (D.D.C. 2007) (*Rooker-Feldman* does not bar federal suit where homeowner was also the plaintiff in the prior state court suit, but claims barred by res judicata), *aff'd*, 2008 WL 4682659 (D.C. Cir. Apr. 8, 2008). *But cf.* Smith v. Provident Consumer Fin. Servs., 2006 WL 1999227 (E.D. Mich. July 17, 2006) (barring claims that homeowners had previously litigated in state court suit they filed; no discussion of fact that they were not the state court defendants).

201 11 U.S.C. §§ 544, 547, 548, 549.

202 National Consumer Law Center, Consumer Bankruptcy Law and Practice § 9.6.1 (9th ed. 2009).

203 11 U.S.C. §§ 1129, 1325. *See also* Woodsbey v. Easy Mortgage (*In re* Woodsbey), 375 B.R. 145 (Bankr. W.D. Pa. 2007) (existence of foreclosure judgment does not prevent bankruptcy court from hearing claims where state law allows debtor to cure mortgage default up to one hour before sheriff's sale).

204 11 U.S.C. §§ 727, 1141, 1328.

bankruptcy court based on substantive rights under the Bankruptcy Code.[205] There is explicit federal statutory authority for bankruptcy courts to hear these claims.

The rule that the doctrine does not apply where the federal plaintiff was not a party to the state court proceeding is also important in the bankruptcy context. The doctrine does not bar a bankruptcy trustee from asserting a claim where the trustee was not a party to the prior state court judgment.[206]

10.6.4.9 Inapplicable to Independent Claims

10.6.4.9.1 When is a claim independent?

Even when no other exception applies, the *Rooker-Feldman* doctrine does not apply if a federal plaintiff presents an independent claim.[207] A claim can be considered independent even if it denies a legal conclusion that a state court has reached in a case to which the federal plaintiff was a party.[208] The case might be governed by res judicata or claim preclusion, but *Rooker-Feldman* neither supplants nor augments those doctrines.[209]

The scope of the independent claim exception is not entirely clear. One of the cases on which the *Rooker-Feldman* doctrine is based, *District of Columbia Court of Appeals v. Feldman*, held that the doctrine prevents federal courts from hearing certain claims that are not appeals but are "inextricably intertwined" with a state court determination.[210] In *Exxon*, the Supreme Court recited this language twice in describing that decision,[211] without clearly endorsing or repudiating it either time.

The *Exxon* court did, however, enunciate two principles that may be roughly equivalent to the "inextricably intertwined" rule. First, language in the decision suggests that two criteria for the application of the *Rooker-Feldman* doctrine are that the injury about which the federal plaintiff complains must have been caused by the state court's ruling and the plaintiff must be seeking relief that would undo that judgment.[212] Conversely, the Court held that the *Rooker-Feldman* doctrine does *not* apply if the federal plaintiff presents some independent claim, even if the claim denies a legal conclusion that a state court has reached in a case to which the plaintiff was a party.[213]

Although some circuits after *Exxon* have continued to apply the "inextricably intertwined" rule,[214] the better view

205 *In re* Sasson, 424 F.3d 864, 871 (9th Cir. 2005); *In re* Gruntz, 202 F.3d 1074 (9th Cir. 2000); *In re* Dunbar, 245 F.3d 1058, 1061–1064 (9th Cir. 2000); Funches v. Household Fin. Consumer Discount Co. (*In re* Funches), 381 B.R. 471 (Bankr. E.D. Pa. 2008) (*Rooker-Feldman* doctrine does not prevent bankruptcy court from avoiding state court foreclosure judgment). *See also In re* Knapper, 407 F.3d 573, 583 n.22 (3d Cir. 2005) (doctrine would not bar claim that is properly based on 11 U.S.C. § 544(b)(1)); *In re* Weinraub, 361 B.R. 586 (Bankr. S.D. Fla. 2007); *In re* Hopkins, 346 B.R. 294 (Bankr. E.D.N.Y. 2006) (*Rooker-Feldman* doctrine does not bar claim that eviction judgment, entered after foreclosure sale, was avoidable transfer). *But cf. In re* Rusch, 2009 WL 1025466 (D.N.J. Jan. 23, 2009) (*Rooker-Feldman* doctrine bars bankruptcy court from vacating default judgment in state court foreclosure action); *In re* Baumgardner, 2007 WL 655308 (Bankr. N.D. Tex. Feb. 27, 2007) (applying *Rooker-Feldman* doctrine to refuse to review state court's determination of ownership of property); *In re* Dunlop, 378 B.R. 85 (Bankr. E.D. Pa. 2007) (*Rooker-Feldman* doctrine prevents bankruptcy courts from serving as appellate courts for state foreclosure proceedings).

206 Ameriquest Mortgage Co. v. Kekauoha-Alisa (*In re* Kekauoha-Alisa), 407 B.R. 442 (B.A.P. 9th Cir. 2009); Prior v. Zerbo (*In re* Zerbo), 397 B.R. 642 (Bankr. E.D.N.Y. 2008).

207 Exxon Mobil Corp. v. Saudi Basic Indus. Corp., 544 U.S. 280, 293, 125 S. Ct. 1517, 161 L. Ed. 2d 454 (2005).

208 Exxon Mobil Corp. v. Saudi Basic Indus. Corp., 544 U.S. 280, 293, 125 S. Ct. 1517, 161 L. Ed. 2d 454 (2005).

209 *Id.*, 544 U.S. at 283–284; Lance v. Dennis, 546 U.S. 459, 126 S. Ct. 1198, 1202, 163 L. Ed. 2d 1059 (2006).

210 460 U.S. 462, 486, 103 S. Ct. 1303, 75 L. Ed. 2d 206 (1983).

211 Exxon Mobil Corp v. Saudi Basic Indus. Corp., 125 S. Ct. 1517, 1523 (2005).

212 Exxon Mobil Corp v. Saudi Basic Indus. Corp., 125 S. Ct. 1524 n.2 (2005) ("the injury of which the petitioners (the losing parties in state court) could have complained in the hypothetical federal suit would have been caused by the state court's invalidation of their mineral leases, and the relief they would have sought would have been to undo the state court's invalidation of the statute"), 1526 (in *Rooker* and *Feldman* cases, "the losing party in state court filed suit in federal court after the state proceedings ended, complaining of an injury caused by the state-court judgment and seeking review and rejection of that judgment"). *See also* Stanley v. Hollingsworth, 307 Fed. Appx. 6 (7th Cir. 2008) (reciting these factors and finding some claims barred and others not barred); Beth-El All Nations Church v. City of Chicago, 486 F.3d 286 (7th Cir. 2007) (*Rooker-Feldman* doctrine bars suit where the injuries the federal plaintiff alleges arose from state court tax foreclosure judgments); Trakansook v. Astoria Fed. Sav. & Loan Ass'n, 2007 WL 1160433 (E.D.N.Y. Apr. 18, 2007) (federal suit that seeks order vacating state court foreclosure judgment seeks review of that judgment even if it is based on different legal theories), *aff'd*, 2008 WL 4962990 (2d Cir. Nov. 21, 2008).

213 Exxon Mobil Corp v. Saudi Basic Indus. Corp., 125 S. Ct. 1527 (2005).

214 Velardo v. Fremont Inv. & Loan, 298 Fed. Appx. 890 (11th Cir. 2008); Dye v. Ameriquest Mortgage Co., 289 Fed. Appx. 941 (7th Cir. 2008); Knapper v. Bankers Trust Co. (*In re* Knapper), 407 F.3d 573 (3d Cir. 2005) (applying "inextricably intertwined" test; *Rooker-Feldman* doctrine bars suit to set aside state foreclosure and sheriff sale on due process grounds); Hoodenpyle v. Deutsche Nat'l Bank Holding Trust, 2009 WL 564278 (D. Colo. Mar. 5, 2009). *See also* Kotsopoulos v. Mortgage Elec. Registration Sys., Inc., 2007 WL 905094 (D.S.C. Mar. 22, 2007) (claim that MERS was not holder in due course and had not loaned money to plaintiffs is barred by *Rooker-Feldman* doctrine because it is inextricably intertwined with state court foreclosure judgment); Chapman v. Delaware County Tax Claim Bur., 2007 WL 2207747 (E.D. Pa. July 24, 2007) (claims for adverse possession and to quiet title are inextricably intertwined with foreclosure judgment; test is whether federal court must determine that the state court judgment was entered erroneously in order to grant the requested relief, or the federal

is that these two principles displace or at least redefine it.[215] A number of courts agree with a Second Circuit opinion that the phrase "inextricably intertwined" has no independent content, but is merely a descriptive label attached to claims that meet the requirements outlined in *Exxon*.[216] Other courts continue to hold that "inextricably intertwined" claims are barred by the doctrine, but define these claims in a fairly narrow way similar to the Supreme Court's definition of independent claims.[217]

court must take an action that would negate the state court's judgment). *Cf.* Beth-El All Nations Church v. City of Chicago, 486 F.3d 286, 292 (7th Cir. 2007) (describing "inextricably intertwined" rule as if it were an independent ground for invoking *Rooker-Feldman* doctrine).

215 The continuing vitality of this *Feldman* rule is thrown into particular doubt by Justice Stevens' opinion commending the Court for "disapprov[ing] of the District Court's resuscitation" of the "incorrectly decided" *Feldman* decision. Lance v. Dennis, 546 U.S. 459, 126 S. Ct. 1198, 1203, 163 L. Ed. 2d 1059 (2006) (Stevens, J., dissenting).

216 Hoblock v. Albany County Bd. of Elections, 422 F.3d 77, 87 (2d Cir. 2005). *Accord* McCormick v. Braverman, 451 F.3d 382, 393, 394–395 (6th Cir. 2006) (citing *Hoblock* with approval; *Exxon* "implicitly repudiated use of the phrase 'inextricably intertwined' to extend *Rooker-Feldman* to situations where the source of the injury was not the state court judgment"); Davani v. Va. Dep't of Transp., 434 F.3d 712, 719 (4th Cir. 2006) ("'inextricably intertwined' language does not create an additional legal test for determining when claims challenging a state-court decision are barred"); Bolden v. City of Topeka, 441 F.3d 1129, 1131 (10th Cir. 2006) (citing *Hoblock* with approval). *See also* Todd v. Weltman, Weinberg & Reis Co., 434 F.3d 432, 437 (6th Cir. 2006) (even if independent claim is inextricably linked to state court decision, preclusion law rather than *Rooker-Feldman* doctrine is correct means of challenging federal claim); Manufactured Home Communities v. City of San Jose, 420 F.3d 1022 (9th Cir. 2005) (inextricably intertwined is not an independent basis for denying federal jurisdiction, but if federal suit is a forbidden de facto appeal, plaintiff cannot litigate issues that are inextricably intertwined with state court judgment); Madura v. Countrywide Home Loans, Inc., 2007 WL 4336094 (M.D. Fla. Dec. 7, 2007) (discussing differences in pre- and post-*Exxon* interpretations; *Rooker-Feldman* doctrine does not bar claims, including TIL rescission, that allege injuries caused by the defendants rather than by the state court foreclosure judgment), *aff'd*, 2009 WL 2488175 (11th Cir. Aug. 17, 2009).

217 Reusser v. Wachovia Bank, 525 F.3d 855, 859 (9th Cir. 2008) (federal suit is a de facto appeal from a state court decision if adjudication of the federal claims would undercut the state court decision or require the district court to interpret the application of state laws or procedural rules); Mo's Express, L.L.C. v. Sopkin, 441 F.3d 1229, 1233, 1237 (10th Cir. 2006) (stating that doctrine bars claims inextricably intertwined with prior state court judgment, but defining these claims as ones where state court judgment actually and proximately caused the injury for which the federal court plaintiff seeks redress); Bear v. Patton, 451 F.3d 639, 642 (10th Cir. 2006) (same); Allen v. Nat'l City Bank, 2007 WL 2341010 (D. Colo. Aug. 14, 2007) (claim that state court judgment was entered in violation of due process alleges an injury that arises from the judgment itself so is barred).

According to the Second Circuit, a claim is independent if a third party's actions are merely ratified, acquiesced in, or left unpunished by the state court judgment. On the other hand, a claim is barred if the injury results from the state court judgment itself, or from a third party's actions that are compelled by the state court judgment.[218] Thus, for example, if a plaintiff seeks a federal court order forbidding a third party from taking an action that a state court has ordered, the doctrine bars the suit.[219] But if the state court judgment merely permits a third party to take a certain action, the *Rooker-Feldman* doctrine does not bar a suit seeking to order the party to take or not to take that action.[220] Likewise, the doctrine will not bar a claim that is based on the manner in which the defendants carried out a state court order.[221] The question is not whether the federal suit seeks to litigate the same claims that were or could have been litigated in state court, but rather whether it seeks redress for injuries caused by the state court decision itself.[222]

The Seventh Circuit has held, in an unpublished decision, that the *Rooker-Feldman* doctrine does not bar a claim arising from an injury that precedes the state court proceedings. Thus, the doctrine did not bar a claim that a creditor had wrongfully force-placed insurance when the homeowner's policy had not lapsed.[223]

10.6.4.9.2 Are TIL rescission claims independent?

In an unpublished decision, the Seventh Circuit held that the *Rooker-Feldman* doctrine would not bar a TIL rescission claim, as the injury was complete at closing when the creditor provided unclear disclosures about the deadline for rescission.[224] A well-reasoned pre-*Exxon* decision supports this view, holding that a TIL rescission claim is independent of a state foreclosure judgment.[225] The court characterized

218 Hoblock v. Albany County Bd. of Elections, 422 F.3d 77, 88 (2d Cir. 2005) (giving examples).

219 *See id.* at 89 (federal suit seeking order requiring elections board to count ballots is not independent claim if state court has ordered board not to count them).

220 Bolden v. City of Topeka, 441 F.3d 1129, 1145 (10th Cir. 2006).

221 Brown v. Varan, 322 Fed. Appx. 453 (7th Cir. 2009) (unpublished) (*Rooker-Feldman* doctrine does not bar claim that eviction pursuant to state court judgment was unlawful while motion for reconsideration was pending in state court, as this is not a collateral attack on the eviction order); Gyadu v. Sheftel, 2007 WL 2154182 (D. Conn. July 23, 2007).

222 Davani v. Va. Dep't of Transp., 434 F.3d 712, 718 (4th Cir. 2006); Turner v. Crawford Square Apts. III, 449 F.3d 542, 547 (3d Cir. 2006) (overlap with claims adjudicated in state court does not mean that *Rooker-Feldman* doctrine applies, but res judicata requires dismissal).

223 Stanley v. Hollingsworth, 307 Fed. Appx. 6 (7th Cir. 2008).

224 Dye v. Ameriquest Mortgage Co., 289 Fed. Appx. 941 (7th Cir. 2008).

225 Lopez v. Delta Funding Corp., No. CV-98-7204, slip op. at 16–17 (E.D.N.Y. June 6, 2000), *available at* www.consumerlaw.org/unreported.

the rescission complaint not as seeking to review the state court foreclosure judgment but as alleging a prior injury that the state court failed to remedy. Further, it held that the injury alleged by the consumers arose out of the defendant's loan agreements themselves and the conduct of the defendants before and during the closing, not from the state court foreclosure judgment. A consumer's TIL rescission claim is not dependent on the commencement of a state court eviction or foreclosure action. It exists whether or not any such action is ever filed. The decision is consistent with the Supreme Court's unequivocal statement that the *Rooker-Feldman* doctrine bars a suit only if the injury complained of was caused by the state court judgment.[226]

That a state court foreclosure judgment should not bar TIL rescission claims is especially clear since a TIL rescission claim survives the entry of a foreclosure judgment and is only extinguished when the home is actually sold.[227] The *Exxon* Court's emphasis on the narrowness of the *Rooker-Feldman* doctrine,[228] and its explicit endorsement of the independent claim exception, give further support to this analysis.

Nonetheless, a number of post-*Exxon* decisions have held that *Rooker-Feldman* is a bar to subject matter jurisdiction over a TIL rescission case brought in federal court after a state court foreclosure judgment.[229] Many of these decisions do not consider whether the TIL rescission claim was an independent claim, but simply rely on pre-*Exxon* decisions. In addition, in many of these cases, the plaintiffs either claimed that the wrongful foreclosure constituted the plaintiff's damages or sought direct relief against enforcement of the state court judgment.

Most of these decisions rely primarily on the view that granting rescission would effectively undo the state court foreclosure judgment. But even if this were correct, the Supreme Court requires not only that the federal case "invite review and rejection" of the state court judgment, but also that it "complain . . . of injuries caused by" the state court judgment.[230] The injury a rescission claim seeks to remedy is not "caused by [the] state-court judgment,"[231] but rather by the lender's actions and inactions at loan closing and in response to the homeowner's rescission notice.[232]

Further, a TIL rescission claim does not necessarily "invit[e] district court review and rejection" of the state court judgment.[233] The consumer could simply seek a ruling from the federal court rescinding the transaction and leave it to the state court to determine any effect on the foreclosure judgment. In addition, if the sale has not yet occurred, enabling the homeowner to retain the home is not at all inconsistent with the foreclosure judgment in states where the homeowner has the right to keep the home by paying the balance due before the sale.[234] In many states this right continues even after the sale,[235] and in a number of states the homeowner also has the right to cure the default before sale by paying just the past-due installments plus permissible costs and fees.[236] A ruling allowing TIL rescission or other claims simply enables the homeowner to exercise rights that the foreclosure judgment preserves.

The argument that TIL and other claims are independent is particularly strong in the foreclosure rescue scam context. Even if a state court has already rendered an eviction judgment, a TIL claim is an independent claim because it is not aimed at the rescuer's right to evict under the lease, but rather at the underlying sale/leaseback transaction.[237]

226 Lance v. Dennis, 546 U.S. 459, 126 S. Ct. 1198, 1201, 163 L. Ed. 2d 1059 (2006); Exxon Mobil Corp v. Saudi Basic Indus. Corp., 544 U.S. 280, 284, 125 S. Ct. 1517, 1521–1522, 161 L. Ed. 2d 454 (2005).

227 Walker v. Contimortgage, 232 B.R. 725 (Bankr. N.D. Ill. 1999).

228 *See* Lance v. Dennis, 546 U.S. 459, 126 S. Ct. 1198, 1201, 163 L. Ed. 2d 1059 (2006) (noting that the Court has never applied the doctrine since *Rooker* and *Feldman* and listing the cases in which the Court rejected the doctrine); Marshall v. Marshall, 547 U.S. 293, 126 S. Ct. 1735, 164 L. Ed. 2d 480 (2006) (Steven, J., concurring in part and concurring in the judgment) (referring to the grave in which *Rooker-Feldman* was buried).

229 *See, e.g.*, Madera v. Ameriquest Mortgage Co. (*In re* Madera), 586 F.3d 228 (3d Cir. 2009) (dismissing TIL rescission claim but addressing merits of TIL damages claim); Velardo v. Fremont Inv. & Loan, 298 Fed. Appx. 890 (11th Cir. 2008); Harper v. Chase Manhattan Bank, 138 Fed. Appx. 130 (11th Cir. 2005) (unpublished) (*Rooker-Feldman* doctrine bars *pro se* TIL suit seeking injunction against enforcement of state court foreclosure judgment; homeowner raised same claims in defense of foreclosure action). *See generally* National Consumer Law Center, Truth in Lending § 8.4.2.4 (6th ed. 2007 and Supp.).

230 *Id.*, 126 S. Ct. at 1201.

231 Exxon Mobil Corp v. Saudi Basic Indus. Corp., 544 U.S. 280, 125 S. Ct. 1517, 1521–1522, 161 L. Ed. 2d 454 (2005).

232 *See, e.g.*, Madura v. Countrywide Home Loans, Inc., 2007 WL 4336094 (M.D. Fla. Dec. 7, 2007) (*Rooker-Feldman* doctrine does not bar claims, including TIL rescission, that allege injuries caused by the defendants rather than by the state court foreclosure judgment), *aff'd*, 2009 WL 2488175 (11th Cir. Aug. 17, 2009).

233 Exxon Mobil Corp v. Saudi Basic Indus. Corp., 544 U.S. 280, 125 S. Ct. 1517, 1521–1522, 161 L. Ed. 2d 454 (2005). *See also* Adkins v. Rumsfeld, 464 F.3d 456, 464 (4th Cir. 2006) (test is whether federal decision would reverse or modify state court judgment, not whether it would upset its enforcement).

234 *See* § 4.2.5, *supra*.

235 *See* § 4.2.6, *supra*.

236 *See* § 4.2.5, *supra*.

237 *See* Brown v. First Nationwide Mortgage Corp., 206 Fed. Appx. 436, 439–440 (6th Cir. 2006) (claim barred by res judicata; reversing application of *Rooker-Feldman* where plaintiff, who asserted TIL and fraud claims, did not directly challenge the state foreclosure judgment but instead complained of the actions of various parties); Brown v. Grant Holding, L.L.C., 394 F. Supp. 2d 1090, 1100 (D. Minn. 2005) (holding *Rooker-Feldman* inapplicable to TILA/HOEPA foreclosure rescue scam case because state housing court only decided whether homeowner could retain possession of the property and could not decide the equitable claim to rescind the sale/leaseback transaction).

10.6.4.9.3 Other claims

A post-*Exxon* decision holds that the doctrine does not bar a claim that a homeowner was denied constitutionally adequate notice of a state condemnation proceeding, because the injury was caused not by the judgment in the state case but by a party to that case.[238] Likewise, claims of fraud, deceptive practices, professional malpractice, and violations of TILA, the Equal Credit Opportunity Act, and the Fair Housing Act, all of which related to the origination of the mortgage, were independent of a state foreclosure judgment so were not barred by the doctrine.[239] Several courts have held that the doctrine does not bar claims based on acts that preceded the state court suit, even if those acts ultimately led to the state court suit.[240] The doctrine did not bar conversion and other claims alleging that the foreclosing creditor's agent unlawfully entered the home and misappropriated the homeowners' personal property while foreclosure proceedings were ongoing, as the homeowners' injury derived from those actions, not the state court judgment.[241] And some courts have held that a claim that a party procured a state court judgment by fraud is an independent claim.[242]

238 Brody v. Village of Port Chester, 2007 WL 704002 (S.D.N.Y. Mar. 7, 2007). *See also* Pittman v. Cuyahoga County Dep't of Children & Family Servs., 241 Fed. Appx. 285 (6th Cir. 2007) (unpublished) (*Rooker-Feldman* doctrine does not bar claims against children's services agency for misrepresenting facts to juvenile court and refusing to recommend that plaintiff be given custody of child); Brown v. First Nationwide Mortgage Corp., 206 Fed. Appx. 436 (6th Cir. 2006) (*Rooker-Feldman* does not bar claims based on opponent's *ex parte* communications and other misconduct in state court proceeding, since injury was caused not by the judgment but by the opponent's acts); Goddard v. Citibank, 2006 WL 842925 (E.D.N.Y. Mar. 27, 2006) (*Rooker-Feldman* doctrine does not bar claims for conversion and intentional infliction of emotional distress caused by opponent's fraud in procuring state court foreclosure judgment, where plaintiff seeks money damages that would not have been available in state court proceeding). *But see* Promiedica Continuing Care Servs. Corp. v. Hillsdale County, 2009 WL 1139587 (W.D. Mich. Apr. 28, 2009) (*Rooker-Feldman* doctrine bars claim based on county treasurer's failure to give proper notice of tax foreclosure, where state court rejected these allegations). *But cf.* Reusser v. Wachovia Bank, 525 F.3d 855 (9th Cir. 2008) (*Rooker-Feldman* doctrine bars claim that bank committed extrinsic fraud in state court post-foreclosure eviction case, where state court had already rejected this claim).

239 Smith v. Encore Credit Corp., 623 F. Supp. 2d 910 (N.D. Ohio 2008) (magistrate's recommendation) (HOEPA, RESPA, TILA, FCRA, UDAP, fraud, state RICO, civil conspiracy, unjust enrichment, and other state claims are all independent claims that are not barred); Council v. Better Homes Depot, Inc., 2006 WL 2376381 (E.D.N.Y. Aug. 16, 2006).

240 Knutson v. City of Fargo, 2010 WL 1427043 (8th Cir. 2010) (*Rooker-Feldman* doctrine does not bar homeowners' claim that city violated § 1983 by failing to reimburse them for damaging their property, even though they had lost a state court suit seeking the same damages, as the injury for which they sought compensation was caused by the city's actions, not by the state court judgment); Turner v. Crawford Square Apts. III, 449 F.3d 542 (3d Cir. 2006) (claim that defendants violated Fair Housing Act by refusing to accept tenant's § 8 benefits not barred under *Rooker-Feldman* doctrine by judgment in eviction case that they brought because of her nonpayment of rent, because injury was caused by acts preceding the judgment rather than by the judgment itself, but claims are barred by res judicata); Zimmerman v. CIT Group, Inc., 2008 WL 5786438 (D. Colo. Oct. 6, 2008) (doctrine does not bar claim that attorney violated FDCPA by improperly filing action and falsely representing character and legal status of debt), *adopted as modified by* 2009 WL 900172 (D. Colo. Mar. 31, 2009) (modifying magistrate's recommendation in part on other grounds); Bush v. Danziger, 2006 WL 3019572 (S.D.N.Y. Oct. 23, 2006) (*Rooker-Feldman* doctrine does not bar claim that defendants acted unlawfully in refusing to reduce public housing tenant's rent and in seeking her eviction, because these acts predate state court eviction suit). *See also* Freedom Mortg. Corp. v. Burnham Mortg., Inc., 569 F.3d 667 (7th Cir. 2009) (*Rooker-Feldman* doctrine does not bar mortgage lender's fraud claim against property flippers even though lender obtained state court foreclosure judgment on the property; the fraud predated the state litigation and was neither addressed nor redressed by the judgment). *But cf.* Trakansook v. Astoria Fed. Sav. & Loan Ass'n, 2007 WL 1160433 (E.D.N.Y. Apr. 18, 2007) (*Rooker-Feldman* doctrine bars challenge to foreclosure judgment even if plaintiff characterizes claim as challenge to creditor's decision to seek that judgment), *aff'd*, 2008 WL 4962990 (2d Cir. Nov. 21, 2008).

241 Burks v. Washington Mut. Bank, 2008 WL 4966656 (E.D. Mich. Nov. 17, 2008).

242 McCormick v. Braverman, 451 F.3d 382, 389 (6th Cir. 2006); Brown v. First Nationwide Mortgage Corp., 206 Fed. Appx. 436 (6th Cir. 2006) (unpublished) (*Rooker-Feldman* doctrine does not apply where plaintiff claims injuries that were caused not by the state court judgment, but by actions, such as *ex parte* communications with the judge, by people involved in state case); Washington v. Wilmore, 407 F.3d 274 (4th Cir. 2005) (claim that witness presented false testimony, which led to plaintiff's state court murder conviction, is independent claim because it challenges means by which conviction was obtained rather than conviction itself, and success would not undo the conviction); Whittiker v. Deutsche Bank Nat'l Trust Co., 605 F. Supp. 2d 914 (N.D. Ohio 2009) (*Rooker-Feldman* doctrine does not bar FDCPA claim based on defendant's provision of false information in state court foreclosure case); Aganos v. GMAC Residential Funding Corp., 2008 WL 4657828, at *4 n.5 (D. Haw. Oct. 22, 2008); Goddard v. Citibank, 2006 WL 842925 (E.D.N.Y. Mar. 27, 2006) (claims based on fraud in procuring state court foreclosure judgment and seeking money damages that were not available in state court proceeding are not barred). *See also* Bernegger v. Washington Mut., F.A., 2008 WL 4722392 (E.D. Wis. Oct. 24, 2008) (*Rooker-Feldman* doctrine does not bar FDCPA claims based on foreclosure attorney's submission of false documents to state court, as injury was complete before state court took any action, but unjust enrichment claim based on attorney's submission of inflated fee bill is barred where it was incorporated into state court judgment); Smith v. ABN AMRO Mortgage Group, Inc., 2007 WL 2029044 (S.D. Ohio July 10, 2007) (*Rooker-Feldman* doctrine does not bar suit that does not seek to overturn state court foreclosure judgment, even though plaintiff sought TRO against sale of home); Brody v. Village of Port Chester, 2007 WL 704002 (S.D.N.Y. Mar. 7, 2007) (federal complaint that opponent provided inadequate notice of state condemnation proceedings not barred because injury was caused by the opponent rather than by the state court

A claim under the Fair Debt Collection Practices Act that a lender falsely represented the amount due after a foreclosure sale was not barred by the *Rooker-Feldman* doctrine, because the consumers were not challenging the validity of their obligations under the state court judgment and the injury they alleged was not caused by that judgment.[243] The Sixth Circuit held that a claim against a collection attorney for filing a false affidavit to initiate a state court garnishment was an independent claim.[244] Nor did the doctrine bar damage claims under the FDCPA and RESPA based on a mortgage holder's manner of servicing a mortgage loan and its failure to respond to a qualified written request, where these claims had not been adjudicated in a state court action that had unsuccessfully sought to enjoin a foreclosure sale.[245]

10.6.5 *Res Judicata and Collateral Estoppel*

Younger abstention, the Anti-Injunction Act, and the *Rooker-Feldman* doctrine all apply only in federal court (although state courts may have similar doctrines). But even if an action is filed in state court, or if a federal case gets beyond those obstacles, the plaintiff may still have to contend with res judicata or collateral estoppel from a prior state eviction or foreclosure judgment. For example, the First Circuit Court of Appeals held that a default judgment in a state court foreclosure action prevented a homeowner from asserting rescission under TILA in federal court.[246] The Full Faith and Credit Clause requires federal courts to give state court judgments the same preclusive effect they would have in state court, so the issue is fundamentally one of state law.[247]

In some states, counterclaims such as TILA are not allowed in eviction or foreclosure proceedings, or those proceedings enjoy summary fast-track dispositions and limited discovery that make it difficult to litigate complicated counterclaims. For those reasons, issue or claim preclusion may not apply to eviction or foreclosure judgments.[248]

---

judgment itself); Mac Pherson v. State Street Bank & Trust Co., 452 F. Supp. 2d 133 (E.D.N.Y. 2006) (due process claim based on inadequate service barred by res judicata and *Rooker-Feldman* doctrine), *aff'd*, 273 Fed. Appx. 61 (2d Cir. 2008) (claim barred by res judicata). *Cf.* Schuh v. Druckman & Sinel, L.L.P., 2008 WL 542504 (S.D.N.Y. Feb. 29, 2008) (magistrate's recommendation) (if the state court judgment produced the plaintiff's injury, claim is barred; if process of procuring the state court judgment caused some independent injury, claim is not barred). *But see* Tal v. Hogan, 453 F.3d 1244 (10th Cir. 2006) (claim that party procured state court judgment by fraud is inextricably intertwined with state court judgment so barred by *Rooker-Feldman* doctrine); Phelps v. Am. Gen. Fin. Servs., 2008 WL 3978318 (E.D. Mich. Aug. 22, 2008) (*Rooker-Feldman* doctrine bars claims based on acts that occurred during state foreclosure proceedings).

243 Schuh v. Druckman & Sinel, L.L.P., 602 F. Supp. 2d 454 (S.D.N.Y. 2009).

244 Todd v. Weltman, Weinberg & Reis Co., 434 F.3d 432, 437 (6th Cir. 2006).

245 Carter v. Countrywide Home Loans, Inc., 2008 WL 4167931 (E.D. Va. Sept. 3, 2008). *But cf.* Andrew v. Ivanhoe Fin., Inc., 2008 WL 2265287 (E.D. Pa. May 30, 2008) (*Rooker-Feldman* doctrine barred rescission claim that was based on creditor's failure to respond to qualified written request).

246 R.G. Fin. Corp. v. Vergara-Nunez, 446 F.3d 178, 187 (1st Cir. 2006). *See also* Stanley v. Hollingsworth, 307 Fed. Appx. 6 (7th Cir. 2008) (*Rooker-Feldman* does not bar claim that creditor wrongfully force placed insurance and other independent claims, but they are barred by claim preclusion); Yeiser v. GMAC Mortgage Corp., 535 F. Supp. 2d 413 (S.D.N.Y. 2008) (finding that RESPA claims which could have been brought in state court foreclosure action were barred by res judicata); Walker v. Seldman, 471 F. Supp. 2d 106 (D.D.C. 2007), *aff'd*, 2008 WL 4682659 (D.C. Cir. Apr. 8, 2008) (*Rooker-Feldman* does not bar federal suit where homeowner was also the plaintiff in prior state court challenge to non-judicial foreclosure, but claims barred by res judicata); Mac Pherson v. State Street Bank & Trust Co., 452 F. Supp. 2d 133 (E.D.N.Y. 2006) (claim based on opponent's misrepresentations to state court in foreclosure case barred by res judicata but not by *Rooker-Feldman* doctrine), *aff'd*, 273 Fed. Appx. 61 (2d Cir. 2008); Council v. Better Homes Depot, Inc., 2006 WL 2376381 (E.D.N.Y. Aug. 16, 2006) (default foreclosure judgment not res judicata as to claims against property flipper and associates who were not parties to that action or in privity with parties, and issues were different; nor does default judgment have collateral estoppel effect); *In re* Rodriguez, 377 B.R. 1 (Bankr. D. P.R. 2007) (stating that RESPA claim not barred by default foreclosure judgment because RESPA violation does not challenge the existence or validity of the mortgage note).

247 Migra v. Warren City Sch. Dist. Bd. of Educ., 465 U.S. 75, 81, 104 S. Ct. 892, 79 L. Ed. 2d 56 (1984); R.G. Fin. Corp. v. Vergara-Nunez, 446 F.3d 178, 182–183 (1st Cir. 2006); Woodsbey v. Easy Mortgage (*In re* Woodsbey), 375 B.R. 145 (Bankr. W.D. Pa. 2007) (existence of foreclosure judgment does not create res judicata bar where state law allows debtor to cure mortgage default up to one hour before sheriff's sale). *See also* Gemini Servs., Inc. v. Mortgage Elec. Registration Sys. (*In re* Gemini Servs., Inc.), 350 B.R. 74, 79–80 (Bankr. S.D. Ohio 2006) (according preclusive effect to state court judgment under the Full Faith and Credit Clause and determining effect of that judgment on chapter 11 case); Smith v. Litton Loan Servicing, L.P., 2005 WL 289927, at *5 (E.D. Pa. Feb. 4, 2005) (unpublished) (holding that plaintiffs' claims were precluded by res judicata under Pennsylvania law, where plaintiffs could have raised those claims in state foreclosure action but did not). *Cf.* Glover v. Countrywide Home Loans, 2006 WL 2192963, at *2 (E.D. Mich. Aug. 2, 2006) (dismissing as claim-precluded homeowner's challenge to foreclosure where a different federal judge had previously dismissed the same claim with prejudice).

248 *See* White v. Long Beach Mortgage, 2007 WL 4079443 (E.D. Pa. Nov. 7, 2007) (res judicata does not prevent federal suit, as counterclaims are permissive rather than compulsory in Pennsylvania foreclosure cases); Brown v. Grant Holding, L.L.C., 394 F. Supp. 2d 1090, 1100 (D. Minn. 2005) (rejecting defendants' res judicata argument where it was unclear whether equitable mortgage counterclaim could have been raised in eviction case and state law favored resolution of equitable claims separate from eviction proceedings); *In re* Weinraub, 2007 WL 473668 (Bankr. S.D. Fla. Feb. 7, 2007) (TIL claims were not compulsory counterclaims in state court eviction proceeding brought by foreclosure rescuer, so not barred by res

Another court has held that an *in rem* mortgage foreclosure judgment does not bar a breach of contract claim for charging excessive and unauthorized fees and failing to properly apply payments.[249] In addition, some courts hold that, while res judicata protects those in privity with a party to the earlier suit, it does not protect a predecessor in interest, such as an entity that assigned its interest in a mortgage before the foreclosure case was filed.[250]

10.6.6 The Bankruptcy Automatic Stay As an Alternative

If an eviction or foreclosure case or some other type of collection action is pending against the homeowner, the consumer should consider bankruptcy court as a forum. In most cases, as soon as a bankruptcy case is filed, all such actions are automatically stayed without the need to consider the impediments to relief discussed above. Using bankruptcy to prevent foreclosure is discussed in detail in Chapter 9, *supra*.

10.7 Mandatory Arbitration Clauses

10.7.1 Introduction

Mandatory arbitration clauses are less pervasive in mortgage loans than in other consumer transactions, but they are still prevalent for certain types of mortgage loans. For example, they are common in certain mortgage loans consummated in 2003 or before—Freddie Mac stopped purchasing mortgages subject to mandatory arbitration as of August 1, 2004, and Fannie Mae stopped purchasing such mortgages effective October 1, 2004. Mandatory arbitration clauses also appear in certain subprime loans originated after those dates where the mortgage was bundled in private label securitizations.

Mandatory arbitration clauses make consumer litigation difficult, restricting class actions, punitive damages, attorney fees, and homeowners' ability to engage in discovery. Arbitration can also be far more costly than a court proceeding, the results are largely secret, and questions have arisen concerning the impartiality of the arbitration forum and arbitrators.

10.7.2 How to Challenge the Enforceability of an Arbitration Requirement

An arbitration requirement is grounded upon an agreement between parties that delineated disputes must be resolved by an arbitration procedure specified in the agreement. The Federal Arbitration Act (FAA) requires that arbitration agreements be enforced.[251] But the federal policy is not that disputes be arbitrated, but that arbitration agreements must be enforced according to their terms.[252] If an arbitration agreement is not an enforceable contract, if a dispute is outside the terms of the agreement, or if the agreement does not apply for any other reason to the consumer's court action, then the arbitration requirement is inapplicable.

The first step in determining the enforceability of an arbitration agreement is to read the arbitration clause. This is particularly important for arbitration clauses found in mortgage loans, many of which pre-date 2004. As a result, they were *not* drafted taking into account recent court precedent as to when an arbitration clause is enforceable. Unlike credit card obligations, mortgage loans cannot be unilaterally amended, so that the pre-2004 language will still be in effect. This presents unique opportunities to challenge such clauses.

The next subsection lists ten challenges to the enforceability of an arbitration requirement in foreclosure litigation. That subsection will not cite to case law, which is both extensive and evolving, but will instead cite to subsections in another NCLC publication, *Consumer Arbitration Agreements* (5th ed. 2007 and Supp.). That treatise contains a detailed analysis of the enforceability of such agreements, and includes sample discovery documents and briefs on an arbitration agreement's enforceability.

10.7.3 Ten Homeowner Responses to an Arbitration Requirement

1. *Proof of the arbitration agreement and the party's standing to enforce it.* When a party seeks to force the consumer into arbitration, that party must produce the actual arbitration agreement to prove there is such a requirement. Review of this language is also essential to a consumer defense because many challenges to the arbitration clause will be based upon the exact language of the agreement.

The arbitration agreement will also not be enforceable if it involves fraud in the factum or if the arbitration clause

judicata); *In re* Cooley, 365 B.R. 464 (Bankr. E.D. Pa. 2007); *In re* Randall, 358 B.R. 145 (Bankr. E.D. Pa. 2006); *In re* Faust, 353 B.R. 94 (Bankr. E.D. Pa. 2006).

249 *In re* Washington, 2007 WL 846658 (E.D. Pa. Mar. 19, 2007) (finding borrower only sued in her capacity as mortgagor of property in foreclosure action; foreclosure action did not constitute *in personam* action of the note).

250 Yeisser v. GMAC Mortgage Corp., 535 F. Supp. 2d 413, 423 (S.D.N.Y. 2008). *See also* Council v. Better Homes Depot, Inc., 2006 WL 2376381 (E.D.N.Y. Aug. 16, 2006) (default foreclosure judgment not res judicata as to claims against property flipper and associates who were not parties to that action or in privity with parties, and issues were different).

251 9 U.S.C. § 2.

252 National Consumer Law Center, Consumer Arbitration Agreements § 7.2 (5th ed. 2007 and Supp.).

was induced by misrepresentation.[253] On the other hand, fraud in the inducement of the loan agreement as a whole is not grounds to challenge the arbitration agreement in court.[254]

An arbitration clause in an initial loan agreement may not apply where that initial loan agreement is superseded by a subsequent refinancing or other, more final agreement that does not contain an arbitration clause[255] The party seeking to enforce the arbitration requirement must also show a right to enforce it. If an agreement is with an originating lender, can a servicer hired by a trustee of a securitization trust enforce the agreement? This may depend on the exact language of the agreement. For example, if a servicer is viewed as an independent contractor instead of an agent, it may not be able to enforce an arbitration agreement that applies to the lender's assignees and agents.[256] On the other hand, if the consumer challenges a party's ownership of the loan, this is a challenge to the loan contract as a whole and not just the arbitration clause, and then the arbitrator resolves this issue.[257]

2. *Class arbitration.* There is growing evidence that corporations fear class arbitration more than a class action in court, and consumer litigants may thus prefer class arbitration over a court class action. Since the Supreme Court's 2003 decision in *Bazzle*,[258] class arbitration before the American Arbitration Association (AAA) and JAMS had become far more common and courts had consistently upheld arbitrators' decisions to allow class arbitration.[259]

The availability of class arbitration though has been muddied by a 2010 Supreme Court decision in *Stolt-Nielsen*.[260] Arbitrators faced with an arbitration agreement that was silent as to whether class arbitration was allowed decided solely on public policy grounds to allow a class-wide procedure. The Court found this to be beyond the arbitrators' powers—arbitrators can only determine if a clause allows class-wide arbitration by interpreting the contract itself. The Court found class arbitration an unusual enough procedure that the arbitrator needs some basis that the procedure is consistent with the parties' intent.

Stolt-Nielsen raises the burden of finding class-arbitration allowed based on a "silent" arbitration agreement, but this burden can be overcome. For example, consider an arbitration clause governed by AAA rules, and that those rules allow the arbitrator to determine if a "silent" clause allows class arbitration. The arbitrator could find this reference to AAA rules sufficient to show that the arbitration clause allows such a procedure. Judicial review of such an arbitrator's decision is very limited.

Other arbitration agreements are not silent as to class arbitration, but explicitly prohibit it. A significant number of courts have found such prohibitions unconscionable, and then either void the whole arbitration requirement or order the case to class-wide arbitration.[261] It is unclear whether *Stolt-Nielsen* will affect this body of law and whether consumers should also seek to reform "silent" arbitration clauses because failure to allow class-wide relief is unconscionable. A discussion as to how class-wide arbitration works is found in NCLC's *Consumer Class Actions* Chapter 3 (7th ed. 2010).

3. *NAF listed as the sole arbitration forum.* The National Arbitration Forum (NAF) is listed as the sole arbitration forum in many arbitration agreements, but the NAF has stopped administering consumer arbitrations. Courts find the selection of NAF to be integral to the agreement so that the arbitration requirement is no longer enforceable, but other courts find selection of NAF to be ancillary, and that the court can appoint an arbitrator if the parties cannot agree on one.[262] AAA is still administering consumer arbitrations, so that this will not be grounds to throw out an arbitration requirement if the agreement allows either NAF or AAA to be the forum.

4. *Where the arbitration clause is unconscionable.* There is an enormous amount of varying case law as to whether an arbitration clause is unconscionable.[263] Consumers will want to show procedural unconscionability (no meaningful choice, standard form adhesion contract, small print, etc.) and also substantive unconscionability, such as that only the homeowner and not the mortgage holder must use arbitration, that important consumer remedies, attorney fees, or the statute of limitations are limited, or that for the particular homeowner the costs of the specific arbitration at issue are prohibitive. If a provision is unconscionable, a court may void the arbitration requirement or only delete the offensive provision.[264]

5. *Is the consumer's claim within the scope of the arbitration clause?* The arbitration clause specifies which disputes must be arbitrated and the homeowner need not arbitrate matters outside the scope of this language. For example, an arbitration clause may state that it does not relate to a creditor's non-judicial foreclosure. Then arguably it should not apply to a court action to enjoin the non-judicial foreclosure.[265]

Much will depend on the clause's exact language.[266] If a clause does not apply to disputes "related" to a loan, but

253 *Id.* §§ 5.2.2.2, 6.7.1
254 *Id.* § 6.7.1.
255 *Id.* § 6.7.4.3.
256 *Id.* § 7.4.
257 Buckeye v. Check Cashing, Inc. v. Cardegna, 546 U.S. 440 (2006).
258 Greentree Fin. Corp. v. Bazzle, 539 U.S. 444 (2003).
259 National Consumer Law Center, Consumer Arbitration Agreements § 3.2.1 (5th ed. 2007 and Supp.).
260 Stolt-Nielsen S.A. v. Animalfeeds Int'l Corp., 2010 WL 1655826 (U.S. Apr. 27, 2010).
261 National Consumer Law Center, Consumer Arbitration Agreements Ch. 6 (5th ed. 2007 and Supp.).
262 National Consumer Law Center, Consumer Arbitration Agreements § 6.6A (Supp.).
263 *Id.* at Ch. 6 (5th ed. 2007 and Supp.).
264 *Id.* § 6.8.
265 *Id.* § 7.3.1.
266 *Id.*

instead "arising under" the loan, then the arbitration clause may not apply to a servicer's tort not arising under the loan.

6. *Where the mortgage holder initiates a judicial foreclosure.* Where a mortgage holder initiates a judicial foreclose, the consumer can certainly raise defenses and almost certainly counterclaims to the action. The consumer need not bring those defenses and counterclaims in a separate arbitration proceeding. Among other reasons, the mortgage holder has waived the arbitration requirement by resorting to a court action.[267]

7. *Is arbitration an appropriate forum to enjoin a non-judicial foreclosure.* Arbitration requirements are enforceable if they offer a practical alternative to a court action to vindicate an individual's rights.[268] Consider an action to temporarily restrain a non-judicial foreclosure. Arbitration requires the homeowner to bring a claim before the designated arbitration forum, whose rules may or may not allow expedited, preliminary, or even equitable relief. Once an arbitrator is appointed and issues a temporary award enjoining the foreclosure, that award is not enforceable until the consumer receives that award and files an action in court to confirm that award. This lengthy process is not a practical alternative to a court temporarily restraining a foreclosure.

8. *Is the litigation in bankruptcy court?* A requirement that a matter be resolved by arbitration may conflict with the Bankruptcy Code's purposes of speedily resolving in one forum all matters concerning a debtor. As a result, a bankruptcy court may have discretion to avoid an arbitration requirement concerning a core proceeding.[269]

9. *Litigation concerning insurance.* FAA preemption of state limits on the enforceability of arbitration clauses does not apply to state insurance statutes. The federal McCarran-Ferguson Act states that federal law cannot impair state law enacted for the purpose of regulating the business of insurance (unless the federal law explicitly relates to the business of insurance, which the FAA does not).[270] In other words, state law limiting arbitration in the business of insurance supersedes the FAA, so that in some states an action concerning credit insurance or other insurance may not have to be arbitrated.

10. *TIL rescission and arbitration.* Under TILA, a home-secured transaction can be rescinded within three days for any reason, or for up to three years if certain disclosures or notices are not provided. To exercise rescission, the consumer simply sends a rescission notice to the creditor. Rescission is self-executing: the security interest is void the obligation to pay finance and other charges is cancelled, and the creditor has the obligation to take various steps, such as returning the homeowner's payments.[271] In addition, if the agreement, including the arbitration clause has been rescinded, then the arbitration clause should no longer be in effect. Litigation following rescission need not be referred to arbitration.

However, when the mortgagee disputes the rescission, a U.S. Supreme Court case indicates that the consumer's action to enforce the rescission is subject to an applicable arbitration requirement.[272] On the other hand, if the mortgagee does not dispute a rescission's effectiveness, the arbitration clause is canceled and does not apply to any subsequent litigation.[273] Mortgagees are less likely to dispute the rescission where the homeowner cancels within the three-day period or where the mortgagee is disputing the tender amount, but not the validity of the rescission. Less clear is the effect on an arbitration requirement where the mortgagee accepts the rescission as proper, but insists on conditional rescission.

10.8 Tax Issues

10.8.1 Overview

In general, a court award or settlement providing for cash or the cancellation of debt is considered taxable income. Exceptions to this general rule occur frequently in mortgage cases.

Whenever the settlement is a recovery of expense, such as payments made, or replaces lost assets, whether loss in value of the home or the loss of physical well-being, the settlement income may be excluded from taxable income, since the settlement does not increase the overall net worth of the individual over what it would have been absent the wrongful acts. Replaced income, such as time off work, on the other hand, is generally taxable, since the underlying income itself would have been taxable. Additional statutory and case law exceptions apply to the treatment of cancelled debt.

If the homeowner took a deduction for the previously-incurred expense repaid in the settlement, however, the homeowner will need to recognize a tax liability to offset that prior deduction, even though the income would otherwise be non-taxable. Examples of prior relevant deductions include a medical expenses deduction for treatment of physical injury or emotional distress or a mortgage interest deduction. Similarly, a taxpayer who receives more than her basis in the home in a settlement reflecting lost value in the home will need to report the excess as a capital gain.[274]

---

267 *Id.* at Ch. 8.

268 *Id.* § 4.2.1.2.

269 *Id.* § 4.2.3.

270 *Id.* § 3.3.4.

271 *See* § 5.6.1, *supra*; National Consumer Law Center, Truth in Lending § 6.6.3 (6th ed. 2007 and Supp.).

272 Buckeye v. Check Cashing, Inc. v. Cardegna, 546 U.S. 440 (2006).

273 Chapman v. Mortgage One Corp., 359 F. Supp. 2d 831 (E.D. Mo. 2005). *See also* National Consumer Law Center, Consumer Arbitration Agreements § 6.7.4.2 (5th ed. 2007 and Supp.).

274 Internal Revenue Service, Publication 4345, Settlements-Taxability.

The following subsections discuss the federal exceptions to the general rule. State taxation law does not always follow the federal scheme; practitioners will need to check what exceptions are available under their state's law. Practitioners should also determine whether or not the discharged debt, even if excluded from income, must be reported. The reporting requirements for cancellation of debt are discussed at §§ 14.6.3.5, 14.6.5 *infra.*

10.8.2 Pain and Suffering Damages

Pain and suffering damages for physical injury are non-taxable,[275] as are medical expenses for emotional distress and mental suffering.[276] Compensation for emotional distress, including physical manifestations of that emotional distress such as insomnia, headaches, and stomach disorders is usually non-taxable.[277]

10.8.3 Multiple and Statutory Damages

Many statutory claims that homeowners raise in defending a foreclosure, such as violations of the Truth in Lending Act, Real Estate Settlement Procedures Act, or state UDAP statute, carry with them the possibility of statutory or multiple damages. In general, statutory damages are taxable, unless state law views them as compensatory. Sometimes state law treats statutory or minimum damages as a proxy for a compensatory award that is difficult to prove. Public policy may require full compensation for the homeowner despite proof problems. If the statute awards minimum or actual damages, whichever is greater, at least the portion of the minimum damages award reflecting actual, non-taxable, damages should be excluded from taxable income.

Where multiple damages are awarded, only the portion over and above the actual damages is necessarily taxable. For example, where treble damages are awarded, two-thirds are clearly taxable, but the other third may not be, depending on the exact nature of the compensated harm.

10.8.4 Damages Relating to Overpayment

When capital is returned, whether by cash payment or cancellation of debt, the resulting benefit to the homeowner is not taxable income.[278] In home defense cases, there may be compensation for routine out-of-pocket expenses, including medical bills, transportation costs, or property damage. Homeowners may also be entitled to a return of other monies wrongfully paid, including a refund of excess interest.

Excess interest may be paid because the rate itself was inflated due to a yield spread premium[279] or because the loan value was inflated. The loan value could be inflated either through excessive fees[280] or by luring the homeowner into overpaying for the home in a property flipping case.[281] Where the homeowners have overpaid, whether through inflated interest or loan value, the difference between what they paid and what they should have paid is return of capital, not income.

10.8.5 When Loan Forgiveness Is Not Income

As discussed fully at § 14.6.3, *infra*, discharged debt, whether discharged by reason of a completed foreclosure sale or a negotiated settlement to litigation, is assumed by the IRS to be taxable income. There are several important exceptions, however, also discussed at § 14.6.3. In many cases, at least a portion of the discharged debt can be legitimately excluded from income.

10.8.6 Taxability of Attorney Fees

The full amount of contingent attorney fees paid as part of a court award or settlement are included in an individual's gross income under the Supreme Court decision in *C.I.R. v. Banks*.[282] The individual can take the attorney fee payment as an itemized deduction on Schedule A of Form 1040, to the extent that the deduction exceeds 2% of the individual's gross income. Under a standard tax calculation this deduction neutralizes much, but not all, of the tax impact of including the contingent fee in the individual's gross income. However, for substantial awards, a further complication may arise in the application of the Alternative Minimum Tax (AMT).

Banks does not address the question of whether the tax treatment of a statutory fee award is similar to a contingent attorney fee award. Though the Supreme Court declined to rule directly on the issue, it suggested that statutory fees

275 26 U.S.C. § 104(a)(2).

276 26 U.S.C. § 105(b); Internal Revenue Service, Publication 4345, Settlements-Taxability.

277 "It is intended that the term emotional distress includes symptoms (e.g., insomnia, headaches, stomach disorders) which may result from such distress." H.R. Conf. Rep. No. 104-737, at 301.2 n.56.

278 *See, e.g.*, Internal Revenue Service, Publication 4345, Settlements-Taxability. *See also* § 14.6.3, *infra* (discussion of cancellation of debt income).

279 For a discussion of yield spread premiums, see §§ 5.3.2.3, 5.9.3, 5.13.6, *supra*.

280 *See* National Consumer Law Center, The Cost of Credit: Regulation, Preemption, and Industry Abuses §§ 11.6.1–11.6.3 (4th ed. 2009 and Supp.) (discussion of equity-stripping refinancings).

281 National Consumer Law Center, The Cost of Credit: Regulation, Preemption, and Industry Abuses § 11.6.6 (4th ed. 2009 and Supp.).

282 C.I.R. v. Banks, 543 U.S. 426 (2005).

may be treated differently. The Court wrote that when statutory fees are greater than the damage award: "Treating the fee award as income to the plaintiff in such cases, it is argued, can lead to the perverse result that the plaintiff loses money by winning the suit. Furthermore, it is urged that treating statutory fee awards as income to plaintiffs would undermine the effectiveness of fee-shifting statutes in deputizing plaintiffs and their lawyers to act as private attorneys general."[283] One subsequent tax court case has found that even fees paid pursuant to a fee-shifting statute are income to the client, at least where those fees are linked to a contingency award agreement between the attorney and the client.[284]

Given that the treatment of statutory fees is unsettled and the potential conflict of interest between an attorney and her client in negotiating the fee claim, practitioners should recommend that clients obtain independent tax advice on the treatment of the attorney fees in any particular case. Where feasible, clients may wish to seek private letter rulings determining the IRS treatment of statutory fees under the particular facts, claims, and retainer at issue. The IRS has tentatively indicated that, where the retainer agreement absolved the client of any obligation to pay legal fees, as do many legal services retainers, payment of statutory fees to the attorneys would not be income to the client.[285] Irrevocable assignment of the attorney fee claim to the attorney by the homeowner prior to commencement of the litigation in general may be helpful,[286] as may cases finding that clients do not own statutory attorney fees.[287] Merely having the fees paid directly to the attorney is insufficient.[288] Fees paid to class counsel in an opt-out class action will be excluded from the income of class members.[289]

283 C.I.R. v. Banks, 543 U.S. 426, 438–439 (2005).

284 Vincent v. C.I.R., 89 T.C.M. (CCH) 1119 (2005).

285 Private Letter Ruling, 2010 WL 15016 (Apr. 16, 2010). Private letter rulings may not be relied on or cited for precedential value. 26 U.S.C. § 6110(k)(3).

286 The United States Solicitor General, representing the IRS in *Banks*, gave qualified endorsement to this strategy in its reply brief: "If such an assignment [of statutory attorney fees to the attorney] is viewed as a transfer of the entirety of the attorney's fee claim to the lawyer, such that the prevailing party retains no meaningful interest in or control over the claim, then it may be possible to view any recovery on that claim as income only of the lawyer." Reply Brief of Petitioner, C.I.R. v. Banks, 2004 WL 2190372 (U.S. Sept. 22, 2004). *But see In re* Equator Corp., 362 B.R. 326, 333 (Bankr. S.D. Tex. 2007) (holding that *Banks* rejects the use of an assignment to prevent attribution of attorney fees as income to the client).

287 *See, e.g.*, Citizens Legal Env't v. Premium Standard Farms, Inc., 397 F.3d 592 (8th Cir. 2005) (plaintiff not entitled to keep statutory attorney fees).

288 I.R.S. Priv. Ltr. Rul. 06-09-014 (Mar. 3, 2006).

289 *See* Treas. Reg. § 1.6041(f)(2), Example 2; I.R.S. Priv. Ltr. Rul. 06-09-014 (Mar. 3, 2006).

10.9 Settlement Issues

10.9.1 Dealing with Multiple Defendants

When multiple defendants are sued, amounts received in settlement with some defendants may be deducted from any court or jury award against a non-settlement defendant.[290] The offset should be limited to amounts received from the defendant; generally, any benefit to a homeowner from nonpayment on a mortgage should not be deducted.[291] The homeowner's attorney should check the jurisdiction's law carefully concerning the manner and form in which the settlement should be documented in order to minimize the effect on the non-settling defendants.

One strategy that may maximize the consumer's total recovery is to stipulate in the settlement agreement that the money is for some specific element of damages that the remaining defendants are not liable for. Examples are the attorney fees to date arising from the independent efforts against the settling defendant,[292] separate damages caused by the settling defendant's independent misconduct,[293] statutory damages, and punitive damages.[294] As punitive damages are based on individual culpability, a payment by one defendant does not reduce the other's liability for punitive damages.[295] Failure to apportion the damages in

290 *See* Neb. Plastics, Inc. v. Holland Colors Ams., Inc., 408 F.3d 410 (8th Cir. 2005) (predicting that Nebraska would require dollar-for-dollar settlement even when additional defendant was intentional tortfeasor); York v. InTrust Bank, N.A., 962 P.2d 405 (Kan. 1998) (settlement with co-defendant applied to offset judgment against remaining defendant for compensatory damages, but not punitive damages). *See also* Zivitiz v. Greenberg, 279 F.3d 536 (7th Cir. 2002) (Ill. law) (no setoff when the damages awarded against non-settling defendant were not for identical injury; Jerome Walert, Annotation, *Contribution Between Joint Tortfeasors As Affected by Settlement by Injured Party by One or More Tortfeasors*, 17 A.L.R. 6th 1 (2006).

291 *See, e.g.*, Ciampi v. Ogden Chrysler Plymouth, 634 N.E.2d 448 (Ill. Ct. App. 1994) (irrelevant in determining offset that the plaintiff had the use of the car for two years without making payments).

292 Wash Trust Co. v. Fatone, 256 A.2d 490 (R.I. 1969). *See also* Beerman v. Toro Mfg. Corp., 1 Haw. App. 111, 615 P.2d 749 (1980) (citing attorney fee for which only one defendant was liable as example of payment that would not count against other defendant's liability).

293 Plath v. Schonrock, 64 P.3d 984 (Mont. 2003) (no setoff when settling defendant's liability was based on separate and distinct claim). *See also* Zivitz v. Greenberg, 279 F.3d 536, 539–540 (7th Cir. 2002); Pasquale v. Speed Prods. Eng'g, 654 N.E.2d 1365 (Ill. 1995).

294 Claims for punitive damages can create interesting settlement dynamics between the defendant and its insurer. Many policies do not cover punitive damages, so the insurer may not be willing to fund a settlement that includes any punitive damages.

295 Beerman v. Toro Mfg. Corp., 615 P.2d 749 (Haw. Ct. App. 1980); Turner v. Firstar Bank, 845 N.E.2d 816 (Ill. App. Ct. 2006) (plaintiff may recover punitive damages from one defendant even though she already recovered full compensatory

a settlement agreement may relieve a defendant of its burden of proving offset.[296]

Another concern is the effect on the jury if the judge allows the admission of evidence of the settlement. If the plaintiff has already recovered a substantial sum from another defendant, the jury may feel that the plaintiff's case no longer has to be taken seriously. If the plaintiff settled with other defendants for a nominal amount, it may devalue the case in the jury's eyes.

Many states follow a rule similar to Rule 408 of the Federal Rules of Evidence, that evidence of compromise or an offer to compromise is not admissible on liability issues.[297] This rule does allow such evidence to be admitted for other purposes, such as proving bias of a witness, negating a contention of undue delay, or proving an effort to obstruct a criminal investigation or prosecution, but courts tend to be reluctant to find it relevant for these purposes.[298] Even if relevant, such evidence can be excluded under Rule 403 (or its state law equivalent) if its value is substantially outweighed by the danger of unfair prejudice, confusion, or similar concerns.[299] If an offset is required because of the settlement, the majority rule is that the jury should still not be informed of the settlement, but the court should handle the offset after the verdict.[300] A motion *in limine* to exclude evidence is recommended. If there is any chance that the evidence will be allowed in, many attorneys recommend alerting the jury to it beforehand, either in *voir dire* or in the opening statement.

Even if the jury is never informed of the terms of the settlement, the "empty chair" effect can be a problem especially if the party who is no longer in the case is the one the jury is likely to perceive as the most culpable. In developing a trial strategy, the plaintiff's attorney should focus on ways to address the jury's discomfort, and should stress the remaining defendant's role in the culpable acts in both the overall scheme and in causing the plaintiff's injuries.

10.9.2 Confidentiality

Settling defendants often request that the settlement prohibit the parties from disclosing the terms of the settlement to anyone. A second, less extreme clause does not prohibit disclosure altogether, but prohibits publicity. Such clauses raise a host of concerns. They enable defendants to cover up massive wrongdoing, and create procedural obstacles if judicial enforcement of the settlement becomes necessary. Confidentiality agreements leave the litigation unsettled because they invite the defendant to sue the plaintiff years later, alleging disclosure of the settlement.

What types of disclosures may be covered and who is subject to nondisclosure provisions vary widely from agreement to agreement. For example, confidentiality agreements may prohibit only disclosure of the amount of settlement, not the fact of settlement, which is a matter of public record in any event. Any confidentiality agreement should also make an exception for evidence that is subpoenaed in another case, to avoid ethical problems. Confidentiality agreements should also contain carve-outs for consultation with tax advisors.

Some defendants may propose confidentiality agreements that cover the attorney as well as the client. These agreements are particularly attractive to defendants because they impede the plaintiff's attorney's representation of other clients against the same defendants. To avoid problems associated with these agreements, some consumer attorneys refuse to sign to any confidentiality agreement that binds them, although the client has freedom to argue that he or she will not disclose the settlement. Another possible step is to insist that any confidentiality clause that applies to the attorney must include language that the nondisclosure agreement is void and unenforceable to the extent that it restricts the attorney's right to practice law.

If a confidentiality clause is included in the settlement agreement its reach should be limited. Tax advisors should be excluded because the settlement may raise tax issues for the homeowner. If the advocate works for a non-profit organization, a carve-out should be created for existing and future funders of the organization. (They will want to know about the work the organization has been doing.) All confidentiality provisions should also have an exemption for a homeowner who is later subpoenaed.

Sometimes creditors are most concerned with not being slandered in the press. If that is the case, the creditor may agree to a joint press release instead of a confidentiality clause. A joint press release allows the creditor to help shape any initial presentation of the facts to the outside

---

damages plus punitive damages from another defendant); York v. InTrust Bank, N.A., 962 P.2d 405 (Kan. 1998); Exxon Corp v. Yarema, 516 A.2d 990 (Md. Ct. Spec. App. 1986) (settlement with other defendants before trial can satisfy compensatory damages but not punitive damages liability of non-settling defendant); Freeman v. Myers, 774 S.W.2d 892 (Mo. Ct. App. 1989); Sanchez v. Clayton, 877 P.2d 567 (N.M. 1994); McGee v. Bruce Hosp. Sys., 545 S.E.2d 286 (S.C. 2001); Gilcrease v. Garlock, Inc., 211 S.W.3d 448 (Tex. App. 2006). *See also* Harriss v. Elliott, 565 N.E.2d 1041 (Ill. App. Ct. 1991) (collecting authority against permitting setoff of punitive damages for public policy reasons).

296 Patton v. Carbondale Clinic, S.C., 641 N.E.2d 427 (Ill. 1994).

297 Rule 408 was amended in 2006 in ways that do not affect this discussion.

298 Graber v. City of Ankeny, 616 N.W.2d 633 (Iowa 2000).

299 Votolato v. Merendi, 747 A.2d 455 (R.I. 2000).

300 Morea v. Cosco, Inc., 422 Mass. 601, 554 N.E.2d 822 (1996); Southeastern Med. Supply, Inc. v. Boyles, Moak & Brickell Ins., Inc., 822 So. 2d 323 (Miss. Ct. App. 2002); Votolato v. Merendi, 747 A.2d 455 (R.I. 2000). *See also* Harriss v. Elliott, 565 N.E.2d 1041 (Ill. App. Ct. 1991). *Cf.* Dynasty Hous., Inc. v. McCollum, 2001 Ala. Civ. App. LEXIS 316 (Ala. Civ. Ct. App. June 22, 2001); Buccaneer Homes v. Pelis, 43 S.W.3d 586 (Tex. App. 2001).

world and to ensure that the press has a designated contact person to call to give the creditor's version of events.

If there is no way to avoid a confidentiality clause, put a price on it. The IRS has in the past attributed the entire monetary value of a settlement to a confidentiality clause.[301] And a settlement so attributed will be treated as taxable income—not a good result for your client. If the creditor wants confidentiality, they should be prepared to pay for it. Document in your agreement or correspondence with the creditor how much was paid for the confidentiality agreement.

It is wise to discuss these issues with the client at the outset of the case, before litigation is commenced. Some attorneys include provisions in their retainer agreements that reflect the understanding that has been worked out with the client about confidentiality clauses. Regardless of the initial discussions with the client, if the client later becomes interested in a settlement that includes a nondisclosure provision, the client should be cautioned about the scope of such provision and the consequences of violating it. Confidentiality agreements place a great and lifelong burden on the client, forcing the client to live under the threat of suit if she ever discloses the settlement or if the defendant ever believes she disclosed it.

A number of federal appellate courts have ruled that a stipulation of settlement that contains a confidentiality clause cannot be approved unless good cause is shown, because such clauses have an adverse impact on the public interest.[302]

10.9.3 Protecting the Consumer's Credit Report

An important element of settlement is protection of the homeowner's credit record. If appropriate, the settlement agreement should provide that the defendant will immediately take all steps necessary to ensure that no credit report or credit reference that is or could be construed as unfavorable to the consumer is made to anyone, and in particular any consumer credit rating agency, with regard to any debts or claims involving the consumer. The agreement should further require the defendant to make a request to each credit reporting agency to whom it furnishes information, asking that the agency delete all references to the alleged debts or claims, and to sign a letter on its letterhead, prepared by the consumer's attorney, stating that its claims against the consumer have been fully released and that any adverse reports should be deleted and deemed unreliable.[303] Deleting the tradeline in this way will remove all history of the debt from the credit reporting system. Depending on the nature of the settlement, homeowners may prefer to have the creditor report all payments made as agreed.[304] A time by which the creditor will transmit the agreed upon correction should be included in the agreement along with a provision requiring that the homeowner's attorney receive a copy of the transmission. It is a good idea to have the homeowner obtain a credit report a month or two after the settlement to make sure the correction have been made as agreed.

If a party fails to complete all the required re-reporting of the debt, there are two ways to proceed: sue the party for breach of contract or have the homeowner dispute the accuracy of the debt with the credit reporting bureaus. A reinvestigation initiated by the homeowner is often the easiest way to clean up the credit report. So long as the creditor does not then verify the disputed debt, the credit reporting bureau should change the reporting to accord with the homeowner's representation that the debt was paid as agreed (or that the tradeline should be deleted). Thus, the final agreement should make clear that the creditor—and its assignees and agents—will not verify the debt in the event of a reinvestigation.

10.9.4 Tax Consequences of Settlement

10.9.4.1 Overview

Settlements in which a homeowner receives money damages or cancellation of debt may result in tax liability. A discussion of the tax treatment of damages, including attorney's fees, which are generally taxable income to the client, may be found at § 10.8, *supra*. Detailed treatment of cancelled debt is found at § 14.6.3, *infra*.

This section highlights two practical areas for consideration when tax liability may result from a settlement agreement: documenting the nature of the damages in the settlement documents and planning for payment of taxes and related expenses in finalizing settlement agreements. In general, practitioners should take care to minimize the tax consequences for clients by documenting potential exclusions from taxable income, ensuring that the client, where appropriate, has competent, independent tax advice, and setting money aside from the settlement to cover payment of

---

301 Amos v. C.I.R., T.C. Memo, 2003-329, 2003 WL 22839795 (Dec. 1, 2003).

302 *See, e.g.*, Citizens First Nat'l Bank v. Cincinnati Ins. Co., 178 F.3d 943 (7th Cir. 1999) (judge must find good cause before approving settlement agreement containing confidentiality clause); Pansy v. Borough of Stroudsburg, 23 F.3d 772 (3d Cir. 1994) (discussing confidentiality agreement, especially in relation to settlement papers that are not filed with the court); City of Hartford v. Chase, 942 F.2d 130 (2d Cir. 1991 (trial court may approve confidentiality order only after very careful, particularized review.).

303 *See* National Consumer Law Center, Fair Credit Reporting § 3.3 (6th ed. 2006 and Supp.) (full discussion of protecting the consumer's credit record as part of a settlement, along with sample language).

304 *See generally* National Consumer Law Center, Fair Credit Reporting § 12.6.4.3 (6th ed. 2006 and Supp.).

taxes and the tax advisor's fees, when necessary. Particularly where a settlement involves cancelled debt, timing of the settlement may preserve or destroy some exclusions from taxable income.[305]

10.9.4.2 Distinguishing Taxable from Non-Taxable Damages

In all cases, attorneys should take care to specify the source of the damages. Replacement for out-of-pocket costs will be non-taxable; replacement for lost income, occasioned by, for example, time off work, will be taxable. Out-of-pocket costs may include repairs made to a home, return of excess interest paid, the inflated value of a purchased home, as well as more mundane out-of-pocket expenses, such as medical bills and transportation costs. When a settlement involves both taxable and non-taxable damages, the documents should specify the percentage of the settlement related to each source of damages. For example, in a Truth in Lending rescission case, practitioners should consider specifying in the settlement agreement the portion of the loan forgiveness related to canceled interest or fees, instead of principal.[306]

The IRS will initially rely on how the settlement agreement allocates the recovery between taxable and non-taxable damages,[307] but the allocation in the settlement agreement is not conclusive.[308] The motivations of the company in settling,[309] the allegations in the taxpayer's complaint, the evidence presented, and arguments made in any court proceeding are all factors in determining the proper allocation.[310] Other factors include jury awards, or any court orders in other cases.[311] Letters discussing the nature and source of damages sought should be preserved for possible later litigation with the IRS.

10.9.4.3 Considering Tax Consequences in Settlement Amounts

The client may want to insist on a higher recovery to offset taxes on the award and any Alternative Minimum Tax (AMT) implications of the attorney fee award.[312] If the client will retain a tax adviser, those fees should be planned for in the settlement. Otherwise, the taxes or fees could erode whatever benefit the client may have otherwise received from the settlement. Some consumers have successfully sought supplements to court-ordered damages to reflect that the consumer will not be made whole because of the tax implications of the award.[313] Because courts have agreed that taxes related to damages may constitute actual damages, homeowners should not hesitate to seek compensation for these obligations.

Some practitioners, with their clients' consent, arrange for payments to tax advisers directly from the settlement proceeds. Others assist their clients in establishing an escrow fund to hold the estimated tax obligation until the taxes are assessed and paid.

10.9.5 Attorney Fees

Defendants often seek to "divide and conquer" by offering a settlement that does not include attorney fees, or includes an inadequate proposal for fees creating a conflict between the homeowner and the homeowner's attorney. This can be a significant problem in foreclosure defense cases where a settlement offer from the defendant may simply provide for a modification of the loan (e.g., write down of principal and/or reduction of interest) without any cash payment. While the Supreme Court has rejected a claim that it was unethical for a defendant to propose a settlement of a civil rights case that required waiver of attorney fees,[314] at least one state court found such a settlement offer unethical in a UDAP case.[315] In many foreclosure defenses cases, fees may be available under statutory claims, particularly pursuant to the Truth in Lending Act. A full discussion of the attorney fees issues in Truth in Lending cases, including availability of fees after settlement, is available in National Consumer Law Center, *Truth in Lending* § 8.9 (6th ed. 2007 and Supp.).

305 *See, e.g.*, § 14.6.4.3, *infra* (in order to exclude cancelled debt in connection with a bankruptcy, the bankruptcy must be filed before the debt is cancelled); § 14.6.4.7, *infra* (exclusion for acquisition indebtedness expires at the end of 2012).

306 *See* § 10.8.4.5, *supra*.

307 *See* Bagley v. Comm'r, 105 T.C. 396 (1995), *aff'd*, 121 F.3d 393 (8th Cir. 1997).

308 Robinson v. Comm'r, 70 F.3d 34, 37 (5th Cir. 1995) (looking past agreement to determine the amount attributable of each type of damage).

309 Knuckles v. Comm'r, 349 F.2d 610, 613 (10th Cir. 1965), *aff'g* T.C. Memo. 1964-33, 23 T.C.M. (CCH) 182 (1964).

310 Threlkeld v. Comm'r, 87 T.C. 1294, 1306 (1986), *aff'd*, 848 F.2d 81 (6th Cir. 1988).

311 Miller v. Comm'r, T.C. Memo. 1993-49, 65 T.C.M. (CCH) 1884 (1993), *supplemented by* T.C. Memo. 1993-558, 66 T.C.M. (CCH) 1568 (1993), *aff'd*, 60 F.3d 823 (4th Cir. 1995).

312 *See* § 10.8.6, *supra* (discussing taxability of attorney fees generally).

313 *See, e.g.*, Blaney v. Int'l Ass'n of Machinists & Aerospace Workers, Dist. No. 160, 55 P.3d 1208 (Wash. Ct. App. 2002) (holding that adverse tax consequences are actual damages and should be awarded based on broad scope of actual damages under state statute and legislative intent to deter misconduct and make victims whole).

314 Evans v. Jeff D., 475 U.S. 717, 106 S. Ct. 1531, 89 L. Ed 2d 747 (1986).

315 Coleman v. Fiore Bros., Inc., 552 A.2d 141 (N.J. 1989).

Problems of settlement offers that do not provide sufficient attorney fees can be minimized by a retainer that unites the homeowner's interest with the attorney's interest. For example, the retainer could provide that, if the case is settled with insufficient provision for fees, the fees are satisfied first out of settlement proceeds. Or it could simply state that the client is responsible to pay the attorney at the agreed rate regardless of whether the case is won or settled. Public interest attorneys who are handling a case without any obligation on the part of the client to pay fees should also have a clear understanding with the client, incorporated in the retainer, about how fee issues will be handled in the event of a settlement. Sample retainer agreements with clients, for both legal services and private attorneys, are found in other NCLC treatises and also on this treatise's companion website.[316]

10.9.6 Protecting Against the Defendant's Bankruptcy

If the defendant is in such bad financial shape that bankruptcy is a possibility, the homeowner's attorney should take special care in handling the settlement.[317] If the defendant files for bankruptcy before paying the agreed settlement amount, that debt may generally be discharged. However, the Supreme Court has ruled that signing a settlement agreement and release does not convert an underlying nondischargeable fraud claim into a dischargeable contract claim.[318] A consumer who has signed a release but has not yet received payment can still challenge the dischargeability of the debt on the ground that the underlying debt was procured by fraud.[319] The Supreme Court did not rule out the possibility that collateral estoppel might prevent the consumer from relitigating the question of fraud. Careful drafting of the release may avoid collateral estoppel problems, but it is safer to condition any release upon receipt of payment. Practitioners should also bear in mind that if home mortgage loans, covered at their inception by the Truth in Lending Act, are sold in a lender's bankruptcy, the purchaser remains subject to any claims and defenses related to the note to the same extent a purchaser outside of bankruptcy would.[320]

In addition, when a defendant files for bankruptcy, the bankruptcy trustee may seek to avoid certain property transfers made by the debtor within ninety days of the filing of the debtor's petition.[321] If the homeowner's attorney receives the settlement amount and forwards it to the homeowner, and the defendant files for bankruptcy within ninety days, the homeowner may be required to return the settlement proceeds to the bankruptcy trustee. Attorneys may want to consider holding settlement proceeds obtained from a defendant teetering on the edge of bankruptcy, with the client's consent, until the ninety-day period passes.

10.9.7 Make Sure the Agreement Is Enforceable

Everything agreed upon must be reduced to writing. Nothing should be left to chance or a promise. Most servicers and lending institutions are big, complex organizations, and any individual representative, lawyer, CEO, frontline worker, or general counsel has only a limited ability to control the other pieces of the organization.

If the terms of the settlement call for the modification of an existing mortgage, the settlement agreement must spell out what happens to all the accounts connected with the loan—escrow and suspense accounts, as well as the principal balance of the loan. The agreement should specify the balance in all accounts and clearly provide that there are no other sums due from the borrower, nor may any other sums be assessed to the borrower's account reflecting any expenses incurred as of the date of the agreement.

If the mortgage is to be released, it may be prudent for the final order to include a judicial deed or a declaration that the mortgage is released. This can eliminate the need to track down a recalcitrant servicer or holder.

In addition, remember that the settling party may or may not own the loan, may never have actually owned the loan, and probably cannot tell you one way or another. In the settlement agreement, bind the current holder, future holders, past holders, and servicers. That may or may not be effective as to other organizations, but it requires the settling party to represent that they have the authority to bind other entities that may have some interest in the note and gives some leverage against that settling party for indemnification if some other creditor shows up in the future and refuses to honor the settlement.

Settlement agreements should provide for attorney fees in the event of a breach and all costs of enforcing the agreement. The homeowner will already be on the hook for attorney fees under the mortgage. Make sure the creditor is as well. This gives some leverage when the servicer or holder fails to release the mortgage as required or to repair

316 *See* National Consumer Law Center, Consumer Class Actions (7th ed. 2010).

317 A more detailed discussion of steps that may be taken to protect consumers when a defendant files bankruptcy is provided in Ch. 17 of National Consumer Law Center, Consumer Bankruptcy Practice (9th ed. 2009).

318 Archer v. Warner, 538 U.S. 314, 123 S. Ct. 1462, 155 L. Ed. 2d 454 (2003).

319 National Consumer Law Center, Consumer Bankruptcy Practice §§ 15.4.3, 18.5.4 (9th ed. 2009).

320 11 U.S.C. § 363(o). *See generally* National Consumer Law Center, Consumer Bankruptcy Law and Practice § 18.9.3 (9th ed. 2009).

321 *See* 11 U.S.C. § 547; National Consumer Law Center, Consumer Bankruptcy Practice § 10.4.2.6.4 (9th ed. 2009).

the clients' credit. An attorney fee clause may speed compliance and may provide the client some redress.

10.9.8 Address the Public Benefit Consequences of the Settlement

Settlements can have significant ramifications for borrowers receiving public benefits. The benefits rules are complex and vary from state to state, and program to program. A public benefits expert should be used to help design a settlement that minimizes the impact on the homeowner.

As a general rule, most programs treat money received as income in the month received and any remaining amount of money at the end of the month as an asset. If the money received is greater than the program's need standard, the program usually will recoup the overpayment of benefits in subsequent months. If the money is not spent down to the program's asset limits within a month, the homeowner risks being terminated from the benefits program. So long as the money is spent down in a month, then, usually the homeowner is at risk for losing only one month of payments—which, depending on the size of the settlement and the amount of public benefits, could be a minor cost or result in a loss of the entire value of the settlement.

At least some of the money received often may be sheltered from offset if paid directly to third parties. Whether this is effective or not depends on the program and the purpose of the payments. Some programs, for example, have in place deeming rules that treat portions of some payments made on behalf of the client to a third party as income, while exempting most of the payment.

In addition, some programs may treat cash payments received in a settlement related to the client's home as replacement of an exempt asset. If this is the case, the entire settlement will be treated as an exempt asset, and there is no need to make settlement payments directly to third parties. Usually, the client will then have ninety days to spend down the funds and convert them to another exempt asset.

10.9.9 Other Considerations

10.9.9.1 Change the Account Number

Most servicers use automated recordkeeping systems. Unless a thorough purge of the existing computer records is done, it is likely that, at some point, when the servicer generates a payment statement or history, some of the forgiven fees in the loan modification may get picked up and swept into the client's current information. Changing the loan's account number helps give the loan a fresh start, without the history of the fees, charges, and principal that have been forgiven in the loan modification.

10.9.9.2 Forbid Future Solicitations of the Borrower

It is likely that the homeowner got into a bad loan because somebody called her up and said that she could get a good deal. When settling a case, consider forbidding future solicitations of the homeowner by the current holder and all of its assignees and agents. This prohibition may give homeowners peace of mind and prevent them from becoming victims all over again.

Chapter 11

Manufactured Home Foreclosures and Repossessions

11.1 Overview

Eighteen million Americans live in manufactured homes.[1] There are currently over eight million manufactured homes in the United States, almost seven million of which are occupied.[2] Many people choose these units because they purport to offer the security and privacy of homeownership at a fraction of a conventional home's upfront cost.[3] Many others do so because they have few other affordable housing options. The median household income of manufactured home residents was $27,452 in 2003, as compared with $44,503 for all households.[4] Many United States armed forces personnel live in manufactured home parks.[5]

In spite of their popularity, manufactured homes often come with hidden costs, some revealing themselves at purchase, others going unnoticed until an owner occupies the home for some time, defaults on a payment, or decides to move. Manufactured homes often depreciate in value over time. They can also sustain serious damage in transit from the manufacturer to the home site and in inclement weather.[6] Once the unit has been delivered to its destination, often a "pad" in a manufactured home park, its wheels are usually removed and adaptations are often made in order to secure it to the ground or pad. For these and other reasons, manufactured homes are not very "mobile," even though they are often referred to as "mobile homes." Moving a manufactured home once it has been secured may be difficult, if not impossible.

Manufactured homes are a relatively recent development in housing. As demand for housing increased in the second half of the twentieth century, travel trailers increasingly began to be used for year-round residences. Soon "mobile homes" were being built that were intended to be permanent housing. There was little regulation of this new form of housing, however, and it was clear that many units had safety and durability issues. These problems prompted Congress to pass the Mobile Home Construction and Safety Standards Act of 1974, directing HUD to promulgate federal construction standards for manufactured homes.[7] Today the term "manufactured home" is typically used to refer to units manufactured to comply with the HUD code, and the term "mobile home" is typically used to refer to homes made prior to June 15, 1976, the effective date of the HUD code.

Despite the creation of the HUD code many consumers continue to experience problems with defects after purchasing manufactured homes.[8] While some of these defects are the result of problems in the design, manufacture, or transport of homes, many defects are the result of improper installation of the home.[9] In an effort to reduce installation problems, Congress mandated in 2000 that HUD develop installation standards for manufactured homes as well as a dispute resolution program.[10]

1 *Dream Home . . . or Nightmare?*, Consumer Rep., Feb. 1998, at 30.

2 American Housing Survey 2005, Table 2-1, Introductory Characteristics—Occupied Units and Table 1A-1. Introductory Characteristics—All Housing Units, *available at* www.census.gov/hhes/www/housing/ahs/ahs.html.

3 The median purchase price for currently occupied homes was $26,370, not including land, American Housing Survey 2005, Table 3-14, Value, Purchase Price, and Source of Down Payment—Owner Occupied Units, *available at* www.census.gov/hhes/www/housing/ahs/ahs.html.

4 American Housing Survey 2005, Table 2-12, Income Characteristics—Occupied Units, *available at* www.census.gov/hhes/www/housing/ahs/ahs.html.

5 Practice Note, 1997 Army Law. 29, 31.

6 *See Dream Home . . . or Nightmare?*, Consumer Rep., Feb. 1998, at 34. *See also* An Assessment of Damage to Manufactured Homes Caused by Hurricane Charley March 31 2005, *available at* www.huduser.org/Publications/pdf/HurricaneCharley04.pdf; David A. Jones & Brad German, *Blowout: South Florida Housing Damage Caused by Hurricane Andrew*, Builder, Feb. 1993, at 276 (noting that 97% of manufactured homes were destroyed in the hurricane, as compared to 10% of conventional single family homes); National Consumer Law Center, NCLC Guide to Mobile Homes (2002).

7 24 C.F.R. pt. 3280.

8 *See* National Consumer Law Center, Consumer Warranty Law Ch. 17 (3d ed. 2006 and Supp.) (discussion manufactured home warranty issues and HUD standards).

9 William Apgar, Allegra Calder, Michael Collins, and Mark Duda, Neighborhood Reinvestment Corporation and Joint Center for Housing Studies, An Examination of Manufactured Housing As a Community and Asset-Building Strategy (Sept. 2002). *See* National Consumer Law Center, Consumer Warranty Law § 17.1.3, 17.7 (3d ed. 2006 and Supp.).

10 Amendments to the National Manufactured Housing Construction and Safety Standards Act in 2000 require the states and

Some consumers who purchase manufactured homes also own the land on which the home is placed. In other cases the units are situated on rented land or in a leased manufactured home park space. The consumer may therefore be answerable to two creditors: the entity that financed the sale of the unit, and the land or park owner. Different rights and remedies attach if the consumer defaults in the obligation to either party. A defaulting consumer may therefore be subject to repossession or foreclosure of the home and eviction from the park at the same time.

Because manufactured homes often depreciate in value, and because park owners frequently impose charges and restrictions (such as the right to refuse potential buyers), it may be hard for a consumer to sell a home for more than a fraction of its purchase price. Furthermore, residents who lease space from park owners are vulnerable to sudden rent increases and charges for utilities and services formerly included in the base rent. The park may become poorly maintained and services may lapse. Finally, there is a critical shortage of park space. If a tenant wishes to leave a bad park rental situation, there may simply be no place else to go. Park owners therefore hold, and exercise, considerable leverage over their tenants.

Consumers usually lack real bargaining power when dealing with park owners. Some states and localities have restricted fees and rent increases, prohibited certain resale restrictions, and enacted disclosure requirements and rules governing evictions.[11] A majority of states have enacted legislation addressing at least some of the problems with parks,[12] but many abuses still are not prohibited. Even in states where protections have been enacted, enforcement of these laws may be sporadic at best, and tenants who cannot afford attorneys may have few means of curbing the abuses they encounter.

This chapter first examines the question whether Article 9 of the Uniform Commercial Code or foreclosure law applies when a debtor defaults on a manufactured home debt.[13] If foreclosure law governs, the foreclosure procedures described in the other chapters of this book will apply. For instances when Article 9 applies, the chapter summarizes the procedures the creditor must follow,[14] and summarizes certain state restrictions on repossession of manufactured homes.[15]

The chapter then examines defenses that consumers may have when a creditor seeks to repossess or foreclose on a manufactured home. First it analyzes federal regulations and state laws that require a creditor, in some circumstances, to offer the debtor an opportunity to cure a default on a manufactured home loan.[16] Then it addresses defenses under the Truth in Lending Act, the Real Estate Settlement Procedures Act (RESPA), state credit laws, and warranty laws;[17] the question whether a manufactured home qualifies for a homestead exemption that would protect it from foreclosure based on a judgment lien;[18] the possibility of a workout or bankruptcy as a means of avoiding loss of the home;[19] and the extent to which seller-related defenses can be asserted against the entity financing the purchase of the home.[20] It concludes with a discussion of special problems that arise because of the relationship of the home to a manufactured home park or the land on which the home is placed.[21]

11.2 Must Foreclosure Procedures Be Followed to Retake Manufactured Home?

11.2.1 Introduction

An initial question whenever a manufactured homeowner is facing the loss of the home is whether foreclosure law or repossession law applies. In nearly all states, manufactured homes are at least initially considered personalty for purposes of secured transactions, and therefore generally subject to replevin or self-help repossession.[22] A manufactured

HUD to develop installation standards within next five years. Pub. L. No. 106-569, tit. VI, § 605, 114 Stat. 2944 (2000) (replacing 42 U.S.C. § 5404). *See* National Consumer Law Center, Consumer Warranty Law § 17.3 (3d ed. 2006 and Supp.).

In 2005, after the Manufactured Housing Consensus Committee made a recommendation, HUD proposed a rule: HUD, Proposed Rule, Model Manufactured Home Installation Standards, 70 Fed. Reg. 21,498 (Apr. 26, 2005). In its December 2006 Semiannual Regulatory Agenda, HUD indicated that final action on the proposed standards should be taken by February 2007. 71 Fed. Reg. 73,401 (Dec. 11, 2006). As of the date of publication of this treatise there has been no final action on the proposed installation standards rule. In mid-2006, HUD proposed a separate rule on enforcement of its installation standards. 71 Fed. Reg. 34,476 (June 14, 2006).

11 *See, e.g.*, Fla. Stat. § 723.037; Mobile Home Anti-Eviction Act, N.J. Stat. Ann. § 2A:18-61.1(f) (West) (unconscionable rent increases not permitted). *See also* Quinn v. Rent Control Bd., 698 N.E.2d 911 (Mass. App. Ct. 1998) (manufactured home rent control survives the abrogation act).

12 *See* National Consumer Law Center, Unfair and Deceptive Acts and Practices § 8.1.2.5.2 (7th ed. 2008 and Supp.).

13 *See* § 11.2, *infra*.

14 *See* § 11.3, *infra*.

15 *See* § 11.4, *infra*.

16 *See* § 11.5, *infra*.

17 *See* §§ 11.6–11.9, *infra*.

18 *See* § 11.10, *infra*.

19 *See* §§ 11.11–11.12, *infra*.

20 *See* § 11.13, *infra*.

21 *See* §§ 11.14–11.15, *infra*.

22 *In re* Onyan, 163 B.R. 21 (Bankr. N.D.N.Y. 1993) (manufactured homes are considered personal property constituting "consumer goods" for purposes of Art. 9); Midland-Guardian Co. v. Hagin, 370 So. 2d 25 (Fla. Dist. Ct. App. 1975) (manufactured home is goods and Article 9 allows secured party to use

home may cease to be personal property when it is annexed to real property.[23] Then the creditor may be required to pursue foreclosure if the buyer defaults. Regardless of whether the home is real or personal property, the secured party cannot use eviction law to regain possession, because the buyer is occupying the manufactured home pursuant to a sale rather than a lease.[24]

If a manufactured home is considered personal property, then it can be bought and sold like other goods. In most states ownership is conveyed by transferring a certificate of title, similar to an automobile title, and security interests are noted on the title. If the home is personal property, a secured party may retake the home through replevin or, in most states, self-help repossession. By contrast, if state real property laws govern, then a deed or mortgage conveying an interest in the land may also convey the structures on it.[25] If the home is considered real property, then security interests are recorded in the local land records and the creditor may be required to use state foreclosure procedures if the debtor defaults.

To determine whether a manufactured home is considered personal property or real property, the first question is whether the state has a statute that governs this issue. There are several different types of state statutes. Many states have statutes that set forth a procedure for a manufactured home to become real property.[26] A few states also have statutes that specify whether a home is considered personalty or realty in a credit transaction.[27] Many states have a statutory scheme that establishes criteria for taxing the home as real property.[28] Some states have no statute at all. In many of the states that do have a statute detailing when a home is, or may become, real property, the statute is often unclear as to whether the home is to be real property for all intents and purposes and whether the statutory method is the only way of converting the home to real property.

In states that do not have a definitive statute, courts generally refer to the law of fixtures and look to a series of factors to determine whether the home has become so attached to the land as to be considered part of the real property.[29] Even in states that have a conversion statute, courts may analyze these factors to buttress the conclusion that a home is or is not real property.

Uncertainty about whether a manufactured home is personalty or realty leaves creditors and consumers vulnerable to confusion.[30] It may be unclear whether foreclosure or repossession procedures must be used to retake the home in the event of a default. If a manufactured home becomes a fixture and therefore part of the real estate, then the security interest should be recorded in the county land records, not

self-help or replevin to obtain possession after default); Griswell v. Columbus Fin. Co., 470 S.E.2d 256 (Ga. Ct. App. 1996) (unless is it is permanently attached to realty, manufactured home is personal property, not real property, so real estate foreclosure law does not apply); Barnett v. First Fed. Sav. & Loan Ass'n of Atlanta, 313 S.E.2d 115 (Ga. Ct. App. 1984) (Article 9 governed manufactured home writ of possession proceeding); Bain v. Community Sales, Inc., 2010 WL 395742 (Mich. Ct. App. Feb. 4, 2010) (for purposes of statute of limitation, manufactured home is personal property until owner follows the procedures outlined in the state conversion statute); Dungan v. Dick Moore, Inc., 463 So. 2d 1094 (Miss. 1985) (Article 9 governs and allows either self-help repossession or replevin to retake vacated manufactured home; debtor has right to redeem, home must be sold pursuant to U.C.C., etc.); White v. Secrest, 467 N.Y.S.2d 954 (County Ct. 1983) (replevin is appropriate remedy if manufactured home is personal property; suit for money damages is an appropriate remedy if replevin cannot be granted because home has become real property); Hensley v. Ray's Motor Co., 580 S.E.2d 721 (N.C. Ct. App. 2003) (for purposes of statute of limitation, manufactured home is personal property governed by U.C.C. unless it is permanently annexed to the land or other circumstances convert it to real property). *See also* Grant v. Gen. Elec. Credit Corp., 764 F.2d 1404, 1407–1408 (11th Cir. 1985) (Ga. law) (Article 9 allows creditor to repossess manufactured home by self help); Green Tree Fin. Servicing Corp. v. Sutton, 650 N.W.2d 228 (Neb. 2002) (upholding ruling allowing creditor's replevy of manufactured home).

23 *See In re* Onyan, 163 B.R. 21, 25 (Bankr. N.D.N.Y. 1993) (construing exemption statute; cost of site preparation was part of purchase price of manufactured home that was permanently attached to the land); *In re* Fink, 4 B.R. 741, 29 U.C.C. Rep. Serv. 1431 (Bankr. W.D.N.Y. 1980) (home ceased to be personalty and became a fixture when it was annexed to real property, so fixture filing was required to perfect security interest); Fuqua Homes, Inc. v. Evanston Bldg. & Loan Co., 370 N.E.2d 780 (Ohio Ct. App. 1977) ("from and after the moment the two [manufactured home] units were joined as one habitation and attached permanently to the foundation, the resulting structure became part of the real estate"; mortgage that bank took on real property after home had already been installed covered the home as well as the land).

24 Branch v. Wesav Fin. Corp., 401 S.E.2d 569 (Ga. Ct. App. 1991); Sanders v. Hughes, 359 S.E.2d 396 (Ga. Ct. App. 1987). *But see* Price v. Miller, 2002 WL 32073789 (Del. Ct. Com. Pl. Dec. 9, 2002) (where state statute defined "an occupant of premises pursuant to a conditional sales agreement" as a tenant, seller must use the eviction procedure prescribed by landlord-tenant law to remove a defaulting buyer); Mix v. Mix, 2005 WL 1940321 (Ohio Ct. App. Aug. 12, 2005) (where secured party caused title to be changed so that secured party was title owner and no longer simply the lien holder and then brought action to evict borrower through action in forcible entry and detainer, failure to bring replevin action was harmless error when borrower left voluntarily before writ of restitution was served).

25 *See In re* Claxton, 239 B.R. 598 (Bankr. N.D. Okla. 1999) (mortgage that bank took on real property after manufactured home had already been installed covered the home as well as the land).

26 *See* § 11.2.3, *infra.*

27 *See* § 11.2.3, *infra.*

28 *See* § 11.2.4, *infra.*

29 *See* § 11.2.5, *infra.*

30 *See* Shoalmire v. U.S. Title of Harrison County, 2010 WL 271302 (Tex. App. Jan. 26, 2010) (describing purchasers' allegation of a failure to disclose that home was a manufactured home and that a security interest against the home itself remained after purchase, despite possible attempts by previous owner to have the home recognized as real property).

on the certificate of title. (Article 9 allows a creditor to file a "fixture filing" in the county land records to perfect a security interest in goods that are or may become fixtures.[31]) But if it is considered personal property, the security interest should be perfected by a notation on the certificate of title if the state issues title for manufactured homes, or, if not, by filing a financing statement.[32] A creditor who has recorded the security interest in the wrong way may not be protected against other claimants.[33]

Bright-line rules created by state statutes that clearly set out how a manufactured home is converted to real property protect secured parties from this uncertainty. A secured party may also seek to protect itself by placing a clause in the contract that the manufactured home will remain personal property regardless of whether it is permanently affixed to real property, unless the secured party consents in writing. Courts have given effect to such clauses, at least in disputes between the parties to the contract.[34] Creditors also often protect themselves by treating a home both as personal property and as a fixture, and perfecting the security interest both through a notation on the title and through a fixture filing in the local land records.[35] To aid lenders, Fannie Mae has assembled a series of letters describing how to convert a manufactured home to real property in each state and to record a mortgage on the land and the home.[36]

11.2.2 *Implications of Treatment of Manufactured Homes As Realty or Personalty*

The determination that a manufactured home is personal or real property can have many implications for both consumers and secured creditors. For issues such as perfection of a security interest, property and sales taxes, exemptions,

31 U.C.C. §§ 9-334, 9-502(b).

32 *See* Mark R. Koontz, *Manufactured Homes Under U.C.C. Revised Article 9: A New Conflict Between Certificates of Title and Financing Statements*, 80 N.C. L. Rev. 1829 (2002).

33 *See, e.g., In re* Oswalt, 318 B.R. 817, 819 (W.D. Mich. 2004) (describing secured creditor's vulnerability before legislative amendments), *aff'd*, 444 F.3d 524 (6th Cir. 2006); *In re* Ritchie, 416 B.R. 638 (B.A.P. 6th Cir. 2009) (lender's security interest in home that was personal property was unperfected and *lis pendens* did not apply leaving lien avoidable by trustee); *In re* Weaver, 69 B.R. 554 (Bankr. W.D. Ky. 1987) (seller's security interest in home that had become a fixture was unperfected where seller did not make a fixture filing); Parsons v. Lender Serv. Inc., 801 P.2d 739, 740–741 (Okla. 1990) (claim of buyer of land has priority over security interest of seller of home where seller did not make fixture filing). *See generally* Mark R. Koontz, *Manufactured Homes Under U.C.C. Revised Article 9: A New Conflict Between Certificates of Title and Financing Statements*, 80 N.C. L. Rev. 1829 (2002) (describing ambiguities and gaps in Article 9's perfection and priority rules for manufactured homes).

A few courts hold that a security interest in a manufactured home must be perfected pursuant to the state's certificate of title law, regardless of whether the home is permanently affixed to land: Hiers v. Bank One, 946 S.W.2d 196 (Ky. Ct. App. 1997) (only means to perfect security interest in manufactured home is by notation on certificate of title, regardless of whether it is permanently affixed to the ground; case was decided before Kentucky enacted manufactured home real property conversion statute); General Elec. Credit Corp. v. Nordmark, 684 P.2d 1 (Or. Ct. App. 1984) (perfection of security interest in manufactured home is by notation on certificate of title, regardless of whether it is permanently affixed to the land; case arose before state adopted title purging law and involved priority dispute between holder of security interest in manufactured home and buyers of land to which it had been attached). *See also In re* Kroskie, 315 F.3d 644 (6th Cir. 2003) (Mich. law) (security interest in manufactured home can be perfected only by notation on title, not mortgage, regardless of permanent attachment to land; decision predates Michigan title-purging law); *In re* Renaud, 302 B.R. 280 (Bankr. E.D. Ark. 2003) (security interest in manufactured home can only be perfected by notation on title, not by recording a mortgage covering the land and the home, even if home is affixed to the land; state title statute has since been amended to create exception when title has been purged).

34 *In re* Thompson, 217 B.R. 375 (B.A.P. 2d Cir. 1998) (giving weight to contract clause that home would remain personal property; home is eligible for cram-down in bankruptcy); Green Tree Credit Corp. v. Thompson (*In re* Thompson), 217 B.R. 375, 378 (B.A.P. 2d Cir. 1998); Homac v. Ft. Wayne Mortgage Co., 577 F. Supp. 1065 (N.D. Ga. 1983) (agreement signed by buyer that manufactured home would remain personalty negates intent to make it part of realty); *In re* Nowlin, 2005 WL 2660377 (E.D. Pa. Oct. 17, 2005) (citing contract clause that home would remain personal property as factor in rejecting creditor's claim that it should be classified as real property for bankruptcy purposes); Lee's Mobile Homes, Inc. v. Grogan, 621 S.W.2d 317 (Mo. Ct. App. 1981) (clause in contract that manufactured home would remain personal property estops buyer from asserting that, because it was installed on permanent foundation, seller could not use replevin to repossess it); Green Tree Fin. Servicing Corp. v. Sutton, 650 N.W.2d 228, 233 (Neb. 2002) (clause will be given effect where rights of third parties are not adversely affected, no statute requires otherwise, and articles are not so completely merged with the realty as to prevent removal without material injury); Pleasant Valley Campground, Inc. v. Rood, 411 A.2d 1104 (N.H. 1980) (giving effect to agreement between parties that manufactured home would be treated as personalty, regardless of whether it was permanently affixed to real estate; contest was between owner of manufactured home and buyer of land at foreclosure sale). *See also* Leader Fed. Bank v. Saunders, 929 P.2d 1343 (Colo. 1997) (buyer who agreed to purge title but did not follow through is estopped from claiming that deed of trust did not convey manufactured home). *But cf.* General Elec. Capital Corp. v. Sohn, 566 So. 2d 841 (Fla. Dist. Ct. App. 1990) (giving no effect to contract's characterization of home as personal property in contest between original secured party and buyer of real estate at tax sale); Parsons v. Lender Service, Inc., 801 P.2d 739 (Okla. Ct. App. 1990) (agreement in contract that manufactured home would remain personal property is not binding on third party).

35 *See* Jacqueline S. Akins, *Fixture Security Interests Under Revised Article 9*, 54 Consumer Fin. L.Q. Rep. 172 (2000).

36 The letters may be found at www.efanniemae.com/sf/guides/ssg/relatedsellinginfo/manufachousing/.

and disclosure requirements, the distinction between real and personal property may be determinative.

The distinction is especially important upon default. Article 9 applies to any transaction that creates a security interest in personal property or fixtures by contract.[37] If a manufactured home is personal property and not a fixture, then it is governed only by Article 9 or other state laws dealing with repossession, not by state foreclosure law.

If the manufactured home is a fixture,[38] then the issue is more complicated. "Fixtures" are defined by the Uniform Commercial Code (UCC) § 9-102(a)(4) as goods that have become so related to particular real property that an interest in them arises under real property law. When an Article 9 security agreement covers goods that have become fixtures, UCC § 9-604(b) allows the creditor to choose between Article 9 remedies and state foreclosure law. Thus, when a manufactured home has become a fixture, the creditor may retake possession of the home, using self-help repossession or a judicial procedure such as replevin if state law makes that procedure available to retake fixtures.[39] Or the creditor may elect to use state foreclosure law. The home may also be subject to foreclosure under a deed of trust or mortgage securing the real property.[40]

The creditor may be unable to use state foreclosure law as a practical matter, however. If the creditor has a security interest in the manufactured home but not a mortgage on the land, foreclosure law may be inapplicable as a matter of state law. It will be a question of state foreclosure law whether a creditor may force the sale of the land if its security interest covers only the manufactured home. If the remedy the secured creditor seeks is removal of the home from the land, the state foreclosure law may not offer this option. Instead, the state foreclosure law may offer only the remedy of selling the real estate, together with any improvements on it, at a foreclosure sale.

Another restriction on the secured creditor's right to take possession of a manufactured home that has become a fixture is that the creditor can remove the home from the land only if its security interest in the home is superior to any mortgage or lien on the land that includes improvements. For example, if a mortgage on the land covers not just the land but all improvements to the land, and the creditor's security interest in the manufactured home is junior to this mortgage, the creditor cannot remove the manufactured home from the land.[41] The fact that the senior mortgage has priority means that if the home and the land are sold upon default, the creditor with the security interest in the manufactured home is limited to any surplus proceeds after the senior mortgage is satisfied. As a result, a creditor who has only a security interest in a manufactured home may be unable to use replevin or self-help repossession if the debtor falls behind on that debt but stays current on a senior mortgage on the land. In addition, if removal of the home damages real property that is owned by someone other than the debtor, or on which someone other than the debtor has a lien, the creditor must reimburse that person for the cost of repair.[42] A fixture filing may create another issue when ownership of the land differs from ownership of the home in that the filing may deter lenders from making loans secured by the land, even if the filing was not authorized by the landowner.[43]

Foreclosure is a more realistic remedy for the secured creditor if it holds a mortgage on the land as well as a security interest in the home. Then the creditor could foreclose on the land and the home together, in which case Article 9 would not apply.[44] In the alternative, Article 9 allows the creditor to proceed under Article 9 against the manufactured home, sell it, and then use state foreclosure law to foreclose on the land separately.[45]

These general rules may be overridden if the state has a statute that specifies a procedure for converting a manufactured home to real property.[46] Some of these statutes specify that, if the home is converted to real property, then foreclosure law or all real estate laws apply. In these states, the creditor would no longer have the option of proceeding under Article 9 to repossess the home. Even in the absence of a conversion statute, some courts hold that a manufactured home is to be treated as real property for all purposes once it is permanently affixed to the land,[47] in which case the creditor's only option may be foreclosure.

There are many cases that address whether a manufactured home has become real property, but almost all involve homestead exemptions, bankruptcy questions, or perfection

37 U.C.C. § 9-109(a).

38 U.C.C. § 9-102(a)(41) defines fixtures as goods that have become so related to particular real property that an interest in them arises under real property law.

39 *See* ATC P'ship v. Town of Windham, 845 A.2d 389 (Conn. 2004) (interpreting statutory replevin procedure not to apply to fixtures).

40 *See* Spencer v. Jameson, 211 P.3d 106 (Idaho 2009) (manufactured home connected to well, septic tank, and utilities was a fixture subject to foreclosure on deeds of trust secured by the real property).

41 U.C.C. § 9-604(c).

42 U.C.C. § 9-604(c). *See* Green Tree Fin. Servicing Corp. v. Sutton, 650 N.W.2d 228 (Neb. 2002).

43 *See* Benizzi v. Bank of Hudson, 855 N.Y.S.2d 764 (N.Y. App. Div. 2008) (denying landowner's summary judgment motion in action seeking have fixture filing held unenforceable).

44 U.C.C. § 9-604(a)(2).

45 U.C.C. § 9-604(a)(1), (b), (c); U.C.C. § 9-604 cmt. 3 ("a security interest in fixtures may be enforced either under real property law or under any of the applicable provisions of Part 6, including sale or other disposition either before or after removal of the fixtures").

46 *See* § 11.2.3, *infra*.

47 *See* Fuqua Homes, Inc. v. Evanston Bldg. & Loan Co., 370 N.E.2d 780 (Ohio Ct. App. 1977) (modular home was converted into real estate and could not be considered a motor vehicle under any provision of law once its two parts were joined and attached to a permanent foundation).

and priority of security interests. Only a few cases have dealt with whether replevin or self-help repossession is precluded once a home has been permanently affixed to the land. In *Lee's Mobile Homes, Inc. v. Grogan*,[48] a debtor argued that a home had become real property, so the creditor could not use replevin to retake it. The court concluded on the facts that the home was still personal property, so did not discuss the question of whether replevin would have been precluded if it had become real property. Similarly, in *Griswell v. Columbus Finance Co.*,[49] a Georgia appellate court found that the debtor's home had not become real property, so rejected the debtor's contention that the state replevin law no longer applied. In *Pokorne Private Capital Group, L.L.C. v. 21st Mortgage Corp.*,[50] self-help repossession was permissible for a home purchased by a dealer and unoccupied. The home had been installed, but not affixed to real property. The court went on to state, however, that had the home been affixed, attempts at self-help repossession would almost certainly have breached the peace.

11.2.3 Manufactured Home Real Property Conversion Statutes

11.2.3.1 Nature and Effect of Manufactured Home Real Property Conversion Statutes

About three-quarters of the states have statutes that set forth a procedure to convert a manufactured home to real property and document that conversion. In states where the method provided by the statute is the only means of converting a manufactured home to real property, the statutes create a bright-line rule: for at least the purposes listed in the statute, and possibly for other purposes as well, public records will show whether the home is real property.

Lenders in these states who want to be able to sell their loans on the secondary market may insist that a home be converted to real property. Fannie Mae, for example, requires a manufactured home to be legally classified as real property, and financing must be secured by a mortgage or deed of trust recorded in the jurisdiction's land records.[51]

The procedure for converting a manufactured home to real property usually involves surrendering the certificate of title or manufacturer's certificate of origin, and filing an affidavit in the local county land records. Typically, the home must be permanently affixed to the land, a concept that is often specifically defined. Some statutes require that the owner of the home must also own the land. Other states also allow a home to be converted to real property if it is permanently affixed to land that the owner is renting, typically requiring that the lease be for a minimum specified period of time. Many such state statutes were created to allow financing of manufactured homes under the former Freddie Mac Leasehold Estate Mortgage Program, under which Freddie Mac would purchase loans on the secondary market that had been made on homes on leased land that were classified as real property. Conversion may be limited to homes that meet certain size criteria.[52]

Conversion statutes have significance in resident-owned communities. If the residents own the park as a cooperative, each homeowner will be renting a lot from the cooperative, so a statute like this may enable them to treat the home as real estate.

Some of the statutes state that once a home is converted to real property, foreclosure law applies. Others achieve the same result by stating that the home, upon conversion, is subject to all laws that apply to real estate.

On the other hand, some conversion statutes say nothing about the implications of the conversion, or state only some effect on the manner in which the home is taxed. The statute may be located among the state's manufactured home statutes, or may be part of the state's motor vehicle, finance, or tax laws. When a statute treats a manufactured home as real property for one purpose, such as taxation, courts are likely to hold that it should be treated as real property for other purposes as well, even if the statute is silent.[53] (Treatment of the home for purposes of a homestead exemption law[54] is distinguishable, however, because of the purpose of those laws to protect debtors and their dependents from destitution and the rule that they are to be liberally construed.[55] Thus, even if a home is treated as personal property for most

48 621 S.W.2d 317 (Mo. Ct. App. 1981).

49 470 S.E.2d 256 (Ga. Ct. App. 1996).

50 2008 WL 963296 (Tex. App. Apr. 10, 2008).

51 Fannie Mae Selling Guide § VII, 102.07.

52 *See, e.g.*, Ohio Rev. Code §§ 3781.06(B)(6)(b), 4503.06, 4505.11.

53 *In re* Cluxton, 327 B.R. 612 (B.A.P. 6th Cir. 2005) (where homeowner followed title purging procedure, home was real estate for purposes of bankruptcy anti-modification rule).

54 *See* § 11.10, *infra*.

55 Green Tree Credit Corp. v. Thompson (*In re* Thompson), 217 B.R. 375 (B.A.P. 2d Cir. 1998) (N.Y. law) (state's inclusion of manufactured homes within homestead exemption does not show intent to classify them as real property for other purposes; home is personal property eligible for cram-down in bankruptcy); Carlson v. Southwest Mobile Homes (*In re* Melvin), 64 B.R. 104 (Bankr. W.D. Mo. 1986) (failure to follow statutory procedure to convert manufactured home to real property does not prevent it from qualifying for homestead exemption; exemption laws are to be liberally construed to preserve shelter for debtors and dependents); Ellis v. Dillon, 345 So. 2d 1241 (La. Ct. App. 1977) (failure to follow statutory procedure for converting manufactured home to real property does not prevent it from qualifying for homestead exemption). *See also In re* Harris, 166 B.R. 163 (Bankr. D. Colo. 1994) (failure to purge title for tax purposes does not prevent court from finding manufactured home to be real property for purposes of exemption statute). *But see In re* White, 287 B.R. 232 (Bankr. E.D. Mo. 2002) (manufactured home did not qualify for homestead exemption where it was not attached to a permanent foundation situated on real estate owned by the owner of the home, as required by statute).

purposes, it may qualify for the homestead exemption because of the liberal construction of homestead exemption laws.)

In states where conversion statutes exist, courts are likely to find that a home continues to be personal property until the statutory procedures are followed. Thus, even if a home is permanently affixed to the land, it may be considered personal property unless the owner has surrendered the title and filed the proper papers to convert it to real property.[56]

Most conversion statutes are carefully written to protect secured parties. Typically the secured party must either release its security interest or accept a mortgage in substitution for the UCC security interest before the state authorities will allow the home to be converted to real property.

In states that use a certificate of title for manufactured homes, conversion statutes generally also prescribe procedures to make sure that the certificate of title is cancelled when the home is converted to real property. Allowing two title documents—the certificate of title and the deed—to coexist would enable an unscrupulous owner to sell the manufactured home twice, assigning the certificate of title to one buyer and conveying a deed to the other.

A state that does not have a title purging statute may still grant requests to cancel a manufactured home's certificate of title. For example, Connecticut formerly issued titles to manufactured homes but no longer does. If a home has a certificate of title, the Department of Motor Vehicles reportedly will grant a request to cancel the title upon a showing that the home is not capable of being operated on a public highway.[57] Other states may have administrative rules allowing cancellation of the title.[58] Even without a title purging statute, a state motor vehicle department may agree to cancel a title if the owner shows that a home no longer meets the jurisdiction's definition of motor vehicle because it has been attached to the land.[59]

A few states specifically forbid title purging. A New York statute provides that the motor vehicle certificate of title for a manufactured home shall not be suspended or revoked because the home has been attached to realty.[60]

11.2.3.2 Listing of State Conversion Statutes

The following states have statutes that specify a procedure for the conversion of a manufactured home to realty for at least some purposes. In the following summaries the terminology of the statutes as to manufactured or mobile homes has been retained.

Alabama: The owner, retail purchaser, or lienholder for original purchaser of a manufactured home not more than twenty years old may apply to cancel the certificate of title or certificate of origin if the home is affixed to real property that the homeowner owns. The ownership of both the home and land must be identical. The owner must submit an application to the state department of revenue, including the certificate of origin or title or a bond in lieu, a release of any liens noted on the title or a bond in lieu, an affidavit executed by all with an ownership interest in the home and realty.[61] If the manufactured home is later detached from the land, the owner must reapply for a new certificate of title.

56 *In re* Nowlin, 321 B.R. 678 (Bankr. E.D. Pa. 2005) (citing fact that owner had not surrendered title as factor in holding that manufactured home was not real property for bankruptcy purposes), *aff'd*, 2005 WL 26660377 (E.D. Pa. Oct. 17, 2005); Beneficial Consumer Discount Co. v. Gerard (*In re* Gerard), 70 B.R. 505 (Bankr. W.D. Pa. 1987) (even if manufactured home is permanently attached to land, rule that security interest is perfected by notation on title continues to apply unless statutory procedure for surrender of title is followed); Leader Fed. Bank v. Saunders, 929 P.2d 1343 (Colo. 1997) (title purging law preempts common law regarding fixtures and is exclusive means of converting manufactured home to real estate; however, here buyer who agreed to purge title but did not follow through is estopped from claiming that deed of trust did not convey manufactured home); ENT Fed. Credit Union v. Chrysler First Fin. Servs. Corp., 826 P.2d 430 (Colo. Ct. App. 1992) (citing fact that owner had not surrendered title in support of conclusion that notation on certificate of title was sufficient to perfect security interest, without fixture filing); Notoco Indus., Inc. v. Powell, 835 So. 2d 835 (La. Ct. App. 2002); Mathieu v. Nettles, 383 So. 2d 1337 (La. Ct. App. 1980); Lee's Mobile Homes, Inc. v. Grogan, 621 S.W.2d 317 (Mo. Ct. App. 1981) (rejecting buyer's argument that seller could not use replevin to recover manufactured home; buyer had agreed it would remain personal property and had not followed title purging procedure); Green Tree Fin. Servicing Corp. v. Sutton, 650 N.W.2d 228 (Neb. 2002) (in priority dispute between financer of manufactured home and third party buyer of land, perfection must be on certificate of title unless owner has followed former statutory procedure to surrender title); Bankamerica Hous. Servs. v. P.D.N. & Assocs., 977 P.2d 396 (Or. Ct. App. 1999). *But see In re* Oswalt, 318 B.R. 817, 819 (W.D. Mich. 2004) (filing of mortgage covering land and manufactured home in county registry of deeds is sufficient to perfect security interest even if title-purging procedure was not followed), *aff'd*, 444 F.3d 524 (6th Cir. 2006); *In re* Sasinouski, 52 B.R. 67 (Bankr. D. Idaho 1985) (even though homeowner did not comply with Idaho title purging statute, land and manufactured home were both encumbered by the deed of trust on land, where deed of trust did not explicitly exclude manufactured home and lender relied upon appraisal that included both the home and land when making the loan); Ford v. Venard, 340 N.W.2d 270 (Iowa 1983) (holding that Iowa's title purging statute was not intended to be the exclusive method to convert manufactured home to real property and that common law methods of converting personal to real property remained).

57 *See* Connecticut information at www.efanniemae.com/sf/guides/ssg/relatedsellinginfo/manufachousing/.

The same site reports that Alaska, Delaware, Illinois, New Jersey, and North Dakota also have informal procedures for surrendering manufactured home titles.

58 *See, e.g.*, N.M. Code R. § 18.19.3.16.

59 *Cf. In re* Wester, 229 B.R. 348 (Bankr. E.D.N.C. 1998) (manufactured home that was permanently affixed to real estate before security interest was granted was not "intended to be operated upon . . . highway" so state law requiring security interest to be perfected by notation on title did not apply).

60 N.Y. Veh. & Traffic Law § 2124.

61 Ala. Code § 32-20-20(b) (effective Jan. 1, 2010).

Manufactured homes more than twenty model years old shall not be required to obtain a certificate of title.[62] This statute is part of the state home certificate of title act and does not state whether the home is treated as real property for foreclosure or other purposes after the title is cancelled.

Arizona: A manufactured home that is permanently affixed, i.e., installed on real property that the homeowner owns,[63] and for which an affidavit of affixture has been recorded, shall be assessed as real property for tax purposes.[64] A manufactured home that is located in a manufactured home park will, along with the leasehold interest, be treated as real property if the owner files an affidavit of affixture with the county recorder and: (1) the home has been installed on the real property with all wheels and axles removed in compliance with local and state installation standards; (2) the owner of the home has entered into a lease of at least twenty years for the lot and the lease specifically permits the recording of an affidavit of affixture; and (3) a memorandum of lease, signed by both landlord and tenant, is recorded that lists specified information.[65] Regardless of whether the home is located in a park, the affidavit of affixture must identify the holder of any security interest in the home that is not terminated by the consent of the secured party, and any such interest survives recordation of the affidavit.[66] When an affidavit of affixture is recorded, the owner must surrender the certificate of title.[67] A lien on a manufactured home for which an affidavit of affixture has been recorded may be perfected either in the manner provided by law for real property or in the manner provided for fixtures.[68]

Arkansas: If a mobile or manufactured home is to be affixed to real estate, the title may be surrendered to the state department of finance and administration for cancellation. After cancellation, a security interest, lien, or encumbrance may be obtained in the same manner as for real property.[69]

California: If a manufactured or mobile home is affixed to a permanent foundation in compliance with state standards,[70] default and sale are governed by California's mortgage foreclosure laws.[71] The homeowner must own the land or be leasing it with a term of at least thirty-five years.[72] Any lienholders must consent to the attachment of the home to the land.[73] The owner must surrender the certificate of title, and a statement that the home has been affixed to real property is to be recorded in the county land records.[74] Once these procedures are completed, the home is deemed a fixture and an improvement to the real property.[75] Default and sale are also governed by the state mortgage foreclosure laws if the creditor has a security interest in the land as well as the home.[76]

Colorado: The owner of a manufactured home, once it is permanently affixed to the ground so that it can no longer be drawn over the public highways, shall file a certificate of permanent location that contains a statement of relinquishment by all secured lenders to release any interest in the home. Homeowners who do not own the land where it is sited must also release any interest in the home unless the property is subject to a lease of at least ten years.[77] Since a homeowner would generally not wish to give up ownership of the home, it is unlikely that homeowners without long-term leases would wish to convert their home to real property. The homeowner then surrenders the certificate of title and applies for purging of the title. The home then becomes real property, and subject to all laws that would apply to real estate.[78] The purchaser of a new manufactured home may use the same procedure to convert the home to real property without a title ever being issued for the home, and instead relying upon the manufacturer's certificate or statement of origin.[79] Although the statute permits conversion of homes placed on land pursuant to long-term leases, this may be problematic as it appears that after conversion the home is taxed as part of the land upon which it sits and so would hold the landowner responsible for taxes for a home he does not own.[80] Upon the filing of a certificate of removal, the statute permits issuance of a new title if the home is removed.[81]

Connecticut: Title conveyances to manufactured homes are recorded on the land records with the town clerk's office of municipality.[82] While the document conveying title to homes on leased land must recite information about the land or park where the home is located,[83] it appears to allow conveyance of homes located upon land owned by the homeowner by deed, and such home would become part of the real property.[84]

62 Ala. Code § 32-20-20(a) (effective Jan. 1, 2010).
63 Ariz. Rev. Stat. Ann. § 42-15201(2).
64 Ariz. Rev. Stat. Ann. § 42-15202.
65 Ariz. Rev. Stat. Ann. § 33-1501. A home recorded as real property under this statute is to be assessed as personal property for tax purposes, however. Ariz. Rev. Stat. § 42-15203(K).
66 Ariz. Rev. Stat. Ann. §§ 33-1501, 42-15203.
67 Ariz. Rev. Stat. Ann. § 28-2063.
68 Ariz. Rev. Stat. Ann. § 42-15205.
69 Ark. Code Ann. §§ 27-14-807, 27-14-1603.
70 Cal. Health & Safety Code § 18551 (West) (includes construction standards, plan approval, etc.).
71 Cal. Health & Safety Code § 18039.1 (West).
72 Cal. Health & Safety Code § 18551(a)(1)(A) (West).
73 Cal. Health & Safety Code § 18551(a)(1)(B) (West).
74 Cal. Health & Safety Code § 18551(a)(2), (3) (West).
75 Cal. Health & Safety Code § 18551(a)(4) (West).
76 Cal. Health & Safety Code § 18039.1 (West).
77 Colo. Rev. Stat. Ann. § 38-29-202 (2)(m).
78 Colo. Rev. Stat. Ann. § 38-29-118 (2).
79 Colo. Rev. Stat. Ann. § 38-29-114.
80 Colo. Rev. Stat. Ann. § 38-29-118 (2).
81 Colo. Rev. Stat. Ann. § 38-29-203.
82 Conn. Gen. Stat. § 21-67a.
83 Conn. Gen. Stat. § 21-67a(c).
84 Connecticut information at www.efanniemae.com/sf/guides/ssg/relatedsellinginfo/manufachousing/.

Florida: The owner of a manufactured home permanently affixed to land owned by the homeowner or in which the homeowner has a recorded leasehold interest of at least thirty years, may retire title to the home.[85] Before title is retired the following documents must be recorded in the official records of the clerk of court in the county where the home is located: (1) the original title to the home, including a statement by any recorded lienholder that the security interest has been released or will be upon retirement of title; (2) legal description of the real property, and if the homeowner's interest in the property is a leasehold, a copy of the lease; and (3) a sworn statement of the owner that he or she owns the home and the real property or leasehold interest. After the title is retired, the home is only conveyed by deed or real estate contract along with the property to which it is affixed.[86] A new title may be obtained if the home is to be removed from the land.[87]

Another Florida statute provides that if the manufactured home was classified as personal property by a seller or lender at the time a security interest in the home was granted, it shall continue to be so classified for all purposes relating to the loan and security agreement.[88]

Georgia: A manufactured or mobile home is personal property unless: (1) the home is or is to be permanently affixed to real property and one or more persons with an ownership interest in the home also has an ownership interest in the real property; and (2) the owner and all holders of security interests sign and file a certificate of permanent location with the clerk of the local superior court and the state revenue commissioner. Once such a certificate has been properly filed, the home is a part of the real property for all legal purposes, including foreclosure.[89]

Idaho: A manufactured home may constitute real property if the home is permanently affixed to a foundation and the running gear is removed. The home must be sited on land that the homeowner owns, is purchasing, or, if the home is being financed in accordance with a federal housing agency's guidelines, is leasing. The homeowner must record with the county recorder a statement of intent to declare the home as real property, and must turn over the certificate of title. Upon exercise of this option, lending institutions may treat the home as real property.[90] Physical removal of the home from the land is then prohibited unless the owner applies to have a new certificate of title issued.[91]

Indiana: If a manufactured home has been attached to real estate by a permanent foundation, the owner may submit the certificate of title and an affidavit to the bureau of motor vehicles.[92] The county recorder is then to record the affidavit in the county real estate records,[93] and the home is thereafter deemed to be an improvement to the real estate.[94]

Iowa: Iowa has separate provisions depending on whether the home is in a manufactured home community. If the home is located in a manufactured home community and installed on a permanent foundation, the owner may surrender the certificate of title to the county treasurer for the purpose of assuring eligibility for federal mortgage lending programs. The title cannot be surrendered if there are unreleased security interests. A foreclosure action on a manufactured home whose title has been surrendered must be conducted as a real estate foreclosure. The owner may reapply for a certificate of title at a later date.[95]

If the home is not in a manufactured home community, it must be placed on a permanent foundation. If a security interest is noted on the title, the homeowner must tender a mortgage on the real estate to the creditor, or the secured party must consent to the conversion, in which case the secured party retains a security interest in the home that is separate from any interest in the land. This statute is a tax law that does not state whether foreclosure law applies after the home is converted to real property.[96]

Kansas: Manufactured homes are not subject to the laws, rules, and regulations applicable to vehicles, including titling and registration requirements and dealer licensing.[97] Rather, after obtaining a manufactured home the new owner is required to get a manufactured home certificate of title.[98] Whenever a manufactured or mobile home is permanently affixed to real property by placement upon a permanent foundation that cannot be removed intact from the land, the owner may apply to have the certificate of title eliminated. The application must include an affidavit signed by the owner and all parties having a security interest in the home. If the application is approved, it is filed in the county registry of deeds. Once the certificate of title is eliminated, ownership of the home is an incident of ownership of the

85 Fla. Stat. § 319.261.
86 Fla. Stat. § 319.261(5).
87 Fla. Stat. § 319.261(6).
88 Fla. Stat. § 320.015.
89 Ga. Code Ann. §§ 8-2-180 to 8-2-183.
90 Idaho Code Ann. §§ 63-304(2), 63-305(1). *Cf. In re* Sasinouski, 52 B.R. 67 (Bankr. Idaho 1985) (even though homeowner did not comply with Idaho title purging statute, land and manufactured home were both encumbered by the deed of trust on land, where deed of trust did not explicitly exclude manufactured home and lender relied upon appraisal that included both the home and land when making the loan); Spencer v. Jameson, 211 P.3d 106 (Idaho 2009) (manufactured home connected to well, septic tank and utilities was a fixture subject to foreclosure on deeds of trust secured by the real property).
91 Idaho Code Ann. § 63-305.
92 Ind. Code § 9-17-6-15.1.
93 Ind. Code § 9-17-6-15.3.
94 Ind. Code § 9-17-6-15.5.
95 Iowa Code § 435.26A.
96 Iowa Code § 435.26. *See also* Ford v. Venard, 340 N.W.2d 270 (Iowa 1983) (holding that Iowa's title purging statute was not intended to be the exclusive method to convert manufactured home to real property and that common-law methods of converting personal to real property remained).
97 Kan. Stat. Ann. § 58-4203.
98 Kan. Stat. Ann. § 58-4204.

land under governing real property law, and the home is subject to a lien only as part of the real property.[99]

Kentucky: When a manufactured home is or is to be permanently affixed to real estate, the owner may file an affidavit of conversion with and surrender the certificate of title to the county clerk, who then is to record the affidavit. The home is then deemed an improvement of the real estate.[100]

Louisiana: A manufactured home is considered immovable when a document describing the home and the land is recorded in the local parish records. The document must include a declaration by the owner of the home and any holder of a security interest in the home that the home is to remain permanently attached to the land. Once this document is recorded, the home is subject to all laws concerning immovable property. After recordation the owner or the owner's agent must file a certified copy with the Secretary of the Department of Public Safety and Corrections who creates an Internet accessible searchable database providing a public record with: the name of the owner of the manufactured home; the date of recording of the act of immobilization; the parish where the act is recorded; the year of manufacture; the name of the manufacturer; the dimensions and the vehicle identification number or numbers of the manufactured home; and the date of the secretary's filing of a copy of the act of immobilization.[101] However, the rights of the holder of a validly recorded chattel mortgage or a security interest perfected under Article 9 of the UCC are unaffected.[102] The owner may reverse the process so that the home is once again treated as movable property by filing another statement of intent and applying for a new certificate of title.[103]

Michigan: The owner of a manufactured home that is affixed to real property in which the owner has an ownership interest may apply for cancellation of the certificate of title. To be considered affixed to the real property, the wheels, towing hitches and running gear must be removed and the home must be attached to a foundation or other support system. The application must include the written consent of each holder of a security interest to termination of the security interest and cancellation of the title. Once the title is cancelled, the manufactured home is considered part of the realty and a lienholder may perfect a new security interest or lien on the manufactured home only in the manner prescribed by the real estate laws.[104] The owner may reapply for a certificate of title at a later date.[105]

In 2003, the Sixth Circuit Court of Appeals held that security interests in manufactured homes in Michigan could be perfected only by recording them on the title, not by recording a traditional mortgage.[106] The legislature responded by amending its titling laws to recognize both methods.[107] It amended the statute again two years later to make this rule retroactive.[108]

Minnesota: When a manufactured home is affixed to real property, and financed by a mortgage on the real property, the owner of the home must surrender the certificate of title to the registrar of motor vehicles for cancellation. The department then is to issue a notice of surrender, which may be recorded in the county recorder's office or the registrar of titles. The statute provides that the manufactured home is then deemed to be an improvement to real property. The department may not cancel the certificate of title, however, if an unsatisfied security interest is noted on it.[109]

Mississippi: A manufactured homeowner or mobile home owner who also owns the land on which the home is located has the option of declaring whether the home is to be classified as personal or real property. To be classified as real property, the wheels and axles must be removed and the home must be anchored and blocked in accord with rules adopted by the commissioner of insurance.[110] A certificate that the home has been classified as real property is then recorded in the county land records,[111] and the home's certificate of title may be sent to the state tax commission for cancellation.[112] The home is then treated as real property

99 Kan. Stat. Ann. § 58-4214.

100 Ky. Rev. Stat. Ann. § 186A.297 (West).

101 La. Rev. Stat. Ann. § 9:1149.4. *See also* La. Rev. Stat. Ann. § 9:1146.3.

102 La. Rev. Stat. Ann. § 9:1149.4.

103 La. Rev. Stat. Ann. § 9:1149.6.

104 Mich. Comp. Laws Ann. § 125.2330i(5) (West).

105 Mich. Comp. Laws Ann. § 125.2330i (West).

106 Boyd v. Chase Manhattan Mortgage Corp. (*In re* Kroskie), 315 F.3d 644 (6th Cir. 2003).

107 Mich. Pub. Act No. 44, S.B. 425 (2003), *enacting* Mich. Comp. Laws Ann. § 125.2330i (West).

108 Mich. Comp. Laws Ann. § 125.2330i (West), *as amended by* Mich. Pub. Act No. 162, H.B. 4484 (2005). *See In re* Ozwalt, 444 F.3d 524 (6th Cir. 2006) (interpreting statute to allow security interest in manufactured home to be perfected by filling of mortgage with county registry, without notation on title, even when transaction occurred before statutory amendments); *In re* Hoggard, 330 B.R. 595, 605 (Bankr. W.D. Mich. 2005) (concluding that 2003 legislation overruled *Kroskie*; also finding security interest in home protected by Revised Article 9's priority rules); Mortgage Elec. Registration Sys. v. Pickrell, 721 N.W.2d 276 (Mich. Ct. App. 2006) (in light of 2005 statutory amendment, creditor has option of perfecting security interest in manufactured home either under the Act or under real estate law, even for home that was affixed to real estate before earlier amendments in 2003). *But cf. In re* Gregory, 316 B.R. 82 (Bankr. W.D. Mich. 2004) (interpreting title purging statute not to have retroactive effect, a conclusion rejected by Sixth Circuit in *In re Ozwalt*, but finding security interest in home protected against bankruptcy trustee's strong-arm power because of Revised Article 9's changes to priority rules).

109 Minn. Stat. § 168A.141. *See also* Minn. Stat. § 273.125 (standards for taxing manufactured homes as real property).

110 Miss. Code Ann. § 27-53-15.

111 *Id. See also* Opinion Miss. Att'y Gen., Miller, No. 2005-0131, 2005 WL 1220419 (Miss. Att'y Gen. Apr. 8, 2005).

112 Miss. Code Ann. § 63-21-30.

for purposes of *ad valorem* taxation, and a security interest in the home and land may be obtained through the use of a mortgage or deed of trust.[113]

Missouri: The owner of a manufactured home may convert it to real property by attaching it to a permanent foundation on real property that the owner of the home owns, and removing or modifying the transportation apparatus so that it is impractical to reconvert it to be readily movable.[114] Unlike the other statutes summarized in this subsection, this statute does not provide for surrender of the title or recordation of a document in the county land records.

Montana: A manufactured home is considered an improvement to real property if the running gear is removed, the home is attached to a permanent foundation on land that is owned or being purchased by the owner of the home (or that is placed on the land with the permission of the landowner), and a statement of intent declaring the manufactured home as an improvement to real property is recorded with the county. The statement of intent must include, *inter alia*, a description of any security interests in the home and approval from all lienholders to eliminate the certificate of title. After these steps are completed, the manufactured home may not be removed from the land unless the owner files a statement of reversal of this declaration. A manufactured home that has been declared an improvement to real property must be treated by lending institutions in the same manner as any other improvement to real property.[115]

Nebraska: The title for a mobile or manufactured home may be canceled if it is affixed to real property in which the owner of the home has any ownership interest. The statute defines ownership interest as fee simple interest, or an interest as a lessee that continues for at least twenty years after the required affidavit. The title is surrendered for cancellation to the county clerk or designated official where the title is issued or to the Department of Motor Vehicles if title is issued by the department. Along with the title to be surrendered an affidavit of affixture on a form provided by the department must be submitted. The form requires among other things, the names and addresses of all owners of the home, a description of the home, the legal description of the real property, a statement that the home is affixed, and the written consent of each lien holder to release its lien and cancel the title. After the title is canceled and the affidavit recorded, the home is treated as part of the real property.[116] The statute also provides a method for returning the home to the status of personal property.[117] For homes affixed to real estate for which a certificate of title was not issued before it was affixed, the homeowner may apply for a certificate of title for surrender and cancellation.[118]

Nevada: A mobile or manufactured home is eligible to become real property if it becomes permanently affixed to land. The owner of the home must either own the land or, if the home is being financed in accordance with the guidelines of a federal housing program, lease it. The owner must record an affidavit of conversion in the county recorder's office, deliver a copy of the affidavit and all documents relating to the home to the manufactured housing division of the state department of business and industry, and pay the current year's personal property tax.[119] (But homes that are sited on lots outside manufactured home parks in accordance with local zoning laws are automatically recorded as real property without the need for an affidavit.[120]) Once the home is converted to real property, it is deemed to be a fixture and an improvement to the real property.[121]

New Hampshire: A manufactured home placed on a site not owned by the homeowner and connected to utilities shall be deemed real estate for the purposes of transfer and shall be subject to attachment, liens, foreclosure, and execution in the same manner as real estate.[122] However, security interests in manufactured housing may also be created and perfected under the UCC as adopted by New Hampshire.[123] The statute does not address homes placed on land owned by the homeowner. Owners of manufactured homes in this situation must rely upon common law to determine if the home becomes real property. New Hampshire also has a statute which allows any lending institution to treat a manufactured home the same as realty for the purposes of securing loans to finance the home. When a lending institution exercises this option, no certificate of title is required, and all of the provisions of real estate law, including conveyances, deeds, and foreclosure, apply to the home. The home must be placed on a foundation or slab and hooked up to all

113 Miss. Code Ann. § 27-53-15.

114 Mo. Rev. Stat. §§ 700.111, 700.010(5) (definition of "manufactured home" as one that is, *inter alia*, readily movable). *See In re* Estate of Parker, 25 S.W.3d 611 (Mo. Ct. App. 2000) (manufactured home not converted to real property when the home was held jointly by married couple and placed on land held by only by one spouse as it was not placed on land held by the owner of the home). *See also* Citizens Nat'l Bank v. Maries Cty. Bank, 244 S.W.3d 266 (Mo. Ct. App. 2008) (despite the fact that the home had been affixed to the consumer's real estate, consumer not entitled to receive manufacturer's statement of origin from floor plan financer that had a perfected security interest in dealer's inventory, when floor plan financer was not paid by dealer).

115 Mont. Code Ann. § 15-1-116.

116 Neb. Rev. Stat. § 60-169.

117 Neb. Rev. Stat. § 60-169.

118 Neb. Rev. Stat. § 60-137.

119 Nev. Rev. Stat. § 361.244. *See In re* Colver, 13 B.R. 521 (Bankr. D. Nev. 1981) (manufactured home placed on land owned by owner of home with its wheels removed remained personal property in absence of compliance with statute and when lender stated in security instrument that home would remain person property over the life of the loan).

120 Nev. Rev. Stat. §§ 278.02095, 361.244(5).

121 Nev. Rev. Stat. § 361.244(3).

122 N.H. Rev. Stat. Ann. § 477:44. *See also* N.H. Rev. Stat. Ann. § 80:18-a (defining "mortgage" for tax collection purposes to include security interests in manufactured housing created and perfected under N.H. Rev. Stat. Ann. § 477:44).

123 N.H. Rev. Stat. Ann. § 477:44 IV.

conventional and necessary utility systems and must be intended to be used as a permanent dwelling unit.[124]

New Jersey: New Jersey requires that all manufactured homes not taxed as real property must have certificates of ownership (titles) issued by the Director of the Division of Motor Vehicles.[125] A manufactured home is taxed as real property when it is affixed to the land by a permanent foundation, or if it is affixed by a nonpermanent foundation and connected to utility systems so as to render it habitable on a permanent basis.[126] However, a manufactured home installed in a park is not taxed as real property.[127] When a mobile or manufactured home is relocated from a park to land which the owner of the home has an interest in or title to, the owner must file a notice with the Director of the Division of Motor Vehicles at least ten days before the move. If the director accepts the notice as complete, the certificate of ownership is canceled on the date of relocation.[128]

North Carolina: A manufactured home qualifies as real property if it is a residential structure; the moving hitch, wheels, and axle have been removed; and the owner either owns the land on which it is located or has a lease of at least twenty years that expressly provides for disposition of the manufactured home upon termination of the lease.[129] The owner of such a home may have the certificate of title cancelled by submitting it, along with an affidavit, to the division of motor vehicles.[130] If the certificate of title shows a security interest that has not been released, the division may not cancel the title without the written consent of all secured parties. The affidavit is then to be filed in the county registry of deeds. Once the certificate of title is cancelled and the affidavit is recorded, the manufactured home becomes an improvement to real property and any lien on the home shall be perfected and given priority in the manner provided for real property liens.[131] An owner who wishes to separate the home from the land after the title has been cancelled can apply for a new certificate of title.

Ohio: To be taxed as real property, a manufactured or mobile home must be affixed to a permanent foundation and located on land that the owner of the home owns.[132] The owner of a home that will be taxed as real property must surrender the certificate of title to the county auditor.[133] The owner must either satisfy any liens on the home, or, with the lienholder's consent, give the lienholder a mortgage on the home and land. Once surrendered, the title is to be deactivated, but it can be reactivated upon application by the owner. These statutes do not state what effect the deactivation of the title has outside the context of taxation, but a bankruptcy case holds that if a home was converted to real property through this procedure for taxation purposes it is also real property for purposes of bankruptcy law.[134]

Oregon: The owner of a manufactured structure, or the dealer selling it, may apply to the county assessor to have the structure recorded in the county deed records. The owner must either own the land on which the structure is located, or hold a recorded lease of twenty years or more that specifically permits the structure to be recorded in the county deed records. The owner must turn over any ownership document for cancellation. The deed records must list any unreleased security interest in the manufactured structure. Once recorded in the deed records, the manufactured structure is subject to the same provisions of law applicable to any other building, housing, or structure on the land, and may be sold separately from the land or leasehold estate only if the owner applies to have it removed from the deed records.[135]

Pennsylvania: Upon application, the department of transportation may cancel a certificate of title for a manufactured home that is affixed to real property.[136] The home must be permanently mounted on a foundation.[137] The owner must complete a form and return it, along with the title, to the department of transportation.[138] If a lien appears on the certificate of title, the title will not be cancelled until the homeowner submits satisfactory evidence that the lien has been recorded against the land.[139] After cancellation, the ownership interest in the manufactured home, together with all liens and encumbrances on it, is transferred to and encumbers the real property.[140]

South Carolina: The owner of a manufactured home may affix the home to real property by installing it in accordance with the state installation standards, removing the wheels, axles, and towing hitch, and filing an affidavit for retirement of title.[141] The owner of the home must either own the land on which it is located or have a leasehold estate of thirty-five years or more in the land. The local register of deeds or

124 N.H. Rev. Stat. Ann. § 384:16-d.
125 N.J. Stat. Ann. §§ 39:10-2, 39:10-6 (West).
126 N.J. Stat. Ann. § 54:4-1.5 (West).
127 N.J. Stat. Ann. § 54:4-1.5 (West).
128 N.J. Stat. Ann. §§ 39:10-2, 39:10-11.1 (West).
129 N.C. Gen. Stat. § 105-273(13).
130 N.C. Gen. Stat. § 20-109.2.
131 N.C. Gen. Stat. §§ 47-20.6, 47-20.7.
132 Ohio Rev. Code Ann. § 4503.06(B)(1), (2) (West).
133 Ohio Rev. Code Ann. § 4505.11 (West).

134 *In re* Cluxton, 327 B.R. 612 (B.A.P. 6th Cir. 2005). *See also In re* Davis, 386 B.R. 182 (B.A.P. 6th Cir. 2008) (for the purpose of determining if home is real property under bankruptcy law, home may be converted by statutory procedure or a traditional fixture analysis); Benner v. Hammond, 673 N.E.2d 205 (Ohio Ct. App. 1996) (holding that home that had title purged under revenue statute and was considered real property under the owner's mortgage was not a "trailer" for the purposes of a restrictive covenant).
135 Or. Rev. Stat. § 446.626. *See also* Or. Rev. Stat. § 446.611 (means of perfecting security interest in manufactured home that still has an ownership document).
136 75 Pa. Cons. Stat. § 1140.
137 Pa. Code tit. 67, § 401.5(a).
138 *Id.*
139 Pa. Code tit. 67, § 401.5(b).
140 75 Pa. Cons. Stat. § 1140.
141 S.C. Code § 56-19-510. *See also* S.C. Code § 56-19-500(1).

clerk of court must then record the affidavit as if it were a deed to real property. Upon completion of this process, the home is to be treated as real property for all purposes except condemnation.[142] The title certificate may be cancelled by presenting it to the division, along with a clocked and stamped copy of the affidavit.[143] Any party listed on the title certificate as having a security interest in the home must either lease the lien or consent to the cancellation of the title.[144] Once a manufactured home has been converted to real property in this manner, a manufactured home severance affidavit must be filed before it can be severed from the land.

South Dakota: If a mobile or manufactured home is fixed to real property, and the owner of the home also owns the land, the owner may request that the title to the home be surrendered.[145] If the owner wants to remove the home from the real property at a later time, the owner may apply to have a title reissued.[146] These statutes are part of the state motor vehicle titling laws and do not state the effect of surrendering the title.

Tennessee: If a manufactured home is affixed to real property, and the ownership of the home is identical to the ownership of the land, the owner may surrender the title to the state department of safety. The owner must submit an affidavit of affixation that, *inter alia*, certifies that all permits required by applicable governmental authorities have been obtained, the foundation system complies with the law and with the manufacturer's specifications, and the wheels and axles have been removed. All lienholders must have released their liens on the home. If the affidavit complies with all the statutory requirements, the county register of deeds is to record it. The home is then subject to taxation as an improvement to the land, but the statute does not specify the effect on foreclosure.[147]

Texas: A manufactured home can be treated as real property, if it is attached to land that the owner of the home owns, or which the owner is leasing under a long-term lease as defined by the state department of housing and community affairs.[148] To be attached to land it must be installed in compliance with state rules and connected to a utility.[149] The owner must file an application for a statement of ownership and location with the department. In addition, each lienholder must either release the lien or give written consent to the conversion of the home to real property.[150] Within sixty days after the department issues a statement of ownership, the owner must file a certified copy in the real property records of the county in which the home is located and notify the department and the tax assessor-collector that the certified copy has been filed.[151] The home is then considered real property for all purposes.[152]

Another Texas statute provides that, if a consumer buys real property and a manufactured home at the same time, and certain other conditions are met, the creditor may elect to treat the home as if it were residential real property for all purposes in connection with the credit transaction.[153] If the creditor so elects, and discloses this election conspicuously to the consumer, then the transaction is considered to be a residential real property transaction for all purposes.[154] Bankruptcy courts seeking to determine if a home is real or personal property have looked only to the statutory conversion process to the exclusion of any general fixture analysis.[155]

Utah: A manufactured or mobile home is considered an improvement to real property if the owner also owns the land to which it is permanently affixed, or leases the land and is financing the home in accordance with federal housing agency guidelines. The owner must surrender the title and complete an affidavit that, *inter alia*, identifies any security interests in the home. The affidavit and the receipt for the surrender of the title are then recorded by the county recorder. The owner may acquire a new title upon removing the manufactured home from the land. Since this statute is part of the state mortgage lending and servicing act, it is likely that it will govern whether foreclosure is the appropriate way for the lender to proceed in the event of default.[156]

Vermont: If a manufactured home is financed while the home is permanently sited in a manner intended for continuous residential occupancy by the owner on land owned by the owner of the home, it shall be financed as a residence.[157] Otherwise a manufactured home may be financed under Vt. Stat. Ann. tit. 9, § 41a(b)(4) or Vt. Stat. Ann. tit. 9, pt. 3, ch. 59, both of which regulate chattel loans.

Virginia: The owner of a manufactured home or house trailer that exceeds the size permitted for highway travel must apply for a title within thirty days after purchase. Once the wheels and other equipment that made the home mobile are removed and the home has been attached to realty, then

142 S.C. Code § 56-19-510.
143 S.C. Code § 56-19-520.
144 *Id.*
145 S.D. Codified Laws § 32-3-3.2.
146 S.D. Codified Laws § 32-3-3.3.
147 Tenn. Code Ann. § 55-3-138. *See also* Tenn. Code Ann. § 55-3-138 (procedure for reapplying for new certificate).
148 Tex. Occ. Code Ann. § 1201.2055 (Vernon).
149 Tex. Occ. Code Ann. § 1201.003(2-a) (Vernon).
150 Tex. Occ. Code Ann. § 1201.2075 (Vernon). *See* Pokorne Private Capital Group, L.L.C. v. 21st Mortgage Corp., 2008 WL 963296 (Tex. App. Apr. 10, 2008) (application for statement of ownership and location was defective when application was filed by previous owner after transfer of home and failed to note existing lien).
151 Tex. Occ. Code Ann. § 1201.2055 (Vernon).
152 *Id. See also* Tex. Prop. Code Ann. § 2.001 (Vernon).
153 Tex. Fin. Code Ann. § 347.455 (Vernon).
154 *Id.*
155 *See, e.g., In re* Lara, 2008 WL 961892 (Bankr. S.D. Tex. Apr. 8, 2008).
156 Utah Code Ann. § 70D-1-20. *See also* Utah Code Ann. § 41-1a-503.
157 Vt. Stat. Ann. tit. 9, § 2603 (b).

the owner may return the title to the department of motor vehicles for cancellation. The home then may be transferred only as real estate is transferred. Any security interest perfected on the title continues despite the cancellation of the title.[158] A bankruptcy court has held that the determination of whether a manufactured home is real or personal property must be made on a case-by-case basis and an owner's failure to comply with the statute, while it might be indicative of the owner's intent that home remain personal property, is not conclusive.[159]

Washington: The owner of a manufactured home that is affixed to land (i.e., installed in accordance with state installation standards[160]) may apply to have the title eliminated. The owner of the home must also own the land on which it is sited, have a lease of thirty-five years or more for the land, or be purchasing the land under a real estate contract.[161] The owner must submit the title and an application, which must identify any security interests, to the department of licensing for approval.[162] After approval, the title is to be cancelled and the approved application is to be recorded in the county real property records.[163] The statute provides that the manufactured home is then to be treated as real property as if it were a site-built structure,[164] except for purposes of taxation.[165] If the title has not been eliminated, the home is not real property.[166] The statute provides a procedure to obtain a new title if the home is to be removed from the land.[167]

West Virginia: The commissioner of motor vehicles may cancel a certificate of title for a mobile or manufactured home that is affixed to real property that the homeowner owns.[168] The owner must submit an application and the certificate of title. The cancellation certificate is then to be recorded in the county deed records. Upon recordation, the statute provides that the home is to be treated for all purposes as an appurtenance to the real estate to which it is affixed.[169]

Wisconsin: The owner of a manufactured home must obtain a certificate of title,[170] unless the owner is not a resident of Wisconsin[171] or the owner intends to make the home a fixture to land in which the homeowner has an ownership or leasehold interest.[172] The leasehold interest must be subject to Wisconsin's real property statutes which exclude leases for a term limited to one year or less.[173]

Wyoming: If a manufactured home is installed on a permanent foundation and is taxable as real property,[174] and all liens have been paid, the certificate of title is to be surrendered to and cancelled by the county clerk.[175]

11.2.4 State Tax Statutes

Many states have statutes that set forth criteria for treating a manufactured home as real property as part of their tax laws.[176] These statutes typically do not require surrender of

158 Va. Code Ann. § 46.2-653.

159 *In re* Banks, 259 B.R. 848 (Bankr. E.D. Va. 2001).

160 Wash. Rev. Code § 65.20.020.

161 Wash. Rev. Code §§ 65.20.020, 65.20.040.

162 Wash. Rev. Code § 65.20.040.

163 Wash. Rev. Code § 65.20.050.

164 *Id. See also* Wash. Rev. Code §§ 65.20.030, 65.20.060 (manufactured home whose title has been eliminated may be conveyed only by deed or real estate contract).

165 Wash. Rev. Code § 65.20.910.

166 Wash. Rev. Code § 65.20.030.

167 Wash. Rev. Code § 65.20.070.

168 W. Va. Code § 17A-3-12b.

169 *Id. See also* W. Va. Code § 15-5-12 (tax statute providing that a manufactured home sited on land owned by someone other than the homeowner is classified as personal property whether or not it is permanently affixed to the land, unless the certificate of title has been cancelled).

170 Wis. Stat. § 101.9203 (1).

171 Wis. Stat. § 101.9203 (3).

172 Wis. Stat. § 101.9203 (4).

173 Wis. Stat. § 706.001.

174 *See* Wyo. Stat. Ann. § 39-15-101(a)(v) (to be real property, must be physically or constructively annexed to the real property and adapted to the use of the real property, and there must be evidence of intent to make it a permanent part of the real property).

175 Wyo. Stat. Ann. § 31-2-502.

176 *See* Alaska Stat. § 29.45.070 (taxation: homes are realty if attached to land or connected to utilities unless expressly classified as personal property by ordinance); Ariz. Rev. Stat. Ann. §§ 42-15201 to 42-15205 (taxation); Ark. Code Ann. § 26-3-203 (taxation); Colo. Rev. Stat. § 42-3-106(6); Conn. Gen. Stat. § 12-63a (manufactured home connected to utilities and used as residence is taxable as real property); Del. Code Ann. tit. 9, § 8351 (statute does not define manufactured homes as real property, but states that they shall be assessed at same tax rate as real estate); Fla. Stat. §§ 193.075 (manufactured home must be taxed as real property if it is permanently affixed to land that the owner of the home owns, i.e., tied down and connected to the normal and usual utilities; similar provision for RVs), 320.015 (taxation; also provides that if a seller or lender characterizes a manufactured home as personal property for purposes of a security interest, it shall remain personal property for those purposes until debt is paid); Idaho Code Ann. §§ 63-303 to 63-305 (taxation); 35 Ill. Comp. Stat. Ann. § 515/1 (manufactured home resting in whole on permanent foundation, with wheels, tongue and hitch removed, is to be assessed and taxed as real property); Ind. Code § 6-1.1-7-1 (taxation); Iowa Code § 435.26 (taxation); Kan. Stat. Ann. § 79-340 (taxation); Ky. Rev. Stat. Ann. § 132.751 (taxation); Me. Rev. Stat. Ann. tit. 36, § 551 (manufactured homes affixed to land, whether or not owned by the homeowner, are taxable as real estate); Md. Code, Tax-Property § 8-234 (West) (manufactured home that is used or usable for residential purposes and permanently attached to land or connected to utility, water, or sewage facilities is taxable as real property unless it is unoccupied and for sale or located temporarily in rented space in trailer park or manufactured home court); Minn. Stat. § 273.125 (taxation); Mo. Rev. Stat. § 137.090 (taxation); Mich. Comp. Laws § 257.801 (taxation); Miss. Code Ann. § 27-53-15 (taxation); Mont. Code Ann. § 15-6-134(1)(b) (taxation); Neb. Rev. Stat. §§ 77-103, 77-3701 (taxation: real property includes manufactured homes not registered for highway use and used or usable for purposes such as residence or office, but not those that are unoccupied and for

the title or provide for recording a home in the local county real estate records. Nonetheless, if a home is treated as real estate for tax purposes, it is more likely that a court will find that it is real estate for other purposes as well.[177]

11.2.5 Whether Manufactured Home Is Treated As Realty in Absence of a State Statute

If there is no state statute which specifically establishes the nature of manufactured homes for purposes of security interests, courts must determine whether a manufactured home remains personal property or has become a fixture. If the home remains personal property, then the only remedies available to the creditor are those provided by Article 9 or state replevin law. If, on the other hand, the home has become a fixture, UCC § 9-604 gives the creditor the option of proceeding either under Article 9 or under the state's real estate law.[178]

Most courts look at several factors to determine whether a manufactured home has become realty. Courts may also refer to these factors even in jurisdictions that have conversion statutes, to buttress their conclusion that the home is or is not real property. The factors include:

- Real or constructive annexation to the real estate in question;
- Appropriation or adaptation to the use or purposes of that part of the realty for which it is connected;
- The intention of the party making the annexation to make a permanent accession to the realty, this intention being inferred from the nature of the chattel, from the relation and situation of the party making the annexation, and from the structure and the purpose for which the annexation has been made; and
- The likelihood that removal would cause substantial injury to the realty.[179]

---

sale); Nev. Rev. Stat. § 361.035 (taxation: incorporates definition in title purging statute); N.H. Rev. Stat. Ann. §§ 72:7-a, 727-b (taxation), 78-B:1 (for purpose of real estate transfer tax, manufactured housing becomes real property when placed on site and tied into utilities); N.J. Stat. Ann. § 54:4-1.5 (West) (manufactured homes are taxed as real property if they are either affixed to the land by a permanent foundation or affixed by a non-permanent foundation and connected to utilities so the home is habitable on a permanent basis, but manufactured home in a park is not taxable as real estate); N.Y. Real Prop. Tax Law § 102(12)(g) (McKinney) (taxation: real property includes manufactured homes unless they are unoccupied and for sale, remain in the jurisdiction for less than sixty days, or are certain small RVs used for purposes such as camping); N.D. Cent. Code § 57-55-10 (personal property tax does not apply to manufactured home that is permanently attached to foundation on land owned by homeowner); Okla. Stat. tit. 68, § 2811 (manufactured home not registered under motor vehicle code is subject to *ad valorem* tax); Or. Rev. Stat. § 308.875 (taxation; statute specifically provides that change for purposes of *ad valorem* taxation does not change status of home with respect to any transactions between the owner and security interest holders or other persons); 72 Pa. Stat. Ann. § 5020-201 (West) (taxation); R.I. Gen. Laws §§ 34-44-4.1 (every deed, instrument, or other writing granting an interest in a mobile or manufactured home must be filed with local recorder of deeds), 44-3-2.2 (towns cannot tax trailer that is registered and taxed as a motor vehicle); S.C. Code Ann. §§ 31-17-310 to 31-17-410 (taxation and licensing); S.D. Codified Laws § 10-9-2 (taxation); Tenn. Code Ann. § 67-5-802 (taxation); Wis. Stat. § 70.043 (manufactured home is an improvement to real property if it is set upon foundation and connected to utilities on land owned by homeowner).

177 *In re* Weaver, 69 B.R. 554 (Bankr. W.D. Ky. 1987) (citing tax law standards as supporting conclusion that manufactured home was fixture for purposes of perfection of security interest). *But see In re* Harris, 166 B.R. 163 (Bankr. D. Colo. 1994) (failure to purge title for tax purposes does not prevent court from finding manufactured home to be real property for purposes of exemption statute). *But cf.* Gen. Elec. Capital Corp. v. Sohn, 566 So. 2d 841 (Fla. Dist. Ct. App. 1990) (classification of manufactured home as realty for tax purposes does not affect seller's or lender's security interest, but applies here because this is a priority dispute between financer of manufactured home and buyer of real estate at tax sale); Onbank & Trust Co. v. Hannold, 684 N.Y.S.2d 677 (App. Div. 1999) (county may institute tax foreclosure on manufactured home as well as the land on which it is sited, regardless of whether home is personalty for other purposes).

178 U.C.C. § 9-604(b). *See* § 11.2.2, *supra*.

179 Cases reciting or applying these factors include: *In re* MBA Poultry, Inc., 291 F.3d 528, 47 U.C.C. Rep. Serv. 2d 1488 (8th Cir. 2002) (Neb. law) (listing the first three factors); *In re* Cluxton, 327 B.R. 612 (B.A.P. 6th Cir. 2005) (reciting first three factors); *In re* Schultz, 2001 Bankr. LEXIS 587, at *15 (Bankr. D.N.H. Apr. 2, 2001); Altegra Credit Co. v. Banks (*In re* Banks), 259 B.R. 848 (Bankr. E.D. Va. 2001) (whether a manufactured home placed upon real property subject to foreclosure has become part of the realty must be decided on a case-by-case basis based on common law doctrine of fixtures, including intent of owner in annexing manufactured home to realty); *In re* Claxton, 239 B.R. 598 (Bankr. N.D. Okla. 1999) (double-wide manufactured home was a fixture and so covered by bank's mortgage on the real property, where it was permanently resting on a concrete foundation, had a stone skirting on three of its four sides, and was surrounded by porches, landscaping and a metal fence); *In re* Painter, 1998 WL 34070559 (Bankr. C.D. Ill. Feb. 27, 1998); *In re* Harris, 166 B.R. 163, 165 (Bankr. D. Colo. 1994) (home was real property for purposes of exemption law where it was attached to sewer, water, and electric systems and the debtor lived there for twelve years and owned the land); *In re* Onyan, 163 B.R. 21, 25 (Bankr. N.D.N.Y. 1993) (construing exemption statute; cost of site preparation was part of purchase price of manufactured home that was permanently attached to the land); *In re* Fink, 4 B.R. 741, 743–744 (Bankr. W.D.N.Y. 1980); Griswell v. Columbus Fin. Co., 470 S.E.2d 256 (Ga. Ct. App. 1996) (unless it is permanently attached to real property, manufactured home is personal property that is subject to replevin); Fuqua Homes, Inc. v. Evanston Bldg. & Loan Co., 370 N.E.2d 780 (Ohio Ct. App. 1977) (ownership dispute between manufacturer of manufactured home and those with interest in the land where it was sited; manufacturer's certificate of ownership not controlling because home had become real property); Parsons v. Lender

There is necessarily some overlap in these factors. For example, the degree to which a manufactured home has been permanently attached to the land or adapted to the use of the real property is often cited as evidence of the party's intention to make a permanent accession.[180] A manufactured home that has been permanently affixed to property is less likely to be removable without causing injury to the realty or the home itself.[181] And, courts have noted, the difficulty of transporting a home based upon its size indicates an intent to have the manufactured home remain indefinitely in one location.[182]

Facts that courts have relied upon in ascertaining whether a manufactured home has been permanently affixed to the land and adapted to the use of the realty include: whether the wheels of the home have been removed,[183] whether the "tongue" or "hitch" used for transporting the home has been removed,[184] whether the structure has been placed on concrete blocks or a foundation with skirting around it,[185] whether it has been connected to a septic system or other utilities,[186] and whether steps or a porch have been attached

---

Serv. Inc., 801 P.2d 739, 13 U.C.C. Rep. Serv. 2d (Okla. Ct. App. 1990); Rourk v. Cameron Appraisal Dist., 131 S.W.3d 285, 296 (Tex. App. 2004) (RVs were not real property for tax purposes); Hartford Nat'l Bank & Trust Co. v. Godin, 398 A.2d 286 (Vt. 1979) (reciting these three factors in dispute between holder of security interest in manufactured home and holder of mortgage on real property; manufactured home became fixture when it was placed on concrete block foundation that was encased in aluminum siding, steps were attached, and it was connected to septic system). *See also In re* Nowlin, 321 B.R. 678 (Bankr. E.D. Pa. 2005) (listing these factors plus whether homeowner owns the land, length of time the home has been attached, etc.), *aff'd,* 2005 WL 2660377 (E.D. Pa. Oct. 17, 2005).

180 *In re* Schultz, 2001 Bankr. LEXIS 587, at *16 (Bankr. D.N.H. Apr. 2, 2001) (fact that parties dug a foundation for manufactured home and connected it to utilities indicated an intention to make permanent attachment).

181 Homac Inc. v. Ft. Wayne Mortgage Co., 577 F. Supp. 1065, 1069 (N.D. Ga. 1983) (court must consider the degree of physical attachment and removability of the article; "wherever the article can be removed without essential injury to the freehold, or the article itself, it is a chattel; otherwise, it is a fixture"); *In re* Fink, 4 B.R. 741 (Bankr. W.D.N.Y. 1980) (finding manufactured home to be a fixture in priority dispute between seller of home and mortgage holder of land, in part because home would have to be dismantled into two parts and the roofing removed to take the home onto highway). *See also* Green Tree Fin. Servicing Corp. v. Sutton, 650 N.W.2d 228 (Neb. 2002) (purchasers of land with manufactured home attached had cause of action for damage to land caused by removal, even though replevin was proper when title records showed properly recorded lien).

182 *In re* Harris, 166 B.R. 163, 165 (Bankr. D. Colo. 1994).

183 George v. Commercial Credit Corp., 440 F.2d 551 (7th Cir. 1971); *In re* Speights, 131 B.R. 205, 207 (N.D. Fla. 1991); *In re* Painter, 1998 WL 34070559 (Bankr. C.D. Ill. Feb. 27, 1998) (home sited on land that homeowners owned was part of realty for bankruptcy purposes where wheels were removed and it was attached to a slab); *In re* Casper, 156 B.R. 794, 800 (Bankr. S.D. Ill. 1993); *In re* Weaver, 69 B.R. 554 (Bankr. W.D. Ky. 1987) (removal of wheels or manufactured parts and placement on permanent, fixed foundation makes home a fixture, so fixture filing is required to perfect security interest); *In re* Gray, 40 B.R. 429 (Bankr. W.D. Okla. 1984) (no permanent foundation and wheels were not removed so manufactured home is not fixture for purposes of perfection rules); Parsons v. Lender Serv. Inc., 801 P.2d 739, 741 (Okla. 1990). *But cf.* BankAmerica Hous. Servs. v. P.D.N. & Assocs., Inc., 977 P.2d 396 (Or. Ct. App. 1999) (fact that wheels had been removed not determinative because under certificate of title statute manufactured home did not lose its status as personalty even if it was affixed to property). *Cf. In re* Nowlin, 321 B.R. 678 (Bankr. E.D. Pa. 2005) (manufactured home was personalty despite removal of wheels where it was placed on concrete blocks on rented land), *aff'd,* 2005 WL 2660377 (E.D. Pa. Oct. 17, 2005).

184 Homac Inc. v. Ft. Wayne Mortgage Co., 577 F. Supp. 1065, 1070 (N.D. Ga. 1983); *In re* Speights, 131 B.R. 205, 206 (N.D. Fla. 1991); Parsons v. Lender Serv. Inc., 801 P.2d 739, 741 (Okla. 1990).

185 *In re* Cluxton, 327 B.R. 612 (B.A.P. 6th Cir. 2005) (placement on concrete block piers sufficient where home was also connected to utilities); *In re* Speights, 131 B.R. 205, 206 (N.D. Fla. 1991); *In re* Schultz, 2001 Bankr. LEXIS 587, at *16–17 (Bankr. D.N.H. Apr. 2, 2001); *In re* Wester, 229 B.R. 348 (Bankr. E.D.N.C. 1998) (deed of trust covered home that had been connected to utilities and attached to owner's land by pouring footers and placing it on brick foundation; since it was not intended for operation on highways security interest did not have to be noted on title); *In re* Painter, 1998 WL 34070559 (Bankr. C.D. Ill. Feb. 27, 1998) (home sited on land that homeowners owned was part of realty for bankruptcy purposes where wheels were removed and it was attached to a slab); *In re* Gray, 40 B.R. 429 (Bankr. W.D. Okla. 1984) (no permanent foundation and wheels were not removed so manufactured home is not fixture for purposes of perfection rules); Corning Bank v. Bank of Rector, 73, 576 S.W.2d 949 (Ark. 1979); Andover Twp. Bd. of Trustees v. O'Brien, 823 N.E.2d 524 (Ohio Ct. App. 2004) (RVs were fixtures and were real property for tax purposes where they were set on pole foundations with concrete bases up to 4 feet below ground level, with roof-overs that prevented removal of RVS, and owners lived there year-round); Parsons v. Lender Serv. Inc., 801 P.2d 739, 740–741 (Okla. 1990) (home placed on poured-concrete footing with concrete blocks running around the full perimeter of the home and brick and mortar skirting).

186 *In re* Cluxton, 327 B.R. 612 (B.A.P. 6th Cir. 2005) (connection to electric and plumbing service sufficient even though home was only placed on concrete block piers); *In re* Schultz, 2001 Bankr. LEXIS 587, at *17 (Bankr. D.N.H. Apr. 2, 2001); *In re* Harris, 166 B.R. 163, 165 (Bankr. D. Colo. 1994) (home was real property for purposes of exemption law where it was attached to sewer, water, and electric systems and the debtor lived there for twelve years and owned the land); *In re* Fink, 4 B.R. 741 (Bankr. W.D.N.Y. 1980); Parsons v. Lender Serv. Inc., 801 P.2d 739, 741 (Okla. 1990) ("The home is hooked-up to gas, electricity, water and telephone lines, and is connected to a septic tank system."). *See also* United States v. Shelby County, Tenn., 385 F. Supp. 1187 (W.D. Tenn. 1974) (manufactured homes that were attached to ground only by cable or anchor that was driven or screwed into ground were personal property for purposes of exemption from local taxation even though they were connected to utilities). *Cf. In re* Nowlin, 321 B.R. 678 (Bankr. E.D. Pa. 2005) (manufactured home was personalty despite connection to utilities where it was placed on concrete blocks on rented land), *aff'd,* 2005 WL 2660377 (E.D. Pa. Oct.

to it.[187] Courts look for "permanent" modifications which are not easily undone. Thus, when a home was perched on cement piers which were not mortared together, rather than being attached to a foundation, the court found that it was not permanently affixed.[188] Where the land would be of little use to the owner without the home, a court held that the home was adapted to the use and enjoyment of the realty.[189]

In some jurisdictions, it is the intent of the manufactured homeowner which is paramount.[190] Thus, even when the purchaser of the home had not connected the home to electricity or installed plumbing, the fact that he intended to do so in order that he could occupy the home as his permanent residence established his intention to install the home as a permanent accession to the real property.[191] Courts will consider a clause in the contract to finance the home stating that the home will remain personal property despite any physical attachment to the land as evidence of intent, but may not find it conclusive.[192]

Another factor cited by courts in many states as pertinent is whether the consumer owns both the realty and the affixed manufactured home.[193] Unity of ownership supports an inference that the manufactured home has become part of the realty.

Most of the cases that apply these factors do not involve the question of whether a secured party should use foreclosure or replevin to retake the home. Instead, they involve disputes between competing claimants to a manufactured home, such as between a secured party whose lien was noted on the title and the buyer of the land on which the home had been permanently installed. Or they involve questions such as taxation or homestead exemptions. Nonetheless, courts may treat these decisions as persuasive in determining whether foreclosure or replevin is the proper procedure for a secured party to recover a manufactured home.

17, 2005); *In re* Gray, 40 B.R. 429 (Bankr. W.D. Okla. 1984) (manufactured home was not a fixture for purposes of perfection rules where wheels had not been removed and it was placed on concrete blocks on rented land, even though it was connected to utilities).

187 *In re* Speights, 131 B.R. 205, 206 (N.D. Fla. 1991) (porch constructed and connected to the manufactured home suggests intention to permanently attach); *In re* Claxton, 239 B.R. 598 (Bankr. N.D. Okla. 1999) (citing addition of porches as support for conclusion that home was real property for question of whether bank's mortgage on the real property covered it); Parsons v. Lender Serv. Inc., 801 P.2d 739, 741 (Okla. 1990) (brick and mortar steps had been constructed at entrance to the home indicating intention to permanently affix). *Cf. In re* Nowlin, 321 B.R. 678 (Bankr. E.D. Pa. 2005) (manufactured home was personalty despite two attached decks where it was placed on concrete blocks on rented land), *aff'd*, 2005 WL 2660377 (E.D. Pa. Oct. 17, 2005).

188 Homac Inc. v. Ft. Wayne Mortgage Co., 577 F. Supp. 1065, 1069–1070 (N.D. Ga. 1983) ("Moreover, it is significant that the concrete blocks composing the piers were not mortared together but merely assembled on top of sixteen-inch square pads of concrete placed in the ground underneath the units. . . . Thus they could be disassembled and loaded directly onto a truck, leaving only the pads to be pried out of the earth. After the first rain filled in the marks left by the pads and the tie-down anchors, only the utility stubs would remain to mark the spot where the manufactured home had been located. In sum, the undisputed facts show that the mobile home could be removed 'without essential injury to the freehold, or the article itself.' "). *See also* United States v. Shelby County, Tenn., 385 F. Supp. 1187 (W.D. Tenn. 1974) (manufactured homes that were attached to ground only by cable or anchor that was driven or screwed into ground were personal property for purposes of exemption from local taxation even though they were connected to utilities). *But see In re* Cluxton, 327 B.R. 612 (B.A.P. 6th Cir. 2005) (placement on concrete block piers sufficient).

189 *In re* Cluxton, 327 B.R. 612 (B.A.P. 6th Cir. 2005). *See also In re* Harris, 166 B.R. 163, 165 (Bankr. D. Colo. 1994) (citing fact that upon removal of home there would be a driveway to nowhere, steps to nowhere, and a bare spot on the land as support for conclusion that home was real property for purposes of exemption statute).

190 *See* Homac Inc. v. Ft. Wayne Mortgage Co., 577 F. Supp. 1065, 1069 (N.D. Ga. 1983) (intention of party more important factor); *In re* Painter, 1998 WL 34070559 (Bankr. C.D. Ill. Feb. 27, 1998) (intent is most important factor, and annexation and adaptability merely bear upon intent).

191 *In re* Onyan, 163 B.R. 21, 26 (Bankr. N.D.N.Y. 1993) (construing exemption statute; cost of site preparation was part of purchase price of manufactured home that was permanently attached to the land).

192 *See In re* Thompson, 217 B.R. 375 (B.A.P. 2d Cir. 1998); Homac Inc. v. Ft. Wayne Mortgage Co., 577 F. Supp. 1065 (N.D. Ga. 1983).

193 Homac Inc. v. Ft. Wayne Mortgage Co., 577 F. Supp. 1065, 1071 (N.D. Ga. 1983); *In re* Nowlin, 321 B.R. 678 (Bankr. E.D. Pa. 2005) (citing fact that home was on rented land as factor in finding it to be personalty); *In re* Schultz, 2001 Bankr. LEXIS 587, at *15 (Bankr. D.N.H. Apr. 2, 2001) (considering several factors including "[t]he relationship between the realty's owner and the person claiming the item"); *In re* Harris, 166 B.R. 163, 165 (Bankr. D. Colo. 1994) ("The Debtor owned the property where the Mobile Home was located. Also, the length of time that the Debtor resided on the property indicates his intent for the structure to be permanent."); *In re* Casper, 156 B.R. 794, 800 (Bankr. S.D. Ill. 1993) ("the relation of the annexer to the realty is significant in discerning intent, as it is presumed that an annexation by one who owns the land is made with the design of its permanent enjoyment with the realty"); Corning Bank v. Bank of Rector, 576 S.W.2d 949, 953 (Ark. 1979) ("The inference is strong, where the party attaching the "fixture" is the owner of the soil, that it was intended to become a part of the soil and not a removable fixture, and to overturn it, there must be strong evidence of a contrary intention manifested by some act or circumstance."). *See also* Rourk v. Cameron Appraisal Dist., 131 S.W.3d 285, 296 (Tex. App. 2004) (there is a presumption that improvements to land made by a tenant are not fixtures), *rev'd on other grounds*, 194 S.W.2d 501 (Tex. 2006) (plaintiffs failed to exhaust administrative remedies). *But cf. In re* Gray, 40 B.R. 429, 434 n.3 (Bankr. W.D. Okla. 1984) (home may be a fixture even if on rented land).

11.3 Repossession and Resale Procedures When Creditor Proceeds Under Article 9

11.3.1 Introduction

If a manufactured home has not become real property, the creditor must proceed under Article 9 or state replevin law to retake the home, and its disposition of the home after retaking it is governed by Article 9. This section provides a brief summary of the most important requirements of Article 9, which are set forth in detail in another treatise in this series.[194]

Article 9 is in effect in all fifty states and the District of Columbia. Many states have adopted non-uniform versions of important provisions of Article 9, however. In addition, many states have non-Article 9 statutes that supplement or override Article 9's requirements for certain types of transactions.[195]

11.3.2 Enforceable Security Interest As Precondition of Repossession

Before there can be any repossession, there must be a valid, enforceable security interest in the collateral. To create an enforceable security interest in a manufactured home under Article 9, the debtor must have signed or otherwise "authenticated"[196] a security agreement that describes the collateral.[197] The agreement must be a written or electronic document and must specifically grant the security interest.[198] Noting the lien on the certificate of title or on a financing statement is insufficient unless that document includes a statement by which the buyer grants the seller a security interest.[199] If the security agreement does not identify the collateral accurately, for example if it lists the wrong serial number, it may not be effective.[200] The security agreement must be signed by the person who owns or has rights in the manufactured home.[201]

194 National Consumer Law Center, Repossessions (6th ed. 2005 and Supp.).

195 *See* National Consumer Law Center, Repossessions Appx. B (6th ed. 2005 and Supp.) (summary of state repossession laws).

196 "Authenticate" is defined by U.C.C. § 9-102(a)(7) to include electronic signatures and similar methods of agreeing to documents.

197 U.C.C. § 9-203(b).

198 *See* National Consumer Law Center, Repossessions § 3.2.2 (6th ed. 2005 and Supp.).

199 *Id.* §§ 3.2.2.2, 3.5.2.

200 *Id.* § 3.2.7.

201 U.C.C. § 9-203(b)(2).

11.3.3 Default

Assuming that there is an enforceable security interest in the home, there must be a default before a creditor can repossess.[202] The Uniform Commercial Code does not define default, leaving the definition to the parties' contract.[203] State law may limit the definition of default, however, and state or federal law may require the creditor to give the debtor a notice of the default and an opportunity to cure it.[204] In addition, if the creditor habitually accepted late payments, and did not give notice to the consumer that it would no longer do so, it may have waived its right to repossess for late payments.[205]

11.3.4 Self-Help Repossession

Article 9 allows the creditor to use self-help to repossess collateral.[206] However, self-help is allowed only if it can be accomplished without breach of the peace.[207] Breach of the peace is very likely if a creditor attempts self-help repossession of an occupied manufactured home, so many creditors seek a judicial order through a replevin action.[208]

The post-repossession requirements of Article 9 apply regardless of whether the creditor retook the manufactured home through self-help repossession or through a judicial action.[209] Thus, creditors recovering the collateral through a replevin action must still dispose of the property according to UCC requirements,[210] just as if the creditor had resorted to self-help repossession.[211]

11.3.5 Debtor's Right of Redemption

After repossession, Article 9 affords the consumer the right to get the collateral back by "redeeming" it.[212] Redemption requires the consumer to pay the full accelerated

202 U.C.C. §§ 9-601, 9-609.

203 U.C.C. § 9-601 cmt. 3.

204 *See* § 11.5, *infra*.

205 *See* National Consumer Law Center, Repossessions § 4.3 (6th ed. 2005 and Supp.).

206 U.C.C. § 9-609.

207 *Id.*

208 *See* §§ 11.1, 11.2, *supra*.

209 U.C.C. §§ 9-609, 9-610 (making no distinction based on whether creditor acquired possession of the collateral through self-help or through replevin). *See* National Consumer Law Center, Repossessions § 5.1.3 (6th ed. 2005 and Supp.).

210 *See* National Consumer Law Center, Repossessions Ch. 10 (6th ed. 2005 and Supp.) (U.C.C. disposition requirements).

211 *See, e.g.*, Royal W. Airway, Inc. v. Valley Bank of Nev., 747 P.2d 895, 5 U.C.C. Rep. Serv. 2d 1170 (Nev. 1987) (creditor responsible for deterioration of airplane seized by sheriff). *See also* BMW Fin. Servs. v. Wheeler, 2001 Conn. Super. LEXIS 709 (Conn. Super. Ct. Mar. 13, 2001) (awarding deficiency judgment to lessor after sale of replevied car).

212 U.C.C. § 9-623.

debt, not just the installments that were past due at the time of repossession, so it is rarely of use to consumers.[213] Some states, however, require the creditor to grant the consumer the right to regain possession of the collateral by paying just the past-due installments.[214]

11.3.6 Secured Party's Sale of the Home

If the consumer does not regain possession of the manufactured home, by redemption or otherwise, in most cases the creditor will sell the home and apply the proceeds to the debt. Article 9 requires the creditor to send the debtor a notice before the sale, containing specified information.[215] While the creditor may choose the manner of sale, all aspects of the sale must be commercially reasonable.[216] If the creditor uses a private sale rather than a public sale, it cannot buy the home itself.[217] Whether the collateral is sold at a public or private sale, Article 9 provides some protection against low-price sales to insiders.[218]

11.3.7 Deficiency or Surplus

The proceeds of the sale are applied first to the expenses of repossessing and selling the home, and then to the debt.[219] If there is money left over, the creditor must pay this surplus to the debtor.[220] If, as is more likely, the proceeds are insufficient to satisfy the debt, the debtor owes the deficiency.[221]

In calculating the deficiency, the debtor must be given credit for any unearned interest and rebates of insurance premiums.[222] The creditor must send the debtor a broad-brush explanation of how the deficiency or surplus was calculated when it pays the surplus to the debtor or demands payment of the deficiency, or the debtor requests an explanation.[223]

213 *See* National Consumer Law Center, Repossessions § 9.3 (6th ed. 2006 and Supp.).

214 *Id.* § 9.2.

215 U.C.C. §§ 9-613, 9-614.

216 U.C.C. § 9-610(b). *See also* LG Enters., Inc. v. Washington Mut. Bank, 2008 WL 1934848 (Wash. Ct. App. May 5, 2008) (dispute between lender and company hired to recondition and sell repossessed manufactured homes provides interesting insight to existing practices).

217 U.C.C. § 9-610(c).

218 U.C.C. § 9-615(f).

219 U.C.C. § 9-615(a).

220 U.C.C. § 9-615(d).

221 *Id.*

222 *See* National Consumer Law Center, Repossessions § 11.3 (6th ed. 2006 and Supp.).

223 U.C.C. § 9-616.

11.3.8 Creditor's Option to Retain Home in Full Satisfaction of Debt

If the debtor has paid less than 60% of the cash price of the home,[224] the seller has the option of keeping the home in full satisfaction of the debt instead of selling it.[225] This option is called strict foreclosure. To exercise this option, the creditor must obtain the debtor's consent, but the debtor's failure to object to a proposal is deemed consent.[226]

If the creditor exercises the option of strict foreclosure, then it simply keeps the manufactured home, and it cannot recover a deficiency.[227] In some circumstances, the creditor's actions, such as using the home or junking it, may amount to a strict foreclosure even though the creditor has not taken any formal steps to propose a strict foreclosure.[228]

11.3.9 Remedies for Violations of Article 9

If the creditor has not complied with Article 9, some courts hold that it is absolutely barred from collecting a deficiency judgment from the debtor. Others adopt a presumption that the value of the collateral equaled the debt, thereby eliminating any deficiency, but allow the creditor to rebut this presumption.[229]

A number of states have statutes that prohibit deficiency judgments in at least some circumstances.[230] Most of these anti-deficiency statutes are limited to transactions involving small dollar amounts, however, so would not apply to manufactured home sales. California prohibits deficiency judgments for manufactured homes unless there is substantial damage beyond wear and tear from normal use.[231]

Article 9 also gives the debtor an affirmative cause of action for any actual damages caused by a violation of its requirements. In the case of a transaction secured by consumer goods such as a manufactured home, if the creditor violates any provision of Part 6 of Article 9, which governs the creditor's remedies upon default, the consumer is entitled at a minimum to statutory damages of the finance charge plus 10% of the cash price or principal.[232] Article 9 also provides a separate $500 statutory damages award for violation of certain other requirements, such as failing to send the explanation of the surplus or deficiency required by UCC § 9-616.[233]

224 U.C.C. § 9-620(e).

225 U.C.C. § 9-620.

226 U.C.C. § 9-620(b), (c).

227 *See* National Consumer Law Center, Repossessions § 9.4 (6th ed. 2006 and Supp.).

228 *See id.* § 12.5.

229 *See id.* § 12.6.

230 *See id.* § 12.4.

231 Cal. Civ. Code § 2983.8 (West); Cal. Heath & Safety Code § 18038.7 (West).

232 U.C.C. § 9-625(c)(2).

233 U.C.C. § 9-625(e), (f). For some violations of § 9-616, the

11.4 State Restrictions on Seizure of Manufactured Homes; Breach of Peace in Repossession

Manufactured homes are exempt from self-help repossession in several states. For example, Minnesota expressly prohibits creditors from utilizing self-help to recover a manufactured home, specifying instead a procedure involving thirty days notice to the debtor and judicial action.[234] A non-uniform provision of Colorado's version of Article 9 allows self-help repossession of a manufactured home without the debtor's consent only if there is clear and convincing evidence that the debtor has vacated the home.[235]

Vermont prohibits self-help repossession of manufactured homes and requires a judicial proceeding.[236] This restriction applies to the holder of a retail installment contract, promissory note, or any other evidence of indebtedness secured by a manufactured home.[237] Wisconsin prohibits creditors from repossessing collateral without a court order unless the debtor voluntarily surrenders the property. There is an exception for motor vehicles, but the term is defined so as to exclude manufactured homes.[238] Louisiana prohibits self-help repossession altogether except for motor vehicles, a term that is defined to exclude manufactured homes.[239] The Navajo Nation prohibits self-help repossession, including repossession of a manufactured home, without first obtaining a court order or written consent of the homeowner.[240]

As a practical matter, the non-voluntary repossession of an occupied manufactured home is virtually certain to violate other laws. It is almost impossible to use self-help to repossess a manufactured home without taking unsecured furniture, clothing, and other personal property located in the home.[241] The Federal Trade Commission's Credit Practices Rule prohibits any creditor from taking a non-possessory, non-purchase money security interest in a consumer's core household goods.[242] Therefore, a creditor cannot claim that this property is collateral that it has a right to repossess.[243]

In addition, a repossessor's entry into the debtor's home is the quintessential breach of the peace, subjecting the creditor to liability for trespass and actual and statutory damages under Article 9 of the Uniform Commercial Code.[244] Self-help repossessions which involve trespass or breach of the peace are always illegal and should be challenged aggressively.[245] Repossessions of homes affixed to the land would be practically impossible without breaching the peace.[246] Repossession could also easily damage personal property such as glassware, lamps, and other breakable items inside the home. If occupants are in the home, repossession is likely to cause substantial distress and possibly injury.[247] For these reasons, many manufactured home creditors avoid self-help repossession of manufactured homes even when state law allows it.

---

consumer must show a pattern or practice of violations.

234 Minn. Stat. § 327.64. *See also* First Nat'l Bank v. Edison Homes, Inc., 415 N.W.2d 442 (Minn. Ct. App. 1987).

235 Colo. Rev. Stat. § 4-9-609.

236 Vt. Stat. Ann. tit. 9, § 2603 (prohibiting use of "prejudgment remedies provided in section 9-503 of Title 9A," which is the section of the former version of Article 9 that allowed self-help repossession).

237 *Id.*

238 Wis. Stat. §§ 218.0101(22), 425.202, 425.206.

239 La. Rev. Stat. Ann. §§ 10:9-609, 9-966, 9-965(C), *referring to* § 32:1252(13).

240 Navajo Nation Code tit. 7 § 621 (2005). *See* Pete v. U.S. Bank, N.A., 2009 WL 532611 (Ariz. Ct. App. Mar. 3, 2009) (upholding default judgment for wrongful repossession against bank acting as an undisclosed principal when home was repossessed without court order or homeowner's authorization).

241 Some state statutes provide debtors a specified amount of time after repossession of a manufactured home to claim personal property seized. *See, e.g.*, La. Rev. Stat. Ann. § 9:5363.1(D) (debtor has twenty-one days from repossession of manufactured home to claim personal property seized). *See also* Dixie Sav. & Loan Ass'n v. Pitre, 751 So. 2d 911 (La. Ct. App. 1999) (damages for wrongful seizure awarded when sheriff seized manufactured home and contents without providing adequate notice to occupant to allow removal of unsecured property); Gaskill v. Doss, 2000 Ohio App. LEXIS 6185 (Ohio Ct. App. Dec. 16, 2000) (affirming award of attorney fees in successful UDAP suit against creditor who lost and damaged buyer's personal property while repossessing manufactured home). *See generally* National Consumer Law Center, Repossessions Ch. 7 (6th ed. 2005 and Supp.).

242 16 C.F.R. § 444.2(a)(4). *See also* Cordell v. Greene Fin., 953 F. Supp. 1391 (M.D. Ala. 1996).

243 *See* National Consumer Law Center, Repossessions Ch. 7 (6th ed. 2005 and Supp.).

244 *See* National Consumer Law Center, Repossessions § 6.4.4.3 (6th ed. 2005 and Supp.).

245 As discussed in National Consumer Law Center, Repossessions §§ 6.3.3, 6.3.4 (6th ed. 2005), self-help repossessions of manufactured homes often involve a trespass or breach of the peace. *See also* Soldal v. Cook County, 506 U.S. 56, 113 S. Ct. 538, 121 L. Ed. 2d 450 (1992) (sheriff's participation in an illegal repossession of a manufactured home constitutes a Fourth Amendment seizure).

246 *See* Pokorne Private Capital Group, L.L.C. v. 21st Mortgage Corp., 2008 WL 963296 (Tex. App. Apr. 10, 2008) (while self-help repossession was permissible for a home that had been installed, but not affixed to real property, the court went on state that had the home been affixed, attempts at self-help repossession would almost certainly have breached the peace).

247 *See In re* Smith, 296 B.R. 46 (Bankr. M.D. Ala. 2003) (granting damages for emotional distress to homeowner who was inside the home when it was repossessed in violation of automatic stay in bankruptcy, requiring her to jump from the moving home to the ground).

11.5 Right to Cure Manufactured Home Default

11.5.1 State Right to Cure Statutes

A number of state statutes provide a right to cure defaults prior to acceleration or repossession for some or all consumer credit transactions. The details vary from state to state and are set out in Appendix B of National Consumer Law Center, *Repossessions* (6th ed. 2005 and Supp.). Even states that do not grant a general right to cure may have a special statute extending that right to manufactured home buyers.[248]

Generally, right to cure laws require the creditor to send a written notice of default and right to cure, and then wait for a specified period before accelerating the note, repossessing the collateral, or seeking court enforcement of the security interest. During that period, the debtor can reinstate the credit transaction as if the default had not occurred merely by paying any back payments plus delinquency charges. The typical statute specifies the number of times in the same credit transaction a debtor is entitled to cure a default.

The scope of any state right to cure law should be carefully checked. The right to cure may apply only when the manufactured home is sold under a retail installment contract that is assigned to a financing company, not when the purchase is financed by a loan. It may apply only to motor vehicles or only to goods other than motor vehicles, and in either case the key question will be whether manufactured homes are considered motor vehicles for purposes of the right to cure statute. It may apply only to manufactured homes that are treated as personalty.

11.5.2 Limited Right to Cure Under Federal Law

Whether a manufactured home is considered realty or personalty, a right to cure the default which supplements or goes beyond state law is potentially available due to regulations of the federal Office of Thrift Supervision.[249] Under these regulations, certain manufactured home creditors who want to take advantage of federal preemption of state interest rate ceilings must afford the consumer a right to cure.

These regulations apply to first mortgages[250] on residential manufactured homes. They apply whether the mortgage was taken as part of a loan or as part of a credit sale.[251] They do not apply, however, when the debtor has abandoned the home.[252]

When these regulations apply, a creditor cannot repossess a home, commence a foreclosure, or accelerate an obligation until thirty days after the creditor sends a notice of default by certified mail, return receipt requested.[253] The notice must state the nature of the default, the action the debtor must take to cure the default, the creditor's intended actions upon the debtor's failure to cure, and the debtor's right to redeem under state law.[254]

The notice, in effect, gives the debtor a second chance, within thirty days of the notice's postmark, to cure any past delinquencies or other default before the total amount due may be accelerated or the home repossessed. To bring the amount current, the debtor needs to pay only the delinquent payments, plus any late or deferral charges.

If the debtor defaults a second time after curing the first default, the creditor must again notify the debtor of the debtor's right to cure. But the debtor is not entitled to notice of default more than twice in any one year period.[255]

It must be stressed that the federal regulations do not require any creditor to grant a right to cure. Only if the creditor seeks protection from state interest rate ceilings must the creditor comply with these regulations. If the creditor fails to afford a right to cure, the consumer's only remedy is to claim that a state interest rate ceiling applies to the transaction. If the creditor exceeded that ceiling, the consumer is entitled to whatever remedy the state interest rate ceiling law provides. This subject is discussed in greater detail in National Consumer Law Center, *Repossessions* § 4.8.3 (6th ed. 2005).

11.6 Truth in Lending Defenses in Manufactured Home Foreclosures

11.6.1 Damages Claims

Truth in Lending claims may be available as defenses or counterclaims in manufactured home foreclosure cases. The

248 *See, e.g.*, Minn. Stat. §§ 327.64, 327.66 (note that Minn. Stat. § 327.63(3) makes this protection inapplicable to a manufactured home that is not encumbered by any security interest when it is affixed to real property, thereby implying that it is applicable to manufactured homes that are encumbered by a security interest when they become affixed to real property); 69 Pa. Stat. Ann. § 623(G) (West) (applies only to installment sale contracts).

249 *See* National Consumer Law Center, Repossessions § 4.8.3 (6th ed. 2005 and Supp.).

250 The term "first mortgage" includes purchase money loans. It also includes other loans taking the manufactured home as security when there is not another mortgage loan already on the home. For example, when a purchase money first mortgage and any other lien on the home is paid off, and then the consumer uses the home as security for an otherwise unrelated loan, that new loan is a first mortgage.

251 12 C.F.R. § 590.2(a).

252 12 C.F.R. § 590.4(h)(1).

253 *Id.*

254 12 C.F.R. § 590.4(h)(2).

255 12 C.F.R. § 590.4(h)(1).

federal Truth in Lending Act (TILA) requires disclosures in any consumer credit transaction.[256]

The disclosures are to be made by the creditor defined as the party to whom the obligation is initially payable.[257] If a manufactured home sale is set up as an installment contract payable to the dealer, which the dealer then assigns to a financer, the dealer is the creditor for TIL purposes. The financer is jointly liable with the dealer for TIL damages if the TIL violations are apparent on the face of the documents assigned.[258] If the financing is set up as a loan, the lender will be the creditor for TIL purposes.[259]

In 2008, the Federal Reserve Board amended its TIL regulations to impose certain substantive requirements on credit, including purchase money credit, that is secured by the consumer's principal dwelling. Restrictions on coercion of appraisers, delays in crediting payments, and pyramiding of late fees went into effect on October 1, 2009.[260] Restrictions on prepayment penalties and lending without regard to repayment ability, and a requirement that escrow accounts be established, apply to certain "higher-priced" mortgage loans, but go into effect for manufactured home credit only on October 1, 2010.[261] Details about these restrictions, what transactions they apply to, and their effective dates, may be found in NCLC's *Truth in Lending*.[262]

The Truth in Lending Act does not apply to transactions in which the amount financed exceeds $25,000, but there is an exception for transactions in which the creditor takes a security interest in real property or in personal property used or expected to be used as the principal dwelling of the consumer.[263] The reference to personal property covers manufactured homes, so the result is that TILA covers credit secured by a manufactured home that is the consumer's principal dwelling regardless of whether the credit exceeds $25,000.

TILA also applies to credit sales of land to consumer buyers. If a combined purchase of a manufactured home and the land on which it will sit is structured as two transactions with two different creditors, there will be potential TIL claims for each transaction.

If the creditor does not comply with TILA, the consumer can sue for actual damages plus attorney fees.[264] Moreover, certain violations lead to statutory damages of double the finance charge.[265] There is a $1000 cap on statutory damages, but the cap is $2000 in the case of a closed-end credit transaction secured by real property or a dwelling,[266] including a manufactured home.[267]

If the creditor files a replevin or foreclosure action to recover a manufactured home, the consumer may be able to raise TIL claims defensively.[268] If the TIL claims equal or exceed the alleged delinquency, the court may find that the creditor does not have grounds for recovery of the home. There is a one-year statute of limitations for TIL damage suits, but TIL damage claims can generally be raised as defenses to the creditor's claim regardless of the statute of limitations.[269]

11.6.2 Rescission

While Truth in Lending damages are an attractive counterclaim that can reduce the alleged delinquency on a manufactured home, the statute also offers a right to rescind that can be an even more powerful tool to prevent foreclosure. Unfortunately, however, the right to rescind applies to only a small subset of credit transactions secured by manufactured homes.

The Truth in Lending Act gives consumers the right to rescind certain home-secured transactions, but this right does not apply when the credit is extended to finance the acquisition of the home,[270] unless the consumer gives a security interest in an existing residence to secure the new extension of credit. In the manufactured home context, the right to rescind would apply if the consumer already owned a manufactured home and refinanced. Given that manufactured homes often depreciate, a more likely scenario may be when consumer already owns a manufactured home on a plot of land and "trades up" for a better manufactured home, giving the creditor a security interest in the land. A home equity loan, home improvement loan, or other non-

256 *See* § 4.11.4, *supra*; National Consumer Law Center, Truth in Lending (6th ed. 2007 and Supp.).

257 15 U.S.C. § 1602(f).

258 15 U.S.C. § 1641. *See* National Consumer Law Center, Truth in Lending § 7.3.10 (6th ed. 2007 and Supp.).

259 *See* National Consumer Law Center, Truth in Lending § 2.3.5 (6th ed. 2007 and Supp.).

260 12 C.F.R. § 226.36. *See* National Consumer Law Center, Truth in Lending § 9.9 (2009 Supp.).

261 12 C.F.R. § 226.35. *See* National Consumer Law Center, Truth in Lending § 9.8 (2009 Supp.).

262 National Consumer Law Center, Truth in Lending §§ 9.8, 9.9 (2009 Supp.).

263 15 U.S.C. § 1603.

264 15 U.S.C. 1640(a). *See* National Consumer Law Center, Truth in Lending (6th ed. 2007 and Supp.) (full discussion of TIL disclosure requirements).

265 15 U.S.C. § 1640.

266 15 U.S.C. § 1640(a)(2)(A)(iii).

267 15 U.S.C. § 1602(v).

268 *See* National Consumer Law Center, Truth in Lending §§ 5.5.5, 5.8.1 (6th ed. 2007 and Supp.).

269 *See* National Consumer Law Center, Truth in Lending § 7.2.5 (6th ed. 2007 and Supp.).

270 *See* 15 U.S.C. §§ 1635(e)(1) (exempting "residential mortgage transactions" from right to rescind), 1602(w) (defining residential mortgage transaction as one "in which a mortgage, deed of trust, purchase money security interest under an installment sales contract, or equivalent consensual security interest is created or retained against the consumer's dwelling to finance the acquisition or initial construction of that dwelling"), 1602(v) (defining dwelling to include a manufactured home). *See also* Official Staff Commentary §§ 226.2(a)(24)-2, (a)(24)-4, (a)(24)-5, 226.23(f)-1 (which flesh out these definitions).

purchase money transaction secured by a manufactured home would also be subject to the right to rescind.

If the creditor is required to afford the consumer a right to rescind, the right normally runs for just three days after consummation of the transaction. The right can be extended for up to three years, however, if the creditor failed to give the consumer certain material Truth in Lending disclosures or proper notice of the right to rescind. If the consumer exercises the right to rescind, the creditor is required to release the mortgage on the property, forgive all finance charges and closing costs, and apply all the consumer's payments toward principal.[271]

The Home Ownership and Equity Protection Act (HOEPA) requires special disclosures and creates special substantive restrictions for certain high-rate home-secured loans. Like the TIL rescission right, it does not apply to credit used to purchase a manufactured home.[272] If a creditor makes a covered loan but does not give the special disclosures, or includes prohibited terms, the consumer has the right to recover enhanced TIL damages and the right to rescind is also extended. The Truth in Lending Act and HOEPA are thoroughly discussed in NCLC's *Truth in Lending*.[273]

11.7 RESPA Defenses in Manufactured Home Foreclosures

The federal Real Estate Settlement Procedures Act (RESPA) can also provide defenses and counterclaims in manufactured home foreclosures. RESPA applies to all loans secured by a first or subordinate lien on residential real property designed principally for the occupancy of one to four families.[274] Unlike the rescission right, it applies to purchase-money credit.

In the manufactured home context, RESPA applies to loans secured by land on which a manufactured home sits or on which a manufactured home will be placed within two years.[275] It thus applies to a loan that finances both land and a manufactured home as a single transaction; a loan to purchase a manufactured home if the loan is secured not only by the home but also by the land on which the home will be placed; and a loan to purchase just the land on which a home will be placed. It does not, however, apply to credit that is secured just by a manufactured home, nor does it cover installment sales.

When RESPA applies, it requires disclosures about closing costs both before and at the time of settlement, notices about escrow accounts and servicing transfers, and the right to obtain account information through a qualified written request. RESPA also prohibits kickbacks and unearned fees for settlement services, charges for preparation of certain documents, and steering of borrowers to a particular title insurance company, and regulates the handling of escrow accounts. Treble damages and attorney fees are available for violation of the anti-kickback provision,[276] and the statute also creates a private cause of action for violations of the anti-steering provision[277] and the servicer obligations.[278]

The closing cost disclosures are particularly helpful as a means of tracing where the money went. Even if there are no RESPA violations, the closing cost disclosures may reveal other causes of action, for example, by demonstrating that the TIL disclosures are inaccurate.

Like TIL damage claims, it should be possible to raise RESPA claims defensively in a replevin or foreclosure action as a means of reducing the alleged delinquency.[279] The mortgage servicing and escrow requirements of RESPA are discussed in more detail in Chapter 8, *supra*, and the other requirements of RESPA are analyzed in NCLC's *The Cost of Credit: Regulation, Preemption, and Industry Abuses* § 12.2.1.[280]

11.8 Defenses Based on State Credit Statutes

Claims and defenses under state credit statutes should also be investigated. Most manufactured home sales are financed and will thus be covered by a state credit statute. If the transaction is set up as an installment sale, with the contract assigned to a financing institution, often there is a retail installment sales act (RISA) or motor vehicle retail installment sales act (MVRISA) that applies. If the transaction is set up as a loan, a different statute will apply. Special attention should be paid to the scope of such statutes because determination of which statute covers manufactured home sales is often difficult. Federal law has also preempted many state credit statutes.[281]

271 There can be other consequences as well, including forfeiture of the right to recover any portion of the principal. *See* National Consumer Law Center, Repossessions § 14.7.3.1 (6th ed. 2005 and Supp.); National Consumer Law Center, Truth in Lending § 6.9.5 (6th ed. 2007 and Supp.).

272 15 U.S.C. § 1602(aa)(1) (excluding "residential mortgage transactions"). *See generally* National Consumer Law Center, Truth in Lending § 9.2.4 (6th ed. 2007 and Supp.).

273 (6th ed. 2007 and Supp.).

274 12 U.S.C. § 2602(1). The loan must also must be made by a federally insured lender or be federally related in one of the other ways spelled out in § 2602. *See* § 8.1.2, *supra*.

275 24 C.F.R. § 3500.5(B)(4).

276 12 U.S.C. § 2607(d)(2)(3).

277 12 U.S.C. § 2608(b).

278 12 U.S.C. § 2605(f).

279 *See* National Consumer Law Center, Repossessions § 5.5.5 (6th ed. 2005 and Supp.).

280 (4th ed. 2009 and Supp.).

281 *See* National Consumer Law Center, The Cost of Credit: Regulation, Preemption, and Industry Abuses Ch. 3 (4th ed. 2009 and Supp.).

Credit statutes often contain, in addition to requirements covering the credit aspects of a transaction, important protections concerning sales provisions, such as prohibiting blanks or waivers of consumer rights in the contract, or requiring that copies of the contract and any credit insurance policy be provided to the consumer. Remedies under credit statutes are often very powerful and can include unenforceability of the obligation. Claims under state credit statutes are discussed in detail in National Consumer Law Center, *The Cost of Credit: Regulation, Preemption, and Industry Abuses*.[282]

11.9 Warranty Defenses

Often the reason a family stops paying on a manufactured home debt is that the home is defective. In such a case, warranty defenses may be available.[283] The buyer may have the right to revoke acceptance of the home and cancel the contract to buy it.[284] Warranty defenses may be asserted against the creditor that financed the sale if it is related to the seller or the seller referred the consumer to it.[285] Federal law sets construction standards for manufactured homes,[286] and about half the states have laws requiring at least a one-year warranty on manufactured homes.[287] Chapter 15 of another National Consumer Law Center treatise, *Consumer Warranty Law* (3d ed. 2006 and Supp.), addresses these and other manufactured home warranty issues in detail.

11.10 Homestead Exemption

Sometimes foreclosure upon a manufactured home is threatened because of a judgment lien rather than a consensual security interest. Whether the debtor can protect the home from judgment execution depends on the language and interpretation of the state homestead exemption statute.

Some state homestead exemptions specifically include manufactured homes.[288] Other states include manufactured homes by providing a homestead exemption for personal property used as a residence,[289] or establish an exemption for manufactured homes separate from the state homestead exemption.[290]

If manufactured homes are not addressed specifically by the state exemption laws, the question will be whether a manufactured home can qualify for a general state homestead exemption. If a home is attached to the land, it may be included in the homestead and exempt from execution of the lien.[291] But even a motor home, travel trailer or other type of recreational vehicle that may not be permanently attached to the land may qualify for a homestead exemption in light of its actual and intended use.[292] Courts also look to the

282 (4th ed. 2009 and Supp.).

283 *See generally* National Consumer Law Center, Consumer Warranty Law Ch. 17 (3d ed. 2006 and Supp.).

284 *Id.* at Ch. 8.

285 *See* National Consumer Law Center, Unfair and Deceptive Acts and Practices § 11.6 (7th ed. 2008 and Supp.).

286 42 U.S.C. §§ 5401–5426. *See* National Consumer Law Center, Consumer Warranty Law § 17.3 (3d ed. 2006 and Supp.) (detailed discussion of federal standards).

287 National Consumer Law Center, Consumer Warranty Law § 17.4.2 (3d ed. 2006 and Supp.).

288 *See, e.g.*, Ariz. Rev. Stat. Ann. § 33-1101(A) (homestead exemption includes the manufactured home and the land on which the manufactured home resides); Fla. Stat. § 222.05; N.Y. C.P.L.R. 5206(a) (McKinney).

289 *See, e.g.*, Me. Rev. Stat. Ann. tit. 14, § 4422(1)(A). *See also In re* Macleod, 295 B.R. 1 (Bankr. D. Me. 2003) (manufactured home used as residence is exempt personal property under Maine statute).

290 *See* Mo. Rev. Stat. § 513.430(1)(6); *In re* White, 287 B.R. 232 (Bankr. E.D. Mo. 2002) (debtor not entitled to homestead exemption as she did not convert her manufactured home from personal property to real property under state law; debtor is entitled to manufactured home exemption).

291 *In re* Thornton, 269 B.R. 682 (Bankr. W.D. Mo. 2001) (home on blocks, with wheels and tires removed and with skirting around it, attached to well and septic system, was real property and qualified for homestead exemption); *In re* Buzzell, 110 B.R. 440 (Bankr. D. Neb. 1990) (manufactured home, which was permanently annexed to the property by means of a wooden addition, qualified for an exemption under state homestead act); Gold v. Schwartz, 774 So. 2d 879 (Fla. Dist. Ct. App. 2001) (manufactured home permanently attached to land qualifies as a homestead). *See also* Colwell v. Royal Int'l Trading Corp., 226 B.R. 714 (Bankr. S.D. Fla. 1998) (married homeowners with two separate manufactured homes, each one held by separate deed and each one living in one home only, were entitled to homestead exemption for both homes pursuant to Florida law), *aff'd*, 196 F.3d 1225 (11th Cir. 1999) (per curiam). *See also* § 11.2, *supra*.

292 *In re* Carlson, 303 B.R. 478 (B.A.P. 10th Cir. 2004) (Utah law) (thirty-two foot trailer located in RV park); *In re* Irwin, 293 B.R. 28 (Bankr. D. Ariz. 2003) (motor home, actually used as the debtor's residence, can qualify for homestead exemption under state law); *In re* Bubnak, 176 B.R. 601 (Bankr. M.D. Fla. 1994) (motor home in park, with permanent utility hookups, had sufficient permanency to qualify as Florida homestead); *In re* Meola, 158 B.R. 881 (Bankr. S.D. Fla. 1993) (travel trailer was a "dwelling house" similar to a manufactured home and qualified as an exempt homestead under state law when it was the debtor's only possession of value and his sole residence for many years); *In re* Mangano, 158 B.R. 532 (Bankr. S.D. Fla. 1993) (motor home's actual and intended use qualified it for a homestead exemption when debtors lived in the motor home, paid rent to the manufactured home park, had no other residence, and the debtors had no license or registration). *See In re* Yettaw, 316 B.R. 560 (Bankr. M.D. Fla. 2004) (debtor, who had sold home and purchased inoperable RV, set up in month-to-month rental space in RV park, could claim homestead). *But see In re* Kelly, 334 B.R. 772 (Bankr. D. Mass. 2005) (debtor who was neither older nor disabled could not claim homestead in manufactured home where term "manufactured homes" added to older and disabled exemption, but not general homestead provision); *In re* Andiorio, 237 B.R. 851 (Bankr. M.D. Fla. 1999) (recreational vehicle that had tires and no permanent

ownership of the underlying land,[293] although some courts have allowed a homestead exemption for a manufactured home even where the homeowner does not own the land.[294] One court has articulated these criteria for a non-traditional homestead: (1) the debtor's intent to make the non-traditional abode his homestead; (2) whether the debtor has no other residence; (3) whether the evidence establishes continuous habitation; (4) whether the debtor maintains at least a possessory right associated with the land establishing a physical presence; (5) whether the non-traditional abode has been physically maintained to allow long-term habitation versus mobility; (6) whether the physical configuration of the abode permits habitation (the physical characteristics of the home are otherwise immaterial).[295]

Even if a manufactured home is classified as personal property for other purposes, it may qualify for a homestead exemption.[296] The purpose of homestead exemption laws is to protect debtors and their dependents from destitution, and they are to be liberally construed to achieve this result.[297]

11.11 Workout Agreements

Workout agreements on manufactured home loans are increasingly possible.[298] Loans on manufactured homes are eligible for modification under the Home Affordable Modification Program (HAMP).[299] As the home is likely to be worth less than the amount due on the loan because of depreciation, lenders may have substantial incentives to work with borrowers in order to avoid large losses in the foreclosure process. The creditor may also be motivated by a desire to avoid a requirement that local tax debts be paid before the home can be resold or to avoid paying fees to get a permit from the local jurisdiction to move the home.

Borrowers facing foreclosure of FHA-insured mortgages on manufactured homes have some protections not available to persons with conventional loans. For example, a lender under these programs must give notice of the default giving the borrower the right within thirty days after the notice to either to cure the default or agree to a modification agreement or repayment plan;[300] and the lender must make reasonable efforts to arrange or hold a face-to-face interview with the homeowner before accelerating the mortgage loan.[301] The lender must also permit reinstatement of the mortgage, even after foreclosure proceedings have been initiated, if the borrower brings the loan current, executes a modification agreement, or agrees to an acceptable repayment plan.[302] Workout options for FHA-insured mortgages are discussed more fully in Chapter 3.

11.12 Using Bankruptcy to Prevent Loss of a Manufactured Home

A bankruptcy filing under chapter 13 will provide a right to cure in installments in the context of a confirmed plan[303] and is a good alternative if a workout cannot be negotiated. Furthermore, if the manufactured home is considered personal property based on state law or the sales contract, the debtor has the right to strip down the secured claim to the value of the collateral and then to pay off the reduced secured claim.[304] The portion of the debt that exceeds the reduced secured claim is treated as unsecured. Any amount of the unsecured portion of the claim that remains unpaid

---

connections to the land, and was maintained for travel, did not qualify for a homestead exemption under Florida law); *In re* Kirby, 223 B.R. 825 (Bankr. M.D. Fla. 1998) (homestead exemption did not protect motor home used as principal residence, where there was no "permanency": motor coach was not attached to land, and debtors neither owned nor leased land in Florida); *In re* Scott, 233 B.R. 32 (Bankr. N.D.N.Y. 1998) (New York homestead may be established in land with a motor home on it, if debtor can show actual physical presence and intent to reside there permanently; not shown here, where period of residence was only a few days, and debtor made no effort to prepare land for long-term residence). *Cf. In re* Norris, 316 B.R. 246 (W.D. Tex. 2004) (houseboat can never be Texas homestead; law requires land or a structure that can be affixed to land), *question certified on appeal*, 413 F.3d 526 (5th Cir. 2005).

293 *In re* Cobbins, 234 B.R. 882 (Bankr. S.D. Miss. 1999) (when defendant did not own land under manufactured home, manufactured home itself did not qualify under the state homestead exemption because defendant was not the landowner), *aff'd*, 227 F.3d 302 (5th Cir. 2000) (unpublished).

294 *In re* Carlson, 303 B.R. 478 (B.A.P. 10th Cir. 2004) (Utah law) (thirty-two foot trailer located in RV park).

295 *See In re* Yettaw, 316 B.R. 560 (Bankr. M.D. Fla. 2004).

296 Green Tree Credit Corp. v. Thompson (*In re* Thompson), 217 B.R. 375 (B.A.P. 2d Cir. 1998) (inclusion of manufactured homes in state homestead exemption law did not make manufactured home real property for bankruptcy purposes). *See also* § 11.2, *supra*.

297 Green Tree Credit Corp. v. Thompson (*In re* Thompson), 217 B.R. 375 (B.A.P. 2d Cir. 1998). *See generally* National Consumer Law Center, Collection Actions Ch. 12 (2008 and Supp.).

298 *See* Ch. 2, *supra*.

299 *See* § 2.8, *supra*.

300 24 C.F.R. § 201.50(b). *See* CitiMortgage, Inc. v. Ferguson, 2008 WL 376380 (Ohio Ct. App. Feb. 7, 2008) (denying summary judgment for lender in foreclosure action based on borrower's statement that lender failed to comply with notice requirement under 24 C.F.R. § 201.50).

301 24 C.F.R. § 201.50(a).

302 24 C.F.R. § 201.50(c).

303 *See* § 9.3, *supra*.

304 *In re* Johnson, 269 B.R. 246 (Bankr. M.D. Ala. 2001); *In re* Stratton, 248 B.R. 177 (Bankr. D. Mont. 2000); *In re* Blevins, 152 B.R. 130 (Bankr. N.D. Tex. 1992) (modification available because manufactured home is personal property); *In re* Plaster, 101 B.R. 696 (Bankr. E.D. Okla. 1989); *In re* Colver, 13 B.R. 521 (Bankr. D. Nev. 1981). *Cf. In re* Speights, 131 B.R. 205 (Bankr. N.D. Fla. 1991) (modification not available because facts establish that home was permanently affixed to the real estate); *In re* Carter, 116 B.R. 156 (Bankr. W.D. Mo. 1990). *See generally* § 9.7, *supra*.

after the debtor completes the chapter 13 plan will be discharged, along with the unpaid portion of other unsecured debts. As manufactured homes often depreciate faster than the debt reduces, the secured portion of the claim will often be far less than the debt.

Amendments made to the Bankruptcy Code by the 2005 Bankruptcy Act[305] define "debtor's principal residence" to mean a residential structure, without regard to whether it is attached to real property.[306] However, the new definition does not appear to prevent strip down of manufactured homes, because no change was made to the Code provision that that protects home secured lenders from modification, 11 U.S.C. § 1322(b)(2). This section remains applicable only to claims secured by real property. While a manufactured home may be the debtor's principal residence under the new definition, it may still be personal property under applicable non-bankruptcy law and therefore the debt would not be secured "only by a security interest in real property" that is the debtor's principal residence.[307] Only if a manufactured home is real property under applicable non-bankruptcy law would the limitations on modification apply, even though the manufactured home is considered the debtor's principal residence. A majority of courts deciding this issue have reached this conclusion.[308] Other exceptions to the anti-modification provision in section 1322(b)(2), which would permit the strip down of a manufactured home security interest, are discussed elsewhere in this treatise.[309]

Another issue that can arise in bankruptcy court is whether the creditor has properly perfected its security interest. Outside of bankruptcy, failure of the creditor to perfect its security interest has no impact on the debtor because the security interest is good against the debtor regardless of perfection.[310] In bankruptcy court, however, the "strong arm" statute[311] gives the trustee the rights of a hypothetical judgment creditor on the date the bankruptcy case was filed. Because a judgment creditor's lien has priority over an unperfected security interest, this means that the trustee can override an unperfected security interest in a manufactured home.[312] The trustee then has to dispose of the collateral but, in some circumstances, the consumer may be able to buy it back from the trustee on better terms than the original contract provided.

11.13 Raising Seller-Related Defenses Against the Foreclosing Creditor

The creditor repossessing or foreclosing on a manufactured home is usually not the same entity that sold the consumer the home. The creditor will nonetheless usually be liable for the consumer's claims against the seller, up to the amount paid by the consumer, because of the contractual language required by the FTC Holder Rule.[313] All assignees of consumer sales contracts have this derivative liability, and purchase-money lenders do also as long as the seller arranged the financing or is affiliated with the lender by common control, contract or business arrangement.[314]

305 Pub. L. No. 109-8 (2005).

306 11 U.S.C. § 101(13A). *See* National Consumer Law Center, Consumer Bankruptcy Law and Practice §§ 11.6.1.2.2.2, 11.6.1.2.2.3, 11.6.1.2.2.4 (9th ed. 2009).

307 11 U.S.C. § 1322(b)(2).

The 2005 Act also attempts to limit strip down rights by adding language at the end of § 1325(a) that removes certain claims based on purchase money security interests from the provisions of §§ 506(a) and 1325(a)(5). However, the first type of purchase money security interest covered by this new language is for a debt incurred within 910 days preceding the filing of the petition, if the collateral consists of a motor vehicle, as defined in 49 U.S.C. § 30102. This language would not include a manufactured home, because a manufactured home does not fit within the referenced definition. The second type of claim encompassed by this new language is a purchase money security interest for a debt incurred within one year preceding the filing of the petition, if the collateral consists of any other thing of value. This could potentially apply to a manufactured home, but the new language does not limit the debtor's right to cure a default on a purchase money mortgage or to otherwise modify a mortgage to the extent the limitation for home secured loans is not applicable. *See* National Consumer Law Center, Consumer Bankruptcy Law and Practice § 11.6.1 (9th ed. 2009).

308 *See In re* Reinhardt, 563 F.3d 558 (6th Cir. 2009); *In re* Ennis, 558 F.3d 343 (4th Cir. 2009); *In re* Coleman, 392 B.R. 767 (B.A.P. 8th Cir. 2008); *In re* Davis, 386 B.R. 182 (B.A.P. 6th Cir. 2008); Green Tree Servicing, L.L.C. v. Harrison, 2009 WL 82565, (W.D. La. Jan. 12, 2009); *In re* Shepherd, 381 B.R. 675 (E.D. Tenn. 2008); Moss v. Greentree-AL, L.L.C., 378 B.R. 655 (S.D. Ala. 2007); *In re* Jordan, 403 B.R. 339 (Bankr. W.D. Pa. 2009); *In re* Oliveira, 378 B.R. 789 (Bankr. E.D. Tex. 2007). *But see In re* Lunger, 370 B.R. 649 (Bankr. M.D. Pa. 2007).

309 *See* § 9.7, *supra*.

310 *See* National Consumer Law Center, Repossessions § 3.2.9 (6th ed. 2005 and Supp.).

311 11 U.S.C. § 544. *See* National Consumer Law Center, Consumer Bankruptcy Law and Practice § 10.4.2.6.2 (9th ed. 2009).

312 *See, e.g.*, Kroskie v. Chase Manhattan Mortgage Corp., 315 F.3d 644 (6th Cir. 2003); *In re* Renaud, 302 B.R. 280 (Bankr. E.D. Ark. 2003); *In re* Trible, 290 B.R. 838 (Bankr. D. Kan. 2003) (creditor's failure to note its lien on manufactured home's certificate of title rendered its security interest in the manufactured home unperfected under state law and subject to avoidance under § 544). *But see In re* Garrett, 276 B.R. 217 (Bankr. E.D. Tenn. 2002) (creditor's lien remained properly perfected following a manufactured home's interstate relocation; the law of the state that issued the certificate continued to govern where the certificate was not surrendered and the home was not registered in the new state at the commencement of the case); *In re* Cassady, 197 B.R. 846 (Bankr. E.D. Tenn. 1996) (creditor properly perfected its security interest in debtor's manufactured home by notation of its lien on the certificate of title even though the home was subsequently attached to the land).

313 16 C.F.R. § 433. *See* BCS Fin. Corp. v. Sorbo, 444 S.E.2d 85 (Ga. Ct. App. 1994). *See generally* National Consumer Law Center, Unfair and Deceptive Acts and Practices § 11.6 (7th ed. 2008 and Supp.).

314 16 C.F.R. § 433.1(d).

The creditor is also, of course, liable for its own wrongful acts. The creditor may have violated a state credit statute, the Truth in Lending Act, or RESPA.[315] It may have violated Article 9 of the UCC or a state law when it repossessed the manufactured home.[316] It may have committed fraud or a UDAP violation in financing the transaction or dealing with the buyers after the sale. In addition, if the loan to purchase the home is insured under the Federal Housing Administration's Title I program,[317] the lender must investigate the manufacturer's record of warranty compliance and obtain certification that the home site meets minimum standards.[318] A lender's failure to comply with these duties may make it fully liable for problems with the home, rather than liable only up to the amount that the consumer has paid as the FTC Holder Rule requires.

11.14 Problems Relating to Manufactured Home Parks

Space in manufactured home parks is often at a premium. A home may lose much of its value if it is sold without an assurance that it can stay on the rented lot in the park. Even if a new buyer has a place to locate the home, moving a manufactured home is costly, runs the risk of damage, and accelerates the home's deterioration even if there are no mishaps in the process of removing, hauling, and re-siting it.

Park owners may exploit these factors as a way of profiting from home repossessions and foreclosures. For example, if the original buyers try to sell the home as a way of avoiding foreclosure and recouping their investment, the park owner may refuse to transfer the lot lease to the new buyer. This can prevent the sale, making it possible for the park owner or the creditor to buy the home at a low price at the foreclosure sale. Then the park owner, either acting for itself or for the creditor, may sell the home to a new buyer or may rent out the home along with the lot. Many parks are owned by or connected with manufactured home dealers and so can replenish their inventory in this manner.

If the state has a comprehensive park statute, it may outlaw restrictions on sale or transfer of homes within the park. It may also prohibit unreasonable refusal by the park to rent to a new buyer.[319]

Even without a specific prohibition in a park statute, there may be ways to attack the park's actions. The park's actions may violate state or federal antitrust laws.[320] If Article 9 governs, the creditor's sale of the home must be commercially reasonable. The park may be closely enough connected to or working closely enough with the creditor that its interference with the consumer's attempts to sell the home may be attributable to the creditor, making the repossession sale commercially unreasonable.[321]

Article 9 also provides some special rules when the collateral is resold to an insider. These rules apply when the buyer of the collateral at the repossession sale is the secured creditor, a party related to the secured creditor,[322] or a secondary obligor.[323] The original dealer is considered a secondary obligor if the secured creditor has a right of recourse against the dealer, i.e., the right to require the dealer to repurchase the obligation if the consumer defaults. If the collateral is sold at the repossession sale to any one of these insiders for a price significantly below the range that an arms-length sale would have produced, then the debtor is entitled to be credited with the price that an arms-length sale would have produced.[324]

11.15 Effect of Default on Debt or Rent for Land on Which Manufactured Home Is Sited

Additional issues may arise as to the land on which the manufactured home rests. If the land is owned by the homeowner, the land may be subject to a mortgage or other liens. The mortgage or lien holder may or may not be the same entity that holds the security interest in the home. In either case, the debt for the land needs to be addressed at the same time as a plan is developed to address the debt on the home.

If the home is attached to the land after the land is purchased, it may become a fixture. Thereafter, the security interests on the land may cover the manufactured home as well. This can come as an unpleasant surprise to a homeowner who is unable to maintain payments on the land but expects to move the home. Generally, the issue will be a question of fact controlled by evidence such as whether the wheels are removed and whether the home is permanently

315 *See* §§ 11.3.3, 11.3.5, *supra*.

316 *See* National Consumer Law Center, Repossessions Ch. 6 (6th ed. 2005 and Supp.).

317 12 U.S.C. § 1703.

318 24 C.F.R. § 201.21(d)(3).

319 *See* Carolyn Carter, Elizabeth De Armond, Jonathan Sheldon, and Odette Williamson, AARP Pub. Policy Inst., Manufactured Housing Community Tenants: Shifting the Balance of Power (2004), *available at* www.aarp.org/research/ppi/liv-com/housing/articles/aresearch-import-871-D18138.html (summarizing state manufactured home park laws and proposing model law); CFED and National Consumer Law Center, Protecting Fundamental Freedoms in Communities (Sept. 2008), *available at* www.consumerlaw.org (click on Homeownership and Consumer Credit, then Manufactured Housing).

320 *Cf.* Russell v. Atkins, 679 A.2d 333 (Vt. 1996). *But cf.* Vermont Mobile Home Owners' Ass'n v. Lapierre, 131 F. Supp. 2d 553 (D. Vt. 2001) (no federal antitrust violation where consumers failed to show economic power in the tying product market or injury from the tying arrangement).

321 *See* § 11.3.6, *supra*.

322 The relationship that is necessary to make a party an insider is defined at U.C.C. § 9-102(a)(62), (63).

323 U.C.C. § 9-615(f).

324 U.C.C. § 9-615(f).

affixed to the ground.[325] In many states, a statute regulates this issue, and the home will remain personalty unless the owner goes through a procedure to surrender the title and record the home in the county land records.[326]

If the manufactured home rests on land which is owned by someone else, it is likely that the homeowner is paying rent, i.e., a fee for occupying the land. This rent must be paid or the homeowner may be evicted. The homeowner may still be liable for rent even after repossession of the home. If the home is repossessed and left on the rental space, the lender may also be responsible for rent and other costs.[327]

Some states strictly regulate park leases and evictions, at minimum requiring that the land or park owner follow certain specific notice procedures prior to commencing eviction proceedings.[328] Because alternative park space is not always readily available, the effect of eviction for nonpayment of ground rent may be loss of the manufactured home as well. In states where park space is at a premium, large ground rent increases or other abusive landlord practices, if unregulated or unchecked, can result in epidemics of evictions. Some legal services attorneys have brought claims against park owners based on unfair trade practice laws, other consumer protection statutes, and common law conversion when rent increases appear to be in bad faith for the purpose of forcing homeowners to abandon valuable manufactured homes.[329]

---

325 *See* § 11.2.5, *supra.*

326 *See* § 11.2.3, *supra.*

327 *See* Green Tree Servicing, L.L.C. v. Futernick, 2009 WL 249474 (Mich. Ct. App. Feb. 3, 2009) (repossessing lender responsible for lot rent and maintenance costs for spaces occupied by homes it has repossessed).

328 *See, e.g.*, Mobile Home Park Act, Colo. Rev. Stat. § 38-12-202(1)(a), (c); N.Y. Real Prop. Law § 233 (McKinney). *See generally* National Consumer Law Center, Unfair and Deceptive Acts and Practices § 8.1.2.5.2 (7th ed. 2008 and Supp.) (listing state manufactured home park laws).

329 *See generally* National Consumer Law Center, Unfair and Deceptive Acts and Practices § 2.2.6 (7th ed. 2008 and Supp.) (discussion of the application of UDAP laws to residential leases and manufactured home parks).

An advocacy approach to these issues may involve legislative or regulatory issues. *See also* Yee v. City of Escondido, 503 U.S. 519, 112 S. Ct. 1522, 118 L. Ed. 2d 153 (1992) (city's manufactured home rent control ordinance and California's manufactured home residency law do not constitute a Fifth Amendment taking).

Chapter 12 Forfeiture of Land Installment Sales Contracts

12.1 Introduction

Land installment sales contracts, sometimes called installment land contracts, land sale contracts, contracts for deed, bonds for deed, or long-term land contracts, are often abusive alternatives to mortgages or deeds of trust.[1] This chapter refers to these contracts as land installment sales contracts, and focuses on the buyer's forfeiture under these contracts.

In a land installment sales contract, the buyer takes possession of the property and makes monthly installment payments of principal and interest to the seller until the principal balance is paid off. The contract term varies, but may exceed twenty years. During the contract period, the buyer is responsible for maintaining the property and for paying the taxes and insurance.[2]

After the contract is signed, the seller continues to hold legal title to the property to secure payment of the purchase price.[3] The buyer is viewed as the property's equitable owner and has possession and full use of the property, so long as the seller's security interest is not impaired.[4]

Land installment sales contracts typically contain forfeiture clauses which provide that "time is of the essence." These clauses purport to allow the seller to forfeit the contract if any payment is missed, retake possession of the property, and keep all payments made as liquidated damages or rent. Upon the seller's exercise of the forfeiture clause, the buyer may be evicted through procedures applicable to tenants.[5] If the buyer has made substantial payments, forfeiture results in a windfall to the seller. In the absence of a contractual forfeiture provision, courts may order that payments already made must be returned to the buyer.[6]

The method by which a contract is foreclosed or "forfeited" depends on state law. Several states regulate land installment sales contracts by statute, detailing procedures for termination, forfeiture, or foreclosure of the contracts.[7] However, in most states, regulation of installment land sales contracts is left to the common law.

In the past, forfeiture clauses of land installment sales contracts were upheld by the courts as written, despite the obvious unfairness to the buyer. More recently, however, courts have begun to question this approach, and are striking clauses that are inherently unfair to the buyer. In addition, some states have enacted legislation to add protections for buyers or to eliminate forfeiture as a remedy altogether.[8] Other states limit forfeiture to situations in which the buyer has abandoned the property or has very little equity in the property. Some courts now require that a property be sold at

---

1 *See, e.g.,* Randall v. Riel, 465 A.2d 505, 507 (N.H. 1983)("The terms 'contract for deed,' 'bond for deed,' and 'installment land contract' are synonymous, and used to describe the most commonly employed mortgage substitute."). *See also* National Consumer Law Center, The Cost of Credit: Regulation, Preemption, and Industry Abuses § 9.4.3.2 (4th ed. 2009 and Supp.).

2 *See, e.g.,* Jackson v. Scheible, 902 N.E.2d 807 (Ind. 2009) (seller has no duty to maintain property up to code standards after entering into two-year installment land sale contact); Graves v. Diehl, 958 S.W.2d 468, 472 (Tex. App. 1997) (equitable interest in property gives land contract vendee standing to bring action against third parties for damage to property); Steiner v. Wisconsin Am. Mut. Ins. Co., 697 N.W.2d 452, 457 (Wis. 2005) (land contract vendee takes on liabilities generally attributed to ownership of real property).

3 *See* Skendzel v. Marshall, 301 N.E.2d 641 (Ind. 1973); Sebastian v. Floyd, 585 S.W.2d 381 (Ky. 1979); Anderson Contracting Co. v. Daugherty, 417 A.2d 1227 (Pa. Super. Ct. 1979). *See generally* Grant Nelson & Dale Whitman, Real Estate Finance Law § 3.26 (4th ed. 2002); Richard R. Powell, The Law of Real Prop. § 84D.01[1] (2002).

4 *See, e.g., In re* Jones, 768 F.2d 923 (7th Cir. 1985); *In re* Griffin, 397 B.R. 356 (Bankr. W.D. Va. 2008) (under Virginia law, judgment lien attached to buyer's equitable interest in the real property being purchased under installment contract); *In re* White, 374 B.R. 257 (Bankr. D. Kan. 2007) (the interest buyer acquires in property under land installment sales contract is sufficient to make a later mortgage debt incurred to pay off the land sales contract a refinancing and not an acquisition loan for purposes of TIL rescission). *See, also In re* Groff, 223 B.R. 697 (Bankr. S.D. Ill. 1998) (chapter 13 debtor may claim homestead exemption in residence being purchased under installment sales contract and avoid judicial lien that impaired the exemption); *In re* Princiotta, 49 B.R. 447 (Bankr. D. Mass. 1985) (same); White v. Brousseau, 566 So. 2d 832 (Fla. Dist. Ct. App. 1990).

5 Long v. Smith, 776 S.W.2d 409 (Mo. Ct. App. 1989).

6 *See, e.g.,* Crowell v. Williams, 615 S.E.2d 797 (Ga. Ct. App. 2005) (buyer's default in payment and seller's attempt to resell property rescinded contract; in absence of forfeiture clause, payments must be returned).

7 *See, e.g.,* Ariz. Rev. Stat. Ann. § 33-741(2); Me. Rev. Stat. Ann. tit. 33, § 481(2); Md. Code Ann., Real Property § 10-101(b) (West); Ohio Rev. Code Ann. § 5313.01(A) (West); Wash. Rev. Code § 61.30.010.

8 *See* § 12.3, *infra.*

a foreclosure sale, with the excess proceeds given to the buyer.[9]

In many states, courts and legislatures have imposed substantive and procedural limits on forfeiture similar to those imposed on mortgages in foreclosure. It is common to require sellers to give notice of a pending forfeiture. The seller must also give the buyer a reasonable chance to cure the default and reinstate the contract or redeem the contract in full.[10]

In addition, a bankruptcy filing may provide an additional avenue of relief for the buyer, whether the court treats the contract as a mortgage or as an executory contract.[11] The bankruptcy stay may also prove helpful, and the buyer may be able to set aside a forfeiture that has already taken place.[12]

Because the law is unsettled as to the buyer's rights under state statutes, common law, and the Bankruptcy Code, both statutory and case law research is necessary to determine what protections are available to a purchaser under a land installment sales contract in a particular state.[13] In addition, absent available consumer protections, litigation challenging forfeitures may be possible based on equitable principles and on due process grounds if state action can be shown.

12.2 Nature of Land Installment Sales Contracts

12.2.1 Legal Obligations of the Parties

Land installment sales contracts are functionally different from leases with an option to buy.[14] The land installment sales contract serves primarily as a financing device, with the seller providing the financing. Similarly, land installment sales contracts differ from the short-term "binder" agreements or "earnest money" contracts that control the relations between a buyer and seller during the relatively short period between the signing of a purchase agreement and a closing, when third party financing typically completes the conveyance. Under the standard land installment sales contract the buyer takes possession of the property upon execution of the agreement and assumes the obligations and benefits of ownership at that time.

The buyer is generally free to transfer the rights under an installment land contract without the prior consent of the seller.[15] Although some courts will give effect to a contract clause forbidding assignment, the seller's acceptance of payments from the assignee may operate as a waiver of the prohibition.[16]

Unsophisticated parties often draft installment land sale contracts. Their documents may fail to meet the formal requirements of the statutes or the common law of a particular jurisdiction. In some cases there may be no written contract at all. Where appropriate, and particularly where there is no evidence of overreaching by one party, courts have implied terms left out of documents or allowed evidence of the parties' conduct to fill in for the deficient terms.[17]

---

9 *See* § 12.4, *infra.*

10 *See* §§ 12.3, 12.4, *infra.*

11 *See* § 12.5, *infra.*

12 *Id.*

13 A state-by-state summary of statutes and selected case law on foreclosure and termination of installment land contracts is provided in Baxter Dunaway, Law of Distressed Real Estate, vol. 2, pt. D, appx. 14A (2009).

14 Bayou Fleet P'ship v. Phillip Family, L.L.C., 976 So. 2d 794 (La. Ct. App. 2008) (summary judgment precluded where there is factual dispute as to whether contract was intended as bond for deed or lease with option to buy); H.J. Bergeron, Inc. v. Parker, 964 So. 2d 1075 (La. Ct. App. 2007) (document labeled "Lease With Option to Purchase" is bond for deed under state statutory definition; seller must give statutory notice of cancellation applicable to a bond for deed); Kopanuk v. AVCP Reg'l Hous. Auth., 902 P.2d 813 (Alaska 1995) (contract creating equitable interest in property was installment land sales contract, not lease); Fadelsak v. Hagley, 2003 WL 21489613 (Ohio Ct. App. June 25, 2003) (contrasting land installment sales contracts and leases with option to buy).

15 Sleeping Indian Ranch, Inc. v. West Ridge Group, L.L.C., 119 P.3d 1062, 1069 (Colo. 2005) (en banc) (installment land contract buyer had right to convey equitable interest in property); Flack v. Laster, 417 A.2d 393 (D.C. 1980) (anti-assignment clause ineffective where vendor acquiesced in assignment by accepting payments from assignee); Carey v. Lincoln Loan Co., 125 P.3d 814 (Or. Ct. App. 2005), *aff'd on other grounds,* 157 P.3d 775 (Or. 2007) (invalidating non-assignment clause of installment sales contract as unconscionable where there was no evidence of commercial need for absolute restriction); Anderson v. Aesoph, 697 N.W.2d 25, 31 (S.D. 2005) (relative to whom buyer conveyed interest in property under installment sales contract may exercise redemption rights); Beren Corp. v. Spader, 255 N.W.2d 247 (Neb. 1977); Brown v. Powell, 648 N.W.2d 329 (S.D. 2002) (vendor waived non-assignment clause by acceptance of payments with knowledge of assignment); Baliles v. Cities Serv. Co., 578 S.W.2d 621 (Tenn. 1979). *Compare* Levine v. First Nat'l Bank of Commerce, 948 So. 2d 1051 (La. 2006) (seller may trigger the due-on-sale clause in its own mortgage by entering into a land installment sales contract).

16 Flack v. Laster, 417 A.2d 393 (D.C. 1980) (anti-assignment clause ineffective where vendor acquiesced in assignment by accepting payments from assignee); Brown v. Powell, 648 N.W.2d 329 (S.D. 2002) (vendor waived non-assignment clause by acceptance of payments with knowledge of assignment).

17 *See, e.g.* Dittrick v. Chalfant, 948 A.2d 400 (Del. Ch. 2007), *aff'd,* 935 A.2d 255 (table), 2007 WL 2697364 (Del. Super. Ct. Sept. 17, 2007) (where parties left the interest rate term out of land sales contract, the court will impute state's statutory default rate of 5% over the federal reserve discount rate as a term of contract); Monea v. Lanci, 2009 WL 4690214 (Ohio Ct. App. Dec. 7, 2009) (reversing summary judgment for eviction where disputed fact questions remained as to whether oral agreement to purchase fell within statute of frauds exception and whether buyer had paid in excess of 20% of purchase price so as to require foreclosure rather than summary eviction); Shimko v. Marks, 632 N.E.2d 990 (Ohio Ct. App. 1993) (doctrine of

Buyers who did not have legal representation when they signed a land installment sales contract may not have known about recording requirements. Under state law, lack of recordation may leave the buyer unprotected against a subsequent purchaser of the property who acquires an interest without notice of the installment contract.[18] Thus, if the seller sells or grants a mortgage in the property to a third party, that party may take the property free and clear of the unrecorded contract buyer's interest. In most cases, however, the third party is deemed to have constructive notice of the legal rights of persons in possession of the property, so cannot claim protection under the state recording statute.[19] At least one state, Maryland, requires that the seller record the contract within fifteen days of its execution. Failure to record the contract gives the buyer the right to cancel the contract and receive a refund of money paid.[20]

12.2.2 Abuses Involving Installment Land Sales Contracts

Buyers often enter into installment land sales contracts because they could not obtain institutional financing or were unable to afford the closing costs and down payment associated with conventional mortgage financing. For sellers, the quick forfeiture remedy can be attractive.[21] Many sellers expect that buyers will be unaware of defenses to forfeiture or will not have access to the legal resources needed to exercise their rights.

While installment land sales contracts are not always abusive, at their worst they can be a vehicle for scams, particularly in neighborhoods where housing values are sinking, or in connection with sales of manufactured housing that is depreciating in value. In these situations the contracts are often the functional equivalent of leases.[22] Sellers anticipate that forfeiture will occur before the buyer builds up any equity. The contract becomes a means of shifting obligations for repairs and taxes on to the party who, for all intents and purposes, is a tenant.[23] Under these circumstances the buyer may be better off seeking to apply unfair and deceptive practices acts and other unconscionability doctrines to challenge purported waivers of the warranty of habitability and other state law tenant protections rather than asserting claims based on property conveyance principles.[24]

Another flagrant misuse of installment land sales contracts involves foreclosure rescue scams.[25] In these transactions homeowners facing foreclosure are solicited to surrender title to their homes in return for a payoff to a foreclosing lender. The property may have a fair market value well above the loan payoff amount. The former homeowner, as a "buyer," then enters into an installment contract to buy the property back from the new owner. The installment payments may be labeled as "rent" and the contract as a "sale/leaseback." The new owner may then seek to declare a default in the agreement, evict the former homeowner, and keep the property. These transactions are in effect exorbitantly high-priced loans that may be attacked on a number of grounds, including as violations of state UDAP statutes, the Truth in Lending Act, and other statutes regulating high cost loans.[26]

---

partial performance and documentation in the form of receipts established existence of installment land sales contract despite parties' failure to comply with statute of frauds); Thornton v. Marcum, 2008 WL 836368 (Tenn. Ct. App. Mar. 31, 2008) (applying doctrine of equitable estoppel to order specific performance of oral installment land sale contract after buyer had made regular payments for three years); Yarto v. Gilliland, 287 S.W.3d 83 (Tex. App. 2009) (enjoining eviction where defendant raised plausible title claim based on oral contract for deed that fell within exception to statute of frauds).

18 In states with a race-notice recording act, the subsequent buyer must also record first to be protected. Richard R. Powell, The Law of Real Prop. § 84D.02[1] (2000).

19 Third parties are deemed to have constructive notice of a possessor's legal rights except in states with pure race recording acts. *Id.*

20 Md. Code Ann., Real Prop. § 10-102(f) (West). *See also* D&Y, Inc. v. Winston, 578 A.2d 1177 (Md. 1990) (buyer may cancel contract and recover all payments if contract not recorded within fifteen-day period, provided that election was made and communicated before recording was actually accomplished); Whitaker v. Whitaker, 901 A.2d 223 (Md. Ct. Spec. App. 2006) (upholding buyer's right under Maryland recording statute to cancel and recover payments minus rental value of property for occupancy period). *But see* Merivale Invs., L.L.C. v. Tuggle, 2009 WL 4727760 (Ohio Ct. App. 2009) (applying Ohio law: seller's failure to record installment land sale contract within twenty days as required by state law did not harm vendee and does not prevent enforcement of contract).

21 *See* Paraguay Place-View Trust v. Gray, 981 P.2d 681, 685 (Colo. Ct. App. 1999); Richard R. Powell, The Law of Real Property § 84D.01[2] (2000); Grant S. Nelson, *The Contract for Deed As a Mortgage: The Case for the Restatement Approach*, 1998 BYU L. Rev. 1111.

22 *See* Eric T. Freyfogle *The Installment Land Contract As Lease: Habitability Protections and the Low-Income Purchaser,* 62 N.Y.U. L. Rev. 293 (May 1987).

23 *See, e.g.,* Jackson v. Scheible, 902 N.E.2d 807 (Ind. 2009) (after entering into two-year installment land sale contact, seller has no duty to maintain property up to code standards).

24 *See* National Consumer Law Center, Unfair and Deceptive Acts and Practices Ch. 8 (7th ed. 2008 and Supp.).

25 *See* National Consumer Law Center, The Cost of Credit: Regulation, Preemption, and Industry Abuses § 11.6.7 (4th ed. 2009 and Supp.).

26 *See, e.g.,* Wilbourn v. Advantage Fin. Partners, L.L.C., 2010 WL 1194950 (N.D. Ill. Mar. 22, 2010) (refusing to dismiss various claims arising out of sale-leaseback scheme, including quiet title, TILA, and state law unconscionability); Foster v. Smith, 2009 WL 703702 (D. Minn. Mar. 16, 2009) (denying lender's summary judgment motion where borrower raised rescission and HOEPA claims related to foreclosure rescue scam); Knapp v. Vandergon, 2009 WL 2602254 (D. Minn. Aug. 21, 2009) (refusing to dismiss equitable mortgage claim); Davis v. Elite Mortgage Servs., Inc., 592 F. Supp. 2d 1052 (N.D. Ill. 2009) (rejecting subsequent mortgage holder's bona fide purchaser defense to homeowner's equitable mortgage action seek-

12.3 Statutory Limitations on Forfeiture

12.3.1 Introduction

Increasingly, states recognize that forfeiture, especially when the buyer has substantial equity in the property, is a harsh remedy. To provide more protection for contract buyers, some states regulate forfeiture by providing guidelines as to when forfeiture is permitted. Other states have enacted laws with protections that are akin to those given to mortgagors. This section focuses on state statutory protections, and the next section will address court decisions protecting contract buyers.

12.3.2 Notice and Right to Cure Requirements

States have enacted legislation which provides a contract buyer with advance notice and an opportunity to cure a default before the contract can be forfeited.[27] The time allotted for buyers to cure the default varies from state to state, but can last as long as a year. In Iowa, for example, the seller must provide written notice of default to the buyer and anyone in possession of the property.[28] The notice must specify the reason for default and state that the buyer has thirty days to cure the default. Under Iowa law, an agreement purporting to waive the right to notice is unenforceable as a matter of public policy.[29]

In some states the length of the grace period is determined by the percentage of the contract price the buyer has already

ing to recover title lost through foreclosure rescue scam); Paulson v. Beliveau, 2008 WL 5104694 (D. Minn. Dec. 1, 2008) (granting partial summary judgment for homeowner in action raising claims for conversion and fraud related to foreclosure rescue scam); Provencher v. T & M Mortgage Solutions, Inc., 2008 WL 2447472 (D. Me. June 18, 2008) (allowing action to proceed under state UDAP statute, equitable mortgage theory, and claims for fraudulent misrepresentation, breach of oral contract, and unconscionability against perpetrators of refinancing scheme using land installment sales contract device to take borrower's home); Jones v. Rees-Max, L.L.C., 514 F. Supp. 2d 1139 (D. Minn. Sept. 17, 2007) (sale-leaseback transaction construed as creating equitable mortgage and not absolute conveyance; court denies broker's motion for summary judgment on TIL/HOEPA claims and finds broker violated Minn. statute regulating "foreclosure purchasers"); Perry v. Queen, 2006 WL 481666 (M.D. Tenn. Feb. 27, 2006) (purported sale/leaseback arrangement was financing transaction subject to Truth in Lending Act; homeowner facing foreclosure gave deed for home worth $94,000 to pay off loan indebtedness of $26,000 with option to buy property back through monthly installment payments); Wilson v. Bel Fury Invs. Group, L.L.C., 2006 WL 297440 (D. Neb. Feb. 6, 2006) (regardless of labels on documents, a sale-leaseback agreement may create a mortgage subject to TILA and HOEPA disclosure requirements, but court declines to grant summary judgment for borrowers due to disputed facts); Rowland v. Haven Props., L.L.C., 2005 WL 1528264 (N.D. Ill. June 24, 2005) (homeowner's claims for violation of, *inter alia*, the Truth in Lending Act, HOEPA, and state consumer fraud act after she deeded away home worth $245,000 in return for payoff of $91,500 mortgage; court rejects defenses that this was merely a sale with a lease back rather than a financing transaction); Bernstein v. New Beginnings Tr., L.L.C., 988 So. 2d 90 (Fla. Dist. Ct. App. 2008) (reversing lower court order evicting former homeowners as lessees after they had entered into sale/leaseback contract on eve of foreclosure sale); Hodges v. Swafford, 863 N.E.2d 881 (Ind. Ct. App. 2007) (finding that arranger of foreclosure rescue scam was "creditor" subject to Truth in Lending Act rescission remedies and that transaction was "high cost loan" subject to limitations on fees and charges under the Home Ownership and Equity Protection Act (HOEPA)), *amended op.*, 868 N.E.2d 1179 (Ind. Ct. App. 2007) (adjusting amounts to be tendered for rescission). *See generally* Daniel. P. Lindsey and Lea A. Weems, *Today's Predatory Lending Tactics Require New Strategies and New Laws: How a Case From Chicago Helped Change Illinois Law*, 13 Public Interest Law Rep. 1 (Winter 2008) (discussing remedies, including equitable mortgage claims, for foreclosure rescue scams); Ch. 15, *infra*.

27 Ariz. Rev. Stat. Ann § 33-741 (length of notice period depends on percentage of purchase price paid); Iowa Code § 656.2 (thirty-day grace period); La. Rev. Stat. Ann. § 9-2941 (buyer may cure within forty-five days of notice of cancellation from seller); Mich. Comp. Laws § 600.5728 (fifteen-day cure period, plus post-judgment redemption periods of varying length depending on percentage of contract price paid); Minn. Stat. § 559.21 (varying notice periods); N.D. Cent. Code §§ 32-18-01 to 32-18-06 (one year grace period); Or. Rev. Stat. § 593.915 (varying notice periods); S.D. Codified Laws §§ 21-50-01 to 21-50-07; Tex. Prop. Code Ann. §§ 5.065–5.066 (Vernon) (varying notice periods); Wash. Rev. Code §§ 61.30.010, 61.30.911 (buyer may redeem or request sale during ninety-day notice period). *See* Upton v. Whitehead, 935 So. 2d 746 (La. Ct. App. 2006) (denying judgment to seller when no evidence of compliance with statutory notice provision), *op. after remand*, 962 So. 2d 1168 (La. Ct. App. 2007) (evicted buyers must be restored to possession and credited for months out of home after eviction based on defective notice); Hall v. Parks, 2009 WL 1393280 (Tex. App. May 19, 2009) (denying forfeiture where no evidence notice of default sent by registered or certified mail as required by state statute); Ward v. Malone, 2007 WL 4260516 (Tex. App. Dec. 6, 2007) (giving notice of right to cure after acceleration instead of before acceleration barred seller from enforcing forfeiture under terms of former Texas statute regulating contracts for deed). *See also In re* Edina Dev. Corp., 370 B.R. 894 (Bankr. D. Minn. 2007) (strictly limiting payment needed for cure to amounts and items required by statute, finding buyer made appropriate tender for cure). *But see* Flynn v. Korneffel, 547 N.W.2d 249 (Mich. 1996) (default amount must actually be paid to seller; deposit of funds in escrow account is not sufficient to redeem); Sitek v. Striker, 764 N.W.2d 585 (Minn. Ct. App. 2009) (state's statutory procedure for termination of contract by deed by serving prescribed notice did not displace court's ability to make judicial determination of forfeiture outside of statutory procedure).

28 Iowa Code § 656.2; Fairfax v. Oaks Dev. Co., 713 N.W.2d 704 (Iowa 2006) (barring forfeiture under Iowa Code § 656.2 because seller did not provide separate copy of the notice of default for both husband and wife buyers).

29 Fritz v. Fritz, 767 N.W.2d 420 (Iowa Ct. App. 2009).

paid.[30] For example, in Ohio, for dwellings on which the contract has been in effect for less than five years, and on which less than 20% of the principal has been paid, forfeiture is authorized only after a thirty day grace period. If the contract has been in effect more than five years and more than 20% of the purchase price has been paid, the contract must be judicially foreclosed, like a mortgage.[31] If the default is not cured by the expiration of the applicable grace period, then the forfeiture can proceed, either judicially or non-judicially, depending on the requirements of state law. By electing to proceed under the Ohio forfeiture remedy, the seller is barred from seeking a deficiency.[32]

12.3.3 Statutes Treating Land Installment Sales Contracts Like Mortgage Loans

Buyers receive the strongest protections under statutes that require foreclosure of installment land sales contracts in the same way mortgages are foreclosed under the state's laws. If the state statute requires only notice of intent to declare a forfeiture and a grace period to pay the arrearage, a seller may proceed with a forfeiture once they it has complied with the notice requirement. By contrast, treatment of an installment land sale contract as a mortgage almost always allows the purchaser an extended redemption period, often of several months, and sometimes even after judgment.[33]

A number of states have adopted legislation which treats some land sales contracts as mortgages.[34] For example, a Maryland statute prohibits forfeiture of a contract to purchase residential property when the buyer is an individual.[35] Instead, the seller must sell the land by a procedure akin to a foreclosure and the buyer is entitled to any surplus realized from the sale.[36]

In Illinois the seller must foreclose the installment contract just like a mortgage, if the contract period is greater than five years and the amount due is less than 80% of the contract price.[37] Otherwise, forfeiture is available after notice, through use of a summary forcible entry and detainer proceeding.[38] In Oklahoma all land installment sales contracts are deemed to be mortgages subject to the same rules of foreclosure as mortgages.[39] In Ohio, if the contract has been in effect more than five years and more than 20% of the purchase price has been paid, the contract must be judicially foreclosed, like a mortgage.[40] Where a state's statutes require the seller to foreclose upon an installment land contact as if it were a mortgage, the buyer must be permitted to exercise any statutory right to redeem that a mortgagor would have.[41] Similarly, when state laws limit deficiency judgments after foreclosures, these restrictions will apply to foreclosures of installment land sales contacts as well.[42]

12.3.4 Other Statutory Protections for Buyers

Several states have adopted statutes that provide additional protections for land installment sales contract buyers. A few states regulate credit terms.[43] Several states require disclosure of the financial terms of these transactions.[44] Texas recently enacted legislation which requires sellers to provide buyers with annual statements disclosing current information such as the amount paid to date, the amount owed, the amounts paid for taxes and insurance, and the number of remaining payments. The statute provides for assessment of penalties against non-complying sellers.[45]

---

30 *See, e.g.*, Ariz. Rev. Stat. Ann. § 33-741 (up to nine months); Minn. Stat. § 559.21 (up to ninety days); Or. Rev. Stat. § 93.915 (up to 120 days); Tex. Prop. Code Ann. §§ 5.065–5.066 (Vernon) (up to sixty days).

31 Ohio Rev. Code Ann. § 5313.07 (West). *See* Waters v. Williams, 2007 WL 172032 (Ohio Ct. App. Jan. 22, 2007) (buyers protected from forfeiture because paid in excess of 20% of original purchase price even though, due to subsequent advances, they had not paid more than 20% of current principal balance).

32 Ohio Rev. Code § 5313.10; Howard v. Temple, 172 Ohio App. 3d 21, 872 N.E.2d 1260 (2007). *See also* Mazur v. Young, 507 F.3d 1013, 1017, 1018 (6th Cir. 2007) (discussing similar provision under Mich. Comp. Laws § 600.5750 which bars a seller's claim for monetary damages under installment land sales contract after entry of judgment in forfeiture action).

33 *See In re* Brown, 249 B.R. 193 (Bankr: N.D. Ill. 2000) (installment land sale contract buyer who filed for chapter 13 bankruptcy relief during statutory post-judgment redemption period may cure default through plan); *In re* Grove, 208 B.R. 845 (Bankr. W.D. Pa. 1997) (same).

34 In Maine a land sales contract must be foreclosed in the same way as a mortgage. Me. Rev. Stat Ann. tit. 33, §§ 481, 482.
In Oklahoma a contract for deed is deemed a mortgage. Okla. Stat. tit. 16, § 11A. *See also* Fla. Stat. § 697.01; Kubany v. Woods, 622 So. 2d 22 (Fla. Dist. Ct. App. 1993) (under Florida law agreement for deed is treated as a mortgage and is subject to same rules of foreclosure as a mortgage).

35 Md. Code Ann., Real Prop. §§ 10-101 to 10-108 (West).

36 Md. Code Ann., Real Prop. §§ 10-101 to 10-108 (West). *See generally* Long v. Burson, 957 A.2d 173, 182–184 (Md. Ct. Spec. App. 2008) (discussing land installment sales contracts as subject to foreclosure procedures under Maryland law).

37 735 Ill. Comp. Stat. 5/15-1106.

38 735 Ill. Comp. Stat. 5/15-1106.

39 Okla. Stat. tit. 16, § 11A.

40 Ohio Rev. Code Ann. § 5313.07 (West).

41 Miles v. Smith, 2006 WL 1793629, at *5 (Cal. Ct. App. June 30, 2006) (unpublished opinion) (buyer under installment land contract has "unconditional right to redeem" regardless of failure to make prior payments due under contract).

42 Peterson v. Hartell, 40 Cal. 3d 102, 115 n.5, 219 Cal. Rptr. 170, 707 P.2d 232 (1985).

43 *See* National Consumer Law Center, The Cost of Credit: Regulation, Preemption, and Industry Abuses § 9.2.3.4 (4th ed. 2009 and Supp.).

44 *Id.*

45 Tex. Prop. Code Ann. § 5077 (Vernon). *See* Flores v. Millen-

12.3.5 Failure to Return a Surplus As an Unfair or Deceptive Practice

The Federal Trade Commission (FTC) has ruled that land installment sales contracts are unfair where the buyer's default results in forfeiture of all payments made to date, even where the sale results in a surplus.[46] While there is no private right of action under the FTC Act, unfair forfeiture practices should be actionable under a state unfair and deceptive practices statute—as long as the statute applies to real estate sales,[47] and as long as the statute prohibits unfair or unconscionable practices.[48]

12.4 Judicial Limitations on Forfeiture

12.4.1 Judicial Treatment of Land Installment Contracts As Mortgages

Absent clear statutory provisions requiring that installment land sale contracts be foreclosed as mortgages, buyers enjoy the strongest protections when court rulings mandate such a requirement.[49] In supporting this type of common law rule, the *Restatement of Property* recognizes that a contract for deed or land installment sales contract creates a mortgage.[50] The *Restatement* position focuses upon the function of a land installment sales contract as a means of securing the sale price of property while granting the essential elements of ownership to the purchaser.

When the installment land contract is treated as the equivalent of a mortgage, the purchaser will benefit from the same rights to cure defaults and redeem from foreclosure as a mortgagor. Some courts require that the land contract purchaser have built up significant equity in the property before the transaction will be treated as a mortgage.[51] However, a purchaser may satisfy this equity requirement by showing appreciation of the property's value, even though substantial payments were never credited to principal.[52]

The Colorado courts have taken a somewhat different approach, applying a set of factors on a case-by-case basis to determine whether a land sales contract will be treated as a mortgage.[53] Other courts require that the seller foreclose

---

nium Interests, Ltd., 185 S.W.3d 427 (Tex. 2006) (buyers need not prove actual harm or injury to recover statutory damages, but court accepts defense of sellers' good faith efforts to comply, three justices dissenting); Nguyen v. Yovan, __ S.W.2d __ , 2009 WL 3152100 (Tex. App. Oct. 1, 2009) (penalties assessed where no evidence showed seller sent annual statements); Henderson v. Love, 181 S.W.3d 810 (Tex. App. 2005) (ruling on constitutionality of statute). *See also In re* Dodson, 2008 WL 4621293 (Bankr. W.D. Tex. Oct. 16, 2008) (seller violated § 5.077 by providing accounting statement that failed to show current status of account, subjecting seller to liquidated damages), *subsequent decision on attorney fees,* 2008 WL 5455409 (Bankr. W.D. Tex. Dec. 22, 2008); Comment, *Contracts for Deed: Extinction Long Overdue*, 37 Tex. Tech L. Rev. 1231 (Summer 2005) (examining Texas legislation).

46 AMREP Corp., 102 F.T.C. 1362 (1983), *aff'd* 768 F.2d 1171 (10th Cir. 1985); Horizon Corp., 97 F.T.C. 464 (1981).

47 *See* National Consumer Law Center, Unfair and Deceptive Acts and Practices § 2.2.5 (7th ed. 2008 and Supp.).

48 *Id.* at Appx. A.

49 *In re* Fox, 83 B.R. 290 (Bankr. E.D. Pa. 1988) (discussing cases on treatment of installment land contracts as mortgages); Petersen v. Hartell, 707 P.2d 232 (Cal. 1985) (installment purchaser may redeem despite long-term default); White v. Brousseau, 566 So. 2d 832 (Fla. Dist. Ct. App. 1990) (a contract for deed is treated as a mortgage and is subject to the same rules of foreclosure); Skendzel v. Marshall, 301 N.E.2d 641 (Ind. 1973) (installment land sales contract is in nature of secured transaction and subject to similar rules for enforcement); Sebastian v. Floyd, 585 S.W.2d 381 (Ky. 1979) (there is no practical distinction between an installment land sales contact and a purchase money mortgage); Mackiewicz v. J.J. & Assocs., 514 N.W.2d 613 (Neb. 1994) (refusing to enforce forfeiture, requiring treatment of land contract as mortgage); Bean v. Walker, 464 N.Y.S.2d 895 (N.Y. App. Div. 1983) (relationship of vendor-vendee under installment land sales contract is substantially the same as that of mortgage holder-mortgagor); Lamberth v. McDaniel, 506 S.E.2d 295 (N.C. Ct. App. 1998) (treating land sales contract as mortgage; contract language cannot waive purchaser's redemption rights); Anderson Contracting Co. v. Daugherty, 417 A.2d 1227 (Pa. Super. Ct. 1979) (Pennsylvania statutes setting forth redemption rights in residential mortgage foreclosures apply to installment land contracts); Andrews v. Nathaniel, 42 V.I. 34 (V.I. 2000) (land installment sales contract should be treated as a mortgage). *See also In re* Smith, 2008 WL 922345 (Bankr. E.D.N.C. Mar. 31, 2008) (contract language cannot waive state law requirement that seller must proceed under foreclosure rules to terminate contract for deed). *But see* Long v. Smith, 776 S.W.2d 409 (Mo. Ct. App. 1989) (Missouri courts do not treat contracts for deed as mortgages).

50 Restatement (Third) of Property (Mortgages) § 3.4(b) (1997). *See also* Grant S. Nelson, *The Contract for Deed As a Mortgage: The Case for the Restatement Approach,* 1998 BYU L. Rev. 1111.

51 *See e.g.* Petersen v. Hartell, 707 P.2d 232 (Cal. 1985); Skendzel v. Marshall, 301 N.E.2d 641 (Ind. 1973); Bean v. Walker, 464 N.Y.S.2d 895 (N.Y. App. Div. 1983).

52 *See* Looney v. Farmers Home Admin., 794 F.2d 310 (7th Cir. 1986) (applying Indiana law and holding that vendor must foreclose land sales contract as mortgage despite buyer's minimal payments applied to principal); Parker v. Camp, 656 N.E.2d 882 (Ind. Ct. App. 1995) (voiding contract provision setting requirement that purchaser pay 75% of sales price before contract will be considered a mortgage). *See also* Call v. LaBrie, 498 N.Y.S.2d 652 (N.Y. App. Div. 1986) (payment of 12% of principal balance over nine years sufficient to convert installment land contract to mortgage).

53 Paraguay Place-View Trust v. Gray, 981 P.2d 681 (Colo. Ct. App. 1999) (to determine whether installment land contract should be treated as a mortgage, court looks at factors such as amount of vendee's equity in property, length of default period, "willfulness" of default, whether improvements made, and whether property maintained); Grombone v. Krekel, 754 P.2d 777 (Colo. Ct. App. 1988) (installment land contract will not be treated as a mortgage where buyers defaulted on virtually all of their contract obligations, made no attempt to cure the defaults, and the buyers' total equity in the property was slightly more than 10% of the purchase price); Woods v. Monticello Dev. Co.,

on a land sale contract if the seller has treated the contract as a mortgage, and grant the defaulting buyer rights akin to those ordinarily provided to a mortgagor under state law.[54] Finally, some courts that decline to equate all land sales contracts with mortgages nevertheless have held as a matter of equity that redemption rights applicable to mortgages must run before the purchaser's rights can be terminated.[55]

12.4.2 *Judicial Creation of Protections Against Forfeiture*

Courts have employed a variety of theories to protect the buyer from forfeiture, some based on mortgage law concepts and related equitable principles.[56] For example, courts have strictly construed any pre-forfeiture notice provisions contained in the contracts against the seller.[57] When the contracts have not provided for pre-forfeiture notice, courts in their equitable discretion have implied a notice obligation.[58]

Similarly, courts have created cure rights allowing the buyer to stop forfeiture by paying the arrearage rather than the full contract debt.[59] The South Dakota Supreme Court, for example, invalidated a forfeiture clause which did not allow the buyer an opportunity to cure the default.[60] Particularly where the contract does not contain an acceleration clause, the buyer should be able to cure by paying only the arrearage at any time until the forfeiture is completed.[61]

Many courts have held that a seller waives the right to exercise the forfeiture clause by continuing to accept late payments after default, especially when the buyer has not been notified of a default.[62] Before forfeiting the contract, a

---

656 P.2d 1324 (Colo. Ct. App. 1982) (record supported denial of redemption, but case remanded for consideration of vendor's waiver of forfeiture by acceptance of late payments).

54 *See In re* Robinson, 2003 WL 22996982 (Bankr. E.D. Pa. Dec. 12, 2003) (the bankruptcy court will give effect to the rights outlined in a notice sent by the seller; the notice, which appeared to have been sent inadvertently, gave the purchaser the same rights as provided a mortgagor under state law including the right to cure the default).

55 *See, e.g.,* Lyons v. Pitts, 923 So. 2d 962 (La. Ct. App. 2006); Jenkins v. Wise, 574 P.2d 1337 (Haw. 1978); Nigh v. Hickman, 538 S.W.2d 936 (Mo. Ct. App. 1976).

56 *See, e.g.,* Jenkins v. Wise, 574 P.2d 1337 (Haw. 1978) (a key determination is whether forfeiture would be harsh and unreasonable under the circumstances); Williams v. Hilycord, 886 N.E.2d 119 (Ind. Ct. App. May 8, 2008) (unpublished) (forfeiture judgment entered by default set aside where buyer's payments totaled 28.5% of purchase price, vendor's security interest in property not jeopardized, and property not abandoned); Dempsey v. Carter, 797 N.E.2d 268 (Ind. Ct. App. 2003) (foreclosure, not forfeiture, is appropriate where purchaser paid more than the minimal contract price and had not committed waste on the property); Jensen v. Schreck, 275 N.W.2d 374 (Iowa 1979) (if forfeiture unconscionable court can prevent forfeiture, but not unconscionable when payments equal only 5% of sale price); Keokuk State Bank v. Eckerly, 354 N.W.2d 785 (Iowa Ct. App. 1984) (when seller also in default, court can prevent forfeiture); Mitchell v. Dahlberg, 547 N.W.2d 74 (Mich. Ct. App. 1996) (prohibiting foreclosure of land contract because of seller's fraud in failure to obtain necessary permits for wastewater discharge and for resort campgrounds); Redmond v. McClelland, 2000 Minn. App. LEXIS 779 (Minn. Ct. App. July 25, 2000); Parrott v. Heller, 557 P.2d 819 (Mont. 1976) (buyers entitled to relief from forfeiture when default was not due to any grossly negligent, willful, or fraudulent breach of duty); Huckins v. Ritter, 661 P.2d 52 (N.M. 1983) (to permit seller to retain $45,000 down payment in addition to regaining possession of property from buyers after seven months is unwarranted). *See also In re* Kingsmore, 295 B.R. 812 (Bankr. D.S.C. 2002) (reviewing the *Lewis* case and concluding that the S.C. Supreme Court did not equate an installment land contract with an equitable mortgage; court did however, recognize right of redemption when equity demands it); Lewis v. Premium Inv. Corp., 568 S.E.2d 361 (S.C. 2002) (holding that an equitable right of redemption exits despite a strict forfeiture provision in an installment land contract).

57 Fajen v. Powlus, 561 P.2d 388 (Idaho 1977) (seller's failure to give required notice waives strict performance of contract as to all defaulted payments until adequate notice is given); Ahrens v. Cottle, 896 P.2d 1127 (Mont. 1995) (forfeiture barred where contract required personal or mail service of notice and vendor posted notice on buyer's door); Reynolds v. Milatzo, 161 P.3d 509 (Wyo. 2007) (contract required seller to deliver notice of forfeiture through escrow agent as well as directly to buyer; seller's omission of delivery through escrow agent barred forfeiture). *See also* Krivins v. Smyers, 1981 WL 3945 (Ohio Ct. App. Apr. 22, 1981) (strictly construing payment schedule language against seller).

58 Martinez v. Martinez, 678 P.2d 1163 (N.M. 1984) (purchaser entitled to notice and a reasonable time of at least thirty days to cure); Elsasser v. Wilcox, 596 P.2d 974 (Or. 1979) (vendor must provide notice and an opportunity to cure); Phair v. Walker, 617 P.2d 616 (Or. Ct. App. 1980) (buyer has right to second notice and reasonable period to cure arrearage after seller's attempt to reinstate strict time for payment under contract); Bankwest v. Groseclose, 535 N.W.2d 860 (S.D. 1995).

59 Allen v. Vaughn, 161 P.3d 1209 (Alaska 2007) (court will imply opportunity to cure, rejecting forfeiture where contact did not explicitly provide for forfeiture remedy); Sindlinger v. Paul, 404 N.W.2d 212 (Mich. 1987); Call v. LaBrie, 498 N.Y.S.2d 652 (N.Y. App. Div. 1986); Shervold v. Schmidt, 359 N.W.2d 361 (N.D. 1984); Elsasser v. Wilcox, 596 P.2d 974 (Or. 1979); BankWest, N.A. v. Groseclose, 535 N.W.2d 860 (S.D. 1995); Call v. Timber Lakes Corp., 567 P.2d 1108 (Utah 1977).

60 Bankwest v. Groseclose, 535 N.W.2d 860 (S.D. 1995).

61 *See, e.g.,* White v. Brousseau, 566 So. 2d 832 (Fla. Dist. Ct. App. 1990); Richard v. Energy Sys. Holding Ltd., 759 P.2d 876 (Idaho 1988); Shervold v. Schmidt, 359 N.W.2d 361 (N.D. 1984).

62 Auernheimer v. Metzen, 783 P.2d 1027 (Or. 1990) (seller waived time is of the essence provision by continuing to accept installment payments without providing notice of default; to reinstate the provision, the seller must to provide notice of default and then allow a reasonable opportunity to cure and advise buyer that timely performance would thereafter be required); Phair v. Walker, 617 P.2d 616 (Or. Ct. App. 1980) (attempt in letter to reinstate strict time requirements of contract was defeated by acceptance of another late payment; buyer has right to second notice and reasonable period to cure arrearage). *See also In re* Draper, 2010 WL 963987 (Bankr. D.N.M. Mar. 12, 2010) (seller's motion for relief from bankruptcy stay denied upon

seller with a pattern of accepting late payments must reinstate the strict time requirements of the contract by providing notice to the buyer that no further late payments will be accepted, and must give the buyer a reasonable time to cure the arrears.[63]

Applying the equitable principles generally recognized in forfeiture cases, the courts will not enforce boilerplate adhesion clauses which purport to bar the purchaser from raising waiver defenses.[64]

Even when the seller has refused late installment payments, the court may rebuff the seller's attempt to forfeit the contract when there was only a short delay in payment of the installment, the seller was not prejudiced by the delay, and the buyer has substantial equity in the property.[65] The doctrine of substantial performance is another equitable principle that courts will apply to deny forfeiture when the buyer's defaults were technical, inadvertent, or unimportant. Under general equitable principles, the seller's breach of its own duties under the contract may also bar the seller from declaring a forfeiture.[66]

In addition, courts have conditioned forfeiture on the seller's return of payments received that exceed the seller's actual damages. Such restitution may be ordered in cases in which the amount retained by the seller is considered unconscionable.[67] In other words, there must be a reasonable relationship between the amount of payments retained and the amount of the vendor's actual damages.[68] In Utah, for

---

finding of waiver of default by seller's acceptance of payments after default declared); Welch v. Cooper, 670 S.W.2d 454 (Ark. Ct. App. 1984) (habitual acceptance of late payments supports finding of waiver); Free v. Free, 936 So. 2d 699 (Fla. Dist. Ct. App. 2006) (purchaser may enforce land contract against vendor despite purchaser's history of untimely payments); Tadros v. Kuzmak, 660 N.E.2d 162 (Ill. App. Ct. 1995) (notice of default for late payments rendered void by vendor's subsequent acceptance of the payments); Keokuk State Bank v. Eckley, 354 N.W.2d 785 (Iowa Ct. App. 1984) (estoppel of forfeiture based on bank's acceptance of five months' late payments); Bailey v. Lilly, 667 P.2d 933 (Mont. 1983) (acceptance of late payments after giving notice of default waived effect of notice); Shervold v. Schmidt, 359 N.W.2d 361 (N.D. 1984) (applying doctrine of estoppel to deny forfeiture where time of essence term waived by conduct); Endres v. Warriner, 307 N.W.2d 146 (S.D. 1981) (waiver found based on conduct; waiver need not be authorized in writing); Williamson v. Wanlass, 545 P.2d 1145 (Utah 1976) (vendor's demand for future strict performance was too vague to reinstate timely payment obligation); Anderson v. Brinkerhoff, 756 P.2d 95 (Utah Ct. App. 1988) (strict compliance with payment terms of contract waived); Reynolds v. Milatzo, 161 P.3d 509 (Wyo. 2007) (sellers will be compensated for monetary loss due to buyers' defaults in paying for insurance, taxes, and other obligations in timely manner, but sellers waived right to declare forfeiture because of the late payments). *See generally* Foundation Prop. Invs., L.L.C. v. CTP, L.L.C., 186 P.3d 766 (Kan. 2008) (collecting cases on lender's waiver of prompt payment by course of conduct as ground for denial of acceleration of mortgage).

63 Nelson v. Butcher, 352 N.E.2d 106 (Ind. Ct. App. 1976); Farmer v. Groves, 555 P.2d 1252 (Or. 1976) (ten days or two weeks notice to cure default was not sufficient when seller accepted late or no payments for six months); Smith by Coe v. Piluso, 719 P.2d 33 (Or. Ct. App. 1986) (time of the essence not term of written contract and parties' conduct never established such a term); 617 P.2d 616 (Or. Ct. App. 1980). *But cf. In re* Guido, 345 B.R. 656 (Bankr. E.D. Ark. 2006) (under Arkansas law, seller may waive its right to declare forfeiture under installment land sales contract by not insisting on strict compliance with the contract terms, but court finds no waiver on facts in this case).

64 *See* Turley v. Staley, __ S.W.3d __, 2009 WL 4667460 (Ark. Ct. App. Dec. 9, 2009) (overturning forfeiture ruling; parties' conduct in accepting late payments trumped non-waiver clause in installment land sale contact); Woods v. Monticello Dev. Co., 656 P.2d 1324 (Colo. Ct. App. 1982) (an anti-waiver clause, like any other term of contract, is subject to modification by course of performance).

65 *See, e.g.*, Harness v. Curtis, 192 S.W.3d 267 (Ark. Ct. App. 2004) (forfeiture denied as inequitable where buyer had been eight days late with installment); McLemore v. McLemore, 827 N.E.2d 1135 (Ind. Ct. App. 2005) (denying forfeiture where buyer had paid 18% of purchase price over three years, and to the extent the buyer's nonpayment of property taxes jeopardized the security property, the seller's interest could be protected adequately through foreclosure); Nigh v. Hickman, 538 S.W.2d 936 (Mo. Ct. App. 1976) (one payment tendered fifteen days late by buyer that had paid almost 35% of purchase price); Cody Discount, Inc. v. Merritt, 629 S.E.2d 697 (S.C. Ct. App. 2006) (rejecting forfeiture as unenforceable penalty and inequitable where seller had accepted late payments in the past and buyer of manufactured home and lot owed only $1000 toward $44,500 purchase price). *See generally* Pardee v. Jolly, 163 Wash. 2d 558, 182 P.3d 967 (2008) (equitable grace period may apply to excuse payment made "a couple of weeks late" so as to avoid forfeiture under real estate contract treated as land sale installment contract).

66 Meyer v. Chieffo, 2008 WL 5235364 (Ohio Ct. App. Dec. 16, 2008) (affirming denial of seller's forcible entry and detainer claim on ground that buyer had legal justification for nonpayment due to seller's failure to correct mold condition in property); Reeder v. Curry, 294 S.W.3d 851 (Tex. App. 2009) (forfeiture rejected as inequitable where buyer did not make two monthly payments after notice of IRS levy on seller). *See generally* Chesson v. Hall, 2007 WL 1964538 (S.D. Tex. July 3, 2007) (sellers' breach of warranty for newly constructed home may excuse buyer's forfeiture under land installment sales contract in cases where homes were not yet built when buyers signed contracts); Fajen v. Powlus, 561 P.2d 388 (Idaho 1977) (vendor may not enforce forfeiture while in noncompliance with title insurance provision of contract); Kim v. Parks, 86 P.3d 63 (Or. Ct. App. 2004) (barring forfeiture where seller materially breached installment land sales contract by failing to perform certain plumbing repairs required by the agreement).

67 Heikkila v. Carver, 378 N.W.2d 214 (S.D. 1985) (to recover restitution, buyer must prove that seller was unjustly enriched).

68 Gomez v. Pagaduan, 613 P.2d 658 (Haw. Ct. App. 1980); Seals v. Sumrall, 887 So. 2d 91 (La. Ct. App. 2004) (seller is entitled to retain damages equal to the fair rental value for period of defaulted buyer's occupancy, but terms of contract allowing seller to retain all sums paid is penal and will not be enforced); Bartholet v. Le Inv., L.C.C., 866 So. 2d 877 (La. Ct. App. 2004) (same). *See also* LaFleur v. Pohronezny, 2009 WL 3366280 (Conn. Super. Ct. Sept. 10, 2009) (enforcing liquidated damages clause after forfeiture where total payments forfeited substantially equaled cumulative value of rentals that would have

example, case law indicates that the court will enforce a forfeiture clause when the amount of the forfeiture does not greatly exceed, or is less than, the amount of damages.[69] When sellers elect to proceed with a forfeiture, the courts strictly limit monetary recovery in accordance with the general law applicable to forfeitures. For example, by canceling the contract through a forfeiture declaration, the seller may lose all claims to recover installments of interest that came due and are unpaid under the contract.[70]

12.5 Using Bankruptcy to Prevent Forfeiture

12.5.1 Can Installment Land Contract Be Treated As Creating a Security Interest?

Many bankruptcy courts have ruled that an installment land sale contract creates a security interest, allowing the debtor to provide for the seller's claim under a chapter 13 plan in any manner that would be appropriate for treatment of a mortgage lender's claim.[71] For example, the debtor may cure a contract arrearage through the life of a chapter 13 plan, in accordance with sections 1322(b)(2), (5) and 1325(a)(5) of the Bankruptcy Code. A chapter 13 debtor may also modify rights of a secured creditor if a security interest was taken in a manufactured home that is defined as personal property under state's law.[72] This modification could substantially reduce principal owed on the obligation. In allowing treatment of the seller's claim as a security interest, the courts focus upon the role of the land sales contract as a financing device.[73]

A number of bankruptcy courts have, however, rejected this view.[74] These courts consider installment land sales contracts to be executory contracts. Bankruptcy Code section 365 applies to executory contracts, typically leases, in bankruptcy.[75] This section requires that debtors assume or reject executory contracts under specific standards and procedures defined in the Code.[76]

It is impossible to reconcile many of the court decisions that have considered whether installment land sale contracts must be treated as secured claims or executory contracts in bankruptcy. Courts relying upon federal law have reached opposite conclusions. For example, some courts find treatment of these contracts as mortgages to be most consistent with the Code's goals of rehabilitation and preservation of the bankruptcy estate.[77] Other courts look to the widely used treatise definition of an executory contact in bankruptcy,[78] then conclude that this definition encompasses installment land contracts.[79] Still other courts focus on state law and

---

been paid for period contract in effect); Crowell v. Williams, 615 S.E.2d 797 (Ga. Ct. App. 2005) (absent an enforceable liquidated damages term in the installment land sales contact, rescission and return of sums paid by the buyer are the appropriate remedies when the buyer can no longer afford payments).

69 Bellon v. Malnar, 808 P.2d 1089 (Utah 1991) (court will enforce forfeiture clause unless it finds forfeiture would be so grossly excessive in relation to loss contemplated by the parties that it would shock the conscience); Perkins v. Spencer, 121 Utah 468, 243 P.2d 446 (1952).

70 Hooker v. Norbu, 899 N.E.2d 655 (Ind. Ct. App. 2008).

71 *See In re* Streets & Beard Farm P'ship, 882 F.2d 233 (7th Cir. 1989); *In re* Frazer, 377 B.R. 621 (B.A.P. 9th Cir. 2007); *In re* Heartline Farms, Inc. v. Daly, 128 B.R. 246 (D. Neb. 1990) (chapter 12), *aff'd* 934 F.2d 985 (8th Cir. 1981); *In re* Kane, 248 B.R. 216 (B.A.P 1st Cir. 2000); *In re* Rehbein, 60 B.R. 436 (B.A.P. 9th Cir. 1986); *In re* Brown, 249 B.R. 193 (Bankr. N.D. Ill. 2000); *In re* Heward Bros., 210 B.R. 475 (Bankr. D. Idaho 1997); *In re* Grove, 208 B.R. 845 (Bankr. W.D. Pa. 1997); *In re* Rowe, 110 B.R. 712 (Bankr. E.D. Pa. 1990); *In re* McDaniel, 89 B.R. 861 (Bankr. E.D. Wash. 1988); *In re* Faiman, 70 B.R. 74 (Bankr. N.D. 1987); *In re* Adolphson, 38 B.R. 776 (Bankr. D. Minn. 1983), *aff'd*, 38 B.R. 780 (D. Minn. 1983); *In re* Patch Graphics, 32 B.R. 373 (Bankr. W.D. Wis. 1983); *In re* Cox, 28 B.R. 588 (Bankr. D. Idaho 1983); *In re* Booth, 19 B.R. 53 (Bankr. D. Utah 1982); *In re* Climer, 10 B.R. 872 (W.D. Tenn. 1977). *See generally* National Consumer Law Center, Consumer Bankruptcy Law and Practice § 12.9.1 (9th ed. 2009).

72 *See In re* Reinhardt, 563 F.3d 558 (6th Cir. 2009); Green Tree Servicing, L.L.C. v. Harrison, 2009 WL 82565, at *2 n.4 (W.D. La. Jan. 12, 2009) (collecting cases). *See also* National Consumer Law Center, Consumer Bankruptcy Law and Practice § 11.6.1.2.2.6 (9th ed. 2009).

73 *See, e.g., In re* Rehbein, 60 B.R. 436, 440 (B.A.P. 9th Cir. 1986) ("Contracts for Deeds are merely a financing arrangement for a sale which has already occurred.").

74 *In re* Terrell, 892 F.2d 469 (6th Cir. 1989); *In re* Speck, 798 F.2d 279 (8th Cir. 1986); Shaw v. Dawson, 48 B.R. 857 (D.N.M. 1985); *In re* Ravenswood Apartments, 338 B.R. 307 (B.A.P. 6th Cir. 2006); *In re* Carson, 286 B.R. 645 (Bankr. E.D. Tenn. 2002); *In re* Walker, 227 B.R. 870 (Bankr. S.D. Ind. 1998); *In re* Scanlon, 80 B.R. 131 (Bankr. S.D. Iowa 1987); *In re* Waldron, 65 B.R. 169 (Bankr. N.D. Tex. 1986); *In re* Vertich, 5 B.R. 684 (Bankr. D.S.D. 1980).

75 11 U.S.C. § 365. *See generally* National Consumer Law Center, Consumer Bankruptcy Law and Practice § 12.9 (9th ed. 2009).

76 11 U.S.C. § 365(b).

77 *In re* Rehbein, 60 B.R. 436 (B.A.P. 9th Cir. 1986); *In re* Fox, 83 B.R. 290 (Bankr. E.D. Pa. 1988); *In re* Booth, 19 B.R. 53 (Bankr. D. Utah 1982) (overriding bankruptcy policies of debtor rehabilitation and benefit to estate require treatment of land sales contracts as mortgages even though considered executory contracts under Utah law).

78 An executory contract is one "under which the obligation of both the bankrupt and the other party to the contract are so far unperformed that the failure of either to complete the performance would constitute a material breach excusing the performance of the other." Vernon Countryman, *Executory Contracts in Bankruptcy*, Part I, 57 Minn. L. Rev. 439, 460 (1973).

79 *See, e.g., In re* Ravenswood Apartments, 338 B.R. 307 (B.A.P. 6th Cir. 2006) (land sales contracts must be regarded as executory contracts because there are significant unperformed obligations on both sides). *See also In re* Griffin, 397 B.R. 356 (Bankr. W.D. Va. 2008) (construing installment land sale contract as executory, but holding that under Virginia law transaction created security interest in property); *In re* Coffelt, 395 B.R. 133 (Bankr. D. Kan. 2008) (contract for deed treated as mort-

follow the state's acknowledged standard for treatment of installment land sales contracts, whether it be as an executory contract or a security device.[80]

Many courts look to a combination of federal and state law. These courts recognize that, while the bankruptcy courts may apply a definition of an executory contract generally accepted by the federal courts, the definition is far too general to be applied without some reference to state law.[81]

12.5.2 Debtor Options If Installment Land Contract Must Be Treated As an Executory Contract in Bankruptcy

Treatment of the installment land contract as a mortgage offers the chapter 13 debtor the most flexible options for curing and reinstating a land sales contract after default. Nevertheless, debtors who face courts that refuse to view the contracts as security instruments still have some recourse for saving their homes. The option for assuming an executory contract under section 365 may offer a viable remedy.

Pursuant to Bankruptcy Code section 1322(b)(7), the chapter 13 debtor may assume an executory contract through the terms of a plan. In order to assume the contract, the debtor must comply with section 365(b). That section requires that the debtor cure any pre-bankruptcy default or provide adequate assurance that the default will be promptly cured, compensate the party to the contract for any actual pecuniary loss resulting from the default, and provide adequate assurance of future performance.[82]

In many cases the home buyer will be able to satisfy the requirements of section 365 through the terms of a plan. Assuming an executory contract through a chapter 13 plan does not place burdens on a debtor that are significantly more onerous than those the debtor would encounter in curing a mortgage default through a plan.

A potential problem that may arise in meeting the executory contract standard is the requirement that the debtor "promptly" cure the default or provide "adequate assurance" that the default will be "promptly" cured.[83] In cases involving home mortgages chapter 13 debtors can typically cure a default over the life of a three- to five-year plan. It is unlikely that courts will consider the cure of an executory contract default over three to five years to be "prompt." However, in the context of curing defaults of long-term leases, such as leases for federally subsidized rental housing, the courts have found cure periods ranging from six months to more than two years acceptable under section 365(b)(1).[84] The nature of the parties' relationship and its expected duration are factors the courts consider in determining a reasonably prompt cure period for an executory contract.[85] Given the long terms of many land sales contracts, purchasers have a valid basis for arguing for lengthy cure periods. A cure period of several years should not appear extravagant given the parties' expectation of the long-term duration of their relationship.

---

gage under Kansas law; trustee may set transfer aside under strong-arm powers where vendor did not comply with recording requirements applicable to mortgages).

80 *In re* Kane 248 B.R. 216 (B.A.P. 1st Cir. 2000), *aff'd on other grounds*, 254 F.3d 325 (1st Cir. 2001); Heartline Farms, Inc. v. Daly, 128 B.R. 246 (D. Neb. 1990) (installment land sales contract treated as mortgage; bankruptcy court would recognize land sales contracts as executory contracts only if Nebraska courts defined them as such); *In re* Drahn, 405 B.R. 470 (Bankr. N.D. Iowa 2009) (although Iowa law considers installment land sale contract to be executory, this rule does not apply to installment contract to purchase manufactured home, defined as personal property under state law); *In re* Carson, 286 B.R. 645 (Bankr. E.D. Tenn. 2002) (Tennessee law considers land sales contracts to be executory contracts); *In re* Walker, 227 B.R. 870 (Bankr. S.D. Ind. 1998) (following Indiana Supreme Court's ruling that installment land sales contracts should be treated as mortgages); *In re* McDaniel, 89 B.R. 861 (Bankr. E.D. Wash. 1988) (no overriding federal interest requires divergence from Washington courts' recognition of land sales contracts as equivalent to mortgages).

81 *In re* Terrell, 892 F.2d 469 (6th Cir. 1989) (land vendor's obligation under Michigan law to convey good title upon full payment is a substantial unperformed obligation, requiring treatment of land sales contract as executory contract under Countryman definition widely used by federal courts); *In re* Streets & Beard Farm P'ship, 882 F.2d 233 (7th Cir. 1989) (under Illinois law the land vendor's only unperformed duty is a ministerial one, to deliver deed upon full payment, placing land sales contract outside of any federal definition of an executory contract).

82 11 U.S.C. § 365(b)(1). *See* National Consumer Law Center, Consumer Bankruptcy Law and Practice § 12.9 (9th ed. 2009).

83 11 U.S.C. § 365(b)(1)(A).

84 *In re* DeCamillo, 206 B.R. 64 (Bankr. D.N.J. 1997) (cure periods of six months to one year acceptable for private unsubsidized residential leases); *In re* Morgan, 181 B.R. 579 (Bankr. N.D. Ala. 1997) (general rule of six months for cure of private unsubsidized apartment leases); *In re* Hall, 202 B.R. 929 (Bankr. W.D. Tenn. 1996) (forty-eight month cure period allowed for subsidized housing lease); *In re* Whitsett, 163 B.R. 752 (Bankr. E.D. Pa. 1994) (one to two years is acceptably prompt cure period for subsidized housing lease).

85 *In re* Reed, 226 B.R. 1 (Bankr. W.D. Ky. 1998); *In re* Trusty, 189 B.R. 977 (Bankr. N.D. Ala. 1995). *See also In re* Coffman, 393 B.R. 829 (Bankr. S.D. Ohio 2008) (cure of automobile lease must be completed by lease termination date as stated in contract); *In re* Brown, 2006 WL 2546824 (Bankr. S.D. Miss. Sept. 1, 2006) (where lease has remaining term of five years, proposed cure within thirteen months from order allowing assumption of lease satisfies "prompt" payment requirement of § 365(b)).

12.5.3 When Is It Too Late to File a Chapter 13 Case to Prevent Forfeiture of an Installment Land Sale Contract?

Regardless of whether the land sales contract is considered a mortgage or an executory contract, the purchaser filing for chapter 13 relief may face the question of when the termination process has gone so far as to preclude a cure or other action to retain rights in the contract through bankruptcy. The key factor will be whether the debtor, at the time the bankruptcy petition was filed, still retained some right under state law to reverse the termination and reinstate the contract.

In one case, an Illinois bankruptcy court looked to the state's forcible entry and detainer statute, which was applicable to termination of the debtor's real estate installment contract.[86] The Illinois statute gave the buyer the opportunity to cure a default in the contract for a limited period after entry of a judgment of possession. Because that period had not yet expired when the debtor filed for bankruptcy relief, the court held that the debtor could cure his contractual default under section 1322(b).[87] Other courts have applied similar reasoning and allowed cure of defaulted installment land sales contracts despite a pre-petition termination, declaration of forfeiture, or entry of judgment.[88]

86 *In re* Brown, 249 B.R. 193 (Bankr. N.D. Ill. 2000).

87 *Id.* 249 B.R. at 198.

88 *See In re* Frazer, 377 B.R. 621 (B.A.P. 9th Cir. 2007) (Bankruptcy Code § 108(b), which provides only a sixty-day extension of time for the debtor to perform certain obligations, does not limit debtor's right to cure a default in a land installment sales contract under a long-term chapter 13 plan of thirty-six to sixty months as allowed by § 1322(b)(3),(5)); *In re* Smith, 2008 WL 922345 (Bankr. E.D.N.C. Mar. 31, 2008) (debtor possessed equitable right to redeem contract for deed despite pre-petition entry of judgment for ejectment; only a foreclosure judgment could properly terminate buyer's interest in property); *In re* Casa Colonial Ltd. P'ship, 375 B.R. 779 (Bankr. E.D. Mich. 2007) (unexpired statutory redemption period following forfeiture judgment and pendency of state court appeal brought debtor's rights under land contract into bankruptcy estate); *In re* Dunn, 2006 WL 3079632 (Bankr. N.D. Ala. Oct. 20, 2006) (debtor may assume bond for title contract under § 365 where vendor waived pre-petition termination by acceptance of payments); *In re* Robinson, 2003 WL 22996982 (Bankr. E.D. Pa. Dec. 12, 2003) (notice sent by seller to buyer allowed for post-judgment cure of land sales contract); *In re* Kingmore, 295 B.R. 812 (Bankr. D.S.C. 2002) (debtor may assume land contract under § 365 because retained redemption right when filed for bankruptcy relief); *In re* Grove, 208 B.R. 845 (Bankr. W.D. Pa. 1997) (under Pennsylvania's mortgage foreclosure law applicable to installment land sales contracts, buyer may cure after entry of judgment); *In re* Nix, 1997 WL 33419263 (Bankr. S.D. Ga. Aug. 26, 2003) (vendor waived pre-petition late payments as ground for termination, allowing debtor to assume contract in chapter 13); *In re* Reichenbach, 219 B.R. 247 (Bankr. E.D. Ark. 1998) (declining to allow post-judgment cure of land sales contract, but giving debtor opportunity to open default judgment in state court, then proceed with cure). *But see In re* Guido, 345 B.R. 656 (Bankr. E.D. Ark. 2006) (state law recognizes waiver of forfeiture by acceptance of late payments, but under facts of this case forfeiture not waived; contract properly canceled pre-petition and debtor may not assume and cure).

12.5.4 Automatic Stay Issues

Section 362(b)(22), added by the 2005 amendments to the Bankruptcy Code, places limitations on the automatic stay of eviction when a pre-petition judgment of possession has been entered against a residential tenant.[89] However, the exception applies only to a debtor who was residing "as a tenant under a lease or rental agreement" and against whom the landlord obtained the pre-petition judgment of possession.[90] The exception should not apply to a purchaser under a land sales contract when that individual is otherwise entitled to cure the default following a pre-petition judgment of possession. The purchaser under a true installment land sales contract is not a "tenant" under a "lease" or "rental agreement."

12.5.5 Setting Aside the Forfeiture

A debtor in bankruptcy may be able to set aside the forfeiture of a land installment sales contract when the remaining debt under the contract is significantly less than the value of the forfeited property. This relief may be available under the Bankruptcy Code's provision for setting aside fraudulent transfers.[91] The Supreme Court in *BFP v. Resolution Trust Corp.*[92] held that the price received at a properly conducted foreclosure sale was the reasonably equivalent value for fraudulent transfer purposes. At least one bankruptcy court has held that the *BFP* ruling does not apply to the forfeiture of installment land sales contracts.[93] The Court relied on the fact that in a forfeiture there is no sale by which the reasonably equivalent value can be measured.[94] If the contract has been in place for a long time, the

89 11 U.S.C. § 362(b)(22). *See* National Consumer Law Center, Consumer Bankruptcy Law and Practice § 9.4.5.6.2 (9th ed. 2009).

90 11 U.S.C. § 362(b)(22).

91 11 U.S.C. § 548.

92 511 U.S. 531, 114 S. Ct. 1757, 128 L. Ed. 2d 556 (1994). See National Consumer Law Center, Repossessions § 8.4.5.4 (6th ed. 2005 and Supp) and National Consumer Law Center, Consumer Bankruptcy Law and Practice § 11.3 (9th ed. 2009) for a discussion of *BFP v. Resolution Trust Corp.*

93 *In re* Grady, 202 B.R. 120 (Bankr. N.D. Iowa 1996). *See also In re* Houston, 385 B.R. 268 (Bankr. N.D. Iowa 2008) (finding constructive fraudulent transfer where, as alternative to forfeiture, buyer reconveyed property to seller for substantially less than reasonable value of cancellation of debt). *But see* McCanna v. Burke, 197 B.R. 333 (D.N.M. 1996); *In re* Vermillion, 176 B.R. 563 (Bankr. D. Or. 1994).

94 *In re* Grady, 202 B.R. 120, 125 (Bankr. N.D. Iowa 1996).

amount remaining due on the contract could be "minuscule and bear no relationship to equivalent value."[95]

In addition, two courts in states where strict foreclosures are the predominate method of foreclosure have held that the *BFP* ruling did not apply to foreclosures that take place without public sales.[96] These courts also noted that the *BFP* ruling was premised upon the occurrence of a public sale which was deemed to establish conclusively that the buyer received reasonably equivalent value for her interest in the property. Land installment contract forfeitures, like strict foreclosures, seldom allow for a public sale. Therefore, the proceedings should be voidable as fraudulent transfers in bankruptcy when the buyer stands to lose significant equity through the forfeiture. In order to use the Bankruptcy Code's fraudulent transfer provision, the transfer must have occurred within two years of the date of the bankruptcy filing.[97] Longer look-back periods may apply under similar state statutes.

95 *Id.*

96 *In re* Chase, 2005 WL 189711 (Bankr D. Vt. Jan. 27, 2005), *later decision,* 328 B.R. 675 (Bankr. D. Vt. 2005); *In re* Fitzgerald, 237 B.R. 252 (Bankr. D. Conn. 1999), *later decision* 255 B.R. 807 (Bankr. D. Conn. 2000).

97 11 U.S.C. § 548(a)(1).

Chapter 13 Tax Liens and Tax Foreclosures

13.1 An Overview of the Process

All states have enacted statutes which authorize both the creation of a lien against real property when taxes on the property are not paid and the enforcement of this lien by a sale of the property. These statutory schemes are not uniform. Nevertheless, enough common features exist to permit some generalizations. While a detailed comparison of state property tax laws is beyond the scope of this treatise, this chapter discusses some of the basic legal principles involved in the real estate tax and enforcement process. It is intended to acquaint the reader with the tax foreclosure process and to suggest strategies which may be available for dealing with tax delinquencies and foreclosures. But more important, it should encourage advocates to examine this area of state law carefully. Procedures exist to protect the rights of homeowners and they should be thoroughly considered.

There are three basic opportunities for intervention in the real estate taxation process. It is possible to object to assessments, assist in seeking tax abatements[1] or compromises, and to contest tax enforcement. The latter may involve objecting to claimed tax liens or affirmative action to prevent, redeem, or set aside sales of property pursuant to a lien.

As with many areas of consumer law, preventing an unmanageable debt from arising in the first instance is the best approach for preventing a tax sale. For that reason, analysis should begin with the assessment process.[2] Tax abatement programs are also discussed below.[3]

While the focus of this section is primarily on *ad valorem*[4] property tax assessment liens and sales, it should be noted that there are other types of governmental liens authorized by state statutes. For example, a municipality may impose a lien for unpaid water and sewer charges or for charges connected with the repair of a building after building code violations were found. The enforcement process of these liens is likely to be similar to the enforcement of regular *ad valorem* property taxes.[5] As with all liens, the rule of thumb is that if there is basis to contest the lien, it is best to do it as early as possible.

1 Appendix F, *infra*, summarizes various state tax abatement laws as a starting point for research.

2 *See* §§ 13.2.1, 13.3.1.2, *infra*.

3 *See* § 13.3.1.3, *infra*.

4 That is, property tax based on the value of the property.

5 *See, e.g.*, Amy Realty v. Gomes, 839 A.2d 1232 (R.I. 2004) (tax sale procedure used for nonpayment of sewer fees).

13.2 Real Property Taxation Process

13.2.1 Property Assessment

The first step in the taxation process is the determination or assessment of the value of the real property, in accordance with the method of valuation used in the jurisdiction.[6] In most jurisdictions these valuations are then reviewed by a board of "equalization" whose role is to insure that similar properties are taxed equally so that the tax burden is distributed evenly. The tax is then levied (or imposed) in proportion to the assessment at a percentage set by statute. State and local law always includes some process for challenging an assessment.[7]

13.2.2 The Tax Lien

13.2.2.1 Priority of Real Estate Tax Liens

If the tax is still not paid within a certain time period, the tax bill becomes a lien on the property. (Often this is the first day of the year following the year in which the tax is

6 Some jurisdictions assess at full value while others use a percentage of full value. *See* Real Estate Tax Appeals, Rohan, vol. 8 § 2.01[3] (1984) (citing U.S. Advisory Commission on Intergovernmental Relations, Significant Features of Fiscal Federalism (1984)).

It should be noted, however, that merely because property is assessed at full value for tax purposes does not mean that the actual tax is higher than the tax in a jurisdiction using a percentage assessment. It is the tax *rate* that determines the amount of the tax. For example, when a full value assessment is used, and the tax rate is 2%, the tax will be lower than if a 60% of value assessment is used with a tax rate of 3.5%. The jurisdiction may gain a psychological advantage, however, by using a percentage assessment. Homeowners who are told that their home was assessed at only 60% of its value may be predisposed to acquiesce to a higher tax.

7 This option is discussed at § 13.3.1.2, *infra*, and should be explored when possible, in a timely manner to prevent improperly inflated or otherwise incorrect values.

assessed.[8]) The lien also typically becomes effective as against fixtures on the property. This may include a manufactured home, if under state law the home is fixed to the land.[9]

By statute, a tax lien almost always has first priority over all other liens, including mortgages, whether created before or after the tax lien.[10] These statutes have been upheld on the grounds that priority is essential to the government collecting the revenue necessary to conduct its business.[11]

Because a tax lien will generally supersede or "prime" any mortgages, mortgage holders in first position will normally insist that taxes be paid through an escrow account established by the lender.[12] The lender then pays the taxes as they come due from funds in the escrow account.[13] Occasionally, the failure of the lender or servicer to make timely or correct disbursements out of escrow to pay taxes will result in a tax lien foreclosure.[14] This problem and others related to escrow accounts are discussed in Chapters 6, 7, and 8, *supra*.

Most mortgage lenders will advance the taxes in order to retain first priority even if they are not receiving payments from the homeowner. In those circumstances, the escrow deficiency becomes part of the mortgage arrears. This means that, on one hand, a tax lien foreclosure is not possible because the taxes have been paid. On the other hand, the mortgage delinquency is exacerbated.[15]

8 *See, e.g.*, Mo. Rev. Stat. § 140.310 (on January 1st any unpaid taxes become a lien on the property); N.M. Stat. § 7-38-48 (unpaid taxes become a lien on January 1st for the tax year for which the taxes are imposed); S.C. Code Ann. § 12-45-70 (taxes are due between 30th of Sept. and 15th of Jan. after their assessment each year).

9 *See* Rochman v. Cape Mercantile Bank & Trust Co., 156 B.R. 794 (Bankr. S.D. Ill. 1993) (manufactured home was fixed to the property and was conveyed with tax deed even though manufactured home was placed on the property after the tax sale); OnBank & Trust Co. v. Hannold, 684 N.Y.S.2d 677 (App. Div. 1999) (home not affixed to land was real property, and not personalty, for tax assessment purposes). *See generally* National Consumer Law Center, Repossessions § 14.13 (6th ed. 2005 and Supp.).

10 *E.g.*, Ky. Rev. Stat. Ann. § 134.420 (West); N.M. Stat. § 7-38-48 (tax lien is the first lien and is paramount to any other interest in the property, perfected or unperfected). *See also* Solarte v. Washington Mut. Bank, 2005 WL 3291813 (Cal. Ct. App. Dec. 6, 2005) (unpublished) (liens for real property taxes have priority over all private liens, regardless of time of creation).

11 *See* ITT Diversified Credit Corp. v. Couch, 669 P.2d 1355 (Colo. 1983) (citing Minneapolis Threshing Mach. Co. v. Roberts County, 34 S.D. at 501, 149 N.W. 163); 72 Am. Jur. 2d *State & Local Taxation* § 898.

12 Mortgage escrow accounting procedures are regulated by the Real Estate Settlement Procedures Act (RESPA). 12 U.S.C. § 2609. *See generally* § 8.3, *supra*.

13 *See generally* Heller v. First Town Mortgage Corp., 1998 WL 614197 (S.D.N.Y. Sept. 14, 1998).

14 Choi v. Chase Manhattan Mortgage Co., 63 F. Supp. 2d 874 (N.D. Ill. 1999) (servicer failed to pay taxes on homeowners' property over two-year period because a tax notification company it contracted with provided erroneous information).

15 *See* Chapters 2, 4, 5, 9, *supra*, 14, *infra* (discussion of the mortgage foreclosure process).

Even when there is no escrow account, a junior mortgage or lien holder may decide to pay a borrower's delinquent tax debt, before or after the tax sale, to avoid losing the priority of its security interest. Most mortgage agreements contain a provision allowing the lender to pay the borrower's taxes and to add any amount paid on the borrower's account to the balance due on the note.[16] Repayment arrangements then must be made with the lender or its servicer rather than with the taxing authority.

If a tax sale process is completed, and the redemption period runs its course, liens junior to the tax lien which generated the sale are extinguished.[17] At least one court has held this to be the case even if the homeowner remains in possession of the property after the end of the redemption period.[18]

13.2.2.2 Lender Liability for Unpaid Taxes

Due to a lender's negligence or malfeasance, a homeowner who is paying real estate taxes in escrow to the mortgage servicer will sometimes nevertheless receive notice of a tax delinquency. Tax payments may have been misdirected, lost, or retained by the servicer. When this occurs, further investigation is necessary to find out whether payments were sent in a timely fashion by the lender.[19]

Upon investigation, any dispute over unpaid taxes may involve three parties: the homeowner, the taxing authority, and the lender or servicer as escrowee. If it can be shown that nonpayment was the result of a mistake by the lender, the lender should be held responsible for late charges, fees, tax penalties and additional interest.[20] If the taxing authorities lost a timely payment, late charges, fees, penalties and interest should be waived.

16 The relevant provision may also be in the promissory note secured by the mortgage.

17 An exception may be liens held by the Federal Deposit Insurance Corporation (FDIC) as receiver due to a protective provision found at 12 U.S.C. § 1825(b)(2). *See, e.g.*, First State Bank-Keene v. Metroplex Petroleum Inc., 155 F.3d 732 (5th Cir. 1998) (sale is valid, but FDIC junior lien not extinguished). *But see* S&R Assocs. v. Lynn Realty Corp., 769 A.2d 413 (N.J. Super. Ct. App. Div. 2001) (valid tax lien entitled to priority over assignee of FDIC's mortgage interest).

18 Hancock Bank v. Ladner, 727 So. 2d 743 (Miss. Ct. App. 1998).

19 *See* § 8.2.2, *supra* (discussion of how to obtain information from a servicer or lender through the use of a "qualified written request" under the Real Estate Settlement Procedures Act (RESPA)).

20 In response to a qualified written response under RESPA disputing improper charges or misapplied payments, the lender or servicer must make any necessary corrections to the borrower's account, including crediting any late charges or penalties resulting from the error. 12 U.S.C. § 2605(e)(2)(A); Reg. X, 24 C.F.R. § 3500.21(e)(3)(i). *See* Ploog v. Homeside Lending, Inc., 2002 U.S. Dist. LEXIS 4646 (N.D. Ill. Mar. 18, 2002) (borrower entitled to actual damages for § 2605(e) violations based on servicer's failure to correct error of paying taxes out of escrow on wrong property); § 8.2.2.2, *supra*.

When the lender fails to make timely tax payments, causes of action against the lender for breach of fiduciary duty as escrowee, breach of contract, negligence and unfair or deceptive acts and practices should be investigated.[21] There have been a few cases of deliberate failure by a lender to make timely tax payments. This may occur because of the lender's insolvency or because the lender prefers to retain the funds in escrow as long as possible to accrue interest.[22] When a lender or servicer deliberately fails to pay property taxes or acts with reckless indifference, and the home is subsequently lost at tax sale, emotional distress and punitive damages may be sought.[23] The borrower may also bring a claim for violation of RESPA under its Servicer Act, section 2605(g), which requires that servicers make payments out of escrow accounts for taxes, insurance premiums, and other charges on a timely basis.[24] Claims for violation of section 2605 must be brought within three years.[25] An individual consumer may recover actual damages, costs and reasonable attorney fees for each violation.[26]

13.2.3 The Tax Sale

If the tax lien is not discharged by payment, the taxing authority will generally initiate a tax sale. The sale process is usually commenced by the filing of a list of delinquent taxes, identifying the taxpayer, the property, and the amount of tax due. The list is recorded and published in the local newspaper. An order of sale is issued to the appropriate government official to conduct the sale.[27] While all states require some form of notice to the taxpayer, the sale in most jurisdictions involves no judicial process.[28]

In some jurisdictions, the property itself is sold at the tax sale, in a process analogous to an execution sale. The property may be sold at auction to the highest bidder, though often it is sold for the amount of unpaid taxes. In states that do not permit the property to be sold for more than the unpaid taxes, there is generally no competitive bidding such as might exist at other auction sales.[29] The proceeds from the sale are then used to satisfy the outstanding tax bill and pay any costs of the sale.[30] Any surplus above the tax obligation and costs should be paid to the former owner or to junior recorded lienholders if required by law. Such surpluses, however, are rare on residential properties, because there is generally little or no competitive bidding.[31]

In other states, something less than full title to the property is initially sold. For example, in Illinois, the purchaser at the tax sale receives a certificate of purchase upon payment of the delinquent taxes and costs.[32] After the expiration of the period of redemption, the certificate holder may obtain the tax deed by initiating an action.[33] In Min-

21 Choi v. Chase Manhattan Mortgage Co., 63 F. Supp. 2d 874 (N.D. Ill. 1999) (home lost to tax foreclosure after servicer failed to make tax payment from borrowers escrow account and then failed to take corrective action to redeem the property; mismanagement of escrow account may give rise to cause of action for breach of fiduciary duty). *See generally* Ch. 7, *supra*; National Consumer Law Center, Unfair and Deceptive Acts and Practices (7th ed. 2008 and Supp.).

22 Escrow funds are invested by most lenders in order to earn interest. The lender or servicer may profit by retaining the difference between the interest paid to the homeowner on the escrow account, if any, and the rate at which the funds are invested. RESPA does not require that interest be paid to the borrower on the escrow account balance, but such interest payments may be required under state law. RESPA does, however, place limitations on the amount that a servicer or lender may require to be paid into an escrow account as a cushion, and requires that any surplus greater than $50 at the time of an escrow account analysis be returned to the borrower. *See* § 8.3, *supra.*

23 *See* Parks v. Wells Fargo Home Mortgage, Inc., 398 F.3d 937 (7th Cir. 2005) (under circumstances in which lender acted quickly to correct error and there was no evidence of malice, jury award of emotional distress and punitive damages vacated; lender's liability limited to actual damages for breach of contract and breach of fiduciary duty claims).

24 12 U.S.C. § 2605(g). *See also* § 8.2.4, *supra.*

25 12 U.S.C. § 2614. *See also* § 8.2.6, *supra.*

26 12 U.S.C. § 2605(f). *See also* § 8.2.6, *supra.*

27 *See, e.g.*, N.M. Stat. § 7-38-65; S.C. Code Ann. § 12-45-180.

28 Some states require the taxing authority to obtain a court order through an *ex parte* proceeding.

29 In these states, when there is more than one bidder on the property, the "highest" bidder may be the purchaser who is willing to accept the smallest proportional share or fraction of the total tax sale interest in exchange for the amount of the unpaid taxes.

30 Most courts have held that a property tax foreclosure is *in rem*, not *in personam*, thus there is no personal liability for any deficiency. *See generally* Mo. Rev. Stat. § 140.640 (personal judgments not authorized); Oberstein v. Adair County Bd. of Review, 318 N.W.2d 817 (Iowa 1982); *In re* McMahon's Estate, 21 N.W.2d 581 (Iowa 1946) (tax on real property ordinarily considered charge on the property and not personal obligation unless statute to the contrary); State v. Rhude & Fryberger, 123 N.W.2d 196 (Minn. 1963); S&R Assocs. v. Lynn Realty Corp., 769 A.2d 413 (N.J. Super. Ct. App. Div. 2001) (tax lien is attached to the realty); McFarland v. Keenan, 84 N.W.2d 884 (S.D. 1957); Real Estate Tax Appeals, Rohan, vol. 8 § 2.01[3] (1984).

A minority of courts have held, however, that property taxes entail a personal obligation on the part of the owner which does not terminate with the sale. *E.g.*, Dillman v. Foster, 656 P.2d 974 (Utah 1982) (under Utah statute although county treasurer may proceed against land to satisfy real estate tax assessment, such in no way mitigates legal obligation imposed on person assessed, under Utah statute).

31 Syntax, Inc. v. Hall, 899 S.W.2d 189 (Tex. 1995) (when tax authority resold property after tax foreclosure sale and before expiration of redemption period it was required to deposit excess proceeds with the court; foreclosed owner may have right to excess proceeds which is not extinguished by the sale).

32 35 Ill. Comp. Stat. §§ 200/21-205, 200/21-240, 200/21-250.

33 35 Ill. Comp. Stat. §§ 220/22-30, 200/22-40. *See* A.P. Properties v. Goshinsky, 186 Ill. 2d 524, 714 N.E.2d 519 (1999) (describing Illinois procedure and holding that purchaser does not have debtor/creditor relationship to taxpayer, so that purchaser could

nesota, a tax judgment is sold. If the property is not redeemed before the expiration of the statutory redemption period, the property forfeits to the purchaser.[34]

In some jurisdictions, there is no sale at all. The taxing authority simply executes its lien by taking the property. For example, in New Hampshire, unpaid taxes become a lien against the property after expiration of a statutory period.[35] The taxpayer and others with a recorded interest in the property are given notice of the lien together with a redemption period of two years and one day to pay off the lien. If the lien is not paid, the town takes the property free and clear of all liens.[36]

Because the property tax lien and sale are entirely created by statute, courts have generally held that all statutory requirements be substantially followed in order to have a valid sale.[37] Thus, the tax itself must be valid. It must be properly levied and it must be properly assessed. Otherwise, the sale may be set aside.[38]

13.2.4 Redemption and Foreclosure

Full rights to the property sold at a tax sale generally do not pass immediately to the purchaser. Rather, the purchaser acquires an interest in the property subject to redemption by the former owner. The former owner has a right to redeem the property by paying to the purchaser the purchase price plus interest within the time period allowed by statute.[39] If the former owner does not redeem within the prescribed period, the purchaser acquires title to the property free and clear of all liens created prior to the sale.[40] In some states the deed is issued to the purchaser automatically upon the expiration of the redemption period; in other states a tax sale purchaser must apply for the deed and then bring a foreclosure action to cut off the right of redemption or an action to quiet title.[41]

13.3 Preventing Property Tax Foreclosures

13.3.1 Minimizing Property Tax Liability

13.3.1.1 Overview

It may be possible to avoid a tax lien and eventual sale by obtaining an abatement, or reduction, of property taxes before the taxes become delinquent. Millions of homeowners pay too much in property taxes either because the assessment of their property is too high or because they have not taken advantage of available tax relief programs or exemptions.[42] By successfully challenging an excessive assessment the homeowner can reduce his or her tax burden accordingly. Special tax abatements can reduce tax liability even further.

13.3.1.2 Challenging the Assessment

13.3.1.2.1 Assessment exceeds taxable value

Subject to the limitations of local statutes and case law, there are basically two grounds on which a property assessment can be contested: the assessment exceeds the property's taxable value, or the property is disproportionately assessed.

In each state, the standard by which a property's taxable value is determined is set by statute. These standards, however, leave much discretion in the hands of the local assessor. States may assess property at "full value,"[43] "actual value,"[44] "fair market value,"[45] or a percentage of full value.[46] Some localities use further classifications, under which different types of property are assessed at different percentages of value. For example, residential property may be valued at a lower percentage of fair market value than commercial property, or vice versa.

---

not object to property transfer under state fraudulent transfer act (UFTA)).

34 Minn. Stat. chs. 280, 281.

35 *See* N.H. Rev. Stat. Ann. § 80:69.

36 N.H. Rev. Stat. Ann. § 80:69.

37 *See, e.g.*, Fidlin v. Collision, 156 N.W.2d 53 (Mich. Ct. App. 1967); VonElbrecht v. Jacobs, 332 S.E.2d 568 (S.C. 1985); C.J.S. *Taxation* § 745.

38 C.J.S. *Taxation* § 754. *See* § 13.3.3, *infra* (discussion of setting aside a completed tax sale).

39 *See* Md. Code Ann., Tax-Prop. § 14-827 (West) (owner has right to redeem until right of redemption has been foreclosed by buyer; buyer can bring foreclosure action not less than one year and not more than two years post sale (§ 14-833)).

40 *See, e.g.*, S.C. Code Ann. § 12-51-130 (tax deed is evidence of good title). *See also* Williams v. McCallum, 917 P.2d 794 (Idaho 1996) (redemption payment tendered one day late was ineffective to redeem property).

41 *See, e.g.*, Md. Code Ann., Tax-Prop. § 14-833 (West) (holder of certificate of sale must bring action to foreclose no sooner than one year after sale and no later than two years after sale). *Cf.* Puget Sound Inv. Group, Inc. v. Bridges, 963 P.2d 944 (Wash. Ct. App. 1998) (holding that under Washington law action to quiet title is necessary after foreclosure of IRS tax lien, ejectment action unavailable).

42 *See generally* Gettle, You Can Get Your Real Estate Taxes Reduced (1977); Chris Black & Gary Chafetz, *Hearing Pledged on Neighborhood Property Values*, Boston Globe, Feb. 1, 1994, at 17 (overassessment based on failure of assessors to take into account large number of foreclosures which reduce market value of all properties).

43 Cal. Rev. & Tax. Code § 401 (West).

44 Iowa Code § 441.21.

45 Vt. Stat. Ann. tit. 32, § 3481.

46 *E.g.*, Conn. Gen. Stat. § 12-62a(b) (70% of true and actual value); Mich. Comp. Laws § 211.27a (50% of true cash value); Nev. Rev. Stat. §§ 361.225, 361.227 (35% of taxable value; taxable value equals full cash value); W. Va. Const. art. X, § 1b (60% of value).

Determining the true value of real property is complicated and requires the consideration of a multitude of factors. Many assessors do not have the time or resources to make accurate assessments, and so rely on outdated data, rules and formulae.[47] A homeowner is entitled to challenge an assessment that is greater than the taxable value as defined by the local statute. To prevail, the homeowner generally would be required to establish a lower value of the property. Expert testimony, while certainly helpful, is not required.[48] The homeowner is competent to testify as to the value of the property from his or her own knowledge of its condition, age, etc.[49]

13.3.1.2.2 Property is disproportionately assessed

An assessment is also subject to challenge on the grounds that the property is disproportionately assessed. That is, the property's assessment is higher than assessments of similar properties in the area. The Equal Protection Clause of the federal Constitution, and similar provisions in state constitutions, prohibit discrimination between persons or property in like situations.[50] Uniformity in the assessment of taxes and equality in the burden of taxation is a fundamental principal of all state taxation.[51] A disproportionate assessment should be reduced so that it is consistent with the assessments of similar properties. To determine whether a property assessment is disproportionate, the assessments of other similar properties should be reviewed at the assessor's office. Property assessments are public records and should be made available to the homeowner upon request.

13.3.1.2.3 Administrative procedures

Each jurisdiction has established administrative procedures for challenging assessments by appeal to a local tax board or agency. Usually such appeals must be filed within a relatively short time after the issuance of the tax bill,[52] and in some states must be accompanied by full payment of the tax, or at least the uncontested amount.[53] Adverse decisions of the administrative body are usually appealable to the state trial court, subject also to statutory time limits. Failure to take advantage of these administrative remedies may bar a later challenge to the assessment.[54] Similarly, failure to pursue available state court remedies may bar a later challenge in federal court under the Tax Injunction Act, which provides that federal district courts shall not enjoin, suspend or refrain the assessment, levy or collection of any tax under state law where a "plain, speedy and efficient" remedy is available in state court.[55] However, the Tax Injunction Act should not deprive a federal district court of subject matter jurisdiction over a homeowner's action alleging improper notice of a tax sale on due process grounds, where the homeowner is not challenging the tax assessment or amounts owed, or the government's authority to collect property taxes and conduct a tax sale.[56]

13.3.1.3 Abatement, Exemption, and Deferral Programs

13.3.1.3.1 Special tax relief programs: overview

Every state has enacted special property tax abatement schemes or exemptions which relieve at least some taxpayers of a portion of their property tax liability by virtue of

47 For example, if the assessment is based on fair market value, this determination should take into account such factors as a high number of foreclosure sales in the area. High foreclosure rates depress market values, but often the number of foreclosures is not taken into account when setting values for assessments, resulting in low-income homeowners paying far too much in property taxes. *See* Chris Black & Gary Chafetz, *Hearing Pledged on Neighborhood Property Values*, Boston Globe, Feb. 1, 1994, at 17.

48 For a case in which the owner prevailed and which contains an exhaustive discussion of the evidence presented by both parties, including formulae used by both parties, see Newbert v. Spagnola, 2006 WL 2062151 (R.I. Super. Ct. July 21, 2006).

49 Joe T. Dehmer Distribs. Inc. v. Temple, 826 F.2d 1463 (5th Cir. 1987); United States v. 3698.63 Acres of Land, 416 F.2d 65, 67 (8th Cir. 1969); United States v. Sowards, 370 F.2d 87 (10th Cir. 1966); Minici v. Orton Crane & Shovel Co., 285 Mass. 499, 503–504 (1934) (owner of property may testify as to its value, as a non-expert, if familiar with its characteristics, actual and potential use).

50 *See generally* C.J.S. *Taxation* § 21.

51 *Id.*

52 *See* City of Danbury v. Dana Inv. Corp., 730 A.2d 1128 (Conn. 1999) (assessment cannot be challenged when tax lien is enforced if deadline for challenging assessment has passed). *See, e.g.*, Ala. Code §§ 40-3-20, 40-3-25 (ten days to object to valuation; adverse decision of board of equalization on objection must be appealed within thirty days); Iowa Code §§ 441.30, 441.37 (must protest assessment between April 16 and May 5 in year of assessment; assessments completed by April 15).

53 *See, e.g.*, Mass. Gen. Laws ch. 59, § 59. *But see In re* Ledgemere, 135 B.R. 193 (Bankr. D. Mass. 1991) (bankruptcy court can determine debtor's tax liability pursuant to 11 U.S.C. § 505 even when debtor failed to file timely appeal of assessment).

54 *See, e.g.*, City of Perth Amboy v. Custom Distrib. Servs., 224 F.3d 235 (3d Cir. 2000) (failure to timely request an offset due to overpayment of taxes bars adjudication of the matter in bankruptcy court).

55 28 U.S.C. § 1341. *See* Maine v. DeVore, 324 F. Supp. 2d 103 (D. Me. 2004).

56 Luessenhop v. Clinton County, New York, 466 F.3d 259 (2d Cir. 2006) (Tax Injunction Act does not bar Federal district courts from adjudicating constitutionality of notice where taxpayers are not seeking to avoid payment of state tax, and the assessment and the authority to collect the same are not disputed); Burns v. Conley, 526 F. Supp. 2d 235 (D.R.I. 2007) (Tax Injunction Act does not deprive court of jurisdiction over state court action challenging tax sale which was removed to federal court by defendant); *In re* Pontes, 310 F. Supp. 2d 447 (D.R.I. 2004) (Tax Injunction Act does not prevent court from invalidating tax sale on due process grounds).

age, disability,[57] income level,[58] or personal status.[59] All states have approved tax relief for older homeowners, and some states extend this relief to older renters as well.[60]

The tax relief provided by these programs can be significant, and should be thoroughly explored for every homeowner. Their benefits are not automatic, however. Most abatement programs require that the homeowner apply for and submit proof of eligibility for the abatement or an exemption.[61] Application must usually be made within a short period after the issuance of the tax bill. These time periods are generally not extendable, and if an application is not timely made, the right to the abatement will be lost.[62] Often homeowners who stand to benefit most are not even aware of these existing programs and so pay more than necessary.[63]

Some states also provide property tax deferrals if hardship is shown.[64] When deferrals apply, the jurisdiction usually retains a tax lien on the property, but will not enforce that lien for a certain period of time, or until occurrence of a specified event such as sale or other property transfer. Interest may or may not accrue on the unpaid taxes during the deferral period depending on the law.

Appendix F, *infra*, summarizes various state tax abatement, exemption, and deferral laws as a starting point for research.

13.3.1.3.2 Types of programs

The extent of any relief available under state programs will depend on the type of program and method of calculating relief. While these programs vary as much as state property tax laws, the following methods are the most widely used.

1. *"Circuit Breaker" Method.* The most common approach is referred to as the "circuit breaker" approach.[65] When a homeowner's property tax bill exceeds a set percentage of household income, the "circuit breaker" goes into effect and relieves the owner of the excess taxes.[66] Often this type of program is administered by the state which grants a credit against income tax liability for the excess property tax.[67]

2. *Fixed Percentage Method.* In other states, qualified households are granted relief from a certain percentage of the tax bill, regardless of the amount.[68]

3. *Homestead Tax Exemption.* Under the third method, a homestead exemption is available to older or low-income homeowners. This exempts a portion of the home's value from taxation until such time as the property ceases to be the owner's primary residence.[69] The homestead exemption usually has a monetary limit which the value of the property cannot exceed.

Even if the homeowner does not qualify under any established criteria for tax relief, some states authorize tax assessors to grant "hardship exemptions."[70] Under these exemptions, a portion of the property is exempted from tax when the owner is unable to pay the full amount of tax because of age, infirmity, or indigence.[71] For example, the New Hampshire abatement statute[72] authorizes the granting of an abatement "as justice requires." This phrase has been

57 *See* Md. Code Ann., Tax-Prop. § 9-102 (West) (relief for disabled renters); N.D. Cent. Code § 57-02-08.1 (relief available for persons over sixty-five or totally disabled with annual income less than $13,500).

58 *See* Md. Code Ann., Tax-Prop., § 9-102 (West) (relief for low-income renters).

59 *E.g.*, Massachusetts grants property tax abatements to the surviving spouse of a firefighter or police officer killed in the line of duty. Mass. Gen. Laws ch. 59, § 5 cl.(42).

60 *See, e.g.*, Md. Code Ann., Tax-Prop. § 9-102 (West).
Some abatement programs have income criteria as well as age. *E.g.*, Md. Code Ann., Tax-Prop. § 9-104 (West) (no property tax credit if annual income exceeds $200,000).

61 *See, e.g.*, *In re* Samaniego, 224 B.R. 154 (Bankr. E.D. Wash. 1998) (right to disability exemption lost by failure to make timely application).

62 *See, e.g.*, Guzman v. Bd. of Assessors, 24 Mass. App. Ct. 118, 120 (1987).

63 According to H. Clyde Reeves, The Role of the State in Property Taxation (1983), at p.xxiv, in Utah slightly more than one half of people eligible for the tax abatement program are taking part in it. The same is true in California, where the complexities of the application procedure has apparently discouraged eligible taxpayers.

64 *See, e.g.*, Cal. Rev. & Tax. Code §§ 20581 to 20622 (West); Colo. Rev. Stat. §§ 39-3.5-101 to 39-3.5-119.

65 Real Estate Tax Appeals § 2.02A. For example, Maryland, Michigan, West Virginia, South Dakota, Vermont, Montana.

66 Real Estate Tax Appeals, Rohan, vol. 8 § 2.01[3] (1984). *See, e.g.*, Ariz. Rev. Stat. Ann. § 42-279; Md. Code Ann., Tax-Prop. § 9-104 (West); W. Va. Code §§ 11-25-1 to 11-25-11.

67 Real Estate Tax Appeals, Rohan, vol. 8 § 2.01[3] (1984).

68 *See, e.g.*, Cal. Rev. & Tax. Code § 20501 (West); Mass Gen. Laws ch. 59, § 5 (older, widowed or orphaned taxpayers exempted to the extent of $2000 in value or $175 in tax if household income is less than $20,000; blind taxpayers exempted to the extent of $5000 or $437.50 in tax; older consumer with limited income receive a $4000 exemption or $350 credit).

69 *See, e.g.*, D.C. Code §§ 47-845, 47-862 (allows a homeowner to defer any taxes in excess of 110% of the prior year's tax bill until the property is sold; deferred taxes become a preferential lien on the property); W. Va. Const. art. X, § 1b-c (first $20,000 of value exempted if owner over 65). *See also* Real Estate Tax Appeals, Rohan, vol. 8 § 202A (1984).

70 Illinois has established an indemnity fund to remedy the harsh results which can result under that state's tax foreclosure process. *See* McClandon v. Rosewell, 701 N.E.2d 150 (Ill. App. Ct. 1998) (tax sale speculator denied relief from fund after purchasing property at tax sale and then losing her interest at subsequent tax sale).

71 *See, e.g.*, Alaska Stat. § 29-45-030(e) ("municipality may, in case of hardship, provide for exemption beyond first $150,000 of assessed value in accordance with regulations of [revenue] department"); Idaho Code Ann. § 63-602AA (exemption based on inability to pay); Mass. Gen. Laws ch. 59, § 5(18).

72 N.H. Rev. Stat. Ann. § 76:17.

interpreted to allow an abatement based on poverty,[73] though the court held that the taxpayer would bear the burden of proving that he or she was unable to pay the tax, which may include showing that it is not reasonable for the taxpayer to relocate, refinance or otherwise obtain additional public benefits.[74]

A few states have also built in protections against rising assessments. For example, in Minnesota an assessment cannot be increased to more than 15% above the prior year's assessment.[75] Florida's constitution was amended to include a similar provision.[76]

And some jurisdictions, by statute, ordinance, or custom, have programs that allow indigent or older taxpayers to perform community work in lieu of paying taxes.[77] These programs may range from performing city or town services (such as doing filing in town offices), to other types of work for community-based organizations. The taxes are paid down at a specified rate in exchange for the work. Always ask if such a program is available in your community, especially for sympathetic cases.

13.3.1.3.3 Seeking tax relief

A common problem in many localities is that taxing authorities never establish a procedure for evaluating and granting the abatements, exemptions or deferrals which are provided under state law. An unrepresented homeowner seeking an abatement may walk into an assessor's office and find that knowledge of state standards for tax relief is nonexistent. Moreover, local hostility to abatements in a town which is having trouble meeting its budget may drive some taxpayers away.

In such localities it may be necessary to educate local authorities about the property tax relief process. Occasionally, that may require legal action, including a mandamus claim, an action for injunctive relief, or in appropriate cases, an action for violation of civil rights.[78]

Alternatively, in most states, there is a process for appealing a decision of the taxing authority to the court system. If there is a high level of hostility in the local assessor's office, it may be a challenge to get a written decision for purposes of appeal. Failure to provide such a decision with findings of fact and conclusions of law may give rise to due process claims under state and federal constitutional standards.

13.3.1.4 Agreement and Compromise

Some states preclude abatements once a homeowner has fallen behind on tax payments.[79] Whether or not an abatement is available, a defaulting taxpayer may be able to reach an agreement with the taxing authority to compromise the outstanding tax bill. Many state legislatures have granted the taxing authority the power to compromise the amount of delinquent taxes,[80] to waive penalties and interest,[81] or to permit a homeowner additional time to cure a tax delinquency.[82] This is an avenue worth exploring, even in conjunction with a challenge to an assessment or an application for a special abatement. Be aware, however, that some states place strict limits on the authority to compromise,[83] while other states do not permit such agreements.[84]

13.3.1.5 Payment in Chapter 13 Bankruptcy

An alternative to the formal compromise process would be a bankruptcy filing. Filing bankruptcy will not only invoke the automatic stay in order to prevent the tax sale process from continuing,[85] but also in a chapter 13 case, the debtor can deal with a tax lien claim by making payments on the claim under a chapter 13 bankruptcy plan.[86] As chapter 13 plans are generally at least thirty-six months and can be as long as sixty months,[87] the debtor may be able to use chapter 13 to obtain a longer time to repay than would be

73 Ansara v. City of Nashua, 118 N.H. 879 (1978); Briggs Petition, 29 N.H. 547 (1854).

74 *Id.*

75 Minn. Stat. § 273.11.

76 Fla. Const. art 7, § 4(1)(A) (increase cannot exceed 3% of prior year's assessment, or the Consumer Price Index). *See also* Md. Code Ann., Tax-Prop. § 9-105 (West) (increase limited to percentage of prior year's assessment).

77 *See, e.g.*, Colo. Rev. Stat. § 39-3.7-101.

78 *See, e.g.*, Osloond v. Farrier, 659 N.W.2d 20 (S.D. 2003) (complaint stated valid due process claim based on tax collector's attempt to conduct tax sale without responding to homeowners' repeated request for assistance in completing application for tax relief and without considering state homestead exemption from tax sales for persons age seventy or older).

79 *See* § 13.3.2.2, *infra*.

80 *See, e.g.*, Mo. Rev. Stat. § 140.120 (county tax commission may compromise back taxes prior to judgment).

81 Tex. Tax Code Ann. § 111.103 (Vernon) (can waive penalties if taxpayer made an effort to comply).

82 N.M. Stat. § 7-38-68 (authorizing tax division to enter into installment agreements, but agreement constitutes an admission of liability); Appeal of Dvorak, 542 A.2d 604 (Pa. Commw. Ct. 1988) (delinquent taxpayer could enter into installment plan to pay balance of taxes due).

83 *See* Tex. Tax Code Ann. § 111.01 (Vernon) (can compromise if cost of collection will exceed amount due and amount due is less than $300).

84 *See, e.g.*, Neb. Const. art. 8, § 4 (except as to taxes delinquent for fifteen years).

85 11 U.S.C. § 362(a); 40235 Wash. St. Corp. v. Lusardi, 329 F.3d 1076 (9th Cir. 2003) (tax foreclosure auction in violation of stay was void even though bankruptcy case later dismissed); *In re* Lambert, 273 B.R. 663 (Bankr. N.D. Fla. 2002). *See* National Consumer Law Center, Consumer Bankruptcy Law and Practice §§ 9.4.3, 9.4.5 (9th ed. 2009).

86 *See* National Consumer Law Center, Consumer Bankruptcy Law and Practice Ch. 11 (9th ed. 2009) (discussion of options for dealing with secured creditors including secured tax creditors).

87 11 U.S.C. § 1322(d).

available by negotiated agreement. However, compliance with other requirements of the bankruptcy law may increase the cost of repayment.[88]

13.3.1.6 Interest on Taxes

If a taxing authority is charging interest on taxes, it is worthwhile checking its statutory authority to do so. In a Pennsylvania case, the court rejected a municipality's attempt to charge 18% interest on taxes under the authority of its home rule charter.[89] The court limited the municipality to a 10% interest rate allowed by a state statute.

In addition, some municipalities sell tax liens and those assignees may charge excessive interest or impose additional fees. Generally, the assignee steps into the shoes of the taxing authority and can only charge the interest and fees authorized by statute.[90]

13.3.1.7 Relief from Tax Sales for Military Personnel

The Servicemembers Civil Relief Act restricts tax sales of real property owned and occupied by a servicemember or her dependents while the servicemember is on active duty.[91] In such cases, non-judicial tax sales are prohibited because tax sales must be approved by court order.[92] In addition, if the taxing authority seeks a judicial order for the sale of the property, the court may stay the tax sale until up to 180 days after the servicemember's period of active duty ends.[93] Regardless of whether a stay was issued, interest on unpaid taxes and assessments is limited to 6%, no penalties can be imposed for nonpayment, and the servicemember has the right to redeem the property for up to 180 days after leaving active duty.[94] All of these rights apply regardless of who owes the taxes or assessments, so they apply if the servicemember's property is subject to tax sale because of a co-owner's unpaid taxes, or because of a prior owner's unpaid water or sewer assessments.

13.3.2 Contesting a Tax Sale

13.3.2.1 Introduction

Once a tax delinquency has occurred, the government will usually proceed to sell the property. To have the best chance of preventing or delaying the sale, the homeowner should act quickly. The grounds on which a homeowner can contest a tax sale, while limited, are well worth exploring.

13.3.2.2 Taxpayer Defenses to a Judicial Tax Foreclosure

When a tax sale is conducted by a judicial process, a taxpayer has an opportunity, through an answer, to raise defenses which challenge the legality or validity of the tax.[95] Defenses include:

- Lack of proper notice and other procedural defects;[96]
- Failure to join necessary parties;[97]
- The property is exempt from taxation.[98] Exempt property includes churches and property of the federal government;
- No law authorizes the tax;
- The official imposing the tax is acting without authority;
- Fees and costs added to the tax bill are unlawful, excessive or unreasonable;[99]

---

88 *See, e.g.*, *In re* Marfin Ready Mix Corp., 220 B.R. 148 (Bankr. E.D.N.Y. 1998) (discussing pre-bankruptcy and post-bankruptcy interest rate requirements for repayment of city real estate tax lien). *See generally* National Consumer Law Center, Consumer Bankruptcy Law and Practice Chs. 11, 12 (9th ed. 2009).

89 Pollice v. Nat'l Tax Funding, 225 F.3d 379 (3d Cir. 2000) (assignee of taxing authority collected unlawfully high interest rates and penalties); *In re* Swinton 287 B.R. 634 (Bankr. W.D. Pa. 2003) (assignee of municipal liens stands in the shoes of municipality and may collect the liens to same extent at the municipality).

90 *See* Pentlong Corp. v. GLS Capital, Inc., 820 A.2d 1240 (Pa. 2003) (assignee of tax liens did not acquire greater rights than municipality and therefore was not entitled to collect attorney fees from taxpayers). *See also* § 13.6, *infra*.

91 50 U.S.C. app. §§ 501–596. *See* Small v. Kulesa, 204 S.W.3d 99 (Ark. Ct. App. 2005) (taxing authority could not conduct tax sale based on tax delinquency of servicemember during period of military service because limitations period for payment of delinquent property taxes before tax sale was tolled). *See also* § 4.9, *supra*.

92 *See* 50 U.S.C. app. § 561.

93 *See* 50 U.S.C. app. § 561(b).

94 *See* 50 U.S.C. app. § 561(c), (d); Conroy v. Aniskoff, 507 U.S. 511, 113 S. Ct. 1562, 123 L. Ed. 2d 229 (1993) (servicemember entitled to suspension of time to redeem property under the Act without need to show that military service prejudiced his ability to redeem title to property).

95 Auditor Gen. v. Smith, 88 N.W.2d 429 (Mich. 1958) (taxpayer's failure to contest a property tax assessment by direct appeal precludes collateral attack on the amount of the assessment, but does not necessarily preclude collateral attack on the validity).

96 *See* § 13.3.4.2, *infra*.

97 *See* Fed. R. Civ. P. 19.

Necessary parties usually include all co-owners, and others with a property interest including lienholders. *E.g.*, City of Middletown v. Meadows Assocs. of Middletown, Inc., 711 A.2d 1 (Conn. Super. Ct. 1998) (condominium unit owners necessary parties to tax foreclosure proceeding involving common elements of condominium).

98 Smith v. Elam, 84 N.W.2d 227 (Minn. 1957).

99 The taxing authority may have the burden of proving that the fees and costs imposed were reasonable. *See* City of Danbury v. Dana Inv. Corp., 776 A.2d 438 (Conn. 2001) (duplicative and unreasonable costs may be challenged). *See also* Pollice v. Nat'l Tax Funding, 225 F.3d 379 (3d Cir. Pa. 2000) (assignee of

- The tax is a result of fraud; or
- The tax has been paid.[100]

Generally, the taxpayer is prohibited from objecting to the valuation of his or her property at this point, when the jurisdiction has established administrative procedures to challenge an assessment and the taxpayer has not pursued an administrative challenge.[101] Two exceptions to this rule are when the valuation (and tax) is the result of fraud,[102] or when the taxpayer was denied access to the administrative process.[103]

13.3.2.3 Enjoining a Sale Occurring Under a Non-Judicial Process

In most states, there is no judicial process prior to a tax sale. In order to prevent a sale in these jurisdictions, the taxpayer must initiate a lawsuit seeking to enjoin the sale. There may, however, be significant procedural obstacles to the maintenance of such an action.

The most common obstacle arises when the taxpayer has failed to exhaust administrative remedies. When the taxpayer's sole complaint is that the tax is excessive in amount, the only remedy is to apply for an abatement in the manner provided by statute and usually the collection of the tax will not be enjoined.[104] While the taxpayer's failure to contest the assessment by direct appeal will usually preclude collateral attack on the amount of the assessment, it does not necessarily preclude attack on the validity of the assessment.[105] Thus, to stop the sale the taxpayer will have to raise a claim of illegality in the assessment or imposition of the tax, or in the collection process. Most courts will enjoin a sale when the tax is not authorized by law or when it is assessed on property not subject to taxation, or when the property has been fraudulently assessed at too high a rate.[106] If statutory procedures have not been followed, any suit challenging the amount of the assessment may be subject to dismissal for failure to exhaust administrative remedies, unless the taxpayer can show that he or she was denied a meaningful opportunity to challenge the assessment administratively,[107] either because of lack of notice or lack of access to the appeal board.

Some states have enacted provisions restricting the authority of courts to enjoin a tax sale. While permitting an injunction when there is no adequate remedy at law, these provisions nevertheless impose a significant procedural impediment to any successful challenge to a tax sale.[108] In these states, the taxpayer would have to pay the disputed tax and then sue for its return.[109] And again, the taxpayer's suit for return of the tax would be subject to any administrative exhaustion requirements.

---

taxing authority collected unlawfully high interest rates and penalties).

100 Bugg v. State Roads Comm'n, 243 A.2d 511 (Md. 1968) (tax sale on which taxes were already paid is invalid and may be collaterally attacked); Smith v. Elam, 84 N.W.2d 227 (Minn. 1957) (defense that property is exempt or that tax has been paid or jurisdictional objections may be raised in delinquent tax proceedings).

101 City of Danbury v. Dana Inv. Corp., 730 A.2d 1128 (Conn. 1999) (assessment cannot be challenged at time tax lien is enforced, if deadline for challenging assessment has passed); State v. Elam, 84 N.W.2d 227 (Minn. 1957) (administrative appeal of assessment is exclusive remedy); City of Bayonne v. Ferenezi, 139 A.2d 315, 316 (N.J. Super. Ct. App. Div. 1958) (in proceeding to foreclose tax sale certificate, question of whether property had been assessed at proper value was immaterial). *But see In re* Ledgemere Land Corp., 135 B.R. 193 (Bankr. D. Mass. 1991) (debtor allowed to contest tax debts in bankruptcy court even though his prior inaction would bar him from contesting them elsewhere).

Also, when the taxpayer is not provided an opportunity to challenge the assessment, the taxpayer can raise the invalidity of the tax as a defense to a tax foreclosure. Griffin v. Cook County, 16 N.E.2d 906 (Ill. 1938).

102 C.J.S. *Taxation* § 774. *But see* Bd. of County Comm'rs of Osage County v. Schmidt, 758 P.2d 254 (Kan. Ct. App. 1988) (taxpayer may not raise allegations of fraud in the valuation or assessment of property for the first time in a tax foreclosure action but must exhaust administrative remedies).

103 Lick v. Dahl, 285 N.W.2d 594 (S.D. 1979) (when taxpayer was notified of increased assessment after the board of supervisors session had ended, court allowed taxpayer to appeal directly to court).

104 *See, e.g.*, Neb. Rev. Stat. § 77-1735 (taxpayer must make a written demand for return of a tax paid within thirty days of payment or be forever barred from contesting the validity of the tax by any legal proceedings); Wis. Stat. § 70.47(7)(a) (to challenge a tax based on valuation of the property or excessive assessment, the taxpayer must first file written objections and appear before a local board of tax equalization); Bd. of County Comm'rs of Osage County v. Schmidt, 785 P.2d 254 (Kan. Ct. App. 1988) (taxpayer must exhaust administrative remedies, statute provides full and adequate remedy to protest tax); Satterfield v. Britton, 78 N.W.2d 817, 822 (Neb. 1956) (taxpayer barred from seeking return of tax when statute requires notice of objection within thirty days of assessment and taxpayer did not file action for three years).

105 State Treasurer v. Eaton, 284 N.W.2d 801 (Mich. Ct. App. 1979) (taxpayer may object to proposed sale on grounds that the taxes are illegal).

106 First Nat'l Bank of White Sulphur Springs v. Bergan, 169 P.2d 233 (Mont. 1946); Paulin v. Town of Danville, 260 A.2d 208 (Vt. 1969) (equity court can issue declaratory judgment when property subject to double assessment of land by two towns because of border dispute).

107 *See, e.g.*, Fisher v. Miller, 218 N.W.2d 821 (Mich. Ct. App. 1974) (when taxpayer's address is known to taxing authorities, notice of increased assessment by publication was insufficient and taxpayer was entitled to judicial review of assessment despite his failure to raise objections administratively); Lick v. Dahl, 285 N.W.2d 594 (S.D. 1979) (when taxpayer was notified of increased assessment after the board of supervisors session had ended, court allowed the taxpayer to appeal assessment directly to court).

108 For example, Virginia and Washington.

109 *See* Satterfield v. Britton, 78 N.W.2d 817, 822 (Neb. 1956)

Another option, and one on which there is little reported case law, is to seek injunctive relief on the ground that the tax creditor is fully and adequately secured by the equity in the property. The argument would be that there is no reason to effect a forfeiture through the tax sale process, as the taxing entity is certain to get its money with interest upon the sale of the property at a later date. This argument has been used successfully in some jurisdictions to prevent mortgage foreclosures, and should apply with equal force to tax sales, because it is even more likely that there will be sufficient equity to protect the lien.

Finally, as discussed above, filing bankruptcy, by virtue of the automatic stay, will automatically prevent the tax sale process from going forward.[110] As most taxing entities hold first position liens, they are generally adequately protected by equity in the property such that they have no entitlement to relief from the stay.[111] In addition, a tax sale or other acts intended to complete transfer of the property under a tax sale procedure may be invalidated if they occur while the automatic stay in bankruptcy is in effect.[112]

13.3.3 Setting Aside a Completed Tax Sale

13.3.3.1 General

Once a tax sale has been completed, homeowners have three options: they can redeem the property by paying the purchase price plus costs; they can do nothing and the tax purchaser's interest will ripen into ownership, or they can attempt to set aside the completed sale. Setting aside foreclosure sales in bankruptcy is treated at § 9.4.4.4, *supra*.[113]

The bases on which a tax sale can be set aside are limited by state laws which restrict certain claims and prescribe short statutes of limitations within which claims can be raised.[114] The rules regarding which claims can be raised and when they can be raised differ from state to state. A generally followed rule is that defects in the foreclosure process which render the sale voidable must be raised within the statutorily prescribed time or be lost; but a tax sale that is void because of illegality is subject to challenge at any time.

This subsection discusses some of the common grounds on which state courts have set aside tax sales and tax deeds.

13.3.3.2 Grounds for Challenging Tax Sales

13.3.3.2.1 Introduction

Because the property tax lien and sale are entirely created by statute, courts have generally held that all statutory requirements must be substantially followed in order to have a valid sale.[115] Typically, a challenge to a completed tax sale arises in one of two ways. After the redemption period has expired, in many states, the tax sale purchaser must request that a tax deed be issued. This request is preceded by a notice to the former owner of the intention to seek a deed.[116] Once the deed is issued, the purchaser brings an action to foreclose the right of redemption or to quiet title.[117] The former owner, who must be made a party to this action, may attempt to challenge the validity of the sale or the deed in this action.

A tax sale may also be invalidated by an action initiated by the taxpayer prior to the expiration of the redemption period. However, any action brought by the taxpayer, as well as any defenses raised in answer to a quiet title action, may be limited by statutory provisions which impose time limitations and restrict the grounds on which a sale can be challenged. Some statutes require that the homeowner tender the redemption amount before bringing an action to

(when a tax imposed is illegal and unauthorized for any purpose, an original action must be brought to recover the tax only by virtue of statutory or constitutional authority; one seeking to recover must show substantial compliance with the statute; taxpayer who did not comply with statutory procedures barred from recovering tax).

110 *See In re* Kane, 254 F.3d 325 (1st Cir. 2001) (town's purported notice of tax foreclosure violated the automatic stay, such that subsequent foreclosure did not affect buyers' interest).

Amendments to the Bankruptcy Code made in 2005 Act impose new restrictions on the application of the automatic stay based on repeat bankruptcy filings. These new provisions must be considered in determining whether the debtor's bankruptcy filing will invoke the automatic stay and stop a pending tax sale. *See* National Consumer Law Center, Consumer Bankruptcy Law and Practice § 9.3.3 (9th ed. 2009).

111 National Consumer Law Center, Consumer Bankruptcy Law and Practice § 9.7.3.2.2 (9th ed. 2009).

112 *In re* Lambert, 273 B.R. 663 (Bankr. N.D. Fla. 2002) (issuance of tax deed related to prepetition tax sale violated automatic stay, was void ab initio, and did not transfer property); *In re* Crosby, 109 B.R. 195 (Bankr. S.D. Miss. 1989) (tax sale was a violation of automatic stay and therefore null and void).

113 The use of § 548(a)(2) of the Bankruptcy Code to set aside tax sales as fraudulent transfers is discussed at § 13.3.3.2.8, *infra*.

114 *See* Wells Fargo Bank, N.A. v. UP Ventures II, L.L.C., 675 S.E.2d 883 (W. Va. 2009) (three-year statute of limitation for bringing action to set aside a tax deed does not violate mortgage holder's due process rights).

115 *See, e.g., In re* Brown, 221 B.R. 849 (Bankr. N.D. Ala. 1998) (sale found void for failing to comply fully with either of two mutually exclusive relevant sale statutes); Fidlin v. Collision, 156 N.W.2d 53 (Mich. Ct. App. 1967); VonElbrecht v. Jacobs, 332 S.E.2d 568 (S.C. 1985); C.J.S. *Taxation* § 745.

116 This notice will usually give the former owner one final opportunity to redeem.

117 *See, e.g.,* Detroit Leasing Co. v. City of Detroit, 2006 WL 1009266 (Mich. Ct. App. Apr. 18, 2006) (quiet title action dismissed because purchaser relied on unsworn affidavit of nonpayment during redemption period which did not strictly comply with statute).

In some states, however, no judicial action is required.

challenge the tax sale.[118] Further, the taxpayer may have to present a legal justification for his or her failure to object sooner, such as the failure to receive notice of earlier proceedings[119] or excusable neglect in failing to respond to earlier proceedings.[120]

The taxpayer may have the burden of proving the irregularity of the tax sale.[121] The grounds on which courts have set aside sales are discussed in the following subsections.

13.3.3.2.2 Defects in the tax lien or in the tax sale process

Statutes governing tax sales and the steps leading up to them must be strictly followed before an owner may be deprived of his or her property by sale.[122] If these steps are not followed, the deed issued from such sale may be set aside.[123] Slight irregularities may not be enough for a court to invalidate a sale,[124] but defects which prejudice the rights of the owner, such as the failure to give proper notice, probably will.[125] Some courts have held that non-compliance with statutory notice requirements renders a tax sale void even if the taxpayer had actual notice of the sale.[126] Defects in the lien itself, such as the absence of the name of

118 *See, e.g.*, *In re* Price, 2006 WL 637831 (11th Cir. Mar. 15, 2006) (homeowner who failed to tender redemption value lacked standing to challenge tax sale based on Georgia statute requiring tender before seeking to "in any way invalidate" a tax sale).

119 Westerheide v. Wilcox, 124 P.2d 409 (Okla. 1942).

120 Bergen-Eastern Corp. v. Koss, 427 A.2d 1132 (N.J. Super. Ct. App. Div. 1981).

121 *See* Giordano v. Gilderdale, 729 So. 2d 760 (La. Ct. App. 1999) (party attacking tax sale bears burden of proving its invalidity); Van Raden Homes, Inc. v. Dakota View Estates, 546 N.W.2d 843 (N.D. 1996). *But see* McGuire v. Rogers, 794 So. 2d 1131 (Ala. Civ. App. 2000) (burden placed on purchaser in tax sale challenge to prove that tax deed is valid by showing that all applicable statutory procedures had been followed).

122 *See, e.g.*, *In re* Brown, 221 B.R. 849 (Bankr. N.D. Ala. 1998) (sale void because time of sale requirements were not met); Wilson v. Daniels, 64 Ark. App. 181, 980 S.W.2d 274 (1998); *In re* Application of County Collector, 692 N.E.2d 1211 (Ill. App. Ct. 1998) (tax deed void when notice omitted complete certificate number; court declines to "open . . . the dike to permit any omission—however minute—of statutorily required information"); Isern v. Summerfield, 956 P.2d 28 (Mont. 1998) (tax sale proceedings demand "punctilious compliance with all statutory procedural requirements"); Van Raden Homes, Inc. v. Dakota View Estates, 546 N.W.2d 843 (N.D. 1996); *In re* Ryan Inv. Co., 517 S.E.2d 692 (S.C. 1999) (tax sale void when notice not sent by restricted delivery, even though postal regulations did not allow mail to a corporation to be sent restricted delivery; only if taxing authority had tried to get post office to deliver notice by restricted delivery would court consider whether alternate methods would be adequate); Rives v. Bulsa, 478 S.E.2d 878 (S.C. Ct. App. 1996); Manji v. Blackwell, 473 S.E.2d 837 (S.C. Ct. App. 1996).

123 Schmidt v. Langel, 874 P.2d 447 (Colo. Ct. App. 1993) (non-compliance with requirements of tax sale statute will serve to void sale); Simes v. Blaser, 592 P.2d 1367 (Idaho 1979) (tax deed void when notice of delinquent taxes sent to only one of two owners listed in recorder's office when statute required that all owners of record be notified); Gradison v. Logan, 190 N.E.2d 29 (Ind. Ct. App. 1963); McQuade v. State, 32 N.W.2d 510 (Mich. 1948); Fulton v. Cornelius, 758 P.2d 312 (N.M. 1988) (validity of tax sale dependent on compliance with statutory and constitutional due process requirements); State *ex rel.* Klineline v. Blackhurst, 749 P.2d 1111 (N.M. 1988) (tax sale statute to be construed strictly like a forfeiture statute); *In re* Tax Sale of 28.8525 Acres, 688 A.2d 1239 (Pa. Commw. Ct. 1997) (tax sale is void without compliance with each of three statutory notice requirements, even if owner has actual notice); Rives v. Bulsa, 478 S.E.2d 878 (S.C. Ct. App. 1996) (tax sale void when property listed, assessed, levied upon, advertised, and sold in name of owner's father rather than owner; whether father was owner's agent was immaterial); Manji v. Blackwell, 473 S.E.2d 837 (S.C. Ct. App. 1996) (tax sale void when notice sent by certified mail but not restricted delivery); Clint Indep. Sch. Dist. v. Cash Invs., Inc., 970 S.W.2d 535 (Tex. 1998) (sale void because sheriff accepted less than minimum required bid).

124 *See, e.g.*, Van Raden Homes, Inc. v. Dakota View Estates, 546 N.W.2d 843 (N.D. 1996) (mere irregularity in notice will not invalidate sale after redemption period passes, as long as notice was given; early mailing and form of notices did not invalidate sale). *But see In re* Application of County Collector, 692 N.E.2d 1211 (Ill. App. Ct. 1998) (tax sale buyer's misstatement of certificate as #25017 instead of #91-0025017 on notice to owner precludes issuance of deed, even though owner was not misled or prejudiced).

125 United States v. Grable, 25 F.3d 298 (6th Cir. 1994) (sale held in wrong place not set aside because no prejudice resulted and because taxpayer's attorney witnessed the sale and did not object); Sienkiewicz v. Palzer, 900 F.2d 206 (9th Cir. 1990) (sale and tax deed void when one co-owner of property was not given notice); Anderson v. Richland County, 711 P.2d 784 (Mont. 1985) (tax deed proceeding void for failure to give proper notice to owner); Garcia v. Ted Parks, L.L.C., 195 P.3d 1269 (Okla. 2008) (tax deed void based on failure to provide actual notice to property owner as required by statute, where process server left notice with son of owner who had merely stopped by his mother's property on way to visit her in the hospital). *Cf.* Wilson v. Daniels, 980 S.W.2d 274 (Ark. Ct. App. 1998) (notice complied with statute as it was mailed to correct address, even though it was returned marked "unclaimed or refused").

126 *See In re* Tax Sale of 28.8525 Acres, 688 A.2d 1239 (Pa. Commw. Ct. 1997) (failure to comply with posting requirements would render sale void even if taxpayer had actual notice; court notes that posting not only notifies taxpayer but also notifies public of opportunity to bid); Robert F. Quinn Trust v. Ruiz, 723 A.2d 1127 (R.I. 1999) (failure to give notice to some persons renders sale invalid even as to others who were properly notified); *In re* Ryan Inv. Co., 517 S.E.2d 692 (S.C. 1999). *But see* Sabbeth v. Tax Claim Bureau, 714 A.2d 514 (Pa. Commw. Ct. 1998) (non-compliance with statutory notice requirements does not render sale void when taxpayer had actual notice). *Cf.* Lyon v. Estate of Newton Cornell, 703 N.Y.S.2d 325 (App. Div. 2000) (non-compliance with statutory notice requirements would not have rendered sale void if owner had actual notice); Van Raden Homes, Inc. v. Dakota View Estates, 546 N.W.2d 843 (N.D. 1996) (omission of names of five of six record owners from published notice not a jurisdictional defect when all six received actual notice by mail); Cruder v. Westmoreland County Tax Claim Bureau, 861 A.2d 411 (Pa. Commw. Ct. 2004) (property owner had actual notice of tax sale).

one of the record owners, should also render the sale invalid.[127]

Some states have passed statutes which provide that failure to strictly comply with the statutory provisions will not affect the validity of the sale.[128] These provisions were enacted in an effort to speed the collection of taxes and to make tax titles easier to establish.[129] However, these statutes should not prevent a challenge based on constitutional grounds, such as one based on the failure to provide adequate notice.[130] An examination of local statutes and case law will reveal which defects affect the validity of the sale and which are treated as mere irregularities. There may also be statutory limits on the time in which claims of defects may be raised.[131] In some states the passage of time cures any defects in the process.

13.3.3.2.3 Taxes are not owed

A tax sale on which taxes were already paid is invalid and may be collaterally attacked.[132] Also if the property is exempt from taxation, any tax sale should be void.[133]

13.3.3.2.4 Fraud in sale process or in the imposition of tax

Fraud in the foreclosure process will render the tax sale void. For example, when the governing statute required the tax sale purchaser to make all reasonable efforts to contact former owners prior to proceeding to foreclose the tax deed, and the purchaser only made efforts to contact one of two former owners, this amounted to constructive fraud and the foreclosure was set aside.[134] When the tax sale purchaser had allegedly promised the owner that he would pay the taxes, summary judgment in favor of the purchaser was reversed.[135]

Fraud in the assessment or imposition of the tax can be raised post sale in most jurisdictions.[136]

13.3.3.2.5 Purchaser's lack of legal authority to bid

If the purchaser at the tax sale is a governmental entity, another question to investigate is whether the purchaser had statutory authority to bid. The state may require public bodies to notify the public and go through various procedures before making major expenditures. There may also be statutory limitations on when a taxing authority can make a bid on a tax debt. While a Texas appellate case found that a taxing authority's purchase of a property at tax sale did not run afoul of these statutes,[137] on other facts such a challenge might be successful.

13.3.3.2.6 Excusable neglect

A taxpayer's excusable neglect in failing to respond to a tax sale foreclosure action may justify setting aside the sale under a rule akin to federal Rule 60(b).[138] For example, in *Bergen-Eastern Corp. v. Koss*,[139] a seventy-four-year-old widow with a history of continuing, serious psychiatric problems received notice of the tax sale but failed to respond until the eviction proceedings. The court ruled that the trial court had the authority to reopen the foreclosure judgment based on excusable neglect, and the owner ten-

---

127 *E.g.*, Town of Pownal v. Anderson, 728 A.2d 1254 (Me. 1999).

128 *See, e.g.*, Ariz. Rev. Stat. Ann. § 42-381 (insubstantial failure to comply with statutory provisions does not affect the validity of the assessment and levy of taxes, nor any tax lien, nor the sale of any tax lien or the foreclosure of the right to redeem by which the tax is enforced).

129 72 Am. Jur. 2d *State and Local Taxation* § 931.

130 *See, e.g.*, Garcia v. Ted Parks, L.L.C., 195 P.3d 1269 (Okla. 2008) (statute which implies that failure to give actual notice to record owner does not affect the validity of tax sale is in conflict with constitutional due process notice requirements). *See also* § 13.3.4, *infra*.

131 *See, e.g.*, Town of Hudson v. Gate City Dev. Corp., 660 A.2d 1100 (N.H. 1995) (statute making tax sale incontestable after ten years precludes all challenges); Van Raden Homes, Inc. v. Dakota View Estates, 546 N.W.2d 843 (N.D. 1996) (only "jurisdictional" defects can be raised after redemption period).

132 Bugg v. State Roads Comm'n, 243 A.2d 511 (Md. 1968); Thomas v. Hardisty, 143 A.2d 618 (Md. 1958).

133 Town of Norwood v. Norwood Civic Ass'n, 165 N.E.2d 124 (Mass. 1960) (taxes void and town cannot foreclose a tax title if taxpayer can establish that its property is exempt from taxation on the date of assessment); Auditor Gen. v. Smith, 88 N.W.2d 429 (Mich. 1958). *But see* Aquarian Church of Universal Serv. v. York County, 44 A.2d 891 (Pa. Commw. Ct. 1985) (statutory remedy of appeal to assessment board is the mandatory and exclusive remedy of persons claiming that real property is exempt from taxation; court refused to enjoin sale when church failed to pursue statutory remedy).

134 Karkenny v. Morgelli, 370 A.2d 137 (Md. Ct. Spec. App. 1977). *See also* Parks v. Wells Fargo Home Mortgage, Inc., 398 F.3d 937 (7th Cir. 2005) (noting that state court had vacated tax sale deed based on actual fraud of purchaser in falsely swearing that she had caused sheriff to personally serve homeowners with statutory notice).

135 Lavidas v. Smith, 987 P.2d 212 (Ariz. Ct. App. 1999).

136 C.J.S. *Taxation* § 774; 72 Am. Jur. 2d *State and Local Taxation* § 1130 (for example, when overassessment intentional or when other property fraudulently omitted from assessment).

137 Bandera Indep. Sch. Dist. v. Hamilton, 2 S.W.3d 367 (Tex. App. 1999).

138 City of Durham v. Keen, 253 S.E.2d 585 (N.C. Ct. App. 1979); Bergen-Eastern Corp. v. Koss, 427 A.2d 1132 (N.J. Super. Ct. App. Div. 1981).

State rules modeled on Rule 60(b) will also impose time limits for the taxpayer to file a motion, and the taxpayer will presumably have to allege a meritorious defense or tender full payment of the delinquent taxes. *See In re* 2435 Plainfield Ave., Inc., 72 F. Supp. 2d 482 (D.N.J. 1999) (taxpayer barred from most grounds for 60(b) relief because motion filed more than one year after tax foreclosure judgment), *aff'd without opinion*, 213 F.3d 629 (3d Cir. 2000).

139 427 A.2d 1132 (N.J. Super. Ct. App. Div. 1981).

dered the full amount of taxes due.[140]

13.3.3.2.7 Equitable grounds

Courts are willing to set aside tax sales on equitable grounds when the taxpayer was misled by the taxing authority. A tax sale was set aside by the court when the taxpayer had made substantial payments of taxes due prior to the sale but allowed the sale to proceed when he did not make full payment or enter into an installment payment plan. The court found that the taxpayer did not understand English well, and set aside the sale on the condition of full payment, because bureau personnel did not take adequate steps to ensure that the owner was not confused as to his rights.[141]

13.3.3.2.8 Inadequacy of price

Except in bankruptcy as discussed below, absent fraud, suppression of bidding at the sale, or other unfairness, the inadequacy of the sale price is usually not enough to invalidate the sale.[142] A price that is grossly inadequate or an inadequate price coupled with some irregularity or unfairness in the foreclosure process may be grounds to set aside a sale under state law.[143]

Prior to the Supreme Court's ruling in *BFP v. Resolution Trust Corp.*[144] when a home was sold at a mortgage foreclosure sale for an amount significantly less than market value, the sale could be set aside as a fraudulent conveyance under section 548(a)(1)(B) of the Bankruptcy Code. In *BFP*, however, the Supreme Court took away this protection for mortgagors in bankruptcy and ruled that the foreclosure sale price was the value of the property for purposes of section 548(a)(1)(B), as long as the foreclosure sale was conducted according to state foreclosure law.[145]

In its opinion, however, the Supreme Court expressly limits its decision to mortgage foreclosures of real estate, stating that "the considerations bearing on other foreclosures and forced sales (to satisfy tax liens, for example) may be different."[146] For tax foreclosures which do not involve a formal sale of the property (i.e., when the purchaser obtains a lien or a certificate rather than an actual deed) the *BFP* analysis should not be relevant.[147] Typically, the purchaser of a tax lien pays only the amount of delinquent taxes, an amount which bears no relationship to the value of the property. For this reason, there is no logical basis on which to conclude that the tax lien purchase price is a "reasonably equivalent value."

Despite the Court's careful effort to distinguish tax sales from mortgage foreclosure sales in *BFP*, some courts have nevertheless applied *BFP* to a tax sale after finding that the sale was noncollusive and regularly conducted in accord with state law.[148] The question may turn on whether applicable state law has protections for owners that are similar to the protections of the foreclosure sale process.[149]

---

140 *Id.*

141 Appeal of Dvorak, 542 A.2d 604 (Pa. Commw. Ct. 1988) (taxpayer was not clearly informed partial payment would not stay the sale; purpose of the real estate tax sale law is not to strip a taxpayer of his property but to insure the collection of taxes; here it was obvious to the bureau personnel that the owner was confused). *But see In re* Sale of Real Estate by Verango County Tax Claim Bureau for 1977 Delinquent Taxes—Sale of 1979, 449 A.2d 879 (Pa. Commw. Ct. 1982) (taxpayer did not read receipt so did not realize taxes had not been paid in full, sale not set aside; dominant purpose of the tax sale law is to provide speedier and more efficient procedures for enforcing tax liens and to improve the quality of titles for tax sales).

142 *In re* 2435 Plainfield Ave., Inc., 72 F. Supp. 2d 482 (D.N.J. 1999) (price disparity does not provide basis for relief from tax foreclosure judgment; debtor could not attack sale under state fraudulent conveyance statute because it excluded tax sales), *aff'd*, 213 F.3d 629 (3d Cir. 2000) (table); City of Durham v. Keen, 253 S.E.2d 585 (N.C. Ct. App. 1979); Patterson v. Goldsmith, 358 S.E.2d 163 (S.C. 1987). *See generally* § 14.2.4, *infra* (discussion of setting aside tax sales in bankruptcy).

143 *See, e.g.*, Alexander v. Phoenix Bond & Indem. Co., 149 F. Supp. 2d 989 (N.D. Ill. 2001) (property owners sufficiently pleaded violation of Sherman Act based on alleged conspiracy by purchasers to fix bid process at tax sales).

144 511 U.S. 531, 114 S. Ct. 1757, 128 L. Ed. 2d 556 (1994).

145 *See* § 14.2.3.3, *infra.*

146 BFP v. Resolution Trust Corp., 511 U.S. at 552 n.3.

147 *In re* Sherman, 223 B.R. 555 (B.A.P. 10th Cir. 1998) (*BFP* does not apply to Wyoming tax sale under statute without a provision for competitive bidding); *In re* Murphy, 331 B.R. 107 (Bankr. S.D.N.Y. 2005) (*BFP* inapplicable where competitive bidding not component of tax sale procedure); *In re* Wentworth, 221 B.R. 316 (Bankr. D. Conn. 1998) (tax transfer of property worth $20,000 to satisfy $1500 lien avoided as constructive fraudulent transfer; *BFP* analysis not relevant to tax lien foreclosure by forfeiture proceeding rather than sale); *In re* Butler, 171 B.R. 321 (Bankr. N.D. Ill. 1994); *In re* McKeever, 132 B.R. 996 (Bankr. N.D. Ill. 1991).

In Illinois, the property transfer is an administrative act based on prior sale of the *tax lien* and a failure to redeem; there is no property sale to which the *BFP* analysis could apply. *See also In re* Grandoe Country Club Co., 252 F.3d 1146 (10th Cir. 2001) (*BFP* analysis applied because tax sale under state law subject to competitive bidding procedure); *In re* Grady, 202 B.R. 120 (Bankr. N.D. Iowa 1996) (*BFP* does not apply to forfeiture of real estate installment sale contract, property interest of $40,000 forfeited to satisfy $16,000 debt under the contract constituted fraudulent transfer).

148 *In re* T.F. Stone Co., 72 F.3d 466 (5th Cir. 1995) (*BFP* analysis applied to state tax sale because there were no bids at an auction conducted in compliance with state law, even though property valued as high as $65,000 was transferred for only $325); Hemstreet v. Brostmeyer, 258 B.R. 134 (Bankr. W.D. Pa. 2001); *In re* Russell-Polk, 200 B.R. 218 (Bankr. E.D. Mo. 1996) (*BFP* analysis applies to tax sales based on similarity between tax lien foreclosures and mortgage foreclosures under Missouri law); *In re* McGrath, 170 B.R. 78 (Bankr. D.N.J. 1994) (applying *BFP* analysis to tax sales).

149 *In re* Washington, 232 B.R. 340 (Bankr. E.D. Va. 1999); *In re* Samaniego, 224 B.R. 154 (Bankr. E.D. Wash. 1998) (application of *BFP* warranted on available facts); *In re* Lord, 179 B.R. 429 (Bankr. E.D. Pa. 1995) (Pennsylvania law affords the same

Uncertainty remains. However, depending on the jurisdiction, debtors may still be able to set aside a tax sale as a fraudulent transfer in bankruptcy, if the transfer occurred less than two years[150] before the filing of the bankruptcy petition,[151] the transfer was for less than a reasonably equivalent value, and was made at a time when the debtor was insolvent.[152] This procedure would be commenced by filing an adversary proceeding.[153] Such an action in bankruptcy court is not barred by the Tax Injunction Act.[154]

13.3.4 Constitutional Challenges to the Sale

13.3.4.1 Sales Subject to Due Process

Because it involves state action, a tax foreclosure is subject to constitutional standards of due process. In this context, due process has been interpreted to require adequate notice and an opportunity to contest the action.[155] Failure to provide due process renders a sale void, passing no title to the purchaser, and subject to collateral attack.[156]

13.3.4.2 Adequate Notice

In 1982, the Supreme Court invalidated the state of Indiana's tax sale procedure on due process grounds because the statute did not provide for actual notice to a mortgage holder of a tax lien foreclosure, but instead permitted notice by publication.[157] The Court ruled that when the mortgage holder's name and address were identified in a publicly recorded mortgage, constructive notice by publication must be supplemented by notice mailed to the mortgage holder's last known address or by personal service.[158] The court recognized the substantial property interest of the mortgage holder which was significantly affected by a tax sale. The court held that in such situations due process requires adequate notice, either by mail "or other means as certain to ensure actual notice."[159] This ruling set the standard by which the notice provisions of state tax foreclosure laws should be judged, not only with respect to mortgage holders but to any person with a protectable interest in the property to be sold, including the owner.

Following the *Mennonite* decision, state courts have struck down laws permitting notice by publication to the property owner,[160] and invalidated sales when the property owner was not notified by mail.[161] When a taxpayer's mailing

---

type of protective procedures to tax sales as mortgage foreclosures so *BFP* applies).

The three relevant factors discussed in the *Lord* decision, notice, opportunity to be heard, and strict adherence to statutory requirements appear to ignore the important question of whether the underlying procedures are designed to generate bidding. Absent procedures designed to encourage bidding, the tax sale is hardly likely to produce the reasonable value of the property. The third *Lord* factor, strict adherence to statutory requirements, seems to be little more than a requirement that the sale be "regularly conducted" consistent with *BFP*. *See also* Hemstreet v. Brostmeyer, 258 B.R. 134 (Bankr. W.D. Pa. 2001) (there is no reason to distinguish between a tax sale or a foreclosure sale under state law).

150 Section 548(a) was amended by the 2005 Bankruptcy Act to extend the look-back period from one year to two years. The two-year period applies to cases filed on or after April 20, 2006. *See* Pub L. No. 109-8, § 1404(b) (2005).

151 There is some dispute as to when the transfer actually occurs for purposes of § 548. *See* Jackson v. Midwest P'ship, 176 B.R. 156 (N.D. Ill. 1994) (sale of tax lien is the transfer of executory interest in property); *In re* Butler, 171 B.R. 321 (Bankr. N.D. Ill. 1994) (sale of tax lien is merely a substitution of creditors).

152 11 U.S.C. § 548. *See generally* National Consumer Law Center, Consumer Bankruptcy Law and Practice § 10.4.2.6.5 (9th ed. 2009).

153 Fed. R. Bankr. P. 7001–7087.

154 *See* 28 U.S.C. § 1341; *In re* Murphy, 331 B.R. 107 (Bankr. S.D.N.Y. 2005). *See also* § 13.3.1.2.3, *supra*.

155 Mennonite Bd. of Missions v. Adams, 462 U.S. 791, 798 (1982) (adequate notice required); Wenatchee Reclamation Dist. v. Mustell, 684 P.2d 1275 (Wash. 1984) (opportunity to contest required).

156 Am. Jur. 2d *State and Local Taxation* § 916; Burns v. Conley, 526 F. Supp. 2d 235 (D.R.I. 2007) (vacating state court decree foreclosing owners' right of redemption where town and tax sale purchaser failed to comply with statutory notice requirements and denied owners their right to due process); Monumental Enters., Inc. v. City of Baltimore, 337 A.2d 176 (Md. Ct. Spec. App. 1975) (finality provisions of tax sale statute cannot operate to give validity to void sale, nor to deny force and effect of due process).

157 Mennonite Bd. of Missions v. Adams, 462 U.S. 791 (1982). *See also* First Nat'l Bank of Eden v. Meyer, 476 N.W.2d 267, 270 (S.D. 1991) (tax deed statute unconstitutional because it did not require that notice be sent to all reasonably ascertainable judgment creditors; citing *Mennonite*).

158 *Mennonite Bd.*, 462 U.S. at 798.

159 *Id.* at 800.

160 Hamilton v. Renewed Hope, Inc., 589 S.E.2d 81 (Ga. 2003) (notice by publication of foreclosure of right to redeem condominium sold at tax sale does not satisfy due process if owner's name and address are "reasonably ascertainable"); LVF Realty Co. v. Harrington, 536 N.Y.S.2d 840 (App. Div. 1989), *appeal dismissed*, 559 N.E.2d 671 (N.Y. 1990) ("where the interest of a property owner will be substantially affected by an act of government and where the owner's name and address are known, due process requires that actual notice be given"); Kahen-Kashi v. Risman, 777 N.Y.S.2d 755 (App. Div. 2004) (local ordinance providing for notice by publication violated due process). *Accord* Quay Dev., Inc. v. Elegante Bldg. Corp., 392 So. 2d 901 (Fla. 1981); Lilly v. Duke, 376 S.E.2d 122 (W. Va. 1988) (posting and publishing of tax foreclosure sale notice was insufficient to satisfy due process rights of property owners whose address was reasonably ascertainable through recorded deed of trust).

161 Brandon Township v. Tomkow, 535 N.W.2d 268 (Mich. Ct. App. 1995) (state statute affording notice and opportunity for hearing only for owners of property worth $1000 or more was unconstitutional); City of Boston v. James, 530 N.E.2d 1254 (Mass. App. Ct. 1988) (municipality must make all reasonable efforts to notify by mail any persons who might have an interest in the land); O'Brien v. Port Lawrence Title & Trust Co., 688 N.E.2d 1136 (Ohio Ct. Com. Pl. Lucas County 1997) (mailed

address is known to taxing authorities,[162] notice by publication only is constitutionally insufficient, and the sale can be attacked by the taxpayer despite a statutory provision that no tax sale shall be set aside except when the tax has been paid or the property is exempt from taxation.[163] Similarly, when notice is sent to the owner's former address after the owner has provided the taxing authority with change of address information, even if this may satisfy statutory notice requirements, adequate notice has not been provided for constitutional due process purposes.[164] Harder issues arise when notice is sent to the taxpayer's last known address, if the taxing authorities could have obtained a better address with reasonable efforts to locate the taxpayer.[165] Due process generally requires that the taxing authority make a reasonable effort to discover the identity and address of a person whose interests are likely to be affected by the tax sale.[166]

In *Plemons v. Gale*,[167] a tax sale purchaser sent a redemption notice to the property owner by certified mail to the property address, which was occupied by tenants, and to the owner's last known address. Each of the notices was returned as undeliverable. In finding that notice was insufficient even though the statutory requirements had been satisfied, the Fourth Circuit held that "when prompt return of an initial mailing makes clear that the original effort at

---

notice of sale to absentee owner at incorrect address insufficient when correct address could have been easily ascertained). *See also* Town of Andover v. State Fin. Servs., 736 N.E.2d 837 (Mass. 2000) (no due process violation when landowner was mailed, but did not receive, notice of sale); Cent. Fisher v. Miller, 218 N.W.2d 821 (Mich. Ct. App. 1974); Vilca v. Village of Port Chester, 681 N.Y.S.2d 291 (App. Div. 1998) (no due process violation when taxing authority mailed notice to empty lot, because taxpayers had actual notice of proceedings); Finnegan v. Seaside Realty Trust, 777 A.2d 548 (R.I. 2001) (lessor's failure to receive notice did not invalidate sale when lessor's option to purchase the property was not recorded and her interest in the property was not readily identifiable to the tax collector or the tax examiner); State Bank v. Dickerson, 2001 Tenn. App. LEXIS 292 (Tenn. Ct. App. Apr. 25, 2001) (sale invalid when lender did not receive notice of sale even though deed of trust was recorded); Pell v. City of Chattanooga, 2000 Tenn. App. LEXIS 302 (Tenn. Ct. App. May 9, 2000) (no due process violation for statute to allow service on owner's spouse instead of owner).

162 Patricia Weingarten Assocs., Inc. v. Jocalbro, Inc., 974 So. 2d 559 (Fla. Dist. Ct. App. 2008).

163 Monumental Enters. Inc. v. City of Baltimore, 337 A.2d 176 (Md. Ct. Spec. App. 1975) (finality provisions of tax sale statute cannot operate to give validity to a void sale, nor to deny in a proper case, the force and effect of the due process provisions of the constitution; here the court did not set aside the sale because taxpayer's failure to get notice was caused by its own neglect).

164 *See, e.g.*, Vosilla v. Rosado, 944 So. 2d 289 (Fla. 2006).

165 *See also* Giordano v. Gilderdale, 729 So. 2d 760 (La. Ct. App. 1999) (sale set aside when notice was mailed to owners' former address, owners had notified sheriff twice of new address, and sheriff's office could not say positively that it had followed its usual procedures for seeking better address); Meadow Farm Realty Corp. v. Pekich, 676 N.Y.S.2d (App. Div. 1998) (mailing to incorrect address insufficient to meet due process); Fernandez v. Tax Claim Bureau of Northampton County, 925 A.2d 207 (Pa. Commw. Ct. 2007) (although county tax bureau took additional steps to locate owner, such as by conducting "Google" search, tax sale held invalid because bureau failed to contact local tax collectors for contact information for owner as required by statute); Warmath v. Payne, 3 S.W.3d 487 (Tenn. Ct. App. 1999) (sale can be set aside on evidence insufficient to establish that notice was mailed in accordance with mandated procedures). *But see* Hutchinson Island Realty, Inc. v. Babcock Ventures, Inc., 867 So. 2d 528 (Fla. Dist. Ct. App. 2004) (tax sale notice sufficient to satisfy due process even though mailed to incorrect address where taxpayer moved without notifying taxing authority); Smith v. Cliffs on the Bay Condo. Ass'n, 617 N.W.2d 536 (Mich. 2000) (taxing authority not required to make inquiries after mail is returned at last known address); Henderson County v. Osteen, 235 S.E.2d 166 (N.C. 1997) (constitutional due process requires only notice to last known address); Hardy v. Moore County, 515 S.E.2d 84 (N.C. Ct. App. 1999) (taxing authority not required to make inquiries after mail is returned at last known address); Amy Realty v. Gomes, 839 A.2d 1232 (R.I. 2004) (notice by certified mail returned unclaimed complied with statutory notification requirements even though municipality knew of another address for landowner because he was paying fees and taxes at that address).

166 Akey v. Clinton County, N.Y., 375 F.3d 231 (2d Cir. 2004) (owner's due process rights violated when county sent tax sale notice to owner's old post office box address after it had switched to a street number system and had failed to update its tax records database; upon return of tax sale notice as undeliverable, due process required county to search for correct address not only in town where property located but also in all towns within the county); Bank of Am. Nat'l Trust & Sav. Ass'n v. Giant Inland Empire R.V. Ctr., Inc., 93 Cal. Rptr. 2d 626 (Cal. Ct. App. 2000) (county had duty to go beyond "lot book report" in seeking mortgage holder's address, especially after original notice was returned marked undeliverable); Hamilton v. Renewed Hope, Inc., 589 S.E.2d 81 (Ga. 2003) (notice by publication of foreclosure of right to redeem did not satisfy due process; summary judgment properly denied because factual issue exists as to whether taxpayer's address could have been ascertained by reasonably diligent efforts); Reeder Assocs. II v. Chicago Belle, Ltd., 778 N.E.2d 828 (Ind. Ct. App. 2002) (due process requires that municipality search its own records and use address for taxpayer in its records rather than address contained in title report that proved to be incorrect); Harrison v. Lenoir, 745 So. 2d 1191 (La. Ct. App. 1999) (sheriff was required to demonstrate further attempts to locate owner after notice was returned stamped "forwarding order expired"); Isern v. Summerfield, 956 P.2d 28 (Mont. 1998) (sale set aside when clerk and recorder could have obtained correct address from county assessor's office located in same building); Parkton Enters., Inc. v. Krulac, 865 A.2d 295 (Pa. Commw. Ct. 2005) (sale set aside because taxing authority failed to take reasonable steps to determine whether there was a new owner of the property). *See also* Bush v. SA Mortgage Serv. Co., 2005 WL 1155851 (E.D. La. May 9, 2005) (allegations in complaint did not sufficiently establish that whereabouts, identity, and property interest of daughter, as heir of owner, were ascertainable through exercise of reasonable diligence, and therefore complaint did not establish that constructive notice was constitutionally deficient).

167 396 F.3d 569 (4th Cir. 2005).

notice has failed, the party charged with notice must make reasonable efforts to learn the correct address before constructive notice will be deemed sufficient."[168]

The *Plemons* court also addressed the degree of follow-up inquiry that was appropriate under the circumstances. The Fourth Circuit rejected the lower court's findings concerning three reasonable alternative methods and held that the tax sale purchaser did not need to consult the telephone directory, ask the tenants at the property, or make inquiries of the mortgagee bank, as such efforts would have been an "exercise in futility" under the circumstances.[169] While some cases may compel more demanding inquiry, the *Plemons* court found that due process requires an "examination (or re-examination) of all available public records when initial mailings have been promptly returned as undeliverable."[170]

In *Jones v. Flowers*,[171] the Supreme Court revisited the issue of adequate notice and attempted to resolve the conflict among the circuit court and state supreme court decisions with respect to the issues presented in *Plemons v. Gale*. The Court in *Jones* addressed the extent to which additional steps are required by due process to provide adequate notice to a property owner before selling property for unpaid taxes after the government becomes aware that an attempt at mailed notice has been returned unclaimed. In *Jones*, an initial certified letter notifying the owner of his tax delinquency and right to redeem was returned as unclaimed. When a notice of public sale was published two years later and no bids were made, a private sale was negotiated by the tax collector as permitted under state law. A second certified letter notifying the owner that the property would be sold if he did not pay the delinquent taxes was also returned unclaimed. After the sale was completed and the thirty-day post-sale redemption period passed, the purchaser sought to evict the occupants of the property. The property owner's daughter, who resided at the property and was served with an unlawful detainer notice, then notified her father. He filed suit in state court alleging that his property had been taken without due process.

The Court held that when mailed notice of a tax sale is returned unclaimed, the state must take additional reasonable steps to attempt to provide notice to the property owner before selling property, "if it is practicable to do so."[172] The Court rejected the state's contentions that it had provided sufficient notice by sending the letter to an address provided by the property owner and which he had an obligation to update, that the property owner was on "inquiry-notice" of tax sales after failing to receive tax bills, and that the property owner should have ensured that occupants of his property notify him of actions against the property.[173] Finally, the Court ruled that follow-up notice before the sale by publication in the newspaper was not constitutionally adequate because it was "possible and practicable to give . . . more adequate warning of the impending tax sale."[174]

Emphasizing that it was not dictating the specific type of additional notice required to be provided in this situation, the Court identified what it considered to be practicable, reasonable steps that could have been taken by the tax collector; it could have resent the notice by regular mail, posted the notice on the front door of the property, and resent the notice addressing it to "occupant."[175] However, the Court ruled that the state was not required to search for the property owner's address in a phonebook or income tax rolls, noting that Arkansas law required the taxpayer to maintain an accurate address with the tax collector. Consequently, the Court found that such an "open-ended search

168 *Id.* at 576.

169 *Id.* at 577.

170 *Id.*

171 547 U.S. 220, 126 S. Ct. 1708, 164 L. Ed. 2d 415 (2006).

172 *Id.* at 1721. *See also* Luessenhop v. Clinton County, New York, 466 F.3d 259 (2d Cir. 2006) (county's attempted notice held to be constitutionally deficient under *Jones* because county made no further attempts to inform homeowners upon receipt of unclaimed notices); Vosilla v. Rosado, 944 So. 2d 289, (Fla. 2006) (where notice of tax deed sale sent to owners' former address complied with state law because owners had provided change of address letters to both the tax collector and court clerk, but not property appraiser as required, notice nevertheless constitutionally deficient because due process required court clerk to take additional reasonable steps in accordance with *Jones* to notify owners prior to selling property, such as by checking to determine whether a change of address had been submitted); Patricia Weingarten Assocs., Inc. v. Jocalbro, Inc., 974 So. 2d 559 (Fla. Dist. Ct. App. Feb. 15, 2008) (finding that additional steps were required when clerk had sent notices by certified mail to four different addresses, all of which were returned unclaimed, but failed to send notice to updated out-of-state address for owner which had been used by tax collector to send tax bills); Edwards v. Neace, 898 N.E.2d 343 (Ind. Ct. App. 2008) (tax deed set aside because owner's correct address could have been discovered upon reasonable inquiry by county auditor); Alexander v. Gross, 996 So. 2d 822 (Miss. Ct. App. 2008) (tax sale void because clerk never sent notice to owners' post office box address, which would have been readily discoverable if diligent search had been conducted). *Cf.* Miner v. Clinton County, N.Y., 541 F.3d 464 (2d Cir. 2008) (distinguishing *Jones* and finding that no additional steps were necessary because record established that taxing authority reasonably believed that notice had reached property owners).

173 *Jones,* 126 S. Ct. at 1718.

174 *Id.* at 1720.

The Court repeated the observation it had made in *Mullane* that " '[c]hance alone' brings a person's attention to 'an advertisement in small type inserted in the back pages of a newspaper. . . .' " *Id., citing* Mullane v. Central Hanover Bank & Trust Co., 339 U.S. 306, 315, 70 S. Ct. 652, 94 L. Ed. 865 (1950).

175 *Jones,* 126 S. Ct. at 1718–1719. *See also* Griffin v. Bierman, 941 A.2d 475 (Md. 2008) (Maryland foreclosure procedure, by requiring alternative steps of sending notice by first-class mail and notice addressed to "occupant," complies with due process and is consistent with *Jones*); *In re* Foreclosure of Lien for Delinquent Taxes by Action in Rem, 2008 WL 697622 (Ohio Ct. App. Mar. 17, 2008) (distinguishing *Jones* and finding that additional steps taken by clerk as required by Ohio law, including additional mailings and notice publication, satisfied due process).

for a new address" imposed burdens on the government "significantly greater" than the "relatively easy" options enumerated by the Court.[176]

The Court in *Jones* additionally observed that the steps it recommended were consistent with what many states require by statute, and suggested that some states go even further in requiring sufficient notice. The Court stated, for example, that a number of states require that notice be given to the occupants of the property.[177] Some states require posting of notice on the property or at the owner's last known address either when the proceedings are commenced,[178] or as an additional step when personal service cannot be accomplished or certified mail is returned.[179] A few states, the Court stated, require a "diligent inquiry to find a property owner's correct address" if mailed notice is returned.[180]

A sale conducted without adequate notice is void for lack of jurisdiction and is subject to collateral attack.[181] Proper notice must be given to each owner and to others with a record interest in the property.[182] Upon death of the taxpayer, the heirs or the estate may be owners entitled to notice if their names and addresses are reasonably ascertainable.[183] Notice is required at each step in the process

176 *Jones,* 126 S. Ct. at 1719. *See also* South Inv. Properties, Inc. v. Icon Invs., L.L.C., 988 So. 2d 1114 (Fla. Dist. Ct. App. 2008) (citing *Jones,* court rejected corporate property owner's argument that notice was defective because clerk had not checked return receipt to determine whether signature was from representative of owner corporation who had authority to accept mail on behalf of corporation); *In re* Application of County Collector for Judgment, Sale Against Lands, Lots Returned Delinquent for Nonpayment of General Taxes and/or Special Assessments, 867 N.E.2d 941 (Ill. Apr. 19, 2007) (on remand after judgment vacated by United States Supreme Court in light of *Jones* opinion, court concluded that returned envelope containing notice with handwritten notation "Person is hospitalized" did not compel under circumstances of case any additional steps by purchaser to obtain owner's address).

177 *See* Cal. Rev. & Tax. Code Ann. § 3704.7 (West); Ga. Code Ann. § 48-4-45(a)(1)(B); 35 Ill. Comp. Stat. §§ 200/21-75(a), 200/22-10, 200/22-15; Me. Rev. Stat. Ann. tit. 36, § 1073; Md. Code Ann., Tax-Prop. § 14-836(b)(4)(i)(2) (West); Mich. Comp. Laws § 211.78i(3); Minn. Stat. § 281.23(6); Mont. Code Ann. § 15-18-212(1)(a), (2)(A); N.D. Cent. Code § 57-28-04(3); Okla. Stat. tit. 68, § 3118(A); S.D. Codified Laws § 10-25-5; Utah Code Ann. § 59-2-1351(2)(a); Wis. Stat. § 75.12(1); Wyo. Stat. Ann. § 39-13-108(e)(v)(B).

178 *See* Del. Code Ann. tit. 9, §§ 8724, 8772; Ga. Code Ann. § 48-4-78(d); Haw. Rev. Stat. § 246-56; Md. Code Ann., Tax-Prop. § 14-836(b)(6); Okla. Stat. tit. 68, § 3118(A).

179 *See* Fla. Stat. § 197.522(2)(a); Minn. Stat. § 281.23(6); S.C. Code Ann. § 12-51-40(c).

180 126 S. Ct. at 1715. *See* Miss. Code Ann. § 27-43-3; Nev. Rev. Stat. § 361.595(3)(b); 72 Pa. Stat. Ann. § 5860.607a (West); R.I. Gen. Laws § 44-9-25.1. *See also* Fernandez v. Tax Claim Bureau of Northampton County, 925 A.2d 207 (Pa. Commw. Ct. 2007) (even though tax claim bureau took additional steps upon return of undelivered notice, including "Google" search on owner, it failed to comply with reasonable efforts requirements under Pennsylvania law which includes contacting the various county tax assessment offices).

181 *See* City of Detroit v. John J. Blake Realty Co., 376 N.W.2d 114 (Mich. Ct. App. 1984) (notice addressed to "occupant" sent to land contract vendee was insufficient when city had access to vendee's name and address, and sale was void); County of Sullivan v. Vaughan, 885 N.Y.S.2d 575 (N.Y. Sullivan County Ct. 2009) (after mailed notice to property owner was returned undeliverable, county failed to give additional adequate notice under the circumstances in that paper notice stapled to a wooden stake in a snow bank at the property was insufficient); Rivera v. Carbon County Tax Claim Bureau, 857 A.2d 208 (Pa. Commw. Ct. 2004) (legal title to property can pass to purchaser after judicial sale only if statutory notice requirements have been met). *See also* Langon v. Reilly, 802 A.2d 951 (D.C. 2002) (sale invalidated, as evidence supported trial court's finding that taxing authority failed to notify owner of tax sale); Anderson v. Richland County, 711 P.2d 784 (Mont. 1985) (tax deed proceeding void for failure to give proper notice to owner).

182 DiVeto v. Kjellgren, 861 A.2d 618 (Me. 2004) (because of confusion in description of property in tax sale notice, which included land not owned by delinquent taxpayer, true owner of property never received proper notice or opportunity to be heard); Lewis v. Columbus Invs., 36 P.3d 75 (Colo. Ct. App. 2000) (upholding taxpayer's challenge to deed on statutory grounds when notice not given to holder of deed of trust); Sines v. Blaser, 592 P.2d 1367 (Idaho 1979) (tax deed void when notice of delinquent taxes given only to one of two owners listed in recorder's office records); Sidun v. Wayne County Treasurer, 751 N.W.2d 453 (Mich. 2008) (sale invalidated when county treasurer failed to notify daughter co-owner after incorrectly assuming that daughter and mother lived together); Brandon Township v. Tomkow, 535 N.W.2d 268 (Mich. Ct. App. 1995) (notice constitutionally inadequate when sent to related corporations but not to record owner); Rebuild Am., Inc. v. Milner, 7 So. 3d 972 (Miss. Ct. App. 2009) (tax sale set aside when notice had been sent to husband, which also contained "et ux" in mailing address, but no separate notice was provided to wife); Garcia v. Ted Parks, L.L.C., 195 P.3d 1269 (Okla. 2008) (tax deed void when process server left notice with son of owner who had merely stopped by his mother's property on way to visit her in the hospital); Robert P. Quinn Trust v. Ruiz, 723 A.2d 1127 (R.I. 1999) (sale void when those holding remainder interests in property did not receive notice, even though notice was given to holder of life estate); Ashness v. Tomasetti, 643 A.2d 802 (R.I. 1994) (failure to notify mortgage holder of foreclosure of sewer tax lien invalidates sale). *See also* Hull v. D'Arcy, 202 P.3d 417 (Wyo. 2009) (evidence failed to establish that husband who had received tax sale notice acted as agent for wife for purposes of receipt of notice). *Cf.* Sienkiewicz v. Palzer, 95 B.R. 139 (B.A.P. 9th Cir. 1988) (co-owner with unrecorded interest not entitled to notice); Sallie v. Tax Sale Investors, Inc., 998 F. Supp. 612 (D. Md. 1998) (tenants with unrecorded lease interest not entitled to notice of sale by mail as a matter of due process); Clallam County v. Folk, 922 P.2d 73 (Wash. 1996) (co-tenant whose property rights were unaffected by tax sale not entitled to notice as a matter of due process).

183 *See* Freeman v. City of Kingsport, 926 S.W.2d 247 (Tenn. Ct. App. 1996) (whether heirs' identity and addresses were ascertainable is a question of fact).

Because due process protects those whose identity and whereabouts are reasonably ascertainable, careful practice upon death of an owner is to notify the taxing authority of the interest and address of the estate or heirs.

which affects the owner's interest.[184] In addition to being served in a manner and form reasonably calculated to reach the interested party, the notice must actually convey the required information.[185] The notice must also be sent far enough in advance of the sale to give the parties a reasonable opportunity to present objections.[186] The owner's awareness that taxes should be due each year does not excuse lack of notice.[187] Notice to a person known to be incompetent and without the protection of a guardian does not satisfy due process.[188] In such a situation, steps must be taken to ensure that meaningful notice is given.

To satisfy due process concerns, the notice should also inform the owner and other interested parties of any rights that exist under the tax sale procedure to avoid a final loss of ownership of the property, such as any post-sale redemption rights. Finding that the right of redemption is a significant property interest entitled to due process protection under the Fourteenth Amendment, a court struck down a Rhode Island tax sale statute for failure to require meaningful notice of the right to redeem property after a tax sale.[189]

Invalidity of a sale for failure to comport with due process should be raised, if possible, before the end of any statutory period to object to the sale. However, expiration of the period to object generally should not preclude late constitutional challenges.[190] If not raised in the trial court in any statutory proceeding to confirm a tax sale or foreclose a right of redemption, the homeowner may be precluded from asserting the constitutional issue on appeal.[191]

13.3.4.3 Full and Adequate Opportunity to Protest

Due process also requires that the taxpayer be given a full and adequate opportunity to contest an assessment before property can be taken by foreclosure.[192] The statutory tax foreclosure scheme of Washington state was ruled unconstitutional for failing to provide a sufficient hearing during which one could contest a sale.[193] The equalization hearing which was afforded by this statute was merely an inquiry into the proper amount of the assessment, and whether foreclosure on that assessment was fair could not be considered.[194] The court ruled that such a hearing was not enough to comport with due process with respect to the foreclosure proceedings.

13.4 Redemption Following Sale

13.4.1 Generally

As discussed earlier in this chapter, tax lien process in most states allows a homeowner to redeem and retain the property for a specified period of time after a tax lien sale is completed.[195] Generally, the homeowner must pay the entire amount of the lien including all unpaid taxes, penalties and interest, plus any costs or expenses incurred by the purchaser in order to effectuate redemption.[196] Under most states' laws, the taxpayer retains the right of possession

184 Westerheide v. Wilcox, 124 P.2d 409 (Okla. 1942) (owners cannot be deprived of right of redemption without due process; required statutory notice of intention to apply for tax deed is vital part of due process). *See also* Yagan v. Bernardi, 684 N.Y.S.2d 117 (App. Div. 1998) ("notice by request" provision applicable to right of redemption found invalid).

185 Covey v. Somers, 351 U.S. 141 (1955); Oakwood Acceptance Corp., L.L.C. v. Massengill, 590 S.E.2d 412 (N.C. Ct. App. 2004) (notice of tax sale's reference to unnamed "Storage Location" failed to meet statute's requirement that "place of sale" be designated).

186 Lyon v. Estate of Newton Cornell, 703 N.Y.S.2d 325 (App. Div. 2000) (notice mailed only eighteen days before sale did not satisfy due process).

187 Harrison v. Lenoir, 745 So. 2d 1191 (La. Ct. App. 1999); Giordano v. MacDonald, 729 So. 2d 760 (La. Ct. App. 1999). *See also* McElvenny v. Bucks County Tax Claim Bureau, 804 A.2d 719 (Pa. Commw. Ct. 2002) (court rejected defense that compliance with notice requirements would not have made a difference in providing actual notice to the owner because due process requires strict adherence to notice requirements regardless of result).

188 Covey v. Somers, 351 U.S. 141 (1955) (tax sale set aside when it was shown that town officials knew taxpayer was incompetent when notice was served and because of his condition was unable to avail himself of the procedure for redemption or answer). *See also* County Collector v. Otsus, 545 N.E.2d 145 (Ill. App. Ct. 1989) (town and purchaser knew or should have known that owner was incompetent).

189 *In re* Pontes, 310 F. Supp. 2d 447 (D.R.I. 2004). *See also* Orange County Comm'r of Fin. v. Helseth, 875 N.Y.S.2d 754, (N.Y. Sup. Ct. 2009) (taxing authority failed to give property owner notice of constitutionally protected right to redemption); Osloond v. Farrier, 659 N.W.2d 20 (S.D. 2003) (complaint stated valid due process claim based on tax collector's attempt to conduct tax sale without responding to homeowners' repeated request for assistance in completing application for tax relief).

190 Sec. First Nat'l Bank v. Murchison, 739 So. 2d 803 (La. Ct. App. 1999) (due process challenge survives expiration of redemption period set by state constitution); Town of N. Reading v. Welch, 711 N.E.2d 603 (Mass. App. Ct. 1999).

Other procedural prerequisites, such as expiration of a statutory period to notify a municipality of a claim against it, also should not obviate a constitutional violation. Yagan v. Bernardi, 684 N.Y.S.2d 117 (App. Div. 1998).

191 Pollard v. Acer Group, 870 A.2d 429 (R.I. 2005) (homeowner waived due process notice claim by failing to assert it in trial court).

192 Wenatchee Reclamation Dist. v. Mustell, 684 P.2d 1275 (Wash. 1984). *See also* Board of County Comm'rs of Osage County v. Schmidt, 758 P.2d 254 (Kan. Ct. App. 1988).

193 *Wentachee Reclamation Dist.*, 684 P.2d at 1280.

194 *Id.* at 1280–1281.

195 *See* § 13.2.4, *supra.*

196 A co-owner with a less than full interest in the property may have to redeem the whole property rather than just his or her partial share. *See* City of Philadelphia v. Keilyk, 551 A.2d 1094 (Pa. Super. Ct. 1988) (owner of one third share could not pay

during the redemption period.

Disputes may arise about the existence of redemption rights at all. Timeliness of redemption is often strictly construed.[197] Once the statutory period is up, redemption rights are terminated. These issues are generally within the jurisdiction of the state's general trial court or a specialized tax commission or court. Strict time limits and requirements to exhaust administrative remedies before proceeding in court may apply. However, in many states, failure to give proper notice of the right of redemption or the actual amount required to redeem can be raised as a defense to termination of the taxpayer's redemption rights.[198] This may include the failure to give notice of any proceeding to foreclose the right of redemption to others having an interest in the property, such as heirs of the property owner.[199]

Similarly, disputes can arise about the manner of redemption. For example, payment in full by certified check may be required.[200] If the redemption amount is tendered by the wrong means, the tax sale purchaser may have the right to reject it. Especially if tender of the redemption amount is at the eleventh hour under the statutory deadline, compliance with all procedural requirements is essential.

Finally, the amount of the redemption obligation may be at issue. The taxpayer may dispute interest, fees, costs and other add-ons to the base amount of the unpaid taxes.[201] Post-sale real estate taxes that have not been secured by lien may also be disputed. As discussed earlier in this chapter, collateral attack on the amount of the unpaid pre-sale taxes may be foreclosed by the sale.[202] However, tender in good faith of an inadequate amount due to confusion or mistake has sometimes been found to be grounds for an equitable extension to pay the remaining balance.[203]

Particularly thorny issues arise when the taxpayer loses the right of possession during the statutory redemption period. The tax sale purchaser buys the right of possession in a few states, subject to the redemption period. If the taxpayer redeems, he or she may regain possession of the property.

If the right of possession is sold, statutes typically require that the value of any improvements made by the tax sale purchaser be included in the redemption amount.[204] Valuing the improvements, particularly if they have been done by the purchasers themselves, can be a long and difficult process requiring court intervention.[205] In addition, the taxpayer may have to seek to evict the purchaser after redemption. An ejectment action or an action to quiet title under state law may be required.

Another set of issues may arise in states in which the title obtained at a tax sale is transferable. If tax title has been transferred after the sale, redemption must typically be made to the new holder of that title.

13.4.2 Borrowing to Effectuate Redemption

One way to effectuate redemption is to borrow to pay necessary amounts. Typically, this would involve obtaining a mortgage and using the proceeds to pay off the tax sale purchaser. The new mortgage holder would obtain first lien position if there are no other (non-tax) liens or mortgages on the property. For older homeowners, options include the possibility of a reverse mortgage.[206]

Certain predatory lenders advertise aggressively to homeowners who own property with outstanding tax liens. These lenders know that financially strapped homeowners may be desperate enough to accept a loan on extortionate terms. In addition, a potential tax sale is often an indication that there is no existing first mortgage (as the first mortgagee would normally pay off any tax liens). Typically this means that there is plenty of equity so that a high-rate loan can be made with little or no risk.[207]

For these reasons, homeowners should exercise care when refinancing their home to address a need to redeem. Shopping for the best available loan terms is essential.

---

one third of the redemption amount to reacquire her one third interest).

197 *See* Cedillo v. Gaitan, 981 S.W.2d 388 (Tex. App. 1998) (expiration of three year limit barred right to recover property).

198 *See* Associated Estates, L.L.C. v. Caldwell, 779 A.2d 939 (D.C. 2000) (tax deed void when notice requirement concerning redemption rights in tax sale statute not strictly followed, regardless of whether record owner actually received redemption notice); Schnitzer v. Rinderer, 17 N.J. Tax 136 (1998) (certificate of redemption based on improper notice of right to redeem was invalid). *See also In re* Pontes, 310 F. Supp. 2d 447 (D.R.I. 2004) (tax sale invalidated on due process grounds when taxing authority failed to give homeowner timely notice of right of redemption and process for exercising redemption).

199 Dillow v. Magraw, 649 A.2d 1157 (Md. Ct. Spec. App. 1994), *aff'd* 671 A.2d 485 (Md. 1996).

200 In some states, where the tax sale purchaser must initiate a court hearing to foreclose the right of redemption, the court may invoke its equitable power to permit the redemption amount to be paid in installments.

201 *See* City of Danbury v. Dana Inv. Corp., 730 A.2d 1128 (Conn. 1999) (duplicative and unreasonable costs may be challenged); Halabu v. Behnke, 541 N.W.2d 285 (Mich. Ct. App. 1995) (failure to serve proper notice tolls running of redemption period, but period is not extended for owner if notice to some other party was defective).

202 *See* § 13.3.2.2, *supra*.

203 *In re* Wells Properties, Inc., 102 B.R. 685 (Bankr. N.D. Ill. 1989).

204 *E.g.*, 53 Pa. Cons. Stat § 7293. *See also* City of Philadelphia v. Watkins, 494 A.2d 1135 (Pa. Super. Ct. 1985) (valuing expenses incurred by purchasers for renovations to determine amount to redeem).

205 These issues can also arise when a facially valid sale is later set aside after expenses have been incurred by the purchasers. *See* Halgus Land Co. v. Holt, 303 A.2d 493 (Pa. Super. Ct. 1973).

206 *See generally* National Consumer Law Center, NCLC Guide to Surviving Debt (2010 ed.).

207 There is no risk to the lender if the full amount advanced can be recovered with interest if foreclosure becomes necessary. The risk is all to the homeowner.

In some cases, a tax sale purchaser may negotiate redemption in installments or may grant time to redeem in excess of the statutory period. Certainly, the terms of a refinancing, including the interest rate, should be no worse than terms which can be obtained from the purchaser. However, fraud by tax sale speculators is also prevalent as discussed below.

13.4.3 Redemption in Bankruptcy

The amount necessary to redeem after a tax sale can also be paid as a secured claim in the chapter 13 bankruptcy process.[208] Several courts have held that because a tax lien is not consensual, the claim associated with the lien can be modified.[209] Thus, for example, a debtor can pay the redemption amount with interest over the duration of a chapter 13 plan even if the plan is completed after the original redemption period expires.[210] Analogous case law allows modification of mortgage debt and payment under a plan completed after the original term of the mortgage has expired.[211]

A few courts have held, based on state law, that the deadline for redemption cannot be extended beyond the tolling period contained in 11 U.S.C. § 108(b).[212] These courts conclude that because the property has been transferred by tax sale under state law and as the remaining redemption right requires a lump sum payment by a date certain, that date certain can only be tolled until sixty days after the bankruptcy filing, and then only if it has not already expired before the bankruptcy filing under state law.[213] When faced with this argument, check your state's law for indicia that the tax sale transfers a lien interest rather than the property itself.[214] Establishing that the tax sale transferred only a lien brings a more significant property right into the bankruptcy estate. Also, if at the time the bankruptcy was filed the tax sale purchaser still needed to take some affirmative step to start the running of the redemption period, the automatic stay will prevent the redemption period from beginning to run.[215]

Whether the property itself or a lien interest in the property is transferred by tax sale under state law, the debtor's bankruptcy filing does bring some interest in the property into the bankruptcy estate until the tax sale process is completed. In states where the property itself is transferred, at least a right of redemption comes into the estate until that right expires.[216] Thus, no matter what the state scheme, filing a bankruptcy case before termination of the redemption period operates as a stay of the tax foreclosure process. The process cannot be completed until the case is over without relief from stay.[217] Whenever possible, chapter 13 debtors should then argue that because a claim based on a tax lien is fully modifiable, it can be paid under 11 U.S.C. § 1325(a)(5) (with present value interest)[218] over the dura-

208 One court has held that a debtor could not redeem in a chapter 13 bankruptcy because the tax sale purchaser was not a creditor of the debtor and so was not bound by the chapter 13 plan. *See In re* Blue, 247 B.R. 748 (Bankr. N.D. Ill. 2000). *In re* Blue is wrongly decided in that it relies on a state court's interpretation of the term "creditor" in a different context and it does not give due weight to the Bankruptcy Code's expansive definition of "claim" in § 101(5) as including a right to an equitable remedy for breach of performance.

209 *See* Rankin v. DeSarno, 89 F.3d 1123 (3d Cir. 1996); *In re* DeMaggio, 175 B.R. 144 (Bankr. D.N.H. 1994). *See also In re* Marfin Ready Mix Corp., 220 B.R. 148 (Bankr. E.D.N.Y. 1998) (statutory tax liens do not constitute security interests and may be modified).

210 Salta Group, Inc. v. McKinney, 380 B.R. 515 (C.D. Ill. 2008) (debtor could modify tax sale purchaser's right to payment before expiration of redemption period by paying off redemption amount through chapter 13 plan); *In re* Hammond, 420 B.R. 633 (Bankr. W.D. Pa. 2009) (debtor could redeem in chapter 13 and could strip down tax lien to value of property); *In re* Kasco, 378 B.R. 207 (Bankr. N.D. Ill. 2007) (stay relief denied because debtor had right to pay off tax sale redemption amount through plan); *In re* Bates, 270 B.R. 455 (Bankr. N.D. Ill. 2001) (when bankruptcy filed prior to expiration of redemption period, claim of tax sale purchaser for redemption amount can be paid under plan and treated like any other secured claim). *See generally* National Consumer Law Center, Consumer Bankruptcy Law and Practice Ch. 11 (9th ed. 2009).

211 National Consumer Law Center, Consumer Bankruptcy Law and Practice § 11.6.2.2 (9th ed. 2009).

212 *See, e.g., In re* Rodgers, 333 F.3d 64 (2d Cir. 2003) (when right to redemption from tax sale expired before bankruptcy petition was filed, automatic stay did not prevent delivery of deed to tax sale purchaser); *In re* Murray, 276 B.R. 869 (Bankr. N.D. Ill. 2002); Matter of Sabec, 137 B.R. 659 (Bankr. W.D. Mich. 1992); Hood v. Hall, 321 Ill. App. 3d 452, 747 N.E.2d 510 (2001) (automatic stay does not toll running of redemption period after tax sale). *Cf. In re* Little, 201 B.R. 98 (Bankr. D.N.J. 1996) (redemption period after mortgage foreclosure sale cannot be extended through end of plan period). *But cf. In re* Tranter, 171 B.R. 256 (Bankr. W.D. Mich. 1994) (state violated automatic stay by taking steps that initiated running of final redemption period).

213 *See* 11 U.S.C. § 108(b).

214 *Compare In re* Halas, 194 B.R. 605 (Bankr. N.D. Ill. 1996) (Ill. law) *with In re* Sabec, 137 B.R. 659 (Bankr. W.D. Mich. 1992) (Mich. law).

215 *In re* Tranter, 171 B.R. 256 (Bankr. W.D. Mich. 1994).

216 *In re* Tranter, 171 B.R. 256 (Bankr. W.D. Mich. 1994) (transfer of property on notice to debtor pursuant to close of redemption period violates automatic stay).

217 *See* Fish Mkt. Nominee Corp. v. Pelofsky, 72 F.3d 4 (1st Cir. 1995); *In re* Dominguez, 312 B.R. 499 (Bankr. S.D.N.Y. 2004) (even though redemption period had expired pre-petition, taxing authority's post-petition acts in obtaining and enforcing default foreclosure judgment violated the automatic stay).

218 *See* Rankin v. DeSarno, 89 F.3d 1123 (3d Cir. 1996) (setting present value rate on real estate tax lien claim at statutory 12% rate). *See also In re* Hammond, 420 B.R. 633 (Bankr. W.D. Pa. 2009) (debtor could redeem in chapter 13 and could strip down tax lien to value of property).

The Supreme Court in Till v. SCS Credit Corp., 124 S. Ct. 1951 (2004), held that a formula method is to be used for calculating interest required under § 1325(a)(5), with the prime rate of interest as the starting point, adjusted by a factor for risk.

tion of the plan. If this argument is not available, the only alternative is to pay the redemption amount before the deadline for redemption (as extended by Bankruptcy Code section 108(b)) expires. A "step-up" payment plan in chapter 13 which uses virtually all of the debtor's disposable income in the first two months of the case to make necessary redemption payments is one possible means of facilitating an otherwise unaffordable redemption.[219]

13.5 Fraud by Tax Sale Speculators

In many communities, there is a group of predatory speculators that seek to profit by manipulating the tax sale process. Some of these speculators buy many properties at tax sale. They then seek to lure unsophisticated homeowners to transfer their redemption rights in exchange for expensive or fraudulent sale-leaseback schemes or high rate loans.[220]

Speculators may also seek to obtain properties at below-market cost and then to resell at a substantial profit. Some of these speculators will do everything possible to frustrate redemption by the taxpayer. Depending on the statutory rules, schemes can include failure to provide required notices, efforts to hide an address which can be used for tendering redemption payments, and misstatements of the redemption amount to frighten homeowners into walking away from their homes.[221]

Remember that homeowners retain their redemption rights even when a tax sale gives a speculator rights in the property. The letter of the law should be enforced against speculators and predatory practices should be challenged in court. Even if there is no way to undo the tax sale itself, the victim may have fraud and other damages claims against the predator.[222]

See National Consumer Law Center, Consumer Bankruptcy Law and Practice § 11.6.1.3.3.5 (9th ed. 2009).

219 Under such a plan, the debtor would not make significant payments to the trustee or other creditors until at least the third month of the plan in order to facilitate redemption of the property before the close of the redemption period. Depending upon the timing of plan confirmation and the creditors to be paid under the plan, this type of chapter 13 plan may not be possible because of an amendment made to § 1325(a)(5) by the 2005 Bankruptcy Act requiring that payments on certain allowed secured claims must be made in equal monthly amounts. *See* National Consumer Law Center, Consumer Bankruptcy Law and Practice § 11.6.1.3.3.3 (9th ed. 2009). Chapter 13 repayment plan options are also discussed in National Consumer Law Center, Consumer Bankruptcy Law and Practice Ch. 12 (9th ed. 2009).

220 *See* § 5.3.6, *supra*, Ch. 15, *infra*.

221 E.g., Parks v. Wells Fargo Home Mortgage, Inc., 398 F.3d 937 (7th Cir. 2005) (noting that state court had vacated tax sale deed based on actual fraud of "tax scavenger" who had falsely verified in state court petition that she had caused sheriff to personally serve homeowners with statutory notice).

222 *Id. See also* National Consumer Law Center, The Cost of Credit: Regulation, Preemption, and Industry Abuses Chs. 11, 12 (4th ed. 2009 and Supp.).

13.6 Private Collection and Enforcement of Tax Liens

Sometimes taxing authorities contract out collection work to independent companies. The question arises whether these companies are governed by state and federal fair debt collection laws. Several courts have held that taxes are not "debts" within the meaning of the federal Fair Debt Collection Practices Act,[223] but state debt collection statutes may have broader coverage. Also, municipal claims other than taxes, e.g., for water and sewer charges, may be considered debts even under the federal statute.[224] If a state or federal debt collection law applies to the collector, consumers have powerful remedies for deceptive or overreaching tactics.[225]

The federal Truth in Lending Act may apply if a creditor agrees to forgo the collection of an existing debt in return for the payment of interest or the establishment of an installment payment schedule.[226] While tax debts may be

223 Pollice v. Nat'l Tax Funding, 225 F.3d 379 (3d Cir. 2000); Staub v. Harris, 626 F.2d 275 (3d Cir. 1980). *See* National Consumer Law Center, Fair Debt Collection § 4.4.2.3 (6th ed. 2008 and Supp.).

Note that officers and employees of states and their political subdivisions are exempt from the federal statute pursuant to 15 U.S.C. § 1692a(6)(C), (8).

224 Piper v. Portnoff Law Assocs., Ltd., 396 F.3d 227 (3d Cir. 2005) (municipal water and sewer services create obligation which is "debt" within meaning of FDCPA; law firm does not obtain exemption from FDCPA coverage by limiting its collection efforts to seeking *in rem* judgment on a municipal lien); Pollice v. Nat'l Tax Funding, 225 F.3d 379 (3d Cir. 2000) (private company that contracted to collect municipal water and sewer debts was covered by FDCPA and violated it by seeking interest and penalties not authorized by law); Albanese v. Portnoff Law Assocs., Ltd., 301 F. Supp. 2d 389 (E.D. Pa. 2004) (municipal liens imposed for nonpayment of trash collection fees are debts under FDCPA); Piper v. Portnoff Law Assocs., 274 F. Supp. 2d 681 (E.D. Pa. 2003) (law firm collecting overdue water bills does not obtain exemption from FDCPA coverage by limiting its collection efforts to *in rem* proceedings); Keauhou Master Homeowner's Ass'n, Inc. v. County of Haw., 87 P.3d 883 (Haw. 2004) (water and sewer obligations owed to county are debts under FDCPA).

225 *See* National Consumer Law Center, Fair Debt Collection (6th ed. 2008 and Supp.). *See also* Piper v. Portnoff Law Assocs., 262 F. Supp. 2d 520 (E.D. Pa. 2003), *aff'd*, 225 F.3d 379 (3d Cir. 2000) (court granted preliminary injunction of sheriff's sale based on likely finding that collection letters on overdue water bill were misleading or deceptive within meaning of FDCPA and that $150 charge for attorney fees to prepare and mail form collection letter was not reasonable under state law).

226 *See* National Consumer Law Center, The Cost of Credit: Regulation, Preemption, and Industry Abuses § 10.5.2.3 (4th ed. 2009 and Supp.) (discussion of the distinction in usury law between a debtor's "detention" of money, which is not a credit transaction, and "forbearance," which does constitute a credit transaction).

excluded from Truth in Lending coverage, other similar municipal claims may not be.[227]

In some states, taxing authorities may sell tax liens to independent companies or "securitize" tax sale or lien certificates. In the securitization process, certificates are bundled and transferred to a trust, which then issues bonds secured by the certificates that are sold as securities to public investors. The trust will typically enter into a contract with a servicer to collect on the certificates. In this situation, the servicer or assignee should be bound by any state laws that would apply to the taxing authority, such as those limiting collection amounts and mandating repayment plans.[228]

227 Pollice v. Nat'l Tax Funding, 225 F.3d 379 (3d Cir. 2000) (collection agency that set up payment plans for municipal claim was covered by TILA to extent it collected water and sewer debts but not tax debts).

228 Varsolona v. Breen Capital Servs. Corp., 853 A.2d 865 (N.J. 2004) (although collection of fees by private servicers on installment payment plans is subject to same restrictions imposed on municipalities and may require lower court on remand to reform contract provisions that are inconsistent with statutory procedures, there was no per se violation of the New Jersey Consumer Fraud Act); Jackson v. HSBC Bank USA, 922 A.2d 750 (N.J. Super. Ct. App. Div. May 4, 2007) (only relief available to plaintiffs is reformation of tax sale certificates in accordance with *Varsolona*); Pentlong Corp. v. GLS Capital, Inc., 820 A.2d 1240 (Pa. 2003) (assignee of tax liens did not acquire greater rights than municipality and therefore was not entitled to collect attorney fees from taxpayers).

Chapter 14 Issues Arising After a Foreclosure Sale

14.1 Re-Purchasing the Home During or After the Foreclosure Sale

14.1.1 Purchasing the Home at the Foreclosure Sale

In every state, the consumer can redeem the home prior to the sale by paying the full amount due including various fees and expenses.[1] In addition, like anyone else, a homeowner can bid on and buy the property at a foreclosure sale. The sale price may be less than the pre-sale redemption amount. Moreover, the foreclosure sale extinguishes junior liens,[2] so that homeowners purchase clear title to their old home, at least until they are sued for a deficiency or new liens are placed on the property.[3]

State law prerequisites to bidding on and purchasing property at a foreclosure sale always include payment of a deposit and payment of the balance within a relatively short time period. This time frame may be so short as to prevent the purchaser to shop for and obtain conventional financing. If the balance is not paid, for whatever reason, most states mandate that the deposit is forfeited and that the property must be resold.

Buying at the foreclosure sale has other negative aspects compared to pre-sale redemption. The homeowner may be outbid at the foreclosure sale, while a foreclosing mortgage holder must accept a redemption offer prior to the sale.[4]

14.1.2 Redeeming the Home After the Foreclosure Sale

14.1.2.1 State Statutes Described

Approximately half the states have foreclosure statutes that provide homeowners with a post-foreclosure sale redemption period—a fixed period of time in which to set the foreclosure sale aside and regain title to the home by paying the foreclosure sale price, interest, and costs of the sale.[5] Some states have more than one redemption law. For example, a state may have one statute that applies to judicial foreclosures, another that applies to non-judicial foreclosures, and a third one that regulates execution of judgment liens against real property. State redemption rights may be preempted if the foreclosure is on a HUD insured or guaranteed mortgage, but only if the mortgage is actually held by HUD and HUD is the foreclosing mortgage holder.[6] Redemption rights following a tax sale are covered at § 13.4, *supra*.

Appendix E, *infra*, provides details on each state's post-redemption right to foreclose. States can be grouped in the following ways. Six states rely primarily upon judicial foreclosures and have a statutory right to redeem after a foreclosure sale:

- Illinois: Redemption until later of seven months after service of complaint or three months after judgment with additional thirty days for a home mortgage if the mortgage holder is the purchaser at sale and the sale price was less than specified amount;
- Iowa: One year under general sale provision;
- Kansas: Twelve months from date of sale;
- Kentucky: One year from date of sale if sale did not

1 *See* § 4.2.6, *supra.*

2 *See* BCGS, L.L.C. v. Jaster, 700 N.E.2d 1075 (Ill. App. Ct. 1998).

3 Similarly, in most states, judgments against the owner can be refiled as liens on the newly acquired property interest.

4 *See* § 14.2, *supra.*

5 *See, e.g., Ex parte* Lynn, 727 So. 2d 90 (Ala. 1999) (construing Alabama's one year redemption period to commence from date purchaser received deed from sheriff); Skelton v. J & G, L.L.C., 922 So. 2d 926 (Ala. Civ. App. 2005) (statute liberally construed in favor of redemption; purchaser's delayed response to request for payout, caused by post office delay, excused former owner from requirement to tender redemption amount when filing for redemption); Riley v. W.R. Holdings, L.L.C., 138 P.3d 316 (Idaho 2006) (redemption amount correctly calculated: foreclosure sale price, plus interest and taxes; purchaser who was not judgment creditor not entitled to attorney fees, nor to sums spent to improve the property); Martin v. Household Fin. Co., 2005 WL 3416140 (Mich. Ct. App. Dec. 13, 2005) (method of calculating redemption amount prescribed by statute: sum paid at foreclosure sale, plus interest and certain costs and fees). *See also* HSBC Bank v. Fenton, 125 P.3d 644 (N.M. Ct. App. 2005) (where former owner and junior lien-holder both seek to redeem property, first to file may redeem); Weldon v. Feldman, 2005 WL 12025 (Wash. Ct. App. Jan. 3, 2005) (unpublished) (when former owner and judgment lienholder each seek to redeem, former owner has priority).

6 *See* 12 U.S.C. §§ 3751–3768; § 3.2.3.1, *supra.*

bring at least two-thirds of property's appraised value;
- North Dakota: Sixty days after sale;
- South Dakota: One year for judicial foreclosures and 180 days for certain power of sale foreclosures if provided in loan documents.[7]

Another eight states where mortgage holders predominately use non-judicial foreclosure have a right to redeem after a foreclosure sale:

- Alabama: One year from date of sale;[8]
- Michigan: Varies from one month to one year depending on size of parcel, number of units, percentage of original loan outstanding;[9]
- Minnesota: One year from sale;
- Missouri: Twelve months from date of sale, but only if mortgage holder acquired the property at sale and homeowner posts bond;
- Montana: Twelve months from sale;
- New Mexico: Nine months from sale;[10]
- Tennessee: Two years, but may be waived by loan documents;
- Wyoming: Three months.[11]

Seven other states have statutes allowing post-sale redemption after judicial foreclosures, but these laws rarely help homeowners because non-judicial foreclosures are the predominate method of foreclosure:

- Alaska: Twelve months for judicial foreclosure and none for power of sale unless loan document authorizes it;
- Arizona: Twelve month redemption from sale after court judgment, none after power of sale foreclosure;
- Arkansas: One year after judicial foreclosure, none for power of sale;
- California: Two year redemption applies in certain judicial foreclosures, if plaintiff seeks deficiency; none for non-judicial foreclosure;
- Michigan: Six months for judicial foreclosure, varying times for non-judicial foreclosure;
- Utah: Six months after judicial foreclosure, none after non-judicial foreclosure sale;
- Washington: Eight months after judicial foreclosure sale, none for deed of trust foreclosure.[12]

Several additional states allow a very limited right to "redeem" for a short period after a judicial foreclosure sale and until certain post-sale formalities are completed, including Florida, North Carolina, Ohio, and South Carolina.[13] The time periods to redeem under these statutes typically run for a matter of weeks.

Where a state provides a post-sale right to redeem. the statute may condition that right in a number of different ways. In Michigan and North Dakota, borrowers have more time to redeem the greater the portion of the underlying debt they have paid.[14] In Illinois, Kansas, and Kentucky, the relation of the foreclosure sale price to the current market value of the property affects the time allowed to redeem.[15] Under statutes such as those in effect in California, Iowa, and New Jersey, the intention of the mortgage holder to pursue a deficiency claim against the homeowner after the sale triggers greater redemption rights.[16]

In states that allow both judicial and non-judicial foreclosure a fairly common development has been to retain the right of redemption as part of the traditional judicial foreclosure practice, but preclude redemption after non-judicial foreclosure sales. Other states, such as Illinois and Missouri, allow more extensive redemption rights if the mortgage holder, rather than a third party, purchases the property at the sale.[17] In a further variation, under some redemption laws, such as those in California and Illinois, homeowners with mortgages used to purchase the property receive greater protections than do homeowners with other types of mortgages.[18]

14.1.2.2 Utility of the Right to Redeem

In general, to successfully exercise the right of a post-sale redemption, the consumer should seek to comply strictly with statutory requirements.[19] Because few financially dis-

7 *See* Appx. E, *infra*.

8 *See Ex parte* Lynn, 727 So. 2d 90 (Ala. 1999) (construing Alabama's one-year redemption period to commence from date purchaser received deed from sheriff); Skelton v. J & G, L.L.C., 922 So. 2d 926 (Ala. Civ. App. 2005) (statute liberally construed in favor of redemption; purchaser's delayed response to request for payout, caused by post office delay, excused former owner from requirement to tender redemption amount when filing for redemption).

9 *See* Martin v. Household Fin. Co., 2005 WL 3416140 (Mich. Ct. App. Dec. 13, 2005) (redemption amount is the sum paid at foreclosure sale, plus interest and certain costs and fees).

10 *See* HSBC Bank v. Fenton, 125 P.3d 644 (N.M. Ct. App. 2005) (where former owner and junior lien-holder both seek to redeem property, first to file may redeem).

11 *See* Appx. E, *infra*.

12 *See* Appx. E, *infra*. See also Weldon v. Feldman, 2005 WL 12025 (Wash. Ct. App. Jan. 3, 2005) (when former owner and judgment lienholder each seek to redeem, former owner has priority).

13 *See* Appx. E, *infra*.

14 *See* Appx. E, *infra*.

15 *See* Appx. E, *infra*.

16 *See* Appx. E, *infra*.

17 *See* Appx. E, *infra*.

18 *See* Appx. E, *infra*.

19 *See* Angeleri v. B. & P. Group, Inc., 2006 WL 2422582 (Mich. Ct. App. Aug. 22, 2006) (strict compliance, but equitable considerations permitted in case of fraud, accident, or mistake); Homestead Sav. Bank v. Norman Nealey Builders, Inc., 2005 WL 2757969 (Mich. Ct. App. Oct. 25, 2005) (error in notice procedure for right to redeem makes sale voidable, not void; court will consider whether harm resulted; where error corrected, and no harm shown, summary judgment for lender affirmed); TCM Properties v. Gunderson, 720 N.W.2d 344

tressed homeowners are able to redeem their homes in a lump sum from existing savings, the redemption right provides the opportunity to sell the home privately, to refinance the debt, or to pay the full claim in bankruptcy.[20]

If the homeowners can find a buyer, they can arrange for the buyer to put up the amount necessary to redeem the home and to pay the homeowner the difference between the negotiated sale price and the redemption amount. This helps to preserve equity that would otherwise be lost in the context of a below market foreclosure sale.

If the homeowners can refinance, they may use the proceeds from the new mortgage to redeem the home, which thereby terminates the foreclosing lender's interest in the home. Careful attention to the details of the refinancing transaction are necessary to avoid desperate choices and scams.

In certain circumstances, a debtor may be able to spread out payments necessary to redeem over the course of a chapter 13 bankruptcy plan.[21] Issues related to redemption rights in bankruptcy are discussed at § 4.2.6, *supra*.

14.2 Setting Aside a Completed Foreclosure Sale

14.2.1 Introduction

Often a homeowner does not seek legal advice until after a foreclosure has been completed. In some cases, the homeowner does not even become aware of the foreclosure until the property has been sold and the new owner brings an eviction action. This subsection summarizes the procedure for setting aside a completed foreclosure and some of the possible grounds for such an action. The procedures to set aside a sale apply whether or not the homeowner was represented by an advocate before or during the sale process.

14.2.2 Procedural Issues

14.2.2.1 Generally

The process required to undo a completed foreclosure will depend on the foreclosure method used by the lender. If the foreclosure was conducted by power of sale, the foreclosed homeowner usually must initiate a suit to set aside or void the sale. Because foreclosure is entirely extra-judicial in most states that allow power of sale foreclosures, there is no existing action in which claims to invalidate the completed foreclosure can be raised. An action to set aside the sale may be filed in state court, or the homeowner can file bankruptcy and seek to set aside the sale in the bankruptcy case.[22]

In a few states that permit power of sale foreclosures, the lender or public official conducting the sale must file a report after the sale with a court. A judicial confirmation process follows. In these states, the homeowner may be allowed to raise objections to the sale in the confirmation process.[23] Failure to do so may preclude later action. In other states, however, the confirmation process is limited to determining whether the sale brought in the fair market value of the property, and the court will not consider other issues.[24]

In states where foreclosure is conducted by a full judicial process, the issues are more complicated. If, under state process, the foreclosure case remains open through completion of the sale process, objections to the validity of the sale may be raised in that case. If, however, the state judicial process terminates with entry of the foreclosure judgment that is not appealed, a party objecting to the sale must either reopen the case or file a separate action to have the sale set aside. One choice or the other may be mandated by statute, rule, or case law. If either option is available, filing a separate action may be preferable if the only issue is the validity of the sale.

Whether the state foreclosure process is judicial or nonjudicial, if an order confirming the completed sale has already been entered,[25] the homeowner may need to reopen the order of confirmation in order to object to the sale. The homeowner's motion to reopen can be litigated in the state

(Minn. Ct. App. 2006) (remand to determine whether mortgagor strictly complied with statute); Bank Ctr. First v. R.C. Transp., L.L.C., 714 N.W.2d 816 (N.D. 2006) (statutory right of redemption can only be exercised within period of time and in manner prescribed by law).

20 Other homeowners have sought creative ways to redeem the property or extend the period of redemption. Anticipating the end of the redemption period, homeowners have sought benefactors, or persons willing to lend a nominal sum of money in exchange for a mortgage on the property. As a junior lienholder, the benefactor-mortgage holder can redeem the property, extend the period of redemption and allow the homeowners time to sell the property and pay off all the liens. Such a strategy is described in TCM Props. v. Gunderson, 720 N.W.2d 344 (Minn. Ct. App. 2006).

21 *But see In re* Snowden, 345 B.R. 607 (Bankr. N.D. Ill. 2006) (right to redeem cannot be stretched to extend throughout the life of a chapter 13 plan).

22 *See* § 14.2.4, *infra* (discussion of setting aside a foreclosure sale in bankruptcy).

23 *See, e.g.*, Bierman v. Hunter, 988 A.2d 530, 538 (Md. Ct. Spec. App. 2010) (homeowner need not file pre-sale injunction, but may raise objections to validity of mortgage, not just irregularities in sale procedure, as objections to judicial ratification of sale).

24 *See, e.g.*, Dorsey v. Mancuso, 547 S.E.2d 787 (Ga. Ct. App. 2001) (confirmation process limited to determining whether sale was properly advertised and brought in fair market value of land).

25 Some "power of sale" states require judicial confirmation of foreclosure sales. *See* Appx. E, *infra*.

court, or, if the homeowner files bankruptcy, can be made in the existing state court foreclosure action then removed to the bankruptcy court to be litigated.[26] In some states, there is a time limit to raise objections to a facially valid sale.[27] Even where state law does not set a specific time limit, laches may preclude an action to set aside a foreclosure sale if the homeowner has failed to act promptly.[28] In most circumstances, the buyer at the foreclosure sale will be a necessary party if the homeowner seeks to set aside the sale.[29]

If the purchaser at the foreclosure sale (who will often be the lender) has already brought an eviction action against the former homeowner and obtained a judgment, the lender may argue that the judgment of eviction is res judicata as to the validity of the foreclosure sale. A judgment in a summary possessory action, however, generally does not resolve any issue of title and therefore should not bar litigation of the validity of a foreclosure.[30] Some state summary process statutes specifically provide that a summary process judgment for possession is not a bar to a later action to recover title.[31]

If the sale is set aside as void, title is normally restored to the homeowner. Mortgage and lien interests on the property are generally restored as if no foreclosure sale has taken place.[32] Further complications may arise in two situations. First, if the sale proceeds are unavailable to be returned to a third party purchaser,[33] the purchaser may be entitled to a lien or other equitable interest in the property. Second, if the property is resold for value after a void sale, the rights of that second purchaser must also be adjudicated.

Once a sale is set aside, the homeowner should generally be able to raise claims against the lender, if any, based on the underlying mortgage.[34] (As discussed above, in a judicial foreclosure state, this may also require reopening or setting aside the foreclosure judgment.) These would include all of the state and federal legal claims discussed in Chapter 5, *supra*, such as usury, truth in lending violations, and consumer fraud (UDAP) claims and procedural defects.

In situations in which the foreclosure purchaser is a third party (not the lender), that third party is likely to be a necessary party to any type of action to set aside the sale under state law. If an action to set aside the sale is brought against a third party purchaser, the homeowners should also name the lender as a defendant so that they can raise any claims they may have against the lender in the same action.

In some cases, the homeowner's goal in setting the sale aside will not be to raise defenses to the underlying mortgage claim but to obtain an opportunity to cure the default or pay off the mortgage in full.[35] Alternatively, a homeowner may wish to obtain a better price for the property either by voluntary sale or a more procedurally fair foreclosure auction.

When the sale cannot be successfully challenged, the homeowner may retain claims for damages against the lender.[36] In some cases these damages may be substantial and may include attorney fee awards. Although these claims may not invalidate the mortgage or the foreclosure, they may create leverage which can be used by the homeowner to reacquire the property from the lender.

14.2.2.2 *Rooker-Feldman* Doctrine

If, following completion of a judicial foreclosure process, the homeowner intends to raise objections concerning the underlying debt, such as TILA or other consumer defenses, the sale must be set aside and the foreclosure judgment must be reopened in the court that entered it. Otherwise, defenses to the debt may be precluded by res judicata or under the *Rooker-Feldman* doctrine.

The *Rooker-Feldman* doctrine bars federal courts from reconsidering state court decisions.[37] If the *Rooker-Feldman* doctrine is applied the claim will be dismissed for want of

---

26 *See* Ingorvaia v. Horton, 816 So. 2d 1256 (Fla. Dist. Ct. App. 2002) (lower court did not abuse discretion in setting aside a sale when mortgage holder did not get notice); National Consumer Law Center, Consumer Bankruptcy Law and Practice Ch. 14 (9th ed. 2009).

27 *See* Independence One Mortgage Corp. v. Gillespie, 672 A.2d 1279 (N.J. Super. Ct. App. Div. 1996) (void sale can be challenged at any time, but voidable sale can only be challenged within time limits set by court rule); Mortgage Elec. Registration Sys., Inc. v. Ralich, 982 A.2d 77 (Pa. Super. Ct. 2009) (unless fraud is alleged, petition to set aside foreclosure sale must be filed before deed is delivered; fraud must be alleged with particularity).

28 *See, e.g.*, Russell v. Argent Mortg. Co., 684 S.E.2d 867 (Ga. 2009).

29 *In re* Foreclosure of a lien by Hunters Creek Townhouse Homeowners Ass'n, Inc., 683 S.E.2d 450 (N.C. Ct. App. 2009). *See also* Shlishey the Best, Inc. v. CitiFinancial Equity Servs., Inc., 14 So. 3d 1271 (Fla. Dist. Ct. App. 2009) (foreclosure sale purchaser was denied due process where creditor obtained *ex parte* order setting aside sale).

30 *See* C.J.S. *Judgments* § 740; Boswell v. Blue Ridge Bank, 2000 U.S. App. LEXIS 29335 (4th Cir. Nov. 16, 2000). *See also* Amresco Residential Mortgage Corp. v. Stange, 631 N.W.2d 444 (Minn. Ct. App. 2001) (mortgagors should bring claim against mortgage holder in a separate action and enjoin prosecution of the eviction proceeding).

31 *See, e.g.*, Mass. Gen. Laws ch. 239, § 7.

32 *See, e.g.*, Williams v. Kimes, 25 S.W.3d 150 (Mo. 2000) (failure to provide notice to contingent remainder holders (heirs) that were known to the trustee invalidated foreclosure sale).

33 For example, the mortgage holder may be a private party that spent the sale proceeds as soon as they were delivered.

34 *See* Young v. 1st Am. Fin. Servs., 977 F. Supp. 38 (D.D.C. 1997) (dispute about validity of sale precluded dismissal of underlying TIL rescission claim).

35 *See* Chs. 2, 4, *supra*.

36 *See* Brown v. Freedman, 474 S.E.2d 73 (Ga. Ct. App. 1996) (breach of duty of good faith and fair dealing gives rise to claim for damages).

37 The *Rooker-Feldman* doctrine arose from the cases of District of Columbia Court of Appeals v. Feldman, 460 U.S. 462, 482–486, 103 S. Ct. 1303, 75 L. Ed. 2d 206 (1983) and Rooker

subject matter jurisdiction. Even without the *Rooker-Feldman* doctrine, res judicata or collateral estoppel may prevent the consumer from litigating issues in federal court that were or could have been raised in the state court proceedings. A federal court is required to give a state court judgment the same preclusive effect as a state court would. A discussion of the *Rooker-Feldman* doctrine is included at § 10.6.4, *supra*, and res judicata is discussed at § 10.6.5, *supra*.

14.2.3 Grounds on Which a Foreclosure May Be Set Aside

14.2.3.1 Overview

In order to recover the property after a foreclosure, a homeowner must be able to assert a legal basis to invalidate the foreclosure sale after a power of sale foreclosure, or to invalidate the judgment or sale after a judicial foreclosure.[38] Generally the homeowner will be required to show some irregularity in the foreclosure process which makes the sale void under state law, or that the sale price was so inadequate that it shocks the conscience. Most claims based on the underlying transaction are lost if not raised before the sale, unless the homeowner can have the sale set aside. In addition, some state statutes provide that a completed sale to a good faith purchaser cuts off the foreclosed homeowner's right to challenge the sale on procedural grounds.[39]

14.2.3.2 Irregularity in the Conduct of the Sale

Each state has its own statutory scheme dictating its foreclosure procedures. Noncompliance with some aspects of this scheme will subject a sale to being set aside, even without proof that the noncompliance affected the outcome of the sale. For example, a state statute may define the conditions under which a lender may conduct a non-judicial foreclosure sale. A sale conducted under circumstances not authorized by the statute will be void.[40] Similarly, when a statute requires notice by advertising, failure to provide the required notice will invalidate the sale.[41] Failure to provide required notice to the borrower and to others with an interest in the property including other lien holders will generally invalidate a sale.[42] Likewise, failure to comply with a

v. Fid. Trust Co., 263 U.S. 413, 44 S. Ct. 149, 68 L. Ed. 362 (1923).

38 *See* Phoenix Holding, L.L.C. v. Martinez, 27 So. 3d 791 (Fla. Dist. Ct. App. 2010) (unfairness alone not grounds to set aside foreclosure sale); Cicoria v. Gazi, 901 So. 2d 282 (Fla. Dist. Ct. App. 2005) (courts may set aside foreclosure sales and allow mortgagors to exercise their statutory right of redemption where there has been some defect in the proceedings regarding notice of the sale date, a very low bid by the purchaser or accident or mistake on the part of the mortgagor or an attorney representing the mortgagor, in failing to attend the foreclosure sale); Deutsche Bank Trust Co. v. Green, 723 N.W.2d 449 (Iowa Ct. App. 2006) (sale set aside where home was sold prior to scheduled foreclosure sale date but the sheriff's office overlooked that information and mistakenly re-sold the home at the foreclosure sale); Keybank Nat'l Assoc. v. Sargent, 758 A.2d 528 (Me. 2000) (any irregularity in the sale following foreclosure will not serve as grounds to set aside the foreclosure judgment if there was no allegation of a defect in the judgment itself). *See generally* Molly F. Jacobson-Greany, *Setting Aside Non-judicial Foreclosure Sales: Extending the Rule to Cover Both Intrinsic and Extrinsic Fraud or Unfairness*, 23 Emory Bankr. Dev. J. (Fall 2006).

39 *See* Taylor v. Just, 59 P.3d 308 (Idaho 2002) (Idaho statute provides that any failure to comply with statutory notice requirements does not affect a sale to a good faith purchaser for value; provision does not apply to homeowner's challenge on the grounds that there was no default).

40 *See, e.g.,* Lee v. HSBC Bank USA 218 P.3d 775 (Haw. 2009) (due to cure of default, mortgagor was no longer in default at time of foreclosure sale, thus sale did not comply with statutory requirements); Staffordshire Invs., Inc. v. Cal-Western Reconveyance Corp., 149 P.3d. 150 (Or. Ct. App. 2006) (foreclosure sale void because statutory requirement for "default" not met once borrower negotiated forbearance agreement with lender before sale). *See also* Davenport v. HSBC Bank, USA, 739 N.W.2d. 383 (Mich. Ct. App. 2007) (successor mortgage holder who did not own interest in mortgage at time of publication of foreclosure notice was not eligible to start the foreclosure, and subsequent sheriff's sale was void).

41 *See, e.g., In re* Gatlin, 357 B.R. 519 (Bankr. W.D. Ark. 2006) (setting aside sale where lender used outdated rural delivery address for property in advertisements and posted notices instead of the property's new 911 street address); Chase v. Morse, 18 Mass. 559, 561 (1905); Moore v. Dick, 187 Mass. 207 (1905) (advertising in the "Lynn Bee" rather than the "Lynn Reporter" was an invalid exercise of the power of sale, even though both papers were published in the same office of the same company). *See also* Deep v. Rose, 364 S.E.2d 228 (Va. 1988) (sale conducted in violation of mandatory time periods contained in statute governing advertisement is void—not voidable; result is to render sale ineffectual, no title passes to purchaser). *But see* Fed. Nat'l Mortgage Ass'n v. N.Y. Fin. & Mortgage, 636 N.Y.S.2d 105 (App. Div. 1995) (attorney's unilateral mistake as to location of foreclosure sale does not provide sufficient basis for invalidating sale, when appellant's attorney was served with notice and notice was proper).

42 *See In re* Kekauoha-Alisa, 394 B.R. 507 (Bankr. D. Haw. 2008 (failure to properly announce postponement of judicial mortgage foreclosure sale grounds to set aside sale), *amended on other grounds by*, 2008 WL 4181347 (Bankr. D. Haw. Sept. 3, 2008); *In re* Kitts, 274 B.R. 491 (Bankr. E.D. Tenn. 2002); Young v. Embley, 143 P.3d 936 (Alaska 2006) (upholding lienholder's challenge to sale based on lack of notice and refusal to allow redemption); Sudhoff v. Federal Nat'l Mortgage Ass'n, 942 So. 2d 425 (2006) (Fla. Dist. Ct. App. 2006) (failure to provide notice to estranged wife, whose name was also on the mortgage, constituted improper notice and justified setting aside foreclosure sale); Federal Home Loan Mortgage Corp. v. Appel, 137 P.3d 429 (Idaho 2006) (sale may be set aside if homeowner did not receive notice of continued sale date after lender obtained relief from bankruptcy stay); Alliance Mortgage Co. v. Pastine, 136 P.3d 457 (Kan. 2006) (setting aside sale for lack of statutorily required notice to junior mortgage holder); Rea v.

material term of the mortgage contract may allow a foreclosure sale to be set aside.[43] For example, the terms of loan documents may prescribe procedures for a non-judicial foreclosure sale that supplement statutory requirements. Because lenders typically draft these documents, the courts will hold the lenders to strict compliance with the terms of their own documents.[44]

In other states, courts are reluctant to set aside a sale based upon violations of foreclosure statutes unless the party challenging the sale can demonstrate that the violation, though technical, resulted in actual prejudice.[45] The homeowner may be required to show that the noncompliance adversely affected the foreclosure sale price, or "chilled bidding."[46] For example, if a foreclosure sale notice incorrectly describes the property or the existing encumbrances, potential bidders may be unwilling to bid for the property or

Fivegees Invs., 2006 WL 1009398 (Mich. Ct. App. Apr. 18, 2006) (failure to provide notice of taxes owed violated homeowner's due process rights and justified setting aside the foreclosure sale); Williams v. Kimes, 25 S.W.3d 150 (Mo. 2000) (failure to provide notice to contingent remainder holders (heirs) that were known to the trustee invalidated foreclosure sale); United States v. Scurry, 940 A.2d 1164 (N.J. 2008) (trial court could not apply doctrine of laches to bar borrower from relief from the sheriff sale when borrower did not receive required notice, had deposited substantial funds with her attorney to cure the arrears, her counsel offered to cure the default and received no reply from the mortgage holder, successful purchaser at the sheriff's sale was the foreclosing mortgage holder, and the property remained vacant and had not been transferred to an innocent third party); Bank of N.Y. v. Vandermeulen, 782 N.Y.S.2d 465 (N.Y. App. Div. 2004) (judgment of foreclosure and sale vacated where summons was not served on mortgagor in the statutorily mandated period); Principal Residential Mortgage, Inc. v. Nash, 606 N.W.2d 120 (N.D. 2000); Ohio Sav. Bank v. Hawley, 2001 Ohio App. LEXIS 702 (Ohio Ct. App. Feb. 16, 2001) (foreclosure sale vacated because mortgagor did not receive actual notice of the sale; notice by publication was inadequate); Mills v. Haggard, 58 S.W.3d 164 (Tex. App. 2001) (failure to send notice to cure). *See also* Meade v. JD Venture Capital, L.L.C., 832 N.Y.S.2d 665 (N.Y. App. Div. 2007) (failure to comply with statutory notice requirements). *But see* Dunn v. Watson, 566 S.E.2d 305 (W. Va. 2002) (homeowner has burden of proof of noncompliance with notice requirements; mere denial that he received the notice of foreclosure sale was insufficient to rebut the presumption of receipt when notice sent by certified mail); Phoenix Holding, L.L.C. v. Martinez, 27 So. 3d 791 (Fla. Dist. Ct. App. 2010) (failure to send notices to the proper address not sufficient grounds to set aside judgment of foreclosure); GMB Fin. Group, Inc. v. Marzano, 899 N.E.2d 298 (Ill. App. Ct. 2008) (failure to provide a additional notice of sale of mortgaged property after original sale postponed more than sixty days did not invalidate sale where mortgagor was personally provided notice of the postponed sale); Wells Fargo Bank Minnesota, N.A. v. Ray, 880 N.Y.S.2d 454 (N.Y. Sup. Ct. 2009) (failure to give proper notice of a foreclosure sale is mere irregularity and not jurisdictional defect; service of the notice of sale is not required on a defendant who is in default for failure to appear).

43 *See* CitiFinancial Mortgage Co. v. Beasley, 2007 WL 77289 (Tenn. Ct. App. Jan. 11, 2007) (foreclosure void because lender conducted sale before expiration of thirty-day cure period provided under deed of trust). *Cf.* Bayview Loan Servicing, L.L.C. v. Simmons 654 S.E.2d 898 (Va. 2008) (failure to provide pre-acceleration notice required by contract meant indebtedness never matured and mortgagor was entitled to damages for lost equity in home).

44 *See* CitiFinancial Mortgage Co. v. Beasley, 2007 WL 77289 (Tenn. Ct. App. Jan. 11, 2007).

45 Knapp v. Doherty, 20 Cal. Rptr. 3d 1 (Cal. Ct. App. 2004) (slight procedural irregularity in sale notice insufficient to set aside sale unless it contributed to inadequate sale price or otherwise injured debtor); Sweet Air Inv., Inc. v. Kenney, 739 N.W.2d 656 (Mich. Ct. App. 2007) (failure to publish notice of adjournment of foreclosure sale not enough to void foreclosure sale absent showing of prejudice); Mortgage Elec. Registration Sys., Inc. v. Schotter, 857 N.Y.S.2d 592 (App. Div. 2008) (publication of sale notice in wrong newspaper was "mere irregularity," denying motion to vacate absent showing of prejudice); Matrix Fin. Servs. Corp. v. McKiernan, 786 N.Y.S.2d 212 (App. Div. 2004) (trivial irregularities in notice of foreclosure sale did not warrant vacating of sale, where appellant failed to establish that substantial right of a party was prejudiced by such irregularities); *In re* Trustee's Sale of Prop. of Brown, 2005 WL 1474042 (Va. Cir. Ct. Mar. 25, 2005) (sale under deed of trust is not invalid on mere technical grounds but only for weighty reasons; a sale not invalid when an unqualified corporation was appointed as a substitute trustee together with a qualified corporation where no party suffered an inequity).

46 *See In re* Townsville, 268 B.R. 95 (Bankr. E.D. Pa. 2001) (notices published three times prior to sale that contained incorrect sales date not sufficient to invalidate sale as there was no evidence that they deterred anyone from bidding or that they negatively affected the sale price of the property); Richardson v. Chase Manhattan Bank, 941 So. 2d 435 (Fla. Dist. Ct. App. 2006) (to prevail on remand homeowner must show that she did not receive notice of sale and that she suffered harm because of the lack of notice); Gilroy v. Ryberg, 667 N.W.2d 544 (Neb. 2003) (trustee violated terms of trust by allowing successful bidder to pay by personal check but homeowner did not establish that defect affected the sale price; party seeking to set aside the sale need not necessarily present direct evidence of prejudice but may meet its burden "by establishing that (1) the defect, by its nature, would have a tendency to result in a reduced sale price and (2) the sale price was inadequate"); Conway v. Eastern Sav. Bank, F.S.B., 2006 WL 3613605 (Tenn. Ct. App. 2006) (no foreclosure set aside where bank failed to comply with statutory advertising provisions, specific facts not pleaded showing owner not given opportunity to cure defect and foreclosure sale price alleged to be insufficient). *See also* Southeast Timberlands, Inc. v. Sec. Nat'l Bank, 469 S.E.2d 454 (Ga. Ct. App. 1996) (error in foreclosure notice regarding amount due on the mortgage did not chill bidding and did not require denial of confirmation because statute did not require notice to state amount due on mortgage); Goldberg v. Frick Elec. Co., 770 A.2d 182 (Md. 2001) (affirming order setting aside sheriff's sale at request of bidder who relied to his detriment on sale notice's misrepresentation of amount of liens on property); J. Ashley Corp. v. Burson, 750 A.2d 618 (Md. Ct. Spec. App. 2000) (confirming sale when borrower did not demonstrate any harm or prejudice resulting from a forty-five minute delay in the start of the sale); Empire of Am. Realty v. Mancine, 656 A.2d 66 (N.J. Super. Ct. Ch. Div. 1994) (setting aside sale when sale held at 11:00 and legislatively prescribed time for sheriff's sale was between 12:00 noon and 5:00 p.m.; this irregularity plus gross inadequacy of the sale price required setting aside the sale).

may bid below the true value. Or, when a statute requires a pre-foreclosure appraisal, an inaccurate appraisal may provide a basis to set aside the sale, if it can be shown that the low appraisal deterred bidders. Other courts may require a homeowner to have offered to cure a default as a precondition to challenging the mortgage holder's compliance with notice provisions in the statute.[47]

14.2.3.3 Inadequacy of Sale Price

14.2.3.3.1 Generally

It is a well-settled rule that mere inadequacy of price will not justify setting aside a foreclosure sale, absent additional circumstances of unfairness or irregularity, unless the sale price is so grossly inadequate as to shock the conscience of the court.[48] A review of decisions from various jurisdictions shows that while it is possible in the rare case to shock the court, it is difficult to get a sale set aside solely on this basis.

For example, in *Federal National Mortgage Ass'n v. Brooks*,[49] the South Carolina Supreme Court found that a price of $875 for a property with $27,000 in equity was not shocking. In *Petition of Nelson*,[50] the Minnesota Supreme Court ruled that the alleged inadequate price of $900 would not justify setting aside an execution sale of property with an assessed value of $100,000.

In a few cases, however, courts have set aside sales when the sale price is less disproportionate. In *Ballentyne v. Smith*[51] the U.S. Supreme Court upheld a lower court's refusal to confirm a sale when the property value was at least seven times the sale price. In *Rife v. Woolfork*,[52] West Virginia's highest court found that a sale price that was one-seventh of the value of the property was sufficiently shocking to set aside the sale. In a Maryland case, a sale was set aside as shocking when the sale price was $2000 and the value of the property was $18,000.[53] A South Carolina appellate court has found shocking to the conscience a sale price of $510 for a property valued at $45,467.[54]

More recently, the Supreme Court of Arizona, in *In re Krohn*,[55] held that a sale of real property under a power of sale in a deed of trust may be set aside solely on the basis that the bid price was grossly inadequate. In that case, the property, with value of $57,500, sold for $10,304.

47 *See* Fordjour v. Fleet Mortgage Group, Inc., 49 Fed. Appx. 130 (9th Cir. 2002) (unpublished); Saldate v. Wilshire Credit Corp. __ F. Supp. 2d __, 2010 WL 624445 (E.D. Cal. Feb. 18, 2010). *See also* Mora v. Superior Court, 2007 WL 215072, at *7 (Cal. Ct. App. Jan. 29, 2007) (unpublished) (noting that any requirement for borrower to tender full indebtedness or arrearage as condition to relief from foreclosure sale is subject to court's equitable discretion).

48 Fed. Deposit Ins. Corp. v. Elder Care Servs., Inc., 82 F.3d 524 (1st Cir. 1996); Cuauhtli v. Chase Home Fin. L.L.C., 2007 WL 548759 (N.D. Tex. Feb. 22, 2007) (grossly inadequate foreclosure sale price insufficient; must also show some impropriety in sale); Baskurt v. Beal, 101 P.3d 1041 (Alaska 2004) (when the inadequacy of the sale price is so gross as to shock the conscience and raise a presumption of fraud or unfairness, or is coupled with other irregularities in the sale procedures, then invalidation of the sale may be justified); *In re* Krohn, 52 P.3d 774 (Ariz. 2002) (sale of real property under power of sale in a deed of trust may be set aside solely on the basis that the bid price was *grossly* inadequate; property with value of $57,500 sold for $10,000 was grossly inadequate); World Sav. & Loan Ass'n v. Amerus Bank, 740 N.E.2d 466 (Ill. App. Ct. 2000); GFS/Morristown, Ltd. P'ship v. Vector Whipany Assocs., 2009 WL 857418 (N.J. Super. Ct. App. Div. Apr. 2, 2009) (affirming foreclosure sale of $18 million commercial property for $100 where mortgage holder was sole bidder and no indication of inequity; judgment was for over $78 million, loan was nonrecourse, and mortgagor had profited from ownership and operation of property); Armstrong v. Csurilla, 817 P.2d 1221 (N.M. 1991); Udall v. T.D. Escrow Servs., Inc., 154 P.3d 882 (Wash. 2007) (auctioneer's mistake in accepting final bid that was $100,000 lower than authorized opening amount was a procedural irregularity, but not sufficient to void sale; insufficiency of price not a procedural irregularity that voids the sale; it is merely a mistake); Manion v. Chase Manhattan Mortgage Corp., 43 P.3d 576, 577 (Wyo. 2002) (fact that there is some inadequacy in the sale price is not sufficient grounds for setting aside a sale when the sale was lawfully made and rightly conducted, with full opportunity for competition in the bidding, and without fraud, partiality, or oppression). *See also* Litke v. Morris, 2006 WL 897961 (N.D. Miss. Apr. 4, 2006) (purchase price of 8% of the home's actual value was grossly inadequate and the foreclosure sale was set aside, but the purchaser was entitled to recovery of the purchase price and amount invested in home repairs); *In re* Schleier, 290 B.R. 45 (Bankr. S.D.N.Y. 2003) (holding foreclosure sale void because of bankruptcy filing minutes before the completion of the sale; further holding that even if the sale was not void for violation of the automatic stay, it would have been set aside on the grounds that the price was grossly inadequate when property sold for $245,000 and evidence established property's value was $1 million); Fagnani v. Fisher, 988 A.2d 1134 (Md. Ct. Spec. App. 2010) (purchase price of $83,800 on property assessed at $327,730 did not shock the conscience); Demuth v. Maryknoll, L.L.C., 2008 WL 5136956 (Minn. Ct. App.2008) (purchase price of $3,196.35 on home with fair market value of $135,000, absent fraud or irregularity, not invalid). *See generally* Osborne on Mortgages § 329 (2d ed. 1970); James Gadsen & Alfred Farha, *Under What Circumstances Can A Foreclosure Sale Be Set Aside Under New York Law?*, N.Y. St. B.J. 42 (May/June 1993) (New York courts have recognized, as general guidelines, that (i) a foreclosure sale will not be set aside for mere inadequacy of price where consideration equal to at least 10% of fair market value was attained; (ii) a sale attaining 10% to 50% of fair market value will be set aside where there is additional evidence of fraud, collusion, mistake, misconduct or exploitive overreaching; and (iii) sales for 50% or more of market value will be upheld. Additional barriers to the exercise of the power to set aside are the intervening rights of independent third parties and the doctrine of laches).

49 405 S.E.2d 604 (S.C. Ct. App. 1991).

50 495 N.W.2d 200 (Minn. 1993).

51 205 U.S. 285 (1907).

52 289 S.E.2d 220 (W. Va. 1982).

53 McCartney v. Frost, 386 A.2d 784 (Md. 1978).

54 Investors Sav. Bank v. Phelps, 397 S.E.2d 780 (S.C. Ct. App. 1990).

55 52 P.3d 774 (Ariz. 2002).

14.2.3.3.2 Inadequate price and irregularity in the conduct of the sale

When a low sale price is coupled with some irregularity in the foreclosure process, courts are more likely to set aside the sale.[56] And, when the sale price is very low, even slight irregularities will be sufficient to justify setting it aside.[57]

Federal National Mortgage Ass'n v. Brooks[58] is one case in point. In this case, the Federal National Mortgage Association (FNMA) sought to foreclose on a property on which it held a second mortgage. FNMA retained an attorney to bid on the property at the sale. On the day of the sale however, the attorney's son became ill and the attorney was unable to attend the sale. He asked his law partner to bid at the sale, but because of a mix-up no bid was entered for FNMA. Instead, a bid of $875 was made by Brooks at the sale and accepted. The next day, FNMA moved to set aside the sale. The value of the foreclosed property was $52,500, subject to a $24,000 first mortgage. The court found that the $875 price was inadequate, but not shockingly so.

The court found irregularities in the conduct of the sale, however, which together with the low price justified voiding the sale. The irregularities upon which the court based its decision were that the referee's notice incorrectly stated that the foreclosure purchaser had thirty days after the sale to pay the purchase price. By law, the purchaser was required to pay within twenty days. Because Brooks did not pay within the twenty days, the sale was defective. What was perhaps the more compelling reason underlying the court's decision, however, was revealed in its discussion of the equities of the case: FNMA had waived a deficiency judgment against the borrower because of the equity in the property. The court concluded that it would be inequitable to allow Brooks to be unjustly enriched at the expense of FNMA.

In *Looper v. Madison Guarantee Savings & Loan Ass'n*,[59] the court affirmed a decision to set aside a foreclosure sale that yielded a sale price of 4.4% of the fair market value, based on the facts that the mortgage holder's lawyer, who was instructed to bid the amount of the foreclosure judgment, was "inadvertently late" for the sale, that the mortgagor would be liable for a huge deficiency judgment had the sale been confirmed, and that the mortgagor was not present at the sale to protect his interests.

Insufficient notice together with a low price may also be enough to set aside a sale. In *Ohio Realty & Investment*

---

56 *See In re* Ryker, 301 B.R. 156 (D.N.J. 2003) (if debtor had standing to bring adversary proceeding challenging sale, then court properly exercised equitable powers, under state law, to set aside sale due to inadequate price as delayed sale was not re-advertised and notice did not specify the actual amount due); Baskurt v. Beal, 101 P.3d 1041, 1046 (Alaska 2004) (setting aside sale where purchase price was less than 15% of sale price and trustee sold two parcels in bulk, when the sale of either parcel alone would likely have generated sufficient proceeds to satisfy amount due; inadequacy of the price coupled with the trustee's unreasonable failure to sell only one parcel justifies invalidating the sale); Lo v. Jensen, 106 Cal. Rptr. 2d 443 (Cal. Ct. App. 2001) (sale set aside because purchasers colluded together to eliminate competition, and they purchased a property valued at over $100,000 for $5412); Alberts v. Fed. Home Loan Mortgage Corp., 673 So. 2d 158 (Fla. Dist. Ct. App. 1996) (setting aside sale on grounds that because of unilateral mistake made by mortgage holder's agent, property was sold for a mere fraction of its fair market value); Aikens v. Wagner, 498 S.E.2d 766 (Ga. Ct. App. 1998) (failure to treat owners fairly or to provide a correct amount due on the mortgage together with low sale price found to be grounds to set aside sale); Nat'l Oil & Gas, Inc. v. Gingrich, 716 N.E.2d 491 (Ind. Ct. App. 1999) (sale set aside when high bidder failed to meet terms of sale and sheriff sold property to next highest bidder without following state mandated procedures for resale); U.S. Bank Nat'l Ass'n v. Hickey, 862 N.Y.S.2d 87 (App. Div. 2008) (sale vacated due to "unconscionably low" sale price and inadequate notice where mortgagors able to refinance and pay off mortgage). *See also* Armstrong v. Csurilla, 817 P.2d 1221 (N.M. 1991) (suggesting that a price range of 10–40% of value may well shock the judicial conscience, and that a price of 40–70% of value, when combined with inequitable conditions, may warrant vacating the sale); Deutsche Bank National Co. v. Butler, 868 A.2d 574 (Pa. Super. Ct. 2005) (foreclosure sale set aside because purchase price was grossly inadequate due to attorney's mistaken failure to increase bidding); Poole v. Jefferson Standard Life Ins. Co., 177 S.E.24 (S.C. 1934) (party not able to place a higher bid because seller not in his office). *Cf.* Burnette v. Wells Fargo Bank, N.A.,2010 WL 1026968 (E.D. Tex. Feb. 16, 2010 (claim of inadequate sale price, violation of terms of deed of trust by appointing substitute trustee and not receiving notice of foreclosure sale sufficient to withstand motion to dismiss). *But see* Griffin v. Shapiro, 857 A.2d 519 (Md. Ct. Spec. App. 2004) (declining to set aside sale where advertisement contained incorrect zip code and sale price represented approximately 45% of property's value based on appraisal and 53% based on tax assessment); Udall v. T.D. Escrow Servs., Inc., 154 P.3d 882 (Wash. 2007) (refusing to invalidate non-judicial foreclosure sale where auctioneer opened with bid that was $100,000 lower than the price the trustee had authorized; the winning bid was $1 over the opening bid but not grossly inadequate).

57 Ballentyne v. Smith, 205 U.S. 285 (1907); Ogden v. First Commercial Mortgage Co., 1999 Ark. App. LEXIS 563 (Ark. Ct. App. Sept. 1, 1999) ($1 sale to homeowner invalidated based on evidence of mistakenly misfiled written bid); Long Beach Mortg. Corp. v. Bebble, 985 So. 2d 611 (Fla. Dist. Ct. App. 2008) (overturning lower court's decision not to set aside foreclosure sale where property sold for 0.2% of its value and no one bid on behalf of mortgage holder who, because of mistake, arrived late to the sale); Empire of Am. Realty v. Mancine, 656 A.2d 66 (N.J. Super. Ct. Ch. Div. 1994); DJBAS Living Trust v. Meinhardt, 755 N.W.2d 501 (S.D. 2008) (upholding set aside of foreclosure sale where mortgage assignee was authorized to bid $100,000 on home that sold for $10,000, arrived late to foreclosure sale).

58 405 S.E.2d 604 (S.C. Ct. App. 1991).

59 729 S.W.2d 156 (Ark. 1987). *See also* Johnson v. Jefferson Standard Life Ins. Co., 429 P.2d 474 (Ariz. Ct. App. 1967) (setting aside sale of property appraised at $73,000 for $5000 where purchaser had persuaded sheriff to dispense with customary reading of sale notice at the sale, and mortgage holder arrived a few minutes late but had been willing to submit a bid of over $55,000).

Corp. v. Southern Bank of West Palm Beach,[60] the Florida court set aside a sale in which the sale was advertised for 11:00 a.m. but actually took place at 2:00 p.m. and a third party was willing to bid 10% more for the property had the sale been conducted on time.

Cooperation among bidders coupled with a grossly inadequate price was enough to set aside a sale in *RSR Investments Inc. v. Barnett Bank of Pinellas*.[61] The only bidders at the sale entered a joint bid of $5000. The value of the property was $107,000. The mortgage holder failed to appear at the sale because of a clerical error. The court found that the amount bid was not just grossly inadequate, "it was sublimely inadequate."[62] It was so low as to raise a presumption of bad faith on the part of the purchasers. The low price coupled with the apparent cooperative rather than competitive bidding justified setting aside the sale.

Finally, inadequate price coupled with actions to frustrate the homeowner's presale redemption right may be sufficient to allow a court to set aside the sale. In *Commercial Credit Loans, Inc. v. Espinoza*,[63] the court concluded that a sale to the lender at a price of about one fifth of value could not be confirmed. In addition to the inadequate price, the court found that the lender had unconscionably frustrated the homeowner's efforts to pay off the debt in full prior to foreclosure. The evidence showed that the lender failed to respond to a Spanish-speaking homeowner's request for information about the amount necessary to cure and the date, time and place of sale. The court ordered the lender to accept the debtor's post-sale cure of the default.

14.2.3.3.3 Inadequate price and unfairness

A mortgage holder or trustee conducting a foreclosure sale is bound to act in good faith and to exercise reasonable diligence to protect the rights of the debtor.[64] When a foreclosure sale yields a price grossly disproportionate to the property's value, it may be an indication of bad faith or lack of reasonable diligence.[65] When a foreclosing mortgage holder also attempts to become the foreclosure purchaser, he will be held to "the strictest good faith and utmost diligence" for the protection of the rights of the debtor.[66] Thus in cases in which the mortgage holder or trustee purchases at its own sale, and then immediately resells the property for a higher price, courts are likely to find a lack of diligence or good faith.[67] The fact that the mortgage holder was able to sell the property for a higher price shortly after a foreclosure sale is strong evidence that the mortgage holder could have gotten a higher price at the foreclosure sale.

The duty of good faith and due diligence may require that the mortgage holder take steps not specifically required by law to get the highest sale price.[68] For example, in *Sandler v. Silk*,[69] the Massachusetts Supreme Judicial Court held that a mortgage holder violated the duty of good faith when it failed to give a junior lienholder notice of a foreclosure sale. The law did not require notice to the lienholder; however, she had specifically requested notice from the mortgage holder. Even though the mortgage holder had complied with all legal notice requirements, it failed to exercise good faith to get the best possible price. The junior lienholder, if

60 300 So. 2d 679 (Fla. 1974).

61 647 So. 2d 874 (Fla. Dist. Ct. App. 1994).

62 *Id.* at 875.

63 689 N.E.2d 282 (Ill. App. Ct. 1997). *See also* Aikens v. Wagner, 498 S.E.2d 766 (Ga. Ct. App. 1998). *But see* Esque Real Estate Holdings, Inc. v. C.H. Consulting, Ltd., 940 So. 2d 1185 (Fla. Dist. Ct. App. 2006) (lender's failure to reply to pre-sale request for redemption figures not considered defect in sale).

64 Williams v. Resolution GGF OY, 630 N.E.2d 581 (Mass. 1994); Sandler v. Silk, 292 Mass. 493, 496 (1935); Lake Hillside Estates Inc. v. Galloway, 473 So. 2d 461 (Miss. 1985); Murphy v. Fin. Dev. Corp., 495 A.2d 1245 (N.H. 1985); Danvers Sav. Bank v. Hammer, 440 A.2d 435 (N.H. 1982). *See* First Fed. Sav. & Loan v. Sharp, 359 S.W.2d 902 (Tex. 1962) (trustee violated duties when he failed to allow high bidder opportunity to produce cash to satisfy bid and instead accepted a lower bid).

Note that this issue frequently arises in cases in which a mortgage holder is seeking to collect a deficiency. Deficiency judgments are discussed at § 14.3, *infra*.

65 *In re* Sharpe, 391 B.R. 117, 156 (Bankr. N.D. Ala. 2008) ("the duty a mortgagee owes a mortgagor in a foreclosure proceeding is one of good faith and fairness, not a general fiduciary duty"); Danvers Sav. Bank v. Hammer, 440 A.2d 435 (N.H. 1982).

66 Union Mkt. Nat'l Bank v. Missuk Derderian, 318 Mass. 578 (1945) (mortgage holder's successful bid at foreclosure was $8500, balance due on the note was $9800, and property was sold for $12,500 two months after the sale).

67 Union Mkt. Nat'l Bank v. Missuk Derderian, 318 Mass. 578 (1945) (mortgage holder's successful bid at foreclosure was $8500, balance due on the note was $9800, and property was sold for $12,500 two months after the sale); Smith v. Haley, 314 S.W.2d 909 (Mo. 1958); Murphy v. Fin. Dev. Corp., 495 A.2d 1245 (N.H. 1985); Danvers Sav. Bank v. Hammer, 440 A.2d 435 (N.H. 1982) (bank bid $100 at foreclosure sale for property valued at $7000, then resold property for $2025). *See also In re* Greenshaw Energy, Inc., 359 B.R. 636 (Bankr. S.D. Tex. 2007) (defects in mailing notices of sale and inaccurate description of property, coupled with lender's purchase at sale of property worth $10 million for $450,000 stated claim for wrongful foreclosure).

68 *In re* Strayton, 360 B.R. 8 (Bankr. D. Mass. Jan. 17, 2007) (enjoining completion of sale where debtor raised substantial questions as to lender's "decidedly minimal" efforts to market property before sale; noting that lender did not work with a broker, did not conduct any marketing research, failed to obtain an inspection or appraisal, and never made arrangements to show property to potential buyers); Brown v. Freedman, 474 S.E.2d 73 (Ga. Ct. App. 1996) (good faith is not limited to provisions of the deed). *See also* Leone v. Fleet Nat'l Bank, 827 N.E.2d 258 (Mass. App. Ct. 2005) (mere compliance with the statutory requirements of notice and advertising without more is not an absolute shield from liability for foreclosing mortgage holders in Massachusetts; but mortgage holder's refusal to postpone foreclosure sale did not amount to a breach of its fiduciary duty on the facts of the case).

69 292 Mass. 493 (1935).

notified, would have attended the sale, and would likely have bid on the property. Under these circumstances the court invalidated the sale.

Also in Massachusetts, a lower court, in *Snowden v. Chase Manhattan Mortgage Corp.*,[70] held that a mortgage holder breached its duty of good faith and reasonable diligence by refusing to grant the homeowner's request to postpone the foreclosure sale in order to give meaningful consideration to a legally binding offer to purchase the property. The prospective purchase would have resulted in full payment for the mortgage holder, including foreclosure costs, and left some funds available for the homeowner. While the case involved a damages claim for wrongful foreclosure, the rationale is equally applicable when the homeowner seeks to set aside the foreclosure sale.

14.2.3.3.4 Practice tips

Few consistent standards emerge from these cases. Courts recognize that they are applying flexible rules: "A price that shocks the conscience of the court can never be reduced to a mathematical formula. It depends on a variety of circumstances: the value of the property, the circumstances surrounding the sale, the price, the rights of the parties participating in the sale, and the harms that may result if the sale is confirmed, to name a few."[71] These are equitable proceedings, and as the Supreme Court stated in *Ballentyne*, "there is a measure of discretion in a court of equity, both as to the manner and conditions of such a [foreclosure] sale, as well as to ordering or refusing a resale."[72] Foreclosure is historically an equitable proceeding intended to protect the debtor by the orderly and legal disposition of his property.[73] It is not an opportunity to procure valuable property at little or no expense.[74] Judicial evaluation of foreclosure sales must be undertaken in light of this general purpose.

It is clear that the court's ultimate conclusion may depend more on the equities of the case than on any other factor. For this reason, advocates should seek to make the homeowner's case as sympathetic as possible. Any potential UDAP[75] violations or fraud by the lender should be included to demonstrate the inequity of the lender's actions. These claims could include UDAP violations committed in the conduct of the sale, as well as in the making of the mortgage itself. A number of reported UDAP cases deal specifically with foreclosures.[76]

Any and every irregularity in the sale should be highlighted for the court, in particular irregularities which may have affected the outcome of the sale. To the extent provable, the disparity between the sale price and property value should be maximized. While proving one of these factors alone may not be enough to set aside a sale, their effect is cumulative.

Advocates should also stress the importance of the state court's function in reviewing foreclosure sale prices. For many years, homeowners in most jurisdictions could have a foreclosure sale set aside as a fraudulent conveyance in bankruptcy law if the property was sold for less than "a reasonably equivalent value."[77] This is no longer the case. In *BFP v. Resolution Trust Corp.*,[78] the Supreme Court ruled that the price obtained at a "regularly conducted, non-collusive foreclosure sale is conclusive as to the value of the property" for the purposes of fraudulent transfer analysis under the Bankruptcy Code. In the Supreme Court's view, at least under bankruptcy law, the foreclosure sale price establishes the value of the property, absent some irregularity in the foreclosure sale.[79] As a result of *BFP*, control of the foreclosure process and foreclosure sale prices now rests almost entirely with the state courts.

In most states, where foreclosures are conducted non-judicially by power of sale, the only safeguards against unfair prices are statutory notice requirements, and the state common law imposing a duty of good faith on the foreclosing mortgage holder. Statutory notice requirements are designed to insure a fair price by attracting the largest number of potential bidders, with the expectation that more bidders will mean higher prices. In reality, however, this purpose is rarely achieved. The mortgage holder may be the only bidder at the foreclosure sale, even when the sale is properly noticed. In light of *BFP*, state courts should be urged to look beyond technical compliance with state foreclosure laws to determine whether the purpose of these laws is being served. That purpose is to insure a fair sale and fair price to protect the rights of the borrower—not to make foreclosure as easy and as profitable as possible for the mortgage holder.[80]

---

70 17 Mass. L. Rptr. 27, 2003 WL 22519518, at *5 (Mass. Super. Ct. 2003) (unreported).

71 Looper v. Madison Guarantee, 729 S.W.2d 156, 157 (Ark. 1987). *Cf.* Smith v. Rusmisell, 517 S.E.2d 494 (W. Va. 1999) (reversing decision setting aside sale at 56% of actual value because the court did not have evidence that the sale price shocked the judicial conscience).

72 Ballentyne v. Smith, 205 U.S. 285, 291 (1907).

73 *In re* Krohn, 203 Ariz. 205, 52 P.3d 774 (Ariz. 2002); Looper v. Madison Guarantee, 729 S.W.2d 156, 157 (Ark. 1987).

74 *In re* Krohn, 52 P.3d 774 (Ariz. 2002) ("[W]indfall profits, like those reaped by bidders paying grossly inadequate prices at foreclosure sales, do not serve the public interest and do no more than legally enrich speculators").

75 Unfair and deceptive acts and practices. *See generally* National Consumer Law Center, Unfair and Deceptive Acts and Practices (7th ed. 2008 and Supp.).

76 *See id.* § 5.1.1.5.6.

77 11 U.S.C. § 548(a)(2). *See, e.g.*, Barrett v. Commonwealth Fed. Sav. & Loan, 939 F.2d 20 (3d Cir. 1991); *In re* Littleton, 888 F.2d 90 (11th Cir. 1989).

The court also noted that it had found no cases in which payment of less that 70% was considered fair equivalent value.

78 511 U.S. 531, 114 S. Ct. 1757, 128 L. Ed. 2d 556 (1994).

79 *See generally* § 14.2.4, *infra*.

80 *See In re* Krohn, 52 P.3d 774 (Ariz. 2002) (courts of equity should assure debtors receive not only procedural but fundamental fairness).

Courts should also be pressed to rigorously enforce the covenant of good faith and due diligence and to invalidate sales made by mortgage holders for their own advantage, without regard for the rights of the debtor.

Finally, it should be noted that even if the foreclosure sale price is not so inadequate that the sale must be set aside, it may nevertheless be sufficiently low to justify the denial of a claim for a deficiency judgment.[81]

14.2.4 Setting Aside a Foreclosure Sale in Bankruptcy

14.2.4.1 Sales That Violate the Automatic Stay

14.2.4.1.1 General

Sales that are conducted in violation of the automatic stay[82] are generally void and can be set aside on that ground alone.[83] This means that any foreclosure sale taken after a bankruptcy filing is without legal effect[84] even sales completed just minutes after a bankruptcy petition is filed.[85] This is true whether or not the seller had knowledge of the stay, though there are limited exceptions to this general rule.[86] If the lender willfully violated the stay, the debtor may be entitled to damages.[87]

81 *See* § 14.3.3, *infra*.

82 11 U.S.C. § 362.

For further discussion of the automatic stay that goes into effect at the time a bankruptcy petition is filed, see generally § 9.3, *supra*, and National Consumer Law Center, Consumer Bankruptcy Law and Practice Ch. 9 (9th ed. 2009).

83 Kalb v. Feuerstein, 308 U.S. 433, 60 S. Ct. 343, 84 L. Ed. 370 (1940); *In re* Cueva, 371 F.3d 232 (5th Cir. 2004); *In re* Mitchell, 279 B.R. 839 (B.A.P. 9th Cir. 2002); *In re* Ford, 296 B.R. 537 (Bankr. N.D. Ga. 2003). *See also* Borg-Warner Acceptance Corp. v. Hall, 685 F.2d 1306 (11th Cir. 1982). *But see In re* Coho Res., Inc., 345 F.3d 338 (5th Cir. 2003) (violations are merely "voidable" and are subject to discretionary "cure" through annulment of stay); *In re* King, 35 B.R. 530 (Bankr. N.D. Ga. 1983) (automatic stay did not void foreclosure sale which occurred an hour after debtor's chapter 13 filing when sale of property by mortgage holder was made to good faith purchasers, who were without knowledge of commencement of chapter 13 case, and who paid fair, equivalent value for property, and no copy of chapter 13 petition was filed in county recording office prior to consummation of foreclosure sale).

84 *E.g.*, 40235 Wash. St. Corp. v. Lusardi, 329 F.3d 1076 (9th Cir. 2003) (tax foreclosure auction in violation of stay was void even though bankruptcy case later dismissed); *In re* Shamblin, 890 F.2d 123 (9th Cir. 1989) (tax sale held in violation of the stay is void); *In re* Ward, 837 F.2d 124 (3d Cir. 1988) (foreclosure sale occurring in violation of the stay is void); *In re* Burg, 295 B.R. 698 (Bankr. W.D.N.Y. 2003) (tax foreclosure sale conducted in violation of automatic stay was void, and did not give purchaser good title to property or any right to obtain relief of the stay for the purpose of evicting the debtor); *In re* Donovan, 266 B.R. 862 (Bankr. S.D. Iowa 2001) (tax deed issued to purchaser at pre-petition tax sale in violation of the stay was void; under state law purchaser does not acquire legal title until tax deed is issued).

85 *See In re* Brown, 311 B.R. 721 (Bankr. W.D. Pa. 2004) (foreclosure sale void because clerk had physical custody of the documents before the sale where paper petition and filing fee handed to court clerk at 9:00 a.m., clerk finished scanning documents and gave the case a number with electronic time stamp as filed at 9:30 a.m., and foreclosure sale took place at 9:15 a.m.); *In re* Schleier, 290 B.R. 45 (Bankr. S.D.N.Y. 2003) (when petition was filed at 9:05 and foreclosure sale completed at 9:15, sale was void; court addressed issue of when "filing" occurs and held that petition is filed when it is the possession of the clerk and is in a condition acceptable for filing; date and time-stamp on a bankruptcy petition creates a rebuttable presumption as to when it was filed, which debtor may rebut with evidence of earlier filing). *But see In re* Sands, 328 B.R. 614 (Bankr. N.D.N.Y. 2005) (stay not in effect to void foreclosure sale when debtor's counsel logged on to CM/ECF eleven minutes before the sale, but all pages not scanned and a "Notice of Electronic Filing" not generated until approximately one hour after the sale).

86 *E.g.*, *In re* Smith, 876 F.2d 524 (6th Cir. 1989) (post-petition sale of repossessed car is void even though bank had no notice of stay); Zestee Foods, Inc. v. Phillips Foods Corp., 536 F.2d 334 (10th Cir. 1976); *In re* Mitchell, 279 B.R. 839 (B.A.P. 9th Cir. 2002) (foreclosure sale conducted in violation of automatic stay was void, and could not be validated by foreclosure sale purchaser's post-petition recording of its deed; § 549 does not protect bona fide purchasers for value when sale is in violation of automatic stay); *In re* Jackson, 392 B.R. 666 (Bankr. S.D. Miss. 2008) (debtor had possessory interest in deceased parent's home under state law; therefore home was part of debtor's bankruptcy estate and post-petition foreclosure sale was voidable despite lack of notice of bankruptcy and sale to third party); *In re* Cooper, 273 B.R. 297 (Bankr. D.D.C. 2002) (under D.C. law, upon default of successful bidder at foreclosure sale, right of redemption revests in debtor, and if debtor then files bankruptcy, a subsequent foreclosure is in violation of the automatic stay, even if mortgage holder was not aware of filing). *See In re* Stockwell, 262 B.R. 275 (Bankr. Vt. 2001) (court validated sale undertaken in violation of automatic stay but debtor's redemption period was reinstated); *In re* Williams, 257 B.R. 297 (Bankr. W.D. Mo. 2001) (court validated sale conducted in violation of the automatic stay because debtor did not act in good faith with respect to the mortgage debt or the foreclosure proceedings). *But see In re* King, 35 B.R. 530 (Bankr. N.D. Ga. 1983) (automatic stay did not void foreclosure sale which occurred an hour after debtor's chapter 13 filing when sale of property by mortgage holder was made to good faith purchasers, who were without knowledge of commencement of chapter 13 case, and who paid fair, equivalent value for property, and no copy of chapter 13 petition was filed in county recording office prior to consummation of foreclosure sale).

87 11 U.S.C. § 362(k). *See In re* Chestnut, 422 F.3d 298 (5th Cir. 2005) (although debtor had only an "arguable claim" to a valid interest in the subject property—a claim which later proved to be meritless—creditor's belief that the property was not part of the bankruptcy estate did not prevent assessment of fines and penalties for willful stay violation in proceeding with the sale while stay in effect); *In re* Noland, 2009 WL 4758651 (Bankr. N.D. Ala. Dec. 7, 2009) (awarding damages where bank initiated foreclosure proceedings post-petition); *In re* Crawford, 388 B.R. 506 (S.D.N.Y. 2008) (mortgage lender could not, by using system of agents and sub-agents, avoid liability for punitive damages related to post-petition foreclosure sale); *In re* Lynn-

Because the sale is void, the law does not require that the sale be set aside by the bankruptcy court. Instead the action to have the sale declared void can be brought as a quiet title action or otherwise in state court. However, because the bankruptcy court has the most experience and interest in vindicating the automatic stay, that forum may provide the best opportunity to pursue this issue.

A few courts have held that a sale held in violation of the stay is voidable rather than void.[88] The majority of the time, this will be a distinction without a difference, because the court will choose to set-aside the voidable action. However, a determination that a sale is voidable rather than void allows the court to ratify the sale, most often by annulling the automatic stay (lifting the stay retroactively).[89] Usually, the courts will do this only on a showing that enforcing the stay would be unfair to the lender for some reason other than the difficulty of undoing the voidable action.[90] For example, the stay has been annulled in a few cases, when the court concluded that the debtor filed bankruptcy and obtained the stay in bad faith.[91]

14.2.4.1.2 Where automatic stay does not apply

Exceptions to the force of an automatic stay are discussed in more detail at § 9.3, *supra*.[92] This subsection provides a brief overview. The Bankruptcy Code generally limits the duration of the automatic stay to thirty days for debtors who had a prior case dismissed within one year before the new filing date.[93] However, debtors who promptly follow mandatory procedural steps and meet a two-tier burden of proof to show good faith in the new filing may obtain an extension

Weaver, 385 B.R. 7 (Bankr. D. Mass. 2008) (five post-petition continuances of foreclosure sale violated automatic stay); *In re* Dawson, 346 B.R. 503 (Bankr. N.D. Cal. 2006) (debtor awarded emotional distress damages); *In re* Kaufman, 315 B.R. 858 (Bankr. N.D. Cal. 2004) (substantial punitive and other damages awarded against a mortgage company that auctioned personal property in the debtor's residence after a foreclosure sale, in violation of stay); *In re* Dominguez, 312 B.R. 499 (Bankr. S.D.N.Y. 2004) (taxing authority willfully violated stay when it obtained post-petition foreclosure judgment without moving for relief from stay, although it had received notice of the debtor-taxpayer's chapter 7 filing; debtor was entitled to damages); *In re* Mauck, 287 B.R. 219 (Bankr. E.D. Mo. 2002) (notice of bankruptcy sent to mortgage servicing agent at address provided for debtor to send payments was sufficient to show that servicing agent, and through it the mortgage holder, were on notice of debtors' chapter 13 filing, such that their subsequent stay violation in mailing debtors a notice of foreclosure was a "willful" violation, for which debtors could recover reasonable attorney fees and costs). *See also In re* Crawford, 388 B.R. 506 (Bankr. S.D.N.Y. 2008) (referee's conduct of foreclosure sale and act of mortgage holder's subagent in making a bid despite knowledge of bankruptcy were willful violations of stay meriting $60,000 punitive damages against mortgage holder, but none against referee due to his legitimate confusion).

88 Easley v. Pettibone Michigan Corp., 990 F.2d 905 (6th Cir. 1993) (actions in violation of stay are voidable and shall be voided absent limited equitable circumstances); *In re* Williams, 257 B.R. 297 (Bankr. W.D. Mo. 2001). *See also* Fed. Deposit Ins. Corp. v. Shearson-American Express, Inc., 996 F.2d 493 (1st Cir. 1993) (even if an attachment violated the stay, an unappealed bankruptcy court order finding that the stay had not been violated was not subject to collateral attack, so that the attachment was deemed valid).

89 *See* Franklin v. Office of Thrift Supervision, 31 F.3d 1020 (10th Cir. 1994) (power to annul stay should rarely be used, probably only in cases of claimants who were honestly ignorant of stay); *In re* Siciliano, 13 F.3d 748 (3d Cir. 1994) (court had authority to annul stay in proper circumstances). *See also In re* Alipio, 380 B.R. 645 (Bankr. D. Conn. 2007) (to receive annulment of stay, creditor must show extreme circumstances and unusually compelling facts); Emigrant Sav. Bank v. Rappaport, 799 N.Y.S.2d 533 (App. Div. 2005) (only bankruptcy court, not state court, has jurisdiction to annul the automatic stay retroactively and validate a foreclosure sale that took place while stay was in effect); Homestead Lending, Inc. v. Watts, 792 N.Y.S.2d 513 (App. Div. 2005) (same).

90 *See In re* Soares, 107 F.3d 969 (1st Cir. 1997) (annulment should not be granted to validate foreclosure when mortgage holder knew of bankruptcy and failed to inform state court); *In re* Williams, 323 B.R. 691, 702 (B.A.P. 9th Cir. 2005) (although stay was annulled retroactively to validate a foreclosure sale, creditor may still be liable for damages under § 362(h) for conducting sale before the annulment order), *aff'd*, 204 Fed. Appx. 582 (9th Cir. Oct. 12, 2006); *In re* Spriggs, 219 B.R. 909 (B.A.P. 10th Cir. 1998) (annulment not granted on equitable grounds, fees for void sale disallowed); *In re* WorldCom, Inc., 325 B.R. 511 (Bankr. S.D.N.Y. 2005) (denying creditor's request for retroactive annulment of stay and discussing significant differences in legal tests for retroactive annulment of stay and termination of stay under § 362(d)); *In re* Adams, 215 B.R. 194 (Bankr. W.D. Mo. 1997) (although creditor innocently violated stay, annulment not granted when relief from the stay would not have been granted had it been sought). *See also In re* Major, 218 B.R. 501 (Bankr. W.D. Mo. 1998) (stay not annulled and creditor not entitled to protection from avoidance of a post-petition transfer under 11 U.S.C. § 549(c)).

91 *See, e.g., In re* Albany Partners, 749 F.2d 670 (11th Cir. 1984); *In re* Bright, 338 B.R. 530 (B.A.P. 1st Cir. 2006) (upholding finding of "unusual and unusually compelling circumstances" justifying annulment of the stay where debtor had failed to disclose her ownership interest in the property in her schedules, innocent third party had purchased the property, and debtor delayed in asserting an objection to the sale); *In re* Fjeldsted, 293 B.R. 12 (B.A.P. 9th Cir. 2003) (citing twelve factors to be considered in determining whether to annul the stay); *In re* Campbell, 356 B.R. 722 (Bankr. W.D. Mo. 2006) (repeat filer acted in bad faith); *In re* Askew, 312 B.R. 274 (Bankr. D.N.J. 2004) (debtor had engaged in repeat filings, stay annulled retroactively); *In re* Duprey, 308 B.R. 843 (Bankr. E.D. Tenn. 2004); *In re* Williams, 257 B.R. 297 (Bankr. W.D. Mo. 2001) (court validated sale conducted in violation of the automatic stay because debtor did not act in good faith with respect to the mortgage debt or the foreclosure proceedings). *See also* Rowe v. Ocwen Sav. Bank & Trust, 220 B.R. 591 (E.D. Tex. 1997) (debtor had filed four previous bankruptcy cases); Vereen v. Deutsche Bank Nat'l Trust Co., 646 S.E.2d 667 (Ga. 2007) (bankruptcy court's annulment of stay, based on finding of debtor's bad faith, retroactively validated sale).

92 See also 24 NCLC REPORTS, Bankruptcy and Foreclosures Ed. (Sept./Oct. 2005).

93 11 U.S.C. § 362(c)(3).

of the stay beyond the initial thirty days.[94] On the other hand, the automatic stay will not go into effect at all for debtors who had two or more cases dismissed within the prior year.[95] Here too, the debtor may move for the imposition of the stay upon showing by clear and convincing evidence that the new filing is in good faith.

Debtors filing for bankruptcy must file with the petition a certificate of timely completion of a briefing from an approved credit counseling agency.[96] The ability to defer or waive this requirement is very limited and noncompliance with this requirement can have severe consequences for a debtor seeking to stay an imminent foreclosure sale. According to some courts, the "dismissal" of a bankruptcy filing for noncompliance with this requirement will burden the debtor with the "repeat filer" limitation on the duration of the automatic stay in a second case filed within a year of the dismissal.[97]

Moreover, there is an issue whether a petition filed without the credit counseling certification triggers the automatic stay.[98] The only certain way to avoid these controversies is to be familiar with the counseling requirement, have the client obtain the briefing pre-petition and file the statement certifying compliance with the petition. Counseling agencies approved by the Office of the U.S. Trustee must make the certifications available at no charge to debtors who cannot afford to pay the cost of the phone, Internet or in-person briefing sessions. Without waiver, the cost of the sessions generally runs about $50 per case.

The automatic stay also will not arise where a debtor files in violation of Bankruptcy Code § 109(g) or of a prior court order limiting the individual's right to bankruptcy protections.[99] Courts can also deny stay protections prospectively on an *in rem* basis for up to two years with respect to a particular property, upon appropriate findings and the recording of the order in the land records.[100] Finally, a new exception to the automatic stay related to voidable post-petition transfers has given rise to some uncertainty as to its meaning and intent.[101]

14.2.4.2 Fraudulent Transfers—11 U.S.C. § 548

For many years and in most jurisdictions, when a home was sold at a foreclosure sale for an amount significantly less than its market value, the homeowner could utilize the trustee's power under 11 U.S.C. § 548(a)(1)(B)[102] (the constructive fraudulent transfer provision of the Code) to have the sale set aside in bankruptcy in most states.[103] Once the sale was set aside the homeowner could either redeem the property through refinancing, raise defenses to the enforcement of the mortgage, or cure the default through chapter 13. Unfortunately, in 1994, the Supreme Court made this much harder to do.

In *BFP v. Resolution Trust Corp.*,[104] the Supreme Court ruled that the price obtained at a "regularly conducted, non-collusive foreclosure sale is conclusive as to the value of the property." The Court concluded that reasonably

94 *See In re* Castaneda, 342 B.R. 90 (Bankr. S.D. Cal. 2006); *In re* Galanis, 334 B.R. 685 (Bankr. D. Utah 2005); *In re* Charles, 334 B.R. 207 (Bankr S.D. Tex. 2005).

95 11 U.S.C. § 362(c)(4).

96 11 U.S.C. § 109(h). *In re* Mitrano, 409 B.R. 812 (E.D. Va. 2009) (outside limited provisions for obtaining waiver or deferment under § 109(h)(2), (3), (4) bankruptcy court did not have discretion to modify the counseling requirement). *See* National Consumer Law Center, Consumer Bankruptcy Law and Practice Ch. 7 (9th ed. 2009) (discussion of the credit counseling requirements).

97 *Compare In re* Ross, 338 B.R. 134 (Bankr. D. Ga. 2006) (filing by ineligible debtor under § 109(h) commences a case that must be "dismissed") *with In re* Elmendorf, 345 B.R. 486 (Bankr. S.D.N.Y. 2006) (court has discretion to "strike" a petition filed by ineligible debtor and treat case as if it never commenced, noting judicial disagreement over issue).

98 *Compare In re* Brown, 342 B.R. 248 (Bankr. D. Md. 2006) (foreclosure sale conducted after petition date and before dismissal of case for noncompliance with § 109(h) was void as conducted in violation of stay) *with In re* Salazar, 339 B.R. 622 (Bankr. S.D. Tex. 2006) (debtor who filed petition without counseling certificate was never eligible to file, and stay never went into effect even temporarily).

99 11 U.S.C. § 362(b)(21).

100 11 U.S.C. § 362(b)(20), (d)(4). *See generally In re* Johnson, 346 B.R. 190 (B.A.P. 9th Cir. 2006) (applying pre-2005 Act law, but noting that new restriction would not apply in the new case before it).

101 11 U.S.C. § 362(b)(24). *See* David A. Young, *Overview of Changes to the Automatic Stay Under the Bankruptcy Abuse and Consumer Protection Act of 2005*, 887 Practicing Law Inst. 441 (2006) (suggesting, without any support from legislative history, that the new subsection was intended to overrule much of the well-established case law holding that post-petition foreclosure sales held in contravention of the stay are void).

However, the legislative history to the 2005 Act suggests that the stay exception in § 362(b)(24) was not so far-reaching and was intended to respond to the decision in Thompson v. Margen (In re McConville), 84 F.3d 340 (9th Cir. 1996). *See* H. Rep. No. 109-31, 109th Cong., 1st Sess. 75–76 (2005).

102 Under section 548(a), a transfer is subject to avoidance as a fraudulent conveyance if it occurred within one year before the bankruptcy case was filed, the debtor received less than a "reasonably equivalent value" from the foreclosure, and:

- The debtor was insolvent on the date of the foreclosure or became insolvent as a result of it; or
- The debtor was engaged in business or was about to engage in a business or transaction with unreasonably small capital; or
- The debtor intended to incur, or believed that he or she would incur, debts beyond his or her ability to pay.

Section 548(a) was amended by the 2005 Bankruptcy Act to extend the look-back period from one year to two years. This amendment is effective for cases filed on or after April 20, 2006. *See* Pub. L. No. 109-8, § 1404(b) (2005).

103 *See* Durrett v. Wash. Nat'l Ins. Co., 621 F.2d 201 (5th Cir. 1980) (foreclosure sale price of 57.7% of property's value not a "fair equivalent value"; the court also noted that it had found no cases in which payment of less than 70% was considered fair equivalent value).

104 511 U.S. 531, 114 S. Ct. 1757, 128 L. Ed. 2d 556 (1994).

equivalent value must take into account the circumstances of the transfer, that is, that the property is subject to a forced sale. Given *BFP*, only if the sale was not regularly conducted or was collusive in some way, may section 548 be invoked to set aside the sale.[105] Additionally, if foreclosure does not involve a sale at all, but rather is a forfeiture of property (such as by strict foreclosure in Connecticut or Vermont), *BFP* should be considered inapplicable.[106]

The Supreme Court expressly limited its holding in *BFP* to foreclosures of real estate, stating that "the considerations bearing on other foreclosures and forced sales (to satisfy tax liens, for example) may be different."[107] For tax foreclosures which do not involve a formal sale of the property (i.e., where the purchaser obtains a lien or a certificate rather than an actual deed), the *BFP* analysis should not be relevant.[108] Typically, the purchaser of a tax lien pays only the amount of delinquent taxes, an amount which bears no relationship to the value of the property. For this reason, there is no logical basis on which to conclude that the tax lien purchase price is a "reasonably equivalent value."

14.2.4.3 Using State Law Invalidity to Set Aside a Sale in Bankruptcy Court

State law may provide alternative grounds which can be used to invalidate a sale in bankruptcy court. A sale which is invalid under state law for any reason is equally invalid in the bankruptcy process. Presumably, if the sale is void or voidable, a declaratory judgment can be obtained that the property involved remains property of the estate.[109] If the grounds which produce state law invalidity also take the sale outside of the protections of *BFP* because it was not "regularly conducted," then the requirements of a fraudulent transfer case can be pleaded in the alternative.[110]

A case decided by the federal bankruptcy court in Massachusetts illustrates the importance of these principles. In *In re Edry*,[111] the bankruptcy court invalidated a foreclosure sale to a third party on the grounds that in conducting the foreclosure sale the bank did not make, in good faith, a diligent effort to protect the interests of the mortgagor, although it complied with the statutory requirements.[112] The court set aside the sale based on its invalidity under state law without evaluating *BFP* or Bankruptcy Code § 548.

The court based its conclusion on several factors, including: the bank's failure to advertise the sale by "display" ads, which were customary in the area; the bank's failure to obtain a current appraisal of the property; the inadequate price obtained at the sale, which was less than 50% of the

105 *See In re* Ryker, 301 B.R. 156 (D.N.J. 2003) (foreclosure sale set aside as fraudulent transfer, though sale was conducted in manner that did not literally violate express requirements of New Jersey law, when as result of postponement of sale and debtor-mortgagor's payment of roughly 75% of mortgage debt, and of mortgage holder's failure to readvertise sale to indicate that such a substantial payment had been made, the notice was rendered defective such that it would deter competitive bidding, and mortgage holder was able to purchase property for amount that was far less than its fair market value). *See also In re* Thorian, 387 B.R. 50 (Bankr. D. Idaho 2008) (failure to provide notice required by deed of trust does not permit avoidance of foreclosure sale unless failure would support invalidation of sale under state law). *See generally* National Consumer Law Center, Consumer Bankruptcy Law and Practice § 10.4.2.6.5 (9th ed. 2009).

106 *See In re* Chase, 328 B.R. 675 (Bankr. D. Vt. 2005) (foreclosure sale conducted in accordance with Vermont's strict foreclosure law does not create presumption of transfer for reasonably equivalent value under *BFP*); *In re* Fitzgerald, 255 B.R. 807 (Bankr. D. Conn. 2000) (*BFP* decision not applicable to strict foreclosure); *In re* Grady, 202 B.R. 120 (Bankr. N.D. Iowa 1996) (*BFP* does not apply to forfeiture of real estate installment sale contract; property interest of $40,000 forfeited to satisfy $16,000 debt under the contract constituted fraudulent transfer). *But see* Talbot v. Fed. Home Loan Mortgage Corp., 254 B.R. 63 (Bankr. D. Conn. 2000) (*BFP* does apply as state's strict foreclosure law is analogous to a foreclosure sale). *See generally* Janet Flaccus, *Pre-Petition and Post-Petition Mortgage Foreclosure and Tax Sales and the Faulty Reasoning of the Supreme Court*, 51 Ark. L. Rev. 25 (1998).

Tax transfers under some states' strict foreclosure procedures also may be challenged. *E.g.*, *In re* Butler, 171 B.R. 321 (Bankr. N.D. Ill. 1994); *In re* McKeever, 132 B.R. 996 (Bankr. N.D. Ill. 1991).

In Illinois, the property transfer is an administrative act based on prior sale of the *tax lien* and a failure to redeem; there is no property sale to which the *BFP* analysis could apply.

107 *BFP*, 114 S. Ct. 1757, at n.3. *But see In re* McGrath, 170 B.R. 78 (Bankr. D.N.J. 1994) (applying *BFP* analysis to tax sales).

108 *E.g.*, *In re* Sherman, 223 B.R. 555 (B.A.P. 10th Cir. 1998) (*BFP* does not apply to Wyoming tax sale when statutory procedure does not provide for competitive bidding); *In re* Butler, 171 B.R. 321 (Bankr. N.D. Ill. 1994); *In re* McKeever, 132 B.R. 996 (Bankr. N.D. Ill. 1991).

In Illinois, the property transfer is an administrative act based on prior sale of the tax lien and a failure to redeem; there is no property sale to which the *BFP* analysis could apply. *See also In re* Grandoe Country Club Co., Ltd., 252 F.3d 1146 (10th Cir. 2001) (*BFP* analysis applied because tax sale under state law subject to competitive bidding procedure).

109 11 U.S.C. § 541.

An adversary proceeding would be required. A turn over order should be requested. The court would have core jurisdiction under 11 U.S.C. § 157(b)(2)(E), (O).

110 *See In re* Fritz, 225 B.R. 218 (E.D. Wash. 1997) (debtor has burden to establish that sale was not "regularly conducted"). *See generally* National Consumer Law Center, Consumer Bankruptcy Law and Practice § 10.4.2.6.5 (9th ed. 2009).

111 201 B.R. 604 (Bankr. D. Mass. 1996) (Queenan, J.).

112 *See also In re* LaPointe, 253 B.R. 496 (D. Mass. 2000) (mortgage holder's failure to use reasonable diligence in conducting sale, by failing to provide notice to a party it knew to be interested in buying property and failing to use customary display advertising, resulted in set-off against deficiency claim for damages caused by mortgage holder's lack of diligence). *Cf. In re* Greenberg, 229 B.R. 544 (B.A.P. 1st Cir. 1999) (sale not set aside on evidence that lender complied with statutory requirements).

property's fair market value. The court concluded that under Massachusetts law, a foreclosing mortgage holder must do more than comply with the procedure prescribed by the statute: "It has been repeatedly held . . . that a mortgagee who attempts to execute a power of sale contained in a mortgage is bound to exercise good faith, and to use reasonable diligence to protect the rights and interests of the mortgagor under the contract. . . . It is his duty, for the benefit of the mortgagor whom he represents, so as to act in the execution of the power as to obtain for the property, as large a price as possible."[113]

In addition to finding that the bank had not fulfilled its duty to the mortgagor, the court held that the high bidder at the foreclosure sale was not a good faith purchaser for value for two reasons. First, the high bidder was an experienced purchaser at foreclosure sales who knew of the usual practice of advertising through display ads.[114]

Second, because the buyer never completed the sales transaction the court concluded that he was not in fact a "purchaser." The bidder had paid a $5000 deposit and had executed a memorandum of sale under which the balance of the purchase price was to be paid within thirty days. Twenty-six days later the mortgagor filed a chapter 13 bankruptcy, and shortly thereafter the bankruptcy judge issued an injunction to prevent the completion of the sale, pending trial.[115] On these grounds, the court invalidated the foreclosure sale.

The state law legal principles which define the duty of a foreclosing mortgage holder, on which *Edry* is based, are widely recognized and are of long standing.[116] Decisions setting aside sales on these grounds are typically very fact specific, suggesting the importance of the advocate's role in identifying irregularities or flaws in the conduct of the sale.[117]

Other examples of defects that may take a case outside the protection of *BFP* may include the failure to adequately notice a postponed sale, or to properly advertise the sale, or any other action which discourages competitive bidding at the sale.[118] Collusion may be shown when the lender has an agreement with the purchaser or with potential bidders which is contrary to the interest of the borrower. Because the mortgage holder has a duty to exercise good faith and diligence in the conducting a foreclosure sale of property,[119] the mortgage holder must remain at arm's length with the buyer.[120]

The difficulty with this type of challenge will be proving that the price actually obtained at the irregular sale was lower than what would have been obtained at a regularly conducted foreclosure sale. Though when the sale price is grossly out of proportion to the property's market value, the homeowner should argue that no regularly conducted sale could yield such a low price.

Given these arguments, foreclosure sales which bring far less than the real value of the property should continue to be carefully evaluated with discovery if necessary. Setting aside the sale can allow a debtor to exempt an interest in the equity and thereby to obtain a resource following bankruptcy. If the debtor is in chapter 13, once the property is recovered for the estate, the debtor can deal with the secured claim by curing the default under the plan.

113 *See* Clark v. Simmons, 23 N.E. 108 (Mass. 1890). "Good faith and reasonable regard for the interest of the mortgagor will not permit him to make a sale when no one will offer a price which another could reasonably think of accepting if he were obliged to sell the property at a day's notice for what it would bring." 23 N.E. at 108.

114 Most often, the buyer at a below market sale is the mortgage holder. Presumably, a mortgage holder cannot be a good faith purchaser in these circumstances.

115 Injunctive relief may be important to prevent completion of sales under state law, but equally important to prevent transfer of property to third parties. A judge may also feel more comfortable setting aside a sale which has not substantially progressed.

116 *See* Johnson v. Jefferson Standard Life Ins. Co., 429 P.2d 474 (Ariz. Ct. App. 1967) (sale of property valued at $73,000 for $5000 was set aside; attorney for mortgage holder arrived eight minutes late with a bid for $56,000, and the purchaser at the sale prevailed upon the deputy sheriff to accept bids without reading notice of sale); MacFarlane v. MacFarlane, 39 So. 995 (Fla. 1905) (when notice of sale was published in a town twenty miles from city where property located and which had a small circulation in the city, and where property located in a city where several newspapers are published, and price bid for property was inadequate (bid was $100, value was $7500), sale set aside); Bon v. Graves, 103 N.E. 1023 (Mass. 1914) (notice placed in newspaper which had limited local circulation, failure to give personal notice to two known potential purchasers, and a price disparity invalidated sale); Ten Hills Co. v. Ten Hills Corp., 5 A.2d 830 (Md. 1939) (trustee, appointed under a mortgage foreclosure decree to sell mortgaged property was bound to exercise same degree of care, diligence and judgment that prudent man of ordinary business experience in selling his own property to best advantage; court found no lack or required care in failure to sell property in lots when mortgagor was unable to sell sufficient lots to pay interest on prior mortgage and taxes); Strawberry Commons Apartment Owners Ass'n, 356 N.W.2d 401 (Minn. Ct. App. 1984) (grossly inadequate price (5% of value), combined with lack of actual notice to owner, excessive attorney fees (fees were $764 and sale price was $1200), and inability of owner to exercise right of redemption due to lack of notice, required setting aside of sale); Gumz v. Chickering, 121 N.W.2d 279 (Wis. 1963) (when highest bid at sale was $87,000, a third party had previously offered to bid $100,000, fair market value was $140,000, and there was confusion about the authority of the bidder, sale must be set aside).

117 *See, e.g.*, Brown v. Freedman, 474 S.E.2d 73 (Ga. Ct. App. 1996) (mortgage holder's failure to tell heir what was owed, fact that mortgage holder took personal property from the home, and purchased property at foreclosure sale for one-fifth of its fair market value, could support finding that he exercised the power of sale unfairly).

118 *See In re* Bundles, 856 F.2d 815, 824 (7th Cir. 1988).

119 Mills v. Mut. Bldg. & Loan Ass'n, 6 S.E.2d 549 (N.C. 1940).

120 Holman v. Ryon, 56 F.2d 307 (D.C. Cir. 1932) (sale by trustee to his wife at less than adequate price is breach of duty).

14.2.4.4 Preferences—11 U.S.C. § 547

With certain exceptions, set forth in Bankruptcy Code § 547(c), the bankruptcy trustee[121] may avoid any transfer of the debtor's property:

- To or for the benefit of a creditor;[122]
- For or on account of an antecedent debt owed by the debtor before such transfer was made;[123]
- Made while the debtor was insolvent;[124]
- Made within ninety days before the date of filing of the petition[125] or between ninety days and one year before the date of filing of the petition, if such creditor, at the time of such transfer was an insider;[126] and
- That enables such creditor to receive more than such creditor would receive if the case were a chapter 7 case, the transfer had not been made, and such creditor received payment of such debt to the extent provided by the provisions of the Code.[127]

121 The debtor's use of § 547(c) is subject to the limitations of § 522(g). *See* National Consumer Law Center, Consumer Bankruptcy Law and Practice § 10.4.2.6.4 (9th ed. 2009).

122 The benefit may be indirect, as when a guarantor benefits from the payment of a debt of the debtor which he or she guaranteed. Because the guarantor would normally have a contingent claim against the debtor for contribution or indemnification in the event the guarantor ultimately paid the debt, the guarantor is a creditor who benefits from the transfer and has therefore received a preference. Levit v. Ingersoll Rand Fin. Corp., 874 F.2d 1186 (7th Cir. 1989) (payments to non-insider creditors made at arms length are preferences subject to one-year limitations period because the payments ultimately benefit insider guarantors); *In re* C-L Cartage Co., 899 F.2d 1490 (6th Cir. 1990) (same); *In re* Robinson Bros. Drilling, 877 F.2d 32 (10th Cir. 1989) (same). *See also In re* Wesley Indus., 30 F.3d 1438 (11th Cir. 1994) (transfer of cash collateral that benefited insider within one year before petition could be a preference).

123 The transfer of a security interest in connection with a car loan, for example, is not on account of an antecedent debt. *In re* McFarland, 131 B.R. 627 (E.D. Tenn. 1990), *aff'd*, 943 F.2d 52 (6th Cir. 1991).

124 Insolvent is defined in 11 U.S.C. § 101(32) in a way that would include virtually all low-income debtors. Under that definition, a debtor is solvent only if his or her assets exclusive of exempt property exceed his or her obligations. *In re* Babiker, 180 B.R. 458 (Bankr. E.D. Va. 1995). *See also In re* Taxman Clothing Co., 905 F.2d 166 (7th Cir. 1990) (costs of sale must be deducted in computing debtor's assets); *In re* Koubourlis, 869 F.2d 1319 (9th Cir. 1989) (creditor must present evidence to rebut presumption of insolvency and cannot simply question debtor's accounting methods); Porter v. Yukon Nat'l Bank, 866 F.2d 355 (10th Cir. 1989) (trustee need not present expert evidence concerning insolvency); *In re* Xonics Photochemical, Inc., 841 F.2d 198 (7th Cir. 1988) (contingent asset or liability must be reduced to its present or expected value for purposes of determining debtor's insolvency).

Under 11 U.S.C. § 547(f), there is a rebuttable presumption that the debtor was insolvent during the ninety days prior to filing a case. Once the presumption is rebutted, the burden of persuasion may shift back to the debtor or trustee. Clay v. Traders Bank of Kansas City, 708 F.2d 1347 (8th Cir. 1983).

125 The ninety-day period is calculated by counting backwards from the petition filing date. *In re* Nelson Co., 959 F.2d 1260 (3d Cir. 1992). The period is not extended just because the final day for filing falls on a weekend or holiday. *In re* Greene, 223 F.3d 1064 (9th Cir. 2000). Conversion from one chapter to another does not start the running of a new preference period. Vogel v. Russell Transfer, Inc., 852 F.2d 797 (4th Cir. 1988). The Code provides that a transfer is perfected only when a bona fide purchaser from the debtor of real property or a judicial lien creditor on a simple contract for personal property or fixtures cannot acquire an interest superior to the trustee. 11 U.S.C. § 547(e). Thus, a transfer of a security interest normally occurs only when it has been perfected. *In re* Nelson Co., 959 F.2d 1260 (3d Cir. 1992) (transfer of judicial lien occurs when judgment is filed and docketed in county where debtor owns property); *In re* Butler, 3 B.R. 182 (Bankr. E.D. Tenn. 1980). *See also* Decatur Contracting v. Belin, Belin & Naddeo, 898 F.2d 339 (3d Cir. 1990). But a belated perfection of a security interest may be deemed under state law to relate back to the date it was granted. *In re* Hesser, 984 F.2d 345 (10th Cir. 1993). For purposes of this section, a transfer made by check is deemed made when the check is honored. Barnhill v. Johnson, 503 U.S. 393, 112 S. Ct. 1386, 118 L. Ed. 2d 39 (1992).

126 Insider is defined at 11 U.S.C. § 101(31) to include relatives of the debtor. Relative is defined at § 101(45). *See In re* Strickland, 230 B.R. 276 (Bankr. E.D. Va. 1999) (boyfriend of debtor's mother not an insider). Many of the cases involving insiders arise from payments on debts guaranteed by insiders. *See In re* Suffola, Inc., 2 F.3d 977 (9th Cir. 1993) (payment to non-insider creditor on debt guaranteed by insider was a payment for the benefit of the insider); *In re* Robinson Bros. Drilling, 877 F.2d 32 (10th Cir. 1989) (payments to non-insider creditors may be avoided as preferential going back one year from date of bankruptcy because debtor's insiders obtained release by virtue of the payments); Levit v. Ingersoll Rand Fin. Corp., 874 F.2d 1186 (7th Cir. 1989) (payments to non-insider creditors may be avoided if made during one-year insider preference period if they benefited insiders who guaranteed the debts being paid). *See also In re* Westex Foods, Inc., 950 F.2d 1187 (5th Cir. 1992) (transfers by debtor garnishee to non-insider creditor in satisfaction of judgment against garnishee's president avoided because they benefited president, who was an insider); *In re* C-L Cartage Co., 899 F.2d 1490 (6th Cir. 1990) (payments made within year before filing to bank in satisfaction of obligation to debtor's president and president's mother were avoidable). The results, but not the reasoning, of many of these cases were overruled by a 1994 amendment creating a new § 550(c), which prohibits recovery of money or property transferred through insider preferences made more than ninety days before the petition from anyone other than the insider creditor who was preferred. However, this amendment does not prevent recovery from a non-insider when an insider was preferred during the ninety days pre-petition, nor does it prevent avoidance of the transfer without an affirmative recovery, which may be all that is necessary if, for example, the transfer was the granting of a lien on property.

127 The date on which the bankruptcy petition is filed rather than the date on which the turnover proceeding is filed is probably the correct date for constructing a hypothetical chapter 7 case to determine how much the creditor would receive. *In re* Tenna Corp., 801 F.2d 819 (6th Cir. 1986). For the purpose of creating a hypothetical distribution, payments which the debtor has voluntarily agreed to make pursuant to a reaffirmation agreement are not included. *In re* Finn, 86 B.R. 902 (Bankr. E.D. Mich. 1988), *rev'd and remanded on other grounds*, 909 F.2d

This section promotes equality among creditors by invalidating pre-bankruptcy seizures or transfers of the debtor's property that would give particular creditors more than they would get in the liquidation distribution scheme of the Code. It also serves to deter creditors from engaging in a race to get at the debtor's property before bankruptcy, because they know that if they do obtain the property and perhaps hasten a bankruptcy, they will only have to surrender it to a trustee exercising the power to avoid preferences.[128]

If a secured creditor forecloses within the preference period and the value of the property foreclosed upon is in excess of the creditor's claim, some bankruptcy courts have held that the foreclosure may be set aside as a preference.[129] The Ninth Circuit Court of Appeals, in *In re Ehring*,[130] ruled that a foreclosure within the ninety days prior to the bankruptcy filing was not a preferential transfer, even though the creditor resold the property for more than $110,000 in excess of the debt within the same ninety-day period.

The debtor in *Ehring* sought to recover the $110,000 as a preference, not to invalidate the sale.[131] The court found that each of the elements of section 547(b) was satisfied, except the requirement that the creditor receive more than it would have in a chapter 7 liquidation.[132] If a third party had outbid the creditor at the foreclosure sale, the court reasoned, there would be no preference because the price paid would not be transferred on account of an antecedent debt.[133] Finding no reason why a creditor should be treated differently than a third party bidder, the court concluded that the foreclosure was not a preference.[134] Furthermore, because the creditor would be allowed to purchase the property at a chapter 7 liquidation sale, the court assumed that the creditor could have purchased the property at the liquidation sale for the same amount it bid at the foreclosure sale, and therefore it did not receive "more" by virtue of the foreclosure.[135]

This reasoning presumes, however, that the liquidation sale in a chapter 7 is like a foreclosure sale, and would have realized the same below market price. When the transfer has resulted in a windfall to the creditor, it is presumably because there is excessive value in the property. That value is exactly what is lost to the estate through a preferential transfer. The trustee has a duty to the unsecured creditors to get the highest price for the property. If the transfer is set aside as preferential, the debtor can either cure the default and pay unsecured creditors the liquidation value of the property in chapter 13 or allow the property to be liquidated and recover the cash value of the property.

14.2.4.5 Sales That Are Not Complete Under State Law

If the debtor retains legal title to the property under state law until an event that occurs after sale such as delivery of the deed or confirmation of the sale, and the debtor files bankruptcy during that period and prior to the necessary event, then the debtor's retained ownership interest comes into the estate.[136] This principle is important because if an

---

903 (6th Cir. 1990). *See also* Rocco v. J.P. Morgan Chase Bank, 255 Fed. Appx. 638 (3d Cir. 2007) (pre-petition sheriff's sale at which mortgage holder purchased house for $1 was not avoidable preference where mortgagors had no equity; mortgagors waived TIL rescission claim by failing to raise it in foreclosure proceeding).

128 H.R. Rep. No. 95-595, at 177–178 (1977).

129 *See In re* Jones, 226 F.3d 917 (7th Cir. 2000)(sale of debtors' home following foreclosure, confirmation of sale, order of distribution, and distribution of the proceeds, all occurring within the ninety-day period, resulted in voidable preference); *In re* Villarreal, 413 B.R. 633 (Bankr. S.D. Tex. 2009) (foreclosure conducted in accordance with state law was a voidable preference because creditor received more than he would have in a chapter 7 liquidation). *See also* Norwest Bank Minn. v. Andrews, 262 B.R. 299 (Bankr. M.D. Pa. 2001) (pre-petition sale may be avoided when secured claim of foreclosing party is substantially less than the fair market value of the property); *In re* Winters, 119 B.R. 283, 284 (Bankr. M.D. Fla. 1990) (when lender purchased property at foreclosure sale for $14,284.26 (the amount of indebtedness) and then sold property for $30,000, foreclosure constituted preferential transfer); *In re* Wheeler, 34 B.R. 818 (Bankr. N.D. Ala. 1983) (FNMA received preferential transfer when it purchased property at foreclosure sale for $15,044.79 and property worth $24,000); *In re* Fountain, 32 B.R. 965, 967–968 (Bankr. W.D. Mo. 1983) (under Bankruptcy Act § 547, when there is equity in property at time of foreclosure, the foreclosure can be set aside as a preference); Basil Mattingly, *Reestablishment of Bankruptcy Review of Oppressive Foreclosure Sales: The Interaction of Avoidance Powers As Applied to Creditor Bid-Ins*, 50 S.C. L. Rev. 363 (1999); Craig A. Averich & Michael Collins, *Avoidance of Foreclosure Sales As Preferential Transfers: Another Serious Threat to Secured Creditors?*, 24 Tex. Tech. Law Rev. 985 (1993). *But see In re* Ehring, 900 F.2d 184 (9th Cir. 1990) (creditor who purchased debtor's house at foreclosure sale did not receive "more" from foreclosure than it would have under chapter 7); *In re* FIBSA Forwarding, Inc., 230 B.R. 334 (Bankr. S.D. Tex. 1999), *aff'd*, 244 B.R. 94 (S.D. Tex 1999) (reaching opposite conclusion, in same judicial district).

130 900 F.2d 184 (9th Cir. 1990). *See also In re* Fibsa Forwarding, Inc., 230 B.R. 334 (Bankr. S.D. Tex. 1999), *aff'd*, 244 B.R. 94 (S.D. Tex. 1999); Chase Manhattan Bank v. Pulcini, 261 B.R. 836 (Bankr. W.D. Pa. 2001) (transaction not avoidable when lender purchased property at a regularly conducted non-collusive sheriff's sale and then sold property to a third party for an amount greater than the amount of its lien). *But see In re* Jones, 226 F.3d 917 (7th Cir. 2000)(sale of debtors' home following foreclosure, confirmation of sale, order of distribution, and distribution of the proceeds, all occurring within the ninety-day period, resulted in voidable preference).

131 *Ehring*, 900 F.2d at 186.

132 *Id.* at 186–188. .

133 *Id.* at 188.

134 *Id.* at 188. ("Since section 547 does not reach a third party purchaser, it is difficult to see why the existence of a preference should turn on the status of the purchaser as creditor.").

135 *Id.* at 189.

136 *In re* Jenkins, 422 B.R. 175 (Bankr. E.D. Ark. 2010) (debtor can cure mortgage default where bankruptcy case was filed before trustee's deed was recorded in connection with foreclosure

auction has been held, but the sale process is not considered complete under state law, a bankruptcy debtor retains an ownership interest and the right to cure the default under 11 U.S.C. § 1322(c)(1).

In addition to the precedents on this issue cited at § 9.4.4, *supra*, an additional argument may be made if the deed generated by the foreclosure sale has not yet been recorded. In many circumstances, the trustee may avoid unrecorded interests in property under the "strong-arm" power granted by 11 U.S.C. § 544(a).[137] By doing so, property comes into the estate free of those interests. If the trustee can avoid the unrecorded interest based on state law, the debtor may claim an exemption in the recovered property.[138]

Additionally, the debtor may exercise the trustee's powers under section 544(a) to avoid involuntary transfers of exempt property when the trustee fails to act.[139] Several courts have allowed trustees or debtors acting in their stead to avoid transfers by foreclosure during the period before the foreclosure deed is recorded.[140] When this opportunity is available, debtors may recover their exempt interest in the property and regain rights that apply to secured claims as if the collateral had never been transferred.[141]

sale); *In re* Gomez, 388 B.R. 279 (Bankr. S.D. Tex. 2008) (debtor's home remained property of bankruptcy estate where bankruptcy petition filed one day after property sold at foreclosure to third party but prior to delivery of mandatory substitute trustee's deed to purchaser; debtor may also avoid sale under 11 U.S.C. § 544). *See* § 9.4.4, *supra*. *See also In re* Brown, 311 B.R. 721 (Bankr. W.D. Pa. 2004) (petition filed a few minutes before sale completed); *In re* Grassie, 293 B.R. 829 (Bankr. D. Mass. 2003) (debtor retains equity of redemption when bankruptcy petition filed minutes after foreclosure sale and memorandum of sale signed by purchaser but before memorandum of sale signed by auctioneer); *In re* Benson, 293 B.R. 234 (Bankr. D. Ariz. 2003) (trustee's sale is not complete until the bid price is paid; so when debtor filed bankruptcy after fall of auctioneer's hammer, but before high bidder paid bid price, bidder's subsequent payment of bid price violated stay, as "act to obtain possession of property of the estate"); *In re* Pellegrino, 284 B.R. 326, 330 (Bankr. D. Conn. 2002) (discussing when debtor's rights in the property are exhausted under strict foreclosure process); *In re* Brown, 282 B.R. 880 (Bankr. E.D. Ark. 2002) (under Arkansas law, judicial foreclosure not complete until sale is confirmed by court, bankruptcy filed after sale but one day before sale was confirmed); *In re* Dow, 250 B.R. 6 (Bankr. D. Mass. 2000) (debtor who filed chapter 13 bankruptcy a few minutes after the sale of her home, but before the mortgage holder signed the memorandum of sale, did not lose ownership in the home as she had a right of redemption under Massachusetts law; the property became part of the estate). *But see In re* Connors, 497 F.3d 314 (3d Cir. 2007) (debtors no longer had right to cure under New Jersey law after hammer fell at foreclosure sale); Colon v. Option One Mortgage Corp., 319 F.3d 912 (7th Cir. 2003) (under Illinois law, chapter 13 debtor's right to cure a mortgage default expires upon completion of the foreclosure sale of the property and does not continue during the period between that sale and the judicial confirmation of that sale by the state court); *In re* Glenn, 760 F.2d 1428 (6th Cir. 1985) (chapter 13 debtor may cure default on mortgage on his principal residence when debt has been accelerated and judgment of foreclosure has been entered provided that no foreclosure sale has taken place; however, once property has been sold, right to cure default and reinstate mortgage ceases); *In re* Froehle, 286 B.R. 94 (B.A.P. 8th Cir. 2002) (redemption period following tax sale under Iowa law not tolled beyond sixty-day period provided for in § 108(b) and debtor may not use cure provisions under chapter 13 to redeem property); *In re* Rossiter, 412 B.R. 677 (D.N.J. 2008) (under New Jersey law, tax sale certificate foreclosure was complete upon the termination of entry of judgment of foreclosure proceeding, not upon sale of the tax certificate); *In re* Williams, 393 B.R. 813 (Bankr. M.D. Ga. 2008) (under Georgia law, debtor's equity of redemption is terminated when the high bid is made at a foreclosure sale); *In re* Tucker, 290 B.R. 134 (Bankr. E.D. Mo. 2003) (under Missouri law, deed of trust foreclosure sale was complete when bid was accepted by trustee and deed was issued to high bidder, though trustee's deed was not recorded prior to commencement of bankruptcy case). *Compare In re* Canney, 284 F.3d 362 (2d Cir. 2002) (under Vermont strict foreclosure law, automatic stay does not permit debtor to redeem property after end of redemption period, except as extended for sixty days by 11 U.S.C. § 108(b) *with In re* Taylor, 286 B.R. 275 (D. Vt. 2002) (applying § 1322(c)(1)in case of strict foreclosure of debtor's primary residence, mortgage holder obtains unencumbered title only when redemption period has passed, and debtor who files a chapter 13 case prior to this point retains right to cure default and reinstate mortgage. *But see In re* Newburn, 2001 WL 101733 (Bankr. N.D. Ill. Feb. 6, 2001) (a right to redeem is not an ownership interest in the property or a right to reinstate the mortgage); *In re* Townsville, 268 B.R. 95 (Bankr. E.D. Pa. 2001); *In re* Bobo, 246 B.R. 453 (Bankr. D.D.C. 2000) (lender granted relief from stay to record deed as sale as completed when gavel fell which was prior to filing petition).

137 *See also In re* Gomez, 388 B.R. 279 (Bankr. S.D. Tex. 2008) (under Texas law, purchaser of debtors' home at prepetition foreclosure sale did not have equitable title and debtors' redemption rights had not expired, where purchaser did not receive trustee's deed prior to filing). *See generally* National Consumer Law Center, Consumer Bankruptcy Law and Practice § 10.4.2.6.2 (9th ed. 2009).

138 11 U.S.C. § 522(g).

This right is available only if the transfer is involuntary—such as a transfer by foreclosure sale. *See generally* National Consumer Law Center, Consumer Bankruptcy Law and Practice § 10.4.2.5 (9th ed. 2009).

139 11 U.S.C. § 522(h).

This principle also applies only to involuntary transfers including foreclosure sales. *See generally* National Consumer Law Center, Consumer Bankruptcy Law and Practice § 10.4.2.2 (9th ed. 2009).

140 *E.g.*, *In re* Beeman, 235 B.R. 519 (Bankr. D.N.H. 1999); *In re* Burns, 183 B.R. 670 (Bankr. D.R.I. 1995); *In re* McDonald, 164 B.R. 325 (Bankr. C.D. Cal. 1994). *Cf. In re* Young, 156 B.R. 282 (Bankr. D. Idaho 1993) (state law provision protecting purchasers at foreclosure sale until recording of foreclosure deed prevents exercise of strong-arm powers).

141 *See* Ch. 9, *supra* (discussion of those rights).

14.3 Deficiency Judgments

14.3.1 Deficiency Judgments Defined

In most states, if the foreclosure sale price is not enough to pay off the loan balance and any allowable foreclosure expenses, the lender may sue the borrower for the balance—the "deficiency." A deficiency judgment can be satisfied by garnishing wages or attaching other non-exempt property. Though a lender may decide not to sue for a deficiency when it seems unlikely that the homeowner will have any assets to satisfy the judgment, foreclosed homeowners should at least be aware of the possibility of a deficiency action after a foreclosure. It is also possible that the right to seek a deficiency will be sold to a debt buyer who may sue on the amount years later.

If the foreclosure sale price bid by a mortgage holder is equal to the amount of the debt plus allowable expenses, the debt is discharged, even if the mortgage holder cannot resell the property for the same amount.[142] The fact that the mortgage holder was not able to inspect the property prior to making its bid is irrelevant.[143]

14.3.2 State Statutory Restrictions on Deficiency Judgments

A number of states have enacted anti-deficiency statutes which prohibit or limit deficiency claims against the former homeowner.[144] Such statutes have been in effect in many parts of the county since the 1930s and courts uphold these state laws against creditor claims that they are unconstitutional infringements of contract rights.[145] The United States Supreme Court has ruled that a state statute which limited a lender's recourse to a post-foreclosure deficiency claim passes constitutional muster even though the statute had been enacted *after* the borrower and lender entered into the loan transaction.[146]

In only fifteen states and the District of Columbia are mortgage holders free to pursue collection of deficiencies against foreclosed homeowners without limitation: Alabama, Delaware, District of Columbia, Illinois, Indiana, Kentucky, Maryland, Massachusetts, Mississippi, Missouri, New Hampshire, Rhode Island, Tennessee, Virginia, West Virginia, and Wyoming.[147] Statutes in the other states prohibit deficiencies outright or impose significant limits upon them. Nevertheless, most anti-deficiency statutes apply only to the foreclosure of purchase money mortgages.[148] Courts will differ as to whether statutory protections against deficiency judgments can be waived.[149]

Twelve states have enacted laws that completely bar deficiencies claims after most, but not all home foreclosures:

- Alaska (after power of sale foreclosure);
- Arizona (most home secured mortgages);
- California (after power of sale foreclosure on home mortgage);
- Hawaii (after power of sale foreclosure of mortgages executed after 1999);
- Minnesota (after power of sale foreclosure if six-month redemption applicable);
- Montana (after power of sale foreclosures);
- Nevada (single family, purchase money mortgages consummated after October 1, 2009);
- North Carolina (for most residential properties, after power of sale foreclosure and also after judicial foreclosures after January 1, 2010);
- North Dakota (for most residential properties);
- Oklahoma (after power of sale foreclosures);
- Oregon (after power of sale foreclosure or after judicial foreclosure of home); and
- Washington (after power of sale foreclosure of residential properties).[150]

In addition, the Uniform Land Security Interest Act (ULSIA) adopted in 1985 and the Uniform Non-Judicial Foreclosure Act promulgated in 2002 include provisions that bar deficiency actions.[151]

---

142 *In re* Morris, 204 B.R. 783, 785 (Bankr. N.D. Ala. 1996).

143 *Id.* (the mortgage holder also sued for pre-foreclosure damage to the property; the court held that it was not entitled to any damages for waste once it acquired the property at foreclosure).

144 *See generally* Appx. E, *infra* (summary of state laws regarding the availability of deficiency judgments).

145 Gelfert v. Nat'l City Bank of N.Y., 313 U.S. 221 (1941); Honeyman v. Jacobs, 306 U.S. 539 (1939). *See also* Lester v. First Am. Bank, Bryan, Tex., 866 S.W.2d 361 (Tex. App. 1993) (upholding Texas deficiency limitation against state constitutional challenge).

146 Gelfert v. Nat'l City Bank of N.Y., 313 U.S. 221 (1941).

147 *See* Appx. E, *infra*.

148 Brumley v. Mallard, Ltd. Liab. Co., 575 S.E.2d 35 (N.C. Ct. App. 2002) (mortgage must state on its face that it is purchase money mortgage in order for anti-deficiency statute to apply), *aff'd*, 580 S.E.2d 691 (N.C. 2003). *See also* Investors Title Ins. Co. v. Sturdivant, 617 S.E.2d 722 (N.C. Ct. App. 2005); Green Park Inn, Inc. v. Moore, 562 S.E.2d 53 (N.C. Ct. App. 2002) (anti-deficiency statute did not apply to long-term lease followed by option to purchase).

149 *Compare* LaSalle Bank Nat'l Ass'n v. Sleutel, 289 F.3d 837 (5th Cir. 2002) *with* Herrera v. LCS Fin. Servs. Corp., 2009 WL 5062192 (N.D. Cal. Dec. 22, 2009) (California Code of Civil Procedure § 580b, state's anti-deficiency statute, cannot be waived by contract); DeBerard Props., Ltd. v. Lim, 85 Cal. Rptr. 2d 292 (Cal. 1999); Cadle Co. II v. Harvey, 100 Cal. Rptr. 2d 150 (Cal. Ct. App. 2000).

150 *See* Appx. E, *infra*.

151 *See* John Mixon & Ira B. Shepard, *Antideficiency Relief for Foreclosed Homeowners: ULSIA Section 511(b)*, 27 Wake Forest L. Rev. 455 (1992); Grant S. Nelson & Dale A. Whitman, *Reforming Foreclosure: The Uniform Nonjudicial Foreclosure Act, 53 Duke L.J. 1399* (2002).

The remaining states are somewhere in the middle, limiting deficiencies, but not prohibiting them. The most common limitation is to require that the fair market value of the property be substituted for the foreclosure sale price when calculating the amount of a deficiency. The "fair value" is not necessarily the sale price, but is an amount that reflects what the property was actually worth, determined in accordance with the statute. The debt owed after foreclosure is then reduced by the larger of the foreclosure sale price or the fair market value of the property. The following twenty states have enacted such laws:

- Colorado (non-judicial foreclosures);
- Connecticut (judicial foreclosures);
- Georgia (non-judicial);
- Idaho (non-judicial);
- Kansas (non-judicial);
- Louisiana (executory process);
- Maine (judicial, when mortgage holder purchases the property);
- Michigan (non-judicial, when mortgage holder purchases the property);
- Nebraska (non-judicial);
- Nevada (non-judicial; applies to the extent to which state's complete ban on deficiencies does not apply to a mortgage);
- New Jersey (judicial);
- New York (judicial);
- Oklahoma (barred in non-judicial, limited to fair market value in judicial);
- Pennsylvania (judicial, when mortgage holder purchases the property);
- South Carolina (judicial);
- South Dakota (non-judicial, when mortgage holder purchases the property);
- Texas (non-judicial);
- Utah (non-judicial);
- Vermont (judicial); and
- Wisconsin (judicial).[152]

Another practice that allows courts in judicial foreclosures to limit deficiency liabilities is the use of an "upset bid" as a threshold to bidding at a foreclosure sale. Under this practice, the court requires a fair market value appraisal before the foreclosure sale and sets an "upset bid," or required minimum bid, based on the appraised value. Arkansas, Louisiana, and Ohio use variations of this practice.[153]

Additional limits on deficiencies come in the form of short statutes of limitations for filing a deficiency lawsuit. Several states, including Connecticut, Georgia, Idaho, Nebraska, New Jersey, Oklahoma, and Utah, set three-month limitation periods for filing mortgage deficiency claims with a court. If the mortgage holder does not begin legal action within this time, its deficiency claim is permanently barred.[154] Under the Montana, Nevada, and New York procedures, the lender must seek the deficiency when it forecloses or in the confirmation of sale proceedings.[155] These timing restrictions effectively prevent lenders from waiting until years later to bring a collection action. Some states also require that borrowers be given additional notice of the lender's intent to seek a deficiency if the sale price does not satisfy the mortgage.[156]

---

152 *See* Appx. E, *infra. Cf.* Dreyfuss v. Union Bank of Cal., 11 P.3d 383 (Cal. 2000) (fair market value credit for property applies only in a subsequent deficiency action and not to subsequent foreclosure on a different parcel of property); Carolina Bank v. Chatham Station, Inc., 651 S.E.2d 386 (N.C. Ct. App. 2007) (the amount yielded at the foreclosure sale is the amount to be used in calculating the deficiency judgment; fact that foreclosing mortgage holder later sold the property for less is irrelevant); First Citizens Bank & Trust Co. v. Cannon, 530 S.E.2d 581 (N.C. Ct. App. 2000) (although husband/debtor successfully pleaded and proved statutory "fair value" defense to deficiency, wife-debtor who did not timely answer deficiency complaint owed deficiency amount by virtue of default judgment).

153 *See* Appx. E, *infra.*

154 *Id. See, e.g.*, Conn. Gen. Stat. § 49-14 (deficiency judgment obtainable thirty days after redemption period expires); Idaho Code § 45-1512 (Michie) (action must be brought within three months of sale). *See also* Business Loan Ctr., L.L.C. v. Nischal, 331 F. Supp. 2d 301 (D.N.J. 2004) (denying deficiency claim because lender failed to obtain judicial confirmation of sale within thirty days as required by Georgia statute). *But see* McCartney v. Integra Nat'l Bank North, 106 F.3d 506, 509 (3d Cir. 1997) (when bankruptcy automatic stay prevented lender from timely completion of prerequisites for filing deficiency action, lender was not barred from pursuing non-discharged deficiency claim after expiration of state six month limit); Fed. Deposit Ins. Corp. v. Hillcrest, 659 A.2d 138 (Conn. 1995) (thirty-day time limit for bringing motion for deficiency judgment was not subject matter jurisdictional and could be waived by consent of the parties; here defendant deemed to have consented to filing of motion after thirty-day period by not objecting when court set deadline for filing).

155 *See* Appx. E, *infra. See also* Iwan Renovations, Inc. v. North Atlanta Nat'l Bank, 673 S.E.2d 632 (Ga. Ct. App. 2009) (finding suit on promissory note secured by second mortgage after non-judicial foreclosure on first mortgage by same lender was attempt to evade judicial confirmation requirement for deficiency judgments; even though two mortgages made at separate times, they were inextricably intertwined); Pines at Setauket v. Retirement Mgmt., 636 N.Y.S.2d 121 (App. Div. 1995).

156 *E.g.*, Mass. Gen. Laws ch. 244, § 17B. *See* Framingham Sav. Bank v. Turk, 664 N.E.2d 472 (Mass. App. Ct. 1996) (lender's failure to serve borrower with formal notice of intent to seek deficiency judgment precluded claim for deficiency judgment; fact that mortgager had actual notice that lender intended to seek deficiency did not cure defect). *See also* Oliver-Mercer Elec. Coop. v. Davis, 696 N.W.2d 924 (N.D. 2005) (lender's failure to comply with statutory notice requirements applicable to non-judicial sales created presumption that the value of the collateral sold equaled the debt). *But see* Bar Harbor Bank & Trust v. The Woods at Moody, L.L.C., 974 A.2d 934, 938–939 (Me. 2009) (deficiency claim not precluded despite lack of strict compliance with statutory notice requirements where bank could

Under Iowa's statute the lender must waive any deficiency claim if it wishes to enforce the borrower's waiver of the post-sale redemption right.[157] New Mexico enacted a unique provision that bars deficiency claims from deeds of trust securing residential loans made to low-income households. The law applies to households whose income was lower than 80% of the state median income for the family's size at the time of the loan application.[158] Florida's statute gives the courts a general discretion to regulate deficiency claims, but does not mandate application of any particular guideline or rule.[159]

California laws provide some of the broadest protections against deficiency claims. Deficiency actions are prohibited in both judicial and non-judicial foreclosures in California when the loan was secured by a residential property containing four or less units. No deficiencies are allowed in connection with power of sale foreclosures, regardless of the type of property involved. For judicial foreclosures of non-residential property, the deficiency is limited by the fair market rule. But for all types of mortgages and foreclosures in California, there is an exception for junior liens if the lien has been voided through foreclosure of a senior lien.[160]

14.3.3 *Judicial Limitations on Deficiency Judgments*

Section 14.2, *supra*, discusses setting aside a foreclosure because of an inadequate sale procedure or price. The same factors can prevent a court from awarding a deficiency judgment. This is particularly the case where a deficiency is sought after a non-judicial foreclosure, where there is no court involvement in the sale. Courts limit deficiency judgments on equitable grounds when the foreclosure sale price is inadequate, the sale was not commercially reasonable, or because of mortgage holder self-dealing.[161]

A mortgage holder or trustee has a duty to use good faith in the conduct of a foreclosure sale.[162] This duty includes using due diligence to obtain a fair price for the borrower's property.[163] When a lender purchases at its own foreclosure sale, it will be held to an even higher standard of utmost diligence for the protection of the rights of the borrower.[164] These provide a basis not only to set aside a sale, but also to deny a deficiency.

Thus in *Pearman v. West Point National Bank*,[165] the Kentucky Court of Appeals ruled that a mortgage holder could not recover a deficiency judgment when the mortgage holder had purchased the property at the foreclosure sale at two-thirds the value of the property and then had contracted to sell the property to a third party for slightly more than the amount of indebtedness one day before the entry of the deficiency judgment. The court held that the mortgage holder breached the covenant of good faith and fair dealing implied in the mortgage contract, and that the breach resulted in the non-enforcement of the deficiency.[166]

In *Wansley v. First National Bank of Vicksburg*,[167] the Mississippi Supreme Court held that a mortgage holder must show more than just a difference between the foreclosure sale price and the amount of indebtedness to be entitled to a deficiency judgment. The mortgage holder seeking a deficiency must satisfy the court that the value of the property was not sufficient to satisfy the debt owed.[168] This

be deemed to have alleged such a claim based on conduct indicating it would seek a deficiency; mortgagors bore responsibility for raising issue of noncompliance as affirmative defense and proving its applicability).

157 *See* Appx. E, *infra*.

158 *Id.*

159 *Id.*

160 Cal. Civ. Proc. Code § 580(b),(d) (West); Georgina W. Kwan, *Mortgagor Protection Laws: A Proposal for Mortgage Foreclosure Reform in Hawaii*, 24 U. Haw. L. Rev. 245, 259–262 (2001).

Note than one court has held that California's anti-deficiency statute does not preclude an action by a mortgage for waste, fraud, and conversion of rents after foreclosure. Evans v. Cal. Trailer Court, Inc., 33 Cal. Rptr. 2d 646 (Cal. Ct. App. 1994).

161 *See* Mortgage Elec. Registration Sys. v. Estrella, 390 F.3d 522 (7th Cir. 2004) (court has discretion to deny lender a deficiency judgment when price shortfall at auction results from negligence of the lender or its agent); *In re* Six, 80 F.3d 452, 456 (11th Cir. 1996). *See also* Nat'l Loan Investors v. LaPointe, 253 B.R. 496 (B.A.P. 1st Cir. 2000) (guarantor may offset the amount of the deficiency with damages she suffered as a result of lender's bad faith in conducting sale); Hartman v. McInnis, 996 So. 2d 704 (Miss. 2007) (every aspect of a foreclosure sale must be commercially reasonable; sale commercially reasonable despite trustee's announcement at the sale that sale would be subject to a senior lien on property); Lost Mountain Dev. Co. v. King, 2006 WL 3740791 (Tenn. Ct. App. Dec. 19, 2006) ("debtor is entitled to present evidence about the fair market value of the property at the time of the sale so as to attempt to overcome the presumption and prove that the price was grossly inadequate").

162 Nat'l Loan Investors v. LaPointe, 253 B.R. 496 (B.A.P. 1st Cir. 2000); Pearman v. W. Point Nat'l Bank, 887 S.W.2d 366 (Ky. Ct. App. 1994); Williams v. Resolution GGF 0Y, 630 N.E.2d 581 (Mass. 1994); Snowden v. Chase Manhattan Mortgage Corp., 2003 WL 22519518 (Mass. Super. Ct. Nov. 5, 2003); Murphy v. Fin. Dev. Corp., 495 A.2d 1245 (N.H. 1985).

163 Murphy v. Fin. Dev. Corp., 495 A.2d 1245 (N.H. 1985). *See also* Snowden v. Chase Manhattan Mortgage Corp., 2003 WL 22519518 (Mass. Super. Ct. Nov. 5, 2003) (lender refused to postpone a foreclosure sale to allow the homeowner to conduct a market sale that would have satisfied the lender's lien and costs and netted the homeowner $50,000 from the equity in his property).

164 Union Mkt. Nat'l Bank v. Missuk Derderian, 62 N.E.2d 661 (Mass. 1945).

165 887 S.W.2d 366 (Ky. Ct. App. 1994).

166 *Id.* at 368. *Cf.* First Nat'l Bank of Southeast Denver v. Blanding, 885 P.2d 324 (Colo. Ct. App. 1994) (lack of good faith bid by mortgage holder requires full adjustment of deficiency, but mortgagor is not entitled to damages for breach of good faith and fair dealing).

167 566 So. 2d 1218, 1224 (Miss. 1990).

168 *Id.* at 1224.

analysis requires a determination of the fair market value of the property and the adequacy of the price obtained at the foreclosure.[169]

An inadequate sale price may not be enough to set aside a sale, but it may be grounds to deny a deficiency judgment.[170] "This is but another way of saying that before we will respect [foreclosure sales] for deficiency purposes, the terms of a foreclosure sale must be *commercially reasonable*."[171] The court reasoned that the UCC requires that the sale of personal property must be commercially reasonable and there is no logical reason to treat real property differently.[172] Thus the court held, "Every aspect of the sale, including the method, advertising, time, place and terms must be commercially reasonable. This is an objective standard."[173]

The rights of bona fide purchasers may be implicated when a court sets aside a foreclosure sale due to inadequacy of the sale price. However, denying or reducing a lender's post-sale deficiency claim does not raise these concerns. Denying the lender's deficiency claim does not impair the bona fide purchaser's title. Therefore, some courts that as a matter of law will not treat inadequacy of price as a ground for setting a foreclosure sale aside will nevertheless permit a debtor to raise the inadequacy and unfairness of a sale price as a defense to a deficiency action.[174]

In addition, even if the court does not ban a deficiency based upon the nature of the foreclosure sale, the consumer can raise counterclaims to the deficiency claim, including those related to the foreclosure. In *Murphy v. Financial Development Corp.*,[175] a New Hampshire court awarded a former homeowner damages in an amount equal to the difference between the foreclosure sale price and the fair market price of the property after the lender purchased the property at the foreclosure sale for the amount due on the note and then sold the property three days later for $11,000 more. The court found that the lender's undeniable knowledge that it could get a higher price for the property is conclusive evidence that the lender has violated its duties of good faith and due diligence (even though it complied with the strict letter of the law).[176] In its opinion the court discusses some of the steps which lenders could and should take to satisfy the duty of the diligence to obtain a fair price.[177] For example, employment of a professional real estate agent to advertise and show the property may be a reasonable method to ensure a fair price.[178]

Other defenses to enforcement of the note and counterclaims against the lender can also be raised in most states to defend against deficiency claims. Usury,[179] warranty, fraud,[180] and many of the consumer defenses discussed elsewhere in this treatise[181] can be pursued. However, in states which have a judicial foreclosure process, certain counterclaims may be precluded by res judicata or the law of the case doctrine, because of the foreclosure judgment.

14.3.4 Creditor Must Prove the Deficiency Amount

When a creditor seeks a deficiency, the creditor must prove its right to that amount. Scrutinizing all aspects of the sale and accounting is critical, particularly in a non-judicial foreclosure state. In a judicial sale, the judgment order itself tells the official how to distribute proceeds from the sale. If the order does not expressly do so, the order will likely direct the official to make a distribution of proceeds according to priorities set forth in a state statute. A judicial foreclosure typically includes a post-sale motion procedure

169 *Id. See also* Hartman v. McInnis, 996 So. 2d 704 (Miss. 2007) (court unable to establish the fair market value of property; simply looking at the property, making vague notes regarding the physical condition of the property, and issuing a value therefrom are insufficient to meet mortgage holder's burden to establish fair market value).

170 566 So. 2d 1218, 1224 (Miss. 1990). *See also* First Nat'l Bank of Southeast Denver v. Blanding, 885 P.2d 324, 327 (Colo. Ct. App. 1994); Haygood v. First Nat'l Bank of New Albany, 517 So. 2d 553 (Miss. 1987); Lake Hillside Estates, Inc. v. Galloway, 473 So. 2d 461, 465 (Miss. 1985). *Cf. In re* Slizyk, 2006 WL 2506489 (Bankr. M.D. Fla. Aug. 28, 2006) (creditor ex-husband not entitled to deficiency judgment where same would be tantamount to a second windfall at expense of debtor ex-wife in addition to first windfall of obtaining property at reduced price; "the amount for which mortgaged property sells at during a properly conducted sale is neither conclusive as to the value of the property nor the right to a deficiency judgment").

171 *Wansley*, 566 So. 2d at 1224. *See also* ROC-Century Assocs. v. Giunta, 658 A.2d 223 (Me. 1995) (when sale of collateral is not in a commercially reasonable manner, a rebuttable presumption is raised that the value of the collateral is equal to the amount of indebtedness; creditor can overcome presumption by presenting evidence of fair and reasonable value and showing that value was less than debt [U.C.C. case]); Hartman v. McInnis, 996 So. 2d 704 (Miss. 2007); Rankin County Bank v. McKinnion, 531 So. 2d 822, 825 (Miss. 1988).

172 *Wansley*, 566 So. 2d at 1225.

173 *Id.* It should be noted that in this case the court found that the foreclosure sale was commercially reasonable.

174 *See e.g.* Lost Mountain Dev. Co. v. King, 2006 WL 3740791 (Tenn. Ct. App. Dec. 19, 2006) (allowing defense to deficiency action based solely on unfairness of sale price, although under Tennessee common law a debtor may not set a sale aside solely on this ground).

175 495 A.2d 1245 (N.H. 1985).

176 *Id.* at 1251.

177 *Id.*

178 *Id.*

179 *Cf.* Ferrigno v. Cromwell Dev. Assocs., 689 A.2d 1150 (Conn. App. Ct. 1997) (usury defense to deficiency claim unavailable because of exception to usury statute for mortgages).

180 *Cf.* U.S. Bank v. Hollo, 2009 WL 5303792 (Conn. Super. Ct. Dec. 2, 2009) (special defenses to foreclosure action do not absolve *pro se* homeowner of liability on note in this case, but court states that allegations regarding conduct (negligent misrepresentation) of mortgage servicer may be considered by court in determining whether deficiency judgment is appropriate).

181 *See* Ch. 5, *supra*.

in which the court must "confirm" the sale, and at which time the homeowner may be able to challenge a proposed deficiency calculation. For example, in Connecticut, Illinois, New York, Ohio, and Vermont, requests to confirm a foreclosure sale are treated as distinct legal proceedings, following specific court rules. The procedures include the opportunity for a hearing and a decision in writing from a judge. In Connecticut the ruling is designated as a "supplemental judgment," and is a separate, appealable court order distinct from the court's earlier foreclosure judgment.

Thus a New York trial court reviewing a foreclosure sale discovered that the mortgage holder had made a claim for $88,000 in attorney fees connected with the foreclosure, a charge not included in the court's earlier foreclosure judgment.[182] The court determined the reasonable attorney fee charge to be only $5000. When a state's laws provide for court procedures to confirm a sale, abuses such as these can be remedied effectively.

In other judicial foreclosure states, after the sale, the mortgage holder or the officer who conducted the sale must file a report describing how any proceeds have been disbursed. The report is a public document filed with the court or county clerk. Under this practice, a court does not routinely review the conduct of the sale or the distribution of proceeds unless a party has formally objected to the officer's report of the sale. Absent objection, the official will distribute proceeds from the sale as described in the report of the sale.

A non-judicial foreclosure proceeds along a very different track. There will have been no prior court ruling that established the amounts owed to the mortgage holder or any other entities claiming shares in the sale proceeds. A neutral public official will not have reviewed the extent or validity of the mortgage holder's claim or the claims of any junior lienholders. A private trustee or the mortgage holder plays a large role in determining the costs of the sale and the extent of any credit against the borrower's debt. This assessment of the borrower's debt by the mortgage holder or trustee will be the initial basis for the deficiency claim. It will also be the amount the mortgage holder reports to the IRS as taxable income to the borrower. As a result, particularly in a non-judicial foreclosure state, the consumer should carefully scrutinize and require substantiation for the mortgage holder's deficiency calculation.

14.3.5 *Deficiency Claims Are Unsecured*

If a family is obligated for a deficiency, keep in mind that this debt generally is not secured by any of the family's remaining property until a judgment lien is obtained.[183] The family at this point could file bankruptcy and discharge the deficiency as an unsecured debt. Moreover, even if the creditor obtains a court judgment for the deficiency, it still cannot seize exempt property to satisfy the deficiency. To the extent the judgment creates a lien which impairs an exemption, it can be avoided in bankruptcy pursuant to section 522(f).[184]

14.4 Claiming a Foreclosure Sale Surplus

14.4.1 *Procedure*

If the foreclosure sale yields more than the amount owed to the foreclosing mortgage holder, a surplus is available for distribution, first to pay off junior liens on the property, and the balance to the former owner. There is significant variation as to the state procedure as to how and when sale proceeds, including surpluses, are distributed.

After the judicial foreclosure sale, in most states the mortgage holder or the officer who conducted the sale must file a report describing how any proceeds have been disbursed. If a surplus remains after paying off the mortgage debt and the costs of the sale, the report will give notice of this sum. The report is a public document filed with the court or county clerk. If there is a surplus to be distributed, the officer pays the surplus funds into court or retains them pending a further order from the court.

A judicial foreclosure typically also includes a post-sale motion procedure in which the court must "confirm" the sale, with notice to all parties.[185] In some states, court review and a hearing are automatic after all foreclosure sales. In other states the matter is set for court review and a hearing only if someone disputes the officer's report, including its proposed distribution of a surplus. When a judge rules in a proceeding to confirm a sale, the judge's order addresses the distribution of any remaining surplus.

The foreclosing mortgage holder and any junior lienholders[186] can file claims subject to objection by the former

182 NYCTL 1998-1 Trust v. Oneg Shabos, Inc., 800 N.Y.S.2d 808 (Sup. Court. 2005).

183 This may not be true in the rare situation that there is other valuable property secured by a mortgage or guarantee. For example, some small business debts are secured by a home mortgage and business property. Similarly, a cosigner may have put up additional security.

184 *See In re* Been, 153 F.3d 1034 (9th Cir. 1998).

185 *See, e.g.*, United States v. Moore, 2006 WL 1144538 (W.D.N.Y. May 1, 2006) (describes N.Y. procedure for allocating surplus).
Separate notice to the parties respecting the confirmation of the sale may not be constitutionally mandated if those parties had received notice of the foreclosure proceeding itself. Galt Alloys v. Keybank, 708 N.E.2d 701 (Ohio 1999). However, some state statutes mandate notice.

186 Properties are sold at foreclosure subject to any senior liens. Junior liens are paid only if there are sufficient sale proceeds after the foreclosing mortgage holder is paid and in most states, only if the junior lienholder affirmatively files a claim. United States v. Hesselbarth, 418 F. Supp. 2d 274 (W.D.N.Y. 2006).

homeowner or others[187] who might also have an interest in the surplus.[188] A junior lienholder may lose its rights to the sale proceeds by failing to participate in the foreclosure proceedings or follow the procedures for claiming a surplus.[189] In other states the foreclosed homeowner can demand an accounting of the sale proceeds and the sale surplus, and can file an action if not satisfied with the response.[190] Other stakeholders, such as the foreclosing mortgage holder or a bankruptcy trustee may bring an action to determine how to distribute the surplus.[191]

On the other hand, particularly in non-judicial foreclosure states, distribution of excess sale proceeds is more informal. The trustee or the mortgage holder's attorney distributes proceeds without any direct court supervision. For example, a Massachusetts homeowner never found out that she was entitled to a $21,000 surplus from a non-judicial foreclosure sale until one year after the sale, when she received a notice from the Internal Revenue Service (IRS) informing her that her former lender had reported the surplus to the government as income to her.[192] A Maine appellate court has held that a seventeen-month delay in filing an accounting and report of sale was reasonable given the lack of any express statutory time frame under the state's foreclosure laws.[193]

Nevertheless, some non-judicial foreclosure states, such as Maryland, New Hampshire, South Dakota, and Washington, require that in all cases in which there is a surplus left after payment of the foreclosing mortgage holder's claim and the costs of sale, the surplus must be transmitted to the local court for further action. In Virginia, the trustee reports to a county commissioner of accounts who reviews the report and sends it on for court review. A judge can confirm or reject the account over a fifteen-day period.

North Carolina's law requires the trustee after a non-judicial foreclosure sale to file a report of the sale with the court within five days of the sale and pay a surplus into court under specific circumstances defined by statute, such as

---

See, e.g., The Huntington Mortgage Co. v. Fed. Deposit Ins. Corp., 2001 WL 1813757 (Mass. Super. Ct. Dec. 20, 2001); 2793 S. 3095 W. v. Munford, 1 P.3d 1116 (Utah Ct. App. 2000); Household Fin. Indus. Loan Co. v. Upton, 6 P.3d 1231 (Wash. Ct. App. 2000).

187 For example, a judgment creditor may have an interest in the proceeds. *See* Bennardo v. Del Monte Caterers, Inc., 811 N.Y.S.2d 434 (N.Y. App. Div. 2006).

A purchaser at a foreclosure sale may also claim a portion of the proceeds as compensation if the former owner does not turn over possession of the property. *See* Legacy Funding L.L.C. v. Cohn, 914 A.2d 760 (Md. 2007) (purchaser may submit a claim for the fair rental value of the property for the time the mortgagor rejected proper demand for possession).

188 For example, a third lienholder might object to the amount claimed by a second lienholder in order to increase its recovery. *See also* Lawyer's Foreclosure Specialists, Inc. v. Schwarz, 2005 WL 3021928 (E.D. Mo. Sept. 25, 2005) (former wife not entitled to surplus where lien for back alimony never attached because never reduced to judgment); Stulz v. Citizen's Bank and Trust Co., 160 S.W.3d 423 (Mo. Ct. App. 2005) (junior lienholder has priority over former owner; junior lien was voluntary assignment of right to surplus, and lien survived bankruptcy); Mortgage Lenders Network U.S.A., Inc. v. Martinez, 819 N.Y.S.2d 849 (table), 2006 WL 1112964 (N.Y. Sup. Ct. Mar. 30, 2006) (mechanic's lien claimant not entitled to surplus; lien invalid because claimant lacked home improvement contractor's license; also failed to comply with lien procedure); Woodside Assurance, Inc. v. N.K. Res., Inc., 175 S.W.3d 421 (Tex. App. 2005) (distribution of surplus from tax sale; one claim is time-barred).

189 United States v. Hesselbarth, 418 F. Supp. 2d 274 (W.D.N.Y. 2006) (only creditors who file and document a claim in surplus money proceeding are entitled to share; creditors who participated in foreclosure but not surplus money proceeding are defaulted); Fidelity Bank v. King, 136 P.3d 465 (Kan. 2006) (junior mortgagee who fails to appear and assert its claim in senior mortgage holder's foreclosure proceeding loses its claim to surplus and becomes unsecured creditor); Casey v. National Info. Servs., Inc., 906 So. 2d 710 (La. Ct. App. 2005) (surplus owed to former owner; creditor lost its claim because it failed to timely "reinscribe" mortgage). *See also* JP Morgan Chase Bank v. U.S. Bank Nat'l Ass'n, 929 So. 2d 651 (Fla. Dist. Ct. App. 2006) (second mortgage holder, which defaulted in proceedings, did not lose right to proceeds); Legacy Funding L.L.C. v. Cohn, 914 A.2d 760 (Md. 2007) (purchaser's claim for a share of surplus proceeds as compensation for mortgagor rejecting proper demand for possession of property should be made in the foreclosure action); Bank of Am., N.A. v. BA Mortgage, L.L.C., 111 P.3d 226 (N.M. Ct. App. 2005) (junior mortgage holder that timely asserted its claims in foreclosure proceeding entitled to surplus, notwithstanding its failure to obtain a judgment on its lien; extensive collection of cases and treatise citations). *But see* B & B Invs. v. Wells Fargo Bank, N.A., 2005 WL 428554 (Cal. Ct. App. Feb. 24, 2005) (unpublished) (creditor that formally notified trustee of its claim before foreclosure sale, but failed to make timely claim in proceeding to determine priorities, allowed to file late on grounds of mistake and excusable neglect); JP Morgan Chase Bank v. U.S. Bank N.A., 929 So. 2d 651 (Fla. Dist. Ct. App. 2006) (distribution to former owner was an error, where second mortgage unsatisfied, even though second mortgage holder defaulted at foreclosure hearing); Franklin Credit Mgmt. Servs. v. Pearlman, 792 N.Y.S.2d 525 (App. Div. 2005) (second mortgage holder that was named party in foreclosure action does not lose right to surplus by failing to file a claim).

190 Duclersaint v. Fed. Nat'l Mortgage Ass'n, 696 N.E.2d 536 (Mass. 1998) (finding that foreclosed homeowner was entitled to surplus from sale, when mortgage holder mistakenly bid more than amount of unpaid mortgage at foreclosure sale; homeowner discovered excess bid when mortgage holder sent a Form 1099A after sale which showed amount of bid).

191 *See, e.g.*, States Res. Co. v. The Architectural Team, Inc., 433 F.3d 73 (1st Cir. 2005) (interpleader action by first mortgage holder; junior mortgage holder counterclaims for UDAP and breach of fiduciary duty, alleging that senior mortgage holder mishandled sale); Wells Fargo Home Mortgage v. Stevenson, 2006 WL 1663342 (N.D. Ga. June 9, 2006) (first mortgage holder interpleads surplus funds, court determines priorities); Lawyer's Foreclosure Specialists, Inc. v. Schwarz, 2005 WL 3021928 (E.D. Mo. Sept. 25, 2005) (interpleader to determine priority of liens on surplus from sale of deceased borrower's realty); *In re* Loewhing, 320 B.R. 281 (Bankr. D.N.J. 2005) (bankruptcy trustee sought declaratory judgment).

192 Duclersaint v. Fed. Nat'l Mortgage Ass'n, 696 N.E.2d 536 (Mass. 1998).

193 Brickyard Ass'n v. Auburn Venture P'ship, 626 A.2d 930 (Me. 1993).

when claims are disputed. Similarly, California and Massachusetts require the trustee to make a report and, under conditions set forth in the statutes, refer certain questions of proposed distribution of proceeds to a court. Michigan requires that the trustee refers the disbursement of the surplus to the court if a junior lienholder makes a claim.

Most other states give a private trustee or the lender substantial discretion in determining when to refer a question over distribution of proceeds to a court. The trustee makes the initial distribution from sale proceeds to cover the foreclosing mortgage holder's claim and the costs of the sale. Then, to the extent proceeds remain, the trustee has the discretion to complete the distribution, including payments to junior lienholders and to the borrower.

The statutes in Arizona, Montana, Nevada, New Mexico, and Utah expressly give the trustee the authority to file an "interpleader" type of legal action in a court. In an interpleader case, the trustee pays the sale proceeds into court so that a judge can decide how the funds should be disbursed. Under most non-judicial foreclosure systems, starting such a proceeding is left to the trustee's discretion. Although a state's foreclosure statutes may not expressly provide for a trustee's authority to start an interpleader action, trustees have the option of resorting to this general type of court proceeding in any jurisdiction when they face disputed or complex claims related to a specific sum of money.

Finally a number of state statutes simply direct the trustee to follow the state's general ranking of priorities in distributing proceeds from a non-judicial foreclosure sale. The distribution takes place entirely outside of court supervision. The priorities are set by statute, or otherwise are part of the state's common law. The statutes in Arkansas, Idaho, Minnesota, Oregon, West Virginia, and Wyoming operate in this manner. Absent a controlling statute defining priorities for distribution, trustees in some states, such as Texas, follow common law rules for distribution of proceeds.

14.4.2 Timelines in Distribution of a Surplus

Most states do not require a surplus to be released by a certain date to the homeowner after a foreclosure sale,[194] but a number of states specify a time period for the official who conducted the foreclosure sale to file a report and accounting of the sale. North Carolina requires that the report be filed within five days of the sale.[195] New York requires that the surplus be paid to court within five days of the sale and the report must be filed within thirty days.[196] Other states require the accounting within ten days or fifteen days.[197] However, many states permit significantly longer times, from thirty days in California, Pennsylvania, and Maryland, to forty-five days in Hawaii, sixty days in West Virginia, and six months in Virginia.[198]

Once homeowners receive a report of the sale, they can decide whether to challenge the report or accept it. Again, local statutes vary in the time limit they set for the consumer to file objections. Once an objection is filed, court calendars may have more to do with the time frame in resolving the objection than do the statutory provisions. When the accounting for a surplus is not disputed, these motions proceed with little delay.

14.4.3 Steps Homeowners Should Take

The former homeowner should evaluate other parties' claims to the surplus. A successful challenge that reduces the amount to which a lienholder is entitled increases the share available to the homeowner, unless even the reduced amount going to junior lienholders uses up all the surplus. In particular, review lienholder claims for fees and costs associated with foreclosure,[199] or a lienholder's failure to properly rebate pre-computed interest or insurance premiums. As described at § 14.4.4, *infra*, a judicial lienholder's priority may be lower than the homeowner's. Moreover, sometimes, a party asserts a right to sale proceeds without even a valid lien.[200]

194 Alabama, Alaska, Arkansas, Colorado, District of Columbia, Delaware, Florida, Georgia, Idaho, Indiana, Iowa, Kansas, Kentucky, Maine, Michigan, Minnesota, Mississippi, Missouri, Montana, Nebraska, Nevada, New Jersey, New Mexico, North Dakota, Oklahoma, Oregon, Rhode Island, South Carolina, Tennessee, Texas, Utah, Washington, and Wisconsin.

195 N.C. Gen. Stat. § 45-21.26.

196 N.Y. Real Prop. Law §§ 1354, 1355 (McKinney).

197 Ariz. Rev. Stat. Ann. § 33-812(B); Wyo. Stat. Ann. § 34-4-104(b); Vt. R. Civ. P. 80.1.

198 *See* Cal. Civ. Code § 2924j (West) (report due within thirty days of issuance of trustee's deed); Haw. Rev. Stat. § 667-33; Va. Code Ann. § 26-15; W. Va. Code § 38-1-8; Md. Civ. R. 14-305; Pa. R. Civ. P. 3136.

199 National City Mortgage Co. v. Stoecker, 888 A.2d 95 (Conn. App. Ct. 2006) (first mortgage holder and foreclosure sale purchaser claimed reimbursement for taxes, water and sewer, property maintenance and post-judgment interest for period between confirmation of sale and expiration of appeals period; amount of debt should be calculated as of the earlier of date title transferred or date by which court ordered it transferred); NYCTL 1 1998 and Bank of New York v. Oneg Shabbos, Inc., 800 N.Y.S.2d 808 (N.Y. Sup. Ct. 2005) (attorney fees reduced from $88,000 to $5000; excessive fees grounds to set aside foreclosure; "broad policy considerations" require that foreclosure fees be kept low, to enable owners to redeem or at least reduce their losses by a surplus). *See also* Bardi v. Morgan, 847 N.Y.S.2d 431 (N.Y. Sup. Ct. 2007) (mortgage holder, who was the successful bidder at the foreclosure sale but defaulted on its closing obligations, cannot continue to charge interest on the mortgage debt and subtract that amount from the surplus funds; interest on the debt is suspended during the period where mortgage holder failed to timely close), *aff'd on other grounds*, 877 N.Y.S.2d 142 (App. Div. 2009).

200 *See* Cal-Western Reconveyance Corp. v. Reed, 62 Cal. Rptr. 3d 244 (Cal. Ct. App. 2007) (wife's claim for a portion of surplus proceeds rejected in absence of valid lien).

In objecting to claims in a court supervised foreclosure sale confirmation process, homeowners must meet any applicable deadlines.[201] If there is no judicial process, an affirmative case must be brought to require the foreclosure trustee or foreclosing mortgage holder to comply with a particular distribution.

Whenever excess sale proceeds are potentially available, the homeowner should keep the relevant court, trustee, or mortgage company informed of the homeowner's current address. It is not uncommon for a family that is forced to relocate by foreclosure not to receive payments due or important notices concerning the distribution of foreclosure proceeds because the family's new address was unknown.

14.4.4 *Relative Rights of Judicial Lien and Homestead Exemption*

While most lienholders take priority over the homeowner as to recovery of the surplus, this is not the case with a judicial lienholder. The debtor's homestead exemption, if provided under state law, should be paid ahead of any claims of judicial lienholders.[202] Consider, for example, a $100,000 surplus, a $50,000 lien following a judgment on credit card debt, and a $90,000 homestead exemption. The first $90,000 goes to the homeowner, since this amount would be exempt if the judicial lienholder tried to foreclose. The remaining $10,000 goes to the judicial lienholder.

In a few states, the right to a homestead exemption must be affirmatively sought by filing a claim. Whether or not an affirmative claim is required, the homeowner must make certain that sale proceeds are appropriately distributed. These issues can be especially complex if the judgment lien applies to only one of two or more joint owners of the foreclosed property. In that case, not only must the exemption be taken into account, but also the value of the relevant fractional shares of property.[203]

14.4.5 *"Surplus Retrieval" Consultants*

During the current foreclosure epidemic a cottage industry of "surplus retrieval" consultants has emerged. These scammers offer a "service" of assisting distressed homeowners through the maze of procedures surrounding a foreclosure sale. The consultants typically end up with a lion's share of any surplus, or simply take money from financially strapped homeowners when there is no likelihood there will ever be a surplus.

Some states, including Maryland and Nevada, recently enacted statutes drafted specifically to regulate the practices of "surplus purchasers."[204] Other states, including California, Colorado, and Florida, include surplus purchasers and their practices within the definition of "foreclosure consultants" who are now subject to state regulation.[205] In other jurisdictions, the state deceptive practices (UDAP) statute should apply.[206]

14.5 Damage Claims for Wrongful Foreclosure

Sections 14.2 and 14.3, *supra*, examined a consumer's right to set aside a foreclosure or to bar a deficiency. A third option is to seek damages for a wrongful foreclosure. In a judicial foreclosure, issues will be raised as to collateral estoppel—that the consumer's damage claims should have been brought in the judicial foreclosure proceeding. No such issues arise where there has been a non-judicial foreclosure. As long as the action is brought within the statute of limitations, the consumer can raise claims against the mortgage holder related to the foreclosure and other matters.

Wrongful foreclosure can be a tort claim—the advantage for such a claim may be the potential for punitive damages. In a number of states the tort is simply called "wrongful foreclosure."[207] Damages have even been awarded for at-

---

201 *Cf. In re* Ferren, 203 F.3d 559 (8th Cir. 2000) (final state court determination of distribution of sale proceeds cannot later be challenged in federal court).

202 *In re* Dezonia, 347 B.R. 920 (Bankr. M.D. Fla. 2006) (borrower entitled to homestead exemption in surplus; Florida homestead survives in proceeds if debtor intends to reinvest in another homestead; intent to reinvest not negated by failure to participate in foreclosure action, where debtor did not expect a surplus); MIDS, Inc. v. Cooney-Ames, 2006 WL 158733 (Cal. Ct. App. Jan. 23, 2006) (California has two homestead exemptions; automatic exemption does not protect surplus; declared exemption does, but liens here had priority over homestead: lien for child support given priority by statute, lien for homeowners' association fees arose at time of purchase, before claim of homestead). *See also In re* Trustee's Sale of Real Property of Ervin, 2006 WL 2397332 (Wash. Ct. App. Aug. 21, 2006) (second deed of trust takes priority over homestead exemption; liens attach to surplus in same order they attached to real property).

203 *See, e.g.*, Johnson v. Cromaz, 1999 Ohio App. LEXIS 6240 (Ohio Ct. App. Dec. 23, 1999) (wife entitled to distribution of proceeds of sale from her unencumbered one-half interest in the property before distribution to husband's judgment creditor). *See also* A Great Mortgage Co. v. Tarlowski, 2006 WL 1320130 (N.J. Super. Ct. Ch. Div. Apr. 28, 2006) (court handling foreclosure orders surplus funds held until family court handling former owners' divorce can determine distribution).

204 Md. Code Ann., Real Prop. §§ 7-301(h), 7-314 (West); Nev Rev. Stat. § 40.463.

205 Cal. Civ. Code § 2945.1(e)(8) (West) (defining surplus recovery as a regulated "service" subject to restrictions under statute applicable to foreclosure consultants); Colo. Rev. Stat. § 6-1103(4)(a)(IX) (including surplus retrieval consultants in scope of regulated foreclosure consultant activities); Fla. Stat. §§ 45.032, 45.034 (regulating contracts to assign sale surpluses).

206 *See* § 15.4.5.5, *infra*.

207 Anokil v. EMC Mortgage Co., 28 Cal. Rptr. 3d 759 (Ct. App. 2005); Sauceda v. GMAC Mortgage. Corp., 268 S.W.3d 135 (Tex. App. 2008); Everson v. Mineola Cmty. Bank, 2006 WL 2106959 (Tex. App. July 31, 2006). *See also* Hamilton v.

tempted wrongful foreclosure.[208] The wrongful foreclosure may also be actionable as another tort, such as fraud,[209] trespass, or conversion.[210] Tort damages will not, however, be available for the wrongful foreclosure itself if the only duties breached arise from the contract.[211] Wrongful foreclosure as a tort is also examined at § 6.4.4.7, *supra*, and tort claims are more generally discussed at § 7.10, *supra*.

Other possible claims relating to the mortgage servicing and foreclosure are examined elsewhere in this treatise:

- Claims under a state unfair and deceptive acts and practices statutes;[212]
- Truth in Lending claims for failure to honor a TIL rescission;[213]
- Fair Debt Collection Practices Act and state debt collection law claims;[214]
- Fair Credit Reporting Act claims for inaccurately furnishing information to reporting agencies;[215]
- Claims under RESPA and state mortgage servicing laws for servicing misconduct;[216]
- Breach of contract and breach of implied covenant of good faith and fair dealing claims;[217] and
- Breach of fiduciary duty claims.[218]

An award of actual damages is often computed as the difference between the fair market value and the foreclosure sale price.[219] Of course, depending on the cause of action, punitive, statutory, or multiple damages may be available, as well as attorney fees.

14.6 Tax Consequences of a Foreclosure Sale: An Introduction

14.6.1 *Foreclosure Sales May Result in Taxable Income*

Loss of a home by foreclosure can result in taxable income to the foreclosed homeowner in two different ways. First, if the foreclosure sale price is more than the homeowner's tax basis in the property, the homeowner may incur a taxable capital gain. Second, if the lender forgives any part of the mortgage debt, including by waiving a deficiency judgment after a foreclosure sale for less than the amount of

---

Willms, 2005 WL 3143712 (E.D. Cal. Nov. 22, 2005) (sale will not be set aside because no evidence that borrower willing or able to tender amount due, but money damages available); Gregorakos v. Wells Fargo Nat'l Ass'n, 647 S.E.2d 289 (Ga. Ct. App. 2007) (to establish a claim for wrongful foreclosure, plaintiff must establish a legal duty owed to it by the foreclosing lender, a breach of that duty, a causal connection between the breach of that duty and the injury it sustained, and damages); Bassett v. Jasper Banking Co., 629 S.E.2d 434 (Ga. Ct. App. 2006) (fact issues whether bank officer knew of borrower's blindness and misled him as to terms of documents; wrongful foreclosure claim depends on outcome of fraud claim); McCarter v. Bankers Trust Co., 543 S.E.2d 755 (Ga. Ct. App. 2000); Katter v. Demoulas, 739 N.E.2d 246 (Mass. 2000); Dobson v. Mortgage Elec. Registration Sys., 259 S.W.3d 19 (Mo. Ct. App. 2008) (claim of wrongful foreclosure sufficient to set aside a sale not the same as a claim to recover damages in tort; tort claim can be asserted when lender had no right to foreclose and plaintiffs must plead and prove that they was not in default). *See generally* 55 Am. Jur. 2d *Mortgages* § 516.

208 *See* Mason v. S. Mortgage Co., 828 So. 2d 735 (Miss. 2002).

209 Jenkins v. WM Specialty Mortgage, L.L.C., 2006 WL 374788 (N.D. Tex. Feb. 17, 2006) (borrower stated common law fraud claim against lender's employee who allegedly made false statements about home equity loan that was later accelerated and posted for foreclosure); Hamilton v. Willms, 2005 WL 3143712 (E.D. Cal. Nov. 22, 2005) (borrower stated claim for promissory fraud; evidence that lender never intended to keep promise to postpone sale in return for $2000 payment; did not come to pick up payment as arranged, then refused to postpone sale for ten minutes while borrower's representative went to nearby bank); Bassett v. Jasper Banking Co., 629 S.E.2d 434 (Ga. Ct. App. 2006) (fact issue whether bank officer knew of borrower's blindness and misled him as to terms of documents).

210 King v. Bank of New York, 2005 WL 2177209 (S.D. Tex. 2005) (borrower stated trespass claim against trustee who initiated eviction after allegedly wrongful foreclosure).

211 UMLIC VP L.L.C. v. T & M Envt'l Sys., Inc., 176 S.W.3d 595 (Tex. App. 2005) (no punitive damages in contract, even if breach is malicious; no independent duty of good faith and fair dealing; no independent cause of action for mental anguish).

212 *See* § 7.2, *supra*. This will depend on the scope of the state's UDAP statute. *Compare* Levine v. First Nat'l Bank of Commerce, 917 So. 2d 1235 (La. Ct. App. 2005) (mortgage foreclosure not exempt transaction "specifically regulated or authorized by the Comptroller of the Currency" because Comptroller had no specific regulations governing this activity; UDAP damages, here $300,000 for mental anguish and humiliation, affirmed) *with* Everson v. Mineola Cmty. Bank, 2006 WL 2106959 (Tex. App. July 31, 2006) (no UDAP claim for wrongful foreclosure or other claims arising from mortgage; mortgage not a good or service within meaning of Texas UDAP statute).

213 *See* § 7.3, *supra*.

214 *See* § 7.4, *supra*.

215 *See* § 7.5, *supra*.

216 *See* § 7.6, Ch. 8, *supra*.

217 *See* §§ 7.7, 7.8, *supra*.

218 *See* § 7.9, *supra*.

219 La Barre v. Shepard, 84 F.3d 496 (1st Cir. 1996); Roylston v. Bank of Am., N.A., 660 S.E.2d 412 (Ga. Ct. App. 2008) (measure of damages is difference between fair market value of property and amount of debt). *See also* Murieta Car Wash, Inc. v. North Country Bank, 2005 WL 2100012 (Cal. Ct. App. Aug. 31, 2005) (measure of damages for wrongful foreclosure is fair market value at time of foreclosure, minus liens and encumbrances); C & K Invs. v. Fiesta Group, Inc., 248 S.W.3d 234 (Tex. App. 2007); UMLIC VP L.L.C. v. T & M Envt'l Sys., Inc., 176 S.W.3d 595 (Tex. App. 2005) (wrongful foreclosure gives rise to cause of action for return of property or for damages; measure of damages is fair market value of property minus balance due on debt; punitive damages not available). *But see* DeGolyer v. Green Tree Servicing, L.L.C., 662 S.E.2d 141 (Ga. Ct. App. 2008) (denying reconsideration and certiorari) (injured party may seek damages for mental anguish in addition to cancellation of the foreclosure in wrongful foreclosure action).

the mortgage debt, the discharged debt is normally included in the borrower's taxable income. Often, borrowers can exclude the discharged debt from taxable income, provided they receive timely advice and file the appropriate documentation with the IRS.

Borrowers can have both capital gains and cancellation of debt income in the same transaction.[220] This double liability happens whenever the amount realized from a foreclosure sale, short sale, or deed in lieu is (1) more than the borrower's basis but (2) less than the outstanding mortgage debt and the lender forgives the difference between the outstanding mortgage debt and the foreclosure sale price.

This subsection provides a brief introduction to some of the practical strategies to address the tax issues that may arise in the foreclosure situation. These issues are complex. Further consultation with an accountant or tax attorney may be necessary to resolve specific taxation issues that arise in a given case. In general, the available free tax-preparation services for low-income or older taxpayers will not be able to help with these issues.[221]

14.6.2 Taxable Gain from the Foreclosure Sale of the Home

14.6.2.1 When Is a Gain Taxable?

For tax purposes, a foreclosure sale is treated the same as a voluntary sale.[222] If the amount realized at the foreclosure sale is greater than the taxpayer's basis in the property, there may be a taxable gain.[223] The gain is recognized when the homeowner's rights are cut off—usually at the foreclosure sale, but potentially at the expiration of the redemption period, if that is in a later tax year.[224] The date of a settlement agreement will trump a later-entered court order.[225]

Most homeowners, and certainly most low-income homeowners, will qualify for the statutory exclusion of capital gains from the sale of a home. Individuals may exclude up to $250,000 and married couples up to $500,000.[226] Only if the homeowners have a great deal of equity or have not lived in the house for at least two of the last five years will they face capital gains taxes.[227]

If the transaction results in a gain for the taxpayer (the amount realized is more than the adjusted basis) above the exclusion, then the gain is subject to tax in accordance with the applicable rates for capital gains.[228] Losses resulting from the foreclosure of a residence, however, are not deductible.[229]

14.6.2.2 Calculating the Amount of the Gain

The gain is measured as the difference between the amount realized at the foreclosure sale and the homeowner's adjusted basis. The homeowner's adjusted basis includes the purchase price of the property, including any purchase money mortgages, plus the cost of any capital improvements made to the property by the homeowner.[230] The basis does not include costs of repairs or maintenance, even if performing the repairs increases the value of the home. Second mortgages are generally not included in the tax basis, except to the extent that the funds are used to make capital improvements.[231]

---

220 *See, e.g.*, Rev. Rul. 90-16, 1990-1 C.B. 12.

221 The IRS only permits the Volunteer Income Tax Assistance sites, and Tax Counseling for the Elderly sites to assist with cancellation of debt reporting if all of the homeowner's discharged debt is eligible for exclusion under the Mortgage Debt Forgiveness Relief Act of 2007. I.R.S. Pub. No. 4555, at 10-22 (2009). Senior staff at the Tax Assistance Centers are permitted to help with other COD issues, but may not assist in key issues, including the insolvency calculation. 2008 National Taxpayer Advocate Annual Report 45-46.

222 Helvering v. Hammel, 311 U.S. 504 (1941);2925 Briarpark, Ltd. v. Comm'r, 163 F.3d 313 (5th Cir. 1999) (foreclosure sale constitutes a "disposition of property" within the meaning of I.R.C. § 1001); Cox v. Comm'r, 68 F.3d 128 (5th Cir. 1995) (same); Lamm v. Commissioner, 873 F.2d 194, 196 (8th Cir. 1989); *In re* Barker, 301 B.R. 892 (Bankr. D. Colo. 2003); Waters v. Commissioner, 2002 WL 1825379 (T.C. May 30, 2002) (the disposition of mortgaged property at a foreclosure sale is treated as a sale or exchange from which the mortgagor may realize gain or loss under I.R.C. § 1001); Danenberg v. Commissioner, 73 T.C. 370 (1980) ("A voluntary sale and a mortgage foreclosure are both 'dispositions' within the scope of the gain or loss provisions of section 1001.").

223 I.R.C. § 1001 (26 U.S.C. § 1001). *See* Cox v. Comm'r, 68 F.3d 128 (5th Cir. 1995) (amount realized under § 1001 from the sale or disposition of property shall be the sum of money received plus the fair market value of any property received).

224 *Compare* Helvering v. Hammel, 311 U.S. 504 (1941) (gain realized upon foreclosure sale); Cox v. Comm'r, 68 F.3d 128 (5th Cir. 1995) (same); *In re* Barker, 301 B.R. 892 (Bankr. D. Colo. 2003)(same) *with* O'Donnell v. Belcher, 414 F.2d 833 (5th Cir. 1969) (discussing tax court finding that gain realized in year right of redemption expired). *See generally* Maule, 590-2d T.M., Taxation of Real Estate Transactions-An Overview.

225 I.R.S. Priv. Ltr. Rul. 2008-44-015 (Oct. 31, 2008).

226 26 U.S.C. § 121 (The Taxpayer Relief Act of 1997, Pub. L. No. 105-34). *See also* I.R.S. Pub. No. 523, Selling Your Home (2009) (discussing rules regarding exclusion from capital gains of proceeds from sale of home).

227 The required two years of ownership and use do not need to be continuous. The exclusion is prorated for homes owned for a shorter period. There are some other exceptions. *See* I.R.S. Pub. No. 523, Selling Your Home (2009).

228 26 U.S.C. §§ 1201–1298 (capital assets generally). *See also* I.R.S. Pub. No. 544, Sales and Other Dispositions of Assets (2009).

If homeowners spread the deduction for points over the life of the mortgage, any remaining undeducted points at the time of a foreclosure sale can be used to offset any taxable gain. *See* I.R.S. Pub. No. 936, Home Mortgage Interest Deduction (2009).

229 26 C.F.R. § 1.165-9(a); I.R.S. Pub. No. 523, Selling Your Home 5 (2009).

230 26 U.S.C. § 1016(a)(1).

231 Woodsam Assocs. v. Commissioner, 198 F.2d 357 (2d Cir. 1952).

The amount realized, for recourse mortgage loans, is the fair market value of the property. Generally, the fair market value of the property will be measured by the net proceeds from the foreclosure sale. The net proceeds are the amount bid at the foreclosure sale plus any cash or property the borrower receives.[232] This is so even if the amount bid at the foreclosure sale is less than the outstanding mortgage debt.[233] If the foreclosure sale bid is higher than the actual fair market value of the property, the taxpayer should produce evidence of the actual fair market value of the property at the time of transfer and may rely on that information to establish the amount realized.[234]

Thus, the amount realized on a deed-in-lieu transaction, for a recourse loan, will be the fair market value of the home, regardless of how much debt is forgiven (the forgiven debt in excess of the fair market value will be cancellation of debt income, discussed at § 14.6.3, *infra).*[235]

For non-recourse loans, the amount realized is the mortgage debt released plus any cash or property received, regardless of the fair market value of the home or the amount bid at the foreclosure sale.[236]

14.6.2.3 Lenders Reporting of the Amount Realized

Lenders should send the taxpayer a Form 1099-A showing the foreclosure bid, the outstanding mortgage debt, and the lender's fair market valuation of the property. If taxpayers disagree with the lender's valuation of the property, they should request that the lender prepare an amended 1099-A. The taxpayers should also be prepared to submit evidence of the actual fair market value. Lenders need not issue a 1099-A in the event that there is cancellation of debt income and a 1099-C is issued.[237] In that case, taxpayers should be able to get the information necessary to figure their capital gains from the 1099-C.

14.6.3 Cancellation of Debt (COD) Income

14.6.3.1 General Rule

Debt is frequently forgiven in connection with short sales, deeds-in-lieu, and other pre-foreclosure workout options or post-foreclosure agreements to forego collection. Debt may also be forgiven by statute if a lender, for example, elects to proceed through a non-judicial foreclosure. Whether forgiven by agreement or by statute, this forgiven debt is taxable as ordinary income unless an exception applies.[238]

The amount of the debt that was canceled, forgiven or discharged is considered cancellation of debt income (COD income).[239] Under the general rule a taxpayer's gross income includes COD income.[240] The rationale for the general rule is based upon the treatment of the loan proceeds when the debtor receives the loan.

When the loan was made, the proceeds were not required to be included in gross income.[241] Though the taxpayer's funds increased, there was a corresponding obligation to repay. The obligation offsets any gain to the taxpayer, thereby justifying the exclusion from gross income.

When the debt is subsequently canceled for anything less than face value, the untaxed funds that were previously offset have (in theory) become newly available to the taxpayer. The cancellation destroys the justification for excluding the loan proceeds from gross income. Therefore, under the general rule, those newly available funds, in the amount of the discharge, are now subject to tax as part of gross income.

14.6.3.2 Determining the Amount of Discharged Debt: Recourse vs. Non-Recourse Debt

The amount of discharged debt subject to inclusion as COD after a foreclosure sale, short sale, or deed-in-lieu is the difference between the amount realized from the disposition of the property, discussed § 14.6. *supra*, and the total amount of debt forgiven. If the lender does not waive the deficiency judgment, no debt is forgiven, and COD income is not triggered.

Forgiveness of debt that is by its terms non-recourse is included in the amount realized and therefore does not upon its discharge in foreclosure or via a deed-in-lieu give rise to discharge of indebtedness income.[242] The existence of an anti-deficiency statute by itself likely does not make the debt non-recourse.[243] Non-recourse debt discharged without surrender or transfer of the property, as through a loan modification or a short payoff via refinancing, does give rise to

232 Maule, 590-2d T.M. Taxation of Real Estate Transactions-An Overview, IV(B)(3)(a).

233 *See, e.g.,* Aizawa v. Comm'r, 29 F.3d 630 (9th Cir. 1994).
The excess of the outstanding mortgage debt over the foreclosure sale bid, if forgiven, is treated as discharge of indebtedness income, discussed at § 14.6.3, *infra.* 26 C.F.R. § 1.1001-2(a)(2).

234 Frazier v. Comm'r, 111 T.C. 243 (1998).

235 26 C.F.R. § 1.1001-2, Example 8.

236 26 U.S.C. § 1001; 26 C.F.R. § 1.1001-2; Rev. Rul. 90-16, 1990-1 C.B. 12.

237 *See* I.R.S. Instr. for Forms 1099-A and 1099-C, at 1, 2 (2010).

238 *See, e.g.,* Higgins v. I.R.S., 403 B.R. 537 (E.D. Tenn. 2009) (finding cancellation of debt income when lender lost right to seek deficiency judgment under Georgia law by failing to timely file for confirmation of foreclosure sale).

239 It is also called cancellation of indebtedness (COI) or discharge of indebtedness (DOI) income.

240 26 U.S.C. § 61(a)(12); United States v. Kirby Lumber Co., 284 U.S. 1 (1931).

241 *See* 26 U.S.C. § 61(a); Comm'r v. Tufts, 461 U.S. 300, 307 (1983).

242 26 C.F.R. § 1.1001-2(a)(1), (c), Example 7.

243 *See In re* Higgins, 403 B.R. 537 (E.D. Tenn. 2009).

discharge of indebtedness income.[244] The treatment of discharged non-recourse debt in a short sale is unsettled.[245]

For a deed-in-lieu, foreclosure sale, or short sale of property secured by recourse debt, the amount of discharged debt is equal to the total indebtedness forgiven, less the fair market value of the property surrendered.[246] Short payoffs via refinancing and loan modifications are treated the same for both recourse and non-recourse debt, with the entire amount of discharged debt treated as COD income, subject to the exclusions, discussed at § 14.6.4, *infra*.

14.6.3.3 Triggering Events: When COD Must Be Reported

Under the IRS regulations, there are eight triggering events that result in a creditor's reporting of COD income for individuals.[247] They are as follows:

- Bankruptcy discharge;[248]
- Foreclosure;
- Expiration of the statute of limitations, including the passing of any appeals period;[249]
- A statutory bar on further collection upon the creditor's election of remedies;
- Cancellation of debt in probate;
- An agreement between the creditor and the borrower;[250]
- The creditor's decision, pursuant to a "defined" policy, which need not be in writing, to cease collection activity on the debt; and
- For creditors that are financial institutions, the passage of three years without payment on the debt and no active collection activity in the previous year, not counting periods of time when the borrower was in bankruptcy or the creditor was otherwise barred from engaging in collection activities.[251]

These events trigger the creditor's obligation to report the discharged debt. The creditor will then report the discharged debt to the IRS and the borrower, using Form 1099-C.

14.6.3.4 When COD Need Not Be Reported

Discharged debt less than $600 need not be reported.[252] Discharged interest and fees also need not be reported,[253] although they may be reported.[254] There is no penalty imposed on creditors for failing to report discharged disputed debt,[255] and creditors should not report debt that was never due and owing.[256] Debt that is discharged by operation of law (other than via one of the triggering events listed above) generally does not need to be reported.[257] Discharge by operation of law can include court decisions and settlement of litigation.[258] This is one basis for excluding debt discharged pursuant to Truth in Lending rescission from taxable income.[259] Creditors also need not report debt discharged in a bankruptcy unless they know (or should know) that the debt was business or investment debt.[260]

14.6.3.5 Form 1099-C

14.6.3.5.1 What is a 1099-C?

Under the Internal Revenue Code, lenders must file Form 1099-C to report most discharged debts.[261] A 1099-A should not be used to report COD, but only the amount realized

244 Rev. Rul. 91-31, 1991-1 C.B. 19 (loan modification); Rev. Rul. 82-202, 1982-2 C.B. 35 (refinancing).

245 *See* I.R.S. Field Service Advisory, 1995 WL 1918329 (Sept. 29, 1995) (discussing the arguments for treating forgiven non-recourse debt either entirely as capital gains or as capital gains and COD income and noting that there are "no settled principles" for dealing with forgiveness of debt in short-sale non-recourse situations).

246 26 C.F.R. § 1.1001-2, Example 8 (deed-in-lieu); Rev. Rul. 82-202, 1982-2 C.B. 35 (refinancing); I.R.S. Field Service Advisory, 1995 WL 1918329 (Sept. 29, 1995) (short sale).

247 26 C.F.R. § 1.6050P-1(b)(2)(i).

248 Debt discharged in a bankruptcy need not be reported unless the creditor knows the debt was business of investment purpose debt. 26 C.F.R. § 1.6050P-1(d)(1)(i).

249 26 C.F.R. § 1.6050P-1(b)(2)(ii).

250 If that agreement merely recognizes that the debt was discharged by operation of law or was never valid, however, the discharged debt may not need to be reported. *See* I.R.S. Priv. Ltr. Rul. 2008-02-012 (Jan. 11, 2008); I.R.S. Priv. Ltr. Rul. 2002-12-004 (Mar. 22, 2002); §§ 14.6.3.4 (discussing when discharged debt need not be reported), 14.6.4.4 (discussing disputed debt exclusion), *infra*.

251 26 C.F.R. § 1.6050P-1(b)(2)(iii).

252 *See* 26 U.S.C. § 6050P(b).

253 26 C.F.R. § 1.6050P-1(d)(2), (d)(3). *See also* § 14.6.4.5, *infra* (discussing exclusion of interest and fees from income).

254 *See* 26 C.F.R. § 1.6050P-1(c).

255 Information Reporting for Discharges of Indebtedness, 61 Fed. Reg. 262, 267 (Jan. 4, 1996).

256 2010 Instructions for Forms 1099-A and 1099-C, at 2. *See also* § 14.6.4.4, *infra* (discussing exclusion of disputed debt).

257 61 Fed. Reg. 262 (Jan. 4, 1996); I.R.S. Priv. Ltr. Rul. 2008-25-045 (May 12, 2008) (finding no need to issue 1099-Cs to servicemembers who exercise their right under the Servicemembers Civil Relief Act to terminate motor vehicle leases early without paying the termination fee).

258 I.R.S. Priv. Ltr. Rul. 2008-02-013 (Jan. 11. 2008) (finding "irrelevant" that the discharge was part of a negotiated settlement without a trial; discharge still by operation of law and therefore not reportable); I.R.S. Priv. Ltr. Rul. 2002-12-004 (Mar. 22, 2002) (finding stipulation to injunction discharge by operation of law).

259 There are at least two other possible bases: the fact that the discharged debt in rescission is interest and fees, also not subject to mandatory reporting, and disputed debt. The treatment of interest and fees is discussed at § 14.6.4.5, *infra*, and the treatment of disputed debt at § 14.6.4.4, *infra*.

260 26 C.F.R. § 1.6050P-1(d)(1).

261 26 C.F.R. § 1.6050P-1(a).

from a transfer of the property.[262] Nonetheless, sometimes a 1099-A will be interpreted by the IRS as reflecting COD income. Some practitioners have reported success in getting the IRS to reverse its position by noting that there was no cancellation of debt separate from the disposal of the property, and that the entire amount of cancelled debt should therefore be treated as a fair market exchange for the property.

Any information provided to the IRS in Form 1099-C must also be furnished to the taxpayer in a written statement.[263] The written statement must be furnished on or before January 31st of the year following the year in which the cancellation was made.[264] The information return requirement is intended to give the IRS notice of transactions that may involve tax consequences and provide the taxpayer with detailed information for her tax reporting. Nearly two million 1099-C's were filed with the IRS in 2008, up nearly twenty percent from 2007.[265]

The IRS automatically checks to see if there is a matching tax return for every 1099-C received.[266] Thus, taxpayers who ignore a 1099-C do so at the peril of receiving an IRS notice of underpayment of tax, coupled with interest and penalties.

Taxpayers should be advised to deal with the reported discharge of debt on their income tax filing, but neither taxpayers nor their advisers should assume that the 1099-C correctly represents the amount of taxable income. Often the 1099-C is wrong and seldom will it include available exclusions. Even if there is significant taxable income, taxpayers can seek a payment plan of up to five years through Form 9465 when necessary.

14.6.3.5.2 The filing of a 1099-C does not mean that tax is owed

The filing of a Form 1099-C does not necessarily reflect a taxable event under the Internal Revenue Code.[267] Lenders often file 1099-C Forms without regard to whether any of the exclusions discussed below applies.[268] In addition, some 1099-C Forms are filed by creditors in error in situations in which filing is not required by the IRS at all. Moreover, the filing of a 1099-C does not mean incontrovertibly that a debt is discharged[269]: it may evince an intention to discharge a debt;[270] it may be filed to comply with the triggering events discussed above;[271] or it may simply be filed in error.[272]

The IRS recommends that taxpayers scrutinize the 1099-Cs they receive and contest the amount of the discharged debt with the lender if it is incorrect.[273] While lenders may vary in their receptivity to recalculating the amount of discharged debt reported, a letter to the lender documenting the inclusion of interest or a miscalculation will do no harm and can be attached to the taxpayer's return as evidence of the true value of the discharged debt.

14.6.3.5.3 Improper filing of a 1099-C; use of a 1099-C to defeat collection actions

Compliance with 1099-C reporting is not a safe harbor from state or federal debt collection practices claims.[274] Intentionally false or misleading 1099-Cs, or the threat of filing a 1099-C, may be grounds for claims based on federal or state fair debt collection practices.[275]

On the other hand, debt collectors are unlikely to be liable to consumers simply for filing a 1099-C in error or with the wrong amounts. Even if the taxpayer has already paid income tax on the discharged debt, a debt collector or creditor can resume collection activity upon filing an

262 2010 Instructions for Forms 1099-A and 1099-C, at 1-2.

263 *See* 26 C.F.R. § 1.6050P-1(f)(2).

264 *See* 26 U.S.C. § 1.6050P-1(f)(3).

265 2009 National Taxpayer Advocate Annual Report 149.

266 2008 National Taxpayer Advocate Annual Report 391 n.5, 395.

267 *See, e.g.,* Owens v. Comm'r, 67 Fed. Appx. 253 (5th Cir. 2003); Sims v. Comm'r, 2002 WL 1825373, at *2 (T.C. June 26, 2002); H.R. Conf. Rep. No. 213, 103d Cong., 1st Sess. 1, 671 (1993) ("[I]nformation returns are required regardless of whether the debtor is subject to tax on the discharged debt. For example, Congress does not expect reporting financial institutions and agencies to determine whether the debtor qualifies for exclusion under section 108.").

268 *See* Wagner v. Client Servs., Inc., 2009 WL 839073 (E.D. Pa. Mar. 26, 2009) (finding FDCPA violation where offer of settlement advised that a if more than $600 in debt was forgiven, a 1099-C would be issued, without a determination as to whether any exclusions would apply).

269 *In re* Zilka, 407 B.R. 684 (Bankr. W.D. Pa. 2009); Lifestyles of Jasper, Inc. v. Gremore, 299 S.W.3d 275 (Ky. Ct. App. 2009); I.R.S. Priv. Ltr. Rul. 2005-0208 (Dec. 30, 2005); I.R.S. Priv. Ltr. Rul. 2005-0207 (Dec. 30, 2005). *But cf.* Amtrust Bank v. Fossett, 224 P.3d 935 (Ariz. Ct. App. 2009) (finding issuance of 1099-C prima facie evidence that the debt was discharged); Franklin Credit Mgmt. Corp. v. Nicholas, 812 A.2d 51, 61 (Conn. App. Ct. 2002) (1099-C signed writing discharging debt).

270 *See, e.g.,* Owens v. Comm'r, 67 Fed. Appx. 253 (5th Cir.2003).

271 *See, e.g.,* Amtrust Bank v. Fossett, 224 P.3d 935 (Ariz. Ct. App. 2009).

272 *See, e.g.,* Franklin Credit Mgmt. Corp. v. Nicholas, 812 A.2d 51, 58 (Conn. App. Ct. 2002).

273 I.R.S. News Release IR-2008-17, Mortgage Workouts, Now Tax-Free for Many Homeowners; Claim Relief on Newly-Revised IRS Form (Feb. 12, 2008), *available at* www.irs.gov/irs/article/0,,id=179073,00.html.

For a critique of the practicality of borrowers disputing the amounts on 1099-Cs with their lenders, see 2007 National Taxpayer Advocate Annual Report 17.

274 I.R.S. Priv. Ltr. Rul. 2005-0208 (Dec. 30, 2005).

275 *See* Kuehn v. Cadle Co., 335 Fed. Appx. 827 (11th Cir. 2009) (finding threat of IRS fine of $50 for failure to provide debt collector with taxpayer's social security number before 1099-C filing requirement triggered a per se violation of the Fair Debt Collections Practices Act). *See generally* National Consumer Law Center, Fair Debt Collection § 1.5.12 (6th ed. 2008 and Supp.).

amended 1099-C.[276] One case even suggested debt collectors could continue with collection activities without amending the 1099-C if the original 1099-C included a statement that debt collection activities would be ongoing.[277] Two IRS private letter rulings give support to this position, by advising that the issuance of a 1099-C does not mean that collection activities must cease.[278]

Nonetheless, depending on the facts and state law, some courts have found that issuance of a 1099-C is at least prima facie evidence that there is no further obligation on the loan.[279]

14.6.3.6 Taxpayer Reporting: Form 982

Individual taxpayers have an independent obligation to report discharge of indebtedness income to the IRS, whether or not the lender issues a 1099-C. Practitioners should advise taxpayers, if there is reportable discharge of indebtedness income, to file a 1040 and attach Form 982 (Reduction of Tax Attributes Due to Discharge of Indebtedness). Form 982 allows taxpayers to claim applicable exclusions from COD income.

Form 982, although recently revised by the IRS, is not user friendly and appears in many respects to be directed only at corporate taxpayers. Individual taxpayers with a discharge of consumer debt need complete only Parts I (identifying the amount of excluded COD income and the basis of the exclusion) and II (the reduction of basis), and only line 10 of Part II. Part III is addressed solely to corporate taxpayers and need not be completed by individual taxpayers. Part I contains check boxes for the bankruptcy, insolvency, and qualified principal residence exceptions. If the taxpayer seeks to exclude the discharged debt for any other reasons, the taxpayer should complete lines 2 and 10a of Form 982 and attach a statement explaining the reason for excluding the discharged debt from taxable income.

IRS Publication 4681, Canceled Debts, Foreclosures, Repossessions, and Abandonment, can be a useful companion to the homeowner or advocate attempting to decode Form 982.

14.6.4 Exclusions from Cancellation of Debt Income

14.6.4.1 Overview

COD income can be excluded from gross income in the following situations: where the consumer is insolvent or has filed bankruptcy, where a debt is disputed or contingent, in the case of interest and fees, under the purchase price infirmity doctrine, and as acquisition indebtedness.[280] A typical consumer might qualify for either of two exceptions involving (1) debt cancellations made while the debtor was insolvent,[281] or (2) discharges made in a bankruptcy case.[282] In addition, forgiven interest or fees for which a deduction could be taken (such as home mortgage interest or points) but has not been, should not be included in COD.[283] Unliquidated, disputed debt or contingent liabilities that are canceled should not be treated as discharge of indebtedness income.

Even if the debt may be excluded from income, that does not absolve the taxpayer of her reporting obligations, discussed at § 14.6.5.1, *infra.*

14.6.4.2 Insolvency Exclusion

COD income is excludable from gross income if the taxpayer is insolvent prior to receiving the discharge, to the extent of the insolvency.[284] Insolvency is defined as an excess of liabilities over the fair market value of assets, as determined immediately prior to the discharge.[285] COD income greater than the insolvency is *not* excludable.

Consider, for example, a taxpayer with assets valued at $18,000 and liabilities of $26,000. This taxpayer is insolvent by $8000. If $6000 of the debt is discharged, the debtor has $6000 worth of COD income. The entire amount of the COD income would be excludable because the amount of the COD income was less than the amount of the initial insolvency.[286]

If, on the other hand, $11,000 of the debt is discharged, only $8000 of the COD income (the amount by which the

276 *See, e.g., In re* Crosby, 261 B.R. 470 (Bankr. D. Kan. 2001). *See generally* National Consumer Law Center, Fair Debt Collection § 1.5.12 (6th ed. 2008 and Supp.).

277 Debt Buyer's Ass'n v. Snow, 481 F. Supp. 2d 1 (D.D.C. 2006).

278 I.R.S. Priv. Ltr. Rul. 2005-0208 (Dec. 30, 2005) ("Section 6050P and the regulations do not prohibit collection activity after a creditor reports by filing a Form 1099-C."); I.R.S. Priv. Ltr. Rul. 2005-0207 (Dec. 30, 2005) ("The Internal Revenue Service does not view a Form 1099-C as an admission by the creditor that it has discharged the debt and can no longer pursue collection.").

279 *See, e.g.,* Amtrust Bank v. Fossett, 224 P.3d 935 (Ariz. Ct. App. 2009); Franklin Credit Mgmt. Corp. v. Nicholas, 812 A.2d 51, 61 (Conn. App. Ct. 2002).

280 See 26 U.S.C. § 108(a). A taxpayer with indebtedness discharged in such circumstances must apply the amount excluded, however, to reduce certain of tax benefits or the basis in property. *See* 26 U.S.C. §§ 108(b)(2), 1017(a).

281 26 U.S.C. § 108(a)(1)(B).

Note that the taxpayer has the burden of proving an exception applies. *See* Danenberg v. Commissioner, 73 T.C. 370 (1980) (exceptions to general rules regarding realization of income are strictly construed).

282 26 U.S.C. § 108(a)(1)(A).

283 26 U.S.C. § 108(e).

284 *See* 26 U.S.C. § 108(a)(1)(B), (d)(3).

285 26 U.S.C. § 108(d)(3).

286 For another example, see Miller v. C.I.C., 2006 WL 1652681 (T.C. June 15, 2006).

debtor was initially insolvent) would be excludable. The debtor would have to include $3000 of the COD income (the amount by which the discharge of debt made the debtor solvent) in gross income.

In determining insolvency, a long-established rule provided that exempt assets did not count as part of the consumer's assets.[287] However, in 1999, the IRS changed its position and issued private letter rulings and technical advisory memoranda stating that even exempt assets should be included in the insolvency equation.[288] A 2001 Tax Court ruling, relying on the legislative history of the 1978 Bankruptcy Reform Act and the 1980 Bankruptcy Tax Act, agreed with the IRS that exempt assets should be included in the insolvency equation.[289] The ruling has not been reviewed by an appellate court, and commentators have criticized it.[290]

Contingent liabilities are counted as liabilities if it is "more likely than not" that the taxpayer will be called upon to pay the obligation in the amount claimed.[291]

In claiming the insolvency exception, taxpayers should make sure to document the insolvency calculation and attach a statement to their return outlining the insolvency calculation.[292] IRS Publication 4681 has a table that may be useful in doing this, or taxpayers may want to attach a credit report to their return.

14.6.4.3 Bankruptcy Exclusion

If the COD occurs in the context of a bankruptcy, the entire amount of COD qualifies for exclusion from gross income.[293] Consumer debtors in bankruptcy are not bound by the limitations on the amount of the insolvency exception, since the bankruptcy exception takes precedence over insolvency.[294] Because of the complete exclusion of COD from income, and the bankruptcy exception for 1099-C reporting,[295] taxpayers facing COD may wish to consider filing bankruptcy.

The timing of the bankruptcy filing is crucial. To qualify for the bankruptcy exclusion, the taxpayer must be under the jurisdiction of a bankruptcy court at the time of the discharge and the discharge must be granted by the court or pursuant to a plan approved by the court.[296] If a debt forgiveness agreement is reached before the filing of the bankruptcy and the insolvency exclusion does not apply, the "taxable event" has occurred and the tax is due. The tax obligation is unlikely to be dischargeable in a later bankruptcy.[297] Similarly, if the bankruptcy is dismissed without a discharge, the bankruptcy exclusion may not be available.[298]

14.6.4.4 Disputed or Contingent Debts

Debt that was never owed or for which repayment was contingent on some future event does not generate COD income upon discharge. For example, the release of a guarantor does not generate COD income to the guarantor.[299] Similarly, if a statute voids the debt, the IRS will generally permit the discharge of that debt to be excluded from income.[300] Thus, the reduction in principal due to a successful Truth in Lending rescission claim should not be included in income. What it means for a debt to have never been owed, or to be contingent, is not always so clear, however.[301]

Cases where the creditor and consumer arrive at a settlement of disputed debt can be particularly tricky. Courts have held that the settlement of a disputed debt by the payment of an amount that is less than the original amount of the debt

287 *See* Marcus Estate v. Comm'r, 34 T.C.M. (CCH) 38 (1975); Cole v. Comm'r, 42 B.T.A. 1110 (1940).

288 Tech. Adv. Mem. 99-35-002; Private Letter Rulings 99-32-019 and 99-32-013.

289 Carlson v. Comm'r, 116 T.C. 87 (2001).

290 *See, e.g.*, Note & Comment, Measuring Assets and Liabilities Under the I.R.C. 108 Insolvency Exclusion, 19 Bank. Dev. J. 429 (2003).

291 Merkel v. Comm'r, 109 T.C. 463 (1997), *aff'd*, 192 F.3d 844 (9th Cir. 1999).

292 2008 National Taxpayer Advocate Annual Report 60.

293 26 U.S.C. § 108(a)(1)(A), (d)(2).

294 *See* 26 U.S.C. § 108(a)(3).

295 26 C.F.R. § 1.6050P-1(d)(1).

296 26 U.S.C. § 108(d)(2). *See also In re* Pflug 146 B.R. 687 (Bankr. E.D. Va. 1992) (citing 11 U.S.C. § 346(j), special tax provisions of the Bankruptcy Code); Schachner v. Comm'r, 2006 WL 3638506 (T.C. Dec. 13, 2006) (finding COD income not excludable under bankruptcy exception where student loan was neither discharged nor eligible for discharge in the bankruptcy case, and was in fact the subject of a finding on non-dischargeability).

The court in *Pflug* noted that the exclusion under the special tax provision includes forgiveness of indebtedness whether or not such indebtedness is "discharged" in the bankruptcy sense. *See also* Notes of Committee on the Judiciary, S. Rep. No. 95-989 (1978).

297 It is likely to create a nondischargeable debt under 11 U.S.C. § 523(a)(1) in chapter 7 cases or to create a priority debt which must be paid in full in chapter 13.

298 Hill v. Comm'r, T.C.M. (RIA) 2009-101 (May 18, 2009).

299 *See, e.g.*, Whitmer v. Comm'r, T.C. Memo. 1996-83.

300 *See, e.g.*, I.R.S. Priv. Ltr. Rul. 2008-25-045 (May 12, 2008) (finding no need to issue 1099-Cs to servicemembers who exercise their right under the Servicemembers Civil Relief Act to terminate motor vehicle leases early without paying the termination fee since there is no income); I.R.S. Priv. Ltr. Rul. 2008-02-012 (Jan. 11, 2008) (finding no reportable discharge of debt when debt canceled under state statute voiding debt in absence of mandated notice); I.R.S. Priv. Ltr. Rul. 2002-12-004 (Mar. 22, 2002) (finding no reportable discharge of debt when debt canceled under state statute forbidding collection of default judgments without inclusion of statutorily mandated notice).

301 *See, e.g.*, I.R.S. Priv. Ltr. Rul. 96-42-041 (July 18, 1996) (contingent liabilities are not included as income, but "gap amounts" under retail installment sales contracts are not contingent liabilities).

does not give rise to COD income.[302] The origins of the doctrine can be traced to the United States Board of Tax Appeals' decision in *Sobel v. Commissioner*.[303] In that case, a New York corporation purchased 100 shares of a bank's stock in exchange for a $21,700 promissory note as payment. When the note matured, the stock was worthless. The taxpayer later sued to rescind the note, arguing that the loan violated the law, and the bank failed to perform certain promises. The parties settled the case, with the taxpayer agreeing to pay half of the note's value. The Board of Tax Appeals found that the taxpayer had not recognized income from discharge of approximately half of his debt as the "release of the note was not the occasion for a freeing of assets and there was no gain."

The Third Circuit adopted this rationale in *Zarin v. Commissioner*.[304] In that case, a taxpayer settled a $3.5 million debt owed to a casino for $500,000. The court found that the debt, a gambling debt, was unenforceable under state law. The taxpayer disputed liability based upon unenforceability and the settlement of $500,000 served to establish the true value of the debt. According the court, under the contested liability doctrine, if a taxpayer in good faith disputed the amount of a debt, a subsequent settlement of the dispute would be treated as the amount of the debt cognizable for tax purposes.

Criticizing *Zarin*, the Tenth Circuit in *Preslar v. Commissioner*[305] held that the disputed debt exception applies only to debts that are not fixed in amount. The loan in *Preslar*, a mortgage loan, was liquidated and as a result any reduction in the amount of the loan would constitute COD income.[306] The court noted that the dispute focused on repayment of the loan and not the amount or validity of the taxpayer's debt. According to the Tenth Circuit, the enforceability of the debt should not affect the tax treatment of the transaction unless the debt is unenforceable as a result of an infirmity (e.g., fraud or material misrepresentation) at the time of its creation.[307]

14.6.4.5 Interest and Fees

In most consumer transactions, only principal amounts canceled are COD income. Canceled interest and fees are generally not counted as income, because such amounts were never available as income to the debtor.[308] The Code specifically excludes as income discharged interest and fees for which the taxpayer would have the right to take a deduction—certainly the case for mortgage interest or points.[309] Fees or interest may also be void under state or federal law, in which case they should never be included in income.[310] Thus, it may be advantageous to draft a settlement agreement to specify that a portion of the loan forgiveness relates to canceled interest or fees instead of to principal.

Truth in Lending rescission of a home mortgage is an important example of a non-taxable event involving forgiven interest and fees. The rescission does not forgive any principal but erases liability for interest and fees. Past payments made toward interest and fees are returned or applied to reduce the principal, and the consumer tenders the net amount financed. The amount saved in interest and fees is not income.

Note, however, if a consumer has taken a deduction for interest payments in previous years, and that interest is subsequently forgiven or refunded to the consumer, the consumer has received a tax benefit. According to one court, the amount previously taken as a deduction becomes income in the current year under the "tax benefit" rule.[311]

14.6.4.6 Purchase Price Infirmity Doctrine

A purchase price reduction is not taxable income if property is bought at an inflated price on credit, and the originating lender or assignee lowers the indebtedness as a direct result of a legitimate argument contesting the purchase price, provided the borrower did not participate in any fraud in agreeing to the purchase price originally.[312]

There is both a common law and statutory basis for this exception. The statutory exception created under 26 U.S.C.

302 Zarin v. Comm'r, 916 F.2d 110 (3d Cir. 1990); Sobel v. Comm'r, 40 B.T.A. 1263 (1939). *See also* I.R.S. Priv. Ltr. Rul. 2008-02-012 (Jan. 11, 2008) (finding it "irrelevant" that debt discharged via settlement instead of through trial where creditor's failure to include statutorily mandated notice voided debt); I.R.S. Priv. Ltr. Rul. 2002-12-004 (Mar. 22, 2002) (no reportable discharged debt where stipulated injunction entered on basis of failure to include statutory notice).

303 40 B.T.A. 1263 (1939).

304 916 F.2d 110 (3d Cir. 1990).

305 167 F.3d 1323 (10th Cir. 1999).

306 The debt in *Preslar* was a $1 million promissory note, given to a bank in connection with the purchase of a ranch that was to be developed by the taxpayer. The bank permitted the taxpayer to repay the loan by assigning the installment sales contract of purchasers of the developed property to the bank at a discount. When the bank became insolvent the FDIC was appointed receiver. The FDIC refused to accept further assignments of the sales contracts as repayment. The taxpayers stopped making payments and sued the FDIC. The parties settled after the FDIC agreed to accept $350,000 in full satisfaction of the debt, which had a balance of nearly $800,000.

307 Preslar v. Comm'r, 167 F.3d 1323 (10th Cir. 1999).

308 *See* 26 C.F.R. § 1.6050P-1(d)(2) (canceled interest need not be reported); § 14.6.3.3, *supra* (discussing COD reporting).

309 26 U.S.C. § 108(a)(e)(2).

310 *See* I.R.S. Priv. Ltr. Rul. 2008-25-045 (May 12, 2008) (finding that the discharge of early termination fees for service members who exercise their right under the Servicemembers Civil Relief Act to terminate motor vehicle leases early is not income, since such fees are illegal under the Act); § 14.6.4.4, *supra*.

311 Schlifke v. Comm'r, 61 T.C.M. (CCH) 1697 (1991).

312 26 U.S.C. § 108 (e)(5); Rev. Rul. 92-99.

§ 108(e)(5)[313] and applies only to agreements between a purchaser and a seller to reduce the debt. Prior to the enactment of the statute, some courts applied the purchase price reduction to third party debt either assumed or incurred in order to purchase the property.[314] It is unclear whether section 108(e)(5) repeals or modifies the common law exception.[315] However, the IRS will treat a debt reduction by a third-party lender as a purchase price adjustment if it based on an infirmity, such as fraud in the original sale.[316]

The purchase price infirmity doctrine can be particularly helpful in property flipping schemes where the house was sold to the homeowner at an inflated price. In these cases, even if the lender had no knowledge of the fraud, if the lender agrees to reduce the debt based on the fact that there was fraud by a third party, that debt reduction should be excludable from gross income.

14.6.4.7 Acquisition Indebtedness

14.6.4.7.1 Overview

For debt discharged from 2007 through 2012, either as a result of the homeowner's financial condition or a decline in the home's value, discharged acquisition indebtedness may be excluded from income, up to $2 million.[317]

Acquisition indebtedness, or qualified principal residence indebtedness, includes loans used to purchase, construct, or substantially improve a taxpayer's principal residence.[318] "Substantial improvements" should include anything that increases the basis in the property.[319] Routine repairs, such as roof repairs, even if long delayed and desperately needed, are not, in the IRS jargon, "substantial improvements" and therefore debt incurred to pay for them likely cannot be credited towards acquisition indebtedness.[320]

Refinanced acquisition indebtedness may also be discharged under this exception, up to the amount of the remaining principal on the loan immediately before the refinancing.[321]

14.6.4.7.2 Ordering rule for home equity debt

A discharge in the case of refinanced home mortgage debt will normally consist of mixed acquisition indebtedness (the principal amount of the old loan) and home equity debt (the fees and remaining principal on the new loan, possibly including such items as consolidated credit card debt).

Under the statute, discharged debt in these circumstances is treated first as home equity debt, which is not eligible for the qualified principal residence exclusion. Only after all of the home equity debt is discharged or paid down, can the debt discharged be treated as qualified principal residence indebtedness, eligible for the exclusion.[322]

An example may be helpful in working through this ordering rule for mixed acquisition and home equity debt. If a taxpayer purchases her home with a $100,000 mortgage, pays $10,000 in principal, and then refinances that loan, consolidating non-mortgage debt, $90,000 of the new loan will be treated as acquisition indebtedness. Suppose the new loan is for $130,000. The home equity debt is then $40,000. If the lender forgives less than $40,000, the entire amount of discharged debt will be treated as home equity debt and not eligible for the qualified principal residence indebtedness exception. If the lender discharges more than $40,000, the amount of discharged debt greater than $40,000 will be treated as acquisition indebtedness and eligible for the qualified principal residence indebtedness exception. So, if the lender discharges $35,000 worth of debt, none of the discharged debt would be treated as acquisition indebtedness. If the lender discharges $45,000 of the debt, $5000 would be treated as acquisition indebtedness. The taxpayer would either need to pay taxes on the first $40,000 discharged (the home equity debt) or make use of a different exclusion from taxable income.

Taxpayers may, if eligible, use the insolvency exception to avoid tax consequences on the discharge of the home equity debt.[323] Thus, in the example above, a taxpayer insolvent before the discharge in the amount of $40,000 or more, would be able to exclude all of the canceled debt from income.

313 (5) Purchase-money debt reduction for solvent debtor treated as price reduction. If—
(A) the debt of a purchaser of property to the seller of such property which arose out of the purchase of such property is reduced,
(B) such reduction does not occur—
(i) in a title 11 case, or
(ii) when the purchaser is insolvent, and
(C) but for this paragraph, such reduction would be treated as income to the purchaser from the discharge of indebtedness.
then such reduction shall be treated as a purchase price adjustment.

314 Comm'r v. Sherman, 135 F.2d 68 (6th Cir. 1943); Hirsch v. Comm'r, 115 F.2d 656 (7th Cir. 1940). *But see* Fifth Ave.-Fourteenth St. Corp. v. Comm'r, 147 F.2d 453 (2d Cir. 1944) (doctrine does not apply to third-party transactions).

315 *See, e.g.*, Preslar v. Comm'r, 167 F.3d 1323 (10th Cir. 1999); Rev. Rul. 92-99, 1992-2 C.B. 35. *See generally* Tatlock, 540-2d T.M., Discharge of Indebtedness, Bankruptcy and Insolvency § II(I).

316 Rev. Rul. 92-99, 1992-2 C.B. 35.

317 26 U.S.C. § 108(a)(1)(E). See generally How Congress Did (or Did Not) Save Your Clients from Foreclosure: The Mortgage Forgiveness Debt Relief Act of 2007, 26 NCLC REPORTS Bankruptcy and Foreclosures Ed. 9 (Nov./Dec. 2007).

318 26 U.S.C. § 163(h)(3)(B).

319 *Cf.* 26 C.F.R. § 1.163-10T.

320 Mertens Law of Fed'l Income Tax'n § 20:10.

321 26 U.S.C. § 163(h)(3)(B); IRS Form 982, at 4.

322 26 U.S.C. § 108(h)(4).

323 IRS Form 982, at 4. *See generally* § 14.6.4.2, *supra* (discussing the insolvency exception).

14.6.5 What to Do If an Exclusion Applies

14.6.5.1 General

When a taxpayer receives a 1099-C, the taxpayer or his or her attorney or accountant must make a independent analysis, distinct from that performed by the creditor, about whether the discharge must be included as part of the taxpayer's gross income, or whether one of the exclusions applies. If the discharged debt is inadvertently included by the taxpayer as income, it will be subject to tax.

Practitioners should provide clients with a letter summarizing any applicable grounds for excluding the COD income from taxable income. If some of the COD income may be excluded for one reason, such as interest and fees, and some for another, such as acquisition indebtedness, the letter should take care to allocate the COD. This letter should include the IRS Circular 230 disclosure, warning that the advice will not necessarily insulate the taxpayer from penalties.[324]

In order to establish the non-taxability of discharged debt with the IRS, the taxpayer must file the long Form 1040 and attach Form 982. Form 982 is discussed in more detail at § 14.6.3.6, *supra.*

14.6.5.2 What to Do If Tax Has Mistakenly Been Paid

A taxpayer who receives a copy of a Form 1099-C may mistakenly report COD income in gross income. If either some or the entire amount of the included COD income was excludable, the IRS is unlikely to catch the error. The taxpayer can, however, remedy the situation.

324 IRS Circular 230 governs practice by attorneys and others in front of the IRS. The regulations contained in IRS Circular 230 can be found at 31 C.F.R. pt. 10. Practice before the IRS in this context includes providing any written advice "having the potential for tax avoidance." 31 C.F.R. § 10.2(a)(4). If the IRS Circular 230 notice is given, then the attorney need not discuss completely all relevant law and all facts (nor confirm the accuracy of the facts). 31 C.F.R. § 10.35. The disclosure language cannot be in a footnote and must be as prominent as any other language in the letter. One version of the disclosure language is the following:

> To ensure compliance with IRS Circular 230, any U.S. federal tax advice provided in this communication is not intended or written to be used, and it cannot be used by the recipient or any other taxpayer (i) for the purpose of avoiding tax penalties that may be imposed on the recipient or any other taxpayer, or (ii) in promoting, marketing or recommending to another party a partnership or other entity, investment plan, arrangement or other transaction addressed herein.

The amount of tax paid on the excludable, yet included, COD income is an overpayment.[325] The debtor can recover the amount of an overpayment, including any interest allowed thereon, as a credit or a refund.[326] A timely[327] written claim must be filed. The consumer debtor can use Form 1040X, the amended U.S. individual income tax return to accomplish the writing requirement.[328]

14.6.5.3 Preventing Submission of a 1099-C Form

A settlement agreement involving debt forgiveness should address whether the creditor will submit a 1099-C Form and in what amount. Settlement agreements should also establish any basis for excluding the discharged debt from income. For example, if the consumer will seek to exclude the discharged debt as qualified principal residence indebtedness, the settlement agreement should specify that the debt is being discharged because of the taxpayer's financial condition or because of a decline in the property value. If the consumer will seek to discharge the debt as disputed, the settlement agreement should recite that the debt is disputed and should not contain any boilerplate language absolving the lender of all wrongdoing.

Practitioners should insist that lenders not report on a 1099-C any amounts not required to be reported, including particularly discharged interest, fees, or debt discharged in a bankruptcy. Creditors should agree to notify taxpayers and their counsel if the IRS or any other taxing authority challenges the reporting of the COD income and provide taxpayers copies of any documents generated or provided in response to the inquiry.

Many attorneys representing foreclosing lenders are willing to be educated on the tax issues in a foreclosure. It is useful to provide them with a letter that explains why the discharge is not taxable and why, in the circumstances of your case, there is no requirement to report the discharged debt to the IRS. Absent "intentional disregard," the penalty for failure to report is $50.[329] Even that penalty will not be imposed if the failure to report was due to "reasonable cause and not willful neglect."[330] Reasonable cause for not reporting should include a good faith belief that the debt is disputed and its discharge does not result in taxable income.

Given the complexity of Form 982 and the lack of pro bono assistance in completing Form 982, consumers are

325 *See* 26 U.S.C. § 6401(c).

326 *See* 26 U.S.C. § 6402.

327 The debtor's claim for credit or refund must generally be filed within the later of three years from the time the return was filed or two years from the time the tax was paid. 26 U.S.C. § 6511(a).

328 26 C.F.R. § 301.6402-3(a)(2).

329 26 U.S.C. § 6721(a)(1).

In the case of intentional disregard, the penalty is 10% of the amount of the discharged debt not reported correctly. 26 U.S.C. § 6721(e)(2).

330 26 U.S.C. § 6724(a).

likely to incur significant costs in challenging 1099-Cs that are issued incorrectly or in an inflated amount. Without guidance from their attorneys, few taxpayers will be aware either of how to report the discharge of indebtedness income or of the applicable exclusions. Consumers who fail to report the discharge of indebtedness income correctly or fail to claim the applicable exceptions can incur steep costs, either in penalties or in overpayment of taxes.

14.7 Rights of Tenants in Possession Following Foreclosure on Their Landlord's Property

14.7.1 Federal Protections

14.7.1.1 Protecting Tenants at Foreclosure Act

In May of 2009, the Protecting Tenants at Foreclosure Act[331] went into effect, although its provisions are scheduled to sunset on December 31, 2012.[332] This Act applies to federally related mortgage loans,[333] and provides all "bona fide" tenants[334] in foreclosed residential properties with certain protections if the lease preceded notice of the foreclosure.[335] Federally related mortgage loans are defined as loans made by federally insured depository lenders (other than for temporary financing, such as a construction loan) or by creditors who make or invest more than one million dollars a year in residential secured loans, HUD-related loans, or loans intended to be sold on the secondary market to Fannie Mae, Ginnie Mae, or Freddie Mac.[336]

The Protecting Tenants at Foreclosure Act actually states that it applies to "any foreclosure on a federally related mortgage loan or on any dwelling or residential real property. . . ."[337] This implies it applies to both federally related mortgage loans and any mortgage on any dwelling or residential real property. At least one court, though, has interpreted the "or" as a scrivener's error.[338]

The Act gives such tenants the right to continue occupying the property through the remaining term of the lease, with the exception that the lease may be terminated upon the provision of ninety days' notice if a buyer intends to occupy the unit as a primary residence.[339] The Act also provides tenants without leases or with leases that are terminable at will under state law the right to ninety days' notice before eviction.[340] Nothing in the new federal law is intended to affect "any federal- or State-subsidized tenancy or any State or local law that provides longer time periods or other additional protections for tenants."[341]

In one case, Bank of America sought unsuccessfully to evade the Act's requirements. It sent a questionnaire to tenants requiring them to respond promptly. When the tenants failed to do so, the bank argued that it could then assume the tenants were not "bona fide" and could immediately evict them. The court had little trouble dismissing this argument.[342]

Where a new owner brings an eviction action in state court, the consumer cannot seek federal court jurisdiction for the case based upon a Protecting Tenants at Foreclosure Act defense. Federal jurisdiction cannot be based upon a defense or counterclaim.[343]

14.7.1.2 Fannie Mae and Freddie Mac Mortgages

In January 2009 both Freddie Mac and Fannie Mae announced programs to rent foreclosed properties on month-to-month leases.[344] Freddie Mac's "REO Rental Initiative" applies to both tenants and former owners in possession at

331 Helping Families Save Their Homes Act of 2009, Pub. L. No. 111-22, §§ 701–704 (2009).

332 *Id.* § 704.

333 *Id.* § 702(a). The Act states that the term "federally-related mortgage loan" has the same meaning as in section 3 of the Real Estate Settlement Procedures Act of 1974, 12 U.S.C. § 2602.

334 A bona fide lease or tenancy is defined as one in which "(1) the mortgagor or the child, spouse, or parent of the mortgagor under the contract is not the tenant; (2) the lease or tenancy was the result of an arms-length transaction; and (3) the lease or tenancy requires the receipt of rent that is not substantially less than fair market rent for the property or the unit's rent is reduced or subsidized due to a Federal, State, or local subsidy." Pub. L. No. 111-22, § 702(b) (2009). *See also* Nott v. Bunson, 2009 WL 3271285 (D. Md. Oct. 9, 2009).

335 *See* U.S. Bank Nat'l Ass'n v. Hurtado, 2010 WL 1444506 (N.Y. Dist. Ct. Apr. 12, 2010) (lease entered into with notice of pending foreclosure).

336 12 U.S.C. § 2602(1)(B).

337 12 U.S.C. § 5220(a).

338 Collado v. Boklari, 892 N.Y.S.2d 731 (Dist. Ct. Nov. 9, 2009).

339 Helping Families Save Their Homes Act of 2009, Pub. L. No. 111-22, § 702(a)(2)(A) (2009).

340 *Id.* § 702(a)(2)(B).

341 *Id. See also* GMAC Mortg., L.L.C. v. Taylor, 2010 WL 702427 (N.Y. Dist. Ct. Mar. 1, 2010) (since the state law applies to all residential properties and the federal Protecting Tenants at Foreclosure Act applies solely to residential properties upon which a federally related loan was foreclosed, the state law "inherently includes a larger universe of tenants" and grants greater additional protection, and therefore is not preempted; however, under facts of case, shorter ten-day notice requirement set forth by state law applied).

342 Bank of America, N.A. v. Owens, 2010 WL 1796984 (N.Y. Cty. Ct. May 5, 2010).

343 Aurora Loan Servs., L.L.C. v. Martinez, 2010 WL 1266887 (N.D. Cal. Mar. 29, 2010); U.S. Nat'l Bank Ass'n v. Garcia, 2009 WL 4048851 (C.D. Cal. Nov. 20, 2009).

344 Not all tenants and owners will be offered leases and it is not clear how long the programs will last. The details of Freddie Mac's program are available at www.freddiemac.com/corporate/buyown/english/avoiding_foreclosure/rental_initiative.html. The details of Fannie Mae's program are available at www.fanniemae.com/newsreleases/2009/4581.jhtml.

the time of the foreclosure. Fannie Mae's "National REO Rental Policy" only applies to tenants.

14.7.1.3 Section 8 Tenants

Section 8 tenants are explicitly protected by the Protecting Tenants at Foreclosure Act. The new owner must honor Section 8 voucher leases and Housing Payment Assistance Payment Contracts that were entered into prior to the foreclosure.[345] Additionally, the Act provides that the fact of foreclosure does not constitute good cause to terminate the lease of a Section 8 tenant unless the new owner intends to use the unit as a primary residence and has provided the tenant with the requisite ninety days' notice.[346]

Section 8 tenants are also protected by other federal law that states that, during the term of the lease, the owner shall not terminate the tenancy except for serious or repeated violation of the terms and conditions of the lease, for violation of applicable law, or for other good cause.[347] HUD regulations also specify that lease termination must be based upon "good cause."[348] This federal law preempts state law that would frustrate the program's objectives by allowing eviction upon the landlord's foreclosure.[349] Of course, state law can provide greater protections. Thus Massachusetts legislation codifies protections for subsidized tenancies by stating explicitly that foreclosure does not affect leases subsidized under state or federal law.[350]

14.7.2 State Law

14.7.2.1 General

The two key predictors under state law as to whether a tenant has rights to remain in the foreclosed property are whether the lease was executed before or after the mortgage and whether a foreclosure is judicial or non-judicial.[351] If a lease was consummated prior to creation of the mortgage, the lease generally is treated as not extinguished by the foreclosure, in both judicial and non-judicial foreclosure states.[352] This is so because the foreclosure purchaser acquires no greater interest than the mortgagor had. The foreclosure purchaser "steps into the shoes" of the foreclosed owner, who had transferred the possessory interest to the tenant and was not entitled to possession of the rental property, by virtue of the lease. However, leases may contain a subordination clause making the lease subordinate to later mortgages in which case the foreclosure will terminate the tenancy.[353]

On the other hand, most courts hold that the non-judicial (or power of sale) foreclosure of a mortgage extinguishes a tenancy entered into *after* execution of the mortgage.[354] A notice requirement in some non-judicial foreclosure states

345 Pub. L. No. 111-22, § 703 (2009).

346 *Id.*

347 *See* 42 U.S.C. § 1437f(o)(7)(C).

348 *See* 24 C.F.R. § 982.310(a), (d).

349 German v. Federal Home Mortgage Corp., 899 F. Supp. 1155, 1162–1165 (S.D.N.Y. 1995) (Section 8 notice and cause requirements apply to successors in interest, even where no payments were received); Webster Bank v. Occhipinti, 1998 WL 846105 (Conn. Super. Ct. Nov. 20, 1998) (in allowing tenant's motion to reopen strict foreclosure judgment, court found that tenant had asserted a valid defense to strict foreclosure; tenant argued that the federal Section 8 program, which permits eviction only under certain circumstances, preempts state common law, which provides that a judgment of strict foreclosure automatically extinguishes any prior tenancies). *See also* Ayers v. Philadelphia Hous. Auth., 908 F.2d 1184, 1192 (3d Cir. 1990) (federal regulations preempt Pennsylvania statute calling for lease termination upon default); Bristol Sav. Bank v. Savinelli, 1996 WL 166396 (Conn. Mar. 21, 1996) (citing EMC Mortgage Corp. v. Smith, Civ. No. 95-04794 (Hous. Ct. Dep't, City of Boston, Mass. Jan. 5, 1996) ("the applicable federal law [for Section 8 tenancy] preempts our common law which permits tenancies to be terminated automatically via foreclosure.")); Federal Home Loan Mortgage Corp. v. Hobbs, Civ. No. 95-04475 (Hous. Ct. Dep't, City of Boston, Mass. Dec. 20, 1995) (termination and notice provisions of Section 8 program preempt state common law rule that tenancies are automatically terminated by operation of law by foreclosure).

It should be noted that in 1998, after these cases were decided, terms of Section 8 leases were modified by 42 U.S.C. § 1437f(o)(7) which required fixed lease terms. These changes, however do not undermine the principle that federal rules governing Section 8 evictions preempt state foreclosure law.

350 *See* Mass. Gen. Laws ch. 186, § 13A.

351 *See generally* Vicki Been & Allegra Glashausser, *Tenants: Innocent Victims of the Nation's Foreclosure Crisis*, 2 Alb. Gov't L. Rev. 1 (2009) (discussing tenants' rights in foreclosure).

352 *See e.g.,* Raiford v. Dep't of Transp., 424 S.E.2d 789 (Ga. Ct. App. 1992) (foreclosure of security deed and sale of property pursuant to power of sale do not divest tenant of her leasehold estate when the lease predates the security deed, as "first in time is first in rank"); Fed. Nat'l Mortgage Ass'n v. Therrian, 678 N.E.2d 193 (Mass. App. Ct. 1997) (possession under lease given prior to execution of mortgage of premises is not extinguished by foreclosure of mortgage); Med Ctr. Bank v. Fleetwood, 854 S.W.2d 278 (Tex. App. 1993) (if lease is executed before deed of trust, lease is superior to deed of trust lien and is not extinguished by foreclosure; purchaser at foreclosure sale becomes new landlord); 55 Am. Jur. 2d *Mortgages* §§ 575, 794 (1971).

Also, for an excellent summary of state law on this issue, see Brief of Appellee, Virginia Mortg. Corp. v. Williams (filed Dec. 22, 1994) (No. 68012), *available at* www.consumerlaw/unreported. *See also* Annot., *Effect of Foreclosure of Mortgage as Terminating Lease*, 14 A.L.R. 658, 664 (1921).

353 *See* 1 Friedman on Leases § 8.1 (5th ed. 2005); Wright v. Home Beneficial Life Ins. Co., 270 S.E.2d 400 (Ga. Ct. App. 1980) (where lease was made "subject to" any future deed to secure debt, lessee becomes tenant at sufferance and interest is terminable by power of sale contained in deed).

354 *See* Burke v. Willard, 137 N.E. 744 (Mass. 1923) (following non-judicial foreclosure there is no privity between the mortgage holder and the tenant of the mortgagor). *See also* Harry B.

may allow tenants to remain in their units for specified periods of time,[355] and the new owner remains subject to state prohibitions on self-help eviction.[356]

In judicial foreclosure states, if the lease is executed after the mortgage, a minority of courts hold that a foreclosure action extinguishes the tenancy, irrespective of whether the tenant is made a party to the foreclosure action.[357] But the majority view is that foreclosure does not extinguish the tenancy if the foreclosing party is on notice of the tenancy, *unless* the tenant is made a party to the foreclosure.[358]

Notice of the tenancy may be either actual or constructive. Even if a lease is not recorded (most residential leases are not), the mortgage holder may be deemed to be on notice because the possession is apparent, or susceptible to ascertainment on reasonable inspection.[359] Thus, when a tenant lives at the property, the lender may be on constructive notice of the tenant's interest in the property, and may be under duty to investigate to ascertain the tenant's claims. If the property is an occupied apartment building with multiple units, the nature of the property alone puts the lender on notice that there are tenants in possession of the property.

The majority rule that requires that tenants be made parties to the foreclosure provides tenants with at least a limited opportunity to defend their interests in the property. The tenant can assert in the foreclosure action any equities which he may have against the former landlord, such as a claim for improvements, or a claim for money damages,[360] or for prepaid rent tendered to the landlord prior to the foreclosure.[361]

14.7.2.2 State "Good Cause" Eviction Statutes

A few states and localities have enacted statutory provisions which limit the grounds on which tenants may be evicted, notwithstanding the expiration of the tenant's lease.[362] These statutes are referred to as "good cause"

Hyde, *The Real Estate Lease As a Credit Instrument*, 20 Bus. Law 359, 388 (1965).

355 For example, in Massachusetts, a tenancy at will survives foreclosure, a lease tenancy is deemed to be a tenancy at will post-foreclosure, and a Section 8 lease survives foreclosure. As a result, the ordinary notice rules for tenants at will and Section 8 tenants (generally thirty days) apply to any eviction post-foreclosure. *See* Mass. Gen. Laws ch. 186, §§ 13, 13A. *See also* Minn. Stat. § 504B.285 (requires that tenants be given two months' written notice to vacate no sooner than one month after the redemption or termination period expires); N.C. Gen. Stat. § 45-21.29 (allows thirty-day notice before order of possession may be issued for properties with at least fifteen units, and notice of ten days for smaller properties, after which sheriff is authorized to remove tenants); Tex. Prop. Code Ann. § 24.005(b) (Vernon) (which entitles tenant to thirty days' notice to vacate where the tenant has paid rent to prior owner or new owner following a request do so).

356 *See, e.g.*, Bank of New York v. Allen, Docket No. 08-SP-0959 (Boston, Mass. Hous. Ct. 2008) (jury verdict for $54,000 based on constructive eviction arising from utility shut-off); Greelish v. Wood, 914 A.2d 1211 (N.H. 2006).

357 *See* Lake v. Avalanche Invs., Inc., 940 So. 2d 1023 (Ala. Civ. App. 2006) (decedent's alleged adopted minor children were not necessary parties in ejectment action brought by purchaser of home at mortgage foreclosure sale; even assuming purchaser shared ownership of the home as tenant in common with decedent's adopted children, a tenant in common could seek to recover entire tract of property from non-title holders and eject them; any possessory interest that alleged adopted children had in the property was independent of interests of occupants named as defendants in ejectment action, and adopted children could assert any claims they might have in a separate action); Balt v. J.S. Funding Corp., 646 N.Y.S.2d 50 (App. Div. 1996) (tenant not indispensable party to a foreclosure action; failure to name tenant does not render foreclosure judgment defective); Dir. of Veterans' Affairs v. Martin, 898 P.2d 230 (Or. Ct. App. 1995) (mortgage holder not required to name tenant as party to foreclosure action; mortgage holder's ejectment action against tenant provided sufficient opportunity to vindicate tenants rights). *See also* Grant S. Nelson & Dale A. Whitman, Real Estate Finance Law § 7.12(4th ed. 2002).

358 *See* Tappin v. Homecomings Fin. Network, Inc., 830 A.2d 711 (Conn. 2003) (purchaser of property at foreclosure sale could not eject tenant who was not joined as a party to foreclosure action and who took possession after *lis pendens* was filed, construing Conn. Gen. Stat. § 49-22(a)); Citizens Bank & Trust v. Bros. Constr. & Mfg., 859 P.2d 394 (Kan. Ct. App. 1993) (bank which has knowledge that lessee is in possession of real estate on which it has a mortgage must join lessee in foreclosure action to foreclose interests of lessee); Grady v. Utica Mut. Ins. Co., 419 N.Y.S.2d 565, 571 (1979) (judgment of foreclosure not conclusive as to nonparties); Empire Sav. Bank v. Towers Co., 387 N.Y.S.2d 138 (1976) (tenant who is not made a party is not affected by judgment of foreclosure); Davis v. Boyajian, Inc., 229 N.E.2d 116 (Ohio C.P. Stark County 1967) (foreclosure could not terminate rights of lessees without making them parties to foreclosure suit).

359 *See* Citizens Bank & Trust v. Bros. Constr. & Mfg., 859 P.2d 394 (Kan. Ct. App. 1993) (knowledge that lessee is in possession of real estate requires bank to join lessee in foreclosure action to foreclose interests of lessee); Freiden v. W. Bank & Trust Co., 50 N.E.2d 369 (Ohio Ct. App. 1943) (those signs which may be seen or ascertained on careful inspection constitute constructive notice).

360 *See* Krochta v. Green, 467 N.Y.S.2d 995, 997 (City Ct. 1983) (where tenant was not made a party to foreclosure action, her right to damages to offset rent overcharge survived foreclosure).

361 *See* Dundee Naval Stores Co. v. McDowell, 33, 61 So. 108, 113 (Fla. 1913) (lessee has right to recoupment for surplus rent tendered).

362 *See, e.g.*, D.C. Code Ann. § 42-3505.1; 735 Ill. Comp. Stat. 5/15-1701 (amended to allow tenants to remain in their apartments for 120 days after order of possession has been filed, or until the end of their lease); N.H. Rev. Stat. § 540:12; N.J. Stat. Ann. §§ 2A:18-61.1 and 2A:50-70 (West); New York City Rent and Eviction Regulations, 9 N.Y. Comp. Codes R. & Regs. §§ 2200.1–2200.17; New York City Rent Stabilization Code, 9 N.Y. Comp. Codes R. & Regs. §§ 2520.1–2520.13.

Additionally many localities have useful municipal "good cause" ordinances. *See, e.g.,* San Francisco Admin. Code § 37.9(a). Absent a "good cause" eviction statute, a tenant can generally be evicted for any reason or no reason, the only restrictions being those contained in the lease. For more comprehensive discussion of the impact of foreclosure on tenants in

eviction statutes. Typically, permissible reasons for eviction include failure to pay rent, breach of a lease, or the commission of an illegal act in the rental unit. The foreclosure and sale of the property usually does not constitute good cause for eviction. Courts in these jurisdictions have held that the eviction restrictions apply to purchasers at foreclosure sales. Thus, in order to evict a tenant the purchaser must establish one of the grounds for eviction specified in the statute.[363] The protections offered by states with "good cause" eviction statutes are only as good as the statutory definition of "good cause." In New Hampshire, N.H. Rev. Stat. § 540:2, for example, includes a category of "other good cause" which includes, but is not limited to, any legitimate business or economic reason.

"Good cause" eviction statutes apply even though the new owner has not accepted or demanded rent, or in any way established a landlord/tenant relationship with the tenant.[364] In *Administrator of Veterans Affairs v. Valentine*,[365] the VA argued that it was not a "landlord," that there was no contractual relationship between it and the tenant, and therefore it was not bound by the eviction control statute. The D.C. Court of Appeals, however, found that the VA fit within the statutory definition of "landlord" because it was the owner of the property. According to the court, the terms "landlord" and "tenant" in the eviction statute should be interpreted with reference to their ordinary meaning and in accordance with the purpose of the statute, to protect renters from evictions, rather than solely in accordance with technical precepts of real property law.

Other state courts have reached similar conclusions. In *Chase Manhattan Bank v. Josephson*,[366] the New Jersey Supreme Court held that "the [Anti-Eviction] Act protects tenants from eviction by foreclosing mortgage holders irrespective of whether their tenancy was established before or after the execution of the mortgage."[367] A Connecticut statute which prohibits the eviction of tenants in buildings of five or more units who are over 62, blind, or physically disabled except for good cause, was held to take precedence over another statutory provision which authorized a mortgage holder to obtain possession of foreclosed property from a mortgagor's tenants in possession.[368]

14.7.2.3 Other State Statutes Offers Protections to Tenants

Recent legislative action in states including California,[369] Illinois,[370] and North Carolina[371] has expanded the notice period for tenants in post-foreclosure evictions. In addition, various legislative measures in states including Missouri,[372]

New York, Massachusetts and New Jersey, see Raun Rasmussen, *The Impact of Foreclosure Proceedings on Residential Tenants*, 28 Clearinghouse Rev. 494 (1994).

363 *See* Gross v. Super. Ct., 217 Cal. Rptr. 284 (Ct. App. 1985) (purchaser of property at foreclosure proceeding, as successor to landlord, was subject to rent-stabilization ordinance, which limited the grounds for eviction); Admin. of Veterans Affairs v. Valentine, 490 A.2d 1165 (D.C. 1985) (statutory eviction restrictions protect tenant of defaulting landlord); Boston Rent Equity Bd. v. Dime Sav. Bank, 611 N.E.2d 245 (Mass. 1993) (foreclosing mortgage holder that purchased property from rent board at foreclosure sale had to obtain certificate of eviction before it could recover possession); Greelish v. Wood, 914 A.2d 1211 (N.H. 2006) (affirming that "good cause" statute applies to post-foreclosure tenancies); Chase Manhattan Bank v. Josephson, 638 A.2d 1301 (N.J. 1994) (New Jersey Anti-Eviction Act applies to foreclosing mortgage holders, protecting tenants from eviction irrespective of whether tenancy was established before or after execution of mortgage); United Institutional Servicing Corp. v. Santiago, 310 N.Y.S.2d 733 (Civ. Ct. 1970) (foreclosure sale did not strip tenants of protection under eviction statute). *But see* Vt. Tenants, Inc. v. Vt. Hous. Fin. Agency, 742 A.2d 745 (Vt. 1999) (state statute which governed landlord-tenant issues did not apply to eviction of tenant following strict foreclosure).

364 *See* Robinson v. First Nat'l Bank of Chicago, 765 A.2d 543 (D.C. 2001) (occupant of home who was tenant of prior owner was entitled to intervene in bank's action after foreclosure for possession of premises brought against prior owner; court must determine whether she is a tenant under the RHA (the good cause eviction statute) and whether she has any right to prevent eviction); Boston Rent Equity Bd. v. Dime Sav. Bank, 611 N.E.2d 245 (Mass. 1993) (determination of tenancy or contractual agreement is not controlling as to whether rent control law requires certificate of eviction); Long Branch Banking Co. v. Howland, 32 A.2d 860 (N.J. Ch. Ct. 1943) (eviction restrictions apply even though technically there was no landlord/tenant relationship); City of New York v. Utsey, 714 N.Y.S.2d 410 (Sup. Ct. 2000) (city which acquired apartment building in tax foreclosure and which acquiesced in continued occupancy by "squatters" was required to serve thirty day notice to quit prior to seeking possession, as squatters' occupancy had ripened into tenancy at will).

365 490 A.2d 1165 (D.C. 1985).

366 638 A.2d 1301 (N.J. 1994).

367 *Id.* at 1314.

368 First Fed. Bank v. Whitney Dev. Corp., 677 A.2d 1363 (Conn. 1996) (in construing Conn. Gen. Stat. § 47A-23c, the court considered the remedial purpose of the statute).

369 *See* Cal. Code Civ. Proc. § 1161(b) (tenant or subtenant in possession of a rental housing unit at the time the property is sold in foreclosure shall be given sixty days' written notice to quit before being removed; law remains in effect until January 1, 2013).

370 *See* 735 Ill. Comp. Stat. 5/15-1701 (now allows tenants to remain in their apartments for 120 days after order of possession has been filed or until the end of their lease).

371 *See* N.C. Gen. Stat. § 45-21.29 (increases notice period before order of possession may be issued for properties with fifteen or more units to thirty days).

372 *See* Mo. Rev. Stat. § 534.030 (new owner of property must give tenant notice that foreclosure sale has occurred; if owner seeks possession, tenant has ten business days from the date of notice to vacate the premises before owner may bring an unlawful detainer action or any other action seeking possession; content of notice is specified in statute).

New Jersey,[373] New York,[374] Virginia,[375] and Wisconsin[376] have been passed to provide various protections for tenants. A Montana statute provides minimal protection for tenants remaining in possession for ten days after foreclosure; they will be considered tenants at will, requiring a thirty-day notice thereafter.[377]

14.7.2.4 Redemption or Purchase by Group of Tenants

In certain states, tenants also have the right to redeem the property by paying the mortgage debt prior to the foreclosure or by paying the foreclosure sale price after the sale when state law provides a statutory right of redemption.[378] While this right may appear at first to be of little value to most tenants, a group of tenants working together with a community group or government housing agency may be able to use the redemption right as a means to obtain mortgage financing to purchase the property.

14.7.3 Rights of Tenants If Their Landlord Files Bankruptcy

In many cases involving foreclosure on a landlord, the landlord files bankruptcy in an effort to retain the property. Most such cases are filed under chapter 7 or 11. Residential property may be transferred away from the current landlord during or immediately after the bankruptcy process. In some situations the transfer will be voluntary and in others required by the court.

A variety of steps may be taken to protect tenants' rights in the bankruptcy process. The Bankruptcy Code includes special protections for tenants when their landlords seek to terminate leases in the bankruptcy process.[379] Federal bankruptcy courts have held that the landlord in bankruptcy cannot compel a sale where adequate protection of a tenant's interest can only be achieved through continued possession of the lease premises.[380] A substantial discussion of tenants' rights as creditors in the bankruptcy process is contained in National Consumer Law Center, *Consumer Bankruptcy Law and Practice* Chapter 17.[381]

14.8 Former Owners in Possession of Property Following Foreclosure

Unless the sale is set aside, the right of a former homeowner to possess the property terminates with the foreclosure sale,[382] ratification,[383] or at the expiration of the re-

373 *See* N.J. Stat. Ann. § 2A:50-70 (in event of foreclosure sale, tenant is entitled to notice within ten business days after transfer of title; notice must be in English and Spanish, and form and content of notice are specified in statute; notice provides that new owner may not evict tenant without "good cause"); violation may result in damages of $2000 plus attorney fees and costs). *See also* N.J. Stat. Ann. § 2A:50-71 (new owner of foreclosed property may not make any communications to induce tenant to vacate property except through "bona fide monetary offer" and may not take actions to place pressure on tenant, during pendency of foreclosure or within one year of transfer of title, to accept any offer to vacate property).

374 N.Y. Real Prop. Acts. Law § 1305 (tenants must be given written notice that they are entitled to remain in premises for the greater of ninety days from date of notice or remainder of lease). *See also* GMAC Mortg., L.L.C. v. Taylor, 2010 WL 702427 (N.Y. Dist. Ct. Mar. 1, 2010) (since the state law applies to all residential properties and the federal Protecting Tenants at Foreclosure Act applies solely to residential properties upon which a federally related loan was foreclosed, the state law "inherently includes a larger universe of tenants" and grants greater additional protection, and therefore is not preempted; however, under facts of case, shorter ten day notice requirement set forth by state law applied).

375 Va. Code Ann. § 55-225.10 (landlord must give written notice to tenant of mortgage default, notice of acceleration, or foreclosure sale within five business days after written notice from the lender is received by the landlord).

376 Wis. Stat. § 846.35 (party bringing foreclosure action must provide tenant with (1)notice no later than five days after action is filed that foreclosure has commenced, (2)notice no later than five days after judgment of foreclosure is entered that such judgment has been made, and (3) notice of the date on which the redemption period ends; violation of notice provisions may result in damages of $250 plus reasonable attorney fees; also, tenant may retain possession for up to two months after end of month in which sale of property is confirmed). *See also* Wis. Stat. § 704.35 (landlord must give tenant notice that foreclosure action has commenced and, if judgment has been entered, notice of date on which redemption period ends).

377 *See* Mont. Code Ann. §§ 71-1-319 (tenants except those prior to trust indenture shall be deemed tenants at will ten days following sale), 70-27-104 (requires thirty-day notice before a tenancy at will may be terminated); Rocky Mountain Bank v. Stuart, 928 P.2d 243 (Mont. 1996) (holding that right to notice can be waived by agreement to vacate after ten days).

378 *Accord* Countrywide Home Loans, Inc. v. Williams, 867 N.Y.S.2d 16 (N.Y. Dist. Ct. 2008) (table). *See, e.g.*, 6280 Ridge Realty L.L.C. v. Goldman, 701 N.Y.S.2d 69 (1999) (tenant has an equitable right to redeem his landlord's mortgage, which is not extinguished if mortgage holder omits tenant as a party in foreclosure action). *See also* Comment, *The Effect of a Mortgage Foreclosure on a Lease Executed Subsequent to the Mortgage*, 17 Wash. L. Rev. 37, 47 (1942); Tiffany & Jones, The Law of Real Property § 1534, at 612 (3d ed. 1939).

379 *See* 11 U.S.C. § 365(h) (if a trustee rejects an unexpired lease of real property under which the debtor is the lessor and if the term of such lease has commenced, the lessee may retain its rights under such lease).

380 *See, e.g.*, *In re* Independence Vill. Inc., 52 B.R. 715, 734 (Bankr. E.D. Mich. 1983) (sale of life care facility did not permit avoidance of residents' possessory interests as protected by 11 U.S.C. § 365(h) as well as state law that states that a tenant cannot be forced to surrender leased premises where there is no provision in the lease allowing for payments).

381 (9th ed. 2009).

382 *See, e.g.*, Murphy v. Countrywide Home Loans, Inc., 199 S.W.3d 441 (Tex. App. 2006) (occupant of property holding over after execution of deed is considered a permissive tenant whose right to possession is inferior to the party holding title).

383 *See, e.g.*, Laney v. State, 842 A.2d 773 (Md. 2004) (foreclosure,

demption period.[384] Procedures will vary depending on whether it was a judicial or non-judicial foreclosure. Often the purchaser at the foreclosure sale (who will often be the lender) will bring an eviction action against the former homeowner and obtain a judgment. In some states, the same summary process that is used to evict tenants will be used to evict the former homeowner.[385] Other states have established a separate procedure for ejecting the former homeowner[386] and may also allow the purchaser to use self-help to gain possession of the property.[387] In some states the former homeowners forfeit their right of redemption if they do not turn over possession of the property.[388] When a former homeowner wishes to challenge the propriety of a foreclosure sale, the proper procedure may be to seek to set aside the foreclosure and not to use that as a defense in an action to evict the former homeowner.[389]

Additionally, purchasers must use the correct procedure to evict former homeowners from the property. In *Attorney General v. Dime Sav. Bank of New York*,[390] for example, the Supreme Judicial Court of Massachusetts ruled that a lender who forecloses on real property by sale may not bring a trespass action against a holdover tenant or mortgagor in possession of the foreclosed property. Instead, it must employ summary process. Similarly, the Maryland Court of Appeals, in *Empire Properties v. Hardy*,[391] overruled attempts by a purchaser to use a forcible entry and detainer action, where the state motion for possession rule dictated the proper judicial procedure the purchaser should pursue to gain possession of the property.

---

sale and ratification cause the mortgagor to lose the right of possession in the property).

384 *See* Broszko v. Principal Mut. Life Ins. Co., 533 N.W.2d 656 (Minn. Ct. App. 1995) (mortgagor of foreclosed property retains the right to possess property until the end of redemption period).

385 *See* Attorney General v. Dime Sav. Bank of New York, 596 N.E.2d 1013 (Mass. 1992) (no reason to distinguish between holdover mortgagors or tenants).

386 *See, e.g.*, Empire Properties v. Hardy, 873 A.2d 1187 (Md. 2005).

387 Laney v. State, 842 A.2d 773 (Md. 2004) (the right of peaceable self-help is a viable mechanism for title owner to obtain possession of property from holdover mortgagor).

388 *See* Jones v. Clausell, 859 So. 2d 1134 (Ala. Ct. App. 2002).

389 *See* Vines v. LaSalle Bank Nat'l Ass'n, 691 S.E.2d 242 (Ga. Ct. App. 2010); Jackman v. LaSalle Bank, N.A., 683 S.E.2d 925 (Ga. Ct. App. 2009).

390 *See* Attorney General v. Dime Sav. Bank of New York, 596 N.E.2d 1013 (Mass. 1992).

391 873 A.2d 1187 (Md. 2005).

Chapter 15 Foreclosure Rescue Scams

15.1 Introduction

Rising foreclosure rates in recent years have brought with them a wave of schemes to take advantage of financially distressed homeowners. A homeowner who is facing foreclosure may be desperate to grab at any hope of saving the home, even if it costs thousands of dollars or put the homeowner's equity at risk. Foreclosure rescue scams come in many variations. Equity stripping schemes are common when the home is worth considerably more than what is due on any outstanding mortgages or liens. Where little equity remains, home scams focus primarily on squeezing additional cash out of the homeowners. Regardless of the type, foreclosure rescue scams have one thing in common: instead of being "rescued," as promised, homeowners end-up worse-off than they were before the transaction having lost their home, their equity, and often additional monies.

Many of the legal theories and strategies used to protect homeowners from foreclosure rescue scams are the same as those used in other consumer protection cases. As a result, more detail on many of the theories discussed in this chapter may be found in other National Consumer Law Center treatises, particularly *Truth in Lending*,[1] *Unfair and Deceptive Acts and Practices*,[2] and *The Cost of Credit: Regulation, Preemption, and Industry Abuses*.[3] Another helpful resource is Prentiss Cox, *Foreclosure Equity Stripping: Legal Theories and Strategies to Attack a Growing Problem*.[4]

Additionally, foreclosure rescue scams are increasingly grabbing the attention of state governments, which have passed a number of laws[5] to combat the scams and have brought a number of enforcement actions.[6] Federal authorities have also been involved, investigating and prosecuting the scams.[7]

This chapter addresses the problem of foreclosure rescue scams and is organized into five substantive sections. Section 15.2 provides a short overview of the predominant types of foreclosure rescue scams. Section 15.3 discusses the initial issues that confront an attorney with a new client: how to recognize a foreclosure rescue scam; what information and documents to obtain from the client; how to investigate the claim; the potential defendants; and the first steps to take to pursue a claim. Section 15.4 discusses the primary legal theories and remedies that are available to attack a foreclosure rescue scam. Section 15.5 discusses the benefits of litigating foreclosure rescue cases in bankruptcy court, and the special issues that arise in that forum. Sample pleadings and other legal materials in foreclosure rescue scam cases are included on the companion website. This treatise's companion website also includes relevant pleadings, discovery, a sample rescission letter, a worksheet for calculating HOEPA points and fees, and computer programs for calculating interest rates. Also, as many of the legal claims used in foreclosure rescue scams are grounded in basic consumer law claims discussed in other NCLC treatises, relevant pleadings, discovery, and legal memoranda useful in these cases are available in the appendices to other treatises, and on *Consumer Law on the Web*.

1 National Consumer Law Center, Truth in Lending (6th ed. 2007 and Supp.).

2 National Consumer Law Center, Unfair and Deceptive Acts and Practices (7th ed. 2008 and Supp.).

3 National Consumer Law Center, The Cost of Credit: Regulation, Preemption, and Industry Abuses (4th ed. 2009 and Supp.).

4 39 Clearinghouse Review Journal of Poverty Law and Policy 607 (Mar.–Apr. 2006).

5 *See* § 15.4.6, *infra.*

6 *See, e.g., Prepared State of the Federal Trade Commission on Foreclosure Rescue Fraud, Hearing Before the Senate Special Committee on Aging*, 110th Cong. (Feb. 13, 2008), *available at* http://aging.senate.gov/hearing_detail.cfm?id=292791& (listing state actions); Press Release, [Illinois Attorney General] Madigan Sues Three Mortgage Rescue Companies (Dec. 21, 2007), *available at* www.illinoisattorneygeneral.gov; Press Release, [Texas] Attorney General Abbott Takes Legal Action Against Foreclosure Rescue Firm's Unlawful Texas Operations (Dec. 14, 2007), *available at* www.oag.state.tx.us; Press Release, Texas Attorney General Abbott Charges Foreclosure Rescue Firm with Operating Unlawful Scam (Sept. 17, 2007), *available at* www.oag.state.tx.us.

7 *See, e.g., Prepared State of the Federal Trade Commission on Foreclosure Rescue Fraud, Hearing Before the Senate Special Committee on Aging*, 110th Cong. (Feb. 13, 2008), *available at* http://aging.senate.gov/hearing_detail.cfm?id=292791&; Press Release, Federal Trade Comm'n, Federal and State Agencies Target Mortgage Foreclosure Rescue and Loan Modification Scams: FTC Leads "Operation Loan Lies" to Stop Fraud and Help Distressed Homeowners (July 15, 2009), *available at* www.ftc.gov/opa/2009/07/loanlies.shtm.

A list of agencies participating in Operation Loan Lies and actions taken as of July 2009 is available at www.ftc.gov/os/2009/07/090715casesummary.pdf.

15.2 What Is a Foreclosure Rescue Scam?

15.2.1 Overview

Foreclosure rescue scams are various types of schemes targeted at homeowners already facing foreclosure and in financial distress.[8] When homeowners have significant equity in their homes or when property values are appreciating, foreclosure rescue scams often focus on obtaining title to the home and robbing homeowners of their equity. When homeowners have little equity, scams center on squeezing upfront fees, often thousand of dollars, from borrowers.

A "rescuer" may identify potential victims through public foreclosure notices in newspapers or at government offices. The homeowner is then contacted by phone, mail, or personal solicitation, with offers to save the home. Television and newspaper advertisements can also lure homeowners to a rescuer.

Foreclosure rescue scams typically come in three varieties. The first might be called "phantom help," where a rescuer charges outrageous fees either for little or no work. Some offer to negotiate loan modifications that never materialize[9] while others may "assist" homeowners in filing for bankruptcy without a proper understanding of the law.[10] Often the foreclosure clock keeps ticking while homeowners wait for rescuers to make good on their promises. Whatever form "phantom help" takes, the homeowner is usually left without enough assistance to save the home, and with little or no time left to seek other assistance.

For example, in *In re McNeal*,[11] the homeowner paid a "foreclosure consultant," $750 to stop the foreclosure of his home. The consultant had spoken to the loan servicer three times and submitted financial information to the servicer, but failed to obtain a loan modification or otherwise stop the foreclosure sale. Consequently, the homeowner filed a chapter 7 bankruptcy to postpone the foreclosure. Finding that the consultant violated California's foreclosure consultant statute,[12] the court awarded the homeowner actual damages of $750 and exemplary damages of $2250.[13]

Another common "phantom help" scenario is exemplified by an operation shut down by the North Carolina Attorney General.[14] The company combed courthouse records for the names of homeowners who were facing foreclosure, then sent them direct mail solicitations claiming they could help avoid foreclosure. When homeowners responded to the mailings, according to the attorney general, the company claimed it had special expertise and a high success rate of saving consumers' homes from foreclosure. The company collected its fee upfront, typically one month's mortgage payment, promising to negotiate with mortgage lenders on the homeowner's behalf. It instructed homeowners not to talk to their mortgage company, urging them to let the "experts" handle all communications. Actually, little or nothing was done to help the homeowners, and they rarely heard from the company after they had paid their money.

The second and third varieties of foreclosure rescue scams are similar—they both involve the transfer of ownership of the home.[15] The second variety involves outright fraud. The homeowners believe they are obtaining refinancing or a new loan and do not realize they are surrendering ownership of the house. The papers accomplishing the transfer may be truly signed by the homeowners, but they are signed in a transaction that is confusing and in which the homeowners are misled about the nature of the papers they are signing. Alternatively, the deed transferring the house may be forged.

The third variety is a bailout that typically involves the homeowners' understanding that they are signing a deed that transfers the ownership of their home, but doing so with the belief that they will be able to regain ownership at a later time. Meanwhile, the homeowners become tenants in their

8 *See* National Consumer Law Center, Desperate Homeowners: Loan Mod Scammers Step In When Loan Services Refuse to Provide Relief (2007), *available at* www.consumerlaw.org/issues/mortgage_servicing/content/LoanModScamsReport0709.pdf; National Consumer Law Center, Dreams Foreclosed: The Rampant Theft of America's Homes Through Equity-Stripping "Foreclosure Rescue" Scams (2005), *available at* www.consumerlaw.org/news/content/ForeclosureReportFinal.pdf.

9 *See* § 15.2.4, *infra.*

10 *See* National Consumer Law Center, Consumer Bankruptcy Law and Practice § 16.6 (9th ed. 2009).

11 286 B.R. 910 (Bankr. N.D. Cal. 2002).

12 Cal. Civ. Code §§ 2945 to 2945.11.

13 *In re* McMeal, 286 B.R. 910, 912 (Bankr. N.D. Cal. 2002). *See also* United States v. Weaver, 290 F.3d 1166 (9th Cir. 2002) (defendants told homeowners that they could register a "common law lien" on the home that would take priority over the mortgage security interest and prevent foreclosure; however, homeowner needed to convey property to a trust to take advantage of the program); *In re* Hennerman, 351 B.R. 143 (Bankr. D. Colo. 2006) (sanctioning bankruptcy petition preparer $9000 and awarding debtor $2300); *In re* Ferguson, 326 B.R. 419 (Bankr. N.D. Ohio 2005) (finding non-attorney "foreclosure consultant" who had entered into pre-petition "foreclosure services agreement" engaged in the unauthorized practice of law and not entitled to payment for illegal services); Fleet v. United States Consumer Council, Inc. 53 B.R. 833 (Bankr. E.D. Pa. 1985); State v. Midland Equities, 458 N.Y.S.2d 126 (N.Y. Sup. Ct. 1982).

14 *See* Press Release, AG Cooper Shuts Down Foreclosure Fraudsters (Aug. 23, 2006), *available at* www.ncdoj.gov/News-and-Alerts/News-Releases-and-Advisories/Press-Releases/AG-Cooper-shuts-down-foreclosure-fraudsters.aspx

15 A related technique for taking control of homes and stripping the equity out of them involves buying distressed mortgage loans from the mortgage holder, and then using foreclosure or the threat of foreclosure to force the homeowner into a disadvantageous transaction. *See, e.g.*, Billingham v. Dornemann, 771 N.E.2d 166 (Mass. App. Ct. 2002). *See also* Harmon v. E.G. Meek, 2008 WL 918513 (Tenn. Ct. App. Apr. 4, 2008) (debt buyer bought note and trust deed, then tried to prevent homeowners from selling home so that he could foreclose on it).

own homes on terms that are often oppressive and unaffordable, ending with their eviction. The rescuer may even renege on promises to pay off the mortgage, leaving the homeowner liable for loans on a house she no longer owns.

Two variations of the repurchase theme, sale-leaseback transactions and *inter vivos* trust transfers, are discussed in more detail in the next two subsections. The remedies for both are similar, generally beginning with showing that the transaction actually was not a sale but an equitable mortgage, and then applying the laws for loans to the transaction.

15.2.2 Sale-Leaseback Schemes

Sale-leaseback schemes encompass a variety of transactions in which homeowners surrender title to their houses with the expectation that they will be able to remain in their homes as renters until they are able to repurchase the property. Invariably, the terms of the deal are so onerous that the buyback becomes impossible. Alternatively, the homeowner's ability to repurchase the property may be cut off by a sale to a bona fide third party purchaser.[16] In either circumstance, the homeowners stand to lose most, if not all, of the equity in their homes. In addition, the homeowners, now tenants in their own houses, may face eviction proceedings for failing to comply with oppressive and unaffordable lease terms.[17] In some cases, these homeowners were defrauded about the deed transfer; others may understand that they were signing a deed but believed that the home would ultimately be "saved." Properly presented challenges to these scams are often successful in defeating these transfers.[18]

The case of *Browner v. District of Columbia* provides an illustrative example of a sale-leaseback transaction.[19] The defendants, Rita Walker and Ferris Browner (doing business as RAW), placed the following advertisement in the "Money to Lend" column of the classified advertisements: "NEED MONEY?—Foreclosure Help." The business also sent letters to homeowners whose homes were being advertised for foreclosure, stating "I'm sorry to read that your property, by order of the court, is being foreclosed upon. We are foreclosure specialists."

In one typical transaction, a homeowner contacted the defendants and was told that RAW would make available $4591.18 to pay a mortgage arrearage and prevent the pending foreclosure of her son's home. In exchange for the monies, the homeowner was required to sign a deed transferring her property to Rita Walker subject to a one-year lease with an option to repurchase. When questioned about the necessity of the deed, RAW assured the homeowner that the deed was merely a technicality, included for the purpose of satisfying the accountant. During the one-year lease, the homeowner was required to pay $375 per month to RAW, in lieu of making $118 monthly mortgage payments. Upon exercising the repurchase option, the homeowner would have been required to repay the $4519.18. At the time of the "sale" to Walker, the property had a market value of $38,185 and was entirely free of debt except for the balance of the first mortgage in the amount of $1600. Thus, the homeowner unwittingly conveyed property worth $38,185 for a total of $6988.18.

The court looked beyond the writings of the parties at the real terms of the transactions and determined that this transaction and others like it were not sales, but loans. Because the effective interest rates on the transactions at issue ranged from 50 to 200%, the court found the defendants guilty of violating the local loan sharking statute.

Similarly, the Nebraska Supreme Court upheld the claims of thirteen homeowners who were induced to enter into fraudulent sale-leaseback deals that allowed rescuers to take the homes for less than full value. The court found that even if the homeowners failed to read the contracts—which allegedly "unmistakably" disclosed the transactions as sales rather than loans—the contracts were not binding because they were induced by fraud.[20]

These decisions are typical of many brought challenging these transactions, in which courts apply principles of equity and rearrange the legal relationship. Section 15.4.1, *infra*, provides a detailed analysis of how this is accomplished.

15.2.3 Inter Vivos *Trusts*

The use of *inter vivos* trusts is a growing form of foreclosure rescue scam.[21] This type of scam is appealing to rescuers because it often requires less money up front than many sale-leaseback transactions, avoids the due-on-sale clause in the homeowner's mortgage and, by creating an "occupancy agreement" rather than a lease, attempts to skirt tenant protections in state laws and local ordinances.[22]

16 *See generally* § 15.4.1.3, *infra* (for strategies to defeat claims of third-party purchasers).

17 *See, e.g.*, *In re* Davis, 169 B.R. 285 (E.D.N.Y. 1994).

In *In re Davis* the lease agreement required monthly rent payments that were clearly unaffordable and required an entire year's rent upon default. Within one month after the sale-leaseback transaction closed and two weeks after the first rental payment was due, the purchaser had perfected a judgment against the former homeowners for a full year's rent and cost and obtained a warrant of eviction for nonpayment of rent.

18 *See generally* § 15.4.1, *infra*.

19 549 A.2d 1107 (D.C. 1988).

20 Eicher v. Mid Am. Fin. Inv. Corp., 702 N.W.2d 792, 803–804 (Neb. 2005).

21 *See, e.g.*, United States v. Weaver, 290 F.3d 1166 (9th Cir. 2002) (criminal prosecution for equity skimming when homeowners transferred title to trust and paid rent to trust in expectation that trust would pay defaulted mortgage); Commonwealth v. Desire, 2007 WL 1302581 (Mass. Super. Ct. Apr. 17, 2007).

22 *See* Garn-St. Germain Depository Institutions Act of 1982, 12 U.S.C. § 1701j-3(d)(8).

In a typical *inter vivos* trust foreclosure scam, the homeowners, knowingly or unknowingly, transfer title of their home to a trust. Initially, as settlors of the trust, the homeowners hold a 100% beneficial interest in the trust. These types of transactions do not require the homeowner's underlying mortgages to be paid off. Instead, this scheme seeks to exploit the exception to the due-on-sale clause for a transfer into an *inter vivos* trust in which the borrower is a beneficiary and which does not affect a transfer of occupancy rights.[23]

Immediately after the creation of the trust, a small beneficial interest (5 to 10%) in the trust is sold to one or more investors.[24] The investor's purchase price for this beneficial interest is typically the amount necessary to bring any delinquent mortgages current.[25] The term of the trust is typically two to three years. At the conclusion of the trust, the house will be sold and the trustee will distribute the proceeds according to the trust documents. The trust documents use complex language to describe the distribution of proceeds, which often results in the investors' getting back about twice as much as they invested plus a percentage of any increased equity.

Under a right of first refusal contained within the trust documents, the homeowners may purchase back their home for fair market value. However, the repurchase agreement requires the homeowners initially to pay the trust the full market value of the home, and only later to receive reimbursement from the trust to compensate them for the equity they already had in the home. This makes repurchase extremely difficult, because the homeowners would have to obtain financing to purchase at full value a home that they already partly own. As a result, these transactions virtually ensure that the homeowners will lose their home as well as much of their equity.

Inter vivos trust schemes also typically have oppressive "occupancy agreements" between the trust and the homeowner (now a tenant). Despite their name, these agreements are essentially leases, and often contain terms that violate state and local laws governing residential leases. Under these agreements, the homeowner pays "rent" to the trustee or a collection service employed by the trustee. The amount of rent is commonly the amount of the mortgage payment plus an additional service fee. Further, the occupancy agreement may contain some or all of the following provisions:

- Failure to make a timely monthly "rent" payment to the trustee constitutes an implied offer to sell the homeowner's beneficial interest in the trust;
- A requirement that homeowners (as tenants) make all necessary repairs, perform all maintenance and maintain homeowner's insurance on the property;
- A provision permitting treble damages in the event that the homeowners (as tenants) hold over beyond the termination of the occupancy agreement;
- Funds paid to a "contingency fund," essentially a security deposit, often in excess of state limits; and
- A provision for a late charge, also exceeding those permitted by state law, in the event monthly payments are not received when due.

Such occupancy agreements, like the trust agreements, are designed to take as much money from the homeowners as possible and to evict them as fast as possible when they fail to make a payment.

A Washington decision describes the use of a trust in a foreclosure rescue scam aimed at homeowners facing tax foreclosure. The rescuer persuaded homeowners to place their homes in a trust, with the rescuer as trustee and co-beneficiary. Upon transfer of title to the trust, the rescuer paid the delinquent property taxes and stopped the tax sale. The land trust and accompanying documents gave the rescuer complete control over the home, even though he paid the homeowners nothing for it. The homeowners had only the right to some percentage of the sale proceeds if the rescuer chose to sell the home, and the right to occupy the property for three years, provided that they paid rent. As a result of a hair trigger default clause, every homeowner who had entered into this deal with the rescuer had defaulted. These deals did not result in homeowners saving their homes, contrary to the rescuer's representations.[26]

15.2.4 Loan Modification Scams

Recently many rescuers have become high-volume, "loan modification specialists." Loan modification scams represent a new variant of the "phantom help" type of foreclosure rescue scam.[27] This scam is most common when borrowers have little or no equity to extract. The pitch by this breed of rescuers is that, for a fee, which can reach several thousand dollars, they will negotiate a loan modification for a financially distressed borrower. The hitch is that the

23 *See* Garn-St. Germain Depository Institutions Act of 1982, 12 U.S.C. § 1701j-3(d)(8).

24 Generally, the beneficial interest transferred to investors will be capped at about 10% to ensure that the original title insurance policy remains effective. Additionally, the transfer of a small beneficial interest may avoid conveyance or transfer taxes.

25 Often the trust accounting will show an "advance" to the homeowner in an amount significantly greater than the amount that was needed to cure the mortgage arrearage. The difference is usually comprised of questionable fees imposed by the trust in connection with the transaction such as documentation, facilitation, transaction, trust set up, or credit counseling fees and a contingency fund.

26 State v. Kaiser, No. 07-2-08789-3 SEA (Super. Ct., King County, Wash. Feb. 6, 2009) (findings of fact and conclusions of law, at ¶¶ 3–10), *later order*, (May 6, 2009), *available at* www.consumerlaw.org/unreported (ordering $3,525,742 restitution to homeowners).

27 *See* § 15.2.1, *supra*.

"work" performed, if any, leads nowhere, with the homeowner out money and time and closer than ever to foreclosure.

One reason that loan modification scams are flourishing is that those who are actually in a position to help—the mortgage servicers and the lenders on whose behalf they are acting—have done an inadequate job of working with homeowners. Servicers have cut costs by relying more on voicemail systems and less on people to assist borrowers, by refusing to respond to borrowers' inquiries, and by failing to resolve borrower disputes. Recent industry efforts to "staff-up" loss mitigation departments have been woefully inadequate. The servicing industry's unresponsiveness to borrowers' inquiries and their inability to provide timely and consistent information to borrowers drives desperate homeowners into the outstretched arms of loan modification scammers.

Saturation marketing by loan modification firms, which is often laced with lies and exaggerations,[28] and pressure tactics play on the desperation and trust of distressed homeowners. These are the same marketing practices that were used to sell the abusive loans that scammers now seek to modify. Many operations have adopted names that imply a government connection.[29]

A number of loan modification scams have involved attorneys. The extent of attorney involvement ranges from nothing more than being a rented name on a scammer's letterhead to forming and operating a modification business under the guise of a law firm.[30] Attorney involvement sometimes serves as a marketing tool, making the business appear more trustworthy or skilled, but without providing any bona fide legal services. In states that fully exempt attorneys from laws restricting loan modification activities, the attorney's involvement may serve to evade the restriction. Typically, in these arrangements, the loan modification work is performed by non-attorneys and must be distinguished from legitimate law practices or nonprofit legal assistance programs where qualified attorneys and paralegals provide bona fide legal assistance.

Most loan modification scams involve taking up-front payments and doing little or nothing for the homeowner. However, other variations on this theme have also been reported:

- Charging a fee to obtain an *un*affordable loan modification;
- Charging exorbitant fees to homeowners attending loan modification seminars;[31]
- Charging thousands of dollars for "loan audits" that are inaccurate, not performed by an attorney, or which are worthless because any potential claims identified are barred by a statute of limitations that has expired.

Ironically, mortgage brokers and other real estate professionals, who saddled borrowers with unsustainable home loans, are now reaping more profit from the same borrowers by promising to fix their bad loans.[32] Indeed many loan modification companies have connections to the defunct subprime mortgage industry.[33] Many loan modification companies recruit mortgage brokers to sell loan modification services.[34]

Even assuming that some of the companies advertising loan modification assistance are not simply out to take homeowners' money, but are engaged in actual attempts to modify the loans, there are serious questions that their businesses are structured in a way that makes it unlikely that any homeowners will benefit. For example, they may work only with homeowners who are in the most serious distress, who are the least likely to have a favorable outcome.[35] Any claims regarding success rates should be regarded with skepticism. Moreover, unlike a nonprofit HUD-approved housing counseling agency, a for-profit loan modification

---

28 Often companies represent themselves as being affiliated with the federal or state governments. *See* John Leland, *Swindlers Find Growing Market in Foreclosures*, New York Times, Jan. 15, 2009, at A1.

29 *See* Press Release, Federal Trade Commission, Federal and State Agencies Crack Down on Mortgage Modification and Foreclosure Rescue Scams (Apr. 6, 2009), *available at* www.ftc.gov/opa/2009/04/hud.shtm.

30 *See* 75 Fed. Reg. 10,707, 10,712 n.68 (Mar. 9, 2010) (describing range of attorney involvement in loan modification activities); Federal Trade Comm'n v. Data Med. Capital, Inc., 2009 WL 2059442 (C.D. Cal. July 13, 2009) (describing attorney involvement).

31 Michale Doyle, *Claims to Fix Mortgages for Fee Set Off Red Flags for the Feds and Cardoza*, Modesto Bee, Oct. 25, 2008, *available at* www.modbee.com/local/story/475093.html (homeowners charged $3500 to attend workshop to resolve delinquent mortgage problems).

32 *See* Alyssa Katz, Predatory Lending with a Smiley Face, Salon.com, Mar. 4, 2009, *available at* www.salon.com/news/feature/2009/03/04/loan_modifications/.

33 For example, BusinessWeek reports that USMAC, which charges clients a non-refundable fee of $3495 to negotiate a loan modification, is owned in part by the president of Citywide Mortgage, a former subprime lender. Robert Berner, *"Help" Can Be Costly*, BusinessWeek, Nov. 11, 2008.

34 *See* Alyssa Katz, Predatory Lending with a Smiley Face, Salon.com, Mar. 4, 2009, *available at* www.salon.com/news/feature/2009/03/04/loan_modifications/ (describing the Loan Processing Center which recruits mortgage brokers from across the country to join the operation); National Foreclosure Prevention Center, *available at* www.ceasemyforeclosure.com/affiliates.php; *Lauren Saunders, National Consumer Law Center, Legislative Solutions for Preventing Loan Modification and Foreclosure Rescue Fraud, U.S. House of Representatives, House Financial Services Committee*

Subcommittee on Housing and Community Opportunity (May 6, 2009), *available at* www.consumerlaw.org (citing specific examples).

35 *See Testimony of Travis B. Plunkett Before the Committee on Commerce, Science, and Transportation of the United States Senate Regarding Consumer Protection and the Credit Crisis* 8–10 (Feb. 26, 2009) (expressing these concerns regarding the debt settlement industry).

consultant is likely to push the homeowner into taking the first modification offered, or to refuse to push for more, even if it offers little chance of actually saving the home.

15.2.5 Short Sale Scams

Information is beginning to surface about a new variety of foreclosure rescue involving the sale of a house that is upside down (that is, more is owed on the house than it is worth). Indeed, some loan modification websites tout their expertise in short sales.

A true short sale is one where the lender agrees to take less than the full amount of the loan in order to clear title and permit the sale to proceed. As long as the lender is part of the process and everyone knows and agrees to the true sale price and the ramifications of a short sale, there is nothing unlawful about a short sale. Like a foreclosure, however, it has an impact on the homeowner's credit report. The lender may also insist that the homeowner remain liable for the deficiency. Even if it is forgiven, the homeowner may owe taxes on the forgiven amount.

In one version of a short sale scam, the realtor and the buyer collude to conceal the full price of the sale from the lender so that they can pocket the difference, often by using option contracts and back-to-back closings. This version is aimed primarily at defrauding the lender, though the homeowner is also hurt by an artificially low sale price, either by being liable on a deficiency or by paying taxes on a higher forgiven balance.[36]

In another version of a short sale scam, the buyer takes over the mortgage without satisfying the due on sale clause and the sale is concealed from the lender.[37] The owner of a We Buy Houses franchise explained at trial that these deals work when the homeowner is only 10% to 15% upside down, because the home is sold to a buyer who is willing to pay a premium above fair market value to avoid a credit check because they cannot qualify for a regular loan.[38] Depending on how the transaction works, the homeowner may be out cash, lose the home, and still end up with a foreclosure on the credit report.

Even assuming that this scheme works for the buyer, whose name is not on the mortgage and whose credit is not at risk, the perils for the homeowner are great. The homeowner remains on the hook for the mortgage if the buyer defaults, risking both a foreclosure on the record and potential liability for any deficiency. Default by the new buyer may be likely, because the buyers that these deals attract are ones who want to avoid a credit check and a substantial down payment. That is, they are seeking the type of "no doc/no money down" loan of the type that led to the foreclosure crisis and is no longer available from regular lenders. The homeowner is also exposed to any other liability, civil or criminal, that comes with violating the due-on-sale clause and actively concealing that sale.

These transactions may begin as traditional loan modification contracts, in which the homeowner pays a fee in the hopes of saving the home. The rescuer may then pressure the homeowner into agreeing to the sale—and into paying a sales commission to the rescuer. Thus, the homeowner has to pay two fees, loses the home, may still have her credit blemished by a foreclosure if the new buyer defaults, and may be exposed to liability for violating the contract.

15.3 Investigating and Preparing a Foreclosure Rescue Scam Case

15.3.1 Recognizing a Foreclosure Rescue Scam

A scam, by its nature, disguises the true intent of the perpetrator. As a result, the victims in some cases may not realize that they have been scammed until they are facing foreclosure or eviction from their own home.

This section and those that follow primarily address cases involving equity-skimming rescue scams. Loan modification scams and other types of "phantom help" are often less complex because they do not involve the transfer of title to the homeowners' property. Despite the simpler nature of

36 *See* Nick & Cindy Davis, Sellers Beware of Short Sale Scams (Apr. 21, 2009), *available at* www.city-data.com/blogs/blog5708-sellers-beware-short-sale-scams.html; Bill Gassett, Short Sale Scammers We Buy Houses (Aug. 14 2008), *available at* http://metrowestmarealestate.blogspot.com/2008/08/short-sale-scammers-we-buy-houses.html; *New "Short Sale" Scam Taking Root?*, St. Petersburg Times, Apr. 22, 2008, *available at* http://blogs.tampabay.com/realestate/2008/04/new-short-sale.html.

37 An article appearing on several real estate investing websites explains how the due on sale clause is avoided. "The game for us is how to transfer ownership to the property without getting caught by the lender." William Bronchick, There's No "Due on Sale" Jail, *available at* www.legalwiz.com/due-on-sale-clause. That article—which predates the foreclosure crisis and the loan modification explosion—explains a scheme in which the property is first transferred to an *inter vivos* trust in the name of the original homeowner, with that homeowner as a beneficiary. That transfer is exempt from the due-on-sale clause under federal law *as long as there is no change in occupancy*. But then, "Sammy Seller quietly assigns his interest under the trust to you [the buyer] (similar to a transfer of stock in a corporation). This assignment is not recorded in any public record. *Sammy moves out and you move in*" (emphasis added). The article—which is aimed at investors, not homeowners—addresses the risks that the parties could be held liable for fraud or other criminal liability, or for civil liability, argues that the risks are not great, and concludes that the transaction "is a risk versus reward gamble."

38 Reporters Transcript, Adversary Proceeding 35–46, *In re* Michelle Perry, No. 08-26905-C-7, (Nunes v. Perry, Adversary No. 08-2463), U.S. Bankruptcy Court (E.D. Cal. Feb. 11, 2009) (on file at National Consumer Law Center).

these later cases, the information in these sections will be useful in obtaining information necessary to prepare such cases.

The following list of questions will help advocates recognize when they are dealing with a foreclosure rescue scam.

Were the homeowners facing foreclosure or otherwise in financial difficulty at the time they transferred their property? Almost all victims of foreclosure rescue scams are facing some type of financial difficulty. Commonly, a foreclosure was imminent. In some cases, homeowners may have been unsuccessful in their attempts to refinance.

Did the homeowner respond to a phone call, letter, posted sign, or other solicitation to get help saving the home or to sell it? Rescuers typically use public records to find names of homeowners facing foreclosure, and then solicit them with promises of help. Many also post flyers that the homeowner may have seen.[39]

Did the homeowner pay upfront fees to someone promising to stop the foreclosure or obtain a loan modification? The success of "phantom help" rescue schemes relies on upfront payments from distressed borrowers.

Were the homeowners instructed to stop communications with their current mortgage company, attorney, or other housing counselor? Homeowners are frequently told to cease all contact with lawyers or their mortgage, and let the rescuers handle the "negotiations." This tactic simultaneously cuts off access to possible refinancing options while running out the clock on ways to prevent the foreclosure.

Did the homeowners convey their property to someone else? The telltale sign of a foreclosure rescue scam is a deed conveying title of the victim's property to the "rescuer" or another party affiliated with the rescuer. The grantee could be a corporation, a trust, an individual unknown to the victim, a long-time acquaintance or even a family member. Remember, rescuers come in all shapes and sizes.

Were the homeowners aware that they executed a deed transferring their property to a third party? In some cases, homeowners are led to believe that they are signing documents for a new loan to bring their mortgage current, when in fact, they deed their home away.

Did the homeowners receive less than fair market value for the transfer of their property? Inadequate consideration is another hallmark of foreclosure rescue scams. These scams depend on equity in the property that can be stripped away when the rescuer refinances or resells the property. Rescuers, if they provide any consideration at all, may pay only a fraction of the value of the home.

Did the homeowners continue to live in their home pursuant to a lease agreement, occupancy agreement or land sales contract? In many foreclosure rescue scams, homeowners surrender title with the expectation that they will be able to remain in their homes. They may sign lease agreements, occupancy agreements, or land sales contracts that permit them to retain possession of their home so long as they pay "rent" to the rescuer. These "rent" payments are often unaffordable and are frequently higher than the homeowners' previous mortgage payments. Homeowners also may continue to have many of the responsibilities of ownership, such as performing property maintenance and making tax payments.

Did the homeowners have an option to repurchase the home sometime in the future? Homeowners who remain in their homes after relinquishing title often believe that they will be able to repurchase the property in the future. There is typically an option or right of repurchase associated with the transaction. However, the option frequently becomes ineffective if the homeowners do not make timely "rent" payments. The repurchase price is almost certainly going to be substantially more than the homeowner originally paid for the home.

Is the "homeowner" facing eviction? One of the key parts of many foreclosure rescue scams is to turn the homeowner into a tenant, who has no claim to the home and can be removed from the home through an eviction action. Especially in a judicial foreclosure state, when a homeowner is facing eviction rather than foreclosure it is a sign of a foreclosure rescue scam.

15.3.2 Gathering Information

15.3.2.1 The Homeowners' Story

The client interview process is important to understanding a foreclosure rescue scam transaction. Homeowners' testimony can make their story come alive. Unfortunately, the speed at which these transactions happen, usually as a result of an impending foreclosure, may leave the consumer confused and unable to remember the details of the transaction. Often, however, they can re-trace their steps and provide at least a general overview of the transaction. Discussing the case in a chronological fashion may also help the homeowner remember what happened next in the sequence of events.

Generally, a good place to start is with some basic facts about the homeowners and the acquisition of their home. After establishing a basic homeownership history, it is useful to know about the homeowners' financial troubles. In part, this conversation is necessary to determine whether the homeowners' financial difficulties were short-term and temporary in nature, or if the homeowners have suffered a more permanent financial setback. A current and future financial picture will be important in evaluating the homeowner's potential remedies.

Next, the homeowner can be walked through the solicitation stage of the scam. What types of solicitations did they receive? Did they make contact with the rescuer in response

39 *See* § 15.3.2.2.2, *infra*.

to such materials? If so, how did they make contact (e.g., telephone, in person, Internet, etc.) and what made this rescuer more attractive than any of the others? This conversation should flow into the initial contact and subsequent contacts that led up to the actual transaction.

In most cases, the homeowners are aware that they signed some document. However, older homeowners may not remember signing any documents. If this is the situation, questions of the homeowner's competency to execute the deed and any other documents should be explored. Whether an individual is competent to execute a deed or other legal document is a question of state law. In general, however, if the homeowner is lacking sufficient mental capacity to understand the nature and significance of the contract, the contract is voidable.[40]

Where homeowners acknowledge executing some documents, it is useful to know the circumstances and setting of the signing. Where was the signing held: in a title insurance company's office or in a fast food restaurant? Who was present? For example, if the notary on the deed is a woman, was a woman in fact present at the signing? What was said? How did the homeowner feel at the time? With respect to the transaction itself, other questions should revolve around the terms of the deal itself. What were the terms of the transaction as understood by the homeowner?

Post-transaction events can be as important as the transaction itself. How did the reality of the transaction stack up to the homeowners' expectations? What caused the homeowner to seek legal advice?

Answers to these and similar questions are likely to yield valuable information about the rescue scam that can be augmented by thoroughly reviewing the "document trail" discussed below.

15.3.2.2 The Document Trail

15.3.2.2.1 The importance of the documents

The documents related to a foreclosure rescue scam can tell a significant part of the story—one that is often more complete than that told by the homeowner. Obtaining any and all paperwork that may exist—from the solicitation materials to deeds and leases to eviction papers—is critical to challenging a foreclosure rescue scam.

It is virtually guaranteed that the written documents will describe a very different transaction from the one that the homeowners tell. The fact that the writings detail a different story does not mean their case will be lost. While the parol evidence rule would traditionally bar the introduction of oral testimony when a writing purports to represent the entire transaction between the parties, this rule does not apply when a court of equity is evaluating the transaction.[41]

All documents obtained should be preserved carefully. Since duplicate or almost-duplicate documents may be obtained from different sources, the documents obtained from each source should be separately labeled and filed. The chain of custody of the documents should be preserved carefully, especially for the documents in the homeowners' possession.

What the homeowners did not receive can be just as important as what they did receive. Being able to prove exactly what documents were and were not in the homeowners' possession at a certain time can turn out to be a key part of a case. For example, many consumers receive a set of papers at closing, keep that set together in the original envelope, and bring it to their attorney's office when they first seek legal advice about the transaction. If the envelope does not contain all the documents that the other parties were required to give the consumer at closing, it is convincing evidence that those documents were not provided. It is a good idea to advise clients to bring in their papers in exactly their original form, without opening any envelopes or rearranging any of the papers. What follows is a discussion of where to find relevant documents, short of formal discovery.

15.3.2.2.2 Solicitation materials

Rescuers often identify distressed homeowners through public foreclosure notices in the newspapers or at government offices. Rescuers then contact the homeowner by phone, personal visit, or card or flyer left at the door. In some cases, homeowners can receive more than fifty offers for assistance within weeks of the initial public foreclosure notice. Some rescuers rely on advertising on the Internet or in local publications. Others plaster posters on telephone poles and bus stops.

The initial solicitation typically revolves around a simple message such as "Stop foreclosure with just one phone call," "I'd like to $ buy $ your house," "You have options," or "Do you need instant debt relief and CASH?" This contact also frequently contains a "time is of the essence" theme, adding a note of urgency to what is already stressful and possibly desperate situation.

---

40 *See* § 5.13.3, *supra*; National Consumer Law Center, Collection Actions § 5.4.1 (2008 and Supp.).

41 *See, e.g.*, Moore v. Cycon Enters., Inc. 2006 WL 2375477 (W.D. Mich. Aug. 16, 2006) (true intention of parties discerned to establish grounds for equitable mortgage; parol evidence does not apply), *later op. on damages and equitable relief at* 2007 WL 475202 (W.D. Mich. Feb. 9, 2007); Woznicki v. Musick, 119 P. 3d 567, 571 (Colo. Ct. App. 2005) ("It is a settled rule and practice of courts of equity to set aside a formal deed . . . upon proof, even by parol evidence, that the conveyance was not a sale, but merely a security for a debt, and therefore a mortgage." Although no equitable mortgage found in this case because jury found intent of the parties showed a sale).

It is important to collect or obtain any solicitation materials used by the rescuer. Solicitation documents can be useful in demonstrating the initial deceptive contact which led the homeowner into the rescue transaction. Sometimes these materials contain written promises or terms that are not embodied in the final transaction.

- Collect any postcards, flyers or letters the client received regarding foreclosure help, even those that may not obviously be from the rescuer.
- Take photographs of any posted sign to which the homeowner responded.
- Print copies of web pages from the rescuer's Internet site. *Keep in mind that Internet sites can change in content from one day to the next.* What you find may not be what your client saw. Further, what you find may not be there tomorrow. Therefore, it is important to print copies of any pages you think relevant the first time you visit the site. If critical incriminating information is on the website, consider consulting a computer expert about preserving a copy of the web content electronically in a way that can be shown to be tamper-proof.
- Obtain a copy of any advertisement the rescuer used to solicit your client. Many local publications will have archives (electronic or paper) of past editions.

15.3.2.2.3 Transaction documents

The number of transaction documents in any given foreclosure rescue scam can vary dramatically. At one end of the spectrum, the homeowner may execute only one document—a deed. At the other end, some scams involve complex trust arrangements that may contain 10 or more different documents.

The most common source of these documents is the homeowners themselves. However, if the homeowner does not have copies, some documents may be obtained from your local land records. In cases where an apparent closing took place, the settlement agent or title company is likely to have copies of the transaction documents. It is important to request copies from the settlement agent even if the homeowner has copies, as the documents the homeowner was given are very likely to be different from those in the settlement agent's files (and this by itself can be helpful in proving the unfairness of the transaction). The identity of the settlement agent can frequently be determined by examining the mortgage or deed of trust in the local land records. Commonly, the first page of the document will have a name and address for returning the original document. In many cases, this will be the settlement agent.

The following is a nonexclusive list of common documents found in foreclosure rescue scams:

- Purchase and Sale Agreement;
- Deed from homeowner to rescuer (or affiliated party);
- HUD-1 settlement statement;[42]
- Copies of actual checks and other proof of disbursements from the proceeds of the transaction (this can generally be obtained from the settlement agent);
- Other real estate sale closing documents;
- Lease, Occupancy Agreement or Land Installment Contract to the homeowner;
- Option to Purchase;
- Power of Attorney.

In addition, a foreclosure rescue transaction in which the homeowner transfers property to an *inter vivos* trust could include some or all of the following:

- Trust Agreement;
- Assignment of Beneficial Interest;
- Beneficiary Agreement;
- Rider to Trust;
- Facilitation Fee Schedule;
- Property Owner Disclosure and Indemnification;
- Investor Disclosure and Indemnification;
- Certification of Trustee Under Trust;
- Trustee Direction Sheet.

15.3.2.2.4 Local land records

Local land records should be checked to determine a number of important facts in the case. They will show whether the homeowner deeded the home to the rescuer or an affiliate of the rescuer, and whether the transferee deeded or mortgaged it to someone else. Assignments of the mortgage may also be found in the local land records. If the rescuer paid off the existing mortgage, there should be a public record of the release of the mortgage. Local land records can also lead to other cases involving the same rescuer, which is critically important to all of these cases.

Typically land transactions are indexed in one of two ways—a grantor-grantee index or a tract index.[43] In many

42 A new factor in some of these scams involves the misstatement—sometimes in large amounts—of the fees and disbursements listed on the HUD-1 form that is to be given to a homeowner at closing. Copies of the actual checks and proof of electronic disbursements—which can generally be obtained from the settlement agent or the title company—are very useful in proving the fraudulent nature of the entire transaction based on the initial deceptions illustrated by these differences in the HUD-1 and the actual disbursement.

43 A grantor-grantee index is typically divided into two parts, one for grantors (the party transferring title to the property) and one for grantees (the party receiving title to the property). Each part is alphabetized by business name or by last name of an individual. In a foreclosure rescue scam, the homeowner will be shown as the grantor and the rescuer as the grantee. When searching for a mortgage, the record owner of the property will be the grantor and the lender will be the grantee. Historical grantee-grantor records are often grouped by year. A tract index lists all the legal transactions pertaining to a piece of property in

cases, the index itself will provide you with some basic information about the transaction. You will want to obtain copies of any relevant documents. The following is a list of documents to look for in the local land records.

- *Deed from homeowner to rescuer (or affiliated party).* You will need to determine whether a deed transferring the property to the rescuer has in fact been recorded. Note that the grantee may be different than the rescuer with whom the homeowner has had contact. If so, the grantee may be affiliated with or conspiring with the rescuer. If the rescuer set up an *inter vivos* trust, there may be a deed from the homeowner to the trust. One type of scam involves the rescuer promising to keep the deed and *not* record it, and then hand it back to the consumer when the consumer has successfully completed the requirements to repurchase the home (which are generally impossible).[44]
- *Any subsequent deeds for or mortgages[45] against the homeowners' property.* You will want to determine whether the rescuer (or affiliated party) remains the current owner of record or whether the property has been deeded to yet another party. It is obviously important to identify all the parties who claim or may claim a current interest in the property, so that they can be included in any litigation on the scam. You will also want to know whether additional liens, securing other loans, have been placed against the property. If the answer is yes to either question, you will need to deal with the issue of whether your client's interest will supersede that of these parties, or whether they will be able to claim they are "bona fide purchasers for value."[46] Additionally, if the rescuer set up an *inter vivos* trust and the home has since been conveyed to a third party, there should be a deed from the trust to the third party.
- *Any other deeds to the rescuer (or affiliated party).* Rescuers generally strike more than once. Other homeowners who have transferred their properties to the rescuer (or an affiliated party) are also likely to be victims of similar scams. These other homeowners can often provide useful information about the rescuer's methods of operation and may also serve as pattern witnesses if the case goes to trial.

  This pattern evidence can be extremely helpful and powerful. It is admissible (1) to show the rescuer's fraudulent intent; (2) to buttress the homeowner's version of the facts by showing a routine practice on the part of the rescuer; (3) to show that the defendants were acting in accordance with a plan, which may help establish the liability of parties who did not deal directly with the homeowner; (4) to show that the homeowners were acting in a reasonable way when they fell for the scam; and (5) to demonstrate the reprehensibility of the defendants' actions, an important factor for punitive damages. Evidence about previous transactions may also show that other defendants knew of the rescuer's fraudulent tactics, thus helping to establish their liability.[47]

  Evidence that the rescuer has engaged in prior transactions is also critical for determining the applicability of the Truth in Lending Act (because a creditor must have made a certain number of loans in the previous year to be covered by the Act, discussed at § 15.4.2.2, *infra*). This evidence may also establish that the rescuer followed a pattern or practice of lending without regard to the homeowner's repayment ability, in violation of the Home Ownership Protection Act.[48]
- *Release or discharge of mortgage.* If the homeowner's mortgage has been released, this shows that the rescuer or someone connected to the rescuer paid it off. If there is no release, then the homeowner's mortgage probably remains a lien on the property. This may be a breach of contract or a fraud if the rescuer promised otherwise. Check the local practice to determine how long it should take for a release to be recorded after a loan is paid in full.
- *Trust documents.* Some foreclosure rescue scams involve homeowners deeding their property to *inter vivos* trusts. In certain states, such a trust is evidenced by a trust agreement recorded with the local land records

15.3.2.2.5 Court records

A good place to start with court records is any pending eviction case against the homeowner and, in a judicial foreclosure state, the documents from the homeowner's foreclosure case. Obtaining information about other lawsuits in which the rescuer (or any other party to the transaction) is involved can also be fruitful. The federal courts and some local courts have an electronic public access service. Courts that have electronic access will generally

one place. This index is typically organized by tract, parcel, plat, block and/or lot number. This information is commonly found in the deed itself, or may be obtained from the property tax assessors office or from the local land records office.

44 *See, e.g.* Smith v. Eisen, 245 S.W.3d 160 (Ark. Ct. App. 2006) (evaluating all oral and written evidence to determine intent of parties in equitable mortgage case).

45 In many foreclosure rescue scams, rescuers drain the equity out of the house by refinancing as soon as they obtain title. The new lender's interest will only take precedence over the homeowner's interest if the lender can be considered a bona fide purchaser. In many situations this is likely not to be the case. *See* § 15.4.1.3, *infra.*

46 *See* § 15.4.1.3, *infra* (full discussion of ways to prove that third parties are not bona fide purchasers for value such that the homeowner's interest will trump any rights they might claim in the property).

47 *See* § 15.4.7.5, *infra.*

48 *See* § 15.4.3.2, *infra.*

allow you to search the index by party name. In local courts that do not have electronic access, you may be thumbing through paper indices or microfiches for case information. Regardless of how you access court records, here are some things to look for:

- *Eviction case against homeowner.* If the homeowner is facing eviction, determine the status of the case and obtain a copy of the case file. This is important not only so that you can take steps to prevent the eviction, discussed at § 15.3.4.2, *infra*, but also because it is not uncommon for the pleadings filed by a rescuer to contain information helpful to the homeowners. For example, the rescuer may have filed a forged lease or a lease containing terms that violate state residential leasing statutes.
- *Other eviction cases filed by the rescuer (or affiliated party).* Like searching for other deeds to the rescuer in the local land records, other eviction cases filed by the rescuer may help you identify other victims. These victims may then be able to provide you with pattern and practice evidence that exposes the transaction as a foreclosure rescue scam and makes it subject to TIL and other legal claims.
- *Other non-eviction cases involving the rescuer (or affiliated party).* A wealth of additional information may be found in non-eviction cases to which the rescuer is a party. Obviously, it is worth checking to see if any other cases have been filed asserting claims associated with a foreclosure rescue scam perpetrated on another homeowner. Other cases to look for are those filed by former employees of the rescuer. Consider searching the local court records for workers' compensation cases, discrimination cases, or any other cases that might have been filed by a disgruntled employee. These employees are often willing to provide very damaging information about the rescuer's operation. A search of the family court records may enable you to locate an ex-spouse who would be able to provide information on the rescuer's business.

15.3.2.2.6 Other documents

15.3.2.2.6.1 General

As discussed below, there are numerous other documents and information that might be helpful to the homeowner's case beyond the transaction documents, land records, and court records.

15.3.2.2.6.2 Payments to rescuer or lender

If the homeowner has been making "rent" payments to the rescuer or has made any other payments to the rescuer, it is useful to obtain evidence of such payments, such as copies of the cancelled checks or money order receipts. In some cases, the homeowners have continued to make payments to mortgage lenders even though they no longer own their homes. Evidence of these payments should also be obtained. The total of these payments will be relevant when calculating damages. They will be also be important in determining what, if anything, the homeowner will have to pay to unwind the transaction.

15.3.2.2.6.3 Rescuer's loan documents

Rescuers frequently cash out the equity in the home by obtaining a bank loan shortly after obtaining title. These loan documents, and loan documents for any other loan obtained by the rescuer, should be collected and reviewed carefully. You should ask for all documents relating to the loan application, the loan processing, the loan underwriting, the loan approval, the settlement of the loan, and the disbursal of loan funds of all parties involved in the loan process. These parties include the rescuer, any partners or investors in the transaction with the rescuer, the broker, originator and lender of the loan, the settlement company closing the loan, as well as the title insurance provider. The documents may demonstrate that the bank had actual or constructive notice of the fraud, or at least a duty of inquiry—any one of which may defeat a claim that the lender is a bona fide purchaser.[49] Prior to the discovery opportunities afforded by litigation, loan documents should be available from the settlement agent. However, if the loan was not part of a "sale transaction" with the homeowner and the homeowner is not a party to the loan in any way, a formal discovery request may be necessary.

15.3.2.2.6.4 Appraisal

An accurate value of the homeowner's property is critical for determining what claims the homeowner may be able to assert as well as what outcomes are realistic for the homeowner. As noted above, a disparity between the fair market value of the property and the consideration provided by the rescuer is common in foreclosure rescue scams. A significant disparity may be a factor in persuading a court that the transaction is unconscionable, that it violates a state foreclosure rescue statute or an unfairness prohibition in a UDAP statute, or that the transaction amounts to an equitable mortgage.[50] A reliable appraisal or broker's price opinion can provide an estimate of the fair market value. The homeowner should obtain an appraisal showing the fair

49 *See* § 15.4.1.3, *infra* (full discussion of ways to prove that third parties are not bona fide purchasers for value such that the homeowner's interest will trump any rights they might claim in the property).

50 *See* §§ 15.3, 15.4.6.1, 15.4.8.2, *infra*.

market value of the home both at the time of the scam and at present.

Where the rescuer has obtained a loan in connection with the transfer of the property, an appraisal may have been done. However, these appraisals should be viewed with caution as, in some cases, they are artificially inflated to allow the rescuer to take out a higher loan amount.

15.3.2.2.6.5 Reports of consumer complaints

Through state freedom of information acts, records of consumer complaints to local consumer protection agencies, attorney general offices, and licensing divisions can be obtained to see whether similar complaints have been made about the rescuer in the past. The Better Business Bureau should also be contacted for copies of any complaints. In addition, the Federal Trade Commission's website has a search function that allows users to identify Federal Trade Commission (FTC) complaints filed against any entity. Even if the FTC has not filed a complaint against an entity, it will provide copies of complaints that consumers have made to it (after redacting identifying information about the complainant) in response to a Freedom of Information Act request.[51]

15.3.2.2.6.6 Corporate and business documents

Every state requires corporations and other businesses to file certain documents at the time the company begins operation in that state and periodically thereafter. The filing typically consists of the articles of incorporation and annual reports. When dealing with corporations, this information is helpful to figure out who stands behind the corporation or business in the event the corporate veil can be pierced or to sue these individuals separately. Further, formal links between the various parties to the transaction can establish a wider net of liability. Some states may permit you to obtain a copy of that part of the company's state tax return that shows the names and addresses of the current officers. Another way to find out who is behind a corporation or other fictitious name is to get the form that the Postal Service requires a person to file when getting a post office box. The form requires a real person and a real address.

15.3.2.2.6.7 Internet searches

Using the Internet and other electronic database services to conduct a search on a topic of interest or to discover information about a particular party to the transaction can prove fruitful. As indicated above, any web pages of note should be printed out immediately and possibly also preserved electronically, as the content of websites can be changed quickly. Be alert for deceptive Internet advertisements or web page designs that use the names of government programs to draw homeowners to the rescuer's website.[52]

15.3.3 *Identifying Possible Defendants*

Rescuers come in all shapes and sizes and rescue scams can involve a number of different players beyond the rescuer. To avoid missing parties, in what can sometimes be complex real estate transactions, it is generally best to cast the liability net as wide as possible to start.

Rescuers and affiliates. First on the list of defendants is the rescuer, or person with whom the homeowners had primary contact, and the grantee to whom the homeowners transferred title to the property. The grantee may be an "investor" or other third party affiliated with the rescuer. Any other individuals affiliated with the rescuer and with whom the homeowners had contact should also be considered potential defendants.

If the rescuer is a corporate entity, consider naming the officers or employees of the rescuer individually. The corporation is likely to have no assets. Many claims, including fraud and unfair and deceptive acts and practices (UDAP) claims, can be asserted against any person who participated in or directed the wrongful acts, regardless of whether the corporate veil is pierced.[53]

Other players in the scheme may include closing agents,[54] appraisers, notaries,[55] and lenders. Even if these parties did not deal directly with the homeowner, they may be liable for conspiring with the rescuer, aiding and abetting the fraud, or knowingly accepting the fruits of the fraud.[56]

---

51 Requests can be emailed to the FTC at foia@ftc.gov. The FTC charges fees for searching its records plus a per-page copying charge.

52 *See* Federal Trade Comm'n v. One or More Unknown Parties Misrepresenting Their Affiliation with the Making Home Affordable Program, 2009 WL 1651270 (D.D.C. May 15, 2009) (enjoining use of paid ads containing links to MakingHomeAffordable.gov).

53 *See* National Consumer Law Center, Unfair and Deceptive Acts and Practices § 11.4 (7th ed. 2008 and Supp.).

54 *See* Proctor v. Metropolitan Money Store Corp., 645 F. Supp. 2d 464 (D. Md. 2009) (denying motion to dismiss RICO claims against settlement agents involved in foreclosure rescue scam); Burkons v. Ticor Title Ins. Co., 813 P.2d 710 (Ariz. 1991) (reversing summary judgment for closing agent in real estate loan swindle where agent knew or should have known of fraud yet failed to disclose it); Mark Props., Inc. v. Nat'l Title Co., 34 P.3d 587 (Nev. 2001) (real estate escrow agent has duty to disclose fraud to parties with whom it has escrow relationship if it is aware of facts and circumstances that a reasonable escrow agent would perceive as evidence of fraud); Childs v. Charske, 822 N.E.2d 853 (Ohio Ct. Com. Pl. 2004) (denying motion to dismiss negligence claim against title agency that allegedly turned blind eye to fraud in real estate flipping scheme).

55 *See* § 15.4.11.2, *infra*.

56 *See* § 15.4.7.7, *infra*.

Parties with potential property interests. Regardless of whether the homeowners' case asserts fraud claims, argues equitable mortgage, or otherwise attempts to quiet title, all parties with potential interests in the property, and their agents, should be joined as defendants, including trustees, buyers, mortgagees, assignees, settlement agents, appraisers, and brokers. Some of these entities may have insurance that will compensate them for any losses they have suffered. For example, a person who has bought the home from the rescuer may have title insurance that will cover the losses suffered because of the homeowner's claim to the home. Insurance coverage of these losses will make it much more likely that the buyer will agree to re-convey the home to the homeowner.

15.3.4 First Steps

15.3.4.1 Need for Quick Action and to Determine the Homeowner's Goals

Time is often of the essence in fighting foreclosure rescue scams. Many times, these cases first present themselves as eviction cases instead of deed theft or foreclosure rescue cases. It is important to act quickly to stop any eviction proceedings and to get a notice of *lis pendens* recorded against the property to preserve the homeowner's remedies, especially as to third parties.

At the same time, it is important to establish the homeowner's goals at an early stage. Is the homeowner's goal to regain the home? If yes, the homeowner needs to have a realistic plan for keeping the home. Does the homeowner have the income necessary to resume regular mortgage payments, pay taxes and insurance, and keep the home in good repair? If the court requires the homeowner to reimburse the rescuer for paying off the delinquency, will the homeowner be able to do this? The homeowner's prospects will be better if there is a likelihood of winning a damage award that will offset all or part of any payment that is necessary to reacquire the home.

Some homeowners may decide that trying to regain the home is not the best plan. The home may be too expensive, or the homeowner may already have relocated and may not want the disruption of another move. In that case, the goal should be to regain the money and home equity lost in the scam.

A third important goal in a foreclosure rescue scam case is to deter fraud. Both the particular rescuer involved in the case and others in the area will take notice of a significant award and may decide that this particular way of making an easy buck is just too risky.

15.3.4.2 Stop Eviction Proceedings

Many foreclosure rescue scam cases initially present themselves as evictions. Homeowners may not know that they have transferred title to their property and may be confused when they receive notice related to eviction proceedings. While state landlord-tenant laws vary widely, most eviction cases proceed much faster than other types of civil cases. Once a judgment against the tenant has been entered, by reason of default or otherwise, removal of the tenant by the sheriff or other government official may occur within days or weeks. In addition, doctrines such as res judicata and *Rooker-Feldman* will be much more serious potential problems if a judgment is entered in an eviction or foreclosure action.[57] Accordingly, the first priority in handling a foreclosure rescue case is often preventing the eviction of the homeowner.

If you are not familiar with the procedures of your local housing court, or the general court handling residential eviction cases, you may want to consider enlisting the help of a housing or tenant lawyer. If a judgment has already been entered, you may want to consider options for removing or reopening it, particularly if it is a default judgment. Some eviction cases may be held over until the title issues are resolved.[58] If the case cannot be stayed and the eviction court is unwilling or unable to consider title issues, consider framing the defense as a challenge to the validity of the lease rather than the title. In other situations, bankruptcy may be an option if a judgment for possession has not been entered.[59]

15.3.4.3 Reviewing the Deed

Deeds should be scrutinized to determine whether the formal requisites were followed. For example, improper acknowledgment of deeds (or mortgages) may affect the validity of the instrument. Other documents to the transaction should be checked as well, but claims related to the formal requirements of deeds often have a very short statute of limitations period (six months or less). It may be helpful to recruit an attorney who specializes in real estate law at an

57 *See* §§ 10.6.4, 10.6.5, *supra.*

58 Beeghly v. Mack, 20 P.3d 610 (Colo. 2001) (in eviction case, when alleged facts raise question of whether deed was an equitable mortgage, ownership issues must be resolved before possession can be determined). *But see* Real Estate Equity Strategies, L.L.C. v. Jones, 720 N.W.2d 352 (Minn. Ct. App. 2006) (upholding trial court's discretionary denial of homeowners' motion for stay of eviction case; they should have sought injunction against the eviction case in the court in which they filed a separate action to set aside the conveyance, and should have filed a *lis pendens* to preserve their claims against third party purchasers; eviction court had jurisdiction to proceed even though homeowners challenged title).

59 *See* § 15.5.2, *infra*; National Consumer Law Center, Consumer Bankruptcy Law and Practice § 9.4.5.6 (9th ed. 2009).

early stage in the case to evaluate these potential claims.

Deed and mortgage fraud cases may involve situations in which the person whom the notary certified as having appeared did not, in fact, appear. Improper notarizations also may result from the notary's acknowledgment of the signature of an imposter or an incompetent person, or even from taking an acknowledgment over the telephone. The homeowners may have been instructed to sign a stack of documents that are then taken elsewhere for notarization. (Ask your client who was present at the time the deed was actually signed, and whether they recall the notary there.) Regardless of the reason for the defective acknowledgment, practitioners should promptly investigate whether such defects may render the instrument invalid.[60]

15.3.4.4 Evaluating Grounds for Rescission/Rescission Notice

The Truth in Lending Act (TILA) and the Home Ownership and Equity Protection Act (HOEPA), discussed at §§ 15.4.2 and 15.4.3, *infra*, allow a homeowner to rescind certain credit transactions that are secured by the home. This right to rescind may be applicable even if the rescuer attempted to structure the transaction as a transfer of ownership of the home rather than as a loan secured by the home. The right to rescind expires after three years in most states, so it is important to evaluate this claim quickly. (Massachusetts has its own TIL-type law that allows rescission up to four years after consummation of the transaction. Maine, Connecticut, Oklahoma, and Wyoming also have state TIL-type laws, so the deadline would be controlled by state law in those states. All of these states have been granted partial exemptions from TILA.[61]) Even if the three-year deadline is not close, exercising the right to rescind by sending a rescission letter may help create a defense to an eviction. It also creates grounds for recording a *lis pendens*, as discussed in the next section.

15.3.4.5 Recording a *Lis Pendens*

In order to cash in on the homeowner's equity, rescuers may attempt to mortgage or resell the home promptly after acquiring it. If the new owner is truly a "bona fide purchaser," the homeowner may not be able to get title to the house back.

The determination of whether the new owner is a bona fide purchaser whose interest in the property trumps the homeowner's largely revolves around whether the purchaser had notice of the homeowner's ongoing claim—although that notice can be actual, constructive, or even simply "inquiry."[62] Therefore, it is generally a good idea to record the homeowner's claim through a *lis pendens* or similar procedure as soon as possible, to eliminate as many of these disputes as possible.[63] *Lis pendens* is the Latin phrase for "a suit pending" and typically refers to a notice filed with the local land records after a case has been filed. Recording a *lis pendens* against a piece of property alerts a potential purchaser or lender that the title of property is in question. The procedure for obtaining and recording a *lis pendens* varies from state to state so be sure to check your state statutes and local court rules for more information.

In a few cases, homeowners have recorded some document other than a *lis pendens* with the local land records. In order to put potential purchasers or mortgage lenders on notice, the homeowner's attorney should make sure that any document that is recorded will be indexed in the same way as a *lis pendens*. Some recording offices have a different indexing system for documents that do not fit into a few standard categories. The goal is to record a document that necessarily puts every potential purchaser or mortgage lender on notice of the homeowner's claims.

15.3.4.6 Evaluating the Competency of the Consumers and Whether or Not They Have Conflicts of Interest

People who are vulnerable, sometimes because of desperation or a trusting nature, but sometimes because of incompetency, are preyed upon by foreclosure rescuers. The attorney should be alert to any questions about the homeowner's competency, and evaluate the need for a guardian *ad litem*.

Another common tactic of foreclosure rescuers is to get members of the homeowner's family involved in the transaction. The rescuer may, for example, have the home transferred to a family member as an intermediate straw party, or misrepresent that family members are living in the home or contributing to housing expenses. Any potential conflicts of interest should be thoroughly explored at the outset of the case. Even if the family members are willing to waive conflicts of interest, it may be wisest to arrange for them to have separate counsel. Otherwise, the defense is likely to try to tar one family member with the misdeeds of others.

---

60 National Consumer Law Center, The Cost of Credit: Regulation, Preemption, and Industry Abuses § 12.10.2.7 (4th ed. 2009 and Supp.).

61 Federal Reserve Board, Official Staff Commentary on Regulation Z, § 226.29(a)-4.

62 *See* § 15.4.1.3, *infra* (discussion on the bona fide purchaser defense).

63 *See* Real Estate Equity Strategies, L.L.C. v. Jones, 720 N.W.2d 352 (Minn. Ct. App. 2006) (upholding trial court's discretionary denial of homeowners' motion for stay of eviction case; they should have sought injunction against the eviction case in the court in which they filed a separate action to set aside the conveyance, and should have filed a *lis pendens* to preserve their claims against third party purchasers); Watson v. Melnikoff, 866 N.Y.S.2d 96 (N.Y. Sup. Ct. May 6, 2008) (table) (voiding lender's mortgage on property where lender made loan to rescuer three days after homeowner filed *lis pendens*).

15.4 Legal Theories to Attack Foreclosure Rescue Scams

15.4.1 Construing the Transaction As a Loan

15.4.1.1 Introduction

A variety of federal and state causes of action, under both statutory and common law, can be used to attack foreclosure rescue scams. Many of these claims begin with the premise that the homeowner's transfer of title to the property, whether in the form of a sale-leaseback or an *inter vivos* trust, was not absolute and was merely intended to provide security for a loan. The equitable mortgage doctrine allows the court to treat the sale as a mortgage in these circumstances.

This recharacterization fits the facts of the typical foreclosure rescue scam: regardless of what the papers actually declare, the homeowner usually intended to maintain possession and long-term ownership of the home, and preserve some of the family's savings built up in the equity of the home, and the transaction with the rescuer was presented as a way of achieving those goals.

Application of the equitable mortgage doctrine means that the homeowner did not lose ownership of the home, but only transferred a security interest, in the transaction with the rescuer. Further, once the transaction is seen as a loan, the homeowner can invoke a variety of state and federal laws applicable to loans, such as state usury laws, state foreclosure laws, the Truth in Lending Act (TILA), and the Home Ownership and Equity Protection Act (HOEPA). The homeowner may have claims such as fraud, RICO, and unfair and deceptive practices that are independent of whether the court treats the transaction with the rescuer as a sale or a mortgage.

15.4.1.2 The Equitable Mortgage Doctrine

Under the common law "equitable mortgage" doctrine,[64] as well as the statutes of some states,[65] courts recognize that "sales" with repurchase options may in fact be loans and that the deeds at issue should be construed as equitable mortgages. The equitable mortgage doctrine has frequently been employed to find that a foreclosure rescue transaction that purports to be a sale is in fact a loan.[66] The question

64 *See, e.g.*, Russell v. Southard, 53 U.S. 139 (1851); Lynch v. Murphy, 161 U.S. 247 (1896); *In re* Cox, 493 F.3d 1336 (11th Cir. 2007) (Georgia law); Restatement (Third) of Property, *Mortgages*, §§ 3.2, 3.3.

The doctrine is normally phrased in terms of a conveyance or deed that appears absolute but was intended as security for performance, or was subject to defeasance. See the annotations and statutory note to the *Restatement* for different formulations of the doctrine.

65 *See, e.g.*, Cadengo v. Consolidated Fund Mgmt., L.L.C., 370 B.R. 681 (Bankr. S.D. Tex. 2007) (discussing Tex. Const. art. XVI, § 50(c)); Cal. Civ. Code § 1695.12; Fla. Stat. Ann. § 697.01; 765 Ill. Comp. Stat. § 905/5; Md. Code Ann., Real Prop. § 7-101; Okla. Stat tit. 46, § 1; N.Y. Real Prop. Law § 320; Restatement (Third) of Property, *Mortgages* §§ 3.2, 3.3 (see annotations and statutory notes for other state laws).

Some states limit application of the doctrine only to the immediate grantee or others with actual notice. *See, e.g.*, Kan. Stat. Ann. § 58-2302; Minn. Stat. Ann. § 507.38.

Other states, while recognizing the equitable mortgage doctrine, limit its usefulness by forbidding consideration of parol evidence, requiring the homeowner's repurchase right to be recorded or executed with the formality of a deed. *See, e.g.*, *In re* Comtois, 363 B.R. 336 (Bankr. D.N.H. 2007) (discussing N.H. Rev. Stat. Ann. § 479).

66 *See, e.g.*, Provencher v. T & M Mortgage Solutions, Inc., 2008 WL 2447472 (D. Me. June 18, 2008) (magistrate's recommended decision) (equitable mortgage adequately pleaded; existence of separate repurchase document does not preclude equitable mortgage); Johnson v. Wheeler, 492 F. Supp. 2d (D. Md. 2007); Stella v. Anderson, 2007 WL 1080309 (D. Minn. Apr. 9, 2007); Moore v. Cycon Enters., Inc. 2006 WL 2375477 (W.D. Mich. Aug. 16, 2006) (finding equitable mortgage after discerning true intention of parties; parol evidence rule does not apply), *later op. on damages and equitable relief at* 2007 WL 475202 (W.D. Mich. Feb. 9, 2007); Perry v. Queen, 2006 WL 481666 (M.D. Tenn. Feb. 27, 2006) (transfer of home created equitable mortgage where consumer was unsophisticated and not represented by counsel, the payment made by the "purchaser" was only 10% of the fair market value of the home, and the mortgage remained in the consumer's name); Wilson v. Bel Fury Invs. Group, L.L.C., 2006 WL 297440 (D. Neb. Feb. 6, 2006) (recognizing equitable mortgage doctrine but denying summary judgment to both sides due to disputes of material fact); Brown v. Grant Holding, L.L.C., 394 F. Supp. 2d 1090 (D. Minn. 2005) (denying summary judgment on question whether transaction constituted an equitable mortgage; evaluating six factors to determine the existence of an equitable mortgage); Rowland v. Haven Properties, L.L.C., 2005 WL 1528264 (N.D. Ill. June 24, 2005) (refusing to dismiss equitable mortgage claim where house worth $245,000 was deeded away for only $91,500 and homeowner alleged fraud and no intent to sell), *later op.*, 2005 WL 2007232 (N.D. Ill. Aug. 11, 2005) (declining to grant preliminary injunction to plaintiff to protect status quo due to factual disputes; listing factors to consider in determining whether transaction constituted an equitable mortgage); Hruby v. Larsen, 2005 WL 1540130 (D. Minn. June 30, 2005) (granting preliminary injunction to maintain status quo; listing elements to prove equitable mortgage and finding that consumers have a likelihood of success on the merits; ordering a bond of $1000 plus monthly payments of $500); O'Brien v. Cleveland, 423 B.R. 477 (Bankr. D.N.J. 2010) (finding transaction to be equitable mortgage and citing National Consumer Law Center, Truth in Lending (6th ed. 2007)); Metcalf v. Bartrand, 491 P.2d 747 (Alaska 1971); Smith v. Eisen, 245 S.W.3d 160 (Ark. Ct. App. 2006) (equitable mortgage must be proven by clear and convincing evidence; court should consider all oral and written evidence and focus on intent of the parties); Robinson v. Builders Supply & Lumber Co., 586 N.E.2d 316 (Ill. App. Ct. 1991) (a deed absolute on its face may be considered an equitable mortgage when parties intend it as security in the nature of a mortgage; where the consideration is grossly inadequate a mortgage is strongly indicated); Carter v. Second

whether the transaction represents a bona fide sale or is a loan depends on the intent of the parties.[67] Specific mortgage-negating language in the documents or the homeowners' knowledge that they were signing a transfer deed is not dispositive of intent.[68] Courts have routinely looked beyond the legal form of these transactions to examine their substance and the circumstances leading up to their execution. Thus, documents that clearly identify a sale and leaseback arrangement are not conclusive if the surrounding circumstances indicate that the homeowner never intended to sell the home and that the transaction should be considered a loan secured by a mortgage.[69] Parol evidence is generally

---

Chance Program, Inc., No. 06 CH 26787 (Cir. Ct., Cook County, Ill. Dec. 23, 2008), *available at* www.consumerlaw.org/unreported (foreclosure rescue transaction was equitable mortgage, not sale); Patterson v. Grace, 661 N.E.2d 580 (Ind. Ct. App. 1996) (finding equitable mortgage where intent of parties was to treat deed transferring ownership as security for a loan, and homeowners remained in exclusive possession, made numerous improvements, and had a right to repurchase); Tullis v. Weeks, 741 N.W.2d 824 (Iowa Ct. App. 2007); London v. Gregory, 2001 WL 726940 (Mich. Ct. App. Feb. 23, 2001) (court of equity has power to reconstrue deed as equitable mortgage); Peterson v. Johnson, 720 N.W.2d 833 (Minn. Ct. App. 2006) (finding equitable mortgage where deed provided as security for loan; remanding for calculation of effective interest rate and balance due on loan; critical factor here was statement in the deed itself that when the loan was repaid the buyer would re-convey land back to seller); Redmond v. McClelland, 2000 Minn. App. LEXIS 779 (Minn. Ct. App. July 25, 2000) (deeds created equitable mortgage even without explicit option to purchase, in light of parties' intent and their relative sophistication); Mortgage Elec. Registration Sys. v. Wilson, 2005 WL 1284047 (N.J. Super. Ct. Ch. Div. May 27, 2005) (reviewing common law rules regarding proving an equitable mortgage; no allegation of usury); Southwell v. Middleton, 851 N.Y.S.2d 74 (N.Y. Sup. Ct. Nov. 16, 2007) (unpublished); Henderson v. Sec. Mortgage & Fin. Co., 273 N.C. 253, 160 S.E.2d 39 (1968); Umpqua Forest Ind. v. Neen'ah-Ore Land Co., 188 Or. 605, 217 P.2d 219 (1950); Swenson v. Mills, 108 P.3d 77 (Or. Ct. App. 2005) (when an absolute deed is accompanied by an option to repurchase, the option weighs in favor of the existence of a mortgage; further evidence in support of mortgage is that purchase price was for only half of property's market value); Long v. Storms, 622 P.2d 731 (Or. Ct. App.), *as modified by* 629 P.2d 827 (Or. Ct. App. 1981); Johnson v. Cherry, 726 S.W.2d 4 (Tex. 1987); Sudderth v. Howard, 560 S.W.2d 511 (Tex. App. 1977); Bown v. Loveland, 678 P.2d 292 (Utah 1984) (construing sale with oral repurchase option as equitable mortgage); Pearson v. Gray, 954 P.2d 343, 345 (Wash. Ct. App. 1998) (loan secured by a quit claim deed, "evinces . . . the granting of an equitable mortgage"); Levy v. Butler, 1998 WL 781146 (Wash. Ct. App. Nov. 9, 1998) (sale with repurchase option coupled with inadequate consideration sufficient to overcome presumption of sale transaction). *But see* Johnson v. Washington, 559 F.3d 238 (4th Cir. 2009) (equitable mortgage under Virginia law requires debtor-creditor relationship as evidenced by a debt owed by the original homeowner to the purchaser; option to repurchase did not constitute such a debt); Franchi v. Farmholme Inc., 191 Conn. 201, 464 A.2d 35 (1983) (sale and leaseback not an equitable mortgage). *But cf. In re* Shewey, 2000 WL 33712477 (Bankr. D. Idaho Apr. 26, 2000) (finding no equitable mortgage where intention of the parties was unclear, lack of consideration for sale was unclear, and terms of the credit were not set out); Woznicki v. Musick, 119 P.3d 567 (Colo. Ct. App. 2005) (no equitable mortgage found where jury found that the intent of the parties was demonstrated that the transaction be a sale); Borden v. Hurley, Civil Action No. C 06-1357 (Circuit Ct., Calvert County, Md. Mar. 28, 2008), *available at* www.consumerlaw.org/unreported (deed of sale is presumed to be absolute conveyance unless clear, unequivocal, and convincing evidence shows it was intended as mortgage; not shown here). *See generally* National Consumer Law Center, The Cost of Credit: Regulation, Preemption, and Industry Abuses § 7.5.2 (4th ed. 2009 and Supp.).

67 *See, e.g., In re* Offshore Dev. Corp., 802 F.2d 1319 (11th Cir. 1986); Redic v. Gary H. Watts Realty Co., 762 F.2d 1181 (4th Cir. 1985); Woods-Tucker Leasing Corp. v. Hutcheson-Ingram Dev. Co., 642 F.2d 744 (5th Cir. 1981); Sachs v. Ginsberg, 87 F.2d 28 (5th Cir. 1936); Jones v. Rees-Max, L.L.C., 514 F. Supp. 2d 1139 (D. Minn. 2007) (fact issue whether parties intended to sell home, as homeowners believed rescuer was offering a service that would enable them to stay in the house, make monthly payments, and repay rescuer; disparity between value of property and price paid also weighs in favor of finding equitable mortgage); Perry v. Queen, 2006 WL 481666 (M.D. Tenn. Feb. 27, 2006); Fox v. Peck Iron & Metal, 25 B.R. 674 (Bankr. S.D. Cal. 1982); Smith v. Eisen, 245 S.W.3d 160 (Ark. Ct. App. 2006) (considering all oral and written evidence to determine intent of parties in equitable mortgage case); Peterson v. Johnson, 720 N.W.2d 833 (Minn. Ct. App. 2006) (finding equitable mortgage where deed was provided as security for loan; remanding for calculation of effective interest rate and balance due on loan); Redmond v. McClelland, 2000 Minn. App. LEXIS 779 (Minn. Ct. App. July 25, 2000); Swenson v. Mills, 108 P.3d 77 (Or. Ct. App. 2005) (when an absolute deed is accompanied by an option to repurchase, the option weighs in favor of the existence of a mortgage; further evidence in support of mortgage is that purchase price was for only half of property's market value); Bantuelle v. Williams, 667 S.W.2d 810 (Tex. 1983). *But see* Bray v. McNeeley, 682 S.W.2d 615 (Tex. App. 1984).

68 *See* Russell v. Southard, 53 U.S. 139 (1851) ("a court of equity does not consider a consent, thus obtained, to be sufficient to fix the rights of the parties. 'Necessitous men,' says the Lord Chancellor, in Vernon v. Bethell, 2 Eden, 113, 'are not, truly speaking, free men; but, to answer a present emergency, will submit to any terms that the crafty may impose upon them.' "); Restatement (Third) of Property, *Mortgages* § 3.3(a) & cmt. D (1997); Josiah Kibe, *Comment: Closing the Door on Unfair Foreclosure Practices in Colorado*, 74 U. Colo. Law Rev. 241, 262 (2003) (collecting statutory citations on admission of parol evidence). *See also* Moore v. Cycon Enters., Inc., 2006 WL 2375477 (W.D. Mich. Aug. 16, 2006) (finding equitable mortgage in light of true intention of parties; parol evidence rule does not apply), *later op. on damages and equitable relief at* 2007 WL 475202 (W.D. Mich. Feb. 9, 2007); Carter v. Second Chance Program, Inc., No. 06 CH 26787 (Cir. Ct., Cook County, Ill. Dec. 23, 2008), *available at* www.consumerlaw.org/unreported. *But see* Missouri v. MWG Prop. Consultants, L.L.C., 2008 WL 2389489 (Mich. Ct. App. June 12, 2008) (unpublished) (taking formalistic view of intent; no equitable mortgage where property owner knew he was relinquishing title, even though parties had agreed to repurchase option).

69 Jones v. Rees-Max, L.L.C., 514 F. Supp. 2d 1139 (D. Minn.

admissible to show these surrounding circumstances.[70] Some states forbid consideration of parol evidence, and may even require the repurchase agreement to be recorded, effectively eliminating the equitable mortgage doctrine.[71] Yet even in those states, the transaction might be considered a loan subject to lending disclosure and usury laws—and may still be voidable—though it is not construed as a mortgage implicating laws limited to mortgage lending.[72]

There are a number of factors that persuade courts that the transaction is actually an equitable mortgage. The legal issue the courts are determining is both the intention of the parties and whether some inequity was involved such that it is appropriate for equitable relief to be provided. Below is a list of factors that courts have used to find that the intention of the parties was in fact to create an equitable mortgage and that equitable relief is appropriate.[73] The presence of just one or more of these factors may be sufficient to establish an equitable mortgage:[74]

- Statements by the homeowner or representations by the purchaser indicating an intention that homeowner continue ownership;[75]
- A substantial disparity between the value received by the homeowner and the actual value of the property;[76]
- Evidence that the payment amount was set at the amount needed to forestall foreclosure, not based on an assessment of the value of the property;[77]
- Existence of an option to repurchase;[78]
- The homeowner's continued possession of the property;[79]

2007) (denying rescuer's motion for summary judgment; statements in documents that no security interest was granted are not dispositive); Smith v. Eisen, 245 S.W.3d 160 (Ark. Ct. App. 2006) (considering all oral and written evidence to determine intent of parties in equitable mortgage case); Browner v. District of Columbia, 549 A.2d 1107 (D.C. 1998); London v. Gregory, 2001 WL 726940 (Mich. Ct. App. Feb. 23, 2001) ("When determining whether to grant equitable relief, the court 'protects the necessitous by looking through the form to the substance of the transaction.' "); Swenson v. Mills, 108 P.3d 77 (Or. Ct. App. 2005) (when an absolute deed is accompanied by an option to repurchase, the option weighs in favor of the existence of a mortgage; further evidence in support of mortgage is that purchase price was for only half of property's market value).

70 Russell v. Southard, 53 U.S. 139 (1851); *In re* Cox, 493 F.3d 1336 (11th Cir. 2007) (Georgia law); Provencher v. T & M Mortgage Solutions, Inc., 2008 WL 2447472 (D. Me. June 18, 2008) (magistrate's recommended decision); McKeeman v. Commercial Credit Equip. Corp., 320 F. Supp. 938 (D. Neb. 1970); Cadengo v. Consolidated Fund Mgmt., L.L.C., 370 B.R. 681 (Bankr. S.D. Tex. 2007); Tullis v. Weeks, 741 N.W.2d 824 (Iowa Ct. App. 2007); Southwell v. Middleton, 851 N.Y.S.2d 74 (N.Y. Sup. Ct. 2007) (unpublished).

71 *See, e.g., In re* Comtois, 363 B.R. 336 (Bankr. D.N.H. 2007) (discussing N.H. Rev. Stat. Ann. § 479).

72 *See In re* Comtois, 363 B.R. 336 (Bankr. D.N.H. 2007) (rejecting claim that transaction was a mortgage, but parties agreed that it was credit and the court found that defendant violated statute requiring interest to be disclosed as an annual rate). *See also In re* Comtois, 2007 WL 1480707 (Bankr. D.N.H. May 18, 2007) (further decision after jury trial, finding that UDAP remedies are available for violating state credit laws).

73 *See, e.g.*, Robinson v. Builders Supply & Lumber Co., 586 N.E.2d 316 (Ill. App. Ct. 1991) (factors are existence of indebtedness, close relationship of parties, prior unsuccessful loan attempts, circumstances surrounding the transaction, disparity of parties' situation, lack of legal assistance, usual type of sale, inadequacy of consideration, manner in which consideration was paid, retention of written evidence of debt, the belief that the debt remains unpaid, an agreement to repurchase, and continued exercise of ownership privileges and responsibilities by the homeowner); Patterson v. Grace, 661 N.E.2d 580 (Ind. Ct. App. 1996) (finding equitable mortgage where parties' intent was to treat deed transferring ownership as security for a loan, and homeowners remained in exclusive possession, made numerous improvements, and had a right to repurchase; listing as factors (1) existence of debt prior to transaction, (2) documents that provide that grantor can redeem by meeting certain conditions, (3) inadequate consideration, (4) grantor paid interest to grantee, (5) grantor retained possession, control and use of property, particularly when no rent was paid, (6) grantor made improvements that a tenant would not likely make, (7) grantee did not exercise ownership or control over property, (8) parties did not intend to extinguish the debt); Peterson v. Johnson, 720 N.W.2d 833 (Minn. Ct. App. 2006) (finding equitable mortgage where deed was provided as security for loan; remanding for calculation of effective interest rate and balance due on loan; critical factor here was statement in the deed itself that when the loan was repaid the buyer would re-convey land back to seller).

74 Woznicki v. Musick, 119 P.3d 567, 571 (Colo. Ct. App. 2005) (no equitable mortgage where jury found intent of the parties showed a sale). *But see* Clemons v. Home Savers, L.L.C., 530 F. Supp. 2d 803 (E.D. Va. 2008) (refusing to consider other factors because an equitable mortgage requires the existence of a debt and homeowner could have vacated the property without owing anything), *aff'd*, 273 Fed. Appx. 296 (4th Cir. 2008) (per curiam).

75 Restatement (Third) of Property, *Mortgages* §§ 3.2(b)(1), 3.3(b)(1) (1997). *See* Tullis v. Weeks, 741 N.W.2d 824 (Iowa Ct. App. 2007).

76 Russell v. Southard, 53 U.S. 139 (1851); *In re* Cox, 493 F.3d 1336 (11th Cir. 2007) (Georgia law); Tullis v. Weeks, 741 N.W.2d 824 (Iowa Ct. App. 2007); Restatement (Third) of Property, *Mortgages* §§ 3.2(b)(2), 3.3(b)(2) & cmt. c (1997). *See, e.g.*, Jones v. Rees-Max, L.L.C., 514 F. Supp. 2d 1139 (D. Minn. 2007); Perry v. Queen, 2006 WL 481666 (M.D. Tenn. Feb. 27, 2006); Browner v. District of Columbia, 549 A.2d 1107 (D.C. 1998); London v. Gregory, 2001 WL 726940 (Mich. Ct. App. Feb. 23, 2001); Howard v. Diolosa, 574 A.2d 995 (N.J. Super. Ct. App. Div. 1990); Bantuelle v. Williams, 667 S.W.2d 810 (Tex. App. 1983); Levy v. Butler, 1998 WL 781146 (Wash. Ct. App. Nov. 9, 1998) (sale with repurchase option coupled with inadequate consideration sufficient to overcome presumption of sale transaction). *But cf.* Johnson v. Washington, 559 F.3d 238 (4th Cir. 2009) (finding disparity between $212,800 sale price and $260,000 contract price insufficient to be persuasive).

77 *In re* Cox, 493 F.3d 1336 (11th Cir. 2007) (Georgia law).

78 Restatement (Third) of Property, *Mortgages* § 3.3(b)(3) (1997).

79 *Id.* §§ 3.2(b)(3), 3.3(b)(4). *See* Tullis v. Weeks, 741 N.W.2d 824 (Iowa Ct. App. 2007). *But cf.* Johnson v. Washington, 559 F.3d 238 (4th Cir. 2009) (continued possession unpersuasive in light of other facts).

- The homeowner's continuing duty to bear ownership responsibilities, such as paying real estate taxes or performing property maintenance;[80]
- Disparity in bargaining power and sophistication, including the homeowner's lack of representation by counsel;[81]
- Evidence showing an irregular purchase process, including the fact that the property was not listed for sale[82] or that the parties did not conduct an appraisal or investigate title;[83]
- Irregularities in the closing or settlement, including unusual payments or the purchaser's failure to contribute funds to the closing;[84] and
- Financial distress of the homeowner, including the imminence of foreclosure and prior unsuccessful attempts to obtain loans.[85]

Many of these factors will be present in most foreclosure rescue scams. The parties—the homeowner and the rescuer—are in grossly different positions of bargaining power. The homeowner is facing a real crisis and has everything to lose. The foreclosure may be the culmination of a series of catastrophic events in the lives of the family—such as job loss, illness, divorce, or death of a family member. The rescuer, on the other hand, is simply looking for a good deal, a quick way to make some money—often quite a lot of money—with relatively little investment and relatively little risk. The rescuer invariably drafts the papers and understands them, while the homeowner often has very little understanding of real estate transactions and is easily misled.

Typically, the homeowner has the burden of demonstrating by clear and convincing evidence that an absolute deed is in fact an equitable mortgage.[86] However, courts have held that a sale with an option to repurchase coupled with a gross disparity between the sale price and the property value without more can satisfy the homeowner's burden.[87] In California, the mere presence of an option to repurchase in an instrument conveying property in foreclosure creates a presumption that the transaction is a loan.[88]

The most direct consequence of an equitable mortgage is that the deed transferring the property from the homeowner is voidable, and the homeowner may be able to assert continuing ownership through a quiet title action.[89] If the

80 Restatement (Third) of Property, *Mortgages* §§ 3.2(b)(4)–(5), 3.3.(b)(5)–(6) (1997); *In re* Cox, 493 F.3d 1336 (11th Cir. 2007) (Georgia law); *In re* Davis, 169 B.R. 285 (E.D.N.Y. 1994) (looking to whether leaseback actually transfers the normal risks and responsibilities of a lease); Moran v. Kenai Towing & Salvage, Inc., 523 P.2d 1237 (Ala. 1974). *Accord* McGill v. Biggs, 434 N.E.2d 772 (Ill. App. Ct. 1982); Howard v. Diolosa, 574 A.2d 995 (N.J. Super. Ct. App. Div. 1990). *Cf.* Carlson v. Bertrand, 2004 WL 3030033 (Minn. Dist. Ct. Mar. 19, 2004) (entering judgment for defendant-purchaser where plaintiff-homeowner failed to demonstrate fraudulent or negligent misrepresentation and where defendant-purchaser had paid off first and second mortgage, made improvements to the property, and paid utility bills owed by the plaintiffs and where the monthly rent payments were lower than the mortgage payments).

81 Perry v. Queen, 2006 WL 481666 (M.D. Tenn. Feb. 27, 2006); Browner v. District of Columbia, 549 A.2d 1107 (D.C. 1998); London v. Gregory, 2001 WL 726940 (Mich. Ct. App. Feb. 23, 2001); Restatement (Third) of Property, *Mortgages* §§ 3.2.(b)(6), 3.3(b)(7) (1997).

In *Browner* the court found that the lender's misconduct was not excused by the fact that the distressed homeowner made an improvident decision. The court made clear that this is precisely the sort of overreaching sought to be curbed by usury laws:

> The purpose of usury laws from time immemorial has been to protect desperately poor people from the consequences of their desperation. Lawmaking authorities in almost all civilizations have recognized that the crush of financial burdens causes people to agree to almost any conditions of the lender and to consent to even the most improvident loans. Lenders, with the money, have all the leverage; borrowers in dire need of money, have none.

Browner, 549 A.2d at 1116. *See also In re* Davis, 169 B.R. 285 (E.D.N.Y. 1994) (equity sellers were people of little means who lacked any real estate experience while equity purchasers were sophisticated and experienced in real estate transactions). *But cf.* Shelton v. Cunningham, 508 P.2d 55 (Ariz. 1973) (finding no equitable mortgage when lender and borrower were both older men with little education).

82 *See, e.g., In re* Davis, 169 B.R. 285 (E.D.N.Y. 1994) (homeowner expressly stated she did not want to sell her home); Browner v. District of Columbia, 549 A.2d 1107 (D.C. 1998) (homeowners had no intent to sell homes); Johnson v. Cherry, 726 S.W.2d 4 (Tex. 1987) (homeowner told real estate agent he was not interested in selling his property).

83 *See, e.g.,* Long v. Storms, 622 P.2d 731 (Or. Ct. App. 1981) (appraisal not conducted until after sale), *as modified by* 629 P.2d 827 (Or. Ct. App. 1981).

84 *See, e.g.,* Johnson v. Wheeler, 492 F. Supp. 2d (D. Md. 2007). *See also* Johnson v. Home Savers Consulting Corp., 2007 WL 925518 (E.D.N.Y. Mar. 23, 2007) (describing irregular payments), *report and recommendation adopted by* 2007 WL 1110612 (E.D.N.Y. Apr. 11, 2007).

85 *See, e.g.,* Perry v. Queen, 2006 WL 481666 (M.D. Tenn. Feb. 27, 2006); Brown v. Grant Holding, L.L.C., 394 F. Supp. 2d 1090 (D. Minn. 2005); McElroy v. Grisham, 810 S.W.2d 933 (Ark. 1991) (seller in dire financial straits, which creditor knew); Browner v. District of Columbia, 549 A.2d 1107 (D.C. 1998) (defendant knew plaintiffs were financially distressed and had been unable to obtain a loan); London v. Gregory, 2001 WL 726940 (Mich. Ct. App. Feb. 23, 2001); Howard v. Diolosa, 574 A.2d 995 (N.J. Super. Ct. App. Div. 1990) (homeowners previously denied four loans by institutional lenders).

86 *See, e.g.,* Mathis v. Perriraz, 2010 WL 56073 (D. Utah Jan. 6, 2010) (discussing types of evidence and prior case law); Robinson v. Builders Supply & Lumber Co., 586 N.E.2d 316 (Ill. App. Ct. 1991); McGill v. Biggs, 105 Ill. App. 3d 706 (1982); Long v. Storms, 622 P.2d 731 (Or. Ct. App. 1981), *as modified by* 629 P.2d 827 (Or. Ct. App. 1981).

87 *See, e.g.,* Koenig v. Van Reken, 279 N.W.2d 590 (Mich. Ct. App. 1979); Levy v. Butler, 1998 WL 781146 (Wash. Ct. App. Nov. 9, 1998).

88 Cal. Civ. Code § 1695.12. *See* Boquilon v. Beckwith, 57 Cal. Rptr. 2d 503 (Cal. Ct. App. 1996).

89 *See, e.g.,* Moore v. Cycon Enters., Inc., 2007 WL 475202 (W.D.

homeowner regains title through a quiet title action, there will still be a debt owed to the rescuer. However, the homeowner may have damage claims to offset the debt that arise from the recharacterization of the transaction as a loan.[90] Even if the homeowner is left owing a debt to the rescuer, the homeowner may be able to save the home by refinancing that debt with a legitimate lender.[91]

15.4.1.3 The Bona Fide Purchaser Defense

Rescuers often sell or encumber the property quickly after gaining title, which may cut off the homeowner's ability to recover the property. Foreclosure rescue transactions would not happen if the rescuers were not able to cash out by taking out a new mortgage or transferring the property to a subsequent buyer, and if these third party buyers or lenders could not get title insurance or close their deals.[92] Unfortunately, the homeowner's ability to get relief may be cut off if the third party is able to assert a defense as a bona fide purchaser or lender.[93] If the deed from the homeowner is actually forged, it is void from the inception and cannot be used to transfer any interest in the property to a third party, even to a bona fide purchaser or lender without notice of the fraud.[94] In some states, a deed can be deemed a forgery if the homeowner was induced to sign it through fraud, deceit, or other misconduct.[95] The difference between "fraud in the factum" and fraud in the inducement is also important because fraud in the factum, like forgery, renders a conveyance void ab initio, even against a bona fide purchaser or lender.[96] Fraud in the inducement, however, only makes the conveyance voidable and will not affect a bona fide third party.[97] Thus, if a rescuer procures an authentic signature by misrepresenting that a document was something other than a deed, the deed is void.[98] Generally, however, if the homeowner signed the deed, knowing it was a deed, it is voidable as to the rescuer but is not void as to a bona fide purchaser or lender.[99] A bona fide purchaser for value of property subject to an equitable mortgage, without notice of such mortgage, takes the property free of the equitable mortgage.[100] However, any purchaser who has notice of the homeowner's claim to ownership may still be subject to the equitable mortgage doctrine. "[N]otice to [the bona fide purchaser], actual or constructive, [is] an element essential to the survival of the [equitable] lien, as against [the bona fide purchaser]."[101] Moreover, suspicious circumstances that

---

Mich. Feb. 9, 2007) (ordering reconveyance of title).

The remedies upon a finding of an equitable mortgage are essentially the same as those upon rescission under TILA. *See* §§ 15.4.2.4.4, 15.4.2.4.5, *infra*.

90 *See, e.g.*, Moore v. Cycon Enters., Inc., 2007 WL 475202 (W.D. Mich. Feb. 9, 2007).

If the transaction was actually a loan, then it is governed by the Truth in Lending Act (*see* § 15.4.2, *infra*), possibly the Home Ownership and Equity Protection Act (*see* § 15.4.3 *infra*), and possibly state usury rules (*see* § 15.4.9, *infra*).

91 In Moore v. Cycon Enters., Inc., 2007 WL 475202 (W.D. Mich. Feb. 9, 2007), the court gave the plaintiff ninety days following expiration of the appeal period to refinance and pay the rescuer back, or face foreclosure by the rescuer.

92 *See* Stith v. Thorne, 488 F. Supp. 2d 534 (E.D. Va. 2007) (observing that other parties provided the rescuers with the necessary funding and facilitated the transaction by providing the documentation and legal appearance, but dismissing certain claims against those third parties due to lack of evidence that they knowingly participated); Commonwealth v. Desire, 2007 WL 1302581 (Mass. Super. Ct. Apr. 17, 2007) (noting number of required participants and the irregularities throughout the process). *But see* Sith v. Thorne, 247 F.R.D. 89 (E.D. Va. 2007) (later decision in same case as discussed above holding that triable issues existed as to whether title company willfully violated state UDAP statute by making payment to rescuer in the absence of written instructions from homeowner, and whether title company used power of attorney to prevent homeowner from seeing the payment).

93 *See, e.g.*, Nichols v. Howard, 2009 WL 1364418 (Cal. Ct. App. May 15, 2009) (unpublished) (finding no remedy under state equity purchaser statute when purchaser mortgaged property to bona fide third party in violation of statute and no proof homeowner could have afforded to perform repurchase agreement); Summage v. Jean, 2007 WL 1288748 (Tex. App. May 3, 2007).

94 *See, e.g.*, Cain v. Bethea, 2007 WL 2859681 (E.D.N.Y. Aug. 17, 2007), *adopted in part and rev'd in part on other grounds* 2007 WL 2846914 (E.D.N.Y. Sept. 26, 2007); Robinson v. Leone, 2007 WL 624690 (Mich. Ct. App. Mar. 1, 2007).

95 *See* Cain v. Bethea, 2007 WL 2859681 (E.D.N.Y. Aug. 17, 2007) (citing cases), *adopted in part and rev'd in part on other grounds* 2007 WL 2846914 (E.D.N.Y. Sept. 26, 2007); Wells Fargo Bank v. Edsall, 880 N.Y.S.2d 877 (N.Y. Sup. Ct. 2009) (deeds that are forged or executed under false pretenses constituting fraud in the factum are void ab initio, and interests of subsequent bona fide purchasers or encumbrancers are not protected, but fraudulently induced deed is merely voidable).

96 Brown v. Carlson, 2009 WL 2914191 (Mass. Super. Ct. Sept. 1, 2009) (discussing fraud in the factum and fraudulent inducement in context of foreclosure rescue scam).

97 Wells Fargo Bank, N.A. v. Robinson, 2009 WL 3210306, at *3 (N.Y. Super. Ct. Oct. 7, 2009).

98 Cain v. Bethea, 2007 WL 2859681 (E.D.N.Y. Aug. 17, 2007) (citing cases), *adopted in part and rev'd in part on other grounds* 2007 WL 2846914 (E.D.N.Y. Sept. 26, 2007) (declining to recommend summary judgment where homeowner claimed that she believed the papers she was signing were a refinance, not a deed).

99 *See* Martinez v. Affordable Hous. Network, Inc., 123 P.3d 1201 (Colo. 2005); Missouri v. MWG Prop. Consultants, L.L.C., 2008 WL 2389489 (Mich. Ct. App. June 12, 2008).

100 Lynch v. Murphy, 161 U.S. 247, 255 (1896); Grant v. Lehtinen, 2003 WL 21961404 (Minn. Ct. App. Aug. 19, 2003) (homeowner's property sold to a neighboring church in breach of repurchase agreement).. *See* Fla. Stat. Ann. § 697.01 (setting forth equitable mortgage rule with exception that "no such conveyance shall be deemed or held to be a mortgage, as against a bona fide purchaser or mortgagee, for value without notice, holding under the grantee"). *Cf.* Foster v. Smith, 2009 WL 703702 (D. Minn. Mar. 16, 2009) (declining to decide whether lender to whom rescuer conveyed a mortgage is bona fide purchaser in absence of factual development).

101 Lynch v. Murphy, 161 U.S. 247, 255 (1896).

may not provide actual notice nevertheless put the purchaser on "inquiry notice" with a duty to investigate further.[102] A claim that a purchaser is a bona fide purchaser is an affirmative defense on which the defendant bears the burden of proof.[103] Thus, A third party who has actual notice, constructive notice, or inquiry notice of the homeowner's claim will not be considered a bona fide purchaser for value.

A purchaser of an interest in real property who has notice in any one of these ways is not considered a bona fide purchaser for value. If the purchaser is not a bona fide purchaser, then the property can still be reclaimed for the benefit of the homeowner.[104] The effect of having notice of a homeowner's claim does not, however, extend to a third party who obtains a lien or title from a bona fide purchaser. Under the shelter rule, "one who is not a bona fide purchaser, but who takes an interest in property from a bona fide purchaser, may be sheltered in the latter's protective status."[105] As a result, a *lis pendens* may not be effective if it is filed after the property has been transferred to a bona fide purchaser, even if the party asserting ownership is a subsequent purchaser with notice based on the *lis pendens*.[106] While the following discussion focuses on sales to third party purchasers, the same principles apply where the rescuer cashes out the equity in the property by obtaining a loan and transfers an interest in the property to a lender as security for the loan.[107]

To ensure that notice is provided to any subsequent purchasers, attorneys representing homeowners should record a *lis pendens* as soon as possible. The *lis pendens* preserves remedies against third party purchasers by clearly and unequivocally putting them on clear and *actual* notice of the questionable circumstances underlying the transfer. However, the failure to record a *lis pendens* does not mean that the third party automatically takes the property free of the homeowner's claims.

Actual notice means just what it sounds like—the third party actually knew the circumstances of the transaction, and thus cannot claim that it did not know of the underlying fraud or equitable mortgage.[108] A court will find constructive notice where a search of the title records would have revealed a defect.[109]

There are several methods of establishing that the purchaser is responsible for at least *inquiring* into the situation to determine if there might be a fraud or equitable mortgage. "Inquiry notice arises when a party becomes aware or should have become aware of certain facts which, if investigated, would reveal the claim of another."[110] Inquiry notice imputes knowledge where the circumstances are such that they would have aroused the suspicions of an ordinary purchaser—however, notice will not be "imputed to a purchaser if a reasonable search would prove, or would have proven, futile."[111] Some states, however, hold that a subsequent purchaser receives good title unless the purchaser had actual notice, not constructive or inquiry notice.[112]

According to the Colorado Supreme Court, "[t]he continued possession of real estate is sufficient to put an interested person on inquiry notice of any legal or equitable claim the person or persons in open, notorious, and exclusive possession of the property may have. . . . [I]t is not too much to ask that a buyer make further inquiries when made aware that the person in physical possession of the property believes they are in fact the true owner of the property. When a reasonable person is made aware that someone in physical possession of property claims ownership, the prudent course of action is to make further investigations."[113]

There are a variety of circumstances, which individually or in combination, may lead a court to place the burden of

---

102 *See* Martinez v. Affordable Housing Network, Inc., 123 P.3d 1201 (Colo. 2005). *See also* Haley v. Corcoran, __ F.2d __, 2009 WL 3163528, at *4 (D. Md. Oct. 2, 2009) (presumption that mortgagee acted in good faith "may be overcome only by showing that the [mortgagee] had knowledge of 'suspicious circumstances' that would give rise to a duty to inquire into previous transactions involving the property.").

103 Davis v. Elite Mortgage Servs., Inc., 592 F. Supp. 2d 1052, 1056 (N.D. Ill. 2009). *But see* Julian v. Buonassissi, 963 A.2d 234, 247 (Md. 2009) (burden of showing that transaction was bona fide shifts to lender only if person alleging fraud shows that grantee had knowledge of suspicious circumstances), *cert. granted*, 970 A.2d 892 (Md. 2009).

104 *See* Martinez v. Affordable Housing Network, Inc., 123 P.3d 1201 (Colo. 2006).

105 Strekal v. Espe, 114 P.3d 67, 75 (Colo. Ct. App. 2004).

106 *See* Deutsche Bank Nat'l Trust Co., Tr. v. Booker, 2010 WL 333718 (D. Md. Jan. 25, 2010) (foreclosing assignee of mortgage was bona fide purchaser even if it obtained interest in property with record notice of homeowner's dispute because assignor was bona fide purchaser of interest in property.).

107 *See* Haley v. Corcoran, 659 F. Supp. 2d 714 (D. Md. 2009) (mortgagee treated as bona fide purchaser if mortgage supported by consideration and taken in good faith).

108 *See* Calvagno v. Bisbal, 430 F. Supp. 2d 95 (E.D.N.Y. 2006) (third party who was informed of serious issues that surrounded the property cannot be a bona fide purchaser); Martinez v. Affordable Housing Network, Inc., 123 P.3d 1201 (Colo. 2005).

109 *See* Martinez v. Affordable Housing Network, Inc., 123 P.3d 1201 (Colo. 2005).

110 Martinez v. Affordable Housing Network, Inc., 123 P.3d 1201, 1206 (Colo. 2005). *See also* Cain v. Bethea, 2007 WL 2859681 (E.D.N.Y. Aug. 17, 2007), *adopted in part and rev'd in part on other grounds* 2007 WL 2846914 (E.D.N.Y. Sept. 26, 2007); Vernier v. Sipe, 2008 WL 400678 (Mich. Ct. App. Feb. 14, 2008); Southwell v. Middleton, 851 N.Y.S.2d 74 (N.Y. Sup. Ct. 2007).

111 Martinez v. Affordable Housing Network, Inc., 123 P.3d 1201, 1206 (Colo. 2005) (once there is a duty to inquire, the purchaser "will be charged with all knowledge that a reasonable investigation would have revealed.").

112 *See, e.g.*, Kan. Stat. Ann. § 58-2302; Minn. Stat. Ann. § 507.38; *In re* Comtois, 363 B.R. 336 (Bankr. D.N.H. 2007) (discussing N.H. Rev. Stat. Ann. § 479).

113 *See* Martinez v. Affordable Housing Network, Inc., 123 P.3d 1201 (Colo. 2005).

further inquiry on to the purchaser:

- The homeowner's continued possession of the property,[114] or conversely the fact that the purchaser did not live in the house;[115]
- A statement by the homeowner to an agent of the purported bona fide purchaser, stating that she owned the house.[116]
- The purchaser's acquisition of title through a quit claim deed, especially if it is one of a series;[117]
- The seller's failure to satisfy the homeowner's recorded mortgages;[118]
- The purchaser's failure to conduct a title search or to obtain title insurance;[119]
- Existence of a *lis pendens*;
- The fact that the purchaser paid significantly less than market value for the property, indicating awareness of title defects (or showing that it was not a bona fide purchase "for value");
- The fact that the purchaser did not contribute funds to the purchase or that the purchaser's closing costs were shifted to the seller;[120]
- Unusual payments or circumstances at the closing that put the purchaser, lender, or title insurer on notice to inquire further;[121]
- Facts indicating that a purported bona fide lender had engaged in a number of other similar transactions under questionable circumstances;[122]
- Any other suspicious circumstances—such as a large discrepancy between the homeowner's original purchase price and the sale price to the rescuer—that would lead a reasonable buyer to inquire further and discover the homeowner's claim.[123]

Some of these factors, such as the homeowner's possession of the property or a *lis pendens*, may be sufficient in and of themselves. Others, such as transfer through a quit claim deed, are not conclusive but may lend support to other evidence. An agent's knowledge of key facts—such as the sale-leaseback arrangement—also can put the principal on notice of facts sufficient to defeat its claim as a bona fide purchaser.[124]

A New York trial court held that a homeowner's allegations regarding the lender's failure to investigate were sufficient to allow a case to proceed. The complaint alleged that the lender, which had extended a loan to the rescuer after the homeowner executed a deed to the rescuer, had failed to verify that the rescuer would be able to make the mortgage

114 Madison v. Gordon, 39 S.W.3d 604, 606 (Tex. 2001) (purchaser is charged with constructive notice of occupant's claims that "the purchaser might have reasonably discovered on proper inquiry" if a court determines that the purchaser had a duty to ascertain the rights of a third-party possessor). *See* Davis v. Elite Mortgage Servs., Inc., 592 F. Supp. 2d 1052 (N.D. Ill. 2009); Martinez v. Affordable Housing Network, Inc., 123 P.3d 1201, 1207 (Colo. 2005). *But see* Left Field Properties, L.L.C. v. Keeney, L.L.C., 2006 WL 630864 (N.J. Super. Ct. App. Div. Mar. 15, 2006) (unpublished) (knowledge that homeowners had lost home through tax sale foreclosure and sheriff's sale insufficient to create inquiry notice); Summage v. Jean, 2007 WL 1288748 (Tex. App. May 3, 2007) (homeowner's continuing possession did not give notice to bona fide lender as buyer provided documents indicating there was a renter).

115 *See* Freddie Mac, Emerging Fraud Trends—Foreclosure Rescue Scheme, Single Family News (June 2007), *available at* www.freddiemac.com/singlefamily/news/newsletter/2007/06/fraud.html (listing red flags for lenders, including borrowers who are purchasing a home as an investment while continuing to rent, purchasing multiple rental properties simultaneously, or purchasing the property as a primary residence when they already own a home of superior value). *But see* Summage v. Jean, 2007 WL 1288748 (Tex. App. May 3, 2007) (homeowner's continuing possession did not give notice bona fide lender as documents indicated there was a renter).

116 LaSalle Bank v. Ferone, 892 N.E.2d 585 (Ill. Ct. App. 2008).

117 *See* Martinez v. Affordable Housing Network, Inc., 123 P.3d 1201, 1207–1208 (Colo. 2005) (observing that conveyance by quitclaim imposes an element of risk on the buyer that, though not dispositive, "is a significant factor to be considered when assessing inquiry notice," and finding two back-to-back quitclaim conveyances particularly unusual); Vernier v. Sipe, 2008 WL 400678 (Mich. Ct. App. Feb. 14, 2008).

118 *See* Martinez v. Affordable Housing Network, Inc., 123 P.3d 1201, 1208 (Colo. 2005).

119 Johnson v. Wheeler, 492 F. Supp. 2d 492(D. Md. 2007); Vernier v. Sipe, 2008 WL 400678 (Mich. Ct. App. Feb. 14, 2008). *See* Martinez v. Affordable Housing Network, Inc., 123 P.3d 1201, 1208 (Colo. 2005).

120 Johnson v. Wheeler, 492 F. Supp. 2d 492(D. Md. 2007); Cain v. Bethea, 2007 WL 2859681 (E.D.N.Y. Aug. 17, 2007), *adopted in part and rev'd in part on other grounds*, 2007 WL 2846914 (E.D.N.Y. Sept. 26, 2007); Freddie Mac, Emerging Fraud Trends—Foreclosure Rescue Scheme, Single Family News (June 2007), *available at* www.freddiemac.com/singlefamily/news/newsletter/2007/06/fraud.html (listing red flags for lenders).

121 Johnson v. Wheeler, 492 F. Supp. 2d 492(D. Md. 2007) (lender insisted on a $100,000 escrow to cover unknown title defects); Cain v. Bethea, 2007 WL 2859681 (E.D.N.Y. Aug. 17, 2007), *adopted in part and rev'd in part on other grounds*, 2007 WL 2846914 (E.D.N.Y. Sept. 26, 2007); Southwell v. Middleton, 851 N.Y.S.2d 74 (N.Y. Sup. Ct. 2007) (unpublished) (issues of fact existed as to whether discrepancies in the closing documents should have put lender's closing representative on inquiry notice).

122 Cain v. Bethea, 2007 WL 2859681 (E.D.N.Y. Aug. 17, 2007), *adopted in part and rev'd in part on other grounds*, 2007 WL 2846914 (E.D.N.Y. Sept. 26, 2007).

123 *See* Davis v. Elite Mortgage Servs., Inc., 592 F. Supp. 2d 1052 (N.D. Ill. 2009) (relying in part on discrepancies in appraisal, title audit, and title policy as to who was living in the property and who was grantee, and homeowner's recorded notice of equitable mortgage, even though it was not recorded in grantor-grantee index); Newman v. 1st 1440 Inv., Inc., 1993 U.S. Dist. LEXIS 354 (N.D. Ill. Jan. 14, 1993); LaSalle Bank v. Ferone, 892 N.E.2d 585 (Ill. App. Ct. 2008) (misrepresentations by rescuer on loan application, coupled with homeowner's statement that she owned the home, put mortgage lender on duty of inquiry).

124 Newman v. 1st 1440 Inv., Inc., 1993 U.S. Dist. LEXIS 354 (N.D. Ill. Jan. 14, 1993). *But see* Stith v. Thorne, 488 F. Supp. 2d 534 (E.D. Va. 2007) (notice "must be clear and strong. . . . A mere suspicion on notice, even though it be a strong suspicion, will not suffice").

payments, verify whether they were licensed as mortgage brokers, or conduct a background investigation of the rescuer and his associates, which would have revealed multiple loans in which one of them was a straw buyer. The court held that a lender has a duty to investigate and ascertain the economic status of the purchaser-mortgagor and whether he or she may be committing a fraud against the seller in the underlying transaction.[125]

The advocate may wish to consult with a real estate expert, or a trust expert if the case involved an *inter vivos* trust, to determine whether the circumstances would arouse suspicion in a reasonable buyer. Real estate practices and customs vary from state to state and from locality to locality, and any departure from standard practices should be suspect. Documents required for a trust also vary from state to state and it is important to determine what documents a reasonable purchaser would inspect and whether there were unusual features of the trust documents that would have alerted a buyer that something was amiss.

For foreclosure rescue scams, the homeowner's continued possession of the property is clearly the most important factor that should put a purchaser on at least inquiry notice. As one court observed, "possession of real estate is sufficient to put an interested person on inquiry notice of any legal or equitable claim the person or persons in open, notorious, and exclusive possession of the property may have. . . . Further, where the party in possession is the sole tenant and lessee, certain circumstances may give arise to a duty to inquire as to their rights as tenants beyond mere possessory rights."[126]

If the rescuer actually forged the deed from the homeowner, then it is void ab initio and not merely voidable. In that case, the rescuer has no title to convey, even to a bona fide purchaser.[127]

Some courts recognize another doctrine, the equitable subrogation doctrine, which may protect a bona fide purchaser or mortgage lender. Under this doctrine, a purchaser or lender that pays off a prior lien on the home is subrogated to the position of that lienholder. The doctrine is intended to avoid unjust enrichment of the homeowner. Thus, for example, if the rescuer obtains a loan of $300,000, and uses $200,000 to satisfy the homeowner's existing mortgage, then the lender is able to assert a $200,000 claim against the homeowner even if the deal is otherwise unwound, as the homeowner received a $200,000 benefit.[128]

Even if the homeowners cannot recover the property from a bona fide purchaser, the equitable mortgage doctrine may still be asserted to pursue monetary claims against the original rescuer.

15.4.2 Truth in Lending

15.4.2.1 Introduction

While the Truth in Lending Act (TILA) is generally a disclosure statute and does not limit the substantive terms of loans, it can be useful in attacking foreclosure rescue scams, because rescuers often structure these transactions as sales and do not provide the disclosures required by TILA.

TILA contains an express cause of action with remedies that include actual and statutory damages and attorney fees. The most important remedy in the foreclosure rescue scam context, however, is the right to rescission, which includes voiding of finance charges and closing costs. TILA also provides the basis for federal jurisdiction, which may or may not be an advantage, depending on the state.

Because TILA only applies to creditors who have a regular business of extending credit, it may not apply to victims of the small time rescuers who populate the foreclosure rescue scam market. A subsection of TILA, however, the Home Ownership and Equity Protection Act (HOEPA), which applies to certain high cost loans, has a looser definition of "creditor," and also provides additional requirements and remedies. HOEPA is discussed at § 15.4.3, *infra*.

15.4.2.2 When Does TILA Apply?

When a sale-leaseback or *inter vivos* trust is found to be a disguised loan, it is subject to disclosure requirements and TIL remedies to the same extent as an explicit secured loan transaction.[129] To fall under TILA, a transaction must in-

125 Mathurin v. Lost & Found Recovery, L.L.C., 854 N.Y.S.2d 629 (N.Y. Sup. Ct. 2008).

126 *See* Martinez v. Affordable Housing Network, Inc., 123 P.3d 1201, 1207 (Colo. 2005).

127 *See* Martinez v. Affordable Housing Network, Inc., 123 P.3d 1201, 1205 (Colo. 2005); M.M.&G., Inc. v. Jackson, 612 A.2d 186 (D.C. 1992); Harding v. Ja Laur Corp., 315 A.2d 132 (Md. Ct. Spec. App. 1974). *See also* Ward v. Gray, 374 A.2d 15 (Del. Super. Ct. 1977) (when there is no jurisdiction to conduct a sale due to fraud or failure to meet notice requirements, the sale is void and any resulting title is a nullity).

128 *See* Johnson v. Melnikoff, 2008 WL 4182397 (N.Y. Sup. Ct. Sept. 11, 2008) (voiding mortgage but applying equitable subrogation doctrine to allow lender from which rescuer obtained secured loan to recover from homeowner the amount it paid on her preexisting mortgage), *aff'd on other grounds*, 882 N.Y.S.2d 914 (App. Div. 2009). *See also* Fremont Inv. & Loan v. Sessions, No. 31105/7 (N.Y. Sup. Ct., Kings Cty. Oct. 28, 2008), *available at* www.consumerlaw.org/unreported (applying equitable subrogation doctrine; lender that made loan to rescuer has claim against homeowners to the extent proceeds were used to pay off existing mortgage).

129 *See, e.g.*, Clemons v. Home Savers, L.L.C., 530 F. Supp. 2d 803 (E.D. Va. 2008) (acknowledging that equitable mortgages are subject to TILA but finding that transaction was not an equitable mortgage), *aff'd*, 273 Fed. Appx. 296 (4th Cir. 2008)(per curiam); Jones v. Rees-Max, L.L.C., 514 F. Supp. 2d 1139 (D.

volve "credit"[130] offered or extended by a "creditor"[131] to a "consumer" (who must be a natural person),[132] primarily for personal, family or household purposes,[133] either subject to a finance charge or payable by written agreement in more than four installments.[134]

Substance governs over form, and state common law or statutory rules governing equitable mortgages can be used to establish that the transaction meets the definition of "credit" for TIL purposes.[135] Once it is established that the transaction is in fact a loan, it is likely that it will meet most of these other criteria.

The most difficult hurdle is establishing that the credit was extended by a "creditor." To meet the TIL definition, a creditor must "regularly" extend consumer credit.[136] In cases of real estate secured loans, "regularly" means six or more loans per year.[137] However, if a high-cost loan that falls under HOEPA[138] is involved, then the creditor need only make two or more mortgages per year, or one such mortgage through a broker, to be considered a creditor for *all* TIL purposes.[139] Searching land and court records may help identify other transactions that can be used to demonstrate that the "rescuer" is a creditor.[140] HOEPA applies to non-purchase money, closed-end credit secured by the homeowner's primary residence. This is the same universe of transactions to which TIL rescission applies, except that TIL rescission applies to open-end as well as closed-end credit.[141]

The "creditor" is the person to whom the obligation is *initially* payable on its face. Arrangers are not covered under TILA. The liability of assignees is discussed at § 15.4.2.6, *infra*. TILA also sets forth several exemptions from its coverage,[142] but a foreclosure rescue transaction is unlikely to fall within any of them.

15.4.2.3 TIL Disclosure Requirements

TILA works primarily by providing standardized definitions of certain loan terms and requiring disclosure of those terms. TILA provides specific definitions and requirements, in some cases quite technical, for the required disclosures.[143] In most foreclosure rescue scams, however, the

Minn. 2007); Stella v. Anderson, 2007 WL 1080309 (D. Minn. Apr. 9, 2007); Moore v. Cycon Enters., Inc., 2006 WL 2375477 (W.D. Mich. Aug. 16, 2006); Wilson v. Bel Fury Inv. Group, 2006 WL 297440, at *5 (D. Neb. Feb. 6, 2006) (No. 8:04CV640); James v. Ragin, 432 F. Supp. 887 (W.D.N.C. 1977); O'Brien v. Cleveland, __ B.R. __, 2010 WL 251600 (Bankr. D.N.J. Jan. 22, 2010) (finding sale-leaseback to be equitable mortgage that violates HOEPA); Eyler v. 3 Vista Court L.L.C. (*In re* Eyler), 2008 WL 4833096 (Bankr. D. Md. Oct. 28, 2008) (although characterized as sale, transaction was loan, and TIL disclosures were required); Carter v. Second Chance Program, Inc., No. 06 CH 26787 (Cir. Ct., Cook County, Ill. Dec. 23, 2008), *available at* www.consumerlaw.org/unreported; Hodges v. Swafford, 863 N.E.2d 881, *reh'g granted, opinion aff'd as amended,* 868 N.E.2d 1179 (Ind. Ct. App. 2007); Long v. Storms, 622 P.2d 731 (Or. 1981) (transaction whereby investor took a deed in exchange for a loan with a repurchase option was an equitable mortgage, or a loan with a security interest; investor found to be creditor subject to Truth in Lending Act and homeowner was entitled to rescind because Truth in Lending disclosures were not made), *as modified by* 629 P.2d 827 (Or. Ct. App. 1981); National Consumer Law Center, Truth in Lending § 6.2.5 (6th ed. 2007 and Supp.). *See also In re* Mattera, 128 B.R. 107 (Bankr. E.D. Pa. 1991). *Cf.* Provencher v. T & M Mortgage Solutions, Inc., 2008 WL 2447472, at *13 (D. Me. June 18, 2008) (magistrate's recommended decision) (recommending dismissal of TIL and HOEPA claims because of inadequate allegations that three-way foreclosure rescue transaction was loan, even though complaint adequately pleaded an equitable mortgage claim), *later op. at* 2008 WL 4857276 (D. Me. Nov. 9, 2008) (allowing plaintiff to file amended complaint containing allegations that correct the pleading deficiencies), *later op. at* 2009 WL 485106 (D. Me. Feb. 25, 2009) (refusing to dismiss amended TIL and HOEPA claims). *But see* Figueroa v. Smith, 2006 WL 4549615 (Bankr. S.D. Fla. Sept. 21, 2006) (finding that loan was from bank to rescuer, not from bank to homeowner, and thus was a purchase-money loan not rescindable under TILA; court failed to recognize that the rescindable loan was the one from the rescuer to homeowner using the deed as collateral, a transaction that was falsely structured as a sale).

130 15 U.S.C. § 1602(e); Reg. Z, 12 C.F.R. § 226.2(a)(14); National Consumer Law Center, Truth in Lending § 2.2.4 (6th ed. 2007 and Supp.).

131 15 U.S.C. § 1602(f); Reg. Z, 12 C.F.R. § 226.2(a)(17)(i); National Consumer Law Center, Truth in Lending § 2.3 (6th ed. 2007 and Supp.).

132 15 U.S.C. § 1602(h); Reg. Z, 12 C.F.R. § 116.2.(a)(11); National Consumer Law Center, Truth in Lending § 2.2.2 (6th ed. 2007 and Supp.).

133 Reg. Z, 12 C.F.R. § 226.2(a)(12); National Consumer Law Center, Truth in Lending §§ 2.2.3, 2.4.2 (6th ed. 2007 and Supp.).

134 15 U.S.C. § 1602(f)(1); Reg. Z. § 226.2(a)(17)(i)(A); National Consumer Law Center, Truth in Lending § 2.3.4 (6th ed. 2007 and Supp.).

135 Reg. Z, 12 C.F.R. § 226.2.(a)(25); Commentary § 226.2(a)(25)-1; Wilson v. Bel Fury Invs. Group, L.L.C., 2006 WL 297440, at *5 (D. Neb. Feb. 6, 2006); Perry v. Queen, 2006 WL 481666 (M.D. Tenn. Feb. 27, 2006) (No. Civ. 3:05-0599); Hruby v. Larsen, 2005 WL 1540130 (D. Minn. June 30, 2005); James v. Ragin, 432 F. Supp. 887 (W.D.N.C. 1977) (sale-leaseback); Long v. Storms, 622 P.2d 731 (Or. Ct. App. 1981) (sale-leaseback), *as modified by* 629 P.2d 827 (Or. Ct. App. 1981); National Consumer Law Center, Truth in Lending §§ 2.1.2, 2.5.4, 6.2.5 (6th ed. 2007 and Supp.).

136 15 U.S.C. § 1602(f); Reg. Z, 12 C.F.R. § 226.2(a)(17)(i).

137 Reg. Z, 12 C.F.R. § 226.17(a), n.3. *See* § 15.3.2.2, *supra* (discussion of records to investigate to obtain evidence of the rescuer's other transactions). *See generally* National Consumer Law Center, Truth in Lending § 2.3.3 (6th ed. 2007 and Supp.).

138 *See* § 15.4.3, *infra* (discussion of HOEPA).

139 15 U.S.C. § 1602(f); Reg. Z, 12 C.F.R. § 226.2 n.3. *See* National Consumer Law Center, Truth in Lending §§ 2.3.6, 9.2.3 (6th ed. 2007 and Supp.).

140 *See* §§ 15.3.2.2.4–15.3.2.2.5, *supra.*

141 *See* § 15.4.2.4.2, *infra.*

142 15 U.S.C. 1603; Reg. Z, 12 C.F.R. § 226.3. *See* National Consumer Law Center, Truth in Lending § 2.4 (6th ed. 2007 and Supp.).

143 In addition to specific definitions, the disclosures must be

technicalities do not matter, because the rescuer structures the transaction as a sale rather than a loan and provides no TIL disclosures at all.

In the case of "closed-end" loans,[144] failure to disclose the following information gives the consumer a right to both actual damages and statutory damages of $400 to $4000 ($200 to $24000 for conduct occurring before July 30, 2008)[145] per transaction for real-estate secured transactions:

- Total finance charge;[146]
- Amount financed;[147]
- Annual percentage rate;[148]
- Payment schedule;[149]
- Total of payments;[150]
- Security interests.[151]

More important than the damages, the failure to disclose any of the items listed above—other than security interests—also gives rise to a right to rescission.

TILA also requires disclosure of a second list of items, violations of which give rise only to actual damages and no right to rescission.[152]

15.4.2.4 The Right of Rescission

15.4.2.4.1 Overview

The right of rescission is the most important remedy TILA provides to attack a foreclosure rescue scam.[153] Rescission can be quite dramatic because it can:

- Completely undo the transaction, eliminate onerous agreements, and void transfer of the property to the rescuer;
- Eliminate the rescuer's ability to use summary eviction proceedings to evict the homeowner from the property;
- Void charges, penalty fees, interest, and other costs, even if already paid; and
- Allow the court to award statutory damages of up to $4000 ($2000 for conduct occurring before July 30, 2008)[154] in the case of closed-end, real-estate-secured loans (in addition to any statutory damages for disclosure violations), if the creditor fails to respond to a proper rescission notice.[155]

The value of rescission to save homeowners from foreclosure rescue scams cannot be overstated. The lender (and assignee) literally must undo the deal if it violated certain requirements. Becoming familiar with the ground rules of rescission is essential in home defense cases.[156]

15.4.2.4.2 What transactions can be rescinded

In addition to TILA's general coverage provisions, only a *non-purchase money security interest* in the consumer's *primary* residence is subject to rescission.[157] This means

---

provided in a timely way, in a form the consumer may keep, before consummation, and in a clear and conspicuous format, segregated from other information. *See* National Consumer Law Center, Truth in Lending §§ 4.2–4.4 (6th ed. 2007 and Supp.).

144 A closed-end loan has a fixed term, as is the case for most foreclosure rescue scams. Different rules apply for open-end loans that, like home equity lines of credit, have no fixed terms and allow the borrower to repay as much or little as he or she decides above a minimum amount.

145 Housing and Economic Recovery Act of 2008, Pub. L. No. 110-289, § 2502(b), 122 Stat. 2654, 2857 (2008) (codified at 15 U.S.C. § 1640(a)(2)(A)(ii)). *See* National Consumer Law Center, Truth in Lending § 8.6.2.1 (6th ed. 2007 and Supp.) (discussing application of 2008 increase in statutory damages).

146 15 U.S.C. § 1638(a)(3); Reg. Z, 12 C.F.R. § 226.18(d). *See* National Consumer Law Center, Truth in Lending Ch. 2, § 4.6.3 (6th ed. 2007 and Supp.).

147 15 U.S.C. § 1638(a)(2)(A); Reg. Z, 12 C.F.R. § 226.18(b). *See* National Consumer Law Center, Truth in Lending § 4.6.2 (6th ed. 2007 and Supp.).

148 15 U.S.C. § 1638(a)(4). *See* National Consumer Law Center, Truth in Lending § 4.6.4 (6th ed. 2007 and Supp.).

149 15 U.S.C. § 1638(a)(6); Reg. Z, 12 C.F.R. § 226.18(g).
The payment schedule includes the number, amount, and timing of payments. *See* National Consumer Law Center, Truth in Lending § 4.6.5 (6th ed. 2007 and Supp.).

150 15 U.S.C. § 1638(a)(5); Reg. Z, 12 C.F.R. § 226.18(h). *See* National Consumer Law Center, Truth in Lending § 4.6.6 (6th ed. 2007 and Supp.).

151 15 U.S.C. § 1638(a)(9); Reg. Z, 12 C.F.R. § 226.18(m). *See* National Consumer Law Center, Truth in Lending § 4.6.7 (6th ed. 2007 and Supp.).

152 This group includes the identity of the creditor, itemization of the amount financed, prepayment penalties, late payment fees, security interest charges, insurance charges and debt cancellation agreement, mortgage lender's assumption policy, a demand feature, and whether certain other information can be found elsewhere. *See* 15 U.S.C. § 1638(a)(1), (a)(2), (a)(10), (a)(11); Reg. Z §§ 226.4(d), (e), 226.17(a)(1) n.38, 226.18(i), (p), (q), 226.20(b); National Consumer Law Center, Truth in Lending §§ 4.7.3–4.7.11 (6th ed. 2007 and Supp.).

153 Moore v. Cycon Enters., Inc., 2006 WL 2375477 (W.D. Mich. Aug. 16, 2006) (TIL rescission allowed against rescuer after transaction recast as a mortgage), *later op. at* 2007 WL 475202 (W.D. Mich. Feb. 9, 2007) (allowing TIL rescission of equitable mortgage and damages).

154 Housing and Economic Recovery Act of 2008, Pub. L. No. 110-289, § 2502(b), 122 Stat. 2654, 2857 (2008) (codified at 15 U.S.C. § 1640(a)(2)(A)(ii)). *See* National Consumer Law Center, Truth in Lending § 8.6.2.1 (6th ed. 2007 and Supp.) (discussing application of 2008 increase in statutory damages).

155 *See* §§ 5.6.3, 5.6.7, *supra*.

156 This subsection provides only a general overview of the rescission remedy. The rescission rules appear in 15 U.S.C. § 1635. Regulation Z and the Official Staff Commentary further flesh out these provisions: Reg. Z, 12 C.F.R. § 226.15 (open-end credit) and § 226.23 (closed-end credit). The relevant Official Staff Commentary is located at Official Staff Commentary §§ 226.15 (open-end credit) and 226.23 (closed-end credit). The statute, regulations, and commentary and extensive analysis can be found in National Consumer Law Center, Truth in Lending (6th ed. 2007 and Supp.).

157 National Consumer Law Center, Truth in Lending § 6.2.1 (6th ed. 2007 and Supp.).

that the mortgage loan in question cannot be the one obtained to purchase the home. Rescission does apply to non-purchase money interests, whether first or second mortgages, home equity loans, bridge loans, home improvement contracts, and liens arising by operation of law.[158] Since foreclosure rescue scams target people who already own their homes, it will usually be clear that the transaction is not a purchase money loan.[159]

15.4.2.4.3 When rescission can be exercised

The homeowner has three business days, including Saturdays,[160] to rescind from the *latest of*:

- Consummation of the transaction;
- Delivery of proper notice of right to rescind;[161] or
- Delivery of all *material* disclosures, correctly made.[162]

The three days begin to run only when all material disclosures and the notice of right to rescind, in the proper form, are received.

If the creditor fails to make the required disclosures or provide notice of the right to rescind, there is a continuing right to rescind for up to *three years from consummation*. Since most foreclosure rescue scams are not styled as loans, the rescuers rarely provide any disclosures, and this three-year rule will normally apply.[163] In addition, in Massachusetts and some other states, rescission under a state TIL law may be permitted defensively by way of recoupment beyond three years.[164]

The right to rescind a loan under TILA is normally extinguished if the consumer's interest in the property is sold or transferred (including by foreclosure sale).[165] This rule does not apply if the transaction is determined to be an equitable mortgage under state law such that any sale or transfer is invalid.[166] As discussed above, there may be issues in applying the equitable mortgage doctrine to a bona fide purchaser who takes title without notice of the equitable mortgage, though the homeowner's continued possession of the property may provide sufficient notice.[167]

For loans that fall under HOEPA,[168] violations of most of the HOEPA protections also trigger the extended three-year right to rescind.

15.4.2.4.4 The three-step rescission process

Rescission works through a sequential, three-step process.

First, the consumer sends *written notice of rescission*, which operates automatically to void the security interest in the real property and to eliminate the consumer's obligation to pay the finance charges (even if accrued) and other charges.[169] In the case of a foreclosure rescue scam, once a sale-leaseback transaction is restructured into a loan, the agreements underlying that transaction would be voided, including any fees or costs the homeowner agreed to pay.

The notice of rescission need not take any special form. Nevertheless, in the case of a foreclosure rescue scam, some explanation is obviously needed since the transaction most likely took the form of a sale or transfer and not of a loan subject to TILA. A sample letter exercising the right to rescission is included on this treatise's companion website. Some courts have held that a complaint filed in court may serve as the notice of rescission, but a separate notice is preferable.[170]

Second, after the notice of rescission has been sent, the creditor or assignee has twenty days to *refund or credit any money paid* (including any money or property given to a third party) and to take steps to *void the security interest*.[171] For a foreclosure rescue scam, this obligation would include the obligation to reconvey the property back to the homeowner and to clear any other clouds or new encumbrances on the homeowner's title.

---

158 *Id.* When the same creditor refinances the loan, rescission applies only to the extent of the new money advanced. *Id.* § 6.2.6.2.

159 *But see* Figueroa v. Smith, 2006 WL 4549615 (Bankr. S.D. Fla. Sept. 21, 2006) (finding that loan was from bank to rescuer, not from bank to homeowner, and thus was a purchase-money loan not rescindable under TILA; court failed to recognize that the rescindable loan was the one from the rescuer to homeowner using the deed as collateral, a transaction that was falsely structured as a sale).

160 Only Sundays and certain specified federal holidays are excluded. Reg. Z, 12 C.F.R. § 226.2(a)(6).

161 Specific rules govern the form of the notice of the right to rescind and the circumstances that make it ineffective or allow the consumer to waive it. National Consumer Law Center, Truth in Lending §§ 6.2.9, 6.4.3, 6.5 (6th ed. 2007 and Supp.).

162 For closed-end loans, the material disclosures are the amount financed, the finance charge, the APR, the payment schedule, and the total of payments. *See* § 15.4.2.3, *supra*.

163 Once the three-year period passes, however, the right to rescind expires and there is generally no right under federal law to raise rescission as a defense to foreclosure even by way of recoupment. There are some potential arguments to get around this rule in certain limited circumstances. *See* National Consumer Law Center, Truth in Lending § 6.3.3 (6th ed. 2007 and Supp.). *See also* Stovall v. Lakanu, 2006 WL 3350686 (D. Minn. Nov. 17, 2006).

164 *See* National Consumer Law Center, Truth in Lending § 6.3.3.3 (6th ed. 2007 and Supp.).

165 *See* National Consumer Law Center, Truth in Lending § 6.3.2.2 (6th ed. 2007 and Supp.).

166 *Id.* § 6.3.2.2.1 & n.238.

167 *See* § 15.4.1.2, *supra*.

168 *See* § 15.4.3, *infra* (discussion of HOEPA).

169 15 U.S.C. § 1635(b); Reg. Z §§ 226.5(d)(1), 226.23(d)(1). *See* National Consumer Law Center, Truth in Lending § 6.6.2 (6th ed. 2007 and Supp.).

170 National Consumer Law Center, Truth in Lending § 6.6.2.1 (6th ed. 2007 and Supp.).

171 15 U.S.C. § 1635(b): Reg. Z §§ 226.15(d)(2), 226.23(d)(2). *See* National Consumer Law Center, Truth in Lending § 6.6.4 (6th ed. 2007 and Supp.).

Third, when the creditor performs its "step 2" obligation, then *the consumer must tender back any money or property received from the creditor*.[172] Although the scope of their modification authority is debatable, most courts have concluded that they have equitable authority to require the consumer to tender before the creditor must perform its obligations, or conversely to modify the tender obligation.[173]

15.4.2.4.5 The consumer's tender obligation

It is important to remember that a homeowner who seeks rescission must be prepared to tender back his or her gains from the transaction, i.e., if the creditor paid off the original mortgage or brought it current, or provided the homeowner with cash. However, the consumer should be able to credit any payments made to the rescuer—whether in the form of rent payments, finance charges, closing costs, or other disguised fees or payments—because rescission voids any obligation to pay those costs. In addition, any closing costs paid to third parties are voided.[174] Finally, any TIL damages to which the consumer is entitled may also be credited against the tender obligation.

Moore v. Cycon Enterprises, Inc.,[175] provides an example of how the tender amount can be calculated in a foreclosure rescue scam case. There, the court found that the sale of the home was really an equitable mortgage, and allowed rescission because the rescuer had not provided the required disclosures to the homeowners. Therefore, the homeowners were no longer liable for any finance charges or any fees and charges paid "to the creditor, paid by the consumer directly to a third party, or passed on from the creditor to the third party."[176] Accordingly, the court eliminated all the charges, totaling over $25,000, that the homeowners had agreed to pay the rescuer. This left only the amount, $190,262.15, that the rescuer had actually paid to the homeowner's mortgagee. Note that the court did not condition the defendant's obligation to reconvey the property on the homeowner's tender. The defendant was given a mortgage on the property, and if the homeowner failed to tender, the defendant would have to commence foreclosure proceedings, which ultimately might provide the homeowner with additional time to refinance.

Next the court reduced the amount due by subtracting two awards of TIL statutory damages—one because of the defendant's failure to provide the notice of the right of rescission, and one because the defendant failed to respond to a valid notice of rescission from the homeowner. Then the court reduced the amount due by the total amounts the homeowner had paid in "rent." Finally the court increased the homeowner's tender amount by the taxes and insurance the defendant had paid on the home. The resulting calculation was:

Principal Amount	$190,262.15
Statutory Damages ($2,000 x 2)	–4,000.00
Prior Rent Credit	–6,706.66
Defendant's Award for Taxes and Ins.	+6,462.27
Tender Amount	*$186,017.76*

The court gave the homeowners 120 days to obtain new financing to pay this tender amount (plus interest that accrued during this period). If the homeowners had won on other claims such as fraud or UDAP violations, the tender amount might have been reduced even more.

The consumer may come up with the tender in a variety of ways. The consumer may be able to refinance elsewhere with an affordable loan, since all interest, closing costs, and credit-related charges are eliminated. (Be sure to look for market rate loans, too.) Elders may wish to explore reverse mortgage options to obtain refinancing funds.[177]

Courts may permit the consumer to repay the tender in installments or allow some time to come up with a payment or refinancing.[178] The consumer may tender in bankruptcy,

172 15 U.S.C. § 1635(b); Reg. Z §§ 226.15(d)(3), 226.23(d)(3). *See* National Consumer Law Center, Truth in Lending §§ 6.6.5, 6.8 (6th ed. 2007 and Supp.).

173 *See* §§ 5.6.3, 5.6.7, *supra*; National Consumer Law Center, Truth in Lending § 6.7 (6th ed. 2007 and Supp.).

TILA does not allow courts to nullify the automatic "step 1" consequences of the rescission notice—voiding of any security interest and cancellation of any charges—although many courts still rely on pre-1980 case law that was in conflict on this point. *See id.* § 6.7.2.

174 This rule is consistent with the equitable rule that the purpose of restitution is simply to prevent the plaintiff's unjust enrichment. Lloyd v. Hoffman, 369 B.R. 549 (Bankr. N.D. Cal. 2007) (rescue scam case), *aff'd*, 2008 WL 298820 (N.D. Cal. Feb. 1, 2008), *aff'd on other grounds*, 572 F.3d 999 (9th Cir. 2009); Restatement (Third) of Restitution § 32 (T.D. No. 3, 2004).

For that reason, the homeowner should get credit for payments made to third parties even if they did not benefit the rescuer. Similarly, the homeowner should be required to reimburse only payments from which he or she benefited, not other expenses of the rescuer. *See* Lloyd v. Hoffman, 369 B.R. 549 (Bankr. N.D. Cal. 2007).

175 2007 WL 475202 (W.D. Mich. Feb. 9, 2007). *See also* Carter v. Second Chance Program, Inc., No. 06 CH 26787 (Cir. Ct., Cook County, Ill. Dec. 23, 2008), *available at* www.consumerlaw.org/unreported (similar calculation); Hodges v. Swafford, 863 N.E.2d 881, *reh'g granted, opinion aff'd as amended*, 868 N.E.2d 1179 (Ind. Ct. App. 2007) (using similar calculation but reducing homeowner's credit for rent paid by amount attributable to taxes and insurance).

176 Moore v. Cycon Enters., Inc., 2007 WL 475202, at *2 (W.D. Mich. Feb. 9, 2007), *citing* Federal Reserve Board, Official Staff Commentary § 226.15(d)(2)-1.

177 *See* National Consumer Law Center, The Cost of Credit: Regulation, Preemption, and Industry Abuses § 6.5 (4th ed. 2009 and Supp.) (discussion of how to assess when a refinancing is a good idea).

178 *See* § 5.6.4, *supra*; National Consumer Law Center, Truth in Lending § 6.7 (6th ed. 2007 and Supp.).

and some courts have treated the creditors as *unsecured* creditors in chapter 13 proceedings.[179]

If the creditor fails to respond to the cancellation notice, the consumer may be forced to file an affirmative action to enforce the rescission right. In bankruptcy proceedings, this may be raised in an adversary proceeding. The creditor's failure to respond gives rise to a claim for statutory damages and actual damages. This is *in addition* to any claim which may be available for other TIL statutory damages.[180]

As soon as the rescission notice is sent, the consumer should start making monthly payments in an affordable amount into an escrow account or some other protected account. These payments will help build up a sum to offer as the tender amount. The consumer's record of regular payments will also be useful in persuading the court to allow the consumer to tender in installments.

Creditors may press the court to require the consumer to tender at an early stage, before the claims have been resolved on the merits. But in most foreclosure rescue scam cases, the homeowner will be asserting not just TIL claims, but also a variety of non-TIL claims that may offer punitive, statutory, or multiple damages. The possibility of a multiple, statutory, or punitive damage award on the homeowner's non-TIL claims is a strong argument why the court should delay any determination of the tender obligation until after trial. After the court resolves all the homeowner's claims, a net amount may be owed to the homeowner. Since rescuers tend to be undercapitalized entrepreneurs, if the homeowner is required to pay the tender amount early the rescuer may disappear with it.

15.4.2.5 Damages and Attorney Fees

TILA gives consumers, with some exceptions, the ability to collect actual damages without any cap and to recover costs and reasonable attorney fees. In addition, consumers may collect statutory damages for certain violations[181] without having to prove actual damages, regardless whether the creditor knew about the violation or whether the consumer was deceived.

In the case of closed-end credit secured by real property, the statute sets statutory damages for disclosure violations between $200 and $2000.[182] In general, the consumer may recover only one statutory recovery per transaction for disclosure violations, even if multiple violations are committed or multiple parties are involved.[183] Separate and apart from disclosure violations, TILA provides statutory damages of $400 to $4000[184] in the case of closed-end real-estate-secured loans, if the creditor fails to respond to a proper rescission notice. Violations of HOEPA prohibitions carry additional statutory penalties.[185]

The limitation period for affirmative damages claims is one year from the date of the violation.[186] Consumers can also assert damage claims defensively by way of recoupment or set-off in an action by the creditor to collect on the alleged debt filed more than a year from the date of the violation.[187] The one-year statute of limitations for damages can also be equitably tolled in the event of fraud.[188]

15.4.2.6 Assignee Liability

Under TILA, assignees are always liable for rescission, to the same extent as the original creditor.[189] However, in order to exercise TIL rescission in the sale-leaseback context, the homeowner must first convince the court to apply the equitable mortgage doctrine to void the transfer deed and convert the sale into a loan subject to TILA.

This might initially appear more difficult if the rescuer has already transferred the property to a third party purchaser. The preliminary conceptual hurdle is then whether the third party should be treated as an assignee of a loan (which the deed has equitably been converted to) or remains a bona fide third party purchaser who takes an interest in the property free of all prior claims. The homeowner will likely have to show that the purchaser had some notice, actual or constructive, or that the facts of the case put the third party on inquiry notice of the suspicious underlying transaction. If the third party is even on inquiry notice, then its claim to the property remains subject to the homeowner's superior rights.[190]

In Hodges v. Swafford, 863 N.E.2d 881, *reh'g granted, opinion aff'd as amended*, 868 N.E.2d 1179 (Ind. Ct. App. 2007), the court ordered the homeowner to execute a promissory note and mortgage in favor of the rescuer, though the appellate court opinion does not reveal the terms of payment.

179 National Consumer Law Center, Truth in Lending § 6.8.4 (6th ed. 2007 and Supp.).

180 *See* § 5.6.7, *supra*.

181 *See* § 15.4.2.3, *supra*.

182 15 U.S.C. § 1640(a)(2)(A)(iii).
The statute is ambiguous on how the court is to determine where in this range to set damages. *See* National Consumer Law Center, Truth in Lending § 8.6.2.1 (6th ed. 2007 and Supp.).

183 15 U.S.C. § 1640(g).
A series of refinancings may be considered multiple transactions, however, allowing one award of statutory damages for the disclosure violations in each refinancing. *See* National Consumer Law Center, Truth in Lending § 8.6.3.1 (6th ed. 2007 and Supp.).

184 $200 to $2000 for conduct prior to July 30, 2008. Housing and Economic Recovery Act of 2008, Pub. L. No. 110-289, § 2502(b), 122 Stat. 2654, 2857 (2008) (codified at 15 U.S.C. § 1640(a)(2)(A)(ii)).

185 *See* § 15.4.3.5, *infra*.

186 15 U.S.C. § 1640(e); National Consumer Law Center, Truth in Lending § 7.2 (6th ed. 2007 and Supp.).

187 15 U.S.C. § 1640(e); National Consumer Law Center, Truth in Lending § 7.2 (6th ed. 2007 and Supp.).

188 *See* National Consumer Law Center, Truth in Lending § 7.2.3 (6th ed. 2007 and Supp.).

189 15 U.S.C. § 1641(c); National Consumer Law Center, Truth in Lending §§ 6.9.2, 7.3 (6th ed. 2007 and Supp.).

190 *See* § 15.4.2.2, *supra*.

In the foreclosure rescue scam context, the homeowner likely still has possession of the property, which should be sufficient to put the purchaser on inquiry notice and defeat a bona fide purchaser defense.[191] In that case, TIL rescission should be available against the assignee/purchaser.[192]

While an assignee has unequivocal responsibility for a rescission claim, its liability for damages depends on whether HOEPA covers the transaction. If only TILA, not HOEPA, applies, the assignee is shielded from TIL liability for damages unless the violation is apparent on face of disclosure documents or other documents assigned.[193] However, as the documents in most foreclosure rescue scam cases are completely void of all loan disclosures—as they are not posed as loans at all, but rather as sales—the absence of correct TIL disclosures will be readily apparent from the face of the documents. Once the hurdle of bona fide purchaser has been made, the third party should be considered an assignee for purposes of TIL damages—as the TIL disclosure violations will be apparent on the documents. If the loan falls under HOEPA, assignees have unequivocal extended liability for damages, regardless of whether the violations are apparent on the face of the documents.[194]

It is always important to marshal evidence showing that the third party had reason to be suspicious of the transaction. The courts have articulated a number of clues that should put third party purchasers on inquiry notice.[195] Evidence along these lines will also be necessary if the homeowner is asserting claims such as fraud directly against the third party purchaser.

15.4.3 Home Ownership and Equity Protection Act

15.4.3.1 Scope

15.4.3.1.1 Overview of HOEPA triggers

In 1994, Congress passed the Home Ownership and Equity Protection Act (HOEPA), designed to prevent some predatory lending practices.[196] HOEPA, which is part of TILA, imposes additional requirements and remedies on loans made at high rates or with excessive costs and fees.

HOEPA applies only to those loans that are subject to rescission under TILA: non-purchase, closed-end credit secured by the homeowner's primary residence.[197] In addition, reverse mortgages are exempted from HOEPA. TILA's general definition of "credit" applies, but the definition of "creditor" is much looser: a creditor need only make two HOEPA loans per year, or one such mortgage through a broker, to be subject to both HOEPA *and* the general TIL provisions.[198] Similarly, once the transaction is viewed as a mortgage and not a sale, courts are willing to find that an individual was acting as a mortgage broker for the purposes of the "creditor" definition regardless of the individual's purported title or role.[199] As with TILA generally, courts will look beyond the form of the transaction and may use the equitable mortgage doctrine to view a sale transaction as a loan.[200] In some states, the position that foreclosure rescue transactions are secured loans governed by HOEPA is additionally supported by the fact that the state foreclosure rescue statute requires the rescuer to abide by HOEPA.[201]

HOEPA protections apply if either of two triggers is met. First, the loan is subject to HOEPA *if the annual percentage rate (APR) exceeds the yield on treasury securities with comparable maturities by more than eight percentage points for a first lien, or ten points for a subordinate lien.*[202] For a sale-leaseback transaction, the time period for a "comparable" treasury maturity can be determined by looking at the terms of the lease, the expiration date of an option to purchase, or the date any balloon payment is due.

Second, the loan is subject to HOEPA if *the total of the points and fees payable at or before closing exceeds 8% of the total loan amount and is over an amount adjusted*

---

191 *See* § 15.4.1.3, *supra.*

192 In Armstrong v. Real Estate Int'l, Ltd., 2006 WL 354983 (E.D.N.Y. Feb. 14, 2006), the court refused to preliminarily enjoin the rescuer from transferring the property because any transferee/assignee would be subject to TIL rescission, and therefore the plaintiff could not show irreparable injury. The court did not discuss the bona fide purchaser defense, but there may have been a *lis pendens* recorded that would have given any purchaser notice.

193 15 U.S.C. § 1641(a).

194 *See* 15.4.3.3, *infra.*

195 *See* 15.4.1.3, *supra.*

196 15 U.S.C. §§ 1602(aa), 1639. Regulations promulgated under HOEPA can be found in Regulation Z, 12 C.F.R. §§ 226.31, 226.32. *See generally* § 5.8, *supra.*

197 *See* §§ 15.4.2.2, 15.4.2.4.1, *supra.*

198 15 U.S.C. § 1602(f); Reg. Z, 12 C.F.R. § 226.2 n.3; National Consumer Law Center, Truth in Lending §§ 2.3.6, 9.2.3 (6th ed. 2007 and Supp.). *See, e.g.*, Hruby v. Larsen, 2005 WL 1540130 (D. Minn. June 30, 2005).

199 Hodges v. Swafford, 863 N.E.2d 881, *reh'g granted, opinion aff'd as amended*, 868 N.E.2d 1179 (Ind. Ct. App. 2007).

200 *See* § 15.4.2.2, *supra.*

201 *See, e.g.*, 2008 Oregon Laws 1st Sp. Sess. Ch. 19 (H.B. 3630), Sec. 9.

202 The relevant rate is the one in effect on the fifteenth day of the month immediately preceding the month in which the application for the extension of credit is received by the creditor. 15 U.S.C. § 1602(aa)(1)(A). In these cases, there is not likely to be a formal "application." The homeowner could argue that the relevant date is the fifteenth day of the month preceding the month in which the rescuer first discussed the transaction, or alternatively, in which the transaction itself occurred.

The rates for comparable treasury bonds can be found on the Federal Reserve's website at www.federalreserve.gov/Releases/H15/data.htm, Scroll down to "treasury constant maturities," find the term of the loan, and click on "Business Day." The length of the contract to repay and "rent" the property is the most likely term to use when selecting the comparable maturity.

annually for inflation ($579 for 2010).[203] "Points and fees" is defined to include all noninterest "finance charges," which in turn are defined as "any charge payable directly or indirectly by the consumer and imposed directly or indirectly by the creditor as an incident to or a condition of the extension of credit."[204] In addition, all compensation paid to mortgage brokers and certain closing costs count as points and fees.[205] Once a foreclosure rescue transaction is reconstructed to be seen as a loan, the costs that the homeowner incurs can be considered to be incident to the extension of credit.

To determine whether a foreclosure rescue transaction meets either of these triggers, one can consider the terms of the repurchase portion of the transaction alone or the unified impact of the sale and the repurchase. When the homeowner's repurchase price is higher than the sale price, the lost equity is arguably a finance charge that should be considered in the calculation.[206]

15.4.3.1.2 Example of APR trigger calculation

The following is an example of how to determine if a foreclosure rescue scam loan exceeds the HOEPA APR trigger. Foreclosure rescue scams are structured in a variety of ways, however, so other ways of determining the APR may be appropriate for a particular case.

Assume that the homeowner fell behind on the mortgage and was $10,000 in arrears, leaving a balance due (including late charges, other charges, and pre-foreclosure costs) of $190,000. A rescuer might pay off this $190,000 balance, and lease the home back to the homeowner at $2500 per month, with an option to repurchase the home at the end of a year for $225,000.[207] The homeowner is thus obligated to pay $232,200 to the rescuer in return for the rescuer's extension of credit in the amount of $190,000.

The annual percentage rate for this loan with this payment schedule is 29.39%.[208] Assuming that the "application" date of the sale-leaseback was June 1, 2006, this APR is well in excess of the HOEPA APR trigger of 14.99% (the Treasury bond rate of 4.99% on the 15th of the prior month plus 10%).[209]

15.4.3.1.3 Example of points and fees trigger calculation

The HOEPA points and fees trigger is based not on the APR but on charges such as prepaid finance charges and broker fees that are paid directly or indirectly by the consumer, at or before closing, as an incident to or a condition of the loan. Certain closing costs can also count toward the points and fees trigger if they are inflated or paid to affiliates, or if the creditor receives a portion of the charge. The rules for determining whether a charge counts toward the points and fees trigger are quite complex and are detailed in NCLC's *Truth in Lending*.[210] A worksheet for calculating HOEPA points and fees is included on the companion website. For most foreclosure rescue transactions, the APR trigger will present a clearer analysis. However, the following example illustrates the application of the points and fees trigger in a hypothetical foreclosure rescue transaction.

Assume a foreclosure rescue transaction in which the rescuer paid off just a $12,000 arrearage, and also charged the homeowner an up-front fee of $500 and required the homeowner to make two additional $400 monthly payments to the rescuer while the rescuer was finalizing the transaction. Assume also that the rescuer required the homeowner to pay $300 for an appraisal before closing, but funneled the money to an appraisal company owned by the rescuer.

All of these up-front charges, totaling $1600, at least arguably count toward the HOEPA points and fees trigger as they were "payable directly or indirectly by the consumer and imposed directly or indirectly by the creditor as an incident to or a condition of the extension of credit."[211] These points and fees would amount to 13.3% of the total loan amount of $12,000,[212] exceeding the HOEPA triggers of $579 (for a 2010 transaction) and 8% of the total loan amount.

---

203 15 U.S.C. § 1602(aa)(1)(B), (aa)(3); Reg. Z, 12 C.F.R. § 226.32(b); 74 Fed. Reg. 40,478 (Aug. 12, 2009).

204 12 C.F.R. §§ 226.32(b), 226.4.

205 12 C.F.R. § 226.32(b).

206 *See* Prentiss Cox, *Foreclosure Equity Stripping: Legal Theories and Strategies to Attack a Growing Problem*, 39 Clearinghouse Review Journal of Poverty Law and Policy 607, 617–618 (Mar.–Apr. 2006) (more detailed discussion of how to calculate these triggers in the context of a foreclosure rescue scam).

207 This is a somewhat simplified version of the transaction described in Moore v. Cycon Enters., Inc., 2006 WL 2375477 (E.D. Mich. Aug. 16, 2006), *later op. at* 2007 WL 475202 (W.D. Mich. Feb. 9, 2007). *See also* Hodges v. Swafford, 863 N.E.2d 881, *reh'g granted, opinion aff'd as amended*, 868 N.E.2d 1179 (Ind. Ct. App. 2007) (employing a similar calculation and finding a 49% finance charge; court included fees to be paid over the life of the loan, not only those due at closing).

208 The APR was calculated using the Irregular Payment tab on the NCLC APR Program included on this treatise's companion website by inserting $190,000 in the "amount financed" box, $255,000 in the "total of payments" box, defining "payment group 1" as having 12 payments of $2500 and clicking "Add Group," defining "payment group 2" as having one payment of $225,000 and clicking "Add Group," and then clicking the "Estimate APR" button.

209 In this example, the 10% APR trigger for junior lien mortgages is used. Since the rescuer only paid the delinquent amount of the existing first mortgage, not the full balance, a conservative approach treats the transaction with the rescuer as a junior lien mortgage loan.

210 National Consumer Law Center, Truth in Lending § 9.2.6 (6th ed. 2007 and Supp.).

211 12 C.F.R. §§ 226.32(b), 226.4.

212 In this example, the homeowner paid the points and fees up front in cash. In a standard mortgage loan, the points and fees are often paid out of the proceeds of the loan and then financed

This example provides a roadmap for calculating the points and fees trigger in the most conservative manner. Alternatively, if the rescuer structures the deal to capture a profit by creating a difference between the homeowner's "sale" price for the property and a much larger "repurchase" price in those cases where there is a "repurchase" contract, the difference arguably is a finance charge and, consequently, a point and fee.[213]

In conventional loans, the charges that count toward the points and fees trigger are usually paid out of the proceeds of the loan at closing (or paid by the lender before closing and then added to the principal of the loan). Sometimes, however, borrowers pay these charges in cash before closing, or bring cash to the closing. With foreclosure rescue scams, the points and fees analysis is clearest if the homeowner made cash payments to the rescuer at or before closing. Charges may also count toward the points and fees trigger if the rescuer paid them at or before closing, and then added them to the amount the consumer agreed to pay to repurchase the home. Foreclosure rescue transactions are structured in a variety of ways, and the analysis of points and fees will depend on the details of the transaction.

15.4.3.2 Substantive Prohibitions

Once a loan is determined to be a high-cost one that meets one of the HOEPA triggers, several additional prohibitions and requirements kick in, beyond those in TILA generally.[214] Most are relevant only to traditional loans, but some are useful in dealing with foreclosure rescue scams.

HOEPA prohibits certain contract terms that Congress determined to be abusive in the high-rate lending context. Among these, *balloon payments* are prohibited unless the loan has a term of five years or more.[215] A lease-purchase arrangement that requires the homeowner to make rent payments for a period of time, followed by a large lump-sum payment to exercise the repurchase option, may violate the balloon payment prohibition.

HOEPA also prohibits certain lender behavior. Of particular note, creditors may not make a HOEPA loan *without regard to ability to repay*, as where the lender looks to the value of the home, rather than the homeowner's monthly income. The Federal Reserve Board made significant amendments to this prohibition in 2008.[216] For transactions in which the creditor received an application prior to October 1, 2009,[217] the prohibition applies only if the creditor engaged in a pattern or practice of this activity. This is a difficult standard to meet, though a pattern or practice may be revealed through discovery of all of the creditor's loans. For transactions prior to the October 1, 2009 effective date, the creditor is presumed to have violated the prohibition if the creditor did not verify and document the borrower's ability to repay with a financial statement and credit report.[218] Foreclosure rescuers usually violate this prohibition since they do not assess ability to repay and do not verify income. The pattern and practice requirement and the presumption have been abolished for transactions after the effective date.

Finally, HOEPA mandates that the consumer receive a special *advance warning at least three business days before the loan consummation*. The lender must warn that the home and any equity in it might be lost in the event of nonpayment, and must disclose, for fixed rate loans, the APR, the amount of regular monthly payments, and any balloon payment.[219] This warning is virtually never made in the context of a foreclosure rescue scam, both because rescuers do not generally structure transactions as loans, and because they often rush the homeowner to complete the transaction quickly, before the homeowner understands the nature of the scam or can obtain advice from a lawyer, friend, or relative.

15.4.3.3 Expanded Assignee Liability

An important aspect of HOEPA is its expanded assignee liability: assignees of covered mortgages are liable for *all* claims and defenses that the consumer could assert against the originator, except to the extent of certain limitations on damages discussed below.[220] This expansion of liability even covers claims and defenses that can be raised against the original lender under common law, statutes, or other theories.

as part of that loan. In that case, the "total loan amount" as defined by HOEPA is the proceeds of the loan minus the points and fees. *See* National Consumer Law Center, Truth in Lending § 9.2.9.6 (6th ed. 2007 and Supp.).

213 *See, e.g.*, Carter v. Second Chance Program, Inc., No. 06 CH 26787 (Cir. Ct., Cook County, Ill. Dec. 23, 2008), *available at* www.consumerlaw.org/unreported (calculating points and fees as difference between amount rescuer paid to satisfy existing mortgage and amount homeowner must pay to repurchase, and finding that HOEPA applies).

214 *See* §§ 5.8.3, 5.8.4, *supra*.

215 Additional prohibitions not discussed in this subsection include prepayment penalties, interest rate increases upon default, negative amortization, prepaid payment, escrows, and due-on-demand clauses. Some of these terms are prohibited for all HOEPA loans, whereas others have exceptions. *See* National Consumer Law Center, Truth in Lending § 9.4 (6th ed. 2007 and Supp.).

216 73 Fed. Reg. 44,522, 44,545–44,546 (July 30, 2008).

217 Official Staff Commentary § 226.1(d)(5)-1; 73 Fed. Reg. 44,522, 44,605 (July 30, 2008).

218 *See* Reg. Z, 12 C.F.R. § 226.34(a)(4); National Consumer Law Center, Truth in Lending § 9.5.2 (6th ed. 2007 and Supp.).

219 Additional requirements for the advance notice are discussed in National Consumer Law Center, Truth in Lending § 9.3 (6th ed. 2007 and Supp.). A recommended model form is contained in Reg. Z Appx. H-16.

220 15 U.S.C. § 1641(d)(1). Assignees are those entities that purchase loans from the original lenders.

An assignee may defeat liability if it legitimately could not have known the assigned mortgage was a covered loan.[221] In the sale-leaseback, there are two facets to this defense.

First, as discussed above, the court must decide whether the assignee had sufficient notice of the true nature of the transaction to be subject to the equitable mortgage doctrine, converting the sale-leaseback into a loan potentially subject to HOEPA.[222]

Second, even if the assignee can be imputed with knowledge that the transaction was a loan, the assignee can defeat liability if it carries the burden of showing that a reasonable person exercising ordinary due diligence could not have determined the transaction was a high-cost loan covered by HOEPA.[223] In the foreclosure rescue scam context, the assignee/purchaser may disavow any knowledge of the details of the original sale-leaseback transaction between the homeowner and the rescuer. To rebut such a claim, the homeowner should seek out evidence of warning signs that, if investigated by a reasonable purchaser, would have revealed the high-cost details that bring the transaction within HOEPA.

Any damage award against the assignee under non-HOEPA/TIL theories that is based on the assignee liability provisions of HOEPA is capped. Damages are limited to the amount of all remaining indebtedness and the total amount already paid by the consumer.[224] When damages are awarded based on TILA and on other claims, the TIL damages must be offset against the damages awarded on the other claims.[225]

15.4.3.4 Remedies

Violations of HOEPA are subject to three remedies.

First, violations of HOEPA trigger actual damages and TIL statutory damages.

Second, HOEPA violations that are "material" (under a common law standard, not the TIL standard) carry enhanced damages of the sum of all finance charges and fees paid by the consumer.[226] In the foreclosure rescue scam context, entering into a sale-leaseback transaction without regard to the homeowner's ability to exercise a repurchase option, or requiring a balloon payment beyond the homeowner's reach, are certainly material violations.

Damage claims have a one-year statute of limitations for affirmative suits, but can be raised at any time defensively.[227]

221 *See* § 5.8.5, *supra*.
222 *See* § 15.4.1.2, *supra*.
223 *Id.*
224 15 U.S.C. § 1641(d)(2)(B).
225 15 U.S.C. § 1641(d)(3). For a discussion of how this cap works, see National Consumer Law Center, Truth in Lending §§ 9.7.5.2–9.7.5.3 (6th ed. 2007 and Supp.).
226 15 U.S.C. § 1640(a).
227 15 U.S.C. § 1640(c).

Third and more important, violations of HOEPA's disclosure provisions and the inclusion of a prohibited term, such as a balloon payment, are deemed "material" under TILA, giving the consumer the right to rescind the transaction for up to three years after it was consummated. Making a loan without regard to ability to pay does not trigger the right to rescind, though it does entitle the homeowner to damages.[228]

15.4.4 *Direct Federal Regulation of Foreclosure Rescuers*

Even though TILA and HOEPA are very important for helping the victims of some foreclosure rescue scams, as of this treatise's print date, the federal government has not yet enacted any legislation or regulations directly addressing foreclosure rescue scams. There are, however, two new rules under consideration that could have a significant impact. The Federal Trade Commission has issued a notice of proposed rulemaking regarding "mortgage assistance relief services" that would prohibit many common forms of misconduct and would ban charging advance fees in a broad range of services offered to distressed homeowners.[229] The Department of Housing and Urban Development has also sought comment on whether loan modification "specialists" should be licensed as loan originators under the Secure and Fair Enforcement for Mortgage Licensing Act of 2008 (the SAFE Act).[230] Future supplements to this treatise will describe these rules in greater detail if they are adopted.

15.4.5 *Unfair and Deceptive Acts and Practices (UDAP) Statutes*

15.4.5.1 Overview of State UDAP Statutes

Foreclosure rescue scams can often be challenged under state unfair and deceptive acts and practices (UDAP) laws.[231]

228 15 U.S.C. § 1639(j); Reg. Z, 12 C.F.R. § 226.23(a) n.48.
229 75 Fed. Reg. 10,707 (Mar. 9, 2010). *See also* Advance Notice of Proposed Rulemaking, 74 Fed. Reg. 26,130 (June 1, 2009).
230 74 Fed. Reg. 66,548 (Dec., 15, 2009); Pub. L. No. 110-289, §§ 1501–1517 (codified at 12 U.S.C. §§ 5101–5116). *See* National Consumer Law Center, The Cost of Credit: Regulation, Preemption, and Industry Abuses 11.6.4.4 (4th ed. 2009 and Supp.).
231 *See, e.g., In re* Comtois, 2007 WL 1480707 (Bankr. D.N.H. May 18, 2007); Pace-Knapp v. Pelascini, 2008 WL 699279 (Wash. Ct. App. Mar. 17, 2008). *See also* §§ 5.5.1, 5.5.2, *supra*.
For more detailed discussion of UDAP laws, see National Consumer Law Center, Unfair and Deceptive Acts and Practices §§ 6.14–6.15 (7th ed. 2008 and Supp.).
Another helpful reference is Prentiss Cox, *Foreclosure Equity Stripping: Legal Theories and Strategies to Attack a Growing Problem*, Clearinghouse Review (Mar.–Apr. 2006) at 607–626.

All fifty states, the District of Columbia, Puerto Rico, Guam, and the Virgin Islands have at least one statute with broad applicability that addresses deception and abuse in the marketplace, and all but Iowa and Puerto Rico afford the consumer a private cause of action.[232] In a majority of states, the UDAP statute prohibits not just deception, but also unfair or unconscionable practices.

The broad, expansive, developing nature of UDAP statutes is their unique strength. When a practice does not fall precisely under a debt collection act, state or federal credit legislation, warranty law, or other statute, UDAP statutes can provide an all-purpose remedy.[233] Almost any abusive business practice aimed at consumers is at least arguably a UDAP violation, unless the trade practice falls clearly outside the scope of the statute.[234] Another important point about UDAP claims is that most courts have held that, since they are not based on breach of contract, they are unaffected by the parol evidence rule or by disclaimers and exculpatory clauses in the contract documents.[235]

A UDAP claim should always be considered when dealing with a foreclosure rescue scam. This section first compares UDAP with fraud claims and then discusses the advantages and disadvantages of UDAP claims as compared to TIL/HOEPA claims. (For a comparison of UDAP claims and claims under state foreclosure rescue statutes, see § 15.4.6.1, *infra*.) This section also discusses the application of UDAP statutes to foreclosure rescue scams, and ends with an overview of UDAP remedies.

15.4.5.2 Comparison of UDAP and Fraud Claims

UDAP claims have a number of advantages when compared to other claims. In contrast to common law fraud, proof of the seller's fraudulent intent or knowledge is not required for a claim under a state UDAP statute. In some cases, consumer reliance, damage, or even actual deception is not a prerequisite to a UDAP action. The standard of proof is typically a preponderance of the evidence, compared with clear and convincing evidence for a fraud claim. Thus, a UDAP claim is a far easier cause of action to prove than common law fraud. The statute of limitations may also be longer, although states differ widely.

Most UDAP statutes offer enhanced damages such as statutory or treble damages, and most offer attorney fees. On the other hand, punitive damages are available for fraud in most states, while only about ten UDAP statutes authorize punitive damages.[236] Combining a fraud claim with a UDAP claim may enable the homeowner to recover punitive damages on the fraud claim and attorney fees on the UDAP claim.[237] A UDAP statute can also supply the remedy for violation of another law that does not contain a private right of action.[238]

A disadvantage of UDAP claims in comparison to fraud claims is that some state UDAP statutes have restrictive coverage provisions. In particular, some UDAP statutes exclude real estate transactions, extensions of credit, or regulated entities such as banks.[239] Even in states that exclude real estate or credit transactions, the practitioner may be able to characterize the transaction with the rescuer as predominantly involving services other than real estate or a loan, however. In addition, entities involved downstream from the rescuer, such as a bank that gives the rescuer a mortgage loan against the home, may have derivative liability for the rescuer's UDAP violations even if they are not covered by the UDAP statute themselves.[240] Nonetheless, the advantage of a fraud claim is that there are few or no limits on the applicability of common law fraud.

Another potential disadvantage of a UDAP claim is that in Colorado, Georgia, Minnesota, Nebraska, New York, South Carolina, and Washington, courts have interpreted the UDAP statute to require the consumer to prove that the challenged practice affects the public interest. Although this should not be difficult in the case of a foreclosure rescue scam, it is not a requirement for a fraud claim. Evidence that the rescuer engaged in similar transactions will help meet

---

The use of UDAP claims to challenge predatory lending is discussed at National Consumer Law Center, Unfair and Deceptive Acts and Practices §§ 6.14, 6.15 (7th ed. 2008 and Supp.); National Consumer Law Center, The Cost of Credit: Regulation, Preemption, and Industry Abuses § 11.6 (4th ed. 2009 and Supp.).

232 These statutes are listed and summarized in National Consumer Law Center, Unfair and Deceptive Acts and Practices Appx. A (7th ed. 2008 and Supp.). Even though Iowa's UDAP statute is generally not privately enforceable, it is possible that it can be raised defensively. *See id.* § 12.2.2.

233 *See, e.g.,* Stith v. Thorne, 247 F.R.D. 89 (E.D. Va. 2007) (finding triable issues under state UDAP claim against title company after dismissing several other claims against the

234 National Consumer Law Center, Unfair and Deceptive Acts and Practices (7th ed. 2008 and Supp.) describes a large body of Federal Trade Commission rules, guides and cases, state regulations and cases, statutory provisions, and other materials that can provide clear guidance in initiating most UDAP claims.

235 National Consumer Law Center, Unfair and Deceptive Acts and Practices § 4.2.19 (7th ed. 2008 and Supp.).

236 National Consumer Law Center, Unfair and Deceptive Acts and Practices § 13.4.3 (7th ed. 2008 and Supp.).

237 *See* Eicher v. Mid Am. Fin. Inv. Corp., 702 N.W.2d 792 (Neb. 2005) (awarding attorney fees under state UDAP statute after awarding other relief on fraud claim against rescuer).

238 *See In re* Comtois, 2007 WL 1480707 (Bankr. D.N.H. May 18, 2007) (using UDAP law to supply remedy for violation of credit disclosure statute).

239 *See* National Consumer Law Center, Unfair and Deceptive Acts and Practices §§ 2.2.1, 2.2.5, 2.3.3 (7th ed. 2008 and Supp.); National Consumer Law Center, Consumer Protection in the States: A 50-State Report on Unfair and Deceptive Acts and Practices Statutes (Feb. 2009), *available at* www.consumerlaw.org (summarizing coverage issues, with detailed state-by-state analysis in appendix).

240 *See* National Consumer Law Center, Unfair and Deceptive Acts and Practices §§ 11.6, 11.7 (7th ed. 2008 and Supp.).

this requirement.[241] Evidence of other transactions is also highly useful for showing intent, seeking punitive damages, and establishing coverage under the Truth in Lending Act, so it is worth developing even where the state UDAP statute does not require a showing of an effect on the public interest.

Nine states—Alabama, California (under one of its UDAP statutes), Georgia, Indiana, Maine, Massachusetts, Texas, West Virginia, and Wyoming—require the consumer to send a notice to the defendant a certain number of days before filing a UDAP action, and Mississippi requires the consumer to utilize an informal dispute resolution procedure before filing suit. If it is necessary to file suit quickly to prevent the rescuer from transferring the property, it may be necessary to omit the UDAP claim at first in these states, and then add it by amendment when the notice period expires. Decisions from the jurisdiction should be consulted to determine the best course of action.

Fraud claims can almost always be tried to a jury, but some states have found no jury trial right for UDAP claims.[242] Even in these states, the fraud and UDAP claims can usually be tried together, with the fraud claims going to the jury and the judge deciding the UDAP claims.[243]

15.4.5.3 Comparison to TILA and HOEPA

UDAP claims are much less technical than Truth in Lending or HOEPA claims. This can be an advantage and a disadvantage. Once an equitable mortgage is established (an intensely factual determination), whether a defendant violated the TILA or HOEPA is usually a very objective determination, suitable for summary judgment. The surrounding circumstances and the underlying fairness or unfairness of the transaction will be only marginally relevant. By contrast, whether a defendant violated a UDAP statute is much more dependent on the facts and nuances of those facts. At trial the practitioner can bring out all the facts and circumstances that show that the transaction was unfair or deceptive.

Another advantage of state UDAP laws is that the consumer need not show that the rescuer engaged in a certain number of credit transactions, as is required under TILA and HOEPA.[244] Some UDAP statutes require a showing that the seller was engaged in trade or commerce, or that the transaction occurred in the ordinary course of the seller's business,[245] but this is a less rigid test.

UDAP statutes also offer much different relief than TILA and HOEPA. Actual damages will be available for all of these claims, but some courts have given a narrow reading to TILA's actual damage provision.[246] Some UDAP statutes explicitly authorize rescission as a remedy, but they lack TILA's step-by-step provisions for unwinding home mortgage transactions. Many UDAP statutes offer multiple, statutory, or punitive damages.

15.4.5.4 Application of Substantive UDAP Standards to Foreclosure Rescue Scams

Most UDAP statutes combine a series of specific prohibitions with a broad, general prohibition of unfair, unconscionable, and/or deceptive practices. Often the rescuer will have violated one of the specific, more clearly defined prohibitions, and in addition the facts will show a violation of the general prohibitions. The broad, flexible prohibitions of most UDAP statutes make them ideal as a way to challenge creative, new forms of abusive business schemes.[247]

The following are some examples of practices prohibited by UDAP statutes that are likely to be present in foreclosure rescue scams:

- The advertising surrounding a foreclosure rescue scheme and the rescuer's sales pitch are likely to run afoul of the UDAP statute's prohibition of deceptive statements. Even if the statements are literally true, they will violate the UDAP statute if their implications are deceptive or if the rescuer has omitted material facts.[248]

241 Phifer v. Home Savers Consulting Corp., 2007 WL 295605 (E.D.N.Y. Jan. 30, 2007) (foreclosure rescue scam has public impact so is covered by N.Y. UDAP statute); Eicher v. Mid Am. Fin. Inv. Corp., 748 N.W.2d 1, 12 (Neb. 2008) (foreclosure rescue scam affects public interest, as defendants "engaged in a pattern of calculated conduct intended to defraud numerous citizens of this state of their homes"); Pace-Knapp v. Pelascini, 2008 WL 699279 (Wash. Ct. App. Mar. 17, 2008) (unpublished) (foreclosure rescue scam affected public interest because scammers engaged in repeat transactions, actively solicited homeowners, and targeted and harmed vulnerable individuals); State v. Kaiser, No. 07-2-08789-3 SEA (Super. Ct., King County, Wash. Feb. 6, 2009) (findings of fact and conclusions of law, at 22) (rescuer's actions met public interest test), *later order*, (May 6, 2009), *available at* www.consumerlaw.org/unreported (ordering $3,525,742 restitution to homeowners).

242 National Consumer Law Center, Unfair and Deceptive Acts and Practices § 12.9.2 (7th ed. 2008 and Supp.).

243 *Id.*

244 *See* § 15.4.2.2, *supra*.

245 *See* National Consumer Law Center, Unfair and Deceptive Acts and Practices § 2.3.4 (7th ed. 2008 and Supp.).

246 *See* National Consumer Law Center, Truth in Lending § 8.5 (6th ed. 2007 and Supp.).

247 *See generally* National Consumer Law Center, Unfair and Deceptive Acts and Practices § 2.1.3, 4.2–4.4 (7th ed. 2008 and Supp.).

248 *See, e.g.*, Griffith v. Barnes, 560 F. Supp. 2d 29 (D.D.C. 2008) (rescuer committed UDAP violations by failing to tell homeowner the potential consequences of failing to comply with the agreement, failing to reveal his sale of the home to a third party and that party's resale of it, and failing to inform her of his intended use of a power of attorney to sell her home); State v. Kaiser, No. 07-2-08789-3 SEA (Super. Ct., King County, Wash. Feb. 6, 2009) (findings of fact and conclusions of law, at ¶ 18) (rescuer violated UDAP statute by omitting material facts,

- A number of UDAP statutes prohibit entering into a transaction knowing that the consumer is unlikely to be able to repay the obligation.[249] Structuring a transaction to create payments and charges that the consumer cannot afford, in order to precipitate a default and foreclosure, will be a UDAP violation in these states and also in states that prohibit unfairness in general.[250] Even in states where the UDAP statute does not include these prohibitions, it is likely that the rescuer misrepresented the nature of the obligations that the homeowner was undertaking.
- Many UDAP statutes specifically prohibit taking advantage of a consumer who is vulnerable because of age, infirmity, illiteracy, educational level, or other causes.[251] Even if the UDAP statute does not contain this prohibition, many decisions require courts to take the consumer's vulnerability into account when assessing whether a statement is deceptive.[252]
- Collecting fees in excess of those allowed by state usury laws may state a UDAP claim.[253] Framing such a violation as a UDAP claim is particularly helpful if the state usury law's remedies are weak or unclear.
- Grossly unfair or unconscionable contract terms may be a UDAP violation in and of themselves.[254]
- Providing misleading HUD-1 settlement statements—as is common in foreclosure rescue scams—can establish a UDAP claim.[255]

This conduct should also be sufficient to satisfy the public interest test required for injunctive relief and in the minority of states that impose a public interest requirement on UDAP actions.[256]

A number of courts have entered UDAP judgments against rescuers. In a private UDAP suit involving a sale-leaseback scheme, a debtor who lost her home to a rescuer won as damages the amount of equity in the home, which the court then trebled.[257] The court held that the rescuer violated the UDAP statute by taking the debtor's home, obtaining her signature on a blank deed, selling the property without returning fair compensation to her, deceptively leading her to believe he was acting in her interests, misrepresenting the import of the agreements she signed, and failing to fulfill his promises. Another court awarded $50,000 punitive damages in a similar sale and leaseback situation based on fraud, breach of fiduciary duty, and UDAP violations.[258]

The Nebraska Supreme Court upheld a finding that a rescuer who misrepresented to homeowners that they were

including that no homeowner had ever successfully repurchased a home and the extent of the rescuer's control over the home), *later order*, (May 6, 2009), *available at* www.consumerlaw.org/unreported (ordering $3,525,742 restitution to homeowners). *See also* National Consumer Law Center, Unfair and Deceptive Acts and Practices §§ 4.2.13, 4.2.14 (7th ed. 2008 and Supp.).

249 *See* National Consumer Law Center, Unfair and Deceptive Acts and Practices § 6.3 (7th ed. 2008 and Supp.).

250 *See, e.g.*, Jackson v. Byrd, 2004 WL 3130653 (D.C. Super. Ct. May 11, 2004) (foreclosure rescue case), *later op.*, 2004 WL 3249693 (D.C. Super. Ct. June 30, 2004) (awarding damages), *later op.*, 2004 WL 3249692 (D.C. Super. Ct. Sept. 2, 2004) (awarding attorney fees), *aff'd*, 902 A.2d 778 (D.C. 2006); Fidelity Fin. Servs. v. Hicks, 574 N.E.2d 15 (Ill. App. Ct. 1991) (allegations of deceptive practices used to make unaffordable loan for home improvements in order to acquire equity in home scam stated a UDAP claim); U.S. Home & Realty Corp. v. Lehnartz, Clearinghouse No. 43,259 (Mich. Dist. Ct. Sept. 30, 1987) (Case No. 87-930), *available at* www.consumerlaw.org/unreported. *But see* Provencher v. T & M Mortgage Solutions, Inc., 2008 WL 2447472, at *13 (D. Me. June 18, 2008) (magistrate's recommended decision) (dismissing claim that rescuers extended loan without regard to homeowner's repayment ability because of lack of proof that transaction was loan), *later op. at* 2008 WL 4857276 (D. Me. Nov. 9, 2008) (allowing plaintiff to file amended complaint containing allegations that correct the pleading deficiencies). *But cf.* Carter v. Second Chance Program, Inc., No. 06 CH 26787 (Cir. Ct., Cook County, Ill. Dec. 23, 2008), *available at* www.consumerlaw.org/unreported (no UDAP violation where homeowner had realistic possibility of repaying and in fact made full payments for seventeen months).

251 *See, e.g.*, Williams v. First Gov't Mortgage & Investors Corp., 225 F.3d 738 (D.C. Cir. 2000); Jackson v. Byrd, 2004 WL 3130653 (D.C. Super. Ct. May 11, 2004) (foreclosure rescue case), *later op.*, 2004 WL 3249693 (D.C. Super. Ct. June 30, 2004) (awarding damages), *later op.*, 2004 WL 3249692 (D.C. Super. Ct. Sept. 2, 2004) (awarding attorney fees), *aff'd*, 902 A.2d 778 (D.C. 2006). *See generally* National Consumer Law Center, Unfair and Deceptive Acts and Practices § 4.4.4 (7th ed. 2008 and Supp.).

252 *See* Billingham v. Dornemann, 771 N.E.2d 166, 178 (Mass. App. Ct. 2002) (foreclosure rescue case). *See generally* National Consumer Law Center, Unfair and Deceptive Acts and Practices § 4.2.11 (7th ed. 2008 and Supp.).

253 *See* National Consumer Law Center, Unfair and Deceptive Acts and Practices § 6.4.4 (7th ed. 2008 and Supp.).

254 State v. Kaiser, No. 07-2-08789-3 SEA (Super. Ct., King County, Wash. Feb. 6, 2009) (findings of fact and conclusions of law, at ¶ 20) (finding rescuer's contracts to violate UDAP statute because they were grossly unfair), *later order*, (May 6, 2009), *available at* www.consumerlaw.org/unreported (ordering $3,525,742 restitution to homeowners).

255 Phifer v. Home Savers Consulting Corp., 2007 WL 295605 (E.D.N.Y. Jan. 30, 2007). *See also* Stith v. Thorne, 247 F.R.D. 89 (E.D. Va. 2007) (holding that triable issues existed as to whether title company willfully violated state UDAP statute by making payment to rescuer in the absence of written instructions from homeowner, and whether title company used a power of attorney to prevent the homeowner from seeing the HUD-1).

256 *See* Federal Trade Comm'n v. Washington Data Res., Inc., 2009 WL 4885033, at *13 (M.D. Fla. Dec. 14, 2009) ("The principal equity . . . is the public interest in protecting consumers from such mortgage foreclosure relief scams. Undoubtedly, this is a significant interest worthy of protection."); National Consumer Law Center, Unfair and Deceptive Acts and Practices § 12.5.3 (7th ed. 2008 and Supp.) (regarding public interest requirement).

257 *In re* Bryant, 111 B.R. 474 (E.D. Pa. 1990).

258 Jeffries v. The Lewis Group (Ill. Cir. Ct. Cook Cty. Oct. 9, 1991), *available at* www.consumerlaw.org/unreported. *See also* R.A. Walker & Assocs., Inc., 3 Trade Reg. Rep. (CCH) ¶ 22,080, F.T.C. File No. 832 3227 (D.D.C. 1983) (issuing preliminary injunction against foreclosure rescue scam).

obtaining loans, when actually they were conveying their homes to the rescuer, violated the state UDAP statute.[259] In another case, a court found a UDAP violation where a consumer, with no one to counsel her, whose sole source of income was Aid to Families with Dependent Children, was pressured into a financing scheme that she did not understand and that was disadvantageous.[260] The uneducated, desperate, low-income borrower "sold" her house for $20,000 and received a repurchase agreement for $32,000 at a variable 9% to 11% rate, which sum included a 20% realty commission.

A District of Columbia trial court found that a rescuer committed numerous deceptive and unconscionable acts. These included failure to disclose the appraised value of the home and that he was the other contracting party and would profit personally from the transaction; presenting himself as helping the homeowner save her home, when his real intention was to acquire the home for a pittance; and acquiring the home at a grossly disproportionate price from an aged and infirm homeowner.[261]

In another case, an entrepreneur bought a delinquent mortgage debt before foreclosure began, then contacted the homeowner, threatened foreclosure, and ultimately browbeat the homeowner into conveying the property to him. A Massachusetts court held that the entrepreneur may have committed UDAP violations by representing to the homeowner that signing the agreements was a mere formality after the homeowner made it clear that he could not afford the payments.[262]

A federal district court in New York awarded damages in a foreclosure rescue scam cased based on both fraud and the New York UDAP statute against a lender who participated in the closing and provided misleading HUD-1 settlement statements for a loan to the rescuer that was secured by the home.[263] Even though the homeowner herself had not relied on the deceptive settlement statement, it enabled the rescuer to obtain the mortgage loans by which the equity was stripped from the home and distributed to the rescuer and his associates. This satisfied the causation requirement of the UDAP statute.[264]

15.4.5.5 UDAP Remedies

The typical UDAP statute offers actual damages plus statutory, multiple, or punitive damages. Actual damages can be substantial. Several decisions have awarded the lost equity in the home as actual damages, and then trebled this amount, where the homeowner was unable to regain the home.[265] Even a homeowner who regains the home may have lost wages and suffered substantial expenses for moving, rent, interest, closing costs, and advice. One court awarded $100,000 in punitive damages under the jurisdiction's UDAP statute.[266] The court found clear and convincing evidence that the rescuers acted with malice, in that they led the homeowner to believe that they would assist her in avoiding foreclosure when they had no intention of doing so. Instead, they obtained title to the home for a fraction of its value, resold it without her knowledge, and extracted substantial equity from it.

Many UDAP statutes either authorize injunctions or authorize "other equitable relief" or "other relief the court deems proper."[267] This broad authority should be aggressively pursued in foreclosure rescue scam cases. It may enable the court to quiet title, order reconveyance of the property, reform the contract, or order the record owner not to reconvey or encumber the property.

A few UDAP statutes explicitly mention rescission as a potential remedy. In other states, general language authorizing other relief or other equitable relief is probably sufficient authority for a rescission order.[268] Since UDAP statutes are intended to liberalize the common law, the court may be willing to dispense with some of the formalities of common law rescission.[269]

---

259 Eicher v. Mid Am. Fin. Inv. Corp., 702 N.W.2d 792 (Neb. 2005). *See also* Pace-Knapp v. Pelascini, 2008 WL 699279 (Wash. Ct. App. Mar. 17, 2008) (plaintiff reasonably interpreted defendant's promises to "save" her home as meaning they would refinance, not buy her house, even though she failed to read the documents or even the titles). *But cf.* Carter v. Second Chance Program, Inc., No. 06 CH 26787 (Cir. Ct., Cook County, Ill. Dec. 23, 2008), *available at* www.consumerlaw.org/unreported (finding no UDAP violation where homeowner knew transaction was a sale-leaseback).

260 U.S. Home & Realty Corp v. Lehnartz, Clearinghouse No. 43,259 (Mich. Dist. Ct. 1987), *available at* www.consumerlaw.org/unreported.

261 Jackson v. Byrd, 2004 WL 3130653 (D.C. Super. Ct. May 11, 2004), *later op.*, 2004 WL 3249693 (D.C. Super. Ct. June 30, 2004) (awarding damages), *later op.*, 2004 WL 3249692 (D.C. Super. Ct. Sept. 2, 2004) (awarding attorney fees), *aff'd*, 902 A.2d 778 (D.C. 2006).

262 Billingham v. Dornemann, 771 N.E.2d 166 (Mass. App. Ct. 2002).

263 Phifer v. Home Savers Consulting Corp., 2007 WL 295605 (E.D.N.Y. Jan. 30, 2007).

264 *But cf.* Cooper v. GGGR Invs., 334 B.R. 179 (E.D. Va. 2005) (denying claim under Virginia's UDAP statute because of lack of proof that plaintiff relied on rescuer's deceptive statements).

265 *In re* Bryant, 111 B.R. 474 (E.D. Pa. 1990) (awarding lost equity as actual damages, trebled); Martinez v. Affordable Hous. Network, Inc., 109 P.3d 983 (Colo. Ct. App. 2004) (awarding lost equity as actual damages, trebled), *rev'd on other grounds*, 123 P.3d 1201 (Colo. 2006) (reversing trial court's determination that buyer of home from rescuer was bona fide purchaser without notice; remanding for trial on quiet title claim). *See also* Eicher v. Mid Am. Fin. Inv. Corp., 702 N.W.2d 792 (Neb. 2005) (affirming award of attorney fees on UDAP claim where damages and rescission were awarded on fraud claim).

266 Griffith v. Barnes, 560 F. Supp. 2d 29 (D.D.C. 2008).

267 *See* National Consumer Law Center, Unfair and Deceptive Acts and Practices § 13.6 (7th ed. 2008 and Supp.).

268 *See id.* § 13.7.

269 *See id.*

Most UDAP statutes provide for an award of attorney fees to a consumer who prevails.[270]

15.4.6 State Foreclosure Rescue Statutes

15.4.6.1 Overview

A number of states have special laws aimed specifically at foreclosure rescue scams.[271] In addition, the Massachusetts Attorney General has issued an regulation under the state's UDAP authority targeting the scams.[272] Michigan has a credit repair statute that is broad enough to encompass foreclosure rescue scams.[273] Florida has a statute that regulates only those who offer to purchase the surplus at a foreclosure sale.[274] As knowledge of the nature of foreclosure rescue scams spreads, more states may adopt such laws, so practitioners should check for recent legislation in their states. These statutes typically forbid certain deceptive or abusive practices, require a right to cancel, and, in most cases, provide special remedies.

These laws have proven helpful in attacking foreclosure rescue scams,[275] though they have not eliminated the scams. NCLC has developed a model state foreclosure rescue statute that builds on the existing approaches and attempts to achieve a more complete remedy.[276]

A significant advantage of asserting a claim under one of these laws is the clear, explicit rules that these laws impose on rescuers. Not only will violation of one of the rules be actionable under the state foreclosure rescue law, but it may also help make a case for fraud or a UDAP violation.

Another advantage of these laws is the relief they provide. They usually authorize attorney fees, and unlike some UDAP statutes these laws typically make an attorney fee award mandatory if the consumer prevails. Their multiple damage provisions may also be mandatory. Many of these statutes also allow the consumer to seek punitive damages, which the state UDAP statute may not allow. In addition, in contrast to some UDAP statutes, these statutes do not require a litigant to send a pre-suit notice or show an impact on the public interest.

Like the Truth in Lending Act, these laws allow consumers to cancel contracts with rescuers. One advantage of cancellation under a state foreclosure rescue law is that most of the state laws do not require the consumer to tender back the amount paid by the rescuer. On the other hand, these state laws tend to be less explicit than TILA about the procedure that the rescuer must follow to cancel the deed, and they provide more protection than TILA for those who buy the home or lend against the home after the rescuer acquires it. Another advantage is that these laws do not generally require that the rescuer have engaged in a certain number of consumer credit transactions in order to qualify for coverage under the law. Massachusetts and the District of Columbia go farther, and completely ban foreclosure rescue transactions, as well as advance fees and advertising for certain foreclosure consulting services.

15.4.6.2 Coverage

The typical statute covers "foreclosure consultants" or some similar term.[277] Most statutes define this term broadly to include anyone who makes an offer, representation, or

270 *See, e.g.*, Eicher v. Mid Am. Fin. Inv. Corp., 748 N.W.2d 1 (Neb. 2008) (awarding fees under UDAP statute to plaintiffs who prevailed on fraud and UDAP claims against foreclosure rescuer); Pace-Knapp v. Pelascini, 2008 WL 699279 (Wash. Ct. App. Mar. 17, 2008) (unpublished) (affirming award of attorney fees on UDAP claim against foreclosure rescue scammer). *See generally* National Consumer Law Center, Unfair and Deceptive Acts and Practices § 13.8 (7th ed. 2008 and Supp.).

271 Cal. Civ. Code §§ 2944.6 to 2944.7, 2945.1 to 2945.11, 1695.1 to 1695.17; Colo. Rev. Stat. §§ 6-1-1101 to 6-1-1120; 2009 Conn. Public Act 208, §§ 23 to 33 (adding foreclosure rescue services and short sale negotiations to scope of debt adjustor license requirement); D.C. Code §§ 42-2431 to 42-2435; Ga. Code Ann. § 10-2-393(b)(20); Haw. Rev. Stat. §§ 480E-1 to 480E-5; Idaho Code §§ 45-1505, 45-1602; 765 Ill. Comp. Stat. §§ 940/1 to 940/65; Ind. Stat. 24-5.5-1-1 to 24-5.5-6-6; Iowa Code §§ 714E.1 to 714E.4, 714F.1 to 714F.9; Md. Code Ann., Real Prop. §§ 7-105(A-1), 7-301 to 7-321; Minn. Stat. Ann. §§ 325N.01 to 325N.18; Mo. Stat. Ann. §§ 407.935 to 407.943; Neb. Rev. Stat. §§ 76-2701 to 76-2728; Nev. Rev. Stat. §§ 645F.300 to 645F.450; N.H. Rev. Stat. §§ 479-B:1 to 479-B:11; New York Real Prop. Law § 265-a; N.C. Gen. Stat. § 14-423 (adding foreclosure assistance to activities covered by state debt adjustment law); 2008 Oregon Laws 1st Sp. Sess. Ch. 19 (H.B. 3630); R.I. Gen. Laws §§ 5-78-1 to 5-79-9; Tenn. Code Ann. §§ 47-18-5401 to 47-19-5402; Va. Code § 59.1-200.1; Wash. Rev. Code §§ 61.34.010 to 61.34.900; Wis. Stat. §§ 846.40 to 846.45.

272 940 Code Mass. Reg. § 25.00.

273 Mich. Comp. Laws §§ 445.1822 to 445.1825.

274 Fla. Stat. §§ 45.031 to 45.035.

275 *See, e.g.*, Johnson v. Wheeler, 492 F. Supp. 2d (D. Md. 2007); Lloyd v. Hoffman, 369 B.R. 549 (Bankr. N.D. Cal. 2007) (permitting homeowner to rescind sale based defendant's failure to put right to cancel next to signature on sale agreement, as required by statute, despite fact that homeowner signed separate notice disclosing right to cancel), *aff'd*, 2008 WL 298820 (N.D. Cal. Feb. 1, 2008), *aff'd on other grounds*, 572 F.3d 999 (9th Cir. 2009); Guest v. Rose, 2007 WL 2758640 (Cal. Ct. App. Sept. 24, 2007).

276 *See* § 15.4.6.6 *infra*.

277 *See* Still v. Arakelyan (*In re* Still), 393 B.R. 896, 915 (Bankr. C.D. Cal. 2008) (finding that defendant met definition); New Towne Props., L.L.C. v. Boyd, No. 2058 (Md. Ct. Spec. App. Oct. 17, 2008), *available at* www.consumerlaw.org/unreported (defendant who entered into sale-leaseback with homeowner and claimed to be able to save home met definition of foreclosure consultant). *But cf.* Holden v. Salvadore, 964 A.2d 508 (R.I. 2009) (where homeowner lost home to foreclosure but then made winning bid at foreclosure sale, person who bought her rights under that bid was not foreclosure consultant, as he did not solicit the homeowner and did not propose to help her avoid foreclosure, which had already occurred).

solicitation to perform, or actually performs any service for compensation that is represented to:

- Stop or postpone a foreclosure sale;
- Obtain forbearance;
- Assist the owner in exercising or getting an extension of a right of reinstatement;
- Assist the owner in obtaining a loan;
- Obtain a waiver of an acceleration clause;
- Lessen the impact of the foreclosure on the owner's credit rating; or
- Save the home from foreclosure.

A solicitation that did not use the words "stop," "postpone," or "save the home" still amounted to a solicitation for foreclosure rescue services where it referred to the remaining redemption period and offered "options to save the equity in your home."[278]

"Service" is typically defined to include providing advice or assistance about foreclosure and serving as an intermediary between the homeowner and creditors.

Maryland's law also covers any person who systematically contacts owners of residences in default to offer foreclosure consulting services.[279] In Michigan, the foreclosure rescue provision is part of the state credit repair law and is much less detailed.[280]

Practitioners in states with foreclosure rescue statutes should evaluate how many of the actors in the scam can be covered by the definition. Many of the subsidiary players in a foreclosure rescue scam may have received compensation and may have represented that their services would help the homeowner obtain a loan, save the home, or stop or delay the sale. Further, even if they do not meet the statutory definition, subsidiary players may be liable on an aiding and abetting theory for the principal's violation of the state foreclosure rescue law.[281] Some courts have used this and other tort doctrines to find subsidiary players liable for violating other consumer protection laws, such as state UDAP laws.[282]

Several of the statutes have separate provisions regulating foreclosure purchasers, i.e., those who obtain a deed to the home with a promise to reconvey it at some future date.[283] New York's law only covers foreclosure purchasers. Maryland explicitly covers surplus buyers, i.e., those who induce homeowners to sign over the surplus proceeds from the foreclosure sale.[284] Florida also has specific provisions for sale of the surplus.[285] In most states, other than Colorado, Iowa, and Nebraska, the general definition of "foreclosure consultant" is broad enough to cover these variations of the scam, and in some states a person can be both a generic foreclosure consultant and one of these specific variants.[286] In Colorado, however, "foreclosure consultant" is defined to exclude those who acquire an interest in the home, so a person cannot fit into both categories.

The statutory exemptions should be examined carefully. The typical statute exempts licensed or chartered lenders, lawyers, licensed debt management services, credit reporting agencies, registered securities advisors and broker-dealers, non-profit organizations, insurance companies, and, in some states, other licensed or regulated entities.[287] Many

278 Jones v. Rees-Max, L.L.C., 514 F. Supp. 2d 1139 (D. Minn. 2007).

279 Md. Code Ann., Real Prop. § 7-301(b)(2).

280 Michigan's law covers stopping, preventing, or delaying a foreclosure, or providing advice or assistance on one of those subjects, as well as obtaining an extension of credit for the homeowner. *See* Mich. Comp. Laws §§ 445.1822 to 445.1825.

281 *See* § 15.4.7.7, *infra.*

282 *See* National Consumer Law Center, Unfair and Deceptive Acts and Practices § 11.1, 11.5.3 (7th ed. 2008 and Supp.).

283 *See, e.g.,* Ga. Code Ann. § 10-1-393(b)(20)(A), (B); 765 Ill. Comp. Stat. ch. 940; Iowa Code §§ 714F.1 to 714F.9; Md. Code Ann., Real Prop. § 7-301(e); Minn. Stat. §§ 325N.10 to 325N.18. *See also* Jones v. Rees-Max, L.L.C., 514 F. Supp. 2d 1139 (D. Minn. 2007) (rescuers met definition of foreclosure purchaser because they had acquired more than one foreclosure reconveyance within twenty-four months); Still v. Arakelyan (*In re* Still), 393 B.R. 896, 915 (Bankr. C.D. Cal. 2008) (mastermind behind foreclosure rescue scheme was not "equity purchaser" because he never took title to the property, but straw buyer he lined up met definition).

284 Md. Code Ann., Real Prop. § 7-301(h). *See also* Cal. Civ. Code § 2945.1(a)(9) (defining "foreclosure consultant" to include people who assist the owner in obtaining the surplus from a foreclosure sale); Colo. Rev. Stat. § 6-1-1103(4)(a)(IX) (defining "foreclosure consultant" to include people who assist the owner in obtaining the surplus from the foreclosure sale); Eyler v. 3 Vista Court L.L.C. (*In re* Eyler), 2008 WL 4833096 (Bankr. D. Md. Oct. 28, 2008) (proposed findings of fact and conclusions of law) (finding that rescuer met definition of foreclosure purchaser); Boquilon v. Beckwith, 49 Cal. App. 4th 1697, 57 Cal. Rptr. 2d 503 (1996) (sale and leaseback arrangement violates California's Home Equity Sales Contract Act).

285 Fla. Stat. §§ 45.032, 45.034.

286 *See, e.g.,* Eyler v. 3 Vista Court L.L.C. (*In re* Eyler), 2008 WL 4833096 (Bankr. D. Md. Oct. 28, 2008) (proposed findings of fact and conclusions of law) (finding that rescuer met both definitions); Segura v. McBride, 7 Cal. Rptr. 2d 436, 5 Cal. App. 4th 1028 (1992).

287 *See* Still v. Arakelyan (*In re* Still), 393 B.R. 896, 915 (Bankr. C.D. Cal. 2008) (foreclosure consultant whose real estate broker license had expired not entitled to exemption even though he was designated licensed officer of a corporation that held an active real estate license; this exemption also applies only if licensed broker makes loan with his own funds, which this defendant did not do); Spencer v. Marshall, 85 Cal. Rptr. 3d 752 (App. 2008) (bankruptcy trustee's approval of sale as sufficient to satisfy obligations to unsecured creditors and bankruptcy court's order allowing debtor to sell home without further order of court did not bring equity purchaser within statutory exception for sale authorized by statute or by order of court); Onofrio v. Rice, 64 Cal. Rptr. 2d 74 (Cal. Ct. App. 1997) (rejecting real estate broker's argument that he fell within statutory exemption); Boquilon v. Beckwith, 57 Cal. Rptr. 2d 503 (Cal. Ct. App. 1996); Parsons v. Abell, Civil No. C-07-3727 (Cir. Ct., Frederick Cty., Md. Mar. 30, 2009), *available at* www.consumerlaw.org/unreported (finding exemption inapplicable to title insurer). *Cf.* Julian v. Buonassissi, 963 A.2d 234, 244 (Md. 2009) (Maryland

of the statutes make it clear that the exemption only applies if the person is acting within the scope of a state license.[288] For example, an attorney would be exempt only while performing work that amounted to the practice of law. Massachusetts and the District of Columbia broadly ban all "foreclosure rescue transactions" entered into for compensation or gain. Massachusetts defines the covered transaction and one that is intended to avoid or delay actual or anticipated foreclosure proceeding and that involves the transfer of title of a home with the homeowner maintaining a legal or equitable interest in the property. The District of Columbia definition covers any transfer of title during or incident to foreclosure, default, or tax sale with the reconveyance, or promise of reconveyance, of an interest back to the homeowner.[289]

15.4.6.3 Right to Cancel

Almost all of the state statutes afford a right to cancel. The typical statute affords the homeowner a three- to ten-day right to cancel any contract with a rescuer, and requires the rescuer to give the homeowner written notice of this right.[290] Failure to provide the notice can—like in TILA—trigger a right to cancel the transaction.

The typical statute is written so that the cancellation period begins to run from the date that the rescuer gives the consumer the notice of the right to cancel and a written contract that complies with the statute. Accordingly, if the consumer was not given these documents, the practitioner should take the position that the right to cancel has not even begun to run.[291] Many decisions interpreting comparable language in state home solicitation statutes have accepted this argument.[292]

Before sending a cancellation notice, the practitioner should ascertain whether the statute obligates the homeowner to tender back funds that the rescuer advanced, and what the implications are if the homeowner fails to make this tender. Maryland requires the homeowner to repay any funds paid or advanced by the foreclosure consultant, foreclosure purchaser, or surplus purchaser within sixty days of cancellation plus 8% interest per annum, though the right to cancel cannot be conditioned on the payment of this money.[293] Oregon has a similar provision, but with 9% interest. Georgia mandates tender by the homeowner of all monies paid to him or her within thirty days of cancellation and is silent on whether the cancellation can be conditioned upon payment. Colorado requires tender within sixty days after cancellation of a foreclosure consulting contract; as to foreclosure purchasers there is no tender obligation, but the foreclosure purchaser is prohibited from paying anything to the homeowner until the cancellation period has passed. New York requires the homeowner, as a condition of reconveyance of title, to tender any consideration received from the foreclosure purchaser. California,[294] Illinois, Michigan, Minnesota, Missouri, Rhode Island, and Washington do not set any tender requirement. If a tender offer is mandatory, the practitioner may still want to send the cancellation notice promptly because of the danger that the rescuer will convey or mortgage the house to an unknowing third party. However, the practitioner and the homeowner should explore financing options immediately.

When the homeowner cancels, most states explicitly protect a good faith mortgagor or purchaser who buys or lends against the home and who does not know of the homeowner's contract with the rescuer or that the rescission period has not expired.[295] In these states, even if the rescuer has

---

foreclosure rescue law does not regulate banks, but bank's interest in the property may be defeated if transaction is void or if bank was not a bona fide purchaser).

288 *See, e.g.*, Johnson v. Wheeler, 492 F. Supp. 2d (D. Md. 2007) (first licensed mortgage broker covered despite statutory exemption; exemption for lender irrelevant if the deed securing its interest was void).

289 D.C. Code § 42-2431(2).

290 Georgia's right to cancel applies only where the foreclosure rescue operator buys the home and the debtor remains in possession of the home. Ga. Code Ann. § 10-1-393(b)(20)(C).

291 New York's statute provides that a noncomplying contract can be rescinded for up to two years after the conveyance is recorded. N.Y. Real Prop. Law § 265-a(8). *See* Eyler v. 3 Vista Court L.L.C. (*In re* Eyler), 2008 WL 4833096 (Bankr. D. Md. Oct. 28, 2008) (proposed findings of fact and conclusions of law) (statutory right to rescind foreclosure rescue transaction never began to run because rescuer failed to give required notice); New Towne Props., L.L.C. v. Boyd, No. 2058 (Md. Ct. Spec. App. Oct. 17, 2008), *available at* www.consumerlaw.org/unreported (three-day rescission period had not begun to run where rescuer failed to give homeowner the statutorily required paperwork). *See also* Lloyd v. Hoffman, 369 B.R. 549 (Bankr. N.D. Cal. 2007) (rejecting defendant's "substantial compliance" argument; time to cancel was extended for failure to put right to cancel next to signature on sale agreement, as required by statute, despite fact that homeowner signed separate notice disclosing right to cancel), *aff'd*, 2008 WL 298820 (N.D. Cal. Feb. 1, 2008).

292 *See* National Consumer Law Center, Unfair and Deceptive Acts and Practices § 9.8.2.6.3 (7th ed. 2008 and Supp.).

293 *See* Eyler v. 3 Vista Court L.L.C. (*In re* Eyler), 2008 WL 4833096 (Bankr. D. Md. Oct. 28, 2008) (proposed findings of fact and conclusions of law) (right to rescind is not conditioned on repayment); New Towne Props., L.L.C. v. Boyd, No. 2058 (Md. Ct. Spec. App. Oct. 17, 2008), slip op. at 8 n.4, *available at* www.consumerlaw.org/unreported (rescission timely and valid despite homeowners' failure to tender).

294 *But cf.* Onofrio v. Rice, 64 Cal. Rptr. 2d 74 (Cal. Ct. App. 1997) (tender required, but homeowners' awards against rescuer may be set off against tender obligation, and no tender is necessary if action attacks validity of underlying debt).

295 *See, e.g.*, Julian v. Buonassissi, 963 A.2d 234, 244–245 (Md. 2009) (failure to provide cancellation notices makes transaction voidable, not void, so bona fide purchaser's interest is unaffected), *cert. granted*, 970 A.2d 892 (Md. 2009); Wells Fargo Bank v. Edsall, 880 N.Y.S.2d 877 (N.Y. Sup. Ct. 2009) (remedies of deed rescission and cancellation are subject to the rights of bona fide purchasers or encumbrancers for value).

already conveyed an interest in the home in an ostensibly arms-length transaction, the practitioner should investigate all information the buyer or lender had about the rescuer and the homeowner. Often the buyer or lender had good reason to suspect that the transaction was irregular.[296]

15.4.6.4 Substantive Prohibitions

The typical foreclosure rescue statute prohibits an array of deceptive, unfair, and abusive practices, so practitioners should check their own statutes carefully. Many prohibit unconscionable contract terms. Some of the statutes prohibit deception in broad terms. Another common provision is a cap on fees or interest rates, or a requirement that a rescuer who purchases the property must pay at least a certain percentage of its fair market value. Massachusetts and the District of Columbia completely ban all foreclosure rescue transactions entered into for profit or gain. Some state foreclosure rescue laws include a requirement that the homeowner receive a notice prior to foreclosure, explaining the foreclosure process and warning the homeowner against foreclosure rescuers.

Most of the statutes prohibit foreclosure consultants from receiving advance fees until all promised work has been completed. Most also prohibit foreclosure rescue consultants from acquiring any interest in the property.[297] Some states, including Minnesota, New York, Rhode Island, and Washington, prohibit eviction of the homeowner unless the foreclosure purchaser has paid the homeowner at least 82% of the home's fair market value.[298]

Some of the states prohibit foreclosure rescue consultants from acquiring any interest in a residence in foreclosure from an owner with whom the consultant has contracted. New York and Rhode Island prohibit eviction of the homeowner unless the foreclosure purchaser has paid the homeowner at least 82% of the home's fair market value.

Some statutes prohibit the rescuer from entering into an agreement to reconvey the home to the homeowner unless the homeowner has a reasonable ability to meet the requirements for reconveyance.[299] Most prohibit other deceptive or abusive practices as well.[300] Many require that a foreclosure rescue contract be in writing, contain all the agreements of the parties, and contain certain terms and disclosures.[301]

15.4.6.5 Remedies

Most of the statutes provide a special private cause of action.[302] Most authorize double or treble damages or punitive damages in addition to actual damages.[303] The typical statute also authorizes attorney fees.[304] Some specifically authorize injunctive relief. Some states provide that a violation is actionable under the state UDAP statute or the state credit repair statute, either as the only remedy or in addition to a special private cause of action. Since the laws generally provide a right to cancel the transaction, which is extended if the rescuer failed to comply with the statute, courts will generally void the deed transferring the property.[305]

296 *But cf.* Julian v. Buonassissi, 963 A.2d 234, 245–246 (Md. 2009) (no evidence that scammers were lender's agents, so their knowledge cannot be attributed to lender; even if they were lender's agents, their interests were adverse to lender so their knowledge cannot be attributed to lender; existence of foreclosure insufficient to put lender on inquiry notice), *cert. granted*, 970 A.2d 892 (Md. 2009).

297 *See, e.g.*, New Towne Props., L.L.C. v. Boyd, No. 2058 (Md. Ct. Spec. App. Oct. 17, 2008), *available at* www.consumerlaw.org/unreported (foreclosure consultant violated Maryland statute when company of which he was the managing member purchased the home); Carter v. Lakenu, 2008 WL 5511073 (Minn. Ct. App. Jan. 20, 2009) (violation established where homeowner conveyed home to foreclosure consultant's wife).

298 *See also* Iowa Code § 714F.8(3)(b); Wis. Stat. § 846.40(8)(b)(2).

299 *See, e.g.*, Jones v. Rees-Max, L.L.C., 514 F. Supp. 2d 1139 (D. Minn. 2007) (applying statutory presumption that rescuer who has not obtained documentation of homeowners' income has violated requirement of verifying that homeowner has reasonable ability to pay for reconveyance); Eyler v. 3 Vista Court L.L.C. (*In re* Eyler), 2008 WL 4833096 (Bankr. D. Md. Oct. 28, 2008) (proposed findings of fact and conclusions of law) (finding violation).

300 *See, e.g.*, Jones v. Rees-Max, L.L.C., 514 F. Supp. 2d 1139 (D. Minn. 2007) (fact question whether rescuer misrepresented monthly rent payment and violated prohibition against representing that he could help homeowners save their home).

301 *See* Jones v. Rees-Max, L.L.C., 514 F. Supp. 2d 1139 (D. Minn. 2007) (finding contract to be noncompliant); Still v. Arakelyan (*In re* Still), 393 B.R. 896, 915 (Bankr. C.D. Cal. 2008) (finding that consultant violated statute by failing to provide written contract; awarding treble damages); Parsons v. Abell, Civil No. C-07-3727 (Cir. Ct., Frederick Cty., Md. Mar. 30, 2009), *available at* www.consumerlaw.org/unreported (finding that rescuers failed to comply with paperwork requirements of Maryland foreclosure rescue law; awarding $354,108 in damages, primarily for emotional distress, and then trebling this amount).

302 *See, e.g.*, Onofrio v. Rice, 64 Cal. Rptr. 2d 74 (Cal. App. Ct. 1997).

303 *See, e.g.*, *In re* McNeal, 286 B.R. 910 (Bankr. N.D. Cal. 2002) (debtor entitled to actual damages in amount of $750 fee he had paid, plus exemplary damages in three times that amount, against foreclosure consultant who charged fee before fully performing the mortgage loan modification and foreclosure sale postponement services for which he was hired, and failed to provide notice in employment agreement of debtor's right to cancel and of statutory restrictions on his ability to collect fee); Parsons v. Abell, Civil No. C-07-3727 (Cir. Ct., Frederick Cty., Md. Mar. 30, 2009), *available at* www.consumerlaw.org/unreported (awarding $354,108 in damages, primarily for emotional distress, and then trebling this amount).

304 Onofrio v. Rice, 64 Cal. Rptr. 2d 74 (Cal. Ct. App. 1997) (affirming award of attorney fees against foreclosure consultant who violated statutory duties).

305 *See, e.g.*, Johnson v. Wheeler, 492 F. Supp. 2d (D. Md. 2007); Lloyd v. Hoffman, 369 B.R. 549 (Bankr. N.D. Cal. 2007), *aff'd*, 2008 WL 298820 (N.D. Cal. Feb. 1, 2008).

In most states, rescuers can also be prosecuted criminally for violations of the statute. The homeowner should consider filing criminal charges. A criminal conviction may prevent the rescuer from defrauding others. Further, the court may order restitution to the homeowner as part of the criminal sentence.

15.4.6.6 NCLC Model State Foreclosure Rescue Statute

NCLC has developed a model state foreclosure rescue statute, which can be found on this treatise's companion website. The model law builds on the existing approaches and attempts to achieve a more complete remedy for combating scams where the rescuer or straw buyer takes title to the property.[306] These different approaches have had some success, though they have not completely stopped foreclosure rescue scams and can be complicated to apply.

The model law builds upon the common law equitable mortgage doctrine,[307] to call a rescue transaction what it is: a loan. Under the equitable mortgage doctrine, a transaction that appears to be an absolute sale but is actually intended to secure repayment is actually a mortgage. The model law deems all rescue transactions to be mortgages: it requires the rescuer to comply with lending laws, deems the rescuer's deed to be merely a mortgage, and deems the rescuer to be merely a lender, with no right to evict or encumber the property.

The model law has the following advantages over the other approaches:

- It is simple to apply.
- It does not send out a mixed message that it is acceptable to take a homeowner's title as long as contract requirements are satisfied.
- It may be more appealing to legislatures that are concerned about banning all foreclosure rescue transactions outright.
- It includes a clear, detailed remedy scheme that none of the existing statutes has, showing precisely how to restructure a transaction that looks like a sale into a loan.
- It provides a workable approach to helping homeowners who received some cash from the rescuer that they cannot afford to pay back immediately.
- It clarifies the warning signs that third party lenders, buyers, title insurers, and escrow companies should look for to ensure that they do not unwittingly enable these scams.

The model law makes clear and explicit what the other statutes leave implicit. Under the existing statutes, once the transaction is found to be unlawful, it is generally necessary to resort to the common law equitable mortgage doctrine or the federal Truth in Lending Act to unwind the transaction. Yet courts are sometimes uncomfortable doing so without clear direction or more recent case law than equitable mortgage cases that could be a century old.

In addition, the model law attempts to achieve a more complete remedy and to stop the scams from happening by depriving scammers of the unwitting assistance of third parties that are critical to the deals. No matter what approach is taken, scammers will violate the law because they are lawbreakers. But even once the scammer is caught, complete relief is often impossible because the home has been encumbered by a new loan from a bona fide lender, or title has been passed to a bona fide purchaser.

The model law specifies the warning signs that should put a third party on notice to inquire into the homeowner's status before getting caught in the middle. Scammers will be unable to complete their transactions if legitimate title or escrow companies will not close their deals, if legitimate lenders will not finance them or enable them to get their money out, and if the scammers cannot flip the properties to legitimate buyers.

The model law's remedy and bona fide purchaser provisions are also adaptable to supplement the existing "regulate it" approach that most states have taken, as well as the "ban it" approach taken by Massachusetts and the District of Columbia.

306 The model law does not address foreclosure consultant scams.

307 *See* § 15.4.1.2, *supra.*

15.4.7 Fraud and Civil Conspiracy

15.4.7.1 Introduction

Claims of fraud and civil conspiracy should always be considered in foreclosure rescue cases. Rescuers commonly rely on false representations to induce homeowners to deed over their homes.

Common law doctrines allow fraud claims to be asserted not only against those who dealt directly with the homeowner, but also against parties who conspired with the rescuer, knowingly accepted the benefits of the fraud, or aided and abetted the rescuer's fraud.[308]

Civil conspiracy, while less well-known than fraud, is recognized as a cause of action in almost all states. It

308 *See, e.g.,* Johnson v. Home Savers Consulting Corp., 2007 WL 925518 (E.D.N.Y. Mar. 23, 2007) (awarding damages for conspiracy to commit fraud but not for fraud because defendant did not deal directly with plaintiff), *report and recommendation adopted by* 2007 WL 1110612 (E.D.N.Y. Apr. 11, 2007); Phifer v. Home Savers Consulting Corp., 2007 WL 295605 (E.D.N.Y. Jan. 30, 2007) (aiding and abetting liability touches everyone who offers substantial assistance in the fraud; in this case, substantial assistance was found from the preparation of a misleading HUD-1 settlement statement); National Consumer Law Center, The Cost of Credit: Regulation, Preemption, and Industry Abuses § 12.10.1 (4th ed. 2009 and Supp.).

provides another way to hold parties liable who enabled the fraud to succeed but did not make fraudulent misrepresentations themselves.

15.4.7.2 Elements of a Fraud Claim

The traditional elements of fraud are a false representation, scienter (i.e., that the defendant made the representation recklessly or with knowledge of its falsity), the defendant's intent that the representation be relied upon, reasonable reliance, and damages resulting from the reliance.[309] These elements make fraud more difficult to establish than a deception claim under a UDAP statute. For example, the consumer often need not prove reliance or intent to deceive under UDAP statutes, and the standard of proof in a UDAP case is a preponderance of the evidence, whereas fraud requires clear and convincing evidence. A number of courts have upheld fraud claims in foreclosure rescue scam cases.[310]

However, the damages available in a fraud case are usually much wider. In particular, fraud damages can include punitive damages in most states, while UDAP statutes rarely authorize more than treble damages. In addition, fraud can be asserted against anyone, while some UDAP statutes have restrictive coverage requirements. Consumer practitioners have also used fraud to reach behind the front person to the financiers who enable predatory lending. Lenders may be the only deep pocket left, and reaching them is also an important way of decreasing the volume of mortgage scams by drying up their funding. The advantages and disadvantages of a fraud claim in comparison to a UDAP claim are discussed in more detail at § 15.4.2.2, *supra*. If common law fraud can be established, it may also be possible to show mail fraud or wire fraud, either of which can be used as a predicate offence for a RICO claim.[311]

Foreclosure rescue scam cases can produce compelling fraud claims. The plaintiffs are often older and vulnerable. The rescuer's fraud is often blatant and heartless. Damages can be significant. Even though fraud is harder to prove than a UDAP claim, practitioners should not shy away from fraud claims in foreclosure rescue cases, particularly since these claims are compelling to juries.

The Nebraska Supreme Court affirmed a judgment of fraud against a rescuer who induced homeowners to sign over deeds to their homes by knowingly misrepresenting that the transactions were loans.[312] While the court's decision does not itemize the relief awarded to the thirteen plaintiffs, it affirmed an award of more than $375,000 in attorney fees on a parallel UDAP claim.

A Colorado Supreme Court decision deals with a rescuer who obtained a quitclaim deed to the home based on certain representations about the steps it would take, but then sold the home. The supreme court affirmed the trial court's conclusion that the rescuer had committed fraud.[313] It also held that the trial court had erred in concluding that the person who bought from the rescuer did not have notice of the homeowners' claim to the home, and remanded the case for a determination about whether the deed was voidable as to the purchaser.

Defendants in foreclosure rescue scam cases are likely to argue that the homeowner's reliance on their misrepresentations was not reasonable. A California court rejected a rescuer's argument that the homeowner knew that she was

309 *See* D. Dobbs, The Law of Torts §§ (2000). *See also* Eicher v. Mid Am. Fin. Inv. Corp., 702 N.W.2d 792, 803 (Neb. 2005) (reciting fraud elements in foreclosure rescue case). *See generally* National Consumer Law Center, Automobile Fraud § 7.2 (3d ed. 2007 and Supp.).

310 *See, e.g.*, Provencher v. T & M Mortgage Solutions, Inc., 2008 WL 2447472 (D. Me. June 18, 2008) (magistrate's recommended decision) (denying motion to dismiss fraud claim based on, *inter alia*, rescuers' misrepresentations that they could not arrange a loan for the homeowner to pay off her mortgage, that she had no choice but to sell her home to the rescuers, that by making seven months of payments she would improve her credit rating and be able to buy back home); Still v. Arakelyan (*In re* Still), 393 B.R. 896, 914–916 (Bankr. C.D. Cal. 2008) (rescuer's representation that only way to save home from foreclosure was to sell it to straw man was fraudulent because actual purpose of sale was to enable rescuer to cash out and take homeowners' equity); Sahni v. Emerald Mortgage Corp., 2008 WL 5394937 (Cal. Ct. App. Nov. 19, 2008) (unpublished) (reversing dismissal of fraud claim; finding plaintiff's allegations sufficiently specific); Martinez v. Affordable Hous. Network, Inc., 123 P.3d 1201 (Colo. 2005); Billingham v. Dornemann, 853 N.E.2d 220 (Mass. App. Ct. 2006) (unpublished); Eicher v. Mid Am. Fin. Inv. Corp., 702 N.W.2d 792 (Neb. 2005); Watson v. Melnikoff, 866 N.Y.S.2d 96 (N.Y. Sup. Ct. May 6, 2008) (table). *See also* Bryan v. Lindsay, 867 N.Y.S.2d 373 (Sup. Ct. 2008) (table, text at 2008 WL 3916011) (denying cross-motions for summary judgment on fraud claim; fact issues as to whether rescuer misrepresented sale as loan transaction). *But see* Southwell v. Middleton, 851 N.Y.S.2d 74 (N.Y. Sup. Ct. 2007) (unpublished) (intention not to perform a contract does not support a fraud claim); Pace-Knapp v. Pelascini, 2008 WL 699279 (Wash. Ct. App. Mar. 17, 2008) (reversing judgment for fraud in the inducement because promises of future performance are not representations of existing fact). *But cf.* Johnson v. Washington, 559 F.3d 238, 245 (4th Cir. 2009) (fraud claim cannot be based on rescuers' statements that they wanted to help homeowner, as these are either accurate or are forward-looking statements of opinion); McMillen v. Kadis (*In re* McMillen), 390 B.R. 1 (Bankr. D. Mass. 2008) (fraud not shown because rescuer did not enter into contract without intent to perform).

311 *See* 18 U.S.C. 1341–1360 (mail fraud and other fraud offences); Proctor v. Metropolitan Money Store Corp., 645 F. Supp. 2d 464, 473–474 (D. Md. 2009) (denying motion to dismiss RICO claim based on mail and wire fraud in "grand mortgage foreclosure rescue scam."). *See also* § 15.4.12, *infra* (discussing RICO claims).

312 Eicher v. Mid Am. Fin. Inv. Corp., 702 N.W.2d 792, 803 (Neb. 2005).

313 Martinez v. Affordable Hous. Network, Inc., 123 P.3d 1201, 1205 (Colo. 2005). *See also In re* Bryant, 111 B.R. 474 (Bankr. E.D. Pa. 1990) (rescuer's actions amounted to common law fraud so violated UDAP statute).

facing foreclosure and in financial distress, so could not have relied on their representations that she would be able to save her home and avoid foreclosure through their intervention: "Indeed, it appears to us that a plaintiff's knowledge that she is in financial distress and is facing foreclosure might make her *more* vulnerable to the kinds of misrepresentations alleged in the operative complaint, not less so."[314]

15.4.7.3 Fraud by Silence

Affirmative misrepresentations are not the only type of fraud that is actionable. Fraud by silence or fraudulent concealment is also recognized as tortious. In general, a party's nondisclosure of material facts is fraudulent if:

- The party has a fiduciary or confidential relationship with the plaintiff;
- Speech is necessary to make full a half-truth;
- One party has superior knowledge or resources regarding the transaction that are not available to the other party, at least in some jurisdictions;
- There is a statutory duty to disclose.[315]

15.4.7.4 Overcoming Exculpatory Contract Clauses

In many foreclosure rescue cases, the homeowners are unaware that the documents they have signed are not loan documents but transfer the home to the rescuer. The Nebraska Supreme Court held that the fact that the documents the homeowners signed were clearly labeled sales to the rescuer rather than loans did not undercut their fraud claims. The court held that even a person who fails to read a contract before signing it is not bound by it if it was procured by fraud.[316]

Similarly, a Massachusetts appellate court held that a merger clause in the homeowner's contract with the rescuer was no defense to fraud.[317] The clause stated that, in deciding to enter into the contract, the homeowner had not relied on any statements or representations by the rescuer. Courts generally agree that the parol evidence rule does not bar evidence of misrepresentations when the claim is based on fraud rather than contract.[318]

15.4.7.5 The Important of Pattern Evidence

Evidence that the rescuer defrauded other homeowners in the same way is powerful. It can confirm in the jury's mind that the defendant is a scoundrel who needs to be punished. Evidence that the rescuer made similar misrepresentations to other people will also make it clearer to the trier of fact that the homeowner is telling the truth. Joining several homeowners in one case was very effective in *Eicher v. Mid America Financial Investment Corp.*,[319] but this evidence can also be introduced when the other homeowners are not parties to the same suit.

Foreclosure rescuers do not usually invent their methods on the spot. They advertise widely and solicit homeowners aggressively with a pitch that follows the same pattern. Thus, pattern evidence can almost always be found. Section 15.3.2.2, *supra*, suggests various ways of finding pattern evidence. Locating other homeowners who have been victimized in the same way should be a high priority.

While evidence of other crimes, wrongs, or acts is not admissible to prove a person's character, there are many other ways to admit it. Under the Federal Rules of Evidence and comparable state rules, evidence of other bad acts *is* admissible to show intent or motive, which is a critical issue in any fraud case. It is also admissible to show knowledge. Since *scienter* is an element of a fraud claim, evidence of the rescuer's other transactions should be admissible on this ground. Pattern evidence will also be admissible against other defendants, for example to show that a purchaser is not a bona fide purchaser without notice, or to show that a third party knowingly accepted the benefits of the fraud. In addition, it is admissible to show habit, routine practice, or absence of mistake or accident, and to support a punitive damages claim.[320]

15.4.7.6 Remedies for Fraud

A homeowner who proves fraud may recover actual damages. Actual damages may consist of the homeowner's lost equity, plus any "rental" payments the homeowner made to the rescuer that exceeded what the homeowner

---

314 Sahni v. Emerald Mortgage Corp., 2008 WL 5394937, at *8 (Cal. Ct. App. Nov. 19, 2008) (unpublished) (emphasis in original).

315 National Consumer Law Center, Automobile Fraud § 7.3.5 (3d ed. 2007 and Supp.).

316 Eicher v. Mid Am. Fin. Inv. Corp., 702 N.W.2d 792, 804 (Neb. 2005), *later appeal*, 748 N.W.2d 1 (Neb. 2008) (general rule that individual who signs contract is presumed to know its contents applies only in absence of fraud; reasonable reliance on misrepresentation that transaction was loan shown despite statement in contract that transaction was sale). *Accord* Still v. Arakelyan (*In re* Still), 393 B.R. 896, 915 (Bankr. C.D. Cal. 2008) (plaintiff's negligence in failing to discover falsity is not defense when misrepresentation was intentional). *But see* Johnson v. Washington, 559 F.3d 238, 245 (4th Cir. 2009) (no fraud where documents plainly stated terms of transaction and corrected any misleading oral statements; homeowners cannot complain when they did not read the documents).

317 Billingham v. Dornemann, 771 N.E.2d 166, 175 (Mass. App. Ct. 2002).

318 *See, e.g.*, Sahni v. Emerald Mortgage Corp., 2008 WL 5394937, at *8 (Cal. Ct. App. Nov. 19, 2008) (unpublished). *See generally* National Consumer Law Center, Automobile Fraud § 7.7.2 (3d ed. 2007 and Supp.).

319 702 N.W.2d 792 (Neb. 2005).

320 Fed. R. Evid. 406. *See* National Consumer Law Center, Automobile Fraud § 9.8.1 (3d ed. 2007 and Supp.).

would have had to pay on the mortgage.[321] Although an independent appraisal is likely to be more persuasive, the homeowner's opinion as to the value of the home is admissible.[322]

The rescuer may argue that the homeowner's losses were caused by factors other than the rescuer's fraud because the homeowners would have lost their homes in any event. The Nebraska Supreme Court rejected this argument in *Eicher v. Mid America Financial Investment Corp*.[323] The plaintiffs there testified that, although their options were limited, they could have considered other alternatives to save their homes if the opportunity with the rescuer had not presented itself. The court accepted these statements as sufficient to establish proximate cause. The court also reversed the denial of damages to a homeowner who paid "rental payments" to the rescuer for two years, but then stopped paying and moved out, after which the original lender foreclosed on the home and sold it. The court held that the fraud was fully perpetrated when the homeowner deeded the home to the rescuer, and his right to recover the equity he lost at that time was unaffected by his later termination of payments and loss of his home to foreclosure.[324]

In a later decision in the same case, the court rejected the rescuer's contention that another one of the plaintiff homeowners suffered no damages because he would have lost the home to foreclosure even if the rescuer had never appeared on the scene. The court held that the rescuer caused the homeowner's loss of equity, and was liable for this damage. Even if the home had gone to foreclosure, the homeowner would likely have been able to recover at least some of the equity.[325]

In almost all states, a homeowner may also recover punitive damages for fraud.[326] States vary in their standards for punitive damages, but typically it is necessary to show some aggravating factors such as malice, oppressiveness, or wantonness.[327]

In the alternative to seeking damages for fraud, the homeowner may rescind the transaction.[328] As a condition of rescission, the homeowner will probably have to tender the actual proceeds received.[329] In addition, a deed may be voidable if fraud is shown.[330]

15.4.7.7 Acceptance of Fruits of Fraud, Civil Conspiracy, Aiding and Abetting

To succeed, foreclosure rescue scams often require the cooperation of more than just the rescuer. Real estate agents, lenders, brokers, appraisers, closing agents, and others may be involved behind the scene. Several theories can impose fraud liability on these less visible participants.[331]

A party who knowingly receives the benefits of a fraud can be held liable for it.[332] This theory of liability is sometimes called "fruits of the fraud" liability. It may amount to ratification of the fraud.[333] For example, a transferee of the home who had reason to know of the fraud may

321 Eicher v. Mid Am. Fin. Inv. Corp., 702 N.W.2d 792, 811 (Neb. 2005). *See* Fleurentin v. McDowell, 2009 WL 2969686 (E.D.N.Y. Sept. 16, 2009) (default judgment explaining calculation of $278,327 in damages from fraud and breach of contract in deed transfer with equitable mortgage). *See also* Eicher v. Mid Am. Fin. Inv. Corp., 748 N.W.2d 1 (Neb. 2008) (subsequent appeal in same action affirming calculation of damages as homeowner's lost equity plus payments made to rescuer, minus payments rescuer made on mortgage).

322 Eicher v. Mid Am. Fin. Inv. Corp., 748 N.W.2d 1 (Neb. 2008).

323 702 N.W.2d 792, 804–805 (Neb. 2005).

324 *Id.* at 811.

325 Eicher v. Mid Am. Fin. Inv. Corp., 748 N.W.2d 1 (Neb. 2008).

326 *See* National Consumer Law Center, Automobile Fraud § 7.11.1 (3d ed. 2007 and Supp.).

327 *Id.*

328 *See* Eicher v. Mid Am. Fin. Inv. Corp., 702 N.W.2d 792 (Neb. 2005) (affirming awards of rescission and damages on fraud claims against rescuer). *But cf.* McMillen v. Kadis (*In re* McMillen), 390 B.R. 1 (Bankr. D. Mass. 2008) (rescission not available where homeowner knew of falsity of rescuer's representations before closing yet opted to proceed with the transaction); Pace-Knapp v. Pelascini, 2008 WL 699279 (Wash. Ct. App. Mar. 17, 2008) (unpublished) (consumer waived right to seek rescission for fraud by remaining in home for two years and signing two lease agreements after discovering that rescuers had acquired her property). *See generally* National Consumer Law Center, Automobile Fraud § 7.11.1 (3d ed. 2007 and Supp.).

329 Martinez v. Affordable Hous. Network, Inc., 123 P.3d 1201 (Colo. 2005) (homeowner who rescinds must tender actual proceeds before bona fide purchaser acquires the home for value without notice; remanding for determination whether this purchaser had notice). *Cf.* Johnson v. Melnikoff, 2008 WL 4182397 (N.Y. Sup. Ct. Sept. 11, 2008) (voiding mortgage but applying equitable subrogation doctrine to allow lender from which rescuer obtained secured loan to recover from homeowner the amount it paid on her preexisting mortgage), *aff'd on other grounds*, 882 N.Y.S.2d 914 (App. Div. 2009).

330 *See, e.g.*, Martinez v. Affordable Hous. Network, Inc., 123 P.3d 1201 (Colo. 2005); Watson v. Melnikoff, 866 N.Y.S.2d 96 (N.Y. Sup. Ct. May 6, 2008) (table) (deed void because procured by fraud; lender's mortgage also void where lender made loan to rescuer three days after homeowners filed *lis pendens*). *But cf.* Missouri v. MWG Prop. Consultants, L.L.C., 2008 WL 2389489 (Mich. Ct. App. June 12, 2008) (refusing to void deed where misrepresentation resulted in wrongful diversion of sale proceeds, not sale of home).

331 *See also* Cain v. Bethea, 2007 WL 2859681 (E.D.N.Y. Aug. 17, 2007) (discussing claims against numerous parties to rescue transaction), *adopted in part and rev'd in part on other grounds* 2007 WL 2846914 (E.D.N.Y. Sept. 26, 2007). *See generally* National Consumer Law Center, The Cost of Credit: Regulation, Preemption, and Industry Abuses § 12.10.1 (4th ed. 2009 and Supp.).

332 *See, e.g.*, Cumis Ins. Soc'y, Inc. v. Peters, 983 F. Supp. 787, 794–795 (N.D. Ill. 1997) (knowing acceptance of fruits of fraud is basis for fraud liability).

333 *See, e.g.*, Duckworth v. Nat'l Bank of Commerce, 656 So. 2d 340 (Ala. 1994) (reversing directed verdict for defendant bank in business fraud case; bank that continued to take payments after learning of forgery, but did not disclose the forgery, may have ratified the forger's fraud).

be liable for fraud even without having ever dealt personally with the homeowner. Other parties, such as closing agents, who profit from the fraud may also be liable.[334]

Civil conspiracy is another means of spreading liability for fraud to all those involved in it. Almost all jurisdictions recognize civil conspiracy as a cause of action.[335] The major benefit of a civil conspiracy claim is that the plaintiff does not have to show that all conspirators committed the tort or committed any unlawful act.[336] Instead, civil conspiracy requires an agreement by two or more persons to perform an unlawful act. The plaintiff must also show some overt act that was accomplished in furtherance of the agreement, and must show damages proximately resulting therefrom.

A third basis for casting fraud liability upon subsidiary players is aiding and abetting.[337] Under this theory, a person who knowingly and substantially assists the principal in performing a fraudulent act that causes injury is liable for the principal's fraud. At the time of providing the assistance, the subsidiary player must be generally aware of his or her role as part of an overall tortious activity.[338] In contrast to civil conspiracy, it is not necessary to show an agreement.[339]

334 *See* Knapp v. Vandergon, 2009 WL 161666 (D. Minn. June 5, 2009) (finding issue of fact regarding whether title company could have participated in joint venture with foreclosure consultant); Cain v. Bethea, 2007 WL 2859681 (E.D.N.Y. Aug. 17, 2007) (refusing to dismiss claims against closing agents), *adopted in part and rev'd in part on other grounds* 2007 WL 2846914 (E.D.N.Y. Sept. 26, 2007); Burkons v. Ticor Title Ins. Co., 813 P.2d 710 (Ariz. 1991) (closing agent may be liable for breach of fiduciary duty if it knows of fraud or is aware of evidence of fraud but does not disclose it); Mark Props., Inc. v. Nat'l Title Co., 34 P.3d 587 (Nev. 2001) (real estate escrow agent has duty to disclose fraud to parties with whom it has escrow relationship if it is aware of facts and circumstances that a reasonable escrow agent would perceive as evidence of fraud).

335 *See, e.g.*, Curriden v. Innovative Mortgage Solutions L.L.C. (*In re* Curriden), 2007 WL 2669431 (Bankr. D.N.J. Sept. 6, 2007) (finding civil conspiracy to deprive debtor of the equity in her home); Eicher v. Mid Am. Fin. Inv. Corp., 748 N.W.2d 1 (Neb. 2008) (upholding civil conspiracy judgment against corporation and its employees who engaged in foreclosure rescue scams). *See generally* National Consumer Law Center, Unfair and Deceptive Acts and Practices § 11.5.3.3 (7th ed. 2008 and Supp.).

336 Sahni v. Emerald Mortgage Corp., 2008 WL 5394937, at *6 (Cal. Ct. App. Nov. 19, 2008) (unpublished) (foreclosure rescue scam plaintiff who alleged conspiracy to commit fraud did not have to allege that each conspirator committed a wrongful act).

337 *See, e.g.*, Cain v. Bethea, 2007 WL 2859681 (E.D.N.Y. Aug. 17, 2007), *adopted in part and rev'd in part on other grounds* 2007 WL 2846914 (E.D.N.Y. Sept. 26, 2007); Phifer v. Home Savers Consulting Corp., 2007 WL 295605 (E.D.N.Y. Jan. 30, 2007) (aiding and abetting liability touches everyone who offers substantial assistance in the fraud; lender's preparation of misleading HUD-1 settlement statement that camouflaged distribution of proceeds was substantial assistance).

338 Halberstam v. Welch, 705 F.2d 472 (D.C. Cir. 1983).

339 *Id.*

15.4.8 Other Common Law Claims

15.4.8.1 Introduction

Common law claims such as unconscionability and breach of fiduciary duty or duty of good faith and fair dealing are often useful in attacking foreclosure rescue scams.[340] These claims offer both advantages and disadvantages over the statutory claims discussed in this section.

15.4.8.2 Unconscionability

The doctrine of unconscionability can be useful in attacking foreclosure rescue agreements, especially where the remedies under a state statute are not adequate or where the transaction is not covered by the UDAP statute. The remedy for unconscionability is usually limited to a defense against the enforcement of the unconscionable contract or terms, and does not normally include restitution or the tort damages available for a fraud claim. Except where it is part of a statute that allows affirmative claims, it usually can only be raised defensively, not affirmatively.[341]

There are five sources of the unconscionability doctrine. First, Article 2 of the Uniform Commercial Code (UCC) allows courts to refuse to enforce unconscionable contracts or clauses,[342] and Article 2A has a similar provision applicable to leases.[343] Since Articles 2 and 2A only apply to sales and leases of goods, however, they are unlikely to be applicable to a foreclosure rescue transaction. Second, in about a third of the states the UDAP statute prohibits unconscionable acts or practices.[344] UDAP statutes vary in their scope,[345] but many will be applicable to foreclosure rescue scams. Third, a number of jurisdictions, particularly those that have consumer credit statutes based on the Uniform Consumer Credit Code, have a non-UCC non-UDAP statute that prohibits unconscionability. These statutes are likely to apply to foreclosure rescue scams. Fourth, many state foreclosure rescue statutes contain their own explicit

340 *See, e.g.*, Rowland v. Haven Properties, L.L.C., 2005 WL 1528264 (N.D. Ill. June 24, 2005) (plaintiff involved in sale-leaseback transaction sufficiently alleged claim for rescission on the basis of duress, fraud or unconscionability); *In re* Davis, 169 B.R. 285 (E.D.N.Y. 1994) (finding sale-leaseback transaction unconscionable and void under New York law).

341 *See* National Consumer Law Center, The Cost of Credit: Regulation, Preemption, and Industry Abuses 12.7.5 (4th ed. 2009 and Supp.). *But see* Swayne v. Beebles Invs., Inc., 891 N.E.2d 1216 (Ohio Ct. App. 2008) (holding foreclosure rescue contract unconscionable in affirmative suit by victim).

342 U.C.C. § 2-302.

343 U.C.C. § 2A-108.

344 *See* National Consumer Law Center, Unfair and Deceptive Acts and Practices § 4.4.1 (7th ed. 2008 and Supp.).

345 *See* § 15.4.5.1, *supra*.

prohibition of unconscionable terms.[346] And, finally, a common law unconscionability doctrine is widely recognized and broadly applicable.[347]

There are two forms of unconscionability: procedural and substantive. Procedural unconscionability involves the bargaining process when the contract was made. The most common type of procedural unconscionability involves oppression or surprise in the bargaining process. Oppression occurs when there is a disparity in bargaining power between the parties.[348] Surprise occurs when creditors hide contract terms from the consumer in fine print or unusually complex clauses. Special vulnerabilities often associated with low-income consumers—such as financial distress or limited education—are also relevant in evaluating procedural unconscionability.[349]

Substantive unconscionability focuses on the content of the contract: whether the contract contains terms that are one-sided and unreasonably, unacceptably or unfairly harsh. Some courts require the consumer to show both substantive and procedural unconscionability to invalidate a term of a contract

Many of the aspects of contracts found to be unconscionable apply to foreclosure rescue scams:

- A grossly excessive price;[350]
- Lack of a substantial benefit for the consumer;[351]
- No reasonable probability of payment in full by the consumer;[352]
- Misleading the consumer into accepting false assurances.[353]

For example, in one case a federal court found enough merit in a homeowner's unconscionability claim to issue a preliminary injunction against a rescuer who lured her into a sale-reconveyance transaction.[354] The court found that the homeowner was not aware of the terms of the reconveyance contract until closing, and even then did not fully comprehend its one-sided nature and the almost certain outcome of the transaction—default and eviction. The reconveyance contract required the homeowner to pay thousands of dollars to the rescuer in unspecified management and yield spread fees; charged her more than triple the actual closing costs; required a $26,000 down payment that she had no ability to make; set her monthly payments at an amount significantly higher than they had been, yet with an interest rate so high that the balance would negatively amortize; imposed prepayment penalties and other terms that would keep her from refinancing or selling the home; and allowed the rescuer to retain all her payments if she defaulted.

In the absence of legislatively prescribed usury ceilings, unconscionability can serve as an outer limit on the price of credit. Even in states where interest rate caps have been removed, courts or sometimes regulators have found excessive rates to be unconscionable, particularly where it can be shown that the borrowers had little choice of credit options.[355]

15.4.8.3 Breach of Duty of Good Faith and Fair Dealing

The duty of good faith and fair dealing between parties to a contract is based both in common law and the UCC.[356] Unlike unconscionability, which is ordinarily determined by looking at contract terms at the time the contract was made, the duty of good faith is imposed on parties to an existing contract. It prevents overreaching in the later stages of the relationship "to prohibit improper behavior in the performance and enforcement" of that contract.[357]

346 *See* § 4.9.4, *supra*.

347 *See generally* National Consumer Law Center, The Cost of Credit: Regulation, Preemption, and Industry Abuses 12.7 (4th ed. 2009 and Supp.).

348 *See, e.g.*, Swayne v. Beebles Invs., Inc., 891 N.E.2d 1216 (Ohio Ct. App. 2008) (loan agreement and later sale-leaseback were procedurally unconscionable in light of great disparity between parties in their knowledge and sophistication).

349 *See* Davis v. Suderov (*In re* Davis), 169 B.R. 285 (E.D.N.Y. 1994) (exceedingly one-sided sale-leaseback agreement was unconscionable where the consumers did not understand it and were under time pressure yet were locked into agreement by having made advance payments to the other party, who was a sophisticated real estate operator); Howard v. Diolosa, 574 A.2d 995 (N.J. Super. Ct. App. Div. 1990) (court refused to enforce sale-leaseback agreement made by desperate homeowners for the sale of a home likely worth over $100,000 for only $25,000.). *See also* Westlake v. Osborne, 713 P.2d 548 (Mont. 1986) (evidence of oppression and unfair surprise required to set aside sale-leaseback agreement, inadequate consideration insufficient basis to set aside contract).

350 *See, e.g.*, Swayne v. Beebles Invs., Inc., 891 N.E.2d 1216 (Ohio Ct. App. 2008) (loan agreement substantively unconscionable where 31% of loan proceeds were allocated to closing costs and fees, and stated APR was 41%; sale-leaseback one year later also unconscionable).

351 *Cf.* Swayne v. Beebles Invs. Inc., 891 N.E.2d 1216 (Ohio Ct. App. 2008) (citing victim's known inability to make required balloon payment as evidence of substantive unconscionability).

352 *See, e.g.*, Swayne v. Beebles Invs., Inc., 891 N.E.2d 1216 (Ohio Ct. App. 2008) (citing victim's known inability to make required balloon payment as evidence of substantive unconscionability).

353 *See generally* National Consumer Law Center, Unfair and Deceptive Acts and Practices § 4.4 (7th ed. 2008 and Supp.); National Consumer Law Center, The Cost of Credit: Regulation, Preemption, and Industry Abuses § 12.7 (4th ed. 2009 and Supp.).

354 Brantley v. Grant Holding, L.L.C., Civil No. 03-6098 (D. Minn. Dec. 23, 2003), *available at* www.consumerlaw.org/unreported.

355 National Consumer Law Center, The Cost of Credit: Regulation, Preemption, and Industry Abuses §§ 11.8.2.4–11.8.8.3 (4th ed. 2009 and Supp.).

356 *Id.* § 11.8.

357 Baldwin v. Laurel Ford Lincoln-Mercury, Inc., 32 F. Supp. 2d 894 (S.D. Miss. 1998); National Consumer Law Center, The Cost of Credit: Regulation, Preemption, and Industry Abuses § 12.8 (4th ed. 2009 and Supp.).

For example, when a rescuer has induced a homeowner into a transaction with a balloon payment with the assurance that refinancing will be available, the refinancing decision may be subject to the duty of good faith and fair dealing.[358] The rescuer may also be bound by this duty when declaring a default on the lease or leaseback agreement.

Breach of this duty constitutes a breach of the contract. Contract remedies, therefore, apply. Some states have held that this duty gives rise to a tort claim as well.[359]

15.4.8.4 Breach of Fiduciary Duty

The existence of a fiduciary or quasi-fiduciary duty gives rise to a duty of fair and honest disclosure of all facts that might influence the consumer's decisions. Fiduciary relationships may be express or implied. An implied duty can arise where the weaker party places trust and confidence in another, who is aware of this trust and takes on the role of advisor.

Breach of a fiduciary duty by failing to disclose all relevant information gives rise to a tort action, which may permit repudiation of the contract as well as damages.[360]

In one case in Ohio, it was the mortgage broker who instigated and perpetrated the foreclosure rescue scam. The court specifically held that with their greater bargaining power, superior business acumen, as well as the circumstances surrounding the transaction, the mortgage brokers in the case had a fiduciary duty to the homeowner.[361] A claim for breach of fiduciary duty has been stated against a real estate agent who arranged a rescue transaction.[362] Another court found the rescuer, a reverend who used a power of attorney to transfer the property first to the church and then to an entity he owned, had a fiduciary duty to the homeowner; under New York law, a power of attorney creates a fiduciary relationship between principal and attorney-in-fact.[363] An attorney who purports to represent the homeowners but is actually complicit in the scam and fails to protect the homeowners' interests violates a fiduciary duty.[364]

Mortgage brokers (including unlicensed individuals performing that role) and real estate agents are often involved in foreclosure rescue scams. These parties may owe a fiduciary duty to the homeowner under state law.[365] Title agents who close foreclosure rescue scam transactions may have a fiduciary duty to disclose fraud to the parties.[366] This duty arises regardless of whether the closing agent has positive proof of the fraud. A closing agent may not "close its eyes in the face of known facts" when it is aware of facts and circumstances that a reasonable closing agent would perceive as evidence of fraud.[367]

15.4.8.5 Intentional Infliction of Emotional Distress

The elements of the tort of intentional infliction of emotional distress are: (1) extreme and outrageous conduct by the defendant with the intention of causing, or reckless disregard of the probability of causing, emotional distress; (2) the plaintiff's suffering severe or extreme emotional distress; and (3) actual and proximate causation.[368] A California court reversed the dismissal of a homeowner's claim for intentional infliction of emotional distress against foreclosure rescuers.[369] The court held that the plaintiff's allegations that the defendants sought her out when she faced foreclosure, promised to help save her home, and ultimately took both her home and her equity, adequately alleged extreme and outrageous conduct.

358 *See* National Consumer Law Center, The Cost of Credit: Regulation, Preemption, and Industry Abuses § 12.8 (4th ed. 2009 and Supp.).

359 *Id.*

360 *See generally* National Consumer Law Center, The Cost of Credit: Regulation, Preemption, and Industry Abuses § 12.9 (4th ed. 2009 and Supp.).

361 Swayne v. Beebles Invs., Inc., 05 CVC-04-4327 (Ohio C.P. Franklin County Nov. 6, 2006), *available at* www.consumerlaw.org/unreported. *But cf.* Clemons v. Home Savers, L.L.C., 2007 WL 2815213 (E.D. Va. Sept. 21, 2007) (rescuer did not owe fiduciary duty to homeowner under Virginia law where there was no special relationship and duties arose solely from contract).

362 *See* Johnson v. Wheeler, 492 F. Supp. 2d (D. Md. 2007).

363 *In re* West, 339 B.R. 557 (Bankr. E.D.N.Y. 2006).

364 Watson v. Melnikoff, 866 N.Y.S.2d 96 (N.Y. Sup. Ct. May 6, 2008) (table).

365 Sahni v. Emerald Mortgage Corp., 2008 WL 5394937 (Cal. Ct. App. Nov. 19, 2008) (unpublished) (complaint adequately alleged that parties who acted as homeowner's mortgage broker and real estate agent breached fiduciary duties, but home buyer did not owe plaintiff a fiduciary duty even though he was a real estate broker, as homeowner was not his client).

366 Burkons v. Ticor Title Ins. Co., 813 P.2d 710 (Ariz. 1991) (reversing judgment for closing agent in real estate loan swindle). *See also* Sahni v. Emerald Mortgage Corp., 2008 WL 5394937, at *10 (Cal. Ct. App. Nov. 19, 2008) (unpublished) (reversing dismissal of complaint; escrow agent owed fiduciary duty to homeowner); Mark Props., Inc. v. Nat'l Title Co., 34 P.3d 587 (Nev. 2001) (real estate escrow agent has duty to disclose fraud to parties with whom it has escrow relationship if it is aware of facts and circumstances that a reasonable escrow agent would perceive as evidence of fraud).

367 Burkons v. Ticor Title Ins. Co., 813 P.2d 710, 718 (Ariz. 1991).

368 Sahni v. Emerald Mortgage Corp., 2008 WL 5394937, at *10 (Cal. Ct. App. Nov. 19, 2008) (unpublished). *See generally* National Consumer Law Center, Fair Debt Collection § 10.2 (6th ed. 2008 and Supp.).

369 Sahni v. Emerald Mortgage Corp., 2008 WL 5394937, at *9–10 (Cal. Ct. App. Nov. 19, 2008) (unpublished). *See* Madlock v. Farmers State Bank, 696 S.W.2d 873 (Mo. Ct. App. 1985) (no recovery for emotional distress from attempted wrongful foreclosure without evidence of bad faith, "malice, willfulness, wantonness, or inhumanity").

15.4.8.6 Other Common Law Claims

Courts have also upheld a claim for conversion against a defendant for exercising unauthorized dominion over the plaintiff's personal property (the proceeds of the sale).[370] Unjust enrichment is another potential claim to force the rescuer to disgorge the proceeds of the sale of the home.[371]

15.4.9 State Credit and Usury Laws

15.4.9.1 State Usury Laws and Their Penalties

Once a transaction is restructured as a loan, state credit and usury laws may apply.[372] State general credit laws may apply even if the state rejects the equitable mortgage doctrine and will not deem the deed to be a mortgage.[373] Moreover, even in states that do not have a usury cap, the transaction may violate laws specifying the form of disclosures for credit.[374] Most states have several different usury statutes.[375] The oldest of these laws are the so-called "general" usury statutes, which purport to set the maximum rate of interest that can be charged in any loan transaction in a jurisdiction. More recent statutes are generally structured as exceptions to the general law and apply only to particular types of transactions. Credit secured by real estate may be separately regulated, and first and junior mortgages may be treated differently. The statutes may also base distinctions on the type of lender, i.e., whether it is a bank, credit union, licensed finance company, or other lender. Thus, it is important to determine which statute applies. Some states have, however, repealed many of their usury ceilings and now allow any interest rate agreed upon by the parties.

After determining which, if any, state usury law applies, the next step is to calculate the actual interest charged. Since foreclosure rescue transactions are typically so one-sided in favor of the rescuer, it is likely that, if the transaction can be characterized as a loan, it will run afoul of any applicable usury statute. The definition of interest is sometimes a complicated issue because it varies from statute to statute, however, so the practitioner will need to be prepared to prove what the interest rate is.

In the case of a foreclosure rescue scam, one way to calculate the interest rate is to treat the amount actually expended by the rescuer as the loan principal. This figure would include amounts the rescuer paid to reinstate or pay off a delinquent mortgage or to pay other charges that relate to the home, such as homeowner's property taxes or insurance premiums. The dollar amount of interest would be calculated as the difference between this figure and the total of all payments the consumer would have to pay to reacquire the home.[376] (State law may, however, allow the lender to collect certain types of fees, such as document preparation fees, and treat them as part of the principal rather than as interest.)

The next step is to convert the dollar amount of interest to a percentage rate. A calculation tool, such as the credit math software included on the companion website to this treatise, should be used for this calculation. Since the typical sale-leaseback requires a large balloon payment after a series of smaller monthly payments, it is important to use a calculation tool that can handle an irregular payment schedule.

---

370 *See* Johnson v. Home Savers Consulting Corp., 2007 WL 925518 (E.D.N.Y. Mar. 23, 2007), *report and recommendation adopted by* 2007 WL 1110612 (E.D.N.Y. Apr. 11, 2007). *But see* Clemons v. Home Savers, L.L.C., 530 F. Supp. 2d 803 (E.D. Va. 2008) (conversion does not apply to theft of money or real property), *aff'd*, 273 Fed. Appx. 296 (2008)(per curiam).

371 Griffith v. Barnes, 560 F. Supp. 2d 29 (D.D.C. 2008) (ordering disgorgement of profits earned by rescuer's sale of residence). *But see* Clemons v. Home Savers, L.L.C., 530 F. Supp. 2d 803 (E.D. Va. 2008) (denying unjust enrichment claim in foreclosure rescue transaction; unjust enrichment does not lie where a contract governs the relationship of the parties), *aff'd mem.*, 273 Fed. Appx. 296 (4th Cir. 2008).

372 McKeeman v. Commercial Credit Equip. Corp., 320 F. Supp. 938 (D. Neb. 1970); Moran v. Kenai Towing and Salvage, Inc., 523 P.2d 1237 (Ala. 1974). *See, e.g.,* McElroy v. Grisham, 810 S.W.2d 933 (Ark. 1991) (sale of property with repurchase option was disguised loan subject to state usury laws). *But see* Holden v. Salvadore, 964 A.2d 508 (R.I. 2009) (finding transaction not a loan under unusual facts: homeowner who had lost home to foreclosure but made winning bid at foreclosure sale assigned her rights under that bid to third party, who believed she was trying to find a buyer and that they would split the sale proceeds). *Cf.* Moore v. Cycon Enters., Inc., 2006 WL 2375477 (W.D. Mich. Aug. 16, 2006); *In re* Comtois, 363 B.R. 336 (Bankr. D.N.H. 2007). *But see* Southwell v. Middleton, 851 N.Y.S.2d 74 (N.Y. Sup. Ct. 2007) (unpublished) (repurchase agreement not considered interest because more akin to a prepayment penalty). *See generally* National Consumer Law Center, The Cost of Credit: Regulation, Preemption, and Industry Abuses §§ 7.5, 9.2.1.4 (4th ed. 2009 and Supp.).

373 *See In re* Comtois, 363 B.R. 336 (Bankr. D.N.H. 2007).

374 *See In re* Comtois, 363 B.R. 336 (Bankr. D.N.H. 2007) (discussing N.H. Rev. Stat. Ann. § 479).

375 A state-by-state list of usury statutes may be found in National Consumer Law Center, The Cost of Credit: Regulation, Preemption, and Industry Abuses Appx. A (4th ed. 2009 and Supp.).

376 *See* Eyler v. 3 Vista Court L.L.C. (*In re* Eyler), 2008 WL 4833096 (Bankr. D. Md. Oct. 28, 2008) (proposed findings of fact and conclusions of law) (foreclosure rescue transaction was usurious loan where it allowed repurchase by Aug. 9, 2005 by payment of $45,000 in addition to the $15,341.32 that rescuer advanced on July 8, 2005, creating an interest rate over 3000%); McElroy v. Grisham, 810 S.W.2d 933 (Ark. 1991) (where owner conveyed property to rescuer for $80,000, with option to repurchase it two years later for $120,000, $40,000 was interest); River Run Props. L.L.C. v. Kappedahl, File No. C2-03-10463, slip op. at 33–35 (Minn. Dist. Ct. July 12, 2004), *available at* www.consumerlaw.org/unreported (principal is amount that rescuer actually paid on existing first mortgage; usury calculation should be based on the difference between the principal and the total of the payments required to reacquire the home).

An example will illustrate this method of calculation.[377] Assume that the homeowner fell behind on the mortgage and was $10,000 in arrears, leaving a balance due (including late charges, other charges, and pre-foreclosure costs) of $190,000. A rescuer might pay off this $190,000 balance, and lease the home back to the homeowner at $2500 per month, with an option to repurchase the home at the end of a year for $225,000.[378] The homeowner is thus obligated to pay $232,200 to the rescuer in return for the rescuer's extension of credit in the amount of $190,000. The annual percentage rate for this loan with this payment schedule is 29.39%.[379]

State usury laws often limit other terms besides interest rates. For example, the usury law may limit points or prohibit balloon payments.[380]

If the case goes to trial, it may be necessary to have an expert witness testify about the effective rate of interest.[381] It should also be noted that the definition of the components of the interest rate in state usury laws may differ from the TIL definition of the components of the finance charge, so state law should be carefully reviewed when calculating the interest rate.

The remedies for usury are determined by individual state statutes.[382] Often the loan will be void as to all or part of the interest, with even double or triple damages, while leaving the principal obligation intact. Some statutes declare usurious loans to be completely void, and may require the return of all monies paid.[383] Equitable remedies, such as enjoining a foreclosure, may also be available.

377 This is the same example as appears at § 15.4.3.1.2, *supra*, as an illustration of the calculation of the HOEPA trigger. However, the interest rate for purposes of a state usury statute and the APR for purposes of TILA are not always the same because of different definitions and exclusions.

378 This is a somewhat simplified version of the transaction described in Moore v. Cycon Enters., Inc., 2006 WL 2375477 (E.D. Mich. Aug. 16, 2006), *later op. at* 2007 WL 475202 (W.D. Mich. Feb. 9, 2007).

379 The APR was calculated using the Irregular Payment tab on the NCLC APR Program included on this treatise's companion website by inserting $190,000 in the "amount financed" box, $255,000 in the "total of payments" box, defining "payment group 1" as having twelve payments of $2500 and clicking "Add Group," defining "payment group 2" as having one payment of $225,000 and clicking "Add Group," and then clicking the "Estimate APR" button.

380 *See, e.g.*, Swayne v. Beebles Invs., Inc., 891 N.E.2d 1216 (Ohio Ct. App. 2008) (rescuer violated state mortgage broker law by arranging a loan with a balloon payment where the loan term was less than five years).

381 For example in Browner v. District of Columbia, 549 A.2d 1107, 1111 (D.C. 1988), the court accepted expert testimony that the sale-leaseback transactions at issue carried effective interest rates of 50% to 200%.

382 *See* § 5.13.5, *supra*.

383 *See, e.g.*, *id.* (voiding the transaction and eliminating rescuer's entitlement to both interest and principal; foreclosure rescue transaction was a usurious loan).

15.4.9.2 Federal Preemption

15.4.9.2.1 Introduction

Before concluding that a rescuer has violated a state usury statute, an essential step is to determine whether the state law has been preempted by federal law. Even though rescuers are typically individuals rather than lending institutions, two of the federal usury preemption laws—the Depository Institutions Deregulation and Monetary Control Act (DIDA) and the Alternative Mortgage Transactions Parity Act (AMTPA)—may apply to them.

15.4.9.2.2 DIDA

The first statute, the Depository Institutions Deregulation and Monetary Control Act (DIDA), covers not only a variety of financial institutions but also any creditor who makes or invests in residential real estate loans or manufactured home credit sales in excess of $1 million per year.[384] Some foreclosure rescuers may meet the $1 million threshold. Only the principal amount of the loan (as determined by the court after finding that the transaction is indeed a loan) should be counted toward the $1 million threshold, however. Thus, if a rescuer pays off a $80,000 mortgage loan, and requires the homeowner to repay $200,000 to reacquire the home, only the $80,000 principal should count toward the $1 million threshold.

To qualify for DIDA preemption, the transaction must involve a *first* lien on residential real property.[385] The lien need not be a *purchase money* lien, however. A rescuer who actually pays off all existing liens on the property (and thus in effect holds a new first lien on the home) may meet this requirement. However, many rescuers pay off only some of the existing liens, pay only the delinquent amount rather than the full debt, or acquire the property subject to all existing liens. In all of these situations, DIDA will not preempt state laws, because the rescuer's lien is junior to these others, and thus is not a first lien.

If DIDA applies, it preempts state laws that limit "the rate or amount of interest, discount points, finance charges, or other charges" on the loan.[386] DIDA does not preempt other consumer protections that may be found in state usury laws, such as restrictions on late charges, balloon payments, and negative amortization.

States have the right to opt out of DIDA preemption, and many have done so, at least in part. Specifically, Colorado, Georgia, Hawaii, Idaho, Iowa, Kansas, Maine, Massachusetts, Minnesota, Nebraska, Nevada, North Carolina, Puerto Rico, South Carolina, and South Dakota have expressly reimposed all or part of their state usury laws.[387]

384 12 U.S.C. § 1735f-5(b).

385 12 U.S.C. § 1735f-7a.

386 *Id.*

387 National Consumer Law Center, The Cost of Credit: Regula-

15.4.9.2.3 AMTPA

The second statute, the Alternative Mortgage Transactions Parity Act (AMTPA), does not affect state interest ceilings on mortgage loans. Instead, it addresses the *structure* of mortgage loans by overriding certain state laws which restrict "creative finance," e.g., laws limiting variable interest rates and balloon payments. These state statutes are replaced, at the option of the lender, by federal regulations. Six states—Arizona, Maine, Massachusetts, New York, South Carolina, and Wisconsin—opted out of AMTPA, so this statute is irrelevant in those states.

AMTPA applies to "housing creditors," which is broadly defined to include any person who regularly makes loans, credit sales, or advances secured by interests in residential real property or a manufactured home.[388] It also includes any transferee of such a lender.[389] AMTPA only applies to these creditors when they are making an "alternative mortgage transaction," defined as one:

- In which the finance charge or interest rate may be adjusted or renegotiated;
- With a balloon payment or a similar structure;
- With any similar type of rate, method of determining return, term, repayment, or other variation not common to traditional fixed rate, fixed term transactions (for example, loans that negatively amortize).[390]

As noted at § 15.4.2.2, *supra*, to bring a rescuer under the Truth in Lending Act it is necessary to show that the rescuer regularly engages in consumer credit transactions. Since AMTPA is applicable only to lenders who "regularly" make home-secured credit transactions, the same evidence that shows that TILA applies will also tend to show that AMTPA preemption is applicable. However, since TILA includes a specific numerical definition of "regularly" and AMTPA does not, it is possible that a court would find that a rescuer met the TIL definition but was not a "housing creditor" for AMTPA purposes.

Assuming that AMTPA applies, the rescuer need not comply with state law, but must comply with federal regulations governing:

- Adjustments to the interest rate, the payment, the balance, or the loan term during the course of the loan.[391] The federal regulations allow adjustments, but require certain safeguards such as use of a readily available and independently verifiable index for interest rate adjustments.[392]
- Disclosures.[393]

The AMTPA regulations formerly preempted state limits on prepayment penalties and late charges for housing creditors, but as of July 1, 2003, they were revised to eliminate this preemption.[394] AMTPA does *not* preempt state licensing laws,[395] state restrictions on attorney fees that the holder can collect in the event of default,[396] or state restrictions on deceptive advertising and practices.[397]

15.4.9.3 Choice of Law Clauses

Another way that a rescuer may try to avoid state credit and usury laws is by purporting to operate under the laws of another state.[398] The rescuer might, for example, insert a clause in the documents the homeowner signs, stating that the transaction will be governed by the laws of some state that imposes few restrictions. Choice of law rules vary from state to state, but such a clause is unlikely to be given effect if the chosen state does not have a substantial relationship to the transaction. Nor will the clause be given effect if the result would be contrary to a fundamental policy of the state with the most significant relation to the transaction. Since rescuers tend to be local entrepreneurs, they are unlikely to be successful in arguing that the transaction has a substantial relationship to any state other than the one where the homeowner lives.

15.4.9.4 Licensing Provisions of State Usury Laws

In addition to interest rate caps, state usury laws may have lender licensing requirements that the rescuer has violated. States typically require a lender other than a bank or credit union to obtain a state license if it wishes to charge more than the legal rate of interest permitted by the general usury statute. The special usury statutes that govern these licensed creditors usually specify the permissible terms of individual credit transactions and include significant penalties for creditors who either fail to obtain a required license or violate their licenses by ignoring statutory consumer protections. Since obtaining the requisite license may be a

tion, Preemption, and Industry Abuses § 3.10.4.1 (4th ed. 2009 and Supp.).

388 12 U.S.C. § 3802(2)(C).

389 12 U.S.C. § 3802(2)(D).

390 12 U.S.C. § 3802(1).

391 12 C.F.R. § 560.220.

392 12 C.F.R. § 560.35.

393 12 C.F.R. § 560.210.

394 12 C.F.R. § 560.220; 67 Fed. Reg. 60,542 (Sept. 26, 2002). *See* National Consumer Law Center, The Cost of Credit: Regulation, Preemption, and Industry Abuses § 3.11.2 (4th ed. 2009 and Supp.).

395 12 U.S.C. § 3802(2).

396 *In re* Jones, 2000 Bankr. LEXIS 1741 (Bankr. E.D.N.C. Dec. 22, 2000).

397 Black v. Fin. Freedom Senior Funding Corp., 112 Cal. Rptr. 2d 445 (Cal. Ct. App. 2001).

398 The effect of choice of law clauses on usury claims is discussed in detail in National Consumer Law Center, The Cost of Credit: Regulation, Preemption, and Industry Abuses § 9.2.9 (4th ed. 2009 and Supp.).

precondition to lending under some special usury statutes, failure to do so may give rise to a usury claim under the statute. Once the transaction has been restructured as an equitable mortgage,[399] the buyer—now deemed a mortgagee—may have also violated state laws regarding licensing of mortgage lenders.[400]

The effects of failure to obtain a proper license vary. Many licensing statutes clearly specify the result of failure to obtain a required license. Sometimes the specified result is to void the transaction in which the unlicensed lender has participated. This is the case with many small loan acts. Other states may provide lesser penalties. Operating without a required license is also a UDAP violation in many states.[401]

Transactions with lenders who are not licensed, but should be, may be void even in the absence of a special statutory provision to that effect. The common law principle that contracts made in violation of regulatory statutes enacted for the protection of the public are rendered null and unenforceable has been applied where creditors failed to comply with appropriate licensing requirements.[402] This general rule applies to licensing statutes enacted for the protection of the public, rather than those enacted merely to raise revenue. Special usury licensing statutes are clearly in the former category, as they are designed to protect borrowers through the strict regulation and supervision of the creditors themselves.

15.4.10 Other State Statutes

15.4.10.1 Introduction

State door-to-door sales laws and state credit repair or credit services laws may provide additional grounds to cancel foreclosure rescue transactions. In some states these laws, especially the credit repair or credit services laws, provide attractive causes of action. One advantage of these laws is that, unlike the Truth in Lending Act, they may not depend on the rescuer's having engaged in a certain number of prior transactions. Since these are state law claims, they also are useful if the consumer prefers to litigate in state court. The statute of limitations may also be longer than for other claims.

One disadvantage of these statutes is that they lack the detailed provisions for unwinding real estate transactions that the Truth in Lending Act provides. These statutes are also less clear as to how they apply to assignees.

15.4.10.2 Door-to-Door Sales Laws

Every state has a door-to-door sales law that gives consumers a right to cancel at least certain types of contracts that are solicited outside the seller's fixed place of business.[403] The typical state statute provides a three-day right to cancel the transaction, and requires the seller to give the consumer notice of this right. A Federal Trade Commission rule also provides a right to cancel sales of goods or services where the seller personally solicits the sale and the buyer's agreement or offer to purchase is made at a place other than the seller's place of business.[404]

Many foreclosure rescue transactions will be subject to the FTC rule or the state law. Foreclosure rescue scams

399 *See* § 15.4.1.2, *supra*.

400 *But see In re* Comtois, 363 B.R. 336 (Bankr. D.N.H. 2007) (since transaction was not a mortgage under New Hampshire statute effectively eliminating the equitable mortgage doctrine, even though it was a loan, buyer/lender did not violate mortgage lender licensing law).

401 National Consumer Law Center, Unfair and Deceptive Acts and Practices § 5.4.8.2 (7th ed. 2008 and Supp.). *See* Susan Martin, *Second Jury Finds Fault with Controversial Foreclosure Rescue Deals*, St. Petersburg Times, Feb. 13, 2010 available at www.tampabay.com/news/courts/civil/second-jury-finds-fault-with-controversial-foreclosure-rescue-deals/1072978# (jury verdict voiding foreclosure rescue sale involving unlicensed real estate broker).

402 National Consumer Law Center, The Cost of Credit: Regulation, Preemption, and Industry Abuses § 10.8.4 (4th ed. 2009 and Supp.).

403 Ala. Code §§ 5-19-1(8), 5-19-12; Alaska Stat. §§ 45.02.350 (door-to-door sales; five-day period), 45.63.030 (telephonic solicitations; seven-day period); Ariz. Rev. Stat. Ann. §§ 44-5001 to 44-5008; Ark. Stat. Ann. §§ 4-89-101 to 4-89-110; Cal. Civ. Code §§ 1689.5 to 1689.14; Colo. Rev. Stat. §§ 5-3-401 to 5-3-405; Conn. Gen. Stat. Ann. §§ 42-134a to 42-143; Del. Code Ann. tit 6, §§ 4401 to 4405; D.C. Code Ann. § 28-3811; Fla. Stat. Ann. §§ 501.021 to 501.055; Ga. Code Ann. § 10-1-6; Haw. Rev. Stat. §§ 481C-1 to 481C-6; Idaho Code §§ 28-43-401 to 28-43-405; 815 Ill. Comp. Stat. Ann. § 505/2B; Ind. Code Ann. §§ 24-4.4-2-501 to 24-4.4-2-502, §§ 24-5-10-1 to 24-5-10-18; Iowa Code Ann. §§ 555A.1 to 555A.6; Kan. Stat. Ann. § 50-640; Ky. Rev. Stat. Ann. §§ 367.410 to 367.460; La. Rev. Stat. Ann. §§ 9:3538 to 9:3541; Me. Rev. Stat. Ann. tit. 32, §§ 4661 to 4670 and tit. 9-A, §§ 3-501 to 3-507; Md. Code Ann., Com. Law §§ 14-301 to 14-306; Mass. Gen. Laws Ann. ch. 93, § 48; Mich. Comp. Laws Ann. §§ 445.111 to 445.117; Minn. Stat. Ann. §§ 325G.06 to 325G.11; Miss. Code Ann. §§ 75-66-1 to 75-66-11; Mo. Rev. Stat. §§ 407.700 to 407.720; Mont. Code Ann. §§ 30-14-501 to 30-14-508; Neb. Rev. Stat. §§ 69-1601 to 69-1607; Nev. Rev. Stat. §§ 598.140 to 598.280 and 598.2801; N.H. Rev. Stat. Ann. §§ 361-B:1 to 361-B:3; N.J. Rev. Stat. Ann. §§ 17:16C-61.1 to 17:16C-61.9; N.M. Stat. Ann. § 57-12-21; N.Y. Pers. Prop. Law §§ 425 to 431; N.C. Gen. Stat. §§ 25A-38 to 25A-42; N.D. Cent. Code §§ 51-18-01 to 51-18-09; Ohio Rev. Code Ann. §§ 1345.21 to 1345.28; Okla. Stat. Ann. tit. 14A, §§ 2-501 to 2-505; Or. Rev. Stat. §§ 83.710 to 83.750; Pa. Stat. Ann. tit. 73, § 201-7; R.I. Gen. Laws §§ 6-28-1 to 6-28-8; S.C. Code Ann. §§ 37-2-501 to 37-2-506; S.D. Comp. Laws Ann. §§ 37-24-5.1 to 37-24-5.7; Tenn. Code Ann. §§ 47-18-701 to 47-18-708; Tex. Bus. & Com. Code Ann. §§ 39.001 to 39.009; Utah Code Ann. §§ 70C-5-101 to 70C-1-105; Vt. Stat. Ann. tit. 9, §§ 2451a, 2454; Va. Code Ann. §§ 59.1-21.1 to 59.1-21.7:1; Wash. Rev. Code Ann. §§ 63.14.040, 63.14.120, 63.14.150, 63.14.154; W. Va. Code §§ 46A-2-132 to 46A-2-135; Wis. Stat. Ann. §§ 423.201 to 423.205; Wyo. Stat. §§ 40-12-104, 40-14-251 to 40-14-255.

404 16 C.F.R. § 429.0(a).

often involve solicitations at the consumer's home, so this element of coverage is satisfied. The services the rescuer is offering must also fall within the state statute or the federal rule. The rescuer is likely to argue that the transaction involved real estate rather than goods or services. Showing that the rescuer promised advice and other efforts that would save the home may establish that the transaction was a mixed transaction that involved not just real estate but also covered services. (Arguing that the transaction involved *only* services, not real estate, may be counterproductive if the homeowner is asserting an equitable mortgage or TIL rescission claim.) Home solicitation sales laws may also be helpful in cases where the rescuer did not acquire the home, but provided advice, referrals, a bankruptcy filing, or similar services.[405]

If the FTC rule or the state statute covers the transaction, but (as is likely) the rescuer failed to give the consumer notice of the right to cancel, a number of decisions hold that the consumer has a continuing right to cancel.[406] At an early stage, after investigating coverage and reviewing the documents, the homeowner's attorney should consider sending the rescuer a notice invoking this right to cancel. The FTC rule requires the seller to honor the buyer's notice of cancellation, and, within ten business days, refund all payments made, return all property traded in, cancel and return any negotiable instruments, and terminate any security interest.[407] While this list of specific steps does not mention voiding of a deed, that step would be encompassed by the requirement to terminate the security interest if the transaction is viewed as a loan.[408]

If the state home solicitation law does not create its own private cause of action, a violation may be actionable under the state UDAP statute. Even without explicit language in the statute, in many states a violation of another consumer protection statute is a per se UDAP violation.[409] There is no private cause of action under the FTC Act to enforce an FTC rule, but in most states violations will also be UDAP violations.[410] In addition, if a statute or the FTC rule affords a right to cancel that the rescuer refuses to recognize, the right to cancel can probably be enforced through a cancellation action in equity or through a declaratory judgment action.[411]

405 *See* § 15.2.1, *supra*.

406 *See* National Consumer Law Center, Unfair and Deceptive Acts and Practices § 9.8.2.6.3 (7th ed. 2008 and Supp.).

407 16 C.F.R. § 429.1(g).

408 *See* § 15.4.1, *supra*.

409 National Consumer Law Center, Unfair and Deceptive Acts and Practices § 3.2.7 (7th ed. 2008 and Supp.).

410 *Id.* §§ 3.2.7, 14.1.

411 *Id.* § 9.8.2.7.

15.4.10.3 State Credit Services or Credit Repair Organization Laws

About three-fourths of the states have credit services or credit repair organization laws.[412] These laws cover organizations that offer to improve a person's credit rating for a fee. Most also cover organizations that offer, for a fee, to obtain an extension of credit for a consumer and that are not licensed or chartered by the state or federal government.[413]

A rescuer who claims to be able to arrange an extension of credit that will enable the consumer to save the home may be covered by the state credit services statute. The key question will be whether the rescuer falls within any of the exceptions set forth in the statute, which usually include licensed real estate agents and attorneys as well as banks, credit unions, and other licensed lenders.

The typical credit repair statute gives the consumer a three- to five-day right to cancel the contract, and requires the organization to give the consumer notice of this right. Many prohibit various deceptive and unfair practices and regulate the terms of the contract.

The breadth of remedies offered by state credit services or credit repair organization laws is their chief advantage. First is the right to cancel. If the rescuer did not give the consumer the required notice of this right, the practitioner should argue that the right to cancel continues indefinitely.[414] The statute may also provide that the consumer's contract with the rescuer is void if the rescuer did not comply with the statute.

The typical statute provides a private cause of action for actual damages, often with a minimum recovery set at the amount paid by the consumer. The measure of actual damages is generally left undefined in these statutes, but could include the value of the equity in the home that the homeowner lost if a causal connection can be established between

412 *See* National Consumer Law Center, Fair Credit Reporting § 3.3 (6th ed. 2006 and Supp.) (state-by-state summaries of state credit repair organization laws).

413 The Arizona, Arkansas, California, Delaware, District of Columbia, Florida, Illinois, Indiana, Kansas, Maryland, Massachusetts, Minnesota, Missouri, Nebraska, Nevada, New Hampshire, North Carolina, Ohio, Oklahoma, Oregon, Pennsylvania, Tennessee, Texas, Utah, Virginia, Washington, West Virginia, and Wisconsin credit services statutes cover entities that offer to obtain extensions of credit for consumers, require a right to cancel, and afford the consumer a private cause of action. Georgia's statute covers entities that offer to obtain extensions of credit but the statute does not afford a right to cancel or a private cause of action. Statutes in Maine and Michigan cover entities that offer to obtain extensions of credit and provide a private right of action but do not require a right to cancel. The Michigan and Washington statutes explicitly include rescuers in the definitions and are discussed at § 15.4.6, *supra*.

414 *See* National Consumer Law Center, Unfair and Deceptive Acts and Practices § 9.8.2.6.3 (7th ed. 2008 and Supp.) (collecting cases holding that consumer has continuing right to cancel under state home solicitation sales statutes if seller fails to give proper notice of right to cancel).

that loss and the violation of the statute. Most authorize punitive damages and attorney fees, and some explicitly provide for injunctive relief.

Many of these statutes explicitly apply their prohibitions not only to the organization itself, but also to its agents and representatives, including independent contractors. Courts have differed on the question whether a claim under the state credit services organization law can be asserted against other entities that are working in tandem with the credit services organization. One decision finds that a lender who prepared a broker agreement for a mortgage broker, and then funded the loan, violated the state credit repair law even though only the broker met the statutory definition of credit services organization.[415] But another decision from the same district holds that others who participate in the scheme with a credit repair organization but do not themselves meet the statutory definition are not subject to the statute.[416]

15.4.11 State Real Estate Requirements

15.4.11.1 Formal Requirements for Deeds

The homeowner's attorney should also check the details of the state's formal requirements for deeds and real estate transactions, since rescuers often cut corners. The deed may be invalid if it is challenged on formal grounds, but there may be a very short deadline for this type of challenge. Showing that the deed is invalid may be the only sure-fire way to void it after the home has been transferred or mortgaged to an innocent third-party. State laws regulating real estate brokers and agents may also be useful. At least one foreclosure rescue transaction has been invalidated because the real estate broker was not properly licensed.[417] State real estate requirements vary from state to state and can be quite technical, so it may be best to get detailed information from the client and then consult with an attorney who has expertise in real estate law.

415 Lewis v. Delta Funding Corp. (*In re* Lewis), 290 B.R. 541 (Bankr. E.D. Pa. 2003).

416 Allen v. Advanta Fin. Corp., 2002 U.S. Dist. LEXIS 11650 (E.D. Pa. Jan. 3, 2002). *See also* Strang v. Wells Fargo Bank, 2005 WL 1655886 (E.D. Pa. July 13, 2005) (lender had no derivative liability under state credit repair law for acts of closing agent and loan broker who were not shown to be covered by that law); Herrod v. First Republic Mortgage Corp., 625 S.E.2d 373 (W. Va. 2005) (lender did not have a legal duty to ensure that independent broker complied with state credit repair law).

417 Susan Martin, *Second Jury Finds Fault with Controversial Foreclosure Rescue Deals*, St. Petersburg Times, Feb. 13, 2010 *available at* www.tampabay.com/news/courts/civil/second-jury-finds-fault-with-controversial-foreclosure-rescue-deals/1072978#.

15.4.11.2 False Notarization

States typically require that signatures on deeds or mortgages be notarized. Defects in the notarization of title documents may affect the validity of the instrument.

Many foreclosure rescue scam cases involve situations in which the person whom the notary certified as having appeared did not, in fact, appear. Borrowers are often instructed to sign a stack of documents that are then taken elsewhere for notarization. Alternatively, improper notarizations may result from the taking of an actual acknowledgment from an imposter, taking an acknowledgment from an incompetent person, or the taking of an acknowledgment over the telephone.

Regardless of the reason for the defective acknowledgment, practitioners should investigate whether such defects render the instrument invalid, providing grounds to void a transfer.[418] Most courts distinguish between defective acknowledgments and failure to acknowledge. Courts are more likely to find instruments valid where the defect is technical in nature, such as use of a notary residing in the wrong county or failure to read the acknowledgment aloud, but will invalidate them when the signatory did not in fact appear before the notary.[419]

In addition to invalidating the deed, the homeowner may be able to seek damages against the notary for false notarization. Notaries are required to perform their duties with honesty, integrity, diligence, and skill.[420] In addition to causes of action under a state UDAP statute or common law theories, such as negligence per se, state statutes may set forth specific causes of action for notary misconduct.[421]

418 *See In re* Miller, 320 B.R. 203 (N.D. Ala. 2006) (stating, but not deciding, mortgage invalid for lack of proper acknowledgment and therefore insufficient to transfer legal title in the collateral to lender); *In re* Fisher, 320 B.R. 52 (E.D. Pa. 2005) (permitting chapter 13 trustee to avoid mortgage where notary was not present to acknowledge mortgagor's identity and voluntary acquiescence to be bound by terms of the agreement); *In re* Bowling, 314 B.R. 127 (Bankr. S.D. Ohio 2004) (same); Goldome Credit Corp. v. Hardy, 503 So. 2d 1227 (Ala. Civ. App. 1987) (affirming trial court's determination that the mortgage not executed before a notary was invalid and setting aside foreclosure). *But see In re* Nichols, 265 B.R. 831 (B.A.P. 10th Cir. 2001) (distinguishing between validity and perfection of improperly notarized mortgage and affirming denial of debtor's motion to avoid mortgagee's lien).

419 *See, e.g., In re* Fisher, 320 B.R. 52 (E.D. Pa. 2005) (deed invalid where notary was not present when documents were signed). *But cf. In re* Biggs, 377 F.3d 515 (6th Cir. 2004) (failure to include mortgagor's name in notarization section rendered the deed of trust invalid under Tennessee law); Poole v. Hyatt, 689 A.2d 82 (Md. 1997) (failure to make oral acknowledgment before notary does not invalidate deed).

420 McComber v. Wells, 72 Cal. App. 4th 512, 85 Cal. Rptr. 2d 376 (1999).

421 *See, e.g.,* Cal. Gov. Code § 8214 ("For the official misconduct or neglect of a notary public, the notary public and the sureties on the notary public's official bond are liable in a civil action to

Notary liability is particularly important because states typically require notaries to be bonded.

The California Court of Appeals has found that a notary who negligently notarizes a trust deed is liable not only for economic damages but also for emotional distress damages, noting "the important function notaries serve in our society."[422] If the false notarization was not a proximate cause of the homeowner's losses, however, courts may be unwilling to award damages.[423] But the false notarization may still provide grounds to invalidate the deed.

15.4.12 RICO

The federal Racketeer Influenced and Corrupt Organizations Act (RICO)[424] provides powerful civil remedies, including attorney fees and treble damages, to victims of a broadly defined range of "racketeering activity" and to those who have been subjected to the collection of an "unlawful debt." "Unlawful debt" includes any usurious debt bearing interest of at least twice the "enforceable rate."

Although RICO is aimed at organized crime, the statute is broadly written to encompass a myriad of fraudulent activities conducted by theoretically "legitimate" organizations and creditors. Therefore, consumers who have been the victim of either fraudulent overcharging or overcharging of at least twice the civil usury rate may wish to consider a RICO claim.[425]

RICO claims have advantages and disadvantages. They offer treble damages, attorney fees, and federal jurisdiction. However, the elements of a RICO claim are complex and rigorous. Courts may be hostile to RICO claims, and many impose special pleading requirements on them. Before making a RICO claim, the homeowner's attorney should evaluate whether the state UDAP statute or a common law fraud claim would offer equivalent relief.

About half the states have their own RICO statutes, and all but a few of these statutes afford a private cause of action.[426] Most are modeled on the federal statute, but some have more relaxed elements. While a federal RICO claim will provide a basis for removing a case to federal court, a claim under a state RICO statute will not, so it is useful if the plaintiff wants to stay in state court. Asserting consumer claims under federal and state RICO statutes is discussed in detail in NCLC's *Unfair and Deceptive Acts and Practices* treatise.[427]

15.4.13 Real Estate Settlement Procedures Act

The federal Real Estate Settlement Procedures Act (RESPA) has also been used to attack foreclosure rescue scams, although RESPA's applicability is complicated and it may ultimately be difficult to use. Two RESPA provisions are potentially helpful. The first prohibits kickbacks pursuant to any referral fee arrangement, and the second prohibits payments unless services were actually performed.[428] In a foreclosure rescue scam, the homeowner's equity is often stripped through payments at settlement to the rescuer, who usually does not take title to the property. These payments are potentially actionable under RESPA.[429]

---

the persons injured thereby for all the damages sustained."); Johnson v. Home Savers Consulting Corp., 2007 WL 925518 (E.D.N.Y. Mar. 23, 2007) (awarding damages against notary for violation of state UDAP law and N.Y. Exec. Law § 135), *report and recommendation adopted by* 2007 WL 1110612 (E.D.N.Y. Apr. 11, 2007).

422 *Id.* at 519, 85 Cal. Rptr. 2d at 380.

423 Davis v. Adoption Auto, 731 F. Supp. 1475 (D. Kan. 1999); Craig v. Metro Bank of Dallas, 601 S.W.2d 734 (Tex. Civ. App. 1980).

424 18 U.S.C. §§ 1961–1968. *See* § 5.13.5, *supra*; National Consumer Law Center, Unfair and Deceptive Acts and Practices §§ 14.2, 14.3 (7th ed. 2008 and Supp.) (extensive analysis of RICO); National Consumer Law Center, The Cost of Credit: Regulation, Preemption, and Industry Abuses § 10.8.5.3 (4th ed. 2009 and Supp.) (overview of using RICO in the credit context).

425 For an overview of using RICO in the credit context, see National Consumer Law Center, The Cost of Credit: Regulation, Preemption, and Industry Abuses § 3.10.4.1 (4th ed. 2009 and Supp.). *See, e.g.*, Proctor v. Metropolitan Money Store Corp., 645 F. Supp. 2d 464 (D. Md. 2009) (RICO claim in foreclosure rescue scam); Eyler v. 3 Vista Court L.L.C. (*In re* Eyler), 2008 WL 4833096 (Bankr. D. Md. Oct. 28, 2008) (proposed findings of fact and conclusions of law) (rescuer violated RICO by seeking to collect debt bearing interest at more than twice lawful rate; awarding treble the homeowner's lost equity). *Cf.* Williams v. Equity Holding Corp., 498 F. Supp. 2d 831 (E.D. Va. 2007) (mail fraud pleaded in foreclosure rescue scam case with sufficient particularity to state RICO claim, but insufficient allegations of pattern).

426 *See, e.g.*, Martinez v. Affordable Hous. Network, Inc., 109 P.3d 983 (Colo. Ct. App. 2004) (affirming jury verdict on state RICO claim against rescuer, but awarding damages only on UDAP claim to avoid duplication), *rev'd on other grounds*, 123 P.3d 1201 (Colo. 2006) (reversing trial court's determination that buyer of home from rescuer was bona fide purchaser without notice; remanding for trial on quiet title claim). *Cf.* Heise v. Porcelli, 2008 WL 2439884 (M.D. Fla. June 13, 2008) (dismissing RICO case with leave to amend; listing specific details that RICO complaint regarding foreclosure rescue scam should have included). *See generally* National Consumer Law Center, Unfair and Deceptive Acts and Practices § 14.3 and Appx. C (7th ed. 2008 and Supp.).

427 National Consumer Law Center, Unfair and Deceptive Acts and Practices §§ 14.2, 14.3 (7th ed. 2008 and Supp.).

428 *See* § 5.9.2, *supra.*

429 *See* Johnson v. Home Savers Consulting Corp., 2007 WL 925518 (E.D.N.Y. Mar. 23, 2007) (awarding damages against attorney who performed no services for homeowner), *report and recommendation adopted by* 2007 WL 1110612 (E.D.N.Y. Apr. 11, 2007). *See also* Sith v. Thorne, 247 F.R.D. 89 (E.D. Va. 2007) (later decision in case discussed below holding that triable issues existed as to whether title company willfully violated state UDAP statute by making payment to rescuer in

However, there are hurdles to asserting a RESPA claim, which were not addressed in the two cases that have addressed RESPA claims. RESPA only applies to "federally related mortgage loans," a term with a special definition under RESPA.[430] The question in the foreclosure rescue scam context is what is the loan that must be federally related—the restructured equitable mortgage between the straw buyer and the homeowner, or the loan from a third party lender to the straw buyer used to finance the transaction?

The equitable mortgage from the straw buyer to the homeowner will not fit the RESPA definition unless the straw buyer makes or invests in more than $1 million a year in residentially secured loans—a threshold that may be possible to show if the straw buyer has been involved in other foreclosure rescue transactions.

The third party loan to the straw buyer is much more likely to be a federally related mortgage loan, but the homeowner may not have standing to raise claims related to the settlement of that loan unless she can argue that the loan should be viewed as one to her. That may be a credible argument since the third party loan is what financed the equitable mortgage to the homeowner, it is encumbering the homeowner's property, and she may ultimately be liable for it if the lender is a bona fide lender.

Nonetheless, advocates should consider a RESPA claim carefully and consider whether the benefits of adding a RESPA claim outweigh the complications that it adds to the case. Regardless whether the homeowner can assert a RESPA claim, misrepresentations on the HUD-1 settlement statement required by RESPA may form part of a UDAP or fraud claim.[431]

the absence of written instructions from homeowner, and whether title company used power of attorney to prevent homeowner from seeing the HUD-1 that revealed the payment); Curriden v. Innovative Mortgage Solutions L.L.C. (*In re* Curriden), 2007 WL 2669431 (Bankr. D.N.J. Sept. 6, 2007) (imposing liability under RESPA for kickbacks in case in which defendants deprived homeowner of her equity). *But see* Stith v. Thorne, 488 F. Supp. 2d 534 (E.D. Va. 2007) (dismissing RESPA claims against title company because no evidence that title company agreed to pay a kickback or to split charges with anyone).

430 *See* 12 U.S.C. § 2602(1)(B); National Consumer Law Center, The Cost of Credit: Regulation, Preemption, and Industry Abuses §§ 12.2.1.1, 12.2.1.2 (4th ed. 2009 and Supp.).

431 *See* Phifer v. Home Savers Consulting Corp., 2007 WL 295605 (E.D.N.Y. Jan. 30, 2007); Sith v. Thorne, 247 F.R.D. 89 (E.D. Va. 2007) (upholding UDAP claim after dismissal of RESPA claim regarding settlement irregularities); § 15.4.5.4, *supra*.

15.5 Challenging Foreclosure Rescue Scams in Bankruptcy

15.5.1 Introduction

Bankruptcy is an important option for victims of foreclosure rescue scams. Bankruptcy may not only provide the victim a fresh financial start, but it may also be a favorable forum for homeowners in their efforts to regain title to their homes. Under the Bankruptcy Code, certain transfers of property made by the debtor may be voided in a bankruptcy proceeding by either the bankruptcy trustee or the debtor. The debtor may also use bankruptcy to stop eviction or foreclosure proceedings initiated by a rescuer or to bring other nonbankruptcy claims against the rescuer.

This section discusses how bankruptcy can be used to challenge foreclosure rescue scams. Most bankruptcy cases are complicated, and those who are not a bankruptcy practitioner should consult with a bankruptcy attorney before filing a case. Chapter 9, *supra*, provides an overview of bankruptcy and discusses selected issues that frequently arise in foreclosure cases. NCLC's *Consumer Bankruptcy Law and Practice*[432] is a comprehensive analysis of bankruptcy law as applied to consumers.

15.5.2 Stopping the Eviction

Many victims of foreclosure rescue scams may only seek legal assistance after the rescuer has initiated an eviction case. In these cases, a critical first step in defending the homeowner will be to stop the eviction process. In most situations, a bankruptcy filing will automatically stop most eviction efforts against the homeowners as well as other creditor actions. However, there are a few exceptions, usually based on prior bankruptcy filings, when the stay may not automatically go into effect or may have a limited duration. There is also a special set of procedures that apply to eviction cases.

If the rescuer has initiated an eviction case against the homeowner, the automatic stay will prevent the rescuer from evicting the homeowner if the bankruptcy case is filed before the state court has entered a judgment for possession against the landlord. If the bankruptcy case is filed after judgment for possession against the homeowner, the full automatic stay will come into effect only for a period of thirty days, and then only if documents are filed with the court certifying that: (1) the debtor has a right to cure the rent default under state law, and (2) the debtor has deposited with the bankruptcy court the rent that will come due during the first thirty days of the bankruptcy case (usually one

432 *See* National Consumer Law Center, Consumer Bankruptcy Law and Practice (9th ed. 2009) (detailed discussion of bankruptcy).

month's rent). To get a stay longer than thirty days, the debtor is required to pay the landlord all of the back rent statement in the judgment for possession. Alternatively, debtors may seek to have these requirements waived under the court's equitable powers.[433]

Because in most cases it is unlikely that victims of foreclosure rescue scams will have the financial resources to pay all the back rent in the judgment for possession within thirty days, the attorney should consider options for removing the judgment or reopening the eviction case before filing for bankruptcy.

15.5.3 Voiding Title Transfers in Foreclosure Rescue Scams

15.5.3.1 Overview

As discussed above, one of the most common indicia of a foreclosure rescue scam is that homeowners transfer their property to the rescuer or a party affiliated with the rescuer. These transactions may give rise to state and federal statutory claims such as unfair and deceptive practices (UDAP) and Truth in Lending (TILA), or common law claims such as fraud, conspiracy, and breach of fiduciary duty. Legal theories for attacking foreclosure rescue scams are discussed at § 15.4, *supra*. However, for homeowners whose primary goal is to regain ownership of their home, bankruptcy may provide an alternative route.

Bankruptcy trustees (and administrators) have the power to avoid or nullify transfers of property pursuant to several sections of the Bankruptcy Code. While these avoidance powers have limitations, they can be extremely powerful in challenging title transfers in foreclosure rescue scams. The Code also permits debtors to utilize the trustee's avoiding powers with some limitations set forth in section 522(g) and 522(h).

While the complex relationship of the bankruptcy provisions used by the debtor to void title transfers may at first appear daunting, especially to nonbankruptcy practitioners, the interplay of the statutes can be reduced to five essential elements. The debtor may avoid a transfer if: (1) the transfer is avoidable by the trustee; (2) the trustee does not attempt to avoid the transfer; (3) the debtor did not conceal the property; (4) the debtor could exempt the property; and (5) the transfer was involuntary. The most difficult hurdle for some victims of foreclosure rescue scams is likely to be demonstrating that the transfer was not voluntary. However, if the homeowner cannot show the last three elements, another option is to persuade the trustee to avoid the transfer, as discussed at § 15.5.3.4, *infra*.

15.5.3.2 Trustees' Powers to Avoid Transfers

15.5.3.2.1 General

The starting point in any avoidance action is a determination of whether the transfer is avoidable by the trustee. As noted above, the bankruptcy trustee may set aside or nullify a wide variety of transfers made by a debtor prior to the commencement of a case. In the foreclosure rescue scam context, the most likely statutory sections to be employed are section 548, dealing with fraudulent transfers, and the "strong arm" powers of section 544.

15.5.3.2.2 Fraudulent transfers

Section 548 of the Bankruptcy Code gives the trustee (and thus the debtor in some instances) the ability to avoid transfers based on either actual or constructive fraud.[434] The trustee may avoid a transfer if the transfer was made within the two years[435] before the case was filed and the transfer meets certain conditions.[436] Specifically, a transfer may be avoided if: (1) the debtor received less than a reasonably equivalent value for the transfer, and (2) the debtor was insolvent on the date of the transfer or became insolvent as a result of the transfer.

Whether a debtor received less than a reasonably equivalent value will depend on the facts and circumstances of each case. The focus of the inquiry is on what the homeowners received in return for what they surrendered. In foreclosure rescue scams, homeowners often receive little or nothing for the equity in their homes. Even where rescuers have cured mortgage arrears, it is doubtful whether such payments are of any benefit to the homeowners who have simultaneously lost title to their homes.[437]

To avoid a transfer under section 548, the debtor must also have been insolvent at the time of transfer or have become insolvent as a result of the transfer. The insolvency inquiry is essentially a balance-sheet test that looks at the difference between the debtor's non-exempt assets and liabilities. Most consumer debtors are insolvent under the Code's definition. For those debtors that may have had non-exempt equity in their homesteads, transferring title to

433 *See In re* Weinraub, 361 B.R. 586 (Bankr. S.D. Fla. 2007) (in light of debtor's allegations that landlord acquired title to their home as a result of a foreclosure rescue scam, court held it had the authority to waive the requirements of §§ 362(b)(22) and 362(l) to preserve the status quo).

434 *See* § 14.2.4.2, *supra* (general discussion of § 548).

435 For cases filed on or before April 20, 2006, fraudulent transfers may only be set aside if the transfer was made within one year prior to the commencement of the case.

436 Foreclosure rescue scams occurring post-petition may be avoided under section 549 using the same principles discussed in these sections. *See In re* Walker, 405 B.R. 300 (Bankr. E.D. Wis. 2009).

437 *See In re* Davis, 148 B.R. 165, 174 (Bankr. E.D.N.Y.), *aff'd*, 169 B.R. 285, 300 (E.D.N.Y. 1994).

their property in a foreclosure rescue scam almost always renders the homeowner insolvent.

15.5.3.2.3 Use of "strong arm clause"

Besides the power to avoid fraudulent transfers under section 548, section 544(b) in combination with state fraudulent transfer laws provides another basis for avoiding title transfers in foreclosure rescue scams.[438] Under almost all state fraudulent transfer laws, a transfer may be deemed fraudulent if: (1) the debtor was insolvent or became insolvent as a result of the transfer, and (2) the conveyance was made without "reasonably equivalent value" or "fair consideration."[439]

Despite their similarities, the right to avoid fraudulent transfers under the Code differs slightly from the right to avoid transfers under state law. Most significantly, state fraudulent transfer laws have a longer "reach-back" period, typically four years. As a result, debtors may use section 544(b) to challenge title transfers outside of the two-year period specified in section 548. Some state laws also provide that a debtor is presumed to be insolvent if he or she is not paying debts as they become due. Under this definition, homeowners who are in financial distress and falling further behind on their mortgage will be presumed to be insolvent.

15.5.3.3 Debtor's Power to Avoid Title Transfers

15.5.3.3.1 General

If the trustee could avoid the title transfer but elects not to do so, the debtor may be able to do so in certain circumstances. Specifically, the debtors may avoid title transfers if they can demonstrate that: (1) the transfer could be avoided by the trustee; (2) the trustee did not attempt to avoid the transfer; (3) the debtor did not conceal the property; (4) the debtor could exempt the property; and (5) the transfer was involuntary.

15.5.3.3.2 Did the debtor conceal the property?

The answer to this question depends largely on whether the debtor has disclosed the property on his or her schedules. Because of the potential consequences of failing to list the property in the schedules, it is always better to be over-inclusive rather than under-inclusive. At a minimum, the causes of action against the rescue scammers should be listed on Schedule B—Personal Property.[440] It may also be prudent to list the property on Schedule A—Real Property with an explanatory note that the debtor had been the title owner of the real property before the transfer, that the debtor believes that the transfer is avoidable, and the debtor retains an equitable interest in the property.

15.5.3.3.3 May the debtor exempt the property?

As a general rule, almost all property in which the debtor has a legal or equitable interest becomes property of the bankruptcy estate at the commencement of a case.[441] However, the Bankruptcy Code permits a debtor to exempt certain property from the estate pursuant to the federal exemptions, as listed in 11 U.S.C. § 522(d), or the applicable state exemptions. For debtors in states that have "opted out" of the federal exemption scheme, only the state law exemptions and exemptions provided by federal non-bankruptcy law are available.[442]

So long as the debtor may exempt some portion of the property, the debtor may avoid transfers of that property using the trustee's powers. The amount recovered up to the amount of the exemption is for the benefit of the debtor, while any amount in excess of the exemption is preserved for the benefit of the estate. So, for example, if the debtor avoids transfer of a $100,000 home that has a $65,000 first mortgage, and there is a $30,000 homestead exemption, the remaining $5000 in equity is preserved for the benefit of the estate. In a chapter 7 bankruptcy, the home may be sold, with the debtor receiving the $30,000 exemption and the remaining $5000 going to unsecured creditors. (The debtor may still be able to save the home, however, by buying out the trustee's interest in the home through refinancing or some other way.) In a chapter 13 bankruptcy, the debtor is required to pay unsecured creditors at least the amount of

---

438 *See* Neese v. Fields (*In re* Fields), 2009 WL 367710 (Bankr. D. Md. Feb. 5, 2009) (awarding judgment to trustee for difference between amount paid for the property by rescuer and amount of loan rescuer obtained; because of rescuer's sale to bona fide purchaser, court cannot avoid homeowner's transfer to rescuer); *In re* Drew, 2006 WL 2403416 (Bankr. D.N.H. Aug. 17, 2006).

439 Almost all state fraudulent transfer laws are based either on the Uniform Fraudulent Conveyance Act, which uses the term "fair consideration," or the more recent Uniform Fraudulent Transfer Act, which uses the term "reasonably equivalent value." Courts have drawn little to no distinction between the "reasonably equivalent value" standard and the "fair consideration" standard. *See, e.g.*, *In re* AppliedTheory Corp., 323 B.R. 838 (Bankr. S.D.N.Y. 2005), *aff'd*, 330 B.R. 362 (S.D.N.Y. 2005); *In re* Tiger Petroleum Co., 319 B.R. 225, 232 (Bankr. N.D. Okla. 2004). *See also* Still v. Arakelyan (*In re* Still), 393 B.R. 896 (Bankr. C.D. Cal. 2008) (finding rescuer's transfer of home to his wife for no consideration to be fraudulent); *In re* Drew, 2006 WL 2403416 (Bankr. D.N.H. Aug. 17, 2006) (consideration equaling 40% of property value at time of transfer did not constitute reasonably equivalent value).

440 Debtors may be judicially estopped from later bringing claims not listed in their schedules. *See, e.g.*, Hamilton v. State Farm Fire & Cas. Co., 270 F.3d 778 (9th Cir. 2001); Wolfork v. Tackett, 273 Ga. 328, 540 S.E.2d 611 (2001).

441 *See* 11 U.S.C. § 541(a)(1).

442 For more information see National Consumer Law Center, Consumer Bankruptcy Law and Practice § 10.2 (9th ed. 2009).

non-exempt assets that would have been distributed to them in a chapter 7 bankruptcy, so the debtor must pay at least $5000 to the unsecured creditors under the plan. (Of course, a debtor who owes less than $5000 to unsecured creditors need only pay them the amount of their debts.)

15.5.3.3.4 Was the transfer involuntary?

The debtor may use the trustee's avoidance powers only where the transfer to be avoided was "involuntary." Neither the term "voluntary" nor "involuntary" is defined in the Bankruptcy Code. Involuntary transfers, however, generally refer to transfers effectuated by operation of law, such as an execution of judgment, repossession, foreclosure, or garnishment. A transfer may also be considered "involuntary" if it resulted from fraud, material misrepresentation, or coercion. According to this standard, a voluntary transfer does not occur where a creditor has concealed or failed to inform a debtor of the essential facts necessary for the debtor to make an intelligent decision on whether to transfer the property to the creditor.

In foreclosure rescue cases where homeowners are led to believe they are taking out a second mortgage or additional financing to cure mortgage arrears, when in reality they are unknowingly transferring title to their home to a third party, the "involuntary" nature of the transaction should not be difficult to establish.[443] Even in cases where homeowners are aware that they are transferring title, it may still be possible to characterize the transaction as involuntary if they did not know all of the material facts of the transaction, misrepresentations were made to them, they faced significant economic coercion as a result of a threatened foreclosure sale, or the closing transaction occurred under tremendous pressure.[444]

443 *See In re* Walker, 405 B.R. 300 (Bankr. E.D. Wis. 2009) (allowing debtor to avoid foreclosure rescue transfer by using § 549 powers pursuant to § 522(h)).

15.5.3.4 Persuading the Trustee to Avoid the Transfer

If the homeowner cannot show all of the elements discussed above, it may be possible to persuade the trustee to avoid the transfer. The advantage of having the trustee avoid the transfer is that the trustee need not show the last three elements: that the debtor did not conceal the property; that the debtor may exempt the property; and that the transfer was involuntary.[445] The trustee is likely to be interested in avoiding the transfer if the home has some non-exempt equity.

If the trustee avoids the transfer, the homeowner will benefit in two ways. First, the homeowner will be able to exempt whatever portion of the home is exempt. Second, if a portion of the home's value is not exempt, it will be under the control of the trustee rather than the rescuer.

In a chapter 13 bankruptcy, the debtor is required to pay the unsecured creditors the amount they would have received in a chapter 7 bankruptcy. Since the amount that unsecured creditors receive in a chapter 7 case is based on the amount of non-exempt assets in the bankruptcy estate, bringing the debtor's non-exempt equity in the home back into the bankruptcy estate increases the amount that will have to be distributed to unsecured creditors in a chapter 13 case.[446]

444 *See In re* Davis, 169 B.R. 285, 295, 298 (E.D.N.Y. 1994).

445 *See In re* Drew, 2006 WL 2403416 (Bankr. D.N.H. Aug. 17, 2006) (chapter 7 trustee sought to avoid transfer and collect damages for violation of state UDAP statute and other common law claims).

446 *See* § 15.5.3.3.3, *supra*.

Appendix A Selected Statutes and Regulations Pertaining to Mortgages Held or Insured by the Federal Government

A.1 Introduction

This appendix contains selected statutes, regulations, and other important documents affecting loans made or guaranteed by the federal government through the Department of Housing and Urban Development (HUD), Department of Veterans Affairs (VA), and the Rural Housing Service (RHS). Each agency has implemented a loss mitigation or foreclosure avoidance program to assist individuals who are delinquent on their mortgages and in danger of foreclosure. The statutes, regulations, or other materials contained in this appendix outline the requirements of those programs, as well as general requirements for servicing such mortgages. The companion website contains additional materials that may be useful to advocates representing consumers facing foreclosure of a federally held or guaranteed loan.

A.2 Loans Insured by the Department of Housing and Urban Development (HUD)

A.2.1 Selected Statutes

TITLE 12. BANKS AND BANKING

CHAPTER 13—NATIONAL HOUSING

SUBCHAPTER II—MORTGAGE INSURANCE

* * *

12 U.S.C. § 1715u. Authority to assist mortgagors in default

(a) Loss mitigation

Upon default or imminent default, as defined by the Secretary of any mortgage insured under this subchapter, mortgagees shall engage in loss mitigation actions for the purpose of providing an alternative to foreclosure (including but not limited to actions such as special forbearance, loan modification, preforeclosure sale, support for borrower housing counseling, subordinate lien resolution, borrower incentives, and deeds in lieu of foreclosure, as required, but not including assignment of mortgages to the Secretary under section 1710(a)(1)(A) of this title) or subsection (c),[1] as provided in regulations by the Secretary.

(b) Payment of partial claim

(1) Establishment of program

The Secretary may establish a program for payment of a partial claim to a mortgagee that agrees to apply the claim amount to payment of a mortgage on a 1- to 4-family residence that is in default or faces imminent default, as defined by the Secretary.

(2) Payments and exceptions

Any payment of a partial claim under the program established in paragraph (1) to a mortgagee shall be made in the sole discretion of the Secretary and on terms and conditions acceptable to the Secretary, except that—

(A) the amount of the payment shall be in an amount determined by the Secretary, not to exceed an amount equivalent to 30 percent of the unpaid principal balance of the mortgage and any costs that are approved by the Secretary;

(B) the amount of the partial claim payment shall first be applied to any arrearage on the mortgage, and may also be applied to achieve principal reduction;

(C) the mortgagor shall agree to repay the amount of the insurance claim to the Secretary upon terms and conditions acceptable to the Secretary;

(D) the Secretary may permit compensation to the mortgagee for lost income on monthly payments, due to a reduction in the interest rate charged on the mortgage;

(E) expenses related to the partial claim or modification may not be charged to the borrower;

(F) loans may be modified to extend the term of the mortgage to a maximum of 40 years from the date of the modification; and

(G) the Secretary may permit incentive payments to the mortgagee, on the borrower's behalf, based on successful performance of a modified mortgage, which shall be used to reduce the amount of principal indebtedness.

(c)(1) Assignment

(A) Program authority

The Secretary may establish a program for assignment to the Secretary, upon request of the mortgagee, of a mortgage on a 1- to 4-family residence insured under this chapter.

(B) Program requirements

The Secretary may accept assignment of a mortgage under this paragraph only if—

(i) the mortgage was in default or facing imminent default, as defined by the Secretary;

1 As in original.

(ii) the mortgagee has modified the mortgage to cure the default and provide for mortgage payments within the reasonable ability of the mortgagor to pay, at interest rates not exceeding current market interest rates; and

(iii) the Secretary arranges for servicing of the assigned mortgage by a mortgagee (which may include the assigning mortgagee) through procedures that the Secretary has determined to be in the best interests of the appropriate insurance fund.

(C) Payment of insurance benefits

Upon accepting assignment of a mortgage under this paragraph, the Secretary may pay insurance benefits to the mortgagee from the appropriate insurance fund, in an amount that the Secretary determines to be appropriate, not to exceed the amount necessary to compensate the mortgagee for the assignment and any losses and expenses resulting from the mortgage modification.

(2) Assignment and loan modification

(A) Authority

The Secretary may encourage loan modifications for eligible delinquent mortgages or mortgages facing imminent default, as defined by the Secretary, through the payment of insurance benefits and assignment of the mortgage to the Secretary and the subsequent modification of the terms of the mortgage according to a loan modification approved by the mortgagee.

(B) Payment of benefits and assignment

In carrying out this paragraph, the Secretary may pay insurance benefits for a mortgage, in the amount determined in accordance with section 1710(a)(5) of this title, without reduction for any amounts modified, but only upon the assignment, transfer, and delivery to the Secretary of all rights, interest, claims, evidence, and records with respect to the mortgage specified in clauses (i) through (iv) of section 1710(a)(1)(A) of this title.

(C) Disposition

After modification of a mortgage pursuant to this paragraph, the Secretary may provide insurance under this subchapter for the mortgage. The Secretary may subsequently—

(i) re-assign the mortgage to the mortgagee under terms and conditions as are agreed to by the mortgagee and the Secretary;

(ii) act as a Government National Mortgage Association issuer, or contract with an entity for such purpose, in order to pool the mortgage into a Government National Mortgage Association security; or

(iii) re-sell the mortgage in accordance with any program that has been established for purchase by the Federal Government of mortgages insured under this subchapter, and the Secretary may coordinate standards for interest rate reductions available for loan modification with interest rates established for such purchase.

(D) Loan servicing

In carrying out this paragraph, the Secretary may require the existing servicer of a mortgage assigned to the Secretary to continue servicing the mortgage as an agent of the Secretary during the period that the Secretary acquires and holds the mortgage for the purpose of modifying the terms of the mortgage, provided that the Secretary compensates the existing servicer appropriately, as such compensation is determined by the Secretary consistent, to the maximum extent possible, with section 1709(b) of this title. If the mortgage is resold pursuant to subparagraph (C)(iii), the Secretary may provide for the existing servicer to continue to service the mortgage or may engage another entity to service the mortgage.

(d) Prohibition of judicial review

No decision by the Secretary to exercise or forego exercising any authority under this section shall be subject to judicial review.

(e) [Repealed.]

(f) Applicability of other laws

No provision of this chapter, or any other law, shall be construed to require the Secretary to provide an alternative to foreclosure for mortgagees with mortgages on 1- to 4-family residences insured by the Secretary under this chapter, or to accept assignments of such mortgages.

[June 27, 1934, ch. 847, tit. II, § 230, *as added* Pub. L. No. 86-372, tit. I, § 114(a), 73 Stat. 662 (Sept. 23, 1959), *and amended* Pub. L. No. 88-560, tit. I, § 104(b), 78 Stat. 770 (Sept. 2, 1964); Pub. L. No. 90-19, § 1(a)(3), 81 Stat. 17 (May 25, 1967); Pub. L. No. 96-399, tit. III, § 341, 94 Stat. 1659 (Oct. 8, 1980); Pub. L. No. 98-181, tit. IV, § 418, 97 Stat. 1212 (Nov. 30, 1983); Pub. L. No. 100-242, tit. IV, § 428, 101 Stat. 1918 (Feb. 5, 1988); Pub. L. No. 102-83, § 5(c)(2), 105 Stat. 406 (Aug. 6, 1991); Pub. L. No. 104-99, tit. IV, § 407(b), 110 Stat. 45 (Jan. 26, 1996); Pub. L. No. 104-134, tit. I, § 101(e) [tit. II, § 221(b)(2)], 110 Stat. 1321–291 (Apr. 26, 1996); [renumbered tit. I] Pub. L. No. 104-140, § 1(a), 110 Stat. 1327 (May 2, 1996); Pub. L. No. 105-276, tit. VI, § 601(f), 112 Stat. 2674 (Oct. 21, 1998); Pub. L. No. 111-22, div. A, tit. II, § 203(d)(1) to (3), 123 Stat. 1645 (May 20, 2009)]

* * *

SUBCHAPTER V—MISCELLANEOUS

* * *

12 U.S.C. § 1735f-14. Civil money penalties against mortgagees, lenders, and other participants in FHA programs

(a) In general

(1) Authority

If a mortgagee approved under the[1] chapter, a lender holding a contract of insurance under subchapter I of this chapter, or a principal, officer, or employee of such mortgagee or lender, or other person or entity participating in either an insured mortgage or subchapter I loan transaction under this chapter or providing assistance to the borrower in connection with any such loan, including sellers of the real estate involved, borrowers, closing agents, title companies, real estate agents, mortgage brokers, appraisers, loan correspondents and dealers, knowingly and materially violates any applicable provision of subsection (b) of this section, the Secretary may impose a civil money penalty on the mortgagee or lender, or such other person or entity, in accordance with this section. The penalty under this paragraph shall be in addition to any other available civil remedy or any available criminal penalty, and may be imposed whether or not the Secretary imposes other administrative sanctions. The penalty shall be in addition to any other available civil remedy or any available

1 [*Editor's Note*: So in original. Probably should be "this."]

criminal penalty, and may be imposed whether or not the Secretary imposes other administrative sanctions.

(2) Amount of penalty

The amount of the penalty, as determined by the Secretary, may not exceed $5,000 for each violation, except that the maximum penalty for all violations by any particular mortgagee or lender or such other person or entity during any 1-year period shall not exceed $1,000,000. Each violation of a[2] the provisions of subsection (b)(1) of this section shall constitute a separate violation with respect to each mortgage or loan application. In the case of a continuing violation, as determined by the Secretary, each day shall constitute a separate violation.

In the case of the mortgagee's failure to engage in loss mitigation activities, as provided in section 536(b)(1)(I) [12 U.S.C. § 1735f-14(b)(1)(I)], the penalty shall be in the amount of three times the amount of any insurance benefits claimed by the mortgagee with respect to any mortgage for which the mortgagee failed to engage in such loss mitigation actions.

(b) Violations for which a penalty may be imposed

(1) Violations

The Secretary may impose a civil money penalty under subsection (a) of this section for any knowing and material violation by a mortgagee or lender or any of its owners, officers, or directors, as follows:

(A) Except where expressly permitted by statute, regulation, or contract approved by the Secretary, transfer of a mortgage insured under this chapter to a mortgagee not approved by the Secretary, or transfer of a loan to a transferee that is not holding a contract of insurance under subchapter I of this chapter.

(B) Failure of a nonsupervised mortgagee, as defined by the Secretary—

(i) to segregate all escrow funds received from a mortgagor for ground rents, taxes, assessments, and insurance premiums; or

(ii) to deposit these funds in a special account with a depository institution whose accounts are insured by the Federal Deposit Insurance Corporation through the Deposit Insurance Fund, or by the National Credit Union Administration.

(C) Use of escrow funds for any purpose other than that for which they were received.

(D) Submission to the Secretary of information that was false, in connection with any mortgage insured under this chapter, or any loan that is covered by a contract of insurance under subchapter I of this chapter.

(E) With respect to an officer, director, principal, or employee—

(i) hiring such an individual whose duties will involve, directly or indirectly, programs administered by the Secretary, while that person was under suspension or withdrawal by the Secretary; or

(ii) retaining in employment such an individual who continues to be involved, directly or indirectly, in programs administered by the Secretary, while that person was under suspension or withdrawal by the Secretary.

(F) Falsely certifying to the Secretary or submitting to the Secretary a false certification by another person or entity.

(G) Failure to comply with an agreement, certification, or condition of approval set forth on, or applicable to—

(i) the application of a mortgagee or lender for approval by the Secretary; or

(ii) the notification by a mortgagee or lender to the Secretary concerning establishment of a branch office.

(H) Violation of any provisions of title I or II of this Act, or any implementing regulation, handbook, or mortgagee letter that is issued under this Act.

(I) Failure to engage in loss mitigation actions as provided in section 230(a) of this Act [12 U.S.C. § 1715u(a)].

(J) Failure to perform a required physical inspection of the mortgaged property.

(K) Violation of section 202(d) of this Act (12 U.S.C. 1708(d)).

(L) Use of "Federal Housing Administration", "Department of Housing and Urban Development", "Government National Mortgage Association", "Ginnie Mae", the acronyms "HUD", "FHA", or "GNMA", or any official seal or logo of the Department of Housing and Urban Development, except as authorized by the Secretary.

(2) The Secretary may impose a civil money penalty under subsection (a) of this section for any knowing and material violation by a principal, officer, or employee of a mortgagee or lender, or other participants in either an insured mortgage or subchapter I loan transaction under this chapter or provision of assistance to the borrower in connection with any such loan, including sellers of the real estate involved, borrowers, closing agents, title companies, real estate agents, mortgage brokers, appraisers, loan correspondents, and dealers for—

(A) submission to the Secretary of information that was false, in connection with any mortgage insured under this chapter, or any loan that is covered by a contract of insurance under subchapter I of this chapter;

(B) falsely certifying to the Secretary or submitting to the Secretary a false certification by another person or entity;

(C) failure by a loan correspondent or dealer to submit to the Secretary information which is required by regulations or directives in connection with any loan that is covered by a contract of insurance under subchapter I of this chapter; or

(D) causing or participating in any of the violations set forth in paragraph (1) of this subsection.

(3) Prohibition Against Misleading Use of Federal Entity Designation

The Secretary may impose a civil money penalty, as adjusted from time to time, under subsection (a) for any use of "Federal Housing Administration", "Department of Housing and Urban Development", "Government National Mortgage Association", "Ginnie Mae", the acronyms "HUD", "FHA", or "GNMA", or any official seal or logo of the Department of Housing and Urban Development, by any person, party, company, firm, partnership, or business, including sellers of real estate, closing agents, title companies, real estate agents, mortgage brokers, appraisers, loan correspondents, and dealers, except as authorized by the Secretary.

(c) Agency procedures

(1) Establishment

The Secretary shall establish standards and procedures governing the imposition of civil money penalties under subsection (a) of this section. These standards and procedures—

(A) shall provide for the Secretary to make the determination to impose the penalty or to use an administrative entity (such as the

---

2 [*Editor's Note*: So in original. "A" probably should not appear.]

Mortgagee Review Board, established pursuant to section 1708(c) of this title) to make the determination;

(B) shall provide for the imposition of a penalty only after the mortgagee or lender or such other person or entity has been given an opportunity for a hearing on the record; and

(C) may provide for review by the Secretary of any determination or order, or interlocutory ruling, arising from a hearing.

(2) Final orders

If no hearing is requested within 15 days of receipt of the notice of opportunity for hearing, the imposition of the penalty shall constitute a final and unappealable determination. If the Secretary reviews the determination or order, the Secretary may affirm, modify, or reverse that determination or order. If the Secretary does not review the determination or order within 90 days of the issuance of the determination or order, the determination or order shall be final.

(3) Factors in determining amount of penalty

In determining the amount of a penalty under subsection (a) of this section, consideration shall be given to such factors as the gravity of the offense, any history of prior offenses (including those before enactment of this section), ability to pay the penalty, injury to the public, benefits received, deterrence of future violations, and such other factors as the Secretary may determine in regulations to be appropriate.

(4) Reviewability of imposition of penalty

The Secretary's determination or order imposing a penalty under subsection (a) of this section shall not be subject to review, except as provided in subsection (d) of this section.

(d) Judicial review of agency determination

(1) In general

After exhausting all administrative remedies established by the Secretary under subsection (c)(1) of this section, a mortgagee or lender or such other person or entity against whom the Secretary has imposed a civil money penalty under subsection (a) of this section may obtain a review of the penalty and such ancillary issues (such as any administrative sanctions under 24 C.F.R. parts 24 and 25) as may be addressed in the notice of determination to impose a penalty under subsection (c)(1)(A) of this section in the appropriate court of appeals of the United States, by filing in such court, within 20 days after the entry of such order or determination, a written petition praying that the Secretary's determination or order be modified or be set aside in whole or in part.

(2) Objections not raised in hearing

The court shall not consider any objection that was not raised in the hearing conducted pursuant to subsection (c)(1) of this section unless a demonstration is made of extraordinary circumstances causing the failure to raise the objection. If any party demonstrates to the satisfaction of the court that additional evidence not presented at the hearing is material and that there were reasonable grounds for the failure to present such evidence at the hearing, the court shall remand the matter to the Secretary for consideration of the additional evidence.

(3) Scope of review

The decisions, findings, and determinations of the Secretary shall be reviewed pursuant to section 706 of Title 5.

(4) Order to pay penalty

Notwithstanding any other provision of law, in any such review, the court shall have the power to order payment of the penalty imposed by the Secretary.

(e) Action to collect penalty

If any mortgagee or lender or such other person or entity fails to comply with the Secretary's determination or order imposing a civil money penalty under subsection (a) of this section, after the determination or order is no longer subject to review as provided by subsections (c)(1) and (d) of this section, the Secretary may request the Attorney General of the United States to bring an action in an appropriate United States district court to obtain a monetary judgment against the mortgagee or lender or such other person or entity and such other relief as may be available. The monetary judgment may, in the court's discretion, include the attorneys fees and other expenses incurred by the United States in connection with the action. In an action under this subsection, the validity and appropriateness of the Secretary's determination or order imposing the penalty shall not be subject to review.

(f) Settlement by Secretary

The Secretary may compromise, modify, or remit any civil money penalty which may be, or has been, imposed under this section.

(g) "Knowingly" defined

For purposes of this section, a person acts knowingly when a person has actual knowledge of acts or should have known of the acts.

(h) Regulations

The Secretary shall issue such regulations as the Secretary deems appropriate to implement this section.

(i) Deposit of penalties in insurance funds

Notwithstanding any other provision of law, all civil money penalties collected under this section shall be deposited in the appropriate insurance fund or funds established under this chapter, as determined by the Secretary.

[June 27, 1934, ch. 847, tit. V, § 536, *as added* Pub. L. No. 101-235, tit. I, § 107(a), 103 Stat. 2000 (Dec. 15, 1989), *and amended* Pub. L. No. 105-65, tit. V, § 553, 111 Stat. 1413 (Oct. 27, 1997); Pub. L. No. 105-276, tit. VI, § 601(g), (h), 112 Stat. 2674 (Oct. 21, 1998); Pub. L. No. 108-447, div. I, tit. II, § 219(a), 118 Stat. 3319 (Dec. 8, 2004); Pub. L. No. 109-171, tit. II, § 2102(b), 120 Stat. 9 (Feb. 8, 2006); Pub. L. No. 109-173, § 9(f)(2), 119 Stat. 3618 (Feb. 15, 2006); Pub. L. No. 111-22, div. A, tit. II, § 203(f), 123 Stat. 1647 (May 20, 2009)]

* * *

A.2.2 Selected Regulations

TITLE 24—HOUSING AND URBAN DEVELOPMENT

SUBTITLE B—REGULATIONS RELATING TO HOUSING AND URBAN DEVELOPMENT

CHAPTER II—OFFICE OF ASSISTANT SECRETARY FOR HOUSING—FEDERAL HOUSING COMMISSIONER, DEPARTMENT OF HOUSING AND URBAN DEVELOPMENT

SUBCHAPTER B—MORTGAGE AND LOAN INSURANCE PROGRAMS UNDER NATIONAL HOUSING ACT AND OTHER AUTHORITIES

PART 203—SINGLE FAMILY MORTGAGE INSURANCE

SUBPART C—SERVICING RESPONSIBILITIES

GENERAL REQUIREMENTS

24 C.F.R. § 203.500 Mortgage servicing generally.

This subpart identifies servicing practices of lending institutions that HUD considers acceptable for mortgages insured by HUD. Failure to comply with this subpart shall not be a basis for denial of insurance benefits, but failure to comply will be cause for imposition of a civil money penalty, including a penalty under § 30.35(c)(2), or withdrawal of HUD's approval of a mortgagee. It is the intent of the Department that no mortgagee shall commence foreclosure or acquire title to a property until the requirements of this subpart have been followed.

[45 Fed. Reg. 29,574 (May 5, 1980); 47 Fed. Reg. 33,254 (Aug. 2, 1982); 50 Fed. Reg. 12,527 (Mar. 29, 1985); 52 Fed. Reg. 6915 (Mar. 5, 1987); 61 Fed. Reg. 35,019 (July 3, 1996); 62 Fed. Reg. 60,129 (Nov. 6, 1997); 70 Fed. Reg. 21,578 (Apr. 26, 2005)]

* * *

MORTGAGEE ACTION AND FORBEARANCE

24 C.F.R. § 203.600 Mortgage collection action.

Subject to the requirements of this subpart, mortgagees shall take prompt action to collect amounts due from mortgagors to minimize the number of accounts in a delinquent or default status. Collection techniques must be adapted to individual differences in mortgagors and take account of the circumstances peculiar to each mortgagor.

[41 Fed. Reg. 49,736 (Nov. 10, 1976)]

24 C.F.R. § 203.602 Delinquency notice to mortgagor.

The mortgagee shall give notice to each mortgagor in default on a form supplied by the Secretary or, if the mortgagee wishes to use its own form, on a form approved by the Secretary, no later than the end of the second month of any delinquency in payments under the mortgage. If an account is reinstated and again becomes delinquent, the delinquency notice shall be sent to the mortgagor again, except that the mortgagee is not required to send a second delinquency notice to the same mortgagor more often than once each six months. The mortgagee may issue additional or more frequent notices of delinquency at its option.

[41 Fed. Reg. 49,736 (Nov. 10, 1976)]

24 C.F.R. § 203.604 Contact with the mortgagor.

(a) [Reserved]

(b) The mortgagee must have a face-to-face interview with the mortgagor, or make a reasonable effort to arrange such a meeting, before three full monthly installments due on the mortgage are unpaid. If default occurs in a repayment plan arranged other than during a personal interview, the mortgagee must have a face-to-face meeting with the mortgagor, or make a reasonable attempt to arrange such a meeting within 30 days after such default and at least 30 days before foreclosure is commenced, or at least 30 days before assignment is requested if the mortgage is insured on Hawaiian home land pursuant to section 247 or Indian land pursuant to section 248 or if assignment is requested under § 203.350(d) for mortgages authorized by section 203(q) of the National Housing Act.

(c) A face-to-face meeting is not required if:

(1) The mortgagor does not reside in the mortgaged property,

(2) The mortgaged property is not within 200 miles of the mortgagee, its servicer, or a branch office of either,

(3) The mortgagor has clearly indicated that he will not cooperate in the interview,

(4) A repayment plan consistent with the mortgagor's circumstances is entered into to bring the mortgagor's account current thus making a meeting unnecessary, and payments thereunder are current, or

(5) A reasonable effort to arrange a meeting is unsuccessful.

(d) A reasonable effort to arrange a face-to-face meeting with the mortgagor shall consist at a minimum of one letter sent to the mortgagor certified by the Postal Service as having been dispatched. Such a reasonable effort to arrange a face-to-face meeting shall also include at least one trip to see the mortgagor at the mortgaged property, unless the mortgaged property is more than 200 miles from the mortgagee, its servicer, or a branch office of either, or it is known that the mortgagor is not residing in the mortgaged property.

(e)(1) For mortgages insured pursuant to section 248 of the National Housing Act, the provisions of paragraphs (b), (c) and (d) of this section are applicable, except that a face-to-face meeting with the mortgagor is required, and a reasonable effort to arrange such a meeting shall include at least one trip to see the mortgagor at the mortgaged property, notwithstanding that such property is more than 200 miles from the mortgagee, its servicer, or a branch office of either. In addition, the mortgagee must document that it has made at least one telephone call to the mortgagor for the purpose of trying to arrange a face-to-face interview. The mortgagee may appoint an agent to perform its responsibilities under this paragraph.

(2) The mortgagee must also:

(i) Inform the mortgagor that HUD will make information regarding the status and payment history of the mortgagor's loan available to local credit bureaus and prospective creditors;

(ii) Inform the mortgagor of other available assistance, if any;

(iii) Inform the mortgagor of the names and addresses of HUD officials to whom further communications may be addressed.

[51 Fed. Reg. 21,873 (June 16, 1986); 52 Fed. Reg. 8068 (Mar. 16, 1987); 52 Fed. Reg. 28,470 (July 30, 1987); 52 Fed. Reg. 48,202 (Dec. 21, 1987); 53 Fed. Reg. 9869 (Mar. 28, 1988); 54 Fed. Reg. 32,971 (Aug. 11, 1989); 61 Fed. Reg. 35,019 (July 3, 1996); 62 Fed. Reg. 60,129 (Nov. 6, 1997)]

24 C.F.R. § 203.605 Loss mitigation performance.

(a) *Duty to mitigate.* Before four full monthly installments due on the mortgage have become unpaid, the mortgagee shall evaluate on a monthly basis all of the loss mitigation techniques provided at § 203.501 to determine which is appropriate. Based upon such evaluations, the mortgagee shall take the appropriate loss mitigation action. Documentation must be maintained for the initial and all subsequent evaluations and resulting loss mitigation actions. Should a claim for mortgage insurance benefits later be filed, the mortgagee shall maintain this documentation in the claim review file under the requirements of § 203.365(c).

(b) *Assessment of mortgagee's loss mitigation performance.*

(1) HUD will measure and advise mortgagees of their loss mitigation performance through the Tier Ranking System (TRS). Under the TRS, HUD will analyze each mortgagee's loss mitigation efforts portfolio-wide on a quarterly basis, based on 12 months of performance, by computing ratios involving loss mitigation attempts, defaults, and claims. Based on the ratios, HUD will group mortgagees in four tiers (Tiers 1, 2, 3, and 4), with Tier 1 representing the highest or best ranking mortgagees and Tier 4 representing the lowest or least satisfactory ranking mortgagees. The precise methodology for calculating the TRS ratios and for determining the tier stratification (or cutoff points) will be provided through Federal Register notice. Notice of future TRS methodology or stratification changes will be published in the Federal Register and will provide a 30-day public comment period.

(2) Before HUD issues each quarterly TRS notice, HUD will review the number of claims paid to the mortgagee. If HUD determines that the lender's low TRS score is the result of a small number of defaults or a small number of foreclosure claims, or both, as defined by notice, HUD may determine not to designate the mortgagee as Tier 3 or Tier 4, and the mortgagee will remain unranked.

(3) Within 30 calendar days after the date of the TRS notice, a mortgagee that scored in Tier 4 may appeal its ranking to the Deputy Assistant Secretary for Single Family or the Deputy Assistant Secretary's designee and request an informal HUD conference. The only basis for appeal by the Tier 4 mortgagee is disagreement with the data used by HUD to calculate the mortgagee's ranking. If HUD determines that the mortgagee's Tier 4 ranking was based on incorrect or incomplete data, the mortgagee's performance will be recalculated and the mortgagee will receive a corrected tier ranking score.

(c) *Assessment of civil money penalty.* A mortgagee that is found to have failed to engage in loss mitigation as required under paragraph (a) of this section shall be liable for a civil money penalty as provided in § 30.35(c) of this title.

[61 Fed. Reg. 35,019 (July 3, 1996); 62 Fed. Reg. 60,129 (Nov. 6, 1997); 70 Fed. Reg. 21,578 (Apr. 26, 2005)]

24 C.F.R. § 203.606 Pre-foreclosure review.

(a) Before initiating foreclosure, the mortgagee must ensure that all servicing requirements of this subpart have been met. The mortgagee may not commence foreclosure for a monetary default unless at least three full monthly installments due under the mortgage are unpaid after application of any partial payments that may have been accepted but not yet applied to the mortgage account. In addition, prior to initiating any action required by law to foreclose the mortgage, the mortgagee shall notify the mortgagor in a format prescribed by the Secretary that the mortgagor is in default and the mortgagee intends to foreclose unless the mortgagor cures the default.

(b) If the mortgagee determines that any of the following conditions has been met, the mortgagee may initiate foreclosure without the delay in foreclosure required by paragraph (a) of this section:

(1) The mortgaged property has been abandoned, or has been vacant for more than 60 days.

(2) The mortgagor, after being clearly advised of the options available for relief, has clearly stated in writing that he or she has no intention of fulfilling his or her obligation under the mortgage.

(3) The mortgaged property is not the mortgagor's principal residence and it is occupied by tenants who are paying rent, but the rental income is not being applied to the mortgage debt.

(4) The property is owned by a corporation or partnership.

[41 Fed. Reg. 49,736 (Nov. 10, 1976), *as amended at* 44 Fed. Reg. 1336 (Jan. 4, 1979); 47 Fed. Reg. 33,254 (July 2, 1982); 47 Fed. Reg. 40,410 (Sept. 14, 1982); 50 Fed. Reg. 12,527 (Mar. 29, 1985); 52 Fed. Reg. 69,15 (Mar. 5, 1987); 61 Fed. Reg. 35,020 (July 3, 1996); 62 Fed. Reg. 60,129 (Nov. 6, 1997)]

24 C.F.R. § 203.608 Reinstatement.

The mortgagee shall permit reinstatement of a mortgage, even after the institution of foreclosure proceedings, if the mortgagor tenders in a lump sum all amounts required to bring the account current, including foreclosure costs and reasonable attorney's fees and expenses properly associated with the foreclosure action, unless: (a) The mortgagee has accepted reinstatement after the institution of foreclosure proceedings within two years immediately preceding the commencement of the current foreclosure action, (b) reinstatement will preclude foreclosure following a subsequent default, or (c) reinstatement will adversely affect the priority of the mortgage lien.

[41 Fed. Reg. 49,736 (Nov. 10, 1976)]

24 C.F.R. § 203.610 Relief for mortgagor in military service.

The mortgagee shall specifically give consideration to affording the mortgagor the benefit of relief authorized by §§ 203.345 and 203.346, if the mortgagor is person in the military service as that term is defined in the Soldiers and Sailors Civil Relief Act of 1940, as amended.

[41 Fed. Reg. 49,736 (Nov. 10, 1976)]

24 C.F.R. § 203.614 Special forbearance.

If the mortgagee finds that a default is due to circumstances beyond the mortgagor's control, as defined by HUD, the mortgagee may grant special forbearance relief to the mortgagor in accordance with the conditions prescribed by HUD.

[60 Fed. Reg. 57,678 (Nov. 16, 1995); 61 Fed. Reg. 35,020 (July 3, 1996); 62 Fed. Reg. 60,129 (Nov. 6, 1997)]

24 C.F.R. § 203.616 Mortgage modification.

The mortgagee may modify a mortgage for the purpose of changing the amortization provisions by recasting the total unpaid amount due for a term not exceeding 360 months. The mortgagee must notify HUD of such modification in a format prescribed by HUD within 30 days of the execution of the modification agreement.

[61 Fed. Reg. 35,020 (July 3, 1996); 62 Fed. Reg. 60,130 (Nov. 6, 1997)]

A.2.3 Selected Mortgagee Letters[1]

Department of Housing and Urban Development, Mortgagee Letter 2000-05 (Jan. 19, 2000)

January 19, 2000

MORTGAGEE LETTER 2000-05

TO: ALL APPROVED MORTGAGEES

ATTENTION: SINGLE FAMILY SERVICING MANAGERS

SUBJECT: LOSS MITIGATION PROGRAM—COMPREHENSIVE CLARIFICATION OF POLICY AND NOTICE OF PROCEDURAL CHANGES

The purpose of this mortgagee letter is to announce clarifications of policy and procedural changes in FHA's Loss Mitigation Program and provide an updated consolidation of the existing program guidance.

BACKGROUND

After April 25, 1996, FHA ceased accepting applications for assignment of insured loans that had gone into default and initiated a comprehensive loss mitigation program to provide relief to borrowers in default. FHA's Loss Mitigation Program returns responsibility for managing loan defaults to mortgagees, and provides financial incentives to recognize them for their efforts. Loss mitigation is considered critical to FHA because it works to fulfill the goal of helping borrowers in default retain home ownership while reducing, or mitigating the economic impact on the insurance fund.

The program includes five strategies to be used by mortgagees as they deem appropriate, based on an individual assessment of the borrower's financial circumstances and the status of the loan. Three of the options ("reinstatement options") promote retention of home ownership, while two assist borrowers in default transition to lower cost housing ("disposition options").

This mortgagee letter provides a complete description of each option, identifies requirements for their use, and describes circumstances in which each may be appropriate. This issuance contains several clarifications of HUD policy. It replaces and supersedes the following mortgagee letters:

Mortgagee letter 97-43, FHA Loss Mitigation—Mortgage Modification Clarification

Mortgagee letter 96-32, Loss Mitigation—Mortgage Modification

Mortgagee letter 96-25, Existing Alternatives to Foreclosure

This mortgagee letter partially supersedes the following mortgagee letters:

Mortgagee letter 96-61, Loss Mitigation Procedures—Special Instructions

(Superseded and replaced, except for the loss mitigation claims instructions, which were changed by Mortgagee letter 99-27.)

Mortgagee letter 97-17, FHA Loss Mitigation—Clarification of Procedures

(Superseded and replaced, except for the model form of note(s) and subordinate mortgage provided, which remain unchanged and are still in effect.)

TABLE OF CONTENTS

EARLY DELINQUENCY (PRIOR TO 90 DAYS DELINQUENT) SERVICING REQUIREMENTS

As stated in Chapter 7 of HUD Handbook 4330.1, REV-5, *Administration of Insured Home Mortgages* (Handbook), the purpose of all collection efforts is to bring a delinquent mortgage current in as short a time as possible. The Handbook describes minimum default servicing requirements to accomplish this objective and expects that the vast majority of one or two payment delinquencies will be addressed by either voluntary reinstatement by mortgagors, or through traditional collection methods outlined in the Handbook, including informal forbearance plans, assumptions, and delinquent refinance.

The Loss Mitigation Program was designed to address serious defaults, those that continue for 90 days or more. However, all efforts taken by a lender in addressing delinquent loans contribute to HUD's goal of home ownership retention and protection of the insurance funds. Many of the most effective loss mitigation actions take place in the early stages of collection.

A. Early Intervention

To meet the procedural requirements of the Loss Mitigation Program (24 CFR 203.355), lenders must become proactive early in the default. The earlier that the lender establishes contact with the borrower, identifies the cause of default and begins to discuss reinstatement options, the more likely it is that the default will be cured and the mortgagor will be able to retain home ownership. Efforts to assist the borrower should begin as soon as the loan becomes delinquent. Mortgagees must make all decisions, particularly discretionary decisions, consistent with Fair Housing and Lending principles.

HUD's minimum collection requirements for borrower contact, described in Chapter 7 of the Handbook, have not changed. However, the time to complete these activities has been compressed due to an acceleration of the foreclosure initiation time limit which, under the revised rule (24 CFR 203.355), has been reduced from nine to six months from the date of default.

B. Cause of Default

HUD does not have a "hardship" test. Lenders may offer FHA relief options to homeowners who have experienced a verifiable loss of income or increase in living expenses to the point where the mortgage payments are no longer sustainable. HUD encourages lenders to develop collection techniques that seek to identify the

1 Mortgagee letters are correspondence from HUD to approved lenders outlining or clarifying policy and procedure regarding the various mortgage programs. Mortgagee letters available at www.hud.gov/offices/hsg/mltrmenu.cfm.

underlying cause of the default at the earliest stages of borrower contact, primarily to determine if the financial problem is permanent or temporary. Borrowers whose ability to support the mortgage debt has been permanently reduced, for example through death, divorce, or permanent disability, are unlikely to reinstate through repayment plans. They should be considered for either loan modification which could provide a permanent reduction in the mortgage payment, or for pre-foreclosure sale which allows borrowers to transition to more affordable housing.

Borrowers who may require credit, legal or employment assistance to resolve temporary financial problems should be referred to housing counseling as quickly as possible.

C. Default Counseling

Borrowers who receive counseling early are much more likely to bring their loans current. Lenders are strongly encouraged to recommend counseling to borrowers and establish working relationships with counseling agencies. At a minimum, the lender must provide the borrower with a copy of the HUD publication PA 426-H, May 19, 1997, *How to Avoid Foreclosure*, no later than the end of the second month of delinquency (24 CFR 203.602). Lenders may make an exception to this requirement if the borrower has filed bankruptcy and, in the opinion of the lender's legal counsel, providing a copy of the HUD pamphlet would be a violation of the bankruptcy stay. This exception must be documented in the servicing file.

D. Informal Forbearance Plans

A verbal repayment agreement with a duration of 3 months or less is considered to be an informal forbearance plan. An informal forbearance plan is the first and best means to ensure that a one or two month delinquency does not escalate beyond the mortgagor's ability to cure. Lenders should avoid use of standard repayment terms, such as requiring all borrowers to make 1 ½ payments per month until reinstatement. Rather, FHA requires lenders to review each mortgagor's financial situation and arrange payment terms consistent with the borrower's ability to pay.

E. Delinquent Refinance

HUD recognizes that there are situations where mortgagors more than two months behind in their payments could cure their default if they were able to refinance the mortgage using their equity to pay off the unpaid balance plus any arrearage. HUD permits lenders to refinance these mortgages under certain circumstances.

Under the Delinquent Refinance Program, the lender must provide an amount equal to one month's mortgage payment, principal, interest, taxes and insurance ("PITI") of the mortgage being refinanced. For detailed instruction regarding delinquent refinances, refer to Mortgagee letter 94-30, dated June 28, 1994, *Refinances of Delinquent Mortgages—Special Instructions*.

F. Sale of the Property

Borrowers who do not have either the ability or willingness to reinstate, but who have sufficient equity to sell their property and use the sale proceeds to repay the arrearage, should be encouraged and assisted by the lender. This assistance may include the additional time provided by an agreement which provides a short term reduction or suspension of payments pending the closing of a sale or loan assumption. Lenders are reminded that any mortgage delinquency must be cured no later than at closing. FHA requirements for assumptions are described in Chapter 6 of the Handbook.

<u>LOSS MITIGATION PROGRAM OVERVIEW</u>

The FHA Loss Mitigation Program delegates to lenders both the authority and the responsibility to utilize actions and strategies to assist borrowers in default in retaining their homes, and/or in reducing losses to FHA's insurance funds. HUD believes that the lender is best positioned to determine which, if any, loss mitigation strategies are appropriate in a given circumstance. Without HUD approval, lenders may, in their sole discretion, utilize any of the loss mitigation options, within the guidelines provided in this document or determined by the Secretary.

Though lenders have great latitude in selecting the loss mitigation strategy appropriate for each borrower, it is critical to understand that **PARTICIPATION IN THE LOSS MITIGATION PROGRAM IS NOT OPTIONAL**. Lenders are required to:

- Consider all reasonable means to address delinquency at the earliest possible moment.
- Inform borrowers of available loss mitigation options and the availability of housing counseling within the second month of delinquency.
- Evaluate each delinquent loan no later than the 90th day of delinquency to determine which loss mitigation option is appropriate.
- Utilize loss mitigation whenever feasible to avoid foreclosure.
- Re-evaluate each loan monthly until reinstatement or foreclosure.
- Report loss mitigation actions through the Single Family Default Monitoring System (SFDMS), (refer to Mortgage Letter 99-9).
- Initiate foreclosure within six months of default unless a loss mitigation option is being pursued and ensure that all actions taken are documented.
- Retain a complete audit trail confirming compliance with all loss mitigation requirements.

Failure to comply with the provisions of the Loss Mitigation Program may result in the loss of incentive compensation and other benefits; reduced reimbursement of foreclosure and acquisition costs; and interest curtailment related to foreclosure delays.

Also, depending upon the severity of the non-compliance, the Department may also refer the lender to the Mortgagee Review Board (MRB) whose sanctions include civil money penalties, indemnification and the termination of the mortgagee's approval to participate in HUD programs.

A. Incentive Fees

In recognition of the effort and administrative expense involved in full implementation of loss mitigation, HUD provides financial incentives to mortgagees who utilize any of the 5 loss mitigation options listed below.

(<u>Reinstatement Options</u>)	
Special Forbearance	$ 100 ($200 for lenders with performance scores in the top 25%)
Loan Modification	$ 500
Partial Claim	$ 250
(<u>Disposition Options</u>)	
Pre-Foreclosure Sale	$ 1,000
Deed-In-Lieu of Foreclosure	$ 250

Additionally, use of any of the options except deed in lieu, extends the time frame requirement to initiate foreclosure or otherwise meet the time frame requirement of 24 CFR 203.355 in the event the workout fails. Use of special forbearance also provides the mortgagee with greater protections against subsequent foreclosure by allowing interest to be calculated more favorably. These benefits are fully described under each option.

B. Performance Measurement

FHA has created a tool to measure lender utilization of the Loss Mitigation Program, and to provide performance-based incentives to mortgagees. The Department intends to score lender performance on an annual basis. Lender performance score results will be used to determine eligibility for some incentive benefits and in selecting lenders for quality assurance reviews. They may also affect a mortgagee's percentage reimbursement for foreclosure expenses. More information on performance scoring is found in Mortgagee Letters 97-21, 98-9 and 99-6.

GENERAL PROGRAM REQUIREMENTS

Both lenders and borrowers have responsibilities under the Loss Mitigation Program. While each option has specific eligibility requirements, there are some policies that apply to all of the options, and some lender requirements which must be met whether or not any of the loss mitigation strategies are used. This section describes these general policies, recommended procedures, and minimum eligibility requirements.

A. Default Status of the Loan

Loss mitigation options are intended to provide relief for borrowers who are currently in default which is defined in 24 CFR 203.330, and in the Handbook as, ". . . a mortgagor's failure to perform under any covenant of the mortgage and the failure continues for 30 days." The lender may make reinstatement options (special forbearance agreements loan modifications and partial claims) available to borrowers whose failure to perform continues for at least 90 days (120 days for partial claims). Disposition options (pre-foreclosure sales and deeds-in lieu of foreclosure) are available immediately upon default, if the cause of the default is incurable, i.e. the borrower has no realistic opportunity to replace the lost income or reduce expenses sufficiently to meet the mortgage obligation.

Any attempt to utilize loss mitigation options by deliberately manufacturing or misrepresenting pertinent facts about a mortgagor's financial or other qualifying status, shall be considered "willful abuse," will disqualify a mortgagor from participation, and could lead to sanctions if perpetrated by a lender.

B. Owner Occupancy

The borrower must occupy the property as a principal residence to be eligible for any of the reinstatement options (special forbearance, loan modification or partial claim). Lenders are authorized to grant reasonable exceptions to non-occupant borrowers seeking relief through pre-foreclosure sale (PFS), or deed-in-lieu of foreclosure (DIL) when it is clear that the subject property was not purchased as a rental investment, or used as a rental for more than 12 months. Justification for the above exceptions must be documented in the claim review file.

If the borrower is a corporation or partnership, a written request for approval must be submitted to:

U.S. Department of Housing and Urban Development
Servicing and Loss Mitigation Division
500 W. Main Street, Suite 400
Oklahoma City, OK 73102

C. Prohibition on Other FHA Loans

The mortgagor may not own other real estate subject to FHA insurance, or have been the mortgagor on prior loans on which an FHA claim has been paid within the past three years. The Credit Alert Interactive Response Systems (CAIVRS) must be used to assist in this determination, prior to use of any of the loss mitigation options.

Lenders are authorized to make reasonable exceptions, for mortgagors who have acquired FHA insured property through inheritance, or for mortgagors who co-signed FHA insured loans to enhance the credit of another borrower. Justification for any exceptions must be documented.

D. Other Eligibility Requirements

FHA has established the following general eligibility restrictions:

- With the exception of special forbearance, loss mitigation options are not available on co-insured loans until the 60th payment has been received.
- Borrowers who have filed bankruptcy are not eligible for any loss mitigation option except partial claim as more fully explained in Section B, page 25. Borrowers who have had a bankruptcy discharged or dismissed may be considered for loss mitigation options including pre-foreclosure sale.
- Loans secured by vacant or abandoned properties are not eligible for reinstatement options, though disposition options may be utilized when properties have been recently vacated by circumstances related to the default, such as job transfer or death. Such circumstances must be documented by the lender in the claim review file.

E. 90 Day Review Requirement

No later than when 3 full monthly installments are due and unpaid, lenders must evaluate each defaulted loan and consider all loss mitigation techniques to determine which, if any, are appropriate (24 CFR 203.605). In order to comply with this 90 day evaluation requirement, lenders must already have contacted the borrower and gathered sufficient information about the borrower's circumstances, intentions and financial condition. Given the normal reticence of most borrowers in financial distress, lenders must be proactive early in the default in order to meet this 90 day deadline. While the lender cannot be responsible if a borrower fails to respond to repeated contacts, claim review files must clearly document aggressive efforts to reach each borrower in default well in advance of the 90 day deadline.

When the cause of the default is curable and the borrower is committed to remaining in the home, HUD expects lenders to consider reinstatement options in the following order:

- Special forbearance
- Loan modification
- Partial claim

When the cause of the default is not curable and/or the borrower is not committed to remaining in the home, HUD expects lenders to consider disposition options in the following order:

- Pre-foreclosure sale
- Deed-in-lieu

F. Option Priority

HUD has established its order of option priority in order to minimize losses to the insurance funds. For example, both a partial claim and a special forbearance will avert a foreclosure and reduce the potential loss to the funds. However, borrower funded reinstatement through a special forbearance plan, is less costly to HUD than a partial claim reinstatement which is funded by FHA. Therefore, HUD requires that lenders determine that a special forbearance is not the best option prior to considering the use of a modification, and that a determination be made that a modification is not the best option prior to considering the use of a partial claim.

However, there will be some situations where a loan modification is clearly the best option, especially when the reduction of the interest rate and/or extension of the loan term yield a sizable reduction of the mortgagor's monthly payment. In these situations, modifications will be preferred over special forbearance. Lenders shall document the reasons why the specific loss mitigation option was chosen in the claim review file.

For the same goal of minimizing loses to HUD's insurance funds, pre-foreclosure sale ("PFS") is preferable to a deed in lieu ("DIL") of foreclosure. In most cases mortgagors are expected to attempt to market the collateral property under the PFS program prior to acceptance of a DIL by the mortgagor.

G. Monthly Evaluation Requirement

As long as the account remains delinquent, the lender must reevaluate the status of each loan monthly following the 90 day review, and is required to maintain documentation of the evaluations. This evaluation may be as simple as noting that the mortgagor is making payments as scheduled if the account is under special forbearance.

H. Evaluation of the Borrower's Financial Condition

To be considered for any of the loss mitigation options, the borrower must provide detailed financial information to the lender. The lender may request that this information be submitted on Form HUD-92068 F, *Request for Financial Information,* or on a similar form provided by the lender. The Department has no objection to situations where a cooperative mortgagor provides complete financial information during a telephone interview. Regardless of how the mortgagor's financial information was secured, the lender must independently verify the financial information by obtaining a credit report, and any other forms of verification the lender deems appropriate.

Regardless of the option under consideration, the lender must analyze the borrower's current and future ability to meet the monthly mortgage obligation, by estimating the borrower's assets and surplus income in the following manner:

- Estimate the borrower's normal monthly living expenses (food, utilities, etc.) including debt service on the mortgage and other scheduled obligations. Make necessary adjustments to reflect increased or decreased expenses for each month of the proposed special forbearance agreement, or in the case of all other options, for a minimum of three months.
- Estimate the borrower's anticipated monthly net income for the same period, making necessary adjustments for income fluctuations.
- Subtract expenses from income to determine the amount of surplus income available each month.
- Divide surplus income by total monthly expenses to determine the **surplus income percentage**.

The lender must use good business judgment to ensure that the workout option selected reasonably reflects the borrower's ability to pay. Borrowers with sufficient surplus income, and/or other assets, must be required to reinstate the debt through a repayment option.

For those situations where the mortgagee's evaluation indicates that the borrower is not eligible for any loss mitigation alternative, and the information relied upon in making this decision was secured from the borrower in a telephone interview, the lender shall advise the borrower in writing of this decision. The lender shall explain the reason for denial and allow the mortgagor at least seven calendar days to submit additional information that may impact upon the mortgagee's evaluation.

In the event a claim for loss is submitted to HUD, the lender must retain the financial analysis and supporting documentation in the claim review file.

I. Combining Options

The loss mitigation options may be used alone or in combination to resolve an existing default, although there are some limitations.

- Special forbearance may be combined with any reinstatement option including delinquent refinance. The combination of options will be sequential, not simultaneous.
- Special forbearance may be used to reinstate a loan prior to an assumption.
- Pre-foreclosure may be combined with a deed-in-lieu provision in the event the property does not sell within the time required.
- Modification may not be combined with a partial claim.

FHA strongly encourages lenders to combine special forbearance plans with modification, or special forbearance plans with partial claim whenever there is any doubt about a borrower's long term income stability. By requiring a borrower to make at least three full monthly payments prior to execution of a modification or partial claim, borrowers demonstrate their ability to support the debt, and FHA is further protected from the risk of workout failure. While this trial period is no guarantee against future default, a borrower's ability to make the first three payments is a strong indication that this is a long term workout option, and not a costly quick-fix.

J. Foreclosure

Lenders may not initiate foreclosure until all loss mitigation options have been considered. Written documentation of this review must be available in all conveyance claim review files (24 CFR 203.605). If the case meets one of the exceptions noted in 24 CFR 203.606, such as abandonment, loss mitigation does not have to be considered prior to initiating foreclosure. However, the claim review file must provide documentation of this finding.

K. Time Requirement to Initiate Action

Lenders must utilize one of the loss mitigation options or initiate foreclosure within six months of the date of default for all mortgages with a default date on or after February 1, 1998 (24 CFR 203.355). FHA considers the lender to have satisfied this requirement if, within the six month time frame, any of the following actions has taken place.

- The loan is reinstated or paid off.
- The borrower executes a special forbearance agreement.
- The loan is modified.
- The loan is reinstated through a partial claim.
- The borrower executes a pre-foreclosure sale agreement.
- The lender executes a deed-in-lieu of foreclosure.
- The lender initiates the first legal action to begin foreclosure.

Lenders must report the action through SFDMS in the month the action occurs or, if after the monthly cut-off date, in the next reporting cycle.

L. Automatic Extensions

If a lender has initiated, but is unable to complete a special forbearance, modification, or partial claim within the six month time limit, the lender is entitled to a 90 day extension of the foreclosure deadline provided the initiative was begun prior to the expiration of the initial six months. Therefore, if there have been no other intervening delays (such as bankruptcy) this "automatic" extension will extend the six month deadline to initiate foreclosure by 90 days. To qualify for the automatic extension, the mortgagee must have completed the loss mitigation evaluation required by 24 CFR 203.605 and have documentation of this analysis in the claim review file. In addition the loss mitigation initiative must be reported on SFDMS, using the appropriate status code. All extensions of time to initiate foreclosure including "automatic extensions" must be properly identified on form HUD-27011, Block 19 on the conveyance claim.

There is no automatic extension provided for completion of a deed-in-lieu, although an extension of time may be requested from the Servicing and Loss Mitigation Office in Oklahoma City. There is also no "automatic extension" for attempting a repayment plan (not special forbearance), a delinquent refinance or an assumption. Lenders must request this extension of time before the expiration of the existing time frame and must explain why an extension of time is necessary.

M. Option Failure

Foreclosure action is suspended during special forbearance and pre-foreclosure sale periods. In the event that these options fail, an additional 90 day extension is provided in which the lender must commence or recommence foreclosure or initiate another loss mitigation option. Failure is defined as:

- Special forbearance—mortgagor fails to perform under the terms of the written special forbearance agreement and the failure continues for 60 days.
- Pre-foreclosure Sale—Either, 4 months from the date of the PFS Agreement (6 months for lenders in the top 25th percentile) if there is no signed contract of sale; or 6 months from the date of the PFS Agreement (8 months for lenders in the top 25th percentile) if there is a signed contract of sale but settlement has not occurred; or the date the lender is notified of the mortgagor's withdrawal; or the date of the letter from the lender to the mortgagor notifying them that participation as been terminated.

N. File Documentation

For each claim filed, the lender must maintain in the claim review file, evidence of compliance with all requirements of the Loss Mitigation Program, as well as supporting documentation including all communication with any HUD office. The mortgagee's regular servicing files should also contain evidence of compliance with the counseling, 90 day review and other requirements of the program for those loans which do not result in a claim.

O. Customer Service

HUD has consolidated all responsibility and authority for management of the Loss Mitigation Program at its Oklahoma City Office. FHA staff in Oklahoma are available to provide customer service to lenders, servicers, counselors and borrowers relative to loss mitigation issues. They have established a toll free number, 888-297-8685 for all inquiries. Written inquiries may be directed to:

U.S. Department of Housing and Urban Development
Servicing and Loss Mitigation Division
500 W. Main Street, Suite 400
Oklahoma City, OK 73102

P. Extensions and Variances

Lenders may request an additional extension of time from the HUD Office in Oklahoma. Each extension request must be submitted on Form HUD-50012, and must be accompanied by a valid justification for the extension.

Additionally, in the new procedures HUD has provided lenders with great flexibility to make exceptions to Department policy when exceptions are deemed to be in the best interest of the Department and the mortgagor. However, if circumstances require a variance not delegated to lenders, written requests should be mailed to the address above.

Q. Option Checklists

Many lenders requested that FHA provide teaching tools to assist in the training of staff unfamiliar with the requirements of the Loss Mitigation Program. In response, FHA has updated the Option Checklists originally published in ML 96-61. The revised checklists, included in the Appendix, highlight the most important eligibility requirements for each loss mitigation option in a convenient, easy to understand format. Use of the checklists is optional. There is no requirement that checklists be delivered to HUD with claims.

SPECIAL FORBEARANCE

A special forbearance is a written repayment agreement between a lender and a mortgagor which contains a plan to reinstate a loan that has been delinquent for at least 90 days. To qualify as a special forbearance and entitle the lender to the incentives afforded under this section, the agreement must provide the mortgagor with relief not typically afforded under an informal forbearance plan (Section D, page 5). Examples of the types of provisions which may be included in a special forbearance agreement include a repayment term of 4 or more months; suspension or reduction of payments for one or more months to allow the borrower to recover from the cause of default; and/or an agreement to allow the borrower to resume making full monthly payments while delaying repayment of the arrearage.

While special forbearance plans have no maximum duration, at no time may the maximum arrearage due under a special forbearance plan exceed the equivalent of 12 months of principal, interest, taxes and insurance ("PITI").

Special forbearance plans must lead to reinstatement of the loan, either by gradually increasing monthly payments in an amount sufficient to repay the arrearage over time, or through resumption of normal payments for a period of time (generally 3 or more months) followed by a loan modification or partial claim. HUD will pay lenders a cash incentive for entering into a special forbearance plan, regardless of the outcome. As an additional incentive, HUD provides increased claim benefits related to the calculation of claimable interest in the event a special forbearance plan fails and a conveyance claim is filed.

To enable lenders to better utilize this option, FHA has reduced its minimum delinquency requirement from 4 months to 90 days. This and other special forbearance requirements are listed below.

A. Loan Default

The loan must be more than 3 months (90 days), but not more than 12 months (365 days) delinquent, and may not be in foreclosure when the special forbearance agreement is executed. Loans that had previously been referred to foreclosure may be removed from foreclosure status prior to execution of a special forbearance. On advice of lender's legal counsel, foreclosure may be suspended subject to the borrower's performance under the terms of the special forbearance agreement, if the suspension, is stipulated in writing in the agreement.

B. Borrower Qualifications

Special forbearance may be offered to borrowers who have recently experienced a verifiable loss of income or increase in living expenses, but who will have sufficient monthly income to correct the delinquency and reinstate the loan within the duration of the plan either through gradual repayment of the arrearage, or through a combination of repayment and modification or partial claim.

The borrower must be an owner occupant, committed to occupy the property as a primary residence during the term of the special forbearance agreement. However, unlike modification and partial claim which require that the borrower have a long term commitment to the home, special forbearance may be used to reinstate a loan to facilitate the eventual sale, or assumption of the property.

C. Property Condition

The lender must conduct any review it deems necessary to verify that the property has no physical conditions which adversely impact the borrower's continued use or ability to support the debt. A borrower will not be able to support payments under a special forbearance plan if the property is in such a deteriorated condition that repairs drain the borrower's monthly resources. An analysis of the borrower's surplus income should consider obvious property maintenance expenses.

If significant deferred maintenance contributed to the cause of the default, it may be appropriate that the special forbearance plan provide a period of mortgage forbearance during which repairs specified in the agreement will be completed at the borrower's expense. If the mortgagee's review identifies a property in extremely poor physical condition, a special forbearance plan, especially one that allows reduction or suspension of payments not tied directly to property repair, may not offer a permanent resolution to the default. Lenders must use good business judgment relative to property condition.

D. Financial Analysis

The lender is required to assess the borrower's ability to repay the default as described in Section H, page 10. HUD expects the lender to project the borrower's surplus monthly income for the duration of the special forbearance period, and to propose repayment terms consistent with the borrower's ability to pay.

The lender must exercise good business judgment to determine that the borrower has the capacity to resume full monthly payments, and eventually reinstate the loan under the terms of the plan. If the financial analysis determines that the borrower does not or will not, in the foreseeable future, have the ability to resume full monthly payments, special forbearance should not be used. The lender should consider other loss mitigation options in the priority detailed in Section F, page 10.

E. Combining Options

Special forbearance may be utilized as a stand alone tool, or combined with a loan modification or partial claim. For example, a borrower may be expected to recover from the cause of the default and resume making full monthly payments, but will not have adequate surplus income to repay the arrearage. In this case, the lender might establish a special forbearance agreement which allows the borrower to demonstrate that he has recovered from the financial problem by making full mortgage payments for a period of 3 or 4 months, at which time the delinquent amount could be capitalized into a modified loan, or paid off through a partial claim promissory note.

F. Required Documentation

A written agreement must be executed by the mortgagor and lender, which clearly defines the term, frequency of payments, and amounts due under the forbearance plan. The agreement must acknowledge previously missed mortgage payments and provide notice that failure to comply with the terms of the special forbearance agreement can result in initiation of foreclosure.

FHA does not dictate a specific format for the agreement, however at a minimum it:

- Must provide the borrower with relief not typically available under an informal forbearance plan.
- Must fully reinstate the loan, except if combined with mortgage modification or partial claim, as in paragraph E, above.
- May not at any time allow the total amount of the arrearage to exceed the equivalent of 12 months PITI. (ARMS, GPMS, and GEMS will be calculated by multiplying 12 times the monthly payment due on the date of default.)
- May not allow for late fees to be assessed while the mortgagor is performing under the terms of a special forbearance plan.
- May allow reasonable foreclosure costs and late fees accrued prior to the execution of the special forbearance agreement to be included as part of the repayment schedule. However, they may only be collected after the loan has been reinstated through payment of all principal, interest, and escrow advances. At no time shall the loan be considered delinquent solely because the borrower has not paid late fees or other foreclosure costs.
- If the special forbearance plan culminates in a modification or partial claim, foreclosure costs and fees may only be collected in accordance with the requirements applicable to those options.
- There is no maximum duration requirement for special forbearance agreements. Lender's are encouraged to allow as much time as is reasonable based on the borrower's ability to repay.

G. Review and Re-negotiation

Lenders must review the status of forbearance plans each month and take appropriate action if the borrower is not complying with the terms of the plan. Plans may be re-negotiated if the borrower's financial circumstances change, however, re-negotiated plans may not exceed HUD's requirement that the loan be no more than 12 months delinquent. Lenders will not be entitled to file a claim for additional special forbearance incentives in the event a plan is re-negotiated.

H. Lender Incentives

FHA believes that well structured special forbearance agreements will resolve the majority of curable loan delinquencies. The Department strongly encourages use of this option and has provided attractive lender incentives.

- First, for every special forbearance agreement executed by a lender, regardless of the outcome, FHA will pay a $100 incentive fee. Lenders, whose overall loss mitigation performance is ranked in the top 25th percentile, will be eligible for incentive payments of $200 per claim.
- Second, when a special forbearance has been utilized and failed, and a conveyance claim is filed, lenders are entitled to collect unpaid interest at the note rate rather than debenture rate of interest.
- Finally, the number of months of interest that may be claimed is computed from the earliest of several dates as provided in 24 CFR 203.402a. This computation generally allows two additional months of interest, than would be payable on a conveyance claim where special forbearance had not been utilized.

These are significant claim benefits, intended to reduce the risk to lenders of offering reduced or suspended payments, and/or longer than normal repayment terms. These incentives are not available with any other loss mitigation option, and, with the exception of the incentive fees, do not apply if the lender files a claim for reimbursement as a result of a modification or partial claim.

I. Filing For Incentive Payment

The lender must file the claim for incentive payment within 60 days of the date of execution of the special forbearance agreement. It is not necessary to submit a copy of the special forbearance agreement or checklist. However, all documentation pertaining to the special forbearance must be retained in the claim review file.

If special forbearance is combined with any other option, the lender is entitled to file a claim for the special forbearance incentive fee, and file a subsequent claim when the other loss mitigation action is finalized.

LOAN MODIFICATION

A loan modification is a permanent change in one or more of the terms of a borrower's loan which if made, allows the loan to be reinstated, and results in a payment the borrower can afford. Modifications may include a change in the interest rate; capitalization of delinquent principal, interest or escrow items; extension of the time available to repay the loan; and/or re-amortization of the balance due.

Modification may be appropriate for borrowers who have experienced a permanent or long term reduction in income or increase in expenses, or have recovered from the cause of the default but do not have sufficient surplus income to repay the arrearage through a repayment plan. To qualify, borrowers must be able to support the monthly mortgage debt after the terms of the loan are modified.

Not all loans are appropriate for modification. Loan characteristics which best support modification include: loans with above market interest rates; lower loan to value ratios; and/or mature terms (loans paid down 10 years or more). The modification tool is valuable when the arrearage can be capitalized into the loan balance, the term extended and/or the interest rate adjusted to current market rate, so that the resulting monthly payment is at a level the borrower can afford.

Modification is most often used to reduce a borrower's payment when the cause of the default is permanent or long term. However, if a borrower has recovered from a short term financial problem and has strong income, a modification may be used to increase the monthly payment slightly, allowing the borrower to repay the arrearage gradually over the life of the loan.

Approximately 96% of all FHA insured loans are securitized in Ginnie Mae guaranteed pools. Prior to modification, but no sooner than the 90th day of default, securitized loans must be purchased from pools. Ginnie Mae has recently streamlined its re-pooling requirements allowing almost all modified FHA loans to be quickly repooled. Details of Ginnie Mae's modification policy are found in the All Participants Letter 96-15, *Pooling FHA Loans That Have Been Modified as a Result of Loss Mitigation Efforts*.

FHA has recently made several changes to its modification program. First, the Department realized that borrowers with below market interest rates were being excluded from the modification program because their loans had to be re-pooled at a discount. When appropriate, lenders may now increase the note interest, not to exceed market rate as defined below in Section F, page 21. Next, to protect borrowers from future payment increases, all modifications must now result in a fully amortizing, fixed rate loan. Adjustable and other variable payment loans will be converted to fixed as a condition of the modification. Finally, the BPO requirement has been eliminated (there is no longer a BPO requirement for any of the reinstatement options). These changes are more fully described below.

A. Loan Delinquency

To modify a defaulted mortgage under the loss mitigation program:

- Three or more full monthly payments must be due and unpaid.
- At least 12 months have elapsed since the origination date of the loan.
- The loan may not be in foreclosure at the time the modification is executed, however, loans removed from foreclosure status may be modified.
- The default must be due to a verifiable loss of income or increase in living expenses.

Note: Loans which are not delinquent but are in danger of imminent default may be modified at the discretion of the lender and insurance coverage will be increased above the original certificate amount as necessary. However, performing loan modifications do not qualify for incentives under the Loss Mitigation Program, and may not meet Ginnie Mae requirements for repooling of modified loans, which requirements are described in Ginnie Mae's All Participants Letter, 96-15.

B. Borrower Qualifications

Modifications may be offered to borrowers who have stabilized, surplus income which, while not sufficient to sustain the original loan and repay the arrearage, is sufficient to support the monthly payment under the modified rate and/or term.

The borrower must be an owner occupant, committed to occupying the property as a primary residence. Modification may not be used as a means to reinstate a loan prior to a sale or assumption.

C. Property Condition

While the modification option does not include a loan-to-value restriction, and no appraisal or broker's price opinion is required, the lender must conduct any review it deems necessary to verify that the property has no physical conditions which adversely impact the borrower's continued use or ability to support the debt.

A borrower may not be able to support payments under a modification if the property is in such a deteriorated condition that repairs drain the borrower's monthly resources. An analysis of the borrower's surplus income should consider anticipated property maintenance expenses. If the mortgagee's inspection identifies a property in extremely poor physical condition, a modification may not offer a permanent resolution to the default.

Costs to complete needed repairs may not be capitalized as part of a modification agreement, nor may a borrower receive any cash back from a modification. Borrowers who have sufficient equity and income to receive cash back should be considered for a delinquent refinance.

D. Financial Analysis

The lender is required to assess the borrower's financial condition as described in Section H, page 10. HUD expects the lender to project the borrower's surplus monthly income for a minimum of three months, and use good business judgment to determine if the borrower has the capacity to repay the arrearage through a repayment or special forbearance plan, before considering modification. If the financial analysis determines that the borrower does not have the ability to support the modified monthly payment, the modification option may not be used.

E. Combining Options

Modification may be utilized as a stand alone tool, or incorporated as part of a repayment, or special forbearance agreement. For example, if a borrower needs time to resolve the default, but will eventually be able to support the debt at the modified rate but no more than that, a repayment plan or special forbearance may culminate in a loan modification. An existing repayment plan, or special forbearance may also be converted to modification if the borrower's circumstances change.

Mortgage modification may not be used in conjunction with a partial claim. If modification is appropriate, it should be used as the primary tool to bring the account current.

F. Allowable Provisions

The following provisions apply to loan modifications:

- All modifications must result in a fixed rate loan. ARM, GPM and GEM mortgages may only be modified to fixed payment, fully amortizing loans.
- The modification must fully reinstate the loan.
- At the lender's discretion, note interest rates may be reduced below market if necessary to resolve the default. Discount fees associated with rate reductions are not reimbursable.
- At the lender's discretion, note interest rates may be increased if supported by the borrower's ability to pay. The maximum interest allowable shall be calculated as 150 basis points above the current FHA debenture interest rate. Debenture interest rates are provided semi-annually through mortgagee letter.
- All or a portion of the PITI arrearage (principal, interest, and escrow items) may be capitalized to the mortgage balance.
- Foreclosure costs, late fees and other administrative expenses may not be capitalized. Lenders may collect the legal and administrative fees (resulting from the canceled foreclosure action), from mortgagors to the extent not reimbursed by HUD, either through a lump sum payment or through a repayment plan separate from, and subordinate to, the modification agreement.
- The modified principal balance may exceed the principal balance at origination.
- The modified principal balance may exceed 100% loan-to-value.
- Lenders may re-amortize the total unpaid amount due over the remaining term of the mortgage, or may extend the term not more than 10 years beyond the original maturity date or 360 months from the due date of the first installment required under the modified mortgage, whichever is less.

G. Lien Status

The lender must ensure first-lien status of the modified mortgage. In satisfying this requirement, the lender must comply with any applicable state or federal laws and regulations.

If title to the property is encumbered with an FHA Title I loan, and the lender servicing the Title II loan has determined that a subordination agreement is necessary, the lender may send a written subordination request to:

U.S. Department of Housing and Urban Development
Home Improvement Branch
451 7th Street, SW, Room 9272
Washington, DC 20410

If title to the property is encumbered with an FHA Title I loan which has been assigned to the Secretary, and the lender servicing the Title II loan has determined that a subordination agreement is necessary, the lender servicing the Title II loan may send a written subordination request to:

HUD Albany Financial Operations Center
Asset Recovery Division
52 Corporate Circle
Albany, NY 12203
(518) 464-4200

H. Required Documentation

FHA does not dictate a specific format for documentation of the modification agreement. The lender is responsible for ensuring that the modification documentation preserves the first lien status of the FHA insured loan. The lender will have to make the determination in accordance with state law as to whether it is necessary to record the Modification Agreement to maintain the first lien requirement.

I. Disclosures

FHA requires lenders to comply with any disclosure or notice requirements applicable under State or Federal law.

J. FHA Mortgage Insurance

Where the loan modification has been processed in accordance with all HUD requirements, the FHA mortgage insurance coverage will be extended to the new principal balance of the loan following modification of eligible loans. Modification has no effect on the one-time MIP or on periodic MIP payments. Monthly MIP payments must be calculated on the original insurance amount.

K. Lender Incentives

FHA will pay lenders a $500 incentive fee for each modification and will reimburse the actual cost of the title search and/or endorsement to the title policy not to exceed $250.00. No other expenses may be included on the claim.

L. Failure

In the event the borrower becomes delinquent following modification, it shall be treated as a new default and serviced accordingly. In the event the loan is foreclosed following modification, the lender must be prepared to deliver a copy of the modification agreement to the Department when a conveyance claim is filed. The lender shall be responsible for maintaining the first lien status of the insured loan subsequent to modification. Any amount of a loan which is not in the first priority position will be considered uninsured and not subject to claim. HUD reserves the right at the time of claim submission to request documentation (legal or otherwise) establishing the first lien status.

M. Limitations on Use

If a loan has been modified or reinstated using a partial claim within the past three years, re-default risk is presumed to increase following a subsequent modification. Prior to granting a modification in this circumstance, the lender must prepare a written justification, and retain a copy along with supporting documents in the claim review file. It is anticipated that this will be a highly unusual occurrence, and that the cause of the second default will be unrelated to the original problem.

N. Filing For Incentive Payment

The lender must file the claim for incentive payment within 60 days of the execution date of the modification agreement. It is not necessary to send a copy of the modification agreement, however, it must be retained in the claim review file and made available to FHA upon request.

FHA will pay lenders a $500 incentive fee for each modification and will reimburse the actual cost of the title search and/or endorsement to the title policy not to exceed $250.00. No other expenses may be included on the claim.

PARTIAL CLAIM

Under the partial claim option, a lender will advance funds on behalf of a borrower in an amount necessary to reinstate a delinquent loan (not to exceed the equivalent of 12 months PITI). The borrower, upon acceptance of the advance, will execute a promissory note and subordinate mortgage payable to HUD. Currently, these promissory or "partial claim" notes carry no interest and are not due and payable until the borrower either pays off the first mortgage or no longer owns the property.

Following reinstatement, the lender will file a "partial" claim for the amount of the advance plus the lender's incentive fee, and forward a copy of the recorded documents to HUD. A contractor retained by HUD will service the partial claim liens.

HUD approval is not required in order for lenders to advance funds and file a partial claim, as long as the requirements detailed in this section are satisfied. This new option provides lenders with a powerful tool to assist borrowers threatened with foreclosure. However, this should be used only if the lender is confident that:

- borrower has the long term financial stability to support the mortgage debt.
- borrower does not have the ability to repay the arrearage through a special forbearance or modification.

There are three notable changes to the partial claim option. First, the seven month delinquency requirement has been eliminated. Partial claims may now be used any time after the fourth month of delinquency, so long as the total arrearage on the loan does not exceed the equivalent of 12 months PITI. Second, the BPO requirement has been eliminated. And the third notable change is that copies of the subordinate lien will not be required to accompany the claim submission. However the original recorded documents will still be required to be submitted.

A. Loan Default

The loan must be at least 4 months (120 days), but no more than 12 months (365 days) delinquent at the time the partial claim note is executed. The loan may not be in foreclosure when the partial claim note is executed. However, a lender may remove a loan from foreclosure if the borrower's financial situation has improved sufficiently to justify a partial claim.

B. Borrower Qualifications

Partial claims may be offered to borrowers who satisfy all of the following requirements:

- Have overcome the cause of the default.
- Have sufficient income to resume monthly mortgage payments.
- Do not have sufficient surplus income to pay the arrearage through a repayment plan.
- A mortgage modification is not appropriate.
- Borrower is owner occupant(s) committed to continuing occupancy of the property as a primary residence. Partial claim may not be used to reinstate a loan prior to a sale or assumption.

A lender may consider a mortgagor who has filed a petition in Bankruptcy Court under Chapter 13 for a partial claim, only after obtaining the approval of the Bankruptcy Court. If the mortgagor has filed a bankruptcy petition under Chapter 7, the lender must obtain Bankruptcy Court approval. and in addition, the mortgagor must reaffirm the debt.

C. Property Condition

There is a change from previous guidance in that a broker's price opinion (BPO) will not be required. While the partial claim option does not include a loan-to-value restriction and no appraisal or broker's price opinion is required, the lender must conduct a review sufficient to verify for FHA that the property has no physical condition(s) which adversely impact the borrower's continued use or ability to support the debt.

A borrower may not be able to support payments under a partial claim if the property is in such a deteriorated condition that repairs drain the borrower's monthly resources. An analysis of the borrower's surplus income should consider anticipated property maintenance expenses. If the mortgagee's inspection identifies a property in extremely poor physical condition, a partial claim may not offer a permanent resolution to the default.

D. Financial Analysis

The lender is required to assess the borrower's financial status as described in Section H, page 10. HUD expects the lender to project the borrower's surplus monthly income for a minimum of three months, and calculate the surplus income percentage.

If the financial analysis determines that the borrower does not have the ability to support the normal monthly payment, the partial claim option may not be used. In no case may partial claim be used if the borrower's surplus income percentage is 0% or less than 0%. If the borrower has low surplus income (\h 5%), lenders are encouraged to combine partial claim with a special forbearance plan allowing the borrower to demonstrate the ability to make payments for a period of 3 or more months prior to origination of the partial claim note.

Lenders must use good business judgment to determine if the borrower has the adequate surplus income to repay the arrearage through special forbearance or mortgage modification before approving a partial claim. Lenders are encouraged to require borrowers to contribute all available funds toward paying down the default, thereby reducing the amount of the partial claim lien.

E. Combining Options

Partial claim may be utilized as a stand alone tool, or incorporated as part of an informal forbearance plan, or special forbearance agreement. For example, if a borrower needs time to resolve the default, but will eventually be able to support the normal monthly payment but no more than that, a repayment plan or special forbearance may culminate in a partial claim. An existing repayment plan or special forbearance may also be converted to partial claim if the borrower's circumstances change. Partial claim may not be used in conjunction with a mortgage modification.

F. Allowable Provisions

The following provisions apply to all partial claim notes:

- The partial claim must fully reinstate the loan.
- The partial claim advance may include only principal, interest and escrow advances required to reinstate the loan.
- In no event may the total arrearage exceed the equivalent of 12 months PITI. The maximum partial claim advance for ARM, GPM, and GEM loans is calculated by adding the specific PITI requirement for each of the monthly installments to be included in the partial claim.
- The lender may not include late fees, legal fees or other administrative expenses in the partial claim note. However, lenders may collect legal and administrative fees (resulting from a canceled foreclosure action) directly from the borrower to the extent not reimbursed by HUD and in accordance with the limitations of Chapter 4 of HB 4330.1 REV-5.
- The lender will record the subordinate mortgage in all jurisdictions except the State of Texas. (In Texas, only a promissory note is required.)
- There is no lien priority requirement for partial claim notes, however the lender must ensure that recordation of the subordinate mortgage does not jeopardize the first lien status of the FHA insured mortgage.
- Payment of a partial claim does not decrease mortgage insurance coverage.

G. Repayment Terms

The partial claim advance will be secured by a note and subordinate mortgage with the following repayment terms.

- The note is interest free. (The Secretary reserves the right to assess interest on partial claim notes originated in the future.)
- The entire principal balance shall be payable as one balloon payment. No monthly or periodic payments are required.
- The note is due at the earlier of 1) payoff of the first mortgage, or 2) when the borrower no longer owns the property.
- There is no prepayment penalty.

Voluntary payments or prepayments should be directed to the following:

U.S. Department of HUD
c/o Clayton National
4 Corporate Drive,
Shelton, CT 06484

H. Required Documentation

A promissory note must be executed in the name of the Secretary and a subordinate mortgage must be obtained and recorded. The lender must include the provisions of HUD's model form of note and subordinate mortgage (as provided in Mortgagee letter 97-17) and make any amendments required by State laws. In the State of Texas only, HUD will accept an unrecorded promissory note. While HUD does not endorse the products or services of vendors, the Department is aware that State specific documents are commercially available. Lenders who take advantage of the convenience of purchasing these documents should review them prior to use.

I. Disclosures

FHA requires lenders to comply with any disclosure or notice requirements applicable under State or Federal law.

J. Lender Incentives

FHA will pay lenders a $250 incentive fee for each partial claim. The borrower may not be charged any additional costs.

K. Failure

In the event the borrower becomes delinquent following reinstatement via a partial claim, it shall be treated as a new default and serviced accordingly.

L. Limitations on Use

If a loan has been modified or reinstated using a partial claim within the past three years, re-default risk is presumed to increase following a subsequent partial claim. Prior to allowing a partial claim in this circumstance, the lender must prepare a written justification, and retain a copy along with supporting documents in the claim review file. It is anticipated that this will be a highly unusual occurrence, and that the cause of the second default will be unrelated to the original problem. There is a lifetime limitation of 12 monthly installments of PITI. Once 12 full monthly installments have been paid, no further partial claims will be honored on a specific case.

M. Claim Filing

The lender must file the claim within 60 days of the date the subordinate lien to HUD is executed. The claim may include the amount of the partial claim note and the $250 incentive fee. No other costs or fees will be paid by HUD.

N. Document Delivery

It is the responsibility of the lender to deliver the original promissory note and recorded mortgage to FHA at the address listed below, as soon as possible but no later than 6 months from the execution date of the partial claim note.

U.S. Department of HUD
c/o Clayton National
4 Corporate Drive,
Shelton, CT 06484

Mortgagee's who fail to deliver original, recorded documents within the time frame specified, will be required to reimburse the Department any incentive fee previously paid for the partial claim. Time extensions may be granted by the Oklahoma City Office of HUD in the event document delivery is delayed by events beyond the control of the lender.

O. Servicing

A contractor selected by HUD will service the partial claim notes. Effective immediately, the following contractor will service the Partial Claim notes:

U.S. Department of HUD
c/o Clayton National
4 Corporate Drive,
Shelton, CT 06484
Telephone: (800) 967-3050

PRE-FORECLOSURE SALE

The pre-foreclosure sale ("PFS") option allows a borrower in default to sell his or her home and use the sale proceeds to satisfy the mortgage debt even if the proceeds are less than the amount owed. This option is appropriate for borrowers whose financial situation requires that they sell their home, but who are unable to sell without FHA relief, because the value of the property has declined to less than the amount owed on the mortgage.

Borrowers must make a commitment to actively market their property for a period of 4 to 6 months, during which time the lender delays foreclosure action. Owner-occupant borrowers who successfully sell to a third party within the required time, are paid a cash consideration up to $1,000. Lenders also receive a $1,000 incentive for successfully avoiding the foreclosure. If the property does not sell, borrowers are encouraged to convey the property to FHA through a deed-in-lieu of foreclosure.

Since PFS was introduced in 1994, it has helped thousands of borrowers in default avoid foreclosure and make a smooth transition to more affordable housing. The changes described below are intended to increase the number of borrowers who can take advantage of the PFS option.

In an effort to open PFS eligibility up to more borrowers, this Mortgagee letter changes two critical ratios used to determine property eligibility and minimum acceptable proceeds. Where Section E(4) of Mortgagee letter 94-45, *HUD's Nationwide Pre-foreclosure Sale Procedure,* established the minimum ratio of appraised value to outstanding mortgage indebtedness at 70%, effective February 1, 2000 the minimum ratio of appraised value to outstanding mortgage indebtedness is 63%. Where Section G(4) of Mortgagee letter 94-45, required minimum acceptable net sales proceeds of 87%, effective February 1, 2000 minimum acceptable net sales proceeds are 82%. **Concurrent with these changes there will be no variances from the above stated ratios.**

Unlike other options, borrowers wishing to participate in the PFS program must submit an *Application to Participate* HUD-90036, along with the financial information required by the lender. The lender will also obtain a recent FHA appraisal and preliminary title report. After reviewing all relevant information, the lender will notify borrowers whether or not they meet the program requirements described below. Acceptance into the program is indicated by issuance by the lender of an *Approval to Participate* HUD-90045.

The forms associated with the PFS program, *Information Sheet* HUD-90035, *Application to Participate* HUD-90036, *Approval to Participate* HUD-90045, and *Variance Request* HUD-90041, are currently being revised to incorporate the ratio changes, provide the disclosure language described above, and to delete references to the assignment program. These forms will be released in a subsequent mortgagee letter. In the meantime, lenders may continue to use current versions of the forms.

A. Loan Default

At the time the pre-foreclosure sale is closed, the loan must be in default (delinquent more than 30 days). Lenders may exercise their discretion to accept applications from borrowers who are facing imminent default, but by the time the pre-foreclosure sale is completed, the loan must be in default. Lenders should document this decision in the claim review file. Under no circumstances shall PFS be available to borrowers who have abandoned their mortgage obligation despite their continued ability to pay.

Home Equity Conversion Mortgages are not eligible pre-foreclosure sale.

B. Borrower Qualifications

The PFS option may be extended to borrowers who satisfy the following requirements:

- Are in default due to a verifiable increase in living expenses or decrease in income.
- Have negative equity of not more than 63% of the outstanding mortgage balance including unpaid principal and accrued interest. (PFS may be considered if the property's appraised value slightly exceeds the mortgage payoff figure, but net proceeds, after deducting the costs of the sale, will fall short of the amount needed to discharge the mortgage by more than $1,000.)
- Occupy the property as a primary residence. Lenders are authorized to grant reasonable exceptions to non-occupant borrowers when it is verifiable that the need to vacate was related to the cause of the default (job loss, transfer, divorce, death), and the subject property was not purchased as a rental investment, or used as a rental for more than 12 months.

C. Application to Participate

Any borrower in default who expresses interest in the pre-foreclosure sale program should be sent a copy of the PFS *Information Sheet*, and *Application to Participate*. Additionally, lenders are encouraged to proactively solicit participation by borrowers who are in default on an FHA insured first mortgage and are unable to cure the default through reinstatement.

By signing and returning the application with the required financial information, borrowers are acknowledging that they have received housing counseling, and are agreeing to:

- List the property with a licensed real estate broker, unrelated to the borrower. The listing agreement must include a specific cancellation clause in the event the terms of a sale are not acceptable to HUD.

- Make a good faith effort to aggressively market the property.
- Perform all normal property maintenance and repairs until closing of the pre-foreclosure sale.

D. Property Value

The lender must obtain a standard FHA appraisal from an appraiser who does not share any interest with the mortgagor or mortgagor's agent. The appraisal must contain both "As Is" and "As Repaired" values for the property, and will be valid for six months. A copy of the appraisal must be shared with the homeowner or sales agent, if requested. Appraisals or opinions of value provided by the borrower, or borrower's real estate agent are not acceptable. The lender must review the appraisal and satisfy itself that the opinion represents the fair market value of the subject property.

E. Property Condition

Properties which have sustained serious damage (fire, flood, earthquake, tornado) are not eligible for PFS if the cost of repair exceeds 10% of the As Repaired appraised value. Lenders may exercise their discretion to accept or reject damaged properties when repair costs are less than the 10% threshold, but should document their decision in the claim review file.

F. Condition of Title

The property must have marketable title. Prior to execution of the *Approval to Participate*, the lender must obtain a title search or preliminary report to verify that the title is not impaired with un-resolvable title problems, or junior liens that cannot be discharged as allowed by HUD. If the lender determines that junior liens and other title issues can be resolved, the borrower may be accepted into the PFS program and resolution of the title issues can be pursued concurrent with marketing.

It is frequently in HUD's interest to aid in the discharge of secondary liens in order to facilitate the sale. Lenders are expected to provide such assistance to the borrower. In some cases junior lien creditors will release a lien in return for a partial cash payment or a promissory note from the borrower. Where the amount required to satisfy or release the lien(s) is in line with the borrower's ability to pay, the borrower should be required to do so. The incentive consideration payable to the borrower should first be applied toward the discharge of liens. If this is not sufficient, the lender can obligate an additional amount not to exceed $1,000 from sale proceeds towards the discharge of liens or encumbrances, if that will result in clear title and allow the sale to proceed. If the borrower has a HUD Title I loan secured by the property, the lender must negotiate a release of the Title I lien in order to proceed with a PFS.

G. Financial Analysis

The lender is required to assess the borrower's financial condition as described in Section H, page 10. HUD expects the lender to project the borrower's surplus monthly income and use good business judgment to determine that the borrower is unable to support the mortgage debt.

H. Approval to Participate

When an application is accepted, the *Approval to Participate* form must be used. The date of this form becomes the starting date of PFS participation. The *Approval to Participate* must include the date by which a signed contract for sale must be obtained, and the minimum acceptable net sales price.

I. Timing of Initiation

The lender must either issue an *Approval to Participate*, commence foreclosure, or initiate another loss mitigation option within 6 months of the date of default, unless the lender qualified for an extension by trying another loss mitigation option.

If the PFS follows a failed special forbearance agreement, the *Approval to Participate* must be granted, or foreclosure or other option initiated within 90 days of the failure. If the PFS follows any other option, the *Approval to Participate* must be granted, or foreclosure or other option initiated within 9 months of the date of default.

J. Duration of the Pre-Foreclosure Sale Period

The pre-foreclosure sale period shall be three months beginning upon lender approval (automatically extended two months for lenders scoring in the top 25th percentile). The lender should review marketing efforts with the mortgagor on a monthly basis. After 90 days without a scheduled closing, the lender must discuss the likelihood of a sale with the real estate broker and make a determination to either end the pre-foreclosure sale period, or extend it for an additional 30 days if a sale is likely. Documentation for this decision should be retained in the claim review file.

If the property is under contract at the end of the marketing period, the lender may extend the PFS period for 60 days not to exceed a total of 6 months (8 months for lenders in the top 25th percentile).

K. Other Lender Responsibilities

The lender is responsible for inspection, protection, and preservation of the property between the 45th day of default and the date of the *Approval to Participate*. Funds expended for preservation and protection will be reimbursed.

L. Early Termination

Borrower participation in the PFS program may be terminated at the discretion of the lender, for any of the following reasons:

- Un-resolvable title problems.
- Determination that the borrower is not acting in good faith to market the property.
- Voluntary withdrawal by the borrower.

M. Failure

Within 90 days of the expiration of the pre-foreclosure sale period (or 6 months of the date of default, whichever is later), if no closing of an approved PFS has occurred, the lender must commence foreclosure or obtain a deed-in-lieu. If the borrower's financial condition has improved to the point that reinstatement is a viable option, the lender may undertake one of the reinstatement loss mitigation tools. However, the lender must fully justify this decision in the claim review file, and must complete the action within the 90 day period.

N. Lender Incentives

FHA will pay lenders an incentive fee of $1,000 for each successful pre-foreclosure sale.

O. Borrower Consideration

Borrowers who successfully sell their properties using this option are relieved of their mortgage obligation, and are entitled to receive consideration in the amount of $750. If the closing occurs within three months of the *Approval to Participate,* the borrower will be entitled to $1,000. Unless the borrower's consideration is required to release junior liens, the borrower may elect to accept cash paid at closing, or may apply some or all of the amount to offset sales costs not paid by FHA, including home warranty plans, optional repairs, and seller's closing expenses.

Borrowers who become good-faith participants in the PFS program shall not be pursued for deficiency judgments by either the lender or the Department in the event that the PFS is unsuccessful and foreclosure occurs.

P. Contract Approval

The lender will have 5 working days from receipt of a signed Contract for Sale, to respond using the *Sale Contract Review* form HUD-90051. The transaction must be an outright sale of the premises. No sale by assumption, regardless of provisions for release of liability, may be considered.

Lenders may approve a sale contract in which the net sales proceeds are at least 82% of As Is appraised value. "Net Sales Proceeds" is defined as the contract price less:

- Sales commission (usually 6% or less).
- Consideration paid to the seller ($750 or $1,000).
- Discharge of junior liens not to exceed $1,000.
- Property repairs required by the appraisal.
- Local/state transfer tax stamps and other customary closing costs including the seller's costs for a title search and title insurance.

Examples of settlement costs which may not be included in the net sales proceeds calculation are:

- Tax service fees and other property transfer costs normally paid by the buyer.
- Home warranty fees.
- Repairs not stipulated in the appraisal.
- Survey costs.
- Lawyer's fees for representing the seller (apart from conducting the settlement or review of documents).

There must not be any hidden terms or special understandings that exist between any of the parties involved in the transaction: buyer, seller, appraiser, sales agent, closing agent, and lender.

Q. Closing and Post Responsibilities

Prior to closing, the lender will provide the closing agent with a *Closing Worksheet,* HUD-90052, which lists all amounts payable out of sale proceeds. Before giving final approval for a closing, the lender must review the HUD-1 to ensure that it complies with earlier closing cost estimates.

A pre-foreclosure sale must be reported to national credit bureaus as a "short sale." Lenders will be responsible for filing information return Form 1099-A with the IRS and reporting any discharge of indebtedness, in accordance with the Internal Revenue Code.

R. Claim Filing

The claim for insurance benefits must be submitted to HUD within 30 days after the date of the PFS closing. HUD will reimburse the lender for reasonable and customary costs of the appraisal, title search (if not included in the settlement statement), and the allowable percentage of legal fees for a foreclosure postponed pending completion of PFS. Disbursements for taxes, assessments, hazard insurance, and other allowable items payable before the date of the PFS closing are reimbursable. FHA will not pay costs related to the property which were incurred after the closing date.

The consideration paid to the borrower and allowable amounts, not to exceed $1,000, paid to release all junior liens should be reflected on the HUD-1 and not included on the claim. The mortgagee's incentive fee shall still be reflected on line 129 of the claim form HUC-27011. (See Mortgagee letter 94-45, *Pre-Foreclosure Sale Program.*)

DEED IN LIEU OF FORECLOSURE

Deed-in-lieu of foreclosure (DIL) is a disposition option in which a borrower voluntarily deeds collateral property to HUD in exchange for a release from all obligations under the mortgage. Though this option results in the borrower losing the property, it is usually preferable to foreclosure because the borrower mitigates the cost and emotional trauma of foreclosure and is eligible to receive borrower's consideration of $500. Also, a DIL is generally less damaging than foreclosure to a borrower's ability to obtain credit in the future. DIL is preferred by HUD because it avoids the time and expense of a legal foreclosure action, and due to the cooperative nature of the transaction, the property is generally in better physical condition at acquisition.

Unlike a legal foreclosure however, acquisition by DIL does not extinguish junior liens or terminate tenancies. Therefore, there is substantial responsibility placed on the lender to determine that the condition of the property and the title meet HUD's minimum requirements. The most significant change in this option is a new requirement that the lender enter into a written agreement with the borrower, stating specific actions the borrower must perform in order to take advantage of this option and receive the financial consideration.

A. Loan Default

Prior to acceptance of the deed conveying the property to HUD, a the loan must be in default (delinquent more than 30 days), and the cause of the default must be determined to be incurable. Lenders may exercise their discretion to enter into DIL agreements with borrowers whose loans are current but are facing imminent default, and should document their decision in the claim review file. The loan must be in default at the time that the DIL is recorded and the property conveyed to HUD. Under no circumstances shall DIL be available to borrowers who have abandoned their mortgage obligation despite their continued ability to pay.

Qualified properties should first be offered for sale through the PFS program. Lenders who elect to accept a DIL without attempting a PFS must provide written justification for their decision in the claim review file.

B. Borrower Qualifications

The DIL option may be extended to borrowers who are unable to continue to support the mortgage debt and who occupy the property as a primary residence.

Lenders are authorized to grant reasonable exceptions to non-occupant borrowers when it is verifiable that the need to vacate was related to the cause of the default (job loss, mandatory job transfer, divorce, death), and the subject property was not purchased as a rental investment, or used as a rental for more than 12 months. However, pursuant to 24 CFR 203.357(b) and (c), lenders must obtain the prior written consent of the Commissioner prior to accepting a DIL from a corporate mortgagor or a mortgagor who owns more than one FHA insured property. To obtain this consent lenders should contact:

U.S. Department of Housing and Urban Development
Servicing and Loss Mitigation Division
500 W. Main Street, Suite 400
Oklahoma City, OK 73102

A DIL may not be considered if HUD has elected to pursue a deficiency judgment against the borrower.

C. Tenant Occupied Properties

HUD will not accept a DIL if the collateral property is occupied at the time of conveyance to the Department, unless HUD determines that the tenancy is in the best interest of the Secretary as defined in 24 CFR 203.671. Lenders should follow the process established in 24 CFR 203.675 to request authorization for an occupied conveyance.

D. Financial Analysis

The lender is required to assess the borrower's financial condition as described in Section H, page 10. HUD expects the lender to project the borrower's surplus monthly income for a minimum of three months and use good business judgment to determine if the borrower has the capacity to support the mortgage debt. Under no circumstances shall deed-in-lieu of foreclosure be available to borrowers who have abandoned their mortgage obligation despite their continued ability to pay. The financial analysis requirement may be waived for borrowers who had previously participated in the PFS program.

E. Condition of Title

Good and marketable title must be conveyed to the Secretary. The lender must complete a title search and may be required to secure release of junior liens and/or endorsements to the title policy. HUD will not accept title subject to most junior liens including IRS liens. However, HUD will allow liens securing repayment of Section 235 assistance payments, partial claim advances and Title I liens.

It is frequently in HUD's interest for the lender to aid in the discharge or discounted payoff of secondary liens. With the borrower's consent, the consideration payable to the borrower may be applied toward discharge of liens if this will result in clear title.

F. Required Documentation

A written DIL agreement must be executed by the mortgagor and lender which contains all of the conditions under which the deed will be accepted, including but not limited to:

- Certification that the borrower does not own any other property subject to a mortgage insured by or held by HUD.
- Specific transfer date.
- Notification that there may be income tax consequences as a result of the DIL.
- Acknowledgment that borrowers who comply with all of the requirements of the agreement shall not be pursued for deficiency judgments.
- A statement describing the general physical condition in which the property will be conveyed.
- Agreement that the borrower will convey the property vacant and free of personal property unless an occupied conveyance has been approved by HUD.
- Itemization of the keys, built-in fixtures and equipment to be delivered by the lender on or before the transfer date.
- Borrower's agreement to provide evidence that certain utilities, assessments and homeowner's association dues are paid in full to the transfer date unless otherwise agreed to by the parties.
- The dollar amount of consideration payable to and/or on behalf of the borrower (not to exceed $500).

FHA does not dictate a specific format for documentation of the deed-in-lieu agreement. The lender is responsible for ensuring that the deed-in-lieu documentation is in compliance with all applicable laws and regulations.

G. Conveyance

The property must be conveyed through a special warranty deed. The original credit instrument must be canceled and surrendered to the borrower, indicating that the mortgage has been satisfied. Whenever possible, title must be conveyed directly from the borrower to HUD. If it is necessary to first convey title to the lender, and then to HUD, the lender must document the reason in the claim review file.

As with all conveyance claims, the lender must record the special warranty deed and deliver the original, recorded deed to the HUD Office having jurisdiction over the subject property within 45 days of the date that good and marketable title was conveyed to the Secretary.

H. Timing

A DIL must be completed or foreclosure initiated within 6 months of the date of default unless the lender qualified for an extension by first trying another loss mitigation option or has received an extension approved by HUD prior to the expiration of the time requirement.

If the DIL follows a failed special forbearance agreement or pre-foreclosure sale, the DIL must be completed or foreclosure initiated within 90 days of the failure. If the DIL follows any other option, it must be completed or foreclosure initiated within 9 months of the date of default. All extensions of time to initiate foreclosure including "automatic extensions" (Section L, page 12) must be properly identified on form HUD-27011, Block 19.

Failure to comply will result in interest curtailment as more fully described in Mortgagee letter 98-7, *FHA Loss Mitigation Program Policy and Procedural Updates*.

I. Lender Incentives

FHA will pay the lender an incentive fee of $250 for administrative expenses. This incentive payment should be claimed on line 129 of form HUD-27011.

J. Borrower Consideration

The borrower is entitled to consideration of $500 upon satisfaction of the requirements of the deed-in-lieu agreement. However, no consideration may be paid if the property is occupied at conveyance.

K. Claim Filing

As with other conveyance claims, the lender is expected to follow the claim instructions detailed in HB 4330.4 REV1 and any updates thereto. Reimbursable expenses include, reimbursement of title costs, the consideration paid to (or on behalf of) the borrower not to exceed $500, and a $250 lender incentive fee.

L. Lender Reporting Requirements

The DIL must be reported to credit reporting bureaus. The lender is also responsible for filing information return Form 1099-A with the IRS, reporting any discharge of indebtedness in accordance with the Internal Revenue Code.

M. Option Not to Convey

The lender may elect not to convey title to HUD and to terminate the contract of mortgage insurance. If this decision is made, HUD must be notified on Form HUD-27050-A.

Sincerely,

____

William C. Apgar
Assistant Secretary for Housing -
Federal Housing Commissioner

APPENDICES

Appendix 1

SPECIAL FORBEARANCE CHECKLIST

Loan Number: ________________ Borrower: ________________________ Date: _____________

Requirement | Verification (Date, Amount, Source of Information etc.)

1. Has the borrower experienced a verifiable loss of income or increase in living expenses?
2. Is the borrower an owner occupant?
3. Did a search of CAIVRS determine that the borrower has no other HUD insured loans or prior loans on which a claim has been paid within the past 3 years?
4. Did the borrower receive the <u>How To Avoid Foreclosure</u> brochure?
5. Will the loan be more than 90 and less than 365 days delinquent on the effective date of the agreement? (show number of days)
6. Did the surplus income analysis to determine the borrower's ability to repay the debt include:
   - a financial statement provided by the borrower?
   - a credit report?
   - income/expense verifications?
   - evidence the borrower can support the payment schedule?
7. The borrower's surplus income percentage is?
8. Has an inspection determined that the property has no adverse conditions affecting continued occupancy?
9. Does the written agreement executed by the borrower:
   - clearly define the terms and frequency of repayment?
   - offer relief not available through a normal repayment plan?
   - state that failure to comply may result in foreclosure?
   - limit the total default to 12 months or less?
10. If the special forbearance agreement culminates in a partial claim or modification, show the proposed date of that action.

Appendix 2

LOAN MODIFICATION CHECKLIST

Loan Number: _______________ Borrower: ______________________________ Date: _________

Requirement — Verification (Date, Amount, Source of Information etc.)

1. Has the borrower experienced a verifiable loss of income or increase in living expenses?
2. Does the borrower have a commitment to continue to occupy the property as his or her primary residence?
3. Did a search of CAIVRS determine that the borrower has no other HUD insured loans or prior loans on which a claim has been paid within the past 3 years?
4. Did the borrower receive the How To Avoid Foreclosure brochure?
5. Will the loan be more than 90 days delinquent on the date of execution and funding? (show number of days)?
6. If this loan had a prior modification or partial claim within the past three years justify the decision to modify now?
7. Did the surplus income analysis to determine the borrower's ability to repay the debt include:
   - a financial statement provided by the borrower?
   - a credit report?
   - income/expense verifications?
   - evidence of the borrower's ability to pay for at least 3 months?
8. The borrower's surplus income percentage is?
9. The default cannot be cured through special forbearance because?
10. Has a title search established first lien status of the modified loan?
    - will release of junior liens be required?
    - will title endorsement be required?
11. Has an inspection determined that the property has no adverse conditions affecting continued occupancy?
12. Does the written modification agreement executed by the borrower:
    - include all advances necessary to reinstate the principal, interest, taxes and insurance?
    - exclude all legal and administrative costs?

Appendix 3

PARTIAL CLAIM CHECKLIST

Loan Number: ________________ Borrower: ______________________________ Date: ____________

Requirement

Verification (Date, Amount, Source of Information etc.)

1. Has the borrower experienced a verifiable loss of income or increase in living expenses?
2. Does the borrower have a commitment to continue to occupy the property as his or her primary residence?
3. Did a search of CAIVRS determine that the borrower has no other HUD insured loans or prior loans on which a claim has been paid within the past 3 years?
4. Did the borrower receive the <u>How To Avoid Foreclosure</u> brochure?
5. Will the loan be more than 120 and less than 365 days delinquent on the date of execution and funding? (show days)
6. If this loan had a prior modification or partial claim within the past three years justify the decision to use a partial claim now?
7. Did the surplus income analysis to determine the borrower's ability to repay the debt include:
   - a financial statement provided by the borrower?
   - a credit report?
   - income/expense verifications?
   - evidence of borrower's ability to pay for at least 3 months?
8. What is the borrower's surplus income percentage? (Is it greater than 0% and less than 17%? show %)
9. Explain why the default cannot be cured through special forbearance?
10. Explain why the default cannot be cured through modification?
11. Has an inspection determined that the property has no adverse conditions affecting continued occupancy?
12. Will the written partial claim note executed by the borrower:
    - fully reinstate the loan?
    - not exceed the equivalent of 12 months PITI?
    - include only principal, interest and escrow advances in the note?

Appendix 4

PRE-FORECLOSURE SALE CHECKLIST

Loan Number: ______________ Borrower: ______________________________ Date: ____________

Requirement — Verification (Date, Amount, Source of Information etc.)

1. Has the borrower experienced an involuntary reduction in income or increase in living expenses?
2. Does the borrower occupy the property as his or her primary residence? If not, explain any variances.
3. Did the borrower sign an Application to Participate HUD-90036, or other disclosure of the availability of reinstatement options?
4. Will the loan be at least 30 days delinquent when the PFS closes? (show number of days)
5. Does a review of CAIVRS indicate that the borrower has no other current FHA loans, or prior loans on which a claim has been paid within the past 3 years? (explain any variances)
6. Does an appraisal completed within the past 6 months show that:
   - the AS IS value is less than the loan amount ? (show Value)
   - the property is worth at least 63% of the unpaid principal balance? (show negative equity ratio)
   - sale proceeds will result in a loss of more than $1,000
   - the property is not seriously damaged?
7. Has a title search been obtained indicating marketable title?
8. Did the surplus income analysis to determine the borrower's inability to repay the debt include:
   - a financial statement provided by the borrower?
   - a credit report?
   - income/expense verifications?
   - the borrower's surplus income percentage? (show %)
9. The PFS agreement, executed by the borrower shows:
   - the end date for marketing is?
   - minimum acceptable net proceeds are?
10. Do Net Sale proceeds equal or exceed 82% of As Is Value? (show %)

Appendix 5

DEED-IN-LIEU OF FORECLOSURE CHECKLIST

Loan Number: ______________ Borrower: ____________________________ Date: ___________

Requirement	Verification (Date, Amount, Source of Information etc.)

1. Has the borrower experienced a verifiable loss of income or increase in living expenses?
2. Does the borrower occupy the property as his or her primary residence? If not, explain any variances.
3. Will the loan be at least 30 days delinquent when the special warranty deed is accepted?
4. Did the borrower receive the <u>How To Avoid Foreclosure</u> brochure?
5. Does a review of CAIVRS indicate that the borrower has no other current FHA loans, or prior loans on which a claim has been paid within the past 3 years? (explain variances)
6. A recent appraisal or BPO indicates the AS IS property value is?
7. If any portion of the property is rented has FHA approved occupied conveyance?
8. Has a title search been obtained showing good and marketable title?
9. Did the surplus income analysis to determine the borrower's inability to repay the debt include:
   - a financial statement provided by the borrower?
   - credit report?
   - income/expense verifications?
   - the borrower's surplus income percentage? (show %)
10. Does a written DIL agreement, executed by the borrower:
    - require the property to be vacant and free of personal property at conveyance?
    - convey title via a special warranty deed in favor of HUD?
    - convey clear title free of junior liens?
    - require the borrower to pay utility bills to the date of conveyance?
    - require the borrower to pay HOA dues or other assessments?
    - advise the borrower to obtain the advice of a tax consultant?

Department of Housing and Urban Development, Mortgagee Letter 2001-14 (May 23, 2001)

May 23, 2001

MORTGAGEE LETTER 2001-14

TO: ALL APPROVED MORTGAGEES

ATTENTION: Single Family Servicing Managers

SUBJECT: FHA Loss Mitigation Clarification of Time Frames

The purpose of this Mortgagee Letter is to clarify the time frame requirements for the FHA Loss Mitigation initiatives. This clarification will address reinstatement loss mitigation claims specifically and will identify several minor procedural changes. These procedural changes shall be applicable for all reinstatement Loss Mitigation claims filed on or after the date of this Mortgagee Letter.

Special Forbearance and Modification

In Mortgagee Letter 00-05, dated January 19, 2000, HUD identified the minimum delinquency for use of both Special Forbearance and Loan Modification as three months. In the discussion regarding Special Forbearance, the Department had also given reference to a minimum delinquency of 90 days. Depending upon interpretation, these instructions appear to be in conflict.

Effective on the date of this Mortgagee Letter, HUD will define the minimum delinquency for both the Special Forbearance initiative and the Loan Modification initiative as three months. Simply stated, **three payments must be due and unpaid**. An example is included in the attachment.

A second problem involving the proper use of Special Forbearance is the maximum delinquency. The change in the maximum delinquency from seven months (as noted in Mortgagee Letter 96-61, dated November 12, 1996) to that of twelve months (as noted in Mortgagee Letter 00-05) was not intended as an automatic extension of the requirement of 24 CFR 203.355. Mortgagees must still take one of the actions required by 24 CFR 203.355 before six months from the date of default to avoid interest curtailment.

The maximum delinquency allowance of twelve months was provided to expand the use of the Special Forbearance initiative. In many cases, mortgagees were barred from initiating foreclosure (or otherwise fulfilling the requirements of 24 CFR 203.355) because of bankruptcy actions. Upon release of bankruptcy, many of those mortgagors had sufficient resources to begin making at least a full mortgage payment, but had arrearages in excess of seven months. By allowing the use of Special Forbearance for such cases, mortgagees would be able to assist more borrowers in saving their homes. An example of this requirement is also included in the attachment.

For cases where the mortgagee was not barred from initiating foreclosure (or otherwise meeting the requirements of 24 CFR 203.355) within six months from the date of default (and no extension was approved), interest will be curtailed on any subsequent conveyance to six months from the date of default regardless of any subsequent Special Forbearance that may have been executed.

An additional issue regarding the maximum time frame relates to accounts where the mortgagee waited until after the first day of the 12th month of delinquency to execute a special forbearance. This situation created both procedural and system related problems as the arrearage appeared to exceed the 12 month maximum. Therefore those Special Forbearance claims could not be processed.

To ensure that all Special Forbearance incentive claims may be processed in a timely manner, the Department will be requesting additional documentation including a copy of the executed forbearance agreement to support those Special Forbearance plans that are executed between the first and the last day of the 12th month of delinquency. These procedures will affect those Special Forbearance claims filed on or after the date of this Mortgagee Letter.

Mortgagees shall continue to file the Special Forbearance claims, preferably via the FHA Connection. As the Department begins processing of the claim, a request will be sent by Claims for the mortgagee to forward supporting documentation (including a copy of the Special Forbearance Agreement and a copy of the loan history). Upon receipt, the claims representative will confirm that the Special Forbearance agreement does not allow the mortgage arrearage to exceed twelve months. **Do not forward any supporting documentation unless requested**. This procedure will ensure that the documentation can be directed to the specific individual that is processing the case.

Partial Claims

In Mortgagee Letter 00-05, dated January 19, 2000, HUD identified the minimum delinquency for a partial claim as four months. In the discussion regarding Partial Claims, the Department had also given reference to a minimum delinquency of 120 days. Depending upon interpretation, these instructions appear to be in conflict.

Effective on the date of this Mortgagee Letter, HUD will define the minimum delinquency for the Partial Claim initiative as four months. **Simply stated, four payments must be due and unpaid**. An example is included in the attachment.

Questions regarding this Mortgagee Letter should be directed to our National Servicing Center at (888) 297-8685.

Sean G. Cassidy
General Deputy Assistant Secretary for Housing-Deputy Federal Housing Commissioner

Attachment

For all examples assume the mortgagor paid the December 1999, installment and failed to make all subsequent payments:

Example 1: Special Forbearance—Minimum Time Requirement

It is now March 2, 2000, and the mortgagor has furnished proof of the job layoff that created a decrease in income. He has also furnished verification from his employer as to when he will return to work full time. Including the March 2000, installment, the account is now three payments due and unpaid. If the borrower is cooperative and returns all requested documentation, the mortgagee need not wait until the last day of the month to enter into a special forbearance with the mortgagor as the account is three payments due and unpaid.

Example 2: Special Forbearance—Maximum Time Requirement

It is now November 2, 2000, and the mortgagor was just released from bankruptcy. The mortgagor filed the bankruptcy in early February 2000, and the mortgagee could not take any action to initiate foreclosure pending the release of bankruptcy. Since being laid off in January 2000, the mortgagor returned to work full time in late October 2000, and may now make a full mortgage payment at a minimum each month. The mortgagee received all required documentation and established a Special Forbearance plan requiring a full payment for the months of January 2001 through March 2001, and a payment and a quarter payment beginning April 1, 2001, until such time as the account is current. This plan would be acceptable because it does not allow the account to become more than 12 payments due and unpaid.

Example 3: Special Forbearance—Maximum Time Requirement

It is now November 2, 2000, and the loan has been sold several times. No servicer took any action to engage in loss mitigation nor did any of the previous servicers request an extension of time. The "ABC" mortgage company just completed an acquisition and found this loan. Upon contact from ABC, the mortgagor was eager to discuss his options.

The mortgagor had encountered several setbacks including a medical emergency involving his child which contributed to an increase in his expenses. He has just begun a new job with good prospects and a raise scheduled for January 1, 2001. It was determined that a Special Forbearance was appropriate because the mortgagor could begin making full monthly mortgage payments in December 2000, with increased payment of one and a quarter payments beginning in February 2001.

This plan would be acceptable because it does not allow the account to become more than 12 payments due and unpaid. However, should this account not reinstate, and it later becomes necessary to foreclose and file a conveyance claim, interest would be curtailed to six months from the date of the original date of default.

Exhibit 4: Partial Claim Time Requirement

It is now April 6, 2000, and the mortgagor furnished documentation of the medical emergency that created both an increase in expenses and a decrease in income. He has also furnished verification from his employer as to when he will begin receiving workman's compensation, which including some supplemental benefits, will provide him with 90% of his former salary for a period of six months during his rehabilitation. His documentation also indicates that he would return to his former position at the end of his rehabilitation. His income will be sufficient to meet a full monthly mortgage payment, but will not be sufficient for any additional to be applied to the arrearage.

A partial claim is appropriate because the account is 4 payments due and unpaid, the mortgagor can begin making regular mortgage payments, but cannot offer any additional sums to be applied towards the arrearage. If the mortgagee is able to complete the partial claim before the end of April, it need not wait until after April 30, 2000, to submit the mortgage insurance claim for the Partial Claim incentive.

Department of Housing and Urban Development, Mortgagee Letter 2002-13 (June 7, 2002)

June 7, 2002

MORTGAGEE LETTER 2002-13

TO: ALL APPROVED MORTGAGEES

ATTENTION: SINGLE FAMILY SERVICING MANAGERS

SUBJECT: Deed-in-Lieu of Foreclosure Consideration Increase and the Authorization to Pay Cash to Occupants for Keys Prior to Eviction

Deed-In-Lieu Consideration

Effective on the date of this Mortgagee Letter, the Department is increasing the consideration for a deed-in-lieu of foreclosure to an amount not to exceed $2,000. The funds may be paid to the borrower upon vacating the property or they may be used to pay off junior liens in order to clear a title. This payment increase amends the policy outlined in Mortgagee Letter 00-05, Loss Mitigation Program—Comprehensive Clarification of Policy and Notice of Procedural Changes, dated January 19, 2000.

Cash For Keys

Effective immediately, the Department authorizes a $1,000 "cash-for-keys" consideration as an alternative to a legal eviction following foreclosure. The consideration represents the savings to the government by avoiding most of the legal expenses associated with an eviction and other property expenses related to delayed possession of properties. Servicers are encouraged to offer up to $1,000 per dwelling, on the condition that the occupant peacefully vacates a property for which the mortgage has been foreclosed. Cash-for-keys may not be utilized in conjunction with deed-in-lieu or pre-foreclosure sale options. Additionally, in jurisdictions with rent control ordinances, lenders must adhere to all applicable laws and regulations.

The cash-for-keys offer should be made available only to occupants who fail to vacate a property after the first notice to quit is delivered and further legal action to evict is imminent. In order to receive the funds, all occupants must vacate the property within 30 days of the cash-for-keys offer. Occupants are required to leave the property in broom-clean condition. All built-in appliances and fixtures must be left in the property. Servicers must inspect the vacant properties prior to releasing the funds to ensure that the occupants have complied with their agreement on the condition of the property. Servicers must maintain documentation for the date and amount of the offer, the occupant's receipt of the funds and agreed upon date of vacancy.

If the cost of eviction in the jurisdiction generally exceeds $1,000 and the servicer determines that $1,000 is not an adequate incentive to avoid eviction, the servicer may contact the marketing and management (M & M) contractor that has jurisdiction over the property to request an increased amount. M & M contractors will refer requests for the over allowable costs to the Government Technical Representative (GTR) with responsibility for the contract area in which the property is located. The Department may develop a list of allowable costs by jurisdiction that will be communicated to servicers in a future mortgagee letter.

Claim Filing

Enter the increased deed-in-lieu and cash-for-keys considerations on form HUD-27011, Single-Family Application for Insurance Benefits, Part D, item 305, Disbursements for HIP, taxes, ground rents and water rates, eviction costs and other disbursements not shown elsewhere.

Sincerely,

John C. Weicher
Assistant Secretary for Housing
Federal Housing Commissioner, H

Department of Housing and Urban Development, Mortgagee Letter 2002-17 (August 29, 2002)

August 29, 2002

MORTGAGEE LETTER 2002-17

TO: ALL APPROVED MORTGAGEES

ATTENTION: Single Family Servicing Managers

SUBJECT: Special Forbearance: Program Changes and Updates

The purpose of this mortgagee letter is to remind lenders of the proper use of the special forbearance agreement as a loss mitigation tool and to introduce several changes in the special forbearance program including new flexibility to utilize special forbearance to assist otherwise creditworthy borrowers who are experiencing temporary unemployment.

Definition and Existing Guidance

A special forbearance is a written repayment agreement between a lender and a mortgagor that contains a plan to reinstate a loan that is a minimum of three payments due and unpaid. To qualify as a special forbearance and entitle the lender to incentives, the agreement must provide the mortgagor with relief not typically afforded under a repayment plan or an informal forbearance plan. Requirements for use of special forbearance are detailed in Mortgagee Letter 2000-05, Loss Mitigation—Comprehensive Clarification of Policy and Notice of Procedural Changes.

This mortgagee letter supersedes the portion of Mortgagee Letter (ML) 2000-05 that addresses Special Forbearance, starting on page 14 through page 18 and those portions of paragraph M on page 13 that pertain to special forbearance. Included in this mortgagee letter are changes and clarifications for most of the sections related to special forbearance in ML 2000-05, but other loss mitigation provisions within ML 2000-05 were left intact. Several additional sections have been provided to clarify time frame and payment application issues. This mortgagee letter does not supersede those portions of Handbook 4330.1 REV-5, paragraph 8-4 that pertain to special forbearance agreements for investors or non-owner occupants.

Changes to and Clarifications to the Special Forbearance Procedures

Type I Special Forbearance

Type I special forbearance is a structured plan that allows a borrower to repay a loan delinquency over time. The plan must provide relief not typically afforded under an informal forbearance or short-term repayment plan including an initial period for financial recovery followed by a payment schedule based on the borrower's ability to repay.

To be considered a valid Type I special forbearance agreement by the Department, a special forbearance agreement must:

- Identify the specific months for which the account is delinquent and note the total arrearage that accrued prior to the beginning of the agreement.
- Must fully reinstate the loan.
- Ensure that the repayment installments required under the terms of the special forbearance are based on the borrower's ability to pay. (Note: the lender must retain in the claim review file, evidence that the lender analyzed the borrower's financial condition as described in paragraph H, page 10 of ML 2000-05, and that the repayment schedule is supported by the financial analysis. (For example, a special forbearance plan may not include a balloon payment unless the borrower's financial analysis indicates the source of the funds for this payment.)
- May allow reasonable foreclosure costs and late fees accrued prior to the execution of the special forbearance agreement to be included as part of the repayment schedule. However, they may only be collected after the loan has been reinstated through payment of all principal, interest, and escrow advances. At no time shall the loan be considered delinquent solely because the borrower has not paid late fees or other foreclosure costs.
- Provide relief that is not typically afforded under an informal forbearance plan, including one or more of the following: (a) suspension or reduction of payments for a period sufficient to allow the borrower to recover from the cause of default; (b) a period during which the borrower is only required to make his/her regular monthly mortgage payment before beginning to repay the arrearage; (c) a repayment period of at least six months.
- Have a minimum duration of four months. There is no maximum length of time to repay the arrearage.
- Not allow late fees to be assessed while the borrower is performing under the terms of a special forbearance plan or allow the loan to be considered delinquent solely because the borrower has not paid late fees or other foreclosure costs.
- Not allow the accrued arrearage to exceed the equivalent of 12 months of principal, interest, taxes and insurance ("PITI"). The twelve months of PITI for ARMS, GPMS, and GEMS will be calculated by multiplying 12 times the monthly payments due on the date of default.
- Allow the borrower to pre-pay the delinquency at any time.
- Maintain a copy of the forbearance agreement that is signed and dated by at least one borrower and by an authorized agent of the lender.

Special Provisions for Type 1 when the Cause of Default is Unemployment

As stated above, the lender is required to make a determination, based on an evaluation of the borrower's financial information that the special forbearance will lead to reinstatement of the loan. When the cause of default is unemployment and the borrower has no immediate prospect of re-employment, it is often not possible for the lender to reach this determination. With this mortgagee letter, HUD is providing additional flexibility for lenders to provide relief to otherwise creditworthy borrowers who have become unemployed and have a reasonable prospect of re-employment in the foreseeable future.

Lenders may now enter into a special forbearance agreement with a borrower who has both a good payment record and a stable employment history, but has not received a commitment of re-employment at the time the lender is reviewing the borrower's financial information. As an indication of the borrower's commitment to retaining homeownership, the borrower should be required to make partial payments in an amount determined by the lender based on the borrower's ability to repay. Further, the borrower must agree to actively seek employment during the term of the reduced payments and to immediately notify the lender when the borrower's employment status changes.

The lender is required to verify the borrower's employment status monthly and renegotiate the terms of the special forbearance plan when the borrower's status changes. As with other Type I special forbearances, the plan must be for a minimum of four months but may be any length. However, at no time may the plan provide for the delinquency to exceed the equivalent of 12 monthly PITI installments.

Type II Special Forbearance

A Type II special forbearance combines a short-term special forbearance plan and a modification or partial claim as a single loss mitigation plan. Lenders should use a Type II special forbearance whenever the loss mitigation evaluation determines that the borrower's best option is either a modification or a partial claim but there is any concern about the borrower's ability or commitment to keep the payments current following reinstatement. Borrower must make at least three full monthly payments prior to execution of a modification or partial claim. Where a short term special forbearance is used to allow borrowers to demonstrate their ability to support the debt, FHA is further protected from the risk of workout failure. Generally, during the trial period the amount of the monthly payment due will not exceed the borrower's normal monthly payment.

To be considered a valid Type II special forbearance agreement by the Department, a special forbearance agreement will contain elements of a Type I, in addition to the following:

- Identify the loss mitigation initiative that will be used

to cure the default, i.e., loan modification or partial claim.

- Not allow late fees to be assessed while the borrower is performing under the terms of a special forbearance plan. Because Type II special forbearance plans culminate in either a loan modification or a partial claim, foreclosure costs and fees may be collected in accordance with the requirements applicable to those options.
- Require a minimum of three monthly installments before the completion of the modification or partial claim.
- A Type II special forbearance is not entitled to receive a special forbearance incentive fee, but may file for the loss mitigation option incentive fee, used to cure the default, when the loss mitigation action is finalized.

Regardless of type, a special forbearance plan must be designed to eventually lead to reinstatement of the loan either directly or in combination with a loan modification or partial claim. While there is no maximum duration requirement for special forbearance agreements and lenders are encouraged to allow as much time for repayment as is reasonable based on the borrower's ability to repay, at no time may the maximum mortgage arrearage due under a special forbearance plan exceed the equivalent of 12 months of principal, interest, taxes and insurance ("PITI").

The special forbearance agreement must be in writing and must be executed by the mortgagor and lender. The agreement must acknowledge previously missed mortgage payments and provide notice that failure to comply with the terms of the special forbearance agreement can result in initiation of foreclosure.

General Requirements

Loan Default

The loan must be at least three months, but not more than 12 months due and unpaid, and may not be in foreclosure when the special forbearance agreement is executed. Loans that had previously been referred to foreclosure may be removed from foreclosure status prior to execution of a special forbearance. On advice of lender's legal counsel, foreclosure may be suspended subject to the borrower's performance under the terms of the special forbearance agreement, if the suspension is stipulated in writing in the agreement.

Borrower Qualifications

Special forbearance may be offered to borrowers who have recently experienced a verifiable loss of income or increase in living expenses, but who have or will have sufficient monthly income to correct the delinquency and reinstate the loan within the duration of the plan either through gradual repayment of the arrearage, or through a combination of repayment and modification or partial claim. Special forbearance should not be offered to borrowers who have repeatedly broken past informal or formal forbearance plans without good cause.

The borrower must be an owner occupant, committed to occupy the property as a primary residence during the term of the special forbearance agreement. However, unlike modification and partial claim, which require that the borrower have a long-term commitment to the home, a special forbearance may be used to reinstate a loan to facilitate the eventual sale, or assumption of the property. HUD Handbook 4330.1, REV-5, Chapter 8 provides additional forbearance relief options for non-owner occupants. Agreements executed per these handbook guidelines are not eligible for special forbearance incentive claim payments.

Property Condition

The lender must conduct any review it deems necessary to verify that the property has no physical conditions which adversely impact the borrower's continued use or ability to support the debt. A borrower will not be able to support payments under a special forbearance plan if the property is in such a deteriorated condition that repairs drain the borrower's monthly resources. An analysis of the borrower's surplus income should consider obvious property maintenance expenses.

If significant deferred maintenance contributed to the cause of the default, it may be appropriate that the special forbearance plan provide a period of mortgage forbearance during which repairs specified in the agreement will be completed at the borrower's expense. If the lender's review identifies a property in extremely poor physical condition, a special forbearance plan, especially one that allows reduction or suspension of payments not tied directly to property repair, may not offer a permanent resolution to the default. Lenders must use good business judgment relative to property condition.

Financial Analysis

The lender is required to assess the borrower's ability to repay the entire delinquency as described in ML 2000-05, section H, page 10. HUD expects the lender to project the borrower's surplus monthly income for the duration of the special forbearance period, and to propose repayment terms consistent with the borrower's ability to pay.

The lender must exercise good business judgment in determining that the borrower has the capacity to resume full monthly payments, and eventually reinstate the loan under the terms of the plan. If the financial analysis reveals that the borrower does not, or has no reasonable expectation that his/her financial situation will recover in the foreseeable future, a Type I special forbearance should not be used. The lender should consider other loss mitigation options in the priority detailed in ML 2000-05, section F, page 10.

Review and Re-negotiation

Lenders must review the status of forbearance plans each month and take appropriate action if the borrower is not complying with the terms of the plan. A system report confirming that the loan is performing under the terms of the forbearance is sufficient to document the lender's compliance with this review requirement except when the cause of the default is unemployment (see, ***Special Provisions for Type 1 when the Cause of Default is Unemployment***). When a lender enters into a special forbearance agreement with a borrower whose continued unemployment is the cause of the default, the lender must document the borrower's employment status monthly and adjust the terms of the plan to reflect changes in income.

Plans may be re-negotiated if the borrower's financial circumstances change. However, re-negotiated plans may not exceed HUD's requirement that the loan be no more than 12 months delinquent. Lenders may only file for the special forbearance incentive claim once per default.

Combining Options

Mortgagee Letter 2000-05 states that a special forbearance (now defined as Type I) can be used alone or combined with any reinstatement option, but that the options would be sequential, not simultaneous. The new Type II special forbearance option that combines special forbearance with either a modification or a partial claim will be considered as a single loss mitigation plan.

Lenders may continue to execute loan modifications and partial claims as stand-alone loss mitigation options; however since the combined Type II option serves to protect FHA from the risk of workout failure, the claim file should provide justification of the lender's decision to skip this option. A Type II special forbearance may not be combined with a delinquent refinance and may not be used to reinstate a loan to facilitate assumption.

Other Provisions

Payment Application

In cases in which the mortgagor is entitled to pre-foreclosure relief (24 CFR 203.606), the lender should be entering into special forbearance and other loss mitigation agreements before foreclosure is considered, and foreclosure costs are incurred. However, in those cases where the borrower brings forth new information after foreclosure has been initiated, lenders are encouraged to evaluate this information and consider all appropriate loss mitigation options. When this reconsideration indicates that it is appropriate to enter into a special forbearance agreement, some special arrangements may need to be made to allow the borrower to repay the foreclosure costs and fees over the term of the forbearance agreement.

In these cases, the borrower will be required to reimburse the lender for only those foreclosure costs accrued to the date the foreclosure was cancelled. Under no circumstances will the borrower be required to pay the lender more than the Department identified as customary and reasonable for claim purposes in the Mortgagee Letter 2001-19, or any subsequent mortgagee letter issued on that subject.

As part of the written special forbearance agreement, the lender and borrower may agree that in addition to the required forbearance installment, the borrower will remit a portion of the foreclosure costs each month. In this instance, the lender must place the foreclosure costs collected each month into a suspense or memo fund account properly identified as belonging to the borrower. When the borrower completes his/her forbearance and the account is current, those funds held in suspense may be released and used to reimburse the lender for foreclosure costs incurred. If the borrower does not complete the special forbearance, all fees held in suspense are to be applied to the borrower's account in the order of priority established in 24 CFR 203.24, before calculating the claim for insurance benefits.

Foreclosure Time Requirements

In cases where foreclosure had begun, but the borrower is given an opportunity to attempt to save his/her home through special forbearance, an extension of time to initiate foreclosure (24 CFR 203.355) may be necessary.

Generally in non-judicial states, the foreclosure action must be cancelled to allow the borrower the opportunity to attempt a special forbearance. 24 CFR 203.355 provides additional time if the lender engages in one of the actions listed, which includes entering into a special forbearance agreement. The regulation does not provide any additional time for the lender if the borrower does not engage in a special forbearance but agrees to a repayment plan instead. In cases with informal forbearance plans, the lender should request an extension of time from the National Servicing Center (NSC). Additional guidance and information can be found on NSC's website at www.hud.gov.

If the case in question is in a judicial foreclosure state it may not be necessary to cancel the foreclosure action, because the lender may be able to temporarily suspend the foreclosure action. In such cases, the lender may be concerned about meeting the reasonable diligence time requirement (24 CFR 203.356). For such cases, the lender should have adequate documentation to support that the borrower provided new information to support that a special forbearance was appropriate after foreclosure was initiated.

The lender's reasonable diligence time frame will be extended for the time the borrower was performing under the terms of the special forbearance agreement as well as an allowance of no more than ninety days (90) to get the foreclosure back on schedule from the date the borrower defaulted under the special forbearance agreement. Additional information on reasonable diligence is found in the Claims Handbook, 4330.4, paragraph 3, page 1-11.

Automatic Extensions

If a lender has initiated, but is unable to complete a special forbearance within the six-month time limit, the lender is entitled to a 90-day extension of the foreclosure deadline provided the initiative was begun prior to the expiration of the initial six months. Therefore, if there have been no other intervening delays (such as bankruptcy) this "automatic" extension will extend the six month deadline to initiate foreclosure by 90 days. To qualify for the automatic extension, the lender must have completed the loss mitigation evaluation required by 24 CFR 203.605 and have documentation of this analysis in the claim review file. In addition, the loss mitigation initiative must be reported to the Single Family Default Monitoring System (SFDMS), using the appropriate status code (09, 12, or 32). All extensions of time to initiate foreclosure including "automatic extensions" must be properly identified on HUD-27011, Block 19 on the conveyance claim.

Option Failure

Foreclosure action is suspended during special forbearance. In the event this option fails, an additional 90-day extension is provided in which the lender must commence or recommence foreclosure or initiate another loss mitigation option.

A special forbearance is considered a failure when any of the following occur:

- The borrower abandons the property;
- The borrower advises the lender that he/she will not follow through and fulfill the terms of the special forbearance agreement; or,
- The borrower allows two installments to become due and unpaid without any advisement to the lender of any problems that rendered the borrower unable to stay current under the terms of the forbearance.

Lender Incentives

FHA believes that well structured special forbearance agreements will resolve the majority of curable loan delinquencies. The Department strongly encourages use of this option and has provided attractive lender incentives.

- First, for each special Type I forbearance agreement executed by a lender, regardless of the outcome, FHA will pay a $100 incentive fee. Lenders whose overall loss mitigation performance is ranked in the top quarter will be eligible for an incentive payment of $200 per Type I special forbearance claim.
- Second, when either a Type I or Type II special forbearance has been utilized and failed, and a conveyance claim is filed, lenders are entitled to collect unpaid interest at the note rate rather than at the debenture rate of interest.
- Finally, the number of months of interest that may be claimed is computed to the earliest of several dates as provided in 24 CFR 203.402a. This computation generally allows two additional months of interest than would be payable on a conveyance claim where special forbearance had not been utilized.

These are significant claim benefits, intended to reduce the risk to lenders of offering reduced or suspended payments, and/or longer than normal repayment terms. These incentives are not available in combination with any other loss mitigation option.

Filing For Incentive Payment

The lender must file the claim for a Type I special forbearance incentive payment within 60 days of the date of execution of the special forbearance agreement. It is not necessary to submit a copy of the special forbearance agreement or checklist. However, all documentation pertaining to the special forbearance must be retained in the claim review file and provided to HUD promptly upon request.

If Type II special forbearance is used, the lender is not entitled to file a claim for the special forbearance incentive fee, but may file for the incentive fee for the loss mitigation option which is used to cure the default when this other loss mitigation action is finalized.

Any questions regarding this mortgagee letter may be directed to HUD's National Servicing Center at (888) 297-8685 or hsg-lossmit@hud.gov. These clarifications and changes in this mortgagee letter are effective immediately.

John C. Weicher
Assistant Secretary for Housing-
Federal Housing Commissioner, H

Department of Housing and Urban Development, Mortgagee Letter 2002-21 (September 26, 2002)

September 26, 2002

MORTGAGEE LETTER 2002-21

TO: ALL APPROVED MORTGAGEES

ATTENTION: Single Family Servicing Managers

SUBJECT: Due Diligence in Acquiring Loans

The purpose of this Mortgagee Letter is to identify and recommend the use of prudent industry practices related to due diligence in the acquisition of whole loans or loan pools.

In recent months, national attention has been drawn to the devastating impact of predatory lending on families who are victimized by a few unscrupulous sellers, appraisers, real estate agents, mortgage originators or investors. The Department believes that no responsible FHA-approved mortgagee would knowingly purchase fraudulently originated loans. Effective due diligence policies, uniformly applied by mortgagees prior to purchase, would cripple the ability of fraudulent lenders to pawn predatory loans off on others in the mortgage industry. If predatory loans cannot be sold, they are unlikely to be made and all borrowers, including FHA borrowers, will be protected.

The Department routinely solicits feedback from lenders regarding the need for clarification of servicing requirements during various industry forums such as servicing conferences. As a result of the national attention on predatory lending, recent industry discussions focused on predatory lending practices and due diligence in the purchase of FHA insured loans. As a follow up to those discussions, several FHA-approved lenders that regularly buy and sell loans provided examples of the quality control procedures used by their firms to review both underwriting and servicing aspects of loan purchase transactions.

Due to the importance of this matter, the Department is considering amending its regulations to require pre-purchase quality control reviews. Until such regulations are issued, the Department will publicize through Mortgagee Letters prudent practices currently being used by the industry.

As such, this letter is the first in a series of Mortgagee Letters on prudent due diligence. Because of its focus on predatory lending, this letter concentrates on due diligence reviews of how loans were originated and underwritten. Future Mortgagee Letters will focus on related matters including prudent due diligence of prior servicing activity. The best practices described herein are provided as guidance to HUD-approved lenders who may find it appropriate or necessary to update their *Quality Control (QC) plan* to include procedures for pre-purchase due diligence of acquired loans. While the Department encourages lenders to review and revise QC plans in accordance with this guidance, the performance of due diligence by asset purchasers is, at present, voluntary.

BACKGROUND

To obtain or maintain approval to participate in HUD mortgage programs, mortgagees are required to "implement a written quality control plan, acceptable to the Secretary, that assures compliance with the regulations and other issuances of the Secretary regarding loan or mortgage origination and servicing" (24 CFR 202.5 (h)). In addition, this written plan must "provide for independent evaluation of the significant information gathered for use in the mortgage credit decisionmaking and loan servicing process for all loans originated or serviced by the mortgagee" (see Chapter 6 (1) of the Mortgagee Approval Handbook, 4060.1 REV-1). This requirement includes loans or loan pools purchased by the mortgagee from unrelated originators.

There are also related requirements regarding the sale of the mortgage in that the purchasing mortgagee succeeds to all rights and becomes bound by all of the obligations of the seller under the contract for mortgage insurance. This would include the originating lender and any successive purchasing lender (see HUD Handbook 4330.1 Rev. 5, Chapter 6).

Prior to closing a portfolio or pool purchase from an independent source, prudent servicers conduct a due diligence review of selected loans within the portfolio. This procedure provides the acquiring servicer the opportunity to measure the credit and collateral risks inherent in the portfolio. Risk might arise from fraudulent transactions, deficient underwriting, defective property condition, inadequate servicing or other factors that may ultimately lead to borrower default or indemnification of the Department.

Just as the written QC plan must identify a specific protocol for on-going review of loans in the lender's portfolio, the plan should also include a documented protocol for due diligence of loans to be acquired. An effective due diligence plan should:

1. Include specific procedures for reviewing the source of the loans;
2. Describe portfolio risk analysis methods;
3. Identify a sampling methodology (random, statistical and or risk targeted sampling);
4. List evaluation criteria for the loan level review; and,
5. Include outcomes if a loan, or a percentage of loans reviewed, is not in compliance with FHA requirements.

Following are examples of best practices for conducting due diligence. These practices are used by many FHA lenders and servicers that routinely purchase whole loans or loan portfolios.

PRE-PURCHASE DUE DILIGENCE

All FHA mortgagees who purchase or anticipate purchasing loans are encouraged to review and update their QC plan to include some or all of the practices described herein.

Review the Source of the Loans

Integrity of source is a critical factor in assessing the risk inherent in any transaction. A thorough review of the reputation, business conduct and practice of the seller is an essential first step in any pre-purchase due-diligence program. Seller review techniques commonly used by FHA lenders are described below. Most of the lenders volunteered that it is their practice to always conduct such reviews prior to a specific purchase transaction and it is their practice to follow up the initial review by conducting additional reviews at routine intervals for a period of time.

1. Utilize a comprehensive questionnaire to be completed by the originating lender or current seller prior to portfolio purchase that fully and completely describes the nature of the seller's business and how it is conducted and fully discloses the seller's current financial condition.
2. Obtain and review a copy of the selling lender/servicer's QC plan and several annual reports.
3. Use HUD's Neighborhood Watch website, which is accessible through the FHA Connection, to screen the originators from whom the seller regularly purchases

loans. See ML 2002-15 for directions on accessing Neighborhood Watch.
4. Establish key questions and responses that are likely to detect fraud or poor business practices and use these questions to conduct interviews with the seller's servicing and collection staff.
5. Audit the seller's origination operations.
6. Check the *Federal Register* to see if the seller has been subject to Mortgagee Review Board actions. Also, use HUD's Neighborhood Watch System as a means of evaluating the originating lender's past performance and to see if HUD has taken any termination actions.

Portfolio Risk Analysis

Portfolio risk analysis looks at performance characteristics of all loans in the transaction. In order to properly measure portfolio risk, the acquiring mortgagee must establish benchmarks for performance characteristics including interest rate, term, collateral type, pre-payment runoff, loan-to-value, delinquency, foreclosure, early payment default, etc. Buyers typically use computer assisted analysis to review all loans in the sale transaction, determine the relative risk and decide if the risk level of the transaction is acceptable before proceeding with further due diligence.

Sampling Methodology

The surest way to know the quality of loans being purchased is to completely re-underwrite each origination file. While this is common for individual loan purchases, it is not economically feasible in large transactions. Pool purchasers typically rely on sampling.

Sampling allows the buyer to conduct a detailed loan level review of a small number of loans in the portfolio and from this review draw conclusions about the overall quality of originations. HUD's Mortgagee Approval Handbook, 4060.1, Rev-1, Chapter 6-1(c), describes sampling techniques relative to quality control reviews. These techniques, including random and statistically valid sampling, may be helpful in establishing a sampling protocol for due diligence reviews.

In addition to sampling, most loan purchasers also target certain loan types or loan characteristics for detailed review. Targeted reviews are conducted on some or all loans that present greater risk potential. FHA lenders report that they commonly conduct targeted reviews using these loan characteristics:

1. Section 203(k) rehabilitation loans (review of initial documentation and current escrow status).
2. Interest rates significantly exceeding the average portfolio rate.
3. Fair Isaac (FICO) scores below acceptable benchmarks established by the purchaser.
4. Loans to non-profit organizations.
5. Loans made based on the credit qualifying of multiple mortgagors to meet minimum income requirements.

Loan Level Review

When conducting loan level due diligence of specific loans, the best practices of many purchasing lenders also include reviewing the following:

1. Verification that each loan in the portfolio/pool is properly insured and that the mortgage insurance certificate has been issued.
2. Verification that the property had not been sold at a significantly lower value within a short time prior to the subject transaction without documentation to support the increased value.
3. Verification that the seller had been the owner of record for some reasonable period of time prior to the subject transaction.
4. Re-calculation of the borrower's qualifying ratios and examination of the validity and sufficiency of the income.
5. Review of the borrower's credit worthiness including:
   - FICO score
   - Credit report and adequacy of supplemental explanations
   - The in-file verification of employment (VOE), Gift Affidavits and other sources of downpayment.
6. Determination that the points and fees charged to the buyer were reasonable based on market conditions at the time of origination and that the rate was fair and appropriate based on the borrower's credit and income.
7. Evaluation of the appraisal to determine that all relevant HUD regulations and guidelines (including HUD Handbooks 4150.1 and 4150.2), were met and followed during the underwriting process.
8. Verification that proper borrower disclosures were provided, that all signatures appear to be genuine and that the file documentation provides no evidence of fraud or poor business practices.

Outcomes

A comprehensive due diligence plan includes planned reactions. It is important that mortgage loan buyers establish risk thresholds and projected outcomes prior to conducting the review so that they know when to walk away from a transaction or an individual loan that presents an unacceptable level of risk. Some common outcomes of pre-purchase due diligence include:

1. Exclusion of one or more individual loans or a cohort of similar loans from the transaction;
2. Providing the seller the opportunity to correct defects;
3. Adjusting pricing to account for the increased risk; or,
4. Cancellation of the sale if the level of non-compliance is significant enough.

Essential to the success of any loan purchase policy is an enforceable loan sale agreement. Typically loan sale agreements provide additional protection for the purchaser by including recourse provisions in the event of contractual default or noncompliance discovered after closing. Recourse may include repurchase of selected loans, indemnity, or other financial remedies for the benefit of the purchaser. HUD encourages use of recourse provisions that require sellers to remedy any loan that is subsequently discovered to have predatory characteristics.

If due diligence is to be an effective protection against predatory lending, purchasers must complete their due diligence review prior to closing the sale transaction. **A rigorous pre-purchase review protects the purchaser and puts sellers on notice that poor quality, predatory or fraudulently originated loans cannot be pawned off on legitimate mortgagees simply based on the strength of the FHA insurance endorsement.**

If during any aspect of a loan sale transaction a mortgagee identifies evidence of potential loan fraud or predatory practices, the Department encourages the mortgagee to notify the seller in writing, listing the loan or loans that appear suspect. If the mortgagee observes what appears to be a fraudulent origination, the mortgagee must report this to the Quality Assurance Division within the Homeownership Center where the loan was originated.

If you have any questions concerning this Mortgagee Letter, please contact the National Servicing Center in Oklahoma City, Oklahoma at 1 (888) 297-8685.

Sincerely,

John C. Weicher
Assistant Secretary for Housing-
Federal Housing Commissioner

Department of Housing and Urban Development, Mortgagee Letter 2003-07 (May 22, 2003)

May 22, 2003

MORTGAGEE LETTER 2003-07

**TO: ALL APPROVED MORTGAGEES
ALL FHA ROSTER APPRAISERS**

SUBJECT: Prohibition of Property Flipping

On May 1, 2003, the Department of Housing and Urban Development published a final rule in *The Federal Register* amending the mortgage insurance regulations to prevent the practice of flipping on properties that will be financed with Federal Housing Administration (FHA) insured mortgages. Property flipping is a practice whereby a recently acquired property is resold for a considerable profit with an artificially inflated value, often abetted by a lender's collusion with the appraiser. These changes to existing credit policies, in effect for all mortgage loan applications signed on or after June 2, 2003, will eliminate the most egregious examples of predatory flips of properties within the FHA mortgage insurance programs and, thus, preclude home purchasers using FHA financing from becoming victims of predatory flipping activity.

This Mortgagee Letter provides a synopsis of the final rule, as well as specific guidance to assist lenders in complying with these new requirements. We urge mortgage lenders and appraisers to review the entire published final rule as well.

Highlights of Final Rule

The final rule requires that: a) only owners of record can sell properties that will be financed using FHA insured mortgages; b) any re-sale of a property may not occur 90 or fewer days from the last sale to be eligible for FHA financing; and c) that for re-sales that occur between 91 and 180 days where the new sales price exceeds the previous sales price by 100 percent or more, FHA will require additional documentation validating the property's value. In addition, the rule provides flexibility for FHA to examine and require additional evidence of appraised value when properties are re-sold within 12 months.

Sale by Owner of Record

To be eligible for a mortgage insured by FHA, the property must be purchased from the owner of record and the transaction may not involve any sale or assignment of the sales contract. This requirement applies to all FHA purchase money mortgages regardless of the time between re-sales.

The mortgage lender must obtain documentation verifying that the seller is the owner of record and submit this to HUD as part of the insurance endorsement binder; it is to be placed behind the appraisal on the left side of the case binder. This documentation may include, but is not limited to, a property sales history report, a copy of the recorded deed from the seller, or other documentation such as a copy of a property tax bill, title commitment or binder, demonstrating the seller's ownership of the property and the date it was acquired.

Re-sales Occurring 90 Days or Less Following Acquisition

If a property is re-sold 90 days or fewer following the date of acquisition by the seller, the property is not eligible for a mortgage insured by FHA. FHA defines the seller's date of acquisition as the date of settlement on the seller's purchase of that property. The re-sale date is the date of execution of the sales contract by the buyer that will result in a mortgage to be insured by FHA.

As an example, a property acquired by the seller is not eligible for a mortgage to be insured for the buyer unless the seller has owned that property for at least 90 days. The seller must also be the owner of record.

Re-sales Occurring Between 91 and 180 Days Following Acquisition

If the re-sale date is between 91 and 180 days following acquisition by the seller, the lender is required to obtain a second appraisal made by another appraiser *if* the resale price is 100 percent or more over the price paid by the seller when the property was acquired.

As an example, if a property is re-sold for $80,000 within six months of the seller's acquisition of that property for $40,000, the mortgage lender must obtain a second independent appraisal supporting the $80,000 sales price. The mortgage lender may also provide documentation showing the costs and extent of rehabilitation that went into the property resulting in the increased value but must still obtain the second appraisal. The cost of the second appraisal may not be charged to the homebuyer.

FHA also reserves the right to revise the re-sale percentage level at which this second appraisal is required by publishing a notice in the Federal Register.

Re-sales Occurring Between 91 Days and 12 Months Following Acquisition

If the re-sale date is more than 90 days after the date of acquisition by the seller but before the end of the twelfth month following the date of acquisition, FHA reserves the right to require additional documentation from the lender to support the re-sale value if the re-sale price is 5 percent or greater than the lowest sales price of the property during the preceding 12 months. At FHA's discretion, such documentation may include, but is not limited to, an appraisal from another appraiser.

FHA will announce its determination to require the additional appraisal and other value documentation, such as an automated valuation method (AVM), through a Federal Register issuance. This requirement may be established either nationwide or on a regional basis, at FHA's discretion.

Exceptions to 90-day Restriction

The final rule exempts properties acquired by an employer or relocation agency in connection with the relocation of an employee from the time restriction on re-sales. Re-sales by HUD under its Real Estate Owned (REO) program are not subject to the time restrictions. However, any subsequent re-sale of such a property must meet the 90-day threshold in order for the mortgage to be eligible as security for FHA insurance. The Homeownership Centers (HOCs) do not have the authority to waive the regulatory requirements set forth in the final rule.

The restrictions established by the final rule are not intended to apply when a builder is selling a newly built home or is building a home for a homebuyer wishing to use FHA-insured financing. HUD will more fully address this issue through issuance of the *Federal Register* notice provided for in § 203.37a(b)(4)(iv) of the final rule.

Date of Property Acquisition Determined by the Appraiser

In addition, mortgage lenders may rely on information provided by the appraiser in compliance with the updated Standard Rule 1-5 of the Uniform Standards of Professional Appraisal Practice (USPAP). This rule requires appraisers to analyze any prior sales of the subject property that occurred within specific time periods, now set for the previous three years for one-to-four family residential properties.

As a result, the information contained on the Uniform Residential Appraisal Report (URAR) describing the Date, Price and Data for Prior Sales for the subject property and the comparables is to include all transactions that occurred *within three years* of the date of the appraisal. Appraisers are responsible for considering and analyzing any prior sales of the property being appraised and the comparables that occurred within three years of the date of the appraisal.

Therefore, provided that the URAR completed by the appraiser shows the most recent sale of the property to have occurred at least one year previously, no additional documentation is required from the mortgage lender. The mortgage lender remains accountable for verifying that the seller is the owner of record and may rely on information developed by the appraiser for this purpose if provided. However, if the lender obtains conflicting information before loan settlement, it must resolve the discrepancy and document the file accordingly.

Summary of Property Flipping Regulations In Effect June 2, 2003

Prior Sale Occurred	0–90 Days	91–180 Days
Eligibility for FHA Financing	**Not Eligible** • Exceptions include relocation agencies and re-sales by employers to employees and sales by HUD of Real Estate Owned. • The HOCs cannot grant exceptions	**Eligible** ***provided:*** • Re-sale price to FHA mortgagors is less than 100% greater than previous sale or • If 100% or more greater than previous sale, second appraisal supports value

If you have any questions regarding this Mortgagee Letter, please contact your Homeownership Center (HOC) in Atlanta (888-696-4687), Denver (800-543-9378), Philadelphia (800-440-8647), or Santa Ana (888-827-5605).

Sincerely,

John C. Weicher
Assistant Secretary for Housing-
Federal Housing Commissioner

Department of Housing and Urban Development, Mortgagee Letter 2003-19 (November 20, 2003)

November 20, 2003

MORTGAGEE LETTER 2003-19

TO: ALL APPROVED MORTGAGEES

ATTENTION: Single Family Servicing Managers

SUBJECT: Partial Claims: Program Changes and Updates

The purpose of this Mortgagee Letter is to remind mortgagees of the proper use of the partial claim as a loss mitigation tool for defaulted FHA mortgagors, and to introduce several changes in the partial claim program which include:

- a reminder that mortgagees shall lose the incentive payment when loss mitigation claims are not submitted within 60 days of the date the partial claim subordinate lien is executed, or where the partial claim security documents are not forwarded timely,
- **a "One-Time Amnesty"** which is being provided to accept all outstanding partial claim related legal documents without penalty;
- additional guidance for calculating pre-foreclosure sale ratios where a partial claim had been provided to the mortgagor in a previous default.

This Mortgagee Letter supersedes the portion of Mortgagee Letter (ML) 2000-05 that addresses partial claims, starting on page 24 through page 29. The other loss mitigation provisions within ML 2000-05 were left intact. Several additional sections have been provided to clarify time frame and address document delivery issues.

Definition and Existing Guidance

Under the partial claim option, a mortgagee will advance funds on behalf of a mortgagor in an amount necessary to reinstate a delinquent loan (not to exceed the equivalent of 12 months worth of principal, interest, taxes, and insurance (PITI)). The mortgagor, upon acceptance of the advance, will execute a promissory note and subordinate mortgage payable to HUD. Currently, these promissory or "partial claim" notes carry no interest and are not due and payable until the mortgagor either pays off the first mortgage or no longer owns the property.

Following reinstatement, the mortgagee will file a partial claim for the amount of the advance plus the mortgagee's incentive fee, and forward a copy of the recorded documents to HUD. A contractor retained by HUD will service the partial claim notes.

HUD approval is not required in order for mortgagees to advance funds and file a partial claim, as long as the requirements detailed in this section are satisfied. This option provides mortgagees with a powerful tool to assist mortgagors threatened with foreclosure. However, this loss mitigation option should be used only if the mortgagee is confident that:

- The mortgagor has the long-term financial stability to support the mortgage debt; and,
- The mortgagor does not have the ability to repay the arrearage through a special forbearance or modification.

A. Loan Default

The loan must be at least four (4) payments due and unpaid, but may not be more than 12 months due and unpaid at the time the partial claim note is executed. The loan may not be in foreclosure when the partial claim note is executed. However, a mortgagee may remove a loan from foreclosure if the mortgagor's financial situation has improved sufficiently to justify a partial claim.

B. Mortgagor Qualifications

Partial claims may be offered to mortgagors who satisfy all of the following requirements:

- Have overcome the cause of the default;
- Have sufficient income to resume monthly mortgage payments;
- Do not have sufficient surplus income to repay the arrearage through a repayment plan;
- A mortgage modification is not appropriate;
- The mortgagor is an owner-occupant(s) committed to continuing occupancy of the property as a primary residence. A partial claim may not be used to reinstate a loan prior to a sale or assumption.

A mortgagee may consider a mortgagor who has filed a petition in Bankruptcy Court under Chapter 13 for a partial claim, only after obtaining the approval of the Bankruptcy Court. If the mortgagor has filed a bankruptcy petition under Chapter 7, the mortgagee must obtain Bankruptcy Court approval. In addition, the mortgagor must reaffirm the debt.

C. Property Condition

While the partial claim option does not include a loan-to-value restriction and no appraisal or broker's price opinion is required, the mortgagee must conduct a review sufficient to verify for FHA that the property has no physical condition(s) which adversely impact the mortgagor's continued use or ability to support the debt.

A mortgagor may not be able to support payments under a partial claim if the property is in such a deteriorated condition that repairs drain the mortgagor's monthly resources. An analysis of the mortgagor's surplus income should consider anticipated property maintenance expenses. If the mortgagee's inspection identifies a property in extremely poor physical condition, a partial claim may not offer a permanent resolution to the default.

D. Financial Analysis

The mortgagee is required to assess the mortgagor's financial status as described in Section H, page 10, of ML 00-05. HUD expects the mortgagee to project the mortgagor's surplus monthly income for a minimum of three months, and calculate the surplus income percentage.

If the financial analysis determines that the mortgagor does not have the ability to support the normal monthly payment, the partial claim option may not be used. In no case may a partial claim be used if the mortgagor's surplus income percentage is 0% or less than 0%. If the mortgagor has low surplus income (\h 5%), mortgagees are encouraged to combine a partial claim with a special forbearance plan allowing the mortgagor to demonstrate the ability to make regular payments for a period of three (3) or more months prior to origination of the partial claim note.

Mortgagees must use good business judgment to determine if the mortgagor has the adequate surplus income to repay the arrearage through a special forbearance or mortgage modification before approving a partial claim. Mortgagees are encouraged to require mortgagors to contribute all available funds toward paying down the default, thereby reducing the amount of the partial claim debt. The lender must retain the financial analysis and supporting documentation in the claim review file that supports the decision that a partial claim was the appropriate loss mitigation option.

E. Combining Options

A partial claim may be utilized as a stand-alone tool, or incorporated as part of a special forbearance agreement. For example, if a mortgagor needs time to resolve the default, but will eventually be able to support the normal monthly payment but no more than that, a repayment plan or special forbearance may culminate in a partial claim. An existing repayment plan or special forbearance may also be converted to partial claim if the mortgagor's circumstances change. A partial claim may not be used in conjunction with a mortgage modification.

On August 29, 2002, the Department published Mortgagee Letter (ML) 2002-17, ***Special Forbearance: Program Changes and Updates*** which provided new guidance for a Type II Special Forbearance. The Type II Special Forbearance combines a short-term special forbearance plan and a modification or partial claim as a single loss mitigation plan. It is an appropriate loss mitigation tool to utilize when there is any concern about the mortgagor's ability or commitment to keep the payments current following reinstatement. For more information on this related issue, please refer to ML 2002-17.

F. Allowable Provisions

The following provisions apply to *all* partial claim notes:

- The partial claim must fully reinstate the loan;
- The partial claim advance may include only principal, interest and escrow advances required to reinstate the loan;
- In no event may the total arrearage exceed the equivalent of 12 months PITI. The maximum partial claim advance for an Adjustable Rate Mortgage (ARM), Graduated Payment Mortgage (GPM), and Growing Equity Mortgage (GEM) loans is calculated by adding the specific PITI requirement for each of the monthly installments to be included in the partial claim.

The mortgagee may not include late fees, legal fees or other administrative expenses in the partial claim note. However, mortgagees may only collect legal costs and fees resulting from a canceled foreclosure action directly from the mortgagor to the extent not reimbursed by HUD and in accordance with HUD limitations. These requirements are provided in Chapter 4 of Handbook 4330.1, REV-5, Administration of Insured Home Mortgages, Mortgagee Letter 2001-19, Single Family Foreclosure Policy and Procedural Changes, or subsequent guidance, if any. As a reminder, under no circumstances will the mortgagor be required to pay the mortgagee more than the Department identified as customary and reasonable for claim purposes.

Although HUD does not prescribe a lien priority requirement for partial claims, the mortgagee must ensure timely recordation of the subordinate mortgage.

G. Repayment Terms

The partial claim advance will be secured by a note and subordinate mortgage with the following repayment terms:

- The note is interest free. (The Secretary reserves the right to assess interest on partial claim notes originated in the future.);
- No monthly or periodic payments are required, however, mortgagors may voluntarily submit partial payments;
- The note is due at the earlier of 1) the payoff of the first mortgage, or 2) when the mortgagor no longer owns the property;
- There is no prepayment penalty;
- A mortgagor is only eligible to apply for a mortgage insurance premium (MIP) refund when the partial claim note has been paid in full;
- The Partial Claim Note and security documents must be payable to HUD;
- Voluntary payments or prepayments should be delivered via a cashier's check or other certified funds to the Department's servicing contractor at the following address.

U.S. Department of HUD
c/o First Madison Services, Inc.
4111 South Darlington
Suite 300
Tulsa, OK 74135

H. Required Documentation

A promissory note must be executed in the name of the Secretary and a subordinate mortgage must be obtained and recorded. The mortgagee must include the provisions of HUD's model form of note and subordinate mortgage (as provided in ML 97-17) and make any amendments required by state laws. While HUD does not endorse the products or services of vendors, the Department is aware that state specific documents are commercially available. Mortgagees who take advantage of the convenience of purchasing these documents should review them prior to use.

I. Disclosures

FHA requires mortgagees to comply with any disclosure or notice requirements applicable under State or Federal law.

J. Use of Pre-Foreclosure Sale where a Partial Claim was provided on an earlier default

Some mortgagees have erroneously failed to include the amount of the Partial Claim when calculating total indebtedness for the purpose of a pre-foreclosure sale. In order to be in compliance, mortgagees must include both the first mortgage and the partial claim amounts to correctly calculate the total outstanding mortgage indebtedness.

K. Loan Payoff or Refinance-Mortgagee Responsibilities

Mortgagees will be responsible for notifying HUD when the first mortgage is being paid in full or refinanced in order for HUD to provide a payoff figure on the Partial Claim. HUD's Servicing Contractor, identified in Section G of this mortgagee letter, should be contacted to request a payoff quote on the outstanding Partial Claim. The purpose of this requirement is to ensure that no partial claim is overlooked when preparations are made to pay the first mortgage in full.

L. Mortgagee Incentives

FHA will pay mortgagees a $250 incentive fee for each partial claim. The mortgagor may not be charged any additional costs for receiving this loss mitigation workout option, however, it is acceptable that legal costs and fees related to a canceled foreclosure action may be collected directly from the mortgagor. Mortgagees are reminded that all such costs must be reflective of work actually completed to the date of the foreclosure cancellation and the attorney fees may not be in excess of the fees that HUD has identified as customary and reasonable for claim purposes. Please refer to Mortgagee Letter 2001-19, issued August 24, 2001, or subsequent issuance, if any, for guidance.

M. Failure by the mortgagor on a Partial Claim

In the event the mortgagor becomes delinquent following reinstatement via a partial claim, it shall be treated as a new default and serviced accordingly.

N. Limitations on Use

If a loan has been modified or reinstated using a partial claim within the past three years, re-default risk is presumed to increase following a subsequent partial claim. Prior to allowing a partial claim in this circumstance, the mortgagee must prepare a written justification, and retain a copy along with supporting documents in the claim review file. It is anticipated that this will be a highly unusual occurrence, and that the cause of the second default will be unrelated to the original problem. There is a lifetime limitation of 12 monthly installments of PITI. **Once 12 full monthly installments have been paid by HUD on a claim type 33 (partial claim) for a given case number, no further partial claims will be honored on a specific case.**

O. Recordation Requirements

Upon execution of a partial claim by a mortgagor, the Department requires that the partial claim security instruments be submitted for recordation to the appropriate jurisdiction within a maximum period of five (5) business days following the execution **AND** prior to filing a claim with HUD.

The responsibility for servicing of the Partial Claim remains with the mortgagee until the security interests are legally recorded in the appropriate jurisdiction.

P. Claim Filing

In accordance with 24 CFR 203.371 (d) "along with the prescribed application for partial claim insurance benefits, the mortgagee shall forward to HUD the original credit and security instruments requirements by paragraph (c) of this section." Provided that the mortgagee has complied with the regulations, the mortgagee must file the claim within 60 days of the date the subordinate lien to HUD is executed. The claim may include the amount of the partial claim note and the $250 incentive fee. HUD will pay no other costs or fees. **Failure to file the claim within 60 days will result in loss of the $250 incentive fee.**

Q. Document Delivery

It is the responsibility of the mortgagee to deliver the original promissory note and recorded mortgage to HUD's servicing contractor's business address listed in Section G of this Mortgagee Letter, as soon as possible, but in any case, no later than six (6) months from the execution date of the partial claim note and security instruments.

HUD expects the mortgagee or its agent to periodically check on the status of all unreturned recorded documents and that mortgagees advise HUD of all such delayed deliveries. Where it appears that recorded documents cannot be forwarded due to delays in the land records office, mortgagees must request an extension of time. HUD's National Servicing Center (NSC) shall grant time extensions in the event document delivery is delayed by events beyond the control of the mortgagee. Except in extreme circumstances, late requests will be denied.

HUD Form 50012 is to be used for extension requests. Box 7, titled "Other" (specify) must be checked and the following wording is recommended for specification purposes: "Requesting an extension of time to return recorded Partial Claim documents to HUD" and must enter the number of days needed. Under the sections "Basis for Extension Request," the mortgagee must indicate the reason for the delay.

R. One-Time Amnesty for accepting outstanding Partial Claim related legal documents without penalty.

HUD shall provide a **"One-Time Amnesty"** to allow mortgagees to submit overdue Partial Claim documents without penalty. The Department is emphasizing HUD's willingness to partner with the mortgage industry on overdue partial claim related legal documents that remain outstanding because of a delay in receipt of recorded documents.

HUD expects mortgagees to exercise prudent and consistent diligence to ensure that all documents are promptly submitted for recordation and are then forwarded to HUD as required. HUD will accept ***without penalty***, all overdue partial claim documents received within *45 days* of the issuance date of this Mortgagee Letter. Once the 45-day grace period has expired, on the 46th day HUD will begin issuing demand letters for the submission of overdue partial claim security instruments and notes and reimbursement of related incentives paid.

Any questions regarding this Mortgagee Letter may be directed to HUD's National Servicing Center (NSC) at (888) 297-8685 or hsg-lossmit@hud.gov. These clarifications are effective immediately.

John C. Weicher
Assistant Secretary for Housing-
Federal Housing Commissioner

Department of Housing and Urban Development, Mortgagee Letter 2004-37 (September 17, 2004)

September 17, 2004

MORTGAGEE LETTER 2004-37

TO: ALL APPROVED MORTGAGEES

SUBJECT: Underwriting and Servicing Policies to Assist Victims of Presidentially-Declared Major Disaster Areas

Flooding and destruction caused by Hurricane Ivan greatly affected portions of Florida and Alabama in September 2004. This Mortgagee Letter is being issued as a reminder to mortgagees of the availability of Federal Housing Administration (FHA) Single Family programs for victims of major disasters, including victims of Tropical Storm Bonnie and Hurricanes Charley and Frances.

When the President declares a disaster, the mortgagee must check with the Federal Emergency Management Agency (FEMA) to obtain the specific affected counties and corresponding declaration dates. This information can be found on the Internet at http://www.fema.gov/disasters or by calling the local FEMA office.

The procedures described in this letter are in effect whenever a disaster is Presidentially-Declared and remain in effect for one year from the date of the President's declaration. Any areas added to the declaration will also be eligible for disaster relief and the same provisions will apply.

I. MORTGAGE ORIGINATIONS

Mortgage Insurance for Disaster Victims

HUD has a special mortgage insurance program under Section 203(h) of the National Housing Act to assist disaster victims. Under this program, individuals or families whose residences were destroyed or damaged to such an extent that reconstruction or replacement is necessary are eligible for 100 percent financing. The requirements for the program are as follows:

- The borrower's previous residence must have been in the disaster area and must have been destroyed or damaged to such an extent that reconstruction or replacement is necessary. The borrower must provide conclusive evidence of the above. Documentation showing a permanent residence in the affected area before the disaster includes a valid driver's license, a voter registration card, utility bills, etc. Documentation regarding destruction of the residence may include an insurance report, an inspection report by an independent fee inspector or government agency, or conclusive photographic evidence showing the destruction or damage. The borrower may have been the owner of the property or a renter of the property affected.
- The borrower is eligible for 100 percent financing of the sales price and no downpayment is required. However, closing cost and prepaid expenses not paid by the seller must be paid by the borrower in cash or through premium pricing.
- Maximum mortgage amounts are the same as for Section 203(b). A list of the mortgage limits can be found on the following website: https://entp.hud.gov/idapp/html/hicostlook.cfm
- The program is limited to one-unit detached homes or units in an approved condominium project. "Spot units" in condominiums are also eligible, subject to the instructions outlined in Mortgagee Letter 96-41. Two, three, and four unit properties may not be purchased under the Section 203(h) program. The mortgage insurance premium is associated with the type of property being purchased, e.g., if the mortgage will be on a one-unit detached property, there will be an upfront mortgage insurance premium of 1.5 percent as well as the annual premium which is collected monthly.
- The borrower's application for mortgage insurance must be submitted to the lender within one year of the

President's declaration of the disaster.

- These mortgages are eligible for processing under the Direct Endorsement program.
- Adjustable rate mortgages (ARMS) may be used with the Section 203(h) program.

Section 203(k) Rehabilitation Mortgages

The requirement for a dwelling to be completed more than one year preceding the date of the application for mortgage insurance under Section 203(k) does not apply to properties in the disaster area. Damaged residences are eligible for Section 203(k) mortgage insurance regardless of the age of the property. The residences need only to have been completed and ready for occupancy for eligibility under Section 203(k). The percentage of financing, however, is determined by the type of mortgage being made, i.e., normal loan-to-value ratios apply to Section 203(k) mortgages made in these areas. The mortgage insurance premium is the same for all other Section 203(k) mortgages.

Construction/Permanent Mortgages

Lenders are encouraged to use the construction/permanent mortgage program in the areas affected. HUD Handbook 4155.1 REV-5 contains complete processing guidelines.

Underwriting

The Department recognizes that victims of a disaster may have to incur debts to replace personal property. Victims of the disaster will be allowed to have a total fixed payment to gross income ratio of 43 percent without compensating factors. The 43 percent ratio can also be exceeded with appropriate compensating factors. This provision will apply to all FHA-insured mortgages regardless of the insurance program.

Disaster victims with Secretary-held mortgages are eligible for new FHA-insured mortgages provided the borrower was current with the forbearance agreement at the time of the disaster and all payments for the preceding twelve months were made within the month due.

Submission of Closed Loans

For lenders located in the areas affected, the Department is extending the time for submission of closed loans for insurance endorsement from 60 days to 90 days after the date of closing. This will provide lenders additional time to locate and reconstruct loan packages where documents may have been destroyed by the disaster.

Endorsement of Delinquent Mortgages

The Homeownership Centers (HOCs) have been granted authority, on a case-by-case basis, to endorse mortgages that are delinquent, provided the delinquency is due to disaster-related circumstances. As a rule, this policy applies to cases where the loan closed before the disaster and the homeowner may have become delinquent in the mortgage payments because of temporary disruptions in employment.

II. MORTGAGE SERVICING

Chapter 14, Federal National Disasters, of HUD Handbook 4330.1 REV-5, *Administration of Insured Home Mortgages*, contains the provisions summarized below.

Moratorium on Foreclosures

A moratorium on foreclosures on property directly affected by the disasters is in effect for a ninety (90) day period from the date the President declared a disaster to have existed. The moratorium applies to the initiation of foreclosures AND foreclosures already in process.

Servicing Actions

In addition to the moratorium, HUD strongly recommends servicing actions for homeowners whose properties were directly affected by the disaster. This includes such actions as special forbearance, mortgage modification, refinancing, and waiver of late charges. HUD also offers a partial claim program to help address problems of unresolved arrearages. Subsequent to the foreclosure moratorium, lenders are encouraged to consider alternatives to foreclosure such as pre-foreclosure sales and deeds in lieu of foreclosure if the homeowner is not in a position to "cure" the mortgage delinquency. Refer to Mortgagee Letter 00-5 for FHA program requirements and incentive payments associated with the above referenced servicing approaches. Further, for loans on properties affected by these disasters, the maximum pre-foreclosure sales period is extended an additional two months, and the minimum appraised as-is value of the property is reduced to 58 percent, without requiring the lender to seek a variance approval from HUD's National Servicing and Loss Mitigation Center in Oklahoma City.

III. DEALING WITH PROPERTY DAMAGE

Mortgagees must follow standard procedures, including assuring that hazard insurance claims are filed and settled expeditiously. Mortgagees must release appropriate proceeds to the mortgagor and must not retain hazard insurance proceeds to make up an existing arrearage without the written consent of the mortgagor.

IV. PROVIDE TEMPORARY HOUSING AND SHELTER

HUD will work with FEMA to identify vacant public housing and HUD-owned properties that can be used as temporary housing for those forced from their homes.

V. THE FEDERAL EMERGENCY MANAGEMENT AGENCY (FEMA) MORTGAGE ASSISTANCE PAYMENTS

Mortgagees must inform mortgagors regarding this program. The following text is an example of what such a notice should include "If a major disaster has occurred, the Federal Emergency Management Agency (FEMA) will publicize a toll-free telephone number in the disaster area. Call that number for information about FEMA's "mortgage assistance program." You may also visit FEMA's temporary Disaster Relief Office in the disaster area or call the permanent FEMA Disaster Relief Office that serves your area."

If you have any questions concerning this Mortgagee Letter, please contact the Homeownership Center in Atlanta at 888-696-4687.

Sincerely,

John C. Weicher
Assistant Secretary for Housing-
Federal Housing Commissioner

Department of Housing and Urban Development, Mortgagee Letter 2005-06 (January 28, 2005)

January 28, 2005

MORTGAGEE LETTER 2005-06

TO: ALL APPROVED MORTGAGEES

SUBJECT: Lender Accountability for Appraisals

This Mortgagee Letter is to remind mortgagees of their responsibilities to obtain high quality appraisals for properties that will be security for FHA-insured mortgages. These responsibilities are contained in an amendment to 24 CFR 203.5 that was published in the Federal Register on July 20, 2004 and which became effective August 19, 2004. This rule also amended 24 CFR 25.9 to make submission of, or causing to be submitted, documentation relating to an appraisal that does not satisfy FHA requirements a ground for administrative action by the Mortgagee Review Board. As explained in the preamble to this final rule, HUD is imposing a standard of accountability to which lenders, sponsor lenders, and loan correspondent lenders will be held that is the same as the standard used to impose civil money penalties for program violations. That standard is one of knowing (actual knowledge) or had reason to know.

HUD handbooks and mortgagee letters specify certain actions that a mortgagee should take to help ensure that appraisals comply with FHA requirements. However, the fact that a mortgagee has taken such actions does not automatically mitigate the standard imposed by this final rule if despite compliance with the requirements, the lender is found to have known or had reason to know about the deficient appraisal.

Background

Since 1991, when passage of Title XI of the Financial Institutions Reform, Recovery and Enforcement Act of 1989 (FIRREA) created systemic state licensure and certification requirements for appraisers, FHA has reiterated the responsibility of lenders to critically review and analyze FHA appraisals. The direction and guidance provided to lenders in previous mortgagee letters included the following:

- "A DE lender that selects its own appraiser must accept responsibility, equally with the appraiser, for the integrity, accuracy and thoroughness of the appraisal and will be held accountable by HUD for the quality of the appraisal."
- "Lenders are reminded that if the appraiser they selected provides a poor or even fraudulent appraisal which leads the Department to insure a mortgage at an inflated amount, the lender is held equally responsible with the appraiser for the violation."
- "Lenders accept responsibility, equally with the appraisers, for the integrity, accuracy and thoroughness of the appraisals, and will be held accountable by HUD"

Handbook 4060.1 REV-1, Change 1, Mortgagee Approval Handbook, dated November 24, 2003, revised and updated the Department's requirements for maintaining and implementing a Quality Control Program for the origination and servicing of HUD/FHA insured mortgages. Chapter 6 contains detailed explanations for quality control plans including appraisal review.

Highlights of Final Rule

The final rule:

a) codifies FHA's requirement that mortgagees are accountable, along with appraisers, for the quality of appraisals on properties securing FHA-insured mortgages;
b) specifically provides that lenders that submit appraisals to HUD which do not meet FHA requirements are subject to the imposition of sanctions by the HUD Mortgagee Review Board;
c) applies to both sponsor lenders that underwrite loans and loan correspondent lenders that originate loans on behalf of their sponsors; and
d) is designed to ensure that lenders are aware of their responsibilities with respect to appraisals and provide homeowners with an accurate statement of the appraised value of their home as well as help assure homeowners that the condition of the home meets FHA standards.
e) clarifies that the standard of accountability to which lenders, sponsor lenders, and loan correspondent lenders will be held is the same as the standard used to impose civil money penalties for program violations, and that standard is one of knowing (actual knowledge) or had reason to know.

Purpose of the Rule

The success of the FHA single family mortgage insurance program, and HUD's ability to safeguard the FHA Insurance Fund, depends significantly on the quality of appraisals on properties that are to be security for insured mortgages. Section 203(b)(2) of the National Housing Act (12 U.S.C. 1709(b)(2)) provides the method for calculating the maximum mortgage amount that FHA can insure. The calculations required by statute are based on the appraised value of the property that is security for the mortgage. If a mortgagor defaults and the mortgagee conveys title to the property in exchange for payment of the mortgage insurance benefits, FHA must then manage and sell the property in order to recoup its insurance loss. If the appraisal was accurate, the loss to FHA will be minimal. If the appraisal was inaccurate, or the appraiser was negligent in reporting readily observable defects, HUD's return on any sale of a property that was overvalued or in poor condition could be significantly reduced, thereby increasing the loss to the FHA Insurance Fund.

If you have any questions concerning this Mortgagee Letter, please contact your local Homeownership Centers in Atlanta (888) 696-4687, Denver (800) 543-9378, Philadelphia (800) 440-8647, or Santa Ana (888) 827-5605 (these are all toll free numbers).

Sincerely,

John C. Weicher
Assistant Secretary for Housing-
Federal Housing Commissioner

Department of Housing and Urban Development Mortgagee Letter 2005-13 (March 21, 2005)

March 21, 2005

MORTGAGEE LETTER 2005-13

TO: ALL APPROVED MORTGAGEES

SUBJECT: Correction to Servicing Guidance for Victims of Presidentially-Declared Major Disaster Areas

The purpose of this Mortgagee Letter is to advise mortgagees that the Federal Emergency Management Agency (FEMA) no longer provides the Mortgage Assistance Payments referred to in Mortgagee Letters 2004-37, 2004-36, and 2004-32. FHA recently became aware that this program was terminated. Mortgagees should no longer refer mortgagors to this program.

If you have any questions concerning this Mortgagee Letter, please contact HUD's National Servicing Center (NSC) at (888) 297-8685.

Sincerely,

John C. Weicher
Assistant Secretary for Housing-
Federal Housing Commissioner

Department of Housing and Urban Development Mortgagee Letter 2005-18 (Apr. 26, 2005)

April 26, 2005

Mortgagee Letter 2005-18

TO: ALL APPROVED MORTGAGEES

ATTENTION: Single Family Servicing Managers

SUBJECT: Success of Loss Mitigation and Increase in Incentive Payments

HUD initiated its loss mitigation program in 1996 in an effort to provide maximum opportunities for Federal Housing Administration (FHA) insured borrowers to retain homeownership. The program delegates loss mitigation responsibility and authority to lenders and cannot be successful without their full participation and cooperation.

Since that time, HUD has seen usage of loss mitigation grow exponentially, especially with home retention options including special forbearance, mortgage modification and partial claim. In fiscal year 2004, the Department paid 84,222 total loss mitigation claims, 78,528 of which were home retention claims. This exceeds the number of foreclosure claims paid during the same period and is a clear indication that FHA lenders are fully committed to curing mortgage default and preventing foreclosure.

Effective use of loss mitigation not only allows families to retain homeownership, it also significantly reduces the financial impact of foreclosure claims against the FHA Insurance Funds. The savings realized through loss mitigation are substantial and ultimately reduce the mortgage insurance premiums paid by all FHA-insured borrowers.

As described in Mortgagee Letter 2000-05, *Loss Mitigation Program—Comprehensive Clarification of Policy and Notice of Procedural Changes*, HUD provides reimbursement of certain costs incurred by lenders in executing loan modification and partial claim loss mitigation options and also provides additional financial incentives for all loss mitigation options. In recognition of the increased costs lenders experience when providing effective default servicing and the savings realized by HUD from this program, the Department is announcing an increase in its loss mitigation incentives and will make these increased incentives available to all lenders that utilize HUD's most powerful home retention options; loan modification and partial claim.

Therefore, effective for loan modifications and partial claims received by HUD on or after June 1, 2005, all lenders will be entitled to claim an additional financial incentive of $250 when submitting a claim type 32 for mortgage modifications, and an additional incentive of $250 when submitting a claim type 33 for partial claims. The total financial incentive that will be payable is $750 for mortgage modifications and $500 for partial claims.

This is in addition to reimbursement of actual allowable expenses, such as the cost of a title search or recording fees, up to the limits provided in Mortgagee Letter *2000-05*. Reimbursements and incentives for other loss mitigation options remain unchanged at this time.

In addition, the Department is announcing another change that will permit more lenders to become eligible for the additional special forbearance and other incentives that lenders have been eligible for based upon their performance. The Department plans to begin using the Loss Mitigation Tier Ranking System (TRS) rather than the Loss Mitigation Performance Assessment (LMPA) as the basis for payment of these additional incentives following the release of TRS Round 20 scores. A subsequent Mortgagee Letter will be issued to advise those lenders scoring in Tier One when they may begin requesting the increased incentives and taking advantage of the other, non-monetary incentives.

Since 1997, HUD has been using the LMPA to measure the loss mitigation performance of lenders and has provided additional loss mitigation incentive payments, certain claim reimbursements, and delegated program authorities to those lenders who scored in the top 25th percentile of this annual performance measure. The Department believes that the information provided by the LMPA is an important measure of lender performance and it will continue to conduct this analysis and publish LMPA scores annually.

The next assessment for the purpose of providing the additional incentives will be tied to the publication of TRS Round 20 scores. This shift to the use of TRS rather than LMPA scores will not penalize any mortgagee that is currently receiving the increased incentives, as the current scoring will continue through the end of the fiscal year.

After publication of TRS Round 20 scores, lenders who rank in Tier One will receive:

1. An additional $100 payment for each Special Forbearance Agreement executed on or after the effective date to be announced by HUD;
2. Pre-foreclosure sale time frames may be extended an additional two months without prior HUD approval; and
3. For loans endorsed on or after February 1, 1998, lenders will be able to claim reimbursement of 75 percent for foreclosure costs (an increase from the current allowance of 66 percent). For loans endorsed prior to February 1, 1998, all lenders will continue to be reimbursed two thirds of the foreclosure costs.

The identity of Tier One lenders in TRS Round 20 will be posted by HUD on its website. The specific site will be announced in a future mortgagee letter but will be accessible through http://www.hud.gov/offices/hsg/sfh/nsc/nschome.cfm.

The Department will continue to publish TRS scores quarterly, but eligibility for performance incentives will be determined on an annual basis using the TRS scores published near the end of each fiscal year. TRS performance scores represent lender performance for the 12-month period prior to issuance.

HUD will continue to use both LMPA and TRS scores in selecting lenders for Quality Assurance reviews. While these scores do not define all aspects related to loss mitigation performance, HUD is confident that they both identify opportunities for improvement in lender performance.

Questions regarding this announcement may be directed to HUD's National Servicing Center toll free at 1-(888) 297-8685.

John C. Weicher
Assistant Secretary for Housing-
Federal Housing Commissioner

Department of Housing and Urban Development Mortgagee Letter 2005-30 (July 12, 2005)

July 12, 2005

MORTGAGEE LETTER 2005-30

TO: All Approved Mortgagees

ATTENTION: Single Family Servicing Managers

SUBJECT: Single Family Foreclosure Policy and Procedural Changes: Reasonable Diligence Requirements; Update to HUD's Schedule of Allowable Attorney Fees; and Update to HUD's Foreclosure Time Frames

This Mortgagee Letter provides updates to HUD's reasonable diligence time frames and the schedule of attorney fees for all jurisdictions.

REASONABLE DILIGENCE REQUIREMENTS AND EFFECTIVE DATES

When foreclosure of a defaulted loan is necessary, HUD regulation 24 CFR 203.356(b) provides that mortgagees "must exercise reasonable diligence in prosecuting the foreclosure proceedings to completion and in acquiring title to and possession of the property." That regulation also states that HUD will make available to mortgagees a time frame that constitutes "reasonable diligence" for each state. This Mortgagee Letter provides an update to the state foreclosure time frames and attorney's fee schedules that were provided in Mortgagee Letter 2001-19, dated

August 24, 2001. The updates are as follows:

Foreclosures

Attachment 1 provides listings of the first legal action necessary to initiate foreclosure on a mortgage and of the typical security instrument used in each state. Reasonable diligence time frames for completing foreclosure and acquisition of title in each state are provided in Attachment 2. These time frames identify the time between the first legal action required by the jurisdiction to commence foreclosure and the date that the foreclosure deed (Sheriff's, Trustee's, etc. or certificate of title) is recorded. Delays in completing foreclosure due to bankruptcy are treated as exceptions and are not included in the time frames.

The revised time frames provided in Attachment 2 will be effective for all cases where the first legal action to initiate foreclosure occurs on or after September 1, 2005.

<u>Acquiring Possession</u>

When a separate legal action is necessary to gain possession following foreclosure, an automatic extension of the reasonable diligence time frame will be allowed for the actual time necessary to complete the possessory action provided that the mortgagee begins such action promptly. Mortgagees must take the first public legal action to initiate the eviction or possessory action within thirty calendar days of foreclosure completion to qualify for this extension of the reasonable diligence time frame.

The Department is not issuing time frames for completing possessory actions because of wide differences in time periods depending upon the location of the property and other factors outside of the mortgagee's control.

<u>Bankruptcies</u>

When a borrower files bankruptcy after foreclosure proceedings have been instituted, an extension of the reasonable diligence time frame for foreclosure and acquisition of the property will be allowed. However, the mortgagee must ensure that all necessary bankruptcy-related legal actions are handled in a timely and effective manner. The case must be promptly referred to a bankruptcy attorney after the bankruptcy is filed and the mortgagee must monitor the action to ensure that the case is timely resolved. The time frame for completing legal action on a bankruptcy will vary based on the chapter under which the bankruptcy is filed.

<u>Chapter 7 Bankruptcy Filings</u>

HUD does not reimburse for legal expenses associated with a current FHA-insured mortgage. Where the mortgagee cannot proceed with foreclosure action because of a Chapter 7 Bankruptcy, the case shall be resolved through dismissal, termination of the automatic stay or trustee abandonment of all interest in the secured property. The mortgagee's claim review file must document that the case was promptly referred to the mortgagee's foreclosure attorney after the bankruptcy filing.

In general, the additional time allowed for the Chapter 7 Bankruptcy delay for meeting the reasonable diligence requirement shall not exceed 90 days from the date of the bankruptcy filing. Any delay beyond 90 days from the date of bankruptcy filing must be supported by documentation that the delay was not due to the failure of the mortgagee to timely notify its bankruptcy attorney or by any failure of the mortgagee's attorney.

<u>Chapter 13 (and Chapter 11 and 12) Bankruptcy Filings</u>

HUD does not reimburse for legal expenses associated with a current FHA-insured mortgage. Where the mortgagee cannot proceed with foreclosure action because of a Chapter 13 (or Chapter 11 or 12) Bankruptcy, the case shall be resolved through dismissal, termination of the automatic stay or trustee abandonment of all interest in the secured property. The mortgagee's claim review file must document that the case was promptly referred to the mortgagee's attorney after the bankruptcy filing.

In addition to prompt and accurate notification to the bankruptcy court, the mortgagee shall closely monitor the payments required by the bankruptcy court. If the borrower becomes 60 days delinquent in payments required under a Chapter 13 (or Chapter 11 or 12) plan, the lender must ensure that prompt legal action is taken to resolve the matter.

In general, the additional time allowed for the Chapter 13 (or Chapter 11 or 12) Bankruptcy delay for meeting the reasonable diligence requirement shall not exceed 90 days from the date of the payments under the bankruptcy plan became 60 days delinquent. Any delay beyond 90 days from the date of the account became 60 days delinquent under the terms of the bankruptcy plan must be supported by documentation that the delay was not due to the failure of the mortgagee to timely notify its bankruptcy attorney or by any failure of the mortgagee's attorney.

<u>Non-compliance</u>

Mortgagees are responsible for "self-curtailment" of interest on single-family claims where reasonable diligence or reporting requirements are not met. Self-curtailment shall be accomplished by identification of the interest curtailment date on Form HUD-27011, Item 31. Explanation and examples are provided in Attachment 4.

<u>SCHEDULE OF ATTORNEY FEES AND EFFECTIVE DATES</u>

The Department has revised the attorney fees that will be considered as reasonable and customary for various legal actions for purposes of calculating the maximum amount HUD will reimburse in an insurance claim. The updated fee schedules are provided in Attachment 3.

These fees cover the customary legal services performed in each type of action. In all cases, the amount claimed for attorney fees shall reasonably relate to the work actually performed. In the event a legal action is stopped for a loss mitigation option, a reinstatement or a payment in full, the attorney fees that the borrower is required to pay shall be commensurate with the work actually completed to that point and the amount charged may not be in excess of the fee that HUD has established as reasonable and customary for claim purposes.

Foreclosures

The update to HUD's Schedule of Attorney Fees, as provided in Attachment 3, will be effective for all cases where the first legal action to initiate foreclosure occurs on or after September 1, 2005. In the interim, mortgagees shall continue to follow the HUD Schedule of Attorney Fees that was issued with Mortgagee Letter 2001-19, dated August 24, 2001.

Bankruptcy Actions

The update to HUD's Schedule of Attorney Fees will be effective for all bankruptcy clearances undertaken on or after September 1, 2005. These fees represent maximum allowable amounts for customary and routine legal services performed in each type of bankruptcy filing. Mortgagee claims for legal fee reimbursement must be reasonably related to the amount of work that the bankruptcy attorney actually performed.

A bankruptcy clearance begins when a petition for release of the bankruptcy stay is submitted to the bankruptcy court. Bankruptcy clearances begun prior to the effective date shall be reimbursed according to HUD's Schedule of Attorney Fees that was issued with Mortgagee Letter 2001-19, dated August 24, 2001.

Possessory Actions (Evictions)

The update to HUD's Schedule of Attorney Fees will be effective for all possessory actions undertaken on or after September 1, 2005. Possessory actions begun prior to the effective date shall be reimbursed according to HUD's Schedule of Attorney Fees that was issued with Mortgagee Letter 2001-19, dated August 24, 2001.

Deeds-in-Lieu of Foreclosure

The update to HUD's Schedule of Attorney Fees will be effective for all deeds-in-lieu recorded in HUD's name on or after September 1, 2005. In the interim, mortgagees shall continue to follow HUD's Schedule of Attorney Fees that was issued with Mortgagee Letter 2001-19, dated August 24, 2001.

Questions regarding this Mortgagee Letter may be directed to HUD's National Servicing Center at (888) 297-8685.

Sincerely,

Brian D. Montgomery
Assistant Secretary for Housing-
Federal Housing Commissioner

Attachments

Attachment 1

Action Considered by the Department of Housing and Urban Development As the First Legal Action to Commence (Institute) Foreclosure

State Code	State	Typical Type of HUD Security Instrument	Normal Method of Foreclosure	First Foreclosure Action
01	Alabama	Mortgage	Non-Judicial	Publication
11	Alaska	Deed of Trust	Non-Judicial	Recording of Notice of Default
02	Arizona	Deed of Trust	Non-Judicial	Recording of Notice of Sale
03	Arkansas	Deed of Trust	Non-Judicial	Recording of Notice of Default
04	California	Deed of Trust	Non-Judicial	Recording of Notice of Default
05	Colorado	Deed of Trust	Non-Judicial	Filing of Foreclosure Documents with Public Trustee
06	Connecticut	Mortgage	Judicial	Delivering Complaint to Sheriff
07	Delaware	Mortgage	Judicial	Complaint
08	District of Columbia	Deed of Trust	Non-Judicial	Recording of Notice of Default
09	Florida	Mortgage	Judicial	Complaint
10	Georgia	Security Deed	Non-Judicial	Publication
83	Guam	Mortgage	Non-Judicial	Posting and Publishing of Notice of Sale
14	Hawaii	Mortgage	Judicial	Complaint
		Mortgage	Non-Judicial	Publication of Notice of Intent to Foreclose
12	Idaho	Deed of Trust	Non-Judicial	Recording of Notice of Default
13	Illinois	Mortgage	Judicial	Complaint
15	Indiana	Mortgage	Judicial	Complaint
16	Iowa	Mortgage	Judicial	Petition
		Deed of Trust	Non-Judicial	Delivering Notice to Clerk
18	Kansas	Mortgage	Judicial	Complaint
20	Kentucky	Mortgage	Judicial	Complaint
22	Louisiana	Mortgage	Judicial	Petition for Executory Process
23	Maine	Mortgage	Judicial	Complaint
24	Maryland	Mortgage	Judicial	Petition in Equity
		Deed of Trust	Non-Judicial	Filing an Order to Docket
25	Massachusetts[1]	Mortgage	Non-Judicial	Filing of Complaint Relative to Servicemembers Civil Relief Act
26	Michigan	Mortgage	Non-Judicial	Publication
27	Minnesota	Mortgage Deed	Non-Judicial	Publication
28	Mississippi	Deed of Trust	Non-Judicial	Publication
29	Missouri	Deed of Trust	Non-Judicial	Publication
31	Montana	Trust Indenture	Non-Judicial	Recording of Notice of Sale
32	Nebraska	Mortgage	Judicial	Petition
		Deed of Trust	Non-Judicial	Publication of Notice of Sale
33	Nevada	Deed of Trust	Non-Judicial	Recording of Notice of Default
34	New Hampshire	Mortgage	Non-Judicial	Publication
35	New Jersey	Mortgage	Judicial	Complaint
36	New Mexico	Mortgage	Judicial	Complaint
37	New York	Mortgage	Judicial	Complaint
38	North Carolina	Deed of Trust	Non-Judicial	Notice of Hearing
40	North Dakota	Mortgage	Judicial	Complaint
41	Ohio	Mortgage Deed	Judicial	Complaint
42	Oklahoma	Mortgage	Judicial	Petition
43	Oregon	Deed of Trust	Non-Judicial	Recording of Notice of Default

State Code	State	Typical Type of HUD Security Instrument	Normal Method of Foreclosure	First Foreclosure Action
44	Pennsylvania	Mortgage	Judicial	Complaint
50	Puerto Rico	Mortgage	Judicial	Complaint
45	Rhode Island	Mortgage	Non-Judicial	Publication
46	South Carolina	Mortgage	Judicial	Complaint
47	South Dakota	Mortgage	Judicial	Complaint
		Deed of Trust	Non-Judicial	Publication of Notice of Sale
48	Tennessee	Deed of Trust	Non-Judicial	Publication
49	Texas	Deed of Trust	Non-Judicial	Posting and Filing of the Notice of Sale
52	Utah	Mortgage	Judicial	Complaint
		Deed of Trust	Non-Judicial	Recording of Notice of Default
53	Vermont	Mortgage	Judicial	Complaint
54	Virginia	Deed of Trust	Non-Judicial	Publication
82	Virgin Islands	Mortgage	Judicial	Complaint
56	Washington	Deed of Trust	Non-Judicial	Recording of Notice of Sale
57	West Virginia	Deed of Trust	Non-Judicial	Publication
58	Wisconsin	Mortgage	Judicial	Complaint
59	Wyoming	Mortgage	Non-Judicial	Publication

Footnote: (1) The mortgagee must first obtain a Judgment from the Land Court certifying that the owners of the property being foreclosed are not entitled to relief under the Servicemembers Civil Relief Act (SCRA).

Attachment 2

HUD REASONABLE DILIGENCE TIME FRAMES (In Months)—Effective 9/1/2005

State	Nonjudicial Foreclosure	Judicial Foreclosure
AK	5	
AL	4	
AR	5	
AZ	4	
CA	7	
CO	7	
CT		9
DC	7	
DE		8
FL		7
GA	4	
GU	10	
HI	4	9
IA	9	17
ID	6	
IL		12
IN		10
KS		9
KY		7
LA		7
MA	8	
MD	6	6
ME		12
MI	9	
MN	10	
MO	3	
MS	4	

State	Nonjudicial Foreclosure	Judicial Foreclosure
MT	7	
NC	5	
ND		8
NE	5	5
NH	4	
NJ		14
NM		7
NV	6	
NY		13
OH		12
OK		7
OR	7	
PA		10
PR		14
RI	3	
SC		7
SD	9	10
TN	4	
TX	3	
UT	5	11
VA	4	
VI		15
VT		14
WA	6	
WI		12
WV	5	
WY	6	

Attachment 3

HUD Schedule of Standard Attorney's Fees – Effective 9/1/2005

STATE	NONJUDICIAL FORECLOSURE	JUDICIAL FORECLOSURE	BANKRUPTCY CLEARANCE	POSSESSORY ACTION	DEED-IN-LIEU
AK	$1,250		Varies[13]	$375	$400
AL	$600[1]		Varies[13]	$375	$400
AR	$650		Varies[13]	$275	$400
AZ	$675		Varies[13]	$275	$400
CA	$650		Varies[13]	$525	$400
CO	$850		Varies[13]	$275	$400
CT		$1,350[2]	Varies[13]	$375	$400
DC	$650[1]		Varies[13]	$375	$400
DE		$1,000	Varies[13]	$325	$400
FL		$1,250	Varies[13]	$375	$400
GA	$650[1,3]		Varies[13]	$375	$400
GU	$1,250		Varies[13]	$375	$400
HI	$1,250	$1,900	Varies[13]	$525	$400
IA	$600	$900	Varies[13]	$325	$400
ID	$650		Varies[13]	$375	$400
IL		$1,150[5]	Varies[13]	$325	$400
IN		$1,050[6]	Varies[13]	$325	$400
KS		$900	Varies[13]	$325	$400
KY		$1,150	Varies[13]	$375	$400
LA		$950	Varies[13]	$325	$400
MA	$1,300		Varies[13]	$625	$400
MD	$850[1,3]	$850	Varies[13]	$375	$400
ME		$1,300	Varies[13]	$525	$400
MI	$700[7]		Varies[13]	$325	$400
MN	$700		Varies[13]	$325	$400
MO	$700		Varies[13]	$325	$400
MS	$600[1]		Varies[13]	$375	$400
MT	$650		Varies[13]	$375	$400
NC	$600[8]		Varies[13]	$375	$400
ND		$950	Varies[13]	$325	$400
NE	$650[9]	$900	Varies[13]	$325	$400
NH	$950		Varies[13]	$425	$400
NJ		$1,350	Varies[13]	$375	$400
NM		$950	Varies[13]	$275	$400
NV	$650		Varies[13]	$375	$400
NY		$1,300[10]	Varies[13]	$725	$400
OH		$1,150	Varies[13]	$325	$400
OK		$950[5]	Varies[13]	$275	$400
OR	$725		Varies[13]	$375	$400
PA		$1,300[11]	Varies[13]	$425	$400
PR		$1,150[12]	Varies[13]	$300	$400
RI	$950		Varies[13]	$525	$400
SC		$850	Varies[13]	$375	$400
SD	$600	$900	Varies[13]	$325	$400
TN	$600[1]		Varies[13]	$375	$400
TX	$600		Varies[13]	$325	$400
UT	$650	$600	Varies[13]	$275	$400
VA	$650[1,3]		Varies[13]	$375	$400

STATE	NONJUDICIAL FORECLOSURE	JUDICIAL FORECLOSURE	BANKRUPTCY CLEARANCE	POSSESSORY ACTION	DEED-IN-LIEU
VI		$1,150	Varies[13]	$300	$400
VT		$1,000	Varies[13]	$375	$400
WA	$725		Varies[13]	$375	$400
WI		$1,150	Varies[13]	$325	$400
WV	$600[1,3]		Varies[13]	$375	$400
WY	$650		Varies[13]	$375	$400

Footnotes:

(1) The fee covers the combined attorney's and notary's fees
(2) This fee applies to strict foreclosures. If the foreclosure orders a Foreclosure by Sale, the fee will be $1,550.
(3) The fee covers both the attorney's fee and the trustee's commission (or statutory fee).
(4) The fee includes reimbursement of any fee for the attorney's certificate of title.
(5) The fee increases by $100 if foreclosure is achieved by summary judgment.
(6) In addition to the allowable foreclosure fee, an auctioneer's fee of up to $250 is allowed for the services of a state licensed auctioneer requested by the lender and approved by the court.
(7) The fee increases to $1,100 for a nonjudicial foreclosure for a case in which the attorney provides services for "proceedings subsequent" that involve registered land.
(8) The fee includes the notary's fee. An additional fee of $250 is allowed for an attorney court appearance for a foreclosure hearing.
(9) This fee relates to the exercise of the power of sale under a deed of trust.
(10) This fee applies to foreclosures other than those conducted in New York City and Long Island. A fee of $1,850 applies to foreclosures conducted in the five boroughs of New York City (Bronx, Brooklyn/Kings, Manhattan, Queens and Staten Island) and in Long Island (Nassau and Suffolk Counties).
(11) The fee covers certain additional legal actions necessary to complete the foreclosure, including motions to postpone or relist a sale and motions to reassess damages.
(12) In addition to the allowable foreclosure fee, $150 is allowed for a notary fee for completed foreclosures. However, if a deed of judicial sale cannot be executed contemporaneously with the foreclosure sale, $300 is allowed for the notary fee.
(13) This fee assumes that all required procedural steps have been completed. The maximum attorney's fee varies based on the chapter under which the bankruptcy action is filed.
- For Chapter 7 bankruptcies, the maximum allowable fee is $650.
- For Chapter 11, 12 and 13 bankruptcies, the maximum allowable fee is $1,000.

Attachment 4

The following examples are provided to illustrate how the date to which debenture interest can be claimed must be calculated. This calculation will take into account the date the first public action to initiate foreclosure was taken and the reporting cycle in which the action was properly reported pursuant to 24 CFR 203.356(a). As provided in Mortgagee Letter 97-18, mortgagees shall be considered to be in compliance with the reporting requirement of 24 CFR 203.356(a) when the case is properly reported to the SFDMS for the reporting cycle (or in the following reporting cycle) in which the first public legal action required to initiate foreclosure is taken.

If one or more time requirements have been missed, the interest curtailment date will be the date of the earliest missed time requirement. Mortgagees shall be responsible for "self curtailment" by identifying the appropriate interest curtailment date on Form HUD-27011, Item 31.

Example 1: Mortgagee fails to initiate foreclosure on a timely basis.

Date of Default	09/01/2003
First public action to foreclose	04/21/2004
SFDMS reflects Status 68 for reporting cycle ending	04/30/2004
SFDMS reflects Status 45 for reporting cycle ending	10/31/2004
Date reflected in item 9 of HUD-27011	11/30/2004
Date reflected in item 10	12/28/2004

Reasonable diligence requirement for the State is six months.

In this example, the mortgagee did not initiate foreclosure within six months of the date of default as required by 24 CFR 203.355(a). The claim system will automatically curtail interest to March 1, 2004, six months from the default date.

Example 2: Mortgagee initiates foreclosure on a timely basis but exceeds the State reasonable diligence time frame for completing the action without a valid, documented reason.

Date of Default	12/01/2003
First public action to foreclose	05/10/2004
SFDMS reflects Status 68 for reporting cycle ending	06/30/2004
SFDMS reflects Status 45 for reporting cycle ending	12/31/2004
Date reflected in item 9 of HUD-27011	01/31/2005
Date reflected in item 10	02/28/2005

Reasonable diligence requirement for the State is six months.

In this example, the mortgagee initiated foreclosure within six months of the date of default as required by 24 CFR 203.355(a) and properly reported the action to SFDMS with Status 68 within the required reporting cycle. However, the reasonable diligence requirement for completing the foreclosure in six months was not met. This requires a curtailment of interest to November 10, 2004 and that date would have to be reflected on Form HUD-27011, Item 31.

Example 3: A timely initiated foreclosure action is delayed by a borrower's Chapter 7 Bankruptcy filing but the mortgagee takes more than 90 days from the date of bankruptcy filing to resolve the case through dismissal, termination of the automatic stay or trustee abandonment of all interest in the secured property and it is not documented that the delay was not due to the failure of the mortgagee to timely notify its bankruptcy attorney or by any failure of the mortgagee's attorney.

Date of Default	12/01/2003
First public action to foreclose	04/12/2004
SFDMS reflects Status 68 for reporting cycle ending	04/30/2004
Date Chapter 7 Bankruptcy filed	05/10/2004
Date reflected in item 21 of HUD-27011	09/15/2004
SFDMS reflects Status 45 for reporting cycle ending	12/31/2004
Date reflected in item 9 of HUD-27011	01/31/2005
Date reflected in item 10	02/28/2005

Reasonable diligence requirement for the State is four months.

In this example, the mortgagee initiated foreclosure within six months of the date of default as required by 24 CFR 203.355(a) and properly reported the action to SFDMS with Status 68 within the required reporting cycle. However, the reasonable diligence requirement for resolving the bankruptcy case and completing the foreclosure was not met. The State reasonable diligence time frame for foreclosure completion is four months and a 90-day extension is authorized for resolving the bankruptcy case. The interest curtailment date for claim purposes would therefore be November 10, 2004 and that date would have to be reflected on Form HUD-27011, Item 31.

Example 4: A timely initiated foreclosure action is delayed by a borrower's Chapter 13 Bankruptcy filing and the borrower subsequently defaults on a confirmed bankruptcy plan. The mortgagee takes more than 90 days from the date plan payments become 60 days delinquent to resolve the case through dismissal, termination of the automatic stay or trustee abandonment of all interest in the secured property and it is not documented that the delay was not due to the failure of the mortgagee to timely notify its bankruptcy attorney or by any failure of the mortgagee's attorney.

Date of Default	04/01/2003
First public action to foreclose	09/09/2003
SFDMS reflects Status 68 for reporting cycle ending	09/30/2003
Date Chapter 13 Bankruptcy filed	10/09/2003
Plan Payments Nov through Feb advance Default Date to	08/01/2003
Date reflected in item 21 of HUD-27011	09/10/2004
SFDMS reflects Status 45 for reporting cycle ending	12/31/2004
Date reflected in item 9 of HUD-27011	01/31/2005
Date reflected in item 10	02/28/2005

Reasonable diligence requirement for the State is five months.

In this example, the mortgagee initiated foreclosure within six months of the date of default as required by 24 CFR 203.355(a) and properly reported the action to SFDMS with Status 68 within the required reporting cycle. However, the reasonable diligence requirement for resolving the Chapter 13 bankruptcy case and completing the foreclosure was not met. Bankruptcy plan payments, due on the first of each month, became 60 days delinquent on April 30, 2004. The mortgagee had a maximum of 90 days from April 30, 2004 to resolve the bankruptcy since no valid reason for further delay was documented. Accordingly, the bankruptcy should have been resolved no later than July 29, 2004, the total authorized delay due to the bankruptcy was 294 days (the bankruptcy filing date of October 9, 2003 through July 29, 2004) and the total time frame allowed for meeting the reasonable diligence requirement was the normal foreclosure time period of five months plus 294 days. The interest curtailment date for claim purposes would therefore be November 29, 2004 and that date would have to be reflected on Form HUD-27011, Item 31.

Example 5: Mortgagee exercises reasonable diligence in completing foreclosure but does not initiate eviction or possessory action within thirty calendar days of foreclosure completion to qualify for extension of the reasonable diligence time frame (Acquiring Possession, page 2, paragraph 1).

Date of Default	12/01/2003
First public action to foreclose	05/10/2004
SFDMS reflects Status 68 for reporting cycle ending	06/30/2004
Foreclosure Completion Date	10/27/2004
Possessory Action Initiated	12/15/2004
Date reflected in item 9 of HUD-27011	01/20/2005
Date reflected in item 10	02/16/2005

Reasonable diligence requirement for the State is six months.

In this example, the mortgagee met the reasonable diligence requirements for initiating, reporting and completing the foreclosure action. However, action to acquire possession of the property was not initiated within thirty calendar days of foreclosure completion. This requires a curtailment of interest to November 26, 2004, the date by which possessory action should have been initiated, and that date would have to be reflected on Form HUD-27011, Item 31.

Example 6: Mortgagee fails to convey the property to HUD within thirty calendar days of acquiring possession and marketable title as required by 24 CFR 203.359.

Date of Default	12/01/2003
First public action to foreclose	05/10/2004
SFDMS reflects Status 68 for reporting cycle ending	06/30/2004
SFDMS reflects Status 45 for reporting cycle ending	10/31/2004
Date reflected in item 9 of HUD-27011	12/29/2004
Date reflected in item 10	02/28/2005

Reasonable diligence requirement for the State is six months.

In this example, the mortgagee exercised reasonable diligence in prosecuting the foreclosure to completion and in acquiring title to and possession of the property. However, it did not meet the requirement to convey the property to HUD within thirty calendar days of acquiring possession and marketable title as required by 24 CFR 203.359. This requires a curtailment of interest to January 28, 2005 and that date would have to be reflected on Form HUD-27011, Item 31.

Department of Housing and Urban Development, Mortgagee Letter 2005-45 (Nov. 22, 2005)

November 22, 2005

MORTGAGEE LETTER 2005-45

TO: ALL APPROVED MORTGAGEES

ATTENTION: Single Family Servicing Managers

SUBJECT: Foreclosure Moratorium Extensions to Assist Victims of Hurricanes Katrina and Rita in Presidentially-Declared Disaster Areas that have counties in Alabama, Louisiana, Mississippi and Texas eligible to receive Individual Assistance.

As a reminder, the Department of Housing and Urban Development (HUD) requires a 90-day moratorium on all foreclosure actions on properties directly affected by Presidentially-declared disasters. The initial moratorium applies to not only new foreclosure initiations, but for all foreclosures in process and has historically applied for both areas declared by FEMA for individual assistance and/or for a public assistance declaration. HUD has provided this guidance in paragraph 14-2 of HUD Handbook, 4330.1, Rev-5, Administration of Insured Home Mortgages, and has repeated it in numerous mortgagee letters. It is also referenced on the following HUD website, http://www.hud.gov/offices/hsg/sfh/nsc/disaster.cfm.

At this time, HUD believes many properties impacted by Hurricanes Katrina and Rita that are in areas declared eligible by FEMA for individual assistance in Alabama, Louisiana, Mississippi, and Texas may need more than the initial 90-day moratorium initiated by the Presidential declaration that began the timeframe. Information on the moratorium was stated on August 31, 2005, in Mortgagee Letter 2005-33, "Underwriting and Servicing Policies to Assist Victims of Presidentially-Declared Major Disaster Areas." As a result of the Department's evaluation of the extreme devastation caused by these disasters, HUD is extending these moratoriums until February 28, 2006, subject to the following restrictions:

1. The extended moratorium will apply only to those counties declared by FEMA to be eligible for individual assistance as a result of Hurricanes Katrina and Rita. Information can be obtained on the Internet at http://www.fema.gov/press/2005/hurricane_season.shtm to determine the counties eligible for individual assistance for the states of Alabama, Louisiana, Mississippi, and Texas or by calling the local FEMA office.

2. The extended moratorium is intended to provide mortgagees additional time in which to confirm the mortgagor's intention and ability to repair the home, retain homeownership and resume making regular mortgage payments. As required in the recently released Mortgagee Letter 2005-41, "Update to General Servicing and Preservation and Protection Requirements for Presidentially-Declared Major Disaster Areas in Alabama, Louisiana, Mississippi and Texas," mortgagees must:

- As quickly as physically possible, assess the status, condition, and damage of the mortgaged property to the extent it is known;
- Locate borrowers and evaluate their short term and long term plans for housing and employment and access to financial services;
- Complete the determination of the borrower(s) hazard and flood insurance coverage;

3. Only properties or mortgagors that are directly affected by the disasters are eligible for the extended moratorium. As soon as information becomes available that indicates that the cause of default is not the result of disaster related property damage or income disruption, mortgagees should document the servicing file with the date this information was confirmed and proceed with foreclosure or initiation of foreclosure actions.

There is no automatic extension of the foreclosure moratorium for properties located outside the individual assistance areas. However, if a mortgagee has been unable to assess property condition or locate a mortgagor in any of the counties designated as Presidentially-declared disaster areas, and they believe it is in the best interest of the government to delay foreclosure or initiation of foreclosure until an assessment can be completed, they may submit form HUD 50012, "Mortgagee's Request for Extension of Time," to HUD's National Servicing Center, as per normal guidelines, indicating the name of the disaster and the reason the extension is needed.

The information collection requirements contained in this document have been approved by the Office of Management and Budget (OMB) under the Paperwork Reduction Act of 1995 (44 U.S.C. 3501–3520) and assigned OMB control numbers 2502-0436, 2502-0523 and 2502-0429. In accordance with the Paperwork Reduction Act, HUD may not conduct or sponsor, and a person is not required to respond to, a collection of information unless the collection displays a currently valid OMB control number.

If you have any questions concerning this Mortgagee Letter, please contact HUD's National Servicing Center at 888-297-8685.

Sincerely,

Brian D. Montgomery
Assistant Secretary for Housing-
Federal Housing Commissioner

Department of Housing and Urban Development Mortgagee Letter 2005-46 (Dec. 1, 2005)

December 1, 2005

MORTGAGEE LETTER 2005-46

TO: ALL APPROVED MORTGAGEES

ATTENTION: Single Family Servicing Managers

SUBJECT: Special Authority for Use of Partial Claims and Loan Modifications to Assist Victims of Hurricanes Katrina, Rita and Wilma in Presidentially-Declared Major Disaster Areas in Alabama, Florida, Louisiana, Mississippi and Texas

Destruction and flooding caused by Hurricanes Katrina, Rita and Wilma have greatly affected portions of Alabama, Florida, Louisiana, Mississippi and Texas. This Mortgagee Letter provides special authority for use of Partial Claims and Loan Modifications to assist borrowers in the areas declared eligible for individual assistance by FEMA who are unable to maintain mortgage obligations due to hurricane related property damage, curtailment of income or increased living expenses. Please refer to http://www.fema.gov/news/disasters.fema for a listing of eligible counties.

Under HUD's loss mitigation program, a mortgagee may advance funds on behalf of a borrower in an amount necessary to reinstate a defaulted loan (not to exceed the equivalent of 12 months worth of principal, interest, taxes, and insurance (PITI)) and file a partial claim for the amount of the advance in accordance with the procedures outlined in Mortgagee Letter 2003-19, dated November 20, 2003. Due to the unusual circumstances relating to Hurricanes Katrina, Rita or Wilma, many FHA-insured borrowers may need earlier access to assistance than is routinely provided under HUD's existing Loss Mitigation Program. Therefore, the Department is authorizing use of a special form of partial claim, which shall be called the FHA Mortgage Assistance Initiative, that will provide more immediate relief to FHA insured borrowers who are temporarily unable to support their mortgage obligations.

Additionally, existing guidance from HUD's Mortgagee Letters 2000-05 and 2003-19, prohibits the use of a partial claim and a loan modification in combination when used to address the same cause of default. Subject to the special conditions noted below, mortgagees may now utilize a partial claim or FHA Mortgage Assistance Initiative and loan modification for the same mortgage to assist a borrower in curing a default whose cause is related to Hurricanes Katrina, Rita or Wilma.

This special authority is available only for the 18-month period effective with the date of this mortgagee letter and is subject to the following requirements:

A. Borrower Qualifications

- The FHA Mortgage Assistance Initiative and the use of a loan modification following a partial claim may be offered to FHA insured borrowers who:
- Live or have full time employment in a county in Alabama, Florida, Louisiana, Mississippi or Texas that has been declared by FEMA to be eligible for individual assistance as a result of Hurricanes Katrina, Rita or Wilma;
- Do not currently have the ability to support their normal monthly mortgage obligation due to a verifiable loss of income or increase in living expenses or property damage to their principal residence attributable to Hurricanes Katrina, Rita or Wilma;
- Own a principal residence that is habitable or can be made habitable;
- Are committed to continuing to occupy the property as a primary residence;
- Have missed at least four but not more than 12 mortgage payments on a FHA insured loan.
- Have not been referred to foreclosure. Loans that were in foreclosure prior to the implementation of the 90-day disaster area foreclosure moratorium announced in ML 2005-33, should be carefully reviewed to determine if the cause of default has been substantially worsened by the hurricane as only borrowers who have experienced hurricane related losses are eligible for this option. Loans that are in foreclosure now or are referred to foreclosure after the expiration of the moratorium must have the foreclosure action terminated prior to execution of the repayment agreement or modification.

B. FHA Mortgage Assistance Initiative

The FHA Mortgage Assistance Initiative option may be offered to borrowers who meet all of the requirements of Section A, are temporarily unable to make their mortgage payments and are expected to have the capacity to resume making full mortgage payments before 12 mortgage payments are due and unpaid. Unlike the existing partial claim, a FHA Mortgage Assistance Initiative may include both the amount needed to cover mortgage obligations currently in default as well as mortgage obligations that will become due and payable (i.e., become "arrearages") before the date the borrower is expected to be able to resume full monthly payments.

As with all partial claims, the account must be in arrears a minimum of four installments. The FHA Mortgage Assistance Initiative will include, in addition to the initial four delinquent installments, only the amount necessary to meet the anticipated need ("arrearages"), not to exceed the equivalent of 12 months of PITI. The mortgagee is requested to perform an escrow analysis prior to filing the claim to ensure that the payment that will be provided by HUD on behalf of the mortgagor represent as accurately as possible the escrow amounts required for taxes and insurance.

Subject to the requirements in this mortgagee letter, mortgagees shall follow the same requirements that were provided in Mortgagee Letters 2000-05 and 2003-19 for evaluation of eligibility, submission of the claim and executing the required security instruments to secure repayment of the funds paid by HUD on behalf of the borrower. In the case of standard partial claims, mortgagees shall use the model forms provided in Mortgagee Letter 97-17. In the case of advanced partial claims, mortgagees shall use the model forms provided in Attachment 1. In either event, mortgagees must make any necessary modifications to the model forms to ensure that the note and mortgage provided to HUD are enforceable. However there are some key differences in that the amount the mortgagee will be able to request in the FHA Mortgage Assistance Initiative as it may include more than the number of installments past due at the time the claim is submitted. In addition, the mortgagor need not immediately resume making regular mortgage payments.

Example 1: The mortgagee makes contact with an affected borrower from the disaster area and is convinced that the borrower wants to return and rebuild, and that property hazard insurance or other funds will be available for the re-construction. The borrower is living in rental housing and cannot make mortgage payments; repairs or re-construction may not start for a number of months, and the borrower may not be able to return to their affected property until some time next summer, but there is good reason to believe that the borrower could return to the property and begin making mortgage payments by September 2006. Assuming that this borrower missed their first mortgage payment in September 2005, they will be eligible for the FHA Mortgage Assistance Initiative after December 2, 2005, when four payments are due and unpaid. If, by the end of December 2005, the mortgagee and borrower have completed the process, then the mortgagee should apply to HUD for a FHA Mortgage Assistance Initiative equal to 12 months PITI.

At that time, the mortgagee will apply three payments to the mortgage arrears, so that at the end of January 2006 the mortgage will remain in default (due for the December and January payments). The balance of the FHA Mortgage Assistance Initiative funds will be held in a special custodial account from which the mortgagee will release and apply one payment to the mortgage account each following month, starting in February 2006, and on the second day of each month. (Additional guidance regarding establishing this custodial account is provided in Attachment 2.)

If the borrower advises the mortgagee that he will return to the property on September 1, 2006, and also confirms that he will make his September 2006 payment timely, the mortgage will still be two months in arrears, with a third payment due-and-payable. The custodial account will have a balance of two months PITI on September 1, 2006. If the borrower makes one month's mortgage payment on September 1, 2006, the mortgagee will apply the remaining two installments from the custodial account on September 2, 2006, bringing the account current. The September installment and all future payments will be the responsibility of the borrower.

Requirements for use of this option:

- Mortgagees may offer more than one partial claim or FHA Mortgage Assistance Initiative to the same borrower, so long as the total amount advanced during the life of the loan does not exceed the equivalent of 12 months worth of PITI However, mortgagees are cautioned, since a loan must be at least four months due and unpaid before a partial claim or FHA Mortgage Assistance Initiative can be utilized, the Department cannot honor either type of partial claim where the arrearage is less than four months.
- The property must be habitable or capable of being repaired. The intent of this special authority is to allow borrowers to retain homeownership. If the insured property has been damaged to the point that it cannot be reconstructed, or the borrower cannot or does not intend to begin reconstruction within 12 months of the date of this Mortgagee Letter, the mortgagee may not offer these special options.
- The repayment terms for a FHA Mortgage Assistance Initiative are the same as those described in ML 2000-05; no interest may be charged on the partial claim amount and repayment is not required until the original (or any modified) balance of the first mortgage is paid in full either through amortization or early payoff.
- Mortgagees may not offer a FHA Mortgage Assistance Initiative within three years of a mortgage modification unless the modification preceded the hurricane and the cause of the new default is clearly hurricane related.

C. Use of Partial Claim Modification

The Department recognizes that some borrowers may, even after returning to work full time, have a permanent reduction in income. After the mortgagee has completed the application of all FHA Mortgage Assistance Initiative funds and the borrower has advised that he or she is unable to resume making the full mortgage payments, it may become necessary for the mortgagee to consider a loan modification. This may be due to the borrower not receiving the same level of income as before the disaster or perhaps a new complication has arisen, such as additional expenses stemming from the disaster.

Upon evaluation of the borrower's financial status where he or she has met all the requirements of Section A and is determined to be financially capable of resuming making the monthly payments as modified, the mortgagee may utilize a loan modification following the use of either a partial claim or a FHA Mortgage Assistance Initiative. As with all loan modifications, the mortgage must be in default. However, for this special use, a loan modification may be completed following the use of either a partial claim or FHA Mortgage Assistance Initiative any time prior to the expiration of the 18-month authority under this mortgagee letter. The one restriction is that all such loan modifications must produce a reduction in the monthly mortgage payment.

Example 2: Following Example 1, the affected borrower missed the first payment in September 2005, then returned to the property by September 1, 2006, and started making full mortgage payments at that time. The mortgagee then applied all payments from the custodial account bringing the account current. However, when the borrower returned to the affected property, repairs or re-construction of the home were not yet complete. After making both the scheduled payments for September, October and November 2006, the contractor disappears after being paid $3,000 toward the next phase of work. The borrower finds another contractor, but then must make an advance payment to the new contractor and, therefore, the $3,000 loss means the borrower cannot make the December or January (2007) mortgage payments. Granted that the borrower can resume full mortgage payments in February 2007, the mortgagee may, at that time, consider a mortgage modification. The mortgage modification may capitalize the two months of arrears, and it may re-amortize the new unpaid balance over 30 years, if the combination of the two will create a monthly payment that is affordable to the affected borrower. To be eligible for an incentive payment, the Department requires that this loan modification produce a reduction in the mortgagor's payment.

Requirements for use of the combination partial claim or FHA Mortgage Assistance Initiative and loan modification option:

- All funds from the partial claim or FHA Mortgage Assistance Initiative must have been applied to the account.
- The modification must reduce the borrower's monthly mortgage payment and must not increase the total PITI. Mortgag-

ees must retain file document demonstrating the benefit of the modification to the borrower.

- Mortgagees must ensure that the FHA-insured mortgage remains in first lien position following any modification. Actual costs to obtain and review title will be reimbursed through the claim up to $250.
- The property must be habitable or capable of being repaired to be habitable. The intent of this special authority is to allow borrowers to retain homeownership. If the property securing the insured loan has been damaged to the point that it cannot be reconstructed, or the borrower cannot or does not intend to begin reconstruction within 12 months of the date of this mortgagee letter, the mortgagee may not offer these special options.
- The repayment terms for a partial claim used in conjunction with a loan modification are the same as those described in ML 2000-05; no interest may be charged on the partial claim amount and repayment is not required until the original (or any modified) balance of the first mortgage is paid in full either through amortization or early payoff.
- The borrower may not be charged any additional costs for receiving this loss mitigation workout option, however, it is acceptable that legal costs and fees related to a canceled foreclosure action may be collected directly from the borrower or be capitalized in conjunction with a loan modification so long as the modified principal and interest (P&I) payment is less than the P&I payment due under the original mortgage terms. Mortgagees are reminded that all such costs must reflect work actually completed to the date of the foreclosure cancellation and the attorney fees may not be in excess of the fees that HUD has identified as customary and reasonable for claim purposes. Please refer to Mortgagee Letters 2001-19, issued August 24, 2001, and 2005-30, issued July 12, 2005 for guidance.

D. Financial Analysis

The mortgagee must assess the borrower's financial situation as described in ML 2000-05, to determine if and when the borrower is expected to have sufficient income to resume full monthly mortgage payments before approving a FHA Mortgage Assistance Initiative or partial claim and loan modification. In addition to the financial analysis requirements described in ML 2000-05, mortgagees should consider expenses related to alternative housing if the insured residence is not habitable, availability and timing of hazard insurance payments and other benefits, delays in returning to full employment and other financial impacts on surplus income that are attributable to Hurricanes Katrina, Rita or Wilma. The financial analysis and documentation supporting the decision to provide partial claim relief must be maintained in the mortgagee's claim review file.

E. Claim Filing and Document Delivery

Mortgagees shall follow existing instructions for filing a partial claim and must file a claim for insurance benefits within 60 days of the date a FHA Mortgage Assistance Initiative or partial claim is executed by the borrower. This will still be considered a claim type 33. The incentive payment for the FHA Mortgage Assistance Initiative is $500, the same as for a Partial Claim.

When the partial claim and loan modification will both be used, a mortgagee must file a separate claim for insurance benefits for both the partial claim and the loan modification and is entitled to receive incentive fees for each action. Mortgagees must file a claim for incentive payment within 60 days of the execution date of the modification agreement. It is not necessary to send a copy of the loan modification, however, it must be retained in the claim review file and made available to FHA upon request. FHA will pay mortgagees a $750 incentive fee for each modification and will reimburse the actual cost of the title search and/or endorsement to the title policy not to exceed $250. No other expenses may be included on the claim.

When filing the claim the mortgagee must include in the "Mortgagee's Comments" section of the claim form, 1) the type of claim—FHA Mortgage Assistance Initiative or loan modification, 2) a brief description of the borrower's entitlement to this special relief—i.e., property zip code or loss of employment in an affected disaster area, 3) reference to other claims on the same mortgage including the total of all partial claim advances to the borrower. This information is especially important to have available in the claim review file for HUD.

While most county or parish recorders' offices in the affected areas have reopened, the Department does recognize that there may be some lengthy delays in receiving recorded documents from some recorders. Mortgagees are asked to request extensions of time to forward the recorded Partial Claim documents whenever there is a delay. All extensions will be approved and are necessary as this process provides for timely notification to HUD of all delays.

F. Remittance

In the event a FHA Mortgage Assistance Initiative agreement is terminated by the mortgagee before all funds have been disbursed (abandonment, condemnation, death), the mortgagee must deliver any undisbursed amounts to HUD's servicing contractor (see below) within five (5) business days of the termination.

Upon payoff or termination of the first mortgage the mortgagee is requested to ensure that amounts due under partial claim are received and remitted to HUD. All funds collected by the mortgagee including voluntary payments received from the borrower, must be delivered to HUD's servicing contractor (see below) within 24 hours from the time of receipt by the mortgagee.

U.S. Department of HUD
c/o Morris Griffin Corp./First Madison Services, Inc.
4111 South Darlington, Suite 300
Tulsa, OK 74135
Phone: 800-967-3050
Alternate phone: 918-879-6921
Fax: 918-270-4213
email address: rtortorici@mgc-fms.com

Please note that additional provisions described in ML 2000-05 and 2003-19 related to Repayment Terms, Option Failure and Disclosures apply also to these special loss mitigation options.

HUD's Office of Inspector General has asked that we remind the industry of the availability the HUD/OIG Hotline. Immediately report any suspicious activity relating to Waste, Fraud, and Abuse to HUD/OIG Hotline at 1-800-347-3735 or Email to hotline@hudoig.gov."

Any questions regarding this Mortgagee Letter may be directed to HUD's National Servicing Center (NSC) at 888-297-8685 or hsg-lossmit@hud.gov.

____

Brian D. Montgomery
Assistant Secretary for Housing-
Federal Housing Commissioner

Attachment 1

FHA Case No.

PROMISSORY NOTE

[Date]

[Property Address]

1. PARTIES

"Borrower" means each person signing at the end of this Note, and the person's successors and assigns. "Secretary" or "Lender" means the Secretary of Housing and Urban Development and its successors and assigns.

2. BORROWER'S PROMISE TO PAY

Borrower promises to pay to the order of Lender, the lesser of U.S. $ [Amount of total advance partial claim to be inserted by Mortgagee] (the "principal sum) or as much of that sum as may be disbursed for the benefit of Borrower(s) by Lender.

3. PROMISE TO PAY SECURED [omit this paragraph in Texas and renumber accordingly]

Borrower's promise to pay is secured by a mortgage, deed of trust or similar security instrument that is dated the same date as this Note and called the "Security Instrument." The Security Instrument protects the Lender from losses, which might result if Borrower defaults under this Note.

4. MANNER OF PAYMENT

(A) Time

On _______, __ [insert maturity date of insured primary mortgage] or, if earlier, when the first of the following events occurs:

(i) Borrower has paid in full all amounts due under the primary Note and related mortgage, deed of trust or similar Security Instruments insured by the Secretary, or

(ii) The maturity date of the primary Note has been accelerated, or

(iii) The primary note and related mortgage, deed of trust or similar Security Instrument are no longer insured by the Secretary, or

(iv) The property is not occupied by the purchaser as his or her principal residence.

(B) Place

Payment shall be made at the Office of Housing FHA-Comptroller, Director of Mortgage Insurance Accounting and Servicing, 451 Seventh Street, SW, Washington, DC 20410 or any such other place as Lender may designate in writing by notice to Borrower.

5. BORROWER'S RIGHT TO REPAY

Borrower has the right to pay the debt evidenced by this Note, in whole or in part, without charge or penalty. If Borrower makes a partial prepayment, there will be no changes in the due date or in the amount of the monthly payment unless Lender agrees in writing to those changes.

6. WAIVERS

Borrower and any other person who has obligations under this Note waive the rights or presentment and notice of dishonor. "Presentment" means the right to require Lender to demand payment of amounts due. "Notice of dishonor" means the right to require Lender to give notice to other persons that amounts due have not been paid.

7. OBLIGATIONS OF PERSONS UNDER THIS NOTE

If more than one person signs this Note, each person is fully and personally obligated to keep all of the promises made in this Note, including the promise to pay the full amount owed. Any person who is a guarantor, surety or endorser of this Note is also obligated to do these things. Any person who takes over these obligations, including the obligations of a guarantor, surety or endorser of this Note, is also obligated to keep all of the promises made in this Note. Lender may enforce its rights under this Note against each person individually or against all signatories together. Any one person signing this Note may be required to pay all the amounts owed under this Note.

BY SIGNING BELOW, Borrower accepts and agrees to the terms and covenants contained in this Note.

____

(SEAL)
Borrower

____

(SEAL)
Borrower

FHA Case No.

SUBORDINATE MORTGAGE

THIS SUBORDINATE MORTGAGE ("Security Instrument") is given on _______, 20__. The Mortgagor is ________. Whose address is _________ ("Borrower"). This Security Instrument is given to the Secretary of Housing and Urban Development, and whose address is 451 Seventh Street, SW, Washington, DC 20410 ("Lender"). Borrower has agreed to repay to Lender, the lesser of U.S. $ [Amount to be inserted by Mortgagee] or as much of that sum as may be disbursed for the benefit of Borrower(s) by Lender. This debt is evidenced by Borrower's note dated the same date as this Security Instrument ("Note"), which provides for the full debt, if not paid earlier, due and payable on _________. This Security Instrument secures to Lender: (a) the repayment of the debt evidenced by the Note, and all renewals, extensions and modifications of the Note; (b) the payment of all other sums, advanced under Paragraph 7 to protect the security of this Security Instrument; and (c) the performance of Borrower's covenants and agreements under this Security Instrument and the Note. For this purpose, Borrower does hereby mortgage, warrant, grant and convey to the Lender, with the power of sale the following described property located in ______ County, State: which has the address of _______________ [Street] _________ [City], _________ [State] ______ [Zip Code], ("Property Address");

TOGETHER WITH all the improvements now or hereafter erected on the property, and all easements, appurtenances, and fixtures now or hereafter a part of the property. All replacements and additions shall also be covered by this Security Instrument. All of the foregoing is referred to in this Security Instrument as the "Property."

BORROWER COVENANTS that Borrower is lawfully seized of the estate hereby conveyed and has the right to mortgage, grant and convey the Property and that the Property is unencumbered, except for encumbrances of record. Borrower warrants and will defend generally the title to the Property against all claims and demands, subject to any encumbrances or record.

THIS SECURITY INSTRUMENT combines uniform covenants for national use and non-uniform covenants with limited variations by jurisdiction to constitute a uniform security instrument covering real property.

Borrower and Lender covenant agree as follows:

UNIFORM COVENANTS.

1. **Payment of Principal.** Borrower shall pay when due the principal of the debt evidenced by the Note.

2. **Borrower Not Released; Forbearance By Lender Not a Waiver.** Extension of the time of payment of the sums secured by this Security Instrument granted by Lender to any successor in interest of Borrower shall not operate to release the liability of the original Borrower or Borrower's successor in interest. Lender shall not be required to commence proceedings against any successor in interest or refuse to extend time for payment or otherwise modify amortization of the sums secured by this Security Instrument by reason of any demand made by the original Borrower or Borrower's successors in interest. Any forbearance by Lender in exercising any right or remedy shall not be a waiver of or preclude the exercise of any right or remedy.

3. **Successors and Assigns Bound; Joint and Several Liability; Co-signers.** The covenants and agreements of this Security Instrument shall bind and benefit the successors and assigns of Lender and Borrower. Borrower's covenants and agreements shall be joint and several. Any Borrower who co-signs this Security Instrument but does not execute the Note: (a) is co-signing this Security Instrument only to mortgage, grant and convey that Borrower's interest in the Property under the terms of this Security Instrument; (b) is not personally obligated to pay the sums secured by this Security Instrument; and (c) agrees that Lender and any other Borrower may agree to extend, modify, forbear or make any accommodations with regard to the term of this Security Instrument or the Note without that Borrower's consent.

4. **Notices.** Any notice to Borrower provided for in this Security Instrument shall be given by delivering it or by mailing it by first class mail unless applicable law requires use of another method. The notice shall be directed to the Property Address or any other address Borrower designates by notice to Lender. Any notice to Lender shall be given by first class mail to: Department of Housing and Urban Development, Attention: Single Family Notes Branch, 451 Seventh Street, SW, Washington, DC 10410 or any address Lender designates by notice to Borrower. Any notice provided for in this Security Instrument shall be deemed to have been given to Borrower or Lender when given as provided in this paragraph.

5. **Governing Law; Severability.** This Security Instrument shall be governed by Federal law and the law of the jurisdiction in which the Property is located. In the event that any provision or clause of this Security Instrument or the Note conflicts with applicable law, such conflict shall not affect other provisions of this Security Instrument or the Note which can be given effect without the conflicting provision. To this end the provisions of this Security Instrument and the Note are declared to be severable.

6. **Borrower's Copy.** Borrower shall be given one conformed copy of the Note and of this Security Instrument.

NON-UNIFORM COVENANTS. Borrower and Lender further covenant and agree as follows:

7. **Acceleration; Remedies.** [State specific language]

If the Lender's interest in this Security Instrument is held by the Secretary and the Secretary requires immediate payment in full under Paragraph 4 [insert Paragraph 3 in Texas] of the Subordinate Note, the Secretary may invoke the nonjudicial power of sale provided in the Single Family Mortgage Foreclosure Act of 1994 ("Act") (12 U.S.C. § 3751 et seq.) by requesting a foreclosure commissioner designated under the Act to commence foreclosure and to sell the Property as provided in the Act. Nothing in the preceding sentence shall deprive the Secretary of any rights otherwise available to a Lender under this paragraph or applicable law.

BY SIGNING BELOW, Borrower accepts and agrees to the terms contained in this Security Instrument and in any rider(s) executed by Borrower and recorded with it.

Witness:

____________________ ____________________ (SEAL)
Borrower

____________________ ____________________ (SEAL)
Borrower

<u>Instructions for Subordinate Model Mortgage Form</u>

<u>Language Preceding Uniform Covenants</u>

Use 1990 FNMA/FHLMC language but: (1) Add a box for the FHA Case No. as shown on the Model Mortgage Form. The Model Mortgage Form uses the FNMA/FHL language for Michigan as an example. The form may Include variations to the standard language that have been approved by FNMA and/or FHLMC. For Maine and New York in which FHMA and FHLMC have approved "plain English" forms, the format and language should Be based on FNMA/FHLMC forms for other sates provided that the language is in conformity with applicable Law. (2) Delete the language "which is organized and existing under the laws of . . ." (3) Delete the language "monthly payments with . . ." and (4) Delete the language "with interest."

<u>Uniform Covenants</u>

The form should designate the paragraphs preceding Paragraph 7 "Uniform Covenants." The text of these Paragraphs must be used as presented in the Model Subordinate Mortgage Form without any change. FNMA/FHLMC language may not be substituted. If change is needed to meet requirements of state or local law or practice, written approval from HUD is needed before the change is made.

<u>Non-Uniform Covenants</u>

The form should designate the paragraphs beginning with Paragraph 7 "Non-Uniform Covenants."

a. The first paragraph under this heading should be the same as under the heading in the FNMA/FHLMC Single Family Mortgage; with appropriate conforming changes to paragraph numbers. The following paragraphs should contain provisions required to adapt the mortgage to the laws and practices of the particular jurisdiction in which the Property is located. The text of these paragraphs should be the same as the FHMA/FHLMC non-uniform covenants for the jurisdiction win which the Property is located. Changes to the FNMA/FHLMLC paragraphs and additional material may be included if needed to conform to requirements of state law or practice.

b. Any special language or notices required be applicable law should appear following the non-uniform covenants using the FNMA/FHLMC Single Family Mortgage Form for the jurisdiction as a guide.

Signatures, etc.
Use the FNMA/FHLMC format at the end of the mortgage except that:

a. Witness lines may be omitted if state and local law does not require witnesses for mortgages.

b. HUD does not require the Borrower's social security number to appear on the mortgage.

Attachment 2

Separate Custodial Account for Advance Partial Claims

The mortgagee is requested to establish a separate custodial account for the purpose of holding funds advanced by the Department of Housing and Urban Development (HUD) through its Advance Partial Claim program. No other funds may be commingled with the Advance Partial Claim funds. The account should be established so that funds may be withdrawn only by the mortgagee, its servicer or HUD. No other entity shall have access to these funds. As required by 24 CFR 202.5 (d), the account must be fully insured by the Federal Deposit Insurance Corporation or the National Credit Union Administration

Upon receipt of the Advance Partial Claim funds, the mortgagee shall apply sufficient installments to leave the account in default. (Two installments are due and unpaid). On the second day of each subsequent month, the mortgagee shall apply one installment to the borrower's arrearage and continue until the borrower resumes making regular payments or until all funds have been applied to the borrower's account. When the borrower resumes making regular mortgage payments, any funds representing past due installments held in the custodial account may be applied to bring the account current. No payments may be applied in advance of the payment due date.

This process will allow the mortgagee to request all funds that will be needed to assist the borrower in one Advance Partial Claim, thereby reducing the administrative burden for the mortgagee, borrower and HUD. By keeping the account technically in default, it also fulfills the statutory requirement of Section 230(b) of the National Housing Act that provides the authority for the Department to offer various loss mitigation initiatives including Partial Claims.

Department of Housing and Urban Development, Mortgagee Letter 2006-05 (Feb. 23, 2006)

February 23, 2006

MORTGAGEE LETTER 2006-05

TO: ALL APPROVED MORTGAGEES

ATTENTION: Single Family Servicing Managers

SUBJECT: Foreclosure Moratorium Extensions to Assist Victims of Hurricanes Katrina, Rita and Wilma

On November 22, 2005, HUD published Mortgagee Letter (ML) 2005-45, Foreclosure Moratorium Extensions to Assist Victims of Hurricanes Katrina and Rita in Presidentially-Declared Disaster Areas that have counties in Alabama, Louisiana, Mississippi, and Texas eligible to receive Individual Assistance. This guidance extended until February 28, 2006, the initial 90-day moratorium on foreclosures of FHA-insured loans in areas impacted by Hurricanes Katrina and Rita.

This forbearance has successfully helped affected borrowers and their mortgagees work through extremely challenging circumstances to obtain available insurance recoveries and explore available alternatives for repairing damaged homes and resolving mortgage defaults. However, due to the magnitude of the storm damage, mortgagees and borrowers may still need additional time to develop and finalize plans for home repair and resumption of mortgage payments. The Department has learned that some borrowers have not received final hazard and flood insurance proceeds. Additionally, borrowers who wish to rebuild and retain homeownership but do not have sufficient insurance proceeds are continuing to explore financing alternatives including Small Business Administration loans and funding through state and local funding sources, including Community Development Block Grant funding that may soon be available. As a result, HUD is extending the foreclosure moratorium for an additional 120 days in those areas eligible for individual assistance, subject to the following restrictions:

1. The extended moratorium will apply to those counties in the states of Alabama, Florida, Louisiana, Mississippi, and Texas declared by FEMA to be eligible for individual assistance as a result of Hurricanes Katrina, Rita or Wilma. Information can be obtained on the Internet at http://www.fema.gov/press/2005/hurricane_season.shtm, or by calling the local FEMA office to determine the counties eligible for individual assistance.

2. On or before March 31, 2006, mortgagees must:

- Assess the status, condition, and habitability of the mortgaged property;
- Establish contact with borrowers and evaluate their short term and long term plans for housing, employment, home repairs and repayment of the mortgage debt;
- Complete a determination of the borrower(s) hazard and flood insurance coverage, property damage and available insurance recoveries;
- Confirm in writing that the borrower intends to work with the mortgagee to develop and implement a plan to repair or rebuild the home and resolve the mortgage delinquency.

3. If, by March 31, 2006, the borrower provides a written commitment to work with the mortgagee to develop and implement a plan to resolve the mortgage delinquency, the time to initiate foreclosure will automatically be extended an additional 90 days to June 30, 2006.

4. The foreclosure moratorium will terminate on March 31, 2006, for all loans where the borrower has not made a written commitment.

5. The written commitment may be an application to utilize one of the FHA loss mitigation options, including Special Forbearance, Mortgage Modification, Partial Claim, Mortgage Assistance Initiative or Deed-In-Lieu of Foreclosure, or it may be a written communication from the borrower delivered by mail, fax or electronic media requesting additional time to work with the mortgagee to resolve the debt.

6. Should a borrower fail to make a written request for additional time to resolve the default on or before the March 31, 2006 deadline, but subsequently notifies the mortgagee of his or her desire to retain homeownership, the mortgagee must fully evaluate the borrower's eligibility for all loss mitigation alternatives and implement the appropriate action.

7. As a reminder, only borrowers who are unable to maintain mortgage obligations due to hurricane related property damage, curtailment of income or increased living expenses are eligible for moratorium relief. Normal timeframes and loss mitigation options apply for borrowers in the individual assistance areas whose cause of default is unrelated to the hurricanes.

There is no automatic extension of the foreclosure moratorium for properties located outside the individual assistance areas. However, if a mortgagee has been unable to assess property condition or contact a borrower in any of the counties designated as Presidentially-declared disaster areas, and they believe it is in the best interest of the government to delay foreclosure or initiation of foreclosure until a loss mitigation assessment can be completed, they may submit form HUD 50012, "Mortgagee's Request for Extension of Time," to HUD's National Servicing Center, as per normal guidelines, indicating the name of the disaster and the reason the extension is needed. Such extension requests should be sent to HUD's National Servicing Center (NSC) at the address below.

U S. Department of Housing and Urban Development
National Servicing Center
Williams Center Tower II
2 West Second Street, Suite 400
Tulsa, Oklahoma 74103
Fax: 918 292-8992
Phone: 888-297-8685

Mortgagees or their servicers are encouraged to consult with their bankruptcy counsel to determine how to permissibly communicate with borrowers in bankruptcy regarding these issues.

Mortgagees and servicers should refer to Mortgagee Letter 2005-33, issued August 31, 2005, and Mortgagee Letter 2005-41, issued October 24, 2005, for current guidance regarding servicing and property preservation and protection matters and to Mortgagee Letter 2005-46, issued December 1, 2005, for details regarding the special FHA Mortgage Assistance Initiative and Mortgage Modification authority.

The Department continues to encourage mortgagees and their servicers not to report delinquencies on loans in the Presidentially-declared disaster areas to credit reporting agencies until and unless a mortgage is referred to foreclosure. However, mortgagees must report all 90-day delinquencies to HUD's Single Family Default Monitoring System (SFDMS) using FHA Connection or EDI. To identify delinquencies caused by property damage and/or natural disasters, HUD has implemented a new Delinquency Status Code and a new Default Reason Code, that are now available for use by mortgagees. The new delinquency status code, Natural Disaster (34), can be used following initial delinquency reporting on a loan that is 90 or more days past due where the property is in a Presidentially-declared disaster area (as defined by FEMA). This code should be used when no other delinquency status code is appropriate (i.e., use status code 34 until the servicer implements a workout option with the borrower or the loan is placed into foreclosure, at which time the loss mitigation or foreclosure action taken would be reported using the appropriate status code). The new default reason code Casualty Loss (19) should be used to report that the delinquency is attributable to the borrower having incurred a sudden, unexpected property loss as the result of an accident, fire, storm, theft, hurricane, earthquake, etc. These new codes must be used immediately.

The information collection requirements contained in this document have been approved by the Office of Management and Budget (OMB) under the Paperwork Reduction Act of 1995 (44 U.S.C. 3501-3520) and assigned OMB control numbers 2502-0436, 2502-0523 and 2502-0429. In accordance with the Paperwork Reduction Act, HUD may not conduct or sponsor, and a person is not required to respond to, a collection of information unless the collection displays a currently valid OMB control number.

If you have any questions concerning this Mortgagee Letter, please contact the National Servicing Center at 888-297-8685.

Sincerely,

____

Brian D. Montgomery
Assistant Secretary for Housing-
Federal Housing Commissioner

Department of Housing and Urban Development, Mortgagee Letter 2006-10 (May 3, 2006)

May 3, 2006

MORTGAGEE LETTER 2006-10

TO: ALL APPROVED MORTGAGEES

ATTENTION: Single Family Servicing Managers

SUBJECT: Special Authority for use of Deed-in-Lieu of Foreclosure to Assist Victims of Hurricanes Katrina, Rita and Wilma in Presidentially-Declared Major Disaster Areas approved for individual assistance in Alabama, Florida, Louisiana, Mississippi and Texas.

Widespread destruction caused by Hurricanes Katrina, Rita and Wilma has created great hardship for many homeowners in the impacted areas. HUD is committed to working with mortgagees to help borrowers affected by the disasters to retain homeownership whenever possible and has provided special authority under Mortgagee Letter 2005-46, dated December 1, 2005, for expanded use of partial claims and loan modifications in cases where borrowers are committed to continued occupancy of the property. Mortgagees are urged to use those special loss mitigation authorities in impacted areas approved for individual disaster assistance to the maximum extent possible under FHA guidelines. However, we recognize that some homes have been seriously damaged and will not be rebuilt. This Mortgagee Letter provides special expanded authority to make it easier for mortgagees to accept voluntary conveyances of property from borrowers in those cases where, due to storm damage, the home is not habitable and will not be restored.

Deed-in-lieu of foreclosure (DIL) is a loss mitigation option in which a borrower voluntarily conveys title to the mortgaged property to either the mortgagee or HUD in exchange for a release from all financial obligations under the mortgage. Many FHA insured mortgagors have homes that were so badly damaged by the hurricanes that they will not be able to rebuild. These mortgagors deserve the opportunity to get out from under the burden of their existing mortgage debt so that they can begin to rebuild their lives. HUD is therefore increasing the borrower consideration and modifying certain program requirements regarding occupancy, property condition and private sale efforts to facilitate DIL acceptance in cases where the home has been seriously damaged and will not be restored to a habitable condition. Additionally, Attachment A of this Mortgagee Letter includes a format for a credit explanation letter that HUD is urging mortgagees to provide on or behalf of DIL borrowers to alleviate adverse credit impacts resulting from these natural disasters.

Effective with the date of this mortgagee letter, mortgagees may utilize the special deed-in-lieu of foreclosure (DIL) authority to assist borrowers with homes in areas approved for individual assistance that have become uninhabitable due to damage caused by Hurricanes Katrina, Rita or Wilma, subject to the special conditions noted below.

Applicable Provisions

1. Eligible Property—The special DIL option may only be offered on property that meets the following criteria:

a. The property is located within a Presidentially-Declared Major Disaster Area in Alabama, Florida, Louisiana, Mississippi and Texas approved for individual assistance, and the home has either;

b. suffered substantial damage attributable to Hurricanes Katrina, Rita or Wilma, or;

c. the cost of estimated storm damage repairs exceeds available hazard and flood insurance recoveries by the greater of $25,000 or 25%.

Substantial damage is defined as homes with storm damage affecting more than 50 percent of the structure or with estimated repair costs that would exceed 50 percent of the home's pre-storm replacement value.

2. Properties Outside Individual Assistance Areas – Mortgages secured by properties within a Presidentially-Declared Major Disaster Area in Alabama, Florida, Louisiana, Mississippi and Texas approved for public assistance may also be eligible for the special DIL option if they meet all other requirements identified herein. Mortgagees may request approval for use of this option by contacting:

U.S. Department of Housing and Urban Development
National Servicing Center-Tulsa
Williams Center Tower II
2 West Second Street, Suite 400
Tulsa, OK 74103
Attn: Program Director
Phone number: (888) 297-8685
Fax number: (918) 292-8992

3. Borrowers—The special DIL option may be extended to individual borrowers who have an FHA-insured mortgage on eligible property, cannot continue to occupy the home as a principal residence due to storm damage and have released available insurance recoveries and Community Development Block Grant funds for home repairs to the mortgagee for application to the mortgage debt.

4. PFS—Qualified properties do not have to be offered for sale through HUD's pre-foreclosure sale program (PFS) before acceptance of a deed-in-lieu as presently required under Mortgagee Letter 00-05, dated January 19, 2000. No justification for the failure to attempt a PFS is required.

5. Conveyance Property Condition—A mortgagee may accept a DIL on an eligible hurricane damaged property and convey the property to HUD without repairing the damage provided that all hazard and flood insurance claims are settled before the conveyance to the Secretary and, pursuant to provisions of 24 CFR 203.379(a)(1), the claim for insurance benefits is reduced by the Secretary's estimate of the cost of repairs or the insurance recovery received by the mortgagee, whichever is greater. In accordance with regulation 24 CFR 203.378(d), this deduction for property damage repairs shall not exceed the amount of the FHA insurance benefit claim.

Standard DIL requirements that the borrower turn the property over to the mortgagee in broom clean condition, remove all personal property and deliver keys and other fixtures to the mortgagee at time of conveyance are waived.

Prior to conveyance of an eligible damaged property, the mortgagee must send a written request for approval of the repair cost estimate to HUD's assigned Management & Marketing (M&M) Contractor along with documentation that the property meets the eligibility criteria of paragraph 1 for the special DIL option. The request should identify the extent and cause of the damage and the amount of any insurance proceeds received or pending and include a copy of a contractor or insurer prepared estimate of the cost of repairing all damage caused by fire, flood, hurricane, earthquake or tornado. Whenever available, the request must also include a copy of the insurer's settlement statement which provides a breakdown of the insurance payment and lists, by item, labor costs, material costs, contractor overhead and profit and the applied sales tax and tax percentage. The Contractor shall review the request and confirm HUD's estimate of the cost of repairing the damage no later than ten (10) calendar days following receipt. Mortgagees may obtain names and contact information for the appropriate M&M contractor at the following website:

http://www.hud.gov/offices/hsg/sfh/reo/mm/mminfo.cfm

6. Demolition Action—If a local government authority has recommended or required that the home be demolished because of substantial damage, significant structural deficiencies and/or the presence of a life threatening hazard and the mortgagee and the borrower agree that the home cannot be rebuilt, the building must be demolished prior to conveyance of the property to HUD.

Prior to demolition, the mortgagee must submit a written approval request to HUD's assigned Management & Marketing (M&M) Contractor as provided in paragraph 5 along with documentation supporting the determination that the home should be demolished. Supporting documentation must include a contractor prepared repair cost estimate and a copy of a letter or notice posted on the property by the unit of local government requiring the demolition. The notice may be described as a Notice of Unsafe Conditions, Notice of Imminent Danger to Collapse, Notice of Pending Demolition or Notice of Condemnation. The M&M Contractor shall review the requests, confirm HUD's estimate of the repair cost and advise the mortgagee whether or not the proposed demolition action should be completed.

In instances where the mortgagee/mortgagor believes that the property should be demolished because of substantial damage, significant structural deficiencies and/or the presence of life threatening hazard, yet the unit of local government has not issued a letter or posted a notice due to the volume of properties damaged as a result of the hurricane, the mortgagees may still submit a request for approval of demolition or make a demolition recommendation. In that instance, the mortgagee must provide a detailed analysis to support the recommendation or demolition request in addition to the required repair cost estimate.

7. Claim Filing—In filing a Part A Claim for insurance benefits, the mortgagee must:

a. Describe the extent of the damage in the mortgagee comments section of Form HUD-27011, Part A;

b. Describe all coverages under property insurance policies that were in place at the time of the disasters and the actions that were taken by the borrower and mortgagee to file and settle property insurance claims for hazard and flood damages and obtain recoveries for all covered losses;

c. Validate that all damage resulted from the hurricane(s) and/or hurricane related flooding and that the home is not habitable;

d. Enter in Part A, item 27, the greater of the hazard and flood insurance recoveries or the HUD approved estimate of the cost of repairs.

If the Part A claim is submitted before proceeds of the agreed insurance settlement are actually received, the mortgagee may use the anticipated recovery amount for purposes of determining the reduction from insurance benefits for the property damage as provided in subparagragh 7(d) above. When the proceeds are received, any necessary adjustment will be made on line 119 of Part B. If the actual proceeds received are less than expected, the mortgagee will be entitled to reimbursement of the difference between the expected proceeds amount and the proceeds actually received only if both are greater than the HUD approved estimate of damage repairs. If actual proceeds received are greater than anticipated, a Part B claim adjustment will be necessary only for the amount by which total recoveries exceed the amount previously credited on the Part A claim.

8. Financial Analysis—Mortgagees must normally obtain information and documentation necessary to assess the borrower's inability to continue to support the mortgage debt as provided in Mortgagee Letter 00-05, dated January 19, 2000. That evaluation is not required where the property has been damaged to the point that it is uninhabitable. Evidence of uninhabitability should be documented in the servicing file.

9. Borrower Consideration—The borrower is entitled to consideration of $5,000 upon satisfaction of the requirements of the deed-in-lieu agreement provided that the property is vacant and clear title is provided. The mortgagee shall pay the borrower consideration and enter the payment amount on form HUD-27011, Single-Family Application for Insurance Benefits, Part D, item 305, Disbursements for HIP, taxes, ground rents and water rates, eviction costs and other disbursements not shown elsewhere. The description field for the payment should identify the qualifying disaster and clearly indicate how the funds were applied. All or part of this consideration may be applied as follows if approved by the borrower in the DIL agreement:

a. Toward discharge or discounted payoff of junior liens as necessary to clear the title.

b. Toward payoff of accrued foreclosure costs and other legal fees actually incurred by the mortgagee not to exceed the reimbursement guidelines specified by HUD in Mortgagee Letter 2005-30, dated July 12, 2005.

c. As a credit against uninsured property repair costs that would normally be deducted from the claim for insurance benefits or the cost of an approved demolition if that expense is not otherwise covered by a local, state or federal entity.

10. Claimable Expenses—Reimbursable expenses include title evidence costs, the consideration paid to (or on behalf of) the borrower, a $250 mortgagee incentive fee for administrative expenses and attorney fees not to exceed $400 for legal services in processing the DIL. The mortgagee may not include in its claim for insurance benefits any foreclosure or legal fees incurred prior to acceptance of the DIL.

11. Tax Consequences—Provisions of the Katrina Emergency Tax Relief Act of 2005 (Public Law 109-73, enacted September 23, 2005), provide relief from the potential federal income tax consequences of debt forgiveness to individuals whose principal residence on August 25, 2005 was located in core disaster areas for Hurricane Katrina only. All borrowers should be advised to obtain independent financial advice about tax consequences of the transaction before executing a DIL.

12. Credit Explanation Letters—The mortgagee shall, in addition to any monetary consideration provided to the borrower, provide the borrower with a credit explanation letter to alleviate potential adverse credit impacts from the DIL action in a format substantially similar to Attachment A.

13. Future Participation in FHA Programs—All borrowers who elect to convey property to HUD via deed in lieu of foreclosure under the special provisions described in this mortgagee letter shall be considered "nonoccupants" under HUD property disposition rules and shall not be eligible to repurchase the same property. Subject to that restriction, they shall not be barred from immediate participation in FHA insured loan and property disposition programs because of the voluntary conveyance. A borrower shall not be ineligible for new FHA-insured financing by reason of a CAIVRS record of a deed-in-lieu claim paid pursuant to this special authority if a credit report shows satisfactory credit prior to the disaster and any derogatory credit subsequent to that date can be related to the effects of the disaster. Mortgagees should refer to Mortgagee Letter 2006-01 dated January 9, 2006 for more specific FHA underwriting guidance to accommodate disaster victims.

14. Other Provisions—All other provisions and requirements of Mortgagee Letter 00-05, dated January 19, 2000 with respect to deeds in lieu of foreclosure shall remain the same. Mortgagees are reminded that the loan must in be in default (30 or more days past due) at the time the voluntary conveyance deed is executed and delivered.

Mortgages are reminded that the primary focus of HUD's loss mitigation efforts is on home retention. Prior to use of this special DIL option, mortgagees must exhaust all loss mitigation home retention options and must support the DIL decision with documentation in the servicing file.

The information collection requirements contained in this document have been approved by the Office of Management and Budget (OMB) under the Paperwork Reduction Act of 1995 (44 U.S.C. 3501-3520) and assigned OMB control numbers 2502-0523 and 2502-0429. In accordance with the Paperwork Reduction Act, HUD may not conduct or sponsor, and a person is not required to respond to, a collection of information unless the collection displays a currently valid OMB control number.

This special authority will expire on March 31, 2007 unless otherwise extended by HUD. Any questions regarding this Mortgagee Letter may be directed to HUD's National Servicing Center (NSC) at (888) 297-8685 or hsg-lossmit@hud.gov.

Sincerely,

____

Brian D. Montgomery
Assistant Secretary for Housing-
Federal Housing Commissioner

Attachment

Attachment A

[Prepare on mortgagee's letterhead and provide to borrower(s). Also provide cover letter explaining that they may wish to send the letter below to credit reporting agencies or other parties that will be considering extending credit to the borrower(s).]

To Whom It May Concern:

Our records indicate that ____________ was the mortgagor of record of an FHA-insured mortgage held by ____________ on the property located at ____________. The FHA Case Number was XXX-XXXXXX-XXX. The original principal balance on this mortgage was $________, with an interest rate of XX%. The date of the first payment due on the mortgage was ________ , with a term of _____ months.

As a result of __ (insert name of declared disaster), the property securing this loan was seriously damaged or destroyed. The damage made the home uninhabitable and it was not financially feasible to repair or rebuild the dwelling. The borrower worked with the mortgage holder to obtain all available hazard and flood insurance recoveries for application to the mortgage debt, voluntarily conveyed title to the property to ____________ on ________ and was granted a release from all remaining financial obligations under the mortgage.

Due to the extreme circumstances resulting from (insert name of declared disaster), both (insert name of mortgagee) and the Department of Housing and Urban Development jointly request that any potential creditors take notice of these circumstances when deciding whether to grant credit to this borrower.

Thank you for your attention to this matter.

Sincerely,
(insert name of mortgagee representative)

Department of Housing and Urban Development Mortgagee Letter 2006-14 (June 8, 2006)

June 8, 2006

MORTGAGEE LETTER 2006-14

TO: ALL APPROVED MORTGAGEES

SUBJECT: Property Flipping Prohibition Amendment

On June 7, 2006, HUD published a final rule in the Federal Register amending regulations at 24 CFR 203.37a prohibiting property flipping in HUD's single-family mortgage insurance programs by providing additional exceptions to the time restrictions on sales. The rule and this mortgagee letter become effective for mortgages endorsed for insurance on or after July 7, 2006. This Mortgagee Letter also rescinds, in their entirety, Mortgagee Letters 2003-07 and 2005-05.

The additional categories of properties exempted from the time restrictions include sales of properties by:

- State and Federally chartered financial Institutions and government-sponsored enterprises (GSEs) (e.g., Fannie Mae and Freddie Mac)
- Local and State government agencies
- Nonprofits approved to purchase HUD REO properties at a discount http://www.hud.gov/offices/hsg/sfh/np/np_hoc.cfm
- Sales of properties within Presidentially-Declared Disaster Areas (upon FHA's announcement of eligibility in a mortgagee letter specific to said disaster)

Prohibition on Property Flipping Described

Property flipping is a practice whereby a property is resold a short period of time after it is purchased by the seller for a considerable profit with an artificially inflated value, often abetted by a lender's collusion with the appraiser. FHA's policy prohibiting property flipping eliminates the most egregious examples of predatory flips of properties within the FHA mortgage insurance programs.

Overview of FHA's Property Flipping Policy

FHA requires that: a) only owners of record may sell properties that will be financed using FHA-insured mortgages; b) any resale of a property may not occur 90 or fewer days from the last sale to be eligible for FHA financing; and c) that for resales that occur between 91 and 180 days where the new sales price exceeds the previous sales price by 100 percent or more, FHA will require additional documentation validating the property's value. FHA also has flexibility to examine and require additional evidence of appraised value when properties are re-sold within 12 months.

Sale by Owner of Record

To be eligible for a mortgage insured by FHA, the property must be purchased from the owner of record and the transaction may not involve any sale or assignment of the sales contract. This requirement applies to all FHA purchase money mortgages regardless of the time between resales.

The mortgage lender must obtain documentation verifying that the seller is the owner of record and submit this to HUD as part of the insurance endorsement binder; it is to be placed behind the appraisal on the left side of the case binder. This documentation may include, but is not limited to, a property sales history report, a copy of the recorded deed from the seller, or other documentation such as a copy of a property tax bill, title commitment or binder, demonstrating the seller's ownership of the property and the date it was acquired. Mortgagees participating in the Lender Insurance program (see ML 2005-36) are to retain this documentation and provide it to FHA upon request.

Resales Occurring 90 Days or Less Following Acquisition

If the owner sells a property within 90 days after the date of acquisition, that property is not eligible security for a mortgage insured by FHA unless it falls within one of the exceptions to the time restrictions on resales set forth in §203.37a(c) of the regulations. FHA defines the seller's date of acquisition as the date of settlement on the seller's purchase of that property. The resale date is the date of execution of the sales contract by the buyer that will result in a mortgage to be insured by FHA.

As an example, a property acquired by the seller is not eligible for a mortgage to be insured for the buyer unless the seller has owned that property for at least 90 days. The seller must also be the owner of record.

Resales Occurring Between 91 and 180 Days Following Acquisition

If the resale date is between 91 and 180 days following acquisition by the seller, the lender is required to obtain a second appraisal made by another appraiser *if* the resale price is 100 percent or more over the price paid by the seller when the property was acquired.

As an example, if a property is resold for $80,000 within six months of the seller's acquisition of that property for $40,000, the mortgage lender must obtain a second independent appraisal supporting the $80,000 sales price. The mortgage lender may also provide documentation showing the costs and extent of rehabilitation that went into the property resulting in the increased value but must still obtain the second appraisal. The cost of the second appraisal may not be charged to the homebuyer.

FHA also reserves the right to revise the resale percentage level at which this second appraisal is required by publishing a notice in the Federal Register.

Resales Occurring Between 91 Days and 12 Months Following Acquisition

If the resale date is more than 90 days after the date of acquisition by the seller but before the end of the twelfth month following the date of acquisition, FHA reserves the right to require additional documentation from the lender to support the resale value if the resale price is 5 percent or greater than the lowest sales price of the property during the preceding 12 months. At FHA's discretion, such documentation may include, but is not limited to, an appraisal from another appraiser.

FHA will announce its determination to require the additional appraisal and other value documentation, such as an automated valuation method (AVM), through a *Federal Register* issuance. This requirement may be established either nationwide or on a regional basis, at FHA's discretion.

Exceptions to 90-day Restriction

The following sales are exempt from the time restrictions provided by §203.37a:

- Sales by HUD of its Real Estate Owned
- Sales by other United States Government agencies of single family properties pursuant to programs operated by these agencies.
- Sales of properties by nonprofits approved to purchase HUD-owned single-family properties at a discount with resale restrictions.
- Sales of properties that are acquired by the sellers by inheritance.
- Sales of properties purchased by employers or relocation agencies in connection with relocations of employees.
- Sales of properties by state and federally charted financial institutions and Government Sponsored Enterprises.
- Sales of properties by local and state government agencies.
- Upon FHA's announcement of eligibility in a notice (i.e., ML), sales of properties located in areas designated by the President as federal disaster areas, will be exempt from the restrictions of the property-flipping rule. The notice will specify how long the exception will be in effect and the specific disaster area affected.

Inapplicability of §203.37a to New Construction

The restrictions in 203.37a are not applicable to a builder selling a newly built home or building a home for a homebuyer wishing to use FHA-insured financing.

Date of Property Acquisition Determined by the Appraiser

Mortgage lenders may rely on information provided by the appraiser in compliance with the updated Standard Rule 1-5 of the Uniform Standards of Professional Appraisal Practice (USPAP). This rule requires appraisers to analyze any prior sales of the subject property that occurred within specific time periods, now set for the previous three years for one-to-four family residential properties.

As a result, the information contained on the Uniform Residential Appraisal Report or other applicable appraisal report form describing the Date, Price and Data for prior Sales is to include all transactions for the subject property within three years of the date of the appraisal and the comparable sales within 12 months of the date of the comparable sale. Appraisers are responsible for considering and analyzing any prior sales of the property being appraised within three years of the date of the appraisal and the comparables that are utilized within 12 months of the date of the comparable sale.

Therefore, provided that the URAR completed by the appraiser shows the most recent sale of the property to have occurred at least one year previously, no additional documentation is required from the mortgage lender. The mortgage lender remains accountable for verifying that the seller is the owner of record and may rely on information developed by the appraiser for this purpose if provided. However, if the lender obtains conflicting information before loan settlement, it must resolve the discrepancy and document the file accordingly.

If you have any questions regarding this Mortgagee Letter, please call 1-800-CALL-FHA.

Sincerely,

Brian D. Montgomery
Assistant Secretary for Housing-
Federal Housing Commissioner

Department of Housing and Urban Development Mortgagee Letter 2006-16 (June 9, 2006)

June 9, 2006

MORTGAGEE LETTER 2006-16

TO: ALL APPROVED MORTGAGEES

ATTENTION: Single Family Servicing Managers

SUBJECT: Mississippi Homeowner Grant Assistance Program

The State of Mississippi has now finalized an action plan for use of Federal Community Development Block Grant (CDBG) funds to assist homeowners who suffered flood damage to their primary residence from Hurricane Katrina. This mortgagee letter provides guidance regarding grant program issues specific to FHA-insured loans.

Under the state plan, eligible homeowners may receive a one-time grant payment, up to a maximum of $150,000, for flood damages not covered by insurance or FEMA grants. An eligible homeowner is one whose home is located outside a FEMA-designated 100-year flood zone, and was flooded as a result of Hurricane Katrina. In exchange for the grant payment, a qualifying homeowner must agree to covenants on their property that establish building code, flood insurance and elevation requirements for them and any future owner of the land and all existing lienholders must subordinate their liens to those covenants. Unpaid and outstanding insurance claims must be subrogated back to the State. After certain deductions, the homeowner has complete discretion of the use of the grant funds, as allowable by State and Federal law.

The Mississippi Development Authority (MDA), which is administering the assistance program, has requested that mortgagees manage the grant closing and funds disbursement process for their customers. Mortgagees that wished to participate were required to sign and return an Opt-In Agreement by the MDA deadline. The Opt-In agreement states that grant managing mortgagees will remit grant funds to the homeowner within five (5) business days and may only reduce the payment by the amount of any past due installments on the Homeowner's mortgage and any taxes due and owing on the Property. However, HUD understands that this agreement does not prohibit homeowners and mortgagees from voluntarily negotiating other arrangements with respect to disbursement of grant funds for home repairs or payoff of mortgage debt.

Subordination Agreements and Disbursement Accounts

HUD has no objection to the subordination of FHA-insured first mortgage liens to the covenants required by the state as a condition for grant awards, and covenant-encumbered title that is otherwise marketable will be acceptable to HUD upon claim, provided that there is no material breach of the covenants as of the date of conveyance of such property to the Secretary that is due to neglect or poor oversight on the part of the mortgagee. HUD recognizes that in order to ensure that there has been no breach of the covenants, mortgagees and homeowners may feel that it is necessary and prudent to enter into disbursement agreements, to which neither HUD nor the State of Mississippi are parties, that allow the mortgagee to escrow grant funds and disburse them in draws as repairs are completed in accordance with covenant requirements.

Secretary Held Liens

HUD may hold a junior lien on some eligible properties as security for a partial claim, mortgage assistance initiative payment or Section 235 subsidy mortgage. Requests to subordinate such liens to the State required covenants should be submitted to HUD's servicing contractor at the address below:

U.S. Department of HUD
c/o Morris Griffin Corp./First Madison Services, Inc.
4111 South Darlington
Suite 300
Tulsa, OK 74135
Phone: 800-967-3050

Any questions regarding this Mortgagee Letter may be directed to HUD's National Servicing Center (NSC) at (888) 297-8685 or hsg-lossmit@hud.gov.

Sincerely,

Brian D. Montgomery
Assistant Secretary for Housing-
Federal Housing Commissioner

Department of Housing and Urban Development Mortgagee Letter 2006-18 (June 30, 2006)

June 30, 2006

MORTGAGEE LETTER 2006-18

TO: ALL APPROVED MORTGAGEES

ATTENTION: Single Family Servicing Managers

SUBJECT: Foreclosure Moratorium Extensions to Assist Borrowers Eligible for Hurricane Grant Funds

This Mortgagee Letter provides a limited extension of the foreclosure moratorium provided by Mortgagee Letter 2006-12, Foreclosure Moratorium Extensions to Assist Victims of Hurricanes Katrina, Rita and Wilma. We have learned that some Mississippi and Louisiana borrowers whose properties were moderately or severely damaged by the hurricanes may be eligible for grant assistance, but have not yet had the opportunity to apply for and receive funds. These grant funds would allow mortgagors to rebuild their homes or, if rebuilding is not feasible, preserve good credit standing by paying off their mortgage debt.

Therefore, for borrowers who may be eligible to apply for Community Development Block Grant (CDBG) funds under either the Mississippi or Louisiana State Programs, HUD is extending the foreclosure moratorium to August 31, 2006. To qualify for this extension, the following criteria must be met:

1. The borrower's mortgaged property must be located in an area eligible for grant assistance. In Mississippi, eligible properties are restricted at this time to those located in Hancock, Harrison, Jackson or Pearl River Counties, which are in the Presidentially declared disaster area. Please refer to ML 2006-16 for further details regarding Mississippi. In Louisiana, this includes properties in any parish designated by FEMA as eligible for individual assistance.

2. The borrower's mortgaged property must have sustained more than $5,000 in hurricane related home damage.

3. On or before June 30, 2006, the borrower must have made a written commitment to work with his or her mortgagee to develop and implement a plan to resolve the mortgage delinquency as described in ML 2006-12.

For mortgages that are no longer covered by a foreclosure moratorium, mortgagees must review each case to confirm that the borrower is not eligible for any of FHA's loss mitigation options prior to initiating foreclosure. In addition to the standard roster of available FHA loss mitigation options, the Department announced in Mortgagee Letter 2005-46, dated

December 1, 2005, an expanded use of partial claims and loan modifications in cases where borrowers are committed to continued occupancy of the property. Mortgagees are urged to use those special loss mitigation authorities in impacted areas approved for individual disaster assistance to the maximum extent possible under FHA guidelines.

Mortgagees are reminded that in accordance with HUD regulation 24 CFR 203.355, they must commence foreclosure or take one of the other options provided by the regulation within the greater of 6 months from the date of default or 90 days from the expiration of action that barred foreclosure. In this case, the limited extension of the foreclosure moratorium is deemed to be HUD's approval to a delay in initiating foreclosure under this regulation.

If further time is needed to take an appropriate action, a mortgagee may request an extension of time by faxing a completed Form HUD-50012 to the National Servicing Center (NSC) at (918) 292-8992 that states the basis for the request and the applicable federal disaster.

The Department continues to encourage mortgagees and their servicers not to report delinquencies on loans in the Presidentially-declared disaster areas to credit reporting agencies until and unless a mortgage is referred to foreclosure. However, mortgagees must report all 90-day delinquencies to HUD's Single Family Default Monitoring System (SFDMS) using FHA Connection or Electronic Default Interchange (EDI). Reporting delinquency data for accounts that are 30 days delinquent does not begin until data for the October 2006 reporting cycle is due to HUD. Data for the October reporting cycle is due between November 1, 2006 and November 7, 2006. For additional guidance, please refer to Mortgagee Letter 2006-15 Future Delinquency Reporting Requirements, dated June 8, 2006.

The information collection requirements contained in this document have been approved by the Office of Management and Budget (OMB) under the Paperwork Reduction Act of 1995 (44 U.S.C. 3501-3520) and assigned OMB control numbers 2502-0436, 2502-0523 and 2502-0429. In accordance with the Paperwork Reduction Act, HUD may not conduct or sponsor, and a person is not required to respond to, a collection of information unless the collection displays a currently valid OMB control number.

If you have any questions concerning this Mortgagee Letter, please contact the National Servicing Center at 888-297-8685.

Sincerely,

Brian D. Montgomery
Assistant Secretary for Housing-
Federal Housing Commissioner

Department of Housing and Urban Development, Mortgagee Letter 2006-28 (Nov. 20, 2006)

November 20, 2006

Mortgagee Letter 2006-28

TO: ALL APPROVED MORTGAGEES

ATTENTION: Single Family Servicing Managers

SUBJECT: Mortgage and Foreclosure Rights of Servicemembers under the Servicemembers Civil Relief Act (SCRA)

This Mortgagee Letter provides information regarding a new legal requirement to notify homeowners in default of the mortgage and foreclosure rights of servicemembers and their dependents under the Servicemembers Civil Relief Act (SCRA). It also provides guidance regarding the implementation of SCRA requirements in servicing FHA-insured mortgages. This guidance supersedes prior Mortgagee letters ML 2003-04, Soldiers' and Sailors' Civil Relief Act and ML 01-22, The Effect of the Soldiers' and Sailors' Civil Relief Act of 1940 on FHA Insured Mortgages. However, the guidance provided in ML 91-20, Effect of the Soldiers' and Sailors' Civil Relief Act of 1940 on FHA Insured Mortgages remains valid with respect to the calculation of Section 235 subsidy.

Section 688 of the National Defense Authorization Act for Fiscal Year 2006 (public law 109-163, enacted January 6, 2006) amended the required content of notifications of homeownership counseling availability under section 106(c)(5)(A)(ii) of the Housing and Urban Development Act (12 U.S.C. 1701x(c)(5)(A)(ii)) and directed HUD to develop and disseminate a format for the required notice.

Servicemembers Civil Relief Act Notice

Pursuant to the statutory amendment, HUD has developed, in consultation with the Departments of Defense and Treasury, the form for the required notice of servicemember rights (Attachment 1). All mortgage loans, including conventional mortgages and mortgages insured by HUD are subject to the notification requirement that became effective June 5, 2006. The notice must:

- Be sent to all homeowners who are in default on a residential mortgage;
- Include the toll-free Military OneSource number to call if servicemembers or their dependents require further assistance (1-800-342-9647); and
- Be made within 45 days from the date a missed payment was due, unless the homeowner pays the overdue amount before the expiration of the 45-day period.

<u>Legal Rights and Protections Under the SCRA Applicable to all Debts</u>

The SCRA states that a debt incurred by a servicemember or spouse jointly, prior to entering military service shall not bear interest at a rate above six percent per year during the period of military service. Interest in excess of six percent per year that would otherwise be incurred during the period of military service is forgiven. Servicemembers become eligible for the interest rate limitation by providing to the mortgagee a written notice, a copy of the military orders calling the servicemember to military service, and any orders further extending military service, not later than 180 days after the date of the servicemember's termination or release from military service. Upon receipt, the mortgagee must limit interest on the obligation to no more than six percent per year effective as of the date on which the servicemember is called to military service. Only a court may grant the mortgagee an exception to the interest rate limitation and then, only if, in the opinion of the court, the ability of the servicemember to pay interest upon the obligation or liability at a rate in excess of six percent per year is not materially affected by reason of the servicemember's military service.

In a legal action to enforce a debt against real estate that is filed during, or within 90 days after the servicemember's military service, a court may stop the proceedings for a period of time, or adjust the debt. In addition, the sale, foreclosure, or seizure of real estate shall not be valid if it occurs during, or within 90 days after the servicemember's military service unless the creditor has obtained a court order approving the sale, foreclosure, or seizure of the real estate.

The SCRA provides some additional legal protections. HUD is not in a position to interpret all the various provisions of the SCRA as they may affect rights between creditors and servicemembers.

Such interpretations should be obtained from the Department of Defense or be determined by the courts.

Reduction of Monthly Payments on FHA-Insured Loans

When, pursuant to the SCRA, interest must be reduced to six percent on an FHA-insured loan, the mortgagee may either calculate interest due for the period of active duty on a per diem basis, or permit the lower interest rate from the first through the last month of military service.

If notified that a mortgagor is on active military duty, the mortgagee must advise the servicemember or representative of the adjusted amount due, provide adjusted coupons or billings, and ensure that the reduced payments are not returned as insufficient.

If the mortgagee was not notified that the mortgagor is on active military duty, but receives a reduced payment that approximates an interest reduction to six percent, an effort should be made to contact the mortgagor or a representative to determine whether the mortgagor is on active duty. If an appropriate explanation is not provided, the mortgagee may return the insufficient payment in accordance with 24 CFR § 203.556.

Section 235 Mortgage Insurance and Assistance Payments Program

A few Section 235 mortgages still have assistance payments from HUD applied to them on behalf of lower-income mortgagors. Assistance for these mortgages may be affected by the six percent interest rate limitation. On all accounts receiving assistance when the note rate of interest exceeds six percent, the amount of assistance must be reanalyzed, and the subsidy amount must be recalculated using the full mortgage payment at a six percent rate when determining the amount of assistance. For some accounts, the interest rate deduction will cause the suspension of assistance for the period of active duty. Whenever an interest rate reduction is made with retroactive effect and the Section 235 assistance is reduced, any over-billed subsidy must be returned to HUD as a refund or adjustment to the subsequent Section 235 monthly billing. When active duty terminates and the note rate resumes, the assistance must be recalculated and restored in accordance with the usual procedures. Any income recertification requests received from mortgagors in accordance with 24 CFR § 235.355 must be processed expeditiously. Please also reference ML 91-20, Effect of the Soldiers' and Sailors' Civil Relief Act of 1940 on FHA Insured Mortgages for additional guidance in calculating Formula 2 subsidy.

HUD Relief Provisions for Servicemembers

FHA regulations contain special relief provisions authorizing postponement of principal payments and foreclosure proceedings for mortgagors in active duty military service as defined in the SCRA. Pursuant to 24 CFR 203.610, the mortgagee shall specifically give consideration to affording the mortgagor relief authorized by 24 CFR 203.345 and 203.346 and covered under the following two paragraphs.

Postponement of Principal Payments

Under 24 CFR 203.345, the mortgagee may, by written agreement with the mortgagor, postpone for the period of military service and for 3 months thereafter any part of the monthly mortgage payment which represents amortization of principal. The agreement shall contain a provision for the resumption of monthly payments after such period in amounts that will completely amortize the mortgage debt within the maturity as provided in the original mortgage. This agreement does not affect the amount of the annual Mortgage Insurance Premium (MIP) that will continue to be calculated in accordance with the original amortization provisions of the mortgage.

Postponement of Foreclosure

Under provisions of 24 CFR 203.346, the period during which the mortgagor is in military service shall be excluded in computing the period during which the mortgagee shall commence foreclosure or acquire the property by other means. Further, postponement or delay in prosecuting foreclosure proceedings during the period the mortgagor is in military service shall not be construed as a failure of the mortgagee to exercise reasonable diligence.

Loss Mitigation

Mortgagees must consider all FHA home retention loss mitigation options for active duty military persons who are in default on an FHA insured loan. These options, including special forbearance, loan modification, and partial claim help protect the servicemember against the risk of foreclosure after the period of service is completed. Mortgagees must also provide delinquent servicemembers with information about pre-foreclosure sale and deed-in-lieu of foreclosure options.

Claims for FHA Insurance Benefits

Debenture interest will not be curtailed because of SCRA-caused delays in initiating or prosecuting foreclosure proceedings. On conveyance claims involving loans subject to SCRA provisions, the Department will pay the applicable debenture interest rate from the date of default to the date the claim is paid unless interest must otherwise be curtailed pursuant to 24 CFR 203.402(k).

Reimbursement of Issuers for Interest Shortfalls on Eligible Loans in Ginnie Mae Mortgage-Backed Securities

Ginnie Mae will reimburse issuers for interest shortfalls attributable to SCRA for all eligible loans. To receive a reimbursement of interest, an issuer must demonstrate that the borrower meets the criteria for a reduction in interest rate. Mortgagees should refer to Chapter 34, Section 34-3 of Ginnie Mae Mortgage-Backed Securities Guide 5500.3, Rev. 1 for further information on obtaining such reimbursement. Links to each chapter of the Ginnie Mae MBS Guide are available at: http://www.ginniemae.gov/guide/guidtoc.asp?subTitle=Issuers

Verification of Military Service

Mortgagees who are otherwise unable to verify a defendant mortgagor's military status may request and obtain a statement as to military service from the Department of Defense pursuant to 50 U.S.C. App. § 582 of the SCRA. To facilitate SCRA searches, the Department of Defense's Manpower Data Center (DMDC) has developed a secure public Internet access system through which any requester can quickly determine whether an individual is currently in the armed forces. The URL for SCRA queries is https://www.dmdc.osd.mil/owa/scra/home. The requester must provide a Social Security number (SSN) and a last name. First name, middle name, birth year, and birth month are optional.

A report is executed by clicking the "LookUp" tab on the query form. If the provided SSN and other identifying information match the name of a person currently on active duty, the DMDC response report will provide the named individual's branch of military service and "begin date" of Active Duty status. If the provided SSN is matched to the name of a person on active duty but the last name and/or birth date entered do not match information recorded for that individual, the DMDC response report page states:

"Based on the social security number you have provided, the individual is currently on Active Duty. However, the name or partial DOB, or both provided do not match the individual against whom the social security number is assigned."

If the DMDC does not have information regarding whether the name of the identified person is on active duty, the response report will only list the supplied name with the text:

"Based on the information you have furnished, the DMDC does not possess any information indicating the individual is currently on active duty."

There is no charge for the online SCRA queries and no authorization, user ID or password is required. Should you require assistance, you may fax a SCRA request to DMDC at 703-696-4156 or call 703-696-6762.

The information collection requirements contained in this document have been approved by the Office of Management and Budget (OMB) under the Paperwork Reduction Act of 1995 (44 U.S.C. 3501-3520) and assigned OMB Control Number 2502-0565. In accordance with the Paperwork Reduction Act, HUD may not conduct or sponsor, and a person is not required to respond to, a collection of information unless the collection displays a currently valid OMB Control Number.

Any questions regarding this Mortgagee Letter may be directed to HUD's National Servicing Center through its toll-free number 1-888-297-8685.

Brian D. Montgomery
Assistant Secretary for Housing-
Federal Housing Commissioner

Attachment

Attachment 1

United States Department of Housing and Urban Development
Servicemembers Civil Relief Act Notice

Legal Rights and Protections Under the SCRA

Servicemembers on "active duty" or "active service," or a dependent of such a servicemember may be entitled to certain legal protections and debt relief pursuant to the Servicemembers Civil Relief Act (50 USC App. §§ 501-596) (SCRA).

Who May Be Entitled to Legal Protections Under the SCRA?

- Active duty members of the Army, Navy, Air Force, Marine Corps, Coast Guard, and active service National Guard;
- Active service members of the commissioned corps of the National Oceanic and Atmospheric Administration;
- Active service members of the commissioned corps of the Public Health Service;
- United States citizens serving with the armed forces of a nation with which the United States is allied in the prosecution of a war or military action; and
- Their spouses.

What Legal Protections Are Servicemembers Entitled To Under the SCRA?

- The SCRA states that, a debt incurred by a servicemember, or servicemember and spouse jointly, prior to entering military service shall not bear interest at a rate above 6 percent during the period of military service.
- The SCRA states that, in a legal action to enforce a debt against real estate that is filed during, or within 90 days after the servicemember's military service, a court may stop the proceedings for a period of time, or adjust the debt. In addition, the sale, foreclosure, or seizure of real estate shall not be valid if it occurs during, or within 90 days after the servicemember's military service unless the creditor has obtained a court order approving the sale, foreclosure, or seizure of the real estate.
- The SCRA contains many other protections besides those applicable to home loans.

How Does A Servicemember or Dependent Request Relief Under the SCRA?

- A servicemember or dependent, or both, may request relief under the SCRA by providing the lender a written notice with a copy of the servicemember's military orders. (Note: Lender should place its name, address and contact information here).

How Does a Servicemember or Dependent Obtain Information About the SCRA?

- The U.S. Department of Defense's information resource is "Military OneSource." Website: www.militaryonesource.com. The toll-free telephone numbers for Military OneSource are: From the United States: 1-800-342-9647. From outside the United States (with applicable access code): 800-3429-6477. International collect: (through long distance operator) 1-484-530-5908.
- Servicemembers and dependents with questions about the SCRA should contact their unit's Judge Advocate, or their installation's Legal Assistance Officer. A military legal assistance office locator for each branch of the armed forces is available at: http://legalassistance.law.af.mil/content/locator.php.

Department of Housing and Urban Development, Mortgagee Letter 2006-29 (Dec 6, 2006)

December 6, 2006

MORTGAGEE LETTER 2006-29

TO: ALL APPROVED MORTGAGEES

ATTENTION: Single Family Servicing Managers

SUBJECT: Louisiana Road Home Program

The State of Louisiana has now finalized an action plan for use of Federal Community Development Block Grant (CDBG) disaster funds to assist homeowners who suffered flood and/or wind damage to their residences from Hurricanes Katrina and/or Rita. This mortgagee letter provides guidance regarding grant program issues specific to FHA-insured loans.

Under the state plan, eligible homeowners may receive a one-time grant payment, up to a maximum of $150,000, for home damages not covered by property insurance, FEMA grants or other

Federal, state or local government programs. In exchange for the grant payment, a qualifying homeowner must agree to covenants and restrictions running with and encumbering the damaged property. Those covenants require flood insurance to be maintained if the property is located in a Special Flood Hazard Area under FEMA Flood Maps, rebuilding and repairs in accordance with applicable housing codes and ordinances, building elevation in accordance with FEMA recommended flood elevations, and homeowner occupancy for three years.

Existing lienholders must subordinate their liens to the state required covenants for the homeowner to be eligible for the Grant award. However, the declaration of covenants generally provides that the covenants shall not be enforced against the mortgagee, FHA, or any subsequent purchaser except to the extent that the subsequent purchaser breaches the covenants.

Subordination Requirement

Given the enforcement exceptions just noted, HUD has no objection to the subordination of FHA-insured first mortgage liens to the covenants required by the state as a condition for grant awards, and covenant-encumbered title that is otherwise good and marketable will be acceptable to HUD upon claim.

Secretary Held Liens

HUD may hold a lien on some eligible properties as security for a partial claim, section 235 subsidy mortgage, HECM mortgage, an assigned FHA mortgage or a property sale under HUD's Good Neighbor Next Door sales program. Requests to subordinate such liens to the State required covenants should be submitted to HUD's servicing contractor at the address below:

U.S. Department of HUD
c/o Morris Griffin Corp./First Madison Services, Inc.
4111 South Darlington, Suite 300
Tulsa, Oklahoma 74135
Phone: (800) 967-3050

The information collection requirements contained in this mortgagee letter have been approved by the Office of Management and Budget (OMB) under the Paperwork Reduction Act of 1995 (44 U.S.C. 3501-3520) and assigned OMB control number 2502-0429. In accordance with the Paperwork Reduction Act, HUD may not conduct or sponsor, and a person is not required to respond to, a collection of information unless the collection displays a currently valid OMB control number.

Any questions regarding this Mortgagee Letter may be directed to HUD's National Servicing Center (NSC) at (888) 297-8685 or hsg-lossmit@hud.gov.

Brian D. Montgomery
Assistant Secretary for Housing-
Federal Housing Commissioner

Department of Housing and Urban Development, Mortgagee Letter 2008-21 (Aug. 14, 2008)

August 14, 2008

MORTGAGEE LETTER 2008-21

TO: ALL APPROVED MORTGAGEES

ATTENTION: Single Family Servicing Managers

SUBJECT: FHA Loss Mitigation Program Updates

The Federal Housing Administration (FHA) is pleased to announce several changes to its Loss Mitigation Program that will strengthen both the Loan Modification and Partial Claim Initiatives.

While these changes are designed to address borrowers who are facing serious defaults, most delinquencies can and should be resolved through early intervention. Mortgagees are reminded of the critical importance of early and constructive contact with delinquent borrowers and the requirement to notify borrowers of the availability of default counseling by HUD-approved counseling agencies.

Loss Mitigation Program Changes

This Mortgagee Letter announces three changes to the existing Loss Mitigation program designed to give mortgagees additional latitude to help borrowers cure defaults and retain homeownership. The changes noted below are effective immediately.

First, with respect to Loan Modifications, mortgagees may use the Treasury 10-year constant maturity as a basis for establishing the maximum interest rate for loan modifications. The maximum interest allowable should be calculated as 200 basis points above the monthly average yield on United States Treasury Securities, adjusted to a constant maturity of 10 years. Mortgagees shall refer to the rate that is in effect as of the date of execution of the loan modification. For information on the 10-year monthly constant maturities, please refer to the statistical release H.15, which is available on the following web site: http://www.federalreserve.gov/releases/h15/data.htm

Next, where loss mitigation is being attempted after foreclosure has been initiated, mortgage servicers and mortgagors have advised that foreclosure related costs and legal fees are often impediments to successful loss mitigation. Many mortgagors who are able to resume making monthly mortgage payments frequently do not have sufficient funds to reimburse the mortgagee the legal fees and foreclosure costs incurred prior to qualifying for loss mitigation and therefore are denied participation.

Effective with this Mortgagee Letter, the Department will begin allowing legal fees and foreclosure costs related to a canceled foreclosure action to be incorporated into either the Loan Modification or the Partial Claim subject to the following requirements. This guidance expands and supersedes, in relevant part, the guidance provided in Loan Modifications section F (page 21) and Partial Claims section F (page 26) of Mortgagee Letter 00-05.

For Loan Modifications, legal fees and related foreclosure costs may now be **capitalized** into the modified principal balance. For Partial Claims (PC), mortgagees may now include legal fees and foreclosure costs related to a canceled foreclosure in the Partial Claim.

Mortgagees are reminded that all such foreclosure costs must reflect work actually completed to the date of the foreclosure cancellation and the attorney fees should not be in excess of the fee schedule that HUD has identified as customary and reasonable for FHA claim reimbursement. Late fees should not be capitalized in a Modification or included in a Partial Claim. As the goal in providing the mortgagor either a Loan Modification or a Partial Claim is to bring the delinquent mortgage current and give the mortgagor a new start, the mortgagee should waive all accrued late fees.

Please refer to Mortgagee Letter 2005-30 (or any subsequent guidance issued by FHA on reasonable and customary foreclosure costs) for the fee schedule for legal fees that HUD has identified as customary and reasonable for FHA claim reimbursement. Lenders should perform a retroactive escrow analysis at the time of the loan modification to ensure that the delinquent payments being capitalized reflect the actual escrow requirements required for those months capitalized.

Finally, in response to the industry's request to provide adequate time for the mortgagee to complete all required actions related to a loan modification, the Department provides the following clarification. When establishing a loan modification, it is acceptable for mortgagees to include all payments due including an additional month in the loan modification.

Consider the following example. The mortgagor is due for the January 2008 and all subsequent payments. The mortgagee completes its loss mitigation evaluation on June 27, 2008. To allow adequate time to complete the loan modification, obtain all required signatures and provide adequate notice to the mortgagor of the new payment, the mortgagee may include the payments due for July 2008 and August 2008 in the loan modification. The mortgagor will begin remitting payments due under the modified mortgage effective with the installment due September 1, 2008.

Any questions regarding this Mortgagee Letter or requirements for use of the partial claim and loan modification authorities may be directed to HUD's National Servicing Center (NSC) at 888-297-8685 or hsg-lossmit@hud.gov.

Sincerely,

Brian D. Montgomery
Assistant Secretary for Housing-
Federal Housing Commissioner

Department of Housing and Urban Development, Mortgagee Letter 2008-27 (Sept. 26, 2008)

September 26, 2008

MORTGAGEE LETTER 2008-27

TO: ALL HUD-APPROVED MORTGAGEES

SUBJECT: Treble Damages for Failure to Engage in Loss Mitigation

The purpose of this Mortgagee Letter is to provide information regarding the Civil Money Penalty that will result in Treble Damages for a mortgagee's failure to engage in loss mitigation.

Treble Damages may be assessed when a mortgagee fails to engage in loss mitigation. On April 26, 2005, the Department published a final rule, "Treble Damages for Failure to Engage in Loss Mitigation", advising the industry of this Civil Money Penalty. A copy of the final rule is available at www.gpoaccess.gov/fr/index.html.

Available Resources to Assist Mortgagees

HUD's National Servicing Center (NSC) is available to assist mortgagees in complying with FHA servicing requirements, including loss mitigation evaluation. The NSC offers Loss Mitigation training to lenders via scheduled classes throughout the year and participates in joint training with regional and national industry groups such as the Mortgage Bankers Association (MBA).

The NSC provides a toll-free telephone line (1-888-297-8685) to provide assistance regarding FHA's Servicing requirements, including HUD's Loss Mitigation Program. This assistance is available to mortgagors and mortgage industry professionals. Information from HUD's National Servicing Center (NSC) is available via the following website: http://www.hud.gov/offices/hsg/sfh/nschome.cfm.

Avoiding Treble Damage Penalty Assessments

There are three key actions that mortgagees must take to help avoid assessment of treble damages for failure to engage in loss mitigation. First, mortgagees must ensure that the loss mitigation evaluations are completed for all delinquent mortgages before four full monthly installments are due and unpaid. Second, mortgagees must ensure that the appropriate action is taken based on these evaluations. Third, mortgagees must maintain documentation of all initial and subsequent loss mitigation evaluations and actions taken.

Failure to Engage in Loss Mitigation

Failure to engage in loss mitigation is defined as:

1. A mortgagee's failure to evaluate a loan for loss mitigation before four full monthly mortgage installments are due and unpaid to determine which, if any, loss mitigation techniques are appropriate (see 24 CFR § 203.605); and/or
2. A subsequent failure to take appropriate loss mitigation action(s).

Mortgagees must be able to provide documentation of their loss mitigation evaluations and actions. Mortgagees will be considered to be in compliance with 24 CFR § 203.501 where plausible loss mitigation options were offered to eligible borrowers. The Department will not consider a mortgagee to have "failed to engage in loss mitigation" where the mortgagee can demonstrate that a borrower was uncooperative or ineligible.

Treble Damages' Assessments

HUD assesses civil money penalties against approved mortgagees through the Mortgagee Review Board (the Board) under 24 C.F.R. Parts 25 and 30. HUD will not assess treble damages for failure to engage in loss mitigation on any loan where the date of default occurred before May 26, 2005, the rule's effective date. If it is determined that civil money penalties for failure to engage in loss mitigation, or other violations of 24 CFR § 30.35 are warranted, the mortgagee will receive a notice from the Board. Mortgagees will have 30 days from receipt of any notice to provide the Board with a written response. If a mortgagee does not respond, the Board will determine the appropriate action to be taken, based upon all available information. Mortgagees may appeal Board determinations to HUD's Office of Administrative Law Judges.

The information collection requirements contained in this document have been approved by the Office of Management and Budget (OMB) under the Paperwork Reduction Act of 1995 (44 U.S.C. 3501-3520) and assigned OMB control numbers 2502-0060, 2502-0523 and 2502-0429. In accordance with the Paperwork Reduction Act, HUD may not conduct or sponsor, and a person is not required to respond to, a collection of information unless the collection displays a currently valid OMB Control Number.

Questions regarding this Mortgagee Letter may be directed to HUD's National Servicing Center at (888) 297-8685.

Sincerely,

Brian D. Montgomery
Assistant Secretary for Housing-
Federal Housing Commissioner

Department of Housing and Urban Development, Mortgagee Letter 2008-32 (Oct. 17, 2008)

October 17, 2008

MORTGAGEE LETTER 2008-32

TO: ALL APPROVED MORTGAGEES

ATTENTION: Single Family Servicing Managers

SUBJECT: Use of FHA Loss Mitigation During Bankruptcy

This Mortgagee Letter updates the Department's position on the use of FHA Loss Mitigation while a borrower is in bankruptcy. The guidance regarding mortgagors in bankruptcy provided on pages 9 and 25 of Mortgagee Letter 2000-05, is superseded by this Mortgagee Letter. Mortgagee Letter 2000-05, generally prohibited mortgagees from offering loss mitigation to a borrower in bankruptcy. That guidance was predicated on the concern that HUD did not want to influence mortgagees to take any action that would be considered by the Bankruptcy Court as a violation of the automatic stay.

The Department was recently approached by the mortgage industry and bankruptcy experts regarding the Department's current guidance on mortgagors in bankruptcy. As a result of these discussions, the Department understands that contact with debtor's counsel or a bankruptcy trustee does not constitute a violation of the automatic stay and that waiting until a bankruptcy is discharged or dismissed before offering loss mitigation may be injurious to the interests of the borrower, the mortgagee and the FHA insurance funds.

Effective immediately, mortgagees must, upon receipt of notice of a bankruptcy filing, send information to debtor's counsel indicating that loss mitigation may be available, and provide instruction sufficient to facilitate workout discussions including documentation requirements, timeframes and servicer contact information. Working through debtor's counsel, mortgagees may offer appropriate loss mitigation options prior to discharge or dismissal, without requiring relief from the automatic stay and in the case of a Chapter 7 bankruptcy, without requiring re-affirmation of the debt. It is strongly recommended that the bankruptcy trustee be copied on all such communications. All loss mitigation actions must be approved by the Bankruptcy Court prior to final execution.

Nothing in this mortgagee letter requires that mortgagees make direct contact with any borrower under bankruptcy protection. However, the information required to file a bankruptcy petition (now a matter of public record) will often include sufficient financial information for the mortgagee to properly evaluate the borrower's eligibility for loss mitigation. Using this financial information, many mortgagees have been able to complete the loss mitigation evaluation before the bankruptcy plan is confirmed and have offered a pre-approved loan modification agreement. For those mortgagors that sought bankruptcy protection solely to avoid foreclosure of their homes, this solution allowed the mortgagor to have the bankruptcy dismissed and begin fresh with a mortgage obligation that is both current and with payments that the mortgagor can afford. For those mortgagors with other financial problems, the resolution of the mortgage problem will put them in a better position to resolve the remaining financial issues.

Where the mortgagor filed the bankruptcy Pro Se, (without an attorney), the Department recommends that information relating to the availability of loss mitigation be provided to the mortgagor with a copy to the bankruptcy trustee. This communication must not infer that it is in any way an attempt to collect a debt. Mortgagees must consult their legal counsel for appropriate language.

The Department cautions mortgagees not to report current loans to HUD's Single Family Default System (SFDMS) simply to alert HUD that a bankruptcy has been filed. Loans must be at least one full payment due and unpaid (30 days delinquent) before reporting to SFDMS is required. Where the mortgagee is successful and is able to utilize loss mitigation on an account in bankruptcy, it must continue to report the appropriate status codes in SFDMS to reflect loss mitigation actions. Please ensure that should the loss mitigation initiative result in reinstatement or payment in full that the appropriate status code is reported to SFDMS.

The information collection requirements contained in this document have been approved by the Office of Management and Budget (OMB) under the Paperwork Reduction Act of 1995 (44 U.S.C. 3501-3520) and assigned OMB control numbers 2502-0429 and 2502-0523. In accordance with the Paperwork Reduction Act, HUD may not conduct or sponsor, and a person is not required to respond to, a collection of information unless the collection displays a currently valid OMB Control Number

Any questions regarding this Mortgagee Letter or requirements for use of the partial claim and loan modification authorities may be directed to HUD's National Servicing Center (NSC) at 888-297-8685 or hsg-lossmit@hud.gov.

Sincerely,

Brian D. Montgomery
Assistant Secretary for Housing-
Federal Housing Commissioner

Department of Housing and Urban Development, Mortgagee Letter 2008-41 (Dec. 19, 2008)

December 19, 2008

MORTGAGEE LETTER 2008-41

TO: ALL APPROVED MORTGAGEES

SUBJECT: Termination of *FHASecure*

While FHA will retain its standard rate-and-term refinance program for borrowers who are current on their existing mortgages, the *FHASecure* program under which FHA was able to insure refinance transactions for borrows delinquent on their mortgages, will terminate on December 31, 2008, as per FHA's initial guidance. Maintaining the program past the original termination date would have a negative financial impact on the MMI Fund that would have to be offset by either substantial across-the-board single family program premium increases or the suspension of FHA's single family insurance programs altogether.

Timing

As of December 31, 2008, FHA will not issue any new case numbers for lenders seeking to refinance borrowers into *FHASecure* loans. Any loans for which the lender has requested a case number and taken a loan application prior to December 31, 2008 may be processed and will be insured by FHA.

Other Refinance Options

Please note: FHA will retain its standard rate-and-term refinance program, as well as cash-out and streamlined refinance products. The standard rate-and-term refinance product is available to borrowers who are current on their existing mortgages. The policy guidance associated with these other refinance programs (Mortgagee Letter 08-40 and 05-43) remain in effect. Further, the HOPE for Homeowners program is available to help borrowers who may be delinquent on their current mortgages. FHA encourages lenders to consider this product for meeting the needs of distressed homeowners.

If you have any questions regarding this Mortgagee Letter, please contact the FHA Resource Center at 1-800-CALL-FHA (1-800-225-5342). Persons with hearing or speech impairments may access this number via TDD/TTY by calling 1-877-TDD-2HUD (1-877-833-2483).

Sincerely,

Brian D. Montgomery
Assistant Secretary for Housing-
Federal Housing Commissioner

Department of Housing and Urban Development, Mortgagee Letter 2008-43 (Dec. 24, 2008)

December 24, 2008

MORTGAGEE LETTER 2008-43

TO: ALL HUD-APPROVED MORTGAGEES

ATTENTION: Single Family Servicing Managers

SUBJECT: Pre-Foreclosure Sale (PFS) Program—Utilizing the PFS Loss Mitigation Option to Assist Families Facing Foreclosure

High foreclosure rates continue to have devastating effects on families and neighborhoods. The Federal Housing Administration (FHA) remains committed to taking actions to help families avoid foreclosure. Since being introduced as a national program in 1994[1], the PFS Program has helped thousands of mortgagors in default to avoid foreclosure and transition to more affordable housing. The PFS Program can help many families who today are facing foreclosure. The PFS loss mitigation option allows a mortgagor in default to sell his or her home and use the sale proceeds in satisfaction of the mortgage debt when the proceeds are less than the amount owed.

This Mortgagee Letter (ML) serves to remind mortgagees of the relief that the PFS Program can bring to borrowers with FHA-insured mortgages. To facilitate greater use of this program, FHA has consolidated in this ML the requirements of the PFS Program that have been issued over the years, and has updated and clarified those requirements where needed, to better address the problems faced by mortgagors today and provide greater flexibility in considering a mortgagor's candidacy for participation in this program.

Key Features of the PFS Program

- Establishing Market Value—Mortgagees are reminded to ensure that properties in the PFS program are sold at or near fair market value as established by an independent appraisal, prepared by an appraiser on the FHA Appraisal Roster.
- Minimum List Price Requirements—Properties offered for sale under the PFS program are to be listed for sale at no less than the "as-is" appraised value as determined by a current FHA appraisal, obtained and reviewed by the mortgagee.
- Negative Equity—The ratio of 63% for the fair market value (FMV) to the outstanding mortgage balance (including unpaid principal and accrued interest) has been updated to address events in the current housing market, and replaced with tiered net sales proceeds.
- Tiered Net Proceeds Requirement—This ML incorporates guidelines for varying minimum net sales proceeds based on the length of time a property has been competitively marketed for sale.
- Marketing Documentation—Prior to accepting a discounted offer, evidence of competitive marketing from the selling broker is to be presented and mortgagees are to retain this documentation in the claim review file.
- Non-owner Occupant Exceptions—Mortgagees are authorized to grant reasonable exceptions to non-occupant mortgagors when documentation indicates a property was not

1 The regulations for the PFS Program are codified in 24 CFR 203.370.

purchased as a rental or used as a rental for more than 18 months, immediately preceding the approval into the PFS program.

- Removal of Repair Limitations—With prior approval from HUD, properties with surchargeable damage (i.e., damage caused by fire, flood, earthquake, hurricane, boiler explosion or mortgagee neglect) may be eligible for the PFS program if funds—sufficient to cover the government's estimated repair costs—are applied to reduce the outstanding debt when a claim is filed.
- Increase in Funds Available for Discharge of Subordinate Liens—In instances where a mortgagor has made an initial contribution/incentive of $750 or $1,000, the amount that can be used from sales proceeds for the discharge of liens or encumbrances (which represent an impediment to conveyance of marketable title) has been raised from $2,000 to $2,500.
- Change in Allowable Closing Costs—Subject to the stated ratios, HUD allows up to 1% of the buyer's mortgage amount for closing costs to be included in the "Seller's Costs" on the HUD-1 for all transactions that involve a new FHA-insured mortgage.

Superseded and Updated Mortgagee Letters and Forms

This ML supersedes in its entirety ML 1994-45, "HUD's Nationwide Pre-Foreclosure Sale (PFS) Procedure". It also supersedes the section (pages 29-35) of ML 2000-05, "Loss Mitigation Program-Comprehensive Clarification of Policy and Notice of Procedural Changes" that describes Pre-Foreclosure Sale requirements.

Additionally, this ML updates, consolidates and/or eliminates the following HUD forms:

Form HUD-90035 (*Information Sheet*) and Form HUD-90036 (*Application to Participate*) have been consolidated to reflect updates made to the program and to delete any reference to HUD's former Assignment Program. The new Form HUD-90035 (*Information/Disclosure*) no longer requires the signature of the party providing homeownership counseling to the mortgagor. Form HUD-90036, *Application to Participate* is obsolete and no longer required.

Form HUD-90038 (*Homeownership Counseling Certificate*) is now obsolete. Form HUD-90054 (*Pre-Foreclosure Sale Data Reporting*) and Form HUD-92068-F (*Mortgage Assignment Program Request for Financials*) were both previously declared obsolete.

Form HUD-90041 (*Request for Variance*) has been slightly modified to reflect the new minimum net sales proceeds of 84%.

Form HUD-90045 (*Approval to Participate*) has been modified to provide a signature block for the mortgagor's signature(s) and new language describing HUD's current PFS Program.

Monitoring of Appraisals

Mortgagees are reminded that HUD performs monitoring reviews of appraisals and holds mortgagees accountable for the quality of appraisals on properties securing FHA-insured mortgages. As such, HUD may request electronically-formatted appraisals to review and ensure their accuracy. Mortgagees who submit appraisals that do not meet HUD's requirements are subject to the imposition of sanctions by the HUD Mortgagee Review Board in accordance with 24 CFR Part § 25.9 (ee) and Part § 203.5 (e)(3).

Information Collection Requirements

Paperwork reduction information collection requirements contained in this document have been approved by the Office of Management and Budget (OMB) under the Paperwork Reduction Act of 1995 (44 U.S.C. 3501-3520) and assigned OMB Control Number 2502-0464. In accordance with the Paperwork Reduction Act, HUD may not conduct or sponsor, and a person is not required to respond to, a collection of information unless the collection displays a currently valid OMB Control Number.

Mortgagees may direct questions or concerns regarding the Department's PFS procedures to the Customer Call Center for HUD's National Servicing Center (NSC). The toll free number is (888) 297-8685. Persons with hearing or speech impairments may reach this number via TDD/TTY by calling 1-877-TDD-2HUD (1-877-833-2483).

Sincerely,

____

Brian D. Montgomery
Assistant Secretary for Housing-
Federal Housing Commissioner

Table of Contents

[*Page numbers omitted.*]

Pre-Foreclosure Sale Introduction

The Pre-Foreclosure Sale (PFS) option allows mortgagors in default (resulting from an adverse and unavoidable financial situation) to sell their home at FMV and use the sale proceeds to satisfy the mortgage debt even if the proceeds are less than the amount owed. This option is appropriate for mortgagors whose financial situation requires that they sell their home, but they are unable to do so without FHA relief because the gross recovery on the sale of their property (i.e., sales price minus sales expenses) is less than the amount owed on the mortgage. HUD's home retention alternatives such as Special Forbearance, Mortgage Modification, or Partial Claim must first be considered and determined unlikely to succeed due to the mortgagor's financial situation. Mortgagees must maintain supporting documentation to demonstrate that a comprehensive review of the mortgagor's financial records was completed, and that the mortgagor did not have sufficient income to sustain the mortgage. Under no circumstances shall the PFS option be made available to mortgagors who have abandoned their mortgage obligation despite their continued ability to pay.

To participate in the program, mortgagors must be willing to make a commitment to actively market their property for a period of 3 months, during which time the mortgagee delays foreclosure action. Mortgagors who successfully sell to a third party within the required time may receive a cash consideration of up to $1,000. Mortgagees also receive a $1,000 incentive for successfully avoiding the foreclosure and complying with all the requirements of this ML. If the property does not sell, mortgagors are encouraged to use the deed-in-lieu of foreclosure (DIL) option, providing the title on the property is marketable. By following procedures and time frames included in this ML, a mortgagee may submit a FHA insurance claim and be compensated for the difference between the sale proceeds and the amount owed on the mortgage (including accrued interest and reimbursable costs).

A PFS sale must be an outright sale of the property. If a foreclosure occurs after the mortgagor unsuccessfully participated in the PFS process in good faith, neither the mortgagee nor HUD will pursue the mortgagor for a deficiency judgment.

Home Equity Conversion Mortgages (HECM) are not eligible for the PFS Program. The Code of Federal Regulations (CFR) provides special provisions for HECM short sales. Mortgagees should refer to 24 CFR Part § 206.125 (c) or contact HUD's NSC at the address below (Attention: HECM Housing Specialist) or email **hecmhelp@hud.gov**.

A. Loan Default

At the time the PFS closes, the loan must be in default (i.e., delinquent more than 30 days). Mortgagees may exercise their discretion to accept applications from mortgagors who are current but facing imminent default. However, by the date the PFS settlement occurs, the loan must be in default. Mortgagees should document this decision in the claim review file.

B. Mortgagor Qualifications

The PFS option may be extended to mortgagors who:

- Are in default as a result of an adverse and unavoidable financial situation. Adverse and unavoidable financial situations may include but are not limited to loss of job or verifiable income reduction and extensive medical expenses;
- Have negative equity as determined by an "as-is" FHA appraisal that indicates a property value less than 100% of the outstanding mortgage balance (including unpaid principal and accrued note rate interest) and any outstanding Partial Claim amounts, which are secured by a subordinate lien and/or a note. A PFS may be considered if the property's "as-is" appraised FMV slightly exceeds the mortgage payoff figure, but gross sales proceeds fall short of the amount needed to discharge the mortgage by more than $1,000;
- Are owner-occupants of a one-to-four unit single-family dwelling with a FHA-insured mortgage under Title II of the National Housing Act. Mortgagees are authorized to grant reasonable exceptions to non-occupant borrowers when it can be demonstrated that the need to vacate was related to the cause of default (e.g., job loss, transfer, divorce, death), and the subject property was not purchased as a rental or used as a rental for more than 18 months prior to the mortgagor's acceptance into the PFS Program;
- Have only one FHA-insured loan. Mortgagees are authorized to make reasonable exceptions for mortgagors who have acquired an FHA-insured property through inheritance or co-signed a FHA-insured loan to further enhance the credit of another mortgagor; or
- Are not a corporation or partnership (i.e., unless a written request to utilize the PFS has been approved by HUD's National Servicing Center (NSC)). Requests for such approvals should be submitted to:

U.S. Department of Housing and Urban Development
National Servicing Center
ATTENTION: Branch Chief
301 NW 6th Street, Suite 200
Oklahoma, OK 73102
Phone Number: (888) 297-8685
Fax Number: (405) 609-8405

C. PFS Program Participation

On the 32nd day but, no later than the 60th day of delinquency, the mortgagee shall send the delinquent borrower a pamphlet (HUD-PA-426, *How to Avoid Foreclosure)* about foreclosure avoidance. This pamphlet provides mortgagors with important information about loss mitigation alternatives, which include the pre-foreclosure sale option.

Mortgagees must inform mortgagors of the full spectrum of foreclosure-avoidance options prior to mortgagors' participation in the PFS Program. The mortgagee shall also advise that default counseling is available and highly recommended, though not required.

A mortgagor who has expressed an interest in the PFS option or who has been identified by the mortgagee as a qualified candidate for the PFS Program must be mailed a copy of the revised Form HUD-90035 (*Information/Disclosure).* Prior to mailing Form HUD-90035, the mortgagee must add its toll-free or collect telephone number to the form. Form HUD-90035 provides the mortgagor with appropriate PFS disclosures, information on housing counseling, and information about tax consequences. This disclosure form, the aforementioned pamphlet, and other HUD forms can be found on HUDclips at: **http://www.hudclips.org.**

D. Financial Analysis

Prior to signing Form HUD-90045 (*Approval to Participate),* the mortgagee must request financial documentation to evaluate the mortgagor's ability to support the mortgage debt. The PFS option may not be offered to mortgagors who have sufficient personal resources to pay off their mortgage commitment.

The mortgagee may prescribe the form that the mortgagor must use to submit its financial information. Mortgagors may provide financial information during a telephone interview, electronically, via the regular mail, or in person. Regardless of how the mortgagor's financial information is obtained, the mortgagee must independently verify the financial information. Mortgagors with surplus income and/or other assets are required to re-pay the indebtedness through the use of a repayment plan.

The mortgagee must analyze the mortgagor's ability to meet the monthly mortgage obligation by:

- Estimating the borrower's fixed monthly expenses (e.g., mortgage payment, food, utilities, car payment, outstanding obligations, etc.);
- Estimating the borrower's anticipated monthly net income (making necessary adjustments for income fluctuations); and
- Subtracting expenses from income to determine the amount of surplus income available each month.

If the mortgagee's evaluation indicates that the mortgagor is not eligible for a PFS or another loss mitigation option, the mortgagee must immediately advise the mortgagor of this decision in writing, explaining the reason for denial and giving the mortgagor at least seven calendar days to respond. In the servicing or claim review file, the mortgagee must maintain all evidence (i.e., supporting documentation, including all communication logs) of compliance with HUD's Loss Mitigation Program requirements.

E. Property Value

Properties offered for sale through the PFS Program are to be listed at no less than the "As Is" value as determined by an appraisal completed in accordance with the requirements of HUD Handbook 4150.2 (Valuation Analysis for Single Family One-to Four-Unit Dwellings). To this end, mortgagees must:

- Obtain a standard electronically-formatted appraisal from an appraiser on FHA's Appraiser Roster. The selected appraiser must not share any business interest with the mortgagor or the mortgagor's agent. Appraisals obtained by the buyer, seller, real estate agent, or other interested parties may not be used to establish the FMV of the property for the PFS Program. It also important to note that:
  1. The appraisal must contain an "as-is" FMV for the subject property;
  2. The appraisal will be valid for six months; and
  3. Distress sales may not be used by the appraiser to establish comparable values unless they represent the only comparables within reasonable proximity of the subject property.
- Provide a copy of the appraisal to the homeowner, sales agent, or HUD, upon request.
- Mortgagees are reminded that in accordance with HUD regulations at 24 CFR Part § 203.365 (c) they are responsible for the accuracy of all documentation used in the PFS decision, including accurate and complete appraisal information.

In an effort to ensure that the most current FMV is used for the PFS, a mortgagee may obtain a new FHA appraisal, even if the property was appraised by an FHA Roster Appraiser within the preceding 6 months.

To be reimbursed through HUD's claim filing process, the cost of the appraisal must be reasonable and customary for the market area where the appraisal is performed. The appraisal must be retained in the claim/servicing file, even if the PFS is not approved or completed.

F. Property Condition

Properties that have sustained damage may be eligible for the PFS option. If the cause of the damage is fire, flood, earthquake, tornado, boiler explosion (for condominium's only) or mortgagee neglect (i.e., surchargeable damages as defined in 24 CFR Part § 203.378) mortgagees must obtain prior approval from the NSC at the address above. Prior to seeking this approval, the mortgagee must obtain the government's estimate of the cost to repair the surchargeable damage by contacting the HUD Management and Marketing (M&M) Contractor with jurisdiction for the geographic area where the property is located. A list of M&M Contractors can be found on the Internet at: http://www.hud.gov/offices/hsg/sfh/reo/mm/mmingo.cfm.

Upon receipt of the government's repair estimate, the mortgagee must submit a Form HUD-90041 (*Request for Variance)* to the NSC to obtain the approval needed to enter into a PFS Agreement with the mortgagor.

In accordance with 24 CFR Part § 203.379 mortgagees are responsible for the cost of surchargeable property damage. If the property is being sold "As Is" subject to the damage, the mortgagee will be required to deduct the government's estimate of the cost of the damage from its PFS claim (See Appendix A—Claim Filing Instructions for Item 109).

If the property is being sold "As Repaired" and funds for surchargeable repairs will be escrowed or provided as a credit to the borrower at closing, the amount of the repair escrow or repair credit is not an allowable settlement cost as defined in Section J of this ML and may not be included in the net sales proceeds calculation.

If the damage is not surchargeable it is not necessary to obtain approval from NSC prior to approving the PFS Agreement. Regardless of the cause of the damage, the mortgagee must work with the mortgagor to file a hazard insurance claim and either use the proceeds to repair the property or adjust the claim by the amount of the insurance settlement (non-surchargeable damage) or the government's repair cost estimate.

Mortgagors are required to disclose any property damage to the mortgagee during the application or after the PFS approval. In the event a property sustains significant damage after a mortgagor has received approval to participate in the PFS program, the mortgagee must re-evaluate the property to determine if it continues to qualify for the PFS Program and terminate participation if the extent of the damage changes the property's FMV.

G. Condition of Title

All properties sold under the PFS Program must have marketable title. Prior to execution of Form HUD-90045 (*Approval to Participate)* the mortgagee must obtain a title search or preliminary report verifying that the title is not impaired with unresolvable title problems or with junior liens that cannot be discharged as permitted by HUD. If the mortgagee determines that these issues can be resolved, the mortgagor may be accepted into the PFS Program and resolution of said issues may be pursued while the property is being marketed.

Frequently, it is in the interest of all parties to facilitate the discharge of secondary liens in order to clear title. In some cases, junior lien holders will release a lien for a partial cash payment or a promissory note from the mortgagor. Mortgagors who have the financial ability to do so must be required to satisfy or obtain release of liens. Additionally, any incentive consideration payable to the mortgagor ($750 to $1,000) may be applied toward discharging liens.

If no other source of funds is available after applying the mortgagor's incentive amount, the mortgagee may obligate up to an additional $1,500—for a total of $2,500—from sale proceeds towards discharging liens or encumbrances to meet all required ratios.

- **Title I Liens**—If the first mortgagee discovers that a mortgagor has a HUD Title I (property improvement) loan secured by the property, the first mortgage holder must contact the Title I subordinate lien holder to advise of the mortgagor's participation in a PFS. The first mortgagee may be required to negotiate the release of the lien in order to proceed with a PFS.

  If the Title I loan has been assigned to HUD, the first mortgagee should contact HUD's Financial Operations Center for guidance. The Center's contact information is as follows:

  U.S. Department of Housing and Urban Development
  Financial Operations Center
  52 Corporate Circle
  Albany, New York 12203.
  1-800-669-5152/ fax (518) 862-2806

Section 235 Recapture—Mortgagors with Section 235 mortgages may be eligible to participate in the PFS Program. However, the mortgagee must first determine if the loan is subject to recapture as referenced in Chapter 11 of HUD Handbook 4330.1, Rev. 4 (*Administration of Insured Home Mortgages*). Generally, if the mortgagor has no equity in the property, there will be no recapture amount owed to HUD under the subsidy provisions of the 235 mortgage. If a recapture amount is owed to HUD after completing the calculation, the mortgagee should contact HUD's NSC prior to approving the PFS.

Partial Claim—The partial claim (unpaid subordinate mortgage) amount must be included in the total delinquency when calculations are made. Any outstanding balance on a partial claim note must be deducted from the net sale proceeds based on the tiered structure of 88%, 86% or the minimum of 84% of "as-is" appraised FMV.

H. Approval to Participate

After determining that a mortgagor and property meet the participation requirements herein, the mortgagee must notify the mortgagor using Form HUD-90045 (*Approval to Participate*). The form shall include the date by which the mortgagor's sales contract must be executed.

I. Participation Requirements

A mortgagor must acknowledge their decision to participate in the PFS program by signing and returning Form HUD-90045 (*Approval to Participate*) to the mortgagee within 7 days of receiving the form. The mortgagor's signature on Form HUD-90045 confirms their agreement to comply with the PFS Program requirements listed below. Mortgagees must monitor the PFS transaction in its entirety to ensure the mortgagors' compliance with these requirements and, should terminate a mortgagor's participation in the PFS Program in the event of noncompliance.

- **Use of Real Estate Broker**—The services of a real estate broker/agent must be retained to market a property within 7 days of the date the approval to participate is granted. The broker/agent must market the property within the pre-established time frame and list the property for the established sales price. The broker/agent selected should have no conflict of interest with the mortgagor, the mortgagee, the appraiser or the purchaser associated with the PFS transaction. Any conflict of interest, appearance of a conflict, or self-dealing by any of the parties to the transaction is strictly prohibited. A broker/agent shall never be permitted to claim a sales commission on a PFS of his or her own property or that of an immediate family member (e.g., spouse, sibling, parent, or child).
- **Pre-Existing Purchasers**—The requirement to engage a real estate professional does not apply if a mortgagor located a buyer for the property prior to being approved to participate in the PFS Program, providing all PFS requirements are met concerning appraisal requirements and minimum ratios for net sales proceeds.
- **Required Listing Disclosure**—The Listing Agreement must include the cancellation clause which reads as follows: "Seller may cancel this Agreement prior to the ending date of the listing period without advance notice to the Broker, and without payment of a commission or any other consideration if the property is conveyed to the mortgage insurer or the mortgage holder. The sale completion is subject to approval by the mortgagee."
- **Property Maintenance**—Until the PFS transaction has closed, the mortgagor must maintain the property in "ready to show" condition, make basic property repairs, and perform all normal property maintenance activities (e.g., interior cleaning, lawn maintenance, etc.).
- **Arms-Length Transaction**—Mortgagors and mortgagees must adhere to ethical standards of conduct in their dealings with all parties involved in a PFS transaction. The PFS must be between two unrelated parties and be characterized by a selling price and other conditions that would prevail in a typical real estate sales transaction.
- **Relocation Services**—A relocation service affiliated with the mortgagor's employer may contribute a fixed sum towards the proceeds of the PFS, without altering the arms- length nature of the sale. This contribution simply reduces the shortfall between the proceeds and the amount owed on the mortgage note. As with any other PFS, such a transaction must result in the outright sale of the property and cancellation of the FHA mortgage insurance.

J. Contract Approval

The mortgagee will have 5 working days from receipt of an executed Contract for Sale to respond back to the mortgagor using the Form HUD-90051 (*Sales Contract Review*). The PFS transaction must be an outright sale of the premises.

No sale by assumption, regardless of provisions for release of liability, may be considered. The contract must not include contingencies that might delay or jeopardize a timely settlement.

Before approving any sales contract, the mortgagee must review the sales documentation to determine that there are no hidden terms or special agreements existing between any of the parties involved in the transaction. Additionally, the mortgagee must determine if the property was marketed at the gross offering price (close to FMV) and the minimum net sales proceeds' requirements (described herein) have been met. The mortgagee will be liable for any insurance claim overpayment on a PFS transaction that closes with net sales proceeds less than the percentages indicated below.

- **Net Sale Proceeds**—Regardless of the property's sale price, a mortgagee may not approve a PFS contract if the net sale proceeds fall below the minimum allowable thresholds stated herein. HUD has established guidelines for varying minimum net sales proceeds based on the length of time a property has been competitively marketed for sale.
  1. For the first 30 days of marketing, mortgagees may only approve offers that will result in minimum net sale proceeds of 88% of the "as-is" appraised FMV.
  2. During the next 30 days of marketing, mortgagees may only approve offers that will result in minimum net sale proceeds of 86% of the "as-is" appraised FMV.
  3. For the duration of the PFS marketing period, mortgagees may only approve offers that will result in minimum net sale proceeds of 84% of the "as-is" appraised FMV.
  4. Mortgagees have the discretion to deny or delay sales where an offer may meet or exceed the 84%, if it is presumed that continued marketing would likely produce a higher sale amount. However, the mortgagee is still limited to 4 to 6 months after the date of the mortgagor's approval to participate in the PFS Program.

Allowable Settlement Costs—The term "Net Sale Proceeds" is defined as the sales price minus closing/settlement costs (i.e., reasonable and customary costs per jurisdiction that are deducted at settlement). Allowable settlement costs include:

1. Sales commission consistent with the prevailing rate but, not to exceed 6%;
2. Real estate taxes prorated to the date of closing;
3. Local/state transfer tax stamps and other closing costs customarily paid by the seller including the seller's costs for a title search and owner's title insurance;
4. Consideration payable to seller of $750 or $1,000 (i.e., if such consideration is not used to discharge junior liens);
5. Up to $2,500 to be used for the discharge of junior liens if closing occurs within 90 days. Within 90 days, the first $1,000 represents the mortgagor's consideration and the additional $1,500 represents FHA's consideration for a total of $2,500. If settlement occurs after 90 days, the first $750 represents the mortgagor's consideration and the additional $1,500 represents FHA's consideration for a total of $2,250;
6. Outstanding partial claim amount. This entire amount must be paid when calculating the net sales proceeds. The seller, buyer, or other interested party may contribute the difference if the net sales proceeds' amount falls below the allowable threshold; and
7. Up to 1% of the buyer's first mortgage amount if the sale includes FHA financing.

Unacceptable Settlement Costs—The following costs may not be included in the net sales proceeds calculation, however, the seller may use their consideration of $750 or $1,000 for these settlement costs.

1. Repair reimbursements or allowances;
2. Home Warranty fees;
3. Discount points or loan fees for non FHA-financing; and
4. Lender's Title Insurance fee.

K. Duration of the Pre-Foreclosure Sale Period

Unless an extension has been approved by NSC, mortgagees have 4 months from the date of the mortgagor's approval to participate in the PFS Program. Mortgagees have a pre-approved extension of 2 additional months to complete the PFS if one of the following exists:

- The mortgagee is in the Tier 1 category under the Department's Tier Ranking System (TRS); or
- There is a signed Contract of Sale, but settlement has not occurred by the end of the fourth month following the date of the mortgagor's approval to participate in the PFS Program.

Mortgagees are reminded that, on a monthly basis, they must review a property's marketing status with the mortgagor and/or real estate broker.

L. Property Inspections

Mortgagees have a responsibility to ensure that insured properties are not subject to abandonment or waste, and are required to conduct property inspections on the 45th day following default if there has been no contact with the mortgagor. Property preservation and protection (P&P) inspections are not required during the PFS period if contact with the mortgagor is maintained, unless there is reason to suspect that the property has become vacant. Inspections to verify occupancy are reimbursable using Part C of the Form HUD-27011 (*Single Family Application for Insurance Benefits*). However, funds expended for P&P work on an occupied property are not reimbursable.

M. Early Termination

A mortgagor may voluntarily terminate participation in the PFS Program at any time. PFS Program participation may also be terminated at the discretion of the mortgagee, for any of the following reasons:

- Un-resolvable title problems;
- Determination that the mortgagor is not acting in good faith to market the property;
- Significant change in property condition or value; and
- Re-evaluation of the information provided by the mortgagor indicates that the case does not qualify for the PFS option.

The mortgagee must forward the mortgagor a date-stamped written explanation for terminating his/her program participation. This letter shall also include the "end-of-participation" date for the mortgagor. The mortgagee must then resume appropriate servicing actions.

N. Failure to Complete a PFS

At the expiration of the PFS period, the mortgagee must re-evaluate available loss mitigation options. If the mortgagor's financial condition has improved to the point that reinstatement is a viable option, the mortgagee may undertake one of the home retention loss mitigation tools. If reinstatement is not feasible, the mortgagee should try to obtain a DIL of foreclosure before commencing foreclosure. An alternate loss mitigation option or first legal action to initiate foreclosure must be completed within 90 days of the expiration of the PFS period. If more than 90 days are needed to complete a DIL or initiate foreclosure or resume foreclosure, mortgagees must follow HUD's standard extension procedures and request an extension from the NSC.

O. Mortgagee Incentive

FHA will pay mortgagees an incentive fee of $1,000 for each completed PFS transaction that complies with all of the requirements in this ML. This fee may be claimed on line 129, Part B of Form HUD-27011.

P. Mortgagor Consideration

Mortgagors, acting in good faith, who successfully sell their properties using this option are relieved of their mortgage obligation and are entitled to a consideration of $750. If the closing occurs within 3 months of the approval to participate, the mortgagor will be entitled to $1,000. Unless the mortgagor's consideration is required to release junior liens, the mortgagor may elect to accept cash paid at closing. The mortgagor may also apply a portion of or the entire amount of consideration to offset sales costs not paid by HUD; including a home warranty plan fee, costs of optional repairs, and buyer's closing expenses. If the PFS is unsuccessful and foreclosure occurs, mortgagors who participate in the PFS Program in good faith will not be pursued for deficiency judgments by the mortgagee or HUD.

Q. Closing and Post Closing Responsibilities

Prior to closing, the mortgagee will provide the closing agent with a Form HUD-90052 (*Closing Worksheet*) which lists all amounts payable from sale proceeds. The closing agent will calculate the actual net sale proceeds and provide a copy of the Form HUD-1 (*Settlement Statement*) to the mortgagee. The mortgagee must review the actual terms of the transaction to ensure that they are in accordance with the earlier estimates prior to granting final approval of the PFS. The mortgagee is required to ensure that:

- The final terms of sale are consistent with the purchase contract;
- Only allowable settlement costs have been deducted from the seller's proceeds;
- The net sales proceeds will be equal to or greater than the allowable thresholds; and
- The Form HUD-90052 is included in the claim/servicing file.

Once the mortgagee gives final approval for the PFS and the settlement occurs, the closing agent must pay the expenses out of the proceeds, and must forward the net sales proceeds to the mortgagee. The closing agent must also forward a copy of the Form HUD-1 to the mortgagee to be included in the claim/servicing file.

A PFS must be reported to national credit bureaus as a "short sale". Mortgagees will be responsible for filing a Form 1099-A (*Acquisition or Abandonment of Secured Property*) with the Internal Revenue Service and reporting any discharge of indebtedness, in accordance with the Internal Revenue Code.

R. Claim Filing

HUD will reimburse the mortgagee for reasonable and customary costs of the appraisal, title search (if not included in the settlement statement), and the allowable percentage of legal fees for a postponed foreclosure, pending completion of the PFS.

Disbursements for taxes, assessments, hazard insurance and other allowable items payable before the date of the PFS closing are reimbursable only if they are not satisfied at closing. HUD will not pay property-related costs which were incurred after the PFS closing date.

HUD will monitor mortgagees by selecting and reviewing appraisals for risk assessment purposes. Electronic appraisals will be reviewed for accuracy and to ensure that FMVs were used in lieu of distressed sale values. HUD is now requiring mortgagees to enter the FMV in Block 30 on Part A of Form HUD-27011.

The consideration paid to the mortgagor and allowable amounts (i.e., which do not exceed $2,500) paid to release all junior liens must be reflected on the Form HUD-1 and must *not* be included on the Form HUD-27011. The mortgagee's incentive fee must be entered on line 129 of Part B of the Form HUD-27011.

Upon receipt of the portion of the sales proceeds designated for mortgage satisfaction, the mortgagee will satisfy the mortgage obligation and file a PFS claim for FHA insurance benefits via Form HUD-27011. The mortgagee must *not* submit an FHA insurance termination to the Department if a PFS claim will be filed.

If the mortgagee began the PFS process timely, then HUD will grant the mortgagee an automatic extension of 90 days after termination of the PFS to initiate another loss mitigation action or undertake the first legal action to institute foreclosure as described in Section "N" of this ML. To receive the extension, the ending date of the terminated or failed PFS transaction must be entered in Block 21 of Part A of the Form HUD-27011. A date that is no more than 90 days after the date listed in Block 21 must be entered in Block 19, to receive this extension. The claim for insurance benefits, (Parts A and B of Form HUD-27011), should be received by HUD within 30 days after the settlement date of the PFS transaction. If the sale proceeds have not been received from the closing agent, an extension must be requested from the NSC. The expiration date of the approved extension must be recorded in Block 20 on Part A of Form HUD-27011.

HUD will hold mortgagees, submitting excessive claims that do not meet the aforementioned required minimum allowable tiered-thresholds of 88%, 86%, or 84%, liable for excessive claim amounts. Claim filing instructions are located in Appendix A and these instructions supersede those found in Chapter 8 of HUD Handbook 4330.1 rev 1 (*FHA Single Family Claims*) For questions about filing a claim, please send an email to FHA_SFClaims@hud.gov. Mortgagees must include their Servicer Number, FHA Case Number, and a keyword phrase, such as "claim filing," "claims status," etc., in the e-mail subject line.

S. Reporting Requirements

Mortgagees are required to update HUD's Single Family Default Monitoring System (SFDMS) with 2 default status codes when utilizing the PFS Program. These codes are as follows:

- Status Code 15 to indicate that the mortgagor has been accepted into the PFS Program; and
- Status Code 17 to indicate that the PFS transaction has been completed.

Mortgagees must update SFDMS with Status Code 15 in the month that the mortgagor is approved to participate in the PFS Program. Mortgagees must continue to report the account under Status Code 15 during the entire time that the mortgagor is participating in the PFS Program. Once a PFS is complete (i.e., settlement has occurred and all funds have been received), mortgagees must report the account as Status Code 17 within 30 days of the PFS closing date. However, if no successful PFS transaction occurs and a DIL is obtained, the account should be reported as Status Code 47 in the month the DIL is *recorded*. Information on additional status codes along with instructions referring to bankruptcy, foreclosure, etc. are included in Mortgagee Letter 2006-15.

Mortgagees will be in compliance with HUD's reporting requirements when reporting codes are entered into the SFDMS within the above-prescribed timeframes. If reporting codes are not provided within the prescribed timeframes, the mortgagee will be subject to interest curtailment. Mortgagees are subject to interest curtailment if they do not initiate the PFS transaction or report the initiation of the PFS transaction to HUD via SFDMS timely.

T. Erroneous Termination of Mortgage Insurance

A mortgagee must not submit a Mortgage Insurance Termination in situations where the mortgagee has filed or intends to file a claim for FHA insurance benefits. HUD can only pay FHA mortgage insurance benefits when the mortgage insurance is in an "active" status. Mortgagees may direct questions or concerns regarding the Department's PFS procedures to the NSC's Customer Service Call Center. The center's toll free number is 1-888-297-8685.

Attachment:
Appendix A—Claim Instructions
Active Forms:
Form HUD-90035 *Information/Disclosure*
Form HUD-90041 *Request for Variance*
Form HUD-90045 *Approval to Participate. Property Sale Information/ Property Occupancy and Maintenance*
Form HUD-90051 *Sales Contract Review*
Form HUD-90052 *Closing Worksheet*
Form HUD-27011 *Single Family Application for Insurance Benefits*

[*These attachments are not reprinted herein. They are available on the website accompanying this treatise and at www.hud.gov/offices/adm/hudclips/letters/mortgagee/2008ml.cfm.*]

Department of Housing and Urban Development, Mortgagee Letter 2009-23 (July 30, 2009)

July 30, 2009

MORTGAGEE LETTER 2009-23

TO: ALL APPROVED MORTGAGEES

SUBJECT: Making Home Affordable Program: FHA's Home Affordable Modification Loss Mitigation Option

On May 20, 2009, the President signed the "Helping Families Save Their Homes Act of 2009." This new law provides the Federal Housing Administration (FHA) with additional loss mitigation authority to assist FHA mortgagors under the Making Home Affordable Program (MHA). The MHA Program is designed to help homeowners retain their homes and to prevent the destructive impact of foreclosures on families and communities.

One key component of MHA provides homeowners the opportunity to reduce their mortgage payments by the use of a loan modification through the Home Affordable Modification Program. When initially introduced to the public, MHA excluded FHA insured mortgages, stating that FHA would develop its own standalone program. This Mortgagee Letter announces a new FHA Loss Mitigation option, the FHA-Home Affordable Modification Program (FHA-HAMP). FHA-HAMP will provide homeowners in default a greater opportunity to reduce their mortgage payments to a sustainable level. This Mortgagee Letter is effective August 15, 2009.

Basic Program Guidelines

The new FHA-HAMP authority will allow the use of a partial claim up to 30 percent of the unpaid principal balance as of the date of default combined with a loan modification. The objective of FHA-HAMP is to assist FHA mortgagors who are in default to modify their mortgage to an affordable payment. According to Mortgagee Letter 2000-05 and subsequent guidance, disposition options (pre-foreclosure sales and deeds-in lieu of foreclosure) are available immediately upon default, if the cause of the default is incurable, i.e. the borrower has no realistic opportunity to replace the lost income or reduce expenses sufficiently to meet the mortgage obligation.

To confirm if the mortgagor is capable of making the new FHA-HAMP payment, the mortgagor must successfully complete a trial payment plan. The trial payment plan shall be for a three month period and the mortgagor must make each scheduled payment on time. The mortgagor's monthly payment required during the trial payment plan must be the amount of the future modified mortgage payment. The Mortgagee must service the mortgage during the trial period in the same manner as it would service a mortgage in forbearance. If the mortgagor does not successfully complete the trial payment plan by making the three payments on time, the mortgagor is no longer eligible for FHA-HAMP. Prior to proceeding to foreclosure, the Mortgagee must re-examine and re-evaluate the borrower's financial condition and confirm that none of FHA's other Loss Mitigation options could assist the mortgagor.

The attachment to this Mortgage Letter supplements program guidelines for FHA-HAMP, including a requirement that the servicer obtain an executed Hardship Affidavit (available at https://www.hmpadmin.com/portal/docs/hamp_borrower/hamphardshipaffidavit.pdf) from every mortgagor and co-mortgagor seeking an FHA-HAMP. FHA-HAMP is a permanent addition to HUD's Loss Mitigation Program as of the date of this Mortgagee Letter.

Debt to Income Ratios

To be eligible under FHA-HAMP, the front end debt to income ratio must be as close as possible, but not less than, 31 percent. This ratio is defined as the total monthly mortgage payment (PITI) for the modified mortgage divided by the mortgagor's gross monthly income (the "Front End Ratio"). The back end debt to income ratio must not exceed 55 percent and is defined as the total monthly mortgage payment plus all recurring monthly debt divided by the mortgagor's gross monthly income (the "Back End Ratio"). Please refer to the sections in the Attachment regarding Underwriting—Front End and Back End Debt to Income Ratios.

Calculation of Maximum Partial Claim Amount under FHA-HAMP

The maximum partial claim amount under FHA-HAMP consists of the sum of (i) arrearages, (ii) legal fees and foreclosure costs related to a canceled foreclosure action and (iii) principal reduction. Arrearages that may be included in the partial claim shall not exceed 12 months of PITI. The maximum partial claim amount under FHA-HAMP is 30 percent of the outstanding principal balance as of the date of default. The principal deferment on the modified mortgage is determined by multiplying the outstanding principal balance by 30 percent and then reducing that amount by arrearages advanced to cure the default for up to 12 months

PITI, and any foreclosure costs incurred to that point subject to the requirements provided in Mortgagee Letter 2008-21. The principal deferment amount for a specific case shall be limited to such an amount that will bring the mortgagor(s) total monthly mortgage payment to 31 percent of gross monthly income.

Example

Mortgagor had a reduction of income and is delinquent 3 full mortgage payments. The unpaid principal balance on the mortgage on the date of default is $150,000 and the monthly payment is $1,220 (consisting of P&I of $920 and escrows, including MIP, of $300). The financial analysis reveals that the mortgagor's gross monthly income is $3,500 and the total monthly other recurring debt payments are $800.

In order to fulfill the 31% Front End Ratio requirement, the mortgagor(s) total monthly mortgage payment would have to be reduced to $1,085 ($3,500 x 31%). Therefore, P&I would have to be reduced to $785 ($1,085 total monthly mortgage payment less $300 escrow and MIP). Assuming that the loan modification will have an interest rate of 6% and a P&I of $785, the new mortgage amount would have to be $130,931, resulting in a principal reduction of $19,069 ($150,000 unpaid principal balance less $130,931). In this example, the mortgagor's Back End ratio is 53.9% ($1,885/ $3,500), which satisfies the 55% Back End Ratio limitation.

In this example, the maximum principal deferment is $41,340 (30% of $150,000, less the $3,660 delinquency, or $45,000—$3,660). However, based on their gross income, mortgagor is eligible only for a principal deferment of $19,069 plus $3,660 arrearages (which would include any foreclosure costs incurred to that point, in accord with Mortgagee Letter 2008-21) for the total Partial Claim of $22,729.

Requirements to Use FHA-HAMP

FHA-HAMP can be utilized only if the mortgagor(s) does not qualify for current loss mitigation home retention options (priority order FHA Special Forbearance, Loan Modification and Partial Claim) under existing guidelines (ML 2008-21, 2003-19, 2002-17, 2000-05). To qualify for the FHA-HAMP program, Mortgagees must evaluate the defaulted mortgage for loss mitigation actions using the aforementioned priority order. According to Mortgagee Letter 2000-05 and subsequent guidance, disposition options (pre-foreclosure sales and deeds-in lieu of foreclosure) are available immediately upon default, if the cause of the default is incurable, i.e. the borrower has no realistic opportunity to replace the lost income or reduce expenses sufficiently to meet the mortgage obligation.

If the mortgagor does not successfully execute the loan modification, the mortgagor is no longer eligible for FHA-HAMP. In such cases, per 24 CFR 203.355, the Mortgagee must re-evaluate the mortgagor's eligibility for the other appropriate loss mitigation actions prior to commencing or continuing a foreclosure.

Mortgagee Incentives

Mortgagees that utilize FHA-HAMP are eligible to receive incentive payments. Mortgagees utilizing this initiative will be allowed to first file for a partial claim (to bring the loan current and defer principal where appropriate), followed by a loan modification claim (claim type 32). Under FHA-HAMP, the Mortgagee may receive an incentive fee of up to $1,250. This total includes $500 for the partial claim and $750 for the loan modification. Mortgagees may also claim up to $250 for reimbursement for a title search and/or recording fees.

Partial Claim Filing and Document Delivery

Mortgagees must file a claim for insurance benefits for the partial claim within the 60-day timeframe stated in ML 2003-19 to receive incentive fees for the FHA-HAMP loss mitigation action. Any previous outstanding partial claim(s) must be subordinated and the mortgage company must provide HUD's Secretary-Held servicing contractor (see 'Remittance' below) with a subordination agreement to request subordination.

Monitoring

FHA will monitor Mortgagees for compliance with the terms of this Mortgagee Letter and will take administrative actions, including sanctions and penalties, against all parties for non-compliance.

Remittance

Please note that all provisions described in the aforementioned existing guidelines, such as Repayment Terms, Option Failure and Disclosures apply also, except as specifically changed under FHA-HAMP.

Mortgagees must forward all required documentation, including subordination requests, and advise all parties to send any payments for the Partial Claims to HUD's Secretary-Held Assets Servicing Contractor which is currently located at:

C&L Service Corp. / Morris-Griffin Corp.
2488 East 81st Street, Suite 700
Tulsa, Oklahoma 74137
Toll Free Phone: (866) 377-8667
Toll Free Fax: (866) 249-0626
Local: (918) 551-5300
Local Fax: (918) 551-5399

Current information about the Secretary-Held Assets Servicing Contractor is located at:

http://www.hud.gov/offices/hsg/sfh/nsc/fmaddr.cfm

Information Collection Requirement

The information collection requirements contained in this document have been approved by the Office of Management and Budget (OMB) under the Paperwork Reduction Act of 1995 (44 U.S.C. 3501-3520) and assigned OMB control numbers 2502-0060, 2502-0523, 2502-0429, and 1505-0216. In accordance with the Paperwork Reduction Act, HUD may not conduct or sponsor, and a person is not required to respond to, a collection of information unless the collection displays a currently valid OMB Control Number.

Any questions regarding this Mortgagee Letter may be directed to HUD's National Servicing Center (NSC) at 888-297-8685 or hsg-lossmit@hud.gov. Persons with hearing or speech impairments may reach this number via TDD/TTY by calling 1-877-TDD-2HUD (1-877-833-2483).

Sincerely,

David H. Stevens
Assistant Secretary for Housing –
Federal Housing Commissioner

Attachment — Guidelines for FHA-HAMP

Guidance	FHA-Home Affordable Modification Program
Eligibility – Mortgagee	The Servicer of the modified FHA-HAMP mortgage must be FHA-Approved.
Eligibility – Mortgagors	The current mortgagor(s) on the existing FHA-insured single family mortgage must be identical to the mortgagor(s) on the HAMP mortgage, except as provided below. All changes in ownership due to death or divorce of the current owners must be supported by legal documentation. The existing FHA-insured mortgage is in default, but is not more than 12 full mortgage payments past due. A default is defined as 1 payment past due more than 30 days. For default calculation purposes, all months are determined to have 30 days. For example, a mortgage due for the July payment is in default on August 1st. The mortgagor(s) must be an owner occupant, have sufficient resources to make the payment on the HAMP mortgage and continue to occupy the home. A new mortgagor may be added to the HAMP mortgage, provided at least one existing mortgagor(s) is retained. The mortgagor must not have intentionally defaulted on their existing mortgage. (Note: Intentionally defaulted means the mortgagor had available funds that could pay their mortgage and other debts without hardship, but failed to pay).
Eligibility – Existing Mortgage	Must be a FHA-insured single family mortgage (1-4 units). Mortgages previously modified under HAMP are ineligible. There is no net present value (NPV) test for eligibility.
Eligibility – Maximum Mortgage Amounts	Not applicable.
Eligibility – Modified Mortgage	The existing FHA-insured mortgage must be re-amortized to a 30-year fixed rate mortgage, and must be modified in compliance with all FHA Mortgage Modification requirements, except those specifically modified under the FHA-HAMP program.
Property Eligibility	The property securing the FHA-insured property must be the mortgagor's primary and only residence; and only single family (1 to 4 unit) properties are eligible.
Interest Rate – Modified New Mortgage	The interest rate must be fixed and meet the guidelines in Mortgagee Letter 2008-21.
Current Loan to Value Requirements Mortgage	None.
Loan Purpose	FHA-HAMP mortgages are required to have a lower monthly principal and interest payment than the unmodified FHA-insured mortgage and are made without an appraisal. All existing subordinate financing must be subordinated to maintain the first lien priority of the HAMP mortgage. For more information, please see ML 2003-19.
Credit History	No minimum credit score required. (Credit report is only used to verify recurring debts.)
Seasoning Requirements on the Existing Mortgage	The first payment due date must be at least 12 months in the past, and at least 4 full mortgage payments must have been paid.
Property Valuation	No appraisal required.
Trial Modification	The Mortgagee must place the mortgagor(s) under a trial modification payment plan for the modified mortgage payment prior to completing the FHA-HAMP. The mortgagor(s) must have made the first three consecutive trial monthly mortgage payments on time before the FHA-HAMP can be completed, and a partial claim filed.
Documentation Requirements	The Mortgagee must obtain the following additional documentation: To be considered for any of the loss mitigation options, the mortgagor must provide detailed financial information to the Mortgagee. Every borrower and co-borrower must sign a hardship affidavit attesting to and describing the hardship. The document to be used is available for download at: https://www.hmpadmin.com/portal/docs/hamp_borrower/hamphardshipaffidavit.pdf The Department has no objection to situations where a cooperative mortgagor provides complete financial information either written or during a telephone interview. Regardless of how the mortgagor's financial information was secured, the Mortgagee must independently verify the financial information by obtaining a credit report (the credit report is not used for credit qualification but Mortgagees are to use for determining indebtedness), and any other forms of verification the Mortgagee deems appropriate.

Guidance	FHA-Home Affordable Modification Program
Underwriting Requirements - General	No Credit Alert Interactive Voice Response System (CAIVRS) review is required, but HUD's Limited Denial of Participation (LDP) and General Services Administration (GSA) exclusion lists are still required checks for all mortgagors. FHA-HAMP processing and underwriting instructions are described below. Where the mortgage is in default and no more than 12 full payments delinquent the Mortgagee combines a partial claim for up to 12 months of arrearages, foreclosure costs, and principal reduction with a modification. Except for the new maximum partial claim amount calculation, the partial claim must meet the requirements of Mortgagee Letters 2000-05, 2003-19 and 2008-21. The mortgagor may not be charged any additional costs for receiving this loss mitigation workout option. On a cancelled foreclosure, Mortgagees are reminded that all such costs must reflect work actually completed to the date of the foreclosure cancellation and the attorney fees may not be in excess of the fees that HUD has identified as customary and reasonable for claim purposes. The financial analysis, Hardship Affidavit, and documentation supporting the decision to provide partial claim relief must be maintained in the mortgagee's claim review file.
Loss Mitigation – Priority Order	FHA-HAMP can only be utilized if the mortgagor(s) does not qualify for current loss mitigation home retention options (FHA Special Forbearance, Loan Modification and Partial Claim) under existing guidelines (ML 2008-21, 2003-19, 2002-17, 2000-05). To qualify for the FHA-HAMP, Mortgagees must utilize its loss mitigation actions using the aforementioned priority order.
Underwriting – Monthly Gross Income	The mortgagor's Monthly Gross Income amount before any payroll deductions includes wages and salaries, overtime pay, commissions, fees, tips, bonuses, housing allowances, other compensation for personal services, Social Security payments, including Social Security received by adults on behalf of minors or by minors intended for their own support, annuities, insurance policies, retirement funds, pensions, disability or death benefits, unemployment benefits, rental income and other income.
Underwriting – Front End Debt to Income Ratio	Front-End ratio is the ratio of PITI to Monthly Gross Income. PITI is defined as principal, interest, taxes and insurance. The Front-End ratio must be as close as possible to, but not less than, 31%.
Underwriting – Back End Debt to Income Ratio	The Back-End ratio is the ratio of the mortgagor's total recurring monthly debts (such as Front-End PITI, payments on all installment debts, monthly payments on all junior liens, alimony, car lease payments, aggregate negative net rental income from all investment properties owned, and monthly mortgage payments for second homes) to the mortgagor's Monthly Gross Income. This ratio must not exceed 55%. The Mortgagee must validate monthly installment, revolving debt and secondary mortgage debt by pulling a credit report for each mortgagor or a joint report for a married couple. The Mortgagee must also consider information obtained from the mortgagor orally or in writing concerning incremental monthly obligations.
Underwriting – Subordinate Financing	Subordinate liens are not included in the Front-End ratio, but they are included in the Back-End ratio.
Underwriting – Upfront Mortgage Insurance Premium	Not applicable.
Underwriting – Annual Premium	Remains the same.
Underwriting – Calculation of Maximum Partial Claim Amount	The maximum one-time only principal reduction on the modification is determined by multiplying the outstanding principal balance of the existing mortgage as of the date of default by 30 percent reduced by (i) arrearage amounts advanced to cure the default for up to 12 months PITI and (ii) allowable foreclosure costs. However, the actual principal reduction amount for a specific case shall be limited to such amount that will bring the mortgagor(s) PITI to an amount not to exceed 31 percent of gross monthly income. Whether or not there are previous Partial Claims for a given case number, the arrearage component of this and any previous Partial Claims cannot exceed the equivalent of 12 months PITI and allowable foreclosure costs. This 12 month PITI maximum is NOT affected by any payments that may have been made to reduce the partial claim mortgage balance.
Partial Claim Guidelines	No interest will accrue on the partial claim. The payment of the partial claim is not due until (i) the maturity of the HAMP mortgage, (ii) a sale of the property, or (iii) a pay-off or refinancing of the HAMP mortgage.

Guidance	FHA-Home Affordable Modification Program
In Foreclosure Process	To ensure that a mortgagor currently in the process of foreclosure has the opportunity to apply, Mortgagees shall not proceed with the foreclosure sale until the mortgagor has been evaluated for the program and, if eligible, an offer to participate in the FHA-HAMP has been made. In the event that the mortgagor does not participate in FHA-HAMP, the Mortgagee must consider the priority order, outlined in "Requirements to Use FHA-HAMP" section of this Mortgagee Letter, prior to proceeding to foreclosure.
90 days Past Due	Ninety day past due mortgages must have been considered for all loss mitigation programs prior to being referred to foreclosure.
Escrows	Mortgagees are required to escrow for mortgagors' real estate taxes and mortgage-related insurance payments.
Unpaid Late Fees Waived	The Mortgagee will waive all late fees.
Credit Report	The Mortgagee will cover the cost of the credit report.
Mortgagee Incentives	Under FHA-HAMP, the Mortgagee may receive an incentive fee of up to $1,250. This total includes $500 for the partial claim and $750 for the loan modification. To receive the incentive payments, the Partial Claim and Loan Modification must meet the requirements of Mortgagee Letters 2008-21, 2003-19, 2002-17, 2000-05, and comply with instructions and requirements in this Mortgagee Letter and Attachment. Mortgagees may also claim up to $250 for reimbursement of title search and/or recording fees.
Mortgagor Cash Contribution	The Mortgagee may not require the mortgagor to contribute cash.
Disclosure	When promoting or describing FHA mortgage options Mortgagees should provide mortgagors with information designed to help them understand the mortgage terms that are being offered. Mortgagees also must provide mortgagors with clear and understandable written information about the terms, costs, and risks of the mortgage in a timely manner to enable mortgagors to make informed decisions. FHA requires Mortgagees to comply with any disclosure or notice requirements applicable under FHA regulations and state or federal law.
Fair Lending	Mortgagees under this program must comply with the Equal Credit Opportunity Act and the Fair Housing Act, which prohibit discrimination on a prohibited basis in connection with mortgage transactions. FHA mortgage programs are subject to the fair lending laws, and Mortgagees should ensure that they do not treat a mortgagor less favorably than other mortgagors on grounds such as race, religion, national origin, sex, marital or familial status (i.e., families with children under age 18 and pregnant women), age, disability, or receipt of public assistance income in connection with any loan modification. These laws also prohibit redlining.
Consumer Inquiries and Complaints	Mortgagees should have procedures and systems in place to be able to respond to inquiries and complaints relating to loan modifications. Mortgagees should ensure that such inquiries and complaints are provided fair consideration, and timely and appropriate responses and resolution.
Case/Mortgage Documentation	Mortgagees will be required to maintain records of key data points for verification/compliance reviews, in accordance with Handbook 4000.2 Rev-3, Paragraph 5-8and Handbook 4155.2, Paragraph 8.B.7.c. Servicing files must be retained for a minimum of the life of the mortgage plus three years, per Handbook 4330.1 Rev-5, paragraph 1-3 E. These documents may include, but are not limited to, mortgagor eligibility, Hardship Affidavit, and qualification and underwriting. Mortgagors will be required to provide declarations under penalty of perjury attesting to the truth of the information that they have provided to the Mortgagee to allow the Mortgagee to determine the mortgagor's eligibility for entry into the FHA–HAMP program.
Anti-Fraud Measures	Measures to prevent and detect fraud, such as documentation and audit requirements are described in Handbook 4060.1, Rev-2. Participating Mortgagees and Mortgagees/investors are not required to modify the mortgage if there is reasonable evidence indicating the mortgagor submitted false or misleading information or otherwise engaged in fraud in connection with the modification. Mortgagees should employ reasonable policies and/or procedures to identify fraud in the modification process.
Data Collection	Mortgagees will continue to be required to collect and transmit mortgagor and property data in order to ensure compliance with the program as well as to measure its effectiveness. Data elements may include data needed to perform underwriting analysis and mortgage terms, and loan level data in order to establish loans for processing during the trial period, to record modification details, and monthly loan activity reports.

Department of Housing and Urban Development, Mortgagee Letter 2009-32 (September 18, 2009)

September 18, 2009

MORTGAGEE LETTER 2009-32

TO: ALL APPROVED MORTGAGEES

SUBJECT: Revised Streamline Refinance Transactions

This Mortgagee Letter provides (1) revised procedures; and (2) reaffirms existing procedures regarding Streamline Refinance transactions. This Mortgagee Letter is effective for new case numbers assigned on or after 60 days from the date of this letter.

Key Revisions:

- Seasoning
- Payment history
- Net tangible benefit for the borrower
- Maximum Combined Loan-to-Value
- New Maximum Mortgage Amount for Streamline Refinances WITHOUT an Appraisal
- Discounts Points no longer included in Existing Debt for Streamline Refinances WITH an Appraisal
- Verification of any assets needed to close
- Certification that borrower is employed and has income
- Elimination of abbreviated Uniform Residential Loan Application (URLA)

I. Revisions for ALL Streamline Refinance Transactions

A. Seasoning

At the time of loan application, the borrower must have made at least 6 payments on the FHA-insured mortgage being refinanced.

B. Payment History

At the time of loan application, the borrower must exhibit an acceptable payment history as described below.

1) For mortgages with less than a 12 months payment history, the borrower must have made all mortgage payments within the month due.

2) For mortgages with a 12 months payment history or greater, the borrower must have:

   a) Experienced no more than *one* 30 day late payment in the preceding 12 months,

   AND

   b) Made all mortgage payments within the month due for the three months prior to the date of loan application.

C. Net Tangible Benefit

The lender must determine that there is a net tangible benefit as a result of the streamline refinance transaction, with or without an appraisal. Net tangible benefit is defined as:

- reduction in the *total* mortgage payment (principal, interest, taxes and insurances, homeowners' association fees, ground rents, special assessments and all subordinate liens),
- refinancing from an adjustable rate mortgage (ARM) to a fixed rate mortgage,

OR

- reducing the term of the mortgage.

Reduction in Total Mortgage Payment: The new total mortgage payment is 5 percent *lower* than the total mortgage payment for the mortgage being refinanced. Example: Total mortgage payment on the existing FHA-insured mortgage is $895; the total mortgage payment for the new FHA-insured mortgage must be $850 or less.

This requirement is applicable when refinancing from a Fixed Rate to Fixed Rate, from an ARM to ARM, from a Graduated Payment Mortgage (GPM) to Fixed Rate, from GPM to ARM, from a 203(k) to 203(b) and from a 235 to 203(b).

Fixed Rate to ARM: Fixed rate mortgages may be refinanced to a one-year ARM provided that the interest rate on the new mortgage is at least 2 percentage points below the interest rate of the current mortgage

ARM to Fixed Rate: The interest rate on the new fixed rate mortgage will be no greater than 2 percentage points above the current rate of the one-year ARM. For hybrid ARMs, the total mortgage payment on the new fixed rate mortgage may not increase by more than 20 percent . Example: total mortgage payment on the hybrid ARM is $895; the total mortgage payment for the new fixed rate mortgage must be $1,074 or less.

Reduction in Term: For transactions that include a reduction in the mortgage term, that loan must be underwritten and closed as a rate and term (no cash-out) refinance transaction.

Investment Properties/Secondary Residences: In addition to meeting the requirement for a reduction in the total mortgage payment, investment properties or secondary residences are *not* eligible for streamline refinancing to ARMs.

D. Certifications and Verifications

When submitting the loan for insurance endorsement, the lender must include a signed and dated cover letter on their letterhead certifying[1] that the borrower is employed and has income at the time of loan application.

If assets are needed to close, the lender must verify and document those assets.

The lenders must also include the pay-off statement in the case binder.

E. Credit Score

If a credit score is available, the lender must enter the credit score into FHA Connection. If more than one credit score is available, lenders must enter all available credit scores.

F. Maximum Combined Loan to Value

If subordinate financing is remaining in place, the maximum combined loan-to-value ratio is 125 percent.

---

1 Title 18 U.S.C. 1014, provides in part that whoever knowingly and willfully makes or uses a document containing any false, fictitious, or fraudulent statement or entry, in any matter in the jurisdiction of any department or agency of the United States, shall be fined not more than $1,000,000 or imprisoned for not more than 30 years or both. In addition, violation of this or others may result in debarment and civil liability for damages suffered by the Department.

- For streamline refinance transactions WITHOUT an appraisal, the CLTV is based on the original appraised value of the property.
- For streamline refinance transactions WITH an appraisal, the CLTV is based on the new appraised value.

G. TOTAL Scorecard

Lenders should not use TOTAL on streamline refinance transactions. If a lender uses TOTAL, that loan must be underwritten and closed as a rate and term (no cash-out) refinance transaction.

H. Uniform Residential Loan Application (URLA)

Mortgagees may no longer use an abbreviated version of the URLA. Due to various disclosure requirements and our longstanding belief that borrowers are best served when certifications they must make are divulged as early as possible in the loan application process, the application for mortgage insurance must be signed and dated by the borrower(s) before the loan is underwritten. Mortgagees are permitted to process and underwrite the loan after the borrowers and interviewer complete the initial URLA and initial form HUD-92900A, HUD/VA Addendume to Uniform Residential Loan Application.

II. <u>Revised Streamline Refinance Transactions WITHOUT an Appraisal</u>

The maximum insurable mortgage cannot exceed:

- The outstanding principal balance[2]

minus the applicable refund of the UFMIP,
PLUS

- The new UFMIP that will be charged on the refinance.

III. <u>Revised Streamline Transaction WITH an Appraisal</u>

The maximum insurable mortgage is the *lower* of:

1) Outstanding principal balance2 *minus* the applicable refund of UFMIP, plus closing costs, prepaid items to establish the escrow account and the new UFMIP that will be charge on the refinance;

OR

2) 97.75 percent of the appraised value of the property plus the new UFMIP that will be charged on the refinance.

Discount points may not be included in the new mortgage. If the borrower has agreed to pay discount points, the lender must verify the borrower has the assets to pay them along with any other financing costs that are not included in the new mortgage amount.

IV. <u>Unchanged Streamline Refinance Transactions</u>

The following on streamline refinance transactions remains unchanged.

• Maximum mortgage limits and maximum mortgage term	4155.1 3.C.2.a and b
• Streamline Refinances for investors/ secondary residences	4155.1 3.C.2.d and e
• Cash back at closing	4155.1 6.C.1.a
• Permissible geographic areas	4155.1 6.C.1.b
• Appraisals	4155.1 6.C.1.c and d
• HUD LDP and GSA exclusion lists	4155.1 6.C.1.e
• Credit Reports	4155.1 6.C.1.f
• Credit Qualifying [except maximum insurable mortgage]	4155.1 6.C.2
• Holding period for assumed loans	4155.1 6.C.3.b
• Adding/Deleting Borrowers	4155.1 6.C.3.d
• Withdrawn Condominium Approval	4155.1 6.C.3.e
• Seven Unit Limitation	4155.1 6.C.3.f
• No Cost Refinances	4155.1 6.C.4.a
• 203(k) to 203(b) [completion of rehabilitation]	4155.1 6.C.4.i
• 235 to 203(b) [overpaid subsidy and junior liens]	4155.1 6.C.4.j

2 The outstanding principal balance may include interest charged by the servicing lender when the payoff is not received on the first day of the month but may not include delinquent interest, late charges or escrow shortages.

If you have any questions regarding this Mortgagee Letter, please contact the FHA Resource Center at 1-800-CALL-FHA (1-800-225-5342). Persons with hearing or speech impairments may access this number via TTD/TTY by calling 1-877-TDD-2HUD (1-877-833-2483).

Sincerely,

David H. Stevens
Assistant Secretary for Housing-
Federal Housing Commissioner

Paperwork Reduction Act

Paperwork reduction information collection requirements contained in this document have been approved by the Office of Management and Budget (OMB) under the Paperwork Reduction Act of 1995 (44 U.S.C. 3501-3520) and assigned OMB control number 2502-0059. In accordance with the Paperwork Reduction Act, HUD may not conduct or sponsor, and a person is not required to respond to, a collection of information unless the collection displays a currently valid OMB Control Number.

Department of Housing and Urban Development, Mortgagee Letter 2009-35 (September 23, 2009)

September 23, 2009

MORTGAGEE LETTER 2009-35

TO: ALL APPROVED MORTGAGEES

SUBJECT: Loan Modifications: FHA Loss Mitigation Incentives—Update

The purpose of this Mortgagee Letter is to update the conditions under which FHA will pay loss mitigation claims for modifications of loans where the current note rate is 50 basis points or more over the current market rate as defined herein. To qualify for the incentive payment and allowable costs on such cases, the modified loan must meet the term and interest rate requirements prescribed in this Mortgagee Letter. These requirements are effective thirty days from the date of this letter.

<u>Background</u>

The recent economic slow-down has increased demand for loss mitigation actions, including but not limited to, loan modifications. Recent industry studies of these loan modifications revealed that borrowers who experienced an increased mortgage payment on a modified loan had a significantly higher re-default rate than borrowers whose loan modification provided a lower payment.

FHA reviewed its recent insured loan modifications and found that, generally, they resulted in higher payments to the borrower. The higher payment was the result of not lowering the interest rate to the current market rate and/or not extending the term to the maximum of thirty years authorized under 24 CFR 203.616. Generally, the loan modifications simply capitalized the past due amounts and allowable charges and did not extend the term of the loan.

Consequently, FHA is updating its term and interest rate requirements for loan modifications to provide for a reduction in the mortgage payment whenever possible and help more mortgagors avoid re-default, (and potential foreclosure). Mortgagees are cautioned that Loan Modifications not meeting FHA's requirements will not be considered as valid loss mitigation actions. Therefore, the workout ratios that the Department uses in determining Tier Ranking Scores will exclude those Loan Modifications not in compliance.

Mortgagee Incentives for Loan Modifications

This Mortgagee Letter clarifies and updates the guidance provided in Mortgagee Letter 2000-05, Loan Modification, section F, Allowable Provisions (pages 21 and 22), and Mortgagee Letter 2008-21, Page 1, and Mortgagee Letter 2009-23, Page 1, with respect to interest rate and term requirements for loan modifications that are eligible for payment of a mortgagee incentive and costs for a title search and/or recording fees on the Loan Modification.

Interest rate and term requirements

In cases where the current note rate is 50 basis points or more over the current market rate:

- The Mortgagee shall reduce the loan modification note rate to the current Market Rate. For purposes of this requirement, the Department shall consider Market Rate to be no more than **50 basis points** greater than the most recent Freddie Mac Weekly Primary Mortgage Market Survey Rate for 30-year fixed-rate conforming mortgages (US average), rounded to the nearest one-eighth of one percent (0.125%), as of the date the Modification Agreement is executed. The weekly survey results are published on the Freddie Mac website at www.freddiemac.com/pmms/ and the Federal Reserve Board includes the average 30-year survey rate in the list of Selected Interest Rates that it publishes weekly in its Statistical Release H.15 at http://www.federalreserve.gov/releases/h15/.
- The Mortgagee must re-amortize the total unpaid amount due over a 360 month period from the due date of the first installment required under the modified mortgage.

Example

The Mortgagee approves a Loan Modification that is executed by the borrower 35 days after the date of this Mortgagee Letter. The current note rate is 7 percent and the most recent Freddie Mac Weekly Primary Mortgage Market Survey Rate for 30-year fixed rate conforming mortgages (US average) as of the Modification date is 5.04 percent. To be eligible for payment of a mortgagee incentive and costs for a title search and/or recording fees on the Loan Modification, the fixed note rate on the modified loan may not exceed 5.50 percent (The Freddie Mac US average rate of 5.04 percent rounded to the nearest eight of a percent plus 50 basis points). The modified mortgage must also re-amortize the total unpaid amount over a 360 month period from the due date of the first installment required under the modified mortgage.

FHA holds servicers accountable for their servicing practices in order to protect the public trust and the FHA Insurance Fund. When a servicer fails to comply with FHA's policies and procedures, FHA will take appropriate action. Servicers that violate FHA program statutes, regulations, handbook requirements and mortgagee letters may be subject to numerous actions including: the repayment of loss mitigation incentives, indemnification, and referral to HUD's Mortgagee Review Board for appropriate sanctions.

Information Collection Requirement

The information collection requirements contained in this document have been approved by the Office of Management and Budget (OMB) under the Paperwork Reduction Act of 1995 (44 U.S.C. 3501-3520) and assigned OMB control numbers 2502-0060, 2502-0523, and 2502-0429. In accordance with the Paperwork Reduction Act, HUD may not conduct or sponsor, and a person is not required to respond to, a collection of information unless the collection displays a currently valid OMB Control Number.

Any questions regarding this Mortgagee Letter may be directed to HUD's National Servicing Center at (888) 297-8685 or hsg-lossmit@hud.gov. Persons with hearing or speech impairments may access this number via TDD/TTY by calling 1-877-TDD-2HUD (1-877-833-2483).

Sincerely,

David H. Stevens
Assistant Secretary for Housing –
Federal Housing Commissioner

A.3 Loans Guaranteed by the Department of Veterans Affairs

A.3.1 Selected Statutes

TITLE 38. VETERANS' BENEFITS

PART III—READJUSTMENT AND RELATED BENEFITS

CHAPTER 37—HOUSING AND SMALL BUSINESS LOANS

SUBCHAPTER II—LOANS

38 U.S.C. § 3710. Purchase or construction of homes

(a) Except as provided in section 3704(c)(2) of this title, any loan to a veteran, if made pursuant to the provisions of this chapter, is automatically guaranteed if such loan is for one or more of the following purposes:

(1) To purchase or construct a dwelling to be owned and occupied by the veteran as a home.

(2) To purchase a farm on which there is a farm residence to be owned and occupied by the veteran as the veteran's home.

(3) To construct on land owned by the veteran a farm residence to be occupied by the veteran as the veteran's home.

(4) To repair, alter, or improve a farm residence or other dwelling owned by the veteran and occupied by the veteran as the veteran's home.

(5) To refinance existing mortgage loans or other liens which are secured of record on a dwelling or farm residence owned and occupied by the veteran as the veteran's home.

(6) To purchase a one-family residential unit in a condominium housing development or project, if such development or project is approved by the Secretary under criteria which the Secretary shall prescribe in regulations.

(7) To improve a dwelling or farm residence owned by the veteran and occupied by the veteran as the veteran's home through energy efficiency improvements, as provided in subsection (d).

(8) To refinance in accordance with subsection (e) of this section an existing loan guaranteed, insured, or made under this chapter.

(9)(A)(i) To purchase a manufactured home to be permanently affixed to a lot that is owned by the veteran.

(ii) To purchase a manufactured home and a lot to which the home will be permanently affixed.

(B)(i) To refinance, in accordance with the terms and conditions applicable under the provisions of subsection (e) of this section (other than paragraph (1)(E) of such subsection) to the guaranty of a loan for the purpose specified in clause (8) of this subsection, an existing loan guaranteed, insured, or made under this chapter that is secured by a manufactured home permanently affixed to a lot that is owned by the veteran.

(ii) To refinance, in accordance with section 3712(a)(5) of this title, an existing loan that was made for the purchase of, and that is secured by, a manufactured home that is permanently affixed to a lot and to purchase the lot to which the manufactured home is affixed.

(10) To purchase a dwelling to be owned and occupied by the veteran as a home and make energy efficiency improvements, as provided in subsection (d).

(11) To refinance in accordance with subsection (e) an existing loan guaranteed, insured, or made under this chapter, and to improve the dwelling securing such loan through energy efficiency improvements, as provided in subsection (d).

(12) With respect to a loan guaranteed after the date of the enactment of this paragraph and before the date that is five years after that date, to purchase stock or membership in a cooperative housing corporation for the purpose of entitling the veteran to occupy for dwelling purposes a single family residential unit in a development, project, or structure owned or leased by such corporation, in accordance with subsection (h).

If there is an indebtedness which is secured by a lien against land owned by the veteran, the proceeds of a loan guaranteed under this section or made under section 3711 of this title for construction of a dwelling or farm residence on such land may be used also to liquidate such lien, but only if the reasonable value of the land is equal to or greater than the amount of the lien.

(b) No loan may be guaranteed under this section or made under section 3711 of this title unless—

(1) the proceeds of such loan will be used to pay for the property purchased, constructed, or improved;

(2) the contemplated terms of payment required in any mortgage to be given in part payment of the purchase price or the construction cost bear a proper relation to the veteran's present and anticipated income and expenses;

(3) the veteran is a satisfactory credit risk, as determined in accordance with the credit underwriting standards established pursuant to subsection (g) of this section;

(4) the nature and condition of the property is such as to be suitable for dwelling purposes;

(5) except in the case of a loan described in clause (7) or (8) of this subsection, the loan to be paid by the veteran for such property or for the cost of construction, repairs, or alterations, does not exceed the reasonable value thereof as determined pursuant to section 3731 of this title;

(6) if the loan is for repair, alteration, or improvement of property, such repair, alteration, or improvement substantially protects or improves the basic livability or utility of such property;

(7) in the case of a loan (other than a loan made for a purpose specified in subsection (a)(8) of this section) that is made to refinance—

(A) a construction loan,

(B) an installment land sales contract, or

(C) a loan assumed by the veteran that provides for a lower interest rate than the loan being refinanced,

the amount of the loan to be guaranteed or made does not exceed the lesser of—

(i) the reasonable value of the dwelling or farm residence securing the loan, as determined pursuant to section 3731 of this title; or

(ii) the sum of the outstanding balance on the loan to be refinanced and the closing costs (including discounts) actually paid by the veteran, as specified by the Secretary in regulations; and

(8) in the case of a loan to refinance a loan (other than a loan or installment sales contract described in clause (7) of this subsection or a loan made for a purpose specified in subsection (a)(8) of this section), the amount of the loan to be guaranteed or made does not exceed 100 percent of the reasonable value of the dwelling or farm residence securing the loan, as determined pursuant to section 3731 of this title.

(c) [Repealed.]

(d)(1) The Secretary shall carry out a program to demonstrate the feasibility of guaranteeing loans for the acquisition of an existing dwelling and the cost of making energy efficiency improvements to the dwelling or for energy efficiency improvements to a dwelling owned and occupied by a veteran. A loan may be guaranteed under this subsection only if it meets the requirements of this chapter, except as those requirements are modified by this subsection.

(2) The cost of energy efficiency measures that may be financed by a loan guaranteed under this section may not exceed the greater of—

(A) the cost of the energy efficiency improvements, up to $3,000; or

(B) $6,000, if the increase in the monthly payment for principal and interest does not exceed the likely reduction in monthly utility costs resulting from the energy efficiency improvements.

(3) Notwithstanding the provisions of section 3703(a)(1)(A) of this title, any loan guaranteed under this subsection shall be guaranteed in an amount equal to the sum of—

(A) the guaranty that would be provided under those provisions for the dwelling without the energy efficiency improvements; and

(B) an amount that bears the same relation to the cost of the energy efficiency improvements as the guaranty referred to in subparagraph (A) bears to the amount of the loan minus the cost of such improvements.

(4) The amount of the veteran's entitlement, calculated in accordance with section 3703(a)(1)(B) of this title, shall not be affected by the amount of the guaranty referred to in paragraph (3)(B).

(5) The Secretary shall take appropriate actions to notify eligible veterans, participating lenders, and interested realtors of the availability of loan guarantees under this subsection and the procedures and requirements that apply to the obtaining of such guarantees.

(6) For the purposes of this subsection:

(A) The term "energy efficiency improvement" includes a solar heating system, a solar heating and cooling system, or a combined solar heating and cooling system, and the application of a residential energy conservation measure.

(B) The term "solar heating" has the meaning given such term in section 3(1) of the Solar Heating and Cooling Demonstration Act of 1974 (42 U.S.C. 5502(1)) and, in addition, includes a passive system based on conductive, convective, or radiant energy transfer.

(C) The terms "solar heating and cooling" and "combined solar heating and cooling" have the meaning given such terms in section 3(2) of the Solar Heating and Cooling Demonstration Act of 1974 (42 U.S.C. 5502(2)) and, in addition, include a passive system based on conductive, convective, or radiant energy transfer.

(D) The term "passive system" includes window and skylight glazing, thermal floors, walls, and roofs, movable insulation panels (when in conjunction with glazing), portions of a residential structure that serve as solar furnaces so as to add heat to the structure, double-pane window insulation, and such other energy-related components as are determined by the Secretary to enhance the natural transfer of energy for the purpose of heating or heating and cooling a residence.

(E) The term "residential energy conservation measure" means—

(i) caulking and weatherstripping of all exterior doors and windows;

(ii) furnace efficiency modifications limited to—

(I) replacement burners, boilers, or furnaces designed to reduce the firing rate or to achieve a reduction in the amount of fuel consumed as a result of increased combustion efficiency,

(II) devices for modifying flue openings which will increase the efficiency of the heating system, and

(III) electrical or mechanical furnace ignition systems which replace standing gas pilot lights;

(iii) clock thermostats;

(iv) ceiling, attic, wall, and floor insulation;

(v) water heater insulation;

(vi) storm windows and doors;

(vii) heat pumps; and

(viii) such other energy conservation measures as the Secretary may identify for the purposes of this subparagraph.

(e)(1) For a loan to be guaranteed for the purpose specified in subsection (a)(8) or for the purpose specified in subsection (a)(11) of this section—

(A) the interest rate of the loan must be less than the interest rate of the loan being refinanced or, in a case in which the loan is a fixed rate loan and the loan being refinanced is an adjustable rate loan, the loan bears interest at a rate that is agreed upon by the veteran and the mortgagee;

(B) the loan must be secured by the same dwelling or farm residence as was the loan being refinanced;

(C) the amount of the loan may not exceed—

(i) an amount equal to the sum of the balance of the loan being refinanced and such closing costs (including any discount permitted pursuant to section 3703(c)(3)(A) of this title) as may be authorized by the Secretary (under regulations which the Secretary shall prescribe) to be included in the loan; or

(ii) in the case of a loan for the purpose specified in subsection (a)(11), an amount equal to the sum of the amount referred to with respect to the loan under clause (i) and the amount specified under subsection (d)(2);

(D) notwithstanding section 3703(a)(1) of this title, the amount of the guaranty of the loan may not exceed the greater of (i) the original guaranty amount of the loan being refinanced, or (ii) 25 percent of the loan;

(E) the term of the loan may not exceed the original term of the loan being refinanced by more than 10 years; and

(F) the veteran must own the dwelling or farm residence securing the loan and—

(i) must occupy such dwelling or residence as such veteran's home;

(ii) must have previously occupied such dwelling or residence as such veteran's home and must certify, in such form as the Secretary shall require, that the veteran has previously so occupied such dwelling or residence; or

(iii) in any case in which a veteran is in active duty status as a member of the Armed Forces and is unable to occupy such residence or dwelling as a home because of such status, the spouse of the veteran must occupy, or must have previously occupied, such dwelling or residence as such spouse's home and must certify such occupancy in such form as the Secretary shall require.

(2) A loan to a veteran may be guaranteed by the Secretary under this chapter for the purpose specified in clause (8) of subsection (a) of this section without regard to the amount of outstanding guaranty entitlement available for use by such veteran, and the amount of such veteran's guaranty entitlement shall not be charged as a result of any guaranty provided for such purpose. For purposes of section 3702(b) of this title, such loan shall be deemed to have been obtained with the guaranty entitlement used to obtain the loan being refinanced.

(3) If a veteran is deceased and if such veteran's surviving spouse was a co-obligor under an existing loan guaranteed, insured, or made under this chapter, such surviving spouse shall, only for the purpose specified in subsection (a)(8) of this section, be deemed to be a veteran eligible for benefits under this chapter.

(f)(1) For a loan to be guaranteed for the purpose specified in subclause (A)(ii) or (B)(ii) of subsection (a)(9) of this section, the purchase of (or the refinancing of a loan secured by) the manufactured home and the lot for that home shall be considered as one loan and must comply with such criteria as may be prescribed by the Secretary in regulations.

(2) A loan may not be guaranteed for the purposes of subsection (a)(9) of this section unless the manufactured home purchased, upon being permanently affixed to the lot, is considered to be real property under the laws of the State where the lot is located.

(g)(1) For the purposes of this subsection, the term "veteran," when used with respect to a loan guaranteed or to be guaranteed under this chapter, includes the veteran's spouse if the spouse is jointly liable with the veteran under the loan.

(2) For the purpose of determining whether a veteran meets the standards referred to in subsection (b)(3) of this section and section 3712(e)(2) of this title, the Secretary shall prescribe regulations which establish—

(A) credit underwriting standards to be used in evaluating loans to be guaranteed under this chapter; and

(B) standards to be used by lenders in obtaining credit information and processing loans to be guaranteed under this chapter.

(3) In the regulations prescribed under paragraph (2) of this subsection, the Secretary shall establish standards that include—

(A) debt-to-income ratios to apply in the case of the veteran applying for the loan;

(B) criteria for evaluating the reliability and stability of the income of the veteran applying for the loan; and

(C) procedures for ascertaining the monthly income required by the veteran to meet the anticipated loan payment terms.

If the procedures described in clause (C) of this paragraph include standards for evaluating residual income, the Secretary shall, in establishing such standards, give appropriate consideration to State statistics (in States as to which the Secretary determines that such statistics are reliable) pertinent to residual income and the cost of living in the State in question rather than in a larger region.

(4)(A) Any lender making a loan under this chapter shall certify, in such form as the Secretary shall prescribe, that the lender has complied with the credit information and loan processing standards established under paragraph (2)(B) of this subsection, and that, to the best of the lender's knowledge and belief, the loan meets the underwriting standards established under paragraph (2)(A) of this subsection.

(B) Any lender who knowingly and willfully makes a false certification under subparagraph (A) of this paragraph shall be liable to the United States Government for a civil penalty equal to two times the amount of the Secretary's loss on the loan involved or to another appropriate amount, not to exceed $10,000, whichever is greater. All determinations necessary to carry out this subparagraph shall be made by the Secretary.

(5) Pursuant to regulations prescribed to carry out this paragraph, the Secretary may, in extraordinary situations, waive the application of the credit underwriting standards established under paragraph (2) of this subsection when the Secretary determines, considering the totality of circumstances, that the veteran is a satisfactory credit risk.

(h)(1) A loan may not be guaranteed under subsection (a)(12) unless—

(A) the development, project, or structure of the cooperative housing corporation complies with such criteria as the Secretary prescribes in regulations; and

(B) the dwelling unit that the purchase of stock or membership in the development, project, or structure of the cooperative housing corporation entitles the purchaser to occupy is a single family residential unit.

(2) In this subsection, the term "cooperative housing corporation" has the meaning given such term in section 216(b)(1) of the Internal Revenue Code of 1986.

(3) When applying the term "value of the property" to a loan guaranteed under subsection (a)(12), such term means the appraised value of the stock or membership entitling the purchaser to the permanent occupancy of the dwelling unit in the development, project, or structure of the cooperative housing corporation.

[Pub. L. No. 85-857, 72 Stat. 1207, § 1810 (Sept. 2, 1958); Pub. L. No. 90-301, §§ 1(a), 2(a), 82 Stat. 113 (May 7, 1968); Pub. L. No. 91-506, § 3, 84 Stat. 1108 (Oct. 23, 1970); Pub. L. No. 93-569, § 3, 88 Stat. 1864 (Dec. 31, 1974); Pub. L. No. 94-324, § 7(11), 90 Stat. 721 (June 30, 1976); Pub. L. No. 95-476, tit. I, §§ 104, 105(a), 92 Stat. 1498, 1499 (Oct. 18, 1978); Pub. L. No. 96-385, tit. IV, §§ 401(a), 402(a), 94 Stat. 1532, 1533 (Oct. 7, 1980); Pub. L. No. 98-223, tit. II, § 205(a), 98 Stat. 42 (Mar. 2, 1984); Pub. L. No. 99-576, tit. IV, § 402(a), (b), 100 Stat. 3280 (Oct. 28, 1986); Pub. L. No. 100-198, §§ 3(a)(2), 7(a), (c), 8(a)(2), 11(b), 13, 101 Stat. 1315, 1318, 1319, 1320, 1325 (Dec. 21, 1987); Pub. L. No. 100-322, tit. IV, § 415(c)(4), 102 Stat. 551 (May 20, 1988); Pub. L. No. 101-237, tit. III, §§ 309, 313(b)(1), 103 Stat. 2075, 2077 (Dec. 18, 1989); renumbered § 3710 and amended Pub. L. No. 102-83, §§ 4(a)(2)(A)(iv), 5(a), (c)(1), 105 Stat. 403, 406 (Aug. 6, 1991); Pub. L. No. 102-547, §§ 6(1), 9(a), (b), 106 Stat. 3636, 3641, 3642 (Oct. 28, 1992); Pub. L. No. 103-446, tit. IX, §§ 904(a), (b), 905, 108 Stat. 4676, 4677 (Nov. 2, 1994); Pub. L. No. 104-110, tit. I, § 101(e), 110 Stat. 768 (Feb. 13, 1996); Pub. L. No. 109-461, tit. V, § 501, 120 Stat. 3431 (Dec. 22, 2006)]

* * *

SUBCHAPTER III-ADMINISTRATIVE PROVISIONS

* * *

38 U.S.C. § 3732. Procedure on default

(a)(1) In the event of default in the payment of any loan guaranteed under this chapter, the holder of the obligation shall notify the Secretary of such default. Upon receipt of such notice, the Secretary may, subject to subsection (c) of this section, pay to such holder the guaranty not in excess of the pro rata portion of the amount originally guaranteed. Except as provided in section 3703(e) of this title, if the Secretary makes such a payment, the Secretary shall be subrogated to the rights of the holder of the obligation to the extent of the amount paid on the guaranty.

(2) Before suit or foreclosure the holder of the obligation shall notify the Secretary of the default, and within thirty days thereafter the Secretary may, at the Secretary's option, pay the holder of the obligation the unpaid balance of the obligation plus accrued interest and receive an assignment of the loan and security. Nothing in this section shall preclude any forebearance for the benefit of the veteran as may be agreed upon by the parties to the loan and approved by the Secretary.

(3) The Secretary may establish the date, not later than the date of judgment and decree of foreclosure or sale, upon which accrual of interest or charges shall cease.

(4)(A) Upon receiving a notice pursuant to paragraph (1) of this subsection, the Secretary shall—

(i) provide the veteran with information and, to the extent feasible, counseling regarding—

(I) alternatives to foreclosure, as appropriate in light of the veteran's particular circumstances, including possible methods of curing the default, conveyance of the property to the Secretary by means of a deed in lieu of foreclosure, and the actions authorized by paragraph (2) of this subsection; and

(II) what the Department of Veterans Affairs' and the veteran's liabilities would be with respect to the loan in the event of foreclosure; and

(ii) advise the veteran regarding the availability of such counseling;

except with respect to loans made by a lender which the Secretary has determined has a demonstrated record of consistently providing timely and accurate information to veterans with respect to such matters.

(B) The Secretary shall, to the extent of the availability of appropriations, ensure that sufficient personnel are available to administer subparagraph (A) of this paragraph effectively and efficiently.

(5) In the event of default in the payment of any loan guaranteed or insured under this chapter in which a partial payment has been tendered by the veteran concerned and refused by the holder, the holder of the obligation shall notify the Secretary as soon as such payment has been refused. The Secretary may require that any such notification include a statement of the circumstances of the default, the amount tendered, the amount of the indebtedness on the date of the tender, and the reasons for the holder's refusal.

(b) With respect to any loan made under section 3711 which has not been sold as provided in subsection (g) of such section, if the Secretary finds, after there has been a default in the payment of any installment of principal or interest owing on such loan, that the default was due to the fact that the veteran who is obligated under the loan has become unemployed as the result of the closing (in whole or in part) of a Federal installation, the Secretary shall (1) extend the time for curing the default to such time as the Secretary determines is necessary and desirable to enable such veteran to complete payments on such loan, including an extension of time beyond the stated maturity thereof, or (2) modify the terms of such loan for the purpose of changing the amortization provisions thereof by recasting, over the remaining term of the loan, or over such longer period as the Secretary may determine, the total unpaid amount then due with the modification to become effective currently or upon the termination of an agreed-upon extension of the period for curing the default.

(c)(1) For purposes of this subsection—

(A) The term "defaulted loan" means a loan that is guaranteed under this chapter, that was made for a purpose described in section 3710(a) of this title, and that is in default.

(B) The term "liquidation sale" means a judicial sale or other disposition of real property to liquidate a defaulted loan that is secured by such property.

(C) The term "net value," with respect to real property, means the amount equal to (i) the fair market value of the property, minus (ii) the total of the amounts which the Secretary estimates the Secretary would incur (if the Secretary were to acquire and dispose of the property) for property taxes, assessments, liens, property maintenance, property improvement, administration, resale (including losses sustained on the resale of the property), and other costs resulting from the acquisition and disposition of the property, excluding any amount attributed to the cost to the Government of borrowing funds.

(D) Except as provided in subparagraph (D) of paragraph (10) of this subsection, the term "total indebtedness," with respect to a defaulted loan, means the amount equal to the total of (i) the unpaid principal of the loan, (ii) the interest on the loan as of the date applicable under paragraph (10) of this subsection, and (iii) such reasonably necessary and proper charges (as specified in the loan instrument and permitted by regulations prescribed by the Secretary to implement this subsection) associated with liquidation of the loan, including advances for taxes, insurance, and maintenance or repair of the real property securing the loan.

(2)(A) Except as provided in subparagraph (B) of this paragraph, this subsection applies to any case in which the holder of a defaulted loan undertakes to liquidate the loan by means of a liquidation sale.

(B) This subsection does not apply to a case in which the Secretary proceeds under subsection (a)(2) of this section.

(3)(A) Before carrying out a liquidation sale of real property securing a defaulted loan, the holder of the loan shall notify the Secretary of the proposed sale. Such notice shall be provided in accordance with regulations prescribed by the Secretary to implement this subsection.

(B) After receiving a notice described in subparagraph (A) of this paragraph, the Secretary shall determine the net value of the property securing the loan and the amount of the total indebtedness under the loan and shall notify the holder of the loan of the determination of such net value.

(4) A case referred to in paragraphs (5), (6), and (7) of this subsection as being described in this paragraph is a case in which the net value of the property securing a defaulted loan exceeds the amount of the total indebtedness under the loan minus the amount guaranteed under this chapter.

(5) In a case described in paragraph (4) of this subsection, if the holder of the defaulted loan acquires the property securing the loan at a liquidation sale for an amount that does not exceed the lesser of the net value of the property or the total indebtedness under the loan—

(A) the holder shall have the option to convey the property to the United States in return for payment by the Secretary of an amount equal to the lesser of such net value or total indebtedness; and

(B) the liability of the United States under the loan guaranty under this chapter shall be limited to the amount of such total indebtedness minus the net value of the property.

(6) In a case described in paragraph (4) of this subsection, if the holder of the defaulted loan does not acquire the property securing the loan at the liquidation sale, the liability of the United States under the loan guaranty under this chapter shall be limited to the amount equal to (A) the amount of such total indebtedness, minus (B) the amount realized by the holder incident to the sale or the net value of the property, whichever is greater.

(7) In a case described in paragraph (4) of this subsection, if the holder of the defaulted loan acquires the property securing the loan at the liquidation sale for an amount that exceeds the lesser of the total indebtedness under the loan or the net value and—

(A)(i) the amount was the minimum amount for which, under applicable State law, the property was permitted to be sold at the liquidation sale, the holder shall have the option to convey the property to the United States in return for payment by the Secretary of an amount equal to the lesser of the amount for which the holder acquired the property or the total indebtedness under the loan; or

(ii) there was no minimum amount for which the property had to be sold at the liquidation sale under applicable State law, the holder shall have the option to convey the property to the United States in return for payment by the Secretary of an amount equal to the lesser of such net value or total indebtedness; and

(B) the liability of the United States under the loan guaranty under this chapter is as provided in paragraph (6) of this subsection.

(8) If the net value of the property securing a defaulted loan is not greater than the amount of the total indebtedness under the loan minus the amount guaranteed under this chapter—

(A) the Secretary may not accept conveyance of the property from the holder of the loan; and

(B) the liability of the United States under the loan guaranty shall be limited to the amount of the total indebtedness under the loan minus the amount realized by the holder of the loan incident to the sale at a liquidation sale of the property.

(9) In no event may the liability of the United States under a guaranteed loan exceed the amount guaranteed with respect to that loan under section 3703(b) of this title. All determinations under this subsection of net value and total indebtedness shall be made by the Secretary.

(10)(A) Except as provided in subparagraphs (B) and (C) of this paragraph, the date referred to in paragraph (1)(D)(ii) of this subsection shall be the date of the liquidation sale of the property securing the loan (or such earlier date following the expiration of a reasonable period of time for such sale to occur as the Secretary may specify pursuant to regulations prescribed by the Secretary to implement this subsection).

(B)(i) Subject to division (ii) of this subparagraph, in any case in which there is a substantial delay in such sale caused by the holder of the loan exercising forebearance at the request of the Secretary, the date referred to in paragraph (1)(D)(ii) of this subsection shall be such date, on or after the date on which forebearance was requested and prior to the date of such sale, as the Secretary specifies pursuant to regulations which the Secretary shall prescribe to implement this paragraph.

(ii) The Secretary may specify a date under subdivision (i) of this subparagraph only if, based on the use of a date so specified for the purposes of such paragraph (1)(D)(ii), the Secretary is authorized, under paragraph (5)(A) or (7)(A) of this subsection, to accept conveyance of the property.

(C) In any case in which there is an excessive delay in such liquidation sale caused—

(i) by the Department of Veterans Affairs (including any delay caused by its failure to provide bidding instructions in a timely fashion); or

(ii) by a voluntary case commenced under title 11, United States Code (relating to bankruptcy);

the date referred to in paragraph (1)(D)(ii) of this subsection shall be a date, earlier than the date of such liquidation sale, which the Secretary specifies pursuant to regulations which the Secretary shall prescribe to implement this paragraph.

(D) For the purpose of determining the liability of the United States under a loan guaranty under paragraphs (5)(B), (6), (7)(B), and (8)(B), the amount of the total indebtedness with respect to such loan guaranty shall include, in any case in which there was an excessive delay caused by the Department of Veterans Affairs in the liquidation sale of the property securing such loan, any interest which had accrued as of the date of such sale and which would not be included, except for this subparagraph, in the calculation of such total indebtedness as a result of the specification of an earlier date under subparagraph (C)(i) of this paragraph.

(11) This subsection shall apply to loans closed before October 1, 2012.

[Pub. L. No. 85-857, 72 Stat. 1212, § 1816(a)–(c)(Sept. 2, 1958); Pub. L. No. 89-117, tit. I, § 107(f), 79 Stat. 460 (Aug. 10, 1965); Pub. L. No. 94-324, § 7(17), 90 Stat. 722 (June 30, 1976); Pub. L. No. 98-369, Div. B, tit. V, § 2512(a), 98 Stat. 1117 (July 18, 1984); Pub. L. No. 100-198, §§ 4(a), 5(a), 101 Stat. 1316 (Dec. 21, 1987); renumbered § 1832 and amended Pub. L. No. 100-322, tit. IV, § 415(b)(1)(A)–(C), (5), 102 Stat. 550, 551 (May 20, 1988); Pub. L. No. 101-237, tit. III, §§ 304(b), 307, 308(a), (b)(1), 313(b)(1), (2), 103 Stat. 2073-2075, 2077 (Dec. 18, 1989); Pub. L. No. 100-322, tit. IV, § 415(b)(5)(C), *as amended* Pub. L. No. 102-54, § 14(g)(1), 105 Stat. 288 (June 13, 1991); Pub. L. No. 102-54, §§ 1, 3(a), 105 Stat. 267 (June 13, 1991); renumbered § 3732 and amended Pub. L. No. 102-83, § 5(a), (c)(1), 105 Stat. 406 (Aug. 6, 1991); Pub. L. No. 103-66, tit. XII, § 12006(a), 107 Stat. 414 (Aug. 10, 1993); Pub. L. No. 103-446, tit. IX, § 907, 108 Stat. 4677 (Nov. 2, 1994); Pub. L. No. 105-33, tit. VIII, § 8013, 111 Stat. 664 (Aug. 5, 1997); Pub. L. No. 106-419, tit. IV, § 402(c), 114 Stat. 1863 (Nov. 1, 2000); Pub. L. No. 107-103, tit. IV, § 405(d), 115 Stat. 994 (Dec. 27, 2001); Pub. L. No. 108-183, tit. IV, § 406, 117 Stat. 2666 (Dec. 16, 2003); Pub. L. No. 109-233, tit. V, § 503(9), 120 Stat. 416 (June 15, 2006)]

* * *

A.3.2 Selected Regulations

A.3.2.1 Introduction

The Department of Veterans Affairs (VA) established a new series of regulations for its Loan Guaranty Program on February 1, 2008.[1] The new rules, established under a new subpart F (§§ 36.4800 to §§ 36.4893, inclusive), are substantively similar to existing regulations in subpart B (§§ 36.4300 to §§ 36.4393, inclusive) with the exception of rules governing a new computer-based loan tracking system. The VA also made several changes to the regulations regarding the servicing and liquidation of loans in default. The new rules will be phased-in over an eleven month period. The servicing industry was divided into several segments, with each segment given a deadline for implementation of the new rules.[2] Servicers who have not yet implemented the new rules will be governed by existing rules under subpart B (§§ 36.4300 to §§ 36.4393, inclusive).

A.3.2.2 Subpart B—Guaranty or Insurance of Loans to Veterans

TITLE 38—PENSIONS, BONUSES, AND VETERANS' RELIEF

CHAPTER I—DEPARTMENT OF VETERANS AFFAIRS

PART 36—LOAN GUARANTY

SUBPART B—GUARANTY OR INSURANCE OF LOANS TO VETERANS

* * *

38 C.F.R. § 36.4313 Advances and other charges.

(a) A holder may advance any amount reasonably necessary and proper for the maintenance or repair of the security, or for the payment of accrued taxes, special assessments, ground or water rents, or premiums on fire or other casualty insurance against loss of or damage to such property and any such advance so made may be added to the guaranteed or insured indebtedness. A holder may also advance the one-half of one percent funding fee due on a transfer under 38 U.S.C. 3714 when this is not paid at the time of transfer. All security instruments for loans to which 38 U.S.C. 3714 applies must include a clause authorizing the collection of an assumption funding fee and an advance for this fee if it is not paid at the time of transfer.

(Authority: 38 U.S.C. 3714)

(b) In addition to advances allowable under paragraph (a) of this section, the holder may charge against the proceeds of the sale of the security; against gross amounts collected; in any accounting to the Secretary after payment of a claim under the guaranty, in the computation of a claim under the guaranty, if lawfully authorized by the loan agreement and subject to § 36.4321(a), or, in the computation of an insurance loss, any of the following items actually paid:

(1) Any expense which is reasonably necessary for preservation of the security,

(2) Court costs in a foreclosure or other proper judicial proceeding involving the security,

(3) Other expenses reasonably necessary for collecting the debt, or repossession or liquidation of the security,

(4) Reasonable trustee's fees or commissions not in excess of those allowed by statute and in no event in excess of 5 percent of the unpaid indebtedness,

(5)(i) Fees for legal services actually performed, not to exceed the reasonable and customary fees for such services in the State where the property is located, as determined by the Secretary.

(ii) In determining what constitutes the reasonable and customary fees for legal services, the Secretary shall review allowances for legal fees in connection with the foreclosure of single-family housing loans, including bankruptcy-related services, issued by HUD, Fannie Mae, and Freddie Mac. The Secretary will review such fees annually and, as the Secretary deems necessary, publish in the Federal Register a table setting forth the amounts the Secretary determines to be reasonable and customary. The table will reflect the primary method for foreclosing in each state, either judicial or non-judicial, with the exception of those States where either judicial or non-judicial is acceptable. The use of a method not authorized in the table will require prior approval from VA. This table will be available throughout the year on a VA controlled Web site, such as at www.homeloans.va.gov.

(iii) If the foreclosure attorney has the discretion to conduct the sale or to name a substitute trustee to conduct the sale, the combined total paid for legal fees under paragraph (b)(5)(i) of this section and trustee's fees pursuant to paragraph (b)(4) of this section shall not exceed the applicable maximum allowance for legal fees established under paragraph (b)(5)(ii) of this section. If the trustee conducting the sale must be a Government official under local law, or if an individual other than the foreclosing attorney (or any employee of that attorney) is appointed as part of judicial proceedings, and local law also establishes the fees payable for the services of the public or judicially appointed trustee, then those fees will not be subject to the maximum established for legal fees under paragraph (b)(5)(ii) of this section and may be included in the total indebtedness.

(6) The cost of a credit report(s) on the debtor(s), which is (are) to be forwarded to the Secretary in connection with the claim,

(7) Reasonable and customary costs of property inspections,

(8) Any other expense or fee that is approved in advance by the Secretary.

(Authority: 38 U.S.C. 3720(a)(3))

(c) Any advances or charges enumerated in paragraph (a) or (b) of this section may be included as specified in the holder's accounting to the Secretary, but they are not chargeable to the debtor unless he or she otherwise be liable therefor.

(d) Advances of the type enumerated in paragraph (a) of this section and any other advances determined to be necessary and proper in order to preserve or protect the security may be authorized by employees designated in § 36.4342(b) in the case of any property constituting the security for a loan acquired by the Secretary or constituting the security for the unpaid balance of the purchase price owing to the Secretary on account of the sale of such property. Such advances shall be secured to the extent legal and practicable by a lien on the property.

(e) Notwithstanding the provisions of paragraph (a) or (b) of this section, holders of condominium loans guaranteed or insured under 38 U.S.C. 3710(a)(6) shall not pay those assessments or charges allocable to the condominium unit which are provided for in the instruments establishing the condominium form of ownership in the absence of the prior approval of the Secretary.

[13 Fed. Reg. 7739, Dec. 15, 1948, *as amended at* 17 Fed. Reg. 9668 (Oct. 25, 1952); 36 Fed. Reg. 320 (Jan. 9, 1971); 40 Fed. Reg. 34,591 (Aug. 18, 1975); 45 Fed. Reg. 38,056 (June 6, 1980); 53 Fed. Reg. 27,049 (July 18, 1988); 53 Fed. Reg. 34,296 (Sept. 6, 1988); 55 Fed. Reg. 37,477 (Sept. 12, 1990); 58 Fed. Reg. 29,116 (May 19, 1993); 59 Fed. Reg. 48,566 (Sept. 22, 1994); 73 Fed. Reg. 6308 (Feb. 1, 2008)]

38 C.F.R. § 36.4314 Extensions and reamortizations.

(a) Provided the debtor(s) is (are) a reasonable credit risk(s), as determined by the holder based upon review of the debtor's (s') creditworthiness, including a review of a current credit report(s) on the debtor(s), the terms of repayment of any loan may by written agreement

---

1 *See* 73 Fed. Reg. 6294 (Feb. 1, 2008) (to be codified at 38 C.F.R. pt. 36).

2 *See* 73 Fed. Reg. 6294 (Feb. 1, 2008); 73 Fed. Reg. 30,505 (June 1, 2008). For a list of servicers and their deadlines for implementing the new rules, go to the VA's website at www.homeloans.va.gov/docs/2007-12-19%20REVISED%20Implementation%20Schedule.xls.

between the holder and the debtor(s), be extended in the event of default, to avoid imminent default, or in any other case where the prior approval of the Secretary is obtained. Except with the prior approval of the Secretary, no such extension shall set a rate of amortization less than that sufficient to fully amortize at least 80 percent of the loan balance so extended within the maximum maturity prescribed for loans of its class.

(b) In the event of a partial prepayment pursuant to § 36.4310, the balance of the indebtedness may, by written agreement between the holder and the debtor(s), be reamortized, provided the reamortization schedule will result in full repayment of the loan within the original maturity, and provided the debtor(s) is (are) reasonable credit risk(s), as determined by the holder based upon review of the debtor's (s') creditworthiness, including a review of a current credit report(s) on the debtor(s).

(c) In the event an additional loan is proposed to be made pursuant to § 36.4351 for the repair, alteration, or improvement of real property on which there is an existing loan guaranteed or insured under 38 U.S.C. Ch. 37, the terms of repayment of the prior loan may, by written agreement between the holder and the debtor, be recast to combine the schedule of repayments on the two loans, provided the entire indebtedness is repayable within the permissible maximum maturity of the original loan.

(d) Unless the prior approval of the Secretary has been obtained, any extension or reamortization agreed to by a holder which relieves any obligor from liability will release the liability of the Secretary under the guaranty or insurance on the entire loan. However, if such release of liability of an obligor results through operation of law by reason of an extension or other act of forbearance, the liability of the Secretary as guarantor or insurer will not be affected thereby, provided the required lien is maintained and the title holder is and will remain liable for the payment of the indebtedness: And further provided, That if such extension or act of forbearance will result in the release of the veteran, all delinquent installments, plus any foreclosure expenses which may have been incurred, shall have been fully paid.

(e) The holder shall promptly forward to the Secretary an advice of the terms of any agreement effecting a reamortization or extension of a guaranteed or insured loan, together with a cop(y)(ies) of the credit report(s) obtained on the debtor(s).

[13 Fed. Reg. 7276 (Nov. 27, 1948), *as amended at* 19 Fed. Reg. 4002 (July 1, 1954); 24 Fed. Reg. 2653 (Apr. 7, 1959); 53 Fed. Reg. 34,296 (Sept. 6, 1988)]

38 C.F.R. § 36.4315 Notice of default and acceptability of partial payments.

(a) *Reporting of defaults.* The holder of any guaranteed or insured loan shall give notice to the Secretary within 45 days after any debtor:

(1) Is in default by reason of nonpayment of any installment for a period of 60 days from the date of first uncured default (see § 36.4301(f)); or

(2) Is in default by failing to comply with any other covenant or obligation of such guaranteed or insured loan which failure persists for a continuing period of 90 days after demand for compliance therewith has been made, except that if the default is due to nonpayment of real estate taxes, the notice shall not be required until the failure to pay when due has persisted for a continuing period of 180 days.

(b) *Partial payments.* A partial payment is a remittance on a loan in default (as defined in § 36.4301(g)) of any amount less than the full amount due under the terms of the loan and security instruments at the time the remittance is tendered.

(1) Except as provided in paragraph (b)(2) of this section, or upon the express waiver of the Secretary, the mortgage holder shall accept any partial payment and either apply it to the mortgagor's account or identify it with the mortgagor's account and hold it in a special account pending disposition. When partial payments held for disposition aggregate a full monthly installment, including escrow, they shall be applied to the mortgagor's account.

(2) A partial payment may be returned to the mortgagor, within 10 calendar days from date of receipt of such payment, with a letter of explanation only if one or more of the following conditions exist:

(i) The property is wholly or partially tenant-occupied and rental payments are not being remitted to the holder for application to the loan account;

(ii) The payment is less than one full monthly installment, including escrows and late charge, if applicable, unless the lesser payment amount has been agreed to under a written repayment plan;

(iii) The payment is less than 50 percent of the total amount then due, unless the lesser payment amount has been agreed to under a written repayment plan;

(iv) The payment is less than the amount agreed to in a written repayment plan;

(v) The amount tendered is in the form of a personal check and the holder has previously notified the mortgagor in writing that only cash or certified remittances are acceptable;

(vi) A delinquency of any amount has continued for at least 6 months since the account first became delinquent and no written repayment plan has been arranged;

(vii) Foreclosure has been commenced by the taking of the first action required for foreclosure under local law;

(viii) The holder's lien position would be jeopardized by acceptance of the partial payment.

(3) A failure by the holder to comply with the provisions of this paragraph may result in a partial or total loss of guaranty or insurance pursuant to § 36.4325(b), but such failure shall not constitute a defense to any legal action to terminate the loan.

[45 Fed. Reg. 31,065 (May 12, 1980)]

38 C.F.R. § 36.4316 Continued default.

(a) In the event any failure of the debtor to discharge the debtor's obligations under the loan continues for a period of 3 months, or for more than 1 month on an extended loan or on a term loan, the holder may at the holder's option then or thereafter give the notice prescribed in § 36.4317.

(b) The notice prescribed in § 36.4317 may be submitted prior to the time prescribed in paragraph (a) of this section in any case where any material prejudice to the rights of the holder or to the Secretary or hazard to the security warrants more prompt action.

[13 Fed. Reg. 7276 (Nov. 27, 1948), *as amended at* 45 Fed. Reg. 31,065 (May 12, 1980); 53 Fed. Reg. 34,296 (Sept. 6, 1988); 61 Fed. Reg. 28,058 (June 4, 1996)]

38 C.F.R. § 36.4317 Notice of intention to foreclose.

(See also § 36.4319.) Except upon the express waiver of the Secretary, a holder shall not begin proceedings in court or give notice of sale under power of sale, or otherwise take steps to terminate the debtor's rights in the security until the expiration of 30 days after delivery by registered mail to the Secretary of a notice of intention to take such action: Provided, That

(a) Immediate action as required under 38 CFR 36.4346 (i), may be taken if the property to be affected thereby has been abandoned by the debtor or has been or may be otherwise subjected to extraordinary waste or hazard, or if there exist conditions justifying the appointment of a receiver for the property (without reference to any contractual provisions for such appointment);

(b) Any right of a holder to repossess personal property may be exercised without prior notice to the Secretary; but notice of any such action taken shall be given by certified mail to the Secretary within ten days thereafter; and

(c) The notice required under this paragraph shall also be provided to the original veteran-borrower and any other liable obligors by certified mail within 30 days after such notice is provided to the Secretary in all cases in which the current owner of the property is not the original veteran-borrower. A failure by the holder to make a good faith effort to comply with the provisions of this subparagraph may result in a partial or total loss of guaranty or insurance pursuant to VA Regulation 36.4325(b), but such failure shall not constitute a defense to any legal action to terminate the loan. A good faith effort will include, but is not limited to:

(1) A search of the holder's automated and physical loan record systems to identify the name and current or last known address of the original veteran and any other liable obligors;

(2) A search of the holder's automated and physical loan record systems to identify sufficient information (e.g., Social Security Number) to perform a routine trace inquiry through a major consumer credit bureau;

(3) Conducting the trace inquiry using an in-house credit reporting terminal;

(4) Obtaining the results of the inquiry;

(5) Mailing the required notices and concurrently providing the Secretary with the names and addresses of all obligors identified and sent notice; and,

(6) Documentation of the holder's records.

[13 Fed. Reg. 7276 (Nov. 27, 1948); 58 Fed. Reg. 29,116 (May 19, 1993)]

38 C.F.R. § 36.4318 Refunding of loans in default.

(a) Upon receiving a notice of default or a notice under § 36.4317, the Secretary may within 30 days thereafter require the holder upon penalty of otherwise losing the guaranty or insurance to transfer and assign the loan and the security therefore to the Secretary or to another designated by the Secretary upon receipt of payment in full of the balance of the indebtedness remaining unpaid to the date of such assignment. Such assignment may be made without recourse but the transferor shall not thereby be relieved from the provisions of § 36.4325.

(b) If the obligation is assigned or transferred to a third party pursuant to paragraph (a) of this section the Secretary may continue in effect the guaranty or insurance issued with respect to the previous loan in such manner as to cover the assignee or transferee.

[13 Fed. Reg. 7276 (Nov. 27, 1948), *as amended at* 45 Fed. Reg. 31,065 (May 12, 1980); 61 Fed. Reg. 28,058 (June 4, 1996)]

* * *

UNDERWRITING STANDARDS, PROCESSING PROCEDURES, AND LENDER RESPONSIBILITY AND CERTIFICATION

* * *

38 C.F.R. § 36.4346 Servicing procedures for holders.

(a) *Establishment of loan servicing program.* The holder of a loan guaranteed or insured by the Secretary shall develop and maintain a loan servicing program which follows accepted industry standards for servicing of similar type conventional loans. The loan servicing program established pursuant to this section may employ different servicing approaches to fit individual borrower circumstances and avoid establishing a fixed routine. However, it must incorporate each of the provisions specified in paragraphs (b) through (l) of this section.

(b) *Procedures for providing information.*

(1) Loan holders shall establish procedures to provide loan information to borrowers, arrange for individual loan consultations upon request and maintain controls to assure prompt responses to inquiries. One or more of the following means of making information readily available to borrowers is required.

(i) An office staffed with trained servicing personnel with access to loan account information located within 200 miles of the property.

(ii) Toll-free telephone service or acceptance of collect telephone calls at an office capable of providing needed information.

(2) All borrowers must be informed of the system available for obtaining answers to loan inquiries, the office from which the needed information may be obtained, and reminded of the system at least annually.

(c) *Statement for income tax purposes.* Within 60 days after the end of each calendar year, the holder shall furnish to the borrower a statement of the interest paid and, if applicable, a statement of the taxes disbursed from the escrow account during the preceding year. At the borrower's request, the holder shall furnish a statement of the escrow account sufficient to enable the borrower to reconcile the account.

(d) *Change of servicing.* Whenever servicing of a loan guaranteed or insured by the Secretary is transferred from one holder to another, notice of such transfer by both the transferor and transferee, the form and content of such notice, the timing of such notice, the treatment of payments during the period of such transfer, and damages and costs for failure to comply with these requirements shall be governed by the pertinent provisions of the Real Estate Settlement Procedures Act as administered by the Department of Housing and Urban Development.

(e) *Escrow accounts.* A holder of a loan guaranteed or insured by the Secretary may collect periodic deposits from the borrower for taxes and/or insurance on the security and maintain a tax and insurance escrow account provided such a requirement is authorized under the terms of the security instruments. In maintaining such accounts, the holder shall comply with the pertinent provisions of the Real Estate Settlement Procedures Act.

(f) *System for servicing delinquent loans.* In addition to the requirements of the Real Estate Settlement Procedures Act, concerning the duties of the loan servicer to respond to borrower inquiries, to protect the borrower's credit rating during a payment dispute period, and to pay damages and costs for noncompliance, holders shall establish a system for servicing delinquent loans which ensures that prompt action is taken to collect amounts due from borrowers and minimize the number of loans in a default status. The holder's servicing system must include the following:

(1) An accounting system which promptly alerts servicing personnel when a loan becomes delinquent;

(2) A collection staff which is trained in techniques of loan servicing and counseling delinquent borrowers to advise borrowers how to cure delinquencies, protect their equity and credit rating and, if the default is insoluble, pursue alternatives to foreclosure;

(3) Procedural guidelines for individual analysis of each delinquency;

(4) Instructions and appropriate controls for sending delinquent notices, assessing late charges, handling partial payments, maintaining servicing histories and evaluating repayment proposals;

(5) Management review procedures for evaluating efforts made to collect the delinquency and the response from the borrower before a decision is made to initiate action to liquidate a loan;

(6) Procedures for reporting delinquencies of 90 days or more and loan terminations to major consumer credit bureaus as specified by the Secretary and for informing borrowers that such action will be taken; and

(7) Controls to ensure that all notices required to be given to the Secretary on delinquent loans are provided timely and in such form as the Secretary shall require.

(g) *Collection actions.*

(1) Holders shall employ collection techniques which provide flexibility to adapt to the individual needs and circumstances of each borrower. A variety of collection techniques may be used based on the holder's determination of the most effective means of contact with borrowers during various stages of delinquency. However, at a minimum the holder's collection procedures must include the following actions:

(i) A written delinquency notice to the borrower(s) requesting immediate payment if a loan installment has not been received within 17 days after the due date. This notice must be mailed no later than the 20th day of the delinquency and state the amount of the payment and of any late charges that are due.

(ii) An effort, concurrent with the written delinquency notice to establish contact with the borrower(s) by telephone. When talking with the borrower(s), the holder should attempt to determine why payment was not made and emphasize the importance of remitting loan installments as they come due.

(iii) A letter to the borrower(s) if payment has not been received within 30 days after it is due and telephone contact could not be made. This letter should emphasize the seriousness of the delinquency and the importance of taking prompt action to resolve the default. It should also notify the borrower(s) that the loan is in default, state the total amount due and advise the borrower(s) how to contact the holder to make arrangements for curing the default.

(iv) In the event the holder has not established contact with the borrower(s) and has not determined the financial circumstances of the borrower(s) or established a reason for the default or obtained agreement to a repayment plan from the borrower(s), then a face-to-face interview with the borrower(s) or a reasonable effort to arrange such a meeting is required.

(2) The holder must provide a valid explanation of any failure to perform these collection actions when reporting loan defaults to the Secretary. A pattern of such failure may be a basis for sanctions under 2 CFR parts 180 and 801.

(h) *Conducting interviews with delinquent borrowers*. When personal contact with the borrower(s) is established, the holder shall solicit sufficient information to properly evaluate the prospects for curing the default and whether the granting of forbearance or other relief assistance would be appropriate. At a minimum, the holder must make a reasonable effort to establish the following:

(1) The reason for the default and whether the reason is a temporary or permanent condition;

(2) The present income and employment of the borrower(s);

(3) The current monthly expenses of the borrower(s) including household and debt obligations;

(4) The current mailing address and telephone number of the borrower(s); and

(5) A realistic and mutually satisfactory arrangement for curing the default.

(i) *Property inspections*.

(1) The holder shall make an inspection of the property securing the loan whenever it becomes aware that the physical condition of the security may be in jeopardy. Unless a repayment agreement is in effect, a property inspection shall also be made at the following times:

(i) Before the 60th day of delinquency or before initiating action to liquidate a loan, whichever is earlier; and,

(ii) At least once each month after liquidation proceedings have been started unless servicing information shows the property remains owner-occupied.

(2) Whenever a holder obtains information which indicates that the property securing the loan is abandoned, it shall make appropriate arrangements to protect the property from vandalism and the elements. Thereafter, the holder shall schedule inspections at least monthly to prevent unnecessary deterioration due to vandalism, or neglect. With respect to any loan more than 30 days delinquent, a property abandonment must be reported to the Secretary and appropriate action initiated under § 36.4317(a) within 15 days after the holder confirms the property is abandoned.

(j) *Collection records*. The holder shall maintain individual file records of collection action on delinquent loans and make such records available to the Secretary for inspection on request. Such collection records shall show:

(1) The dates and content of letters and notices which were mailed to the borrower(s);

(2) Dated summaries of each personal servicing contact and the result of same;

(3) The indicated reason(s) for default; and,

(4) The date and result of each property inspection.

(k) *Reporting to the Secretary*. A summary of collection efforts, the information obtained through such efforts and the holder's evaluation of the reason for the default and prospects for resolution of the default must be included in any notice provided to the Secretary pursuant to §§ 36.4315 and 36.4317.

(l) *Quality control procedures*. No later than 180 days after the effective date of this regulation, each loan holder shall establish internal controls to periodically assess the quality of the servicing performed on loans guaranteed by the Secretary and assure that all requirements of this section are being met. Those procedures must provide for a review of the holder's servicing activities at least annually and include an evaluation of delinquency and foreclosure rates on loans in its portfolio which are guaranteed by the Secretary. As part of its evaluation of delinquency and foreclosure rates, the holder shall:

(1) Collect and maintain appropriate data on delinquency and foreclosure rates to enable the holder to evaluate effectiveness of its collection efforts;

(2) Determine how its VA delinquency and foreclosure rates compare with rates in reports published by the industry, investors and others; and,

(3) Analyze significant variances between its foreclosure and delinquency rates and those found in available reports and publications and take appropriate corrective action.

(m) Holders shall provide available statistical data on delinquency and foreclosure rates and their analysis of such data to the Secretary upon request.

[58 Fed. Reg. 29,117 (May 19, 1993); 61 Fed. Reg. 28,058 (June 4, 1996); 72 Fed. Reg. 30,242 (May 31, 2007)]

* * *

A.3.2.3 Subpart F—Guaranty or Insurance of Loans to Veterans with Electronic Reporting

SUBPART F—GUARANTY OR INSURANCE OF LOANS TO VETERANS WITH ELECTRONIC REPORTING

* * *

38 C.F.R. § 36.4807 Interest rate reduction refinancing loan.

(a) Pursuant to 38 U.S.C. 3710(a)(8), (a)(9)(B)(i), and (a)(11), a veteran may refinance an existing VA guaranteed, insured, or direct loan to reduce the interest rate payable on the existing loan provided that all of the following requirements are met:

(1) The new loan must be secured by the same dwelling or farm residence as the loan being refinanced.

(2) The veteran owns the dwelling or farm residence securing the loan and

(i) Occupies the dwelling or residence as his or her home; or

(ii) Previously occupied the dwelling or residence as his or her home and certifies, in such form as the Secretary shall require, that he or she has previously occupied the dwelling or residence as a home; or

(iii) In a case in which the veteran is or was unable to occupy the residence or dwelling as a home because the veteran was on active duty status as a member of the Armed Forces, the spouse of the veteran occupies, or previously occupied, the dwelling or residence as the spouse's home and certifies to that occupancy in such form as the Secretary shall require.

(Authority: 38 U.S.C. 3710(e)(1))

(3) The monthly principal and interest payment on the new loan is lower than the principal and interest payment on the loan being refinanced; or the term of the new loan is shorter than the term of the loan being refinanced; or the new loan is a fixed-rate loan that refinances a VA-guaranteed adjustable rate mortgage; or the increase in the monthly payments on the loan results from the inclusion of energy efficient improvements, as provided by § 36.4839(a)(4); or the Secretary approves the loan in advance after determining that the new loan is necessary to prevent imminent foreclosure and the veteran qualifies for the new loan under the credit standards contained in § 36.4840.

(4) The amount of the refinancing loan does not exceed:

(i) An amount equal to the balance of the loan being refinanced, which is not delinquent, except as provided in paragraph (a)(5) of this section, plus closing costs authorized by § 36.4813(d) and a discount not to exceed 2 percent of the loan amount; or

(ii) In the case of a loan to refinance an existing VA-guaranteed or direct loan and to improve the dwelling securing such loan through energy efficient improvements, the amount referred to with respect to the loan under paragraph (a)(4)(i) of this section, plus the amount authorized by § 36.4839(a)(4).

(Authority: 38 U.S.C. 3703, 3710)

(5) If the loan being refinanced is delinquent (delinquent means that a scheduled monthly payment of principal and interest is more than 30 days past due), the new loan will be guaranteed only if the Secretary approves it in advance after determining that the borrower, through the lender, has provided reasons for the loan deficiency, has provided information to establish that the cause of the delinquency has been corrected, and qualifies for the loan under the credit standards contained in § 36.4840. In such cases, the term "balance of the loan being refinanced" shall include any past due installments, plus allowable late charges.

(6) The dollar amount of guaranty on the 38 U.S.C. 3710(a)(8) or (a)(9)(B)(i) loan does not exceed the greater of the original guaranty amount of the loan being refinanced or 25 percent of the new loan.

(7) The term of the refinancing loan (38 U.S.C. 3710(a)(8)) may not exceed the original term of the loan being refinanced plus ten years, or the maximum loan term allowed under 38 U.S.C. 3703(d)(1), whichever is less. For manufactured home loans that were previously guaranteed under 38 U.S.C. 3712, the loan term, if being refinanced under 38 U.S.C. 3710(a)(9)(B)(i), may exceed the original term of the loan but may not exceed the maximum loan term allowed under 38 U.S.C. 3703(d)(1).

(Authority: 38 U.S.C. 3703(c)(1), 3710(e)(1))

(b) Notwithstanding any other regulatory provision, the interest rate reduction refinancing loan may be guaranteed without regard to the amount of guaranty entitlement available for use by the veteran, and the amount of the veteran's remaining guaranty entitlement, if any, shall not be charged for an interest rate reduction refinancing loan. The interest rate reduction refinancing loan will be guaranteed with the lesser of the entitlement used by the veteran to obtain the loan being refinanced or the amount of the guaranty as calculated under § 36.4802(a). The veteran's loan guaranty entitlement originally used for a purpose as enumerated in 38 U.S.C. 3710(a)(1) through (7) and (a)(9)(A)(i) and (ii) and subsequently transferred to an interest rate reduction refinancing loan (38 U.S.C. 3710(a)(8) or (a)(9)(B)(i)) shall be eligible for restoration when the interest rate reduction refinancing loan or subsequent interest rate reduction refinancing loans on the same property meets the requirements of § 36.4802(h).

(Authority: 38 U.S.C. 3703(a))

(c) Title to the estate which is refinanced for the purpose of an interest rate reduction must be in conformity with § 36.4854.

(Authority: 38 U.S.C. 3710(a)(8), (a)(9)(B)(i) and (e))

(The Office of Management and Budget has approved the information collection requirements in this section under control number 2900-0601.)

[73 Fed. Reg. 6319 (Feb. 1, 2008)]

* * *

38 C.F.R. § 36.4814 Advances and other charges.

(a) A holder may advance any amount reasonably necessary and proper for the maintenance or repair of the security, or for the payment of accrued taxes, special assessments, ground or water rents, or premiums on fire or other casualty insurance against loss of or damage to such property and any such advance so made may be added to the guaranteed or insured indebtedness. A holder may also advance the one-half of one percent funding fee due on a transfer under 38 U.S.C. 3714 when this is not paid at the time of transfer. All security instruments for loans to which 38 U.S.C. 3714 applies must include a clause authorizing the collection of an assumption funding fee and an advance for this fee if it is not paid at the time of transfer.

(Authority: 38 U.S.C. 3703, 3714, 3732)

(b) In addition to advances allowable under paragraph (a) of this section, the holder may charge against the proceeds of the sale of the security; may charge against gross amounts collected; may include in any accounting to the Secretary after payment of a claim under the guaranty; may include in the computation of a claim under the guaranty, if lawfully authorized by the loan agreement and subject to § 36.4824(a); or, may include in the computation of an insurance loss, any of the following items actually paid:

(1) Any expense which is reasonably necessary for preservation of the security;

(2) Court costs in a foreclosure or other proper judicial proceeding involving the security;

(3) Other expenses reasonably necessary for collecting the debt, or repossession or liquidation of the security;

(4) Reasonable trustee's fees or commissions not in excess of those allowed by statute and in no event in excess of 5 percent of the unpaid indebtedness;

(5)(i) Fees for legal services actually performed, not to exceed the reasonable and customary fees for such services in the State where the property is located, as determined by the Secretary.

(ii) In determining what constitutes the reasonable and customary fees for legal services, the Secretary shall review allowances for legal fees in connection with the foreclosure of single-family housing loans, including bankruptcy-related services, issued by HUD, Fannie Mae, and Freddie Mac. The Secretary will review such fees annually and, as the Secretary deems necessary, publish in the Federal Register a table setting forth the amounts the Secretary determines to be reasonable and customary. The table will reflect the primary method for foreclosing in each state, either judicial or non-judicial, with the exception of those States where either judicial or non-judicial is acceptable. The use of a method not authorized in the table will require prior approval from VA. This table will be available throughout the year on a VA controlled Web site, such as at http://www.homeloans.va.gov.

(iii) If the foreclosure attorney has the discretion to conduct the sale or to name a substitute trustee to conduct the sale, the combined total paid for legal fees under paragraph (b)(5)(i) of this section and trustee's fees pursuant to paragraph (b)(4) of this section shall not exceed the applicable maximum allowance for legal fees established under paragraph (b)(5)(ii) of this section. If the trustee conducting the sale must be a Government official under local law, or if an individual other than the foreclosing attorney (or any employee of that attorney) is appointed as part of judicial proceedings, and local law also establishes the fees payable for the services of the public or judicially appointed trustee, then those fees will not be subject to the maximum established for legal fees under paragraph (b)(5)(ii) of this section and may be included in the total indebtedness.

(6) The cost of a credit report(s) on the debtor(s), which is (are) to be forwarded to the Secretary in connection with the claim;

(7) Reasonable and customary costs of property inspections;

(8) Any other expense or fee that is approved in advance by the Secretary.

(Authority: 38 U.S.C. 3720(a)(3), 3732)

(c) Any advances or charges enumerated in paragraph (a) or (b) of this section may be included as specified in the holder's accounting to the Secretary, but they are not chargeable to the debtor unless he or she otherwise be liable therefor.

(d) Advances of the type enumerated in paragraph (a) of this section and any other advances determined by VA to be necessary and proper in order to preserve or protect the security may be authorized by employees designated in § 36.4845(b) in the case of any property constituting the security for a loan acquired by the Secretary or constituting the security for the unpaid balance of the purchase price owing to the Secretary on account of the sale of such property. Such advances shall be secured to the extent legal and practicable by a lien on the property.

(e) Notwithstanding the provisions of paragraph (a) or (b) of this section, holders of condominium loans guaranteed or insured under 38 U.S.C. 3710(a)(6) shall not pay those assessments or charges allocable to the condominium unit which are provided for in the instruments establishing the condominium form of ownership in the absence of the prior approval of the Secretary.

(f)(1) Fees and charges otherwise allowable by this section that accrue after the date specified in paragraph (f)(2) of this section may not be included in a claim under the guaranty.

(2) The date referenced in paragraph (f)(1) of this section will be computed by adding 210 calendar days to the due date of the last paid installment, plus the reasonable period that the Secretary has determined, pursuant to § 36.4822(a), it should have taken to complete the foreclosure. There will also be added to the time period specified in the previous sentence such additional time as the Secretary determines was reasonably necessary to complete the foreclosure if the Secretary determines the holder was unable to complete the foreclosure within the time specified in that section due to Bankruptcy proceedings, appeal of the foreclosure by the debtor, the holder granting forbearance in excess of 30 days at the request of the Secretary, or other factors beyond the control of the holder.

(Authority: 38 U.S.C. 3703(c), 3720, 3732)

[73 Fed. Reg. 6324, 6325 (Feb. 1, 2008)]

38 C.F.R. § 36.4815 Loan modifications.

(a) Subject to the provisions of this section, the terms of any guaranteed loan may be modified by written agreement between the holder and the borrower, without prior approval of the Secretary, if all of the following conditions are met:

(1) The loan is in default;

(2) The event or circumstances that caused the default has been or will be resolved and it is not expected to re-occur;

(3) The obligor is considered to be a reasonable credit risk, based on a review by the holder of the obligor's creditworthiness under the criteria specified in § 36.4840, including a current credit report. The fact of the recent default will not preclude the holder from determining the obligor is now a satisfactory credit risk provided the holder determines that the obligor is able to resume regular mortgage installments when the modification becomes effective based upon a review of the obligor's current and anticipated income, expenses, and other obligations as provided in § 36.4840;

(4) At least 12 monthly payments have been paid since the closing date of the loan;

(5) The current owner(s) is obligated to repay the loan, and is party to the loan modification agreement; and

(6) The loan will be reinstated to performing status by virtue of the loan modification.

(b) Without the prior approval of the Secretary, a loan can be modified no more than once in a 3-year period and no more than three times during the life of the loan.

(c) All modified loans must bear a fixed-rate of interest, which may not exceed the Government National Mortgage Association (GNMA) current month coupon rate that is closest to par (100) plus 50 basis points. The rate shall be determined as of the close of business the last business day of the month preceding the date the holder approved the loan modification.

(d) The unpaid balance of the modified loan may be re-amortized over the remaining life of the loan. The loan term may extend the maturity date to the shorter of:

(1) 360 months from the due date of the first installment required under the modification, or

(2) 120 months after the original maturity date of the loan.

(e) Only unpaid principal; accrued interest; deficits in the taxes and insurance impound accounts; and advances required to preserve the lien position, such as homeowner association fees, special assessments, water and sewer liens, etc., may be included in the modified indebtedness. Late fees and other charges may not be capitalized.

(f) Holders shall not charge a processing fee under any circumstances to complete a loan modification. However, late fees and any other actual costs incurred and legally chargeable, including but not limited to the cost of a title insurance policy for the modified loan, but which cannot be capitalized in the modified indebtedness, may be collected directly from the borrower as part of the modification process.

(g) Holders will ensure the first lien status of the modified loan.

(h) The dollar amount of the guaranty may not exceed the greater of:

(1) The original guaranty amount of the loan being modified (but if the modified loan amount is less than the original loan amount, then the amount of guaranty will be equal to the original guaranty percentage applied to the modified loan), or

(2) 25 percent of the loan being modified subject to the statutory maximum specified at 38 U.S.C. 3703(a)(1)(B).

(i) The obligor may not receive any cash back from the modification.

(j) This section does not create a right of a borrower to have a loan modified, but simply authorizes the loan holder to modify a loan in certain situations without the prior approval of the Secretary.

(Authority: 38 U.S.C. 3703(c)(1), 3720)

[73 Fed. Reg. 6325 (Feb. 1, 2008)]

38 C.F.R. § 36.4816 Acceptability of partial payments.

A partial payment is a remittance by or on behalf of the borrower on a loan in default (as defined in § 36.4801) of any amount less than the full amount due under the terms of the loan and security instruments at the time the remittance is tendered.

(a) Except as provided in paragraph (b) of this section, or upon the express waiver of the Secretary, the mortgage holder shall accept any partial payment and either apply it to the mortgagor's account or identify it with the mortgagor's account and hold it in a special account pending disposition. When partial payments held for disposition aggregate a full monthly installment, including escrow, they shall be applied to the mortgagor's account.

(b) A partial payment may be returned to the mortgagor, within 10 calendar days from date of receipt of such payment, with a letter of explanation only if one or more of the following conditions exist:

(1) The property is wholly or partially tenant-occupied and rental payments are not being remitted to the holder for application to the loan account;

(2) The payment is less than one full monthly installment, including escrows and late charge, if applicable, unless the lesser payment amount has been agreed to under a documented repayment plan;

(3) The payment is less than 50 percent of the total amount then due, unless the lesser payment amount has been agreed to under a documented repayment plan;

(4) The payment is less than the amount agreed to in a documented repayment plan;

(5) The amount tendered is in the form of a personal check and the holder has previously notified the mortgagor in writing that only cash or certified remittances are acceptable;

(6) A delinquency of any amount has continued for at least 6 months since the account first became delinquent and no written repayment plan has been arranged;

(7) Foreclosure has been commenced by the taking of the first action required for foreclosure under local law; or

(8) The holder's lien position would be jeopardized by acceptance of the partial payment.

(c) A failure by the holder to comply with the provisions of this paragraph may result in a partial or total loss of guaranty or insurance pursuant to § 36.4828(b), but such failure shall not constitute a defense to any legal action to terminate the loan.

(Authority: 38 U.S.C. 3703(c)(1))

[73 Fed. Reg. 6325, 6326 (Feb. 1, 2008)]

* * *

38 C.F.R. § 36.4819 Servicer loss-mitigation options and incentives.

(a) The Secretary will pay a servicer in tiers one, two, or three an incentive payment for each of the following successful loss-mitigation options or alternatives to foreclosure completed: repayment plans, special forbearance agreements, loan modifications, compromise sales, and deeds-in-lieu of foreclosure. Only one incentive payment will be made with respect to any default required to be reported to the Secretary pursuant to § 36.4817(c). No incentive payment will be made to a servicer in tier four. The options and alternatives are listed in paragraph (b) of this section from top to bottom in their preferred order of consideration (i.e., a hierarchy for review), but VA recognizes that individual circumstances may lead to "out of the ordinary" considerations.

(b) The amount of the incentive payment is as follows:

Tier ranking	One	Two	Three	Four
Repayment Plan	$200	$160	$120	$0
Special Forbearance	200	160	120	0
Loan Modification	700	500	300	0
Compromise Sale	1,000	800	600	0
Deed in Lieu of Foreclosure	350	250	150	0

(c) For purposes of this section, a loss-mitigation option or alternative to foreclosure will be deemed successfully completed as follows:

(1) With respect to a repayment plan (as defined in § 36.4801), when the loan reinstates;

(2) With respect to special forbearance (as defined in § 36.4801), when the loan reinstates. If a repayment plan is developed at the end of the forbearance period, then the special forbearance is not eligible for an incentive payment, although the subsequent repayment plan may be eligible upon loan reinstatement;

(3) With respect to a loan modification, when the modification is executed and the loan reinstates;

(4) With respect to a compromise sale, when the claim under guaranty is filed; or

(5) With respect to a deed-in-lieu of foreclosure, when the claim under guaranty is filed.

(d) Incentive payments with respect to repayment plans, special forbearances and loan modifications shall be made no less frequently than monthly. For all other successful loss-mitigation options, incentives shall be paid in the final claim payment.

(e) The Secretary shall reserve the right to stop an incentive payment to a servicer if the servicer fails to perform adequate servicing.

(Authority: 38 U.S.C. 3703(c), 3720, 3722)

(The Office of Management and Budget has approved the information collection requirements in this section under control number 2900-0021.)

[73 Fed. Reg. 6327 (Feb. 1, 2008)]

38 C.F.R. § 36.4820 Refunding of loans in default.

(a) Upon receiving a notice of default or a notice under § 36.4817, the Secretary may require the holder upon penalty of otherwise losing the guaranty or insurance to transfer and assign the loan and the security therefore to the Secretary or to another designated by the Secretary upon receipt of payment in full of the balance of the indebtedness remaining unpaid to the date of such assignment. Such assignment may be made without recourse but the transferor shall not thereby be relieved from the provisions of § 36.4828.

(b) If the obligation is assigned or transferred to a third party pursuant to paragraph (a) of this section the Secretary may continue in effect the guaranty or insurance issued with respect to the previous loan in such manner as to cover the assignee or transferee.

(c) Servicers must deliver to the Secretary all legal documents, including but not limited to proper loan assignments, required as evidence of proper loan transfer within 60 calendar days from the date that VA sends notice to the servicer that VA has decided to refund a loan under this section. Servicers exhibiting a continued failure to provide timely loan transfer documentation may, at the discretion of the Secretary and following advance notice to the servicer, be subject to temporary suspension of all property acquisition and claim payments until all deficiencies identified in the notice provided to the servicer have been corrected.

(Authority: 38 U.S.C. 3703(c) and 3732(a))

(The Office of Management and Budget has approved the information collection requirements in this section under control number 2900-0362.)

[73 Fed. Reg. 6327, 6328 (Feb. 1, 2008)]

* * *

38 C.F.R. § 36.4850 Servicing procedures for holders.

(a) *Establishment of loan servicing program.* The holder of a loan guaranteed or insured by the Secretary shall develop and maintain a loan servicing program which follows accepted industry standards for servicing of similar type conventional loans. The loan servicing program established pursuant to this section may employ different servicing approaches to fit individual borrower circumstances and avoid establishing a fixed routine. However, it must incorporate each of the provisions specified in paragraphs (b) through (l) of this section.

(b) *Procedures for providing information.* (1) Loan holders shall establish procedures to provide loan information to borrowers, arrange for individual loan consultations upon request and maintain controls to assure prompt responses to inquiries. One or more of the following means of making information readily available to borrowers is required.

(i) An office staffed with trained servicing personnel with access to loan account information located within 200 miles of the property.

(ii) Toll-free telephone service or acceptance of collect telephone calls at an office capable of providing needed information.

(2) All borrowers must be informed of the system available for obtaining answers to loan inquiries, the office from which the needed information may be obtained, and reminded of the system at least annually.

(c) *Statement for income tax purposes.* Before February 1st of each calendar year, the holder shall furnish to the borrower a statement of the interest paid and, if applicable, a statement of the taxes disbursed from the escrow account during the preceding year. At the borrower's request, the holder shall furnish a statement of the escrow account sufficient to enable the borrower to reconcile the account.

(d) *Change of servicing.* Whenever servicing of a loan guaranteed or insured by the Secretary is transferred from one holder to another, notice of such transfer by both the transferor and transferee, the form and content of such notice, the timing of such notice, the treatment of payments during the period of such transfer, and damages and costs for failure to comply with these requirements shall be governed by the pertinent provisions of the Real Estate Settlement Procedures Act as administered by the Department of Housing and Urban Development.

(e) *Escrow accounts.* A holder of a loan guaranteed or insured by the Secretary may collect periodic deposits from the borrower for taxes and/or insurance on the security and maintain a tax and insurance escrow account provided such a requirement is authorized under the terms of the security instruments. In maintaining such accounts, the holder shall comply with the pertinent provisions of the Real Estate Settlement Procedures Act.

(f) *System for servicing delinquent loans.* In addition to the requirements of the Real Estate Settlement Procedures Act, concerning the duties of the loan servicer to respond to borrower inquiries, to protect the borrower's credit rating during a payment dispute period, and to pay damages and costs for noncompliance, holders shall establish a system for servicing delinquent loans which ensures that prompt action is taken to collect amounts due from borrowers and minimize the number of loans in a default status. The holder's servicing system must include the following:

(1) An accounting system which promptly alerts servicing personnel when a loan becomes delinquent;

(2) A collection staff which is trained in techniques of loan servicing and counseling delinquent borrowers to advise borrowers how to cure delinquencies, protect their equity and credit rating and, if the default is insoluble, pursue alternatives to foreclosure;

(3) Procedural guidelines for individual analysis of each delinquency;

(4) Instructions and appropriate controls for sending delinquent notices, assessing late charges, handling partial payments, maintaining servicing histories and evaluating repayment proposals;

(5) Management review procedures for evaluating efforts made to collect the delinquency and the response from the borrower before a decision is made to initiate action to liquidate a loan;

(6) Procedures for reporting delinquencies of 90 days or more and loan terminations to major consumer credit bureaus as specified by the Secretary and for informing borrowers that such action will be taken; and

(7) Controls to ensure that all notices required to be given to the Secretary on delinquent loans are provided timely and in such form as the Secretary shall require.

(g) *Collection actions.* (1) Holders shall employ collection techniques which provide flexibility to adapt to the individual needs and circumstances of each borrower. A variety of collection techniques may be used based on the holder's determination of the most effective means of contact with borrowers during various stages of delinquency. However, at a minimum the holder's collection procedures must include the following actions:

(i) An effort, concurrent with the initial late payment notice to establish contact with the borrower(s) by telephone. When talking with the borrower(s), the holder should attempt to determine why payment was not made and emphasize the importance of remitting loan installments as they come due.

(ii) A letter to the borrower(s) if payment has not been received within 30 days after it is due and telephone contact could not be made. This letter should emphasize the seriousness of the delinquency and the importance of taking prompt action to resolve the default. It should also notify the borrower(s) that the loan is in default, state the total amount due and advise the borrower(s) how to contact the holder to make arrangements for curing the default.

(iii) In the event the holder has not established contact with the borrower(s) and has not determined the financial circumstances of the borrower(s) or established a reason for the default or obtained agreement to a repayment plan from the borrower(s), then a face-to-face interview with the borrower(s) or a reasonable effort to arrange such a meeting is required.

(iv)(A) A letter to the borrower if payment has not been received:

(1) In the case of a default occurring within the first 6 months following loan closing or the execution of a modification agreement pursuant to § 36.4815, within 45 calendar days after such payment was due; or

(2) In the case of any other default, within 75 calendar days after such payment was due.

(B) The letter required by paragraph (g)(1)(iv)(A) must be mailed no later than 7 calendar days after the payment is delinquent for the time period stated in paragraph (g)(1)(iv)(A) and shall:

(1) Provide the borrower with a toll-free telephone number and, if available, an e-mail address for contacting the servicer;

(2) Explain loss mitigation options available to the borrower;

(3) Emphasize that the intent of servicing is to retain home ownership whenever possible; and

(4) Contain the following language:

> The delinquency of your mortgage loan is a serious matter that could result in the loss of your home. If you are the veteran whose entitlement was used to obtain this loan, you can also lose your entitlement to a future VA home loan guaranty. If you are not already working with us to resolve the delinquency, please call us to discuss your workout options. You may be able to make special payment arrangements that will reinstate your loan. You may also qualify for a repayment plan or loan modification.
>
> VA has guaranteed a portion of your loan and wants to ensure that you receive every reasonable opportunity to bring your loan current and retain your home. VA can also answer any questions you have regarding your entitlement. If you have access to the Internet and would like to obtain more information, you may access the VA web site at *www.va.gov*. You may also learn where to speak to a VA Loan Administration representative by calling 1-800-827-1000.

(2) The holder must provide a valid explanation of any failure to perform these collection actions when reporting loan defaults to the Secretary. A pattern of such failure may be a basis for sanctions under 2 CFR parts 180 and 801.

(h) *Conducting interviews with delinquent borrowers.* When personal contact with the borrower(s) is established, the holder shall solicit sufficient information to properly evaluate the prospects for curing the default and whether the granting of forbearance or other relief assistance would be appropriate. At a minimum, the holder must make a reasonable effort to establish the following:

(1) The reason for the default and whether the reason is a temporary or permanent condition;

(2) The present income and employment of the borrower(s);

(3) The current monthly expenses of the borrower(s) including household and debt obligations;

(4) The current mailing address and telephone number of the borrower(s); and

(5) A realistic and mutually satisfactory arrangement for curing the default.

(i) *Property inspections.* (1) The holder shall make an inspection of the property securing the loan whenever it becomes aware that the physical condition of the security may be in jeopardy. Unless a repayment agreement is in effect, a property inspection shall also be made at the following times:

(i) Before the 60th day of delinquency or before initiating action to liquidate a loan, whichever is earlier; and

(ii) At least once each month after liquidation proceedings have been started unless servicing information shows the property remains owner-occupied.

(2) Whenever a holder obtains information which indicates that the property securing the loan is abandoned, it shall make appropriate arrangements to protect the property from vandalism and the elements. Thereafter, the holder shall schedule inspections at least monthly to prevent unnecessary deterioration due to vandalism, or neglect. With respect to any loan more than 60 calendar days delinquent, if the property is abandoned, this fact must be reported to the Secretary as required in § 36.4817(c)(10) and immediate action should be initiated by the servicer to terminate the loan once the abandonment has been confirmed.

(j) *Collection records.* The holder shall maintain individual file records of collection action on delinquent loans and make such records available to the Secretary for inspection on request. Such collection records shall show:

(1) The dates and content of letters and notices which were mailed to the borrower(s);

(2) Dated summaries of each personal servicing contact and the result of same;

(3) The indicated reason(s) for default; and

(4) The date and result of each property inspection.

(k) *Quality control procedures.* No later than 180 days after the effective date of this regulation, each loan holder shall establish internal controls to periodically assess the quality of the servicing performed on loans guaranteed by the Secretary and assure that all requirements of this section are being met. Those procedures must provide for a review of the holder's servicing activities at least annually and include an evaluation of delinquency and foreclosure rates on loans in its portfolio which are guaranteed by the Secretary. As part of its evaluation of delinquency and foreclosure rates, the holder shall:

(1) Collect and maintain appropriate data on delinquency and foreclosure rates to enable the holder to evaluate effectiveness of its collection efforts;

(2) Determine how its VA delinquency and foreclosure rates compare with rates in reports published by the industry, investors and others; and,

(3) Analyze significant variances between its foreclosure and delinquency rates and those found in available reports and publications and take appropriate corrective action.

(*l*) *Provision of Data.* Holders shall provide available statistical data on delinquency and foreclosure rates and their analysis of such data to the Secretary upon request.

(Authority 38 U.S.C. 3703(c)(1))

(The Office of Management and Budget has approved the information collection requirements in this section under Control Number 2900-0530.)

[73 Fed. Reg. 6350–6352 (Feb. 1, 2008)]

* * *

A.3.3 VA Guaranty Loans Foreclosure Fee Schedule and Time Frames

A.3.3.1 VA Legal Services Fee Table

Jurisdiction	Non-judicial foreclosure	Judicial foreclosure	Deed-in-lieu of foreclosure	Foreclosure restart fee [2]	Chapter 13 release [3]	Chapter 7 release [3]
Alabama	550	N/A	350	350	850	650
Alaska	1200	N/A	350	350	850	650
Arizona	625	N/A	350	350	850	650
Arkansas	750	N/A	350	350	850	650
California	600	N/A	350	350	850	650
Colorado	800	N/A	350	350	850	650
Connecticut	N/A	1250	350	350	850	650
Delaware	N/A	950	350	350	850	650
District of Columbia	600	N/A	350	350	850	650
Florida	N/A	1200	350	350	850	650
Georgia	600	N/A	350	350	850	650
Guam	1200	N/A	350	350	850	650
Hawaii	N/A	1850	350	350	850	650
Idaho	600	N/A	350	350	850	650
Illinois	N/A	1100	350	350	850	650
Indiana	N/A	1000	350	350	850	650
Iowa	550	850	350	350	850	650
Kansas	N/A	850	350	350	850	650
Kentucky	N/A	1100	350	350	850	650
Louisiana	N/A	900	350	350	850	650
Maine	N/A	1250	350	350	850	650
Maryland	800	N/A	350	350	850	650
Massachusetts	N/A	1250	350	350	850	650
Michigan	650	N/A	350	350	850	650
Minnesota	650	N/A	350	350	850	650
Mississippi	550	N/A	350	350	850	650
Missouri	650	N/A	350	350	850	650
Montana	600	N/A	350	350	850	650
Nebraska	600	850	350	350	850	650
Nevada	600	N/A	350	350	850	650
New Hampshire	900	N/A	350	350	850	650
New Jersey	N/A	1300	350	350	850	650
New Mexico	N/A	900	350	350	850	650
New York—Western Counties [1]	N/A	1250	350	350	850	650
New York—Eastern Counties	N/A	1800	350	350	850	650
North Carolina	550	N/A	350	350	850	650
North Dakota	N/A	900	350	350	850	650
Ohio	N/A	1100	350	350	850	650
Oklahoma	N/A	900	350	350	850	650
Oregon	675	N/A	350	350	850	650
Pennsylvania	N/A	1250	350	350	850	650
Puerto Rico	N/A	1100	350	350	850	650
Rhode Island	900	N/A	350	350	850	650
South Carolina	N/A	850	350	350	850	650
South Dakota	650	850	350	350	850	650
Tennessee	550	N/A	350	350	850	650
Texas	550	N/A	350	350	850	650
Utah	600	N/A	350	350	850	650
Vermont	N/A	950	350	350	850	650
Virginia	600	N/A	350	350	850	650
Virgin Islands	N/A	1100	350	350	850	650
Washington	675	N/A	350	350	850	650
West Virginia	550	N/A	350	350	850	650
Wisconsin	N/A	1100	350	350	850	650
Wyoming	600	N/A	350	350	850	650

[1] Western Counties of New York are: Allegany, Cattaraugus, Chautauqua, Erie, Genesee, Livingston, Monroe, Niagara, Ontario, Orleans, Steuben, Wayne, Wyoming, and Yates. The remaining counties are in Eastern New York.

[2] When a foreclosure is stopped due to circumstances beyond control of the holder or its attorney (including, but not limited to bankruptcy, VA-requested delay, property damage, hazardous conditions, condemnation, natural disaster, property seizure, or relief under the Servicemembers Civil Relief Act) and then restarted, VA will allow the restart fee in addition to the base foreclosure attorney fee.

[3] For each additional relief of stay under either chapter, VA will pay $250.

A.3.3.2 VA Foreclosure Timeframes

Jurisdiction	Procedure	Final event	Time frame (calendar days)
Alabama	Non-Judicial	Sale	60
Alaska	Non-Judicial	Sale	120
Arizona	Non-Judicial	Sale	120
Arkansas	Non-Judicial	Sale	90
California	Non-Judicial	Sale	150
Colorado	Non-Judicial	Sale	150
Connecticut	Judicial	Sale (Vesting Date)	180
Delaware	Judicial	Confirmation/Ratification	240
District of Columbia	Non-Judicial	Sale	60
Florida	Judicial	Confirmation/Ratification	150
Georgia	Non-Judicial	Sale	90
Guam	Non-Judicial	Sale	180
Hawaii	Judicial	Confirmation	240
Idaho	Non-Judicial	Sale	180
Illinois	Judicial	Sale	300
Indiana	Judicial	Sale	270
Iowa	Judicial	Sale	180
	Non-Judicial	Sale (Filing of Affidavit)	60
Kansas	Judicial	Sale	150
Kentucky	Judicial	Confirmation	150
Louisiana	Judicial	Sale	180
Maine	Judicial	Sale	300
Maryland	Non-Judicial	Ratification Date	90
Massachusetts	Judicial Order	Sale	180
Michigan	Non-Judicial	Sale	90
Minnesota	Non-Judicial	Sale	90
Mississippi	Non-Judicial	Sale	90
Missouri	Non-Judicial	Sale	60
Montana	Non-Judicial	Sale	150
Nebraska	Judicial	Confirmation	180
	Non-Judicial	Sale	120
Nevada	Non-Judicial	Sale	150
New Hampshire	Non-Judicial	Sale	90
New Jersey	Judicial	Sale	300
New Mexico	Judicial	Confirmation	180
New York—Western Counties [1]	Judicial	Sale	240
New York—Eastern Counties	Judicial	Sale	270
North Carolina	Non-Judicial	Sale	120
North Dakota	Judicial	Sale	240
Ohio	Judicial	Confirmation	360
Oklahoma	Judicial	Confirmation	210
Oregon	Non-Judicial	Sale	150
Pennsylvania	Judicial	Sale	270
Puerto Rico	Judicial	Confirmation	450
Rhode Island	Non-Judicial	Sale	90
South Carolina	Judicial	Sale	180
South Dakota	Judicial	Sale	150
	Non-Judicial	Sale	90
Tennessee	Non-Judicial	Sale	60
Texas	Non-Judicial	Sale	90
Utah	Non-Judicial	Sale	150
Vermont	Judicial	Sale	300
Virginia	Non-Judicial	Sale	60
Virgin Islands	Judicial	Sale	540
Washington	Non-Judicial	Sale	150
West Virginia	Non-Judicial	Sale	60
Wisconsin	Judicial—Abandoned	Confirmation	210
	Judicial—Tenant Occupied	Confirmation	240
	Judicial—Owner Occupied	Confirmation	330
Wyoming	Non-Judicial	Sale	90

[1] Western Counties of New York are: Allegany, Cattaraugus, Chautauqua, Erie, Genesee, Livingston, Monroe, Niagara, Ontario, Orleans, Steuben, Wayne, Wyoming, and Yates. The remaining counties are in Eastern New York.

A.3.3.3 VA Making Home Affordable Program

Veterans Benefits Administration
Department of Veterans Affairs
Washington, DC 20420

Circular 26-10-02
January 8, 2010

VA MAKING HOME AFFORDABLE PROGRAM

1. PURPOSE. This circular provides authority and instructions for modifying VA-guaranteed home loans in accordance with the President's Making Home Affordable (MHA) program. These new procedures will be effective February 1, 2010.

2. BACKGROUND. VA has a longstanding policy of encouraging servicers to work with veteran borrowers to explore all reasonable options to help them retain their homes, or when that is not feasible, to mitigate losses by pursuing alternatives to foreclosure. In an effort to help homeowners avoid foreclosure, the President announced the MHA program to make home loans more affordable. Two main features are the Home Affordable Refinance Program (HARP) and the Home Affordable Modification Program (HAMP). HARP was introduced to help borrowers refinance at lower interest rates despite high loan-to-value (LTV) ratios, and provides relief similar to VA's existing Interest Rate Reduction Refinancing Loan (IRRRL) program. HAMP was introduced to avoid foreclosures by modifying loans to increase affordability relative to borrower income. Under HAMP, an affordable modification is defined as a new monthly mortgage payment (including principal, interest, property taxes, insurance, and condominium or homeowners' association fees (PITIA)) that is no greater than 31 percent of the borrower's monthly gross income. HAMP requires a two-step process for modifications that includes: a Trial Period Plan, where the borrower makes the proposed new modified mortgage payment for 3 months; and, after determination of eligibility for HAMP, an Agreement outlining the terms of the final modification. This circular explains how VA loans fit into the MHA program.

3. GUIDANCE TO SERVICERS

a. VA HAMP. VA expects servicers to exert all reasonable efforts to assist veteran borrowers in retaining ownership of their homes or mitigating losses when retention is not possible. Before considering VA HAMP, servicers must first evaluate defaulted mortgages for traditional loss mitigation actions cited in Title 38, Code of Federal Regulations, section 36.4819 (38 CFR 36.4819); i.e., repayment plans, special forbearances, traditional loan modifications. If the payments are affordable, then the traditional loss mitigation option will be used to help the veteran retain the home and avoid foreclosure. If none of the traditional home retention loss mitigation options provide an affordable payment, the servicer must evaluate the loan for a VA HAMP modification prior to deciding that the default is insoluble and exploring alternatives to foreclosure. VA expects servicers to complete all loss mitigation activities, including review for HAMP modifications, expeditiously, as interest on any claim under guaranty on an unsuccessful case is limited to 210 days from the due date of the last paid installment plus the published timeframe for foreclosure in the State where the security is located. This circular provides servicers with temporary authority to modify VA-guaranteed loans in a manner similar to HAMP. This VA HAMP authority can be utilized only if the following three requirements are met: 1) borrower does not qualify for traditional home retention loss mitigation, 2) the property is the borrower's primary residence, and 3) the VA HAMP modification is agreed upon by December 31, 2012 (current HAMP expiration date). The VA guaranty amount on a HAMP modification will be calculated pursuant to 38 CFR 36.4815, which could increase the maximum guaranty amount on the modified loan.

b. Servicer Completes Net Present Value (NPV) Calculation for VA HAMP. To determine if a default is insoluble, the servicer must perform a two-step NPV evaluation that will establish veteran borrower qualification for VA HAMP. This is necessary to ensure a veteran receives appropriate consideration for loan modification, even when the VA guaranty makes foreclosure a more financially attractive option for a servicer. The VA-Guaranteed Loan NPV model will assume that the loan is guaranteed by VA, with the customary claim and acquisition payments. The Conventional Loan NPV model assumes that the loan is not guaranteed by VA, and that no guaranty claim or acquisition is payable. Both NPV models require that all parameters, other than the existence of the VA guaranty, be identical (e.g., discount rate, default rate, standard VA modification incentive, etc.). Guidance regarding NPV models can be found at the HAMP website, www.hmpadmin.com. Based on the outcome of these model calculations, the servicer will take the appropriate action, as detailed in the table below.

SCENARIO	VA-GUARANTEED LOAN NPV TEST	CONVENTIONAL LOAN NPV TEST	SERVICER ACTION
A	Favor Modification	Not Needed	Execute VA HAMP modification pursuant to U.S. Department of Treasury's HAMP guidelines. For current loans, follow instructions in subparagraph d below.
B	Reject Modification	Favor Modification	Loan may be eligible for VA Refund (purchase). The servicer is required to notify VA so refunding may be considered. For current loans, follow instructions in subparagraph d below. For delinquent loans, follow instructions in subparagraph e below.
C	Reject Modification	Reject Modification	Explore short sale, deed in lieu, or proceed with foreclosure.

c. Servicer Authority to Complete VA HAMP Modifications. If the loan meets HAMP eligibility requirements, the servicer must execute the modification pursuant to the HAMP guidelines located at www.hmpadmin.com with the following exceptions:

(1) Standard VA servicer incentives apply.

(2) VA-guaranteed home loans are not eligible for any MHA incentives issued by the U.S. Department of Treasury at this time.

(3) VA will not pay incentives for any modification completed on a current loan.

(4) VA will not pay borrower incentives.

(5) Servicer Participation Agreements are not required.

d. Modification of Current Loans. Current loans may not be solicited for VA HAMP modification, as they should be considered for refinancing with programs such as VA's IRRRL. However, if a veteran borrower contacts a servicer to advise of "imminent danger of default", the loan may be evaluated under the VA HAMP guidelines. Modification of current loans requires VA prior approval. See Circular 26-09-17, Interim Process for Pre-Approval of Loan Modifications on Current Loans, issued October 1, 2009, for instructions on seeking prior approval to modify current loans.

e. Referral to VA for Refunding Consideration. When the table in subparagraph b above indicates that the loan may be eligible for VA refunding consideration, the servicer will e-mail the VALERI-assigned VA technician about the potential refunding. Servicers must also copy a VA Servicing Officer (SO) at the same Regional Loan Center (RLC) on the e-mail, in case the technician is unavailable for an extended period of time. The case information in VALERI lists the assigned VA technician, and servicers should refer to the VA Regional Loan Center Contact Information (by clicking the VALERI link at www.homeloans.va.gov) to obtain the name of an SO. The servicer will upload to VALERI all available and relevant information required under HAMP, including the data used in the servicer's NPV calculation. Relevant information includes, but is not limited to, the total eligible indebtedness, the borrowers' expected gross monthly income, and the expected monthly escrow amount. The VA technician will e-mail the servicer within 7 calendar days with a determination of whether or not VA will proceed with refunding consideration. VA will reimburse additional interest accrued in accordance with existing policies. If insufficient documentation is provided to make a determination, the servicer may be liable for accrued interest during VA's further development.

4. GUIDANCE TO VA STAFF

a. VA Refunding with HAMP Modifications. A VA technician will receive an e-mail from a servicer after it has analyzed a loan under the HAMP guidelines and believes refunding may be appropriate according to the table in paragraph 3b. If the servicer has provided all available and relevant information (including the data used in the NPV calculation), the VA technician will e-mail the servicer within 7 calendar days as to whether or not VA will proceed with refunding consideration. After this preliminary review, in instances where a decision is made not to proceed with refunding consideration, SO approval must be obtained prior to notifying the servicer. However, SO approval is not required in instances when refunding consideration will proceed. All refund recommendations must be thoroughly documented. If VA will not refund the loan, the technician will notify the servicer to pursue loss mitigation alternatives or foreclosure. If a decision is made to continue with refunding consideration, the technician will open the "review refund" process and proceed with refunding as usual. VA will reimburse additional interest accrued in accordance with existing policies.

b. VA NPV Model for Refunding. During the refunding review, the technician must utilize a newly introduced VA NPV refunding model available on the VA Intranet. The technician will input income and other required data and calculate the adjusted interest rate, term, and principal deferment for a loan modification needed to achieve a monthly mortgage payment (PITIA) of no greater than 31 percent of the borrower's gross income. The VA HAMP refunding program provides for a fixed interest rate, with a floor of two percent for the life of the loan; a maximum term of up to 40 years; and principal deferment when appropriate. The U.S. Department of Treasury directive describes principal deferment as a non-interest bearing and non-amortizing amount, which is essentially a balloon payment fully due and payable upon the earliest of: the transfer of the property, the payoff of the interest bearing unpaid principal balance, or the maturity of the loan.

c. Special Considerations. If the initial VA NPV analysis indicates the loan should not be refunded, the technician will thoroughly review the case and clearly document any special circumstances that could justify approval of the refunding. For example, if the present default was caused by unique circumstances beyond the veteran's control that have been resolved or will clearly soon be resolved, the technician may recommend approval to the SO with documentation to justify not following the initial analysis. RLC management may contact VA Central Office for guidance in unusual situations.

d. Benefits of VA Refunding to Servicers and Veterans. If a loan cannot be modified by the servicer under HAMP, but is refunded by VA, the servicer is essentially paid in full for the loan and the veteran receives a fresh start with affordable payments. Unlike the HAMP program, VA refunds does not have a 3-month trial period because the VA modification agreement immediately changes the installment amount to begin the fresh start sooner. Additionally, VA will not increase the interest rate after 5 years; instead the loan will retain the lower refunded rate for the life of the modification.

5. QUESTIONS. Questions may be directed to Mike Frueh at mike.frueh@va.gov.

6. RESCISSION: This circular is rescinded January 1, 2014.

By Direction of the Under Secretary for Benefits
Mark Bologna, Director
Loan Guaranty Service

Distribution: CO: RPC 2024
SS (26A1) FLD: VBAFS, 1 each (Reproduce and distribute based on RPC 2024)

(LOCAL REPRODUCTION AUTHORIZED)

A.3.3.4 Policy on Loan Modifications

Veterans Benefits Administration — Circular 26-09-17
Department of Veterans Affairs — Change 1
Washington, DC 20420 — January 11, 2010

INTERIM PROCESS FOR PRE-APPROVAL OF LOAN MODIFICATIONS ON CURRENT LOANS

1. PURPOSE. The purpose of this change is to extend the rescission date of the basic circular to coincide with the rescission date of Circular 26-10-2.

2. Therefore, Circular 26-09-17 is changed as follows:

Page 2, paragraph 6: Delete "January 1, 2012." And insert "January 1, 2014."

By Direction of the Under Secretary for Benefits

Mark Bologna, Director
Loan Guaranty Service

Distribution: CO: RPC 2024
SS (26A1) FLD: VBAFS, 1 each (Reproduce and distribute based on RPC 2024)

(LOCAL REPRODUCTION AUTHORIZED)

A.3.4 VA Guaranty Policy Regarding Natural Disasters

VA Loan Guaranty Policy Regarding Natural Disasters

In the event that there is a declaration of a major disaster, the following is an outline of VA requirements regarding loans secured by properties in areas designated by Federal authorities as a result of a natural disaster such as hurricanes, tropical storms, tornadoes, etc. When the President declares a disaster, lenders and servicers must check with the Federal Emergency Management Agency (FEMA) to obtain the specific counties and corresponding declaration dates. In addition, lenders and servicers should check with FEMA for any amendments. This information can be found on the Internet at www.fema.gov/disasters or by calling the local FEMA office.

1. ***Loan Origination Issues***

a. **Loan Closed Prior to Disaster.** Any loan closed prior to the date of the declared disaster is eligible for VA Guaranty without regard to the disaster. The "Loan Servicing and Claims" information in paragraph 2 applies to these cases.

b. **Property Appraised Prior to Disaster.** For a loan on a property appraised on or before the date of the declared disaster and not closed prior to that date to be eligible for VA guaranty:

1) **Certifications.** Both of the following certifications must be submitted with the guaranty request:

a) **Lender Certification**—This is to affirm that the property which is security for VA loan number ________ has been inspected to ensure that it was either not damaged in the recently declared disaster or has been restored to its pre-disaster condition or better.

____________ ____________ _____
(Lender Signature) (Lender Title) (Date)

b) **Veteran Certification**—I have inspected the property located at [rule; 10] and find its condition now to be acceptable to me. I understand that I will not be charged for any disaster-related expenses and now wish to close the loan.

____________ _____
(Veteran Signature) (Date)

2) **VA Loan Summary Sheet.** The "Remarks" section of VA Form 26-0286, VA Loan Summary Sheet must be annotated "Lender and Veteran Disaster Certifications Enclosed." Additionally, if local law requires the property to be inspected and approved by the local building inspection authority, a copy of the appropriate local report(s) must be provided. Neither VA nor the veteran purchaser shall bear the expense of any disaster-related inspection or repairs.

3) **Decline in Value.** If there is an indication that the property, despite repairs, will be worth less at the time of loan closing than it was at the time of appraisal, then the lender must have the VA fee appraiser update the original value estimate. The payment of the appraiser's fee for that service will be a contractual matter between the buyer and seller. If the property value has decreased, the loan amount must be reduced accordingly.

4) **Employment/Income Certification.** The lender should ascertain prior to closing that the veteran's employment and income have not changed since the loan application. If at the time of closing the veteran is no longer employed or family income has been reduced, this information should be reported to VA or the automatic underwriter, as appropriate, for evaluation prior to closing the loan.

2. Loan Servicing and Claims Issues

a. **Assistance to Homeowners.** VA encourages holders of guaranteed loans in disaster areas to extend every possible forbearance to borrowers in distress through no fault of their own. VA Regulations regarding "Reapplication of Prepayments" (38 CFR 36.4310), "Advances" (38 CFR 36.4313). "Extensions and Reamortizations" (38 CFR 36.4314) and "Supplement Loans" (38 CFR 36.4355) may be of assistance in appropriate cases. It is the loan holder's responsibility to inspect damage to properties, counsel borrowers concerning assistance that may be available to them and provide the applicable Regional Loan Center with a report that outlines the findings and actions for each damaged property. Loan holders should contact the appropriate Regional Loan Center before consenting to an insurance adjustment where the proceeds will not be sufficient to pay the loan balance or restore the security.

b. **VA Bulletin for Borrowers.** Please include a copy of the attached "VA Loan Guaranty Benefits" paper in any correspondence you send borrowers in the disaster areas. The information provided here should be beneficial to all parties involved.

c. **Moratorium on Foreclosures.** Although the loan holder is ultimately responsible for determining when to initiate foreclosure and for completing termination action, VA requests that holders establish a 90-day moratorium from the date of the declared disaster on initiating new foreclosures in the disaster areas. Since VA is requesting this, the provisions of 38 CFR 36.4319(f) will not be applied by VA during the moratorium to loans secured by properties in the disaster areas. Also, the period of the moratorium will be considered "VA-requested forbearance" for purposes of the no-bid avoidance provisions of 38 CFR 36.4321. There are two exceptions to the 90-day moratorium on new foreclosures:

1) When a default is clearly insoluble and there is no likelihood of reinstatement and the holder requests and receives VA prior approval to initiate foreclosure during the period of the moratorium; or

2) When a foreclosure sale, the product of an insoluble default which occurred prior to the disaster, was already scheduled. The sale should be delayed only to the extent necessary to determine whether the liquidation appraisal remains accurate and for such time as it may take for the holder to obtain acceptable hazard insurance loss settlement for purposes of 38 CFR 36.4326.

d. **Insurance Requirements.** VA Regulations (38 CFR 36.4326) require that lenders and holders ensure that homes financed with the assistance of VA-guaranteed loans be sufficiently insured against hazards (including flooding, where appropriate). Insurance proceeds are to be applied to the restoration of the security or to the loan balance. The burden of proof is upon the lender or holder to establish that no increase in VA's ultimate liability is attributable to the failure of the lender or holder to have the property properly insured, or to properly apply an insurance loss settlement.

Holders are reminded that hazard insurance policies are not to be canceled in the event of a foreclosure sale if the property is to be conveyed to VA. The policies are to be endorsed to the Secretary of Veterans Affairs.

Any case-specific Appraisal, Loan Production and/or Loan Administration issues may be directed to the appropriate Regional Loan Center.

VA LOAN GUARANTY BENEFITS

This bulletin is distributed by the Department of Veterans Affairs to provide information during major disasters. The information given below is primarily for homeowners whose loans are guaranteed by VA.

Contact Your Mortgage Company

Contact your lender as soon as possible regarding your loss. ***You are not excused from making your regular monthly loan payments even if your home is not habitable.*** You should discuss forbearance or possible extension or modification of your loan if you are unable to make your payments on time. You should also have your lender explain procedures regarding insurance loss checks and repairs to your property, payment to contractors, etc.

Contact Your Insurance Company or Agent

File insurance loss claims as soon as possible. However, ***do not make a hasty settlement on insurance.*** When the property is damaged but repairable, attempt to get the engineer's office of your local government to make an inspection for ***structural damage.*** If possible, get at least two estimates from licensed contractors for cost of repairs or rebuilding. Insurance checks for personal property and living expenses should be made payable to you only. Checks for damage to your home should be made payable to you and your mortgage company.

Contact FEMA (Federal Emergency Management Agency)

You begin the disaster application process by calling FEMA's toll free number 1-800-621-FEMA (3362), or 1-800-462-7585 (TTY) for the hearing and speech impaired. In order to receive the maximum assistance, you must register with FEMA before their deadline expires. You cannot obtain assistance for uninsured losses or damages to your home from the Small Business Administration (SBA) or any other disaster recovery agency if you have not registered with FEMA. More information can be found at the FEMA website, www.fema.gov. Be sure to check every source for maximum assistance including the SBA. ***Do not pay your loan in full*** before checking with SBA on a loan for the uninsured portion of your loss. Low interest loans, cash grants, and housing assistance may be available from agencies associated with the disaster recovery effort.

Check Other Sources of Help

Veterans should contact local offices of the American Legion, Veterans of Foreign Wars, Disabled American Veterans (DAV), or other veterans organizations to see if special assistance may be available, even to non-members of the organization.

Change your Address

If you are receiving a monthly benefit check from VA or another source, and you will not be able to receive mail at your regular address, notify your local post office and VA Regional Office of your change of address. For information on VA benefits other than home loans, call 1-800-827-1000.

A.4 Loans Held by the Rural Housing Service (formerly the Farmers Home Administration)

A.4.1 Selected Statutes

TITLE 42. THE PUBLIC HEALTH AND WELFARE

CHAPTER 8A—SLUM CLEARANCE, URBAN RENEWAL, AND FARM HOUSING

SUBCHAPTER III—FARM HOUSING

42 U.S.C. § 1471. Financial assistance by Secretary of Agriculture

(a) Authorization and purposes of assistance

The Secretary of Agriculture (hereinafter referred to as the "Secretary") is authorized, subject to the terms and conditions of this subchapter, to extend financial assistance, through the Farmers Home Administration, (1) to owners of farms in the United States and in the Territories of Alaska and Hawaii and in the Commonwealth of Puerto Rico, the Virgin Islands, the territories and possessions of the United States, and the Trust Territory of the Pacific Islands, to enable them to construct, improve, alter, repair, or replace dwellings and other farm buildings on their farms, and to purchase buildings and land constituting a minimum adequate site, in order to provide them, their tenants, lessees, sharecroppers, and laborers with decent, safe, and sanitary living conditions and adequate farm buildings as specified in this subchapter, and (2) to owners of other real estate in rural areas for the construction, improvement, alteration, or repair of dwellings, related facilities, and farm buildings and to rural residents, including persons who reside in reservations or villages of Indian tribes, for such purposes and for the purchase of buildings and the purchase of land constituting a minimum adequate site, in order to enable them to provide dwellings and related facilities for their own use and buildings adequate for their farming operations, and (3) to elderly or handicapped persons or families who are or will be the owners of land in rural areas for the construction, improvement, alteration, or repair of dwellings and related facilities, the purchase of dwellings and related facilities and the purchase of land constituting a minimum adequate site, in order to provide them with adequate dwellings and related facilities for their own use, and (4) to an owner described in clause (1), (2), or (3) for refinancing indebtedness which—

(A) was incurred for an eligible purpose described in such clause, and

(B)(i) if not refinanced, is likely to result (because of circumstances beyond the control of the applicant) at an early date in the loss of the applicant's necessary dwelling or essential farm service buildings, or

(ii) if combined (in the case of a dwelling that the Secretary finds not to be decent, safe, and sanitary) with a loan for improvement, rehabilitation, or repairs and not refinanced, is likely to result in the applicant's continuing to be deprived of a decent, safe, and sanitary dwelling.

(5)[1] Definitions.—For purposes of this subchapter, the terms "repair," "repairs," "rehabilitate," and "rehabilitation" include measures to evaluate and reduce lead-based paint hazards, as such terms are defined in section 4851b of this title.

(b) Definitions

(1) For the purpose of this subchapter, the term "farm" shall mean a parcel or parcels of land operated as a single unit which is used for the production of one or more agricultural commodities and which customarily produces or is capable of producing such commodities for sale and for home use of a gross annual value of not less than the equivalent of a gross annual value of $400 in 1944, as determined by the Secretary. The Secretary shall promptly determine whether any parcel or parcels of land constitute a farm for the purposes of this subchapter whenever requested to do so by any interested Federal, State, or local public agency, and his determination shall be conclusive.

(2) For the purposes of this subchapter, the terms "owner" and "mortgage" shall be deemed to include, respectively, the lessee of, and other security interest in, any leasehold interest which the Secretary determines has an unexpired term (A) in the case of a loan, for a period sufficiently beyond the repayment period of the loan to provide adequate security and a reasonable probability of accomplishing the objectives for which the loan is made, and (B) in the case of a grant for a period sufficient to accomplish the objectives for which the grant is made.

(3) For the purposes of this subchapter, the term "elderly or handicapped persons or families" means families which consist of two or more persons, the head of which (or his or her spouse) is at least sixty-two years of age or is handicapped. Such term also means a single person who is at least sixty-two years of age or is handicapped. A person shall be considered handicapped if such person is determined, pursuant to regulations issued by the Secretary, to have an impairment which (A) is expected to be of long-continued and indefinite duration, (B) substantially impedes his ability to live independently, and (C) is of such a nature that such ability could be improved by more suitable housing conditions, or if such person has a developmental disability as defined in section 15002 of this title. The Secretary shall prescribe such regulations as may be necessary to prevent abuses in determining, under the definitions contained in this paragraph, eligibility of families and persons for admission to and occupancy of housing constructed with assistance under this subchapter. Notwithstanding the preceding provisions of this paragraph, such term also includes two or more elderly (sixty-two years of age or over) or handicapped persons living together, one or more such persons living with another person who is determined (under regulations prescribed by the Secretary) to be essential to the care or well-being of such persons, and the surviving member or members of any family described in the first sentence of this paragraph who were living, in a unit assisted under this subchapter, with the deceased member of the family at the time of his or her death.

(4) For the purpose of this subchapter, the terms "low income families or persons" and "very low-income families or persons" means those families and persons whose incomes do not exceed the respective levels established for lower income families and very low-income families under the United States Housing Act of 1937 [42 U.S.C. § 1437 et seq.]. Notwithstanding the preceding sentence, the maximum income levels established for purposes of this subchapter for such families and persons in the Virgin Islands shall not be less than the highest such levels established for purposes of this subchapter for such families and persons in American Samoa, Guam, the Northern Mariana Islands, and the Trust Territory of the Pacific Islands. The temporary absence of a child from the home due to placement in foster care should not be considered in considering family composition and family size.

(5)(A) For the purpose of this subchapter, the terms "income" and "adjusted income" have the meanings given by sections 3(b)(4) and 3(b)(5), respectively, of the United States Housing Act of 1937 [42 U.S.C. § 1437a(b)(4), (5)].

(B) For purposes of this subchapter, the term "income" does not include dividends received from the Alaska Permanent Fund by a person who was under the age of 18 years when that person qualified for the dividend.

(6) For the purposes of this subchapter, the term "Indian tribe" means any Indian tribe, band, group, and nation, including Alaska Indians, Aleuts, and Eskimos, and any Alaskan Native Village, of the United States, which is considered an eligible recipient under the Indian Self-Determination and Education Assistance Act (Public Law 93-638) [25 U.S.C. § 450 et seq.] or was considered an eligible recipient under chapter 67 of Title 31 prior to repeal of such chapter.

(7) For the purposes of this subchapter, the term "rural resident" shall include a family or a person who is a renter of a dwelling unit in a rural area.

(8) For the purposes of this subchapter, the term "adequate dwelling" means a decent, safe, and sanitary dwelling unit.

1 [*Editor's Note*: So in original. Paragraphs (1) to (4) were not enacted.]

(c) Conditions of eligibility

In order to be eligible for the assistance authorized by subsection (a) of this section, the applicant must show (1) that he is the owner of a farm which is without a decent, safe, and sanitary dwelling for himself and his family and necessary resident farm labor, or for the family of the operating tenant, lessee, or sharecropper, or without other farm buildings adequate for the type of farming in which he engages or desires to engage, or that he is the owner of other real estate in a rural area or a rural resident without an adequate dwelling or related facilities for his own use or buildings adequate for his farming operations, or that the applicant is an elderly or handicapped person or family in a rural area without an adequate dwelling or related facility for its own use, or that he is the owner of a farm or other real estate in a rural area who needs refinancing of indebtedness described in clause (4) of subsection (a) of this section; (2) that he is without sufficient resources to provide the necessary housing and buildings on his own account; and (3) that he is unable to secure the credit necessary for such housing and buildings from other sources upon terms and conditions which he could reasonably be expected to fulfill. If an applicant is a State or local public agency or Indian tribe—

(A) the provisions of clause (3) shall not apply to its application; and

(B) the applicant shall be eligible to participate in any program under this subchapter if the persons or families to be served by the applicant with the assistance being sought would be eligible to participate in such program.

(d) Additional definitions

As used in this subchapter (except in sections 1473 and 1474(b) of this title) the terms "farm," "farm dwelling," and "farm housing" shall include dwellings or other essential buildings of eligible applicants.

(e) Prepayment of taxes, insurance, and other expenses; advances to account of borrower; interest, time for repayment

The Secretary shall establish procedures under which borrowers under this subchapter are required to make periodic payments for the purpose of taxes, insurance, and other necessary expenses as the Secretary may deem appropriate. Notwithstanding any other provision of law, such payments shall not be considered public funds. The Secretary shall direct the disbursement of the funds at the appropriate time or times for the purposes for which the funds were escrowed. The Secretary shall pay the same rate of interest on escrowed funds as is required to be paid on escrowed funds held by other lenders in any State where State law requires payment of interest on escrowed funds, subject to appropriations to the extent that additional budget authority is necessary to carry out this sentence. If the prepayments made by the borrower are not sufficient to pay the amount due, advances may be made by the Secretary to pay the costs in full, which advances shall be charged to the account of the borrower, bear interest, and be payable in a timely fashion as determined by the Secretary. The Secretary shall notify a borrower in writing when loan payments are delinquent.

(f) Increase in loan limits

With respect to any limitation on the amount of any loan which may be made, insured, or guaranteed under this subchapter for the purchase of a dwelling unit, the Secretary may increase such amount by up to 20 percent if such increase is necessary to account for the increased cost of the dwelling unit due to the installation of a solar energy system (as defined in subparagraph (3) of the last paragraph of section 1703(a) of Title 12) therein.

(g) Avoidance of involuntary displacement of families and businesses

The programs authorized by this subchapter shall be carried out, consistent with program goals and objectives, so that the involuntary displacement of families and businesses is avoided.

(h) Eligibility of resident aliens

The Secretary may not restrict the availability of assistance under this subchapter for any alien for whom assistance may not be restricted under section 1436a of this title.

(i) Loan packaging by nonprofit organizations as a "development cost"

For the purposes of this subchapter, the term "development cost" shall include the packaging of loan and grant applications and actions related thereto by public and private nonprofit organizations tax exempt under Title 26.

(j) Program transfers

Notwithstanding any other provision of law, the Secretary shall not transfer any program authorized by this subchapter to the Rural Development Administration.

[July 15, 1949, ch. 338, tit. V, § 501, 63 Stat. 432; Pub. L. No. 87-70, tit. VIII, §§ 801(a), 803, 75 Stat. 186 (June 30, 1961); Pub. L. No. 87- 723, § 4(a)(1), 76 Stat. 670 (Sept. 28, 1962); Pub. L. No. 89-117, tit. X, § 1001, 79 Stat. 497 (Aug. 10, 1965); Pub. L. No. 89-754, tit. VIII, §§ 801, 807, 80 Stat. 1282 (Nov. 3, 1966); Pub. L. No. 91-609, tit. VIII, § 802, 84 Stat. 1806 (Dec. 31, 1970); Pub. L. No. 93-383, tit. V, §§ 501–503, 505(a), 520, 88 Stat. 692, 693, 699 (Aug. 22, 1974); Pub. L. No. 95-128, tit. V, §§ 503, 507(a)(1), (2), (b), 91 Stat. 1139, 1140, 1141 (Oct. 12, 1977); Pub. L. No. 95-619, tit. II, § 248(c), 92 Stat. 3235 (Nov. 9, 1978); Pub. L. No. 96-153, tit. V, §§ 502(b), 506, 93 Stat. 1134, 1136 (Dec. 21, 1979); Pub. L. No. 96-399, tit. V, §§ 506, 507(a), (h), 512, 94 Stat. 1669–1671 (Oct. 8, 1980); Pub. L. No. 98-181, tit. V, § 502, 97 Stat. 1240 (Nov. 30, 1983); Pub. L. No. 98-479, tit. I, § 105(a), tit. II, § 203(d)(3), 98 Stat. 2226, 2229 (Oct. 17, 1984); Pub. L. No. 99-272, tit. XIV, § 14001(b)(3), 100 Stat. 328 (Apr. 7, 1986); Pub. L. No. 100-242, tit. III, §§ 302(a), (b)(1), 303, 315, 316(a), 101 Stat. 1893, 1894, 1897 (Feb. 5, 1988); Pub. L. No. 101-625, tit. VII, §§ 702, 703, 104 Stat. 4282, 4283 (Nov. 28, 1990); Pub. L. No. 102-550, tit. VII, § 714, tit. X, § 1012(m), 106 Stat. 3842, 3907 (Oct. 28, 1992); Pub. L. No. 104-193, tit. IV, § 441(b), 110 Stat. 2276 (Aug. 22, 1996); Pub. L. No. 106-402, tit. IV, § 401(b)(8), 114 Stat. 1738 (Oct. 30, 2000); Pub. L. No. 107-76, tit. VII, § 752, 115 Stat. 740 (Nov. 28, 2001); Pub. L. No. 108-199, div. A, tit. VII, § 768, 118 Stat. 40 (Jan. 23, 2004)]

42 U.S.C. § 1472. Loans for housing and buildings on adequate farms

(a) Terms of loan

(1) If the Secretary determines that an applicant is eligible for assistance as provided in section 1471 of this title and that the applicant has the ability to repay in full the sum to be loaned, with interest, giving due consideration to the income and earning capacity of the applicant and his family from the farm and other sources, and the maintenance of a reasonable standard of living for the owner and the occupants of said farm, a loan may be made by the Secretary to said applicant for a period of not to exceed thirty-three years from the making of the loan with interest. The Secretary may accept the personal liability of any person with adequate repayment ability who will cosign the applicant's note to compensate for any deficiency in the applicant's repayment ability. At the borrower's option, the borrower may prepay to the Secretary as escrow agent, on terms and conditions prescribed by him, such taxes, insurance, and other expenses as the Secretary may require in accordance with section 1471(e) of this title.

(2) The Secretary may extend the period of any loan made under this section if the Secretary determines that such extension is necessary to permit the making of such loan to any person whose income does not exceed 60 per centum of the median income for the area and who would otherwise be denied such loan because the payments required under a shorter period would exceed the financial capacity of such person. The aggregate period for which any loan may be extended under this paragraph may not exceed 5 years.

(3)(A) Notwithstanding any other provision of this subchapter, a loan may be made under this section for the purchase of a dwelling located on land owned by a community land trust, if the borrower and the loan otherwise meet the requirements applicable to loans under this section.

(B) For purposes of this paragraph, the term "community land trust" means a community housing development organization as such term is defined in section 12704 of this title (except that the requirements under section 12704(6)(C) of this title and section 12704(6)(D) of this title shall not apply for purposes of this paragraph)—

(i) that is not sponsored by a for-profit organization;

(ii) that is established to carry out the activities under clause (iii);

(iii) that—

(I) acquires parcels of land, held in perpetuity, primarily for conveyance under long-term ground leases;

(II) transfers ownership of any structural improvements located on such leased parcels to the lessees; and

(III) retains a preemptive option to purchase any such structural improvement at a price determined by formula that is designed to ensure that the improvement remains affordable to low- and moderate-income families in perpetuity; and

(iv) that has its corporate membership open to any adult resident of a particular geographic area specified in the bylaws of the organization.

(b) Provisions of loan instrument

The instruments under which the loan is made and the security given shall—

(1) provide for security upon the applicant's equity in the farm or such other security or collateral, if any, as may be found necessary by the Secretary reasonably to assure repayment of the indebtedness;

(2) provide for the repayment of principal and interest in accordance with schedules and repayment plans prescribed by the Secretary, except that any prepayment of a loan made or insured under section 1484 or 1485 of this title shall be subject to the provisions of subsection (c) of this section;

(3) except for guaranteed loans, contain the agreement of the borrower that he will, at the request of the Secretary, proceed with diligence to refinance the balance of the indebtedness through cooperative or other responsible private credit sources whenever the Secretary determines, in the light of the borrower's circumstances, including his earning capacity and the income from the farm, that he is able to do so upon reasonable terms and conditions;

(4) be in such form and contain such covenants as the Secretary shall prescribe to secure the payment of the loan with interest, protect the security, and assure that the farm will be maintained in repair and that waste and exhaustion of the farm will be prevented.

(c) Prepayment and refinancing provisions

(1)(A) The Secretary may not accept an offer to prepay, or request refinancing in accordance with subsection (b)(3) of this section of, any loan made or insured under section 1484 or 1485 of this title pursuant to a contract entered into after December 21, 1979, but before December 15, 1989, unless the Secretary takes appropriate action which will obligate the borrower (and successors in interest thereof) to utilize the assisted housing and related facilities for the purposes specified in section 1484 or 1485 of this title, as the case may be, for a period of—

(i) fifteen years from the date on which the loan was made in the case of a loan made or insured pursuant to a contract entered into after December 21, 1979, but before December 15, 1989, and utilized for housing and related facilities which have not received assistance under section 1490a(a)(1)(B), (a)(2), or (5) of this title or section 1437f of this title; or

(ii) twenty years from the date on which the loan was made in the case of any other such loan;

or until the Secretary determines (prior to the end of such period) that there is no longer a need for such housing and related facilities to be so utilized or that Federal or other financial assistance provided to the residents of such housing will no longer be provided.

(B) The Secretary may not accept an offer to prepay, or request refinancing in accordance with subsection (b)(3) of this section of, any initial loan made or insured under section 1485 of this title pursuant to a contract entered into on or after December 15, 1989.

(2) If any loan which was made or insured under section 1484 or 1485 of this title pursuant to a contract entered into prior to December 15, 1989, is prepaid or refinanced on or after October 8, 1980, and tenants of the housing and related facilities financed with such loan are displaced due to a change in the use of the housing, or to an increase in rental or other charges, as a result of such prepayment or refinancing, the Secretary shall provide such tenants a priority for relocation in alternative housing assisted pursuant to this subchapter.

(3) Notice of offer to prepay

Not less than 30 days after receiving an offer to prepay any loan made or insured under section 1484 or 1485 of this title, the Secretary shall provide written notice of the offer or request to the tenants of the housing and related facilities involved, to interested nonprofit organizations, and to any appropriate State and local agencies.

(4)(A) Agreement by borrower to extend low income use

Before accepting any offer to prepay, or requesting refinancing in accordance with subsection (b)(3) of this section of, any loan made or insured under section 1484 or 1485 of this title pursuant to a contract entered into prior to December 15, 1989, the Secretary shall make reasonable efforts to enter into an agreement with the borrower under which the borrower will make a binding commitment to extend the low income use of the assisted housing and related facilities involved for not less than the 20-year period beginning on the date on which the agreement is executed.

(B) Assistance available to borrower to extend low income use

To the extent of amounts provided in appropriation Acts, the agreement under subparagraph (A) may provide for 1 or more of the following forms of assistance that the Secretary, after taking into account local market conditions, determines to be necessary to extend the low income use of the housing and related facilities involved:

(i) Increase in the rate of return on investment.

(ii) Reduction of the interest rate on the loan through the provision of interest credits under section 1490a(a)(1)(B) of this title, or additional assistance or an increase in assistance provided under section 1490a(a)(5) of this title.

(iii) Additional rental assistance, or an increase in assistance provided under existing contracts, under section 1490a(a)(2) or 1490a(a)(5) of this title or under section 1437f of this title.

(iv) An equity loan to the borrower under paragraphs (1) and (2) of section 1485(c) of this title or under paragraphs (1) and (2) of section 1484(j) of this title, except that an equity loan referred to in this clause may not be made available after August 6, 1996, unless the Secretary determines that the other incentives available under this subparagraph are not adequate to provide a fair return on the investment of the borrower, to prevent prepayment of the loan insured under section 1484 or 1485 of this title, or to prevent the displacement of tenants of the housing for which the loan was made.

(v) Incremental rental assistance in connection with loans under clauses (ii) and (iv) to the extent necessary to avoid increases in the rental payments of current tenants not receiving rental assistance under section 1490a(a)(2) of this title or under section 1437f of this title, or current tenants of projects not assisted under section 1490a(a)(5) of this title.

(vi) In the case of a project that has received rental assistance under section 1437f of this title, permitting the owner to receive rent in excess of the amount determined necessary by the Secretary to defray the cost of long-term repair or maintenance of such a project.

(C) Approval of assistance

The Secretary may approve assistance under subparagraph (B) for assisted housing only if the restrictive period has expired for any loan for the housing made or insured under section 1484 or 1485 of this title pursuant to a contract entered into after December 21, 1979, but before December 15, 1989, and the Secretary determines that the combination of assistance provided—

(i) is necessary to provide a fair return on the investment of the borrower; and

(ii) is the least costly alternative for the Federal Government that is consistent with carrying out the purposes of this subsection.

(5)(A) Offer to sell to nonprofit organizations and public agencies

(i) In general

If the Secretary determines after a reasonable period that an agreement will not be entered into with a borrower under paragraph (4), the Secretary shall require the borrower (except as provided in subparagraph (G)) to offer to sell the assisted housing and related facilities involved to any qualified nonprofit organization or public agency at a fair market value determined by 2 independent appraisers, one of whom shall be selected by the Secretary and one of whom shall be selected by the borrower. If the 2 appraisers fail to agree on the fair market value, the Secretary and the borrower shall jointly select a third appraiser, whose appraisal shall be binding on the Secretary and the borrower.

(ii) Period for which requirement applicable

If, upon the expiration of 180 days after an offer is made to sell housing and related facilities under clause (i), no qualified nonprofit organization or public agency has made a bona fide offer to purchase, the Secretary may accept the offer to prepay, or may request refinancing in accordance with subsection (b)(3) of this section of, the loan. This clause shall apply only when funds are available for purposes of carrying out a transfer under this paragraph.

(B) Qualified nonprofit organizations and public agencies

(i) Local nonprofit organization or public agency

A local nonprofit organization or public agency may purchase housing and related facilities under this paragraph only if—

(I) the organization or agency is determined by the Secretary to be capable of managing the housing and related facilities (either directly or through a contract) for the remaining useful life of the housing and related facilities; and

(II) the organization or agency has entered into an agreement that obligates it (and successors in interest thereof) to maintain the housing and related facilities as affordable for very low-income families or persons and low income families or persons for the remaining useful life of the housing and related facilities.

(ii) National or regional nonprofit organization

If the Secretary determines that there is no local nonprofit organization or public agency qualified to purchase the housing and related facilities involved, the Secretary shall require the borrower to offer to sell the assisted housing and related facilities to an existing qualified national or regional nonprofit organization.

(iii) Selection of qualified purchaser

The Secretary shall promulgate regulations that establish criteria for selecting a qualified nonprofit organization or public agency to purchase housing and related facilities when more than 1 such organization or agency has made a bona fide offer. Such regulations shall give a priority to those organizations or agencies with the greatest experience in developing or managing low income housing or community development projects and with the longest record of service to the community.

(C) Financing of sale

To facilitate the sale described in subparagraph (A), the Secretary shall—

(i) to the extent provided in appropriation Acts, make an advance to the nonprofit organization or public agency whose offer to purchase is accepted under this paragraph to cover any direct costs (other than the purchase price) incurred by the organization or agency in purchasing and assuming responsibility for the housing and related facilities involved;

(ii) approve the assumption, by the nonprofit organization or public agency involved, of the loan made or insured under section 1484 or 1485 of this title;

(iii) to the extent provided in appropriation Acts, transfer any rental assistance payments that are received under section 1490a(a)(2)(A) of this title or under section 1437f of this title, or any assistance payments received under section 1490a(a)(5) of this title, with respect to the housing and related facilities involved; and

(iv) to the extent provided in appropriation Acts, provide a loan under section 1485(c)(3) of this title to the nonprofit organization or public agency whose offer to purchase is accepted under this paragraph to enable the organization or agency to purchase the housing and related facilities involved.

(D) Rent limitation and assistance

The Secretary shall, to the extent provided in appropriation Acts, provide to each nonprofit organization or public agency purchasing housing and related facilities under this paragraph financial assistance (in the form of monthly payments or forgiveness of debt) in an amount necessary to ensure that the monthly rent payment made by each low income family or person residing in the housing does not exceed the maximum rent permitted under section 1490a(a)(2)(A) of this title or, in the case of housing assisted under section 1490a(a)(5) of this title, does not exceed the rents established for the project under such section.

(E) Restriction on subsequent transfers

Except as provided in subparagraph (B)(ii), the Secretary may not approve the transfer of any housing and related facilities purchased under this paragraph during the remaining useful life of the housing and related facilities, unless the Secretary determines that—

(i) the transfer will further the provision of housing and related facilities for low income families or persons; or

(ii) there is no longer a need for such housing and related facilities by low income families or persons.

(F) General restriction on prepayments and refinancings

Following the transfer of the maximum number of dwelling units set forth in subparagraph (H)(i) in any fiscal year or the maximum number of dwelling units for which budget authority is available in any fiscal year, the Secretary may not accept in such fiscal year any offer to prepay, or request refinancing in accordance with subsection (b)(3) of this section of, any loan made or insured under section 1484 or 1485 of this title pursuant to a contract entered into prior to December 15, 1989, except in accordance with subparagraph (G). The limitation established in this subparagraph shall not apply to an offer to prepay, or request to refinance, if, following the date on which such offer or request is made (or following February 5, 1988, whichever occurs later) a 15-month period expires during which no budget authority is available to carry out this paragraph. For purposes of this subparagraph, the Secretary shall allocate budget authority under this paragraph in the order in which offers to prepay, or request to refinance, are made.

(G) Exception

This paragraph shall not apply to any offer to prepay, or any request to refinance in accordance with subsection (b)(3) of this section, any loan made or insured under section 1484 or 1485 of this title pursuant to a contract entered into prior to December 15, 1989, if—

(i) the borrower enters into an agreement with the Secretary that obligates the borrower (and successors in interest thereof)—

(I) to utilize the assisted housing and related facilities for the purposes specified in section 1484 or 1485 of this title, as the case may be, for a period determined by the Secretary (but not less than the period described in paragraph (1)(B) calculated from the date on which the loan is made or insured); and

(II) upon termination of the period described in paragraph (1)(B), to offer to sell the assisted housing and related facilities to a qualified nonprofit organization or public agency in accordance with this paragraph; or

(ii) the Secretary determines that housing opportunities of minorities will not be materially affected as a result of the prepayment or refinancing, and that—

(I) the borrower (and any successor in interest thereof) are obligated to ensure that tenants of the housing and related facilities financed with the loan will not be displaced due to a change in the use of the housing, or to an increase in rental or other charges, as a result of the prepayment or refinancing; or

(II) there is an adequate supply of safe, decent, and affordable rental housing within the market area of the housing and related facilities and sufficient actions have been taken to ensure that the rental housing will be made available to each tenant upon displacement.

(H) Funding

(i) Budget limitation

Not more than 5,000 dwelling units may be transferred under this paragraph in any fiscal year, and the budget authority that may be provided under this paragraph for any fiscal year may not exceed the amounts required to carry out this paragraph with respect to such number.

(ii) Reimbursement of rural housing insurance fund

There are authorized to be appropriated to the Rural Housing Insurance Fund such sums as may be necessary to reimburse the Fund for financial assistance provided under this paragraph, paragraph (4), and section 1487(j)(7) of this title.

(I) Definitions

For purposes of this paragraph:

(i) Local nonprofit organization

The term "local nonprofit organization" means a nonprofit organization that—

(I) has a broad based board reflecting various interests in the community or trade area; and

(II) is a not-for-profit charitable organization whose principal purposes include developing or managing low income housing or community development projects.

(ii) Nonprofit organization

The term "nonprofit organization" means any private organization—

(I) no part of the net earnings of which inures to the benefit of any member, founder, contributor, or individual;

(II) that is approved by the Secretary as to financial responsibility; and

(III) that does not have among its officers or directorate persons or parties with a material interest (or persons or parties related to any person or party with such an interest) in loans financed under section 1485 of this title that have been prepaid.

(J) Regulations

Notwithstanding section 1490n of this title, the Secretary shall issue final regulations to carry out this paragraph not later than 60 days after February 5, 1988. The Secretary shall provide for the regulations to take effect not later than 45 days after the date on which the regulations are issued.

(d) Dwelling units available to very low-income families or persons

On and after November 30, 1983—

(1) not less than 40 percent of the funds approved in appropriation Acts for use under this section shall be set aside and made available only for very low-income families or persons; and

(2) not less than 30 percent of the funds allocated to each State under this section shall be available only for very low-income families or persons.

(e) Manufactured homes; qualifications for loans made or insured; energy conservation requirements

(1) A loan which may be made or insured under this section with respect to housing shall be made or insured with respect to a manufactured home or with respect to a manufactured home and lot, whether such home or such home and lot is real property, personal property, or mixed real and personal property, if—

(A) the manufactured home meets the standards prescribed pursuant to title VI of the Housing and Community Development Act of 1974 [42 U.S.C. § 5401 et seq.];

(B) the manufactured home, or the manufactured home and lot, meets the installation, structural, and site requirements which would apply under title II of the National Housing Act [12 U.S.C. § 1707 et seq.]; and

(C) the manufactured home meets the energy conserving requirements established under paragraph (2), or until the energy conserving requirements are established under paragraph (2), the manufactured home meets the energy conserving requirements applicable to housing other than manufactured housing financed under this subchapter.

(2) Energy conserving requirements established by the Secretary for the purpose of paragraph (1)(C) shall—

(A) reduce the operating costs for a borrower by maximizing the energy savings and be cost-effective over the life of the manufactured home or the term of the loan, whichever is shorter, taking into account variations in climate, types of energy used, the cost to modify the home to meet such requirements, and the estimated value of the energy saved over the term of the mortgage; and

(B) be established so that the increase in the annual loan payment resulting from the added energy conserving requirements in excess of those required by the standards prescribed under title VI of the Housing and Community Development Act of 1974 [42 U.S.C. § 5401 et seq.] shall not exceed the projected savings in annual energy costs.

(3) A loan that may be made or insured under this section with respect to a manufactured home on a permanent foundation, or a manufactured home on a permanent foundation and a lot, shall be repayable over the same period as would be applicable under section 203(b) of the National Housing Act [12 U.S.C. § 1709(b)].

(f) Remote rural areas

(1) Loan supplements

The Secretary may supplement any loan under this section to finance housing located in a remote rural area or on tribal allotted or Indian trust land with a grant in an amount not greater than the amount by which the reasonable land acquisition and construction costs of the security property exceeds the appraised value of such property.

(2) Prohibition

The Secretary may not refuse to make, insure, or guarantee a loan that otherwise meets the requirements under this section solely on the basis that the housing involved is located in an area that is excessively rural in character or excessively remote or on tribal allotted or Indian trust land.

(g) Deferred mortgage demonstration

(1) Authority

With respect to families or persons otherwise eligible for assistance under subsection (d) of this section but having incomes below the amount determined to qualify for a loan under this section, the Secretary may defer mortgage payments beyond the amount affordable at 1 percent interest, taking into consideration income, taxes and insurance. Deferred mortgage payments shall be converted to payment status when the ability of the borrower to repay improves. Deferred amounts shall not exceed 25 percent of the amount of the payment due at 1 percent interest and shall be subject to recapture.

(2) Interest

Interest on principal deferred shall be set at 1 percent and any interest payments deferred under this subsection shall not be treated as principal in calculating indebtedness.

(3) Funding

Subject to approval in appropriations Acts, not more than 10 percent of the amount approved for each of fiscal years 1993 and 1994 for loans under this section may be used to carry out this subsection.

(h) Doug Bereuter Section 502 Single Family Housing Loan Guarantee Program

(1) Short title

This subsection may be cited as the "Doug Bereuter Section 502 Single Family Housing Loan Guarantee Act."

(2) Authority

The Secretary shall, to the extent provided in appropriation Acts, provide guaranteed loans in accordance with this section, section 1487(d) of this title, and the last sentence of section 1490a(a)(1)(A) of this title, except as modified by the provisions of this subsection. Loans shall be guaranteed under this subsection in an amount equal to 90 percent of the loan.

(3) Eligible borrowers

Loans guaranteed pursuant to this subsection shall be made only to borrowers who are low or moderate income families or persons, whose incomes do not exceed 115 percent of the median income of the area, as determined by the Secretary.

(4) Eligible housing

Loans may be guaranteed pursuant to this subsection only if the loan is used to acquire or construct a single-family residence that is—

(A) to be used as the principal residence of the borrower;

(B) eligible for assistance under this section, section 203(b) of the National Housing Act [12 U.S.C. § 1709(b)], or chapter 37 of Title 38; and

(C) located in a rural area.

(5) Priority and counseling for first-time homebuyers

(A) In providing guaranteed loans under this subsection, the Secretary shall give priority to first-time homebuyers (as defined in paragraph (17)).

(B) The Secretary may require that, as a condition of receiving a guaranteed loan pursuant to this subsection, a borrower who is a first-time homebuyer successfully complete a program of homeownership counseling under section 1701x(a)(1)(iii) of Title 12 and obtain certification from the provider of the program that the borrower is adequately prepared for the obligations of homeownership.

(6) Eligible lenders

Guaranteed loans pursuant to this subsection may be made only by lenders approved by and meeting qualifications established by the Secretary.

(7) Loan terms

Loans guaranteed pursuant to this subsection shall—

(A) be made for a term not to exceed 30 years;

(B) involve a rate of interest that is fixed over the term of the loan and does not exceed the rate for loans guaranteed under chapter 37 of Title 38 or comparable loans in the area that are not guaranteed; and

(C) involve a principal obligation (including initial service charges, appraisal, inspection, and other fees as the Secretary may approve)—

(i) for a first-time homebuyer, in any amount not in excess of 100 percent of the appraised value of the property as of the date the loan is accepted or the acquisition cost of the property, whichever is less, plus the guarantee fee as authorized by subsection (h)(7)[2] of this section; and

(ii) for any borrower other than a first-time homebuyer, in an amount not in excess of the percentage of the property or the acquisition cost of the property that the Secretary shall determine, such percentage or cost in any event not to exceed 100 percent of the appraised value of the property as of the date the loan is accepted or the acquisition cost of the property, whichever is less, plus the guarantee fee as authorized by subsection (h)(7)[3] of this section.

(8) Guarantee fee

With respect to a guaranteed loan under this subsection, the Secretary may collect from the lender at the time of issuance of the guarantee a fee equal to not more than 1 percent of the principal obligation of the loan.

(9) Refinancing

Any guaranteed loan under this subsection may be refinanced and extended in accordance with terms and conditions that the Secretary shall prescribe, but in no event for an additional amount or term which exceeds the limitations under this subsection.

(10) Nonassumption

Notwithstanding the transfer of property for which a guaranteed loan under this subsection was made, the borrower of a guaranteed loan under this subsection may not be relieved of liability with respect to the loan.

(11) Geographical targeting

In providing guaranteed loans under this subsection, the Secretary shall establish standards to target and give priority to areas that have a demonstrated need for additional sources of mortgage financing for low and moderate income families.

(12) Allocation

The Secretary shall provide that, in each fiscal year, guaranteed loans under this subsection shall be allocated among the States on the basis of the need of eligible borrowers in each State for such loans in comparison with the need of eligible borrowers for such loans among all States.

(13) Loss Mitigation

Upon default or imminent default of any mortgage guaranteed under this subsection, mortgagees shall engage in loss mitigation actions for the purpose of providing an alternative to foreclosure (including actions such as special forbearance, loan modification, pre-foreclosure sale, deed in lieu of foreclosure, as required, support for borrower housing counseling, subordinate lien resolution, and borrower relocation), as provided for by the Secretary.

(14) Payment of Partial Claims and Mortgage Modifications

The Secretary may authorize the modification of mortgages, and establish a program for payment of a partial claim to a mortgagee that agrees to apply the claim amount to payment of a mortgage on a 1- to 4-family residence, for mortgages that are in default or face imminent default, as defined by the Secretary. Any payment under such program directed to the mortgagee shall be made at the sole discretion of the Secretary and on terms and conditions acceptable to the Secretary, except that—

(A) the amount of the partial claim payment shall be in an amount determined by the Secretary, and shall not exceed an amount equivalent to 30 percent of the unpaid principal balance of the mortgage and any costs that are approved by the Secretary;

(B) the amount of the partial claim payment shall be applied first to any outstanding indebtedness on the mortgage, including any arrearage, but may also include principal reduction;

(C) the mortgagor shall agree to repay the amount of the partial claim to the Secretary upon terms and conditions acceptable to the Secretary;

(D) expenses related to a partial claim or modification are not to be charged to the borrower;

(E) the Secretary may authorize compensation to the mortgagee for lost income on monthly mortgage payments due to interest rate reduction;

(F) the Secretary may reimburse the mortgagee from the appropriate guaranty fund in connection with any activities that the mortgagee is required to undertake concerning repayment by the mortgagor of the amount owed to the Secretary;

(G) the Secretary may authorize payments to the mortgagee on behalf of the borrower, under such terms and conditions as are defined by the Secretary, based on successful performance under the terms of the mortgage modification, which shall be used to reduce the principal obligation under the modified mortgage; and

(H) the Secretary may authorize the modification of mortgages with terms extended up to 40 years from the date of modification.

---

2 [*Editor's Note*: So in original. Should probably read "subsection (h)(8)."]

3 [*Editor's Note*: So in original. Should probably read "subsection (h)(8)."]

(15) Assignment

(A) Program Authority

The Secretary may establish a program for assignment to the Secretary, upon request of the mortgagee, of a mortgage on a 1- to 4-family residence guaranteed under this chapter.

(B) Program Requirements

(i) In General

The Secretary may encourage loan modifications for eligible delinquent mortgages or mortgages facing imminent default, as defined by the Secretary, through the payment of the guaranty and assignment of the mortgage to the Secretary and the subsequent modification of the terms of the mortgage according to a loan modification approved under this section.

(ii) Acceptance of Assignment

The Secretary may accept assignment of a mortgage under a program under this subsection only if—

(I) the mortgage is in default or facing imminent default;

(II) the mortgagee has modified the mortgage or qualified the mortgage for modification sufficient to cure the default and provide for mortgage payments the mortgagor is reasonably able to pay, at interest rates not exceeding current market interest rates; and

(III) the Secretary arranges for servicing of the assigned mortgage by a mortgagee (which may include the assigning mortgagee) through procedures that the Secretary has determined to be in the best interests of the appropriate guaranty fund.

(C) Payment of Guaranty

Under the program under this paragraph, the Secretary may pay the guaranty for a mortgage, in the amount determined in accordance with paragraph (2), without reduction for any amounts modified, but only upon the assignment, transfer, and delivery to the Secretary of all rights, interest, claims, evidence, and records with respect to the mortgage, as defined by the Secretary.

(D) Disposition

After modification of a mortgage pursuant to this paragraph, and assignment of the mortgage, the Secretary may provide guarantees under this subsection for the mortgage. The Secretary may subsequently—

(i) re-assign the mortgage to the mortgagee under terms and conditions as are agreed to by the mortgagee and the Secretary;

(ii) act as a Government National Mortgage Association issuer, or contract with an entity for such purpose, in order to pool the mortgage into a Government National Mortgage Association security; or

(iii) re-sell the mortgage in accordance with any program that has been established for purchase by the Federal Government of mortgages insured under this title, and the Secretary may coordinate standards for interest rate reductions available for loan modification with interest rates established for such purchase.

(E) Loan Servicing

In carrying out the program under this subsection, the Secretary may require the existing servicer of a mortgage assigned to the Secretary under the program to continue servicing the mortgage as an agent of the Secretary during the period that the Secretary acquires and holds the mortgage for the purpose of modifying the terms of the mortgage. If the mortgage is resold pursuant to subparagraph (D)(iii), the Secretary may provide for the existing servicer to continue to service the mortgage or may engage another entity to service the mortgage.

(16) Definitions

For purposes of this subsection:

(A) The term "displaced homemaker" means an individual who—

(i) is an adult;

(ii) has not worked full-time full-year in the labor force for a number of years but has, during such years, worked primarily without remuneration to care for the home and family; and

(iii) is unemployed or underemployed and is experiencing difficulty in obtaining or upgrading employment.

(B) The term "first-time homebuyer" means any individual who (and whose spouse) has had no present ownership in a principal residence during the 3-year period ending on the date of purchase of the property acquired with a guaranteed loan under this subsection except that—

(i) any individual who is a displaced homemaker may not be excluded from consideration as a first-time homebuyer under this subparagraph on the basis that the individual, while a homemaker, owned a home with his or her spouse or resided in a home owned by the spouse; and

(ii) any individual who is a single parent may not be excluded from consideration as a first-time homebuyer under this subparagraph on the basis that the individual, while married, owned a home with his or her spouse or resided in a home owned by the spouse.

(C) The term "single parent" means an individual who—

(i) is unmarried or legally separated from a spouse; and

(ii)(I) has 1 or more minor children for whom the individual has custody or joint custody; or

(II) is pregnant.

(D) The term "State" means the States of the United States, the Commonwealth of Puerto Rico, the District of Columbia, the Commonwealth of the Northern Mariana Islands, Guam, the Virgin Islands, American Samoa, the Trust Territories of the Pacific, and any other possession of the United States.

(17) Guarantees for refinancing loans

(A) In general

Upon the request of the borrower, the Secretary shall, to the extent provided in appropriation Acts and subject to subparagraph (F), guarantee a loan that is made to refinance an existing loan that is made under this section or guaranteed under this subsection, and that the Secretary determines complies with the requirements of this paragraph.

(B) Interest rate

To be eligible for a guarantee under this paragraph, the refinancing loan shall have a rate of interest that is fixed over the term of the loan and does not exceed the interest rate of the loan being refinanced.

(C) Security

To be eligible for a guarantee under this paragraph, the refinancing loan shall be secured by the same single-family residence as was the loan being refinanced, which shall be owned by the borrower and occupied by the borrower as the principal residence of the borrower.

(D) Amount

To be eligible for a guarantee under this paragraph, the principal obligation under the refinancing loan shall not exceed an amount equal to the sum of the balance of the loan being refinanced and such closing costs as may be authorized by the Secretary, which shall include a discount not exceeding 200 basis points and an origination fee not exceeding such amount as the Secretary shall prescribe.

(E) Other requirements

The provisions of the last sentence of paragraph (2) and paragraphs (3), (6), (7)(A), (8), (10), (13), and (14) shall apply to loans guaranteed under this paragraph, and no other provisions of paragraphs (2) through (15) shall apply to such loans.

(F) Authority to establish limitation

The Secretary may establish limitations on the number of loans guaranteed under this paragraph, which shall be based on market conditions and other factors as the Secretary considers appropriate.

[July 15, 1949, ch. 338, tit. V, § 502, 63 Stat. 433; Pub. L. No. 87-70, tit. VIII, § 801(b), 75 Stat. 186 (June 30, 1961); Pub. L. No. 87-723, § 4(a)(2), 76 Stat. 671 (Sept. 28, 1962); Pub. L. No. 89-117, tit. X, § 1002, 79 Stat. 497 (Aug. 10, 1965); Pub. L. No. 89-754, tit. VIII, § 802, 80 Stat. 1282 (Nov. 3, 1966); Pub. L. No. 93-383, tit. V, § 505(b), 88 Stat. 693 (Aug. 22, 1974); Pub. L. No. 95-128, tit. V, § 502(a), 91 Stat. 1139 (Oct. 12, 1977); Pub. L. No. 96-153, tit. V, § 503, 93 Stat. 1134 (Dec. 21, 1979); Pub. L. No. 96-399, tit. V, § 514(a), 94 Stat. 1671 (Oct. 8, 1980); Pub. L. No. 98-181, tit. V, § 503(a), (d), 97 Stat. 1240, 1241 (Nov. 30, 1983); Pub. L. No. 98-479, tit. I, § 105(b)(1), 98 Stat. 2226 (Oct. 17, 1984); Pub. L. No. 100-242, tit. II, § 241, tit. III, § 314, 101 Stat. 1886, 1897 (Feb. 5, 1988); Pub. L. No. 100-628, tit. X, § 1028, 102 Stat. 3271 (Nov. 7, 1988); Pub. L. No. 101-235, tit. II, § 206, 103 Stat. 2041 (Dec. 15, 1989); Pub. L. No. 101-625, tit. VII, §§ 704(a), 705(a), 706(b), 719(b), 104 Stat. 4283, 4284, 4297 (Nov. 28, 1990); Pub. L. No. 102-142, tit. VII, § 743(b), 105 Stat. 915 (Oct. 28, 1991); Pub. L. No. 102-550, tit. VII, §§ 701(g), 702(a), 703, 704, 712(a), (b), 106 Stat. 3834, 3835, 3841 (Oct. 28, 1992); Pub. L. No. 104-180, tit. VII, § 734(c)(3)(A), (B), 110 Stat. 1602 (Aug. 6, 1996); Pub. L. No. 105-276, tit. V, § 599C(e)(2)(A), (f), 112 Stat. 2662, 2663 (Oct. 21, 1998); Pub. L. No. 106-569, tit. VII, § 701, 114 Stat. 3013 (Dec. 27, 2000); Pub. L. No. 108-285, § 3(b), (c), 118 Stat. 917 (Aug. 2, 2004); Pub. L. No. 108-447, Div. A, tit. VII, § 726(b), 118 Stat. 2842 (Dec. 8, 2004); Pub. L. No. 111-22, div. A, tit. I, § 101(a), (b), 123 Stat. 1633, 1635 (May 20, 2009)]

* * *

A.4.2 Selected Regulations

TITLE 7—AGRICULTURE

SUBTITLE B—REGULATIONS OF THE DEPARTMENT OF AGRICULTURE

CHAPTER XXXV—RURAL HOUSING SERVICE, DEPARTMENT OF AGRICULTURE

PART 3550—DIRECT SINGLE FAMILY HOUSING LOANS AND GRANTS

SUBPART A—GENERAL

* * *

7 C.F.R. § 3550.4 Reviews and appeals.

Whenever RHS makes a decision that is adverse to a participant, RHS will provide the participant with written notice of such adverse decision and the participant's rights to a USDA National Appeals Division hearing in accordance with 7 CFR part 11. Any adverse decision, whether appealable or non-appealable may be reviewed by the next-level RHS supervisor.

[61 Fed. Reg. 59,779 (Nov. 22, 1996)]

* * *

SUBPART B—SECTION 502 ORIGINATION

* * *

§ 3550.68 Payment subsidies.

RHS administers three types of payment subsidies: interest credit, payment assistance method 1, and payment assistance method 2. Payment subsidies are subject to recapture when the borrower transfers title or ceases to occupy the property.

(a) *Eligibility for payment subsidy.*

(1) Applicants or borrowers who receive loans on program terms are eligible to receive payment subsidy if they personally occupy the property and have adjusted income at or below the applicable moderate-income limit.

(2) Payment subsidy may be granted for initial loans or subsequent loans made in conjunction with an assumption only if the term of the loan is 25 years or more.

(3) Payment subsidy may be granted for subsequent loans not made in conjunction with an assumption if the initial loan was for a term of 25 years or more.

(b) *Determining type of payment subsidy.*

(1) A borrower currently receiving interest credit will continue to receive it for the initial loan and for any subsequent loan for as long as the borrower is eligible for and remains on interest credit.

(2) A borrower currently receiving payment assistance using payment assistance method 1 will continue to receive it for the initial loan and for any subsequent loan for as long as the borrower is eligible for and remains on payment assistance method 1.

(3) A borrower who has never received payment subsidy, or who has stopped receiving interest credit or payment assistance method 1, and at a later date again qualifies for a payment subsidy, will receive payment assistance method 2.

(4) A borrower may not opt to change payment assistance methods.

(c) *Calculation of payment assistance.* Regardless of the method used, payment assistance may not exceed the amount necessary if the loan were amortized at an interest rate of one percent.

(1) *Payment Assistance Method 2.* The amount of payment assistance granted is the lesser of the difference between:

(i) The annualized promissory note installments for the combined RHS loan and eligible leveraged loans plus the cost of taxes and insurance less twenty-four percent of the borrower's adjusted income, or

(ii) The annualized promissory note installment for the RHS loan less amount the borrower would pay if the loan were amortized at an interest rate of one percent.

(2) *Payment Assistance Method 1.* The amount of payment assistance granted is the difference between the annualized note rate installment as prescribed on the promissory note and the lesser of:

(i) The floor payment, which is defined as a minimum percentage of adjusted income that the borrower must pay for PITI: 22 percent for very low-income borrowers, 24 percent for low-income borrowers with adjusted income below 65 percent of area adjusted median, and 26 percent for low-income borrowers with adjusted incomes between 65 and 80 percent of area adjusted median; or

(ii) The annualized note rate installment and the payment at the equivalent interest rate, which is determined by a comparison of the borrower's adjusted income to the adjusted median income for the area in which the security property is located. The following chart is used to determine the equivalent interest rate.

When the applicant's adjusted income is:

Percentage of Median Income and the Equivalent Interest Rate

Equal to or more than:	BUT less than:	THEN the equivalent interest rate is*
00%	50.01 of adjusted median income	1%
50.01%	55 of adjusted median income	2%
55%	60 of adjusted median income	3%
60%	65 of adjusted median income	4%
65%	70 of adjusted median income	5%
70%	75 of adjusted median income	6%
75%	80.01 of adjusted median income	6.5%
80.01%	90 of adjusted median income	7.5%
90%	100 of adjusted median income	8.5%
100%	110% of adjusted median income	9%
110%	Or more than adjusted median income	9.5%

* Or note rate, whichever is less; in no case will the equivalent interest rate be less than one percent.

(d) *Calculation of interest credit.* The amount of interest credit granted is the difference between the note rate installment as prescribed on the promissory note and the greater of:

(1) Twenty percent of the borrower's adjusted income less the cost of real estate taxes and insurance, or

(2) The amount the borrower would pay if the loan were amortized at an interest rate of 1 percent.

(e) *Annual review.* The borrower's income will be reviewed annually to determine whether the borrower is eligible for continued payment subsidy. The borrower must notify RHS whenever an adult member of the household changes or obtains employment, there is a change in household composition, or if income increases by at least 10 percent so that RHS can determine whether a review of the borrower's circumstances is required.

[72 Fed. Reg. 73,255 (Dec. 27, 2007)]

7 C.F.R. § 3550.69 Deferred mortgage payments.

For qualified borrowers, RHS may defer up to 25 percent of the monthly principal and interest payment at 1 percent for up to 15 years. This assistance may be granted only at initial loan closing and is reviewed annually. Deferred mortgage payments are subject to recapture when the borrower transfers title or ceases to occupy the property.

(a) *Eligibility.* In order to qualify for deferred mortgage payments, all of the following must be true:

(1) The applicants adjusted income at the time of initial loan approval does not exceed the applicable very low-income limits.

(2) The loan term is 38 years, or 30 years for a manufactured home.

(3) The applicant's payments for principal and interest, calculated at a one percent interest rate for the maximum allowable term, plus estimated costs for taxes and insurance exceeds:

(i) For applicants receiving payment assistance, 29 percent of the applicants repayment income by more than $10 per month; or

(ii) For applicants receiving interest credit, 20 percent of adjusted income by more than $10 per month.

(b) *Amount and terms.*

(1) The amount of the mortgage payment to be deferred will be the difference between the applicants payment for principal and interest, calculated at one percent interest for the maximum allowable term, plus estimated costs for taxes and insurance and:

(i) For applicants receiving payment assistance, 29 percent of the applicants repayment income.

(ii) For applicants receiving interest credit, 20 percent of adjusted income.

(2) Deferred mortgage payment agreements will be effective for a 12-month period.

(3) Deferred mortgage assistance may be continued for up to 15 years after loan closing. Once a borrower becomes ineligible for deferred mortgage assistance, the borrower can never again receive deferred mortgage assistance.

(c) *Annual review.* The borrower's income, taxes, and insurance will be reviewed annually to determine eligibility for continued deferred mortgage assistance. The borrower must notify RHS whenever an adult member of the household changes or obtains employment or if income increases by at least 10 percent so that RHS can determine whether a review of the borrower's circumstances is required.

[61 Fed. Reg. 59,779 (Nov. 22, 1996)]

* * *

SUBPART E—SPECIAL SERVICING

* * *

7 C.F.R. § 3550.204 Payment assistance.

Borrowers who are eligible may be offered payment assistance in accordance with subpart B of this part. Borrowers who are not eligible for payment assistance because the loan was approved before August 1, 1968, or the loan was made on above-moderate or nonprogram (NP) terms, may refinance the loan in order to obtain payment assistance if:

(a) The borrower is eligible to receive a loan with payment assistance;

(b) Due to circumstances beyond the borrower's control, the borrower is in danger of losing the property; and

(c) The property is program-eligible.

[61 Fed. Reg. 59,779 (Nov. 22, 1996)]

7 C.F.R. § 3550.205 Delinquency workout agreements.

Borrowers with past due accounts may be offered the opportunity to avoid liquidation by entering into a delinquency workout agreement that specifies a plan for bringing the account current. To receive a delinquency workout agreement, the following requirements apply:

(a) A borrower who is able to do so will be required to pay the past-due amount in a single payment.

(b) A borrower who is unable to pay the past-due amount in a single payment must pay monthly all scheduled payments plus an agreed upon additional amount that brings the account current within 2 years or the remaining term of the loan, whichever is shorter.

(c) If a borrower becomes more than 30 days past due under the terms of a delinquency workout agreement, RHS may cancel the agreement.

[61 Fed. Reg. 59,779 (Nov. 22, 1996)]

* * *

7 C.F.R. § 3550.207 Payment moratorium.

RHS may defer a borrowers scheduled payments for up to 2 years. NP borrowers are not eligible for a payment moratorium.

(a) *Borrower eligibility*. For a borrower to be eligible for a moratorium, all of the following conditions must be met:

(1) Due to circumstances beyond the borrower's control, the borrower is temporarily unable to continue making scheduled payments because:

(i) The borrower's repayment income fell by at least 20 percent within the past 12 months;

(ii) The borrower must pay unexpected and unreimbursed expenses resulting from the illness, injury, or death of the borrower or a family member; or

(iii) The borrower must pay unexpected and unreimbursed expenses resulting from damage to the security property in cases where adequate hazard insurance was not available or was prohibitively expensive.

(2) The borrower occupies the dwelling, unless RHS determines that it is uninhabitable.

(3) The borrower's account is not currently accelerated.

(b) *Reviews of borrower eligibility*.

(1) Periodically RHS may require the borrower to submit financial information to demonstrate that the moratorium should be continued. The moratorium may be canceled if:

(i) The borrower does not respond to a request for financial information;

(ii) RHS receives information indicating that the moratorium is no longer required; or

(iii) In the case of a moratorium granted to pay unexpected or unreimbursed expenses, the borrower cannot show that an amount at least equal to the deferred payments has been applied toward the expenses.

(2) At least 30 days before the moratorium is scheduled to expire, RHS will require the borrower to provide financial information needed to determine whether the borrower is able to resume making scheduled payments.

(c) *Resumption of scheduled payments*. When the borrower is able to resume scheduled payments, the loan will be reamortized to include the amount deferred during the moratorium and the borrower will be required to escrow. If the new monthly payment, after consideration of the maximum amount of payment subsidy available to the borrower, exceeds the borrower's repayment ability, all or part of the interest that has accrued during the moratorium may be forgiven.

(d) *Borrowers unable to resume scheduled payments*. If even after all appropriate servicing actions have been taken the borrower is unable to resume making scheduled payments after 2 consecutive years of being on a moratorium, the account will be liquidated.

[61 Fed. Reg. 59,779 (Nov. 22, 1996)]

7 C.F.R. § 3550.208 Reamortization using promissory note interest rate.

Reamortization using the promissory note interest rate may be authorized when RHS determines that reamortization is required to enable the borrower to meet scheduled obligations, and only if the Government's lien priority is not adversely affected.

(a) *Permitted uses*. Reamortization at the promissory note interest rate may be used to accomplish a variety of servicing actions, including to:

(1) Repay unauthorized assistance due to inaccurate information.

(2) Repay principal and interest accrued and advances made during a moratorium.

(3) Bring current an account under a delinquency workout agreement after the borrower has demonstrated the willingness and ability to meet the terms of the loan and delinquency workout agreement and reamortization is in the borrower's and Government's best interests.

(4) Bring a delinquent account current in the case of an assumption where the due on sale clause is not triggered as described in § 3550.163(c).

(5) Cover the remaining debt when a portion of the security property is being transferred but the acquisition price does not cover the outstanding debt. The remaining balance will be reamortized for a period not to exceed 10 years or the final due date of the note being reamortized, whichever is sooner.

(6) Bring an account current where the National Appeals Division (NAD) reverses an adverse action, the borrower has adequate repayment ability, and RHS determines the reamortization is in the best interests of the Government and the borrower.

(b) *Payment term of reamortized loan*. Except as noted in paragraph (a)(5) of this section, the term of the reamortized loan may be extended to the maximum term for which the borrower was eligible at the time the loan was originally made, less the number of years the loan has been outstanding. In all cases, the term must not exceed the remaining security life of the property.

[67 Fed. Reg. 78,332 (Dec. 24, 2002)]

* * *

7 C.F.R. § 3550.211 Liquidation.

(a) *Policy*. When RHS determines that a borrower is unable or unwilling to meet loan obligations, RHS may accelerate the loan and, if necessary, acquire the security property. The borrower is responsible for all expenses associated with liquidation and acquisition. If the account is satisfied in full, the borrower will be released from liability. If the account is not satisfied in full, RHS may pursue any deficiency unless the borrower received a moratorium at any time during the life of the loan and faithfully tried to repay the loan.

(b) *Tribal allotted or trust land*. Liquidations involving a security interest in tribal allotted or trust land shall only be pursued after offering to transfer the account to an eligible tribal member, the tribe, or the Indian Housing Authority. Forced liquidation of RHS security interests in Indian trust lands or on tribal allotted land will be recommended only after the State Director has determined it is in the best interest of the Government.

(c) *Acceleration and foreclosure*. If RHS determines that foreclosure is in the best interest of the Government, RHS will send an acceleration notice to each borrower and any cosigner.

(d) *Voluntary liquidation*. Borrowers may voluntarily liquidate through:

(1) *Refinancing or sale*. The borrower may refinance or sell the security property for at least net recovery value and apply the proceeds to the account.

(2) *Deed in lieu of foreclosure*. RHS may accept a deed in lieu of foreclosure to convey title to the security property only after the debt has been accelerated and when it is in the Government's best interest.

(3) *Offer by third party*. If a junior lienholder or cosigner makes an offer in the amount of at least the net recovery value, RHS may assign the note and mortgage.

(e) *Bankruptcy*.

(1) When a petition in bankruptcy is filed by a borrower after acceleration, collection actions and foreclosure actions are suspended in accordance with the provisions of the Bankruptcy Code.

(2) RHS may accept conveyance of security property by the trustee in bankruptcy if the Bankruptcy Court has approved the transaction, RHS determines the conveyance is in the best interest of the Government, and RHS will acquire title free of all liens and encumbrances except RHS liens.

(3) Whenever possible in a Chapter 7 Bankruptcy, a reaffirmation agreement will be signed by the borrower and approved by the court prior to discharge, if RHS decides to continue with the borrower.

(f) *Junior lienholder foreclosure*. When a junior lienholder foreclosure does not result in payment in full of the RHS debt but the property is sold subject to the RHS lien, RHS may liquidate the account unless the new owner is eligible to assume the RHS debt and actually assumes the RHS debt.

(g) *Payment subsidy*. If the borrower is receiving payment subsidy, the payment subsidy agreement will not be canceled when the debt is accelerated, but will not be renewed unless the account is reinstated.

(h) *Eligibility for special servicing actions*. A borrower is not eligible for special servicing actions once the account has been accelerated.

(i) *Reporting*. RHS may report to IRS and credit reporting agencies any debt settled through liquidation.

[67 Fed. Reg. 78,332 (Dec. 24, 2002)]

* * *

A.5 Loans Guaranteed by the Rural Housing Service

A.5.1 Selected Regulations

TITLE 7—AGRICULTURE

* * *

Subtitle B—Regulations of the Department of Agriculture

* * *

CHAPTER XVIII—RURAL HOUSING SERVICE, RURAL BUSINESS-COOPERATIVE SERVICE, RURAL UTILITIES SERVICE, AND FARM SERVICE AGENCY, DEPARTMENT OF AGRICULTURE

* * *

SUBCHAPTER H—PROGRAM REGULATIONS

PART 1980—GENERAL

* * *

Subpart D—Rural Housing Loans

* * *

7 C.F.R. § 1980.371 Defaults by the borrower.

Default occurs when the borrower fails to perform under any covenant of the mortgage or Deed of Trust and the failure continues for 30 days. The Lender will negotiate in good faith in an attempt to resolve any problem. The borrower must be given a reasonable opportunity to bring the account current before any foreclosure proceedings are started.

(a) The Lender must make a reasonable attempt to contact the borrower if the payment is not received by the 20th day after it is due.

(b) The Lender must make a reasonable attempt to arrange and hold an interview with the borrower for the purpose of resolving the delinquent account before the loan becomes 60 days delinquent. Reasonable effort consists of not less than one letter sent to the borrower at the property address via certified mail or similar method which the borrower refuses to accept or fails to respond.

(c) If the Lender is unable to make contact with the borrower, the Lender must determine whether the property has been abandoned and the value of the security is in jeopardy before the account becomes two payments delinquent.

(d) When the loan becomes three payments delinquent, the Lender must report borrower delinquencies to credit repositories and make a decision with regard to liquidation of the account. The Lender may proceed with liquidation of the account unless there are extenuating circumstances.

7 C.F.R. § 1980.372 Protective advances.

Protective advances must constitute an indebtedness of the borrower to the Lender and be secured by the security instrument. Protective advances are advances made for expenses of an emergency nature necessary to preserve or protect the physical security. Attorney fees are not a protective advance. The Lender will not make protective advances in lieu of an additional loan. In order to assure that a protective advance over $500 will be included in the loss payment, Lenders are encouraged to obtain prior RHS approval.

* * *

7 C.F.R. § 1980.374 Liquidation.

If the Lender concludes the liquidation of a guaranteed loan account is necessary because of one or more defaults or third party actions that the borrower cannot or will not cure or eliminate within a reasonable period of time, the Lender will notify RHS of the decision to liquidate. Initiation of foreclosure begins with the first public action required by law such as filing a complaint or petition, recording a notice of default, or publication of a notice of sale. Foreclosure must be initiated within 90 days of the date the decision to liquidate is made unless the foreclosure has been delayed by law. When there is a legal delay (such as bankruptcy), foreclosure must be started within 60 days after it becomes possible to do so.

(a) *Expeditious liquidation.* Once the decision to liquidate has been made, the Lender must proceed in an expeditious manner. Lenders must exercise due diligence in completing the foreclosure process. Lenders are expected to complete foreclosure within the time frames that are reasonable for the state in which the property is located.

(b) *Maximum collection.* The Lender is expected to make the maximum collection possible on the indebtedness. The Lender will consider the possibility of recovery of any deficiency apart from the acquisition or sale of collateral. The Lender will submit a recommendation on such recovery considering the borrower's assets and ability to pay, prospects of future recovery, the costs of pursuing such recovery, recommendation for obtaining a judgment, and the collectability of a judgment in view of the borrower's assets.

(c) *Allowable liquidation costs.* Certain reasonable liquidation costs (costs similar to those charged for like services in the area) will be allowed during the liquidation process. No in-house expenses of the Lender will be allowed including, but not limited to, employee salaries, staff lawyers, travel, and overhead. Liquidation costs are deducted from the gross sales proceeds of the collateral when the Lender has conducted the liquidation.

(d) *Servicing plan.* The Lender must submit a servicing plan to RHS when the account is 90 days delinquent and a method other than foreclosure is recommended to resolve delinquency. RHS encourages Lenders and delinquent borrowers to explore an acceptable alternative to foreclosure to reduce loss and expenses of foreclosure. Although prior approval is not required in all cases, the Agency may reject a plan that does not protect the Government's interest.

(1) *Continuation with the borrower.* The Lender may continue with the borrower when a clear and realistic plan to eliminate the delinquency is presented. The Lender must fully document the borrower's prospects of success and make this information available to RHS upon request.

(2) *Voluntary liquidation.* RHS may accept the Lender's plan to use voluntary liquidation when the plan clearly addresses the responsibilities of the parties, the Lender maintains oversight of the progress of the sale, the property is listed for sale at a price in line with its market value (if there is not already a bona fide purchaser for the dwelling), and the expected cost to the Government is the same as or less than the cost of foreclosure.

(3) *Deed-in-lieu of foreclosure.* The Lender may take a deed-in-lieu of foreclosure from the borrower when it will not result in a cost to the Government in excess of that expected for foreclosure.

(4) *Other methods.* RHS may accept a proposal submitted by the Lender that is not specifically addressed in but is consistent with the provisions of this subpart if the Lender fully documents how the proposal will result in a savings to the Government.

(e) *Handling shared equity.* Interest assistance payments made under § 1980.390 of this subpart will not be subject to shared equity if the loan is liquidated in accordance with the Lender Agreement unless:

(1) The property is sold at or prior to foreclosure for an amount exceeding the Lender's unpaid balance and costs of foreclosure, or

(2) A junior lienholder takes over the Lender's loan.

7 C.F.R. § 1980.375 Reinstatement of the borrower's account.

The Lender may reinstate an account when all delinquent payments and any funds that were advanced to pay authorized expenses are paid or as required under state law. When the Lender wishes to consider other offers by the borrower to bring the account current, the Lender must obtain RHS concurrence.

* * *

7 C.F.R. § 1980.390 Interest assistance.

In order to assist low-income borrowers in the repayment of the loan, RHS is authorized to provide interest assistance payments subject to the availability of funds. Regardless of what date a borrower's loan payment is due each month, interest assistance payments will be made by RHS directly to the Lender on or before the 15th day of the month in which the borrower's payment is due.

(a) *Policy.* It is the policy of RHS to grant interest assistance on guaranteed loans to low-income borrowers to assist them in obtaining and retaining decent, safe, and sanitary dwellings and related facilities as long as the borrower remains eligible for payments when funds are available for interest assistance. Interest assistance must be established for the borrower at the time the loan guarantee is authorized.

(b) *Processing interest assistance agreements.* The Lender will process the interest assistance agreement and submit it to RHS for approval.

(1) RHS will reimburse the Lender in the amounts authorized in exhibit D of FmHA Instruction 1980-D (available in any RHS office) for the cost of processing the agreement. The fee will be paid upon receipt of a valid agreement which has been coded as requiring a processing fee payment. The processing fee is payable when:

(i) A new agreement is made with the borrower except at the time of loan closing.

(ii) The borrower had an agreement for the previous year and a new agreement is made for the current year.

(iii) The borrower is eligible for but not presently on interest assistance and enters into a new interest assistance agreement.

(iv) The borrower has a change in circumstances which requires a revision to the current agreement. When the change in circumstances results in an agreement with less than 90 days remaining, the agreement for the subsequent year will be prepared at the same time. This action is considered one agreement.

(2) A processing fee will not be paid when the revision to an existing agreement is required due to an error on the part of the Lender or the borrower.

(c) *Amount of interest assistance.*

(1) The amount of interest assistance granted will be the difference between the monthly installment due on the promissory note eligible for interest assistance and the amount the borrower would pay if the note were amortized at the rate corresponding to the borrower's income range as outlined in the master interest assistance agreement.

(2) The basis for the amount of interest assistance for each loan is determined by the amount of interest assistance authorized to the Agency as shown in exhibit D of FmHA Instruction 1980-D (available in any RHS office) and the note interest rate.

(3) A borrower receiving a loan in a high cost area will be granted an additional 1 percent interest assistance in order to assist the borrower up to the maximum rate in exhibit D of FmHA Instruction 1980-D (available in any RHS office).

(i) The Administrator may designate an area as a high cost area for interest assistance purposes. Such designation may be granted when the State Director makes a written request for it and provides documentation that low-income borrowers in the area could not afford to purchase a dwelling under the interest assistance table in exhibit D of FmHA Instruction 1980-D (available in any RHS office). The area must also be designated by HUD as a high cost area. The amount of additional interest assistance for high cost areas is 1 percent; however, in no case will more interest assistance be granted than the amount necessary to reach the lowest floor rate in exhibit D of FmHA Instruction 1980-D (available in any RHS office).

(ii) The change in a designation to (or from) a high cost area will not affect existing loans. An individual's loan eligibility for high cost designation is determined at the time of issuance of the conditional commitment for loan guarantee.

(d) *Shared equity.* Prior to loan closing, the Lender will advise the applicant that interest assistance is subject to equity sharing.

(e) *Eligibility.* To be eligible for interest assistance, a borrower must personally occupy the dwelling and must meet the following additional requirements:

(1) *Initial loans.* Interest assistance may be granted at the time the loan note guarantee is issued, or an assumption is processed in accordance with § 1980.366, when:

(i) The borrower's adjusted income at the time of loan guarantee approval did not exceed the applicable low-income limit, the loan guarantee was funded from interest assisted guaranteed loan funds, and a master interest assistance agreement was completed at closing if the borrower is ever to receive interest assistance.

(ii) The borrower's net family assets do not exceed the maximum allowable amount as per exhibit D of FmHA Instruction 1980-D (available in any RHS office) unless an exception is authorized. The calculation of net family assets will exclude the value of the dwelling and a minimum adequate dwelling site, cash on hand which will be used to reduce the amount of the loan, and household goods and personal automobiles and the debts against them. The Lender may request an exception at the time the initial application is submitted to RHS for a loan guarantee. For the purpose of determining whether an exception is justified, consideration will be given to the nature of the assets upon which a borrower is currently dependent for a livelihood or which could be used to reduce or eliminate the need for interest assistance.

(iii) The loan was approved as a subsidized guaranteed loan on or after April 17, 1991.

(iv) The amount of interest assistance will be $20 or more per month in accordance with the provisions of paragraph (c)(1) of this section. Interest assistance in amounts of less than $20 per month will not be granted.

(2) *Existing loans.* Interest assistance may be granted at any time after loan closing if:

(i) The requirements of paragraphs (e)(1)(i), (e)(1)(iii), and (e)(1)(iv) of this section are met.

(ii) The borrower's adjusted annual income does not exceed the low-income limit.

(iii) The borrower requests interest assistance through the Lender or the Lender determines that interest assistance is needed to enable the borrower to repay the loan.

(iv) The Lender processes the interest assistance agreement and submits it to RHS for approval.

(f) *Processing interest assistance.* The Lender will process interest assistance agreements in accordance with this section. The interest assistance agreement will be executed by the Lender and borrower and forwarded to RHS for approval.

(1) *Amount of interest assistance.* The amount of interest assistance for which a borrower is eligible will be determined by use of the interest assistance agreement as outlined in paragraph (c) of this section.

(i) *Determination of income.* The Lender is responsible for determining the borrower's annual and adjusted annual income as outlined in §§ 1980.347 and 1980.348 of this subpart. Income of all persons occupying the dwelling will be verified in accordance with § 1980.347 of this subpart.

(ii) *Effective period.* Annual interest assistance agreements will be for a 12-month period.

(2) *Interest assistance agreements.* The master interest assistance agreement will be executed for each qualifying loan at loan closing provided funds are available for interest assistance at the time the guarantee is issued. This agreement establishes the conditions and maximum amounts of interest assistance for the life of the loan. Each year, an annual interest assistance agreement will be used to determine the amount of interest assistance for the coming 12 months.

(i) The Lender will determine the borrower's adjusted annual income, document the calculations, and complete the interest assistance agreement form.

(ii) The borrower will review the interest assistance agreement form and sign the form signifying that all information is correct as shown.

(iii) If the information contained on the interest assistance agreement appears correct, RHS will approve the agreement and make monthly payments to the Lender on behalf of the borrower.

(iv) When the borrower's income is within the low-income limits but the provisions of paragraphs (e)(1)(ii) or (e)(1)(iv) of this section preclude granting interest assistance, the master interest assistance agreement must be executed if the borrower desires to be considered for interest assistance at a later date due to a change in circumstances.

(g) *Interest assistance modification.* A change in the borrower's circumstances after the effective date of the Annual Interest Assistance Agreement will be handled as follows:

(1) RHS required modifications before expiration. The borrower is responsible for reporting any increases in income exceeding $100 per month to the Lender. The Lender is not responsible for monitoring the borrower's income. The Lender must process a revised interest assistance agreement when a reported increase in the borrower's income results in the need for less interest assistance in accordance with paragraph (c) of this section.

(2) *Additional interest assistance before expiration.* The borrower may request and the Lender may process a modification of the interest assistance agreement and submit the modified agreement to RHS when:

(i) The borrower's adjusted annual income decreases by more than $100 per month;

(ii) The interest assistance calculation per paragraph (c) of this section indicates that the borrower is eligible for an additional $20 interest assistance per month; and

(iii) There are interest assistance funds available if the amount needed by the borrower exceeds the initial floor rate established at the time the loan was closed per paragraph (c) of this section.

(3) *Other changes in the borrower's circumstances.* When one coborrower has left the dwelling, interest assistance based on the remaining coborrower's income may be extended if:

(i) The remaining coborrower is occupying the dwelling, owns a legal interest in the property, and is liable for the debt;

(ii) The remaining coborrower certifies as to who lives in the house;

(iii) Separation is not due only to work assignment or military orders; and

(iv) The remaining coborrower is informed and agrees that should the coborrower begin to live in the dwelling, that coborrower's income will then be counted toward annual income and interest assistance may be reduced or canceled.

(4) *Effect of modification.* An interest assistance agreement modified as per paragraph (g)(1), (g)(2), or (g)(3) of this section is valid for the remainder of the agreement period.

(5) *Correction of interest assistance agreement.* When an error by RHS or the Lender resulted in too little interest assistance being granted, a corrected agreement will be prepared effective the date of the error if the error results in granting $20 or more per month less interest assistance than the borrower was eligible to receive. The Lender must return any overpayment made by the borrower unless an agreement is reached to apply the funds to the loan as an extra payment.

(h) *Eligibility review.* Borrowers receiving interest assistance will be reviewed annually within 30 to 60 days prior to the anniversary date of the loan. All existing agreements must be reviewed and processed for the upcoming 12 months during the review period. Interest assistance will not be renewed if the amount that the borrower qualifies for is less than $20 per month.

(1) The Lender will obtain written verification of the income of each borrower and all adult members of the borrower's household and conduct the review.

(i) *Borrower responsibility.* The borrower will:

(A) Report the income of each adult member of the household to the Lender;

(B) Assure that each household member has provided sufficient information on that person's income for the Lender to conduct the review; and

(C) Cooperate in the Lender's efforts to verify income.

(ii) [Reserved]

(2) *Processing interest assistance renewals not reviewed during the review period.* The Lender may process interest assistance renewals not completed during the review period as follows:

(i) The amount of interest assistance will be based on the borrower's current annual income.

(ii) The effective date will be:

(A) The expiration period of the previous interest assistance agreement if the RHS approval official determines failure to renew was the fault of RHS or the Lender.

(B) The next payment due date following approval in all other cases.

(3) *Interest assistance form.* Interest assistance payments will not be made after the expiration date unless RHS receives and approves a new interest assistance agreement form.

(i) Cancellation of interest assistance.

(1) An existing interest assistance agreement will be canceled under the following circumstances:

(i) When the borrower has never occupied the dwelling, the interest assistance will be canceled as of the date of issuance of the guarantee. The Lender will refund all interest assistance payments to RHS.

(ii) The cancellation will be effective on the date on which the earliest action occurs which causes the cancellation or the date the Lender became aware of the situation if the date cannot be determined when:

(A) The borrower ceases to occupy, sells, or conveys title to the dwelling.

(B) The borrower has received improper interest assistance and a corrected agreement will not be submitted.

(C) The borrower has had an increase in income and is no longer eligible for interest assistance.

(D) The security is acquired by the Lender.

(E) The Lender formally declares the loan to be in default and accelerates the loan.

(2) [Reserved]

(j) *Overpayment.* When the Lender becomes aware of circumstances that have resulted in an overpayment of interest assistance for any reason, except as provided in paragraph (k) of this section, the following actions will be taken:

(1) The Lender will immediately notify RHS.

(2) The borrower will be notified and the interest assistance agreement will be corrected.

(3) A repayment agreement acceptable to RHS will be reached.

(k) *Unauthorized use of loan funds.* When RHS becomes aware that the Lender allowed loan funds to be used for unauthorized purposes, interest assistance paid on said amounts will be promptly repaid by the Lender. The Lender may work out a repayment agreement with the borrower but is expected to make every effort to minimize the adverse impact on the borrower's repayment ability.

(*l*) *Appeals.* All applicants/borrowers and Lenders may appeal adverse determinations in accordance with § 1980.399 when RHS denies, reduces, cancels, or refuses to renew interest assistance.

(m) *Reinstatement of interest assistance.* The RHS approval official may authorize reinstatement of the borrower's interest assistance if it was canceled because the loan was accelerated and if the acceleration was withdrawn with RHS approval.

7 C.F.R. § 1980.391 Equity sharing.

The policy of RHS is to collect all or a portion of interest assistance granted on a guaranteed RH loan when any of the events described in paragraph (a) of this section occur, if any equity exists in the security.

(a) *Determining the amount of shared equity.* The RHS approval official will calculate shared equity when a borrower's account is settled by payment-in-full (including refinancing) of the outstanding indebtedness, the transfer of title, or when the borrower ceases to occupy the property. The calculation of shared equity when the account is in liquidation will be handled in accordance with § 1980.374(e).

(1) *How to calculate.* The amount of shared equity will be based on the amount of interest assistance granted on the loan, the appreciation in property value between the closing date of the

loan and the date the account is satisfied or acquired by the Lender via liquidation action, the period of time the loan is outstanding, the amount of original equity the borrower has in the property, and the value of capital improvements to the property. Shared equity will be the lesser of the interest assistance granted or the amount of value appreciation available for shared equity. Value appreciation available for shared equity means the market value of the property less all debts secured by prior liens, sales expenses, any original borrower equity, principal reduction, and value added by any capital improvements.

(i) *Market value.* Market value of the property as of the date the loan is to be paid in full or the date the borrower ceases to occupy and will be documented by one of the following:

(A) A sales contract which reasonably represents the fair market value based on the Lender's and RHS approval official's knowledge of the property and the area.

(B) Lender's appraisal when the loan will be refinanced provided the appraisal reasonably represents the fair market value.

(C) If the items listed in either paragraph (a)(1)(i)(A) or (a)(1)(i)(B) of this section are not available, another current appraisal, if readily available, when the appraiser meets the qualifications of § 1980.334.

(D) When the account is being paid off from insurance proceeds, the most recent appraisal available if the Lender or RHS can document that it represents an accurate indication of the value at the time the dwelling was damaged or destroyed. If not, the best information available will be used to determine the market value. The RHS approval official will interview the borrower to determine the extent of improvements, if any, and the general condition of the property at the time of loss. The amount of the insurance payment is generally a good indication of value; however, tax records or comparable sales will be considered.

(E) RHS appraisal, with prior approval of the State Director.

(ii) *Prior liens.* Prior liens refers to the amount of liens that are prior to the Lender's liens and include, but may not be limited to, prior mortgages, and real estate taxes and assessments levied against the property.

(iii) *Sale/refinancing expenses.* Sale/refinancing expenses include, but are not limited to, expenses commonly associated with the sale or refinancing of real estate that are not reimbursed, such as sales commissions, advertising costs, recording fees, pro rata taxes, points based on the current interest rate, appraisal fees, transfer tax, deed preparation fee, loan origination fee, etc. In refinancing situations, only those expenses necessary to finance the amount of the current RHS debt are allowed. Shared equity may be calculated using estimated expenses if actual expenses cannot be obtained and the RHS approval official is satisfied with the estimated amount and the prorating of the expenses are accurate for this transaction.

(iv) *Original borrower equity.* Original equity consists of a contribution by the borrower that reduces the amount of the loan below the market value. The contribution may be in the form of cash and/or value of the lot if the home was constructed on the borrower's property.

(v) *Capital improvements.* Capital improvements will be considered to the extent that they do not exceed market value contribution as indicated by a sales comparison analysis. Generally, the value added by improvements will be the difference in market value at the time of sale and market value without capital improvements. Cost of the improvement will not be considered, only contribution to value. Maintenance cost and replacement of short-lived depreciable items are normal expenses associated with home ownership and are not considered capital improvements.

(2) *Other considerations.*

(i) *Overpayments of interest assistance.* When RHS has overpaid interest assistance and the overpaid amounts remain uncollected at the time shared equity is calculated, the overpaid amount will be added to shared equity.

(ii) *Multiple loans.* When a borrower has more than one loan and elects to pay only some of the loans, shared equity will not be calculated unless the remaining loan is not subject to shared equity. Shared equity will be calculated when the account is paid in full taking into consideration all of the interest assistance granted on the account.

(b) *Miscellaneous provisions*—

(1) *Changes in terms.* Shared equity will not be calculated when an account is reamortized.

(2) *Junior liens.* Junior liens are not considered in the shared equity calculation. In the event a junior lienholder forecloses, the RHS approval official will calculate shared equity before providing the lienholder with a pay-off figure, which is in addition to any amounts still due the Lender on the loan in the same manner as paragraph (a) of this section.

(c) *Affordable housing proposals.* Shared equity under an affordable housing innovation (such as limited equity or a state or county sponsored shared equity) will be calculated in accordance with this subpart unless prior written approval is obtained from RHS. Proposals that deviate from this subpart must be reviewed and approved in the National office prior to issuance of the loan note guarantee.

7 C.F.R. § 1980.392 Mortgage Credit Certificates (MCCs) and Funded Buydown Accounts.

(a) *MCCs.* MCCs are authorized under the Tax Reform Act of 1986 and allow the borrower to receive a Federal tax credit for a percentage of their mortgage interest payment. They may be used by RHS guaranteed RH borrowers to improve their repayment ability for the loan. MCCs impact on the borrower's tax liability. MCCs may be used with interest assisted loans when the amount of the tax credit is based on the amount of interest actually paid by the borrower. MCCs are subject to shared equity of a portion of any "gain" realized on the property when sold within 10 years after purchase. If the loan is also an RHS interest assisted loan, RHS shall receive priority for shared equity repayment. Income taxes are complex issues; RHS employees and Lenders are not expected to be able to identify all issues impacting the borrower's taxes. Lenders should encourage borrowers to consult with a tax advisor.

(1) When the Lender is participating in an MCC program the amount of the tax credit is considered as an additional resource available for repayment of the loan when the credit is taken on a monthly basis from withholding.

(2) The Lender will submit a copy of the MCC and a copy of the applicant's Form IRS W-4, "Employee's Withholding Allowance Certificate," along with the other materials for the loan guarantee request. The amount of tax credit is limited to the applicant's maximum tax liability.

(i) The MCC must show the rate of credit allowed.

(ii) The Form IRS W-4 must reflect that the borrower is taking the tax credit on a monthly basis.

(iii) The Lender will certify that the borrower has completed and processed all of the necessary documents to obtain the tax credit in accordance with this section.

(b) *Funded buydown accounts.* A funded buydown account is a prepaid arrangement between a builder or a seller and a Lender that is designed to improve applicant's repayment ability. Funded buydown accounts are permitted when the Lender obtains prior RHS concurrence. RHS will consider buydown accounts when there are compensating factors which indicate the borrower's ability to meet the expected increases in loan payment. The seller, Lender or other third party must place funds in an escrow account with monthly releases scheduled directly to the Lender to reduce the borrower's monthly payment during the early years of the loan. The maximum reduction which may be considered is 2 percent below the note rate, even though the actual buydown may be for more. Reductions in buydown assistance may not result in an increase in the interest rate paid by the borrower of more than 1 percent per year. The borrower shall not be required to repay escrowed buydown funds. Funds must be escrowed with a state or federally supervised Lender. Funded buydown accounts must be fully funded for the buydown period. Buydown periods must be at least 12 months for each 1 percent of the buydown.

* * *

7 C.F.R. § 1980.399 Appeals.

The borrower and the Lender respectively can appeal an RHS administrative decision that directly and adversely impacts them. Decisions made by the Lender are not covered by this paragraph even if RHS concurrence is required before the Lender can proceed. Appeals will be conducted in accordance with the rules of the National Appeals Division, USDA.

(a) *Appealable decisions.*

(1) The borrower and the Lender must jointly execute the written request for an alleged adverse decision made by RHS. The Lender need not be an active participant in the appeal process.

(2) The Lender only may appeal cases where RHS has denied or reduced the amount of a loss payment to the Lender.

(b) *Nonappealable decisions.*

(1) The Lender's decision as to whether to make a loan is not subject to appeal.

(2) The Lender's decision to deny servicing relief is not subject to appeal.

(3) The Lender's decision to accelerate the account is not subject to appeal.

A.5.2 Selected Administrative Notices

RD AN No 4429. (1980-D)
April 14, 2009

TO: State Directors
Rural Development

ATTENTION: Rural Housing Program Directors,
Guaranteed Rural Housing Specialists,
Rural Development Managers, and
Area Directors

FROM: James C. Alsop ***(Signed by Thomas E. Hannah)***
Acting Administrator
Housing and Community Facilities Programs

SUBJECT: Single Family Housing Guaranteed Loan Program Acceptable Liquidation Fees and Costs

PURPOSE/INTENDED OUTCOME:

The purpose of this Administrative Notice (AN) is to amend the guidelines regarding reimbursement of attorney and trustee fees incurred for liquidated single family housing loans guaranteed by Single Family Housing Guaranteed Loan Program (SFHGLP).

COMPARISON WITH PREVIOUS AN:

This AN replaces AN 4341 (1980-D) dated March 14, 2008, which expires on March 31, 2009. The Schedule of Standard Attorney/Trustee's Fees for the SFHGLP has been updated in order to align with the Schedule of Standard Attorney's Fees established by Housing and Urban Development (HUD).

BACKGROUND:

SFHGLP regulations authorize the reimbursement of liquidation fees and costs that are actually paid by the lender, for liquidated loans, that result in a loss to the lender within the limits of the guarantee.

EXPIRATION DATE: March 31, 2010

FILING INSTRUCTIONS: Preceding RD Instruction 1980-D

RD Instruction 1980-D, section 1980.374(c) states that the Agency will allow "reasonable" liquidation costs similar to those charged for like services in the area. In 1994, the Federal Housing Authority (FHA) began utilizing Fannie Mae's Schedule of Standard Attorney/Trustee's Fees until FHA established its own fee schedule in September 1998. The SFHGLP will adhere to the Schedule of Standard Attorney/Trustee's Fees published by HUD for foreclosure, deed-in-lieu of foreclosure and bankruptcy.

IMPLEMENTATION RESPONSIBILITIES:

It is not the Agency's intent to regulate the amounts that lenders pay for services performed, but to limit the extent to which the SFHGLP reimburses the lender for attorney fees incurred. The SFHGLP will use HUD's current Schedule of Standard Attorney/Trustee's Fees as the basis for determining reasonable and customary attorney fees. The Schedule of Standard Attorney/Trustee's Fees became effective for all SFHGLP loans where the first legal action required initiating foreclosure; the petition for bankruptcy release, or the date the deed-in-lieu of foreclosure is executed on or after February 1, 2003. Fees higher than the published amounts may be appropriate, in cases such as contested foreclosures, required probate procedures, etc., and are subject to approval by the Agency approval official on a case-by-case basis. Justification for higher fees must be documented in the file.

It is important to make the distinction between attorney/trustee fees and attorney/trustee costs. Typically, the fee for the service performed by the attorney is listed separately on the attorney's invoice from the actual costs involved in the liquidation proceedings. A complete list of allowable liquidation costs would not be practical, since procedural requirements vary by jurisdiction. Generally, the SFHGLP will reimburse a lender for costs, which must be paid to public officials such as sheriffs, clerks of court or recorders of deeds, as well as other costs, required by law (i.e., private service of process and required publications).

RD Instruction 1980-D, section 1980.374(c) states that in-house expenses of the lender will not be allowed during the liquidation process. Employee salaries, staff attorneys and overhead charges are considered examples of in-house expenses. Overhead expenses include, but are not limited to, items such as telephone calls, photocopying charges, overnight mail fees and postage (not including certified or registered mailings required by law). Typical overhead costs are inherent to the foreclosure process and payment of these expenses is not reimbursable.

Outsourcing of services, such as document preparation, are customary in the industry and are also considered as attorney's overhead. These fees are allowed as a separate expense *only* if the attorney fee is reduced in a proportionate amount to the document preparation fee that is charged.

Example:

- State = Tennessee
- Acceptable Foreclosure Attorney Fee = $600
- $475 Attorney fee invoiced
- $125 Outsourced Document Preparation Fee
- $600 Total of fees charged

In the above example, the foreclosure attorney has chosen to outsource a portion of his service to a contractor. The total fee charged to the lender is the same as if the attorney's firm had performed this function. This is considered an acceptable fee that is eligible for reimbursement.

If a foreclosure proceeding is interrupted due to a bankruptcy filed by the borrower, or if a deed-in-lieu of foreclosure or pre-foreclosure sale is accepted prior to the completion of the foreclosure, a maximum of 75% of the allowable attorney fee and all actual foreclosure costs incurred will be reimbursed. If state statute requires that the foreclosure be restarted from the beginning, after a bankruptcy is dismissed or relief from stay is granted, the lender will be reimbursed for 100% of allowable foreclosure attorney fees and costs incurred after the bankruptcy stay is lifted. If state statute does not require that the foreclosure be restarted from the beginning, reimbursement of all foreclosure attorney fees incurred both before and after the bankruptcy is limited to the amount listed on the Schedule of Standard Attorney/Trustee's Fees.

It is important to keep in mind that the maximum allowable bankruptcy fees cover the entry of an appearance, request for service, preparation and filing of the proof of claim, objections to the proof of claim, detailed review and analysis of the plan, objection to confirmation of the plan, reaffirmation of the debt, attendance at any meeting of creditors (when attendance is appropriate), motions for relief and/or motions to dismiss, and any other customary services performed in a bankruptcy matter. In establishing the maximum allowable fees, it was presumed that attendance would be required for up to two court hearings and for all necessary meetings of creditors. The fee will vary depending on the chapter under which the bankruptcy is filed.

Although maximum allowable bankruptcy fees are established, reimbursement of attorney's fees that have been prorated to reasonably relate to the amount of legal work actually performed by the bankruptcy attorney will be allowed. If the attorney has not completed the majority of legal services taken into consideration in the maximum allowable fee, the attorney's fee should be prorated to reflect the amount of work actually performed by the attorney. For example, if a case is referred to the attorney solely for filing a proof of claim or a motion for relief, the full maximum allowable bankruptcy fee cannot be reimbursed.

Generally, attorney fees will not be reimbursed that exceed the maximum allowable bankruptcy fees which cover the customary and routine legal services performed in each type of bankruptcy filing. However, when encountering situations whereby expenses for additional legal work beyond those pleadings and hearings that are considered in establishing the maximum allowable fee schedule, as long as the work is necessary to protect the interests of the Agency, additional reimbursement may be justified. Examples of additional reimbursements are:

- Additional attorney's fees of up to $250 for each additional motion, response, or other pleading (such as a new request or a second request to lift a bankruptcy stay), if attendance at a court hearing is not required.
- Additional attorney's fees of up to $500 ($250 for a pleading + $250 for a hearing), if attendance at a single hearing on an additional pleading is required.
- Additional attorney's fees of up to $100 for each continued court hearing on a pleading (beyond the two hearings that were taken into consideration in the maximum allowable fee and the first hearing on the pleading).

It is the responsibility of the lender to present sufficient documentation for justification of additional fees exceeding the maximum allowable bankruptcy fees noted in Attachment 1. Fees may be reimbursed for such fees and costs to the extent that services to protect the interests of the Agency were actually rendered; and, the fees and costs charged for them are reasonable and necessary and comply with the guidelines set forth.

The Agency will not reimburse any attorney fees or costs incurred for a prior liquidation action that has been reinstated by the borrower or for which the foreclosed property is redeemed. Attorney fees and costs should be included in the amount collected from the borrower with the reinstatement or foreclosure redemption.

The foreclosure fees in Attachment 1 list the attorney or trustee fee limits allowed for each SFHGLP recommended method of foreclosure listed in the most recent AN published on *"Single Family Housing Guaranteed Loan Program Acceptable Foreclosure Time Frames."* In States where more than one foreclosure method is available, the limits listed are based on the method that is most cost effective in reducing legal fees and interest expense. The Agency does not intend to prohibit the payment of attorney fees and costs where the lender obtains title through a method of foreclosure other than what is recommended. However, the Agency approval official must determine whether the foreclosure method chosen by the lender was in the best interest of the government. For example, the recommended foreclosure method in some States is nonjudicial. However, judicial foreclosures are required to preserve the rights of a deficiency judgment. If the lender can demonstrate that the recovery of a deficiency judgment is expected, the foreclosure method should be considered acceptable and reasonable attorney fees and costs reimbursed within the limits of the guarantee.

During lender compliance reviews, files should be reviewed in an effort to ensure that lenders are complying with the fee limit requirements. Lenders that are determined to be out of compliance should be counseled on the provisions of the regulations and monitored closely for future compliance.

Questions about this AN may be directed to Stuart Walden (202.690.4507) or Debbie Terrell (918.534.3254), of the Single Family Housing Guaranteed Loan Division; or, by email at stuart.walden@wdc.usda.gov or debra.terrell@wdc.usda.gov. All ANs are available at the Rural Development website http://www.rurdev.usda.gov/regs.

Attachment

Attachment 1

Schedule of Standard Attorney/Trustee's Fees

STATE	NON-JUDICIAL FORECLOSURE	JUDICIAL FORE-CLOSURE	BANKRUPTCY CLEARANCE	POSSESSORY ACTION	DEED-IN-LIEU
AK	$1,250		Varies[13]	$375	$400
AL	$600[1]		Varies[13]	$375	$400
AR	$650		Varies[13]	$275	$400
AZ	$675		Varies[13]	$275	$400
CA	$650		Varies[13]	$525	$400
CO	$850		Varies[13]	$275	$400
CT		$1,350[2]	Varies[13]	$375	$400
DC	$650[1]		Varies[13]	$375	$400
DE		$1,000	Varies[13]	$325	$400
FL		$1,250	Varies[13]	$375	$400
GA	$650[1,3]		Varies[13]	$375	$400
GU	$1,250		Varies[13]	$375	$400
HI	$1,250	$1,900	Varies[13]	$525	$400
IA	$600	$900	Varies[13]	$325	$400
ID	$650		Varies[13]	$375	$400
IL		$1,150[5]	Varies[13]	$325	$400
IN		$1,050[6]	Varies[13]	$325	$400
KS		$900	Varies[13]	$325	$400
KY		$1,150	Varies[13]	$375	$400
LA		$950	Varies[13]	$325	$400
MA	$1,300		Varies[13]	$625	$400
MD	$850[1,3]	$850	Varies[13]	$375	$400
ME		$1,300	Varies[13]	$525	$400
MI	$700[7]		Varies[13]	$325	$400
MN	$700		Varies[13]	$325	$400
MO	$700		Varies[13]	$325	$400
MS	$600[1]		Varies[13]	$375	$400
MT	$650		Varies[13]	$375	$400
NC	$600[8]		Varies[13]	$375	$400
ND		$950	Varies[13]	$325	$400
NE	$650[9]	$900	Varies[13]	$325	$400
NH	$950		Varies[13]	$425	$400
NJ		$1,350	Varies[13]	$375	$400
NM		$950	Varies[13]	$275	$400
NV	$650		Varies[13]	$375	$400
NY		$1,300[10]	Varies[13]	$725	$400
OH		$1,150	Varies[13]	$325	$400
OK		$950[5]	Varies[13]	$275	$400
OR	$725		Varies[13]	$375	$400
PA		$1,300[11]	Varies[13]	$425	$400
PR		$1,150[12]	Varies[13]	$300	$400
RI	$950		Varies[13]	$525	$400
SC		$850	Varies[13]	$375	$400
SD	$600	$900	Varies[13]	$325	$400
TN	$600[1]		Varies[13]	$375	$400
TX	$600		Varies[13]	$325	$400
UT	$650	$600	Varies[13]	$275	$400
VA	$650[1,3]		Varies[13]	$375	$400
VI		$1,150	Varies[13]	$300	$400
VT		$1,000	Varies[13]	$375	$400
WA	$725		Varies[13]	$375	$400
WI		$1,150	Varies[13]	$325	$400
WV	$600[1,3]		Varies[13]	$375	$400
WY	$650		Varies[13]	$375	$400

Footnotes:

(1) The fee covers the combined attorney's and notary's fees.
(2) This fee applies to strict foreclosures. If the foreclosure orders a Foreclosure by Sale, the fee will be $1,550.
(3) The fee covers both the attorney's fee and the trustee's commission (or statutory fee).
(4) The fee includes reimbursement of any fee for the attorney's certificate of title.
(5) The fee increases by $100 if foreclosure is achieved by summary judgment.
(6) In addition to the allowable foreclosure fee, an auctioneer's fee of up to $250 is allowed for the services of a state licensed auctioneer requested by the lender and approved by the court.
(7) The fee increases to $1,100 for a non-judicial foreclosure for a case in which the attorney provides services for "proceedings subsequent" that involve registered land.
(8) The fee includes the notary's fee. An additional fee of $250 is allowed for an attorney court appearance for a foreclosure hearing.
(9) This fee relates to the exercise of the power of sale under a deed of trust.
(10) This fee applies to foreclosures other than those conducted in New York City and Long Island. A fee of $1,850 applies to foreclosures conducted in the five boroughs of New York City (Bronx, Brooklyn/Kings, Manhattan, Queens and Staten Island) and in Long Island (Nassau and Suffolk Counties).
(11) The fee covers certain additional legal actions necessary to complete the foreclosure, including motions to postpone or relist a sale and motions to reassess damages.
(12) In addition to the allowable foreclosure fee, $150 is allowed for a notary fee for completed foreclosures. However, if a deed of judicial sale cannot be executed contemporaneously with the foreclosure sale, $300 is allowed for the notary fee.
(13) This fee assumes that all required procedural steps have been completed. The maximum attorney's fee varies based on the chapter under which the bankruptcy action is filed.
- For Chapter 7 bankruptcies, the maximum allowable fee is $650.
- For Chapter 11, 12, and 13 bankruptcies, the maximum allowable fee is $1,000

RD AN No. 4434 (1980-D)
April 30, 2009

TO: State Directors
Rural Development

ATTENTION: Rural Housing Program Directors,
Guaranteed Rural Housing Specialists,
Area Directors and Area Managers

FROM: James C. Alsop ***(Signed by James C. Alsop)***
Acting Administrator
Rural Housing Service

SUBJECT: Single Family Guaranteed Rural Housing Loan Program
Acceptable Foreclosure Time Frames

PURPOSE/INTENDED OUTCOME:

The purpose of this Administrative Notice (AN) is to clarify and standardize the acceptable foreclosure time frame by State for Single Family Housing Loans Guaranteed by the Single Family Housing Guaranteed Loan Program (SFHGLP).

COMPARISON WITH PREVIOUS AN:

This AN replaces RD AN No. 4342 (1980-D), which expired on March 31, 2009. The acceptable foreclosure timelines in 21 States have been increased.

EXPIRATION DATE: April 30, 2010

FILING INSTRUCTIONS: Preceding RD Instruction 1980-D

BACKGROUND:

This AN provides consistency in the treatment of loss claim interest reductions resulting from untimely foreclosure initiation or completion. RD Instruction 1980-D, Section 1980.371(d), states that lenders must make a decision regarding liquidation by the time the loan is three payments past due. RD Instruction 1980-D, section 1980.374 states that foreclosure must be initiated within 90 days of the date the decision to liquidate is made unless the foreclosure has been delayed by law or an alternative to foreclosure is recommended to resolve the delinquency. Initiation of foreclosure begins with the first public action required by law, such as filing a Complaint or Petition, recording a Notice of Default, or publication of a Notice of Sale. RD Instruction 1980-D provides no guidance as to what is considered a reasonable time frame in which to complete a foreclosure in the state where the property is located. Previously, some State Offices had developed and implemented their own foreclosure time frames by which to curtail interest on loss claims. This AN establishes state specific guidance for time frames for completing foreclosure actions initiated after the date of this notice.

The SFHGLP adheres to Freddie Mac's foreclosure time frames. These time frames are measured from the first legal action (which is in accordance with RD Instruction 1980-D) to the foreclosure sale date, which is when the 6-month REO marketing period begins. Basic time frames of foreclosure processes most commonly utilized by private attorneys in state courts compare favorably to the Freddie Mac time frames. Additionally, Freddie Mac measures time frames in days as opposed to months, making compliance determinations and interest reduction calculations easier.

IMPLEMENTATION RESPONSIBILITIES:

The SFHGLP will use the foreclosure time frames as prescribed in Attachment 1, when determining whether a lender has exercised diligence in completing the foreclosure process. Differences in state procedures will affect the length of time required to complete foreclosure, therefore, the time frame will depend on the location of the property.

Attachment 1 also lists the recommended method of foreclosure and the first public action required by law to initiate each foreclosure method. In states where more than one foreclosure method is available but only one option is listed, the Agency chose the method that is most cost effective in reducing legal fees and accrued interest expense. The Agency does not intend to prohibit the payment of claims where the lender obtains title through a method of foreclosure other than what is recommended. However, the Agency office processing the loss claim request must determine whether the foreclosure method chosen by the lender was in the best interest of the Federal Government. For example, if the recommended foreclosure method is non-judicial, but judicial foreclosures are required to preserve the lender's right to a deficiency judgment, the lender may demonstrate that recovery on a deficiency judgment is expected after considering the time and cost of litigation. In such case, the judicial foreclosure method should be considered acceptable.

SFHGLP foreclosure time frames start with the date of the first legal action required by law, end with the foreclosure sale date, and do not include post-sale redemption periods or sale confirmations. Since redemption periods may be adjusted under some state laws based on the circumstances surrounding a property, such as the amount of unpaid principal still owed or the occupancy status of the property, reasonable time frames for redemption periods and sale confirmations should be established on a case-by case basis in accordance with state law. Reimbursement of accrued interest may be reduced in accordance with RD Instruction 1980-D, Section 1980.376(b), for each day that the foreclosure continues past the prescribed time frame unless the lender presents a valid reason that justifies the delay.

Lenders and the Agency must ensure that staff members are familiar with state guidelines related to foreclosures. Exceptions to the foreclosure time frame, which cause delays beyond the lender's control must be documented and submitted with the claim package. Examples of such circumstances include bankruptcy petitions filed after foreclosure initiation, contested foreclosures, and court scheduling delays or delays in obtaining service. Supporting documentation includes attorney correspondence or copies of court records. Lenders are responsible for including documentation to support the first public action and the foreclosure sale date in the claim package provided to the Agency office responsible for processing the claim.

The lender may be authorized a 60-day extension to the allowable time frame for compliance with state law when a bankruptcy delays the completion of foreclosure. To determine the impact of a bankruptcy filing on the foreclosure time frame, the total number of days from first action to foreclosure sale will be calculated. The total number of days between the bankruptcy filing date and the date of bankruptcy release or dismissal for each applicable bankruptcy case will then be subtracted from the total number of foreclosure days. The resulting number of days will be compared to the SFHGLP foreclosure time frame plus an automatic 60-day extension to determine if time frame was met.

Example -

Property State—Georgia

RHS Time Frame – 150 Days

	Date	Number of Days from Foreclosure Initiation
1st Publication Held	2/6/08	0
Bankruptcy Filed	3/1/08	23
Bankruptcy Released	9/14/08	220
Foreclosure Sale Republished	10/6/08	242
Foreclosure Sale Held	1/15/09	343

The total number of days between first publication and the foreclosure sale date is 343 days. The total number of days between bankruptcy filing and bankruptcy release was 197 days. The number of foreclosure days (343) minus the number of bankruptcy days (197) equals 146. The SFHGLP time frame for Georgia is 150 days. In this example, it is not required to add the 60-day extension to bring the time frame to 210 days. This example demonstrates that the foreclosure was pursued diligently and the delay resulted from the state requirement to republish the foreclosure sale. As a result, the lender is not penalized for not meeting the time frame.

Each Rural Development State Office is responsible for notifying state-approved lenders of the revised foreclosure time frame requirements. The National Office will advise nationally-approved lenders concurrent with the issuance of this AN.

In addition, during lender compliance reviews, files should continue to be reviewed in an effort to ensure that lenders are complying with the foreclosure requirements. Lenders that are determined to be out of compliance or that use Attorneys who are consistently out of compliance should be counseled on the provisions of the regulations and should be monitored closely for future compliance.

Questions about this AN may be directed to Stuart Walden or Debbie Terrell of the Single Family Housing Guaranteed Loan Division, USDA, Rural Housing Service, 1400 Independence Avenue, SW, Washington, DC 20250-0784. The contact telephone number is (202) 720-1452; or, via e-mail: stuart.walden@wdc.usda.gov or debra.terrell@wdc.usda.gov.

Attachment

State	Days[1] from Foreclosure Initiation to Foreclosure Sale	Foreclosure Method	Initiation of Foreclosure Document
Alabama	150	Non-judicial	Publication
Alaska	150	Non-judicial	Recording of Notice of Default
Arizona	150	Non-judicial	Recording of Notice of Sale
Arkansas	150	Non-judicial	Recording of Notice of Default
California	150	Non-judicial	Recording of Notice of Default
Colorado	165	Non-judicial	Filing of Foreclosure Docs with Public Trustee
Connecticut	220	Judicial	Delivery of Complaint to Sheriff
Delaware	250	Judicial	Complaint Filed
Florida	170	Judicial	Complaint Filed
Georgia	150	Non-judicial	Publication
Guam	250	Non-judicial	Recording of Notice of Default
Hawaii	150	Non-judicial	Publication of Notice of Intent to Foreclose
Idaho	190	Non-judicial	Recording of Notice of Default
Illinois	275	Judicial	Complaint Filed
Indiana	265	Judicial	Complaint Filed
Iowa[2]	315	Judicial	Complaint Filed
Kansas	180	Judicial	Petition Filed
Kentucky	265	Judicial	Complaint Filed
Louisiana	220	Judicial	Petition for Executory Process
Maine	355	Judicial	Complaint Filed
Maryland	150	Judicial	Filing an Order to Docket
Massachusetts	195	Non-Judicial	Filing Complaint Relative to Soldier's and Sailor's Relief Act
Michigan	150	Non-judicial	Publication
Minnesota	150	Non-judicial	Publication
Mississippi	150	Non-judicial	Publication
Missouri	150	Non-judicial	Publication
Montana	205	Non-judicial	Recording of Notice of Sale
Nebraska	155	Non-judicial	Filing of Notice of Default
Nevada	155	Non-judicial	Recording of Notice of Default
New Hampshire	150	Non-judicial	Publication
New Jersey	300	Judicial	Complaint Filed
New Mexico	250	Judicial	Complaint Filed
New York	280	Judicial	Complaint Filed
North Carolina	150	Non-judicial	Notice of Hearing
North Dakota	190	Judicial	Complaint Filed
Ohio	265	Judicial	Complaint Filed
Oklahoma	250	Judicial	Petition Filed
Oregon	180	Non-judicial	Recording of Notice of Default
Pennsylvania	300	Judicial	Complaint Filed
Puerto Rico	375	Judicial	Complaint Filed
Rhode Island	150	Non-judicial	Publication
South Carolina	215	Judicial	Complaint Filed
South Dakota	205	Judicial	Complaint Filed
Tennessee	150	Non-judicial	Publication
Texas	150	Non-judicial	Posting and Filing of Notice of Sale
Utah	165	Non-judicial	Recording of Notice of Sale
Vermont	360	Judicial	Complaint Filed
Virgin Islands	325	Judicial	Complaint Filed
Virginia	150	Non-judicial	Publication
Washington	160	Non-judicial	Recording of Notice of Default
West Virginia	150	Non-judicial	Publication
Wisconsin	310	Judicial	Complaint Filed
Wyoming	150	Non-judicial	Publication

1 State foreclosure time frames are in calendar days.

2 State time frame represents the standard elapsed time for a judicial foreclosure without redemption. A longer time frame may be allowed if a borrower files a written demand to delay the sale.

A.6 Hope for Homeowners

A.6.1 Overview

HOPE for Homeowners (H4H), a program authorizing the FHA to insure loans made to refinance homeowners into thirty year fixed-rate mortgages, was created by the Housing and Economic Recovery Act of 2008. Under this temporary program, the principal balance and interest rate for an eligible homeowner is reduced through refinancing into an affordable FHA-insured loan based on current property values. The Helping Families Save Their Home Act of 2009 made key changes to the program and those changes are effective for loans made on or after January 1, 2010.

A.6.2 Statute

TITLE 12—BANKS AND BANKING

CHAPTER 13—NATIONAL HOUSING

SUBCHAPTER II—MORTGAGE INSURANCE

12 U.S.C. § 1715z-23. HOPE for Homeowners Program

(a) Establishment

There is established in the Federal Housing Administration a HOPE for Homeowners Program.

(b) Purpose

The purpose of the HOPE for Homeowners Program is—

(1) to create an FHA program, participation in which is voluntary on the part of homeowners and existing loan holders to insure refinanced loans for distressed borrowers to support long-term, sustainable homeownership;

(2) to allow homeowners to avoid foreclosure by reducing the principle balance outstanding, and interest rate charged, on their mortgages;

(3) to help stabilize and provide confidence in mortgage markets by bringing transparency to the value of assets based on mortgage assets;

(4) to target mortgage assistance under this section to homeowners for their principal residence;

(5) to enhance the administrative capacity of the FHA to carry out its expanded role under the HOPE for Homeowners Program;

(6) to ensure the HOPE for Homeowners Program remains in effect only for as long as is necessary to provide stability to the housing market; and

(7) to provide servicers of delinquent mortgages with additional methods and approaches to avoid foreclosure.

(c) Establishment and implementation of program requirements

(1) Duties of Secretary

In order to carry out the purposes of the HOPE for Homeowners Program, the Secretary, after consultation with the Board, shall—

(A) establish requirements and standards for the program consistent with section 203(b) to the maximum extent possible; and

(B) prescribe such regulations and provide such guidance as may be necessary or appropriate to implement such requirements and standards.

(2) Duties of the Secretary

In carrying out any of the program requirements or standards established under paragraph (1), the Secretary may issue such interim guidance and mortgagee letters as the Secretary determines necessary or appropriate.

(3) Duties of Board

The Board shall advise the Secretary regarding the establishment and implementation of the HOPE for Homeowners Program.

(d) Insurance of mortgages

The Secretary is authorized upon application of a mortgagee to make commitments to insure or to insure any eligible mortgage that has been refinanced in a manner meeting the requirements under subsection (e).

(e) Requirements of insured mortgages

To be eligible for insurance under this section, a refinanced eligible mortgage shall comply with all of the following requirements:

(1) Borrower Certification

(A) No Intentional Default or False Information

The mortgagor shall provide a certification to the Secretary that the mortgagor has not intentionally defaulted on the existing mortgage or mortgages or any other substantial debt within the last 5 years and has not knowingly, or willfully and with actual knowledge, furnished material information known to be false for the purpose of obtaining the eligible mortgage to be insured and has not been convicted under Federal or State law for fraud during the 10-year period ending upon the insurance of the mortgage under this section.

(B) Liability for Repayment

The mortgagor shall agree in writing that the mortgagor shall be liable to repay to the Secretary any direct financial benefit achieved from the reduction of indebtedness on the existing mortgage or mortgages on the residence refinanced under this section derived from misrepresentations made by the mortgagor in the certifications and documentation required under this paragraph, subject to the discretion of the Secretary.

(C) Current Borrower Debt-to-Income Ratio

As of the date of application for a commitment to insure or insurance under this section, the mortgagor shall have had, or thereafter is likely to have, due to the terms of the mortgage being reset, a ratio of mortgage debt to income, taking into consideration all existing mortgages of that mortgagor at such time, greater than 31 percent (or such higher amount as the Secretary determines appropriate).

(2) Determination of principal obligation amount

The principal obligation amount of the refinanced eligible mortgage to be insured shall—

(A) be determined by the reasonable ability of the mortgagor to make his or her mortgage payments, as such ability is determined by the Secretary pursuant to section 1709(b)(4) of this title or by any other underwriting standards established by the Secretary; and

(B) not exceed 90 percent of the appraised value of the property to which such mortgage relates (or such higher percentage as the Secretary determines, in the discretion of the Secretary).

(3) Required waiver of prepayment penalties and fees
All penalties for prepayment or refinancing of the eligible mortgage, and all fees and penalties related to default or delinquency on the eligible mortgage, shall be waived or forgiven.

(4) Extinguishment of subordinate liens

(A) Required agreement
All holders of outstanding mortgage liens on the property to which the eligible mortgage relates shall agree to accept the proceeds of the insured loan and any payments made under this paragraph, as payment in full of all indebtedness under the eligible mortgage, and all encumbrances related to such eligible mortgage shall be removed. The Secretary may take such actions, as may be necessary and appropriate to facilitate coordination and agreement between the holders of the existing senior mortgage and any existing subordinate mortgages, taking into consideration the subordinate lien status of such subordinate mortgages. Such actions may include making payments, which shall be accepted as payment in full of all indebtedness under the eligible mortgage, to any holder of an existing subordinate mortgage, in lieu of any future appreciation payments authorized under subparagraph (B).

(B) Shared appreciation

(i) In general
The Secretary may establish standards and policies that will allow for the payment to the holder of any existing subordinate mortgage of a portion of any future appreciation in the property secured by such eligible mortgage that is owed to the Secretary pursuant to subsection (k).

(ii) Factors
In establishing the standards and policies required under clause (i), the Secretary shall take into consideration—

(I) the status of any subordinate mortgage;

(II) the outstanding principal balance of and accrued interest on the existing senior mortgage and any outstanding subordinate mortgages;

(III) the extent to which the current appraised value of the property securing a subordinate mortgage is less than the outstanding principal balance and accrued interest on any other liens that are senior to such subordinate mortgage; and

(IV) such other factors as the Secretary determines to be appropriate.

(C) Voluntary program
This paragraph may not be construed to require any holder of any existing mortgage to participate in the program under this section generally, or with respect to any particular loan.

(5) Term of mortgage
The refinanced eligible mortgage to be insured shall—

(A) bear interest at a single rate that is fixed for the entire term of the mortgage; and

(B) have a maturity of not less than 30 years from the date of the beginning of amortization of such refinanced eligible mortgage.

(6) Maximum loan amount
The principal obligation amount of the eligible mortgage to be insured shall not exceed 132 percent of the dollar amount limitation in effect for 2007 under section 1454(a)(2) of this title for a property of the applicable size.

(7) Prohibition on second liens
A mortgagor may not grant a new second lien on the mortgaged property during the first 5 years of the term of the mortgage insured under this section, except as the Secretary determines to be necessary to ensure the maintenance of property standards.

(8) Appraisals
Any appraisal conducted in connection with a mortgage insured under this section shall—

(A) be based on the current value of the property;

(B) be conducted in accordance with title XI of the Financial Institutions Reform, Recovery, and Enforcement Act of 1989 (12 U.S.C. 3331 *et seq.*);

(C) be completed by an appraiser who meets the competency requirements of the Uniform Standards of Professional Appraisal Practice;

(D) be wholly consistent with the appraisal standards, practices, and procedures under section 1708(e) of this title that apply to all loans insured under this chapter; and

(E) comply with the requirements of subsection (g) of this section (relating to appraisal independence).

(9) Documentation and verification of income
In complying with the FHA underwriting requirements under the HOPE for Homeowners Program under this section, the mortgagee shall document and verify the income of the mortgagor or non-filing status in accordance with procedures and standards that the Secretary shall establish (provided that such procedures and standards are consistent with section 1709(b) to the maximum extent possible) which may include requiring the mortgagee to procure a copy of the income tax returns from the Internal Revenue Service, for the two most recent years for which the filing deadline for such years has passed.

(10) Mortgage fraud

(A) Prohibition
The mortgagor shall no have been convicted under Federal or State law for fraud during the 10-year period ending upon the insurance of the mortgage under this section.

(B) Duty of Mortgagee
The duty of the mortgagee to ensure that the mortgagor is in compliance with the prohibition under subparagraph (A) shall be satisfied if the mortgagee makes a good faith effort to determine that the mortgagor has not been convicted under Federal or State law for fraud during the period described in subparagraph (A).

(11) Primary residence
The mortgagor shall provide documentation satisfactory in the determination of the Secretary to prove that the residence covered by the mortgage to be insured under this section is occupied by the mortgagor as the primary residence of the mortgagor, and that such residence is the only residence in which the mortgagor has any present ownership interest, except that the Secretary may provide exceptions to such latter requirement (relating to present ownership interest) for any mortgagor who has inherited a property.

(12) Ban on Millionaires
The mortgagor shall not have a net worth, as of the date the mortgagor first applies for a mortgage to be insured under the Program under this section, that exceeds $1,000,000.

(f) Study of auction or bulk refinance program

(1) Study

The Board shall conduct a study of the need for and efficacy of an auction or bulk refinancing mechanism to facilitate refinancing of existing residential mortgages that are at risk for foreclosure into mortgages insured under this section. The study shall identify and examine various options for mechanisms under which lenders and servicers of such mortgages may make bids for forward commitments for such insurance in an expedited manner.

(2) Content

(A) Analysis

The study required under paragraph (1) shall analyze—

(i) the feasibility of establishing a mechanism that would facilitate the more rapid refinancing of borrowers at risk of foreclosure into performing mortgages insured under this section;

(ii) whether such a mechanism would provide an effective and efficient mechanism to reduce foreclosures on qualified existing mortgages;

(iii) whether the use of an auction or bulk refinance program is necessary to stabilize the housing market and reduce the impact of turmoil in that market on the economy of the United States;

(iv) whether there are other mechanisms or authority that would be useful to reduce foreclosure; and

(v) and any other factors that the Board considers relevant.

(B) Determinations

To the extent that the Board finds that a facility of the type described in subparagraph (A) is feasible and useful, the study shall—

(i) determine and identify any additional authority or resources needed to establish and operate such a mechanism;

(ii) determine whether there is a need for additional authority with respect to the loan underwriting criteria established in this section or with respect to eligibility of participating borrowers, lenders, or holders of liens;

(iii) determine whether such underwriting criteria should be established on the basis of individual loans, in the aggregate, or otherwise to facilitate the goal of refinancing borrowers at risk of foreclosure into viable loans insured under this section.

(3) Report

Not later than the expiration of the 60-day period beginning on July 30, 2008, the Board shall submit a report regarding the results of the study conducted under this subsection to the Committee on Financial Services of the House of Representatives and the Committee on Banking, Housing, and Urban Affairs of the Senate. The report shall include a detailed description of the analysis required under paragraph (2)(A) and of the determinations made pursuant to paragraph (2)(B), and shall include any other findings and recommendations of the Board pursuant to the study, including identifying various options for mechanisms described in paragraph (1).

(g) Appraisal independence

(1) Prohibitions on interested parties in a real estate transaction

No mortgage lender, mortgage broker, mortgage banker, real estate broker, appraisal management company, employee of an appraisal management company, nor any other person with an interest in a real estate transaction involving an appraisal in connection with a mortgage insured under this section shall improperly influence, or attempt to improperly influence, through coercion, extortion, collusion, compensation, instruction, inducement, intimidation, nonpayment for services rendered, or bribery, the development, reporting, result, or review of a real estate appraisal sought in connection with the mortgage.

(2) Civil monetary penalties

The Secretary may impose a civil money penalty for any knowing and material violation of paragraph (1) under the same terms and conditions as are authorized in section 1735f-14(a) of this title.

(h) Standards to protect against adverse selection

(1) In general

The Secretary shall, by rule or order, establish standards and policies to require the underwriter of the insured loan to provide such representations and warranties as the Secretary considers necessary or appropriate to enforce compliance with all underwriting and appraisal standards of the HOPE for Homeowners Program.

(2) Exclusion for violations

The Secretary shall not pay insurance benefits to a mortgagee who violates the representations and warranties, as established under paragraph (1), or in any case in which a mortgagor fails to make the first payment on a refinanced eligible mortgage.

(3) Other authority

The Secretary may establish such other standards or policies as necessary to protect against adverse selection, including requiring loans identified by the Secretary as higher risk loans to demonstrate payment performance for a reasonable period of time prior to being insured under the program.

(i) Premiums

(1) Premiums

For each refinanced eligible mortgage insured under this section, the Secretary shall establish and collect—

(A) at the time of insurance, a single premium payment in an amount not more than 3 percent of the amount of the original insured principal obligation of the refinanced eligible mortgage, which shall be paid from the proceeds of the mortgage being insured under this section, through the reduction of the amount of indebtedness that existed on the eligible mortgage prior to refinancing; and

(B) in addition to the premium required under paragraph (1), an annual premium in an amount not more than 1.5 percent of the amount of the remaining insured principal balance of the mortgage.

(2) Considerations

In setting the premium under this subsection, the Secretary shall consider—

(A) the financial integrity of the HOPE for Homeowners Program; and

(B) the purposes of the HOPE for Homeowners Program described in subsection (b).

(j) Origination fees and interest rate

The Secretary shall establish—

(1) a reasonable limitation on origination fees for refinanced eligible mortgages insured under this section; and

(2) procedures to ensure that interest rates on such mortgages shall be commensurate with market rate interest rates on such types of loans.

(k) Exit Fee

(1) Five-year phase-in for equity as a result of sale or refinancing

For each eligible mortgage insured under this section, the Secretary and the mortgagor of such mortgage shall, upon any sale or disposition of the property to which such mortgage relates, or upon the subsequent refinancing of such mortgage, be entitled to the following with respect to any equity created as a direct result of the mortgage being insured under this section:

(A) If such sale or refinancing occurs during the period that begins on the date that such mortgage is insured and ends 1 year after such date of insurance, the Secretary shall be entitled to 100 percent of such equity.

(B) If such sale or refinancing occurs during the period that begins 1 year after such date of insurance and ends 2 years after such date of insurance, the Secretary shall be entitled to 90 percent of such equity and the mortgagor shall be entitled to 10 percent of such equity.

(C) If such sale or refinancing occurs during the period that begins 2 years after such date of insurance and ends 3 years after such date of insurance, the Secretary shall be entitled to 80 percent of such equity and the mortgagor shall be entitled to 20 percent of such equity.

(D) If such sale or refinancing occurs during the period that begins 3 years after such date of insurance and ends 4 years after such date of insurance, the Secretary shall be entitled to 70 percent of such equity and the mortgagor shall be entitled to 30 percent of such equity.

(E) If such sale or refinancing occurs during the period that begins 4 years after such date of insurance and ends 5 years after such date of insurance, the Secretary shall be entitled to 60 percent of such equity and the mortgagor shall be entitled to 40 percent of such equity.

(F) If such sale or refinancing occurs during any period that begins 5 years after such date of insurance, the Secretary shall be entitled to 50 percent of such equity and the mortgagor shall be entitled to 50 percent of such equity.

(2) Appreciation in value

For each eligible mortgage insured under this section, the Secretary may, upon any sale or disposition of the property to which the mortgage relates, be entitled to up to 50 percent of appreciation, up to the appraised value of the home at the time when the mortgage being refinanced under this section was originally made. The Secretary may share any amounts received under this paragraph with or assign the rights of any amounts due to the Secretary to the holder of the existing senior mortgage on the eligible mortgage, the holder of any existing subordinate mortgage on the eligible mortgage, or both.

(*l*) Establishment of HOPE Fund

(1) In general

There is established in the Federal Housing Administration a revolving fund to be known as the Home Ownership Preservation Entity Fund, which shall be used by the Secretary for carrying out the mortgage insurance obligations under this section.

(2) Management of Fund

The HOPE Fund shall be administered and managed by the Secretary, who shall establish reasonable and prudent criteria for the management and operation of any amounts in the HOPE Fund.

(m) Limitation on aggregate insurance authority

The aggregate original principal obligation of all mortgages insured under this section may not exceed $300,000,000,000.

(n) Reports by Secretary

The Secretary shall submit monthly reports to the Congress identifying the progress of the HOPE for Homeowners Program, which shall contain the following information for each month:

(1) The number of new mortgages insured under this section, including the location of the properties subject to such mortgages by census tract.

(2) The aggregate principal obligation of new mortgages insured under this section.

(3) The average amount by which the principle balance outstanding on mortgages insured this section was reduced.

(4) The amount of premiums collected for insurance of mortgages under this section.

(5) The claim and loss rates for mortgages insured under this section.

(6) Any other information that the Board considers appropriate.

(o) Required outreach efforts

The Secretary shall carry out outreach efforts to ensure that homeowners, lenders, and the general public are aware of the opportunities for assistance available under this section.

(p) Enhancement of FHA capacity

The Secretary shall take such actions as may be necessary to—

(1) contract for the establishment of underwriting criteria, automated underwriting systems, pricing standards, and other factors relating to eligibility for mortgages insured under this section;

(2) contract for independent quality reviews of underwriting, including appraisal reviews and fraud detection, of mortgages insured under this section or pools of such mortgages; and

(3) increase personnel of the Department as necessary to process or monitor the processing of mortgages insured under this section.

(q) GNMA commitment authority

(1) Guarantees

The Secretary shall take such actions as may be necessary to ensure that securities based on and backed by a trust or pool composed of mortgages insured under this section are available to be guaranteed by the Government National Mortgage Association as to the timely payment of principal and interest.

(2) Guarantee authority

To carry out the purposes of section 1721 of this title, the Government National Mortgage Association may enter into new commitments to issue guarantees of securities based on or backed by mortgages insured under this section, not exceeding $300,000,000,000. The amount of authority provided under the preceding sentence to enter into new commitments to issue guarantees is in addition to any amount of authority to make new commitments to issue guarantees that is provided to the Association under any other provision of law.

(r) Sunset

The Secretary may not enter into any new commitment to insure any refinanced eligible mortgage, or newly insure any refinanced eligible mortgage pursuant to this section before October 1, 2008 or after September 30, 2011.

(s) Definitions

For purposes of this section, the following definitions shall apply:

(1) Approved financial institution or mortgagee

The term "approved financial institution or mortgagee" means a financial institution or mortgagee approved by the Secretary under section 1709 of this title as responsible and able to service mortgages responsibly.

(2) Board

The term "Board" means the Advisory Board for the HOPE for Homeowners Program. The Board shall be composed of the Secretary, the Secretary of the Treasury, the Chairperson of the Board of Governors of the Federal Reserve System, and the Chairperson of the Board of Directors of the Federal Deposit Insurance Corporation, or their designees.

(3) Eligible mortgage

The term "eligible mortgage" means a mortgage—

(A) the mortgagor of which—

(i) occupies such property as his or her principal residence; and

(ii) cannot, subject to such standards established by the Secretary, afford his or her mortgage payments; and

(B) originated on or before January 1, 2008.

(4) Existing senior mortgage

The term "existing senior mortgage" means, with respect to a mortgage insured under this section, the existing mortgage that has superior priority.

(5) Existing subordinate mortgage

The term "existing subordinate mortgage" means, with respect to a mortgage insured under this section, an existing mortgage that has subordinate priority to the existing senior mortgage.

(6) HOPE for Homeowners Program

The term "HOPE for Homeowners Program" means the program established under this section.

(7) Secretary

The term "Secretary" means the Secretary of Housing and Urban Development, except where specifically provided otherwise.

(t) Requirements related to the Board

(1) Compensation, actual, necessary, and transportation expenses

(A) Federal employees

A member of the Board who is an officer or employee of the Federal Government shall serve without additional pay (or benefits in the nature of compensation) for service as a member of the Board.

(B) Travel expenses

Members of the Board shall be entitled to receive travel expenses, including per diem in lieu of subsistence, equivalent to those set forth in subchapter I of chapter 57 of Title 5.

(2) Bylaws

The Board may prescribe, amend, and repeal such bylaws as may be necessary for carrying out the functions of the Board.

(3) Quorum

A majority of the Board shall constitute a quorum.

(4) Staff; experts and consultants

(A) Detail of Government employees

Upon request of the Board, any Federal Government employee may be detailed to the Board without reimbursement, and such detail shall be without interruption or loss of civil service status or privilege.

(B) Experts and consultants

The Board shall procure the services of experts and consultants as the Board considers appropriate.

(u) Rule of construction related to voluntary nature of the program

This section shall not be construed to require that any approved financial institution or mortgagee participate in any activity authorized under this section, including any activity related to the refinancing of an eligible mortgage.

(v) Rule of construction related to insurance of mortgages

Except as otherwise provided for in this section or by action of the Secretary, the provisions and requirements of section 1709(b) of this title shall apply with respect to the insurance of any eligible mortgage under this section. The Secretary shall conform documents, forms, and procedures for mortgages insured under this section to those in place for mortgages insured under section 203(b) to the maximum extent possible consistent with the requirements of this section.

(w) HOPE Bonds

(1) Issuance and repayment of Bonds

Notwithstanding section 661c(b) of Title 2, the Secretary of the Treasury shall—

(A) subject to such terms and conditions as the Secretary of the Treasury deems necessary, issue Federal credit instruments, to be known as "HOPE Bonds", that are callable at the discretion of the Secretary of the Treasury and do not, in the aggregate, exceed the amount specified in subsection (m);

(B) provide the subsidy amounts necessary for loan guarantees under the HOPE for Homeowners Program, not to exceed the amount specified in subsection (m), in accordance with the provisions of the Federal Credit Reform Act of 1990 (2 U.S.C. 661 *et seq.*), except as provided in this paragraph; and

(C) use the proceeds from HOPE Bonds only to pay for the net costs to the Federal Government of the HOPE for Homeowners Program, including administrative costs and payments pursuant to subsection (e)(4)(A).

(2) Reimbursements to Treasury

Funds received pursuant to section 4568(b) of this title shall be used to reimburse the Secretary of the Treasury for amounts borrowed under paragraph (1).

(3) Use of reserve fund

If the net cost to the Federal Government for the HOPE for Homeowners Program exceeds the amount of funds received under paragraph (2), remaining debts of the HOPE for Homeowners Program shall be paid from amounts deposited into the fund established by the Secretary under section 4567(e) of this title remaining amounts in such fund to be used to reduce the National debt.

(4) Reduction of National debt

Amounts collected under the HOPE for Homeowners Program in accordance with subsections (i) and (k) in excess of the net cost to the Federal Government for such Program shall be used to reduce the National debt.

(X) Payments to Servicers and Originators

The Secretary may establish a payment to the

(1) servicer of the existing senior mortgage or existing subordinate mortgage for every loan insured under the HOPE for Homeowners Program; and

(2) originator of each new loan insured under the HOPE for Homeowners Program.

(Y) Auctions
The Secretary, with the concurrence of the Board, shall, if feasible, establish a structure and organize procedures for an auction to refinance eligible mortgages on a wholesale or bulk basis.

[June 27, 1934, ch. 847, tit. II, § 257, *as added* Pub. L. No. 110-289, div. A, tit. III, § 1402, 122 Stat. 2809 (July 30, 2008), *and amended* Pub. L. No. 110-343, div. A, tit. I, § 124, 122 Stat. 3791 (Oct. 3, 2008); Pub. L. No. 111-22, div. A, tit. II, § 202(a), 123 Stat. 1640 (May 20, 2009)]

A.6.3 Regulations

TITLE 24—HOUSING AND URBAN DEVELOPMENT
SUBTITLE B—REGULATIONS RELATING TO HOUSING AND URBAN DEVELOPMENT
CHAPTER XXIV—BOARD OF DIRECTORS OF THE HOPE FOR HOMEOWNERS PROGRAM
PART 4000—BOARD OF DIRECTORS OF THE HOPE FOR HOMEOWNERS PROGRAM

Authority: 5 U.S.C. 552; 12 U.S.C. 1715z-22.

PART 4001—HOPE FOR HOMEOWNERS PROGRAM

Authority: 12 U.S.C. 1701z-22.

* * *

PART 4000—BOARD OF DIRECTORS OF THE HOPE FOR HOMEOWNERS PROGRAM

Authority: 5 U.S.C. 552; 12 U.S.C. 1715z-22.

24 C.F.R. § 4000.1 Purpose and scope.

This subpart establishes the Board's procedures governing access to records of the Board under the Freedom of Information Act (5 U.S.C. 552).

[74 Fed. Reg. 7813 (Feb. 20, 2009)]

24 C.F.R. § 4000.2 Freedom of Information Act.

(a) *In general.* While the Board is not part of the Department of Housing and Urban Development ("HUD"), the Board follows the regulations promulgated by HUD at subparts A and B ("FOIA Disclosure Information") of part 15 ("Public access to HUD records under the Freedom of Information Act and testimony and production of information by HUD employees") of Title 24 ("Housing and Urban Development") of the Code of Federal Regulations ("CFR"), except as otherwise provided in this section. Any reference in 24 CFR 15.1 through 15.112 to "HUD" shall be construed to refer to the Board. In the event that the regulations at subparts A and B of part 15 of title 24 of the CFR subsequently are amended by HUD, the Board will follow those amended regulations. The following additional information is provided to implement 24 CFR 15.1 through 15.112 as such sections apply to the Board.

(b) *Requests for information.* All requests to the Board for access to records of the Board should be directed to the attention of the Board at the U.S. Department of Housing and Urban Development (HUD), Freedom of Information Act Office, 451 Seventh Street, SW., Room 10139, Washington, DC 20410-3000 (HUD Headquarters), where the Board maintains its principal place of business. Requestors should follow the directions for requesting records as provided in the regulations in 24 CFR part 15, subpart B. The public reading rooms for the Board are the reading rooms located at HUD Headquarters in Washington, DC. Due to security measures at HUD Headquarters, an advance appointment to review the public comments must be scheduled by calling the FOIA Office at 202-708-3054 (this is not a toll-free number).

(c) *Requests for records.* Initial determinations whether to grant requests for records of the Board will be made by the Secretary of the Board or the designee of such official. Requests for records by mail should be addressed to the same address as that provided in paragraph (a) of this section.

(d) *Administrative appeal of initial determination to deny records.*

(1) Appellate determinations with respect to the records of the Board will be made by an official, designated by the Executive Director of the Board, who had no involvement in the initial determination of the request for records that is the subject of the appeal.

(2) Appellate determinations with respect to requests for expedited processing shall be made by the Secretary of the Board or the designee of such official.

(3) Appeals should be addressed to the address provided in paragraph (a) of this section.

(e) *Delivery of process.* Service of process will be received by Counselor to the Board or the designee of such official and shall be delivered to the address provided in paragraph (a) of this section to the attention of Counselor to the Board.

[74 Fed. Reg. 7813 (Feb. 20, 2009)]

PART 4001—HOPE FOR HOMEOWNERS PROGRAM

Authority: 12 U.S.C. 1701z-22.

Subpart A—HOPE for Homeowners Program—General Requirements

24 C.F.R. § 4001.01 Purpose of program.

The HOPE for Homeowners Program is a temporary program authorized by section 257 of the National Housing Act, established within the Federal Housing Administration (FHA) of the Department of Housing and Urban Development (HUD) that offers homeowners and existing loan holders (or servicers acting on their behalf) FHA insurance on refinanced loans for distressed borrowers to support long-term sustainable homeownership by, among other things, allowing homeowners to avoid foreclosure. The HOPE for Homeowners Program is administered by HUD through FHA.

[73 Fed. Reg. 58,421 (Oct. 6, 2008); 74 Fed. Reg. 7813 (Feb. 20, 2009)]

24 C.F.R. § 4001.03 Requirements and delegated authority.

(a) *Core requirements.* This subpart establishes the core requirements for the HOPE for Homeowners Program that have been adopted by the Board of Directors (Board) for the HOPE for Homeowners Program (Program). In addition to the core requirements, codified in this subpart, the Board of Directors may adopt and issue additional requirements, standards and policies through non-codified regulations, including through order, Federal Register notice, or other statement, such as a mortgagee letter, to be issued and implemented by FHA.

(b) *Basic Program parameters.*

(1) FHA is authorized to insure eligible refinanced mortgages under the Program commencing no earlier than October 1, 2008. The authority to insure additional mortgages under the Program expires September 30, 2011.

(2) Under this Program, an eligible mortgagor may obtain a refinancing of his or her existing mortgage(s) with a new mortgage loan insured by FHA, subject to conditions and restrictions specified in section 257 of the National Housing Act and requirements established by the Board.

(c) *Delegated authority.* HUD is statutorily charged with administering, through FHA, the Program. In carrying out the Program requirements established by the Board, FHA is directed to issue such interim guidance and mortgagee letters as FHA determines necessary or appropriate, within the parameters of the requirements, standards and policies adopted by the Board. In addition to FHA's statutory charge, the Board of Directors authorizes FHA to address unique or case-by-case situations as may be encountered by FHA in carrying out the Program, and to take such action as may be necessary to implement the Board's requirements. This delegated implementing authority includes, but is not limited to, specifying application forms, mortgage application procedures, certifications or other assurances, and other information collection requirements, subject to such rules, standards and policies as the Board may adopt.

(d) *Other applicable requirements.* Except as may be otherwise provided by the Board, the provisions and requirements in the FHA regulations in 24 CFR part 203, which are generally applicable to all FHA-insured single family mortgage insurance programs, also apply with respect to the insurance of a refinanced eligible mortgage under the Program.

[73 Fed. Reg. 58,421 (Oct. 6, 2008)]

24 C.F.R. § 4001.05 Approval of mortgagees.

(a) *Eligibility.* In order for a mortgage to be eligible for insurance under this part, the mortgagee originating the mortgage loan and seeking mortgage insurance under this part shall have been approved by the Secretary pursuant to 24 CFR part 202.

(b) *Mortgagee whose loan is to be refinanced.* A mortgagee holding or servicing an eligible mortgage to be refinanced and insured under section 257 of the National Housing Act is not required to be an approved mortgagee as required in paragraph (a) of this section, unless it seeks to be the originator of the refinanced mortgage to be insured by FHA.

[73 Fed. Reg. 58,421 (Oct. 6, 2008)]

24 C.F.R. § 4001.07 Definitions.

As used in this part and in the Program, the following definitions apply.

Act means the National Housing Act (12 U.S.C. 1701 *et seq.*).

Allowable closing costs mean charges, fees and discounts that the mortgagee may collect from the mortgagor as provided in 24 CFR 203.27(a).

Board means the Board of Directors for the HOPE for Homeowners Program, which is comprised of the Secretary of HUD, the Secretary of the Treasury, the Chairman of the Board of Governors of the Federal Reserve System (Federal Reserve Board), and the Chairperson of the Board of Directors of the Federal Deposit Insurance Corporation or the designees of each such individual.

Capital improvements means a repair, renovation, or addition to a property that significantly enhances the value of the property, but does not include expenses for interior decor, landscape maintenance, or normal maintenance or replacement expenses.

Contract of insurance means the agreement by which FHA provides mortgage insurance to a mortgagee.

Default and delinquency fees means late charges contained in a mortgage/security instrument for the late or non-receipt of payments from mortgagors after the date upon which payment is due, including charges imposed by the mortgagee for the return of payments on the mortgage due to non-sufficient funds.

Direct financial benefit, as used in section 257(e)(1)(A)(ii)(II) of the Act, consists of the greater of two factors:

(1) The amount of initial equity the mortgagor has in the property at the closing for the Program mortgage as determined under § 4001.118; and

(2) The total amount that the existing senior mortgage and all existing subordinate mortgages on the property have been written down.

Disposition means any transaction that results in whole or partial transfer of title of a property other than—

(1) A sale of the property; or

(2) Any transaction or transfer specified in 12 U.S.C. § 1701j-3(d)(1) through (8).

Eligible Mortgage means a mortgage as defined in § 4001.104.

Existing senior mortgage means an eligible mortgage that has superior priority and is being refinanced by a mortgage insured under section 257 of the Act.

Existing subordinate mortgage means a mortgage that is subordinate in priority to an eligible mortgage which is being refinanced by a mortgage insured under section 257 of the Act.

FHA means the Federal Housing Administration.

HOPE for Homeowners Program (or Program) means the program established under section 257 of the Act.

HUD means the Department of Housing and Urban Development.

Intentionally defaulted for purposes of section 257(e)(1)(A) of the Act means the mortgagor:

(1) Knowingly failed to make payment on the mortgage or debt;

(2) Had available funds at the time payment on the mortgage or debt was due that could pay the mortgage or debt without undue hardship; and

(3) The debt was not subject to a bona fide dispute.

Mortgage has the same meaning as provided in 24 CFR 203.17(a)(1).

Mortgagee has the same meaning as provided in 24 CFR 203.251(f).

Mortgagor has the same meaning as provided in 24 CFR 203.251(e).

Premium pricing means the price for the sale of a mortgage loan with an above market rate of interest.

Prepayment penalties mean such amounts as defined in 12 CFR 226.32(d)(6) of the Federal Reserve Board's Regulation Z (Truth in Lending).

Primary residence means the dwelling where the mortgagor maintains his or her permanent place of abode and typically spends the majority of the calendar year. A mortgagor can only have one primary residence.

Program mortgage means the mortgage into which the existing senior mortgage is refinanced.

Related party of a person means any of the following or another person acting on behalf of the person or any of the following—

(1) The person's father, mother, stepfather, stepmother, brother, sister, stepbrother, stepsister, son, daughter, stepson, stepdaughter, grandparent, grandson, granddaughter, father-in-law, mother-in-law, brother-in-law, sister-in-law, son-in-law, daughter-in-law, the spouse of any of the foregoing, and the person's spouse;

(2) Any entity of which 25 percent or more of any class of voting securities is owned, controlled or held in the aggregate by the person or the persons referred to in paragraph (1); and

(3) Any entity of which the person or any person referred to in paragraph (1) serves as a trustee, general partner, limited partner, managing member, or director.

Secretary means the Secretary of Housing and Urban Development.

Total monthly mortgage payment means the sum of:

(1) Principal and interest, as determined on a fully indexed and fully amortized basis; and

(2) *Escrowed amounts.*

(i) The monthly required amount collected by or on behalf of the mortgagee for real estate taxes, premiums for required hazard and mortgage insurance, homeowners' association dues, ground rent, special assessments, water and sewer charges and other similar charges required by the note or security instrument; or

(ii) For mortgages not subject to escrow deposits, 1/12 of the estimated annual costs for items listed in paragraph (2)(i) of this definition.

[73 Fed. Reg. 58,421 (Oct. 6, 2008); 74 Fed. Reg. 621 (Jan. 7, 2009)]

Subpart B—Eligibility Requirements and Underwriting Procedures

24 C.F.R. § 4001.102 Cross-reference.

(a) All of the provisions of 24 CFR part 203, subpart A, concerning eligibility requirements of mortgages covering one-family dwellings under section 203 of the National Housing Act (12 U.S.C. 1709) apply to mortgages on one-family dwellings to be insured under section 257 of the National Housing Act (12 U.S.C. 1701z-22), except the following provisions: 203.7 Commitment Process; 203.10 Informed consumer choice for prospective FHA mortgagors; 203.12 Mortgage insurance on proposed or new subdivisions; 203.14 Builder's warranty; 203.16 Certificate and contract regarding use of dwelling for transient or hotel purposes; 203.17(d) Maturity; 203.18 Maximum mortgage amounts; 203.18a Solar-energy system; 203.18b Increased mortgage amount; 203.18c One-time or up-front MIP excluded from limitations on maximum mortgage amounts; 203.18d Minimum principal loan amount; 203.19 Mortgagor's minimum investment; 203.20 Agreed interest rate; 203.29 Eligible mortgage in Alaska, Guam, Hawaii or the Virgin Islands; 203.32 Mortgage lien; 203.37a Sale of property; 203.42 Rental properties; 203.43 Eligibility of miscellaneous types of mortgages; 203.43a Eligibility of mortgages covering housing in certain neighborhoods; 203.43d Eligibility of mortgages in certain communities; 203.43e Eligibility of mortgages covering houses in federally impacted areas; 203.43g Eligibility of mortgages in certain communities; 203.43h Eligibility of mortgages on Indian land insured pursuant to section 248 of the National Housing Act; 203.43i Eligibility of mortgages on Hawaiian Home Lands insured pursuant to section 247 of the National Housing Act; 203.43j Eligibility of mortgages on Allegany Reservation of Seneca Nation Indians; 203.44 Eligibility of advances; 203.45 Eligibility of graduated payment mortgages; 203.47 Eligibility of growing equity mortgages; 203.49 Eligibility of adjustable rate mortgages; 203.50 Eligibility of rehabilitation loans; 203.51 Applicability; and 203.200-203.209 Insured Ten-Year Protection Plans (Plan).

(b) For the purposes of this subpart, all references in 24 CFR part 203, subpart A, to section 203 of the Act shall be construed to refer to section 257 of the Act. Any references in 24 CFR part 203, subpart A, to the "Mutual Mortgage Insurance Fund" shall be deemed to be to the Home Ownership Preservation Entity Fund, and any references to "the Commissioner" shall be deemed to be to the Board or the Commissioner (as the context may require).

(c) If there is any conflict in the application of any requirement of 24 CFR part 203, subpart A, to this part the provisions of this part shall control.

[73 Fed. Reg. 58,422 (Oct. 6, 2008); 74 Fed. Reg. 621 (Jan. 7, 2009)]

24 C.F.R. § 4001.104 Eligible mortgages.

A mortgage eligible to be refinanced under section 257 of the Act must:

(a) Have been originated on or before January 1, 2008;

(b) Be secured by a property owned and occupied by the mortgagor as his or her primary residence, and be the only residence in which the mortgagor has any present ownership interest; and

(c) Meet such other requirements as the Board may adopt.

[73 Fed. Reg. 58,422 (Oct. 6, 2008)]

24 C.F.R. § 4001.106 Eligible mortgagors.

A mortgagor shall be eligible to refinance his or her existing mortgages under section 257 of the Act only if:

(a)(1) The mortgagor had, on March 1, 2008, a total monthly mortgage payment (based on mortgages outstanding on March 1, 2008) of more than 31 percent of the mortgagor's monthly gross income; or

(2) If the mortgagor's existing senior mortgage or existing subordinate mortgage, if any, is an adjustable-rate mortgage that by its terms resets after March 1, 2008, the mortgagor has a total monthly mortgage payment (based on mortgages outstanding on March 1, 2008) of more than 31 percent of the mortgagor's monthly gross income calculated as of the date the mortgagor first applies for the Program mortgage;

(b) The mortgagor does not have an ownership interest in any other residential property;

(c) The mortgagor has not been convicted of fraud under federal or state law in the past 10 years;

(d) The mortgagor certifies that the mortgagor has not intentionally defaulted on any mortgage or debt and has not knowingly, or willfully and with actual knowledge, furnished material information known to be false for purposes of obtaining any Program mortgage; and

(e) The mortgagor meets such other requirements as the Board may adopt.

[73 Fed. Reg. 58,422 (Oct. 6, 2008); 74 Fed. Reg. 621 (Jan. 7, 2009)]

24 C.F.R. § 4001.108 Eligible properties.

(a) A mortgage may be insured under the Program only if the property that is to be the security for the mortgage is a 1-to-4 unit residence.

(b) The following property types are eligible to secure a mortgage insured under the Program:

(1) Detached and semi-detached dwellings;

(2) A condominium unit;

(3) A cooperative unit; or

(4) A manufactured home that is permanently affixed to realty and is treated as realty under applicable state law except state taxation law.

[73 Fed. Reg. 58,422 (Oct. 6, 2008); 74 Fed. Reg. 621 (Jan. 7, 2009)]

24 C.F.R. § 4001.110 Underwriting.

A mortgage may be insured under the Program only if the following conditions are met:

(a) *Loan-to-value and income thresholds.* The loan-to-value (LTV), payment-to-income, and debt-to-income ratios of the Program mortgage do not exceed the thresholds set forth in either paragraph (a)(1) or (a)(2) of this section.

(1) *Program mortgage with LTV ratio of 90 percent or less.*

(i) The initial principal balance of the Program mortgage as a percentage of the current appraised value of the property does not exceed 90 percent;

(ii) The total monthly mortgage payment of the mortgagor under the Program mortgage does not exceed 38 percent of the mortgagor's monthly gross income; and

(iii) The sum of the total monthly mortgage payment under the Program mortgage and all monthly recurring expenses of the mortgagor does not exceed 50 percent of the mortgagor's monthly gross income.

(2) *Program mortgage with up to 96.5 percent LTV.*

(i) The initial principal balance of the Program mortgage as a percentage of the current appraised value of the property does not exceed 96.5 percent;

(ii) The total monthly mortgage payment of the mortgagor under the Program mortgage does not exceed 31 percent of the mortgagor's monthly gross income; and

(iii) The sum of the total monthly mortgage payment under the Program mortgage and all monthly recurring expenses of the mortgagor does not exceed 43 percent of the mortgagor's monthly gross income.

(b) *Past credit performance.* The mortgagor must have made at least six full payments on the existing senior mortgage being refinanced under the Program.

(c) The Program mortgage shall have a maturity of not less than 30 years and not more than 40 years from the date of origination.

(d) *Non-occupant co-borrowers.* A mortgage loan may be insured by the FHA under the Program, even if one of the mortgagors on the loan (i.e., a co-signer) does not reside at the residence securing the loan, provided that the non-resident mortgagor relinquishes all interests in the property that is to be security for the mortgage before an application is submitted for FHA insurance under the Program.

(e) *Amount of new mortgage payment.* The mortgagor's total monthly payment on the mortgage to be insured under the Program must not be greater than the mortgagor's aggregate total monthly mortgage payment under the mortgagor's existing senior mortgage and all existing subordinate mortgages.

(f) *Limit on origination fees.* Mortgagees may charge and collect from mortgagors allowable closing costs.

[73 Fed. Reg. 58,422 (Oct. 6, 2008); 74 Fed. Reg. 621 (Jan. 7, 2009)]

24 C.F.R. § 4001.112 Income verification.

The mortgagee shall use FHA's procedures to verify the mortgagor's income and shall comply with the following additional requirements:

(a) The mortgagee shall document and verify the income of the mortgagor by obtaining a transcript of the borrower's Federal income tax returns or a copy of the borrower's Federal income tax returns obtained directly from the Internal Revenue Service for the most recent two years; and

(b) The mortgagee shall document and verify the mortgagor's income in any case in which the mortgagor has not filed a Federal income tax return.

[73 Fed. Reg. 58,423 (Oct. 6, 2008)]

24 C.F.R. § 4001.114 Appraisal.

(a) The property shall be appraised by an appraiser on the FHA Appraiser Roster.

(b) An appraisal of a property to be security for a Program mortgage shall be conducted in accordance with Uniform Standards of Professional Appraisal Practice (USPAP) but dated no more than 90 days from the date on which the mortgage transaction is closed, except as otherwise provided by the Board.

(c) The mortgagee must inform the appraiser that copies of the appraisal may be shared with holders and servicers of existing subordinate mortgages.

[73 Fed. Reg. 58,423 (Oct. 6, 2008)]

24 C.F.R. § 4001.116 Representations and prohibitions.

(a) *Underwriting and appraisal standards.* In order for the Program mortgage to be eligible for insurance under the Program, the underwriter and the mortgagee must provide certifications, in a format approved by the FHA, that the mortgage is in compliance with the underwriting and the appraisal standards set forth in this part, and that it meets all requirements applicable to the Program. FHA may require additional certifications by the mortgagee to ensure compliance with such additional standards as the FHA deems necessary given the specific mortgage transaction presented.

(b) *Mortgagor's liability for repayment.*

(1) The mortgagor shall provide a certification to FHA that the mortgagor has not:

(i) Intentionally defaulted on the mortgagor's existing mortgage(s), or any other debt; or

(ii) Knowingly or willfully and with actual knowledge furnished material information known to be false for the purpose of obtaining the mortgagor's existing mortgage(s).

(2) The mortgagor shall provide any other certifications that FHA may otherwise require.

(3) A mortgagor obligated under a Program mortgage shall agree in writing, on a form approved by the Board, to be liable to pay to FHA any Direct Financial Benefit achieved from the reduction of indebtedness on the existing senior and subordinate mortgages that are being refinanced under the Program if he or she makes a false statement or other misrepresentation in the

certifications and documentation required for Program eligibility, including but not limited to the certifications required under section 257(e)(1)(A)(i) of the Act.

(c) *Mortgagee in violation of Program requirements.*

(1) If the mortgagee holds a Program mortgage that it originated and/or underwrote, and FHA finds that the mortgagee violated the Program requirements, FHA is prohibited from paying FHA insurance benefits to that mortgagee.

(2) If the mortgagee no longer holds the Program mortgage that it originated and/or underwrote, FHA will pay the insurance claim to the mortgagee presently holding the Program mortgage (if all other requirements of the contract for mortgage insurance are met and the present holder did not participate in the violation of Program requirements) and shall seek indemnification from the non-holding mortgagee.

(d) *FHA insurance.* A mortgage is eligible for insurance if the mortgagee submits a complete case binder within such time period as the Board prescribes. The binder shall include evidence acceptable to the Board that the mortgage is current.

(e) *Mortgagor failure to make first mortgage payment.* FHA shall not pay a mortgage insurance claim to any mortgagee if the first total monthly mortgage payment is not made within 120 days from the date of closing of the mortgage. The mortgagee shall not, directly or indirectly, make all or a part of the first total monthly mortgage payment on behalf of the mortgagor. The mortgagee is prohibited from escrowing funds at closing for all or part of the first total monthly mortgage payment.

[73 Fed. Reg. 58,423 (Oct. 6, 2008); 74 Fed. Reg. 621 (Jan. 7, 2009)]

24 C.F.R. § 4001.118 Equity sharing.

(a) *Initial Equity.* For purposes of section 257(k)(1) of the Act, the initial equity created as a direct result of the origination of a Program mortgage on a property, as calculated by the Program mortgage lender, shall equal:

(1) The lesser of—

(i) The appraised value of the property that was used at the time of origination of the Program mortgage to underwrite the mortgage and to determine compliance with the maximum loan-to-value ratio at origination established by section 257(e)(2)(B) of the Act; or

(ii) The outstanding amount due under all existing senior mortgages, existing subordinate mortgages, and non-mortgage liens on the property; less

(2) The original principal amount of the Program mortgage on the property.

(b) *FHA's interest.* Upon the sale or disposition of a property or Program mortgage refinancing, FHA shall calculate and be entitled to receive the portion of the initial equity (as defined by paragraph (a) of this section) set forth in section 257(k)(1) of the Act, subject to such standards and policies as the Board may establish.

[73 Fed. Reg. 58,423 (Oct. 6, 2008); 74 Fed. Reg. 621 (Jan. 7, 2009)]

24 C.F.R. § 4001.120 Appreciation sharing or upfront payment.

(a) *Calculation of appreciation.* For purposes of section 257(k)(2) of the Act, the amount of the appreciation in value of a property securing a Program mortgage that occurs between the date the mortgage was insured under section 257 of the Act and the date of any subsequent sale or disposition of the property shall be equal to the following, as such amounts of appreciation may be established to the satisfaction of FHA:

(1) In the case of—

(i) A sale of the property to one or more persons none of which is a related party of the mortgagor, the gross proceeds from the sale of the property; or

(ii) A disposition of the property or the sale of the property to a related party of the mortgagor, the current appraised value of the property at the time of the disposition or sale; less

(2) The amount of closing costs, as adopted by the Board, incurred by the mortgagor(s) in connection with such sale or disposition, if any; less

(3) Seventy-five percent, as may be modified by the Board, of the actual expenditures for Capital Improvements made by the mortgagor(s) after the date of origination of the Program mortgage; and less

(4) The appraised value of the property that was used at the time of origination of the Program mortgage to underwrite that mortgage and determine compliance with the maximum loan-to-value ratio at origination established by section 257(e)(2)(B) of the Act.

(b) *HUD's interest in appreciation.* Upon sale or disposition of a property securing a Program mortgage, FHA shall be entitled to receive an amount equal to 50 percent of the appreciation in value of the property calculated in accordance with paragraph (a) of this section.

(c) *Eligibility of subordinate mortgage holders to receive a portion of appreciation in value.* The persons or entities that hold, on the date of origination of a Program mortgage, an existing subordinate mortgage on the property shall be eligible to receive a portion of FHA's interest in the appreciation in value of the property, as determined in accordance with the provisions of this section and such additional standards and policies that the Board may establish, if:

(1) The existing subordinate mortgage was originated on or before January 1, 2008;

(2) The amount of the unpaid principal and interest on such existing subordinate mortgage, as of the first day of the month in which the mortgagor made application for the Program mortgage, is at least $2,500; and

(3) Each person holding such existing subordinate mortgage agrees, in connection with the origination of the Program mortgage, to fully release:

(i) The mortgagor(s) from any indebtedness under the existing subordinate mortgage; and

(ii) The holder's mortgage lien on the property.

(d) *Shared appreciation interest of subordinate mortgage holders.*

(1) *In general.* The eligible holder(s) of an existing subordinate mortgage on a property securing a Program mortgage shall be eligible to receive, subject to paragraph (c)(3) of this section, an interest in FHA's interest in the appreciation in the value of such property up to the amount set forth in the Appendix to this part.

(2) *Form.* The interest of an eligible holder of an existing subordinate mortgage under paragraph (d) of this section is evidenced in a shared appreciation certificate or other documentation to be issued by, or on behalf of, HUD.

(3) *Multiple subordinate liens.* If there is more than one eligible existing subordinate mortgage on a property securing a Program mortgage, the interests of such eligible existing subordinate mortgages under paragraph (d)(1) of this section shall have priority among each other in the same order of priority that existed among the existing subordinate mortgages on the date of origination of the Program mortgage.

(4) *Distribution of appreciation interest to subordinate mortgage holders.* Upon the sale or disposition of a property securing a Program mortgage other than sale or disposition related to a default, any proceeds due to FHA as a result of the appreciation in value of the property (as calculated in accordance with paragraph (a) of this section) shall be distributed:

(i) First to the holders of any shared appreciation certificate or other documentation issued by HUD with respect to the property, if any, in accordance with paragraphs (d)(1), (d)(2), and (d)(3) of this section; and

(ii) The remaining amounts, if any, will be retained by FHA.

(e) *Election to receive upfront payment in lieu of a share of appreciation.* Upon meeting the requirements of paragraph (c) of this section, the eligible holder(s) of an existing subordinate mortgage on a property securing a Program mortgage may elect to receive, contemporaneously with the origination of the Program mortgage, a payment from FHA in an aggregate amount determined in accordance with the formula provided in Appendix A to this part in lieu of any right to receive a portion of FHA's 50 percent interest in the future appreciation in the appraised value of such property under paragraph (c) of this section.

[73 Fed. Reg. 58,424 (Oct. 6, 2008); 74 Fed. Reg. 621 (Jan. 7, 2009)]

24 C.F.R. § 4001.122 Fees and closing costs.

(a) The holder or servicer of the existing senior and subordinate mortgages shall either forgive or waive all prepayment penalties and delinquency and default fees.

(b) Allowable closing costs incurred in connection with the refinancing and insurance of a mortgage under the Program can be paid from the following sources:

(1) The mortgagor's assets;

(2) The mortgagee holding or servicing the existing senior and subordinate mortgage or the mortgagee originating the Program mortgage;

(3) Premium pricing by the mortgagee providing the Program mortgage;

(4) Financed as part of the Program mortgage provided that the mortgage amount is adjusted accordingly, and the loan-to-value ratio does not exceed 90 percent (including the up-front premium required under § 4001.203(a)(1));

(5) A Federal, state, county or parish, or municipal program; or

(6) Such other sources as the Board may permit.

[73 Fed. Reg. 58,424 (Oct. 6, 2008)]

Subpart C—Rights and Obligations Under the Contract of Insurance

24 C.F.R. § 4001.201 Cross-reference.

(a) All of the provisions of 24 CFR part 203, subpart B, covering mortgages insured under section 203 of the Act shall apply to mortgages insured under section 257 of the Act, *except the following sections*: 203.256 Insurance of open-end advances; 203.259a Scope; 203.260 Amount of insurance premium; 203.261 Calculation of periodic MIP (periodic MIP); 203.270 Open-end insurance charges; 203.280 One-time of Up-front MIP; 203.281 Calculation of one-time MIP; 203.283 Refund of one-time MIP; 203.284 Calculation of up-front and annual MIP on or after July 1, 1991; 203.285 Fifteen year mortgages: calculation of up-front and annual MIP on or after December 26, 1992; 203.415-203.417 Certificate of Claim; 203.420-203.427 Mutual Mortgage Insurance Fund and Distributive Shares; 203.436 Claim procedures—graduated payment mortgages; 203.438 Mortgages on Indian land insured pursuant to section 248 of the National Housing Act; 203.439 Mortgages on Hawaiian home lands insured pursuant to section 247 of the National Housing Act; 203.439a Mortgages on property in Allegheny Reservation of Seneca Nation of Indians authorized by section 203(q) of the National Housing Act; and 203.440-203.495 Rehabilitation Loans.

(b) For the purposes of this subpart, all references in 24 CFR part 203, subpart B, to section 203 of the Act shall be construed to refer to section 257 of the Act. Any references in 24 CFR part 203, subpart B, to the "Mutual Mortgage Insurance Fund" shall be deemed to be to the Home Ownership Preservation Entity Fund, and any references to "the Commissioner" shall be deemed to be to the Board or the Commissioner (as the context may require).

(c) If there is any conflict in the application of any requirement of 24 CFR part 203, subpart B, to this part 4001, the provisions of part 4001 shall control.

[73 Fed. Reg. 58,424 (Oct. 6, 2008)]

24 C.F.R. § 4001.203 Calculation of upfront and annual mortgage insurance premiums for Program mortgages.

(a) *Applicable premiums.* Any mortgage presented for endorsement under section 257 on or after October 1, 2008, and prior to September 30, 2011, shall be subject to the following requirements:

(1) *Upfront premium.* FHA shall establish and collect a single premium payment equal to 3 percent of the amount of the original insured principal obligation of the Program mortgage.

(2) *Annual premium.* In addition to the premium under paragraph (a)(1) of this section, FHA shall establish and collect an annual premium payment in an amount equal to 1.5 percent of the amount of the remaining insured principal balance of the Program mortgage.

(b) *Proceeds for payment of the upfront premium.* The up-front premium shall be paid with proceeds from the Program mortgage through a reduction of the amount of indebtedness that existed on the eligible mortgage prior to its being refinanced.

[73 Fed. Reg. 58,425 (Oct. 6, 2008)]

Subpart D—Servicing Responsibilities

24 C.F.R. § 4001.301 Cross-reference.

(a) All of the provisions of 24 CFR part 203, subpart C, covering mortgages insured under section 203 of the Act shall apply to mortgages insured under section 257 of the Act, *except as follows*: 203.664 Processing defaulted mortgages on property located on Indian land; 203.665 Processing defaulted mortgages on property located on Hawaiian home lands; 203.666 Processing defaulted mortgages on property in Allegany Reservation of Seneca Nation of Indians; and 203-670-203.681 Occupied Conveyance.

(b) For the purposes of this subpart, all references in 24 CFR part 203, subpart C, to section 203 of the Act shall be construed to refer to section 257 of the Act. Any references in 24 CFR part 203, subpart C, to the "Mutual Mortgage Insurance Fund" shall be deemed to be to the Home Ownership Preservation Entity Fund, and any references to "the Commissioner" shall be deemed to be to the Board or the Commissioner (as the context may require).

(c) If there is any conflict in the application of any requirement of 24 CFR part 203, subpart C, to this part 4001, the provisions of part 4001 shall control.

[73 Fed. Reg. 58,425 (Oct. 6, 2008)]

24 C.F.R. § 4001.303 Prohibition on subordinate liens during first five years.

(a) *Prohibition on subordinate liens during first five years.* Except as provided in paragraph (b) of this section, a mortgagor shall not, during the first 5 years of the term of the mortgagor's Program mortgage, incur any debt, take any action, or fail to take any action that would have the direct result of causing a lien to be placed on the property securing the Program mortgage if such lien would be subordinate to the Program mortgage.

(b) *Property preservation exception.* Paragraph (a) of this section shall not prevent a mortgagor on the Program mortgage from incurring new mortgage debt secured by a lien on the property securing the Program mortgage that is subordinate to the Program mortgage if:

(1) The proceeds of the new mortgage debt are necessary to ensure the maintenance of property standards, including health and safety standards;

(2) Repair or remediation of the condition would preserve or increase the property's value;

(3) The cost of the proposed repair or remediation is reasonable for the geographic market area;

(4) The results of the repair or remediation are not primarily cosmetic;

(5) The repair or remediation does not represent routine maintenance;

(6) The new mortgage debt is closed-end credit, as defined in § 226.2 of the Federal Reserve Board's Regulation Z (12 CFR 226.2); and

(7) The sum of the unpaid principal balance and accrued and unpaid interest on the Program mortgage and the original principal balance of the new mortgage debt:

(i) Does not exceed 95 percent of the estimated appraised value of the property securing the Program mortgage after completion of the proposed repair or remediation; and

(ii) Is less than:

(A) The estimated appraised value of the property securing the Program mortgage after completion of the proposed repair or remediation; less

(B) FHA's proportionate share of the initial equity created upon origination of the Program mortgage as determined pursuant to the schedule set forth in section 257(k)(1) of the Act as if a sale of the property had occurred on the date of origination of the new mortgage debt.

[73 Fed. Reg. 58,425 (Oct. 6, 2008)]

Subpart E—Enforcement

Mortgagor False Information

24 C.F.R. § 4001.401 Notice of false information from mortgagor-procedure.

(a) If FHA finds that the mortgagor has made a false certification or provided false information via any means, including but not limited to false documentation, FHA shall inform the mortgagor, in writing or any other acceptable format, of such fact.

(b) The notice shall be sent to the mortgagor's last known address by both certified and ordinary mail. The notice shall state with specificity the misrepresentation or false statement made by the mortgagor. The notice shall include a request for repayment of the Direct Financial Benefit that the mortgagor is deemed to have received, as determined by FHA, by the refinancing of the eligible mortgage and subordinate mortgages. This does not preclude HUD or the United States from bringing any other action that they may be authorized to bring.

(c) The mortgagor may request a hearing before a Hearing Officer. The hearing will be conducted in accordance with the provisions of 24 CFR part 26, subpart A, except as modified by this section. Requests for a hearing must be made within 45 days from the date of the false information notice.

[73 Fed. Reg. 58,425 (Oct. 6, 2008)]

Appraiser Independence

24 C.F.R. § 4001.403 Prohibitions on interested parties in insured mortgage transaction.

(a) A mortgage lender, mortgage broker, mortgage banker, real estate broker, appraisal management company or employee thereof, and any person with an interest in a real estate transaction involving an appraisal conducted as part of the process for insuring a mortgage under section 257 of the Act shall not improperly influence or attempt to improperly influence through any means, including but not limited to coercion, extortion, collusion, compensation, instruction, inducement, intimidation, nonpayment for services rendered, or bribery, the development, reporting, result or review of a real estate appraisal sought in connection with the origination, processing and closing of the mortgage for insurance.

(b) HUD may, pursuant to its authority under section 536(a) of the Act, bring an action to impose a civil money penalty for a violation of paragraph (a) of this section.

(c) The authority to bring a civil money penalty under this section shall not preclude HUD from bringing any other action that HUD may be authorized to bring for a violation of paragraph (a) of this section.

[73 Fed. Reg. 58,425 (Oct. 6, 2008)]

Mortgagees

24 C.F.R. § 4001.405 Mortgagees.

(a) FHA is authorized by the Board to engage in monitoring activities to ensure mortgagee compliance with the requirements of this Program. The Mortgagee Review Board at HUD is authorized by the Board to impose sanctions and civil money penalties against mortgagees that violate program requirements under this part. The authority of the Mortgagee Review Board to impose sanctions and civil penalties shall not preclude HUD from bringing any other action that HUD may be authorized to bring.

(b) Nonpayment of mortgage insurance claims for reasons established in § 4001.16 shall not preclude the Mortgagee Review Board or HUD from bringing any action against the mortgagee that the Mortgagee Review Board or HUD are authorized to bring.

(c) The mortgagee may request a hearing before a Hearing Officer. The hearing will be conducted in accordance with the provisions of 24 CFR part 26, subpart A, except as modified by this section. Requests for a hearing must be made within 45 days from the date of the false information notice.

[73 Fed. Reg. 58,426 (Oct. 6, 2008)]

Appendix A to Part 4001—Calculation of Upfront Payment or Future Appreciation Payment

Subordinate mortgage lien holder's cumulative combined loan-to-value ratio	Upfront payment option Percent of unpaid principal and interest that lien holder is eligible to receive # (percent)	Future appreciation option* Percent of unpaid principal and interest that lien holder is eligible to receive # (percent)
>135%	3	9%
<=135%	4	12%

* A payment to a subordinate mortgage lien holder will depend on actual appreciation of the property as determined in accordance with 24 CFR 4001.120. Payment will be made according to the subordinate lien holder's position of priority in relation to the property at the time the Program mortgage is originated.

Payment will be based upon principal and interest as of the first day of the month in which the borrower made application for the Program mortgage, calculated at the pre-default contract rate of interest.

[73 Fed. Reg. 58,426 (Oct. 6, 2008); 74 Fed. Reg. 622 (Jan. 7, 2009)]

A.6.4 Selected Mortgagee Letters

Department of Housing and Urban Development, Mortgagee Letter 2009-43 (October 20, 2009)

October 20, 2009

MORTGAGEE LETTER 2009-43

TO: ALL APPROVED MORTGAGEES

SUBJECT: HOPE for Homeowners Program – Comprehensive Guidance

The Helping Families Save Their Homes Act of 2009 amends the National Housing Act, providing for key changes in the HOPE for Homeowners (H4H) Program. The H4H Program is effective for endorsements on or before September 30, 2011. This Mortgagee Letter supersedes in their entirety Mortgagee Letters 2008-29, 2008-30 and 2009-03 and is effective for endorsements on or after January 1, 2010.

Key changes to the H4H Program:

- Borrowers are ineligible if their net worth exceeds $1,000,000,
- Borrowers must not have defaulted on any substantial debt in the last 5 years,
- The age of appraisal now follows standard FHA guidance,

- Reduced mortgage insurance premiums,
- Revised loan-to-value and debt-to-income ratios,
- Maximum loan-to-value excludes the Upfront Mortgage Insurance Premium,
- Eliminated requirement for obtaining most recent two year tax returns,
- Eliminated special lender and underwriter certification,
- Exit Premium replaces Shared Equity,
- Shared Appreciation feature eliminated,
- New note and mortgage replaces previous shared equity and shared appreciation notes and mortgages, and
- Lenders must submit 5 test cases for pre-closing review by FHA.

Contents:

PART I. ORIGINATION GUIDANCE

A. Determining Eligibility

Borrower Eligibility

Mortgage Status: Borrowers are eligible for this Program, if:

- They have not intentionally defaulted on their existing mortgage(s) or any other substantial debt in the last 5 years (Intentionally defaulted means the borrower had available funds that could pay the mortgage and other debts without hardship. Debts subject to a documented bona fide dispute may be excluded. Substantial debt is any amount in excess of $100,000.)

AND

- If delinquent on their mortgage, have made a minimum of six (6) full payments during the life of the existing senior mortgage (full payment is defined as what was acceptable to the lender for meeting the monthly payment obligation under the terms and conditions of the mortgage).
- Borrowers in bankruptcy are not precluded by FHA requirements from participating in the H4H program.

Principal Residence: Borrowers must reside in the property securing the loan being refinanced, and may not have an ownership interest in other residential real estate (except for any inherited properties), including second homes and/or rental properties.

Net Worth: No individual borrower may have a net worth in excess of $1,000,000 at the time of the loan application, excluding assets in Qualified Retirement Plan accounts. Qualified Retirement Plans include, but are not limited to, IRA plans, 401(k) plans, the Thrift Savings Plan, Keogh plans, 403(b) plans, and 457 (b) plans. Use the items in Section VI. Assets and Liabilities of the Uniform Residential Loan Application to assist in determining an individual borrower's net worth, except for vested interest and retirement funds.

Fraud Convictions: Borrowers must certify they have not been convicted of fraud under state and Federal laws in the last 10 years.

False Information: Borrowers must certify that they did not knowingly or willfully provide material false information to obtain the new mortgage under the H4H program.

Mortgage Payment-to-Income: As of the date of the loan application for the new H4H mortgage, the borrower shall have had or thereafter be likely to have due to the terms of the mortgage being reset, an aggregate monthly mortgage payment-to-income ratio (DTI) on all existing mortgages greater than 31 percent of the borrower's gross monthly income. The monthly mortgage payment is defined as the fully-indexed and fully-amortized Principal, Interest, Taxes and Insurance (PITI) payment (this includes principal and interest, taxes and insurances, homeowners' association fees, ground rents, special assessments and all subordinate liens). When calculating the mortgage payment-to-income ratio at the time of loan application the lender should:

1. Analyze the employment and income documentation it will use to qualify the borrower for the new H4H loan;
2. Obtain from the servicer(s) the total monthly mortgage payment[3] due at the time of loan application, including any amounts due on subordinate liens; and
3. For mortgages without escrows, obtain tax and insurance information from the borrower. If the borrower does not provide insurance information, then the servicer of the mortgage should estimate the monthly cost of hazard insurance (and flood insurance, if applicable) based on the property's location and the rate in effect at the time of loan application. If the borrower does not provide real estate tax information, the lender should obtain it from public records.

Mortgage Eligibility

Origination Date: The mortgage being refinanced must have been originated on or before January 1, 2008.

Primary Mortgage: Each holder of an existing primary mortgage being refinanced must:

- Waive all prepayment penalties and late payment fees (including insufficient funds fees) on the mortgage. Prepayment penalties are defined in the Federal Reserve Board's Regulation Z (Truth in Lending), 12 CFR 226.32(d)(6);
- Agree to accept the proceeds of the new H4H mortgage as payment in full, *and*
- Release their outstanding mortgage liens.

Subordinate Mortgage: Each holder of an existing subordinate mortgage must:

- Waive all prepayment penalties and late payment fees (including insufficient funds fees) on the mortgage. Prepayment penalties are defined in the Federal Reserve Board's Regulation Z (Truth in Lending), 12 CFR 226.32(d)(6);
- Agree to accept the upfront payment as payment in full; *and*
- Release their outstanding mortgage liens.

3 When calculating the fully indexed total monthly mortgage payment as of a certain date lenders should use the index rate prevailing on the date of loan application, plus the margin applicable after the expiration of any introductory interest rate, if any. The fully amortizing payment is based on the term of the loan, e.g., for a 2/28 loan the amortization schedule would be based on 30 years.

Mortgage Type: Any type of mortgage is eligible for refinancing under the H4H Program, including conventional (prime, Alt-A, subprime) or government-backed (FHA, VA, or Rural Development), fixed-rate or an adjustable rate mortgage; and

Payment Characteristics: The mortgage being refinanced may have a variety of payment characteristics, including interest only, payment option, negative amortization and/or any other exotic features.

Property Eligibility

Only Residence: The property must be the borrower's primary and only residence in which they have an ownership interest (if there are non-occupant co-borrowers, they will need to quit claim their interest in the property prior to the occupying co-borrowers applying for the H4H Program);

- An exception is provided for borrowers who—due to inheritance—have an ownership interest in other residential property.

Number of Units: One- to four-unit properties are eligible, including condominium units, cooperative units and manufactured housing permanently affixed and classified as real estate.

B. Consumer Protections and Disclosures

Although counseling is not required as a condition of insurance endorsement, borrowers should be strongly encouraged to contact and work with a housing counseling agency. The lender must provide to the borrower(s) the HOPE for Homeowners Consumer Disclosure and Certification Form at the time of initial loan application for the Program. This certification and disclosure form must be signed and dated by the borrower at the time of execution of the initial Universal Residential Loan Application (URLA) and HUD/VA Addendum to the URLA [see Exhibit A].

Typically, borrowers execute a final URLA and a final Addendum to the URLA at the time of closing. Borrowers will also need to sign and date the HOPE for Homeowners Consumer Disclosure and Certification Form at the time of closing.

To ensure that parties on title (e.g., non-borrowing spouse) are aware of and understand how they could be affected by the unique features of the HOPE for Homeowners Program, they should receive and sign either the initial or final HOPE for Homeowners Consumer Disclosure and Certification Form.

C. Appraisals

The appraisal for the H4H mortgage must be performed by an appraiser on the FHA Appraiser Roster and conducted using FHA guidelines, which can be found in the Resources box at http://www.hud.gov/groups/appraisers.cfm. For case numbers assigned on or before December 31, 2009, the validity period of the appraisal is 180 days. For case numbers assigned on or after January 1, 2010, the validity period of the appraisal is 120 days.

Prevailing Appraised Value

If an appraisal is ordered by the current lender or servicer and a new appraisal is ordered by a different lender that will originate the new loan under this Program, the value provided in the appraisal ordered by the new lender will prevail as the appraisal accepted for obtaining FHA insurance.

Appraisal Practices in Declining Markets

Although there is no standard industry definition, for purposes of performing appraisals of properties that are to be collateral for FHA insured mortgages, a declining market is considered to be any neighborhood, market area, or region that demonstrates a decline in prices or deterioration in other market conditions as evidenced by an oversupply of existing inventory or extended marketing times. A declining trend in the market will be identified by the conclusions of the Market Conditions Addendum (Fannie Mae Form 1004MC/ Freddie Mac Form 71, released November 2008). The appraiser must provide a summary comment and provide support for all conclusions relating to the trend of the current market. See Mortgagee Letter 2009-09 for more guidance.

Lender Responsibilities

Lenders are responsible for properly reviewing the appraisal and determining if the appraised value used to determine the mortgage amount is accurate and adequately supports the value conclusion. (See 24 CFR 203.5(c)(3)).

Lenders are reminded that if the appraiser they selected provides a poor or fraudulent appraisal that leads FHA to insure a mortgage at an inflated amount, the lender is held responsible, equally with the appraiser, if the lender knew or should have known that there were problems with the integrity, accuracy and thoroughness of an appraisal submitted to FHA for mortgage insurance purposes.

Pressure on Appraisers and Conflicts of Interest

Lenders and appraisers must avoid conflicts of interest which affect, either in reality or in appearance, the credibility of the appraisal. A lender may not choose an appraiser that has any interest, direct or indirect, in the property being appraised. Instances of undue pressure or influence on an appraiser reported to FHA may result in appropriate sanctions against the lender involved.

D. Term and Interest Rate on the H4H Mortgage

Only 30-year term, fixed-rate mortgages may be offered under this Program. While the interest rate on the new mortgage is to be negotiated between the borrower and the lender, lenders should offer rates that are commensurate with interest rates on similar types of loans, if any (not considering the annual premium in that comparison).

E. Mortgage Insurance Premiums

The Upfront Mortgage Insurance Premium (UFMIP) is 2.00 percent of the base loan amount (loan amount excluding UFMIP) regardless of the loan-to-value (LTV) ratio. The Annual premium (collected monthly) is .75 percent of the base loan amount. Cancellation of the annual premium will follow standard FHA guidelines [HUD Handbook 4155.2 7.3.c.].

F. Calculating the Maximum Mortgage Amount

The amount of the H4H mortgage may not exceed a nationwide maximum mortgage limit as follows:

One-unit $550,440
Two-units $704,682
Three-units $851,796
Four-units $1,058,574

For a three- or four-unit property, lenders are reminded of FHA's standard policy requiring those properties to be self-sufficient [HUD Handbook 4155.1 2.B.4].

Maximum Loan-to-Value

The status of the mortgage being refinanced will determine the maximum loan-to-value ratio on the new H4H mortgage.

Borrowers Current on Their Mortgage: The maximum loan-to-value ratio on the new H4H mortgage is 105 percent of current appraised value (excluding UFMIP). The debt-to-income ratios for qualifying the borrower will follow standard FHA policy, including the use of compensating factors to exceed them [HUD Handbook 4155.1 4.F.3].

Borrowers Delinquent on Their Mortgage: There are two alternative loan-to-value (LTV) and debt-to-income (DTI) methodologies to qualify borrowers for the program:

1. A maximum LTV of 96.5 percent of current appraised value (excluding UFMIP) provided the borrower's mortgage payment-to-income ratio and a total debt-to-income ratio under the new Program mortgage do not exceed 31 percent and 43 percent, respectively, *or*
2. A maximum LTV of 90 percent of current appraised value (excluding UFMIP), the borrower's mortgage payment-to-income ratio and a total debt-to-income ratio may be up to 38 percent and 50 percent, respectively.

Borrowers with Credit Scores Below 500: the maximum loan-to-value ratio on the new H4H mortgage is 90 percent of current appraised value.

Mortgage Proceeds: The proceeds from the new H4H mortgage will be applied to the existing primary mortgage, and extinguish all mortgage-related debts under all existing mortgages including:

- Advances by existing lenders/servicers for taxes, hazard insurance and/or mortgage insurance; and
- Out of pocket third party legal expenses of the existing lenders/servicers associated with foreclosures and preservation and protection (See Mortgagee Letters 2007-03 and 2005-30).

Closing Costs and Prepaid Items

Standard FHA policy regarding closing costs is applicable, including the 1 percent cap on origination fees. The origination fee compensates the lender for administrative costs in originating and closing the loan. The origination fee covers administrative costs for taking the loan application, evaluating, preparing and submitting a proposed mortgage loan. The origination fee cannot be supplemented by other fees to cover these administrative costs, such as "application or processing" fees or broker fees. The origination fee cannot exceed the greater of $20 or one percent of the original principal amount of the mortgage (excluding any UFMIP).

FHA does not require that closing costs and prepaid items come only from the borrower's own assets, giving lenders and borrowers the flexibility to determine which of the following options (or combination of options) should be used to pay these costs:

- Borrowers pay closing costs and prepaid items from their own assets;
- The closing costs and prepaid items may be financed into the mortgage provided the LTV does not exceed the applicable percent (90 or 96.5 excluding UFMIP) for borrowers delinquent on their mortgage or 105 percent (excluding UFMIP) for borrowers current on their mortgage;
- The servicing lender, originating lender and/or a third party (e.g., family member, a Federal, state or local Program, charitable organization) may pay the closing costs and prepaid items; and/or
- The originating lender may pay the borrower's closing costs and prepaid items through premium pricing. [HUD Handbook 4155.1 5.A.2.i]

G. Underwriting the Mortgage and Qualifying the Borrower

For analytical purposes, FHA requires all approved lenders to use FHA's TOTAL Mortgage Scorecard (TOTAL). Regardless of the risk classification obtained from TOTAL for each mortgage originated under the H4H Program, the underwriter must:

- Determine that the borrower's total monthly mortgage payment on the new H4H loan *is less than* the borrower's aggregate total monthly mortgage payment on his or her existing (non-H4H) mortgage(s), including any subordinate mortgage liens, based on a fully-indexed, fully-amortizing PITI payment.
- Determine that the borrower has the capacity to repay the new H4H loan using the appropriate debt-to-income ratios described below.

Property Condition

While appraisers should report all readily observable property deficiencies in the appraisal, underwriters are reminded to use their professional judgment and rely on prudent underwriting practices in determining when a property condition poses a threat to the safety of an occupant and/or jeopardizes the soundness of structural integrity of the property. Examples of property conditions that may represent a risk to health and safety of the occupants or soundness of the property include but are not limited to:

- Inadequate access/egress from bedrooms to the exterior of the home
- Leaking or worn out roofs
- Evidence of structural damage
- Exterior and interior defective paint surfaces in homes constructed pre-1978

Other readily observable property deficiencies that are minor property conditions such as (but not limited to) missing hand rails, trip hazards, damaged plaster, and poor workmanship may be waived by the underwriter.

Credit

While the intent of the program is to assist borrowers by refinancing them into a safe and affordable FHA-insured mortgage by focusing on their capacity to repay the new H4H mortgage rather than their past credit performance, there are a few credit-related items that should be addressed.

***Credit Alert Interactive Voice Response System* (CAIVRS)**

Lenders must use CAIVRS to screen all borrowers involved in the new H4H mortgage. Borrowers are generally not eligible for a new H4H mortgage if CAIVRS indicates they are presently delinquent on a Federal debt, or have had a claim paid within the previous three years on a loan made and insured on their behalf by HUD. Under certain circumstances, lenders may make exceptions. See HUD Handbook 4155.1 4.A.7.f and 4.A.8.e for more information.

Judgments, Tax Liens and Recurring Obligations

- Judgments do not need to be paid off if they do not or will not affect title, such as civil and/or medical judgments. However, a payment plan must be in place and included in the borrower's qualifying ratios.
- Judgments and/or tax liens against the subject property must be released and extinguished by the time of or at closing. A common mechanism for achieving these releases is for the primary lien holder to write down the existing mortgage to accommodate including of these items in the new H4H mortgage.
- Underwriters should not automatically reject borrowers for making their mortgage payment their first priority at the expense of meeting other recurring obligations in a timely manner.

Gaps in Employment

For borrowers who have experienced gaps in employment (including self-employed borrowers), the income from the current job may be considered effective and stable provided the borrower has been employed – at the time of loan application – in the current job for at least three months or more, regardless of whether the new employment would be considered the same line of work as previously held employment.

Borrowers Current on Their Mortgage

- For LTVs greater than 97.75 percent, determine that the borrower has made all mortgage payments within the month due for the 12 month period preceding the date of loan application.
- Determine that the mortgage payment-to-income and total debt-to-income ratios do not exceed 31 percent and 43 percent respectively. Exceeding these ratios is acceptable only if strong compensating factors are documented [HUD Handbook 4155.1 4.F.3.a]. For borrowers with limited recurring expenses, greater latitude is permissible on the *mortgage* payment-to-income ratio than the total debt-to-income ratio.
- Non-occupant *co-signers* (i.e., borrowers who do not hold ownership interest in the property) may be added for the new H4H mortgage in order to supplement income and meet the debt-to-income ratios.

Borrowers Delinquent on Their Mortgage

- For a mortgage LTV up to 96.5 percent, excluding UFMIP, determine that the mortgage payment-to-income and total debt-to-income ratios are at, or below, 31 percent and 43 percent respectively. For a mortgage LTV up to 90 percent, determine that the mortgage payment-to-income and total debt-to-income ratios are at, or below, 38 percent and 50 percent, respectively.
- Non-occupant *co-signers* (i.e., borrowers who do not hold ownership interest in the property) may be added in order to supplement income and meet the debt-to-income ratios.

Borrowers with Credit Scores Below 500

- Determine that the mortgage payment-to-income and total debt-to-income ratios are at, or below, 38 percent and 50 percent, respectively (maximum LTV up to 90 percent).
- Non-occupant *co-signers* (i.e., borrowers who do not hold ownership interest in the property) may be added in order to supplement income and meet the debt-to-income ratios.

H. <u>Documentation Requirements</u>

In addition to the standard documentation requirements found in HUD Handbook 4155.2 3.C, the following additional documentation for H4H loans must be included in the case binder on the right hand side. This additional documentation will also become a part of the pre-endorsement review conducted by FHA staff (Direct Endorsement Program) or the lender (Lender Insurance Program). Exhibit B is a suggested pre-endorsement review checklist for FHA staff and lenders to use. For lenders that submit electronic case binders, this information must be a new index labeled H4H.

- **Prior Mortgage Origination Date:** Evidence the mortgage(s) being refinanced was originated on/before January 1, 2008, such as a HUD-1 Settlement Statement the mortgage payment history from the servicer, or the Note.
- **Payment History:** If delinquent at the time of the refinance, evidence that the borrower made 6 full payments during the life of the first mortgage loan being refinanced, such as the mortgage payment history from the servicer.
- **Prior Total Mortgage Payment:** Evidence that the prior aggregate mortgage payment DTI was more than 31 percent as of the date of loan application.
- **Primary Residence:** Evidence that the property is the borrower's primary residence, such as a Federal or state tax return, driver's license and/or voter registration card.
- **HOPE for Homeowners Consumer Disclosure and Certifications:** The initial and final HOPE for Homeowners Consumer Disclosure and Certifications, signed and dated by the borrower(s), along with the initial and final URLA and Addendum to the URLA.
- **Conviction of Fraud:** The HOPE for Homeowners Consumer Disclosure and Certifications provided by the borrower serves as documentation for meeting this eligibility requirement.
- **First Payment Made:** Evidence that the first payment on the new mortgage was made by the borrower and not by any interested party to the transaction, not from the loan proceeds and not escrowed at closing (e.g. cancelled check, cashier's check with corresponding bank statement showing available funds).
- **Net Worth:** Evidence that any individual borrower's net worth does not exceed $1,000,000, excluding assets in Qualified Retirement Plans accounts. Qualified Retirement Plans include, but are not limited to, IRA plans, the Thrift Savings Plan, 401(k) plans, Keogh plans, 403 (b) plans, and 457 (b) plans. Use the items in Section VI. Assets and Liabilities of the Uniform Residential Loan Application to assist in determining an individual borrower's net worth, except for vested interest and retirement funds.

I. Prohibition Against Subordinate Financing

Under the H4H Program, borrowers are prohibited from taking out new subordinate liens for the first 5 years of the mortgage except when necessary to ensure maintenance of property standards. Therefore, during the first 5 years of the mortgage, FHA will permit a subordinate mortgage lien only if the proceeds are essential to preserve and protect the property, and:

- The condition to be repaired represents a health and safety hazard and/or the failure to make the repair will cause the property condition to deteriorate;
- The cost of the proposed repair is reasonable for the geographic market area as determined by HUD's residential property management contractor;
- The repairs are not primarily cosmetic and do not represent routine maintenance; and
- The financing is a closed-end loan under Federal Reserve Board's Regulation Z.

When a subordinate lien is made to protect and preserve the property, HUD will subordinate the Exit Premium Mortgage (EPM) to the new subordinate lien HUD will not subordinate its initial equity to any subordinate financing – either within the first 5 years or thereafter – except liens as described above or for FHA loss mitigation actions (mortgage modifications and partial claims).

J. Exit Premium

As a condition of the H4H mortgage, the borrower must share with HUD a portion of the initial equity. Initial equity is the lesser of:

- The appraised value at the time of the H4H loan origination less the original principal balance on the H4H mortgage, *OR*
- The outstanding amount due under all existing mortgages less the original principal balance on the H4H mortgage.

The originating lender will prepare an Exit Premium note and mortgage (EPM) using the format attached as Exhibit C. A dollar amount equaling the initial equity will be inserted in the EPM. The EPM will be executed by the borrower and recorded with all other loan documents in second lien position.

The Act provides that, in the event of refinance, sale or other disposition, HUD is entitled to receive the following percentage of initial equity:

During Year 1 100% of equity is paid to FHA
During Year 2 90% of equity is paid to FHA
During Year 3 80% of equity is paid to FHA
During Year 4 70% of equity is paid to FHA
During Year 5 60% of equity is paid to FHA
After Year 5 50% of equity is paid to FHA

Example: Appraised value is $200,000, which is less than the outstanding amount due under all existing mortgages less the original principal balance on the H4H mortgage. The loan-to-value on the H4H mortgage is 90%, or $180,000. The equity amount that would be stated in the EPM is $20,000. If the borrower refinanced during Year 2, $18,000 in initial equity is paid to FHA.

Originating EPM liens

In addition to other origination actions, the originating lender of a H4H mortgage will complete actions necessary to determine and document a borrower's commitment to share equity as required under section 257 of the National Housing Act, as well as the commitment of existing lien holders to waive all rights to collect existing debt and to release the lien. The originating lender will:

- Identify all existing lien holders through review of the borrower's loan application and by obtaining a preliminary title report,
- Request that all existing lien holders provide a payoff statement itemizing unpaid principal, unpaid accrued interest, daily interest calculation, and allowable costs advanced on behalf of the borrower (e.g., taxes, insurance, legal fees, etc.),
- Refer the borrower to the HOPE for Homeowners Consumer Disclosure and Certifications he or she signed at the time of initial loan application (Exhibit A), and
- Provide the borrower copies of all payoff statements for review, requesting that the borrower notify the originating lender within 5 business days of receipt of any discrepancies noted on the payoff statements.

Absent any challenge from the borrower regarding a payoff amount, the originating lender will:

- Determine the dollar amount of borrower's initial equity as described in the example above,
- Prepare and cause the borrower to execute the EPM for the H4H mortgage,
- Record the EPM with other loan documents,
- Register the H4H security instrument in the Mortgage Electronic Registration System (MERS) as MERS Original Mortgages, and
- Deliver the original EPM note and recorded mortgage to HUD's servicing contractor at the address below and retain copies in the servicing file.

Document Delivery

Following funding of the H4H mortgage, the originating lender will record the EPM mortgage documents in the public records of the county in which the property is located and will deliver the original EPM note and original recorded mortgage documents to HUD at the address listed below no later than 15 business days from the date of endorsement. Time extensions may be granted by the National Servicing Center (NSC) in the event document delivery is delayed by events beyond the control of the lender.

U.S. Department of HUD
c/o C&L Service Corporation / Morris-Griffin Corporation
2488 East 81st Street, Suite 700
Tulsa, Oklahoma 74137

Other documentation requirements include a copy of the HUD-1 settlement statement, and a copy of the appraisal that was completed in order to establish the amount of the H4H mortgage. HUD accepts certified copies of the recorded mortgage when the original recorded documents are not available. The EPM note and mortgage will be serviced by HUD.

K. First Payment Default and Submission of Case Binders for Endorsement

Lenders are not eligible for claim payment if the first mortgage payment is not received within 120 days of loan closing. FHA does not prohibit lenders from requesting borrowers to bring the first mortgage payment on the new H4H mortgage to closing.

The endorsement process for the H4H Program conforms to existing FHA standards with the following exceptions:

- Lenders must include evidence in the case binder that the borrower made the first payment *from their own funds* within 120 days of the closing on the H4H loan;
- Lenders must certify that the loan is current at the time of submission *and* that they did not bring the loan current to make it eligible for insurance.

Unendorsed Loans

In the event an H4H loan is not endorsed for FHA insurance, HUD will execute and record a release of the EPM. HUD will not reimburse the originating lender for any upfront payment advanced to a subordinate lien holder and will have no liability to provide any payment to primary and/or subordinate lien holders who elected the future appreciation option.

The originating lender will receive a refund of the upfront mortgage insurance premium and any periodic mortgage insurance premiums (MIP) received by HUD. If the originating lender funded an upfront payment to subordinate lien holders in lieu of future appreciation, the originating lender may apply the refunded MIP first to reimburse itself for any amount advanced to a prior subordinate lien holder(s) as an upfront payment and will apply any remainder in accordance with normal servicing guidance. If the unendorsed H4H loan included a future appreciation option, HUD will notify the prior primary and subordinate lien holder(s) that the agreement is void and request its return.

L. Extinguishment of Subordinate Liens

All existing mortgage lien holders must waive all rights to collect existing debt. To facilitate this agreement among lien holders, HUD may offer an upfront payment to qualifying subordinate lien holders in exchange for releasing their liens. Subordinate lien holders whose write off is less than $2,500 will not receive the opportunity for an upfront payment.

Part II provides instructions on determining dollar amounts for an upfront payment.

PART II. UPFRONT PAYMENT TO SUBORDINATE LIEN HOLDERS

In exchange for a full release of liens and the release of the borrower from all indebtedness under the related subordinate mortgage, a subordinate mortgage lien holder may choose to receive a cash payment equal to a percentage of the total principal and accrued interest they are writing off.

Upfront payments for subordinate lien holders are based on the number of days the subordinate lien is past due at the time of the loan application and its cumulative loan-to-value position. In accordance with the chart below, subordinate lien holders may receive an upfront payment equivalent to the percentage of the total principal and accrued interest they are writing off. Lenders must use the Upfront Payment Worksheet (Exhibit D) to determine the amount of the upfront payment to a subordinate lien holder.

	Days Past Due			
Cumulative LTV	Paid within month due	30-59	60-89	90+
<90.00	0.50	0.40	0.28	0.09
90.01 – 100.00	0.45	0.36	0.26	0.06
100.01 – 125.00	0.35	0.28	0.20	0.03
125.01 – 150.00	0.20	0.16	0.11	0.03
>150.00	0.10	0.08	0.03	0.03

In the event that a subordinate lien holder elects the upfront payment:

- Not less than ten (10) business days prior to the scheduled date of closing the H4H loan, the originating lender will send an Upfront Payment Worksheet for each eligible subordinate mortgage lien, executed by the subordinate lien holder and the originating lender, to the National Servicing Center at the address provided above.
- Not less than five (5) business days prior to closing, the NSC will notify the originating lender of discrepancies noted on the Upfront Payment Worksheet, if any, and request corrections prior to closing.
- The originating lender will provide instructions to the closing agent to pay the calculated upfront payment(s) reflected on the Upfront Payment Worksheet previously provided to the NSC.
- The originating lender will advance funds in the amount of the new mortgage *and* the amount necessary to pay the upfront payment(s) to the subordinate lien holder(s) that have chosen this option.
- Within 15 days of receipt by the NSC of the EPM Note, Mortgage and other required documents, HUD will automatically reimburse the originating lender the amount of the upfront payment(s) on endorsed loans.

PART III. SERVICING GUIDANCE

A. Refinancing

Refinancing of an H4H mortgage will be permitted subject to the guidelines established in this section. In the event of any refinance of the H4H mortgage, the borrower must pay to HUD its full equity interest as stated in the EPM. H4H mortgages may not be refinanced using the FHA streamline process. Refinancing into another conventional loan product is permitted subject to the following restrictions:

No earlier than 12 months from the date of closing on the H4H mortgage, the borrower may refinance if:

- The refinance results in a 30 year amortizing fixed-rate loan with a principal and interest payment that is lower than the P&I payment due on the existing H4H mortgage,
- The proceeds from the refinance are sufficient to pay off the percent of initial equity due to HUD, and
- The cash received by or on behalf of the borrower is limited to the borrower's applicable percentage of initial equity created by the H4H loan as stated in the EPM any earned equity the borrower has accrued, and any appreciation.

B. Default and Loss Mitigation

Lender must follow the same documentation and reporting guidelines when providing loss mitigation to borrowers with H4H mortgages that apply to FHA-insured mortgages. HUD's Loss Mitigation Program allows for the following special considerations when evaluating an H4H borrower for loss mitigation.

Loss Mitigation Options

Special Forbearance: Follow existing Program guidance.

Loan Modification: HUD will subordinate the EPM to any modification of an H4H mortgage completed in accordance with HUD's Loss Mitigation Program.

Partial Claim: A partial claim note does not require subordination of the EPM.

Pre-Foreclosure Sale: The lender will include the total dollar amount of the EPM in the total debt calculation for the negative equity ratio calculations in addition to any existing Partial Claim. Net proceeds must fit into the eighty-two percent (82%) requirement and up to $2,000 can be used to pay off any junior property preservation lien. If a junior property preservation lien does not exist, the borrower is not eligible for the $2,000.

Deed-In-Lieu (DIL): HUD will accept a DIL subject to the EPM lien and will allow up to $2,000 to be used to satisfy a junior property preservation lien.

Voluntary Termination of Insurance

Section 229 of the National Housing Act, as implemented by the H4H Regulations, provides that the Secretary shall terminate any insurance contract upon request by the mortgagor and the mortgagee. In the event the borrower and mortgagee mutually request termination of insurance and the request is granted, annual mortgage insurance premiums will no longer be due and payable to HUD. However, the borrower will not be entitled to a refund of any upfront mortgage insurance premium received by HUD and will remain obligated for the exit premium and appreciation mortgages, that can be discharged only as provided in other sections of this guidance.

C. Sale and Payoff

Upon sale or other disposition (transfer of title without sale) of the property securing a H4H mortgage, the borrower must satisfy HUD's equity interest (if not already satisfied through refinance). Upon receipt of a payoff request, HUD will calculate the payoff amount for its equity interest and issue a payoff demand to the closing agent. HUD is entitled to its respective percentage of the initial equity amount as stated in the EPM even if there are no net proceeds or net proceeds are negative.

PART IV. SECONDARY MARKET

H4H mortgages can be securitized in Ginnie Mae MBS. Due to the special characteristics of the underlying H4H mortgages, they are pooled separately from standard MBS in Ginnie Mae II pools designated with the MFS pool type (APM 08-18). Ginnie Mae will monitor the performance of H4H loans and pools and may take into consideration the fact that a Ginnie Mae issuer's portfolio of mortgage loans includes H4H loans when Ginnie Mae reviews issuer compliance with the delinquency thresholds as set forth in Chapter 18 of the Ginnie Mae MBS Guide, "Mortgage Delinquency and Default". See APM 09-01 for further information on this policy.

PART V. PRE-CLOSING REVIEW

Given the uniqueness and risk associated with the HOPE for Homeowners (H4H) program, mortgagees that want to offer this program must submit a minimum of 5 cases for pre-closing review. One hundred percent of the loans insured under the H4H program will be subject to Post Endorsement Technical Reviews.

A. Processing Applications While in Pre-Closing Review Status

Mortgagees in pre-closing review status for the H4H program may take applications from borrowers, order case numbers and appraisals, order credit reports, obtain verifications of deposit and employment, and otherwise process the application in accordance with all Direct Endorsement policies and guidelines up to the point of closing the loan. The loan package must be submitted to HUD at that point for an underwriting review.

Lenders must submit their first five (5) H4H loans for pre-closing review. If the lender is given permission to close on all of these first 5 loans, they are released from pre-closing status and granted unconditional approval to underwrite H4H loans.

If one or more of these first 5 loans exhibits significant deficiencies, the lender will be required to submit a total of ten (10) acceptable H4H loans prior to being released from pre-closing status and granted unconditional approval to underwrite H4H loans. Significant deficiencies include – but are not limited to – lack of appropriate signatures and certifications, insufficient supporting documentation regarding the payment history on the prior mortgage, the prior mortgage payment not exceeding 31 percent, and lack of evidence that the first payment was made from the borrower's own funds.

If the lender is unable to submit 10 acceptable H4H loans within 180 days of entering pre-closing status, the lender can no longer offer the H4H program.

Submitting Pre-Closing Review Cases

Due to the huge volume of cases which pass through the Homeownership Centers, it is easy for pre-closing review cases to be misdirected. To avoid this problem, ***please clearly indicate each H4H pre-closing loan in large block letters on the case binder*** and send the case binders to the attention of the appropriate Homeownership Center.

HUD retains the case binder for all pre-closing review cases. These case binders will not be returned to the lender, even where the case is rejected. If lenders believe that they will need the originals of any documents submitted, either to satisfy investor requirements or for other reasons, it is recommended that they submit copies to the Homeownership Center. Copies are acceptable provided that they are legible, and accompanied by signed individual or blanket certifications that the documents are true copies.

Since the quality of the lender's submissions and underwriting directly impact the successful completion of the pre-closing review, before submitting pre-closing review cases, lenders should carefully review them for completeness and clarity. Lenders should ensure that all necessary documents are in the case binder, and that they are consistent with the information provided on the Loan Transmittal. Effective income for qualifying on the new loan must be appropriately determined and verified. Missing documents and inconsistencies will result in rejections and/or "Unacceptable" ratings.

B. HUD Processing of Pre-Closing Review Cases

The processing of pre-closing review cases is a priority but please do not telephone or contact the Homeownership Center for status reports until four working days have passed.

Upon the completion of the pre-closing review, the lender will be notified in writing whether it may proceed with closing. Until system modifications to FHA Connection are completed, lenders will also be notified in writing of deficiencies in the file and how they may be corrected.

Lenders are cautioned not to schedule closings too closely after the submission of pre-closing review cases. There is no guarantee that permission to close on the loan will be given at all, or that it will necessarily be issued in time to meet a specified closing date.

C. Submission of Closing Packages for Endorsement

Following permission to proceed with closing and the actual closing of the loan in accordance with outstanding Direct Endorsement policies and procedures, the closing package should be submitted to HUD for insurance endorsement. Upon receipt, HUD will merge the closing documents with the loan package submitted for pre-closing review, and process the loan for endorsement. Immediately following endorsement, the merged case file will be forwarded to a federal records center. Again, certified true copies of documents are acceptable. To ensure proper handling, mortgagees should ***clearly mark the closing package as an insert "Closing Package" for H4H loan.***

PART VI. MONITORING AND PROGRAM COMPLIANCE

A. Monitoring

Current monitoring practices (such as the Post Endorsement Technical Reviews, Appraiser Watch, and Lender Monitoring Reviews), will be used to monitor lenders and appraisers participating in the H4H Program as well as loan performance. If a serious violation of H4H or existing FHA Program requirements is discovered, FHA's standard indemnification procedures and claim payment procedures apply, i.e., holders of FHA insurance benefits who were not a party to the violation will be paid a claim and the deficiency or loss to FHA will be pursued under the indemnification agreement with the lender responsible for the violation.

H4H mortgages will not be included in HUD's performance analysis of a lender's compare ratio with respect to the Credit-Watch Termination Initiative. However, FHA will develop a separate module in Neighborhood Watch to display a lender's performance compare ratio for H4H loans

If you have any questions regarding this Mortgagee Letter, please call the FHA Resource Center at 1-800-CALLFHA (1-800-225-5342). Persons with hearing or speech impairments may access this number via TDD/TTY by calling 1-877-TDD-2HUD (1-877-833-2483).

Sincerely,

David H. Stevens,
Assistant Secretary for Housing-
Federal Housing Commissioner

Exhibit A

HOPE for Homeowners Consumer Disclosure and Certification Form

U.S. Department of Housing and Urban Development

Federal Housing Administration

OMB Approval No. XXXX-XXXX (exp. XX/XX/XXXX)

I M P O R T A N T

Mortgages made under the FHA's HOPE for Homeowners Program have some special restrictions. If you refinance your home through this program:

1. You must share with FHA a portion of any newly equity created by your new HOPE for Homeowners mortgage, as described below.
2. You cannot take out a second mortgage, home equity loan, or home equity line of credit for the first five years you have your new loan, except under certain circumstances for emergency repairs.
3. You will pay an upfront mortgage insurance premium of 2% and a 0.75% annual mortgage insurance premium on the current principal balance of your new mortgage. The annual premium will be included in your monthly payments.
4. To apply for a mortgage under the HOPE for Homeowners Program, you must certify that the Borrower Certification statements below are true. There are serious penalties if you provide false information.

Equity Sharing Requirements. I/we agree to share the initial equity created at the beginning of this mortgage with FHA. Initial equity is the difference between the appraised value of the home at the time of the new HOPE for Homeowners mortgage (or the amount owed on my/our existing mortgage, if that is less), and the initial balance on my/our HOPE for Homeowners mortgage.

If I/we sell or refinance my/our home, I/we agree to share the newly created equity with FHA according to the following schedule:

If I/we sell or refinance:	FHA will receive:
During year 1	100% of initial created equity
During year 2	90% of initial created equity
During year 3	80% of initial created equity
During year 4	70% of initial created equity
During year 5	60% of initial created equity
After year 5	50% of initial created equity

Understanding Shared Equity. As an example, say you have no equity in your home. You have one mortgage for $200,000 and the appraisal report just said your home is worth $200,000. If your new HOPE for Homeowners mortgage is for $180,000, the amount of newly created equity is $20,000. This newly created equity is what you must share with FHA when you later decide to move or refinance.

Continuing the example, if you decide to move three years after receiving your new HOPE for Homeowners mortgage, at closing, FHA will receive $16,000 (80%), and you will be entitled to the remaining $4,000. Remember, this is equity that you did not have prior to receiving your new HOPE for Homeowners mortgage.

Borrower Certification. I/we certify that I/we have read the above restrictions. If I/we are offered and accept a mortgage under FHA's HOPE for Homeowners Program, I/we understand that I/we will be agreeing to be bound by these restrictions on the new mortgage for as long as we hold that mortgage.

Furthermore, I/we certify:

- I/we have not intentionally defaulted on my/our mortgage or any other substantial debt (any amount greater than $100,000) in the last 5 years. An intentional default is defined as a default that occurred when a borrower had readily available funds at the time a mortgage payment or other debt was due, such that the borrower could have paid the mortgage or other debt without undue hardship.
- I/we have not been convicted of fraud under federal or state law in the past 10 years. I/we agree that FHA may perform routine background checks, including automated searches of federal, state, and county databases, to confirm that I/we have not been convicted of fraud.
- I/we have not knowingly, or willfully and with actual knowledge, furnished material false information for the purpose of obtaining my/our new HOPE for Homeowners mortgage.
- If I/we make any willful false statement in this certification or any other documentation I/we provide for Program eligibility, I/we may be punished with fines or imprisonment of up to 5 years, or both, under section 1001 of title 18, United States Code, and I/we also may be subject to civil and/or administrative penalties and sanctions.

I/we understand that if I/we misrepresent or falsify anything in this statement or any other documentation I/we provide for Program eligibility, and I/we refinance through this program, I/we will be liable to repay the Federal Housing Administration any direct financial benefit I/we gain from the reduction of debt on my/our existing mortgage(s).

Signature Date

Signature Date

Previous editions are obsolete. Page 1 of 2 Form **HUD-XXXXX** (XX/XXXX)

The originating lender is not responsible for verifying certifications made by the Borrower(s) in this document.

The information collection requirements contained in this document have been submitted to the Office of Management and Budget (OMB) under the Paperwork Reduction Act of 1995 (44 U.S.C. 3501-3520) and are pending an OMB control number. In accordance with the Paperwork Reduction Act, HUD may not conduct or sponsor, and a person is not required to respond to, a collection of information unless the collection displays a currently valid OMB control number.

Exhibit B

LENDER INSURANCE PROGRAM
MODEL PRE-INSURANCE REVIEW

U.S. Department of Housing
and Urban Development

See second page for Public Burden

Office of Housing - Federal Housing Commissioner

CASE NUMBER: ______________________________ REVIEWED BY: __________________________________

RIGHT SIDE OF BINDER:
(Note: This does not represent a stacking order)

1. A R **AUTOMATED UNDERWRITING FEEDBACK CERTIFICATE/FINDINGS REPORT**

2. A R **FIRST-TIME HOME BUYER COUNSELING CERTIFICATE** (Hawaiian Homeland Loans only)

3. A R **LATE REQUEST FOR ENDORSEMENT CERTIFICATION** (ML 05-23)

4. A R **MORTGAGE CREDIT ANALYSIS WORKSHEET (HUD 92900-WS OR HUD 92900-PUR) OR FHA LOAN UNDERWRITING AND TRANSMITTAL SUMMARY (HUD-92900-LT)**
   Signed & dated by DE Underwriter and reflects U/W ID#
   AUS loans should reflect the system used and appropriate ID #. A DE Underwriter DOES NOT need to sign.
   IF APPLICABLE: 203K Worksheet (HUD 92700), EEM worksheet, 203h documentation

5. A R **NOTE** (Include Note for Secondary Mortgage when applicable):
   Certified true copy unless there is a blanket certification in the file
   Contains all 9 paragraphs of model note
   Signed/conformed/executed
   Mortgage amount is not higher than approved (92900-WS or PUR #3c & page 3 of HUD 92900-A)
   Term of mortgage is the same as approved (92900-WS or PUR #7) Maximum term is 360 months
   Property Address same as on URAR and reflects correct FHA case number and ADP Code
   Applicable Allonges/Agreements (796 Buydown, 203K Rehabilitation Loan agreements, etc.)

6. A R **SECURITY INSTRUMENT** (Include Security Instrument for Secondary Mortgage when applicable):
   Certified true copy unless there is a blanket certification in the file
   Signed/conformed/executed
   Paragraph 9 (Grounds for Acceleration)
   Paragraph 18 (Foreclosure Procedures)
   Property Address same as on URAR
   Applicable Riders (PUD, CONDO, ARM, 203k, etc)

7. A R **HUD-1 SETTLEMENT STATEMENT & ADDENDUM**
   Addenda signed by Borrower, Seller and Settlement Agent – required on all purchase transactions (NOTE: HUD, as the seller, does not sign on REO Sales)
   Legible copies of pages 1 and 2 of the HUD-1 or HUD-1A should be provided
   NOTE: Refinance HUD-1 may be a one-page form (HUD-1A); an addendum is not required
   Do not issue a Notice of Return (NOR) because of missing signatures on either purchase or refinance transactions.

8. A R **UNIFORM RESIDENTIAL LOAN APPLICATION** (URLA) Signed and dated by all borrowers

9. A R **ADDENDUM TO URLA (HUD 92900-A, PAGES 1, 2, 3 & 4)**
   Completed, signed and dated by appropriate parties
   Page 3 signed by DE Underwriter or identified as AUS with appropriate ID

10. A R **CREDIT REPORT(S)**

11. A R **ASSET VERIFICATION**--VOD and/or bank statements

12. A R **GIFT LETTER** (if gift is shown on Mortgage Credit Analysis Worksheet)
   NOTE: AUS Accept: does not need a letter; gift may be noted on the application (URLA) in-lieu-of a gift letter

13. A R **INCOME VERIFICATION**--May be any of the following: Written or Verbal VOE and pay stub, Federal Tax Returns, Evidence of Pension/Retirement

14. A R **EVIDENCE OF SOCIAL SECURITY NUMBER** (Copy of Social Security Card, pay stub, W-2, etc.)

LENDER INSURANCE PROGRAM
MODEL PRE-INSURANCE REVIEW

See second page for Public Burden

U.S. Department of Housing and Urban Development

Office of Housing - Federal Housing Commissioner

CASE NUMBER: ______________________ REVIEWED BY: ______________________

ADDITIONAL REVIEW SPECIFIC TO THE HOPE FOR HOMEOWNERS PROGRAM

RIGHT SIDE OF BINDER:
(Note: This does not represent a stacking order)

1. A R **PRIOR MORTGAGE ORIGINATION DATE**
Evidence the mortgage being refinanced was originated on/before January 1, 2008, such as a HUD-1 Settlement Statement, the mortgage payment history from the servicer, or the Note.

2. A R **PAYMENT HISTORY**
If delinquent at time of refinance, evidence that the borrower made 6 full payments during the life of the loan being refinanced, such as the mortgage payment history from the servicer.

3. A R **PRIOR MORTGAGE PAYMENT**
   - Evidence that the prior total mortgage payment DTI was >31% at the time of loan application, including any subordinate liens.
   - For estimated escrow accounts, documentation for the cost of insurances as well public record information for taxes.

4. A R **PRIMARY RESIDENCE**
Evidence that the property is the borrower's primary residence, such as Federal or state tax returns, driver's license and/or voter registration card. If borrower owns other property, evidence that it was inherited.

5. A R **HOPE FOR HOMEOWNERS CONSUMER DISCLOSURE AND CERTIFICATIONS**
The initial ***and*** final HOPE for Homeowners Consumer Disclosure and Certifications as well as the initial URLA and Addendum to the URLA.

6. A R **FIRST PAYMENT MADE**
Evidence that the first payment on the new mortgage was made by the borrower and not by any interested party to the transaction, from the loan proceeds or escrowed at closing (e.g. cancelled checks, cashiers check with corresponding bank statement showing funds available).

7. A R **EXIT PREMIUM NOTE AND SECURITY INSTRUMENTS**
Signed/conformed/executed
Property address same as on URAR and reflects correct FHA case number

LENDER INSURANCE PROGRAM
PRE-ENDORSEMENT REVIEW
(Non-HECM files)

U.S. Department of Housing
and Urban Development

See second page for Public Burden

Office of Housing Federal Housing Commissioner

CASE NUMBER: ____________________ REVIEWED BY: ____________________

LEFT SIDE OF BINDER:
(Note: This does not represent a stacking order)

15. A R **IF APPLICABLE: MORTGAGEE ASSURANCE OF COMPLETION (HUD 92300)** Completed & Signed

16. A R **COMPLIANCE INSPECTION REPORT (HUD 92051),** Countersigned by DE Underwriter, or evidence repair requirements or certifications have been completed. Local government or professional tradesman inspection may be acceptable.

17. A R **IF APPLICABLE: (Existing Properties) WOOD DESTROYING INSECT INFESTATION REPORT,** Form NPMA-33 or State mandated infestation report.

18. A R **IF APPLICABLE: LOCAL HEALTH AUTHORITY'S APPROVAL** for individual water and/or sewer systems.

19. A R **NEW CONSTRUCTION EXHIBITS:**
Builder's Certification (HUD 92541): Completed & Signed
Builder's One-Year Warranty (HUD 92544)
As applicable:
- An early start letter
- Evidence of a 10-year warranty
- 3 inspections completed by local authority
- Building Permit and CO
- FHA Compliance Inspector (footings, frame & final)

(NOTE: Manufactured Homes require only 2 inspections by FHA Compliance Inspector)
As applicable: Subterranean Termite Treatment Report - NPCA-99a and NPCA-99b

20. A R **STATEMENT OF APPRAISED VALUE (HUD 92800.5B)**

21. A R **IF APPLICABLE: ENGINEER'S CERTIFICATE FOR MANUFACTURED HOUSING FOUNDATION**

22. A R **REAL ESTATE APPRAISAL:** Correct appraisal form utilized/Completed/signed/dated by appraiser
- Form 1004 for single unit properties.
- Form 1025 for 2-4 unit properties.
- Form 1073 for Condos.
- Form 1004c for Manufactured Homes.

If MAR documentation: HUD-91322 and HUD-91322.3, including all attachments and amendments
If VA issued NOV/MNOV documentation: including all attachments and endorsements

23. A R **SPECIALIZED ELIGIBILITY DOCUMENTS (SUCH AS, BUT NOT LIMITED TO)**:
203(k): Rehabilitation Agreement, Plans, Work Write-ups, Cost Estimates, and Initial Draw Request
Form HUD-92561—Borrower's Contract with Respect to Hotel and Transient Use of Property (2-4 units)
Condominiums: Verification regarding 51% owner occupancy. Spot Condo documentation (if spot approval)

This information is required to determine the eligibility of loans for FHA mortgage insurance. Lenders are not required to use this format when conducting a pre-endorsement review under the Lender Insurance program. This format is provided to illustrate what should be included in a pre-endorsement review under the Lender Insurance program. Section 256 of the National Housing Act [12 U.S.C 1715z-21] allows for delegation of authority to endorse FHA mortgage loans without a pre-endorsement review conducted by FHA. Lenders approved to participate in this program will conduct their own pre-insurance review. The public reporting burden for this collection of information is estimated to average 15 minutes per response, including time for reviewing instructions, searching existing data sources, gathering and maintaining data needed, and completing and reviewing the collection of information. This agency may not conduct or sponsor, and a person is not required to respond to a collection of information unless that collection displays a valid OMB control number.

Exhibit C

+

EXIT PREMIUM NOTE

______________, 20____

[Property Address]

[insert identifying number for administrative tracking of note]

THIS NOTE (the "Note") is given on ______________ ____, 20___ by and between **[Borrower's Name]** (whether one or more person, hereinafter referred to as **"Borrower"**) and the **Secretary of Housing and Urban Development,** whose address is 451 Seventh Street, S.W., Washington, D.C., 20410 (hereinafter referred to as the **"Lender"**).

DEFINITIONS

A. **Event of Default.**

The term "Event of Default" shall mean any misrepresentation(s) made by the Borrower in the HOPE for Homeowners Consumer Disclosure and Certification.

B. **Initial Equity.**

In the event of the occurrence of a Maturity Event or an Event of Default, the Property's Initial Equity is in the amount of ______________ ($_____). **[Insert amount equivalent to: The lesser of--(i) the appraised value of the Property that was used at the time of origination of the HOPE for Homeowners (H4H) Mortgage to underwrite the mortgage and to determine compliance with the maximum loan-to-value ratio at origination established by 12 U.S.C. § 1715z-23(e)(2)(B); or (ii) the outstanding amount due under all existing senior mortgages, existing subordinate mortgages, and non-mortgage liens on the Property; *minus* the original principal amount of the H4H Mortgage.]**

C. **Maturity Event.**

The refinance of the H4H Mortgage, a sale or any other disposition of all or any part of the Property (including the sale or disposition of a beneficial interest in the Property or foreclosure by a senior mortgagee) where there has been no refinance of the H4H Mortgage prior to such sale or disposition.

A Maturity Event shall not include the following:

(a) a transfer by devise, descent, or operation of law on the death of a joint tenant or tenant by the entirety;

(b) the granting of a leasehold interest of three (3) years or less not containing an option to purchase;

(c) a transfer to a relative resulting from the death of the Borrower;

(d) a transfer where the spouse or children of the Borrower become an owner of the property;

(e) a transfer resulting from a decree of a dissolution of marriage, legal separation agreement, or from an incidental property settlement agreement, by which the spouse of the Borrower becomes an owner of the property; or

(f) a transfer into an *inter vivos* trust in which the borrower is and remains a beneficiary and which does not relate to a transfer of rights of occupancy in the property.

RECITALS

R1. The Borrower has chosen to participate in the HOPE for Homeowners program as established by Title IV of the Housing and Economic Recovery Act of 2008 (the "H4H Program") as amended by the Emergency Economic Stabilization Act of 2008 and the Helping Families Save Their Homes Act of 2009.

R2. As a participant in the H4H Program, the Borrower has a Federal Housing Administration (FHA) insured first mortgage of even date herewith in the amount of ____________ **[Insert amount of the H4H Mortgage]** with ______________ **[Insert First Lienholder Name]** secured by the Property as defined herein (the "H4H Mortgage").

R3. Pursuant to the terms and conditions of the H4H Program, the Borrower shall grant the Lender an equity interest in the Property by executing this Note and an Exit Premium Mortgage (the "EPM") of even date herewith with the EPM to be secured by a second priority lien against the Property.

NOW, THEREFORE, in exchange of good and valuable consideration, the receipt and legal sufficiency of which are hereby acknowledged and the mutual covenants herein contained, the parties do hereby agree as follows:

1. **Borrower's Promise to Pay**.

Upon the occurrence of a Maturity Event, the Borrower hereby promises to pay to the order of the Lender principal based on Initial Equity pursuant to the following schedule:

(a) If the Maturity Event occurs during the period that begins on the date the H4H Mortgage becomes FHA-insured (the "Date of Insurance") and ends one (1) year after the Date of Insurance, the Borrower shall pay the Lender one hundred percent (100%) of Initial Equity.

(b) If the Maturity Event occurs during the period that begins one (1) year following the Date of Insurance and ends two (2) years after such Date of Insurance, the Borrower shall pay the Lender ninety percent (90%) of Initial Equity.

(c) If the Maturity Event occurs during the period that begins two (2) years following the Date of Insurance and ends three (3) years after such Date of Insurance, the Borrower shall pay the Lender eighty percent (80%) of Initial Equity.

(d) If the Maturity Event occurs during the period that begins three (3) years following the Date of Insurance and ends four (4) years after such Date of Insurance, the Borrower shall pay the Lender seventy percent (70%) of Initial Equity.

(e) If the Maturity Event occurs during the period that begins four (4) years following the Date of Insurance and ends five (5) years after such Date of Insurance, the Borrower shall pay the Lender sixty percent (60%) of Initial Equity.

(f) If the Maturity Event occurs during any period that begins five (5) years following the Date of Insurance, the Borrower shall pay the Lender fifty percent (50%) of Initial Equity.

2. **H4H Mortgage Not Eligible for Insurance**. Lender agrees that if the H4H Mortgage is determined to be ineligible for insurance under the National Housing Act, the Note shall be void and the Lender shall execute and record a release for the EPM. A written statement of any authorized agent of the Lender dated subsequent to the date hereof, declining to insure the H4H Mortgage, shall be deemed conclusive proof of such ineligibility.

3. **Interest**. This Note shall not bear interest unless the principal amount due upon occurrence of a Maturity Event is not paid to Lender. If principal amount due is not paid, the principal sum due pursuant Paragraph 1 of this Note shall bear interest from the date of the Maturity Event at the rate of the current value of funds to the United States Treasury in effect on the date of the Maturity Event. The current value of funds rate is prescribed and published by the Secretary of the Treasury in the Federal Register and the Treasury Fiscal Requirements Manual Bulletins.

4. **Mortgage**. This Note is secured by an EPM, deed of trust, or similar security instrument of even date herewith between Borrower and Lender (the "Security

Instrument"). The Security Instrument encumbers certain real property located at **[Insert Property Address]** (the "Property Address") and more fully described in the Security Instrument (the "Property").

5. **Payment**.

(a) No regular monthly payments are due under this Note. A payment is due upon the occurrence of a Maturity Event pursuant to the terms and schedule provided in Paragraph 1 of this Note.

This Note is a deferred contingent liability. Principal and any interest on this Note and all other sums, which may or shall become due under this Note and the Security Instrument, shall be due and payable upon the occurrence of the Maturity Event (Maturity Date) if (1) not otherwise satisfied in accordance with the provisions of the Security Instrument, or (2) there is an Event of Default.

(b) Payment shall be made at Single Family Notes/H4H, PO Box 105053, Atlanta, GA 30348-5053, or at such place as Lender may designate in writing by notice to Borrower.

6. **Prepayment**. Borrower shall not have the right to prepay this Note, in whole or in part.

7. **Grounds for Acceleration of Debt and Event of Default**.

Upon the occurrence of an Event of Default, Lender may declare, without notice, immediately due and payable the principal and interest equivalent to the amount of Initial Equity due on this Note and all other sums which may or shall become due under the EPM or this Note.

8. **Payment of Lender's Costs and Expenses**. If Lender has required immediate payment in full, as described above, Lender may require Borrower to pay costs and expenses including reasonable and customary attorney's fees for enforcing this Note to the extent not prohibited by applicable law. Such fees and costs shall bear interest from the date of disbursement at a rate of the current value of funds to the United States Treasury in effect on the date of the date of disbursement and, at the option of Lender, shall be immediately due and payable. The current value of funds rate is prescribed and published by the Secretary of the Treasury in the Federal Register and the Treasury Fiscal Requirements Manual Bulletins.

9. **Modifications**. This Note shall not be modified, amended, changed, discharged, or terminated orally. This Note may only be modified, amended, changed, discharged, or terminated by an agreement in writing signed by the party against whom enforcement of such modification, amendment, change, discharge, or termination is sought.

10. **Notices.** Any notice to Borrower provided for in this Note shall be given by delivering it or by mailing it by first class mail unless applicable law requires use of

another method. The notice shall be directed to the Property Address or any other address Borrower designates by notice to Lender. Any notice to Lender shall be given by first class mail to Lender's address stated herein or any address Lender designates by notice to Borrower. Any notice provided for in this Note shall be deemed to have been given to Borrower or Lender when given as provided in this paragraph.

11. **Time of the Essence**. Time is of the essence as to all dates set forth herein.

12. **Waivers**. Borrower and all endorsers, sureties and guarantors jointly and severally waive presentation for payment, demand for payment, notice of nonpayment, notice of protest, notice of dishonor, protest, notice of protest, and any and all lack of diligence or delays in collection or enforcement of this Note.

13. **Successors and Assigns Bound**. The covenants and agreements of this Note shall bind and benefit the successors and assigns of Lender and Borrower. The covenants and agreements of Borrower under this Note are not assignable without the prior written consent of Lender.

14. **Governing Law; Severability**. This Note shall be governed by Federal law. In the event that any provision or clause of this Note or the Security Instrument conflicts with applicable law, such conflict shall not affect other provisions of this Note or the Security Instrument which can be given effect without the conflicting provision. To this end the provisions of this Note and the Security Instrument are declared to be severable.

15. **Authority to Execute**. The representative of Borrower executing this Note represents that he/she has full power, authority and legal right to execute and deliver this Note and that the debt hereunder constitutes a valid and binding obligation of Borrower.

BY SIGNING BELOW, Borrower accepts and agrees under seal to the terms and covenants contained in this Note.

BORROWER:

By:__________________________(SEAL)

Name:__________________________

By:__________________________(SEAL)

Name:__________________________

[NOTE: THE FOLLOWING IS A SAMPLE MODEL MORTGAGE FORM THAT IS NOT ADAPTED FOR STATE LAW. THE FHA-APPROVED MORTGAGEE EXTENDING THE FIRST MORTGAGE IS RESPONSIBLE FOR ADAPTING PROVISIONS WITHIN THIS MODEL FORM TO STATE LAW ON BEHALF OF HUD. THE GENERAL SUBSTANCE OF EACH PROVISION SHOULD NOT CHANGE FROM THE MODEL FORM. IF THERE IS A CONFLICT BETWEEN SUBSTANTIVE CONTENT OF A PARTICULAR PROVISION AND STATE LAW, THE MORTGAGEE SHALL CONTACT FHA FOR FURTHER GUIDANCE.]

After Recording Return To:

[Insert where to return recorded document]

________________**[Space Above This Line For Recording Data]**____________

[insert identifying number for administrative tracking of mortgage]

EXIT PREMIUM MORTGAGE

THIS EXIT PREMIUM MORTGAGE (the "EPM") is given on ____________ ____, 20___ by and between ________________**[Insert Borrower's Name]** (whether one or more person, hereinafter referred to as **"Borrower"**) and the **Secretary of Housing and Urban Development,** whose address is 451 Seventh Street, S.W., Washington, D.C., 20410 (hereinafter referred to as the **"Lender"**). **[Insert the following language if the EPM is registered with MERS...** "with **Mortgage Electronic Registration Systems, Inc.**, organized and existing under the laws of Delaware, with an address and telephone number of P.O. Box 2026, Flint, Michigan 48501-2026, tel. (888) 679-MERS ("**MERS**") acting solely as a nominee for Lender and Lender's successors and assigns. **FOR PURPOSES OF RECORDING THIS MORTGAGE, MERS IS THE MORTGAGEE OF RECORD."]**

DEFINITIONS

A. **Event of Default.**

The term "Event of Default" shall mean any misrepresentation(s) made by the Borrower on the HOPE for Homeowners Consumer Disclosure and Certification.

B. **Initial Equity.**

In the event of the occurrence of an Maturity Event or an Event of Default, the Property's Initial Equity is in the amount of ____________________ ($_____). **[Insert amount equivalent to: The lesser of--(i) the appraised value of the Property that was used at the time of origination of the HOPE for Homeowners (H4H) Mortgage to underwrite the mortgage and to determine compliance with the maximum loan-to-value ratio at origination established**

by 12 U.S.C. § 1715z-23(e)(2)(B); or (ii) the outstanding amount due under all existing senior mortgages, existing subordinate mortgages, and non-mortgage liens on the Property; *minus* the original principal amount of the H4H Mortgage.]

C. **Maturity Event.**

The refinance of the H4H Mortgage, a sale or any other disposition of all or any part of the Property (including the sale or disposition of a beneficial interest in the Property or foreclosure by a senior mortgagee) where there has been no refinance of the H4H Mortgage prior to such sale or disposition.

A Maturity Event shall not include the following:

(a) a transfer by devise, descent, or operation of law on the death of a joint tenant or tenant by the entirety;

(b) the granting of a leasehold interest of three (3) years or less not containing an option to purchase;

(c) a transfer to a relative resulting from the death of the Borrower;

(d) a transfer where the spouse or children of the Borrower become an owner of the property;

(e) a transfer resulting from a decree of a dissolution of marriage, legal separation agreement, or from an incidental property settlement agreement, by which the spouse of the Borrower becomes an owner of the property; or

(f) a transfer into an *inter vivos* trust in which the borrower is and remains a beneficiary and which does not relate to a transfer of rights of occupancy in the property.

RECITALS

R1. Borrower is the owner of property located in ________ County, ____________ more particularly described on **Schedule A** annexed hereto which has the address of _________________________ [Street], ____________, ____________, ____________ [Zip code], (the "Property Address").

R2. The Borrower has chosen to participate in the HOPE for Homeowners program as established by Title IV of the Housing and Economic Recovery Act of 2008 as amended by the Emergency Economic Stabilization Act of 2008 and the Helping Families Save Their Homes Act of 2009 (the "H4H Program").

R3. As a participant in the HOPE Program, the Borrower has a Federal Housing Administration (FHA) first mortgage of even date herewith in the amount of ________**[Insert amount of the H4H Mortgage]** with ________ **[Insert First Lienholder Name]** secured by the Property as defined herein (the "H4H

Mortgage").

R4. Pursuant to the terms and conditions of the H4H Program, the Borrower shall grant the Lender an equity and appreciation interest in the Property by executing an Exit Premium Note (the "Note") and this EPM of even date herewith with this EPM to be secured by a second priority lien against the Property.

NOW, THEREFORE, in exchange of good and valuable consideration, the receipt and legal sufficiency of which are hereby acknowledged and the mutual covenants herein contained, the parties do hereby agree as follows:

1. Borrower promises to pay the principal sum stipulated in the Note and all other sums which may or shall become due under this EPM or the Note, upon the occurrence of a Maturity Event (the "Maturity Date"), if (a) not otherwise satisfied in accordance with the provisions of this EPM or (b) there is an Event of Default.

2. This EPM secures (a) the repayment of the debt evidenced by the Note; (b) the performance of Borrower's promises and agreements under this EPM and the Note. For this purpose, Borrower hereby mortgages, warrants, grants, and conveys to Lender a security interest, with power of sale, in the Property;

TOGETHER WITH all the improvements now or hereafter erected on the property, and all easements, appurtenances, and fixtures now or hereafter a part of the property. All replacements and additions shall also be covered by this EPM.

BORROWER COVENANTS that Borrower is lawfully seized of the estate hereby conveyed and has the right to mortgage, grant and convey the Property and that the Property is unencumbered, except for encumbrances of record. Borrower warrants and will defend generally the title to the Property against all claims and demands, subject to any encumbrances of record.

UNIFORM COVENANTS

1. Payment of Principal and Interest.

Upon the occurrence of a Maturity Event, the Borrower hereby promises to pay to the order of the Lender principal based on Initial Equity pursuant to the following schedule:

(A) If the Exit Premium Maturity Event occurs during the period that begins on the date the H4H Mortgage becomes FHA-insured (the "Date of Insurance") and ends one (1) year after the Date of Insurance, the Borrower shall pay the Lender one hundred percent (100%) of Initial Equity.

(B) If the Maturity Event occurs during the period that begins one (1) year following the Date of Insurance and ends two (2) years after such Date of

Insurance, the Borrower shall pay the Lender ninety percent (90%) of Initial Equity.

(C) If the Maturity Event occurs during the period that begins two (2) years following the Date of Insurance and ends three (3) years after such Date of Insurance, the Borrower shall pay the Lender eighty percent (80%) of Initial Equity.

(D) If the Maturity Event occurs during the period that begins three (3) years following the Date of Insurance and ends four (4) years after such Date of Insurance, the Borrower shall pay the Lender seventy percent (70%) of Initial Equity.

(E) If the Maturity Event occurs during the period that begins four (4) years following the Date of Insurance and ends five (5) years after such Date of Insurance, the Borrower shall pay the Lender sixty percent (60%) of Initial Equity.

(F) If the Maturity Event occurs during any period that begins five (5) years following the Date of Insurance, the Borrower shall pay the Lender fifty percent (50%) of Initial Equity.

The Note shall not bear interest unless the principal amount due upon occurrence of a Maturity Event is not paid to Lender. If the principal amount due is not paid, the principal sum due pursuant Paragraph 1 of the Note shall bear interest from the date of the Maturity Event at the rate of the current value of funds to the United States Treasury in effect on the date of the Maturity Event. The current value of funds rate is prescribed and published by the Secretary of the Treasury in the Federal Register and the Treasury Fiscal Requirements Manual Bulletins.

Lender agrees that if the H4H Mortgage is determined to be ineligible for insurance under the National Housing Act, the Note shall be void and the Lender shall execute and record a release for the EPM. A written statement of any authorized agent of the Lender dated subsequent to the date hereof, declining to insure the H4H Mortgage, shall be deemed conclusive proof of such ineligibility.

4. **Payment of Taxes, Insurance, and Other Charges**. Borrower shall pay all (a) taxes and special assessments levied or to be levied against the Property; (b) leasehold payments or ground rents on the Property; (c) Community Association Dues, Fees, and Assessments, (c) governmental or municipal charges, fines, and impositions; (d) other items which can attain priority over this Security Instrument as a lien or encumbrance on the Property. The phrase “Community Association Dues, Fees, and Assessments” means all dues, fees, assessments and other charges that are imposed on Borrower or the Property by a condominium association, homeowners association or similar organization. Borrower shall pay these obligations on time directly to the entity

owed the payment. If failure to pay would adversely affect Lender's interest in the Property, upon Lender's request, Borrower shall promptly furnish to Lender receipts evidencing these payments.

If Borrower fails to make these payments, fails to perform any other covenants and agreements contained in this EPM, or there is a legal proceeding that may significantly affect Lender's rights in the Property (such as a proceeding in bankruptcy, for condemnation, or to enforce laws or regulations), then Lender may do and pay whatever is necessary to protect the value of the Property and Lender's rights in the Property, including payment of taxes and hazard insurance.

Any amounts disbursed by Lender under this paragraph shall become an additional debt of Borrower and be secured by this EPM. These amounts shall bear interest from the date of disbursement at a rate of the current value of funds to the United States Treasury in effect on the date of the date of disbursement and, at the option of Lender, shall be immediately due and payable. The current value of funds rate is prescribed and published by the Secretary of the Treasury in the Federal Register and the Treasury Fiscal Requirements Manual Bulletins.

Borrower shall promptly discharge any lien which has priority over this EPM or is subordinate to this EPM unless the lien has priority as provided in Paragraph 9. If Lender determines that any part of the Property is subject to a lien that may either attain priority over this EPM or be subordinate to this EPM, Lender may give Borrower a notice identifying the lien. Borrower shall satisfy the lien or take one or more of the actions set forth above within ten (10) days of the giving of notice.

5. **Fire, Flood and Other Hazard Insurance.** Borrower shall insure all improvements on the Property, whether now in existence or subsequently erected, against any hazards, casualties, and contingencies, including fire, for which Lender requires insurance. This insurance shall be maintained in the amounts and for the periods that Lender requires. Borrower shall also insure all improvements on the Property, whether now in existence or subsequently erected, against loss by floods to the extent required by the Lender. All insurance shall be carried with companies approved by Lender. The insurance policies and any renewals shall be held by Lender and shall include loss payable clauses in favor of, and in a form acceptable to, Lender.

If any improvement is located within the special flood hazard area, Borrower shall obtain flood insurance covering all improvements on the property, whether now in existence or subsequently erected, in an amount equal to (a) the value of the Property, or (b) the maximum limit of coverage made available under the National Flood Insurance Act of 1968, whichever is less. If any improvement on the Property is located within a special flood hazard area, Borrower shall insure all improvements on the Property, whether now in existence or subsequently erected, against loss by floods to the extent required by law. The insurance policies and any renewals, regardless of whether such policies and renewals are required by Lender, shall include loss payable clauses in favor of, and in a form acceptable to, Lender.

In the event of loss, Borrower shall give Lender immediate notice by mail. Lender may make proof of loss if not made promptly by Borrower. Each insurance company concerned is hereby authorized and directed to make payment for such loss directly to Lender, instead of to Borrower and to Lender jointly. All or any part of the insurance proceeds may be applied by Lender, at its option, either (a) to the reduction of the indebtedness under the Note and this EPM, or (b) to the restoration or repair of the damaged Property. Any excess insurance proceeds over an amount required to pay all outstanding indebtedness under the Note and this EPM shall be paid to the entity legally entitled thereto.

In the event of foreclosure of this EPM or other transfer of title to the Property that extinguishes the indebtedness, all rights, title and interests of Borrower in and to insurance policies in force shall pass to the purchaser.

6. **Maintenance and Protection of Property**. Borrower shall not commit, or permit, any waste on, destruction to, or damage to the Property. Borrower shall not allow the Property to deteriorate, reasonable wear and tear excepted. Borrower shall, at all times, maintain the Property. Borrower shall comply with all applicable Federal, state, and local statutes, ordinances, codes, regulations, requirements, and restrictive covenants, if any, upon the use of the Property. Borrower shall, to the satisfaction of Lender, promptly repair or replace any of the Property damaged by fire or other casualty. Lender and its representatives shall have the right to inspect the Property from time to time at any reasonable hour.

7. **Occupancy, Preservation, Maintenance and Protection of the Property; Borrower's Loan Application; Leaseholds.** Borrower shall occupy, establish, and use the Property as Borrower's principal residence upon execution of this EPM and shall continue to occupy the Property as Borrower's principal residence unless Lender determines that requirement will cause undue hardship for Borrower or unless extenuating circumstances exist which are beyond Borrower's control. Borrower shall notify Lender of any extenuating circumstances. Lender may inspect the Property if the Property is vacant or abandoned or the loan is in default. Lender may take reasonable action to protect and preserve such vacant or abandoned property. Borrower shall also be in default if Borrower, during the loan application process, gave materially false or inaccurate information or statements to Lender (or failed to provide Lender with any material information) in connection with the loan evidenced by the Note, including, but not limited to, representations concerning Borrower's occupancy of the Property as a principal residence. If this EPM is on a leasehold, Borrower shall comply with the provisions of the lease. If Borrower acquires fee title to the Property, the leasehold and fee title shall not be merged unless Lender agrees to the merger in writing.

8. **Prepayment; Release of Security Instrument**. Borrower shall not have the right to prepay the Note. The Note shall be considered satisfied and this EPM shall be released only upon receipt of principal and interest pursuant to Paragraph 1 and 2 of the Note.

9. **Priorities**. Notwithstanding any other provision to the contrary, this EPM is superior to all liens on the Property, other than the HOPE Mortgage. Additionally, during the first five (5) years of the HOPE Mortgage, the Borrower shall not grant any junior lien interest in the Property unless the Borrower obtains the Lender's prior express written consent to grant a security interest in the Property to secure a loan that is essential to preserve, protect, and repair the Property (the "P&P Loan") and fulfills the following criteria:

(A) the condition to be repaired represents a health or safety hazard;

(B) failure to make the repair will cause the property condition to deteriorate;

(C) the cost of the proposed repair is reasonable for the geographic market area;

(D) the repairs are not primarily cosmetic and do not represent routine maintenance;

(E) the P&P Loan is a closed-end loan under Federal Reserve Board's Regulation Z;

10. **Fees**. Lender may collect fees and charges authorized by this EPM or the Note.

11. **Grounds for Acceleration of Debt and Event of Default**.Upon the occurrence of an Event of Default, Lender may declare, without notice, immediately due and payable the principal and interest equivalent to the amount of Initial Equity due on the Note and all other sums which may or shall become due under this EPM or the Note.

12. **Time of the Essence**. Time is of the essence as to all dates set forth herein.

13. **Waivers**. Borrower and all endorsers, sureties and guarantors jointly and severally waive presentation for payment, demand for payment, notice of nonpayment, notice of protest, notice of dishonor, protest, notice of protest, and any and all lack of diligence or delays in collection or enforcement of this EPM.

14. **Successors and Assigns Bound**. The covenants and agreements of this EPM shall bind and benefit the successors and assigns of Lender. The covenants and agreements of Borrower under this Note are not assignable without the prior express written consent of Lender. Borrower's covenants and agreements shall be joint and several.

15. **Modifications**. This EPM shall not be modified, amended, changed, discharged, or terminated orally. This EPM may only be modified, amended, changed, discharged, or terminated by an agreement in writing signed by the party against whom

enforcement of such modification, amendment, change, discharge, or termination is sought.

16. **Notices.** Any notice to Borrower provided for in this EPM shall be given by delivering it or by mailing it by first class mail unless applicable law requires use of another method. The notice shall be directed to the Property Address or any other address Borrower designates by notice to Lender. Any notice to Lender shall be given by first class mail to Lender's address stated herein or any address Lender designates by notice to Borrower. Any notice provided for in this EPM shall be deemed to have been given to Borrower or Lender when given as provided in this paragraph.

17. **Governing Law; Severability**. This EPM shall be governed by Federal law. In the event that any provision or clause of this EPM or the Note conflicts with applicable law, such conflict shall not affect other provisions of this EPM or the Note which can be given effect without the conflicting provision. To this end the provisions of this EPM and the Note are declared to be severable.

18. **Copy of Mortgage**. Borrower acknowledges that he/she has received a true copy of this EPM, read this EPM, and executed this EPM as of the date at the top of the first page.

19. **Hazardous Substances**. Borrower shall not cause or permit the presence, use, disposal, storage, or release of any Hazardous Substances on or in the Property. Borrower shall not do, nor allow anyone else to do, anything affecting the Property that is in violation of any Environmental Law. The preceding two sentences shall not apply to the presence, use, or storage on the Property of small quantities of Hazardous Substances that are generally recognized to be appropriate to normal residential uses and to maintenance of the Property.

Borrower shall promptly give Lender written notice of any investigation, claim, demand, lawsuit or other action by any governmental or regulatory agency or private party involving the Property and any Hazardous Substance or Environmental Law of which Borrower has actual knowledge. If Borrower learns, or is notified by any governmental or regulatory authority, that any removal or other remediation of any Hazardous Substances affecting the Property is necessary, Borrower shall promptly take all necessary remedial actions in accordance with Environmental Law.

As used in this paragraph, "Hazardous Substances" are those substances defined as toxic or hazardous substances by Environmental Law and the following substances: gasoline, kerosene, other flammable or toxic petroleum products, toxic pesticides and herbicides, volatile solvents, materials containing asbestos or formaldehyde, and radioactive materials. As used in this paragraph "Environmental Law" means Federal law and laws of the jurisdiction where the Property is located that relate to health, safety or environmental protection.

20. **Authority to Execute**. The Borrower executing this EPM represents that he/she has full power, authority and legal right to execute and deliver this EPM and that the debt secured hereunder constitutes a valid and binding obligation of Borrower

NON-UNIFORM COVENANTS.

Borrower and Lender further covenant and agree as follows:

21. **Foreclosure Procedure**. If Lender requires immediate payment in full under Paragraph 11, Lender may invoke the power of sale and any other remedies permitted by applicable law.

If Lender invokes the power of sale, Lender shall give notice of sale to Borrower in the manner provided in Paragraph 16. Lender shall publish and post the notice of sale, and the Property shall be sold in the manner prescribed by applicable law. Lender or its designee may purchase the Property at any sale. The proceeds of the sale shall be applied in the following order: (a) to all expenses of the sale, including, but not limited to, reasonable attorney's fees; (b) to all sums secured by this EPM; and (c) any excess to the person or persons legally entitled to it.

[**The following language is mandatory in all cases**.] If the Lender's interest in this EPM is held by the Secretary of Housing and Urban Development (the Secretary) and the Secretary requires immediate payment in full under Paragraph 12, the Secretary may invoke the nonjudicial power of sale provided in the Single Family Mortgage Foreclosure Act of 1994 ("Act") (12 U.S.C. 3751 et seq.) by requesting a foreclosure commissioner designated under the Act to commence foreclosure and to sell the Property as provided in the Act. Nothing in the preceding sentence shall deprive the Secretary of any rights otherwise available to a Lender under this Paragraph or applicable law.

22. **Riders to this EPM**. The following Riders are to be executed by Borrower [check box as applicable] and the covenants of each such Rider shall be incorporated into and shall amend and supplement the covenants and agreements of this EPM:

☐ Other [specify]:

____

BY SIGNING BELOW, Borrower accepts and agrees under seal to the terms contained in this Security Instrument and in any Rider(s) executed by Borrower and recorded with it.

Witnesses: BORROWER:

_________________ By:_______________________(SEAL)

Name:____________________________

____________________ By:____________________(SEAL)

Name:____________________

______________[Space Below This Line for Acknowledgement]______________

State of ____________________)
) ss.:
County of ____________________)

On the <<DAY>> day of <<MONTH>>, in the year <<YEAR>>, before me, the undersigned, a Notary Public in and for said State, personally appeared <<BORROWER>>, personally known to me or proved to me on the basis of satisfactory evidence to be the individual whose name is subscribed to the within instrument and acknowledged to me that s/he executed the same in her/his capacity, and that by her/his signature on the instrument, the individual, or the person or entity on behalf of which the individual acted, executed the instrument.

____
Notary Public

SCHEDULE A

[Insert legal description of property]

Exhibit D

HOPE for Homeowners Subordinate Lien Upfront Payment Worksheet

U.S. Department of Housing and Urban Development

Federal Housing Administration

OMB Approval No. XXXX-XXXX (exp. XX/XX/XXXX)

Borrower(s) Name	FHA Case Number
Property Address	Appraised Value
Originating Lender Name	Appraisal Date

First Lien Holder Name	Third Lien Holder Name (if any)
Second Lien Holder Name	Fourth Lien Holder Name (if any)

	First Lien	Second Lien	Third Lien (if any)	Fourth Lien (if any)	Line Total
1. **Principal** *					
2. **Accrued Interest** *					
3. **Amount Owed** (Line 1 + Line 2)					
4. **LTV** (Line 3 ÷ Appraised Value)					
5. **Cumulative LTV** **					
6. **Days Past Due**					
7. **Upfront Payment Factor**					
8. **Upfront Payment** (Line 3 × Line 7)					

Instructions. In accordance with the chart to the right, subordinate lien holders may receive an upfront payment equal to a percentage of the principal and accrued interest they are writing off. The Upfront Payment Factor for each subordinate lien is based on the number of days the lien is past due at the time of HOPE for Homeowners loan application and the lien's Cumulative Loan-to-Value Ratio (Cumulative LTV).

UPFRONT PAYMENT FACTORS		**Days Past Due (#)**			
		0 - 29	**30 - 59**	**60 - 89**	**90 +**
Cumulative LTV (%)	**≤ 90.00**	0.50	0.40	0.28	0.09
	90.01 - 100.00	0.45	0.36	0.26	0.06
	100.01 - 125.00	0.35	0.28	0.20	0.03
	125.01 - 150.00	0.20	0.16	0.11	0.03
	> 150.00	0.10	0.08	0.03	0.03

* When completing the above worksheet, use the principal and accrued interest amounts as of the first day of the month in which the HOPE for Homeowners loan application was made, with interest calculated at the pre-default contract rate.

** A lien's Cumulative LTV is the sum of its LTV and the LTVs of all more senior liens. For instance, the Cumulative LTV of a third lien equals the sum of the third's LTV, the second's LTV, and the first's LTV. When complete, the Total of Line 4 should approximately equal to the Cumulative LTV of the most junior loan. (Unavoidable rounding errors caused by working with decimals may prevent the two boxes from matching exactly.)

Subordinate Lien Holder Authorized Signature	Title	Date
Subordinate Lien Holder Address		Telephone
Originating Lender Authorized Signature	Title	Date

The information collection requirements contained in this document have been submitted to the Office of Management and Budget (OMB) under the Paperwork Reduction Act of 1995 (44 U.S.C. 3501-3520) and are pending an OMB control number. In accordance with the Paperwork Reduction Act, HUD may not conduct or sponsor, and a person is not required to respond to, a collection of information unless the collection displays a currently valid OMB control number.

Previous editions are obsolete. Page 1 of 2 Form **HUD-XXXXX** (XX/XXXX)

EXAMPLE OF A COMPLETED
SUBORDINATE LIEN UPFRONT PAYMENT WORKSHEET

This is an example of a properly completed Subordinate Lien Upfront Payment Worksheet, in a case where there is only one subordinate lien. (If there was a second subordinate lien (a third lien), the Third Lien column of the Worksheet would also be completed.)

The example property is currently appraised at $100,000 with a primary lien of $105,000 ($95,000 principal and $5,000 accrued interest) and a subordinate lien of $18,000 ($17,000 principal and $1,000 accrued interest). The subordinate lien is 32 days past due at the time of application.

Given this information, the Subordinate Lien Upfront Payment Worksheet is completed as follows:

	First Lien	Second Lien	Third Lien (if any)	Fourth Lien (if any)	Line Total
1. **Principal**	$95,000	$17,000			$112,000
2. **Accrued Interest**	$5,000	$1,000			$6,000
3. **Amount Owed** (Line 1 + Line 2)	$105,000	$18,000			$123,000
4. **LTV** (Line 3 ÷ Appraised Value)	105%	18%			123%
5. **Cumulative LTV**	105%	123%			
6. **Days Past Due**		32			
7. **Upfront Payment Factor**		0.28			
8. **Upfront Payment** (Line 3 × Line 7)		$5,040			$5,040

Calculating Cumulative LTV. The Cumulative LTV (Row 5) for a first lien equals its LTV (Row 4). For a second lien, the Cumulative LTV equal the first lien's LTV plus the second lien's LTV. In this example, the second lien's Cumulative LTV is 105% plus 18%, or 123%.

If the example property had a third lien, the third lien's Cumulative LTV would be calculated as 105% plus 18%, plus the third lien's LTV.

Determining Upfront Payment Factor. Use a subordinate lien's Cumulative LTV (Row 5) and its Days Past Due (Row 6) to determine the appropriate Upfront Payment Factor on the "Upfront Payment Factors" chart, on page one of this form. In this example, the second lien's Upfront Payment Factor of 0.28 is determined as follows:

UPFRONT PAYMENT FACTORS		Days Past Due (#)			
		0 - 29	**30 - 59**	**60 - 89**	**90 +**
Cumulative LTV (%)	**≤ 90.00**	0.50	0.40	0.28	0.09
	90.01 - 100.00	0.45	0.36	0.26	0.06
	100.01 - 125.00	0.35	0.28	0.20	0.03
	125.01 - 150.00	0.20	0.16	0.11	0.03
	> 150.00	0.10	0.08	0.03	0.03

If the example property had a third lien, its Upfront Payment Factor would be determined in the same manner, using the third lien's Cumulative LTV and Days Past Due.

Appendix B Federal Agency Guidelines on Workouts Including Loan Modifications

This appendix collects program guidelines or statements of policy issued by federal agencies, including the Department of Treasury, regarding efforts the financial industry should take to help borrowers in default or at risk of default on their mortgage. Details of federal government's primary anti-foreclosure initiative, the Home Affordable Modification Program (HAMP), are included at B.3, *infra*. HAMP was modeled, in part, on a loan modification program developed by the FDIC. Details on the FDIC's program are included at B.1 and B.2, *infra* along with a link to the program's website.

B.1 Federal Financial Agencies' Statement on Loss Mitigation

Statement on Loss Mitigation Strategies for Servicers of Residential Mortgages

The Federal Deposit Insurance Corporation, Board of Governors of the Federal Reserve System, Office of the Comptroller of the Currency, Office of Thrift Supervision, National Credit Union Administration, and Conference of State Bank Supervisors (CSBS) encourage federally regulated institutions[1] and state-supervised entities that service mortgage loans (collectively referred to as "servicers") to pursue strategies to mitigate losses while preserving homeownership to the extent possible and appropriate.

Previously, in April 2007, the federal financial agencies issued a *Statement on Working with Mortgage Borrowers* and followed this with the July 2007 *Statement on Subprime Mortgage Lending*. Both interagency statements encouraged federally regulated institutions to work constructively with residential borrowers at risk of default and to consider prudent workout arrangements that avoid unnecessary foreclosures. In these statements, the federal financial agencies stated that prudent workout arrangements that are consistent with safe and sound lending practices are generally in the long-term best interest of both the financial institution and the borrower. CSBS, the American Association of Residential Mortgage Regulators (AARMR), and the National Association of Consumer Credit Administrators developed a parallel *Statement on Subprime Mortgage Lending* that applies to state-supervised mortgage brokers and lenders. In June 2007, CSBS and AARMR issued a consumer alert and an industry letter to address resetting mortgage loans.

These previous statements focused on residential loans retained by federally regulated institutions and state-supervised entities. However, many subprime and other mortgage loans have been transferred into securitization trusts. Servicing for these securitized loans is governed by the terms of contract documents, typically referred to as Pooling and Servicing Agreements. A significant number of adjustable-rate mortgages are scheduled to reset in the coming months. As indicated in the *Statement on Subprime Mortgage Lending* and the October 2006 *Interagency Guidance on Nontraditional Mortgage Product Risks*, these resets may result in a significant payment shock to the borrower, which can increase the likelihood of default.

Servicers of securitized mortgages should review the governing documents for the securitization trusts to determine the full extent of their authority to restructure loans that are delinquent or in default or are in imminent risk of default. The governing documents may allow servicers to proactively contact borrowers at risk of default, assess whether default is reasonably foreseeable, and, if so, apply loss mitigation strategies designed to achieve sustainable mortgage obligations. The Securities and Exchange Commission (SEC) has provided clarification that entering into loan restructurings or modifications when default is reasonably foreseeable does not preclude an institution from continuing to treat serviced mortgages as off-balance sheet exposures.[2] Also, the federal financial agencies and CSBS

1 For purposes of this Statement, the term "federally regulated institutions" refers to state- and nationally-chartered banks and their subsidiaries; bank holding companies and their nonbank subsidiaries; savings associations and their subsidiaries; savings and loan holding companies and their subsidiaries; and credit unions.

2 In general, default could be considered "reasonably foreseeable" when a lender has made actual contact with the borrower, has assessed the borrower's ability to pay, and has a reasonable

understand that the Department of Treasury has indicated that servicers of loans in qualifying securitization vehicles may modify the terms of the loans before an actual delinquency or default when default is reasonably foreseeable, consistent with Real Estate Mortgage Investment Conduit tax rules.[3]

Servicers are encouraged to use the authority that they have under the governing securitization documents to take appropriate steps when an increased risk of default is identified, including:

- proactively identifying borrowers at heightened risk of delinquency or default, such as those with impending interest rate resets;
- contacting borrowers to assess their ability to repay;
- assessing whether there is a reasonable basis to conclude that default is "reasonably foreseeable"; and
- exploring, where appropriate, a loss mitigation strategy that avoids foreclosure or other actions that result in a loss of homeownership.

Loss mitigation techniques that preserve homeownership are generally less costly than foreclosure, particularly when applied before default. Prudent loss mitigation strategies may include loan modifications; deferral of payments; extension of loan maturities; conversion of adjustable-rate mortgages into fixed-rate or fully indexed, fully amortizing adjustable-rate mortgages; capitalization of delinquent amounts; or any combination of these. As one example, servicers have been converting hybrid adjustable-rate mortgages into fixed-rate loans. Where appropriate, servicers are encouraged to apply loss mitigation techniques that result in mortgage obligations that the borrower can meet in a sustained manner over the long term.

In evaluating loss mitigation techniques, servicers should consider the borrower's ability to repay the modified obligation to final maturity according to its terms, taking into account the borrower's total monthly housing-related payments (including principal, interest, taxes, and insurance, commonly referred to as "PITI") as a percentage of the borrower's gross monthly income (referred to as the debt-to-income or "DTI" ratio). Attention should also be given to the borrower's other obligations and resources, as well as additional factors that could affect the borrower's capacity and propensity to repay. Servicers have indicated that a borrower with a high DTI ratio is more likely to encounter difficulties in meeting mortgage obligations.

Some loan modifications or other strategies, such as a reduction or forgiveness of principal, may result in additional tax liabilities for the borrower that should be included in any assessment of the borrower's ability to meet future obligations.

When appropriate, servicers are encouraged to refer borrowers to qualified non-profit and other homeownership counseling services and/or to government programs, such as those administered by the Federal Housing Administration, which may be able to work with all parties to avoid unnecessary foreclosures. When considering and implementing loss mitigation strategies, servicers are expected to treat consumers fairly and to adhere to all applicable legal requirements.

basis to conclude that the borrower will be unable to continue to make mortgage payments in the foreseeable future. See the attachment to the July 24, 2007, letter from SEC Chairman Cox to Chairman Frank, House Committee on Financial Services.

3 *See* 26 CFR 1.860G-2(b)(3)(i).

B.2 FDIC Loan Modification Program

The FDIC developed its loan modification program in an attempt to streamline and standardize the mortgage industry's approach to modifying mortgages. The model is based on the loan modification program the agency developed when it took over Indy Mac Federal Bank. To assist lenders and servicers in adopting the program, the FDIC published a guide describing the program, and a set of standard documents and marketing materials, including a sample loan modification agreement. Excerpts from the FDIC loan modification guide are reprinted below. The complete guide can be found on this treatise's companion website.

The FDIC has also developed a calculator to conduct the net present value (NPV) analysis. The calculator is available on this treatise's companion website as well as the FDIC's website at www.fdic.gov/consumers/loans/loanmod/NPV.xls.

Program

II. Program

Key objectives

- Systematic determination of borrower specific modification terms using a standardized NPV test to minimize losses on distressed mortgages.
- Target distressed borrowers. Modifications may be available for loans that are at least 60 days delinquent or where default is reasonably foreseeable.[1]
- Implement modification program that can be used across a broad range of investors.

Step 1: Determine Eligibility

Servicers typically manage loans for other investors, including Government Sponsored Enterprises (GSEs), private investors owning securities collateralized by the mortgages, and whole loan investors. Each investor type has different standards for approving loan modification. The GSEs have authorized loss mitigation programs for seriously delinquent loans, however some loans owned by the GSEs may be modified based on eligibility standards similar to those used for private investors. The GSEs recently announced the adoption of more streamlined modification plans that apply many of the features of the FDIC Loan Modification Program model.

Loans serviced for private investors are governed by servicing contracts which often contain a standard clause allowing the servicer to modify seriously delinquent or defaulted mortgages, or mortgages where default is "reasonably foreseeable".[2] This even holds true for complex private label securitizations with many tranches and investors.

Loans subject to these contracts are typically eligible for modification given:

- The loan is at least 60 days delinquent where the loan is considered one day delinquent on the day following the next payment due date.
- Foreclosure sale is not imminent and the borrower is currently not in bankruptcy, or has not been discharged from Chapter 7 bankruptcy since the loan was originated.
- The loan was not originated as a second home or an investment property.

Loans sold whole to individual investors often require a case-by-case approach. These loans are subject to both servicing and securitization contracts. The Appendix contains guidelines on how to evaluate whole loan servicing agreements.

[1] Due to contractual restrictions in IndyMac's pooling and servicing agreements, IndyMac Federal Bank has not modified securitized loans where default is reasonably foreseeable. Most other agreements do allow modification of such loans.

[2] See the *American Securitization Forum's Streamlined Foreclosure and Loss Avoidance Framework for Securitized Mortgage Loans*, Issued Dec. 6, 2007 and revised July 8, 2008.

Program (Continued)

FDIC

Step 2: Calculate an "Affordable" Payment

In order to calculate an affordable payment, recent financial income information must be available for the borrower. Efforts to contact the borrower via special mailings, calling campaigns, email, and other outreach methods are used.

The FDIC Loan Modification Program calculates the modified principal, interest, taxes, and insurance (PITI) payment per a borrower specific HTI ratio of no more than 38 percent. Housing expenses on a PITI basis may include:

- The modified principal and interest payment for the subject loan, as applicable,
- Real estate taxes,
- Property hazard, flood, and mortgage insurance premiums,
- Leasehold estate payments, and
- Homeowners' association (HOA) dues.

Industry standards set forth by certain FHA lending programs indicate a mortgage payment based on a 31 percent to 38 percent HTI ratio is affordable. The FDIC Loan Modification Program follows these origination standards as illustrated below.

Example of HTI ratio calculation

Monthly Gross Income
$3,618 - Borrower 1
$2,756 - Borrower 2
$6,374 - Total Monthly Gross Income

PITI Payment Determination
$6,374 x **38%** = $2,422

Monthly Housing Expense
$2,422 - Maximum Total Monthly Housing Expense
$ - 364 - Taxes, hazard, flood, and mortgage insurance, etc.
$ - 85 - HOA dues
$1,973 - Maximum modified principal and interest payment

Total HTI Ratio
$2,422 / $6,374 = **38%**

Program (Continued)

FDIC

If the initial modification calculation at 38 percent does not decrease the borrower's payment by 10 percent or more, the HTI ratio is lowered to 35 percent and then lowered to 31 percent to achieve the 10 percent savings. In cases where a 10 percent reduction can not be achieved, the 31 percent HTI ratio is used for affordability.

Step 3: Determine the "Total Debt" by capitalizing certain costs in the unpaid principal balance

- Delinquent interest, taxes, and insurance escrows and
- Third party fees such as foreclosure attorney or trustee fees and property preservation costs.

Step 4: Solve for "Affordable Payment" through a three step waterfall process

1) **Interest Rate Reduction**: Cap the life-of-loan interest rate at the Freddie Mac Weekly Survey rate as of the week of the modification offer, then reduce the interest rate incrementally to as low as 3 percent to achieve the "affordable" payment per the adjusted unpaid principal balance (UPB) and remaining amortization term. An interest rate floor of 3 percent will enable the borrower to maintain approximately a 38 percent HTI ratio throughout the life of the loan, assuming modest borrower earnings growth commensurate with the inflation rate. The reduced rate remains in effect for 5 years. After this period, the interest rate increases by not more than one percent annually until the Freddie Mac Weekly Survey rate is achieved. If the "affordable" modified PITI payment amount has not been achieved, proceed to the next step.

2) **Extend Amortization Term**: For loans with an original term of 30 years, re-amortize the adjusted UPB at the reduced interest rate (3 percent floor) over an extended amortization term of 40 years from the original first payment date. For securitized loans, the amortization will be extended to 40 years from the original first payment date, but the maturity date will not change, resulting in a balloon payment. For loans with an original term of less than 30 years, extend the amortization period for only 10 years. If the modified PITI payment amount has not been achieved, proceed to the next step.

3) **Partial Principal Forbearance**: Reduce the adjusted UPB for amortization purposes and amortize over a 40 year period at the reduced interest rate (3 percent floor). This process splits the debt into an interest-bearing, amortizing portion and a zero percent, zero payment portion of the loan. The repayment of the "postponed" principal will be due when the loan is paid in full. For loans within securitizations, this principal forbearance should be passed as a write-off of principal to the trust, with any future collections at time of pay-off submitted to the trust as a recovery.

Program (Continued)

FDIC

Step 5: Apply the NPV Tool

Run the modified loans through the NPV Tool in order to ensure that the modified payment creates a positive economic scenario for the investor.

Step 6: Market via systematic "bulk" approach

A bulk modification model processes large segments of delinquent loans with recent borrower financial information on file. The model performs automated loan-level underwriting based on the existing loan terms and recent financial information obtained from the customer, which is verified prior to completing the modification. The bulk modification process establishes modification eligibility and modification terms as detailed in the previous steps, then uses a traditional marketing approach to provide the borrower with an easy to follow, pre-populated modification offer. The marketing materials also instruct the borrower to either contact the servicer with questions or just send in the signed documents and the first payment to complete the modification offer. The modification offer explicitly states the amount of the borrower's new monthly principal and interest payment as follows:

Reduce your monthly payment of principal and interest to $x,xxx.xx and bring your loan current!

While some borrowers may appear to have the capacity to pay, their ability to do so may be inhibited by other debt obligations. Bankers and servicers should consider establishing relationships with community groups willing to contact and provide credit counseling to these borrowers. Entering into compensation agreements with local non-profit organizations with HUD-approved counselors also may assist in contacting borrowers, obtaining the requisite financial information, and completing the modification. Compensation should be based on a borrower contact and modification completion. For example, IndyMac Federal Bank pays participating community groups $150 for borrower contact and counseling services, and an additional $350 once the loan modification is completed. A copy of a counseling compensation agreement is provided in the Appendix.

NPV Test

FDIC

NPV Test

Once the modification terms are established, the impact of the modification concessions to the investor are compared to the estimated loss given foreclosure. If the modification is less costly than foreclosure, it is approved. This test ensures that modifications mitigate the loss for investors. This diagram illustrates the NPV test:

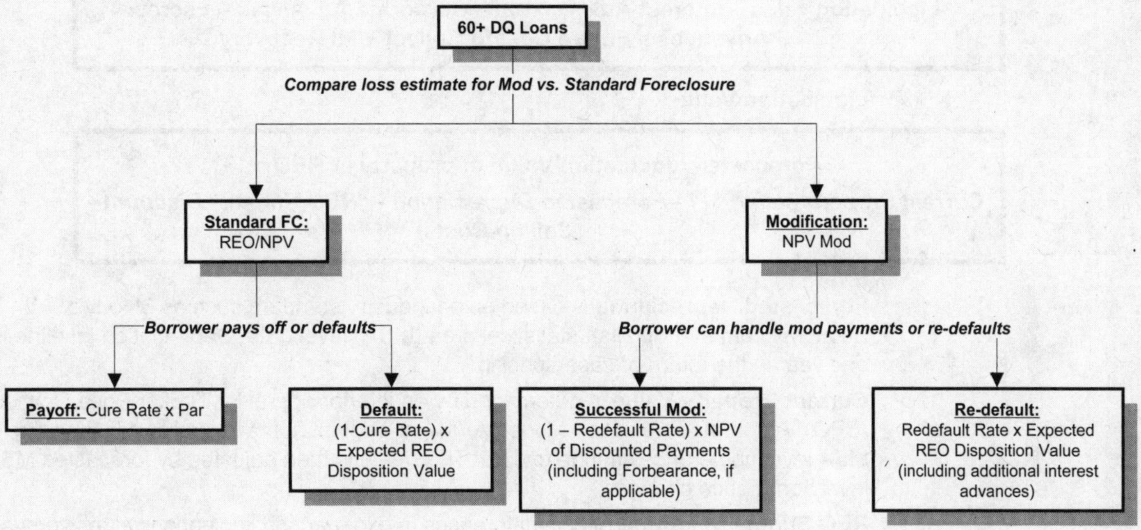

NPV Test

FDIC

➢ **The formula used to estimate the cost of foreclosure is:**

Loan Value = Cure Rate * Par + (1 – Cure Rate) * Expected REO Disposition Value

Description of the formula terms:

➢ **Cure rate** is based on recent industry or servicer data. It is based on a combination of delinquency status, combined loan-to-value (LTV), FICO and original income documentation. A 12 month cure period is used.

➢ **Expected REO Disposition Value**:

Liquidation value – Interest Adv/Accrual – Corporate Advances – Escrow Advances – Future Cost to Collect + MI Recovery

➢ **Liquidation Value:**

Forecasted Liquidation Value of property at REO = ***Current Property Value * (1 - Forecasted Depreciation - "REO Stigma" Discount – Selling Costs)***

➢ **Forecasted Depreciation** is based on an industry standard such as Moody's Economy.com metropolitan statistical area (MSA) level data. Depreciation timeline is one year in the future or case-specific.

➢ **Current Property Value** is determined by an interior appraisal, Broker Price Opinion (BPO), Automated Valuation Model (AVM), or original appraisal value adjusted by MSA level home price change to date. This value is then adjusted by forecasted MSA level home price changes.

➢ **REO Stigma Discount** reflects differences in experienced liquidation values versus estimated property values.

➢ **Selling Costs** include 10 percent for broker commission, potential repairs and maintenance costs.

➢ **Interest Advances/Accruals** includes delinquent interest advanced (securitized/sold loans) or accrued (owned loans).

➢ **Corporate Advances** include non-escrow advances already made on the borrowers behalf.

➢ **Escrow Advances** already made on the borrowers behalf.

➢ **Future Cost to Collect** is an estimate of future interest accruals, T&I payments, and FC expenses.

➢ **MI Recovery (if applicable)** is estimated based on MI coverage percentage adjusted for possible MI claim denial.

NPV Test (Continued)

FDIC

- **The formula used to estimate the cost of modification is:**

> **Loan Value = (1 – Redefault Rate) x NPV of Discounted Payments + Redefault Rate x (REO Disposition Value + Additional Accrued Costs)**

Description of the formula terms:

- **Re-default rate** is estimated per historical re-default experience for other modification programs and a program specific projection.
- **NPV of discounted payments** is the net present value of the adjusted UPB (cash outflow) and the modified payment stream (cash inflow) discounted at the Freddie Mac Weekly Survey rate as of the week of the modification offer. An NPV example is provided in the Appendix.
- **REO disposition value** (see above).
- **Additional costs** include 9 additional months of accrued interest, taxes, and insurance payments plus additional forecasted home price depreciation, as applicable.[3]

[3] Currently, the Case-Shiller forecast provided by Moody's Economy.com projects that home prices will reach their trough in about one year from today, which also is equivalent to the base case timetable for REO disposition in the NPV Tool. This means that delaying foreclosure will not lead to further home price declines at REO disposition for most geographical areas.

NPV Test (Continued)

FDIC

In Addition to Updated Liquidation Value, a Servicer must Formally Backtest Servicer and/or Portfolio Specific Assumptions and Regularly Update Assumptions Based on Industry Standards

1. **Forecasted Depreciation** (industry standard)
   - Updated monthly to incorporate latest home price data.
2. **Cure Rates** (servicer and/or portfolio specific)
   - Updated quarterly and based on 12 month history (to adjust for current credit environment). Suggested cure factors include the current delinquency status of the loan, combined LTV, borrower FICO, and original income documentation.
3. **REO Stigma** (servicer and/or portfolio specific)
   - Updated monthly to incorporate latest experience by region.
4. **Re-default Rate** (servicer and/or portfolio specific)
   - Based on past re-default experience for other modification programs and a program specific projection. The servicer should carefully monitor and incorporate the program's actual re-default rate.
5. **Discount Rate** (both industry standard and servicer and/or portfolio specific)
   - Freddie Mac Weekly Survey rate as of the week of the modification offer is used to discount the modified payment cashflow. A required return methodology is used to discount the estimated foreclosure value.
6. **Prepayment rate** (servicer and/or portfolio specific)
   - The model assumes a voluntary prepayment rate of zero.

Process

FDIC

III. Process

Key Objectives

- Leverage large scale modification offer/delivery process.
- Give collections and loss mitigation staff the ability to offer tailored solutions based on borrower need, willingness and ability to pay, balanced with investor guidelines and a formal NPV test.
- Streamline paperwork and income verification process.
- Establish a protocol for community group referrals.

Once eligibility is established, the loan modification offer is based on the borrowers income information. For borrowers with recent income information on file, a firm offer may be extended, contingent on income verification. However, verified income may be different from that on file and tolerance for some variation should be established. For borrowers with no recent income information on file, a conditional offer may be extended, contingent on income verification. This type of offer should use a more rigorous verification process requiring both tax returns and recent pay stub information.

For both firm and conditional modification offers, the key to program success is a scalable offer delivery process, which immediately provides the borrower with modification terms and instructions.

Process (Continued)

Offer/Delivery process – Two-Tiered Approach:

1. **Bulk Approach**: Loans processed through the bulk modification process are sent a pre-approved offer with pre-populated modification documents, income verification forms and informational material. This modification package provides the borrower with a custom modification offer and instructions to complete the modification with a quick one-touch close. Modification paperwork is handled via an automated process. The modification agreement is pre-populated and the loans are pre-qualified; as a result, the operations process is simplified to collecting the modification agreements, verifying income documentation, and completing system updates to ensure the borrower receives modified terms on the next statement.

2. **Point of Sale Approach**: Use of traditional inbound and outbound customer service and collection staff should allow borrowers to obtain fast and customized solutions. Loss mitigation staff require access to a modification tool which allows the collector to discuss all viable workout options before proceeding with an offer. For example, a delinquent borrower calls collections and is unable to afford the current mortgage payment. The collector enters the borrower's information into a desktop tool which immediately provides the collector with possible workout solutions such as modification, short sale, and cash for keys programs. If the modification is NPV positive, the collector informs the borrower of modification eligibility, collects the first modified payment, updates the system, and either generates the modification documents from the system, or includes borrower in the next bulk mailing.

   One of the Benefits: Saying "Yes" to the borrower and providing the reduced modified payment amount motivates the borrower to finish submitting the final documentation needed to complete the modification. Once the borrower verbally accepts the modified payment, the collector initiates a 60-day payment plan at the new amount and takes the paperwork off the foreclosure path. When the documents are received and income is verified, modification changes are processed permanently in the system.

   Community group referrals should be prioritized through a dedicated hotline and email address. Groups with a relationship with the servicer should be trained on the specific information required to complete the modification. This provides another venue to streamline the paperwork processing.

Process (Continued)

FDIC

Income Verification

Income verification minimizes re-default and ensures the affordability standard is uniformly implemented. The gross monthly income for all borrowers who have signed the mortgage note must be supported by either last years tax returns or recent pay stubs. A dedicated underwriting group reconciles verbal financial information on file to documented income.

B.3 Making Home Affordable Modification Program

B.3.1 Overview

The Home Affordable Modification Program (HAMP) was developed as part of the Making Home Affordable Modification Program by the U.S. Department of Treasury to help homeowners who are in default or at risk of defaulting on their mortgage with lowering their monthly payment to an affordable level. The program also aims to standardize the mortgage industry's practice regarding loan modifications. To achieve that goal, Treasury published program guidelines and model forms for lenders and servicers to adopt. Detailed guidelines and a list of participating servicers and lenders are available on Treasury's website at www.financialstability.gov and on the program's administrative website for servicers at www.hmpadmin.com. The most detailed program guidelines are contained in the Supplemental Directives and FAQs. These documents are available on the servicer's administrative website. Major changes in the program are outlined in these documents and advocates are advised check the administrative website frequently to ensure that they have the most up-to-date program guidelines.

B.3.2 Supplemental Directive 09-01: Introduction of the Home Affordable Modification Guidelines

Supplemental Directive 09-01 **April 6, 2009**

Introduction of the Home Affordable Modification Program

Background

On February 18, 2009, President Obama announced the Homeowner Affordability and Stability Plan to help up to 7 to 9 million families restructure or refinance their mortgages to avoid foreclosure. As part of this plan, the Treasury Department (Treasury) announced a national modification program aimed at helping 3 to 4 million at-risk homeowners—both those who are in default and those who are at imminent risk of default—by reducing monthly payments to sustainable levels. On March 4, 2009, the Treasury issued uniform guidance for loan modifications across the mortgage industry. This Supplemental Directive provides additional guidance to servicers for adoption and implementation of the Home Affordable Modification program (HAMP) for mortgage loans that are not owned or guaranteed by Fannie Mae or Freddie Mac (Non-GSE Mortgages).

Under the HAMP, a servicer will use a uniform loan modification process to provide a borrower with sustainable monthly payments. The guidelines set forth in this document apply to all eligible mortgage loans secured by one- to four-unit owner-occupied single-family properties.

In order for a servicer to participate in the HAMP with respect to Non-GSE Mortgages, the servicer must execute a servicer participation agreement and related documents (Servicer Participation Agreement) with Fannie Mae in its capacity as financial agent for the United States (as designated by Treasury) on or before December 31, 2009. The Servicer Participation Agreement will govern servicer participation in the HAMP program for all Non-GSE Mortgages. Servicers of mortgage loans that are owned or guaranteed by Fannie Mae or Freddie Mac should refer to the HAMP announcement issued by the applicable GSE.

The HAMP reflects usual and customary industry standards for mortgage loan modifications contained in typical servicing agreements, including pooling and servicing agreements (PSAs) governing private label securitizations. As detailed in the Servicer Participation Agreement, participating servicers are required to consider <u>all</u> eligible mortgage loans unless prohibited by the rules of the applicable PSA and/or other investor servicing agreements. Participating servicers are required to use reasonable efforts to remove any prohibitions and obtain waivers or approvals from all necessary parties in order to carry out any modification under the HAMP.

To help servicers implement the HAMP, this Supplemental Directive covers the following topics:

- HAMP Eligibility
- Underwriting
- Modification Process
- Reporting Requirements
- Fees and Compensation
- Compliance

<u>HAMP Eligibility</u>

A Non-GSE Mortgage is eligible for the HAMP if the servicer verifies that all of the following criteria are met:

- The mortgage loan is a first lien mortgage loan originated on or before January 1, 2009.
- The mortgage loan has not been previously modified under the HAMP.
- The mortgage loan is delinquent or default is reasonably foreseeable; loans currently in foreclosure are eligible.
- The mortgage loan is secured by a one- to four-unit property, one unit of which is the borrower's principal residence. Cooperative share mortgages and mortgage loans secured by condominium units are eligible for the HAMP. Loans secured by manufactured housing units are eligible for the HAMP.

- The property securing the mortgage loan must not be vacant or condemned.
- The borrower documents a financial hardship and represents that (s)he does not have sufficient liquid assets to make the monthly mortgage payments by completing a Home Affordable Modification Program Hardship Affidavit and provides the required income documentation. The documentation supporting income may not be more than 90 days old (as of the date the servicer is determining HAMP eligibility).
- The borrower has a monthly mortgage payment ratio of greater than 31 percent.
- A borrower in active litigation regarding the mortgage loan is eligible for the HAMP.
- The servicer may not require a borrower to waive legal rights as a condition of the HAMP.
- A borrower actively involved in a bankruptcy proceeding is eligible for the HAMP at the servicer's discretion. Borrowers who have received a Chapter 7 bankruptcy discharge in a case involving the first lien mortgage who did not reaffirm the mortgage debt under applicable law are eligible, provided the Home Affordable Modification Trial Period Plan and Home Affordable Modification Agreement are revised as outlined in the *Acceptable Revisions to HAMP Documents* section of this Supplemental Directive.
- The borrower agrees to set up an escrow account for taxes and hazard and flood insurance prior to the beginning of the trial period if one does not currently exist.
- Borrowers may be accepted into the program if a fully executed Home Affordable Modification Trial Period Plan is in the servicer's possession on December 31, 2012.
- The current unpaid principal balance (UPB) of the mortgage loan prior to capitalization must be no greater than:

  o 1 Unit: $729,750
  o 2 Units: $934,200
  o 3 Units: $1,129,250
  o 4 Units: $1,403,400

Note: Mortgage loans insured, guaranteed or held by a federal government agency (e.g., FHA, HUD, VA and Rural Development) may be eligible for the HAMP, subject to guidance issued by the relevant agency. Further details regarding inclusion of these loans in the HAMP will be provided in a subsequent Supplemental Directive.

The HAMP documents are available through www.financialstability.gov. Documents include the Home Affordable Modification Trial Period Plan (hereinafter referred to as Trial Period Plan), the Home Affordable Modification Agreement (hereinafter referred to as the Agreement), the Home Affordable Modification Program Hardship Affidavit (hereinafter referred to as the Hardship Affidavit) and various cover letters.

Underwriting

Hardship Affidavit

Every borrower and co-borrower seeking a modification, whether in default or not, must sign a Hardship Affidavit that attests to and describes one or more of the following types of hardship:

1. A reduction in or loss of income that was supporting the mortgage.
2. A change in household financial circumstances.
3. A recent or upcoming increase in the monthly mortgage payment.
4. An increase in other expenses.
5. A lack of sufficient cash reserves to maintain payment on the mortgage and cover basic living expenses at the same time. Cash reserves include assets such as cash, savings, money market funds, marketable stocks or bonds (excluding retirement accounts and assets that serve as emergency fund—generally equal to three times the borrower's monthly debt payments).
6. Excessive monthly debt payments and overextension with creditors, e.g., the borrower was required to use credit cards, a home equity loan, or other credit to make the mortgage payment.
7. Other reasons for hardship detailed by the borrower.

Note: The borrower is not required to have the Hardship Affidavit notarized.

Reasonably Foreseeable (Imminent) Default

A borrower that is current or less than 60 days delinquent who contacts the servicer for a modification, appears potentially eligible for a modification, and claims a hardship must be screened for imminent default. The servicer must make a determination as to whether a payment default is imminent based on the servicer's standards for imminent default and consistent with applicable contractual agreements and accounting standards. If the servicer determines that default is imminent, the servicer must apply the Net Present Value test.

In the process of making its imminent default determination, the servicer must evaluate the borrower's financial condition in light of the borrower's hardship as well as inquire as to the condition of and circumstances affecting the property securing the mortgage loan. The servicer must consider the borrower's financial condition, liquid assets, liabilities, combined monthly income from wages and all other identified sources of income, monthly obligations (including personal debts, revolving accounts, and installment loans), and a reasonable allowance for living expenses such as food, utilities, etc. The hardship and financial condition of the borrower shall be verified through documentation.

Documenting the Reason for and Timing of Imminent Default

A servicer must document in its servicing system the basis for its determination that a payment default is imminent and retain all documentation used to reach its conclusion. The servicer's documentation must also include information on the borrower's financial condition as well as the condition and circumstances of the property securing the mortgage loan.

Net Present Value (NPV) Test

All loans that meet the HAMP eligibility criteria and are either deemed to be in imminent default (as described above) or 60 or more days delinquent must be evaluated using a standardized NPV test that compares the NPV result for a modification to the NPV result for no modification. If the NPV result for the modification scenario is greater than the NPV result for no modification, the result is deemed "positive" and the servicer MUST offer the modification. If the NPV result for no modification is greater than NPV result for the modification scenario, the modification result is deemed "negative" and the servicer has the option of performing the modification in its discretion. For mortgages serviced on behalf of a third party investor for which the modification result is deemed "negative," however, the servicer may not perform the modification without express permission of the investor. If a modification is not pursued when the NPV result is "negative," the servicer must consider the borrower for other foreclosure prevention options, including alternative modification programs, deeds-in-lieu, and preforeclosure sale programs.

Whether or not a modification is pursued, the servicer MUST maintain detailed documentation of the NPV model used, all NPV inputs and assumptions and the NPV results.

Fannie Mae has developed a software application for servicers to submit loan files to the NPV calculator. The software application is available on the Home Affordable Modification servicer web portal accessible through www.financialstability.gov. On this portal, servicers will have access to the NPV calculator tool as well as detailed guidelines for submitting proposed modification data.

Servicers having at least a $40 billion servicing book will have the option to create a version of the NPV calculator that uses a set of cure rates and redefault rates estimated based on the experience of their own portfolios, taking into consideration, if feasible, current LTV, current monthly mortgage payment, current credit score, delinquency status and other loan or borrower attributes. Detailed guidance on required inputs for custom NPV calculations is forthcoming.

For mortgages serviced on behalf of a third party investor, the servicer must use a discount rate at least as high as the rate used on the servicer's own portfolio, but in no event higher than the maximum rate permitted under the HAMP.

To obtain a property valuation input for the NPV calculator, servicers may use either an automated valuation model (AVM), provided that the AVM renders a reliable confidence score, or a broker's price opinion (BPO). A servicer may use an AVM provided by one of the GSEs. As an alternative, servicers may rely on their internal AVM provided that:

(i) the servicer is subject to supervision by a Federal regulatory agency;
(ii) the servicer's primary Federal regulatory agency has reviewed the model; and
(iii) the AVM renders a reliable confidence score.

If a GSE AVM or the servicer AVM is unable to render a value with a reliable confidence score, the servicer must obtain an assessment of the property value utilizing a BPO or a property valuation method acceptable to the servicer's Federal regulatory supervisor. Such assessment must be rendered in accordance with the Interagency Appraisal and Evaluation Guidelines (as if such guidelines apply to loan modifications). In all cases, the property valuation used cannot be more than 90 days old.

Verifying Borrower Income and Occupancy Status

Servicers may use recent verbal financial information obtained from the borrower and any co-borrower 90 days or less from the date the servicer is determining HAMP eligibility to assess the borrower's eligibility. The servicer may rely on this information to prepare and send to the borrower a solicitation for the HAMP and an offer of a Trial Period Plan. When the borrower returns the Trial Period Plan and related documents, the servicer must review them to verify the borrower's financial information and eligibility—except that documentation of income may not be more than 90 days old as of the determination of eligibility.

As an alternative, a servicer may require a borrower to submit the required documentation to verify the borrower's eligibility and income prior to preparing a Trial Period Plan. Upon receipt of the documentation and determination of the borrower's eligibility, a servicer may prepare and send to the borrower a letter indicating that the borrower is eligible for the HAMP together with a Trial Period Plan.

The borrower will only qualify for the HAMP if the verified income documentation confirms that the monthly mortgage payment ratio prior to the modification is greater than 31 percent. The "monthly mortgage payment ratio" is the ratio of the borrower's current monthly mortgage payment to the borrower's monthly gross income (or the borrowers' combined monthly gross income in the case of co-borrowers). The "monthly mortgage payment" includes the monthly payment of principal, interest, property taxes, hazard insurance, flood insurance, condominium association fees and homeowner's association fees, as applicable (including any escrow payment shortage amounts subject to a repayment plan). When determining a borrower's monthly mortgage payment ratio, servicers must adjust the borrower's current mortgage payment to include, as applicable, property taxes, hazard insurance, flood insurance, condominium association fees and homeowner's association fees if these expenses are not already included in the borrower's payment. The monthly mortgage payment does not include mortgage insurance premium payments or payments due to holders of subordinate liens.

With respect to adjustable rate loans where there is a rate reset scheduled within 120 days after the date of the evaluation (a "Reset ARM"), the monthly mortgage payment used to determine eligibility will be the greater of (i) the borrower's current scheduled monthly mortgage payment or (ii) a fully amortizing monthly mortgage payment based on the note reset rate using the index value as of the date of the evaluation (the "Reset Interest Rate"). With respect to adjustable rate loans that reset more than 120 days after the date of the evaluation, the borrower's current scheduled monthly mortgage payment will be used to determine eligibility.

The borrower's "monthly gross income" is the borrower's income amount before any payroll deductions and includes wages and salaries, overtime pay, commissions, fees, tips, bonuses, housing allowances, other compensation for personal services, Social Security payments, including Social Security received by adults on behalf of minors or by minors intended for their own support, and monthly income from annuities, insurance policies, retirement funds, pensions, disability or death benefits, unemployment benefits, rental income and other income. If only net income is available, the servicer must multiply the net income amount by 1.25 to estimate the monthly gross income.

Servicers should include non-borrower household income in monthly gross income if it is voluntarily provided by the borrower and if there is documentary evidence that the income has been, and reasonably can continue to be, relied upon to support the mortgage payment. All non-borrower household income included in monthly gross income must be documented and verified by the servicer using the same standards for verifying a borrower's income.

The servicer may not require a borrower to make an up-front cash contribution (other than the first trial period payment) for the borrower to be considered for the HAMP. The HAMP documents instruct the borrower (the term "borrower" includes any co-borrower) to provide the following financial information to the servicer:

If the borrower is employed:

- A signed copy of the most recently filed federal income tax return, including all schedules and forms, if available,
- A signed IRS Form 4506-T (Request for Transcript of Tax Return), and
- Copies of the two most recent paystubs indicating year-to-date earnings.
- For additional income such as bonuses, commissions, fees, housing allowances, tips and overtime, a servicer must obtain a letter from the employer or other reliable third-party documentation indicating that the income will in all probability continue.

If the borrower is self-employed:

- A signed copy of the most recent federal income tax return, including all schedules and forms, if available,
- A signed IRS Form 4506-T (Request for Transcript of Tax Return), and
- The most recent quarterly or year-to-date profit and loss statement for each self-employed borrower.
- Other reliable third-party documentation the borrower voluntarily provides.

Note: For both a salaried or a self-employed borrower, if the borrower does not provide a signed copy of the most recently filed federal income tax return, or if the Compliance Agent so requires, the servicer must submit the Form 4506-T to the IRS to request a transcript of the return.

If the borrower elects to use alimony or child support income to qualify, acceptable documentation includes:

- Photocopies of the divorce decree, separation agreement, or other type of legal written agreement or court decree that provides for the payment of alimony or child support and states the amount of the award and the period of time over which it will be received. Servicers must determine that the income will continue for at least three years.
- Documents supplying reasonably reliable evidence of full, regular and timely payments, such as deposit slips, bank statements or signed federal income tax returns.

If the borrower has other income such as social security, disability or death benefits, or a pension:

- Acceptable documentation includes letters, exhibits, a disability policy or benefits statement from the provider that states the amount, frequency, and duration of the benefit. The servicer must determine that the income will continue for at least three years.
- The servicer must obtain copies of signed federal income tax returns, IRS W-2 forms, or copies of the two most recent bank statements.

If the borrower receives public assistance or collects unemployment:

- Acceptable documentation includes letters, exhibits or a benefits statement from the provider that states the amount, frequency, and duration of the benefit. The servicer must determine that the income will continue for at least nine months.

If the borrower has rental income, acceptable documentation includes:

- Copies of all pages from the borrower's most recent two years of signed federal income tax returns and Schedule E—Supplemental Income and Loss. The monthly net rental income to be calculated for HAMP purposes equals 75 percent of the gross rent, with the remaining 25 percent considered vacancy loss and maintenance expense.

A servicer must confirm that the property securing the mortgage loan is the borrower's primary residence as evidenced by the most recent signed federal income tax return (or transcript of tax return obtained from the IRS), a credit report and one other form of documentation that would supply reasonable evidence that the property is the borrower's primary residence (such as utility bills in the borrower's name).

A servicer is not required to modify a mortgage loan if there is reasonable evidence indicating the borrower submitted false or misleading information or otherwise engaged in fraud in connection with the modification.

Standard Modification Waterfall

Servicers are required to consider a borrower for a refinance through the Hope for Homeowners program when feasible. Consideration for a Hope for Homeowners refinance should not delay eligible borrowers from receiving a modification offer and beginning the trial period. Servicers must use the modification options listed below to begin the HAMP modification and work to complete the Hope for Homeowners refinance during the trial period.

Servicers must apply the modification steps enumerated below in the stated order of succession until the borrower's monthly mortgage payment ratio is reduced as close as possible to 31 percent, without going below 31 percent (the "target monthly mortgage payment ratio"). If the applicable PSA or other investor servicing agreement prohibits the servicer from taking a modification step, the servicer may seek approval for an exception.

Servicers are not precluded under the HAMP from agreeing to a modification that reduces the borrower's monthly mortgage payment ratio below 31% as long as the modification otherwise complies with the HAMP requirements. Similarly and where otherwise permitted by the applicable PSA or other investor servicing contract, servicers are not precluded under the HAMP from agreeing to a modification where the interest rate does not step up after five years, or where additional principal forbearance is substituted for extending the term as needed to achieve the target monthly mortgage payment ratio of 31%, so long as the modification otherwise complies with HAMP requirements. However, borrower, servicer and investor incentive payments for these modifications will be paid based on modification terms that reflect the target monthly mortgage payment ratio and standard modification terms.

Note: If a borrower has an adjustable-rate mortgage (ARM) or interest-only mortgage, the existing interest rate will convert to a fixed interest rate, fully amortizing loan.

Step 1: Capitalize accrued interest, out-of-pocket escrow advances to third parties, and any required escrow advances that will be paid to third parties by the servicer during the trial period and servicing advances (costs and expenses incurred in performing its servicing obligation, such as those related to preservation and protection of the security property and the enforcement of the mortgage) paid to third parties in the ordinary course of business and not retained by the servicer, if allowed by state law. The servicer should capitalize only those third party delinquency fees that are reasonable and necessary. Fees permitted by Fannie Mae and Freddie Mac for GSE loans shall be considered evidence of fees that would be reasonable for non-GSE loans. Late fees may not be capitalized and must be waived if the borrower satisfies all conditions of the Trial Period Plan.

Step 2: Reduce the interest rate. If the loan is a fixed rate mortgage or an adjustable-rate mortgage, then the starting interest rate is the current interest rate. If the loan is a Reset ARM, the starting interest rate is the Reset Interest Rate.

Reduce the starting interest rate in increments of .125 percent to get as close as possible to the target monthly mortgage payment ratio. The interest rate floor in all cases is 2.0 percent.

- If the resulting rate is below the Interest Rate Cap, this reduced rate will be in effect for the first five years followed by annual increases of one percent per year (or such lesser amount as may be needed) until the interest rate reaches the Interest Rate Cap, at which time it will be fixed for the remaining loan term.
- If the resulting rate exceeds the Interest Rate Cap, then that rate is the permanent rate.

The "Interest Rate Cap" is the Freddie Mac Weekly Primary Mortgage Market Survey (PMMS) Rate for 30-year fixed rate conforming loans, rounded to the nearest 0.125 percent, as of the date that the Agreement is prepared.

Step 3: If necessary, extend the term and reamortize the mortgage loan by up to 480 months from the modification effective date (i.e., the first day of the month following the end of the trial period) to achieve the target monthly mortgage payment ratio. If a term extension is not permitted under the applicable PSA or other investor servicing agreement, reamortize the mortgage loan based upon an amortization schedule of up to 480 months with a balloon payment due at maturity. Negative amortization after the effective date of the modification is prohibited.

Step 4: If necessary, the servicer must provide for principal forbearance to achieve the target monthly mortgage payment ratio. The principal forbearance amount is non-interest bearing and non-amortizing. The amount of principal forbearance will result in a balloon payment fully due and payable upon the earliest of the borrower's transfer of the property, payoff of the interest bearing unpaid principal balance, or maturity of the mortgage loan. The modified interest bearing balance (i.e., the unpaid principal balance excluding the deferred principal balloon amount) must create a current mark-to-market LTV (current LTV based upon the new valuation) greater than or equal to 100 percent if the result of the NPV test is negative and the servicer elects to perform the modification.

There is no requirement to forgive principal under the HAMP. However, servicers may forgive principal to achieve the target monthly mortgage payment ratio on a standalone basis or before any step in the standard waterfall process set forth above. If principal is forgiven, subsequent steps in the standard waterfall may not be skipped. If principal is forgiven and the interest rate is not reduced, the existing rate will be fixed and treated as the modified rate for the purposes of the Interest Rate Cap.

Verifying Monthly Gross Expenses

A servicer must obtain a credit report for each borrower or a joint report for a married couple who are co-borrowers to validate installment debt and other liens. In addition, a servicer must consider information concerning monthly obligations obtained from the borrower either orally or in writing. The "monthly gross expenses" equal the sum of the following monthly charges:

- The monthly mortgage payment, taxes, property insurance, homeowner's or condominium association fee payments and assessments related to the property whether or not they are included in the mortgage payment.
- Any mortgage insurance premiums.
- Monthly payments on all closed-end subordinate mortgages.
- Payments on all installment debts with more than ten months of payments remaining, including debts that are in a period of either deferment or forbearance. When payments on an installment debt are not on the credit report or are listed as deferred, the servicer must obtain documentation to support the payment amount included in the monthly debt payment. If no monthly payment is reported on a student loan that is deferred or is in forbearance, the servicer must obtain documentation verifying the proposed monthly payment amount, or use a minimum of 1.5 percent of the balance.
- Monthly payment on revolving or open-end accounts, regardless of the balance. In the absence of a stated payment, the payment will be calculated by multiplying the outstanding balance by 3 percent.
- Monthly payment on a Home Equity Line of Credit (HELOC) must be included in the payment ratio using the minimum monthly payment reported on the credit report. If the HELOC has a balance but no monthly payment is reported, the servicer must obtain documentation verifying the payment amount, or use a minimum of one percent of the balance.
- Alimony, child support and separate maintenance payments with more than ten months of payments remaining, if supplied by the borrower.
- Car lease payments, regardless of the number of payments remaining.
- Aggregate negative net rental income from all investment properties owned, if supplied by the borrower.
- Monthly mortgage payment for second home (principal, interest, taxes and insurance and, when applicable, leasehold payments, homeowner association dues, condominium unit or cooperative unit maintenance fees (excluding unit utility charges)).

Total Monthly Debt Ratio

The borrower's total monthly debt ratio ("back-end ratio") is the ratio of the borrower's monthly gross expenses divided by the borrower's monthly gross income. Servicers will be required to send the Home Affordable Modification Program Counseling Letter to borrowers with a post-HAMP modification back-end ratio equal to or greater than 55 percent. The letter states the borrower must work with a HUD-approved housing counselor on a plan to reduce their total indebtedness below 55 percent. The letter also describes the availability and advantages of counseling and provides a list of local HUD-approved housing counseling agencies and directs the borrower to the appropriate HUD website where such information is located. The borrower must represent in writing in the HAMP documents that (s)he will obtain such counseling.

Face-to-face counseling is encouraged; however, telephone counseling is also permitted from HUD-approved housing counselors provided it covers the same topics as face-to-face sessions. Telephone counseling sessions provide flexibility to borrowers who are unable to attend face-to-face sessions or who do not have an eligible provider within their area.

A list of approved housing counseling agencies is available at http://www.hud.gov/offices/hsg/sfh/hcc/fc/ or by calling the toll-free housing counseling telephone referral service at 1-800-569-4287. A servicer must retain in its mortgage files evidence of the borrower notification. There is no charge to either borrowers or servicers for this counseling.

Mortgages with No Due-on-Sale Provision

If a mortgage that is not subject to a due-on-sale provision receives an HAMP, the borrower agrees that the HAMP will cancel the assumability feature of that mortgage.

Escrow Accounts

All of the borrower's monthly payments must include a monthly escrow amount unless prohibited by applicable law. The servicer must assume full responsibility for administering the borrower's escrow deposit account in accordance with the mortgage documents and all applicable laws and regulations. If the mortgage loan being considered for the HAMP is a non-escrowed mortgage loan, the servicer must establish an escrow deposit account prior to the beginning of the trial period. Servicers who do not have this capacity must implement an escrow process within six months of signing the Servicer Participation Agreement. However, the servicer must ensure that the trial payments include escrow amounts and must place the escrow funds into a separate account identified for escrow deposits.

Servicers are encouraged to perform an escrow analysis prior to establishing the trial period payment. When performing an escrow analysis, servicers should take into consideration tax and insurance premiums that may come due during the trial period. When the borrower's escrow account does not have sufficient funds to cover an expense and the servicer advances the funds necessary to pay an expense to a third party, the amount of the servicer advance that is paid to a third party may be capitalized.

In the event the initial escrow analysis identifies a shortage—a deficiency in the escrow deposits needed to pay all future tax and insurance payments—the servicer must take steps to eliminate the shortage. Any actions taken by the servicer to eliminate the escrow shortage must be in compliance with applicable laws, rules and regulations, including, but not limited to, the Real Estate Settlement Procedures Act and the Truth in Lending Act.

Compliance with Applicable Laws

Each servicer (and any subservicer it uses) must be aware of, and in full compliance with, all federal, state, and local laws (including statutes, regulations, ordinances, administrative rules and orders that have the effect of law, and judicial rulings and opinions)—including, but not limited to, the following laws that apply to any of its practices related to the HAMP:

- Section 5 of the Federal Trade Commission Act, which prohibits unfair or deceptive acts or practices.
- The Equal Credit Opportunity Act and the Fair Housing Act, which prohibit discrimination on a prohibited basis in connection with mortgage transactions. Loan modification programs are subject to the fair lending laws, and servicers and lenders should ensure that they do not treat a borrower less favorably than other borrowers on grounds such as race, religion, national origin, sex, marital or familial status, age, handicap, or receipt of public assistance income in connection with any loan modification. These laws also prohibit redlining.
- The Real Estate Settlement Procedures Act, which imposes certain disclosure requirements and restrictions relating to transfers of the servicing of certain loans and escrow accounts.
- The Fair Debt Collection Practices Act, which restricts certain abusive debt collection practices by collectors of debts, other than the creditor, owed or due to another.

Modification Process

Borrower Solicitation

Servicers should follow their existing practices, including complying with any express contractual restrictions, with respect to solicitation of borrowers for modifications.

A servicer may receive calls from current or delinquent borrowers directly inquiring about the availability of the HAMP. In that case, the servicer should work with the borrower to obtain the borrower's financial and hardship information and to determine if the HAMP is appropriate. If the servicer concludes a current borrower is in danger of imminent default, the servicer must consider an HAMP modification.

When discussing the HAMP, the servicer should provide the borrower with information designed to help them understand the modification terms that are being offered and the modification process. Such communication should help minimize potential borrower confusion, foster good customer relations, and improve legal compliance and reduce other risks in connection with the transaction. A servicer also must provide a borrower with clear and understandable written information about the material terms, costs, and risks of the modified mortgage loan in a timely manner to enable borrowers to make informed decisions. The servicer should inform the borrower during discussions that the successful completion of a modification under the HAMP will cancel any assumption feature, variable or step-rate feature, or enhanced payment options in the borrower's existing loan, at the time the loan is modified.

Servicers must have adequate staffing, resources, and facilities for receiving and processing the HAMP documents and any requested information that is submitted by borrowers. Servicers must also have procedures and systems in place to be able to respond to inquiries and complaints about the HAMP. Servicers should ensure that such inquiries and complaints are provided fair consideration, and timely and appropriate responses and resolution.

Document Retention

Servicers must retain all documents and information received during the process of determining borrower eligibility, including borrower income verification, total monthly mortgage payment and total monthly gross debt payment calculations, NPV calculations (assumptions, inputs and outputs), evidence of application of each step of the standard waterfall, escrow analysis, escrow advances, and escrow set-up. The servicers must retain all documents and information related to the monthly payments during and after the trial period, as well as incentive payment calculations and such other required documents.

Servicers must retain detailed records of borrower solicitations or borrower-initiated inquiries regarding the HAMP, the outcome of the evaluation for modification under the HAMP and specific justification with supporting details if the request for modification under the HAMP was denied. Records must also be retained to document the reason(s) for a trial modification failure. If an HAMP modification is not pursued when the NPV result is "negative," the servicer must document its consideration of other foreclosure prevention options. If a borrower under an HAMP modification loses good standing, the servicer must retain documentation of its consideration of the borrower for other loss mitigation alternatives.

Servicers must retain required documents for a period of seven years from the date of the document collection.

Temporary Suspension of Foreclosure Proceedings

To ensure that a borrower currently at risk of foreclosure has the opportunity to apply for the HAMP, servicers should not proceed with a foreclosure sale until the borrower has been evaluated for the program and, if eligible, an offer to participate in the HAMP has been made. Servicers must use reasonable efforts to contact borrowers facing foreclosure to determine their eligibility for the HAMP, including in-person contacts at the servicer's discretion. Servicers must not conduct foreclosure sales on loans previously referred to foreclosure or refer new loans to foreclosure during the 30-day period that the borrower has to submit documents evidencing an intent to accept the Trial Period Plan offer. Except as noted herein, any foreclosure sale will be suspended for the duration of the Trial Period Plan, including any period of time between the borrower's execution of the Trial Period Plan and the Trial Period Plan effective date.

However, borrowers in Georgia, Hawaii, Missouri, and Virginia will be considered to have failed the trial period if they are not current under the terms of the Trial Period Plan as of the date that the foreclosure sale is scheduled. Accordingly, servicers of HAMP loans secured by properties in these states may proceed with the foreclosure sale if the borrower has not made the trial period payments required to be made through the end of the month preceding the month in which the foreclosure sale is scheduled to occur.

Mortgage Insurer Approval

If applicable, a servicer must obtain mortgage insurer approval for HAMP modifications. Servicers should consult their mortgage insurance providers for specific processes related to the reporting of modified terms, payment of premiums, payment of claims, and other operational matters in connection with mortgage loans modified under the HAMP.

Executing the HAMP Documents

Servicers must use a two-step process for HAMP modifications. Step one involves providing a Trial Period Plan outlining the terms of the trial period, and step two involves providing the borrower with an Agreement that outlines the terms of the final modification.

In step one, the servicer should instruct the borrower to return the signed Trial Period Plan, together with a signed Hardship Affidavit and income verification documents (if not previously obtained from the borrower), and the first trial period payment (when not using automated drafting arrangements), to the servicer within 30 calendar days after the Trial Period Plan is sent by the servicer. The servicer is encouraged to contact the borrower before the expiration of the 30-day period if the borrower has not yet responded to encourage submission of the material. The servicer may, in its discretion, consider the offer of a Trial Period Plan to have expired at the end of 60 days if the borrower has not submitted both an executed Trial Period Plan and complete documentation as required under the Trial Period Plan. If the borrower's submission is incomplete, the servicer should work with the borrower to complete the Trial Period Plan submission. Note: The borrower is not required to have the Hardship Affidavit notarized.

Upon receipt of the Trial Period Plan from the borrower, the servicer must confirm that the borrower meets the underwriting and eligibility criteria. Once the servicer makes this determination and has received good funds for the first month's trial payment, the servicer should sign and immediately return an executed copy of the Trial Period Plan to the borrower. Payments made by the borrower under the terms of the Trial Period Plan will count toward successful completion irrespective of the date of the executed copy of the Trial Period Plan.

If the servicer determines that the borrower does not meet the underwriting and eligibility standards of the HAMP after the borrower has submitted a signed Trial Period Plan to the servicer, the servicer should promptly communicate that determination to the borrower in writing and consider the borrower for another foreclosure prevention alternative.

In step two, servicers must calculate the terms of the modification using verified income, taking into consideration amounts to be capitalized during the trial period. Servicers are encouraged to wait to send the Agreement to the borrower for execution until after receipt of the second to the last payment under the trial period. Note: the borrower is not required to have the Agreement notarized.

Servicers are reminded that all HAMP documentation must be signed by an authorized representative of the servicer and reflect the actual date of signature by the servicer's representative.

Acceptable Revisions to HAMP Documents

Servicers are strongly encouraged to use the HAMP documents available through www.financialstability.gov. Should a servicer decide to revise the HAMP documents or draft its own HAMP documents, it must obtain prior written approval from Treasury or Fannie Mae with the exception of the following circumstances:

- The servicer must revise the HAMP documents as necessary to comply with Federal, State and local law. For example, in the event that the HAMP results in a principal forbearance, servicers are obligated to modify the uniform instrument to comply with laws and regulations governing balloon disclosures.
- The servicer may include, as necessary, conditional language in HAMP offers and modification agreements indicating that the HAMP will not be implemented unless the servicer receives an acceptable title endorsement, or similar title insurance product, or subordination agreements from other existing lien holders, as necessary, to ensure that the modified mortgage loan retains its first lien position and is fully enforceable.
- If the borrower previously received a Chapter 7 bankruptcy discharge but did not reaffirm the mortgage debt under applicable law, the following language must be inserted in Section 1 of the Trial Period Plan and Section 1 of the Agreement: "I was discharged in a Chapter 7 bankruptcy proceeding subsequent to the execution of the Loan Documents. Based on this representation, Lender agrees that I will not have personal liability on the debt pursuant to this Agreement."
- The servicer may include language in the HAMP cover letter providing instructions for borrowers who elect to use an automated payment method to make the trial period payments.

Unless a borrower or co-borrower is deceased or a borrower and a co-borrower are divorced, all parties who signed the original loan documents or their duly authorized representative(s) must execute the HAMP documents. If a borrower and a co-borrower are divorced and the property has been transferred to one spouse in the divorce decree, the spouse who no longer has an interest in the property is not required to execute the HAMP documents. Servicers may evaluate requests on a case-by-case basis when the borrower is unable to sign due to circumstances such as mental incapacity, military deployment, etc. Furthermore, a borrower may elect to add a new co-borrower.

Use of Electronic Records

Electronic records for HAMP are acceptable as long as the electronic record complies with applicable law.

Assignment to MERS

If the original mortgage loan was registered with Mortgage Electronic Registration Systems, Inc. (MERS) and the originator elected to name MERS as the original mortgagee of record, solely as nominee for the lender named in the security instrument and the note, the servicer MUST make the following changes to the Agreement:

> (a) Insert a new definition under the "Property Address" definition on page 1, which reads as follows:
>
> "MERS" is Mortgage Electronic Registration Systems, Inc. MERS is a separate corporation that is acting solely as a nominee for lender and lender's successors and assigns. MERS is the mortgagee under the Mortgage. MERS is organized and existing under the laws of Delaware, and has an address and telephone number of P.O. Box 2026, Flint, MI 48501-2026, (888) 679-MERS.
>
> (b) Add as section 4.I.:
>
> That MERS holds only legal title to the interests granted by the borrower in the mortgage, but, if necessary to comply with law or custom, MERS (as nominee for lender and lender's successors and assigns) has the right: to exercise any or all of those interests, including, but not limited to, the right to foreclose and sell the Property; and to take any action required of lender including, but not limited to, releasing and canceling the mortgage loan.
>
> (c) MERS must be added to the signature lines at the end of the Agreement, as follows:
>
> ____________________________
>
> Mortgage Electronic Registration Systems, Inc.—Nominee for Lender

The servicer may execute the Agreement on behalf of MERS and, if applicable, submit it for recordation.

Trial Payment Period

Servicers may use recent verbal financial information to prepare and offer a Trial Period Plan. Servicers are not required to verify financial information prior to the effective date of the trial period. The servicer must service the mortgage loan during the trial period in the same manner as it would service a loan in forbearance.

The trial period is three months in duration (or longer if necessary to comply with applicable contractual obligations). The borrower must be current under the terms of the Trial Period Plan at the end of the trial period to receive a permanent loan modification. Current in this context is defined as the borrower having made all required trial period payments no later than 30 days from the date the final payment is due.

The effective date of the trial period will be set forth in the Trial Period Plan. In most cases, the effective date is the first day of the month following the servicer's mailing of the offer for the Trial Period Plan. The trial period extends for two (or more if necessary to comply with applicable contractual obligations) additional payments after the effective date.

Servicers are encouraged to require automated payment methods, such as automatic payment drafting. If automatic payment drafting is required, it must be used by all HAMP borrowers, unless a borrower opts out.

If the verified income evidenced by the borrower's documentation exceeds the initial income information used by the servicer to place the borrower in the trial period by more than 25 percent, the borrower must be reevaluated based on the program eligibility and underwriting requirements. If this reevaluation determines that the borrower is still eligible, new documents must be prepared and the borrower must restart the trial period.

If the verified income evidenced by the borrower's documentation is less than the initial income information used by the servicer to place the borrower in the trial period, or if the verified income exceeds the initial income information by 25 percent or less, and the borrower is still eligible, then the trial period will not restart and the trial period payments will not change; provided, that verified income will be used to calculate the monthly mortgage payment under the Agreement. (If, based on verified income the result of the NPV test is "negative" for modification, the servicer is not obligated to perform the modification.) However, if the servicer determines the borrower is not eligible for the HAMP based on verified income, the servicer must notify the borrower of that determination and that any trial period payments made by the borrower will be applied to the mortgage loan in accordance with the borrower's current loan documents.

If a servicer has information that the borrower does not meet all of the eligibility criteria for the HAMP (e.g., because the borrower has moved out of the house) the servicer should explore other foreclosure prevention alternatives prior to resuming or initiating foreclosure.

Note that under the terms of the Agreement, trial payments should be applied when they equal a full contractual payment (determined as of the time the HAMP is offered).

If the borrower complies with the terms and conditions of the Trial Period Plan, the loan modification will become effective on the first day of the month following the trial period as specified in the Trial Period Plan. However, because the monthly payment under the Agreement will be based on verified income documentation, the monthly payment due under the Agreement may differ from the payment amount due under the Trial Period Plan.

Use of Suspense Accounts and Application of Payments

If permitted by the applicable loan documents, servicers may accept and hold as "unapplied funds" (held in a T&I custodial account) amounts received which do not constitute a full monthly, contractual principal, interest, tax and insurance (PITI) payment. However, when the total of the reduced payments held as "unapplied funds" is equal to a full PITI payment, the servicer is required to apply all full payments to the mortgage loan.

Any unapplied funds remaining at the end of the trial payment period that do not constitute a full monthly, contractual principal, interest, tax and insurance payment should be applied to reduce any amounts that would otherwise be capitalized onto the principal balance.

If a principal curtailment is received on a loan that has a principal forbearance, servicers are instructed to apply the principal curtailment to the interest bearing UPB. If, however, the principal curtailment amount is greater than or equal to the interest bearing UPB, then the curtailment should be applied to the principal forbearance portion. If the curtailment satisfies the principal forbearance portion, any remaining funds should then be applied to the interest bearing UPB.

Recording the Modification

For all mortgage loans that are modified pursuant to the HAMP, the servicer must follow investor guidance with respect to ensuring that the modified mortgage loan retains its first lien position and is fully enforceable.

Monthly Statements

For modifications that include principal forbearance, servicers are encouraged to include the amount of the gross UPB on the borrower's monthly payment statement. In addition, the borrower should receive information on a monthly basis regarding the accrual of "pay for performance" principal balance reduction payments.

Redefault and Loss of Good Standing

If, following a successful trial period, a borrower defaults on a loan modification executed under the HAMP (three monthly payments are due and unpaid on the last day of the third month), the loan is no longer considered to be in "good standing." Once lost, good standing cannot be restored even if the borrower subsequently cures the default. A loan that is not in good standing is not eligible to receive borrower, servicer or investor incentives and reimbursements and these payments will no longer accrue for that mortgage. Further, the mortgage is not eligible for another HAMP modification.

In the event a borrower defaults, the servicer must work with the borrower to cure the modified loan, or if that is not feasible, evaluate the borrower for any other available loss mitigation alternatives prior to commencing foreclosure proceedings. The servicer must retain documentation of its consideration of the borrower for other loss mitigation alternatives.

Reporting Requirements

Each servicer will be required to register with Fannie Mae to participate in the HAMP. Fannie Mae will provide an HAMP Registration form to facilitate registration.

Additionally, servicers will be required to provide periodic HAMP loan level data to Fannie Mae. The data must be accurate, complete, and in agreement with the servicer's records. Data should be reported by a servicer at the start of the modification trial period and during the modification trial period, for loan set up of the approved modification, and monthly after the modification is set up on Fannie Mae's system. Servicers will be required to submit three separate data files as described below.

Note: The following data files can be delivered through a data collection tool on the servicer web portal available through www.financialstability.gov. Detailed guidelines for submitting data files are available at the servicer web portal. For those servicers who cannot use this process, an alternate process to submit data via a spreadsheet will be made available. More information on the alternative process for submitting data in a spreadsheet will be provided in the future.

Trial Period

Servicers will be required to provide loan level data in order to establish loans for processing during the HAMP trial period. See Exhibit A for trial period set up attributes.

In addition, servicers will be required to report activity during the HAMP trial period in order to substantiate the receipt of proceeds during the trial period and to record modification details. See Exhibit B for trial period reporting attributes.

Loan Setup

A one time loan set up is required to establish the approved modified HAMP loan on Fannie Mae's system. The file layout is the same that is used for establishing loans for processing during the trial period. See Exhibit A for loan set up attributes.

Servicers are required to provide the set up file the business day after the modification closes. The set up file should reflect the status of the loan after the final trial period payment is applied. The set up file will contain data for the current reporting period (e.g., prior month balances).

Monthly Loan Activity Reporting

The month after the loan set up file is provided, servicers must begin reporting activity on all HAMP loans on a monthly basis (e.g., loan set up file provided in July, the first loan activity report is due in August for July activity). See Exhibit C for monthly reporting attributes.

The HAMP loan activity report (LAR) is due by the 4th business day each month. Servicers will have until the 15th calendar day of each month to clear up any edits and have a final LAR reported to Fannie Mae. The Fannie Mae system will validate that the borrower payment has been made as expected and that the last paid installment (LPI) date is current before accruing the appropriate monthly compensation due.

If a loan becomes past due (the LPI date does not advance), the monthly compensation on that loan will not be accrued. If the loan is brought current, compensation will not be caught up (e.g., if a loan was two months past due, and then the borrower makes the payments and brings the loan current, the annual compensation provided would be for ten months. The two months of compensation associated with the period of delinquency is not recoverable).

Additional Data Requirements

Additional data elements must be collected and reported as specified in Exhibit D. Some of these elements must be collected for all completed modifications regardless of the date of completion; guidance for collecting these elements will be forthcoming shortly. The requirement to collect these elements for trial modifications and for loans evaluated for a modification will be phased in as specified in Exhibit D.

Reporting to Mortgage Insurers

Servicers must maintain their mortgage insurance processes and comply with all reporting required by the mortgage insurer for loans modified under the HAMP. Servicers should consult with the mortgage insurer for specific processes related to the reporting of modified terms, payment of premiums, payment of claims, and other operational matters in connection with mortgage loans modified under the HAMP.

Servicers are required to report successful HAMP modifications and the terms of those modifications to the appropriate mortgage insurers, if applicable, within 30 days following the end of the trial period and in accordance with procedures that currently exist or may be agreed to between servicers and the mortgage insurers.

Servicers must include the mortgage insurance premium in the borrower's modified payment, and must ensure that any existing mortgage insurance is maintained. Among other things, the servicer must ensure that the mortgage insurance premium is paid. In addition, servicers must adapt their systems to ensure proper reporting of modified loan terms and avoid impairing coverage for any existing mortgage insurance. For example, in the event that the modification includes principal forbearance, servicers must continue to pay the correct mortgage insurance premiums based on the gross UPB, including any principal forbearance amount, must include the gross UPB in their delinquency reporting to the mortgage insurer, and must ensure any principal forbearance does not erroneously trigger automatic mortgage insurance cancellation or termination.

Transfers of Servicing

When a transfer of servicing includes mortgages modified under the HAMP, the transferor servicer must provide special notification to the transferee servicer. Specifically, the transferor servicer must advise the transferee servicer that loans modified under the HAMP are part of the portfolio being transferred and must confirm that the transferee servicer is aware of the special requirements for these loans, and agrees to assume the additional responsibilities associated with servicing them. A required form of assignment and assumption agreement must be used and is a part of the Servicer Participation Agreement.

Credit Bureau Reporting

The servicer should continue to report a "full-file" status report to the four major credit repositories for each loan under the HAMP in accordance with the Fair Credit Reporting Act and credit bureau requirements as provided by the Consumer Data Industry Association (the "CDIA") on the basis of the following: (i) for borrowers who are current when they enter the trial period, the servicer should report the borrower current but on a modified payment if the borrower makes timely payments by the 30th day of each trial period month at the modified amount during the trial period, as well as report the modification when completed, and (ii) for borrowers who are delinquent when they enter the trial period, the servicer should continue to report in such a manner that accurately reflects the borrower's delinquency and workout status following usual and customary reporting standards, as well as report the modification when completed. More detailed guidance on these reporting requirements will be published by the CDIA.

"Full-file" reporting means that the servicer must describe the exact status of each mortgage it is servicing as of the last business day of each month.

Fees and Compensation

Late Fees

All late charges, penalties, stop-payment fees, or similar fees must be waived upon successful completion of the trial period.

Administrative Costs

Servicers may not charge the borrower to cover the administrative processing costs incurred in connection with a HAMP. The servicer must pay any actual out-of-pocket expenses such as any required notary fees, recordation fees, title costs, property valuation fees, credit report fees, or other allowable and documented expenses. Servicers will not be reimbursed for the cost of the credit report(s).

Incentive Compensation

No incentives of any kind will be paid if (i) the servicer has not executed the Servicer Participation Agreement, or (ii) the borrower's monthly mortgage payment ratio starts below 31 percent prior to the implementation of the HAMP. The calculation and payment of all incentive compensation will be based strictly on the borrower's verified income. Each servicer must promptly apply or remit, as applicable, all borrower and investor compensation it receives with respect to any modified loan.

With respect to payment of any incentive that is predicated on a six percent reduction in the borrower's monthly mortgage payment, the reduction will be calculated by comparing the monthly mortgage payment used to determine eligibility (adjusted as applicable to include property taxes, hazard insurance, flood insurance, condominium association fees and homeowner's association fees) and the borrower's payment under HAMP.

The amount of funds available to pay servicer, borrower and investor compensation in connection with each servicer's modifications will be capped pursuant to each servicer's Servicer Participation Agreement (Program Participation Cap). Treasury will establish each servicer's initial Program Participation Cap by estimating the number of

HAMP modifications expected to be performed by each servicer during the term of the HAMP. The Program Participation Cap could be adjusted based on Treasury's full book analysis of the servicer's loans.

The funds remaining available for a servicer's modifications under that servicer's Program Participation Cap will be reduced by the maximum amount of compensation payments potentially payable with respect to each loan modification upon entering into a trial period. In the event the compensation actually paid with respect to a loan modification is less than the maximum amount of compensation payments potentially payable, the funds remaining available for a servicer's modifications under the HAMP will be increased by the difference between such amounts.

Treasury may, from time to time and in its sole discretion, revise a servicer's Program Participation Cap. Fannie Mae will provide written notification to a servicer of all changes made to the servicer's Program Participation Cap. Once a servicer's Program Participation Cap is reached, a servicer must not enter into any agreements with borrowers intended to result in new loan modifications, and no payments will be made with respect to any new loan modifications.

Servicer Incentive Compensation

A servicer will receive compensation of $1,000 for each completed modification under the HAMP. In addition, if a borrower was current under the original mortgage loan, a servicer will receive an additional compensation amount of $500. All such servicer incentive compensation shall be earned and payable once the borrower successfully completes the trial payment period, provided that the servicer has signed and delivered to Fannie Mae a Servicer Participation Agreement, any related documentation and any required servicer or loan set up data prior to the effective date of the loan modification.

If a particular borrower's monthly mortgage payment (principal, interest, taxes, all related property insurance and homeowner's or condominium association fees but excluding mortgage insurance) is reduced through the HAMP by six percent or more, a servicer will also receive an annual "pay for success" fee for a period of three years. The fee will be equal to the lesser of: (i) $1,000 ($83.33/month), or (ii) one-half of the reduction in the borrower's annualized monthly payment. The "pay for success" fee will be payable annually for each of the first three years after the anniversary of the month in which a Trial Period Plan was executed. If the loan ceases to be in good standing, the servicer will cease to be eligible for any further incentive payments after that time, even if the borrower subsequently cures his or her delinquency.

Borrower's Incentive Compensation

To provide an additional incentive for borrowers to keep their modified loan current, borrowers whose monthly mortgage payment (principal, interest, taxes, all related property insurance and homeowner's or condominium association fees but excluding mortgage insurance) is reduced through the HAMP by six percent or more and who make timely monthly payments will earn an annual "pay for performance" principal balance reduction payment equal to the lesser of: (i) $1,000 ($83.33/month), or (ii) one-half of the reduction in the borrower's annualized monthly payment for each month a timely payment is made. A borrower can earn the right to receive a "pay for performance" principal balance reduction payment for payments made during the first five years following execution of the Agreement provided the loan continues to be in good standing as of the date the payment is made. The "pay for performance" principal balance reduction payment will accrue monthly but will be applied annually for each of the five years in which this incentive payment accrues, prior to the first payment due date after the anniversary of the month in which the Trial Period Plan was executed. This payment will be paid to the mortgage servicer to be applied first towards reducing the interest bearing UPB on the mortgage loan and then to any principal forbearance amount (if applicable). Any applicable prepayment penalties on partial principal prepayments made by the government must be waived. Borrower incentive payments do not accrue during the Trial Period; however, on the first month of the modification, the borrower will accrue incentive payments equal to the number of months in the trial period.

If and when the loan ceases to be in good standing, the borrower will cease to be eligible for any further incentive payments after that time, even if the borrower subsequently cures his or her delinquency. The borrower will lose his or her right to any accrued incentive compensation when the loan ceases to be in good standing.

Investor Payment Reduction Cost Share and Up Front Incentives

If the target monthly mortgage payment ratio is achieved, investors in Non-GSE Mortgages are entitled to payment reduction cost share compensation. This compensation equals one-half of the dollar difference between the borrower's monthly payment under the modification at the target monthly mortgage payment ratio and the lesser of (i) what the borrower's monthly payment would be at a 38 percent monthly mortgage payment ratio; or (ii) the borrower's pre-modification monthly payment. Payment reduction cost share compensation shall accrue monthly as the borrower makes each payment so long as the loan is in good standing as defined in these guidelines. This compensation will be provided for up to five years or until the loan is paid off, whichever is earlier.

Additionally, investors will receive a one-time incentive of $1,500 for each Agreement executed with a borrower who was current prior to the start of the Trial Period Plan. The one-time incentive is conditional upon at least a six percent reduction in the borrower's monthly mortgage payment. Neither the payment reduction share nor the up-front incentive shall be payable if the Trial Period Plan is not successfully completed.

Compliance

Servicers must comply with the HAMP requirements and must document the execution of loan evaluation, loan modification and accounting processes. Servicers must develop and execute a quality assurance program that includes either a statistically based (with a 95 percent confidence level) or a ten percent stratified sample of loans modified, drawn within 30-45 days of final modification and reported on within 30-45 days of review. In addition, a trending analysis must be performed on a rolling 12-month basis.

Treasury has selected Freddie Mac to serve as its compliance agent for the HAMP. In its role as compliance agent, Freddie Mac will utilize Freddie Mac employees and contractors to conduct independent compliance assessments. In addition, loan level data will be reviewed for eligibility and fraud.

The scope of the assessments will include, among other things, an evaluation of documented evidence to confirm adherence (e.g., accuracy and timeliness) to HAMP requirements with respect to the following:

- Evaluation of Borrower and Property Eligibility
- Compliance with Underwriting Guidelines
- Execution of NPV/Waterfall processes
- Completion of Borrower Incentive Payments
- Investor Subsidy Calculations
- Data Integrity

The review will also evaluate the effectiveness of the servicer's quality assurance program; such evaluation will include, without limitation, the timing and size of the sample selection, the scope of the quality assurance reviews, and the reporting and remediation process.

There will be two types of compliance assessments: on-site and remote. Both on-site and remote reviews will consist of the following activities (among others): notification, scheduling, self assessments, documentation submission, interviews, file reviews, and reporting.

For on-site reviews, Freddie Mac will strive to provide the servicer with (i) a 30-day advance notification of a pending review and (ii) subsequent confirmation of the dates of the review. However, Freddie Mac reserves the right to arrive at the servicer's site unannounced. Freddie Mac will request the servicer to make available documentation, including, without limitation, policies and procedures, management reports, loan files and a risk control self assessment ready for review. Additionally, Freddie Mac may request additional loan files during the review. Interviews will usually be conducted in-person.

During the review window, Freddie Mac will review loan files and other requested documentation to evaluate compliance with HAMP terms. Upon the completion of the review, Freddie Mac will conduct an exit interview with the servicer to discuss preliminary assessment results.

For remote reviews, Freddie Mac will request the servicer to send documentation, including, without limitation, policies and procedures, management reports, loan files and a risk control self assessment within 30 days of the request. In addition, time will be scheduled for phone interviews, including a results summary call after the compliance review is completed to discuss preliminary results.

The targeted time frame for publishing the servicer assessment report is 30 days after the completion of the review. Treasury will receive a copy of the report five business days prior to the release of the report to the servicer.

There will be an issue/resolution appeal process for servicer assessments. Servicers will be able to submit concerns or disputes to an independent quality assurance team within Freddie Mac.

A draft rating and implication methodology for the compliance assessments will be published in a subsequent Supplemental Directive and servicer feedback will be solicited prior to the finalization of the methodology.

[*Editor's Note: The following Exhibits are not reprinted herein. Exhibits are reprinted in full on this treatise's companion website.*]

Exhibit A: HAMP Trial Modification and Official Modification Loan Setup Data Elements
Exhibit B: HAMP Monthly Trial Data Collection Elements
Exhibit C: Monthly Loan Activity Records
Exhibit D: HAMP Additional Data Requirements

B.3.3 Supplemental Directive 09-03: Home Affordable Modification Program—Trial Period Guidance

Supplemental Directive 09-03 July 6, 2009

Home Affordable Modification Program—Trial Period Guidance

In Supplemental Directive 09-01, the Treasury Department (Treasury) announced the eligibility, underwriting and servicing requirements for the Home Affordable Modification Program (HAMP). Under the HAMP, servicers apply a uniform loan modification process to provide eligible borrowers with sustainable monthly payments for their first lien mortgage loans. This Supplemental Directive provides additional guidance with respect to the commencement of the trial period and the reporting requirements for trial period and loan set up. This Supplemental Directive also provides servicers with a new option with respect to the commencement of the modification.

Commencement of Trial Period

A borrower's trial period starts on the Trial Period Plan Effective Date, which is a field in the Trial Period Plan that is completed by the servicer. If the servicer transmits the Trial Period Plan to the borrower on or before the 15th day of a calendar month, then the servicer should insert the first day of the next month as the Trial Period Plan Effective Date. If the servicer transmits the Trial Period Plan to the borrower after the 15th day of a calendar month, the servicer should use the first day of the month after the next month as the Trial Period Plan Effective Date. This determination should be based on the date of the cover letter used to transmit the Trial Period Plan to the borrower.

For example, if the servicer completes the Trial Period Plan and transmits it to the borrower on June 2nd, the servicer should use July 1st as the Trial Period Plan Effective Date. If the servicer completes the Trial Period Plan and transmits it to the borrower on June 27th, the servicer should use August 1st as the Trial Period Plan Effective Date.

The date that the first trial period payment is due under the terms of the Trial Period Plan must be the same date as the Trial Period Plan Effective Date. The servicer must receive the borrower's first trial period payment on or before the last day of the month in which the Trial Period Plan Effective Date occurs ("Trial Period Offer Deadline"). The servicer must consider the Trial Period Plan offer to have expired if the servicer does not receive the borrower's first trial period payment by the Trial Period Offer Deadline. Servicers are reminded, as provided in Supplemental Directive 09-01, that the servicer may, in its discretion, consider the offer of a Trial Period Plan to have expired at the end of 60 days if the borrower has not submitted both an executed Trial Period Plan and complete documentation as required under the Trial Period Plan. Further, a servicer must not execute the Trial Period Plan or return it to the borrower until after confirming the borrower meets all eligibility criteria based on the borrower's verified documentation.

Trial Period and Loan Set Up Reporting Requirements

The servicer should begin trial period reporting once the servicer receives the borrower's first trial period payment (as long as that payment is received by the servicer on or before the last day of the month in which the Trial Period Plan Effective Date occurs), regardless of whether the servicer has received an executed copy of the Trial Period Plan or the required income verification documentation from the borrower. The servicer must provide to Fannie Mae, as program administrator, the trial period set up attributes set forth in Appendix A of the HAMP Servicer Reporting Requirements available on www.HMPadmin.com no later than the fourth business day of the month immediately following the month in which the Trial Period Plan Effective Date occurs. For example, if the Trial Period Plan Effective Date is July 1st and the servicer receives the borrower's first trial period payment on or before July 31st (including payments received by the servicer prior to July 1st), the servicer must report to Fannie Mae the trial period set up attributes by the fourth business day of August.

Notwithstanding the guidance provided in Supplemental Directive 09-01 regarding the timing of the loan set up reporting requirement relating to a modification, the servicer is required to provide to Fannie Mae, as program administrator, the loan set up attributes set forth in Appendix A of the HAMP Servicer Reporting Requirements available on www.HMPadmin.com no later than the fourth business day of the month in which the modification is effective. For example, if a modification is effective as of September 1st, the servicer must provide to Fannie Mae the loan set up attributes no later than the fourth business day of September.

Commencement of Modification

A servicer should prepare the HAMP modification agreement (the "Agreement") in order to allow sufficient processing time for the modification to become effective on the first day of the month following the final trial period month. However, in the event the borrower does not pay the final trial period payment on or before the due date set forth in Section 2 of the Trial Period Plan, then the servicer may, at its option, complete the Agreement such that the modification becomes effective on the first day of the second month following the final trial period month. In either instance, the modification effective date and the due date for the first payment under the Agreement must be the same date. A servicer must treat all borrowers the same in applying this option by selecting, in its discretion and evidenced by a written policy, the date by which the final Trial Period Payment must be submitted before the servicer applies this option ("cutoff date"). The cutoff date must be after the due date for the final trial period payment as set forth in Section 2 of the Trial Period Plan.

If the servicer elects this option, the borrower will not be required to make an additional trial period payment during the month (the "interim month") in between the final trial period month and the month in which the modification becomes effective. For example, if the last trial period month is March and the servicer elects the option described above, the borrower is not required to make any payment during April, and the modification becomes effective, and the first payment under the Agreement is due, on May 1st.

Neither the borrower nor the servicer will be entitled to accrue incentive compensation for the interim month if the borrower does not make a trial period payment during the interim month. The servicer must modify the Home Affordable Modification Agreement Cover Letter to inform the borrower about (i) the delay of the modification effective date by one month and (ii) the effects of the interim month and the delay in the effective date of the Agreement, including, but not limited to, the delay in the effective date of the modified interest rate, the increase in the delinquent interest capitalized, and the loss of one month's accrual of the incentive payment if the borrower does not make an additional trial period payment.

The servicer should report the length of the trial period on the loan set up record, excluding the interim month if the borrower does not make an additional trial period payment, and including the interim month if the borrower does make an additional trial period payment. As provided above, the servicer must provide to Fannie Mae, as program administrator, the loan set up attributes set forth in Appendix A of the HAMP Servicer Reporting Requirements available on www.HMPadmin.com no later than the fourth business day of the month in which the modification is effective. The effects of the interim month and attendant capitalization on the terms of the modification agreement may not alter the servicer's previous determination of the borrower's eligibility.

B.3.4 Supplemental Directive 09-08: Home Affordable Modification Program-Borrower Notices

Supplemental Directive 09-08 November 3, 2009

Home Affordable Modification Program – Borrower Notices

Background

In Supplemental Directive 09-01, the Treasury Department (Treasury) announced the eligibility, underwriting and servicing requirements for the Home Affordable Modification Program (HAMP). Under HAMP, servicers apply a uniform loan modification process to provide eligible borrowers with sustainable monthly payments for their first lien mortgage loans. While HAMP program guidelines are intended to reach a broad range of at-risk borrowers, there will be loans that cannot be approved for a HAMP Trial Period Plan (Trial Period Plan) or official HAMP modification, and there will be borrowers who choose not to accept a Trial Period Plan or official HAMP modification offer. In such cases, borrowers must be informed in writing of the reasoning for servicer determinations regarding program eligibility.

This Supplemental Directive provides guidance to servicers of first lien mortgage loans that are not owned or guaranteed by Fannie Mae or Freddie Mac (Non-GSE Mortgages). Servicers of mortgage loans that are owned or guaranteed by Fannie Mae or Freddie Mac should refer to the related HAMP guidelines issued by the applicable GSE.

Servicers participating in HAMP with respect to Non-GSE Mortgages are required to execute a Servicer Participation Agreement, through which they are contractually obligated to "perform the services required under the Program Documentation and the Agreement in accordance with the practices, high professional standards of care, and degree of attention used in a well managed [servicing] operation". That high standard of care is considered to include providing borrowers with timely and accurate written communication about the modification process, including but not limited to, notice that a borrower will not be offered a HAMP modification. This Supplemental Directive provides servicers with additional guidance related to the format, content and timing of notices that must be provided to borrowers requesting consideration for a HAMP modification (Borrower Notices). This Supplemental Directive is effective January 1, 2010; however, servicers are encouraged to implement this guidance as soon as possible.

Borrower Notices

A servicer must send a Borrower Notice to every borrower that has been evaluated for HAMP but is not offered a Trial Period Plan, is not offered an official HAMP modification, or is at risk of losing eligibility for HAMP because they have failed to provide required financial documentation. The written notices must comply with all laws, rules and regulations including but not limited to, the Equal Credit Opportunity Act, when applicable to the transaction.

Evaluation for HAMP. Supplemental Directive 09-06 announced additional data reporting requirements that are triggered when a mortgage loan is evaluated for HAMP. It provided that a mortgage is evaluated for HAMP when one of the following events has occurred:

- A borrower has submitted a written request (either hardcopy or electronic submission) for consideration for a HAMP modification that includes, at a minimum, current borrower income and a reason for default or explanation of hardship, as applicable; or
- A borrower has verbally provided sufficient financial and other data to allow the servicer to complete a Net Present Value (NPV) analysis; or
- A borrower has been offered a Trial Period Plan.

When a borrower is evaluated for HAMP and the borrower is not offered a Trial Period Plan or official HAMP modification, servicers are required to provide data specified in Schedule IV of Supplemental Directive 09-06 (Schedule IV) to Fannie Mae as Treasury's program administrator. The data reporting requirements in Schedule IV are designed to document the disposition of borrowers evaluated for HAMP.

Whenever a servicer is required to provide data specified in Schedule IV, the servicer must also comply with the requirements in this Supplemental Directive and send the appropriate Borrower Notice. With the exception of the Notice of Incomplete Information, all Borrower Notices must be mailed no later than 10 business days following the date of the servicer's determination that a Trial Period Plan or official HAMP modification will not be offered. Borrower Notices may be sent electronically only if the borrower has previously agreed to exchange correspondence relating to the modification with the Servicer electronically.

Content of Borrower Notices. The content of the Borrower Notices will vary depending on the information intended to be conveyed or the determination made by the servicer. All Borrower Notices must be written in clear, non-technical language, with acronyms and industry terms such as "NPV" explained in a manner that is easily understandable. The explanation(s) should relate to one or more of the Not Approved/Not Accepted reason codes specified in Schedule IV. Model clauses for reasons that relate to the codes in Schedule IV are attached as Exhibit A. Use of the model clauses is optional; however, they illustrate a level of specificity that is deemed to be in compliance with the language requirements of this Supplemental Directive.

- *Non-Approval*—for borrowers not approved for a Trial Period Plan or official HAMP modification, this notice must provide the primary reason or reasons for the non-approval. The notice must also describe other foreclosure alternatives for which the borrower may be eligible, if any, including but not limited to other modification programs, short sale and/or deed in lieu or forbearance, and identify the steps the borrower must take in order to be considered for those options. If the servicer has already approved the borrower for another foreclosure alternative, information necessary to participate in or complete the alternative should be included. Whenever a non-government foreclosure prevention option is discussed, the notice should be clear that the borrower was considered for but is not eligible for HAMP.

  When the borrower is not approved for a HAMP modification because the transaction is NPV negative, the notice must, in addition to an explanation of NPV, include a list of certain input fields that are considered in the NPV decision and a statement that the borrower may, within 30 calendar days of the date of the notice, request the date the NPV calculation was completed and the values used to populate the NPV input fields defined in Exhibit A. The purpose of providing this information is to allow the borrower the opportunity to correct values that may impact the analysis of the borrower's eligibility.

  If the borrower, or the borrower's authorized representative, requests the specific NPV values orally or in writing within 30 calendar days from the date of the notice, the servicer must provide them to the borrower within 10 calendar days of the request. If the loan is scheduled for foreclosure sale when the borrower requests the NPV values, the servicer may not complete the foreclosure sale until 30 calendar days after the servicer delivers the NPV values to the borrower. This will allow the borrower time to make a request to correct any values that may have been inaccurate.

  Upon written receipt from the borrower of evidence that one or more of the NPV values is inaccurate, the servicer must verify the evidence and if accurate must re-run the NPV calculation if the correction is material and is likely to change the NPV outcome. Other values not affected by the correction do not need to be changed from the first NPV calculation. If the borrower identifies inaccuracies in the NPV values, the servicer must suspend the foreclosure sale until the inaccuracies are reconciled. Servicers are not required to provide the numeric NPV results or NPV input values not enumerated in Exhibit A.
- *Payment Default During the Trial Period Plan*—this notice informs the borrower that the borrower failed to make all the trial period payments by the end of the Trial Period Plan and is in default. The notice must also describe other foreclosure alternatives for which the borrower may be eligible, if any, including but not limited to other modification programs, short sale and/or deed in lieu or forbearance and identify the steps the borrower must take in order to be considered for these options. If the servicer has already approved the borrower for another foreclosure alternative, information necessary to participate in or complete the alternative should be included. Whenever a non-government foreclosure prevention option is discussed, the notice should be clear that the borrower was considered for but is not eligible for HAMP.
- *Loan Paid Off or Reinstated*—this notice confirms that the subject loan was paid off or reinstated and must provide the payoff or reinstatement date. If the loan was reinstated this notice must include a statement that the borrower may contact the servicer to request reconsideration under HAMP if they experience a subsequent financial hardship.
- *Withdrawal of Request or Non-Acceptance of Offer*—this notice confirms that the borrower withdrew the request for consideration for either a Trial Period Plan or HAMP modification or did not accept a either a Trial Period Plan or a HAMP modification offer. Failure to make the first trial period payment in a timely manner is considered non-acceptance of the Trial Period Plan.
- *Incomplete Information*—this notice provides a list of the financial verification documents the servicer previ-

ously requested from the borrower but has not received. Servicers must develop and implement outreach procedures to obtain financial information from borrowers who do not provide verification documentation in a timely manner. As part of these procedures, the servicer must mail the borrower a notice listing all documents needed to complete the evaluation and a date by which the information must be received before the borrower becomes ineligible for HAMP. If the borrower fails to provide all required verification documents by the date provided, the servicer will declare the borrower ineligible for a modification and send the borrower a Non-Approval Notice.

When used to determine if a borrower is qualified for a verified income Trial Period Plan, the servicer must send the notice to the borrower no earlier than 30 days after the date of the first written request for documentation and not less than 30 days before the servicer discontinues its evaluation for HAMP. When used in conjunction with a Trial Period Plan based on stated income, the servicer must send the notice not less than 30 calendar days prior to the expiration of a Trial Period Plan.

As provided in Supplemental Directive 09-01, a servicer that offers a Trial Period Plan to a borrower based on stated income must obtain financial documentation in order to verify the borrower's eligibility for a HAMP modification. Supplemental Directive 09-01 provides that the servicer may, in its discretion, consider the offer of a Trial Period Plan to have expired at the end of 60 days if the borrower has not submitted the required documentation. The servicer must consider the Trial Period Plan to have expired if the borrower has not submitted the required documentation by the end of the trial period.

All Borrower Notices must also include the following:

- A toll-free number through which the borrower can reach a servicer representative capable of providing specific details about the contents of the Borrower Notice and reasons for a non-approval determination.
- The HOPE Hotline Number (888-995-HOPE), with an explanation that the borrower can seek assistance at no charge from HUD-approved housing counselors and can request assistance in understanding the Borrower Notice by asking for MHA HELP.
- Any information, disclosures or notices required by the borrower's mortgage documents and applicable federal, state and local law.

Compliance

Treasury has selected Freddie Mac to serve as its compliance agent for HAMP. Supplemental Directive 09-01 describes the overall roles and responsibilities of servicers and the compliance agent in performing servicer reviews and oversight, which are unchanged by this Supplemental Directive. As compliance agent, Freddie Mac will examine the expanded reporting codes provided to Treasury, the content and distribution of Borrower Notices sent to borrowers, and the responsiveness of the servicer's customer service hotline for borrowers seeking additional detail about the information contained in the Borrower Notice. Servicers are expected to retain in the borrower file a copy of the Borrower Notice(s) sent to the borrower. The review will also confirm the existence and evaluate the effectiveness of the servicer's quality assurance program as it relates to the notification process and customer service hotline. Such evaluation will include, without limitation, the timing and size of the sample selection, the scope of the quality assurance reviews, and the reporting and remediation process.

Exhibit A

Model Clauses for Borrower Notices

The model clauses in this exhibit provide sample language that may be used to communicate the status of a borrower's request for a Home Affordable Modification. The model clauses relate to the Not Approved/Not Accepted reason codes in Schedule IV of Supplemental directive 09-06. Use of the model clauses is optional, however, they illustrate a level of specificity that is deemed to be in compliance with language requirements of the program.

Non Approval Notice

1. **Ineligible Mortgage.** We are unable to offer you a Home Affordable Modification because your loan did not meet one or more of the basic eligibility criteria of the Home Affordable Modification Program.
   - ☐ You did not obtain your loan on or before January 1, 2009.
   - ☐ Your loan with us is not a first lien mortgage.
   - ☐ The current unpaid principal balance on your loan is higher than the program limit. ($729,750 for a one unit property, $934,200 for a two unit property, $1,129,250 for a three unit property and $1,403,400 for a four unit property).

2. **Ineligible Borrower.** We are unable to offer you a Home Affordable Modification because your current monthly housing expense, which includes the monthly principal and interest payment on your first lien mortgage loan plus property taxes, hazard insurance and homeowner's dues (if any) is less than or equal to 31% of your gross monthly income (your income before taxes and other deductions) which, (select one) [you told us is $ _________] OR [we verified as $ _________]. Your housing expense must be greater than 31% of your gross monthly income to be eligible for a Home Affordable Modification. If you believe this verified income is incorrect, please contact us at the number provided below.

3. **Property Not Owner Occupied.** We are unable to offer you a Home Affordable Modification because you do not live in the property as your primary residence.

4. **Ineligible Property.** We are unable to offer a Home Affordable Modification because your property:
   - ☐ Is vacant
   - ☐ Has been condemned.
   - ☐ Has more than four dwelling units.

5. **Investor Guarantor Not Participating.** We are unable to offer you a Home Affordable Modification because:
   - ☐ We service your loan on behalf of an investor or group of investors that has not given us the contractual authority to modify your loan under the Home Affordable Modification Program.
   - ☐ Your loan is insured by a private mortgage insurance company that has not approved a modification under the Home Affordable Modification Program.
   - ☐ Your loan is guaranteed and the guarantor has not approved a modification under the Home Affordable Modification Program.

6. **Bankruptcy Court Declined.** We are unable to offer you a Home Affordable Modification because you have filed for bankruptcy protection and the proposed modified loan terms were not approved by the Bankruptcy Court. You may wish to contact your bankruptcy counsel or trustee to discuss this decision.

7. **Negative NPV.** The Home Affordable Modification Program requires a calculation of the net present value (NPV) of a modification using a formula developed by the Department of the Treasury. The NPV calculation requires us to input certain financial information about your income and your loan including the factors listed below. When combined with other data in the Treasury model, these inputs estimate the cash flow the investor (owner) of your loan is likely to receive if the loan is modified and the investor's cash flow if the loan is not modified. Based on the NPV results the owner of your loan has not approved a modification.

   If we receive a request from you within 30 calendar days from the date of this letter, we will provide you with the date the NPV calculation was completed and the input values noted below. If, within 30 calendar days of receiving this information you provide us with evidence that any of these input values are inaccurate, and those inaccuracies are material, for example a significant difference in your gross monthly income or an inaccurate zip code, we will conduct a new NPV evaluation. While there is no guarantee that a new NPV evaluation will result in the owner of your loan approving a modification, we want to ensure that the NPV evaluation is based on accurate information.

   Available NPV Inputs
   - a. Unpaid balance on the original loan as of [Data Collection Date]
   - b. Interest rate before modification as of [Data Collection Date].
   - c. Months delinquent as of [Data Collection Date]
   - d. Next ARM reset date (if applicable)
   - e. Next ARM reset rate (if applicable)
   - f. Principal and interest payment before modification
   - g. Monthly insurance payment
   - h. Monthly real estate taxes
   - i. Monthly HOA fees (if applicable)
   - j. Monthly gross income
   - k. Borrower's Total Monthly Obligations
   - l. Borrower FICO
   - m. Co-borrower FICO (if applicable)
   - n. Zip Code
   - o. State

8. **Default Not Imminent.** We are unable to offer you a Home Affordable Modification because you are current on your mortgage loan and after reviewing the financial information you provided us we have determined that you are not at risk of default because:
   - ☐ You have not documented a financial hardship that has reduced your income or increased your expenses, thereby impacting your ability to pay your mortgage as agreed.
   - ☐ You have sufficient net income to pay your current mortgage payment.
   - ☐ You have the ability to pay your current mortgage payment using cash reserves or other assets.

9. **Excessive Forbearance.** We are unable to offer you a Home Affordable Modification because we are unable to create an affordable payment equal to 31% of your reported monthly gross income without changing the terms of your loan beyond the requirements of the program.

10. **Previous HAMP Modification.** We are unable to offer you a Home Affordable Modification because your loan was previously modified under the Home Affordable Modification Program. The program does not allow more than one modification.

11. **Request Incomplete.** We are unable to offer you a Home Affordable Modification because you did not provide us with the documents we requested. A notice which listed the specific documents we needed and the time frame required to provide them was sent to you more than 30 days ago.

12. **Trial Plan Default.** We are unable to offer you a Home Affordable Modification because you did not make all of the required Trial Period Plan payments by the end of the trial period.

Loan Paid Off or Reinstated. We are not considering your request for a modification because:

- ☐ Your loan was paid in full on ____________.
- ☐ Your loan was reinstated on ____________ and you no longer appear to be in need of modification. If you feel that you are at risk of default please contact us to discuss your eligibility and qualification for a Home Affordable Modification.

Offer Not Accepted by Borrower / Request Withdrawn. We are not considering your request for a modification because:

- ☐ After being offered a Trial Period Plan or Home Affordable Modification you notified us on _______ that you did not wish to accept the offer.
- ☐ After initially asking to be considered for a Home Affordable Modification you withdrew that request on _______ .

Incomplete Information Notice. We cannot continue to review your request for a Home Affordable Modification because:

- ☐ You are currently in a Trial Period Plan, however you have not provided all of the documentation we previously requested. If we do not receive the required documents by [insert expiration date of Trial Period Plan but no less than 30 days from the date of the letter] we will terminate your Trial Period Plan and may resume other means to collect any amounts due on your account. The documents we need are: [Insert list of required documents]
- ☐ You have requested consideration for a Trial Period Plan, however, you have not provided all of the documentation we previously requested. If we do not receive the required documents by [insert date no less than 30 days from the date of the letter] we will consider that you have withdrawn your request for a modification and may resume other means to collect any amounts due on your account. The documents we need are: [Insert list of required documents.]

B.3.5 Supplemental Directive 09-09 Revised: Introduction of the Home Affordable Foreclosure Alternatives—Short Sale and Deed-in-Lieu of Foreclosure

Supplemental Directive 09-09 Revised **March 26, 2010**

Home Affordable Foreclosure Alternatives—Short Sale and Deed-in-Lieu of Foreclosure Update

Background

In Supplemental Directive 09-01, the Treasury Department (Treasury) announced the eligibility, underwriting and servicing requirements for the Home Affordable Modification Program (HAMP). Under HAMP, the servicers apply a uniform loan modification process to provide eligible borrowers with sustainable monthly payments for their first lien mortgage loans. While HAMP program guidelines are intended to reach a broad range of at-risk borrowers, it is expected that servicers will encounter situations where they are unable to approve a HAMP modification request, a HAMP modification is offered and not accepted by the borrower, or the borrower falls out of a HAMP modification. In these instances, the borrower may benefit from an alternative that helps the borrower transition to more affordable housing and avoid the stigma of a foreclosure.

This Supplemental Directive replaces in its entirety Supplemental Directive 09-09 and is effective as of April 5, 2010.

This Supplemental Directive provides guidance to servicers for adoption and implementation of the Home Affordable Foreclosure Alternatives Program (HAFA). HAFA is part of HAMP and provides financial incentives to servicers and borrowers who utilize a short sale or a deed-in-lieu to avoid a foreclosure on an eligible loan under HAMP. Both of these foreclosure alternatives reduce the need for potentially lengthy and expensive foreclosure proceedings. The options help preserve the condition and value of the property by minimizing the time a property is vacant and subject to vandalism and deterioration. In addition, these options generally provide a substantially better outcome than a foreclosure sale for borrowers, investors and communities. This Supplemental Directive provides guidance to servicers for adoption and implementation of HAFA for first lien mortgage loans that are not owned or guaranteed by Fannie Mae or Freddie Mac (Non-GSE Mortgages). In order for a servicer to participate in HAFA for Non-GSE Mortgages, the servicer must execute a servicer participation agreement and related documents (SPA) with Fannie Mae in its capacity as financial agent for the United States (as designated by Treasury) to participate in HAMP on or before October 3, 2010. In certain circumstances, Supplemental Directive 09-01 requires participating servicers to consider borrowers for other foreclosure prevention options, including short sale and deed-in-lieu programs. As a result, servicers already participating in HAMP must follow the guidance set forth in this Supplemental Directive, which provides servicers with the option to determine the extent to which short sales or deeds-in-lieu will be offered under this program. Servicers of mortgage loans that are owned or guaranteed by Fannie Mae or Freddie Mac should refer to the HAFA announcement issued by the applicable GSE. A loan must be HAMP eligible and meet the other requirements stated herein to be eligible for incentive compensation under HAFA.

A servicer may elect to implement this Supplemental Directive prior to April 5, 2010, provided that the servicer is able to collect and report all required information as described in the *Reporting Requirements* section of this Supplemental Directive. Borrowers may be accepted into HAFA if a Short Sale Agreement or DIL Agreement, as described in this Supplemental Directive, is fully-executed by the borrower and received by the servicer on or before December 31, 2012.

To help servicers implement HAFA, this Supplemental Directive covers the following topics:

- Foreclosure Alternatives
- HAFA Consideration
- Evaluation
- Short Sale
- Deed-in-Lieu
- General Terms and Conditions
- Incentive Compensation
- Standard Form Documents
- Reporting Requirements
- Compliance

Foreclosure Alternatives

In a short sale, the servicer allows the borrower to list and sell the mortgaged property with the understanding that the net proceeds from the sale may be less than the total amount due on the mortgage. The short sale must be an arm's length transaction with the net sale proceeds (after deductions for reasonable and customary selling costs) being applied to a discounted ("short") mortgage payoff acceptable to the servicer. The servicer accepts the short payoff in full satisfaction of the total amount due on the first mortgage.

In a deed-in-lieu of foreclosure (DIL), the borrower voluntarily transfers ownership of the mortgaged property to the servicer in full satisfaction of the total amount due on the first mortgage. The servicer's willingness to approve and accept a DIL is contingent upon the borrower's ability to provide marketable title, free and clear of mortgages, liens and encumbrances. Generally, servicers require the borrower to make a good faith effort to sell the property through a short sale before agreeing to accept the DIL. However, under circumstances acceptable to the investor, the servicer may accept a DIL without the borrower first attempting to sell the property. With either the HAFA short sale or DIL, the servicer may not require a cash contribution or promissory note from the borrower and must forfeit the ability to pursue a deficiency judgment against the borrower.

Short sales and DILs are complex transactions involving coordination and cooperation among a number of parties including, but not limited to, servicers, appraisers, borrowers (sellers), buyers, real estate brokers and agents, title agencies, and often mortgage insurance companies and subordinate and other lien holders. The HAFA program simplifies and streamlines the use of short sales and DIL options by incorporating the following unique features:

- Complements HAMP by providing viable alternatives for borrowers who are HAMP eligible.
- Utilizes borrower financial and hardship information collected in conjunction with HAMP, eliminating the need for additional eligibility analysis.
- Allows the borrower to receive pre-approved short sale terms prior to the property listing.
- Prohibits the servicer from requiring, as a condition of approving the short sale, a reduction in the real estate commission agreed upon in the listing agreement.
- Requires that borrowers be fully released from future liability for the debt.
- Uses standard processes, documents and timeframes.
- Provides financial incentives to borrowers, servicers and investors.

HAFA Consideration

Each participating servicer must develop a written policy, consistent with investor guidelines, that describes the basis on which the servicer will offer the HAFA program to borrowers. This policy may incorporate such factors as the severity of the loss involved, local market conditions, the timing of pending foreclosure actions and borrower motivation and cooperation.

Servicers may not solicit a borrower for HAFA until the borrower has been evaluated for a HAMP modification in accordance with the provisions of Supplemental Directive 09-01 and any supplemental HAMP guidance. Borrowers that meet the eligibility criteria for HAMP but who are not offered a Trial Period Plan, do not successfully complete a Trial Period Plan, or default on a HAMP modification should first be considered for other loan modification or retention programs offered by the servicer prior to being evaluated for HAFA.

In accordance with the provisions of Supplemental Directive 09-01, a loan meets the basic eligibility criteria if all of the following conditions are met:

- The property is the borrower's principal residence, except that the property can be vacant up to 90 days prior to the date of the Short Sale Agreement (SSA), Alternative Request for Approval of Short Sale (Alternative (RASS) or DIL Agreement if the borrower provides documentation that the borrower was required to relocate at least 100 miles from the property to accept new employment or was transferred by the current employer and there is no evidence indicating that the borrower has purchased a one- to four-unit property 90 days prior to the date of the SSA, Alternative RASS or DIL Agreement;
- The mortgage loan is a first lien mortgage originated on or before January 1, 2009;
- The mortgage is delinquent or default is reasonably foreseeable;

- The current unpaid principal balance is equal to or less than $729,750[1]; and
- The borrower's total monthly mortgage payment (as defined in Supplemental Directive 09-01) exceeds 31 percent of the borrower's gross income.

Pursuant to the servicer's policy, every potentially eligible borrower must be considered for HAFA before the borrower's loan is referred to foreclosure or the servicer allows a pending foreclosure sale to be conducted. Servicers must consider possible HAMP eligible borrowers for HAFA within 30 calendar days of the date the borrower:

- Does not qualify for a Trial Period Plan;
- Does not successfully complete a Trial Period Plan;
- Is delinquent on a HAMP modification by missing at least two consecutive payments; or
- Requests a short sale or DIL.

The date and outcome of the HAFA consideration must be documented in the servicer's file.

When a borrower, who was not previously evaluated for a HAMP modification, requests a short sale or DIL, the servicer must determine the basic eligibility of the borrower as described in the *HAFA Consideration* section of this Supplemental Directive. In addition, the servicer must obtain a completed Request for Modification and Affidavit (RMA)[2] and evidence of the borrower's income sufficient to determine that the borrower meets the 31 percent income eligibility requirement and has experienced a hardship. The servicer is not required to obtain an IRS Form 4506-T nor 4506-EZ, unless it is necessary to verify the borrower's income; to evaluate the mortgage loan using the NPV test; or, to apply the standard modification waterfall set out in Supplemental Directive 09-01. The servicer must notify the borrower verbally or in writing of the availability of a HAMP modification and allow the borrower 14 calendar days from the date of the notification to contact the servicer by verbal or written communication and request consideration for a HAMP modification. If the borrower does not wish to be considered for a modification, this does not trigger a non-approval notice under Supplemental Directive 09-08, *Borrower Notices*.

Borrowers in active Chapter 7 or Chapter 13 bankruptcy cases must be considered for HAFA if the borrower,[3] borrower's counsel or bankruptcy trustee submits a request to the servicer. With the borrower's permission, a bankruptcy trustee may contact the servicer to request a short sale or DIL under HAFA. Servicers are not required to solicit these borrowers proactively for HAFA. The servicer and its counsel must work with the borrower or borrower's counsel to obtain any court and/or trustee approvals required in accordance with local court rules and procedures. Servicers should extend HAFA timeframes as necessary to accommodate delays in obtaining court approvals or receiving any periodic payment when they are made to a trustee.

Evaluation

If the servicer determines that a borrower is eligible for a HAFA offer based on its written policy and this Supplemental Directive, the servicer must follow the steps below to determine if a short sale or DIL offer will be extended to the borrower.

Borrower Solicitation and Response. If the servicer has not already discussed a short sale or DIL with the borrower, the servicer must proactively notify the borrower in writing of the availability of these options and allow the borrower 14 calendar days from the date of the notification to contact the servicer by verbal or written communication and request consideration under HAFA. If the borrower fails to contact the servicer within the timeframe or at any time indicates that he or she is not interested in these options, the servicer has no further obligation to extend a HAFA offer.

Expected Recovery through Foreclosure and Disposition. Though not a HAFA requirement, it is expected that servicers will, in accordance with investor guidelines, perform a financial analysis to determine if a short sale or DIL is in the best interest of the investor, guarantor and/or mortgage insurer. The results of any analysis must be retained in the servicing file. The HAMP base NPV model does not project investor cash flows from either a short sale or DIL and should be used only to determine borrower eligibility for a HAMP modification.

Use of Borrower Financial Information. Verified borrower financial information obtained in conjunction with HAMP may be relied upon to determine a borrower's eligibility for HAFA. If financial and hardship information is documented and verified, no additional financial or hardship assessment is required by HAFA. However, in accordance with investor guidelines, the servicer may request updated financial information to evaluate the borrower. If a borrower was evaluated for HAMP based on verbal financial data, the servicer may send the borrower a Short Sale Agreement (SSA) and must require the borrower to deliver the financial information required under HAMP when the borrower returns the executed SSA. The servicer must verify a borrower's financial information through documen-

1 This amount refers to 1 unit properties. Higher amounts apply to 2 to 4 unit dwellings. *See* Supplemental Directive 09-01.

2 Servicers may elect to use a proprietary financial information form substantially similar to the RMA and a hardship affidavit in lieu of the RMA.

3 Where the borrower filed the bankruptcy pro se, (without an attorney), it is recommended that the servicer provide information relating to the availability of a HAMP modification and foreclosure alternatives to the borrower with a copy to the bankruptcy trustee. This communication should not imply that it is in any way an attempt to collect a debt. Servicers must consult their legal counsel for appropriate language.

tation and obtain a signed Hardship Affidavit prior to approving a short sale or accepting a DIL under HAFA.

Property Valuation. The servicer must, independent of the borrower and any other parties to the transaction, assess the current value of the property in accordance with the investor's guidelines. The servicer may not require the borrower to pay in advance for the valuation, but may add the cost to the outstanding debt in accordance with the borrower's mortgage documents and applicable law in the event the short sale or DIL is not completed.

Review of Title. The servicer must review readily available information provided by the borrower, the borrower's credit report, the loan file or other sources to identify subordinate liens and other claims on title to determine if the borrower will be able to deliver clear, marketable title to a prospective purchaser or the investor. Although not required by HAFA, the servicer may order a title search or preliminary title report. The servicer may not charge the borrower in advance for any cost incurred in the title review, but may add the cost to the outstanding debt in accordance with the borrower's mortgage documents and applicable law in the event the short sale or DIL is not completed.

Borrower Notice. When a HAFA short sale or DIL is not available, the servicer must communicate this decision in writing to any borrower that requested consideration. The notice must explain why a short sale or DIL under HAFA cannot be offered, provide a toll free telephone number that the customer may call to discuss the decision and otherwise comply with the notice requirements of Supplemental Directive 09-08, *Borrower Notices*.

Short Sale

The HAFA short sale process employs standard form documents and defined performance timeframes to facilitate clear communication between the parties to the listing and sale transaction. Servicers must adhere to the following guidelines in connection with the issuance of an SSA.

Minimum Acceptable Net Proceeds. Prior to approving a borrower to participate in a HAFA short sale, the servicer must determine the minimum acceptable net proceeds (minimum net) that the investor will accept from the transaction. Each servicer must develop a written policy, consistent with investor guidelines, that describes the basis on which the minimum net will be determined. However, the minimum net proceeds must be at least equal to or less than the list price minus the sum of allowable costs that may be deducted from gross sale proceeds (or the acceptable sale proceeds). This policy may incorporate such factors as local market conditions, customary transactional costs of such sales, and the amounts that may be required to release any subordinate liens on the property. A servicer's policy for determining the minimum net must be consistently applied for all loans serviced for that investor. The minimum net may be expressed as a fixed dollar amount, as a percentage of the current market value of the property, or as a percentage of the list price as approved by the servicer. Once determined, the servicer must document the minimum net in the servicing file for each property subject to HAFA. After signing an SSA, the servicer may not increase the minimum net requirement until the initial SSA termination date is reached (not less than 120 calendar days). Subsequent changes to the minimum net when the SSA is extended must be documented.

Allowable Transaction Costs. In determining the minimum net, the servicer must consider reasonable and customary real estate transaction costs for the community in which the property is located and determine which of these costs the servicer or investor is willing to pay from sale proceeds. The servicer must describe the costs that may be deducted from the gross sale proceeds in the SSA.

Short Sale Agreement. The HAFA SSA, which is attached as Exhibit A, outlines the roles and responsibilities of the servicer and borrower in the short sale listing process and provides key marketing terms, such as a list price or acceptable sale proceeds and the duration of the SSA. The HAFA Request for Approval of a Short Sale (RASS), which must accompany the SSA, is attached as Exhibit A1. The RASS is submitted to the servicer when an offer is received to provide the terms and conditions of the short sale and together with the sales contract, provides settlement instructions to the settlement agent. Either proactively, or at the request of an eligible borrower, the servicer will prepare and send an SSA to the borrower after determining that the proposed sale is in the best interest of the investor. A borrower may not participate in a HAMP Trial Period Plan and agree to a HAFA SSA simultaneously. The servicer will also provide the borrower a RASS, pre-populated with contact information for the servicer, the property address and the loan number.

In the event that a borrower has an executed sales contract and requests the servicer to approve a short sale under HAFA before an SSA has been executed, the servicer must evaluate the borrower for HAFA as described in the Alternative Request for Approval of a Short Sale (Alternative RASS) section.

While servicers may amend the terms of the SSA in accordance with investor requirements, applicable laws or local real estate practice, at a minimum the SSA must include the following:

- A fixed termination date not less than 120 calendar days from the effective date of the SSA ("Effective Date"). The Effective Date must be stated in the SSA and is the date the SSA is mailed to the borrower. The term of the SSA may be extended at the discretion of the servicer up to a total term of 12 months if agreed to by the borrower, in accordance with the requirements of the investor.

- A requirement that the property be listed with a licensed real estate professional who is regularly doing business in the community where the property is located.
- Either a list price approved by the servicer or the acceptable sale proceeds, expressed as a net amount after subtracting allowable costs that the servicer will accept from the transaction.
- The amount of closing costs or other expenses the servicer will permit to be deducted from the gross sale proceeds expressed as a dollar amount, a percentage of the list price or a list by category of reasonable closing costs and other expenses that the servicer will permit to be deducted from the gross sale proceeds.
- The amount of the real estate commission that may be paid, not to exceed 6% of the contract sales price, and when applicable, notification that the servicer retained a contractor to assist the listing broker with the transaction along with the payment amount (expressed as a fixed dollar amount or percentage of the contract sales price) if paid from sale proceeds.
- A statement by the borrower authorizing the servicer to communicate the borrower's personal financial information to other parties (including Treasury and its agents) as necessary to complete the transaction.
- Cancellation and contingency clauses that must be included in listing and sale agreements notifying prospective purchasers that the sale is subject to approval by the servicer and/or third parties.
- Notice that the sale must represent an arm's length transaction and that the purchaser may not sell the property within 90 calendar days of closing, including certification language regarding the arm's length transaction that must be included in the sales contract.
- An agreement that upon successful closing of a short sale acceptable to the servicer, the borrower will be released from all liability for repayment of the first mortgage debt.
- An agreement that upon successful closing of a short sale acceptable to the servicer the borrower will be entitled to a relocation incentive of $3,000, which will be deducted from the gross sale proceeds at closing.
- Notice that the servicer will allow a portion of gross sale proceeds to be paid to subordinate lien holders in exchange for release and full satisfaction of their liens.
- Notice that a short sale may have income tax consequences and/or may have a derogatory impact on the borrower's credit score and a recommendation that the borrower seek professional advice regarding these matters.
- The amount of the monthly mortgage payment, if any, that the borrower will be required to pay during the term of the SSA, which amount must not exceed 31% of the borrower's gross monthly income.
- An agreement that so long as the borrower performs in accordance with the terms of the SSA, the servicer will not complete a foreclosure sale.
- Terms under which the SSA can be terminated.

Borrower Obligations. The borrower must sign and return the SSA within 14 calendar days from its Effective Date along with a copy of the real estate broker listing agreement and information regarding any subordinate liens. In returning and signing the SSA the borrower agrees to:

- Provide all information and sign documents required to verify program eligibility.
- Cooperate with the listing broker to actively market the property and respond to servicer inquiries.
- Maintain the interior and exterior of the property in a manner that facilitates marketability.
- Work to clear any liens or other impediments to title that would prevent conveyance.
- Make the monthly payment stipulated in the SSA, if applicable.

Monitoring Marketing Activity / Cause for Termination. During the term of the SSA, the servicer may terminate the SSA before its expiration due to any of the following events:

- The borrower's financial situation improves significantly, the borrower qualifies for a modification, or the borrower brings the account current or pays the mortgage in full.
- The borrower or the listing broker fails to act in good faith in listing, marketing and/or closing the sale, or otherwise fails to abide by the terms of the SSA.
- A significant change occurs to the property condition and/or value.
- There is evidence of fraud or misrepresentation.
- The borrower files for bankruptcy and the Bankruptcy Court declines to approve the SSA.
- Litigation is initiated or threatened that could affect title to the property or interfere with a valid conveyance.
- The borrower fails to make the monthly payment stipulated in the SSA, if applicable.

Request for Approval of Short Sale. Within three business days following receipt of an executed purchase offer, the borrower or the listing broker should deliver to the servicer a completed RASS describing the terms of the sale transaction. With the RASS, the borrower must submit to the servicer:

- A copy of the executed sales contract and all addenda.
- Buyer's documentation of funds or buyer's pre-approval or commitment letter on letterhead from a lender.
- All information regarding the status of subordinate liens and/or negotiations with subordinate lien holders.

Approval or Disapproval of Sale. Within ten business days of receipt of the RASS and all required attachments, the servicer must indicate its approval or disapproval of the proposed sale by signing the appropriate section of the RASS and mailing it to the borrower.

The servicer must approve a RASS if the net sale proceeds available for payment to the servicer equal or exceed the minimum net determined by the servicer prior to the execution or extension of the SSA and all other sales terms and conditions in the SSA have been met. Additionally, the servicer may not require, as a condition of approving a short sale, a reduction in the real estate commission below the commission stated in the SSA.

The servicer may require that the sale closing take place within a reasonable period following acceptance of the RASS, but in no event may the servicer require that a transaction close in less than 45 calendar days from the date of the sales contract without the consent of the borrower.

Alternative Request for Approval of Short Sale. If the borrower has an executed sales contract and requests the servicer to approve a short sale under HAFA before an SSA has been executed, then the borrower must submit the request to the servicer in the form of the Alternative Request for Approval of Short Sale (Alternative RASS), attached as Exhibit B. Upon receipt of the Alternative RASS, the servicer must determine the basic eligibility of the borrower as described in the *HAFA Consideration* section of this Supplemental Directive. If the borrower appears to be eligible and was not previously considered for a Trial Period Plan, the servicer must notify the borrower verbally or in writing of the availability of a HAMP modification and allow the borrower 14 calendar days from the date of the notification to contact the servicer by verbal or written communication and request consideration for a HAMP modification.

If the borrower does not wish to be considered for a modification, this does not trigger a nonapproval notice under Supplemental Directive 09-08, *Borrower Notices* and the servicer may consider the Alternative RASS in accordance with this Supplemental Directive without first having to enter into a SSA with the borrower. In such cases, the servicer should obtain a completed RMA[4] and evidence of income prior to completing the short sale. The IRS Form 4506-T or 4506-EZ is not required, unless it is necessary to verify the borrower's income and the servicer is not required to evaluate the mortgage loan using the NPV test or to apply the standard modification waterfall set out in Supplemental Directive 09-01. If the servicer approves the short sale using the Alternative RASS, the loan will qualify for HAFA program incentives.

4 Servicers may elect to use a proprietary financial information form substantially similar to the RMA and a hardship affidavit in lieu of the RMA.

Deed-in-Lieu

In accordance with investor requirements, servicers have the discretion to accept a HAFA DIL, which requires a full release of the debt and waiver of all claims against the borrower. The borrower must agree to vacate the property by a date certain, leave the property in broom clean condition and deliver clear, marketable title.

Typically, servicers require that the borrower make a good faith effort to list and market the property before the servicer will agree to accept a DIL. Under circumstances acceptable to the investor, servicers may agree to accept a DIL without requiring a marketing period. In either circumstance, the transaction will be eligible for incentives as described in the *Incentive Compensation* section of this Supplemental Directive if the borrower meets the HAFA eligibility criteria.

SSA. The SSA contains optional DIL language that may be included or deleted by the servicer prior to execution of the SSA. If the DIL language is included, the investor is obligated to accept a DIL in accordance with the terms of the SSA if the term of the SSA expires without resulting in a sale of the property. If the servicer offers the DIL option separately from the SSA or without a marketing period, the servicer must provide the Deed-in-Lieu Agreement form ("DIL Agreement"), attached as Exhibit C.

DIL Terms. The following terms apply to a HAFA DIL:

- **Marketable Title.** The borrower must be able to convey clear, marketable title to the servicer or investor. The requirements for extinguishment of subordinate liens as described in the *Release of Subordinate Liens* section of this Supplemental Directive apply to DIL transactions.
- **Written Agreement.** The conditions for acceptance of a DIL must be in writing and signed by both the servicer and borrower. They may be set forth in the SSA if approved with the short sale, or in the DIL Agreement.
- **Vacancy Date.** The SSA or DIL Agreement must specify the date by which the borrower must vacate the property, which in no event shall be less than 30 calendar days from the date of the termination date of the SSA or the date of a separate DIL Agreement, unless the borrower voluntarily agrees to an earlier date.
- **Relocation Assistance.** Borrowers who participate in a HAFA DIL transaction are eligible for $3,000 in relocation assistance as described in the *Incentive Compensation* section of this Supplemental Directive.

General Terms and Conditions

Suspension of Foreclosure Sales. At the servicer's discretion, the servicer may initiate foreclosure or continue with an existing foreclosure proceeding during the HAFA process, but may not complete a foreclosure sale:

- While determining the borrower's eligibility and qualification for HAFA.
- While awaiting the timely return of a fully executed SSA.
- During the term of a fully executed SSA.
- Pending transfer of property ownership based on an approved sales contract per the RASS or Alternative RASS.
- Pending transfer of property ownership via a DIL by the date specified in the SSA or DIL Agreement.

Payment Forbearance. The servicer will identify in the SSA, Alternative RASS or DIL Agreement the amount of the monthly mortgage payment, if any, that the borrower is required to make during the term of the applicable agreement and pending transfer of property ownership, as applicable. In no event may the amount of the borrower's monthly payment exceed the equivalent of 31 percent of the borrower's gross monthly income. Servicers must develop a written policy in accordance with investor requirements that identifies the circumstances under which they will require monthly payments and how that payment will be determined. Any requirement for the borrower to make monthly payments must be in accordance with applicable laws, rules and regulations.

Release of Subordinate Liens. It is the responsibility of the borrower to deliver clear marketable title to the purchaser or investor and to work with the listing broker, settlement agent and/or lien holders to clear title impediments. The servicer may, but is not required to, negotiate with subordinate lien holders on behalf of the borrower. The servicer, on behalf of the investor, will authorize the settlement agent to allow a portion of the gross sale proceeds as payment(s) to subordinate mortgage/lien holder(s) in exchange for a lien release and full release of borrower liability. Each lien holder, in order of priority, may be paid no more than six percent (6%) of the unpaid principal balance of their loan, until the $6,000 aggregate cap is reached. Payments will be made at closing from the gross sale proceeds and must be reflected on the HUD-1 Settlement Statement. Investors are eligible for incentive reimbursement for up to one-third of the cost to extinguish subordinate liens as described in the *Incentive Compensation* section of this Supplemental Directive.

Prior to releasing any funds to subordinate mortgage/lien holder(s), the servicer through its agent must obtain written commitment from the subordinate lien holder that it will release the borrower from all claims and liability relating to the subordinate lien in exchange for receiving the agreed upon payoff amount. Although servicers have discretion to draft policies and procedures for ensuring that the commitment of subordinate lien holders is documented prior to closing and such documentation is retained in the servicing file, they would be in compliance with HAFA guidelines if they further required the closing attorney or agent to either confirm that they are in receipt of this commitment from subordinate lien holders on the HUD-1 Settlement Statement, or request that a copy of the written commitment provided by the subordinate lien holder be sent to the servicer with the HUD-1 Settlement Statement which is provided in advance of the closing.

Subordinate mortgage/lien holder(s) may not require contributions from either the real estate agent or borrower as a condition for releasing its lien and releasing the borrower from personal liability. In addition, any payments to subordinate mortgage/lien holder(s) related to the short sale or DIL must be reflected on the HUD-1 Settlement Statement, as applicable.

Release of First Mortgage Lien. The servicer should follow local or state laws or regulations to time the release of its first mortgage lien after receipt of sale proceeds from a short sale or delivery of the deed and property in a DIL transaction. If local or state law does not require release within a specified time from the date the servicer receives payment and satisfies the mortgage, the servicer must release it first mortgage lien within 30 business days. Additionally, the investor must waive all rights to seek a deficiency judgment and may not require the borrower to sign a promissory note for the deficiency.

Borrower Fees. Servicers may not charge the borrower any administrative processing fees in connection with HAFA. The servicer must pay all out-of-pocket expenses, including but not limited to notary fees, recordation fees, release fees, title costs, property valuation fees, credit report fees, or other allowable and documented expenses, but the servicer may add these costs to the outstanding debt in accordance with borrower's mortgage documents and applicable laws in the event the short sale or DIL is not completed. Servicers may require borrowers to waive reimbursement of any remaining escrow, buy down funds or prepaid items, and assign any insurance proceeds to the investor, if applicable. Those funds will not be applied to reduce the total net proceeds from the sale.

Mortgage Insurer Approval. For loans that have mortgage insurance coverage, the servicer/investor must obtain mortgage insurer approval for HAFA foreclosure alternatives. A mortgage loan does not qualify for HAFA unless the mortgage insurer waives any right to collect additional sums (cash contribution or a promissory note) from the borrower.

Incentive Compensation

Treasury will provide reimbursements and incentives as set forth below. However, no incentives will be paid to the borrower, servicer or investor if the net proceeds from a sale exceed the total amount due on the first mortgage when title is transferred. The amount of any contribution paid by a mortgage insurer or other provider of credit enhancement shall not be considered in determining whether the mortgage was paid in full and whether servicers are eligible for such incentive compensation.

Borrowers, servicers and investors will be eligible for HAFA incentives upon successful completion of the short sale or DIL if an SSA, Alternative RASS or DIL Agreement, as applicable, was executed on or before December 31, 2012. Servicers will be reimbursed by Treasury upon reporting the completed HAFA transaction as described in the *Reporting Requirements* section of this Supplemental Directive. For a short sale or DIL, incentives will be paid as follows:

Borrower Relocation Assistance. Following the successful closing of a short sale or DIL, the borrower shall be entitled to an incentive payment of $3,000 to assist with relocation expenses. In a short sale transaction, the servicer must instruct the settlement agent to pay the borrower from sale proceeds at the same time that all other payments, including the payoff to the servicer, are disbursed by the settlement agent. The amount paid to the borrower must appear on the HUD-1 Settlement Statement.

If the servicer conducts a formal closing for a DIL transaction and the borrower has vacated the property, the borrower relocation incentive of $3,000 must be paid at closing and reflected on the HUD-1 Settlement Statement. If at the time of closing the borrower has not vacated the property, the servicer must mail a check to the borrower within five business days of the borrower's vacancy and delivery of keys to the servicer or the servicer's agent. Similarly, if the DIL transaction is not conducted as a formal closing, the servicer must mail a check to the borrower within five business days from the later of the borrower's execution of the deed or the borrower's vacancy and delivery of keys to the servicer or servicer's agent.

Servicers will be reimbursed for the full amount of this incentive payment after the HAFA transaction is reported as described in *Reporting Requirements* section of this Supplemental Directive.

Servicer Incentive. The servicer will be paid $1,500 to cover administrative and processing costs for a short sale or DIL completed in accordance with the requirements of HAFA and the applicable documents. Investors may elect to pay additional incentive compensation to servicers which will not affect the HAFA servicer incentive.

Investor Reimbursement for Subordinate Lien Releases. The investor will be paid a maximum of $2,000 for allowing a portion of the short-sale proceeds to be distributed to or paid to subordinate lien holders. This reimbursement will be earned on a one-for-three matching basis. For each three dollars an investor pays to secure release of a subordinate lien, the investor will be entitled to one dollar of reimbursement up to the maximum reimbursement of $2,000. To receive an incentive, subordinate lien holders must agree to release their liens and waive all future claims against the borrower. The servicer is not responsible for any future actions or claims against the borrower by such subordinate lien holders or creditors.

Standard Form Documents

Servicers are required to use the HAFA documents attached to this Supplemental Directive or forms that are substantially similar in content to the forms provided, except that the servicer may amend the terms of the SSA or DIL Agreement in accordance with investor requirements, applicable laws or local real estate practice and may customize the forms with servicer specific logos. This Supplemental Directive increases incentives provided in Supplemental Directive 09-09, which may impact servicers' HAFA documents, therefore, servicers may manually note changes to their existing HAFA documents until their current supply of forms are exhausted, however, use of the revised HAFA documents or forms that are substantially similar in content is required by June 1, 2010.

Document Retention. Servicers must retain all documents and information received during the process of determining borrower eligibility and qualification for HAFA.

For a period of seven years from the date of the document collection, servicers must retain detailed records of borrower solicitations or borrower-initiated inquiries regarding HAFA, the outcome of the evaluation for foreclosure alternatives under HAFA and specific justification with supporting details if foreclosure alternatives were denied. Records must also be retained to document the reasons for termination of the SSA or expiration of HAFA transactions without a completed short sale or acceptance of a DIL.

Signatures and Electronic Documents. All HAFA documentation must be signed by an authorized representative of the servicer and reflect the actual date of signature by the servicer's representative.

Unless a borrower or co-borrower is deceased or a borrower and a co-borrower are divorced, all parties who signed the original loan documents or their duly authorized representatives must execute the HAFA documents. If a borrower and a co-borrower are divorced and the property has been transferred to one spouse in the divorce decree, the spouse who no longer has an interest in the property is not required to execute the HAFA documents. Servicers may evaluate requests on a case-by-case basis when the borrower is unable to sign due to circumstances such as mental incapacity or military deployment.

Any party to a document utilized in HAFA may, subject to applicable law and any investor requirements or restrictions, prepare, sign and send the document through electronic means provided: (a) appropriate technology is used to store an authentic record of the executed document and the technology otherwise ensures the security, confidentiality and privacy of the transaction, (b) the document is enforceable under applicable law, (c) the servicer obtains the borrower's consent to use electronic means to enter into the document, (d) the servicer ensures that the borrower is able to retain a copy of the document and provides a copy to the borrower that the borrower may download, store and print, and (e) the borrower, at any time, may elect to enter into the document through paper means or to receive a paper copy of the document.

Reporting Requirements

As a condition to receiving the incentive payments offered through HAFA, servicers are required to provide periodic HAFA loan level data to Fannie Mae, in its capacity as program administrator. The data submitted must be accurate, complete, timely, and agree with the servicer's records. Data will be reported by a servicer at key milestones in the transaction:

- **Notification**—when the SSA or DIL Agreement is signed and executed, or updated following an extension of the marketing terms;
- **Short Sale/DIL Loan Set Up**—at the transfer of property ownership (closing of a short sale or acceptance of DIL); and/or
- **Termination**—when the SSA or DIL Agreement expires or when the SSA or DIL Agreement is terminated by the servicer.

Each milestone is a separate data transmission and must be reported no later than the fourth business day of the month following the event. The required data elements are attached to this Supplemental Directive as Exhibit D. In addition, HAFA reporting requirements will be posted on the servicer web portal at www.hmpadmin.com. Note also that the reporting information required under Supplemental Directive 09-06 must be provided by the servicer for all HAFA transactions.

The HAFA reporting and payment processes are currently under development by Fannie Mae, in its capacity as program administrator. Subsequent guidance will be provided describing when the HAFA reporting and processes will be available. Servicers will not be required to report HAFA data until the reporting process is in place, but in this interim period servicers must collect and store information on all HAFA transactions so that the necessary data can be reported when the processes become available. In addition, HAFA incentives will not be paid until the payment process is available; borrowers, servicers and investors will be reimbursed for all incentives relating to HAFA transactions closed prior to the reporting and payment processes becoming available.

Credit Bureau Reporting. The servicer should continue to report a "full file" status to the major credit repositories for each loan under the HAFA program in accordance with the Fair Credit Reporting Act and the Consumer Data Industry Association's ("CDIA's") Metro 2 Format credit bureau requirements. "Full file" reporting means that the servicer must describe the exact status of each mortgage it is servicing as of the last business day of each month. The Payment Rating code should be the code that properly identifies whether the account is current or past due within the activity period being reported—prior to completion of the HAFA transaction. Because CDIA's Metro 2 format does not provide an Account Status Code allowable value for a short sale, a short sale should identified with the reporting of Special Comment Code "AU". The information below is consistent with "CDIA Mortgage and Home Equity Reporting Guidelines in Response to Current Financial Conditions" (May 2009).

Reporting should be as follows:

Short Sales

- Account Status Code = 13 (paid or closed/zero balance)
- Payment Rating = 0, 1, 2, 3, 4, 5, or 6
- Special Comment Code = AU (account paid in full for less than the full balance)
- Current Balance = $0
- Amount Past Due = $0
- Date Closed = MMDDYYYY
- Date of Last Payment = MMDDYYYY

Deed-in-Lieu

- Account Status Code = 89 (deed-in-lieu of foreclosure on a defaulted loan)
- Payment Rating = 0, 1, 2, 3, 4, 5, or 6
- Current Balance = $0
- Amount Past Due = $0
- Date Closed = MMDDYYYY
- Date of Last Payment = MMDDYYYY

Compliance

Servicers must comply with the HAFA short sale and DIL requirements specified in this Supplemental Directive and any subsequent policy guidance. Servicers must have adequate staffing and resources for responding to borrower requests for participation, for receiving and processing HAFA documents in accordance with program guidelines and for ensuring that inquiries and complaints about HAFA receive fair consideration, along with timely and appropriate response and resolution.

Treasury has selected Freddie Mac to serve as its compliance agent for HAFA. In its role as compliance agent, Freddie Mac will utilize Freddie Mac employees and contractors to conduct independent compliance assessments. The scope of the assessments will include, among other things, an evaluation of documented evidence to confirm adherence (e.g., accuracy and timeliness) to HAFA requirements with respect to the following:

- Assessment of the process for evaluating and approving borrowers for a HAFA short sale or DIL.
- Adherence to the standard policies and guidelines for completing HAFA short sales and DIL and consistent application of same.
- Determining fair market value, recommended list price, approved sale proceeds and approved minimum net proceeds, as applicable.
- Guidelines for allowable payoffs to junior lien holders.
- Use of standard documents and document retention.
- Completion of borrower, servicer and investor incentive payments.

The review will also confirm the existence and evaluate the effectiveness of the servicer's quality assurance program; such evaluation will include, without limitation, the timing and size of the sample selection, the scope of the quality assurance reviews, and the reporting and remediation process.

There will be two types of compliance assessments: on-site and remote. Both on-site and remote reviews will include the following activities (among others): notification, scheduling, self assessments, documentation submission, interviews, file reviews, and reporting.

For on-site reviews, Freddie Mac will strive to provide the servicer with (i) a 30-day advance notification of a pending review and (ii) subsequent confirmation of the dates of the review; however, Freddie Mac reserves the right to arrive at the servicer's site unannounced. Freddie Mac will request the servicer to make available documentation, including, without limitation, policies and procedures, management reports, loan files and a risk control self assessment ready for review. Moreover, Freddie Mac may request additional loan files during the review. Interviews will usually be conducted in-person.

During the review window, Freddie Mac will review loan files and other requested documentation to evaluate compliance with HAFA terms. Upon the completion of the review, Freddie Mac will conduct an exit interview with the servicer to discuss preliminary assessment results.

For remote reviews, Freddie Mac will request the servicer to send documentation, including, without limitation, policies and procedures, management reports, loan files and a risk control self assessment within 30 calendar days of the request. In addition, time will be scheduled for phone interviews, including a results summary call after the compliance review is completed to discuss preliminary results.

The targeted time frame for publishing the servicer assessment report is 30 calendar days after the completion of the review. Treasury will receive a copy of the report five business days prior to the release of the report to the servicer. There will be an issue/resolution appeal process for servicer assessments. Servicers will be able to submit concerns or disputes to an independent quality assurance team within Freddie Mac.

A draft rating and implication methodology for the compliance assessments will be published in a subsequent Supplemental Directive and servicer feedback will be solicited prior to the finalization of the methodology.

[*Editor's Note: The following Exhibits are not reprinted herein. Exhibits are reprinted in full on this treatise's companion website.*]

Exhibit A: Short Sale Agreement
Exhibit A1: Request for Approval of Short Sale
Exhibit B: Alternative Request for Approval of Short Sale
Exhibit C: DIL Agreement
Exhibit D: HAFA Data Elements

B.3.6 Supplemental Directive 10-01: Home Affordable Modification Program—Program Update and Resolution of Active Trial Modifications

Supplemental Directive 10-01 January 28, 2010

Home Affordable Modification Program—Program Update and Resolution of Active Trial Modifications

Background

In Supplemental Directive 09-01, the Treasury Department (Treasury) announced the eligibility, underwriting and servicing requirements for the Home Affordable Modification Program (HAMP). Under HAMP, servicers apply a uniform loan modification process to provide eligible borrowers with sustainable monthly payments for their first lien mortgage loans. This Supplemental Directive amends key features of the program. A significant program change is a requirement for full verification of borrower eligibility prior to offering a trial period plan. Effective for all HAMP trial period plans with effective dates on or after June 1, 2010, a servicer may only offer a borrower a trial period plan based on verified income documentation in accordance with this Supplemental Directive.

This Supplemental Directive also provides guidance to assist servicers in making HAMP eligibility determinations for borrowers currently in active trial period plans, including those borrowers subject to the temporary review period required by Supplemental Directive 09-10.

This Supplemental Directive provides guidance to servicers of first mortgage loans that are not owned or guaranteed by Fannie Mae or Freddie Mac (Non-GSE Mortgages). Servicers of first mortgage loans that are owned or guaranteed by Fannie Mae or Freddie Mac should refer to the related HAMP guidelines issued by the applicable GSE.

Requesting Consideration for Modification

Supplemental Directive 09-01 gave servicers the option of placing a borrower into a trial period plan based on verbal financial information obtained from the borrower, subject to later verification during the trial period. Effective for all trial period plans with effective dates on or after June 1, 2010, a servicer may evaluate a borrower for HAMP only after the servicer receives the following documents, subsequently referred to as the "Initial Package". The Initial Package includes:

- Request for Modification and Affidavit (RMA) Form,
- IRS Form 4506-T or 4506T-EZ, and
- Evidence of Income

Request for Modification and Affidavit (RMA) Form

The RMA Form provides the servicer with borrower and co-borrower financial information including the cause of the borrower's hardship. The financial information and hardship sections of the RMA must be completed and executed by the borrower and, if applicable, the coborrower. The RMA also solicits data related to the race, ethnicity and gender of the borrower and co-borrower, referred to as Government Monitoring Data (GMD). The borrower and coborrower are not required to provide GMD. Servicers may not refuse to accept an RMA because the borrower or co-borrower did not complete this section. The RMA is available to servicers on www.HMPadmin.com.

Servicers may require use of the RMA by all borrowers requesting consideration for HAMP or may continue to use other proprietary financial information forms that are substantially similar in content to the RMA. When provided by or on behalf of the borrower, the RMA form must be accepted by servicers in lieu of any servicer specific form(s). When the RMA is not used, servicers must obtain an executed MHA Hardship Affidavit, a standalone version of which is available on www.HMPadmin.com. Servicers may also incorporate all of the information on this standalone affidavit into their own form. Throughout this Supplemental Directive, the term RMA is used to indicate both the HAMP RMA form and servicer proprietary forms substituted for the RMA.

IRS Form 4506-T/4506T-EZ

All borrowers must provide a signed and completed IRS 4506-T/4506T-EZ (Request for Transcript of Tax Return).[1] While either form is acceptable, use of Form 4506T-EZ is encouraged because of its relative simplicity. Both forms are available on www.HMPadmin.com. Borrowers may access Form 4506T-EZ in either English or Spanish on www.MakingHomeAffordable.gov. After completion, the borrower must print, sign and send the form to his or her servicer.

Evidence of Income

The Initial Package must also include the borrower's income verification documentation described in the "Borrower Income/Asset Documentation and Verification of Eligibility" section of this Supplemental Directive. The income evidence and financial information provided by the borrower may not be more than 90 days old as of the date the Initial Package is received by the servicer.

Acknowledgment and Review of Initial Package

Within 10 business days following receipt of an Initial Package, the servicer must acknowledge in writing the borrower's request for HAMP participation by sending the borrower confirmation that the Initial Package was received, and a description of the servicer's evaluation process and timeline. If the Initial Package is received from the borrower via e-mail, the servicer may e-mail the acknowledgment. Servicers must maintain evidence of the date of receipt of the borrower's Initial Package in its records.

Within 30 calendar days from the date an Initial Package is received, the servicer must review the documentation provided by the borrower for completeness. If the documentation is incomplete, the servicer must send the borrower an Incomplete Information Notice in accordance with the guidance set forth in the "Incomplete Information Notice" section below. If the borrower's documentation is complete, the servicer must either:

- Send the borrower a Trial Period Plan Notice; or
- Make a determination that the borrower is not eligible for HAMP and communicate this determination to the borrower in accordance with the Borrower Notice guidance provided in Supplemental Directive 09-08.

A single written communication sent within 10 days of receipt of a borrower's request for HAMP participation may also include, at the servicer's discretion, the results of its review of the Initial Package. Servicers are reminded that Supplemental Directive 09-01 generally prohibits servicers from proceeding with a foreclosure sale for any potentially eligible mortgage loan until the borrower has been evaluated for eligibility under HAMP and has been determined to be ineligible or has declined a trial period plan offer.

Incomplete Information Notice

If the servicer receives an incomplete Initial Package or needs additional documentation to verify the borrower's eligibility and income, the servicer must send the borrower an Incomplete Information Notice that lists the additional required verification documentation. The Incomplete Infor-

1 IRS Form 4506T-EZ may not be applicable to borrowers that do not file federal income tax returns on a calendar year basis, borrowers that do not file federal income tax returns using Form 1040 and borrowers that have not filed a federal income tax return. Servicers should obtain a signed and completed IRS Form 4506-T from these borrowers.

mation Notice must include a specific date by which the documentation must be received, which must be no less than 30 calendar days from the date of the notice. If the documents are not received by the date specified in the notice, the servicer must make one additional attempt to contact the borrower in writing regarding the incomplete documents. This additional notice must include the specific date by which the documentation must be received, which must be no less than 15 calendar days from the date of the second notice. If a borrower is unresponsive to these requests for documentation the servicer may discontinue document collection efforts and determine the borrower to be ineligible for HAMP. If the borrower is determined to be ineligible for HAMP, the servicer must communicate this determination to the borrower in accordance with the Borrower Notice guidance provided in Supplemental Directive 09-08.

Trial Period Plan Approval

Within 30 calendar days following receipt of an Initial Package or complete verification documents, the servicer must complete its verification and evaluate the borrower's eligibility for HAMP and, if the borrower is qualified, send the borrower a Trial Period Plan Notice. If the borrower is determined to be ineligible for HAMP, the servicer must communicate this determination to the borrower in accordance with the Borrower Notice guidance provided in Supplemental Directive 09-08. Servicers are reminded that Supplemental Directive 09-01 prohibits servicers from initiating a new foreclosure action while a borrower is in a trial period plan.

Consideration for Alternative Loss Mitigation Options

When a borrower is determined to be ineligible for a HAMP modification, the servicer is required to consider that borrower for all other available loss mitigation options, including but not limited to refinance, forbearance, non-HAMP modifications and, to the extent a borrower does not qualify for a home retention alternative, Home Affordable Foreclosure Alternatives (short sales or deeds in lieu of foreclosure) under Supplemental Directive 09-09. As required in Supplemental Directive 09-08, available loss mitigation options should be described in the Non-Approval Notice.

Continued Eligibility for HAMP

A borrower who has been evaluated for HAMP but does not meet the minimum eligibility criteria described in the "HAMP Eligibility" section of Supplemental Directive 09-01 or who meets the minimum eligibility criteria but is not qualified for HAMP by virtue of a negative NPV result, excessive forbearance or other financial reason, may request reconsideration for HAMP at a future time if they experience a change in circumstance.

Borrower Income/Asset Documentation and Verification of Eligibility

Servicers should request that the borrower provide the income verification documentation listed below but may, consistent with contractual requirements, substitute other reliable forms of verification when appropriate. Servicers are responsible for determining that any information provided by the borrower and which is needed to evaluate the borrower's qualification for HAMP is complete and accurate. When evaluating a borrower's eligibility for HAMP, servicers should use good business judgment consistent with the judgment employed when modifying mortgage loans held in their own portfolio. This guidance, which is effective as of the date of this Supplemental Directive, supersedes the "Borrower Income/Asset Documentation and Verification" section in Supplemental Directive 09-07 and applies both to evaluation of borrowers currently in active trial period plans as well as to evaluation of borrowers being evaluated for verified income trial period plans.

- **Employment Income.** Copies of two recent pay stubs, not more than 90 days old at time of submission, indicating year-to-date earnings.
  a. Servicers may accept pay stubs that are not consecutive if, in the business judgment of the servicer, it is evident that the borrower's income has been accurately established.
  b. When two pay stubs indicate different periodic income, servicers may use year-to-date earnings to determine the average periodic income, and account for any non-periodic income reflected in either of the pay stubs.
  c. When verifying annualized income based on the year-to-date earnings reflected on pay stubs, servicers may, in their business judgment, make adjustments when it is likely that sources of additional income (bonus, commissions, etc.) are not likely to continue.
- **Self-employment Income.** The most recent quarterly or year-to-date profit and loss statement for each self-employed borrower. Audited financial statements are not required.
- **Other earned income** (e.g., bonus, commission, fee, housing allowance, tips, overtime). Reliable third party documentation describing the nature of the income (e.g. an employment contract or printouts documenting tip income).
- **Benefit Income** (e.g., social security, disability, death benefits, pension, public assistance, adoption assistance). Evidence of (i) the amount and frequency of the benefits such as letters, exhibits, a disability policy or benefits statement from the provider, and (ii) receipt of payment, such as copies of the two most recent bank statements or deposit advices showing deposit amounts.

If a benefits statement is not available, servicers may rely only on receipt of payment evidence, if it is clear that the borrower's entitlement is ongoing.

- **Unemployment Benefits.** Evidence of the amount, frequency and duration of the benefits (usually obtained through a monetary determination letter). The unemployment income must continue for at least nine months from the date of the application. The duration of benefit eligibility—including federal and state extensions—may be evidenced by a screenshot or printout from the Department of Labor UI benefit tool, which is available at http://www.ows.doleta.gov/unemploy/ben_entitle.asp.
- **Rental income.** Rental income is generally documented through the Schedule E—Supplemental Income and Loss, for the most recent tax year.
  a. When Schedule E is not available to document rental income because the property was not previously rented, servicers may accept a current lease agreement and bank statements or cancelled rent checks.
  b. If the borrower is using income from the rental of a portion of the borrower's principal residence, the income may be calculated at 75 percent of the monthly gross rental income, with the remaining 25 percent considered vacancy loss and maintenance expense.
  c. If the borrower is using rental income from properties other than the borrower's principal residence, the income to be calculated for HAMP purposes should be 75 percent of the monthly gross rental income, reduced by the monthly debt service on the property (i.e., principal, interest, taxes, insurance, including mortgage insurance, and association fees), if applicable.
- **Alimony, Separation Maintenance, and Child Support Income.** Borrowers are not required to use alimony, separation maintenance or child support income to qualify for HAMP. However, if the borrower chooses to provide this income, it should be documented with (i) copies of the divorce decree, separation agreement or other legal written agreement filed with a court, or a court decree that provides for the payment of alimony or child support and states the amount of the award and the period of time over which it will be received, and (ii) evidence of receipt of payment, such as copies of the two most recent bank statements or deposit advices showing deposit amounts. If the borrower voluntarily provides such income, and that income renders the borrower ineligible for a HAMP offer, the servicer is allowed to remove that income from consideration and re-evaluate the borrower for HAMP eligibility.
- **20% Threshold for Passive and Non-Wage Income.** Notwithstanding the foregoing, passive and non-wage income (including rental, part-time employment, bonus/tip, investment and benefit income) does not have to be documented if the borrower declares such income and it constitutes less than 20% of the borrower's total income.
- **Non-Borrower Income.** Servicers should include non-borrower household income in monthly gross income if it is voluntarily provided by the borrower and if, in the servicer's business judgment, that the income reasonably can continue to be relied upon to support the mortgage payment. Non-borrower household income included in the monthly gross income must be documented and verified by the servicer using the same standards for verifying a borrower's income.

Association Fees

If a borrower has indicated that there are association fees, but has not been able to provide written documentation to verify the fees, the servicer may rely on the information provided by the borrower if the servicer has made reasonable efforts to obtain the association fee information in writing.

Principal Forbearance Limitation

Effective as of the date of this Supplemental Directive, with respect to both "positive" and "negative" NPV results, servicers are not required to forbear more than the greater of (i) 30 percent of the unpaid principal balance of the mortgage loan (after any capitalization under Step 1 of the standard modification waterfall) or (ii) an amount resulting in a modified interest-bearing balance that would create a current mark-to-market loan-to-value ratio equal to 100 percent. If the borrower's monthly mortgage payment cannot be reduced to the target monthly mortgage payment ratio of 31 percent unless the servicer forbears more than the amounts described above, the servicer may consider the borrower ineligible for a HAMP modification. However, servicers are permitted, in accordance with existing servicing agreements and investor guidelines, to forbear principal in excess of the amounts described above in order to achieve the target monthly mortgage payment ratio of 31 percent for both NPV-positive and NPV-negative loans.

In the event a servicer elects to forbear principal in an amount resulting in a modified interest-bearing balance that would create a current mark-to-market loan-to-value ratio less than 100 percent in negative NPV situations, the servicer should ignore the error code and the flag for excessive forbearance that is returned by the current version of the NPV model. Updates will be made to the NPV model in the future to eliminate this error code.

IRS Form 4506-T/4506T-EZ

All borrowers must provide a signed and completed IRS Form 4506-T/4506T-EZ (Request for Transcript of Tax Return) with the Initial Package, and the servicer must submit the borrower's Form 4506-T/4506T-EZ to the IRS for processing unless the borrower provides a signed copy of his or her most recent federal income tax return, including all schedules and forms. Servicers should review the tax information and use good business judgment to determine whether any discrepancies exist. If the servicer determines that discrepancies relevant to the HAMP decision exist, the servicer must reasonably reconcile the discrepancies.

Credit Report and Occupancy Verification

For all borrowers, the servicer must obtain a credit report for each borrower or a joint report for a married couple who are co-borrowers to validate installment debt and other liens as described on page 10 of Supplemental Directive 09-01. Servicers should use the credit report to confirm that the property securing the mortgage loan is the borrower's principal residence. If the credit report is inconsistent with other information provided by the borrower, the servicer must use good business judgment in reconciling the inconsistency.

Property Valuation Documentation

Servicers must obtain a property valuation input for the NPV model using an automated valuation model (AVM), provided that the AVM renders a reliable confidence score, a broker's price opinion (BPO), or an appraisal. A servicer may use an AVM provided by one of the GSEs. As an alternative, servicers may rely on their internal AVM provided:

- The servicer is subject to supervision by a Federal regulatory agency;
- The servicer's primary Federal regulatory agency has reviewed the model; and
- The AVM renders a reliable confidence score.

If a GSE AVM is unable to render a value with a reliable confidence score, or the servicer AVM does not meet the requirements above, the servicer must obtain an assessment of the property value utilizing a BPO, an appraisal or a property valuation method documented as acceptable to the servicer's Federal regulatory supervisor. Such assessment must be rendered in accordance with the Interagency Appraisal and Evaluation Guidelines (as if such guidelines apply to loan modifications). In all cases, the property valuation used cannot be more than 90 days old as of the date the servicer first evaluates the borrower for a HAMP trial period plan using the NPV model.

Document Perfection

Servicers must use good business judgment when determining the level of perfection of the verification documents. Servicers may elect to accept documents with imperfections (blank fields, erasures, use of correction tape, inaccurate dates, etc.) if the servicer determines that the imperfections are immaterial to the business decision, are not indicative of fraud and do not impact the servicer's ability to verify the completeness and accuracy of the borrower's financial representations.

Borrower Signatures

Unless a borrower or co-borrower is deceased or divorced, all parties who signed the original loan documents or their duly authorized representative(s) should sign the HAMP documents. However, servicers may encounter circumstances where a co-borrower signature is not obtainable, for reasons such as mental incapacity, military deployment or contested divorce. Servicers should use good business judgment, in accordance with existing servicing agreements and investor guidelines, when determining whether to accept a document without a co-borrower's signature.

Electronic Submission

For all documents required by Treasury (other than for IRS Form 4506-T/4506T-EZ), electronic submission and signatures are acceptable.

Fraud Detection

Servicers should not modify a mortgage loan if there is reasonable evidence indicating the borrower submitted income information that is false or misleading or if the borrower otherwise engaged in fraud in connection with the modification.

Conversion from Trial to Permanent Modification

Servicers must use a two-step process for HAMP modifications. Following underwriting and a determination that the borrower qualifies for a HAMP trial modification, servicers will place qualified borrowers in a trial period plan by preparing and sending a Trial Period Plan Notice to the borrower describing the terms of the trial modification and the payment due dates. Borrowers who make all trial period payments timely and who satisfy all other trial period requirements will be offered a permanent HAMP modification.

Step 1: Trial Period Plan Start

The trial period is three months in duration (or longer if necessary to comply with applicable contractual obligations). Borrowers are not required to sign or return the Trial Period Plan Notice. Servicers should retain a copy of the Trial Period Plan Notice in the borrower file and note the date that it was sent to the borrower. Receipt of the first payment due under the trial period plan on or before the last day of the month in which the first payment is due is evidence of the borrower's acceptance of the trial period plan and its terms and conditions. The effective date of the trial period will be set forth in the trial period plan and is the first day of the month in which the first trial period plan payment is due.

Step 2: Conversion to Permanent

The borrower must be current under the terms of the trial period plan at the end of the trial period to receive a permanent loan modification. "Current" in this context is defined as the borrower having made each required trial period payment by the last day of the month in which it is due. Borrowers who fail to make current trial period payments are considered to have failed the trial period and are not eligible for a HAMP modification. Servicers are instructed to use good business judgment in determining whether trial period payments were received timely or if mitigating circumstances caused the payment to be late. Exceptions should be documented in the servicing record.

Resolution of Active Trial Modifications

In Supplemental Directive 09-10, Treasury implemented a temporary review period for all active HAMP trial modifications scheduled to expire on or before January 31, 2010. During this temporary review period, servicers were not permitted to cancel an active HAMP trial modification for any reason other than failure to meet the HAMP property eligibility requirements. Servicers were also required to send written notification to all borrowers to inform them of their current modification status and provide borrowers with the opportunity to remedy any documentation or payment deficiencies. Following this required notice and cure period, servicers should make final determinations for all active HAMP trial modifications subject to Supplemental Directive 09-10 in accordance with the guidelines set forth below.

In addition, servicers have initiated trial period plans based on verbal income information that are not subject to the temporary review period required by Supplemental Directive 09-10 (and may continue to do so for trial period plans with effective dates prior to June 1, 2010). Servicers should make final determinations for such trial modifications upon the expiration of the applicable trial period in accordance with the guidelines set forth below.

- If the borrower has not made all required trial period payments, or has not submitted any income verification documentation, the servicer must find the borrower ineligible for a permanent HAMP modification and cancel the HAMP trial modification from the Treasury system of record. When a HAMP trial modification is cancelled, the servicer must consider the borrower for other available foreclosure prevention alternatives and send the borrower the appropriate Borrower Notice in accordance with Supplemental Directive 09-08.
- If the borrower has submitted all required trial period payments, and the borrower has submitted some form of income documentation, the servicer must evaluate the borrower, determine whether the borrower is eligible for a permanent HAMP modification, and promptly communicate the eligibility determination to the borrower. If the income documentation is insufficient to make a HAMP decision, and the servicer is unable to obtain the required documentation from the borrower, the servicer must find the borrower ineligible for a permanent HAMP modification and cancel the HAMP trial modification from the Treasury system of record. When a HAMP trial modification is cancelled, the servicer must consider the borrower for other available foreclosure prevention alternatives and send the borrower the appropriate Borrower Notice in accordance with Supplemental Directive 09-08.

If the borrower has not submitted or signed a Hardship Affidavit but has made all required trial period payments and is otherwise eligible for a HAMP modification, the servicer may approve the borrower for a modification, send the Hardship Affidavit to the borrower with the Home Affordable Modification Agreement and instruct the borrower to execute and return both as a condition of the permanent HAMP modification.

If the borrower has not submitted a signed and completed Form 4506-T or 4506T-EZ but has submitted the most recent tax return (including all applicable schedules), has made all required trial period payments and is otherwise eligible for a HAMP modification, the servicer may approve the borrower for a modification, send the Form 4506-T or 4506T-EZ, as applicable, to the borrower with the Home Affordable Modification Agreement and instruct the borrower to execute and return both as a condition of the permanent HAMP modification.

Supplemental Directive 09-01 requires servicers to reevaluate a loan using the NPV model if the borrower's documented income differs from the stated income used in the borrower's initial qualifying NPV test. With respect to trial period plans with effective dates prior to June 1, 2010, servicers may elect, in accordance with existing servicing agreements and investor guidelines, to offer the borrower a permanent HAMP modification without performing an additional NPV evaluation based on the borrower's verified income documentation. If the servicer elects not to perform an additional NPV evaluation in this situation, the servicer should enter the trial period values for NPV Date and NPV Value when reporting the official loan set up file to the Treasury system of record.

In situations where servicers reevaluate a loan using the NPV model based on the borrower's verified income documentation, servicers are reminded that they should test a borrower using the same major version of the NPV model that was used to test the loan for trial modification eligibility. Detailed versioning requirements are included in the Base NPV Model Documentation, which is available at www.HMPadmin.com, and in Exhibit A to this Supplemental Directive.

All active HAMP trial modifications scheduled for cancellation due to an NPV negative result based on an NPV re-testing procedure that was not fully consistent with the HAMP versioning requirements must be re-tested in accordance with the versioning requirements prior to the servicer cancelling the trial modification.

Documentation Requirements

Servicers are required to maintain appropriate documentary evidence of their HAMP-related activities, and to provide that documentary evidence upon request to Freddie Mac as the Compliance Agent for Treasury. Documentation should be maintained by the servicer for all HAMP activities, including, but not limited to, the following:

- The servicer's process for pre-screening non-performing loans against the basic HAMP requirements;
- The servicer's process for evaluating investor willingness to participate in HAMP and attempts to obtain waivers on specific loans;
- Phone contact with borrowers relating to HAMP;
- All written communications that relate to or mention HAMP;
- Policies and procedures that include HAMP-related activities;
- Training materials relating to HAMP;
- Any reports, memoranda, or other documentation relating to HAMP; and
- The decision-making process when applying good business judgment in accordance with HAMP and, where applicable, reference the servicer's associated policies and procedures.

For phone contact with borrowers related to HAMP, well-documented servicer system notes (including but not limited to date, names of contact persons, and a summary of the conversation) will constitute appropriate documentation. Written correspondence should be retained in an accessible manner and made available upon request by the Compliance Agent.

EXHIBIT A
NPV VERSIONING REQUIREMENTS

Detailed versioning requirements are included in the Base NPV Model Documentation, which is available at www.HMPadmin.com. These requirements include:

- Ensuring that the same major model version is used for repeat NPV tests as was used to qualify the borrower for a HAMP trial modification. For example:
  a. If the borrower was qualified using any sub-version of a HAMP major model version on the portal, the borrower should be re-tested using at least the same HAMP major model version (and are encouraged to re-test using the specific model release (e.g. 3.x) if possible). For borrowers initially tested on the portal, the portal automatically sorts borrowers into the appropriate model version based on the NPV Run Date.
  b. If the borrower was tested on a proprietary model or a recoded version of the base model before September 1, 2009, the borrower should be re-tested using that proprietary model or recoded version. If that model is no longer operational and the servicer must use a different model for subsequent tests, any re-test results used for the decision must be adjusted so that the borrower is insulated, as much as is possible, from NPV changes resulting purely from differences in the models. Servicers who have implemented a proprietary NPV model or are operating a recoded version of the base model should refer to the version control guidance issued on October 16, 2009 by Treasury's Compliance Agent for further details regarding treatment of these loans.
- Ensuring that all NPV inputs remain constant when the borrower is retested, except (i) those that were found to be incorrect at the time of the initial NPV evaluation and (ii) inputs that have been updated based on the borrower's income documentation. Inputs that may be updated based on the borrower's documentation are limited to the following:
  a. Association Dues/Fees before Modification
  b. Monthly Hazard and Flood Insurance
  c. Monthly Real Estate Taxes
  d. Monthly Gross Income
  e. Unpaid Principal Balance After Modification (interest-bearing UPB)
  f. Principal Forbearance Amount
  g. Interest Rate After Modification
  h. Amortization Term After Modification
  i. Principal and Interest Payment After Modification

  Inputs that may not change regardless of their evolution since the trial's initiation include:
  a. Unpaid Principal Balance Before Modification
  b. Borrower FICO and Co-borrower FICO
  c. Property Value
  d. Interest Rate Before Modification
  e. Term Before Modification
  f. Monthly Principal and Interest Payments Before Modification
  g. Months Past Due
  h. ARM Reset Rate and ARM Reset Date
  i. Data Collection Date
  j. Imminent Default Status
  k. NPV Run Date
  l. Advances/Escrow
  m. Discount Rate Risk Premium (spread of discount rate over PMMS rate)
- Servicers who have implemented a proprietary NPV model or are operating a recoded version of the base model must ensure that all economic inputs remain constant from the first to subsequent tests. Inputs that should be held constant include the PMMS rate and all quarterly input tables.

B.3.7 Supplemental Directive 10-02: Home Affordable Modification Program—Borrower Outreach and Communication

Supplemental Directive 10-02 March 24, 2010

Home Affordable Modification Program—Borrower Outreach and Communication

Background

In Supplemental Directive 09-01, the Treasury Department (Treasury) announced the eligibility, underwriting and servicing requirements for the Home Affordable Modification Program (HAMP). Under HAMP, servicers apply a uniform loan modification process to provide eligible borrowers with sustainable monthly payments for their first lien mortgage loans. This Supplemental Directive represents an ongoing effort to improve program effectiveness by amending policies and procedures related to borrower outreach and communication, especially with respect to the initiation and continuation of foreclosure actions and extending HAMP benefits to borrowers who have filed for bankruptcy court protection. These changes become effective on June 1, 2010. The changes set forth herein do not abridge a servicer's ability to service delinquent loans in accordance with industry standards.

The significant changes described in this Supplemental Directive include:

- Clarification of the requirement to solicit proactively all borrowers whose first mortgage loans are potentially eligible for HAMP and who have two or more payments due and unpaid. Reasonable solicitation efforts are defined.
- Prohibition against referral to foreclosure until either: (i) a borrower has been evaluated and determined to be ineligible for HAMP; or (ii) reasonable solicitation efforts have failed.
- A requirement that a servicer, in certain specific circumstances, allow a 30-day borrower response period following issuance of a Non-Approval Notice before a foreclosure sale may be conducted.
- A requirement that a servicer provide a written certification to the foreclosure attorney or trustee stating that a borrower is not HAMP-eligible before a foreclosure sale may be conducted.
- A requirement that servicers must consider borrowers in active bankruptcy for HAMP if a request is received from the borrower, borrower's counsel or bankruptcy trustee.
- Clarification of the requirement that servicers use reasonable efforts to obtain approval from investors to participate in HAMP.

This Supplemental Directive provides guidance to servicers of first lien mortgage loans that are not owned or guaranteed by Fannie Mae or Freddie Mac (Non-GSE Mortgages). Servicers of first lien mortgage loans that are owned or guaranteed by Fannie Mae or Freddie Mac should refer to the related HAMP guidelines issued by the applicable GSE.

Borrower Communication

Borrower Solicitation

Each servicer must have clear and comprehensive internal written policies for identification and solicitation of borrowers who are potentially eligible for HAMP based on information in the servicer's possession. These procedures should follow investor guidelines and comply with all contractual restrictions and with applicable laws, rules and regulations, including, but not limited to, the Fair Debt Collection Practices Act.

Servicers must pre-screen all first lien mortgage loans where two or more payments are due and unpaid to determine if they meet the basic criteria for consideration under HAMP (one-to-four unit residential property, occupied by the borrower as his or her principal residence, not vacant or condemned, originated on or before January 1, 2009, unpaid principal balance does not exceed $729,750[1] and not previously modified under HAMP). Servicers must proactively solicit for HAMP any borrower whose loan passes this pre-screen, unless the servicer has documented that the investor is not willing to participate in HAMP pursuant to the "Investor Solicitation" section of this Supplemental Directive.

Solicitation must include written communication clearly describing HAMP. Use of the form of solicitation letter available on www.HMPadmin.com shall satisfy this requirement. The servicer's HAMP solicitation may also identify other options potentially available to help the borrower cure the delinquency and retain homeownership. A servicer is deemed to have made a "Reasonable Effort" to solicit a borrower if over a period of at least 30 calendar days: (1) the servicer makes a minimum of four telephone calls to the last known phone numbers of record, at different times of the day; and (2) the servicer sends two written notices to the last address of record by sending one letter via certified/express mail or via overnight delivery service (such as Federal Express or UPS) with return receipt/delivery confirmation and one letter via regular mail. Any contact with eligible borrowers, whether by telephone, mail or otherwise, must (1) advise borrowers that they may be eligible for HAMP; (2) clearly describe the Initial Package required to be submitted by the borrower pursuant to Supplemental Directive 10-01 and state what other information the servicer needs to complete the HAMP analysis; (3) provide a toll-free tele-

1 Maximum loan limit for one unit dwelling. 2 units—$934,200; 3 units—$1,129,250; 4 units—$1,404,400.

phone number through which the borrower can reach a servicer representative; and (4) identify any unique requirements the servicer may have established for submission of an Initial Package received later than 30 business days prior to a scheduled foreclosure sale date. All contact attempts must be documented in the servicing file. If the servicer has documentation evidencing that it satisfied the Reasonable Effort standard for HAMP prior to the effective date of this Supplemental Directive, re-solicitation of the borrower is not required.

Successful efforts by a servicer to communicate with the borrower or co-borrower about resolution of the delinquency are termed "right party contact" for purposes of this Supplemental Directive. If right party contact is established and the borrower expresses an interest in HAMP, the servicer must send a written communication to the borrower via regular or electronic mail that clearly describes the Initial Package required to be submitted by the borrower to request a HAMP modification. The communication should:

- Describe the income evidence required to be evaluated for HAMP;
- Provide the Request for Modification and Affidavit (RMA) (or other proprietary financial information form substantially similar in content to the RMA and, if necessary, a Hardship Affidavit); and
- Include an Internal Revenue Service (IRS) Form 4506T-EZ (or IRS Form 4506-T, if necessary).

The communication should also include clear language stating that during the HAMP evaluation the home will not: (i) be referred to foreclosure; or (ii) be sold at a foreclosure sale if the foreclosure process has already been initiated. In the communication, the servicer must include a specific date by which the Initial Package must be returned, which must be no less than 15 calendar days from the date of the communication. Electronic mail for this purpose may only be sent to an email address provided by the borrower when right party contact was made. Such email address must be documented in the servicing file.

If right party contact is established prior to satisfaction of the Reasonable Effort standard, the servicer must continue to take steps to satisfy the Reasonable Effort standard until the Initial Package is submitted by the borrower.

If right party contact is established but the borrower does not submit an Initial Package, the servicer must resend the Initial Package communication. Again, the servicer must include a specific date by which the Initial Package must be returned, which must be no less than 15 calendar days from the date of the second communication. If the borrower does not respond by providing an Initial Package within the required time period set forth in the second communication, the servicer may determine the borrower to be ineligible for HAMP.

If right party contact is established but the borrower submits an incomplete Initial Package within the required time period, the servicer must comply with the Incomplete Information Notice requirements set forth in Supplemental Directive 10-01. If the borrower does not respond to either the 30-day Incomplete Information Notice or the 15-day Incomplete Information Notice by providing a complete Initial Package within the required time period, the servicer may determine the borrower to be ineligible for HAMP.

The servicer is not required to send an Initial Package if, as a result of discussions with the borrower, the servicer determines that the borrower does not meet the basic eligibility criteria for HAMP as described in Supplemental Directive 09-01, or the servicer determines that the borrower's monthly mortgage obligation (including principal interest, taxes, insurance and homeowner's association fee, if applicable) is substantially less than 31% of the borrower's gross monthly income. Such decision must be documented in the applicable servicing file.

Other Borrower Communication

As set forth in Supplemental Directives 09-07 and 10-01, servicers must acknowledge the Initial Package within 10 business days of receipt through a written communication to the borrower that includes a description of the servicer's evaluation process and timeline. Additionally, the communication must include clear language that states that during the HAMP evaluation the home will not: (i) be referred to foreclosure; or (ii) be sold at a foreclosure sale if the foreclosure process has already been initiated. If the Initial Package is received from the borrower via email, the servicer may email the acknowledgement to the same email address from which the Initial Package was received or other email address designated by the borrower in the Initial Package.

Servicer communications should provide the borrower with clear written information designed to help the borrower understand the modification process in accordance with Supplemental Directive 09-01. These communications must provide a toll-free telephone number where the borrower can reach a representative of the servicer capable of providing specific details about the HAMP modification process. The hours of operation for the toll-free telephone number should be listed.

Servicers must have adequate staffing, written procedures, resources and facilities for receipt, management, retention and retrieval of borrower documents to ensure that borrowers are not required to submit multiple copies of documents. Servicers must accept the RMA and other required verification documents submitted on behalf of borrowers by HUD-approved housing counseling agencies, non-profit consumer advocacy organizations, legal guardians, powers of attorney or legal counsel when the borrower has provided written authorization or provides written authorization contemporaneously with the submission of the RMA. The borrower is considered to have provided written authorization if a copy of the power of attorney, order of guardianship, or other legal papers authorizing the third party to act on behalf of the borrower are provided. Written authorization may be supplanted by the legal documents authorizing a third party to act more generally on behalf of the borrower in cases of disability or borrowers unavailable due to active duty military service.

Servicers must have written procedures and personnel in place to provide timely and appropriate responses to borrower inquiries and complaints in connection with HAMP within the timelines specified in this and previous Supplemental Directives. These procedures must include a process through which borrowers may escalate disagreements to a supervisory level, where a separate review of the borrower's eligibility or qualification can be performed.

Foreclosure Actions

The following guidance replaces in its entirety the guidance set forth on page 14 of Supplemental Directive 09-01 under the heading "Temporary Suspension of Foreclosure Proceedings".

Prohibition on Referral and Sale

A servicer may not refer any loan to foreclosure or conduct a scheduled foreclosure sale *unless* and *until* at least one of the following circumstances exists:

- The borrower is evaluated for HAMP and is determined to be ineligible for the program; or
- The borrower is offered a trial period plan, but fails to make a trial period payment by the last day of the month in which such payment is due; or
- The servicer has established right party contact, has sent at least two written requests asking the borrower to supply required information in accordance with this Supplemental Directive and has otherwise satisfied the Reasonable Effort solicitation standard, and the borrower failed to respond by the dates indicated in those requests; or
- The servicer has satisfied the Reasonable Effort solicitation standard without establishing right party contact; or
- The borrower or co-borrower states he or she is not interested in pursuing a HAMP modification and such statement is reflected by the servicer in their servicing system.

Borrower Response Period

Supplemental Directive 09-08 describes circumstances in which a written Non-Approval Notice must be provided to borrowers who have not been approved for HAMP. The servicer may not conduct a foreclosure sale within the 30 calendar days after the date of a Non-Approval Notice or any longer period required to review supplemental material provided by the borrower in response to a Non-Approval Notice unless the reason for non-approval is (1) ineligible mortgage, (2) ineligible property, (3) offer not accepted by borrower/request withdrawn or (4) the loan was previously modified under HAMP.

A model clause describing these rights is attached as Exhibit A. Use of the model clause is optional; however, it illustrates the level of specificity that is deemed to be in compliance with the language requirements of this Supplemental Directive.

Halt of Existing Foreclosure Actions During a Trial Period Based on Verified Income

With respect to a borrower who submits a request for HAMP consideration after a loan has been referred to foreclosure, the servicer shall, immediately upon the borrower's acceptance of a trial period plan based on verified income as described in Supplemental Directive 10-01 and for the duration of the trial period, take those actions within its authority that are necessary to halt further activity and events in the foreclosure process, whether judicial or non-judicial, including but not limited to refraining from scheduling a sale or causing a judgment to be entered.

The servicer shall not be in violation of this instruction to the extent that: (a) a court with jurisdiction over the foreclosure proceeding (if any), or the bankruptcy court in a bankruptcy case, or the public official charged with carrying out the activity or event, fails or refuses to halt some or all activities or events in the matter after the servicer has made reasonable efforts to move the court or request the public official for a cessation of the activity or event; (b) the servicer must take some action to protect the interests of the owner, investor, guarantor or servicer of the loan in response to action taken by the borrower or other parties in the foreclosure process; or (c) there is not sufficient time following the borrower's acceptance of the trial period plan for the servicer to halt the activity or event, provided that in no event shall the servicer permit a sale to go forward. The servicer must document in the servicing file if any of the foregoing exceptions to the requirement to halt an existing foreclosure action are applicable.

Deadline for Suspension of Foreclosure Sales

When a borrower submits a request for HAMP consideration after a foreclosure sale date has been scheduled and the request is received no later than midnight of the seventh business day prior to the foreclosure sale date (the "Deadline"), the servicer must suspend the sale as necessary to evaluate the borrower for HAMP. Servicers are not required to suspend a foreclosure sale when: (1) a request for HAMP consideration is received after the Deadline; (2) a borrower received a HAMP modification and lost good standing; (3) a borrower received a HAMP offer and made the first payment under the trial period plan, but did not make a subsequent payment by the applicable deadline; or (4) a borrower was evaluated based upon an Initial Package and determined to be ineligible under HAMP requirements.

The servicer shall not be in violation of this instruction to the extent that a court with jurisdiction over the foreclosure proceeding (if any), or the bankruptcy court in a bankruptcy case, or the public official charged with carrying out the activity or event, fails or refuses to halt the sale after the servicer has made reasonable efforts to move the court or request the public official for a cessation of the sale. The servicer must document in the servicing file if the foregoing exception to the requirement to suspend an existing foreclosure sale is applicable.

A borrower will be deemed to have requested consideration for HAMP when a complete Initial Package (i.e., RMA, Form 4506T-EZ, required evidence of income) is received by the servicer or its foreclosure attorney/trustee prior to the Deadline. However, the servicer may establish additional requirements for requests received later than 30 calendar days prior to a scheduled foreclosure sale date, including, for example, a requirement that a complete Initial Package be delivered through certified/express delivery mail with return receipt/delivery confirmation to either the servicer or the foreclosure attorney/foreclosure trustee. These requirements must be posted on the servicer's website and communicated to the borrower in writing in accordance with the Borrower Solicitation requirements of this Supplemental Directive or through other written communication.

If the borrower contacts the servicer prior to the Deadline, the servicer must inform the borrower of the Deadline and any submission requirements.

Mitigating Foreclosure Impact

The servicer must take the following action to mitigate foreclosure impact:

- **Simultaneous Trial Period Plan and Foreclosure Explanation.** When a borrower is simultaneously in foreclosure and is either being evaluated for HAMP or is in a trial period plan, the servicer must provide the borrower with a written notification that explains, in clear language, the concurrent modification and foreclosure processes and that states that even though certain foreclosure activities may continue, the home will not be sold at a foreclosure sale while the borrower is being considered for HAMP or while the borrower is making payments under a trial period plan. Model language for this notification is attached as Exhibit B. Use of the model language is optional; however, it illustrates the level of specificity that is deemed to be in compliance with the language requirements of this Supplemental Directive.
- **Foreclosure Attorney/Trustee Communication.** Servicers must develop and implement written policies and procedures to provide notification to their foreclosure attorney/trustee regarding a borrower's HAMP status, including whether the borrower is potentially eligible for HAMP (and is subject to the Borrower Solicitation requirements of this Supplemental Directive), and whether the borrower is being evaluated for, or is currently in, a HAMP trial period plan. Servicers must ensure that their foreclosure attorney/trustee adheres to all of the requirements of this Supplemental Directive with respect to referral to foreclosure, stay of foreclosure actions and suspension of foreclosure sales.
- **Certification Prior to Foreclosure Sale.** Servicers must develop and implement written procedures applicable to all loans that are potentially eligible for HAMP (and are subject to the Borrower Solicitation requirements of this Supplemental Directive) that require the servicer to provide to the foreclosure attorney/trustee a written certification that (i) one of the five circumstances under the "Prohibition on Referral and Sale" section of this Supplemental Directive exists, and (ii) all other available loss mitigation alternatives have been exhausted and a non-foreclosure outcome could not be reached. This certification must be provided no sooner than seven business days prior to the scheduled foreclosure sale date (the Deadline) or any extension thereof.

Borrowers in Bankruptcy

Borrowers in active Chapter 7 or Chapter 13 bankruptcy cases must be considered for HAMP if the borrower,[2] borrower's counsel or bankruptcy trustee submits a request to the servicer. With the borrower's permission, a bankruptcy trustee may contact the servicer to request a HAMP modification. Servicers are not required to solicit these borrowers proactively for HAMP. Borrowers who are in a trial period plan and subsequently file for bankruptcy may not be denied a HAMP modification on the basis of the bankruptcy filing. The servicer and its counsel must work with the borrower or borrower's counsel to obtain any court and/or trustee approvals required in accordance with local court rules and procedures. Servicers should extend the trial period plan as necessary to accommodate delays in obtaining court approvals or receiving a full remittance of the borrower's trial period payments when they are made to a trustee, but they are not required to extend the trial period beyond two months, resulting in a total five-month trial period. In the event of a trial period extension, the borrower shall make a trial period payment for each month of the trial period, including any extension month.

When a borrower in an active Chapter 13 bankruptcy is in a trial period plan and the borrower has made post-petition payments on the first lien mortgage in the amount required

2 Where the borrower filed the bankruptcy pro se, (without an attorney), it is recommended that the servicer provide information relating to the availability of a HAMP modification to the borrower with a copy to the bankruptcy trustee. This communication should not imply that it is in any way an attempt to collect a debt. Servicers must consult their legal counsel for appropriate language.

by the trial period plan, a servicer must not object to confirmation of a borrower's Chapter 13 plan, move for relief from the automatic bankruptcy stay, or move for dismissal of the Chapter 13 case on the basis that the borrower paid only the amounts due under the trial period plan, as opposed to the non-modified mortgage payments.

Borrowers who have received a Chapter 7 bankruptcy discharge in a case involving the first lien mortgage who did not reaffirm the mortgage debt under applicable law are eligible for HAMP. The following language must be inserted in Section 1 of the Home Affordable Modification Agreement:

> "I was discharged in a Chapter 7 bankruptcy proceeding subsequent to the execution of the Loan Documents. Based on this representation, Lender agrees that I will not have personal liability on the debt pursuant to this Agreement."

Substitution of Income Documents

When a borrower is in an active Chapter 7 or Chapter 13 bankruptcy, the servicer may accept copies of the bankruptcy schedules and tax returns (if returns are required to be filed) in lieu of the RMA and Form 4506T-EZ, and may use this information to determine borrower eligibility (with the income documentation). Servicers should request the schedules and tax returns from the borrower, borrower's counsel or bankruptcy court. If the bankruptcy schedules are greater than 90 days old as of the date that such schedules are received by the servicer, the borrower must provide updated evidence of income to determine HAMP eligibility. Additionally, either directly or through counsel, borrowers must provide a completed and executed Hardship Affidavit (or RMA).

Waiver of Trial Period Plan

Pending development of systems capability, and at the discretion of the servicer, borrowers in an active Chapter 13 bankruptcy who are determined to be eligible for HAMP may be converted to a permanent modification without completing a trial period plan if:

- The borrower makes all post-petition payments on their first lien mortgage loan due prior to the effective date of the Home Affordable Modification Agreement, and at least three of those payments are equal to or greater than the proposed modified payment;
- The modification is approved by the bankruptcy court, if required; and
- The trial period plan waiver is permitted by the applicable investor guidelines.

When payments under a bankruptcy plan are used in lieu of a trial period in accordance with these guidelines, the servicer and borrower will be eligible to accrue "pay for success" and "pay for performance" incentives for the length of a standard HAMP trial period.

Changes to several data reporting attributes under HAMP will be required to enable servicers to report a bankruptcy plan in lieu of a HAMP trial period. Servicers should look for a full description and detail of the data attributes for bankruptcy reporting to be posted on www.HMPadmin.com. Servicers may not exercise this waiver authority until the data elements are posted and the system capability exists to support this policy change.

Continued HAMP Eligibility

Servicers are reminded of those situations when a borrower may seek reconsideration for a HAMP modification. As stated in Supplemental Directive 10-01, a borrower who has been evaluated for HAMP but does not meet the minimum eligibility criteria described in the "HAMP Eligibility" section of Supplemental Directive 09-01 or who meets the minimum eligibility criteria but is not qualified for HAMP by virtue of a negative NPV result, excessive forbearance or other financial reason, may request reconsideration for HAMP at any time prior to the Deadline if they experience a change in circumstance. In these cases, the servicer is obligated to consider the borrower's request pursuant to its obligations under the Servicer Participation Agreement (SPA).

A servicer's SPA obligation to offer the borrower a HAMP modification is considered satisfied, and the borrower is not eligible for a subsequent HAMP offer, if the borrower either (1) received a HAMP modification and lost good standing, or (2) the borrower received a HAMP offer and either failed to make one or more payments under trial period plan by the last day of the month in which it was due, or if applicable, failed to provide all required documents by the end of the trial period.

Servicing Transfers of Loans in Foreclosure

The servicer may transfer a loan free and clear of all HAMP-related obligations under the SPA if one of the five circumstances under the "Prohibition on Referral and Sale" section of this Supplemental Directive exists with respect to such loan, and any applicable response period has elapsed, unless a borrower with continued HAMP eligibility requests consideration prior to the effective date of the servicing transfer. Such loans are not required to be transferred pursuant to the form of Assignment and Assumption Agreement attached as Exhibit D to the Servicer Participation Agreement. Servicers should refer to the "Transfers of Servicing" section of Supplemental Directive 09-01 for guidance regarding servicing transfers of loans modified pursuant to HAMP.

Investor Solicitation

Within 90 days of executing a Servicer Participation Agreement (SPA), the servicer must review all servicing agreements to determine investor participation in the program. Within 30 days of identifying an investor as a non-participant, the servicer will contact the investor in writing at least once, encouraging the investor to permit modifications under HAMP.

Within 60 calendar days following the effective date of this Supplemental Directive, participating servicers must, if they have not already done so, provide to Fannie Mae, as Treasury's Program Administrator: (1) the number of investors for whom it services loans; (2) a list of those investors who do not participate in HAMP; and (3) the number of loans serviced for each investor that does not participate in HAMP. Servicers that execute a SPA after the date of this Supplemental Directive must provide the investor participation list to Fannie Mae, as Treasury's program administrator, within 120 days of SPA execution.

Servicers are required to notify Fannie Mae, as Treasury's Program Administrator, of changes to the Investor Participation List within 30 calendar days of any change.

Documentation

Servicers are required to maintain appropriate documentary evidence of their HAMP-related activities, and to provide that documentary evidence upon request to Freddie Mac as the Compliance Agent for Treasury. As Compliance Agent, Freddie Mac will incorporate the additional requirements articulated in this Supplemental Directive into its compliance program. Servicers must maintain documentation in well-documented servicer system notes or in loan files for all HAMP activities addressed in this Supplemental Directive, including, but not limited to, the following:

- All HAMP related communications, whether verbal or written, with or to the borrower or trusted advisor (including but not limited to the dates of communications, names of contact person(s), and a summary of the conversation), including any email correspondence to or from the borrower.
- Pre-screening of loans for HAMP prior to referring any loan to foreclosure or conducting scheduled foreclosure sales.
- Postponement of scheduled foreclosure sales in applicable scenarios.
- Substitution of income documents for borrowers in active Chapter 7 or Chapter 13 bankruptcy.
- Waiver of the trial period plan for borrowers in active Chapter 13 bankruptcy.
- Policies and procedures required by this Supplemental Directive.
- Certification prior to foreclosure sale.
- Evidence of assessment of investor willingness to participate in HAMP and any specific outreach to investors on either a portfolio or loan-by-loan basis, including copies of any contracts with investors relied upon in denying HAMP modifications. This should include, where applicable, documentation relating to specific parameters or limitations on participation required by investors for steps in the waterfall.
- Evidence of receipt of the Initial Package from a borrower.

EXHIBIT A
BORROWER RESPONSE PERIOD

The model clause in this exhibit provides sample language that may be used to explain the borrower response period that exists after a borrower is issued a Non-Approval Notice unless the reason for non-approval is (1) ineligible mortgage, (2) ineligible property, (3) offer not accepted by borrower/request withdrawn or (4) the loan was previously modified under HAMP. Use of the model clause is optional; however, it illustrates a level of specificity that is deemed to be in compliance with language requirements of this Supplemental Directive.

> You have 30 calendar days from the date of this notice to contact [name of servicer] to discuss the reason for non-approval for a HAMP modification or to discuss alternative loss mitigation options that may be available to you. Your loan may be referred to foreclosure during this time, or any pending foreclosure action may continue. However, **no foreclosure sale will be conducted and you will not lose your home** during this 30-day period [or any longer period required for us to review supplemental material you may provide in response to this Notice].

EXHIBIT B
MODEL SIMULTANEOUS TRIAL PLAN-FORECLOSURE PROCESS EXPLANATION

[Servicer Logo]

[Date]

[Name]
[Address 1]
[Address 2]

Dear [borrower and co-borrower name(s)]:

We are committed to helping you retain your home. That's why we are currently evaluating your mortgage for eligibility in the Home Affordable Modification Program ("HAMP") which would modify the terms of your loan and make your mortgage payments more affordable. Your loan has been previously referred to foreclosure and we will continue the foreclosure process while we evaluate your loan for HAMP. However, **no foreclosure sale will be conducted and you will not lose your home** during the HAMP evaluation.

HAMP Eligibility

- If you are eligible for HAMP, you will enter into a "trial period". You will receive a Trial Period Plan Notice which will contain a new trial payment amount (this will temporarily replace your current mortgage payment during the HAMP trial period). To accept the Trial Period Plan, you must make your first trial payment by the specified due date. Once you accept, we will halt the foreclosure process as long as you continue to make your required trial plan payments.
- If you do not qualify for HAMP, or if you fail to comply with the terms of the Trial Period Plan, you will be sent a Non-Approval Notice. In most cases, you will have 30 days to review the reason for non-approval and contact us to discuss any concerns you may have. During this 30-day review period, we may continue with the pending foreclosure action, but **no foreclosure sale will be conducted and you will not lose your home.**

Important—Do not ignore any foreclosure notices.

The HAMP evaluation and the process of foreclosure may proceed at the same time. You may receive foreclosure/eviction notices—delivered by mail or in person—or you may see steps being taken to proceed with a foreclosure sale of your home. While you will not lose your home during the HAMP evaluation, to protect your rights under applicable foreclosure law, you may need to respond to these foreclosure notices or take other actions. If you have any questions about the foreclosure process and the evaluation of your HAMP request, contact us at [XXX.XXX.XXXX]. If you do not understand the legal consequences of the foreclosure, you are also encouraged to contact a lawyer or housing counselor for assistance.

Questions

Call **XXX.XXX.XXXX** if you cannot afford to make your trial period payments, but want to remain in your home. Or if you have decided to leave your home, contact us—we have other options that may be able to help you avoid foreclosure. Additionally, if you have any questions about the foreclosure (or other legal notices that you receive), please call us for assistance. You can also call the Homeowners HOPE Hotline at 1-888-995-HOPE (4673) if you need further counseling. They offer free HUD-certified counseling services in English and Spanish, and can help answer any questions you have.

Sincerely,
[Servicer Contact Person Name]
[Servicer Contact Person Title]
[Servicer Name]

B.3.8 Supplemental Directive 10-04: Home Affordable Unemployment Program Background

Supplemental Directive 10-04 **May 11, 2010**

Home Affordable Unemployment Program

Background

In Supplemental Directive 09-01, the Treasury Department (Treasury) announced the eligibility, underwriting and servicing requirements for the Home Affordable Modification Program (HAMP). Under HAMP, servicers apply a uniform loan modification process to provide eligible borrowers with sustainable monthly housing payments. This Supplemental Directive provides servicers flexibility to provide assistance to borrowers whose hardship is related to unemployment. When a borrower is unemployed, a HAMP trial period plan or permanent HAMP modification may not be appropriate, and in some cases, the borrower may not have the ability to make the required payments.

This Supplemental Directive requires servicers to consider eligible borrowers for the Home Affordable Unemployment Program (UP), which grants borrowers a forbearance plan during which regular monthly mortgage payments are reduced or suspended. Borrowers will be evaluated for HAMP at the earlier of re-employment or 30 days prior to the expiration of the UP forbearance plan.

This Supplemental Directive provides guidance to servicers of first lien mortgage loans that are not owned or guaranteed by Fannie Mae or Freddie Mac (Non-GSE Mortgages) or insured or guaranteed by a federal agency, such as the Federal Housing Administration (FHA), and is effective for all participating servicers on July 1, 2010. However, servicers may begin to offer UP earlier so long as all unemployed borrowers that are potentially eligible are considered for UP as of the date the servicer begins offering UP. Servicers that have executed a servicer participation agreement and related documents (SPA) must follow the guidance set forth in this Supplemental Directive. Servicers of first lien mortgage loans that are owned or guaranteed by Fannie Mae or Freddie Mac should refer to relevant guidance issued by the applicable GSE.

Help for Unemployed Borrowers

This guidance replaces the language under the heading "Unemployment Benefits" in the "Borrower Income/Asset Documentation and Verification of Eligibility" section of Supplemental Directive 10-01. A borrower who is unemployed and requests assistance under HAMP must be evaluated for and, if qualified, receive an UP forbearance plan before the borrower may be considered for HAMP. For borrowers being considered for trial period plans with effective dates on or after July 1, 2010, servicers may no longer consider unemployment insurance benefits as a source of income when evaluating borrowers for HAMP. For purposes of this Supplemental Directive, the term "borrower" includes any co-borrower.

UP Forbearance Plan Eligibility

Servicers are required to offer an UP forbearance plan to a borrower who meets the following HAMP minimum eligibility criteria:

- The mortgage loan is secured by a one- to four-unit property, one unit of which is the borrower's principal residence.
- The mortgage loan is a first lien mortgage loan originated on or before January 1, 2009.
- The current unpaid principal balance of the mortgage loan is equal to or less than $729,750.[1]
- The mortgage loan is delinquent or default is reasonably foreseeable.
- The mortgage loan has not been previously modified under HAMP and the borrower has not previously received an UP forbearance period.

Additional UP forbearance plan eligibility requirements include that the borrower:

- Makes a request before the first mortgage lien is seriously delinquent (before three monthly payments are due and unpaid). A request for UP may be made by phone, mail or email. Servicers must document the date of the UP request in the servicing file and, within 10 business days, confirm the receipt of the request with the borrower via mail or return email.
- Is unemployed at the date of the request for UP and is able to document that he or she will receive unemployment benefits in the month of the Forbearance Period Effective Date (defined below) even if his or her unemployment benefit eligibility is scheduled to expire before the end of the UP forbearance period.

The servicer may, pursuant to investor or regulator guidelines, require a borrower to have received unemployment benefits for up to three months before the forbearance period will begin. A borrower who has received unemployment benefits for less than the minimum time period required by the servicer may request consideration for an UP forbearance plan; however, the forbearance period will not begin until after the borrower has received unemployment benefits as required by the servicer. Servicers must have written procedures for determining when a borrower must be in receipt of up to three months of unemployment benefits and must consistently apply those procedures.

To be eligible for HAMP, a borrower's total monthly mortgage payment (principal, interest, taxes, insurance and association fees, if any) prior to the modification must exceed 31 percent of the borrower's gross income. To streamline the delivery of unemployment assistance, a servicer may waive this criterion for UP forbearance plan eligibility. However, servicers are not required to offer an UP forbearance plan to borrowers whose total monthly mortgage payment is less than or equal to 31 percent of the borrower's monthly gross income, including unemployment benefits. Servicers are not required to offer an UP forbearance plan if a household member that is not a borrower becomes unemployed, even if that income contributed to the mortgage payment.

Unemployed borrowers who do not meet the eligibility criteria for an UP forbearance plan should be evaluated for other proprietary forbearance programs. Borrowers that are not offered any type of forbearance plan must be evaluated for HAMP, excluding from monthly gross income unemployment benefits and any other temporary sources of income related to unemployment, such as severance payments. If the borrower is not eligible for HAMP, the servicer must send the borrower a Non-Approval Notice in accordance with Supplemental Directive 09-08 and describe other foreclosure alternatives for which the borrower may be eligible, including but not limited to the Home Affordable Foreclosure Alternatives Program (HAFA) or other short sale or deed-in-lieu programs.

A borrower in a permanent HAMP modification that becomes unemployed is not eligible for an UP forbearance plan. A borrower who was previously determined to be ineligible for a HAMP modification may request consideration for an UP forbearance plan if the borrower meets all of the eligibility requirements.

Conversion from HAMP Trial Period Plan to an UP Forbearance Plan

A borrower who is currently in a HAMP trial period plan and becomes unemployed may seek consideration under UP if the borrower was not seriously delinquent (as defined above) as of the first payment due date of the HAMP trial period plan. A servicer may not require an unemployed borrower in a trial period plan to convert to an UP forbearance plan. However, upon receipt of a request for consideration for an UP forbearance plan by an unemployed borrower in a trial period plan and evidence that the borrower is or will be eligible for unemployment benefits, the servicer must cancel the trial period plan and follow the guidance for establishing the Forbearance Period Effective Date, as described below. The servicer may not impose a waiting period before commencement of the forbearance plan by requiring the borrower to be in receipt of unemployment benefit for a longer period than required by UP. If following an UP forbearance plan the borrower is determined to again be eligible for HAMP, the borrower must

1 This amount refers to 1 unit properties. Higher amounts apply to 2 to 4 unit dwellings. *See* Supplemental Directive 09-01.

complete a new HAMP trial period plan. To determine eligibility, the borrower will be required to submit complete and updated HAMP documentation (including the RMA and updated proof of income), but will not be required to re-submit IRS Form 4506T-EZ if the servicer has already obtained a tax transcript for the most recent tax year.

UP Forbearance Plan Terms

The minimum UP forbearance period is the lesser of three months or upon notification that the borrower has become re-employed. Servicers should establish procedures for tracking borrowers' employment status and include any applicable borrower instructions in the Forbearance Plan Notice (FPN); as described below. Servicers may extend the minimum forbearance period in increments at the servicer's discretion, in accordance with investor and regulatory guidelines. Any borrower eligibility review or recertification documentation requirements that may apply after the initial forbearance period are at the servicer's discretion, in accordance with investor and regulatory guidelines.

During the UP forbearance plan, the borrower's monthly mortgage payment must be reduced to an amount that is no more than 31 percent of the borrower's gross monthly household income. In determining gross monthly income, the servicer may rely on stated income provided by the borrower or may require documentation of income. At the discretion of the servicer, the borrower's monthly mortgage payments may be suspended in full. The payment amount, if any, will be determined by the servicer in accordance with investor and regulator guidelines and applicable laws and regulations. Servicers must have written procedures for determining when a payment will be required during an UP forbearance plan and how the payment amount will be determined, and must consistently apply those procedures.

Commencement of UP Forbearance Plan

A borrower's UP forbearance plan starts on the Forbearance Period Effective Date. If the servicer transmits the FPN, to the borrower on or before the 15th day of a calendar month, then the servicer should insert the first day of the next month as the Forbearance Period Effective Date. If the servicer transmits the FPN to the borrower after the 15th day of a calendar month, the servicer may, as an alternative, use the first day of the month after the next month as the Forbearance Period Effective Date. Servicers who elect this alternative and require the borrower to have received unemployment benefits for up to three months should factor the additional month towards meeting the established requirement for unemployment benefits so that the forbearance period may begin immediately after meeting the requirement and must do so consistently for all borrowers in accordance with written policies and procedures. This determination should be based on the date that the FPN is sent to the borrower.

If the servicer requires a reduced monthly payment, the servicer must receive the borrower's reduced payment on or before the last day of the month in which it is due. If the borrower fails to make timely payments, the UP forbearance plan may be canceled and the borrower is not eligible for HAMP consideration. Servicers are instructed to use good business judgment in determining whether UP forbearance payments were received timely or if mitigating circumstances caused the payment to be late. Exceptions should be documented by the servicer.

Notices

After receiving the borrower's documentation of unemployment benefits the servicer is required to determine the borrower's eligibility for UP and mail an FPN or a Non-Approval Notice within 10 business days following the date of the servicer's determination. For existing UP forbearance plans, at least 30 days prior to the expiration date, the servicer is required to determine if an extension will be provided and mail an FPN, as applicable, within 10 day business days following the determination. A Non-Approval Notice is not required when an extension is not granted.

If a borrower is eligible for UP and any extension thereof, the FPN should describe the terms and conditions of the initial UP forbearance plan or extension, which at a minimum must include the following:

- Duration of the forbearance plan along with the Forbearance Period Effective Date and the expiration date;
- Periodic payment amount, if any;
- Brief explanation regarding what will occur when the borrower is re-employed or when the forbearance plan expires; and
- Borrower's responsibility to provide updates to his or her employment status during the forbearance plan, if applicable.

Borrowers are not required to sign or return the FPN. However, servicers may require the borrower to execute and return a written forbearance plan agreement if required by investor guidelines. Servicers should retain a copy of the FPN in the applicable servicing file and note the date that it was sent to the borrower.

If a borrower is determined to be ineligible for forbearance, servicers must communicate this determination to the borrower in writing along with the primary reason for ineligibility. The notice must also describe other foreclosure alternatives for which the borrower may be eligible, if any, including but not limited to HAMP, other home retention programs, HAFA or other short sale or deed-in-lieu programs, and identify the steps the borrower must take in order to be considered for those options. Servicers may use the applicable non-approval model clause provided in Supplemental Directive 09-08. Model clauses specific to UP are attached as Exhibit B. Use of the model clauses is optional; however, they illustrate a level of specificity that is deemed to be in compliance with the language requirements of this Supplemental Directive.

Late Fees

Late charges may accrue while the servicer is determining borrower eligibility for an UP forbearance plan and during the forbearance period. However, a servicer must not collect late charges from the borrower during the forbearance period. Additionally, all accrued and unpaid late charges must be waived in the event the borrower receives a permanent HAMP modification.

Transition from Forbearance to HAMP

At the earlier of 30 days following notification that the borrower has found employment or 30 days prior to expiration of the a forbearance period, the servicer must provide a HAMP eligible borrower with an Initial Package of HAMP documents and, upon receipt of the completed Initial Package from the borrower, must evaluate the borrower for HAMP. Both the borrower and servicer must adhere to the timing and notice requirements in Supplemental Directive 10-02. The servicer may extend the forbearance period by a maximum of 30 days as needed to allow the borrower time to submit the needed documentation. If the borrower is determined to be ineligible for HAMP or other home retention options, the borrower must be considered for other foreclosure alternatives, such as HAFA or other short sale and deed-in-lieu programs.

When evaluating a borrower for HAMP and calculating the borrower's total monthly mortgage payment ratio prior to the modification, the borrower's monthly gross income must include the new employment income as verified by an offer letter, first pay stub or other documentation consistent with the judgment employed by servicers when modifying mortgage loans held in their own portfolio. Any missed payments prior to and during the UP forbearance plan should be capitalized as part of the standard HAMP modification process.

Suspension of Foreclosure Actions

Servicers may not refer any loan to foreclosure or conduct a scheduled foreclosure sale in the following circumstances:

- While the borrower is being evaluated for UP; evaluation begins when a borrower makes a request for UP;
- After the servicer mails the FPN even if the servicer requires the borrower to be in receipt of up to three months of unemployment benefits before commencement of the forbearance plan;
- During the initial UP forbearance plan or any extension thereof; and
- Following the UP forbearance plan while the borrower is being evaluated for or participating in HAMP or HAFA.

In addition, servicers are reminded of the solicitation and foreclosure provisions in Supplemental Directive 10-02.

Reporting Requirements

During the UP forbearance plan, servicers are required to provide monthly UP forbearance plan summary level data to Fannie Mae, in its capacity as program administrator. A list of the required summary level data, which may be updated periodically on www.HMPadmin.com, is listed in Exhibit A. The data submitted must be accurate, complete, timely, and agree with the servicer's records.

As discussed previously, a borrower in an active HAMP trial period plan is eligible for an UP forbearance plan. However, a borrower may not simultaneously be in a HAMP trial period plan and an UP forbearance plan. Active trial period plans must be canceled in the Treasury system of record in the month in which the UP forbearance plan becomes effective. Thirty days prior to the expiration of the UP forbearance plan or when the borrower becomes re-employed, eligible borrowers may transition from an UP forbearance plan into a HAMP trial. Servicers are required to provide loan level reporting at the following key transition milestones:

- Exit from HAMP trial period plan to an UP forbearance plan—Servicers are required to submit applicable data pursuant to Supplemental Directive 09-06 including a Trial Fallout Reason Code indicating that the borrower is entering into an UP forbearance plan.
- Transition from an UP forbearance plan to HAMP Trial—If the borrower transitions from an UP forbearance plan into a HAMP trial period plan, servicers are required to submit a HAMP trial set up transaction with attributes indicating that the borrower had an UP forbearance plan.

Changes to several data reporting attributes under HAMP are required to enable servicers to report an exit from HAMP to an UP forbearance plan and a transition from an UP forbearance plan to a HAMP trial period plan. All UP forbearance plan reporting requirements and any updates will be posted on the servicer web portal at www.HMPadmin.com.

Credit Reporting

The servicer should continue to report a "full-file" status report to the four major credit repositories for each loan in a UP forbearance plan in accordance with the Fair Credit Reporting Act and credit bureau requirements as provided by the Consumer Data Industry Association (the "CDIA").

Compliance

Freddie Mac is Treasury's compliance agent for HAMP. Supplemental Directive 09-01 describes the overall roles and responsibilities of both servicers and the compliance agent in performing servicer reviews and oversight, which are unchanged by this Supplemental Directive. As compliance agent, Freddie Mac will incorporate an evaluation of UP implementation, processes, and controls into its servicer reviews. It is anticipated that the compliance agent will require a copy of servicers' written policies and procedures in addition to other information which may be requested from the compliance agent to perform its compliance reviews.

Documentation Requirements

Servicers are required to maintain appropriate documentary evidence of their HAMP-related activities, and to provide that documentary evidence upon request to Freddie Mac as the Compliance Agent for Treasury. With respect to UP forbearance plans, documentation that should be maintained by the servicer includes, but is not limited to, the following:

- Written policies and procedures relating to UP forbearance plans, including:
  - Determining eligibility for the program including: unemployment status, any requirement for receipt of unemployment benefits prior to commencement of the forbearance period, duration and status of unemployment benefits; waiver of the 31 percent mortgage payment ratio threshold, and forbearance term extension criteria;
  - Determining any borrower eligibility recertification and re-employment status;
  - Determining when an UP forbearance plan requires a payment and how the payment amount is determined;
  - Canceling any existing HAMP trial modifications determined to be eligible for an UP forbearance plan; and
- The decision-making process when applying discretion or business judgment as outlined in this Supplemental Directive.

For phone contact with borrowers related to UP forbearance plans, well-documented servicer system notes (including but not limited to date, names of contact persons, and a summary of the conversation) will constitute appropriate documentation. Written correspondence should be retained in an accessible manner and made available upon request by the Compliance Agent.

Exhibit A
Monthly Survey Information
For All Loans that Enter an UP Forbearance Plan

Data Description	**Initiated in Current Month**	**Cumulative**
1. Active UP Forbearance Plans (FP) including any extensions		
2. Active UP FP by investor a. PLS b. Portfolio		
3. Active UP FP by Source a. New request b. Cancelled HAMP trial period plan		
4. UP FP Payments a. FP with no payment required b. FP with some payment required c. Average payment reduction (%)		
5. Completed UP FP a. Ended as a result of Reemployment b. FP Term expired 5(a) + 5(b) must equal total		
6. Disposition of Completed UP FP a. Hardship resolved through re-employment b. HAMP Trial offered c. Other mod offered d. Short Sale offered e. DIL offered f. Foreclosure pending g. Reinstatement h. Other		
7. Duration of Completed UP FP a. Average b. Segregation by term (*optional*) i. 3 months ii. > 3—6 months iii. > 6—9 months iv. > 9 months		
8. UP FP Cancelations as a result of non-payment or borrower non-compliance.		
9. UP FP by State *(optional)* A separate state chart will be provided for this reporting		
Survey data may change		

Exhibit B
Model Clauses

The model clauses in this exhibit provide sample language that may be used to communicate the status of a borrower's request for the Home Affordable Unemployment Program. The model clauses are in addition to the existing model clauses provided in Supplemental Directive 09-08 that relate to the Not Approved/Not Accepted reason codes in *Schedule IV* of Supplemental Directive 09-06. Use of the model clauses is optional; however, they illustrate a level of specificity that is deemed to be in compliance with language requirements of the program.

Non Approval Notice

1. **Unemployment Program.** We are unable to offer you a forbearance plan under the Home Affordable Unemployment Program because:

- ☐ As of the date of your request, you did not provide us with documentation that you are receiving or will receive unemployment benefits [*insert only if applicable:* for at least ______ months].
- ☐ As of the date of your request, your loan was delinquent by three or more monthly mortgage payments.
- ☐ Your total monthly mortgage payment is less than or equal to 31 percent of the household monthly gross income, including unemployment benefits.

B.3.9 Home Affordable Modification Program Base Net Present Value (NPV) Model Specifications

This subsection reprints an overview of the HAMP Base Net Present Value (NPV) Model Specifications. For more detail, see this treatise's companion website which reprints the Home Affordable Modification Program, Base Net Present Value (NPV) Model v3.0 Model Documentation (Dec. 8, 2009).

HOME AFFORDABLE MODIFICATION PROGRAM BASE NET PRESENT VALUE (NPV)MODEL SPECIFICATIONS

UPDATED: JUNE 11, 2009

Overview

As a part of the Making Home Affordable Program, we are providing standardized guidance and a base net present value (NPV) model described herein that any servicer who participates in the Home Affordable Modification Program (HAMP) can use or, if eligible, customize into a proprietary NPV model. The base NPV model is illustrative of an NPV model that meets the specifications put forward under the Making Home Affordable Program. Servicers are not precluded from using the illustrative model for making program NPV determinations. It is our expectation that servicers may use the Base NPV Model Documentation to customize the model based on their individual portfolio experience—all within the standardized guidelines put forward for the model under the program. The base NPV model will provide consistency in NPV calculations for the Home Affordable Modification Program and help the industry move toward a more standard process for evaluating the NPV of mortgages for purposes of making modifications.

A participating servicer in the Home Affordable Modification Program must modify any loan that meets the program's eligibility criteria if the modification tests "positive" for NPV. When mortgage modifications have a positive NPV, it is in the best interests of lenders, servicers, investors, and borrowers to modify mortgages to reduce the risk of foreclosure. The Home Affordable Modification Program increases the potential number of mortgage modifications that will have a positive NPV, resulting in more servicers modifying mortgages, and keeping more Americans in their homes. The Home Affordable Modification Program specifies a precise method for determining NPV and provides a base NPV model that any servicer can use or customize into a proprietary NPV model that satisfies all of the program's methodological requirements.

Under the program, a defined set of parameters for the base NPV model can be customized for each servicer. Every servicer is given discretion, within specified limits, to choose a discount rate. In addition, larger servicers are given discretion to develop portfolio-specific default rates. These customization capabilities are built into the base NPV model to preserve the ability of servicers, lenders, and investors to tailor the base NPV model to reflect the unique characteristics of the loans that they service or own, and to incorporate knowledge gained from years of working with those particular groups of mortgages. For other servicers, the baseline parameters can provide a sufficient NPV tool to evaluate loans being considered for modification.

Net Present Value of Modification

In general, NPV refers to the value today of a cash-generating investment—such as a bond or mortgage loan. When an investor is faced with a choice between two alternative investments—specifically, between the timing and amounts of the cash flows for each investment—the investor obviously prefers the choice that has a higher present value.

In the context of a mortgage borrower who has become distressed, the investor—or a third party servicer, acting on behalf of the investor—faces a choice of whether to modify the mortgage or leave it as-is. Each choice generates expected cash flows, and the present values of these two cash flows are likely to be different. If the loan is modified, there is a greater chance that the borrower will eventually be able to repay the loan in full. If not, there is a higher likelihood that the loan will go to foreclosure, and the investor will absorb the associated losses. If the NPV of the modified loan is higher than the NPV of the loan as-is, a modification is said to be "NPV positive."

The Making Home Affordable Program is structured to produce modifications that are more likely to test NPV positive, increasing the number of modifications that will be done and keeping more Americans in their homes. It does this, first, by lowering the probability that borrowers will default by making borrower payments more affordable and, second, by providing incentive payments that are added to cash flows received by lenders (or investors).

If a borrower meets the eligibility criteria for the Home Affordable Modification Program, a servicer will adjust the terms of the borrower's loan (modify the loan) to reduce the borrower's payment to the program's target front-end debt-to-income (DTI) ratio of 31 percent. At a 31 percent DTI, the borrower will have a monthly mortgage payment that is more affordable over the long term, so that the borrower will be more able to afford to stay in his or her home.

Servicers must reduce payments in the precise manner specified by the Making Home Affordable Program (the "Standard Waterfall"), starting with reducing the interest rate on the mortgage. Once the servicer knows which loan terms will change, the servicer is ready to run an NPV model calculation. If the expected value to the lender of the loan after a HAMP modification exceeds the expected value of the same loan to the lender if it is not modified, then the NPV test result is positive and the servicer must modify the loan.

Requiring servicers to modify all NPV-positive loans ensures that there is help for all distressed borrowers when an objective test demonstrates the modification will benefit both the borrower and the investor. The program does not require the servicer to modify the loan if the modification tests negative, though the servicer must consider other ways to prevent foreclosure.

The Base NPV Model

The program supplies a base NPV model that any servicer may use to satisfy the requirement to modify all eligible loans that test NPV positive for modification. Large servicers—those having a book of business exceeding $40 billion—have some discretion to customize the base NPV model with respect to two important inputs, the expected default rates for loans that are not modified and the re-default rates for loans that are modified, as discussed further below.

Both the base NPV model and a servicer's proprietary customized version will:

1. Compute the net present value of the mortgage assuming it is not modified.
   a. Determine the probability that the mortgage defaults.
   b. Project the future cash flows of the mortgage if it defaults and the present value of these cash flows.
   c. Project the future expected cash flows of the mortgage if it does not default and the present value of these cash flows.
   d. Take the probability weighted average of the two present values.
2. In the same manner, compute the net present value of the mortgage assuming it is modified, incorporating the effects on cash flows and performance of the modification terms and subsidies provided by the Home Affordable Modification Program.
3. Compare the two present values to determine if the HAMP modification is NPV positive.

An NPV model used in the HAMP takes into account the principal factors that can influence these cash flows, including:

1. The value of the home relative to the size of the mortgage.
2. The likelihood that the loan will be foreclosed on.
3. Trends in home prices.
4. The cost of foreclosure, including:
   a. legal expenses,
   b. lost interest during the time required to complete the foreclosure action,
   c. property maintenance costs, and
   d. expenses involved in reselling the property.
5. The cost of conducting a modification, including:
   a. a lower monthly payment from the borrower,
   b. the likelihood a borrower will default even after the loan is modified,
   c. financial incentives provided by the government, and
   d. the likelihood that a loan will be paid off before its term expires (prepayment probability).

The base NPV model was designed by an expert working group including the Department of the Treasury, the Federal Deposit Insurance Corp., the Federal Housing Finance Agency, Fannie Mae, and Freddie Mac. It was designed specifically for the Home Affordable Modification Program. The base NPV model reflects aggregate data across many servicers, as well as the professional judgment of the working group.

Individual servicers have their own unique experience with the loans they service. The program permits servicers to customize the base NPV model to reflect that unique experience, within certain constraints and guidelines. As a result of customization, servicer NPV results and resulting modification decisions will likely vary even when borrowers' circumstances appear to be similar, but the results will be more accurate and provide a better gauge of appropriate modifications.

Key Parameters of the Base NPV Model and Customization of Inputs

Below is a summary of important parameters used in the Home Affordable Modification Program base NPV model, and the extent to which servicers may customize the parameters of the base NPV model.

Discount Rate: For a firm that owns a mortgage loan (the investor), the mortgage is a series of future cash payments expected from the borrower. But the promise of a payment in the future is worth less to an investor than cash today. How much less will depend on the discount rate—the higher the discount rate, the less a future payment is worth to an investor today. For example, a $1,000 payment in one year would be worth about $950 today using a 5 percent discount rate, and that same $1,000 payment in a year would be worth about $800 today using a 25 percent discount rate. In the base NPV model, all servicers are permitted limited discretion to adjust the discount rate by up to 250 basis points because different investors may place different values on future payments versus payments received today.

The discount rate the servicer uses may be as low as Freddie Mac's Primary Mortgage Market Survey (PMMS) weekly rate for 30-year fixed-rate conforming loans, and as high as the PMMS weekly rate plus 250 basis points. (To find the current PMMS go to http://www.freddiemac.com/pmms.) With respect to loans that are not owned or guaranteed by Fannie Mae or Freddie Mac, the servicer may apply a single discount rate or two discount rates, one for loans in its own portfolio and another for loans serviced for all other investors. However, in no case may a servicer use a higher discount rate for loans in its own portfolio than the rate used for loans it services for other investors. With respect to loans owned or guaranteed by Fannie Mae or Freddie Mac, the servicer must apply the rate specified in Fannie Mae and Freddie Mac guidance.

Whatever discount rate the servicer chooses to use must be applied to both cash flows—that is, to the cash flows if the loan is modified under the Home Affordable Modification Program, as well as the cash flows if the loan is not modified.

Default Rates: The base NPV model projects default rates in two scenarios. It projects the probability of default if the loan is not modified and the probability of default if the loan is modified. Default rates depend on a number of variables particular to the loan. In general, however, the default rate is assumed to vary based on the credit quality of the borrower, the borrower's debt burden, the loan-to-value (LTV) of the home at the time of modification, and whether the loan is modified earlier or later in the delinquency cycle.

In the base NPV model, the default rates are generated by a model based on the performance of GSE and non-GSE loans. As Home Affordable Modification Program performance data become available, the base NPV model will be updated to reflect actual program experience.

Large servicers—those with a book exceeding $40 billion—may customize the base NPV model to use modeled default rates that reflect their own portfolio experience. These customized default rate models must be empirically validated where possible, commercially reasonable, and will be subject to review and oversight by program monitors.

Default rates may vary significantly from one large servicer to another based on differences in their portfolios. Therefore, allowing servicers flexibility to use rates that reflect their own portfolio experience should result in more accurate evaluations of proposed modifications.

Home Prices: Future increases or decreases in home prices impact a borrower's willingness to stay in a house and potential financial loss in the event of foreclosure. A servicer must use the home price projection provided in the base NPV model. A servicer does not have discretion to substitute a different projection. The home price projection for the program has been made available by FHFA exclusively for this program, is based on data from a broad cross section of mortgage transactions, and will be updated quarterly. The projection is not based on the FHFA House Price Index and does not represent an official forecast of FHFA or any other government agency.

REO Discount: Foreclosed or real estate owned (REO) properties generally sell for less than similar, non-distressed assets. This is referred to as the REO Discount and it recognizes the deterioration in perceived value that buyers often place on a home that has been foreclosed. The REO Discount is worse in some markets than in others. The REO Discount values used in the base NPV model are based on an analysis of sale prices of foreclosed homes sold by Fannie Mae and Freddie Mac. REO Discount values vary by state and home price. Servicers are not permitted to change the REO assumptions in the base NPV model.

B.3.10 Servicer Participation Agreement

COMMITMENT TO PURCHASE FINANCIAL INSTRUMENT
and
SERVICER PARTICIPATION AGREEMENT

This Commitment to Purchase Financial Instrument and Servicer Participation Agreement (the "Commitment") is entered into as of the Effective Date, by and between Federal National Mortgage Association, a federally chartered corporation, as financial agent of the United States ("Fannie Mae"), and the undersigned party ("Servicer"). Capitalized terms used, but not defined contextually, shall have the meanings ascribed to them in Section 12 below.

Recitals

WHEREAS, the U.S. Department of the Treasury (the "Treasury") has established a Making Home Affordable Program pursuant to section 101 and 109 of the Emergency Economic Stabilization Act of 2008 (the "Act"), as section 109 of the Act has been amended by section 7002 of the American Recovery and Reinvestment Act of 2009;

WHEREAS, the Treasury has established a variety of programs (the "Programs") under the Act to stabilize the housing market by facilitating first lien mortgage loan modifications, facilitating second lien mortgage loan modifications and extinguishments, providing home price decline protection incentives, encouraging foreclosure alternatives, such as short sales and deeds in lieu of foreclosure, and making other foreclosure prevention services available to the marketplace (collectively, the "Services");

WHEREAS, the Programs may include Services relating to FHA, VA and USDA loans;

WHEREAS, Fannie Mae has been designated by the Treasury as a financial agent of the United States in connection with the implementation of the Programs; all references to Fannie Mae in the Agreement shall be in its capacity as financial agent of the United States;

WHEREAS, Fannie Mae will fulfill the roles of administrator and record keeper for the Programs, and in conjunction therewith must standardize certain mortgage modification and foreclosure prevention practices and procedures as they relate to the Programs, consistent with the Act and in accordance with the directives of, and guidance provided by, the Treasury;

WHEREAS, Federal Home Loan Mortgage Corporation ("Freddie Mac") has been designated by the Treasury as a financial agent of the United States and will fulfill a compliance role in connection with the Programs; all references to Freddie Mac in the Agreement shall be in its capacity as compliance agent of the Programs;

WHEREAS, all Fannie Mae and Freddie Mac approved servicers are being directed through their respective servicing guides and bulletins to implement the Programs with respect to mortgage loans owned, securitized, or guaranteed by Fannie Mae or Freddie Mac (the "GSE Loans"); accordingly, this Agreement does not apply to the GSE Loans;

WHEREAS, all other servicers, as well as Fannie Mae and Freddie Mac approved servicers, that wish to participate in the Programs with respect to loans that are not GSE Loans (collectively, "Participating Servicers") must agree to certain terms and conditions relating to the respective roles and responsibilities of participants and other financial agents of the government; and

WHEREAS, Servicer wishes to participate in the Programs as a Participating Servicer on the terms and subject to the conditions set forth herein.

Accordingly, in consideration of the representations, warranties, and mutual agreements set forth herein and for other good and valuable consideration, the receipt and sufficiency of which are hereby acknowledged, Fannie Mae and Servicer agree as follows.

Agreement

1. Services

A. Contemporaneously with the execution and delivery of this Commitment and the Financial Instrument, Servicer will execute and deliver to Fannie Mae one or more schedules describing the Services to be performed by Servicer pursuant to this Agreement, effective as of the Effective Date of the Agreement (each, a "Service Schedule" or an "Initial Service Schedule" and, collectively, the "Initial Service Schedules"). After the Effective Date of the Agreement, Servicer may opt-in to any additional initiatives offered by Treasury in connection with the Programs by executing and delivering to Fannie Mae one or more additional Service Schedules describing the Services relating to such initiatives (each, a "Service Schedule" or an "Additional Service Schedule" and, collectively, the "Additional Service Schedules") (the Initial Service Schedules and the Additional Service Schedules, collectively, the "Service Schedules"). All Service Schedules that are executed and delivered to Fannie Mae by Servicer from time to time will be numbered sequentially (e.g. Service Schedule A-1; Service Schedule A-2; Service Schedule A-3; et seq.) and are referenced herein, collectively, as Exhibit A; Exhibit A is hereby incorporated into the Commitment by this reference.

B. Subject to Section 10.C., Servicer shall perform the Services described in (i) the Financial Instrument attached hereto as Exhibit B (the "Financial Instrument"); (ii) the Service Schedules attached hereto, collectively, as Exhibit A; (iii) the guidelines and procedures issued by the Treasury with respect to the Programs outlined in the Service Schedules (the "Program Guidelines"); and (iv) any supplemental documentation, instructions, bulletins, frequently asked questions, letters, directives, or other communications, including, but not limited to, business continuity requirements, compliance requirements, performance requirements and related remedies, issued by the Treasury, Fannie Mae, or Freddie Mac in order to change, or further describe or clarify the scope of, the rights and duties of the Participating Servicers in connection with the Programs outlined in the Service Schedules (the "Supplemental Directives" and, together with the Program Guidelines, the "Program Documentation"). The Program Documentation will be available to all Participating Servicers at www.HMPadmin.com; for the avoidance of doubt, the term "Program Documentation" includes all of the Program Guidelines and Supplemental Directives issued by Treasury and made available to Participating Servicers at www.HMPadmin.com prior to the Effective Date of the Agreement. The Program Documentation, as the same may be modified or amended from time to time in accordance with Section 10 below, is hereby incorporated into the Commitment by this reference.

C. Servicer's representations and warranties, and acknowledgement of and agreement to fulfill or satisfy certain duties and obligations, with respect to its participation in the Programs and under the Agreement are set forth in the Financial Instrument. Servicer's certification as to its continuing compliance with, and the truth and accuracy of, the representations and warranties set forth in the Financial Instrument will be provided annually in the form attached hereto as Exhibit C (the "Certification"), beginning on June 1, 2010 and again on June 1 of each year thereafter during the Term (as defined below) and upon the execution and delivery by Servicer of any Additional Service Schedule during the Term.

D. The recitals set forth above are hereby incorporated herein by this reference.

2. Authority and Agreement to Participate in Programs

A. Servicer shall perform the Services for all mortgage loans it services, whether it services such mortgage loans for its own account or for the account of another party, including any holders of mortgage-backed securities (each such other party, an "Investor").

B. Fannie Mae acknowledges that Servicer may service mortgage loans for its own account or for the account of one or more Investors and may be subject to restrictions set forth in pooling and servicing agreements or other servicing contracts governing Servicer's servicing of a mortgage loan; Servicer shall use reasonable efforts to remove all prohibitions or impediments to its authority, and use reasonable efforts to obtain all third party consents, waivers and delegations that are required, by contract or law, in order to perform the Services.

C. Notwithstanding subsection B., if (x) Servicer is unable to obtain all necessary consents, waivers and delegations for performing any Services under the Programs, or (y) the pooling and servicing agreement or other servicing contract governing Servicer's servicing of a mortgage loan prohibits Servicer from performing such Services for that mortgage loan, Servicer shall not be required to perform such Services with respect to that mortgage loan and shall not receive all or any portion of the Purchase Price (defined below) otherwise payable for such Services with respect to such loan.

D. Notwithstanding anything to the contrary contained herein, the Agreement does not apply to GSE Loans. Servicers are directed to the servicing guides and bulletins issued by Fannie Mae and Freddie Mac, respectively, concerning the Programs as applied to GSE Loans.

E. Servicer's performance of the Services and implementation of the Programs shall be subject to review by Freddie Mac and its agents and designees as more fully set forth in the Agreement.

3. Set Up; Prerequisite to Payment

Servicer will provide to Fannie Mae: (a) the set up information required by the Program Documentation and any ancillary or administrative information requested by Fannie Mae in order to process Servicer's participation in the Programs as a Participating Servicer on or before the Effective Date of the Agreement as to the Initial Service Schedules that are executed and delivered contemporaneously herewith, and on or before the effective date of the Additional Service Schedules (if any) executed and delivered after the Effective Date of the Agreement; and (b) the data elements for each mortgage obligation, property, or borrower eligible for the Programs as and when described in the Program Documentation and the Financial Instrument. Purchase Price payments will not be remitted pursuant to Section 4 with respect to Services for which the required data elements have not been provided.

4. Agreement to Purchase Financial Instrument; Payment of Purchase Price

A. Fannie Mae, in its capacity as a financial agent of the United States, agrees to purchase, and Servicer agrees to sell to Fannie Mae, in such capacity, the Financial Instrument that is executed and delivered by Servicer to Fannie Mae in the form attached hereto as Exhibit B, in consideration for the payment by Fannie Mae, as agent, of the Purchase Price.

B. The conditions precedent to the payment by Fannie Mae of the Purchase Price with respect to the Services described on the Initial Service Schedules are: (a) the execution and delivery of the Commitment, the Initial Service Schedules, and the Financial Instrument by Servicer to Fannie Mae; (b) the execution and delivery of the Commitment and the Initial Service Schedules by Fannie Mae to Servicer; (c) the delivery of copies of the fully executed Commitment, Initial Service Schedules and Financial Instrument to Treasury on the Effective Date of the Agreement; (d) the performance by Servicer of the Services described in the Agreement, in accordance with the terms and conditions thereof, to the reasonable satisfaction of Fannie Mae and Freddie Mac; and (e) the satisfaction by Servicer of such other obligations as are set forth in the Agreement.

C. The conditions precedent to the payment by Fannie Mae of the Purchase Price with respect to the Services described on the Additional Service Schedules (if any) are: (a) the execution and delivery of the Additional Service Schedules and the Certification by Servicer to Fannie Mae; (b) the execution and delivery of the Additional Service Schedules by Fannie Mae to Servicer; (c) the delivery of copies of the fully executed Additional Service Schedules to Treasury; (d) the performance by Servicer of the Services described in the Agreement, in accordance with the terms and conditions thereof, to the reasonable satisfaction of Fannie Mae and Freddie Mac; and (e) the satisfaction by Servicer of such other obligations as are set forth in the Agreement.

D. Solely in its capacity as the financial agent of the United States, and subject to subsection E. below, Fannie Mae shall remit all payments described in the Program Documentation to Servicer for the account or credit of Servicer, Investors and borrowers, in each case in accordance with the Program Documentation (all such payments, collectively, the "Purchase Price"); all payments remitted to Servicer for the credit or account of third parties under the Program Documentation shall be applied by Servicer as required by the Program Documentation. Fannie Mae shall have no liability to Servicer with respect to the payment of the Purchase Price, unless and until: (a) Servicer and all other interested parties have satisfied all pre-requisites set forth herein and in the Program Documentation relating to the applicable Program payment structure, including, but not limited to, the delivery of all data elements required by Section 3 of this Commitment; and (b) the Treasury has provided funds to Fannie Mae for remittance to Servicer, together with written direction to remit the funds to Servicer in accordance with the Program Documentation.

E. The Purchase Price will be paid to Servicer by Fannie Mae as the financial agent of the United States as and when described herein and in the Program Documentation in consideration for the execution and delivery of the Financial Instrument by Servicer on or before the Effective Date of the Agreement, upon the satisfaction of the conditions precedent to payment described in this Section 4.

F. The value of the Agreement is limited to [INSERT DOLLAR AMOUNT] (the "Program Participation Cap"). Accordingly, the aggregate Purchase Price payable to Servicer under the Agreement with respect to all Services described on all of the Service Schedules that are executed and delivered in connection with the Agreement may not exceed the amount of the Program Participation Cap. For each Service to be performed by Servicer, the aggregate remaining Purchase Price available to be paid to Servicer under the Agreement will be reduced by the maximum Purchase Price potentially payable with respect to that Service. In the event the Purchase Price actually paid with respect to that Service is less than the maximum Purchase Price potentially payable, the aggregate remaining Purchase Price available to be paid to Servicer under the Agreement will be increased by the difference between such amounts. Notwithstanding the foregoing, no agreements with any party that may result in a new payment obligation under the Programs will be effected under the Agreement, and no payments will be made with respect to any new Services, from and after the date on which the aggregate Purchase Price paid or payable to Servicer under the Agreement equals the Program Participation Cap. Treasury may, from time to time in its sole discretion, adjust the amount of the Program Participation Cap. Servicer will be notified of all adjustments to the Program Participation Cap in writing by Fannie Mae.

G. Servicer shall maintain complete and accurate records of, and supporting documentation for, all Services provided in connection with the Programs including, but not limited to, data relating to borrower payments (e.g., principal, interest, taxes, homeowner's insurance, hazard insurance, flood insurance and homeowner's association and/or condo fees), delinquencies and the terms of each agreement executed under the Programs (e.g., trial modification agreements, loan modification agreements and extinguishment agreements), which will be relied upon by Fannie Mae when calculating, as financial agent for the United States, the Purchase Price to be paid by the Treasury through Fannie Mae or any other financial agent. Servicer agrees to provide Fannie Mae and Freddie Mac with documentation (including copies of executed borrower agreements) and other information with respect to any amounts paid by the Treasury as may be reasonably requested by such parties. In the event of a discrepancy or error in the amount of the Purchase Price paid hereunder, at Fannie Mae's election, (x) Servicer shall remit to Fannie Mae the amount of any overpayment within thirty (30) days of receiving a refund request from Fannie Mae, or (y) Fannie Mae may immediately offset the amount of the overpayment against other amounts due and payable to Servicer by Fannie Mae, as financial agent of the United States, upon written notice to Servicer. Servicer shall still be obligated to credit to the respective accounts of Investors and borrowers any portion of the Purchase Price to which they are entitled (if any) notwithstanding such offset unless otherwise directed by Fannie Mae.

H. At the election and upon the direction of the Treasury and with prior written notice to Servicer, Fannie Mae may deduct from any amount to be paid to Servicer any amount that Servicer, Investor, or borrower is obligated to reimburse or pay to the United States government, provided, however, that any amount withheld under this subsection H. will be withheld only from the amounts payable to, or for the account or credit of, the party which is liable for the obligation to the United States government.

5. Term

A. New Services may be undertaken by Servicer as described in the Financial Instrument and the Program Documentation from and after the Effective Date until December 31, 2012 (the "Initial Term"), subject to one or more extensions of the Initial Term by the Treasury, or earlier termination of the Agreement by Fannie Mae pursuant to the provisions hereof, or earlier suspension or termination of one or more of the Programs by the Treasury, provided, however, no new Services may be undertaken by Servicer, and Servicer will have no further obligation to perform any Services under this Agreement, from and after the date on which the Program Participation Cap is reached.

B. Servicer shall perform the Services described in the Program Documentation in accordance with the terms and conditions of the Agreement during the Initial Term and any extensions thereof (the Initial Term, together with all extensions thereof, if any, the "Term"), and during such additional period as may be necessary to: (i) comply with all data collection, retention and reporting requirements specified in the Program Documentation during and for the periods set forth therein; and (ii) complete all Services that were initiated by Servicer, including, but not limited to, the completion of all documentation relating thereto, during the Term. Servicer agrees that it will work diligently to complete all Services as soon as reasonably possible after the end of the Term or earlier termination.

C. Notwithstanding Sections 5.A. and 5.B., if the Servicer has elected to participate in the Second Lien Modification Program by executing and delivering to Fannie Mae a Service Schedule relating thereto, the Servicer in its discretion, may elect to opt out of the Second Lien Modification Program on an annual basis by providing notice to Fannie Mae in accordance with Section 9 hereof within 30 days following the anniversary of the Effective Date of the Service Schedule for the Second Lien Modification Program. Following the Servicer's election to opt out of the Second Lien Modification Program, the Servicer will not be required to perform any Services for any new mortgage loans under the Second Lien Modification Program; however, the Servicer must continue to perform any Services for any mortgage loan for which it had already begun performing Services prior to electing to opt out of the Second Lien Modification Program.

D. The Agreement, or any of the Programs implemented under the Agreement, may be terminated by Fannie Mae or Servicer prior to the end of the Term pursuant to Section 6 below.

6. Defaults, Acts of Bad Faith and Early Termination; Remedies for and Effects of Defaults, Acts of Bad Faith and Early Termination; Opportunity to Cure

A. The following constitute events of default by Servicer under the Agreement (each, an "Event of Default" and, collectively, "Events of Default"):

(1) Servicer fails to perform or comply with any of its material obligations under the Agreement, including, but not limited to, circumstances in which Servicer fails to ensure that all eligibility criteria and other conditions precedent specified in applicable Program Documentation are satisfied prior to effectuating any Services in connection with any of the Programs.

(2) Servicer: (a) ceases to do business as a going concern; (b) makes a general assignment for the benefit of, or enters into any arrangement with creditors in lieu thereof; (c) admits in writing its inability to pay its debts as they become due; (d) files a voluntary petition under any bankruptcy or insolvency law or files a voluntary petition under the reorganization or arrangement provisions of the laws of the United States or any other jurisdiction; (e) authorizes, applies for or consents to the appointment of a trustee or liquidator of all or substantially all of its assets; (f) has any substantial part of its property subjected to a levy, seizure, assignment or sale for or by any creditor or governmental agency; or (g) enters into an agreement or resolution to take any of the foregoing actions.

5

(3) Servicer, any employee or contractor of Servicer, or any employee or contractor of Servicers' contractors, commits a grossly negligent, willful or intentional, or reckless act (including, but not limited to, misrepresentation or fraud) in connection with any of the Programs or the Agreement.

(4) Any representation, warranty, or covenant made by Servicer in the Agreement or any Certification is or becomes materially false, misleading, incorrect, or incomplete.

(5) An evaluation of performance that includes any specific findings by Freddie Mac, in its sole discretion, that Servicer's performance under any performance criteria established pursuant to applicable Program Documentation is materially insufficient, or any failure by Servicer to comply with any directive issued by Fannie Mae or Freddie Mac with respect to documents or data requested, findings made, or remedies established, by Fannie Mae and/or Freddie Mac in conjunction with such performance criteria or other Program requirements.

B. Fannie Mae may take any, all, or none of the following actions upon an Event of Default by Servicer under the Agreement:

(1) Fannie Mae may: (i) withhold some or all of the Servicer's portion of the Purchase Price until, in Fannie Mae's determination, Servicer has cured the default; and (ii) choose to utilize alternative means of paying any portion of the Purchase Price for the credit or account of borrowers and Investors and delay paying such portion pending adoption of such alternative means.

(2) Fannie Mae may: (i) reduce the amounts payable to Servicer under Section 4; and/or (ii) obtain repayment of prior payments made to Servicer under Section 4, provided, however, Fannie Mae will seek to obtain repayment of prior payments made under Section 4 only with respect to Services that are determined by Fannie Mae or Freddie Mac to have been impacted by, or that Fannie Mae or Freddie Mac believes may have been, or may be, impacted by, the Event of Default giving rise to the remedy.

(3) Fannie Mae may require Servicer to submit to additional Program administrator oversight, including, but not limited to, additional compliance controls and quality control reviews.

(4) Fannie Mae may terminate the Agreement and cease its performance hereunder, or cease its performance hereunder as to any Program in which Servicer is a participant.

(5) Fannie Mae may require Servicer to submit to information and reporting with respect to its financial condition and ability to continue to meet its obligations under the Agreement.

C. The following constitute acts of bad faith of Investors and borrowers in connection with the Programs (each, an "Act of Bad Faith" and, collectively, "Acts of Bad Faith"): an Investor or borrower commits a grossly negligent, willful or intentional, or reckless act (including, but not limited to, misrepresentation or fraud) in connection with any of the Programs (including, but not limited to, in connection with such Investor's or borrower's response to Program questionnaires, the execution or delivery to Servicer, Fannie Mae, or Treasury of any of the agreements relating to such Investor's or borrower's participation in any of the Programs and the production of supporting documentation therefor and in connection with any audit or review by Freddie Mac for Investor or borrower compliance with the Programs). For brevity, any such Investor or borrower is referred to in this subsection as a "defaulting party" or as a "defaulting" Investor or borrower and the Act of Bad Faith by such Investor or borrower as a "default."

D. Fannie Mae may take any, all, or none of the following actions if an Act of Bad Faith involving an Investor or a borrower occurs, or is reasonably believed by Fannie Mae to have occurred, in connection with any of the Programs:

6

(1) Fannie Mae may withhold all or any portion of the Purchase Price payable to, or for the credit or account of, the defaulting party until, in Fannie Mae's determination, the default has been cured or otherwise remedied to Fannie Mae's satisfaction.

(2) Fannie Mae may: (i) reduce the amounts payable to Servicer for the credit, or account of, the defaulting party under Section 4; and/or (ii) obtain repayment of prior payments made to or for the credit or account of the defaulting party under Section 4. Servicer will reasonably cooperate with, and provide reasonable support and assistance to, Fannie Mae and Freddie Mac in connection with their respective roles and, in Fannie Mae's case, in connection with its efforts to obtain repayment of prior payments made to Investors and borrowers as provided in this subsection.

(3) Fannie Mae may require Servicer to submit to additional Program administrator oversight, including, but not limited to, additional compliance controls and quality control reviews.

(4) Fannie Mae may cease its performance hereunder as to some or all of the Services subject to the Agreement that relate to the defaulting Investor or borrower.

(5) Fannie Mae may terminate the Agreement and cease its performance hereunder if Acts of Bad Faith occur on a recurring basis, are widespread among the Investor or borrower bases served by Servicer, or occur in combination or in connection with one or more Events of Default by Servicer.

E. In addition to the termination rights set forth above, Fannie Mae may terminate the Agreement or any Program implemented under the Agreement immediately upon written notice to Servicer:

(1) at the direction of the Treasury;

(2) in the event of a merger, acquisition, or other change of control of Servicer;

(3) in the event that a receiver, liquidator, trustee, or other custodian is appointed for the Servicer; or

(4) in the event that a material term of the Agreement is determined to be prohibited or unenforceable as referred to in Section 11.C.

F. The Agreement will terminate automatically:

(1) in the event that the Financial Agency Agreement, dated February 18, 2009, by and between Fannie Mae and the Treasury is terminated; or

(2) upon the expiration or termination of all of the Programs implemented under the Agreement.

G. The effects of the expiration or termination of the Agreement are as follows:

(1) In the event that the Agreement expires at the end of the Initial Term or any extension thereof pursuant to Section 5, or in the event that the Agreement expires or is terminated pursuant to Section 6.E. or 6.F., Fannie Mae shall, solely in its capacity as the financial agent of the United States, continue to remit all amounts that are properly payable pursuant to Section 4 to Servicer in accordance with the Program Documentation until paid in full, provided, however, that Purchase Price payments will be made only with

7

respect to Services that were performed in accordance with the applicable Program Documentation prior to the date of expiration or termination and that do not exceed the Program Participation Cap.

(2) In the event that the Agreement is terminated in connection with an Event of Default by Servicer, no compensation with respect to any Service will be paid to Servicer for the account of the Servicer subsequent to termination; Fannie Mae's only continuing obligations as financial agent of the United States subsequent to termination will be to remit all payments that are properly payable pursuant to Section 4 to Servicer (or, at Fannie Mae's discretion, an alternative provider) for the account of borrowers and Investors in accordance with the Program Documentation until paid in full.

(3) In the event that the Agreement is terminated in connection with an Act of Bad Faith by an Investor or a borrower, no compensation with respect to any Services will be paid to Servicer for the credit or account of the defaulting Investor or borrower subsequent to termination; Fannie Mae's only continuing obligation as financial agent of the United States subsequent to termination will be to remit all payments that are properly payable pursuant to Section 4 to Servicer for the credit or account of non-defaulting parties as described in the applicable Program Documentation until paid in full. For the avoidance of doubt, if the Act of Bad Faith resulting in the termination of the Agreement occurs in connection with an Event of Default of Servicer, no compensation with respect to any Service will be paid to Servicer for the account of the Servicer subsequent to termination.

H. Fannie Mae, in its capacity as the financial agent of the United States, may reduce the amounts payable to Servicer under Section 4, or obtain repayment of prior payments made under Section 4, in connection with: (a) an evaluation of Servicer's performance that includes any specific findings by Freddie Mac that Servicer's performance under any performance criteria established pursuant to the Program Documentation is materially insufficient, or (b) any failure by Servicer to comply materially with any directive issued by Fannie Mae or Freddie Mac with respect to documents or data requested, findings made, or remedies established, by Fannie Mae and/or Freddie Mac in conjunction with such performance criteria or other Program requirements; provided, however, Fannie Mae will seek to obtain repayment of prior payments made under Section 4 only with respect to Services that are determined by Fannie Mae or Freddie Mac to have been impacted by, or that Fannie Mae or Freddie Mac believes may have been, or may be, impacted by, the findings giving rise to this remedy. Fannie Mae may initially avail itself of this remedy in lieu of a specific declaration of an Event of Default, provided, however, that doing so shall not preclude Fannie Mae from later declaring an Event of Default or exercising any other rights or remedies otherwise available to it under this Section 6, or at law or in equity, in connection with the event giving rise to this remedy, or any future events giving rise to this remedy.

I. The remedies available to Fannie Mae upon an Event of Default and an Act of Bad Faith under this Section are cumulative and not exclusive; further, these remedies are in addition to, and not in lieu of, any other remedies available to Fannie Mae at law or in equity.

J. In the event of the expiration or termination of the Agreement or any Program implemented under the Agreement under any circumstances, Servicer and Fannie Mae agree to cooperate with one another on an ongoing basis to ensure an effective and orderly transition or resolution of the Services, including the provision of any information, reporting, records and data required by Fannie Mae and Freddie Mac.

K. If an Event of Default under Section 6.A.1., Section 6.A.4., or Section 6.A.5. occurs and Fannie Mae determines, in its sole discretion, that the Event of Default is curable and elects to exercise its right to terminate the Agreement, Fannie Mae will provide written notice of the Event of Default to Servicer and the Agreement will terminate automatically thirty (30) days after Servicer's receipt of such notice, if the Event of Default is not cured by Servicer to the reasonable satisfaction of Fannie Mae prior to the end of such thirty (30) day period. If Fannie Mae determines, in its sole discretion, that an Event of Default under Section 6.A.1., Section 6.A.4., or Section 6.A.5. is not curable, or if an Event of Default under Section 6.A.2. or Section 6.A.3.

occurs, and Fannie Mae elects to exercise its right to terminate the Agreement under Section 6.B.4., Fannie Mae will provide written notice of termination to the Servicer on or before the effective date of the termination.

7. Disputes

Fannie Mae and Servicer agree that it is in their mutual interest to resolve disputes by agreement. If a dispute arises under the Agreement, the parties will use all reasonable efforts to promptly resolve the dispute by mutual agreement. If a dispute cannot be resolved informally by mutual agreement at the lowest possible level, the dispute shall be referred up the respective chain of command of each party in an attempt to resolve the matter. This will be done in an expeditious manner. Servicer shall continue diligent performance of the Services pending resolution of any dispute. Fannie Mae and Servicer reserve the right to pursue other legal or equitable rights they may have concerning any dispute. However, the parties agree to take all reasonable steps to resolve disputes internally before commencing legal proceedings.

8. Transfer or Assignment; Mergers, Acquisitions and Changes of Control; Effects of Assignment

A. Mortgage loans and servicing rights are freely transferable under this Agreement, subject to: (i) the contractual requirements regarding notice and the execution and delivery of the Assignment and Assumption Agreement, in the form of Exhibit D, set forth in Sections 8 and 9 hereof, and (ii) any restrictions under applicable Federal, state and local laws, regulations, regulatory guidance, statutes, ordinances, codes and requirements. Servicer must provide written notice to Fannie Mae and Freddie Mac pursuant to Section 9 below of: (i) any transfers or assignments of mortgage loans, or servicing rights relating to mortgage loans, that are 60 or more days delinquent and otherwise eligible for consideration or process under one or more of the Programs at the time of transfer or assignment, or for which the Servicer is performing Services at the time of transfer or assignment (collectively, "Eligible Loans"); and (ii) any other transfers or assignments of Servicer's rights and obligations relating to Eligible Loans under this Agreement, including, but not limited to, transfers or assignments of any rights or obligations relating to Eligible Loans under this Agreement that occur in connection with the merger, acquisition, or other change of control of Servicer. Such notice must include payment instructions for payments to be made to the transferee or assignee of the Eligible Loans, servicing rights or other rights and obligations subject to the notice (if applicable), and, subject to Section 8.B. below, evidence of the assumption by such transferee or assignee of the Eligible Loans, servicing rights or other rights and obligations that are transferred, in the form of Exhibit D (the "Assignment and Assumption Agreement"). Servicer acknowledges that Fannie Mae will continue to remit payments to Servicer in accordance with Section 4 for Services relating to mortgage loans, servicing rights or other rights and obligations that have been assigned or transferred, and that Servicer will be liable for underpayments, overpayments and misdirected payments, unless and until such notice and an executed Assignment and Assumption Agreement are provided to Fannie Mae and Freddie Mac.

B. Servicer shall notify Fannie Mae as soon as legally possible of any proposed merger, acquisition, or other change of control of Servicer, and of any financial and operational circumstances which may impair Servicer's ability to perform its obligations under the Agreement, in accordance with Sections 8 and 9, provided, however, that Servicer need not execute and deliver an Assignment and Assumption Agreement in the form of Exhibit D in the event that the assignment and assumption occur by operation of law in connection with a merger, acquisition, or other change of control of Servicer and are effective as to all of Servicer's rights and obligations under this Agreement with respect to all of the mortgage loans it services.

C. The effects of transfers and assignments under this Agreement are as follows:

(1) If the Servicer transfers or assigns all or any portion of its portfolio of mortgage loans or servicing rights to a third party pursuant to an Assignment and Assumption Agreement, only the Eligible Loans must be identified on a schedule to the Assignment and Assumption Agreement. The transferee or assignee of Servicer's mortgage loans and servicing rights must assume Servicer's obligations under this Agreement only with respect to Eligible Loans, subject to the Service Schedules and the Program Documentation applicable to the Programs in which Servicer agreed to participate prior to the transfer or assignment. Any mortgage loans or servicing rights that (I) are not Eligible Loans at the time of the transfer or assignment, (II)

are a part of the transferee's or assignee's existing portfolio prior to the transfer or assignment, or (III) become a part of the transferee's or assignee's portfolio subsequent to such transfer or assignment will become subject to the Programs only if the transferee or assignee has itself executed a Commitment to Purchase Financial Instrument and Servicer Participation Agreement separate and apart from the transfer or assignment involving Servicer and, then, only in accordance therewith.

(2) If the Servicer transfers or assigns its portfolio of mortgage loans and servicing rights to a third party in connection with a merger, acquisition, or other change of control and the transfer or assignment is effective by operation of law, the transferee or assignee of such mortgage loans and servicing rights must provide servicing with respect to all such mortgage loans and servicing rights (regardless of status at the time of transfer or assignment with respect to Program eligibility) in accordance with this Agreement, subject to the Service Schedules and the Program Documentation applicable to the Programs in which Servicer agreed to participate prior to the transfer or assignment. Any mortgage loans or servicing rights that (I) are a part of the transferee's or assignee's existing portfolio prior to the transfer or assignment, or (II) become a part of the transferee's or assignee's portfolio subsequent to such transfer or assignment will become subject to the Programs only if the transferee or assignee has itself executed a Commitment to Purchase Financial Instrument and Servicer Participation Agreement separate and apart from the transfer or assignment involving Servicer and, then, only in accordance therewith.

(3) Servicer may not transfer or assign any mortgage loans or servicing rights to any third party in a manner that is intended to circumvent, or has the effect of circumventing, Servicer's obligations under this Agreement.

9. Notices

All legal notices under the Agreement shall be in writing and referred to each party's point of contact identified below at the address listed below, or to such other point of contact at such other address as may be designated in writing by such party. All such notices under the Agreement shall be considered received: (a) when personally delivered; (b) when delivered by commercial overnight courier with verification receipt; (c) when sent by confirmed facsimile; or (d) three (3) days after having been sent, postage prepaid, via certified mail, return receipt requested. Notices shall not be made or delivered in electronic form, except as provided in Section 12.B. below, provided, however, that the party giving the notice may send an e-mail to the party receiving the notice advising that party that a notice has been sent by means permitted under this Section.

To Servicer:

[INSERT SERVICER CONTACT INFORMATION FOR LEGAL NOTICES – INCLUDE EMAIL]

To Fannie Mae:

[INSERT FANNIE MAE CONTACT INFORMATION FOR LEGAL NOTICES – INCLUDE EMAIL]

To Treasury:

[INSERT TREASURY CONTACT INFORMATION FOR LEGAL NOTICES – INCLUDE EMAIL]

To Freddie Mac:

[INSERT FREDDIE MAC CONTACT INFORMATION FOR LEGAL NOTICES – INCLUDE EMAIL]

10. Modifications

A. Subject to Sections 10.B. and 10.C., modifications to the Agreement shall be in writing and signed by Fannie Mae and Servicer.

B. Fannie Mae and the Treasury each reserve the right to unilaterally modify or supplement the terms and provisions of the Program Documentation that relate (as determined by Fannie Mae or the Treasury, in their reasonable discretion) to the compliance and performance requirements of the Programs, and related remedies established by Freddie Mac, and/or to technical, administrative, or procedural matters or compliance and reporting requirements that may impact the administration of the Programs.

C. Notwithstanding Sections 10.A. and 10.B., any modification to the Program Documentation that materially impacts the borrower eligibility requirements, the amount of payments of the Purchase Price to be made to Participating Servicers, Investors and borrowers under any of the Programs in which Servicer participates, or the rights, duties, or obligations of Participating Servicers, Investors or borrowers in connection with any of the Programs in which Servicer participates (each, a "Program Modification" and, collectively, the "Program Modifications") shall be effective only on a prospective basis; Participating Servicers will be afforded the opportunity to opt-out of a modified Program when Program Modifications are published with respect to the Services to be performed by Servicer in connection with the modified Program on or after the effective date of the Program Modification, at Servicer's discretion. Opt-out procedures, including, but not limited to, the time and process for notification of election to opt-out and the window for such election, will be set forth in the Program Documentation describing the Program Modification, provided, however, that Servicer will be given at least thirty (30) days to elect to opt-out of a Program Modification. For the avoidance of doubt, during the period during which Servicer may elect to opt-out of a Program Modification and after any such opt-out is elected by Servicer, Servicer will continue to perform the Services described in the Financial Instrument and the Program Documentation (as the Program Documentation existed immediately prior to the publication of the Program Modification prompting the opt-out) with respect to any Services that Servicer had already begun to perform prior to the opt-out.

11. Miscellaneous

A. The Agreement shall be governed by and construed under Federal law and not the law of any state or locality, without reference to or application of the conflicts of law principles. Any and all disputes between the parties that cannot be settled by mutual agreement shall be resolved solely and exclusively in the United States Federal courts located within the District of Columbia. Both parties consent to the jurisdiction and venue of such courts and irrevocably waive any objections thereto.

B. The Agreement is not a Federal procurement contract and is therefore not subject to the provisions of the Federal Property and Administrative Services Act (41 U.S.C. §§ 251-260), the Federal Acquisition Regulations (48 CFR Chapter 1), or any other Federal procurement law.

C. Any provision of the Agreement that is determined to be prohibited or unenforceable in any jurisdiction shall, as to such jurisdiction, be ineffective to the extent of such prohibition or unenforceability without invalidating the remaining provisions of the Agreement, and no such prohibition or unenforceability in any jurisdiction shall invalidate such provision in any other jurisdiction.

D. Failure on the part of Fannie Mae to insist upon strict compliance with any of the terms hereof shall not be deemed a waiver, nor will any waiver hereunder at any time be deemed a waiver at any other time. No waiver will be valid unless in writing and signed by an authorized officer of Fannie Mae. No failure by Fannie Mae to exercise any right, remedy, or power hereunder will operate as a waiver thereof. The rights, remedies, and powers provided herein are cumulative and not exhaustive of any rights, remedies, and powers provided by law.

E. The Agreement shall inure to the benefit of and be binding upon the parties to the Agreement and their permitted successors-in-interest.

F. The Commitment, the Service Schedule(s) and the Assignment and Assumption Agreement (if applicable) may be executed in two or more counterparts (and by different parties on separate counterparts), each of which shall be an original, but all of which together shall constitute one and the same instrument.

G. The Commitment, together with the Service Schedule(s), the Financial Instrument, the Certifications, the Assignment and Assumption Agreement (if applicable) and the Program Documentation, constitutes the entire agreement of the parties with respect to the subject matter hereof. In the event of a conflict between any of the foregoing documents and the Program Documentation, the Program Documentation shall prevail. In the event of a conflict between the Program Guidelines and the Supplemental Directives, the Program Guidelines shall prevail.

H. Any provisions of the Agreement (including all documents incorporated by reference thereto) that contemplate their continuing effectiveness, including, but not limited to, Sections 4, 5.B., 6, 8, 9, 11 and 12 of the Commitment, and Sections 2, 3, 5, 7, 8, 9 and 10 of the Financial Instrument, and any other provisions (or portions thereof) in the Agreement that relate to, or may impact, the ability of Fannie Mae and Freddie Mac to fulfill their responsibilities as agents of the United States in connection with the Programs, shall survive the expiration or termination of the Agreement.

12. Defined Terms; Incorporation by Reference

A. All references to the "Agreement" necessarily include, in all instances, the Commitment and all documents incorporated into the Commitment by reference, whether or not so noted contextually, and all amendments and modifications thereto. Specific references throughout the Agreement to individual documents that are incorporated by reference into the Commitment are not inclusive of any other documents that are incorporated by reference, unless so noted contextually.

B. The term "Effective Date" means the date on which Fannie Mae transmits a copy of the fully executed Commitment, Initial Service Schedule(s) and Financial Instrument to Treasury and Servicer with a completed cover sheet, in the form attached hereto as Exhibit E (the "Cover Sheet"); the Agreement shall be effective on the Effective Date. Any Additional Service Schedules that are executed and delivered to Fannie Mae after the Effective Date of the Agreement shall be also be accompanied by a completed Cover Sheet and shall be effective on the effective date or dates set forth therein. All executed documents and accompanying Cover Sheets will be faxed, emailed, or made available through other electronic means to Treasury and Servicer in accordance with Section 9.

C. The Program Documentation and Exhibit A – Service Schedule(s) (Service Schedule A-1, et seq.), Exhibit B – Form of Financial Instrument, Exhibit C – Form of Certification, Exhibit D – Form of Assignment and Assumption Agreement and Exhibit E – Form of Cover Sheet (in each case, in form and, upon completion, in substance), including all amendments and modifications thereto, are incorporated into this Commitment by this reference and given the same force and effect as though fully set forth herein.

[SIGNATURE PAGE FOLLOWS; REMAINDER OF PAGE INTENTIONALLY LEFT BLANK]

12

In Witness Whereof, Servicer and Fannie Mae by their duly authorized officials hereby execute and deliver this Commitment to Purchase Financial Instrument and Servicer Participation Agreement as of the Effective Date.

SERVICER: [INSERT FULL LEGAL NAME OF SERVICER]	**FANNIE MAE**, solely as Financial Agent of the United States
By:____________________	By:____________________
Name:____________________	Name:____________________
Title:____________________	Title:____________________
Date:____________________	Date:____________________

EXHIBITS

Exhibit A	Service Schedule(s)
Exhibit B	Form of Financial Instrument
Exhibit C	Form of Certification
Exhibit D	Form of Assignment and Assumption Agreement
Exhibit E	Form of Cover Sheet

EXHIBIT A

SERVICE SCHEDULE(S)

The attached Service Schedules together comprise Exhibit A to that certain Commitment to Purchase Financial Instrument and Servicer Participation Agreement (the "Commitment"), entered into as of the Effective Date, by and between Federal National Mortgage Association ("Fannie Mae"), a federally chartered corporation, acting as financial agent of the United States, and the undersigned party ("Servicer").

Each of the Service Schedules attached hereto is effective as of the Effective Date, or on such other date or dates as may be specified therein. All of the capitalized terms that are used but not defined in the Service Schedules shall have the meanings ascribed to them in the Commitment.

Exhibit A is deemed to be amended to include all Additional Service Schedules (if any) that are executed and delivered by the parties after the Effective Date in accordance with the Agreement, without any further action on the part of the parties hereto.

SERVICE SCHEDULE A-[INSERT NUMBER]

This Service Schedule is appended to that certain Commitment to Purchase Financial Instrument and Servicer Participation Agreement (the "Commitment"), entered into as of the Effective Date, by and between Federal National Mortgage Association ("Fannie Mae"), a federally chartered corporation, acting as financial agent of the United States, and the undersigned party ("Servicer"), and, together with all other Services Schedules appended thereto (if any), constitutes Exhibit A to the Commitment.

All of the capitalized terms that are used but not defined below shall have the meanings ascribed to them in the Commitment or in applicable Program Documentation.

1. **Program Name:**

Servicer hereby elects to participate in the following Program(s):

Home Affordable Modification Program (HAMP)

2. **Description of Program Services:**

All services required to be performed by a participating servicer as set forth in the Program Documentation for the Home Affordable Modification Program under the Emergency Economic Stabilization Act of 2008, as amended, including, but not limited to, obligations relating to the modification of first lien mortgage loans and the provision of loan modification and foreclosure prevention services relating thereto.

3. **Effective date of Service Schedule:**

[OPTION A:]This Service Schedule is executed and delivered contemporaneously with the Commitment; accordingly, the effective date of this Service Schedule is the Effective Date of the Agreement.

[OPTION B:]This Service Schedule is effective as of [INSERT DATE].

In Witness Whereof, Servicer and Fannie Mae by their duly authorized officials hereby execute and deliver this Service Schedule as of the effective date of the Service Schedule set forth above.

SERVICER: [INSERT FULL LEGAL NAME OF SERVICER]

By:____________________________
Name:__________________________
Title:___________________________
Date:___________________________

FANNIE MAE, solely as Financial Agent of the United States

By:____________________________
Name:__________________________
Title:___________________________
Date:___________________________

SERVICE SCHEDULE A-[INSERT NUMBER]

This Service Schedule is appended to that certain Commitment to Purchase Financial Instrument and Servicer Participation Agreement (the "Commitment"), entered into as of the Effective Date, by and between Federal National Mortgage Association ("Fannie Mae"), a federally chartered corporation, acting as financial agent of the United States, and the undersigned party ("Servicer"), and, together with all other Services Schedules appended thereto (if any), constitutes Exhibit A to the Commitment.

All of the capitalized terms that are used but not defined below shall have the meanings ascribed to them in the Commitment or in applicable Program Documentation.

1. **Program Name:**

Servicer hereby elects to participate in the following Program(s):

Second Lien Modification Program

2. **Description of Program Services:**

All services required to be performed by a participating servicer as set forth in the Program Documentation for the Second Lien Modification Program under the Emergency Economic Stabilization Act of 2008, as amended, including, but not limited to, obligations relating to the modification or extinguishment of second lien mortgage loans and the provision of loan modification and foreclosure prevention services relating thereto.

3. **Effective date of Service Schedule:**

[OPTION A:]This Service Schedule is executed and delivered contemporaneously with the Commitment; accordingly, the effective date of this Service Schedule is the Effective Date of the Agreement.

[OPTION B:]This Service Schedule is effective as of [INSERT DATE].

In Witness Whereof, Servicer and Fannie Mae by their duly authorized officials hereby execute and deliver this Service Schedule as of the effective date of the Service Schedule set forth above.

SERVICER: [INSERT FULL LEGAL NAME OF SERVICER]

By:____________________
Name:____________________
Title:____________________
Date:____________________

FANNIE MAE, solely as Financial Agent of the United States

By:____________________
Name:____________________
Title:____________________
Date:____________________

A-2

SERVICE SCHEDULE A-[INSERT NUMBER]

This Service Schedule is appended to that certain Amended and Restated Commitment to Purchase Financial Instrument and Servicer Participation Agreement (the "Commitment"), entered into as of the Effective Date, by and between Federal National Mortgage Association ("Fannie Mae"), a federally chartered corporation, acting as financial agent of the United States, and the undersigned party ("Servicer"), and, together with all other Services Schedules appended thereto (if any), constitutes Exhibit A to the Commitment.

All of the capitalized terms that are used but not defined below shall have the meanings ascribed to them in the Commitment or in applicable Program Documentation.

1. **Program Name:**

Servicer hereby elects to participate in the following Program(s):

Treasury Federal Housing Administration - Home Affordable Modification Program (Treasury FHA-HAMP)

2. **Description of Program Services:**

All services required to be performed by a participating servicer relating to Treasury FHA-HAMP, as set forth in guidance issued by the Federal Housing Administration from time to time; including Mortgagee Letter 2009-23, 2009-35, 2009-39, 2010-04 and 2010-10, and in the Program Documentation for including Treasury FHA-HAMP in the Home Affordable Modification Program under the Emergency Economic Stabilization Act of 2008, as amended, including, but not limited to, obligations relating to the modification of first lien mortgage loans insured by the Federal Housing Administration and the provision of loan modification and foreclosure prevention services relating thereto.

3. **Effective date of Service Schedule:**

[OPTION A:]This Service Schedule is executed and delivered contemporaneously with the Commitment; accordingly, the effective date of this Service Schedule is the Effective Date of the Agreement.

[OPTION B:]This Service Schedule is effective as of [INSERT DATE].

In Witness Whereof, Servicer and Fannie Mae by their duly authorized officials hereby execute and deliver this Service Schedule as of the effective date of the Service Schedule set forth above.

SERVICER: [INSERT FULL LEGAL NAME OF SERVICER]

By:____________________
Name:____________________
Title:____________________
Date:____________________

FANNIE MAE, solely as Financial Agent of the United States

By:____________________
Name:____________________
Title:____________________
Date:____________________

EXHIBIT B

FORM OF FINANCIAL INSTRUMENT

FINANCIAL INSTRUMENT

This Financial Instrument is delivered as provided in Section 1 of the Commitment to Purchase Financial Instrument and Servicer Participation Agreement (the "Commitment"), entered into as of the Effective Date, by and between Federal National Mortgage Association ("Fannie Mae"), a federally chartered corporation, acting as financial agent of the United States, and the undersigned party ("Servicer"). This Financial Instrument is effective as of the Effective Date. All of the capitalized terms that are used but not defined herein shall have the meanings ascribed to them in the Commitment.

For good and valuable consideration, the receipt and sufficiency of which is hereby acknowledged, Servicer agrees as follows:

1. Purchase Price Consideration; Services. This Financial Instrument is being purchased by Fannie Mae pursuant to Section 4 of the Commitment in consideration for the payment by Fannie Mae, in its capacity as a financial agent of the United States, of various payments detailed in the Program Documentation and referred to collectively in the Commitment as the "Purchase Price."

   (a) The conditions precedent to the payment by Fannie Mae of the Purchase Price with respect to the Services described on the Initial Service Schedules are: (i) the execution and delivery of this Financial Instrument, the Commitment and the Initial Service Schedules by Servicer to Fannie Mae; (ii) the execution and delivery of the Commitment and the Initial Service Schedules by Fannie Mae to Servicer; (iii) the delivery of copies of the fully executed Commitment, Initial Service Schedules and Financial Instrument to Treasury on the Effective Date of the Agreement; (iv) the performance by Servicer of the Services described in the Agreement; and (v) the satisfaction by Servicer of such other obligations as are set forth in the Agreement. Servicer shall perform all Services in consideration for the Purchase Price in accordance with the terms and conditions of the Agreement, to the reasonable satisfaction of Fannie Mae and Freddie Mac.

   (b) The conditions precedent to the payment by Fannie Mae of the Purchase Price with respect to the Services described on the Additional Service Schedules (if any) are: (i) the execution and delivery of the Additional Service Schedules and the Certification by Servicer to Fannie Mae; (ii) the execution and delivery of the Additional Service Schedules by Fannie Mae to Servicer; (iii) the delivery of copies of the fully executed Additional Service Schedules to Treasury; (iv) the performance by Servicer of the Services described in the Agreement, in accordance with the terms and conditions thereof, to the reasonable satisfaction of Fannie Mae and Freddie Mac; and (v) the satisfaction by Servicer of such other obligations as are set forth in the Agreement.

2. Authority and Agreement to Participate in Program. Subject to the limitations set forth in Section 2 of the Agreement, Servicer shall use reasonable efforts to remove all prohibitions or impediments to its authority and to obtain all third party consents, waivers and delegations that are required, by contract or law, in order to perform the Services.

3. Audits, Reporting and Data Retention.

   (a) Freddie Mac, the Federal Housing Finance Agency and other parties designated by the Treasury or applicable law shall have the right during normal business hours to conduct unannounced, informal onsite visits and to conduct formal onsite and offsite physical, personnel and information technology testing, security reviews, and audits of Servicer and to examine all books, records and data related to the Services provided and Purchase Price received in connection with each of the Programs in which Servicer participates on thirty (30) days' prior written notice.

B-1

(b) Servicer will collect, record, retain and provide to Treasury, Fannie Mae and Freddie Mac all data, information and documentation relating to the Programs in which Servicer participates as required by applicable Program Documentation. All such data, information and documentation must be provided to the Treasury, Fannie Mae and Freddie Mac as, when and in the manner specified in applicable Program Documentation. In addition, Servicer shall provide copies of executed contracts and tapes of loan pools related to the Programs for review upon request.

(c) Servicer shall promptly take corrective and remedial actions associated with reporting and reviews as directed by Fannie Mae or Freddie Mac and provide to Fannie Mae and Freddie Mac such evidence of the effective implementation of corrective and remedial actions as Fannie Mae and Freddie Mac shall reasonably require. Freddie Mac may conduct additional reviews based on its findings and the corrective actions taken by Servicer.

(d) In addition to any other obligation to retain financial and accounting records that may be imposed by Federal or state law, Servicer shall retain all information described in Section 3(b), and all data, books, reports, documents, audit logs and records, including electronic records, related to the performance of Services in connection with the Programs. In addition, Servicer shall maintain a copy of all computer systems and application software necessary to review and analyze these electronic records. Unless otherwise directed by Fannie Mae or Freddie Mac, Servicer shall retain these records for at least 7 years from the date the data or record was created, or for such longer period as may be required pursuant to applicable law. Fannie Mae or Freddie Mac may also notify Servicer from time to time of any additional record retention requirements resulting from litigation and regulatory investigations in which the Treasury or any agents of the United States may have an interest, and Servicer agrees to comply with these litigation and regulatory investigations requirements.

4. Internal Control Program.

(a) Servicer shall develop, enforce and review on a quarterly basis for effectiveness an internal control program designed to: (i) ensure effective delivery of Services in connection with the Programs in which Servicer participates and compliance with applicable Program Documentation; (ii) effectively monitor and detect loan modification fraud; and (iii) effectively monitor compliance with applicable consumer protection and fair lending laws. The internal control program must include documentation of the control objectives for Program activities, the associated control techniques, and mechanisms for testing and validating the controls.

(b) Servicer shall provide Freddie Mac with access to all internal control reviews and reports that relate to Services under the Programs performed by Servicer and its independent auditing firm to enable Freddie Mac to fulfill its duties as a compliance agent of the United States; a copy of the reviews and reports will be provided to Fannie Mae for record keeping and other administrative purposes.

5. Representations, Warranties and Covenants. Servicer makes the following representations, warranties and covenants to Fannie Mae, Freddie Mac and the Treasury, the truth and accuracy of which are continuing obligations of Servicer. In the event that any of the representations, warranties, or covenants made herein cease to be true and correct, Servicer agrees to notify Fannie Mae and Freddie Mac immediately.

(a) Servicer is established under the laws of the United States or any state, territory, or possession of the United States or the District of Columbia, and has significant operations in the United States. Servicer has full corporate power and authority to enter into, execute, and deliver the Agreement and to perform its obligations hereunder and has all licenses necessary to carry on its business as now being conducted and as contemplated by the Agreement.

(b) Servicer is in compliance with, and covenants that all Services will be performed in compliance with, all applicable Federal, state and local laws, regulations, regulatory guidance, statutes, ordinances, codes and requirements, including, but not limited to, the Truth in Lending Act, 15 USC 1601 § et seq., the Home Ownership and Equity Protection Act, 15 USC § 1639, the Federal Trade Commission Act, 15 USC § 41 et seq., the Equal Credit Opportunity Act, 15 USC § 701 et seq., the Fair Credit Reporting Act, 15 USC § 1681 et seq., the Fair Housing Act and other Federal and state laws designed to prevent unfair, discriminatory or predatory lending practices and all applicable laws governing tenant rights. Subject to the following sentence, Servicer has obtained or made, or will obtain or make, all governmental approvals or registrations required under law and has obtained or will obtain all consents necessary to authorize the performance of its obligations under the Programs in which Servicer participates and the Agreement. The performance of Services under the Agreement will not conflict with, or be prohibited in any way by, any other agreement or statutory restriction by which Servicer is bound, provided, however, that Fannie Mae acknowledges and agrees that this representation and warranty is qualified solely by and to the extent of any contractual limitations established under applicable pooling and servicing agreements and other servicing contracts to which Servicer is subject. Servicer is not aware of any other legal or financial impediments to performing its obligations under the Programs in which Servicer participates or the Agreement and shall promptly notify Fannie Mae of any financial and/or operational impediments which may impair its ability to perform its obligations under such Programs or the Agreement. Servicer is not delinquent on any Federal tax obligation or any other debt owed to the United States or collected by the United States for the benefit of others, excluding any debt or obligation that is being contested in good faith.

(c) Servicer covenants that: (i) it will perform its obligations in accordance with the Agreement and will promptly provide such performance reporting as Fannie Mae may reasonably require; (ii) all Services will be offered to borrowers, fully documented and serviced , or otherwise performed, in accordance with the applicable Program Documentation; and (iii) all data, collection information and other information reported by Servicer to Fannie Mae and Freddie Mac under the Agreement, including, but not limited to, information that is relied upon by Fannie Mae or Freddie Mac in calculating the Purchase Price or in performing any compliance review will be true, complete and accurate in all material respects, and consistent with all relevant business records, as and when provided.

(d) Servicer covenants that it will: (i) perform the Services required under the Program Documentation and the Agreement in accordance with the practices, high professional standards of care, and degree of attention used in a well-managed operation, and no less than that which the Servicer exercises for itself under similar circumstances; and (ii) use qualified individuals with suitable training, education, experience and skills to perform the Services. Servicer acknowledges that Program participation may require changes to, or the augmentation of, its systems, staffing and procedures, and covenants and agrees to take all actions necessary to ensure it has the capacity to implement the Programs in which it participates in accordance with the Agreement.

(e) Servicer covenants that it will comply with all regulations on conflicts of interest that are applicable to Servicer in connection with the conduct of its business and all conflicts of interest and non-disclosure obligations and restrictions and related mitigation procedures set forth in the Program Documentation (if any), as they relate to the Programs in which Servicer participates.

(f) Servicer acknowledges that the provision of false or misleading information to Fannie Mae or Freddie Mac in connection with any of the Programs or pursuant to the Agreement may constitute a violation of: (a) Federal criminal law involving fraud, conflict of interest, bribery, or gratuity violations found in Title 18 of the United States Code; or (b) the civil False Claims Act (31 U.S.C. §§ 3729-3733). Servicer covenants to disclose to Fannie Mae and Freddie Mac any credible evidence, in connection with the Services, that a management official, employee, or contractor of Servicer has committed, or may have committed, a violation of the referenced statutes.

(g) Servicer covenants to disclose to Fannie Mae and Freddie Mac any other facts or information that the Treasury, Fannie Mae or Freddie Mac should reasonably expect to know about Servicer and its contractors to help protect the reputational interests of the Treasury, Fannie Mae and Freddie Mac in managing and monitoring the Programs in which Servicer participates.

(h) Servicer covenants that it will timely inform Fannie Mae and Freddie Mac of any anticipated Event of Default and of any Act of Bad Faith of which it becomes aware.

(i) Servicer acknowledges that Fannie Mae or Freddie Mac may be required to assist the Treasury with responses to the Privacy Act of 1974 (the "Privacy Act"), 5 USC § 552a, inquiries from borrowers and Freedom of Information Act, 5 USC § 552, inquiries from other parties, as well as formal inquiries from Congressional committees and members, the Government Accounting Office, Inspectors General and other government entities, as well as media and consumer advocacy group inquiries about the Programs and their effectiveness. Servicer covenants that it will respond promptly and accurately to all search requests made by Fannie Mae or Freddie Mac, comply with any related procedures which Fannie Mae or Freddie Mac may establish, and provide related training to employees and contractors. In connection with Privacy Act inquiries, Servicer covenants that it will provide updated and corrected information as appropriate about borrowers' records to ensure that any system of record maintained by Fannie Mae on behalf of the Treasury is accurate and complete.

(j) Servicer acknowledges that Fannie Mae is required to develop and implement customer service call centers to respond to borrowers' and other parties' inquiries regarding the Programs, which may require additional support from Servicer. Servicer covenants that it will provide such additional customer service call support as Fannie Mae reasonably determines is necessary to support the Programs in which Servicer participates.

(k) Servicer acknowledges that Fannie Mae and/or Freddie Mac are required to develop and implement practices to monitor and detect loan modification fraud and to monitor compliance with applicable consumer protection and fair lending laws. Servicer covenants that it will fully and promptly cooperate with Fannie Mae's inquiries about loan modification fraud and legal compliance and comply with any anti-fraud and legal compliance procedures which Fannie Mae and/or Freddie Mac may require. Servicer covenants that it will develop and implement an internal control program to monitor and detect loan modification fraud and to monitor compliance with applicable consumer protection and fair lending laws, among other things, as provided in Section 4 of this Financial Instrument and acknowledges that the internal control program will be monitored, as provided in such Section.

(l) Servicer shall sign and deliver a Certification to Fannie Mae and Freddie Mac beginning on June 1, 2010 and again on June 1 of each year thereafter during the Term, and upon the execution and delivery by Servicer of Additional Service Schedule(s) (if any) during the Term, in each case in the form attached as Exhibit C to the Agreement.

(m) Solely if Servicer has elected to participate in the Second Lien Modification Program by executing and delivering to Fannie Mae a Service Schedule relating thereto, Servicer represents, warrants and covenants that each mortgage loan it modifies under the Second Lien Modification Program is, or will be at the time of modification, a lien that is second in priority relative to the first lien that was modified under the Programs.

6. Use of Contractors. Servicer is responsible for the supervision and management of any contractor that assists in the performance of Services in connection with the Programs in which Servicer participates. Servicer shall remove and replace any contractor that fails to perform. Servicer shall ensure that all of its contractors comply with the terms and provisions of the Agreement. Servicer shall be responsible for the acts or omissions of its contractors as if the acts or omissions were by the Servicer.

7. Data Rights.

(a) For purposes of this Section, the following definitions apply:

(i) "Data" means any recorded information, regardless of form or the media on which it may be recorded, regarding any of the Services provided in connection with the Programs.

(ii) "Limited Rights" means non-exclusive rights to, without limitation, use, copy, maintain, modify, enhance, disclose, reproduce, prepare derivative works, and distribute, in any manner, for any purpose related to the administration, activities, review, or audit of, or public reporting regarding, the Programs and to permit others to do so in connection therewith.

(iii) "NPI" means nonpublic personal information, as defined under the GLB.

(iv) "GLB" means the Gramm-Leach-Bliley Act, 15 U.S.C. 6801-6809.

(b) Subject to Section 7(c) below, Treasury, Fannie Mae and Freddie Mac shall have Limited Rights, with respect to all Data produced, developed, or obtained by Servicer or a contractor of Servicer in connection with the Programs, provided, however, that NPI will not be transferred by Fannie Mae in violation of the GLB and, provided, further, that Servicer acknowledges and agrees that any use of NPI by, the distribution of NPI to, or the transfer of NPI among, Federal, state and local government organizations and agencies does not constitute a violation of the GLB for purposes of the Agreement. If requested, such Data shall be made available to the Treasury, Fannie Mae, or Freddie Mac upon request, or as and when directed by the Program Documentation relating to the Programs in which Servicer participates, in industry standard useable format.

(c) Servicer expressly consents to the publication of its name as a participant in the Programs listed on the Service Schedules, and the use and publication of Servicer's Data, subject to applicable state and federal laws regarding confidentiality, in any form and on any media utilized by Treasury, Fannie Mae or Freddie Mac, including, but not limited to, on any website or webpage hosted by Treasury, Fannie Mae, or Freddie Mac, in connection with such Programs, provided that no Data placed in the public domain: (i) will contain the name, social security number, or street address of any borrower or other information that would allow the borrower to be identified; or, (ii) will, if presented in a form that links the Servicer with the Data, include (x) information other than program performance and participation related statistics, such as the number of modifications or extinguishments, performance of modifications, characteristics of the modified loans, or program compensation or fees, or (y) any information about any borrower other than creditworthiness characteristics such as debt, income, and credit score. In any Data provided to an enforcement or supervisory agency with jurisdiction over the Servicer, these limitations on borrower information shall not apply.

8. Publicity and Disclosure.

(a) Servicer shall not make use of any Treasury name, symbol, emblem, program name, or product name, in any advertising, signage, promotional material, press release, Web page, publication, or media interview, without the prior written consent of the Treasury.

(b) Servicer shall not publish, or cause to have published, or make public use of Fannie Mae's name, logos, trademarks, or any information about its relationship with Fannie Mae without the prior written permission of Fannie Mae, which permission may be withdrawn at any time in Fannie Mae's sole discretion.

(c) Servicer shall not publish, or cause to have published, or make public use of Freddie Mac's name (i.e., "Freddie Mac" or "Federal Home Loan Mortgage Corporation"), logos, trademarks, or any information about its relationship with Freddie Mac without the prior written permission of Freddie Mac, which permission may be withdrawn at any time in Freddie Mac's sole discretion.

9. Limitation of Liability. IN NO EVENT SHALL FANNIE MAE, THE TREASURY, OR FREDDIE MAC, OR THEIR RESPECTIVE OFFICERS, DIRECTORS, EMPLOYEES, AGENTS OR AFFILIATES BE LIABLE TO SERVICER WITH RESPECT TO ANY OF THE PROGRAMS OR THE AGREEMENT, OR FOR ANY ACT OR OMISSION OCCURRING IN CONNECTION WITH THE FOREGOING, FOR ANY DAMAGES OF ANY KIND, INCLUDING, BUT NOT LIMITED TO DIRECT DAMAGES, INDIRECT DAMAGES, LOST PROFITS, LOSS OF BUSINESS, OR OTHER INCIDENTAL, CONSEQUENTIAL, SPECIAL OR PUNITIVE DAMAGES OF ANY NATURE OR UNDER ANY LEGAL THEORY WHATSOEVER, EVEN IF ADVISED OF THE POSSIBILITY OF SUCH DAMAGES AND REGARDLESS OF WHETHER OR NOT THE DAMAGES WERE REASONABLY FORESEEABLE; PROVIDED, HOWEVER, THAT THIS PROVISION SHALL NOT LIMIT FANNIE MAE'S OBLIGATION TO REMIT PURCHASE PRICE PAYMENTS TO SERVICER IN ITS CAPACITY AS FINANCIAL AGENT OF THE UNITED STATES IN ACCORDANCE WITH THE AGREEMENT.

10. Indemnification. Servicer shall indemnify, hold harmless, and pay for the defense of Fannie Mae, the Treasury and Freddie Mac, and their respective officers, directors, employees, agents and affiliates against all claims, liabilities, costs, damages, judgments, suits, actions, losses and expenses, including reasonable attorneys' fees and costs of suit, arising out of or resulting from: (a) Servicer's breach of Section 5 (Representations, Warranties and Covenants) of this Financial Instrument; (b) Servicer's negligence, willful misconduct or failure to perform its obligations under the Agreement; or (c) any injuries to persons (including death) or damages to property caused by the negligent or willful acts or omissions of Servicer or its contractors. Servicer shall not settle any suit or claim regarding any of the foregoing without Fannie Mae's prior written consent if such settlement would be adverse to Fannie Mae's interest, or the interests of the Treasury or Freddie Mac. Servicer agrees to pay or reimburse all costs that may be incurred by Fannie Mae and Freddie Mac in enforcing this indemnity, including attorneys' fees.

IN WITNESS WHEREOF, Servicer hereby executes this Financial Instrument on the date set forth below.

[INSERT FULL LEGAL NAME OF SERVICER]:

____

[Name of Authorized Official] Date

[Title of Authorized Official]

EXHIBIT C

FORM OF CERTIFICATION

<u>CERTIFICATION</u>

This Certification is delivered as provided in Section 1.C. of the Commitment to Purchase Financial Instrument and Servicer Participation Agreement (the "<u>Commitment</u>"), effective as of [INSERT], by and between Federal National Mortgage Association ("<u>Fannie Mae</u>"), a federally chartered corporation, acting as financial agent of the United States, and the undersigned party ("<u>Servicer</u>"). All terms used, but not defined herein, shall have the meanings ascribed to them in the Commitment.

Servicer hereby certifies, as of [INSERT DATE ON WHICH CERTIFICATION IS GIVEN], that:

1. Servicer is established under the laws of the United States or any state, territory, or possession of the United States or the District of Columbia, and has significant operations in the United States. Servicer had full corporate power and authority to enter into, execute, and deliver the Agreement and to perform its obligations hereunder and has all licenses necessary to carry on its business as now being conducted and as contemplated by the Agreement.

2. Servicer is in compliance with, and certifies that all Services have been performed in compliance with, all applicable Federal, state and local laws, regulations, regulatory guidance, statutes, ordinances, codes and requirements, including, but not limited to, the Truth in Lending Act, 15 USC 1601 § et seq., the Home Ownership and Equity Protection Act, 15 USC § 1639, the Federal Trade Commission Act, 15 USC § 41 et seq., the Equal Credit Opportunity Act, 15 USC § 701 et seq., the Fair Credit Reporting Act, 15 USC § 1681 et seq., the Fair Housing Act and other Federal and state laws designed to prevent unfair, discriminatory or predatory lending practices and all applicable laws governing tenant rights. Subject to the following sentence, Servicer has obtained or made all governmental approvals or registrations required under law and has obtained all consents necessary to authorize the performance of its obligations under the Programs in which Servicer participated and the Agreement. The performance of Services under the Agreement has not conflicted with, or been prohibited in any way by, any other agreement or statutory restriction by which Servicer is bound, except to the extent of any contractual limitations under applicable pooling and servicing agreements and other servicing contracts to which Servicer is subject. Servicer is not aware of any other legal or financial impediments to performing its obligations under the Programs or the Agreement and has promptly notified Fannie Mae of any financial and/or operational impediments which may impair its ability to perform its obligations under the Programs or the Agreement. Servicer is not delinquent on any Federal tax obligation or any other debt owed to the United States or collected by the United States for the benefit of others, excluding any debts or obligations that are being contested in good faith.

3. (i) Servicer has performed its obligations in accordance with the Agreement and has promptly provided such performance reporting as Fannie Mae and Freddie Mac have reasonably required; (ii) all Services have been offered by Servicer to borrowers, fully documented and serviced by Servicer in accordance with the applicable Program Documentation; and (iii) all data, collection information and other information reported by Servicer to Fannie Mae and Freddie Mac under the Agreement, including, but not limited to, information that was relied upon by Fannie Mae and Freddie Mac in calculating the Purchase Price and in performing any compliance review, was true, complete and accurate in all material respects, and consistent with all relevant business records, as and when provided.

4. Servicer has: (i) performed the Services required under the Program Documentation and the Agreement in accordance with the practices, high professional standards of care, and degree of attention used in a well-managed operation, and no less than that which the Servicer exercises for itself under similar circumstances; and (ii) used qualified individuals with suitable training, education, experience and skills to perform the Services. Servicer acknowledges that Program participation required changes to, or the augmentation of, its systems, staffing and procedures; Servicer took all actions necessary to ensure that it had the capacity to implement the Programs in which it participated in accordance with the Agreement.

5. Servicer has complied with all regulations on conflicts of interest that are applicable to Servicer in connection with the conduct of its business and all conflicts of interest and non-disclosure obligations and restrictions and related mitigation procedures set forth in the Program Documentation (if any), as they related to the Programs in which Servicer participated.

6. Servicer acknowledges that the provision of false or misleading information to Fannie Mae or Freddie Mac in connection with the Programs or pursuant to the Agreement may constitute a violation of: (a) Federal criminal law involving fraud, conflict of interest, bribery, or gratuity violations found in Title 18 of the United States Code; or (b) the civil False Claims Act (31 U.S.C. §§ 3729-3733). Servicer has disclosed to Fannie Mae and Freddie Mac any credible evidence, in connection with the Services, that a management official, employee, or contractor of Servicer has committed, or may have committed, a violation of the referenced statutes.

7. Servicer has disclosed to Fannie Mae and Freddie Mac any other facts or information that the Treasury, Fannie Mae or Freddie Mac should reasonably expect to know about Servicer and its contractors to help protect the reputational interests of the Treasury, Fannie Mae and Freddie Mac in managing and monitoring the Programs.

8. Servicer acknowledges that Fannie Mae and Freddie Mac may be required to assist the Treasury with responses to the Privacy Act of 1974 (the "Privacy Act"), 5 USC § 552a, inquiries from borrowers and Freedom of Information Act, 5 USC § 552, inquiries from other parties, as well as formal inquiries from Congressional committees and members, the Government Accounting Office, Inspectors General and other government entities, as well as media and consumer advocacy group inquiries about the Programs and their effectiveness. Servicer has responded promptly and accurately to all search requests made by Fannie Mae and Freddie Mac, complied with any related procedures which Fannie Mae and Freddie Mac have established, and provided related training to employees and contractors. In connection with Privacy Act inquiries, Servicer has provided updated and corrected information as appropriate about borrowers' records to ensure that any system of record maintained by Fannie Mae on behalf of the Treasury is accurate and complete.

9. Servicer acknowledges that Fannie Mae is required to develop and implement customer service call centers to respond to borrowers' and other parties' inquiries regarding the Programs in which Servicer participates, which may require additional support from Servicer. Servicer has provided such additional customer service call support as Fannie Mae has reasonably requested to support such Programs.

10. Servicer acknowledges that Fannie Mae and/or Freddie Mac are required to develop and implement practices to monitor and detect loan modification fraud and to monitor compliance with applicable consumer protection and fair lending laws. Servicer has fully and promptly cooperated with Fannie Mae's inquiries about loan modification fraud and legal compliance and has complied with any anti-fraud and legal compliance procedures which Fannie Mae and/or Freddie Mac have required. Servicer has developed and implemented an internal control program to monitor and detect loan modification fraud and to monitor compliance with applicable consumer protection and fair lending laws, among other things, as provided in Section 4 of the Financial Instrument.

11. Solely if Servicer has elected to participate in the Second Lien Modification Program by executing and delivering to Fannie Mae a Service Schedule relating thereto, Servicer acknowledges that each mortgage loan it modified under the Second Lien Modification Program was, at the time of modification, second in priority relative to the first lien that was modified under the Programs.

In the event that any of the certifications made herein are discovered not to be true and correct, Servicer agrees to notify Fannie Mae and Freddie Mac immediately.

[INSERT FULL LEGAL NAME OF SERVICER]:

____________________________ ____________________

[Name of Authorized Official] Date
[Title of Authorized Official]

EXHIBIT D

FORM OF ASSIGNMENT AND ASSUMPTION AGREEMENT

ASSIGNMENT AND ASSUMPTION AGREEMENT

This Assignment and Assumption Agreement (the "Assignment and Assumption Agreement") is entered into as of [INSERT DATE] by and between [INSERT FULL LEGAL NAME OF ASSIGNOR] ("Assignor") and [INSERT FULL LEGAL NAME OF ASSIGNEE] ("Assignee"). All terms used, but not defined, herein shall have the meanings ascribed to them in the Underlying Agreement (defined below).

WHEREAS, Assignor and Federal National Mortgage Association, a federally chartered corporation, as financial agent of the United States ("Fannie Mae"), are parties to a Commitment to Purchase Financial Instrument and Servicer Participation Agreement, a complete copy of which (including all exhibits, amendments and modifications thereto) is attached hereto and incorporated herein by this reference (the "Underlying Agreement");

WHEREAS, Assignor has agreed to assign to Assignee all of its rights and obligations under the Underlying Agreement with respect to the Eligible Loans that are identified on the schedule attached hereto as Schedule 1 (collectively, the "Assigned Rights and Obligations"); and

WHEREAS, Assignee has agreed to assume the Assigned Rights and Obligations.

NOW, THEREFORE, for good and valuable consideration, the receipt and sufficiency of which are hereby acknowledged, the parties hereto agree as follows:

1. Assignment. Assignor hereby assigns to Assignee all of Assignor's rights and obligations under the Underlying Agreement with respect to the Assigned Rights and Obligations.

2. Assumption. Assignee hereby accepts the foregoing assignment and assumes all of the rights and obligations of Assignor under the Underlying Agreement with respect to the Assigned Rights and Obligations.

3. Effective Date. The date on which the assignment and assumption of rights and obligations under the Underlying Agreement is effective is [INSERT EFFECTIVE DATE OF ASSIGNMENT/ASSUMPTION].

4. Successors. All future transfers and assignments of the Assigned Rights and Obligations transferred and assigned hereby are subject to the transfer and assignment provisions of the Underlying Agreement. This Assignment and Assumption Agreement shall inure to the benefit of, and be binding upon, the permitted successors and assigns of the parties hereto.

5. Counterparts. This Assignment and Assumption Agreement may be executed in counterparts, each of which shall be an original, but all of which together constitute one and the same instrument.

IN WITNESS WHEREOF, Assignor and Assignee, by their duly authorized officials, hereby execute and deliver this Assignment and Assumption Agreement, together with Schedule 1, effective as of the date set forth in Section 3 above.

ASSIGNOR: [INSERT FULL LEGAL NAME OF ASSIGNOR]

By:____________________________________
Name:__________________________________
Title:__________________________________
Date:__________________________________

ASSIGNEE: [INSERT FULL LEGAL NAME OF ASSIGNEE]

By:____________________________________
Name:__________________________________
Title:__________________________________
Date:__________________________________

D-2

SCHEDULE 1

To

ASSIGNMENT AND ASSUMPTION AGREEMENT

EXHIBIT E

FORM OF COVER SHEET

Cover Sheet for Transmission of Commitment to Purchase Financial Instrument and Servicer Participation Agreement and Related Documents

To: [INSERT FULL LEGAL NAME OF SERVICER] ("Servicer"), [INSERT SERVICER CONTACT]

From: Federal National Mortgage Association, a federally chartered corporation, as financial agent of the United States ("Fannie Mae")

Copy To: The U.S. Department of the Treasury, [INSERT TREASURY CONTACT]

Date: [INSERT DATE OF TRANSMISSION]

Method of Transmission: [Facsimile to [INSERT FAX NUMBER OF SERVICER]] [[Email with PDF file attached to [INSERT SERVICER EMAIL ADDRESS][Specify other method of electronic delivery]]

NOTICE

[IF THIS TRANSMISSION OCCURS UPON EXECUTION OF COMMITMENT:]This transmission constitutes notice to Servicer that the Commitment to Purchase Financial Instrument and Servicer Participation Agreement, by and between Fannie Mae and Servicer (the "Commitment") and the Service Schedule(s) and Financial Instrument attached thereto have been fully executed and are effective as of the date of this transmission. The date of this transmission shall be the "Effective Date" of the Commitment, the Service Schedule(s) and the Financial Instrument.

[IF THIS TRANSMISSION OCCURS IN CONNECTION WITH DELIVERY OF ADDITIONAL SERVICE SCHEDULES:] This transmission constitutes notice to Servicer that Additional Service Schedule(s) and a Certification have been delivered by Servicer to Fannie Mae, pursuant to Section 4 of the Commitment to Purchase Financial Instrument and Servicer Participation Agreement, by and between Fannie Mae and Servicer (the "Commitment"). The Additional Service Schedule(s) and the Certification attached hereto have been fully executed and are effective as of the date set forth in the Additional Service Schedule(s).

Copies of the fully executed Additional Service Schedule(s) and the Certification are attached to this transmission for your records.

B.3.11 Home Affordable Modification Program Request for Modification and Affidavit (RMA)

Making Home Affordable Program
Request For Modification and Affidavit (RMA)

MAKING HOME AFFORDABLE.GOV

REQUEST FOR MODIFICATION AND AFFIDAVIT (RMA) page 1 | COMPLETE ALL THREE PAGES OF THIS FORM

Loan I.D. Number______________________ Servicer______________________

BORROWER		CO-BORROWER	
Borrower's name		Co-borrower's name	
Social Security number	Date of birth	Social Security number	Date of birth
Home phone number with area code		Home phone number with area code	
Cell or work number with area code		Cell or work number with area code	

I want to:	☐ Keep the Property	☐ Sell the Property	
The property is my:	☐ Primary Residence	☐ Second Home	☐ Investment
The property is:	☐ Owner Occupied	☐ Renter Occupied	☐ Vacant

Mailing address

Property address (if same as mailing address, just write same) E-mail address

Is the property listed for sale? ☐ Yes ☐ No
Have you received an offer on the property? ☐ Yes ☐ No
Date of offer ________ *Amount of offer $*________________
Agent's Name: ______________________
Agent's Phone Number: ______________________
For Sale by Owner? ☐ Yes ☐ No

Have you contacted a credit-counseling agency for help ☐ Yes ☐ No
If yes, please complete the following:
Counselor's Name: ______________________
Agency Name: ______________________
Counselor's Phone Number: ______________________
Counselor's E-mail: ______________________

Who pays the real estate tax bill on your property?
☐ I do ☐ Lender does ☐ Paid by condo or HOA
Are the taxes current? ☐ Yes ☐ No
Condominium or HOA Fees ☐ Yes ☐ No $ ____________
Paid to: ______________________

Who pays the hazard insurance premium for your property?
☐ I do ☐ Lender does ☐ Paid by Condo or HOA
Is the policy current? ☐ Yes ☐ No
Name of Insurance Co.: ______________________
Insurance Co. Tel #: ______________________

Have you filed for bankruptcy? ☐ Yes ☐ No If yes: ☐ Chapter 7 ☐ Chapter 13 *Filing Date:*______________
Has your bankruptcy been discharged? ☐ Yes ☐ No *Bankruptcy case number* ______________________

Additional Liens/Mortgages or Judgments on this property:

Lien Holder's Name/Servicer	Balance	Contact Number	Loan Number

HARDSHIP AFFIDAVIT

I (We) am/are requesting review under the Making Home Affordable program.
I am having difficulty making my monthly payment because of financial difficulties created by (check all that apply):

☐ My household income has been reduced. For example: unemployment, underemployment, reduced pay or hours, decline in business earnings, death, disability or divorce of a borrower or co-borrower.	☐ My monthly debt payments are excessive and I am overextended with my creditors. Debt includes credit cards, home equity or other debt.
☐ My expenses have increased. For example: monthly mortgage payment reset, high medical or health care costs, uninsured losses, increased utilities or property taxes.	☐ My cash reserves, including all liquid assets, are insufficient to maintain my current mortgage payment and cover basic living expenses at the same time.

☐ Other:

Explanation (continue on back of page 3 if necessary): ______________________

REQUEST FOR MODIFICATION AND AFFIDAVIT (RMA) page 2 | COMPLETE ALL THREE PAGES OF THIS FORM

INCOME/EXPENSES FOR HOUSEHOLD[1]

Number of People in Household:

Monthly Household Income		Monthly Household Expenses/Debt		Household Assets	
Monthly Gross Wages	$	First Mortgage Payment	$	Checking Account(s)	$
Overtime	$	Second Mortgage Payment	$	Checking Account(s)	$
Child Support / Alimony / Separation[2]	$	Insurance	$	Savings/ Money Market	$
Social Security/SSDI	$	Property Taxes	$	CDs	$
Other monthly income from pensions, annuities or retirement plans	$	Credit Cards / Installment Loan(s) (total minimum payment per month)	$	Stocks / Bonds	$
Tips, commissions, bonus and self-employed income	$	Alimony, child support payments	$	Other Cash on Hand	$
Rents Received	$	Net Rental Expenses	$	Other Real Estate (estimated value)	$
Unemployment Income	$	HOA/Condo Fees/Property Maintenance	$	Other ____________	$
Food Stamps/Welfare	$	Car Payments	$	Other ____________	$
Other (investment income, royalties, interest, dividends etc.)	$	Other ____________ ____________	$	Do not include the value of life insurance or retirement plans when calculating assets (401k, pension funds, annuities, IRAs, Keogh plans, etc.)	
Total (Gross Income)	**$**	***Total Debt/Expenses***	**$**	***Total Assets***	**$**

INCOME MUST BE DOCUMENTED

[1]Include combined income and expenses from the borrower and co-borrower (if any). If you include income and expenses from a household member who is not a borrower, please specify using the back of this form if necessary.

[2]You are not required to disclose Child Support, Alimony or Separation Maintenance income, unless you choose to have it considered by your servicer.

INFORMATION FOR GOVERNMENT MONITORING PURPOSES

The following information is requested by the federal government in order to monitor compliance with federal statutes that prohibit discrimination in housing. **You are not required to furnish this information, but are encouraged to do so. The law provides that a lender or servicer may not discriminate either on the basis of this information, or on whether you choose to furnish it.** If you furnish the information, please provide both ethnicity and race. For race, you may check more than one designation. If you do not furnish ethnicity, race, or sex, the lender or servicer is required to note the information on the basis of visual observation or surname if you have made this request for a loan modification in person. **If you do not wish to furnish the information, please check the box below.**

BORROWER	☐ I do not wish to furnish this information	CO-BORROWER	☐ I do not wish to furnish this information
Ethnicity:	☐ Hispanic or Latino ☐ Not Hispanic or Latino	*Ethnicity:*	☐ Hispanic or Latino ☐ Not Hispanic or Latino
Race:	☐ American Indian or Alaska Native ☐ Asian ☐ Black or African American ☐ Native Hawaiian or Other Pacific Islander ☐ White	*Race:*	☐ American Indian or Alaska Native ☐ Asian ☐ Black or African American ☐ Native Hawaiian or Other Pacific Islander ☐ White
Sex:	☐ Female ☐ Male	*Sex:*	☐ Female ☐ Male

To be completed by interviewer		Name/Address of Interviewer's Employer
This request was taken by: ☐ Face-to-face interview ☐ Mail ☐ Telephone ☐ Internet	*Interviewer's Name (print or type) & ID Number* *Interviewer's Signature* *Date* *Interviewer's Phone Number (include area code)*	

page 2 of 3 ▶

REQUEST FOR MODIFICATION AND AFFIDAVIT (RMA) page 3 | COMPLETE ALL THREE PAGES OF THIS FORM

ACKNOWLEDGEMENT AND AGREEMENT

In making this request for consideration under the Making Home Affordable Program, I certify under penalty of perjury:

1. That all of the information in this document is truthful and the event(s) identified on page 1 is/are the reason that I need to request a modification of the terms of my mortgage loan, short sale or deed-in-lieu of foreclosure.
2. I understand that the Servicer, the U.S. Department of the Treasury, or their agents may investigate the accuracy of my statements and may require me to provide supporting documentation. I also understand that knowingly submitting false information may violate Federal law.
3. I understand the Servicer will pull a current credit report on all borrowers obligated on the Note.
4. I understand that if I have intentionally defaulted on my existing mortgage, engaged in fraud or misrepresented any fact(s) in connection with this document, the Servicer may cancel any Agreement under Making Home Affordable and may pursue foreclosure on my home.
5. That: my property is owner-occupied; I intend to reside in this property for the next twelve months; I have not received a condemnation notice; and there has been no change in the ownership of the Property since I signed the documents for the mortgage that I want to modify.
6. I am willing to provide all requested documents and to respond to all Servicer questions in a timely manner.
7. I understand that the Servicer will use the information in this document to evaluate my eligibility for a loan modification or short sale or deed-in-lieu of foreclosure, but the Servicer is not obligated to offer me assistance based solely on the statements in this document.
8. I am willing to commit to credit counseling if it is determined that my financial hardship is related to excessive debt.
9. I understand that the Servicer will collect and record personal information, including, but not limited to, my name, address, telephone number, social security number, credit score, income, payment history, government monitoring information, and information about account balances and activity. I understand and consent to the disclosure of my personal information and the terms of any Making Home Affordable Agreement by Servicer to (a) the U.S. Department of the Treasury, (b) Fannie Mae and Freddie Mac in connection with their responsibilities under the Homeowner Affordability and Stability Plan; (c) any investor, insurer, guarantor or servicer that owns, insures, guarantees or services my first lien or subordinate lien (if applicable) mortgage loan(s); (d) companies that perform support services in conjunction with Making Home Affordable; and (e) any HUD-certified housing counselor.

▶ ______________________________ ______________

Borrower Signature Date

▶ ______________________________ ______________

Co-Borrower Signature Date

HOMEOWNER'S HOTLINE

If you have questions about this document or the modification process, please call your servicer.

If you have questions about the program that your servicer cannot answer or need further counseling, you can call the Homeowner's HOPE™ Hotline at 1-888-995-HOPE (4673). The Hotline can help with questions about the program and offers free HUD-certified counseling services in English and Spanish.

888-995-HOPE™
Homeowner's HOPE™ Hotline

NOTICE TO BORROWERS

Be advised that by signing this document you understand that any documents and information you submit to your servicer in connection with the Making Home Affordable Program are under penalty of perjury. Any misstatement of material fact made in the completion of these documents including but not limited to misstatement regarding your occupancy in your home, hardship circumstances, and/or income, expenses, or assets will subject you to potential criminal investigation and prosecution for the following crimes: perjury, false statements, mail fraud, and wire fraud. The information contained in these documents is subject to examination and verification. Any potential misrepresentation will be referred to the appropriate law enforcement authority for investigation and prosecution. By signing this document you certify, represent and agree that: "Under penalty of perjury, all documents and information I have provided to Lender in connection with the Making Home Affordable Program, including the documents and information regarding my eligibility for the program, are true and correct."

If you are aware of fraud, waste, abuse, mismanagement or misrepresentations affiliated with the Troubled Asset Relief Program, please contact the SIGTARP Hotline by calling 1-877-SIG-2009 (toll-free), 202-622-4559 (fax), or www.sigtarp.gov. Mail can be sent to Hotline Office of the Special Inspector General for Troubled Asset Relief Program, 1801 L St. NW, Washington, DC 20220.

THE DEPARTMENT OF THE TREASURY 1789

page 3 of 3

B.3.12 Home Affordable Modification Program Hardship Affidavit

Making Home Affordable Program
Hardship Affidavit

MAKING HOME AFFORDABLE.GOV

HARDSHIP AFFIDAVIT page 1 — COMPLETE ALL TWO PAGES OF THIS FORM

Loan I.D. Number______________________ Servicer______________________

BORROWER		CO-BORROWER	
Borrower's name		Co-borrower's name	
Social Security number	Date of birth	Social Security number	Date of birth

Property address (include city, state and zip):

I want to:	☐ Keep the Property	☐ Sell the Property	
The property is my:	☐ Primary Residence	☐ Second Home	☐ Investment Property
The property is:	☐ Owner Occupied	☐ Renter Occupied	☐ Vacant

HARDSHIP AFFIDAVIT

I (We) am/are requesting review under the Making Home Affordable program.
I am having difficulty making my monthly payment because of financial difficulties created by (check all that apply):

☐ My household income has been reduced. For example: unemployment, underemployment, reduced pay or hours, decline in business earnings, death, disability or divorce of a borrower or co-borrower.

☐ My monthly debt payments are excessive and I am overextended with my creditors. Debt includes credit cards, home equity or other debt.

☐ My expenses have increased. For example: monthly mortgage payment reset, high medical or health care costs, uninsured losses, increased utilities or property taxes.

☐ My cash reserves, including all liquid assets, are insufficient to maintain my current mortgage payment and cover basic living expenses at the same time.

☐ Other:

Explanation (continue on back of page 2 if necessary): ______________________

Have you filed for bankruptcy? ☐ Yes ☐ No If yes: ☐ Chapter 7 ☐ Chapter 13 *Filing Date:*______________
Has your bankruptcy been discharged? ☐ Yes ☐ No *Bankruptcy case number* ______________

INFORMATION FOR GOVERNMENT MONITORING PURPOSES

The following information is requested by the federal government in order to monitor compliance with federal statutes that prohibit discrimination in housing. **You are not required to furnish this information, but are encouraged to do so. The law provides that a lender or servicer may not discriminate either on the basis of this information, or on whether you choose to furnish it.** If you furnish the information, please provide both ethnicity and race. For race, you may check more than one designation. If you do not furnish ethnicity, race, or sex, the lender or servicer is required to note the information on the basis of visual observation or surname if you have made this request for a loan modification in person. **If you do not wish to furnish the information, please check the box below.**

BORROWER	☐ I do not wish to furnish this information	CO-BORROWER	☐ I do not wish to furnish this information
Ethnicity:	☐ Hispanic or Latino ☐ Not Hispanic or Latino	*Ethnicity:*	☐ Hispanic or Latino ☐ Not Hispanic or Latino
Race:	☐ American Indian or Alaska Native ☐ Asian ☐ Black or African American ☐ Native Hawaiian or Other Pacific Islander ☐ White	*Race:*	☐ American Indian or Alaska Native ☐ Asian ☐ Black or African American ☐ Native Hawaiian or Other Pacific Islander ☐ White
Sex:	☐ Female ☐ Male	*Sex:*	☐ Female ☐ Male

To be completed by interviewer		Name/Address of Interviewer's Employer
This request was taken by: ☐ Face-to-face interview ☐ Mail ☐ Telephone ☐ Internet	*Interviewer's Name (print or type) & ID Number* *Interviewer's Signature* *Date* *Interviewer's Phone Number (include area code)*	

HARDSHIP AFFIDAVIT page 2 | COMPLETE ALL TWO PAGES OF THIS FORM

ACKNOWLEDGEMENT AND AGREEMENT

In making this request for consideration under the Making Home Affordable Program, I certify under penalty of perjury:

1. That all of the information in this document is truthful and the event(s) identified on page 1 is/are the reason that I need to request a modification of the terms of my mortgage loan, short sale or deed-in-lieu of foreclosure.
2. I understand that the Servicer, the U.S. Department of the Treasury, or their agents may investigate the accuracy of my statements, may require me to provide supporting documentation. I also understand that knowingly submitting false information may violate Federal law.
3. I understand the Servicer will pull a current credit report on all borrowers obligated on the Note.
4. I understand that if I have intentionally defaulted on my existing mortgage, engaged in fraud or misrepresented any fact(s) in connection with this document, the Servicer may cancel any Agreement under Making Home Affordable and may pursue foreclosure on my home.
5. That: my property is owner-occupied; I intend to reside in this property for the next twelve months; I have not received a condemnation notice; and there has been no change in the ownership of the Property since I signed the documents for the mortgage that I want to modify.
6. I am willing to provide all requested documents and to respond to all Servicer questions in a timely manner.
7. I understand that the Servicer will use the information in this document to evaluate my eligibility for a loan modification or short sale or deed-in-lieu of foreclosure, but the Servicer is not obligated to offer me assistance based solely on the statements in this document.
8. I am willing to commit to credit counseling if it is determined that my financial hardship is related to excessive debt.
9. I understand that the Servicer will collect and record personal information, including, but not limited to, my name, address, telephone number, social security number, credit score, income, payment history, government monitoring information, and information about account balances and activity. I understand and consent to the disclosure of my personal information and the terms of any Making Home Affordable Agreement by Servicer to (a) the U.S. Department of the Treasury, (b) Fannie Mae and Freddie Mac in connection with their responsibilities under the Homeowner Affordability and Stability Plan; (c) any investor, insurer, guarantor or servicer that owns, insures, guarantees or services my first lien or subordinate lien (if applicable) mortgage loan(s); (d) companies that perform support services in conjunction with Making Home Affordable; and (e) any HUD-certified housing counselor.

▶ ______________________________ ______________

Borrower Signature Date

▶ ______________________________ ______________

Co-Borrower Signature Date

HOMEOWNER'S HOTLINE

If you have questions about this document or the modification process, please call your servicer.

If you have questions about the program that your servicer cannot answer or need further counseling, you can call the Homeowner's HOPE™ Hotline at 1-888-995-HOPE (4673). The Hotline can help with questions about the program and offers free HUD-certified counseling services in English and Spanish.

888-995-HOPE™
Homeowner's HOPE™ Hotline

NOTICE TO BORROWERS

Be advised that by signing this document you understand that any documents and information you submit to your servicer in connection with the Making Home Affordable Program are under penalty of perjury. Any misstatement of material fact made in the completion of these documents including but not limited to misstatement regarding your occupancy in your home, hardship circumstances, and/or income, expenses, or assets will subject you to potential criminal investigation and prosecution for the following crimes: perjury, false statements, mail fraud, and wire fraud. The information contained in these documents is subject to examination and verification. Any potential misrepresentation will be referred to the appropriate law enforcement authority for investigation and prosecution. By signing this document you certify, represent and agree that: "Under penalty of perjury, all documents and information I have provided to Lender in connection with the Making Home Affordable Program, including the documents and information regarding my eligibility for the program, are true and correct."

If you are aware of fraud, waste, abuse, mismanagement or misrepresentations affiliated with the Troubled Asset Relief Program, please contact the SIGTARP Hotline by calling 1-877-SIG-2009 (toll-free), 202-622-4559 (fax), or www.sigtarp.gov. Mail can be sent to Hotline Office of the Special Inspector General for Troubled Asset Relief Program, 1801 L St. NW, Washington, DC 20220.

THE DEPARTMENT OF THE TREASURY 1789

page 2 of 2

B.3.13 Home Affordable Modification Program Trial Period Plan Notice

HELPING YOU STAY IN YOUR HOME. MAKING HOME AFFORDABLE[SM]

[Servicer Logo]

You may be able to make your payments more affordable!
Call 1.8XX.XXX.XXX for Immediate Assistance.

[Date]
[Name]
[Address 1]
[Address 2]

Dear ______________________ [Loan number]

Congratulations! You are approved to enter into a trial period plan under the Home Affordable Modification Program. This is the first step toward qualifying for more affordable mortgage payments. Please read this letter so that you understand all the steps you need to take to modify your mortgage payments.

What you need to do...

To accept this offer, you must make new monthly "trial period payments" in place of your normal monthly mortgage payment. Send in your monthly trial period payments—instead of your normal monthly mortgage payment—as follows:

1st payment: $X,XXX.XX by XX/01/XX
2nd payment: $X,XXX.XX by XX/01/XX
3rd payment: $X,XXX.XX by XX/01/XX

If you do not make each trial period payment in the month in which it is due, your loan will not be modified under the Home Affordable Modification Program.

In addition to making your trial period payments on time, you must send copies of all the documents that are noted on the attached checklist no later than ____________ so that we can verify the financial information you already provided to us (use the return envelope provided for your convenience). **If the documents are not received by [insert the due date again], this offer will end and your loan will not be modified.**

After all trial period payments are timely made and you have submitted all the required documents, your mortgage would then be permanently modified if you qualify. (Your existing loan and loan requirements remain in effect and unchanged during the trial period.) If you have any questions or if you cannot afford the trial period payments shown above but want to remain in your home, or if you have decided to leave your home but still want to avoid foreclosure, please call us at **1.8XX.XXX.XXXX** as we may be able to help you.

Sincerely,

[Servicer Contact Person Name]
[Servicer Contact Person Title]
[Servicer Name]

Attachments: (1) Checklist; (2) Frequently Asked Questions and (3) Additional Trial Period Plan Information and Legal Notices

The *Making Home Affordable Program* was created to help millions of homeowners refinance or modify their mortgages. As part of this program, we – your mortgage servicer – and the Federal Government are working to offer you options to help you stay in your home.

COMPLETE YOUR CHECKLIST This is the information we need to help you modify your mortgage payments.

Review and Complete—All Four Steps (If Applicable)
❑ 1. Send your first trial period mortgage payment of $ ________, **AND**
❑ 2. Complete and sign (by all borrowers) the enclosed [*Select one* MHA Request for Modification & Affidavit (RMA) OR MHA Hardship Affidavit form], **AND** ***You must only complete and sign this form if it is enclosed in this package.***
❑ 3. Sign and date a copy of the enclosed IRS Form 4506-T (Request for Transcript of Tax Return) or the 4506T-EZ (Short Form Request for Individual Tax Return Transcript) for each borrower (borrowers who filed a Form 1040 series on a calendar-year basis may use Form 4506T-EZ in place of Form 4506-T). Borrowers who filed their tax returns jointly may send in one IRS Form 4506-T/4506T-EZ signed and dated by both of the joint filers **AND** ***You must only complete and sign this form if it is enclosed in this package.***
❑ 4. Return the required income documentation. This documentation includes: **For each borrower who receives a salary or hourly wages—** • Copy of your two most recent pay stubs that show year-to-date earnings **For each borrower who is self-employed—** • Most recent quarterly or year-to-date profit/loss statement. **For each borrower who has income such as social security, disability or death benefits, pension, adoption assistance, public assistance, or unemployment—** • Copy of benefits statement or letter from the provider that states the amount, frequency and duration of the benefit, and • Two most recent bank statements showing receipt of such payment. **For each borrower who is relying on alimony, child support or separation maintenance as qualifying income*—** • Copy of divorce decree, separation agreement, other written agreement filed with the court, or decree that states the amount and period of time over which it will be received, and • Two most recent bank statements showing receipt of such payment. *You are not required to disclose child support, alimony or separation maintenance income, unless you choose to have it considered by your servicer. **For each borrower who has rental income or if you are current on your mortgage payments:** • Copies of the most recently filed signed federal tax return with all schedules, including the Schedule E—Supplemental Income and Loss (servicer can also request through IRS). **For each borrower who has non-wage income (part time employment, bonuses, tips and investment income):** • Copy of documentation describing the nature of the income (e.g. an employment contract or printouts documenting tip income) *If you have other types of income, cannot locate the required documents, or have questions*

about the paperwork required, please contact us at [1.8XX.XXX.XXXX].

Important Information

Keep a copy of all documents for your records. Don't send original income documentation.

If you do not make your trial period payments or do not provide all required, signed and completed documentation for each borrower on time, **we will not be able to determine if you qualify for the Home Affordable Modification Program.**

If you have further questions about this trial period plan or the program, please call us at XXX-XXX-XXXX.

If you would like to speak with a counselor about this program, call the Homeowner's HOPE™ Hotline 1-888-995-HOPE (4673). The Homeowner's HOPE™ Hotline offers free HUD-certified counseling services and is available 24/7 in English and Spanish. Other languages are available by appointment.

FREQUENTLY ASKED QUESTIONS Get the answers you need to some of the most common questions.

Q. What else should I know about this offer?

- If you make your new payments timely and submit the paperwork by the deadline, **we will not conduct a foreclosure sale.**
- You will not be charged any fees for this Trial Period Plan or final modification.
- If your loan is modified, we will waive all unpaid late charges.
- Your credit score may be affected by accepting a trial period plan or modification. For more information about your credit score, go to http://www.ftc.gov/bcp/edu/pubs/consumer/credit/cre24.shtm.
- You may be required to attend credit counseling.

Q. Why is there a trial period?

The trial period offers you immediate payment relief (and could prevent a foreclosure sale) while we process your paperwork to determine if you qualify for a permanent loan modification. It also gives you time to make sure you can manage the lower monthly mortgage payment. Note: This is only a temporary Trial Period Plan. Your existing loan and loan requirements remain in effect and unchanged during the trial period.

Q. How was my new payment in the trial period determined?

Your trial period payment is approximately 31% of your total gross monthly income, which you told us was $________. The new payment includes principal and interest and an escrow amount of $________ to pay property taxes, insurance and other permissible escrow fees. If we were able to modify your loan today, based on the information you gave us, we estimate your modified interest rate would be ____%. If we modify your loan permanently after the trial period, the interest rate may be different due to a variety of factors that affect the terms of your final modification. If you did not have an escrow account before, the timing of your tax and insurance bills may require that you make a payment to cover any such bills when they come due. This is known as an escrow shortage. Your loan has an escrow shortage of $_______; this can either be paid in a lump sum when the loan is modified or over the next ____ years (or ______ months). If you wish to pay the total shortage as a lump sum, please contact us.

Q. What happens if my verified income is different from the amount I told you verbally?

During the trial period, we will verify your income based on the documentation you must provide. Your verified income will determine your eligibility for a permanent modification and its final terms. If your verified income is significantly higher than the income you told us, you may have to restart your trial period with a higher payment based on that higher income. Also, if your verified income is different from the amount you gave us verbally, you may no longer be eligible for a Home Affordable Modification.

Q. When will I know if my loan can be modified permanently and how will the modified loan balance be determined?

Once we confirm you are eligible for a Home Affordable Modification and you make all of your trial period payments on time, we will send you a modification agreement detailing the terms of the modified loan. Any difference between the amount of the trial period payments and your regular mortgage payments will be added to the balance of your loan along with any other past due amounts as permitted by your loan documents. While this will increase the total amount that you owe, it should not significantly change the amount of your modified mortgage payment as that is determined based on your total monthly gross income, not your loan balance.

FREQUENTLY ASKED QUESTIONS Get the answers you need to some of the most common questions.

Q. Are there incentives that I may qualify for if I am current with my new payments?

Once your loan is modified, you can earn a pay-for-success incentive for every month that you make on-time payments beginning with the trial period payments. Depending on your modified monthly payment, you may accrue up to $1,000 each year for five years for a total of $5,000. This important benefit, *which will be applied to your principal balance each year after the anniversary date of your first trial period payment due date,* will help you earn equity in your home by reducing the amount that you owe. However, you must remain current on your loan. You will lose this benefit if your modified loan becomes 90 days delinquent at any time during this five year period. If you lose this benefit, you will lose all accrued, unapplied incentive payments.

Q. Will my interest rate and principal and interest payment be fixed after my loan is permanently modified?

Once your loan is modified, your interest rate and monthly principal and interest payment will be fixed for the life of your mortgage **unless** your initial modified interest rate is below current market interest rates. In that case, the below market interest rate will be fixed for five years. At the end of the fifth year, your interest rate may increase by 1% per year until it reaches a cap. The cap will equal the market rate of interest being charged by mortgage lenders on the day your modification agreement is prepared (the Freddie Mac Primary Mortgage Market Survey Rate for 30-year, fixed-rate conforming mortgages). Once your interest rate reaches the cap it will be fixed for the remaining life of your loan. Like your trial period payment, your new monthly payment will also include an escrow for property taxes, hazard insurance and other escrowed expenses. If the cost of your homeowners insurance, property tax assessment or other escrowed expenses increases, your monthly payment will increase as well.

Q. What if I other questions about Home Affordable Modification that cannot be answered by my mortgage servicer?

888-995-HOPE™
Homeowner's HOPE™ Hotline

Call the Homeowner's HOPE™ Hotline at **1-888-995-HOPE (4673).** This Hotline can help with questions about the program and offers access to free HUD-certified counseling services in English and Spanish.

Q. What if I am aware of fraud, waste, mismanagement or misrepresentations affiliated with the Troubled Asset Relief Program?

Please contact SIGTARP at 1.877.SIG.2009 (toll-free), 202.622.4559 (fax) or www.sigtarp

Mail can be sent to: Hotline Office of the Special Inspector General for Troubled Asset Relief Program, 1801 L Street NW, Washington, DC 20220.

IMPORTANT PROGRAM INFO Here's additional information you need to know about the Home Affordable Modification Program.

Additional Trial Period Plan Information and Legal Notices

The terms of your trial period plan below are effective on the day you make your first trial period payment, provided you have paid it on or before [Month XX, 20XX]. You and we agree that:

We will not proceed to foreclosure sale during the trial period, provided you are complying with the terms of the trial period plan, except as detailed below:

- During the trial period, any pending foreclosure action or proceeding will not be dismissed and may be immediately resumed if you fail to comply with the terms of the trial period plan or do not qualify for a modification. A new notice of default, notice of intent to accelerate, notice of acceleration, or similar notice will not be necessary to continue the foreclosure action (foreclosure notices). You waive any and all rights to receive such foreclosure notices to the extent permitted by applicable law. However, if your property is located in Georgia, Hawaii, Missouri, or Virginia and a foreclosure sale is currently scheduled, the foreclosure sale will not be suspended and foreclosure may proceed if you do not make each and every trial period payment that is due through the end of the month preceding the month in which the foreclosure sale is scheduled to occur. For example, if a foreclosure sale is scheduled in February and you do not make your January and any earlier required trial period payment by the end of January, the foreclosure sale may proceed in these four states. If a foreclosure sale occurs pursuant to this provision, the trial period plan will be deemed to have terminated.

During the trial period, we may accept and post your trial period payments to your account and it will not affect foreclosure proceedings that have already been started.

- The servicer's acceptance and posting of your new payment during the trial period will not be deemed a waiver of the acceleration of your loan or foreclosure action and related activities, and shall not constitute a cure of your default under your loan unless such payments are sufficient to completely cure your entire default under your loan.

If your monthly payment did not include escrows for taxes and insurance, you are now required to do so:

- You agree that any prior waiver that allowed you to pay directly for taxes and insurance is revoked. You agree to establish an escrow account and to pay required escrows into that account.

Your current loan documents remain in effect; however, you may make the trial period payment instead of the payment required under your loan documents:

- You agree that all terms and provisions of your current mortgage note and mortgage security instrument remain in full force and effect and you will comply with those terms; and that nothing in the trial period plan shall be understood or construed to be a satisfaction or release in whole or in part of the obligations contained in the loan documents.

Page 7 of 7

B.3.14 Other Home Affordable Modification Program Documents

The following is a list of other documents that are available on the Home Affordable Modification Program's administrative website for servicers at www.hmpadmin.com.

- Supplemental Directive 09-02: Fair Housing Obligations Under the Home Affordable Modification Program;
- Supplemental Directive 09-04: Home Affordable Modification Program-Home Price Decline Protection Incentives;
- Supplemental Directive 09-05: Introduction of the Second Lien Modification Program;
- Supplemental Directive 09-06: Home Affordable Modification Program-Data Collection and Reporting Requirements Guidance;
- Supplemental Directive 09-07: Home Affordable Modification Program-Streamlined Borrower Evaluation Process;
- Supplemental Directive 09-10: Home Affordable Modification Program—Temporary Review Period for Active Trial Modifications Scheduled to Expire on or Before January 31, 2010;
- Supplemental Documentation—Frequently Asked Questions—Home Affordable Modification Program—2009–2010 Conversion Campaign;
- Supplemental Documantation—Frequently Asked Questions—Home Affordable Modification Program;
- Home Affordable Modification Program Base Net Present Value (NPV) Model v.3.0 Model Documentation.

Appendix C Federal Mortgage Servicing Law

C.1 Introduction

This appendix contains selected provisions of the Real Estate Settlements Procedures Act (RESPA) and Regulation X that pertain to mortgage servicing. Other sections of RESPA and Regulation X are reprinted in Appendix C of National Consumer Law Center, *The Cost of Credit: Regulation and Legal Challenges* (4th ed. 2009 and Supp.). In addition, this appendix includes selected provisions of the Truth in Lending Act and Regulation Z, and the Servicemembers Civil Relief Act, that relate to certain servicing practices and the requirements for disclosure of change in ownership of mortgage loans.

C.2 Selected Provisions of the Real Estate Settlements Procedures Act, 12 U.S.C. §§ 2601–2617

TITLE 12. BANKS AND BANKING
CHAPTER 27—REAL ESTATE SETTLEMENT PROCEDURES

* * *

12 U.S.C. § 2602. Definitions

For purposes of this chapter—

(1) the term "federally related mortgage loan" includes any loan (other than temporary financing such as a construction loan) which—

(A) is secured by a first or subordinate lien on residential real property (including individual units of condominiums and cooperatives) designed principally for the occupancy of from one to four families, including any such secured loan, the proceeds of which are used to prepay or pay off an existing loan secured by the same property; and

(B)(i) is made in whole or in part by any lender the deposits or accounts of which are insured by any agency of the Federal Government, or is made in whole or in part by any lender which is regulated by any agency of the Federal Government, or

(ii) is made in whole or in part, or insured, guaranteed, supplemented, or assisted in any way, by the Secretary or any other officer or agency of the Federal Government or under or in connection with a housing or urban development program administered by the Secretary or a housing or related program administered by any other such officer or agency; or

(iii) is intended to be sold by the originating lender to the Federal National Mortgage Association, the Government National Mortgage Association, the Federal Home Loan Mortgage Corporation, or a financial institution from which it is to be purchased by the Federal Home Loan Mortgage Corporation; or

(iv) is made in whole or in part by any "creditor," as defined in section 1602(f) of Title 15, who makes or invests in residential real estate loans aggregating more than $1,000,000 per year, except that for the purpose of this chapter, the term "creditor" does not include any agency or instrumentality of any State;

(2) the term "thing of value" includes any payment, advance, funds, loan, service, or other consideration;

(3) the term "settlement services" includes any service provided in connection with a real estate settlement including, but not limited to, the following: title searches, title examinations, the provision of title certificates, title insurance, services rendered by an attorney, the preparation of documents, property surveys, the rendering of credit reports or appraisals, pest and fungus inspections, services rendered by a real estate agent or broker, the origination of a federally related mortgage loan (including, but not limited to, the taking of loan applications, loan processing, and the underwriting and funding of loans), and the handling of the processing, and closing or settlement;

(4) the term "title company" means any institution which is qualified to issue title insurance, directly or through its agents, and also refers to any duly authorized agent of a title company;

(5) the term "person" includes individuals, corporations, associations, partnerships, and trusts;

(6) the term "Secretary" means the Secretary of Housing and Urban Development;

(7) the term "affiliated business arrangement" means an arrangement in which (A) a person who is in a position to refer business incident to or a part of a real estate settlement service involving a federally related mortgage loan, or an associate of such person, has either an affiliate relationship with or a direct or beneficial ownership interest of more than 1 percent in a provider of settlement services; and (B) either of such persons directly or indirectly refers such business to that provider or affirmatively influences the selection of that provider; and

(8) the term "associate" means one who has one or more of the following relationships with a person in a position to refer settlement business: (A) a spouse, parent, or child of such person; (B) a corporation or business entity that controls, is controlled by, or is under common control with such person; (C) an employer, officer, director, partner, franchisor, or franchisee of such person; or (D) anyone who has an agreement, arrangement, or understanding, with such person, the purpose or substantial effect of which is to enable the person in a position to refer settlement business to benefit financially from the referrals of such business.

[Pub. L. No. 93-533, § 3, 88 Stat. 1724 (Dec. 22, 1974); Pub. L. No. 94-205, § 2, 89 Stat. 1157 (Jan. 2, 1976); Pub. L. No. 98-181, tit. IV, § 461(a), 97 Stat. 1230 (Nov. 30, 1983); Pub. L. No. 102-550, tit. IX, § 908(a), (b), 106 Stat. 3873 (Oct. 28, 1992); Pub. L. No. 104-208, div. A, tit. II, § 2103(c)(1), 110 Stat. 3009–400 (Sept. 30, 1996)]

* * *

12 U.S.C. § 2605. Servicing of mortgage loans and administration of escrow accounts

(a) Disclosure to applicant relating to assignment, sale, or transfer of loan servicing

Each person who makes a federally related mortgage loan shall disclose to each person who applies for the loan, at the time of application for the loan, whether the servicing of the loan may be assigned, sold, or transferred to any other person at any time while the loan is outstanding.

(b) Notice by transferor of loan servicing at time of transfer

(1) Notice requirement

Each servicer of any federally related mortgage loan shall notify the borrower in writing of any assignment, sale, or transfer of the servicing of the loan to any other person.

(2) Time of notice

(A) In general

Except as provided under subparagraphs (B) and (C), the notice required under paragraph (1) shall be made to the borrower not less than 15 days before the effective date of transfer of the servicing of the mortgage loan (with respect to which such notice is made).

(B) Exception for certain proceedings

The notice required under paragraph (1) shall be made to the borrower not more than 30 days after the effective date of assignment, sale, or transfer of the servicing of the mortgage loan (with respect to which such notice is made) in any case in which the assignment, sale, or transfer of the servicing of the mortgage loan is preceded by—

(i) termination of the contract for servicing the loan for cause;

(ii) commencement of proceedings for bankruptcy of the servicer; or

(iii) commencement of proceedings by the Federal Deposit Insurance Corporation or the Resolution Trust Corporation for conservatorship or receivership of the servicer (or an entity by which the servicer is owned or controlled).

(C) Exception for notice provided at closing

The provisions of subparagraphs (A) and (B) shall not apply to any assignment, sale, or transfer of the servicing of any mortgage loan if the person who makes the loan provides to the borrower, at settlement (with respect to the property for which the mortgage loan is made), written notice under paragraph (3) of such transfer.

(3) Contents of notice

The notice required under paragraph (1) shall include the following information:

(A) The effective date of transfer of the servicing described in such paragraph.

(B) The name, address, and toll-free or collect call telephone number of the transferee servicer.

(C) A toll-free or collect call telephone number for (i) an individual employed by the transferor servicer, or (ii) the department of the transferor servicer, that can be contacted by the borrower to answer inquiries relating to the transfer of servicing.

(D) The name and toll-free or collect call telephone number for (i) an individual employed by the transferee servicer, or (ii) the department of the transferee servicer, that can be contacted by the borrower to answer inquiries relating to the transfer of servicing.

(E) The date on which the transferor servicer who is servicing the mortgage loan before the assignment, sale, or transfer will cease to accept payments relating to the loan and the date on which the transferee servicer will begin to accept such payments.

(F) Any information concerning the effect the transfer may have, if any, on the terms of or the continued availability of mortgage life or disability insurance or any other type of optional insurance and what action, if any, the borrower must take to maintain coverage.

(G) A statement that the assignment, sale, or transfer of the servicing of the mortgage loan does not affect any term or condition of the security instruments other than terms directly related to the servicing of such loan.

(c) Notice by transferee of loan servicing at time of transfer

(1) Notice requirement

Each transferee servicer to whom the servicing of any federally related mortgage loan is assigned, sold, or transferred shall notify the borrower of any such assignment, sale, or transfer.

(2) Time of notice

(A) In general

Except as provided in subparagraphs (B) and (C), the notice required under paragraph (1) shall be made to the borrower not more than 15 days after the effective date of transfer of the servicing of the mortgage loan (with respect to which such notice is made).

(B) Exception for certain proceedings

The notice required under paragraph (1) shall be made to the borrower not more than 30 days after the effective date of assignment, sale, or transfer of the servicing of the mortgage loan (with respect to which such notice is made) in any case in which the assignment, sale, or transfer of the servicing of the mortgage loan is preceded by—

(i) termination of the contract for servicing the loan for cause;

(ii) commencement of proceedings for bankruptcy of the servicer; or

(iii) commencement of proceedings by the Federal Deposit Insurance Corporation or the Resolution Trust Corporation for conservatorship or receivership of the servicer (or an entity by which the servicer is owned or controlled).

(C) Exception for notice provided at closing

The provisions of subparagraphs (A) and (B) shall not apply to any assignment, sale, or transfer of the servicing of any mortgage loan if the person who makes the loan provides to the borrower, at settlement (with respect to the property for which the mortgage loan is made), written notice under paragraph (3) of such transfer.

(3) Contents of notice

Any notice required under paragraph (1) shall include the information described in subsection (b)(3) of this section.

(d) Treatment of loan payments during transfer period

During the 60-day period beginning on the effective date of transfer of the servicing of any federally related mortgage loan, a late fee may not be imposed on the borrower with respect to any payment on such loan and no such payment may be treated as late for any other purposes, if the payment is received by the transferor servicer (rather than the transferee servicer who should properly receive payment) before the due date applicable to such payment.

(e) Duty of loan servicer to respond to borrower inquiries

(1) Notice of receipt of inquiry

(A) In general

If any servicer of a federally related mortgage loan receives a qualified written request from the borrower (or an agent of the borrower) for information relating to the servicing of such loan, the servicer shall provide a written response acknowledging receipt of the correspondence within 20 days (excluding legal public holidays, Saturdays, and Sundays) unless the action requested is taken within such period.

(B) Qualified written request

For purposes of this subsection, a qualified written request shall be a written correspondence, other than notice on a payment coupon or other payment medium supplied by the servicer, that—

(i) includes, or otherwise enables the servicer to identify, the name and account of the borrower; and

(ii) includes a statement of the reasons for the belief of the borrower, to the extent applicable, that the account is in error or provides sufficient detail to the servicer regarding other information sought by the borrower.

(2) Action with respect to inquiry

Not later than 60 days (excluding legal public holidays, Saturdays, and Sundays) after the receipt from any borrower of any qualified written request under paragraph (1) and, if applicable, before taking any action with respect to the inquiry of the borrower, the servicer shall—

(A) make appropriate corrections in the account of the borrower, including the crediting of any late charges or penalties, and transmit to the borrower a written notification of such correction (which shall include the name and telephone number of a representative of the servicer who can provide assistance to the borrower);

(B) after conducting an investigation, provide the borrower with a written explanation or clarification that includes—

(i) to the extent applicable, a statement of the reasons for which the servicer believes the account of the borrower is correct as determined by the servicer; and

(ii) the name and telephone number of an individual employed by, or the office or department of, the servicer who can provide assistance to the borrower; or

(C) after conducting an investigation, provide the borrower with a written explanation or clarification that includes—

(i) information requested by the borrower or an explanation of why the information requested is unavailable or cannot be obtained by the servicer; and

(ii) the name and telephone number of an individual employed by, or the office or department of, the servicer who can provide assistance to the borrower.

(3) Protection of credit rating

During the 60-day period beginning on the date of the servicer's receipt from any borrower of a qualified written request relating to a dispute regarding the borrower's payments, a servicer may not provide information regarding any overdue payment, owed by such borrower and relating to such period or qualified written request, to any consumer reporting agency (as such term is defined under section 1681a of Title 15).

(f) Damages and costs

Whoever fails to comply with any provision of this section shall be liable to the borrower for each such failure in the following amounts:

(1) Individuals

In the case of any action by an individual, an amount equal to the sum of—

(A) any actual damages to the borrower as a result of the failure; and

(B) any additional damages, as the court may allow, in the case of a pattern or practice of noncompliance with the requirements of this section, in an amount not to exceed $1,000.

(2) Class actions

In the case of a class action, an amount equal to the sum of—

(A) any actual damages to each of the borrowers in the class as a result of the failure; and

(B) any additional damages, as the court may allow, in the case of a pattern or practice of noncompliance with the requirements of this section, in an amount not greater than $1,000 for each member of the class, except that the total amount of damages under this subparagraph in any class action may not exceed the lesser of—

(i) $500,000; or

(ii) 1 percent of the net worth of the servicer.

(3) Costs

In addition to the amounts under paragraph (1) or (2), in the case of any successful action under this section, the costs of the action, together with any attorneys fees incurred in connection with such action as the court may determine to be reasonable under the circumstances.

(4) Nonliability

A transferor or transferee servicer shall not be liable under this subsection for any failure to comply with any requirement under this section if, within 60 days after discovering an error (whether pursuant to a final written examination report or the servicer's own procedures) and before the commencement of an action under this subsection and the receipt of written notice of the error from the borrower, the servicer notifies the person concerned of the error and makes whatever adjustments are necessary in the appropriate account to ensure that the person will not be required to pay an amount in excess of any amount that the person otherwise would have paid.

(g) Administration of escrow accounts

If the terms of any federally related mortgage loan require the borrower to make payments to the servicer of the loan for deposit into an escrow account for the purpose of assuring payment of taxes, insurance premiums, and other charges with respect to the property, the servicer shall make payments from the escrow account for such taxes, insurance premiums, and other charges in a timely manner as such payments become due.

(h) Preemption of conflicting State laws

Notwithstanding any provision of any law or regulation of any State, a person who makes a federally related mortgage loan or a servicer shall be considered to have complied with the provisions of any such State law or regulation requiring notice to a borrower at the time of application for a loan or transfer of the servicing of a loan if such person or servicer complies with the requirements under this section regarding timing, content, and procedures for notification of the borrower.

(i) Definitions

For purposes of this section:

(1) Effective date of transfer

The term "effective date of transfer" means the date on which the mortgage payment of a borrower is first due to the transferee servicer of a mortgage loan pursuant to the assignment, sale, or transfer of the servicing of the mortgage loan.

(2) Servicer

The term "servicer" means the person responsible for servicing of a loan (including the person who makes or holds a loan if such person also services the loan). The term does not include—

(A) the Federal Deposit Insurance Corporation or the Resolution Trust Corporation, in connection with assets acquired, assigned, sold, or transferred pursuant to section 1823(c) of this title or as receiver or conservator of an insured depository institution; and

(B) the Government National Mortgage Association, the Federal National Mortgage Association, the Federal Home Loan Mortgage Corporation, the Resolution Trust Corporation, or the Federal Deposit Insurance Corporation, in any case in which the assignment, sale, or transfer of the servicing of the mortgage loan is preceded by—

(i) termination of the contract for servicing the loan for cause;

(ii) commencement of proceedings for bankruptcy of the servicer; or

(iii) commencement of proceedings by the Federal Deposit Insurance Corporation or the Resolution Trust Corporation for conservatorship or receivership of the servicer (or an entity by which the servicer is owned or controlled).

(3) Servicing

The term "servicing" means receiving any scheduled periodic payments from a borrower pursuant to the terms of any loan, including amounts for escrow accounts described in section 2609 of this title, and making the payments of principal and interest and such other payments with respect to the amounts received from the borrower as may be required pursuant to the terms of the loan.

(j) Transition

(1) Originator liability

A person who makes a federally related mortgage loan shall not be liable to a borrower because of a failure of such person to comply with subsection (a) of this section with respect to an application for a loan made by the borrower before the regulations referred to in paragraph (3) take effect.

(2) Servicer liability

A servicer of a federally related mortgage loan shall not be liable to a borrower because of a failure of the servicer to perform any duty under subsection (b), (c), (d), or (e) of this section that arises before the regulations referred to in paragraph (3) take effect.

(3) Regulations and effective date

The Secretary shall, by regulations that shall take effect not later than April 20, 1991, establish any requirements necessary to carry out this section. Such regulations shall include the model disclosure statement required under subsection (a)(2) of this section.

[Pub. L. No. 93-533, § 6, *as added* Pub. L. No. 101-625, tit. IX, § 941, 104 Stat. 4405 (Nov. 28, 1990), *and amended* Pub. L. No. 102-27, tit. III, § 312(a), 105 Stat. 154 (Apr. 10, 1991); Pub. L. No. 103-325, tit. III, § 345, 108 Stat. 2239 (Sept. 23, 1994); Pub. L. No. 104-208, div. A, tit. II, § 2103(a), 110 Stat. 3009–399 (Sept. 30, 1996)]

12 U.S.C. § 2606. Exempted transactions

(a) In general

This chapter does not apply to credit transactions involving extensions of credit—

(1) primarily for business, commercial, or agricultural purposes; or

(2) to government or governmental agencies or instrumentalities.

(b) Interpretation

In prescribing regulations under section 2617(a) of this title, the Secretary shall ensure that, with respect to subsection (a) of this section, the exemption for credit transactions involving extensions of credit primarily for business, commercial, or agricultural purposes, as provided in subsection (a)(1) of this section shall be the same as the exemption for such credit transactions under 1603(1) of Title 15.

[Pub. L. No. 93-533, § 7, *as added* Pub. L. No. 103-325, tit. III, § 312, 108 Stat. 2221 (Sept. 23, 1994), *and amended* Pub. L. No. 104-208, div. A, tit. II, § 2103(b), 110 Stat. 3009–399 (Sept. 30, 1996)]

* * *

12 U.S.C. § 2609. Limitation on requirement of advance deposits in escrow accounts

(a) In general

A lender, in connection with a federally related mortgage loan, may not require the borrower or prospective borrower—

(1) to deposit in any escrow account which may be established in connection with such loan for the purpose of assuring payment of taxes, insurance premiums, or other charges with respect to the property, in connection with the settlement, an aggregate sum (for such purpose) in excess of a sum that will be sufficient to pay such taxes, insurance premiums and other charges attributable to the period beginning on the last date on which each such charge would have been paid under the normal lending practice of the lender and local custom, provided that the selection of each such date constitutes prudent lending practice, and ending on the due date of its first full installment payment under the mortgage, plus one-sixth of the estimated total amount of such taxes, insurance premiums and other charges to be paid on dates, as provided above, during the ensuing twelve-month period; or

(2) to deposit in any such escrow account in any month beginning with the first full installment payment under the mortgage a sum (for the purpose of assuring payment of taxes, insurance premiums and other charges with respect to the property) in excess of the sum of (A) one-twelfth of the total amount of the estimated taxes, insurance premiums and other charges which are reasonably anticipated to be paid on dates during the ensuing twelve months which dates are in accordance with the normal lending practice of the lender and local custom, provided that the selection of each such date constitutes prudent lending practice, plus (B) such amount as is necessary to maintain an additional balance in such escrow account not to exceed one-sixth of the estimated total amount of such taxes, insurance premiums and other charges to be paid on dates, as provided above, during the ensuing twelve-month period: Provided, however, That in the event the lender determines there will be or is a deficiency he shall not be prohibited from requiring additional monthly deposits in such escrow account to avoid or eliminate such deficiency.

(b) Notification of shortage in escrow account

If the terms of any federally related mortgage loan require the borrower to make payments to the servicer (as the term is defined in section 2605(i) of this title) of the loan for deposit into an escrow account for the purpose of assuring payment of taxes, insurance premiums, and other charges with respect to the property, the servicer shall notify the borrower not less than annually of any shortage of funds in the escrow account.

(c) Escrow account statements

(1) Initial statement

(A) In general

Any servicer that has established an escrow account in connection with a federally related mortgage loan shall submit to the borrower for which the escrow account has been established a statement clearly itemizing the estimated taxes, insurance premiums, and other charges that are reasonably anticipated to be paid from the escrow account during the first 12 months after the establishment of the account and the anticipated dates of such payments.

(B) Time of submission

The statement required under subparagraph (A) shall be submitted to the borrower at closing with respect to the property for which the mortgage loan is made or not later than the expiration of the 45-day period beginning on the date of the establishment of the escrow account.

(C) Initial statement at closing

Any servicer may submit the statement required under subparagraph (A) to the borrower at closing and may incorporate such statement in the uniform settlement statement required under section 2603 of this title. The Secretary shall issue regulations prescribing any changes necessary to the uniform settlement statement under section 2603 of this title that specify how the statement required under subparagraph (A) of this section shall be incorporated in the uniform settlement statement.

(2) Annual statement

(A) In general

Any servicer that has established or continued an escrow account in connection with a federally related mortgage loan shall submit to the borrower for which the escrow account has been established or continued a statement clearly itemizing, for each period described in subparagraph (B) (during which the servicer services the escrow account), the amount of the borrower's current monthly payment, the portion of the monthly payment being placed in the escrow account, the total amount paid into the escrow account during the period, the total amount paid out of the escrow account during the period for taxes, insurance premiums, and other charges (as separately identified), and the balance in the escrow account at the conclusion of the period.

(B) Time of submission

The statement required under subparagraph (A) shall be submitted to the borrower not less than once for each 12-month period, the first such period beginning on the first January 1st that occurs after November 28, 1990, and shall be submitted not more than 30 days after the conclusion of each such 1-year period.

(d) Penalties

(1) In general

In the case of each failure to submit a statement to a borrower as required under subsection (c) of this section, the Secretary shall assess to the lender or escrow servicer failing to submit the statement a civil penalty of $50 for each such failure, but the total amount imposed on such lender or escrow servicer for all such failures during any 12-month period referred to in subsection (b)[1] of this section may not exceed $100,000.

(2) Intentional violations

If any failure to which paragraph (1) applies is due to intentional disregard of the requirement to submit the statement, then, with respect to such failure—

(A) the penalty imposed under paragraph (1) shall be $100; and

(B) in the case of any penalty determined under subparagraph (A), the $100,000 limitation under paragraph (1) shall not apply.

[Pub. L. No. 93-533, § 10, 88 Stat. 1728 (Dec. 22, 1974); Pub. L. No. 94-205, § 8, 89 Stat. 1158 (Jan. 2, 1976); Pub. L. No. 101-625, tit. IX, § 942(a), 104 Stat. 4411 (Nov. 28, 1990); Pub. L. No. 104-208, div. A, tit. II, § 2103(g)(2), 110 Stat. 3009–401 (Sept. 30, 1996)]

12 U.S.C. § 2610. Prohibition of fees for preparation of truth-in-lending, uniform settlement, and escrow account statements

No fee shall be imposed or charge made upon any other person (as a part of settlement costs or otherwise) by a lender in connection with a federally related mortgage loan made by it (or a loan for the purchase of a mobile home), or by a servicer (as the term is defined under section 2605(i) of this title), for or on account of the preparation and submission by such lender or servicer of the statement or statements required (in connection with such loan) by sections 2603 and 2609(c) of this title or by the Truth in Lending Act [15 U.S.C. § 1601 et seq.].

[Pub. L. No. 93-533, § 12, 88 Stat. 1729 (Dec. 22, 1974); Pub. L. No. 101-625, tit. IX, § 942(b), 104 Stat. 4412 (Nov. 28, 1990)]

* * *

1 [*Editor's Note*: So in original. Probably should be subsection "(c)."]

12 U.S.C. § 2614. Jurisdiction of courts; limitations

Any action pursuant to the provisions of section 2605, 2607, or 2608 of this title may be brought in the United States district court or in any other court of competent jurisdiction, for the district in which the property involved is located, or where the violation is alleged to have occurred, within 3 years in the case of a violation of section 2605 of this title and 1 year in the case of a violation of section 2607 or 2608 of this title from the date of the occurrence of the violation, except that actions brought by the Secretary, the Attorney General of any State, or the insurance commissioner of any State may be brought within 3 years from the date of the occurrence of the violation.

[Pub. L. No. 93-533, § 16, 88 Stat. 1731 (Dec. 22, 1974); Pub. L. No. 98-181, tit. IV, § 461(d), 97 Stat. 1232 (Nov. 30, 1983); Pub. L. No. 104-208, div. A, tit. II, § 2103(e), 110 Stat. 3009–400 (Sept. 30, 1996)]

12 U.S.C. § 2615. Contracts and liens; validity

Nothing in this chapter shall affect the validity or enforceability of any sale or contract for the sale of real property or any loan, loan agreement, mortgage, or lien made or arising in connection with a federally related mortgage loan.

[Pub. L. No. 93-533, § 17, 88 Stat. 1731 (Dec. 22, 1974)]

12 U.S.C. § 2616. State laws unaffected; inconsistent Federal and State provisions

This chapter does not annul, alter, or affect, or exempt any person subject to the provisions of this chapter from complying with, the laws of any State with respect to settlement practices, except to the extent that those laws are inconsistent with any provision of this chapter, and then only to the extent of the inconsistency. The Secretary is authorized to determine whether such inconsistencies exist. The Secretary may not determine that any State law is inconsistent with any provision of this chapter if the Secretary determines that such law gives greater protection to the consumer. In making these determinations the Secretary shall consult with the appropriate Federal agencies.

[Pub. L. No. 93-533, § 18, 88 Stat. 1731 (Dec. 22, 1974); Pub. L. No. 94-205, § 9, 89 Stat. 1159 (Jan. 2, 1976)]

* * *

C.3 Selected RESPA Regulations: Regulation X, 24 C.F.R. Part 3500

TITLE 24—HOUSING AND URBAN DEVELOPMENT

SUBTITLE B—REGULATIONS RELATING TO HOUSING AND URBAN DEVELOPMENT

CHAPTER XX—OFFICE OF ASSISTANT SECRETARY FOR HOUSING—FEDERAL HOUSING COMMISSIONER, DEPARTMENT OF HOUSING AND URBAN DEVELOPMENT

PART 3500—REAL ESTATE SETTLEMENT PROCEDURES ACT

* * *

24 C.F.R. § 3500.2 Definitions.

(a) *Statutory terms.* All terms defined in RESPA (12 U.S.C. 2602) are used in accordance with their statutory meaning unless otherwise defined in paragraph (b) of this section or elsewhere in this part.

(b) *Other terms.* As used in this part:

Application means the submission of a borrower's financial information in anticipation of a credit decision relating to a federally related mortgage loan, which shall include the borrower's name, the borrower's monthly income, the borrower's social security number to obtain a credit report, the property address, an estimate of the value of the property, the mortgage loan amount sought, and any other information deemed necessary by the loan originator. An application may either be in writing or electronically submitted, including a written record of an oral application.

Balloon payment has the same meaning as "balloon payment" under Regulation Z (12 CFR part 226).

Changed circumstances means:

(1)(i) Acts of God, war, disaster, or other emergency;

(ii) Information particular to the borrower or transaction that was relied on in providing the GFE and that changes or is found to be inaccurate after the GFE has been provided. This may include information about the credit quality of the borrower, the amount of the loan, the estimated value of the property, or any other information that was used in providing the GFE;

(iii) New information particular to the borrower or transaction that was not relied on in providing the GFE; or

(iv) Other circumstances that are particular to the borrower or transaction, including boundary disputes, the need for flood insurance, or environmental problems.

(2) Changed circumstances do not include:

(i) The borrower's name, the borrower's monthly income, the property address, an estimate of the value of the property, the mortgage loan amount sought, and any information contained in any credit report obtained by the loan originator prior to providing the GFE, unless the information changes or is found to be inaccurate after the GFE has been provided; or

(ii) Market price fluctuations by themselves.

Business day means a day on which the offices of the business entity are open to the public for carrying on substantially all of the entity's business functions.

Dealer means, in the case of property improvement loans, a seller, contractor, or supplier of goods or services. In the case of manufactured home loans, "dealer" means one who engages in the business of manufactured home retail sales.

Dealer loan or dealer consumer credit contract means, generally, any arrangement in which a dealer assists the borrower in obtaining a federally related mortgage loan from the funding lender and then assigns the dealer's legal interests to the funding lender and receives the net proceeds of the loan. The funding lender is the lender for the purposes of the disclosure requirements of this part. If a dealer is a "creditor" as defined under the definition of "federally related mortgage loan" in this part, the dealer is the lender for purposes of this part.

Effective date of transfer is defined in section 6(i)(1) of RESPA (12 U.S.C. 2605(i)(1)). In the case of a home equity conversion mortgage or reverse mortgage as referenced in this section, the effective date of transfer is the transfer date agreed upon by the transferee servicer and the transferor servicer.

Federally related mortgage loan or mortgage loan means as follows:

(1) Any loan (other than temporary financing, such as a construction loan):

(i) That is secured by a first or subordinate lien on residential real property, including a refinancing of any secured loan on residential real property upon which there is either:

(A) Located or, following settlement, will be constructed using proceeds of the loan, a structure or structures designed principally for occupancy of from one to four families (including individual units of condominiums and cooperatives and including any related interests, such as a share in the cooperative or right to occupancy of the unit); or

(B) Located or, following settlement, will be placed using proceeds of the loan, a manufactured home; and

(ii) For which one of the following paragraphs applies. The loan:

(A) Is made in whole or in part by any lender that is either regulated by or whose deposits or accounts are insured by any agency of the Federal Government;

(B) Is made in whole or in part, or is insured, guaranteed, supplemented, or assisted in any way:

(1) By the Secretary or any other officer or agency of the Federal Government; or

(2) Under or in connection with a housing or urban development program administered by the Secretary or a housing or related program administered by any other officer or agency of the Federal Government;

(C) Is intended to be sold by the originating lender to the Federal National Mortgage Association, the Government National Mortgage Association, the Federal Home Loan Mortgage Corporation (or its successors), or a financial institution from which the loan is to be purchased by the Federal Home Loan Mortgage Corporation (or its successors);

(D) Is made in whole or in part by a "creditor," as defined in section 103(f) of the Consumer Credit Protection Act (15 U.S.C. 1602(f)), that makes or invests in residential real estate loans aggregating more than $1,000,000 per year. For purposes of this definition, the term "creditor" does not include any agency or instrumentality of any State, and the term "residential real estate loan" means any loan secured by residential real property, including single-family and multifamily residential property;

(E) Is originated either by a dealer or, if the obligation is to be assigned to any maker of mortgage loans specified in paragraphs (1)(ii)(A) through (D) of this definition, by a mortgage broker; or

(F) Is the subject of a home equity conversion mortgage, also frequently called a "reverse mortgage," issued by any maker of mortgage loans specified in paragraphs (1)(ii)(A) through (D) of this definition.

(2) Any installment sales contract, land contract, or contract for deed on otherwise qualifying residential property is a federally related mortgage loan if the contract is funded in whole or in part by proceeds of a loan made by any maker of mortgage loans specified in paragraphs (1)(ii)(A) through (D) of this definition.

(3) If the residential real property securing a mortgage loan is not located in a State, the loan is not a federally related mortgage loan.

Good faith estimate or *GFE* means an estimate of settlement charges a borrower is likely to incur, as a dollar amount, and related loan information, based upon common practice and experience in the locality of the mortgaged property, as provided on the form prescribed in § 3500.7 and prepared in accordance with the Instructions in Appendix C to this part.

HUD-1 or HUD-1A settlement statement (also HUD-1 or HUD-1A) means the statement that is prescribed by the Secretary in this part for setting forth settlement charges in connection with either the purchase or the refinancing (or other subordinate lien transaction) of 1- to 4-family residential property.

Lender means, generally, the secured creditor or creditors named in the debt obligation and document creating the lien. For loans originated by a mortgage broker that closes a federally related mortgage loan in its own name in a table funding transaction, the lender is the person to whom the obligation is initially assigned at or after settlement. A lender, in connection with dealer loans, is the lender to whom the loan is assigned, unless the dealer meets the definition of creditor as defined under "federally related mortgage loan" in this section. See also § 3500.5(b)(7), secondary market transactions.

[Editor's Note: HUD promulgated the following change to this subsection but stayed its effective date. It is possible that the proposed change may be withdrawn. Check for developments in the Federal Register. Add to subsection (b):

Loan originator means a lender or mortgage broker.

Managerial employee *means an employee of a settlement service provider who does not routinely deal directly with consumers, and who either hires, directs, assigns, promotes, or rewards other employees or independent contractors, or is in a position to formulate, determine, or influence the policies of the employer. Neither the term "managerial employee" nor the term "employee" includes independent contractors, but a managerial employee may hold a real estate brokerage or agency license.*]

Manufactured home is defined in § 3280.2 of this title.

Mortgage broker means a person (not an employee of a lender) or entity that renders origination services and serves as an intermediary between a borrower and a lender in a transaction involving a federally related mortgage loan, including such a person or entity that closes the loan in its own name in a table funded transaction. A loan correspondent approved under 24 CFR 202.8 for Federal Housing Administration programs is a mortgage broker for purposes of this part.

Mortgaged property means the real property that is security for the federally related mortgage loan.

Origination service means any service involved in the creation of a mortgage loan, including but not limited to the taking of the loan application, loan processing, and the underwriting and funding of the loan, and the processing and administrative services required to perform these functions.

Person is defined in section 3(5) of RESPA (12 U.S.C. 2602(5)).

Prepayment penalty has the same meaning as "prepayment penalty" under Regulation Z (12 CFR part 226).

Public Guidance Documents means documents that HUD has published in the Federal Register, and that it may amend from time-to-time by publication in the Federal Register. These documents are also available from HUD at the address indicated in 24 CFR 3500.3.

Refinancing means a transaction in which an existing obligation that was subject to a secured lien on residential real property is satisfied and replaced by a new obligation undertaken by the same borrower and with the same or a new lender. The following shall not be treated as a refinancing, even when the existing obligation is satisfied and replaced by a new obligation with the same lender (this definition of "refinancing" as to transactions with the same lender is similar to Regulation Z, 12 CFR 226.20(a)):

(1) A renewal of a single payment obligation with no change in the original terms;

(2) A reduction in the annual percentage rate as computed under the Truth in Lending Act with a corresponding change in the payment schedule;

(3) An agreement involving a court proceeding;

(4) A workout agreement, in which a change in the payment schedule or change in collateral requirements is agreed to as a result of the consumer's default or delinquency, unless the rate is increased or the new amount financed exceeds the unpaid balance plus earned finance charges and premiums for continuation of allowable insurance; and

(5) The renewal of optional insurance purchased by the consumer that is added to an existing transaction, if disclosures relating to the initial purchase were provided.

Regulation Z means the regulations issued by the Board of Governors of the Federal Reserve System (12 CFR part 226) to implement the Federal Truth in Lending Act (15 U.S.C. 1601 et seq.), and includes the Commentary on Regulation Z.

Required use means a situation in which a person must use a particular provider of a settlement service in order to have access to some distinct service or property, and the person will pay for the settlement service of the particular provider or will pay a charge attributable, in whole or in part, to the settlement service. However, the offering of a package (or combination of settlement services) or the offering of discounts or rebates to consumers for the purchase of multiple settlement services does not constitute a required use. Any package or discount must be optional to the purchaser. The discount must be a true discount below the prices that are otherwise generally available, and must not be made up by higher costs elsewhere in the settlement process.

RESPA means the Real Estate Settlement Procedures Act of 1974, 12 U.S.C. 2601 et seq.

Servicer means the person responsible for the servicing of a mortgage loan (including the person who makes or holds a mortgage loan if such person also services the mortgage loan). The term does not include:

(1) The Federal Deposit Insurance Corporation (FDIC) or the Resolution Trust Corporation (RTC), in connection with assets acquired, assigned, sold, or transferred pursuant to section 13(c) of the Federal Deposit Insurance Act or as receiver or conservator of an insured depository institution; and

(2) The Federal National Mortgage Corporation (FNMA); the Federal Home Loan Mortgage Corporation (Freddie Mac); the RTC; the FDIC; HUD, including the Government National Mortgage Association (GNMA) and the Federal Housing Administration (FHA) (including cases in which a mortgage insured under the National Housing Act (12 U.S.C. 1701 et seq.) is assigned to HUD); the National Credit Union Administration (NCUA); the Farmers Home Administration or its successor agency under Public Law 103-354 (FmHA); and the Department of Veterans Affairs (VA), in any case in which the assignment, sale, or transfer of the servicing of the mortgage loan is preceded by termination of the contract for servicing the loan for cause, commencement of proceedings for bankruptcy of the servicer, or commencement of proceedings by the FDIC or RTC for conservatorship or receivership of the servicer (or an entity by which the servicer is owned or controlled).

Servicing means receiving any scheduled periodic payments from a borrower pursuant to the terms of any mortgage loan, including amounts for escrow accounts under section 10 of RESPA (12 U.S.C. 2609), and making the payments to the owner of the loan or other third parties of principal and interest and such other payments with respect to the amounts received from the borrower as may be required pursuant to the terms of the mortgage servicing loan documents or servicing contract. In the case of a home equity conversion mortgage or reverse mortgage as referenced in this section, servicing includes making payments to the borrower.

Settlement means the process of executing legally binding documents regarding a lien on property that is subject to a federally related mortgage loan. This process may also be called "closing" or "escrow" in different jurisdictions.

Settlement service means any service provided in connection with a prospective or actual settlement, including, but not limited to, any one or more of the following:

(1) Origination of a federally related mortgage loan (including, but not limited to, the taking of loan applications, loan processing, and the underwriting and funding of such loans);

(2) Rendering of services by a mortgage broker (including counseling, taking of applications, obtaining verifications and appraisals, and other loan processing and origination services, and communicating with the borrower and lender);

(3) Provision of any services related to the origination, processing or funding of a federally related mortgage loan;

(4) Provision of title services, including title searches, title examinations, abstract preparation, insurability determinations, and the issuance of title commitments and title insurance policies;

(5) Rendering of services by an attorney;

(6) Preparation of documents, including notarization, delivery, and recordation;

(7) Rendering of credit reports and appraisals;

(8) Rendering of inspections, including inspections required by applicable law or any inspections required by the sales contract or mortgage documents prior to transfer of title;

(9) Conducting of settlement by a settlement agent and any related services;

(10) Provision of services involving mortgage insurance;

(11) Provision of services involving hazard, flood, or other casualty insurance or homeowner's warranties;

(12) Provision of services involving mortgage life, disability, or similar insurance designed to pay a mortgage loan upon disability or death of a borrower, but only if such insurance is required by the lender as a condition of the loan;

(13) Provision of services involving real property taxes or any other assessments or charges on the real property;

(14) Rendering of services by a real estate agent or real estate broker; and

(15) Provision of any other services for which a settlement service provider requires a borrower or seller to pay.

Special information booklet means the booklet prepared by the Secretary pursuant to section 5 of RESPA (12 U.S.C. 2604) to help persons understand the nature and costs of settlement services. The Secretary publishes the form of the special information booklet in the Federal Register. The Secretary may issue or approve additional booklets or alternative booklets by publication of a Notice in the Federal Register.

State means any State of the United States, the District of Columbia, the Commonwealth of Puerto Rico, and any territory or possession of the United States.

Table funding means a settlement at which a loan is funded by a contemporaneous advance of loan funds and an assignment of the loan to the person advancing the funds. A table-funded transaction is not a secondary market transaction (see § 3500.5(b)(7)).

Third party means a settlement service provider other than a loan originator.

Title company means any institution, or its duly authorized agent, that is qualified to issue title insurance.

Title service means any service involved in the provision of title insurance (lender's or owner's policy), including but not limited to: title examination and evaluation; preparation and issuance of title commitment; clearance of underwriting objections; preparation and issuance of a title insurance policy or policies; and the processing and administrative services required to perform these functions. The term also includes the service of conducting a settlement.

Tolerance means the maximum amount by which the charge for a category or categories of settlement costs may exceed the amount of the estimate for such category or categories on a GFE.

[57 Fed. Reg. 56,857 (Dec. 1, 1992); 59 Fed. Reg. 65,11 (Feb. 10, 1994); 59 Fed. Reg. 14,749 (March 30, 1994); 59 Fed. Reg. 65,448 (Dec. 19, 1994); 60 Fed. Reg. 14,636 (March 20, 1995); 61 Fed. Reg. 13,233 (March 26, 1996); 61 Fed. Reg. 29,252 (June 7, 1996); 61 Fed. Reg. 51,782 (Oct. 4, 1996); 61 Fed. Reg. 58,475 (Nov. 15, 1996); 62 Fed. Reg. 20,088 (April 24, 1997); 73 Fed. Reg. 68,239 (Nov. 17, 2008); 73 Fed. Reg. 68,240 (Nov. 17, 2008); 74 Fed. Reg. 2369 (Jan. 15, 2009); 74 Fed. Reg. 10,173 (Mar. 10, 2009); 74 Fed. Reg. 22,826 (May 15, 2009)]

* * *

24 C.F.R. § 3500.4 Reliance upon rule, regulation or interpretation by HUD.

(a) *Rule, regulation or interpretation.*—

(1) For purposes of sections 19 (a) and (b) of RESPA (12 U.S.C. 2617 (a) and (b)) only the following constitute a rule, regulation or interpretation of the Secretary:

(i) All provisions, including appendices, of this part. Any other document referred to in this part is not incorporated in this part unless it is specifically set out in this part;

(ii) Any other document that is published in the Federal Register by the Secretary and states that it is an "interpretation," "interpretive rule," "commentary," or a "statement of policy" for purposes of section 19(a) of RESPA. Such documents will be prepared by HUD staff and counsel. Such documents may be revoked or amended by a subsequent document published in the *Federal Register* by the Secretary.

(2) A "rule, regulation, or interpretation thereof by the Secretary" for purposes of section 19(b) of RESPA (12 U.S.C. 2617(b)) shall not include the special information booklet prescribed by the Secretary or any other statement

or issuance, whether oral or written, by an officer or representative of the Department of Housing and Urban Development (HUD), letter or memorandum by the Secretary, General Counsel, any Assistant Secretary or other officer or employee of HUD, preamble to a regulation or other issuance of HUD, Public Guidance Document, report to Congress, pleading, affidavit or other document in litigation, pamphlet, handbook, guide, telegraphic communication, explanation, instructions to forms, speech or other material of any nature which is not specifically included in paragraph (a)(1) of this section.

(b) *Unofficial interpretations; staff discretion.* In response to requests for interpretation of matters not adequately covered by this part or by an official interpretation issued under paragraph (a)(1)(ii) of this section, unofficial staff interpretations may be provided at the discretion of HUD staff or counsel. Written requests for such interpretations should be directed to the address indicated in § 3500.3. Such interpretations provide no protection under section 19(b) of RESPA (12 U.S.C. 2617(b)). Ordinarily, staff or counsel will not issue unofficial interpretations on matters adequately covered by this Part or by official interpretations or commentaries issued under paragraph (a)(1)(ii) of this section.

(c) All informal counsel's opinions and staff interpretations issued before November 2, 1992, were withdrawn as of that date. Courts and administrative agencies, however, may use previous opinions to determine the validity of conduct under the previous Regulation X.

[61 Fed. Reg. 13,233 (March 26, 1996)]

24 C.F.R. § 3500.5 Coverage of RESPA.

(a) *Applicability.* RESPA and this part apply to all federally related mortgage loans, except for the exemptions provided in paragraph (b) of this section.

(b) *Exemptions.*

(1) A loan on property of 25 acres or more.

(2) *Business purpose loans.* An extension of credit primarily for a business, commercial, or agricultural purpose, as defined by Regulation Z, 12 CFR 226.3(a)(1). Persons may rely on Regulation Z in determining whether the exemption applies.

(3) *Temporary financing.* Temporary financing, such as a construction loan. The exemption for temporary financing does not apply to a loan made to finance construction of 1- to 4-family residential property if the loan is used as, or may be converted to, permanent financing by the same lender or is used to finance transfer of title to the first user. If a lender issues a commitment for permanent financing, with or without conditions, the loan is covered by this part. Any construction loan for new or rehabilitated 1- to 4-family residential property, other than a loan to a bona fide builder (a person who regularly constructs 1- to 4-family residential structures for sale or lease), is subject to this part if its term is for two years or more. A "bridge loan" or "swing loan" in which a lender takes a security interest in otherwise covered 1- to 4-family residential property is not covered by RESPA and this part.

(4) *Vacant land.* Any loan secured by vacant or unimproved property, unless within two years from the date of the settlement of the loan, a structure or a manufactured home will be constructed or placed on the real property using the loan proceeds. If a loan for a structure or manufactured home to be placed on vacant or unimproved property will be secured by a lien on that property, the transaction is covered by this part.

(5) *Assumption without lender approval.* Any assumption in which the lender does not have the right expressly to approve a subsequent person as the borrower on an existing federally related mortgage loan. Any assumption in which the lender's permission is both required and obtained is covered by RESPA and this part, whether or not the lender charges a fee for the assumption.

(6) *Loan conversions.* Any conversion of a federally related mortgage loan to different terms that are consistent with provisions of the original mortgage instrument, as long as a new note is not required, even if the lender charges an additional fee for the conversion.

(7) *Secondary market transactions.* A bona fide transfer of a loan obligation in the secondary market is not covered by RESPA and this part, except as set forth in section 6 of RESPA (12 U.S.C. 2605) and § 3500.21. In determining what constitutes a bona fide transfer, HUD will consider the real source of funding and the real interest of the funding lender. Mortgage broker transactions that are table-funded are not secondary market transactions. Neither the creation of a dealer loan or dealer consumer credit contract, nor the first assignment of such loan or contract to a lender, is a secondary market transaction (see § 3500.2).

[59 Fed. Reg. 6512 (Feb. 10, 1994); 59 Fed. Reg. 14,749 (March 30, 1994); 61 Fed. Reg. 13,233 (March 26, 1996); 61 Fed. Reg. 58,475 (Nov. 15, 1996)]

* * *

24 C.F.R. § 3500.12 No fee.

No fee shall be imposed or charge made upon any other person, as a part of settlement costs or otherwise, by a lender in connection with a federally related mortgage loan made by it (or a loan for the purchase of a manufactured home), or by a servicer (as that term is defined under 12 U.S.C. 2605(i)(2)) for or on account of the preparation and distribution of the HUD-1 or HUD-1A settlement statement, escrow account statements required pursuant to section 10 of RESPA (12 U.S.C. 2609), or statements required by the Truth in Lending Act, 15 U.S.C. 1601 et seq.

[59 Fed. Reg. 6515 (Feb. 10, 1994); 61 Fed. Reg. 13,233 (March 26, 1996)]

24 C.F.R. § 3500.13 Relation to State laws.

(a) State laws that are inconsistent with RESPA or this part are preempted to the extent of the inconsistency. However, RESPA and these regulations do not annul, alter, affect, or exempt any person subject to their provisions from complying with the laws of any State with respect to settlement practices, except to the extent of the inconsistency.

(b) Upon request by any person, the Secretary is authorized to determine if inconsistencies with State law exist; in doing so, the Secretary shall consult with appropriate Federal agencies.

(1) The Secretary may not determine that a State law or regulation is inconsistent with any provision of RESPA or this part, if the Secretary determines that such law or regulation gives greater protection to the consumer.

(2) In determining whether provisions of State law or regulations concerning affiliated business arrangements are inconsistent with RESPA or this part, the Secretary may not construe those provisions that impose more stringent limitations on affiliated business arrangements as inconsistent with RESPA so long as they give more protection to consumers and/or competition.

(c) Any person may request the Secretary to determine whether an inconsistency exists by submitting to the address indicated in § 3500.3, a copy of the State law in question, any other law or judicial or administrative opinion that implements, interprets or applies the relevant provision, and an explanation of the possible inconsistency. A determination by the Secretary that an inconsistency with State law exists will be made by publication of a notice in the Federal Register. "Law" as used in this section includes regulations and any enactment which has the force and effect of law and is issued by a State or any political subdivision of a State.

(d) A specific preemption of conflicting State laws regarding notices and disclosures of mortgage servicing transfers is set forth in § 3500.21(h).

[57 Fed. Reg. 56,857 (Dec. 1, 1992); 61 Fed. Reg. 13,233 (March 26, 1996); 61 Fed. Reg. 58,476 (Nov. 15, 1996)]

* * *

24 C.F.R. § 3500.17 Escrow accounts.

(a) *General.* This section sets out the requirements for an escrow account that a lender establishes in connection with a federally related mortgage loan. It sets limits for escrow accounts using calculations based on monthly payments and disbursements within a calendar year. If an escrow account involves biweekly or any other payment period, the requirements in this section shall be modified accordingly. A HUD Public Guidance Document entitled "Biweekly Payments—Example" provides examples of biweekly accounting and a HUD Public Guidance Document entitled "Annual Escrow Account Disclosure Statement—Example" provides examples of a 3-year accounting cycle that may be used in accordance with paragraph (c)(9) of this section. A HUD Public Guidance Document entitled "Consumer Disclosure for Voluntary Escrow Account Payments" provides a model disclosure format that originators and servicers are encouraged, but not required, to provide to consumers when the originator or servicer anticipates a substantial increase in disbursements from the escrow account after the first year of the loan. The disclosures in that model format may be combined with or included in the Initial Escrow Account Statement required in § 3500.17(g).

(b) *Definitions*. As used in this section:

Aggregate (or) composite analysis, hereafter called *aggregate analysis*, means an accounting method a servicer uses in conducting an escrow account analysis by computing the sufficiency of escrow account funds by analyzing the account as a whole. Appendix E to this part sets forth examples of aggregate escrow account analyses.

Annual escrow account statement means a statement containing all of the information set forth in § 3500.17(i). As noted in § 3500.17(i), a servicer shall submit an annual escrow account statement to the borrower within 30 calendar days of the end of the escrow account computation year, after conducting an escrow account analysis.

Cushion or reserve (hereafter cushion) means funds that a servicer may require a borrower to pay into an escrow account to cover unanticipated disbursements or disbursements made before the borrower's payments are available in the account, as limited by § 3500.17(c).

Deficiency is the amount of a negative balance in an escrow account. As noted in § 3500.17(f), if a servicer advances funds for a borrower, then the servicer must perform an escrow account analysis before seeking repayment of the deficiency.

Delivery means the placing of a document in the United States mail, first-class postage paid, addressed to the last known address of the recipient. Hand delivery also constitutes delivery.

Disbursement date means the date on which the servicer actually pays an escrow item from the escrow account.

Escrow account means any account that a servicer establishes or controls on behalf of a borrower to pay taxes, insurance premiums (including flood insurance), or other charges with respect to a federally related mortgage loan, including charges that the borrower and servicer have voluntarily agreed that the servicer should collect and pay. The definition encompasses any account established for this purpose, including a "trust account," "reserve account," "impound account," or other term in different localities. An "escrow account" includes any arrangement where the servicer adds a portion of the borrower's payments to principal and subsequently deducts from principal the disbursements for escrow account items. For purposes of this section, the term "escrow account" excludes any account that is under the borrower's total control.

Escrow account analysis means the accounting that a servicer conducts in the form of a trial running balance for an escrow account to:

(1) Determine the appropriate target balances;

(2) Compute the borrower's monthly payments for the next escrow account computation year and any deposits needed to establish or maintain the account; and

(3) Determine whether shortages, surpluses or deficiencies exist.

Escrow account computation year is a 12-month period that a servicer establishes for the escrow account beginning with the borrower's initial payment date. The term includes each 12-month period thereafter, unless a servicer chooses to issue a short year statement under the conditions stated in § 3500.17(i)(4).

Escrow account item or *separate item* means any separate expenditure category, such as "taxes" or "insurance," for which funds are collected in the escrow account for disbursement. An escrow account item with installment payments, such as local property taxes, remains one escrow account item regardless of multiple disbursement dates to the tax authority.

Initial escrow account statement means the first disclosure statement that the servicer delivers to the borrower concerning the borrower's escrow account. The initial escrow account statement shall meet the requirements of § 3500.17(g) and be in substantially the format set forth in § 3500.17(h).

Installment payment means one of two or more payments payable on an escrow account item during an escrow account computation year. An example of an installment payment is where a jurisdiction bills quarterly for taxes.

Payment due date means the date each month when the borrower's monthly payment to an escrow account is due to the servicer. The initial payment date is the borrower's first payment due date to an escrow account.

Penalty means a late charge imposed by the payee for paying after the disbursement is due. It does not include any additional charge or fee imposed by the payee associated with choosing installment payments as opposed to annual payments or for choosing one installment plan over another.

Pre-accrual is a practice some servicers use to require borrowers to deposit funds, needed for disbursement and maintenance of a cushion, in the escrow account some period before the disbursement date. Pre-accrual is subject to the limitations of § 3500.17(c).

Shortage means an amount by which a current escrow account balance falls short of the target balance at the time of escrow analysis.

Single-item analysis means an accounting method servicers use in conducting an escrow account analysis by computing the sufficiency of escrow account funds by considering each escrow item separately. Appendix E to this part sets forth examples of single-item analysis.

Submission (of an escrow account statement) means the delivery of the statement.

Surplus means an amount by which the current escrow account balance exceeds the target balance for the account.

System of recordkeeping means the servicer's method of keeping information that reflects the facts relating to that servicer's handling of the borrower's escrow account, including, but not limited to, the payment of amounts from the escrow account and the submission of initial and annual escrow account statements to borrowers.

Target balance means the estimated month end balance in an escrow account that is just sufficient to cover the remaining disbursements from the escrow account in the escrow account computation year, taking into account the remaining scheduled periodic payments, and a cushion, if any.

Trial running balance means the accounting process that derives the target balances over the course of an escrow account computation year. Section 3500.17(d) provides a description of the steps involved in performing a trial running balance.

(c) *Limits on payments to escrow accounts.*

(1) A lender or servicer (hereafter servicer) shall not require a borrower to deposit into any escrow account, created in connection with a federally related mortgage loan, more than the following amounts:

(i) *Charges at settlement or upon creation of an escrow account.* At the time a servicer creates an escrow account for a borrower, the servicer may charge the borrower an amount sufficient to pay the charges respecting the mortgaged property, such as taxes and insurance, which are attributable to the period from the date such payment(s) were last paid until the initial payment date. The "amount sufficient to pay" is computed so that the lowest month end target balance projected for the escrow account computation year is zero (-0-) (see Step 2 in Appendix E to this part). In addition, the servicer may charge the borrower a cushion that shall be no greater than one-sixth (1/6) of the estimated total annual payments from the escrow account.

(ii) *Charges during the life of the escrow account.* Throughout the life of an escrow account, the servicer may charge the borrower a monthly sum equal to one-twelfth (1/12) of the total annual escrow payments which the servicer reasonably anticipates paying from the account. In addition, the servicer may add an amount to maintain a cushion no greater than one-sixth (1/6) of the estimated total annual payments from the account. However, if a servicer determines through an escrow account analysis that there is a shortage or deficiency, the servicer may require the borrower to pay additional deposits to make up the shortage or eliminate the deficiency, subject to the limitations set forth in § 3500.17(f).

(2) *Escrow analysis at creation of escrow account.* Before establishing an escrow account, the servicer must conduct an escrow account analysis to determine the amount the borrower must deposit into the escrow account (subject to the limitations of paragraph (c)(1)(i) of this section), and the amount of the borrower's periodic payments into the escrow account (subject to the limitations of paragraph (c)(1)(ii) of this section). In conducting the escrow account analysis, the servicer must estimate the disbursement amounts according to paragraph (c)(7) of this section. Pursuant to paragraph (k) of this section, the servicer must use a date on or before the deadline to avoid a penalty as the disbursement date for the escrow item and comply with any other requirements of paragraph (k) of this section. Upon completing the initial escrow account analysis, the servicer must prepare and deliver an initial escrow account statement to the borrower, as set forth in paragraph (g) of this section. The servicer must use the escrow account analysis to determine whether a surplus, shortage, or deficiency exists and must make any adjustments to the account pursuant to paragraph (f) of this section.

(3) *Subsequent escrow account analyses.* For each escrow account, the servicer must conduct an escrow account analysis at the completion of the escrow account computation year to determine the borrower's monthly escrow account payments for the next computation year, subject to the limitations of paragraph (c)(1)(ii) of this section. In conducting the escrow account analysis, the servicer must estimate the disbursement amounts according to paragraph (c)(7) of this section. Pursuant to paragraph (k) of this section, the servicer must use a date on or before the deadline to avoid a penalty as the disbursement date for the escrow item and comply with any other requirements of paragraph (k) of this section. The servicer must use the escrow account analysis to determine whether a surplus, shortage, or deficiency exists, and must make any adjustments to the account pursuant to paragraph (f) of this section. Upon completing an escrow account analysis, the servicer must prepare and submit an annual escrow account statement to the borrower, as set forth in paragraph (i) of this section.

(4) *Aggregate accounting required.* All servicers must use the aggregate accounting method in conducting escrow account analyses.

(5) *Cushion.* The cushion must be no greater than one-sixth (1/6) of the estimated total annual disbursements from the escrow account.

(6) *Restrictions on pre-accrual.* A servicer must not practice pre-accrual.

(7) *Servicer estimates of disbursement amounts.* To conduct an escrow account analysis, the servicer shall estimate the amount of escrow account items to be disbursed. If the servicer knows the charge for an escrow item in the next computation year, then the servicer shall use that amount in estimating disbursement amounts. If the charge is unknown to the servicer, the servicer may base the estimate on the preceding year's charge, or the preceding year's charge as modified by an amount not exceeding the most recent year's change in the national Consumer Price Index for all urban consumers (CPI, all items). In cases of unassessed new construction, the servicer may base an estimate on the assessment of comparable residential property in the market area.

(8) *Provisions in mortgage documents.* The servicer must examine the mortgage loan documents to determine the applicable cushion for each escrow account. If the mortgage loan documents provide for lower cushion limits, then the terms of the loan documents apply. Where the terms of any mortgage loan document allow greater payments to an escrow account than allowed by this section, then this section controls the applicable limits. Where the mortgage loan documents do not specifically establish an escrow account, whether a servicer may establish an escrow account for the loan is a matter for determination by other Federal or State law. If the mortgage loan document is silent on the escrow account limits and a servicer establishes an escrow account under other Federal or State law, then the limitations of this section apply unless applicable Federal or State law provides for a lower amount. If the loan documents provide for escrow accounts up to the RESPA limits, then the servicer may require the maximum amounts consistent with this section, unless an applicable Federal or State law sets a lesser amount.

(9) *Assessments for periods longer than one year.* Some escrow account items may be billed for periods longer than one year. For example, servicers may need to collect flood insurance or water purification escrow funds for payment every three years. In such cases, the servicer shall estimate the borrower's payments for a full cycle of disbursements. For a flood insurance premium payable every 3 years, the servicer shall collect the payments reflecting 36 equal monthly amounts. For two out of the three years, however, the account balance may not reach its low monthly balance because the low point will be on a three-year cycle, as compared to an annual one. The annual escrow account statement shall explain this situation (see example in the HUD Public Guidance Document entitled "Annual Escrow Account Disclosure Statement—Example," available in accordance with § 3500.3).

(d) *Methods of escrow account analysis.*

(1) The following sets forth the steps servicers must use to determine whether their use of aggregate analysis conforms with the limitations in § 3500.17(c)(1). The steps set forth in this section result in maximum limits. Servicers may use accounting procedures that result in lower target balances. In particular, servicers may use a cushion less than the permissible cushion or no cushion at all. This section does not require the use of a cushion.

(2) *Aggregate analysis.*

(i) In conducting the escrow account analysis using aggregate analysis, the target balances may not exceed the balances computed according to the following arithmetic operations:

(A) The servicer first projects a trial balance for the account as a whole over the next computation year (a trial running balance). In doing so the servicer assumes that it will make estimated disbursements on or before the earlier of the deadline to take advantage of discounts, if available, or the deadline to avoid a penalty. The servicer does not use pre-accrual on these disbursement dates. The servicer also assumes that the borrower will make monthly payments equal to one-twelfth of the estimated total annual escrow account disbursements.

(B) The servicer then examines the monthly trial balances and adds to the first monthly balance an amount just sufficient to bring the lowest monthly trial balance to zero, and adjusts all other monthly balances accordingly.

(C) The servicer then adds to the monthly balances the permissible cushion. The cushion is two months of the borrower's escrow payments to the servicer or a lesser amount specified by State law or the mortgage document (net of any increases or decreases because of prior year shortages or surpluses, respectively).

(ii) *Lowest monthly balance.* Under aggregate analysis, the lowest monthly target balance for the account shall be less than or equal to one-sixth of the estimated total annual escrow account disbursements or a lesser amount specified by State law or the mortgage document. The target balances that the servicer derives using these steps yield the maximum limit for the escrow account. Appendix E to this part illustrates these steps.

(e) *Transfer of servicing.*

(1) If the new servicer changes either the monthly payment amount or the accounting method used by the transferor (old) servicer, then the new servicer shall provide the borrower with an initial escrow account statement within 60 days of the date of servicing transfer.

(i) Where a new servicer provides an initial escrow account statement upon the transfer of servicing, the new servicer shall use the effective date of the transfer of servicing to establish the new escrow account computation year.

(ii) Where the new servicer retains the monthly payments and accounting method used by the transferor servicer, then the new servicer may continue to use the escrow account computation year established by the transferor servicer or may choose to establish a different computation year using a short-year statement. At the completion of the escrow account computation year or any short year, the new servicer shall perform an escrow analysis and provide the borrower with an annual escrow account statement.

(2) The new servicer shall treat shortages, surpluses and deficiencies in the transferred escrow account according to the procedures set forth in § 3500.17(f).

(3) A pre-rule account remains a pre-rule account upon the transfer of servicing to a new servicer so long as the transfer occurs before the conversion date.

(f) *Shortages, surpluses, and deficiencies requirements.*

(1) *Escrow account analysis.* For each escrow account, the servicer shall conduct an escrow account analysis to determine whether a surplus, shortage or deficiency exists.

(i) As noted in § 3500.17(c) (2) and (3), the servicer shall conduct an escrow account analysis upon establishing an escrow account and at completion of the escrow account computation year.

(ii) The servicer may conduct an escrow account analysis at other times during the escrow computation year. If a servicer advances funds in paying a disbursement, which is not the result of a borrower's payment default under the underlying mortgage document, then the servicer shall conduct an escrow account analysis to determine the extent of the deficiency before seeking repayment of the funds from the borrower under this paragraph (f).

(2) *Surpluses.*

(i) If an escrow account analysis discloses a surplus, the servicer shall, within 30 days from the date of the analysis, refund the surplus to the borrower if the surplus is greater than or equal to 50 dollars ($50). If the surplus is less than 50 dollars ($50), the servicer may refund such amount to the borrower, or credit such amount against the next year's escrow payments.

(ii) These provisions regarding surpluses apply if the borrower is current at the time of the escrow account analysis. A borrower is current if the servicer receives the borrower's payments within 30 days of the payment due date. If the servicer does not receive the borrower's payment within 30 days of the payment due date, then the servicer may retain the surplus in the escrow account pursuant to the terms of the mortgage loan documents.

(iii) After an initial or annual escrow analysis has been performed, the servicer and the borrower may enter into a voluntary agreement for the forthcoming escrow accounting year for the borrower to deposit funds into the escrow account for that year greater than the limits established under paragraph (c) of this section. Such an agreement shall cover only one escrow accounting year, but a new voluntary agreement may be entered into after the next escrow analysis is performed. The voluntary agreement may not alter how surpluses are to be treated when the next escrow analysis is performed at the end of the escrow accounting year covered by the voluntary agreement.

(3) *Shortages.*

(i) If an escrow account analysis discloses a shortage of less than one month's escrow account payment, then the servicer has three possible courses of action:

(A) The servicer may allow a shortage to exist and do nothing to change it;

(B) The servicer may require the borrower to repay the shortage amount within 30 days; or

(C) The servicer may require the borrower to repay the shortage amount in equal monthly payments over at least a 12-month period.

(ii) If an escrow account analysis discloses a shortage that is greater than or equal to one month's escrow account payment, then the servicer has two possible courses of action:

(A) The servicer may allow a shortage to exist and do nothing to change it; or

(B) The servicer may require the borrower to repay the shortage in equal monthly payments over at least a 12-month period.

(4) *Deficiency.* If the escrow account analysis confirms a deficiency, then the servicer may require the borrower to pay additional monthly deposits to the account to eliminate the deficiency.

(i) If the deficiency is less than one month's escrow account payment, then the servicer:

(A) May allow the deficiency to exist and do nothing to change it;

(B) May require the borrower to repay the deficiency within 30 days; or

(C) May require the borrower to repay the deficiency in 2 or more equal monthly payments.

(ii) If the deficiency is greater than or equal to 1 month's escrow payment, the servicer may allow the deficiency to exist and do nothing to change it or may require the borrower to repay the deficiency in two or more equal monthly payments.

(iii) These provisions regarding deficiencies apply if the borrower is current at the time of the escrow account analysis. A borrower is current if the servicer receives the borrower's payments within 30 days of the payment due date. If the servicer does not receive the borrower's payment within 30 days of the payment due date, then the servicer may recover the deficiency pursuant to the terms of the mortgage loan documents.

(5) *Notice of Shortage or Deficiency in Escrow Account.* The servicer shall notify the borrower at least once during the escrow account computation year if there is a shortage or deficiency in the escrow account. The notice may be part of the annual escrow account statement or it may be a separate document.

(g) *Initial Escrow Account Statement.*

(1) *Submission at settlement, or within 45 calendar days of settlement.* As noted in § 3500.17(c)(2), the servicer shall conduct an escrow account analysis before establishing an escrow account to determine the amount the borrower shall deposit into the escrow account, subject to the limitations of § 3500.17(c)(1)(i). After conducting the escrow account analysis for each escrow account, the servicer shall submit an initial escrow account statement to the borrower at settlement or within 45 calendar days of settlement for escrow accounts that are established as a condition of the loan.

(i) The initial escrow account statement shall include the amount of the borrower's monthly mortgage payment and the portion of the monthly payment going into the escrow account and shall itemize the estimated taxes, insurance premiums, and other charges that the servicer reasonably anticipates to be paid from the escrow account during the escrow account computation year and the anticipated disbursement dates of those charges. The initial escrow account statement shall indicate the amount that the servicer selects as a cushion. The statement shall include a trial running balance for the account.

(ii) Pursuant to § 3500.17(h)(2), the servicer may incorporate the initial escrow account statement into the HUD-1 or HUD-1A settlement statement. If the servicer does not incorporate the initial escrow account statement into the HUD-1 or HUD-1A settlement statement, then the servicer shall submit the initial escrow account statement to the borrower as a separate document.

(2) *Time of submission of initial escrow account statement for an escrow account established after settlement.* For escrow accounts established after settlement (and which are not a condition of the loan), a servicer shall submit an initial escrow account statement to a borrower within 45 calendar days of the date of establishment of the escrow account.

(h) *Format for initial escrow account statement.*

(1) The format and a completed example for an initial escrow account statement are set out in HUD Public Guidance Documents entitled "Initial Escrow Account Disclosure Statement—Format" and "Initial Escrow Account Disclosure Statement—Example," available in accordance with § 3500.3.

(2) *Incorporation of initial escrow account statement into HUD-1 or HUD-1A settlement statement.* Pursuant to § 3500.9(a)(11), a servicer may add the initial escrow account statement to the HUD-1 or HUD-1A settlement statement. The servicer may include the initial escrow account statement in the basic text or may attach the initial escrow account statement as an additional page to the HUD-1 or HUD-1A settlement statement.

(3) *Identification of payees.* The initial escrow account statement need not identify a specific payee by name if it provides sufficient information to identify the use of the funds. For example, appropriate entries include: county taxes, hazard insurance, condominium dues, etc. If a particular payee, such as a taxing body, receives more than one payment during the escrow account computation year, the statement shall indicate each payment and disbursement date. If there are several taxing authorities or insurers, the statement shall identify each taxing body or insurer (e.g., "City Taxes," "School Taxes," "Hazard Insurance," or "Flood Insurance," etc.).

(i) *Annual escrow account statements.* For each escrow account, a servicer shall submit an annual escrow account statement to the borrower within 30 days of the completion of the escrow account computation year. The servicer shall also submit to the borrower the previous year's projection or initial escrow account statement. The servicer shall conduct an escrow account analysis before submitting an annual escrow account statement to the borrower.

(1) *Contents of annual escrow account statement.* The annual escrow account statement shall provide an account history, reflecting the activity in the escrow account during the escrow account computation year, and a projection of the activity in the account for the next year. In preparing the statement, the servicer may assume scheduled payments and disbursements will be made for the final 2 months of the escrow account computation year. The annual escrow account statement must include, at a minimum, the following (the items in paragraphs (i)(1)(i) through (i)(1)(iv) must be clearly itemized):

(i) The amount of the borrower's current monthly mortgage payment and the portion of the monthly payment going into the escrow account;

(ii) The amount of the past year's monthly mortgage payment and the portion of the monthly payment that went into the escrow account;

(iii) The total amount paid into the escrow account during the past computation year;

(iv) The total amount paid out of the escrow account during the same period for taxes, insurance premiums, and other charges (as separately identified);

(v) The balance in the escrow account at the end of the period;

(vi) An explanation of how any surplus is being handled by the servicer;

(vii) An explanation of how any shortage or deficiency is to be paid by the borrower; and

(viii) If applicable, the reason(s) why the estimated low monthly balance was not reached, as indicated by noting differences between the most recent account history and last year's projection. HUD Public Guidance Documents entitled "Annual Escrow Account Disclosure Statement—Format" and "Annual Escrow Account Disclosure Statement—Example" set forth an acceptable format and methodology for conveying this information.

(2) *No annual statements in the case of default, foreclosure, or bankruptcy.* This paragraph (i)(2) contains an exemption from the provisions of § 3500.17(i)(1). If at the time the servicer conducts the escrow account analysis the borrower is more than 30 days overdue, then the servicer is exempt from the requirements of submitting an annual escrow account statement to the borrower under § 3500.17(i). This exemption also applies in situations where the servicer has brought an action for foreclosure under the underlying mortgage loan, or where the borrower is in bankruptcy proceedings. If the servicer does not issue an annual statement pursuant to this exemption and the loan subsequently is reinstated or otherwise becomes current, the servicer shall provide a history of the account since the last annual statement (which may be longer than 1 year) within 90 days of the date the account became current.

(3) *Delivery with other material.* The servicer may deliver the annual escrow account statement to the borrower with other statements or materials, including the Substitute 1098, which is provided for federal income tax purposes.

(4) *Short year statements.* A servicer may issue a short year annual escrow account statement ("short year statement") to change one escrow account computation year to another. By using a short year statement a servicer may adjust its production schedule or alter the escrow account computation year for the escrow account.

(i) *Effect of short year statement.* The short year statement shall end the "escrow account computation year" for the escrow account and establish the beginning date of the new escrow account computation year. The servicer shall deliver the short year statement to the borrower within 60 days from the end of the short year.

(ii) *Short year statement upon servicing transfer.* Upon the transfer of servicing, the transferor (old) servicer shall submit a short year statement to the borrower within 60 days of the effective date of transfer.

(iii) *Short year statement upon loan payoff.* If a borrower pays off a mortgage loan during the escrow account computation year, the servicer shall submit a short year statement to the borrower within 60 days after receiving the pay-off funds.

(j) *Formats for annual escrow account statement.* The formats and completed examples for annual escrow account statements using single-item analysis (pre-rule accounts) and aggregate analysis are set out in HUD Public Guidance Documents entitled "Annual Escrow Account Disclosure Statement—Format" and "Annual Escrow Account Disclosure Statement—Example."

(k) *Timely payments.*

(1) If the terms of any federally related mortgage loan require the borrower to make payments to an escrow account, the servicer must pay the disbursements in a timely manner, that is, on or before the deadline to avoid a penalty, as long as the borrower's payment is not more than 30 days overdue.

(2) The servicer must advance funds to make disbursements in a timely manner as long as the borrower's payment is not more than 30 days overdue. Upon advancing funds to pay a disbursement, the servicer may seek repayment from the borrower for the deficiency pursuant to paragraph (f) of this section.

(3) For the payment of property taxes from the escrow account, if a taxing jurisdiction offers a servicer a choice between annual and installment disbursements, the servicer must also comply with this paragraph (k)(3). If the taxing jurisdiction neither offers a discount for disbursements on a lump sum annual basis nor imposes any additional charge or fee for installment disbursements, the servicer must make disbursements on an installment basis. If, however, the taxing jurisdiction offers a discount for disbursements on a lump sum annual basis or imposes any additional charge or fee for installment disbursements, the servicer may at the servicer's discretion (but is not required by RESPA to), make lump sum annual disbursements in order to take advantage of the discount for the borrower or avoid the additional charge or fee for installments, as long as such method of disbursement complies with paragraphs (k)(1) and (k)(2) of this section. HUD encourages, but does not require, the servicer to follow the preference of the borrower, if such preference is known to the servicer.

(4) Notwithstanding paragraph (k)(3) of this section, a servicer and borrower may mutually agree, on an individual case basis, to a different disbursement basis (installment or annual) or disbursement date for property taxes from that required under paragraph (k)(3) of this section, so long as the agreement meets the requirements of paragraphs (k)(1) and (k)(2) of this section. The borrower must voluntarily agree; neither loan approval nor any term of the loan may be conditioned on the borrower's agreeing to a different disbursement basis or disbursement date.

(l) *System of recordkeeping.*

(1) Each servicer shall keep records, which may involve electronic storage, microfiche storage, or any method of computerized storage, so long as the information is easily retrievable, reflecting the servicer's handling of each borrower's escrow account. The servicer's records shall include, but not be limited to, the payment of amounts into and from the escrow account and the submission of initial and annual escrow account statements to the borrower.

(2) The servicer responsible for servicing the borrower's escrow account shall maintain the records for that account for a period of at least five years after the servicer last serviced the escrow account.

(3) A servicer shall provide the Secretary with information contained in the servicer's records for a specific escrow account, or for a number or class of escrow accounts, within 30 days of the Secretary's written request for the information. The servicer shall convert any information contained in electronic storage, microfiche or computerized storage to paper copies for review by the Secretary.

(i) To aid in investigations, the Secretary may also issue an administrative subpoena for the production of documents, and for the testimony of such witnesses as the Secretary deems advisable.

(ii) If the subpoenaed party refuses to obey the Secretary's administrative subpoena, the Secretary is authorized to seek a court order requiring compliance with the subpoena from any United States district court. Failure to obey such an order of the court may be punished as contempt of court.

(4) Borrowers may seek information contained in the servicer's records by complying with the provisions set forth in 12 U.S.C. 2605(e) and § 3500.21(f).

(5) After receiving a request (by letter or subpoena) from the Department for information relating to whether a servicer submitted an escrow account statement to the borrower, the servicer shall respond within 30 days. If the servicer is unable to provide the Department with such information, the Secretary shall deem that lack of information to be evidence of the servicer's failure to submit the statement to the borrower.

(m) *Penalties.*

(1) A servicer's failure to submit to a borrower an initial or annual escrow account statement meeting the requirements of this part shall constitute a violation of section 10(d) of RESPA (12 U.S.C. 2609(d)) and this section. For each such violation, the Secretary shall assess a civil penalty of 75 dollars ($75), except that the total of the assessed penalties shall not exceed $130,000 for any one servicer for violations that occur during any consecutive 12-month period.

(2) Violations described in paragraph (m)(1) of this section do not require any proof of intent. However, if a lender or servicer is shown to have intentionally disregarded the requirements that it submit the escrow account statement to the borrower, then the Secretary shall assess a civil penalty of $110 for each violation, with no limit on the total amount of the penalty.

(n) *Civil penalties procedures.* The following procedures shall apply whenever the Department seeks to impose a civil money penalty for violation of section 10(c) of RESPA (12 U.S.C. 2609(c)):

(1) *Purpose and scope.* This paragraph (n) explains the procedures by which the Secretary may impose penalties under 12 U.S.C. 2609(d). These procedures include administrative hearings, judicial review, and collection of penalties. This paragraph (n) governs penalties imposed under 12 U.S.C. 2609(d) and, when noted, adopts those portions of 24 CFR part 30 that apply to all other civil penalty proceedings initiated by the Secretary.

(2) *Authority.* The Secretary has the authority to impose civil penalties under section 10(d) of RESPA (12 U.S.C. 2609(d)).

(3) *Notice of intent to impose civil money penalties.* Whenever the Secretary intends to impose a civil money penalty for violations of section 10(c) of RESPA (12 U.S.C. 2609(c)), the responsible program official, or his or her designee, shall serve a written Notice of Intent to Impose Civil Money Penalties (Notice of Intent) upon any servicer on which the Secretary intends to impose the penalty. A copy of the Notice of Intent must be filed with the Docket Clerk, Office of Administrative Law Judges, at the address provided in the Notice of Intent.

The Notice of Intent will provide:

(i) A short, plain statement of the facts upon which the Secretary has determined that a civil money penalty should be imposed, including a brief description of the specific violations under 12 U.S.C. 2609(c) with which the servicer is charged and whether such violations are believed to be intentional or unintentional in nature, or a combination thereof;

(ii) The amount of the civil money penalty that the Secretary intends to impose and whether the limitations in 12 U.S.C. 2609(d)(1), apply;

(iii) The right of the servicer to a hearing on the record to appeal the Secretary's preliminary determination to impose a civil penalty;

(iv) The procedures to appeal the penalty;

(v) The consequences of failure to appeal the penalty; and

(vi) The name, address, and telephone number of the representative of the Department, and the address of the Docket Clerk, Office of Administrative Law Judges, should the servicer decide to appeal the penalty.

(4) *Appeal procedures.*

(i) *Answer.* To appeal the imposition of a penalty, a servicer shall, within 30 days after receiving service of the Notice of Intent, file a written Answer with the Docket Clerk, Office of Administrative Law Judges, Department of Housing and Urban Development, at the address provided in the Notice of Intent. The Answer shall include a statement that the servicer admits, denies, or does not have (and is unable to obtain) sufficient information to admit or deny each allegation made in the Notice of Intent. A statement of lack of information shall have the effect of a denial. Any allegation that is not denied shall be deemed admitted. Failure to submit an Answer within the required period of time will result in a decision by the Administrative Law Judge based upon the Department's submission of evidence in the Notice of Intent.

(ii) *Submission of evidence.* A servicer that receives the Notice of Intent has a right to present evidence. Evidence must be submitted within 45 calendar days from the date of service of the Notice of Intent, or by such other time as may be established by the Administrative Law Judge (ALJ). The servicer's failure to submit evidence within the required period of time will result in a decision by the Administrative Law Judge based upon the Department's submission of evidence in the Notice of Intent. The servicer may present evidence of the following:

(A) The servicer did submit the required escrow account statement(s) to the borrower(s); or

(B) Even if the servicer did not submit the required statement(s), that the failure was not the result of an intentional disregard of the requirements of RESPA (for purposes of determining the penalty).

(iii) *Review of the record.* The Administrative Law Judge will review the evidence submitted by the servicer, if any, and that submitted by the Department. The Administrative Law Judge shall make a determination based upon a review of the written record, except that the Administrative Law Judge may order an oral hearing if he or she finds that the determination turns on the credibility or veracity of a witness, or that the matter cannot be resolved by review of the documentary evidence. If the Administrative Law Judge decides that an oral hearing is appropriate, then the procedural rules set forth at 24 CFR part 30 shall apply, to the extent that they are not inconsistent with this section.

(iv) *Burden of Proof.* The burden of proof or the burden of going forward with the evidence shall be upon the proponent of an action. The Department's submission of evidence that the servicer's system of records lacks information that the servicer submitted the escrow account statement(s) to the borrower(s) shall satisfy the Department's burden. Upon the Department's presentation of evidence of this lack of information in the servicer's system of records, the burden of proof shifts from the Secretary to the servicer to provide evidence that it submitted the statement(s) to the borrower.

(v) *Standard of Proof.* The standard of proof shall be the preponderance of the evidence.

(5) *Determination of the Administrative Law Judge.*

(i) Following the hearing or the review of the written record, the Administrative Law Judge shall issue a decision that shall contain findings of fact, conclusions of law, and the amount of any penalties imposed. The decision shall include a determination of whether the servicer has failed to submit any required statements and, if so, whether the servicer's failure was the result of an intentional disregard for the law's requirements.

(ii) The Administrative Law Judge shall issue the decision to all parties within 30 days of the submission of the evidence or the post-hearing briefs, whichever is the last to occur.

(iii) The decision of the Administrative Law Judge shall constitute the final decision of the Department and shall be final and binding on the parties.

(6) *Judicial review.*

(i) A person against whom the Department has imposed a civil money penalty under this part may obtain a review of the Department's final decision by filing a written petition for a review of the record with the appropriate United States district court.

(ii) The petition must be filed within 30 days after the decision is filed with the Docket Clerk, Office of Administrative Law Judges.

(7) *Collection of penalties.*

(i) If any person fails to comply with the Department's final decision imposing a civil money penalty, the Secretary, if the time for judicial review of the decision has expired, may request the Attorney General to bring an action in an appropriate United States district court to obtain a judgment against the person that has failed to comply with the Department's final decision.

(ii) In any such collection action, the validity and appropriateness of the Department's final decision imposing the civil penalty shall not be subject to review in the district court.

(iii) The Secretary may obtain such other relief as may be available, including attorney fees and other expenses in connection with the collection action.

(iv) Interest on and other charges for any unpaid penalty may be assessed in accordance with 31 U.S.C. 3717.

(8) *Offset.* In addition to any other rights as a creditor, the Secretary may seek to collect a civil money penalty through administrative offset.

(9) At any time before the decision of the Administrative Law Judge, the Secretary and the servicer may enter into an administrative settlement. The settlement may include provisions for interest, attorney's fees, and costs related to the proceeding. Such settlement will terminate the appearance before the Administrative Law Judge.

(o) *Discretionary payments.* Any borrower's discretionary payment (such as credit life or disability insurance) made as part of a monthly mortgage payment is to be noted on the initial and annual statements. If a discretionary payment is established or terminated during the escrow account computation year, this change should be noted on the next annual statement. A discretionary payment is not part of the escrow account unless the payment is required by the lender, in accordance with the definition of "settlement service" in § 3500.2, or the servicer chooses to place the discretionary payment in the escrow account. If a servicer has not established an escrow account for a federally related mortgage loan and only receives payments for discretionary items, this section is not applicable.

[59 Fed. Reg. 53,902 (Oct. 26, 1994); 60 Fed. Reg. 8816 (Feb. 15, 1995); 60 Fed. Reg. 24,735 (May 9, 1995); 61 Fed. Reg. 13,233 (March 26, 1996); 61 Fed. Reg. 29,252 (June 7, 1996); 61 Fed. Reg. 46,510 (Sept. 3, 1996); 61 Fed. Reg. 50,219 (Sept. 24, 1996); 61 Fed. Reg. 51,782 (Oct. 4, 1996); 61 Fed. Reg. 58,476 (Nov. 15, 1996); 63 Fed. Reg. 32,36 (Jan. 21, 1998); 68 Fed. Reg. 12,789 (Mar. 17, 2003); 72 Fed. Reg. 5589 (Feb. 6, 2007); 73 Fed. Reg. 68,242 (Nov. 17, 2008); 74 Fed. Reg. 4636 (Jan. 26, 2009)]

* * *

24 C.F.R. § 3500.19 Enforcement.

(a) *Enforcement policy.* It is the policy of the Secretary regarding RESPA enforcement matters to cooperate with Federal, State, or local agencies having supervisory powers over lenders or other persons with responsibilities under RESPA. Federal agencies with supervisory powers over lenders may use their powers to require compliance with RESPA. In addition, failure to comply with RESPA may be grounds for administrative action by the Secretary under 2 CFR part 2424 concerning debarment, suspension, ineligibility of contractors and grantees, or under part 25 of this title concerning the HUD Mortgagee Review Board. Nothing in this paragraph is a limitation on any other form of enforcement that may be legally available.

(b) *Servicing Disclosure Statement; Requirements.* (1) At the time an application for a mortgage servicing loan is submitted, or within 3 business days after submission of the application, the lender, mortgage broker who anticipates using table funding, or dealer who anticipates a first lien dealer loan shall provide to each person who applies for such a loan a Servicing Disclosure Statement. A format for the Servicing Disclosure Statement appears as Appendix MS-1 to this part. The specific language of the Servicing Disclosure Statement is not required to be used. The information set forth in "Instructions to Preparer" on the Servicing Disclosure Statement need not be included with the information given to applicants, and material in square brackets is optional or alternative language. The model format may be annotated with additional information that clarifies or enhances the model language. The lender, table funding mortgage broker, or dealer should use the language that best describes the particular circumstances.

(2) The Servicing Disclosure Statement must indicate whether the servicing of the loan may be assigned, sold, or transferred to any other person at any time while the loan is outstanding. If the lender, table funding mortgage broker, or dealer in a first lien dealer loan will engage in the servicing of the mortgage loan for which the applicant has applied, the disclosure may consist of a statement that the entity will service such loan and does not intend to sell, transfer, or assign the servicing of the loan. If the lender, table funding mortgage broker, or dealer in a first lien dealer loan will not engage in the servicing of the mortgage loan for which the applicant has applied, the disclosure may consist of a statement that such entity intends to assign, sell, or transfer servicing of such mortgage loan before the first payment is due. In all other instances, the disclosure must state that the servicing of the loan may be assigned, sold or transferred while the loan is outstanding.

(c) *Servicing Disclosure Statement; Delivery.* The lender, table funding mortgage broker, or dealer that anticipates a first lien dealer loan shall deliver the Servicing Disclosure Statement within 3 business days from receipt of the application by hand delivery, by placing it in the mail, or, if the applicant agrees, by fax, e-mail, or other electronic means. In the event the borrower is denied credit within the 3 business-day period, no servicing disclosure statement is required to be delivered. If co-applicants indicate the same address on their application, one copy delivered to that address is sufficient. If different addresses are shown by co-applicants on the application, a copy must be delivered to each of the co-applicants.

(d) *Investigations.* The procedures for investigations and investigational proceedings are set forth in 24 CFR part 3800.

[59 Fed. Reg. 65,448 (Dec. 19, 1994); 61 Fed. Reg. 10,442 (March 13, 1996); 61 Fed. Reg. 13,233 (March 26, 1996); 72 Fed. Reg. 73,484 (Dec. 27, 2007); 73 Fed. Reg. 68,242 (Nov. 17, 2008)]

* * *

24 C.F.R. § 3500.21 Mortgage servicing transfers.

(a) *Definitions.* As used in this section:

Master servicer means the owner of the right to perform servicing, which may actually perform the servicing itself or may do so through a subservicer.

Mortgage servicing loan means a federally related mortgage loan, as that term is defined in § 3500.2, subject to the exemptions in § 3500.5, when the mortgage loan is secured by a first lien. The definition does not include subordinate lien loans or open-end lines of credit (home equity plans) covered by the Truth in Lending Act and Regulation Z, including open-end lines of credit secured by a first lien.

Qualified written request means a written correspondence from the borrower to the servicer prepared in accordance with paragraph (e)(2) of this section.

Subservicer means a servicer who does not own the right to perform servicing, but who does so on behalf of the master servicer.

Transferee servicer means a servicer who obtains or who will obtain the right to perform servicing functions pursuant to an agreement or understanding.

Transferor servicer means a servicer, including a table funding mortgage broker or dealer on a first lien dealer loan, who transfers or will transfer the right to perform servicing functions pursuant to an agreement or understanding.

(b) *Servicing Disclosure Statement and Applicant Acknowledgement; requirements.*

(1) At the time an application for a mortgage servicing loan is submitted, or within 3 business days after submission of the application, the lender, mortgage broker who anticipates using table funding, or dealer who anticipates a first lien dealer loan shall provide to each person who applies for such a loan a Servicing Disclosure Statement. This requirement shall not apply when the application for credit is turned down within three business days after receipt of the application. A format for the Servicing Disclosure Statement appears as Appendix MS-1 to this part. Except as provided in paragraph (b)(2) of this section, the specific language of the Servicing Disclosure Statement is not required to be used, but the Servicing Disclosure Statement must include the information set out in paragraph (b)(3) of this section, including the statement of the borrower's rights in connection with complaint resolution. The information set forth in Instructions to Preparer on the Servicing Disclosure Statement need not be included on the form given to applicants, and material in square brackets is optional or alternative language.

(2) The Applicant's Acknowledgement portion of the Servicing Disclosure Statement in the format stated is mandatory. Additional lines may be added to accommodate more than two applicants.

(3) The Servicing Disclosure Statement must contain the following information, except as provided in paragraph (b)(3)(ii) of this section:

(i) Whether the servicing of the loan may be assigned, sold or transferred to any other person at any time while the loan is outstanding. If the lender, table funding mortgage broker, or dealer in a first lien dealer loan does not engage in the servicing of any mortgage servicing loans, the disclosure may consist of a statement to the effect that there is a current intention to assign, sell, or transfer servicing of the loan.

(ii) The percentages (rounded to the nearest quartile (25%)) of mortgage servicing loans originated by the lender in each calendar year for which servicing has been assigned, sold, or transferred for such calendar year. Compliance with this paragraph (b)(3)(ii) is not required if the lender, table funding mortgage broker, or dealer on a first lien dealer loan chooses option B in the model format in paragraph (b)(4) of this section, including in square brackets the language "[and have not serviced mortgage loans in the last three years.]." The percentages shall be provided as follows:

(A) This information shall be set out for the most recent three calendar years completed, with percentages as of the end of each year. This information shall be updated in the disclosure no later than March 31 of the next calendar year. Each percentage should be obtained by using as the numerator the number of mortgage servicing loans originated during the calendar year for which servicing is transferred within the calendar year and, as the denominator, the total number of mortgage servicing loans originated in the calendar year. If the volume of transfers is less than 12.5 percent, the word "nominal" or the actual percentage amount of servicing transfers may be used.

(B) This statistical information does not have to include the assignment, sale, or transfer of mortgage loan servicing by the lender to an affiliate or subsidiary of the lender. However, lenders may voluntarily include transfers to an affiliate or subsidiary. The lender should indicate whether the percentages provided include assignments, sales, or transfers to affiliates or subsidiaries.

(C) In the alternative, if applicable, the following statement may be substituted for the statistical information required to be provided in accordance with paragraph (b)(3)(ii) of this section: "We have previously assigned, sold, or transferred the servicing of federally related mortgage loans."

(iii) The best available estimate of the percentage (0 to 25 percent, 26 to 50 percent, 51 to 75 percent, or 76 to 100 percent) of all loans to be made during the 12-month period beginning on the date of origination for which the servicing may be assigned, sold, or transferred. Each percentage should be obtained by using as the numerator the estimated number of mortgage servicing loans that will be originated for which servicing may be transferred within the 12-month period and, as the denominator, the estimated total number of mortgage servicing loans that will be originated in the 12-month period.

(A) If the lender, mortgage broker, or dealer anticipates that no loan servicing will be sold during the calendar year, the word "none" may be substituted for "0 to 25 percent." If it is anticipated that all loan servicing will be sold during the calendar year, the word "all" may be substituted for "76 to 100 percent."

(B) This statistical information does not have to include the estimated assignment, sale, or transfer of mortgage loan servicing to an affiliate or subsidiary of that person. However, this information may be provided voluntarily. The Servicing Disclosure Statements should indicate whether the percentages provided include assignments, sales or transfers to affiliates or subsidiaries.

(iv) The information set out in paragraphs (d) and (e) of this section.

(v) A written acknowledgement that the applicant (and any co-applicant) has/have read and understood the disclosure, and understand that the disclosure is a required part of the mortgage application. This acknowledgement shall be evidenced by the signature of the applicant and any co-applicant.

(4) The following is a model format, which includes several options, for complying with the requirements of paragraph (b)(3) of this section. The model format may be annotated with additional information that clarifies or enhances the model language. The lender or table funding mortgage broker (or dealer) should use the language that best describes the particular circumstances.

(i) *Model Format*: The following is the best estimate of what will happen to the servicing of your mortgage loan:

(A) *Option A*. We may assign, sell, or transfer the servicing of your loan while the loan is outstanding. [We are able to service your loan[.][,] and we [will] [will not] [haven't decided whether to] service your loan.]; or

(B) *Option B*. We do not service mortgage loans[.][,] [and have not serviced mortgage loans in the past three years.] We presently intend to assign, sell, or transfer the servicing of your mortgage loan. You will be informed about your servicer.

(C) As appropriate, the following paragraph may be used:
We assign, sell, or transfer the servicing of some of our loans while the loans are outstanding, depending on the type of loan and other factors. For the program for which you have applied, we expect to [assign, sell, or transfer all of the mortgage servicing][retain all of the mortgage servicing] [assign, sell, or transfer ______ % of the mortgage servicing].

(ii) [Reserved]

(c) *Servicing Disclosure Statement and Applicant Acknowledgement; delivery*. The lender, table funding mortgage broker, or dealer that anticipates a first lien dealer loan shall deliver Servicing Disclosure Statements to each applicant for mortgage servicing loans. Each applicant or co-applicant must sign an Acknowledgement of receipt of the Servicing Disclosure Statement before settlement.

(1) In the case of a face-to-face interview with one or more applicants, the Servicing Disclosure Statement shall be delivered at the time of application. An applicant present at the interview may sign the Acknowledgment on his or her own behalf at that time. An applicant present at the interview also may accept delivery of the Servicing Disclosure Statement on behalf of the other applicants.

(2) If there is no face-to-face interview, the Servicing Disclosure Statement shall be delivered by placing it in the mail, with prepaid first-class postage, within 3 business days from receipt of the application. If co-applicants indicate the same address on their application, one copy delivered to that address is sufficient. If different addresses are shown by co-applicants on the application, a copy must be delivered to each of the co-applicants.

(3) The signed Applicant Acknowledgment(s) shall be retained for a period of 5 years after the date of settlement as part of the loan file for every settled loan. There is no requirement for retention of Applicant Acknowledgment(s) if the loan is not settled.

(d) *Notices of Transfer; loan servicing—*

(1) *Requirement for notice.*

(i) Except as provided in this paragraph (d)(1)(i) or paragraph (d)(1)(ii) of this section, each transferor servicer and transferee servicer of any mortgage servicing loan shall deliver to the borrower a written Notice of Transfer, containing the information described in paragraph (d)(3) of this section, of any assignment, sale, or transfer of the servicing of the loan. The following transfers are not considered an assignment, sale, or transfer of mortgage loan servicing for purposes of this requirement if there is no change in the payee, address to which payment must be delivered, account number, or amount of payment due:

(A) Transfers between affiliates;

(B) Transfers resulting from mergers or acquisitions of servicers or subservicers; and

(C) Transfers between master servicers, where the subservicer remains the same.

(ii) The Federal Housing Administration (FHA) is not required under paragraph (d) of this section to submit to the borrower a Notice of Transfer in cases where a mortgage insured under the National Housing Act is assigned to FHA.

(2) *Time of notice.*

(i) Except as provided in paragraph (d)(2)(ii) of this section:

(A) The transferor servicer shall deliver the Notice of Transfer to the borrower not less than 15 days before the effective date of the transfer of the servicing of the mortgage servicing loan;

(B) The transferee servicer shall deliver the Notice of Transfer to the borrower not more than 15 days after the effective date of the transfer; and

(C) The transferor and transferee servicers may combine their notices into one notice, which shall be delivered to the borrower not less than 15 days before the effective date of the transfer of the servicing of the mortgage servicing loan.

(ii) The Notice of Transfer shall be delivered to the borrower by the transferor servicer or the transferee servicer not more than 30 days after the effective date of the transfer of the servicing of the mortgage servicing loan in any case in which the transfer of servicing is preceded by:

(A) Termination of the contract for servicing the loan for cause;

(B) Commencement of proceedings for bankruptcy of the servicer; or

(C) Commencement of proceedings by the Federal Deposit Insurance Corporation (FDIC) or the Resolution Trust Corporation (RTC) for conservatorship or receivership of the servicer or an entity that owns or controls the servicer.

(iii) Notices of Transfer delivered at settlement by the transferor servicer and transferee servicer, whether as separate notices or as a combined notice, will satisfy the timing requirements of paragraph (d)(2) of this section.

(3) *Notices of Transfer; contents.* The Notices of Transfer required under paragraph (d) of this section shall include the following information:

(i) The effective date of the transfer of servicing;

(ii) The name, consumer inquiry addresses (including, at the option of the servicer, a separate address where qualified written requests must be sent), and a toll-free or collect-call telephone number for an employee or department of the transferee servicer;

(iii) A toll-free or collect-call telephone number for an employee or department of the transferor servicer that can be contacted by the borrower for answers to servicing transfer inquiries;

(iv) The date on which the transferor servicer will cease to accept payments relating to the loan and the date on which the transferee servicer will begin to accept such payments. These dates shall either be the same or consecutive days;

(v) Information concerning any effect the transfer may have on the terms or the continued availability of mortgage life or disability insurance, or any other type of optional insurance, and any action the borrower must take to maintain coverage;

(vi) A statement that the transfer of servicing does not affect any other term or condition of the mortgage documents, other than terms directly related to the servicing of the loan; and

(vii) A statement of the borrower's rights in connection with complaint resolution, including the information set forth in paragraph (e) of this section. Appendix MS-2 of this part illustrates a statement satisfactory to the Secretary.

(4) *Notices of Transfer; sample notice.* Sample language that may be used to comply with the requirements of paragraph (d) of this section is set out in Appendix MS-2 of this part. Minor modifications to the sample language may be made to meet the particular circumstances of the servicer, but the substance of the sample language shall not be omitted or substantially altered.

(5) *Consumer protection during transfer of servicing.* During the 60-day period beginning on the effective date of transfer of the servicing of any mortgage servicing loan, if the transferor servicer (rather than the transferee servicer that should properly receive payment on the loan) receives payment on or before the applicable due date (including any grace period allowed under the loan documents), a late fee may not be imposed on the borrower with respect to that payment and the payment may not be treated as late for any other purposes.

(e) *Duty of loan servicer to respond to borrower inquiries.*

(1) *Notice of receipt of inquiry.* Within 20 business days of a servicer of a mortgage servicing loan receiving a qualified written request from the borrower for information relating to the servicing of the loan, the servicer shall provide to the borrower a written response acknowledging receipt of the qualified written response. This requirement shall not apply if the action requested by the borrower is taken within that period and the borrower is notified of that action in accordance with the paragraph (f)(3) of this section. By notice either included in the Notice of Transfer or separately delivered by first-class mail, postage prepaid, a servicer may establish a separate and exclusive office and address for the receipt and handling of qualified written requests.

(2) *Qualified written request; defined.*

(i) For purposes of paragraph (e) of this section, a qualified written request means a written correspondence (other than notice on a payment coupon or other payment medium supplied by the servicer) that includes, or otherwise enables the servicer to identify, the name and account of the borrower, and includes a statement of the reasons that the borrower believes the account is in error, if applicable, or that provides sufficient detail to the servicer regarding information relating to the servicing of the loan sought by the borrower.

(ii) A written request does not constitute a qualified written request if it is delivered to a servicer more than 1 year after either the date of transfer of servicing or the date that the mortgage servicing loan amount was paid in full, whichever date is applicable.

(3) *Action with respect to the inquiry.* Not later than 60 business days after receiving a qualified written request from the borrower, and, if applicable, before taking any action with respect to the inquiry, the servicer shall:

(i) Make appropriate corrections in the account of the borrower, including the crediting of any late charges or penalties, and transmit to the borrower a written notification of the correction. This written notification shall include the name and telephone number of a representative of the servicer who can provide assistance to the borrower; or

(ii) After conducting an investigation, provide the borrower with a written explanation or clarification that includes:

(A) To the extent applicable, a statement of the servicer's reasons for concluding the account is correct and the name and telephone number of an employee, office, or department of the servicer that can provide assistance to the borrower; or

(B) Information requested by the borrower, or an explanation of why the information requested is unavailable or cannot be obtained by the servicer, and the name and telephone number of an employee, office, or department of the servicer that can provide assistance to the borrower.

(4) *Protection of credit rating.*

(i) During the 60-business day period beginning on the date of the servicer receiving from a borrower a qualified written request relating to a dispute on the borrower's payments, a servicer may not provide adverse information regarding any payment that is the subject of the qualified written request to any consumer reporting agency (as that term is defined in section 603 of the Fair Credit Reporting Act, 15 U.S.C. 1681a).

(ii) In accordance with section 17 of RESPA (12 U.S.C. 2615), the protection of credit rating provision of paragraph (e)(4)(i) of this section does not impede a lender or servicer from pursuing any of its remedies, including initiating foreclosure, allowed by the underlying mortgage loan instruments.

(f) *Damages and costs.*

(1) Whoever fails to comply with any provision of this section shall be liable to the borrower for each failure in the following amounts:

(i) *Individuals.* In the case of any action by an individual, an amount equal to the sum of any actual damages sustained by the individual as the result of the failure and, when there is a pattern or practice of noncompliance with the requirements of this section, any additional damages in an amount not to exceed $1,000.

(ii) *Class Actions.* In the case of a class action, an amount equal to the sum of any actual damages to each borrower in the class that result from the failure and, when there is a pattern or practice of noncompliance with the requirements of this section, any additional damages in an amount not greater than $1,000 for each class member. However, the total amount of any additional damages in a class action may not exceed the lesser of § 500,000 or 1 percent of the net worth of the servicer.

(iii) *Costs.* In addition, in the case of any successful action under paragraph (f) of this section, the costs of the action and any reasonable attorneys' fees incurred in connection with the action.

(2) *Nonliability.* A transferor or transferee servicer shall not be liable for any failure to comply with the requirements of this section, if within 60 days after discovering an error (whether pursuant to a final written examination report or the servicer's own procedures) and before commencement of an action under this section and the receipt of written notice of the error from the borrower, the servicer notifies the person concerned of the error and makes whatever adjust-

ments are necessary in the appropriate account to ensure that the person will not be required to pay an amount in excess of any amount that the person otherwise would have paid.

(g) *Timely payments by servicer.* If the terms of any mortgage servicing loan require the borrower to make payments to the servicer of the loan for deposit into an escrow account for the purpose of assuring payment of taxes, insurance premiums, and other charges with respect to the mortgaged property, the servicer shall make payments from the escrow account in a timely manner for the taxes, insurance premiums, and other charges as the payments become due, as governed by the requirements in § 3500.17(k).

(h) *Preemption of State laws.* A lender who makes a mortgage servicing loan or a servicer shall be considered to have complied with the provisions of any State law or regulation requiring notice to a borrower at the time of application for a loan or transfer of servicing of a loan if the lender or servicer complies with the requirements of this section. Any State law requiring notice to the borrower at the time of application or at the time of transfer of servicing of the loan is preempted, and there shall be no additional borrower disclosure requirements. Provisions of State law, such as those requiring additional notices to insurance companies or taxing authorities, are not preempted by section 6 of RESPA or this section, and this additional information may be added to a notice prepared under this section, if the procedure is allowable under State law.

[59 Fed. Reg. 65,448 (Dec. 19, 1994); 60 Fed. Reg. 2642 (Jan. 10, 1995); 60 Fed. Reg. 14,636 (March 20, 1995); 61 Fed. Reg. 13,233 (March 26, 1996)]

* * *

Appendix E to Part 3500—Arithmetic Steps

I. Example Illustrating Aggregate Analysis

ASSUMPTIONS:

Disbursements:
- $360 for school taxes disbursed on September 20
- $1,200 for county property taxes:
- $500 disbursed on July 25
- $700 disbursed on December 10

Cushion: One-sixth of estimated annual disbursements
Settlement: May 15
First Payment: July 1

Step 1—Initial Trial Balance

	Aggregate		
	pmt	disb	bal
Jun	0	0	0
Jul	130	500	-370
Aug	130	0	-240
Sep	130	360	-470
Oct	130	0	-340
Nov	130	0	-210
Dec	130	700	-780
Jan	130	0	-650
Feb	130	0	-520
Mar	130	0	-390
Apr	130	0	-260
May	130	0	-130
Jun	130	0	0

Step 2—Adjusted Trial Balance
[Increase monthly balances to eliminate negative balances]

	Aggregate		
	pmt	disb	bal
Jun	0	0	780
Jul	130	500	410
Aug	130	0	540
Sep	130	360	310
Oct	130	0	440
Nov	130	0	570
Dec	130	700	0
Jan	130	0	130
Feb	130	0	260
Mar	130	0	390
Apr	130	0	520
May	130	0	650
Jun	130	0	780

Step 3—Trial Balance With Cushion

	Aggregate		
	pmt	disb	bal
Jun	0	0	1040
Jul	130	500	670
Aug	130	0	800
Sep	130	360	570
Oct	130	0	700
Nov	130	0	830
Dec	130	700	260
Jan	130	0	390
Feb	130	0	520
Mar	130	0	650
Apr	130	0	780
May	130	0	910
Jun	130	0	1040

II. Example Illustrating Single-Item Analysis (Existing Accounts)

ASSUMPTIONS:

Disbursements:

$360 for school taxes disbursed on September 20

$1,200 for county property taxes:

$500 disbursed on July 25

$700 disbursed on December 10

Cushion: One-sixth of estimated annual disbursements

Settlement: May 15

First Payment: July 1

Step 1—Initial Trial Balance

	Single-item					
	Taxes			School taxes		
	pmt	disb	bal	pmt	disb	bal
June	0	0	0	0	0	0
July	100	500	-400	30	0	30
August	100	0	-300	30	0	60
September	100	0	-200	30	360	-270
October	100	0	-100	30	0	-240
November	100	0	0	30	0	-210
December	100	700	-600	30	0	-180
January	100	0	-500	30	0	-150
February	100	0	-400	30	0	-120
March	100	0	-300	30	0	-90
April	100	0	-200	30	0	-60
May	100	0	-100	30	0	-30
June	100	0	0	30	0	0

Step 2—Adjusted Trial Balance
(Increase Monthly Balances To Eliminate Negative Balances)

	Single-item					
	Taxes			School taxes		
	pmt	disb	bal	pmt	disb	bal
Jun	0	0	600	0	0	270
Jul	100	500	200	30	0	300
Aug	100	0	300	30	0	330
Sep	100	0	400	30	360	0
Oct	100	0	500	30	0	30
Nov	100	0	600	30	0	60
Dec	100	700	0	30	0	90
Jan	100	0	100	30	0	120
Feb	100	0	200	30	0	150
Mar	100	0	300	30	0	180
Apr	100	0	400	30	0	210
May	100	0	500	30	0	240
Jun	100	0	600	30	0	270

Step 3—Trial Balance With Cushion

	Single-Item					
	Taxes			School taxes		
	pmt	disb	bal	pmt	disb	bal
Jun	0	0	800	0	0	330
Jul	100	500	400	30	0	360
Aug	100	0	500	30	0	390
Sep	100	0	600	30	360	60
Oct	100	0	700	30	0	90
Nov	100	0	800	30	0	120
Dec	100	700	200	30	0	150
Jan	100	0	300	30	0	180
Feb	100	0	400	30	0	210
Mar	100	0	500	30	0	240
Apr	100	0	600	30	0	270
May	100	0	700	30	0	300
Jun	100	0	800	30	0	330

[59 Fed. Reg. 53,908 (Oct. 26, 1994); 60 Fed. Reg. 8816 (Feb. 15, 1995); 61 Fed. Reg. 29,255 (June 7, 1996); 61 Fed. Reg. 51,782 (Oct. 4, 1996); 61 Fed. Reg. 58,479 (Nov. 15, 1996); 73 Fed. Reg. 68,259 (Nov. 17, 2008)]

C.4 Selected Provisions of Regulation Z, 12 C.F.R. Part 226

Title 12—Banks and Banking

Chapter II—Federal Reserve System

Subchapter A—Board of Governors of the Federal Reserve System

Part 226—Truth in Lending (Regulation Z)

Subpart E—Special Rules for Certain Home Mortgage Transactions

12 C.F.R. § 226.36 Prohibited acts or practices in connection with credit secured by a consumer's principal dwelling.

[*This section was added by 73 Fed. Reg. 44,604 (July 30, 2008) and is effective Oct. 1, 2009.*]

(a) *Mortgage broker defined.* For purposes of this section, the term "mortgage broker" means a person, other than an employee of a creditor, who for compensation or other monetary gain, or in expectation of compensation or other monetary gain, arranges, negotiates, or otherwise obtains an extension of consumer credit for another person. The term includes a person meeting this definition, even if the consumer credit obligation is initially payable to such person, unless the person provides the funds for the transaction at consummation out of the person's own resources, out of deposits held by the person, or by drawing on a bona fide warehouse line of credit.

(b) *Misrepresentation of value of consumer's dwelling*—

(1) *Coercion of appraiser.* In connection with a consumer credit transaction secured by a consumer's principal dwelling, no creditor or mortgage broker, and no affiliate of a creditor or mortgage broker shall directly or indirectly coerce, influence, or otherwise encourage an appraiser to misstate or misrepresent the value of such dwelling.

(i) Examples of actions that violate this paragraph (b)(1) include:

(A) Implying to an appraiser that current or future retention of the appraiser depends on the amount at which the appraiser values a consumer's principal dwelling;

(B) Excluding an appraiser from consideration for future engagement because the appraiser reports a value of a consumer's principal dwelling that does not meet or exceed a minimum threshold;

(C) Telling an appraiser a minimum reported value of a consumer's principal dwelling that is needed to approve the loan;

(D) Failing to compensate an appraiser because the appraiser does not value a consumer's principal dwelling at or above a certain amount; and

(E) Conditioning an appraiser's compensation on loan consummation.

(ii) Examples of actions that do not violate this paragraph (b)(1) include:

(A) Asking an appraiser to consider additional information about a consumer's principal dwelling or about comparable properties;

(B) Requesting that an appraiser provide additional information about the basis for a valuation;

(C) Requesting that an appraiser correct factual errors in a valuation;

(D) Obtaining multiple appraisals of a consumer's principal dwelling, so long as the creditor adheres to a policy of selecting the most reliable appraisal, rather than the appraisal that states the highest value;

(E) Withholding compensation from an appraiser for breach of contract or substandard performance of services as provided by contract; and

(F) Taking action permitted or required by applicable federal or state statute, regulation, or agency guidance.

(2) *When extension of credit prohibited.* In connection with a consumer credit transaction secured by a consumer's principal dwelling, a creditor who knows, at or before loan consummation, of a violation of paragraph (b)(1) of this section in connection with an appraisal shall not extend credit based on such appraisal unless the creditor documents that it has acted with reasonable diligence to determine that the appraisal does not materially misstate or misrepresent the value of such dwelling.

(3) *Appraiser defined.* As used in this paragraph (b), an appraiser is a person who engages in the business of providing assessments of the value of dwellings. The term "appraiser" includes persons that employ, refer, or manage appraisers and affiliates of such persons.

(c) *Servicing practices.*

(1) In connection with a consumer credit transaction secured by a consumer's principal dwelling, no servicer shall—

(i) Fail to credit a payment to the consumer's loan account as of the date of receipt, except when a delay in crediting does not result in any charge to the consumer or in the reporting of negative information to a consumer reporting agency, or except as provided in paragraph (c)(2) of this section;

(ii) Impose on the consumer any late fee or delinquency charge in connection with a payment, when the only delinquency is attributable to late fees or delinquency charges assessed on an earlier payment, and the payment is otherwise a full payment for the applicable period and is paid on its due date or within any applicable grace period; or

(iii) Fail to provide, within a reasonable time after receiving a request from the consumer or any person acting on behalf of the consumer, an accurate statement of the total outstanding balance that would be required to satisfy the consumer's obligation in full as of a specified date.

(2) If a servicer specifies in writing requirements for the consumer to follow in making payments, but accepts a payment that does not conform to the requirements, the servicer shall credit the payment as of 5 days after receipt.

(3) For purposes of this paragraph (c), the terms "servicer" and "servicing" have the same meanings as provided in 24 CFR 3500.2(b), as amended.

(d) This section does not apply to a home equity line of credit subject to § 226.5b.

[73 Fed. Reg. 44,604 (July 30, 2008)]

C.5 Selected Provisions of the Servicemembers Civil Relief Act

50 U.S.C. App. §§ 501–596

[As enacted by Pub. L. No. 108-189, 117 Stat. 2835 (2003), unless otherwise noted.]

TITLE 50 APPENDIX—WAR AND NATIONAL DEFENSE

Servicemembers Civil Relief Act

* * *

Title I—General Provisions

§ 511. Definitions
§ 512. Jurisdiction and applicability of Act
§ 513. Protection of persons secondarily liable
§ 514. Extension of protections to citizens serving with allied forces

* * *

* * *

Title I—General Provisions

50 U.S.C. App. § 511. Definitions

For the purposes of this Act:

(1) Servicemember

The term "servicemember" means a member of the uniformed services, as that term is defined in section 101(a)(5) of title 10, United States Code.

(2) Military service

The term "military service" means—

(A) in the case of a servicemember who is a member of the Army, Navy, Air Force, Marine Corps, or Coast Guard—

(i) active duty, as defined in section 101(d)(1) of title 10, United States Code, and

(ii) in the case of a member of the National Guard, includes service under a call to active service authorized by the President or the Secretary of Defense for a period of more than 30 consecutive days under section 502(f) of title 32, United States Code, for purposes of responding to a national emergency declared by the President and supported by Federal funds;

(B) in the case of a servicemember who is a commissioned officer of the Public Health Service or the National Oceanic and Atmospheric Administration, active service; and

(C) any period during which a servicemember is absent from duty on account of sickness, wounds, leave, or other lawful cause.

(3) Period of military service

The term "period of military service" means the period beginning on the date on which a servicemember enters military service and ending on the date on which the servicemember is released from military service or dies while in military service.

(4) Dependent

The term "dependent," with respect to a servicemember, means—

(A) the servicemember's spouse;

(B) the servicemember's child (as defined in section 101(4) of title 38, United States Code); or

(C) an individual for whom the servicemember provided more than one-half of the individual's support for 180 days immediately preceding an application for relief under this Act.

(5) Court

The term "court" means a court or an administrative agency of the United States or of any State (including any political subdivision of a State), whether or not a court or administrative agency of record.

(6) State

The term "State" includes—

(A) a commonwealth, territory, or possession of the United States; and

(B) the District of Columbia.

(7) Secretary concerned

The term "Secretary concerned"—

(A) with respect to a member of the armed forces, has the meaning given that term in section 101(a)(9) of title 10, United States Code;

(B) with respect to a commissioned officer of the Public Health Service, means the Secretary of Health and Human Services; and

(C) with respect to a commissioned officer of the National Oceanic and Atmospheric Administration, means the Secretary of Commerce.

(8) Motor vehicle

The term "motor vehicle" has the meaning given that term in section 30102(a)(6) of title 49, United States Code.

(9) Judgment

The term "judgment" means any judgment, decree, order, or ruling, final or temporary.

[As amended by Pub. L. No. 108-454, 118 Stat. 3624 (2004).]

50 U.S.C. App. § 512. Jurisdiction and applicability of Act

(a) Jurisdiction

This Act applies to—

(1) the United States;

(2) each of the States, including the political subdivisions thereof; and

(3) all territory subject to the jurisdiction of the United States.

(b) Applicability to proceedings

This Act applies to any judicial or administrative proceeding commenced in any court or agency in any jurisdiction subject to this Act. This Act does not apply to criminal proceedings.

(c) Court in which application may be made

When under this Act any application is required to be made to a court in which no proceeding has already been commenced with respect to the matter, such application may be made to any court which would otherwise have jurisdiction over the matter.

50 U.S.C. App. § 513. Protection of persons secondarily liable

(a) Extension of protection when actions stayed, postponed, or suspended

Whenever pursuant to this Act a court stays, postpones, or suspends (1) the enforcement of an obligation or liability, (2) the prosecution of a suit or proceeding, (3) the entry or enforcement of an order, writ, judgment, or decree, or (4) the performance of any other act, the court may likewise grant such a stay, postponement, or suspension to a surety, guarantor, endorser, accommodation maker, comaker, or other person who is or may be primarily or secondarily subject to the obligation or liability the performance or enforcement of which is stayed, postponed, or suspended.

(b) Vacation or set-aside of judgments

When a judgment or decree is vacated or set aside, in whole or in part, pursuant to this Act, the court may also set aside or vacate, as the case may be, the judgment or decree as to a surety, guarantor, endorser, accommodation maker, comaker, or other person who is or may be primarily or secondarily liable on the contract or liability for the enforcement of the judgment or decree.

(c) Bail bond not to be enforced during period of military service

A court may not enforce a bail bond during the period of military service of the principal on the bond when military service prevents the surety from obtaining the attendance of the principal. The court may discharge the surety and exonerate the bail, in accordance with principles of equity and justice, during or after the period of military service of the principal.

(d) Waiver of rights

(1) Waivers not precluded

This Act does not prevent a waiver in writing by a surety, guarantor, endorser, accommodation maker, comaker, or other person (whether primarily or secondarily liable on an obligation or liability) of the protections provided under subsections (a) and (b). Any such waiver is effective only if it is executed as an instrument separate from the obligation or liability with respect to which it applies.

(2) Waiver invalidated upon entrance to military service

If a waiver under paragraph (1) is executed by an individual who after the execution of the waiver enters military service, or by a dependent of an individual who after the execution of the waiver enters military service, the waiver is not valid after the beginning of the period of such military service unless the waiver was executed by such individual or dependent during the period specified in section 106 [section 516 of this Appendix].

50 U.S.C. App. § 514. Extension of protections to citizens serving with allied forces

A citizen of the United States who is serving with the forces of a nation with which the United States is allied in the prosecution of a war or military action is entitled to the relief and protections provided under this Act if that service with the allied force is similar to military service as defined in this Act. The relief and protections provided to such citizen shall terminate on the date of discharge or release from such service.

* * *

50 U.S.C. App. § 516. Extension of rights and protections to reserves ordered to report for military service and to persons ordered to report for induction

(a) Reserves ordered to report for military service

A member of a reserve component who is ordered to report for military service is entitled to the rights and protections of this title and titles II and III [of this Appendix] during the period beginning on the date of the member's receipt of the order and ending on the date on which the member reports for military service (or, if the order is revoked before the member so reports, or the date on which the order is revoked).

(b) Persons ordered to report for induction

A person who has been ordered to report for induction under the Military Selective Service Act (50 U.S.C. App. 451 et seq.) is entitled to the rights and protections provided a servicemember under this title and titles II and III [of this Appendix] during the period beginning on the date of receipt of the order for induction and ending on the date on which the person reports for induction (or, if the order to report for induction is revoked before the date on which the person reports for induction, on the date on which the order is revoked).

50 U.S.C. App. § 517. Waiver of rights pursuant to written agreement

(a) In general

A servicemember may waive any of the rights and protections provided by this Act. In the case of a waiver that permits an action described in subsection (b), the waiver is effective only if made pursuant to a written agreement of the parties that is executed during or after the servicemember's period of military service. The written agreement shall specify the legal instrument to which the waiver applies and, if the servicemember is not a party to that instrument, the servicemember concerned. Any such waiver that applies to an action listed in subsection (b) of this section is effective only if it is in writing and is executed as an instrument separate from the obligation or liability to which it applies.

(b) Actions requiring waivers in writing

The requirement in subsection (a) for a written waiver applies to the following:

(1) The modification, termination, or cancellation of—

(A) a contract, lease, or bailment; or

(B) an obligation secured by a mortgage, trust, deed, lien, or other security in the nature of a mortgage.

(2) The repossession, retention, foreclosure, sale, forfeiture, or taking possession of property that—

(A) is security for any obligation; or

(B) was purchased or received under a contract, lease, or bailment.

(c) Prominent display of certain contract rights waivers

Any waiver in writing of a right or protection provided by this Act [sections 501 to 596 of this Appendix] that applies to a contract, lease, or similar legal instrument must be in at least 12 point type.

(d) Coverage of periods after orders received

For the purposes of this section—

(1) a person to whom section 106 [section 516 of this Appendix] applies shall be considered to be a servicemember; and

(2) the period with respect to such a person specified in subsection (a) or (b), as the case may be, of section 106 [section 516 of this Appendix] shall be considered to be a period of military service.

[As amended by Pub. L. No. 108-454, 118 Stat. 3624 (2004).]

50 U.S.C. App. § 518. Exercise of rights under Act not to affect certain future financial transactions

Application by a servicemember for, or receipt by a servicemember of, a stay, postponement, or suspension pursuant to this Act in the payment of a tax, fine, penalty, insurance premium, or other civil obligation or liability of that servicemember shall not itself (without regard to other considerations) provide the basis for any of the following:

(1) A determination by a lender or other person that the servicemember is unable to pay the civil obligation or liability in accordance with its terms.

(2) With respect to a credit transaction between a creditor and the servicemember—

(A) a denial or revocation of credit by the creditor;

(B) a change by the creditor in the terms of an existing credit arrangement; or

(C) a refusal by the creditor to grant credit to the servicemember in substantially the amount or on substantially the terms requested.

(3) An adverse report relating to the creditworthiness of the servicemember by or to a person engaged in the practice of assembling or evaluating consumer credit information.

(4) A refusal by an insurer to insure the servicemember.

(5) An annotation in a servicemember's record by a creditor or a person engaged in the practice of assembling or evaluating consumer credit information, identifying the servicemember as a member of the National Guard or a reserve component.

(6) A change in the terms offered or conditions required for the issuance of insurance.

50 U.S.C. App. § 519. Legal representatives

(a) Representative

A legal representative of a servicemember for purposes of this Act [sections 501 to 596 of this Appendix] is either of the following:

(1) An attorney acting on the behalf of a servicemember.

(2) An individual possessing a power of attorney.

(b) Application

Whenever the term "servicemember" is used in this Act [sections 501 to 596 of this Appendix], such term shall be treated as including a reference to a legal representative of the servicemember.

Title II—General Relief

50 U.S.C. App. § 521. Protection of servicemembers against default judgments

(a) Applicability of section

This section applies to any civil action or proceeding, including any child custody proceeding, in which the defendant does not make an appearance.

(b) Affidavit requirement

(1) Plaintiff to file affidavit

In any action or proceeding covered by this section, the court, before entering judgment for the plaintiff, shall require the plaintiff to file with the court an affidavit—

(A) stating whether or not the defendant is in military service and showing necessary facts to support the affidavit; or

(B) if the plaintiff is unable to determine whether or not the defendant is in military service, stating that the plaintiff is unable to determine whether or not the defendant is in military service.

(2) Appointment of attorney to represent defendant in military service

If in an action covered by this section it appears that the defendant is in military service, the court may not enter a judgment until after the court appoints an attorney to represent the defendant. If an attorney appointed under this section to represent a servicemember cannot locate the servicemember, actions by the attorney in the case shall not waive any defense of the servicemember or otherwise bind the servicemember.

(3) Defendant's military status not ascertained by affidavit

If based upon the affidavits filed in such an action, the court is unable to determine whether the defendant is in military service, the court, before entering judgment, may require the plaintiff to file a bond in an amount approved by the court. If the defendant is later found to be in military service, the bond shall be available to indemnify the defendant against any loss or damage the defendant may suffer by reason of any judgment for the plaintiff against the defendant, should the judgment be set aside in whole or in part. The bond shall remain in effect until expiration of the time for appeal and setting aside of a judgment under applicable Federal or State law or regulation or under any applicable ordinance of a political subdivision of a State. The court may issue such orders or enter such judgments as the court determines necessary to protect the rights of the defendant under this Act.

(4) Satisfaction of requirement for affidavit

The requirement for an affidavit under paragraph (1) may be satisfied by a statement, declaration, verification, or certificate, in writing, subscribed and certified or declared to be true under penalty of perjury.

(c) Penalty for making or using false affidavit

A person who makes or uses an affidavit permitted under subsection (b) (or a statement, declaration, verification, or certificate as authorized under subsection (b)(4)) knowing it to be false, shall be fined as provided in title 18, United States Code, or imprisoned for not more than one year, or both.

(d) Stay of proceedings

In an action covered by this section in which the defendant is in military service, the court shall grant a stay of proceedings for a minimum period of 90 days under this subsection upon application of counsel, or on the court's own motion, if the court determines that—

(1) there may be a defense to the action and a defense cannot be presented without the presence of the defendant; or

(2) after due diligence, counsel has been unable to contact the defendant or otherwise determine if a meritorious defense exists.

(e) Inapplicability of section 202 procedures

A stay of proceedings under subsection (d) shall not be controlled by procedures or requirements under section 202 [section 522 of this Appendix].

(f) Section 202 protection

If a servicemember who is a defendant in an action covered by this section receives actual notice of the action, the servicemember may request a stay of proceeding under section 202 [section 522 of this Appendix].

(g) Vacation or setting aside of default judgments

(1) Authority for court to vacate or set aside judgment

If a default judgment is entered in an action covered by this section against a servicemember during the servicemember's period of military service (or within 60 days after termination of or release from such military service), the court entering the judgment shall, upon application by or on behalf of the servicemember, reopen the judgment for the purpose of allowing the servicemember to defend the action if it appears that—

(A) the servicemember was materially affected by reason of that military service in making a defense to the action; and

(B) the servicemember has a meritorious or legal defense to the action or some part of it.

(2) Time for filing application

An application under this subsection must be filed not later than 90 days after the date of the termination of or release from military service.

(h) Protection of bona fide purchaser

If a court vacates, sets aside, or reverses a default judgment against a servicemember and the vacating, setting aside, or reversing is because of a provision of this Act, that action shall not impair a right or title acquired by a bona fide purchaser for value under the default judgment.

[As amended by Pub. L. No. 110-181, 122 Stat. 128 (2008).]

50 U.S.C. App. § 522. Stay of proceedings when servicemember has notice

(a) Applicability of section

This section applies to any civil action or proceeding, including any child custody proceeding, in which the plaintiff or defendant at the time of filing an application under this section—

(1) is in military service or is within 90 days after termination of or release from military service; and

(2) has received notice of the action or proceeding.

(b) Stay of proceedings

(1) Authority for stay

At any stage before final judgment in a civil action or proceeding in which a servicemember described in subsection (a) is a party, the court may on its own motion and shall, upon application by the servicemember, stay the action for a period of not less than 90 days, if the conditions in paragraph (2) are met.

(2) Conditions for stay

An application for a stay under paragraph (1) shall include the following:

(A) A letter or other communication setting forth facts stating the manner in which current military duty requirements materially affect the servicemember's ability to appear and stating a date when the servicemember will be available to appear.

(B) A letter or other communication from the servicemember's commanding officer stating that the servicemember's current military duty prevents appearance and that military leave is not authorized for the servicemember at the time of the letter.

(c) Application not a waiver of defenses

An application for a stay under this section does not constitute an appearance for jurisdictional purposes and does not constitute a waiver of any substantive or procedural defense (including a defense relating to lack of personal jurisdiction).

(d) Additional stay

(1) Application

A servicemember who is granted a stay of a civil action or proceeding under subsection (b) may apply for an additional stay based on continuing material affect of military duty on the servicemember's ability to appear. Such an application may be made by the servicemember at the time of the initial application under subsection (b) or when it appears that the servicemember is unavailable to prosecute or defend the action. The same information required under subsection (b)(2) shall be included in an application under this subsection.

(2) Appointment of counsel when additional stay refused
If the court refuses to grant an additional stay of proceedings under paragraph (1), the court shall appoint counsel to represent the servicemember in the action or proceeding.

(e) Coordination with section 201 [section 521 of this Appendix]
A servicemember who applies for a stay under this section and is unsuccessful may not seek the protections afforded by section 201 [section 521 of this Appendix].

(f) Inapplicability to section 301 [section 531 of this Appendix]
The protections of this section do not apply to section 301 [section 531 of this Appendix].

[As amended by Pub. L. No. 108-454, 118 Stat. 3624 (2004) and by Pub. L. No. 110-181, 122 Stat. 128 (2008).]

50 U.S.C. App. § 523. Fines and penalties under contracts

(a) Prohibition of penalties
When an action for compliance with the terms of a contract is stayed pursuant to this Act, a penalty shall not accrue for failure to comply with the terms of the contract during the period of the stay.

(b) Reduction or waiver of fines or penalties
If a servicemember fails to perform an obligation arising under a contract and a penalty is incurred arising from that nonperformance, a court may reduce or waive the fine or penalty if—

(1) the servicemember was in military service at the time the fine or penalty was incurred; and

(2) the ability of the servicemember to perform the obligation was materially affected by such military service.

* * *

50 U.S.C. App. § 525. Duration and term of stays; codefendants not in service

(a) Period of stay
A stay of an action, proceeding, attachment, or execution made pursuant to the provisions of this Act by a court may be ordered for the period of military service and 90 days thereafter, or for any part of that period. The court may set the terms and amounts for such installment payments as is considered reasonable by the court.

(b) Codefendants
If the servicemember is a codefendant with others who are not in military service and who are not entitled to the relief and protections provided under this Act, the plaintiff may proceed against those other defendants with the approval of the court.

(c) Inapplicability of section
This section does not apply to sections 202 and 701 [sections 522 and 591 of this Appendix].

50 U.S.C. App. § 526. Statute of limitations

(a) Tolling of statutes of limitation during military service
The period of a servicemember's military service may not be included in computing any period limited by law, regulation, or order for the bringing of any action or proceeding in a court, or in any board, bureau, commission, department, or other agency of a State (or political subdivision of a State) or the United States by or against the servicemember or the servicemember's heirs, executors, administrators, or assigns.

(b) Redemption of real property
A period of military service may not be included in computing any period provided by law for the redemption of real property sold or forfeited to enforce an obligation, tax, or assessment.

(c) Inapplicability to internal revenue laws
This section does not apply to any period of limitation prescribed by or under the internal revenue laws of the United States.

50 U.S.C. App. § 527. Maximum rate of interest on debts incurred before military service

(a) Interest rate limitation

(1) Limitation to 6 percent
An obligation or liability bearing interest at a rate in excess of 6 percent per year that is incurred by a servicemember, or the servicemember and the servicemember's spouse jointly, before the servicemember enters military service shall not bear interest at a rate in excess of 6 percent—

(A) during the period of military service and one year thereafter, in the case of an obligation or liability consisting of a mortgage, trust deed, or other security in the nature of a mortgage; or

(B) during the period of military service, in the case of any other obligation or liability.

(2) Forgiveness of interest in excess of 6 percent
Interest at a rate in excess of 6 percent per year that would otherwise be incurred but for the prohibition in paragraph (1) is forgiven.

(3) Prevention of acceleration of principal
The amount of any periodic payment due from a servicemember under the terms of the instrument that created an obligation or liability covered by this section shall be reduced by the amount of the interest forgiven under paragraph (2) that is allocable to the period for which such payment is made.

(b) Implementation of limitation

(1) Written notice to creditor
In order for an obligation or liability of a servicemember to be subject to the interest rate limitation in subsection (a), the servicemember shall provide to the creditor written notice and a copy of the military orders calling the servicemember to military service and any orders further extending military service, not later than 180 days after the date of the servicemember's termination or release from military service.

(2) Limitation effective as of date of order to active duty

Upon receipt of written notice and a copy of orders calling a servicemember to military service, the creditor shall treat the debt in accordance with subsection (a), effective as of the date on which the servicemember is called to military service.

(c) Creditor protection

A court may grant a creditor relief from the limitations of this section if, in the opinion of the court, the ability of the servicemember to pay interest upon the obligation or liability at a rate in excess of 6 percent per year is not materially affected by reason of the servicemember's military service.

(d) Definitions

In this section:

(1) Interest

The term "interest" includes service charges, renewal charges, fees, or any other charges (except bona fide insurance) with respect to an obligation or liability.

(2) Obligation or liability

The term "obligation or liability" includes an obligation or liability consisting of a mortgage, trust deed, or other security in the nature of a mortgage.

(e) Penalty

Whoever knowingly violates subsection (a) shall be fined as provided in title 18, United States Code, imprisoned for not more than one year, or both.

(f) Preservation of other remedies

The penalties provided under subsection (e) are in addition to and do not preclude any other remedy available under law to a person claiming relief under this section, including any award for consequential or punitive damages.

[As amended by Pub. L. No. 110-289, § 2203(b), 122 Stat. 2849 (2008) and by Pub. L. No. 110-389, § 807, 122 Stat. 4189 (2008).]

Title III—Rent, Installment Contracts, Mortgages, Liens, Assignment, Leases

50 U.S.C. App. § 531. Evictions and distress

(a) Court-ordered eviction

(1) In general

Except by court order, a landlord (or another person with paramount title) may not—

(A) evict a servicemember, or the dependents of a servicemember, during a period of military service of the servicemember, from premises—

(i) that are occupied or intended to be occupied primarily as a residence; and

(ii) for which the monthly rent does not exceed $2,400, as adjusted under paragraph (2) for years after 2003; or

(B) subject such premises to a distress during the period of military service.

(2) Housing price inflation adjustment

(A) For calendar years beginning with 2004, the amount in effect under paragraph (1)(A)(ii) shall be increased by the housing price inflation adjustment for the calendar year involved.

(B) For purposes of this paragraph—

(i) The housing price inflation adjustment for any calendar year is the percentage change (if any) by which—

(I) the CPI housing component for November of the preceding calendar year, exceeds

(II) the CPI housing component for November of 1984.

(ii) The term "CPI housing component" means the index published by the Bureau of Labor Statistics of the Department of Labor known as the Consumer Price Index, All Urban Consumers, Rent of Primary Residence, U.S. City Average.

(3) Publication of housing price inflation adjustment

The Secretary of Defense shall cause to be published in the Federal Register each year the amount in effect under paragraph (1)(A)(ii) for that year following the housing price inflation adjustment for that year pursuant to paragraph (2). Such publication shall be made for a year not later than 60 days after such adjustment is made for that year.

(b) Stay of execution

(1) Court authority

Upon an application for eviction or distress with respect to premises covered by this section, the court may on its own motion and shall, if a request is made by or on behalf of a servicemember whose ability to pay the agreed rent is materially affected by military service—

(A) stay the proceedings for a period of 90 days, unless in the opinion of the court, justice and equity require a longer or shorter period of time; or

(B) adjust the obligation under the lease to preserve the interests of all parties.

(2) Relief to landlord

If a stay is granted under paragraph (1), the court may grant to the landlord (or other person with paramount title) such relief as equity may require.

(c) Penalties

(1) Misdemeanor

Except as provided in subsection (a), a person who knowingly takes part in an eviction or distress described in subsection (a), or who knowingly attempts to do so, shall be fined as provided in title 18, United States Code, or imprisoned for not more than one year, or both.

(2) Preservation of other remedies and rights

The remedies and rights provided under this section are in addition to and do not preclude any remedy for wrongful conversion (or wrongful eviction) otherwise available under the law to the person claiming relief under this section, including any award for consequential and punitive damages.

(d) Rent allotment from pay of servicemember

To the extent required by a court order related to property which is the subject of a court action under this section, the Secretary concerned shall make an allotment from the pay of a servicemember to satisfy the terms of such order, except that any such allotment shall be subject to regulations prescribed by the Secretary concerned establishing the maximum amount of pay of servicemembers that may be allotted under this subsection.

(e) Limitation of applicability

Section 202 [section 522 of this Appendix] is not applicable to this section.

50 U.S.C. App. § 532. Protection under installment contracts for purchase or lease

(a) Protection upon breach of contract

(1) Protection after entering military service

After a servicemember enters military service, a contract by the servicemember for—

(A) the purchase of real or personal property (including a motor vehicle); or

(B) the lease or bailment of such property,

may not be rescinded or terminated for a breach of terms of the contract occurring before or during that person's military service, nor may the property be repossessed for such breach without a court order.

(2) Applicability

This section applies only to a contract for which a deposit or installment has been paid by the servicemember before the servicemember enters military service.

(b) Penalties

(1) Misdemeanor

A person who knowingly resumes possession of property in violation of subsection (a), or in violation of section 107 of this Act [section 517 of this Appendix], or who knowingly attempts to do so, shall be fined as provided in title 18, United States Code, or imprisoned for not more than one year, or both.

(2) Preservation of other remedies and rights

The remedies and rights provided under this section are in addition to and do not preclude any remedy for wrongful conversion otherwise available under law to the person claiming relief under this section, including any award for consequential and punitive damages.

(c) Authority of court

In a hearing based on this section, the court—

(1) may order repayment to the servicemember of all or part of the prior installments or deposits as a condition of terminating the contract and resuming possession of the property;

(2) may, on its own motion, and shall on application by a servicemember when the servicemember's ability to comply with the contract is materially affected by military service, stay the proceedings for a period of time as, in the opinion of the court, justice and equity require; or

(3) may make other disposition as is equitable to preserve the interests of all parties.

50 U.S.C. App. § 533. Mortgages and trust deeds

(a) Mortgage as security

This section applies only to an obligation on real or personal property owned by a servicemember that—

(1) originated before the period of the servicemember's military service and for which the servicemember is still obligated; and

(2) is secured by a mortgage, trust deed, or other security in the nature of a mortgage.

(b) Stay of proceedings and adjustment of obligation

In an action filed during, or within 9 months[1] after, a servicemember's period of military service to enforce an obligation described in subsection (a), the court may after a hearing and on its own motion and shall upon application by a servicemember when the servicemember's ability to comply with the obligation is materially affected by military service—

(1) stay the proceedings for a period of time as justice and equity require, or

(2) adjust the obligation to preserve the interests of all parties.

(c) Sale or foreclosure

A sale, foreclosure, or seizure of property for a breach of an obligation described in subsection (a) shall not be valid if made during, or within 9 months[2] after, the period of the servicemember's military service except—

(1) upon a court order granted before such sale, foreclosure, or seizure with a return made and approved by the court; or

(2) if made pursuant to an agreement as provided in section 107 [section 517 of this Appendix].

(d) Penalties

(1) Misdemeanor

A person who knowingly makes or causes to be made a sale, foreclosure, or seizure of property that is prohibited by subsection (c), or who knowingly attempts to do so, shall be fined as provided in title 18, United States Code, or imprisoned for not more than one year, or both.

(2) Preservation of other remedies

The remedies and rights provided under this section are in addition to and do not preclude any remedy for wrongful conversion otherwise available under law to the person claiming relief under this section, including consequential and punitive damages.

[As amended by Pub. L. No. 110-289, § 2203(a), 122 Stat. 2849 (2008).]

50 U.S.C. App. § 534. Settlement of stayed cases relating to personal property

(a) Appraisal of property

When a stay is granted pursuant to this Act in a proceeding to foreclose a mortgage on or to repossess personal property, or to rescind or terminate a contract for the purchase of personal property, the court may appoint three disinterested parties to appraise the property.

---

1 *Editor's Note*: This amendment, made by Pub. L. No. 110-289, 122 Stat. 2849 (2008), is effective for the period July 30, 2008 until December 31, 2010. The period will return to 90 days on January 1, 2011.

2 *Editor's Note*: This amendment, made by Pub. L. No. 110-289, 122 Stat. 2849 (2008), is effective for the period July 30, 2008 until December 31, 2010. The period will return to 90 days on January 1, 2011.

(b) Equity payment
Based on the appraisal, and if undue hardship to the servicemember's dependents will not result, the court may order that the amount of the servicemember's equity in the property be paid to the servicemember, or the servicemember's dependents, as a condition of foreclosing the mortgage, repossessing the property, or rescinding or terminating the contract.

* * *

50 U.S.C. App. § 538. Extension of protections to dependents

Upon application to a court, a dependent of a servicemember is entitled to the protections of this title if the dependent's ability to comply with a lease, contract, bailment, or other obligation is materially affected by reason of the servicemember's military service.

* * *

Title V—Taxes and Public Lands

50 U.S.C. App. § 561. Taxes respecting personal property, money, credits, and real property

(a) Application
This section applies in any case in which a tax or assessment, whether general or special (other than a tax on personal income), falls due and remains unpaid before or during a period of military service with respect to a servicemember's—
(1) personal property (including motor vehicles); or
(2) real property occupied for dwelling, professional, business, or agricultural purposes by a servicemember or the servicemember's dependents or employees—
(A) before the servicemember's entry into military service; and
(B) during the time the tax or assessment remains unpaid.

(b) Sale of property
(1) Limitation on sale of property to enforce tax assessment
Property described in subsection (a) may not be sold to enforce the collection of such tax or assessment except by court order and upon the determination by the court that military service does not materially affect the servicemember's ability to pay the unpaid tax or assessment.
(2) Stay of court proceedings
A court may stay a proceeding to enforce the collection of such tax or assessment, or sale of such property, during a period of military service of the servicemember and for a period not more than 180 days after the termination of, or release of the servicemember from, military service.

(c) Redemption
When property described in subsection (a) is sold or forfeited to enforce the collection of a tax or assessment, a servicemember shall have the right to redeem or commence an action to redeem the servicemember's property during the period of military service or within 180 days after termination of or release from military service. This subsection may not be construed to shorten any period provided by the law of a State (including any political subdivision of a State) for redemption.

(d) Interest on tax or assessment
Whenever a servicemember does not pay a tax or assessment on property described in subsection (a) when due, the amount of the tax or assessment due and unpaid shall bear interest until paid at the rate of 6 percent per year. An additional penalty or interest shall not be incurred by reason of nonpayment. A lien for such unpaid tax or assessment may include interest under this subsection.

(e) Joint ownership application
This section applies to all forms of property described in subsection (a) owned individually by a servicemember or jointly by a servicemember and a dependent or dependents.

* * *

Title VII—Further Relief

50 U.S.C. App. § 591. Anticipatory relief

(a) Application for relief
A servicemember may, during military service or within 180 days of termination of or release from military service, apply to a court for relief—
(1) from any obligation or liability incurred by the servicemember before the servicemember's military service; or
(2) from a tax or assessment falling due before or during the servicemember's military service.

(b) Tax liability or assessment
In a case covered by subsection (a), the court may, if the ability of the servicemember to comply with the terms of such obligation or liability or pay such tax or assessment has been materially affected by reason of military service, after appropriate notice and hearing, grant the following relief:
(1) Stay of enforcement of real estate contracts
(A) In the case of an obligation payable in installments under a contract for the purchase of real estate, or secured by a mortgage or other instrument in the nature of a mortgage upon real estate, the court may grant a stay of the enforcement of the obligation—
(i) during the servicemember's period of military service; and
(ii) from the date of termination of or release from military service, or from the date of application if made after termination of or release from military service.
(B) Any stay under this paragraph shall be—
(i) for a period equal to the remaining life of the installment contract or other instrument, plus a period of time equal to the period of military service of the servicemember, or any part of such combined period; and

(ii) subject to payment of the balance of the principal and accumulated interest due and unpaid at the date of termination or release from the applicant's military service or from the date of application in equal installments during the combined period at the rate of interest on the unpaid balance prescribed in the contract or other instrument evidencing the obligation, and subject to other terms as may be equitable.

(2) Stay of enforcement of other contracts

(A) In the case of any other obligation, liability, tax, or assessment, the court may grant a stay of enforcement—

(i) during the servicemember's military service; and

(ii) from the date of termination of or release from military service, or from the date of application if made after termination or release from military service.

(B) Any stay under this paragraph shall be—

(i) for a period of time equal to the period of the servicemember's military service or any part of such period; and

(ii) subject to payment of the balance of principal and accumulated interest due and unpaid at the date of termination or release from military service, or the date of application, in equal periodic installments during this extended period at the rate of interest as may be prescribed for this obligation, liability, tax, or assessment, if paid when due, and subject to other terms as may be equitable.

(c) Affect of stay on fine or penalty

When a court grants a stay under this section, a fine or penalty shall not accrue on the obligation, liability, tax, or assessment for the period of compliance with the terms and conditions of the stay.

Appendix D Summary of State Mortgage Servicing, Payoff Statement, and Mortgage Discharge Laws

This appendix is a summary of individual state laws relating to the servicing of mortgages. Appendix D.1 summarizes state laws that apply generally to servicing. It includes state laws that require notice of the transfer of servicing, plus state restrictions on escrow accounts, including required notices and requirements relating to the payment of interest and handling of funds in the account. It also summarizes state laws giving borrowers the right to make inquiries about their mortgage or escrow account. (State laws that require a prompt response to payoff statement requests are summarized in Appendix D.2, however.) It concludes with a description of servicing requirements found in any high-cost loan law in the state.

In recent years, some states have enacted laws requiring servicers to engage in loss mitigation before foreclosing on a consumer's home mortgage, and to participate in mediation programs and mandatory conferences. These laws are not collected in Appendix D but are summarized in Appendix E.2, *infra*.

Appendix D.2 summarizes one particular type of law: state laws that require a prompt response when a mortgage debtor requests a payoff statement. Appendix D.3 summarizes state laws that require lenders to record a satisfaction or discharge of the mortgage promptly after payoff.

Practitioners should use this appendix for easy reference to the laws of their state, and to compare their state's laws with those of other states. But practitioners should not use these summaries to the exclusion of the actual statutory and regulatory materials. Note also that this appendix only analyzes the statutory language itself, and does not include judicial interpretations of that language. In addition, because state servicing laws are typically not codified as part of a single statutory scheme and are often scattered among several different statutes, this appendix does not purport to provide a comprehensive summary of all state servicing laws.

As in all areas of state regulation of lenders, practitioners should be aware that some or all of the provisions in these state servicing statutes or regulations may not apply to a particular entity either by the terms of statute itself or as a result of federal preemption. A discussion of federal preemption of state servicing laws can be found in §§ 8.3.1, and 8.4, *supra*.

D.1 State Mortgage Servicing Laws

ALASKA

Alaska Stat. § 18.56.135

Scope: Mortgage loans purchased by the Alaska Housing Finance Corporation (AHFC) under a residential loan program authorized by this statute and serviced by an institution other than the AHFC.

Exclusions: None specified.

Transfer Notice Requirements: Transferor lender must notify borrower within ten days of actual sale date of servicing. Notification must include name, address, and telephone number of person who will assume responsibility for servicing and accept payments; detailed written financial breakdown of the loan, including interest rate, monthly payment, and current escrow balance. Transferee servicer shall, within twenty days after due date of first payment, notify borrower of the name, address and phone number of the person who can provide information about the servicing of the loan, and any changes regarding loan escrow amount or loan servicing requirements, including interest rate, monthly payment, and current escrow balance.

Borrower Inquiries: Servicer must respond within fifteen days to written request for information. Response must include telephone number of representative who can assist borrower.

Escrow Requirements:

Restrictions: None specified.

Recordkeeping and notice: If funds in escrow insufficient, must promptly notify borrower.
Handling of funds: Must make tax and insurance payments in timely manner; if funds in escrow insufficient, may make payment on behalf of borrower.
Interest: None specified.
Additional Requirements: Transferee servicer shall provide corrected coupon or payment books, if used.
Private Remedies: None specified.
State Remedies: None specified.
Special Servicing Requirements for High-Cost Loans: None.

ARIZONA

Ariz. Rev. Stat. Ann. § 6-946 (Mortgage Bankers); Ariz. Rev. Stat. Ann. § 33-747

Scope: Mortgage bankers, defined as persons who for compensation, directly or indirectly make or negotiate, or offer to make or negotiate, mortgage loans or mortgage banking loans. § 6-941.
Exclusions: Persons regulated under other state or federal law, such as banks, trust companies, savings and loan associations, credit unions, insurance companies; lawyers not principally engaged in mortgage banking; certain nonprofit corporations; certain small investors not in business of mortgage banking. § 6-942.
Transfer Notice Requirements: At time of closing, mortgage banker must provide all disclosures required by RESPA. § 6-946; *see also* § 6-906 (same provision applicable to mortgage brokers).
Borrower Inquiries: Not specified, but see Appx. D.2, *infra*, for payoff statement requirements.
Escrow Requirements:
Restrictions: Estimated payments shall be such that the amount collected during each period will approximate the actual amount due for each category of payment (taxes, insurance premiums, and other charges).
Recordkeeping and notice: All periodic payments out of escrow shall be accounted for annually to the borrower. § 6-946.
Handling of funds: Mortgage banker shall promptly pay all periodic payments to the extent monies have been collected for payment. § 6-946.
Interest: None specified.
Additional Requirements: Separate statute covering contract for deed transactions provides that lender may replace account servicing agent at any time, by sending written notice, in prescribed form, to borrower, old servicer, and new servicer, and recording the change with the deed. Required notification includes only name and address of servicer, and description of property. § 33-747.
Private Remedies: None specified.
State Remedies: None specified.
Special Servicing Requirements for High-Cost Loans: None.

ARKANSAS

Ark. Code Ann. §§ 23-39-501 to 23-39-518 (Fair Mortgage Lending Act)

Scope: Mortgage bankers, defined as persons who engage in the business of making loans primarily secured by mortgage, deed of trust, reverse mortgage, or other equivalent consensual security interest on real property. Mortgage servicers, defined as persons who, under contract with mortgage banker, receive payments from borrowers for mortgage loan, or taxes and insurance associated with mortgage loan. § 23-39-502.
Exclusions: State or federally chartered banks, credit unions, trust companies, industrial loan companies, small business investment corporations, real estate investment trusts, certain real estate brokers, nonprofit corporations, attorneys, and government agencies, lenders, servicers, etc. whose only loans in Arkansas are nonresidential (i.e., other than one-to-four family residential). § 23-39-502.
Transfer Notice Requirements: None specified.
Borrower Inquiries: Not specified.
Escrow Requirements:
Restrictions: None specified.
Recordkeeping and notice: None specified.
Handling of funds: Mortgage bankers and servicers must maintain segregated escrow account, in a federally insured financial institution. § 23-39-511. Must safeguard and account for any money received for, from, or on account of the borrower, or not entitled to retain; must follow reasonable instructions from the borrower; must not fail to disburse funds in accordance with agreement to service mortgage loan. §§ 23-39-510, 23-39-513.
Interest: None specified.
Additional Requirements: Credit union must maintain escrow account as a segregated bank account for payment of taxes and casualty insurance on mortgaged property; must maintain detailed ledger accounts for each escrow account. 003-14-001 Ark. Code R. §16(G). Mortgage bankers and servicers shall submit audited financial statements for prior fiscal year with annual license renewal. § 23-39-506. Managing principal officer shall have at least three years experience and meet other requirements set by commissioner. § 23-39-508.
Private Remedies: None specified.
State Remedies: Mortgage bankers and servicers licensed by Arkansas Securities Commission, which is empowered to: deny, revoke, or suspend licenses; issue cease and desist orders; sue for administrative penalties of up to $10,000 ($25,000 if cease and desist order violated) or for other relief, including an accounting, disgorgement, or declaratory judgment; refer criminal matters to prosecutor. § 23-39-514.
Special Servicing Requirements for High-Cost Loans: Ark. Code Ann. §§ 23-53-101 to 23-53-106 prohibit increasing interest rates upon default on payments.

CALIFORNIA

Cal. Civ. Code §§ 2937, 2954 to 2954.8 (West)

Scope: Transfer requirements apply to transferor of servicing of mortgage or deed of trust secured by real property located in state containing one to four residential units. § 2937. Escrow requirements apply to lenders or purchasers (and their agents) of obligations secured by real property containing a single-family, owner-occupied dwelling. § 2954. Provisions of § 2954.2 apply to mortgagees of real property containing a one to four family residence.
Exclusions: "Servicing agent" does not include a trustee exercising a power of sale pursuant to a deed of trust. § 2937.
Transfer Notice Requirements: Transferor and transferee of servicing must notify borrower (or subsequent obligor) before borrower becomes obligated to make payments to new servicer (if a notice

of default has been recorded or a judicial foreclosure is in progress, should notify the attorney named in the notice of default or foreclosure). Notice to borrower must include name and address of new servicing agent; date the transfer will take place; address to which payments should be sent; due date of next payment. Transferor must notify new servicing agent about existing insurance policies servicer is responsible for maintaining, including flood and hazard insurance. Borrower not liable for amounts paid to former servicer prior to borrower's receipt of notice of the transfer, or for late charges if these payments were otherwise on time. § 2937.

Borrower Inquiries: Borrower may request additional account statements (discussed below). See also Appx. D.2, *infra*, for payoff statement requirements.

Escrow Requirements:

Restrictions: Escrow may be required only for loan insured or guaranteed by certain government agencies, or loan of more than ninety percent of sale price, or where all combined loans exceed eighty percent of home value, or after borrower has missed two tax payments, or where loan is made in compliance with Regulation Z requirements for high-priced home loans regardless of whether loan is high priced, or when home is refinanced or modified under a home preservation program. If escrow used in absence of these conditions, borrower must be told it is voluntary. § 2954. May not require deposits in escrow account in excess of that permitted by RESPA or reasonably necessary to pay taxes or insurance premiums as they become due. Excess must be refunded within thirty days, unless parties agree otherwise. Additional payments may be required to make up deficiencies. § 2954.1.

Recordkeeping and Notice: Itemized annual accounting must be provided free within sixty days of end of calendar year; information includes accounting of moneys received, credited, or disbursed for principal, interest, late charges, and payment of taxes and insurance. Additional accounting statements at borrower's request, for prescribed fees—$.50 each for statements requested in advance on a monthly basis, $1 when requested for only one month, $5 for single cumulative statement. Borrower must be notified of availability of additional statements. No increase in monthly payments permitted until borrower has been given an itemized accounting, listing the new payment amount and explanation of reasons for increase. §§ 2954, 2954.2.

Handling of funds: Payments shall be made promptly to ensure that insurance remains in force and tax payments are not delinquent. § 2954.1.

Interest: Financial institutions must pay two percent interest on funds held in escrow accounts for one to four family residences, and must not charge any fee for maintaining escrow account that will result in payment of less than two percent interest on monies held in escrow accounts. Interest shall be credited to borrower's account annually or upon termination of account. § 2954.8.

Private Mortgage Insurance Requirements: If private mortgage insurance is required, lender must notify borrower within thirty days after close of escrow of the conditions under which cancellation is possible, the information needed to communicate with lender and insurer, and the procedure for cancellation. Thereafter, lender must provide annual notice that cancellation may be possible, and an address and phone number for inquiries. This information may be included in the annual accounting required by § 2954.2. Private mortgage insurance on a loan for personal, family or household purposes secured by an owner-occupied one to four unit dwelling may be cancelled by a request in writing two years after origination if the loan balance is not more than 75%, no required payment has been more than thirty days late in the past twenty-four months, and no other default has been recorded. Within thirty days after cancellation, insurer must refund any unused premium to person designated by insured. These sections do not apply to loans such as FHA and VA that require insurance for the life of the mortgage. Cal. Ins. Code §§ 117, 12640.02; Cal. Civ. Code §§ 2954.6 through 2954.7.

Additional Requirements: None specified.

Private Remedies: Any person harmed by violation of escrow requirements may sue for actual damages and injunctive relief. §§ 2954, 2954.1. Any person harmed by violation of private mortgage insurance requirements has a cause of action for injunctive relief, treble damages, costs and reasonable attorney fees. Cal. Civ. Code § 2954.6.

State Remedies: Willful and repeated violations of escrow requirements punishable by fines of $50 to $200. § 2954.

Special Servicing Requirements for High-Cost Loans: Cal. Fin. Code §§ 4970, 4973 prohibit increasing interest rates upon default on payments. *See also* Cal. Civ. Code § 1916.7 (adjustable rate loan requirements).

COLORADO

Colo. Rev. Stat. §§ 38-40-103, 38-40-104

Scope: Any person who regularly engages in the collection of payments on mortgages and deeds of trust.

Exclusions: None specified.

Transfer Notice Requirements: Not more than twenty days after transfer of servicing, transferor must notify borrower of name, address, and telephone number of new servicer. Borrower may continue sending payments to former servicer until new servicer provides same notice. Transferor shall forward to new servicer any payments received and due after the date of transfer.

Borrower Inquiries: Servicer must respond within twenty days to borrower's written request for information about loan that is readily available to servicer from its books and records and does not constitute giving of legal advice. Response must include servicer's phone number. See also Appx. D.2, *infra*, for payoff statement requirements.

Escrow Requirements:

Restrictions: None specified.

Recordkeeping and notice: Servicer must provide borrower with annual summary of loan activity, including but not limited to, total amount of principal and interest paid on the loan in that calendar year.

Handling of funds: Servicer must pay taxes when due, if funds for full payment of taxes are in escrow.

Interest: None specified.

Additional Requirements: Servicer shall promptly credit all payments received and perform all duties as required by law or the mortgage or deed of trust.

Private Remedies: Borrower aggrieved by violation of section, if violation not remedied in timely, reasonable and good faith manner, after good faith effort to resolve dispute made by borrower, may bring an action for actual damages plus $1000 statutory damages (if actual damages have occurred), costs, and reasonable

attorney fees. Servicer who fails to timely pay taxes from escrow liable for any interest and late fees resulting from late payment.
State Remedies: None specified.
Special Servicing Requirements for High-Cost Loans: Colo. Rev. Stat. §§ 5-3.5-101 to 5-3.5-201 prohibit increasing interest rates upon default on payments.

CONNECTICUT

Conn. Gen. Stat. §§ 36a-715 to 36a-719, 49-2a to 49-2c

Scope: Servicing of loan or extension of credit which is secured by a first mortgage upon any interest in one to four family residential owner-occupied real property not subject to any prior mortgages. Includes the renewal or refinancing of an existing first mortgage loan.
Exclusions: None specified.
Transfer Notice Requirements: None specified. Separate statute covering assignment of mortgage (not transfer of servicing) requires that transferor notify borrower in proper form (recording of assignment not sufficient) and that borrower may continue to pay transferor until proper notice provided. § 49-10.
Borrower Inquiries: Not specified, but see Appx. D.2, *infra*, for payoff statement requirements.
Escrow Requirements:

Restrictions: None specified.
Recordkeeping and notice: Borrower must be provided notice without charge stating amounts to be paid into escrow sufficient for payment of taxes and insurance when due. § 36a-716.
Handling of funds: Taxes and insurance premiums must be paid when due, provided sufficient funds are in account, and bills received at least fifteen days before due date. If amount in escrow account insufficient after borrower has paid amounts requested by servicer, servicer must pay taxes and insurance from its own funds. In such case, servicer must give borrower option to pay shortage over period of not less than one year, and servicer may not charge interest on the shortage during that year. § 36a-716. Connecticut Housing Finance Authority (CHFA) loans must provide for monthly payments into escrow, and must reserve amounts sufficient to pay estimated amounts for taxes and insurance when due. Conn. Agencies Regs. § 8-248E-27.
Interest: Lender or servicer must pay interest on funds held in escrow for taxes and insurance. Rate set by Banking Commissioner based on Federal Reserve Board deposit index, except shall not be less than 1.5%. § 49-2a (exceptions set out in § 49-2c). CHFA loans must pay at least four percent interest on escrow account. § 8-248E-27.

Private Mortgage Insurance Requirements: Lender who requires private mortgage insurance on a loan for personal, family, or household purposes, secured by a owner-occupied one-to-four unit residence, must disclose at time application is filed that this insurance is required, that its purpose is to protect the lender, the conditions under which borrower may cancel, and a good-faith estimate of initial and monthly costs. This may be included in a RESPA good faith estimate. These disclosures are not required for loans such as FHA or VA that require insurance for the life of the loan. Conn. Gen. Stat. §§ 36a-725 and -726.
Additional Requirements: None specified.
Private Remedies: Mortgage servicer is liable for any penalties, interest, or late fees resulting from late payments of taxes and insurance in violation of § 36a-716, and for actual damages, including losses that should have been covered by insurance that was allowed to lapse, plus costs and reasonable attorney fees. § 36a-717.
State Remedies: Banking commissioner may order restitution or issue cease and desist orders. § 36a-718. Lender or servicer can be fined not more than $100 per violation for failure to pay interest on escrow accounts. § 49-2a.
Special Servicing Requirements for High-Cost Loans: Conn. Gen. Stat. §§ 36a-746 to 36a-746g prohibit increasing interest rates upon default on payments or charging fees for loan modification.

DELAWARE

Del. Code Ann. tit. 5, §§ 2302(8), 2303, 2313(c)

Scope: Not specified.
Exclusions: None specified.
Transfer Notice Requirements: None specified.
Borrower Inquiries: Not specified.
Escrow Requirements:

Restrictions: None specified.
Recordkeeping and notice: None specified.
Handling of funds: None specified.
Interest: None specified.

Additional Requirements: Del. Code Ann. tit. 5, § 2303 requires "accelerated mortgage payment providers," defined by § 2302(8) to mean "any person who, in accordance with a written contract, receives funds from a mortgagor to transmit, on behalf of such mortgagor, to a lender or servicer in order to exceed regularly scheduled minimum payment obligations under the terms of the indebtedness" to be licensed. Accelerated mortgage payment providers shall provide an annual statement to a mortgagor of the transmittals, which shall identify the dates and amounts received for transmission, the dates and amounts of transmittals made to the lender, and the name and address of the lender or recipient of such transmittals.
Private Remedies: None specified.
State Remedies: None specified.
Special Servicing Requirements for High-Cost Loans: None specified.

DISTRICT OF COLUMBIA

D.C. Code § 26-1115

Scope: Mortgage lenders, defined as persons who make loans, primarily for personal, family, or household use, secured by a mortgage, deed of trust, or other equivalent consensual security interest on a dwelling, or who service mortgage loans for others by receiving payments from borrowers for distribution. § 26-1101.
Exclusions: Banks and various other regulated financial institutions, insurance companies, various government agencies, certain nonprofit corporations, loans to family members, seller financed transactions, lawyers and realtors when acting as such and not principally in the business of brokering loans, and registered mortgage loan originators. § 26-1102.
Transfer Notice Requirements: None specified.
Borrower Inquiries: Not specified.
Escrow Requirements:

Restrictions: Borrower who has made down payment of twenty percent or more of purchase price, or who has equity of twenty percent or more of fair market value, may not be required to place funds in escrow account. Such borrowers must be notified at closing of their right to pay taxes and insurance directly. Lender may, in case of default during term of loan, and in exchange for not exercising its rights, require an escrow for taxes or insurance payments. Escrow may not be required for subordinate loan, unless there is no escrow for superior loan. § 26-1115.

Recordkeeping and notice: None specified.

Handling of funds: Escrow funds must be kept in separate account. § 26-1115.

Interest: None specified.

Additional Requirements: None specified.

Private Remedies: None specified.

State Remedies: Requirements administered by superintendent of banks, who is empowered to suspend and revoke licenses, issue orders against licensees or persons required to be licensed, impose penalties of up to $25,000 for violation of orders, or refer cases to corporation counsel for court action for damages and restitution. § 26-1118.

Special Servicing Requirements for High-Cost Loans: D.C. Code Ann. §§ 26-1152.01 to 26-1152.23 prohibit increasing interest rates upon default on payments, oppressive or unfair mandatory arbitration clauses, negative amortization, and advance payments.

FLORIDA

Fla. Stat. § 501.137

Scope: Lenders whose loans are secured by real property in state, who hold escrow funds for payment of taxes or insurance premiums.

Exclusions: None specified.

Transfer Notice Requirements: None specified.

Borrower Inquiries: Not specified.

Escrow Requirements:

Restrictions: None specified.

Recordkeeping and notice: Borrower shall be provided with annual statement of escrow account. If deficiency in escrow account occurs, must notify borrower within fifteen days after receipt of notification that any tax or insurance premium is due.

Handling of funds: Payments shall be made promptly, if funds available, so as to obtain maximum tax discounts and prevent cancellation of insurance.

Interest: None specified.

Additional Requirements: Fla. Stat. Ann. § 494.0061[1] requires mortgage lenders, defined by § 494.001(4)[2] to include servicers, to be licensed.

Private Remedies: If lender negligently fails to pay taxes or insurance premiums, at time when funds in account are sufficient, and borrower suffers a loss as a result, lender is liable for such loss. In case of loss resulting from lack of insurance coverage, liability limited to coverage limits of policy that was allowed to lapse. If lender negligently fails to pay insurance premium, but premium is not more than ninety days overdue, insurer must reinstate, retroactive to date of cancellation, and lender must reimburse borrower for any fees or penalties. If premium is more than ninety days overdue, and insurer refuses to reinstate, lender must pay borrower the difference between the cost of the old policy and that of a comparable new policy for a period of two years, plus costs and attorney fees.

State Remedies: None specified.

Special Servicing Requirements for High-Cost Loans: Fla. Stat. Ann. §§ 494.0078 to 494.00791 prohibit increasing interest rates upon default on payments or charging fees for loan modification.

GEORGIA

Ga. Code Ann. §§ 7-1-1000 to 7-1-1002, 7-6A-1 to 7-6A-13

Scope: Not specified.

Exclusions: None specified.

Transfer Notice Requirements: None specified.

Borrower Inquiries: Not specified.

Escrow Requirements:

Restrictions: None specified.

Recordkeeping and notice: None specified.

Handling of funds: Not specified.

Interest: None specified.

Additional Requirements: Ga. Code Ann. § 7-1-1002 requires mortgage lenders, defined by § 7-1-1000(20) to include servicers, to be licensed. (§ 7-1-1001 exempts banks, credit unions, and a variety of other entities.)

Private Remedies: None specified.

State Remedies: None specified.

Special Servicing Requirements for High-Cost Loans: Ga. Code Ann. §§ 7- 6A-1 to 7-6A-13 prohibits increasing interest rates upon default on payments or charging fees for loan modification. It also restricts the amount and timing of late fees, requires the homeowner to be afforded the opportunity to cure a default up until the home is transferred by foreclosure sale, and requires notice of intent to foreclose to be sent to the homeowner by certified mail at least fourteen days before publication of the legal advertisement required by statute.

HAWAII

Haw. Rev. Stat. §§ 454M-5 to 454M-6 (effective July 1, 2010)

Scope: Mortgage servicers, defined as persons responsible for receiving any scheduled periodic payments on residential mortgage loans, including amounts for escrow accounts under RESPA, and for making other payments; includes making payments to borrowers on reverse mortgages. § 454M-1.

Exclusions: Banks and other federally regulated or operated institutions, trust companies, credit unions, insurance companies, and licensed financial service loan companies and persons making five or fewer mortgage loans. § 454M-3.

Transfer Notice Requirements: At acceptance of servicing rights, mortgage servicers must disclose any notice required by RESPA, a schedule of ranges and categories of fees and costs for servicing activities, and a notice that complaints may be submitted to the commissioner of financial institutions. § 454M-5.

---

1 Fla. Stat. Ann. § 494.0061 is repealed effective October 1, 2010, and is being replaced by 494.00611 (which is effective October 1, 2010).

2 Fla. Stat. Ann. § 494.001 is amended effective October 1, 2010, at which time the correct reference will be subsection 19, not subsection 4.

Borrower Inquiries: Not specified.
Escrow Requirements:
Restrictions: None specified.
Recordkeeping and notice: None specified.
Handling of funds: None specified.
Interest: Not specified.
Additional Requirements: Mortgage loan originators, those who take mortgage applications or negotiate terms, must be licensed. § 454F-1. Mortgage loan servicers must also be licensed. § 454M-2. Mortgage loan servicers must, in the event of a delinquency or other default, act in good faith to inform the borrower of the facts concerning the delinquency or default, and, if the borrower replies, negotiate with the borrower to attempt a resolution or workout relating to the delinquency. § 454M-5.
Private Remedies: None specified.
State Remedies: Commissioner may investigate and conduct hearings on violations, deny licenses of mortgage servicers, issue fines of up to $5000 or report violations to HUD. §§ 454M-7, 454M-8, 454M-10.
Special Servicing Requirements for High-Cost Loans: None specified.

IDAHO

Idaho Code Ann. §§ 26-2802 to 26-2809

Scope: Mortgage company, defined as person who makes, services, buys, or sells residential mortgage loans. § 26-2802.
Exclusions: Banks, licensed lenders, credit unions, government entities, licensed real estate professionals, and owners who sell property but give credit secured by that property. § 26-2803.
Transfer Notice Requirements: Mortgage company must notify borrower within fifteen days after it assigns note and does not retain servicing. Mortgage company that purchases or receives assignment of note with servicing must provide borrower a written statement within thirty days describing policies relating to escrow account. § 26-2809.
Borrower Inquiries: Additional account statement must be provided within thirty days of written request. Fee may be charged for statement other than annual statement. § 26-2808.
Escrow Requirements:
Restrictions: Mortgage company may not keep more than 120% of amount necessary to pay estimated taxes and insurance premiums in escrow account. If borrower notifies company that amount held is excessive, company must either return excess within thirty days or explain why amount being reserved is reasonable and necessary. Director of Department of Finance after administrative hearing may order mortgage company to reduce escrow reserve requirements for such accounts. § 26-2807.
Recordkeeping and notice: Annual statement must be provided free of charge showing all payments made or credited, total unpaid balance, disposition of all escrow funds, balance of escrow account, and any penalties or interest because of failure to pay taxes on time. § 26-2808. Mortgage company must clearly disclose to borrowers all requirements for escrow accounts. § 26-2807.
Handling of funds: None specified.
Interest: None specified.
Additional Requirements: None specified.
Private Remedies: None specified.
State Remedies: Department of Finance empowered to issue cease and desist orders, or bring court action for injunction, penalties (up to $5000 per violation), costs, and "other appropriate remedies." § 26-2806.
Special Servicing Requirements for High-Cost Loans: None.

ILLINOIS

205 Ill. Comp. Stat. 5/48.2 (Illinois Banking Act); 205 Ill. Comp. Stat. 635/3-7 (Residential Mortgage License Act); 765 Ill. Comp. Stat. 910/1 to 910/15 (Mortgage Escrow Account Act); 765 Ill. Comp. Stat. 915/1 (Mortgage Tax Escrow Act)

Scope:
Illinois Banking Act: Residential mortgages.
Residential Mortgage License Act: Licensees engaged in brokering, funding, originating, servicing, or purchasing residential loans, defined as mortgages on real property located in state improved by one to four family dwelling, used wholly or partly as a residence, or subject to regulations of Commissioner of Banks and Real Estate, unimproved property upon which such buildings are to be constructed.
Mortgage Escrow Account Act: Mortgage lenders, which include banks, savings and loan associations, and any person that lends money for the purpose of enabling another to purchase a residence or that services such loan. Applies to escrow accounts and escrow-like arrangements for single family owner-occupied residences.
Exclusions:
Illinois Banking Act: None specified.
Residential Mortgage License Act: Numerous exclusions including banks, savings and loan associations, consumer loan licensees, and entities engaged solely in commercial mortgage lending.
Mortgage Escrow Acts: Not applicable to lender using capitalization method of accounting for receipt of payments for taxes. 765 Ill. Comp. Stat. 910/10.
Transfer Notice Requirements:
Illinois Banking Act: Lender must notify borrower within forty-five days of transfer, by certified mail, return receipt requested, of name and address of transferee; name, address, and phone number for borrower inquiries; name and address to which next three payments are to be submitted to the transferee, and the amount of next three payments. If further transfers made, or the above information changes, borrower must be notified within forty-five days. 205 Ill. Comp. Stat. 5/48.2(e)(2), (3).
Residential Mortgage License Act: When servicing transferred, notice shall be given at time of transfer and shall include information on where and to whom to address questions about mortgage; the name, address, and telephone number to whom at least next three months payments are to be sent, and the amount required for these three payments. See also Residential Mortgage Servicing Act regulations, Ill. Admin. Code tit. 38, §§ 1050.810 to 1050.850, which require that borrower be notified at time of closing that if servicing is transferred, notice shall be provided by both transferor and transferee. Borrower must be provided with a toll-free number at which to verify a notice of transfer. If licensee is party to large transfer of servicing it must ensure that sufficient staff and facilities are available to prevent inconvenience to borrowers. In addition to

notifying the borrower, transferor must promptly notify the insurance company and taxing authority of the change, and notify the transferee of the escrow balance and other information. Transferee must provide borrower with any coupons or payment books required, respond promptly to inquiries, and "exercise forbearance when sorting out transfer related problems, including but not limited to delinquency and assessment of late charges."

Borrower Inquiries:

Residential Mortgage License Act: Licensee must maintain toll-free telephone number or other toll-free arrangement for borrower inquiries. Ill. Admin. Code tit. 38, § 1050.850.

Escrow Requirements:

Illinois Banking Act: None specified.

Residential Mortgage License Act:

Restrictions: Commissioner may promulgate rules. 205 Ill. Comp. Stat. 635/3-9; *see* Ill. Admin. Code tit. 38, §§ 1050.830 to 1050.850.

Recordkeeping and notice: Borrower should receive thirty days notice of payment change, along with plain English explanation of how the new amount was calculated. Account analysis shall be done at least once every year. Ill. Admin. Code tit. 38, § 1050.830. If mortgage is in first-lien position and lender requires escrow, borrower must be provided with Escrow Account Disclosure Agreement. Ill. Admin. Code tit. 38, § 1050.1360.

Handling of funds: Tax or insurance bills received thirty days before penalty date or due date should be paid before that date. Ill. Admin. Code tit. 38, § 1050.830.

Interest: No.

Mortgage Escrow Acts:

Restrictions: In lieu of an escrow account, borrower may pledge an interest bearing time deposit with the lender in amount sufficient to cover anticipated taxes. When mortgage is reduced to sixty-five percent of its original amount, and if borrower is not in default, lender must inform borrower of option to terminate escrow account (not applicable to government insured or guaranteed loans that require an escrow). After terminating escrow if borrower fails to furnish proof of tax payment lender may reestablish escrow following reasonable effort to verify nonpayment. Escrow for single-family residence may not (except during first year of mortgage's life) contain an amount greater than 150% of the previous year's real assessed property tax.

Recordkeeping and notice: Borrower must be notified at time of closing of the provisions of act. See also Ill. Admin. Code tit. 38, §§ 1050.1350 and 1050.1360 for details of information to be provided. When lender pays property tax from escrow account, must give written notice within forty-five days of amount paid, date of payment, and index or account number or property description used for tax assessment purposes. In lieu of this information, lender may give written notice of a means of communication—including phone, fax, e-mail, Internet or "other means"—where borrower can obtain the information.

Handling of funds: None specified.

Interest: None specified.

Additional Requirements:

Residential Mortgage License Act: Licensee shall make good faith effort to credit payments to mortgage account on same calendar date payments received. Ill. Admin. Code tit. 38, § 1050.840.

Private Remedies:

Illinois Banking Act: None specified.

Residential Mortgage License Act: None specified.

Mortgage Escrow Acts: Borrower may bring action for actual damages based on lender's noncompliance with provisions of act. 765 Ill. Comp. Stat. 910/9.

State Remedies: None specified.

Special Servicing Requirements for High-Cost Loans: 815 Ill. Comp. Stat. 137/1 to 137/175 restricts the amount and timing of late fees.

INDIANA

Ind. Code §§ 24-9-4-1 to 24-9-4-12

Scope: Not specified.

Exclusions: None specified.

Transfer Notice Requirements: None specified.

Borrower Inquiries: Not specified.

Escrow Requirements:

Restrictions: None specified.

Recordkeeping and notice: None specified.

Handling of funds: None specified.

Interest: None specified.

Additional Requirements: None specified.

Private Remedies: None specified.

State Remedies: None specified.

Special Servicing Requirements for High-Cost Loans: Ind. Code §§ 24-9-4-1 to 24-9-4-12 prohibit increasing interest rates upon default on payments and charging fees for loan modification.

IOWA

Iowa Code § 535B.11 (Mortgage Bankers and Brokers); Iowa Code § 524.905 (State Banks); Iowa Code § 533.315 (Credit Unions); Iowa Code §§ 534.202, 534.206 (Savings and Loan Associations); Iowa Code § 536A.20 (Industrial Loan Companies)

Scope:

Mortgage Bankers and Brokers: Anyone who makes, originates, services, arranges, or negotiates four or more residential mortgage loans in one year. Residential real property includes owner-occupied one or two family dwellings occupied or intended to be occupied for residential purposes. State banks, credit unions, savings and loan associations, and licensed industrial loan companies covered under separate statutes.

Exclusions:

Mortgage Bankers and Brokers: Natural person who services less than fifteen mortgage loans, and does not sell or transfer loans.

Transfer Notice Requirements:

Mortgage Bankers and Brokers: Transferor shall send notice to borrower, within fifteen calendar days of transfer, providing names and addresses of former and new servicer; effective date of transfer; statement concerning the effect of the transfer on terms and conditions of mortgage; address to which payments should be submitted for next three months; name and address of person to whom questions may be directed.

Borrower Inquiries: Not specified, but see Appx. D.2, *infra*, for payoff statement requirements.
Escrow Requirements:
Mortgage Bankers and Brokers:
Restrictions: None specified.
Recordkeeping and notice: Perform yearly escrow analysis, and provide legible copy to borrower. If there is a change in the payment amount, must notify borrower at least twenty days before date of change. Summary of analysis must include name and address of mortgagor and mortgagee; balance in escrow account at beginning of year; aggregate amount of deposits during year; aggregate amount of withdrawals from escrow account for payments of principal, interest, insurance, taxes, and other withdrawals; summary of loan principal for the year including the amount of principal outstanding at beginning and end of year.
Handling of funds: Pay taxes and insurance before due date. Lender is responsible for late penalties incurred as a result of lender's failure to meet due dates, unless borrower failed to timely remit statement of amount due to lender.
Interest: None specified.
State Banks, Credit Unions, Savings and Loan Associations, Industrial Loan Companies:
Restrictions: May require monthly escrow payments of one-twelfth of the estimated yearly tax, special assessment, and insurance payments.
Recordkeeping and notice: Must provide written annual account of all transactions on loan and escrow account. Must be delivered within thirty days of end of year (parties may agree to a year reporting period other than a calendar year), and include substantially the same items as required of mortgage bankers (see above). *See also* Iowa Admin. Code r. 197-12.4(534) (at time of loan application, savings and loan association must inform borrower whether an escrow will be required, its purpose, and the method of calculating payments).
Handling of funds: None specified.
Interest: Must pay interest at the same rate paid to depositors on ordinary savings accounts (industrial loan companies shall pay lowest rate paid to holders of its thrift certificates).
Additional Requirements: Execute and deliver release after payoff; provide to borrower upon request copy of abstract of title in lender's possession. § 535B.11.
Private Remedies: None specified.
State Remedies: Superintendent of banking has power, after hearing, to issue cease and desist orders, and may request attorney general to bring civil enforcement action seeking injunctive relief, restitution to borrower, and costs and attorney fees. The attorney general may also sue under the deceptive practices statute. § 535B.13.
Special Servicing Requirements for High-Cost Loans: None.

KANSAS

Kan. Stat. Ann. §§ 58-2337 to 58-2341

Scope: Loans secured by real estate on which is located, or will be located pursuant to a home loan, a dwelling or dwellings for not more than four families.
Exclusions: None specified.
Transfer Notice Requirements: Transferor lender must notify borrower, within ten business days after transfer of servicing, of name, address, and phone number of new servicer. Upon borrower's request, notice must provide detailed written financial breakdown, including interest rate, monthly payment amount, and current escrow balance.
Borrower Inquiries: Transferee lender or servicer must respond within fifteen business days to borrower's written request for information. Response must include telephone number of representative who can assist borrower.
Escrow Requirements:
Restrictions: None specified.
Recordkeeping and notice: Transferee lender or servicer must provide annual escrow summary on or before February 15, including amount of each transaction, and purpose for which money spent.
Handling of funds: None specified.
Interest: None specified.
Additional Requirements: None specified.
Private Remedies: If transferor lender fails to comply with transfer notice requirements, or transferee lender or servicer fails to comply with annual escrow account summary requirements, and noncompliance was due to failure to exercise reasonable care, lender or servicer is liable for actual damages plus $100 per occurrence.
State Remedies: None specified.
Special Servicing Requirements for High-Cost Loans: None.

KENTUCKY

Ky. Rev. Stat. Ann. §§ 286.8-010 to 286.8-990 (West); *see also* Ky. Rev. Stat. Ann. § 360.100 (West) (High-Cost Home Loans)

Scope: Mortgage loan companies and loan brokers, defined to include any person servicing mortgage loans. § 286.010(19), (20).
Exclusions: Financial institutions such as banks, credit unions, industrial loan companies regulated under other statutes, realtors, natural persons lending to family members without compensation, natural persons making loans secured by a dwelling that is the natural person's residence.
Transfer Notice Requirements: None specified.
Borrower Inquiries: Upon reasonable notice, account to borrower for funds paid into escrow for taxes and insurance payments. § 286.8-130. For high-cost home loans as defined by statute, § 360.100 prohibits lenders from charging for the first request of each calendar year for a written payoff calculation, but thereafter may charge a reasonable fee not to exceed $10 or actual costs, whichever is greater, per payoff statement request.
Escrow Requirements:
Restrictions: None specified.
Recordkeeping and notice: Upon reasonable notice, account to commissioner for all funds in company's escrow account. § 286.8-130.
Handling of funds: Deposit all escrow payments in an FDIC-insured account, separate from lender's own funds. Promptly credit borrower's payments into account, and pay taxes and insurance premiums in timely fashion, not later than statutory or contractual deadlines. § 286.8-130.
Interest: Interest earned on escrow account shall belong to borrower, and shall be applied to expenses to be paid from escrow account. § 286.8-130.

Additional Requirements: License; surety bond; escrow account funds shall not be subject to execution or attachment on any claim against lender. § 286.8-130.
Private Remedies: None specified.
State Remedies: Commissioner of financial institutions may impose penalties of $1000 to $5000. Any person who knowingly engages in residential mortgage lending without a license or registration is guilty of a Class A misdemeanor. § 286.8-990.
Special Servicing Requirements for High-Cost Loans: Ky. Rev. Stat. Ann. § 360.100 prohibits increasing interest rates upon default on payments or charging fees for loan modification. It also restricts the amount and timing of late fees.

MAINE

Me. Rev. Stat. Ann. tit. 9-A, § 2-310 (Supervised Lenders); Me. Rev. Stat. Ann. tit. 9-A, §§ 9-304 to 9-305-A (First-Lien Mortgages); Me. Rev. Stat. Ann. tit. 9-B, § 429 (Financial Institutions; Escrow Accounts)

Scope:
Supervised Lenders: Consumer loans with finance charges that exceed 12 1/4% per year, secured by mortgage on real estate.
First-Lien Mortgages: Transactions secured by first lien on real estate.
Financial Institutions: Financial institutions, credit unions, and supervised lenders and their assignees. Mortgages on owner-occupied one to four unit real property. Escrow account means account established by agreement under which borrower pays lender sums to be used for taxes or insurance. Tit. 9-B, § 429.
Exclusions:
Financial Institutions: Transactions for which payment of interest on escrow accounts is forbidden by federal law. Tit. 9-B, § 429.
Transfer Notice Requirements:
Supervised Lenders and First-Lien Mortgages: Loan may not be assigned unless either the lender retains servicing and has a place of business in state, or maintains a toll-free phone number or other free means of oral communication, or the assignee or servicing agent maintains such a toll-free number or free means of oral communication. The telephone number must be disclosed to borrowers in the coupon book, or on periodic statements, and must be staffed during normal business hours to enable borrower to communicate with lender, assignee, or servicer about loan. Tit. 9-A, § 2-310; tit. 9-B, § 304.
Financial Institutions: None specified.
Borrower Inquiries: Not specified, but see Appx. D.2, *infra*, for payoff statement requirements.
Escrow Requirements:
First-Lien Mortgages:
Restrictions: None specified.
Recordkeeping and notice: None specified.
Handling of funds: Make prompt payments of taxes and insurance premiums. Creditor, assignee or servicer who fails to do so must rectify the results of the late payment, including correcting the consumer's credit report and causing the discharge of any liens.
Interest: Interest shall be paid at least quarterly, at rate of not less than three percent per year. Interest may not be reduced by charges for service or maintenance of account. Tit. 9-A, § 305; tit. 9-B, § 429; *see also* tit. 33, § 504.
Financial Institutions:
Restrictions: None specified.
Recordkeeping and notice: None specified.
Handling of funds: None specified.
Interest: Interest on required escrow accounts shall be paid at least quarterly, at a rate not less than 50% of the one-year Treasury note rate, or the rate of a comparable instrument if the one-year Treasury note is not offered, as published in a financial newspaper of national circulation, as of the first business day of the year in which the quarterly interest or dividend is paid. Interest may not be reduced by charges for service or maintenance of account. Tit. 9-B, § 429; *see also* tit. 33, § 504.
Additional Requirements: None specified.
Private Remedies: Creditor, assignee or servicer who fails to make timely payments from escrow for taxes or insurance premiums is liable to consumer for actual damages. Must also rectify the results of late payment, by correcting consumer's credit report and causing the discharge of any liens.
State Remedies:
Supervised Lenders and First-Lien Mortgages: Provisions are part of the Maine Consumer Credit Code.
Financial Institutions: None specified.
Special Servicing Requirements for High-Cost Loans: None.

MARYLAND

Md. Code Ann., Com. Law §§ 12-109 to 12-109.2, 12-1026 (West) (Escrow); Md. Code Ann., Com. Law § 13-316 (West) (Mortgage Servicing)

Scope: Mortgage, deed of trust, or lien secured by one to four family residential real estate located in state.
Exclusions: Escrow provisions in § 12-109 and § 12-1026 do not apply if loan purchased by out-of-state lender through Freddie Mac, Fannie Mae, or Ginnie Mae.
Transfer Notice Requirements: Within seven days after acquiring servicing, new servicer must notify borrower of name, address, and telephone number of new servicer; address payments are to be sent to; principal and escrow balances; telephone number of contact person for complaints and inquiries; statement that servicer's violation of statute will result in liability. § 13-316.
Borrower Inquiries: Servicer shall designate contact person who shall respond to written complaints or inquiries in writing within fifteen days. Must provide toll-free number for borrower inquiries during business hours. § 13-316.
Escrow Requirements:
Restrictions: If balance in escrow account exceeds amount provided for in contract, lender must give borrower the option of receiving a refund (to be made within sixty days of request for refund), applying excess to interest or principal, or leaving excess in escrow account.
Recordkeeping and notice: Borrower must be provided with annual statement of escrow balance.
Handling of funds: Taxes and insurance premiums shall be timely paid, provided borrower has paid sufficient amount, and servicer is in possession of tax bill or tax notice. Lender may not impose service charge or collection fee for escrow account on a

first mortgage. Escrow funds may not be commingled with lender's own funds.

Interest: Interest must be paid on escrow accounts at greater of three percent or the amount paid on the institution's regular passbook savings accounts. Interest to be paid annually by crediting escrow account. §§ 12-109, 12-1026.

Private Mortgage Insurance Requirements: If a banking institution holds a first mortgage on residential property, and a private mortgage insurance company partially insures the mortgage, lender shall eliminate all charges to the borrower for private mortgage insurance when the mortgage is reduced to the level at which the Homeowners Protection Act of 1998 requires termination of private mortgage insurance. Md. Code Ann. Fin. Inst. § 5-508.

Additional Requirements: Funds in escrow account may not be used to reduce principal or pay interest or other loan charges, except upon foreclosure or agreement with borrower. §§ 12-109.1, 12-1026. Md. Code, Fin. Inst. § 11-504 requires mortgage lenders, defined by § 11-501(i) to include servicers, to be licensed. (§ 11-501(i) exempts certain depository institutions and a variety of other entities.)

Private Remedies: Borrower may bring action for economic damages caused by violation of § 13-316, in addition to any other available remedies (such as under UDAP statute).

State Remedies: None specified, but provisions part of state deceptive practices (UDAP) statute.

Special Servicing Requirements for High-Cost Loans: None.

MASSACHUSETTS

761 Mass. Code Regs. §§ 21.18, 22.18, 22.23

Scope: Massachusetts Home Mortgage Finance Agency mortgage loans.

Exclusions: None specified.

Transfer Notice Requirements: None specified.

Borrower Inquiries: Not specified, but see Appx. D.2, *infra*, for payoff statement requirements.

Escrow Requirements:

Restrictions: Mortgage loan must provide for collection of escrow payments to maximum extent permitted by RESPA, except that escrow for hazard insurance not required.

Recordkeeping and notice: Servicer shall maintain adequate records of escrow payments, and recompute escrow payment annually.

Handling of funds: Escrow funds must be kept in insured bank account. Servicer must obtain bills for taxes and insurance and pay them prior to penalty or termination date. If funds in escrow exceed amount needed to pay estimated taxes and insurance, servicer must either repay to borrower or credit funds against monthly installments of escrow payments. If funds insufficient for payment of taxes or insurance, servicer should seek to obtain necessary sums from borrower. If borrower fails to remit, if time insufficient, or if account is in foreclosure, servicer must pay out of own funds, and sum will be added to loan balance, and is payable by borrower on demand with interest.

Interest: None specified.

Additional Requirements: Mass. Gen. Laws ch. 93, § 24A requires third party loan servicers to be registered and debt collectors to be licensed, with exceptions for banks, credit unions, and a variety of other institutions.

Private Remedies: None specified.

State Remedies: None specified.

Special Servicing Requirements for High-Cost Loans: Mass. Gen. Laws ch. 183C, §§ 1 to 19 prohibit increasing interest rates upon default on payments or charging fees for loan modification.

MICHIGAN

Mich. Comp. Laws §§ 445.1651 to 445.1684 (Mortgage Lenders, Brokers and Servicers Licensing Act); Mich. Comp. Laws § 565.161 (Escrow Statements) to 565.164 (Escrow Adjustments)

Scope:

Mortgage Lenders, Brokers and Servicers Licensing Act: Persons who make or offer to make, or service or offer to service, a loan secured by a first mortgage on real property located in state used, or improved to be used, as dwelling for four or fewer families. § 445.1651a.

Conveyances: Applies to all conveyances of real property.

Exclusions:

Mortgage Lenders, Brokers and Servicers Licensing Act: Numerous including depository financial institutions, certain lawyers and realtors, certain nonprofit corporations, persons who make or service ten or fewer mortgage loans per year. § 445.1675.

Conveyances: None specified.

Transfer Notice Requirements: None specified.

Borrower Inquiries:

Mortgage Lenders, Brokers and Servicers Licensing Act: Servicer must, within twenty-five days of written request, furnish a ledger history of the account, showing the date and amount of all payments made or credited to the account in the previous twelve-month period (but not for period in excess of preceding twelve-month period), and the total unpaid balance. Servicer shall not charge for providing one ledger history upon written request in a twelve-month period. § 445.1674.

Conveyances: None specified.

Escrow Requirements:

Mortgage Lenders, Brokers and Servicers Licensing Act: None specified (annual mortgage account notice discussed below).

Conveyances:

Restrictions: None specified.

Recordkeeping and notice: If loan requires payments into escrow for taxes, improvements or insurance, lender or servicer must furnish, within sixty days of end of calendar year, an account statement showing beginning balance in escrow account, all funds received, itemized statement of disbursements, and ending balance (not required if monthly billing forms disclose the escrow balance and expenditures for taxes). §§ 565.161, 565.162.

Handling of funds: None specified.

Interest: None specified.

Additional Requirements:

Mortgage Lenders, Brokers and Servicers Licensing Act: Servicer shall furnish annually to borrower a statement of mortgage account showing the unpaid principal balance, interest paid, and amounts paid into and disbursed from escrow during the preceding twelve-month period. Servicer shall not charge for providing annual statement. § 445.1674.

Conveyances: None specified.

Private Remedies:

Mortgage Lenders, Brokers and Servicers Licensing Act: Borrower may sue for declaratory judgment, injunction, actual damages or $250 (whichever is greater, except award shall not exceed actual damages if noncompliance was not willful, intentional, or result of gross negligence), attorney fees, and costs. Class actions permitted. § 445.1681.

Conveyances: If there are sufficient funds in escrow account and lender or servicer fails to pay taxes when due, lender or servicer is liable for any penalties or fees resulting from the nonpayment. § 565.163.

State Remedies:

Mortgage Lenders, Brokers and Servicers Licensing Act: Servicing provisions are part of extensive scheme for regulating mortgage brokers, lenders and servicers; the commissioner of financial services is empowered to revoke and suspend licenses, issue cease and desist orders, and impose penalties. "Any person," including a prosecutor or the attorney general, may sue for declaratory judgment, injunction, and greater of actual damages or $250. *See* §§ 445.1661 to 445.1684. Section 445.1679 also provides for civil fines of up to $30,000 if violations are found to not be a result of error.

Conveyances: None specified.

Special Servicing Requirements for High-Cost Loans: None.

MINNESOTA

Minn. Stat. §§ 47.205 (Servicers); Minn. Stat. § 47.20(9) (Escrow)

Scope: Servicing of mortgage loans financing one to four family owner-occupied residences.

Exclusions: None specified.

Transfer Notice Requirements: Transferor lender must notify borrower no more than ten days after transfer of servicing. Notification must include name, address, and telephone number of new servicer and also include a detailed written financial breakdown, including but not limited to, interest rate, monthly payment amount, and current escrow balance. Transferee lender or new servicer shall issue corrected coupon or payment books, if used, and shall provide notification to borrower within twenty days after first payment is due of the name, address, and telephone number of the person from whom the borrower can receive information regarding the servicing of the loan, and shall inform borrower of any changes made regarding the mortgage escrow account or servicing requirements including, but not limited to, interest rate, monthly payment amount, and current escrow balance.

Borrower Inquiries: Transferee lender or new servicer shall respond within fifteen business days to a written request for information from borrower. Written response must include the telephone number of the company representative who can assist the borrower.

Escrow Requirements:

Restrictions: None specified.

Recordkeeping and notice: Lender shall promptly notify borrower of shortage of funds in escrow account. For loans on which escrow not required by law or regulation, or by HUD, FHA or VA, or required because original loan was for more than 80% of appraised value of the unit, borrower must be notified at closing of the right to discontinue the escrow after five years, if no payment was more than thirty days delinquent during the preceding year. If this is the case, borrower must be notified again within sixty days after the fifth anniversary. (For loans prior to Jan. 1, 1998, the period is seven years.) Mortgagee may not charge a fee for maintaining the escrow, or for allowing discontinuance. If borrower discontinues, mortgagee must refund any funds remaining in the account to borrower.

Handling of funds: Lender or servicer must make payments for taxes or insurance from escrow accounts in a timely manner as obligations become due provided that sufficient funds exist in account. If there is a shortage of funds in escrow account, lender or servicer must notify borrower of the shortage and may make payments on behalf of borrower to cover escrow disbursements.

Interest: None specified.

Additional Requirements: Borrower may cancel private mortgage insurance if outstanding balance is not more than 80% of fair market value, as determined by a professional appraisal within ninety days before the request to cancel; no payment was sixty or more days late during the twelve month period beginning twenty-four months before the date of the request, or more than thirty days late during the twelve months prior to the request; the mortgage was made at least twenty-four months prior to the request; the property is owner-occupied; and the mortgage has not been pooled with other mortgages as collateral for certain bonds of state or its subdivisions. Borrowers must receive annual notice of this right to cancel. Within thirty days of receipt of written request, lender must either request insurer to cancel; request additional information from borrower if needed to enable servicer to determine whether borrower is eligible to cancel; or provide borrower with written notice of reasons for servicer's refusal to cancel. If private mortgage insurance is cancelled, refund of unearned premiums should go to the borrower or other person who actually paid the premiums. Minn. Stat. § 47.207. In addition, Minn. Stat. § 58.04 requires residential mortgage loan servicers to be licensed, with exceptions for banks, credit unions, certain loan originators, and a variety of other entities, and § 58.13(9) generally prohibits servicers from making false or misleading statements or representations.

Private Remedies: Actual damages, plus statutory damages of $500 per occurrence if violation due to the lender's failure to exercise reasonable care.

State Remedies: Willful and repeated violation of banking statute is a felony. § 47.26.

Special Servicing Requirements for High-Cost Loans: None.

MISSISSIPPI

Miss. Code Ann. §§ 81-18-1 to 81-18-61 (Mortgage Consumer Protection Law)

[Note that this statute is repealed effective July 1, 2010.]

Scope: Mortgages on one to four unit residences occupied by natural person(s). Mortgage lenders including servicers. § 81-18-3(s).

Exclusions: Numerous exclusions including banks, credit unions, various other entities regulated under other statutes, government entities, certain nonprofit corporations.

Transfer Notice Requirements: None specified.

Borrower Inquiries: Not specified, but see Appx. D.2, *infra*, for payoff statement requirements.

Escrow Requirements:

Restrictions: None specified.

Recordkeeping and notice: Upon reasonable request, lender must account to debtor for funds paid into escrow account for taxes or insurance.
Handling of funds: Escrow funds must be deposited in FDIC-insured account, separate from funds of lender.
Interest: None specified.
Additional Requirements: License (§ 81-18-7), recordkeeping (§ 81-18-21), surety bond of $150,000 (§ 81-18-11(b)).
Private Remedies: None specified.
State Remedies: Provisions are part of a regulatory program administered by the commissioner of banking and consumer finance, who has the power to suspend or revoke licenses, issue cease and desist orders, and impose penalties.
Special Servicing Requirements for High-Cost Loans: None.

MISSOURI

Mo. Rev. Stat. § 443.861 (Transfer of Servicing Rights); Mo. Rev. Stat. § 443.865 (Escrow and Transfer Provisions of Residential Mortgage Broker License Act)

Scope: Brokering, funding, originating, servicing, or purchasing of loans made to individuals for personal, family, or household purposes, secured by mortgage on residential real property.
Exclusions: Numerous exclusions including banks, insurance companies, certain mortgage bankers supervised by federal entities, persons making loans from own funds for investment purposes.
Transfer Notice Requirements: Notice must be given to borrower simultaneously with transfer stating where and to whom to address questions; exact name, address, and telephone number of entity at least next three payments are to be submitted to; and total amount required for each of these payments. § 443.861.
Borrower Inquiries: Not specified.
Escrow Requirements:
Restrictions: None specified.
Recordkeeping and notice: Director may promulgate regulations for handling of escrow accounts by licensees. § 443.865. Rules require that if an escrow agreement is required, a written Escrow Account Disclosure Agreement must be executed at closing. Compliance with applicable federal law is deemed compliance with rule. *See* Mo. Code Regs. Ann. tit. 20, § 1140-30.110.
Handling of funds: Mortgage servicers must pay property taxes from escrow accounts (as defined in 24 C.F.R. § 3500.17) in one annual payment before January 1 of the year following the year for which the tax is levied. § 443.453.
Interest: None specified.
Additional Requirements: Include: license; surety bond; maintenance of full-service office; annual audit.
Private Remedies: None specified.
State Remedies: Provisions are part of a licensing program administered by the director of the Division of Finance, who has the power to suspend and revoke licenses, or to ask attorney general to sue to enjoin violations.
Special Servicing Requirements for High-Cost Loans: None.

MONTANA

Mont. Code Ann. §§ 32-9-145, 71-1-113 to 71-1-115

Scope: Mortgage lenders: entities that close loans, on any real property located in the state of Montana upon which is constructed a dwelling or upon which a dwelling is intended to be built within a two-year period, advance funds, offer to advance funds, or commit to advancing funds for a mortgage loan applicant. § 32-9-103. Lending institutions. § 71-1-113.
Exclusions: Government agencies, banks, pension plans, certain nonprofits, attorneys, accountants, individuals negotiating terms for family members, individuals offering financing on the sale of their own property, and persons performing brokerage activities not agents or compensated by mortgage lenders or brokers. § 32-9-104.
Transfer Notice Requirements: None specified.
Borrower Inquiries: Not specified.
Escrow Requirements:
Restrictions: Accounting for escrow funds must be performed in compliance with the aggregate accounting rules established in Regulation X, 24 C.F.R.§ 3500, and in compliance with § 71-1-115. § 32-9-145. If a lending institution requires a borrower under a mortgage or trust indenture to make payment into a reserve fund for future payment of property taxes, insurance premiums, and other expenses, the amount of funds on reserve may not exceed 110% of the projected amount needed to pay those expenses. § 71-1-113.
Recordkeeping and notice: Lending institutions shall keep an itemized record of each payment entered into a reserve fund and each disbursement, and shall annually mail a statement of total receipts and disbursements to each borrower. § 71-1-115.
Handling of funds: Money received from a borrower must be considered as held in trust immediately upon receipt and be placed in a depository institution prior to the end of the third business day following receipt. Funds must be placed in a separate account only for borrower's funds and be designated and maintained only for the benefit of borrowers. Escrow funds may not be commingled with any other funds. Money maintained in an escrow fund account is exempt from execution, attachment, or garnishment. § 32-9-145.
Interest: None specified.
Additional Requirements: Registration and license.
Private Remedies: None specified.
State Remedies: None specified.
Special Servicing Requirements for High-Cost Loans: None specified.

NEBRASKA

Neb. Rev. Stat. §§ 45-711, 45-713 (Transfer of Servicing); Neb. Rev. Stat. § 45-101.05 (Escrows)

Scope: Transfer of servicing provisions apply to licensed mortgage bankers (defined by § 45-702 to include servicers): persons who, for compensation, directly or indirectly make, negotiate, acquire, sell, or arrange for residential mortgage loans. A residential mortgage loan is any loan or extension of credit (including refinancing and assumption of prior loans or contracts of sale) secured by a lien on an owner-occupied one to four family dwelling used as a residence, whether or not the dwelling is attached to real property. Escrow provisions of § 45-101.05 apply to mortgage loans generally.
Exclusions: Financial institutions, bank holding companies, insurance companies, realtors, attorneys in ordinary course of practice

(not actively and principally in business of negotiating mortgage loans), and individuals negotiating terms on their residences or on behalf of family members. § 45-703.

Transfer Notice Requirements: Not less than fifteen days before effective date of transfer, transferor shall notify borrower in writing of the date of the transfer; the name, address, and phone number of the transferee; instructions concerning payments made before and after the date of the transfer. Notice not required if transferor provides borrower with this information at time of closing. § 45-739.

Borrower Inquiries: Mortgage bankers must maintain a toll-free number or accept collect calls from borrowers. Message service that does not allow the option of personal contact does not satisfy this requirement. If mortgage banker ceases to service mortgage loans, must continue to provide toll-free number or accept collect calls for twelve months. § 45-737. See also Appx. D.2, *infra*, for payoff statement requirement.

Escrow Requirements:

Restrictions: At closing borrower may not be required to deposit more than the total amount of taxes and insurance due from the date when the last payment of taxes and insurance premiums would have been paid until the date of the first payment on the mortgage, plus a cushion of one-sixth of the estimated total annual payments from the date of settlement. Thereafter borrower may not be required to deposit in one month more than one-twelfth of the estimated tax and insurance payments, plus a cushion of one-sixth of the estimated payments. If a shortage exists or there will be a deficiency, lender may require additional payments into escrow account in pro rata portions, corresponding to the number of months from the time when the deficiency is discovered until the due date of the tax or insurance payments. § 45-101.05.

Recordkeeping and notice: If escrow amount insufficient to pay taxes or insurance when due, mortgage bankers must give notice to borrower, at least fifteen days before due date. At least once per year, must perform complete escrow analysis, and provide detailed report without charge to borrower. If amount of escrow payments will change, must notify borrower at least twenty days before change becomes effective. § 45-737.

Handling of funds: Mortgage bankers must disburse tax and insurance payments on or before due date, unless funds insufficient and borrower has not paid, after being given at least fifteen days notice. § 45-737.

Interest: None specified.

Additional Requirements: Registration, license, bond.

Private Remedies: Mortgage banker is liable for any penalty incurred by borrower for failure to timely disburse tax or insurance payments, unless banker can show that funds were insufficient, and borrower failed to remit after being given fifteen days notice. § 45-737. Except where expressly authorized, there is no private right of action for violation of the Mortgage Bankers Licensing and Registration Act. § 45-746.

State Remedies: Provisions are part of a licensing scheme administered by the Department of Banking and Finance, which is empowered to revoke or suspend licenses, issue cease and desist orders, and impose administrative fines of up to $5000 per violation. Director may ask attorney general to bring civil enforcement proceeding for injunctive relief, restitution to aggrieved borrower and costs of investigation and prosecution. *See* §§ 45-742, 45-743, 45-744. Violation of § 45-101.05 is a Class IV misdemeanor. § 45-101.07.

Special Servicing Requirements for High-Cost Loans: None.

NEVADA

Nev. Rev. Stat. §§ 645A.010 to 645A.230 (Escrow Agents); Nev. Rev. Stat. § 645B.170 (Mortgage Brokers and Agents); Nev. Rev. Stat. § 645E.430 (Mortgage Bankers)

Scope: Mortgage brokers, mortgage agents, and mortgage bankers.

Exclusions: Numerous including banks, finance companies, insurance companies regulated under other state or federal laws, lenders whose loans are approved under certain federal programs, certain lawyers and realtors, sellers of real property who offer credit secured by property sold.

Transfer Notice Requirements: None specified.

Borrower Inquiries: Not specified.

Escrow Requirements:

Restrictions: Payments required to be made into escrow account shall be in amount reasonably necessary to pay obligations as they become due.

Recordkeeping and notice: Account to the debtor upon reasonable notice for any funds paid into escrow account. Conduct annual account review and, within thirty days after completion of review, notify borrower of the amount by which the contributions exceed the amount reasonably necessary to pay annual obligations. Within twenty days borrower may specify the disposition of the excess funds. If borrower does not specify, excess shall remain in escrow account.

Handling of funds: Escrow funds must be kept in FDIC-insured account, separate from lender's own funds. Taxes and insurance must be paid in timely fashion to avoid insurance being canceled or taxes becoming delinquent. If deficiency exists, may request additional funds from borrower.

Interest: None specified.

Additional Requirements: License (§ 645A.210), surety bond (§ 645A.041).

Private Remedies: None specified. *See* § 645B.0145.

State Remedies: Violation is a misdemeanor (if more than $1000 involved, it is a Class D felony).

Special Servicing Requirements for High-Cost Loans: None.

NEW HAMPSHIRE

N.H. Rev. Stat. Ann. § 397-A:15-a (Nondepository First Mortgage Bankers); N.H. Rev. Stat. Ann. §§ 397-B:1 to 397-B:10 (Mortgage Loan Servicers); N.H. Rev. Stat. Ann. § 384:16-c (Banks)

Scope:

Nondepository First Mortgage Bankers and Mortgage Loan Services: The servicing provisions of chapter 397-A apply to "licensees," which is defined to include mortgage bankers and brokers. § 397-A:1.

Banks: Generally applies to state banks, savings banks or institutions for savings, trust companies, banking companies and all similar corporations, building and loan associations, and credit unions. § 384:1.

Exclusions:

Nondepository First Mortgage Bankers: Numerous exclusions including any bank, trust company, savings and loan association, credit union, thrift company, attorney not actively and principally engaged in the business of negotiating first mortgage loans, individual negotiating loan terms for family members or for a loan secured by their own dwelling. § 397-A:4.

Mortgage Loan Servicers: State or federally chartered banks, savings and loan associations, credit unions. § 397-B:10.

Transfer Notice Requirements: None specified.

Borrower Inquiries:

Nondepository First Mortgage Bankers: Borrower complaints naming licensed bank or mortgage servicing company filed in writing with bank commissioner shall be forwarded to licensee within ten days by banking department. Bank or servicer must within thirty days of receipt of complaint send written acknowledgment to borrower and banking department. Within sixty days following receipt of complaint, either make appropriate corrections to account and provide borrower and department with written notification of corrections or provide written explanation setting forth reason why licensee believes actions are correct. Response shall include documentary evidence. § 397-A:15-a. See also Appx. D.2, *infra*, for payoff statement requirements.

Mortgage Loan Servicers: Same provisions applicable to mortgage servicing companies pursuant to § 397-B:7.

Escrow Requirements:

Mortgage Loan Servicers:

Restrictions: None specified.

Recordkeeping and notice: Servicer at its own expense must notify borrower of amounts necessary to ensure sufficient funds will be available in account to timely pay taxes and insurance premiums.

Handling of funds: Taxes and insurance premiums shall be paid when due, provided bills have been received fifteen days before due date, and sufficient funds are in account. If borrower has made the requested escrow payments but there are insufficient funds in account, servicer shall pay taxes and insurance premiums out of its own funds, and give borrower option to pay deficiency over twelve months, without charging interest on the deficiency. § 397-B:5.

Interest: None specified.

Banks:

Restrictions: None specified.

Recordkeeping and notice: None specified.

Handling of funds: None specified.

Interest: Banks requiring escrow accounts for taxes and insurance on mortgaged property must pay interest at minimum rate established by banking commissioner, which shall be one percent below mean interest rate paid by state chartered banks on regular savings accounts. § 384:16-c. Same requirement for mortgage companies not subject to § 384:16-c on loans which finance acquisition of single-family homes. § 384:16-e. *See also* N.H. Code Admin. R. Ann. Ban 2506.01 (mortgage companies must pay interest on escrow accounts).

Additional Requirements: Mortgage servicing companies required to register with the banking department. § 397-B:4. Banking department authorized to conduct public and private investigations of servicing companies. § 397-B:9.

Private Remedies:

Mortgage Loan Servicers: Servicers liable for penalties and interest resulting from late payment of escrow charges, actual damages, costs, and reasonable attorney fees. Actual damages includes any losses which should have been covered by insurance had the servicer not allowed policy to lapse. § 397-B:6.

State Remedies:

Mortgage Loan Servicers: Bank commissioner may request that attorney general seek injunction to enjoin violations. May be subject to administrative fine up to $2500 for each knowing violation of any rule or order of commissioner; $1500 for each negligent violation. § 397-B:6.

Special Servicing Requirements for High-Cost Loans: None.

NEW JERSEY

N.J. Stat. Ann. §§ 17:16F-15 to 17:16F-26 (West); *see also* N.J. Stat. Ann. § 46:10B-25 (West)

Scope: Mortgage loans made to individuals for personal, family, or household purposes, secured by a structure containing not more than six dwelling units (parts of structure may be used for nonresidential purposes).

Exclusions: Transfer of servicing, after termination for cause or bankruptcy of prior servicer, to Ginnie Mae, Freddie Mac, Fannie Mae, Resolution Trust Corp., or FDIC.

Transfer Notice Requirements: Transferor must notify tax collector of sale or assignment of servicing not more than forty-five days after transfer, or not less than ten days before taxes due, whichever is earlier. Notification on form approved by commissioner. Transferor must forward tax bill and stubs to transferee. Transferee must notify tax collector (same time frame), including information concerning its procedure for responding to questions regarding escrow accounts. Transferee must provide corrected coupon or payment books, if used, within twenty days after first escrow payment is due. § 17:16F-17.

Borrower Inquiries: None specified, but see Appx. D.2, *infra*, for payoff statement requirements.

Escrow Requirements:

Restrictions: None specified.

Recordkeeping and notice: Borrower shall be promptly notified of any shortage, and notified within thirty days if escrow account charged any late payment fee.

Handling of funds: Tax and insurance payments shall be made before amount due becomes delinquent, if sufficient funds in escrow. Servicer permitted but not required to make payments to cover escrow disbursements if funds in account insufficient. Servicer may not charge borrower for penalties or interest for late payment of amounts payable from escrow, unless charge caused by borrower's error or omission. If servicer fails to pay taxes within twenty days of receiving notice from tax collector of tax delinquency, borrower may pay them and send copy of paid bill to servicer; servicer must credit the amount paid including any interest to the escrow account and borrower may stop making further escrow payments until amount paid by borrower to tax authorities is restored to account. If servicer fails to correct a tax delinquency within thirty days of notice of tax sale, borrower may arrange to pay taxes directly to tax collector, and may notify servicer that borrower has made arrangements to pay future payments of taxes and insurance directly and that escrow account shall be terminated. Within ten days of receipt of paid tax bill and notice of escrow termination, servicer must remit to borrower the funds in the escrow account. If, after termination, borrower fails to pay taxes or insurance, servicer may pay them directly and recover amount from borrower with interest.

Interest: None specified.

Additional Requirements: Servicer may not charge borrower for duplicate tax bill unless original was sent to borrower and borrower failed to forward it. § 17:16F-19. Tax collector must notify borrower if servicer's failure to pay taxes subjects property to tax sale. § 17:16F-24. For home loans as defined by statute, § 46:10B-25 requires payments to be posted on the date received.

Private Remedies: If violation of escrow disbursement requirements is not remedied in reasonable, timely manner, after good faith efforts to resolve dispute, borrower has right of action for actual damages (plus an additional $500 if actual damages awarded), costs, and reasonable attorneys fees. § 17:16F-18. If property is subject to tax sale, and borrower's name appears in the notice, borrower may sue for actual damages, including the cost of printing a correction in the newspapers that published the notice, plus costs and attorney fees. § 17:16F-26.

State Remedies: None specified. Regulatory scheme administered by the commissioner of community affairs. *See* N.J. Admin. Code tit. 5, §§ 33-4.5 to 33-4.10.

Special Servicing Requirements for High-Cost Loans: N.J. Stat. Ann. § 46:10B-26 prohibits increasing interest rates upon default on payments or charging fees for loan modification. It also restricts the amount and timing of late fees.

NEW MEXICO

N.M. Stat. § 48-7-8 (Mortgage Escrow Funds)

Scope: Real property mortgages.

Exclusions: None specified.

Transfer Notice Requirements: None specified.

Borrower Inquiries: Not specified.

Escrow Requirements:

Restrictions: Sum exceeding two months escrow payments plus the pro rata accrual for taxes, insurance premiums and other required charges shall, upon demand of the borrower (but not more than once per year), be credited to the principal on the mortgage within sixty days of the demand.

Recordkeeping and notice: None specified.

Handling of funds: None specified.

Interest: None specified (see penalty provision below).

Additional Requirements: None specified.

Private Remedies: If excess sum in escrow not credited to principal upon demand, penalty of six percent interest per year on excess accumulation shall be payable to the borrower.

State Remedies: None specified.

Special Servicing Requirements for High-Cost Loans: See N.M. Stat. Ann. §§ 58-21A-1 to 58-21A-14. Prohibited practices include: increasing interest rates upon default on payments; charging fees for loan modification that are not bona fide, reasonable, and actual; and charging more than seventy-five dollars to defer any payment due under the terms of a loan. § 58-21A-4. The amount and timing of late fees are also restricted and notice of default and a right to cure before foreclosure is required. § 58-21A-6.

NEW YORK

N.Y. Banking Law § 6-k (McKinney) (Real Property Insurance Escrow Accounts); N.Y. Gen. Oblig. Law § 5-601 (McKinney); N.Y. Real Prop. Tax Law §§ 952 to 959 (McKinney) (Real Property Tax Escrow Accounts)

Scope: Provisions dealing with real property insurance escrow accounts apply to any bank, trust company, national bank, state or federal savings and loan association, credit union, or any other entity which maintains escrow account in relation to mortgages on one to four family residences located in state. § 6-k. Other provisions apply to same entities in relation to mortgages on one to six family residences located in state. §§ 5-601, 952.

Exclusions: None specified.

Transfer Notice Requirements: Transferee must provide written notice no later than ten business days after transfer, including name, address, and telephone number of transferee. §§ 6-k, 953.

Borrower Inquiries: At borrower's request, transferor must advise borrower of the amount of money in the escrow account at the time of transfer. §§ 6-k, 953. See also Appx. D.2, *infra*, for payoff statement requirements.

Escrow Requirements:

Restrictions: No entity may impose a service charge or other fee for maintenance of escrow account. §§ 5-601, 953.

Recordkeeping and notice: At time when account is established, borrower to be provided with prescribed notice. Annual account analysis shall be provided without charge to borrower, which shall include beginning and ending balance, interest earned, and amount of insurance premiums and taxes paid. At borrower's request, must provide without charge the date(s) of the insurance and tax payments. Required information may be provided in notices sent pursuant to other state or federal law. After loan is paid off, borrower must be notified no later than thirty days after final payment that escrow is being terminated, that borrower is now responsible for insurance and tax payments, and the name, address, and telephone number of the insurance company and tax collector. §§ 6-k, 953.

Handling of funds: Escrow funds must be deposited in FDIC-insured account. Account may be debited for insurance premiums and taxes only if actual payment is made within twenty-one days after the debit. Payments for insurance and taxes must be made out of escrow in a timely manner. If insurance bill is sent to borrower, failure to timely forward it excuses the servicer from liability for late payments.

Interest: Interest shall be provided at no less than the minimum rate of interest as set by banking board regulation. § 5-601.

Private Mortgage Insurance Requirements: Borrower may not be required to pay, directly or indirectly, for mortgage guarantee insurance after unpaid principal is 75% or less of appraised value at time loan was made, or such higher percentage as banking board may, by regulation, determine. (For loans pursuant to N.Y. mortgage agency's forward commitment program, percentage is 60%.) N.Y. Ins. Law § 6503(d) through (f).

Additional Requirements: Tax collector shall mail to borrower a receipt no later than three weeks after taxes have been paid by servicer. § 955.

Private Remedies: Lender or servicer who fails to make timely payments for insurance and taxes is liable for amount of premiums and taxes and all penalties and interest imposed thereon. §§ 6-k, 955. In addition, if payments for insurance premiums have not been made for thirty days after due date, or if payments for taxes have not been made for 180 days after due date, and borrower has made required payments into escrow account, borrower may be awarded, if court finds that failure to comply was due to negligence or intentional acts, injunctive relief and liquidated damages of three times the amount of the premium or taxes (but not more than $6000). §§ 6-k, 956. Lender or servicer shall also be liable for all actual damages for failure to make timely payment of insurance premiums. § 6-k. Lender or servicer who fails to provide proper notice to borrower after escrow account closed when loan is paid off is liable for interest and penalties charged to borrower for late payment of property taxes. § 953.

State Remedies: Regulatory scheme administered by the superintendent of banks. Attorney general may sue to enforce escrow provisions of Real Property Tax Law. For repeated fraudulent or illegal acts in violation of certain sections, court may impose civil penalty up to $1000 per violation. Bona fide error defense available. § 957.

Special Servicing Requirements for High-Cost Loans: N.Y. Banking Law § 6-l prohibits increasing interest rates upon default on payment and fees for modification or deferral.

NORTH CAROLINA

N.C. Gen. Stat. §§ 45-90 to 45-95; § 24-1.1E

Scope: "Home loans," defined as loans secured by real property in North Carolina used or intended to be used as a dwelling. "Servicers" as defined in RESPA, 12 U.S.C. § 2605(i). § 45-90.

Exclusions: Attorney who, in the practice of law or performing as a trustee, accepts payments related to a loan closing, default, foreclosure, or settlement of a dispute or legal claim related to a loan. § 45-90.

Transfer Notice Requirements: None specified.

Borrower Inquiries: Servicer must provide a written statement within ten business days in response to a borrower request for information and/or account dispute. Servicer must provide the requested information and/or documents (including items listed in § 45-93 if requested) within twenty-five business days of receipt of request, and shall promptly correct account errors. Borrower entitled to one response statement in any six-month period free of charge, and additional statements shall be provided if borrower pays reasonable charge not to exceed $25. § 45-93. *See also* Appx. D.2, *infra* (payoff statement requirements).

Escrow Requirements:

Restrictions: None specified.

Recordkeeping and notice: None specified.

Handling of funds: Servicer shall collect and make payments from escrow account in timely manner, so as to ensure that no late penalties are assessed or other negative consequences result. This provision applies even if loan is delinquent or in default unless servicer has reasonable basis to believe that recovery of funds will not be possible or if loan is more than ninety days in default. § 45-92.

Interest: None specified.

Additional Requirements: Fees incurred by servicer must be assessed within forty-five days (or if foreclosure attorney or trustee fees, within forty-five days of being charged) and explained clearly and conspicuously in a statement servicer must mail to borrower within thirty days after assessing the fee. If procedure is not followed, servicer is not entitled to the fee. Payments to servicer must be accepted and credited within one business day, provided that borrower has made the full contractual payment and servicer has sufficient information to credit the account. Borrower must be notified within ten business days if payment is not credited, and advised of reasons why not credited. All fees charged by servicer must be permitted under applicable law and the contracts between the parties. These provisions apply regardless of whether loan is considered in default or borrower is in bankruptcy or borrower has been in bankruptcy. § 45-91.

Private Remedies: In addition to equitable remedies and other remedies at law, borrower injured by violation of Act may bring an action for recovery of actual damages, including reasonable attorney fees. At least thirty days before borrower brings civil action for damages, borrower shall notify servicer in writing of any claimed errors or disputes that are basis of the action. Servicer will not be liable if: (1) violation was not intentional or the result of bad faith; and (2) within thirty days after discovering or being notified of an error, and prior to legal action by borrower, the servicer corrected the error and compensated borrower for any fees or charges incurred by borrower as a result of the violation. § 45-94.

State Remedies: Commissioner of Banks and Attorney General may enforce provisions.

Special Servicing Requirements for High-Cost Loans: N.C. Gen. Stat. § 24-1.1E prohibits the lender in its sole discretion to accelerate the indebtedness, balloon payments more than twice as large as the average of earlier scheduled payments, negative amortization, financing of fees or charges, increasing interest rates upon default on payments, or charging fees for loan modification or deferrals.

NORTH DAKOTA

N.D. Cent. Code §§ 47-10.2-01 to 47-10.2-05 (Escrow Accounts); N.D. Cent. Code § 6-08-29

Scope: Escrow account statute applies to servicers who maintain escrow accounts for a "secondary residential mortgagee," defined as an out-of-state successor mortgagee who purchases interest in a first lien mortgage on property located in state that is borrower's principal residence (not including mobile homes). § 47-10.2-01. Other provisions apply generally to banking institutions, savings and loan associations, and credit unions making mortgages on residential property.

Exclusions: None specified.

Transfer Notice Requirements: None specified.

Borrower Inquiries: None specified, but see Appx. D.2, *infra*, for payoff statement requirements.

Escrow Requirements:

Restrictions: None specified.

Recordkeeping and notice: Servicer must provide written notification to borrower, on or before March 1 of the following year, of any excess amount in escrow account (defined as any amount received in a calendar year in excess of $300 plus the amount needed to pay taxes and insurance premiums during the calendar year). § 47-10.2-02. Borrower may elect within thirty days after date of notice to either receive a refund of all or part of the excess amount or leave the excess in the escrow account; servicer must comply with borrower's request within thirty days of election. § 47-10.2-03. Annual statement shall be provided showing in detail all debits and credits on the account. §§ 6-08-29.

Handling of funds: Borrower may instruct servicer by December 1, if there are sufficient funds in escrow, on timing of tax payments to be made out of escrow, for example, whether taxes should be paid when due, by December 31, or by February 15 so as to qualify for early payment discount. § 47-10.2-04.

Interest: None specified.

Additional Requirements: None specified.

Private Remedies: Escrow agent who disregards timely instructions for payment of taxes is liable for $500 plus actual damages, costs, and reasonable attorney fees. § 47-10.2-04. Servicer who fails to respond to pay-off request by depositing answer in mail or personally delivering it within seven days of request is liable to borrower for all damages resulting from delay. § 35-03-18.

State Remedies: None specified.

Special Servicing Requirements for High-Cost Loans: None.

OHIO

Ohio Rev. Code Ann. § 1349.27 (West)

Scope: Not specified.

Exclusions: None specified.

Transfer Notice Requirements: None specified.

Borrower Inquiries: Not specified.

Escrow Requirements:

Restrictions: None specified.

Recordkeeping and notice: None specified.

Handling of funds: None specified.

Interest: None specified.

Additional Requirements: None specified.

Private Remedies: None specified.

State Remedies: None specified.

Special Servicing Requirements For High-Cost Loans: Ohio Rev. Code Ann. § 1349.27 prohibits increasing interest rates upon default on payments.

OREGON

Or. Rev. Stat. §§ 86.205 to 86.275

Scope: Lenders making loans of $100,000 or less, secured by real property occupied by borrower and located within state, including multi-family property. Definition of lenders includes holders. § 86.205.

Exclusions: None specified.

Transfer Notice Requirements: None specified.

Borrower Inquiries: Not specified.

Escrow Requirements:

Restrictions: At settlement, borrower may not be required to deposit more than the estimated amount of taxes and insurance due and payable on date of settlement, and the pro rata portion thereof that has accrued, plus one-sixth of the estimated amount of such charges that will be due within one year after settlement. After settlement, borrower may not be required in any one month to deposit more than one-sixth of total estimated charges to be due within subsequent twelve months. If lender determines that there will be a deficiency, it may require deposit of pro rata amounts needed to make up deficiency by due date. If loan subject to RESPA, compliance with RESPA and Reg. X shall be deemed compliance with statute. § 86.240. Lender may not impose a service charge for any required escrow account. § 86.250.

Recordkeeping and notice: If escrow not required by loan terms, borrower and lender may agree that escrow account will be maintained. Borrower must be notified in writing before entering into voluntary escrow arrangement that it is not condition of loan agreement, whether interest will be paid and at what rate, and whether borrower will be charged for the escrow services (charge may not exceed the amount of interest income earned on account). § 86.255.

Handling of funds: Lender must pay escrow charges on or before due dates, and in case of taxes, in time to qualify for any discounts authorized under state law. If lender fails to timely pay taxes, lender must credit the amount of any lost discount to borrower's escrow account. § 86.260.

Interest: Interest shall be provided on any required escrow accounts at rate not less than "discount rate," which is based on ninety-one-day Treasury bills, less 100 basis points. Interest shall be paid quarterly by crediting escrow account. § 86.245.

Private Mortgage Insurance Requirements: Mortgagor may not be required to pay, directly or indirectly, the cost of mortgage insurance on a loan secured by a junior lien, if the indebtedness evidenced by the loan, combined with mortgage and loan amounts at the time the loan is made is less than 60% of the fair market value of the property at the time the loan is made. Or. Rev. Stat. § 742.282.

Additional Requirements: See Or. Admin. R. 274-020-0388 and 274-045-0150, covering escrow accounts on Veteran's Loans administered by the state Department of Veteran's Affairs (cushion of one-sixth of the estimated amount due permitted; annual account analysis must be conducted and borrower notified of amount of any surplus, shortage, or deficiency, and the new amount of escrow payment; if there is a deficiency, director may advance the funds and increase the escrow payments or, if borrower chooses, may repay as lump sum; surplus of $25 or more must be refunded to borrower).

Private Remedies: If lender willfully fails to timely pay taxes, or upon discovery of noncompliance fails to credit amount of lost tax discount, borrower has cause of action to recover an amount equal to fifteen times the amount of the lost discount, plus any interest that accrued on the unpaid taxes, and attorney fees to prevailing party. § 86.260. Any violation of escrow provisions also renders the escrow requirement voidable at borrower's option and renders lender liable to borrower for the greater of actual damages or $100, costs, and reasonable attorney fees at trial and on appeal if borrower gives written demand at least ten days before filing suit. No attorney fees shall be awarded if lender tenders an amount not less that the damages awarded to borrower. § 86.265.

State Remedies: None specified.

Special Servicing Requirements for High-Cost Loans: None.

PENNSYLVANIA

63 Pa. Stat. Ann. §§ 456.501 to 456.524 (West)

Scope: Not specified.

Exclusions: None specified.

Transfer Notice Requirements: None specified.

Borrower Inquiries: Not specified.

Escrow Requirements:

Restrictions: None specified.

Recordkeeping and notice: None specified.

Handling of funds: None specified.

Interest: None specified.

Additional Requirements: None specified.
Private Remedies: None specified.
State Remedies: None specified.
Special Servicing Requirements for High-Cost Loans: 63 Pa. Stat. Ann. §§ 456.501 to 456.524 prohibits increasing interest rates upon default on payments.

PUERTO RICO

P.R. Laws Ann. tit. 7, §§ 1051, 1057a

Scope: Persons engaged in the granting of mortgage loans to finance or refinance the acquisition of real property; definition includes servicing. § 1051.
Exclusions: Banks, certain insurance companies and very small lenders (portfolio less than $100,000). § 1052.
Transfer Notice Requirements: None specified.
Borrower Inquiries: None specified.
Escrow Requirements:
Restrictions: "Concessionaires" (licensees) under the Mortgage Institutions Act are prohibited from "mak[ing] excessive collections to be withheld in escrow accounts for the lender to have more protection in the mortgage loan." § 1057a(13).
Recordkeeping and notice: None specified.
Handling of Funds: None specified.
Interest: None specified.
Additional Requirements: None specified.
Private Remedies: None specified.
State Remedies: Fines, possible criminal actions, injunction, revocation, suspension. § 1061.
Special Servicing Requirements for High-Cost Loans: None.

RHODE ISLAND

R.I. Gen. Laws § 19-9-2 (Escrow Accounts); R.I. Gen. Laws § 34-26-2

Scope: Any regulated financial institution and any person who makes or negotiates loans secured by owner-occupied one to four family residences. § 19-9-1.
Exclusions: Mortgages insured or guaranteed by Veterans Admin., Federal Housing Admin., Farmers Home Loan Admin., or private mortgage insurer licensed to do business in state. § 19-9-2.
Transfer Notice Requirements: None specified.
Borrower Inquiries: None specified, but see Appx. D.2, *infra*, for payoff statement requirements.
Escrow Requirement:
Restrictions: Lender holding borrower's funds in escrow for payment of taxes may not charge an annual "tax service fee" or other annual fee for ascertaining whether taxes have been paid. § 19-9-2.
Recordkeeping and notice: None specified.
Handling of funds: Within thirty days after mortgage satisfied, lender must disburse to borrower any funds held in the escrow account. § 34-26-2.
Interest: Lender shall pay or credit interest on funds in escrow account at rate equal to the rate paid to mortgagee on its regular savings account, if offered, and otherwise at a rate not less than the prevailing market rate of interest for regular savings accounts. Credit of interest accrues on daily basis and shall be made annually on December 31. § 19-9-2. *See also* 02-010-017 R.I. Code R. § 98-9.
Additional Requirements: None specified.
Private Remedies: None specified.
State Remedies: Lender who fails to pay interest on escrow account or charges unlawful tax service fee shall be fined no more than $100 per violation. § 19-9-2.
Special Servicing Requirements for High-Cost Loans: R.I. Gen. Laws § 34-25.2-1 to 34-25.2-15 prohibits increasing interest rates upon default on payments or charging fees for modification or deferrals. It also restricts the amount and timing of late fees.

SOUTH CAROLINA

S.C. Code Ann. §§ 37-23-10 to 37-23-60

Scope: Not specified.
Exclusions: None specified.
Transfer Notice Requirements: None specified.
Borrower Inquiries: Not specified.
Escrow Requirements:
Restrictions: None specified.
Recordkeeping and notice: None specified.
Handling of funds: None specified.
Interest: None specified.
Additional Requirements: None specified.
Private Remedies: None specified.
State Remedies: None specified.
Special Servicing Requirements for High-Cost Loans: S.C. Code Ann. §§ 37-23-10 to 37-23-60 prohibit increasing interest rates upon default on payments or charging fees for loan modification.

TENNESSEE

Tenn. Comp. R. & Regs. 0180-17-.03

Scope: Transferor and transferee of servicing rights under a mortgage loan.
Exclusions: None specified.
Transfer Notice Requirements: Transferor must give notice, at least ten days before due date of first payment due after transfer of servicing rights, of name and address to which future payments are to be made. Until notice given, borrower may continue sending payments to transferor, and may not be charged by either transferor or transferee for any nonpayment or late payment penalties based on continuation of payments to transferor.
Borrower Inquiries: Not specified, but see Appx. D.2, *infra*, for payoff statement requirements.
Escrow Requirements: None specified.
Additional Requirements: Tenn. Code Ann. § 45-13-201 requires mortgage loan servicers to be licensed, with exceptions for banks, credit unions, and a variety of other entities.
Private Remedies: None specified.
State Remedies: None specified.
Special Servicing Requirements for High-Cost Loans: Tenn. Code Ann. § 45-20-103 prohibits increasing interest rates upon default on payments. It also restricts the amount and timing of late fees.

TEXAS

Tex. Fin. Code Ann. §§ 343.201 to 343.206 (Vernon)

Scope: Not specified.
Exclusions: None specified.

Transfer Notice Requirements: None specified.
Borrower Inquiries: Not specified.
Escrow Requirements:
Restrictions: None specified.
Recordkeeping and notice: None specified.
Handling of funds: None specified.
Interest: None specified.
Additional Requirements: None specified.
Private Remedies: None specified.
State Remedies: None specified.
Special Servicing Requirements for High-Cost Loans: Tex. Fin. Code §§ 343.201 to 343.206 restrict use of balloon payments, and prohibit negative amortization, prepayment penalties, and charges for services or products not provided.

UTAH

Utah Code Ann. §§ 70D-1-102 to 70D-2-304 (Mortgage Lending and Servicing); Utah Code Ann. §§ 7-17-1 to 7-17-10 (Reserve Accounts)

Scope:
Mortgage Lending and Servicing: Loans made for personal, family, or household purposes and secured by a mortgage on real property located in state. § 70D-1-102.
Reserve Accounts: Lenders who make or hold loans secured by owner-occupied one to four family residential property, including mortgages, trust deeds, and conditional land sales contracts. § 7-17-2.
Exclusions:
Mortgage Lending and Servicing: Loans made by an individual to a family member, and loans covered by Utah Code Ann. Title 70C. Persons who make five or fewer mortgage loans per year; lawyers and realtors; government agencies; certain nonprofit corporations; and mortgage loans of two years or less. §§ 70D-2-102, 70D-2-103.
Reserve Accounts: Certain provisions not applicable to accounts established prior to July 1, 1979.
Transfer Notice Requirements: Mortgage lender or broker must give applicant a written notice disclosing, if such is the case, that the loan or the servicing may be sold or assigned. At closing, lender must notify borrower of the name of the initial servicer, and the address to which payments should be made. If servicing is transferred, both transferor and transferee must notify borrower at least ten days before due date of first payment after transfer. Transferor must also disclose (unless it regularly provides the information in monthly statements) the date and amount of all payments made within the previous twelve-month period, the balance in the escrow account, and the total unpaid balance of the mortgage loan. If a payment is misdirected because of an error in giving the required notices, no late charges may be imposed. § 70D-2-303.
Borrower Inquiries: Within fifteen days after receipt of written request (unless servicer regularly provides the information in monthly statements), servicer must provide a statement of account with date and amount of all payments credited within past twelve months, balance in escrow account, and total unpaid balance on mortgage loan. First two statements within twelve months must be provided free of charge; may charge reasonable fee for additional statements. § 70D-2-304.
Escrow Requirements:
Reserve Accounts:
Restrictions: At closing, may not require deposit of more than estimated total of taxes and insurance premiums that will be due at closing, and the pro rata portion thereof which has accrued, plus a cushion of one-sixth of the estimated amount of escrow charges that will be due during the twelve months following closing. For any month thereafter, may not require more than one-twelfth of the estimated annual amount of escrow charges due, plus enough to maintain the one-sixth cushion (as deposited at closing). § 7-17-7.
Recordkeeping and notice: Annual statement shall be provided without charge within sixty days after end of calendar year, showing money received for interest and principal, and payments to and disbursements from any escrow account. § 7-17-5. If lender does not require reserve account, must inform borrower of following options: 1) borrower may elect to maintain a voluntary non-interest bearing escrow account to be serviced by lender at no charge to borrower, or 2) borrower may manage payment of tax and insurance payments on own account. (This requirement does not apply to loans made, renewed or modified on or after May 6, 2002.) § 7-17-4.
Handling of funds: Taxes, insurance premiums and other charges shall be timely paid out of escrow, if sufficient funds in escrow. § 7-17-6. If lender estimates there will be a deficiency on due date, it may require additional deposits based on a pro rata portion of the deficiency for the number of months from date deficiency discovered to the due date for the charges. If lender determines there is a deficiency after the due date, it may bill the borrower for the deficiency, or add the sum to the principal, or require additional monthly deposits in the escrow account for up to twelve months to make up the deficiency. Lender may exercise default remedies under loan agreement if borrower fails to pay any amount billed to recover a deficiency. If failure to pay persists for thirty days after notice, lender no longer required to pay interest on escrow account. § 7-17-7.
Interest: If escrow account required, interest shall be credited to the account on a yearly basis as of December 31, at the rate of either: 5 ½%; the average of weighted cost of funds index published by Federal Home Loan Bank, less 1 ½%; or the statement savings rate or share account rate offered to public by depository institution holding escrow account. Interest not required to be paid if escrow required by government insurer or guarantor, if the principal of loan exceeds eighty percent of appraised value of property, or if payment of interest is prohibited by federal law or regulation. § 7-17-3.
Additional Requirements: Lender or servicer must credit to borrower's account any payment received as of the date it is received or by next banking day, unless: payment is insufficient to pay principal, interest, late charges, and escrow reserves then due; loan has been referred to an attorney because of default; or payment is received at address other than payment address specified by lender. § 70D-2-303. Lender may not charge service fee for administration of reserve accounts. § 7-17-3.
Private Remedies:
Mortgage Lenders and Servicers: Any mortgage lender, broker, or servicer who violates provisions is liable to injured party for

actual damages. Prevailing party entitled to costs and attorney fees. § 70D-2-501.

Reserve Accounts: Lender liable for all damages resulting from negligent failure to make timely payments of taxes, insurance premiums, and other charges out of escrow. Borrower's failure to timely deliver tax or insurance bills sent to borrower will relieve lender from liability. § 7-17-6. In addition, lender who violates other provisions is liable for greater of actual damages or $100. Prevailing party may be awarded costs and attorney fees. Bona fide error defense (notwithstanding maintenance of procedures to avoid errors) available to lender. No liability if, upon being given notice of borrower's claim not less than thirty days before action filed, lender tenders (prior to commencement of action) not less than the amount of damages awarded. Action must be bought within one year after date of violation. Escrow account maintained in violation of the act is voidable at option of borrower. § 7-17-8.

State Remedies:

Mortgage Lenders and Servicers: Willful violation of provisions is class A misdemeanor. § 70D-2-501. Provisions enforced by the Department of Financial Institutions, which is empowered to issue cease and desist orders, but may not award damages or penalties. § 70D-2-504. Department commissioner may also bring an action in state court for violations of chapter 70D. § 70D-2-502.

Special Servicing Requirements for High-Cost Loans: None.

VERMONT

Vt. Stat. Ann. tit. 8, § 10404

Scope: Lender or servicer who requires periodic payments by borrower into an escrow account on a loan secured by residential real estate occupied by borrower.

Exclusions: None specified.

Transfer Notice Requirements: None specified.

Borrower Inquiries: Not specified, but see Appx. D.2, *infra*, for payoff statement requirements.

Escrow Requirements:

Restrictions: Lender shall not require aggregate annual deposits greater than estimated total annual taxes, insurance premiums, and other charges plus one-twelfth of that total, or monthly payments greater than one-twelfth of reasonably anticipated annual charges plus an amount sufficient to provide an additional account balance no greater than one-twelfth of that total.

Recordkeeping and notice: Lender shall provide annually, or upon request of the borrower, financial statements relating to the escrow account in manner and form approved by the commissioner. Lender may not charge for preparation or transmittal of statements.

Handling of funds: Lender must make timely payments out of escrow and is primarily responsible for payment of escrow charges and any late penalties resulting from late payment of such charges. Escrow account funds must be kept in a FDIC-insured institution.

Interest: Interest shall be paid at the rate provided for regular savings accounts in the institution where account kept, or otherwise at rate not less than prevailing market rate for regular savings accounts offered by local banks. Interest shall be calculated based on average monthly balance and credited to account on first day of each quarter. No interest shall be paid if lender requires escrow account because borrower has failed, within past year, to make timely payment of taxes and insurance.

Additional Requirements: None specified.

Private Remedies: Aggrieved borrower may bring action for injunctive relief, actual damages, three times amount of interest not paid on escrow balance, plus costs and reasonable attorney fees.

State Remedies: Commissioner of banking may bring action for injunctive relief, restitution, administrative costs, and attorney fees.

Special Servicing Requirements for High-Cost Loans: None.

VIRGIN ISLANDS

V.I. Code Ann. tit. 9, §§ 66, 67 (Banks and Foreign Banks); V.I. Code Ann. tit. 9, §§ 361, 363, 375 (Mortgage Lenders and Brokers)

Scope: §§ 66 and 67 cover banks and foreign banks. Tit. 9, §§ 1–2. §§ 361, 363, and 375 cover mortgage lenders (defined to include servicers). *See* § 361.

Exclusions: National banks are excluded by tit. 9, § 1 from §§ 66 and 67. A variety of depository institutions and certain other entities are excluded from §§ 363 and 375 by tit. 9, § 362.

Transfer Notice Requirements: None specified.

Borrower Inquiries: Not specified.

Escrow Requirements:

Restrictions: None specified by §§ 66 and 67. § 375 prohibits mortgage lenders from requiring escrow account on subordinate mortgage loan unless no escrow account is being maintained for the superior mortgage loan.

Recordkeeping and notice: If escrow required for taxes, insurance or other purposes, must provide annual statement within sixty days after end of calendar year. Must include beginning balance, total receipts, itemized statement of expenditures, ending balance and accrued interest. Not required if monthly billing statements or passbook provide this information. § 66.

Handling of funds: Not specified by §§ 66 and 67, but § 375 requires escrow accounts to be segregated from mortgage lender's accounts.

Interest: Must pay interest on the average quarterly balance of the escrow account at the prevailing rate for the bank's passbook savings accounts. § 67.

Additional Requirements: None specified by §§ 66 and 67, but §§ 361 and 363 require covered mortgage lenders, defined to include servicers, to be licensed.

Private Remedies: None specified.

State Remedies: Fine of up to $25 per account per day for failure to credit interest to escrow accounts. § 67.

Special Servicing Requirements for High-Cost Loans: None.

VIRGINIA

Va. Code Ann. § 6.1-423

Scope: Lenders and brokers who originate, make, or negotiate a mortgage loan, which is a loan to an individual for personal, family, or household purposes secured by a mortgage or deed of trust on a one to four family residential property located in state, including renewal and refinancing. § 6.1-409.

Exclusions: Various financial institutions and other entities regulated under other sections of statute or authorized to engage in business as a bank, savings institution, or credit union; lenders making three or fewer mortgage loans in any twelve-month period; federal and state government agencies; certain quasi-governmental agencies; certain realtors and lawyers; nonprofit corporations. § 6.1-411. Definition of mortgage loan excludes loans to buyers made by sellers, loans to those related to lender by blood or marriage, loans to bona fide employees of the lender, and loans secured by a mortgage or deed of trust upon any interest in a more than four-family residential property used for a commercial or agricultural purpose. § 6.1-409.
Transfer Notice Requirements: At least ten days before due date of first payment affected by the transfer, transferor must notify borrower of name and address to which future payments are to be sent. Borrower may continue sending payments to old servicer until this notice is given. *See* 10 Va. Admin. Code § 5-160-20.
Borrower Inquiries: Not specified, but see Appx. D.2, *infra*, for payoff statement requirements.
Escrow Requirements:
Restrictions: Lender may not require escrow account on subordinate mortgage unless no escrow account is being maintained for superior mortgage loan. *See also* § 6.1-237.7 (same requirement for industrial loan companies).
Recordkeeping and notice: Lender must notify insurance company within thirty days after lender changes its billing address, or sixty days before renewal date of insurance policy, whichever is later.
Handling of funds: Escrow funds must be kept in accounts segregated from accounts of lender, not commingled with other funds of lender. *See also* §§ 6.1-237.7 (same requirement for industrial loan companies); 6.1-2.8 (lender is liable to borrow if it fails to make timely payment of taxes or insurance from escrow).
Interest: None specified.
Private Mortgage Insurance Requirements: Lender that requires private mortgage insurance as prerequisite for lending must return to person who paid premium any sum not used to secure insurance. Va. Stat. Ann. § 6.1-2.9:1.
Additional Requirements: None specified.
Private Remedies: Nothing in article precludes borrower who suffers loss as a result of violation from bringing action for damages, restitution, and attorney fees as provided by statute, except if consumer receives restitution as a result of attorney general's action; borrower who suffers loss as result of broker's breach of duty in § 6.1-422 may bring an action against such broker to recover actual damages, attorney fees, and court costs. § 6.1-431.
State Remedies: Commissioner of Bureau of Financial Institutions empowered to issue implementing regulations. *See* 10 Va. Admin. Code §§ 5-160-10 to 5-160-60. State Corporation Commission empowered to suspend or revoke licenses, issue cease and desist orders, impose administrative fines up to $2500, or refer cases to the attorney general for court action for injunction and restitution. *See* Va. Code Ann. §§ 6.1-425 to 6.1-430 (Michie).
Special Servicing Requirements for High-Cost Loans: None.

WASHINGTON

Wash. Rev. Code §§ 19.148.010 to 19.148.900 (Mortgage Loan Servicing)

Scope: Loans used to finance the acquisition of an owner-occupied one to four family residence located in state.
Exclusions: None specified.
Transfer Notice Requirements: At or before closing, lender must inform borrower if servicing is subject to sale, transfer, or assignment. If lender who did not make this disclosure merges with another institution, so that transfer becomes possible, lender must make disclosure within thirty days of the merger. If servicing is transferred, transferee servicer must notify borrower at least thirty days before due date of first payment after transfer of the name, address, and phone number of company division that can provide information about the loan, and advise borrower of any changes in servicing requirements, including interest rate, monthly payment, and escrow balance.
Borrower Inquiries: Transferee servicer must respond in writing within fifteen days of receipt of written request for information from borrower. Response must include telephone number of company division that can assist the borrower.
Escrow Requirements: None specified.
Additional Requirements: Transferee servicer must issue new coupon or payment books, if used and necessary.
Private Remedies: Injured party may bring action for actual damages, costs, and reasonable attorney fees.
State Remedies: None specified.
Special Servicing Requirements for High-Cost Loans: None.

WEST VIRGINIA

W. Va. Code §§ 31-17-1 to 31-17-20 (Mortgage Loans)

Scope: Any person who services mortgages is included in definition of "lender." § 31-17-1(i). "Servicing" a loan is defined in § 31-17-1(n).
Exclusions: Authorized banks, other licensed lenders, and insurance companies, parties supervised or licensed by federal agency; other person and entity exemptions noted in § 31-17-2.
Transfer Notice Requirements: None specified.
Borrower Inquiries: Holder of a primary or subordinate mortgage loan instrument shall deliver to the borrower, within ten business days from and after receipt of written request, a statement of the borrower's account, free of charge once each year and not more than three dollars for each additional statement. *See also* Appx. D.2, *infra* (payoff statement requirements).
Escrow Requirements: None specified.
Additional Requirements: License; surety bond; annual financial statements; minimum amount of available funds; requirements as to record keeping, disclosures, advertising, fees, and terms of mortgage instruments, and prohibitions of misrepresentation.
Private Remedies: Actions for damages, costs and attorney fees; loan cancellation; right to cause of action cannot be waived. § 31-17-17.
State Remedies: Injunctions; license suspension or revocation; fines, and imprisonment.

WISCONSIN

Wis. Stat. § 138.052

Scope: Loans secured by first lien mortgage, made or refinanced after Nov. 1, 1981, on one to four family dwelling which is borrower's principal place of residence.
Exclusions: Manufactured or mobile home transactions; loans insured or committed to be insured by U.S. Department of Housing and Urban Development; loans insured, guaranteed, or committed to be insured or guaranteed pursuant to 38 U.S.C. §§ 1801–1827 (Veterans Administration) or 7 U.S.C. §§ 1921–1995 (Rural Housing Service).
Transfer Notice Requirements: Within fifteen working days after transfer of servicing, lender shall notify borrower in writing of the name, address, and telephone number of new servicer.
Borrower Inquiries: Lender or servicer must respond to inquiries within fifteen days. See also Appx. D.2, *infra*, for payoff statement requirements.
Escrow Requirements:
Restrictions: None specified.
Recordkeeping and notice: If escrow is required, lender must provide before the loan closing a written notice to borrower stating that borrower may require payments to be made out of escrow based on several specified options and the responsibilities of the borrower and servicer in exercising and carrying out those options.
Handling of funds: If borrower provides written notice to servicer specifying the method of making payments out of escrow for taxes based on available options, servicer must comply with election unless borrower is not current with loan payments. If servicer fails to comply with election, borrower may establish an escrow account in a financial institution of the borrower's choice.
Interest: Interest shall be paid on escrow funds at rate set by division of banking.
Additional Requirements: Lender or servicer must treat payment by check or other negotiable instrument as made on date when check is physically received.
Private Remedies: Borrower may sue for $500 plus actual damages, costs, and reasonable attorney fees. No liability if unintentional mistake corrected by lender after demand.
State Remedies: None specified.
Special Servicing Requirements for High-Cost Loans: Wis. Stat. §§ 428.202 to 428.211 prohibit increasing interest rates upon default on payments, the amount of balloon payments, and negative amortization.

D.2 Payoff Statement Requirements

Alabama

Requirements: None.

Alaska

Requirements: None.

Arizona

Ariz. Rev. Stat. Ann. § 33-715

Requirements: Where failure to provide statement fourteen days after written demand, liability for $500 damages plus any actual damages. Holder may charge no more than $30 fee for statement.

Arkansas

Requirements: None.

California

Cal. Civ. Code § 2943 (West)

Requirements: Where failure to provide statement twenty-one days after written demand, liability for $300 damages plus any actual damages; liability may recur after six-month period. Holder may charge no more than $30 fee for statement.

Colorado

Colo. Rev. Stat. § 5-3.5-103(h)

Requirements: For specified loans as defined in § 5-3.5-101(2), statement required no more than five business days after written request. No fee allowed for payoff quote. For enforcement see § 5-3.5-201.

Connecticut

Conn. Gen. Stat. § 49-10a

Requirements: Payoff statement or reinstatement payment statement required on date requested by mortgagor as long as mortgagee has seven business days in which to reply. No fee allowed unless agreed upon for expedited reply. For non-compliance, no interest accrual allowed for period after which statement was due.

Delaware

Requirements: None.

District of Columbia

Requirements: None.

Florida

Fla. Stat. Ann. § 701.04 (West)

Requirements: Within fourteen days of written request, holder is to deliver estoppel letter indicating unpaid balance.

Georgia

Ga. Code Ann. § 7-6A-3

Requirements: Payoff balance due no later than five days after request. Fee allowed up to $10.

Hawaii

Requirements: None.

Idaho

Idaho Code Ann. § 26-2808

Requirements: Borrower may request from mortgage company at any time a statement of account's payments and "total unpaid balance," to be delivered within thirty days of written request; fee may be charged.

Illinois

735 Ill. Comp. Stat. 5/15-1505.5 (West)

Requirements: In a foreclosure action, upon mortgagor's written demand, mortgagee or mortgagee's agent shall prepare an accurate payoff demand statement within ten business days after receipt of demand. No fee for first payoff demand statement. One who willfully fails to deliver statement is liable for actual damages or $500 if no actual damages are sustained. 735 Ill. Comp. Stat. 5/15-1505.5.

Indiana

Ind. Code § 24-4.5-2-209 (Consumer Credit Code)

Requirements: If noncompliance within ten days of first written request, creditor or mortgage servicer is liable for $100; within ten days of second request, liable for the greater of $100 or the interest due from date of first request until date of compliance. *Cf.* § 24-4.5-2-104(2)(b) as to applicability to mortgages.

Iowa

Iowa Code § 535B.11(4)

Requirements: Party servicing mortgage must respond in writing within ten business days to written request for payoff information.

Kansas

Requirements: None.

Kentucky

Ky. Rev. Stat. Ann. § 286.8-220(2)(e) (West)

Requirements: Upon receipt of written request, it is unlawful to delay beyond five business days issuance of written payoff statement. State may seek fine; willful violation is felony. § 286.8-990.

Louisiana

La. Rev. Stat. Ann. § 6:1096 (H)

Requirements: Statement due within five days of written request. Reasonable fee allowed for second request within a year.

Maine

Me. Rev. Stat. Ann. tit. 9-A, § 9-305-B (First Lien Mortgages)

Requirements: Creditor, assignee, or servicer shall provide within three business days of request a precise figure as of date certain and computation method for ascertaining figure after date certain. No charges for first two requests within a year; maximum $5.00 charge for subsequent requests. Civil action allowed seeking damages for noncompliance, no less than $250 and no more than $1000, plus costs and attorney fees. § 9-405. Fines and criminal penalties for knowing and willful violations. § 9-407.

Maryland

Requirements: None.

Massachusetts

Mass. Gen. Laws ch. 183, § 54D

Requirements: Mortgagor, holder, or servicer shall provide within five business days of receipt of request a precise figure as of date certain and computation method for ascertaining figure after date certain. No fee for first request within each six-month period. Liability for noncompliance: the greater of $500 or actual damages; costs and attorney fees.

Michigan

Requirements: None.

Mississippi

Miss. Code Ann. § 81-18-27(1), (*l*)

Requirements: It is prohibited to not respond within three days to oral or written request for payoff amount from borrower or authorized third party. Section 81-18-51 provides that statute sunsets July 1, 2010.

Missouri

Requirements: None.

Montana

Requirements: None.

Nebraska

Neb. Rev. Stat. § 45-737(6)

Requirements: Licensee must answer within ten days of receipt of written request without charge; fee up to $10 allowed where request is within sixty days of prior fulfilled request. Violation may lead to injunction or fines.

Nevada

Requirements: None.

New Hampshire

N.H. Rev. Stat. Ann. § 397-A:15(V)

Requirements: Payoff amount as of specific date, with a daily interest rate charge, to be provided within five days of receipt of written request. Penalties: misdemeanor, fines, license revocation or suspension. § 397-A:21.

New Jersey

N.J. Stat. Ann. § 46:10B-25(f) (West)

Requirements: Payoff amount to be provided by seven days after request; no fee.

New Mexico

Requirements: None.

New York

N.Y. Real Prop. Law § 274-a(2) (McKinney)

Requirements: Holder, assigns, or persons to whom payments are required to be made must provide payoff statement within thirty days of bona fide written request as specified; noncompliance results in liability for actual damages.

North Carolina

N.C. Gen. Stat. § 45-36.7

Requirements: Borrower may request statement for a specified date not more than thirty days after request given; creditor to deliver statement within ten days of request. For noncompliance creditor is liable for actual damages and, if those are unpaid within thirty days of receipt of demand, costs and attorney fees.

North Dakota

N.D. Cent. Code § 35-03-18

Requirements: Mortgage servicer upon written request must provide amount for date specified as to payoff amount and escrow accounts. No fee. If noncompliance within seven days of receipt of request and if closing postponed due to delay, servicer liable for resulting damages.

Ohio

Requirements: None.

Oklahoma

Requirements: None.

Oregon

Requirements: None.

Pennsylvania

Requirements: None.

Rhode Island

R.I. Gen. Laws § 19-9-9

Requirements: Owner or servicer of loan must provide payoff within three business days of written or telefaxed request.

South Carolina

Requirements: None.

South Dakota

Requirements: None.

Tennessee

Requirements: None.

Texas

Requirements: None.

Utah

Requirements: None.

Vermont

Vt. Stat. Ann. tit. 27, § 464

Requirements: Payoff statement to be mailed or delivered within five days of request; holder or any authorized servicer's liability in civil action for noncompliance: $25 per day up to $5000, consequential and punitive damages, costs, and attorney fees. *See also* tit. 8, § 2232a(c).

Virginia

Va. Code Ann. § 6.1-330.82

Requirements: The holder shall mail or deliver written statement of the amount to the property owner or his designee within ten business days of the receipt of a written request such party or his designee.

West Virginia

W. Va. Code § 31-17-9(d)

Requirements: Holder shall provide without charge to the borrower within three business days after receipt of the borrower's written request, a payoff statement in manner requested by borrower.

Wisconsin

Wis. Stat. § 422.306(2) (Consumer Credit Transactions)

Requirements: Regarding mortgages on real property, required statement need specify dates and payments received and charges imposed during the previous twelve months, and the unpaid balance remaining at the time of the statement. No charge for one such statement once every twelve months. Additional statements shall be furnished if the customer pays reasonable fees.

Wyoming

Requirements: None.

D.3 Mortgage Discharge Laws

Alabama

Ala. Code §§ 35-10-27, 35-10-30

Requirements: $200 penalty upon failure to record satisfaction after thirty days from written request.

Alaska

Alaska Stat. § 34.20.050

Requirements: After ten days written request to discharge, mortgage holder who refuses or neglects to discharge is liable for $300 damages plus any damages resulting from refusal or neglect.

Arizona

Ariz. Rev. Stat. Ann. § 33-712

Requirements: Any person receiving satisfaction of mortgage is liable for actual damages upon failure to record within thirty days; after continuing failure for a further thirty days following a written request, liability is for $1000 plus any actual damages. Mortgagor may obtain payoff deed from a title insurer in specified manner if mortgage holder (including "account servicing agent") fails to provide such after sixty days from date of full payment. § 33-750.

Arkansas

Ark. Code Ann. § 23-39-513(2)

Requirements: Improper refusal to issue satisfaction or release is prohibited practice. *See* Appx. D.1, *State Remedies, supra.*

California

Cal. Civ. Code § 2941 (West)

Requirements: Mortgagee or assignee receiving satisfaction of mortgage is liable for actual damages and $500 upon failure to record within thirty days or, after recording, failure to honor written request to deliver original note to mortgagor.

Colorado

Requirements: None.

Connecticut

Conn. Gen. Stat. § 49-8

Requirements: If release is not delivered within sixty days of satisfaction, mortgage holder is liable the greater of actual damages or $200 per week after the sixty-day period up to a maximum of $5000, plus costs and attorney fees. Mortgagor may have satisfaction recorded by duly appointed officer if mortgagee fails to record such within sixty days of payment. § 49-8a.

Delaware

Del. Code Ann. tit. 25, § 2111

Requirements: Holder is to have satisfaction recorded within sixty days of performance; debtor is responsible for any recording fees. Upon holder's non-compliance, debtor is entitled to send notice demanding recording of satisfaction. For willful non-compliance, holder shall be "fined not more than $1,000 for each such failure together with assessed costs, for each failure, not to exceed $1,000." Recorder shall file complaint with attorney general's office as to non-compliance. Debtor may also seek actual damages, minimally $10, up to $500, or a greater amount if so proven. § 2114. Section 2120 provides a procedure whereby an attorney authorized to practice law in the state may record a request for satisfaction after paying in full a debt owed by a debtor to a creditor who holds a mortgage on the debtor's property.

District of Columbia

Requirements: None.

Florida

Fla. Stat. Ann. §§ 701.03, 701.04 (West)

Requirements: Within sixty days of full payment, holder must cancel as required by law and must deliver to payor recorded satisfaction.

Georgia

Ga. Code Ann. § 7-1-1013(4)

Requirements: Improper refusal to issue a satisfaction of loan is a prohibited act. Violation is misdemeanor subject to imprisonment or fine no greater than $1000. § 7-1-1019

Hawaii

Haw. Rev. Stat. § 506-8

Requirements: Where failure to provide release within sixty days of written request, holder is liable for treble damages, costs, and attorney fees.

Idaho

Idaho Code Ann. § 45-915

Requirements: Upon demand, holder must immediately deliver certificate of satisfaction or have it recorded; liability for non-compliance is damages plus $100.

Illinois

765 Ill. Comp. Stat. Ann. §§ 905/2, 905/4 (West)

Requirements: Where failure to provide release within one month of payment, holder liable for $200 and attorney fees in civil action.

Indiana

Ind. Code §§ 32-29-1-6, 32-29-1-7, 32-29-11-1

Requirements: Upon mortgagor's request mortgagee shall release, discharge, and enter satisfaction in record or deliver to mortgagor certificate of satisfaction to be recorded. *Cf.* § 24-4.5-2-104(2)(b) as to applicability to mortgages.

Iowa

Iowa Code § 535B.11(5)

Requirements: Release to be delivered within forty-five days of payment; debtor may notify state administrator of noncompliance; if holder fails to deliver release within fifteen days of administrator's notice, liable for $50 for each day of delinquency after the fifteen days.

Kansas

Kan. Stat. Ann. § 58-2309a

Requirements: Mortgagee or assignee who fails to enter satisfaction, within twenty days of written demand by certified or registered mail, is liable in civil action for $500 and any proven additional damages plus attorney fees.

Kentucky

Ky. Rev. Stat. Ann. § 382.365 (West)

Requirements: Release of lien required within thirty days of satisfaction. Where noncompliance without good cause follows written request made in person or by certified mail, final lien holder or assignee liable for attorney fees and damages, the amount dependent on time elapsed from date of notice.

Louisiana

La. Rev. Stat. Ann. § 9:5385

Requirements: Mortgagee or servicing agent or any holder to produce instrument for release within thirty days of written demand; noncompliance results in liability for damages and attorney fees. Mortgagee to deliver documentation for cancellation of mortgage to mortgagor within sixty days of payment; upon failure to do so mortgagor may proceed to have satisfaction recorded by submission of affidavit by authorized party and fifteen-day written notice to mortgagee. § 9:5167.1.

Maine

Me. Rev. Stat. Ann. tit. 9-A, § 9-307(3) (First Lien Mortgages)

Requirements: Creditor shall deliver written evidence of payment in full within thirty days of satisfaction. Civil action allowed seeking damages for noncompliance, no less than $250 and no more than $1000, plus costs and attorney fees. § 9-405. Fines and criminal penalties for knowing and willful violations. § 9-407. Mortgagor may have discharge recorded by attorney's submission of affidavit. Tit. 33, § 553-A.

Maryland

Md. Code Ann., Comm. Law § 12-1024 (West)

Requirements: Credit grantor to record or provide in recordable form release within a reasonable time after satisfaction.

Massachusetts

Mass. Gen. Laws ch. 183, § 55

Requirements: Within forty-five days of payment, holder must record discharge and provide copy of discharge to payoff agent, or provide discharge for recording with a notice as specified. Liability for noncompliance: only actual damages if compliance within thirty days of written demand for compliance; the greater of $2500 or actual damages, costs and attorney fees. Defenses available to holder are specified. Discharge by affidavit of attorney is available where noncompliance.

Michigan

Mich. Comp. Laws § 565.44

Requirements: Upon payment and request, holder must register discharge within sixty days (seventy-five days for period prior to Dec. 27, 2006), liability for non-compliance is $1000 plus actual damages; court may award double damages in civil action.

Minnesota

Minn. Stat. § 47.208

Requirements: Any holder is to deliver satisfaction to payer within forty-five days of payment and of receipt of written request; liability to payer for noncompliance is civil penalty up to $500 and actual damages. *See also* § 507.41 (liability for actual damages if failure to discharge within ten days of written request).

Mississippi

Miss. Code Ann. § 81-18-27(d)

Requirements: Improper refusal to issue satisfaction is prohibited. Section 81-18-51 provides that statute sunsets July 1, 2010.

Missouri

Mo. Rev. Stat. §§ 443.130, 443.170

Requirements: If no release submitted for recording within forty-five days of written request by certified mail, return receipt requested, mortgagee is liable for the lesser of the amount of $300 for each day after the 45th day that release is not recorded or 10% of the loan amount, plus court costs and attorney fees. Upon failure to provide release within thirty days, holder's personal representative is liable for 10% of mortgage amount.

Montana

Mont. Code Ann. § 71-1-212

Requirements: Where failure to deliver certificate of release within ninety days after request, mortgagee, representative, or assignee is liable for $500 and actual damages.

Nebraska

Neb. Rev. Stat. §§ 76-252, 45-737(7)

Requirements: Where failure to deliver certificate of release in recordable form within sixty days after written request, mortgagee or party licensed as mortgage banker (*see* § 45-702) is liable for the greater of $5000 or actual damages, plus attorney fees and costs.

Nevada

Requirements: None.

New Hampshire

N.H. Rev. Stat. Ann. § 397-A:15(VII)

Requirements: Upon full payment of second mortgage loans, holder is to release or provide evidence for release; if holder has original note, must be returned to borrower upon written request within reasonable time period. Penalties: misdemeanor, fines, license revocation or suspension. § 397-A:21.

New Jersey

N.J. Stat. Ann. § 46:18-11.2 (West)

Requirements: Upon satisfaction, mortgagee, agents, or assignees shall within twenty days notify mortgagor of the right to demand that mortgage be canceled upon mortgagor's payment of recording fee; within thirty days of receipt of fee, mortgagee to record cancellation. Upon failure mortgagor to deliver notice of noncompliance, fifteen days after receipt of notice, mortgagee's liability is $50 per day up to $1000; if 20 day notice of action provided, mortgagee may also be liable for costs and attorney fees. §§ 46:18-11.3, 46:18-11.4.

New Mexico

N.M. Stat. §§ 48-7-4, 48-7-4.1, 48-7-5

Requirements: Upon full satisfaction it is the mortgagee's duty to have release recorded. Penalty is a fine of at least $10 and no more than $25; also liability in civil action to clear title for costs and attorney fees. If noncompliance ninety days after payment, title insurer may have release recorded.

New York

N.Y. Real Prop. Law § 275 (McKinney)

Requirements: Upon satisfaction holder must have release recorded within thirty days. Liability for noncompliance: $500 if after thirty days, $1000 if after sixty days; $1500 if after ninety days.

North Carolina

N.C. Gen. Sat. § 45-36.9

Requirements: Creditor or servicer must record satisfaction within thirty days after full payment; liable for actual but not punitive damages for failure to do so, plus $1000 and attorney fees if creditor does not record satisfaction within thirty days of debtor's demand. A different statute, N.C. Gen. Stat. § 45-36.3, applies only to satisfactions that occur before October 1, 2005.

North Dakota

N.D. Cent. Code § 35-03-16

Requirements: Discharge to be recorded by mortgagee or its representative within thirty days of discharge being signed.

Ohio

Ohio Rev. Code Ann. § 5301.36 (West)

Requirements: Satisfaction to be recorded by mortgagee within ninety days of payment; liability for noncompliance is $250 damages in legal action plus any other legal remedy available to mortgagor.

Oklahoma

Okla. Stat. tit. 46, § 15

Requirements: Holder to file release within fifty days of satisfaction; upon failure to do so mortgagor may request in writing a release. Upon noncompliance within ten days after request, holder is liable in civil action to mortgagor for 1% of principal per day, not to exceed $100, for each day after ten-day period; total penalty not to exceed principal amount.

Oregon

Or. Rev. Stat. § 86.140

Requirements: Upon failure to discharge mortgage within thirty days of request, mortgagee or assignee is liable for actual damages plus $500, recoverable in action at law.

Pennsylvania

21 Pa. Stat. Ann. §§ 681, 682 (West)

Requirements: Upon full payment, mortgagee to enter satisfaction. Upon failure to do so within forty-five days of request, mortgagor is entitled in legal actions to any amount of damages not exceeding the mortgage-money.

Rhode Island

R.I. Gen. Laws §§ 34-26-2, **34-26-5**

Requirements: Upon full payment, mortgagee, successor, or assignee is to enter within thirty days satisfaction or execute release. Liability for noncompliance within ten days of a request for discharge: actual damages in civil action, triple costs, and attorney fees.

South Carolina

S.C. Code Ann. §§ 29-3-310, 29-3-320

Requirements: Upon full payment and delivery of request, holder is within three months to provide mortgagor proof of satisfaction or is to record release with option of charging mortgagor up to $25 recording fee. Liability for noncompliance: damages of the lesser of one half of the debt amount or $25,000, actual damages, costs, and attorney fees. Successful suit also will result in court order to have satisfaction entered by court officer

South Dakota

S.D. Codified Laws § 44-3-8

Requirements: Holder shall deliver satisfaction within thirty days of full payment. Immediately upon payment or thereafter, where mortgagor delivers written request, holder obliged to deliver within ten days of receipt of the written request a release sufficient to cancel lien. Upon noncompliance after the ten days, holder is liable for actual damages, attorney fees, and an additional $100.

Tennessee

Tenn. Code Ann. § 66-25-102

Requirements: Holder is liable for $100 after forty-five days from written request; upon noncompliance thirty days after second request, $1000; if action instituted to collect forfeitures, holder liable for expenses, costs, and attorney fees.

Texas

Requirements: None.

Utah

Utah Code Ann. § 57-1-38

Requirements: Servicer or lender failing to release security interest within ninety days of final payment is liable for the greater of $1000 or treble the actual damages, plus expenses, costs, and attorney fees.

Vermont

Vt. Stat. Ann. tit. 27, § 464

Requirements: Holder and any servicer must, within thirty days of payment, execute and deliver valid discharge; holder's or any authorized servicer's liability in civil action for noncompliance: $25 per day up to $5000, consequential and punitive damages, costs, and attorney fees. *See also* tit. 8, § 2232a(e).

Virginia

Va. Code Ann. §§ 55-66.3, 55-66.5

Requirements: If the lien creditor has not, within ninety days after payment, either provided the certificate of satisfaction or delivered it to the clerk's office with the necessary fee for filing, creditor shall forfeit $500 to borrower. Following the ninety-day period, if the amount forfeited is not paid within ten business days after written demand for payment is sent, the lien creditor shall pay costs and attorney fees. After twenty days notice to holder, owner may apply to court for release; costs and attorney fees may be awarded.

Virgin Islands

V.I. Code Ann. tit. 28, § 128

Requirements: If no discharge within ten days of written request, mortgagee, representative, or assignee is liable for $100 damages, and also for actual damages occasioned by such neglect or refusal, to be recovered in an action.

Washington

Wash. Rev. Code § 61.16.030

Requirements: Upon failure to acknowledge satisfaction as provided by statute sixty days from the date of request, the mortgagee shall forfeit and pay to the mortgagor damages and attorney fees; court in action for damages shall issue an order directing the immediate recording of discharge.

West Virginia

W. Va. Code §§ 31-17-9(c), 38-12-1(a)

Requirements: Release shall be executed and furnished to the debtor within thirty days after the debt has been satisfied. Upon noncompliance, borrower may seek court order for release, with holder liable for costs and attorney fees. § 38-12-10.

Wisconsin

Wis. Stat. § 422.306(4) (Consumer Credit Transactions)

Requirements: Within forty-five days after payment the creditor shall give or forward to the customer instruments which acknowledge payment in full and evidence of release of any recorded lien on real estate.

Wyoming

Wyo. Stat. Ann. § 34-1-132

Requirements: Mortgagee or holders, including servicing agents, within thirty days of receipt of written request for discharge, shall execute release. Liability for noncompliance: actual damages plus special damages of 1/10 of 1% of principal, not to exceed $100 per day after thirty-day period. Mortgagee of record liable for same damages if failure to provide name and address of current holder within sixty days of the written request.

Appendix E Summary of State Foreclosure Laws

This appendix is a state-by-state summary of foreclosure laws. Practitioners should use this for easy reference to the foreclosure laws of their state, and to compare their state's laws with those of other states. However, this summary should not be used instead of the actual statutory materials. Note also that this appendix analyzes only the statutory language itself, and does not include judicial interpretation of that language. The practitioner will have to research state court decisions (some of which are referenced in the chapters of this manual) for judicial interpretation of statutory provisions. Practitioners should also be aware that local custom, which generally is not reflected in the statute, may affect the way in which foreclosures are conducted in a jurisdiction. For this reason, local resources and materials must be consulted.

A note on the categories within each summary: the "preforeclosure notice" category refers generally to the notice of sale and notice of default, if required. It does not refer to notice of the commencement of a court action, though such notice would always be required under court rules governing service of process. The "number of notices" category refers to whether the state requires a separate notice of default in addition to a notice of sale.

ALABAMA

Ala. Code §§ 35-10-1 to 35-10-30, §§ 6-5-247 to 6-5-256

Most Common Method of Foreclosure: Non-judicial; Power of sale in mortgage.

Preforeclosure Notice:

Number of Notices: One: Notice of sale.

Amount of Notice Required: Thirty days prior to sale.

Content of Notice: Time, place, and terms of sale.

Method of Service: By publication once a week for three consecutive weeks, unless the loan documents set additional requirements.

Redemption: Within one year after foreclosure, by paying the purchase price to the buyer plus interest and costs, but borrower loses the right to redeem if he or she does not surrender possession within ten days after written demand for possession by the buyer.

Deficiency: A deficiency judgment is obtainable.

Post-Sale Provisions Regarding Proceeds: No statutory procedures for accounting for proceeds and return of surplus.

ALASKA

Alaska Stat. § 34.20.070

Most Common Method of Foreclosure: Non-judicial; Power of sale in deed of trust.

Preforeclosure Notice:

Number of Notices: One: Notice of default and sale.

Amount of Notice Required: Notice is to be served not less than thirty days after default and not less than three months before sale.

Content of Notice: a) Name of trustor; b) book and page where trust deed is recorded, or the serial number assigned to the trust deed by the recorder; c) description of the property, including property's street address if there is one; d) statement that breach has occurred; e) nature of the breach; f) sum owing; and g) date, time, and place of sale.

Method of Service: By certified mail on the borrower and occupant.

Right to Cure Default/Reinstate: Can cure any time before the sale, but the lender can refuse to accept payment if two prior Notices of Default and Sale have been recorded. Must pay attorney fees and costs actually incurred in order to cure.

Redemption: No right of redemption after sale if a non-judicial foreclosure. § 34.20.090.

Deficiency: No deficiency judgment after a foreclosure by power of sale. § 34.20.100.

Post-Sale Provisions Regarding Proceeds: No statutory procedures for disbursement of proceeds and return of surplus after power of sale foreclosure.

ARIZONA

Ariz. Rev. Stat. Ann. §§ 33-741 to 33-749, 33-801 to 33-821

Most Common Method of Foreclosure: Non-judicial; Power of sale in deed of trust. (Judicial foreclosure for some existing mortgages, which were common prior to 1971.)

Foreclosure by Power of Sale Permitted?: On deeds of trust only. § 33-807.

Judicial Foreclosure Procedure: After expiration of the forfeiture period, the mortgagee must bring action in superior court in the county where the property is located.

Preforeclosure Notice:

Number of Notices: *For a power of sale, one notice*: Notice of sale. A power of sale cannot be exercised before the expiration of ninety days from the recording of the notice of sale. § 33-807. *For a judicial foreclosure, one notice*: Notice of election to forfeit.

Amount of Notice Required: For foreclosure of deed of trust: sale may take place on the 91st day (not a Sunday or legal holiday) after the recording of the notice of sale. § 33-807. If judicial foreclosure, notice must be recorded twenty days before forfeiture. The mortgagee can enforce forfeiture only after the expiration of the following periods after the date monies are due: thirty days if less than twenty percent of the purchase price is paid; sixty days if greater than or equal to twenty percent and less than thirty percent of the purchase price is paid; 120 days if greater than or equal to thirty percent and less than fifty percent or more of the purchase price is paid; nine months if fifty percent or more of the purchase price is paid. § 33-742.

Content of Notice: See Statutory forms §§ 33-743(B) and 33-808. For judicial foreclosure, notice of intent must state how to reinstate and the deadline for reinstatement. § 33-743(F). Notice of trustee's sale includes the date, time and place of sale, description of the property, original, principal balance, and information about the trustee and beneficiary, including the trustee's phone number and the number of the state or federal licensing body which regulates the trustee. § 33-808. Must be mailed to borrower within five days of recording of notice of sale.

Method of Service: For a power of sale, the foreclosure notice must be recorded in the applicable court recorder's office, published in a newspaper at least once a week for four consecutive weeks, posted twenty days before the sale on the property, and mailed by registered or certified mail to the owner of record or other person who has recorded a request for notice prior to the recording of the notice of sale. §§ 33-808, 33-809. For a judicial foreclosure, by in-hand delivery or by first-class mail. § 33-743.

Right to Cure Default/Reinstate: For a power of sale foreclosure, up to 5:00 p.m. on the last day, other than a Saturday or legal holiday, before the sale date or the filing of an action to foreclose the trust deed. § 33-813. For a judicial foreclosure, up to twenty days after service of the notice of intent to forfeit.

Redemption: No redemption after power of sale foreclosure. For a judicial foreclosure, can redeem judgment prior to the sale if the property is not abandoned. § 33-726. After sale in judicial foreclosure, judgment debtor may redeem within six months after the sale date, or within thirty days after the sale date if the property was abandoned. § 12-1282.

Post-Sale Provisions Regarding Proceeds: For a power of sale foreclosure, must notify borrower within fifteen days after sale if there are surplus proceeds. § 33-812(B).

Deficiency: No deficiency claim allowed if either a single one-family or a single two-family dwelling of two and one-half acres or less is sold pursuant to power of sale. § 33-814G.

ARKANSAS

Ark. Code Ann. §§ 18-49-101 to 18-49-106, §§ 18-50-101 to 18-50-116

Most Common Method of Foreclosure: Non-judicial; Power of sale in mortgage (except for agricultural land).

Judicial Foreclosure Procedure: *See* §§ 18-49-101 to 18-49-106.

Preforeclosure Notice:

Number of Notices: One: Notice of default and intention to sell; must be recorded.

Amount of Notice Required: Notice must be mailed, by certified and first-class mail, within thirty days of recording (§ 18-50-104) and published once a week for four weeks prior to date of sale. Notice must also be posted in the courthouse and on the Internet. § 18-50-105. Trustee must also file affidavit of mailing with recorder of deeds prior to or on date of sale. § 18-50-106. If judicial foreclosure, single notice must be published once at least ten days prior to sale. § 18-49-104.

Content of Notice: a) Names of parties; b) description of the property; c) book and page where mortgage is recorded; d) default; e) amount owing; f) statement that you may lose your property if you do not take immediate action; and g) time, date, and place of sale. § 18-50-104.

Method of Service: By mail and by publication.

Right to Cure Default/Reinstate: Up to the time of the sale, but must pay costs and attorney fees actually incurred. § 18-50-114.

Redemption: If a judicial foreclosure, within one year by payment of the purchase price plus interest and the costs of the sale. Right of redemption may be waived in mortgage. § 18-49-106. No redemption if foreclosed by power of sale.

Post-Sale Provisions Regarding Proceeds: Proceeds are applied to the expenses of the sale, mortgage debt, and other recorded liens, with any surplus to the mortgagor. § 18-50-109.

Deficiency: No bids for less than two-thirds of entire indebtedness can be accepted. § 18-50-107. A deficiency judgment is limited to the lesser of the indebtedness minus the fair market value or the indebtedness minus the sale price of the property. § 18-50-112. Action for a deficiency after a non-judicial foreclosure must be brought within one year of date of sale.

High-Cost Home Loans: Intentional violation of the Arkansas Home Loan Protection Act, Ark. Code Ann. §§ 23-53-101 through 106, renders the loan agreement void. The creditor may not collect any principal, interest, or other fees, and the borrower can recover payments made. Ark. Code Ann. § 23-53-106. A borrower may raise violations of the Act against an assignee (unless the assignee can show that it took certain precautions to avoid accepting assignments of high-cost home loans) as a defense by recoupment or setoff in a collection action, or to obtain possession of the home. § 23-53-105. TILA right of rescission and other remedies provided by the Act are available to the borrower by way of recoupment against a party foreclosing, at any time during life of the loan. Ark. Code Ann. § 23-53-106.

CALIFORNIA

Cal. Civ. Code §§ 2924 to 2924*l*; Cal. Civ. Proc. Code §§ 580a to 580d (West)

Most Common Method of Foreclosure: Non-judicial; Power of sale in deed of trust.

Judicial Foreclosure Procedure: *See* Cal. Civ. Proc. Code, §§ 725a to 730.5 (West). Generally judicial foreclosure used only if there are problems requiring court resolution or if likelihood for recovery of deficiency judgment.

Preforeclosure Notice:

Number of Notices: Two: Notice of default and notice of sale.

Amount of Notice Required: For a notice of default, three months. For a notice of sale, twenty days.

Content of Notice: *Notice of default*: a) Identify the mortgage; b) nature of the breach; c) election to sell to satisfy obligation; and d) notice of right to cure, if curable. Notice must be filed in the county where the mortgaged property is located. *Notice of Sale*: a) Time and place of sale; and b) total amount due plus a reasonable estimate of costs and expenses. Cal. Civ. Code § 2924c. Name, in-state street address, and toll-free or instate telephone number of the trustee or its agent. Street address or legal description of property. If personal property or fixtures are to be sold, these must be described. Cal. Civ. Code § 2924f.

Method of Service: By certified or registered mail, and by regular first-class mail and by publication once a week for three weeks, beginning twenty days before the sale, in a newspaper of general circulation, and posting in a public place and in a conspicuous place on the property. Notice of sale must also be recorded. Cal. Civ. Code § 2924b.

Right to Cure Default/Reinstate: Can cure within five days before the sale. Cal. Civ. Code § 2924c.

Redemption: None, unless there is a deficiency judgment. (See above for restrictions on deficiencies.) Two-year right of redemption if court grants deficiency judgment. Cal. Civ. Proc. Code § 729.010.

Post-Sale Provisions Regarding Proceeds: Within thirty days of sale, the trustee must give notice of any surplus to anyone who may have a claim on the proceeds. Claims are to be sent to the trustee to determine priority. If the trustee cannot resolve the claims within ninety days, then the court will. If there are no disputes, the claims must be paid within thirty days. Cal. Civ. Code § 2924j.

Deficiency: No deficiency upon power of sale foreclosure. Cal. Civ. Proc. Code § 580d. No deficiency upon judicial foreclosure of purchase money mortgage on owner-occupied dwelling with four or fewer units, or for failure to complete purchase by contract for deed. Cal. Civ. Proc. Code § 580b. When deficiencies are permitted, amount is limited by the fair market value of the property. Cal. Civ. Proc. Code §§ 580a, 726(b).

High-Cost Home Loans: A provision in a loan agreement that violates enumerated subsections of the high-cost home loan act is unenforceable against borrower. The listed subsections forbid, *inter alia*, call provisions and balloon payments. The court may reform the loan terms to conform to the statute. Cal. Fin. Code §§ 4973, 4978.

Miscellaneous: Special notice is required under the Unruh Act for deeds of trust, where the security interest is a single-family owner-occupied residence and it secures the obligation under the Unruh Retail Installment Sales Act (§§ 1801 to 1812.20). Cal. Civ. Code § 2924f. Notice to occupants/tenants regarding effect of foreclosure is required. Cal. Civ. Code § 2924.8.

Special Temporary Provision Mandating Pre-Foreclosure Loss Mitigation Contact: Effective September 6, 2008 for loans made between January 1, 2003 and December 31, 2007 mortgagee cannot file notice of default until thirty days after contacting borrower to explore options to avoid foreclosure. Must advise borrower of opportunity for conference with mortgagee and schedule conference within fourteen days of request. Notice of default must include declaration of compliance with this provision. Cal. Civ. Code § 2923.5. Legislature has issued declaration supporting loan modifications, but not mandating it. Cal. Civ. Code § 2923.6.

Special Temporary Provision Authorizing Delay of Foreclosure Sale: Statute requires ninety-day delay after filing notice of default and before sale in order to allow servicer to review borrower for loan modification. Delay does not apply if servicer has been exempted from provision by Commissioner of Corporations. Commissioner exempts servicers based on showing they have a loan modification review process that complies with standards in statute. Effective May 21, 2009 to Jan. 1, 2011 for loans recorded Jan. 1, 2003 to Jan. 1, 2008. Cal. Civ. Code § 2923.52-53.

COLORADO

Colo. Rev. Stat. §§ 38-38-100.3 to 38-38-114

Most Common Method of Foreclosure: Power of sale by a public trustee, with court supervision.

Preforeclosure Notice:

Number of Notices: Two: Notice of motion pursuant to Colo. R. Civ. P. 120 for court order to authorize sale. § 38-38-105; Colo. R. Civ. P. 120. Combined notice of sale, right to cure, and right to redeem—but this must be mailed twice, once within twenty days after recording the notice of election and demand, and once forty-five to sixty days before the first scheduled date of sale. § 38-38-103. Effective June 2008, thirty days before mortgagee files notice of election and demand, must mail borrower notice with state hotline information and give direct number to mortgagee's loss mitigation office. § 38-38-102.5.

Amount of Notice Required: *Notice of Motion*: Fifteen days prior to hearing date. Hearing date not later than the day prior to which an effective notice to cure may be filed pursuant to § 38-38-104. Colo. R. Civ. P. 120. *Combined Notice*: By mail, within twenty days after recording notice of election and demand, and between forty-five and sixty days before first scheduled sale date. It must also be published once a week for four weeks between sixty and forty-five days prior to first scheduled sale date. § 38-38-103.

Content of Notice: *Notice of Election and Demand*: Names of grantors, beneficiaries or grantees, and holder; date of deed of trust; information about recordation of deed of trust; original principal balance; current principal balance; description of the property; statement whether holder is foreclosing on all or part of the property; statement of the violation of the note or deed of trust on which the foreclosure is based; and name, address, and bar number of holder's attorney (§ 38-38-101); plus supporting documents. *Notice to homeowner*: All of the above, plus a statement about deadline for notice of intent to cure and notice of intent to redeem; the name, address, and telephone number of each attorney for holder; the date and place of sale; and a statement that the lien being foreclosed may not be a first lien. § 38-38-103. *Notice of motion*: Description of the instrument, the property, and the default; time and place of hearing; right to file responses; last date for responses; right to move hearing to county where property is located (if motion was filed elsewhere); return address of moving party. Colo. R. Civ. P. 120.

Pre-Foreclosure Requirement Regarding Standing: When electing to publish property for sale holder must file with public trustee the evidence of ownership of the debt, including documentation of indorsements and assignments.

Method of Service: *Notice of motion*: Mail and posting. Colo. R. Civ. P. 120. *Combined notice*: By publication and by mail.

Right to Cure Default/Reinstate: Up to noon of the day before the sale, but must give fifteen-day prior notice of intent to cure. Holder must respond with cure amount statement within ten days of receipt of borrower's notice of intent to cure (or by eight calendar days before the sale), otherwise sale continued on week-to-week basis until holder provides the statement. § 38-38-104.

Redemption: By lienholders only within specified periods. § 38-38-302.

Post-Sale Provisions Regarding Proceeds: Excess proceeds go to creditors in order of priority, with any balance to the mortgagor. § 38-38-111.

Deficiency: § 38-38-106 states that owner may raise as defense that minimum bid based on fair market value of property was not made by the holder or its attorney prior to sale.

Foreclosure Deferment: Effective June 2, 2009, borrower may request deferment of foreclosure sale for up to ninety days to allow consideration of loan modification. Borrower must request deferment through a housing counselor within twenty days of posting of notice of opportunity to request deferment. Counselor makes initial determination that borrower qualifies for deferment. If eligible for deferment, foreclosure sale is continued until counselor certifies termination of deferment. Deferment terminates automatically after ninety calendar days or at next scheduled sale date after end of ninety-day period. Counselor uses FDIC net present value calculation in reviewing eligibility for deferment. Homeowner may be required to pay two-thirds of scheduled monthly principal and interest payment in order to maintain deferment. § 38-38-801 to 38-38-805.

CONNECTICUT

Conn. Gen. Stat. §§ 49-1 to 49-31j; Conn. Rules Superior Ct. Rules 23-16 to 23-19.

Most Common Method of Foreclosure: Strict foreclosure (no sale). If the strict foreclosure process is used, the court gives the mortgagor a period of time to pay the debt; if the mortgagor does not do so within the specified period of time, title vests in mortgagee. § 49-24. The court may also require appraisal, and on basis of appraisal may order foreclosure by sale. See § 49-25 for sale procedure.

Judicial Foreclosure Procedure: Strict foreclosure is commenced by filing of Writ, Summons, and Complaint, as in any other civil action. Must serve all junior lienholders. Lender must provide notice to homeowner of statutory protections from foreclosure at time the action commences. § 49-31e.

Redemption: If the court orders foreclosure by sale, the redemption period is set by the court. § 49-19. Mortgagor can stay sale by paying the judgment amount with interest and costs before the sale takes place. § 49-25. An encumbrancer can redeem.

Deficiency: A deficiency judgment is obtainable within thirty days after the redemption period expires (§ 49-14), and after a court hearing.

Miscellaneous: Mortgagee must respond within seven days to written request of mortgagor for reinstatement or payoff figure. Sanctions can be imposed for noncompliance. §49-10a. The mortgagor, if underemployed or unemployed, can apply for protection from foreclosure and the court can restructure the debt. But the mortgagor cannot raise a defense to foreclosure and file for protection. § 49-31f. *See* § 8-265dd (Emergency Mortgage Assistance Program).

Post-Sale Provisions Regarding Proceeds: Proceeds must be brought into court to be disposed of pursuant to a supplemental judgment. § 49-27.

Mediation Requirements: Legislation effective July 1, 2008 to July 1, 2010 directs Court Administrator for state to implement statewide foreclosure mediation program. No judgment may be entered for ninety-day period after return date on summons and complaint to allow for completion of mediation. § 49-31*l*; 8-265ee. *See* Ch. 4, *supra* (description of Connecticut foreclosure mediation program).

DELAWARE

Del. Code Ann. tit. 10, § 5061

Most Common Method of Foreclosure: Judicial.

Foreclosure by Power of Sale Permitted?: No.

Judicial Foreclosure Procedure: *Scire facias*/Order to show cause why the mortgaged premises should not be seized upon breach of a condition. Writ served like a summons. Twenty days to answer. Notice of Sale:

Number of Notices: One.

Amount of Notice Required: Ten days pre-sale.

Content of Notice: a) Day, hour, and place of sale; b) what land and tenements are to be sold; and c) where they lie.

Method of Service: By posting in ten places and delivery by the sheriff to the defendant, and by publication in a newspaper two weeks prior to sale. Del. Code Ann. tit. 10, § 4973.

Right to Cure Default/Reinstate: None.

Redemption: Once the sale is confirmed by the court, no redemption.

Post-Sale Provisions Regarding Proceeds: Court must confirm sale. Surplus goes to the mortgagor/owner. Del. Code Ann. tit. 10, §§ 5061, 5065–5067.

Deficiency: To obtain a deficiency judgment, must file suit on the note. No deficiency in *scire facias* action.

Miscellaneous: Sale must be confirmed by the court. Once confirmed, no redemption. No counterclaims or set-offs allowed in *scire facias* action.

Foreclosure Mediation: By administrative order of August 31, 2009 the president judge of Delaware Superior Courts implemented a statewide foreclosure mediation program. Borrowers may elect to participate in mediation within fifteen days of service of summons and complaint. *See* Ch. 4, *supra*.

DISTRICT OF COLUMBIA

D.C. Code §§ 42-815, 42-816

Most Common Method of Foreclosure: Power of sale.

Preforeclosure Notice:

Number of Notices: One.

Amount of Notice Required: Thirty days prior to sale.

Content of Notice: Amount of loan and amount of default, and date, time, and place of sale and such other information as required by D.C. regulations.

Method of Service: By registered or certified mail.
Right to Cure Default/Reinstate: Up to five days before the sale, once in two consecutive years. § 42-815.01.
Redemption: None after a power of sale foreclosure.
Deficiency: A deficiency judgment is obtainable. If judicial foreclosure action brought, deficiency judgment may be entered in that action. § 42-816.

FLORIDA

Fla. Stat. Ann. §§ 702.01 to 702.10, 45.031 and 45.0315 (West)

Most Common Method of Foreclosure: Judicial action. The mortgagee can request the issuance of an order to show cause to the mortgagor why final judgment of foreclosure should not be entered. § 702.10.
Foreclosure by Power of Sale Permitted?: No.
Judicial Foreclosure Procedure: File complaint in equity. If a show cause order is requested, a hearing may be held twenty-one days after in-hand service or thirty-one days after the first publication date. Defendant may file a defensive motion but no answer is valid unless it is verified. Sale is made by the clerk no less than twenty days after the final decree. After the sale, the clerk must file a certification of sale indicating the highest bidder and amount of the bid. If there are no objections within ten days, the clerk files the certificate of title. § 45.031.
Notice of Sale:
Number of Notices: One.
Amount of Notice Required: Notice must be published in a newspaper for two consecutive weeks with the second publication at least five days before the sale date. §§ 45.031, 702.035.
Content of Notice: a) Description of the property; b) time and place of sale; and c) statement that sale will be made pursuant to decree of foreclosure, giving the docket number of the case, name of the case, where pending, and name of the clerk making the sale. The homeowner must also be advised of the existence of a homestead tax exemption and how to claim it, warned about possible scams involving the assignment of rights or sale of the home, and advised to consult a lawyer or legal aid office.
Method of Service: By publication.
Redemption: Until later of the date the clerk files the certificate of sale or as specified in judgment.
Post-Sale Provisions Regarding Proceeds: Disbursed by the clerk according to the final decree. Must file a report after disbursement. Sale confirmed if no objections in sixty days. § 45.031 to 45.0315.
Deficiency: Can include a deficiency action in a foreclosure action, but must have in-hand service on the defendant to pursue a deficiency. The court has discretion as to a deficiency decree. §§ 702.06, 45.031(8). Even if a default judgment is entered on the foreclosure, the defendant is entitled, by case law, to a jury trial on the amount of the deficiency.
High-Cost Home Loans: Under the Florida Fair Lending Act, Fla. Stat. Ann. §§ 494.0078 to 494.00797, the lender must mail a notice of the right to cure default forty-five days before filing a foreclosure action. If the amount necessary to cure the default will change during the forty-five-day period, the notice must include information sufficient to calculate the amount during that period. The notice must also include the date by which payment must be made (not less than forty-five days from the notice), the name, address and telephone number of a contact to pay or dispute the defaulted amount, and the consequences of failure to cure. § 494.00794.
Mediation Provisions: Pursuant to Fla. Rule of Judicial Administration No. 2.215(b)(2), the chief judge of a judicial circuit may issue an administrative order requiring mediation of residential foreclosure cases. Several chief judges have issued orders providing for mediation of residential foreclosures in their courts, including the 1st, 9th, 11th, 12th, 18th,and 19th judicial circuits. Courts may stay proceedings while the mediation takes place under local rules. The Florida Supreme Court issued an administrative order on December 28, 2009 establishing guidelines for statewide foreclosure mediation. Guidelines include requirement that plaintiff provide documentary evidence of ownership interest in note and mortgage. *See* Ch. 4, *supra* (reviewing foreclosure mediation programs).

GEORGIA

Ga. Code Ann. §§ 44-14-160 to 44-14-191

Most Common Method of Foreclosure: Power of sale.
Preforeclosure Notice:
Number of Notices: One: Notice of sale.
Amount of Notice Required: By mail, fifteen days prior to sale. Additional notice by advertising may be required. § 44-14-162.2.
Method of Service: By registered or certified mail or statutory overnight delivery.
Post-Sale Provisions Regarding Proceeds: After the foreclosing mortgagee is paid, surplus goes to the mortgagor.
Deficiency: No deficiency judgment unless the mortgagee makes a report of the sale to the court within thirty days after the sale for confirmation of sale, and the sale is confirmed. The court will not confirm the sale unless it is satisfied that the property brought its true market value. § 44-14-191.
High-Cost Home Loans: Loans covered by the Georgia Fair Lending Act, Ga. Code Ann. §§ 7-6A-1 to 7-6A-11, require additional notices. Notice of intent to foreclose must be provided fourteen days prior to publication of advertisement required by § 44-14-162. Before foreclosure action is filed, lender must send notice of right to cure. Borrower can cure the default and reinstate up until the time of sale. The Act limits the fees, including attorney fees, that can be charged to reinstate the loan. § 7-6A-5. In an action to enjoin foreclosure or to keep or regain possession of the home, assignees of high-cost home loans are subject to all affirmative claims and any defenses with respect to the loan that the borrower could assert against the creditor of the loan, unless the assignee exercised reasonable diligence at the time of the purchase of the loan to avoid purchasing or taking assignment of high-cost home loans. The borrower may assert against the creditor all claims and defenses that the borrower may have against the seller or home improvement contractor. § 7-6A-6.

GUAM

Guam Code Ann. tit. 7, §§ 24101, 24104 to 24105, 24107, 23113, 23124

Most Common Method of Foreclosure: Judicial foreclosure.
Judicial Foreclosure Procedure: All foreclosures must be brought in superior court.
Preforeclosure Notice:
Number of Notices: Notice of sale.

Amount of Notice Required: Twenty days prior to the sale.
Content of Notice: Time, place of sale, description of the property and terms of the sale.
Method of Service: By posting in three public places in city or town where property located and publication once a week for a period of at least twenty days prior to sale.
Redemption: Within one year after foreclosure by paying the purchase price, plus interest of one percent per month and any taxes, improvements and costs arising since foreclosure.
Post-Sale Provisions Regarding Proceeds: Surplus, if any, goes to mortgagor. § 24105.
Deficiency: Deficiency judgment is available. § 24107.

HAWAII

Haw. Rev. Stat. §§ 667-1 to 667-42

Most Common Method of Foreclosure: Power of sale. Two alternative processes: § 667-5 and the more recent §§ 667-21 to 667-42, an alternate power of sale process that applies to mortgages containing power of sale executed after July 1, 1999. In the summaries that follow, these will be referred to as standard and alternate.
Judicial Foreclosure Procedure: Complaint filed in circuit court. § 667-1.
Preforeclosure Notice:
Number of Notices: *Standard*: One: Notice of sale. *Alternate*: Two: notice of default and notice of sale.
Amount of Notice Required: *Standard*: Three weeks. *Alternate*: Notice of default, sixty days. *Notice of sale*: Same as standard.
Content of Notice: *Standard*: Description of property; time and place of sale. § 667-7. *Alternate*: *Notice of default*: Names and addresses of mortgagor and mortgagee; description of property; nature of default; if nonpayment of money, detailed itemization of amount needed to cure; warning that acceleration will take place if not cured by specified date; contact information of person representing the mortgagee; description of the foreclosure process; notice that if borrower consents, public showing of property will be arranged; and form for borrower consent to showing. § 667-22. *Notice of sale*: Date, time, and place of sale, and of open house showings, if any; unpaid balance on mortgage; description of property; names of mortgagor, mortgagee, and junior creditors; contact information of person conducting sale; terms and conditions of sale; notice that the default may be cured and the mortgage reinstated up to three business days before the sale by paying the delinquent amount plus costs and fees incurred by the mortgagee, and that there is no right to redeem thereafter. § 667-27.
Method of Service: *Standard*: Newspaper publication once in three successive weeks, with third publication not less than fourteen days before sale; posting on property not less than twenty-one days before sale. § 667-5. *Alternate*: Notice of default must be served, defined to mean service that complies with rules of civil procedure. §§ 667-22, 667-21. Notice of sale must be mailed or delivered to borrower and junior creditors, and posted and published as for the standard notice of sale. § 667-27.
Right to Cure Default/Reinstate: *Standard*: None. *Alternate*: Sixty days from notice of default. (Notice must specify in detail what must be done to cure.) If default is cured, mortgage is reinstated; if not, creditor may proceed to public sale. § 667-22 and 667-24. May cure up to three business days before sale date by paying delinquent amount, plus costs and fees actually incurred by mortgagee because of default and proposed sale. § 667-27.
Redemption: None.
Post-Sale Provisions Regarding Proceeds: Affidavit of sale must be recorded thirty days after sale. § 667.3. Surplus proceeds paid to borrower. § 667-10.
Deficiency: *Standard*: Allowed. *Alternate*: Barred. § 667-38.
Miscellaneous: *Alternate*: If borrower consents, lender must conduct two open house public showings before the public sale. § 667-26. After an "Alternate" power of sale public sale, foreclosing mortgagee must file and record an affidavit, with copies of the various notices attached, describing the sale process. §§ 667-32, 667-33. The borrower, mortgagor, and certain creditors may appeal to the circuit court within thirty days. § 667-35. If no appeal is taken, the sale is conclusively presumed to have been legal, fair, and reasonable, and the purchase price to be the fair market value. § 667-34.

IDAHO

Idaho Code Ann. §§ 45-1505 to 45-1515

Most Common Method of Foreclosure: Power of sale.
Preforeclosure Notice:
Number of Notices: One: Notice of default sale.
Amount of Notice Required: One hundred twenty days prior to sale.
Content of Notice: a) Set forth default; b) names of parties to the deed of trust; c) description of the property; d) book and page number of recorded deed; e) sum owing; f) default; and g) date, time, and place of sale; h) a statutorily prescribed notice describing the foreclosure procedure, warning about the danger of foreclosure rescue scams, advising the homeowner to promptly consult a lawyer or financial professional, and disclosing the five-day cooling-off period for certain foreclosure rescue transactions. § 45-1505.
Method of Service: By registered or certified mail to the owner; by in-hand service on an adult occupant 120 days prior to the sale (at least three attempts at service must be made and server must post copy in conspicuous place on each attempt); and by publication four times with the final publication at least thirty days prior to the sale.
Right to Cure Default/Reinstate: Can cure within 115 days of the filing of Notice of default and sale. Must pay costs and fees actually incurred; trustee fees regulated by statute. § 45-1506(12).
Redemption: None. § 45-1508.
Post-Sale Provisions Regarding Proceeds: Proceeds are applied to the sale expenses, the debt of the foreclosing creditor, other liens, and then any surplus goes to the debtor. § 45-1507.
Deficiency: Amount of a deficiency judgment is limited by the fair market value at the date of sale, as found by the court. § 45-1512. Action must be brought within three months after the sale.

ILLINOIS

735 Ill. Comp. Stat. 5/15-1501 to 5/15-1605

Most Common Method of Foreclosure: Judicial.
Foreclosure by Power of Sale Permitted?: No. 735 Ill. Comp. Stat.

§ 5/15-1405.
Judicial Foreclosure Procedure: Initiated by complaint or counterclaim which meets requirements of § 5/15-1504. Must record notice of foreclosure, which must include information regarding the pending foreclosure, like a *lis pendens*. § 5/15-1503. Effective January 1, 2009 there is a requirement for plain language information about borrower's legal rights to be listed on the summons. 735 Ill. Comp. Stat. § 5/15-1504. After judgment, the sale is conducted by a judge or sheriff.
Notice of Sale:
Number of Notices: One.
Amount of Notice Required: Not more than forty-five days and not less than seven days pre-sale. § 5/15-1507.
Content of Notice: a) Name, address, and phone number of person to contact for information; b) common address and description of the property; c) legal description of the property; d) description of improvements; e) times for inspection; f) time and place of sale; g) terms of sale; h) the case title, case number, and court in which foreclosure was filed; and i) such other information as ordered by the court. § 5/15-1507.
Method of Service: By publication for three consecutive weeks, once per week, with the first notice published not more than forty-five days prior to the sale and last notice not less than seven days pre-sale.
Right to Cure Default/Reinstate: Ninety days from the date of service of the complaint. 735 Ill. Comp. Stat. § 5/15-1602.
Redemption: Generally, until the later of seven months after service of complaint or three months after the entry of judgment of foreclosure. Special right to redeem residential real estate, if the purchaser was the mortgagee, and the sale price was less than the amount specified in § 1603(d), then borrower may redeem for thirty days after confirmation by paying the sale price plus certain prescribed costs and interest. *See* 735 Ill. Comp. Stat. §§ 5/15-1603 to 5/15-1604.
Post-Sale Provisions Regarding Proceeds: The person conducting the sale must file a report of sale with the court. The court then conducts a hearing to confirm the sale. §§ 5/15-1508, 5/15-1512.
Deficiency: A deficiency judgment is obtainable. § 5/15-1508. Surplus is held by a person appointed by the court until the court orders distribution.
High-Cost Home Loans: Under the High Risk Home Loan Act, 815 Ill. Comp. Stat. §§ 137/1 to 137/175, lender must send credit counseling notice to borrower who has been delinquent more than thirty days. If the lender is notified in writing by an approved credit counselor within fifteen days after mailing that the borrower is seeking approved credit counseling, the lender may not initiate foreclosure action until thirty days after the date of such notice, unless the parties have otherwise entered into a written debt management plan within the thirty-day period. § 137/100. Lender of a high-risk loan with legal right of foreclosure must use judicial foreclosure proceedings. Before filing foreclosure action, lender must give at least thirty-day notice of right to cure default, including sufficient information for borrower to calculate amount necessary to cure default if amount will change during thirty-day period due to permitted late fees or daily interest. The notice must also include deadline for curing default (not less than thirty days), consequences of failure to cure, and the names, addresses and telephone numbers of persons to contact to pay or dispute the default. § 137/105. If a provision of a loan agreement violates the Act, that provision is unenforceable against the borrower. (The statute forbids, *inter alia*, call provisions and balloon payments.) Borrower may raise violations of Act against assignee (unless the assignee exercises due diligence and takes other precautions to avoid accepting assignment of high-cost home loans) as claims or defenses in foreclosure or collection actions, or in actions to enjoin foreclosure or regain possession. § 137/135.
Miscellaneous: Statewide database to be established for predatory lending information, requiring lenders to submit data subject to guidelines to be implemented. 765 Ill. Comp. Stat. § 77/70 to 77/73. Legislation effective in 2008 regulates broad range of mortgage lending practices, requiring verification of ability to repay, establishing broker duty to borrower, restricting prepayment penalties, and prohibiting equity stripping and loan flipping. 205 Ill. Comp. Stat. 635/5-1, *et seq.*
Notices to Occupants/Tenants: Prior to collecting rents, foreclosing mortgagee required to provide notice containing identifying information to occupants. 735 Ill. Comp. Stat. § 15-1703. *See also* 735 Ill. Comp. Stat. § 15-1701(regulating continued occupancy of tenants after foreclosure).

INDIANA

Ind. Code §§ 32-30-10-1 to 32-30-10-14, 32-29-1-1 to 32-29-1-11, 32-29-7-1 to 32-29-7-14

Most Common Method of Foreclosure: Judicial.
Foreclosure by Power of Sale Permitted?: No. § 32-29-1-3.
Judicial Foreclosure Procedure: "One action" state. § 32-30-10-10. The complaint is filed in equity in the circuit court where the property is located. The sale is conducted by a sheriff, or by an auctioneer if the court orders. Waiting periods between filing and sale: three months for mortgages signed on or after July 1, 1975; six months for mortgages signed after Dec. 30, 1957 but before July 1, 1975; twelve months for mortgages signed before Jan. 1, 1958. Waiting periods can be waived, but if waived, no deficiency judgment.
Notice of Sale:
Number of Notices: One.
Amount of Notice Required: Publication once per week for three consecutive weeks, with the first advertisement at least thirty days prior to the sale and copy served on borrower at time of first advertisement.
Content of Notice: Location of property, and common description. § 32-29-7-3.
Method of Service: By advertisement, by posting at the door of the courthouse, and by service upon the owner in accordance with Indiana Rules of Procedure governing service of process.
Right to Cure Default/Reinstate: If before final judgment any interest or installment of principal are due, but no other installments are due, and defendant pays the principal and interest, plus costs at any time before judgment, the foreclosure must be dismissed. If this sum is paid after final judgment, the proceedings must be stayed. Stay can be lifted if a subsequent installment is missed. § 32-30-10-11.
Redemption: Before the sale, by payment to clerk or sheriff, of the amount of the judgment, plus certain costs and interest. No redemption after sale. §§ 32-29-7-7, 32-29-7-13, and 32-30-10-5.
Post-Sale Provisions Regarding Proceeds: Sheriff pays proceeds to

court. Proceeds applied to sale expenses, taxes, amount of redemption where certificate of sale outstanding, payment of principal, interest, residue secured by mortgage and not due, surplus to debtor, heirs, or assigns per court. §§ 32-30-10-14, 32-29-7-9 (statutory order of distribution of proceeds).

Deficiency: A deficiency judgment is obtainable if there is a written agreement, and if the applicable waiting period for execution of judgment is not waived. §§ 32-29-7-5, 32-30-10-7.

High-Cost Home Loans: Borrower may cure default by tendering amount or performance required by mortgage at any time before transfer of title pursuant to foreclosure, judicial proceeding and sale, or otherwise. § 24-9-5-2. Lender with right to foreclose must use the judicial foreclosure procedure of the state in which the property securing the loan is located. § 24-9-5-3. Borrower in foreclosure may raise violations of high-cost home loan statute against lender or subsequent holder or assignee as claim, counterclaim, or defense, or in an action to enjoin foreclosure or preserve or regain possession. § 24-9-5-1.

Pre-Foreclosure Notice: Plaintiff must send notice warning homeowner of foreclosure rescue scams and giving housing counselor contact information thirty days before filing complaint. § 24-5.5-3-1.

Foreclosure Conferences: Applicable to foreclosure actions filed after June 30, 2009. *See* Ch. 4, *supra*.

IOWA

Iowa Code §§ 654.1 to 654.26

Most Common Method of Foreclosure: Judicial.

Foreclosure by Power of Sale Permitted?: No (§ 654.1), except as provided in § 654.18 (Alternative Non-judicial Voluntary Foreclosure Procedure) or § 655A (Non-judicial Foreclosure of Nonagricultural Mortgages). The mortgagee waives the deficiency if an alternative procedure is used.

Judicial Foreclosure Procedure: The complaint is filed in equity, served personally; "one action" state.

Notice of Sale:

- *Number of Notices*: One.
- *Amount of Notice Required*: Four weeks prior to the sale.
- *Content of Notice*: Time and place of sale.
- *Method of Service*: By posting in three public places, and by publication in a newspaper.

Right to Cure Default/Reinstate: As to agricultural land, once in twelve months, up to forty-five days after the notice of default is given. As to nonagricultural land, the borrower has thirty days to cure the default. Notice must state that mortgagor has right to cure. §§ 654.2A to 654.2D.

Redemption: Waived if an alternative procedure is used. § 654.18. One year if a judicial foreclosure.

Post-Sale Provisions Regarding Proceeds: Surplus is paid to the mortgagor. §§ 654.5 and 654.7.

Deficiency: Limited in certain cases by § 654.26. No deficiency if non-judicial foreclosure procedure is used under § 655A. Mortgage may provide for six-month redemption period if mortgagee waives deficiency and mortgagor does not exercise right to delay foreclosure. § 628.26.

Miscellaneous: An agricultural land mortgagor has a right of first refusal after recording of the sheriff's deed. § 654.16A. See § 654.16 for other special protections for farms. In a foreclosure of non-agricultural land without redemption, the mortgagee can elect foreclosure without redemption, but the mortgagor can request a delay of the sale if it is a primary residence. § 654.20. A mortgagor can apply for a continuance if default is admitted and the default is due to climatic conditions, or if the governor declares a state of economic emergency. The moratorium can last one to two years. § 654.15 (moratorium statute). See §§ 654.2A to 654.2D for special rules relating to agricultural property, and §§ 654A.1 to 654A.16 for farm mediation program.

KANSAS

Kan. Stat. Ann. § 60-2410

Most Common Method of Foreclosure: Judicial.

Foreclosure by Power of Sale Permitted?: No.

Judicial Foreclosure Procedure: Complaint filed in local district court. If personal service, mortgagor has twenty days to respond. If service by publication, mortgagor has forty-one days.

Notice of Sale: An officer gives public notice of the time and place of the sale once a week for three weeks by advertisement, with the last publication not less than seven days and not more than fourteen days prior to the sale. The sale must be confirmed by the court.

Redemption: An owner can redeem within twelve months of the sale or less if the property was abandoned, or three months if less than one-third of original debt has been paid; twelve months if all mortgages on property total less than one-third of market value of property for the amount paid by the purchaser and interest, costs, and taxes. § 60-2414. The three-month redemption period may be extended for another three months if owner loses primary source of income after foreclosure.

Deficiency: The court can deny confirmation of sale for an inadequate price, or set an upset price. § 60-2415.

Post-Sale Provisions Regarding Proceeds: Court must confirm sale and the proposed distribution of proceeds. § 60-2415.

KENTUCKY

Ky. Rev. Stat. Ann. §§ 426.525 to 426.720 (West)

Most Common Method of Foreclosure: Judicial.

Foreclosure by Power of Sale Permitted?: No. § 426.525.

Judicial Foreclosure Procedure: Complaint filed in circuit court. Defendants have twenty days to respond from date of service.

Preforeclosure Notice:

- *Number of Notices*: One.
- *Amount of Notice Required*: If by advertisement, once per week for three consecutive weeks. If by posting, fifteen days preceding the sale.
- *Content of Notice*: Time, place, and terms of sale, and description of the property.
- *Method of Service*: By posting on the courthouse door and three other places.

Redemption: Within one year, if the sale does not bring at least two-thirds of the property's appraised value. To redeem, must pay original purchase money and ten percent interest. §§ 426.530, 426.220.

Post-Sale Provisions Regarding Proceeds: Court must confirm sale. Surplus goes to the defendant. § 426.500.

Deficiency: A deficiency judgment is obtainable if the borrower is served in-hand or fails to answer.

High-Cost Home Loans: Lenders must provide notice of default and right to cure thirty days prior to initiation of foreclosure for loans covered by Ky. Rev. Stat. Ann. § 360.100. The notice should contain the amount needed to cure the default, the date payment is due, and, if amount needed to cure will change, information sufficient to enable borrower to calculate daily change.
Miscellaneous: The commissioner or officer who makes the sale must report the sale price to the court and the sale must be confirmed by the court. § 426.540. Land must be appraised before the sale.

LOUISIANA

La. Code Civ. Proc. Ann. arts. 3721 to 3753, 2631 to 2772

Most Common Method of Foreclosure: Judicial.
Judicial Foreclosure Procedure: By "executory proceeding" (arts. 2631 to 2724) or "ordinary proceeding" (art. 3722). Nearly all foreclosures are by executory proceeding. Under executory process, the mortgagor confesses judgment in the mortgage in the event he does not make required payments. Upon the filing of a petition, with the mortgage attached, the court can order issuance of writ of seizure of sale. La. Code Civ. Proc. Ann. art. 2638. Defenses may be raised through an injunction, or suspensive appeal.
Preforeclosure Notice: Notice of sale is contained in the petition for executory process which is posted on the property. Notice of seizure must be published at least twice, and not less than three days after the debtor has been served with written notice of seizure.
Redemption: No right of redemption.
Deficiency: A deficiency judgment is only obtainable in an ordinary proceeding or in an executory proceeding if the property has been appraised in accordance with La. Code Civ. Proc. Ann. art. 2723.
Miscellaneous: See Patrick S. Ottinger, *Enforcement of Real Mortgages by Executory Process*, 51 La. L. Rev. 87 (1990), for more information on executory process.
Post-Sale Provisions Regarding Proceeds: Sheriff distributes proceeds according to statutory priorities. La. Code of Civ. Pro. art. 2373.

MAINE

Me. Rev. Stat. Ann. tit. 14, §§ 6101 to 6325

Most Common Method of Foreclosure: Judicial/strict foreclosure.
Foreclosure by Power of Sale Permitted?: No, except against a corporation or partnership or limited liability company. § 6203-A.
Judicial Foreclosure Procedure: File complaint in superior court. The court must determine after a hearing whether a breach has occurred. Process is to be served in accordance with Maine Rules of Civil Procedure.
Notice of Sale: Sale follows the expiration of the period of redemption.

Number of Notices: One.
Amount of Notice Required: By publication once per week for three consecutive weeks, with the first publication not more than ninety days after the expiration of the period of redemption, and by mail thirty days before sale for foreclosures after January 1, 1995. Sale shall be held not less than thirty days and not more than forty-five days after the date of the first publication. § 6323.
Method of Service: By publication.

Right to Cure Default/Reinstate: Within thirty-five days of notice of default. Amount required to cure can include reasonable attorney fees. § 6111. Note that the acceptance of payments by the holder after the commencement of foreclosure proceedings and before the expiration of the right of redemption is a waiver of foreclosure, unless the parties agree otherwise in writing, or the payment is returned within ten days. § 6321. The mortgagee and mortgagor may enter into an agreement for payments to be accepted to bring the mortgage current, with the foreclosure process being stayed so long as the payments are current. § 6321.
Reporting: Mortgagees must report data about foreclosure actions to Department of Professional and Financial Regulation, Bureau of Consumer Credit Protection. § 6111.
Redemption: For mortgages executed after October 1, 1975, ninety days from the date of judgment, by paying the judgment amount with interest. (For older mortgages, one year, unless the mortgage provides otherwise.) § 6322.
Post-Sale Provisions Regarding Proceeds: The mortgagee must distribute proceeds per the judgment and must file a report with the court and mail a copy to the mortgagor. Parties have thirty days to file objections to accounting. Any surplus is paid to the mortgagor. § 6324.
Deficiency: Limited to the amount established as of the date of the sale (§ 6323), and by the fair market value as of the date of the sale if the mortgagee is the purchaser. § 6324.
High-Cost Loan Law: Statute expanded in 2007 to require income documentation and analysis of borrower's ability to repay; prohibits financing of points and fees and bars prepayment penalties on high-cost loans. Allows for assignee liability for violations of high-cost home loan rules. For most loans secured by principal dwellings, prohibits loan flipping, encouraging default, and sets limits on recourse to late fees. Me. Rev. Stat. Ann. tit. 9-A, §§ 8-103(1-A), 8-206-A to 8-206-G.
Foreclosure Mediation: Statewide program for foreclosure mediation effective January 1, 2010. § 6231-A. *See* Ch. 4, *supra*.

MARYLAND

Md. Code Ann. Real Prop. §§ 7-105 to 7-105.8, and Maryland Rules 14-201 to 14-209, and 14-305 to 14-306

Most Common Method of Foreclosure: Power of sale with court supervision.
Preforeclosure Notice:

Number of Notices: Three: Notice of intent, order to docket, and notice of sale.
Amount of Notice Required: Notice of intent to foreclose must be filed forty-five days before filing action. § 7-105.1(c)(1). (Foreclosure action may not be filed in court until the later of ninety days after default or forty-five days after notice of intent. § 7-105.1(b)(1)). The secured party may petition a court to waive these time and notice requirements if: (1) the loan was obtained by fraud or deception; (2) no payments have ever been made; (3) the property has been destroyed; or (4) default occurred after the stay had been lifted in a bankruptcy. If the petition is granted, the secured party may foreclose at any time after default. § 7-105.1(b)(2). Order to docket must be served at least forty-five days before foreclosure. Notice of sale must be published not less than fifteen days before sale date. § 7-105.1(g).

Content of Notice: Notice of intent must include the amount needed to cure and reinstate (including past-due payments, penalties, and fees), names and phone numbers of the secured party, the servicer (if any), and an agent of the secured party who is authorized to modify the terms of the loan. § 7-105.1(c)(4). Order to docket (or complaint for judicial foreclosure) must provide an affidavit stating date and nature of default, the license number of mortgage originator and lender, the date and nature of the default, the date that the notice of intent was provided, the amount needed to reinstate; an original or certified copy of the mortgage or deed of trust, note (and affidavit of ownership), and any assignments; a non-military affidavit (pursuant to the Servicemembers Civil Relief Act); and a prescribed form, notifying the borrower—in considerable detail—about the right to cure/reinstate, the availability of assistance, the risks of fraudulent rescue operations, and various alternatives to foreclosure. § 7-105.1(d). Notice of sale must include the time, place, and terms of the proposed sale. § 7-105.1(g).

Method of Service: Notice of intent must be sent certified mail, return receipt requested, *and* first-class mail. A copy must be sent to the Commissioner of Financial Regulation. § 7-105.1(c)(3). Personal service of an order to docket or foreclosure complaint must be attempted. § 7-105.1(c)(4). If two attempts fail, court may authorize service by certified and first-class mail and posting on the property. Notice of sale must be published in a newspaper of general circulation for three successive weeks, the first publication not less than fifteen days before the sale, and the last not more than one week before, and served on the record owner by certified *and* first-class mail not less than thirty nor more than ten days before the sale. §§ 7-105.1(g), 7-105.2(c). Notice must also be provided to holders of subordinate interests, including condo and homeowners' associations. § 7-105.3.

Right to Cure Default/Reinstate: Yes. By paying all past-due payments, penalties, and fees, up to one business day before the sale. The secured party or its agent must provide the borrower's attorney, within a reasonable time, with the amount needed to reinstate, and instructions for delivering the payment. § 7-105.1(h).

Redemption: No right of redemption after sale.

Deficiency: Yes. Rule 14-208(b). If proceeds insufficient, creditor may sue for deficiency within three years after ratification of auditor's report.

Post-Sale Provisions Regarding Proceeds: An audit is required when court ratifies sale. Md. Rule 14-207(d) and 14-305, 14-306. Parties may file exceptions within 30 days of filing of report of sale.

Miscellaneous: Record owner may file action for failure to make sale in compliance with statute within three years after ratification of sale. § 7-105.1(i). Other Maryland statutes that protect homeowners facing foreclosure: Protection of Homeowners in Foreclosure Act, §§ 7-301 to 7-325. Requires licensing and regulation of foreclosure consultants; regulates certain transactions involving residences in default; provides five-day rescission period; requires notice to former owners who become tenants. Maryland Mortgage Fraud Protection Act, §§ 7-401 to 7-409.

MASSACHUSETTS

Mass. Gen. Laws ch. 244, §§ 14, 17B, 18, 35A

Most Common Method of Foreclosure: Power of sale.

Preforeclosure Notice:

Number of Notices: Two: Notice of default and right to cure and notice of sale.

Amount of Notice Required: Notice of default and right to cure, ninety days. Mass. Gen. Laws ch. 244, § 35A. Notice of sale to owner no later than fourteen days before sale date and by publication three successive weeks.

Content of Notice: *Notice of default and right to cure*: Nature of default; right to cure; amount needed to cure; deadline for cure; name, address, and toll-free or local phone number of person to whom payment should be made; name and address of mortgagee or holder; phone number of representative of mortgagee whom borrower should contact if borrower disagrees with conclusion that default has occurred or the amount needed to cure; names of current or former broker and loan originator; local or toll-free number for borrower to seek assistance from Mass. Housing Finance Agency or the division of banks. Mass. Gen. Laws ch. 244, § 35A.

Notice of sale: a) Date, time, place, and terms of sale; b) name of mortgagor; and c) description of the property.

Method of Service: Notice of default and right to cure, mailing to address "last known to" mortgagee or holder. Mass. Gen. Laws ch. 244, § 35A. *Notice of sale*: By registered or certified mail, or by publication.

Right to Cure Default/Reinstate: For owner-occupied dwelling with four or fewer units, ninety-day right to cure, by paying full amount due without acceleration of unpaid balance. Cure amount may include late fees, as permitted by Mass. Gen. Laws ch. 183, § 59 (which requires a fifteen-day grace period, limits late fees to 3% of the delinquent amount, not including estimated taxes, and forbids pyramiding of late fees) and per diem interest, but may not include a fee for the right to cure, or attorney fees incurred before or during the cure period. Right may be exercised once in five years. Mortgagee or holder may not accelerate until ninety days after notice of default and right to cure. Mass. Gen. Laws ch. 244, § 35A.

Redemption: None after the sale if sold pursuant to power of sale in mortgage deed or if buyer in possession of land for three years.

Post-Sale Provisions Regarding Proceedings: Mortgagee must notify the commissioner of banks of the date of the foreclosure sale and the purchase price, and must file a copy of the notice of default and right to cure. Mass. Gen. Laws ch. 244, § 35A. Within sixty days after sale, holder or its representative must provide former homeowner with a detailed accounting for the proceeds. Mass. Gen. Laws ch. 183, § 27.

Deficiency: A deficiency judgment is obtainable. Notice of intent to seek a deficiency must be given with the notice of sale. Notice of sale must be served twenty-one days prior to the sale if a deficiency judgment is to be sought.

High-Cost Home Loans: Under the Predatory Home Loan Practices Act, Mass. Gen. Laws ch. 183C, §§ 1–19, before accelerating loan for default a lender must notify the consumer in writing and offer a reasonable opportunity to pay outstanding balance. Mass. Gen. Laws ch. 183C, § 9. High-cost home loan made without compliance with counseling requirements is unenforceable. Mass. Gen. Laws ch. 183C, § 3. Court that finds violation of home loan statute has power to rescind high-cost home loan, bar lender from collecting, enjoin judicial or non-judicial foreclosure or other lender action, reform the terms of a high-cost home mortgage, enjoin other prohibited conduct, and provide other relief. Mass. Gen. Laws ch. 183C, § 18. Borrower in foreclosure may raise

violations of the statute against assignee (unless the assignee exercises due diligence and takes other precautions to avoid accepting assignment of high-cost home loans) as a defense or counterclaim, or in an action to enjoin foreclosure or preserve or regain possession. Mass. Gen. Laws ch. 183C, § 15.
Miscellaneous: Notice of postponement of the sale, if any, is not required. Most foreclosure sales are held after a judicial process in land court to determine that the mortgagor is not a soldier or sailor on active duty overseas. No other defenses may be raised in this judicial proceeding. Commissioner of banks shall maintain a foreclosure database. Mass. Gen. Laws ch. 244, § 14A.

MICHIGAN

Mich. Comp. Laws §§ 600.3101 to 600.3180, 600.3201 to 600.3280

Most Common Method of Foreclosure: Power of sale. The party foreclosing must be either the owner of the indebtedness or of an interest in the indebtedness secured by the mortgage or the servicing agent of the mortgage. If the party foreclosing is not the original mortgagee, a record chain of title must exist prior to the sale date evidencing the assignment of the mortgage to the party foreclosing. § 600.3204.
Preforeclosure Notice:
Number of Notices: One.
Amount of Notice Required: If by publication, once per week for four consecutive weeks. If by posting, within fifteen days of the first advertisement.
Content of Notice: a) Names of mortgagor, mortgagee, and assignee if any; b) date of mortgage and date recorded; c) amount due; d) description of the premises; and e) length of redemption period.
Method of Service: By publication and by posting.
Redemption: Redemption periods are determined by the number of units, number of acres, and percentage of original loan outstanding and whether property is abandoned. Times vary from one month to one year. *See* § 600.3240.
Deficiency: If the mortgagee is, directly or indirectly, the purchaser at a sale pursuant to a power of sale, then the debtor may raise as defense or setoff that the value of the property at the time of sale was equal to the debt, or that the sale price was substantially less than the property's true value. § 600.3280.
Post-Sale Provisions Regarding Proceeds: After satisfying mortgage debt and costs of sale, individual who conducted sale disburses any surplus to borrower; but if receives notice of claims by lienholders, may refer to court for determination of payment rights. § 600.3252.
Foreclosure Conferences: Effective for two years from July 5, 2009, foreclosure sale may be stayed for up to ninety days to allow for conference to consider loan modification. §§ 600.3204, 600.3205a–d. *See* Ch. 4, *supra*.

MINNESOTA

Minn. Stat. §§ 580.01 to 580.30

Most Common Method of Foreclosure: Power of sale.
Preforeclosure Notice:
Number of Notices: Two: Notice of sale and foreclosure advice notice, but the latter is to be delivered with the former. §§ 47.20 (right to cure before acceleration), 580.021, 580.022 (notice and form to encourage use of counseling services).
Amount of Notice Required: Four weeks prior to the sale for service on the occupant. Published notice must be published six weeks before the sale. The foreclosure advice notice must be delivered with the notice of sale and with each subsequent written communication regarding the foreclosure up to the day of redemption.
Content of Notice: *Notice of sale*: a) Name of mortgagor and mortgagee and original amount of mortgage; b) date of mortgage, when and where recorded; c) amount due; d) description of the premises; e) time and place of sale; f) time for redemption; and g) the mortgagee's right to reduce the redemption period under the statute. The foreclosure advice notice advises mortgagors to call the Minnesota Housing Finance Agency for more assistance and requires that mortgage holder respond within fifteen days to counselors' requests for specific information. §§ 580.021 and 580.022.
Method of Service: By service on the occupant like a summons, or by publication in a newspaper.
Right to Cure Default/Reinstate: Borrower has the right to reinstate up to time of sale by bringing the loan current including foreclosure fees and costs. § 580.30.
Redemption: Twelve months or six months, depending on date of mortgage, whether property is agricultural, and number of acres. § 580.23. Borrower is entitled to possession during the redemption period.
Deficiency: Limited by the fair market value, as determined by a jury. No deficiency is available if non-judicial foreclosure is used and six-month redemption period is applicable. § 582.30(2). For certain agricultural land, deficiency is limited by fair market value, as determined by a jury. § 582.30(3).
Post-Sale Provisions Regarding Proceeds: Mortgagee distributes proceeds in priority defined by statute and any remaining surplus to mortgagor. § 580.90.
Miscellaneous: "Mortgage Originator and Servicer Licensing Act" prohibits originator and servicer from making residential mortgage loans without verifying borrower's ability to repay; applies net tangible benefit standard to refinancings; restricts prepayment penalties and negatively amortizing loans; requires brokers to act in best interest of borrowers. Minn. Stat. §§ 58.02, 58.03, 58.15, 58.16, 58.137.

MISSISSIPPI

Miss. Code Ann. §§ 89-1-55 to 89-1-59

Most Common Method of Foreclosure: Power of sale.
Preforeclosure Notice:
Number of Notices: One: Notice of sale.
Amount of Notice Required: If by advertisement, three consecutive weeks before the sale.
Content of Notice: Name of the original mortgagor, terms and place of sale.
Method of Service: By advertisement, and by posting on the courthouse door.
Right to Cure Default/Reinstate: Up to the date of the sale by paying delinquent amount and certain fees and costs.
Redemption: None.
Post-Sale Provisions Regarding Proceeds: Surplus goes to the

mortgagor after junior lienholders are paid.
Deficiency: May be obtained in proceeding filed within one year from sale date. If mortgagee is high bidder at sale, deficiency may be denied if bid at sale is not reasonable.
Miscellaneous: The governor can declare a disaster and impose a moratorium on foreclosures for up to two years. § 89-1-301.

MISSOURI

Mo. Rev. Stat. §§ 443.290 to 443.453

Most Common Method of Foreclosure: Power of sale.
Preforeclosure Notice:
Number of Notices: One.
Amount of Notice Required: Twenty days.
Content of Notice: a) Date, book, and page of record of mortgage; b) grantor; c) date, time, terms, and place of sale; and d) description of the property. § 443.320.
Method of Service: By publication, and by registered or certified mail to the record owner. § 443.325.
Redemption: Foreclosure under a power of sale forecloses equity of redemption unless the lender is the purchaser. If the lender is the purchaser, can redeem up to one year after the sale, so long as notice of intent to redeem is given within ten days before the sale. § 443.410. Mortgagor must satisfy the bond requirements of§ 443.420.
Notification requirement for tenants: § 534.030.
Deficiency: May be obtained by mortgagee.

MONTANA

Mont. Code Ann. §§ 71-1-222 to 71-1-235, 71-1-301 to 71-1-321 (Small Tract Financing Act)

Most Common Method of Foreclosure: Power of sale.
Preforeclosure Notice:
Number of Notices: One: Notice of sale.
Amount of Notice Required: Thirty days. § 71-1-224. 120 days for Small Tract Financing Act. § 71-1-315.
Content of Notice: Not indicated. For Small Tract Financing Act (applies to parcels of 40 acres or less), parties names; book and page on which mortgage recorded; description of property; nature of default; amount owing; and time, place, and date of sale. § 71-1-313.
Method of Service: By advertisement thirty days prior to the sale; by posting in five conspicuous places; and by in-person service thirty days pre-sale on the occupant, mortgagor, and persons claiming interest of record. § 71-1-224. For Small Tract Financing Act, registered or certified mail to borrower, and certain other interested persons, 120 days before sale; posting on property twenty days before sale; publication for three successive weeks, with last publication at least twenty days before sale. § 71-1-315.
Right to Cure Default/Reinstate: Under the Small Tract Financing Act, may cure at any time prior to the sale; applies to deeds of trust on property of less than forty acres. § 71-1-312.
Redemption: One year after the sale by paying the amount of the purchase and costs. Under judicial procedure, the mortgagor retains possession during the redemption period if the property is a home. § 71-1-229. *See* §§ 25-13-802, 25-13-821. Under the Small Tract Financing Act (power of sale foreclosure), purchaser is entitled to possession ten days after sale. No right of redemption. §§ 71-1-318, 71-1-319.
Post-Sale Provisions Regarding Proceeds: Surplus is deposited with the court. The court directs distribution. § 71-1-225. Under small-tract procedure trustee distributes proceeds along statutory priorities. May deposit proceeds with county treasurer and allow court to decide disputed claims. § 71-1-316.
Deficiency: A deficiency judgment is not allowed on a foreclosure of a purchase price mortgage unless judicial foreclosure process is used. §§ 71-1-232, 71-1-317.

NEBRASKA

Neb. Rev. Stat. §§ 76-1005 to 76-1018 (power of sale); 25-2137 to 25-2155 (judicial)

Most Common Method of Foreclosure: Power of sale.
Preforeclosure Notice:
Number of Notices: Two: Notice of default and notice of sale. § 76-1006.
Amount of Notice Required: Notice of default, one month before notice of sale (two if agricultural property). § 76-1006. Notice of sale, approximately six weeks (publication for five successive weeks, the last at least ten days before sale). § 76-1007.
Content of Notice: *Notice of default*: Names of parties, book and page or computer reference where deed recorded, description of property, nature of default, and intent to sell. § 76-1006. *Notice of sale*: description of property, time and place of sale. § 76-1007.
Method of Service: Registered or certified mail to borrower and other persons who requested notice. Notice of default must be recorded. Notice of sale must be published for five successive weeks, with the last publication at least ten days before sale. §§ 76-1006 to 76-1008.
Right to Cure Default/Reinstate: One month after filing of notice of default (two for agricultural land), by paying the delinquent amount, plus costs and fees actually incurred, up to the greater of $50 or 1% of the delinquent amount. § 76-1012.
Redemption: No. Trustee's deed gives title without right of redemption. § 76-1010.
Post-Sale Provisions Regarding Proceeds: Trustee applies proceeds to debt, and various costs and fees actually incurred; surplus to the person entitled to it. § 76-1011.
Deficiency: Creditor must bring action within three months after sale. Deficiency limited to the lesser of the difference between the amount owed and the fair market value of the property, or the difference between the indebtedness and the sale price. § 76-1013.

NEVADA

Nev. Rev. Stat. § 107.080 and 40.455 to 40.463

Most Common Method of Foreclosure: Power of sale for deeds of trust.
Preforeclosure Notice:
Number of Notices: Two: Notice of default (breach) and election to sell; and notice of sale.
Amount of Notice Required: For notice of default (breach), three months. For notice of sale, three weeks.
Content of Notice: *Notice of default*: Must describe default and may contain notice of intent to accelerate entire unpaid balance

if permitted by secured obligation. Notice of default also must be recorded. *Notice of sale*: Must state time and place of sale and must be published once per week for three weeks.

Method of Service: *Notice of default*: By mail to the grantor and owner on the date the notice is recorded; and, within ten days of recording of notice, by mail to each person who filed a request for a copy and to each "person with an interest" subordinate to the deed of trust. *Notice of sale*: By mail within twenty days before the date of sale set forth in the notice of sale, posting in three places, and publication for three consecutive weeks. § 107.080(4).

Right to Cure Default/Reinstate: Borrower may cure until five days before the sale date by payment of the arrearage, costs, and fees. § 40.430.

Redemption: None for non-judicial foreclosures.

Deficiency: Limited to the lesser of (i) the amount by which the amount of the secured debt exceeds the fair market value of the property as determined by the court, or (ii) the difference between the amount for which the property was sold and the amount of the secured debt, with interest from the date of sale. § 40.459. But, for purchase money loans for a single family residence occupied continuously by the borrowers, deficiencies prohibited (applies to obligations incurred after October 1, 2009). § 40.455.

Post-Sale Provisions Regarding Proceeds: Trustee distributes proceeds under statutory guidelines, with surplus to debtor, but may refer for interpleader action if there are disputed claims. § 40.462. Contract with third party to assist debtor in recovering proceeds of foreclosure sale which do not comply with statute are void; fee charged to debtor must be reasonable. § 40.463.

High-Cost Home Loans: Power of sale under trust agreement entered into on or after October 1, 2003, and subject to § 152 of the Home Ownership and Equity Protection Act of 1994 and applicable federal regulations, requires additional notice at least sixty days before date of sale. The notice, which must be personally served unless otherwise directed by a court, must include applicable telephone numbers and addresses for offices of consumer credit counseling, attorney general, division of financial institutions, legal services, and lender. Date of sale may not be less than thirty days after date of most recently filed action, if any, claiming unfair lending practice in connection with the trust agreement. §§ 107.080, 107.085. Court that finds violation of high-cost home loan statute (Nev. Rev. Stat. §§ 598D.010 through 598D.150) has power to award equitable remedy and may cure any existing default and cancel a pending foreclosure sale, trustee's sale, or other sale to enforce the agreement. If damages are awarded (statute allows three times actual damages) borrower has a defense against the unpaid obligation up to the amount of the damages. § 598D.110.

Foreclosure Mediation: Effective July 1, 2009 Assembly Bill 149 created system of judicially supervised foreclosure mediation, available at borrower's request. Generally amending procedures at § 107.080. *See* Ch. 4, *supra*.

NEW HAMPSHIRE

N.H. Rev. Stat. Ann. § 479:25

Most Common Method of Foreclosure: Power of sale.

Preforeclosure Notice:

Number of Notices: One.[1]

Amount of Notice Required: If to the mortgagor, in hand or by certified or registered mail twenty-five days before the sale. If by publication, once per week for three consecutive weeks with the first publication not less than twenty days prior to the sale. Also, any grantee with an interest in the property recorded at least thirty days prior to the sale must get twenty-five days' notice.

Content of Notice: a) Date, time, and place of sale; b) location of the property; c) date of mortgage; d) volume and page number where mortgage is recorded; e) terms of sale; f) that the mortgagor has the right to petition the court, with notice to the mortgagee and posting of bonds as the court may require, to enjoin the sale; and g) that failure to take action will bar any action based on the validity of the foreclosure.

Method of Service: By hand or by registered or certified mail, and by publication in a newspaper of general circulation published in the county where the town is located.

Redemption: Up to the time of sale, by paying the full amount due plus costs. § 479:18.

Post-Sale Provisions Regarding Proceeds: The seller must record the deed and affidavit of compliance within sixty days of the sale. § 479:26. Trustee must report to court within ten days after sale. Court may confirm sale or order a resale. § 479.23, 479.24.

Deficiency: May be obtained in action filed after sale.

Miscellaneous: The mortgagee has a duty of good faith and due diligence in the conduct of the sale. If the duty is violated, the borrower may be able to get damages equal to the difference between the sale price and the fair market value. *Murphy v. Fin. Dev. Co.*, 126 N.H. 536 (1985).

NEW JERSEY

N.J. Stat. Ann. §§ 2A:50-1 to 2A:50-21, 2A:50-53 to 2A:50-62 (residential mortgage only) (West)

Most Common Method of Foreclosure: Suit in equity.

Foreclosure by Power of Sale Permitted?: No, in most circumstances (§§ 2A:50-2.2, 2A:50-2.3); can waive the right to a judicial foreclosure if the property is non-residential; is not one-, two-, three-, or four-family in which the borrower lives; is a second mortgage; and if the lender is a bank.

Judicial Foreclosure Procedure: Can get judgment to foreclose in whole or in part. Set-offs allowed. Sale is by the sheriff (§ 2A:50-19); the sheriff must make a report of the sale. The court must confirm the sale. The mortgagor has ten days after the sale to object. Rule 4:65-5.

Preforeclosure Notice:

Number of Notices: One.

Amount of Notice Required: Thirty days before taking any legal action, by registered or certified mail, return receipt requested. § 2A:50-56 (residential mortgages only).

Content of Notice: Include obligation, nature of default, right to cure, how to cure, time to cure, that the lender intends to foreclose if default is not cured, advise the mortgagor to seek legal counsel, the availability of financial assistance programs,

1 If the mortgage is a second mortgage, the borrower must be served with a notice of intent to foreclose fifteen days before commencement of the foreclosure proceedings. N.H. Rev. Stat. Ann. § 397-A:16-a.

the lender's address and telephone number, description of the property. Sheriff sale purchaser must provide notice with statutory content to tenants. § 2A:50-70.

Method of Service of Notice of Sale: By posting on the property and in the county office four times for four weeks, or by advertisement in two newspapers and mailed to the mortgagor and other parties. Record *lis pendens*.

Right to Cure Default/Reinstate: Up to date of final judgment by tendering amount due before default, perform any obligations necessary, pay costs, and contractual late charges. May reinstate only once in eighteen months. § 2A:50-57 (residential mortgages only). Final judgment of foreclosure of residential mortgage may be delayed if debtor certifies that there is a reasonable likelihood that debtor will be able to provide payment necessary to cure the default within forty-five days. § 2A:50-58.

Post-Sale Provisions Regarding Proceeds: Surplus is deposited with the court and paid to persons entitled to it as determined by the court. § 2A:50-37.

Redemption: If creditor sues for and recovers a deficiency, the foreclosure and sale is opened, and debtor may redeem by paying the full amount of the judgment, with interest, costs and reasonable expenses. Action for redemption must be brought within six months after judgment for deficiency. § 2A:50-4.

Deficiency: No personal deficiency judgment in foreclosure actions or execution thereon for balance due. Deficiency judgment is obtainable in an action on the note after foreclosure (which shall reopen the foreclosure and sale). Judgment is limited by the fair market value. Action for a deficiency judgment must be brought within three months. § 2A:50-1.

High-Cost Home Loans: High-cost home loans covered under the Home Ownership Security Act, N.J. Stat. Ann. §§ 46:10B-22 to 10B-35 (West), must use judicial foreclosure procedures. N.J. Stat. Ann. § 46:10B-26(k) (West). "Save New Jersey Homes Act of 2008" effective from September 15, 2008 through January 1, 2011 applies to ARM loans. § 46:10B-36 to 46:10B-42. Statute sets requirement for disclosures related to interest rates and changes, with a special notice to borrower of intent to foreclose. § 46:10B-41. Also authorizes borrower to request period of extension of foreclosure of up to three years, with allowance for lender to modify loan.

Mediation Procedures: In October 2008, the New Jersey Supreme Court initiated a program to require mediation in residential foreclosure cases. Mediation is mandatory if homeowner files an answer or at any time homeowner requests a stay for mediation. *See* Ch. 4, *supra*. Legislation approved in January 2009 creates funding for the mediation system. In December 2008, legislature enacted "Mortgage Stabilization and Relief Act," which will provide financial assistance to facilitate loan modifications.

Six-Month Foreclosure Forbearance Period for Certain Loans: Borrowers may request six-month period of forbearance, during which foreclosure cannot proceed, in order to pursue mediation. Applicable loans must be "high risk mortgages" defined by statute. These include loans with various onerous provisions, including reset terms that increase the initial interest rate by two or more percentage points, prepayment penalties, an interest only feature, negative amortization, or "pick a payment" options. In effect for two years from the July 2, 2009 effective date. § 46:10B-50.

Statute of Limitations: Foreclosure action cannot be commenced later than the earliest of six years from the date set for final payment, thirty-six years from recording of mortgage, or twenty years from date of default. § 2A:50-56.1.

NEW MEXICO

N.M. Stat. Ann. §§ 48-7-1 to 48-7-24, 39-5-1 to 39-5-23, 48-10-1 to 48-10-21 (power of sale) (West)

Note: The power of sale statute was amended in 2006 to remove the prohibition on powers of sale in residential deeds of trust. As power of sale is likely to be the more common method for post-2006 contracts, both procedures are summarized.

Most Common Method of Foreclosure: Judicial. Required for residential loans. § 58-21A-6E.

Foreclosure by Power of Sale Permitted?: Yes, for loans not covered by "Home Loan Protection" statute. § 58-21A-3J.

Right to Cure: Before filing judicial foreclosure complaint mortgagee must provide borrower with notice of right to cure for at least a thirty-day period by paying arrearage, interest and late fees. Borrower may also cure after complaint filed until title is transferred by means of foreclosure sale. No attorney fees may be assessed in connection with cure within thirty days of pre-complaint notice. Attorney fees in excess of $100 may not be charged in curing a default prior to filing of a complaint. § 58-21A-6.

Judicial Foreclosure Procedure: Sale may not take place until thirty days after judgment. The sale is conducted by the sheriff. Before the sale, the sheriff must have the property appraised. The property cannot sell for less than two-thirds of its appraised value. § 39-5-5. See also § 39-5-14 regarding "reoffer of unsold property."

Preforeclosure Notice:

Number of Notices: One: Notice of sale.

Amount of Notice Required: *Judicial*: If by publication, for four weeks preceding the sale. § 39-5-3. *Power of sale*: Recording of notice of sale at least ninety days before sale. § 48-10-10.

Content of Notice: *Judicial*: a) Title of the case in which foreclosure judgment is obtained; b) date of judgment; c) amount of judgment; d) description of the property; and e) time and conditions of sale. Notice may be in English or Spanish; the sheriff must determine which will be most effective to give the most extensive notice. § 39-5-1. *Power of sale*: Time and place of sale, legal description and street address of property. Notice sent to borrower within five days after recording of notice of sale must include nature of the breach, and intent to sell. § 48-10-11.

Method of Service: *Judicial*: By publication, or by posting in six of the most public places in the county. § 39-5-1. *Power of sale*: By publication (same as judicial), recording and certified or regular mail to borrower, junior encumbrancers, and anyone who has recorded a request for notice. §§ 48-10-11, 48-10-12.

Redemption: *Judicial*: After judgment and before sale (which must be at least thirty days after judgment), may pay amount of judgment plus costs of sale. § 39-5-17. Within nine months of the sale, by paying the purchaser the purchase price plus certain taxes, costs, fees, and 10% interest or by paying this amount into court. §§ 39-5-18, 39-5-21. For certain old mortgages (pre-1957) the parties may shorten the redemption period to one month, but court may extend this period. §§ 39-5-18 and 39-5-19. *Power of sale*: Nine months after trustees sale, by same amount as for judicial.

§ 48-10-16.
Deficiency: Deficiency not barred after judicial foreclosure, but property cannot be sold for less than two-thirds of its appraised value. § 39-5-5. No provision regarding deficiency upon judicial foreclosure. *Power of sale*: Creditor may sue for deficiency within six years after judgment. No deficiency judgment after power of sale foreclosure on property occupied by low-income household. § 48-10-17. Low-income defined as less than 80% of state median for household size based on loan application income.
Post-Sale Provisions Regarding Proceeds: Trustee distributes along statutory priorities, may deposit surplus with clerk of court for judicial determination of distribution; surplus to mortgagor. § 48-10-15.
High-Cost Home Loans: The Home Loan Protection Act, N.M. Stat. Ann. §§ 58-21A-1 to 58-21A-14, requires lenders to provide notice of right to cure prior to filing a foreclosure action for loans covered by the Act. The notice should contain the amount needed to cure the default and, if amount needed to cure will change, information sufficient to enable borrower to calculate daily change. Borrowers are given thirty days from delivery of notice to cure the default. Lenders must use judicial foreclosure procedures. Borrower in foreclosure may raise violations of the Act against an assignee (unless the assignee exercises due diligence and takes other precautions to avoid accepting assignment of high-cost home loans) as counterclaim or defense, or in action to enjoin foreclosure or preserve or retain possession of the home. N.M. Stat. § 58-21A-11.
Miscellaneous: A deed of trust can be foreclosed by a power of sale under the Deeds of Trust Act, but the Act only applies to commercial deeds of trust of $500,000 or more. §§ 48-10-1 to 48-10-21. Prepayment penalty prohibited. § 48-7-19.

NEW YORK

N.Y. Real Prop. Acts. Law §§ 1301 to 1391 (McKinney)

Most Common Method of Foreclosure: Judicial.
Foreclosure by Power of Sale Permitted?: Statute authorizing non-judicial foreclosure of non-residential properties expired July 1, 2009. N.Y. Real Prop. Acts. Law § 1401.
Judicial Foreclosure Procedure: Must name all the parties with an interest in the property or a lien. § 1311. Complaint must specify the basis for the standing of the named plaintiff to proceed with action. § 1303. *Lis pendens* also must be filed. For residential mortgages, notices served with summons and complaint must briefly describe the foreclosure process, warn of homesaver scams, and provide contact information for banking department, which will provide information about public and private sources of information and assistance. §§ 1303, 1320.
Pre-Foreclosure Notice: At least ninety days before filing foreclosure action the foreclosing entity must serve homeowner with notice containing specified content. Notice advises recipient of nature of action and encourages efforts to settle dispute before legal action begins. As of January 2010, notice requirement applies to most home loans in state, not only to subprime and non-traditional loans. Notice requirement in effect until January 14, 2015. N.Y. Real Prop. Acts. Law § 1304. Additional notice of legal options and explanation of foreclosure procedure must be served with summons and complaint. N.Y. Real Prop. Acts. Law § 1303.
Notice of Sale:
Method of Service: By advertisement.
Right to Cure Default/Reinstate: Can pay the amount due into the court any time before the final judgment and the case will be dismissed; after judgment, but before the sale, the proceedings shall be stayed upon payment of arrearages.[2] § 1341.
Redemption: None after the sale.
Post-Sale Provisions Regarding Proceeds: An officer must make a report to the court within thirty days of sale, and surplus must be paid to the court within five days of receipt. The sale must be confirmed by the court. § 1354 to 1355. The court's order directs the distribution of proceeds.
Deficiency: A deficiency judgment is obtainable if the defendant was served in-hand or appears in the action. Limited by the market value of the property. § 1371.
Notice to Tenants: Tenants to receive notice of rights in foreclosure within ten days of service of summons and complaint on homeowner. N.Y. Real Prop. Acts. Law § 1303. Subject to limited exceptions, foreclosing entity must provide written notice to tenants of right to continued occupancy for greater of ninety days from date notice mailed or remainder of lease term. N.Y. Real Prop. Acts. Law § 1305.
High-Cost Home Loans: Foreclosure complaint of high-cost home loan must contain, and lender must prove, allegation that plaintiff lender has complied with law relating to such loans, N.Y. Banking Law § 6-*l*, and to lenders of such loans. N.Y. Banking Law § 595-a; N.Y. Real Prop. Acts. Law § 1302. An intentional violation of the high-cost home loan statute voids the transaction and bars the lender from collecting. N.Y. Banking Law § 6-*l*. The loan may be rescinded for a violation of the law, whether the violation is raised as an affirmative claim or a defense. Rescission is available as a defense without time limitation. A borrower in foreclosure may raise against assignee any claim to recoupment or defenses to payment, based on violation of this statute, that could be raised against the original lender. N.Y. Banking Law § 6-*l*(10)–(12); N.Y. Real Prop. Acts. Law § 1302.
Mandatory Settlement Conferences: New York Civil Practice Rule 3408, effective September 1, 2008, required a settlement conference for a residential foreclosure action involving a high-cost home loan. The rule was amended in December 2009 to make the settlement conference mandatory for all residential foreclosures. *See* Ch. 4, *supra*. A conference must be scheduled within sixty days of service of complaint. Provision is effective until Feb. 13, 2015.

NORTH CAROLINA

N.C. Gen. Stat. §§ 45-21.1 to 45-21.38

Most Common Method of Foreclosure: Power of sale with prior hearing before clerk.
Preforeclosure Notice:
Number of Notices: Four: Preforeclosure notice; notice of default; notice of hearing; and notice of sale.
Amount of Notice Required: For notice of default, thirty days before notice of hearing. For notice of hearing, ten days before

2 However, upon subsequent default by the defendant, the court can order enforcement of the judgment. *But see* Fed. Nat'l Mortgage Ass'n v. Miller, 123 Misc. 2d 431, 473 N.Y.S.2d 743 (Sup. Ct. 1984) (effect of acceleration clause).

the hearing. For notice of sale, twenty days before the sale for service on the debtor. § 45-21.16.

Content of Notice: *Preforeclosure Notice*: At least forty-five days before initiating foreclosure, mortgage holder must provide notice informing homeowner of amount owed, specify contacts with mortgagee where homeowner can obtain more information, and give information about housing counselors. § 53-243.11(21). Additional notice requirements, including advising of loss mitigation contacts, apply for high-cost loans. § 45-102. *Notice of Default*: Amount of principal and interest due, the interest rate, and any other sums claimed to be due. § 45-21.16(c). *Notice of hearing*: a) Description of the property, date and original amount of mortgage, and the book and page where recorded; b) name and address of holder; c) nature of default; d) whether mortgage has been accelerated; e) any right to cure; f) right of debtor to appear before the clerk to show cause why foreclosure should not be allowed; g) that if foreclosure is consummated, debtor will be evicted; and h) other miscellaneous information, including whether any requests for information, pursuant to § 45-88, have been made to the lender or servicer and whether the requests have been complied with. § 45-21.16. Must confirm that notice of default mailed. Must certify that loan is not subprime, as defined in § 45-101. Copy of notice must be filed with administrative office of courts. *Notice of sale*: a) Description of instrument (mortgage); b) date, time, and place of sale; c) description of the property; and d) terms of sale. For residential property with less than fifteen units, certain notices to tenants are also required. § 45-21.16A. Clerk must make determination, either at hearing or on the basis of affidavit submitted by foreclosing entity, that loss mitigation options have been considered. The clerk may continue the hearing for up to sixty days from the date scheduled for the original hearing if it appears that further consideration of loss mitigation options may resolve the matter without a foreclosure sale. § 45-21.16C.

Method of Service: For a notice of hearing, by service on the debtor like a summons. For a notice of sale, by posting fifteen days prior to the sale; by publishing in a newspaper once per week for two consecutive weeks, with the date of the last publication not less than ten days before the sale; and by regular mail to the debtor. § 45-21.17.

Redemption: By payment of amount of obligation in full, plus expenses of sale or proposed sale, before sale or within ten days thereafter. §§ 45-21.20, 45-21.27.

Post-Sale Provisions Regarding Proceeds: Preliminary report of sale due five days from sale. § 45-21.26. Final report of the sale must be filed with the clerk within thirty days of the receipt of sale proceeds. The report must include proof of notice. § 45-21.33. Surplus proceeds go to the person entitled to them, if known; if not known, the proceeds are paid to the court clerk for determination. § 45-21.31.

Deficiency: The mortgagor can show the fair market value of the property as a defense in a deficiency action. § 45-21.36. No deficiency judgment on foreclosure by power of sale of purchase money mortgage. § 45-21.38. Under 2009 enactment applicable to certain mortgages and deeds of trust recorded prior to January 1, 2010, no deficiency may be claimed after power of sale foreclosure when borrower resided in property at time of sale. § 45-21.38A(d)(1). For certain mortgages and deeds of trust recorded on or after January 1, 2010, no deficiency when borrower resided in property at time of sale, whether judicial or power of sale foreclosure. § 45-21.38A(d)(2).

High-Cost Loans: Prohibits, *inter alia*, making high-cost loans without a certification from a housing counselor that the borrower received counseling on the appropriateness of the loan. Also requires income documentation and ability to repay analysis for certain high-cost loans; prohibits yield spread premiums in subprime loans. §§ 24-1.1E and 24-1.1F.

Miscellaneous: See § 45-21.34 for enjoining a mortgage sale or confirmation thereof. Upset bids are allowed. Note that issues at clerk's hearing are limited to whether there was a valid debt, whether a default has occurred, whether holder has right to foreclose, and whether proper notice was given. Other defenses must be raised in action to enjoin foreclosure. Commissioner of Banks to require servicers and brokers to provide data on range of fees, charges, and other characteristics of loans. § 53-243.10. Commissioner may suspend foreclosure up to sixty days upon evidence of violation of servicer obligations. §§ 53-243.12, 45-21.16B, 45-104, and 45-105. Fees associated with foreclosure are subject to disclosure and limitations under § 45-91. Clerk of court may stay foreclosure upon notice of violation from Commissioner of Banks. § 45-21.16B.

NORTH DAKOTA

N.D. Cent. Code §§ 32-19-01 to 32-19-41

Most Common Method of Foreclosure: Judicial.

Foreclosure by Power of Sale Permitted?: No, except mortgages held by the state which contain a power of sale. § 35-22-01.

Judicial Foreclosure Procedure: Action is brought in district court. The complaint must state whether the plaintiff will seek a deficiency judgment. The sale is made by the sheriff.

Preforeclosure Notice:

Number of Notices: Three: Notice of intent (§ 32-19-20), summons and complaint (§ 32-19-36), notice of sale (§ 32-19-08).

Amount of Notice Required: For notice of intent, not less than thirty nor more than ninety days before filing of foreclosure. § 32-19-20. For notice of sale, if by advertisement, once per week for three consecutive weeks with the last publication to be at least ten days prior to the sale.

Content of Notice: Notice of intent; description of property; date and amount of mortgage; itemized statement of cure amount (principal, interest, advances for taxes, insurance maintenance); and statement that if default is not cured within thirty days, foreclosure action will be filed. § 32-19-21. Summons and complaint, identify the mortgage being foreclosed, establish the redemption period, and state whether a deficiency (if available) is being sought. § 32-19-04.

Method of Service: Notice of intent may be served by mail. § 32-19-22. Summons must be served as required in rules of civil procedure. § 32-19-36. Notice of sale, by advertisement, if a newspaper is printed in the county, otherwise by posting on the courthouse door and five other places. A sale made without the required notice must be set aside. § 28-23-04.

Right to Cure Default/Reinstate: Can cure default within thirty days of notice of intent to foreclose. Notice of default must include statement of amounts needed to cure. § 32-19-28.

After judgment, but before the sale, the defendant can bring into court the amount due and the proceedings will be stayed, but the

court can enforce the judgment if the defendant subsequently defaults in payments.[3]
Redemption: Within sixty days, but one year for agricultural land. The period of redemption begins at the time of the filing of the foreclosure action or at the time of first publication of the foreclosure notice. §§ 32-19-18, 28-24-02.
Post-Sale Provisions Regarding Proceeds: Any surplus after payment of the debt and costs shall be brought into court for the defendant, subject to the order of the court. § 32-19-10.
Deficiency: No deficiency for foreclosure of residential property of four or fewer units up to forty contiguous acres; may obtain deficiency judgment for agricultural land of more than 40 acres, but must be based on fair market value; for other properties, deficiency judgments may be based on appraised value. § 32-19-03.
Miscellaneous: § 15-07-10: Authorizes original mortgagor to repurchase non-grant lands following foreclosure by matching highest bid within one hour after sale.

OHIO

Ohio Rev. Code Ann. §§ 2323.07, 5301.39, 5721.18 (West)

Most Common Method of Foreclosure: Judicial.
Foreclosure by Power of Sale Permitted?: No. *See Etna Coal & Iron v. Marting*, 14 O.F.D. 325.
Judicial Foreclosure Procedure: The lender must sue the borrower in the county where the property is located to obtain a foreclosure order. Service of foreclosure complaint is generally by certified mail. Ohio Civil Rule 4.1(A). Must have the property appraised and the property must be offered for sale at not less than two-thirds the appraised value. The sale is conducted by the sheriff.
Preforeclosure Notice:
Number of Notices: One.
Amount of Notice Required: Thirty days by advertisement, once per week for three consecutive weeks.
Redemption: Up to the confirmation of sale by paying the full amount of the judgment and costs. § 2329.33.
Post-Sale Provisions Regarding Proceeds: Notice to borrower within 90 days of sale indicating any surplus. § 2329.31. Sale must be confirmed by the court. § 2329.44.
Deficiency: A deficiency judgment is allowed, but void after two years from the confirmation of sale. § 2329.08. Property cannot be sold for less than two-thirds of appraised fair market value. §§ 2329.20, 2329.17.
Mediation programs: In 2008, the Chief Justice of the Ohio Supreme Court promulgated general guidelines for county courts of common pleas to implement residential foreclosure mediation programs. Several county courts have implemented local programs, including Cuyahoga, Franklin, Lucas, and Summit counties. Generally, a defendant may request an extension of time to answer a complaint while court orders case to proceed under rules for judicial mediation. *See* Ch. 4, *supra* (describing Ohio foreclosure mediation programs).
Miscellaneous: State statute regulates points and fees, restricts prepayment penalties, and mandates counseling before loan with debt-to-income ratio over 50% can be made. Also directs state UDAP statute to apply to certain lending practices such as failure to consider ability to repay. Other provisions regulate appraisers and brokers. Ohio Rev. Code §§ 1345.01 to 1345.03.

OKLAHOMA

Okla. Stat. tit. 12, §§ 686, 764 to 765, 773; Okla. Stat. tit. 46, §§ 41 to 49

Most Common Method of Foreclosure: Judicial.
Foreclosure by Power of Sale Permitted?: Yes, but may not be used against a homestead, if the homeowner chooses to require judicial foreclosure, nor may it be used to foreclose a lien for an extension of credit primarily for agricultural purposes. Judgment is required. Okla. Stat. tit. 46, § 43(A)(2).
Judicial Foreclosure Procedure: "One action" state. Complaint is filed in equity.
Preforeclosure Notice: Executed by the sheriff. Okla. Stat. tit. 12, § 764. But see Okla. Stat. tit. 46, §§ 40 to 49 (Power of Sale Act), although the Act does not apply to a homestead if the mortgagor elects judicial foreclosure pursuant to Okla. Stat. tit. 46, § 43A(2)(b).
Number of Notices: *Judicial*: One. Okla. Stat. tit. 12, § 764. *Power of sale*: Two: Notice of intent and notice of sale. Okla. Stat. tit. 46, §§ 44, 45.
Amount of Notice Required: *Judicial*: By mailing, at least ten days prior to the sale and by publication, beginning at least thirty days prior to the sale. Okla. Stat. tit. 12, § 764. *Power of sale*: Two: Notice of intent and notice of sale. Okla. Stat. tit. 46, §§ 44, 45.
Content of Notice: *Judicial*: Legal description of the property, and time and place of sale. Okla. Stat. tit. 12, § 764. *Power of sale*: *Notice of intent*: Name and address of mortgagee, description of default, availability of right to cure, amount needed to cure, that foreclosure will occur if default not cured, and the debtor should consult an attorney. Okla. Stat. tit. 46, § 44. *Notice of sale*: Nature of default, description of property, time and place of sale, notice of right to redeem, and notice that if property is homestead, debtor may elect judicial foreclosure up to ten days before sale. Okla. Stat. tit. 46, § 45.
Method of Service: *Judicial*: By first-class mail to the judgment debtor and other lienholders. By publication of notice for two consecutive weeks, beginning thirty days prior to the sale, Okla. Stat. tit. 12, § 764. Power of sale, notice of intent, certified mail. Okla. Stat. tit. 46, § 44. Notice of sale, by personal service, and by publication. Okla. Stat. tit. 46, § 45.
Right to Cure Default/Reinstate: If a power of sale is used, can cure within thirty-five days of notice of intent to foreclose, but not more than four times in twenty-four months if property is homestead, otherwise three times. Okla. Stat. tit. 46, § 44.
Redemption: Up to the confirmation of sale. Okla. Stat. tit. 42, §§ 18 to 20, tit. 46, § 43(B).
Post-Sale Provisions Regarding Proceeds: Judicial sale: Any surplus must be paid to the defendant on demand. Okla. Stat. tit. 12, §§ 765 and 773 (confirmation hearing and objections). Power of sale: surplus to former owner. Okla. Stat. tit. 46, § 48.
Deficiency: A deficiency judgment is limited by the market value of the property on the date of sale. Okla. Stat. tit. 12, § 686. After the sale, notice of the confirmation hearing must be given to all persons who received the notice of sale. Objections may be filed.

3 *But see* Metro. Bld'g & Loan Ass'n v. Weinberger, 67 N.D. 627, 275 N.W. 638 (1937) (section does not apply to mortgages which have been accelerated).

Okla. Stat. tit. 12, § 765. The mortgagee must move for a deficiency judgment within ninety days of sale. Okla. Stat. tit. 12, § 686. If the debtor allows the foreclosure to proceed under power of sale, and gives timely notice that the property is homestead and that he or she elects against a deficiency judgment, then no deficiency judgment. Okla. Stat. tit. 46, § 43.

OREGON

Or. Rev. Stat. §§ 86.735 to 86.795

Most Common Method of Foreclosure: Power of sale for deeds of trust.

Preforeclosure Notice:

Number of Notices: Two: Notice of default and notice of sale. Notice of default must be recorded.

Amount of Notice Required: For notice of sale, 120 days prior to sale. For publication, once per week for four consecutive weeks with the last publication more than twenty days pre-sale.

Content of Notice: a) Names of parties; b) description of the property; c) where deed of trust is recorded; d) nature of default; e) sum owing; f) election to sell; g) date, time, and place of sale; and h) right to reinstatement up to five days before sale by curing default.

Method of Service: By publication, and by both first-class and certified mail to the grantor and occupant. Notice of sale must be personally served on occupant. If personal service cannot be accomplished, then by posting on the premises. § 86.750.

Right to Cure Default/Reinstate: Up to five days before the sale. Limits on costs for a residential mortgage (e.g., total of both trustee's fees and attorney fees shall be amount actually charged or $1000, whichever is less). § 86.753. Up to fifteen days before the sale, the mortgagee must provide a detailed written statement to the mortgagor, upon request, of the amount needed to cure. §§ 86.757, 86.759.

Redemption: None after sale. § 86.770(1).

Post-Sale Provisions Regarding Proceeds: Any surplus proceeds go to the grantor. § 86.765.

Deficiency: No deficiency on power of sale foreclosure. No deficiency after judicial foreclosure of residential mortgage. § 86.770(2).

Notice to Tenants: Purchaser must give thirty- or sixty-day notice, depending on nature of tenancy, in order to terminate leases of residential tenants. §§ 86.755(5)(c), 86.745 (notice to tenants).

Notice of Procedure to Request Loan Modification: On or before date of recording notice of default, the trustee must serve borrower with notice of proposed action, amount due and options for stopping sale. § 86.737. The notice informs borrower of procedures for requesting a loan modification and conferring with lender. Borrower has thirty days to apply for a loan modification. An affidavit verifying service of notice and compliance with loan modification review requirement must be recorded on or before date the trustee conducts sale. These requirements effective until Jan. 2, 2012. § 86.750(4), (5). *See* Ch. 4, *supra* (discussing foreclosure mediation and conference requirements).

PENNSYLVANIA

35 Pa. Stat. Ann. §§ 1680.402c to 1680.409c (West); 41 Pa. Stat. Ann. §§ 403 to 404 (West); Pa. R. Civ. P. 1141 to 1150

Most Common Method of Foreclosure: Judicial.

Judicial Foreclosure Procedure: Action commenced by filing a complaint in court of common pleas. Must serve the owner as well as the occupant of the property.

Preforeclosure Notice: *See* 41 Pa. Stat. Ann. § 403.

Number of Notices: Two: 1) Notice of right to apply to Pennsylvania Housing Finance Agency for Assistance. 35 Pa. Stat. Ann. § 1680.403c. But note that the provisions of this article do not apply if the agency officially declares that it has not funds available for emergency assistance. 35 Pa. Stat. Ann. § 1680.409c. 2) Notice of intention to foreclose. 41 Pa. Stat. Ann. § 403. For form of notice, see 10 Pa. Code § 7.4.

Amount of Notice Required: Thirty days.

Content of Notice: a) Particular obligation or real estate security interest; b) nature of claimed default; c) right to cure default and how to cure; d) precise sum of money needed to cure; e) time to cure; f) method by which debtor's ownership or possession may be terminated; and g) right of debtor to sell or refinance. 41 Pa. Stat. Ann. § 403(c). Attorney fees limited to $50 if no foreclosure complaint filed. 41 Pa. Stat. Ann. § 406(3).

Method of Service: By certified or registered mail to the owner's last known address and to the property.

Right to Cure Default/Reinstate: Up to one hour before the bidding, but not more than three times in one year, by paying the amount due and costs. 41 Pa. Stat. Ann. § 404.

Redemption: None after the sale.

Deficiency: A deficiency judgment is allowed in a separate action filed after completion of sale. If judgment creditor is directly or indirectly the purchaser, limited by fair market value of property. 42 Pa. Cons. Stat. Ann. 8103(a).

Post-Sale Provisions Regarding Proceeds: Sheriff files proposed schedule of distribution of proceeds within thirty days of sale. Distribution of proceeds after ten days if no objection; if objection, sheriff refers to court.

Mediation Programs: The Philadelphia Common Pleas Court instituted a "Residential Mortgage Foreclosure Diversion Pilot Program" in April 2008. The court's order stays sheriff sales pending conciliation conferences; the mortgage holder must certify completion of conciliation before a sale can proceed. The Allegheny County court issued a mediation order in December 2008 under which mortgagees must file certification of participation in conciliation. Mortgagees must respond to homeowners, proposals, and sales stayed until conciliation process completed. A number of other Pennsylvania county courts, including Bucks, Butler, Fayette, Lackawanna, Northampton, and Somerset counties, have implemented various forms of mediation or conference requirements for foreclosure cases. *See* Ch. 4 (discussing foreclosure mediation and conference requirements).

PUERTO RICO

P.R. Laws Ann. tit. 30, §§ 2701 to 2725

Most Common Method of Foreclosure: Summary procedure (§ 2701) or judicial action (P.R. R. Civ. P. 51.8).

Preforeclosure Notice: Debtor must be given twenty days to cure default before the procedure can be initiated. § 2703. Demand made by certified mail. Cure amount does not include attorney fees.

Foreclosure Process: Foreclosure procedure initiated by filing a brief which meets requirements of § 2706. It then gives debtor thirty days to pay off any claims plus fees and costs. § 2710.

Debtor can submit deposition of objections within first twenty days of the thirty days of demand for payment. § 2706. Court can hold hearing on defenses within ten days of service thereof.

After thirty days pass and objections resolved, property can be sold at auction by marshal. § 2719. Marshal must issue edict of date, time, place of auction. §§ 2720, 2721.

Redemption: There is no statutory right to redeem after sale. § 2710.

Post-Sale Provisions Regarding Proceeds: Sale must then be confirmed by court. § 2725. The court orders distribution of proceeds. § 2726.

RHODE ISLAND

R.I. Gen. Laws §§ 34-27-1 to 34-27-5, 34-25.2-1 to 34-25.2-15

Most Common Method of Foreclosure: Power of sale.

Preforeclosure Notice:

Number of Notices: Two.

Preforeclosure Counseling Notice: No less than forty-five days before initiating foreclosure, mortgagee must serve borrower with notice describing counseling available through HUD-approved agencies. Failure to comply with this notice requirement renders a foreclosure void. The mortgagee must include in the foreclosure deed an affidavit of compliance with this requirement. § 34-27-3.1 (effective Jan. 5, 2010).

Notice of Sale: By mail, thirty days prior to the first publication and by publication, twenty-one days and must publish three times. § 34-27-4.

Content of Notice: Date, time, and place of sale. § 34-11-22.

Method of Service: By certified mail and by publication.

Redemption: Up to three years after the sale by filing a lawsuit. § 34-23-3.

Deficiency: A deficiency judgment is obtainable.

Post-Sale Provisions Regarding Proceeds: Trustee makes distribution to mortgagee and pays expenses of sale and taxes; pays surplus to mortgagor. § 34-11-22.

High-Cost Home Loans: Limited application based on definition of covered loans. Forbids, *inter alia*, flipping, call provisions, balloon payments, negative amortization, and default interest rates. Requires credit counseling and reasonable belief by creditor that borrower will be able to repay. Restricts late payment charges. Assignees liable, unless they can show reasonable procedures and due diligence to avoid taking assignment of high-cost home loans. §§ 34-25.2-1 to 34-25.2-15.

SOUTH CAROLINA

S.C. Code Ann. §§ 15-39-610, 15-39-650, 15-39-660, 29-3-630 to 29-3-790

Most Common Method of Foreclosure: Judicial.

Judicial Foreclosure Procedure: In any action, the plaintiff must establish the amount of the debt. Notice is given as in any civil action.

Preforeclosure Notice:

Number of Notices: One.

Amount of Notice Required: If by advertisement, for three weeks prior to the sale.

Content of Notice: a) Property to be sold; b) time and place of sale; and c) name of plaintiff and defendant.

Method of Service: By advertisement in a newspaper, and by posting in three public places.

Redemption: None after foreclosure.

Deficiency: Upset bids are accepted within thirty days of sale. § 15-39-720. Deficiency judgments are allowed (§ 29-3-660), but the defendant can ask the court for an order of appraisal within thirty days of the sale. When appraisal has been requested and performed, deficiency limited to excess of debt over appraised value.

Post-Sale Provisions Regarding Proceeds: Court's foreclosure decree sets out order for payment of claims. §§ 29-3-630 and 29-3-650.

High-Cost Home Loans: If, before the maturity date of the debt, the court finds a violation of the high-cost home loans statute, S.C. Code Ann. §§ 37-23-10 through 37-23-85, it may refuse to enforce the agreement, or the term or part that was unlawful, or rewrite the agreement to eliminate the unlawful part. S.C. Code Ann. § 37-23-50. In an action to collect the debt, borrower may raise a violation of this statute as a matter of defense by recoupment or setoff. S.C. Code Ann. § 37-23-50.

Administrative Order on HAMP Compliance and Foreclosures: On May 22, 2009 the South Carolina Supreme Court issued an administrative order which requires that an entity filing a foreclosure complaint verify by affidavit how it complied with any obligation it had to review the homeowner for a HAMP loan modification. A copy of the order is available at www.judicial.state.sc.us/courtOrders/displayOrder.cfm?orderNo=2009-05-22-01.

SOUTH DAKOTA

S.D. Codified Laws §§ 21-48-1 to 21-48-26

Most Common Method of Foreclosure: Power of sale. See §§ 21-47-1 to 21-47-25 for the judicial foreclosure procedure; see also §§ 21-48A-1 to 21-48A-5 for non-judicial voluntary foreclosure.

Preforeclosure Notice:

Number of Notices: One.

Amount of Notice Required: By publication, four weeks. Written notice to be served twenty-one days prior to sale. § 21-48-6.1.

Content of Notice: a) Names of mortgagor and mortgagee; b) date of mortgage; c) amount due; d) description of the property; e) time and place of sale; f) debtor's right to apply for judicial foreclosure action; g) description of default; and h) names and addresses of all persons claiming a recorded interest in the property. § 21-48-6.

Method of Service: By publication once per week for four consecutive weeks.

Right to Cure Default/Reinstate: None for power of sale foreclosure. In foreclosure by action, debtor may cure default and stay the proceedings by paying into court the amount then due, with costs and disbursements. §§ 21-47-8 to 21-47-10.

Redemption: None after a power of sale foreclosure. But see §§ 21-49-11 to 21-49-40 for "Short Term Redemption Mortgages" (one-year redemption after judgment, but may vary depending upon document terms).

Deficiency: A deficiency judgment is limited by the true market value of the property if mortgagee, payee, or other holder purchases the property directly or indirectly. § 21-48-14. If debtor and

creditor agree to a voluntary foreclosure pursuant to §§ 21-48A-1 to 21-48A-5, there is no deficiency and no surplus. § 21-48A-1. A judicial foreclosure bars a deficiency, except as provided in §§ 21-47-16, § 21-47-17. These latter statutes allow court to consider property's value in setting deficiency debt.
Miscellaneous: After commencement of foreclosure by a power of sale, the mortgagor can require a mortgagee to foreclose by action by making an application to the court. No reasons need be given. § 21-48-9.
Post-Sale Provisions Regarding Proceeds: Any surplus is paid into court; junior lienholders and borrower receive payments to extent proceeds available. §§ 21-48-16 and 21-47-18.

TENNESSEE

Tenn. Code Ann. §§ 35-5-101 to 35-5-111, 66-8-101 to 66-8-103

Most Common Method of Foreclosure: Power of sale.
Preforeclosure Notice:
Number of Notices: One: Notice of sale.
Amount of Notice Required: Notice to be sent to debtor by registered mail, return receipt requested, on or before the first publication date. § 35-5-101(e). If by publication, twenty days. If by posting, thirty days. Must publish three times with the first notice at least twenty days prior to the sale.
Content of Notice: a) Names of parties; b) description of the land; c) time and place of sale; and d) identification of any federal or state liens. § 35-5-104.
Method of Service: By publication or by posting; service on homeowner by registered or certified mail.
Redemption: Up to two years. §§ 66-8-101, 66-8-102. But right can be waived by provision in mortgage or deed of trust. §§ 66-8-102, 66-8-103.
Deficiency: A deficiency judgment is obtainable.
High-Cost Home Loans: Tennessee Home Loan Protection Act, §§ 45-20-101 to 45-20-111 forbids, *inter alia*, flipping, acceleration at will, balloon payments, and negative amortization, and requires a good faith belief by lender in borrower's ability to repay. Section 45-20-104 provides a right to cure and reinstate up to three business days before foreclosure sale. Borrower must be given notice of this right thirty days before publication of the notice of foreclosure: nature of default, amount needed to cure, deadline to cure, and contact information for lender.
Miscellaneous: The sale is neither voidable nor void if the notice provisions are not complied with. The trustee could be guilty of misdemeanor, however. §§ 35-5-106, 35-5-107.

TEXAS

Tex. Prop. Code Ann. § 51.002 (Vernon)

Most Common Method of Foreclosure: Power of sale.
Preforeclosure Notice:
Number of Notices: Two: Notice of default and opportunity to cure (with twenty days to cure) and notice of sale (for residential mortgage foreclosures only).
Amount of Notice Required: Twenty-one days prior to sale.
Content of Notice: Earliest time of sale, and place of sale.
Method of Service: By certified mail and by posting on the courthouse door.
Right to Cure Default/Reinstate: Can cure within twenty days of the notice of default. § 51.002(d).
Redemption: No right of redemption.
Deficiency: A deficiency action must be brought within two years of the sale. The borrower can ask the court to determine the fair market value. If the court determines that the fair market value is greater than the sale price, the borrower is entitled to an offset. § 51.003.
Miscellaneous: Note special provision regarding deed-in-lieu. § 51.006. Foreclosure of certain loans secured by a lien on a homestead is prohibited by Tex. Const. art. 16, § 50, except when certain requirements are met. These requirements include foreclosure only by court order. Tex. Const. art. 16, § 50(a)(6).

UTAH

Utah Code Ann. §§ 57-1-19, 57-1-23 to 57-1-34, 78-37-1 to 78-37-9 (judicial foreclosure); Utah R. Civ. P. 69(i), (j)

Most Common Method of Foreclosure: Power of sale.
Preforeclosure Notice:
Number of Notices: Two: Notice of default and notice of sale.
Amount of Notice Required: *Notice of Default*: Must be recorded at least three months prior to sale. Must be mailed to mortgagor by certified or registered mail within ten days after recording. §§ 57-1-24 and 57-1-25. *Non-judicial Foreclosure Procedure*: Notice of sale describing the property and time and place of sale must be published three times for three consecutive weeks, and last date of publication must be at least ten days prior to sale, posted in a conspicuous place on the property and in the county recorder's office at least twenty days prior to sale.
Right to Cure Default/Reinstate: Within three months of the filing of the notice of default. § 57-1-31.
Redemption: No post-sale right to redeem after power of sale foreclosure.
Post-Sale Provisions Regarding Proceeds: Trustee applies proceeds in statutorily prescribed order; surplus to debtor. § 57-1-29. Court may direct that any surplus be deposited in the court, to be distributed as the court directs. § 78-37-4.
Deficiency: Action for deficiency must be brought within three months after sale. Amount of deficiency is limited to the difference between the debt (including various costs, fees, etc.) and the fair market value. § 57-1-32.

VERMONT

Vt. Stat. Ann. tit. 12, §§ 4523 to 4533a; Vt. R. Civ. P. 80.1.

Most Common Method of Foreclosure: Judicial (strict foreclosure).
Foreclosure by Power of Sale Permitted?: Yes, if a power of sale is contained in the mortgage. Vt. Stat. Ann. tit. 12, § 4531a; *see* Vt. Stat. Ann. tit. 12, § 4532. Power of sale foreclosure not available for owner-occupied one- or two-unit dwelling. § 4531a(a).
Judicial Foreclosure Procedure: Filing of complaint complying with Vt. R. Civ. P. 80.1. Complaint is served in accordance with Vt. R. Civ. P. 4. (Note that residential tenants must also be notified. § 2523.) Judicial foreclosure is ordinarily strict foreclosure—that is, the property is awarded to the creditor without a sale, and the mortgagor retains any surplus value in the property over the mortgage debt. Under recent amendments, the court may forego a sale and allow strict foreclosure only if it finds "based on competent evidence" that there is no value in the property in excess of

the plaintiff's claim. § 4528(b). Accounting must be submitted to the court; the court makes a finding as to principal, interest, and costs due. The court then issues a writ of possession to the mortgagee and the mortgagee takes the property free and clear of the interests of any named defendants. §§ 4531-33, Vt. R. Civ. P. 80.1. When filing a foreclosure action the plaintiff must file a statement with the Vermont Commissioner of Banking identifying the current owner of the mortgage, the original lender and the servicer. Vt. Stat. Ann. tit. 12, § 4532a.

Preforeclosure Notice:

Number of Notices: Two: Notice of intent to foreclose and notice of sale (power of sale foreclosure).

Amount of Notice Required: *Notice of intent*: Thirty days prior to notice of sale. *Notice of sale*: Sixty days prior to sale.

Content of Notice: *Notice of intent*: The mortgage to be foreclosed, the condition claimed to have been breached, whether debt has been accelerated, amount to be paid or other action necessary to cure, time to cure, intention to foreclose by power of sale, and right to notice of sale. *Notice of sale*: Legal description of premises, terms of sale, right to redeem, right to redemption, and time and place of sale.

Method of Service: Registered or certified mail. Notice of sale must also be recorded, and must be published once a week for three weeks in newspaper of general circulation.

Redemption: Six months from date of decree, but court has discretion to shorten this period. § 4528. If a sale is ordered, mortgagor may redeem until time of sale. § 4532. Sale may not take place until seven months from date of service of complaint if property is one- or two- unit dwelling, but court may reduce time if waste is shown. § 4531a.

Post-Sale Provisions Regarding Proceeds: After a court-ordered sale, seller must report to the court within ten days. The court can confirm or set aside the sale. § 4533. If there is a surplus, the order of confirmation should order the distribution to lienholders, etc., with the surplus to the debtor. Vt. R. Civ. P. 80.1(j)(1).

Deficiency: In a strict foreclosure without a sale the mortgagee must plead claim for deficiency and obtain separate judgment, limited by fair market value of property. In judicial foreclosure with a sale, mortgagee must ask for deficiency in complaint; debt limited by fair market value if mortgagee buys at sale. Vt. R. Civ. P. 80.1(j)(2), Reporter's Note to Rule 80.1, 1982 amendments.

VIRGINIA

Va. Code Ann. §§ 55-59 to 55-66.6

Most Common Method of Foreclosure: Power of sale.

Preforeclosure Notice:

Number of Notices: One.

Amount of Notice Required: For service by mail, fourteen days. For publication, if the deed of trust does not establish advertising requirements, four weeks if published weekly or five consecutive days if published daily; if the deed of trust does provide for advertising, then as provided—but not less than two weeks if published weekly or three consecutive days if published daily. Serving the statutory notice creates rebuttable presumption that foreclosing lienholder complied with any requirements as to notice of default contained in deed of trust. §§ 55-59.2, 55-59.1.

Content of Notice: a) Time, date, and place of sale; b) terms of sale; c) names of trustees; d) description and location of property; and e) contact information for person who can respond to inquiries about the sale. §§ 55-59.3, 55-62.

Method of Service: By in-hand delivery, or by mail and publication.

Redemption: No right of redemption for a non-judicial foreclosure.

Deficiency: A deficiency judgment is obtainable.

Post-Sale Provisions Regarding Proceeds: Within six months of sale trustee must account for proceeds to the commissioner of accounts where deed was recorded. § 26-15. Commissioner must report to the court. Judge must review report within fifteen days and may confirm report or decline to do so. Report final if no objection in fifteen days. § 26-33. Surplus to borrower. §§ 26-15 and 55-59.4(3).

High-Cost Loan Law: Prohibits refinancing within twelve months unless in borrower's best interest. Va. Code Ann. § 6.1-422. Amendments in 2008 require mortgagee to give notice of right to cure at least ten days before sending acceleration notice. Notice of right to cure must contain information on contacts for obtaining loan account information from lender, with additional thirty days' delay of foreclosure if homeowner responds to the notice. Lender required to make good faith attempts at loss mitigation. § 55-59.1:1.

VIRGIN ISLANDS

V.I. Code Ann. tit. 5, §§ 484, 492 to 496; V.I. Code Ann. tit. 28, §§ 531 to 538.

Most Common Method of Foreclosure: Judicial. V.I. Code Ann. tit. 28, § 531 provides that liens on real property, except for judgment liens, whether created by a mortgage or otherwise "shall be foreclosed, and the property adjudged to be sold to satisfy the debt secured thereby, by an action of an equitable nature."

Preforeclosure Notice:

Number of Notices: Notice of sale.

Amount of Notice Required: Written or printed notice, posted in a public place or near office of court clerk and published once a week for four weeks prior to the sale in a newspaper in the judicial division in which the sale is to take place.

Content of Notice of Sale: Time, place of sale, and description of the property.

Method of Service: Publication.

Right to Cure Default/Reinstate: Up to time of sale. V.I. Code Ann. tit. 28, § 538.

Redemption: Within six months after the order of confirmation of sale by payment of the purchase amount plus interest at the legal rate and any taxes that the purchaser may have paid. V.I. Code Ann. tit. 28, § 535; V.I. Code Ann. tit. 5, §§ 492, 493, 496.

Post-Sale Provisions Regarding Proceeds: Sale of real property must be confirmed by court. Judgment debtor has five days to object. Proceeds are paid into court. Debtor who waives objections receives any surplus before confirmation. V.I. Code Ann. tit. 5, § 489.

Deficiency: A deficiency appears to be available—but creditor must sue on the note or other evidence of debt in the same action as it seeks foreclosure. V.I. Code Ann. tit. 28, § 531.

WASHINGTON

Wash. Rev. Code §§ 61.24.020 to 61.24.140

Most Common Method of Foreclosure: Power of sale on deed of trust.[4]

Preforeclosure Notice:

Number of Notices: Two: Notice of default and notice of sale. § 61.24.030.

Amount of Notice Required: For a notice of default, thirty days before notice of sale recorded. § 61.24.030. For a notice of sale, ninety days. § 61.24.040. Note that sale may not take place less than 190 days after default.

Content of Notice: *Notice of default*: a) Description of the property; b) where instrument is recorded; c) nature of default; d) itemized account of arrears; e) itemized account of other charges; f) total amount necessary to reinstate; g) that failure to cure within thirty days will result in foreclosure sale in 120 days; h) effect of foreclosure; and i) that mortgagor has recourse to courts. *Notice of sale*: a) Description of property; b) time, date, and place of sale; c) where deed of trust is recorded; d) amount in arrears; e) total sum owing; f) terms of sale; g) effect of foreclosure; h) that mortgagor can file court action; and i) reinstatement rights, including deadline. For owner-occupied residential property, an additional statement at the beginning of the notice is required, warning that the process can lead to loss of the home, pointing out alternatives (paying or disputing amount owed, selling or refinancing, seeking private or government assistance, bankruptcy), warning of the danger of home-saver scams, and advising of the existence of counseling and legal services.

Method of Service: For a notice of default, by registered or certified mail and first-class mail, by posting, or by personal service. For a notice of sale, by registered or certified mail and first-class mail, by posting on a conspicuous place, or by in-person service on the occupant.

Right to Cure Default/Reinstate: Up to eleven days before the sale by paying principal and interest due and reasonable expenses and fees actually incurred. §§ 61.24.040, 61.24.090.

Post-Sale Provisions Regarding Proceeds: The trustee deposits notice of proceeds with the clerk and the court determines distribution. § 61.24.080.

Redemption: No redemption right after non-judicial foreclosure. § 61.24.050. Eight months for judicial foreclosure. § 6.23.020.

Deficiency: No deficiency decree if the foreclosure is by power of sale. § 61.24.100. A deficiency may be obtained in the event of judicial foreclosure.

Notice to Tenants: A tenant or subtenant of residential real property at time of foreclosure sale must be given sixty days' written notice to vacate before the tenant may be evicted through an unlawful detainer action. § 61.24.146.

Certification of Loss Mitigation Efforts: A notice of default filed under § 61.24.030 must include a declaration ("Foreclosure Loss Mitigation Form") that the beneficiary contacted the borrower to assess loss mitigation options or attempted with due diligence to make contact and was unsuccessful. The requirement applies to deeds of trust on residential properties made from Jan. 1, 2003 to Dec. 31, 2007. The provision is to be in effect from July 26, 2009 to Dec. 31, 2012. § 61.24.031.

WEST VIRGINIA

W. Va. Code §§ 38-1-3 to 38-1-15

Most Common Method of Foreclosure: Power of sale.

Preforeclosure Notice:

Number of Notices: One.

Amount of Notice Required: If to the mortgagor, within a reasonable time before the sale. If to any subordinate lienholder, at least twenty days prior to the sale.

Content of Notice: a) Time and place of sale; b) names of parties to the deed; c) date of the deed; d) office and book in which it is recorded; e) description of the property; and f) terms of sale.

Method of Service: By publication, and by certified mail return receipt requested.

Right to Cure Default/Reinstate: For ten days after the notice of right to cure is served; the notice of right to cure can be served five days after the default. No right to cure if in default and notice is served three or more times. § 46A-2-106.

Redemption: None if the sale is confirmed.

Post-Sale Provisions Regarding Proceeds: Surplus sale proceeds go to the mortgagor. § 38-1-7. Return of account must be made within two months after the sale or the trustee forfeits its commission. § 38-1-8.

Miscellaneous: See § 38-1-14 for special provisions regarding foreclosure of a credit line for a deed of trust.

WISCONSIN

Wis. Stat. §§ 846.01 to 846.25

Most Common Method of Foreclosure: Judicial.

Judicial Foreclosure Procedure: The court enters judgment and orders the sale. The sale cannot take place for one year after judgment (§ 846.10), unless the mortgagee waives the right to a deficiency judgment on a property of less than twenty acres, in which case the property can be sold six months after judgment. § 846.101. If the property is abandoned, it can be sold two months after judgment. § 846.102.

Pre-Foreclosure Sale Notice: Given by the sheriff or referee making the sale. § 846.16.

Number of Notices: One.

Amount of Notice Required: If by publication, six weeks. If by posting, three weeks. § 815.31.

Content of Notice: Time and place of sale, and description of the property.

Method of Service: If by publication, once per week for six weeks. If by posting, in three places three weeks prior to the sale. § 815.31.

Right to Cure Default/Reinstate: Can cure by bringing the amount due into the court before judgment and the case will be dismissed. After judgment, can bring amount due into the court and the proceedings will be stayed, but the court may enforce judgment upon subsequent default. § 846.05.

Redemption: Can redeem any time before the sale by paying amount of judgment plus interest. § 846.13.

Deficiency: A deficiency judgment is obtainable and must be pled in foreclosure action. § 846.04. Before confirming a sale and

4 Power of sale foreclosure is not available for agricultural or farm land. Wash. Rev. Code § 61.24.030.

rendering a deficiency judgment, court must be satisfied that the fair market value of the premises sold has been credited on the debt. § 846.165. If mortgagee waives deficiency, redemption period shortened from twelve to six months. § 846.101.
Post-Sale Provisions Regarding Proceeds: After payment of mortgagee's debt, court must approve disbursement of surplus to the parties entitled to payment. § 846.08, 846.10(3).
High-Cost Home Loans: Wis. Stat. §§ 428.202 to 428.211. Prohibits, among other things, balloon payments, acceleration at will, negative amortization, interest rates on default, certain pre-payment requirements, flipping, misrepresentations, and recommending that customer default on existing loan. Requires lender to consider borrower's ability to repay, regulates form of payment of loan proceeds to home-improvement contractors, and prohibits finance of certain types of credit insurance products through loan proceeds.

WYOMING

Wyo. Stat. Ann. §§ 34-4-101 to 34-4-113 (power of sale), 1-18-101 to 1-18-114 (judicial sale)

Most Common Method of Foreclosure: Power of sale.
Preforeclosure Notice:
Number of Notices: Two: Notice of intent to foreclose and notice of sale.
Amount of Notice Required: Notice of intent to foreclose must be served by certified mail ten days before beginning publication. § 34-4-103. Notice of sale must be published four weeks prior to the sale. Prior to the first publication, a copy of the notice of sale must be served by certified mail upon the record owner, the person in possession if different than the record owner, and holders of recorded mortgages and liens which appear of record at least twenty-five days before the sale date. § 34-4-104.
Content of Notice: a) Name of mortgagor and mortgagee; b) date of mortgage and when recorded; c) amount due under mortgage; d) description of the property; e) terms of sale; and f) a statement that "The property being foreclosed upon may be subject to other liens and encumbrances that will not be extinguished at the sale and any prospective purchaser should research the status of title before submitting a bid." § 34-4-105. *Cf.* § 1-18-101(b).
Method of Service: By publication and by certified mail with return receipt requested. Must also serve notice on the person in possession of the property if different than the record owner.
Redemption: Within three months from date of sale. § 1-18-103.
Post-Sale Provisions Regarding Proceeds: Surplus goes to the mortgagor on demand. For foreclosures and execution sales commenced on or after July 1, 2005, proceeds are paid in the following order: a) reasonable collection and enforcement expenses, and mortgagee's attorney fees and legal expenses to the extent provided by law, b) satisfaction of the obligations secured by the mortgage being foreclosed; c) satisfaction of subordinate or junior mortgages or liens; and d) surplus proceeds to the mortgagor. §§ 34-4-104, 34-4-113, 1-18-113.
Deficiency: A deficiency judgment is obtainable if a separate written agreement obligates the mortgagor. § 34-4-113(c).

Appendix F Summary of State Real Estate Tax Abatement Laws

Every state has enacted special property tax abatement schemes or exemptions which relieve at least some taxpayers of a portion of their property tax liability by virtue of age, disability, income level, or personal status. All states have approved tax relief for older homeowners, and some states extend this relief to older renters as well. The abatements provided by these programs can be significant, and should be thoroughly explored for every homeowner. Their benefits are not automatic, however. Most abatement programs require that the homeowner apply for and submit proof of eligibility for an abatement or an exemption. Application must usually be made within a short period after the issuance of the tax bill. These time periods are generally not extendable, if an application is not timely made, the right to the abatement will be lost. Often homeowners who stand to benefit most are not even aware of these existing programs and so pay more than necessary.

This appendix summarizes and abridges state tax abatement laws. Refer to the statutory citations for more information. Careful research may turn up additional laws which apply on a state or local basis. In addition, in some communities, there may be formal or informal policies to negate or postpone tax enforcement proceedings for older taxpayers or taxpayers experiencing a hardship. Check for this possibility by contacting the taxing authorities directly.

ALABAMA

Ala. Code §§ 40-9-1 to 40-9-33

Elder and Disabled Exemption: The principal residence, plus up to 160 acres adjacent thereto, of any person who is age sixty-five or older, with a net income of $7500 or less is exempt from local property taxes. § 40-9-21.

Homestead: Homestead is exempt up to $4000 in assessed value if owner is not sixty-five or older. § 40-9-19(a). Homestead of elder (over sixty-five) or disabled or blind person entitled to exemption of up to $2000 in assessed value, but localities can enact higher exemption up to $4000. Elder (over sixty-five) with income of less than $12,000, or blind or disabled persons entitled to exemption up to $5000. These exemptions do not apply to county-wide and school district taxes levied for school purposes. Municipalities may, however, allow an exemption from school district taxes for elder and disabled homeowners. § 40-9-19.1.

Veterans: Home of veteran (purchased pursuant to 38 U.S.C. § 701 and Chapter 12) is exempt from all *ad valorem* property taxes as long as home is occupied by veteran or surviving spouse. § 40-9-20.

ALASKA

Alaska Stat. §§ 29.45.030, 29.45.040, 09.38.010

Elder and Disabled Veterans Exemption: The principal residence of a resident sixty-five or older, a disabled person, or a resident at least sixty years old who is the widow or widower of either is exempt from local property taxes on the first $150,000 of the assessed value of the real property. § 29.45.030(e). By ordinance approved by the voters, a municipality may exempt from taxation the assessed value of such property exceeding $150,000. § 29.45.050(i).

Elder and Disabled Veterans Tax Equivalency Payment: A resident sixty-five or older, a disabled person, or a resident at least sixty years old who is the widow or widower of either and who rents a permanent place of abode is eligible to apply for a tax equivalency payment. § 29.45.040.

Homestead: A person is entitled to a homestead exemption not exceeding $54,000 of the value of the principal residence of that person or that person's dependents. § 09.38.010.

ARIZONA

Ariz. Rev. Stat. Ann. §§ 43-1072, 42-11111, 42-17301 to 42-17313

Elder: Residents who are at least sixty-five, have a sufficiently low-income, and paid property taxes or rent, are entitled to an income tax credit. § 43-1072. Property tax deferral is available for residents who are at least seventy, are low-income, own no other real property, meet certain residency requirements, and whose home is valued at not more than $150,000. §§ 42-17301 to 42-17313.

Disabled: Property of qualified disabled persons exempt from tax.

Ariz. Const. art. 9, § 2.2; Ariz. Rev. Stat. § 42-11111.
Veterans: Property of qualified honorably discharged veterans and widows exempt from taxes. Ariz. Const. art. 9, §§ 2, 2.1.

ARKANSAS

Ark. Code Ann. §§ 26-3-301 to 26-3-310

Disabled Veterans and Their Surviving Spouses and Minor Dependent Children: Disabled veteran is exempt from all state taxes on his homestead. § 26-3-306(a)(1)(A). Upon the death of the veteran, his surviving spouse and minor children are entitled to the exemption. § 26-3-306(a)(1)(B)(i). The surviving spouse and minor dependent children of a member of the armed forces killed within the scope of military duties are entitled to the exemption. Protects spouse until he or she remarries. The surviving spouse of either a disabled veteran who has since died or a service member killed while on active duty may reinstate the property tax exemption if his or her subsequent marriage terminates. Protects children until they reach the age of majority.

CALIFORNIA

Cal. Const. art. XIII, § 3(k); Cal. Rev. & Tax. Code § 218 (West)

Homestead: $7000 of the full value of a resident's principal residence is exempt from taxation. Cal. Const. art. XIII, § 3(k); Cal. Rev. & Tax. Code § 218.
Elder: Owners and renters who are at least sixty-two, and who have a gross household income below $35,251, are eligible for property tax assistance on those taxes paid on the first $34,000 in assessed value. Cal. Rev. & Tax. Code §§ 20501–20564. There is also a provision for property tax postponement. Cal. Rev. & Tax. Code §§ 20581–20622. The income limitation is adjusted annually for inflation.
Disabled: Disabled are eligible for the same property tax assistance as elders (Cal. Rev. & Tax. Code §§ 20501–20564), as well as property tax postponement (Cal. Rev. & Tax. Code §§ 20581–20622).
Veterans: Principal residences of disabled veterans and those who died while on active duty are exempt from taxation up to a dollar amount which depends on a variety of factors. Cal. Rev. & Tax. Code § 205.5. Surviving spouses of disabled veterans are eligible for the same exemptions. Cal. Rev. & Tax. Code § 205.5.

COLORADO

Colo. Rev. Stat. §§ 39-31-101 to 39-31-104

Elder: Residents who are at least sixty-five, and meet other criteria, are eligible for a grant to assist with real property taxes. §§ 39-31-101 to 39-31-104. Also, residents who are at least sixty-five may be eligible to defer taxes on their homestead. §§ 39-3.5-101 to 39-3.5-117. The Colorado legislature has also provided for the creation of Property Tax Work-off Programs for elders. §§ 39-3.7-101 to 39-3.7-102.

CONNECTICUT

Conn. Gen. Stat. §§ 12-1 to 12-170dd

General: All residents are eligible for an income tax credit for a portion of the amount of their property tax paid on their primary residence. § 12-704c. A municipality may abate the property taxes on any residence which exceed 8% of the resident's income. § 12-124a. Also, § 12-62d provided that a municipality may provide for property tax relief following tax rate evaluations which raise the tax rate to at least 1.5% of the market value of residences but in 2006 this section was repealed "effective July 1, 2006, and applicable to assessment years commenting on or after October 1, 2010."
Elder: Homeowners who are at least sixty-five, and meet certain other qualifications, are eligible for property tax relief. §§ 12-170aa to 12-170dd. A number of other statutes provide for further property tax relief for elders. §§ 12-129b, 12-129.
Disabled: Disabled persons are eligible for the same property tax relief as elders. §§ 12-170aa to 12-170dd. Disabled persons who meet certain other criteria are eligible for other exemptions. §§ 12-81(17), 12-81(20) (disabled veterans), 12-81(21) (disabled veterans), 12-81(55), 12-81i, 12-81j.
Veterans: Veterans and their surviving spouses, children, and parents may be eligible for property tax exemptions. §§ 12-81(19) to 12-81(26), 12-81f, 12-81g, 12-82, 12-93a.

DELAWARE

Del. Code Ann. tit. 9, §§ 8131 to 8141, 8363

Elder: Elder (sixty-five and over) homeowners with income of not more than $3000 per year are entitled to an exemption from taxation of $5000 of assessed value. [Note: statute states it does not apply to property taxes levied by a municipality.] This exemption also provides relief from mobile home taxes.

DISTRICT OF COLUMBIA

D.C. Code §§ 47-849 to 47-850.04, 47-863

General: For single family residential property and property with not more than five dwelling units, which includes the principal dwelling place of the owner, $64,000 (increased annually based on cost-of-living adjustments) is deducted from the estimated market value in calculating tax. § 47-850(a).
Elder: All "Class 1" property owners sixty-five and older whose annual household income is less than $100,000 shall be eligible for a 50% decrease in property tax liability. § 47-863. Class 1 property is property occupied by the owner and contains not more than five dwelling units.

FLORIDA

Fla. Stat. §§ 196.001 to 196.32

Homesteads: Homesteads exempted from all taxation up to a certain amount in assessed value. § 196.031. Additional exemptions available under § 196.031(d). Residents eligible for homestead exemptions may also be eligible to defer property taxes on their residence. §§ 197.242 to 197.262.
Elder: Amount of assessed value eligible for homestead exemption expanded for residents sixty-five or older. §§ 196.031, 196.075.
Disabled: Amount of assessed value eligible for homestead exemption expanded for totally and permanently disabled residents. §§ 196.031, 196.101.
Disabled Veterans and Their Surviving Spouses: Up to $5000 of property exempt from taxation for veterans having at least 10%

disability obtained under certain conditions. § 196.24. Unmarried surviving spouse of at least five years entitled to same exemption. § 196.24. Homestead owned and used by veteran with service-connected, total, and permanent disability or veteran who dies of service-connected causes while on active duty is exempt from taxation. § 196.081. Surviving spouse eligible for the same homestead exemption under specified circumstances. § 196.081. Partially or totally disabled veterans of age sixty-five or older entitled to discount on *ad valorem* tax on owned and occupied homestead under specified conditions. § 196.082. Additional exemptions for certain veterans in wheelchairs and surviving spouse. § 196.091.

GEORGIA

Ga. Code Ann. §§ 48-5-40 to 48-5-56

Homestead: Homestead exemption allowed up to $2000 in assessed value. § 48-5-44.
Elder: There are a number of provisions for homestead exemptions for elders (§§ 48-5-47, 48-5-47.1, 48-5-48.3 (effective Jan. 1, 2007), 48-5-52), as well as deferrals. §§ 48-5-72, 48-5-72.1.
Disabled: Homestead exemptions for qualified disabled veterans and the unremarried surviving spouse or minor children of disabled veterans. Ga. Code Ann. § 48-5-48.

GUAM

Guam Code Ann. tit. 11, §§ 24110, 24402 to 24404

Elder: Elder persons (55 years or older) receive 80% abatement of tax on principal residence owned for five consecutive years or more. Property valuation frozen at amount assessed in first year of eligibility. §§ 24110, 24113.
Homestead Exemption: For purposes of assessing real property, homeowner entitled to exemption on the first $50,000 of the appraised value of improvements. Exemption limited to one home for any one owner. §§ 24402, 24404.
Disabled: Permanently disabled receive 80% abatement for principal residence of 5-year duration. §§ 24112, 24113.

HAWAII

Haw. Rev. Stat. §§ 246-1 to 246-63

General: Principal residence exempt from property taxes for up to $12,000 in assessed value. § 246-26.
Elder: Homes of residents aged sixty to sixty-nine are entitled to double the exemption (up to $24,000), and homes of residents seventy and over are entitled to two and one-half times the exemption ($30,000). § 246-26(d).
Disabled: Disabled persons are entitled to real property tax exemptions up to a taxable value of $15,000. § 246-31. Qualified disabled veterans are exempted from all property taxes. § 246-29.
Miscellaneous: Eligible low-income renters are eligible for an income tax credit. § 235-55.7.

IDAHO

Idaho Code Ann. §§ 55-1001 to 55-1011, 63-602AA, 63-602G

Homestead: The dwelling house or mobile home in which the owner resides or intends to reside, or unimproved land regardless of size and owned with the intent of placing such a residence thereon, is exempt from taxation but the exemption amount shall not exceed the lesser of the (i) total net value of the land, mobile home and improvements, or (ii) $100,000. §§ 55-1001, 55-1003.
Residential Improvements: The lesser of the first $75,000 (amount to be adjusted to reflect cost-of-living fluctuations) or 50% of the market value for assessment purposes of residential improvements to an owner-occupied residence is exempt from property taxation. § 63-602G.
Undue Hardship: Persons owning real property may be relieved from paying all or a part of their property tax upon a showing of undue hardship. § 63-602AA.

ILLINOIS

320 Ill. Comp. Stat. 25/1 to 25/13, 30/1 to 30/8, 35 Ill. Comp. Stat. §§ 200/15-167 to 200/15-185

Homestead: (35 Ill. Comp. Stat. 200/15-167 to 200/15-185): Owner-occupied residential real estate is entitled to a general exemption in the form of a reduction in the assessed value of the property. There are special provisions for the home of returning veterans, disabled persons, persons sixty-five years of age or older, and long-time occupants of a homestead. Also provides for freeze in assessed value of homestead for certain older consumers meeting income limits. Home of a disabled veteran or spouse or unmarried surviving spouse of the veteran is exempt up to $70,000, plus there is a standard disabled veteran exemption of $5000. There is also a four-year exemption of up to $75,000 of value added by home improvements or by rebuilding due to a catastrophic event.
Tax Relief: (320 Ill. Comp. Stat. 25/4): Persons sixty-five and over and disabled persons within statutory income limitations (e.g., $36,740 for a three person household in grant year 2009) are entitled to a "grant" in the amount by which their property taxes for the year exceed 3.5% of their household income. For 2009 claim year applications submitted during 2010, household must have annual income of less than $45,657 for household with three persons or more. Maximum amount of grant is $700, less 4.5% of household income.
Tax Deferral: (320 Ill. Comp. Stat. 30/1 to 30/8): Taxpayers sixty-five years or older with an income of not more than $40,000 ($50,000 for 2006 and after) can apply for deferral of all or part of the property taxes on their residence. Deferral claimed plus interest cannot exceed 80% of the taxpayer's equity in the property. If the taxes deferred equal 80%, the taxpayer must pay interest each year at 6%. Upon the death of the taxpayer, taxes plus interest become due from the taxpayer's heirs, unless the heir is a surviving spouse. If the heir is the surviving spouse, the deferral can be continued. Otherwise, the heirs must pay the taxes. If the taxes are not paid, then the town can foreclose.

INDIANA

Ind. Code §§ 6-1.1-12-1 to 6-1.1-12-42

Elder: Persons over age sixty-five with income not more than $25,000, and whose home is valued at not more than $182,430, are entitled to a deduction of the lesser of half the assessed value or $12,480. Explicitly applies to mobile homes. Surviving spouse covered if age sixty or over. § 6-1.1-12-9.
Blind and Disabled Persons: Persons with income of not more

than $17,000 are entitled to a deduction from the assessed value of $12,480. § 6-1.1-12-11.

Disabled Veterans or Surviving Spouses: If totally disabled (or has 10% disability and is at least sixty-two years old), entitled to a $12,480 deduction unless value of property exceeds $143,160. This deduction may be used with other deductions, except World War I deduction. § 6-1.1-12-14.

Partially Disabled Veterans and Surviving Spouses: Entitled to $24,960 exemption where individual has a service-connected disability of at least 10% and served in a war. § 6-1.1-12-13.

IOWA

Iowa Code §§ 425.1 to 425.40

Homestead: Homeowners are entitled to a credit against the actual levy (tax) on the first $4850 of actual value for the homestead. § 425.1.

Elder and Disabled: In addition to the homestead exemption, older persons (sixty-five and over) and totally disabled persons are entitled to a credit or reimbursement for taxes paid based on the income schedule contained in § 425.23. Example of credit: if income is $0 to $8499.99, credit is 100% of taxes paid; if income is $8500 to $9499.99, credit is 85% of taxes paid. These amounts are adjusted for inflation. §§ 425.16 to 425.40.

KANSAS

Kan. Stat. Ann. §§ 79-4501 to 79-4531

Homestead: Persons 55 or older, disabled, disabled veteran, unremarried surviving spouse of disabled veteran, surviving spouse of active duty military personnel who died in the line of duty, or persons having dependent children under the age of eighteen are entitled to tax refund (on income taxes) for property taxes paid according to the schedule contained in § 79-4508 to be adjusted for cost-of living increases annually. § 79-4502. The maximum refund is $700. § 79-4509.

KENTUCKY

Ky. Rev. Stat. Ann. § 132.810 (West)

Elder and Disabled: Homeowners age sixty-five or older, or persons who are totally disabled are entitled to a $6500 exemption on their personal residence, based on purchasing power of 1972 dollar. § 132.810. Per statute, amount of exemption is to be adjusted for increases in the cost-of-living.

LOUISIANA

La. Rev. Stat. Ann. § 47:1703

Homestead: Pursuant to Section 20 of Article VII of the La. Constitution, $7500 of the assessed value of a homestead is exempt.

MAINE

Me. Rev. Stat. Ann. tit. 36, §§ 841, 6251

Infirmity or Poverty: An assessor may grant an abatement based on his judgment, either on his own knowledge or on written application. Assessor must notify persons who have expressed an inability to pay their taxes of the right to request an abatement within three years of the imposition of the tax.

Widows and Children of Veterans: Unremarried widows and children of veterans may be granted such abatement as the assessor deems proper, within one year of the imposition of the tax.

Homestead: Elders may be eligible for deferral of property taxes based upon income. § 6251.

MARYLAND

Md. Code Ann., Tax-Prop. §§ 9-101, 9-104, 9-105 (West)

Elder and Disabled Veterans: (§ 9-104): Persons over age seventy and disabled veterans are entitled to a credit against their property tax, the amount of which is a percentage of their income. The percentage is graduated by income level, see § 9-104(g)(2) for table of percentages. No credits for property owners with income greater than $200,000. Surviving spouse of disabled veteran is entitled to credit up until spouse remarries.

General/Homestead: (§ 9-105): For all homesteads, owner is entitled to a tax credit against property tax which is calculated as follows:

For the State Property Tax: 1) multiplying the prior year's assessment by 110%; 2) subtracting that amount from the current year's assessment; 3) if the difference is a positive number, multiplying the difference by the applicable state tax rate for the current year.

For the County or Municipal Property Tax: 1) multiplying the current year's assessment by the percentage established by the county or municipality; 2) subtracting that amount from the current year's assessment; 3) if the difference is a positive number, multiplying the difference by the applicable county or municipal tax rate for the current year.

MASSACHUSETTS

Mass. Gen. Laws ch. 59, § 5

Elder, Widowed, or Orphaned Taxpayers: Entitled to exemption, either to the extent of $2000 in property value or $175 in tax, if the household income is less than $20,000. (clause 17). These amounts are adjusted annually according to the consumer price index. (clause 17E). Assessors may provide additional abatements to those taxpayers who by reason of age, infirmity, poverty, or hardship relating to a change to active military status, the assessors judge are "unable to contribute fully." Tax deferral also available for persons over sixty-five. (clauses 41 to 41D).

Blind: Entitled to exemption to the extent of the $5000 value or $437.50 in tax. (clause 37).

Elder with Limited Income: Entitled to an exemption of $4000 or a $350 credit.

Veterans: Disabled (10% or more) or recipient of Purple Heart. Surviving spouses. Parents of soldiers or sailors killed in wartime service. Certain surviving spouses of World War I veterans. Greater of $2000 in valuation or $400 in tax. For veterans with certain injuries, or certain medal recipients, exemptions of $4000 or $750, or $8000 or $1250. Disabled veterans in "specially adapted housing": $10,000 or $950. One-hundred percent disabled veterans: $10,000 or $1500. (clauses 22 to 22E).

Miscellaneous: Surviving spouses of firefighters and police killed in the line of duty are entitled to an abatement. Mass. Gen. Laws ch. 59, § 5 cl. 42.

MICHIGAN

Mich. Comp. Laws §§ 211.1 to 211.7ff

Low-Income: Homestead is eligible for exemption from taxation in whole or in part, based on guidelines developed by local assessing unit. § 211.7u. Local guidelines may not set income limitations below the federal poverty line.
Disabled Veterans and Their Surviving Spouses: Disabled veterans living in housing specially adapted with the aid of certain federal financial assistance are exempt from all taxation on their homestead. Upon the death of the veteran, a surviving spouse is entitled to the exemption until remarriage. § 211.7b.

MINNESOTA

Minn. Stat. § 290A.04

General Property Tax Relief: Taxpayers are allowed a refund of property taxes paid in the amount by which the property taxes exceed a specified percentage of income. The percentage varies by income level. Income limit is $77,520 per year. In addition, if property taxes increase in one year more than 12% or $100, the owner is entitled to an additional refund on the increase over the greater of 12% or $100. Maximum additional refund is $1000.

MISSISSIPPI

Miss. Code Ann. §§ 27-33-3, 27-33-67 to 27-33-79

Homestead: Taxpayers under sixty-five are entitled to an exemption on their homestead based on assessed value, up to a maximum exemption of $300 for those counties which have completed their update of *ad valorem* taxation, and $240 for counties without completed updates.
Elder Homestead: Taxpayers over age sixty-five, and certain totally disabled persons, are entitled to an exemption to the extent of $7500 of assessed value in those counties which have completed their update of *ad valorem* taxation, and $6000 in counties without completed updates.

MISSOURI

Mo. Rev. Stat. §§ 135.010 to 135.035

Elder: Persons sixty-five and over, with income of $27,500 or less, or $30,000 or less if homestead is owned and occupied for the entire year, are entitled to a tax credit for income taxes based on the amount by which their total property tax exceeds a certain percentage of their income. Refer to tables at § 135.030 for percentages and credit amounts. Eligibility described in § 135.010(1), (2).
Surviving Spouse of Public Safety Officer: The surviving spouse of a public safety officer killed in the line of duty is entitled to an income tax credit equal to the amount of property taxes due on his or her homestead. If the credit exceeds the amount of income taxes due, the excess is considered an overpayment. The surviving spouse is entitled to this exemption from the year the officer is killed until the year the surviving spouse remarries. § 135.090.

MONTANA

Mont. Code Ann. § 15-6-211

Low-Income Deceased and Disabled Veterans: Exemption for unmarried surviving spouse of veteran killed on duty or veteran with 100% service-connected disability. Percentage of exempt amount homeowner is entitled to claim is based on income.

NEBRASKA

Neb. Rev. Stat. §§ 77-3501 to 77-3530, 77-4209 to 77-4212

Homestead: Exempt amount for homestead is the lesser of (a) the taxable value of the homestead or (b) 80% of the average assessed value of single family residential property in the homeowner's county of residence, or $40,000 for low-income, and $50,000 for disabled and veterans, whichever is greater. § 77-3501.01. Percentage of exempt amount homeowner is entitled to claim is based on income. For example, if income is between $0 and $19,200 for a single claimant or $22,500 for a married or closely related claimant, homeowner is entitled to claim 100% of the exempt amount. § 77-3507. Homeowners are also eligible for a property tax credit based on the value of their land and the county in which it is located. §§ 77-4209 to 77-4212. Homeowners eligible for an exemption are still entitled to this credit, but the combined tax relief cannot exceed total tax liability.
Disabled: Disabled persons and veterans entitled to exemption based on income and subject to maximum exempt amount. §§ 77-3508, 77-3509. Exemption reduced if homestead value exceeds certain amounts. § 77-3506.03

NEVADA

Nev. Rev. Stat. §§ 361.080 to 361.159

Surviving Spouses: Exemption for widows or widowers not to exceed $1000, the amount to be adjusted annually based on CPI percentage increase. § 361.080.
Blind: Exemption not to exceed $3000, the amount to be adjusted annually based on CPI percentage increase. Medical verification is required. § 361.085.
Veterans: Exemption of $2000, the amount to be adjusted annually based on CPI percentage increase. Does not extend to family of veterans. § 361.090.
Disabled Veterans: Exemption for veterans with service-connected permanent disabilities and unremarried surviving spouses. Amount of exemption varies based on percentage of disability. Maximum of $20,000, adjusted each year starting with fiscal year 2005–2006 to reflect CPI increases. § 361.091.

NEW HAMPSHIRE

N.H. Rev. Stat. Ann. § 76:16

General: Selectmen or assessors may abate any tax assessed for good cause shown. Any person aggrieved by the assessment of a tax may apply in writing for abatement by March 1 of the year following the notice of the imposition of the tax. Poverty or inability to pay is good cause. *See* Brigg's Petition, 29 N.H. 547 (1854). Tax deferral is available for those over sixty-five who have owned home for at least five consecutive years, and for disabled persons who have owned home for at least one year, if assessors believe that tax would cause undue hardship or possible loss of property. N.H. Rev. Stat. Ann. § 72:38-a.

NEW JERSEY

N.J. Stat. Ann. §§ 54:4-3.30, 54:4-8.11, 54:4-8.57 to 54:4-8.63 (West)

General: Formerly two kinds of exemption were provided, homestead and N.J. Saver, but the latter was folded into the former in 2004. Homestead rebate or credit is calculated as a percentage of property taxes owed, not to exceed $10,000. Applicable percentage is determined by gross income. §§ 54:4-8.57 to 8.75.
Elder, Blind, or Disabled Citizens: Entitled to greater of either general homestead credit or amount by which property taxes exceed 5% of gross income, but within annually-adjusted income ranges. $250 deduction. § 54:4-8.59.
Veterans: Property of certain totally disabled veterans and surviving spouses, and spouses of veterans killed on active service, is exempt from taxation. § 54:4-3.30. *Hennefield v. Town of Montclair*, 22 N.J. Tax 166 (Mar. 15, 2005) recognized a previous version of § 54:4-3.30 as unconstitutional, and held that, despite its references to marriage, same-sex couples in domestic partnerships were entitled to equal benefits under the law.

NEW MEXICO

N.M. Const. art. VIII, §§ 5, 15; N.M. Stat. §§ 7-37-4 to 7-37-5.1, 42-10-9 to 42-10-13

Homestead: Each person has a homestead exemption of $60,000 from attachment, execution, or foreclosure by judgment creditors for property the person owns and occupies. Joint owners are each entitled to the full exemption of $60,000. N.M. Stat. § 42-10-9. Exemption does not apply to taxes, garnishment, recorded liens of mortgagees or lessors, or mechanics and materialmen liens. N.M. Stat. § 42-10-11.
Head of Family: $2000 of the taxable value of the residential real property of the head of the family is exempt from property tax. "Head of the family" includes one spouse in a joint household, a widow or widower, a head of household providing more than 50% support to any related person, a single person, or a condominium association member or like entity paying property tax through the association. N.M. Const. art. VIII, § 5; N.M. Stat. § 7-37-4.
Veterans and Their Surviving Unmarried Spouses: Up to $4000 of the taxable value of property owned by veteran, surviving unmarried spouse, or held in a grantor trust under Internal Revenue Code §§ 671–677. Veteran or surviving spouse must be a New Mexico resident. Exemption is $3000 for 2004 taxes and $3500 for 2005 taxes.
Disabled Veterans and Their Surviving Spouses: Property of veteran having "one hundred percent permanent and total service-connected disability" is fully exempt from tax if it is occupied as disabled veteran's principal place of residence. Property held in a grantor trust under Internal Revenue Code §§ 671–677 by disabled veteran or surviving spouse is exempt if additional conditions met. N.M. Stat. § 7-37-5.1.

NEW YORK

N.Y. Real Prop. Tax Law §§ 458 to 460, 466 to 467 (McKinney)

Elder: (sixty-five and older) Property is exempt from taxation to the extent of 50% of the assessed value, provided that the governing board of the municipality adopts a local law enacting exemption. Exemption is subject to income limitations, see § 467(b)(1). Municipality must send notice of the exemption to residents. § 467(4).
Veterans: Property of disabled veteran which has been adapted using federal grant for that purpose is totally exempt. Certain other property of veterans is exempt up to $5000. § 458. Alternative exemptions for veterans, with amount varying according to whether veteran served in combat, and whether disabled (rate of exemption tied to percentage of disability). Municipalities may, within limits, increase or decrease the amount of these exemptions, or refuse to grant them. § 458-a.
Disabled: Municipalities may grant exemptions for improvements to property necessary to accommodate disabled resident. § 459. Property of disabled persons with limited income is 50% exempt from municipal taxation, including taxation by other taxing entities (counties, school districts, etc.). § 459-c.
Volunteer Firefighters or Ambulance Workers: Certain counties may allow exemptions of up to 10% to certain volunteer firefighters or ambulance workers. § 466-b.
Physically Disabled Crime Victims: Any improvements to real property used to facilitate and accommodate the use of such real property by physically disabled victims of crime are exempt from taxation. § 459-b.
Clergy: Any real property owned by clergy engaged in work assigned by the church or denomination of which he is a member is exempt to the extent of $1500 of value. § 460.

NORTH CAROLINA

N.C. Gen. Stat. §§ 105-277.1, 105-277.1B

Elder or Disabled: For persons over sixty-five or disabled, with an income of $25,000 per year or less through July 1, 2008 (subject to cost of living adjustments in subsequent years), the greater of $25,000 or 50% of the appraised value of permanent residence is excluded from taxation. For qualifying persons who have owned the property as a permanent residence for at least five consecutive years and occupied the property for at least five years, the income limit is increased to 150% of the standard levels under the "homestead circuit breaker." § 105-277.1B. Certain percentages of taxes due can also be deferred under the homestead circuit breaker. Those persons who qualify for both the regular exemption and the circuit breaker have the choice of participating in either program, though if a property is owned by multiple owners, all owners must meet the qualification criteria to participate in the circuit breaker. If the property is owned by husband and wife as tenants in the entirety, only one spouse has to meet the occupation requirement and the age or disability requirement.

NORTH DAKOTA

N.D. Cent. Code §§ 57-02-08.1, 57-38-01.29

Homestead: Maximum credit of $500 for individuals and $1000 for married couples. Only authorized for years 2007 and 2008. § 57-38-01.29.
Elder or Disabled with Limited Income: Persons sixty-five and older and persons permanently and totally disabled, unless household assets exceed $75,000 (excluding homestead value up to $100,000), with income of $26,000 or less receive a reduction in the assessment of the taxable value of their homestead. Reduction is based on income. For example, if income is less than $18,000,

then reduction is 100% of taxable valuation, up to a maximum of $4,500 of taxable valuation. See provision for percentages. § 57-02-08.1.

OHIO

Ohio Rev. Code Ann. §§ 323.151 to 323.159 (West)

Disabled, Elder, and Surviving Spouse of Disabled or Elder Person: Homestead exemption allows qualifying homeowners who are sixty-five years or older or permanently and totally disabled (and their surviving spouses if they are at least fifty-nine but not sixty-five or more years of age on the date the deceased spouse dies), regardless of income, to exempt $25,000 of a home's market value from property taxation and a reduction in the assessment and effective tax rate. § 323.152.

OKLAHOMA

Okla. Stat. tit. 68, §§ 2904 to 2906, 2888 to 2890; Okla. Stat. tit. 31, § 2

Elder and Disabled Persons: A person sixty-five years or older or a totally disabled person who is also a head of household, a resident of the state during the entire preceding year, and whose gross household income does not exceed $12,000 may file for relief from property tax. Okla. Stat. tit. 68, §§ 2904–2906.
Rural and Urban Homesteads: Any single person of legal age, a married couple and their minor child or children, or the minor child or children of a deceased person (residing together or separated), or a surviving spouse is entitled to a homestead exemption from *ad valorem* taxes of $1000 of assessed value. Heads of households whose gross household income did not exceed $20,000 in the preceding year are entitled to an additional $1000 exemption. A rural homestead may not exceed 160 acres of land and improvements, and an urban homestead may not exceed one acre. If more than 25% of the square footage of the improved property claimed as an urban homestead is used for business purposes, the homestead exemption is limited to $5000. Okla. Stat. tit. 31, § 2; Okla. Stat. tit. 68, §§ 2888–2890.

OREGON

Or. Rev. Stat. § 307.250

Disabled Veterans: Exemption not to exceed $15,000 for certain disabled veterans and unremarried surviving spouses. Exemption is $18,000 if disability is service-connected. Since July 1, 2000, exemption each year is 103% of previous year's exemption.

PENNSYLVANIA

72 Pa. Stat. Ann. §§ 4751-21 to 4751-26 (West)

Elder: Persons age sixty-five or over are entitled to a tax rebate for property taxes paid, according to a schedule which is based on income and amount paid. Schedule at § 4751-24.

PUERTO RICO

P.R. Laws Ann. tit. 29, § 814

Veterans: Property tax exemption of up to $5000 of assessed value of property for period of ten years. Subject to certain restrictions, injured veterans' primary residence exempt from property tax. Subject to certain restrictions, property tax exemption on the first $50,000 of the appraised value of the property for disabled veterans who receive disability compensation of 50% or more from the Veterans Administration.

RHODE ISLAND

R.I. Gen. Laws §§ 44-3-4 to 44-3-52

Totally Disabled: City or town council may freeze tax rate and valuation for totally disabled persons. Applicant must meet established income requirements of the locality. §§ 44-3-15, 44-3-16.
Visually Impaired: Exemption of $6000 for the visually impaired, with some variations as to the amount of the exemption by town. § 44-3-12. Towns may increase this exemption up to $22,500. If a town does not increase exemption over $6000, exemption must increase, whenever town increases tax rate, by the same percentage as the tax rate.
Elder: Towns and municipalities may by local ordinance provide for the freezing of the rate and valuation of taxes of persons age sixty-five and older subject to income requirements set by towns. § 44-3-16. Some towns have exemptions of varying amounts rather than a freeze. § 44-3-13. Advocates should check the statute for particular towns.
Veterans: Veterans of foreign wars, or their surviving spouses, are provided with general and property-specific tax exemptions, generally for $1000 and $10,000, respectively, though local municipalities can depart from those levels. § 44-3-4. A number of local municipalities provide additional veterans exemptions, sometimes at significantly higher levels. Parents of veterans who died during service are entitled to a $3000 exemption, though local municipalities can depart from that level, upward or downward. § 44-3-5.
Low-Income: Exemption from taxation for any person who in the judgment of the assessor is unable from "infirmity or poverty" to pay the property tax. § 44-3-3(16).

SOUTH CAROLINA

S.C. Code Ann. §§ 12-37-210 to 12-37-450

Elder or Disabled: The first $50,000 of the fair market value of the dwelling place of a person who is sixty-five or older or disabled or blind is exempt. Explicitly includes mobile home on property of another. § 12-37-250. Surviving spouses of eligible persons are entitled to the same exemption so long as they receive fee simple title or a life estate of the dwelling place within nine months of their spouse's death, they do not remarry, and they use the dwelling place as their permanent home and legal residence.
Veterans Exemptions: If 100% disabled, dwelling house and one acre of land totally exempt. Also protects surviving spouses of totally disabled veterans or veterans killed in action. Same exemption for police and firefighters suffering total service-connected disability and for any veteran who received Medal of Honor or was a prisoner of war during WWI, WWII, Korea, or Vietnam. Same exemption for paraplegic or hemiplegic persons. § 12-37-220.

SOUTH DAKOTA

S.D. Codified Laws §§ 10-6B-1 to 10-6B-15

Elder and Disabled: (if adopted by local tax board) Elder and disabled persons are entitled to a property tax reduction based on income. For example, if a family's household income is between $0 and $5640, then property taxes are reduced by 55%; if income is between $5641 and $5758, then taxes are reduced by 53%. Maximum income is $7765 for family, $5758 for single person. Certain low-income elders and low-income disabled persons are eligible for a freeze of their tax assessments (owners of single family homes, with income of $14,000 or less for single person, $17,500 for family). These figures are adjusted annually for change in the consumer price index.

TENNESSEE

Tenn. Code Ann. §§ 67-5-701 to 67-5-705

Elder Low-Income: Low-income elder homeowners pay no taxes on the first $25,000 of value, subject to income limitations. Income limit $24,000 (2007). § 67-5-702. Income limitation will be adjusted according to the cost of living increases for Social Security.
Disabled: Disabled persons pay no taxes on the first $25,000 of value, subject to income limitations. Income limit for 2007 was $24,000. § 67-5-703. Income limitation will be adjusted according to the cost of living increases for Social Security.
Disabled Veteran: Disabled veterans pay no taxes on the first $175,000 of fair market value of property. § 67-5-704. Surviving spouses of disabled veterans and veterans who died in combat are entitled to the same exemption, so long as they do not remarry. Surviving spouses of veterans who died in combat must have exclusive use and ownership of the property.
Tax Freeze for Elders: Towns may adopt a resolution which freezes the tax level applied to the primary residences of elder persons (over sixty-four) at the level of the year the town enrolled in the program, the year in which the person turned sixty-five, or the year the person purchased the property, whichever is later. Income limit for participation is the greater of either the limit for general elder tax relief ($24,000 for 2007), or the weighted average of the median incomes for people aged sixty-five to seventy-four and people seventy-five and over in the county where the property is located, as determined by the decennial census. The base tax level is increased based on increases in the assessed property value and improvements made to the property. § 67-5-705.

TEXAS

Tex. Tax Code Ann. §§ 11.13, 11.131, 11.22, 11.26, 11.432 (Vernon)

Homestead: Owner is entitled to exemption from county taxation of $3000 of the assessed value of residence, and exemption of $15,000 of appraised value from school district taxation. § 11.13. Special application and eligibility requirements apply for manufactured homes. § 11.432.
Elder and Disabled: Entitled to an additional $10,000 exemption from school district taxation. (Exemption amount may be increased by the governing tax body.) There are also limitations on the ability of school districts to raise taxes on persons that qualify for this exemption. § 11.26. Certain surviving spouses are also covered.
Disabled Veterans: Veterans who are totally disabled due to a service-connected disability are entitled to an exemption from taxation of the total appraised value of the homestead residence. § 11.131. Partially disabled veterans are entitled to an exemption of $12,000 of assessed value of property if sixty-five or older, blind in one or both eyes, or without use of one or more limbs. Other disabled veterans entitled to exemption ranging from $5000 to $12,000 depending upon disability rating. Surviving spouse of disabled veteran is also entitled to exemption as long as spouse remains unmarried. Surviving spouse of individual who dies while on active duty as a member of the armed forces is entitled to exemption of $5000 as long as spouse remains unmarried. § 11.22.

UTAH

Utah Code Ann. §§ 59-2-1104 to 59-2-1220

Disabled Veterans: The first $200,000 of taxable value of property is exempt for veterans who are 100% disabled due to a service-related injury. For lesser disabilities, the exemption will be the same percentage of $200,000, that is, a 50% disability confers an exemption of $100,000. Also applies to unremarried surviving spouses and minor orphans. § 59-2-1104.
Blind Persons: Tax exemption for the first $11,500 of property owned by blind persons. Also applies to unremarried surviving spouses and minor orphans. Must file application for exemption each year with verification by doctor. § 59-2-1106.
Low-Income: Counties have discretion to remit or abate taxes of any low-income person in an amount not to exceed the amount of the homeowner's credit for the lowest household income bracket under § 59-2-1208 or not more than 50% of total tax assessed for that year, whichever is less. § 59-2-1107. Individuals under sixty-five qualify only if disabled or can show extreme hardship. § 59-2-1109. Counties may also defer taxes for low-income persons. Deferred taxes continue to accumulate with interest as lien against property. Individuals under age sixty-five qualify only if disabled or can show extreme hardship. §§ 59-2-1108, 59-2-1109.

VERMONT

Vt. Stat. Ann. tit. 24, § 1535

General: The board of assessors may abate in whole or in part the taxes of persons who are unable to pay. § 1535(a).

VIRGIN ISLANDS

V.I. Code Ann. tit. 33, § 2305

Homestead: Property owners and their spouses are entitled to a $400 tax credit. Exemption from real property taxes for principal residence up to the first $20,000 of the assessed value.
Elder: Residents sixty and older whose gross individual income does not exceed $30,000 and gross household income does not exceed $50,000, are entitled to a tax credit of $500.
Disabled: Persons with disabilities, as determined by the Social Security Administration, whose gross individual income does not exceed $30,000 and gross household income does not exceed $50,000, are entitled to a $500 tax credit.
Veterans: Veterans and widows of veterans are entitled to a $650 tax credit. Subject to certain restrictions, veterans who have permanent and total disability due to certain injuries are completely exempt from property taxes.
Restrictions: Tax credits, other than the homestead credit, are

exclusive, not cumulative. Residents claiming the homestead credit can also claim one, and only one, additional credit if eligible. Also, real property owners, with certain limited exceptions, are required to pay a minimum annual tax of $300 on residential real property.

VIRGINIA

Va. Code Ann. §§ 58.1-3200 to 58.1-3228

Elder or Disabled: Localities may by ordinance provide for exemptions from, deferral of, or combination program of exemptions from taxation of real estate of persons at least sixty-five years of age or disabled. § 58.1-3210. Or exemptions may be provided for value of property that represents the increase in value from the year such person reached age sixty-five or the ordinance became effective, whichever is later. Localities may also adopt, by ordinance, tax exemptions or deferrals for properties jointly owned by two or more people, not all of whom have to be sixty-five or disabled, subject to combined financial worth limitations that vary based on locale, and income limitations. § 58.1-3211.1. Such exemptions do not apply to properties jointly owned by a husband and wife and no one else.
Restrictions: Applies to persons whose income is less than $50,000 per year or the income limit for the family to qualify for federal housing assistance as published by HUD. § 58.1-3211. Up to $10,000 in income may be excluded if the owner is permanently disabled. Also, financial worth (excluding value of the property) cannot exceed $200,000. § 58.1-3211(2). Listed towns can increase the income and financial worth limits to $75,000 per year, and $540,000.
Other Exemptions: Localities may adopt partial exemptions for substantial rehabilitation, renovation or replacement of property in certain areas. § 58.1-3220. Or for the abatement of taxes on buildings that were razed or destroyed or damaged by circumstances beyond the owner's control. § 58.1-3222.

WASHINGTON

Wash. Rev. Code §§ 84.36.381, 84.38.030

Elders and Veterans: Exemption for sixty-one or older and veterans with 100% service-connected disability. Surviving spouse or domestic partner if fifty-seven or older and spouse or domestic partner was receiving exemption at time of death. Amount of exemption is based on income. Property tax deferral up to 80% of equity value of home is available to persons who will reach age sixty by the end of the year in which they apply, have a combined income of $40,000 or less, and otherwise meet the requirements for an exemption. § 84.38.030.
Disabled: Exemption for persons retired due to disability, and surviving spouses or domestic partners. Amount of exemption varies depending on income.

WEST VIRGINIA

W. Va. Code §§ 11-6B-1 to 11-6B-12

Elder or Disabled: First $20,000 of value exempt from homestead when owner is sixty-five or older, or is disabled, and has been resident of West Virginia for two years. § 11-6B-3.

WISCONSIN

Wis. Stat. §§ 234.621 to 234.625

Elder: Persons sixty and older with income of not more than $20,000, may apply for loans to pay for property taxes and special assessments in the amount of the property taxes at prime plus 1%. The loan is due upon the death of the taxpayer or transfer of the property. The loan creates a lien on the property for the amount of the loan. §§ 234.622 to 234.625.

WYOMING

Wyo. Stat. Ann. §§ 39-11-105, 39-13-105, 39-13-109

Veteran Exemption: War veterans and veterans with disabilities who are bona fide residents for at least three years at the time of claiming the exemption are entitled to an annual exemption from property tax of $3000 of the assessed value. §§ 39-11-105(a)(xxiv), 39-13-105. A surviving spouse is entitled to the same exemption so long as he or she is unmarried. § 39-13-105(a)(v). The exemption applies only to the principal residence of the veteran or qualifying surviving spouse and can be claimed in only one county. § 39-13-105(c)(iv), (v).
Improvements for Disabled Access: Any improvement to residential property making an entrance to or common facilities within the property accessible to a disabled person is exempt from property tax. § 39-11-105(a)(xxxii).
Homestead Tax Credit: Persons occupying a homestead as a principal residence are entitled to a specified property tax credit depending on the size of the property, the assessed value, and whether the land upon which the dwelling is located

is owned by the same person owning the dwelling. § 39-13-109(d)(i)(A), (E), (F).
Property Tax Relief Program: Repealed effective January 1, 2008.

Appendix G Summary of State Condominium Laws

This appendix is a summary of state laws governing the foreclosure of condominium assessment liens. It describes the method of foreclosure, the scope of the lien, required notices, permitted fees and interest, and the right, if available, to challenge the lien. It also describes the right of the unit owner to redeem the condominium unit after a sale.

In several states condominiums are governed by more than one statute. The most modern statutes, so-called common interest ownership statutes, cover condominiums, co-operatives, and planned communities. This appendix cites all condominium-related statutes and summarizes the provisions of the most current statutes. Older statutes often contain little or no discussion of lien assessment or foreclosure. The sections of the newest statutes that deal with this topic often apply to all condominiums, even those created before the statute's effective date. The appendix does not cite timeshare statutes, which may include specific provisions regarding foreclosure of timeshare assessment liens. (*See, e.g.*, Louisiana Timesharing Act, La. Rev. Stat. Ann. §§ 9:1131.1 to 1131.30.) Advocates are advised to check the applicability section of each statute carefully to determine the scope of its coverage.

Please note that this appendix analyzes statutory language and does not include actual statutory or regulatory material. Practitioners should augment their research by reading the actual statutes, regulations, and court decisions interpreting the statute.

ALABAMA

Ala. Code §§ 35-8A-101 to 35-8A-417 (Uniform Condominium Act); Ala. Code §§ 35-8-1 to 35-8-22 (Condominium Ownership Act)

Applicability: The Uniform Condominium Act, Ala. Code §§ 35-8A-101 to 35-8A-417, applies to condominiums created after January 1, 1991. With limited exception (*see* §§ 35-8A-302(a)(10) and 35-8A-315), the provisions of the Uniform Condominium Act summarized below also apply to condominiums created before the effective date.

Method of Foreclosure: The lien may be foreclosed in the same manner as a mortgage on real estate. § 35-8A-316(a).

Notices: Before foreclosing, the condominium association must give "reasonable advance notice" to the unit owner and all lienholders of record. § 35-8A-316(a). Any unit owner, mortgagee, or prospective purchaser or lender may request a written statement from the association, setting forth the amount of assessments, fees, interest and late charges due. (Association may charge $10 for this statement.) Failure to provide this statement within ten days of request will extinguish any lien, but not discharge the unit owner's debt. § 35-8A-316(h).

Interest, Fees & Costs: Any judgment or decree in an action to enforce this section, or to collect assessments or fines, must provide costs and reasonable attorney fees for prevailing party. § 35-8A-316(g). The condominium association may impose charges for late payment of assessments or fines for violation of rules. § 35-8A-302(a)(11). Past-due assessments bear interest at the rate set by the association, not exceeding 18% per year. § 35-8A-315(b).

Scope of Lien: The association has a lien for all assessments or fines, from the time the assessment or fine becomes due. If an assessment is payable in installments, the association has a lien for the entire amount when the first installment becomes due. § 35-8A-316(a).

Ability to Contest Lien: Not specified.

Lien Extinguished: A lien is extinguished if proceedings to enforce it are not instituted within three years after the full amount of the assessment becomes due. § 35-8A-316(e).

Explicit Right of Redemption: Not specified.

ALASKA

Alaska Stat. §§ 34.08.010 to 34.08.995 (Common Interest Ownership Act); Alaska Stat. §§ 34.07.010 to 34.07.460 (Horizontal Property Regimes Act)

Applicability: The Common Interest Ownership Act, Alaska Stat. §§ 34.08.010 to 34.08.995, applies to condominiums created after January 1, 1986. Communities with limited expenses are exempt from many portions of the statute.

Method of Foreclosure: The association's lien is foreclosed by the procedure set forth in § 34.35.005 for liens on real estate. § 34.08.470(j)(1).

Notices: The association, within ten days after written request by the unit owner, must provide a written statement, in recordable form, setting forth the amount of unpaid assessments. § 34.08.470(h).

Interest, Fees & Costs: The unit owners' association may impose reasonable charges for late payment of assessments. § 34.08.320(a)(11). Overdue assessments bear interest at the rate set by the association, not to exceed 18% per year. § 34.08.460(b). Section 34.35.005 (foreclosure of liens on real estate) provides for reasonable attorney fees.
Scope of Lien: The condominium association has a lien for all assessments, fines, charges, fees, late charges and interest, from the time the assessment or fine becomes due. If an assessment is payable in installments, the association has a lien for the full amount, from the time the first installment becomes due. § 34.08.470(a). The lien is not subject to the homestead exemption. § 34.08.470(b).
Ability to Contest Lien: Not specified.
Lien Extinguished: A lien for an unpaid assessment is extinguished if proceedings to enforce it are not brought within three years of the date the assessment became due. § 34.08.470(e).
Explicit Right of Redemption: Not specified.

ARIZONA

Ariz. Rev. Stat. Ann. §§ 33-1201 to 33-1270 (Condominium Act)

Applicability: Arizona's Condominium Act, Ariz. Rev. Stat. §§ 33-1201 to 33-1270, applies to condominiums created within the state without regard to the date the condominium was created. § 33-1201.
Method of Foreclosure: A lien for assessments, or for late fees, costs and attorney fees incurred with respect to assessments, may be foreclosed like a mortgage on real estate, but only if owner has been delinquent in payment of amounts secured by the lien (excluding reasonable collection and attorney fees, charges for late payment, and costs incurred with respect to those assessments) for a period of one year or in the amount of $1200 or more, whichever occurs first. A lien for other fees, penalties, etc. is created only after judgment in a civil action, and may not be foreclosed. It becomes effective only upon transfer of the property. § 33-1256(A).
Notices: Upon written request, the condominium association must provide the unit owner, escrow agent, lienholder or owner's designee with a written statement of the amount of unpaid assessments. Failure to furnish this statement within fifteen days will extinguish any lien for the assessments. § 33-1256(I).
Interest, Fees & Costs: A judgment or decree under this section must include costs and reasonable attorney fees for the prevailing party. § 33-1256(H). Past-due assessments bear interest at a rate established by the board, subject to the condominium documents. § 33-1255(B). The association has power to establish late fees for assessments. § 33-1242(A)(11).
Scope of Lien: A condominium association has a lien for unpaid assessments, and for late fees, costs and reasonable attorney fees incurred with respect to assessments. This lien exists from the time the assessment becomes due. If the assessment is payable in installments, the association has a lien for the entire amount when the first installment becomes due. § 33-1256(A).
Ability to Contest Lien: Not found.
Lien Extinguished: A lien for unpaid assessments is extinguished if enforcement proceedings are not instituted within three years after the full amount of the assessment becomes due. § 33-1256(F).
Explicit Right of Redemption: Not specified.

ARKANSAS

Ark. Code Ann. §§ 18-13-101 to 18-13-120 (Horizontal Property Act)

Method of Foreclosure: Not specified.
Notices: Not specified.
Interest, Fees & Costs: Not specified.
Scope of Lien: Not specified.
Ability to Contest Lien: Not specified.
Lien Extinguished: Not specified.
Explicit Right of Redemption: Not specified.

CALIFORNIA

Cal. Civ. Code §§ 1350 to 1378 (West) (Common Interest Developments)

Applicability: California's statute was recently amended and some procedures described below (i.e., notice, meeting with the board to discuss debt) apply only to liens recorded after January 1, 2003.
Method of Foreclosure: Thirty days after a lien is recorded, it may be enforced in any manner permitted by law, including judicial sale, or sale by trustee named in notice of lien, following procedures for power of sale foreclosure of mortgage or deed of trust. §§ 1367(e), 1367.1(g). For liens recorded on and after January 1, 2006, an association must use a small claims action instead of judicial or non-judicial foreclosure to enforce the lien if the amount of the delinquent assessment (excluding accelerated assessments, late charges, fees, attorney fees, interest and costs of collection) is less than $1800. For delinquent assessments greater than $1800 or more than twelve months delinquent, the association may use judicial or non-judicial foreclosure subject to conditions set forth in § 1367.4. § 1367.4.
Notices: Thirty days before recording a lien, the association must notify the unit owner, in writing, by certified mail, explaining the collection and lien enforcement procedures of the association, including the owner's right to inspect the association records, a warning in 14-point capitals that the owner's interest may be sold without court action, and an itemized statement of the amount due, including the method of calculation of late charges, costs, etc., a statement that the owner will not be liable if it is determined that the assessment was timely paid, notification of the right to request a meeting with the board. §§ 1367(a), 1367.1(a). Notice of a delinquent assessment must be recorded with the county recorder. §§ 1367(b), 1367.1(d). Notice must be mailed to all record owners of unit owner's interest within ten days after recording. If the delinquent sum is paid, association must record satisfaction and release of lien within twenty-one days. §§ 1367(b), 1367.1(d). If a lien was recorded in error, the party who recorded it shall, within twenty-one days, record the release or rescission, and provide a declaration to the owner stating that the lien was recorded in error. § 1367.1(i).
Interest, Fees & Costs: If an assessment is paid late (i.e., fifteen days after due date, unless declaration provides longer time period) the association may charge reasonable collection costs, including reasonable attorney fees; late charge of the greater of $10 or 10% of the delinquent assessment (unless the declaration provides for a lesser amount); interest not to exceed 12% per year, commencing thirty days after assessment becomes due. § 1366.
Scope of Lien: Regular or special assessments, plus late fees,

reasonable costs of collection, and interest. Also penalties imposed to pay for repair of damage caused by unit owner or owner's guests or tenants. Lien becomes effective when recorded. Other monetary penalties, except late payment fees, do not give rise to liens. §§ 1367(b), (c) and 1367.1(d), (e).
Ability to Contest Lien: The owner may submit a request to meet with the board to discuss a payment plan. The board must inform the owner of the standards for payment plans, if any. The board, or a committee designated by the board, must meet with the owner within forty-five days of a request mailed within fifteen days of the postmark of the notice. § 1367.1(c)(3). Prior to recording a lien for delinquent assessments, an association must offer the owner and, if so requested by the owner, participate in dispute resolution pursuant to association's "meet and confer" program required in §§ 1363.810–1363.850. § 1367.1(a)(1)(A). Prior to initiating a foreclosure, an association must also offer such a "meet and confer" program, or an alternative dispute resolution with a neutral third party pursuant to §§ 1369.510–1369.590. The decision to pursue dispute resolution or a particular type of alternative dispute resolution shall be the owner's choice, except that binding arbitration is not available if the association intends to initiate a judicial foreclosure. § 1367.1(c)(1)(B).
Lien Extinguished: Not specified.
Explicit Right of Redemption: A non-judicial foreclosure is subject to a right of redemption which expire ninety days after the sale, and the notice of sale must include statement regarding right of redemption. § 1367.4(c)(4).

COLORADO

Colo. Rev. Stat. §§ 38-33.3-101 to 38-33.3-319 (Common Interest Ownership Act); Colo. Rev. Stat. §§ 38-33-101 to 38-33-113 (Condominium Ownership Act)

Applicability: The Common Interest Ownership Act, Colo. Rev. Stat. §§ 38-33.3-101 to 38-33.3-319 (which covers condominiums, co-operatives, and planned communities), applies to condominiums created after July 1, 1992. However, § 38-33.3-316 of the Common Interest Ownership Act apples to all condominiums, including those created before the effective date.
Method of Foreclosure: The lien is foreclosed like a mortgage of real estate. § 38-33.3-316(11).
Notices: The association must furnish, upon written request by unit owner or holder of security interest, a statement of the assessments due. If the association fails to respond within fourteen days, it cannot enforce its lien as to any assessments due at the date of the request. § 38-33.3-316(8).
Interest, Fees & Costs: The association may impose charges for late payment of assessments, and recover reasonable attorney fees and other legal costs of collection, whether or not suit was initiated. § 38-33.3-123(1)(a). The association may not fine any unit owner for an alleged violation unless the association has adopted a written policy governing the imposition of fines that includes a fair and impartial fact-finding process. § 38-33.3-209.5. Past-due assessments bear interest at a rate set by the association, not to exceed 21% per year. § 38-33.3-315(2). The association is entitled to costs and reasonable attorney fees in an action brought by the association under this section. § 38-33.3-316(7).
Scope of Lien: The association has a statutory lien for assessments and fines, including late charges, attorney fees and interest. If an assessment is payable in installments, each installment is a lien from the time it becomes due. § 38-33.3-316(1).
Ability to Contest Lien: Not specified.
Lien Extinguished: A lien for unpaid assessments is extinguished if enforcement proceedings are not instituted within six years after the full amount becomes due. § 38-33.3-316(5).
Explicit Right of Redemption: Not specified.

CONNECTICUT

Conn. Gen. Stat. §§ 47-200 to 47-299 (Common Interest Ownership Act); Conn. Gen. Stat. §§ 47-68a to 47-90c (Condominium Act)

Applicability: The Common Interest Ownership Act, Conn. Gen. Stat. §§ 47-200 to 47-299 (covers condominiums, co-operatives and planned communities), applies to condominiums created after January 1, 1984. Except for § 47-257, the provisions of the Common Interest Ownership Act summarized below also apply to condominiums created before the effective date.
Method of Foreclosure: Same as mortgage of real property. § 47-258(j). An association may not commence an action to foreclose unless: (1) the unit owner owes a sum equal to at least two months of common expense assessments; (2) the association has made a demand for payment in a record; and (3) the executive board has either voted to commence foreclosure specifically against that unit or has adopted a standard procedure that provides for foreclosure against that unit. § 47-258(m).
Notices: Within ten days after a request made in a record by a unit owner, the association must provide a written statement of the amount of unpaid assessments due on a unit. § 47-258(h).
Interest, Fees & Costs: The association may charge interest on any past-due assessments at the rate set by the association, not exceeding 18% per year. § 47-257(b). The association may impose late fees, interest, or both on late payments of assessments. § 47-244(11). A judgment or decree under this section must include costs and reasonable attorney fees for the prevailing party. § 47-258(g).
Scope of Lien: Reasonable attorney fees and costs, assessments, fines, late charges, fees and interest. If assessment is due in installments, the full amount becomes a lien when the first installment is due. § 47-258(a).
Ability to Contest Lien: Not specified.
Lien Extinguished: A lien for unpaid assessments expires if enforcement proceedings are not brought within three years after entire amount becomes due. In case of owner's bankruptcy, this limitation period is tolled until thirty days after the automatic stay is lifted. § 47-258(e).
Explicit Right of Redemption: Not specified.

DELAWARE

Del. Code Ann. tit. 25, §§ 2201 to 2243 (Unit Property Act)

Method of Foreclosure: A judgment against a unit and its owner is enforceable in the same manner as is otherwise provided by law. Tit. 25, § 2234. The association must obtain a judgment before the assessment is considered a lien.
Notices: Not specified.
Interest, Fees & Costs: Overdue assessments may bear interest at a rate of up to 18% per year, starting thirty days after the due date.

Tit. 25, § 2233.
Scope of Lien: Assessments are the personal liability of the unit owner. Tit. 25, § 2233.
Ability to Contest Lien: Not specified.
Lien Extinguished: Not specified.
Explicit Right of Redemption: Not specified.

DISTRICT OF COLUMBIA

D.C. Code §§ 42-1901.01 to 42-1904.18 (Condominiums); D.C. Code § 42-2001 to 42-2051 (Horizontal Property Regimes)

Applicability: The District of Columbia's condominium statute, D.C. Code Ann. § 42-1901.01 to 42-1904.18, applies to condominiums created after March 29, 1977. With limited exception (i.e., § 42-1903.12), the provisions of the statute cited below also apply to condominiums created before the effective date.
Method of Foreclosure: Association may foreclose by power of sale. § 42-1903.13(c)(1).
Notices: Thirty days before foreclosure sale, association must send notice to unit owner at address of unit, and any other address designated by owner, with a copy to the Mayor or his designated agent. The notice must state that if the assessment, interest and late charge are not paid within thirty days after mailing date of notice, the unit will be sold, and the date, time and place of the sale. The association must also publish notice of the public sale in a newspaper at least three times during the fifteen days before the sale. § 42-1903.13(c)(4), (5). Upon written request, a unit owner or purchaser is entitled to a recordable statement, setting forth the amount of assessments due. Failure to furnish the statement within ten days will extinguish the lien. § 42-1903.13(h).
Interest, Fees & Costs: Any judgment to enforce § 42-1903.13 shall include costs and attorney fees. § 42-1903.13(f). Past-due assessments bear interest at the lesser of 10% per year, or the maximum permitted rate for first mortgages, starting fifteen days after the assessment is due. § 42-1903.12(e). The association may impose late payment fees. § 42-1903.08(a)(11).
Scope of Lien: Assessments are a lien from the time they become due. If due in installments, association has a lien for entire amount when first installment becomes due. §§ 42-1903.13(a), 42-2016.
Ability to Contest Lien: Not specified.
Lien Extinguished: A lien for assessments or installments, and late charges and interest, will lapse if enforcement proceedings are not brought within three years after the assessment or installment becomes due. § 42-1903.13(e).
Explicit Right of Redemption: Not specified.
Miscellaneous: Unit owner has right to cure default at any time prior to foreclosure sale, by tendering payment in full for assessments, late charges, interest, costs and attorney fees. § 42-1903.13(c)(2).

FLORIDA

Fla. Stat. Ann. §§ 718.101 to 718.622 (West) (Condominium Act); Fla. Stat. Ann. §§ 721.80 to 721.86 (West) (Timeshare Lien Foreclosure Act); Fla. Stat. Ann. §§ 721.01 to 721.32 (West) (Vacation Plan and Timesharing Act)

Applicability: A timeshare plan subject to both the Vacation Plan and Timesharing Act, Fla. Stat. Ann. §§ 721.01 to 721.32, and the Condominium Act, §§ 718.101 to 718.622, must meet the requirements of both chapters, with limited exception. § 721.03(3). In the event of a conflict between the two chapters, the provisions of chapter 721 prevail. § 721.03(2).
Method of Foreclosure: The association's lien may be foreclosed in the same manner as a mortgage on real property. § 718.116(6)(a). The Timeshare Lien Foreclosure Act authorizes the consolidation of foreclosure proceedings against up to fifteen timeshare estates when the action is filed by a single plaintiff against a single timeshare property, the default and remedy provisions in the operative documents are substantially the same for each defendant, and the nature of the alleged defaults are the same for each defendant. A court must sever for trial any count of the complaint to which a defendant raises a timely defense or counterclaim. § 721.83.
Notices: Except as otherwise provided, no lien may be filed against a unit owner until thirty days after the date on which a notice of intent to file a lien has been delivered by certified mail, return receipt requested, and by first-class U.S. mail to the owner's last known address. § 718.121(4). No foreclosure judgment may be entered until at least thirty days after the association gives written notice to the unit owner of its intention to foreclose its lien. If this notice is not given at least thirty days before the foreclosure action is filed, and if the unpaid assessments, including those coming due after the claim of lien is recorded, are paid before the entry of a final judgment of foreclosure, the association shall not recover attorney fees or costs. The notice requirement is satisfied if the unit owner records a notice of contest of the lien. The notice requirement does not apply if an action to foreclose a mortgage on the condominium unit is pending before any court; if the rights of the association would be affected by such foreclosure; and if actual, constructive, or substitute service of process has been made on the unit owner. § 718.116(6)(b).
Interest, Fees & Costs: Assessments which are not paid when due bear interest at the rate provided in the declaration, from the due date until paid. This rate may not exceed the rate allowed by law, and, if no rate is provided in the declaration, interest shall accrue at the rate of 18% per year. Also, if the declaration or bylaws provide, the association may charge an administrative late fee in addition to interest, in an amount not to exceed the greater of $25 or 5% of each installment of the assessment for each delinquent installment that the payment is late. The association may recover reasonable attorney fees and costs. § 718.116(3).
Scope of Lien: The claim of lien secures all unpaid assessments which are due and which may accrue subsequent to the recording of the claim of lien and prior to the entry of a certificate of title, as well as interest and all reasonable costs and attorney fees incurred by the association incident to the collection process. § 718.116(5)(b).
Ability to Contest Lien: By recording a Notice of Contest of Lien, a unit owner may require the association to enforce a recorded claim of lien against his or her condominium parcel. § 718.116(5)(c).
Lien Extinguished: Lien effective for one year after the claim of lien is recorded unless, within that time, an action to enforce the lien is started. The one-year period is automatically extended for any length of time during which the association is prevented from filing a foreclosure action by an automatic stay resulting from a bankruptcy petition filed by the parcel owner or any other person claiming an interest in the parcel. § 718.116(5)(b).
Explicit Right of Redemption: Not specified.

GEORGIA

Ga. Code Ann. §§ 44-3-70 to 44-3-116 (Condominium Act); Ga. Code Ann. §§ 44-3-220 to 44-3-235 (Property Owners' Association Act); Apartment Ownership Act, Ga. L. 1963, p.561

Applicability: The Apartment Ownership Act applies to condominiums created prior to October 1, 1975 unless instruments creating such a condominium are amended to be subject to the Condominium Act. § 44-3-113. The Property Owners' Association Act, Ga. Code Ann. §§ 44-3-220 to 44-3-235, is not applicable to associations created pursuant to the Condominium Act unless the development created under the former includes a condominium. § 44-3-235(b).
Method of Foreclosure: In the same manner as other liens for the improvement of real property. §§ 44-3-109(c), 44-3-232(c).
Notices: Thirty days notice by certified mail or statutory overnight delivery, return receipt requested, at the address of the unit and any other address designated by the unit owner, stating the amount due, with interest and late charges. No foreclosure action against a lien shall be permitted unless the amount of the lien is at least $2000. §§ 44-3-109(c), 44-3-232(c). Upon written request, any owner, mortgagee, or prospective purchaser or lender is entitled to a written statement setting forth the amount due for assessments, etc. Failure to furnish this statement within five days of receipt of the request will extinguish the lien. §§ 44-3-109(d), 44-3-232(d).
Interest, Fees & Costs: Lien will include late charges of the greater of $10 or 10% of the amount due, 10% interest from the time the assessment became due, collection costs including court costs, reasonable attorney fees actually incurred, expenses of sale, and of protection or preservation of the unit pending sale, and fair rental value from the time the action is instituted until the date of sale or other satisfaction of the judgment. §§ 44-3-109(b), 44-3-232(b).
Scope of Lien: Assessments, fines and reasonable charges for materials or services furnished to owner by the association are a lien on the unit from the time they become due. §§ 44-3-109(a), 44-3-232.
Ability to Contest Lien: Not specified.
Lien Extinguished: The lien will lapse if no enforcement action is instituted within four years after the assessment or installment became due. §§ 44-3-109(c), 44-3-232(c).
Explicit Right of Redemption: Not specified.

GUAM

Guam Code Ann. tit. 21, §§ 45124 to 45155 (Horizontal Property Act)

Method of Foreclosure: Manager or board of directors may foreclose in the same manner as a mortgage on real property. In such a foreclosure, unit owner shall be required to pay reasonable rental if so provided in the bylaws, and plaintiff is entitled to appointment of receiver to collect the same. § 45124.
Notices: Not specified.
Interest, Fees & Costs: Not specified.
Scope of Lien: All sums assessed but unpaid for share of common expenses. § 45124.
Ability to Contest Lien: Not specified.
Lien Extinguished: Not specified.
Explicit Right of Redemption: Not specified.
Miscellaneous: Suit for a money judgment for unpaid common expenses may be brought without foreclosing or waiving the lien. § 45124.

HAWAII

Haw. Rev. Stat. §§ 514A-1 to 514A-135 (Condominium Property Act); Haw. Rev. Stat. §§ 514B-1 to 514B-163 (Condominium Property Act)

Applicability: Hawaii recently revised its condominium law. The Condominium Property Act, Haw. Rev. Stat. §§ 514B-1 to 514B-163, applies to all condominiums created after July 1, 2006. Chapter 514A, also entitled the Condominium Property Act, applies only to condominiums created prior to July 1, 2006, except as provided in §§ 514B-22 and 514B-23.
Method of Foreclosure: The lien may be foreclosed by action, or by non-judicial or power of sale foreclosure, as provided in real property chapter 667. § 514B-146(a)(2). *See also* Haw. Rev. Stat. §§ 667-1 to 667-51.
Notices: The association may impose late fees. If it wishes to take late fees, fines, interest or legal fees out of future common expense payments, it must adopt and distribute to all owners a policy that permits this. § 514B-105(c).
Interest, Fees & Costs: The association may impose charges and penalties, including late fees and interest. § 514B-104(a)(11). Past-due assessments bear interest at the rate set by the association, not to exceed 18% per year. § 514B-144(b). The association is entitled to reasonable collection expenses, including attorney fees, for collecting delinquent assessments, foreclosing a lien, and enforcing rules. Attorney fees to prevailing party. § 514B-157.
Scope of Lien: All sums assessed by the association but unpaid are a lien against the unit. § 514B-146(a).
Ability to Contest Lien: Chapter 514B provides that owner who first pays full amount of assessment may file in small claims court or require association to mediate dispute concerning amount or validity of amount claimed by association. If parties are unable to resolve dispute through mediation, then either party may file for arbitration. §§ 514B-146(c), (d).
Lien Extinguished: Not specified.
Explicit Right of Redemption: Not specified.

IDAHO

Idaho Code Ann. §§ 55-1501 to 55-1527 (Condominium Property Act)

Method of Foreclosure: The lien may be foreclosed by power of sale, in the same way as a deed of trust, or any other method permitted by law. § 55-1518.
Notices: Each unit owner is entitled, on ten days notice, to a statement of account, setting forth any unpaid assessments or other charges. The management may charge a reasonable fee to provide this information. § 55-1507(h). The association must record a lien with the county recorder which specifies the amount of assessment and other charges due, a description of the unit, and the name of the owner. If the amount due is paid, the association must record the satisfaction and release of the lien. § 55-1518.
Interest, Fees & Costs: Not specified, but § 55-1518, defining lien, refers to penalties, interest, cost and attorney fees.
Scope of Lien: Unpaid assessments, including penalties, interest, costs and attorney fees. § 55-1518.

Ability to Contest Lien: Not specified.
Lien Extinguished: Lien is extinguished if no enforcement is initiated within one year after recording, but association may extend the period by one year, by recording a written extension. § 55-1518.
Explicit Right of Redemption: Not specified.

ILLINOIS

765 Ill. Comp. Stat. 605/1 to 605/32 (Condominium Property Act)

Method of Foreclosure: After a lien has been recorded, it may be foreclosed by an action, in the same way as a mortgage of real estate. 765 Ill. Comp. Stat. 605/9(h).
Notices: Lien must be recorded. 765 Ill. Comp. Stat. 605/9(h).
Interest, Fees & Costs: Attorney fees are specifically permitted. 765 Ill. Comp. Stat. 605/9.2(b). Board of managers may impose late fees and fines. 765 Ill. Comp. Stat. 605/18.4(l).
Scope of Lien: Unpaid assessments or fines, with interest, late charges, reasonable attorney fees and costs of collection. 765 Ill. Comp. Stat. 605/9(g)(1).
Ability to Contest Lien: Not specified.
Lien Extinguished: Not specified.
Explicit Right of Redemption: Not specified.

INDIANA

Ind. Code §§ 32-25-1-1 to 32-25-9-2 (Condominiums)

Method of Foreclosure: The lien may be filed and foreclosed by suit, like a mechanic's and materialman's lien. § 32-25-6-3(b).
Notices: Not specified.
Interest, Fees & Costs: Not specified.
Scope of Lien: Unpaid common expense assessments become a lien at the time of assessment. § 32-25-6-3(a).
Ability to Contest Lien: Not specified.
Lien Extinguished: Not specified.
Explicit Right of Redemption: Not specified.
Miscellaneous: The association may bring an action to recover a money judgment for unpaid common expenses without foreclosing or waiving the lien.

IOWA

Iowa Code §§ 499B.1 to 499B.20 (Horizontal Property Act)

Method of Foreclosure: The lien may be foreclosed by suit in the same manner as a mortgage of real property. § 499B.17.
Notices: Not specified.
Interest, Fees & Costs: Not specified.
Scope of Lien: The council has a lien for all unpaid common expense assessments. § 499B.17.
Ability to Contest Lien: Not specified.
Lien Extinguished: Not specified.
Explicit Right of Redemption: Not specified.
Miscellaneous: The council may bring an action to recover a money judgment for unpaid common expenses without foreclosing or waiving the lien. § 499B.17.

KANSAS

Kan. Stat. Ann. §§ 58-3101 to 58-3129 (Apartment Ownership Act); Kan. Stat. Ann. §§ 58-3701 to 58-3713 (Townhouse Ownership Act)

Method of Foreclosure: Lien may be foreclosed by suit, in the same manner as a mortgage of real property. §§ 58-3123(a), 58-3710.
Notices: Not specified.
Interest, Fees & Costs: Not specified.
Scope of Lien: All sums assessed but unpaid for common expenses are a lien against the unit. §§ 58-3123(a), 58-3710.
Ability to Contest Lien: Not specified.
Lien Extinguished: Not specified.
Explicit Right of Redemption: Not specified.
Miscellaneous: The association may bring an action to recover a money judgment for unpaid common expenses without foreclosing or waiving the lien. §§ 58-3123(a), 58-3710.

KENTUCKY

Ky. Rev. Stat. Ann. §§ 381.805 to 381.910 (West) (Horizontal Property Law)

Method of Foreclosure: The lien may be foreclosed by suit, in the same manner as a mortgage on real property. § 381.883.
Notices: Not specified.
Interest, Fees & Costs: Not specified.
Scope of Lien: All sums assessed for common expenses and unpaid are a lien on the unit. § 381.883.
Ability to Contest Lien: Not specified.
Lien Extinguished: Not specified.
Explicit Right of Redemption: Not specified.
Miscellaneous: A suit to recover a money judgment for unpaid common expenses is maintainable without lien enforcement or waiving the lien. § 381.883.

LOUISIANA

La. Rev. Stat. Ann. §§ 9:1121.101 to 9:1124.115 (Condominium Act)

Method of Foreclosure: Not specified.
Notices: The association must record a "claim of privilege," a description of the unit, the name of the owner, the amount due, and the date when it became due. § 9:1123.115(A)(2). At least seven days before recording the claim, the association must serve on the unit owner, by personal service or registered or certified mail, a detailed sworn statement of its claim that includes the date the assessment became delinquent or accelerated. § 9:1123.115(A)(3).
Interest, Fees & Costs: The unit owners' association may impose late payment fees and fines for violations of rules. § 9:1123.102(11). The lien includes attorney fees if these are provided for in the declaration, and interest either at the rate set by the declaration, or, if no rate is set, at the legal rate. § 9:1123.115(A).
Scope of Lien: The association has a "privilege" on the unit for unpaid or accelerated assessments, interest, and reasonable attorney fees. If unit owner fails to timely pay assessments for six months or more during any eight-month period, the association may accelerate assessment on common elements for twelve-month period and file a privilege for same after notice to owner under § 9:1123.115(A)(3). § 9:1123.115(A)1. Interest on unpaid assessments may be charged at the rate set in the declaration, or if no rate is provided, at the legal interest rate. § 9:1123.115(A)(1). The

association has a separate privilege for the share of assessments attributable to utility service. This privilege is enforced in the same way as the privilege established by § 9:1123.115. § 9:1123.116.
Ability to Contest Lien: Not specified.
Lien Extinguished: The "privilege" is extinguished if a notice of filing suit is not recorded within one year after the recording of the claim. § 9:1123.115(B).
Explicit Right of Redemption: Not specified.

MAINE

Me. Rev. Stat. Ann. tit. 33, §§ 1601-101 to 1604-118 (Condominium Act); Me. Rev. Stat. Ann. tit. 33, §§ 560 to 587 (Unit Ownership Act)

Applicability: The Condominium Act, Me. Rev. Stat. Ann. tit. 33, §§ 1601 to 1604-118, applies to condominiums created after January 1, 1983. Section 1603-116 of the Condominium Act apples to all condominiums, including those created before the effective date.
Method of Foreclosure: The lien may be foreclosed like a mortgage on real estate. § 1603-116(a).
Notices: Within ten days after a written request, the association must provide the owner with a recordable written statement of the amount of unpaid assessments due for the unit. § 1603-116(h).
Interest, Fees & Costs: The association may impose fees for late payments, or fines for violation of rules. § 1603-102(a)(11). A judgment or decree in any action to enforce this section must include costs and reasonable attorney fees for the prevailing party. § 1603-116(g).
Scope of Lien: The association has a lien for assessments, including late charges, interest and fines, from the time they become due. If the assessment is payable in installments, the full amount is a lien from the time the first installment is due. § 1603-116(a).
Ability to Contest Lien: Not specified.
Lien Extinguished: A lien is extinguished if enforcement proceedings are not brought within three years after the full amount of the assessments became due. § 1603-116(e).
Explicit Right of Redemption: Not specified.

MARYLAND

Md. Code Ann., Real Prop. §§ 11-101 to 11-143 (West) (Condominium Act); *see also* Md. Code Ann., Real Prop. §§ 14-201 to 14-206 (West) (Contract Lien Act)

Method of Foreclosure: Liens may be created following the procedures of the Contract Lien Act. § 11-110(d). The Contract Lien Act, Real Prop. §§ 14-201 to 14-206, covers liens created by contracts recorded with land records (i.e., condominium declarations, time-shares, etc.) and provides for notice and hearing. § 14-203. These liens may be foreclosed like a real property mortgage containing a power of sale. § 14-204.
Notices: If an installment is fifteen days late, the association may accelerate the entire year's assessment. Within fifteen days after the due date, the association must notify the unit owner that it will accelerate if the installment is not paid within fifteen days of the notice. § 11-110(e)(3). Notice of intent to impose lien must be given as required by the Contract Lien Act, § 14-203.
Interest, Fees & Costs: The association may impose late payment fees, or fines for violation of rules. § 11-109(d)(16). Overdue assessments bear interest at 18% per year unless a lower rate is specified in the bylaws. For assessments that remain unpaid for fifteen days, the association may impose a late charge of the greater of $15 or 10% of the amount due. § 11-110(e).
Scope of Lien: Assessments, including interest, late charges, costs and attorney fees, may be enforced by imposition of a lien pursuant to Contract Lien Act (Real Prop. Law § 14-201 to 14-206). § 11-110(d).
Ability to Contest Lien: As provided for in Contract Lien Act, § 14-203.
Lien Extinguished: Contract Lien Act requires that notice of intent to impose a lien must be furnished within two years of contract breach. § 14-203. Action to foreclose the lien must be brought within twelve years after recording. § 14-204(c).
Explicit Right of Redemption: Not specified.

MASSACHUSETTS

Mass. Gen. Laws ch. 183A, §§ 1 to 22 (Condominiums)

Method of Foreclosure: The lien is foreclosed as provided for in ch. 254, §§ 5, 5A. Ch. 183A, § 6(c). The association must file a civil action to enforce the lien. Ch. 254, § 5.
Notices: When an assessment has been delinquent for sixty days, the association must send notice, by certified and first class mail, to the unit owner, stating the amount of the delinquency. If a condominium unit is being rented, the association may, twenty-five days after an assessment is due, notify the owner that it intends to collect rent from the tenant. Ch. 183A, § 6(c). Within ten days of a written request, the association must provide a statement in recordable form, setting forth the amount due for unpaid assessments. Ch. 183A, § 6(d).
Interest, Fees & Costs: The association may impose fines, late charges, interest, reasonable costs of collection, including court costs and attorney fees. Ch. 183A, § 6a(a)(ii). The association may impose charges or charge interest for late payment, and impose fines for violations of rules.
Scope of Lien: The association has a lien for common expense assessments, including interest, late fees, and costs of collection, or for assessments against an individual owner for expenses caused by misconduct of the owner or the owner's tenants or guests, from the time the assessments are due. Ch. 183A, § 6(a).
Ability to Contest Lien: In a civil action as required by ch. 254, § 5.
Lien Extinguished: Not specified.
Explicit Right of Redemption: Not specified.

MICHIGAN

Mich. Comp. Laws §§ 559.101 to 559.276 (Condominium Act)

Method of Foreclosure: The lien may be foreclosed by advertisement or by action, like a real estate mortgage. § 559.208(1), (2).
Notices: Notice of intent to foreclose must be recorded in registry of deeds, and served on unit owner by first class mail ten days before commencement of foreclosure proceedings. Notice must include description of unit, name of owner, and amounts due (exclusive of interest, costs, attorney fees or future assessments). § 559.208(3).
Interest, Fees & Costs: In foreclosure, the association is entitled to reasonable interest, expenses, costs and attorney fees. § 559.208(2).
Scope of Lien: The association has a lien for unpaid assessments,

including interest, collection and late charges, and attorney fees, for fines, as provided for in condominium documents, and for sums advanced to pay taxes or other liens to protect the association's lien. § 559.208(a).
Ability to Contest Lien: Not specified.
Lien Extinguished: Not specified.
Explicit Right of Redemption: Redemption period is six months from date of sale, unless the property was abandoned, in which case it is one month. § 559.208(2).

MINNESOTA

Minn. Stat. §§ 515B.1-101 to 515B.4-118 (Common Interest Ownership Act); Minn. Stat. §§ 515.01 to 515.29 (Condominium Act); Minn. Stat. §§ 515A.1-101 to 515A.4-118 (Uniform Condominium Act)

Applicability: Minnesota has three condominium laws. The Common Interest Ownership Act, Minn. Stat. §§ 515B.1-101 to 515B.4-118, which covers condominiums, co-operatives and planned communities, applies to all condominiums created after June 1, 1994. Some provisions of the older acts still apply to condominiums created before 1994. The provisions of the Common Interest Ownership Act summarized below apply to all condominiums, including those created before the effective date.
Method of Foreclosure: The lien may be foreclosed by power of sale or by action, like a real property mortgage. § 515B.3-116.
Notices: Within ten business days after a written request, the association must furnish the owner with a statement in recordable form setting forth the amount of unpaid assessments. § 515B.3-116(g). If an installment of an assessment is more than sixty days overdue, and the association wishes to accelerate the entire amount of the assessment, it must give ten days written notice to the unit owner. § 515B.3-115(h).
Interest, Fees & Costs: The association may impose late payment charges, and fines for violations of rules. § 515B.3-102(a)(11). Reasonable attorney fees for collection of assessments or for enforcement of this chapter against an owner may be assessed against the unit. § 515B.3-115(e)(4). In foreclosure, the association is entitled to costs and disbursements of foreclosure, and attorney fees as provided for in the declaration (in foreclosure by sale) or determined by the court (in foreclosure by action). § 515B.3-116(h)(4).
Scope of Lien: The association has a lien for unpaid assessments, including fees, charges, late charges, fines and interest, and reasonable attorney fees. If an assessment is paid in installments, the association has a lien for the entire amount as soon as the first installment is due. §§ 515B.3-115(e)(4), (5) and 116(a).
Ability to Contest Lien: Not specified.
Lien Extinguished: The lien is barred if enforcement action is not brought within three years after the last installment of the assessment became due. § 515B.3-116(d).
Explicit Right of Redemption: Redemption period is six months from date of sale, or "a lesser period authorized by law." § 515B.3-116(h)(4).

MISSISSIPPI

Miss. Code Ann. §§ 89-9-1 to 89-9-37 (Condominium Law)

Method of Foreclosure: The lien may be foreclosed by power of sale, like a mortgage or deed of trust (*see* § 89-1-55) or "in any other manner permitted by law." § 89-9-21.
Notices: The lien becomes effective when recorded. § 89-9-21.
Interest, Fees & Costs: Lien for unpaid assessments may include interest, costs, penalties and attorney fees. § 89-9-21.
Scope of Lien: The association has a lien for assessments, including interest, costs, penalties and attorney fees, if provided for in the declaration. This amount becomes a lien when recorded. § 89-9-21.
Ability to Contest Lien: Not specified.
Lien Extinguished: Lien is extinguished if no enforcement proceeding is brought within one year after recording; association may obtain a one-year extension by recording written extension. § 89-9-21.
Explicit Right of Redemption: Not specified.

MISSOURI

Mo. Rev. Stat. § 448.1-101 to 448.4-120 (Uniform Condominium Act); Mo. Rev. Stat. § 448.005 to 448.210 (Condominium Property Act)

Applicability: The Uniform Condominium Act applies to condominiums created after September 28, 1993. The provisions of the Uniform Condominium Act summarized below also apply to condominiums created before the effective date.
Method of Foreclosure: The lien may be foreclosed like a real estate mortgage, or a power of sale pursuant to chapter 443. § 448.3-116(1).
Notices: Within ten business days of a written request, the association must furnish the owner with a recordable statement of the amount of unpaid assessments on the unit. § 448.3-116(8).
Interest, Fees & Costs: The association may impose late payment charges, or fines for violations of rules. § 448.3-102(1)(11). A judgment or decree in an action to enforce this section must include costs and attorney fees for the prevailing party. § 448.3-116(7)
Scope of Lien: The association has a lien for unpaid assessments, including fees, charges, late charges, fines and interest. If the assessment is payable in installments, the entire sum is a lien from the time the first installment becomes due. § 448.3-116(1).
Ability to Contest Lien: Not specified.
Lien Extinguished: The lien is extinguished if enforcement proceedings are not brought within three years after the full amount of the assessments becomes due. § 448.3-116(5).
Explicit Right of Redemption: Not specified.

MONTANA

Mont. Code Ann. §§ 70-23-101 to 70-23-902 (Unit Ownership Act)

Method of Foreclosure: The lien is foreclosed like a lien created by title 71, chapter 3, part 5 (construction liens). § 70-23-608. *See also* Mont. Code Ann. §§ 71-3-521 to 7-3-563.
Notices: A claim of lien must be recorded, including a statement of the amount due, the name of the owner, and a description of the property. § 70-23-607(2), (3).
Interest, Fees & Costs: Not specified.
Scope of Lien: If the association furnishes to any unit any services, labor or material lawfully chargeable as common expenses, it has

a lien for the reasonable value of such common expenses. § 70-23-607(1).
Ability to Contest Lien: Not specified.
Lien Extinguished: Not specified.
Explicit Right of Redemption: Not specified.

NEBRASKA

Neb. Rev. Stat. §§ 76-825 to 76-894 (Condominium Act); Neb. Rev. Stat. §§ 76-801 to 76-823 (Condominium Property Act)

Applicability: The Condominium Act, Neb. Rev. Stat. §§ 76-825 to 76-894, applies to condominiums created after January 1, 1984. Section 76-874 of the Condominium Act applies to all condominiums, including those created before the effective date.
Method of Foreclosure: The lien may be foreclosed like a mortgage on real estate. § 76-874(a).
Notices: Notice of the dollar amount of the lien must be recorded in the office where mortgages are recorded. The association must give reasonable notice to all lienholders whose interest will be affected. § 76-874(a). Within ten business days of a written request, the association must provide a unit owner with a recordable statement of the amount of assessments due on the unit. § 76-874(g).
Interest, Fees & Costs: The association may impose late charges, and fines for violations of rules. § 76-860(a)(11). A judgment or decree in any action brought under this section must include costs and reasonable attorney fees for the prevailing party. § 76-874(f).
Scope of Lien: The association has a lien for assessments, including fees, charges, late charges, fines and interest. If the assessment is to be paid in installments, it may be a lien from the time the first installment is due and the assessment is recorded. § 76-874(a).
Ability to Contest Lien: Not specified.
Lien Extinguished: A lien for unpaid assessments is extinguished if enforcement proceedings are not brought within three years after the full amount of the assessments became due. § 76-874(d).
Explicit Right of Redemption: Not specified.

NEVADA

Nev. Rev. Stat. §§ 116.001 to 116.795 (Uniform Common-Interest Ownership Act); Nev. Rev. Stat. §§ 117.010 to 117.110 (Condominium Act)

Applicability: The Uniform Common Interest Ownership Act, Nev. Rev. Stat. §§ 116.001 to 116.795, applies to condominiums created after January 1, 1992. With limited exception, the Act also applies to condominiums created before 1992. *See, e.g.*, §§ 116.1201(2)(d), 116.1203.
Method of Foreclosure: The Uniform Common Interest Ownership Act outlines the procedure for foreclosure. The association may sell the unit after it complies with notice requirements, and the owner fails to pay the amount of the lien, including the costs, fees and expenses of enforcement, within ninety days after the later of the date of recording of the notice of default or the date when notice of default was mailed to the owner. The association may not foreclose for an unpaid fine or penalty unless the violation threatened the health, safety or welfare of the residents of the community. § 116.31162. Sale is by public auction to the highest bidder. § 116.31164(2).
Notices: Before foreclosing, the association must send notice to the unit owner, by certified or registered mail, return receipt requested. Not less than thirty days after mailing the notice, the association must record a notice of default and intent to sell. Both these notices must include a description of the property, the name of the owner, and the amount due. § 116.31162. Before selling the unit, the association must give notice of the time and place of the sale to the unit owner, lienholders or purchaser (if known) and the ombudsman, and must publish notice in the newspaper. § 116.311635.
Interest, Fees & Costs: The association may impose late payment charges, and various fines and penalties. § 116.3102(k), (l), (m). A judgment or decree in an action to enforce this section must include costs and reasonable attorney fees for the prevailing party. § 116.3116(7). Within ten business days of a written request, the association must provide the unit owner with a statement, in recordable form, of the amount of unpaid assessments against the unit. § 116.3116(8).
Scope of Lien: The association has a lien for construction penalties and assessments, including penalties, fees, charges, late charges, fines and interest. If an assessment is due in installments, the full amount is a lien from the time the first installment becomes due. § 116.3116(1).
Ability to Contest Lien: If the association's board is discussing an alleged violation of the rules, including the failure to pay an assessment, the unit owner who may be sanctioned is entitled to appear and testify at the hearing, and may request a public hearing. § 116.31085(4), (5).
Lien Extinguished: A lien for unpaid assessments is extinguished if enforcement proceedings are not instituted within three years after the full amount of the assessment becomes due. § 116.3116(5)
Explicit Right of Redemption: Before sale, unit owner may prevent sale by paying the amount due, including costs, fees and expenses of enforcement within ninety days after notice of the intent to sell. § 116.31162. No right of redemption after a sale that conforms to the requirements of §§ 116.31162–116.31164, 116.31166.

NEW HAMPSHIRE

N.H. Rev. Stat. Ann. §§ 356-B:1 to 356-B:69 (Condominium Act)

Method of Foreclosure: The association must bring an action to enforce the lien. § 356-B:46(IV), (VII).
Notices: Within six months after an assessment becomes due, the association must perfect its lien by recording a memorandum containing a description of the property, the name of the owner, the amount due, and the date of issuance of the memorandum. § 356-B:46 (III). Within ten days after a written request, the association must furnish to a unit owner or prospective purchaser a recordable statement of the amount due on the unit. Failure to do so will extinguish the lien. (The association may charge $10 for the statement.) § 356-B:46(VIII). If the association seeks to collect rent from a delinquent owner's tenant, it must give the owner thirty-days notice (measured from the date of mailing). § 356-B:46-a.
Interest, Fees & Costs: The judgment or decree in a suit to enforce this section must include costs and attorney fees, and interest at the maximum lawful rate from the time the assessment became due. § 356-B:46(V).
Scope of Lien: The association has a lien on the unit for unpaid assessments. § 356-B:46(I).

Ability to Contest Lien: Not specified.
Lien Extinguished: No suit to enforce a lien may be brought after six years from the time the lien is perfected; the lien is extinguished. (A petition to enforce is sufficient to constitute institution of suit.) § 356-B:46(IV).
Explicit Right of Redemption: Not specified.
Miscellaneous: The Condominium Act supersedes the previous law, N.H. Rev. Stat. Ann. §§ 479-A:1 to 479-A:28, the New Hampshire Unit Ownership of Real Property Act. However, portions of the old law may apply to condominiums established before September 10, 1977. § 356-B:2. *See also* Neumann v. Village of Winnipesaukee Timeshare Owners' Assoc., 147 N.H. 111, 784 A.2d 699 (N.H. 2001).

NEW JERSEY

N.J. Stat. Ann. §§ 46:8B-1 to 46:8B-38 (West) (Condominium Act); N.J. Stat. Ann. §§ 46:8A-1 to 46:8A-28 (West) (Horizontal Property Act)

Applicability: The Condominium Act, N.J. Stat. Ann. §§ 46:8B-1 to 46:8B-38 (West), was effective on January 7, 1970. The Horizontal Property Act continues to govern all property created pursuant to it, unless there is a waiver of the regime as provided in § 46:8A-12. § 46:8B-2.
Method of Foreclosure: Liens may be foreclosed by suit, in the same manner as a foreclosure of a mortgage on real property. § 46:8B-21(f).
Notices: The lien becomes effective upon the recording of a claim of lien including a description of the property, the name of the owner, the amount due, and the date it became due. § 46:8B-21(a). Within ten days of request, the association must provide to an owner, prospective purchaser or lien-holder a statement of the amount due. § 46:8B-21(d).
Interest, Fees & Costs: The association may charge interest, late fees and reasonable attorney fees, if authorized by the master deed or bylaws. § 46:8B-15(e). Common expense assessments bear interest from the due date, at the legal interest rate, unless a lower rate is set by the association. § 46:8B-17.
Scope of Lien: The association has a lien for unpaid assessments including interest and any late fees, fines and attorney fees authorized by the bylaws or master deed. The association may not, however, record a lien for a sum which consists only of late fees. §§ 46:8B-17, 46:8B-21(a).
Ability to Contest Lien: Not specified.
Lien Extinguished: Not specified, but the lien loses its limited priority status sixty months after filing. § 46:8B-21(b)(4), (5).
Explicit Right of Redemption: Not specified.

NEW MEXICO

N.M. Stat. Ann. §§ 47-7A-1 to 47-7D-20 (West) (Condominium Act); N.M. Stat. Ann. §§ 47-7-1 to 47-7-28 (West) (Building Unit Ownership Act)

Applicability: The Condominium Act, N.M. Stat. Ann. §§ 47-7A-1 to 47-7D-20 (Michie), applies to all condominiums created after 1982. The Building Unit Ownership Act, N.M. Stat. Ann. §§ 47-7-1 to 47-7-28 (Michie), was not repealed and older condominiums are still covered by that act, unless the association's board passes a resolution making themselves subject to the new act.
Method of Foreclosure: The lien may be foreclosed like a mortgage on real estate. § 47-7C-16(A). Recordation of condominium declaration constitutes record notice and perfection of the lien. § 47-7C-16(C).
Notices: Within ten business days after a written request, the association must provide the owner with a statement of the amount due on the unit. § 47-7C-16(G).
Interest, Fees & Costs: The association has power to impose late charges and fines for violation of rules. § 47-7C-2(A)(11). Past-due assessments bear interest at a rate set by the association, not to exceed 18% per year. § 47-7C-15(B). A judgment or decree in any action to enforce this section may include costs and reasonable attorney fees for the prevailing party. § 47-7C-16(F).
Scope of Lien: The association has a lien for past-due assessments, including fees, charges, late charges, fines and interest. If an assessment is payable in installments, the entire amount is a lien from the time the first installment is due. § 47-7C-16(A).
Ability to Contest Lien: Not specified.
Lien Extinguished: The lien is extinguished if enforcement proceedings are not instituted within three years after the full amount of the assessment became due. § 47-7C-16(D).
Explicit Right of Redemption: Not specified.

NEW YORK

N.Y. Real Prop. Law §§ 339-d to 339-kk (McKinney) (Condominium Act)

Method of Foreclosure: The lien may be foreclosed by suit, like a mortgage of real property. § 339-aa.
Notices: The board must record a verified notice of lien, with a description of the property, the owner's name, the amount and purpose for which due, and the date it became due. § 339-aa.
Interest, Fees & Costs: Lien for assessments includes interest. § 339-z.
Scope of Lien: The board has a lien for unpaid common charges and interest. § 339-z.
Ability to Contest Lien: Not specified.
Lien Extinguished: Lien expires six years after date of filing. § 339-aa.
Explicit Right of Redemption: Not specified.

NORTH CAROLINA

N.C. Gen. Stat. §§ 47C-1-101 to 47C-4-120 (Condominium Act); N.C. Gen. Stat. §§ 47A-1 to 47A-37 (Unit Ownership Act)

Applicability: The Condominium Act, N.C. Gen. Stat. §§ 47C-1-101 to 47C-4-120, applies to condominiums created after October 1, 1986. With the exception of § 47C-3-115, the provisions of the Act cited below also apply to condominiums created before 1986.
Method of Foreclosure: The lien may be foreclosed by power of sale, like a real estate mortgage. § 47C-3-116(a). Lien for fines, interest thereon, or attorney fees incurred solely in connection with fines is enforced by judicial foreclosure. § 47C-3-116(a1).
Notices: The lien must be recorded with the clerk of the superior court, stating the association name and address, name of record owner at time of filing, lot description, and amount due. § 47C-3-116(a), (g). No fewer than fifteen days prior to filing the lien, the association shall mail a statement of the assessment amount due by first-class mail to the physical address of the unit and the unit

owner's address of record. §§ 47C-3-116(a), 47F-3-116(a). The claim must include a specific statement (language specified in statute) and an attached certificate of service attesting to the attempt of service. §§ 47C-3-116(g), 47F-3-116(g).
Interest, Fees & Costs: The association may impose late charges not exceeding greater of $20 per month or 10% of any unpaid assessment installment, and reasonable fines (not to exceed $100) for violations of rules, bylaws, etc. § 47C-3-102(a)(11). Past-due assessments bear interest at a rate set by the association, not to exceed 18% per year. § 47C-3-115(b). A judgment or decree in any proceeding to enforce this section must include costs and reasonable attorney fees for the prevailing party. § 47C-3-116(e).
Scope of Lien: The association has a lien for assessments, including fees, charges, late charges fines and interest, which remain unpaid for thirty days. § 47C-3-116(a).
Ability to Contest Lien: Not specified.
Lien Extinguished: The lien is extinguished if enforcement proceedings are not brought within three years of its docketing with the court clerk. § 47C-3-116(c).
Explicit Right of Redemption: Not specified.

NORTH DAKOTA

N.D. Cent. Code §§ 47-04.1-01 to 47-04.1-15 (Condominium Ownership of Real Property)

Method of Foreclosure: Not specified.
Notices: The lien becomes effective when the administrative body records a notice of assessment, including the name of the owner and the amount due. § 47-04.1-11.
Interest, Fees & Costs: Lien may include interest, costs and penalties. § 47-04.1-11.
Scope of Lien: A reasonable common expense assessment, including interest, costs and penalties, is a lien on the unit. § 47-04.1-11.
Ability to Contest Lien: Not specified.
Lien Extinguished: Not specified.
Explicit Right of Redemption: Not specified.

OHIO

Ohio Rev. Code Ann. §§ 5311.01 to 5311.27 (West) (Condominium Property)

Method of Foreclosure: The association must bring an action to foreclose on the lien. *See* § 5311.18.
Notices: The lien becomes effective when a certificate of lien is recorded, with a description of the unit, the owner's name, and the amount due (subject to later adjustments for interest, costs, etc.). § 5311.18(A)(3).
Interest, Fees & Costs: The association may impose interest, late charges and returned check charges, and "enforcement assessments" for violations of rules, etc., and may adopt rules concerning the collection of delinquent payments. § 5311.081(B)(12), (13).
Scope of Lien: The association has a lien for unpaid assessments, including interest, administrative late fees, enforcement assessments, and any collection costs, attorney fees and paralegal fees incurred by the association. § 5311.18(A).
Ability to Contest Lien: A unit owner who believes that part of the common expenses were improperly charged may bring an action to discharge the lien in common pleas court. The court may order a discharge of all or part of the lien. § 5311.18(C).
Lien Extinguished: The lien is valid for five years from the date of filing. § 5311.18(A)(4).
Explicit Right of Redemption: Not specified.

OKLAHOMA

Okla. Stat. tit. 60, §§ 501 to 530 (Unit Ownership Estate Act)

Method of Foreclosure: The lien may be foreclosed by suit, like a mortgage of real property. § 524(b).
Notices: Not specified.
Interest, Fees & Costs: Not specified.
Scope of Lien: The association has a lien for unpaid common expense assessments. § 524(a).
Ability to Contest Lien: Not specified.
Lien Extinguished: Not specified.
Explicit Right of Redemption: Not specified.

OREGON

Or. Rev. Stat. §§ 100.005 to 100.990 (Condominium Act)

Method of Foreclosure: The lien is foreclosed like a construction lien. § 100.450(4); *see* Or. Rev. Stat. § 87.010 (Entitlement to Construction Liens).
Notices: Before foreclosing, the association must record a claim of lien including a description of the unit, the name of the owner, and the amount presently due, with a statement that future unpaid assessments will continue to accumulate with interest. § 100.450(2), (3).
Interest, Fees & Costs: The association has the power to impose charges for late payment of assessments, attorney fees for collection of assessments, and fines for violation of rules. (A schedule of fines for various violations must be established, and communicated to all unit owners, and an opportunity for alternate dispute resolution provided before any litigation or administrative proceeding to collect a fine.) § 100.405(4)(k), (11). In any action to foreclose a lien or collect assessments, prevailing party is entitled to reasonable attorney fees at trial and on appeal. § 100.470.
Scope of Lien: The association has a lien for unpaid assessments, including interest, late charges, attorney fees, costs or other amounts levied under the declaration or bylaws. § 100.450(1), (5).
Ability to Contest Lien: Not specified.
Lien Extinguished: The lien remains in force for six years after the date when the last unpaid assessment became due. § 100.450(4)(a).
Explicit Right of Redemption: Not specified.

PENNSYLVANIA

68 Pa. Cons. Stat. §§ 3101 to 3414 (Uniform Condominium Act)

Method of Foreclosure: The lien may be foreclosed like a mortgage of real property. § 3315(a).
Notices: Within ten business days after a written request, the association must provide a unit owner with a statement of unpaid assessments levied against the unit, and any credits or surplus in favor of the unit. § 3315(g).
Interest, Fees & Costs: The association may impose late fees, and fines for violation of rules. § 3302(a)(11). Past-due assessments may bear interest at a rate set by the association, not to exceed 15%

per year. § 3314(b). A judgment or decree in any proceeding to enforce this section must provide costs and reasonable attorney fees to the prevailing party. § 3315(f).
Scope of Lien: The association has a lien for unpaid assessments and fines, including fees, charges, late charges, interest, and reasonable costs, including legal fees, incurred by the association in collection or enforcement. If an assessment is due in installments, the association has a lien when the first installment becomes due. § 3315(a).
Ability to Contest Lien: Not specified.
Lien Extinguished: A lien is extinguished if enforcement proceedings are not begun within three years after the assessments became payable. § 3315(d).
Explicit Right of Redemption: Not specified.

PUERTO RICO

P.R. Laws Ann. tit. 31, §§ 1291 to 1294e (Horizontal Property)

Method of Foreclosure: Not specified.
Notices: Association must give fifteen days notice, certified mail return receipt requested, before suing for unpaid assessments. § 1293c.
Interest, Fees & Costs: Delinquent assessments bear interest at the maximum legal rate. After default in three consecutive installments, an additional penalty of 1% per month of the total amount owed may be imposed. § 1293c.
Scope of Lien: For common expense assessments and other "legally agreed upon" expenses. §§ 1293e, 1293c.
Ability to Contest Lien: Not specified.
Lien Extinguished: Not specified.
Explicit Right of Redemption: Not specified.

RHODE ISLAND

R.I. Gen. Laws §§ 34-36.1-1.01 to 34-36.1-4.20 (Condominium Law); R.I. Gen. Laws §§ 34-36-1 to 34-36-39 (Condominium Ownership Law)

Applicability: Rhode Island's Condominium Law, R.I. Gen. Laws §§ 34-36.1-1.01 to 34-36.1-4.20, applies to condominium established after July 1, 1982. With limited exception (e.g., § 34-36.1-3.15 on interest rates) the provisions of the Condominium Law summarized below apply also apply to condominiums established before July 1, 1982.
Method of Foreclosure: The association may sell the unit at public auction, after giving the required notices. § 34-36.1-3.21(a)(1).
Notices: Before foreclosure, the association must first give written notice, certified mail, return receipt requested, to the owner at his or her last known address and to the holder of the first mortgage or deed of trust of record at the address for service required by § 34-36.1-3.16(b)(4). At least twenty days after mailing this notice, the association must publish notice in a newspaper for two successive weeks. The date of sale must be at least fifteen days after the publication of the first notice. § 34-36.1-3.21(a)(2). Within ten business days of receipt of a written request, the association must provide a unit owner or first mortgage holder with a recordable written statement of the amount of unpaid assessments due on the unit. 34-36.1-3.16(h). Within seven days after the foreclosure sale, the association shall send an additional written notice to the holder of the first mortgage or deed of trust of record as provided in § 34-36.1-3.16(b)(4) by certified mail, return receipt requested, and first class mail, identifying the name of the highest bidder and the amount of the bid. § 34-36.1-3.21(a)(4).
Interest, Fees & Costs: The association has the power to impose charges for late payment of assessments, and fines for violation of rules. § 34-36.1-3.02(a)(11). Past-due assessments bear interest at a rate established by the association, not to exceed 21% per year. § 34-36.1-3.15(b)(1). A judgment or decree in any action to enforce this section must provide costs and reasonable attorney fees for the prevailing party. § 34-36.1-3.16(g). The unit owner is liable for all reasonable expenses, including attorney fees, incurred by the association in collecting delinquent assessments, and any payments for taxes or on superior liens, paid by the association to protect its lien. § 34-36.1-3.16(i).
Scope of Lien: The association has a lien for unpaid assessments, including fees, charges, late charges, fines, interest, collection expenses, and sums expended by the association for taxes or superior liens in order to protect their lien. If the assessment is due in installments, the full amount is a lien from the time the first assessment becomes due. § 34-36.1-3.16(a), (i).
Ability to Contest Lien: Not specified.
Lien Extinguished: A lien for unpaid assessments is extinguished if enforcement proceedings are not instituted within six years after the full amount of the assessment became due. § 34-36.1-3.16(e).
Explicit Right of Redemption: Any foreclosure sale held by the association is subject to a thirty day right of redemption running in favor of the holder of the first mortgage or deed of trust of record. This right must be exercised by paying the full amount of assessments due together with all attorney fees and costs incurred by the association in connection with the collection and foreclosure process within thirty days of the date of the post-foreclosure sale notice sent by the association. Otherwise, the right of redemption terminates thirty days from the date of the post-foreclosure sale notice. § 34-36.1-3.21(c).

SOUTH CAROLINA

S.C. Code Ann. §§ 27-31-10 to 27-31-440 (Horizontal Property Act)

Method of Foreclosure: The lien may be foreclosed by suit, like a mortgage of real property. § 27-31-210(a).
Notices: Not specified.
Interest, Fees & Costs: Not specified.
Scope of Lien: The association has a lien for unpaid common expense assessments. § 27-31-210(a).
Ability to Contest Lien: Not specified.
Lien Extinguished: Not specified.
Explicit Right of Redemption: Not specified.

SOUTH DAKOTA

S.D. Codified Laws §§ 43-15A-1 to 43-15A-30 (Condominiums)

Method of Foreclosure: Not specified.
Notices: Not specified.
Interest, Fees & Costs: Not specified.
Scope of Lien: Not specified.
Ability to Contest Lien: Not specified.
Lien Extinguished: Not specified.
Explicit Right of Redemption: Not specified.

TENNESSEE

Tenn. Code Ann. §§ 66-27-201 to 66-27-507 (Tennessee Condominium Act of 2008)

Applicability: The Tennessee Condominium Act of 2008 (Tenn. Code Ann. §§ 66-27-201 to 66-27-507) replaces the Horizontal Property Act (Tenn. Code Ann. §§ 66-27-101 to 66-27-123) and applies to all condominiums created after January 1, 2009. The provisions of the Act summarized below also apply to condominiums created before 2009, but only with respect to events and circumstances arising after January 1, 2009.
Method of Foreclosure: The lien may be foreclosed by judicial action or in like manner as a deed of trust with power of sale after giving the required notices. § 66-27-415(a)(1). *See also* § 35-5-101.
Notices: Within seven days after receipt of a written request, the association must provide the unit owner, or holder of any mortgage or deed of trust encumbering such unit, a written statement of the amount due. § 66-27-415(h).
Interest, Fees & Costs: The association has the power to impose charges for late payment of assessments and levy reasonable fines for violations of rules. § 66-27-402(11). A judgment or decree in a foreclosure action must include costs and reasonable attorney fees for the prevailing party. § 66-27-415(g).
Scope of Lien: The association has a lien on a unit for any assessment levied against that unit or fines imposed against its unit owner from the time the assessment or fine becomes due. § 66-27-415(a)(1). Unless the declaration provides otherwise, fees, charges, late charges, and interest are enforceable as assessments. If an assessment is payable in installments, the full amount of the assessment is a lien from the time the first installment becomes due. § 66-27-415(a)(1)(D).
Ability to Contest Lien: Not specified.
Lien Extinguished: A lien for unpaid assessments is extinguished if enforcement proceedings are not instituted within six years after the date the lien for the assessment becomes effective. § 66-27-415(e).
Explicit Right of Redemption: Not specified.

TEXAS

Tex. Prop. Code Ann. §§ 82.001 to 82.164 (Vernon) (Uniform Condominium Act); Tex. Prop. Code Ann. §§ 81.001 to 81.210 (Vernon) (Condominium Act)

Applicability: The Uniform Condominium Act, Tex. Prop. Code Ann. §§ 82.001 to 82.164, applies to condominiums created after January 1, 1994. The provisions of the Uniform Condominium Act summarized below also apply to condominiums created before 1994. § 82.002.
Method of Foreclosure: The lien may be foreclosed judicially or by power of sale, like a real estate mortgage. § 82.113(d), (e). *See also* § 51.002.
Notices: Not specified.
Interest, Fees & Costs: The association has power to impose interest and late payment charges for late payment of assessments, returned check fees, and fines for violation of rules, and to adopt rules for the collection of delinquent assessments. § 82.102(a)(12), (13).
Scope of Lien: The association has a lien on the unit, and on rents and insurance proceeds "relating to" the unit, for assessments, which include regular and special assessments, dues, fees, charges, interest, late fees, fines, collection costs, attorney fees, and any other amount due to the association by the unit owner or levied against the unit by the association. § 82.113(a). The association may not, however, foreclose a lien for assessments consisting solely of fines. § 82.113(e). If, on January 1, 1994, a unit is the homestead of the unit owner and is subject to a declaration that does not contain a valid assessment lien against the unit, the lien provided by this section does not attach against the unit until the unit ceases to be the homestead of the person owning it on January 1, 1994. § 82.113(k).
Ability to Contest Lien: Not specified.
Lien Extinguished: Not specified.
Explicit Right of Redemption: At any time before a non-judicial foreclosure sale, the owner may avoid foreclosure by paying all amounts due the association. § 82.113(j). If the association purchases the unit at the foreclosure sale, the former owner may redeem within ninety days, by paying all amounts due the association at the time of the foreclosure sale, interest from the date of foreclosure sale to the date of redemption at the rate provided by the declaration for delinquent assessments, reasonable attorney fees and costs incurred by the association in foreclosing the lien, any assessment levied against the unit by the association after the foreclosure sale, and any reasonable cost incurred by the association as owner of the unit, including costs of maintenance and leasing. During the ninety-day redemption period, the association may not transfer the unit to anyone other than a redeeming owner. § 82.113(g).

UTAH

Utah Code Ann. §§ 57-8-1 to 57-8-38 (Condominium Ownership Act)

Method of Foreclosure: The lien may be foreclosed by sale or judicial foreclosure, like a mortgage or deed of trust, or in any other manner permitted by law. § 57-8-20(4)(b).
Notices: Management committee must record notice of lien. § 57-8-20(4)(a). Within ten days after written request, the committee must provide the unit owner with a statement of unpaid assessments. The association may charge up to $10 for this statement. § 57-8-20(7).
Interest, Fees & Costs: In a foreclosure, the unit owner is liable for costs and expenses, including reasonable attorney fees. § 57-8-20(2).
Scope of Lien: The committee has a lien for unpaid assessments, including costs of collection and reasonable attorney fees, whether or not suit is brought. § 57-8-20(2).
Ability to Contest Lien: Limited. The Act provides for notice and a hearing if the association seeks to terminate utilities or access to recreational facilities for failure to pay assessments. § 57-8-20(5).
Lien Extinguished: Not specified.
Explicit Right of Redemption: Not specified.

VERMONT

Vt. Stat. Ann. tit. 27A, §§ 1-101 to 4-120 (Uniform Common Interest Ownership Act); Vt. Stat. Ann. tit. 27, §§ 1301 to 1365 (Condominium Ownership Act)

Applicability: The Uniform Common Interest Ownership Act, Vt.

Stat. Ann. tit. 27A, §§ 1-101 to 4-120, applies to condominiums created after the Act's effective date, January 1, 1999. Communities with twenty-four or fewer units or annual assessments of less than $300 are not subject to all of the Act's provisions. §§ 1-203, 1-204. With limited exception (*see, e.g.*, § 3-115(b) regarding interest rate) the provisions of the Uniform Common Interest Ownership Act summarized below apply to condominiums created before the effective date.
Method of Foreclosure: The lien may be foreclosed pursuant to title 12, § 4531a (power of sale foreclosure of real estate mortgages). Title 27A, § 3-116(i).
Notices: Within ten business days after receipt of a written request, the association must provide the unit owner with a recordable statement of the amount due. Title 27A, § 3-116(h).
Interest, Fees & Costs: The association has the power to impose charges for late payment of assessments, and fines for violation of rules. Title 27A, § 3-102(a)(11). Past-due assessments bear interest at a rate set by the association, not to exceed the legal rate. Title 276A, § 3-115(b). A judgment or decree in any action brought under any provision of this section must include costs and reasonable attorney fees for the prevailing party. Title 27A, § 3-116(g).
Scope of Lien: The association has a lien for unpaid assessments, including fees, charges, late charges, fines and interest. If an assessment is payable in installments, the full amount is a lien from the time the first assessment becomes due. Title 27A, § 3-116(a).
Ability to Contest Lien: Not specified.
Lien Extinguished: A lien for unpaid assessments is extinguished if enforcement proceedings are not begun within three years after the full amount of the assessment becomes due. Title 27A, § 3-116(e).
Explicit Right of Redemption: Not specified.

VIRGIN ISLANDS

V.I. Code Ann. tit. 28, §§ 901 to 927 (Condominium Act)

Method of Foreclosure: The lien may be foreclosed by suit, like a mortgage of real property. § 922(a).
Notices: Not specified.
Interest, Fees & Costs: Not specified.
Scope of Lien: The association has a lien for unpaid common expense assessments. § 922(a).
Ability to Contest Lien: Not specified.
Lien Extinguished: Not specified.
Explicit Right of Redemption: Not specified.

VIRGINIA

Va. Code Ann. §§ 55-79.39 to 55-79.103 (Condominium Act); Va. Code Ann. §§ 55-79.1 to 55-79.38 (Horizontal Property Act)

Applicability: The Condominium Act (Va. Code. Ann. §§ 55-79.39 to 55-79.103) supersedes the Horizontal Property Act (Va. Code Ann. §§ 55-79.1 to 55-79.38) and applies to all condominiums established after July 1, 1974.
Method of Foreclosure: The association may foreclose by a non-judicial foreclosure sale, after giving the required notices. The statute prescribes detailed requirements for notice and the conduct of the sale. § 55-79.84(I).
Notices: Lien is perfected by recording memorandum of lien within ninety days from the time the assessment becomes due. The memorandum must include a description of the property, the name of the owner, the amount due, and the date of issuance of the memorandum. § 55-79.84(B), (C). Before advertising a foreclosure sale, the association must give the owner notice of the amount owed for the perfected lien, the action required to satisfy the debt, a date not less than sixty days from the date of notice by which the debt must be satisfied, a warning that if the debt is not satisfied, the unit must be sold, and notice of the owner's right to bring a court action to challenge the debt. § 55-79.84(I)(1). After the expiration of the sixty days, the association must record the name of the trustee appointed to carry out the sale. § 55-79.84(2). The association must give notice by certified or registered mail, at least fourteen days before the proposed sale, of the time and place of the sale, to the unit owner and any lienholder or assignee whose interest was recorded at least thirty days before the proposed sale. § 55-79.84(I)(4). The statute provides standards for newspaper advertisement. Failure to comply with these requirements will render the sale, upon petition, voidable by a court. § 55-79.84(I)(5) to (7). A unit owner, or a prospective purchaser who has entered into a contract, is entitled to a recordable statement from the association of the amount due. Failure to provide this statement within ten business days of a written request will extinguish the lien. The association may charge $10 for this statement. § 55-79.84(H).
Interest, Fees & Costs: In any action brought pursuant to this section, the judgment or decree shall include costs and reasonable attorney fees. If the association prevails, it is entitled to interest at the judgment rate from the time each sum became due. § 55-79.84(E).
Scope of Lien: The association has a lien for unpaid assessments. § 55-79.84(A).
Ability to Contest Lien: The unit owner may bring a court action in circuit court to assert the non-existence of the debt, or any other defense to the sale. § 55-79.84(I)(1).
Lien Extinguished: The lien is extinguished if action to enforce is not brought within thirty-six months from the recording of the lien. § 55-79.84(D).
Explicit Right of Redemption: The unit owner may prevent the sale by paying, before the date of the sale, the sum secured by the lien, plus all costs and expenses incurred in perfecting and enforcing the lien, including but not limited to advertising costs and reasonable attorney fees. § 55-79.84(I)(3).

WASHINGTON

Wash. Rev. Code §§ 64.34.010 to 64.34.950 (Condominium Act); Wash. Rev. Code §§ 64.32.010 to 64.32.920 (Horizontal Property Regimes Act)

Applicability: The Condominium Act, Wash. Rev. Code Ann. §§ 64.34.010 to 65.34.950, applies to condominiums created after July 1, 1990. The sections of the Condominium Act summarized below also apply to condominiums created before the effective date. § 64.34.010.
Method of Foreclosure: The lien may be enforced judicially or by non-judicial sale if the declaration provides a power of sale. § 64.34.364(9).
Notices: Within fifteen days of a written request, the association must provide the unit owner or mortgagee with a statement of the amount due on the unit. § 64.34.364(15).

Interest, Fees & Costs: The association has the power to impose charges for late payments of assessments, and fines for violation of rules. §§ 64.34.304(1)(k), 64.34.364(13). Delinquent assessments bear interest at a rate set by the association, or if no rate is set, at the maximum rate permitted by § 19.52.020. § 64.34.360(2). The association is entitled to costs and reasonable attorney fees incurred for collection of delinquent assessments, whether or not a suit is commenced or prosecuted to judgment. The association is entitled to appellate costs and attorney fees if it prevails. § 64.34.364(14).
Scope of Lien: The association has a lien for unpaid assessments from the time they come due. § 64.34.364(1).
Ability to Contest Lien: Not specified.
Lien Extinguished: The lien, and the personal liability it secures, is extinguished if proceedings to enforce the lien or collect the debt are not brought within three years after the assessment became due. § 64.34.364(8).
Explicit Right of Redemption: Not specified.

WEST VIRGINIA

W. Va. Code §§ 36B-1-101 to 36B-4-120 (Uniform Common Ownership Interest Act); W. Va. Code §§ 36A-1-1 to 36A-8-3 (Condominiums and Unit Property Act)

Applicability: The Uniform Common Ownership Interest Act, W. Va. Code §§ 36B-1-101 to 36B-4-120, applies to condominiums created after the effective date (1986). With limited exception (§ 36B-3-115(b) regarding interest rate) the provisions of the Uniform Common Interest Ownership Act summarized below apply to condominiums created before the effective date. § 36B-1-204.
Method of Foreclosure: Not specified.
Notices: To perfect its lien, the association must give notice to the unit owner, by registered or certified mail, return receipt requested, or as provided in § 56-2-1 (pleading and practice—service of notices), and must record a notice of lien, including a description of the unit, the owner's name, the amount due, and the date of recording. § 36B-3-116(h). Within ten business days of a written request, the association must provide the unit owner with a recordable statement of the amount due on the unit. § 36B-3-116(g).
Interest, Fees & Costs: The association may impose charges for late payment of assessments, or fines for violations of rules. § 36B-3-102(a)(11). Past-due assessments bear interest at the rate set by the association, not to exceed 18% per year. § 36B-3-115(b). A judgment or decree in any action brought under this section must include costs and reasonable attorney fees for the prevailing party. § 36B-3-116(f).
Scope of Lien: The association has a lien for assessments, including fees, charges, late charges, fines and interest, from the time the assessment becomes due. If the assessment is due in installments, the entire amount is a lien from the time the first installment is due. § 36B-3-116(a).
Ability to Contest Lien: Not specified.
Lien Extinguished: A lien for unpaid assessments is extinguished if enforcement proceedings are not begun within three years after the full amount of the assessments became due. § 36B-3-116(d).
Explicit Right of Redemption: Not specified.

WISCONSIN

Wis. Stat. §§ 703.01 to 703.38 (Condominium Ownership Act)

Method of Foreclosure: The lien may be enforced and foreclosed like a mortgage of real property. § 703.165(7).
Notices: The association must record a notice of lien within two years after the assessment becomes due, including a description of the unit, the name of the owner, the amount due, and the period for which it is due. § 703.165(3), (8). Before initiating a foreclosure action, the association must give the owner ten days notice, by registered mail, return receipt requested. § 703.165(7). Within ten business days after a written request, a grantee is entitled to a statement from the association of the amount due for the unit. Failure to provide this statement will extinguish any lien that has not been recorded. § 703.165(4).
Interest, Fees & Costs: Unpaid assessments bear interest at a rate set by the association, not to exceed the maximum rate permitted by law. § 703.165(6).
Scope of Lien: Unpaid assessments for common expenses or fines, plus interest and actual costs of collection, are a lien against the unit from the time the assessments become due if a statement of condominium lien is recorded within two years after the due date. § 703.165(3).
Ability to Contest Lien: Not specified.
Lien Extinguished: Action must be brought within three years after recording of condominium lien. § 703.165(7).
Explicit Right of Redemption: Not specified.

WYOMING

Wyo. Stat. Ann. §§ 34-20-101 to 34-20-104 (Condominium Ownership)

Method of Foreclosure: Not specified.
Notices: Not specified.
Interest, Fees & Costs: Not specified.
Scope of Lien: Not specified.
Ability to Contest Lien: Not specified.
Lien Extinguished: Not specified.
Explicit Right of Redemption: Not specified.

Appendix H Sample Foreclosure Prevention Counseling Forms and Practice Aids

This appendix contains sample forms that can be adapted for use by attorneys or housing advocates seeking to assist borrowers in default on their mortgage. Some of these forms were developed for non-lawyer housing counselors, but may be used by others to evaluate whether a homeowner has the long-term financial wherewithal to retain a home when legal defenses are raised. The other forms included in this appendix are samples of common mortgage-related documents.

Section H.1 of this appendix contains sample foreclosure prevention counseling forms:

Form 1: Sample Foreclosure Prevention Intake Form

Form 1 is designed to be filled in by an advocate or intake worker based on information supplied by the client. The form provides a complete overview of a homeowner's finances in order to help an advocate determine what foreclosure prevention strategies are possible.

Form 2: Sample Authorization to Release Information

In order to present a client's full range of foreclosure prevention options, an advocate generally must obtain information about the amount of money the loan servicer claims is due. Due to valid privacy concerns for borrowers, very few servicers will release information to an advocate without written authorization from the borrower. Form 2 is a sample client authorization form. This form should be sent by facsimile to the loan servicer with Form 3 requesting the necessary information.

Form 3: Information Request for Loan Servicer

Form 3 is a sample form that is useful for obtaining necessary information from a loan servicer about the status of a client's loan. The information provided on this form helps determine the amounts that the servicer believes are needed to cure or pay-off the loan. In some cases, obtaining this information will crystallize a dispute the borrower may have concerning the amount due on the loan. Many potential issues about amounts that may be improperly claimed due by a loan servicer are addressed in Chapter 6, *supra*.

Form 4: Sample Loan Modification Forms

The forms included in this section are sample loan modification agreements used by the industry, including Fannie Mae and Freddie Mac. Although these are copies of forms that are currently used, the industry is constantly revising and updating these documents. Advocates should check Fannie Mae and Freddie Mac's servicing guidelines or other industry publications for the latest versions.

Section H.2 of this appendix contains sample qualified written requests:

Form 5: Sample Qualified Written Request Under RESPA

Form 5 is a sample "qualified written request" for information under the Real Estate Settlement Procedures Act (RESPA). A section of RESPA, 12 U.S.C. § 2605, provides a procedure and a remedy to obtain information from a loan servicer that fails to provide it under a more informal request. This form is an example of a "qualified written request" that meets the requirements of the law. For more information, see Ch. 2, § 8.2.2, *supra*. Form 5 is a sample "qualified written request" that is designed for use directly by consumer borrowers. For sample qualified written requests which may be used by attorneys representing borrowers see Forms 6 and 7 below.

Forms 6 and 7: Sample Qualified Written Requests Under RESPA for Use by Attorneys

The forms included in this section are sample "qualified written requests" that are designed for use directly by attorneys representing borrowers. Form 7 is a qualified written request that can be sent after a client has filed for bankruptcy.

Section H.3 of this appendix contains sample mortgage and servicing forms:

Form 8: Sample Mortgage

Forms 8 is a sample mortgage that is based on the Uniform Instruments provided by Fannie Mae and Freddie Mac for the origination of single-family residential mortgage loans in all States and U.S. Territories. State specific versions of the Fannie Mae/Freddie Mac mortgages and deeds of trusts are available at www.freddiemac.com/uniform/.

Form 9: Sample Promissory Note-Fixed Rate Mortgage

Form 9 is Fannie Mae and Freddie Mac's uniform multistate promissory note for fixed-rate loans. State specific versions of the promissory note is available at www.freddiemac.com/uniform/.

Form 10: Sample Promissory Note-Adjustable Rate Mortgage

Form 10 is Fannie Mae and Freddie Mac's uniform multistate promissory note for adjustable rate loans using the one year Treasury Index. State specific versions of adjustable rate promissory note (using other indices) are available at www.freddiemac.com/uniform/.

Form 11: Sample Change Rate Notice for ARM

Forms 11 is a sample Change Rate Notice for an adjustable rate mortgage.

Form 12: Sample Annual Escrow Account Statement

Forms 12 is a sample Annual Escrow Account Statement as required under RESPA, 12 U.S.C. § 2605. See §§ 8.3.3.2, *supra* for a discussion of this form.

Form 13: Sample Notice As to Change of Servicer

Forms 13 is a sample Notice as to Change of Servicer as required under RESPA, 12 U.S.C. § 2605. See §§ 8.2.3, *supra* for a discussion of this form.

H.1 Sample Foreclosure Prevention Counseling Forms

H.1.1 Sample Foreclosure Prevention Intake Form

I. CLIENT INFORMATION

Date:________

Name(s)

Address

Home Phone
Work Phone
Best Times to Reach
Marital Status
Spouse (if any)
Children (names and ages)

Others in Household:

II. INFORMATION ABOUT HOME BEING FORECLOSED

Address of Property If Different from Above	
Names of all Co-owners w/ Address if Different	
Year Purchased	
Original Purchase Price	
Estimate of Current Value	
Number of Rooms	
Owner Occupant?	At purchase? Yes___ No___ Now? Yes___ No___
Multi-Family Home?	Yes___ No ___ Name of tenants Rent received
Condition	Exc____ Good___ Fair___ Poor___
Major repairs needed	Describe
Number of Mortgages	
Other Liens	

Notes:

III. MORTGAGE INFORMATION

Part 1

Information on Delinquent Mortgage (some info may be filled in after initial client interview when records are obtained):

Type of Mortgage	Purchase Money ____ Refinance ___ Home Equity Loan ___ Debt Consolidation ___ Other ___
Year of Mortgage	
Original Amount	
Has client brought original loan papers	Yes ___ No ___
Current Lender or Servicer	
Address of Current Lender or Servicer Phone: Fax: Contact Person	
Loan Account Number	
Investor/Insurer	HUD Insured ___ VA ___ FmHA/RHS ___ Fannie Mae ___ Freddie Mac ___ PMI ______________________ Other
Term of mortgage (in months)	
Interest Rate	
Principal and Interest Payment (monthly)	
Tax and Insurance Payment (monthly)	
Total Monthly Payment	
Months Behind	
Total arrears including costs	
Current Principal Balance	

Pay-off Amount	

Reason for Default:

Client's Statement of Objectives and Plan:

Notes:

Part 2

Other Mortgages and Liens:

Yes___ No___

Describe:

Is Client In Default?/ Status/Amount of Monthly Payment:

IMPORTANT NOTE: If there are other mortgages, obtain information in Part 1 (above) for each on separate form.

IV. HOUSEHOLD FINANCIAL INFO

INCOME BUDGET FOR HOUSEHOLD				
SOURCE OF INCOME	**LAST MO. ACTUAL**	**THIS MO. EXPECTED**	**THIS MO. ACTUAL**	**ADJUSTED MONTHLY**
Employment	$	$	$	$
Overtime				
Child Support/Alimony				
Pension				
Interest				
Public Benefits				
Dividends				
Trust Payments				
Royalties				
Rents Received				
Other (List)				
TOTAL (MONTHLY)	**$**	**$**	**$**	**$**

NOTES/ANTICIPATED CHANGES:

EXPENSE BUDGET FOR HOUSEHOLD				
TYPE OF EXPENSE	**LAST MO. ACTUAL**	**THIS MO. EXPECTED**	**THIS MO. ACTUAL**	**ADJUSTED MONTHLY**
Payroll Deductions	$	$	$	$
Income Tax Withheld				
Social Security				
FICA				
Wage Garnishments				
Credit Union				
Other				
Home Related Expenses				
Mortgage or Rent				
Second Mortgage				
Third Mortgage				
Real Estate Taxes				
Insurance				
Condo Fees & Assessments				
Mobile Home Lot Rent				

Home Maintenance/Upkeep				
Utilities				
Gas				
Electric				
Oil				
Water/Sewer				
Telephone				
Other				
Food				
Clothing				
Laundry and Cleaning				
Medical				
Current Needs				
Prescriptions				
Dental				
Other				
Transportation				
Auto Payments				
Car Insurance				
Gas and Maintenance				
Public Transportation				
Life Insurance				
Alimony or Support Paid				
School Expenses				
Recreation				
Charity/Church				
Student Loan Payments				
Amounts Owed on Debts				
Credit Card				
Credit Card				
Credit Card				
Medical Bill				
Medical Bill				
Other Back Bills (List)				
Cosigned Debts				
Business Debts (List)				
Other Expenses (List)				
Miscellaneous				
TOTAL				

Other Important Debt Issues:

Wage Garnishments Pending	Yes___	No___
Court Cases Pending	Yes___	No___
Utility Shut-offs	Yes___	No___
Car Loan Defaults or Repossessions	Yes___	No___
Tax Debts	Yes___	No___
Student Loan Debts	Yes___	No___

Other:

Notes/Anticipated Changes:

Describe Assets and Other Resources:

Savings	Yes___	No___	Amount $________
Court Cases Pending Against Others	Yes___	No___	Value $________
Anticipated Tax Refunds	Yes___	No___	Amount $________
Assets Which Can Be Sold	Yes___	No___	Value $________
Pension or Retirement Funds	Yes___	No___	Value $________

Other Assets and Notes:

INCOME AND EXPENSE TOTALS

	Last Mo. Actual	This Mo. Expected	This Mo. Actual	Adjusted Expected
A. Total Projected Monthly Income				
B. Total Projected Monthly Expenses				
Excess Income or Shortfall (A minus B)				

Notes:

V. OTHER INFORMATION

1. Have client(s) made an effort to arrange a workout on their own? What result?

2. Has the client filed bankruptcy? If so when? Current status of case if still pending? If bankruptcy is over, what result?

3. Other issues which came up during interview.

4. Questions and open issues that must be resolved.

H.1.2 Sample Authorization to Release Information

TO: Handout Mortgage Co.
[Address]
Attention: Loss Mitigation Department

RE: Account No:[Account Number]
Borrowers: Sam and Sally Consumer
Prop. Address: 2321 Westmoreland Ave.
Wheeling, West Virginia 26211

AUTHORIZATION TO RELEASE INFORMATION

Dear Sir or Madam:

We are working with the Neighborhood House Counseling Service, West Virginia (a HUD certified counseling agency) on a plan to resolve our mortgage delinquency. We hereby authorize you to release any and all information concerning our account to the Neighborhood House Counseling Service at their request.

We further authorize you to discuss our case with [Counselor 1] or [Counselor 2]. They are working to help us address our financial problems and to propose a loss mitigation plan which is within your guidelines.

At present, we request that you fill out the request for loan information which accompanies this letter. Please return it to [Counselor 1] by fax ([Fax Number]) no later than Friday, February 26, 2010. You may release additional information to the Neighborhood House Counseling Service in the future without further authorization.[1]

Thank you in advance for your assistance.

Very truly yours,

Sam and Sally Consumer
[Date]
[Phone Number]

---

[1] If required by the servicer a sentence may be added which states, "This Authorization to Release Information expires ____ days for the date shown below.

H.1.3 Information Request for Loan Servicer

Borrower(s)______________________________ Loan #:__________________

Address____

Pursuant to the attached authorization by the borrower, please supply the following information about the above referenced account. The information will be used to help the borrower propose a loss mitigation plan, if possible.

Mortgage Investor:________________________Investor Loan #: _______________
Mortgage Insurance Company: ____________________________

♦ **Loan Payment Info**:

Current Interest Rate: __________%
Monthly Principal & Interest Payment: __________
Monthly Escrow payment: __________
Total Monthly Mortgage Payment: __________

♦ **Amount of Arrears:**

Due For (Earliest unpaid installment): __________
Late Charges Due: __________
Foreclosure Fees & Costs Due: __________
Other Unpaid Charges: __________

Balance In Suspense Account: __________

TOTAL ARREARS (as of ________) $_________

♦ **Total Balance Due on Loan:**

Unpaid Principal Balance: __________
Past Due Interest: __________
Unpaid Escrow: __________

TOTAL AMOUNT DUE ON LOAN (PAY-OFF) (as-of _______) $_________
Per Diem Interest: _________

Date Of Most Recent BPO / Appraisal: ____________ Value:_______
Other Comments:

FORECLOSURE STATUS:____
SALE DATE (IF SCHEDULED):____

H.1.4 Sample Loan Modification Forms

Below are samples of loan modification agreements used by the industry including agreements used by Fannie Mae, Freddie Mac and the FDIC. Although these are copies of forms that are currently used, the industry is constantly revising and updating these documents. Attorneys should check Fannie Mae and Freddie Mac servicing guidelines or other industry publications for the latest version.

H.1.4.1 Fannie Mae Loan Modification Agreement

FannieMae.

Date	
Fannie Mae Loan Number	FHA/VA/MI Case Number
Mortgagor (or Trustor)	
Property Address	

Agreement for Modification or Extension of a Mortgage

The Mortgagor (or Trustor) identified above (hereinafter referred to as the "Mortgagor") does hereby apply for ________________________ of the payment provisions of the above-referenced mortgage loan ("Modification" or "Extension") covering an indebtedness owing from the Mortgagor to Fannie Mae (hereinafter referred to as "Mortgagee"), evidenced by a note (or bond) and secured by a real property mortgage or trust deed (said note or bond and real property mortgage or trust deed are hereinafter referred to as the "Mortgage"), and the Mortgagor represents and agrees as follows:

(1) Mortgagor is now the owner and holder of the real property encumbered by said Mortgage, recorded in the public records in the County of ____________________, State of ________________, in book ________, page ________, or document or file number ________________.

(2) Under the terms of said Mortgage, there remains unpaid as of the first day of the month in which this Agreement is made, the sum of $ ________________ of principal, $ ________________ of interest thereon, $ ________________ of advances made by the Mortgagee thereunder, and $ ________________ of interest on such advances, aggregating a total sum of $ ________________ for which amount the Mortgagor is indebted to the Mortgagee under said Mortgage, which is a valid lien.

(3) Mortgagor hereby deposits with the Mortgagee, if such deposit is required by the Mortgagee, the sum of $ ________________, which is to be applied to the present balance due on the principal of said Mortgage (including advances, if any), and the sum of $ ________________, which is to be applied to the delinquent interest due on the said principal (and advances, if any), with the application of said deposited amounts to be made as of the effective date of this Agreement. If the modification or extension is not agreed to by Mortgagee, said deposited amounts shall be returned to Mortgagor.

(4) Mortgagor agrees the terms of said Mortgage are modified or extended relative to the payment of the said indebtedness by providing for payment of the balance of the principal, including any unpaid interest due thereon (after the aforementioned deposits, if any, have been applied thereto) as follows: Said total balance of $ ________________ is to be paid, plus interest on the unpaid balance at a rate of ________% per annum (with such rate changing periodically if required by the provisions of the mortgage note), in equal monthly installments of $ ________________ (excluding the sums required to be deposited for the payment of insurance. taxes. etc.). The first of said installments shall become due and payable on the ________ day of ____________________, ________, and the remaining installments, as they may be changed periodically if required by the provisions of the mortgage note, successively on the ______ day of each and every month thereafter, until said mortgage indebtedness is fully paid, except that, if not sooner paid, the final payment of principal and interest shall be due and payable on the ________ day of ____________________, ________, which is the present or extended maturity date.

(5) Mortgagor agrees to make the payments as specified in Paragraph (4) hereof and understands and agrees that:
(a) All the rights and remedies, stipulations, and conditions contained in said Mortgage relating to default in the making of payments under the Mortgage shall also apply to default in the making of said modified payments hereunder.
(b) All covenants, agreements, stipulations, and conditions in said Mortgage shall be and remain in full force and effect, except as herein modified, and none of the Mortgagor's obligations or liabilities under said Mortgage shall be diminished or released by any provisions hereof, nor shall this Agreement in any way impair, diminish, or affect any of the Mortgagee's rights under or remedies on the Mortgage, whether such rights or remedies arise thereunder or by operation of law. Also, all rights of recourse to which the Mortgagee is presently entitled against any property or any other persons in any way obligated for, or liable on, the Mortgage are expressly reserved by the Mortgagee.

(c) All costs and expenses incurred by Mortgagee in connection with this Agreement, including recording fees, title examination, and attorney's fees, shall be paid by the Mortgagor and shall be secured by said Mortgage, unless stipulated otherwise by Mortgagee.
(d) Mortgagee agrees to make and execute such other documents or papers as may be necessary or required to effectuate the terms and conditions of this Agreement which, if approved and accepted by Mortgagee, shall bind and inure to the heirs, executors, administrators, and assigns of the Mortgagor.

(6) For the purposes of inducing and influencing the Mortgagee to execute this Agreement, the undersigned Mortgagor represents of his or her own knowledge that the names of all owners or other persons having an interest in the mortgaged property are as follows:

Name

____________________ ____________________

____________________ ____________________

All such persons identified above are of legal age, and none is under any legal disability, except as follows:

____________________ ____________________

____________________ ____________________

* Witnessed by:	Executed by:
____________(SEAL) (Witness)	____________(SEAL) (Mortgagor)
____________(SEAL) (Witness)	____________(SEAL) (Mortgagor)

*ACKNOWLEDGMENT
The undersigned, being obligated for the payment of the above-described Mortgage indebtedness, hereby consents to the execution of this Agreement between the Mortgagor therein described and the Mortgagee, and further consents to any modification or extension of the Mortgage under said Agreement.

* Witnessed by:	Executed by:
____________(SEAL) (Witness)	____________(SEAL) (Mortgagor)
____________(SEAL) (Witness)	____________(SEAL) (Mortgagor)

AGREED TO BY:

(Mortgage Servicer)	(Mortgagee of Record)
(Authorized Representative)	(Authorized Representative)
(Date)	(Date)

* The execution of this Agreement should be witnessed and the appropriate acknowledgement clause should be added, if these are requirements under local law. In addition, if required under local law or practice, this Agreement should be filed for record.

H.1.4.2 Freddie Mac Loan Modification Agreement

Loan #: _______________

This document was prepared by:

____

After recording please return to:

____

THIS MODIFICATION IS TO BE EXECUTED IN DUPLICATE ORIGINALS. ONE ORIGINAL IS TO BE AFFIXED TO THE ORIGINAL NOTE AND ONE ORIGINAL IS TO BE RECORDED IN THE LAND RECORDS WHERE THE SECURITY INSTRUMENT IS RECORDED.

LOAN MODIFICATION AGREEMENT

This Loan Modification Agreement ("Modification"), is effective _______, 20__, between _______________ ("Borrower") and _______________ ("Lender"), and amends and supplements (1) the Note (the "Note") made by the Borrower, dated _______ , 20__, in the original principal sum of U.S. $_____, and (2) the Mortgage, Deed of Trust or Deed to Secure Debt (the "Security Instrument"), recorded on ________ , 20__ as Document No. _______ in Book or Liber _____, at page(s) _____ , of the _______________ Records of__________ [County and state, or other jurisdiction]. The Security Instrument, which was entered into as security for the performance of the Note, encumbers the real and personal property described in the Security Instrument (and defined in the Security Instrument as the "Property"), which is located at _______________ .

That real property is described as follows:

The Borrower has requested that the Lender modify the terms of the Note and Security Instrument. The Lender has agreed to do so pursuant to the terms and conditions stated in this Modification. In consideration of the agreements made in this Modification, and other good and valuable consideration which the parties agree they have received, the Borrower and Lender agree to modify the terms of the Note and Security Instrument as follows. The Borrower and the Lender agree that the provisions of this Modification supersede and replace any inconsistent provisions set forth in the Note and Security Instrument.

1. The Borrower represents that the Borrower __ is, __ is not, the occupant of the Property.

2. The Borrower acknowledges that interest has accrued but not been paid and the Lender has incurred, paid or otherwise advanced taxes, insurance premiums and other expenses necessary to protect or enforce its interest in the Note and the Security Instrument, and that such interest, costs and expenses, in the total amount of $_______, have been added to the indebtedness under the terms of the Note and Security Instrument. As of ________, 20__, the amount, including such amounts which have been added to the indebtedness (if any), payable under the Note and Security Instrument (the "Unpaid Principal Balance") is U.S. $ ________.

3. The Borrower promises to pay the Unpaid Principal Balance, plus interest, to the order of the Lender, until the Unpaid Principal Balance has been paid. Interest will be charged on the Unpaid Principal Balance at the yearly rate of __ %, beginning ________, 20__. The Borrower promises to make monthly payments of principal and interest of U.S. $________, beginning on the __ day of _________, 20__, and continuing thereafter on the same day of each succeeding month. If on _________ , 20__ (the "Modified Maturity Date"), the Borrower still owes amounts under the Note and the Security Instrument, as amended by this Modification, the Borrower will pay these amounts in full on the Modified Maturity Date. The Borrower will make such payments at ___________ _______________ or at such other place as the Lender may require.

4. Except to the extent that they are modified by this Modification, the Borrower will comply with all of the covenants, agreements, and requirements of the Note and the Security Instrument, including without limitation, the Borrower's covenants and agreements to make all payments of taxes, insurance premiums, assessments, escrow items, impounds, and all other payments that the Borrower is obligated to make under the Security Instrument.

5. Nothing in this Modification shall be understood or construed to be a satisfaction or release in whole or in part of the Note and Security Instrument. Except as otherwise specifically provided in this Modification, the Note and Security Instrument will remain unchanged and in full effect, and the Borrower and Lender will be bound by, and comply with, all of the terms and provisions thereof, as amended by this Modification.

6. If one or more riders are executed by the Borrower and recorded together with this Modification, the covenants and agreements of each such rider shall be incorporated into and shall amend and supplement the covenants and agreements of this Modification as if the rider(s) were a part of this Modification. [Check applicable box(es)]

7. If one or more riders are executed by the Borrower and recorded together with this Modification, the covenants and agreements of each such rider shall be incorporated into and shall amend and supplement the covenants and agreements of this Modification as if the rider(s) were a part of this Modification. [Check applicable box(es)]

[ ] 1–4 Family Rider—Assignment of Rents
[ ] Modification Due on Transfer Rider
[ ] Bankruptcy Rider
[ ] Other Rider

[To be signed by all Borrowers, endorsers, guarantors, sureties, and other parties signing the Note or Security Instrument].

__________ ______________________________ (Seal)
Date - Borrower

__________ ______________________________ (Seal)
Date - Borrower

__________ ______________________________ (Seal)
Date - Borrower

_______________________ (Seal)
Date _______________ - Borrower

____
Date _______________ - Lender

By: _______________

[Space Below This Line for Acknowledgment in Accordance with Laws of Jurisdiction]

MULTISTATE DELINQUENT LOAN MODIFICATION—Single-Family

H.1.4.3 Sample Modification Due on Transfer Rider

Modification Due on Transfer Rider

THIS MODIFICATION DUE ON TRANSFER RIDER, effective the _____ day of __________, 20__, is incorporated into and shall be deemed to amend and supplement the Loan Modification Agreement of the same date made by __________ (the "Borrower") and __________ (the "Lender") covering the Property described in the Loan Modification Agreement located at:

____

____

In addition to the covenants and agreements made in the Loan Modification Agreement, the Borrower and Lender covenant and agree as follows:

A. Notwithstanding any other covenant, agreement or provision of the Note and Security Instrument, as defined in the Loan Modification Agreement, the Borrower agrees as follows:

Transfer of the Property or a Beneficial Interest in Borrower. If all or any part of the Property or any interest in it is sold or transferred (or if a beneficial interest in Borrower is sold or transferred and Borrower is not a natural person) without Lender's prior written consent, Lender may, at its option, require immediate payment-in-full of all sums secured by the Security Instrument. However, this option shall not be exercised by Lender if exercise is prohibited by federal law as of the date of the Loan Modification Agreement.

If Lender exercises this option, Lender shall give Borrower notice of acceleration. The notice shall provide a period of not less than 30 days from the date the notice is delivered or mailed within which Borrower must pay all sums secured by the Security Instrument. If Borrower fails to pay these sums prior to the expiration of this period, Lender may invoke any remedies permitted by the Security Instrument without further notice or demand on Borrower.

B. Except as otherwise specifically provided in this Modification Due On Transfer Rider, the Loan Modification Agreement, the Note and Security Instrument will remain unchanged and in full effect.

_______________ _______________________ (Seal)
Date - Borrower

_______________ _______________________ (Seal)
Date - Borrower

_______________ [Name of Lender]
Date By: _______________________

H.1.4.4 Sample Modification Bankruptcy Disclosure Rider

Modification Bankruptcy Disclosure Rider

THIS MODIFICATION BANKRUPTCY RIDER, effective the _____ day of __________, 20__, is incorporated into and shall be deemed to amend and supplement the Loan Modification Agreement of the same date made by __________ (the "Borrower") and __________ (the "Lender") covering the property described in the Loan Modification Agreement located at: __________.

In addition to the covenants and agreements made in the Loan Modification Agreement, the Borrower and Lender covenant and agree as follows:

Borrower represents that Borrower was discharged in a Chapter 7 bankruptcy proceeding subsequent to the execution of the Note and Security Instrument. Borrower and Lender acknowledge and agree that the Loan Modification Agreement does not affect the discharge of the Borrower's personal liability on the debt.

_______________ _______________ -Seal Borrower
Date

_______________ _______________ -Seal Borrower
Date

_______________ By: _______________
Date

H.1.4.5 Sample Assignment of Rents

1–4 Family Modification Agreement Rider
Assignment of Rents

THIS 1–4 FAMILY MODIFICATION AGREEMENT RIDER ASSIGNMENT OF RENTS ("1–4 Family Rider") effective the __ day of __________, 20__, is incorporated into that certain Loan Modification Agreement (the "Modification") of the same date made by __________ (the "Borrower") and is incorporated into and amends and supplements the Security Instrument executed by Borrower to secure the Note. The Security Instrument covers the Property as defined and described in the Security Instrument and located at:

____
[Property Address]

1–4 FAMILY COVENANTS. In addition to the covenants and agreements made in the Security Instrument, Borrower and Lender further covenant and agree as follows:

A. ADDITIONAL PROPERTY SUBJECT TO THE SECURITY INSTRUMENT. In addition to the Property described in the Security Instrument, the following items are added to the Property description, and shall also constitute the Property covered by the Security Instrument: building materials, appliances and goods of every nature whatsoever now or hereafter located in, on, or used, or intended to be used in connection with the Property, including, but not limited to, those for the purposes of supplying or distributing heating, cooling, electricity, gas, water, air and light, fire prevention and extinguishing apparatus, security and access control apparatus, plumbing, bath tubs, water heaters, water closets, sinks, ranges, stoves, refrigerators, dishwashers, disposals, washers, dryers, awnings, storm windows, storm doors, screens, blinds, shades, curtains and curtain rods, attached mirrors, cabinets, paneling and attached floor coverings now or hereafter attached to the Property, all of which, including replacements and additions thereto, shall be deemed to be and remain a part of the Property covered by the Security Instrument. All of the foregoing together with the Property described in the Security Instrument (or the leasehold estate if the Security Instrument is on a leasehold) are referred to in this 1–4 Family Rider and the Security Instrument as the "Property."

B. USE OF PROPERTY; COMPLIANCE WITH LAW. Borrower shall not seek, agree to or make a change in the use of the Property or its zoning classification, unless Lender has agreed in writing to the change. Borrower shall comply with all laws, ordinances, regulations and requirements of any governmental body applicable to the Property.

C. SUBORDINATE LIENS. Except as permitted by federal law, Borrower shall not allow any lien inferior to the Security Instrument to be perfected against the Property without Lender's prior written permission.

D. RENT LOSS INSURANCE. Borrower shall maintain insurance against rent loss in addition to the other hazards for which insurance is required by Uniform Covenant 5 of the Security Instrument.

E. "BORROWER'S RIGHT TO REINSTATE" DELETED. Uniform Covenant 18 of the Security Instrument is deleted.

F. BORROWER'S OCCUPANCY. Unless Lender and Borrower otherwise agree in writing, the first sentence in Uniform Covenant 6 of the Security Instrument concerning Borrower's occupancy of the Property is deleted. All remaining covenants and agreements set forth in Uniform Covenant 6 of the Security Instrument shall remain in effect.

G. ASSIGNMENT OF LEASES. Upon Lender's request, Borrower shall assign to Lender all leases of the Property and all security deposits made in connection with leases of the Property. Upon the assignment, Lender shall have the right to modify, extend or terminate the existing leases and to execute new leases, in Lender's sole discretion. As used in this paragraph G, the word "lease" shall mean "sublease" if the Security Instrument is on a leasehold.

H. ASSIGNMENT OF RENTS; APPOINTMENT OF RECEIVER; LENDER IN POSSESSION. Borrower absolutely and unconditionally assigns and transfers to Lender all the rents revenues ("Rents") of the Property, regardless of to whom the Rents of the Property are payable. Borrower authorizes Lender or Lender's agents to collect the Rents, and agrees that each tenant of the Property shall pay the Rents to Lender or Lender's agents. However, Borrower shall receive the Rents until (i) Lender has given Borrower notice of default pursuant to paragraph 21 of the Security Instrument and (ii) Lender has given notice to the tenant(s) that the Rents are to be paid to Lender or Lender's agent. This assignment of Rents constitutes an absolute assignment and not an assignment for additional security only.

If Lender gives notice of default to Borrower: (i) all Rents received by Borrower shall be held by Borrower as trustee for the benefit of Lender only, to be applied to the sums secured by the Security Instrument; (ii) Lender shall be entitled to collect and receive all of the Rents of the Property; (iii) Borrower agrees that each tenant of the Property shall pay all Rents due and unpaid to Lender or Lender's agents upon Lender's written demand to the tenant; (iv) unless applicable law provides otherwise, all Rents collected by Lender or Lender's agents shall be applied first to the costs of taking control of and managing the Property and collecting the Rents, including but not limited to, attorney's fees, receiver's fees, premiums on receiver's bonds, repair and maintenance costs, insurance premiums, taxes, assessments and other charges on the Property, and then to the sum secured by the Security Instrument; (v) Lender, Lender's agents or any judicially appointed receiver shall be liable to account for only those rents actually received; and (vi) Lender shall be entitled to have a receiver appointed to take possession of and manage the Property and collect the Rents and profits derived from the Property without any showing as to the inadequacy of the Property as security.

If the Rents of the Property are not sufficient to cover the costs of taking control of and managing the Property and of collecting the Rents, any funds expended by Lender for such purposes shall become indebtedness of Borrower to Lender secured by the Security Instrument pursuant to Uniform Covenant 7 of the Security Instrument.

Borrower represents and warrants that Borrower has not executed any prior assignment of the Rents and has not and will not perform any act that would prevent Lender from exercising its rights under this paragraph.

Lender, or Lender's agents or a judicially appointed receiver, shall not be required to enter upon, take control of or maintain the Property before or after giving notice of default to Borrower. However, Lender, or Lender's agents or a judicially appointed receiver, may do so at any time when a default occurs. Any application of Rents shall not cure or waive any default or invalidate any other right or remedy of Lender. This assignment of Rents of the Property shall terminate when all the sums secured by the Security Instrument are paid in full.

I. CROSS-DEFAULT PROVISION. Borrower's default or breach under any note or agreement in which Lender has an interest shall be a breach under the Security Instrument and Lender may invoke any of the remedies permitted by the Security Instrument.

J. **PRIOR ASSIGNMENT OF RENTS.** This 1–4 Family Rider supersedes the provisions of any previous 1–4 Family Rider Assignment of Rents (a "Previous Assignment") executed by Borrower pertaining to the Property. If a Previous Assignment has been executed by the Borrower, then the assignment and lien granted in the assignment of Rents contained in Paragraph H of this 1–4 Family Rider shall relate back in time to the date and priority of any such Previous Assignment.

K. **CAPITALIZED TERMS.** Capitalized terms used in this 1–4 Family Rider shall have the meanings ascribed to them in the Modification except as otherwise specifically set forth in this 1–4 Family Rider.

BY SIGNING BELOW, Borrower accepts and agrees to the terms and provisions contained in this 1–4 Family Rider.

_________ (Seal)
Date - Borrower

_________ (Seal)
Date - Borrower

______ [Name of Lender]
Date By: ____________

H.2 Sample Qualified Written Requests

H.2.1 Sample Qualified Written Request Under RESPA for Use by Consumers

Joe & Sally Consumer
[Address]

January 1, 2010

VIA CERTIFIED MAIL
USA Federal Bank, FSB
[Address]

Attn: Mortgage Loan Accounting Department [or Borrower Inquiry Department]

Re: Loan # 99999999
Joe and Sally Consumer
[Address]

Dear Sir or Madam:

USA Federal Bank, FSB is the servicer of our mortgage loan at the above address. We dispute the amount that you claim is owed according to the Monthly Billing Statement and request that you send us information about the fees, costs, and escrow accounting on our loan. This is a "qualified written request" pursuant to the Real Estate Settlement and Procedures Act (section 2605(e)).

Specifically, we are requesting the following information:

1. A complete payment history which lists the dates and amounts of all the payments we have made on the loan to date, and shows how each payment was applied or credited (whether to principal, interest, escrow, suspense, or some other treatment);
2. A breakdown of the amount of claimed arrears or delinquencies on our account, including an itemization of all fees and charges you claim are currently due;
3. An explanation of how the amount due of [amount] on the Monthly Billing Statement dated [date] was calculated and an explanation of why this amount was increased to [amount] in the most recent Statement [or foreclosure notice] dated [date];
4. The payment dates, purpose of payment, and recipient of any and all foreclosure fees and costs that have been charged to our account;
5. The payment dates, purpose of payment, and recipient of all escrow items charged to our account since [date USA Federal Bank took over the servicing];
6. A breakdown of the current escrow charge showing how it is calculated and the reasons for any increase within the last 24 months;
7. A copy of any annual escrow statements, and notices of a shortage, deficiency, or surplus, sent to us within the last three (3) years; and
8. The current balance in any suspense account as of [date] and the reason why such funds were deposited in the account.

Thank you for taking the time to acknowledge and answer this request as required by the Real Estate Settlement and Procedures Act (section 2605(e)).

Very truly yours,

Joe & Sally Consumer

H.2.2 Sample Qualified Written Requests Under RESPA for Use by Attorneys

H.2.2.1 General

[Date]

[Mortgage Co. or Servicer]

RE: *[Name of Mortgagor]*
[Mortgagor's Address]
[Acct. No. ________]

To Whom It May Concern:

Please treat this letter as a **"qualified written request"** under the Real Estate Settlement Procedures Act, 12 U.S.C. § 2605(e). This request is made on behalf of my client, *[client]*, based on her dispute of the amount alleged to be due and owing contained in the *[servicer's]* notice of default. Specifically, I am requesting a breakdown of the following information:

1. The monthly principal and interest payment, and monthly escrow payment from *[date]* to *[date]*.

2. The total amount, separately listed and identified, for any unpaid principal, interest, escrow charges, and other charges due and owing as of *[date]*.

3. The total amount paid by *[client]* on the mortgage account as of the date of the notice of default.

4. For each payment received from [*date*] to [*date*], indicate the amount of the payment, the date received, the date posted to the account, how the payment was applied or credited (indicating the portion, if any, applied or credited to principal, interest, escrow, suspense or other treatment), and the month to which the payment was applied. If interest is calculated using a daily accrual accounting method, indicate for each payment the number of days that lapsed from the prior payment application date.

5. The amount, payment date, purpose, and recipient of all foreclosure expenses, late charges, NSF check charges, appraisal fees, property inspection/preservation fees, force placed insurance charges, legal fees, bankruptcy/proof of claim fees, recoverable corporate advances, and other expenses or costs that have been charged and/or assessed to [*client's*] mortgage account from [*date*] to [*date*].

6. The amount, payment date, purpose, and recipient of all escrow account items, including but not limited to taxes, water and sewer charges, and insurance premiums, charged and/or assessed to [*client's*] mortgage account from [*date*] to [*date*].

7. A breakdown of the current escrow account payment showing how it was calculated and the reasons for any increase or decrease in the months prior to [*date*]. Indicate the date when the last escrow account analysis was conducted on the mortgage account.

8. The balance in the escrow account as of [*date*].

9. The balance in any suspense account as of [*date*] and the reason why such funds were deposited in said account.

10. The current interest rate on [*client's*] mortgage account.

To the extent that [*servicer*] has charged to the [*client's*] mortgage account any late fees appraisal fees, broker price opinion fees, property inspection/preservation fees, legal fees, recoverable corporate advances, and other fees or costs in connection with the notice of default and [*servicer's*] claim that the account is in default, [client] disputes such fees and costs and specifically requests that the account be corrected to delete such fees and costs.

Finally, if you are not the current holder of the note and mortgage relating to [*client's*] mortgage account, please provide the name and address of said holder and indicate your relationship to this entity. Also, please indicate the date when you began servicing [*client's*] mortgage account, and if you acquired the servicing rights in this mortgage account following a transfer of servicing from another servicer, state the name of the prior servicer and the effective date of the transfer of servicing to [*servicer*].

Thank you for taking the time to acknowledge and answer this request as required by the Real Estate Settlement Procedures Act (§ 2605(e)).

Very truly yours,

[*signature*]
Attorney for Debtor

H.2.2.2 Bankruptcy

[*Date*]
[*Mortgage Co. or Servicer*]
RE: [*Debtor*]
[*Debtor's Address*]
[*SSN:*]
[*Bk. No.:*]
[*File Date:*]
[*Acct. No.*]

To Whom It May Concern:

Please treat this letter as a **"qualified written request"** under the Real Estate Settlement Procedures Act, 12 U.S.C. § 2605(e). This request is made on behalf of my client, [*client*], based on her dispute of the amount alleged to be due and owing contained in the [*servicer's*] notice of default and/or proof of claim filed in [*client's*] Chapter 13 bankruptcy. Specifically, I am requesting a breakdown of the following pre-bankruptcy and post-bankruptcy information:

1. The monthly principal and interest payment, and monthly escrow payment prior to [*date of bk. filing*].

2. The monthly principal and interest payment, and monthly escrow payment subsequent to [*date of bk. filing*].

3. The total unpaid principal, interest and escrow balances due and owing as of [*date of bk. filing*].

4. For each payment received during the 18 months prior to [*date of bk. filing*], indicate the amount of the payment, the date received, the date posted to the account, how the payment was applied or credited (indicating the portion, if any, applied or credited to principal, interest, escrow or suspense), and the month to which the payment was applied. If interest is calculated using a daily accrual accounting method, indicate for each payment the number of days that lapsed from the prior payment application date.

5. The amount, payment date, purpose, and recipient of all foreclosure expenses, late charges, NSF check charges, appraisal fees, property inspection/preservation fees, force placed insurance charges, legal fees, recoverable corporate advances, and other expenses or costs that have been charged and/or assessed to [*client's*] mortgage account in the 18 months prior to [*date of bk. filing*].

6. The amount, payment date, purpose, and recipient of all foreclosure expenses, late charges, NSF check charges, appraisal fees, property inspection/preservation fees, force placed insurance charges, legal fees, bankruptcy/proof of claim fees, recoverable corporate advances, and other expenses or costs that have been charged and/or assessed to [*client's*] mortgage account subsequent to [*date of bk. filing*].

7. The amount, payment date, purpose, and recipient of all escrow account items, including but not limited to taxes, water and sewer charges, and insurance premiums, charged and/or assessed to [*client's*] mortgage account in the 18 months prior to [*date of bk. filing*].

8. A breakdown of the current escrow account payment showing how it was calculated and the reasons for any increase or decrease in the 18 months prior to [*date of bk. filing*].

9. The balance in the escrow account as of [*date of bk. filing*].

10. The balance in any suspense account as of [date of bk. filing] and the reason why such funds were deposited in said account.

11. The current interest rate on [*client's*] mortgage account.

To the extent that [servicer] has charged to the [client's] mortgage account, subsequent to [date of bk. filing], any appraisal fees, broker price opinion fees, property inspection/preservation, legal fees, bankruptcy/proof of claim fees, recoverable corporate advances, and other fees or costs that were not disclosed to [client] and approved by the bankruptcy court, [client] disputes such fees and costs and requests that the account be corrected to delete such fees and costs.

Finally, if you are not the current holder of the note and mortgage relating to [*client's*] mortgage account, please provide the name and address of said holder and indicate your relationship to this entity.

Thank you for taking the time to acknowledge and answer this request as required by the Real Estate Settlement Procedures Act (sec. 2605(e)).

Very truly yours,

[*signature*]

Attorney for Debtor

H.3 Sample Mortgage and Servicing Forms

H.3.1 Sample Mortgage

MORTGAGE

DEFINITIONS

Words used in multiple sections of this document are defined below and other words are defined in Sections 3, 11, 13, 18, 20 and 21. Certain rules regarding the usage of words used in this document are also provided in Section 16.

(A) "Security Instrument" means this document, which is dated ____________________, ____________, together with all Riders to this document.

(B) "Borrower" is ____________________. Borrower is the mortgagor under this Security Instrument.

(C) "Lender" is ____________________. Lender is a ____________________ organized and existing under the laws of ____________________. Lender's address is ____________________. Lender is the mortgagee under this Security Instrument.

(D) "Note" means the promissory note signed by Borrower and dated ____________________, ____________. The Note states that Borrower owes Lender ____________________ Dollars (U.S. $____________________) plus interest. Borrower has promised to pay this debt in regular Periodic Payments and to pay the debt in full not later than ____________________.

(E) "Property" means the property that is described below under the heading "Transfer of Rights in the Property."

(F) "Loan" means the debt evidenced by the Note, plus interest, any prepayment charges and late charges due under the Note, and all sums due under this Security Instrument, plus interest.

(G) "Riders" means all Riders to this Security Instrument that are executed by Borrower. The following Riders are to be executed by Borrower [check box as applicable]:

☐ Adjustable Rate Rider	☐ Planned Unit
☐ Condominium Rider	☐ Development Rider
☐ Second Home Rider	☐ Other(s) [specify]
☐ Balloon Rider	____________________
☐ 1–4 Family Rider	☐ Biweekly Payment Rider

(H) "Applicable Law" means all controlling applicable federal, state and local statutes, regulations, ordinances and administrative rules and orders (that have the effect of law) as well as all applicable final, non-appealable judicial opinions.

(I) "Community Association Dues, Fees, and Assessments" means all dues, fees, assessments and other charges that are imposed on Borrower or the Property by a condominium association, homeowners association or similar organization.

(J) "Electronic Funds Transfer" means any transfer of funds, other than a transaction originated by check, draft, or similar paper instrument, which is initiated through an electronic terminal, telephonic instrument, computer, or magnetic tape so as to order, instruct, or authorize a financial institution to debit or credit an account. Such term includes, but is not limited to, point-of-sale transfers, automated teller machine transactions, transfers initiated by telephone, wire transfers, and automated clearinghouse transfers.

(K) "Escrow Items" means those items that are described in Section 3.

(L) "Miscellaneous Proceeds" means any compensation, settlement, award of damages, or proceeds paid by any third party (other than insurance proceeds paid under the coverages described in Section 5) for: (i) damage to, or destruction of, the Property; (ii) condemnation or other taking of all or any part of the Property; (iii) conveyance in lieu of condemnation; or (iv) misrepresentations of, or omissions as to, the value and/or condition of the Property.

(M) "Mortgage Insurance" means insurance protecting Lender against the nonpayment of, or default on, the Loan.

(N) "Periodic Payment" means the regularly scheduled amount due for (i) principal and interest under the Note, plus (ii) any amounts under Section 3 of this Security Instrument.

(O) "RESPA" means the Real Estate Settlement Procedures Act (12 U.S.C. § 2601 et seq.) and its implementing regulation, Regulation X (24 C.F.R. Part 3500), as they might be amended from time to time, or any additional or successor legislation or regulation that governs the same subject matter. As used in this Security Instrument, "RESPA" refers to all requirements and restrictions that are imposed in regard to a "federally related mortgage loan" even if the Loan does not qualify as a "federally related mortgage loan" under RESPA.

(P) "Successor in Interest of Borrower" means any party that has taken title to the Property, whether or not that party has assumed Borrower's obligations under the Note and/or this Security Instrument.

TRANSFER OF RIGHTS IN THE PROPERTY

This Security Instrument secures to Lender: (i) the repayment of the Loan, and all renewals, extensions and modifications of the Note; and (ii) the performance of Borrower's covenants and agreements under this Security Instrument and the Note. For this purpose, Borrower does hereby mortgage, grant and convey to Lender and Lender's successors and assigns, with power of sale, the following described property located in the ____________________ [Type of Recording Jurisdiction] of ______________________ [Name of Recording Jurisdiction] which currently has the address of ______________________ [Street] ______________________ [City], Massachusetts ________ [Zip Code] ("Property Address"):

TOGETHER WITH all the improvements now or hereafter erected on the property, and all easements, appurtenances, and fixtures now or hereafter a part of the property. All replacements and additions shall also be covered by this Security Instrument. All of the foregoing is referred to in this Security Instrument as the "Property."

BORROWER COVENANTS that Borrower is lawfully seised of the estate hereby conveyed and has the right to mortgage, grant and convey the Property and that the Property is unencumbered, except for encumbrances of record. Borrower warrants and will defend generally the title to the Property against all claims and demands, subject to any encumbrances of record.

THIS SECURITY INSTRUMENT combines uniform covenants for national use and non-uniform covenants with limited variations by jurisdiction to constitute a uniform security instrument covering real property.

UNIFORM COVENANTS. Borrower and Lender covenant and agree as follows:

1. Payment of Principal, Interest, Escrow Items, Prepayment Charges, and Late Charges. Borrower shall pay when due the principal of, and interest on, the debt evidenced by the Note and any prepayment charges and late charges due under the Note. Borrower shall also pay funds for Escrow Items pursuant to Section 3. Payments due under the Note and this Security Instrument shall be made in U.S. currency. However, if any check or other instrument received by Lender as payment under the Note or this Security Instrument is returned to Lender unpaid, Lender may require that any or all subsequent payments due under the Note and this Security Instrument be made in one or more of the following forms, as selected by Lender: (a) cash; (b) money order; (c) certified check, bank check, treasurer's check or cashier's check, provided any such check is drawn upon an institution whose deposits are insured by a federal agency, instrumentality, or entity; or (d) Electronic Funds Transfer.

Payments are deemed received by Lender when received at the location designated in the Note or at such other location as may be designated by Lender in accordance with the notice provisions in Section 15. Lender may return any payment or partial payment if the payment or partial payments are insufficient to bring the Loan current. Lender may accept any payment or partial payment insufficient to bring the Loan current, without waiver of any rights hereunder or prejudice to its rights to refuse such payment or partial payments in the future, but Lender is not obligated to apply such payments at the time such payments are accepted. If each Periodic Payment is applied as of its scheduled due date, then Lender need not pay interest on unapplied funds. Lender may hold such unapplied funds until Borrower makes payment to bring the Loan current. If Borrower does not do so within a reasonable period of time, Lender shall either apply such funds or return them to Borrower. If not applied earlier, such funds will be applied to the outstanding principal balance under the Note immediately prior to foreclosure. No offset or claim which Borrower might have now or in the future against Lender shall relieve Borrower from making payments due under the Note and this Security Instrument or performing the covenants and agreements secured by this Security Instrument.

2. Application of Payments or Proceeds. Except as otherwise described in this Section 2, all payments accepted and applied by Lender shall be applied in the following order of priority: (a) interest due under the Note; (b) principal due under the Note; (c) amounts due under Section 3. Such payments shall be applied to each Periodic Payment in the order in which it became due. Any remaining amounts shall be applied first to late charges, second to any other amounts due under this Security Instrument, and then to reduce the principal balance of the Note.

If Lender receives a payment from Borrower for a delinquent Periodic Payment which includes a sufficient amount to pay any late charge due, the payment may be applied to the delinquent payment and the late charge. If more than one Periodic Payment is outstanding, Lender may apply any payment received from Borrower to the repayment of the Periodic Payments if, and to the extent that, each payment can be paid in full. To the extent that any excess exists after the payment is applied to the full payment of one or more Periodic Payments, such excess may be applied to any late charges due. Voluntary prepayments shall be applied first to any prepayment charges and then as described in the Note.

Any application of payments, insurance proceeds, or Miscellaneous Proceeds to principal due under the Note shall not extend or postpone the due date, or change the amount, of the Periodic Payments.

3. Funds for Escrow Items. Borrower shall pay to Lender on the day Periodic Payments are due under the Note, until the Note is paid in full, a sum (the "Funds") to provide for payment of amounts due for: (a) taxes and assessments and other items which can attain priority over this Security Instrument as a lien or encumbrance on the Property; (b) leasehold payments or ground rents on the Property, if any; (c) premiums for any and all insurance required by Lender under Section 5; and (d) Mortgage Insurance premiums, if any, or any sums payable by Borrower to Lender in lieu of the payment of Mortgage Insurance premiums in accordance with the provisions of Section 10. These items are called "Escrow Items." At origination or at any time during the term of the Loan, Lender may require that Community Association Dues, Fees, and Assessments, if any, be escrowed by Borrower, and such dues, fees and assessments shall be an Escrow Item. Borrower shall promptly furnish to Lender all notices of amounts to be paid under this Section. Borrower shall pay Lender the Funds for Escrow Items unless Lender waives Borrower's obligation to pay the Funds for any or all Escrow Items. Lender may waive Borrower's obligation to pay to Lender Funds for any or all Escrow Items at any time. Any such waiver may only be in writing. In the event of such waiver, Borrower shall pay directly, when and where payable, the amounts due for any Escrow Items for which payment of Funds has been waived by Lender and, if Lender requires, shall furnish to Lender receipts evidencing such payment within such time period as Lender may require. Borrower's obligation to make such payments and to provide receipts shall for all purposes be deemed to be a covenant and agreement contained in this Security Instrument, as the phrase "covenant and agreement" is used in Section 9. If Borrower is obligated to pay Escrow Items directly, pursuant to a waiver, and Borrower fails to pay the amount due for an Escrow Item, Lender may exercise its rights under Section 9 and pay such amount and Borrower shall then be obligated under

Section 9 to repay to Lender any such amount. Lender may revoke the waiver as to any or all Escrow Items at any time by a notice given in accordance with Section 15 and, upon such revocation, Borrower shall pay to Lender all Funds, and in such amounts, that are then required under this Section 3.

Lender may, at any time, collect and hold Funds in an amount (a) sufficient to permit Lender to apply the Funds at the time specified under RESPA, and (b) not to exceed the maximum amount a lender can require under RESPA. Lender shall estimate the amount of Funds due on the basis of current data and reasonable estimates of expenditures of future Escrow Items or otherwise in accordance with Applicable Law.

The Funds shall be held in an institution whose deposits are insured by a federal agency, instrumentality, or entity (including Lender, if Lender is an institution whose deposits are so insured) or in any Federal Home Loan Bank. Lender shall apply the Funds to pay the Escrow Items no later than the time specified under RESPA. Lender shall not charge Borrower for holding and applying the Funds, annually analyzing the escrow account, or verifying the Escrow Items, unless Lender pays Borrower interest on the Funds and Applicable Law permits Lender to make such a charge. Unless an agreement is made in writing or Applicable Law requires interest to be paid on the Funds, Lender shall not be required to pay Borrower any interest or earnings on the Funds. Borrower and Lender can agree in writing, however, that interest shall be paid on the Funds. Lender shall give to Borrower, without charge, an annual accounting of the Funds as required by RESPA. If there is a surplus of Funds held in escrow, as defined under RESPA, Lender shall account to Borrower for the excess funds in accordance with RESPA.

If there is a shortage of Funds held in escrow, as defined under RESPA, Lender shall notify Borrower as required by RESPA, and Borrower shall pay to Lender the amount necessary to make up the shortage in accordance with RESPA, but in no more than 12 monthly payments. If there is a deficiency of Funds held in escrow, as defined under RESPA, Lender shall notify Borrower as required by RESPA, and Borrower shall pay to Lender the amount necessary to make up the deficiency in accordance with RESPA, but in no more than 12 monthly payments.

Upon payment in full of all sums secured by this Security Instrument, Lender shall promptly refund to Borrower any Funds held by Lender.

4. Charges; Liens. Borrower shall pay all taxes, assessments, charges, fines, and impositions attributable to the Property which can attain priority over this Security Instrument, leasehold payments or ground rents on the Property, if any, and Community Association Dues, Fees, and Assessments, if any. To the extent that these items are Escrow Items, Borrower shall pay them in the manner provided in Section 3.

Borrower shall promptly discharge any lien which has priority over this Security Instrument unless Borrower: (a) agrees in writing to the payment of the obligation secured by the lien in a manner acceptable to Lender, but only so long as Borrower is performing such agreement; (b) contests the lien in good faith by, or defends against enforcement of the lien in, legal proceedings which in Lender's opinion operate to prevent the enforcement of the lien while those proceedings are pending, but only until such proceedings are concluded; or (c) secures from the holder of the lien an agreement satisfactory to Lender subordinating the lien to this Security Instrument. If Lender determines that any part of the Property is subject to a lien which can attain priority over this Security Instrument, Lender may give Borrower a notice identifying the lien. Within 10 days of the date on which that notice is given, Borrower shall satisfy the lien or take one or more of the actions set forth above in this Section 4.

Lender may require Borrower to pay a one-time charge for a real estate tax verification and/or reporting service used by Lender in connection with this Loan.

5. Property Insurance. Borrower shall keep the improvements now existing or hereafter erected on the Property insured against loss by fire, hazards included within the term "extended coverage," and any other hazards including, but not limited to, earthquakes and floods, for which Lender requires insurance. This insurance shall be maintained in the amounts (including deductible levels) and for the periods that Lender requires. What Lender requires pursuant to the preceding sentences can change during the term of the Loan. The insurance carrier providing the insurance shall be chosen by Borrower subject to Lender's right to disapprove Borrower's choice, which right shall not be exercised unreasonably. Lender may require Borrower to pay, in connection with this Loan, either: (a) a one-time charge for flood zone determination, certification and tracking services; or (b) a one-time charge for flood zone determination and certification services and subsequent charges each time remappings or similar changes occur which reasonably might affect such determination or certification. Borrower shall also be responsible for the payment of any fees imposed by the Federal Emergency Management Agency in connection with the review of any flood zone determination resulting from an objection by Borrower.

If Borrower fails to maintain any of the coverages described above, Lender may obtain insurance coverage, at Lender's option and Borrower's expense. Lender is under no obligation to purchase any particular type or amount of coverage. Therefore, such coverage shall cover Lender, but might or might not protect Borrower, Borrower's equity in the Property, or the contents of the Property, against any risk, hazard or liability and might provide greater or lesser coverage than was previously in effect. Borrower acknowledges that the cost of the insurance coverage so obtained might significantly exceed the cost of insurance that Borrower could have obtained. Any amounts disbursed by Lender under this Section 5 shall become additional debt of Borrower secured by this Security Instrument. These amounts shall bear interest at the Note rate from the date of disbursement and shall be payable, with such interest, upon notice from Lender to Borrower requesting payment.

All insurance policies required by Lender and renewals of such policies shall be subject to Lender's right to disapprove such policies, shall include a standard mortgage clause, and shall name Lender as mortgagee and/or as an additional loss payee. Lender shall have the right to hold the policies and renewal certificates. If Lender requires, Borrower shall promptly give to Lender all receipts of paid premiums and renewal notices. If Borrower obtains any form of insurance coverage, not otherwise required by Lender, for damage to, or destruction of, the Property, such policy shall include a standard mortgage clause and shall name Lender as mortgagee and/or as an additional loss payee.

In the event of loss, Borrower shall give prompt notice to the insurance carrier and Lender. Lender may make proof of loss if not made promptly by Borrower. Unless Lender and Borrower otherwise agree in writing, any insurance proceeds, whether or not the underlying insurance was required by Lender, shall be applied to restoration or repair of the Property, if the restoration or repair is economically feasible and Lender's security is not lessened. During such repair and restoration period, Lender shall have the right to hold such insurance proceeds until Lender has had an opportunity to inspect such Property to ensure the work has been completed to Lender's satisfaction, provided that such inspection shall be undertaken promptly. Lender may disburse proceeds for the repairs and restoration in a single payment or in a series of progress payments as the work is completed. Unless an agreement is made in writing or Applicable Law requires interest to be paid on such insurance proceeds, Lender shall not be required to pay Borrower any interest or earnings on such proceeds. Fees for public adjusters, or other third parties, retained by Borrower shall not be paid out of the insurance proceeds and shall be the sole obligation of Borrower. If the restoration or repair is not economically feasible or Lender's security would be lessened, the insurance proceeds shall be applied to the sums secured by this Security Instrument, whether or not then due, with the excess, if any, paid to Borrower. Such insurance proceeds shall be applied in the order provided for in Section 2.

If Borrower abandons the Property, Lender may file, negotiate and settle any available insurance claim and related matters. If Borrower does not respond within 30 days to a notice from Lender that the insurance carrier has offered to settle a claim, then Lender may negotiate and settle the claim. The 30-day period will begin when the notice is given. In either event, or if Lender acquires the Property under Section 22 or otherwise, Borrower hereby assigns to Lender (a) Borrower's rights to any insurance proceeds in an amount not to exceed the amounts unpaid under the Note or this Security Instrument, and (b) any other of Borrower's rights (other than the right to any refund of unearned premiums paid by Borrower) under all insurance policies covering the Property, insofar as such rights are applicable to the coverage of the Property. Lender may use the insurance proceeds either to repair or restore the Property or to pay amounts unpaid under the Note or this Security Instrument, whether or not then due.

6. Occupancy. Borrower shall occupy, establish, and use the Property as Borrower's principal residence within 60 days after the execution of this Security Instrument and shall continue to occupy the Property as Borrower's principal residence for at least one year after the date of occupancy, unless Lender otherwise agrees in writing, which consent shall not be unreasonably withheld, or unless extenuating circumstances exist which are beyond Borrower's control.

7. Preservation, Maintenance and Protection of the Property; Inspections. Borrower shall not destroy, damage or impair the Property, allow the Property to deteriorate or commit waste on the Property. Whether or not Borrower is residing in the Property, Borrower shall maintain the Property in order to prevent the Property from deteriorating or decreasing in value due to its condition. Unless it is determined pursuant to Section 5 that repair or restoration is not economically feasible, Borrower shall promptly repair the Property if damaged to avoid further deterioration or damage. If insurance or condemnation proceeds are paid in connection with damage to, or the taking of, the Property, Borrower shall be responsible for repairing or restoring the Property only if Lender has released proceeds for such purposes. Lender may disburse proceeds for the repairs and restoration in a single payment or in a series of progress payments as the work is completed. If the insurance or condemnation proceeds are not sufficient to repair or restore the Property, Borrower is not relieved of Borrower's obligation for the completion of such repair or restoration.

Lender or its agent may make reasonable entries upon and inspections of the Property. If it has reasonable cause, Lender may inspect the interior of the improvements on the Property. Lender shall give Borrower notice at the time of or prior to such an interior inspection specifying such reasonable cause.

8. Borrower's Loan Application. Borrower shall be in default if, during the Loan application process, Borrower or any persons or entities acting at the direction of Borrower or with Borrower's knowledge or consent gave materially false, misleading, or inaccurate information or statements to Lender (or failed to provide Lender with material information) in connection with the Loan. Material representations include, but are not limited to, representations concerning Borrower's occupancy of the Property as Borrower's principal residence.

9. Protection of Lender's Interest in the Property and Rights Under this Security Instrument. If (a) Borrower fails to perform the covenants and agreements contained in this Security Instrument, (b) there is a legal proceeding that might significantly affect Lender's interest in the Property and/or rights under this Security Instrument (such as a proceeding in bankruptcy, probate, for condemnation or forfeiture, for enforcement of a lien which may attain priority over this Security Instrument or to enforce laws or regulations), or (c) Borrower has abandoned the Property, then Lender may do and pay for whatever is reasonable or appropriate to protect Lender's interest in the Property and rights under this Security Instrument, including protecting and/or assessing the value of the Property, and securing and/or repairing the Property. Lender's actions can include, but are not limited to: (a) paying any sums secured by a lien which has priority over this Security Instrument; (b) appearing in court; and (c) paying reasonable attorneys' fees to protect its interest in the Property and/or rights under this Security Instrument, including its secured position in a bankruptcy proceeding. Securing the Property includes, but is not limited to, entering the Property to make repairs, change locks, replace or board up doors and windows, drain water from pipes, eliminate building or other code violations or dangerous conditions, and have utilities turned on or off. Although Lender may take action under this Section 9, Lender does not have to do so and is not under any duty or obligation to do so. It is agreed that Lender incurs no liability for not taking any or all actions authorized under this Section 9.

Any amounts disbursed by Lender under this Section 9 shall become additional debt of Borrower secured by this Security Instrument. These amounts shall bear interest at the Note rate from the date of disbursement and shall be payable, with such interest, upon notice from Lender to Borrower requesting payment.

If this Security Instrument is on a leasehold, Borrower shall comply with all the provisions of the lease. If Borrower acquires fee title to the Property, the leasehold and the fee title shall not merge unless Lender agrees to the merger in writing.

10. Mortgage Insurance. If Lender required Mortgage Insurance as a condition of making the Loan, Borrower shall pay the premiums required to maintain the Mortgage Insurance in effect. If, for any reason, the Mortgage Insurance coverage required by Lender ceases to be available from the mortgage insurer that previously provided such insurance and Borrower was required to make separately designated payments toward the premiums for Mortgage Insurance, Borrower shall pay the premiums required to obtain coverage substantially equivalent to the Mortgage Insurance previously in effect, at a cost substantially equivalent to the cost to Borrower of the Mortgage Insurance previously in effect, from an alternate mortgage insurer selected by Lender. If substantially equivalent Mortgage Insurance coverage is not available, Borrower shall continue to pay to Lender the amount of the separately designated payments that were due when the insurance coverage ceased to be in effect. Lender will accept, use and retain these payments as a non-refundable loss reserve in lieu of Mortgage Insurance. Such loss reserve shall be non-refundable, notwithstanding the fact that the Loan is ultimately paid in full, and Lender shall not be required to pay Borrower any interest or earnings on such loss reserve. Lender can no longer require loss reserve payments if Mortgage Insurance coverage (in the amount and for the period that Lender requires) provided by an insurer selected by Lender again becomes available, is obtained, and Lender requires separately designated payments toward the premiums for Mortgage Insurance. If Lender required Mortgage Insurance as a condition of making the Loan and Borrower was required to make separately designated payments toward the premiums for Mortgage Insurance, Borrower shall pay the premiums required to maintain Mortgage Insurance in effect, or to provide a non-refundable loss reserve, until Lender's requirement for Mortgage Insurance ends in accordance with any written agreement between Borrower and Lender providing for such termination or until termination is required by Applicable Law. Nothing in this Section 10 affects Borrower's obligation to pay interest at the rate provided in the Note.

Mortgage Insurance reimburses Lender (or any entity that purchases the Note) for certain losses it may incur if Borrower does not repay the Loan as agreed. Borrower is not a party to the Mortgage Insurance.

Mortgage insurers evaluate their total risk on all such insurance in force from time to time, and may enter into agreements with other parties that share or modify their risk, or reduce losses. These agreements are on terms and conditions that are satisfactory to the mortgage insurer and the other party (or parties) to these agreements. These agreements may require the mortgage insurer to make payments using any source of funds that the mortgage insurer may have available (which may include funds obtained from Mortgage Insurance premiums).

As a result of these agreements, Lender, any purchaser of the Note, another insurer, any reinsurer, any other entity, or any affiliate of any of the foregoing, may receive (directly or indirectly) amounts that derive from (or might be characterized as) a portion of Borrower's payments for Mortgage Insurance, in exchange for sharing or modifying the mortgage insurer's risk, or reducing losses. If such agreement provides that an affiliate of Lender takes a share of the insurer's risk in exchange for a share of the premiums paid to the insurer, the arrangement is often termed "captive reinsurance." Further:

(a) Any such agreements will not affect the amounts that Borrower has agreed to pay for Mortgage Insurance, or any other terms of the Loan. Such agreements will not increase the amount Borrower will owe for Mortgage Insurance, and they will not entitle Borrower to any refund.

(b) Any such agreements will not affect the rights Borrower has—if any—with respect to the Mortgage Insurance under the Homeowners Protection Act of 1998 or any other law. These rights may include the right to receive certain disclosures, to request and obtain cancellation of the Mortgage Insurance, to have the Mortgage Insurance terminated automatically, and/or to receive a refund of any Mortgage Insurance premiums that were unearned at the time of such cancellation or termination.

11. Assignment of Miscellaneous Proceeds; Forfeiture. All Miscellaneous Proceeds are hereby assigned to and shall be paid to Lender.

If the Property is damaged, such Miscellaneous Proceeds shall be applied to restoration or repair of the Property, if the restoration or repair is economically feasible and Lender's security is not lessened. During such repair and restoration period, Lender shall have the right to hold such Miscellaneous Proceeds until Lender has had an opportunity to inspect such Property to ensure the work has been completed to Lender's satisfaction, provided that such inspection shall be undertaken promptly. Lender may pay for the repairs and restoration in a single disbursement or in a series of progress payments as the work is completed. Unless an agreement is made in writing or Applicable Law requires interest to be paid on such Miscellaneous Proceeds, Lender shall not be required to pay Borrower any interest or earnings on such Miscellaneous Proceeds. If the restoration or repair is not economically feasible or Lender's security would be lessened, the Miscellaneous Proceeds shall be applied to the sums secured by this Security Instrument, whether or not then due, with the excess, if any, paid to Borrower. Such Miscellaneous Proceeds shall be applied in the order provided for in Section 2.

In the event of a total taking, destruction, or loss in value of the Property, the Miscellaneous Proceeds shall be applied to the sums secured by this Security Instrument, whether or not then due, with the excess, if any, paid to Borrower.

In the event of a partial taking, destruction, or loss in value of the Property in which the fair market value of the Property immediately before the partial taking, destruction, or loss in value is equal to or greater than the amount of the sums secured by this Security Instrument immediately before the partial taking, destruction, or loss in value, unless Borrower and Lender otherwise agree in writing, the sums secured by this Security Instrument shall be reduced by the amount of the Miscellaneous Proceeds multiplied by the following fraction: (a) the total amount of the sums secured immediately before the partial taking, destruction, or loss in value divided by (b) the fair market value of the Property immediately before the partial taking, destruction, or loss in value. Any balance shall be paid to Borrower.

In the event of a partial taking, destruction, or loss in value of the Property in which the fair market value of the Property immediately before the partial taking, destruction, or loss in value is less than the amount of the sums secured immediately before the partial taking, destruction, or loss in value, unless Borrower and Lender otherwise agree in writing, the Miscellaneous Proceeds shall be applied to the sums secured by this Security Instrument whether or not the sums are then due.

If the Property is abandoned by Borrower, or if, after notice by Lender to Borrower that the Opposing Party (as defined in the next sentence) offers to make an award to settle a claim for damages, Borrower fails to respond to Lender within 30 days after the date the notice is given, Lender is authorized to collect and apply the Miscellaneous Proceeds either to restoration or repair of the Property or to the sums secured by this Security Instrument, whether or not then due. "Opposing Party" means the third party that owes

Borrower Miscellaneous Proceeds or the party against whom Borrower has a right of action in regard to Miscellaneous Proceeds.

Borrower shall be in default if any action or proceeding, whether civil or criminal, is begun that, in Lender's judgment, could result in forfeiture of the Property or other material impairment of Lender's interest in the Property or rights under this Security Instrument. Borrower can cure such a default and, if acceleration has occurred, reinstate as provided in Section 19, by causing the action or proceeding to be dismissed with a ruling that, in Lender's judgment, precludes forfeiture of the Property or other material impairment of Lender's interest in the Property or rights under this Security Instrument. The proceeds of any award or claim for damages that are attributable to the impairment of Lender's interest in the Property are hereby assigned and shall be paid to Lender.

All Miscellaneous Proceeds that are not applied to restoration or repair of the Property shall be applied in the order provided for in Section 2.

12. Borrower Not Released; Forbearance By Lender Not a Waiver. Extension of the time for payment or modification of amortization of the sums secured by this Security Instrument granted by Lender to Borrower or any Successor in Interest of Borrower shall not operate to release the liability of Borrower or any Successors in Interest of Borrower. Lender shall not be required to commence proceedings against any Successor in Interest of Borrower or to refuse to extend time for payment or otherwise modify amortization of the sums secured by this Security Instrument by reason of any demand made by the original Borrower or any Successors in Interest of Borrower. Any forbearance by Lender in exercising any right or remedy including, without limitation, Lender's acceptance of payments from third persons, entities or Successors in Interest of Borrower or in amounts less than the amount then due, shall not be a waiver of or preclude the exercise of any right or remedy.

13. Joint and Several Liability; Co-signers; Successors and Assigns Bound. Borrower covenants and agrees that Borrower's obligations and liability shall be joint and several. However, any Borrower who co-signs this Security Instrument but does not execute the Note (a "co-signer"): (a) is co-signing this Security Instrument only to mortgage, grant and convey the co-signer's interest in the Property under the terms of this Security Instrument; (b) is not personally obligated to pay the sums secured by this Security Instrument; and (c) agrees that Lender and any other Borrower can agree to extend, modify, forbear or make any accommodations with regard to the terms of this Security Instrument or the Note without the co-signer's consent.

Subject to the provisions of Section 18, any Successor in Interest of Borrower who assumes Borrower's obligations under this Security Instrument in writing, and is approved by Lender, shall obtain all of Borrower's rights and benefits under this Security Instrument. Borrower shall not be released from Borrower's obligations and liability under this Security Instrument unless Lender agrees to such release in writing. The covenants and agreements of this Security Instrument shall bind (except as provided in Section 20) and benefit the successors and assigns of Lender.

14. Loan Charges. Lender may charge Borrower fees for services performed in connection with Borrower's default, for the purpose of protecting Lender's interest in the Property and rights under this Security Instrument, including, but not limited to, attorneys' fees, property inspection and valuation fees. In regard to any other fees, the absence of express authority in this Security Instrument to charge a specific fee to Borrower shall not be construed as a prohibition on the charging of such fee. Lender may not charge fees that are expressly prohibited by this Security Instrument or by Applicable Law.

If the Loan is subject to a law which sets maximum loan charges, and that law is finally interpreted so that the interest or other loan charges collected or to be collected in connection with the Loan exceed the permitted limits, then: (a) any such loan charge shall be reduced by the amount necessary to reduce the charge to the permitted limit; and (b) any sums already collected from Borrower which exceeded permitted limits will be refunded to Borrower. Lender may choose to make this refund by reducing the principal owed under the Note or by making a direct payment to Borrower. If a refund reduces principal, the reduction will be treated as a partial prepayment without any prepayment charge (whether or not a prepayment charge is provided for under the Note). Borrower's acceptance of any such refund made by direct payment to Borrower will constitute a waiver of any right of action Borrower might have arising out of such overcharge.

15. Notices. All notices given by Borrower or Lender in connection with this Security Instrument must be in writing. Any notice to Borrower in connection with this Security Instrument shall be deemed to have been given to Borrower when mailed by first class mail or when actually delivered to Borrower's notice address if sent by other means. Notice to any one Borrower shall constitute notice to all Borrowers unless Applicable Law expressly requires otherwise. The notice address shall be the Property Address unless Borrower has designated a substitute notice address by notice to Lender. Borrower shall promptly notify Lender of Borrower's change of address. If Lender specifies a procedure for reporting Borrower's change of address, then Borrower shall only report a change of address through that specified procedure. There may be only one designated notice address under this Security Instrument at any one time. Any notice to Lender shall be given by delivering it or by mailing it by first class mail to Lender's address stated herein unless Lender has designated another address by notice to Borrower. Any notice in connection with this Security Instrument shall not be deemed to have been given to Lender until actually received by Lender. If any notice required by this Security Instrument is also required under Applicable Law, the Applicable Law requirement will satisfy the corresponding requirement under this Security Instrument.

16. Governing Law; Severability; Rules of Construction. This Security Instrument shall be governed by federal law and the law of the jurisdiction in which the Property is located. All rights and obligations contained in this Security Instrument are subject to any requirements and limitations of Applicable Law. Applicable Law might explicitly or implicitly allow the parties to agree by contract or it might be silent, but such silence shall not be construed as a prohibition against agreement by contract. In the event that any provision or clause of this Security Instrument or the Note conflicts with Applicable Law, such conflict shall not affect other provisions of this Security Instrument or the Note which can be given effect without the conflicting provision.

As used in this Security Instrument: (a) words of the masculine gender shall mean and include corresponding neuter words or words of the feminine gender; (b) words in the singular shall mean and include the plural and vice versa; and (c) the word "may" gives sole discretion without any obligation to take any action.

17. Borrower's Copy. Borrower shall be given one copy of the Note and of this Security Instrument.

18. Transfer of the Property or a Beneficial Interest in Borrower. As used in this Section 18, "Interest in the Property" means any legal or beneficial interest in the Property, including, but not limited to, those beneficial interests transferred in a bond for deed, contract for deed, installment sales contract or escrow agreement, the intent of which is the transfer of title by Borrower at a future date to a purchaser.

If all or any part of the Property or any Interest in the Property is sold or transferred (or if Borrower is not a natural person and a beneficial interest in Borrower is sold or transferred) without Lender's prior written consent, Lender may require immediate payment in full of all sums secured by this Security Instrument. However, this option shall not be exercised by Lender if such exercise is prohibited by Applicable Law.

If Lender exercises this option, Lender shall give Borrower notice of acceleration. The notice shall provide a period of not less than 30 days from the date the notice is given in accordance with Section 15 within which Borrower must pay all sums secured by this Security Instrument. If Borrower fails to pay these sums prior to the expiration of this period, Lender may invoke any remedies permitted by this Security Instrument without further notice or demand on Borrower.

19. Borrower's Right to Reinstate After Acceleration. If Borrower meets certain conditions, Borrower shall have the right to have enforcement of this Security Instrument discontinued at any time prior to the earliest of: (a) five days before sale of the Property pursuant to any power of sale contained in this Security Instrument; (b) such other period as Applicable Law might specify for the termination of Borrower's right to reinstate; or (c) entry of a judgment enforcing this Security Instrument. Those conditions are that Borrower: (a) pays Lender all sums which then would be due under this Security Instrument and the Note as if no acceleration had occurred; (b) cures any default of any other covenants or agreements; (c) pays all expenses incurred in enforcing this Security Instrument, including, but not limited to, reasonable attorneys' fees, property inspection and valuation fees, and other fees incurred for the purpose of protecting Lender's interest in the Property and rights under this Security Instrument; and (d) takes such action as Lender may reasonably require to assure that Lender's interest in the Property and rights under this Security Instrument, and Borrower's obligation to pay the sums secured by this Security Instrument, shall continue unchanged. Lender may require that Borrower pay such reinstatement sums and expenses in one or more of the following forms, as selected by Lender: (a) cash; (b) money order; (c) certified check, bank check, treasurer's check or cashier's check, provided any such check is drawn upon an institution whose deposits are insured by a federal agency, instrumentality or entity; or (d) Electronic Funds Transfer. Upon reinstatement by Borrower, this Security Instrument and obligations secured hereby shall remain fully effective as if no acceleration had occurred. However, this right to reinstate shall not apply in the case of acceleration under Section 18.

20. Sale of Note; Change of Loan Servicer; Notice of Grievance. The Note or a partial interest in the Note (together with this Security Instrument) can be sold one or more times without prior notice to Borrower. A sale might result in a change in the entity (known as the "Loan Servicer") that collects Periodic Payments due under the Note and this Security Instrument and performs other mortgage loan servicing obligations under the Note, this Security Instrument, and Applicable Law. There also might be one or more changes of the Loan Servicer unrelated to a sale of the Note. If there is a change of the Loan Servicer, Borrower will be given written notice of the change which will state the name and address of the new Loan Servicer, the address to which payments should be made and any other information RESPA requires in connection with a notice of transfer of servicing. If the Note is sold and thereafter the Loan is serviced by a Loan Servicer other than the purchaser of the Note, the mortgage loan servicing obligations to Borrower will remain with the Loan Servicer or be transferred to a successor Loan Servicer and are not assumed by the Note purchaser unless otherwise provided by the Note purchaser.

Neither Borrower nor Lender may commence, join, or be joined to any judicial action (as either an individual litigant or the member of a class) that arises from the other party's actions pursuant to this Security Instrument or that alleges that the other party has breached any provision of, or any duty owed by reason of, this Security Instrument, until such Borrower or Lender has notified the other party (with such notice given in compliance with the requirements of Section 15) of such alleged breach and afforded the other party hereto a reasonable period after the giving of such notice to take corrective action. If Applicable Law provides a time period which must elapse before certain action can be taken, that time period will be deemed to be reasonable for purposes of this paragraph. The notice of acceleration and opportunity to cure given to Borrower pursuant to Section 22 and the notice of acceleration given to Borrower pursuant to Section 18 shall be deemed to satisfy the notice and opportunity to take corrective action provisions of this Section 20.

21. Hazardous Substances. As used in this Section 21: (a) "Hazardous Substances" are those substances defined as toxic or hazardous substances, pollutants, or wastes by Environmental Law and the following substances: gasoline, kerosene, other flammable or toxic petroleum products, toxic pesticides and herbicides, volatile solvents, materials containing asbestos or formaldehyde, and radioactive materials; (b) "Environmental Law" means federal laws and laws of the jurisdiction where the Property is located that relate to health, safety or environmental protection; (c) "Environmental Cleanup" includes any response action, remedial action, or removal action, as defined in Environmental Law; and (d) an "Environmental Condition" means a condition that can cause, contribute to, or otherwise trigger an Environmental Cleanup.

Borrower shall not cause or permit the presence, use, disposal, storage, or release of any Hazardous Substances, or threaten to release any Hazardous Substances, on or in the Property. Borrower shall not do, nor allow anyone else to do, anything affecting the Property (a) that is in violation of any Environmental Law, (b) which creates an Environmental Condition, or (c) which, due to the presence, use, or release of a Hazardous Substance, creates a condition that adversely affects the value of the Property. The preceding two sentences shall not apply to the presence, use, or storage on the Property of small quantities of Hazardous Substances that are generally recognized to be appropriate to normal residential uses and to maintenance of the Property (including, but not limited to, hazardous substances in consumer products).

Borrower shall promptly give Lender written notice of (a) any investigation, claim, demand, lawsuit or other action by any governmental or regulatory agency or private party involving the Property and any Hazardous Substance or Environmental Law of which Borrower has actual knowledge, (b) any Environmental Condition, including but not limited to, any spilling, leaking, discharge, release or threat of release of any Hazardous Substance, and (c) any condition caused by the presence, use or release of a Hazardous Substance which adversely affects the value of the Property. If Borrower learns, or is notified by any governmental or regulatory authority, or any private party, that any removal or other remediation of any Hazardous Substance affecting the Property is necessary, Borrower shall promptly take all necessary remedial actions in accordance with Environmental Law. Nothing herein shall create any obligation on Lender for an Environmental Cleanup.

NON-UNIFORM COVENANTS. Borrower and Lender further covenant and agree as follows:

22. Acceleration; Remedies. Lender shall give notice to Borrower prior to acceleration following Borrower's breach of any covenant or agreement in this Security Instrument (but not prior to acceleration under Section 18 unless Applicable Law provides otherwise). The notice shall specify: (a) the default; (b) the action required to cure the default; (c) a date, not less than 30 days from the date the notice is given to Borrower, by which the default must be cured; and (d) that failure to cure the default on or before the date specified in the notice may result in acceleration of the sums secured by this Security Instrument and sale of the Property. The notice shall further inform Borrower of the right to reinstate after acceleration and the right to bring a court action to assert the non-existence of a default or any other defense of Borrower to acceleration and sale. If the default is not cured on or before the date specified in the notice, Lender at its option may require immediate payment in full of all sums secured by this Security Instrument without further demand and may invoke the STATUTORY POWER OF SALE and any other remedies permitted by Applicable Law. Lender shall be entitled to collect all expenses incurred in pursuing the remedies provided in this Section 22, including, but not limited to, reasonable attorneys' fees and costs of title evidence.

If Lender invokes the STATUTORY POWER OF SALE, Lender shall mail a copy of a notice of sale to Borrower, and to other persons prescribed by Applicable Law, in the manner provided by Applicable Law. Lender shall publish the notice of sale, and the Property shall be sold in the manner prescribed by Applicable Law. Lender or its designee may purchase the Property at any sale. The proceeds of the sale shall be applied in the following order: (a) to all expenses of the sale, including, but not limited to, reasonable attorneys' fees; (b) to all sums secured by this Security Instrument; and (c) any excess to the person or persons legally entitled to it.

23. Release. Upon payment of all sums secured by this Security Instrument, Lender shall discharge this Security Instrument. Borrower shall pay any recordation costs. Lender may charge Borrower a fee for releasing this Security Instrument, but only if the fee is paid to a third party for services rendered and the charging of the fee is permitted under Applicable Law.

24. Waivers. Borrower waives all rights of homestead exemption in the Property and relinquishes all rights of curtesy and dower in the Property. BY SIGNING BELOW, Borrower accepts and agrees to the terms and covenants contained in this Security Instrument and in any Rider executed by Borrower and recorded with it.

Witnesses:

H.3.2 Sample Promissory Note—Fixed Rate Mortgage

NOTE

1. BORROWER'S PROMISE TO PAY

In return for a loan that I have received, I promise to pay U.S. $ ____________ (this amount is called "Principal"), plus interest, to the order of the Lender. The Lender is ______________________________. I will make all payments under this Note in the form of cash, check or money order.

I understand that the Lender may transfer this Note. The Lender or anyone who takes this Note by transfer and who is entitled to receive payments under this Note is called the "Note Holder."

2. INTEREST

Interest will be charged on unpaid principal until the full amount of Principal has been paid. I will pay interest at a yearly rate of ______ %.

The interest rate required by this Section 2 is the rate I will pay both before and after any default described in Section 6(B) of this Note.

3. PAYMENTS

(A) Time and Place of Payments

I will pay principal and interest by making a payment every month.

I will make my monthly payment on the __________ day of each month beginning on ______________ , ________ . I will make these payments every month until I have paid all of the principal and interest and any other charges described below that I may owe under this Note. Each monthly payment will be applied as of its scheduled due date and will be applied to interest before Principal. If, on ______________, 20_____, I still owe amounts under this Note, I will pay those amounts in full on that date, which is called the "Maturity Date."

I will make my monthly payments at ______________ or at a different place if required by the Note Holder.

(B) Amount of Monthly Payments

My monthly payment will be in the amount of U.S. $______ .

4. BORROWER'S RIGHT TO PREPAY

I have the right to make payments of Principal at any time before they are due. A payment of Principal only is known as a "Prepayment." When I make a Prepayment, I will tell the Note Holder in writing that I am doing so. I may not designate a payment as a Prepayment if I have not made all the monthly payments due under the Note.

I may make a full Prepayment or partial Prepayments without paying a Prepayment charge. The Note Holder will use my Prepayments to reduce the amount of Principal that I owe under this Note. However, the Note Holder may apply my Prepayment to the accrued and unpaid interest on the Prepayment amount, before applying my Prepayment to reduce the Principal amount of the Note. If I make a partial Prepayment, there will be no changes in the due date or in the amount of my monthly payment unless the Note Holder agrees in writing to those changes.

5. LOAN CHARGES

If a law, which applies to this loan and which sets maximum loan charges, is finally interpreted so that the interest or other loan charges collected or to be collected in connection with this loan exceed the permitted limits, then: (a) any such loan charge shall be reduced by the amount necessary to reduce the charge to the permitted limit; and (b) any sums already collected from me which exceeded permitted limits will be refunded to me. The Note Holder may choose to make this refund by reducing the Principal I owe under this Note or by making a direct payment to me. If a refund reduces Principal, the reduction will be treated as a partial Prepayment.

6. BORROWER'S FAILURE TO PAY AS REQUIRED

(A) Late Charge for Overdue Payments

If the Note Holder has not received the full amount of any monthly payment by the end of __________ calendar days after the date it is due, I will pay a late charge to the Note Holder. The amount of the charge will be __________ % of my overdue payment of principal and interest. I will pay this late charge promptly but only once on each late payment.

(B) Default

If I do not pay the full amount of each monthly payment on the date it is due, I will be in default.

(C) Notice of Default

If I am in default, the Note Holder may send me a written notice telling me that if I do not pay the overdue amount by a certain date, the Note Holder may require me to pay immediately the full amount of Principal which has not been paid and all the interest that I owe on that amount. That date must be at least 30 days after the date on which the notice is mailed to me or delivered by other means.

(D) No Waiver By Note Holder

Even if, at a time when I am in default, the Note Holder does not require me to pay immediately in full as described above, the Note Holder will still have the right to do so if I am in default at a later time.

(E) Payment of Note Holder's Costs and Expenses

If the Note Holder has required me to pay immediately in full as described above, the Note Holder will have the right to be paid back by me for all of its costs and expenses in enforcing this Note to the extent not prohibited by applicable law. Those expenses include, for example, reasonable attorneys' fees.

7. GIVING OF NOTICES

Unless applicable law requires a different method, any notice that must be given to me under this Note will be given by delivering it or by mailing it by first class mail to me at the Property Address above or at a different address if I give the Note Holder a notice of my different address.

Any notice that must be given to the Note Holder under this Note will be given by delivering it or by mailing it by first class mail to the Note Holder at the address stated in Section 3(A) above or at a different address if I am given a notice of that different address.

8. OBLIGATIONS OF PERSONS UNDER THIS NOTE

If more than one person signs this Note, each person is fully and personally obligated to keep all of the promises made in this Note, including the promise to pay the full amount owed. Any person who is a guarantor, surety or endorser of this Note is also obligated to do these things. Any person who takes over these obligations, including the obligations of a guarantor, surety or endorser of this Note, is also obligated to keep all of the promises made in this Note. The Note Holder may enforce its rights under this Note against each person individually or against all of us together. This means that any one of us may be required to pay all of the amounts owed under this Note.

9. WAIVERS

I and any other person who has obligations under this Note waive the rights of Presentment and Notice of Dishonor. "Presentment" means the right to require the Note Holder to demand payment of amounts due. "Notice of Dishonor" means the right to require the Note Holder to give notice to other persons that amounts due have not been paid.

10. UNIFORM SECURED NOTE

This Note is a uniform instrument with limited variations in some jurisdictions. In addition to the protections given to the Note Holder under this Note, a Mortgage, Deed of Trust, or Security Deed (the "Security Instrument"), dated the same date as this Note, protects the Note Holder from possible losses which might result if I do not keep the promises which I make in this Note. That Security Instrument describes how and under what conditions I may be required to make immediate payment in full of all amounts I owe under this Note. Some of those conditions are described as follows:

If all or any part of the Property or any Interest in the Property is sold or transferred (or if Borrower is not a natural person and a beneficial interest in Borrower is sold or transferred) without Lender's prior written consent, Lender may require immediate payment in full of all sums secured by this Security Instrument. However, this option shall not be exercised by Lender if such exercise is prohibited by Applicable Law.

If Lender exercises this option, Lender shall give Borrower notice of acceleration. The notice shall provide a period of not less than 30 days from the date the notice is given in accordance with Section 15 within which Borrower must pay all sums secured by this Security Instrument. If Borrower fails to pay these sums prior to the expiration of this period, Lender may invoke any remedies permitted by this Security Instrument without further notice or demand on Borrower.

WITNESS THE HAND(S) AND SEAL(S) OF THE UNDERSIGNED.

H.3.3 Sample Promissory Note—Adjustable Rate Mortgage

ADJUSTABLE RATE NOTE

(1 Year Treasury Index—Rate Caps)

THIS NOTE CONTAINS PROVISIONS ALLOWING FOR CHANGES IN MY INTEREST RATE AND MY MONTHLY PAYMENT. THIS NOTE LIMITS THE AMOUNT MY INTEREST RATE CAN CHANGE AT ANY ONE TIME AND THE MAXIMUM RATE I MUST PAY.

1. BORROWER'S PROMISE TO PAY

In return for a loan that I have received, I promise to pay U.S. $__________ (this amount is called "Principal"), plus interest, to the order of the Lender. The Lender is __________ . I will make all payments under this Note in the form of cash, check or money order.

I understand that the Lender may transfer this Note. The Lender or anyone who takes this Note by transfer and who is entitled to receive payments under this Note is called the "Note Holder."

2. INTEREST

Interest will be charged on unpaid principal until the full amount of Principal has been paid. I will pay interest at a yearly rate of _______ %.

The interest rate I will pay will change in accordance with Section 4 of this Note. The interest rate required by this Section 2 and Section 4 of this Note is the rate I will pay both before and after any default described in Section 7(B) of this Note.

3. PAYMENTS

(A) Time and Place of Payments

I will pay principal and interest by making a payment every month.

I will make my monthly payment on the first day of each month beginning on ____________ , ____________ . I will make these payments every month until I have paid all of the principal and interest and any other charges described below that I may owe under this Note. Each monthly payment will be applied as of its scheduled due date and will be applied to interest before Principal. If, on __________ , 20________, I still owe amounts under this Note, I will pay those amounts in full on that date, which is called the "Maturity Date."

I will make my monthly payments at__________ or at a different place if required by the Note Holder.

(B) Amount of My Initial Monthly Payments

Each of my initial monthly payments will be in the amount of U.S. $ ______________. This amount may change.

(C) Monthly Payment Changes

Changes in my monthly payment will reflect changes in the unpaid principal of my loan and in the interest rate that I must pay. The Note Holder will determine my new interest rate and the changed amount of my monthly payment in accordance with Section 4 of this Note.

4. INTEREST RATE AND MONTHLY PAYMENT CHANGES

(A) Change Dates

The interest rate I will pay may change on the first day of ______________ , ______________ , and on that day every 12th month thereafter. Each date on which my interest rate could change is called a "Change Date."

(B) The Index

Beginning with the first Change Date, my interest rate will be based on an Index. The "Index" is the weekly average yield on United States Treasury securities adjusted to a constant maturity of one year, as made available by the Federal Reserve Board. The most recent Index figure available as of the date 45 days before each Change Date is called the "Current Index."

If the Index is no longer available, the Note Holder will choose a new index which is based upon comparable information. The Note Holder will give me notice of this choice.

(C) Calculation of Changes

Before each Change Date, the Note Holder will calculate my new interest rate by adding ______________ percentage points (______________ %) to the Current Index. The Note Holder will then round the result of this addition to the nearest one-eighth of one percentage point (0.125%). Subject to the limits stated in Section 4(D) below, this rounded amount will be my new interest rate until the next Change Date.

The Note Holder will then determine the amount of the monthly payment that would be sufficient to repay the unpaid principal that I am expected to owe at the Change Date in full on the Maturity Date at my new interest rate in substantially equal payments. The result of this calculation will be the new amount of my monthly payment.

(D) Limits on Interest Rate Changes

The interest rate I am required to pay at the first Change Date will not be greater than ______________ % or less than ______________ %. Thereafter, my interest rate will never be increased or decreased on any single Change Date by more than one percentage point (1.0%) from the rate of interest I have been paying for the preceding 12 months. My interest rate will never be greater than ______________ %.

(E) Effective Date of Changes

My new interest rate will become effective on each Change Date. I will pay the amount of my new monthly payment beginning on the first monthly payment date after the Change Date until the amount of my monthly payment changes again.

(F) Notice of Changes

The Note Holder will deliver or mail to me a notice of any changes in my interest rate and the amount of my monthly payment before the effective date of any change. The notice will include information required by law to be given to me and also the title and telephone number of a person who will answer any question I may have regarding the notice.

5. BORROWER'S RIGHT TO PREPAY

I have the right to make payments of Principal at any time before they are due. A payment of Principal only is known as a "Prepayment." When I make a Prepayment, I will tell the Note Holder in writing that I am doing so. I may not designate a payment as a Prepayment if I have not made all the monthly payments due under the Note.

I may make a full Prepayment or partial Prepayments without paying a Prepayment charge. The Note Holder will use my Prepayments to reduce the amount of Principal that I owe under this Note. However, the Note Holder may apply my Prepayment to the accrued and unpaid interest on the Prepayment amount, before applying my Prepayment to reduce the Principal amount of the Note. If I make a partial Prepayment, there will be no changes in the due dates of my monthly payment unless the Note Holder agrees in writing to those changes. My partial Prepayment may reduce the amount of my monthly payments after the first Change Date following my partial Prepayment. However, any reduction due to my partial Prepayment may be offset by an interest rate increase.

6. LOAN CHARGES

If a law, which applies to this loan and which sets maximum loan charges, is finally interpreted so that the interest or other loan charges collected or to be collected in connection with this loan exceed the permitted limits, then: (a) any such loan charge shall be reduced by the amount necessary to reduce the charge to the permitted limit; and (b) any sums already collected from me which exceeded permitted limits will be refunded to me. The Note Holder may choose to make this refund by reducing the Principal I owe under this Note or by making a direct payment to me. If a refund reduces Principal, the reduction will be treated as a partial Prepayment.

7. BORROWER'S FAILURE TO PAY AS REQUIRED

(A) Late Charges for Overdue Payments

If the Note Holder has not received the full amount of any monthly payment by the end of ______________ calendar days after the date it is due, I will pay a late charge to the Note Holder. The amount of the charge will be ______________ % of my overdue payment of principal and interest. I will pay this late charge promptly but only once on each late payment.

(B) Default

If I do not pay the full amount of each monthly payment on the date it is due, I will be in default.

(C) Notice of Default

If I am in default, the Note Holder may send me a written notice telling me that if I do not pay the overdue amount by a certain date, the Note Holder may require me to pay immediately the full amount of Principal which has not been paid and all the interest that I owe on that amount. That date must be at least 30 days after the date on which the notice is mailed to me or delivered by other means.

(D) No Waiver By Note Holder

Even if, at a time when I am in default, the Note Holder does not require me to pay immediately in full as described above, the Note Holder will still have the right to do so if I am in default at a later time.

(E) Payment of Note Holder's Costs and Expenses

If the Note Holder has required me to pay immediately in full as described above, the Note Holder will have the right to be paid back by me for all of its costs and expenses in enforcing this Note to the extent not prohibited by applicable law. Those expenses include, for example, reasonable attorneys' fees.

8. GIVING OF NOTICES

Unless applicable law requires a different method, any notice that must be given to me under this Note will be given by delivering it or by mailing it by first class mail to me at the Property Address above or at a different address if I give the Note Holder a notice of my different address.

Any notice that must be given to the Note Holder under this Note will be given by delivering it or by mailing it by first class mail to the Note Holder at the address stated in Section 3(A) above or at a different address if I am given a notice of that different address.

9. OBLIGATIONS OF PERSONS UNDER THIS NOTE

If more than one person signs this Note, each person is fully and personally obligated to keep all of the promises made in this Note, including the promise to pay the full amount owed. Any person who is a guarantor, surety or endorser of this Note is also obligated to do these things. Any person who takes over these obligations, including the obligations of a guarantor, surety or endorser of this Note, is also obligated to keep all of the promises made in this Note. The Note Holder may enforce its rights under this Note against each person individually or against all of us together. This means that any one of us may be required to pay all of the amounts owed under this Note.

10. WAIVERS

I and any other person who has obligations under this Note waive the rights of Presentment and Notice of Dishonor. "Presentment" means the right to require the Note Holder to demand payment of amounts due. "Notice of Dishonor" means the right to require the Note Holder to give notice to other persons that amounts due have not been paid.

11. UNIFORM SECURED NOTE

This Note is a uniform instrument with limited variations in some jurisdictions. In addition to the protections given to the Note Holder under this Note, a Mortgage, Deed of Trust, or Security Deed (the "Security Instrument"), dated the same date as this Note, protects the Note Holder from possible losses which might result if I do not keep the promises which I make in this Note. That Security Instrument describes how and under what conditions I may be required to make immediate payment in full of all amounts I owe under this Note. Some of those conditions are described as follows:

> If all or any part of the Property or any Interest in the Property is sold or transferred (or if Borrower is not a natural person and a beneficial interest in Borrower is sold or transferred) without Lender's prior written consent, Lender may require immediate payment in full of all sums secured by this Security Instrument. However, this option shall not be exercised by Lender if such exercise is prohibited by Applicable Law. Lender also shall not exercise this option if: (a) Borrower causes to be submitted to Lender information required by Lender to evaluate the intended transferee as if a new loan were being made to the transferee; and (b) Lender reasonably determines that Lender's security will not be impaired by the loan assumption and that the risk of a breach of any covenant or agreement in this Security Instrument is acceptable to Lender.
>
> To the extent permitted by Applicable Law, Lender may charge a reasonable fee as a condition to Lender's consent to the loan assumption. Lender may also require the transferee to sign an assumption agreement that is acceptable to Lender and that obligates the transferee to keep all the promises and agreements made in the Note and in this Security Instrument. Borrower will continue to be obligated under the Note and this Security Instrument unless Lender releases Borrower in writing.
>
> If Lender exercises the option to require immediate payment in full, Lender shall give Borrower notice of acceleration. The notice shall provide a period of not less than 30 days from the date the notice is given in accordance with Section 15 within which Borrower must pay all sums secured by this Security Instrument. If Borrower fails to pay these sums prior to the expiration of this period, Lender may invoke any remedies permitted by this Security Instrument without further notice or demand on Borrower.

WITNESS THE HAND(S) AND SEAL(S) OF THE UNDERSIGNED.

H.3.4 Sample Change Rate Notice for ARM

[Mortgage Company]

January 17, 2009

Loan: [NUMBER]

Dear: [NAME]

Effective with your 03-01-09 payment the interest rate on your mortgage loan will be adjusted, as required by your Mortgage Mote. Please refer to your Note for details on how we are required to compute your new rate, or call our Customer service Department at 1-800-555-5555.

Your current interest rate of 11.10000% was based on the index rate of 1.98375%. Your new interest rate of 11.10000% is based on the new index of 1.43000%, then added to your margin of 5.95000%. The result was then rounded as specified in your Note.

In conjunction with the interest rate change, your Principal and Interest payment will also be adjusted as specified by your Note. Your Principal and Interest payment will be $459.97 effective with your 03-01-09 payment. Your new total payment, including your monthly escrow deposit, will be $530.55. Your new Principal and Interest amount was based on a projected principal balance of $47,209.37.

These changes will be reflected on your Monthly Statement when the 03-01-09 payment is due. If you have any questions regarding this change, please Contact our Customer Service Department, toll-free, at 1-800-555-5555.

Sincerely,

[Mortgage Company]

H.3.5 Sample Annual Escrow Account Statement

[Bank Name]
Customer Service:
Toll free 1.800.555.5555 Se habla espanol
TDD Dial 7-1-1 for relay assistance

Annual Escrow
Account Statement
Statement Date: November 08, 2009
Review Period: January 2009 to December 2009
Your Loan Number:

What is an escrow account?

A portion of each of your monthly home loan payments goes into an escrow account. This money is used to pay items such as your property taxes and insurance premiums when they are due.

In accordance with federal guidelines, we review your Escrow Account at least one time each year to ensure that we are collecting enough money to make all required payments. This document is a review of your Escrow Account activity since your last analysis.

Monthly Home Loan Payment

	Current	New Payment (effective 01/01/10) if you select Option A below	New Payment (effective 01/01/10) if you select Option B below
Principal & Interest	1,337.13	1.337.13	1,337.13
Escrow Account Deposit	247.86	324.45*	324.45*
Plus: Account Balancer/Shortage	0.00	0.00	146.79**
Total Payment Amount	1,584.99	1,661.58	1,808.37

Your new total payment includes an updated monthly escrow deposit, based on projected amounts to be paid from your Escrow Account, of $324.45* and, if applicable, an amount needed to repay the escrow shortage of $146.79**.

Please review the detailed information provided on the back of this page.

Here are your shortage repayment options. You may select one of the following options:

Option A: Pay Entire Shortage Now
* Pay the entire $1,761.47 escrow account shortage using the Escrow Account Balancer Payment Coupon below for a new total payment of $1,661.58. **See chart above.**
* Pay a portion of your shortage—every $12 paid reduces your total payment by $1.
*** NOTE: The new payment amount will be effective the month after the shortage amount is received. Any remaining increase in the escrow payment is to cover the projected increase in your bills for the upcoming years.**

Option B: Pay Shortage Over 12 Months
Pay the $1,761.47 escrow account shortage in 12 Account Balancer payments of $146.79 each. To choose this option, no action is required. The 12 payments will be automatically added to your home loan payment for January 2010 through December 2010.
If you select this option, your new monthly home loan payment (effective 01/01/07) will be $1,808.37. See chart above.

ANTICIPATED ESCROW ACCOUNT PAYMENTS

This section reflects the escrow activity that is expected to occur in the next 12 months. The *Total Tax and Insurance Monthly Payment Amount* at the bottom of this chart is your new monthly escrow deposit, as listed on Page 1 of this statement.

TAX

Item	Annual Expense	Anticipated Date(s) of Payment
COUNTY TAX	$ 2,909.37	DECEMBER 10

INSURANCE

Item	Annual Expense	Anticipated Date(s) of Payment
FIRE/HOMEOWN	$ 984.00	MARCH 10

TOTAL TAX AND INSURANCE
MONTHLY PAYMENT AMOUNT = $324.45

Balancing Your Escrow Account
The front of this statement shows that you have an Escrow Account Shortage of $1,761.47. How was this determined?

Your previous year's activity is used to estimate the deposit and disbursement activity in your Escrow Account and project your *lowest account balance* for the year ahead. Your projected *lowest account balance* is compared to your *minimum required balance* as shown in the *Escrow Account Balancer* below these paragraphs. This determines the amount required to bring your Escrow Account into balance.

Since taxes and insurance premiums often go up, we require that you maintain a *minimum required balance* in your account at all times to prevent a negative balance in your account.

As shown in the information in the box and graph below, you will reach your *lowest account balance* of -$1,112.57 in March 07. This is subtracted from your *minimum required balance* of $648.90 resulting in an Escrow Account Shortage of $1,761.47.

In order to pay your Escrow Account Shortage and bring your account into balance, you may pay the $1,761.47 shortage in full (Option A on front) or pay the shortage over 12 months (Option B on front). It's your choice.

Escrow Account Balancer

Minimum Required Balance	$648.90
Less: Lowest Account Balance (Mar 10)	–$1,112.57
Annual Account Balancer/Shortage	$1,765.47
Monthly Account Balancer/Shortage	146.79

Projected Escrow Account Balance
The graph below shows your projected Escrow Account Balance for the next 12 months with your new monthly Escrow Account Deposit of $324.45 and the "Anticipated Escrow Account Payments" chart shown on the next page. Your projected beginning escrow balance of -$1,101.92 is based on anticipated deposits and disbursements.

Escrow Account History for the Prior Payment Period
The following is a comparison of the anticipated and actual Escrow Account activity for the previous payment period. Anticipated amounts are taken from your last analysis. Your most recent monthly payment during the past year was $1,584.99, of which $1,337.13 was for principal and interest and $247.86 went into your Escrow Account.

At the time of your last analysis, your anticipated lowest balance was $495.72. In reviewing your account activity, your actual low escrow balance was -$1,101.92.

NOTE: An asterisk (*) in the chart below indicates a difference between what actually occurred and what was anticipated. This difference may be due to a change in Escrow items such as an increase in your insurance premium or a change in the due date of your property tax. Insurance and Tax payments may be disbursed before their due dates to allow for more mail and posting time at the insurance company or tax office. An "E" in the chart below indicates expected activity.

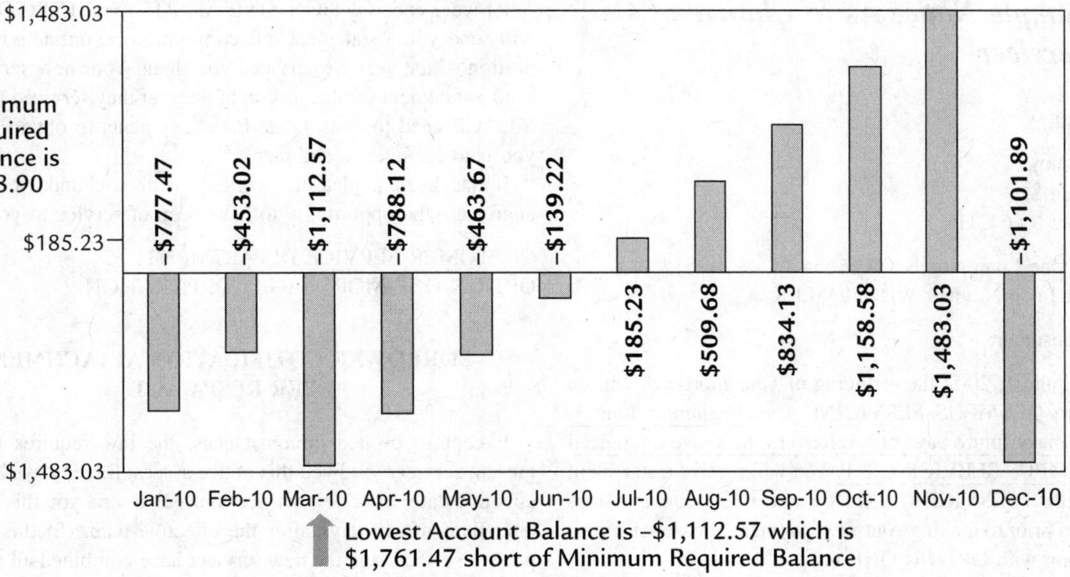

	Deposits to Escrow (credits to Escrow)		Payments from Escrow (debits from Escrow)			Escrow Balance	
Month	**Anticipated**	**Actual**	**Anticipated**	**Actual**	**Description**	**Projected**	**Actual**
Jan 09	247.86	247.86				611.14	–182.87
Feb 09	247.86	247.86				859.00	64.99
Mar 09	247.86	247.86	859.00	984.00*	FIRE/HOMEOWN	1,106.86	312.85
Apr 09	247.86	247.86				495.72	423.29
May 09	247.86	247.86				743.58	–175.43
Jun 09	247.86	247.86				991.44	72.43
Jul 09	247.86	247.86				1,239.30	320.29
Aug 09	247.86	247.86				1,487.16	568.15
Sep 09	247.86	247.86				1,735.02	816.01
Oct 09	247.86	247.86				1,982.88	1,063.87
Nov 09	247.86	247.86				2,230.74	1,311.73
Dec 09	247.86	247.86E	2,115.36	2,909.37	COUNTY TAX	2,478.60	1,559.59
						611.10	–1,101.92
	2,974.32	**2,974.32**	**2,974.36**	**3,893.37**			

H.3.6 Sample Notice As to Change of Servicer

January 1, 2009

Patrick Consumer
33 West Main St.
Kansas City, MO 64111

Re: Option One Loan Number 6066654
Investor Loan Number WDO5945LEK

Dear Mr. Consumer:

Effective June 1, 2002 the servicing of your mortgage will be transferred to OLYMPUS SERVICING L.P. Beginning June 1, 2002 please make future payments related to the above referenced loan to OLYMPUS SERVICING L.P. You will receive a statement from OLYMPUS SERVICING L.P. However, if the statement does not reach you prior to making your next payment, please send your payment along with OPTION ONE coupon to:

PAYMENTS	CORRESPONDENCE
OLYMPUS SERVICING L.P.	OLYMPUS SERVICING L.P.
P.O. Box 660720	9600 Great Hills Trail, 200W
Dallas, TX 75266-0720	Austin, TX 78759

Thereafter, payments should be directed to the payment address on your billing statement.

On June 1, 2002 Option One Mortgage Corporation will cease to accept payments related to this loan. If your mortgage payment is being drafted, you should notify your bank of the transfer. The new servicer will inform you of their method of accepting payments.

Any payments received by OPTION ONE MORTGAGE CORPORATION after the transfer will be forwarded to the new servicer. On June 1, 2002 OLYMPUS SERVICING L.P. will begin accepting your payments.

On or after June 1, 2002 you may contact OLYMPUS SERVICING L.P. Customer Service Department at (800) 671-0252, if you have any questions concerning your account. Their hours are 8:00 a.m. to 8:00 p.m. Monday through Friday, and 8:00 a.m. to 2:00 p.m. on Saturdays (CST).

Prior to June 1, 2002 you may contact the OPTION ONE MORTGAGE CORPORATION, Customer Service Department at (800) 648-9605, if you have any questions concerning your account. Our hours are 7:30 a.m. to 6:00 p.m. Monday through Thursday, and Friday 7:00 a.m. to 5:00 p.m. (PST).

At year-end, OPTION ONE MORTGAGE CORPORATION will send you a statement reflecting your account activity for the portion of the year we serviced your loan. Your new servicer will send a statement for the portion of the year they serviced your loan. You will need to consolidate both statements to obtain the totals you paid for interest and taxes.

It has been a pleasure working with you and we sincerely appreciate the opportunity to have been of service to you.

CUSTOMER SERVICE DEPARTMENT
OPTION ONE MORTGAGE CORPORATION

BORROWER NOTIFICATION ATTACHMENT PER RESPA ACT

Except in limited circumstances, the law requires that your present servicer send you this notice at least fifteen days before the effective date. Your new servicer must also send you this notice no later than fifteen days after the effective date. (In this case the present servicer and the new servicer have combined all necessary information in this one notice.)

You should also be aware of the following information, which is set out in more detail in Section 6 of RESPA (12 U.S.C. § 2605).

During the sixty-day period following the effective date of the transfer of loan servicing, a loan payment received by your old servicer before its due date may not be treated by the new loan servicer as late, and a late fee may not be imposed on you.

Section 6 of RESPA (12 U.S.C. § 2605) gives you certain consumer rights. If you send a "qualified written request" to your loan servicer concerning the servicing of your loan, your servicer must provide you with a written acknowledgment within twenty business days of receipt of your request. A "qualified written request" is a written correspondence, other than notice on a payment coupon or other medium supplied by the servicer, which includes your name and account number, and your reasons for the request. Not later than sixty business days after receiving your request, your servicer must make any appropriate corrections to your account, and must provide you with written clarification regarding any dispute. During this sixty-day period, your servicer may not provide information to a consumer reporting agency concerning any overdue payment related to such period or qualified written request.

Section 6 of RESPA also provides for damages and costs for individuals or classes of individuals in circumstances where servicers are shown to have violated the requirements of the Section. You should seek legal advice if you believe your rights have been violated.

Appendix I

Sample Foreclosure Pleadings and Other Litigation Documents

I.1 Introduction

This appendix contains several sample pleadings used in foreclosure related actions. The pleadings are from actual cases and have been drafted by experienced attorneys. However, the pleadings in the text are for demonstration purposes only. Foreclosure is governed by local law and thus many of the pleadings contain state-specific legal claims. The pleadings and other documents must be adapted by a competent professional to fit the circumstances of a given case and the requirements of local rules and practice.

This appendix contains the following pleadings:

1 Advocates need to be particularly alert to changes in rules governing the HAMP program, keeping in mind that the pleadings reproduced here were drafted during the first year of the program's existence. These pleadings may reflect rules that to some extent have been updated or may eventually be superseded.

I.2 Answers to Judicial Foreclosures

I.2.1 Answer with Counterclaims Regarding Management of Escrow Account

IN THE UNITED STATES DISTRICT COURT
FOR THE EASTERN DISTRICT OF PENNSYLVANIA

CMT MORTGAGE CORPORATION, S/B/M TO CMT MORTGAGE COMPANY	)
Plaintiff,	)
v.	)
[Consumer],	)
Defendant.	)

FIRST AMENDED ANSWER AND AMENDED COUNTERCLAIMS

Defendant [Consumer], by and through his attorney, [Attorney], Esquire, hereby files the following Answer to Plaintiff's Complaint and states as follows:

1. Admitted.
2. Admitted.
3. Admitted.
4. Admitted.
5. Denied. The allegations contained in Paragraph 5 are conclusions of law to which no responsive pleading is required and the same are therefore denied. In the alternative, the Mortgage is not in default because Defendant did not fail to make timely payments on his mortgage. The Mortgagee and its agents failed to accept the mortgage payments.
6. Denied. Defendant is not in default of the loan; therefore, the principal is not owed. Defendant does not owe the interest because Plaintiff improperly applied payments and Plaintiff refused to accept payments properly tendered. Regarding the attorney's fee, after reasonable investigation, Defendant is without sufficient information to form a belief as to the truth of this averment. Defendant does not owe late charges because Defendant tendered payment in a timely manner. There is no deficiency in Defendant's escrow account. Upon information and belief, there should be a credit to the escrow account.
7. Denied. The allegations contained in Paragraph 5 are conclusions of law to which no responsive pleading is required and the same is therefore denied.
8. Admitted.
9. Denied. The allegations contained in Paragraph 5 are conclusions of law to which no responsive pleading is required and the same is therefore denied.

WHEREFORE, Defendant respectfully requests that this Honorable Court dismiss with prejudice Plaintiff's claims against him.

IT IS FURTHER REQUESTED that this Honorable Court deny the relief requested and prayers for relief presented by Plaintiff and against Defendant in their entirety, with prejudice.

FIRST DEFENSE

10. Defendant incorporates herein by reference each and every response and allegation in the preceding Paragraphs as if the same were hereby set forth.

11. Plaintiff's Complaint fails to set forth any causes of actions for which relief may be granted.

SECOND DEFENSE

12. Plaintiff's claims are barred by doctrine of estoppel.

THIRD DEFENSE

13. Plaintiff's claims are barred by the doctrine of waiver.

FOURTH DEFENSE

14. Plaintiff's claims are barred by the doctrine of payment.

FIFTH DEFENSE

15. Plaintiff's claims are barred by the doctrine of unclean hands.

SIXTH DEFENSE

16. Plaintiff's claims are barred by the doctrine of fraud, based on the facts set forth in the counterclaims below. Defendant incorporates by reference each and every response and allegation in the paragraphs following as if the same were hereby set forth.

17. Defendant reserves the right to introduce any and all such further defenses that may arise during discovery and up to and including time of trial.

WHEREFORE, Defendant respectfully requests that this Honorable Court dismiss with prejudice Plaintiff's claims against him.

IT IS FURTHER REQUESTED that this Honorable Court deny the relief requested and prayers for relief presented by Plaintiff and against Defendant in their entirety, with prejudice.

COUNTERCLAIMS

18. Defendant incorporates herein by reference each and every response and allegation in the preceding Paragraphs as if the same were hereby set forth.

19. Plaintiff has overcharged Defendant's account for payments of taxes that do not exist, resulting in a demand for increased monthly payments from Defendant.

20. Plaintiff reported to Defendant in August 2003 that the 2002–2003 school taxes in the amount of $2,430.75 were paid on August 1, 2003.

21. Upon information and belief, Plaintiff did not pay the 2003 school taxes until June 2, 2004.

22. In or about March 2004, a tax lien was placed against the property for the 2003 school taxes.

23. Upon information and belief, on June 2, 2004, Lester County Tax Authority received $1,394.89 for payment for school district tax lien against Defendant's property.

24. Plaintiff, in statements sent to Defendant beginning in

August 2003, represented to Defendant that he would be responsible for a deficiency in his escrow account in the amount of $850.96.

25. Plaintiff increased Defendant's monthly payments from $652.62 to $890.90.

26. Plaintiff represented that the increase was to make up the escrow deficiency.

27. Upon receiving the notice of the increased escrow charges, Defendant contacted Plaintiff by telephone and challenged the escrow charges.

28. Within a month, Defendant sent a written challenge of the escrow charges to Plaintiff.

29. Approximately a month after the written challenge to the escrow charges, Defendant again contacted Plaintiff by telephone.

30. Plaintiff's representative acknowledged that the escrow account had errors, and stated that she would correct the escrow charges.

31. Defendant continued to pay Plaintiff the monthly payment of $652.62 per month.

32. Plaintiff held the $656.62 paid by Defendant in a suspense account until the account reached $890.96.

33. Late fees were charged to Defendant while the money was held in the suspense account.

34. In or about August 2004, Plaintiff refused Defendant's payments.

35. Plaintiff continues to refuse Defendants payments.

36. Plaintiff charged Defendant's escrow account $326.08 for the February 2004 county tax payment.

37. Upon Information and belief, in February 2004 Plaintiff paid the county taxes of $159.84.

38. In April 2004 Plaintiff charged Defendant's escrow account $1,191.57 for "county tax pd."

39. Upon information and belief, no payment was made to the county taxing authority in April 2004.

40. In May 2004 Plaintiff charged Defendant's escrow account $1,191.57 for "school tax pd."

41. Upon information and belief, no payment was made to the school taxing authority in May 2004.

42. In June 2004, Plaintiff reported that it received $1,191.57 refunded from Lester County Tax Authority.

43. Plaintiff credited the refunded $1,191.57 to Defendant's escrow account.

44. On August 6, 2004, Plaintiff charged Defendant's escrow account for "school tax pd." the amount of $2,669.53.

45. Upon information and belief, Plaintiff did not pay the school taxing authority $2,669.53 in August 2004.

46. On August 6, 2004, Plaintiff also charged Defendant's escrow account for "school tax pd." the amount of $1,282.49.

47. Upon information and belief, on August 23, 2004, the school district received $1,282.45 in full payment for the 2004 school year.

48. As of August 16, 2004, Plaintiff reported Defendant's escrow account was deficient $4,109.53.

49. Overall, Plaintiff reported that it distributed $9,091.99 from Defendant's escrow account, and that it paid a net amount of $7,9000.42 from Defendant's escrow account.

50. Overall, Plaintiff actually paid $2,837.18 for Defendant's escrow account.

Count I—Unfair Trade Practices

51. Defendant incorporates herein by reference each and every response and allegation in the preceding Paragraphs as if the same were hereby set forth.

52. Plaintiff misrepresented to Defendant the amount of county and school taxes due.

53. Plaintiff misrepresented the amount required to satisfy the charges that were likely to be paid by the escrow account.

54. Plaintiff misrepresented the monthly amount Defendant would need to pay into the escrow account.

55. Plaintiff misrepresented the balance of the escrow account.

56. Plaintiff misrepresented that the payments to the taxing authority were made when they were not.

57. Plaintiff made the misrepresentations to Defendant falsely, with knowledge of its falsity, or with recklessness as to whether the misrepresentations were true or false.

58. Plaintiff made the misrepresentations with the intent of misleading Defendant into relying on the statements.

59. Defendant justifiably relied upon Plaintiff's representations.

60. As a result of Plaintiff's misrepresentations, Defendant has suffered and continues to suffer financial harm including but not limited to:

a. Increased interest expenses on his mortgage;
b. Improperly charged late fees on his mortgage;
c. Interest on the property tax payments;
d. Damage to his credit report and credit score; and
e. Attorney's fees and costs associated with attempting to correct this dispute.

61. Plaintiff engaged in fraudulent or deceptive conduct which had a likelihood of creating confusion or misunderstanding in violation of the Unfair Trade Practices and Consumer Protection Law, 73 P.S. § 201-3.

WHEREFORE, Defendant respectfully requests that this Honorable Court enter judgment for Defendant and against Plaintiff for the following:

A. Declaratory judgment that Plaintiff's conduct violated Unfair Trade Practices and Consumer Protection Law, 73 P.S. § 201-1, *et seq.*;
B. Award actual damages;
C. Award statutory damages pursuant to 73 P.S. § 201-9.2;
D. Award costs and attorney's fees; and
E. Grant such other relief as the Court may deem just and proper.

Count II—Breach of Contract

62. Defendant incorporates herein by reference each and every response and allegation in the preceding Paragraphs as if the same were hereby set forth.

63. Defendant entered into a mortgage and note with Plaintiff's predecessor in interest.

64. As part of the agreement, Plaintiff promised to maintain an escrow account for Defendant for the purpose of distributing taxes.

65. Plaintiff overcharged Defendant's escrow account over a period of more than one year.

66. Plaintiff refused Defendant's monthly payments.

67. As a result of Plaintiff's failure to perform in accordance with the contract, Defendant has suffered and continues to suffer financial harm including but not limited to:

a. Increased interest expenses on his mortgage;
b. Improperly charged late fees on his mortgage;
c. Interest on the property tax payments;
d. Damage to his credit report and credit score; and
e. Attorney's fees and costs associated with attempting to correct this dispute.

WHEREFORE, Defendant respectfully requests that this Honorable Court enter judgment for Defendant and against Plaintiff for the following:

A. Award actual damages;
B. Award costs and attorney's fees; and
C. Grant such other relief as the Court may deem just and proper.

Count III—Breach of Fiduciary Duty

68. Defendant incorporates herein by reference each and every response and allegation in the preceding Paragraphs as if the same were hereby set forth.

69. Defendant entered into a mortgage and note with Plaintiff's predecessor in interest.

70. Plaintiff at all times relevant hereto agreed to act as escrow holder and depository with respect to the monies paid by Defendant pursuant to the agreement.

71. As escrow agent and depository, Plaintiff was the agent for Defendant and owed a fiduciary duty to him.

72. Plaintiff's overcharging of and misadministration of the escrow account constituted breaches of Plaintiff's fiduciary duty to Defendant.

73. As a result of Plaintiff's breaches of its fiduciary duties to Defendant, Defendant has suffered and continues to suffer financial harm including but not limited to:

a. Increased interest expenses on his mortgage;
b. Improperly charged late fees on his mortgage;
c. Interest on the property tax payments;
d. Damage to his credit report and credit score; and
e. Attorney's fees and costs associated with attempting to correct this dispute.

WHEREFORE, Defendant respectfully requests that this Honorable Court enter judgment for Defendant and against Plaintiff for the following:

B. Award actual damages;
C. Award punitive damages;
D. Award costs and attorney's fees; and
E. Grant such other relief as the Court may deem just and proper.

Count IV—Unlawful Debt Collection Practices

74. Defendant incorporates herein by reference each and every response and allegation in the preceding Paragraphs as if the same were hereby set forth.

75. In the alternative, upon information and belief, Plaintiff was acting as a debt collector to collect the debt allegedly owed or due to another.

76. Plaintiff, by overcharging Defendant's escrow account, falsely represented the amount of the debt necessary to cure the deficiency of the escrow account in violation of 15 U.S.C. § 1692e(2)(A).

77. Plaintiff, by initiating this action after wrongfully refusing the Defendant's tender of payment, falsely represented the character, amount, or legal status of the debt in violation of 15 U.S.C. § 1692e(2)(A).

78. Plaintiff, by failing to report the disputed debt as disputed to credit reporting bureaus, communicated credit information which was known or which should have been known as false in violation of 15 U.S.C. § 1692e(8).

79. Plaintiff, by continuing to charge late fees and interest, and by holding Defendant's payments in a suspense account, failed to cease collection on a disputed debt in violation of 15 U.S.C. § 1692g(b).

80. As a result of Plaintiff's unlawful debt collections practices, Defendant has suffered and continues to suffer financial harm including but not limited to:

a. Increased interest expenses on his mortgage;
b. Improperly charged late fees on his mortgage;
c. Interest on the property tax payments;
d. Damage to his credit report and credit score; and
e. Attorney's fees and costs associated with attempting to correct this dispute.

WHEREFORE, Defendant respectfully requests that this Honorable Court enter judgment for Defendant and against Plaintiff for the following:

B. Declaratory judgment that Plaintiff's conduct violated the Fair Debt Collection Practices Act, 15 U.S.C. § 1692, *et seq.;*
C. Award actual damages;
D. Award statutory damages pursuant to 15 U.S.C. § 1692k;
E. Award costs and attorney's fees pursuant to 15 U.S.C. § 1692k; and
F. Grant such other relief as the Court may deem just and proper.

Count V—Real Estate Settlement Procedures Act Violations

81. Defendant incorporates herein by reference each and every response and allegation in the preceding Paragraphs as if the same were hereby set forth.

82. Plaintiff serviced a federally related mortgage loan for Defendant.

83. Plaintiff, in servicing the mortgage loan, was under an obligation to submit to Defendant a statement clearly itemizing the estimated taxes to be paid with the escrow funds.

84. Plaintiff engaged in a pattern or practice of failing to make payment from the escrow account in a timely manner in violation of 12 U.S.C. § 2605.

85. As a result of Plaintiff's improper servicing of the escrow account, Defendant has suffered and continues to suffer financial harm including but not limited to:

a. Increased interest expenses on his mortgage;
b. Improperly charged late fees on his mortgage;
c. Interest on the property tax payments;
d. Damage to his credit report and credit score; and
e. Attorney's fees and costs associated with attempting to correct this dispute.

WHEREFORE, Defendant respectfully requests that this Honorable Court enter judgment for Defendant and against Plaintiff for the following:

B. Declaratory judgment that plaintiff's conduct violated the Real Estate Settlement Procedures Act, 12 U.S.C. § 2601, *et seq.;*

C. Award actual damages;
D. Award statutory damages pursuant to 12 U.S.C. § 2605(f);
E. Award costs and attorney's fees pursuant to 12 U.S.C. § 2605(f); and
F. Grant other such relief as the Court may deem just and proper.

Respectfully Submitted,
Attorney for Defendant

I.2.2 *Answer with TILA and RESPA Affirmative Defenses*

IN THE CIRCUIT COURT OF COOK COUNTY, ILLINOIS
COUNTY DEPARTMENT, CHANCERY DIVISION

________________)	
CHANCE BANK OF TEXAS,)	
Plaintiff,)	
)	
v.)	No. 00 CH 0000
)	
BERNICE HOMEOWNER,)	
Defendant,)	
________________)	

SECOND AMENDED ANSWER AND AFFIRMATIVE DEFENSES TO COMPLAINT TO FORECLOSE MORTGAGE

Now comes Defendant, by and through her attorneys, and answers Plaintiff's Complaint, as follows:

[*Answers 1-6 omitted.*]

WHEREFORE, Defendant prays that this Court enter an Order: Dismissing the Complaint in this case with prejudice and entering judgment in favor of Defendant and against Plaintiff.

AFFIRMATIVE DEFENSES

Statement of Facts

1. Ms. Homeowner is a 72-year-old woman who has owned the property at 1234 W. Main Street (hereinafter, "the home") for over thirty years.

2. The home was purchased for approximately $20,000 in 1970.

3. At all relevant times, Ms. Homeowner has resided in the home with her sons and grandchildren.

4. Ms. Homeowner, as a senior citizen with limited education and income, but substantial equity in her home, was a prime target for predatory mortgage lenders and brokers.

5. Ms. Homeowner was an unsophisticated borrower who did not understand many of the basic terms and costs of a typical mortgage loan transaction. For example, between 1995 and 1999, Ms. Homeowner entered into at least 4 costly home refinance loans as follows:

a. In July, 1995, Ms. Homeowner entered into a mortgage loan with Option One Mortgage Corporation, for a $48,750 loan amount at 12.85% Annual Percentage Rate, with closing costs of $4111.

b. In November, 1996, Ms. Homeowner refinanced the Option One loan with The Money Store, which paid off approximately $58,142 to Option One, paid off a few small credit card debts, and which purportedly gave her $16,327 cash to perform certain home improvements. She was charged approximately $7300 in closing costs for this loan, including almost $6000 in broker fees on a loan of approximately $80,000.

c. In April or May, 1997, Ms. Homeowner refinanced the Money Store loan with a mortgage lender/broker called Midwest America Financial Corp. Midwest paid The Money Store some $84,000, and charged Ms. Homeowner approximately $4000 in closing costs, a portion of which she was required to pay at the closing. The resulting loan was about $90,000, at 12.9% interest, with payments of $922 per month and a balloon after 15 years. In this transaction, Ms. Homeowner had received a preliminary Truth In Lending Disclosure which substantially differed from the final loan terms, but did not realize the discrepancy due to her unsophistication.

d. In May, 1999, Ms. Homeowner took the loan presently at issue, described in more detail below, with a principal balance of $120,000 and monthly payments exceeding 80% of her total household monthly income.

e. In the space of four years, therefore, Ms. Homeowner increased the indebtedness secured by her home from $48,750 to $120,000, and paid over $20,000 in closing costs and mortgage fees (not counting regular interest on the loans), but received the benefit of only about $19,000 at most.

6. Each of the foregoing loans substantially reduced Ms. Homeowner's equity in her home and increased her monthly mortgage payments without providing her with a proportionate economic benefit.

7. In February 1999, Ms. Homeowner received a phone solicitation from Victory Mortgage ("Victory"), a mortgage broker. Victory explained to Ms. Homeowner that it could offer her a new loan that would reduce her mortgage payments and provide her with some extra cash.

8. Because Ms. Homeowner was struggling to make her monthly mortgage payments of approximately $990 a month and because she needed about $1600 to repair her roof, she agreed to meet with Victory.

9. Soon thereafter, a male Victory agent visited Ms. Homeowner at her home. Victory's agent repeated the assertions about the loan's benefits and urged Ms. Homeowner to complete loan application documents. In reliance on Victory's promises that the loan would provide her with additional cash and lower her monthly mortgage payments, Ms. Homeowner signed these documents.

10. In or around March 1999, Ms. Homeowner went to the office of Victory Mortgage near Central and Lawrence Avenue in Chicago and met with its agent, Wendy Smith. Ms. Smith again promised Ms. Homeowner that Victory could provide a new mortgage loan that would reduce her mortgage payments and provide her with the cash to repair her leaking roof.

11. In reliance on Ms. Smith's assertions, Ms. Homeowner completed additional documents relating to the loan application.

12. Subsequently, a Victory agent named Mira James contacted Ms. Homeowner and informed her that her loan was ready to close. On or about May 27, 1999, Ms. Homeowner went to an office in downtown Chicago where the closing was completed.

13. At the closing, Ms. Homeowner was presented with a

myriad of loan documents to sign. A man showed Ms. Homeowner the documents and told her where to sign them. He stated that she did not need to read the documents because the signing was a mere formality. Ms. Homeowner, with limited education and little ability to understand the complicated financial documents placed before her, signed all the documents. Mira James was present at the closing.

14. Upon completing the closing, Ms. Homeowner asked Mira James when she would receive the funds to repair her roof. James informed her that the loan they had arranged for her was insufficient to provide her with the $1600 in cash she had requested. Instead, James stated that Victory would to pay Ms. Homeowner's first monthly mortgage payment.

15. A few days later, James called Ms. Homeowner and said that Victory would not make the payment because they had just discovered some unpaid back taxes. Ms. Homeowner did not understand this because her previous mortgage company was supposed to pay the property taxes, and she was unaware of any tax arrearage.

16. The mortgage documents created a loan transaction between Ms. Homeowner and Saxon Mortgage, Inc. ("Saxon") for the principal amount of $120,000 with an Annual Percentage Rate of 12.042%.

17. On information and belief, Saxon reviewed Ms. Homeowner's application and prepared all the documents in connection with the loan. Moreover, Saxon had an arrangement or agreement with Victory whereby Victory referred borrowers to Saxon for mortgage loans. Therefore, Saxon authorized, approved, and/or ratified each document and procedure employed by Victory in connection with the making of the loan.

18. The transaction created a 15-year loan which increased Ms. Homeowner's mortgage payments to $1142.79 (excluding taxes and insurance) with a balloon payment in the 180th month (when Ms. Homeowner is 84) of $101,686.62.

19. The loan also carried a prepayment penalty which would require Ms. Homeowner to pay an amount equal to six months interest if she paid off the loan within five years.

20. Ms. Homeowner had no idea that she would still owe $101,686.62 after making payments for fifteen years and would not have agreed to the loan had she known.

21. Ms. Homeowner relied on Victory's representation that the loan would provide her with $1600 for the roof and would lower the monthly payment and interest rate. She would not have entered into the transaction had she been aware of the true nature of the loan.

22. Ms. Homeowner's reliance was reasonable under all of the circumstances, given her advanced age, limited education and lack of financial sophistication, and the fact that Victory was a professional mortgage broker which undertook to assist and advise Ms. Homeowner in obtaining a loan.

23. According to the Itemization of Amount Financed attached to the Truth In Lending Statement, Victory received $7800 from the loan proceeds for arranging the loan.

24. Victory received at least $5597 from the loan proceeds.

25. Victory received an additional payment of $3750 from Saxon, denominated "Broker's Compensation."

26. On information and belief, based on counsel's familiarity with mortgage industry practices, the $3750 was measured or calculated based on the rate of interest which Victory was able to get Ms. Homeowner to sign for, *i.e.*, Victory's compensation was increased by an amount corresponding to a higher rate of interest on the loan. The higher the rate, the more Victory could receive. Such a payment is sometimes known in the mortgage industry as a "yield spread premium."

27. As part of the transaction, Ms. Homeowner paid thousands of dollars in fees to the mortgage broker for obtaining a balloon loan with an interest rate of 11%, that increased her mortgage payments without providing her with any real economic benefit.

28. On information and belief, based on counsel's familiarity with the mortgage industry, the 11% interest rate exceeded Saxon's par rate on 15 year balloon loans for borrowers with similar credit histories to Ms. Homeowner's.

29. Victory was more than adequately compensated for its services by Ms. Homeowner from the loan proceeds. The mortgage broker provided no goods or services for the additional "yield spread premium" fee.

30. Ms. Homeowner received no real economic benefit from this transaction.

31. With respect to the loan transaction, Saxon was a "creditor" as that term is defined in the Truth-in-Lending Act, 15 U.S.C. § 1602(f), and Regulation Z, 12 C.F.R. § 226.2(a)(17).[1]

32. The transaction between Saxon and Ms. Homeowner was a "consumer credit transaction" as that term is defined in the Truth-in-Lending Act, 15 U.S.C. § 1602(h), and Regulation Z, 12 C.F.R. § 226.2(a).

33. The transaction between Saxon and Ms. Homeowner was a "closed-end credit transaction" as the term is defined in 12 C.F.R. § 226.2(10), and is subject to the requirements for such transactions set forth in 15 U.S.C. § 1638 and 12 C.F.R. §§ 226.17-226.24.

34. The transaction between Saxon and Ms. Homeowner was one in which a security interest was taken in Ms. Homeowner's principal place of residence.

35. The transaction between Saxon and Ms. Homeowner was for the principal amount of $120,000.

36. The transaction between Saxon and Ms. Homeowner was for the Amount Financed of $111,705.66.

37. As such, the "total loan amount" for the transaction, as defined in 15 U.S.C. § 1602(aa)(1)(B) and 12 C.F.R. § 226.32(a)(1)(ii) was therefore a maximum of $111,705.66.

38. The total points and fees paid by Ms. Homeowner in connection with the loan exceeded 8% of the total loan amount.

39. When the total points and fees are greater than 8% of the total loan amount, the mortgage is defined as a high rate mortgage pursuant to 15 U.S.C. § 1602(aa).

40. The transaction between Saxon and Ms. Homeowner was therefore a high rate mortgage.

41. Ms. Homeowner has suffered economic and emotional damages as a result of the Third-Party Defendants' conduct described herein. She is faced with the possible loss of her home of over thirty years.

First Affirmative Defense

Plaintiff's Assignor's Failure to Provide Required Truth in Lending Disclosures

42. As described above, the transaction between plaintiff's assignor and Ms. Homeowner was a high rate mortgage. 15 U.S.C. § 1602(aa)(1)(B).

1 [*Editor's Note*: Citations throughout answer as in original.]

43. The transaction of May 27, 2000, between plaintiff's assignor and Ms. Homeowner, was therefore one in which the provisions of 15 U.S.C. § 1639 and 12 C.F.R. § 226.32 were applicable.

44. Plaintiff's assignor violated the Truth-in-Lending, *inter alia*,

a. by failing to provide the disclosures to the consumer required by 15 U.S.C. §§ 1639(a)(1) and (a)(2)(A) and 12 C.F.R. § 226.32(c)(1)–(3);

b. by failing to provide the above disclosures to the consumer required at least three business days prior to the consummation of the transaction, in violation of 15 U.S.C. §§ 1639(b)(1) and 12 C.F.R. § 226.31(c).

c. by failing to provide accurate disclosures as required by 15 U.S.C. § 1638(a), and Reg. Z §§ 226.17 and 226.18.

45. The failure to comply with any provision of 15 U.S.C. § 1639 is deemed a failure to deliver material disclosures for the purpose of 15 U.S.C. § 1635. *See* 15 U.S.C. § 1639(j).

46. Pursuant to the Truth-in-Lending Act, Ms. Homeowner, had an absolute right to cancel the transaction for three business days after the transaction, or within three days of receiving proper disclosures from the plaintiff, after which she would not be responsible for any charge or penalty.

47. Plaintiff's assignor's violations of 15 U.S.C. §§ 1638, 1639 and 12 C.F.R. §§ 226.17, 226.18, 226.31 and 226.32, which are considered to be a failure to give all material disclosures, give rise to a continuing right of rescission on the part of Ms. Homeowner.

48. Ms. Homeowner hereby elects to rescind the transaction between herself and plaintiff's assignor, pursuant to her continuing right of rescission.

49. When a consumer elects to rescind pursuant to the Truth-in-Lending Act, any security interest taken in connection with the transaction becomes void. 15 U.S.C. § 1635(b).

50. When a consumer elects to rescind pursuant to the Truth-in-Lending Act, the consumer is not liable for any finance or other charge. 15 U.S.C. § 1635(b).

51. The mortgage that is the subject of this foreclosure action was taken in connection with the transaction that Ms. Homeowner has elected to rescind.

52. Since the mortgage is now void, this foreclosure case is due to be dismissed.

WHEREFORE, Ms. Homeowner prays that this Court dismiss plaintiff's complaint, with prejudice.

Second Affirmative Defense

Recoupment for Violation of the Real Estate Settlement and Procedures Act

53. The transaction between plaintiff's assignor and Ms. Homeowner was a "federally related mortgage loan" as that term is defined in the Real Estate Settlement and Procedures Act ("RESPA"), 12 U.S.C. § 2602(1).

54. Plaintiff's assignor's funding and origination of this transaction are "settlement services" as that term is defined in RESPA, 12 U.S.C. § 2601(3).

55. As part of the transaction, Ms. Homeowner paid fees to the mortgage broker of at least $________ for obtaining a balloon loan with an interest rate of 11%, that increased her mortgage payments without providing her with any real economic benefit.

56. This interest rate exceeded plaintiff's assignor's par rate on 15 year balloon loans.

57. In exchange for submitting an above par rate loan, plaintiff's assignor paid the mortgage broker $3,750. This payment was in addition to the money paid by Ms. Homeowner, and was not for any services provided by the mortgage broker to plaintiff's assignor or Ms. Homeowner.

58. The mortgage broker was more than adequately compensated for its services by Ms. Homeowner.

59. The mortgage broker provided no goods or services for this fee.

60. Plaintiff's assignor's payment of this fee to the mortgage broker violates RESPA's prohibition against providers of settlement services from paying referral fees and kickbacks. 12 U.S.C. § 2607.

61. Plaintiff's violation of RESPA is a violation that subjects Plaintiff to a civil penalty of three times the amount of any charge paid for settlement services. 12 U.S.C. § 2607(d)(2).

WHEREFORE, Bernice Homeowner, prays that this Court dismiss plaintiff's complaint, with prejudice, or, in the alternative, reduce the amount owed by Ms. Homeowner by the amount of damages available under RESPA.

Third Affirmative Defense

Illinois Consumer Fraud and Deceptive Practices Act

62. Ms. Homeowner realleges paragraphs 1–50.

63. This defense is asserted pursuant to the Illinois Consumer Fraud and Deceptive Business Practices Act, 815 ILCS § 505 *et seq.*

64. Victory Mortgage, Wendy Mead, Mira James, and other unidentified employees and/or agents of Victory Mortgage made misrepresentations to Ms. Homeowner, as set forth above, including but not limited to statements that they would act in her best interest, obtain a loan which would be to her benefit, lower her monthly payment, and provide additional cash to repair her roof.

65. Victory and its agents or employees also misrepresented the amount it was charging Ms. Homeowner for its purported services.

66. Saxon (plaintiff's assignor) misrepresented the terms and finance charges imposed on the loan.

67. Saxon's closing agent misrepresented the import and contents of the documents which he asked Ms. Homeowner to sign, and concealed the terms of the loan while requiring Ms. Homeowner to sign the documents.

68. Saxon and Victory entered into a conspiracy to defraud Ms. Homeowner by agreeing to the payment of a kickback (the "yield spread premium") from Saxon to Victory for the purpose of getting Ms. Homeowner to accept the loan at a higher rate than Saxon was prepared to impose, without disclosing to Ms. Homeowner the purpose and nature of the kickback.

69. The misrepresentations were material in nature, as they concerned the basic terms and benefits of the loan.

70. Victory and its employee agents knew that their representations were false at the time they were made.

71. Saxon knew that its Truth In Lending disclosures were inaccurate. Saxon's agent knew that representations to Ms. Homeowner at the closing were false.

72. The misrepresentations and omissions were made with the

intent to induce Ms. Homeowner's reliance and thereby to enter into the transaction.

73. Ms. Homeowner reasonably relied on Saxon's and Victory's misrepresentations to her detriment.

74. Plaintiff's assignor is a mortgage company with extensive experience and sophistication in transactions involving residential mortgages.

75. Conversely, Ms. Homeowner is a single family homeowner who is inexperienced and unsophisticated in matters involving consumer lending.

76. The fees charged to Ms. Homeowner far exceed the fees normally charged to consumers in home mortgage transactions.

77. In addition to the fees paid by Ms. Homeowner for the loan, plaintiff's assignor paid an illegal kickback to the mortgage broker of $3750 in violation of RESPA.

78. Furthermore, plaintiff's assignor failed to properly notify Ms. Homeowner about the high cost nature of the loan, and failed to provide accurate Truth In Lending disclosures.

79. Finally, the mortgage that plaintiff's assignor entered into with Ms. Homeowner increased her monthly mortgage payments by more than $150, left her with a balloon payment of $101,686.62 due when she is 84 years old and provided her with absolutely no real economic benefit.

80. Plaintiff's assignor's practices as described above are unfair, immoral, unethical, and unscrupulous.

81. Theses practices offend public policy.

82. As a result of plaintiff's assignor's unfair practices, in violation of the Consumer Fraud Act, 815 ILCS § 505, Ms. Homeowner suffered substantial injury in that she is now faced with the loss of her home.

83. Plaintiff, as holder of a high cost loan, is liable for all claims and defenses that can be raised against its assignor. 15 U.S.C. § 1641(d)(1).

84. On information and belief, based on documents found in plaintiff's loan files, plaintiff knew that the terms of the loan had been misrepresented to Ms. Homeowner.

85. Plaintiff knew that the Truth In Lending disclosures given to Ms. Homeowner were inaccurate. Such inaccuracy was apparent on the face of the documents assigned to plaintiff.

WHEREFORE, Bernice Homeowner prays that this Court dismiss Plaintiff's Complaint with prejudice, or in the alternative, reduce the amount owed by Ms. Homeowner by the amount of damages available under the CFA.

Fourth Affirmative Defense

Common Law Fraud

86. Ms. Homeowner incorporates paragraphs 1–74 above by reference herein.

87. Victory Mortgage, Wendy Mead, Mira James, and other unidentified employees and/or agents of Victory Mortgage made misrepresentations to Ms. Homeowner, as set forth above, including but not limited to statements that they would act in her best interest, obtain a loan which would be to her benefit, lower her monthly payment, and provide additional cash to repair her roof.

88. Victory and its agents or employees also misrepresented the amount it was charging Ms. Homeowner for its purported services.

89. Saxon (plaintiff's assignor) misrepresented the terms and finance charges imposed on the loan.

90. Saxon's closing agent misrepresented the import and contents of the documents which he asked Ms. Homeowner to sign, and concealed the terms of the loan while requiring Ms. Homeowner to sign the documents.

91. Saxon and Victory entered into a conspiracy to defraud Ms. Homeowner by agreeing to the payment of a kickback (the "yield spread premium") from Saxon to Victory for the purpose of getting Ms. Homeowner to accept the loan at a higher rate than Saxon was prepared to impose, without disclosing to Ms. Homeowner the purpose and nature of the kickback.

92. The misrepresentations were material in nature, as they concerned the basic terms and benefits of the loan.

93. Victory and its employee agents knew that their representations were false at the time they were made.

94. Saxon knew that its Truth In Lending disclosures were inaccurate. Saxon's agent knew that representations to Ms. Homeowner at the closing were false.

95. The misrepresentations and omissions were made with the intent to induce Ms. Homeowner's reliance and thereby to enter into the transaction.

96. Ms. Homeowner reasonably relied on Saxon's and Victory's misrepresentations to her detriment.

97. Plaintiff knew that the loan terms had been misrepresented to Ms. Homeowner, and knew that the Truth In Lending disclosures given to Ms. Homeowner were inaccurate. Such inaccuracy was apparent on the face of the documents assigned to plaintiff.

98. Plaintiff accepted assignment of the note with notice that the documents contained therein were inaccurate and that the loan violated TILA and RESPA. Therefore plaintiff is subject to the defense of fraud raised herein.

99. Plaintiff, as holder of a high cost loan, is liable for all claims and defenses that can be raised against its assignor. 15 U.S.C. § 1641(d)(1).

WHEREFORE, Bernice Homeowner prays that this Court dismiss Plaintiff's Complaint with prejudice, or in the alternative, reduce the amount owed by Ms. Homeowner by the amount of her damages.

Fifth Affirmative Defense

Violation of the Illinois Interest Act

100. This defense is asserted pursuant to the Illinois Interest Act, 815 ILCS § 205.

101. The loan entered by plaintiff's assignor and Ms. Homeowner on May 27, 1999, was for the stated sum of $120,000.

102. The stated interest rate on the loan entered by plaintiff's assignor and Ms. Homeowner was 11.00%.

103. In addition to the stated interest, plaintiff's assignor charged Ms. Homeowner at least $12,044.34 in points and fees.

104. The points and fees paid by Ms. Homeowner are 10.04% of the principal amount of $120,000.

105. The points and fees charged to Ms. Homeowner are therefore in excess of 3% of the principal amount of the loan.

106. The loan made by plaintiff's assignor to Ms. Homeowner is secured by her home, which is residential real estate in the state of Illinois.

107. The loan requires the payment of interest at an interest rate in excess of 8% per annum. Section 4.1a of the Illinois Interest Act, 815 ILCS § 205/4.1a(f), limits the amount of certain charges,

including "points" "service charge" "discounts" "commission" or otherwise, in the case of loans with an interest rate in excess of 8% per annum that are secured by residential real estate, to not more than 3% of the principal amount.

108. Plaintiff's actions as described in paragraphs 66–71 above were done "knowingly" as that term is used in Section 6 of the Interest Act. 815 ILCS, § 205/6. A knowing violation of the Interest Act subjects the offender to a penalty of twice the total of all interest, discount and charges determined by the loan contract or paid by the obligor, whichever is greater. 815 ILCS § 205/6.

109. The total of all interest, discounts, and charges determined by the loan contract in connection with the transaction far exceeds the payoff balance owed by Ms. Homeowner.

110. Pursuant to Section 6 of the Interest Act, Plaintiff's statutory liability is not less than twice the total of all interest, discounts or charges determined by the loan contract. Ms Homeowner is therefore entitled to a complete set-off against all amounts that Plaintiff claims are due, under the terms of the Mortgage. 815 ILCS § 205/6.

WHEREFORE, Bernice Homeowner prays that this Honorable Court dismiss plaintiff's complaint with prejudice.

____

Attorney for the Defendant

I.2.3 Motion to Dismiss (on Standing Grounds) and in the Alternative to Stay Judicial Foreclosure for Review for HAMP Loan Modification

IN THE CIRCUIT COURT, FOURTH JUDICIAL CIRCUIT, IN AND FOR DUVAL COUNTY, FLORIDA

________________________)
U.S. BANK, NATIONAL)
ASSOCIATION)
Plaintiff,)
)
v.)
)
WILLIAM M. HOMEOWNER)
and MICHELE L.)
HOMEOWNER et al.,)
Defendants.)
________________________)

DEFENDANTS, WILLIAM M. HOMEOWNER AND MICHELE L. HOMEOWNER'S MOTION TO DISMISS PLAINTIFF'S COMPLAINT TO FORECLOSE MORTGAGE, *OR IN THE ALTERNATIVE, MOTION TO STAY THE SUBJECT LAWSUIT*

The Defendants, William M. Homeowner and Michele L. Homeowner (hereinafter "the Homeowners" or "Defendants,") by and through their undersigned counsel, file this their Motion to Dismiss Plaintiff's Complaint to Foreclose Mortgage, or in the Alternative, Motion to Stay the Subject Lawsuit pursuant to Rules 1.130, 1.210(a), 1.140(b) (6), 1.140(e), *Fla. R. Civ. P.*, and state in support thereof:

MOTION TO DISMISS FOR LACK OF STANDING
Failure to Consistently Allege Ownership of Subject Mortgage and Mortgage Note

1. Plaintiff, U.S. BANK, NATIONAL ASSOCIATION (hereinafter "U.S. Bank" or "Plaintiff"), filed the subject action on May 21, 2009 concerning the Homeowners' 2006 purchase money, Fannie Mae mortgage.

2. Plaintiff alleges in its complaint it is the servicer for the owner and is acting on behalf of the owner with authority to do so and is the present "designated holder."

3. Rule 1.210(a) of the Florida Rules of Civil Procedure provides, in pertinent part:

> Every action may be prosecuted in the name of the real party in interest, but a personal representative, administrator, guardian, trustee of an express trust, a party with whom or in whose name a contract has been made for the benefit of another, or a party expressly authorized by statute may sue in that person's own name without joining the party for whose benefit the action is brought. . . .

4. In Florida, the prosecution of a residential mortgage foreclosure action must be by the owner and holder of the mortgage and the note. Plaintiff does not allege that it owns or holds the note and, in fact, alleges that another unnamed entity is both the owner and the holder. *Your Construction Center, Inc. v. Gross*, 316 So. 2d 596 (Fla. 4th DCA 1975, *Greenwald v. Triple D Properties, Inc.*, 424 So. 2d 185, 187 (Fla. 4th DCA 1983). However, the Second and Third District Courts of Appeal have ruled that merely being the holder of the note provides no standing to seek enforcement in a foreclosure action if the holder is acting for the real party in interest. *Mortgage Electronic Registration Systems v. Revoredo*, 955 So. 2d 33 (Fla. 3d DCA 2007); *Mortgage Electronic Registration Systems, Inc. v. Azize*, 965 So. 2d 151 (FlA.2d DCA 2007).

5. Standing requires that the party prosecuting the action have a sufficient stake in the outcome and that the party bringing the claim be recognized in the law as being a real party in interest entitled to bring the claim. This entitlement to prosecute a claim in Florida court rests exclusively in those persons granted by substantive law, the power to enforce the claim. *Kumar Corp. v. Nopal Lines, Ltd., et al*, 462 So. 2d 1178, (Fla. 3d DCA 1985). A plaintiff's lack of standing at the commencement of a case is a fault that cannot be cured by gaining standing after the case has been filed. *Progressive Express Ins. Co. v. McGrath Community Chiropractic*, 913 So. 2d 1281, 1285 (FlA.2d DCA 2005).

6. Parties may rely on the "relation back" rule when asserting standing. *Progressive*, supra. When applying the "relation back" rule, the party who did not have standing at the time the action was filed may amend their statement of claim to show that they acquired standing that "related back to the original statement of claim." Id. at 1285-1286; *Fla.R.Civ.P.* 1.190(c). However, this rule does not allow a party to establish the right to maintain an action retroactively by acquiring standing after the fact. *Progressive*, 913 So. 2d at 1285 (citing *Jeff-Ray Corp. v. Jacobson*, 566 So. 2d 885, 886 (Fla. 4th DCA 1990) (finding that "the assignee of a mortgage could not maintain the mortgage foreclosure action because the assignment was dated four months after the action was filed, if the plaintiff wished to proceed on the assignment, it must file a new complaint.")

Alternative Motion to Stay this Foreclosure Lawsuit

7. Plaintiff has no right to pursue this foreclosure at this time because it has failed to provide the mandatory pre-foreclosure, default servicing required because U.S. Bancorp, parent company of U.S. Bank, National Association, received 6.6 billion dollars in Troubled Asset Relief Plan ("TARP") funds under the Economic Stabilization Act of 2008 ("EESA"), according to the United States Department of the Treasury § 105(a) Troubled Asset Relief Program (TARP) Report to Congress for the period April 1, 2009—April 30, 2009.

8. The purpose of the TARP funds as stated in Public Law 110-343 known as the Economic Stabilization Act of 2008 is as stated below:

> SEC. 2. PURPOSES
> The purposes of this Act are—
> (1) to immediately provide authority and facilities that the Secretary of the Treasury can use to restore liquidity and stability to the financial system of the United States; and
> (2) to ensure that such authority and such facilities are used in a manner that
> (A) protects home values, college funds, retirement accounts, and life savings;
> (B) preserves homeownership and promotes jobs and economic growth;
> (C) maximizes overall returns to the taxpayers of the United States; and
> (D) provides public accountability for the exercise of such authority.

9. In implementing the Act, the United States Treasury has instituted a number of programs, including the Making Home Affordable Act, Capital Purchase Program and Capital Assistance Program among others. See *http://www.financialstability.gov/roadtostability/programs.htm*

10. Pursuant to the plans and the authority provided by H.R. 1424 Title I § 109-110, the United States Treasury has ordered as follows:

> Mortgage Foreclosure Mitigation: All recipients of capital investments under the Financial Stability Plan will be required to commit to participate in mortgage foreclosure mitigation programs consistent with guidelines Treasury released as part of its Making Home Affordable mortgage modification program.

www.financialstability.gov/about/transparencyaccountability.html (April 16, 2009).

11. If U.S. Bank can prove it is the owner and holder of the subject note and mortgage, as a recipient of TARP funds, it is subject to the U.S. Treasury loan modification program guidelines for the Making Home Affordable Program which require "Any foreclosure action . . . be temporarily suspended during the trial period, or while borrowers are considered for alternative foreclosure prevention options. In the event that the Home Affordable Modification or alternative foreclosure options fail, the foreclosure action may be resumed."

12. Plaintiff has committed in the Securities Purchase Agreement of its Home Affordable Modification Program, to "expand the flow of credit to U.S. consumers and businesses on competitive terms to promote the sustained growth and vitality of the U.S. economy." Also, "the Company agrees to work diligently, under existing programs, to modify the terms of residential mortgages as appropriate to strengthen the health of the U.S. economy."

13. U.S. Bank has already been remunerated for its troubled assets, has sought and been given taxpayer money and agreed to undertake meaningful loan modification with their clients who are facing foreclosure in return for billions of taxpayer dollars. Plaintiff has taken the money and now seeks to recover again from the homeowner through foreclosure even though it has not complied with the loss mitigation requirements as required by TARP.

14. Further Plaintiff has no right to pursue this foreclosure because it has failed to provide the mandatory, pre-foreclosure default servicing required in the subject Fannie Mae insured residential mortgage in accordance with the controlling Fannie Mae single family loan servicing guidelines, orders and regulations prior to filing this foreclosure action. See *www.efanniemae.com/sf/guides/ssg/annltrs/pdf/2009/0905.pdf.*

15. Defendants have the right to participate in a meaningful repayment plan, forbearance, loan modification, and/or other foreclosure prevention loan services from Plaintiff pursuant to and in accordance with Fannie Mae orders and guidelines before the commencement or initiation of this foreclosure action.

16. According to the Fannie Mae Servicing Guide, "All Fannie Mae-approved servicers must participate in the program for all eligible Fannie Mae portfolio mortgage loans and MBS pool mortgage loans guaranteed by Fannie Mae." The Guide later notes, "To ensure that a borrower currently at risk of foreclosure has the opportunity to apply for the HAMP, servicers should not proceed with a foreclosure sale until the borrower has been evaluated for the program and, if eligible, an offer to participate in the HAMP has been made. Servicers must use reasonable efforts to contact borrowers facing foreclosure to determine their eligibility for the HAMP, including in-person contacts at the servicer's discretion." Guidelines pages 1 and 16.

17. The Fannie Mae Servicing Guide also states, "If a servicer has information that the borrower does not meet all of the eligibility criteria for the HAMP (e.g., because the borrower has moved out of the house) the servicer should explore other foreclosure prevention alternatives prior to resuming or initiating foreclosure." Fannie Mae has instituted the new HomeSaver Forbearance as a loss mitigation option for borrowers who do not qualify for HAMP but who are in default or for whom default is imminent. Guidelines page 17.

18. Defendants are being denied and deprived by Plaintiff of their right to access the required mortgage servicing. Defendants are being illegally subjected by the Plaintiff to this foreclosure action, being forced to defend the same and they are being charged illegal court costs and related fees, and attorney fees. Defendants are having their credit slandered and negatively affected, all of which constitutes irreparable harm to these Defendants for the purpose of injunctive relief.

19. As a proximate result of the Plaintiff's unlawful actions, Defendants continue to suffer the irreparable harm described above for which monetary compensation is inadequate.

20. Defendants have a right to access the foreclosure prevention servicing prescribed by the EESA and Fannie Mae laws, regulations, orders and guidelines which are being denied to them by the Plaintiff.

23. There is a substantial likelihood that Defendants would have been able to avoid foreclosure had Plaintiff not illegally filed the subject action.

WHEREFORE, Defendants, William M. Homeowner and Michele L. Homeowner, request this court dismiss the Plaintiff's Complaint to Foreclose Mortgage or, alternatively, to stay this action until Plaintiff complies with its obligations either under EESA or the Fannie Mae servicing regulations and guidelines for an award of attorney's fees and for all other relief to which these Defendants prove themselves entitled.

Respectfully submitted,
[Attorney for Defendants]
[Date]

I.3 Complaint to Enjoin Non-Judicial Foreclosure and for Damages (Massachusetts)

COMMONWEALTH OF MASSACHUSETTS
SUPERIOR COURT

Ellen Lee Consumer,	)	
Plaintiff,	)	
v.	)	
EAZ Credit Corporation, Limited Mortgage Group, Inc. and Dutch Bank National Trust Company, as Trustee for the registered holders of Bravo Mortgage Asset Trust 20001, Bravo Mortgage Asset Backed PassThrough Certificates, Series 20001	)	COMPLAINT SEEKING DAMAGES AND EQUITABLE RELIEF INCLUDING INJUNCTIVE RELIEF TO STOP FORECLOSURE
Defendants.	)	

I. PRELIMINARY STATEMENT

1. Plaintiff, Ellen Lee Consumer, ("Ms. Consumer"), has lived in her Somerville home her entire life—64 years. The circumstances leading to Ms. Consumer's financial struggles began when she refinanced her home loan with EAZ Credit Corporation, ("EAZ"), brokered by Limited Mortgage Group ("Limited"). In this refinancing, EAZ charged high closing costs and misrepresented loan terms, preventing Ms. Consumer from understanding the cost of the loan she received. In doing so, EAZ violated the consumer protection statute M.G.L. c. 93A ("c. 93A"), together with that law's implementing regulations, including 940 C.M.R. §§ 3.01 *et seq.*, 6.01 *et seq.*, and 8.01 *et seq.*, as well as the common law.

2. In addition, EAZ refinanced Ms. Consumer's previous home loan with Old Century Mortgage against her best interest, in violation of M.G.L. c. 183 § 28C. Among other things, the EAZ refinance increased Ms. Consumer's interest rate by a point and a half and changed the rate from fixed to adjustable, thereby increasing Ms. Consumer's monthly mortgage payments by over $1,000.00 per month.

3. Ms. Consumer was no longer able to make the high monthly payments required by the EAZ loan when a heart illness with which she had been struggling for years increased in severity and prevented her from working. Ms. Consumer had a heart transplant in 1995 and suffers from seizures, cardiac arrest and congestive heart failure. It is likely that this is a terminal illness. Her daughter, Laura Consumer, rents the apartment below Ms. Consumer in the property and is instrumental in Ms. Consumer's care.

4. Dutch Bank, as trustee, has begun foreclosure proceedings on behalf of a securitization trust. There is currently a foreclosure sale date set on Ms. Consumer's property for December 21, 2007 at 1:00 p.m.—just four days before Christmas.

5. A true and correct copy of the Legal Notice sent to Ms. Consumer informing her of the foreclosure is attached as *Exhibit A*.

II. JURISDICTION AND VENUE

6. This court has jurisdiction over this matter and this Defendant pursuant to M.G.L. c. 223A, § 3, c. 212, § 4 and c. 214, § 1.

7. Venue lies in this county pursuant to M.G.L. c. 223, § 8.

III. PARTIES

8. Ms. Consumer is a natural person who resides at 100 Main Street, Somerville, Massachusetts 02143.

9. EAZ is a mortgage lender with its principal place of business located at 1000 Aston Parkway, Suite 100, Irvine, California 92606.

10. Limited is a mortgage broker that acted as EAZ's agent for the purpose of disclosing loan information. It has a principal place of business located at 100 Arcadia Street, Unit 0, Boston, Massachusetts 02127.

11. Dutch Bank National Trust Company, as Trustee for the registered holders of Bravo Mortgage Asset Trust 2000-1, Bravo Mortgage Asset Backed Pass-Through Certificates, Series 2000-1, ("Dutch Bank") has its principal place of business located at 1000 West Street, Santa Ana, California 92705.

IV. FACTS

12. Ms. Consumer is an unsophisticated borrower with little experience in real estate transactions or mortgage finance.

13. Ms. Consumer acquired her home at 100 Main Street in Somerville (the "Somerville Residence") in 1976 when her parents passed away.

14. Ms. Consumer has lived in her Somerville Residence for her entire life—64 years.

Old Century Mortgage Loan

15. Before refinancing with EAZ, Ms. Consumer had a loan on better terms with Old Century Mortgage (the "Old Century Mortgage" loan).

16. The Old Century Mortgage loan had a term of 360 months, a fixed interest rate of 7.70%, and an annual percentage rate ("APR") of 7.876%.

17. Ms. Consumer's monthly payment on the Old Century Mortgage loan was fixed at $4,634.25.

18. Limited, as broker for the Old Century Mortgage loan, received a 1.25% loan origination fee, amounting to $8,125.00, plus a $9,750.00 yield spread premium.

19. A true and correct copy of Ms. Consumer's Truth In Lending disclosure for the Old Century Mortgage loan is attached hereto as *Exhibit B*.

20. A true and correct copy of Ms. Consumer's fixed rate Note for the Old Century Mortgage loan is attached hereto as *Exhibit C*.

21. A true and correct copy of Ms. Consumer's HUD1 Settlement Statement for the Old Century Mortgage loan is attached hereto as *Exhibit D*.

EAZ Loan

22. In or about May 2005, Ms. Consumer spoke with Steve DelRio, a Limited representative acting as EAZ's agent, who claimed that he could refinance Ms. Consumer's Old Century Mortgage loan at a lower rate and that the new loan would pay off all of her debts.

23. Instead, the EAZ loan had an adjustable interest rate of 9.91% and an APR of 10.164%, increasing Ms. Consumer's monthly payments by over $1,000.00—to $5,646.00 per month.

24. According to the Truth In Lending Disclosure, Ms. Consumer's monthly payments on the EAZ loan increased to $6,166.49 per month as of December 1, 2007.

25. Limited received a $3,750.00 broker fee and a $6,900.00 "rebate" in the transaction, as well as a $500.00 processing fee.

26. In addition, EAZ received a $440.00 underwriting fee and a $475.00 administration fee in the transaction.

27. By contrast, Ms. Consumer received only $853.74 in cash from the transaction.

28. The Good Faith Estimate ("GFE") Limited prepared and Ms. Consumer received for the EAZ loan disclosed only a $6,900.00 "loan origination fee," and did not disclose any broker's fees.

29. A true and correct copy of Ms. Consumer's Truth In Lending disclosure for the EAZ loan is attached hereto as *Exhibit E*.

30. A true and correct copy of Ms. Consumer's adjustable rate Note for the EAZ loan is attached hereto as *Exhibit F*.

31. A true and correct copy of Ms. Consumer's HUD1 Settlement Statement for the EAZ loan is attached hereto as *Exhibit G*.

32. A true and correct copy of Ms. Consumer's GFE is attached hereto as *Exhibit H*.

33. A true and correct copy of Ms. Consumer's Mortgage granting a power of sale to EAZ is attached hereto as *Exhibit I*.

34. Approximately one year into the EAZ loan, Ms. Consumer fell behind as she was unable to afford the high monthly payments.

35. In June, 2007, Ms. Consumer suffered from cardiac arrest and was no longer able to work.

36. In September, 2007, Dutch Bank began foreclosure proceedings on the mortgage.

37. On information and belief, Dutch Bank does not hold any interest in the mortgage because it has not received assignment from the mortgagee. No assignment to Dutch Bank appears of record in the registry.

38. Dutch Bank lacks authority to act under the power of sale.

Emergency Legislation Governing Foreclosure Proceedings

39. On November 30, 2007, Governor Patrick signed emergency legislation to assist borrowers facing foreclosure and to provide special protections for sub-prime borrowers.

40. A true and correct copy of the legislation is attached as *Exhibit J*.

41. A true and correct copy of the press release announcing the enactment is attached as *Exhibit K*.

42. Section 11 of the legislation provides as follows:

SECTION 11. Said Chapter 244 is hereby further amended by inserting after section 35 the following section:—

> Section 35A. (a) Any mortgagor of residential real property located in the Commonwealth consisting of a dwelling house with accommodations for 4 or less separate households and occupied in whole or in part by the mortgagor, shall have a 90 day right to cure a default of a required payment as provided in such residential mortgage or note secured by such residential real property by full payment of all amounts that are due without acceleration of the maturity of the unpaid balance of such mortgage. The right to cure a default of a required payment shall be granted once during any 5 year period, regardless of the mortgage holder.
>
> (b) The mortgagee, or anyone holding thereunder, shall not accelerate maturity of the unpaid balance of such mortgage obligation or otherwise enforce the mortgage because of a default consisting of the mortgagor's failure to make any such payment in subsection (a) by any method authorized by this chapter or any other law until at least 90 days after the date a written notice is given by the mortgagee to the mortgagor.
>
> Said notice shall be deemed to be delivered to the mortgagor when delivered to the mortgagor or when mailed to the mortgagor at the mortgagor's address last known to the mortgagee or anyone holding thereunder.

43. Section 21 of the legislation makes Section 11 effective as of *May 1, 2007*—a retroactive effect consistent with the legislation's emergency preamble.

44. 100 Main Street, Somerville, Massachusetts, the property in question, is a residential real property located in the Commonwealth consisting of a dwelling house with accommodations for 4 or less separate households and is occupied in whole or in part by the mortgagor.

45. Section 11(c) of the legislation requires notices to borrowers containing information about the nature of the delinquency, together with a 90-day right to cure.

46. Ms. Consumer has not received a notice that conforms to the requirements of the law.

47. The law prohibits the mortgagee or anyone holding under the mortgage from foreclosing until no less than 90 days after the notice is sent.

48. Ms. Consumer has not had 90 days to cure as required by the law.

49. On December 4, 2007, Plaintiff, by counsel, contacted foreclosure counsel for Dutch Bank to request a temporary delay of foreclosure to address the requirements of the new law and/or to permit this matter to be heard. The request was refused.

COUNT I: PRELIMINARY AND PERMANENT INJUNCTIVE RELIEF (As Against EAZ and Dutch Bank)

50. Ms. Consumer repeats and realleges all paragraphs above as if set forth fully herein.

51. On information and belief, Dutch Bank does not have the right to act pursuant to the power of sale, because it is not an assignee of the mortgagee.

52. On information and belief, the Legal Notice provided to Ms. Consumer pursuant to G.L. c. 144, § 14 is not valid because at the time it was sent, Dutch Bank was not an assignee of the mortgagee and had no power to act on behalf of the mortgagee under the statute.

53. Dutch Bank cannot conduct a valid sale of the residence under Massachusetts' law.

54. Neither Dutch Bank, nor any party acting on its behalf, sent the notice required by the statute attached as Exhibit J and described more fully in paragraphs 39 to 43 above.

55. Absent the required notice, Dutch Bank cannot enforce the power of sale.

56. Dutch Bank's foreclosure, if allowed to proceed, would cause Ms. Consumer irreparable harm.

57. The balance of hardships tips decidedly in favor of Ms. Consumer, because absent injunctive relief, she will lose her home of 64 years, and may lose accumulated equity and/or the right to raise claims and defenses to enforcement of the mortgage as set forth hereunder.

58. Preliminary and permanent injunctive relief is consistent with the public interest, because it will prevent a wrongful foreclosure and because it effectuates the purposes of recently enacted statutory law.

59. Absent injunctive relief, there is substantial likelihood that neither EAZ nor Dutch Bank will conform its conduct to the law.

COUNT II: VIOLATION OF CHAPTER 93A AND ITS IMPLEMENTING REGULATIONS (As Against EAZ and Limited)

60. Ms. Consumer repeats and realleges all paragraphs above as if set forth fully herein.

61. EAZ and Limited have violated c. 93A and its implementing regulations by utilizing terms and practices that were unfair, deceptive, and/or unconscionable. These violations included, without limitation:

a. Employing a bait and switch strategy using Limited as its agent by offering Ms. Consumer a mortgage on favorable terms prior to closing and then offering a different mortgage loan product at closing in violation of 940 C.M.R. §§ 8.04(4) and 8.06(1) and c. 93A § 2;

b. Using Limited as its agent, promising to refinance Ms. Consumer's mortgage on more favorable terms to induce her to close the loan in violation of 940 C.M.R. § 8.06(1) and c. 93A § 2;

c. Making a loan on terms that were unfair and deceptive in light of its hidden advantages to EAZ and its hidden costs to Ms. Consumer, including, without limitation, using unjustified and undisclosed broker's fees as a means to create a hidden advantage in refinancing the loan in violation of 940 C.M.R. §§ 3.04, 3.05, 3.13, and 6.05, M.G.L. c. 183 § 63 and c. 93A § 2;

d. Providing a confusing variable rate provision in the loan designed to protect EAZ if rates increase from those in place when the loan is made without providing a benefit to Ms. Consumer when rates decline; and

e. Failing to make disclosures that comply with 940 C.M.R. § 8.05(2).

62. EAZ's conduct was willful or knowing within the meaning of c. 93A, § 2.

63. Limited's conduct was willful or knowing within the meaning of c. 93A, § 2.

64. Ms. Consumer was injured and suffered damages by virtue of the violations.

65. The demand letter requirement under c. 93A § 9 does not apply to EAZ or Limited because Ms. Consumer is asserting her claims defensively against the foreclosure action.

66. The demand letter requirement under c. 93A § 9 does not apply to EAZ because EAZ does not maintain a place of business and/or does not keep assets within the Commonwealth.

COUNT III: M.G.L. c. 183 § 28C (As Against EAZ and Limited)

67. Ms. Consumer repeats and realleges all paragraphs above as if set forth fully herein.

68. EAZ refinanced Ms. Consumer's home loan within 60 months of the Old Century Mortgage loan.

69. Ms. Consumer acquired the EAZ loan for personal, family or household use.

70. The EAZ loan is secured by a mortgage on the Somerville Residence.

71. The EAZ refinance was not in Ms. Consumer's best interest, within the meaning of M.G.L. c. 183, § 28C for the following reasons:

a. Ms. Consumer's initial monthly principal and interest payments increased by over $1,000.00;

b. Ms. Consumer's 30 year fixed loan became a variable 2/28 loan;

c. Ms. Consumer's APR increased substantially; and

d. The costs and fees associated with the refinance were significantly higher than the amount of cash Ms. Consumer received in the transaction.

72. EAZ and Limited knew that the refinance loan was not in Ms. Consumer's interest, but proceeded in light of high fees and profits to them.

73. As a result of the EAZ refinance, Ms. Consumer has been damaged and is entitled to relief sufficient to conform the loan to the better terms of the Old Century Mortgage loan and to a declaration that EAZ knowingly refinanced her mortgage loan against her best interest.

COUNT IV: CLAIMS FOR UNCONSCIONABILITY AND/OR ILLEGALITY

74. Ms. Consumer repeats and realleges all paragraphs above as if set forth fully herein.

75. Contract terms that violate either a statute or a validly enacted regulation are void as against public policy.

76. Contract terms that violate either a statute or a validly enacted regulation are unconscionable and unenforceable.

77. The terms of the EAZ loan violate the Attorney General's regulations, 940 C.M.R. §§ 3.01 *et seq.,* 6.01 *et seq*., 8.01 *et seq.* and M.G.L. c. 183 § 28C.

78. To accomplish the purposes of the Attorney General's regulations, 940 C.M.R. §§ 3.01 *et seq.,* 6.01 *et seq*., 8.01 *et seq.,* which are to protect borrowers from predatory lending, it is necessary to void the EAZ mortgage.

79. To accomplish the purpose of M.G.L. c. 183 § 28C, which is to prevent lenders from refinancing borrowers' home loans against their best interest, it is necessary to void the EAZ mortgage.

80. The extent of EAZ's illegal behavior is extreme enough to warrant voiding the mortgage.

81. There is a strong public policy underlying the Attorney General's regulations, 940 C.M.R. §§ 3.01 *et seq.,* 6.01 *et seq*., 8.01 *et seq.* and M.G.L. c. 183 § 28C, which is to protect borrowers from predatory lending and to help borrowers avoid foreclosure.

82. The effectuation of the public policies underlying the Attorney General's regulations, 940 C.M.R. §§ 3.01 *et seq.,* 6.01 *et seq*., 8.01 *et seq.* and M.G.L. c. 183 § 28C would be defeated absent a sanction that voids the mortgage.

83. Ms. Consumer is entitled to relief from the unconscionable and/or illegal contract terms including but not limited to cancellation of the loan contract and/or refund of unjustified broker's fees.

COUNT V: BREACH OF CONTRACT (As Against EAZ)

84. Ms. Consumer repeats and realleges all paragraphs above as if set forth fully herein.

85. EAZ, using Limited as its agent, offered Ms. Consumer different terms in its oral and written disclosures than the ones it offered at closing.

86. To the extent that EAZ offered terms to Ms. Consumer prior to closing, EAZ formed contracts with Ms. Consumer to provide those promised terms.

87. Promised terms included, without limitation: lower monthly payments and a better interest rate.

88. By delivering different terms at closing than the ones initially promised, EAZ breached its contracts with Ms. Consumer.

89. EAZ's conduct caused Ms. Consumer irreparable harm including, without limitation, increasing the amount of monthly payments owed to unaffordable levels thereby putting her at imminent risk of foreclosure.

90. EAZ's conduct increased the cost of the loan to the Ms. Consumer.

91. Ms. Consumer is therefore entitled to damages and equitable remedies for EAZ's breach of the loan contract.

COUNT VI: INTENTIONAL MISREPRESENTATION (As Against EAZ and Limited)

92. Ms. Consumer repeats and realleges all paragraphs above as if set forth fully herein.

93. EAZ and Limited made misrepresentations to Ms. Consumer, upon which Ms. Consumer relied to her detriment.

94. EAZ's and Limited's misrepresentations included, without limitation:

a. making preliminary oral and written disclosures pertaining to the settlement charges of the loan and;

b. promising that the new loan would lower Ms. Consumer's monthly payments.

95. EAZ and Limited made these misrepresentations to induce Ms. Consumer to enter into refinancing agreements with them.

96. EAZ's and Limited's practices caused Ms. Consumer harm including, without limitation, increasing the amount of monthly payments owed to an unaffordable level thereby putting Ms. Consumer at imminent risk of foreclosure.

97. Ms. Consumer is entitled to damages and equitable remedies for EAZ's and Limited's intentional misrepresentations.

COUNT VII: BREACH OF THE COVENANT OF GOOD FAITH AND FAIR DEALING

98. Ms. Consumer repeats and realleges all paragraphs above as if set forth fully herein.

99. The contracts between Ms. Consumer and EAZ included a duty of good faith and fair dealing. Pursuant to an implied covenant in the subject contracts, EAZ had a duty not to do anything which would deprive Ms. Consumer of the benefits of those contracts, and had a duty to do everything that the contracts presupposed each of the parties would do to accomplish the purpose or purposes of the subject contracts.

100. EAZ acted in breach of the implied covenant of good faith and fair dealing, and its duties thereunder, when it offered terms to Ms. Consumer prior to closing, and failed to provide those promised terms.

101. As a result of EAZ's wrongful conduct, Ms. Consumer has suffered and continues to suffer economic losses and other damages.

COUNT VIII: UNJUST ENRICHMENT (As Against EAZ and Limited)

102. Ms. Consumer repeats and realleges all paragraphs above as if set forth fully herein.

103. By their wrongful acts and omissions, including but not limited to making predatory and unfair mortgage loans described herein, EAZ and Limited have been unjustly enriched at the expense of Ms. Consumer, and thus Ms. Consumer has been unjustly deprived.

104. By reason of the foregoing, Ms. Consumer seeks restitution from EAZ and Limited, and an order of this Court disgorging all profits, benefits, and other compensation obtained by EAZ and Limited from their wrongful conduct.

REQUESTED RELIEF

WHEREFORE, Ms. Consumer respectfully requests that this honorable Court:

a.) provide preliminary and permanent injunctive relief to prevent the December 21, 2007 foreclosure sale;
b.) provide injunctive relief conforming the EAZ loan to the better terms of the Old Century Mortgage loan;
c.) declare that EAZ knowingly refinanced her mortgage loan against her best interest;
d.) award damages pursuant to G.L. c. 93A;
e.) award Ms. Consumer her reasonable attorneys' fees and costs; and
f.) grant such relief as the Court deems appropriate and just.

Respectfully Submitted,
Attorneys for Consumer

I.4 Pleadings to Enjoin Non-Judicial Foreclosure (North Carolina)

I.4.1 Temporary Restraining Order

STATE OF NORTH CAROLINA
IN THE GENERAL COURT OF JUSTICE
COUNTY OF NEW HANOVER
SUPERIOR COURT DIVISION

______________________)
Jane Consumer John Consumer,)
Plaintiffs)
)
v.)
)
Easy Mortgage, ABC Lender,)
and Ed Smith, in his capacity as)
Substitute Trustee,)
Defendants.)
______________________)

TEMPORARY RESTRAINING ORDER

THIS MATTER, having been heard on Plaintiffs' Motion For Temporary Restraining Order and the Court being sufficiently advised, and it appearing to the Court that the Plaintiffs will suffer immediate and irreparable harm by virtue of losing title to their land through foreclosure sale by defendants and Ed Smith, in his capacity as Substitute Trustee, their agents or assigns, that the potential injury to the Plaintiffs is of such a nature that compensation alone will not make Plaintiffs whole, that the relative hardships pertaining to the relief requested are weighted in favor of the Plaintiffs, and that time is of the essence;

FURTHER, the Court finds grounds for this Order to be granted without notice to the adverse parties, for the reasons and the efforts to give notice as cited in Plaintiffs' Motion for Temporary Restraining Order;

IT IS HEREBY ORDERED, that defendant and Ed Smith, Substitute Trustee, in that Special Proceeding __ SP _____, their agents, servants or employees are hereby enjoined from further foreclosure proceedings toward the sale of Plaintiffs' home and are ordered not to conduct the foreclosure sale otherwise ordered in __ SP _____.

A Bond in the amount of $___________ is appropriate for purposes of addressing the harm likely to be suffered by the parties restrained and for all purposes otherwise required by law. The Bond shall be posted as a condition to this Order becoming effective.

This Order shall expire on the_____ day of _________, _______.

This the __ day of_________, _____.

I.4.2 Memorandum for Preliminary Injunction and Proposed Order

STATE OF NORTH CAROLINA
IN THE GENERAL COURT OF JUSTICE
COUNTY OF NEW HANOVER
SUPERIOR COURT DIVISION

______________________)
Jane Consumer John Consumer,)
Plaintiffs)
)
v.)
)
)
Easy Mortgage, ABC Lender,)
and Ed Smith, in his capacity as)
Substitute Trustee,)
Defendants.)
______________________)

MEMORANDUM IN SUPPORT OF PLAINTIFFS' MOTION FOR PRELIMINARY INJUNCTION

NATURE OF THE ACTION

Plaintiffs seek a Preliminary Injunction restraining defendant and its Substitute Trustee(s) from proceeding toward foreclosure of their home through the mortgage loan plaintiffs Jane and John Consumer obtained from [mortgage lender and broker]. *(Summarize the claims against the lender and mortgage broker arising from this mortgage loan transaction).*

Plaintiffs are confronted with foreclosure of their home due to the mortgage loan arranged by defendants [mortgage lender and broker]. Plaintiffs contend that defendants acted unlawfully in connection with the mortgage loan and plaintiffs seek protection from the Court in the form of injunctive relief, restraining the foreclosure while the claims asserted herein are determined by the Court.

ARGUMENT

I. A PRELIMINARY INJUNCTION SHOULD BE ISSUED TO PRESERVE THE STATUS QUO.

Plaintiffs have requested that this Court enter a preliminary injunction prohibiting defendant from proceeding with foreclosure. North Carolina foreclosure statutes specifically provide that foreclosure sales may be enjoined, and that legal and equitable reasons for opposing foreclosure should be raised in an injunction proceeding. G.S. 45-21.34; *In re Foreclosure of Goforth Properties, Inc.*, 334 N.C. 369, 374; 432 S.E.2d 855, 858 (1993). *Cf.*, G.S. 45-21.16(d). All benefit of the doubt should be accorded the plaintiffs in these actions. As the North Carolina Supreme Court emphasized in *Princeton Realty Corp. v. Kalman*, 272 N.C. 201, 159 S.E.2d 193, 196 (1967): "It is generally proper, when the parties are at issue concerning the legal or equitable right, to grant an interlocutory injunction to preserve the right in status quo until the determination of the controversy. . . ." The standards for the issuance of a preliminary injunction in the Fourth Circuit are outlined in *Multi-Channel TV Cable Co. v. Charlottesville Quality Operating Cable Co.*, 22 F.3d 546, 551–53 (4th Cir. 1994).

In the case at bar, plaintiffs have alleged several separate claims for relief against the defendants. Should plaintiffs prevail on any one of these grounds, the rights of the note holder, borrower and homeowners will be altered such that foreclosure or acceleration of the note prior to the Court's determination of these claims is inappropriate and would deprive plaintiffs of meaningful access to relief.

II. *PLAINTIFFS ARE LIKELY TO PREVAIL ON THE MERITS OF THEIR CASE.*

A. THE EXCESSIVE FEES CHARGED TO PLAINTIFF ON THE MORTGAGE CONSTITUTE AN UNFAIR AND DECEPTIVE TRADE PRACTICE.

The plaintiffs have alleged in the Complaint that the fees charged in connection with his mortgage loan were excessive. In connection with the mortgage loan, the following fees were charged and collected:

Appraisal fee to Triangle Appraisal Service	300.00
Credit report	6.00
Broker fee	7,705.50
Flood certifax Fee	14.00
Tax certification fee	46.00
Broker Service Comp.*	3,300.00
Settlement or closing fee	65.00
Abstract or title search	525.00
Title insurance	106.40

*Paid at closing

A creditor violates unfair practices laws when it over-reaches in a loan transaction by charging high fees and high interest rates under oppressive circumstances. *Jungkurth v. Eastern Financial Services, Inc.,* 74 B.R. 323, 335–36 (Bankr. E.D. Pa. 1987) (involving more specific statutory prohibitions than in G.S. 75-1.1); *Family Financial Services, Inc. v. Spencer,* 41 Conn. App. 754, 677 A.2d 479, 488 (1996).

Charging interest in excess of state law is a violation of New Hampshire unfair trade practices law. *In Re Arsenault*, 184 B.R. 864, 874 (Bankr. D.N.H. 1995). Double charging for certain closing costs can be deceptive. *Therrien v. Resource Financial Group*, 704 F. Supp. 322, 328 (D.N.H. 1989).

Defendant's role as a fiduciary causes the imposition of the fees to breach both defendant's duty to "fully reveal the nature and extent of [its] fees to the client for whom he acts," *Rushing v. Stephanus*, 64 Wash.2d 607, 393, P.2d 281 (S. Ct. Wash. 1964), and its "duty to deal fairly with the principal in all transactions between them." *Armstrong v. Republic Realty Mortgage Corporation*, 631 F.2d 1344, 1349 (8th Cir. 1980). Where a fiduciary relationship exists, the "defendants [have] the burden of showing that they did not take advantage of plaintiffs and handled the transactions in a fair, open and honest manner." *Sanders v. Spaulding and Perkins, Ltd.*, 82 N.C. App. 680, 347 S.E.2d 866, 867. *See also McNeill*, 223 N.C. 178, 25 S.E.2d 615 (1943); *Smith v. Moore*, 149 N.C. 185, 62 S.E. 892 (1908). The fiduciary's duty of disclosure is a duty to disclose "all" material facts and to make "full" disclosure.

C. THE MORTGAGE FEES VIOLATE CHAPTER 24.

i. The Lender's Imposition Of Any Charges Above Those Specifically Allowed By Chapter 24 Causes The Loans To Be Usurious.

N.C.G.S. § 24-8 specifically states that "[n]o lender shall charge or receive from any borrower . . . in connection with a loan . . . any sum of money, thing of value or other consideration other than that which is pledged as security . . . , together with fees and interest provided for in Chapter 24 or Chapter 53 of the North Carolina General Statutes. . . ." It was on the basis of this statute and this analysis that the N.C. Supreme Court found the loan to be usurious in *Kessing v. National Mortgage Corporation*, 278 N.C. 523, 180 S.E.2d 823 (1971). Subsequently, the N.C. Court of Appeals applied the same rationale to find a loan usurious in the case of *Bagri v. Desai*, 83 N.C. App. 150, 349 S.E.2d 309 (1986). Both courts interpreted N.C.G.S. § 24-8 to mean that when the lender charged anything other than that which was specifically allowed in Chapters 24 and 53, the loan was usurious.

The concept that various charges, when combined with the actual interest charged, cause the loan to be usurious is not new in North Carolina. There are numerous cases so holding. In *Henderson v. Security Mortgage and Finance Co.*, 273 N.C. 253, 160 S.E.2d 39 (1968), the Supreme Court held that an illegal commission charged made the loan usurious. In *Kessing v. National Mortgage Corporation, supra,* the Supreme Court used the same analysis to disallow a requirement imposed upon the borrower as a condition of the loan that a percentage of the value of the borrower's partnership be transferred to the lender. Citing from the 1927 opinion of the Supreme Court of *Ripple v. Mortgage and Acceptance Corp.*, 193 N.C. 422, 137 S.E. 156, the Supreme Court held in *Kessing* that:

> . . . Where a transaction is in reality a loan of money, whatever may be its form, and the lender charges for the use of his money *a sum in excess of interest at the legal rate, by whatever name the charge may be called, the transaction will be held to be usurious*. The law considers the substance and not the mere form or outward appearance of the transaction in order to determine what it in reality is. If this were not so, the usury laws of the State would easily be evaded by lenders of money who would exact from borrowers with impunity compensation for money loaned in excess of interest at the legal rate.

278 N.C. at 531, 180 S.E.2d at 828 (quoting from *Ripple*; emphasis added).

Chapter 24 of the North Carolina General Statutes sets out the current fees and charges, and other terms, that lenders can require of borrowers in this state.

ii. The Lender Violated Chapter 24 in Origination of Loan

Fees charged or received by third parties in connection with plaintiffs' mortgage loan constituted (i) unreasonable compensation for loan-related goods, products, and services, or (ii) compensation for which no loan-related goods and products are provided or for which no or only nominal loan-related services are performed.

The loan was: a "high-cost home loan" which did not exceed the lesser of (i) the conforming loan size limit for a single family dwelling as established by FNMA or (ii) three hundred thousand dollars; and was incurred by natural persons primarily for personal, family, or household purposes; purposes; and was secured by a deed of trust against property occupied the borrower's principal dwelling as defined in N.C.G.S. 24-1.1E. The loan was made without the borrowers being advised that the loan was a high cost loan. The loan was made without certification from a counselor approved by the North Carolina Housing Finance Agency that the borrowers received counseling on the advisability of the loan transaction and the appropriate loan for the borrowers. The loan financed directly or indirectly fees and charges to third parties.

The loan charges violate limitations and requirements of Chapter 24, including, but not limited to, those set out in N.C.G.S. 24-1.1E, 24-8, 24-10, 24-10.1 and are otherwise contrary to public policy.

D. MORTGAGE BROKER BREACHED ITS DUTIES OF LOYALTY IN CONNECTION WITH THE MORTGAGE.

III. INJURY.

There are several grounds on which the injury sustained by reason of the foreclosure would be irreparable. Real property is unique. *E.g., Mauney v. Morris*, 73 N.C. App. 589, 591, 327 S.E.2d 248 (1985). If the foreclosure is allowed to proceed, plaintiffs will have no ability to reacquire this unique real property that is the subject of this foreclosure. Intangible damages arise from a person being subject to a foreclosure, such as loss of credit standing, and loss of reputation and standing in the community.

STATE OF NORTH CAROLINA
IN THE GENERAL COURT OF JUSTICE
COUNTY OF NEW HANOVER
SUPERIOR COURT DIVISION

__________________________)
__________________)
Plaintiffs)
)
v.)
)
__________________, in their)
capacities as Substitute Trustee,)
Defendants.)
__________________________)

PRELIMINARY INJUNCTION ORDER

THIS CAUSE having come on to be heard before the undersigned Superior Court Judge on Motion of Plaintiffs for Preliminary Injunction, the Court finds that Plaintiffs have shown the following through their Complaint, Affidavit and the oral argument of Counsel at the hearing of this Motion: claims which have a substantial likelihood of success on the merits; that Plaintiffs will suffer immediate and irreparable harm by virtue of losing title to their land through foreclosure sale; that the potential injury to the Plaintiffs is of such a nature that compensation alone will not make Plaintiffs whole; that the restraint ordered imposes no undue burden, or risk of harm to Defendants; that balancing the risk of harm between the parties favors injunctive relief in favor of Plaintiffs, that time is of the essence; and that the bond of $_____ posted by the Plaintiffs on________ , will adequately protect Defendants from any reasonable risk of harm by the restraint ordered while the underlying claims determining the rights of the parties are decided.

IT IS THEREFORE ORDERED that Defendants are prohibited from pursuing further foreclosure proceedings toward the sale of Plaintiffs' property until such time as Plaintiffs' claims are resolved and the Court makes a full determination of the respective rights of the parties.

This the _____ day of ________,______ .

I.4.3 Notice of Appeal and Order of Bond on Appeal

SUPERIOR COURT JUDGE PRESIDING
STATE OF NORTH CAROLINA
IN THE GENERAL COURT OF JUSTICE

______________________________)
In the Matter of the foreclosure of)
a Deed of Trust executed by)
_____ in the original amount of)
$_____ dated _____, recorded)
in Book _____, and re-recorded)
in Book _____ County)
Registry, _____ Substitute)
Trustee)
______________________________)

NOTICE OF APPEAL

Respondents _____, by and through undersigned counsel and pursuant to N.C.G.S. § 45-21.16(d1), herby give Notice of Appeal from that Order allowing foreclosure sale entered in this action by the Clerk of Superior Court on _____.

WHEREFORE, Respondents request the following:

1. That the Superior Court place this action on its Civil Calendar for hearing and determination before a Superior Court Judge.
2. That pursuant to N.C.G.S. §§ 1-301.1 and 45-21.16(e), all parties to this cause be given an opportunity to be heard.
3. That pursuant to N.C.G.S. § 1-301.1, the Superior Court Judge proceed to hear and determine all matters in controversy in this action.

Respectfully submitted this the_____ day of __________.

SUPERIOR COURT JUDGE PRESIDING
STATE OF NORTH CAROLINA
IN THE GENERAL COURT OF JUSTICE

______________________________)
In the Matter of the foreclosure of)
a Deed of Trust executed by)
_____ in the original amount of)
$_____ dated _____, recorded)
in Book _____, and re-recorded)
in Book _____ County)
Registry, _____ Substitute)
Trustee)
______________________________)

ORDER OF BOND ON APPEAL

THIS MATTER, coming before the undersigned Clerk of Superior Court upon the Notice of Appeal by Respondents _____, pursuant to N.C.G.S. § 45-21.16(d1) and after consideration of sufficient surety as adequate to protect the Petitioners from any probable loss by reason of appeal;

IT IS HEREBY ORDERED:

1.) The Order allowing foreclosure sale as entered in this action on _____ and the foreclosure proceeding are stayed upon posting of the bond set forth below and disposition of this appeal by the Superior Court Judge.

2.) Respondents are ordered to post a bond of $_____ on or before _____, to protect Petitioners' interest pursuant to N.C.G.S.§ 45-21.16 and as a condition to this Order becoming effective.

This the __ day of _____, _____.

CLERK OF SUPERIOR COURT

I.5 Pleadings to Enjoin Non-Judicial Foreclosure by Servicer Who Failed to Review for HAMP Modification[2]

I.5.1 Complaint

DISTRICT COURT
_________ COUNTY, COLORADO

______________________________)
EMILY E. HOMEOWNER)
)
v.)
)
[Defendant 3] CORPORATION,)
and)
[Defendant 2] MORTGAGE,)
INC., and)
[Defendant 1] MORTGAGE,)
and)
[TRUSTEE] COUNTY)
PUBLIC TRUSTEE)
______________________________)

VERIFIED COMPLAINT

NOW COMES Plaintiff, Emily E. Homeowner, through her undersigned counsel, and hereby brings claims for against the aforementioned parties for injunctive relief. Plaintiff states the following:

THE PARTIES

1. Plaintiff Emily E. Homeowner owns her home located at [Address].

2. Defendant [Defendant 1] serviced plaintiff's mortgage loan until July 1, 2009. *See* Exhibit C.

3. Defendant [Defendant 2] Mortgage, Inc. ("[Defendant 2]") has serviced plaintiff's mortgage loan since July 1, 2009. [Defendant 2] is in receipt of plaintiff's application for a loan modification but has not yet responded to this application.

---

2 Advocates need to be particularly alert to changes in rules governing the HAMP program, keeping in mind that the pleadings reproduced here were drafted during the first year of the program's existence. These pleadings may reflect rules that to some extent have been updated or may eventually be superseded.

4. Defendant [Defendant 3] Corporation ("[Defendant 3]") claims to own the Note securing plaintiff's mortgage loan.

5. Defendant [Trustee], the ________ County Public Trustee, has scheduled plaintiff's home to be sold at foreclosure on November 4, 2009.

STATEMENT OF FACTS

6. On July 6, 2009, [Defendant 3] filed a foreclosure action with the ________ County Public Trustee against Plaintiff's home, foreclosure number [Number]. *See* Exhibit A.

7. Plaintiff does not contest that her mortgage loan was then in default. The default arose after Plaintiff's husband and co-borrower, Heath Homeowner, was convicted of domestic assault and was incarcerated. *See* Exhibit B at 11.

8. As a result of the conviction, Ms. Homeowner not only lost her husband's income, but suffered impacts on her health and spent considerable time and energy on legal proceedings. However, she continued working full time and does so to this day.

9. Plaintiff has now filed for a divorce from Mr. Homeowner. Mr. Homeowner remains incarcerated to this date and Plaintiff continues to be unable to make her monthly mortgage payment of $937.00, which is about 40% of her monthly income.

10. Shortly after her default, Plaintiff diligently began working with her then-servicer, [Defendant 1], to reach a modification or workout agreement that would allow her to make a monthly payment she could afford.

11. On April 13, 2009, [Defendant 1] entered into a Servicer Participation Agreement (the "SPA") with Fannie Mae (acting as an agent of the federal government) in which it agreed to apply the Treasury Department's Home Affordable Modification Program ("HAMP") to all loans it services. *See* Exhibit E.

12. The HAMP program was developed by the United States Department of the Treasury ("Treasury") pursuant to its authority under the federal Troubled Asset Relief Program. *See* Emergency Economic Stabilization Act of 2008, Pub. L. No. 110-343, § 101, 122 Stat. 3765 (Oct. 3, 2008) ("EESA"). As described on the federal government's Making Home Affordable website, HAMP "commits $75 billion to keep up to 3 to 4 million Americans in their homes by preventing avoidable foreclosures." About Making Home Affordable, *http://makinghomeaffordable.gov/about.html* (last visited 10/26/09).

13. Fannie Mae enters contracts with servicers under the program on behalf of Treasury, in its capacity as an agent of the federal government. *See* EESA § 101(c)(3).

14. Under the terms of the HAMP program and pursuant to the SPA, [Defendant 1] agreed to evaluate all borrowers in default or at risk of default to see whether accepting reduced monthly mortgage payments set at 31% of the borrower's income would ultimately prove more beneficial to the owner of the loan than foreclosing on the property.

15. One of the primary duties of HAMP servicers is an agreement to suspend all pending foreclosure proceedings until HAMP analysis is complete.

16. [Defendant 1] further agreed to offer a 3-month HAMP Trial Period at the new payment level to all borrowers meeting certain requirements (discussed below) who pass this "Net Present Value" ("NPV") test.

17. Finally, [Defendant 1] agreed that once a trial period is offered, the new loan terms creating a 31% payment will become effective as a loan modification if the borrower successfully makes all payments.

18. When [Defendant 1] received Plaintiff's request for a modification, [Defendant 1] requested that Plaintiff send the required documentation to analyze her eligibility for a HAMP modification.

19. On May 13, 2009, Plaintiff sent a fax to [Defendant 1] which included every document [Defendant 1] had requested. *See* Exhibit B.

20. Before Plaintiff received any response to her request for a modification and supporting documentation, the servicing of her loan was transferred to [Defendant 2] effective July 1, 2009. *See* Exhibit C.

21. When Plaintiff heard of the transfer, she immediately contacted [Defendant 2]'s loss mitigation department to inquire about the status of her HAMP modification request. [Defendant 2] requested that Plaintiff consult a housing counseling agency, and she did so promptly. *See* Exhibit G.

22. Finally, in late August or early September 2009, plaintiff received a documentation request from [Defendant 2]. She promptly faxed all requested documents on September 16, 2009. *See* Exhibit D.

23. Since sending this documentation, Plaintiff has received no further response from [Defendant 2]. The foreclosure sale of her property is still scheduled for November 4, 2009. *See* Exhibit I.

FIRST CLAIM: BREACH OF CONTRACT

24. Although plaintiff complied with the borrower documentation requirements of HAMP, [Defendant 1] never completed the contractually required analysis to determine whether she was entitled to a HAMP trial period.

25. Although Plaintiff complied with the borrower documentation requirements of HAMP a second time, [Defendant 2] has not yet completed the contractually required analysis to determine whether she is entitled to a HAMP trial period.

26. Despite clear HAMP provisions to the contrary, defendants have allowed Plaintiff's home to remain in foreclosure pending analysis of her request for a HAMP modification.

27. Defendants [Defendant 1] and [Defendant 2] have therefore breached their contractual duties under the SPA and AAA.

28. Because the HAMP program exists for the purpose of benefitting borrowers who face foreclosure, Plaintiff may enforce these contractual duties as a third party beneficiary to the SPA and AAA.

WHEREFORE, Plaintiff prays for the following relief:

A. An order enjoining the Public Trustee from selling Plaintiff's house on November 4, 2009, until such time as defendant [Defendant 2] has complied with all HAMP requirements regarding her loan.

B. An order enjoining defendants [Defendant 3] and [Defendant 2] from pursuing foreclosure of Plaintiff's property until such time as defendant [Defendant 2] has complied with all HAMP requirements regarding her loan.

C. An order requiring [Defendant 3] and [Defendant 2] to remove all fees, charges, and interest arising from the wrongfully-instituted foreclosure proceeding, and associated delays, from Plaintiff's account.

Respectfully submitted,
[Attorney for Plaintiff]
[Date]

EXHIBITS
[*Not reprinted herein*]

Exhibit A: Notice of Election & Demand
Exhibit B: [Defendant 1] Modification Documentation
Exhibit C: Letters Confirming Transfer of Servicing
Exhibit D: [Defendant 2] Modification Documentation
Exhibit E: Servicer Participation Agreement
Exhibit F: NPV Spreadsheet
Exhibit G: Housing Counseling Documentation
Exhibit H: Foreclosures Near Plaintiff's Address
Exhibit I: _______ County Public Trustee Webpage—Foreclosure Listing

I.5.2 *Motion for Temporary Restraining Order*

DISTRICT COURT
_______ COUNTY, COLORADO

EMILY E. HOMEOWNER	)
v.	)
[Defendant 3] CORPORATION, and [Defendant 2] MORTGAGE, INC., and [Defendant 1] MORTGAGE, and [Trustee] _______ COUNTY PUBLIC TRUSTEE	)

MOTION FOR TEMPORARY RESTRAINING ORDER

Plaintiff Emily E. Homeowner, through counsel pursuant to C.R.C.P. 65(d), moves the Court to issue a temporary restraining order, ordering defendants [Defendant 3] Corporation, [Defendant 2] Mortgage, Inc., [Defendant 1] Mortgage, and the Public Trustee to cease and desist from selling her home at foreclosure.

Plaintiff has commenced this action by filing the attached Verified Complaint alleging a state law breach of contract claim. As a court of general jurisdiction, this Court has jurisdiction over her claim.

This motion is supported by the verified complaint with exhibits, the accompanying memorandum brief, and the affidavit in support of motion for temporary restraining order, which are all incorporated by reference.

WHEREFORE, Plaintiff requests that the Court enter its Temporary Restraining Order:

G. Ordering the Public Trustee to refrain from selling Plaintiff's house on November 4, 2009, and until the merits of Plaintiff's Motion for Preliminary Injunction are determined.
H. Ordering defendants [Defendant 3] and [Defendant 2] from pursuing foreclosure of Plaintiff's property on November 4, 2009, and until the merits of Plaintiff's Motion for Preliminary Injunction are determined.
I. Order defendants [Defendant 3] and [Defendant 2] to refrain from charging additional foreclosure-related fees to Plaintiff's account until the merits of Plaintiff's Motion for Preliminary Injunction are determined.

Respectfully submitted,
[Attorney for Plaintiff]
[Date]

I.5.3 *Memorandum in Support of Motion for Temporary Restraining Order*

DISTRICT COURT
_______ COUNTY, COLORADO

EMILY E. HOMEOWNER	)
v.	)
[Defendant 3] CORPORATION, and [Defendant 2] MORTGAGE, INC., and [Defendant 1] MORTGAGE, and [Trustee] _______ COUNTY PUBLIC TRUSTEE	)

MEMORANDUM AND BRIEF IN SUPPORT OF MOTION FOR TEMPORARY RESTRAINING ORDER

NOW COMES the Plaintiff, Emily E. Homeowner, by and through counsel, pursuant to Colo. R. Civ. P. 65(b), and submits this Memorandum in support of his Motion for Temporary Restraining Order. In support of her request, Plaintiff states the following:

I. PLAINTIFF SATISFIES THE REQUIREMENTS FOR ISSUANCE OF A TEMPORARY RESTRAINING ORDER WITHOUT NOTICE TO THE DEFENDANTS

Rule 65(b) of the Colorado Rules of Civil Procedure provides for the issuance of a restraining order without written or oral notice to the adverse party or his attorney if "(1) [i]t clearly appears from specific facts shown by affidavit or by the verified complaint or by testimony that immediate and irreparable injury, loss, or damage will result to the applicant before the adverse party or his attorney can be heard in opposition, and (2) the applicant's attorney certifies to the court in writing or on the record the efforts, if any, which have been made to give the notice and the reasons supporting his claim that notice should not be required." Colo. R. Civ. P. 65(b).

A. PLAINTIFF WILL SUFFER AN IMMEDIATE AND IRREPARABLE INJURY IF HER HOME IS FORECLOSED BEFORE A HEARING ON HER MOTION FOR PRELIMINARY INJUNCTION

Plaintiff will permanently lose her ownership interest in the subject property unless Defendants are ordered to refrain from selling Plaintiff's home at foreclosure pending a hearing and resolution of Plaintiff's Complaint. The loss of their home would be devastating to Plaintiff and her two children, as detailed in the accompanying Affidavit. First, Plaintiff would lose the equity she has built in her home. Second, Plaintiff and her children would be without a place to live, and Plaintiff fears difficulty securing an affordable rental. This hardship is particularly severe for Plaintiff's daughter, who has undergone the trauma of sexual abuse by her father and would be unusually harmed by further upheaval.

B. EFFORTS HAVE BEEN MADE TO GIVE NOTICE TO DEFENDANTS OF PLAINTIFF'S CLAIM

Undersigned counsel has spoken with counsel for [Defendant 3] Corporation in the instant foreclosure proceeding, [Attorney] of [Firm], and notified him of the imminent filing of Plaintiff's claim. Counsel first wrote to [Attorney] on October 16, 2009, requesting that his client voluntarily suspend the sale pending HAMP compliance. [Attorney] indicated by letter of October 23, 2009 that he had sought instruction from his client regarding whether to postpone sale. Counsel then contacted [Attorney] by fax on October 27, 2009 to inform him that this lawsuit would be filed if his client did not voluntarily forestall sale by 5:00 p.m. on October 28, 2009. [Attorney] notified counsel in the afternoon that his client would be unlikely to meet that deadline, and nothing further was received by 5:00.

In addition, [Attorney] stated in his letter and in person that his client was in contact with its servicer, [Defendant 2], regarding Plaintiff's modification request. Accordingly, counsel believes that [Defendant 2] is also on notice of Plaintiff's claim. Further notice should not be required due to the extremely urgent timeline involved.

Respectfully submitted,
[Attorney for Plaintiff]
[Date]

I.5.4 Affidavit in Support of Motion for Temporary Restraining Order

DISTRICT COURT
_______ COUNTY, COLORADO

______________________	)
EMILY E. HOMEOWNER	)
	)
v.	)
	)
[Defendant 3] CORPORATION, and	)
[Defendant 2] MORTGAGE, INC., and	)
[Defendant 1] MORTGAGE, and	)
[Trustee] _______ COUNTY PUBLIC TRUSTEE	)
______________________	)

AFFIDAVIT OF EMILY E. HOMEOWNER

I, Emily E. Homeowner, Plaintiff, having been duly sworn, state the following:

1. I am the Plaintiff in this case and am over 18 years of age.
2. I am the owner of the property at [Address] and occupy it as my sole residence. My two children, a friend, and his son also occupy the property.
3. One of the named defendants in this case, [Defendant 3] Corporation ("[Defendant 3]"), has commenced a foreclosure action against my residence, which I discovered when I received a notice from the Public Trustee.
4. A foreclosure sale is presently scheduled to be held by defendant _______ County Public Trustee on November 4, 2009 at 10:00 a.m.
5. I fell behind on my mortgage when my husband was convicted of domestic assault and sent to federal prison.
6. The relief that I am seeking in this case is an opportunity to be evaluated for a loan modification pursuant to the terms of an agreement entered into by my former loan servicer, [Defendant 1] Mortgage ("[Defendant 1]"), under the federal Home Affordable Modification Program ("HAMP"), which is binding on my current loan servicer, [Defendant 2] Mortgage, Inc. ("[Defendant 2]").
7. It is my understanding that if I were evaluated for a modification under HAMP, I would likely qualify for a trial loan modification.
8. My claims against the defendants are more fully detailed in my Verified Complaint, filed contemporaneously with this Affidavit, which initiates a breach of contract action against them. The facts therein are true to the best of my knowledge.
9. If my house is sold at foreclosure sale, I will be unable to obtain the relief I am seeking at the time the merits of my case are heard, as I will no longer own my home.
10. I am of limited income and receive approximately $2,348 per month.
11. If my home is sold at foreclosure sale, my two children and I will be homeless and I believe we will have difficulty securing a

rental due to my income and the presence of a foreclosure on my credit record.

12. In addition, if our home is sold, my daughter will face further upheaval, which will be damaging to her health and well-being.

13. I currently owe $94,711.06 on my mortgage. I believe my home is worth $120,000. This may be an underestimate as Zillow.com estimates the value of my home at $150,500 and the tax-assessed value of my home is $137,751. Thus, if my home is foreclosed I will lose equity I have built in it.

Respectfully submitted,
[Attorney for Plaintiff]
[Date]

I.5.5 Proposed Temporary Restraining Order

DISTRICT COURT
_______ COUNTY, COLORADO

_____________________)
EMILY E. HOMEOWNER)
)
v.)
)
[Defendant 3] CORPORATION,)
and)
[Defendant 2] MORTGAGE,)
INC., and)
[Defendant 1] MORTGAGE,)
and)
[Trustee] _______ COUNTY)
PUBLIC TRUSTEE)
_____________________)

ORDER GRANTING TEMPORARY RESTRAINING ORDER

THE COURT having considered Plaintiff's Verified Complaint, Motion for Temporary Restraining Order and the supporting affidavit, testimony and exhibits, and being sufficiently advised in the premises and it appearing to the Court that unless a Temporary Restraining Order is issued by this Court, that Plaintiff will suffer immediate and irreparable loss in that she will lose any rights to the property after March 16, 2010—

IT IS ORDERED that Defendants, their agents, employees and attorneys, and those persons having active participation with them who receive actual notice of this Order, be and are hereby ordered to take all actions necessary to halt the sale of Plaintiff's property and the accrual of continued fees, charges, and interest on her mortgage account.

IT IS FURTHER ORDERED that Defendants are to appear before the Court within ten (10) days and show cause, if there is any, why the Temporary Restraining Order should not be converted to a Preliminary Injunction.

IT IS FURTHER ORDERED that:

1. Defendant's Motion for Preliminary Injunction must be heard by this Court on or before ____________, 2009.
2. This Temporary Restraining Order shall be immediately served upon issuance on all affected parties.

This Temporary Restraining Order is issued on ____________, 2009 at __________ AM/PM, at____________, Colorado.

BY THE COURT:
DISTRICT COURT JUDGE

I.5.6 Motion for Waiver of Additional Security in Support of Motion for Temporary Restraining Order

DISTRICT COURT
_______ COUNTY, COLORADO

_____________________)
EMILY E. Homeowner)
)
v.)
)
[Defendant 3] CORPORATION,)
and)
[Defendant 2] MORTGAGE,)
INC., and)
[Defendant 1] MORTGAGE,)
and)
[Trustee] _______ COUNTY)
PUBLIC TRUSTEE)
_____________________)

MOTION FOR WAIVER OF ADDITIONAL SECURITY REQUIREMENT

Pursuant to Rule 65(c) of the Colorado Rules of Civil Procedure, Plaintiff requests that the security required as a prerequisite to the issuance of the injunctive relief be waived or fixed at a nominal sum so as to reflect the equities involved in the present matter and to assure the Plaintiff an effective opportunity to redress her grievances and secure relief from Defendant's acts and omissions. In support of this motion, Plaintiff states the following:

1. Rule 65(c) states that no restraining order or preliminary injunction shall issue except upon the giving of security by the applicant.

2. The purpose of this provision is to enable a restrained or enjoined party to secure indemnification for the costs and pecuniary injury that may accrue during the period in which a wrongfully issued equitable order remains in effect.

3. In this case, because defendants may simply sell Plaintiff's house at foreclosure sale once any wrongfully granted injunctive relief is lifted, Defendants' existing security interest in Plaintiff's home provides sufficient protection from any harm arising from an erroneous injunction.

4. As detailed in her Affidavit, Plaintiff's home contains equity beyond the amount required to repay her mortgage obligation and foreclosure costs.

5. Accordingly, Defendants can recover any damages suffered due to wrongfully granted injunctive relief from the proceeds of the sale of plaintiff's home.

6. Plaintiff is willing to consent to an expedited trial schedule to

minimize any harm to Defendants from wrongfully granted injunctive relief.

7. Plaintiff is proceeding in forma pauperis and any further security obligation would be a hardship to her.

8. Plaintiff therefore prays that the court will consider her home as adequate security against any damages suffered by Defendants due to wrongfully granted injunctive relief, and require no further security bond.

Respectfully submitted,
[Attorney for Plaintiff]
[Date]

I.5.7 Motion for Preliminary Injunction

DISTRICT COURT
_______ COUNTY, COLORADO

EMILY E. HOMEOWNER	)
v.	)
[DEFENDANT 3] CORPORATION, AND [DEFENDANT 2] MORTGAGE, INC., AND [DEFENDANT 1] MORTGAGE, AND [TRUSTEE]_______ COUNTY PUBLIC TRUSTEE	)

MOTION FOR PRELIMINARY INJUNCTION

NOW COMES Plaintiff, Emily E. Homeowner, by and through counsel, pursuant to Colo. R. Civ. P. 65(a) & (d), and hereby moves the court for a preliminary injunction pending trial on the merits of her Verified Complaint against Defendants, for the reasons detailed in the accompanying memorandum and brief.

WHEREFORE, Plaintiff requests that the Court enter its Preliminary Injunction:

D. Ordering the Public Trustee to refrain from selling Plaintiff's house on November 4, 2009, and until the merits of Plaintiff's Verified Complaint are determined.

E. Ordering defendants [Defendant 3] and [Defendant 2] to refrain from pursuing foreclosure of Plaintiff's property on November 4, 2009, and until the merits of Plaintiff's Verified Complaint are determined.

F. Ordering defendants [Defendant 3] and [Defendant 2] to refrain from charging additional foreclosure-related fees to Plaintiff's account until the merits of Plaintiff's Verified Complaint are determined.

Respectfully submitted,
[Attorney for Plaintiff]
[Date]

I.5.8 Memorandum in Support of Motion for Preliminary Injunction

DISTRICT COURT
_______ COUNTY, COLORADO

EMILY E. HOMEOWNER	)
v.	)
[DEFENDANT 3] CORPORATION, AND [DEFENDANT 2] MORTGAGE, INC., AND [DEFENDANT 1] MORTGAGE, AND [TRUSTEE]_______ COUNTY PUBLIC TRUSTEE	)

MEMORANDUM AND BRIEF IN SUPPORT OF MOTION FOR PRELIMINARY INJUNCTION

NOW COMES the Plaintiff, Emily E. Homeowner, by and through counsel, pursuant to Colo. R. Civ. P. 65(a) & (d), and submits this Memorandum in support of her Motion for Preliminary Injunction. In support of her request, Plaintiff states the following:

I. FACTUAL BACKGROUND

On July 6, 2009, defendant [Defendant 3] Corporation filed a Notice of Election and Demand for Sale against Plaintiff with the _______ County Public Trustee's Office, thus initiating foreclosure sale number [Number]. Plaintiff does not contest that her mortgage loan was then in default. The default arose after Plaintiff's husband and co-borrower, Heath Homeowner, was convicted in April 2008 of domestic assault. As a result of the conviction, Ms. Homeowner not only lost her husband's income, but suffered impacts on her health and that of her daughter, and spent considerable time and energy on legal proceedings. Although she was initially able to make her mortgage payments by working a part-time job in addition to her full-time job and by accepting a renter, these solutions were unsustainable, particularly once her renter lost his job in August 2008. Plaintiff fell behind on her mortgage payments in September 2008. Plaintiff has now filed for a divorce from Mr. Homeowner, who remains incarcerated to this date. Plaintiff continues to be unable to make her monthly mortgage payment of $937.00.

Shortly after her default, Plaintiff diligently began working with her then-servicer, [Defendant 1] Mortgage ("[Defendant 1]"), to reach a modification or workout agreement that would allow her to make a monthly payment she could afford. On April 13, 2009, [Defendant 1] entered into a Servicer Participation Agreement (the "SPA") with Fannie Mae (acting as an agent of the federal government) in which it agreed to apply the Treasury Department's Home Affordable Modification Program ("HAMP") to all loans it services. Pursuant to this agreement, [Defendant 1] agreed to evaluate all borrowers in default or at risk of default to see whether adjusting the loan's terms to create monthly mortgage payments set at 31% of the borrower's income would prove more beneficial to the owner of the loan than foreclosing on the property, as determined by applying a "Net Present Value" ("NPV") calculation.[3] [Defendant 1] further agreed to offer a 3-month HAMP Trial Period at the new payment level to all borrowers meeting certain requirements (discussed below) who pass the NPV test. Finally, [Defendant 1] agreed that once a trial period is offered and a borrower successfully makes the trial payments, new loan terms creating a 31% payment will become permanently effective as a loan modification. 31% of Plaintiff's monthly income would be $727.88, a considerable reduction from her current $937.00 payment.

Accordingly, when [Defendant 1] received plaintiff's request for a modification, [Defendant 1] requested that Plaintiff send the required documentation to analyze her eligibility for a HAMP modification.[4] On May 13, 2009, Plaintiff sent a fax to [Defendant 1] which included every document [Defendant 1] had requested.[5] But before Plaintiff received any response to her request for a modification and supporting documentation, the servicing of her loan was transferred to [Defendant 2] Mortgage, Inc. ("[Defendant 2]") effective July 1, 2009.

When Plaintiff heard of the transfer, she immediately contacted [Defendant 2]'s loss mitigation department to inquire about the status of her HAMP modification request. She was instructed to meet with a housing counseling service to seek assistance in obtaining a modification from her servicer, and did so promptly, on July 13, 2009. *See* Exhibit G to Verified Complaint. Finally, in late August or early September 2009, plaintiff received a documentation request from [Defendant 2]. She promptly faxed all requested documents on September 16, 2009. Since sending this documentation, Plaintiff has received no further response from [Defendant 2]. Her foreclosure sale is still scheduled for November 4, 2009.

3 Servicers must reach a 31% payment by engaging in a "standard modification waterfall" of changes to the loan terms—first, capitalizing all accrued interest and third-party escrow advances; second, reducing the interest rate stepwise as low as 2% (the rate then increases back to the current Freddie Mac PMMS over several years); third, extending the repayment and amortization term on the loan as long as forty years; and finally, deferring principal. *See* Supplemental Directive 09-01, at 8-10.

4 [Defendant 1] sent this request using a form modeled on that created by the Treasury Department specifically for HAMP. *Compare* Exhibit X at 1-4 (modification documentation sent to [Defendant 1]) *with* Home Affordable Modification Trial Period Plan Cover Letter, *available at* www.hmpadmin.com/portal/programs/hamp_borrower.html (follow link) (last visited 10/26/09) *and* Home Affordable Modification Program Hardship Affidavit, *available at* www.hmpadmin.com/portal/docs/hamp_borrower/hamphardshipaffidavit.pdf (last visited 10/26/09).

5 The copy of the fax which plaintiff saved in her files, attached to the verified complaint as Exhibit B, is missing 17 pages because plaintiff removed her copy of her 2008 federal tax return, which is exactly 17 pages long. Her federal tax return is attached to the verified complaint as part of Exhibit D, her modification documentation packet to [Defendant 2]. [*Editor's Note: Exhibits are not reprinted herein.*]

II. PLAINTIFF MEETS THE REQUIREMENTS FOR ISSUANCE OF A PRELIMINARY INJUNCTION

"The grant or denial of a preliminary injunction is a decision which lies within the sound discretion of the trial court." *Rathke v. MacFarlane*, 648 P.2d 648, 653 (Colo. 1982). "In exercising its discretion the trial court must find among other elements that the moving party has demonstrated a reasonable probability of success on the underlying merits, that the balance of equities favors the injunction, and that the granting of the injunction will not disserve the public interest." *Kourlis v. District Court*, 930 P.2d 1329, 1332 n.9 (Colo. 1997) (*citing Rathke*, 648 P.2d at 653-54). Plaintiff meets each of these requirements.

A. PLAINTIFF HAS A REASONABLE PROBABILITY OF SUCCESS ON THE MERITS

Plaintiff has sued the defendants on the basis that they have breached the SPA and [Defendant 1]'s related assumption agreement with [Defendant 2], contracts to which she is a third-party beneficiary.

1. [Defendant 1] was contractually bound to consider Plaintiff's loan for a HAMP modification

The HAMP program was developed by the United States Department of the Treasury ("Treasury") pursuant to its authority under the federal Troubled Asset Relief Program. See Emergency Economic Stabilization Act of 2008, Pub. L. No. 110-343, § 101, 122 Stat. 3765 (Oct. 3, 2008) ("EESA"). As described on the federal government's Making Home Affordable website, HAMP "commits $75 billion to keep up to 3 to 4 million Americans in their homes by preventing avoidable foreclosures." About Making Home Affordable, http://makinghomeaffordable.gov/about.html (last visited 10/26/09). Fannie Mae enters contracts with servicers to participate in the program on behalf of Treasury, in its capacity as an agent of the federal government. See EESA § 101(c)(3); SPA at 1 ("Fannie Mae has been designated by the Treasury as a financial agent of the United States in connection with the implementation of the Program.").

A servicer's duties under an SPA, stated most simply, are to "perform the loan modification and other foreclosure prevention services" the program makes available to borrowers. SPA § 1(A). To meet this objective, the SPA binds servicers to obey existing and future "Supplemental Directives" published by Treasury further fleshing out the HAMP program.[6] Treasury published the first Supplemental Directive on April 6, 2009, one week before [Defendant 1] signed the SPA. Supplemental Directive 09-01: Introduction to the HAMP Program, *available at* https://www.hmpadmin.com/portal/docs/hamp_servicer/sd0901.pdf (April

6 Section 1(A) of the SPA provides that "Servicer shall perform the loan modification and other foreclosure prevention services described in (i) the Financial Instrument . . . (ii) the Program guidelines and procedures issued by the Treasury . . . and (iii) any supplemental documentation, instructions, bulletins, letters, directives or other communications . . . issued by the Treasury, Fannie Mae, or Freddie Mac in order to change, or further describe or clarify the scope of, the rights and duties of the Participating Servicers in connection with the Program (the "Supplemental Directives" . . .)." SPA § 1(A).

6, 2009) (hereinafter "Supplemental Directive 09-01"). It has since published six more directives. To clarify these documents, Treasury maintains a "Frequently Asked Questions" document answering servicer questions. Supplemental Documentation—Frequently Asked Questions, *available at* https://www.hmpadmin.com/portal/docs/hamp_servicer/hampfaqs.pdf (August 19, 2009) (hereinafter "FAQ"). Finally, Treasury has provided a comprehensive, regularly updated checklist for servicers. Checklist for Getting Started and Participating in HAMP for Non-GSE Loans at 1, *available at* https://www.hmpadmin.com/portal/docs/hamp_servicer/hampchecklist.pdf (last updated 10/14/09) (hereinafter "Checklist"). While the Supplemental Guidelines as updated by the FAQ govern in the event of a conflict with the checklist,[7] the checklist helps to consolidate in one document a description of the entire program as it is intended to function.

These documents make clear that participating servicers are *required* to make a threshold eligibility determination for any borrower who contacts the servicer requesting consideration, as Plaintiff has. *See* FAQ at 2 (once a borrower contacts the servicer about HAMP, "[p]articipating servicers are required to validate the homeowner's eligibility for HAMP and capacity to pay"); Checklist at 2-3 (servicers must "[c]onsider borrowers whose loans are in default" as "potential candidates for HAMP," and must then "review available information" to determine whether the remaining eligibility criteria are met). Next, if the borrower proves eligible for the program, servicers are *required* to analyze the present value of HAMP payments versus foreclosure. Supplemental Directive 09-01 at 4 ("All loans that meet the HAMP eligibility criteria and are . . . 60 or more days delinquent must be evaluated using a standardized NPV test that compares the NPV result for a modification to the NPV result for no modification."). If a loan passes this test, the servicer is *required* to offer a HAMP Trial Period and, assuming payments are made successfully, a final HAMP loan modification. Supplemental Directive 09-01 at 15 ("Once the servicer makes [the eligibility and NPV] determination and has received good funds for the first month's trial payment, the servicer should sign and immediately return an executed copy of the Trial Period Plan to the borrower."); 18 ("If the borrower complies with the terms and conditions of the Trial Period Plan, the loan modification will become effective on the first day of the month following the trial period.").

Plaintiff's loan was plainly eligible to be considered for participation as of July 1, 2009, and continues to be eligible.[8] To qualify for HAMP analysis, a borrower must hold a loan which (1) was originated on or before January 1, 2009; (2) has not previously been modified under HAMP; (3) is delinquent or at risk of imminent default; (4) secures a one-to-four unit property encompassing the borrower's principal residence; and (5) is not vacant or condemned. In addition, the borrower must have a mortgage payment that is more than 31% of her monthly income, and must have experienced some financial hardship (including reduced income or excessive monthly debt payments) leaving her without sufficient liquidity to make the current payment. *Id.* at 2. As demonstrated by Exhibits B and D to the Verified Complaint, Plaintiff satisfies each of these requirements. Moreover, at the time of the transfer to [Defendant 2] on July 1, Plaintiff had requested a modification from [Defendant 1] and had provided documentation supporting her eligibility.

7 At the bottom of page 1 of the Checklist is a disclaimer stating: "While every effort has been made to ensure the reliability of the content of this checklist, the provisions of the Supplemental Directives (as further supplemented or clarified in FAQs) govern, and must be adhered to in the event of any conflict." Home Affordable Modification Program (HAMP): Checklist at 1.

8 Moreover, as discussed below, our analysis indicates that plaintiff's loan is likely to be NPV-positive and qualify her for a Trial Period Plan once it is properly considered for modification. *See* Exhibit F to the verified complaint. However, we are unable to perfectly replicate the NPV test developed by Treasury for HAMP use, as this is not made available except to servicers.

2. As [Defendant 1]'s assignee, [Defendant 2] is contractually bound to consider Plaintiff's loan for a HAMP modification

Section 8 of the SPA provides that [Defendant 1] must give notice to Fannie Mae and Freddie Mac of "any transfers or assignment of mortgage loans subject to this Agreement," and "[s]uch notice must include . . . evidence of the assumption by such transferee or assignee of the mortgage loans or other rights and obligations that are transferred, in the form of Exhibit C (the "Assignment and Assumption Agreement"). The section goes on to provide that "[a]ny purported transfer or assignment of mortgage loans or other rights or obligations under the Agreement in violation of this Section is void." SPA § 8(A). In turn, Exhibit C, the model Assignment and Assumption Agreement ("AAA"), incorporates the SPA by reference and assigns to the assignee "all of Assignor's rights and obligations under the [SPA] with respect to" those mortgage loans identified as HAMP-eligible. SPA Exhibit C.[9]

Thus, assuming that it complied with the SPA in this regard, [Defendant 1] contracted with [Defendant 2] to assume [Defendant

9 Since [Defendant 1] signed its SPA, Fannie Mae and the Treasury Department have made certain modifications to the standard Servicer Participation Agreement. These modifications further clarify the federal government's intent to bind all assignees. As revised, section 8(A) now provides that notice must be given to Fannie Mae and Freddie Mac of the assignment of "mortgage loans, or servicing rights relating to mortgage loans, that are 60 or more days delinquent and otherwise eligible for consideration or process under one or more of the Programs at the time of transfer or assignment, or for which the Servicer is performing Services at the time of transfer or assignment (collectively, "Eligible Loans")." Moreover, a new subsection of section 8 now provides:

> If the Servicer transfers or assigns all or any portion of its portfolio of mortgage loans or servicing rights to a third party pursuant to an Assignment and Assumption Agreement, only the Eligible Loans must be identified on a schedule to the Assignment and Assumption Agreement. *The transferee or assignee of Servicer's mortgage loans and servicing rights must assume Servicer's obligations under this Agreement only with respect to Eligible Loans*, subject to the Service Schedules and the Program Documentation applicable to the Programs in which Servicer agreed to participate prior to the transfer or assignment.

Servicer Participation Agreement § 8(C)(i) (last updated 8/28/09), *available at* www.hmpadmin.com/portal/docs/hamp_servicer/servicerparticipationagreement.pdf (last visited 10/22/09) (emphasis added).

1]'s HAMP duties for those loans for which [Defendant 2] became servicer on July 1, 2009, including Plaintiff's.[10] [Defendant 2], in turn, agreed to be bound by the SPA in its servicing of those loans.

3. Defendants are contractually bound to halt the foreclosure sale of Plaintiff's home until they have made a determination of HAMP eligibility and considered Plaintiff for other available modifications

One of the primary duties of HAMP servicers is an agreement to suspend all pending foreclosure proceedings until HAMP analysis is complete:

> To ensure that a borrower currently at risk of foreclosure has the opportunity to apply for the HAMP, *servicers should not proceed with a foreclosure sale until the borrower has been evaluated for the program and, if eligible, an offer to participate in the HAMP has been made.* Servicers must use reasonable efforts to contact borrowers facing foreclosure to determine their eligibility for the HAMP, including in-person contacts at the servicer's discretion. Servicers must not conduct foreclosure sales on loans previously referred to foreclosure or refer new loans to foreclosure during the 30-day period that the borrower has to submit documents evidencing an intent to accept the Trial Period Plan offer.

Supplemental Directive 09-01 at 14. Elsewhere, the Directive stresses that, "[a]s detailed in the Servicer Participation Agreement, participating servicers are required to consider *all* eligible mortgage loans unless prohibited by the rules of the applicable . . . investor servicing agreements." *Id.* at 1.

Under the terms of the SPA and AAA, then, Plaintiff is clearly entitled to a suspension of the foreclosure sale currently scheduled for November 4, 2009, until such time as defendants have analyzed her loan to determine whether it passed the NPV test; notified her of such determination; and either (1) offered her a HAMP trial period or (2) considered her for other available foreclosure prevention options. *See* Supplemental Directive 09-01 at 4 ("If a modification is not pursued when the NPV result is "negative," the servicer must consider the borrower for other foreclosure prevention options, including alternative modification programs, deeds-in-lieu, and preforeclosure sale programs.").

4. Plaintiff is a third-party beneficiary of the SPA and AAA

"A person not a party to an express contract may bring an action on such contract if the parties to the agreement intended to benefit the non-party, provided that the benefit claimed is a direct and not merely an incidental benefit of the contract." *E.B. Roberts Constr. Co. v. Concrete Contractors, Inc.*, 704 P.2d 859, 865 (Colo. 1985) (citations omitted); *see also Jefferson County School Dist. No. R-1 v. Shorey*, 826 P.2d 830, 843 (Colo. 1992) (employees may sue to enforce a collective bargaining agreement); *Clark v. State Farm Mut. Auto. Ins. Co.*, 319 F.3d 1234, 1241 (10th Cir. Colo. 2003) ("In Colorado, a pedestrian to whom PIP benefits are payable is a third-party beneficiary of the policy and has standing to bring reformation and contract claims against the insurer."). "While the intent to benefit the non-party need not be expressly recited in the contract, the intent must be apparent from the terms of the agreement, the surrounding circumstances, or both." *E.B. Roberts Constr. Co.*, 704 P.2d at 865.[11]

The HAMP program and the SPAs creating it are manifestly intended to benefit defaulting borrowers—indeed, this is the reason for the program's existence. Supplemental Directive 09-01, which is incorporated into the SPA, states:

> On February 18, 2009, President Obama announced the Homeowner Affordability and Stability Plan to help up to 7 to 9 million families restructure or refinance their mortgages to avoid foreclosure. As part of this plan, the Treasury Department (Treasury) announced *a national modification program aimed at helping 3 to 4 million at-risk homeowners*—both those who are in default and those who are at imminent risk of default—by reducing monthly payments to sustainable levels.

Supplemental Directive 09-01 at 1 (emphasis added). Similarly, the Making Home Affordable website introduces HAMP as a plan to "help . . . Americans reduce their monthly mortgage payments to more affordable levels" by "preventing avoidable foreclosures." About Making Home Affordable, *supra*. As described in more detail on a borrower FAQ page:

> *The Program helps borrowers who are struggling to keep their loans current or who are already behind on their mortgage payments.* By providing mortgage loan servicers with financial incentives to modify existing first lien mortgages, the Treasury hopes to *help homeowners avoid foreclosure* regardless of who owns or guarantees the mortgage.

10 As discussed *supra*, later revisions to the SPA have clarified the parties' intent regarding what loans assumed by an assignee servicer must be considered for HAMP. The revisions sensibly limit such loans to those which are sixty days delinquent. Even if this limitation is read into the SPA signed by GMAC, plaintiff's loan had been in default for nine months at the time of the transfer, and, indeed, was already under consideration for modification. Thus, under any feasible definition of the category of loans which MGC agreed to analyze for a modification, hers qualifies.

11 Although section 11(A) of the SPA states that it "shall be governed by and construed under Federal law and not the law of any state or locality," "[a] choice of law clause, like an arbitration clause, is a contractual right that cannot ordinarily be invoked by or against a party who did not sign the contract in which the provision appears," subject to possible exceptions based on a close relationship between the third party and the contracting parties which are not applicable here. Cooper v. Meridian Yachts, Ltd., 575 F.3d 1151, 1169 (11th Cir. Fla. 2009). At any rate, to determine the federal common law "we may look to general principles for interpreting contracts." County of Santa Clara v. Astra USA, Inc., 540 F.3d 1094, 1100 (9th Cir. 2008) (quotations, citations, and alterations omitted). As stated in the Restatement (Second) of Contracts, those principles are the same in all relevant respects as Colorado's rule. *See* Restatement (Second) of Contracts §§ 302 and cmt. d, 304. *See also* Montana v. United States, 124 F.3d 1269, 1273 (Fed. Cir. 1997).

Borrower Frequently Asked Questions, http://makinghome affordable.gov/borrower-faqs.html#b1 (last visited 10/26/09) (emphases added). In addition, although the legislation underpinning HAMP—the Emergency Economic Stabilization Act—is necessarily vague and general given its sweeping aims, the statute specifically requires the Secretary of the Treasury to consider "the need to help families keep their homes and to stabilize communities" in utilizing his TARP authority. EESA § 103(3).

There is another major indication that Fannie Mae, the "promisee" who bargained for the servicers' promises to participate in HAMP, intends that *all* borrowers whose loans are eligible should receive the benefit of the program. Fannie Mae recently sued under HAMP to enjoin *all* pending foreclosures in the state of South Carolina until borrowers could uniformly be considered under the program. The South Carolina Supreme Court granted the injunction and created procedures for judges in the state to ensure that no foreclosure occurs until the servicer has complied with HAMP. *See* Administrative Order Re: Mortgage Foreclosures and the Home Affordable Modification Program (HMP), 2009-05-22-01 (S.C. May 22, 2009), *available at* http://www.judicial.state.sc.us/courtOrders/displayOrder.cfm?orderNo=2009-05-22-01.

Finally, to the extent there is any doubt that borrowers are intended beneficiaries of HAMP, the commentary to the Restatement explains that "[i]n cases of doubt, the question whether such an intention is to be attributed to the promisee may be influenced by the likelihood that recognition of the right will further the legitimate expectations of the promisee, make available a simple and convenient procedure for enforcement, or protect the beneficiary in his reasonable reliance on the promise." Restatement (Second) of Contracts, § 304 cmt. e. It is apparent that the federal government lacks the resources to enforce servicer agreements as to every defaulting borrower around the nation, and that third-party suits will prove the most "simple and convenient procedure for enforcement."

Thus, the available evidence regarding the intent of Fannie Mae and [Defendant 1] compels the conclusion that Plaintiff is an intended third-party beneficiary of the SPA. [Defendant 2], in turn, presumably contracted in an AAA to assume *all* of [Defendant 1]'s obligations under the SPA. The AAA incorporates the SPA by reference. Because the intent to benefit borrowers is apparent from the text of the SPA, the Supplemental Directives, and the surrounding circumstances, [Defendant 2] and [Defendant 1] also intended to benefit these third-party beneficiaries when they entered into an AAA, and Plaintiff may enforce the AAA, SPA, and Supplemental Directives against [Defendant 2].

B. PLAINTIFF WILL SUFFER AN IRREPARABLE INJURY IF HER HOME IS ALLOWED TO BE SOLD AT FORECLOSURE

Needless to say, the loss of their home would be devastating to Plaintiff and her two children, as detailed in her Affidavit accompanying her Motion for Temporary Restraining Order. First, Plaintiff would lose the equity she has built in her home. Second, Plaintiff and her children would be without a place to live, and plaintiff fears she will have difficulty securing an affordable rental. This hardship is particularly severe for Plaintiff's teenage daughter, who has undergone a traumatic experience in recent years and would be unusually harmed by further upheaval, such as moving to a new residence.

In addition, our analysis indicates that the loss of plaintiff's home is probably avoidable through the HAMP program, such that engaging in the HAMP analysis to which Plaintiff is entitled would result not merely in a delay of an inevitable foreclosure, but in a successful HAMP modification. This conclusion is based on a preliminary analysis of the Net Present Value of a HAMP-modified loan versus a foreclosure. Although no parties other than servicers and the federal government have access to the HAMP NPV formula, Treasury officials have indicated that the formula is based on a similar formula used by the FDIC in other contexts. *E.g.* Assistant Secretary for Financial Institutions Michael S. Barr Written Testimony on Stabilizing the Housing Market before the House Financial Services Committee at 3 (September 9, 2009), *available at http://www.house.gov/apps/list/hearing/financialsvcs_dem/barr_-_treasury.pdf*. A worksheet implementing the FDIC formula is available online at http://www.fdic.gov/consumers/loans/loanmod/loanmodguide.html (click on "Net Present Value Worksheet).

Exhibit F to the Verified Complaint shows the results of an NPV analysis of Plaintiff's loan using the FDIC worksheet, based on the same information she sent to [Defendant 2] as support for her request for a modification. As the exhibit shows, at least using the FDIC formulation of NPV, plaintiff comes up "NPV positive." If this result were the same under the HAMP formula, she would meet all requirements to receive a HAMP trial period of three payments set at 31% of her income, and would receive a final loan modification assuming she made these payments. Accordingly, a preliminary injunction may be the difference between retaining her property permanently, and losing it permanently.

C. PLAINTIFF HAS NO REMEDY AT LAW

Because a foreclosed homeowner has no right to redeem after a foreclosure sale is complete, *see* Colo. Rev. Stat. Title 38, Article 38, and foreclosure sales are typically not rescinded for reasons other than irregularities in the sale itself, *see Mt. Carbon Metro Dist. v. Lake George Co.*, 847 P.2d 254, 257 (Colo. Ct. App. 1993), Plaintiff will be left without any legal remedy if her home is sold.

D. THE INTEREST OF THE PUBLIC STRONGLY FAVORS ALLOWING THE OPPORTUNITY TO NEGOTIATE A MODIFICATION

A recent study by the Center for Responsible Lending estimates that in 2009, foreclosures in Colorado will lead to a decline of *$5.9 billion* in the contribution of housing to the state economy. Center for Responsible Lender, Colorado Foreclosures: Impact & Opportunities (January 2009), *available at* www.responsiblelending.org/mortgage-lending/tools-resources/factsheets/co-foreclosure-factsheet.pdf. High foreclosure rates also influence crime rates. *See, e.g.*, Sheriff Ted Mink, Foreclosed Homes and Their Impact on Neighborhoods (April 2008), *available at* http://www.co.jefferson.co.us/sheriff/sheriff_T62_R241.htm (detailing specific crime effects of foreclosures in nearby Jefferson County).

The [Metro] area, where Plaintiff's home is located, is particularly hard-hit, absorbing a larger decline in housing prices than other metropolitan areas in the state. *Id.* Indeed, a search on *www.realtytrac.com* for Plaintiff's address revealed a staggering 202 properties subject to recent or pending foreclosure sale within the three square miles surrounding Plaintiff's home. *See* Exhibit H to the Verified Complaint.

Finally, the relief plaintiff requests would permanently forestall a sale *only* if a loan modification turns out to be NPV-positive; that is, more beneficial to investors than foreclosure over the long term. This built-in safeguard belies any argument that a loss to investors might outweigh the potential impact of a foreclosure on Plaintiff's community.

E. THE BALANCE OF EQUITIES STRONGLY FAVORS ALLOWING PLAINTIFF AND [Defendant 2] AN OPPORTUNITY TO NEGOTIATE A HAMP MODIFICATION

For the same reason that it would be strange to argue that there is any benefit to the public from foreclosing on Plaintiff's home on November 4, it would be peculiar indeed for Defendants to argue that the equities favor some interest of theirs over the Plaintiff's interest in remaining in her home: Foreclosure will be permanently forestalled *only if* the HAMP NPV analysis proves that a loan modification would result in overall greater value to the investor in Plaintiff's loan than would a foreclosure.[12] The NPV test is sophisticated and accounts for factors such as the likelihood of a future default if the loan is modified and the time a home is likely to spend on the market before resale if the foreclosure goes forward. *See* Exhibit F to the Verified Complaint. Thus, it does a good job of safeguarding defendants' interests simply by its mere application.

The equities favor an injunction for other reasons as well. The hardship to a family that is evicted from their home simply does not compare to a financial loss on a mortgage loan absorbed by vast lending and servicing corporations. Moreover, unlike [Defendant 1] and [Defendant 2], Plaintiff has diligently pursued the possibility of modification for months, sending paperwork promptly, keeping careful records, and meeting with a housing counselor. *See* Exhibits B, D, and G to the Verified Complaint. Responsibility for the delay in assessing her HAMP eligibility lies squarely with the defendants.

F. ENJOINING THE SCHEDULE FORECLOSURE SALE WILL PRESERVE THE STATUS QUO ANTE

As the parties currently stand, Plaintiff owns her home and owes [Defendant 3] mortgage arrears and associated fees. [Defendant 3], in turns, claims to own the Note securing her mortgage. Plaintiff is in the process of being considered for a loan modification by [Defendant 3]'s servicer, [Defendant 2]. A foreclosure sale would permanently and irrevocably upend this state of affairs, ending Plaintiff's interest in her property and her opportunity to obtain an affordable mortgage loan, as well as defendants' opportunity to save money on a modification that is NPV-positive. The addition of ongoing foreclosure-related fees to Plaintiff's mortgage account also disrupts the status quo by increasing her debt to defendants [Defendant 3] and [Defendant 2].

For the foregoing reasons, Plaintiff satisfies all requirements for a preliminary injunction suspending the foreclosure sale of her home until she can be analyzed for participation in the HAMP program.

12 HAMP does obligate the servicer to consider plaintiff's loan for other foreclosure prevention options if her loan should fail the NPV test; however, it does not obligate the servicer to select any particular option.

Respectfully submitted,
[Attorney for Plaintiff]
[Date]

I.6 Pleadings to Enjoin Non-Judicial Foreclosure Borrower in Temporary HAMP Modification

I.6.1 Complaint

IN THE DISTRICT COURT OF
THE FOURTH JUDICIAL DISTRICT STATE OF IDAHO,
IN AND FOR THE COUNTY OF ADA

EDIS HOMEOWNER and MELSIA HOMEOWNER, husband and wife,
Plaintiffs

v.

METLIFE BANK, N.A., d/b/a METLIFE HOME LOANS, a national banking association; TRANSNATION TITLE AND ESCROW, INC., d/b/a FIDELITY NATIONAL TITLE COMPANY OF IDAHO, a foreign corporation; and GORILLA CAPITAL OF ADA COUNTY 8, L.L.C., an Idaho limited liability company,
Defendants.

VERIFIED COMPLAINT AND DEMAND FOR JURY TRIAL

The plaintiffs, Edis and Melsia Homeowner, by and through their attorney Richard Alan Eppink of Idaho Legal Aid Services, Inc., complain against the defendants and for their claims for relief allege:

1. The plaintiffs, refugees resettled here from Bosnia and Herzegovina, bring this action to prevent their family from being turned out of their home as a result of an improper trustee's sale. They ask this Court to void and annul that sale, to enjoin compliance with state foreclosure and federal Home Affordable Modification Program ("HAMP") requirements, and to be made whole for violations of law and other requirements.

PARTIES AND JURISDICTION

2. Plaintiffs EDIS HOMEOWNER ("Edis") and MELSIA HOMEOWNER ("Melsia") (collectively, "the Homeowners"), husband and wife, were resettled with their family by the United States of America in 2000 as refugees from the nation of Bosnia and Herzegovina, escaping from the former Socialist Federal

Republic of Yugoslavia. They were resettled to Boise, Idaho, where in July 2001 they bought their first home in America. In fall 2006 they sold that home and upgraded to a larger one for their family, which home is now the focus of this action. Edis and Melsia have made a home there since then with their three children and Edis's disabled, 71-year-old mother, Nadia Homeowner, also a Bosnian refugee.

3. Defendant METLIFE BANK, N.A., ("Metlife") doing business as METLIFE HOME LOANS, is a national banking association and a division of Metlife, Inc., a Delaware corporation. Metlife serviced the Homeowners' debt on their home, on information and belief as servicer for "Fannie Mae," the Federal National Mortgage Association. Metlife transacts business within the State of Idaho and, on information and belief, owns and possesses real property situate within the State of Idaho.

4. Defendant TRANSNATION TITLE AND ESCROW, INC., ("Transnation") doing business as FIDELITY NATIONAL TITLE COMPANY OF IDAHO, is a Delaware corporation that transacts business within the State of Idaho. Transnation purports to be the trustee who conducted the trustee's sale at which the Homeowners' home was sold.

5. Defendant GORILLA CAPITAL OF ADA COUNTY 8, L.L.C., ("Gorilla") is an Idaho limited liability company, organized in January 2010, that transacts business within the State of Idaho and, on information and belief, owns and possesses real property situate within the State of Idaho. Gorilla purports to have been the buyer at the trustee's sale at which the Homeowners' home was sold. A principal member of Gorilla is Gorilla Capital, Inc., on information and belief an Oregon corporation doing business under various names in Arizona, Florida, Washington, Oregon, and Idaho. On information and belief, Gorilla's and Gorilla Capital, Inc.'s primary business strategy involves purchasing family homes at deep discounts in irregular or otherwise underbid foreclosure and trustee's sales, then rapidly evicting the occupant family and flipping the property into the private market.

6. The Homeowners claim and pray for an amount for damages in these causes that exceeds the jurisdictional limit for this Court and pray for other relief within the jurisdiction of this Court.

GENERAL ALLEGATIONS

The Home, Metlife's Statements, and Improper Trustee's Sale

7. The Homeowners purchased a home for their family in September 2006. Their home consists of real property, improved with a single family house and other improvements, situated in Ada County, Idaho, described as "[Plat Description]," and located at and more commonly referred to as [Address]. The real property and improvements will be referred to as "home" throughout this Complaint. At that time the Homeowners executed as grantors and trustors, two deeds of trust concerning the home and securing the debt they had incurred to purchase it.

8. The Homeowners have resided, with their three minor children and Edis's mother, at the home at all times since then. They have no other home or residence. Edis has invested approximately $30,000.00 in improvements on the property, including hardwood floors, granite countertops, and a patio; and another approximately $30,000.00 of his own labor in installing those improvements.

9. In August 2007, the Homeowners refinanced the debts they had incurred to purchase the home. As part of the refinancing, the home was reconveyed to the Homeowners from the trusts under the two prior deeds of trust, and the Homeowners as grantors and trustors executed a new, single deed of trust concerning the home, securing the new debt they had incurred (the "home loan"). The lender for the refinance was First Horizon Home Loans, a division of First Tennessee Bank, N.A.

10. In or about June 2008, Metlife acquired the residential mortgage origination and servicing business of First Tennessee Bank, N.A., including First Horizon Home Loans and, on information and belief, the contracts and other assets related to the servicing of the Homeowners' home loan.

11. On information and belief, sometime after June 2008, Metlife began servicing the Homeowners' home loan.

12. Accordingly, sometime after June 2008, the Homeowners began receiving statements and payment coupons about the home loan from Metlife, and the Homeowners began sending their monthly payments on the home loan to Metlife.

13. After the refinance, the Homeowners had a total monthly payment of $1,684.78 on the home loan. Edis was self-employed in construction and stone masonry, and the impact in 2008 and 2009 of a severe national and local economic downturn substantially reduced the Homeowners' income. Edis's income for 2008 was barely half of his income in 2007. With reduced income, it became hard for the Homeowners to make the $1,696.33 monthly payment each month.

14. The Homeowners were able to make their payments for January and February 2009 on time. But on or about April 7, 2009, they faxed an application for a loan modification or workout to Metlife. The application consisted of a completed "Hardship Letter" form explaining some of the hardships that would prevent them from making timely payment, along with a completed "Borrower Financial Statement" form, and several attachments.

15. On April 10, 2009, the Homeowners also sent, by Express Mail, that same application for a loan modification to Metlife, which received it on April 13, 2009.

16. On or about May 8, 2009, the Homeowners received from a letter from Metlife, stating in part that "You may be eligible for the Home Affordable Modification program, part of the initiative announced by President Obama to help homeowners. As your mortgage loan servicer, we will work with you in an effort to make your mortgage payment affordable" and that "If you do not qualify for a loan modification under this program . . . we will work with you to explore other options available to help you keep your home or ease your transition to a new home." The letter asked the Homeowners to phone Metlife. A true copy of that letter is attached to this Complaint as "Exhibit A" and incorporated into this Complaint as thought fully set forth here.

17. On or about the same day, May 8, 2009, Edis phoned Metlife and was told Metlife would mail the Homeowners a loan modification offer.

18. On or about May 29, 2009, the Homeowners mailed to Metlife a check for $3,512.30, which was returned to them by Metlife on or about June 9, 2009. Metlife provided no reason why the check was returned. A true copy of Metlife's letter to the Homeowners (with handwritten annotation by the Homeowners) giving no reason for the return of the check is attached to this Complaint as "Exhibit B" and incorporated into this Complaint as thought fully set forth here.

19. On or about June 22, 2009, the Homeowners finally received the loan modification offer that Metlife told Edis on or about May

8, 2009, that it would mail. The offer included a letter from Metlife, dated June 19, 2009, to the Homeowners, requesting acceptance of the offer no later than July 19, 2009, and stating in part that "We have enclosed a customized Home Affordable Modification Trial Period Plan" and again that "If you do not qualify for a loan modification under this program . . . we will work with you to explore other options available to help you keep your home or ease your transition to a new home." An enclosure that accompanied the letter stated that "As long as you comply with the terms of the Trial Period Plan, we will not start foreclosure proceedings or conduct a foreclosure sale if foreclosure proceedings have started." Also included, as stated, was a "Home Affordable Modification Trial Period Plan" ("HAMP Plan"). True copies of this letter (with handwritten annotation by the Homeowners) and related enclosures that accompanied it are attached to this Complaint as "Exhibit C" and incorporated into this Complaint as thought fully set forth here.

20. On June 25, 2009, the Homeowners sent all materials requested by Metlife to Metlife, as well as the HAMP Plan, which they had executed. A true copy of the HAMP Plan is attached to this Complaint as "Exhibit D" and incorporated into this Complaint as thought fully set forth here.

21. The same day, June 25, 2009, Edis phoned Metlife and asked why Metlife had returned the Homeowners' check for $3,512.30. Metlife told Edis that he was entering HAMP and that everything was okay.

22. Under the HAMP Plan, the Homeowners' monthly payment on the home loan was reduced to $1,052.68 for a three month trial period. After the trial period, under the HAMP Plan, if the Homeowners complied with the plan, Metlife would send the Homeowners a "Modification Agreement" for their signature which would reflect the new payment amount and waive any unpaid late charges already accrued.

23. On or about July 7, 2009, the Homeowners timely mailed and made their first payment under the HAMP Plan.

24. On or about July 13, 2009, the Homeowners received a copy of a "Notice of Trustee's Sale" concerning the home loan and their home. On or about the same day, Edis phoned Metlife and asked its agent, Jessica, about that notice. Metlife told Edis not to worry about the letter because the Homeowners had entered HAMP and that the Homeowners could throw the notice away.

25. On or about July 17, 2009, just before the Homeowners' first HAMP Plan payment was due, Edis phoned Metlife and asked if it had received his first HAMP Plan payment. Metlife told Edis that it had received the payment.

26. On or about July 21, 2009, the Homeowners timely mailed and made their second payment under the HAMP Plan.

27. On or about August 5, 2009, Metlife mailed to the Homeowners a letter "RE: SPECIAL FOREBEARANCE AGREEMENT" stating in part that "Metlife Home Loans is in receipt of your signed Special Forebearance Agreement. . . ." A true copy of this letter is attached to this Complaint as "Exhibit E" and incorporated into this Complaint as thought fully set forth here.

28. On or about August 17, 2009, the Homeowners timely mailed and made their third payment under the HAMP Plan.

29. On or about September 22, 2009, Edis phoned Metlife and asked why he had not received a modification agreement for the Homeowners' signature, under the HAMP Plan. Metlife told Edis that Metlife was still processing the Homeowners' case. Metlife also told Edis to continue making a total payment of $1,052.68 each month while Metlife continued to process the Homeowners' case.

30. On or about the same day, September 22, 2009, the Homeowners mailed and made a fourth payment of $1,052.68 to Metlife, as Metlife had instructed Edis.

31. On or about October 31, 2009, the Homeowners mailed and made a fifth payment of $1,052.68 to Metlife, as Metlife had instructed Edis.

32. On or about November 9, 2009, the Homeowners received a letter from Metlife's agent, First American LMS, asking for another Hardship Affidavit from the Homeowners, along with a completed Financial Disclosure Form and copies of pay stubs. The Homeowners faxed all requested materials to Metlife's agent on or about November 11, 2009.

33. On or about November 23, 2009, Metlife or its agent phoned Edis and requested that he provide copies of his pay stubs again. Edis faxed them as requested the same day.

34. On or about December 7, 2009, the Homeowners mailed and made a sixth payment of $1,052.68 to Metlife, as Metlife had instructed Edis.

35. On or about January 9, 2010, the Homeowners mailed and made a seventh payment of $1,052.68 to Metlife, as Metlife had instructed Edis.

36. On or about February 8, 2010, the Homeowners mailed and made an eighth payment of $1,052.68 to Metlife, as Metlife had instructed Edis.

37. On or about the same day, February 8, 2010, Metlife phoned Edis and requested that he provide copies of his pay stubs—again—and copies of recent bank statements. On or about February 9, 2010, the Homeowners faxed all requested materials to Metlife.

38. On or about February 16, 2010, the Homeowners received notice from Metlife stating in part that it "cannot accept this payment because it doesn't represent the total amount that is due on your account. The total amount due is $16,200.18." A true copy of this letter (with handwritten annotations by the Homeowners or their friend) is attached to this Complaint as "Exhibit F" and incorporated into this Complaint as though fully set forth here.

39. On or about the next day, February 17, 2010, Edis attempted for most of the morning to reach Metlife by phone, but his call was never answered by a human being. Edis therefore traveled to the nearest Metlife office, in Eagle, Idaho. There, a human being, Michelle, on information and belief tried to reach another Metlife employee several times, finally connecting them to another Metlife employee who asked the Homeowners to provide a letter stating that they were not renting the home and to provide copies of their pay stubs, again. On or about the same day, the Homeowners faxed all the materials Metlife had requested.

40. On or about March 4, 2010, the Homeowners received a letter from Metlife "Re: Foreclosure Process to Begin" that stated in part "you have defaulted on the Forebearance [sic] Agreement (the 'Agreement') that was entered into to assist you in bringing your loan current." A true copy of this letter is attached to this Complaint as "Exhibit G" and incorporated into this Complaint as though fully set forth here. On or about the same day, the Homeowners phoned Metlife and spoke to Chanelle. Metlife told the Homeowners that Metlife was still processing the Homeowners' HAMP modification and asked the Homeowners to phone again on March 10, 2010.

41. On or about March 8, 2010, the Homeowners phoned Metlife and spoke to Derek. Metlife told the Homeowners that

their case had been transferred to a different department and that the trustee's sale on the home had been postponed. Metlife told the Homeowners to phone again in two to three weeks. The Homeowners asked if they should send payment (again) for February, or for March, but Metlife told them not to send any payment.

42. On information and belief, on March 12, 2010, Transnation conducted a trustee's sale of the home, at which Gorilla placed a bid of $111,201.00. On information and belief, Gorilla had "inquiry notice" of potential defects in the trustee's sale process.

43. At that March 12, 2010, trustee's sale, on information and belief Metlife did not make a credit bid in the total amount it was owed on the home loan, but instead made a credit bid of $111,200.00.

44. On March 12, 2010, Mike Thomas, an agent of Gorilla, visited Edis at the home and told Edis that Gorilla had purchased the home that day. On March 13, 2010, Mike Thomas as Gorilla's agent again visited Edis at the home and tried to give him $500.00 to immediately vacate the home.

45. On or about March 16, 2010, Edis phoned the Idaho Attorney General's office and then Metlife. Metlife told Edis that it would call him back. The same day, Metlife phoned Edis and asked him—yet again—to provide copies of his pay stubs. The Homeowners faxed the requested materials the same day.

46. On March 12, 2010, Gorilla had commenced an action in the Fourth Judicial District Court of the State of Idaho alleging unlawful detainer of the home by the Homeowners. That action is proceeding before the magistrate division of this Court under Ada County case no. [Case Number]. On March 25, 2010, the parties to that action—Gorilla and the Homeowners—stipulated to continue further proceedings in the case until April 6, 2010.

The Home Affordable Modification Program

47. The economic downturn in the United States has resulted in millions of homeowners falling behind in their mortgage payments, and facing foreclosure and the risk of losing their homes.

48. In early 2009, the Obama administration took action to stem the tide of what had become a national foreclosure crisis, through enactment of the Homeowner Affordability and Stability Plan ("HASP"). HASP is authorized by the Emergency Economic Stabilization Act of 2008 and was developed "to provide assistance for up to 7 to 9 million homeowners by reducing monthly mortgage payments to sustainably affordable levels, preventing avoidable foreclosures and helping millions of Americans keep [their] homes." (U.S. Dep't of Treasury, 100 Days Progress Report, at 4 (Apr. 29, 2009) (available at http://www.treas.gov/press/releases/reports/100daysreport_042909.pdf).)

49. As part of HASP, Treasury established the Home Affordable Modification Program. HAMP's primary purpose is to assist the millions of homeowners in default or at imminent risk of default on their home mortgages "by establishing a standardized and streamlined process for servicers (including lenders or investors that service their own loans) to follow in evaluating and conducting modifications of existing mortgages, and by providing meaningful incentives to servicers, investors and borrowers to encourage loan modifications." (Financial Stability Oversight Board, Quarterly Report to Congress Pursuant to § 104(g) of the Emergency Economic Stabilization Act of 2008, at 31 (Mar. 31, 2009).) Treasury has committed $50 billion to finance modifications under HAMP. Funding for HAMP began on April 13, 2009.

50. HAMP is governed by documents issued by Treasury and designated in the HAMP These documents include uniform "Home Affordable Modification Program Guidelines" for modifying loans under HAMP (the "Guidelines"); subsequent Supplemental Directives; and "Frequently Asked Questions" ("FAQs") intended to further clarify HAMP program requirements.

51. HAMP provides homeowners with significant benefits. Principally, the reduction of borrowers' monthly loan payments to affordable and sustainable levels is intended to allow borrowers to avoid foreclosure and retain their home. HAMP accomplishes these goals by reducing borrowers' monthly payments toward principal, interest, taxes and insurance to 31% of their gross income. In addition, HAMP provides reductions in mortgage principal for five years to borrowers who remain current in their modified payments.

52. HAMP also offers homeowners protection against foreclosure. No foreclosure proceedings may be commenced against homeowners so long as they meet the HAMP minimum eligibility requirements and are being assessed for modification, and any foreclosure proceedings commenced before they were considered for HAMP modifications are to be suspended.

53. Homeowners also are protected from having mortgage servicers condition a loan modification upon waiver of the borrower's legal rights—a common demand from servicers in non-HAMP loan modification or forbearance programs—or a cash contribution from the borrower in addition to the trial modification loan payments.

54. Servicers handling loans owned by "Fannie Mae, the Federal National Mortgage Association, ("Fannie Mae servicers") are required to participate in HAMP for all eligible Fannie Mae portfolio mortgage loans and MBS pool mortgage loans guaranteed by Fannie Mae.

55. On information and belief, at all relevant times the Homeowners' home loan has been an eligible Fannie Mae portfolio mortgage loan or MBS pool mortgage loan guaranteed by Fannie Mae.

56. For Fannie Mae servicers, HAMP is additionally governed by documents issued by Fannie Mae. These documents include the Fannie Mae "Servicing Guide" and "Announcements" that amend and modify the Servicing Guide. Copies of three of these Announcements, Announcements 09-05R, 09-25, and 09-31, concerning HAMP, are attached to this Complaint as "Exhibit H" and incorporated into this Complaint as thought fully set forth here.

57. Under the governing guidelines and documents, HAMP reduces an eligible borrower's monthly payments toward principal, interest, taxes and insurance to 31% of the borrower's gross income.

58. HAMP requires that "[f]oreclosure actions . . ., including initiation of new foreclosure actions, must be postponed for all borrowers that meet the minimum HAMP eligibility criteria." (Frequently Asked Questions, at 2 (August 19, 2009).) Further, under HAMP a servicer "must not conduct foreclosure sales on loans previously referred to foreclosure or refer new loans to foreclosure during the 30-day period that the borrower has to submit documents evidencing an intent to accept the Trial Period Plan offer. (Supp. Direct. 09-01, at 14 (available at https://www.hmpadmin.com/portal/docs/hamp_servicer/sd0901.pdf).)

59. HAMP also prohibits foreclosure sales during the three-month trial period preceding any permanent loan modification.

60. Even if a borrower defaults after receiving a permanent

HAMP modification, under HAMP a servicer "must work with the borrower to cure the modified loan, or if that is not feasible, evaluate the borrower for any other available loss mitigation alternatives prior to commencing foreclosure proceedings." (*Id.* at 19.)

61. Moreover, because an eligible borrower who is not offered a HAMP modification must be considered for "other foreclosure prevention alternatives, including alternative modification programs, deed-in-lieu and short sale programs," HAMP requires that "[a]ny foreclosure action will be temporarily suspended . . . while borrowers are considered for alternative foreclosure prevention options." (Guidelines, at 3, 6 (available at http://www.treas.gov/press/releases/reports/modification_program_guidelines.pdf).)

CLAIMS FOR RELIEF AGAINST DEFENDANT METLIFE BANK, N.A.

62. The plaintiffs incorporate by reference all allegations contained in the paragraphs above as if set forth again in each of the claims for relief set forth below.

Breach of Contract

63. Metlife offered to enter into a contractual relationship with the Homeowners through its offer of the HAMP Plan.

64. The Homeowners accepted Metlife's offer by signing the HAMP Plan, returning the signed HAMP Plan to Metlife, and making the necessary payments under the HAMP Plan.

65. Metlife breached its contract by failing to provide the Homeowners with a permanent loan modification after they made three timely payments under the HAMP Plan.

66. The Homeowners were damaged as a proximate result of Metlife's breach of contract.

Breach of the Covenant of Good Faith and Fair Dealing

67. Every contact has an implied covenant of good faith and fair dealing that neither party will do anything that will have the effect of destroying or injuring the right of the other party to receive the benefit of the contract.

68. Metlife breached the covenant of good faith and fair dealing by failing to offer the Homeowners a permanent modification after even eight months of timely HAMP Plan payments.

69. The Homeowners were damaged as a proximate result of Metlife's breach of the covenant of good faith and fair dealing.

Promissory Estoppel

70. The Homeowners justifiably relied on Metlife's statements that no trustee's sale would be held and that they would be able to lower their monthly mortgage payments permanently if they made the three payments for the HAMP Plan and otherwise complied with Metlife's requests under HAMP. As a result, the Homeowners made eight payments for the HAMP Plan.

71. The Homeowners' reliance was to their substantial economic detriment as they forwent other opportunities, including seeking another type of loan modification or refinancing their home loan, and because they now must take extraordinary actions to annul and void an improperly held trustee's sale of their home.

72. The Homeowners did not know and could not know that Metlife's statements were false and misleading.

73. Metlife did see and should have reasonably foreseen that the Homeowners relied and would rely upon Metlife's statements.

74. Under the facts and circumstances of this case, justice requires the enforcement of Metlife's promises and representations.

75. The Homeowners are entitled to enforcement of Metlife's promises and representations from the HAMP Plan and Metlife is liable to the Homeowners for actual damages.

Fraud

76. During the duration of the Homeowners communication with Metlife about their hardship, modification of the home loan, HAMP, the HAMP Plan, and "foreclosure" by trustee's sale, Metlife stated to the Homeowners among other things that it was processing the Homeowners' HAMP case and modification and that no trustee's sale or other foreclosure sale would occur, including representing to the Homeowners on March 8, 2010, that any foreclosure sale was postponed.

77. These statements made by Metlife were false.

78. Metlife knew these statements were false or was unaware at the time it made them that they were false.

79. These statements made by Metlife were material.

80. Metlife made these statements to the Homeowners with the intent that the Homeowners rely on them, to their detriment.

81. The Homeowners had no way to determine that Metlife's statements were false.

82. The Homeowners did in fact rely upon Metlife's statements and made payments under the HAMP Plan.

83. Metlife nevertheless caused the home to be sold at the purported March 12, 2010, trustee's sale and caused damages to the Homeowners.

CLAIMS FOR RELIEF AGAINST DEFENDANT TRANSNATION TITLE AND ESCROW, INC.

84. The plaintiffs incorporate by reference all allegations contained in the paragraphs above as if set forth again in each of the claims for relief set forth below.

Declaratory Judgment

85. At the time of the purported trustee's sale on March 12, 2010, the Homeowners were not in default of the deed of trust or any related promissory note.

86. At the time of the purported trustee's sale on March 12, 2010, the Homeowners had entered into an accord, novation, or other modification of relevant contracts and no sale could have lawfully been conducted or any trustee's deed issued.

87. The purported trustee's sale could not have been conducted in conformance with federal law, HAMP, Idaho law, including the requirements of I.C. § 45-1505, or the due process requirements of the constitutions of the United States and the State of Idaho.

88. The Homeowners are entitled to have the trustee's deed issued on or about March 12, 2010, concerning the home annulled and voided.

89. The Homeowners are entitled to an order requiring Transnation to take such actions as are necessary to complete the set aside, reversal, annulment, and avoidance of the March 12, 2010, trustee's sale.

CLAIMS FOR RELIEF AGAINST DEFENDANT GORILLA CAPITAL OF ADA COUNTY 8, L.L.C.

90. The plaintiffs incorporate by reference all allegations contained in the paragraphs above as if set forth again in each of the claims for relief set forth below.

Quiet Title

91. At the time of the purported trustee's sale on March 12, 2010, the Homeowners were not in default of the deed of trust or any related promissory note.

92. At the time of the purported trustee's sale on March 12, 2010, the Homeowners had entered into an accord, novation, or other modification of relevant contracts and no sale could have lawfully been conducted or any trustee's deed issued.

93. The purported trustee's sale could not have been conducted in conformance with federal law, HAMP, Idaho law, including the requirements of I.C. § 45-1505, or the due process requirements of the constitutions of the United States and the State of Idaho. On information and belief, Gorilla had "inquiry notice" of potential defects in the trustee's sale process.

94. The Homeowners are entitled to have the trustee's deed issued on or about March 12, 2010, concerning the home annulled and voided.

95. The Homeowners are entitled to be declared the rightful owner of the home, subject to the August 2007 deed of trust.

96. Gorilla, and its officers, servants, employees, attorneys, and all those in active concert or participation with them, should be enjoined from proceeding by process of law or otherwise from attempting to dispossess the Homeowners until their right of ownership is determined by this Court in this case. Gorilla should accordingly be enjoined from proceeding in Ada County case no. [Number], before the magistrate division of this Court, or in any other action to dispossess the Homeowners, until further order of this Court.

DEMAND FOR JURY TRIAL

The plaintiffs hereby demand trial by a jury composed of no less than twelve (12) persons on all issues so triable, pursuant to Rule 38, *Idaho Rules of Civil Procedure*.

PRAYER FOR RELIEF

WHEREFORE the plaintiffs pray for judgment against the defendants as follows:

1. That the March 12, 2010, trustee's sale be set aside, reversed, annulled, and voided.
2. That Gorilla, and its officers, servants, employees, attorneys, and all those in active concert or participation with them, be prohibited by preliminary injunction from proceeding by process of law or otherwise from attempting to dispossess the Homeowners until their right of ownership is determined by this Court in this case. Gorilla should accordingly be enjoined from proceeding in Ada County case no. [Number], before the magistrate division of this Court, or in any other action to dispossess the Homeowners, until further order of this Court.
3. That the Homeowners be declared the rightful owners of the home, subject to the August 2007 deed of trust.
4. That the trustee's deed issued on or about March 12, 2010, concerning the home annulled and voided.
5. That Transnation be ordered to take such actions as are necessary to complete the set aside, reversal, annulment, and avoidance of the March 12, 2010, trustee's sale.
6. That the Court award damages against Metlife for an amount to be proved at trial, alleged for the purposes of default to be at least $150,000.
7. For a reasonable attorney's fee and all costs of suit, in the amount of $2,500.00 in the case of default.
8. For such other relief as the Court deems just.

Respectfully submitted,
[Attorney for Plaintiff]
[Date]

I.6.2 Motion for Preliminary Injunction

IN THE DISTRICT COURT OF
THE FOURTH JUDICIAL DISTRICT STATE OF IDAHO,
IN AND FOR THE COUNTY OF ADA

____________________________)
EDIS HOMEOWNER and)
MELSIA HOMEOWNER,)
husband and wife,)
Plaintiffs,)
)
v.)
)
METLIFE BANK, N.A., d/b/a)
METLIFE HOME LOANS, a)
national banking association;)
TRANSNATION TITLE AND)
ESCROW, INC., d/b/a)
FIDELITY NATIONAL TITLE)
COMPANY OF IDAHO, a)
foreign corporation; and)
GORILLA CAPITAL OF ADA)
COUNTY 8, L.L.C., an Idaho)
limited liability company,)
Defendants.)
____________________________)

MOTION FOR A PRELIMINARY INJUNCTION

The plaintiffs, by and through their attorney, Richard Alan Eppink of Idaho Legal Aid Services, Inc., and respectfully move this Court, under Rule 65, *Idaho Rules of Civil Procedure*, for a preliminary injunction, temporarily enjoining defendant GORILLA CAPITAL OF ADA COUNTY 8, L.L.C., ("Gorilla") and its officers, servants, employees, attorneys, and all those in active concert or participation with them, from:

1. Proceeding by process of law or otherwise in any attempt to interfere with the plaintiffs' possession or use of their home (described below) until their right of ownership is determined by this Court in this case, or further order of this Court. Gorilla should accordingly be enjoined from proceeding in Ada County case no. [Number], before the magistrate division of this Court, or in any other action to dispossess the Homeowners, until further order of this Court, concerning the Homeowners' home, described as "[Plat

Description]" and located at and more commonly referred to as [Address].

2. Conveying, contracting for sale, or otherwise transferring the real property described as "[Plat Description]" and located at and more commonly referred to as [Address], until the plaintiffs' right of ownership is determined by this Court in this case, or further order of this Court.

This motion is made on the following grounds and for the following reasons:

1. That if Gorilla commits or continues any attempts to interfere with the plaintiffs' use or possession of their home, or conveys, contracts for sale, or otherwise transfers any of its purported interests in their home, it will produce great and irreparable injury to the plaintiff; and

2. That Gorilla is trying to evict the plaintiffs, in violation of the plaintiff's rights and which would render judgment in the plaintiffs' favor ineffectual.

This Motion is based upon the facts set out in the plaintiffs' Verified Complaint, the plaintiff's Request for Judicial Notice, the Affidavit of Richard Alan Eppink, and the brief in its support, filed along with this motion. Oral argument *is* requested.

WHEREFORE, the plaintiffs respectfully ask this Court for a preliminary injunction of the effect described above.

Respectfully submitted,
[Attorney for Plaintiff]
[Date]

I.6.3 Memorandum in Support of Motion for Preliminary Injunction

IN THE DISTRICT COURT OF
THE FOURTH JUDICIAL DISTRICT STATE OF IDAHO,
IN AND FOR THE COUNTY OF ADA

EDIS HOMEOWNER and
MELSIA HOMEOWNER,
husband and wife,
Plaintiffs,

v.

METLIFE BANK, N.A., d/b/a
METLIFE HOME LOANS, a
national banking association;
TRANSNATION TITLE AND
ESCROW, INC., d/b/a
FIDELITY NATIONAL TITLE
COMPANY OF IDAHO, a
foreign corporation; and
GORILLA CAPITAL OF ADA
COUNTY 8, L.L.C., an Idaho
limited liability company,
Defendants.

BRIEF IN SUPPORT OF MOTION FOR A PRELIMINARY INJUNCTION

The plaintiffs, Edis and Melsia Homeowner ("the Homeowners"), through their attorney Richard Alan Eppink of Idaho Legal Aid Services, Inc., submit the following brief in support of their Motion for a Preliminary Injunction and show this Court:

I. A SUMMARY OF THE VERIFIED COMPLAINT AND OTHER FACTS

This action and the plaintiffs' Motion for a Preliminary Injunction are, at their essence, about the Homeowners right to remain in their home.[13] To ensure any final determination about the Homeowners' ownership and right to remain has any meaningful effect, the Homeowners must prevent defendant Gorilla Capital of Ada County 8, L.L.C., ("Gorilla"), which claims an interest in their home adverse to them, from using its purported interest to dispossess the Homeowners or interfere with other essential "sticks in the bundle of rights that are commonly characterized as property." *Dolan v. City of Tigard*, 512 U.S. 374, 384 (1994).

Gorilla is a business association that, as the Homeowners understand it, seeks profit from buying family homes significantly under market value at foreclosure sales in several states, including Idaho, and then tries to quickly "flip" those homes by selling them in the private market. (Complaint ¶ 5; Aff. of Richard Alan Eppink at Ex. 3.) Gorilla has purported, including in an action under I.C. § 6-310 praying for immediate restitution of the home from the Homeowners, to have acquired the home at foreclosure auction. (Request for Judicial Notice ¶ 4 & Ex. 3.) The Homeowners, however, purchased the home in 2006, refinancing it in 2007 with the help of a lender, and have since invested about $30,000 into further improvements to the property and $30,000 of their own labor in installing those improvements. (Complaint ¶¶ 8, 9.)

When, during 2008 and 2009, the Homeowners' income decreased substantially, they began having trouble making monthly payments on the obligation secured by the home, and they sought help from their lender and mortgage servicer in avoiding default on the obligation. (Complaint ¶¶ 13, 14.) Fortunately, in early 2009, the federal executive branch took actions to stifle an emerging national foreclosure crisis and established the Home Affordable Modification Program ("HAMP")[14], which established a "standardized and streamlined process for servicers . . . to follow in evaluating and conducting modifications of exiting mortgages." Financial Stability Oversight Board, Quarterly Report to Congress Pursuant to § 104(g) of the Emergency Economic Stabilization Act of 2008, at 31 (Mar. 31, 2009). HAMP is governed by guidelines, directives, and other guidance promulgated by the U.S. Department of the Treasury. Mortgage servicers handling loans owned by the Federal National Mortgage Association ("Fannie Mae") are

13 The Homeowners' make their home upon real property and improvements on it, described as "Lot 3 in Block 2 of Legacy Park Subdivision, according to the Plat thereof, filed in [Book of Plats Page Numbers], Records of Ada County, Idaho," and located at and more commonly referred to as [Address].

14 HAMP is a part of the federal executive's Homeowner Affordability and Stability Plan, authorized by the Emergency Economic Stabilization Act of 2008, often referred to popularly as the "bailout." Pub. L. No. 110-343 div. A, 122 Stat. 3765 (Oct. 3, 2008).

required to participate in HAMP for all eligible Fannie Mae portfolio mortgage loans and MBS pool mortgage loans guaranteed by Fannie Mae. Fannie Mae, Announcement 09-05R at 1 (Apr. 21, 2009) (Complaint Ex. H).

In April 2009, the Homeowners applied to their mortgage servicer, Metlife Bank, N.A., doing business as Metlife Home Loans ("Metlife"), for a modification of their home loan. On May 8, 2009, Metlife began considering them for HAMP, making the Homeowners a HAMP Plan offer on June 19, 2009. (Complaint ¶¶ 14, 19, Ex. C.) A central protection for borrowers under HAMP is the requirement that servicers put off foreclosure while HAMP consideration or agreements are underway. Both under the Treasury HAMP directives and Fannie Mae's own HAMP directives, servicers are prohibited from commencing the foreclosure process for 30 days after the borrower has received a HAMP Plan offer. Fannie Mae, Announcement 09-05R at 16 ("Servicers must not conduct foreclosure sales on mortgage loans previously referred to foreclosure or refer new mortgage loans to foreclosure during the 30-day period that the borrower has to submit documents evidencing an intent to accept the Trial Period Plan offer" (emphasis in original)); U.S. Dep't of Treasury, HAMP Supplemental Directive 09-01, at 14 (Apr. 6, 2009).

Patently violating the federal HAMP requirements, Metlife started the foreclosure process against the Homeowners just 17 days after the Homeowners received Metlife's HAMP Plan offer and just two weeks after the Homeowners sent the accepted, executed HAMP Plan back to Metlife. (Request for Judicial Notice ¶ 1 & Ex. 1.) That is, on July 9, 2010, Metlife recorded, with the Ada County Recorder, a "Notice of Default and Election to Sell Under Deed of Trust." (*Id.*) Yet, ironically, the Homeowners sent their first HAMP Plan payment to Metlife two days before, which it accepted. (Complaint ¶ 23.)

Over the course of the next eight months, Metlife continued to accept the Homeowners' HAMP Plan payments. Not only did it accept them, it repeatedly told the Homeowners that it was still processing their HAMP Plan and that the Homeowners should continue to send HAMP Plan payments. (Complaint ¶¶ 29–39.) Despite those apparently false statements, Metlife proceeded with a trustee's sale, further violating the federal HAMP requirements. For, even if Metlife could somehow demonstrate that the Homeowners were ineligible for HAMP, it did not consider the Homeowners for "other foreclosure prevention alternatives, including alternative modification programs," during which consideration Metlife would have still been required under HAMP to further suspend any foreclosure action. (*See* Complaint ¶¶ 40–44); U.S. Dep't of Treasury, HAMP Guidelines 3, 6 (Mar. 4, 2009).

The same day as the invalid March 12, 2010, trustee's sale, Gorilla commenced an I.C. § 6-310 action to evict the Homeowners, under Ada County case no. [Number]. (Request for Judicial Notice ¶ 4 & Ex. 3; Complaint ¶ 46.) The Homeowners are now therefore at imminent risk of eviction from their home, sold in violation of HAMP, I.C. § 45-1505, and other requirements. Moreover, Gorilla is now marketing the Homeowners' home for sale. (Aff. of Richard Alan Eppink ¶ 4.) Metlife, for its part, has now acknowledged that despite that the Homeowners were not declined for modification assistance, it nevertheless inexplicably permitted their home to be sold at foreclosure sale. (Aff. of Richard Alan Eppink at Ex. 2.)

II. STANDARDS

The Homeowners want to preserve the *status quo* of their home, and their undisturbed residence in it, with a temporary injunction under I.R.C.P. 65. Under I.R.C.P. 65 (e), this Court may use a temporary injunction for that purpose where it appears to the Court

> that commission or continuance of some act during the litigation would produce . . . great or irreparable injury to the plaintiff," I.R.C.P. 65(e)(2); or
>
> that the defendant is doing . . . or is about to do . . . some act in violation of the plaintiff's rights . . . tending to render the judgment ineffectual," I.R.C.P. 65(e)(3).

The decision to grant the plaintiffs' motion is within this Court's sound discretion. *Brady v. City of Homedale*, 130 Idaho 569, 572, 944 P.2d 704, 707 (1997). In cases, like this one, where ownership of real property is at issue, "questions of title will not be passed upon although rights will be protected *pendente lite* even though the title is doubtful." *Rowland v. Kellogg Power & Water Co.*, 40 Idaho 216, 225, 233 P. 869, 872 (1925). In applying for this injunction, the Homeowners don't have to make out a case at this stage that would entitle them to inevitable relief after final hearing; rather, "[i]f complainant has made out a prima facie case or if from the pleadings and the conflicting affidavits it appears to the court that a case is presented proper for its investigation on a final hearing, a preliminary injunction may issue to maintain the *status quo*." *Id.*, 40 Idaho at 225, 233 P. at 872.

III. EVICTION OF THE HOMEOWNERS OR CONVEYANCE OF THE HOME WOULD IRREPARABLY HARM THE HOMEOWNERS AND RENDER THE RELIEF THEY PRAY FOR INEFFECTUAL

Here, very simply, the Homeowners want to stay in the home they've made for themselves and their family since 2006, at least until this Court figures out who owns it. The defendant Gorilla of Ada County 8, L.L.C., purports to have purchased it at a trustee's sale. (Complaint ¶¶ 5, 44). The Homeowners have made complaint in this case detailing the events that preceded that trustee's sale, and how the sale was improperly held. Noncompliance with the nonjudicial foreclosure process and requirements (beyond mere violation of the procedural requirements set out at I.C. § 45-1506 *if* a court determines that the winning bidder was a good faith purchaser) voids the sale. *Taylor v. Just*, 138 Idaho 137, 142, 59 P.3d 308, 313 (2002); *cf. Fed. Home Loan Mortg. Corp. v. Appel*, 143 Idaho 42, 47, 137 P.3d 429, 434 (2006) ("status as a bona fide purchaser or a purchaser in good faith, at least in the context of a nonjudicial foreclosure sale, is generally not available where a purchaser is on inquiry notice of a potential defect of statutory notice provisions"). This Court must require strict compliance with the terms of the deed of trust foreclosure statutes. *Sec. Pac. Fin. Corp. v. Bishop*, 109 Idaho 25, 27, 704 P.2d 357, 359 (Ct. App. 1985).

This Court should find no surprise that the Homeowners ask it to keep them in their home until investigation and discovery in this case are completed, and all facts brought to light in final hearing. For "the law of England has so particular and tender a regard to the immunity of a man's house, that it stiles it his castle, and will never suffer it to be violated with impunity." 4 Sir William Blackstone, Commentaries on the Laws of England 175 (Wayne Morrison ed., Cavendish 2001) (1769). The modern law of America, as well, recognizes that "[w]e have, after all, lived our whole national history with an understanding of 'the ancient adage that a man's house is his castle [to the point that t]he poorest man may in his cottage bid defiance to all the forces of the Crown.' " *Georgia v. Randolph*, 547 U.S. 103, 115 (2006) (quoting *Miller v. United States*, 357 U.S. 301, 307 (1958). Indeed, a modern study of those displaced from their homes found in them a "grief response showing most of the characteristics of grief and mourning for a lost person" and noted that "relocation was a crisis with potential danger to mental health for many people." Marc Fried, Grieving for a Lost Home: Psychological Costs of Relocation, in Urban Renewal: The Record and the Controversy 359, 361, 377 (James Q. Wilson, ed., 1966). Accordingly, courts of this state generally presume that "[n]o amount of money, it is said, can compensate for the loss of an unique tract of land." *Wood v. Simonson*, 108 Idaho 699, 702, 701 P.2d 319, 322 (Ct. App. 1985).

Permitting Gorilla to evict the Homeowners and their family while this case awaits trial will mean the Homeowners likely never make it their home again. Gorilla is in the business of flipping foreclosed homes into the private market. (Complaint ¶ 5; Aff. of Richard Alan Eppink at Ex. 3.) By the time this case reaches its conclusion, if the Homeowners are displaced through Gorilla's efforts, the property almost certainly have been conveyed at least once, and likely occupied by another family. The Homeowners' damage, in loss of their home, will be irreparable and tremendous.

Likewise, eviction of the Homeowners during the course of this litigation would render judgment in their favor ineffectual. They would be displaced from a home likely already sold to another, which would violate their rights: not only to due process of law as their complaint to quiet title against Gorilla under I.C. § 6-401 is considered by this Court, but to the home itself, as the complaint sufficiently alleges their right to the home due to an invalid trustee's sale. It appears unmistakable, even at this early stage:

1. that Metlife offered a HAMP Plan to the Homeowners on or about June 19, 2010 (Complaint ¶ 19 & Ex. C);
2. that its offer told the Homeowners that "we will not start foreclosure proceedings" (*Id.*);
3. that its offer said that because that is a requirement of the United States Department of Treasury's HAMP directives (Complaint ¶ 58; HAMP Supp. Direct. 09-01 at 14 (available at https://hmpadmin.com/portal/docs/hamp_servicer/sd0901.pdf)); and
4. yet Metlife started foreclosure proceedings anyway, just 19 days later, by recording a Notice of Default against the Homeowners with the Ada County Recorder on July 9, 2010 (Req. for Judicial Notice, ¶ 1 & Ex. 1).

By that time, the Homeowners had already accepted Metlife's offer (on June 25, 2009) and, ironically, mailed their first check in performance of the agreement on July 7, 2009, two days before Metlife violated the agreement and federal HAMP requirements by starting the foreclosure process. Metlife itself now acknowledges as much, stating to Idaho's Office of the Attorney General that the Homeowners were not declined for modification yet the foreclosure sale went forward anyway. (Aff. of Richard Alan Eppink at Ex. 2.)

The Homeowners were therefore not in default. No other Notice of Default was ever recorded. (Request for Judicial Notice ¶ 2). Therefore, it appears certain that the trustee's sale was void. *Taylor*, 138 Idaho at 140, 59 P.3d at 311; *see also* I.R.C.P. 65(e)(3). As to Gorilla, even had it made perfunctory inquiry concerning the property it would have had notice of defects in the foreclosure process; and our courts hold trustee's sale buyers to inquiry notice of such defects. *Fed. Home Loan Mortg. Corp.*, 143 Idaho at 47, 137 P.3d at 434. Gorilla, in its own promotional website, insists that it completes "extensive value assessment, property inspection and title research" and that "[f]or every home we buy, we look at over 150 properties that don't make the cut." (Aff. of Richard Alan Eppink at Ex.3.)

A Gorilla conveyance or a Gorilla eviction of the Homeowners would therefore violate their rights and obviously render judgment quieting title in their favor ineffectual. This Court should preserve the *status quo* to prevent irreparable harm by keeping the Homeowners and their family in their home. *See, e.g., Martenson v. RG Fin.*, No.CV09-1314-PHX-NVW, 2010 U.S. Dist. LEXIS 11921, at *28 (D. Ariz. Jan. 22, 2010) (issuing preliminary injunction to prevent post-foreclosure eviction, upon $100.00 security).

IV. THE HOME ITSELF PROVIDES SUFFICIENT SECURITY FOR GORILLA

As both Gorilla, should it contest this action, and the Homeowners will be fighting over the possession of a home of unclear title, this Court naturally should hold that unclear title as security under I.R.C.P. 65(c). Even if Gorilla's alleged purchase of title were confirmed in this action, it will then own a home with an assessed value of $191,900 that it acquired for $111,201. (Complaint ¶ 42; Request for Judicial Notice ¶ 3 & Ex. 2.) That is, some $80,000 of security for Gorilla likely rests in the home itself, protecting Gorilla from any damages, costs, and fees it may later allege it incurred under this Court's injunction. Accordingly, with the home given as security, the Court might appropriately enter an order prohibiting the Homeowners from maliciously damaging it during this litigation, and allowing Gorilla to show during the course of the litigation, through competent assessment or appraisal, that the security has become insufficient by depreciation.

V. CONCLUSION

For all the reasons cited herein, the plaintiffs' Motion for a Preliminary Injunction should be GRANTED.

Respectfully submitted,
[Attorney for Plaintiff]
[Date]

I.7 Complaint to Enforce Permanent Modification for Borrower in Trial HAMP Modifcation

IN THE COURT OF COMMON PLEAS
LUCAS COUNTY, OHIO

Victoria Homeowner	)
Plaintiff,	)
v.	)
Wells Fargo Bank, N.A.	)
Defendant	)

COMPLAINT WITH JURY DEMAND ENDORSED HEREIN

INTRODUCTION

1. This is an action for breach of contract, breach of the duty of good faith and fair dealing, and promissory arising from the actions of Defendant Wells Fargo Bank, N.A. ("Wells Fargo") towards Plaintiff Victoria Homeowner ("Ms. Homeowner") under the Home Affordable Modification Plan ("HAMP").

2. Wells Fargo offered Ms. Homeowner a Trial Period Plan under HAMP in which she would make three monthly payments and, if Ms. Homeowner's situation did not change, Wells Fargo would offer a permanent loan modification.

3. Ms. Homeowner accepted Wells Fargo's offer. Since then Ms. Homeowner has made seven payments under the Trial Period Plan and complied with all other HAMP criteria. To date, Wells Fargo has not offered Ms. Homeowner a permanent loan modification.

4. Ms. Homeowner files this action because Wells Fargo has failed to comply with its contractual duties and Ms. Homeowner now faces the prospect of losing her home.

PARTIES

5. Plaintiff Victoria Homeowner is a 67-year-old widow, mother, and foster mother who resides in Lucas County, Ohio. She has lived at [Address] in Toledo since 2005.

6. Defendant Wells Fargo is a foreign corporation authorized to do business in Ohio. Wells Fargo services residential mortgage loans, including the mortgage loan that Ms. Homeowner has on her property.

JURISDICTION AND VENUE

7. Jurisdiction and venue are appropriate in this Court because Ms. Homeowner lives in Lucas County, Ohio, and Wells Fargo regularly conducts business in Lucas County, Ohio.

FACTS

The HAMP Program

8. The United States Department of the Treasury created the Home Affordable Modification Program (HAMP) pursuant to its authority under the Troubled Assets Relief Program to help at-risk homeowners avoid foreclosure by restructuring their mortgages. See Emergency Economic Stabilization Act of 2008, Pub. L. No. 110-343, § 101, 122 Stat. 3765 (October 3, 2008) ("ESSA"). Under the terms of HAMP, the Treasury Department provides financial incentives for lenders to reduce homeowners' monthly mortgage payments to sustainable levels.

9. To participate in HAMP, servicers enter into a contract with Fannie Mae in its capacity as an agent of the United States. See ESSA § 101(c)(3).

10. Wells Fargo signed a "Servicer Participation Agreement for the Home Affordable Modification Program" ("the HAMP contract") with Fannie Mae on April 13, 2009 (attached as Exhibit A).

11. [Omitted.]

Wells Fargo's Duties Under HAMP

12. Once Wells Fargo signed its contract with Fannie Mae to participate in HAMP, it was required to review all mortgage loans that are in default or in imminent risk of default.

13. The HAMP contract is supplemented by Supplemental Guidelines, which are incorporated by reference in § 1(A) of the HAMP contract.

13. [Omitted.]

14. Under HAMP directives, "participating servicers are required to consider all eligible mortgage loans unless prohibited by the rules of the applicable [Pooling and Servicing Agreement] and/or other investor servicing agreements." See Supplemental Directive 09-01 at page 1 (attached as Exhibit B) (emphasis in original).

15. Wells Fargo's obligations under HAMP are clear. First, Wells Fargo must make a threshold determination of whether the borrower meets basic eligibility criteria for the program. These criteria include a determination that there is no previous HAMP modification of the mortgage, the borrower is in default or likely to default, the borrower lives in the home, the current monthly payments are above 31% of the borrower's gross income, and the borrower is experiencing financial hardship. Id. at 2-3.

16. Next, if the borrower meets these basic eligibility criteria, Wells Fargo is required to conduct "waterfall" test. The waterfall test requires Wells Fargo to take a series of steps, such as reducing the interest rate and extending the term of the loan, to adjust the borrower's monthly payments of principal, interest, taxes, and insurance to no more than 31% of the borrower's monthly gross household income. Id. at 8.

17. Wells Fargo then completes a "net present value" ("NPV") test then looks to see if these modified terms would put the investor in a better financial outcome than if the house proceeded to foreclosure. If the NPV test yields a "positive" outcome (i.e., the value of completing a modification exceeds the value of foreclosing on the property), Wells Fargo is required to offer a trial modification under HAMP. Id. at 4, 15. If the NPV test yields a "negative" outcome (i.e., the value of completing a modification is less than the value of foreclosing on the property), Wells Fargo is required to consider the borrower for other foreclosure prevention measures. Id. at 4.

18. Borrowers make three payments under a "Trial Period Plan." "If the borrower complies with the terms and conditions of the Trial Period Plan, the loan modification will become effective on the first day of the month following the trial period as specified

in the Trial Period Plan." Id. at 18.

19. During the Trial Period Plan, Wells Fargo verifies the borrower's income to set the monthly payment amount in the permanent loan modification. Id.

20. According to Supplemental Directive 09-01, if the borrower's income is verified and "if the borrower complies with the terms and conditions of the Trial Period Plan, the loan modification will become effective on the first day of the month following the trial period as specified in the Trial Period Plan." Id.

Wells Fargo's Series of Unreasonable Workout Offers

21. Wells Fargo and Ms. Homeowner were originally parties to a foreclosure action, Case No. [Number]. That case was dismissed without prejudice on February 18, 2009 after this Court granted Ms. Homeowner's Motion to Dismiss.

22. In early 2009, Wells Fargo requested financial information from Ms. Homeowner. She submitted the requested information through her attorney on January 14, 2009. A Wells Fargo employee confirmed that he received the financial information and stated that the submitted information was "all I need."

23. In April 2009, Wells Fargo offered a payment plan that included Ms. Homeowner paying the delinquency over eighteen months. This plan would have raised her monthly mortgage payments during that time from approximately $1,638.99 to nearly $2,600.00 per month. Ms. Homeowner rejected this offer because the monthly payment would have been approximately 89% of her monthly gross income.

24. On April 22, 2009, Ms. Homeowner received a letter from Wells Fargo requesting updated financial information. On May 4, 2009, Ms. Homeowner submitted the requested financial information through her attorney. Ms. Homeowner submitted additional information on May 8, 2009 at the request of Wells Fargo.

25. In May 2009, Wells Fargo requested updated bank statements from Ms. Homeowner. She submitted the requested information through her attorney on May 22, 2009.

26. On June 23, 2009, Wells Fargo offered a payment plan in which Ms. Homeowner would pay approximately $1,600.00 per month for three months and then a balloon payment of approximately $18,000.00. Ms. Homeowner rejected this offer because the balloon payment would have been unaffordable.

27. On July 16, 2009, Wells Fargo called Ms. Homeowner and asked that she resend the previously-submitted financial information. She resent the financial information that day through her attorney.

28. On July 22, 2009, Wells Fargo offered Ms. Homeowner a forbearance plan. Under that plan, Ms. Homeowner would make six monthly payments of $1,365.52, a balloon payment of $26,426.56 due on February 1, 2010, and then resume her mortgage payments. Ms. Homeowner rejected this offer because the balloon payment would have been unaffordable.

Wells Fargo's HAMP Modification Offer

29. On July 31, 2009, Wells Fargo offered Ms. Homeowner a Trial Period Plan under the HAMP program (attached as Exhibit C). Under the Trial Period Plan, Ms. Homeowner would make three monthly payments of $1,280.43. If her financial situation did not change and she made her three payments on time, Wells Fargo would then offer Ms. Homeowner a permanent loan modification.

30. Ms. Homeowner's mortgage satisfies the "threshold determination" criteria for a HAMP modification.

31. The three Trial Period Plan payments were due on August 30, 2009, October 1, 2009, and November 1, 2009.

32. Ms. Homeowner accepted the Trial Period Plan by signing the Trial Period Plan (attached as Exhibit D), sending in the completed paperwork including updated financial information, and sending the first payment on August 12, 2009.

33. Ms. Homeowner submitted the October 1, 2009 payment on September 19, 2009.

34. Ms. Homeowner submitted the November 1, 2009 payment on October 19, 2009.

35. Despite making the three monthly payments on time and her financial situation not changing, Ms. Homeowner did not receive a permanent loan modification offer from Wells Fargo.

36. Since Wells Fargo had not offered Ms. Homeowner a permanent loan modification, she continued making payments at the Trial Period Plan payment amount. She submitted the December 1, 2009 payment November 21, 2009.

37. Ms. Homeowner submitted the January 1, 2010 payment on December 22, 2010.

38. Ms. Homeowner submitted the February 1, 2010 payment on January 25, 2010.

39. Ms. Homeowner submitted the March 1, 2010 payment on February 18, 2010.

40. Despite making seven monthly payments, complying with all other aspects of HAMP, and repeatedly inquiring about the status of a permanent loan modification, Ms. Homeowner has not received an offer of a permanent loan modification from Wells Fargo.

Injury Caused to Ms. Homeowner

41. Despite Ms. Homeowner's timely payments, Wells Fargo claims Ms. Homeowner is in default of the Trial Period Plan and has threatened foreclosure against Ms. Homeowner.

42. During the seven months of the Trial Period Plan, Wells Fargo has reported Ms. Homeowner as "delinquent" to the credit reporting agencies, further damaging her credit rating.

CAUSES OF ACTION
First Claim—Breach of Contract

43. The allegations of all other paragraphs and claims in this pleading are fully incorporated as if fully rewritten herein.

44. Wells Fargo offered to enter into a contractual relationship with Ms. Homeowner through its offer of the Trial Period Plan.

45. Ms. Homeowner accepted Wells Fargo's offer by signing the Trial Period Plan, returning the signed Trial Period Plan to Wells Fargo, and making the necessary payments under the Trial Period Plan.

46. Wells Fargo breached its contract by failing to provide Ms. Homeowner with a permanent loan modification after she made three timely payments under the Trial Period Plan.

47. Ms. Homeowner was damaged as a proximate result of Wells Fargo's breach of contract.

Second Claim—Breach of Duty of Good Faith and Fair Dealing

48. The allegations of all other paragraphs and claims in this pleading are fully incorporated as if fully rewritten herein.

49. Every contact has an implied duty of good faith and fair dealing that neither party will do anything that will have the effect of destroying or injuring the right of the other party to receive the benefit of the contract.

50. Wells Fargo breached its duty of good faith and fair dealing by failing to offer Ms. Homeowner a permanent modification after seven months of timely payments.

51. Ms. Homeowner was damaged as a proximate result of Wells Fargo's breach of its duty of good faith and fair dealing.

Third Claim—Promissory Estoppel

52. The allegations of all other paragraphs and claims in this pleading are fully incorporated as if fully rewritten herein.

53. Ms. Homeowner reasonably relied on Wells Fargo's statements that she would be able to lower her monthly mortgage payments permanently if she made the three payments for the Trial Period Plan and otherwise complied with Wells Fargo's requests under HAMP. As a result, Ms. Homeowner made the seven payments for the Trial Period Plan.

54. Ms. Homeowner's reliance was to her detriment as she forwent other opportunities, including seeking another type of loan modification or refinancing the existing loan.

55. Ms. Homeowner did not know and could not know that Wells Fargo's statements were misleading.

56. Under the facts and circumstances of this case, justice requires the enforcement of Wells Fargo's promises and representations.

57. Ms. Homeowner is entitled to enforcement of Wells Fargo's promises and representations from the Trial Period Plan and Wells Fargo is liable to Ms. Homeowner for actual damages.

REQUEST FOR RELIEF

WHEREFORE, Plaintiff Victoria Homeowner respectfully prays that this Court award relief and damages as follow:

a. For the claim of breach of contract,
   i. Award actual damages;
   ii. Award compensatory damages; and
   iii. Require that Defendant fulfill its obligations under the contract.
b. For the claim of breach of duty of good faith and fair dealing,
   i. Award actual damages;
   ii. Declare that Defendant breached its duty of good faith and fair dealing;
   iii. Require that Defendant fulfill its obligations under the contract; and
   iv. Enjoin Defendant from attempting to foreclose on Plaintiff's home until Defendant fulfills its obligations under the contract and offers a permanent loan modification.
c. For the claim of promissory estoppel,
   i. Award actual damages; and
   ii. Enforce Defendant's promises and representations.
d. Such other relief as this Court finds equitable and just.

JURY DEMAND

Plaintiff Victoria Homeowner hereby demands trial by jury on all issues triable of right by a jury in this action.

Respectfully submitted,
[Attorney for Plaintiff]
[Date]

I.8 Pleadings Related to Standing and Servicer Misconduct

I.8.1 Answer to Judicial Foreclosure

IN THE CIRCUIT COURT, FOURTH
JUDICIAL CIRCUIT, IN AND FOR
DUVAL COUNTY, FLORIDA

_______________________)
GMAC MORTGAGE, L.L.C.)
Plaintiff/Counterclaim)
Defendant,)
)
v.)
)
CARRIE Homeowner, et al.,)
Defendant/Counterclaim)
Plaintiff.)
)
v.)
)
LAW OFFICES OF DAVID J.)
STERN, a Florida Professional)
Association,)
Counterclaim Defendant,)
_______________________)

DEFENDANT'S ANSWER, AMENDED AFFIRMATIVE DEFENSES, AND AMENDED COUNTERCLAIMS IN RESPONSE TO PLAINTIFF'S COMPLAINT

Defendant CARRIE Homeowner, (hereinafter "Defendant" or "Ms. Homeowner") by and through undersigned counsel files this her Answer, Amended Affirmative Defenses and Amended Counterclaims in response to the Complaint to Foreclose Mortgage and to Enforce Lost Loan Documents filed by Plaintiff, GMAC MORTGAGE, L.L.C. (hereinafter "Plaintiff" or "GMAC"), and says:

ANSWER

1. Ms. Homeowner admits the allegations contained in Paragraphs 1, 2 and 15 of Plaintiff's complaint for jurisdictional purposes only, however, does not admit Plaintiff is entitled to the relief sought therein.

2. Ms. Homeowner admits the allegations contained in 3 and 6 of Plaintiff's complaint.

3. As to Paragraphs 4 and 5 of Plaintiff's complaint, Ms. Homeowner admits the mortgage was recorded on September 4, 2001 in Official Records Book [Number] at page [Number] of the

public record of Duval County, Florida. However, Defendant denies the mortgage was properly assigned to GMAC MORTGAGE, LCC and denies Plaintiff owns and holds the note and mortgage.

4. Ms. Homeowner denies the allegations contained in Paragraphs 7, 8, 10, and 12 of Plaintiff's Complaint, Defendant is without specific knowledge and therefore denies the allegation contained in these paragraphs.

5. As to the allegations contained in Paragraph 9 of Plaintiff's complaint, Ms. Homeowner denies Plaintiff has the right to declare the full amount due and payable.

6. As to Paragraphs 11, 12, 13 and 14, Defendant is without specific knowledge regarding the allegations contained therein and therefore denies the same.

7. As to Paragraphs 16, 17, 18, 19, and 20, Defendant denies each of these paragraphs and denies the subject mortgage note is a negotiable instrument and therefore denies Plaintiff has the right to enforce the promissory note as requested in Count Two.

AFFIRMATIVE DEFENSES

First Affirmative Defense—Lack of Subject Matter Jurisdiction

8. Rule 1.210(a) Fla.R.Civ.P., provides in pertinent part:

> Every action may be prosecuted in the name of the real party in interest, but a personal representative, administrator, guardian, trustee of an express trust, a party with whom or in whose name a contract has been made for the benefit of another, or a party expressly authorized by statute may sue in that person's own name without joining the party for whose benefit the action is brought.

9. The prosecution of a residential mortgage foreclosure action must be by the owner and holder of the mortgage and the note. Plaintiff is not entitled to maintain an action if it does not own and hold the note which is purportedly secured by the subject mortgage. *Your Construction Center, Inc. v. Gross*, 316 So. 2d 596 (Fl. 4th DCA 1975); *Greenwald v. Triple D Properties, Inc.*, 424 So. 2d 185, 187 (Fla. 4th DCA 1983).

10. Plaintiff filed this action on October 1, 2008 and provided the following documents in support of its claim of standing:

a. The subject mortgage and note listing the lender as Taylor, Bean & Whitaker Mortgage Corp. and;

b. A promissory note filed on April 28, 2009 and endorsed to GMAC Mortgage Company in an undated endorsement and then endorsed in blank by Plaintiff in an endorsement that is also undated.

11. On April 28, 2009, Plaintiff filed an "Assignment of Note" executed by Beth [Brown], an employee of Stern, as Assistant Secretary of Mortgage Electronic Registration Systems, Inc. ("MERS") purportedly transferring the subject mortgage from MERS residing or located at c/o GMAC Mortgage, L.L.C., to GMAC Mortgage, L.L.C. The assignment was dated November 7, 2008 and purportedly effective September 11, 2008.

12. The plaintiff's lack of standing at the commencement of a case is a fault that cannot be cured by gaining standing after the case has been filed. *Progressive Express Ins. Co. v. McGrath Community Chiropractic*, 913 So. 2d 1281, 1285 (FlA.2d DCA 2005). If Plaintiff was without standing when the suit was filed then a new lawsuit must be filed. *Progressive*, 913 So. 2d at 1285 (citing *Jeff Ray Corp. v. Jacobson*, 566 So. 2d 885, 886 (Fla. 4th DCA 1990) (the assignee of a mortgage could not maintain the mortgage foreclosure action because the assignment was dated four months after the action was filed, if the plaintiff wished to proceed on the assignment, it must file a new complaint).

13. Plaintiff may rely on the "relation back" rule when asserting standing. *Progressive*, supra. When applying the "relation back" rule the party who did not have standing at the time the action was filed may amend their statement of claim to show that they acquired standing that "related back to the original statement of claim." Id. at 1285, 1286. However, this rule does not allow a party to establish the right to maintain an action retroactively by acquiring standing after the fact. *Progressive,* 913 So. 2d at 1285.

Second Affirmative Defense—Failure of Condition Precedent FHA HAMP Programs

14. On April 13, 2009, GMAC Mortgage L.L.C. received approximately $2.1 billion in incentive payments under the Making Home Affordable Program. Pursuant to the program agreements and the authority provided by H.R. 1424 Title I § 109-110, the United States Treasury has ordered as follows:

> Mortgage Foreclosure Mitigation: All recipients of capital investments under the Financial Stability Plan will be required to commit to participate in mortgage foreclosure mitigation programs consistent with guidelines Treasury released as part of its Making Home Affordable mortgage modification program.

See www.financialstability.gov/about/transparencyaccountability.html (April 16, 2009). Plaintiff is required to allow Ms. Homeowner to participate in the mandatory loan modification application process and has failed to do so.

15. The purpose of the TARP funds as stated in Public Law 110-343 known as the Economic Stabilization Act of 2008 is as stated below:

> SEC. 2. PURPOSES
>
> The purposes of this Act are—
>
> (1) To immediately provide authority and facilities that the Secretary of the Treasury can use to restore liquidity and stability to the financial system of the United States; and
>
> (2) To ensure that such authority and such facilities are used in a manner that
>
> (A) Protects home values, college funds, retirement accounts, and life savings;
>
> (B) Preserves homeownership and promotes jobs and economic growth;
>
> (C) Maximizes overall returns to the taxpayers of the United States; and
>
> (D) Provides public accountability for the exercise of such authority.

16. In implementing the Act, the United States Treasury has instituted a number of programs, including the Making Home Affordable Act, Capital Purchase Program and Capital Assistance Program among others. See www.financialstability.gov/roadtostability/programs.htm.

17. If Plaintiff can prove it is the owner and holder of the subject note and mortgage, as a recipient of TARP funds, it is subject to the U.S. Treasury loan modification program guidelines for the Making Home Affordable Program which require "Any foreclosure action . . . be temporarily suspended during the trial period, or while borrowers are considered for alternative foreclosure prevention options. In the event that the Home Affordable Modification or alternative foreclosure options fail, the foreclosure action may be resumed."

18. Plaintiff has committed in the Securities Purchase Agreement to "expand the flow of credit to U.S. consumers and businesses on competitive terms to promote the sustained growth and vitality of the U.S. economy." Also, "the Company agrees to work diligently, under existing programs, to modify the terms of residential mortgages as appropriate to strengthen the health of the U.S. economy."

19. Plaintiff has already been remunerated for its troubled assets, has sought and been given taxpayer money and agreed to undertake meaningful loan modification with their clients who are facing foreclosure in return for billions of taxpayer dollars. Plaintiff has taken the money and now seeks to recover again from the homeowner through foreclosure even though it has not complied with the loss mitigation requirements as required by TARP.

20. In addition, because Ms. Homeowner's loan is an FHA-insured loan, GMAC was required to comply with the payment forbearance, mortgage modification, and other foreclosure prevention loan servicing or collection requirements imposed on GMAC and the subject FHA mortgage by federal regulations promulgated by HUD, pursuant to the National Housing Act, 12 U.S.C. § 1710(a). These requirements must be followed before a mortgagee may commence foreclosure. 24 C.F.R. Part 203(C), Servicing Responsibilities Mortgagee Action and Forbearance and Paragraph 9(a) of the subject mortgage and Paragraph 6(B) of the subject note. (Lender may, except as limited by regulations issued by the Secretary in the case of payment default. . . .")

21. GMAC is required by HUD regulations to ensure that all of the servicing requirements of 24 C.F.R. Part 203(C) have been met before initiating foreclosure. 24 C.F.R.§ 203.606.

22. According to the regulations and terms of the subject note and mortgage Plaintiff is required to adapt effective collection techniques designed to meet Ms. Homeowner's individual differences and take account of their peculiar circumstances to minimize the default in their mortgage payments as required by 24 C.F.R. § 203.600.

23. GMAC failed to make any reasonable efforts as required by federal regulations and the terms of her note and mortgage to arrange a face to face meeting with Ms. Homeowner before three full monthly installments were unpaid to discuss his circumstances and possible foreclosure avoidance. 24 C.F.R. § 203.604.

24. GMAC failed to inform Ms. Homeowner that it would make loan status and payment information available to local credit bureaus and prospective creditors, failed to inform Ms. Homeowner of other assistance, and failed to inform her of the names and addresses of HUD officials to whom further communication could be addressed as required by federal law and the terms of her note and mortgage. 24 C.F.R. § 203.604.

25. GMAC is required under federal law to adapt its collection and loan servicing practices to Ms. Homeowner's individual circumstances and to re-evaluate these techniques each month after default and GMAC failed to do so.

26. GMAC failed to perform its servicing duty to Ms. Homeowner to manage the subject mortgage as required by FHA's special foreclosure prevention workout programs which must include and allow for the restructuring of the loan whereby the borrower pays out the delinquency in installments or advances to bring the mortgage current.

27. GMAC further denied Ms. Homeowner access to a repayment plan or special forbearance in the form of a written agreement that would reduce or suspend their monthly mortgage payments for a specific period to allow her time to recover from the financial hardship she was suffering through no fault of her own. Such a plan can involve changing one or more terms of the subject mortgage in order to help Ms. Homeowner bring the claimed default current, and thereby prevent foreclosure.

28. GMAC's failure to comply with the FHA repayment plan or special forbearance workout programs denied Ms. Homeowner the required access to explore alternatives to avoid foreclosure prior to the addition of additional foreclosure fees and costs.

29. Ms. Homeowner is being denied and deprived by Plaintiff of his right to access the required mortgage servicing. Plaintiff is illegally subjecting her to this foreclosure action, thereby forcing her to defend the same while charging illegal court costs, other related fees, and attorney fees. Ms. Homeowner is having her credit slandered and negatively affected, all of which constitutes irreparable harm to her the purpose of injunctive relief.

30. As a proximate result of the Plaintiff's unlawful actions, Ms. Homeowner continues to suffer the irreparable harm described above for which monetary compensation is inadequate.

31. Ms. Homeowner has the right to access the foreclosure prevention servicing prescribed by the EESA and FHA laws, regulations, orders and guidelines which are being denied to her by the Plaintiff, therefore GMAC should stay the prosecution of this mortgage foreclosure lawsuit and analyze her ability to avoid foreclosure through the modification of her mortgage.

Third Affirmative—Defense Violations of the Federal Fair Debt Collection Practices Act

32. Ms. Homeowner realleges the allegations contained in paragraphs 49 through 74, below, inclusive, and Count One of her Counterclaims and incorporate the same herein by reference.

33. Plaintiff violated the Federal Fair Debt Collection Practices Act in the course if its collection of Ms. Homeowner's consumer mortgage transaction as is more particularly described below.

34. Based upon Plaintiff's violations of this Florida consumer collection law it is not entitled to the equitable remedy of foreclosure.

Fourth Affirmative Defense—Violations of the Florida Deceptive and Unfair Trade Practices Act

35. Ms. Homeowner realleges the allegations contained in paragraphs 49 through 53 and 55 through 74, below, inclusive, and Count Two of her Counterclaims and incorporate the same herein by reference.

36. Plaintiff violated the Florida Deceptive and Unfair Trade Practices Act in the servicing and collection of Ms. Homeowner's consumer mortgage transaction as is more particularly described in her Counterclaims below.

37. Plaintiff is not entitled to the equitable remedy of foreclo-

sure as a result of its violations of this Florida consumer credit protection statute.

Fifth Affirmative Defense—Breach of Contract

38. Plaintiff engaged in practices and omissions in the servicing and collection of Ms. Homeowner's consumer mortgage transaction as is more particularly described in Paragraphs 55 through 74 below.

39. Paragraph 9(a) of the subject mortgage sets the prerequisites for foreclosure

> Lender may, except as limited by regulations issued by the Secretary in the case of payment default. . . ."

This section refers to the federal regulations more particularly set out below which the lender must follow prior to filing a foreclosure lawsuit.

40. Paragraph 6(B) of the subject note provides

> If Borrower defaults by failing to pay in full any monthly payment, then Lender may, except as limited by regulations of the Secretary in the case of payment defaults, require immediate payment in full of the principal balance remaining due and all accrued interest. Lender may choose not to exercise this option without waiving it right in the event of any subsequent default. In many circumstances regulations issued by the Secretary will limit Lender's rights to require immediate payment in full in the case of payment defaults. This Note does not authorize acceleration when not permitted by HUD regulations.

41. Plaintiff is not entitled to the equitable remedy of foreclosure as a result of its breach of the subject mortgage and note.

Sixth Affirmative Defense—Fraud and Misrepresentation

42. Defendant realleges all paragraphs in her First Affirmative Defense and Paragraphs 49 through 53 and 55 through 74.

43. Plaintiff engaged in a number of knowing fraudulent acts, specifically:

a. Plaintiff filed and continues to maintain this action even thought it knew it did not have standing at the time the lawsuit was filed and then proceeded to manufacture an assignment of mortgage to give the impression it had and does have standing;

b. Plaintiff knew that it prematurely brought suit before completing the required FHA pre-suit loss mitigation options prior to bringing the subject foreclosure and has failed to consider Ms. Homeowner for the requisite loan modification required for consumers' whose lenders/servicers received TARP funds under the Making Home Affordable Program.

44. The preceding acts of fraud and misrepresentation concern material pre-suit collection requirements and material fabrication of non-litigation documents all of which are material to Ms. Homeowner and this case.

45. Plaintiff intended reliance on it acts of acts of fraud and misrepresentation by the Defendant and this Court.

46. Defendant and this Court have reasonably relied on Plaintiff's false representations.

47. As a result of its fraudulent actions and misrepresentations, Plaintiff is not entitled to any relief, equitable or otherwise.

WHEREFORE, Ms. Homeowner requests her Answer and Affirmative Defenses be deemed sufficient; that this Court deny the Plaintiff's Complaint to Foreclose Mortgage and grant such other and further relief as this Court deems just and equitable.

AMENDED COUNTERCLAIMS

The Counterclaim Plaintiff/Defendant, CARRIE Homeowner, (hereinafter "Ms. Homeowner") files this amended complaint and sues the Counterclaim Defendant/Plaintiff, GMAC MORTGAGE, L.L.C. (hereinafter "GMAC") and pursuant to Rules 1.170(h) and 1.190(a), Fla.R.Civ.P., Non-Party Counterclaim Defendant, the Law Offices of David J. Stern (hereinafter "Stern") and alleges:

Jurisdictional Allegations

48. This Court has jurisdiction over these Counterclaims as they arise out of the mortgage loan transaction which is the subject of GMAC's Complaint to Foreclose Mortgage.

Factual Allegations
Creation of False Documents

49. Ms. Homeowner executed a note and mortgage on August 22, 2001 payable to Taylor, Bean & Whitaker Mortgage Corp.

50. On October 1, 2008, Stern's office filed the subject foreclosure lawsuit on behalf of its client GMAC. At the time Stern's office filed this action to present, GMAC did not and does not have sufficient documentation to establish it is the proper party to bring this action and the documentation upon which Plaintiff relies for standing was improperly manufactured by GMAC's counsel acting on its behalf as its authorized agent.

51. Stern and GMAC provided the following documents in support of GMAC's claim it is the proper party to bring this foreclosure lawsuit:

a. The subject mortgage and note listing the lender as Taylor, Bean & Whitaker Mortgage Corp.; and

b. A promissory note filed on April 28, 2009 and endorsed to GMAC Mortgage Company in an undated endorsement and then endorsed in blank by Plaintiff in an endorsement that is also undated.

52. On April 28, 2009, Plaintiff filed an "Assignment of Note" executed by Beth [Brown], an employee of Stern, as Assistant Secretary of Mortgage Electronic Registration Systems, Inc. ("MERS") purportedly transferring the subject mortgage from MERS residing or located at c/o GMAC Mortgage, L.L.C., to GMAC Mortgage, L.L.C. The assignment was dated November 7, 2008 and purportedly effective September 11, 2008.

53. On June 3, 2009, counsel for Ms. Homeowner took Ms. [Brown]'s deposition and determined:

a. Ms. [Brown] was employed by Stern at the time she executed the subject assignment and affidavit in support of summary judgment and executed these documents as a routine part of her day to day activities at the request of her employer;

b. She did not review any of the underlying title or other documents prior to executing the assignment and affidavit in support of summary judgment;

c. She did not hold any positions with Taylor, Bean and Whitaker Mortgage Company, MERS or GMAC;

d. She did not have any knowledge of the title documents relating to Taylor, Bean and Whitaker Mortgage or the accounting documents of GMAC;

e. She did not have any knowledge about MERS business practices and had never spoken with any one from MERS.

In other words, Stern and GMAC created false documents to make it appear GMAC is the proper party to bring this action.

54. On November 14, 2008, Beth [Brown] executed a false affidavit in support of her firm's client, GMAC's, motion for Summary Judgment. She testified she did not have any knowledge of the underlying data to support an y of the figure she included in the affidavit in support of summary judgment; did not review any documents or records such as account histories, statements or other documents prior to executing the affidavit; and did not know how the information was gathered or who prepared the numbers contained in the affidavit.

Failure to Provide FHA Pre-Foreclosure Loss Mitigation

55. Ms. Homeowner fell behind in her monthly payments for reasons beyond her control because her financial circumstances changed.

56. Despite her changed financial circumstances, Ms. Homeowner continued to try and make payments each month. Each time her payments were past due, Ms. Homeowner would contact GMAC to ask for a repayment arrangement.

57. When Ms. Homeowner contacted GMAC, she was told she would have to qualify for a repayment agreement. The amount Ms. Homeowner was told she would have to pay to become current on the loan was unaffordable based on her circumstances. Ms. Homeowner did her best to make the required payment.

58. Because Ms. Homeowner's loan is an FHA-insured loan, GMAC was required to comply with the payment forbearance, mortgage modification, and other foreclosure prevention loan servicing or collection requirements imposed on GMAC and the subject FHA mortgage by federal regulations promulgated by HUD, pursuant to the National Housing Act, 12 U.S.C. § 1710(a). These requirements must be followed before a mortgagee may commence foreclosure. 24 C.F.R. Part 203(C), Servicing Responsibilities Mortgagee Action and Forbearance and Paragraph 9(a) of the subject mortgage and Paragraph 6(B) of the subject note. (Lender may, except as limited by regulations issued by the Secretary in the case of payment default. . . .")

59. GMAC is required by HUD regulations to ensure that all of the servicing requirements of 24 C.F.R. Part 203(C) have been met before initiating foreclosure. 24 C.F.R.§ 203.606.

60. According to the regulations and terms of the subject note and mortgage Plaintiff is required to adapt effective collection techniques designed to meet Ms. Homeowner's individual differences and take account of their peculiar circumstances to minimize the default in their mortgage payments as required by 24 C.F.R. § 203.600.

61. GMAC failed to make any reasonable efforts as required by federal regulations and the terms of her note and mortgage to arrange a face to face meeting with Ms. Homeowner before three full monthly installments were unpaid to discuss his circumstances and possible foreclosure avoidance. 24 C.F.R. § 203.604.

62. GMAC failed to inform Ms. Homeowner that it would make loan status and payment information available to local credit bureaus and prospective creditors, failed to inform Ms. Homeowner of other assistance, and failed to inform her of the names and addresses of HUD officials to whom further communication could be addressed as required by federal law and the terms of her note and mortgage. 24 C.F.R. § 203.604.

63. GMAC is required under federal law to adapt its collection and loan servicing practices to Ms. Homeowner's individual circumstances and to re-evaluate these techniques each month after default and GMAC failed to do so. 24 C.F.R. § 203.605.

64. GMAC failed to perform its servicing duty to Ms. Homeowner to manage the subject mortgage as required by FHA's special foreclosure prevention workout programs which must include and allow for the restructuring of the loan whereby the borrower pays out the delinquency in installments or advances to bring the mortgage current.

65. GMAC further denied Ms. Homeowner access to a repayment plan or special forbearance in the form of a written agreement that would reduce or suspend their monthly mortgage payments for a specific period to allow her time to recover from the financial hardship she was suffering through no fault of her own. Such a plan can involve changing one or more terms of the subject mortgage in order to help Ms. Homeowner bring the claimed default current, and thereby prevent foreclosure.

66. GMAC's failure to comply with the FHA repayment plan or special forbearance workout programs denied Ms. Homeowner the required access to explore alternatives to avoid foreclosure prior to the addition of additional foreclosure fees and costs.

Failure to Provide HAMP Loan Modification Options

67. In addition, on April 13, 2009, GMAC Mortgage L.L.C. received $2.1 billion in incentive payments under the Making Home Affordable Program. Pursuant to the plans and the authority provided by H.R. 1424 Title I § 109-110, the United States Treasury has ordered as follows:

> Mortgage Foreclosure Mitigation: All recipients of capital investments under the Financial Stability Plan will be required to commit to participate in mortgage foreclosure mitigation programs consistent with guidelines Treasury released as part of its Making Home Affordable mortgage modification program.

See www.financialstability.gov/about/transparencyaccountability.html (April 16, 2009). Plaintiff is required to allowing Ms. Homeowner to participate in the mandatory loan modification application process and has failed to do so.

68. The purpose of the TARP funds as stated in Public Law 110-343 known as the Economic Stabilization Act of 2008 is as stated below:

> SEC. 2. PURPOSES
>
> The purposes of this Act are—
>
> (1) To immediately provide authority and facilities that the Secretary of the Treasury can use to restore liquidity and stability to the financial system of the United States; and
>
> (2) To ensure that such authority and such facilities are used in a manner that
>
> (A) Protects home values, college funds, retirement accounts, and life savings;

(B) Preserves homeownership and promotes jobs and economic growth;

(C) Maximizes overall returns to the taxpayers of the United States; and

(D) Provides public accountability for the exercise of such authority.

69. In implementing the Act, the United States Treasury has instituted a number of programs, including the Making Home Affordable Act, Capital Purchase Program and Capital Assistance Program among others. See http://www.financialstability.gov/roadtostability/programs.htm.

70. If Plaintiff can prove it is the owner and holder of the subject note and mortgage, as a recipient of TARP funds, it is subject to the U.S. Treasury loan modification program guidelines for the Making Home Affordable Program which require "Any foreclosure action . . . be temporarily suspended during the trial period, or while borrowers are considered for alternative foreclosure prevention options. In the event that the Home Affordable Modification or alternative foreclosure options fail, the foreclosure action may be resumed."

71. Plaintiff has committed in the Securities Purchase Agreement to "expand the flow of credit to U.S. consumers and businesses on competitive terms to promote the sustained growth and vitality of the U.S. economy." Also, "the Company agrees to work diligently, under existing programs, to modify the terms of residential mortgages as appropriate to strengthen the health of the U.S. economy."

72. Plaintiff has already been remunerated for its troubled assets, has sought and been given taxpayer money and agreed to undertake meaningful loan modification with their clients who are facing foreclosure in return for billions of taxpayer dollars. Plaintiff has taken the money and now seeks to recover again from the homeowner through foreclosure even though it has not complied with the loss mitigation requirements as required by TARP.

73. GMAC failed to comply with its mortgage servicing responsibilities under the terms of the subject FHA mortgage and as a participant in the TARP/HAMP program. As a proximate result, Ms. Homeowner's delinquency has been improperly inflated by mortgage foreclosure filing, service and other fees and inspections and by foreclosure attorneys' fees that Ms. Homeowner cannot afford to pay. Therefore, Ms. Homeowner remains at the risk of losing her home.

74. GMAC filed the subject lawsuit without first allowing Ms. Homeowner the right to pursue the federally-required loan modification and loss mitigation opportunities.

Count One—Federal Fair Debt Collection Practices Act

75. Ms. Homeowner realleges the allegations contained in 49 through 74 above and incorporate the same herein by reference.

76. Ms. Homeowner brings this action against GMAC and Stern seeking statutory damages for its violations of the Federal Fair Debt Collections Practices Act, 15 U.S.C. § 1692, et seq. ("FDCPA").

77. The FDCPA was enacted to protect all consumers from debt collectors who seek to collect debts through illegal means and who engage in unfair and/or deceptive practices during the collection of a debt.

78. Ms. Homeowner is a "consumer" within the meaning of FDCPA, 15 U.S.C. § 1692a(3).

79. GMAC and Stern have engaged in collection of "debts" as this phrase is defined by 15 U.S.C. § 1692a(5) allegedly owed by Ms. Homeowner. GMAC through its authorized agent, Stern sought to foreclose upon the subject mortgage and in addition sought an accounting of the monetary sums due to GMAC and requested the Court find Ms. Homeowner responsible for paying these sums and be ordered to pay the amounts to GMAC. GMAC through its authorized agent, Stern requested this Court to enter a deficiency judgment be entered if applicable.

80. GMAC and Stern are "debt collectors" within the meaning of FDCPA, 15 U.S.C. § 1692a(6).

81. On November 7, 2008, GMAC and Stern created an Assignment executed by Beth [Brown], an employee of Stern, as Assistant Secretary of Mortgage Electronic Registration Systems, Inc. ("MERS") purportedly transferring the subject mortgage from MERS residing or located at c/o GMAC Mortgage, L.L.C., to GMAC Mortgage, L.L.C. Even though the assignment was dated November 7, 2008 and purportedly effective September 11, 2008. Ms. [Brown] also executed an Affidavit in Support of Plaintiff's Motion for Summary Judgment on November 13, 2008.

82. On June 3, 2009, counsel for Ms. Homeowner took Ms. [Brown]'s deposition and determined:

a. Ms. [Brown] was employed by Stern at the time she executed the subject assignment and affidavit in support of summary judgment and executed these documents as a routine part of her day to day activities at the request of her employer;

b. She did not review any of the underlying title or other documents prior to executing the subject assignment;

c. She did not hold any positions with Taylor, Bean and Whitaker Mortgage Company, MERS or GMAC;

d. She did not have any knowledge of the title documents relating to Taylor, Bean and Whitaker Mortgage or the accounting documents of GMAC;

e. She did not have any knowledge about MERS business practices and had never spoken with any one from MERS

f. She did not have any knowledge of the underlying data to support an y of the figure she included in the affidavit in support of summary judgment;

g. She did not review any documents or records such as account histories, statements or other documents prior to executing the affidavit; and

h. She did not know how the information was gathered or who prepared the numbers contained in the affidavit.

In other words, in November, 2008 Stern and GMAC created false documents to make it appear GMAC is the proper party to bring this action and in support of its request for the entry of a summary judgment.

83. GMAC and Stern knew they should not falsify assignments and affidavits. GMAC and Stern falsely represented that the assignments and affidavits were valid in violation of 15 U.S.C. § 1692e(10) and 15 U.S.C. § 1692f.

84. As a result of these FDCPA violations, Ms. Homeowner has been subjected to false and illegal collection activities, and has therefore been harmed.

85. It has been necessary for Ms. Homeowner to retain Jacksonville Area Legal Aid, Inc., a nonprofit law firm which provides free legal services to the indigent and working poor, to prosecute civil litigation based upon the Act. Her counsel has incurred and

will incur costs and other related expenses in prosecuting this action and her counsel is entitled to reimbursement of their costs and attorneys fee's pursuant to 15 U.S.C. § 1692k(3).

Wherefore, Ms. Homeowner requests this Court to enter a judgment against GMAC and Stern as follows:

(1) Award actual and statutory damages pursuant to 15 U.S.C. § 1692k(a) against Stern for violations of the Federal Fair Debt Collection Practices Act; and

(2) Other and further relief as may be deemed just and proper.

Count Two—Florida Deceptive and Unfair Trade Practices Act

86. This is an action for injunctive and declaratory relief pursuant to the Florida Deceptive and Unfair Trade Practices Act, Florida Statutes §§ 501.201, *Fla. Stat.* et seq. (hereinafter "the Act") and Chapter 86, *Fla.Stat.*

87. The provisions of the Act are to be liberally construed to promote the following policies:

a. To simplify, clarify, and modernize the law governing consumer protection, unfair methods of competition, and unconscionable, deceptive, and unfair trade practices; and

b. To protect the consuming public and legitimate business enterprises from those who engage in unfair methods of competition, or unconscionable, deceptive, or unfair acts or practices in the conduct of any trade or commerce. § 501.202(1) and (2), Fla. Stat.

88. At all times relevant hereto, Ms. Homeowner was a "consumer" as defined by § 501.203 (7), Fla. Stat.

89. At all times relevant hereto, GMAC and Stern were engaged in "trade or commerce" as defined by § 501.203 (8), *Fla. Stat.*

90. The Act makes unlawful "[u]nfair methods of competition, unconscionable acts or practices, and unfair or deceptive acts or practices in the conduct of any trade or commerce." § 501.204 (1), Fla. Stat.

91. GMAC and Stern created an Assignment executed by Beth [Brown], an employee of Stern, as Assistant Secretary of Mortgage Electronic Registration Systems, Inc. ("MERS") purportedly transferring the subject mortgage from MERS residing or located at c/o GMAC Mortgage, L.L.C., to GMAC Mortgage, L.L.C. The assignment was dated November 7, 2008 and purportedly effective September 11, 2008.

92. On June 3, 2009, counsel for Ms. Homeowner took Ms. [Brown]'s deposition and determined:

a. Ms. [Brown] was employed by Stern at the time she executed the subject assignment and she executed the assignment as a routine part of her day to day activities at the request of her employer;

b. She did not review any of the underlying title or other documents prior to executing the subject assignment;

c. She did not hold any positions with Taylor, Bean and Whitaker Mortgage Company, MERS or GMAC;

d. She did not have any knowledge of the title documents relating to Taylor, Bean and Whitaker Mortgage or the accounting documents of GMAC; and

e. She did not have any knowledge about MERS business practices and had never spoken with any one from MERS.

93. Stern and GMAC violated the Act by engaging in unfair and deceptive acts and practices including, but not limited to: (a) failing to provide Ms. Homeowner with the pre-foreclosure, loss mitigation opportunities required by the subject note and mortgage, regulations and federal law and regulations and (b) preparing and executing a false and improper assignment signed by an Stern employee to create the illusion that GMAC owns the subject mortgage.

94. Stern and GMAC knew or should have known the assignment created to give the illusion that GMAC owns the subject mortgage was unauthorized and invalid. This assignment was created by Stern on GMAC's behalf and with its acceptance and approval.

95. Stern and GMAC's actions as set forth in Paragraphs 55 through 74, 92, and 93 above represent a bona fide, actual, present and ascertained controversy relating to Stern and GMAC's routine practice as described in these Paragraphs.

96. Ms. Homeowner had and has a right and privilege to participate in loan modification and loss mitigation options prior to the foreclosure of her home.

97. Ms. Homeowner has a right and privilege to know if the Plaintiff is the true and unquestioned owner and holder of the subject consumer mortgage and note and to confirm the transfer of property rights in her home were completed in accordance with applicable law.

98. Ms. Homeowner has a right to and privilege for her consumer mortgage loan to proceed in litigation without unverified and/or false testimony and documents being filed in pursuit thereof.

99. Ms. Homeowner has a right and privilege to not be subjected to illegal, abusive and/or improper use of process and she has an actual, present and antagonistic interest in the collection of the subject mortgage as her home is the subject of the above-styled mortgage foreclosure lawsuit.

100. As a direct result of Sterns and GMAC's actions, Ms. Homeowner has been damaged as she is in danger of losing her home and the equity she has established in her home. Because of the premature filing of the foreclosure lawsuit the amounts necessary to reinstate the subject loan have been increased to an amount she can not afford. Additionally, she has not been afforded an opportunity for loan modification as required by the HAMP program.

101. Stern and GMAC violated the act by engaging the following acts of unconscionable conduct, or unfair/deceptive practices in the conduct of trade or commerce:

a. Stern and GMAC claimed and continues to claim GMAC is the owner and holder of the subject note and mortgage even thought they knew this status was based upon falsified documents created and executed to give the illusion that GMAC owns the subject mortgage;

b. GMAC knew that it prematurely brought suit before exploring the required FHA pre-suit loss mitigation options prior to bringing the subject foreclosure and knows it is continuing the subject lawsuit without allowing Ms. Homeowner to participate in the HAMP program.

102. Pursuant to § 768.72 (2002), Fla. Stat., Ms. Homeowner reserves the right to amend this complaint to add a prayer for punitive damages upon a showing by evidence in the record providing a basis for recovery of such damages.

103. Ms. Homeowner has been required to retain the services of the undersigned counsel to pursue her claims against Plaintiff for violations of the Act. Counsel will incur costs and attorney's fees as a result of their representation of Ms. Homeowner.

WHEREFORE, Ms. Homeowner requests this Court enter a

judgment against Stern and GMAC pursuant to the Act as follows:

(1) Declare Stern and GMAC's practices to be in violation of the Act as provided by the Act § 501.211(1), Fla. Stat.

(2) Declare GMAC is without standing in this case and to provide Ms. Homeowner with access to the special servicing provided by FHA guidelines;

(3) Enjoin GMAC and Stern from engaging in deceptive and unfair trade practices as provided by § 501.211(1), Fla. Stat. and enjoin them from creating and using falsified assignments and to enjoin GMAC and Stern from charging foreclosure fees and costs in connection with foreclosure commenced and pursued prior to or without the requisite pre-foreclosure loss mitigation and/or loan modification opportunities;

(4) Award attorney's fees and costs to Ms. Homeowner's counsel pursuant to the Act; and

(5) Grant such other and further relief as this Court deems equitable.

Count Three—Abuse of Legal Process

104. This is an action for injunctive and declaratory relief and for damages based upon GMAC and Stern's abuse of the legal process in connection with the subject foreclosure lawsuit.

105. On October 1, 2008, Stern's office filed the subject foreclosure lawsuit on behalf of its client GMAC. At the time Stern's office filed this action to present, GMAC did not and does not have sufficient documentation to establish it is the proper party to bring this action and the documentation upon which GMAC relies for standing was improperly manufactured by Stern acting on its behalf as its authorized agent, GMAC.

106. Stern and GMAC provided the following documents in support of GMAC claim it is the proper party to bring this foreclosure lawsuit:

a. The subject mortgage and note listing the lender as Taylor, Bean & Whitaker Mortgage Corp.; and

b. A promissory note filed on April 28, 2009 and endorsed to GMAC Mortgage Company in an undated endorsement and then endorsed in blank by Plaintiff in an endorsement that is also undated.

107. On November 14, 2008, Beth [Brown] executed a false affidavit in support of her firm's client, GMAC's, motion for Summary Judgment. She testified she did not have any knowledge of the underlying data to support an y of the figure she included in the affidavit in support of summary judgment; did not review any documents or records such as account histories, statements or other documents prior to executing the affidavit; and did not know how the information was gathered or who prepared the numbers contained in the affidavit.

108. On June 3, 2009, counsel for Ms. Homeowner took Ms. [Brown]'s deposition and determined:

a. Ms. [Brown] was employed by Stern at the time she executed the subject assignment and affidavit in support of summary judgment and executed these documents as a routine part of her day to day activities at the request of her employer;

b. She did not review any of the underlying title or other documents prior to executing the subject assignment;

c. She did not hold any positions with Taylor, Bean and Whitaker Mortgage Company, MERS or GMAC;

d. She did not have any knowledge of the title documents relating to Taylor, Bean and Whitaker Mortgage or the accounting documents of GMAC;

e. She did not have any knowledge about MERS business practices and had never spoken with any one from MERS;

f. She did not have any knowledge of the underlying data to support an y of the figure she included in the affidavit in support of summary judgment;

g. She did not review any documents or records such as account histories, statements or other documents prior to executing the affidavit; and

h. She did not know how the information was gathered or who prepared the numbers contained in the affidavit.

109. Stern and GMAC created false documents in an effort to obtain a foreclosure final judgment against Ms. Homeowner. These documents include an assignment of mortgage which GMAC and Stern intended to make it appear to the Court that GMAC was and is the proper party to bring this action. In fact, the assignor did not work for the assignor or MERS and had no information, personal or otherwise, relating to the information contained in the assignment including the effective date.

110. Stern and GMAC also created a false affidavit in support it GMAC's motion for summary judgment by having one of Stern's employees without the requisite knowledge of the status of the account and utilized this affidavit in the legal process to falsely represent to the Court Stern's employee has the authority to execute the affidavit and had conducted the necessary research to determine the amounts due on the subject mortgage and had reviewed the information necessary to execute the affidavit. See *In re Stewart*, 391 B.R. 327, 338-339 (Bkrtcy. E.D. La. 2008); *Wells Fargo Bank, N.A. v. Jones*, 391 B.R. 577 (Bkrtcy E.D. La 2008).

111. GMAC and Stern utilized the assignment and affidavit in the legal process to falsely represent to the Court that GMAC had and has the requisite standing to bring this mortgage foreclosure lawsuit and the sums due and which should be included in the foreclosure final judgment.

112. By creating and utilizing the false assignment and affidavit, GMAC and Stern misused legal process and the Court system to promote their best interests by misleading the Court as to GMAC right to bring the subject mortgage foreclosure lawsuit and by misleading the Court as to the legitimacy of the sworn statements in the summary judgment affidavit.

113. GMAC and Stern should not have abused the foreclosure process by filing false documents to support their claim that GMAC was the proper party to bring this action and by falsely supporting GMAC's motion for summary judgment with an affidavit that was based upon insufficient knowledge of the facts contained therein.

114. GMAC and Stern's actions were willful and constituted an intentional misuse of process in an effort to wrongfully foreclose upon Ms. Homeowner's home.

115. Therefore, GMAC and Stern misused civil legal process against Ms. Homeowner in an effort to accomplish the foreclosure upon her home based upon false documents.

116. Pursuant to § 768.72 (2002), Fla. Stat., Ms. Homeowner reserves the right to amend this complaint to add a prayer for punitive damages upon a showing by evidence in the record providing a basis for recovery of such damages.

WHEREFORE, Ms. Homeowner requests actual and special

damages against GMAC and Stern, jointly and severally for abuse of legal process.

DEMAND FOR JURY TRIAL

Ms. Homeowner demands a trial by jury on all issues so triable.

Respectfully submitted,
[Attorney for Ms. Homeowner]
[Date]

I.8.2 Complaint in Response to Nonjudicial Foreclosure

This complaint raises affirmative claims and defenses to a wrongful foreclosure based on a civil conspiracy to engage in predatory lending, misapplication of payments and assessment of improper servicing charges, lack of standing based a defective assignment from MERS, and failure to offer a HAMP modification or loss mitigation required by the PSA. It includes claims based on assignee and joint venture liability.

IN THE CIRCUIT COURT OF
LEE COUNTY, ALABAMA

____________________	)
OLIVER [CONSUMER], NORA [CONSUMER], STEVEN [CONSUMER],	)
Plaintiffs,	)
v.	)
The Bank of New York Mellon, in its Individual capacity, The Bank of New York Mellon, in its capacity as trustee of the [securitized trust], Bank of America as successor in interest to Countrywide Home Loans, Bank of America Home Loan Servicing as successor in interest to Countrywide Home Loan Servicing, Inc. Merscorp, Inc.; Mortgage Electronic Registration System, Inc.; and [fictitious defendants No. 1 to 11],	)
Defendants	)
____________________	)

COMPLAINT

STATEMENT OF THE PARTIES

1. The Plaintiffs are each adult resident citizens of the Lee County, Alabama and are each over the age of nineteen years.

2. The Defendant Bank of New York Mellon, individually, is a foreign corporation doing business by agent in Lee County, Alabama at all times material to this complaint.

3. The Defendant Bank of New York Mellon, as trustee, is a foreign corporation doing business by agent in Lee County, Alabama at all times material to this complaint and is the Trustee under the Pooling and Servicing Agreement for CWABS, Inc. Asset Backed Certificate Series 2005-13 a corporate trust authorized and existing under the Laws of the State of New York which is a special purpose vehicle or "SPV" in industry parlance, which purchases mortgages and then sells securities backed by the income from the mortgages purchased to the secondary bond market and various investors including institutions, governments and individuals all over the world.

4. The Defendant Bank of America is the successor in interest to Countrywide Home Loans as its purchaser and is a foreign corporation doing business by agent in Lee County, Alabama.

5. The Defendant Bank of America Home Loan Servicing is a foreign corporation doing business in Lee County, Alabama and is the successor in interest to Countrywide Home Loan Servicing as its purchaser.

6. The Defendant MERSCORP, Inc. is the parent corporation of Mortgage Electronic Registration Systems, Inc. or MERS and is a foreign corporation doing business by agent in Lee County, Alabama at all times material hereto.

7. The Defendant Mortgage Electronic Registration Systems is a foreign corporation doing business by agent in Lee County, Alabama at all times material hereto.

8. The Fictitious defendants are identified as No. 1, whether singular or plural, that entity who or which sold the specific mortgage product to the Plaintiffs which is made the basis of this lawsuit; No. 2, whether singular or plural, that entity who or which, as an agent, servant or employee provided funding for the mortgage product sold to the plaintiffs made the basis of this lawsuit; No. 3, whether singular or plural, Plaintiffs hereby intending to designate that entity or individual or those entities or individuals who provided funding for the loan made the basis of this suit at each step of the securitization process; No. 4, whether singular or plural, that entity who individual who or which, through agents or otherwise, marketed to Plaintiffs the particular mortgage product made the basis of this lawsuit; No. 5, whether singular or plural, Plaintiffs hereby intending to designate those persons or entities who control the mortgage foreclosure process for this loan and who determine, direct and control the manner in which the foreclosure process is undertaken No. 6, whether singular or plural, that entity or individual who or which authorized and ratified the actions of the persons or entities responsible for the manner in which the foreclosure process is undertaken by various defendants to this action including the fictitious defendant No. 5; No. 7 are those entities or individuals who are responsible for producing and providing documents used to foreclose upon the Plaintiffs and who in fact provide the documents without regard to their veracity; No. 8, whether singular or plural, that entity who or which, as described above, is the predecessor corporation of any of the entities described above or in the body of the complaint; and No. 9, whether singular or plural, that entity who or which, as described above, is the successor corporation of any of the entities described herein; and No. 10 whether singular or plural, that entity who or which had any involvement with the origination, servicing, or foreclosure upon said mortgage loan of the plaintiffs No. 11 whether singular or plural are those persons or entities who are subsidiaries or affiliates or joint venturers of the Fictitious Party Defendants herein who are otherwise unknown at this time or, if

their names are known at this time, their identities as proper party defendants are not known to the plaintiff at this time, and their true names will be substituted by amendment when ascertained.

JURISDICTION

9. Jurisdiction is proper in the Circuit Court of Lee County. The underlying action is based upon a contract executed in Lee County, Alabama. The action is brought to enjoin a foreclosure instituted in Lee County, and is in the nature of a counterclaim to that foreclosure action. The action is brought to enforce the contractual remedies allowed in paragraph 22 of the mortgage document. The action seeks damages in contract and tort for the actions of the defendants with respect to their origination, servicing and foreclosure on the loan in question.

VENUE

10. Venue is proper in this Court as the plaintiff is a citizen of Lee County and all of or substantially all of the wrongs complained of occurred in this County.

STATEMENT OF FACTS

11. The defendant Bank of America Home Loan Servicing contacted the plaintiff Steve [Consumer] through its counsel sometime on or about April 21, 2009 and notified the Plaintiff Steven [Consumer] that they were accelerating the promissory note executed by him and intended to foreclose upon the property located at [Address] on July 26, 2009.

12. The Loan secured by said mortgage has an alleged amount due exceeding $400,000. This is due upon a parcel of real estate that according to a recent appraisal was worth no more than $250,000. The subject property has a home constructed on it which was built in 1949 and is without many modern amenities including central heat and air.

13. At the time of the origination of this loan (approximately July 2005) Steve [Consumer] was self employed in the lawn care business. His parents, Oliver and Nora [Consumer], signatories to the mortgage documents, are and all times material hereto were elderly, disabled and on a fixed income. The financial information available in the form of tax returns for 2005 indicate that Steven [Consumer]'s net income for the tax filing due for April 15, 2005 was less than $2,000. Assuming from the tax records filed that all categories of wages listed in the schedules were paid to Steve [Consumer] his gross income could not have exceeded $55,000. The mortgage payment due to make the basic principal and interest payments under the loan would have exceeded 58% of Steve [Consumer]'s gross monthly income assuming that his income was annualized.

14. The plaintiff's financial information was available to the defendants and the defendants knew or should have known of the income of the plaintiffs at the time of making the loan and further knew or should have known that the plaintiff Steven [Consumer] was not qualified for the subject loan, but based upon its greed for fees and charges and origination payments, approved the loan and steered the plaintiff to a loan that was high cost, predatory and not suitable for the plaintiff.

15. The loan when made was predatory in the sense that the loan was not suitable or affordable for the plaintiff, that the loan made far exceeded the value of the property and was designed to enrich the defendants at the consumers expense and to steer the plaintiff into a loan that the plaintiff neither wanted or needed based upon the plaintiffs financial situation.

16. The loan when made was structured to extract the maximum amount of fees and to be as costly and expensive to the plaintiff as possible for the benefit of the defendants who were engaged in a civil conspiracy to make predatory and high cost loans which were unaffordable and to sell them into the secondary market to unsuspecting investors through the process of securitization.

17. The loan when made was made without considering the plaintiff's ability to pay and without considering the plaintiff's financial situation and in violation of the industry standards for underwriting and in violation of the underwriting rules established and stated for the SPV or trust which allegedly owns the loan in question.

18. The defendants are engaged in and have engaged in a civil conspiracy to engage in illegal predatory lending and there is a demonstrable pattern and practice of predatory lending by these defendants.

19. Some of the characteristics of the predatory loans and actions of the defendants are: making loans based on the value of the homes involved in the transaction, failing to consider the ability of the consumer to repay the loan, making loans without documenting the ability of the consumer to repay the loans, including predatory terms in the loan such as a prepayment penalty, an adjustable rate that only increases and never decreases, making and originating loans that have no net benefit to the consumer and making loans that are unaffordable when made.

20. The loan made to the plaintiff was unaffordable when made and was made in violation of the defendant's own underwriting guidelines and regulatory guidance provided by federal regulatory authorities and was predatory in nature.

21. The actions of the defendant in this respect are taken in violation of applicable regulatory guidance and give rise to common law claims of negligence, wantonness, unjust enrichment, unconscionability and suppression.

22. The plaintiffs allege that when this loan was originated by the defendants that they engaged in conduct that was negligent, wanton, and unconscionable and included acts that were unfair and deceptive including but not limited to each of the following: the defendant underwrote the loan in violation of its own stated underwriting guidelines mandated by the appropriate federal regulatory authorities, took advantage of its superior bargaining power and position to steer the plaintiff into a loan which was not suitable for him and which had the practical effect of increasing his costs of credit and did so with knowledge that the loan was unaffordable and predatory. The act of originating this loan was driven by the defendants' financial incentives and the loan was made without properly considering whether the type of loan made to the plaintiff was suitable for his purposes and needs but instead steered the plaintiff to a loan which was the most profitable for the participants to the predatory lending conspiracy. The defendants violated their own "best practices" and regulatory guidelines to make the loan and the marketing and origination of the loan was premised in unfair and deceptive acts prohibited by federal regulatory authorities. The acts of the defendants in this respect are taken in violation of law.

23. Further, once the defendants began to service the subject loan they serviced the loan in a negligent or wanton manner and in

violation of the note and mortgage between the parties. That is to say that the defendants engaged in some or all of the following practices with respect to the mortgage account: the defendants misapplied payments to the account, marked up charges to the account, improperly placed payments in suspense and failed to credit the payments to the account, made illegal, unauthorized or improper charges to the account in violation of law, the security instruments and/or various regulatory guidelines, paid one charge for a service to the account (for example, attorney's fees, Broker price opinions, property inspection charges, force placed insurance) but charged the account a higher amount than paid for the service in violation of the law, the security instruments and/or various regulatory guidelines, instituted an accounting system in the form of its mortgage servicing software which created artificial, false or bogus defaults on the account for the purpose of imposing fees and charges to the account of the plaintiff and which paid the defendants fees before applying payments to principal and interest in violation of the mortgage payment covenant as contained in the security instrument.

24. When the loan progressed to a state of default, the defendants assured the plaintiffs that they would engage in loss mitigation and would not foreclose. Despite these mitigation assurances from that entity known as Bank of America Home Loan Servicing; the defendants continued with the foreclosure sale against the plaintiff's property.

25. The plaintiffs allege that the defendants lack standing to foreclose in that they have no present legal right to enforce the security agreement that underlies the foreclosure action.

26. The defendant Bank of New York Mellon as trustee for CWABS, Inc. Asset Backed Certificate Series 2005-13 alleges that it is the assignee of the mortgage in question and the owner of the debt and that as such it has the present legal right to foreclose.

27. The plaintiffs allege, upon information and belief, that the alleged assignment as between MERS and Bank of New York Mellon as trustee for CWABS, Inc. Asset Backed Certificate Series 2005-13 is defective, void, or otherwise unenforceable as to the security instrument in question in this case.

28. Further, the plaintiffs allege that the uniform mortgage instrument provides them with the right to make any claim that they may have which offsets or defeats the claims of the defendants with respect to their allegations of default and entitlement to foreclosure.

29. The defendants are engaged in and have engaged in a pattern and practice of falsifying loan transactions and in particular assignments of mortgages for the purpose of enabling its joint venturers and co-conspirators to foreclose on property of unsuspecting or unknowing consumers illegally and without legal standing to foreclose.

30. The defendants are engaged in a joint venture as defined by Alabama law and as such are liable jointly and severally for the actions of all members of the joint venture.

31. As a result of the actions of the defendants the plaintiffs have been injured and harmed in that they have suffered financial loss, damage to their reputation and suffered mental anguish.

32. The plaintiffs claim from the defendants all damages allowed by law in the present action.

AFFIRMATIVE DEFENSES TO THE UNDERLYING FORECLOSURE ACTION

33. The plaintiffs allege that acceleration was improper and in violation of the parties contract.

34. The plaintiffs allege that the defendant failed to offer a modification agreement which would have cured any alleged default and would have been an absolute defense to foreclosure as required by their acceptance of federal bailout funds pursuant to HAMP, TARP and guidance from the Treasury Department.

35. The plaintiffs allege that the defendants failed to comply with applicable mortgage servicing regulations, guidelines and agreements and as such a condition precedent to acceleration and foreclosure has been violated requiring the dismissal of the underlying foreclosure action.

36. The plaintiffs allege that the servicer of the loan failed to offer pre-foreclosure loss mitigation as required by the agreements between the trustee and the servicer. This document is called a Pooling and Servicing Agreement or a PSA, in industry parlance, which requires that the servicer take certain actions to prevent foreclosure before acceleration of the loan and foreclosure. This failure requires that the underlying action seeking foreclosure be dismissed or abated until such time as the servicer complies with these requirements.

37. The plaintiffs allege that the trustee lacks standing to initiate a foreclosure action. As grounds therefore, the plaintiffs are willing to provide at an evidentiary hearing, proof of said lack of standing to foreclose.

38. The mortgage assignment portending to transfer the mortgage to the trustee is void, voidable, illegal, without legal effect and is otherwise invalid and unenforceable as a matter of law.

COUNT ONE
Respondeat Superior Liability

39. The plaintiffs reallege all prior paragraphs as if set out here in full.

40. The Defendant Bank of New York Mellon, a defendant in this action hired, directed, or controlled the actions of Bank of America, as successor in interest to Countrywide in its capacity of originator and servicer of the mortgage loan in this case.

41. Bank of America, who is also a defendant in this action, serves at the pleasure of both the Trust and Trustee and/or is a part of a joint venture with the Trust and Trustee in this action. Bank of America and Bank of New York Mellon and various fictitious defendants to this action are alleged, upon information and belief, to be engaged in a civil conspiracy to engage in conduct which is unlawful for the purpose of unjustly enriching the members or participants in the joint venture or civil conspiracy.

42. The Bank of New York Mellon is liable in tort for all of the wrongful actions of its agents, employees, joint venturers or servants, Bank of America and various fictitious defendants.

43. As a result of the wrongful actions described herein the plaintiffs have been injured and damaged and claim all damages allowable under law for these actions.

Second Cause of Action
Negligent or Wanton Hiring, Supervision, Training or Retention

44. The Plaintiffs reallege all prior paragraphs as if set out here in full.

45. The Bank of New York Mellon negligently or wantonly hired, trained, supervised or retained the defendant, Bank of America and various fictitious defendants described herein.

46. As a result of this negligence or wantonness, depending on evidence adduced, the Plaintiffs were injured and damaged by the actions of Bank of America and the various fictitious defendants.

47. As a result, the Bank of New York Mellon is liable for all damages proximately and directly flowing from actions of its agents, employees, joint venturers or servants, Bank of America and various fictitious defendants.

Third Cause of Action
Joint Venture Liability

48. The Plaintiffs reallege all prior paragraphs as if set out here in full.

49. The Defendants in this action are part of a joint venture as defined by controlling law.

50. As a member of that joint venture, the defendants are liable to the Plaintiffs for any tortious actions of any member of the joint venture against the defendants.

51. As a result thereof, the Plaintiffs reallege in its entirety the entire complaint against the defendants herein.

52. As a result of the actions of the joint venturers, the plaintiffs have been injured and damaged as heretofore alleged.

53. The Plaintiffs claim all damages as allowed by law for the wrongful acts of the joint venturers against them.

Fourth Claim for Relief
(Breach of Contract)

54. The Plaintiffs reallege all prior paragraphs of the pleading as if set out here in full.

55. Plaintiffs are parties to a contract for a mortgage on the Plaintiffs' property.

56. Upon information and belief, the mortgage that is the subject of this lawsuit was "securitized' by one or more of the defendants.

57. The subject mortgage, once securitized, became subject to a contract between the Trustee of the special purpose entity (or trust) and its successors and assigns. This Contract is commonly referred to as a "Pooling and Servicing Agreement" (hereinafter "PSA"). The PSA is the document which creates the Trust which allegedly holds the loans forming the pool or trust assets.

58. Under the provisions of the PSA, the servicer is required to actively engage in "loss mitigation" under their agreement with the Trust to prevent the foreclosure of the property and to provide for income to the trust in the form of payments by the borrowers on the mortgage. The Plaintiffs in this case are an intended Third Party Beneficiary of the PSA.

59. The actions and conduct of the defendants in applying to the mortgage illegal, unauthorized charges, creating a false or exaggerated default, failing to engage in loss mitigation and attempting to foreclose on the property of the Plaintiffs are breaches of the mortgage or note and of the PSA of which the Plaintiffs are a third party beneficiary.

60. As a result thereof, the defendants are liable for all natural, proximate and consequential damages of their breach of contract.

Fifth Cause of Action
(Unjust Enrichment)

61. The Plaintiffs adopt and reallege all prior paragraphs as if set out here in full.

62. The actions of the defendants in underwriting, selling and originating an unaffordable mortgage to the Plaintiffs for the sole purpose of generating fees and commissions and which violated applicable laws and regulations resulted in the defendants being unjustly enriched.

63. As a result of the defendants' unjust enrichment, the Plaintiffs have been injured and damaged in that the Plaintiffs were sold a mortgage loan which the defendants knew or should have known was unaffordable when made and was made without considering the ability of the Plaintiffs to pay and afforded them no tangible benefit resulting in financial and emotional damages including mental anguish.

64. The Plaintiffs claim all damages allowable under law as a result of the defendants' wrongful conduct and unjust enrichment.

SIXTH CAUSE OF ACTION
NEGLIGENCE OR WANTONNESS PER SE

65. The Plaintiffs adopt and reallege all prior paragraphs as if set out here in full.

66. Each of the following actions of the defendants are instances of conduct previously banned as unfair and deceptive by federal regulatory authorities governing the actions of these defendants, which were engaged in by the defendants in this case:

67. Making a loan based on the value of the collateral.

a. Making a loan that the lender knew or should have known was unaffordable when made.
b. Making a loan without considering the borrowers ability to repay.
c. Making a loan without considering the borrowers sources of income.
d. Making a high cost loan to a borrower when the underlying loan was already in default.
e. Making a loan for the purposes of equity stripping.
f. Making a loan a 100% refinance when a second mortgage or home equity loan would have served the same purpose.
g. Making a loan that was stated income, no documentation loan in addition to having other predatory characteristics such as a prepayment penalty and an adjustable rate and a high cost.
h. Making a loan designed to avoid the HOEPA triggers set out in the TILA.
i. Failing to properly oversee its agents, employees, vendors and associates who broker loans for them to prevent predatory lending practices by them.

68. As a result of violating these and/or other and additional federal regulations with respect to the making of this loan, the third party defendants are liable to the Plaintiffs under the theories of negligence per se or wantonness per se depending upon evidenced adduced.

69. As a result of the negligence or wantonness per se the Plaintiffs claim all damages allowed by law.

SEVENTH CAUSE OF ACTION CIVIL CONSPIRACY

70. Plaintiffs adopt and reallege all prior paragraphs as if set out here in full.

71. The defendants engaged in an unlawful combination and conspiracy to originate and service a mortgage loan through a pattern and practice of predatory lending and to conceal this unlawful activity for the purpose of unjustly enriching the joint venturers and conspirators. To accomplish the purposes of the civil conspiracy the members of the conspiracy engaged in conduct against the plaintiffs as set out herein which includes actions that give rise to claims of negligence, wantonness, suppression, unjust enrichment, forgery, unfair and deceptive acts and practices and actions which violate regulatory guidance promulgated by national banking and lending authorities.

72. As a result of this civil conspiracy, civil wrongs were committed against the Plaintiffs and other consumers. The motivation for the civil conspiracy was the defendants' greed.

73. As a result of the civil conspiracy the Plaintiffs were injured and damaged and claim all damages allowed by law.

EIGHT CAUSE OF ACTION NEGLIGENCE

74. The plaintiffs reallege all prior paragraphs as if set out here in full.

75. The defendants owed a fiduciary duty to the plaintiffs to properly collect payments, distribute payments, debit the mortgage account and credit the mortgage account in accordance with the mortgage payment covenant contained in the mortgage. Defendants also owed the plaintiffs a duty not to assess illegal, unauthorized or improper charges and to service the mortgage of the plaintiffs in a commercially reasonable manner so as to not create a false default or a default not based in fact.

76. The defendants breached their duty to the plaintiffs by not properly crediting the account or distributing the payments appropriately and by applying to the account charges which are illegal, unauthorized or improper and servicing the loan in a manner that is commercially unreasonable and by creating a false default or exacerbating a default for the purposes of unjustly enriching the defendants.

77. The defendants' breach proximately caused injury and damage to the plaintiffs, including emotional and financial injuries and the plaintiffs claim all damages allowed by law for their injuries.

NINTH CAUSE OF ACTION WANTONNESS

78. The plaintiffs reallege all prior paragraphs as if set out here in full.

79. The defendants engaged in wanton conduct in that the defendants consciously misapplied payments made on the account and added false and bogus charges to the account in an attempt to create a "false" delinquency so that the defendants could wrongfully declare the loan to be in default. The actions of the defendants were taken with reckless indifference to the consequences to the plaintiffs, knowing full well that the defendants' actions would produce injury and harm to the plaintiffs.

80. The defendants knew that these actions were likely to result in injury to the plaintiffs including financial and emotional injuries and mental anguish.

81. As a proximate result of the defendants' wantonness the plaintiffs were injured and harmed and suffered financial injury and emotional damages and the plaintiffs claim all damages allowed by law for those injuries.

TENTH CAUSE OF ACTION UNJUST ENRICHMENT

82. The plaintiffs adopt and reallege all prior paragraphs as if set out here in full.

83. The actions of the defendants in applying charges to the mortgage account of the plaintiff which was either illegal, wrong in character, wrong in amount, unauthorized, or otherwise improper resulted in the defendant being unjustly enriched.

84. As a result of the defendants' unjust enrichment, the plaintiffs have been injured and damaged in that the plaintiffs have been forced to pay charges that were illegal, wrong in character, wrong in amount, unauthorized, or otherwise improper under threat of foreclosure by the defendants.

85. The plaintiffs claim all damages allowable under law as a result of the defendants' wrongful conduct and unjust enrichment.

ELEVENTH CAUSE OF ACTION WRONGFUL FORECLOSURE

86. The plaintiffs reallege all prior paragraphs as if set out here in full.

87. The defendants have initiated a foreclosure proceeding against the plaintiffs in violation of law.

88. The initiation of the foreclosure proceeding by the defendants was either negligent, wanton or intentional, depending on proof adduced at trial.

89. As a result thereof, the defendants are liable for all natural, proximate and consequential damages due to its actions including an award of punitive damages upon a proper evidentiary showing.

TWELFTH CAUSE OF ACTION PETITION FOR AN EX PARTE TEMPORARY RESTRAINING ORDER

90. The plaintiffs adopt and reallege all prior paragraphs of this pleading as if set out here in full.

91. A Temporary Restraining Order is an equitable remedy that the Circuit Court has the power and authority to grant.

92. The purpose of a Temporary Restraining Order (hereinafter TRO) is to preserve the status quo ante until a final determination has been made on the merits.

93. A TRO may be granted without notice if it clearly appears from specific facts shown by a verified pleading or affidavit that immediate and irreparable harm will result before the adverse party or his attorney can be heard in opposition is notified.

94. In the present case, the defendants have published the plaintiffs' home for foreclosure sale to occur on July 26, 2009.

95. Unless a TRO is entered in the present case, the plaintiffs will be deprived of their property without the Circuit Court having an opportunity to review or rule upon the substantive allegations of the complaint.

96. The Petitioners allege that immediate and irreparable harm will result if the defendants are allowed to complete the foreclosure.

97. The Petitioners aver that the legal remedy available is inadequate to prevent the foreclosure without the intervention of the Court.

98. The Petitioners aver that a property right exists in the home.

99. The Petitioners aver that there is no default on the home other than a false or bogus default created by the defendants.

100. The Petitioners aver that the foreclosing entity lacks standing to pursue foreclosure in the present case and that to allow it to foreclose could cause the petitioners to lose the home without being relieved of the contractual obligation on the debt.

101. The Petitioners request that the Court enter a temporary injunction until such time as the Court can determine from the evidence in the case if the Defendants have a legal right to foreclose on the Plaintiffs' property.

102. The Petitioners show unto the Court that enforcement is feasible as the Court has jurisdiction of this matter and has in personam jurisdiction over the parties.

103. The Petitioner further alleges that the hardships are balanced in this matter and that the Defendants have no meritorious defense to the best of the Petitioners' knowledge and belief. Further, the defendants are protected equitably in that the home in question is occupied and the home is maintained and not suffering waste or neglect.

104. The Petitioners pray that this Court will issue an ex parte TRO until such time as this Court may take up this matter.

105. The Petitioners further pray that this Court would grant the relief requested and issue a Temporary Restraining Order enjoining the foreclosure sale from being conducted as scheduled until such time as the merits of the plaintiffs' complaint can be heard by the Court after the taking of evidence.

WHEREFORE, the Plaintiffs having set forth their claims for relief against the Defendants respectfully pray of the Court as follows:

A. That the Plaintiffs have and recover against the Defendants a sum to be determined by a jury of actual damages;
B. That the Plaintiffs have and recover against the Defendants a sum to be determined by a jury of punitive damages;
C. That the Defendants be enjoined from continuing with the foreclosure sale temporarily but until such time as the material averments of the Plaintiffs' complaint have been heard.
D. That the Plaintiffs have such other and further relief as the Court may deem just and proper in the circumstances.

Respectfully submitted,
[Attorney for Plaintiff]
[Date]

I.8.3 Request for Admissions to Foreclosing Lender

IN THE UNITED STATES BANKRUPTCY COURT
WESTERN DISTRICT OF NORTH CAROLINA
SHELBY DIVISION

______________________)
IN THE MATTER OF:)
Debtor)
Plaintiff)
)
v.) Adv. Proc.
)
)
Defendant)
______________________)

DEFENDANT'S FIRST REQUEST FOR ADMISSIONS (PROOF OF OWNERSHIP OF THE MORTGAGE NOTE and PROPER TRANSFERS)

Pursuant to Rule 36 of the Federal Rules of Civil Procedure, which is made applicable to this Adversary Proceeding by Rule 7036 of the Federal Rules of Bankruptcy Procedure, Debtor/Defendant hereby demands that the Plaintiff, within thirty (30) days after service hereof, admit or specifically deny for the purposes of the above-captioned Adversary Proceeding and subject to all pertinent objections as to admissibility which may be interposed during further proceedings, the truth of the following facts.

In the event that any request is denied in whole or in part, you should set forth the reasons for such denial and identify the persons having knowledge thereof and the documents relating thereto.

DEFINITIONS

A. "You" means the Plaintiff ________.
B. "Debtor/Defendant" means ________.
C. "You" or "Your" means Plaintiff ____________, its agents, employees, attorneys, servants, predecessors and/or successors in interest and all others acting on its behalf.
D. "Original Mortgage Note" means the promissory note in the amount of $________, dated ________, and signed by Debtor/Defendant.

REQUEST FOR ADMISSIONS

1. Referring to the original mortgage note which is the subject of Plaintiff's Motion for Relief from Stay, the full name of the original Lender listed on the said note in the amount of $ ________, dated ________, and signed by Debtor/Defendant is ____________.

Response:

2. Plaintiff is not the lender named in the original mortgage note which is the subject of this case.

Response:

3. Plaintiff is not the holder of the original mortgage note.

Response:

4. Plaintiff is not the owner of the original mortgage note.
Response:

5. The original lender has not transferred possession of the original mortgage note or any rights thereunder to Plaintiff.
Response:

6. Plaintiff is not in possession of the original mortgage note.
Response:

7. The original mortgage note has not been lost or destroyed.
Response:

8. The original lender has not filed an affidavit attesting to the loss of the original mortgage note or its destruction.
Response:

9. Plaintiff does not have a signed Power of Attorney authorizing it to file any type of affidavit attesting to the loss of the original mortgage note or its destruction.
Response:

10. Plaintiff never had possession of the original mortgage note before it was allegedly lost.
Response:

11. Plaintiff has no actual knowledge as to who lost the original mortgage note.
Response:

12. The original mortgage note in this case is part of a securitized trust composed of more than one mortgage loan.
Response:

13. The securitized trust was created by a Pooling and Servicing Agreement.
Response:

14. The Pooling and Servicing Agreement includes mandatory rules as to the time for the transfer of all original mortgage notes and security instruments (mortgages and deeds of trust) to the Master Document Custodian for the Trust.
Response:

15. The original mortgage note was in fact transferred and delivered to the Master Document Custodian for the Trust.
Response:

16. The original mortgage note was received by the Master Document Custodian for the Trust prior to the final date for the delivery of the same as set forth in the conveyancing rules of the Pooling and Servicing Agreement.
Response:

17. The Master Document Custodian filed a written report with the Trustee for the securitized trust in which it attested to the actual possession and custody of the original mortgage note in this case.
Response:

18. If the original mortgage note in this case included an allonge, then the said allonge was permanently affixed to the said note.
Response:

19. An allonge cannot be permanently affixed to a mortgage note by way of a paper clip, staple or scotch tape.
Response:

20. An allonge was affixed to the original mortgage note in this case because there was insufficient room at the bottom or foot of the original mortgage note for any endorsements.
Response:

21. The named Depositor for the securitized trust in this case actually transferred the original mortgage note to the Master Document Custodian for the trust.
Response:

22. The Sponsor for the securitized trust in this case actually transferred the original mortgage note to the Depositor for the trust.
Response:

23. The Originator for the mortgage loan in this case transferred the original mortgage note to the Sponsor for the securitized trust.
Response:

24. The Master Document Custodian for the securitized trust in this case verified in writing to the Trustee for the trust that it had confirmed an unbroken chain of transfers and deliveries of the original mortgage note from the Originator to the Sponsor, from the Sponsor to the Depositor, from the Depositor to the Trustee for the trust, and from the Trustee to the Master Document Custodian for the trust.
Response:

25. The Trustee for the securitized trust in this case is the lawful owner and possessor of the original mortgage note.
Response:

26. No party, other than the Trustee for the securitized trust in this case, has any legal claims or rights in the original mortgage note.
Response:

27. Any and all documents that purport to transfer the original mortgage note from the Originator to you would not be consistent with the mandatory conveyancing rules in the Pooling and Servicing Agreement for the trust that actually owns the original mortgage note.
Response:

28. MERS has never claimed any beneficial rights or any form of ownership rights in the original mortgage note.
Response:

29. MERS is not the holder of the original mortgage note in this case.
Response:

30. Any rights MERS may have had in the original mortgage note were transferred to the Master Document Custodian for the securitized trust when the trust was formed or shortly thereafter.
Response:

31. MERS has no business records as to the receipt of any payments on the original mortgage note.
Response:

32. MERS has no business records as to the application of payments on the original mortgage note.
Response:

33. MERS has on employees who have ever serviced the original mortgage loan in this case.
Response:

34. As between MERS and the Trustee for the securitized trust, the Trustee has all rights of ownership and possession with respect to the original mortgage note.
Response:

35. The securitized trust that owns the original mortgage note in this case issued bonds to various parties who thereby acquired an ownership interest in the corpus of the trust.
Response:

36. The corpus of the trust consisted and does consist of original mortgage notes such as the note in this case.
Response:

37. The bonds issued by the trust were rated by Fitch, Moody's or Standard & Poor's.
Response:

38. The investment-grade bonds issued by the trust could not have been sold without such ratings by Fitch, Moody's or Standard & Poor's.
Response:

39. In rating the bonds, Fitch, Moody's or Standard & Poor's represented and confirmed to the potential bond buyers that the Master Document Custodian actually had physical possession of all original mortgage notes to be delivered to the trust, including the note in this case.
Response:

40. In rating the bonds, Fitch, Moody's or Standard & Poor's represented and confirmed to the potential bond buyers that all of the original mortgage notes had been properly transferred and delivered to the Master Document Custodian in an unbroken chain of transfers and deliveries from the originator to the intermediate parties and from such parties to the said Master Document Custodian for the trust.
Response:

41. In rating the bonds, Fitch, Moody's or Standard & Poor's represented and confirmed to the potential investment-grade bond buyers that all of the original mortgage notes had been transferred to the trust in true sales from each party in the chain of transfers and deliveries.
Response:

42. The Prospectus for the trust in this case represents that the mortgage loans are owned by the trust and are bankruptcy remote from any claims against the originators of the said loans.
Response:

43. The Prospectus for the trust in this case represents that each transfer and delivery of the original mortgage notes from the originator to the sponsor, from the sponsor to the depositor and from the depositor to the Master Document Custodian for the trust was a true and arms-length sale.
Response:

43. The Prospectus for the trust in this case represents that the trust is the lawful owner and possessor of all original mortgage notes included in the trust, including the original mortgage loan in this case.
Response:

Respectfully submitted,
[Attorney for Debtor]
[Date]

I.8.4 Interrogatories, Requests for Admissions to Foreclosing Trust

PLAINTIFF'S INTERROGATORIES AND REQUEST FOR PRODUCTION TO DEFENDANT (XYZ) TRUST

DEFINITION OF TERMS

1. The term "plaintiff" or "plaintiffs" means the party identified as such in this pleading.

2. The term "defendant or defendants" means any or all of the parties to this litigation who are delineated as defendants in these pleadings and their subsidiaries, affiliates, any successors and assigns, and predecessors, and includes every officer, director, partner, agent, employee, attorney, servant, or any other person presently or formerly acting for or on behalf of said entity.

3. The term "document" is used in its customary broad sense to include, by way of illustration only and not by way of limitation, all written or graphic matter of every kind or description, whether printed or reproduced by any process, or written and/or produced by hand, whether final or draft, original or reproduction, whether or not claimed to be privileged or otherwise subject to exclusion from discovery, whether in the actual or constructive possession, custody or control of the defendant, including: letters correspondence, memoranda or transcripts of telephone or personal conversations, microfilm, microfiche, telegrams, books, magazines, newspapers, advertisements, periodicals, bulletins, circulars, brochures, pamphlets, statements, notices, advertising layouts, trade letters, press releases, reports, rules, regulations, directives, teletype or telefax messages, minutes or records of meetings, interoffice communications, financial statements, ledgers, books of account, proposals, prospectuses, offers, invoices, orders, receipts, working papers, desk calendars, appointment books, diaries, routing slips, time sheets, logs, movies, tapes (or visual or audio reproduction), records, drawings, blueprints, sketches, plans, graphs, charts, photographs, shipping papers, purchase orders, phonograph records, phono-records, data processing paper results, data printouts and computations (both in existence and stored in memory components), transcripts of oral statements or testimony, reports and/or summaries of interviews, reports and/or summaries of investigations, opinions or reports of consultants, forecasts, opinions of counsel, court papers and any and all other data compilations or information resources from which information can be obtained or translated, if necessary, through detection devices into reasonably usable form, or material similar to any "document" as used herein. "Document" as used herein also includes the original of any document in whatever form or medium it may exist, and all copies of each such document bearing, on any sheet or side thereof, any marks, including by way of illustration only and not by way of limitation, initials, stamped indicia, any comment or notation, or any character not a part of the original text, or any reproduction thereof.

4. The term "communication" means any contact, oral or

written, formal or informal, at any time or place, under any circumstances, in any manner, whereby a statement of any nature is transmitted or transferred, and shall include, without limitation, any documents containing, constituting reflecting, memorializing, referring or relating to any such contact.

5. The word "or" means and/or and should be read both ways so as to encompass both constructions and calls for documents to be produced responsive to both constructions.

6. The term "representative" refers to any employee, agent, attorney or accountant.

7. The term "person" means natural person, proprietorships, partnerships, groups, corporations, associations, societies, organizations, or government bodies or any other individual or entity.

8. The term "identify" when used in connection with a natural person means to set forth the full name, title, present business address and present business affiliation of said person.

9. The term "identify" when used in connection with a person which is a proprietorship, partnership, corporation, or other organization means to set forth the full name and present business address of that dealership, proprietorship, partnership, corporation, or other organization.

10. The term "identify" when used with reference to a document means to state the date and author (and, if different, the signer or signers), the addresses of the author(s), signer(s), or any individual(s) receiving copies, the type of document (e.g., letter, memorandum, chart), and its present or last known location or custodian.

11. The term "identify" when used with reference to an agreement, contract, understanding or communication means, in addition to Definition 10 above: (a) to state whether it was written or oral, to identify the parties thereto, the place where it was made or occurred, and the date or dates thereof; (b) to identify the parties thereto, the place where it was made or occurred, and the date or dates thereof; (c) to identify the persons who negotiated or had any role in suggesting, framing or drafting the terms of the agreement, contract or understanding or who participated therein; and (d) to state the substance of the communication, agreement, contract or understanding.

12. The term "identify" when used with reference to a meeting, incident, occurrence or conversation means to state its date, place and subjects covered, to identify its participants and to identify all documents reporting upon or otherwise recording or referring to anything that transpired at such meetings.

13. The term "the transaction" or "the transactions" or "account" or "accounts" when used herein without qualifications means the transactions and accounts between and among the Debtors and the named defendants in all related activities and agents or assigns of either party.

14. The term "Note" shall refer to the Mortgage Promissory Note executed by the plaintiffs in connection with the mortgage loan transaction that is the subject of this litigation.

15. The term "Mortgage" shall refer to the Document filed in the Records of the Probate Judge's Office for the County in which the Real Property that is the subject of this litigation is located which is alleged to secure one of the defendants' alleged lien against the Real Property.

16. The term "Real Property" shall refer to the Real Property and improvements that is the subject of this litigation.

17. The term "present" means up to and including the date of your final response to these interrogatories and requests for production of documents.

18. The term "relating to" or "relates to" means regarding, reflecting, discussing, describing, containing, identifying, analyzing, studying, reporting, commenting, evidencing, constituting, revealing, setting forth, considering, recommending, questioning, disputing contesting, correcting, construing, mentioning, associated with, referring to, alluding to, or pertaining to, in whole or in part.

19. The singular shall be construed to include the plural, and the plural shall be construed to include the singular.

20. The masculine includes the feminine, and the feminine includes the masculine.

21. The word "and" shall be construed to include the word "or," and the word "or" shall be construed to include the word "and."

22. The word "each" shall be construed to include the word "every," and the word "every" shall be construed to include the word "each."

23. The word "any" shall be construed to include the word "all," and the word "all" shall be construed to include the word "any."

II. INSTRUCTIONS

1. The time period for which production of documents and things requested shall be from the date of origination of the mortgage loan that is the subject of this litigation until the date of your responses unless otherwise specified.

2. Each of the following requests is continuing, and in the event that at any later date you obtain or discover any additional document responsive to any request, you shall submit such document promptly.

3. If an objection is made to any request herein, all documents covered by the request not subject to the objection should be produced. Similarly, if an objection is made to production of a document, the portion(s) of that document not subject to objection should be produced with the portion(s) objected to deleted and indicated clearly.

4. Each document is to be produced in its entirety even if only a portion of the document is related to the identified subject matter and without abbreviation, editing, or expurgation and including all appendices, tables, or other attachments. If an appendix, table, or other attachment is not presented with the original but is attached to a copy thereof or is otherwise available, it should be submitted and clearly marked to indicate the document to which it corresponds. With the exception of privileged material, no document or portion thereof should be masked or deleted in any manner. To the extent possible, documents should be produced in the same order and arrangement as in the file form which they are taken.

5. Unless otherwise requested, in lieu of producing original documents, you may produce photocopies, provided that you shall retain the original documents and produce them to the plaintiffs upon request. Further, copies of original documents may be submitted in lieu of originals only if they are true, correct, and complete copies of the original documents, and their submission constitutes a waiver of any claim as to the authenticity of the copy should it be necessary to introduce such copy into evidence in any legal proceeding. *Please provide color copies of any document originally produced in color or containing type, writing, or other*

marks in any color other than black.

6. Documents that may be responsive to more than one request need not be submitted more than once; however, such documents should be so identified.

7. All headings herein are included only for organization purposes and should not be construed as being part of any request, or as limiting any request in any manner.

III. PRIVILEGE

If any document would be required to be produced in response to any request except for the fact that a privilege against production is claimed, set forth for each such document:

1. Its date, title, type of document (memorandum, letter, e-mail, electronic communication, data file, data image, etc.), and length;

2. Its preparer, sender, addressee, recipient and anyone who received a copy of that document when it was originally disseminated;

3. A general description of its subject matter (without revealing the information as to which any privilege is claimed);

4. The exact grounds upon which the objection to production is based;

5. The identity of all persons, in addition to those identified as required by section 2 herein, known to you who have seen or had access to the document;

6. The identity of all parties who have had custody or possession of the document and at what periods of time; and

7. The identity of the person now in possession of the document.

IV. DOCUMENTS NO LONGER IN EXISTENCE OR NO LONGER UNDER YOUR POSSESSION, CUSTODY OR CONTROL

If any document, requested herein was at one time in existence and under your possession, custody or control but has since been lost, discarded or destroyed or has been removed from your possession, custody or control, then with respect to each such document:

1. Identify and describe such document by date, title and type of document;

2. State when each such document was most recently in your possession or subject to your control and what disposition was made of such document, including an identification of the person, if any, presently in possession or control of such document if such document has not been lost or destroyed;

3. Please identify all of your systems that contained at one time images of the originals of such documents, where such images are stored, how they are stored, and produce a copy of your document retention and document destruction policy;

4. Please state where you maintain copies of all documents in the event of a mass disaster and identify all documents at such location and how they are stored at such location;

5. State the name, title, and location of each party who conducted a search for any lost documents in this case and describe in detail the nature and extent of each search and produce all reports, findings or search results generated by said parties;

6. State the full name and address of the Master Document Custodian for the original loan documents in this case and produce all records related to such documents in the possession of the said Custodian and all documents, reports, or forms produced by said Custodian with respect to all of the documents related to the securitization of the mortgage note in this case;

7. State when any such lost document was transferred or destroyed, identify the person who transferred or destroyed such document and the persons who authorized or directed that the document be transferred or destroyed or having knowledge of its transfer or destruction and state the reason such document was transferred or destroyed; and

8. Identify all persons having knowledge of the contents of any lost or destroyed documents.

V. ORGANIZATION

Pursuant to the Alabama Rules of Civil Procedure it is requested that the documents produced be organized and labeled so as to correspond with the categories of this request for production.

VI. INTERROGATORIES

Question No. 1:

Do you agree that the pooling and servicing agreement dated September 1, 2005 is the agreement which created this trust? If your answer to the foregoing is in the negative please explain in detail how this trust was created including in your answer a statement of where, when and how the trust was formed and pursuant to what law was the trust formed.

Response:

Question No. 2:

Please state the name and address of the depositor to this Pooling and Servicing Agreement.

Response:

Question No. 3:

Please state the name and address of the master servicer to this Pooling and Servicing Agreement.

Response:

Question No. 4:

Please state the name and address of the trustee to this Pooling and Servicing Agreement.

Response:

Question No. 5:

Please state the custodian for this trust including their name, address and contact information.

Response:

Question No. 6:

Please state the name, address and contact information of the master servicer to this trust.

Response:

Question No. 7:

Please state the primary purpose for the formation of this trust.

Response:

Question No. 8:

Please state the cut off date for this trust.

Response:

Question No. 9:

Do you agree that this trust is formed and governed under the laws of the State of New York?

Response:

Question No. 10:

If you do not agree please state in detail every reason that you disagree and provide any documentation, evidence, or other explanatory materials in support of your position.

Response:

Question No. 11:

Please state the name and address of every person who has signed any document under oath for filing with the Internal Revenue Service or the Securities and Exchange Commission regarding this trust. For each such person identified please provide:

a) That person's name, address and contact information if they are employed by any party who executed the Pooling and Servicing Agreement.
b) If they are not employed by a party who executed the Pooling and Servicing Agreement please state the name of their employer at the time in which they executed the subject documents with the Internal Revenue Service and/or the Securities and Exchange Commission.

Response:

Question No. 12:

Please identify every attorney or law firm who provided an Opinion of Counsel to any party who executed the Pooling and Servicing Agreement for this Trust with respect to any action on behalf of this trust at any time since its formation with respect to any issue which the Pooling and Servicing Agreement requires any party to the agreement to obtain an Opinion of Counsel. This request should be interpreted as requesting:

a) The name of any attorney who provided an opinion of counsel;
b) The Firm who employed the attorney;
c) The last available contact information for the attorney in the possession of the respondent including name, address, phone number(s), facsimile numbers and email addresses.

Response:

Question No. 13:

Please produce every opinion of counsel received by any party to the Pooling and Servicing Agreement for this Trust in the possession of the Trust or reasonably available to the Trust through the parties to the Pooling and Servicing Agreement with respect to any matter involving any action on behalf of this trust at any time since its formation with respect to any issue which the Pooling and Servicing Agreement requires any party to the agreement to obtain an Opinion of Counsel.

Response:

Question No. 14:

Please identify every accountant or accounting firm who provided any Opinion as to the compliance with the REMIC provisions of the United States Tax Code to either the Trust or any Party to the Pooling and Servicing Agreement which formed the Trust at any time since the formation of the Trust. This request should be interpreted as requesting:

a) The name of any accountant who provided any opinion as referenced in the question;
b) The Firm who employed the accountant;
c) The last available contact information for the accountant in the possession of the respondent including the accountant's name, address, phone number(s), facsimile numbers and email addresses.

Response:

Question No. 15:

Please produce a copy of every opinion received from an Accountant or Accounting Firm as to the compliance with the REMIC provisions of the United States Tax Code to either the Trust or any Party to the Pooling and Servicing Agreement which formed the Trust at any time since the formation of the Trust.

Response:

Question No. 16:

Please Identify every "Certifying Officer" as that term is defined in the Pooling and Servicing Agreement, who has certified any act of the trust whether that officer is employed by the servicer, the trustee, the depositor, the originator, or any agent or employee of any of those parties. For each such officer please provide:

a) Their last known address and phone number as well as any other contact information available to the Trust or any party to the Trust Agreement (the PSA).
b) The complete employment file (excluding dates of birth and social security numbers) of each certifying officer.
c) List each act certified and the officer who certified the act and to whom the act was certified (i.e. the Internal Revenue Service, The SEC, etc.).
d) Provide a complete copy of each responsive certification.

Response:

Question No. 17:

Please produce a copy of the mortgage loan purchase agreement executed by each signatory to that agreement.

Response:

Question No. 18:

Please produce a copy of the mortgage note including any indorsements upon said promissory note as well as any tender and delivery receipts or other evidences of transfer and receipt as between the originator and any other party to the securitization agreement which allegedly ultimately resulted in the sale of this promissory note to this Trust. If there are any documents which purport to transfer the promissory note between the Originator and any other entity please provide the following information also:

a) The identity (including their name, last known address, last available contact information and employer and title at the time of the act described) of any person who executed any indorsement, allonge, transfer authorization or acknowledgement, bailment letter, delivery guarantee, delivery receipt, acknowledgement, bailee letter, or any other type of delivery confirmation.
b) The date upon which the document(s) requested was executed.
c) Any forms, resolutions, or grants of authority empowering the person executing the documents to undertake the transfer of the promissory notes on behalf of the entity transferring the promissory notes.

Response:

Question No. 19:

Please produce a complete copy of any prospectus or free writing prospectus filed with the SEC or prepared or produced on behalf of trust. This should also include any supplements to any prospectus so identified.

Response:

Question No. 20:

Please list the name of every seller as that term is defined by the trust Pooling and Servicing Agreement who has sold any mortgage loan to this trust.

Response:

Question No. 21:

Please state the start up day of this trust.

Response:

Question No. 22:

Please identify every person or entity who has served as the "tax matters person" for this trust include in your answer their name, address and last know contact information including phone numbers, fax numbers and any email addresses known or reasonably available to the respondent.

Response:

Question No. 23:

Please identify the individual or entity who has executed any Internal Revenue Service Form 1066, U. S. Real Estate Mortgage Investment Conduit income tax return, including Schedule Q thereto, as well as any other forms required under applicable tax law for this trust at any time since its inception or creation through the present day. This information should include the current or last known contact information including the name, address, phone or fax numbers and any email addresses known or reasonably available to the respondent for the person so identified.

Response:

Question No. 24:

Please produce any and all executed exhibits to the pooling and servicing agreement as part of your production of the pooling and servicing agreement in this case.

Response:

Question No. 25:

Please produce any correspondence or communication of any kind between any of the parties to the Pooling and Servicing Agreement regarding any matter in any way related to the trust, the trust agreement, or the oversight, maintenance and administration of the trust and its assets.

Response:

Question No. 26:

Please state whether or not there has been a servicing transfer with respect to this trust.

Response:

Question No. 27:

Please produce a full and complete copy of the mortgage file with respect to the Plaintiff's loan.

Response:

Question No. 28:

Please state the closing date for this trust.

Response:

Question No. 29:

Please identify any entity, individual or party who has an agreement of any kind, type or nature with the Trust for any

Response:

Question No. 30:

Please identify the NIMS Insurer for this Trust. This information should include the current or last known contact information including the name, address, phone or fax numbers and any email addresses known or reasonably available to the respondent for the person or entity so identified.

Response:

Question No. 31:

Please identify every form of insurance, overcollateralization, payment guarantee, swap, interest rate swap, credit enhancement or any other form of payment guarantee, protection against default, or derivative which in any manner insures, attempts to insure, guarantees or attempts to guarantee payments to the certificate holders of the Trust as set forth in the Pooling and Servicing Agreement or any agreement that is executed between the Trust and any other entity as a result of the creation of the trust.

Response:

Question No. 32:

For each item or agreement identified in the previous question please identify the parties to that agreement, produce an executed copy of the agreement and describe in plain English what the agreement addresses and the protection, guarantee or insurance provided by the agreement.

Response:

Question No. 33:

Identify all parties answering or assisting in providing answers to these interrogatories and request for production and for each such party include the current or last known contact information including the name, address, phone or fax numbers and any email addresses known or reasonably available to the respondent.

Response:

Question No. 34:

Please identify who is currently in possession of the promissory note that is the subject of this litigation and where said promissory note is physically located. Your identification should include the name, address, phone or fax numbers and any email addresses known or reasonably available to the respondent.

Response:

Question No. 35:

Identify all securitizations known to you to have been made by where the assets of the trust included home mortgage loans originated or purchased by Option One Mortgage Corporation at any time from the origination of the loan that is the subject of this litigation until the present day.

Response:

I.8.5 Motion to Dismiss Complaint for Lack of Standing

________________________)

IN THE COMMON PLEAS COURT OF OTTAWA COUNTY, OHIO CIVIL DIVISION

________________________)
Deutsche Bank Trust Company)
Americas, as Indenture Trustee)
for Saxon Asset Securities Trust)
20063)
Plaintiff,)
)
v.)
)
Christopher L. Homeowner, et)
al.)
Defendants)
________________________)

MOTION TO DISMISS OF DEFENDANTS CHRISTOPHER L. HOMEOWNER AND EMILYE L. HOMEOWNER

Defendants Christopher L. Homeowner and Emilye L. Homeowner, by and through counsel, move this Court to dismiss the Complaint in Foreclosure. When Plaintiff filed its Complaint in Foreclosure, it had not acquired the necessary rights in the Note and Mortgage at issue. Thus, for the second time in six months, a subsidiary of Deutsche Bank has filed a foreclosure against Mr. and Mrs. Homeowner prior to obtaining the necessary rights in the Note and Mortgage at issue. As a result, Plaintiff was not a real party in interest pursuant to Civ. R. 17(A), did not have standing to file its Complaint in Foreclosure, and had no ability to invoke the jurisdiction of this Court.

MEMORANDUM IN SUPPORT
Statement of Facts

Defendants Christopher L. Homeowner and Emilye L. Homeowner (collectively "Mr. and Mrs. Homeowner") have owned the property located at [Address] in Port Clinton since 2002.

This is the second foreclosure filing against Mr. and Mrs. Homeowner in the past six months. The first case was dismissed by this Court, sua sponte, on April 14, 2009 because the plaintiff—also a subsidiary of Deutsche Bank that was represented by The Law Offices of John D. Clunk—was unable to follow this Court's requirement that "a foreclosure plaintiff must provide documentation that it is the owner and holder of the note and mortgage as of the date the foreclosure action is filed." See Deutsche Bank National Trust Co. v. [Homeowner], Case No. 08-CV-712E, "Judgment Entry," attached as Exhibit A.

In this case, Plaintiff Deutsche Bank Trust Company Americas, as Indenture Trustee for Saxon Asset Securities Trust 2006-3 is seeking to foreclosure on the home owned by Mr. and Mrs. Homeowner. Plaintiff filed its Complaint in Foreclosure on May 5, 2009. On May 11, 2009, six days after filing its Complaint in Foreclosure, Deutsche Bank National Trust Company, as Trustee for Saxon Asset Securities Trust 2006-3 (the plaintiff in the 2008 foreclosure case), assigned the Note and Mortgage to Plaintiff Deutsche Bank Trust Company Americas, as Indenture Trustee for Saxon Asset Securities Trust 2006-3 ("hereinafter "Deutsche Bank Americas"). See Assignment of Note and Mortgage, attached as Exhibit B. On May 18, 2009, this Court ordered, sua sponte, for Plaintiff to show how it acquired its rights in the property. On June 8, 2009, Plaintiffs filed its "Notice of Compliance with Court Order Dated May 18, 2009," which included the December 19, 2008 assignment and the May 11, 2009 assignment. See Exhibits B and C of "Plaintiff's Notice of Compliance with Court Order Dated May 18, 2009." These documents show that Plaintiff received its rights in the Note and Mortgage on May 11, 2009, six days after it filed this action.

Law and Argument

I. This Court's Recent Ruling in a Previous Foreclosure Action Against Defendants Requires Dismissal in the Present Action

The legal issue over whether a foreclosing party can acquire the note and mortgage after filing a foreclosure action was addressed by this Court in the previous foreclosure action against the Homeowners. In dismissing this case, this Court made the law clear:

> A foreclosure plaintiff . . . especially one who is not identified on the note and/or mortgage at issue, must attach to its complaint documentation demonstrating that it is the owner and holder of the note and mortgage upon which suit is filed. In other words, a foreclosure plaintiff must provide documentation that it is the owner and holder of the note and mortgage as of the date the foreclosure action is filed.

Deutsche Bank National Trust Co. v. [Homeowner], Case No. 08-CV-712E, "Judgment Entry," attached as Exhibit A (citations omitted) (hereinafter "2008 Foreclosure Case"). The legal issues in the 2008 Foreclosure Case and the present case are identical. Since a foreclosing party has once again failed to meet this basic requirement prior to filing a foreclosure against Mr. and Mrs. Homeowner, the Homeowners ask that this Court dismiss this action.

II. Plaintiff Was Not a Real Party in Interest at the Time the Complaint Was Filed; Therefore, the Complaint Must Be Dismissed

The Complaint in Foreclosure made several statements involving Plaintiff's alleged rights in the Note and Mortgage at issue. Plaintiff stated that it "is due upon a certain promissory note the sum of $63,365.78." Complaint in Foreclosure, ¶ 1. Plaintiff "has declared said debt to be immediately due and payable." Id. Further, Plaintiff stated that it "is entitled to foreclosure of said mortgage." Complaint in Foreclosure, ¶ 3.

A simple analysis of these documents shows that Plaintiff's assertions as to its rights in the Note and Mortgage, as stated in the

Complaint in Foreclosure, are false. On May 11, 2009, six days *after* Plaintiff filed its Complaint in Foreclosure, Plaintiff was assigned the Note and Mortgage at issue (attached as "Exhibit B"). Thus, when Plaintiff filed its Complaint in Foreclosure, it had no legal rights in the Note or Mortgage.

Besides this Court's ruling in the 2008 Foreclosure Case, there are several other recent Ohio cases with very similar facts in which the foreclosing plaintiff's case was dismissed. First, the First Appellate District of Ohio upheld a decision by the trial court dismissing the foreclosure complaint because the plaintiff could not show that it was assigned the note and mortgage prior to the filing of the complaint. Wells Fargo Bank v. Byrd (1st App. Dist. Hamilton Cty.), 2008 Ohio 4603 (attached as "Appendix A"). In Byrd, the court held that "the trial court properly dismissed the foreclosure complaint filed by [plaintiff] in this case because, at the time the complaint was filed, [plaintiff] did not own the mortgage that was the basis for the suit." Id at ¶23. The holding in Byrd is clear: you cannot file a foreclosure suit if you do not own the mortgage at the time the complaint was filed and acquiring the mortgage by assignment after the suit was filed does not cure the underlying jurisdictional defect. Id at ¶23.

In Wells Fargo Bank v. Heiskell, the Court of Common Pleas in Franklin County dismissed the action because the foreclosing plaintiff was not a real party in interest at the time it filed the foreclosure complaint. Case No. 02CVE-10-11149, January 28, 2003 (attached as "Appendix B"). In Heiskell, the court reasoned,

> [A]t the time Plaintiff filed the above-captioned matter it was not the real party in interest because it was not the holder of the promissory note and mortgage. As a result, the Court finds that at the time the above-captioned matter was commenced Plaintiff did not have a cause of action against Defendant.

Id. at 2.

Other courts in Ohio have held that when a plaintiff files an action on a debt it does not own, even if it later obtains the mortgage, dismissal is appropriate. In DLJ Mortgage Capital Inc. v. Bazzy, the Court of Common Pleas in Montgomery County granted the defendant's motion to dismiss because the foreclosing plaintiff was assigned the mortgage after it filed the complaint. Case No. 02-4316, May 16, 2003 (attached as "Appendix C"). The assignment to plaintiff was made after the Complaint was filed but before the defendant's objection was raised. Id at 5. In dismissing the foreclosure case based on this late assignment, the court found that the plaintiff "failed to establish that it is a real party in interest as required under Civ. R. 17(A), and as such, lacks standing to invoke the jurisdiction of this Court." The court continued by stating,

> This Court refuses to apply Civ. R. 17(A) in a way that would encourage—much less reward—what can be at best deemed gross inaccuracies within the Complaint. . . . . This Court refuses to allow a party to "correct" a clearly false pleading by relying on Civ. R. 17(A).

Id.

In Manufacturer's Trader's Trust v. White, the Court of Common Pleas in Franklin County dismissed the action on similar grounds. In reaching its decision, the court stated, "The uncontradicted evidence is that, at the time of filling of the complaint, Plaintiff was not the real party in interest and therefore had no standing to bring the action. The Court therefore concludes that dismissal is proper." Case No. 02CV-7179, April 17, 2003, page 2 (attached as "Appendix D"), citing O'Brien v. University Tenant's Union, Inc. (1975), 42 Ohio St. 2d 242.

In Deutsche Bank Trust Co. v. Wright, a case with very similar facts, "Plaintiff filed its Complaint before formal assignment of the interest." Case No. G-4801-CI-0200802217-000, Nov. 18, 2008, page 3 (attached as "Appendix E"). The Court of Common Pleas in Lucas County dismissed this case because Plaintiff "failed to demonstrate it is the real party in interest" based on Civ. R. 17(A). Id at 3-4.

Finally, in Wells Fargo Bank, N.A. v. Homeowner, another case with similar facts, the Court of Common Pleas in Lucas County dismissed the case because "Plaintiff, Wells Fargo Bank, N.A. was not a real party in interest at the time the Complaint in Foreclosure was filed and therefore lacked standing and capacity to bring this action." Case. No. G-4801-CI-0200806622-000, Feb. 26, 2008, (attached as "Appendix F").

These cases make it clear that a foreclosure complaint should be dismissed if the plaintiff does not own the note and mortgage at the time it filed the complaint. In the present case, Plaintiff—based on documents it filed in this case—did not own the Note and Mortgage when it filed its Complaint in Foreclosure. As a result, this Court should dismiss this action.

III. This Case Should Be Dismissed Because Plaintiff Lacks Standing to File its Complaint

The doctrine of standing operates to ensure actual adversity between the plaintiff and defendant. To have standing, a plaintiff must establish (1) an injury-in-fact; (2) caused by the defendant's conduct; and (3) redressability via a favorable decision. Bourke v. Carnahan (10th Dist. Franklin Cty. 2005), 163 Ohio App. 3d 818, ¶10.

Standing is a threshold issue that courts must decide prior to addressing the merits of a claim. Cuyahoga County Bd. of Comm'rs v. State of Ohio (2006), 112 Ohio St. 3d 59, ¶22. "[B]efore an Ohio court can consider the merits of a legal claim, the person seeking relief must establish standing to sue." Ohio Contractors Assn. v. Bicking (1994), 71 Ohio St. 3d 318, 320. Thus, the party seeking relief bears the burden of establishing its standing. Id.

In a recent case with similar facts and upon a similar motion to dismiss, the Court of Common Pleas in Lucas County recently dismissed the foreclosure action. In Wells Fargo Bank, N.A. v. Hissa, the mortgage was not assigned until three days after the foreclosure complaint was filed. In dismissing this case, this Court stated that the foreclosing plaintiff "cannot cure its lack of standing by subsequently obtaining an interest in the mortgage." Case No. CI 08-6993, February 25, 2009 (attached as "Appendix G").

Further, the appellate court in Byrd addressed the standing issue, holding, "in a foreclosure action, a bank that was not the mortgagee when suit was filed cannot cure its lack of standing by subsequently obtaining an interest in the mortgage." Id at ¶16.

Here, similar to Hissa and Byrd, Plaintiff lacks standing because, when it filed its Complaint, it was not the holder of both the Note and Mortgage at issue. Plaintiff is not named in either instrument attached to the Complaint, and there are no assignments attached to the Complaint or any subsequent filings that were timely executed and that result in valid assignment of both the Note and Mortgage to Plaintiff prior to the filing of this action. Thus, on the face of the Complaint, Plaintiff lacks standing to bring or maintain this case.[15] See Byrd at ¶16. See also In re Foreclosure Cases (N.D. Ohio Oct. 31, 2007), Case No. 1:07CV2282 et al, 2007 U.S. Dist. Lexis 840112 (attached as "Appendix H"); In re Foreclosure Cases (S.D. Ohio Nov. 15, 2007), 521 F. Supp. 2d 650.[16] Additionally, a plaintiff in a foreclosure action cannot cure its lack of standing by subsequently obtaining an interest in the mortgage. Byrd at ¶16; Hissa at 2. Thus, since Plaintiff had no standing to bring this action, this case should be dismissed.

IV. This Court Does Not Have Jurisdiction to Hear This Case Because Plaintiff Cannot Establish the Existence of an Actual Controversy

The Ohio Constitution provides, "The courts of common pleas and divisions thereof shall have such original jurisdiction over all justiciable matters . . . as may be provided by law." Ohio Const. Art. IV, § 4(B) (emphasis added). Accordingly, a prerequisite to this Court's jurisdiction is the existence of a "justiciable matter."

As stated above in Section I, supra, Plaintiff had no legal interest in the Note and Mortgage at the time it filed the Complaint. Absent an actual controversy, there is no justiciable matter sufficient to invoke this Court's jurisdiction. In State ex rel. Barclays Bank PLC v. Court of Common Pleas of Hamilton County, the Supreme Court held, "the presence of a disagreement, however sharp and acrimonious it may be, is insufficient to create an actual controversy if the parties to the action do not have adverse legal interests." State ex rel. Barclays Bank PLC v. Court of Common Pleas of Hamilton County (1996), 74 Ohio St. 3d 536. In that case, the investors failed to name the beneficiary as a defendant and thus there was no actual controversy between the parties and therefore no jurisdiction. Id at 542-543.

Barclays establishes that when a plaintiff sues the wrong party, the court lacks jurisdiction because there is no actual controversy between the parties. Just the same, when the wrong plaintiff brings an action, no actual controversy exists. Because jurisdiction addresses a court's power to address a case, the proper remedy when a court lacks jurisdiction is to dismiss the complaint. Civ. R. 12(H)(3). The issue of jurisdiction cannot be waived, and therefore may be raised at any time. Cleveland Elec. Illum. Co. v. Lake County Bd. of Revision (2002), 96 Ohio St. 3d 165, ¶16; H.R. Options, Inc. v. Zaino (2004), 100 Ohio St. 3d 373, ¶8. In addition, courts may address the issue of jurisdiction sua sponte. Rinehart v. Dillard (10th Dist. Franklin Cty. 2007), 2007 Ohio 4310, ¶17.

In Byrd, supra, the court addressed this jurisdictional issue in detail. The court initially discussed the real party in interest, jurisdictional, and standing issues concurrently, stating, "A party lacks standing to invoke the jurisdiction of a court unless he has, in an individual or a representative capacity, some real interest in the subject matter of the action." Id at ¶9. The court concluded, "Acquiring the mortgage by assignment after the suit was commenced could not have cured the jurisdictional defect arising from the fact that, at the time the lawsuit was filed, [Plaintiff] Wells Fargo had no claim against the Byrds." Id at ¶23.

Because Plaintiff lacks standing in this case, the constitutional jurisdictional prerequisite of an actual controversy is also lacking. Accordingly, under Article IV, Section 4(B) of the Ohio Constitution, this Court lacks jurisdiction of this case and the case should be dismissed pursuant to Civ. R. 12(H)(3).

V. Conclusion

The pattern exhibited by Deutsche Bank is troubling. For the second time in six months, a subsidiary of Deutsche Bank has filed a foreclosure against Mr. and Mrs. Homeowner via counsel from The Law Offices of John D. Clunk. For the second time in six months, the party attempting to foreclosure on Mr. and Mrs. Homeowner did not acquire its rights in the Note and Mortgage until after it filed the foreclosure action.

Because Plaintiff was not assigned any rights in the Note or Mortgage until after it commenced this action, Plaintiff was not a real party in interest at the time it filed the Complaint, had no standing to file its Complaint, and did not have the ability to invoke the jurisdiction of this Court. For this and all of the above reasons, Plaintiff's Complaint must be dismissed.

REQUEST FOR RELIEF

WHEREFORE, for the reasons stated above, Defendants request this Court to dismiss Plaintiff's Complaint with prejudice due to a second instance in which a subsidiary of Deutsche Bank failed to show that is was a real party in interest when it filed a foreclosure action against Defendants; alternatively dismiss Plaintiff's Complaint with prejudice due to Plaintiff's failure to show that it is a real party in interest; alternatively dismiss Plaintiff's Complaint with prejudice due to Plaintiff's failure to establish standing; or alternatively dismiss Plaintiff's Complaint due to a lack of jurisdiction over the matter.

Respectfully submitted,
[Attorney for Defendants]
[Date]

---

15 The fact that plaintiff brought this action when it had no right to do so, and that plaintiff would present such documents to a court to create the illusion of standing, is not surprising for a number of reasons. Katherine Porter, Associate Professor of Law at the University of Iowa, recently completed a study on behalf of the National Conference of Bankruptcy Judges based on original data in 1700 chapter 13 bankruptcy cases. As Professor Porter argues, as a matter of equity as well as equal protection of the law, plaintiff and others seeking to foreclose mortgages should not be allowed to benefit from participation in this pervasive disregard for the requirements of the civil rules and local rules of court that results in the widespread gross mistake and disregard of the law. Porter, Katherine M., *Misbehavior and Mistake in Bankruptcy Mortgage Claims*, 87 Tex. L. Rev. 121 (2008), *available at* http://papers.ssrn.com/sol3/papers.cfm?abstract_id=1027961.

16 While neither these decisions nor the Federal Rules of Civil Procedure are binding, these cases from Ohio's federal courts are insightful into the issues surrounding whether a foreclosing party is a real party in interest. In addition, this Court cited the *In re Foreclosure Cases* decision in its Judgment Entry from the 2008 Foreclosure Case.

I.9 Action Against Mortgage Servicer for an Accounting and for Violation of RESPA and FDCPA

I.9.1 Complaint

UNITED STATES DISTRICT COURT
EASTERN DISTRICT OF PENNSYLVANIA

Andrea Consumer,
Plaintiff

v.

LINTON LOAN SERVICING LP

COMPLAINT

1. This is an action by a low-income homeowner against a mortgage servicing company seeking a proper accounting of her mortgage and statutory damages under the Fair Debt Collection Practices Act and the Real Estate Settlement Procedures Act.

2. Jurisdiction over this matter is conferred upon this Court by 12 U.S.C. 2614, 15 U.S.C. 1692 and 28 U.S.C. 1331. The court has supplemental jurisdiction over her state law claims.

3. Venue lies in this judicial district in that the events which gave rise to this claim occurred here and the property which is the subject of the action is situated within this district.

4. Plaintiff Mrs. Consumer is a natural person residing at [Address].

5. The Defendant, Linton Loan Servicing, LP ("Linton"), is a corporation with its principal offices at 500 West Central Drive, Houston Texas. Linton is the servicing agent for the holder of Mrs. Consumer's mortgage. The mortgage on Mrs. Consumer's home is held by WFM Bank Minnesota, NA as the trustee for an investor-owned trust that holds a large pool of mortgage loans sold by Owens Federal Savings Bank.

6. Andrea Consumer and her husband, Joe Consumer, purchased their home in North Philadelphia in 1984.

7. In December 1998 Mr. and Mrs. Consumer refinanced their mortgage and entered into a loan with Pier, Inc., trading as Sunnyside Mortgage Company. The mortgage was later sold to Owens Federal Savings Bank, who in turn sold it to WFM Bank of Minnesota, trustee. Owens continued to service the mortgage.

8. Mrs. Consumer eventually filed a civil suit against Owens, seeking to rescind the 1998 loan and seeking other relief.

9. The civil suit against Owens was settled by a December 2000 settlement and loan modification agreement that, among other things, called for Owens to reduce the loan principal to $25,984 and the interest rate to 8%, and for Mrs. Consumer to make monthly payments of principal and interest of $190.66. A copy of the December 2000 loan modification agreement is attached as Exhibit "A."

10. At some time on or about April 29, 2002 the servicing of the mortgage loan was transferred from Owens Federal Savings Bank to Defendant Linton.

11. Shortly after the servicing transfer, Linton demanded that Mrs. Consumer make monthly payments of $394.79, which was the payment prior to the December 2000 modification.

12. On May 21, 2002, Mrs. Consumer, through her lawyer, reminded Linton of the terms of the loan modification, including the $190.66 payment amount, enclosed another copy of the modification agreement, and asked Linton to correct Mrs. Consumer's account records accordingly.

13. Nevertheless, Linton failed and refused to revise its account records to reflect the loan modification agreement.

14. On or about July 21, 2004 Linton mailed a statement to Mrs. Consumer incorrectly asserting that the mortgage payments were delinquent.

15. On or about August 10, 2004 Mrs. Consumer wrote to Linton disputing the alleged delinquency and asking Linton to correct its account records to reflect that her payments of $190.66 were paid up to date.

16. On August 18, 2004 Linton acknowledged Mrs. Consumer's written request for account information and adjustments. On or about October 8, 2004, Linton wrote to Mrs. Consumer acknowledging the loan modification and asserting that Linton's records had been updated to reflect the loan modification. The same letter stated that Mrs. Consumer's payment was in fact $190.66, and was due for October 1, 2004, in other words, her payments were current.

17. Mrs. Consumer subsequently received a letter dated September 22, 2004, asserting that she had an escrow deficit of $5285.17, and that effective November 1, 2004 her mortgage payment would increase to 455.8 (sic).

18. At about the same time in September 2004 Mrs. Consumer received her monthly statement dated September 15, 2004 showing the amount due by October 1 as $190.66. This statement also, however, reflected an escrow deficit of $5,285.17 and "other fees due" of $40,927.12. No explanation was provided for the escrow deficit or the other fees.

19. In November, 2004, Mrs. Consumer received a letter from Linton asserting that her loan was past due for November and December, 2004, and that the total due was $1461. No explanation was provided for this curious arithmetic. Meanwhile Mrs. Consumer continued sending the $190.66 monthly payments to Linton.

20. In December 2004 Mrs. Consumer received her monthly statement dated December 15 which called for a current payment amount of $666.96, and a total amount due by January 1 2005 of $2,118.43. The "other fees due" had increased slightly to $40,936.12.

21. Mrs. Consumer received another letter from Linton dated January 5, 2005 asserting that she owed three payments, and must send $2,127.96 "today." This amount was apparently calculated on the same basis as the December statement amount, with the January 17 late fee added in advance. A copy of the January 5 letter is attached as Exhibit "B." This letter also falsely stated or implied that foreclosure was imminent and could begin "immediately" or "today" if payment was not made.

22. Also dated January 5, 2005 were two additional letters sent by Linton. One, entitled "Notice of Default and Intent to Accelerate," demanded $2,127.96, and stated that after 45 days Linton could accelerate the mortgage balance and foreclose the property. This letter is attached as Exhibit "C."

23. The other January 5, 2005 letter, entitled "Appendix A," is similar to the notice required by Pennsylvania law prior to fore-

closure. This letter is attached as Exhibit "D."

24. Exhibit D says that the monthly payments due were in the amount of $455.80 each, contradicting the statements calling for $666.96. Exhibit D also contains mathematically inconsistent amounts needed to be paid by Mrs. Consumer, on page three. The letter asserts that three payments of $455.80 are due, plus $19.06 in late charges and $319.18 in deferred late charges. These amounts total $1705.64. However the total amount demanded is $2,127.96.

25. Mrs. Consumer received another letter dated January 27, 2005, purporting to respond to her attorney's written request for account information. Exhibit "E." The January 27 letter states that the payment amount is $666.96 effective October 1, and is attributable to advances for insurance and taxes. The letter includes an escrow analysis that makes reference to an annual payment of $417.39 for insurance, but does not explain the escrow deficit in excess of $5,000.

26. It is mathematically impossible for annual insurance payments of $417.39 from 2002 to 2004 to accumulate to a deficit of $5,000. Mrs. Consumer pays her own real estate taxes, which are about $500 per year. Even if Linton had paid the taxes from 2002 through 2004, that would account only for $1,500 of the asserted escrow advances.

27. The January 27 letter also includes a payment history, but only from September 2004 through December 2004. The history printout included is incomprehensible, does not identify transactions as payments, advances or charges, does not begin to address the questions and concerns expressed by Mrs. Consumer and her attorney, and is completely unresponsive to her qualified written requests, which asked for an explanation of the $5,000 escrow deficit.

28. On or about May 13, 2005 Linton, through its attorneys Utrech Law Office, P.C., mailed a "Reinstatement Quote" to Mrs. Consumer. The May 13, 2005 reinstatement is attached as Exhibit "F." The total amount claimed to be due is shown as $47,103.60. This document calls for monthly payments of $362.61, an amount that does not correspond to the $190.66 payment for principal and interest, the $666.96 payment shown on the December statement, or the $455.80 referred to on Exhibit D.

29. Exhibit E includes a demand for payment for numerous inspections of the property, despite the fact that Mrs. Consumer has been in constant communication with Linton, has a working telephone, and Linton has no basis to believe there is any danger of the property being abandoned.

30. Exhibit E includes a demand for $400 for a BPO, that is, a broker price opinion. This amount is not properly chargeable to Mrs. Consumer under the contract or Pennsylvania law.

31. Having no way to determine the correct amount due, Mrs. Consumer sent $1,400 to Linton on May 6, 2005 (enough to cover the principal and interest payments due from November 2004 through May 2005) in an effort to show her good faith and desire to maintain her mortgage payments.

32. Linton has, for the past two years, provided Mrs. Consumer with inconsistent, incomprehensible statements and correspondence and has made it impossible for her to maintain her monthly mortgage payments. To the extent Linton has made advances for taxes and insurance Linton has failed to identify the amounts advanced in a clear and simple manner and to establish a reasonable plan for Mrs. Consumer to repay those amounts.

33. Mrs. Consumer has suffered severe emotional distress and anxiety as a result of Linton's conduct, and has expended money to travel to and from her attorney's office and to copy documents in her vain efforts to resolve this account dispute.

COUNT I—FAIR DEBT COLLECTION PRACTICES ACT

34. Linton was a debt collector within the meaning of the Fair Debt Collection Practices Act (FDCPA), 15 U.S.C. 1692a, at the time it became the servicing agent for Mrs. Consumer's loan, in that it regularly collects debts owed to another, and the debt was asserted by Linton to be contractually in default at the time it became the servicer of the debt.

35. Each of the letters described above incorrectly stated the amount and the status of Mrs. Consumer's debt.

36. Linton failed to provide verification of the alleged debt to Mrs. Consumer in response to her timely written request for such written verification.

37. Due to the repeated and continuing violations of the FDCPA, Mrs. Consumer is entitled to actual and statutory damages under 15. U.S.C. 1692k.

COUNT II—RESPA

38. Linton is a servicer of a federally related mortgage loan within the meaning of the Real Estate Settlement Procedures Act (RESPA), 12 U.S.C. § 2605.

39. Each of Mrs. Consumer's (and her attorney's) written requests for information about her account and correction of Linton's numerous errors were "qualified written requests" within the meaning of RESPA.

40. Linton failed to respond in a proper and timely way to Mrs. Consumer's "qualified written requests" for information about, and corrections to, her mortgage account, in violation of 12 U.S.C. § 2605(e).

COUNT III—PENNSYLVANIA ACT 6 of 1974

41. Mrs. Consumer's mortgage is a "residential mortgage obligation" covered by Pennsylvania Act 6 of 1974, 41 Pa. Stat. 101-605.

42. Linton has repeatedly failed to provide Mrs. Consumer with an accurate notice of the amount required to cure her mortgage default, as required by 41 P.S. 403, and has improperly demanded payment of improper amounts and has thwarted her right to cure her default, under 41 P.S. 404, and has applied some of her payments to amounts not due under her mortgage and Act 6.

WHEREFORE, Plaintiff requests judgment in her favor and against Linton for three times the amount of the illegal charges.

COUNT IV—PENNSYLVANIA CONSUMER PROTECTION LAW

43. Linton's conduct described above constituted unfair and deceptive acts and practices, as defined by 73 Pa. Stat. § 201-2(4).

44. Mrs. Consumer has suffered an ascertainable loss of money as a result of Linton's unfair and deceptive practices.

WHEREFORE, Plaintiff requests that the court enter judgment in her favor and against defendants, for a proper accounting and application of her mortgage payments and for actual, statutory, treble and/or punitive damages, and attorney's fees and costs, along with any other and further relief as the court deems just and proper.

Attorney for Plaintiff

I.9.2 Plaintiffs Proposed Findings of Fact and Conclusions of Law

UNITED STATES DISTRICT COURT
EASTERN DISTRICT OF PENNSYLVANIA

Andrea Consumer,
Plaintiff
v.
LINTON LOAN SERVICING LP

PLAINTIFF'S PROPOSED FINDINGS OF FACT AND CONCLUSIONS OF LAW

FINDINGS OF FACT

1. This is an action by a low-income homeowner against a mortgage servicing company seeking an accounting of her mortgage and statutory damages under the Fair Debt Collection Practices Act and the Real Estate Settlement Procedures Act and state law.

2. Plaintiff Andrea Consumer is a natural person residing at [Address].

3. The Defendant, Linton Loan Servicing, LP ("Linton"), is a corporation with its principal offices at 500 West Central Drive, Houston Texas. Linton is the servicing agent for the holder of Ms. Consumer's mortgage. The mortgage on Ms. Consumer's home is held by WFM Bank Minnesota, NA as the trustee for an investor-owned trust that holds a large pool of mortgage loans.

4. Andrea Consumer and her husband, William Consumer, purchased their home in North Philadelphia in 1984.

5. In December 1998 Mr. and Mrs. Consumer refinanced their mortgage and entered into a loan with Pier, Inc., trading as Sunnyside Mortgage Company. The mortgage was later sold to Owens Federal Savings Bank, who in turn sold it to WFM Bank of Minnesota, trustee. Owens continued to service the mortgage.

6. Mrs. Consumer eventually filed a civil suit against Owens, seeking to rescind the 1998 loan and seeking other relief.

7. The civil suit against Owens was settled by a December 2000 settlement and loan modification agreement ("the 2000 modification") that, among other things, called for Owens to reduce the loan principal to $25,984 and the interest rate to 8%, and for Mrs. Consumer to make monthly payments of principal and interest of $190.66. Exhibit 1.

8. On April 29, 2002 the servicing of the mortgage loan was transferred from Owens Federal Savings Bank to Defendant Linton. Exhibit 2.

9. For a period of 29 months, from April 29, 2002, through at least September 2004, Linton failed and refused to adjust its records to reflect the 2000 modification, and as a result continued demanding monthly payments ranging from $343 to $666 or more from Mrs. Consumer, contrary to the terms of the modification. As a result Mrs. Consumer received dozens of letters, account statements and telephone calls from Linton that completely misrepresented the amounts she owed.

10. Linton appears to have corrected the loan principal and interest rate by the end of September 2004. Exhibit 8, 9. However, Linton continued demanding repayment by Mrs. Consumer of legal fees incurred by Owens prior to the 2000 modification, contrary to the terms of the modification agreement. (Exhibit 3, entry dated 10/21/2004).

11. On May 9, 2002, Linton sent Ms. Consumer a letter demanding that Mrs. Consumer make monthly payments of $394.79, which was the payment prior to the 2000 modification, and asserting that she was past due for payments since September 2000. Exhibit 2.

12. On May 21, 2002, Mrs. Consumer, through her lawyer, faxed a letter to Linton calling attention to the terms of the loan modification, including the $190.66 payment amount, enclosing another copy of the 2000 modification agreement, and asking Linton to correct Mrs. Consumer's account records accordingly. These documents were received on the same day by Linton. Exhibit 1.

13. On October 25, 2002 Linton mailed a "adjustable rate mortgage loan adjustment notice" asserting that the principal balance was $33,126.86 and the new monthly payment would be $343.74, based on an interest rate of 11.875%, considerably in excess of the amounts provided for in the 2000 modification. Exhibit 4.

14. Linton also mailed rate adjustment notice letters to Mrs. Consumer on April 30, 2003, October 24, 2003, and April 26, 2004, each of which incorrectly stated that Mrs. Consumer's mortgage bore an adjustable interest rate based on the original Note, instead of the fixed 8% rate called for in the 2000 modification. Exhibit 3.

15. Linton mailed a monthly billing statement on April 14, 2004, May 14, 2004, June 14, 2004, July 15, 2004, August 13, 2004, and September 15, 2004, none of which reflected the lower interest rate and payment provided for in the 2000 modification. See Exhibit 3, entries for corresponding dates.

16. On or about August 10, 2004 Mrs. Consumer wrote to Linton disputing the alleged delinquency and asking Linton to correct its account records to reflect that her payments were to be $190.66, and not $343.74 (or whatever amounts Linton was demanding based on the adjustable rate Note.) Exhibit 5.

17. On August 18, 2004 Linton acknowledged Mrs. Consumer's written request for account information and adjustments. Exhibit 6.

18. On September 3, 2004 and again on September 16, 2004, Linton wrote to Mrs. Consumer acknowledging the loan modification and asserting that Linton's records had been updated to reflect the loan modification. The September 16 letter stated that Mrs. Consumer's payment was in fact $190.66, and was due for October 1, 2004, in other words, her payments were current. Exhibits 8, 9.

19. However, Mrs. Consumer then received a letter dated September 22, 2004, asserting that she had an escrow deficit of $5285.17, and that effective November 1, 2004 her mortgage payment would increase to 455.8 (sic). Exhibit 11.

20. The September 22, 2004 letter was incorrect. As of that date, Linton had made the following payments for taxes and insurance on Mrs. Consumer's property:

a. $528.66 insurance premium September 5, 2002
b. $417.61 insurance premium May 28, 2003
c. $417.39 insurance premium May 10, 2004
d. $2,965.28 real estate taxes paid on January 29, 2004 [nb]
Total:$4,328.94 (Defendant's Exhibit D15)

21. At about the same time in September 2004 Mrs. Consumer received her monthly statement dated September 15, 2004 showing the amount due by October 1 as $190.66. This statement also, however, reflected an escrow deficit of $5,285.17 and "other fees due" of $40,927.12. No explanation was provided for the escrow deficit or the other fees. Exhibit 12.

22. On December 6, 2004 Linton sent Mrs. Consumer a letter saying she was past due for two months, and owed a total of $1,451.47. Exhibit 13. This was clearly inconsistent with the September notices referring to a payment of $455 to recover the tax and insurance advances.

23. Also in December 2004 Mrs. Consumer received her monthly statement dated December 15 which called for a current payment amount of $666.96, and a total amount due by January 1 2005 of $2,118.43. The "other fees due" had increased slightly to $40,936.12. Exhibit 14.

24. Mrs. Consumer received another letter from Linton dated January 5, 2005 asserting that she owed three payments, and must send $2,127.96 "today." Exhibit 15. This amount was apparently calculated on the same basis as the December statement amount, with the January 17 late fee added in advance. Exhibit 15 also falsely stated or implied that foreclosure was imminent and could begin "immediately" or "today" if payment was not made. Pennsylvania law requires a 30-day notice prior to foreclosure, and also prohibits foreclosure for up to 90 days if a homeowner applies for emergency mortgage assistance. 41 Pa. Stat. § 403, 35 Pa. Stat. § 1680.403c.

25. Also dated January 5, 2005 were two additional letters sent by Linton. One, entitled "Notice of Default and Intent to Accelerate," demanded $2,127.96, and stated that after 45 days Linton could accelerate the mortgage balance and foreclose the property. Exhibit 16.

26. The other January 5, 2005 letter, entitled "Appendix A," is similar to the notice required by Pennsylvania law prior to foreclosure. Exhibit 17.

27. Exhibit 17 says that the monthly payments due were in the amount of $455.80 each, contradicting the statements calling for $666.96. Exhibit 17 also contains mathematically inconsistent amounts needed to be paid by Mrs. Consumer, on page three. The letter asserts that three payments of $455.80 are due, plus $19.06 in late charges and $319.18 in deferred late charges. These amounts total $1705.64. However the total amount demanded is $2,127.96.

28. Although Exhibit 17 demands $319.18 in deferred late charges, other letters sent by Linton (Exhibits 8 and 19) state or suggest that Linton was waiving the late charges.

29. Mrs. Consumer received another letter dated January 27, 2005, purporting to respond to her attorney's written request for account information. Exhibit 19. The January 27 letter states that the payment amount is $666.96 effective October 1, and is attributable to advances for insurance and taxes. The letter includes an escrow analysis that makes reference to an annual payment of $417.39 for insurance, but does not explain the escrow deficit in excess of $5,000.

30. The January 27 letter also includes a payment history, but only from September 2004 through December 2004. The history printout included is incomprehensible, does not identify transactions as payments, advances or charges, does not begin to address the questions and concerns expressed by Mrs. Consumer and her attorney, and is completely unresponsive to her qualified written requests, which asked for an explanation of the $5,000 escrow deficit and all other amounts demanded, as well as an account history from 2002.

31. In the five months *after* September 2004, when Linton had allegedly corrected Ms. Consumer's account to reflect the loan modification agreement, Ms. Consumer received conflicting notices demanding three different monthly payment amounts, escrow advances that were not due, and a mysterious $40,936 fee balance.

32. Mrs. Consumer was understandably confused and upset during this period and frustrated in her attempts to determine in telephone conversations with Linton exactly what she owed and why.

33. On or about May 13, 2005 Linton, through its attorneys Utrech Law Office, P.C., mailed a "Reinstatement Quote" to Mrs. Consumer. Exhibit 22. The total amount claimed to be due is shown as $47,103.60. This document calls for monthly payments of $362.61, an amount that does not correspond to the $190.66 payment for principal and interest, the $666.96 payment shown on the December statement, or the $455.80 referred to on Exhibit 17, i.e. a fourth conflicting amount for her monthly payment.

34. Exhibit 22 includes a demand for payment for numerous inspections of the property, despite the fact that Mrs. Consumer has been in constant communication with Linton, has a working telephone, and Linton has no basis to believe there is any danger of the property being abandoned.

35. Exhibit 22 includes a demand for $400 for a BPO, that is, a broker price opinion. This amount is not properly chargeable to Mrs. Consumer under the contract or Pennsylvania law, because it was not a reasonable and necessary cost of foreclosure, incurred after the mailing of a proper 30-day notice of intent to foreclose, 41 Pa. Stat. §§ 403, 406.

36. Having no way to determine the correct amount due, Mrs. Consumer sent a certified check for $1400 to Linton on May 6, 2005 (enough to cover the seven principal and interest payments due from November 2004 through May 2005) in an effort to show her good faith and desire to maintain her mortgage payments. This payment was later refused by Linton.

37. To the present date it does not appear that Linton properly adjusted Mrs. Consumer's account, retroactively to January 2001, the effective date of the loan modification agreement. As a result, payments made and accepted from January 2001 to the present may have been applied improperly.

38. Linton has, for the past two years, provided Mrs. Consumer with inconsistent, incomprehensible statements and correspondence and has made it impossible for her to maintain her monthly mortgage payments.

39. To the extent Linton has made advances for taxes and insurance, Linton has failed to identify these amounts advanced in a clear and simple notice and payment demand, and has failed to establish a reasonable plan for Mrs. Consumer to repay those amounts.

40. Mrs. Consumer has suffered severe confusion, frustration, emotional distress, loss of sleep, anxiety and fear of losing her home as a result of Linton's conduct, continuously during the nearly four years from May 2002 to the present.

CONCLUSIONS OF LAW

41. Jurisdiction over this matter is conferred upon this Court by 12 U.S.C. § 2614, 15 U.S.C. § 1692 and 28 U.S.C. §§ 1331. The court has supplemental jurisdiction over the state law claims.

COUNT I—FAIR DEBT COLLECTION PRACTICES ACT

42. Linton was a debt collector within the meaning of the Fair Debt Collection Practices Act ("FDCPA"), 15 U.S.C. 1692a, at the time it became the servicing agent for Mrs. Consumer's loan, in that it regularly collected debts owed to another.

43. The FDCPA coverage exception for servicers of debts that are not past due does not apply to Linton. 15 U.S.C. 1692a(6)(F)(iii). Linton asserted in its initial communication with Mrs. Consumer that her payments were seriously past due. Exhibit 2. Whether Linton was correct or not, the assertion of a default is sufficient to bring Linton under the FDCPA. *Schlosser v. Fairbanks Capital Corp.*, 323 F.3d 534 (7th Cir. 2003).

44. Each of the letters described above incorrectly stated the amount and the status of Mrs. Consumer's debt.

45. In particular, the four rate adjustment letters dated October 25, 2002, April 30, 2003, October 24, 2003, and April 26, 2004, the six monthly statements mailed in 2004 (including Exhibits 12 and 14), and the ten letters and notices (Exhibits 11-13, 15-17, 19-22) for a total of twenty written communications to Mrs. Consumer, each constituted a separate violation of 15 U.S.C. § 1692e.

46. Linton failed to provide verification of the alleged debt to Mrs. Consumer in response to her timely written request for such written verification, in violation of 15 U.S.C. § 1692g(b).

47. Although the statute of limitations under the Federal statute is one year, encompassing the written communication and other conduct from June 2004 to the present, Pennsylvania's Fair Credit Extension Uniformity Act, 73 Pa. Stat. §§ 2270.1 to 2270.6, imposes the same requirements on debt collectors as the federal law. 73 Pa. Stat. § 2270.4(A). A violation of the Pennsylvania debt collection provisions is *per se* a violation of the Pennsylvania Consumer Protection Law, 73 Pa. Stat. §§ 201-9.2, 2270.6(A). The statute of limitations for private actions under the Consumer Protection law is six years. *Gabriel v. O'Hara*, 368 Pa. Super. 383, 534 A.2d 488 (1987).

48. Because of the difficulty of quantifying the misapplication of Mrs. Consumer's payments by Linton throughout the three year period at issue, it is appropriate to award the $100 minimum damages under the Pennsylvania Consumer Protection Law for each of the incorrect and misleading communications, for a total of $2,000. *See In re Koresko*, 91 B.R. 689 (Bankr. E.D. Pa. 1988).

49. Due to the repeated and continuing violations of the FDCPA, Mrs. Consumer is entitled to actual and statutory damages under 15. U.S.C. 1692k, as follows:

A) $1,000 statutory damages under the FDCPA,
B) actual damages of $ __ for anxiety and emotional distress suffered from 2002 to the present,
C) minimum statutory damages under the Pennsylvania Fair Credit Extension Uniformity Act and the Consumer Protection Law of $100 for each violation, for a total of $2,000, and
D) reasonable attorneys fees and costs.

COUNT II—RESPA

50. Linton is a servicer of a federally related mortgage loan within the meaning of the Real Estate Settlement Procedures Act ("RESPA"), 12 U.S.C. § 2605.

51. The May 21, 2002 letter to Linton was a "qualified written request" to Linton, within the meaning of 12 U.S.C. § 2605(e)(1)(B) and was received on that date by Linton.

52. Linton failed to make appropriate corrections to the account within 60 days, and failed to notify Ms. Consumer of any corrections, as required by 12 U.S.C. 2605(e)(2).

53. Each of Mrs. Consumer's (and her attorney's) subsequent written requests for information about her account and correction of Linton's numerous errors were "qualified written requests" within the meaning of RESPA, including, among others, the January 13, 2005 letter to Linton, Exhibit 18.

54. Linton failed to respond in a proper and timely way to Mrs. Consumer's "qualified written requests" for information about, and corrections to, her mortgage account, in violation of 12 U.S.C. § 2605(e).

55. As a result of a pattern or practice of noncompliance with the servicing provisions of RESPA, Linton is liable to Mrs. Consumer for actual damages in the amount of $ __ and statutory damages of $1,000. 12 U.S.C. § 2605(f)(1).

COUNT III—PENNSYLVANIA ACT 6 of 1974

56. Mrs. Consumer's mortgage is a "residential mortgage obligation" covered by Pennsylvania Act 6 of 1974, 41 Pa. Stat. §§ 101-605.

57. Linton has repeatedly failed to provide Mrs. Consumer with an accurate notice of the amount required to cure her mortgage default, as required by 41 P.S. § 403, has improperly demanded payment of amounts not due, and has thwarted her right to cure her default, under 41 P.S. § 404.

58. The excess charges to Mrs. Consumer's account include $319.18 in late charges caused by Linton's failure to implement the loan modification, Exhibit 17 page 3, the $400 "BPO" fee and $70 in inspection fees, Exhibit 22.

59. Linton is therefore liable to Mrs. Consumer for three times the excess charges, 41 P.S. 502, or $2,367.54, together with reasonable attorney's fees and costs.

COUNT IV—PENNSYLVANIA CONSUMER PROTECTION LAW

60. Linton's conduct described above constituted unfair and deceptive acts and practices, as defined by 73 Pa. Stat. § 201-2(4).

61. Mrs. Consumer has suffered an ascertainable loss of money as a result of Linton's unfair and deceptive practices.

62. Mrs. Consumer is entitled to recover three times her actual damages, or $ __, together with reasonable attorney's fees and costs, 73 Pa. Stat. § 201-9.2.

63. The Pennsylvania Consumer Protection Law also authorizes an award to an aggrieved consumer of "other appropriate relief," which in this case includes a full and complete accounting of her mortgage account by Linton, together with all adjustments necessary to reflect the terms of the 2000 modification agreement, effective January 2001, to remove all late charges, and any other fee or charge of any kind, apart from the agreed reduced principal, interest from January 2001, and actual payments of real estate taxes and insurance made by Linton since January 2001.

64. The relief to be awarded the plaintiff can be summarized as follows:

a. $1,000 statutory damages under the FDCPA,

b. $2,000 for the twenty violations of the Pennsylvania debt collection statute,
c. $1,000 statutory damages for violating RESPA,
d. $2,367.54 in treble damages under Pennsylvania Act 6 of 1974,
e. $ actual damages for emotional distress,
f. an injunction directing Linton to analyze Mrs. Consumer's account retroactive to the date of the 2000 loan modification agreement, to reapply her payments properly under that agreement, to remove all fees or charges imposed by Linton or the previous servicer, including any attorney's fees or foreclosure costs, and to discuss with Mrs. Consumer and establish a reasonable repayment schedule for any taxes and insurance advances made by Linton from 2002 to the present (which may include setting off the damage award to Mrs. Consumer against these amounts due),
g. and reasonable attorney's fees and costs, in an amount to be determined after submission of an appropriate motion by the Plaintiff.

Respectfully submitted, Attorney for Plaintiff

I.10 Pleadings Related to Broker and Loan Origination Abuses

I.10.1 Complaint

STATE OF NORTH CAROLINA ORANGE COUNTY
IN THE GENERAL COURT OF JUSTICE
SUPERIOR COURT DIVISION

________________________	)	
BETTY CONSUMER,	)	
Plaintiff,	)	
	)	
v.	)	
	)	
R & B FUNDING GROUP,	)	
INC., d/b/a National Builders,	)	02-CVS-0000
J.P. MORGAN CHASE BANK,	)	02-SP-000
as Trustee, ROYAL	)	(Jury Trial Requested)
MORTGAGE & FINANCIAL	)	
SERVICE CENTERS, INC.,	)	
and ELIZABETH B. WELD	)	
and DAVID W. SMITH, as	)	
Substitute Trustees,	)	
Defendants.	)	
________________________	)	

COMPLAINT

Plaintiff, complaining of the defendants and in support of her motion for injunctive relief, alleges as follows:

Nature of Action

1. Plaintiff brings this action for damages and to enjoin a foreclosure proceeding instituted against her by the current holder of her mortgage loan, J.P. Morgan Chase Bank. She contends that the originator of the loan in question, R & B Funding Group, Inc. acted unlawfully in connection with the origination of a mortgage loan made to her in April, 2002 by failing to comply with North Carolina laws prohibiting the financing of fees in excess of five percent of the loan amount, and by failing to ensure that she was provided with financial counseling prior to consummating this "high cost" loan. Plaintiff further contends that Royal Mortgage & Financial Service Centers, Inc. which served as her mortgage broker, breached its fiduciary duty to her. Plaintiff further alleges that the practices of R & B Funding Group, Inc. as well as Royal Mortgage & Financial Service Centers, Inc. constituted unfair and deceptive practices.

Parties

2. Plaintiff is a citizen and resident of the town of Consumerville in Orange County, North Carolina.

3. Defendant, R & B Funding Group, Inc., D/B/A National Builders (hereinafter "R & B") is, upon information and belief, a North Carolina Corporation and originated Plaintiff's mortgage loan together with a mortgage broker, Royal Mortgage & Financial Service Centers, Inc., pursuant to arrangements made by R & B.

4. Defendant, J.P. Morgan Chase Bank (hereinafter "J.P. Morgan"), is, upon information and belief, the creditor and/or the trust administrator of a trust that is assignee of Plaintiff's loan, or otherwise holds Plaintiff's loan.

5. Defendant Royal Mortgage & Financial Service Centers, Inc. (hereinafter "Royal Mortgage"), is, upon information and belief, a corporation organized under the laws of North Carolina and performed mortgage brokerage and/or loan origination services pursuant to arrangements made by R & B at times pertinent to the events referenced in this complaint.

6. Defendants Elizabeth B. Weld and David W. Smith are parties to this action only in their capacity as Substitute Trustees of Plaintiff's Deed of Trust, and the only relief sought against Defendant Weld and/or Smith is injunctive relief enjoining foreclosure of the deed of trust.

Factual Allegations

7. Plaintiff Betty Consumer is an 82-year-old widow. She is in failing health and has limited understanding of financial transactions, including the instant transaction.

8. Consumer lives in a modest home on Main Road in Consumerville, in Orange County, North Carolina. She and her late husband purchased this home almost fifty years ago, and she has lived there ever since.

9. In the spring of 2002, Consumer's son, John Consumer, contacted a mortgage broker about refinancing Consumer's existing mortgage. At that time, Consumer's home was secured by a mortgage with Bank of America, Inc.

10. On information and belief, John Consumer contacted an individual named Steve Smith, who, upon information and belief, was employed by Defendant mortgage broker Royal Mortgage.

11. Sometime in March or April 2002, Steve Smith contacted Consumer by calling her on the telephone and informed her that he would arrange for the refinancing of Plaintiff's home loan.

12. Steve Smith took information from Plaintiff over the telephone concerning her finances, and upon information and belief,

prepared loan application documents for Plaintiff in order to secure a loan with Defendant R & B.

13. At all times relevant hereto, Steve Smith was an employee and agent of defendant Royal Mortgage.

14. Upon information and belief, all contacts with Steve Smith and/or Royal Mortgage, were transacted over the telephone.

15. On approximately April 18, 2002, a loan closing was conducted in Consumer's living room. On information and belief, a representative from the law firm of Brock, Scott & Ingersoll went to Consumer's home and asked her to sign many documents. Upon information and belief, Defendant R & B, and not Consumer, selected this law firm to be the settlement agent in this transaction.

16. At the time that the loan closed, Consumer signed a HUD-1 Settlement Statement dated April 18, 2002, which listed the various loan related expenses.

17. The amount of the loan was $37,000.00.

18. Among the various fees charged in connection with Plaintiff's loan included a "loan origination fee" of $395, a "mortgage broker fee" of $1424.50, a "settlement fee" of $100, a "title search" fee of $425, a "lender amount" of $35, and a "doc prep" fee of $100.

19. According to the Federal Truth-in-Lending Act Disclosure Statement signed at the closing, Consumer was to pay monthly payments of $298.50 for 30 years. The total of payments as disclosed is $107,460.00.

20. The total of points and fees paid by plaintiffs at or before the loan closing exceeded 5% of the "total loan amount," as that term is defined by N.C.G.S. 24-1.1E,[17] and were financed within the loan.

21. The loan was secured against title to plaintiff's principal dwelling, located at Main Road, Consumerville, North Carolina, by a Deed of Trust which is recorded in Book 00 at Page 00 of the Orange County Registry.

22. The proceeds of the loan were primarily for personal, family, or household purposes.

23. Plaintiff was not advised that the loan was a "high cost-home loan" as defined in N.C.G.S. 24-1.1E.

24. Upon information and belief, no party to the transaction received a certification from a counselor approved by the North Carolina Housing Finance Agency verifying that plaintiff had been counseled as to the advisability of the loan transaction.

25. Plaintiff was not counseled by a counselor approved by the North Carolina Housing Finance Agency as to the advisability of the loan transaction.

26. Defendant, R & B had a duty to inform plaintiff that the loan transaction was a "high-cost home loan" and, as such, that this loan required the various counseling protections and safeguards embraced by Chapter 24 of the North Carolina General Statutes.

27. Defendant, R & B breached this duty and the plaintiff was directly, proximately and foreseeably damaged by the breach of this duty.

28. Upon information and belief, defendant Royal Mortgage did not provide bona fide or legitimate mortgage broker services to plaintiff, even though plaintiff was charged $1424.50 by defendant, Royal Mortgage, for mortgage broker services.

29. The loan transaction in question was intended to refinance Plaintiff's then existing first mortgage with Bank of America in the amount of $26,635.37, as indicated by line 1513 on the HUD-1 Settlement Statement. On information and belief, a check was disbursed by the closing agent three days after the loan closing to Bank of America, but said check was neither cashed nor applied to Plaintiff's mortgage account at Bank of America. Bank of America did not satisfy the deed of trust, but instead continued to withdraw monthly payments from Plaintiff's checking account and applied them to her old mortgage account. Plaintiff attempted to make payments to the servicer of the mortgage that is the subject of this action, but as money was being withdrawn from her checking account each month by Bank of America, her checks on the new mortgage bounced.

30. On or about October 17, 2002, Defendant J.P. Morgan Chase Bank as Trustee, through its substitute trustee, Defendants Weld and/or Smith, filed a foreclosure action against the plaintiff, alleging that the plaintiff is in default in payments under the terms of the April 2002 loan contract. The foreclosure action is filed as 02 SP 000.

31. Plaintiff, who is unsophisticated, did not realize the bank's error. After getting several collection calls and letters, she finally sought the help of a social worker from the Orange County Department of Aging, who in turn sought assistance from the North Carolina Attorney General's Consumer Protection Division. As a result of these inquiries, the closing agent resubmitted a check to Bank of America on October 29, 2002, and upon information and belief, Plaintiff's prior mortgage was satisfied shortly thereafter.

32. Despite being apprised of the circumstances surrounding the failure of the April 2002 lender to pay off Plaintiff's prior mortgage, the substitute trustee refused to delay or stop the foreclosure proceedings. The foreclosure hearing before the clerk was scheduled for November 18, 2002.

Count One

VIOLATION OF CHAPTER 24 OF THE NORTH CAROLINA GENERAL STATUTES

(Against Defendant R & B, and against J.P. Morgan Chase Bank as Trustee in its capacity as assignee or holder of interest in Plaintiff's loan)

33. All paragraphs of this complaint are incorporated herein as if fully restated.

34. The loan transaction in question was: a "high-cost home loan" which did not exceed the lesser of (i) the conforming loan size limit for a single family dwelling as established by FNMA or (ii) three hundred thousand dollars; and was incurred by natural persons primarily for personal, family, or household purposes; and was secured by a deed of trust against property occupied as the borrower's principal dwelling as defined in N.C.G.S. 24-1.1E. With willful and corrupt intent, the lender, Defendant, R & B, and/or its agents, made and/or arranged the loan without the counseling required under Chapter 24 of the North Carolina General Statutes and specifically under N.C.G.S. 24-1.1E9(c). The loan was made without certification from a counselor approved by the North Carolina Housing Finance Agency that the borrowers received counseling on the advisability of the loan transaction and the appropriate loan for the borrowers. These acts and practices entitle Plaintiff to the remedies set out in N.C.G.S. 24-1.1E9d. Defendant R & B, together with Defendants J.P. Morgan, as Trustee, are liable as holders of interests in Plaintiff's loan.

17 [*Editor's Note*: Citations throughout complaint as in original.]

Count Two

UNFAIR AND DECEPTIVE ACTS AND PRACTICES AS DEFINED IN N.C.G.S. 75-1.1

(Against Defendant R & B, and against J.P. Morgan Chase Bank as Trustee in its capacity as assignee or holder of interest in Plaintiff's loan)

35. All paragraphs of this complaint are incorporated herein as if fully restated.

36. Defendants' acts as described above, and particularly those acts specifically set out in Count One, proximately damaged Plaintiff, are in and affecting commerce, violate public policy, have the capacity to deceive an ordinary consumer, are unscrupulous, immoral, and oppressive, and constitute unfair and deceptive trade practices under N.C.G.S. 75-1.1, thereby entitling Plaintiff to three times her actual damages plus a reasonable attorney's fee pursuant to N.C.G.S. 75-16 and 75-16.1. The remedy requested pursuant to this count which relates to acts or practices described in Count One is plead in the alternative to the relief requested pursuant to Count One, as prescribed in N.C.G.S. 24-1.1E(d). Defendant R & B, together with Defendants J.P. Morgan are liable as holders of interests in Plaintiff's loan.

Count Three

BREACH OF FIDUCIARY DUTIES

(Against Defendant Royal Mortgage)

37. All paragraphs of this complaint are incorporated herein as if fully restated.

38. Defendant, Royal Mortgage, upon information and belief, was the employer of and had as its agent Steve Smith, who solicited and intentionally induced the trust, confidence and reliance of Plaintiff as her mortgage loan counselor and guide, and Smith and Royal Mortgage occupied the position of Plaintiff's mortgage broker. The position of trust, confidence and reliance that Steve Smith and Royal Mortgage occupied with respect to Plaintiff and the position they occupied as Plaintiff's mortgage broker created fiduciary duties owed by Smith and Royal Mortgage to Plaintiff which were breached by the conduct set forth above, that was done for the sake of self dealing and unjustified profits taken by Smith and Royal Mortgage through the broker fee of $1424.50.

39. Plaintiff is entitled to remedies that include imposition of a constructive trust upon the proceeds of the transaction as were paid to Defendant, Royal Mortgage and Steve Smith, to an order requiring disgorgement of all proceeds paid to Royal Mortgage and Smith and to other legal and equitable remedies to be imposed jointly and severally upon Defendant Royal Mortgage.

Count Four

UNFAIR AND DECEPTIVE ACTS AND PRACTICES AS DEFINED IN N.C.G.S. 75-1.1

(Against Defendant Royal Mortgage)

40. All paragraphs of this complaint are incorporated herein as if fully restated.

41. The acts of Defendant Royal Mortgage as described above, and particularly those acts specifically set out in Count Three, proximately damaged plaintiff, are in and affecting commerce, violate public policy, have the capacity to deceive an ordinary consumer, are unscrupulous, immoral, and oppressive, and constitute unfair and deceptive trade practices under N.C.G.S. § 75-1.1, thereby entitling plaintiff to three times her actual damages plus a reasonable attorney's fee pursuant to N.C.G.S. §§ 75-16 and 75-16.1.

Request for Relief

WHEREFORE, Plaintiff requests:

1. That Plaintiff be awarded, pursuant to Count One, monetary damages in the amount of double recovery of any interest paid on this loan together with a Declaratory Order that the remaining interest due under the loan is forfeited.

2. That Plaintiff be awarded, pursuant to Count Two, three times her actual damages plus a reasonable attorney's fee pursuant to N.C.G.S. 75-16 and 75-16.1, upon the condition that the remedy pursuant to Count Two, is in the alternative to the relief requested pursuant to Count One, as may be required by N.C.G.S. 24-1.1E(d);

3. That Plaintiff be awarded, pursuant to Counts Three, an Order that Defendant Royal Mortgage disgorge and pay to Plaintiff all proceeds paid to it and by any party in connection with the transaction.

4. That Plaintiff be awarded, pursuant to Count Four, three times her actual damages plus a reasonable attorney's fee to be paid by Defendant Royal Mortgage;

5. That the foreclosure action brought by the substitute trustees on behalf of Defendant JP Morgan Chase Bank against the Plaintiff be temporarily and preliminary enjoined pending a final adjudication of this action;

6. That the Court award such other relief as it deems just and proper;

7. That this case be tried by a jury.

This the ________ day of November, 2002.

I.10.2 Memorandum in Support of Motion for Preliminary Injunction

STATE OF NORTH CAROLINA ORANGE COUNTY
IN THE GENERAL COURT OF JUSTICE
SUPERIOR COURT DIVISION

BETTY CONSUMER, Plaintiff,	)	
v.	)	
R & B FUNDING GROUP, INC., d/b/a National Builders, J.P. MORGAN CHASE BANK, as Trustee, ROYAL MORTGAGE & FINANCIAL SERVICE CENTERS, INC., and ELIZABETH B. WELD and DAVID W. SMITH, as Substitute Trustees Defendants.	)	02-CVS-0000 02-SP-000

PLAINTIFF'S MEMORANDUM IN SUPPORT OF MOTION FOR PRELIMINARY INJUNCTION

Facts

Plaintiff is an unsophisticated, 82-year-old widow. She lives in a modest home on Main Road in Carrboro, in Orange County, North Carolina where she has lived since she and her late husband purchased it almost fifty years ago. In the spring of 2002, Consumer's son contacted a mortgage broker employed by Defendant Royal Mortgage about refinancing Consumer's existing mortgage with Bank of America. This mortgage broker called Consumer, took the necessary information from Consumer over the phone and prepared the loan application documents that eventually secured a loan by Consumer with Defendant R & B Funding Group (hereinafter R & B) on approximately April 18, 2002 when the attorneys conducting the closing appeared at Consumer's residence to obtain her signature. Defendant R & B rather Consumer selected the law firm that settled this transaction. When the loan was closed, Consumer signed a HUD-1 Settlement Statement, a copy of which is attached to the complaint. According to the Statement, in addition to the loan amount of $37,000.00 and Consumer was financed a "loan origination fee" of $395, a "mortgage broker fee" of $1424.50, a "settlement fee" of $100, a "title search" fee of $425, a "lender amount" of $35, and a "doc prep" fee of $100. According to the Federal Truth-in-Lending Act Disclosure Statement Consumer also signed at the closing, Consumer was to pay monthly payments of $298.50 for 30 years. The total of payments as disclosed is $107,460.00.

The total of these fees paid by Consumer exceeded 5% of the "total loan amount," as defined by N.C. Gen. Stat. 24-1.1E[18] and such fees were financed within her loan. Consumer was not advised that the loan was a "high cost-home loan" as defined in N.C. Gen. Stat. 24-1.1E and was not provided the requisite counseling required by the statute as to the advisability of the loan transaction.

The loan transaction in question was intended to refinance Plaintiff's then existing first mortgage with Bank of America in the amount of $26,635.37. Her deed of trust, however, for reasons unknown to Consumer, was not satisfied. Bank of America continued to withdraw monthly payments from Plaintiff's checking account and applied them to her old mortgage account. As a result of these automatic monthly withdrawals, Consumer was unable, due to her limited fixed income, to pay on her new mortgage that is the subject of this action. Plaintiff, who is unsophisticated, did not realize the bank's error. After getting several collection calls and letters, she finally sought the help of a social worker from the Orange County Department of Aging, who in turn sought assistance from the North Carolina Attorney General's Consumer Protection Division. As a result of these inquiries, the closing agent resubmitted a check to Bank of America on October 29, 2002, and upon information and belief, Plaintiff's prior mortgage was satisfied shortly thereafter.

On October 17, 2002, a foreclosure action was filed against Consumer, alleging that the plaintiff is in default in payments under the terms of the April 2002 loan contract. Despite being apprised of the circumstances surrounding the failure of the April 2002 lender to pay off Plaintiff's prior mortgage, the substitute trustee refused to delay or stop the foreclosure proceedings. The foreclosure hearing before the clerk was scheduled for November 18, 2002, and an order allowing the sale to proceed was entered that day. A sale of Consumer's property is scheduled for ________.

Argument

STANDARD FOR ENJOINING FORECLOSURE ACTIONS

The statutory scheme of the foreclosure proceedings, N.C. Gen. Stat. 45-21.1 *et seq.* requires the Court to grant a restraining order when there is bona fide controversy as to the debt which should be resolved before a foreclosure sale. The hearing provided for in N.C. Gen. Stat. 45-21.16 is designed to be a summary proceeding, at which the mortgagor may only contest four narrow factual issues (existence of a valid debt, existence of default, trustee's right to foreclose, and sufficiency of the notice). It was not intended to settle all matters in controversy between the parties. *Golf Vistas, Inc. v. Mortgage Investors,* 39 N.C. App. 230, 249 S.E.2d 815 (1978). If a mortgagor feels that equitable or legal defenses to the foreclosure exist, they should be asserted in an action to enjoin the foreclosure sale under N.C. Gen. Stat. 45-21.34. *In re Helms*, 55 N.C. App. 68, 284 S.E.2d 553 (1981), *cert. denied*, 305 N.C. 300, 291 S.E.2d 149 (1982). This statute permits any owner of real estate to apply to a Superior Court judge to enjoin a foreclosure sale "upon any legal or equitable ground which the Court may deem sufficient." N.C. Gen. Stat. 45-21.34. Otherwise, a mortgagor will lose his property interest without a full opportunity to defend and could suffer irreparable loss.

The standard against which a request for a preliminary injunction to enjoin a foreclosure sale is measured is clear:

> It is the rule with us that in actions of this character, the main purpose of which is to obtain a

18 [*Editor's Note*: Citations throughout memorandum as in original.]

> permanent injunction, if the evidence raises serious question as to the existence of facts which make for Plaintiff's right, and sufficient to establish it, a preliminary restraining order will be continued to the hearing. If the Plaintiff has shown probable cause or it can reasonably be seen that he will be able to make out his case at the final hearing, the injunction will be continued. . . .

Little v. Wachovia Bank and Trust Co. 208 N.C. 726, 182 S.E. 491 (1935).

All benefit of the doubt should be accorded to the Plaintiffs in these actions. As the Supreme Court emphasized in *Princeton Realty Corp. v. Kalman*, 272 N.C. 201, 159 S.E.2d 193, 196 (1967):

> It is generally proper, when the parties are at issue concerning the legal or equitable right, to grant an interlocutory injunction to preserve the right in status quo until the termination of the controversy, and especially is this the rule when the principal relief sought is in itself an injunction, because a dissolution of a pending interlocutory injunction, or the refusal of one. . . . will virtually decide the case upon its merits, and deprive the Plaintiff of all remedy or relief, even though he should be afterwards able to show ever so good a case.

The courts have granted injunctions against a foreclosure sale when there is a serious question as to the amount due or to default. The concern of the court in equity is to preserve the status quo. Moreover, the courts have held the dissolution of an injunction or restraining order before trial on the merits to be reversible error. See, e.g., *Princeton Realty Corp. v. Kalman,* 272 N.C. 201, 159 S.E.2d 193 (1967) (the lower court erred in dissolving a temporary restraining order prior to a final hearing on the merits when a serious question as to default coupled with a reasonable apprehension of irreparable injury to the plaintiff exists and when the record indicates the existence of a bona fide controversy in which plaintiff may prevail); *Golf Vistas, Inc. v. Mortgage Investors, supra* (the trustor is entitled to restrain the foreclosure proceeding pursuant to N.C. Gen. Stat. 45-21.34 where questions are raised to default and partial release); *Superscope, Inc. v. Kincaid,* 56 N.C. App. 673, 289 S.E.2d 595 (1982) (when the record reveals a bona fide controversy that should be resolved before the foreclosure sale of corporate property, an order denying a preliminary injunction is reversed).

PLAINTIFF HAS RAISED SUBSTANTIAL CLAIMS AGAINST THE DEFENDANTS

In the case at bar, the Plaintiff has alleged several separate claims for relief against the Defendants. In 1999, the North Carolina General Assembly enacted Plaintiff's First Cause of Action in her Complaint asserts a claim and seeks damages for Defendant R & B's violation of Chapter 24 of the North Carolina General Statutes, specifically N.C. Gen. Stat. 24-1.1E(c)1. Plaintiff's Second Cause of Action asserts a claim and seeks damages for Defendant R & B's unfair and deceptive trade practices. Plaintiff bases both claims upon R & B's financing of fees in excess of five percent of the loan amount and failure to ensure that Plaintiff receive financial counseling prior to consummating a high-cost home loan. Plaintiff also asserts claims and seeks damages for Defendant Royal Mortgage's breach of fiduciary duty and unfair and deceptive trade practices. Should Plaintiff prevail on any one of these grounds, the foreclosure action should be permanently enjoined. Clearly the Plaintiff has raised "serious questions" and established "probable cause" to allow the injunction prohibiting the foreclosure sale to continue until a full trial on the merits of Plaintiffs' numerous claims can be heard.

DEFENDANT'S VIOLATION OF CHAPTER 24 OF THE NORTH CAROLINA GENERAL STATUTES

A lender's financing of fees in excess of five percent of the loan amount is a legal defense to foreclosure. N.C. Gen. Stat. 24-1.1E(c)(3) provides,

> In making a high-cost home loan, a lender may not directly or indirectly finance: a. Any prepayment fees or penalties payable by the borrower in a refinancing transaction if the lender or an affiliate of the lender is the noteholder of the note being refinanced; b. Any points and fees; or c. Any other charges payable to third parties.

Given evidence contained in the attached HUD1 Settlement Statement, attached to Plaintiff's complaint, of points and fees paid by Plaintiff, their inclusion within refinanced amount and their sum as exceeding five percent of the loan amount, Plaintiff submits that there is a substantial likelihood that she will prevail on the merits of her claim that Defendant R & B refinanced points and fees in excess of five percent of loan amount within Plaintiff's loan.

A lender's failure to ensure that a borrower receive financial counseling prior to consummating a high-cost home loan is a violation of North Carolina's predatory lending act. N.C. Gen. Stat. 24-1.1E(c)(1) provides, "A lender may not make a high-cost home without first receiving certification from a counselor approved by the North Carolina Housing Finance Agency that the borrower has received counseling on the advisability of the loan transaction and the appropriate loan for the borrower." Given Plaintiff was not advised that the loan was a "high-cost home loan" or counseled by a counselor approved by the North Carolina Housing Finance Agency as to the advisability of the loan transaction, Plaintiff submits that there is a substantial likelihood that she will prevail on the merits of her claim that Defendant R & B failed to ensure that she receive financial counseling prior to consummating her high-cost home loan.

DEFENDANT ROYAL MORTGAGE BREACHED FIDUCIARY DUTIES TO PLAINTIFF

Plaintiff has alleged that Defendant Royal Mortgage owed Plaintiff a fiduciary duty by its position as registered mortgage broker/lender. In *Johnson v. Insurance Company*, 300 N.C. 247, 266 S.E.2d 610 (1980), the Supreme Court described the nature of the relationship between borrower and mortgage broker. The court noted that "the broker is manifestly engaged in the business of selling his services in procuring a loan which is most favorable to the needs and resources of the potential borrower, who, in turn, has sought to obtain a broker who can best represent his interests in securing proper financing." *Id.*, at 261-62. The Court further noted that "an exchange of value does occur as the result of this process of securing broker as the representative of the potential borrower." *Id.* Plaintiff has alleged that these fiduciary duties were breached by Defendant Royal Mortgage's inducing Plaintiff to enter into a loan contract when they knew or should have known of Plaintiff's lack of capacity, and by inducing her to enter into a loan contract with high points and fees. Mortgage Broker Registration Act, N.C. Gen. Stat. 53-238 against Defendant. Plaintiff has also alleged that both Defendants have committed unfair and deceptive trade practices in conjunction with entering into this loan transaction.

Conclusion

Plaintiff contends that he states a meritorious equitable defense to Defendants R & B and Royal Mortgage's claim that she is liable for payment under the promissory note. She has raised several defenses and claims with respect to the transaction. For these reasons, Plaintiffs respectfully request that a preliminary injunction be issued enjoining the foreclosure proceeding pending a final adjudication of this action.

This, the ________ day of ____________ 1999

I.10.3 Discovery Requests and Request to Admit to Lender

IN THE CIRCUIT COURT OF COOK COUNTY, ILLINOIS
COUNTY DEPARTMENT, CHANCERY DIVISION

________________	)	
CHANCE BANK OF TEXAS,	)	
Plaintiff,	)	
	)	
v.	)	No. 00 CH 0000
	)	
BERNICE HOMEOWNER,	)	
Defendant.	)	
________________	)	

BERNICE HOMEOWNER'S FIRST DISCOVERY REQUEST

Defendant, Bernice Homeowner, hereby requests that plaintiff Chance Bank of Texas ("Chance"), respond to the following interrogatories and document requests within 28 days after service hereof, in accordance with Illinois Supreme Court Rule 201.[19]

Unless otherwise stated, the time period of these requests is from January, 1999, to the present.

Instructions and Definitions

A. Throughout this request, "You" or "Your" refers to the answering party or parties, and their owners, officers, agents, representatives, independent contractors, employees, attorneys, and/or anyone acting on their behalf.

B. Please furnish all information in your possession and control. If you cannot answer the requests in full after exercising due diligence to secure the information to do so, state the answer to the extent possible specifying your inability to answer the remainder, and state whatever information or knowledge you have concerning the unanswered portion.

C. Each request and interrogatory is considered continuing, and if you obtain information which renders its answers or any of them incomplete or inaccurate, you are obligated to serve amended answers on the undersigned.

D. Insofar as may be applicable, and except as otherwise indicated, the term "document" or "documents" shall refer to any and all writings and recorded materials, of any kind whatsoever, that is or has been in your possession, control or custody or of which you have knowledge, whether originals or copies, including but not limited to contracts, documents, notes, rough drafts, inter-office memoranda, memoranda for the files, letters, research materials, correspondence, logs, diaries, forms, bank statements, tax returns, card files, books of account, journals, ledgers, invoices, blueprints, diagrams, drawings, computer print-outs, discs or tapes, reports, surveys, statistical computations, studies, pictures, maps, graphs, charts, minutes, manuals, pamphlets, or books of any nature or kind whatsoever; and all other materials handwritten, printed, typed, mimeographed, photocopied or otherwise reproduced; and slides or motion pictures, television tapes; all tape recordings (whether for computer, audio or visual replay) or other written, printed or recorded matter or tangible things on which words, phrases, symbols or information are affixed.

E. A request to "identify" a document is a request to state (insofar as may be applicable):

1. The date of such document.
2. The type of document or written communication it is.
3. The names and present addresses of the person or persons who prepared such document and of the signers, senders and addressees of such document.
4. The name of any principal whom or which the signers, senders and preparers of such document were thereby representing.
5. The present location of such document.
6. The name and present address of the person now having custody of the document.
7. Whether you possess or control the original or a copy thereof and if so, the location and name of the custodian of such original or copy.
8. A brief description of the contents of such document.

F. A request to "describe" any oral statement or communication is a request to state:

1. The name and present address of each individual making such statement or communication.
2. The name of any principal or employer whom or which such individual was thereby representing and the position in which such individual was then employed or engaged by such principal or employee.
3. The name and present address of the individual or individuals to whom the oral statement or communication was made, and the name of any principal or employer whom such person or persons were representing at the time of and in connection with such oral statement or communication, as well as the employment position in which they were then employed or engaged.
4. The names and present addresses of any other individuals present when such oral statement or communication was

19 [*Editor's Note*: Citations throughout discovery and requests for admissions as in original.]

made or who heard or acknowledged hearing the same.

5. The place where such oral statement or communication was made.
6. A brief description of the contents of such oral statement or communication.

G. A request to "cite" portions or provisions of any document is a request to state, insofar as applicable with reference to such portion or provision, the title, date, division, page, sheet, charge order number, and such other information as may be necessary to accurately locate the portion or provision referenced.

H. The term "person" shall include a natural person, partnership, corporation, association, or other group however organized.

I. Whenever a request is made to "identify" a natural person, it shall mean to supply all of the following information:

1. His/her full name.
2. His/her employer and position at the time.
3. The name of any person or entity (natural or artificial) whom she/he is claimed to have represented in connection with the matter to which the interrogatory relates.
4. His/her last known address, telephone number, and employer.
5. His/her present employer.

J. A request to "explain fully" any answer, denial or claim is a request (insofar as may be applicable) to:

1. State fully and specifically each fact and/or contention in support of your answer, denial or claim; and
2. For each such fact or contention, to identify each person who has knowledge relative to that fact or contention, each document that tends to support that fact or contention; and each document that tends to dispute that fact or contention.

K. Unless otherwise specified, the terms "subject account" or "subject transaction" means the transaction(s) described in the complaint(s), including any prior or ongoing contract or communication relating to the transaction and/or account, up to and including the date of your answers to these interrogatories. Specifically, "subject transaction" includes each and every agreement, contract, communication or transaction between Ms. Homeowner and Chance and/or its assignor (Saxon Mortgage), agents, representatives and employees, between Chance and its assignor, and between Ms. Homeowner and Victory Mortgage and/or its agents, representatives and employees.

L. A request in any of the enclosed interrogatories to "identify" any document is a request to attach said document to answers to these interrogatories. If documents are attached to answers to these interrogatories, they must be marked to identify which interrogatory they refer to. In identifying documents you are also requested to produce, you need to supply only so much of the requested information as is not readily apparent from the face of the document.

If any paragraph of this request is believed to be ambiguous or unduly burdensome, please contact the undersigned and an effort will be made to remedy the problem.

Requests to Admit

1. Defendant, Bernice Homeowner, (hereinafter "Ms. Homeowner") is a 70-year-old woman who has owned the property at 1234 W. Main Street (hereinafter "home") since 1970.

2. Ms. Homeowner currently resides in the home with her two sons and four grandchildren.

3. At the time of the subject transaction, Ms. Homeowner, was a senior citizen with limited education and income, but substantial equity in her home.

4. Between 1995 and 1998, Ms. Homeowner entered into at least 3 home refinance loans. Each loan substantially reduced Ms. Homeowner's equity in her home and increased her monthly mortgage payments without providing her with a proportionate economic benefit.

5. In February 1999, Ms. Homeowner received a phone solicitation from Victory Mortgage ("Victory"), a mortgage broker.

6. Some time thereafter, a Victory Mortgage agent visited Ms. Homeowner at her home, where Ms. Homeowner signed documents in connection with a loan application.

7. On or about May 27, 1999, the loan closing was completed at the offices of Victory Mortgage, where Ms. Homeowner signed numerous documents in connection with the transaction.

8. The loan did not provide for a cash payment to Ms. Homeowner in the amount of $1600 or any other amount.

9. Ms. Homeowner did not receive any disbursement from the subject loan.

10. Victory Mortgage did not pay the first monthly payment on the subject loan.

11. Victory Mortgage received at least $7800 in connection with the subject transaction.

12. Victory Mortgage received at least $7532 in connection with the subject transaction.

13. Victory Mortgage received at least $7032 in connection with the subject transaction.

14. Victory Mortgage received at least $7032 from the loan proceeds in connection with the subject transaction.

15. Victory Mortgage received a payment of $3750 from Saxon in connection with the subject transaction.

16. The amount of the $3750 payment from Saxon to Victory Mortgage was based on or calculated from the interest rate of the loan.

17. The $3750 payment from Saxon to Victory Mortgage would have been lower if the interest rate of the subject loan was lower.

18. As a normal industry practice, "Broker Compensation" payments by mortgage lenders to mortgage brokers paid outside closing are based on the size of the interest rate, i.e., the Broker Compensation may be higher if the interest rate is higher.

19. As a normal industry practice, "Broker Compensation" payments by mortgage lenders to mortgage brokers paid outside closing may be referred to by one or more of the following terms: "yield spread premiums," "yield spread," fee, "yield differential," "service release fee," "service release premium," "bonus upsell points," and/or "back-end points."

20. Victory Mortgage received a total of at least $10,782 in connection with the subject transaction.

21. Victory Mortgage provided no goods or services of value to Ms. Homeowner in connection with the subject transaction.

22. The Truth In Lending Disclosure issued in connection with Ms. Homeowner's loan accurately states that the Amount Financed was $111,705.66.

23. The Truth In Lending Statement issued in connection with the subject transaction did not accurately disclose the Amount Financed.

24. The "total loan amount" for the transaction, as defined in 15 U.S.C. § 1602(aa)(1)(B) and 12 C.F.R. § 226.32(a)(1)(ii), was not more than $111,705.66.

25. The points and fees disclosed by plaintiff's assignor in the Itemization of Amount Financed was $8294.34.

26. The prepaid finance charges disclosed by plaintiff's assignor in the Itemization of Amount Financed was $8294.34.

27. The "broker's origination fee" was $7800, as disclosed in the Itemization of Amount Financed issued in connection with he subject transaction.

28. The total points and fees imposed in connection with the subject loan transaction was $12,044.34.

29. The total points and fees were at least 10.78% of the total loan amount.

30. The interest rate on the subject transaction was above the par rate of plaintiff's assignor at the time of the transaction.

31. The interest rate on the subject transaction was above Chance's par rate for borrowers similarly situated to Ms. Homeowner at the time of the transaction.

32. No Truth In Lending Act disclosures were provided to Ms. Homeowner prior to her signing the loan documents.

33. Plaintiff's assignor did not provide Ms. Homeowner with any Truth In Lending disclosures three days prior to the time when she signed the loan documents.

Interrogatories

1. State the name, job title, and business address of each person providing information in response to these discovery requests.

2. Provide the following information for all employees and agents of Chance and/or its assignor and/or Victory Mortgage who had any involvement in the transaction with plaintiff or in the administration of her account, including but not limited the origination, underwriting, disbursement and assignment of the subject account: full name, present or last known home and business addresses and telephone numbers; date first employed by you; whether presently employed by you; all job title(s) and dates during which each job was held; and if not presently employed, Social Security number and exact date of birth. State, generally, each individual's involvement (*e.g.*, preparation of documents, notarizing signatures, approval of financing terms, communications with the borrower; sending of notices, disbursement of funds, etc.).

3. State the date and subject matter of each communication (oral or written): (a) between or among any of the parties to this action, and (b) between you and any other person or entity (other than your counsel), relating to the subject account and/or transaction. Identify all documents reflecting or relating to such communications, including but not limited to letters, faxes, notes, internal memoranda, calendars, computer data, and credit applications, etc.

4. State the date and amount of each payment (a) disbursed from the loan proceeds of the subject transaction and/or account; (b) received by you from anyone in connection with the subject account; and (c) paid to or received by anyone else in connection with the subject account (regardless of whether the payment came from the loan proceeds or another source). Identify the payor and payee of each such payment made or received, including but not limited to payments made to brokers, appraisers, title companies, credit reporting agencies, couriers and contractors, and identify all documents relating to same, including all canceled checks and receipts.

5. Describe your policy and practice relating to the origination, approval or underwriting, preparation, disbursement and acceptance of assignment of a residential mortgage loan such as the subject transaction(s), including but not limited to all agreements with brokers, lenders, title companies, assignors, etc. Identify all documents relating to or reflecting such policy, practices and agreements, including all documentation required to be in assigned account files, and all forms given or sent to borrowers, information or forms which borrowers are requested to provide in order to obtain a loan, and all instructions, policy and procedure manuals, memoranda and guidelines given to brokers, title companies, lenders and/or closing agents, and any persons who review account files for approval and/or acceptance of assignment.

6. If your response to any of the foregoing Requests To Admit is anything other than an unqualified admission, state in detail all facts upon which you rely on in denying the request, state whether any investigation was made to determine your response and describe any such investigation, and identify all documents reviewed or relied upon.

7. If you are declining to produce any document or respond to any paragraph in whole or in part because of a claim of privilege, please: identify the subject matter, type (e.g., letter, memorandum), date, and author of the privileged communication or information, all persons that prepared or sent it, and all recipients or addressees; identify each person to whom the contents of each such communication or item of information have heretofore been disclosed, orally or in writing; state what privilege is claimed; and state the basis upon which the privilege is claimed.

8. If any document requested was, but no longer is, in your possession or subject to your control, please state: the date of its disposition; the manner of its disposition (e.g., lost, destroyed, or transferred to a third party); and an explanation if the circumstances surrounding the disposition of the document.

9. With respect to each expert or opinion witness whom you will or may call upon to give evidence in connection with this case, please state: his or her name, address, telephone number, occupation, and current employment; the subject matter of his or her expertise; any matters which you contend qualify him or her as an expert; the substance of all facts and opinions to which he or she could testify if called as a witness; a summary of the grounds for each such opinion, and identify all documents, reports or statements made by any such expert.

10. Describe and define all charges listed in Exhibits A, B and C to Homeowner's Affirmative Defenses, and explain any discrepancies in the listed figures, *i.e.*, explain why the Itemization of Amount Financed states that the Broker's Origination Fee was $7800, and that $500 was paid to Thomas Appraisals, while the HUD-1 Settlement Statement states that a $7032.63 "loan origination fee" plus $500 for an appraisal was paid to Victory Mortgage.

11. If you believe that other or different amounts were paid to Victory Mortgage in connection with the subject transaction (other than what is disclosed in the Exhibits to Homeowner's Affirmative Defenses), please state what amounts were paid and explain the discrepancy. Identify each and every service or goods you believe were provided by Victory Mortgage to Ms. Homeowner in connection with the transaction and the reasonable fair market value of those goods and services.

12. State the amount that you believe is the "total loan amount" and the total "points and fees" involved in the subject transaction and explain how you arrived at those figures.

13. Explain the basis and/or the manner in which the payments

made to Victory Mortgage were calculated (e.g., percentage of loan amount, interest rate of loan, specific services provided).

14. State the name, residence and business addresses and phone numbers, and job position of all person(s) and/or entities not identified in response to any preceding Interrogatory, who had any involvement in or has knowledge of any facts relating to matters alleged in Homeowner's Affirmative Defenses, and/or who may testify as witnesses at the trial or any hearing hereof. Identify each and every written or recorded statement made by such potential witnesses.

15. Identify all agreements between Chance and Saxon Mortgage. State the number of residential mortgage loans assigned by Saxon to Chance in the last three years, and identify those in which Victory Mortgage was the broker. Of these loans, state how many were in default of at least one month, within the first three years after they were made. State whether Chance has received any complaints (oral or written, whether or not filed with any judicial or administrative forum or consumer protection agency) from other borrowers in transactions in which either Saxon or Victory Mortgage was involved, and identify all individuals who made such complaints.

Requests for Production of Documents

1. Please produce all documents (including all computer or digital media-stored data) relating to Ms. Homeowner, the property located at 1234 W. Main Street, Chicago, Illinois, and the subject transaction and/or account, or which are indexed, filed or retrievable under her name or any number, symbol, designation or code (such as a transaction number or Social Security number) assigned to her or to the subject transaction(s), including but not limited to all documents relating to the origination, approval, disbursement, assignment and administration of the loan(s), all agreements between Chance and Saxon, and all correspondence related to the subject transaction.

2. All documents relating or referring to your policy and practice relating to the origination, approval or underwriting, preparation, disbursement and acceptance of assignment of a residential mortgage loan such as the subject transaction(s), including but not limited to all agreements with brokers, lenders, title companies, assignors, etc. Identify all documents relating to or reflecting such policy, practices and agreements, including all documentation required to be in assigned account files, and all instructions, policy and procedure manuals, memoranda and guidelines given to brokers, title companies, lenders, closing agents, and/or any persons who review account files for approval and/or acceptance of assignment.

3. All documents relating to any judicial or administrative proceeding, public or private consumer protection agency or office, and all customer complaints in which Chance, Saxon or Victory Mortgage were alleged to have made misrepresentations or violated any consumer protection statutes, rules or regulations relating to mortgages, mortgage brokers, or consumer credit.

4. Copies of all insurance policies which may afford coverage as to the matters complained of, or under which a claim was made. Include any policy which refers to consumer protection coverage and any comprehensive general liability policy.

5. All documents identified in response to the above Interrogatories, and all documents referred to or reviewed in preparing the response to the above Interrogatories, not otherwise called for in these document production requests.

I.10.4 Interrogatories and Requests for Production of Documents to Broker

STATE OF NORTH CAROLINA ORANGE COUNTY
IN THE GENERAL COURT OF JUSTICE
SUPERIOR COURT DIVISION

BETTY CONSUMER,	)	
Plaintiff,	)	
v.	)	
R & B FUNDING GROUP, INC., d/b/a National Builders, J.P. MORGAN CHASE BANK, as Trustee, ROYAL MORTGAGE & FINANCIAL SERVICE CENTERS, INC., and ELIZABETH B. WELD and DAVID W. SMITH, as Substitute Trustees,	)	02-CVS-0000 02-SP-000
Defendants.	)	

PLAINTIFF'S FIRST SET OF INTERROGATORIES TO DEFENDANT

TO: Royal Mortgage & Financial Service Centers, Inc.
c/o Joe Broker
Post Office Drawer 123
Raleigh, NC

YOU ARE REQUIRED, pursuant to North Carolina Rule of Civil Procedure 33,[20] to answer, completely, in writing, and under oath, the following interrogatories, and to return your answers to these interrogatories to Plaintiff's attorneys at the addresses indicated below, within thirty days of the date of service of these interrogatories.

Pursuant to North Carolina Rule of Civil Procedure 34, Plaintiff requests that Defendant produce the following documents for inspection and copying at the office of Plaintiff's attorney within thirty days of this request. In the alternative, Defendant may provide Plaintiff with legible copies of the requested documents.

A. In answering these interrogatories, furnish all information which is available to you, including information which is in the possession of your attorneys, employees or agents of Royal Mortgage & Financial Service Centers, Inc., and not merely such information known of your own personal knowledge.

B. If you cannot answer any of the interrogatories in full, after exercising due diligence to do so, state your inability and answer to the extent possible, state reasons for your inability to answer the remainder (including a list of the sources which were consulted for a response) and state whatever information or knowledge you have concerning the unanswered portions.

C. Each interrogatory is considered continuing, and if you

20 [*Editor's Note*: Citations throughout discovery as in original.]

obtain information which renders its answer or one of them incomplete or inaccurate, you are obligated to serve amended or supplementary answers on the undersigned.

D. For the purposes of these interrogatories, "identify," when used with reference to a document or documents, means to state as applicable, the type of document (e.g., installment contract, credit application, letter, memorandum, notes, etc.); the date of the document; the name, address and phone number of its present custodian; and, if a document is no longer in existence, the date and circumstances under which it was destroyed or lost.

E. For the purposes of these interrogatories, the terms "document" or "documents" refer to all writings and recorded materials, of any kind, that are or have been in possession, control or custody of Defendant or of which Defendant has knowledge, whether originals or copies. Such writings or recordings include, but are not limited to, contracts, documents, notes, rough drafts, inter-office memoranda, memoranda for the files, letters, research materials, correspondence, logs, diaries, forms, bank statements, tax invoices, diagrams, drawings, computer printouts or tapes, reports, statistical computations, studies, graphs, charts, minutes, manuals, pamphlets, or books of all nature and kind whether handwritten, typed, printed, mimeographed, photocopied or otherwise reproduced, all tape recordings (whether for computer, audio or visual replay) or other written, printed and recorded matter of tangible things on which words, phrases, symbols or information are recorded.

F. For the purposes of these interrogatories, "identify," when used with reference to a person, means to provide the following information for each person:

1. Full name;
2. Whether such person is or was ever an employee of Defendant;
3. Social security number;
4. Job title;
5. Date of initial employment;
6. Professional licenses held;
7. Whether the person has terminated employment with Defendant and, if so, the date each person terminated employment; and
8. The last known address of each person.

G. For the purposes of these interrogatories, "loan transaction" refers to the loan transaction entered into between Plaintiff and Defendant R & B Funding Group, Inc., on approximately April 18, 2002.

I. For the purposes of these Interrogatories, the term "Defendant" refers to Royal Mortgage and Financial Service Centers, Inc.

J. For the purposes of these Interrogatories, the term "high-cost loan" refers to a mortgage loan for more than $20,000, the total points and fees for which exceeds 5% of the total loan amount.

Interrogatories

1. Identify the person(s) who answered or participated in answering each of these interrogatories for Defendant. Include the position held by the respondent for Defendant, including the length of time the respondent has held this position, and the duties performed for Defendant.

2. Please state the Defendant's correct legal name.

3. Please state any other names which the Defendant uses to identify itself, whether such names are registered with any official, and the date and place of such registration.

4. Please identify each person who has knowledge of the facts and/or who participated in the loan transaction, including, but not limited to, the person who reviewed the credit application, processed the application, determined the terms of the financing agreement, performed the calculations in arriving at the terms of the financing agreement, and prepared any documents in connection with this transaction.

5. State whether any commission or other special remuneration was paid to any employee of Defendant as a result of the loan transaction.

6. For each commission or other remuneration stated in response to the preceding interrogatory, state:

a. The date each commission or other remuneration was paid;
b. The amount of commission or other remuneration; and
c. How the amount of each commission or other remuneration was determined.

7. Please identify the location of the closing or settlement of the loan transaction.

8. Please identify each person who was present at the closing or settlement of the loan transaction.

9. Identify all documents prepared for or by, received by, or signed by Plaintiff relating to the loan transaction and state:

a. The order in which those documents were signed by Plaintiff;
b. Which of the documents contained blanks or were not completed at the time they were signed by Plaintiff, and which portions were left blank or incomplete;
c. When and by whom the blanks or partially completed forms were filled in or completed; and
d. The date(s) each was signed by Defendant and by Plaintiff.

10. State whether the Plaintiff was advised by the Defendant that the loan obtained by Plaintiff during this loan transaction was a high-cost home loan.

11. If the answer to the preceding interrogatory is yes, describe how and when Plaintiff was so advised.

12. Did the Defendant receive certification from a counselor approved by the North Carolina Housing Finance Agency that the borrower has received counseling on the advisability of the loan transaction and the appropriate loan for the borrower, before making its loan to the Plaintiff?

13. Please state whether the Defendant provides training to new employees involved in brokering loans.

a. If so, describe the training content, time and duration.
b. If so, describe all documents and audio or visual materials used in such training.
c. If so, identify each person involved in providing such training.

14. Please state the total amount that Plaintiff has paid to Defendant either directly or indirectly in connection with the transaction in question. Identify each payment individually and state the date of each payment.

15. Please state how long Steve Smith was employed by Defendant. If he is no longer employed, state the reason. Please state his social security number and current address and telephone number.

16. If it is the contention of the Defendant that the Plaintiff received a net tangible benefit as a result of the loan transaction, please describe to the best extent possible the facts that support that contention.

17. Describe fully all the duties that Defendant performed for or on behalf of Plaintiff.

18. Identify any document that you rely on in support of your second defense (Motion to Compel Arbitration).

19. Describe fully all facts that support your contention that Plaintiff has failed to state a claim upon which relief can be granted.

20. Describe fully all facts that support your contention that the doctrine of laches applies as a defense to Plaintiff's complaint.

21. Describe fully all facts that support your contention that the doctrine of waiver and estoppel apply as defenses to Plaintiff's complaint.

22. Describe fully all facts that support your contention that the applicable statute of limitations period ended before Plaintiff entered her complaint.

23. Describe fully all facts that support your contention that the appropriate venue for this action is Wake County.

Requests for Production

1. All disclosure statements or other notices given by the Defendant to the Plaintiff regarding the loan transaction.

2. All documents provided by the Defendant to the Plaintiff describing the terms of the loan transaction.

3. The loan application, loan worksheet, application worksheet or other document used in considering the application of the Plaintiff for a loan in connection with the loan transaction that occurred on April 18, 2002.

4. All written communications either by or to the Plaintiff in connection with the loan transaction.

5. All telephone log sheets, internal memoranda, notes or other documents prepared or reflecting activity on the Plaintiff's account in connection with the loan transaction.

6. All documents recording, reflecting or otherwise relating to visits which the Defendant or its agents made to Plaintiff's home in connection with the loan transaction.

7. All documents you rely on for payment of document preparation fees in connection with the loan transaction.

8. All correspondence between Defendant and R & B Funding Group, Inc.

9. All contracts or agreements you entered into with Plaintiff relating to this loan transaction.

10. A copy of the outside and inside front and back of the file folder on the Plaintiff's loan folder.

11. All documents reflecting commission and/or bonuses paid to any individual including, but not limited to, payments to your employees, agents and any loan broker in connection with the loan transaction.

12. Any and all documents which you intend to use or introduce at trial.

This is the ________ day of January, 2003.

I.10.5 Interrogatories and Request for Production of Documents to Lender

STATE OF NORTH CAROLINA ORANGE COUNTY
IN THE GENERAL COURT OF JUSTICE
SUPERIOR COURT DIVISION

BETTY CONSUMER, Plaintiff, v. R & B FUNDING GROUP, INC., D/B/A National Builders, J.P. MORGAN CHASE BANK, as Trustee, ROYAL MORTGAGE & FINANCIAL SERVICE CENTERS, INC., and ELIZABETH B. WELD and DAVID W. SMITH, as Substitute Trustees Defendants.	02-CVS-0000 02-SP-000

PLAINTIFF'S FIRST SET OF INTERROGATORIES AND REQUEST FOR PRODUCTION OF DOCUMENTS

TO: R & B Funding Group, Inc.
c/o Joe Lender
P.O. Box 11111
Durham, NC

YOU ARE REQUIRED, pursuant to North Carolina Rule of Civil Procedure 33,* * * to answer, completely, in writing, and under oath, the following interrogatories, and to return your answers to these interrogatories to Plaintiff's attorneys at the addresses indicated below, within thirty days of the date of service of these interrogatories.

Pursuant to North Carolina Rule of Civil Procedure 34, Plaintiff requests that Defendant produce the following documents for inspection and copying at the office of Plaintiff's attorney within thirty days of this request. In the alternative, Defendant may provide Plaintiff with legible copies of the requested documents.

A. In answering these interrogatories, furnish all information which is available to you, including information which is in the possession of your attorneys, employees or agents of R & B Funding Group, Inc., and not merely such information known of your own personal knowledge.

B. If you cannot answer any of the interrogatories in full, after exercising due diligence to do so, state your inability and answer to the extent possible, state reasons for your inability to answer the remainder (including a list of the sources which were consulted for a response) and state whatever information or knowledge you have concerning the unanswered portions.

C. Each interrogatory is considered continuing, and if you obtain information which renders its answer or one of them incomplete or inaccurate, you are obligated to serve amended or supplementary answers on the undersigned.

D. For the purposes of these interrogatories, "identify," when used with reference to a document or documents, means to state as applicable, the type of document (e.g., installment contract, credit application, letter, memorandum, notes, etc.); the date of the document; the name, address and phone number of its present custodian; and, if a document is no longer in existence, the date and circumstances under which it was destroyed or lost.

E. For the purposes of these interrogatories, the terms "document" or "documents" refer to all writings and recorded materials, of any kind, that are or have been in possession, control or custody of Defendant or of which Defendant has knowledge, whether originals or copies. Such writings or recordings include, but are not limited to, contracts, documents, notes, rough drafts, inter-office memoranda, memoranda for the files, letters, research materials, correspondence, logs, diaries, forms, bank statements, tax invoices, diagrams, drawings, computer printouts or tapes, reports, statistical computations, studies, graphs, charts, minutes, manuals, pamphlets, or books of all nature and kind whether handwritten, typed, printed, mimeographed, photocopied or otherwise reproduced, all tape recordings (whether for computer, audio or visual replay) or other written, printed and recorded matter of tangible things on which words, phrases, symbols or information are recorded.

F. For the purposes of these interrogatories, "identify," when used with reference to a person, means to provide the following information for each person:

1. Full name;
2. Whether such person is or was ever an employee of Defendant;
3. Social security number;
4. Job title;
5. Date of initial employment;
6. Professional licenses held;
7. Whether the person has terminated employment with Defendant and, if so, the date each person terminated employment; and
8. The last known address of each person.

G. For the purposes of these interrogatories, "loan transaction" refers to the loan transaction entered into between Plaintiff and Defendant R & B Funding Group, Inc., on approximately April 18, 2002.

I. For the purposes of these Interrogatories, the term "Defendant" refers to R & B Funding Group, Inc.

J. For the purposes of these Interrogatories, the term "high-cost loan" refers to a mortgage loan for more than $20,000, the total points and fees for which exceeds 5% of the total loan amount.

Interrogatories

1. Identify the person(s) who answered or participated in answering each of these interrogatories for Defendant. Include the position held by the respondent for Defendant, including the length of time the respondent has held this position, and the duties performed for Defendant.

2. Please state the Defendant's correct legal name.

3. Please state any other names which the Defendant uses to identify itself, whether such names are registered with any official, and the date and place of such registration.

4. Please identify each person who has knowledge of the facts and/or who participated in the loan transaction, including, but not limited to, the person who reviewed the credit application, processed the application, determined the terms of the financing agreement, performed the calculations in arriving at the terms of the financing agreement, and prepared any documents in connection with this transaction.

5. State whether any commission or other special remuneration was paid to any employee as a result of the loan transaction.

6. For each commission or other remuneration stated in response to the immediately preceding interrogatory, state:

a. The date each commission or other remuneration was paid;
b. The amount of commission or other remuneration; and
c. How the amount of each commission or other remuneration was determined.

7. State whether any commission or other special remuneration was paid to any employee as a result of the loan transaction.

8. For each commission or other remuneration stated in response to the immediately preceding interrogatory, state:

a. The date each commission or other remuneration was paid;
b. The amount of commission or other remuneration; and
c. How the amount of each commission or other remuneration was determined.

9. Please identify the location of the closing or settlement of the loan transaction.

10. Please identify each person who was present at the closing or settlement of the loan transaction.

11. Please state whether the Plaintiff was granted the right to select the attorney that served as the settlement agent in the loan transaction from an approved list or otherwise.

12. Identify all documents prepared for or by, received by, or signed by Plaintiff relating to the loan transaction and state:

a. The order in which those documents were signed by Plaintiff;
b. Which of the documents contained blanks or were not completed at the time they were signed by Plaintiff, and which portions were left blank or incomplete;
c. When and by whom the blanks or partially completed forms were filled in or completed; and
d. The date(s) each was signed by Defendant and by Plaintiff.

13. At the time of the loan transaction, describe Defendant's policy, if any, with respect to determining whether a borrower received a benefit from refinancing an existing loan with a new *high-cost home* loan. Explain fully the criteria the Defendant applied in determining which customers received a tangible net benefit.

14. State whether the Plaintiff was advised that the loan she was getting was a high-cost home loan. If so, describe how, by whom and when she was so advised.

15. State whether Defendant received certification from a counselor approved by the North Carolina Housing Finance Agency that the borrower has received counseling on the advisability of the loan transaction and the appropriate loan for the borrower, before making its loan to the Plaintiff.

16. Please describe how Defendant determined the finance charges to be imposed in the loan transaction.

17. Please state whether the Defendant provided training on the new provisions of North Carolina's restrictions on high cost home loans to employees involved in originating mortgage loans in North Carolina during the time period from January, 2000 to the present.

a. If so, describe the training content, time and duration.
b. If so, describe all documents and audio or visual materials used in such training.

c. If so, identify each person involved in providing such training.

18. Please state the total amount that Plaintiff has paid to Defendant in connection with the transaction in question. Identify each payment individually and state the date of each payment.

19. Please describe the steps taken by the Defendant to pay off the mortgage loan that Plaintiff had with Bank of America, account no. 0000-0000-000, at the time she entered into this loan transaction.

20. If it is the contention of the Defendant that the Plaintiff received a net tangible benefit as a result of the loan transaction, please describe to the best extent possible the facts that support that contention.

21. For each year beginning with 2000 to the present, state the following:

a. The total number of mortgage loans entered into by the Defendant's branch office that originated Plaintiff's loan;
b. The total number of mortgage loans entered into by the Defendant's branch referenced above in which a high-cost home loan was procured by a borrower;
c. The total income, commission, or other remuneration received by employees of Defendant as a result of the origination of loans in North Carolina;
d. The total number of branch offices owned by Defendant R & B Funding Group, Inc.

22. Please identify the entity to which Defendant sold, assigned or otherwise transferred Plaintiff's loan, and the date on which the sale or assignment occurred. State the remuneration received by Defendant for selling, assigning, or transferring Plaintiff's loan.

23. Describe to the fullest extent you can what the "Loan Origination Fee" charged to Plaintiff in connection with this loan transaction in the amount of $395.00 was used for.

24. Describe to the fullest extent you can what the "Mortgage Broker Fee" charged to Plaintiff in connection with this loan transaction in the amount of $1424.50 was used for.

25. Describe to the fullest extent you can what the "Settlement or Closing Fee" charged to Plaintiff in connection with this loan transaction in the amount of $100.00 was used for.

26. Describe to the fullest extent you can what the "Title Search" fee charged to Plaintiff in the amount of $425.00 was used for.

27. Describe to the fullest extent you can what the "Lender Notification Fee," charged to Plaintiff in connection with this loan transaction in the amount of $35.00 was used for.

28. Describe to the fullest extent you can what the "Document Prep." Fee, charged to Plaintiff in connection with this loan transaction in the amount of $100.00 was used for.

29. If it is the Defendant's contention that any of the following fees should not be included in calculating the "high cost home loan" threshold contained in § 24-1.1E(a)(6), please state, to the fullest extent you can, all the facts which support your contention:

a. Loan Origination Fee in the amount of $395.00;
b. Mortgage Broker Fee in the amount of $1424.50;
c. Document Fee in the amount of $35.00.

Requests for Production

1. All disclosure statements or other notices given by the Defendant to the Plaintiff regarding the loan transaction.

2. All documents provided by the Defendant to the Plaintiff describing the terms of the loan transaction.

3. The notice(s) of right to cancel given to the Plaintiff in connection with the loan transaction.

4. The loan application, loan worksheet, application worksheet or other document used in considering the application of the Plaintiff for a loan in connection with the loan transaction that occurred on April 18, 2002.

5. The settlement statement, commitment letter and any worksheet or other document used to prepare the federal disclosure statement in the loan transaction.

6. All written communications either by or to the Plaintiff in connection with the loan transaction.

7. All written communications either by or to any other Defendant in the present case in connection with the loan transaction.

8. All telephone log sheets, internal memoranda, notes or other documents prepared or reflecting activity on the Plaintiff's account in connection with the loan transaction.

9. All documents recording, reflecting or otherwise relating to visits which the Defendant or its agents made to Plaintiff's home in connection with the loan transaction.

10. All documents that reflect payment of a $35.00 Document Fee to Document Systems (as indicated on line 808 of Plaintiff's HUD-1 Settlement Statement).

11. All documents that reflect fees, commissions or other payment made to any party, including the Plaintiff, in connection with the loan transaction, including but not limited to, contracts, bills, cancelled checks and other back-up documentation for such payment.

12. All documents relating to any fees, commission or payments received by the Defendant in connection with the loan transaction from the Plaintiff.

13. All documents relating to any fees, commission or payments received by the Defendant in connection with the loan transaction from anyone other than the Plaintiff.

14. All contracts, agreements, correspondence, records of communication or other documents reflecting interaction with any loan broker who was paid in the loan transaction.

15. All materials used by Defendant since January 1, 1998 to train its staff in conducting due diligence or otherwise reviewing loan files before acquiring loans.

16. All documents relating to any internal inspection procedures you used at the time of the loan transaction to insure that your employees or agents were complying with the new limitations on high cost home loans set forth by § 24-1.1E of the North Carolina General Statutes.

17. A copy of the outside and inside front and back of the file folder on the Plaintiff's loan account.

18. Copies of both sides of each and every check issued or received in connection with the loan transaction.

19. All documents reflecting commission and/or bonuses paid to any individual including, but not limited to, payments to your employees, agents and any loan broker in connection with the loan transaction.

20. All documents related in any way to any criteria or system used to determine the Plaintiff's credit worthiness.

21. All documents used in choosing, determining, setting, changing or adjusting the interest rate in the transaction, including any documents related to how the amount of the interest rate relates to the Plaintiff's individual circumstances.

22. Any and all documents contained in Plaintiff's loan file.

23. Any and all documents which you intend to use or introduce at trial.

This is the ________ day of March, 2003.

I.11 Sample Complaint for Fraud Against Home Improvement Contractor

IN THE CIRCUIT COURT
ST. CLAIR COUNTY, ILLINOIS

SENTEX HOME EQUITY CORP. PLAINTIFF,	)	
v.	)	
HATTIE O. CONSUMER, DEFENDANT,	)	No. 99-CH-0000
v.	)	
STANLEY DARROW, DEFENDANT.	)	

THIRD-PARTY COMPLAINT

Now comes the Defendant, Hattie O. Consumer, by her attorney, and for her complaint for damages states as follows.

Factual Allegations

1. The Defendant, Hattie Consumer, is a natural person currently residing at 123 Main Street, East Cupcake, IL. Ms. Consumer is an 82 year old disabled widow with an eighth grade education. Her total monthly income is $520 month, from Social Security, a pension, and Supplemental Security Income.

2. Ms. Consumer has lived in her home since 1977, when she began buying it under a bond-for-deed from Sieron-Fauss Associates. She received a quit-claim deed to the property in 1990. Ms. Consumer has no other debt and had never before taken out a home equity loan.

3. Defendant Stanley Darrow is a natural person, engaged in the construction business. Sometimes Defendant Darrow uses the name "Windell Darrow Construction Company," although, upon information and belief, no such company is registered to do business in Illinois.

4. In the fall of 1998, Ms. Consumer contacted Defendant Stanley Darrow about making repairs to her home. Defendant Darrow agreed to repair her roof, her kitchen floor, and front porch.

5. Defendant Darrow and Ms. Consumer never signed a written contract. Defendant Darrow agreed and contracted to perform the work listed in paragraph 4 in exchange for $7000.

6. Defendant Darrow told Ms. Consumer that he could get her a loan to pay for the home repairs. Defendant Darrow told Ms. Consumer that she would have to pay no more than $150 a month on the loan.

7. Upon information and belief, Defendant Darrow did arrange a loan for Ms. Consumer.

8. The loan Defendant Darrow arranged for Ms. Consumer was with Sentex Home Equity Corporation. It had a principal of $16,000, with stated interest 13.35%. Ms. Consumer paid over $1000 in points and fees out of the loan principal at the closing.

9. Upon information and belief, Defendant Darrow had an undisclosed business relationship with Plaintiff Sentex.

10. On January 14, 1999, Ms. Consumer received a phone call from Defendant Darrow, informing her that she needed to go to the closing the next day. Defendant Darrow picked up Ms. Consumer and took her to the closing.

11. On January 15, 1999, at the East Cupcake office of Nations Title, Ms. Consumer executed a note and mortgage against her home for the purpose of securing funds to pay for the repairs to her home. The only debt paid off by the loan was a sewer lien of approximately $972. Upon information and belief, all loan documents and closing instructions had been prepared by Plaintiff Sentex the previous day and sent via facsimile to Nations Title.

12. Defendant Consumer signed all loan documents, including the mortgage creating a security interest against her home, on January 15, 1999. No documents were provided to Ms. Consumer before the closing.

13. When she was signing the loan documents, Ms. Consumer noticed that the monthly principal and interest payment was $206.14, or nearly 40% of her income. Ms. Consumer told the closing agent and Defendant Darrow that she would not be able to pay that much monthly, and could only pay $150, the amount she and Defendant Darrow had agreed upon.

14. A few days after the closing, Defendant Darrow called Ms. Consumer and informed her that she needed to sign the check. Defendant Darrow picked Ms. Consumer up, took her to a bank, and turned over to her $600 in proceeds from the loan. Upon information and belief, Defendant Darrow kept possession of $12,735.66, the balance of the funds provided under the loan.

15. Defendant Darrow did fix the roof, but did not fix either the porch or kitchen floor. Defendant Darrow also failed to remove all of his trash from the property. Ms. Consumer has not heard from Defendant Darrow since he initially worked on her home. Defendant Darrow has not returned Ms. Consumer's repeated phone calls.

16. On or about March 9, 2000, Ms. Consumer's attorney wrote to Defendant Darrow demanding that the work be completed and the excess funds returned. A copy of that letter is attached as Exhibit A. Defendant Darrow never responded to that letter.

17. Defendant Darrow's work on the roof was substandard. Large portions of the roof have begun to buckle and warp. Proper venting was not installed, in violation of the Building and Occupancy Code, as adopted by the East Cupcake City Council. Soffit and fascia boards were not primed and painted. Drip edges were not installed properly. Defendant Darrow also failed to obtain any permits for the work from the East Cupcake Building Department.

Count I
FRAUD

Defendant Consumer repeats and reaffirms each and every allegation set forth in paragraphs 1 through 17 as if fully set forth herein.

18. Defendant Stanley Darrow knowingly made false statements

of material fact regarding the terms of the mortgage.

19. At the time Defendant Darrow made these statements, they were false, since the loan payment was more than the $150 promised.

20. Defendant Stanley Darrow knowingly made false statements of material fact as to the home repair contract with Ms. Consumer.

21. At the time Defendant Darrow made these statements, they were false, since the repairs were not completed, the repairs that were completed were not completed in compliance with city codes, and Mr. Darrow accepted more than the bargained-for consideration.

22. Defendant Stanley Darrow offered these statements as fact, not opinion, with the intent to induce Defendant to enter into the mortgage loan and provide the funds to him.

23. Ms. Consumer reasonably relied on Defendant Darrow's statements in signing the loan documents and turning over the funds obtained under the mortgage loan to him with the belief that her roof, porch, and kitchen would be properly repaired according to the terms of their agreement.

24. Had Ms. Consumer known the monthly payment that would be required under the loan, she would not have agreed to enter into it.

25. Had Ms. Consumer known that the repairs would not be completed and that those repairs that were completed would not be performed in substantial compliance with city code, she would not have entered into the contract for home repairs with Defendant Darrow.

26. As a result of Ms. Consumer's reliance on Defendant Darrow's statements, Ms. Consumer suffered damages in that she now faces the foreclosure of her home and no significant repairs have been performed on it.

WHEREFORE, Defendant Hattie Consumer prays that this Court

a. Award damages to be established at trial, and
b. Award such other relief as this Court deems just and proper.

Count II
CREDIT SERVICES ORGANIZATION ACT

Plaintiff repeats and reaffirms each and every allegation set forth in paragraphs 1 through 26 as if fully set forth herein.

27. Defendant is a "credit services organization" within the meaning of the Credit Services Organization Act, 815 ILCS 605/3 (d).[21]

28. Defendant deceived Plaintiff into obtaining a loan

a. By not registering as a credit services organization as the Act requires under ILCS 605/9;
b. By not providing Ms. Consumer with a consumer statement before accepting payment as required under 815 ILCS 605/6;
c. By not using a written contract as outlined in 815 605/7;
d. By making misleading or untrue statements to lending companies concerning Ms. Consumer's financial situation; and
e. By deceiving Ms. Consumer as to the cost and terms of the mortgage loan.

29. By reasons of the aforesaid violations of the Credit Services Organization Act, Defendant is liable to Plaintiff in the amount of actual damages to be established at trial in accordance with 815 ILCS 605/11.

WHEREFORE, Plaintiff prays that this Court

a. Award actual damages to be established at trial pursuant to 815 ILCS 605/11.
b. Award such other relief as this Court deems just and proper.

Count III
CONSUMER FRAUD AND DECEPTIVE BUSINESS PRACTICES ACT

Defendant repeats and reaffirms each and every allegation set forth in paragraphs 1 through 29 as if fully set forth herein.

30. Defendant Darrow is engaged in "trade" or "commerce" within the meaning of the Consumer Fraud and Deceptive Business Practices Act, 815 ILCS 505/1(f).

31. Defendant Darrow deceived Ms. Consumer, intending that Ms. Consumer rely on his deceptions and execute a mortgage on her home, through the following and other unfair practices:

a. By willfully and with a reckless indifference for Ms. Consumer's rights failing to provide her with notice of her rights under the Federal Trade Commission's Rule Concerning the Preservation of Consumer's Claims and Defenses, 16 C.F.R. § 433;
b. By violating the Credit Services Organizations Act, 815 ILCS 605/1 *et seq.*;
c. By obtaining credit for Ms. Consumer without being licensed as a broker;
d. By willfully and with a reckless indifference for Ms. Consumer's rights procuring credit for Ms. Consumer beyond her ability to repay;
e. By misrepresenting the quantity of work he would perform under the home repair contract;
f. By misrepresenting the quality of work he would perform under the home repair contract;
g. By misrepresenting the amount he would charge for the work under the home repair contract;
h. By failing to get required building permits for the work performed on her home; and
i. By refusing to provide Ms. Consumer with a written contract.

32. Defendant Darrow engaged in this conduct willfully, in violation of public policy, and with the intent that Ms. Consumer would rely on his misrepresentations and enter into a mortgage loan on her home and provide him with the proceeds of that loan.

33. When Ms. Consumer entered into the loan transaction, she did so under the understanding that she could only pay $150 a month and that all monies were to go to Defendant Darrow for repairs to her home. Ms. Consumer believed that Defendant Darrow would perform all promised work in a professional manner.

34. By reason of the aforesaid violations of the Consumer Fraud and Deceptive Business Practices Act, Defendant is liable to Plaintiff in the amount of actual damages to be established at trial in accordance with 815 ILCS 505/10a.

WHEREFORE, Plaintiff prays that this Court

a. Award actual damages to be established at trial pursuant to with 815 ILCS 505/10a;
b. Award such other relief as this Court deems just and proper.

---

21 [*Editor's Note*: Citations throughout complaint as in original.]

Appendix J Glossaries

J.1 Generalized Glossary

Compliments of AFFIL partners: Center for Responsible Lending and the National Consumer Law Center

Italicized words are separately defined within this subsection.

Acceleration. When a *creditor* claims the total balance of a loan is due immediately. This can not usually occur unless you have fallen behind on payments. In the case of a home mortgage, receipt of a letter stating that a loan has been "accelerated" is normally an important warning sign of foreclosure.

Accord and Satisfaction. This is the legal term which applies when you make clear that you consider your payment the full and final resolution of a disputed debt. If the creditor accepts the payment, the law treats that acceptance as the final payment of the debt.

Adjustable Rate Mortgage (ARM). A mortgage in which the interest rate can be adjusted at specified intervals by a given formula using an index and margin.

Amortize. This means to pay off a loan with regular payments. Part of each payment is applied to principal and to interest. At the end of the term, the loan is paid in full. There is no balloon payment.

Amount Financed. The amount of money you are getting in a loan, calculated under rules required by federal law. This is the amount of money you are borrowing after deduction of certain loan charges that the *Truth in Lending Act* defines as *finance charges*, i.e., *principal* minus finance charges. You should think of the amount financed as the real amount you are borrowing. You will find the amount financed for a loan on the *disclosure statement* that is given to you when the loan papers are signed.

Annual Percentage Rate. The interest rate on a loan expressed under rules required by federal law. It is more accurate to look at the annual percentage rate (as opposed to the stated interest rate) to determine the true cost of a loan, because it tells you the full cost of the loan including many of the lender's fees. You will find the annual percentage rate for a loan on the *disclosure statement* that is given to you when the loan papers are signed.

Answer. In a lawsuit, this is a legal document that the *defendant* must file to respond to the claims being raised. There are often short time deadlines to file an answer. Failure to file an answer can result in a *default judgment*.

Appraisal. An estimate of the value of property made by a qualified professional called an "appraiser." Appraisals vary in price depending upon whether it contains a full report with a market analysis involving comparable sales or a simple "drive by."

Arbitration. See *Mandatory Arbitration*.

Arrears. The total amount you are behind on a debt. Usually the amount of all back payments plus any collection costs.

Assignee. When a mortgage is transferred from one party to another (usually because the loan is purchased for investment purposes), the party that assumes ownership of the mortgage, as well as the rights and responsibilities attached to that mortgage, is known as the "assignee." An assignee may receive all or part of a security interest.

Assignee Liability. A legal term that means that the purchaser of a loan may be held liable for legal claims against the original lender. Typically, the original lenders sell loans in the secondary market after the loan closes. If a predatory lending claim arises, assignee liability ensures that the borrower can pursue legal action. Assignee liability also encourages loan purchasers to conduct thorough due diligence.

Assignment. The transfer of a mortgage or deed of trust to another party usually evidenced by a document showing that the current mortgage holder (assignor) assigned its rights to the new holder (assignee).

Attachment. A legal process that allows a creditor to "attach" a *lien* to property that you own. Depending on state law, almost any kind of property may be subject to attachment, including your home, automobile, bank accounts, and wages. Once a *lien* is attached to the property, you may face further collection action on that property, including *execution, garnishment* or *foreclosure*.

Automatic Stay. An automatic end to creditor collection activity. Filing bankruptcy is the only way to get this protection. If the *debtor* filed other bankruptcy cases that were dismissed within the previous twelve months, however, she may not get an automatic stay or it may only last for the first thirty days of the bankruptcy case.

Auto/Car Title Loan. A short term loan secured by a borrower's car title. A typical car title loan has a triple-digit annual interest rate, requires repayment within one month, and is made for much less than the value of the car. Many borrowers who cannot afford to pay off their loans repeatedly extend them for additional fees. In some states, lenders are allowed to keep the surplus from the sale of the car if the borrower defaults on payment.

Balloon Payment. A large lump-sum *payment* that is due as the last payment on a loan. Often used by lenders as a way to make monthly payments artificially low.

Bank. A financial institution that accepts deposits, makes loans, and performs other services for its customers. According to Robert Frost, "a bank is a place where they lend you an umbrella in fair weather and ask you for it back when it begins to rain."

Bankruptcy. A legal process available in all states that allows you to address your debt problems according to a set of special rules while getting protection from continued collection activity. See also *Liquidation* and *Reorganization*.

Bond. Amounts required by a court order to protect a party to a lawsuit while the case proceeds. A bond may be required in some circumstances to pursue an appeal.

Bounce Loans. A short-term loan granted by a bank to cover an overdraft incurred by using either paper check or debit cards. Banks charge high penalty fees for each overdraft, ranging from $20 to $35 per overdraft plus a per-day fee of $2 to $5 at some banks until the account is brought to a positive balance. With "bounce loan" programs, banks pay themselves back the amount of the overdraft and fees out of the next deposit. See *Overdraft Loan*.

Broker's Price Opinion. An evaluation of property value typically based on a drive-by exterior examination, public data sources, and recent comparable sales, that is obtained by a *servicer* as an alternative to a full appraisal after a loan is in default or when the loan is being modified.

Cap. A ceiling that limits how much the interest rate on the loan may be adjusted. There are periodic caps, which limit how much the interest may be adjusted per period, and a lifetime cap, which limits how much the interest rate may be adjusted over the life of the loan.

Capitalization. Capitalization occurs when items owed on a loan are treated as part of a new principal balance. When *arrears* are "capitalized," the amount of the arrears is included in the principal before the interest rate is applied. Often, capitalization and *reamortization* go hand in hand. If the arrears are "capitalized" and the loan is "reamortized," your lender will recalculate your payment using the existing interest rate and the new principal balance.

Chapter 7 Bankruptcy. See *Liquidation*.

Chapter 13 Bankruptcy. See *Reorganization*.

Check Cashing. Service offered by alternative financial institutions to people who do not have access to mainstream banking services. Although the fees can be high (typically 3% of the check value), unlike predatory payday lending, the practice generally does not encourage a cycle of debt.

Closed-End Loan. A loan with a fixed term.

Closing. The process of signing loan papers which obligate the borrower to repay a loan. This term is associated with the signing of a mortgage loan. It is also called the settlement.

Closing Agent. The mortgage closing or settlement is usually conducted by an agent for the lender. This person is called the closing agent. Often this agent is an attorney.

Closing Costs. These are costs related to the financing and title transfer of real estate. They include expenses such as points, taxes, title insurance, mortgage insurance, commissions, and fees.

Collateral. Property put up to secure a loan. If you have given a creditor collateral, that creditor can normally take and sell the collateral if you are not able to repay the loan. A creditor with collateral is normally known as a "*secured creditor*."

Commitment. An agreement, often in writing, between a lender and a borrower to loan money at a future date subject to the completion of paperwork or compliance with stated conditions. The commitment may guarantee an interest rate or other terms until a future date. See *Lock*.

Complaint. A document beginning a lawsuit. A complaint normally includes a statement of all of the claims being raised by the person bringing the lawsuit.

Conventional Loan. A loan issued to a borrower with an excellent or very good credit rating. Conventional loans do not include those insured by the federal government, such as the Federal Housing or Veterans Administrations, or subprime loans.

Cosigner. A person who agrees to be responsible for someone else's debt. A cosigner is normally responsible for paying back a debt just as if he or she had received the money.

Counterclaim. A response to a lawsuit in which the person being sued raises legal claims against the person (or business) which started the case. For example, if you are sued by an automobile seller who claims you did not pay for a car, you might counterclaim that the car was a "lemon."

Credit Bureau. Also called consumer reporting agency or credit reporting agency. This is a company that receives information about a consumer's credit history and keeps records that are available to those seeking data about that consumer.

Credit Insurance. Insurance designed to pay off a borrower's mortgage debt if the borrower dies or is otherwise incapable of meeting the loan obligation. When sold in a "single premium" or "lump sum," all premiums are charged in advance and typically added to the loan balance, increasing the overall cost by requiring the borrower to pay interest on the premiums over the life of the loan. Since single-premium credit insurance has fallen into disfavor, lenders have introduced analogous products such as "debt cancellation" contracts.

Credit Report. Also called a consumer report or a credit record. A report documenting the credit history and current status of a borrower's monthly payment obligations and containing public information such as bankruptcies, court *judgments*, and tax liens.

Credit Score. A credit score (sometimes called a "FICO" score) is a number that summarizes your credit history. The score is based on a number of factors, including how well debts have been paid off, current levels of debt, types of credit, and length of credit history. Lenders use credit scores to decide who qualifies for a loan and how much the loan should cost. Scores generally range from 350 to 900; most lenders consider a score over 660 to be very good.

Creditor. Also called a lender. Any person or business to whom you owe money.

Cure a Default. If you have defaulted on a debt, this is a process for correcting the *default*. Most often, a "cure" refers to getting caught up on missed payments (paying the *arrears*). A cure may also be called *reinstatement*.

Debt Collector. The most common use of this term applies to anyone who collects debts. However, under the federal *Fair Debt Collection Practices Act* "FDCPA," the term "debt collector" only applies to collection agencies and lawyers (or their employees) that are collecting debts for others. State laws may cover other types of collectors.

Debt Consolidation. Refinancing debt into a new loan. In the mortgage lending context, relatively short-term, unsecured debt often is rolled into long-term mortgage loans, putting the home at greater risk.

Debt-to-Income Ratio. The relationship between the consumer's monthly debt payments and the monthly income, expressed as a ratio. Lenders will often set a maximum debt-to-income ratio and usually do not make loans to consumers whose ratios exceed the lender's standard.

Debt Management Plan. Debt management plans are offered by many credit counseling agencies. Through debt management plans (DMPs), consumers send the credit counseling agency a monthly payment, which the agency then distributes to the consumer's creditors. In return, the consumer is supposed to get a break, usually in the form of creditor agreements to waive fees and to lower interest rates.

Debtor. Any person who owes money to another. In *bankruptcy*, the term "debtor" refers to the person who begins a bankruptcy case.

Debtor's Examination. Also known as "post-judgment process," "asset examination," and "supplementary process." This is normally a court ordered proceeding in which a debtor must appear in court or in an attorney's office to answer questions about current income and assets from which a *judgment* may be collected. In many states, failure to appear at a debtor's examination can result in an arrest warrant.

Debt Settlement. Negotiation and settlement services are different from debt management services (see *Debt Management Plan*) mainly because the debt settlement agencies do not send regular monthly payments to creditors. Instead, these agencies generally maintain a consumer's funds in separate accounts, holding the money until the agency believes it can settle a consumer's debts for less than the full amount owed.

Deed. A deed is an instrument that transfers ownership from the seller to the buyer upon the closing of the sale.

Deed in Lieu. An agreement to turn real estate over to a lender as an alternative to *foreclosure*.

Deed of Trust. In some states, this is the term used for a pledge of real estate as *collateral*. It is similar to a *mortgage*.

Default. Failing to meet the requirements of an agreement. Most defaults involve failure to make required payments. However, other types of defaults are possible, including failure to maintain necessary insurance and failure to keep *collateral* in proper condition.

Default Judgment. A *judgment* in a lawsuit against a party who did not meet legal requirements in connection with the case. The most common reason for a default judgment is failing to file an *answer* or other necessary papers before deadlines specified by law.

Default Rate. The interest rate the creditor will charge once the borrower defaults on the loan. If a default interest rate is listed in a loan contract, it is always higher than the contract interest rate.

Defendant. In a lawsuit, this is the person or business that is being sued.

Defense. A legal reason why a court should not award any or all of what is requested in a lawsuit. For example, a statement that the money is not owed is a defense to a collection lawsuit.

Deficiency. The amount a debtor owes a creditor on a debt after the creditor seizes and sells the *collateral*. A deficiency arises when the collateral is sold for less than the amount of the debt. Normally, a creditor must bring a lawsuit to collect a deficiency.

Deposition. A proceeding in a legal case in which a person is asked questions about relevant facts (usually in a lawyer's office) and gives sworn answers under oath. Your deposition may be required if you start a lawsuit or if one is filed against you. Your lawyer may require depositions of others. Depositions are a normal part of the *discovery* process used to prepare for a court trial.

Deregulation. The process started in the 1980s of loosening or eliminating regulation of the lending industry. Deregulation resulted, in part, in the removal of usury caps and borrower protections. Since then, abusive lending practices have increased.

Discharge. A document that ends a debtor's legally enforceable obligation to pay a debt. It is common to get a discharge of a mortgage debt after the mortgage is fully paid off. In addition, most bankruptcies result in a discharge at the end of the case that applies to many debts.

Disclosure Statement. This term is commonly used to refer to the document that explains loan terms according to the *Truth in Lending Act*.

Discount Fee. See *Points*.

Discovery. This term covers a variety of legal processes by which the parties to a lawsuit obtain information from each other and documents related to the case.

Down Payment. Money paid to make up the difference between the purchase price and the mortgage amount. Down payments are usually 20% of the sale price on *conventional loans*.

Equity. Your equity in property is the amount of cash you would keep if you sold property and paid off all of the liens on that property. For example, if you own a house worth $100,000, but you owe $60,000 on your original mortgage and $10,000 on a second mortgage, you have $30,000 in equity. The same principle applies to cars and other types of property.

Equity Stripping. Loan terms on mortgages (usually refinances) designed to maximize the lender's revenues by increasing the borrower's loan balance; this practice reduces the borrower's equity in the home. Equity stripping may occur in various ways, but the most common is charging excessive fees that are financed as part of the new loan.

Escrow. Amounts set aside for a particular purpose. A formal escrow usually requires a legal agreement that covers permissible usage of the escrow and how and where the money is to be kept. One type of escrow is money you pay to your mortgage company to cover taxes and insurance. Escrow is also used when you have a dispute with a creditor. You may choose to set up an escrow to pay the debt in the event you lose the dispute.

Escrow Closing or Settlement. The occasion where the purchase of a home is financed or a non-purchase money loan (see *Home Equity Loan*) and *mortgage* is signed, the buyer pays the mortgage, and closing costs are paid.

Eviction. A legal process terminating the right to occupy a home, apartment or business property. State law eviction proceedings are required before putting someone out.

Execution. The process of enforcing a court judgment by taking property from the *defendant*. Execution of a judgment of *eviction*, for example, involves the sheriff or a public official putting the tenants out. Execution of a *judgment lien* involves seizing and selling the property subject to the lien.

Exempt Property. Property that the law allows you to keep when you are being faced with collection on an *unsecured debt*. In *bankruptcy*, exempt property is protected from sale to satisfy the claims of creditors. Your exemption applies to your *equity* in the property after deduction for the amounts you owe to pay *liens* on that property.

Exemptions. These are laws that give you the right to keep your *exempt property*.

Exploding ARM (Adjustable Rate Mortgage). A common type of "hybrid" ARM in the subprime market that includes both a fixed and adjustable interest rate component. A "2/28" hybrid ARM comes with an initial short-term fixed interest rate for two years, followed by rate adjustments, generally in six-month increments for the remainder of the loan's term. Typically the introductory rate is artificially low, giving homeowners a dramatic increase in housing costs after the introductory period expires.

Fair Credit Reporting Act. A federal (national) law that regulates *credit bureaus* and the use of credit reports.

Fair Debt Collection Practices Act. A federal (national) law that governs the conduct of debt collectors and that prevents many abusive collection tactics.

Fannie Mae. See *Federal National Mortgage Association.*

Federal Deposit Insurance Corporation (FDIC). An independent agency created by Congress in 1933 to maintain financial stability and public confidence in the nation's banking system. The FDIC insures deposits in banks and thrift institutions for up to $100,000. The agency also directly examines and supervises about 5300 banks and savings banks, more than half of the institutions in the U.S. banking system.

Federal Housing Administration (FHA). One of the agencies of the federal government that insures first mortgage lenders against loss when a loan is made following FHA regulations. The FHA does not lend money; it only insures the loan.

Federal Law. A law of the United states that applies throughout the country. The *bankruptcy* law is an example of a federal law.

Federal National Mortgage Association (Fannie Mae) and Federal Home Mortgage Corporation (Freddie Mac). A high percentage of mortgages are now held by investors. The two largest investors that purchase mortgages on the secondary market are Fannie Mae and Freddie Mac. These "government sponsored enterprises" were created by Congress to provide liquidity or capital in the housing market by purchasing mortgages. This helps put money back into the hands of the originating lender so that new loans can be made. The originating lender must follow certain guidelines specified by Freddie Mac and Fannie Mae when qualifying the borrower for a loan, commonly called *underwriting* guidelines.

Federal Reserve Board (Fed). The central bank of the United States. It was created by Congress to provide the nation with a safer, more flexible, and more stable monetary and financial system. Its central agency conducts US monetary policy, and its twelve regional banks support and regulate commercial banks and thrifts.

Fee. Any charge added to a loan.

Finance Charge. The amount of money a loan will cost you expressed as a dollar figure. The finance charge includes the interest together with certain other loan charges specified by the *Truth in Lending Act*. You will find the loan's finance charge on the *disclosure statement* given to you when you sign the loan papers.

Finance Company. A company engaged in making loans to individuals or businesses. Unlike a bank, it does not receive deposits from the public.

Fixed Rate Mortgage. A mortgage on which the interest rate is set for the term of the loan.

Flipping. The practice of refinancing a loan without providing a net benefit to the homeowner. Although some borrowers may receive cash as a result of flipped loans, the benefit of this compensation may be outweighed by the costs of losing equity or taking on unaffordable debt. See *Property Flipping*.

Force Placed Insurance. The insurance policy your lender will "force" you to purchase if your insurance is cancelled or if your lender does not have proof of your insurance coverage. Force placed insurance is very expensive.

Foreclosure. A legal process to terminate your ownership of real estate that is *collateral* for a debt, based on a *mortgage* or *deed of trust*. In some states, foreclosure involves a court proceeding ("judicial foreclosure"), while in others foreclosure occurs by creditor action alone ("non-judicial foreclosure").

Foreclosure Rescue Scam. This scam targets those who have fallen behind on their mortgage payments. A con artist promises to help consumers save their home but is actually intent on stealing the home or most of its accumulated equity.

Fraudulent Transfer. Giving away property to keep it out of the hands of creditors. The law allows *creditors* to sue to get the property back.

Freddie Mac. See *Federal Home Mortgage Corporation.*

Fully Indexed Rate. The interest rate on an adjustable rate mortgage that is calculated by adding the margin to the index at the time the loan is originated. Historically, lenders have underwritten mortgages to the fully indexed rate. During the subprime lending boom, some lenders underwrote mortgages to the initial interest rate, also called a "teaser" rate, which generally is less than the fully indexed rate and does not reflect the risk that the interest rate will increase when the margin is added to the index. The fully indexed rate also does not fully reflect the risk of an increase in the interest rate. It is not the maximum rate that can be charged on the note, but rather reflects what the interest rate would have been at the time the loan was made based solely on the index at that time and the stated margin.

Garnishment. A *creditor's* seizure, to satisfy a debt, of property belonging to the *debtor* that is in the possession of a third party. Usually a court has to authorize the seizure in advance. An example would be seizure of money in your bank account to repay a court judgment. Wages owed to you can also be garnished in many states.

Ginnie Mae. See *Government National Mortgage Association.*

Good Faith Estimate (GFE). An itemization of the estimated closing costs. Lenders or brokers must provide this list to the loan applicant for a mortgage loan within three business days after receipt of the application. The GFE is intended to assure that consumers have adequate information about closing costs early on to enable them to shop for those, as well as interest rates. This disclosure is required by the Real Estate Settlement Procedures Act.

Government Mortgage Guarantors. There are special government programs that provide mortgage insurance or guarantees to lenders who make purchase-money mortgage loans to homebuyers who meet certain criteria. These programs are offered through the federal government (the Federal Housing Administration, part of the Department of Housing and Urban Development; the Rural Housing Service, part of the Department of Agriculture; and the Veterans Administration) or by a state housing finance agency. In addition to the insurance, these loans come with an obligation on the part of the insured lenders to work with homeowners to cure defaults.

Government National Mortgage Association (Ginnie Mae). It is a quasi-governmental agency that guarantees pools of Federal Housing Administration (FHA) and Veteran Administration (VA) insured-loans that had been securitized for investment purposes.

Guarantor. A person who agrees to pay another person's debt in the event that he or she does not pay. The term guarantor is often used interchangeably with *cosigner*, even though there are some minor legal distinctions in the collection process.

Hazard Insurance. Insurance that covers property loss or damage, usually paid for by borrowers and required when obtaining a mortgage.

Holder. The mortgage holder "owns" the borrowers' mortgage. Since many mortgages are assigned by the originator to a purchaser on the secondary market, very often the mortgage holder will not be the bank or mortgage company who made the loan.

Home Equity Loan. Generally, this term is used to describe any mortgage loan that is not used to finance the purchase of the home.

Home Ownership and Equity Protection Act (HOEPA). This is a federal (national) law that provides special protection to homeowners when they obtain home mortgage loans at high interest rates or with high fees.

Homestead Exemption. The right, available in most states and in the *bankruptcy* process, to treat your residence as *exempt property* that can not be sold to satisfy the claims of *unsecured creditors*. In most states, the homestead exemption covers a certain dollar amount of your equity in your residence. A home can not normally be sold to pay claims of your creditors unless your equity in the home exceeds the amount of the exemption. A homestead exemption will not normally protect you from *foreclosure* when you have voluntarily pledged your home as *collateral*.

Index. A published rate often used to establish the interest rate charged on adjustable rate mortgages or to compare investment returns. Examples of commonly used indexes include Treasury bill rates, the prime rate, LIBOR (the London Interbank Offered Rate), and the Eleventh District Cost-of-Funds Index (issued by the San Francisco Federal Home Loan Bank).

Interest. Is the cost of borrowing money over time. Interest rates are expressed as a percentage.

Investor. A company that invests in mortgages that other companies have originated. They purchase the mortgage for a set amount and collect monthly payments, usually through a servicer.

Insolvent. A person or business that does not have sufficient assets to pay its debts.

Judgment. A determination by a court as to the outcome of a lawsuit, including any amounts owed.

Judgment Lien. A *lien* that attaches to property as the result of a *judgment*. For example, if you lose a collection lawsuit, the creditor normally has the right to an *attachment* on any real estate that you own.

Judgment-Proof. This term is applied to people or businesses with property of minimal value, which can be entirely protected by *exemptions*. If you are judgment-proof, it is difficult or sometimes impossible for any creditor to force you to pay a debt.

Kickback. Money paid by one of the settlement service providers, e.g., the lender, title company, or closing attorney, for referring a customer.

Lemon Law. This is a state law that gives you protection if you purchase an automobile that does not work properly and can not easily be fixed. Most lemon laws only apply to new cars, but some also apply to used cars.

Levy. A process, in some states, for *attachment* of a *judgment lien* and/or *execution* of that *lien*.

Lien. Also called a "security interest," it is a legal interest taken by creditors in your property to secure repayment of a debt. A lien can be created voluntarily in connection with a loan, such as when you pledge real estate by giving a creditor a *mortgage* or *deed of trust*. A lien can also be created without your consent by *attachment* based on a court order. A creditor with a lien is called a *secured creditor*.

Liquidation. Sale of property to pay creditors. The term is also used as a shorthand name for the chapter 7 bankruptcy process, even though property is not always sold in that bankruptcy process.

Lis Pendens. A notice, recorded in the chain of title to real property, required or permitted in some states to warn all persons that certain property is the subject of litigation and that any interests in the real property acquired during the pendency of the suit are subject to its outcome.

Loan Application. A standard form that creditors use to obtain personal and financial information from a borrower before deciding whether to make a loan.

Loan Term. The loan term is the length of time before the loan is due to be repaid in full. Most mortgage loans have fifteen or thirty-year terms. Many predatory consumer loans (payday loans, car title loans, refund anticipation loans) have very short loan terms, which increase the APR earned by the lender and/or pressure consumers into extending their loans at additional fees.

Loan-to-Value Ratio (LTV). The relationship, expressed as a percentage, between the loan amount and the value of the property securing the loan. The more equity in the property, the lower the percentage. Conversely, the less equity, the higher the percentage. A "high LTV loan" is one made with little or no equity in the property to secure the loan in the event of foreclosure. Conventional lenders require an LTV of, at most, 80%. *Subprime* lenders usually prefer a lower LTV, in the 70–75% range.

Lock. The *interest* rate selected by the borrower at a certain time during the loan process that is guaranteed by the lender for a specific number of days. This is called "locking" the rate. Once the rate is locked, neither the lender nor the borrower can change it.

Mandatory Arbitration. A clause in a loan contract that requires the borrower to use arbitration to resolve any legal disputes that arise from the loan. Mandatory arbitration typically means borrowers lose their right to pursue legal actions, including any appeals, in a court of law. Evidence indicates that arbitration is often costly for borrowers and may reduce their chances of receiving a fair outcome. Borrowers often are unaware that a mandatory arbitration agreement has been included in their home documents.

Margin. The number added to the index to determine the interest rate on an adjustable rate mortgage. For example, if the index rate is 6%, and the current note rate is 8.75%, the margin is 2.75%.

Market Value. The highest price one would pay and the lowest price the seller would accept on a property. Market value may be different from the price a property could actually be sold for at a given time.

Mortgage. An agreement in which a property owner grants a *creditor* the right to satisfy a debt by selling the real property in the event of a *default.*

Mortgage-Backed Security. A type of investment backed by pools of mortgage loans, with payments on the underlying mortgages generating the return to investors. By selling mortgages in the secondary mortgage market, where they are collected and packaged as investments, lenders are able to generate more funds for future lending.

Mortgage Broker. An individual who offers to arrange financing for a homeowner. In theory, the broker operates as the agent for the homeowner, seeking the best product. States vary as to whether or not the brokers are regulated.

Mortgagee. The entity that obtains a security interest in the real property of another, usually the lender.

Mortgage Insurance. See *Private Mortgage Insurance.*

Mortgage Servicer. A bank, mortgage company, or a similar business that communicates with property owners concerning their *mortgage* loans. The servicer usually works for another company that owns the mortgage. It may accept and record payments, negotiate *workouts*, and supervise the *foreclosure* process in the event of a *default.*

Mortgagor. The owner of real property who grants a *mortgage* to another, usually a lender.

Negative Amortization. Negative amortization occurs when your payments do not cover the amount of interest due for that payment period. For example, if you have a $50,000 loan at 10% interest for fifteen years and make monthly payments of $400 a month, that loan will negatively amortize. At the end of the fifteen years, even if you make all of your payments, you will still owe more than $50,000. Negative amortization is usually associated with a large *balloon payment* due in the last month of the loan.

Negative Equity. Negative *equity* arises when the value of an item of property you own is less than the total you owe on all the liens on that property. For example, if you own a home worth $100,000 and borrow $125,000 to consolidate debts, you have negative equity of $25,000.

Non-Purchase Money Security Interest. A non-purchase money security interest arises when you agree to give a lender collateral that was not purchased with money from that loan. For example, a finance company may insist that you give a lawn mower or living room set as collateral for a loan you take out to pay for car repairs.

Non-Sufficient Funds (NSF). Fees are charged for non-sufficient funds (NSF) when a checking account is overdrawn. The threat of these charges contribute to the pressure payday borrowers are under to renew loans and pay repeated fees. NSF fees differ from overdraft fees, which are charged for the extension of a loan using bank funds to cover the amount you would have overdrawn.

Note. This term is commonly used as a name for a contract involving the loan of money.

Notice of Right to Cancel. This document explains your right to cancel a loan in some circumstances. You should receive such a notice in connection with most door-to-door sales and for *mortgage* loans that are not used to buy your residence.

Notice to Quit. In most states, this is a notice given by an owner of property (usually a landlord) demanding that a tenant leave within a specified period of time or face eviction proceedings.

Office of the Comptroller of the Currency (OCC). Charters, regulates and supervises all national banks. It also supervises all federal branches and agencies of foreign banks.

Office of Thrift Supervision (OTS). The successor thrift regulator to the Federal Home Loan Bank Board and a division within the Treasury Department. The OTS is responsible for the examination and regulation of federally chartered and state chartered savings associations.

Open-Ended Loan. A loan without a definite term or end date.

Origination Fee. A fee paid to a lender for processing a loan application. It is stated as a percentage of the mortgage amount, or "points."

Originator. The lender who makes the loan and whose name is on the loan documents.

Overdraft Loan. Overdraft loans, also called bounce-check protection or courtesy overdraft protection, are a form of high-cost, short-term credit, wherein financial institutions cover their customers' overdrafts when they have a negative balance, and then charge them a fee. These loans have been exempted from interest rate disclosure requirements and can contribute to a devastating cycle of debt. See *Bounce Loan*.

Payday Loan. (Also called "cash advances," "deferred presentment," "deferred deposits" or "check loans.") Payday loan customers write the lender a post-dated check or sign an authorization for the lender to take money out of an account electronically for a certain amount. The amount on the check equals the amount borrowed plus a fee that is either a percentage of the full amount of the check or a flat dollar amount. The check (or debit agreement) is then held for up to a month, usually until the customer's next payday or receipt of a government check. At the end of the agreed time period, the customer must either pay back the full amount of the check (more than what the lender gave out), allow the check to be cashed, or pay another fee to extend the loan. Most payday borrowers get caught in a debt trap, unable to pay off the loan in the two-week term, and so are compelled to avoid default by paying repeated high fees for no new money.

Payment Option ARM (Adjustable Rate Mortgage). A mortgage that allows a number of different payment options each month, including very minimal payments. The minimum payment option can be less than the interest accruing on the loan, resulting in negative amortization.

Payment Shock. An unmanageable rise in a consumer's monthly mortgage payment, typically the result of an increase in the interest rate on an ARM loan. For example, a 2% bump in a loan's interest rate can increase the consumer's monthly payment 24%.

Personal Property. Property other than real estate.

PITI. Principal + Interest + Taxes + Insurance. The total monthly mortgage expense.

Plaintiff. This is a person or business that begins a lawsuit.

Points/Loan Discount Points. A cost of the credit imposed by the lender. Points are prepaid in cash or financed as part of the loan principal. Each point is equal to 1% of the loan amount (e.g., two points on a $100,000 mortgage would cost $2000). Generally in the conventional loan market and sometimes in the subprime market, points are paid to lower the loan's interest rate. In that event, the points are called discount points.

Power of Sale Clause. A provision in a mortgage or deed of trust permitting the *mortgagee* or trustee to sell the property without court authority if the payments are not made.

Predatory Lending. A term for a variety of lending practices that strip wealth or income from borrowers. Predatory loans typically are much more expensive than justified by the risk associated with the loan. Characteristics of predatory loans may include, but are not limited to, excessive or hidden fees, charges for unnecessary products, high interest rates, terms designed to trap borrowers in debt, fraud, and refinances that do not provide any net benefit to the borrower.

Preemption. A term used when one law or rule directly overrides an existing law or rule. Preemption provisions in a federal law generally displace state laws governing the same topic. In the area of predatory lending, federal preemption would nullify many state protections for homeowners and prevent states from addressing local predatory lending issues as they arise. Banks and other depository institutions claim broad preemption of state laws.

Prepayment. Paying off all or part of the loan balance before it is due.

Prepayment Penalty. A fee charged by a lender if the borrower pays the loan off early. The lender's rationale for imposing prepayment penalties is to cover the loss of costs advanced by the lender at the time of origination. Mortgage loans with prepayment penalties often include a yield spread premium payment by the lender to the broker.

Pre-Sale. Sale of property in anticipation of *foreclosure* or *repossession*, usually with the lender's consent. A pre-sale is likely to lead to a higher sale price than foreclosure or repossession.

Principal. The amount borrowed.

Private Mortgage Insurance (PMI). Insurance provided by non-government insurers that protects lenders against loss if a borrower defaults. This insurance is usually required when a borrower makes less than a 20% down payment. When the borrower's equity in the property equals 20%, she may request the insurance be canceled.

Processing Fee. A charge imposed by a creditor to process or handle a loan application.

Property Flipping. Property flipping scams typically involve speculators who buy dilapidated residential properties at low prices and resell them at huge markups to unsophisticated (and often first-time) homebuyers. Falsified *appraisals* are often the linchpin of property flipping scams.

Property Inspection Fee. A charge imposed by a servicer for inspections (usually drive-bys) to determine the physical condition or occupancy status of mortgaged property, often charged repeatedly once an account is placed in default status.

Pro Se. (Also called "pro per.") Representing yourself (without an attorney) in a legal case or bankruptcy proceeding.

Punitive Damages. Special damages that are sometimes awarded in court to punish a party which is responsible for serious misconduct.

Purchase Money Mortgage. The mortgage loan obtained to purchase a home.

Purchase Money Security Interest. A lien on property that arises when you agree to allow a lender to take as collateral the property you are purchasing with the loan.

Reaffirmation. An agreement in the *bankruptcy* process to pay back a debt that would otherwise be *discharged* in bankruptcy. Most reaffirmation agreements are a bad idea.

Real Estate Settlement Procedures Act (RESPA). The purpose of this *federal law* is to protect consumers from unnecessarily high settlement charges and certain abusive practices that have developed in the residential real estate market. The law requires disclosures before and at the *closing*, as well as periodically throughout the term of the *mortgage* loan. The disclosures address settlement costs, servicing transfers, and escrows. RESPA also prohibits kickbacks and fee-splitting between settlement servicer providers.

Reamortization. When a loan is reamortized, your payment is recalculated based on loan terms that are different from the original terms. For example, if you have paid for five years on a ten-year loan, your lender might consider starting the ten-year period again and recalculating your payments. This will lower your payments. Similarly, your *arrears* may be *capitalized* (included in the principal) and your loan reamortized to reflect the higher principal balance on which interest is accruing.

Redeem. Recovering *collateral* from a *creditor* by paying the entire amount you owe whether past due or not.

Redlining. In the mortgage lending context, the practice of denying the extension of credit to residents of a specific geographic area due to their race, ethnicity, age, or sex.

Refinancing. The process of paying off current debts by borrowing new money either from an existing *creditor* or a new creditor.

Refund Anticipation Loan. See *Tax Refund Anticipation Loans.*

Registry of Deeds. Also called Land Records or Recorder's Office. These offices are located in every county. Real property deeds, mortgages or deeds of trust, assignments, liens, and other documents affecting real property are filed in these offices.

Reinstatement. The process of remedying a *default* so that the lender will treat you as if you had never fallen behind. See *Curing a Default.*

Renewal. In some states, regulations limit the number of times a single payday loan can be extended or "rolled over." Payday lenders accomplish the same effect with loan renewals, also known as "back-to-back transactions." In a renewal transaction, the borrower pays off an existing payday loan in order to open another one (either immediately or after a cooling-off period). The borrower gets no new money, but pays another fee for the new loan.

Rent-to-Own. Rent-to-own companies "rent" merchandise to a consumer for a stated period, after which the consumer owns the merchandise. A consumer would pay over four times the value of the merchandise under a typical contract. The company is not required to disclose interest rates, although the transaction is much like a loan in that the company may levy unlimited finance charges for late payments, and may repossess the merchandise.

Reorganization (Chapter 13 Bankruptcy). This is a bankruptcy process to get relief from debts by making court-supervised payments over a period of time. The alternative is usually *liquidation* under chapter 7.

Replevin. The legal process in which a creditor seeks to recover *personal property* on which it claims a *lien*. Replevin is often threatened, but rarely occurs.

Repossession. (Often called "self-help repossession.") Seizure by the creditor of *collateral* after the debtor's *default*, usually without court supervision or permission. Repossession is most common in connection with car loans.

Rescission. This is a right under some laws to cancel a contract or loan. The most common example of rescission arises in home equity loan transactions. You have the right to rescind that loan within the first three business days after the loan is signed. In some cases, if the *creditor* has violated the law, your right to rescind may continue after the three-day period is up.

Retaliatory Eviction. An *eviction* where a landlord seeks to punish a tenant for exercising his or her legal rights (such as complaining to the building inspector or forming a tenant's organization).

Reverse Mortgage. A *refinancing* option usually available only to older homeowners who have built up substantial equity in their property. In a reverse mortgage, money is drawn based on the value of the property without an immediate repayment obligation, because the lender expects repayment by sale of the property at some point in the future.

Reverse Redlining. The practice of extending credit on unfair terms to those in certain communities based upon race, ethnicity, sex, or age.

Rollover. Rollovers are common practice in payday lending. Payday loan terms are typically two weeks, but borrowers are flipped into rollovers: they pay another fee to keep the loan outstanding in an extension. Many borrowers pay a high fee every payday without ever paying down the principal or receiving new money, and end up paying many times the original loan amount in fees. See also *Renewal.*

Sale-Leaseback. An early form of payday lending circumvention, in which a payday lender avoids legal restrictions by claiming the loan they make is payment for an item the borrower owns, but pretends to "sell" to the lender, who then "leases" it back to the borrower for a fee. The "sale" proceeds are the loan, and the fee is the interest. Also commonly used in car title lending.

Satisfaction. This is a legal document that states that a debt has been fully paid or that partial payment has been accepted as payment in full. A satisfaction is a type of *discharge.*

Secondary Market. This term describes the phenomenon where originating lenders sell their loans to buyers (often called investors), usually in bulk. This enables mortgage companies specializing in home equity lending to operate with a small capital base. They can obtain a line of credit from a major bank, originate loans, and then obtain money to make new loans by selling them to investors. The secondary market includes "wholesale" lenders who buy loans from small lenders, and the securitization market, where mortgage loans are pooled and sold to investors.

Secured Credit Cards. A credit card for which the card issuer requires that the card holder place a certain amount of money in a bank account with the card issuer. If the debtor does not repay the credit card, the card issuer can seize the money in the bank account.

Secured Creditor. Any *creditor* that has *collateral* for a debt.

Secured Debt. A debt for which the *creditor* has *collateral* in the form of a *mortgage*, *lien*, or *security interest* in certain items of property. The creditor can seize the property (*collateral*) if the *debtor defaults* in repayment of the debt.

Securitization. It is the process of investing in and providing capital for the creation of mortgage loans. This process brings together a variety of entities to accomplish these goals. Loans are pooled and assigned to a trustee that supervises the servicer of the loans and distributes the monthly returns to the securities holders. The pools of loans are sometimes insured and they are rated by the various bond-rating agencies. An investment firm invites investors to buy certificates or mortgage-backed securities that pay an attractive interest rate over a specific term. Investors are compensated through interest payments that are often guaranteed by bond insurance companies. The borrower's monthly payments on the loan cover both the return to the investors and a profit to the lender. The risk of loss to the investors is negligible given insurance and recourse agreements between the trustee and the lender. Creating capital flow in this way for subprime lenders only took off following 1994.

Security Interest. See *Lien*.

Self-Help Repossession. This is a process by which a *creditor* that has taken property as *collateral* can *repossess* the property without first getting court permission.

Servicer. See *Mortgage Servicer*.

Settlement. The closing of a mortgage loan. Also, the delivery of a loan or security to a buyer.

Settlement Statement ("the HUD-1"). The Real Estate Settlement Procedures Act requires lenders to give this disclosure at closing, or one day in advance of closing if the consumer requests it. It should be the final statement of settlement costs. The RESPA disclosure focuses on closing costs as a dollar amount.

Short Sale. A type of *pre-sale* in which the *creditor* agrees to let you sell property (usually real estate) for less than the full amount owed and to accept the proceeds of the sale as full *satisfaction* of the debt.

Short-Term credit. Payday lenders and purveyors of overdraft loans, car title loans and refund anticipation loans offer extremely short-term credit, typically a few days to one month, and charge interest rates in the triple digits. The excessive charges far outweigh the risks associated with these loans.

State Law. A law passed by an individual state that only applies to transactions in that state.

Statute. Another word for a law passed by a state or federal legislative body. Laws enacted by local bodies, such as city councils, usually are called ordinances.

Steering. The practice of routing certain borrowers to lenders that charge higher fees or interest rates than the borrowers' credit histories warrant.

Subpoena. A document that is normally issued by a court in connection with a lawsuit, and that directs your attendance in a court or law office at a particular time. A subpoena may require production of documents related to the case.

Subprime Loan. A loan that is more expensive than a comparable prime loan. Subprime lending is generally defined as less than "A" (i.e. prime) lending. This type of lending is designed to provide credit to borrowers with no credit history or past credit problems at a higher cost than conventional "A" mortgage loans. Most of the predatory mortgage lending occurs in the subprime market.

Summons. (Also called "original notice" or "notice of suit.") This is a document that is provided at the beginning of the lawsuit to tell the *defendant* what is being requested and what must be done to respond to the *complaint*. The term "summons" is also sometimes used interchangeably with *subpoena* for other legal papers that direct a person to be at a particular place at a particular time.

Table-Funded Transaction. Is one where the nominal lender is actually originating the loan for another entity whose money is used to fund the loan. The loan will be transferred within a relatively short period of time after the *closing* to the lender who funded the loan.

Targeting. A practice in which lenders specifically market high-cost or predatory loans to potential customers based on factors such as race, ethnicity, or age. Targeting is a form of discrimination because it targets minorities and other populations and exploits them by offering loans with abusive terms and conditions.

Tax Refund Anticipation Loan. A loan to the *debtor* to be repaid out of the debtor's tax refund. The refund is often then sent directly to the lender. These loans can be very expensive.

Tax Service Fee. The fee charged by a lender for a report about whether the borrower is or has been delinquent on the payment of taxes.

Title. A legal document establishing the right of ownership.

Title Insurance. Insurance to protect the lender (lender's policy) or the buyer (buyer's policy) against loss arising from disputes over ownership or a property.

Title Search. A check of the title records to ensure that the seller is the legal owner of the property and that there are no outstanding liens or other claims on the property.

Triple-Digit Interest. Payday and overdraft loans typically carry triple digit interest rates. The annual percentage rate (APR) for payday and other predatory consumer loans generally exceeds 400%.

Trustee. A trustee is a person or business that is responsible for managing assets for others. In *bankruptcy*, the trustee is a person appointed to administer the bankruptcy case and its assets to maximize the recovery for unsecured creditors.

Truth in Lending Act (TILA). A federal (national) law that requires that most lenders, when they make a loan, provide standard form disclosures of the cost and payment terms of the loan.

Unsecured Creditor. A *creditor* that has no *collateral* for the debt owed.

Underwriting. The process of applying established lending criteria to the qualifications of a particular loan applicant.

Underwriting Fee. A fee charged by a creditor to perform *underwriting*.

Unsecured Creditor. A creditor that has no *collateral* for the debt owed.

Unsecured Debt. A debt that does not involve *collateral*.

Usury. The practice of lending money and charging the borrower interest, especially at an exorbitant or illegally high rate. Examples include *payday*, *overdraft*, and *auto title loans*. Payday loans typically carry an annual percentage rate (APR) of over 400%, sometimes exceeding 1000%. Societies and religions throughout history have banned or limited the charging of interest on loans. Click here to read about the History of Usury.

Variable Rate. Interest rate that changes periodically in relation to an index.

Variable Rate Mortgage. This is a mortgage loan on which the interest rate can change over time. The changes can affect the amount of your monthly payments.

Wage Assignment. An agreement to have wages paid to a person other than yourself. For example, some people assign a portion of their wages to be paid directly to cover a credit union bill.

Wage Garnishment. *Garnishment* of the *debtor*'s wages from the debtor's employer.

Warranty. Goods or services you purchase contain explicit and/or implicit promises (called warranties) that the goods or services sold will meet certain standards. A seller's failure to live up to warranties often can be a *defense* to repayment of the debt.

Workout. This term covers a variety of negotiated agreements you might arrange with *creditors* to address a debt you are having trouble paying. Most commonly, the term is used with respect to agreements with a *mortgage* lender to restructure a loan to avoid *foreclosure*.

Yield Spread Premiums (YSP). A fee from a lender to a loan broker paid when the broker arranges a loan where the interest rate on the loan is inflated to an amount higher than the "par" rate. The par rate is the base rate at which the lender will make a loan to borrower on a given day.

J.2 Specialized Glossary of Mortgage Servicing Terms

The following is a glossary of terms related to the servicing of consumer mortgages. Advocates may find this glossary helpful in understanding mortgage escrow statements, loan histories, and other client account documents obtained through discovery or in response to a qualified written request under the Real Estate Settlement Procedures Act (RESPA). It includes abbreviations that commonly appear on account statements. However, these account documents often contain numerical codes and other cryptic notations used by servicers to designate particular account transactions. When possible, advocates should request that account histories and statements be provided in a complete and comprehensible format in which all codes are translated, or request that a separate explanation of all transaction codes used by the servicer be provided. The companion website to this handbook includes a list of transaction codes widely used in the mortgage servicing industry. For a more generalized glossary of mortgage terms, see J.1, *supra*.

Abbreviations	
Adj	Adjustment
Bal	Interest Short
Bk	Bankruptcy
Bnkrpcy	Bankruptcy
BPO	Broker's Price Opinion
Corp Adv	Corporate Advance
DDLPI	Due Date of Last Paid Installment
DFRD	Deferred Charge
Disb	Disbursement
Esc Adv	Escrow Advance
Esc Bal	Escrow Balance
Esc Int	Interest on Escrow
Exp Adv	Expense Advance
Fee Cde	Fee Code
Fl. Ins.	Flood Insurance
Haz Ins	Hazard Premium
Insp	Property Inspection Fee
Int	Interest Payment
Int Arr	Interest Short
Int Sh	Interest Short
MERS	Mortgage Electronic Registration System
MIN	Mortgage Identification Number
MIP	Mortgage Insurance Premium
Misc Adj	Adjustment
Misc Susp	Suspense Account
NSF Chk Chg	Returned Check Fee
NSF Fee	Returned Check Fee
PMI	Private Mortgage Insurance
Pmt Amt	Payment Amount
Prin	Principal
REO	Real Estate Owned
Stat Exp	Statutory Expense
Susp	Suspense Account
Susp Bal	Suspense Balance
Tran	Fee Code

Acceleration. Action by lender/servicer to declare entire mortgage amount due before maturity date based on specific conditions listed in mortgage, such as payment default.

Accrued Interest. Interest earned for the period of time that has elapsed since interest was last paid.

Adjustment (Adj; Misc Adj). Change to prior account treatment of payment or expense, including reallocation of funds held in suspense account. Also may refer to change in loan terms.

Related terms: Late Charge Adjustment; Miscellaneous Adjustment; Miscellaneous Corporate Adjustments

Attorney Advance. Disbursement for attorney fees, often for collection and foreclosure services on account in default, to be recovered from borrower if permitted under mortgage.

Related terms: Corporate Advance

Bankruptcy (Bk; Bnkrpcy). Bankruptcy filed by borrower, often resulting in internal transfer of servicing to servicer's bankruptcy department or to default servicer.

Bankruptcy Fee. Fee charged to borrower by lender or servicer as a result of bankruptcy filing by borrower, often a flat fee included in amount owed listed on proof of claim filed by servicer in chapter 13 or added to account as recoverable expense or corporate advance without notice to borrower or bankruptcy court approval.
Related terms: Bankruptcy Monitoring Fee; Proof of Claim (POC) Fee

Broker's Price Opinion (BPO). Evaluation of property value typically based on drive-by exterior examination, public data sources, and recent comparable sales, obtained by servicer as alternative to full appraisal after loan is placed in default status or upon loan modification.

Capitalization. Addition of certain amounts to the outstanding principal balance, which may occur, for example, as part of loan modification.
Related terms: Modification

Corporate Advance (Corp Adv). Disbursement for servicing-related expenses (not escrow expenses) paid with servicer funds rather than escrow funds, to be recovered from borrower. May include foreclosure expenses, attorney fees, bankruptcy fees, force placed insurance, and so forth.
Related terms: Expense Advance; Corporate Recoverable Advances

Coupon Payment. Regularly scheduled mortgage payment made in amount reflected on payment coupon, typically sent by borrower to servicer's payment processing center.
Related terms: Lock Box Payment

Cushion. An additional sum of money required by lender to be paid into escrow account as part of monthly escrow payment to protect lender against increases in escrow expenses.
Related terms: Reserve

Daily Accrual Accounting. Method of calculating earned interest on a daily basis, if provided for in note and permitted by state law. Interest is computed at the contract rate on the unpaid balance on the account based on the number of days that lapse from the date prior payment received to the date current payment received.
Related terms: Simple Interest Loan

Default Servicer. Servicer of subprime, home equity, non-performing and other loans in which increased default-related activities are anticipated.
Related terms: Subservicer; Special Servicer

Deferred Charge (DFRD). Charge assessed to account but not initially collected, typically resulting from acceptance of installment payment that does not include, for example, amount for late charge or NSF fee.
Related terms: Deferred Late Charge; Late Charge Assessed; Deferred NSF Charge

Demand Letter. Letter notifying borrower of a delinquency or default, possibly a notice of intent to foreclose.
Related terms: Notice of Intent to Foreclose

Demand Letter Assessment. Fee for sending the demand letter or notice of intent to foreclose.

Disbursement (Disb). Use of funds to pay for servicing-related charges and expenses, including payments made out of escrow.
Related terms: Escrow Disbursement

Due Date. Date on which borrower's monthly installment of principal, interest, and escrow (if applicable) is due as stated in note.

Due Date of Last Paid Installment (DDLPI). Due date of the last fully paid monthly installment of principal, interest, and escrow (if applicable); not the date on which such payment was credited or date of next scheduled installment.

Escrow Account. Trust account into which a borrower's funds are deposited and held to pay taxes, insurance premiums, and other escrow expenses.
Related terms: Trust Account; Impound Account

Escrow Advance (Esc Adv). Disbursement for escrow expense paid with servicer funds at time when insufficient funds in borrower's escrow account, to be recovered from borrower as escrow shortage or deficiency.
Related terms: Expense Advance; Escrow Advance Repayment

Escrow Balance (Esc Bal). Amount of funds remaining in escrow account.

Escrow Deficiency. Amount of a negative balance in an escrow account at the time of an escrow analysis, resulting from escrow advances.

Escrow Payment. Portion of borrower's monthly mortgage payment held by the servicer in escrow account to pay for taxes, insurance premiums, or other escrow items as they become due.

Escrow Shortage. Amount by which current escrow account balance falls short of the projected target balance at the time of an escrow analysis.

Escrow Surplus. Amount by which current escrow account balance exceeds the projected target balance at the time of an escrow analysis.

Expense Advance (Exp Adv). May be either corporate advance or escrow advance (see definitions above).

Fax Fee. Fee charged to borrower for transmitting payoff statement via facsimile. Usually charged in addition to payoff fee.
Related terms: Payoff Fee

Fee Code (Fee Cde; Tran). Numerical code used by servicer to designate type of account transaction.
Related terms: Transaction Code

Flood Insurance (Fl. Ins.). Unlike a standard hazard insurance policy, flood insurance cover losses to property caused by flooding. Homeowners with property in high-risk areas may be required by the lender to obtain and maintain flood insurance coverage on the property.

Forbearance. Plan to cure default that may involve temporary suspension of payments or repayment plan based on modified payment amount (with portion paid towards past due amount), extending typically for three to twelve months.
Related terms: Loss Mitigation Option; Workout Plan

Force Placed Insurance. Hazard insurance or flood insurance purchased by servicer on borrower's home (generally covering only lender's interest) when policy purchased directly by borrower on non-escrow mortgage account has lapsed, when servicer contends that borrower has failed to provide proof of insurance coverage, or when account is in default.

Hazard Premium (Haz Ins). Premium for hazard insurance on borrower's home.

Interest on Escrow (Esc Int). Interest earned on funds held in escrow account paid either directly to borrower or credited to escrow account.

Interest Payment (Int). Portion of borrower payment applied to mortgage interest.

Interest Short (Int Sh; Int Arr; Bal). Earned interest remaining unpaid after application of mortgage payment, typically reflected on account history as negative balance. Frequently occurs on loans with negative amortization or when irregular payments made under daily accrual accounting method.
Related terms: Accrued but Unpaid Interest; Interest Shortfall

Irregular Payment. Mortgage payment made in amount or at time different than regularly scheduled payment under terms of note.
Related terms: Non-coupon Payment

Late Charge Assessed. Fee charged to borrower's account when payment made after due date (usually fifteen days after due date).
Related terms: Late Charge Adjustment; Deferred Late Charge

Loan Modification. Agreement to permanently change one or more terms of original mortgage (e.g., change in interest rate, payment amount, term, or capitalization of arrears over extended term) as means to resolve default or to settle litigation between parties.
Related terms: Loss Mitigation Option; Workout Plan

Lock Box Payment. Borrower payment sent to designated address (usually post office box) at the servicer's payment processing center (servicer may outsource service to third-party company who collects mail directed to post office box and deposits funds to servicer's bank account).
Related terms: Coupon Payment

Master Servicer. Servicer responsible for protecting interests of mortgage-backed securities' certificate holders and oversight of primary servicers.
Related terms: Primary Servicer

Mortgage Electronic Registration System (MERS). Electronic registry system for tracking ownership of individual mortgages, servicing rights, and security interests used by MERS members.

Mortgage Identification Number (MIN). Number assigned to a mortgage that is registered with MERS (see definition above) and used for identification and various other purposes for life of mortgage.

Mortgage Insurance Premium (MIP). Payment of private mortgage insurance (PMI) premium (see definition for PMI).

Partial Payment. Payment that is less than total amount due. Servicer will return to borrower or accept and either apply to account or hold as unapplied (typically in suspense account).
Related terms: Unapplied Payment; Payment Shortage

Partial Reinstatement. Change in account status from default to current based on borrower payment of less than total amount due and completion of repayment plan for remaining arrearage.
Related terms: Reinstatement; Full Reinstatement

Payment Amount (Pmt Amt). Regular installment payment amount, which includes principal, interest and, if applicable, escrow.

Pay-Off Fee. Fee charged to borrower for providing statement of amount required to pay off loan.
Related terms: Fax Fee

Primary Servicer. Servicer responsible for payment collection, cash management, escrow administration, and loan reporting to mortgage-backed securities' trustees and certificate holders. Some functions may be delegated to subservicer.
Related terms: Master Servicer

Principal (Prin). Sum of money outstanding on mortgage upon which interest is payable.

Principal Payment. Portion of borrower payment applied to mortgage principal.

Private Mortgage Insurance (PMI). Insurance to protect lender against loss if borrower defaults. Similar to insurance by government entities such as FHA, except issued by private mortgage insurance company. Premium is paid by borrower as part of monthly mortgage payment.

Property Inspection Fee (Insp). Fee charged to borrower for inspections (usually drive-by) to determine the physical condition or occupancy status of mortgage property, often imposed repeatedly once account is placed in default status.
Related terms: Property Preservation Fee

Property Preservation Disbursement. Disbursement by servicer for securing, winterizing, and repairing property that has been foreclosed (real estate owned). May also refer to fees for property inspections, broker price opinions, and foreclosure expenses.

Recovery. Distribution of borrower payment or funds to servicer as reimbursement of escrow, corporate, or other advances.
Related terms: Escrow Advance Recovery

Redistribution. Application of payment or other posting to two or more accounts.

Refund. Funds returned to borrower, often following escrow account analysis showing surplus.

Returned Check Fee (NSF Fee; NSF Chk Chg). Charge imposed for bounced check.
Related terms: Non-sufficient Fund Fee; Deferred Charge

Real Estate Owned (REO). Property acquired by lender as a result of foreclosure or deed in lieu of foreclosure.

Reinstatement. Change in account status from default to current, typically upon acceptance of all payments due (full reinstatement).
Related terms: Full Reinstatement; Partial Reinstatement

Repayment. Disbursement to servicer as recovery of corporate or escrow advance.

Reserve. An additional sum of money required by lender to be paid into escrow account as part of monthly escrow payment to protect lender against increases in escrow expenses.
Related terms: Cushion

Reversal. Removal of previously imposed charge or reapplication of previously credited payment. Generally involves two-step accounting process in which item is reversed in one transaction and reapplied in another transaction.
Related terms: NSF Reversal

Servicing Advances. Funds advanced by servicer under terms of agreement with lender to cover servicing costs and expenses as they occur.

Short Payment. Payment made in less than full monthly amount due under the loan payment schedule, often held in suspense account until full amount received.
Related terms: Irregular Payment

SpeedPay Fee. Fee charged for making electronic payment.

Statutory Expense (Stat Exp). Any tax, special assessment, or other charge imposed by federal, state, or local taxing authority or other governmental entity. Generally does not refer to taxes paid through escrow account but rather corporate advances to cover such charges when account is in default or property facing tax sale, or following a foreclosure.

Subservicer. Servicer who does not own the right to perform servicing, but who does so on behalf of the master or primary servicer.
Related terms: Special Servicer; Default Servicer

Suspense Account (Susp; Misc Susp). Catch-all account used as place to temporarily put funds that are in "suspense" until servicer makes decision on how to permanently allocate or apply, often used to hold less than full installment payments or payments received while account in default.
Related terms: Corporate Suspense Account; Suspense Activity; Partial Payment; Unapplied Payment; Unapplied Funds

Suspense Balance (Susp Bal). Amount of funds held in suspense account.
Related terms: Unapplied Funds

Tax Penalty. Interest, late charge, or other penalty imposed by taxing authority for late payment of taxes.

Transaction Date. Date reflected on payment or account history showing time when servicer completed account transaction or took other action.

Transaction Description. Notation on payment or account history often in code describing nature of, or reason for, application of payment, disbursement, or other servicer action.

Trustee Suspense Account. Suspense account used by servicer to hold payments received from chapter 13 bankruptcy trustee pursuant to borrower's chapter 13 plan providing for cure of prepetition mortgage arrearages.

Unapplied Payment. Payment that is less than total amount due. Servicer will return to borrower or hold as unapplied (typically in suspense account).
Related terms: Partial Payment; Payment Shortage

Unapplied Funds. Portion of partial payment remaining after accepted by servicer and applied to one or more full installments, typically held in suspense account until enough funds received to make full installment.
Related terms: Partial Payment

Appendix K

Finding Pleadings, Primary Sources on the Companion Website

Foreclosures includes free access to its companion website, which remains free with continued subscription to this title. The companion websites includes all appendices found in *Foreclosures* plus approximately 200 sample pleadings and 150 primary source documents—statutes, regulations, agency interpretations, forms, pleadings, handbooks, reports, and much more—all easily located with flexible, powerful search tools. Documents are in PDF format and the pleadings are also in Word format.

This appendix describes the documents found on the companion website, how to access them, and how to print, download them onto your computer, or copy-paste them into a word processing file.

K.1 Pleadings and Primary Sources Found on the Companion Website

This website contains over 350 foreclosure-related files, including all of the treatise's appendices and many additional pleadings and primary sources. The website contains sample mortgage foreclosure counseling forms and sample qualified written requests, and extensive primary source materials concerning HUD, VA, and Rural Housing Service, and reverse mortgages—federal statutes, regulations, handbooks, loss mitigation guidelines, and key agency letters. The website also includes extensive materials concerning FDIC and HAMP loan modifications, and selected RESPA statutory and regulatory provisions, and other key documents concerning mortgage servicing. The website also includes summaries of state mortgage servicing, foreclosure, right to cure, condominium, and real estate tax abatement laws.

Of special note are over 150 sample mortgage foreclosure pleadings, including all pleadings found in the manual and many additional pleadings relating to injunction against sale, federally financed housing, RESPA, HOEPA, HAMP loan modifications, fraud and UDAP claims, land installment sales contracts, TIL rescission, and bankruptcy. The website also includes a number of pleadings relating to foreclosure rescue scams and debt collection litigation, and two different Windows-based credit math programs, which compute APRs, generate amortization tables, and calculate Rule of 78 rebates

The website does *not* contain the full text of the manual chapters. See K.5, *infra* about using Internet-based keyword searches to pinpoint page numbers in the manual where topics are discussed.

K.2 How to Access the Website

One-time registration is required to access the companion website. Once registered, a user subsequently logging in will be granted immediate access to all the websites he or she is authorized to use. For example, one username and password allows a subscriber to four NCLC titles to access all four companion websites.

To register for the first time, go to www.consumerlaw.org/webaccess, click "New users click here to register, go to www.consumerlaw.org/webaccess, and click "New users click here to register." Enter the Companion Website Registration Number found on the packing statement or invoice accompanying this publication. Then enter the requested information and click Enter. An e-mail address may be used for the username or a different username may be chosen.

Subscribers do *not* need to register more than once. If subscribers purchase additional NCLC titles later, they will automatically be given access to the corresponding companion websites. Registering a second time with the same registration number overrides a prior username and password.

Once registered, click on the login link at **www.consumerlaw.org/webaccess**, enter the username and password, and select the Foreclosures website from the list of authorized websites.

An alternate login method may be particularly useful for libraries, legal aid offices, or law firms that subscribe to the entire set of NCLC manuals. Simply e-mail publications@nclc.org with a list or range of static IP addresses for which access should be permitted. Users from those addresses can then go to www.consumerlaw.org/ipaccess to be granted access *without* entering a username and password.

Once logged in, users can click the "My Account" link on the left toolbar to change their personal information. We also encourage users who find any mistakes to notify us using the "Report Errors" button, also on the left toolbar. At minimum, **use of the companion websites with Internet Explorer requires Adobe Reader 7.0 or later or Adobe Acrobat 7.0 or later. Users of other browsers, or those experiencing problems with the websites, should download the latest version of the free Adobe Reader (currently 9.0) from Adobe's website at www.adobe.com.** A link to Adobe's site is provided on the NCLC companion website login page.

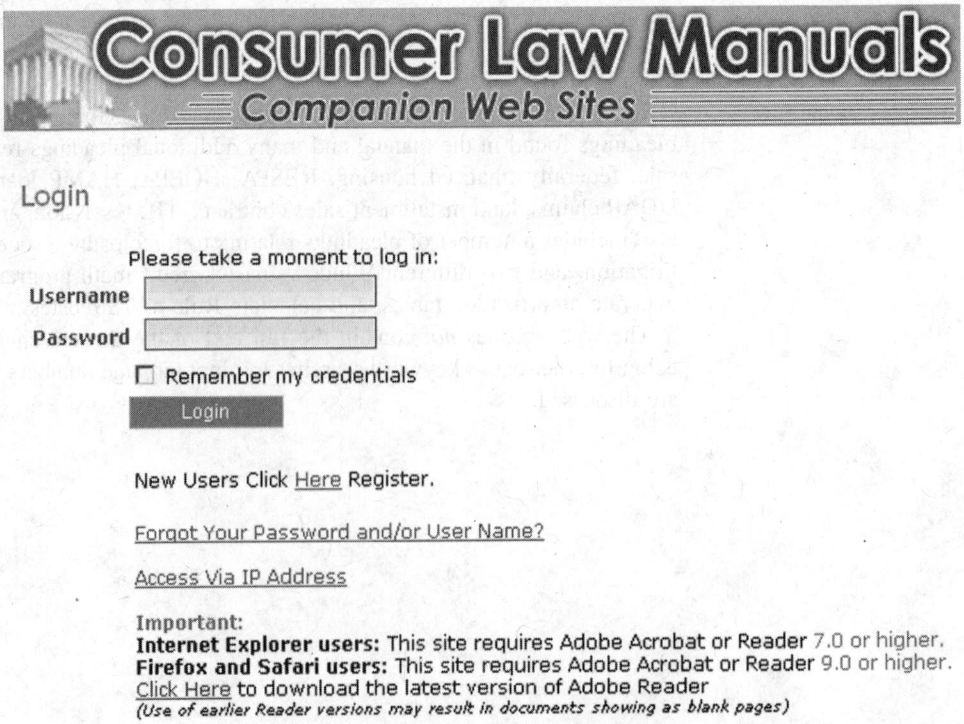

K.3 Locating Documents on the Website

The companion website provides three options to locate documents.

1. The search page (the home page) uses keyword searches to find documents—full text searches of all documents on the website or searches just on the documents' titles.

- Narrow the search to documents of a certain type (such as federal regulations or pleadings) by making a selection from the "Document Type" menu, and then perform a full text or document title search.
- To locate a specific appendix section, select the appendix section number (e.g., A.2.3) or a partial identifier (e.g., A) in the search page's "Appendix" drop-down fields.
- Click Search Hints for a quick reference to special search operators, wildcards, shortcuts, and complex searches. Read this closely, as syntax and search operators may be slightly different from those of other websites.

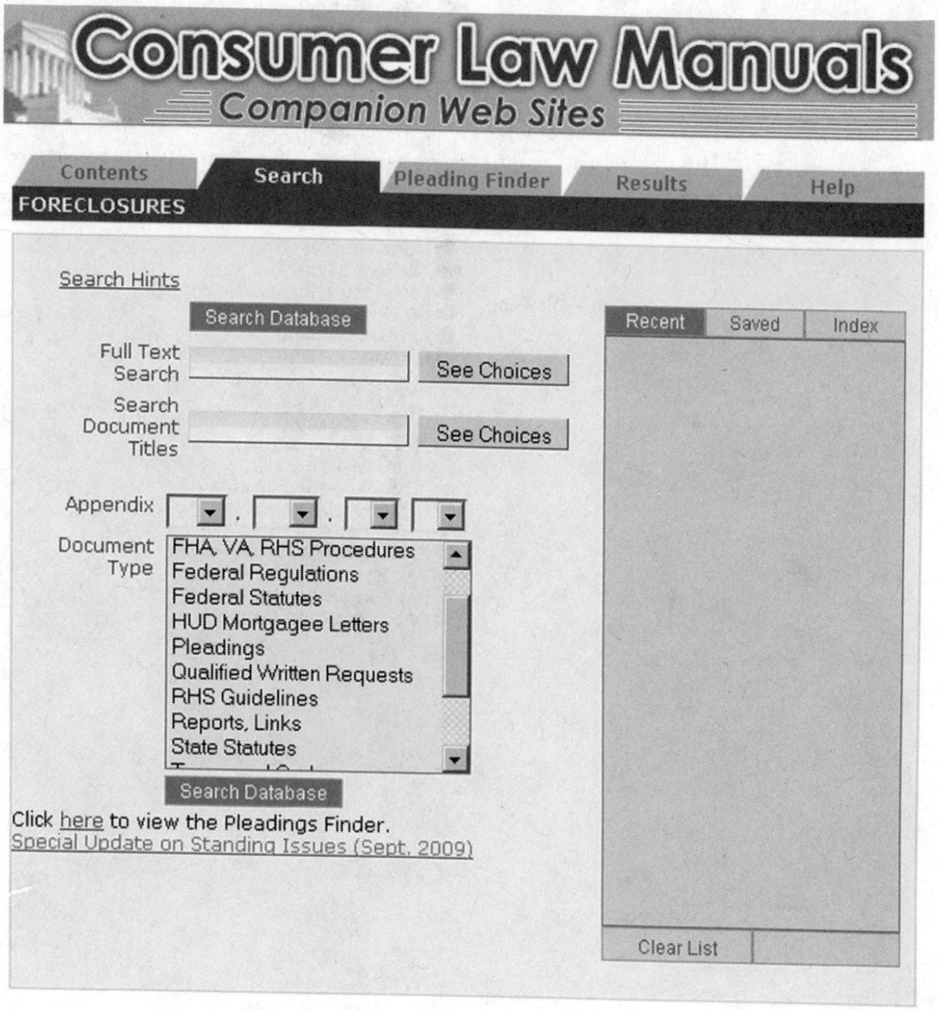

2. The contents page (click on the "Contents" tab at the top of the page) is a traditional "branching" table of contents. Click a branch to expand it into a list of sub-branches or documents. Each document appears once on this contents tree.

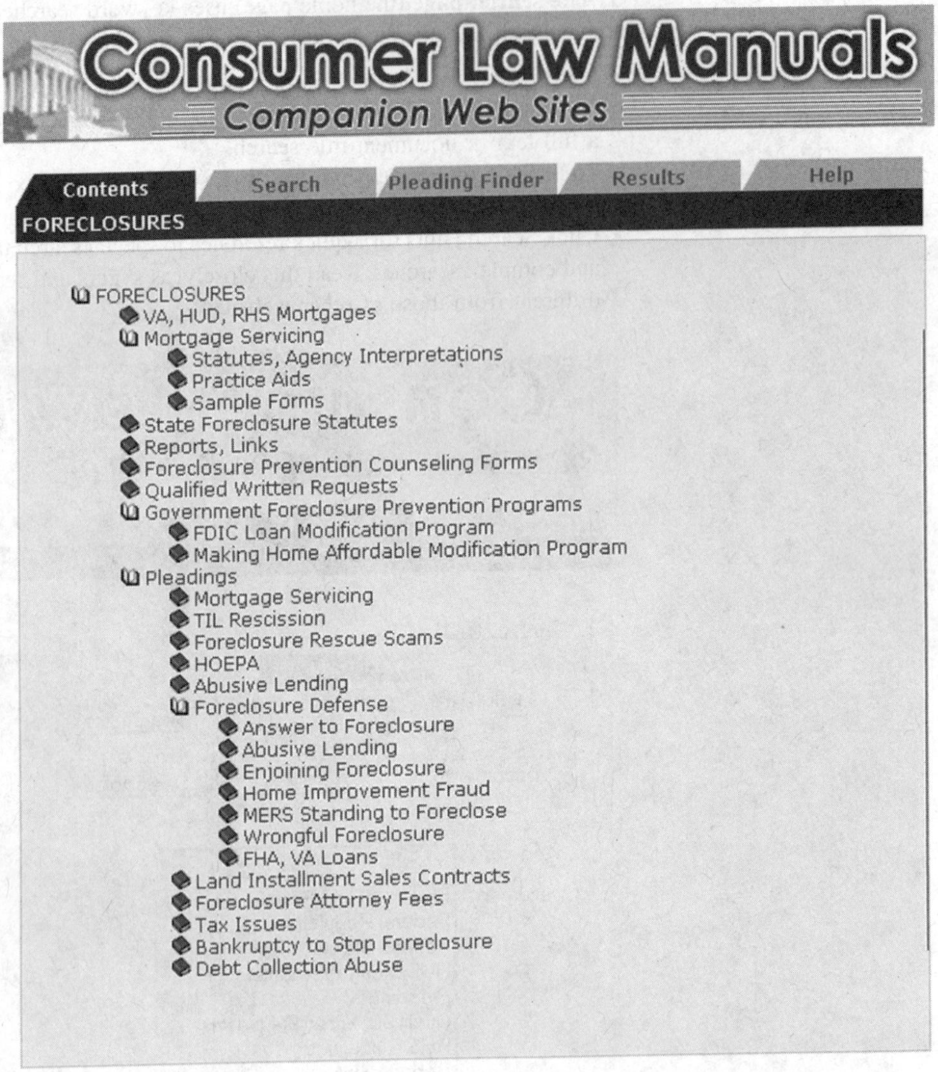

3. The pleading finder page (click on the "Pleading Finder" tab at the top of the page) allows pleadings to be located using one or more menus, such as "Type of Pleading-General" or "Subject." For many users, this will be the preferred method of finding a pleading. More than one item can be selected from a menu, using the Ctrl key. For example, make one selection from "Type of Pleading—General," one from "Subject," and three from "Legal Claims" to locate all pleadings of that type and subject that contain one or more of the three legal claims selected. If this search produces insufficient results, deselect "Subject" and/or "Legal Claims" to find pleadings of that type in any subject area or based upon any legal claim.

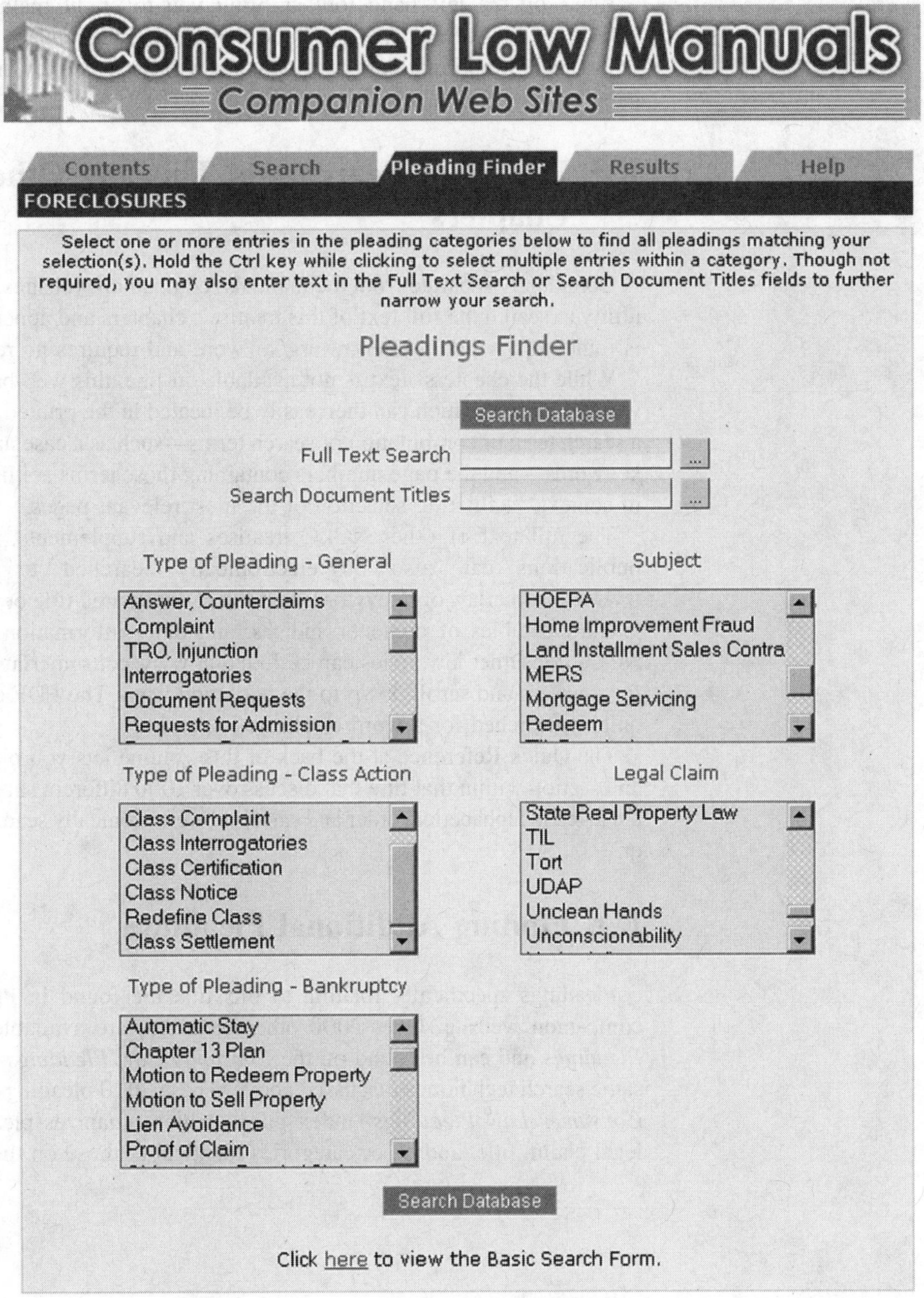

K.4 How to Use the Documents, Find Word Versions, and Locate Additional Features

All documents on the website are in PDF format, and can be printed, downloaded onto your computer, or cut and pasted into a word processing document. Pleadings and certain other documents also are available in Word format, facilitating the opening of entire documents in a word processor. After opening the selected PDF file, click at the top of the page on "Word Version, if available." If a Word version is listed as available, click "DOC Download Document" to save the Word file to your computer.

Links on the left hand toolbar bring you to credit math software, search tips, other websites, tables of contents and indices of all NCLC manuals, and other practice aids. Links to especially important new developments will be placed toward the bottom of the "Search" page.

K.5 Electronic Searches of This and Other NCLC Titles' Chapters

Completely separate from the manuals' companion websites, NCLC offers a handy on-line utility to search the full text of this treatise's chapters and appendices. This free search utility is found at www.consumerlaw.org/keyword and requires no registration or login.

While the chapters' text is not available on-line, this web-based search engine will find a word or phrase, which can then easily be located in the printed manual. Select this title, enter a search term or combination of search terms—such as a case name, a regulation cite, or other keywords—and the page numbers containing those terms are listed. Search results are shown in context, facilitating selection of the most relevant pages.

The full text of other NCLC treatises and supplements, *NCLC REPORTS*, and other publications can also be electronically searched to locate relevant topics at www.consumerlaw.org/keyword. Just select the desired title or search across all NCLC titles.

Current tables of contents, indices, and other information for all eighteen titles in the NCLC consumer law series can be found at www.consumerlaw.org/shop. Click *Publications for Lawyers* and scroll down to the book you want. The PDF documents found there can be quickly searched for a word or phrase.

The Quick Reference at the back of this volume lets you pinpoint the correct NCLC title and section within that title that discuss over 1000 different subject areas. These subject areas are listed in alphabetical order and can also be electronically searched at www.consumerlaw.org/qr.

K.6 Finding Additional Pleadings

Pleadings specifically relating to this title are found in PDF and Word format on the companion website. Over 2000 other pleadings are available at NCLC's *Consumer Law Pleadings* and can be found on the *Consumer Law Pleadings* companion website using the same search techniques discussed above. These 2000 pleadings can also be pinpointed using *Consumer Law Pleadings*' index guide, which organizes pleadings by type, subject area, legal claim, title, and other categories identical to those on the website.

Appendix L

Helpful Websites

[*This list is not exhaustive, just illustrative.*]

Mortgage Industry

Federal National Mortgage Association (Fannie Mae):
www.efanniemae.com/sf/guides/ssg/index.jsp

The Fannie Mae *Single-Family Servicing Guide* is available by following the links at this site.

Federal Home Loan Mortgage Corporation (Freddie Mac):
www.freddiemac.com

This site has bulletins and other notices that Freddie Mac issues to servicers. To access Freddie Mac's Single-Family Seller/Servicer Guide follow the links at http://freddiemac.com/sell/guide/.

Government National Mortgage Association (Ginnie Mae):
www.ginniemae.gov

Ginnie Mae is a government corporation which guarantees mortgage-backed securities composed of FHA-insured or VA-guaranteed mortgage loans that are issued by private lenders.

Federal Housing Finance Agency:
www.fhfa.gov/

The Federal Housing Finance Agency (FHFA) is a new agency, formed by the merger of the Office of Federal Housing Enterprise Oversight, the Federal Housing Finance Board and the U.S. Department of Housing and Urban Development government-sponsored enterprise mission team. FHFA regulates Fannie Mae, Freddie Mac, and the twelve Federal Home Loan Banks.

PMI:
www.pmigroup.com

A private mortgage insurer.

MGIC:
http://mgic.com

A private mortgage insurer.

U.S. Foreclosure Network (USFN):
www.usfn.org

A national association of foreclosure attorneys.

Mortgage Bankers Association:
www.mbaa.org

A national association representing the real estate finance industry.

Mortgage Electronic Registration System:
www.mersinc.org

MERS is a registration system created by the real estate finance industry to track mortgage ownership and servicing rights.

Current Mortgage Rates in the Prime Market:
www.bankrate.com
Shows the rates a homeowner might get in a refinancing.

American Securitization Forum
www.americansecuritization.com/

Foreclosure Prevention Initiatives

FDIC Loan Modification Program:
www.fdic.gov/consumers/loans/loanmod/loanmodguide.html
This website has information on the modification program the FDIC developed for the financial services industry. The website includes a worksheet to calculate net present value.

Home Affordable Modification Program:
www.hmpadmin.com/portal/index.html
This is the administrative website for servicers created by the Department of Treasury.

Making Home Affordable Program:
http://makinghomeaffordable.gov/modification_eligibility.html
The general website for the Making Home Affordable Program.

National Community Reinvestment Coalition:
www.fairlending.com/
NCRC is a national nonprofit that seeks fair and equal access to credit and banking services and products for all racial and ethnic groups. The organization runs a National Homeownership Sustainability Fund to refinance troubled loans.

Government Sites

U.S. Census Bureau, American Housing Survey:
www.census.gov/hhes/www/housing/ahs/ahs.html

U.S. Department of Housing and Urban Development:
www.hud.gov
This site includes HUDClips which has access to all mortgagee letters, handbooks and regulations.

USDA Rural Housing Service:
www.rurdev.usda.gov/rhs
Information on the direct and guarantee loan programs. Decisions by the USDA's National Appeals Division are available at www.nad.usda.gov/.

U.S. Department of Veteran's Affairs:
www.homeloans.va.gov/
The Home Loan Guaranty Services website.

Federal Trade Commission:
www.ftc.gov/bcp/menus/consumer/credit.shtm
FTC publications on consumer credit rights.

Federal Emergency Management Agency:
www.fema.gov/

Federal Deposit Insurance Corporation:
www.fdic.gov/index.html

Federal Reserve Statistical Release:
http://federalreserve.gov/releases/h15/data.htm#top
This Federal Reserve website provides historical data on treasury bond rates which is needed for calculating the APR trigger on loans governed by the Home Ownership and Equity Protection Act (HOEPA).

Internal Revenue Service:
www.irs.gov
An IRS site that is helpful in answering basic tax filing and other questions.

Office of the Comptroller of Currency:
www.occ.treas.gov/aboutocc.htm

Office of Thrift Supervision:
www.ots.treas.gov/

U.S. Securities and Exchange Commission:
www.sec.gov
At the SEC's website you can search for company filings using EDGAR.

Credit Bureaus (and to order credit reports):

Equifax:
www.equifax.com

Experian (formerly TRW):
www.experian.com

TransUnion:
www.transunion.com

To order free reports:
www.annualcreditreport.com

General Consumer and Legal Sites

AARP:
www.aarp.org.
This website provides information about elder-related issues, including many consumer issues such as reverse mortgages and predatory lending. AARP's model state law on Home Improvement Financing is available at www.aarp.org/research/legis-polit/legislation/aresearch-import-165-D17165.html.

AFFIL:
www.affil.org
An organization designed to draw national attention to the problems with the lending industry in America.

American Bankruptcy Institute:
www.abiworld.org
This website provides bankruptcy information for consumers and lawyers.

Better Business Bureau:
www.bbb.org
You can check on a businesses' complaint record or file a complaint on-line.

Consumer Federation of America:
www.consumerfed.org

A membership organization that advocates for consumers. The website also has educational information for consumers and all of the reports on different topics written by CFA staff.

Consumers Union:
www.consumersunion.org

Consumers Union, publisher of *Consumer Reports*, is an independent, nonprofit testing and information organization serving consumers. The website includes information on a wide range of consumer topics.

National Association of Consumer Advocates:
www.naca.net

Provides a listing of consumer attorney members throughout the country, divided by practice area. Also includes updated information on hot consumer topics and other events.

National Association of Consumer Bankruptcy Attorneys:
www.nacba.org

Contains general information about consumer bankruptcy issues as well as referrals to bankruptcy attorneys nationwide.

National Consumer Law Center:
www.consumerlaw.org

Updated to include information on key developments in consumer law, NCLC comments to regulatory and legislative proposals, and investigative reports on a variety of consumer credit topics. Also includes information on how to order NCLC publications, including books, periodicals and consumer education materials.

Penn State Dickinson School of Law Bankruptcy Pro Bono Directory:
www.dsl.psu.edu.

The "publications" section of this website contains a directory of national bankruptcy pro bono programs sorted by state.

Other

Center for Responsible Lending:
www.responsiblelending.org/

Fairbanks Settlement Information:
www.nclc.org/issues/cocounseling/examples_litigation.shtml#fairbanks

Fitch Ratings:
www.fitchratings.com/

National Community Reinvestment Coalition:
www.ncrc.org/

National Rural Housing Coalition:
www.nrhcweb.org

Neighborhood Reinvestment Corporation:
www.nw.org/network/home.asp

Minnesota Mortgage Foreclosure Prevention Association:
www.mmfpa.org

Securities Industry and Financial Markets Association:
www.sifma.org/

Index

References are to sections

References are to sections

References are to sections

References are to sections

References are to sections

References are to sections

References are to sections

References are to sections

References are to sections

References are to sections

References are to sections

References are to sections

References are to sections

References are to sections

References are to sections

References are to sections

References are to sections

References are to sections

References are to sections

Quick Reference to the Consumer Credit and Sales Legal Practice Series

References are to sections in *all* manuals in NCLC's Consumer Credit and Sales Legal Practice Series. References followed by "S" appear only in a Supplement.

Readers should also consider another search option available at ***www.consumerlaw.org/keyword***. There, users can search all eighteen NCLC treatises for a case name, party name, statutory or regulatory citation, or *any* other word, phrase, or combination of terms. The search engine provides the title, page number and context of every occurrence of that word or phrase within each of the NCLC treatises. Further search instructions and tips are provided on the website.

The Quick Reference to the Consumer Credit and Sales Legal Practice Series pinpoints where to find specific topics analyzed in the NCLC treatises. References are to individual treatise or supplement sections. For more information on these volumes, see *What Your Library Should Contain* at the beginning of this volume, or go to www.consumerlaw.org.

This Quick Reference is a speedy means to locate key terms in the appropriate NCLC treatise. More detailed indexes are found at the end of the individual NCLC volumes. Both the detailed contents pages and the detailed indexes for each treatise are also available on NCLC's website, www.consumerlaw.org.

NCLC *strongly recommends,* when searching for PLEADINGS on a particular subject, that users refer to the *Index Guide* accompanying *Consumer Law Pleadings*, and *not* to this Quick Reference. Another option is to search for pleadings directly on *Consumer Law Pleadings*, using the finding tools that are provided on the website.

The finding tools found on NCLC's companion websites are also an effective means to find statutes, regulations, agency interpretations, legislative history, and other primary source material found in manual appendices and on NCLC's companion websites. Other search options are detailed at page ix, *supra*: *About the Companion Website, Other Search Options.*

Abbreviations

AUS	=	Access to Utility Service (4th ed. 2008 and 2010 Supp.)
Auto	=	Automobile Fraud (3d ed. 2007 and 2010 Supp.)
Arbit	=	Consumer Arbitration Agreements (5th ed. 2007 and 2009 Supp.)
Coll	=	Collection Actions (2008 and 2010 Supp.)
CBPL	=	Consumer Banking and Payments Law (4th ed. 2009 and 2010 Supp.)
Bankr	=	Consumer Bankruptcy Law and Practice (9th ed. 2009)
CCA	=	Consumer Class Actions (7th ed. 2010)
CLP	=	Consumer Law Pleadings, Numbers One Through Fifteen (2009)
COC	=	The Cost of Credit (4th ed. 2009 and 2010 Supp.)
CD	=	Credit Discrimination (5th ed. 2009 and 2010 Supp.)
FCR	=	Fair Credit Reporting (6th ed. 2006 and 2009 Supp.)
FDC	=	Fair Debt Collection (6th ed. 2008 and 2010 Supp.)
Fore	=	Foreclosures (3d ed. 2010)
Repo	=	Repossessions (6th ed. 2005 and 2009 Supp.)
Stud	=	Student Loan Law (3d ed. 2006 and 2009 Supp.)
TIL	=	Truth in Lending (6th ed. 2007 and 2009 Supp.)
UDAP	=	Unfair and Deceptive Acts and Practices (7th ed. 2008 and 2009 Supp.)
Warr	=	Consumer Warranty Law (4th ed. 2010)

References are to sections in *all* manuals in NCLC's Consumer Credit and Sales Legal Practice Series

References are to sections in *all* manuals in NCLC's Consumer Credit and Sales Legal Practice Series

References are to sections in *all* manuals in NCLC's Consumer Credit and Sales Legal Practice Series

References are to sections in *all* manuals in NCLC's Consumer Credit and Sales Legal Practice Series

References are to sections in *all* manuals in NCLC's Consumer Credit and Sales Legal Practice Series

References are to sections in *all* manuals in NCLC's Consumer Credit and Sales Legal Practice Series

References are to sections in *all* manuals in NCLC's Consumer Credit and Sales Legal Practice Series

References are to sections in *all* manuals in NCLC's Consumer Credit and Sales Legal Practice Series

References are to sections in *all* manuals in NCLC's Consumer Credit and Sales Legal Practice Series

References are to sections in *all* manuals in NCLC's Consumer Credit and Sales Legal Practice Series

References are to sections in *all* manuals in NCLC's Consumer Credit and Sales Legal Practice Series

NOTES

NOTES

NOTES